OFFICIAL TOURIST BOARD GUIDE

Self Catering

Contents

Further information

Useful indexes

VisitBritain

VisitBritain is the organisation created to market Britain to the rest of the world, and England to the British.

Formed by the merger of the British Tourist Authority and the English Tourism Council, its mission is to build the value of tourism by creating world-class destination brands and marketing campaigns.

It will also build partnerships with – and provide insights to – other organisations which have a stake in British and English tourism.

Guernsey and Jersey are not drawn to scale

Botany Bay, Kent

How to use this guide

This official VisitBritain guide is packed with information from where to stay, to how to get there and what to see. In fact, everything you need to know to enjoy England and the Channel Islands.

Choose from a wide range of quality-assessed accommodation to suit all budgets and tastes. This guide contains a comprehensive listing of all self-catering properties participating in VisitBritain's Enjoy England Quality Rose assessment scheme, including serviced apartments, boat accommodation and approved caravans.

Each property has been visited annually by professional assessors who apply nationally agreed standards so that you can book with confidence knowing your accommodation has been checked and rated for quality.

Regional tourism contacts and tourist information centres are listed – contact them for further information. You'll also find **events, travel information, maps** and useful **indexes**.

Check out the places to visit in each region, from towns and cities to spectacular coast and countryside, plus historic homes, castles and great family attractions! Regional maps show selected destinations as well as National Trails and sections of the National Cycle Network. For even more ideas go online at enjoyengland.com, jersey.com and visitguernsey.com.

Business travellers will find that city-centre serviced apartments are an excellent alternative to hotel accommodation, offering hotel services such as daily cleaning, concierge and business centre services but with an individual kitchen and lounge area.

Finding accommodation is easy...

1. REGIONAL SECTIONS

The guide is divided into regions (see page 3) and accommodation is listed alphabetically by place name within each region.

Start your search for accommodation in these sections. For an even wider choice in England, turn to the listings starting on page 483 where you will find ALL Enjoy England assessed self-catering holiday homes, including those that have not taken a paid entry.

2. COLOUR MAPS

Use the colour maps, starting on page 30, to pinpoint the location of all accommodation featured in the regional sections.

Then refer to the place index at the back of the guide to find the page number. The index also includes tourism areas such as the New Forest and the Cotswolds.

3. INDEXES

The indexes, listed on page 771, make it easy to find accommodation that matches specific requirements; for example, properites suitable for guests with disabilities or those that have an outdoor pool. And if you know the name of the establishment, use the property index.

Accommodation entries explained

Each accommodation entry contains detailed information to help you decide if it is right for you. This has been provided by proprietors and our aim is to ensure that it is as objective and factual as possible.

1 Listing under town or village with map reference

2 Quality rating

3 Classification

4 Number of units and how many they sleep

5 Prices per unit per week for low and high season

6 Establishment name, village/town and booking details

7 Indicates when the establishment is open and payment accepted

8 Website information (web addresses are shown without the prefix www.)

9 Accommodation details

10 Walkers, cyclists, pets and families welcome

11 Accessible rating where applicable

12 Special promotions

13 Travel directions

14 At-a-glance facility symbols

Key to symbols

Information about many of the accommodation services and facilities is given in the form of symbols.

Unit

- TV
- Satellite/cable channels
- Telephone
- DVD player
- Games console
- Microwave
- Dishwasher
- Freezer
- Hairdryer
- Washing machine in all units
- Linen provided
- Linen available for hire
- Towels provided
- Smoking units available
- Daily servicing of unit
- Garden/patio
- Barbecue
- Real log/coal fire

General

- Children welcome (a number following gives minimum age)
- Cots
- Highchairs
- Parking next to unit
- Laundry facilities
- Weekend/mid-week bookings
- Pets welcome by arrangement

Leisure

- Swimming pool – indoor
- Swimming pool – outdoor
- Games room
- Tennis court(s)
- Riding/pony-trekking nearby
- Fishing nearby
- Access to golf
- Cycle hire nearby

National Accessible Scheme

The National Accessible Scheme includes standards for hearing and visual impairment as well as mobility impairment – see pages 14-15 for further information.

Welcome schemes

Walkers, cyclists, families and pet owners are warmly welcomed where you see these signs – see page 12 for further information.

Ratings and awards at a glance

Reliable, rigorous, easy to use – look out for the following ratings and awards to help you choose with confidence.

Star ratings

Establishments are awarded a rating of one to five stars based on a combination of quality of facilities and services provided. Put simply, **the more stars, the higher the quality and the greater the range of facilities and level of service.**

The process to arrive at a star rating is very thorough. National tourist board professional assessors visit establishments annually and work to strict criteria to check the available facilities. A quality score is awarded for every aspect of the layout and design of the accommodation, the ease of use of all the appliances, the comfort of the beds, the range and quality of the kitchen equipment and, most importantly, the cleanliness. They also score the range and presentation of visitor information provided.

From January 2006, all the national assessing bodies (VisitBritain, VisitScotland, Visit Wales, Jersey Tourism and VisitGuernsey) have operated to a common set of standards, giving holidaymakers and travellers a clear guide on exactly what to expect at each level (see page 773).

For information on awards see overleaf

Ratings made easy

★
Simple, practical, no frills

★★
Well presented and well run

★★★
Good level of quality and comfort

★★★★
Excellent standard throughout

★★★★★
Exceptional with a degree of luxury

For full details of the quality assessment schemes, go online at **enjoyengland.com/quality**

Some self-catering establishments offer a choice of accommodation units that may have different star ratings. In this case, the entry shows the range available.

Enjoy England Awards for Excellence

The prestigious and coveted Enjoy England Awards for Excellence showcase the very best in English tourism. Run by VisitBritain in association with England's regions, they include a Self-Catering Holiday of the Year category (see page 16).

Welcome schemes

Enjoy England runs four special Welcome schemes: Cyclists Welcome, Walkers Welcome, Welcome Pets! and Families Welcome. Scheme participants actively encourage these types of visitors and make special provision to ensure a welcoming, comfortable stay (see page 12).

National Accessible Scheme

Establishments with a National Accessible Scheme rating have been thoroughly assessed to set criteria and provide access to facilities and services for guests with visual, hearing or mobility impairment (see page 14).

Visitor Attraction Quality Assurance

Attractions participating in this scheme are visited every year by a professional assessor and must achieve high standards in all aspects of the visitor experience to receive this Enjoy England award. The assessment focuses on the nature of the welcome, hospitality, services and presentation as well as the standards of toilets, shop and café where provided.

What to expect

All self-catering accommodation that is awarded a star rating will meet the minimum standards – so you can be confident that you will find the basic services that you would expect, such as:

- Clear information prior to booking on all aspects of the accommodation including location, facilities, prices, deposit, policies on smoking, children and cancellation etc
- No shared facilities, with the exception of a laundry room in multi-unit sites
- All appliances and furnishings will meet product safety standards for self-catering accommodation, particularly regarding fire safety
- At least one smoke alarm in the unit and a fire blanket in the kitchen
- Clear information on emergency procedures, including who to contact
- Contact details for the local doctor, dentist, chemist etc
- All statutory obligations will be met including an annual gas check and public liability insurance.

Certain additional facilities and services are required at the higher star levels, some of which may be important to you:

TWO-STARs must provide ★★

- Single beds a minimum of 3ft wide and double beds a minimum of 4ft 6in.

THREE-STARs must provide ★★★

- Bed linen (with or without additional charge).

FOUR-STARs must provide ★★★★

- All advertised sleeping space in bedrooms (unless a studio)
- Bed linen included in the hire charge and beds are made up for arrival.

FIVE-STARs must provide ★★★★★

- Full-size beds, including those for children
- At least two of the following items: tumble-dryer, telephone, Hi-Fi, video, DVD.

Some self-catering establishments offer a choice of accommodation units that may have different star ratings. In this case, the entry shows the range available.

A special welcome

To help make your selection of accommodation easier VisitBritain has four special Welcome schemes which accommodation in England can be assessed to. Owners participating in these schemes go the extra mile to welcome walkers, cyclists, families or pet owners and provide additional facilities and services to make your stay even more comfortable.

Families Welcome

If you are searching for a great family break look out for the Families Welcome sign. The sign indicates that the proprietor offers additional facilities and services catering for a range of ages and family units. For families with young children, the accommodation will have special facilities such as cots and highchairs, storage for push-chairs and somewhere to heat baby food or milk. Where meals are provided, children's choices will be clearly indicated, with healthy options available.They'll also have information on local walks, attractions, activities or events suitable for children, as well as local child-friendly pubs and restaurants. Not all accommodation is able to cater for all ages or combinations of family units, so do check when you book.

Welcome Pets!

Want to travel with your faithful companion? Look out for accommodation displaying the Welcome Pets! sign. Participants in this scheme go out of their way to meet the needs of guests bringing dogs, cats and/or small birds. In addition to providing water and food bowls, torches or nightlights, spare leads and pet washing facilities, they'll buy in food on request, and offer toys, treats and bedding. They'll also have information on pet-friendly attractions, pubs, restaurants and recreation. Of course, not everyone is able to offer suitable facilities for every pet, so do check if there are any restrictions on the type, size and number of animals when you book.

Walkers Welcome

If walking is your passion seek out accommodation participating in the Walkers Welcome scheme. Facilities include a place for drying clothes and boots, maps and books for reference and a first-aid kit. Packed breakfasts and lunch are available on request in hotels and guesthouses, and you have the option to pre-order basic groceries in self-catering accommodation. A wide range of information is provided including public transport, weather, local restaurants and attractions, details of the nearest bank and all night chemists.

Cyclists Welcome

If you like to explore by bike seek out accommodation displaying the Cyclists Welcome symbol. Facilities include a lockable undercover area and a place to dry outdoor clothing and footwear, an evening meal if there are no eating facilities available within one mile, and a packed breakfast or lunch on request. Information is also provided on cycle hire and cycle repair shops, maps and books for reference, weather and details of the nearest bank and all night chemists and more.

For further information go online at enjoyengland.com/quality

Classifications explained

Self-catering holiday homes differ in style and the rating scheme covers a range of accommodation. Every year more than 11,000 different properties in England are assessed. They must all be self-contained and have a kitchen, so there is always the option of eating in.

Holiday cottages, houses and lodges

Choose from cosy country cottages, smart town-centre apartments, seaside villas, grand country houses for large family gatherings, and even quirky conversions of windmills, railway carriages and lighthouses. Most take bookings by the week, generally from a Friday or Saturday, but short breaks are increasingly offered, particularly outside the main season.

Holiday cottage agencies

Our assessors also work with a number of agencies, ranging from small, local organisations that specialise in one particular area, to large Britain-wide operators who can help locate a holiday cottage anywhere in the country. In every case procedures and processes have been checked. Some agencies organise their own assessments, but the majority use national tourist board quality standards and are gradually bringing all their properties into the star-rating scheme. If you are looking for accommodation during a peak period and for a specific week, it is worth contacting an agency first (see page 478).

Serviced apartments

City-centre serviced apartments are an excellent alternative to hotel accommodation, offering hotel services such as daily cleaning, concierge and business centre services, but with a kitchen and lounge area that allow you to eat in and relax when you choose. A telephone and Internet access tend to be standard. Prices are generally based on the property, so they often represent excellent value for money for families and larger groups. They are also particularly suitable for business travellers who appreciate the extra space, privacy and flexibility. Serviced apartments tend to accept bookings for any length of period, and many are operated by agencies whose in-depth knowledge and choice of properties makes searching easier at busy times.

Boat accommodation

Select from quality-assessed Narrowboats, Cruisers and Hotel Boats. Boat accommodation is explained fully on page 767.

Approved caravan holiday homes

Individual caravans assessed to minimum standards, but without a star rating.

National Accessible Scheme

Finding suitable accommodation is not always easy, especially if you have to seek out rooms with level entry or specially adapted bathrooms. Use the National Accessible Scheme to help you make your choice.

Proprietors of accommodation taking part in the National Accessible Scheme have gone out of their way to ensure a comfortable stay for guests with special hearing, visual or mobility needs. These exceptional places are full of extra touches to make everyone's visit trouble-free, from handrails, ramps and step-free entrances (ideal for buggies too) to level-access showers and colour contrast in the bathrooms.

Appropriate National Accessible Scheme symbols are included in the guide entries (shown opposite). If you have additional needs or special requirements we strongly recommend that you make sure these can be met by your chosen establishment before you confirm your reservation. The index at the back of the guide gives a list of establishments that have received a National Accessible rating.

For a wider selection of accessible accommodation, order a copy of the *Easy Access Britain* guide featuring almost 500 places to stay. It is available from Tourism for All for £9.99 (plus P&P). Alternatively, visit tourismforall.org.uk for a directory of National Accessible Scheme and Tourism for All members.

The criteria VisitBritain and national/regional tourism organisations have adopted do not necessarily conform to British Standards or to Building Regulations. They reflect what the organisations understand to be acceptable to meet the practical needs of guests with mobility or sensory impairments and encourage the industry to increase access to all.

tourismforall

The National Accessible Scheme forms part of the Tourism for All campaign that is being promoted by VisitBritain and national/regional tourism organisations. Additional help and guidance on finding suitable holiday accommodation can be obtained from:

Tourism for All
c/o Vitalise, Shap Road Industrial Estate, Kendal LA9 6NZ

information helpline 0845 124 9971
reservations 0845 124 9973
(lines open 9-5 Mon-Fri)

f (01539) 735567

e info@tourismforall.org.uk

w tourismforall.org.uk

England

Mobility Impairment Symbols

Typically suitable for a person with sufficient mobility to climb a flight of steps but who would benefit from fixtures and fittings to aid balance.

Typically suitable for a person with restricted walking ability and for those who may need to use a wheelchair some of the time and can negotiate a maximum of three steps.

Typically suitable for a person who depends on the use of a wheelchair and transfers unaided to and from the wheelchair in a seated position. This person may be an independent traveller.

Typically suitable for a person who depends on the use of a wheelchair and needs assistance when transferring to and from the wheelchair in a seated position.

EXCEPTIONAL

EXCEPTIONAL

Access Exceptional is awarded to establishments that meet the requirements of independent wheelchair users or assisted wheelchair users shown above and also fulfil more demanding requirements with reference to the British Standards BS8300:2001.

Visual Impairment Symbols

1 Typically provides key additional services and facilities to meet the needs of visually impaired guests.

2 Typically provides a higher level of additional services and facilities to meet the needs of visually impaired guests.

Hearing Impairment Symbols

1 Typically provides key additional services and facilities to meet the needs of guests with hearing impairment.

2 Typically provides a higher level of additional services and facilities to meet the needs of guests with hearing impairment.

Enjoy England Awards for Excellence

Enjoy England Awards for Excellence are all about telling the world what a fantastic place England is to visit, whether it's for a day trip, a weekend break or a fortnight's holiday.

Organised by VisitBritain and sponsored by The Caravan Club, The Enjoy England Awards for Excellence are the annual accolades for English tourism, recognising the best places to stay and visit. Now in their 20th year, the Awards are known throughout the industry, promoting healthy competition and high standards. Competition is fierce, and entries are submitted to regional tourism organisations across England before being short-listed for the national finals, culminating in an Awards ceremony held in April each year.

enjoyEngland®
Awards for **Excellence**

There are fifteen categories, from visitor attractions and hotels to self-catering accommodation and caravan parks. This year's winners include a country house hotel in the Yorkshire Dales, Europe's largest free airshow in Sunderland, an environmentally sustainable villa and restaurant in Norfolk and a children's attraction and story centre in Buckinghamshire. Seek them out and experience them for yourself – you won't be disappointed.

The complete list of winners can be found online at enjoyengland.com.

Self-Catering Holiday of the Year 2008

GOLD WINNERS

The Mill Granary Cottages, Ingleton, near Darlington, Durham ★★★★★

Stone Cottage, Patterdale, near Penrith, Cumbria ★★★★★

SILVER WINNER

Compton Pool Farm, Marldon, near Paignton, Devon ★★★★★

Clockwise: Stone Cottage; The Mill Granary Cottages; Compton Pool Farm

Stone Cottage

Judges praised the dedicated owners for their hard work in maintaining such an exceptionally high-quality product.

The Mill Granary Cottages

These luxurious stone-built granary cottages offer outstanding accommodation with spectacular views. Both cottages combine many original features with modern furnishings and state-of-the-art facilities. With mobility 2 access ratings, they are also suitable for people with restricted mobility. Situated in Lower Teesdale, near Darlington in Durham, it's a great location for exploring the Pennines, the Dales and the region's great heritage sites.

The Mill Granary sleeps eight to ten people (plus cots) in four bedrooms. With its large kitchen, big comfy sofas and ample accommodation, it's ideal for large family groups or two families. To keep the kids entertained there's swings and slides as well as an indoor play area with table tennis.

The single-storey Mill Byre has an open plan kitchen and lounge giving the cottage a modern, contemporary feel. Four bedrooms can accommodate up to seven guests and a cot is also available. Visit any time of the year – the Range cooker and log burning stove make this a cosy retreat.

If you fancy a night off from the kitchen you can order a wide selection of delicious home cooked suppers.

t (01325) 730339
w millgranary.co.uk

Stone Cottage

This boutique five-star cottage is in the heart of some of the best walking country in the Lake District National Park, in the tiny hamlet of Deepdale near Ullswater. It sleeps six plus a baby in four individually designed bedrooms – all with wonderful views. Stone Cottage is a great place to unwind with walks from the door and wildlife in the garden.

Antique and contemporary furnishings combine with designer fabrics to create a calm and under-stated atmosphere. Little touches are everywhere, from candles and luxury toiletries in the bathroom to a baby bath, logs for the open fire and free wireless broadband. The very well-equipped kitchen will keep even the most adventurous cook happy and for those that like home entertainment there's a wide screen tv with freesat channels and a dvd player.

You can order provisions in advance – from wild boar Cumberland sausages to luxury hampers. And if you have a special occasion to celebrate, take advantage of their private chef service. Activity days can be organised on request, too, from fly fishing to inspirational cooking!

t (017684) 82647
w lakelandstonecottage.co.uk

Family fun

Kids and weather. They change mood from one moment to the next. Fortunately, that's also one of the most striking things about this country's great outdoors and attractions: you just step across the threshold and its landscapes and entertainment venues offer all the varied play potential you need to fill holidays, sunny afternoons or rainy weekends.

So, there you are on the beach building sandcastles, paddling, eating ice cream and basking in the warm memory that you'll take home. You watch the teenagers hanging out with their surfboards, part of the family outing but doing their own thing. There's something for all ages and that's priceless in every sense of the word. Next time, maybe picnicking in woods, leaping through treetops on an aerial adventure, or getting your hands on heritage – whatever makes everyone happy.

Then it rains and you want to stay indoors. London's Science Museum is free, like a good number of England's top attractions, and that pleases Money Bags. Everyone immediately vanishes into one of the galleries: in Who Am I? you're morphing your face older and younger, in another you're discovering how to forecast weather, which could be useful for planning your next trip!

Anticipate the family's next mood. Animal magic at Chester Zoo, following Harry Potter to Alnwick Castle, or screaming your heads off at Drayton Manor Theme Park in Staffordshire? There's always another boredom-buster just around the corner.

For lots more great ideas visit enjoyEngland.com/ideas

Clockwise: Botany Bay, Kent; Blackpool Pleasure Beach, Lancashire; Wookey Hole Caves and Papermill, near Wells; Woburn Safari Park, Bedfordshire

Clockwise: Whinstone Lee Tor, Peak District, Derbyshire; Waterhead, Cumbria; Porlock Bay, Somerset; North York Moors

greatideas

Rural escapes

Take one of hundreds of footpaths along the eastern end of Hope Valley in the Peak District and you'll find yourself at Stanage Edge. The wind whips around the gritstone outcrop, but all you can think about are the exhilarating panoramic views. Just a five-minute walk from the roadside car park, what a reward!

Ramble, cycle, relax over a picnic – in Britain's national parks you're quickly a world away from the day-to-day routine. Sea views across Porlock Bay, Exmoor, or purple waves of heather on the North York Moors work the yin and yang magic of nature. Wander with ponies on Dartmoor, enjoy the people-free hillsides of the Cheviots in Northumberland. What a sense of complete escape!

For a different experience follow the footpaths and cycleways to East Lancashire's Panopticons: gateway landmarks to magnificent countryside. Discover Burnley's huge Singing Ringing Tree crooning its low, mysterious song at Crown Point, or the striking steel Halo at Top o' Slate in Rossendale. They're fun, imaginative and easy to reach.

England boasts an astonishing diversity of natural wonders on the doorstep. From the flat waterscapes of the Norfolk Broads to the jutting peaks of the Lake District, from the ancient woodlands of the New Forest to Dorset's fossil-jewelled Jurassic Coast – there's scenery and breathing spaces to suit every activity and mood.

This is our natural heritage, shaped by primeval forces and just waiting to be explored. Step out and do so: you'll return with happily weary legs, a ravenous appetite and that wonderful tingling sensation on your face from a day in the fresh air.

For lots more great ideas visit enjoyEngland.com/ideas

Clockwise: At Bristol, Bristol; the British Museum, London; NewcastleGateshead; Spinnaker Tower, Portsmouth

greatideas

City breaks

Cities today exude confidence. It's a self-belief that comes from bold investment. And as you gaze up at yet another remarkable new building that demands your attention and sparks your imagination, you realize that nowhere is this confidence more visible than in the architecture of the now.

Architects have done us proud in this country. Many of our cities are studded with gleaming out-of-this-world structures that find the fulcrum between form and function. And today you've taken time out to see the Lowry Museum in Manchester's Salford Quays. Just glimpsing the metal hull of the building from a distance makes you speed your step. Somehow, the thrilling combination of stainless steel and glass makes this inspirational waterside building a fitting home for the world's greatest collection of Lowry works.

It's just the kind of landmark building that you can seek out in many English cities these days. Portsmouth Harbour's 170-metre Spinnaker Tower, in the design of a billowing sail, conjures thoughts of sea breezes. So you take the lift to its Crow's Nest view deck, open to the elements, and see for miles, wind in your hair. Wembley Stadium, Gateshead Millennium Bridge, each one is a vigorous marriage of art and purpose.

Why not set a day aside, fish out your A to Z, and go on a safari of spectacular structures in a city near to (or far from) you.

For lots more great ideas visit enjoyEngland.com/ideas

greatideas

Food and drink

A quiet revolution has been simmering away in Britain. Fresh, locally-sourced and organic ingredients have become the order of the day. From bustling farmers' markets to family kitchens turning out hand-made puddings, jams and breads, dining in or out, you'll more than likely be presented with fresh wholesome food cooked with passion.

Start with the famous Ludlow Food Festival and follow the little-known Sausage Trail, an event in which the town's five independent butchers create new sausage varieties and vie for the crown of People's Choice. You'll find everything from organic rare breeds sausages to the Shropshire Sizzler – a rich blend of local pork, peaches and blue cheese. Take some back to base and spark up the barbie for a fantastic feast.

Fancy lunch while out exploring? Three cheers for the gastropub where high quality cooked-from-scratch bistro meals are served at bar room prices. As you tuck into a crisp salad and garlic mayo (made with free range eggs, of course) you begin to wonder if Chicken in a Basket wasn't just a bad dream.

At the charming Waffle House in St Alban's you can't help but admire the blend of inventiveness, quality produce and sheer dedication that goes into the cooking. Here you'll find waffles of every conceivable shape and size, served with freshly made toppings such as chilli con carne as well as an endless choice of sweet varieties.

The good news is, you'll find places like this all over Britain: it's a foodies' heaven.

For lots more great ideas visit enjoyEngland.com/ideas

Clockwise: Ludlow, Shropshire; Constantine Bay, Cornwall; Canterbury, Kent; tempting dessert

Reg Martin & Sons

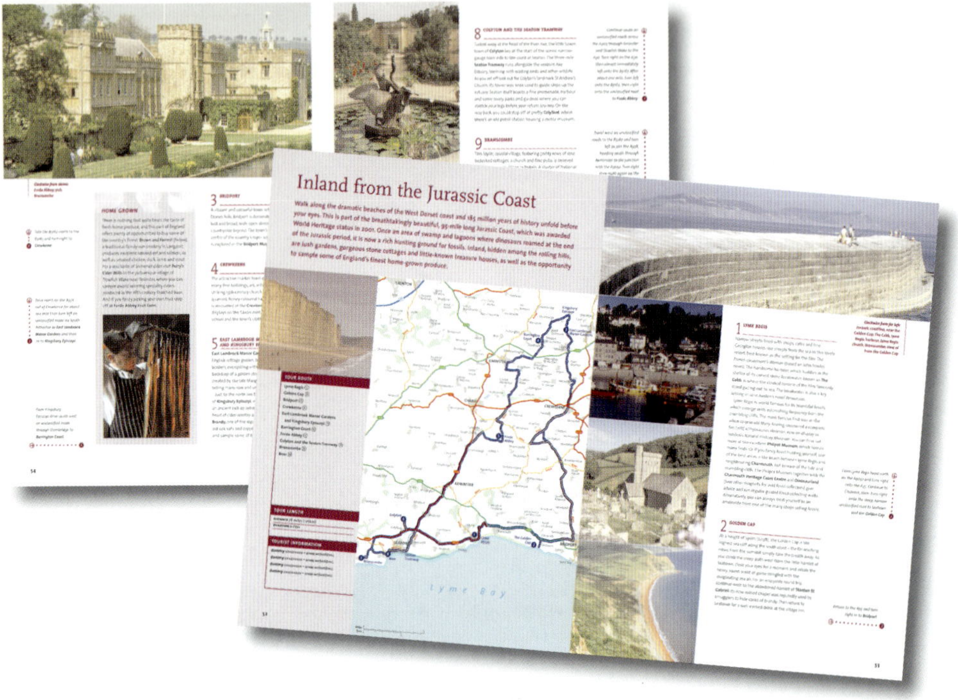

Take a tour of England

VisitBritain presents a series of **three** inspirational touring guides to the regions of England: South and South West, Northern England and Central England.

Each guide takes you on a fascinating journey through stunning countryside and coastlines, picturesque villages and lively market towns, historic houses and gardens.

- Easy-to-use maps
- Clear directions to follow the route
- Lively descriptions of all the places for you to discover
- Stunning photographs bring each area to life

Touring Central England – £14.99
Touring Northern England – £14.99
Touring South and South West England – £14.99
plus postage and handling

Now available in good bookshops.
For special offers on VisitBritain publications, please visit **enjoyenglanddirect.com**

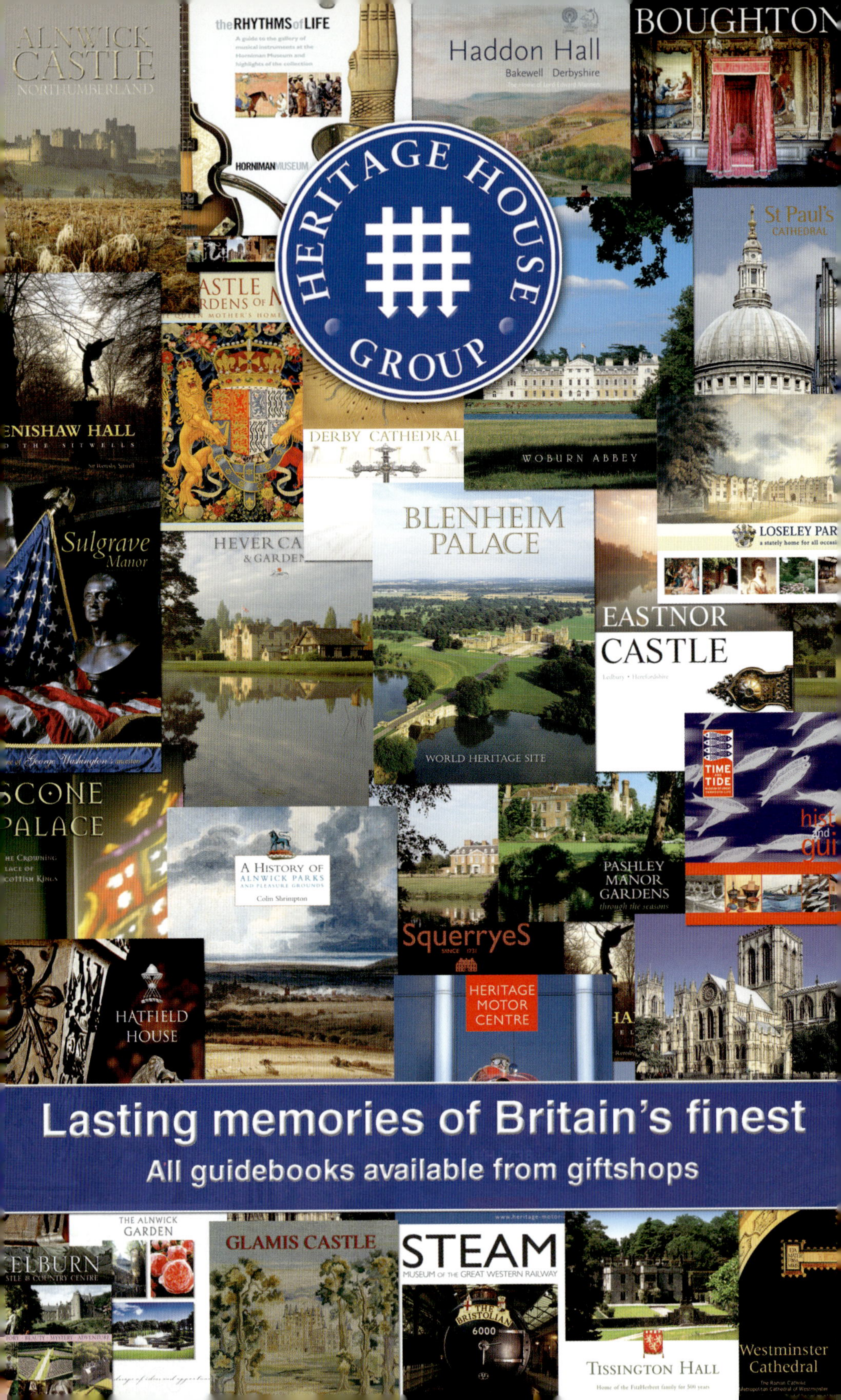

Location Maps

Every place name featured in the regional accommodation sections of this Enjoy England guide has a map reference to help you locate it on the maps which follow. For example, to find Colchester, Essex, which has 'Map ref 3B2', turn to Map 3 and refer to grid square B2.

All place names appearing in the regional sections are shown with orange circles on the maps. This enables you to find other places in your chosen area which may have suitable accommodation – the place index (at the back of this guide) gives page numbers.

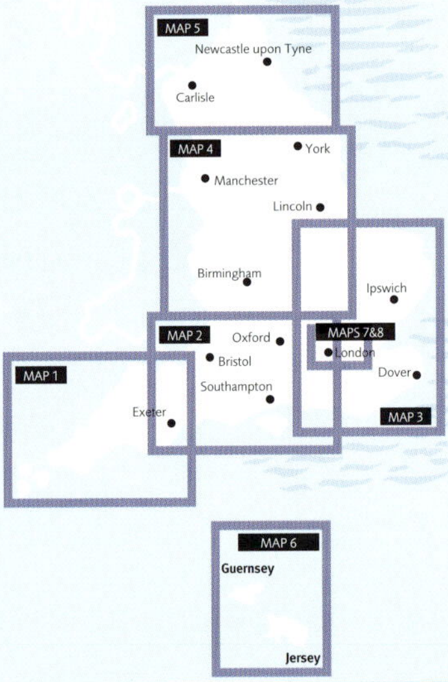

Key to regions: South West England

C
D
BRISTOL CHANNEL
ENGLISH CHANNEL
Weston-super-Mare
Lympsham
Burnham-on-Sea
Cheddar
Lynton
Combe Martin
Lee
Mortehoe
Woolacombe
Berrynarbor
Croyde
Porlock
Bratton
Minehead
Blue Anchor
Simonsbath
EXMOOR NATIONAL PARK
Exford
Sampford Brett
Luxborough
SOMERSET
Burrowbridge
Taunton
Stoke St Gregory
Barnstaple
Brayford
Westward Ho!
Swimbridge
Filleigh
North Molton
Dulverton
Bampton
Bideford
Yarnscombe
Great Torrington
King's Nympton
Chulmleigh
Stoke sub Hamdon
South Petherton
Culmhead
Churchinford
Otterford
Ilminster
Poughill
Bude
DEVON
Holsworthy
Okehampton
Broadclyst
Whimple
Honiton
Axminster
Charmouth
Crackington Haven
Exeter
Exeter International
Colyton
Lyme Regis
Seatown
Seaton
Sidmouth
Longdown
Launceston
Lifton
Altarnun
Moretonhampstead
DARTMOOR NATIONAL PARK
Bovey Tracey
Teigngrace
Dawlish Warren
Dawlish
Tavistock
St Neot
Liskeard
Ashburton
Dartmeet
Maidencombe
Torquay
Paignton
Brixham
Lanreath-by-Looe
East Looe
Looe
Plymouth
Plymouth City
Portwrinkle
Rame
Stoke Gabriel
Modbury
Mothecombe
Dartmouth
Bigbury-on-Sea
ROSCOFF
SANTANDER
0
25 Miles
0
40 Km
N

Map 2

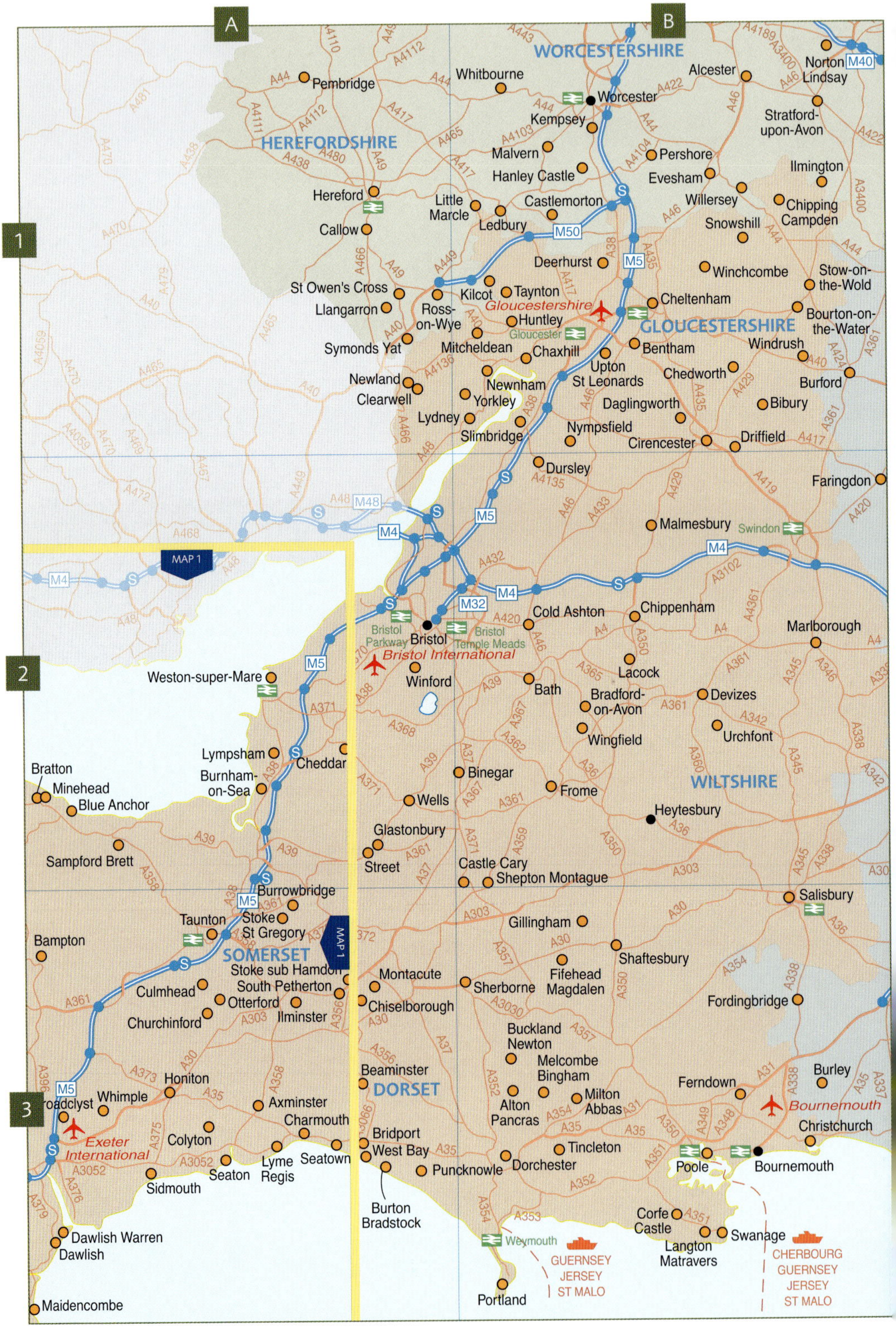

Key to regions: South West England Central England South East England

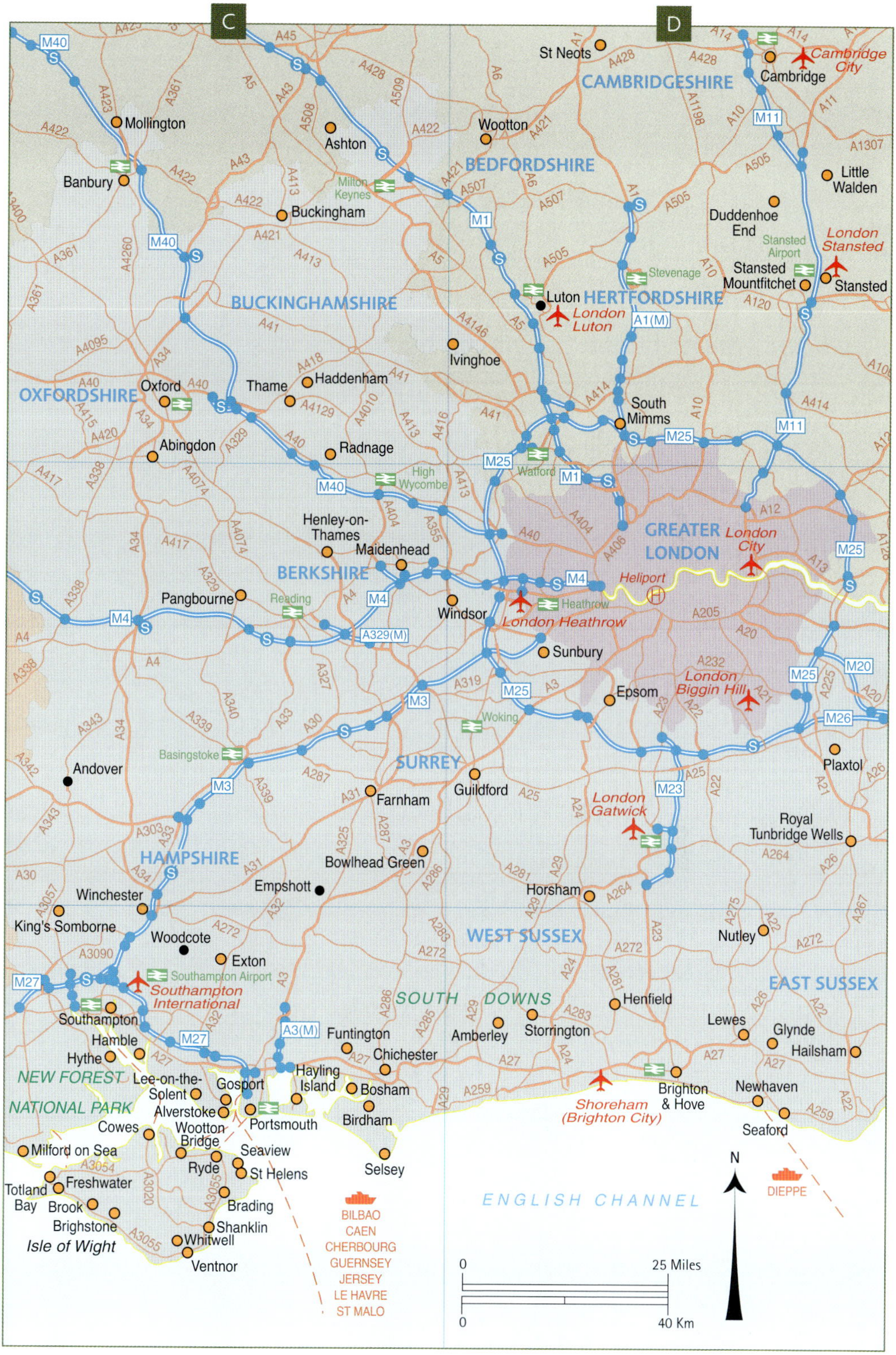

London

Orange circles indicate accommodation within the regional sections of this guide

Map 3

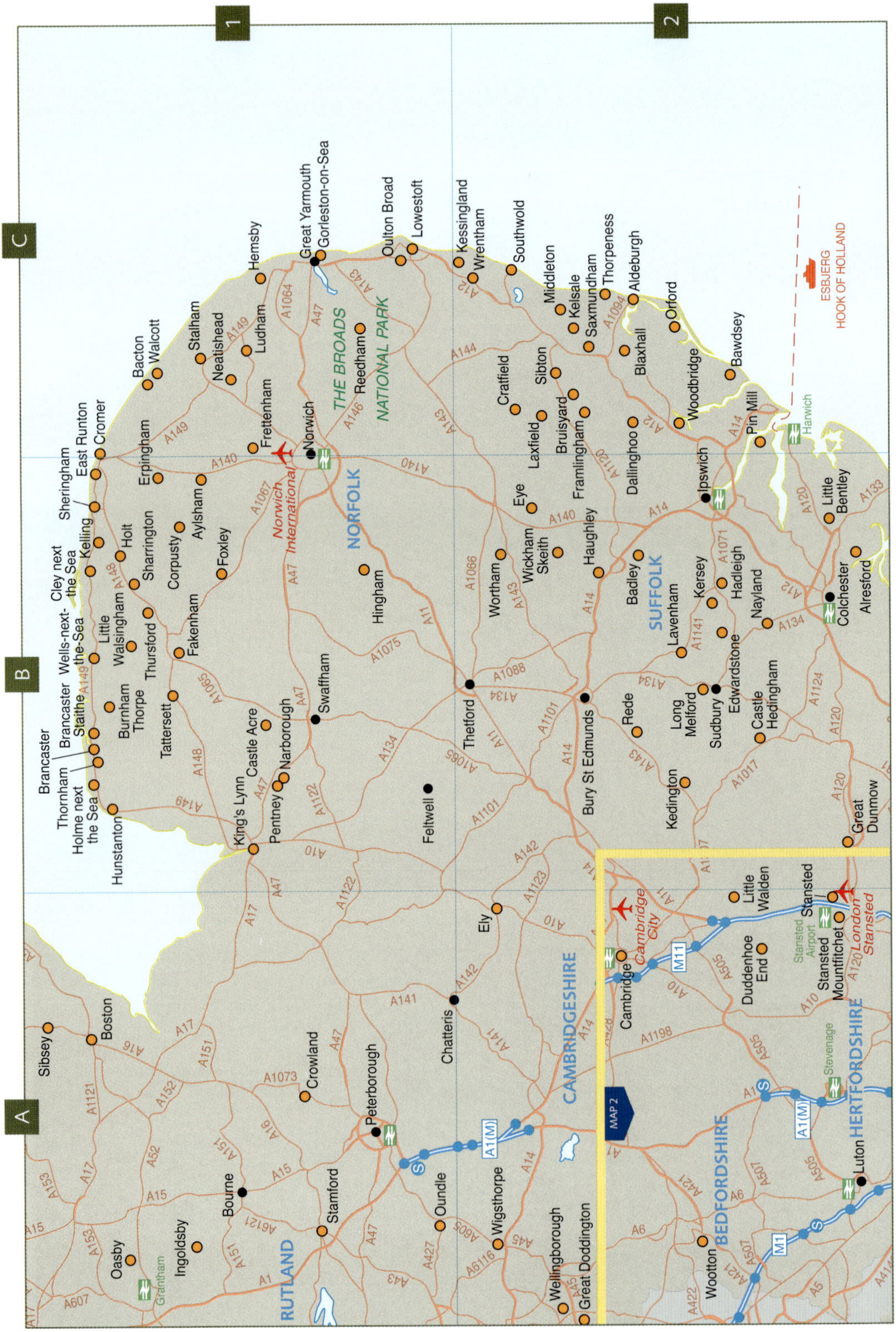

Key to regions: Central England | South East England | London

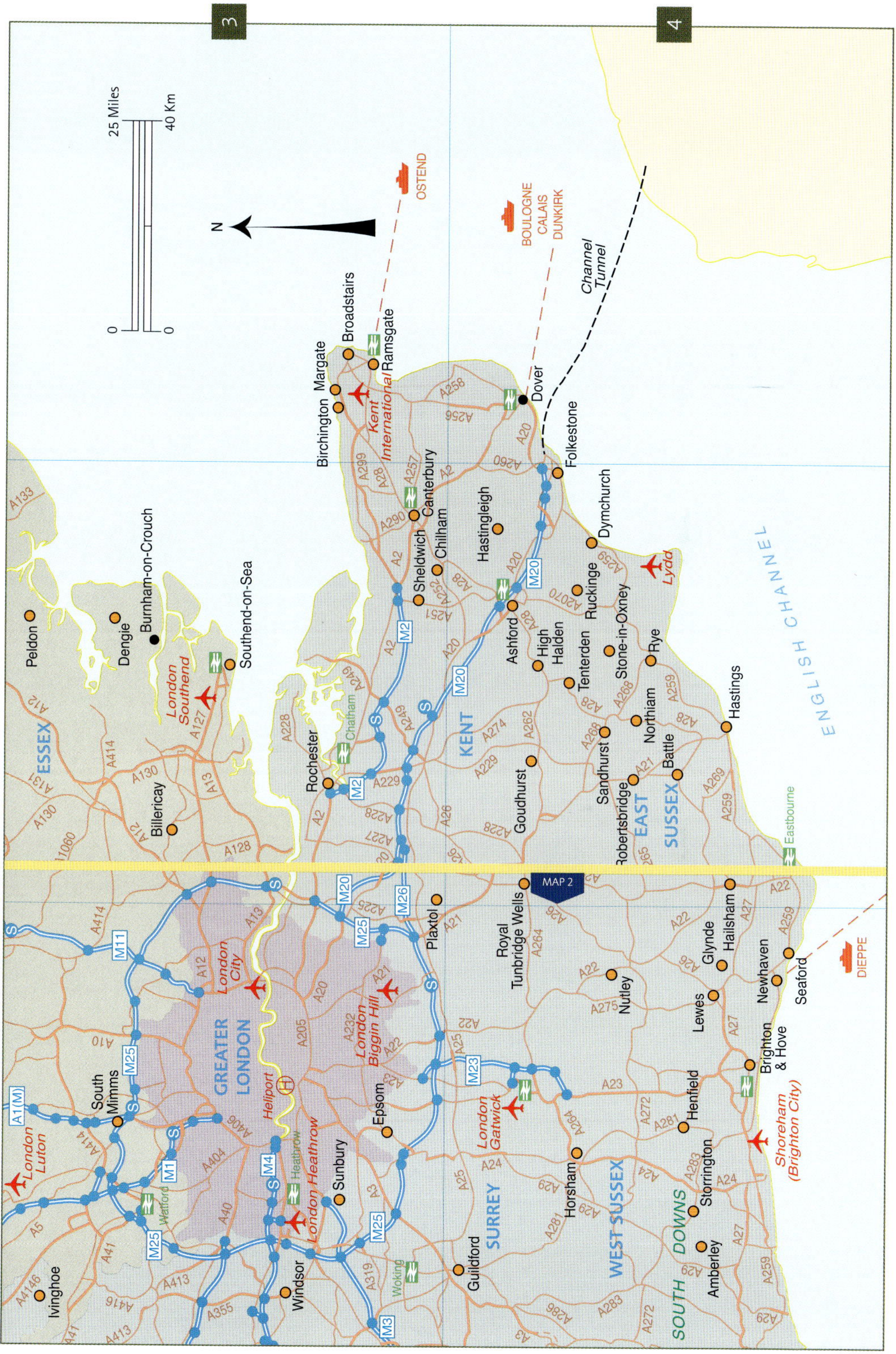
3
4
25 Miles
40 Km
0
0
N
OSTEND
BOULOGNE
CALAIS
DUNKIRK
Channel Tunnel
Broadstairs
Ramsgate
Margate
Birchington
Kent International
Dover
Folkestone
Canterbury
Chilham
Sheldwich
Hastingleigh
Dymchurch
Lydd
Ruckinge
Ashford
High Halden
Tenterden
Stone-in-Oxney
Rye
Northiam
Sandhurst
Hastings
ENGLISH CHANNEL
Battle
Robertsbridge
EAST SUSSEX
Goudhurst
KENT
Chatham
Rochester
Eastbourne
Peldon
Dengie
Burnham-on-Crouch
Southend-on-Sea
London Southend
ESSEX
Billericay
MAP 2
Royal Tunbridge Wells
Plaxtol
Hailsham
Glynde
Newhaven
Seaford
DIEPPE
Lewes
Nutley
Brighton & Hove
Shoreham (Brighton City)
Henfield
Storrington
Amberley
SOUTH DOWNS
WEST SUSSEX
Horsham
London Gatwick
SURREY
Guildford
Woking
Epsom
London Biggin Hill
GREATER LONDON
London City
Heliport
Heathrow
London Heathrow
Sunbury
Windsor
South Mimms
Watford
London Luton
Ivinghoe

Map 4

Key to regions: Northern England Central England

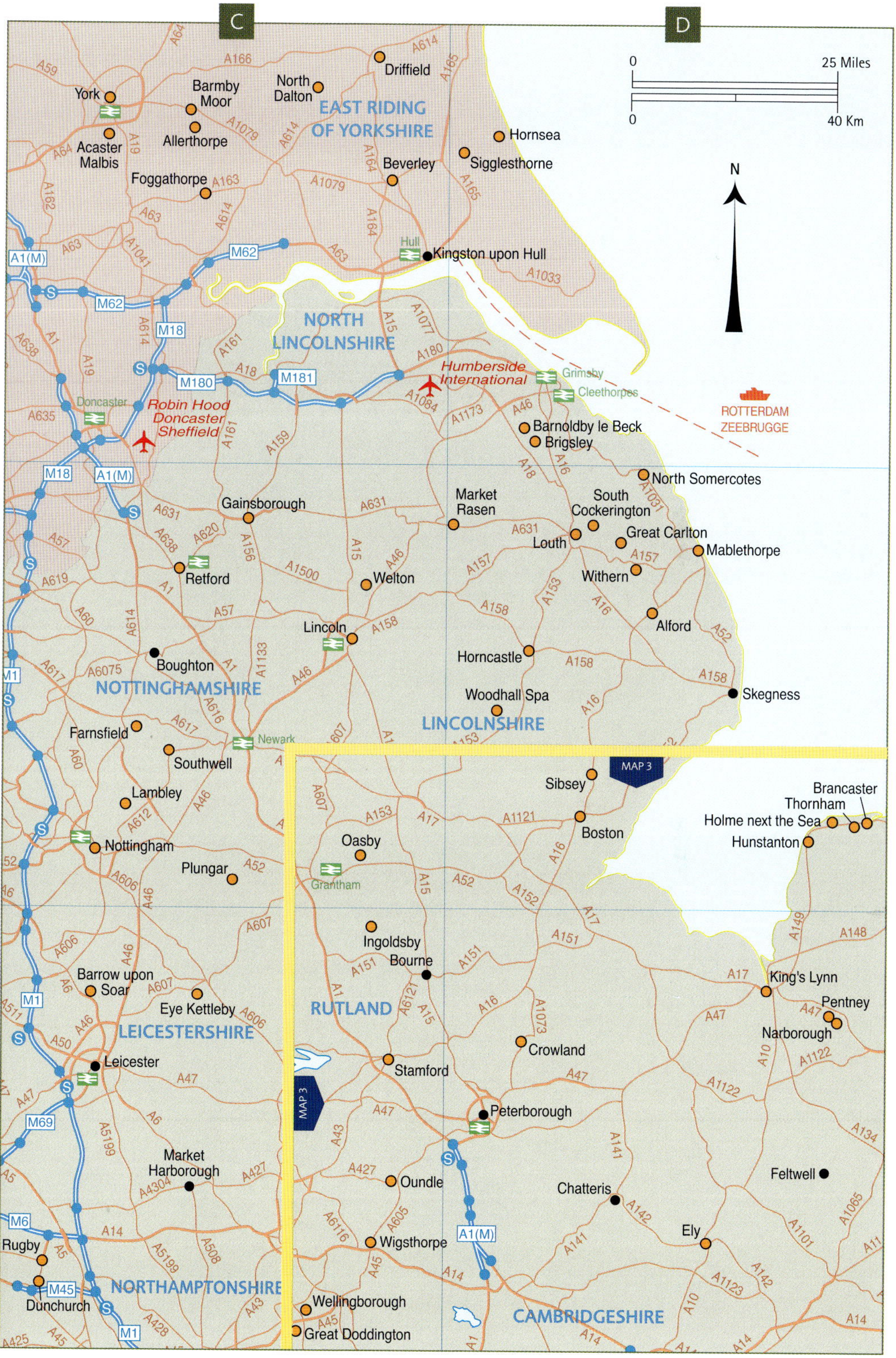

Orange circles indicate accommodation within the regional sections of this guide

Map 5

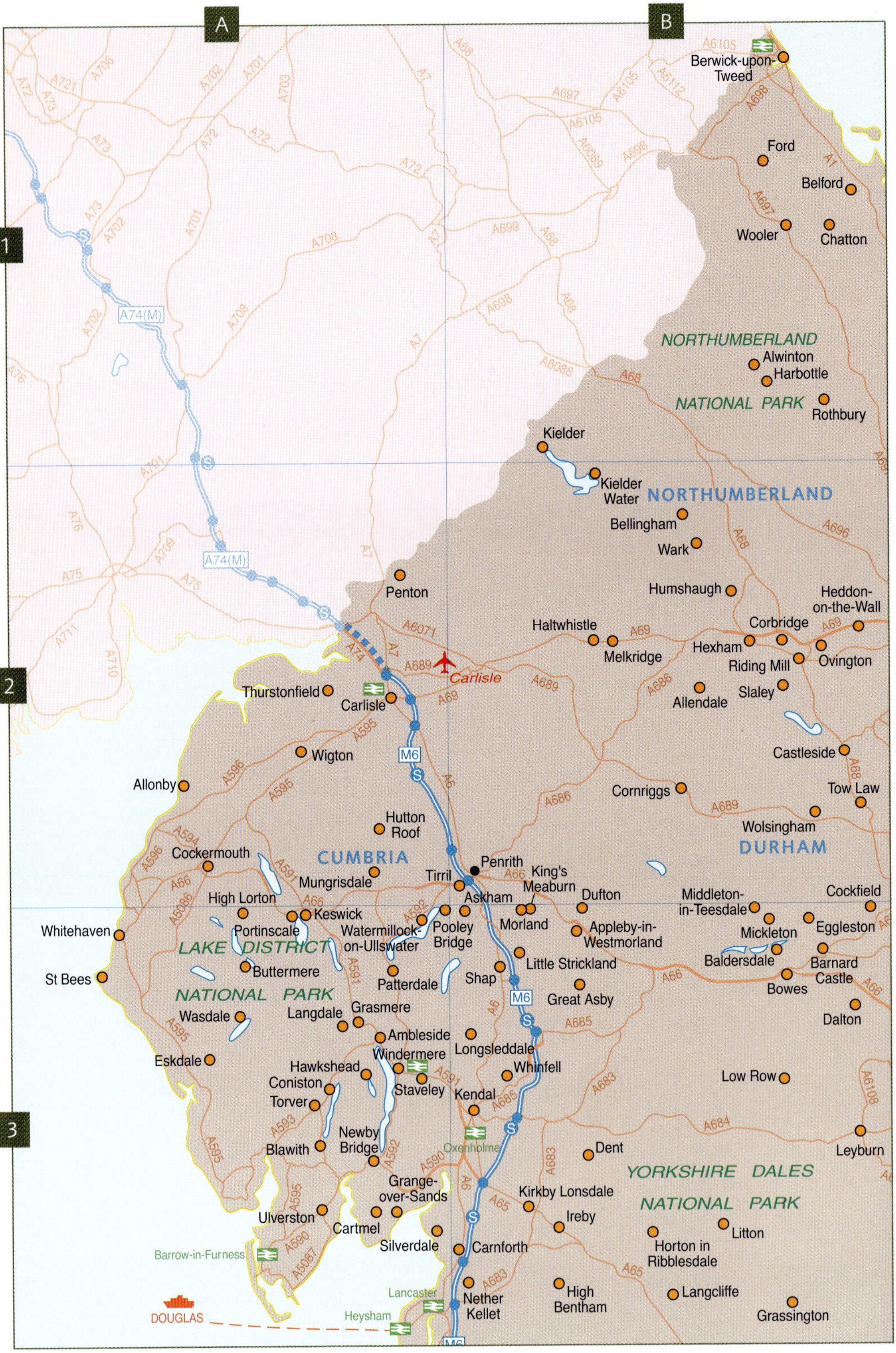

Key to regions: Northern England

Orange circles indicate accommodation within the regional sections of this guide

Map 6

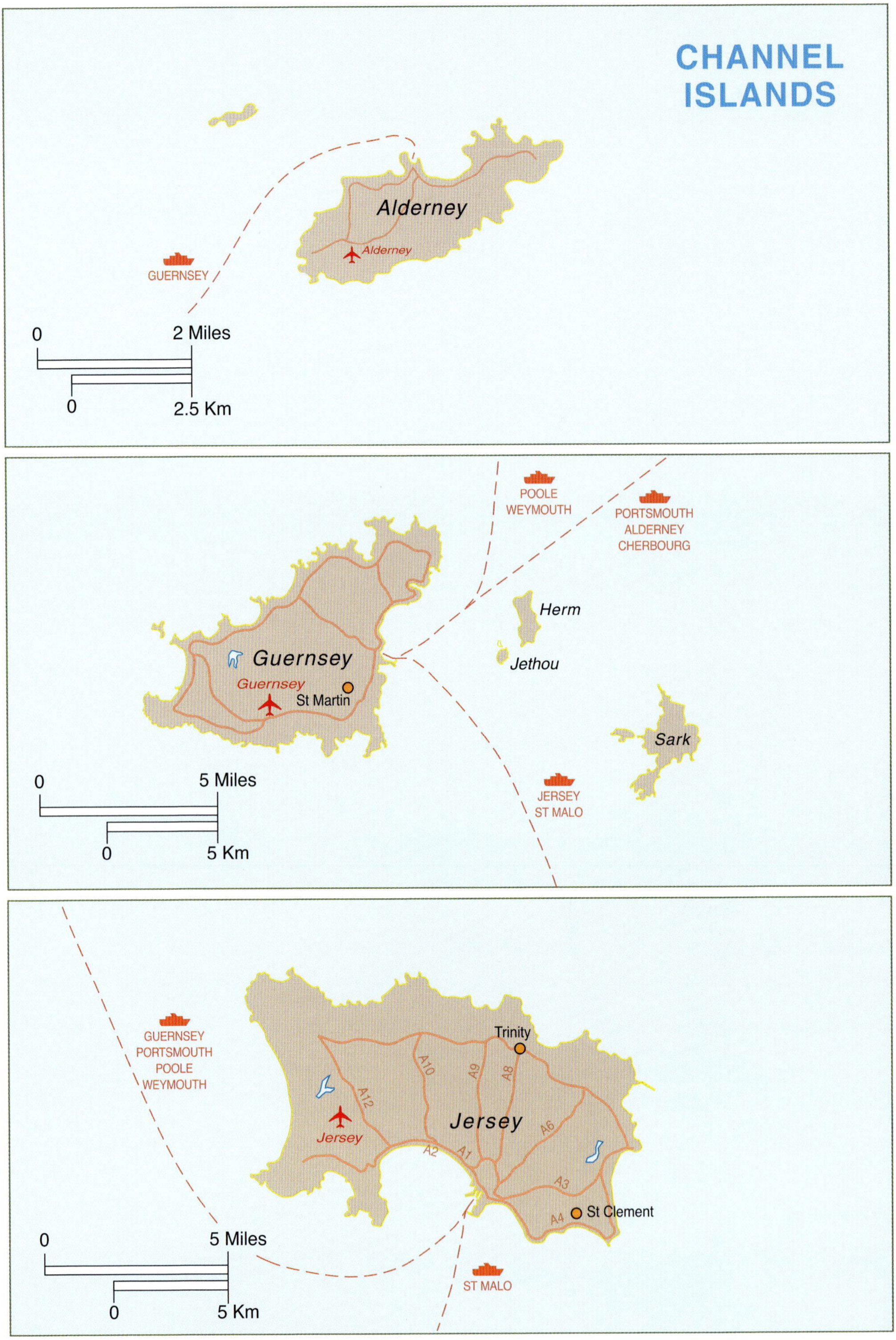

Key to regions: Channel Islands

Orange circles indicate accommodation within the regional sections of this guide

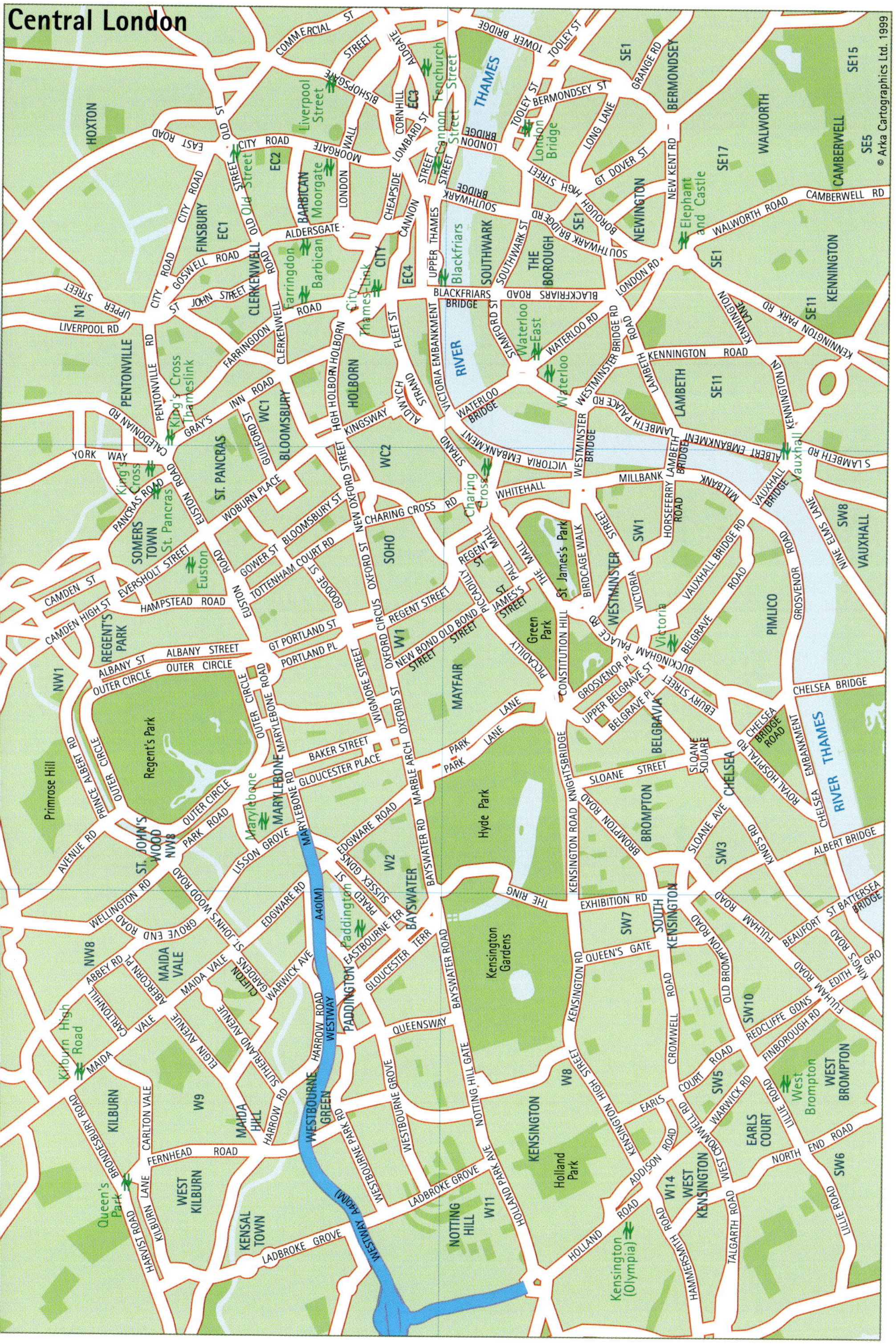
Central London
© Arka Cartographics Ltd. 1999
HOXTON
N1
FINSBURY
EC1
EC2
EC3
EC4
CLERKENWELL
PENTONVILLE
BARBICAN
HOLBORN
BLOOMSBURY
WC1
WC2
ST. PANCRAS
SOMERS TOWN
REGENT'S PARK
NW1
NW8
Primrose Hill
Regent's Park
ST. JOHN'S WOOD
MARYLEBONE
SOHO
MAYFAIR
W1
W2
BAYSWATER
Hyde Park
Kensington Gardens
MAIDA VALE
MAIDA HILL
KILBURN
WEST KILBURN
W9
KENSAL TOWN
NOTTING HILL
W11
KENSINGTON
W8
Holland Park
W14
WEST KENSINGTON
EARLS COURT
SW5
SW6
SW7
SW3
SW10
SOUTH KENSINGTON
BROMPTON
WEST BROMPTON
CHELSEA
BELGRAVIA
PIMLICO
WESTMINSTER
SW1
SW8
VAUXHALL
LAMBETH
SE11
KENNINGTON
SE1
SE5
SE15
SE17
CAMBERWELL
WALWORTH
NEWINGTON
BERMONDSEY
SOUTHWARK
THE BOROUGH
CITY
Green Park
St James's Park
RIVER THAMES
THAMES
Liverpool Street
Fenchurch Street
Cannon Street
Moorgate
Old Street
Barbican
Farringdon
City Thameslink
Blackfriars
London Bridge
Waterloo East
Waterloo
Elephant and Castle
Charing Cross
King's Cross Thameslink
King's Cross
St. Pancras
Euston
Marylebone
Paddington
Victoria
Vauxhall
Kilburn High Road
Queen's Park
Kensington (Olympia)
West Brompton
WESTWAY (A40(M))
A40(M)
TOWER BRIDGE
LONDON BRIDGE
SOUTHWARK BRIDGE
BLACKFRIARS BRIDGE
WATERLOO BRIDGE
WESTMINSTER BRIDGE
LAMBETH BRIDGE
VAUXHALL BRIDGE
CHELSEA BRIDGE
ALBERT BRIDGE
BATTERSEA BRIDGE
CITY ROAD
EUSTON ROAD
MARYLEBONE ROAD
OXFORD ST
REGENT STREET
PICCADILLY
EDGWARE ROAD
BAYSWATER ROAD
KENSINGTON ROAD
BROMPTON ROAD
KING'S RD
FULHAM ROAD
CROMWELL ROAD
HOLLAND PARK AVE
LADBROKE GROVE
HARROW ROAD
CAMDEN HIGH ST
HAMPSTEAD ROAD
TOTTENHAM COURT RD
CHARING CROSS RD
KINGSWAY
STRAND
WHITEHALL
VICTORIA EMBANKMENT
ALBERT EMBANKMENT
CHELSEA EMBANKMENT
MILLBANK
KENNINGTON ROAD
WALWORTH ROAD
CAMBERWELL RD
NEW KENT RD
BLACKFRIARS ROAD
WATERLOO RD
PARK LANE
BAKER STREET
SLOANE STREET

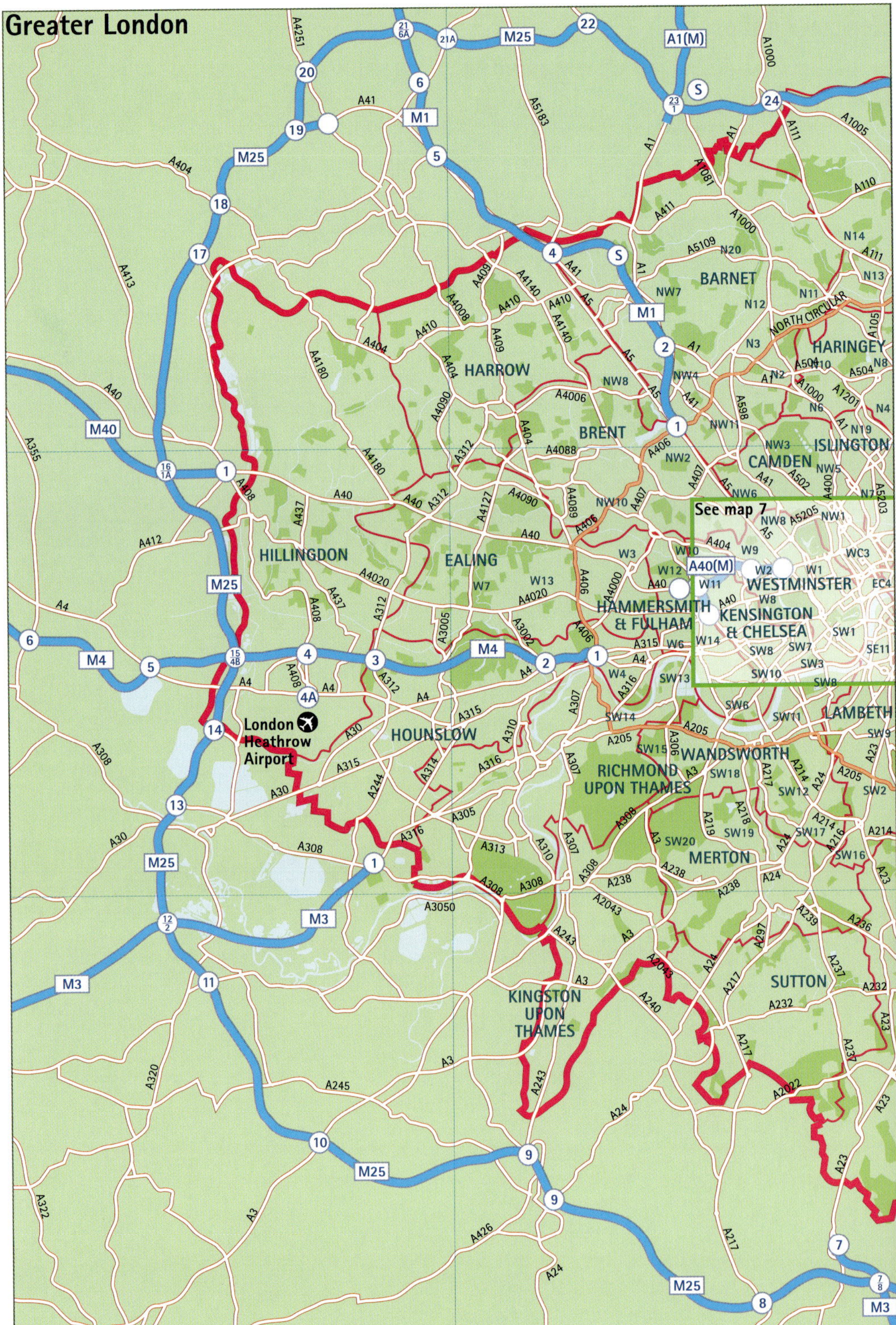
Greater London
See map 7
BARNET
HARINGEY
HARROW
BRENT
CAMDEN
ISLINGTON
HILLINGDON
EALING
WESTMINSTER
HAMMERSMITH & FULHAM
KENSINGTON & CHELSEA
HOUNSLOW
LAMBETH
WANDSWORTH
RICHMOND UPON THAMES
MERTON
SUTTON
KINGSTON UPON THAMES
London Heathrow Airport
NORTH CIRCULAR
M25
M1
M40
M4
M3
A1(M)
A40(M)
NW1
NW2
NW3
NW4
NW5
NW6
NW7
NW8
NW10
NW11
N2
N3
N6
N8
N10
N11
N12
N13
N14
N19
N20
W1
W2
W3
W4
W6
W7
W8
W9
W10
W11
W12
W13
W14
WC3
EC4
SW1
SW2
SW3
SW6
SW7
SW8
SW9
SW10
SW11
SW12
SW13
SW14
SW15
SW16
SW17
SW18
SW19
SW20
SE11

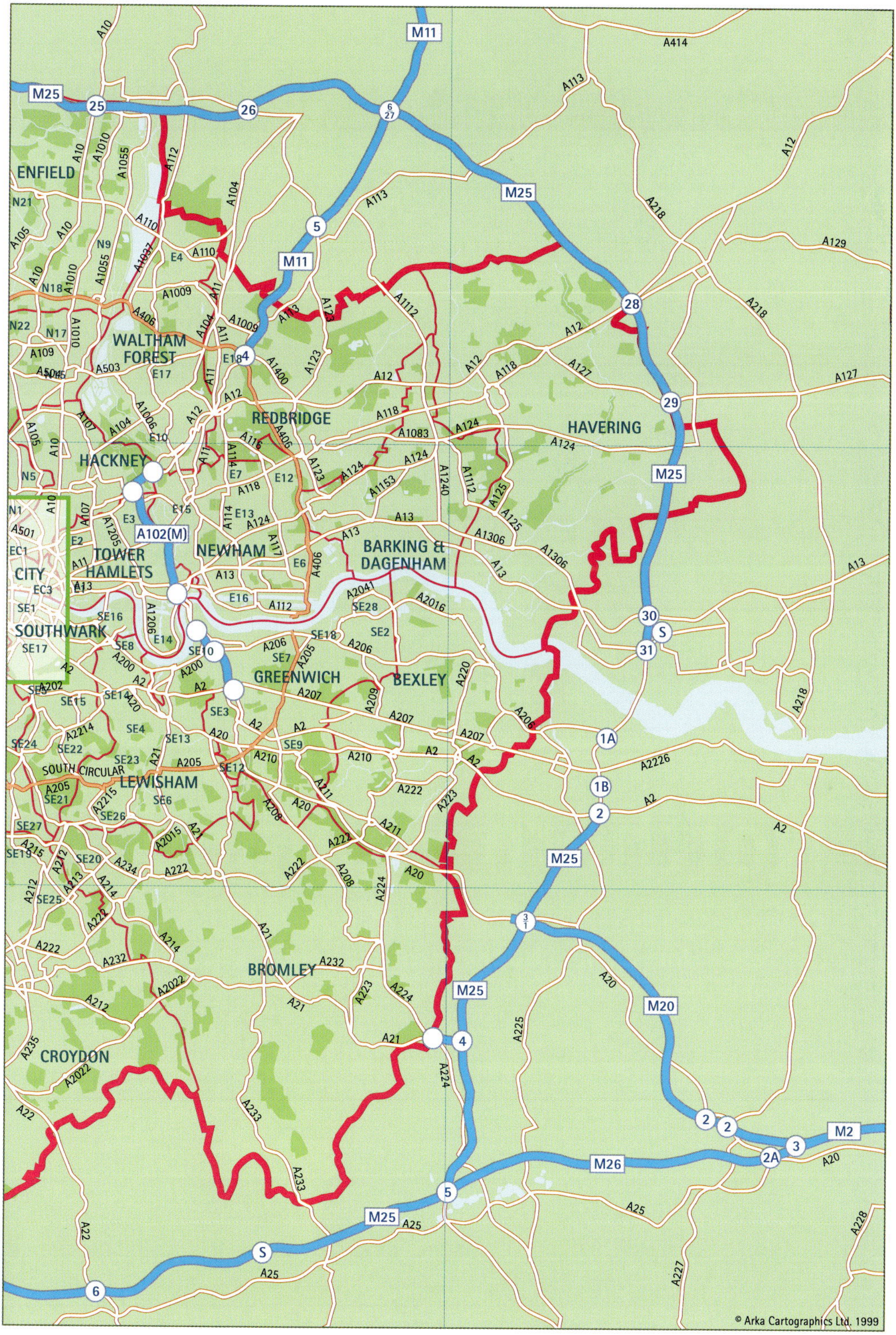
ENFIELD
WALTHAM FOREST
REDBRIDGE
HAVERING
HACKNEY
NEWHAM
TOWER HAMLETS
CITY
SOUTHWARK
BARKING & DAGENHAM
GREENWICH
BEXLEY
LEWISHAM
BROMLEY
CROYDON
M25
M11
M20
M26
M2
A102(M)
SOUTH CIRCULAR

Northern England

Cheshire, Cumbria, Durham, Greater Manchester, Lancashire, Merseyside, Northumberland, Tees Valley, Tyne and Wear, Yorkshire

Clockwise: Bamburgh Castle, Northumberland; Liverpool; North Yorkshire Moors Railway

Great days out

Explore windswept moors and breathtaking coastlines. Admire mirrored-glass lakes and magnificent cathedrals. Discover pioneering industrial heritage and cutting-edge cities. Northern England is a proud fusion of history, dramatic landscapes and modern culture – not forgetting fun-filled seaside resorts!

Relive the revolution

Where did the Industrial Revolution gather pace? In Northern England, of course! Experience its legacy in so many ways. At **Beamish Museum**, a town, colliery village and farm have been recreated using authentic early 19th and 20thC buildings – get around by tramcar and chat to costumed interpreters. Children love living history this way. Hear vivid tales at the **National Coal Mining Museum for England** at Wakefield, put on hat, belt and battery and tour underground with an experienced miner. Clamber onto historic craft at **The National Waterways Museum**, Ellesmere Port. Or maybe trains are more your style? Go spotting at **Locomotion, The National Railway Museum** in Shildon, one of the oldest railway towns in the world. Steaming Days get dads as excited as the kids.

Natural highs

Wide-open spaces abound in the National Parks – Yorkshire alone has over 1,000 square miles to explore. Escape and hear your laughter in the breeze as you fly a kite from high on the **North York Moors**. You can always pick up tips from the professionals at Sunderland International Kite Festival. **The Lake District and Cumbria** have inspired poets, painters and climbers, and Wastwater was recently voted 'Britain's favourite view'. Enjoy it at ground level or hike up Scafell Pike, England's highest peak, for a stunning aerial picture. You'll also feel on top of the world cycling or walking to **East Lancashire's Panopticons**, a series of innovative structures pointing the way to panoramic countryside: Halo, illuminating the Rossendale night sky, is simply breathtaking.

For more firsts and highs, ramble the **North Pennines Area of Outstanding Natural Beauty**, Britain's first geopark. Weardale and Teesdale are renowned for dazzling waterfalls – aptly named **High Force** is England's highest. Build castles along rippled-sand beaches, such as Spittal and St Aidans, in the North East. Board a boat to **Holy Island** to learn the secrets of the Lindisfarne Gospels. And remember the binoculars on the **Farne Islands** – home to hundreds of thousands of puffins and dewy-eyed grey seals.

Wastwater, Cumbria

Join the Romans

Pace along **Hadrian's Wall** in the footsteps of soldiers nearly two millennia ago. Built in just six years, it runs for an amazing 73 miles. **Chesters** is Britain's best-preserved Roman cavalry fort and you can find out more about Romans in the region at **Tullie House**

Left to right: Alnwick Castle, Northumberland; York Minster

why not... cycle the shoreline of Coniston Water, perfect for easygoing family rides?

Museum and Art Gallery, Carlisle. In the walled city of Chester, Britain's best-preserved Roman town, visit the partially excavated amphitheatre or the **Dewa Roman Experience** where you can step aboard a Roman galley, stroll a reconstructed street and handle 'dig' discoveries.

Grand designs

Northern England has more than its fair share of remarkable buildings. Please the children with a visit to **Alnwick Castle**, aka Hogwarts in the first Harry Potter films. They'll be enthralled by one of the world's largest treehouses, too. **Tatton Park** in Cheshire is among the most complete historic estates, featuring a mansion, gardens, farm, Tudor Old Hall, deer park and speciality shops. And **Castle Howard**, near York, sets an impressive standard in home décor with its Canalettos, Holbeins and Gainsboroughs. Seek green-fingered inspiration at **Sheffield's Winter Garden**, which grows more than 2,500 plants from around the world in a huge temperate glasshouse the size of 5,000 domestic greenhouses!

Tiptoe beneath the towering vaulted ceilings of **York Minster**, the largest medieval Gothic cathedral in Northern Europe and home to glittering stained glass collections. Durham City's medieval cobbled streets are crowned by the magnificent towers of **Durham Castle and Cathedral** – 'the best cathedral on planet earth', according to travel writer Bill Bryson. And now's the time to discover the twin **Anglo-Saxon monasteries at Wearmouth and Jarrow**, the UK's nomination for World Heritage Status in 2009.

Young hearts and minds

Candyfloss and sticky rock, thrills and spills – **Blackpool** is your dream ticket for family fun. Book ringside seats at the **Tower Circus**, and gasp in amazement as international artists

Blackpool

perform superhuman feats. Hop onto sock-popping rides at **Camelot Theme Park** near Chorley or **Go Ape!** in Grizedale Forest on rope bridges and Tarzan swings. Then stimulate the brain cells at **Rotherham's Magna** on an elemental interactive adventure through fire, earth, air and water. Or take the plunge at **The Deep** in Hull and come nose to nose with sharks in the submarium.

Modern city culture

There's also plenty to keep pulses racing in Northern England's dynamic cities where regeneration is the name of the game. Enjoy the renaissance of **NewcastleGateshead**, highlighted by the stunning architecture of the **Gateshead Millennium Bridge**. New artists at the **Baltic Centre for Contemporary Art** keep pushing the boundaries. Explore **Liverpool** and **Manchester**, both vibrant club scenes – of the soccer and night-time variety. Liverpool, revered birthplace of The Beatles, is still sparking from its European Capital of Culture 2008 status. Tour the revitalised **Albert Dock** along the World Heritage waterfront and sample the contemporary art of **Tate Liverpool**.

why not... join a ghost walk around York, claimed as Europe's most haunted city?

In **Manchester** head for **Salford Quays** and **The Lowry**, the inspirational waterfront centre for the visual arts and entertainment. The daring aluminium **Imperial War Museum North** designed by Daniel Libeskind is a showstopper, one of Manchester's many free museums. Next up: **Leeds** has a new must-see **City Museum** featuring an astounding Treasures Gallery. Middlesbrough, though not a city, also beckons with the recently opened **Middlesbrough Institute of Modern Art** housing works by Tracey Emin and other headline names.

Clockwise: NewcastleGateshead; The Deep, Hull; The Lowry, Manchester

Destinations

Berwick-upon-Tweed

England's northernmost town guards the mouth of the River Tweed. Marvel at some of the finest 16thC city walls in Europe, built by Elizabeth I to protect the town. Visit Bamburgh Castle and the beautiful gardens at Alnwick. Roam magnificent Heritage coastline and see Holy Island and the fairytale Lindisfarne Castle.

Bamburgh near Berwick-upon-Tweed

Blackpool

Britain's favourite holiday resort. Experience thrills and excitement at the Pleasure Beach, take tea in the magnificent Tower Ballroom, or stroll the seven miles of sandy beaches. Blackpool offers you world-class shows, cosmopolitan restaurants, vibrant nightlife, an active sports scene and breathtakingly beautiful scenery on the doorstep.

Chester

Experience one of Europe's top heritage cities. Walk the unique city walls, then visit the famous Rows, unique two-tiered galleries, to shop for everything from antiques to high fashion. Stroll along the banks of the beautiful River Dee, explore the Roman amphitheatre, and spend a day at Chester's famous Roodee Racecourse.

Cumbria – The Lake District

With breathtaking mountains and sparkling lakes, the unsurpassed scenery of Cumbria – The Lake District has inspired writers and poets across the ages. Explore the best walking and climbing routes that England has to offer, and see for yourself 'Britain's favourite view'. Take a lake cruise, visit wonderful homes and gardens or simply enjoy the views.

Durham

Described by Bill Bryson as 'a perfect little city.' Explore majestic Durham Cathedral, a World Heritage Site, and thought by many to be the finest Norman church architecture in England. Visit the tombs of St Cuthbert and the Venerable Bede. Take a coffee in the cobbled Market Place and enjoy the stunning floral displays, or walk down to the riverbank for magnificent views.

Hull

Enjoy the invigorating yet relaxing atmosphere that only a waterfront city can offer. Visit the Museum Quarter linking four of Hull's eight free museums. Don't miss 'The Deep', home to 40 sharks and one of the most spectacular sea-life attractions in the world. Marvel at the engineering of the Humber Bridge and, after dark, experience Hull's very own café bar culture.

Leeds

Rich local history, world-class sport, outstanding museums and galleries, and diverse year-round entertainment, that's Leeds. It's a shopaholic's dream, from the elegant Corn Exchange to the exquisite Victoria Quarter, not to mention the only Harvey Nichols outside London. See opera and dance at the Opera North and Northern Ballet and explore the Yorkshire Dales right on the doorstep.

National Park
Area of Outstanding Natural Beauty
Heritage Coast
National Trails
nationaltrail.co.uk
Sections of the
National Cycle Network
nationalcyclenetwork.org.uk
Berwick-upon-Tweed
Holy Island/
Lindisfarne
Bamburgh
Northumberland
Coast
Wooler
Alnwick
PENNINE
WAY
NORTHUMBERLAND
Kielder Water
and Forest Park
Druridge
Druridge
Bay
Bellingham
HADRIAN'S
WALL PATH
Tynemouth
South Shields
Solway
Coast
Carlisle
Newcastle
Gateshead
Sunderland
Silloth
Derwent
Reservoir
Durham
North
Pennines
Stanhope
Maryport
Penrith
Hartlepool
Middleton-
in-Teesdale
Stockton-
on-Tees
Middlesbrough
Workington
Keswick
Saltburn-by-the-Sea
Whitehaven
Barnard
Castle
Darlington
Whitby
Kirkby
Stephen
LAKE DISTRICT
Ambleside
Dalegarth
Windermere
NORTH YORK
MOORS
CLEVELAND
WAY
Scarborough
Ravenglass
Filey
Helmsley
YORKSHIRE
DALES
Grange-
over-Sands
Kirkby
Lonsdale
Ulverston
Arnside &
Silverdale
Barrow-
in-Furness
DALES WAY
Ripon
Howardian
Hills
Nidderdale
Bridlington
Harrogate
Lancaster
Forest of
Bowland
York
YORKSHIRE
WOLDS WAY
Skipton
Ilkley
Haworth
Leeds
Blackpool
Bradford
Hull
Preston
Blackburn
Withernsea
Wakefield
Huddersfield
Southport
Halifax
Chorley
Barnsley
PENNINE
BRIDLEWAY
PEAK
DISTRICT
Doncaster
Manchester
Liverpool
Rotherham
Sheffield
Neston
Ellesmere Port
Knutsford
Chester
Macclesfield
Nantwich
0
50 miles
0
75 kms

Durham

Liverpool

Experience the unique atmosphere of Liverpool. The birthplace of the Beatles and European Capital of Culture 2008 offers you more theatres, museums and galleries than any UK city outside London. Its history as one of the world's great ports has left a remarkable legacy of art and architecture to explore, not forgetting, the city's famous sporting pedigree. So if it's Strawberry Fields, Premiership football or Europe's finest culture you're looking for, it has to be Liverpool.

Manchester

Explore a city that has reinvented itself as a truly contemporary metropolis. You'll find modern landmark buildings, a wealth of art and culture, great bars and world-class hospitality. There's every experience imaginable, from fine dining and top-class theatre, to major sporting events and year-round festivals. It's a shopping destination in its own right, rivalling that of the capital, with top stores and chic boutiques.

Clockwise: Chester; Leeds; Martindale, Cumbria

NewcastleGateshead

Must-see attractions including the award-winning Gateshead Millennium Bridge, the Baltic Centre for Contemporary Art and the magnificent new Sage Gateshead, a stunning Sir Norman Foster building, with billowing curves of glass and steel catering for every genre of music. Rich in culture, architecture and history and with a great reputation for style, shopping and nightlife, the variety of life in NewcastleGateshead surprises even the most well travelled visitor.

Whitby

With its quaint cobbled streets and picturesque houses standing on the steep slopes of the River Esk, Whitby is dominated by its cliff top Abbey. Explore one of Britain's finest stretches of coastline. Climb the steps to the parish church of St Mary, whose churchyard inspired Bram Stocker's 'Dracula'. Then down to the historic quayside of this 1,000-year-old port and celebrate the town's seafaring tradition at the Captain Cook Festival, named in honour of Whitby's most famous son.

York

Visit award-winning attractions including the magnificent York Minster, and the world's biggest and best railway museum. Let 21stC technology transport you back to the Viking age at Jorvik, and wander through the terrifying York Dungeon. Pedestrianised streets make York an ideal city to explore on foot. Follow the city's specialist shopping trails '5 Routes to Shopping Heaven', or browse the specialist antique and book dealers.

For lots more great ideas visit enjoyEngland.com/destinations

Visitor attractions

Family and Fun

Aquarium of the Lakes
Lakeside, Cumbria
(015395) 30153
aquariumofthelakes.co.uk
Freshwater aquarium complete with underwater viewing tunnel.

Beamish, The North of England Open Air Museum
Beamish, Durham
(0191) 370 4000
beamish.org.uk
Award-winning open-air museum of working life.

Blackpool Tower & Circus
Blackpool, Lancashire
(01253) 622242
blackpooltower.co.uk
Entertainment for all ages, night and day.

Blue Planet Aquarium
Ellesmere Port, Cheshire
(0151) 357 8804
blueplanetaquarium.com
Underwater adventure in the UK's largest aquarium.

Chester Zoo
Chester, Cheshire
(01244) 380280
chesterzoo.org
Meet over 7,000 animals and 500 species.

Darlington Railway Centre and Museum
Darlington, Durham
(01325) 460532
drcm.org.uk
See, touch and feel living railway heritage.

The Deep
Hull, East Yorkshire
(01482) 381000
thedeep.co.uk
One of the world's most spectacular aquariums.

Hartlepool's Maritime Experience
Hartlepool, Durham
(01429) 860077
hartlepoolsmaritimeexperience.com
Authentic reconstruction of an 18thC seaport.

JORVIK Viking Centre
York, North Yorkshire
(01904) 543400
jorvik-viking-centre.co.uk
Meet the Vikings, face-to-face.

Killhope, The North of England Lead Mining Museum
Cowshill, Durham
(01388) 537505
durham.gov.uk/killhope
Award-winning underground experience.

Liverpool Football Club Museum and Stadium Tour
Liverpool
(0151) 260 6677
liverpoolfc.tv
Touch the famous 'This is Anfield' sign!

Locomotion: The National Railway Museum at Shildon
Shildon, Durham
(01388) 777999
locomotion.uk.com
Historic buildings and vehicles celebrate railway heritage.

Magna Science Adventure Centre
Rotherham, South Yorkshire
(01709) 720002
visitmagna.co.uk
An unforgettable, interactive science adventure.

Manchester United Museum & Tour
Manchester
0870 442 1994
manutd.com
Official tour of the 'Theatre of Dreams'.

Merseyside Maritime Museum
Liverpool
(0151) 478 4499
merseysidemaritimemuseum.org.uk
Liverpool's seafaring heritage brought to life.

MOSI (Museum of Science and Industry)
Manchester
(0161) 832 2244
mosi.org.uk
Five historic buildings packed with fascinating displays.

The National Waterways Museum
Ellesmere Port, Cheshire
(0151) 355 5017
nwm.org.uk
Britain's largest collection of inland waterway craft.

Nature's World
Middlesbrough
(01642) 594895
naturesworld.org.uk
Pioneering eco-garden of the future.

Saltburn Smugglers Heritage Centre
Saltburn-by-the-Sea, Tees Valley
(01287) 625252
redcar-cleveland.gov.uk/leisure
Meet costumed characters in ancient fishermens' cottages.

Seven Stories, The Centre for Children's Books
Newcastle upon Tyne, Tyne and Wear
0845 271 0777
sevenstories.org.uk
Britain's first centre dedicated to children's literature.

Yorkshire Waterways Museum
Goole, East Yorkshire
(01405) 768730
waterwaysmuseum.org.uk
Museum, adventure centre and nature trail.

Heritage

Alnwick Castle
Alnwick, Northumberland
(01665) 510777
alnwickcastle.com
Dazzling medieval castle with glorious state rooms.

Arley Hall & Gardens
Northwich, Cheshire
(01565) 777353
arleyhallandgardens.com
Charming stately home and award-winning gardens.

Bamburgh Castle
Bamburgh, Northumberland
(01668) 214515
bamburghcastle.com
Imposing castle in dramatic coastal setting.

Beeston Castle
Beeston, Cheshire
(01829) 260464
english-heritage.org.uk
13thC castle with views over eight counties.

Belsay Hall, Castle and Gardens
Newcastle upon Tyne, Tyne and Wear
(01661) 881636
english-heritage.org.uk
Medieval castle, 17thC manor and gardens.

Brodsworth Hall and Gardens
Doncaster, South Yorkshire
(01302) 724969
english-heritage.org.uk
Italianate house with marvellous labyrinthine gardens.

Castle Howard
York, North Yorkshire
(01653) 648444
castlehoward.co.uk
Magnificent 18thC house in stunning parkland.

Chester Cathedral
Chester, Cheshire
(01244) 324756
chestercathedral.com
Medieval cathedral with spectacular carved choir stalls.

Durham Castle
Durham
(0191) 334 3800
durhamcastle.com
Superb Norman castle in World Heritage Site.

Fountains Abbey and Studley Royal Water Garden
Ripon, North Yorkshire
(01765) 608888
fountainsabbey.org.uk
12thC monastic ruin with captivating landscaped gardens.

Harewood House
Harewood, West Yorkshire
(0113) 218 1010
harewood.org
Stunning architecture and exquisite Adam interiors.

Holker Hall and Gardens
Cark in Cartmel, Cumbria
(015395) 58328
holker-hall.co.uk
Magnificent Neo-Elizabethan mansion and award-winning gardens.

Levens Hall & Gardens
Levens, Cumbria
(015395) 60321
levenshall.co.uk
Elizabethan mansion and world-famous topiary gardens.

Lyme Park
Disley, Cheshire
(01663) 766492
nationaltrust.org.uk
Tudor house transformed into an Italianate palace.

National Coal Mining Museum for England
Wakefield, West Yorkshire
(01924) 848806
ncm.org.uk
Award-winning museum of the English coalfields.

Newby Hall & Gardens
Ripon, North Yorkshire
0845 450 4068
newbyhall.com
One of England's renowned Adam houses.

North Yorkshire Moors Railway
Pickering, North Yorkshire
(01751) 472508
nymr.co.uk
Nostalgic steam excursions through spectacular landscapes.

Ripley Castle
Ripley, North Yorkshire
(01423) 770152
ripleycastle.co.uk
Medieval castle set in a delightful estate.

Sewerby Hall and Gardens
Sewerby, East Yorkshire
(01262) 673769
sewerby-hall.co.uk
Country house and gardens in cliff-top location.

Speke Hall, Garden and Estate
Speke, Merseyside
(0151) 427 7231
nationaltrust.org.uk
Wonderful, rambling Tudor mansion with Victorian interiors.

Indoors

1853 Gallery
Shipley, West Yorkshire
(01274) 531163
saltsmill.org.uk
Works by Hockney in historic mill buildings.

BALTIC Centre for Contemporary Art
Gateshead, Tyne and Wear
(0191) 478 1810
balticmill.com
Dynamic international art.

The Bowes Museum
Barnard Castle, Durham
(01833) 690606
thebowesmuseum.org.uk
Outstanding European fine and decorative arts.

Captain Cook Birthplace Museum
Middlesbrough
(01642) 311211
captcook-ne.co.uk
Learn about Cook's life.

Discovery Museum
Newcastle upon Tyne, Tyne and Wear
(0191) 232 6789
twmuseums.org.uk/discovery
The history of Tyneside brought to life.

Imperial War Museum North
Manchester
(0161) 836 4000
iwm.org.uk
Dynamic displays reflecting the impact of war.

Jodrell Bank Visitor Centre
Holmes Chapel, Cheshire
(01477) 571339
jb.man.ac.uk/scicen
Home of the world-famous Lovell Telescope.

Leeds City Art Gallery
Leeds, West Yorkshire
(0113) 247 8256
leeds.gov.uk/artgallery
Remarkable collection of 20thC British art.

The Lowry
Salford, Manchester
(0161) 876 2000
thelowry.com
World-renowned art gallery, exhibitions and theatre.

Millennium Galleries
Sheffield, South Yorkshire
(0114) 278 2600
sheffieldgalleries.org.uk
Vibrant galleries of arts, craft and design.

mima, Middlesbrough Institute of Modern Art
Middlesbrough
(01642) 726720
visitmima.com
Inspiring modern and contemporary art.

National Glass Centre
Sunderland, Tyne and Wear
(0191) 515 5555
nationalglasscentre.com
Stunning displays and live glass-blowing.

National Media Museum
Bradford, West Yorkshire
0870 701 0200
nationalmediamuseum.org.uk
Seven-floor gallery featuring giant IMAX screen.

Royal Armouries Museum
Leeds, West Yorkshire
(0113) 220 1916
royalarmouries.org
Thrilling entertainment and world-famous arms collection.

Tullie House Museum and Art Gallery
Large Visitor Attraction of the Year - Silver
Carlisle, Cumbria
(01228) 618718
tulliehouse.co.uk
Jacobean house, Pre-Raphaelite art and interactive fun.

South Shields Museum and Art Gallery
South Shields, Tyne and Wear
(0191) 456 8740
twmuseums.org.uk/southshields
Explore the history of South Tyneside.

Sunderland Museum and Winter Gardens
Sunderland, Tyne and Wear
(0191) 553 2323
twmuseums.org.uk/sunderland
Stunning winter gardens and imaginative galleries.

Tate Liverpool
Liverpool
(0151) 702 7400
tate.org.uk/liverpool
Housing the National Collection of Modern Art.

Thackray Museum
Leeds, West Yorkshire
(0113) 244 4343
thackraymuseum.org
Experience Victorian slums, explore the human body.

The Whitworth Art Gallery
Manchester
(0161) 275 7450
whitworth.man.ac.uk
Internationally famous collection of British watercolours.

World Museum Liverpool
Liverpool
(0151) 478 4393
liverpoolmuseums.org.uk
Featuring the award-winning Natural History Centre.

The World of Glass
St Helens, Merseyside
(01744) 22766
worldofglass.com
Live glass-blowing and multi-media shows.

Outdoors

Chesters Roman Fort (Hadrian's Wall)
Chollerford, Northumberland
(01434) 681379
english-heritage.org.uk
The best-preserved Roman cavalry fort in Britain.

Go Ape! High Wire Forest Adventure – Grizedale
Grizedale, Cumbria
0845 643 9215
goape.co.uk
High-adrenaline adventure in the trees.

Go Ape! High Wire Forest Adventure – Dalby
Low Dalby, North Yorkshire
0845 643 9215
goape.co.uk
Exhilarating course of bridges, swings and slides.

Hadrian's Wall Path National Trail
Hexham, Northumberland
(01434) 322002
nationaltrail.co.uk/hadrianswall
84-mile trail stretching from coast to coast.

Kielder Castle Forest Park Centre
Kielder, Northumberland
(01434) 250209
forestry.gov.uk
Visitor centre for England's largest forest.

National Wildflower Centre
Liverpool
(0151) 738 1913
nwc.org.uk
A peaceful haven with seasonal wildflower displays.

RHS Garden Harlow Carr
Harrogate, North Yorkshire
(01423) 565418
rhs.org.uk/harlowcarr
Spectacular 58-acre garden with year-round interest.

RSPB Blacktoft Sands Nature Reserve
Whitgift, East Yorkshire
(01405) 704665
rspb.org.uk
Spot avocets, bitterns and marsh harriers.

Windermere Lake Cruises
Lakeside, Cumbria
(015394) 43360
windermere-lakecruises.co.uk
Sail the Lakes on launches and steamers.

WWT Washington Wetland Centre
Washington, Tyne and Wear
(0191) 416 5454
wwt.org.uk
100-acre conservation site with diverse wildlife.

Yorkshire Sculpture Park
Wakefield, West Yorkshire
(01924) 832631
ysp.co.uk
Browse art alfresco on beautiful 18thC parkland.

ASSURANCE OF A GREAT DAY OUT
Attractions with this sign participate in the Visitor Attraction Quality Assurance Scheme which recognises high standards in all aspects of the visitor experience.

Events 2009

Bradford International Film Festival
Bradford
bradfordfilmfestival.org.uk
Feb - Mar

Jorvik Viking Festival
York
jorvik-viking-centre.co.uk
18 - 22 Feb

John Smith's Grand National
Liverpool
aintree.co.uk
2 - 4 Apr

Chester Food and Drink Festival 2009
Chester
chesterfoodanddrink.com
10 - 13 Apr

Arley Horse Trials and Country Fair 2009
Northwich
arleyhallandgardens.com
16 - 17 May

Great Yorkshire Show
Harrogate
greatyorkshireshow.co.uk
Jul

Sunderland International Air Show
Sunderland
sunderland-airshow.com
25 - 26 Jul

Stockton International Riverside Festival
Stockton
sirf.co.uk
29 Jul - 2 Aug

St Leger Festival
Doncaster
doncaster-racecourse.co.uk
Sep

Regional contacts and information

For more information on accommodation, attractions, activities, events and holidays in Northern England, contact one of the following regional or local tourism organisations. Their websites have a wealth of information and many produce free publications to help you get the most out of your visit.

England's Northwest

There are various publications and guides about England's Northwest available from the following Tourist Boards or by logging on to **visitenglandsnorthwest.com** or calling **0845 600 6040**:

Visit Chester and Cheshire
Chester Railway Station, 1st Floor, West Wing Offices, Station Road, Chester CH1 3NT
t (01244) 405600
t 0845 073 1324 (accommodation booking)
e info@visitchesterandcheshire.co.uk
w visitchester.com or visitcheshire.com

Cumbria Tourism
Windermere Road, Staveley, Kendal LA8 9PL
t (015398) 22222
e info@cumbriatourism.org
w golakes.co.uk

The Lancashire and Blackpool Tourist Board
St George's House, St George's Street
Chorley PR7 2AA
t (01257) 226600 (Brochure request)
e info@visitlancashire.com
w visitlancashire.com

Visit Manchester – The Tourist Board For Greater Manchester
Carver's Warehouse, 77 Dale Street
Manchester M2 2HG
t 0161 237 1010
t 0871 222 8223 (information and brochure request)
e touristinformation@visitmanchester.com
w visitmanchester.com

The Mersey Partnership – The Tourist Board for the Liverpool City Region
12 Princes Parade, Liverpool L3 1BG
t (0151) 233 2008 (information enquiries)
t 0844 870 0123 (accommodation booking)
e info@visitliverpool.com (accommodation enquiries)
e 08place@liverpool.gov.uk (information enquiries)
w visitliverpool.com

Clockwise: Arley Hall and Gardens, Cheshire; Ilkley Moor, Yorkshire; Beamish, Durham

Yorkshire

The following publications are available from the Yorkshire Tourist Board by logging on to **yorkshire.com** or calling **0844 888 5123**:

- **Yorkshire Accommodation Guide 2009**
  Information on Yorkshire, including hotels, self catering, camping and caravan parks.

- **Make Yorkshire Yours Magazine**
  This entertaining magazine is full of articles and features about what's happening in Yorkshire, including where to go and what to do.

North East

Log on to the North East England website at **visitnortheastengland.com** for further information on accommodation, attractions, events and special offers throughout the region. A range of free guides are available for you to order online or by calling **0870 160 1781**:

- **Holiday and Short Breaks Guide**
  Information on North East England, including hotels, bed and breakfast, self-catering, caravan and camping parks and accessible accommodation as well as events and attractions throughout the region.

- **Cycling Guide**
  A guide to day rides, traffic-free trails and challenging cycling routes.

- **Gardens Guide**
  A guide to the region's most inspirational gardens.

- **Walking Guide**
  Circular trails and long distance routes through breathtaking countryside.

Tourist Information Centres

When you arrive at your destination, visit an Official Partner Tourist Information Centre for quality assured help with accommodation and information about local attractions and events, or email your request before you go. To search for attractions and Tourist Information Centres on the move just text INFO to 62233, and a web link will be sent to your mobile phone. To find a Tourist Information Centre by region visit enjoyEngland.com/find-tic.

Accrington	Town Hall, Blackburn Rd	(01254) 872595	tourism@hyndburnbc.gov.uk
Alnwick	2 The Shambles	(01665) 511333	alnwicktic@alnwick.gov.uk
Altrincham	20 Stamford New Road	(0161) 912 5931	tourist.information@trafford.gov.uk
Ashton-under-Lyne	Wellington Road	(0161) 343 4343	tourist.information@tameside.gov.uk
Aysgarth Falls	Aysgarth Falls National Park Centre	(01969) 662910	aysgarth@ytbtic.co.uk
Barnard Castle	Flatts Road	(01833) 690909	tourism@teesdale.gov.uk
Barnoldswick	Fernlea Avenue	(01282) 666704	tourist.info@pendle.gov.uk
Barrow-in-Furness	Duke Street	(01229) 876505	touristinfo@barrowbc.gov.uk
Batley	Bradford Road	(01924) 426670	batley@ytbtic.co.uk
Beverley	34 Butcher Row	(01482) 391672	beverley.tic@eastriding .gov.uk
Blackburn	50-54 Church Street	(01254) 53277	visit@blackburn.gov.uk
Blackpool	1 Clifton Street	(01253) 478222	tic@blackpool.gov.uk
Bolton	Le Mans Crescent	(01204) 334321	tourist.info@bolton.gov.uk
Bowness	Glebe Road	(015394) 42895	bownesstic@lake-district.gov.uk
Bradford	Centenary Square	(01274) 433678	tourist.information@bradford.gov.uk
Bridlington	25 Prince Street	(01262) 673474	bridlington.tic@eastriding.gov.uk
Brigg	Market Place	(01652) 657053	brigg.tic@northlincs.gov.uk
Burnley	Croft Street	(01282) 664421	tic@burnley.gov.uk
Bury	Market Street	(0161) 253 5111	touristinformation@bury.gov.uk
Carlisle	Greenmarket	(01228) 625600	tourism@carlisle-city.gov.uk
Chester (Town Hall)	Northgate Street	(01244) 402111	tis@chester.gov.uk
Cleethorpes	42-43 Alexandra Road	(01472) 323111	cleetic@nelincs.gov.uk
Cleveleys	Victoria Square	(01253) 853378	cleveleystic@wyrebc.gov.uk
Clitheroe	12-14 Market Place	(01200) 425566	tourism@ribblevalley.gov.uk
Congleton	High Street	(01260) 271095	tourism@congleton.gov.uk
Coniston	Ruskin Avenue	(015394) 41533	mail@conistontic.org
Danby	Lodge Lane	(01439) 772737	moorscentre@northyorkmoors-npa.gov.uk
Darlington	13 Horsemarket	(01325) 388666	tic@darlington.gov.uk
Doncaster	38-40 High Street	(01302) 734309	tourist.information@doncaster.gov.uk

Durham	2 Millennium Place	(0191) 384 3720	touristinfo@durhamcity.gov.uk
Ellesmere Port	Kinsey Road	(0151) 356 7879	cheshireoaks.cc@visitor-centre.net
Filey*	The Evron Centre, John Street	(01723) 383637	fileytic@scarborough.gov.uk
Fleetwood	The Esplanade	(01253) 773953	fleetwoodtic@wyrebc.gov.uk
Garstang	High Street	(01995) 602125	garstangtic@wyrebc.gov.uk
Grassington	Colvend, Hebden Road	(01756) 751690	grassington@ytbtic.co.uk
Guisborough	Church Street	(01287) 633801	guisborough_tic@redcar-cleveland.gov.uk
Halifax	Piece Hall	(01422) 368725	halifax@ytbtic.co.uk
Harrogate	Crescent Road	(01423) 537300	tic@harrogate.gov.uk
Hartlepool	Church Square	(01429) 869706	hpooltic@hartlepool.gov.uk
Hawes	Station Yard	(01969) 666210	hawes@ytbtic.co.uk
Haworth	2/4 West Lane	(01535) 642329	haworth@ytbtic.co.uk
Hebden Bridge	New Road	(01422) 843831	hebdenbridge@ytbtic.co.uk
Helmsley	Helmsley Castle	(01439) 770173	helmsley@ytbtic.co.uk
Hexham	Wentworth Car Park	(01434) 652220	hexham.tic@tynedale.gov.uk
Holmfirth	49-51 Huddersfield Road	(01484) 222444	holmfirth.tic@kirklees.gov.uk
Hornsea*	120 Newbegin	(01964) 536404	hornsea.tic@eastriding.gov.uk
Huddersfield	3 Albion Street	(01484) 223200	huddersfield.tic@kirklees.gov.uk
Hull	1 Paragon Street	(01482) 223559	tourist.information@hullcc.gov.uk
Humber Bridge	Ferriby Road	(01482) 640852	humberbridge.tic@eastriding.gov.uk
Ilkley	Station Rd	(01943) 602319	ilkley@ytbtic.co.uk
Kendal	Highgate	(01539 725758	kendaltic@southlakeland.gov.uk
Keswick	Market Square	(017687) 72645	keswicktic@lake-district.gov.uk
Knaresborough	9 Castle Courtyard	0845 389 0177	kntic@harrogate.gov.uk
Knutsford	Toft Road	(01565) 632611	ktic@macclesfield.gov.uk
Lancaster	29 Castle Hill	(01524) 32878	lancastertic@lancaster.gov.uk
Leeds	The Arcade, City Station	(0113) 242 5242	tourinfo@leeds.gov.uk
Leeming Bar	The Yorkshire Maid, The Great North Road	(01677 424262	leeming@ytbtic.co.uk

Left to right: Holker Hall and Gardens, Cumbria; Locomotion: The National Railway Museum, Durham

Leyburn	Railway Street	(01969) 623069	leyburn@ytbtic.co.uk
Liverpool 08 Place	Whitechapel	(0151) 233 2459	contact@liverpool.08.com
Liverpool John Lennon Airport	Speke Hall Avenue	0906 680 6886**	info@visitliverpool.com
Lytham St Annes	67 St Annes Road West	(01253) 725610	touristinformation@fylde.gov.uk
Macclesfield	Town Hall	(01625) 504114	informationcentre@macclesfield.gov.uk
Malham	National Park Centre	(01969) 652380	malham@ytbtic.co.uk
Malton	58 Market Place	(01653) 600048	maltontic@btconnect.com
Manchester Visitor Information Centre	Lloyd St	0871 222 8223	touristinformation@marketing-manchester.co.uk
Morecambe	Marine Road Central	(01524) 582808	morecambetic@lancaster.gov.uk
Morpeth	Bridge Street	(01670) 500700	tourism@castlemorpeth.gov.uk
Nantwich	Market Street	(01270) 537359	touristi@crewe-nantwich.gov.uk
Newcastle-upon-Tyne	8-9 Central Arcade	(0191) 277 8000	tourist.info@newcastle.gov.uk
Northwich	1 The Arcade	(01606) 353534	tourism@valeroyal.gov.uk
Oldham	12 Albion Street	(0161) 627 1024	ecs.tourist@oldham.gov.uk
Otley	Nelson Street	(01943) 462485	otleytic@leedslearning.net
Pateley Bridge*	18 High Street	0845 389 0177	pbtic@harrogate.gov.uk
Pendle Heritage Centre	Park Hill	(01282) 661701	heritage.centre@pendle.gov.uk
Penrith	Middlegate	(01768) 867466	pen.tic@eden.gov.uk
Pickering	The Ropery	(01751) 473791	pickering@ytbtic.co.uk
Preston	Lancaster Road	(01772) 253731	tourism@preston.gov.uk
Redcar	Esplanade	(01642) 471921	redcar_tic@redcar-cleveland.gov.uk
Reeth	Hudson House, The Green	(01748) 884059	reeth@ytbtic.co.uk
Richmond	Victoria Road	(01748) 828742	richmond@ytbtic.co.uk
Ripon	Minster Road	(01765) 604625	ripontic@harrogate.gov.uk
Rochdale	The Esplanade	(01706) 924928	tic@link4life.org
Rotherham	40 Bridgegate	(01709) 835904	tic@rotherham.gov.uk
St Helens	The World of Glass	(01744) 755150	info@sthelenstic.com
Salford	The Lowry, Pier 8	(0161) 848 8601	tic@salford.gov.uk
Saltburn-by-the-Sea	3 Station Buildings	(01287) 622422	saltburn_tic@redcar-cleveland.gov.uk
Scarborough	Brunswick Shopping Centre	(01723) 383636	tourismbureau@scarborough.gov.uk
Scarborough (Harbourside)	Sandside	(01723) 383636	harboursidetic@scarborough.gov.uk
Settle	Cheapside	(01729) 825192	settle@ytbtic.co.uk
Sheffield	14 Norfolk Row	(0114) 2211900	visitor@sheffield.gov.uk
Skipton	35 Coach Street	(01756) 792809	skipton@ytbtic.co.uk
Stockport	30 Market Place	(0161) 474 4444	tourist.information@stockport.gov.uk
Sunderland	50 Fawcett Street	(0191) 553 2000	tourist.info@sunderland.gov.uk
Sutton Bank	Sutton Bank Visitor Centre	(01845) 597426	suttonbank@ytbtic.co.uk

Thirsk	49 Market Place	(01845) 522755	thirsktic@hambleton.gov.uk
Todmorden	15 Burnley Road	(01706) 818181	todmorden@ytbtic.co.uk
Wakefield	9 The Bull Ring	0845 601 8353	tic@wakefield.gov.uk
Warrington	Academy Way	(01925) 428585	informationcentre@warrington.gov.uk
Wetherby	17 Westgate	(01937) 582151	wetherbytic@leedslearning.net
Whitby	Langborne Road	(01723) 383637	whitbytic@scarborough.gov.uk
Whitehaven	Market Place	(01946) 598914	tic@copelandbc.gov.uk
Wigan	62 Wallgate	(01942) 825677	tic@wlct.org
Wilmslow	Rectory Fields	(01625) 522275	i.hillaby@macclesfield.gov.uk
Windermere	Victoria Street	(015394) 46499	windermeretic@southlakeland.gov.uk
Withernsea*	131 Queen Street	(01964) 615683	withernsea.tic@eastriding.gov.uk
York (De Grey Rooms)	Exhibition Square	(01904) 550099	info@visityork.org
York (Railway Station)	Station Road	(01904) 550099	info@visityork.org

*seasonal opening

**calls to this number are charged at premium rate

Clockwise: High Force, Durham; Royal Armouries Museum, Yorkshire; Manchester United Museum and Tour

where to stay in
Northern England

All place names in the blue bands are shown on the maps at the front of this guide.

A complete listing of all Enjoy England assessed accommodation covered by this guide appears at the back.

Accommodation symbols

Symbols give useful information about services and facilities. On page 7 you can find a key to these symbols.

ACASTER MALBIS, North Yorkshire Map ref 4C1

★★★★
SELF CATERING

Units **1**
Sleeps **1–6**

LOW SEASON PER WK
Min £400.00

HIGH SEASON PER WK
Max £700.00

10% discount for multiple-week bookings.

Orchard Lodge, Acaster Malbis, York

contact Ms Bridget Karn, Mount Pleasant House, Acaster Malbis YO23 2UP **t** (01904) 700924 & 07766 352049 **e** bridget@orchardlodgeyork.co.uk

orchardlodgeyork.co.uk REAL-TIME BOOKING

open All year
payment Cash, cheques
nearest shop 3 miles
nearest pub 1 mile

Scandinavian log cabin offering a high specification with double and twin bedrooms, both with en suite (bathroom and shower room). There is also a double sofa bed in the lounge, allowing six people to stay comfortably. The cabin is designed for relaxation and leisure, sitting in a secluded landscape of fields and orchard.

ONLINE MAP

Unit General P S
Leisure

ACKLINGTON, Northumberland Map ref 5C1

★★★★
SELF CATERING

Units **11**
Sleeps **2–8**

LOW SEASON PER WK
£200.00–£550.00

HIGH SEASON PER WK
£400.00–£1,152.00

Bank House Holiday Cottages, Guyzance, Acklington

contact Mr Steven Stone, 1 Whalton Park, Morpeth NE61 3TU **t** 07525 615411
e info@bankhouseholidaycottages.co.uk

bankhouseholidaycottages.co.uk GUEST REVIEWS • SPECIAL OFFERS • REAL-TIME BOOKING

open All year except January
payment Credit/debit cards, cash, cheques
nearest shop 3 miles
nearest pub 3 miles

A range of one, two, three and four-bedroom beautifully converted stone buildings, complete with original farmhouse, set in a natural woodland setting close to beautiful Northumbrian coastline.

SAT NAV *NE65 9AP* **ONLINE MAP**

Unit General P S

AISKEW, North Yorkshire Map ref 5C3

★★★
SELF CATERING

Units 4
Sleeps 2–6

LOW SEASON PER WK
£219.00–£261.00

HIGH SEASON PER WK
£340.00–£500.00

Off-peak short breaks by arrangement.

Courtyard Cottages, Aiskew, Bedale

contact Mr & Mrs James & Jill Cartman, Courtyard Cottages, The Nurseries, Aiskew, Bedale DL8 1BN
t (01677) 423689 **e** jill@courtyardcottages.net

courtyardcottages.net

open All year
payment Credit/debit cards, cash, cheques, euros
nearest shop 1 mile
nearest pub 1 mile

These delightful old brick and cobble cottages with beamed ceilings combine local country craftsmanship with all modern facilities. Overlooking colourful courtyard gardens. Quiet, secure, yet only five minutes' walk from the old market town of Bedale with its wide main street and cobbled parking. James Herriot's 'Gateway to the Dales'.

ONLINE MAP

Unit General Leisure

Don't forget www.

Web addresses throughout this guide are shown without the prefix www. Please include www. in the address line of your browser. If a web address does not follow this style it is shown in full.

ALLENDALE, Northumberland Map ref 5B2

★★★★
SELF CATERING

Units 1
Sleeps 6

LOW SEASON PER WK
£550.00

HIGH SEASON PER WK
£790.00

Fell View Cottage, Hexham

contact Mr & Mrs Colin & Carole Verne-Jones, 69 Buckinghamshire Road, Durham DH1 2BE
t (0191) 386 9045 **e** colin.verne-jones@fellviewcottage.co.uk

fellviewcottage.co.uk GUEST REVIEWS · SPECIAL OFFERS

open All year
payment Cash, cheques
nearest shop 1.5 miles
nearest pub 1.5 miles

Rebuilt barn, now detached, three-bedroom stone cottage in Area of Outstanding Natural Beauty with wonderful unrestricted views of the Allendale Valley and beyond. Built to the highest possible standards of a traditional Northumberland cottage, it has a large master bedroom with a king-size bed and two further twin bedrooms.

ONLINE MAP

Unit General P Leisure

ALLERTHORPE, East Riding of Yorkshire Map ref 4C1

★★★★
SELF CATERING

Units 1
Sleeps 4–6

LOW SEASON PER WK
£350.00–£400.00

HIGH SEASON PER WK
£450.00–£550.00

Free access to grounds of Allerthorpe Lakeland Park.

Manderlay, Allerthorpe Lakeland Park, York

t (01759) 301444 **e** info@allerthorpelakelandpark.co.uk

allerthorpelakelandpark.co.uk

open All year except Christmas and New Year
payment Credit/debit cards, cash, cheques
nearest shop 2 miles
nearest pub 0.75 miles

Brand new luxury apartment tastefully decorated to highest standards. Consists of master bedroom, second room with twin single beds and bunk bed. Family bathroom with large shower. Contemporary living room provides seating, flat-screen TV, dining table and modern fitted kitchenette. Spectacular views of lake and surrounding grounds.

Unit General P Leisure

ALLONBY, Cumbria Map ref 5A2

★★★★
SELF CATERING

Units 1
Sleeps 2–14

LOW SEASON PER WK
£700.00–£740.00

HIGH SEASON PER WK
£780.00–£800.00

Crookhurst Farm, Allonby, Maryport

contact Brenda Wilson, Crookhurst Farm, c/o Bowscale Farm, Allonby, Maryport CA15 6RB
t (01900) 881228 & 07773 047591 **e** brenda@crookhurst.com

crookhurst.com SPECIAL OFFERS

Crookhurst is a working farm set in open countryside, 0.5 miles from the picturesque village on the Solway coast. The farmhouse provides spacious group accommodation in a cosy homely environment.

open All year
payment Cash, cheques
nearest shop 0.5 miles
nearest pub 0.5 miles

Unit General P Leisure

What shall we do today?

For ideas on places to visit, see the beginning of this regional section or go online at enjoyengland.com.

ALNMOUTH, Northumberland Map ref 5C1

★★★★★
SELF CATERING

Units 1
Sleeps 1–7

LOW SEASON PER WK
Min £550.00

HIGH SEASON PER WK
Max £1,275.00

Low-season short breaks available by arrangement, within one month of booking.

Paradise Lodge, Alnmouth, Alnwick

contact Ms Sandra MacDonald, Heavenly Holiday Homes, Durham House, 33a Old Elvet, Durham DH1 3HN **t** (0191) 384 3904 & 07971 538316 **e** sa@heavenlyholidayhomes.co.uk

heavenlyholidayhomes.co.uk GUEST REVIEWS • SPECIAL OFFERS • REAL-TIME BOOKING

open All year
payment Credit/debit cards, cash, cheques
nearest shop less than 0.5 miles
nearest pub less than 0.5 miles

Exceptional and individual Victorian renovation in Alnmouth's prime seaside location. Light-filled and spacious, this fabulous property's bay windows have window seats and comfy chairs to take full advantage of the fantastic panoramic sea and estuary views. Furnished and equipped to the highest standards. Welcome hamper. True luxury.

ONLINE MAP

Unit TV SC DVD General P Leisure

ALNMOUTH, Northumberland Map ref 5C1

★★★
SELF CATERING

Units 1
Sleeps 4

LOW SEASON PER WK
£260.00–£575.00

HIGH SEASON PER WK
£260.00–£575.00

Platone, Alnmouth

contact Mr & Mrs J & B Galbraith, 3 Hipsburn Steadings, Lesbury, Alnwick NE66 3QP
t (01665) 830084 **e** jandbgalbraith@tiscali.co.uk

northumberlandcottages.co.uk

Charming, well-equipped cottage situated in heart of Alnmouth village. Accommodation comprises lobby, galley kitchen, sitting room, two bedrooms, bathroom, patio garden, parking space.

open All year
payment Cash, cheques
nearest shop less than 0.5 miles
nearest pub less than 0.5 miles

Unit TV SC DVD General P

ALNMOUTH, Northumberland Map ref 5C1

★★–★★★
SELF CATERING

Units 4
Sleeps 5

LOW SEASON PER WK
£220.00–£280.00

HIGH SEASON PER WK
£250.00–£300.00

Wooden Farm Holiday Cottages, Alnmouth

contact Mr Gordon Farr, Wooden Farm Holiday Cottages, Lesbury, Alnmouth, Alnwick NE66 2TW
t (01665) 830342

Stone-built cottages in a quiet farm setting, overlooking the coast and the picturesque village of Alnmouth. Only four miles from Alnwick Castle and Gardens.

open All year
payment Cash, cheques
nearest shop 1 mile
nearest pub 1 mile

Unit TV General P Leisure

ALNWICK, Northumberland Map ref 5C1

★★★★
SELF CATERING

Units 2
Sleeps 3–4

LOW SEASON PER WK
£225.00–£500.00

HIGH SEASON PER WK
£450.00–£650.00

29 Bondgate Within, Alnwick

contact Mr Toby Wilkie-Smith, Ridley Properties, 27 Ridley Place, Newcastle-upon-Tyne NE1 8JN
t (0191) 230 5471 **e** toby@daviesbellreed.co.uk

open All year
payment Cash, cheques
nearest shop less than 0.5 miles
nearest pub less than 0.5 miles

Two excellent two-bedroom period stone properties located in the heart of this thriving market town, minutes from pubs and restaurants. Flat A sleeps four and Flat B sleeps three.

Unit TV DVD General P Leisure

For **key to symbols** see page 7

ALNWICK, Northumberland Map ref 5C1

★★★
SELF CATERING

Units 3
Sleeps 4–10

LOW SEASON PER WK
£250.00–£350.00

HIGH SEASON PER WK
£350.00–£600.00

The Harehope Estate welcomes dogs and horses. We have outside kennels and stables with grazing.

Harehope Estate, Alnwick

contact Ms Alison Wrangham, Harehope Hall, Eglingham, Alnwick NE66 2DP **t** (01668) 217329
e aliwrangham@btconnect.com

open All year
payment Cash, cheques
nearest shop 4 miles
nearest pub 2 miles

Enjoy a real rural retreat with wonderful walking on your doorstep when you stay in the spacious wing of our large, secluded country house or two idyllic riverside cottages. Beautiful views of the Cheviot hills and just half an hour's drive to many wonderful beaches.

Unit General P Leisure

ALWINTON, Northumberland Map ref 5B1

★★★★
SELF CATERING

Units 1
Sleeps 3

LOW SEASON PER WK
Min £225.00

HIGH SEASON PER WK
Max £550.00

WALKERS WELCOME CYCLISTS WELCOME

Fellside Cottage, Alwinton

contact Mrs Denise Straughan, Fellside Cottage, Bedlington Lane Farm, Bedlington NE22 6AA
t (01670) 823042 **e** stay@fellsidecottcheviots.co.uk

fellsidecottcheviots.co.uk

Cosy cottage nestling in the beautiful Upper Coquet Valley. Fully furnished and equipped to a high standard. Open fire. Lovely garden and patio. Enjoy the peace and stunning surroundings. A walker's paradise.

open All year
payment Cash, cheques
nearest shop 10 miles
nearest pub less than 0.5 miles

Unit TV SC DVD General P S
Leisure

AMBLESIDE, Cumbria Map ref 5A3

★★★
SELF CATERING

Units 1
Sleeps 5

LOW SEASON PER WK
£311.00–£412.00

HIGH SEASON PER WK
£470.00–£597.00

Dower House Cottage, Ambleside

contact Mrs Margaret Rigg, The Dower House, Wray Castle, Ambleside LA22 0JA **t** (015394) 33211

Self-catering cottage with two bedrooms, large kitchen, dining room, large sitting room, bathroom. French windows opening onto terrace and gardens.

open All year
payment Cash, cheques
nearest shop 4 miles
nearest pub 2.5 miles

Unit TV General P Leisure

AMBLESIDE, Cumbria Map ref 5A3

★★★★-★★★★★
SELF CATERING

Units **26**
Sleeps **2–6**

LOW SEASON PER WK
Min £340.00

HIGH SEASON PER WK
Min £495.00

Midweek 4 nights for the price of 3. Weekends, Fri and Sat nights subject to availability.

Kirkstone Foot Apartments, Ambleside

contact Mrs J Tunnicliff, Kirkstone Foot Apartments Limited, Kirkstone Pass Road, Ambleside LA22 9EH **t** (015394) 32232 **e** enquiries@kirkstonefoot.co.uk

kirkstonefoot.co.uk

open All year
payment Credit/debit cards, cash, cheques

Superior, luxury holiday cottages and apartments set amongst two acres of beautiful, landscaped grounds, yet only a two-minute stroll from the centre of Ambleside.

Unit TV DVD General P S Leisure

AMBLESIDE, Cumbria Map ref 5A3

★★★-★★★★
SELF CATERING

Units **10**
Sleeps **2–8**

LOW SEASON PER WK
£240.00–£575.00

HIGH SEASON PER WK
£595.00–£855.00

The Lakelands, Ambleside

contact Jackie Kingdom, The Lakelands, Lower Gale, Ambleside LA22 0BD **t** (015394) 33777 **e** lakeland@globalnet.co.uk

the-lakelands.com

Self-catering apartments at The Lakelands, set in a unique position overlooking Ambleside with unspoilt views of the surrounding fells. Furnished with quality in mind. Private leisure centre available for use of guests.

open All year
payment Credit/debit cards, cash, cheques
nearest shop less than 0.5 miles
nearest pub less than 0.5 miles

Unit TV General P Leisure

AMBLESIDE, Cumbria Map ref 5A3

★★★★-★★★★★
SELF CATERING

Units **100**
Sleeps **4–8**

LOW SEASON PER WK
£490.00–£1,000.00

HIGH SEASON PER WK
£910.00–£1,900.00

Langdale Estate Lodges, Langdale

contact Self Catering, The Langdale Estate, Great Langdale, Ambleside LA22 9JD **t** (015394) 38012 **e** selfcatering@langdale.co.uk

langdale.co.uk SPECIAL OFFERS

open All year
payment Credit/debit cards, cash, cheques
nearest shop less than 0.5 miles
nearest pub less than 0.5 miles

Langdale's famous Scandinavian lodges offer exceptional modern comfort with the convenience of having all the facilities you will ever need right on your doorstep. Each lodge is carefully positioned to give a high degree of privacy: some overlook waterways and ponds, others afford views of wooded glades or spectacular fells.

ONLINE MAP

Unit TV SC DVD SH General P S
Leisure

What do the star ratings mean?

Detailed information about star ratings can be found at the back of this guide.

AMBLESIDE, Cumbria Map ref 5A3

★★★
SELF CATERING

Units 1
Sleeps 4

LOW SEASON PER WK
£300.00–£370.00

HIGH SEASON PER WK
£410.00–£580.00

North Syke, Ambleside

contact Christine Fagg, North Syke Holiday Home, North Road, Ambleside LA22 9DT
t 07870 576466 **e** chris@northsyke.co.uk

northsyke.co.uk

A warm, welcoming listed 1741 cottage. Secluded location tucked away in old Ambleside, offering a rare combination of peace and close proximity to village shops, restaurants, pubs, cinema and major walks or gentle strolls.

open All year
payment Cash, cheques
nearest shop less than 0.5 miles
nearest pub less than 0.5 miles

Unit General
Leisure

AMBLESIDE, Cumbria Map ref 5A3

★★★
SERVICED APARTMENTS

Units 20
Sleeps 2–6

LOW SEASON PER WK
£450.00–£550.00

HIGH SEASON PER WK
£550.00–£700.00

Hotel rooms: we offer 5 nights for 4 during Jan, Feb, Mar, Oct, Nov, Dec.

Quaysiders Club, Ambleside

t (015394) 33969 **e** ian@quaysiders.co.uk

quaysiders.co.uk REAL-TIME BOOKING

open All year
payment Credit/debit cards, cash, cheques
nearest shop 0.5 miles
nearest pub 0.5 miles

High-class self-catering apartments and hotel rooms opposite Lake Windermere in Ambleside. Apartments rented by the week from Saturday to Saturday. Hotel rooms rented by the night. Bookings can be made direct from our website.

ONLINE MAP

Unit General
Leisure

AMBLESIDE, Cumbria Map ref 5A3

★★★★
SELF CATERING

Units 1
Sleeps 6

LOW SEASON PER WK
£400.00–£500.00

HIGH SEASON PER WK
£600.00–£700.00

Wayside Cottage, Clappersgate, Ambleside

contact Dennis Leech, 22 Styvechale Avenue, Coventry CV5 6DX **t** (024) 7667 7549 & 07712 353201 **e** waysidecottage@lineone.net

waysidecottage.co.uk

open All year
payment Cheques
nearest shop 1 mile
nearest pub 1 mile

An attractive 17thC cottage completely modernised to a high standard of comfort, makes an ideal base for a holiday with many beautiful walks from the door and the amenities of Ambleside only a twenty-minute walk away.

SAT NAV *LA22 9LE* **ONLINE MAP**

Unit General Leisure

Place index

If you know where you want to stay, the index by place name at the back of the guide will give you the page number listing accommodation in your chosen town, city or village. Check out the other useful indexes too.

APPLEBY-IN-WESTMORLAND, Cumbria Map ref 5B3

★★★
SELF CATERING

Units 7
Sleeps 2–7

LOW SEASON PER WK
£220.00–£450.00

HIGH SEASON PER WK
£250.00–£530.00

Short breaks available Oct-Mar and at other times subject to availability. Minimum 2-night stay. Contact us for prices.

Milburn Grange Holiday Cottages, Knock, Appleby-in-Westmorland

contact Russell & Debbie Clark, Milburn Grange Holiday Cottages, Milburn Grange, Knock, Appleby-in-Westmorland CA16 6DR **t** (017683) 61867 **e** holidays@milburngrange.co.uk

milburngrange.co.uk GUEST REVIEWS • SPECIAL OFFERS • REAL-TIME BOOKING

open All year
payment Credit/debit cards, cash, cheques
nearest shop 0.5 miles
nearest pub 2 miles

Nestling at the foot of the Pennines and enjoying uninterrupted views of the Lakeland fells, our cosy cottages offer a high standard of accommodation and are open all year. The seven cottages can sleep from two to seven people with large groups of up to 29 people accommodated.

ONLINE MAP

Unit General
Leisure

APPLEBY-IN-WESTMORLAND, Cumbria Map ref 5B3

★★★
SELF CATERING

Units 1
Sleeps 2–4

LOW SEASON PER WK
£135.00–£185.00

HIGH SEASON PER WK
£190.00–£300.00

Wray Cottage, Appleby-in-Westmorland

contact Mrs Cowey, The Hunting House, Great Asby, Appleby-in-Westmorland CA16 6HD
t (017683) 52485

Quiet situation in conservation area. All on one level. Private garden. One bedroom, sofa bed in lounge/diner. Ideal centre, on Westmoorland Way, for walking, sightseeing; easy reach of Lakes and Dales.

open All year
payment Cash, cheques
nearest shop 5 miles
nearest pub less than 0.5 miles

Unit General Leisure

ASKHAM, Cumbria Map ref 5B3

★★★★
SELF CATERING

Units 1
Sleeps 4

LOW SEASON PER WK
Min £325.00

HIGH SEASON PER WK
Max £600.00

Short breaks (3 nights minimum) available. Discount for 2-person occupancy.

Sycamore Barn Holiday Cottage, Ullswater

contact Ellen Pickup, Sycamore Barn Holiday Cottage, Sycamore House, Askham CA10 2PF
t (01931) 712410 **e** sycamorehousebarn@btinternet.com

sycamorehousebarn.com

open All year
payment Credit/debit cards, cash, cheques
nearest shop less than 0.5 miles
nearest pub less than 0.5 miles

Sycamore Barn is a high quality, beautifully furnished barn conversion attached to the owners' 18thC house situated in the pretty village of Askham, a conservation area on the Lowther Estate, in the Lake District National Park. Double bedroom (en suite shower room), twin bedroom (mezzanine with en suite bathroom). Excellent walking area.

SAT NAV *CA10 2PF*

Unit General Leisure

Check the maps for accommodation locations

Colour maps at the front pinpoint all the places where accommodation is featured within the regional sections of this guide. Pick your location and then refer to the the place index at the back to find the page number.

BALDERSDALE, Durham Map ref 5B3

★★★★
SELF CATERING

Units 1
Sleeps 4

LOW SEASON PER WK
£250.00–£350.00

HIGH SEASON PER WK
£375.00–£450.00

Clove Lodge Cottage, Baldersdale

contact Mrs Caroline Carter, Clove Lodge Cottage, Baldersdale DL12 9UP **t** (01833) 650030
e carolinecarter69@aol.com

clovelodge.co.uk

A stone-built Victorian cottage in a spectacular location on the Pennine Way. Ideal for sightseeing, walking, wildlife and relaxation.

open All year except Christmas and New Year
payment Cash, cheques
nearest shop 7 miles
nearest pub 7 miles

Unit General Leisure

BAMBURGH, Northumberland Map ref 5C1

★★★★
SELF CATERING

Units 1
Sleeps 4

LOW SEASON PER WK
Min £280.00

HIGH SEASON PER WK
Max £630.00

The Cottage, Bamburgh

contact Mrs Turnbull, 1 Friars Court, Bamburgh NE69 7AE **t** (01668) 214494
e theturnbulls2k@btinternet.com

holidaynorthumbria.co.uk

Charming, quality accommodation minutes from a beautiful sandy beach, with wonderful views of the magnificent Bamburgh Castle. Large, private gardens and parking.

open All year
payment Cash, cheques
nearest shop 0.5 miles
nearest pub 0.5 miles

Unit General

BAMBURGH, Northumberland Map ref 5C1

★★★★★
SELF CATERING

Units 2
Sleeps 2–8

LOW SEASON PER WK
£375.00–£895.00

HIGH SEASON PER WK
£525.00–£1,575.00

Short breaks available Nov-Mar.

Glebe House and Glebe Cottage, Bamburgh

contact Mrs Maria Eliana Robinson, EMR Properties, The Glebe, Radcliffe Road, Bamburgh NE69 7AE
t (01668) 214456 **e** stay@bamburghglebe.co.uk

bamburghglebe.co.uk

open All year
payment Cash, cheques
nearest shop less than 0.5 miles
nearest pub less than 0.5 miles

This lovely 18thC vicarage has stunning views of church, castle and sea. Spacious and well furnished with full central heating included. First-class kitchen. Children and household pets welcome. Large, peaceful, private gardens. An ideal base for walking and exploring Northumberland's Heritage Coast.

Unit General Leisure

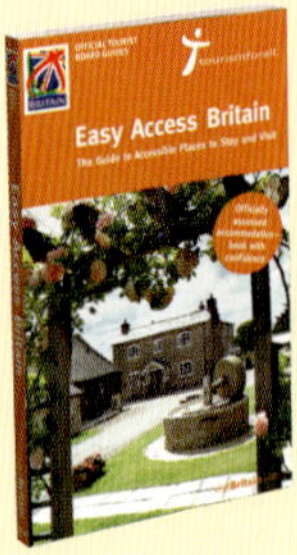

Where can I find accessible accommodation?

If you have special hearing, visual or mobility needs, there's an index of National Accessible Scheme participants featured in this guide. For more accessible accommodation buy a copy of Easy Access Britain available online at visitbritaindirect.com, and from Tourism for All on 0845 124 997 or visit tourismforall.org.uk.

BAMBURGH, Northumberland Map ref 5C1

★★★★
SELF CATERING

Units 16
Sleeps 2–6

LOW SEASON PER WK
£259.00–£466.00

HIGH SEASON PER WK
£420.00–£776.00

Outchester & Ross Farm Cottages, Belford

contact Mrs Shirley McKie, 1 Cragview Road, Belford NE70 7NT **t** (01668) 213336
e enquiry@rosscottages.co.uk

rosscottages.co.uk

open All year
payment Cash, cheques
nearest shop 3 miles
nearest pub 3 miles

Outchester and Ross are both in unique, secluded coastal locations in one of the most beautiful areas of Northumberland between Bamburgh and Holy Island. Our cottages are warm, comfortable and well equipped – each double glazed and with its own private garden. Relax completely and just enjoy being here.

Unit General P Leisure

BAMBURGH, Northumberland Map ref 5C1

★★★
SELF CATERING

Units 5
Sleeps 2–5

LOW SEASON PER WK
£210.00–£275.00

HIGH SEASON PER WK
£520.00–£700.00

Point Cottages, Bamburgh

contact Mrs Sanderson, 30 The Oval, Benton, Newcastle upon Tyne NE12 9PP **t** (0191) 266 2800
e info@bamburgh-cottages.co.uk

bamburgh-cottages.co.uk

Cluster of cottages with fine sea views to Lindisfarne, the Farne Islands and Bamburgh Castle. Adjacent to golf course. Furnished to a high standard. Large garden.

open All year
payment Cash, cheques
nearest shop 1 mile
nearest pub 1 mile

Unit General P S Leisure

BAMBURGH, Northumberland Map ref 5C1

★★★★–★★★★★
SELF CATERING

Units 6
Sleeps 2–10

LOW SEASON PER WK
£195.00–£720.00

HIGH SEASON PER WK
£365.00–£1,800.00

AONB Award for Excellence in Facilities. Short breaks Nov-Mar. Access to Seafield Health and Beauty Club.

Springhill Farm Holiday Accommodation, Seahouses, Bamburgh

contact Mrs Julie & Miss Sarah Gregory, Springhill Farm Holiday Accommodation, Springhill Farm, Seahouses NE68 7UR **t** (01665) 721820 **e** enquiries@springhill-farm.co.uk

springhill-farm.co.uk SPECIAL OFFERS

open All year
payment Credit/debit cards, cash, cheques
nearest shop 0.5 miles
nearest pub 0.5 miles

Beautifully converted traditional barns and original farm cottages. All designed to exceptional standards, decorated and finished with both modern and traditional furniture and appliances, aimed to balance character with functionality for all of your holiday needs. Only half a mile from the outstanding Heritage Coast running between Bamburgh and Seahouses.

ONLINE MAP

Unit General P S
Leisure

Need some ideas?

Big city buzz or peaceful panoramas? Take a fresh look at England and you may be surprised at what's right on your doorstep. Explore the diversity online at enjoyengland.com

BAMBURGH, Northumberland Map ref 5C1

★★★★-★★★★★
SELF CATERING

Units **3**
Sleeps **2–28**

LOW SEASON PER WK
£221.00–£1,666.00

HIGH SEASON PER WK
£394.00–£2,362.00

Short breaks available all year. Weekend breaks, 3 nights, Fri-Mon. Midweek breaks, 4 nights, Mon-Fri.

Waren Lea Hall, Bamburgh

contact Carolynn Croisdale-Appleby, Abbotsholme, Hervines Road, Amersham HP6 5HS
t (01494) 725194 & 07901 716136 **e** croisdaleappleby@aol.com

selfcateringluxury.co.uk

open All year
payment Cash, cheques
nearest shop 1.5 miles
nearest pub 1.5 miles

Imposing, spacious country house on shore of Budle Bay at Waren Mill near Bamburgh in two acres of waters-edge parkland. Breathtaking views of Lindisfarne and Cheviots. Holiday homes can be booked individually or together and sleep 14, 10 and 4 guests. Waren Lea Hall enjoys an unrivalled location with easy access for walking, golf, fishing etc.

Unit General P Leisure

BARMBY MOOR, East Riding of Yorkshire Map ref 4C1

★★★★
SELF CATERING

Units **1**
Sleeps **1–6**

LOW SEASON PER WK
£375.00–£400.00

HIGH SEASON PER WK
£440.00–£600.00

Short breaks (3 days), bookable 28 days in advance, 60% normal weekly rate.

FAMILIES WELCOME PETS! WELCOME

Northwood Coach House, York

contact Ann Gregory, Northwood Coach House, St Helens Square, Barmby Moor YO42 4HF
t (01759) 302305 **e** annjgregory@hotmail.com

northwoodcoachhouse.co.uk

open All year
payment Cash, cheques, euros
nearest shop less than 0.5 miles
nearest pub less than 0.5 miles

This pretty, three-bedroomed, converted Victorian coach house overlooks open countryside. Warm and cosy in winter, it is ideally situated in a picturesque village on the edge of the Wolds, only 12 miles from York and convenient for the coast and moors. Pubs, shops and restaurants nearby.

Unit General P Leisure

BARNARD CASTLE, Durham Map ref 5B3

★★★★
SELF CATERING

Units **1**
Sleeps **1–4**

LOW SEASON PER WK
£420.00

HIGH SEASON PER WK
£420.00

Cheeseborough House, Barnard Castle

contact Mr & Mrs Ian & Eva Reid, Cheeseborough House, 34 The Bank, Barnard Castle DL12 8PN
t (01833) 631304 **e** enquiries@number34.com

cheeseboroughs.co.uk

Beautifully restored 18thC weaver's house, full of old features. Two double bedrooms (en suite), secluded patio garden, close to town facilities.

open All year
payment Cash, cheques
nearest shop less than 0.5 miles
nearest pub less than 0.5 miles

Unit General P Leisure

Where can I get help and advice?

Tourist Information Centres offer friendly help with accommodation and holiday ideas as well as suggestions of places to visit and things to do. You'll find contact details at the beginning of each regional section.

BEADNELL, Northumberland Map ref 5C1

★★★★
SELF CATERING

Units 1
Sleeps 1–6

LOW SEASON PER WK
£370.00–£503.00

HIGH SEASON PER WK
£636.00–£850.00

Shore Cottage, Beadnell

contact Mrs Lesley Barnett, North East Coast Holidays, 7 Alnside Court, Alnwick NE66 3PD
t (01665) 833233 **e** d_barnettuk@yahoo.co.uk

open All year
payment Cash, cheques
nearest shop 1 mile
nearest pub 1 mile

Three-bedroom bungalow two minutes from beach. One double and two single bedrooms, two beds in each. Large lounge/diner with wood-burning stove. En suite shower room and fully fitted bathroom. Large enclosed garden with table and chairs.

Unit General P

BEADNELL, Northumberland Map ref 5C1

★★★
SELF CATERING

Units 7
Sleeps 2–5

LOW SEASON PER WK
£170.00–£200.00

HIGH SEASON PER WK
£400.00–£460.00

Town Farm Cottages, Beadnell

Heritage Coast Holidays, Unit 6g, Greensfield Court, Greensfield Industrial Estate, Alnwick NE66 2DE
t (01665) 604935 **e** info@heritagecoastholidays.co.uk

heritagecoastholidays.co.uk

open All year
payment Credit/debit cards, cash, cheques, euros
nearest shop less than 0.5 miles
nearest pub less than 0.5 miles

Located on the Heritage Coast at Beadnell, these cottages and apartments are converted from a 17thC coach house and stables. Superbly positioned within the village and just a short walk from a magnificent beach. The accommodation is very well equipped and has full central heating. Ideally located for exploring the beautiful Northumberland coastline.

Unit General P Leisure

BELFORD, Northumberland Map ref 5B1

★★★-★★★★
SELF CATERING

Units 3
Sleeps 2–6

LOW SEASON PER WK
Min £200.00

HIGH SEASON PER WK
Max £530.00

Fenham le Moor Cottages, Belford

contact Mrs Katie Burn, Fenham-le-Moor, Belford NE70 7PN **t** (01668) 213247
e enquiries@fenham-le-moor.co.uk

fenham-le-moor.co.uk

Comfortably furnished cottages and open-plan studio on working farm, overlooking the Lindisfarne Nature Reserve. A unique situation for birdwatching and walking, with views over to Holy Island.

open All year
payment Cash, cheques
nearest shop 4 miles
nearest pub 4 miles

Unit General P Leisure

It's all quality-assessed accommodation

Our commitment to quality involves wide-ranging accommodation assessment. Ratings and awards were correct at the time of going to press but may change following a new assessment. Please check at time of booking.

BELFORD, Northumberland Map ref 5B1

★★★
SELF CATERING

Units 3
Sleeps 2–6

LOW SEASON PER WK
Min £150.00

HIGH SEASON PER WK
Max £445.00

Swinhoe Farm Cottages and Riding Centre, Belford

contact Mrs Valerie Nixon, Swinhoe Farm Cottages and Riding Centre, Swinhoe Farm House, Swinhoe, Belford NE70 7LJ **t** (01668) 213370 **e** valerie@swinhoecottages.co.uk

swinhoecottages.co.uk

Well-equipped cottages on working farm. Many walks including St Cuthbert's Cave. Approximately 10 minutes' drive from Bamburgh, with its sandy beaches, and Holy Island. Riding centre on farm.

open All year
payment Cash, cheques
nearest shop 3 miles
nearest pub 3 miles

Unit General P Leisure

BELLINGHAM, Northumberland Map ref 5B2

★★★★
SELF CATERING

Units 3
Sleeps 2–6

LOW SEASON PER WK
£260.00–£350.00

HIGH SEASON PER WK
£410.00–£500.00

3- and 4-day bookings accepted – from £120.

Riverdale Court, Hexham

contact Mr & Mrs John & Iben Cocker, Bellingham, Hexham NE48 2JT **t** (01434) 220254
e reservations@riverdalehallhotel.co.uk

riverdalehallhotel.co.uk

open All year
payment Credit/debit cards, cash, cheques
nearest shop 0.5 miles
nearest pub less than 0.5 miles

Nestling alongside Riverdale Hall Hotel with splendid views over the North Tyne river and Dunterley Fells (Pennine Way). Guests have free use of hotel pool, sauna and cricket field. There is a charge for salmon fishing. All apartments have either a balcony or patio area.

Unit General P S
Leisure

BERWICK-UPON-TWEED, Northumberland Map ref 5B1

★★★
SELF CATERING

Units 1
Sleeps 1–5

LOW SEASON PER WK
£170.00–£190.00

HIGH SEASON PER WK
£200.00–£350.00

Broadstone Cottage, Norham, Berwick-upon-Tweed

contact Mr Edward Chantler, Broadstone Farm, Maidstone ME17 2AT **t** (01622) 850207

Village cottage. Ideal centre for touring, walking and fishing holidays. Twenty minutes to beach. Shops and pubs nearby. Full central heating. Bathroom with shower. One double, one twin.

open All year
payment Cash, cheques

Unit General P

BERWICK-UPON-TWEED, Northumberland Map ref 5B1

★★★★★
SELF CATERING

Units 4
Sleeps 1–4

LOW SEASON PER WK
£295.00–£395.00

HIGH SEASON PER WK
£395.00–£595.00

Various special rates available for flexible short breaks. Details available on request, or visit our website.

Composers at Woodlands, Berwick-upon-Tweed

contact Mr & Mrs Martin & Dee Colam, Composers at Woodlands, Woodlands, Scremerston, Berwick-upon-Tweed TD15 2QU **t** (01289) 332599 **e** info@composers-woodlands.co.uk

composers-woodlands.co.uk SPECIAL OFFERS • REAL-TIME BOOKING

open All year
payment Credit/debit cards, cash, cheques, euros
nearest shop 2 miles
nearest pub 2 miles

Luxury properties, tastefully furnished and immaculately maintained to highest standard. Fully fitted kitchens equipped with everything you could need, double and twin-bedded rooms, sumptuous bathroom suite with bath and walk-in shower. Lounge with leather sofas, writing desk, digital television and audio radio/CD. Simply perfect accommodation in tranquil surroundings.

SAT NAV *TD15 2QU* **ONLINE MAP**

Unit TV General P S Leisure

BERWICK-UPON-TWEED, Northumberland Map ref 5B1

★★★★
SELF CATERING

Units 1
Sleeps 6

LOW SEASON PER WK
£285.00–£401.00

HIGH SEASON PER WK
£322.00–£551.00

Smiddy Cottage, Berwick-upon-Tweed

contact Mrs June Simpson, Smiddy Cottage, Forgeway, Main Street, Horncliffe, Berwick-upon-Tweed TD15 2XW **t** (01289) 386411 **e** june@smiddycottage.co.uk

smiddycottage.co.uk

Converted blacksmith's shop in quiet village on English/Scottish border. Five miles from coast. Ideal for walking and fishing.

open All year
payment Cash, cheques
nearest shop 4 miles
nearest pub less than 0.5 miles

Unit TV General P

BEVERLEY, East Riding of Yorkshire Map ref 4C1

★★★★
SELF CATERING

Units 1
Sleeps 4

LOW SEASON PER WK
Min £275.00

HIGH SEASON PER WK
Max £370.00

The Cottage, Beverley

contact Kenneth Hearne, The Cottage, 25 Allhallows Road, Walkington HU17 8SH **t** (01482) 868310 **e** knhearne@talk21.com

akcottage.com

Cottage with two bedrooms (one double, one twin). Furnished to a very high standard. All mod cons and safety requirements. Private parking. Rural, picturesque environment.

open All year
payment Cash, cheques
nearest shop less than 0.5 miles
nearest pub less than 0.5 miles

Unit TV General 5 P Leisure

BEVERLEY, East Riding of Yorkshire Map ref 4C1

★★★★★
SELF CATERING

Units 1
Sleeps 2–12

LOW SEASON PER WK
£250.00–£900.00

HIGH SEASON PER WK
£350.00–£2,000.00

High Farm Country Park, Beverley

contact Lisa Johnson, High Farm Country Park, Beverley HU17 9SL **t** (01964) 543243 **e** info@highfarmcountrypark.co.uk

highfarmcountrypark.co.uk

Set around a beautiful courtyard with separate patio areas. Cottage can be booked as a whole or split into three units. En suite bathrooms, Freeview TV, luxury kitchens and leather sofas.

open All year
payment Credit/debit cards, cash, cheques
nearest shop 3 miles
nearest pub 1 mile

Unit TV General P S Leisure

BLAWITH, Cumbria Map ref 5A3

★★★★
SELF CATERING

Units 1
Sleeps 1–4

LOW SEASON PER WK
£225.00–£275.00

HIGH SEASON PER WK
£300.00–£375.00

Birchbank Cottage, Blawith

contact Linda Nicholson, Birchbank, Blawith, Ulverston LA12 8EW **t** (01229) 885277
e birchbank@btinternet.com

birchbank.co.uk

Relax and unwind in this lovely beamed cottage on a Lakeland sheep farm between Coniston Water and the Duddon Estuary. Cumbria Way 0.5 miles. One double, one twin. Linen and electricity included.

open All year
payment Cash, cheques
nearest shop 4 miles
nearest pub 4 miles

Unit General P Leisure

BOSTON SPA, West Yorkshire Map ref 4B1

★★★★
SELF CATERING

Units 1
Sleeps 3–6

LOW SEASON PER WK
£375.00

HIGH SEASON PER WK
£525.00

Short breaks (minimum 2 nights) available – please contact us for prices.

Skye Cottage, Boston Spa, Wetherby

contact Mr and Mrs David and Anne Watts, 20 Church Street, Boston Spa, Wetherby LS23 6DN
t 07941 353 202 **e** info@cosyhaven.co.uk

cosyhaven.co.uk GUEST REVIEWS • SPECIAL OFFERS

open All year
payment Cash, cheques, euros
nearest shop less than 0.5 miles
nearest pub less than 0.5 miles

Skye Cottage, a 19thC stone cottage with charisma, has two bedrooms (king with beamed ceiling, small double), well-equipped kitchen and dining room, patio/garden with barbecue and seating for six. Sleeps four (plus two). Flat-screen TV, DVD, MP3 docking and free Wi-Fi. You may not want to leave.

SAT NAV *LS23 6DN* **ONLINE MAP**

Unit General Leisure

BOWES, Durham Map ref 5B3

★★★★
SELF CATERING

Units 5
Sleeps 2–4

LOW SEASON PER WK
£165.00–£220.00

HIGH SEASON PER WK
£270.00–£360.00

Short breaks (3 nights) available from £125 for a 2-bedded cottage to £260 for a 4-bedded cottage.

Mellwaters Barn, Bowes, Barnard Castle

contact Mr Andrew Tavener, East Mellwaters Farm, Stainmore Road, Barnard Castle DL12 9RH
t (01833) 628181 **e** mellwatersbarn@aol.com

mellwatersbarn.co.uk

open All year
payment Cash, cheques
nearest shop 5 miles
nearest pub 1 mile

Wake up to wildlife on the edge of England's last wilderness, with quiet country roads and magnificent scenery. These spacious and airy cottages are fully equipped and are designed to give maximum possible access. Some cottages can be joined together for larger parties. Prices include everything except food.

Unit General P Leisure

Using map references

Map references refer to the colour maps at the front of this guide.

BOYNTON, East Riding of Yorkshire Map ref 5D3

★★★★
SELF CATERING

Units 1
Sleeps 4

LOW SEASON PER WK
£280.00–£350.00

HIGH SEASON PER WK
£350.00–£450.00

No 8 Boynton, Bridlington

contact Elizabeth Myhill, Glebe Farm, Rudston YO25 4UG **t** (01262) 420201
e djwilson.farm@tiscali.co.uk

no8boynton.co.uk GUEST REVIEWS

Delightful whitewashed country cottage. Original features, beautiful antique furniture. Fully equipped and centrally heated. Own garden and parking. Close to country houses, coastal resorts and RSPB reserve. Welcome refreshments provided.

open All year
payment Cash, cheques
nearest shop 3 miles
nearest pub 3 miles

Unit General P Leisure

BRIDLINGTON, East Riding of Yorkshire Map ref 5D3

★★★
SELF CATERING

Units 2
Sleeps 4

LOW SEASON PER WK
£215.00–£380.00

HIGH SEASON PER WK
£410.00–£494.00

East Coast Holiday Cottages, Bridlington

contact Cynthia Dean, East Coast Holiday Cottages, 23 Scarborough Crescent YO16 7PA
t 0845 863 9743 **e** eastcoastholidaycottages@hotmail.com

eastcoastholidaycottages.co.uk

East Coast Holiday Cottages has two bungalows in Sewerby village near the sea with lovely cliff-top walks, Sewerby Hall and Park and land train to Bridlington, one mile away. Pets are welcome in both bungalows.

open All year
payment Cash, cheques
nearest pub less than 0.5 miles

Unit General P Leisure

BRIDLINGTON, East Riding of Yorkshire Map ref 5D3

★★–★★★
SELF CATERING

Units 8
Sleeps 2–6

LOW SEASON PER WK
£140.00–£210.00

HIGH SEASON PER WK
£210.00–£420.00

Hemsley Holiday Flats, Bridlington

contact Mr E Halliday, Helmsley Holiday Flats, 5 Alexandra Drive, Bridlington YO15 2HZ
t (01262) 672603

open All year
payment Cash, cheques
nearest shop 0.5 miles
nearest pub 0.5 miles

Enjoying a quiet location on a private road overlooking the North Bay seafront, bowling green and Flamborough Head. Accommodation is self-contained with fridge, cooker and colour TV. Licensed residents' lounge. Scooter hire. Scooter- and wheelchair-charging facilities. Close to shops, cafes, and the Leisure World complex. Dogs welcome by arrangement. Private parking. Ground-floor bungalow available.

Unit General P

For **key to symbols** see page 7

BRINSCALL, Lancashire Map ref 4A1

★★★
SELF CATERING

Units 1
Sleeps 5–8

LOW SEASON PER WK
£375.00

HIGH SEASON PER WK
£475.00

Part- and midweek bookings accepted.

Moors View Cottage, Chorley

contact Mrs Sheila Smith, Moors View Cottage, Four Seasons Guest House, Thornton FY5 1EP
t (01253) 853537 & 07747 808406 **e** fourseasonsguesthouse@talktalk.net

open All year
payment Cash, cheques, euros
nearest shop less than 0.5 miles
nearest pub less than 0.5 miles

Situated amid lovely countryside adjacent to canal, motorways, market towns and coast, this fully equipped cottage comprises two bedrooms and excellent bed-settee, luxury bathroom, separate shower and toilet, large through lounge and dining area, oak kitchen, off-road parking, large rear garden and sun room. Fuel, power and linen included.

Unit General P Leisure

BUTTERMERE, Cumbria Map ref 5A3

★★★★
SELF CATERING

Units 6
Sleeps 2–6

LOW SEASON PER WK
Min £280.00

HIGH SEASON PER WK
Max £745.00

Any reservations of 4 or more nights DB&B receive a further night on the same basis free. Please refer to website for last-minute offers.

Bridge Hotel & Self Catering Apartments, Buttermere

contact John McGuire, Bridge Hotel & Self Catering Apartments, Buttermere, Nr Keswick CA13 9UZ
t (017687) 70252 **e** enquiries@bridge-hotel.com

bridge-hotel.com SPECIAL OFFERS

open All year
payment Credit/debit cards, cash, cheques, euros
nearest shop less than 0.5 miles
nearest pub less than 0.5 miles

Superbly situated and surrounded by fells, six apartments disposed over two floors; three lower have one bedroom, sleeping up to four; three upper have two bedrooms, two bathrooms, and sleep up to six. Included are dishwashers, fridges/freezers, ovens, toasters, microwaves, TV, DVD, linen, towels and car parking. Hotel bars offer drinks and good food.

Unit General P
Leisure

CARLISLE, Cumbria Map ref 5A2

★★★★
SELF CATERING

Units 1
Sleeps 1–4

LOW SEASON PER WK
£260.00–£320.00

HIGH SEASON PER WK
£355.00–£460.00

West Cottage, Cumwhinton, Carlisle

contact Mrs Allison Stamper, West Cottage, Cringles, Cumwhinton CA4 8DL **t** (01228) 561600

A spacious, tastefully furnished and well-equipped cottage adjoining a Georgian listed house in a village location three miles from historic Carlisle city. Shop, post office and pub in village.

open All year
payment Cash, cheques
nearest shop less than 0.5 miles
nearest pub less than 0.5 miles

Unit General P
Leisure

Remember to check when booking

Please remember that all information in this guide has been supplied by the proprietors well in advance of publication. Since changes do sometimes occur it's a good idea to check details at the time of booking.

CARNFORTH, Lancashire Map ref 5B3

★★★
SELF CATERING

Units 2
Sleeps 4–6

LOW SEASON PER WK
£270.00–£320.00

HIGH SEASON PER WK
£340.00–£480.00

Old Waterslack Farm Cottages and Caravans, Silverdale, Nr Carnforth

contact Sam Riseborough, Old Waterslack Farm Cottages and Caravans, Silverdale, Carnforth LA5 0UH **t** (01524) 720833 **e** bnhevey@tiscali.co.uk

oldwaterslackfarmholidaycottages.co.uk

open All year
payment Cash, cheques
nearest shop 1 mile
nearest pub 1 mile

Two high-quality holiday cottages on the outskirts of the beautiful village of Silverdale. Well-appointed accommodation in tranquil, scenic surroundings, one mile from village with shops, post office and pubs. Shippen sleeps six, Coach House sleeps four. Excellent walking country – as gentle or strenuous as you like! Historic Lancaster and Kendal easily accessible.

Unit TV SC DVD General P S
Leisure

CARTMEL, Cumbria Map ref 5A3

★★★★
SELF CATERING

Units 1
Sleeps 7–9

LOW SEASON PER WK
£340.00–£535.00

HIGH SEASON PER WK
£675.00–£1,150.00

WALKERS WELCOME · CYCLISTS WELCOME

The Hayloft, Nr Cartmel, Grange-over-Sands

contact Carrie Tomlinson, c/o Highfield, Arkholme, Carnforth LA6 1AU **t** (01524) 221390 **e** hayloft.info@virgin.net

hayloftcottageholidays.co.uk GUEST REVIEWS · SPECIAL OFFERS

The Hayloft is a luxury barn conversion in south Lakeland's stunning Cartmel Peninsula. It features three bedrooms, including a four-poster bed, jacuzzi bathroom, galleried lounge, games room and enclosed garden.

open All year
payment Cheques
nearest shop 0.5 miles
nearest pub less than 0.5 miles

Unit TV DVD General P S
Leisure

CARTMEL, Cumbria Map ref 5A3

★★★–★★★★
SELF CATERING

Units 7
Sleeps 1–18

LOW SEASON PER WK
£240.00–£350.00

HIGH SEASON PER WK
£400.00–£780.00

Short breaks available from Nov-Easter and throughout the year if availability allows.

Longlands at Cartmel, Grange-over-Sands

contact Martin Ainscough, Longlands at Cartmel, Cartmel, Grange-over-Sands LA11 6HG **t** (015395) 36475 **e** longlands@cartmel.com

cartmel.com SPECIAL OFFERS

open All year
payment Cash, cheques
nearest shop 1 mile
nearest pub 1 mile

Extremely well-equipped cottages, furnished to a very high standard, set in a courtyard behind a beautiful Georgian house set in parkland on the side of Hampsfell outside Cartmel. Restored walled garden. Great walks, and superb pubs and restaurants in the village.

Unit TV DVD General S Leisure

Has every property been assessed?

All accommodation in this guide has been rated for quality, or is awaiting assessment, by a professional national tourist board assessor.

For **key to symbols** see page 7

CASTLESIDE, Durham Map ref 5B2

★★–★★★
SELF CATERING

Units 5
Sleeps 1–11

LOW SEASON PER WK
£225.00–£700.00

HIGH SEASON PER WK
£250.00–£750.00

Short breaks of 3 nights often available – call for details.

Derwent Grange Cottages, Consett

contact Mr & Mrs Elliot, Derwent Grange Farm, Castleside, Consett DH8 9BN **t** (01207) 508358
e ekelliot@aol.com

derwentgrange.co.uk

open All year
payment Cash, cheques
nearest shop 1 mile
nearest pub 1 mile

Charming cottages converted from farm buildings, set on a working sheep farm, providing a serene, relaxing holiday. Access to wonderful countryside and tourist attractions. Friendly hosts. Accommodation caters for singles, couples or families and all linen and heating is included. Laundry facilities are available.

Unit General P Leisure

CASTLESIDE, Durham Map ref 5B2

★★★★
SELF CATERING

Units 1
Sleeps 1–4

LOW SEASON PER WK
£250.00–£300.00

HIGH SEASON PER WK
£300.00–£350.00

Jasmine Cottage, Castleside, Consett

contact Mrs Margaret Steel, Jasmine Cottage, Pondfield Villa Farm, Millershill Lane, Consett DH8 9HF **t** (01207) 582703 **e** k.a.steel@btinternet.com

pondfieldvillacottage.co.uk

open All year
payment Cash, cheques
nearest shop 2 miles
nearest pub 2 miles

Well-equipped comfortable cottage set in open countryside, close to A68 and local facilities. The cottage is on one level, has a modern kitchen and two bedrooms with en suite. Ideal base to visit Durham, Roman Wall, Beamish Museum, Newcastle, MetroCentre, or relax in the garden or patio. Parking for two cars.

SAT NAV *DH8 9HF*

Unit General P Leisure

CHATTON, Northumberland Map ref 5B1

★★★
SELF CATERING

Units 1
Sleeps 2

LOW SEASON PER WK
£150.00–£240.00

HIGH SEASON PER WK
£260.00–£340.00

Percy Cottage, Alnwick

contact Mrs Helen Reed-Jones, The Property Investments, Jamarus Lodge, Kirknewton, Wooler NE71 6XF **t** (01668) 216556 **e** tonyreedjones@aol.com

percycottage.co.uk

Attractive stone cottage set in village of Chatton, beautifully refurbished and offering spacious, well-equipped accommodation.

open All year
payment Cash, cheques
nearest shop less than 0.5 miles
nearest pub less than 0.5 miles

Unit General P

CYCLISTS WELCOME

Fancy a cycling holiday?

For a fabulous freewheeling break, seek out accommodation participating in our Cyclists Welcome scheme. Look out for the symbol and plan your route online at nationalcyclenetwork.org.

CHESTER, Cheshire Map ref 4A2

★★★
SELF CATERING

Units 1
Sleeps 1–4

LOW SEASON PER WK
£150.00–£200.00

HIGH SEASON PER WK
£200.00–£250.00

Kingswood Coach House, Chester

contact Mrs C Perry, Kingswood Coach House, Kingswood, Parkgate Road, Chester CH1 6JS
t (01244) 851204 **e** caroline.m.perry@btopenworld.com

Ideal for couples. Large bedroom, fitted kitchen, living room, toilet and shower. Garden and patio, off-road parking. Close to bus route. Near Wales and Wirral.

open All year
payment Cash, cheques
nearest shop 2 miles
nearest pub less than 0.5 miles

Unit General P Leisure

CHESTER, Cheshire Map ref 4A2

★★★
SELF CATERING

Units 2
Sleeps 5

LOW SEASON PER WK
£200.00–£420.00

HIGH SEASON PER WK
£230.00–£560.00

Spireview Apartment, Chester

contact Mr Michael Pimlott, 14 Beckenham Road, Wallasey CH45 2NZ **t** 07800 123964
e corkeyhomes@hotmail.com

corkeyhomes.co.uk REAL-TIME BOOKING

This spacious apartment has two double bedrooms (one has an en suite bathroom). There is a separate bathroom and a very large kitchen/living room with a balcony and views towards the city walls.

open All year
payment Cheques
nearest shop 0.5 miles
nearest pub less than 0.5 miles

Unit General P

CHESTER, Cheshire Map ref 4A2

★★★★
SELF CATERING

Units 1
Sleeps 1–4

LOW SEASON PER WK
Min £400.00

HIGH SEASON PER WK
Min £570.00

Wharton Lock Apartment & Balcony, Chester

contact Mrs Sandra Jeffrey, Chester Canalside Holidays, Chester CH2 3DH **t** (01244) 312788
e rentals@stayinchester.com

stayinchester.com GUEST REVIEWS • SPECIAL OFFERS • REAL-TIME BOOKING

Luxury apartment with private canalside balcony in Chester, five minutes' walk to city centre. King-size and twin bedrooms, two bathrooms, parking, Wi-Fi. Romantic breaks, family holidays, business trips.

open All year
payment Credit/debit cards, cash, cheques, euros
nearest shop less than 0.5 miles
nearest pub less than 0.5 miles

Unit General P Leisure

CHOP GATE, North Yorkshire Map ref 5C3

★★★★
SELF CATERING

Units 1
Sleeps 2–7

LOW SEASON PER WK
£325.00–£400.00

HIGH SEASON PER WK
£400.00–£500.00

Broadfields Cottage, Chop Gate

contact Mrs Judith Staples, Broadfields Cottage, Broadfields, Chop Gate, Middlesborough TS9 7JB
t (01642) 778384 **e** wkstaples@broadfields.orangehome.co.uk

open All year
payment Cash, cheques
nearest shop 2 miles
nearest pub 1 mile

Charming stone-built four-bedroomed country cottage adjoining owners' house. One double, one three-quarter, one bunk bed and one single. Two bathrooms. Wood-burning stove in living room. Outstanding views all around. Excellent walking country.

Unit General P Leisure

Where are the maps?

Colour maps can be found at the front of the guide. They pinpoint the location of all accommodation found in the regional sections.

CLITHEROE, Lancashire Map ref 4A1

★★★
SELF CATERING

Units 1
Sleeps 1–2

LOW SEASON PER WK
£140.00–£160.00

HIGH SEASON PER WK
£170.00–£220.00

Weavers Cottage, West Bradford, Clitheroe

contact Mr & Mrs Andrew & Susan Mackenzie, Brook House, Clitheroe Road, West Bradford, Clitheroe BB7 4TA **t** (01200) 443122 & 07709 923715 **e** rafmack@hotmail.com

Small, detached, restored 18thC weaver's cottage, two miles Clitheroe, providing studio accommodation. Off-road parking, beautiful gardens, private patio. Ideal for walking, birdwatching in Forest of Bowland. Dogs welcome.

open All year
payment Cash, cheques
nearest shop 2 miles
nearest pub 1 mile

Unit General P Leisure

COCKERMOUTH, Cumbria Map ref 5A2

★★★
SELF CATERING

Units 1
Sleeps 1–5

LOW SEASON PER WK
Max £275.00

HIGH SEASON PER WK
Max £350.00

37 Kirkgate, Cockermouth

contact Nelson & Val Chicken, 39 Kirkgate, Cockermouth CA13 9PJ **t** (01900) 823236
e valandnelson@btopenworld.com

37kirkgate.com

An ideal base for touring Cumbria, this spacious and comfortable three-bedroomed Georgian house overlooks the tree-lined, cobbled area of Kirkgate.

open All year
payment Cash, cheques
nearest shop less than 0.5 miles
nearest pub less than 0.5 miles

Unit General P Leisure

COCKERMOUTH, Cumbria Map ref 5A2

★★★
SELF CATERING

Units 1
Sleeps 4–6

LOW SEASON PER WK
£320.00–£390.00

HIGH SEASON PER WK
£450.00–£680.00

3-night breaks available Oct-Mar. 20% discount for 2 people, depending on season.

The Stables, Dean, Workington

contact Veronica Roper, Sunnyside, Gib Lane, Hoghton PR5 0RS **t** (01254) 852027 & 07901 913812
e veronica@vroper.fsnet.co.uk

vholidays.moonfruit.com GUEST REVIEWS • SPECIAL OFFERS • REAL-TIME BOOKING

open All year
payment Cash, cheques, euros
nearest shop 5 miles
nearest pub less than 0.5 miles

Delightful and very comfortable 18thC cottage with inglenooks, exposed beams and log fire – an excellent base at any time of year. Dean is a peaceful village, ideally situated for exploring the Northern Lakes, West Cumbria, Carlisle, the Solway Coast and the Scottish Borders. Secluded garden – perfect for relaxing. Walking, cycling, golf, fishing. Ospreys nearby.

SAT NAV *CA14 4TH*

Unit General P Leisure

COCKFIELD, Durham Map ref 5B3

★★★★
SELF CATERING

Units 2
Sleeps 4–5

LOW SEASON PER WK
Min £160.00

HIGH SEASON PER WK
Max £340.00

Midweek and weekend breaks available out of season. Open Christmas and New Year.

Stonecroft and Swallows Nest, Bishop Auckland

contact Mrs Alison Tallentire, Low Lands Farm, Bishop Auckland DL13 5AW **t** (01388) 718251
e info@farmholidaysuk.com

farmholidaysuk.com

open All year
payment Cash, cheques
nearest shop 1 mile
nearest pub 1 mile

Award-winning cottages on a working livestock farm. Both cottages beautifully renovated and decorated to an exceptionally high standard. Beams, log fires, gas barbecue, own gardens and parking. Close to Durham City, Northumberland, Lakes, Hadrian's Wall. Pets and children most welcome, childminding available. Children's equipment, fuels, electric, linens and towels all included.

Unit General P Leisure

CONGLETON, Cheshire Map ref 4B2

★★
SELF CATERING

Units 1
Sleeps 2–10

LOW SEASON PER WK
£333.00–£840.00

HIGH SEASON PER WK
£644.00–£875.00

Broomfield Barns, Congleton

contact Ms Anita Lockett, Broomfield Barns, Broomfield House, Trap Road, Congleton CW12 2LT
t (01260) 224581

broomfieldbarns.com SPECIAL OFFERS

Broomfield Barn provides self-catering accommodation for up to ten people. Located in the heart of the Cheshire countryside with easy access to the Derbyshire hills.

open All year except July
payment Cash, cheques
nearest shop 5 miles
nearest pub 0.5 miles

Unit General P S Leisure

CONISTON, Cumbria Map ref 5A3

★★★★
SELF CATERING

Units 2
Sleeps 6

LOW SEASON PER WK
Min £325.00

HIGH SEASON PER WK
Max £525.00

Short breaks available.

1 and 2 Ash Gill Cottages, Torver, Coniston

contact Dorothy Cowburn, Lyndene, Pope Lane, Whitestake, Preston PR4 4JR **t** (01772) 612832

open All year
payment Cash, cheques
nearest shop 3 miles
nearest pub less than 0.5 miles

Set amidst the rolling hills surrounding Coniston Water, the houses are equipped to the highest standard. Ample parking, gardens and patios. Central heating throughout for the cooler months. Excellent base for walking, touring, watersports and pony-trekking. Sorry, no pets.

Unit General 3 P S Leisure

WALKERS WELCOME WELCOME WALKERS

Do you like walking?

Walkers feel at home in accommodation participating in our Walkers Welcome scheme. Look out for the symbol. Consider walking all or part of a long-distance route – go online at nationaltrail.co.uk.

CONISTON, Cumbria Map ref 5A3

★★★
SELF CATERING

Units 1
Sleeps 4–5

LOW SEASON PER WK
Min £250.00

HIGH SEASON PER WK
Max £490.00

Shelt Gill, Coniston

contact Rosalind Dean, Shelt Gill, c/o 9 The Fairway, Sheffield S10 4LX **t** 0845 009 3998
e holiday@sheltgill.co.uk

sheltgill.co.uk

Medieval cottage with a view of Lake Coniston from the timbered living room. There is a stream in the garden and easy access to hill walks.

open All year
payment Cash, cheques, euros
nearest shop 1 mile
nearest pub less than 0.5 miles

Unit General P Leisure

CORBRIDGE, Northumberland Map ref 5B2

★★★★
SELF CATERING

Units 1
Sleeps 5

LOW SEASON PER WK
£300.00–£350.00

HIGH SEASON PER WK
£400.00

April Cottage, Corbridge

contact Mrs Kate Dean, 21 Woodland Close, Chelford, Macclesfield SK11 9BZ **t** (01625) 861718
e peterandkatedean@btopenworld.com

aprilcottagecorbridge.co.uk

open All year
payment Cash, cheques
nearest shop less than 0.5 miles
nearest pub less than 0.5 miles

19thC cottage in centre of village, with enclosed garden. Near to Hadrian's Wall and the Roman camps. Within easy reach of Northumbrian coast and castles, Kielder Forest and Northumberland National Park. There are good shops and food outlets plus proximity of historic Newcastle with its bridges, the Sage and Baltic galleries.

ONLINE MAP

WALKERS WELCOME

Unit General Leisure

CORBRIDGE, Northumberland Map ref 5B2

★★★
SELF CATERING

Units 2
Sleeps 4–5

LOW SEASON PER WK
£235.00–£300.00

HIGH SEASON PER WK
£325.00–£425.00

The Hayes, Corbridge

contact Mrs Monica Matthews, The Hayes, Newcastle Road, Corbridge NE45 5LP **t** (01434) 632010
e camon@surfree.co.uk

hayes-corbridge.co.uk

Two stone cottages, converted from former stables. Set in a small courtyard, in spacious grounds of large country house on the outskirts of historic village near Hadrian's Wall. Easy access A68/A69.

open All year
payment Credit/debit cards, cash, cheques
nearest shop 0.5 miles
nearest pub 0.5 miles

Unit General P S Leisure

What do the star ratings mean?

For a detailed explanation of the quality and facilities represented by the stars, please refer to the information pages at the back of this guide.

CORBRIDGE, Northumberland Map ref 5B2

★★★★
SELF CATERING

Units 1
Sleeps 6

LOW SEASON PER WK
£250.00–£350.00

HIGH SEASON PER WK
£350.00–£550.00

Weekends available.

Oswald Cottage, Corbridge

contact Mrs Hannah Harriman, Oswald Cottage, Swarden House, Kyloe House Farm, Eachwick, Newcastle upon Tyne NE18 0BB **t** (01661) 852909 **e** hannahharriman@btinternet.com

open All year
payment Cash, cheques
nearest shop less than 0.5 miles
nearest pub less than 0.5 miles

Exceptional 18thC double-fronted large stone cottage. Carved external Latin inscription 'To the good all things are good' reflects interior ambience. Beams and open fire. In heart of historic village but quiet. Stone's throw from river and superb local shops. Lovely patio garden. Perfect, winter or summer.

Unit TV General 5 S

CORBRIDGE, Northumberland Map ref 5B2

★★★
SELF CATERING

Units 1
Sleeps 4

LOW SEASON PER WK
£110.00–£200.00

HIGH SEASON PER WK
£250.00–£280.00

West Fell Cottage, Corbridge

contact Mrs Joan Smith, West Fell Cottage, Ladycutter Lane, Corbridge NE45 5RZ **t** (01434) 632044 **e** westfell@hotmail.co.uk

Two-bedroom farm cottage near Dilston Castle, convenient for Corbridge and the Roman Wall.

open All year
payment Cash, cheques
nearest shop 1.5 miles
nearest pub 0.75 miles

Unit TV DVD General P Leisure

CORNRIGGS, Durham Map ref 5B2

★★★★★
SELF CATERING

Units 2
Sleeps 2–6

LOW SEASON PER WK
£310.00–£380.00

HIGH SEASON PER WK
£450.00–£560.00

Cornriggs Cottages, Cowshill in Weardale, Bishop Auckland

contact Mr & Mrs Harry and Janet Elliott, Cornriggs Cottages, c/o Low Cornriggs Farm, Cornriggs, Cowshill DL13 1AQ **t** (01388) 537600 & 07818 843159 **e** cornriggsfarm@btconnect.com

britnett.net/lowcornriggsfarm SPECIAL OFFERS · REAL-TIME BOOKING

open All year
payment Credit/debit cards, cash, cheques, euros
nearest shop 4 miles
nearest pub 1 mile

Two beautiful, large, luxury cottages in the heart of Weardale. Working hill farm with wildflower meadows, spectacular views, quiet roads. Wake up to the sound of birdsong. Each cottage has three bedrooms, two en suite bathrooms and an accessible wc and shower, fitted kitchen and dining area, lounge, patio, garden and safe play area.

SAT NAV *DL13 1AQ* **ONLINE MAP**

1
WALKERS WELCOME · CYCLISTS WELCOME · FAMILIES WELCOME

Unit TV DVD General P S Leisure

PETS! WELCOME WELCOME PETS!

Where is my pet welcome?

Want to take your cherished companion with you on holiday? Proprietors participating in our Welcome Pets! scheme go out of their way to make special provision for you and your pet. Look out for the symbol.

CRAMLINGTON, Northumberland Map ref 5C2

★★★★
SELF CATERING

Units 9
Sleeps 2–36

LOW SEASON PER WK
£290.00–£590.00

HIGH SEASON PER WK
£430.00–£870.00

3-4-night stays welcomed, all year round.

Burradon Farm Houses & Cottages, Cramlington

contact Mrs Judith Younger, Burradon Farm Houses & Cottages, Burradon Farm, Cramlington NE23 7ND **t** (0191) 268 3203 **e** judy@burradonfarm.co.uk

burradonfarm.co.uk REAL-TIME BOOKING

open All year
payment Credit/debit cards, cash, cheques
nearest shop 0.5 miles
nearest pub 0.5 miles

Burradon Farm is located only a few miles from the spectacular Northumbrian coastline and within easy reach of the cultural heritage and dynamic centre which is Newcastle-upon-Tyne. The new barn conversions have become characterful, high-quality houses and cottages boasting every amenity and facility to ensure an enjoyable visit. Dishwasher in houses. Wi-Fi internet connection.

ONLINE MAP

Unit TV DVD General P S Leisure

CRASTER, Northumberland Map ref 5C1

★★★★
SELF CATERING

Units 1
Sleeps 8

LOW SEASON PER WK
Max £750.00

HIGH SEASON PER WK
Max £1,750.00

Craster Tower Penthouse Apartment, Alnwick

contact Mrs Fiona Craster, Craster Tower, Alnwick NE66 3SS **t** (01665) 576674
e stay@crastertower.co.uk

crastertower.co.uk REAL-TIME BOOKING

Spacious penthouse apartment in historic Craster Tower, close to picturesque fishing village. Sleeps eight. Centrally heated plus log-burning stove. Two bathrooms and additional shower room.

open All year
payment Credit/debit cards, cash, cheques, euros
nearest shop less than 0.5 miles
nearest pub 0.5 miles

Unit TV DVD General P S
Leisure

CREWE, Cheshire Map ref 4A2

★★★
SELF CATERING

Units 2
Sleeps 2–6

LOW SEASON PER WK
Min £300.00

HIGH SEASON PER WK
Max £400.00

Bank Farm Cottages, Crewe

contact Mrs Ann Vaughan, Newcastle Road, Crewe CW2 5JG **t** (01270) 841809

Charming holiday cottages created from Victorian farm buildings, furnished to a high standard. Full gas central heating, washing machines, microwaves. Ample parking. Excellent base for North Wales potteries.

open All year
payment Cash, cheques, euros
nearest shop 1 mile
nearest pub 0.5 miles

Unit TV General P Leisure

DALTON, North Yorkshire Map ref 5B3

★★★
SELF CATERING

Units 1
Sleeps 4

LOW SEASON PER WK
£200.00–£300.00

HIGH SEASON PER WK
£300.00–£420.00

Keepers Cottage, Dalton

contact Dorothy Lewis, Keepers Cottage, Dalton Hall, Dalton, Richmond DL11 7GU
t (01833) 621446 **e** dorothy.lewis@cottagesnorthyorkshire.co.uk

Lovingly restored Georgian gamekeeper's cottage. Lounge, eat-in kitchen, two bedrooms. Beautiful views across open countryside.

open All year
payment Cash, cheques
nearest shop 8 miles
nearest pub 0.5 miles

Unit TV General P S Leisure

What if I need to cancel?

It's advisable to check the proprietor's cancellation policy at the time of booking in case you have to change your plans.

DANBY, North Yorkshire Map ref 5C3

★★
SELF CATERING

Units 1
Sleeps 1–7

LOW SEASON PER WK
£190.00–£290.00

HIGH SEASON PER WK
£220.00–£330.00

Clitherbecks Farm, Danby, Whitby

contact Mrs Catherine Harland, Clitherbecks Farm, Danby YO21 2NT **t** (01287) 660321
e nharland@clitherbecks.freeserve.co.uk

clitherbecks.freeserve.co.uk

open All year
payment Cash, cheques
nearest shop 2 miles
nearest pub 1 mile

Neil and Cathy Harland welcome you to Clitherbecks Farm, one mile from Danby and directly north from the National Park Moors Centre. Accommodation for seven people in two bedrooms in the farmhouse. You have your own entrance through a fenced garden. Seasonal produce available from this traditional hill farm.

SAT NAV *YO21 2NT*

Unit General P Leisure

DARLINGTON, Tees Valley Map ref 5C3

★★★
SELF CATERING

Units 1
Sleeps 4

LOW SEASON PER WK
£260.00–£280.00

HIGH SEASON PER WK
£280.00–£330.00

Pegasus Cottage, Darlington

contact Mr & Mrs Stuart and Denise Chapman, Pegasus Cottage, 4 Tees View, Hurworth Place, Darlington DL2 2DH **t** (01325) 722542 **e** stuart1948@msn.com

pegasuscottage.co.uk

Converted stable block of a Grade II Listed building, c1850. Local mayor's Design Award winner 1995. Set in small village three miles from Darlington.

open All year
payment Credit/debit cards, cash, cheques
nearest shop 1 mile
nearest pub less than 0.5 miles

Unit General P Leisure

DELPH, Greater Manchester Map ref 4B1

★★★★
SELF CATERING

Units 2
Sleeps 2–6

LOW SEASON PER WK
£250.00–£350.00

HIGH SEASON PER WK
£300.00–£400.00

The Stables, Delph, Oldham

contact Mrs G Whipp, Sandbed Farm Cottage, Sandbed Lane, Delph, Oldham OL3 5UZ
t (01457) 871668 **e** gwyneth.whipp@btinternet.com

saddleworthcottages.co.uk

Luxury modern conversion of stables into two self-contained units in rural and historic area, known as Saddleworth. One family room plus sofa bed and two twin rooms plus sofa bed.

open All year
payment Cash, cheques, euros
nearest shop 0.5 miles
nearest pub 0.5 miles

Unit General P

DENT, Cumbria Map ref 5B3

★★★
SELF CATERING

Units 2
Sleeps 4

LOW SEASON PER WK
£220.00–£265.00

HIGH SEASON PER WK
£265.00–£350.00

Short breaks from Oct-Mar, weekend or midweek. Any combination, subject to availability.

Middleton's Cottage and Fountain Cottage, Dent, Sedbergh

contact Mr & Mrs Ayers, Middleton's Cottage and Fountain Cottage, The Old Rectory, Polegate BN26 5RB **t** (01323) 870032 **e** candpayers@mistral.co.uk

dentcottages.co.uk

open All year
payment Cash, cheques
nearest shop less than 0.5 miles
nearest pub less than 0.5 miles

Modernised mid-17thC cottages in centre of small, quaint village, comfortably furnished and decorated to high standards. Quiet, unspoilt Dentdale offers a good base for walking, touring and exploring the Yorkshire Dales or the Lake District, with Kendal and Hawes nearby. Brochure available.

Unit General

DRIFFIELD, East Riding of Yorkshire Map ref 4C1

★★★
SELF CATERING

Units 2
Sleeps 1–5

LOW SEASON PER WK
£195.00–£295.00

HIGH SEASON PER WK
£295.00–£495.00

Manor Farm Cottages, North Dalton, Driffield

contact Antony & Jennie Byass, Manor Farm Cottages, North Dalton Manor, Driffield YO25 9UX **t** (01377) 217324 **e** lanpulse@aol.com

yorkshirewoldsholidaycottages.com

Fully modernised Georgian cottages in pretty village. Ideal for exploring York, Beverley and east coast. Moors and many stately homes within easy driving distance. Good pubs serving food nearby.

open All year
payment Cash, cheques
nearest shop 2 miles
nearest pub 2 miles

Unit General Leisure

DUFTON, Cumbria Map ref 5B3

★★★★
SELF CATERING

Units 2
Sleeps 2–8

LOW SEASON PER WK
Min £400.00

HIGH SEASON PER WK
Max £700.00

Brow Farm Bed & Breakfast, Appleby-in-Westmorland

contact Mrs Wendy Swinbank, Brow Farm Bed & Breakfast, Dufton, Appleby-in-Westmorland CA16 6DF **t** (017683) 52865 **e** stay@browfarm.com

browfarm.com

open All year
payment Credit/debit cards, cash, cheques
nearest shop 0.5 miles
nearest pub 0.5 miles

New barn conversion creating two self-catering cottages. Both well equipped and finished to a high standard. Set in picturesque village at the foot of Pennines. Good area for walking and touring Lake District and Yorkshire Dales.

Unit General

Looking for an ideal family break?

For accommodation offering additional facilities and services for a range of ages and family units, look out for the Families Welcome symbol. Owners of these properties will go out of their way to welcome families.

DURHAM Map ref 5C2

★★★★
SELF CATERING

Units 1
Sleeps 4

LOW SEASON PER WK
£350.00–£450.00

HIGH SEASON PER WK
£450.00–£550.00

Apt 19 Freemans Quay, Walkergate, Durham

contact G S Hall, Garden Cottage, Southill Hall, Plawsworth DH3 4EQ **t** (0191) 387 3001
e graham375@btinternet.com

New luxury two-bedroom, two-bathroom apartment with balcony and secure parking in the heart of Durham city centre.

open All year
payment Cash, cheques, euros
nearest shop less than 0.5 miles
nearest pub less than 0.5 miles

Unit TV DVD General P

DURHAM Map ref 5C2

★★★★
SELF CATERING

Units 1
Sleeps 1–5

LOW SEASON PER WK
£560.00–£700.00

City of Durham Freemans Quay Apartment, Durham

contact Mrs Marcia Watson, 1 Freemans Quay, Millennium Place, Durham DH1 1WA
t (01388) 812429 & 07779 729388 **e** info@cityofdurhamapartment.co.uk

cityofdurhamapartment.co.uk SPECIAL OFFERS · REAL-TIME BOOKING

City of Durham Freemans Quay Apartment is a luxurious two-bedroomed, two-bathroomed fully serviced self-catering accommodation in the heart of Durham City.

open All year
payment Credit/debit cards, cash, cheques
nearest shop less than 0.5 miles
nearest pub less than 0.5 miles

Unit TV SC DVD General P S

DURHAM Map ref 5C2

★★★★
SELF CATERING

Units 1
Sleeps 2–4

LOW SEASON PER WK
£250.00–£300.00

HIGH SEASON PER WK
£300.00–£380.00

The Old Power House, Chester-le-Street

contact Mrs Anne Hall, Garden Cottage, Southill Hall, Chester-le-Street DH3 4EQ **t** (0191) 387 3001
e graham375@btinternet.com

theoldpowerhouse.co.uk

Redeveloped power house in walled garden of old hall, providing compact two-bedroomed country cottage. Three-acre landscaped gardens. Idyllic location midway between Durham (three miles) and Chester-le-Street. Newcastle and MetroCentre (Gateshead) 25 minutes.

open All year
payment Cash, cheques, euros
nearest shop 2 miles
nearest pub 1 mile

Unit TV DVD General P

DURHAM Map ref 5C2

★★★★
SELF CATERING

Units 1
Sleeps 10

LOW SEASON PER WK
£1,000.00–£1,250.00

HIGH SEASON PER WK
£1,250.00–£1,500.00

Ramside Farmhouse, Durham

contact Ms Katherine Hunt, Ramside Farmhouse, Carrville, Durham DH1 1TD **t** (0191) 386 5282
e reservations@ramsidehallhotel.co.uk

ramsidehallhotel.co.uk SPECIAL OFFERS · REAL-TIME BOOKING

Ramside Farmhouse is situated in the middle of the glorious Ramside Golf Course, with its own walled garden. The interior is superb. Five double bedrooms, three bathrooms, lounge with real fire, country kitchen/pantry.

open All year
payment Credit/debit cards
nearest shop less than 0.5 miles
nearest pub less than 0.5 miles

Unit TV SC DVD General P S
Leisure

Using map references

The map references refer to the colour maps at the front of this guide. The first figure is the map number, the letter and figure that follow indicate the grid reference on the map.

EASBY, North Yorkshire Map ref 5C3

★★★★★
SELF CATERING

Units **1**
Sleeps **6**

LOW SEASON PER WK
£420.00–£590.00

HIGH SEASON PER WK
£590.00–£760.00

Short breaks available Oct-Mar.

Abbey House, Richmond

contact John Martin, The Old Stables, Easby, Richmond DL10 7EU **t** (01748) 825298
e easbycottages@hotmail.co.uk

open All year
payment Cash, cheques, euros
nearest shop 1 mile
nearest pub 1 mile

13thC cottage which has been sympathetically refurbished to provide high quality accommodation consisting of three en suite double bedrooms, large comfortable lounge, cloakroom and fully equipped kitchen/diner opening onto large enclosed courtyard. Fishing rights from the garden. The property provides a truly peaceful and idyllic retreat.

Unit General P Leisure

EGGLESTON, Durham Map ref 5B3

★★★★
SELF CATERING

Units **1**

LOW SEASON PER WK
£320.00–£380.00

HIGH SEASON PER WK
£380.00–£810.00

Stable Court, Barnard Castle

contact Mrs J D Broughton, Holt Road, Swanton Novers, Melton Constable NR24 2NW
t (01263) 862500

open All year
payment Cash, cheques
nearest shop 5 miles
nearest pub 2 miles

Set high in the beautiful Teesdale Valley with outstanding views and spacious accommodation. A holiday offering country living, peace and tranquillity within easy reach of many places of interest and activities. Lovely walks from the property. Picturesque Cotherstone and Eggleston offer pubs and shop. Historic market town of Barnard Castle four miles.

Unit General

EGTON BRIDGE, North Yorkshire Map ref 5D3

★★★–★★★★
SELF CATERING

Units **3**
Sleeps **2–4**

LOW SEASON PER WK
£194.00–£324.00

HIGH SEASON PER WK
£324.00–£595.00

Broom House Cottages, Egton Bridge, Whitby

contact David & Maria White, Broom Cottage, Whitby YO21 1XD **t** (01947) 895279
e mw@broom-house.co.uk

egton-bridge.co.uk GUEST REVIEWS • SPECIAL OFFERS • REAL-TIME BOOKING

open All year
payment Credit/debit cards, cash, cheques
nearest shop 2 miles
nearest pub 0.75 miles

Recently refurbished stone cottages situated in Egton Bridge village in the beautiful Esk Valley, in the North York Moors National Park. Excellent walking etc. Shop and pub within walking distance. Visit website for more details.

ONLINE MAP

Unit General P Leisure

EGTON BRIDGE, North Yorkshire Map ref 5D3

★★★
SELF CATERING

Units 1
Sleeps 1–4

LOW SEASON PER WK
Max £250.00

HIGH SEASON PER WK
Max £365.00

Key Green Farmhouse Annexe, Egton Bridge, Whitby

contact Mr and Mrs Kate & Ian Johnson, Key Green Farmhouse, Egton Bridge, Whitby YO22 5AX
t (01947) 895601 **e** keygreenfarmhouse@yahoo.co.uk

keygreenfarmhouse.co.uk

One-bedroom farmhouse annexe in the North York Moors, ideal location for walking and relaxing. Within easy reach of local shops and pubs.

open All year
payment Cash, cheques
nearest shop 2 miles
nearest pub less than 0.5 miles

Unit General P Leisure

EMBLETON, Northumberland Map ref 5C1

★★★★★
SELF CATERING

Units 7
Sleeps 2–8

LOW SEASON PER WK
£220.00–£400.00

HIGH SEASON PER WK
£550.00–£1,700.00

Winter short breaks with wildlife walks. Fishing on private lake included in price. Fully inclusive prices with logs, electricity, linen, towels.

Doxford Cottages, Embleton

contact Ms Sue Pringle, Doxford Cottages, Doxford Estate, Chathill NE67 5DW **t** (01665) 589393
e stay@doxfordcottages.co.uk

doxfordcottages.co.uk GUEST REVIEWS • SPECIAL OFFERS • REAL-TIME BOOKING

open All year
payment Credit/debit cards, cash, cheques
nearest shop 2 miles
nearest pub 2 miles

Superb location on 2,500-acre estate near Beadnell. Luxurious cottages, a perfect retreat with south-facing terraces opening to lawns with views of Doxford Lake. The cottages have granite worktops, oak furniture and modern kitchens; Sky TV, CD and DVD, radios and broadband. Great comfort and style for the perfect holiday.

SAT NAV *NE67 5DW* **ONLINE MAP**

Unit General P S
Leisure

EMBLETON, Northumberland Map ref 5C1

★★★–★★★★
SELF CATERING

Units 9
Sleeps 2–7

LOW SEASON PER WK
£175.00–£225.00

HIGH SEASON PER WK
£350.00–£600.00

3-night stays available Oct-Mar (excl Christmas and New Year).

Doxford Farm Cottages, Chathill

contact Mrs Sarah Shell, Doxford Farm, Doxford, Chathill NE67 5DY **t** (01665) 579348 & (01665) 579477 **e** doxfordfarm@hotmail.com

doxfordfarmcottages.com

open All year
payment Credit/debit cards, cash, cheques
nearest shop 4 miles
nearest pub 4 miles

Well equipped cottages on a working farm in wooded countryside four miles from sea. Central heating, open fires. Wildlife trails and woodland walks. Ideal base for Northumberland's castles, coastline and Alnwick Gardens.

Unit General P S
Leisure

Looking for a wide range of facilities?

More stars means higher quality accommodation plus a greater range of facilities and services.

ESKDALE, Cumbria Map ref 5A3

★★★★
SELF CATERING

Units **4**
Sleeps **1–5**

LOW SEASON PER WK
£250.00–£280.00

HIGH SEASON PER WK
£320.00–£500.00

Flexible short breaks available Nov-Feb. Any combination of days to suit your plans.

The Chalets, Eskdale

contact Lisa Borrowdale & Philip Hayden, The Chalets, Boot, Eskdale CA19 1TF **t** (019467) 23128
e info@thechalets.co.uk

thechalets.co.uk

open All year
payment Cash, cheques
nearest shop 1 mile
nearest pub less than 0.5 miles

In a peaceful and untouched part of the Lake District, surrounded by stunning scenery, The Chalets have four immaculately presented cottages. Each has two bedrooms, a modern kitchen and pristine bathroom; large living/dining area; mature south facing riverside gardens. BBQ facilities, charming pubs and spectacular walks. Two chalets sleep five and two sleep four.

Unit General P Leisure

ESKDALE, Cumbria Map ref 5A3

★★★★
SELF CATERING

Units **1**
Sleeps **2–6**

LOW SEASON PER WK
£300.00–£405.00

HIGH SEASON PER WK
£440.00–£530.00

Old Brantrake, Eskdale

contact Mr & Mrs Tyson, Brant Rake, Eskdale CA19 1TT **t** (019467) 23340

open All year
payment Cash, cheques
nearest shop 1.5 miles
nearest pub 0.75 miles

17thC listed farmhouse in a quiet rural setting; ideal for walking, exploring the central fells or touring. Restored to high standard, three bedrooms, with two WCs, bath and shower, modern kitchen and woodfire. In winter, short lets (minimum three nights) are also available. Brochure.

Unit General P Leisure

ESKDALE, Cumbria Map ref 5A3

★★★★
SELF CATERING

Units **1**
Sleeps **2–4**

LOW SEASON PER WK
£255.00–£355.00

HIGH SEASON PER WK
£400.00–£465.00

Randle How, Eskdale Green

contact Susan Wedley, Randle How, c/o Long Yocking How, Eskdale Green, Holmrook CA19 1UA
t (01946) 723126 **e** jswedley@btinternet.com

3randlehowselfcatering.com

open All year
payment Cash, cheques
nearest shop 0.5 miles
nearest pub 0.5 miles

Cosy 18thC cottage in a quiet lane, with modern facilities and a well-equipped kitchen. Log fires, full central heating and large attractive garden. An ideal all-year location for walking or touring holidays in the western lakes. Five minutes from the village shop and the Ravenglass and Eskdale railway.

Unit General P

What shall we do today?

For ideas on places to visit, see the beginning of this regional section or go online at enjoyengland.com.

FILEY, North Yorkshire Map ref 5D3

★★★★★
SELF CATERING

Units 22
Sleeps 2–6

LOW SEASON PER WK
£350.00–£450.00

HIGH SEASON PER WK
£550.00–£750.00

Some apartments designated for short breaks only. See website for booking and more.

5 Leys Holiday Accommodation, Filey

contact Mrs Sonia Suggars, 5 Leys Holiday Accommodation, 7-10 The Beach, Filey YO14 9LA
t 0845 094 5051 **e** info@5leys.co.uk

5leys.co.uk SPECIAL OFFERS • REAL-TIME BOOKING

open All year
payment Credit/debit cards, cash, cheques
nearest shop 1 mile
nearest pub less than 0.5 miles

5 Leys Holiday Accommodation is ideally located only seven metres away from award-winning sands. An on-site bar and restaurants allows guests to choose between booking a table and preparing a meal in their own luxury suite/apartment. We are five minutes' walk from the town centre where you will find an array of shops, bars and restaurants.

SAT NAV *YO14 9LA* **ONLINE MAP**

Unit General Leisure

FILEY, North Yorkshire Map ref 5D3

★★★
SELF CATERING

Units 5
Sleeps 1–5

LOW SEASON PER WK
£295.00–£385.00

HIGH SEASON PER WK
£475.00–£585.00

The Cottages, Filey

contact Mr & Mrs David Teet, The Cottages, Muston Grange Farm, Muston Road, Filey YO14 0HU
t (01723) 516620

open All year
payment Cash, cheques, euros
nearest shop 1 mile
nearest pub 1 mile

Range of converted farm buildings providing quality accommodation in private courtyard setting. One cottage suitable for wheelchair access. Twenty minutes' walk to beach or town. Ideal spot for Yorkshire's attractions and countryside.

Unit General Leisure

FLOCKTON, West Yorkshire Map ref 4B1

★★★★★
SELF CATERING

Units 1
Sleeps 6

LOW SEASON PER WK
£460.00

HIGH SEASON PER WK
£660.00–£860.00

2 The Lodge, Beaconsfield Farm, Paul Lane, Flockton Moor, Wakefield

contact Mr & Mrs Dale, 3 The Lodge, Beaconsfield Farm, Paul Lane, Flockton Moor, Wakefield WF4 4BP **t** 07798 698 226 & (01924) 849226 **e** enquiries@thelodgeatflocktonmoor.co.uk

thelodgeatflocktonmoor.co.uk

Luxurious four-bedroom, two-bathroom, barn conversion with outstanding panoramic views over open countryside and across to the Pennines.

open All year
payment Cash, cheques
nearest shop 2 miles
nearest pub 1 mile

Unit General Leisure

What if I need to cancel?

It is advisable to check the proprietor's cancellation policy in case you have to change your plans at a later date.

For **key to symbols** see page 7

FOGGATHORPE, East Riding of Yorkshire Map ref 4C1

★★★★
SELF CATERING

Units **1**
Sleeps **2–4**

LOW SEASON PER WK
£200.00–£350.00

HIGH SEASON PER WK
£300.00–£750.00

Yellowtop Country Park, Foggathorpe

contact Paula Jessop, Yellowtop Country Park, Foggathorpe, York YO8 6PZ **t** (01430) 860461
e paulayellowtop@aol.com

yellowtopcountry.co.uk SPECIAL OFFERS • REAL-TIME BOOKING

open All year
payment Credit/debit cards, cash, cheques, euros
nearest shop 2 miles
nearest pub 2 miles

Situated at the foot of the Yorkshire Wolds between York and beautiful Beverley, surrounded by attractive market towns. Offering famous Yorkshire hospitality. Excellent coarse fishing. Lovely walks on and off-site. Wi-Fi hot spot. Pretty local village, just two miles away, hosts a good selection of pubs and eateries.

ONLINE MAP

Unit General Leisure

FOLLIFOOT, North Yorkshire Map ref 4B1

★★★★★
SELF CATERING

Units **5**
Sleeps **4–6**

HIGH SEASON PER WK
£1,050.00–£1,200.00

Please visit the website for our special offers.

Repton Green, Rudding Park, Harrogate

Repton Green, Rudding Park, Follifoot, Harrogate HG3 1JH **t** (01423) 871350
e reservations@ruddingpark.com

reptongreen.com

payment Credit/debit cards, cash, cheques, euros
nearest shop less than 0.5 miles
nearest pub less than 0.5 miles

Exclusive self-catering lodges furnished and equipped to the highest standard, set beside Rudding Park's championship golf course. Enjoy the peaceful surroundings of 300 acres of parkland with the spa town of Harrogate only three miles away. Open all year except February.

ONLINE MAP

Unit General P S
Leisure

FORD, Northumberland Map ref 5B1

★★★–★★★★★
SELF CATERING

Units **2**
Sleeps **2–13**

LOW SEASON PER WK
Min £330.00

HIGH SEASON PER WK
Min £532.00

Weekend and short breaks, min 2 nights, available throughout the year.

Ford Castle, Ford

contact Mrs Karen Bartlett, Ford Castle, Ford TD15 2PX **t** (01890) 820257
e kbartlett@northumberland.gov.uk

open All year
payment Credit/debit cards, cash, cheques
nearest shop less than 0.5 miles
nearest pub 1.8 miles

Ford Castle is a residential activity centre, dating back to the 14th century, with two self-catering properties within the grounds. The Flag Tower has been refurbished to a very high standard. The Clock Tower cottage has three bedrooms, one with en suite facilities.

Unit General Leisure

FORTON, Lancashire Map ref 4A1

★–★★★
SELF CATERING

Units 3
Sleeps 1–6

LOW SEASON PER WK
£350.00–£700.00

HIGH SEASON PER WK
£450.00–£800.00

Cleveley Mere Fishing & Lodges, Forton, Preston

contact Peter & Lynne Brown, Cleveley Mere Fishing Lodges, Cleveley Lodge, Forton PR3 1BY
t (01524) 793644

cleveleymere.com REAL-TIME BOOKING

open All year
payment Cash, cheques
nearest shop 1.5 miles
nearest pub 1.5 miles

Cleveley Mere lies in the scenic Wyre Valley and has three self-contained lodges overlooking a beautiful, peaceful, 23-acre trout lake set in a private nature reserve and surrounded by fields, woodlands and River Wyre, with magnificent views of the neighbouring fells. Short breaks or weekly breaks available.

ONLINE MAP

Unit General P Leisure

GAINFORD, Durham Map ref 5C3

★★★
SELF CATERING

Units 1
Sleeps 6

LOW SEASON PER WK
Min £250.00

HIGH SEASON PER WK
Max £410.00

Low Green Cottage, Darlington

contact Mrs Barbara McLean, 84 Montalbo Road, Barnard Castle DL12 8BP **t** (01833) 637594
e info@lowgreencottage.co.uk

lowgreencottage.co.uk REAL-TIME BOOKING

A two-bedroomed, two-bathroomed comfortable Victorian cottage sleeping four to six, overlooking the delightful village green of Gainford. Within easy walking distance of local shops, cafe and restaurant.

open All year
payment Cash, cheques, euros

Unit General P Leisure

GARSTANG, Lancashire Map ref 4A1

★★★
SELF CATERING

Units 2
Sleeps 2–5

LOW SEASON PER WK
£220.00–£320.00

HIGH SEASON PER WK
£290.00–£420.00

Knotts Hey Cottages, Bilsborrow, Preston

contact Mr Collinson, Knotts Hey Cottages, Stanzaker Hall Drive, Catterall, Preston PR3 0PB
t (01995) 640519 **e** holidays@brockcottages.co.uk

brockcottages.co.uk

Secluded Knotts Hey Cottages in the heart of north west Lancashire within easy access of Lakes, Dales, Bowland, and Fylde Coast. Open-plan cottages, two double bed and one double bed, all en suite.

open All year
payment Cash, cheques, euros
nearest shop 1 mile
nearest pub 2 miles

Unit General P Leisure

GILLAMOOR, North Yorkshire Map ref 5C3

★★★★★
SELF CATERING

Units 1
Sleeps 4

LOW SEASON PER WK
£420.00–£450.00

HIGH SEASON PER WK
£460.00–£765.00

Hen House, Gillamoor, Kirkbymoorside

contact Maria Demkowicz, Church View, Main Street, Gillamoor YO62 7HX **t** 07786 885093
e maria@henhousecottage.co.uk

henhousecottage.co.uk

open All year
payment Cash, cheques
nearest shop 3 miles
nearest pub less than 0.5 miles

Stone single-storey cottage with secluded garden and superb views. Twin and king-size or two king-size bedrooms, one en suite plus wetroom. Recently renovated, beautifully decorated and furnished. Woodburner, central heating, private parking for two cars. Quiet village location. Beautiful walking country, perfect for rest and relaxation.

SAT NAV *YO62 7HX*

Unit TV SC DVD General P

GILLING WEST, North Yorkshire Map ref 5C3

★★★★–★★★★★
SELF CATERING

Units 5
Sleeps 2–10

LOW SEASON PER WK
£185.00–£900.00

HIGH SEASON PER WK
£320.00–£2,500.00

Gilling Old Mill Cottages, Richmond

contact Hugh, Joyce and Neville Bird, Gilling Old Mill, Waters Lane, Gilling West, Richmond DL10 5JD **t** (01748) 822771 **e** admin@yorkshiredales-cottages.com

yorkshiredales-cottages.com SPECIAL OFFERS

open All year
payment Credit/debit cards, cash, cheques
nearest shop less than 0.5 miles
nearest pub less than 0.5 miles

Magnificent range of cottages converted from traditional stone farm buildings, situated on the edge of the North Yorkshire dales near Richmond. Comfortably furnished and well equipped, they are ideal for a relaxing holiday. Good walking area and well placed to visit major attractions of the North East.

ONLINE MAP

Unit TV DVD General P Leisure

GRANGE-OVER-SANDS, Cumbria Map ref 5A3

★★★
SELF CATERING

Units 1
Sleeps 2–4

LOW SEASON PER WK
£350.00–£375.00

HIGH SEASON PER WK
£375.00–£475.00

Cornerways Bungalow, Grange-over-Sands

contact Eunice Rigg, Cornerways Bungalow & Greaves Farm, Prospect House, Barber Green, Grange-over-Sands LA11 6HU **t** (015395) 36329 & (015395) 36587

Pleasant bungalow in quiet situation, with double and twin bedroom. All-round views, private garden with parking. Ideal base for touring Lake District. Personal supervision.

open March to October
payment Cash, cheques
nearest shop 2 miles
nearest pub 2 miles

Unit TV General 4 P

Place index

If you know where you want to stay, the index by place name at the back of the guide will give you the page number listing accommodation in your chosen town, city or village. Check out the other useful indexes too.

GRANGE-OVER-SANDS, Cumbria Map ref 5A3

★★★
SELF CATERING

Units **1**
Sleeps **1–6**

LOW SEASON PER WK
£300.00–£350.00

HIGH SEASON PER WK
£350.00–£500.00

Open all year round. 3-night stays (minimum) available Nov-mid-Mar; also 7 days over New Year.

Dyer Dene, Grange-over-Sands

contact Mrs Andrews, Dyer Dene, c/o 121 Dorchester Road, Garstang PR3 1FE **t** (01995) 602769
e dyerdene@fish.co.uk

dyerdene.com

open All year
payment Cash, cheques
nearest shop 2 miles
nearest pub 1 mile

Comfortable cottage in tranquil valley. Beautiful views and excellent local walking. Garage-cum-games room and gardens. Open fire in sitting room. New conservatory. Ideal for children. Winter daily rate £50.00.

ONLINE MAP

Unit General Leisure

GRASMERE, Cumbria Map ref 5A3

★★★
SELF CATERING

Units **1**
Sleeps **1–12**

LOW SEASON PER WK
£300.00–£870.00

HIGH SEASON PER WK
£300.00–£2,080.00

Late-availability offers are available on our website or by telephone. 10% discount for return guests.

Bramrigg House, Grasmere

contact Lana Thorne, Lake District Inns and Cottages, Thirlmere, Keswick CA12 4TN **t** 05006 00725
e stay@lakedistrictinns.co.uk

lakedistrictinns.co.uk SPECIAL OFFERS · REAL-TIME BOOKING

open All year
payment Credit/debit cards, cash, cheques
nearest shop 0.5 miles
nearest pub 0.5 miles

This early 1900s Lakeland house has been extended and modernised to create a wonderful home in the Lake District National Park. Bramrigg House is located just a ten-minute walk from the picturesque village of Grasmere. One of the finest holiday homes available in the Lake District.

SAT NAV *LA22 9QG*

Unit General
Leisure

GRASMERE, Cumbria Map ref 5A3

★★★★
SELF CATERING

Units **3**
Sleeps **2–5**

LOW SEASON PER WK
£303.00–£340.00

HIGH SEASON PER WK
£502.00–£670.00

A week booked in the year allows 10% off a second week booked in Mar (excl Easter holidays).

Broadrayne Farm Cottages, Grasmere

contact Mr Bev Dennison & Mrs Jo Dennison Drake, Broadrayne Farm, Grasmere, Ambleside LA22 9RU **t** (015394) 35055 **e** jo@grasmere-accommodation.co.uk

grasmere-accommodation.co.uk

open All year
payment Cash, cheques
nearest shop 1.3 miles
nearest pub 0.5 miles

With dramatic mountains, rolling fells, glorious lakes and peaceful valleys, Broadrayne Farm is at the heart of the Lake District, superbly located for wonderful views. The traditional farm properties have been lovingly renovated with today's creature comforts, including open coal fires, central heating and off-street parking. Pets welcome by arrangement.

SAT NAV *LA22 9RU* **ONLINE MAP**

Unit General
Leisure

GRASSINGTON, North Yorkshire Map ref 5B3

★★★★
SELF CATERING

Units 1
Sleeps 1–4

LOW SEASON PER WK
£270.00–£295.50

HIGH SEASON PER WK
£495.00–£522.50

The Barn, Grassington

contact Gail Evans, The Barn, c/o 8 Sedber Lane, Grassington BD23 5LQ **t** (01756) 753390
e grassington@art-by-gail.uk

dalestay.co.uk/thebarn

The Barn is a luxury, self-catering cottage, situated in a private fold, yards from Grassington's cobbled square. The location is tranquil, sheltered and convenient with a delightful, enclosed garden.

open All year
payment Cash, cheques
nearest shop less than 0.5 miles
nearest pub less than 0.5 miles

Unit General 10 P Leisure

GREAT ASBY, Cumbria Map ref 5B3

★★★★
SELF CATERING

Units 3
Sleeps 2–5

LOW SEASON PER WK
£250.00–£375.00

HIGH SEASON PER WK
Max £475.00

Four nights for the price of three.

Scalebeck Holiday Cottages, Great Asby, Appleby-in-Westmorland

contact Mr K J Budding, Scalebeck Holiday Cottages, Scalebeck, Appleby-in-Westmorland CA16 6TF
t (017683) 51006 **e** mail@scalebeckholidaycottages.com

scalebeckholidaycottages.co.uk

open All year
payment Credit/debit cards, cash, cheques
nearest shop 5 miles
nearest pub 1 mile

Three well-appointed self-catering cottages sleeping two to five in 17thC barn conversion. Secluded, quiet valley, abundant wildlife. Ideal base to explore Lakes and Dales. Non-smokers, pets welcome, games room with table tennis and pool table. Gas central heating, open all year. Gas, electricity, bed linen and towels included.

Unit General P Leisure

HALIFAX, West Yorkshire Map ref 4B1

★★★★
SELF CATERING

Units 2
Sleeps 2–4

LOW SEASON PER WK
£305.00–£320.00

HIGH SEASON PER WK
£365.00–£460.00

Short breaks available, minimum 3 nights. Check our website for late availability.

Cherry Tree Cottages, Barkisland, Nr Halifax

contact Stan & Elaine Shaw, Cherry Tree Cottages, Wall Nook, Barkisland, Halifax HX4 0BL
t (01422) 372662 **e** cherrytree@yorkshire-cottages.co.uk

yorkshire-cottages.co.uk SPECIAL OFFERS · REAL-TIME BOOKING

open All year
payment Credit/debit cards, cash, cheques
nearest shop 1 mile
nearest pub less than 0.5 miles

Warm, comfortable, stone-built cottages set in two acres of natural woodland/heather garden with superb Pennine views and direct access to open countryside and footpaths. Close to a quiet Calderdale village with good pubs and restaurants nearby. Ideal location for exploring Brontë Country and Pennine Yorkshire. Pets and children welcome. Wireless internet access.

SAT NAV *HX4 0BL* **ONLINE MAP**

Unit General P Leisure

Has every property been assessed?

All accommodation in this guide has been rated for quality, or is awaiting assessment, by a professional national tourist board assessor.

HALTWHISTLE, Northumberland Map ref 5B2

★★★
SELF CATERING

Units 1
Sleeps 1–5

LOW SEASON PER WK
£200.00–£300.00

HIGH SEASON PER WK
£250.00–£350.00

Whitchester Farm Cottage, Haltwhistle

contact Mr J M Hall, Whitchester Farm Cottage, Whitchester, Haltwhistle NE49 0NF
t (01434) 322855 **e** whitchester@ukonline.co.uk

whitchester.co.uk

Farm cottage on working dairy farm in Roman Wall area. The accommodation comprises two bedrooms, shower room with wc, living room, kitchen and utility room.

open All year
payment Cash, cheques
nearest shop 1 mile
nearest pub 1 mile

Unit General P Leisure

HAMSTERLEY FOREST

See under Barnard Castle, Tow Law, Wolsingham

HARBOTTLE, Northumberland Map ref 5B1

★★★
SELF CATERING

Units 1
Sleeps 1–3

LOW SEASON PER WK
£195.00–£235.00

HIGH SEASON PER WK
£300.00–£395.00

Brackenlea Cottage, Rothbury

contact Mr & Mrs John & Helen Dalrymple, 15 Wellway Court, Morpeth NE61 1BW
t (01670) 519629 **e** info@brackenleacottage.co.uk

brackenleacottage.co.uk

open All year
payment Cash, cheques
nearest shop 10 miles
nearest pub less than 0.5 miles

Charming, luxury, well appointed two-bedroom corner terraced stone cottage located in the lovely village of Harbottle in the Northumberland National Park. Ideally situated for the beautiful Northumberland Moors, and in easy reach of Alnwick, the spectacular Northumberland coast and the Scottish Borders.

Unit General P S Leisure

HARROGATE, North Yorkshire Map ref 4B1

★★★★
SELF CATERING

Units 14
Sleeps 2–4

LOW SEASON PER WK
£375.00–£535.00

HIGH SEASON PER WK
£420.00–£610.00

Short breaks available from £70pn, minimum 2 nights.

Ashness Apartments, Harrogate

contact Mr Spinlove & Miss H Spinlove, Ashness Apartments, 15 St Marys Avenue HG2 0LP
t (01423) 526894 **e** office@ashness.com

ashness.com

open All year
payment Credit/debit cards, cash, cheques

High-quality apartments, superbly situated in a nice, quiet road of fine Victorian townhouses very near the town centre of Harrogate. Excellent shops, restaurants and cafes are a short walk away through Montpellier Gardens with the Stray and Valley Gardens just around the corner.

ONLINE MAP

Unit General P S

Do you have access needs?

Look for the National Accessible Scheme symbols if you have special hearing, visual or mobility needs. An index of accommodation participating in the scheme can be found at the back of this guide.

HARROGATE, North Yorkshire Map ref 4B1

★★★★
SELF CATERING

Units **1**
Sleeps **1–5**

LOW SEASON PER WK
£300.00–£400.00

HIGH SEASON PER WK
£350.00–£450.00

Ashrigg, Harrogate

contact Mr & Mrs Peter & Angela Holt, 39 Spring Lane, Harrogate HG3 1NP **t** (01423) 871177 **e** pholt@westrigg.freeserve.co.uk

ashrigg.co.uk

Fully furnished/equipped first-floor apartment. One double, one twin and one single. Full central heating, fully fitted kitchen. Garden for guests' use. Off-road parking.

open All year
payment Cash, cheques
nearest shop less than 0.5 miles
nearest pub less than 0.5 miles

Unit TV DVD General P S

HARROGATE, North Yorkshire Map ref 4B1

★★★★
SELF CATERING

Units **10**
Sleeps **2–8**

LOW SEASON PER WK
£330.00–£530.00

HIGH SEASON PER WK
£630.00–£930.00

Short breaks at 70% of weekly rate.

Brimham Rocks Cottages, Harrogate

contact Chris & Deborah Gray, Brimham Rocks Cottages, High North Farm, Harrogate HG3 5EY **t** (01765) 620284 **e** brimhamrc@yahoo.co.uk

brimham.co.uk

open All year
payment Cash, cheques
nearest shop 3 miles
nearest pub 1.5 miles

Found on the edge of the Dales, these cosy and comfortable country cottages are ideally located to explore Harrogate, York, Ripon, Knaresborough, Leeds and surrounding areas. Many have private garden and hot tubs, complemented by the indoor heated swimming pool and games room. You and your pets can be sure of a warm welcome.

Unit TV DVD General P S Leisure

HARROGATE, North Yorkshire Map ref 4B1

★★★★
SELF CATERING

Units **3**
Sleeps **2–5**

LOW SEASON PER WK
£240.00–£325.00

HIGH SEASON PER WK
£395.00–£580.00

Dinmore Cottages, Burnt Yates, Harrogate

contact Denise Wales, Dinmore Cottages, Dinmore House, Pateley Bridge Road, Burnt Yates HG3 3ET **t** (01423) 770860 **e** aib@dinmore-cottages.freeserve.co.uk

dinmore-cottages.co.uk

open All year
payment Credit/debit cards, cash, cheques, euros
nearest shop 3 miles
nearest pub 1 mile

Award-winning Dales cottages converted from 17thC farmstead. Peaceful situation, breathtaking views over Nidderdale, a protected Area of Outstanding Natural Beauty. Only seven miles to spa town of Harrogate, close to York and Herriot Country. Ideal for walkers and birdwatchers and for touring and sightseeing in the Yorkshire Dales.

Unit TV General P Leisure

Check the maps for accommodation locations

Colour maps at the front pinpoint all the places where accommodation is featured within the regional sections of this guide. Pick your location and then refer to the place index at the back to find the page number.

HARROGATE, North Yorkshire Map ref 4B1

★★★★
SELF CATERING

Units 1
Sleeps 6

LOW SEASON PER WK
Min £300.00

HIGH SEASON PER WK
Max £750.00

Regent Cottage, Harrogate

contact Robert Blake, 1a Moorfield Road IP12 4JN **t** (01394) 382565
e robert@blake4110.fsbusiness.co.uk

We offer comfortable accommodation for adults. With three bedrooms, one en suite, sitting-room and kitchen/diner. Parking. Within easy walking distance of town centre. Illustrated brochure available.

open All year
payment Cash, cheques
nearest shop less than 0.5 miles
nearest pub less than 0.5 miles

Unit General 10 P

HARROGATE, North Yorkshire Map ref 4B1

★★★-★★★★
SELF CATERING

Units 4
Sleeps 2–10

LOW SEASON PER WK
£295.00–£700.00

HIGH SEASON PER WK
£395.00–£950.00

Rudding Estate Cottages, Harrogate

Rudding Park Estate Ltd, Haggs Farm, Haggs Road, Harrogate HG3 1EQ **t** (01423) 844844
e info@rudding.com

rudding.com/cottages GUEST REVIEWS • SPECIAL OFFERS • REAL-TIME BOOKING

open March to October
payment Credit/debit cards, cash, cheques
nearest shop 1 mile
nearest pub 1 mile

Just three miles from central Harrogate and one mile from picturesque Follifoot village, these private country-estate cottages are surrounded by fields and woodland. Each well-equipped and comfortable cottage has lovely views, gardens and car parking. Pets are welcome, and ground-floor accommodation is available.

SAT NAV *HG3 1DQ* **ONLINE MAP**

Unit General P Leisure

HARROGATE, North Yorkshire Map ref 4B1

★★★★★
SELF CATERING

Units 2
Sleeps 2–4

LOW SEASON PER WK
£1,155.00

HIGH SEASON PER WK
£1,155.00

Rudding Gates, Follifoot

contact Jan Mackaness, Rudding Park Estate Ltd, Haggs Farm, Haggs Road, Follifoot HG3 1EQ
t (01423) 844844 **e** info@rudding.com

rudding.com/gates GUEST REVIEWS • SPECIAL OFFERS • REAL-TIME BOOKING

open All year
payment Credit/debit cards, cash, cheques
nearest shop less than 0.5 miles
nearest pub less than 0.5 miles

These award-winning gatehouse apartments in Follifoot, just three miles from central Harrogate, provide the very latest in luxury self-catering accommodation. Decorated and equipped to the highest standard, they are the perfect destination for special holidays and indulgent weekend breaks. Each apartment has two en suite bedrooms, private parking and pretty walled gardens.

SAT NAV *HG3 1DT* **ONLINE MAP**

Unit General P Leisure

HARROGATE, North Yorkshire Map ref 4B1

★★★
SELF CATERING

Units 12
Sleeps 2–7

LOW SEASON PER WK
Min £330.00

HIGH SEASON PER WK
Max £973.00

Receive £20 off your booking if you mention this advert when making your reservation.

Rudding Holiday Park, Harrogate

Rudding Holiday Park, Follifoot, Harrogate HG3 1JH **t** (01423) 870439
e holiday-park@ruddingpark.com

ruddingpark.com SPECIAL OFFERS

open All year
payment Credit/debit cards, cash, cheques, euros
nearest shop less than 0.5 miles
nearest pub less than 0.5 miles

Choose from our traditional stone-built houses in the beautiful grounds of Rudding Park or our timber lodges, set in delightful woodland clearings, many overlooking a small lake. Three miles south of Harrogate, Deer House family pub, shop, swimming pool, children's playground, games room, 18-hole golf course, 6-hole short course and driving range.

ONLINE MAP

Unit General P Leisure

HAWKSHEAD, Cumbria Map ref 5A3

★★★
SELF CATERING

Units 10
Sleeps 2–6

LOW SEASON PER WK
Min £252.00

HIGH SEASON PER WK
Max £575.00

The Croft Holiday Flats, Hawkshead, Ambleside

contact Mrs Barr, The Croft Holiday Flats, North Lonsdale Road, Hawkshead LA22 0NX
t (015394) 36374 **e** enquiries@hawkshead-croft.com

hawkshead-croft.com

Large house, with garden and private parking, converted into holiday flats. In village of Hawkshead on B5286 from Ambleside.

open All year
payment Credit/debit cards, cash, cheques

Unit General P Leisure

HAWKSHEAD, Cumbria Map ref 5A3

★★★
SELF CATERING

Units 1

LOW SEASON PER WK
£235.00–£285.00

HIGH SEASON PER WK
£335.00–£455.00

Meadow View, Ambleside

Blakes Cottages, Earby, Barnoldswick BB94 0AA **t** 0870 336 7777

blakes.cottages.co.uk

Three-hundred-year-old cottage in the centre of Hawkshead. Entrance hall, bathroom, twin bedroom, double bedroom with wash basin and separate wc, kitchen and living accommodation. Central heating.

open All year
payment Credit/debit cards, cash, cheques
nearest shop less than 0.5 miles
nearest pub less than 0.5 miles

Unit General 11 P Leisure

Country Code always follow the Country Code

- Be safe – plan ahead and follow any signs
- Leave gates and property as you find them
- Protect plants and animals, and take your litter home
- Keep dogs under close control
- Consider other people

HAWORTH, West Yorkshire Map ref 4B1

★★★★–★★★★★
SELF CATERING

Units 9
Sleeps 1–7

LOW SEASON PER WK
£290.00–£520.00

HIGH SEASON PER WK
£365.00–£730.00

Short breaks our speciality: 3-night weekend and 4-night midweek (excl Bank Holidays).

Hewenden Mill Cottages, Cullingworth

contact Janet Emanuel, Hewenden Mill Cottages, Cullingworth BD13 5BP **t** (01535) 274259
e info@hewendenmillcottages.co.uk

hewendenmillcottages.co.uk SPECIAL OFFERS · REAL-TIME BOOKING

open All year
payment Credit/debit cards, cash, cheques
nearest shop 1 mile
nearest pub 1 mile

Ideally placed in the heart of heritage-rich Brontë Country, our luxury accommodation provides the perfect place to relax and unwind. Set within eleven acres of ancient woodland, the mill and mill workers' cottages have been sympathetically converted into luxurious self-catering apartments and houses. Visit our website for an online tour, availability and booking.

ONLINE MAP

Unit General P Leisure

HAWORTH, West Yorkshire Map ref 4B1

★★★
SELF CATERING

Units 2
Sleeps 2–5

LOW SEASON PER WK
£175.00–£230.00

HIGH SEASON PER WK
£220.00–£350.00

Weavers Cottage and Loft, Haworth

contact Gaye Bond, Weavers Cottage & Weavers Loft, 10 & 8 Mill Hill, Haworth BD22 8QT
t (01535) 211184 **e** g.j.bond@blueyonder.co.uk

weaverscottage-web.co.uk

The weavers' cottage and loft, built in 1780, is a Grade II Listed building of special historic interest. There are many original features including mullion windows.

open All year
payment Cash, cheques
nearest shop less than 0.5 miles
nearest pub less than 0.5 miles

Unit General P

HEBDEN BRIDGE, West Yorkshire Map ref 4B1

★★★
SELF CATERING

Units 1
Sleeps 1–2

LOW SEASON PER WK
£200.00–£300.00

HIGH SEASON PER WK
£250.00–£400.00

The Garden House, Hebden Bridge

contact Mr Martin Robinson, The Garden House, Manor House, Blackshawhead, Hebden Bridge HX7 7JR **t** (01422) 842794 **e** manorhousestudio@talktalk.net

manorhousestudio.co.uk

Twenty-first-century extension to 16thC hall house, set in large tranquil landscaped garden. Galleried bedroom with twin beds. Well-appointed living room with fitted kitchen area. Luxurious shower room. Terrace. Views over Upper Calderdale.

open All year except Christmas and New Year
payment Cash, cheques
nearest shop 1 mile
nearest pub 1 mile

Unit General P Leisure

HEDDON-ON-THE-WALL, Northumberland Map ref 5B2

★★★
SELF CATERING

Units 1
Sleeps 2–7

LOW SEASON PER WK
£290.00–£315.00

HIGH SEASON PER WK
£450.00–£485.00

2 East Town House, Newcastle upon Tyne

contact Mr & Mrs Ridley and Beryl Amos, 1 East Town House, Heddon-on-the-Wall, Newcastle upon Tyne NE15 0DR **t** (01661) 852277

open All year
payment Cash, cheques
nearest shop less than 0.5 miles
nearest pub less than 0.5 miles

Stone-built, well-equipped house furnished to a high standard, in historic village on Hadrian's Wall. Only six miles to Newcastle, 20 minutes from Hexham.

Unit General P Leisure

HELMSLEY, North Yorkshire Map ref 5C3

★★★★
SELF CATERING

Units 1
Sleeps 1–4

LOW SEASON PER WK
Min £210.00

HIGH SEASON PER WK
£305.00–£385.00

Townend Cottage, Beadlam

contact Mrs Margaret Begg, Townend Farmhouse, High Lane, Beadlam, Nawton, York YO62 7SY
t (01439) 770103 **e** margaret.begg@ukgateway.net

visityorkshire.com

open All year
payment Cash, cheques
nearest shop 3 miles
nearest pub less than 0.5 miles

Originally part of an 18thC farmhouse, this is a very warm, comfortable, two-bedroomed stone cottage with oak beams. Situated off the main road in a village three miles from the charming market town of Helmsley. Ideal for walking or touring Moors, coast and York. Central heating and log fire included in price.

Unit General P

HEXHAM, Northumberland Map ref 5B2

★★★★★
SELF CATERING

Units 1
Sleeps 5

LOW SEASON PER WK
£700.00

HIGH SEASON PER WK
£700.00

Any number of nights available (minimum 2).

Chapel House, Steel, Hexham

contact Mrs Joan Liddle, Chapel House, Peth Head Cottage, Juniper, Hexham NE47 0LA
t (01434) 673286 **e** info@chapel-house.info

chapel-house.info

open All year
payment Credit/debit cards, cash, cheques, euros
nearest shop 4 miles
nearest pub 2 miles

Lovely secluded detached cottage with wonderful views and sunny south-facing garden. Spacious open plan living area featuring oil-fired Aga and inglenook fireplace with woodburning stove. Any number of nights available (minimum two).

Unit General P Leisure

HEXHAM, Northumberland Map ref 5B2

★★★★★
SELF CATERING

Units 1
Sleeps 3

LOW SEASON PER WK
£265.00–£325.00

HIGH SEASON PER WK
£385.00–£460.00

Holy Island House, Hexham

contact Mrs Judith Youens, Holy Island House, Gilesgate, Hexham NE46 3QL **t** (01434) 609386
e stay@holyislandhouse.co.uk

holyislandhouse.co.uk

open March to October
payment Cash, cheques

An 18thC wing of 17thC listed building. Beamed ceilings, flagged floors, feature fireplaces, period furnishings. Kitchen, living/dining room, single and double bedroom, bath with shower over, parking and small patio. Close to town centre, award-winning park and Hexham Abbey. Accommodates up to three guests.

Unit TV General 12 P S

HEXHAM, Northumberland Map ref 5B2

★★★★
SELF CATERING

Units 3
Sleeps 1–5

LOW SEASON PER WK
£210.00–£395.00

HIGH SEASON PER WK
£280.00–£500.00

Old Church Cottages, Chollerton, Hexham

contact Mrs Marilyn Framrose, Old Church Cottage, Chollerton, Hexham NE46 4TF
t (01434) 681930 **e** mframrose@chollerton-oldchurch.co.uk

chollerton-oldchurch.co.uk GUEST REVIEWS • SPECIAL OFFERS • REAL-TIME BOOKING

Beautiful converted country church: two two-bedroom apartments and double studio apartment. Spacious gardens with patio, seating, pond and barbecue. Local bus. Superb restaurants. Two miles from Hadrian's Wall, convenient for Newcastle, Alnwick, Scottish Borders.

open All year
payment Credit/debit cards, cash, cheques, euros
nearest shop 1 mile
nearest pub 1 mile

Unit TV General P S Leisure

HEXHAM, Northumberland Map ref 5B2

★★★
SELF CATERING

Units 1
Sleeps 2

LOW SEASON PER WK
£175.00–£225.00

HIGH SEASON PER WK
£225.00–£275.00

WALKERS WELCOME CYCLISTS WELCOME

Rosebank Cottage, Fourstones

contact Mrs Francine Jukes, Appletree Cottage, Fourstones, Hexham NE47 5DF **t** (01434) 674634
e info@rosebankcottage.co.uk

rosebankcottage.co.uk

Enjoy high-quality accommodation in a traditional stone cottage with breathtaking views of South Tyne Valley. Ideal for walkers, sleeps two plus sofa bed. Terrific base for exploring Hadrian's Wall Country.

open All year
payment Cash, cheques, euros
nearest shop less than 0.5 miles
nearest pub less than 0.5 miles

Unit TV DVD General P S Leisure

Check the maps for accommodation locations

Colour maps at the front pinpoint all the cities, towns and villages where you will find accommodation entries in the regional sections. Pick your location and then refer to the place index at the back to find the page number.

HEXHAM, Northumberland Map ref 5B2

★★★★
SELF CATERING

Units 2
Sleeps 2–4

LOW SEASON PER WK
£280.00–£380.00

HIGH SEASON PER WK
£380.00–£480.00

Special-price weeks available Nov–Mar.

Sammy's Place/Broadway Apartment, Hexham

contact Mr & Mrs Ian and Susan Sibbald, 9 Charlton Close, Beaumont Park, Hexham NE46 2QF
t (01434) 604143 & 07903 038623 **e** sammys-place@hotmail.com

sammyshideaway.com

open All year
payment Cash, cheques
nearest shop less than 0.5 miles
nearest pub less than 0.5 miles

Beautifully appointed self-catering apartments, ideal for couples, individuals and families. Situated in and around the heart of Hexham, Hadrian's Wall Country. Single level, one double, one twin, both en suite. Linen, towels, Sky TV, cooker, microwave, dishwasher, washer/dryer, fridge/freezer. Cot and highchair available. No pets/smoking.

SAT NAV *NE46 2EA*

Unit General Leisure

HIGH BENTHAM, North Yorkshire Map ref 5B3

★★★★
SELF CATERING

Units 1
Sleeps 1–4

HIGH SEASON PER WK
£190.00–£270.00

Holmes Farm Cottage, Lancaster

contact Mrs Story, Holmes Farm Cottage, Holmes Farm, Lower Bentham, Lancaster LA2 7DE
t (015242) 61198 **e** lucy@clucy.demon.co.uk

holmesfarmcottage.co.uk

open All year
payment Cash, cheques
nearest shop 1 mile
nearest pub 0.5 miles

Tastefully converted stone cottage with large, landscaped garden, surrounded by 127 acres of beautiful pastureland. Ideal base for visiting Lake District, Dales and coast.

Unit General Leisure

HIGH LORTON, Cumbria Map ref 5A3

★★★
SELF CATERING

Units 3
Sleeps 2–8

LOW SEASON PER WK
£210.00–£560.00

HIGH SEASON PER WK
£320.00–£820.00

High Swinside Holiday Cottages, High Lorton

contact Mr Jacques Hankin, High Swinside Holiday Cottages, High Swinside Farm, High Lorton, Cockermouth CA13 9UA **t** (01900) 85206 **e** bookings@highswinside.demon.co.uk

highswinside.demon.co.uk

open All year
payment Cash, cheques
nearest shop 2 miles
nearest pub 2 miles

Former hill farm, overlooking Lorton Vale with stunning views and offering peace and tranquillity. Well-equipped cottages. Large groups (up to 14) can be catered for. Children welcome. Beams and log fires, together with meal service, make for a wonderful stay. Full details on our website.

ONLINE MAP

Unit General Leisure

HIGH LORTON, Cumbria Map ref 5A3

★★★★★
SELF CATERING

Units 1
Sleeps 2

LOW SEASON PER WK
£350.00–£400.00

HIGH SEASON PER WK
£450.00–£500.00

Short breaks available Nov-Mar: 4-night stay.

Holemire Barn, Cockermouth

contact Angela Fearfield, Holemire Barn, Holemire House, Cockermouth CA13 9TX **t** (01900) 85225
e enquiries@lakelandbarn.co.uk

lakelandbarn.co.uk REAL-TIME BOOKING

open All year
payment Cash, cheques
nearest shop less than 0.5 miles
nearest pub less than 0.5 miles

Traditional Lakeland barn with exposed beams, converted to quality accommodation. In beautiful Lorton Vale, overlooking local fells. Close to Keswick and northern Lakes. Warm in winter, light and sunny in summer. Situated in the midst of superb walking country. A wealth of garden birds and ospreys nesting close by. Red squirrels in garden.

ONLINE MAP

Unit TV DVD General P Leisure

HOLMBRIDGE, West Yorkshire Map ref 4B1

★★★
SELF CATERING

Units 1
Sleeps 4

LOW SEASON PER WK
£250.00–£350.00

HIGH SEASON PER WK
£295.00–£400.00

Heselwood Cottage, Holmfirth

contact Mr & Mrs Chris & Jenny Brook, 195 Woodhead Road, Holmbridge, Holmfirth HD9 2NW
t (01484) 685175 **e** jenandchris@heselwoodcottage.co.uk

heselwoodcottage.co.uk

Charming cottage in country village location. Comprising one double, one twin room, bathroom, lounge/diner, kitchen. Use of picturesque garden.

open All year
payment Cash, cheques
nearest shop less than 0.5 miles
nearest pub less than 0.5 miles

Unit TV DVD General S

HOLMFIRTH, West Yorkshire Map ref 4B1

★★★★
SELF CATERING

Units 1
Sleeps 6

LOW SEASON PER WK
Min £400.00

HIGH SEASON PER WK
Max £650.00

Book 2 weeks and get a 5% discount.

Manor Farm Cottage, Upper Denby, Huddersfield

contact Mrs C E Crossland, 37 Bank Lane, Huddersfield HD8 8UT **t** (01484) 864722
e manorfarmcottage@btinternet.com

manorfarmcottage.com GUEST REVIEWS · SPECIAL OFFERS

open All year
payment Cash, cheques
nearest shop 1.5 miles
nearest pub less than 0.5 miles

This beautiful Grade II Listed 17thC farmhouse cottage provides high quality accommodation combining original features with new fixtures and fittings. Sleeps up to six people in one double bedroom and one family bedroom. Secure parking. Garden with patio and barbecue. Excellent walking country. Many places of interest within easy reach.

ONLINE MAP

Unit TV DVD General P Leisure

Where can I get help and advice?

Tourist Information Centres offer friendly help with accommodation and holiday ideas as well as suggestions of places to visit and things to do. You'll find contact details at the beginning of each regional section.

HOLMFIRTH, West Yorkshire Map ref 4B1

★★★★
SELF CATERING

Units 1
Sleeps 1–5

LOW SEASON PER WK
£200.00–£270.00

HIGH SEASON PER WK
£220.00–£400.00

Mytholmbridge Studio Cottage, Holmfirth

contact Sue Clay, Luke Lane, Holmfirth HD9 7TB **t** (01484) 686642 **e** sue@mytholmbridge.co.uk

mytholmbridge.co.uk

Secluded 250-year-old stone barn situated in 'Last of the Summer Wine' country. Original beams retained within the contemporary open space. Light, spacious living area. Garden, large car park, close to local amenities.

open All year
payment Credit/debit cards, cash, cheques, euros
nearest shop less than 0.5 miles
nearest pub less than 0.5 miles

Unit General P Leisure

HOLY ISLAND, Northumberland Map ref 5C1

★★★
SELF CATERING

Units 2
Sleeps 4

LOW SEASON PER WK
£230.00–£350.00

HIGH SEASON PER WK
£350.00–£560.00

Farne Court Cottage, Farne View Cottage, Holy Island

contact Mrs Batty, Waterside House, Dalton, Lockerbie DG11 1AT **t** (01387) 840122
e angelabatty@btinternet.com

18thC stone cottages with courtyard, private garden and parking. Very well equipped and furnished. Cosy in winter (woodburner). Close to beach and castle.

open All year
payment Cash, cheques
nearest shop less than 0.5 miles
nearest pub less than 0.5 miles

Unit General P Leisure

HOLY ISLAND, Northumberland Map ref 5C1

★★★
SELF CATERING

Units 1
Sleeps 8

LOW SEASON PER WK
Min £475.00

HIGH SEASON PER WK
Max £920.00

Links View, Holy Island

contact Rachel Pain, **e** linksviewholyisland@yahoo.co.uk

lindisfarne.org.uk/links-view

A Grade II Listed house in Holy Island village offering self-catering holiday accommodation.

open All year
payment Cash, cheques
nearest shop less than 0.5 miles
nearest pub less than 0.5 miles

Unit General P

HORNSEA, East Riding of Yorkshire Map ref 4D1

★★★
SELF CATERING

Units 1
Sleeps 1–4

LOW SEASON PER WK
£275.00–£300.00

HIGH SEASON PER WK
£375.00–£450.00

Cherry Tree, Hornsea

contact Mrs Rita Leonard, Cherry Tree, Cowden Parva Farm, Main Road Cowden, Hull HU11 4UG
t (01964) 527245 & 07720 349716 **e** leonardritaruth@yahoo.co.uk

Cosy holiday home, Hornsea, East Yorkshire coast. Bungalow with quality fixtures and fittings, large conservatory, gas, electricity and all linens, parking off-road. Quiet cul-de-sac off town centre. Large lake.

open All year
payment Cash, cheques, euros
nearest shop less than 0.5 miles
nearest pub less than 0.5 miles

Unit General P
Leisure

HORTON IN RIBBLESDALE, North Yorkshire Map ref 5B3

★★★
SELF CATERING

Units 1
Sleeps 1–5

LOW SEASON PER WK
£280.00–£320.00

HIGH SEASON PER WK
£320.00–£380.00

Blind Beck Holiday Cottage, Settle

contact Heather Huddleston, Blind Beck Holiday Cottage, Horton in Ribblesdale BD24 0HT
t (01729) 860396 **e** h.huddleston@daelnet.co.uk

blindbeck.co.uk

This 17thC cottage is full of character. Located in the centre of the Three Peaks area and near the Settle-Carlisle railway.

open All year
payment Cash, cheques
nearest shop 0.5 miles
nearest pub 0.5 miles

Unit General P

HUMSHAUGH, Northumberland Map ref 5B2

★★★
SELF CATERING

Units 1
Sleeps 3

LOW SEASON PER WK
Max £200.00

HIGH SEASON PER WK
Max £250.00

East Farm Cottage, Hexham

contact Mrs Gwen Dodds, East Farm House, Humshaugh, Hexham NE46 4AT **t** (01434) 689150
e charles.dodds2@btopenworld.com

Listed 18thC cottage. Lounge and kitchen with dining area on ground floor. Two bedrooms (double and single) and bathroom on first floor.

open All year
payment Cash, cheques
nearest shop less than 0.5 miles
nearest pub 0.5 miles

Unit General P S

HUNMANBY, North Yorkshire Map ref 5D3

★★★★
SELF CATERING

Units 1
Sleeps 5

LOW SEASON PER WK
£200.00–£300.00

HIGH SEASON PER WK
£350.00–£500.00

Short breaks also available.

Aislaby Cottage, Hunmanby, Nr Filey

contact Suzanne Watkinson, 12 Lombard Street, Rawdon, Leeds LS19 6BW **t** (0113) 250 1407
e richard.watkinson4@btinternet.com

open All year
payment Cash, cheques
nearest shop less than 0.5 miles
nearest pub less than 0.5 miles

Aislaby Cottage is located close to shops, pubs, takeaways, restaurants, golf, tennis and gymnasium. Ten minutes' drive from beaches at Filey, Hunmanby Gap and Reighton Sands. Safe, enclosed garden with hardwood furniture, LCD TV, DVD, woodburning stove, dishwasher and washing machine. Linen and towels included. No smoking, no pets.

Unit General S

HUTTON-LE-HOLE, North Yorkshire Map ref 5C3

★★★★
SELF CATERING

Units 2
Sleeps 2–10

LOW SEASON PER WK
Min £295.00

HIGH SEASON PER WK
Max £495.00

The Green, Hutton-le-Hole, York

t (020) 8892 9132 **e** info@thegreen.eu

thegreen.eu

open All year
payment Cash, cheques
nearest shop 3 miles
nearest pub less than 0.5 miles

With views over the village green from every bedroom and sitting room, this unique holiday home is ideal for exploring the Yorkshire moors and coastal towns with Castle Howard and York a short drive away. Our spacious, newly refurbished apartments sleep between two and ten people in comfort. Dogs welcome.

Unit General P Leisure

HUTTON ROOF, Cumbria Map ref 5A2

★★★★★
SELF CATERING

Units 4
Sleeps 1–20

LOW SEASON PER WK
Min £400.00

HIGH SEASON PER WK
Max £1,695.00

Carrock Cottages, Penrith

contact Malcolm & Gillian Iredale, Carrock Cottages, Carrock House, How Hill, Hutton Roof CA11 0XY **t** (017684) 84111 **e** info@carrockcottages.co.uk

carrockcottages.co.uk REAL-TIME BOOKING

payment Credit/debit cards, cash, cheques
nearest shop 5 miles
nearest pub 5 miles

Award-winning luxury cottages in quiet, rural location near lovely villages of Hesket Newmarket, Caldbeck and Greystoke. Explore northern Lake District or head north to historic Carlisle and on to Hadrian's Wall. Restaurants, fell-walking and other activities. Warm welcome guaranteed. Internet access, digital TV/DVD players. Prices differ at Christmas, New Year and Easter.

SAT NAV *CA11 0XY*

Unit General P S
Leisure

IREBY, Lancashire Map ref 5B3

★★★★
SELF CATERING

Units 1
Sleeps 4

LOW SEASON PER WK
£275.00–£360.00

Springfield, Carnforth

contact Miss Heather Bavin, Bainbridge House, High Barn Road, Ireby, Carnforth LA6 2JY
t (01524) 242501 **e** heather.bavin@btinternet.com

visitnorthlancashire.co.uk

Renovated 19thC cottage with two double bedrooms, situated in quiet hamlet. Ideal for away-from-it-all holidays. Open fire. Sun lounge. Welcome hamper for stays of one week or more. Off-peak short breaks.

open All year
payment Cash, cheques
nearest shop 1.5 miles
nearest pub 2 miles

Unit General P S Leisure

KENDAL, Cumbria Map ref 5B3

★★★★
SELF CATERING

Units 4
Sleeps 2–18

LOW SEASON PER WK
£210.00–£240.00

HIGH SEASON PER WK
£255.00–£420.00

Short breaks from 2 nights available most of the year, prices from £100.

Shaw End Mansion, Kendal

contact Mr & Mrs Robinson, Haveriggs Farm, Kendal LA8 9EF **t** (01539) 824220
e robinson@fieldendholidays.co.uk

fieldendholidays.co.uk SPECIAL OFFERS · REAL-TIME BOOKING

open All year
payment Credit/debit cards, cash, cheques
nearest shop 3 miles
nearest pub 3 miles

Shaw End Mansion is set on a 200-acre farm in a beautiful location. Shaw End – a restored Georgian house – contains spacious and elegant apartments with fantastic views and walks from the doorstep. Why not rent the whole house, which is ideal for weddings and parties.

Unit General P S Leisure

It's all quality-assessed accommodation

Our commitment to quality involves wide-ranging accommodation assessment. Ratings and awards were correct at the time of going to press but may change following a new assessment. Please check at time of booking.

KESWICK, Cumbria Map ref 5A3

★★★★
SELF CATERING

Units **4**
Sleeps **2–16**

LOW SEASON PER WK
£195.00–£750.00

HIGH SEASON PER WK
£380.00–£1,450.00

Brackenrigg, Keswick

contact Judy & Harry Marsland, Naddle, Keswick CA12 4TF **t** (017687) 72258
e info@brackenrigg.com

brackenrigg.com SPECIAL OFFERS

Stunning location near Keswick and Grasmere, magnificent views of Helvellyn and Blencathra, gardens and woodland pathways to explore, delightful walking straight from your door, four beautiful cottages for two-sixteen persons.

open All year
payment Credit/debit cards, cash, cheques
nearest shop 3 miles
nearest pub 2 miles

Unit General P Leisure

KESWICK, Cumbria Map ref 5A3

★★★★★
SELF CATERING

Units **2**
Sleeps **1–2**

LOW SEASON PER WK
£340.00–£390.00

HIGH SEASON PER WK
£440.00–£490.00

Any 3 consecutive days at a cost of £80pn reducing to £60pn during winter months, subject to availability.

The Coach House & Derwent Cottage Mews, Keswick

contact Sue Newman, Derwent Cottage, Portinscale, Keswick CA12 5RF **t** (017687) 74838

derwentcottage.co.uk

open All year
payment Credit/debit cards, cash, cheques
nearest shop 1 mile
nearest pub less than 0.5 miles

Derwent Cottage Mews and Coach House are both one-bedroom apartments, decorated to a high standard and fully equipped. Both have access to the garden, the Coach House having double doors opening out from the living room onto an awning-covered patio. Derwent Cottage is set back from the road in its own grounds, one mile from Keswick.

Unit General P

KESWICK, Cumbria Map ref 5A3

★★★
SELF CATERING

Units **1**
Sleeps **1–4**

LOW SEASON PER WK
Min £200.00

HIGH SEASON PER WK
Max £360.00

Short breaks welcome, out of season only, from Nov-Apr.

The Cottage, Keswick

contact Mrs Margaret Beaty, The Cottage, Birkrigg, Newlands Valley, Keswick CA12 5TS
t (017687) 78278

open All year
payment Cash, cheques
nearest shop 3 miles
nearest pub 2 miles

Cosy, comfortable, oak-beamed cottage, converted from a stable, nestled between the farm guesthouse and adjoining barn. Very pleasantly situated five miles from Keswick in a peaceful valley with excellent view of the surrounding range of mountains. Ideal for fell-walking. Lounge, kitchen, one double room, one twin room, shower/toilet.

Unit General 2 P

Remember to check when booking

Please remember that all information in this guide has been supplied by the proprietors well in advance of publication. Since changes do sometimes occur it's a good idea to check details at the time of booking.

KESWICK, Cumbria Map ref 5A3

★★★
SELF CATERING

Units 1
Sleeps 2–4

LOW SEASON PER WK
£250.00–£2,000.00

Short breaks and holidays brochure available offering a wide range of 2 – 7 night packages throughout the year.

The Cottage Suite, Keswick

contact Lynne Watkins, The Skiddaw Hotel, Main Street, Keswick CA12 5BN **t** (017687) 72071
e info@skiddawhotel.co.uk

skiddawhotel.co.uk

open All year
payment Credit/debit cards, cash, cheques
nearest shop less than 0.5 miles
nearest pub less than 0.5 miles

A two-bedroomed (one twin, one double) Victorian cottage, refurbished sparing no expense, offering comfort, elegance, private parking. Situated at the rear of Skiddaw Hotel. The kitchen offers modern facilities. The sitting room and bedrooms boast flat screen televisions. A variety of welcome packs are available. Free use of nearby leisure facilities.

Unit General P Leisure

KESWICK, Cumbria Map ref 5A3

★★★★
SELF CATERING

Units 5
Sleeps 2–8

LOW SEASON PER WK
£290.00–£555.00

HIGH SEASON PER WK
£455.00–£1,035.00

Short breaks Nov-Mar and at other times at short notice. Special 2-person rates.

Croft House Holidays, Keswick

contact Mrs Boniface, Croft House Holidays, Croft House, Applethwaite, Keswick CA12 4PN
t (017687) 73693 **e** holidays@crofthouselakes.co.uk

crofthouselakes.co.uk GUEST REVIEWS • SPECIAL OFFERS

open All year
payment Cash, cheques
nearest shop 1 mile
nearest pub 1 mile

Escape to stunning, panoramic views of Derwentwater and Borrowdale. Peaceful, rural locations in Applethwaite village, one mile from Keswick. Cottage for four and ground-floor apartment for two in a Victorian country house. Two further cottages for four and six and spacious detached barn conversion for eight with snooker room.

ONLINE MAP

Unit General P Leisure

KESWICK, Cumbria Map ref 5A3

★★★
SELF CATERING

Units 3
Sleeps 2–12

LOW SEASON PER WK
£260.00–£360.00

HIGH SEASON PER WK
£370.00–£550.00

Short breaks available all year. Please enquire for availability and prices.

Hillside, Keswick

contact Dr & Mrs M J & D J Wright, Fisherfield, New Road, Portinscale, Keswick CA12 5TX
t (017687) 80256 **e** info@keswick-hillside-apts.co.uk

keswickhillsideapartments.co.uk

open All year
payment Cash, cheques
nearest shop less than 0.5 miles
nearest pub less than 0.5 miles

Three very comfortable, clean, self-catering apartments, sleeping two-twelve guests. Located away from the busy centre yet within short walking distance of local amenities, facilities and walks. Rental costs are for each apartment and include electricity and heating, making Hillside a competitive and flexible alternative to B&B. Free parking facilities.

ONLINE MAP

Unit General Leisure

KIELDER, Northumberland Map ref 5B1

★★★★–★★★★★
SELF CATERING

Units 32
Sleeps 2–6

LOW SEASON PER WK
£180.00–£360.00

HIGH SEASON PER WK
£400.00–£950.00

Kielder Lodges, Kielder Water and Forest Park

Leaplish Waterside Park, Kielder Water and Forest Park NE48 1BT **t** (01434) 250294
e kielder.holidays@nwl.co.uk

nwl.co.uk/kielder

Scandinavian-style luxury lodges, situated in peaceful surroundings. An excellent centre for touring Scottish Borders and Hadrian's Roman Wall Country.

open February to December
payment Credit/debit cards, cash, cheques
nearest shop less than 0.5 miles
nearest pub less than 0.5 miles

Unit General Leisure

KIELDER FOREST

See under Bellingham, Kielder, Kielder Water, Wark

KIELDER WATER, Northumberland Map ref 5B2

★★★★★
SELF CATERING

Units 4
Sleeps 1–6

LOW SEASON PER WK
£200.00–£300.00

HIGH SEASON PER WK
£500.00–£800.00

Short breaks, golf, riding, pamper, fine dining, special celebrations/ weddings. Sleeps 14 if rented as a whole.

Falstone Barns, Nr Kielder Water and Forest Park, Hexham

contact Mrs Nicolette Forster, Falstone Barns, Falstone Farm, Falstone, Hexham NE48 1AA
t (01434) 240251 & 07891 817185 **e** info@falstonebarns.com

falstonebarns.com SPECIAL OFFERS • REAL-TIME BOOKING

open All year
payment Credit/debit cards, cash, cheques
nearest shop less than 0.5 miles
nearest pub less than 0.5 miles

Barn conversions near Kielder Water offering luxurious themed holiday apartments; set in 38 acres of private estate, offering tailor-made holidays.

SAT NAV *NE48 1AA*

Unit General
Leisure

KING'S MEABURN, Cumbria Map ref 5B3

★★★★–★★★★★
SELF CATERING

Units 5
Sleeps 3–6

LOW SEASON PER WK
£195.00–£540.00

HIGH SEASON PER WK
£305.00–£750.00

Short breaks available Oct-Mar (excl Christmas and New Year). Minimum 2 nights.

Lyvennet Cottages, Penrith

contact Margaret, Wendy & Janet Addison, Lyvennet Cottages, Keld Farm, King's Meaburn, Penrith CA10 3BS **t** (01931) 714226 **e** wendyaddison@yahoo.com

lyvennetcottages.co.uk

open All year
payment Cash, cheques
nearest shop 5 miles
nearest pub less than 0.5 miles

Five attractive cottages and stunning mill conversion. Furnished to a high standard in peaceful village, overlooking the beautiful Lyvennet valley and Lakeland hills. Open fires, linen and fuel provided. Free double-bank fishing, pets welcome. Ideally situated for an active or touring holiday. Bring your horse on holiday. Livery/grass available.

Unit General Leisure

What do the star ratings mean?

Detailed information about star ratings can be found at the back of this guide.

KIRBY MISPERTON, North Yorkshire Map ref 5D3

APPROVED CARAVAN HOLIDAY HOME

Units **2**
Sleeps **2–4**

LOW SEASON PER WK
£150.00–£220.00

HIGH SEASON PER WK
£220.00–£280.00

Lendales Farm, Malton

contact Mr Scaling, Lendales Farm, Malton YO17 6XR **t** (01653) 668220 **e** avvq77@dsl.pipex.com

lendalesfarm.co.uk REAL-TIME BOOKING

Family-run mixed working farm. Situated in quiet country site. Spacious four-berth caravan holiday homes with decking. Excellent for exploring Ryedale and beyond. Something to suit all ages.

payment Cash, cheques
nearest shop 2.5 miles
nearest pub 0.5 miles

Unit General 4 P Leisure

KIRKBY LONSDALE, Cumbria Map ref 5B3

★★★★
SELF CATERING

Units **3**

LOW SEASON PER WK
£260.00–£360.00

HIGH SEASON PER WK
£425.00–£500.00

Short breaks, subject to availability, (excl Christmas and New Year). Pets welcome.

Sellet Hall Cottages, Carnforth, Kirkby Lonsdale

contact Mrs Hall, Sellet Hall Cottages, Sellet Hall, Carnforth LA6 2QF **t** (01524) 271865
e sellethall@hotmail.com

sellethall.com

open All year
payment Cash, cheques

Unique cottages converted from 17thC barn set in the grounds of Sellet Hall, surrounded by open countryside and complemented by far-distance views over the Lune Valley, Trough of Bowland and Yorkshire Dales. All have log fires, fitted kitchens, dishwasher, microwave etc. Own gardens, patio and parking.

Unit General P Leisure

KIRKBY MALZEARD, North Yorkshire Map ref 5C3

★★★★
SELF CATERING

Units **1**
Sleeps **6**

LOW SEASON PER WK
£300.00–£370.00

HIGH SEASON PER WK
£430.00–£580.00

WALKERS WELCOME CYCLISTS WELCOME

Alma Cottage, Kirkby Malzeard, Ripon

contact Mrs Janet Barclay, 12 St Stephen's Road, Cold Norton, Chelmsford CM3 6JE
t (01621) 828576 **e** janet@lbarclay.demon.co.uk

almacottage.co.uk GUEST REVIEWS

Comfortable three-bedroom period cottage in stone terrace of friendly Nidderdale village. Ideal for dales, moors, walking, cycling, riding, sightseeing and birdwatching. Walled garden, secure garage, one double, two twins.

open All year
payment Cash, cheques
nearest shop less than 0.5 miles
nearest pub less than 0.5 miles

Unit General P S Leisure

KIRKBYMOORSIDE, North Yorkshire Map ref 5C3

★★★★
SELF CATERING

Units 2
Sleeps 2–4

LOW SEASON PER WK
£275.00–£350.00

HIGH SEASON PER WK
£350.00–£395.00

The Cornmill, Kirkbymoorside

contact Chris & Karen Tinkler, The Cornmill, Kirkby Mills, Kirkbymoorside YO62 6NP
t (01751) 432000 **e** cornmill@kirbymills.demon.co.uk

kirbymills.demon.co.uk REAL-TIME BOOKING

open All year
payment Credit/debit cards, cash, cheques
nearest shop 0.5 miles
nearest pub 0.75 miles

Sympathetically restored stable mews cottages in 18thC watermill complex on the River Dove. Well-appointed accommodation with linen and towels, TV, video, mini hi-fi and central heating included. Bed and bath downstairs, living room upstairs. Garden and barbecue. Meals in the millhouse by arrangement.

SAT NAV *YO62 6NP*

Unit TV General P Leisure

KIRKBYMOORSIDE, North Yorkshire Map ref 5C3

★★★★
SELF CATERING

Units 2
Sleeps 4

LOW SEASON PER WK
£250.00–£380.00

HIGH SEASON PER WK
£390.00–£460.00

Short breaks available Nov-Mar – 3-night stay (excluding Christmas and half-terms).

Surprise View Cottage & Field Barn Cottage, Kirkbymoorside

contact Mrs Ruth Wass, Sinnington Lodge, Sinnington, York YO62 6RB **t** (01751) 431345
e info@surpriseviewcottages.co.uk

surpriseviewcottages.co.uk

open All year
payment Cash, cheques
nearest shop 3 miles
nearest pub 1 mile

Historic barn conversions on farmstead (originally an old mill and tannery) giving panoramic views over moorland edge, and immediate access to field and woodland walks. Warm, roomy accommodation with excellent-quality furnishings and fittings. A wealth of beams and original stone and brick features. 'Comfort' is the key word.

Unit TV DVD General P
Leisure

KNARESBOROUGH, North Yorkshire Map ref 4B1

★★★
SELF CATERING

Units 1
Sleeps 2

LOW SEASON PER WK
£180.00–£200.00

HIGH SEASON PER WK
£200.00–£220.00

Garden Apartment, Knaresborough

contact Antje Rowinski, Garden Apartment, 3 Aspin Way, Knaresborough HG5 8HL
t (01423) 860463 **e** david.rowinski@ntlworld.com

Located in the picturesque market town of Knaresborough, a short walk to the market square with shops, pubs and restaurants. An ideal position to visit Harrogate, York, Leeds, the Dales and Yorkshire coastline.

open All year
payment Cash, cheques, euros
nearest shop less than 0.5 miles
nearest pub 0.5 miles

Unit TV General P Leisure

CYCLISTS WELCOME

Fancy a cycling holiday?

For a fabulous freewheeling break, seek out accommodation participating in our Cyclists Welcome scheme. Look out for the symbol and plan your route online at nationalcyclenetwork.org.

KNARESBOROUGH, North Yorkshire Map ref 4B1

★★★★
SELF CATERING

Units 1
Sleeps 1–2

LOW SEASON PER WK
£295.00–£325.00

HIGH SEASON PER WK
£260.00–£295.00

Short breaks available. 3-night stays Oct-Mar.

The Granary, Knaresborough

contact Mrs Rachel Thornton, Gibbet House Farm, Farnham Lane, Knaresborough HG5 9JP
t (01423) 862325 & 07970 000068

open All year
payment Cash, cheques, euros
nearest shop 1.5 miles
nearest pub 1.5 miles

Traditional, converted granary adjacent to farmhouse. Situated in 30 acres of parkland with stunning views of the Nidderdale Valley. Furnished to a high standard. Five miles Harrogate, two miles Knaresborough. Central for Dales, Yorkshire coast, Herriot and Heartbeat Country. The perfect setting for a peaceful and comfortable holiday.

Unit General P Leisure

LANGCLIFFE, North Yorkshire Map ref 5B3

★★★
SELF CATERING

Units 1
Sleeps 4

LOW SEASON PER WK
£160.00–£200.00

HIGH SEASON PER WK
£270.00–£300.00

Bear Cottage, Langcliffe, Nr Settle

contact Mr D Widdop, 1 St Johns Row, Langcliffe BD24 9NJ **t** (01729) 824363
e jayne.craig2@btopenworld.com

bear-cottage.com

An early 19thC terraced cottage in a small picturesque village overlooking Langcliffe village green. It has a warm, cosy feel, tucked away to the side of the old chapel.

open All year
payment Cash, cheques
nearest shop 1 mile
nearest pub 1 mile

Unit General 5 P Leisure

LANGDALE, Cumbria Map ref 5A3

★★★–★★★★★
SELF CATERING

Units 2
Sleeps 2–10

LOW SEASON PER WK
£250.00–£850.00

HIGH SEASON PER WK
£380.00–£2,050.00

4-night winter midweek breaks for the price of 2 (Garden Cottage £140, Meadow Bank £320).

Meadow Bank, Ambleside

contact Patricia Locke, Langdale Cottages, 13 Park Road, Hale, Altrincham WA15 9NL
t (0161) 928 6953 **e** patricia.locke@btinternet.com

langdale-cottages.co.uk SPECIAL OFFERS

open All year
payment Cash, cheques
nearest shop less than 0.5 miles
nearest pub less than 0.5 miles

In the centre of the unspoilt village of Elterwater, Meadow Bank has fine views towards the beck and fells. It is an exceptional property, completely renovated and beautifully furnished throughout. The house has four bedrooms and three bathrooms. There is also the Garden Cottage. Leisure club facilities are included.

Unit General P Leisure

Do you like walking?

Walkers feel at home in accommodation participating in our Walkers Welcome scheme. Look out for the symbol. Consider walking all or part of a long-distance route – go online at nationaltrail.co.uk.

LASTINGHAM, North Yorkshire Map ref 5C3

★★★★
SELF CATERING

Units 1
Sleeps 1–5

LOW SEASON PER WK
£250.00–£285.00

HIGH SEASON PER WK
£385.00–£425.00

Old Reading Room, Lastingham, York

contact Reservations, Lastingham Grange, Lastingham, North Yorkshire YO62 6TH **t** (01751) 417345
e reservations@lastinghamgrange.com

lastinghamgrange.com REAL-TIME BOOKING

A charming three-bedroom cottage located in the historic village of Lastingham on the edge of the North York Moors. A peaceful backwater in the heart of the National Park.

open All year
payment Credit/debit cards, cash, cheques, euros
nearest shop 5 miles
nearest pub less than 0.5 miles

Unit General P Leisure

LEEDS BRADFORD INTERNATIONAL AIRPORT

See under Otley

LEYBURN, North Yorkshire Map ref 5B3

★★★
SELF CATERING

Units 6
Sleeps 2–6

LOW SEASON PER WK
£175.00–£230.00

HIGH SEASON PER WK
£230.00–£350.00

Short breaks available Oct-Apr.

Dales View Holiday Homes, Leyburn

contact Messrs John Chilton, Dales View Holiday Homes, Jenkins Garth, Leyburn DL8 5SP
t (01969) 623707 & (01969) 622808 **e** bookings@daleshols.co.uk

daleshols.co.uk SPECIAL OFFERS · REAL-TIME BOOKING

open All year
payment Cash, cheques
nearest shop less than 0.5 miles
nearest pub less than 0.5 miles

Stone-built period cottages and self-contained apartments form a secluded courtyard only 80m from Leyburn marketplace. Ideal touring and walking centre for the Dales. Comfortable, well-maintained properties, heated throughout winter. Private parking, garden and play area. Some properties with panoramic views over Wensleydale.

Unit General P

LITTLE STRICKLAND, Cumbria Map ref 5B3

★★★★
SELF CATERING

Units 1
Sleeps 2–3

LOW SEASON PER WK
£225.00–£250.00

HIGH SEASON PER WK
£250.00–£325.00

Spring Bank, Penrith

contact Mrs J Ostle, Spring Bank, Little Strickland, c/o Meadowfield, Penrith CA10 3EG
t (01931) 716246 **e** springbank17@hotmail.com

holidaycumbria.co.uk SPECIAL OFFERS

Spacious, king-/twin-bedded bungalow in quiet location. Easy access to Lakes, Dales and Eden Valley. Satisfied clients reflect quality accommodation/location. All facilities, kitchen/diner, garden, rural views. Brochure available.

open All year
payment Cash, cheques
nearest shop 3 miles
nearest pub 2 miles

Unit General P

PETS! WELCOME

Where is my pet welcome?

Want to take your cherished companion with you on holiday? Proprietors participating in our Welcome Pets! scheme go out of their way to make special provision for you and your pet. Look out for the symbol.

LITTON, North Yorkshire Map ref 5B3

★★★–★★★★★
SELF CATERING

Units 9
Sleeps 2–14

LOW SEASON PER WK
£230.00–£920.00

HIGH SEASON PER WK
£360.00–£1,550.00

Stonelands, Litton, Skipton

contact Brenda Cowan, Stonelands Farm Yard Cottages, Stonelands, Litton BD23 5QH
t (01756) 770293 **e** stonelandsfarm@aol.com

stonelandscottages.com

open All year
payment Credit/debit cards, cash, cheques
nearest shop 7 miles
nearest pub 0.5 miles

A friendly welcome awaits you at our charming award-winning stone barn conversion, set amidst our working hill farm. Relax in a tranquil setting amid breathtaking views, with four-poster beds, spa baths and exposed beams. Indoor heated swimming pool, sauna and children's play area. Short breaks all year. Private parking.

Unit TV General P S Leisure

LIVERPOOL, Merseyside Map ref 4A2

★★★
SERVICED APARTMENTS

Units 6
Sleeps 2–6

HIGH SEASON PER WK
Max £455.00

Weekly and monthly discounts are available. Please enquire with your requests.

International Inn Serviced Apartments, Liverpool

contact Leah Williams, 4 South Hunter Street, Off Hardman Street, Liverpool L1 9JG
t (0151) 709 8135 **e** info@internationalinn.co.uk

internationalinnapartments.co.uk GUEST REVIEWS • REAL-TIME BOOKING

open All year except Christmas
payment Credit/debit cards, cash, cheques
nearest shop less than 0.5 miles
nearest pub less than 0.5 miles

The award-winning International Inn offers private self-catering apartments in the heart of Liverpool's historic cultural quarter. Tastefully furnished, high standard accommodation with all the facilities required to enjoy your visit in comfort and privacy. The optimum choice for business or pleasure city breaks. The ideal option for longer stays in Liverpool.

ONLINE MAP

Unit TV DVD General S

LIVERPOOL, Merseyside Map ref 4A2

★★★★
SELF CATERING

Units 2
Sleeps 4–6

LOW SEASON PER WK
£500.00

HIGH SEASON PER WK
£600.00

Port Sunlight Village Trust, Port Sunlight, Wirral

contact Mrs Sandra Nicholls, 95 Greendale Road, Port Sunlight, Wirral CH62 4XE **t** (0151) 644 4801
e s.nicholls@portsunlightvillage.com

portsunlightvillage.com

open All year
payment Credit/debit cards, cash, cheques
nearest shop 0.5 miles
nearest pub 0.5 miles

Grade II Listed cottages located in the heart of Port Sunlight garden village amid picturesque surroundings. Within easy reach of Chester, Liverpool and North Wales.

Unit TV DVD General P S Leisure

LIVERPOOL, Merseyside Map ref 4A2

★★★★
SELF CATERING

Units 2
Sleeps 1–8

LOW SEASON PER WK
£400.00–£600.00

HIGH SEASON PER WK
£500.00–£600.00

Trafalgar Warehouse Apartments, Liverpool

contact Mr Ray Gibson, Trafalgar Warehouse Apartments, Appt 9/10, 17-19 Lord Nelson Street, Liverpool L3 5QB **t** 07715 118419

trafalgarwarehouseapartments.co.uk GUEST REVIEWS

Fully furnished, open-plan apartments with character features and contemporary fittings. Two double beds in each apartment, one of which is on the mezzanine floor. Luxurious bathroom with jacuzzi.

open All year
payment Credit/debit cards, cash, cheques, euros
nearest shop less than 0.5 miles
nearest pub less than 0.5 miles

Unit General

LOCKTON, North Yorkshire Map ref 5D3

★★★
SELF CATERING

Units 1
Sleeps 2–4

LOW SEASON PER WK
£295.00

HIGH SEASON PER WK
£325.00

Nov-Apr weekend and midweek breaks available including welcome pack.

The Little Barn, Pickering

contact Mr James Fisk, The Little Barn, The Courtyard, Ivy Cottage, Lockton YO18 7PY
t (01751) 460325 **e** judi@btinternet.com

open All year
payment Cash, cheques
nearest shop less than 0.5 miles
nearest pub 0.5 miles

This delightful 17thC barn has oak beams throughout and has been tastefully modernised. Perfectly situated in a spacious garden, with both moors and Dalby Forest on its doorstep, it also offers stabling, grazing and secure lock-up for tack and bicycles. Ideal for steam train, 'Heartbeat' country, historic York and east coast.

Unit General Leisure

LONGHORSLEY, Northumberland Map ref 5C1

★★★★–★★★★★
SELF CATERING

Units 15
Sleeps 2–7

LOW SEASON PER WK
£275.00–£565.00

HIGH SEASON PER WK
£500.00–£1,565.00

Winter weekend spa breaks available with a full range of treatments available 7 days a week.

Beacon Hill Farm Holidays, Longhorsley, Morpeth

contact Mr Alun Moore, Beacon Hill Farm, Beacon Hill, Longhorsley, Morpeth NE65 8QW
t (01670) 780900 & 07802 517121 **e** alun@beaconhill.co.uk

beaconhill.co.uk GUEST REVIEWS · SPECIAL OFFERS · REAL-TIME BOOKING

open All year
payment Credit/debit cards, cash, cheques
nearest shop 2 miles
nearest pub 2 miles

Luxury self-catering cottages situated on a beautiful farm with outstanding views of the Northumbrian hills and coast. Explore Northumberland from this award-winning base. Perfectly located for beaches, castles and National Trust properties. Walk through the landscaped gardens to a spa with pool, sauna, jacuzzi and gym.

ONLINE MAP

Unit General
Leisure

FAMILIES WELCOME WELCOME FAMILIES

Looking for an ideal family break?

For accommodation offering additional facilities and services for a range of ages and family units, look out for the Families Welcome symbol. Owners of these properties will go out of their way to welcome families.

LONGHORSLEY, Northumberland Map ref 5C1

★★★★
SELF CATERING

Units 1
Sleeps 8

LOW SEASON PER WK
£500.00–£850.00

HIGH SEASON PER WK
£975.00–£1,250.00

West Moor Farm Cottage, Longhorsley

contact Mrs Carolyn Raven, West Moor Farm Cottage, West Moor Farm, Longhorsley NE65 8QX
t 07816 245678 **e** info@westmoorfarm.co.uk

westmoorfarm.co.uk

open All year
payment Cash, cheques, euros
nearest shop 1.5 miles
nearest pub 1.5 miles

This four-bedroom cottage with views over the Cheviots has been described as having the wow factor! On site is a livery/trekking yard. We welcome pets and encourage horse-owners to bring their animals on holiday too. Many bridleways/footpaths and beaches, plus golf courses. Please take a look at the virtual tour on our website.

Unit TV DVD General P S
Leisure

LONGSLEDDALE, Cumbria Map ref 5B3

★★★
SELF CATERING

Units 1
Sleeps 2

LOW SEASON PER WK
£160.00–£250.00

HIGH SEASON PER WK
£250.00–£260.00

The Coach House, Kendal

contact Jenny Farmer, The Coach House, c/o Capplebarrow House, Longsleddale, Kendal LA8 9BB
t (01539) 823686 **e** jenyfarmer@aol.com

capplebarrowcoachhouse.co.uk

Stone-built, converted coach house with ground-floor shower room and bedroom and open staircase to first-floor kitchen and lounge. Excellent views. Located in peaceful, picturesque valley.

open All year
payment Cash, cheques
nearest shop 6 miles
nearest pub 7 miles

Unit TV SC DVD General P S

LOW ROW, North Yorkshire Map ref 5B3

★★★★
SELF CATERING

Units 1
Sleeps 1–2

LOW SEASON PER WK
£250.00–£265.00

HIGH SEASON PER WK
£330.00–£410.00

Curlew Cottage, Low Row, Richmond

contact Mrs Rachel Browning, 8 Hyperion Drive, Rochester ME2 3RG **t** (01634) 725273
e hillsr1@hotmail.com

curlew-cottage.org.uk

Curlew Cottage is a delightful one-bedroom Grade II Listed 18thC former lead miner's cottage, commanding spectacular views over Swaledale in the heart of the Yorkshire Dales National Park.

open All year
payment Cheques
nearest shop 4 miles
nearest pub 0.5 miles

Unit TV DVD General P S Leisure

Don't forget www.

Web addresses throughout this guide are shown without the prefix www. Please include www. in the address line of your browser. If a web address does not follow this style it is shown in full.

LUDDENDEN, West Yorkshire Map ref 4B1

★★★★
SELF CATERING

Units 1
Sleeps 2

LOW SEASON PER WK
£200.00–£300.00

HIGH SEASON PER WK
£300.00–£400.00

Folly Too, Luddenden, Halifax

contact Mrs Gail Rowe, 4 Box House, Old Lane, Luddenden HX2 6QA **t** (01422) 881166
e follytoo@hotmail.com

follytoo.com REAL-TIME BOOKING

open All year
payment Cash, cheques
nearest shop 0.5 miles
nearest pub less than 0.5 miles

Original weaver's cottage situated in the heart of the stunning conservation village of Luddenden in the Calder Valley. Spectacular views, charm and comfort – 'that's a promise'.

SAT NAV *HX2 6PZ* **ONLINE MAP**

Unit General P S

LYTHAM ST ANNES, Lancashire Map ref 4A1

★★★★
SELF CATERING

Units 1
Sleeps 1–5

LOW SEASON PER WK
£225.00–£380.00

HIGH SEASON PER WK
£380.00–£520.00

Ribble Way walking, Ribble Estuary birdwatching, Christmas and New Year.

Lytham Holiday Cottage, Lytham

contact Mr & Mrs Llewellyn, 5 Rosewood Close, Lytham St Annes FY8 4PE **t** (01253) 739598 & 07941 866447 **e** cottage@llewellyns.freeserve.co.uk

freewebs.com/lytham-holiday-cottage SPECIAL OFFERS

open All year
payment Cash, cheques, euros
nearest shop less than 0.5 miles
nearest pub less than 0.5 miles

Modern mews cottage, two bedrooms, one king-double, one twin (sleeps four/five with cot or foldaway bed), lounge, dining/kitchen, jacuzzi bathroom, cot, highchair. Freeview TV, DVD recorder. Electric cooker, gas hob. Dishwasher, fridge-freezer, microwave, washing machine. 0.25 miles Lytham Green, 0.5 miles town centre. Rear garden, barbecue and furniture. Parking.

SAT NAV *FY8 5AU*

Unit General P S

LYTHAM ST ANNES, Lancashire Map ref 4A1

★★★
SELF CATERING

Units 4
Sleeps 1–5

LOW SEASON PER WK
£220.00–£280.00

HIGH SEASON PER WK
£250.00–£310.00

Merlewood Holiday Apartments, Lytham St Annes

contact Mrs Sharon Iqbal, Merlewood Holiday Apartments, 383 Clifton Drive North, Lytham St Annes FY8 2PA **t** (01253) 726082

merlewoodapartments.co.uk

Self-contained apartments for couples/families. Separate kitchens and bedrooms, sea views, 50yds from promenade and town centre. Private parking.

open All year
payment Cash, cheques

Unit General P S

MACCLESFIELD, Cheshire Map ref 4B2

★★★★
SELF CATERING

Units 2
Sleeps 4–10

LOW SEASON PER WK
£250.00–£450.00

HIGH SEASON PER WK
£450.00–£550.00

Common Barn Cottages, Rainow, Macclesfield

contact Geoff & Rona Cooper, Common Barn Self-Catering Cottages, Common Barn Farm, Smith Lane, Rainow, Macclesfield SK10 5XJ **t** (01625) 574878 **e** g_greengrass@hotmail.com

commonbarnfarm.co.uk GUEST REVIEWS

open All year
payment Credit/debit cards, cash, cheques
nearest shop 3 miles
nearest pub 0.5 miles

A superb barn conversion situated on a working sheep/hill farm 1,250ft above sea level. Set amongst the rolling hills of the Peak District National Park with breathtaking views of the Cheshire plain and across to the Welsh mountains. We have wireless broadband available. Luxury underfloor heating.

ONLINE MAP

Unit General P Leisure

MACCLESFIELD, Cheshire Map ref 4B2

★★★
SELF CATERING

Units 1
Sleeps 6

LOW SEASON PER WK
£175.00–£190.00

HIGH SEASON PER WK
£190.00–£280.00

Mill House Farm Cottage, Macclesfield

contact Mrs Lynne Whittaker, Mill House Farm Cottage, Mill House Farm, Macclesfield SK11 0NZ **t** (01260) 226265 **e** lynne_whittaker@yahoo.co.uk

geocities.com/farm_cottage

Comfortable, spacious cottage on 130-acre dairy farm bordering the Peak District. Beautiful surrounding countryside and convenient for Alton Towers, Potteries, Chester, Manchester Airport.

open All year except Christmas and New Year
payment Cash, cheques
nearest shop 5 miles
nearest pub 0.5 miles

Unit General P S Leisure

MALTON, North Yorkshire Map ref 5D3

★★★★
SELF CATERING

Units 1
Sleeps 4

LOW SEASON PER WK
Min £278.00

HIGH SEASON PER WK
Max £550.00

Short breaks offered throughout the year subject to availability. Discounts offered for early bookings and consecutive weeks. See website for details.

Easthorpe Lodge, Easthorpe

contact Mrs Rebecca A Carrie, **t** (01944) 710429 **e** info@easthorpelodge.co.uk

easthorpelodge.co.uk GUEST REVIEWS · SPECIAL OFFERS

open All year
payment Credit/debit cards, cash, cheques
nearest shop 2 miles
nearest pub 1.5 miles

Charming, rural, 19thC stone cottage with garden. Double and twin rooms on ground floor. Three miles from Castle Howard. Perfect for exploring North York Moors, York, Whitby and the East Coast. Walks from doorstep. Near delightful market towns of Malton, Pickering and Helmsley. Newly refurbished in 2007/2008 to a high standard. Extra sofa bed in sitting room, cot available.

ONLINE MAP

WALKERS WELCOME · CYCLISTS WELCOME · FAMILIES WELCOME

Unit General P S
Leisure

Using map references

Map references refer to the colour maps at the front of this guide.

MALTON, North Yorkshire Map ref 5D3

★★★★
SELF CATERING

Units **1**
Sleeps **2–3**

LOW SEASON PER WK
£205.00–£275.00

HIGH SEASON PER WK
£305.00–£355.00

Midweek and weekend breaks generally available.

Swans Nest Cottage, Malton

contact Yvonne Dickinson, Swans Nest Cottage, Abbotts Farm House, Ryton YO17 6SA
t (01653) 694970 **e** swansnestcottage@hotmail.com

cottageguide.co.uk/swansnestcottage

open All year
payment Credit/debit cards, cash, cheques, euros
nearest shop 5 miles
nearest pub 2.5 miles

Cosy, two-bedroomed old farm cottage caringly modernised. In the heart of rural Ryedale, central to North York Moors, Yorkshire Wolds, east coast and York. Price includes logs and coal.

Unit General 3 P

MALTON, North Yorkshire Map ref 5D3

★★★★
SELF CATERING

Units **1**
Sleeps **1–4**

LOW SEASON PER WK
£204.00–£249.00

HIGH SEASON PER WK
£283.00–£442.00

£25 discount for stays of 2 weeks or longer.

Walnut Garth, Nr Malton

t 07766 208348 **e** cas@walnutgarth.co.uk

walnutgarth.co.uk GUEST REVIEWS

open All year
payment Cash, cheques
nearest shop less than 0.5 miles
nearest pub less than 0.5 miles

Tastefully decorated, two-bedroom cottage furnished to a high standard with all modern conveniences. Walnut Garth is set in the grounds of owner's property at edge of village, yet only two miles from market town of Malton and excellent selection of local amenities and attractions. Easy access to York and coast.

ONLINE MAP

Unit General P Leisure

MELKRIDGE, Northumberland Map ref 5B2

★★★★
SELF CATERING

Units **1**
Sleeps **1–4**

LOW SEASON PER WK
£225.00–£305.00

HIGH SEASON PER WK
£365.00–£410.00

Old Brewery Cottage, Haltwhistle

contact Mrs Jacqueline Robson, Old Brewery Cottage, Melkridge, Haltwhistle NE49 0LT
t (01434) 320063 **e** jacqueline141778@aol.com

oldbrewerycottage.com REAL-TIME BOOKING

Cottage comprising kitchen/dining room, lounge, two double bedrooms and bathroom with private area and parking.

open All year
payment Credit/debit cards, cash, cheques
nearest shop 2 miles
nearest pub 2 miles

Unit General P

What if I need to cancel?

It is advisable to check the proprietor's cancellation policy in case you have to change your plans at a later date.

MICKLETON, Durham Map ref 5B3

★★★★
SELF CATERING

Units 1
Sleeps 1–4

LOW SEASON PER WK
£215.00–£230.00

HIGH SEASON PER WK
£330.00–£345.00

Short breaks available.

The Old Dairy, Mickleton, Barnard Castle

contact Mrs Tracey Cooke, West Pasture Farm, Kelton Road, Mickleton, Barnard Castle DL12 0PW
t (01833) 640248 **e** tcookes@sky.com

teesdaleholidaycottages.co.uk

open All year
payment Cash, cheques
nearest shop 1.5 miles
nearest pub 1.5 miles

Set in the heart of the North Pennines, on the side of Grassholme Reservoir, surrounded by woods, fells and fields, this two-bedroom converted dairy is a haven for those wanting to escape the hustle and bustle of everyday living. Perfect for walking, fishing, cycling, sailing or just relaxing.

Unit General P S Leisure

MIDDLEHAM, North Yorkshire Map ref 5C3

★★★★★
SELF CATERING

Units 1
Sleeps 4

LOW SEASON PER WK
Min £395.00

HIGH SEASON PER WK
Max £485.00

WALKERS WELCOME CYCLISTS WELCOME

Demonicus Cottage, Middleham

contact Ms Joan Macbeth, 48 Hazelwood Avenue, Newcastle upon Tyne NE2 3HX
t (0191) 239 9366 **e** joan@middlehamcottage.com

middlehamcottage.com

A delightful 18thC dales cottage overlooking the market square of this historic village. Recently renovated, and furnished and equipped to an exceptionally high standard. Sleeps four.

open All year
payment Cash, cheques
nearest shop less than 0.5 miles
nearest pub less than 0.5 miles

Unit General P S Leisure

MIDDLEHAM, North Yorkshire Map ref 5C3

★★★★
SELF CATERING

Units 1
Sleeps 1–5

LOW SEASON PER WK
Min £322.00

HIGH SEASON PER WK
Min £491.00

Middle Cottage, Middleham, Leyburn

contact Mrs Jennie Perren, 2 North Park Grove, Roundhay, Leeds LS8 1JJ **t** (0113) 237 1817
e jennifer.perren@btinternet.com

yorkshire-dales-holiday-cottage.co.uk

Sitting room with dining area, kitchen, three bedrooms, bathroom with shower. Electric heating, garden to the rear, parking 200yds.

open All year
payment Cash, cheques
nearest shop less than 0.5 miles
nearest pub less than 0.5 miles

Unit General S Leisure

MIDDLETON-IN-TEESDALE, Durham Map ref 5B3

★★★★
SELF CATERING

Units 1
Sleeps 6

LOW SEASON PER WK
£280.00–£300.00

HIGH SEASON PER WK
£290.00–£530.00

The Barn, Middleton-in-Teesdale, Barnard Castle

contact Mr Alan Kitchener, 2 Westwood Way, Boston Spa, Wetherby LS23 6DX **t** (01937) 844657
e alan.kitchener@ntlworld.com

Newly converted barn with well equipped kitchen/diner. Large lounge, three double bedrooms with twin beds. Bathroom plus shower room. Large, private rear garden with extensive off-road parking.

open All year
payment Cash, cheques
nearest shop 4 miles
nearest pub less than 0.5 miles

Unit General P S Leisure

MIDDLETON-IN-TEESDALE, Durham Map ref 5B3

★★★
SELF CATERING

Units 1
Sleeps 2–6

LOW SEASON PER WK
Min £175.00

HIGH SEASON PER WK
Max £395.00

Country Cottage, Middleton-in-Teesdale

contact Mr Burman, 1 Thorn Road, Stockport SK7 1HG **t** (0161) 860 7123
e enquiries@robinburman.com

Two-hundred-year-old cottage in quiet, peaceful location with superb views, surrounded by farmland. Excellent walking countryside.

open All year
payment Cheques
nearest shop 1.6 miles
nearest pub 1.6 miles

Unit General Leisure

MIDDLETON-IN-TEESDALE, Durham Map ref 5B3

★★★
SELF CATERING

Units 1
Sleeps 2

LOW SEASON PER WK
£120.00–£140.00

HIGH SEASON PER WK
£150.00–£200.00

Firethorn Cottage, 33 Town End, Middleton-in-Teesdale

contact Mrs June Thompson, Cutbush Farmhouse, Hardingham Road, Hingham, Norwich NR9 4LY
t (01953) 850364

Stone-built lead miner's cottage, one up/one down, flagstone floors, traditional rag rugs, beamed ceilings. Superb walking, fishing, pubs and restaurants. Night storage heaters. Refrigerator.

open All year
payment Cash, cheques

Unit General

MORLAND, Cumbria Map ref 5B3

★★★★★
SELF CATERING

Units 4
Sleeps 1–20

LOW SEASON PER WK
£2,409.00–£3,882.00

HIGH SEASON PER WK
£4,927.00–£6,971.00

Morland Hall, Penrith

Morland Hall, Morland, Penrith CA10 3BB **t** (01931) 714715 **e** info@morlandhall.co.uk

morlandhall.co.uk SPECIAL OFFERS • REAL-TIME BOOKING

Morland Hall and three beautifully presented self-catering houses nestle in the glorious countryside of the Eden Valley surrounded by 15 acres of private parkland.

open All year
payment Credit/debit cards, cash, cheques, euros
nearest shop 1 mile
nearest pub 1 mile

Unit General P
Leisure

MORPETH, Northumberland Map ref 5C2

★★★
SELF CATERING

Units 1
Sleeps 4

LOW SEASON PER WK
£325.00–£375.00

HIGH SEASON PER WK
£375.00–£450.00

Meldon Park, Morpeth

contact Mrs Cookson, Meldon Park, Morpeth NE61 3SW **t** (01670) 772433
e mrscookson@compuserve.com

cottageguide.co.uk/meldonpark

Stunning, unique and peaceful location in rural Northumberland, centrally located for city, hills and coast. One double and one twin room, log-burning stove, central heating, spacious gardens and unrivalled views.

open All year
payment Cash, cheques
nearest shop 5 miles
nearest pub 0.5 miles

Unit General P Leisure

Place index

If you know where you want to stay, the index by place name at the back of the guide will give you the page number listing accommodation in your chosen town, city or village. Check out the other useful indexes too.

For **key to symbols** see page 7

MORPETH, Northumberland Map ref 5C2

★★–★★★★★
SELF CATERING

Units 16
Sleeps 4–10

LOW SEASON PER WK
£240.00–£450.00

HIGH SEASON PER WK
£350.00–£850.00

Micklewood Park, Morpeth

contact Mr Mark Towers, Micklewood Park at Longhirst, Longhirst, Morpeth NE61 3LL
t (01670) 794530

micklewoodpark.co.uk

Five/six-bedroomed houses set in woodland grounds of listed country house. Fully fitted kitchen, shower and bathroom, two toilets and dining room.

open All year
payment Credit/debit cards, cash, cheques
nearest shop 3 miles
nearest pub 3 miles

Unit General Leisure

MUNGRISDALE, Cumbria Map ref 5A2

★★★★
SELF CATERING

Units 5
Sleeps 2–7

LOW SEASON PER WK
£275.00–£450.00

HIGH SEASON PER WK
£350.00–£650.00

Near Howe Cottages, Penrith

contact Steve & Jill Woolley, Near Howe Cottages, Near Howe, Mungrisdale, Penrith CA11 0SH
t (017687) 79678 **e** enquiries@nearhowe.co.uk

nearhowe.co.uk GUEST REVIEWS • REAL-TIME BOOKING

open All year
payment Cash, cheques, euros
nearest shop 5 miles
nearest pub 2 miles

The ideal answer for a stress-free, away-from-it-all holiday, set amidst 350 acres of open moorland. All cottages have spectacular views over the Cumbrian Fells. Large garden with relaxation areas. Easily accessible, yet isolated enough to ensure peace and tranquillity.

ONLINE MAP

Unit General Leisure

NETHER KELLET, Lancashire Map ref 5B3

★★★
SELF CATERING

Units 1
Sleeps 3–4

LOW SEASON PER WK
Min £155.00

HIGH SEASON PER WK
Min £235.00

The Apartment, Nether Kellet

contact Mr Richardson, The Apartment, 10 Meadowcroft, Carnforth LA6 1HN **t** (01524) 734969 & (01524) 736331

One-bedroomed, self-contained flat with extensive, private gardens in peaceful, rural village. Secluded cul-de-sac location.

open All year
payment Cash, cheques
nearest shop less than 0.5 miles
nearest pub less than 0.5 miles

Unit General Leisure

NEWBY BRIDGE, Cumbria Map ref 5A3

★★★★
SELF CATERING

Units 1
Sleeps 2–4

LOW SEASON PER WK
£290.00–£400.00

HIGH SEASON PER WK
£400.00–£520.00

Woodland Cottage, Newby Bridge

contact Mr Newton, Newby Bridge Country Caravan Park, c/o Fellside Lodge, Canny Hill LA12 8NF
t (015395) 31030 **e** info@cumbriancaravans.co.uk

cumbriancaravans.co.uk GUEST REVIEWS

Detached cottage with two en suite bedrooms, in own private gardens within the award-winning Newby Bridge Caravan Park. All on one level.

open All year except Christmas and New Year
payment Credit/debit cards, cash, cheques, euros
nearest shop less than 0.5 miles
nearest pub 1 mile

Unit General Leisure

NEWCASTLE UPON TYNE, Tyne and Wear Map ref 5C2

★★★
SELF CATERING

Units 1
Sleeps 1–4

LOW SEASON PER WK
£230.00–£350.00

HIGH SEASON PER WK
£230.00–£350.00

135 Audley Road, Newcastle upon Tyne

contact Miss Linda Wright, 137 Audley Road, South Gosforth, Newcastle upon Tyne NE3 1QH
t (0191) 285 6374

audleyender.fsnet.co.uk

Self-contained flat, close to shops and Metro, with easy access to city centre. All amenities.

payment Cash, cheques
nearest shop less than 0.5 miles
nearest pub less than 0.5 miles

Unit General

NEWTON-BY-THE-SEA, Northumberland Map ref 5C1

★★★★
SELF CATERING

Units 5
Sleeps 2–8

LOW SEASON PER WK
£290.00–£400.00

HIGH SEASON PER WK
£630.00–£950.00

Link House Farm Holiday Cottages, Newton-by-the-Sea, Alnwick

contact Mrs Jayne Hellmann, Link House Farm Holiday Cottages, Link House Farm, Newton-by-the-Sea, Alnwick NE66 3ED **t** (01665) 576820 **e** jayne@linkhousefarm.com

linkhousefarm.com

open All year
payment Cash, cheques
nearest shop 2.5 miles
nearest pub 0.5 miles

Secluded, quality stone-built, converted cottages on a working farm. One minute's walk from picturesque sandy beach. Two to four bedroom accommodation. Ideal for families and couples. Good central base for touring, sightseeing and walking, or just 'getting away'. Playground and football area. Peacocks. Sorry, no pets.

ONLINE MAP

Unit General P S Leisure

NEWTON-BY-THE-SEA, Northumberland Map ref 5C1

★★★★
SELF CATERING

Units 1
Sleeps 2–6

LOW SEASON PER WK
£295.00–£445.00

HIGH SEASON PER WK
£370.00–£670.00

Seawinds, Alnwick

contact Mrs Jo Leiper, Bygate, Black Heddon, Newcastle upon Tyne NE20 0JJ **t** (01661) 881506
e stay@buston.co.uk

buston.co.uk

open All year
payment Cash, cheques
nearest shop 3 miles
nearest pub less than 0.5 miles

Situated within the picturesque village of Low Newton-by-the-Sea, this former fisherman's cottage is just 200m from a beautiful sandy beach which is part of Northumberland's Heritage Coast area. A high-quality cottage offering many home comforts, making it an exceptional base from which to discover the many secrets of the surrounding area.

Unit General P Leisure

Remember to check when booking

Please remember that all information in this guide has been supplied by the proprietors well in advance of publication. Since changes do sometimes occur it's a good idea to check details at the time of booking.

NEWTON-ON-RAWCLIFFE, North Yorkshire Map ref 5D3

★★★★
SELF CATERING

Units 3
Sleeps 4–7

LOW SEASON PER WK
£395.00–£495.00

HIGH SEASON PER WK
£555.00–£645.00

Short breaks available, three nights – flexible – except at peak periods.

Keldlands Farm Cottages, Newton-on-Rawcliffe, Pickering

contact Jill Thomas, Holiday Homes in Yorkshire, PO Box 9, Thirsk, North Yorkshire YO7 2YZ
t (01845) 597660 **e** info@keldlandsfarmcottages.co.uk

keldlandsfarmcottages.co.uk

open All year
payment Credit/debit cards, cash, cheques
nearest shop 3 miles
nearest pub 1 mile

Three stone-built, beamed cottages, extensively renovated and equipped to a high standard. Two two-bedroom fully en suite cottages and one three-bedroom fully en suite. Double and single beds, fully flexible. Hot tubs, sauna and games room with pool table. A peaceful hideaway close to all the North Yorkshire attractions.

SAT NAV *YO18 8JP*

Unit General
Leisure

NORTH DALTON, East Riding of Yorkshire Map ref 4C1

★★★
SELF CATERING

Units 1
Sleeps 3–4

LOW SEASON PER WK
£200.00–£315.00

HIGH SEASON PER WK
£330.00–£410.00

Short breaks available, 2 nights (excl Christmas, New Year, Easter and Bank Holidays).

Old Cobbler's Cottage, Driffield, North Dalton

contact Chris Wade, Waterfront Cottages, 2 Star Row, North Dalton, Driffield YO25 9UX
t (01377) 217662 & 07801 124264 **e** chris.wade@adastra-music.co.uk

waterfrontcottages.co.uk

open All year
payment Credit/debit cards, cash, cheques
nearest shop 1.5 miles
nearest pub less than 0.5 miles

19thC, mid-terraced, oak-beamed cottage overlooking picturesque pond in a peaceful and friendly farming village, between York and Yorkshire's Heritage Coast. Ideally located for walking, visiting the coast, historic houses, races at York and Beverley or just relaxing. Excellent inn/restaurant adjacent, shops 1.5 miles. Pets welcome.

Unit General Leisure

NORTHWICH, Cheshire Map ref 4A2

★★★–★★★★
SELF CATERING

Units 5
Sleeps 2–3

LOW SEASON PER WK
£350.00

HIGH SEASON PER WK
£350.00

Yew Tree Farm Apartments, Davenham, Northwich

Yew Tree Farm Apartments, Davenham Road, Billinge Green, Northwich CW9 7RZ **t** (01606) 334770 & 07794 906601 **e** ade@yewtreeapartments.co.uk

yewtreeapartments.co.uk

Converted barn, luxury self-catering apartments one mile from Davenham, near Northwich, overlooking large lake and open countryside. CCTV. Apartments sleep two/three. Very quiet location. 20 minutes M6 junction 19.

open All year
payment Credit/debit cards, cash, cheques
nearest shop less than 0.5 miles
nearest pub 1 mile

Unit General

Has every property been assessed?

All accommodation in this guide has been rated for quality, or is awaiting assessment, by a professional national tourist board assessor.

OSGODBY, North Yorkshire Map ref 5D3

★★★★
SELF CATERING

Units 2
Sleeps 4

LOW SEASON PER WK
£240.00–£360.00

HIGH SEASON PER WK
£380.00–£540.00

Out-of-season or last-minute short breaks welcome but must phone to book these.

Seaviews Too, Scarborough

contact Mrs Rebekah Manning, 15 Southwold Crescent, Eastfield, Scarborough YO11 3RF
t (01723) 586243 & 07972 754789 **e** seaviewstoo@btinternet.com

seaviewstoo.plus.com

open All year
payment Cash, cheques

Stunning sea views in every direction from these two immaculate semi-detached bungalows, which stand in a small, private development adjacent to the Cleveland Way cliff-top walk. Comfortably furnished, well-equipped accommodation comprising open-plan lounge/dining room, two double bedrooms, modern kitchen, bathroom with power-shower. Peaceful surroundings.

SAT NAV *YO11 3JT*

Unit TV SC DVD General

OTLEY, West Yorkshire Map ref 4B1

★★★★
SELF CATERING

Units 1
Sleeps 13

LOW SEASON PER WK
£700.00–£900.00

HIGH SEASON PER WK
£800.00–£1,200.00

WALKERS WELCOME · CYCLISTS WELCOME · FAMILIES WELCOME · PETS! WELCOME

The Birches, Otley

contact Liz Burrows, The Old Rectory, The Green, Guiseley LS20 9BB **t** 07799 142745
e lzburrows@aol.com

chevinvista.co.uk

open All year
payment Cash, cheques
nearest shop 1 mile
nearest pub 1 mile

Large seven-bedroomed detached property. Four doubles, two singles, one bunk room, each with LCD TV and Sky link. Property has two lounges, large kitchen/diner with spectacular views and balcony off, and games room with full-size pool table. Located next to Chevin Forest.

Unit TV SC DVD General P S
Leisure

OVINGTON, Northumberland Map ref 5B2

★★★★
SELF CATERING

Units 1
Sleeps 2–4

LOW SEASON PER WK
£280.00–£350.00

HIGH SEASON PER WK
£350.00–£425.00

Westgarth Cottage, Ovington, Prudhoe

contact Mrs Claire Graham, Stonecroft, Ovington, Prudhoe NE42 6EB **t** (01661) 832202
e west.cape@btinternet.com

west-cape-northumberland.co.uk

Attractive stone-built cottage in a small, peaceful village surrounded by beautiful countryside, near the historic towns of Hexham and Corbridge.

open All year
payment Cash, cheques
nearest shop less than 0.5 miles
nearest pub 1 mile

Unit TV DVD General 5 P

Check the maps for accommodation locations

Colour maps at the front pinpoint all the places where accommodation is featured within the regional sections of this guide. Pick your location and then refer to the place index at the back to find the page number.

OXENHOPE, West Yorkshire Map ref 4B1

★★★★★
SELF CATERING

Units 1
Sleeps 1–2

LOW SEASON PER WK
£177.00–£237.00

HIGH SEASON PER WK
£282.00–£393.00

Honeysuckle Cottage, Oxenhope, Keighley

contact Mrs Susan Mytum, Hardnaze Farm, Hardnaze Lane, Oxenhope, Keighley BD22 9QN
t (01535) 645500 **e** suemytum@btinternet.com

hardnaze.co.uk

In beautiful open countryside two miles from Haworth, home of the Brontës, a newly converted, luxury, one-bedroomed cottage on a small working farm. Modern dining kitchen, lounge with french windows onto patio. Spectacular views.

open All year
payment Cash, cheques
nearest shop 2 miles
nearest pub less than 0.5 miles

Unit General P

OXENHOPE, West Yorkshire Map ref 4B1

★★★
SELF CATERING

Units 1
Sleeps 2–3

LOW SEASON PER WK
£100.00–£120.00

HIGH SEASON PER WK
£180.00–£200.00

Yate Cottage, Oxenhope, Keighley

contact Mrs Jean M M Dunn, Yate House, Yate Cottage, Yate Lane, Oxenhope, Keighley BD22 9HL
t (01535) 643638 **e** jeanandhugh@dunnyate.freeserve.co.uk

uk-holiday-cottages.co.uk/yatecottage

18thC cottage adjoining Yate House, a 'yeoman' house of striking architectural appearance. South-facing view over beautiful garden to hills. No short breaks.

open All year except Christmas and New Year
payment Cash, cheques
nearest shop less than 0.5 miles
nearest pub less than 0.5 miles

Unit General 8 P

PATELEY BRIDGE, North Yorkshire Map ref 5C3

★★★★
SELF CATERING & SERVICED APARTMENTS

Units 4
Sleeps 2–10

LOW SEASON PER WK
£195.00–£385.00

HIGH SEASON PER WK
£300.00–£750.00

Short breaks available.

Helme Pasture, Old Spring Wood, Harrogate

contact Mrs Rosemary Helme, Hartwith Bank, Summerbridge, Harrogate HG3 4DR
t (01423) 780279 **e** helmepasture@btinternet.com

helmepasture.co.uk SPECIAL OFFERS • REAL-TIME BOOKING

open All year
payment Credit/debit cards, cash, cheques, euros
nearest shop less than 0.5 miles
nearest pub less than 0.5 miles

Scandinavian lodges and converted Dales barn. Award-winning conservation woodland. Holiday in tranquil surroundings. Country walks. Close to a multitude of attractions including Fountains Abbey, castles, Yorkshire villages and floral towns – Harrogate, Skipton, Ripon, York. Traditional markets. Pet-friendly, laundry facilities, and a warm family welcome.

SAT NAV *HG3 4DR*

Unit General P Leisure

PATELEY BRIDGE, North Yorkshire Map ref 5C3

★★★★
SELF CATERING

Units 1
Sleeps 3

LOW SEASON PER WK
£200.00–£235.00

HIGH SEASON PER WK
£235.00–£395.00

North Oaks Farm Cottages, Pateley Bridge

contact Sue Loveless, 1 and 2 North Oaks Farm Cottages, North Oaks Farm, Fellbeck HG3 5EP
t (01423) 712446 **e** cottages@loveless.co.uk

northoakscottages.co.uk

Cottages on a former farm. Large dining-room/lounge, kitchen with oak units. Upstairs has a double bedroom, a single bedroom and a bathroom. Garden with views of Brimham Rocks and Pateley Moor.

open All year
payment Credit/debit cards, cash, cheques, euros
nearest shop 3 miles
nearest pub 1 mile

Unit General P Leisure

PATRICK BROMPTON, North Yorkshire Map ref 5C3

★★★★ SELF CATERING

Units 1
Sleeps 4

LOW SEASON PER WK
£220.00–£320.00

HIGH SEASON PER WK
£340.00–£420.00

The Parlour, Patrick Brompton

contact Mrs D Bratley, Butterwell Farm, Patrick Brompton DL8 1LN **t** (01677) 450229
e theparlour@butterwellfarm.com

Recently converted barn with original features, on working farm. Luxurious, spacious accommodation. Gateway to the Dales, lovely views, lots of pubs, restaurants and activities nearby. All rooms ground-level.

open All year
payment Cash, cheques
nearest shop 2 miles
nearest pub 0.5 miles

Unit General Leisure

PATTERDALE, Cumbria Map ref 5A3

★★★★ SELF CATERING

Units 1
Sleeps 12–15

LOW SEASON PER WK
£1,270.00–£1,500.00

HIGH SEASON PER WK
£1,980.00–£2,200.00

Broad How, Patterdale

Country Holidays **t** 0870 192 1617

countryholidays2007.co.uk

open All year
payment Credit/debit cards, cash, cheques
nearest shop less than 0.5 miles
nearest pub less than 0.5 miles

Beautiful, large, 1850s family house, sensitively and comfortably modernised. Log fire, piano, pool table, books and games. In stunning Lakeland scenery, one mile from Ullswater with its steamer service (April to October), sailing, swimming etc. Marvellous fell walking, and within easy reach of small towns for non-walkers. Property number 8478.

Unit General
Leisure

PENTON, Cumbria Map ref 5A2

★★★ SELF CATERING

Units 2
Sleeps 2–4

LOW SEASON PER WK
£230.00–£250.00

HIGH SEASON PER WK
£380.00–£395.00

Liddel Park Country Cottages, Carlisle

contact Brian Wicklow, Liddel Park Country Cottages, Catlowdy, Penton, Carlisle CA6 5QW
t (01228) 577440 **e** holiday@liddelpark.co.uk

liddelpark.co.uk REAL-TIME BOOKING

Peace and tranquillity in a forest setting with abundance of wildlife. Ideal base for exploring England's Border Country, Hadrian's Wall and the Northern Lake District. Fishing available on local rivers.

open All year
payment Cash, cheques
nearest shop 7 miles
nearest pub 2 miles

Unit General Leisure

PICKERING, North Yorkshire Map ref 5D3

★★★★-★★★★★
SELF CATERING

Units 8
Sleeps 2–10

LOW SEASON PER WK
£255.00–£855.00

HIGH SEASON PER WK
£365.00–£1,850.00

Four-times winner of Yorkshire Tourist Board's Self-Catering Holiday of the Year award.

Beech Farm Cottages, Wrelton, Nr Pickering

contact Mrs Rooney Massara, Beech Farm Cottages, Main Street, Wrelton, Pickering YO18 8PG
t (01751) 476612 & (01751) 476612 **e** massara@beechfarm.com

beechfarm.com GUEST REVIEWS • SPECIAL OFFERS • REAL-TIME BOOKING

open All year
payment Credit/debit cards, cash, cheques, euros
nearest shop 2 miles
nearest pub less than 0.5 miles

Award-winning, luxury stone cottages with heated indoor pool, sauna, children's play area, gardens and paddock. Horse, pony and llama in field. Delightful location in quiet village on edge of North York Moors National Park. Also convenient for coast and York. The cottages are in a courtyard setting backing onto fields. Brochure available or please phone.

SAT NAV *YO18 8PG* **ONLINE MAP**

Unit General
Leisure

PICKERING, North Yorkshire Map ref 5D3

★★★★
SELF CATERING

Units 1
Sleeps 4

LOW SEASON PER WK
Min £250.00

HIGH SEASON PER WK
Max £500.00

High Kingthorpe Lodges, Pickering

contact John Tunnicliffe, High Kingthorpe Lodges, Riseborough Hagg Farm, Marton Road, Pickering YO18 8LR **t** (01751) 476457 **e** info@kingthorpe.com

kingthorpe.com

open All year
payment Cash, cheques
nearest shop 2 miles
nearest pub 1 mile

High Kingthorpe Lodge is a stunning log cabin located in the North York Moors National Park. The lodge nestles on the edge of 400 acres of privately owned woodland with breathtaking views of the valley, where the Pickering to Grosmont steam railway winds its way to 'Heartbeat' country.

Unit General

PICKERING, North Yorkshire Map ref 5D3

★★★★
SELF CATERING

Units 11
Sleeps 4–12

LOW SEASON PER WK
£380.00–£750.00

HIGH SEASON PER WK
£500.00–£1,717.20

Hungate Cottages, Pickering

contact Mr Richard Robertson, Hungate Cottages, Recreation Road, Pickering YO18 7ET
t (01751) 476382 **e** holidays@hungatecottages.co.uk

hungatecottages.co.uk REAL-TIME BOOKING

open All year
payment Credit/debit cards, cash, cheques, euros
nearest shop less than 0.5 miles
nearest pub less than 0.5 miles

Luxury, highly individual holiday cottages which have the unique appeal of being a short walk from the town centre, whilst retaining the tranquillity and peacefulness of the countryside. Easy access to the Moors, York, Castle Howard, steam railway and the beautiful port towns of Whitby and Scarborough. See website for further information.

Unit General
Leisure

PICKERING, North Yorkshire Map ref 5D3

★★★★
SELF CATERING

Units 9
Sleeps 2–8

LOW SEASON PER WK
£195.00–£430.00

HIGH SEASON PER WK
£500.00–£1,090.00

Senior citizen and 2-person discounts. Short breaks.

Keld Head Farm Cottages, Pickering

contact Julian & Penny Fearn, Keld Head Farm Cottages, Keld Head, Pickering YO18 8LL
t (01751) 473974 **e** julian@keldheadcottages.com

keldheadcottages.com SPECIAL OFFERS

open All year
payment Credit/debit cards, cash, cheques, euros
nearest shop less than 0.5 miles
nearest pub 0.5 miles

On the edge of Pickering, in open countryside overlooking fields where sheep and cows graze. Beautiful, spacious, character stone cottages with pantile roofs, traditional stone fireplaces and beamed ceilings, tastefully furnished with the emphasis on comfort and relaxation. Some rooms with four-poster beds. Award-winning gardens with garden house. York, moors and coast easily accessible.

ONLINE MAP

Unit General P Leisure

PICKERING, North Yorkshire Map ref 5D3

★★★★
SELF CATERING

Units 4
Sleeps 1–6

LOW SEASON PER WK
£250.00–£370.00

HIGH SEASON PER WK
£450.00–£835.00

Low season short breaks: 2 or 3 nights over the weekend and 4 nights for the price of 3 midweek.

Mel House Cottages, Pickering

contact John and Penny Wicks, Let's Holiday, Mel House, Pickering YO18 8QA **t** (01751) 475396
e holiday@letsholiday.com

letsholiday.com SPECIAL OFFERS

open All year
payment Credit/debit cards, cash, cheques
nearest shop 4 miles
nearest pub less than 0.5 miles

Comfortable and fully equipped offering indoor pool, spa and sauna, and set in extensive level grounds at the heart of our National Park village. Paddocks and stabling for DIY livery. Village pub, play area and duck pond nearby. Perfect for exploring North York Moors, the coast and City of York.

ONLINE MAP

Unit General P Leisure

PICKERING, North Yorkshire Map ref 5D3

★★★★
SELF CATERING

Units 13
Sleeps 2–7

LOW SEASON PER WK
£250.00–£550.00

HIGH SEASON PER WK
£400.00–£820.00

PETS! WELCOME

North Yorkshire Cottages, Pickering

contact Mrs Elaine Bedford, North Yorkshire Cottages, 117 Eastgate, Pickering YO18 7DW
t (01751) 476653 **e** vbenq@northyorkshirecottages.co.uk

northyorkshirecottages.co.uk/vbenq.aspx SPECIAL OFFERS · REAL-TIME BOOKING

A collection of luxury cottages in and around Pickering. All individually developed to maximise period charm and modern-day luxury. 'Your retreat in the heart of North Yorkshire.'

open All year
payment Credit/debit cards, cash, cheques
nearest shop less than 0.5 miles
nearest pub less than 0.5 miles

Unit General P
Leisure

PICKERING, North Yorkshire Map ref 5D3

★★★
SELF CATERING

Units 2
Sleeps 2

LOW SEASON PER WK
Min £200.00

HIGH SEASON PER WK
Min £330.00

Short breaks, last-minute bargains.

The Old Forge Cottages, Pickering

contact Judy French, The Old Forge, Wilton, Pickering YO18 7JY **t** (01751) 477399
e theoldforge1@aol.com

forgecottages.co.uk GUEST REVIEWS • SPECIAL OFFERS

open All year
payment Cash, cheques
nearest shop 1 mile
nearest pub 1 mile

Cosy cottages for two, all year round. Forge stable conversions providing comfortable, well-equipped accommodation with patio and barbecue. Private parking, easy access to bus route. Local attractions include steam railway, Dalby Forest, Yorkshire Moors, Eden Camp, Flamingo Land and Langdale Quest.

ONLINE MAP

Unit TV DVD General P S Leisure

PICKERING, North Yorkshire Map ref 5D3

★★★★
SELF CATERING

Units 5
Sleeps 4–8

LOW SEASON PER WK
£250.00–£600.00

HIGH SEASON PER WK
£470.00–£1,000.00

Stainers Farm Cottages, Malton

contact Jackie Smith, Stainers Farm Cottages, Stainers Farm, Little Barugh YO17 6UY
t (01653) 668224 **e** info@stainersfarm.co.uk

stainersfarm.co.uk

Newly renovated country cottages with individual character and charm in a peaceful rural setting with wonderful views of open countryside.

open All year except January
payment Cash, cheques
nearest shop 5 miles
nearest pub 1.5 miles

Unit TV DVD General S

PONTELAND, Northumberland Map ref 5C2

★★★
SELF CATERING

Units 2
Sleeps 4

LOW SEASON PER WK
£206.00–£398.00

HIGH SEASON PER WK
£358.00–£500.00

The Old Stables and The Old Tack Room, Newcastle upon Tyne

contact Miss Clare Stephenson, The Old Stables and The Old Tack Room, North Road, Newcastle upon Tyne NE20 9UR **t** (01661) 822188 & 07786 537424 **e** elandgreen@msn.com

elandfarm.co.uk

Conversion of farm buildings. Both sleep four – one double and one twin in each. On 200-acre grassland farm.

open All year
payment Cash, cheques
nearest shop 0.5 miles
nearest pub 0.5 miles

Unit TV DVD General P S Leisure

POOLEY BRIDGE, Cumbria Map ref 5A3

★★★★
SELF CATERING

Units 1
Sleeps 4

LOW SEASON PER WK
Max £340.00

HIGH SEASON PER WK
Max £575.00

The Steading, Great Strickland, Penrith

contact Mr and Mrs Yates, Yates Estates, 12 Mallard Road, Mountsorrel LE12 7FR **t** (0116) 237 6453
e enquiries@yatesestates.co.uk

yatesestates.co.uk GUEST REVIEWS • SPECIAL OFFERS

Stylishly refurbished barn, combining rustic charm with modern comforts. Spacious yet cosy, log-burner, beams, private garden. Tranquil village with pub. Easy access to popular tourist destinations. Two-person discounts.

open All year
payment Credit/debit cards, cheques
nearest shop 2.5 miles
nearest pub less than 0.5 miles

Unit TV DVD General P S Leisure

Where are the maps?

Colour maps can be found at the front of the guide. They pinpoint the location of all accommodation found in the regional sections.

PORTINSCALE, Cumbria Map ref 5A3

★★★★
SELF CATERING

Units 1
Sleeps 2–8

LOW SEASON PER WK
£350.00–£480.00

HIGH SEASON PER WK
£510.00–£580.00

Short breaks available Jan-Mar, Nov-Dec.

Woodside, Portinscale, Keswick

contact Mr Paul Carter, Woodside, Low Portinscale, Portinscale, Keswick CA12 5RP
t (017687) 72702 & 07979 206925 **e** paulandrew40@hotmail.com

keswickcharactercottages.co.uk

open All year
payment Cheques
nearest shop 1.5 miles
nearest pub less than 0.5 miles

Four-bedroom, end of terrace, recently renovated, Lakeland cottage sleeping eight. Stunning views of Skiddaw, parking for two cars, garden with large deck. Ideal base for exploring the Northern fells. Ideal for families, well-behaved dogs welcome.

SAT NAV *CA12 5RP*

Unit General P Leisure

RIBBLE VALLEY

See under Clitheroe, Slaidburn

RICHMOND, North Yorkshire Map ref 5C3

★★★★
SELF CATERING

Units 1
Sleeps 2–4

LOW SEASON PER WK
Max £250.00

HIGH SEASON PER WK
Max £370.00

Bookings taken for 3-7nights out of season if available. Price from £50 per night.

Coach House, Whashton, Richmond

contact Mrs Fairlie Turnbull, Coach House, New Skeeby Grange, Skeeby, Richmond DL10 5ED
t (01748) 822276 **e** gandmf@tiscali.co.uk

newskeebygrange.co.uk

open All year
payment Cash, cheques
nearest shop 3 miles
nearest pub 1.5 miles

Oak-beamed coach house on our family working farm three miles from historic Richmond, gateway to Swaledale. Both bedrooms have a wonderful view over our farmland and the hills beyond. A small patio opens out from the sitting room, where you can dine and enjoy a glass of wine in the sunshine!

SAT NAV *DL11 7JS*

Unit General P Leisure

RIDING MILL, Northumberland Map ref 5B2

★★★
SELF CATERING

Units 1
Sleeps 2

LOW SEASON PER WK
£205.00–£235.00

HIGH SEASON PER WK
£265.00–£350.00

Morningside Cottage, Riding Mill

contact Mr Gerald & Dorothea Weldon, Morningside Cottage, Morningside, Riding Mill NE44 6HL
t (01434) 682350 **e** dorotheaweldon@fsmail.net

morningside-cottage.co.uk

This attached cottage is primarily for two adults but two children can also be accommodated on a sofa bed. Freeview television. Village pub and restaurant only 200yds.

open All year
payment Cash, cheques
nearest shop less than 0.5 miles
nearest pub less than 0.5 miles

Unit General P Leisure

Where can I get help and advice?

Tourist Information Centres offer friendly help with accommodation and holiday ideas as well as suggestions of places to visit and things to do. You'll find contact details at the beginning of each regional section.

RIPON, North Yorkshire Map ref 5C3

★★★★★
SELF CATERING

Units 1
Sleeps 6

LOW SEASON PER WK
£355.00–£430.00

HIGH SEASON PER WK
Max £688.00

Short breaks available except in high season. Special rates for two-person occupancy.

Waterfront House, Ripon

contact Mrs C E Braddon, Waterfront House, Chantry Bells, Chantry Court, Ripley, Harrogate HG3 3AD **t** (01423) 770704 **e** chris1.braddon@virgin.net

dalesholidayripon.co.uk

open All year
payment Cash, cheques
nearest shop 0.5 miles
nearest pub less than 0.5 miles

Superb location. Luxury property with excellent facilities. Sleeps six. One double four-poster with en suite and two twins with house bathroom. South-facing balcony overlooking peaceful canal basin. Short walk to river bank, cathedral, market place, pubs and restaurants. Ideal for exploring the Yorkshire Dales and North York Moors.

Unit General 6 P Leisure

ROCHDALE, Greater Manchester Map ref 4B1

★★★
SELF CATERING

Units 1
Sleeps 5

LOW SEASON PER WK
£250.00–£300.00

HIGH SEASON PER WK
£300.00–£350.00

Pennine Cottages, Wardle, Rochdale

contact Mrs Joy Mitchell, 2 Pennine Cottages, Lower House Lane, Wardle, Rochdale OL12 9PL
t (01706) 379632

hometown.aol.co.uk/penninecottage

Stone-built farm cottage on a working sheep farm. Three bedrooms. Baby facilities on request, at no extra charge. Quiet location, excellent views.

open All year
payment Cash, cheques
nearest shop 1 mile
nearest pub 1 mile

Unit General P Leisure

ROSEDALE ABBEY, North Yorkshire Map ref 5C3

★★★★
SELF CATERING

Units 5
Sleeps 2–4

LOW SEASON PER WK
£160.00–£300.00

HIGH SEASON PER WK
£190.00–£599.00

See website for special promotions.

Rosedale Abbey Holiday Cottages, Rosedale Abbey, Pickering

contact Mrs D Collins, Rosedale Abbey Caravan Park, Rosedale Abbey, Pickering YO18 8SA
t (01751) 417272 **e** rosedalecaravanpark@moorsweb.co.uk

rosedaleholidaycottages.co.uk SPECIAL OFFERS

open All year
payment Credit/debit cards, cash, cheques
nearest shop less than 0.5 miles
nearest pub less than 0.5 miles

The cottages and apartments are immaculately presented, beautifully furnished and equipped to a very high standard. In peaceful village setting nestling in the North York Moors National Park. Ideal walking country within easy reach of Yorkshire's Heritage Coast.

SAT NAV *YO18 8SA*

Unit General P

It's all quality-assessed accommodation

Our commitment to quality involves wide-ranging accommodation assessment. Ratings and awards were correct at the time of going to press but may change following a new assessment. Please check at time of booking.

ROSEDALE ABBEY, North Yorkshire Map ref 5C3

★★★★
SELF CATERING

Units 1
Sleeps 2–8

LOW SEASON PER WK
£300.00–£550.00

HIGH SEASON PER WK
£550.00–£850.00

Woodlea, Pickering

contact Pauline Belt, PO Box 63, Tadcaster LS24 9WN **t** (01937) 831290
e p.belt@daviscoleman.com

rosedaleholidaycottage.co.uk

open All year
payment Cash, cheques
nearest shop 0.75 miles
nearest pub 0.5 miles

Delightful house with stunning views. Three twin bedrooms and one double. Beautiful, well-maintained garden. New kitchen recently fitted. Log fire in the lounge. Village shop, pubs and restaurants within five minutes' walk. Many places of interest within easy reach.

Unit General P Leisure

ROTHBURY, Northumberland Map ref 5B1

★★★★
SELF CATERING

Units 1
Sleeps 6

LOW SEASON PER WK
Min £395.00

HIGH SEASON PER WK
Max £510.00

Clervaux, Rothbury

contact Mrs Kathryn Reynalds, Kyloe, Hillside West, Rothbury, Morpeth NE65 7YN
t (01669) 620784 **e** clervaux.rothbury@hotmail.co.uk

clervaux.co.uk

Clervaux will accommodate six people and cot. Master double bedroom with en suite shower/wc. Twin room in newly converted attic. Single bedroom with additional hideaway bed. Recently refurbished. Stunning views. Woodburning stove.

open All year
payment Cash, cheques
nearest shop 1 mile
nearest pub 1 mile

Unit General P Leisure

ROTHBURY, Northumberland Map ref 5B1

★★★★
SELF CATERING

Units 1
Sleeps 6

LOW SEASON PER WK
£246.00–£371.00

HIGH SEASON PER WK
£473.00–£600.00

3-night breaks available. Nov-Mar inclusive.

Whitton Lodge, Rothbury

contact Mrs Maggie Monaghan, Whitton Grange, Whitton, Morpeth NE65 7RL **t** (01669) 620929
e maggie.monaghan@btinternet.com

cottage-northumberland.co.uk

open All year
payment Cash, cheques
nearest shop 0.6 miles
nearest pub 0.6 miles

Listed lodge and garden. Idyllic, peaceful setting. Stunning views over Coquetdale. Continually updated. Children welcome. No pets. Non-smoking. Ten-minute walk to Rothbury with excellent shopping and eating. The recently restored grange Edwardian gardens will be a delight to gardeners, and may be viewed by arrangement with the owners. Walkers and cyclists welcome.

Unit General P Leisure

Remember to check when booking

Please remember that all information in this guide has been supplied by the proprietors well in advance of publication. Since changes do sometimes occur it's a good idea to check details at the time of booking.

ST BEES, Cumbria Map ref 5A3

★★★
SELF CATERING

Units 2
Sleeps 4–5

LOW SEASON PER WK
£250.00–£350.00

HIGH SEASON PER WK
£400.00–£600.00

Springbank Farm Lodges, St Bees

contact Carole Woodman, Springbank Farm, High Walton, St Bees CA22 2TY **t** (01946) 822375
e stevewoodman@talk21.com

springbanklodges.co.uk GUEST REVIEWS • SPECIAL OFFERS • REAL-TIME BOOKING

open All year
payment Credit/debit cards, cash, cheques, euros
nearest shop 1 mile
nearest pub 1 mile

New luxury two-bedroomed log cabins, en suite, fully fitted kitchen, open-plan lounge/dining area, separate wet room. Balcony with spectacular open views. Tranquil farm setting. Rare breeds, farm walks, children's play area. Close to beach and the mystical Western Lakes. Wheelchair-friendly with ample parking.

SAT NAV *CA22 2TY* **ONLINE MAP**

Unit General Leisure

ST BEES, Cumbria Map ref 5A3

★★★★
SELF CATERING

Units 1
Sleeps 6

LOW SEASON PER WK
Min £325.00

HIGH SEASON PER WK
Max £425.00

Tarn Flatt Cottage, Whitehaven

contact Janice Telfer, Tarn Flatt Cottage, Tarn Flatt Hall, Sandwith CA28 9UX **t** (01946) 692162
e stay@tarnflattfarm.co.uk

tarnflattfarm.co.uk

Three-bedroom accommodation on a working farm. Quiet location. Sea views.

open All year
payment Cash, cheques
nearest shop 2 miles
nearest pub 1 mile

Unit General Leisure

SANDSEND, North Yorkshire Map ref 5D3

★★★★–★★★★★
SELF CATERING

Units 9
Sleeps 2–9

LOW SEASON PER WK
£320.00–£505.00

HIGH SEASON PER WK
£585.00–£1,095.00

Short breaks available from Sep–May. We offer a 10% reduction for last-minute bookings and recommendations.

Raithwaite Hall, Whitby

contact Amanda Pearson, Raithwaite Hall, Sandsend, Whitby YO21 3ST **t** (01947) 893284
e admin@raithwaite.co.uk

raithwaite.co.uk SPECIAL OFFERS

open All year
payment Credit/debit cards, cash, cheques
nearest shop less than 0.5 miles
nearest pub less than 0.5 miles

Luxury stone cottages in a secluded woodland retreat just a short walk from three miles of golden sands. These extremely comfortable cottages have been converted to the highest standard offering well-equipped modern facilities, making this the ideal location for a peaceful and relaxing holiday.

SAT NAV *YO21 3ST* **ONLINE MAP**

Unit General
Leisure

CYCLISTS WELCOME

Fancy a cycling holiday?

For a fabulous freewheeling break, seek out accommodation participating in our Cyclists Welcome scheme. Look out for the symbol and plan your route online at nationalcyclenetwork.org.

SCARBOROUGH, North Yorkshire Map ref 5D3

★★–★★★
SELF CATERING

Units 4
Sleeps 1–5

LOW SEASON PER WK
£140.00–£240.00

HIGH SEASON PER WK
£240.00–£300.00

Parade Holiday Flats, Scarborough

contact Sue Sayers, 12 Belle Vue Parade, Scarborough YO11 1SU **t** (01723) 374307
e suesayers@tesco.net

Spacious, modern, clean one-bedroomed, self-contained flats situated close to the town centre. Each flat furnished to high standards. Ground-floor bedroom available. Easy access to railway station, shops and beaches.

open June to September
payment Cash, cheques
nearest shop less than 0.5 miles
nearest pub less than 0.5 miles

Unit General P

SCARBOROUGH, North Yorkshire Map ref 5D3

★★★★
SELF CATERING

Units 1
Sleeps 4

LOW SEASON PER WK
£240.00–£340.00

HIGH SEASON PER WK
£370.00–£550.00

Sea Vista Holiday Bungalow, Cayton Bay, Scarborough

contact Mr & Mrs A Roper, Merlewood, Bradford Road, Bingley BD16 1TT **t** (01274) 564741
e info@sea-vista.com

sea-vista.com

Two-double-bedroom bungalow on coast near Scarborough. Fantastic sea views from Scarborough Castle to cliffs of Cayton Bay. Adjacent to Cleveland Way. Comfortably furnished with good-quality, new furniture.

open All year
payment Cheques
nearest shop 0.5 miles
nearest pub 0.5 miles

Unit General 8

SCARBOROUGH, North Yorkshire Map ref 5D3

★★★–★★★★
SELF CATERING

Units 3
Sleeps 1–4

LOW SEASON PER WK
£240.00–£305.00

HIGH SEASON PER WK
£460.00–£580.00

3-night and last-minute breaks available Oct–Mar.

Smugglers Rock Cottages, Ravenscar, Scarborough

contact Mrs Sharon Gregson, Staintondale Road, Ravenscar YO13 0ER **t** (01723) 870044
e info@smugglersrock.co.uk

smugglersrock.co.uk REAL-TIME BOOKING

open All year
payment Credit/debit cards, cash, cheques
nearest shop 2 miles
nearest pub 2 miles

Beautiful cottages in Ravenscar (southern end of Robin Hood's Bay) furnished to a very high standard with panoramic views of the National Park and sea. Fully equipped for maximum comfort and relaxation. The cottages are an ideal base for country and coastal holidays. Friendly farm animals. Bed and breakfast also available.

SAT NAV *YO13 0ER* **ONLINE MAP**

Unit General P S
Leisure

SEAHOUSES, Northumberland Map ref 5C1

★★★★
SELF CATERING

Units 1
Sleeps 1–6

LOW SEASON PER WK
£250.00–£525.00

HIGH SEASON PER WK
£525.00

The Lobster Pots, Seahouses

contact Mrs Julia Steel, 10 Crofters Lea, Leeds LS19 7WE **t** (0113) 239 1130
e julia@thelobsterpots.co.uk

thelobsterpots.co.uk GUEST REVIEWS · SPECIAL OFFERS

Beautifully furnished holiday home with sea views. Situated only five minutes' walk from breathtaking coastline. Ideal for children, with enclosed garden and toys. Dogs welcome.

open All year
payment Cash, cheques
nearest shop 0.5 miles
nearest pub 0.5 miles

Unit SC General P S
Leisure

For **key to symbols** see page 7

SEAHOUSES, Northumberland Map ref 5C1

★★★
SELF CATERING

Units 2
Sleeps 1–4

LOW SEASON PER WK
£250.00–£325.00

HIGH SEASON PER WK
£325.00–£550.00

North East Coast Holidays, Seahouses

contact Mrs Lesley Barnett, 7 Alnside Court, Lesbury, Alnwick NE66 3PD **t** (01665) 833233
e d_barnettuk@yahoo.co.uk

northeastcoastholidays.co.uk

open All year
payment Cash, cheques
nearest shop 1 mile
nearest pub 1 mile

Comfortable, well-equipped, two-bedroom cottages close to sea, beaches and golf courses. These cottages are the perfect base to explore Northumberland. Own garden and parking. Linen included. Families welcome. Non-smoking. Sea views. Houses next door to each other (ideal for two families).

Unit TV DVD P S General Leisure

SEAHOUSES, Northumberland Map ref 5C1

★★★
SELF CATERING

Units 1
Sleeps 1–4

HIGH SEASON PER WK
Max £460.00

Peregrine, Seahouses

contact Mr Chris Dempsey, Kimmerghame Mains Farmhosue, Duns TD11 3LU **t** (01361) 882536 & 07711 182761 **e** linda@gpm-marketing.co.uk

Peregrine is stone-built (1845), within the old Seahouses fishing village, close to the harbour, and is double-glazed, with night storage heaters.

open All year
payment Cheques
nearest shop 0.5 miles
nearest pub less than 0.5 miles

Unit TV DVD General S Leisure

SEAHOUSES, Northumberland Map ref 5C1

★★★★
SELF CATERING

Units 1
Sleeps 1–6

HIGH SEASON PER WK
Max £480.00

Sparrowhawk, Seahouses

contact Mr Chris Dempsey, Kimmerghame Mains Farmhouse, Duns TD11 3LU **t** (01361) 882536
e linda@gpm-marketing.co.uk

Sparrowhawk is a modern, three-bedroom terraced house in the newer part of Seahouses. Full double-glazing and night storage heaters plus gardens and off-street parking.

open All year
payment Cheques
nearest shop 0.75 miles
nearest pub 0.75 miles

Unit TV DVD General P S Leisure

SHAP, Cumbria Map ref 5B3

★★★★
SELF CATERING

Units 1
Sleeps 6

LOW SEASON PER WK
£280.00

HIGH SEASON PER WK
£460.00

The Stable, Crosby Ravensworth, Penrith

contact Mrs Christine Jackson, Wickerslack Farm, Crosby Ravensworth, Penrith CA10 2LN
t (01931) 715236

Recently renovated, clean, warm and cosy cottage. Peaceful, rural setting with superb views. Four-poster, king-size and twin bedrooms (all on ground and first floor), two bathrooms. Patio and barbecue. Breakfasts available in the farmhouse.

open All year
payment Cash, cheques
nearest shop 3 miles
nearest pub 2 miles

Unit TV DVD General P S

What if I need to cancel?

It's advisable to check the proprietor's cancellation policy at the time of booking in case you have to change your plans.

SHEFFIELD, South Yorkshire Map ref 4B2

★★★
SELF CATERING

Units 1
Sleeps 4

LOW SEASON PER WK
£175.00

HIGH SEASON PER WK
£175.00

The Flat, Sheffield

contact Margaret Cox, The Flat, 152 Whirlowdale Road S7 2NL **t** (0114) 221 5553

Self-contained flat with own door and stairs. Attached to owners' property on the south west edge of Sheffield. One bedroom with double bed. Double sofa bed in sitting room.

open All year except Christmas and New Year
payment Cash, cheques
nearest shop 1 mile
nearest pub 0.5 miles

Unit General P Leisure

SHEFFIELD, South Yorkshire Map ref 4B2

★★-★★★
SELF CATERING

Units 5
Sleeps 2–6

LOW SEASON PER WK
£150.00–£350.00

HIGH SEASON PER WK
£200.00–£400.00

Short breaks and special promotions, please call for details.

Foxholes Farm, Low Bradfield, Sheffield

contact Rachel Hague, Foxholes Farm, Sheffield S6 6HY **t** (0114) 285 1383 & 07917 030602
e foxholes.farm@tiscali.co.uk

foxholesfarm.co.uk

open All year
payment Cash, cheques
nearest shop 0.5 miles
nearest pub 0.5 miles

The converted Grade II Listed buildings house the cottages, three of which have a double room and a twin room, one a double room and a single room, and the other a double room. All units have fitted kitchens, lounge area, bathroom and some also have a double sofa bed.

SAT NAV *S6 6HY*

Unit General P Leisure

SIGGLESTHORNE, East Riding of Yorkshire Map ref 4D1

★★★★
SELF CATERING

Units 1
Sleeps 1–4

LOW SEASON PER WK
£200.00–£250.00

HIGH SEASON PER WK
£300.00–£370.00

Peggy's Cottage, Hornsea

contact Ms Jude Collingwood, Peggy's Cottage, Hall Farm, Hull HU11 5QH **t** (01964) 535395
e p.collingwood@btinternet.com

Once a stable, now a comfortable and pretty cottage enjoying a peaceful, rural setting four miles from the sea and Hornsea Mere.

open All year
payment Cash, cheques, euros
nearest shop 4 miles
nearest pub 1 mile

Unit General P Leisure

SILVERDALE, Lancashire Map ref 5A3

★★★★-★★★★★
SELF CATERING

Units 2
Sleeps 1–8

LOW SEASON PER WK
£365.00–£595.00

HIGH SEASON PER WK
£395.00–£675.00

Short breaks available Nov-Mar (weekends and midweek).

Wolf House Cottages, Silverdale, Nr Arnside

t (01524) 701573 **e** enquiries@wolfhousecottages.co.uk

wolfhousecottages.co.uk

open All year
payment Cash, cheques
nearest shop 1 mile
nearest pub 1 mile

Detached, beautifully furnished cottages with private gardens and stunning views over fields or Morecambe Bay in an Area of Outstanding Natural Beauty. Owners have lifetime interest in the arts, crafts and environment. Walks and cycle rides from the doorstep, close to RSPB reserve, Lake District, Yorkshire Dales and Forest of Bowland.

Unit General P Leisure

For **key to symbols** see page 7

SKIPTON, North Yorkshire Map ref 4B1

★★★–★★★★★
SELF CATERING

Units 7
Sleeps 1–4

LOW SEASON PER WK
£150.00–£260.00

HIGH SEASON PER WK
£230.00–£400.00

Cawder Hall Cottages, Skipton

contact Graham Pearson, Cawder Hall Cottages, Cawder Lane, Skipton BD23 2TD **t** (01756) 791579
e info@cawderhallcottages.co.uk

cawderhallcottages.co.uk

open All year
payment Credit/debit cards, cash, cheques
nearest shop 1 mile
nearest pub 0.5 miles

Peaceful, tastefully converted farm cottages in open countryside, one mile from castle and historic market town of Skipton. Suitable for disabled.

Unit General P Leisure

SKIPTON, North Yorkshire Map ref 4B1

★★★★
SELF CATERING

Units 1
Sleeps 14

LOW SEASON PER WK
£600.00–£800.00

HIGH SEASON PER WK
£900.00–£1,300.00

Craven House, Skipton

contact Mrs Joanne Rushton, Milton Street, Skipton BD23 2ED **t** (01756) 794657
e joanne@craven-house.co.uk

craven-house.co.uk SPECIAL OFFERS

Large Victorian terrace in market town of Skipton, accommodating 14 people in seven bedrooms; three rooms en suite, three house bathrooms.

open All year
payment Cash, cheques, euros
nearest shop less than 0.5 miles
nearest pub less than 0.5 miles

Unit General Leisure

SLAIDBURN, Lancashire Map ref 4A1

★★★
SELF CATERING

Units 2
Sleeps 5–14

LOW SEASON PER WK
£239.00–£369.00

HIGH SEASON PER WK
£463.00–£739.00

3-night stays available all year except Jul, Aug, Christmas and New Year.

Laythams Farm Cottages, Clitheroe

contact Mr Ian Roger Driver, Laythams Farm Cottages, 1 Laythams Farm, Back Lane, Slaidburn, Clitheroe BB7 3AJ **t** (01200) 446454 **e** idriver@nildram.co.uk

laythamsfarmcottages.co.uk SPECIAL OFFERS

open All year except Christmas and New Year
payment Cash, cheques
nearest shop 2 miles
nearest pub 2 miles

This 16thC Pennine longhouse is in the birdwatcher's and walker's paradise of the Forest of Bowland. The kitchen and dining/pool room are downstairs whilst upstairs is the lounge with open fire and grand piano. Another smaller cottage is available and the two can be connected for larger parties.

SAT NAV *BB7 3AJ* **ONLINE MAP**

Unit General P
Leisure

SLALEY, Northumberland Map ref 5B2

★★★
SELF CATERING

Units 1
Sleeps 1–5

LOW SEASON PER WK
£250.00–£280.00

HIGH SEASON PER WK
£280.00–£300.00

Combhills Farm, Hexham

contact Mrs Ogle, Combhills Farm, Slaley, Hexham NE47 0AQ **t** (01434) 673475
e margaret@ogle.entadsl.com

Comfortable, well-equipped, centrally heated cottage on working family farm. Centrally located for Newcastle, Durham, MetroCentre and Hadrian's Wall. Beautiful countryside for walking. Ample parking.

open All year
payment Cash, cheques
nearest shop 0.5 miles
nearest pub 0.5 miles

Unit General P

SOUTHPORT, Merseyside Map ref 4A1

★★★★
SELF CATERING

Units 2
Sleeps 1–6

LOW SEASON PER WK
£195.00–£375.00

HIGH SEASON PER WK
£260.00–£450.00

Martin Lane Farmhouse Holiday Cottages, Burscough

contact Mrs Stubbs, Martin Lane Farmhouse Holiday Cottages, Ormskirk L40 8JH **t** (01704) 893527
e mlfhc@btinternet.com

martinlanefarmhouse.btinternet.co.uk REAL-TIME BOOKING

open All year
payment Cash, cheques, euros
nearest shop 4 miles
nearest pub less than 0.5 miles

Beautiful, award-winning country cottages, nestling in the rich arable farmland of West Lancashire and just four miles from Southport and the seaside. Our cottages have a friendly, relaxed, family atmosphere. The ideal base for visiting all the North West's major attractions.

Unit General P Leisure

WALKERS WELCOME

Do you like walking?

Walkers feel at home in accommodation participating in our Walkers Welcome scheme. Look out for the symbol. Consider walking all or part of a long-distance route – go online at nationaltrail.co.uk.

SOUTHPORT, Merseyside Map ref 4A1

★★★
SELF CATERING

Units 5
Sleeps 2–6

LOW SEASON PER WK
Min £170.00

HIGH SEASON PER WK
Max £340.00

Sandy Brook Farm, Southport

contact Mr Core, Sandy Brook Farm, 52 Wyke Cop Road, Scarisbrick, Southport PR8 5LR
t (01704) 880337 & 07719 468712 **e** sandybrookfarm@lycos.co.uk

sandybrookfarm.co.uk

Converted barn offering self-catering apartments furnished in traditional style with all modern amenities. Three-and-a-half miles from Southport in rural area of Scarisbrick. Adapted apartment for disabled guests.

open All year
payment Cash, cheques
nearest shop 2 miles
nearest pub 1 mile

Unit General P Leisure

STAINTONDALE, North Yorkshire Map ref 5D3

★★★
SELF CATERING

Units 4
Sleeps 1–6

LOW SEASON PER WK
£175.00–£260.00

HIGH SEASON PER WK
£290.00–£470.00

White Hall Farm Holiday Cottages, Scarborough

contact Mr & Mrs James and Celia White, White Hall Farm Holiday Cottages, White Hall Farm, Scarborough YO13 0EY **t** (01723) 870234 **e** celia@white66.fsbusiness.co.uk

whitehallcottages.co.uk

open All year
payment Cash, cheques
nearest shop 6 miles
nearest pub 4 miles

Peace and tranquillity found on our 130-acre sheep farm with stunning coastal and rural views. Walks from your door amid woodland, streams and coastal path. Home from home, well-equipped, welcoming cottages, which are separate from the farm. Ideally located to explore North Yorkshire. Dogs/horses made welcome.

SAT NAV *YO13 0EY*

Unit General P S Leisure

STAITHES, North Yorkshire Map ref 5C3

★★★
SELF CATERING

Units 1
Sleeps 5

LOW SEASON PER WK
£265.00–£365.00

HIGH SEASON PER WK
£355.00–£595.00

Pennysteel Cottage, Staithes

contact Chris Wade, Waterfront Cottages, 2 Star Row, North Dalton, Driffield YO25 9UX
t (01377) 217662 & 07801 124264 **e** chris.wade@adastra-music.co.uk

waterfrontcottages.co.uk

open All year
payment Credit/debit cards, cash, cheques
nearest shop less than 0.5 miles
nearest pub less than 0.5 miles

Old fisherman's cottage of unique character with beamed ceilings, wood-panelled walls and wood-burning stove. All windows and terrace overlook the picturesque harbour of Staithes. Ideal for the coast and walking. Top-quality restaurant, pub serving food, cafes, art gallery and craft and local shops all within a few yards.

Unit General Leisure

PETS! WELCOME WELCOME PETS!

Where is my pet welcome?

Want to take your cherished companion with you on holiday? Proprietors participating in our Welcome Pets! scheme go out of their way to make special provision for you and your pet. Look out for the symbol.

STAVELEY, Cumbria Map ref 5A3

★★★
SELF CATERING

Units 4
Sleeps 2–5

LOW SEASON PER WK
£260.00–£300.00

HIGH SEASON PER WK
£400.00–£560.00

Brunt Knott Farm Holiday Cottages, Kendal

contact William & Margaret Beck, Brunt Knott Farm Holiday Cottages, Brunt Knott Farm, Kendal LA8 9QX **t** (01539) 821030 **e** margaret@bruntknott.demon.co.uk

bruntknott.demon.co.uk

open All year
payment Cash, cheques
nearest shop 1.5 miles
nearest pub 1.5 miles

Cosy cottages on small, secluded, 17thC hill farm. Peaceful, elevated, fellside location with superb panoramic views over Lakeland fells. Five miles from Windermere/Kendal. Cycling/lovely walks from your doorstep. Central heating. Three cottages with wood-burner/open fire. Parking. Laundry facilities. Winter short breaks available. Brochure available.

Unit General P S Leisure

THIRSK, North Yorkshire Map ref 5C3

★★★★
SELF CATERING

Units 1
Sleeps 2–4

LOW SEASON PER WK
£200.00–£250.00

HIGH SEASON PER WK
£300.00–£350.00

The Garden Cottage, Rainton, Thirsk

contact Mr Yates, Nursery Garden Holiday Home Park, Baldersby Park, Rainton, Thirsk YO7 3PG **t** (01845) 577277 **e** nurserygardencp@talk21.com

nurserygarden.co.uk

Ground-floor single-storey, very well equipped one-bedroomed semi-detached cottage, recently refurbished to a very high standard. Rural setting with convenient access from major road links. Off-road parking.

open All year
payment Cash, cheques
nearest shop 1 mile
nearest pub 1 mile

Unit TV DVD General 12 P Leisure

THIRSK, North Yorkshire Map ref 5C3

★★★
SELF CATERING

Units 1
Sleeps 2–4

LOW SEASON PER WK
£100.00–£200.00

HIGH SEASON PER WK
£250.00–£300.00

Pasture House Farm, Thirsk

contact Mr Arthur Bierton, Pasture House Farm, Stockton Road, Thirsk YO7 2LT **t** (01845) 522791

Single-storey cottage consisting of one double bedroom, living room with kitchen to one side, bathroom with shower. Can sleep four with bed settee. Parking.

open All year
payment Cash, cheques, euros
nearest shop 2 miles
nearest pub 1 mile

Unit TV DVD General P S Leisure

For **key to symbols** see page 7

THORNLEY, Lancashire Map ref 4A1

★★★★
SELF CATERING

Units **2**
Sleeps **4–10**

LOW SEASON PER WK
£260.00–£510.00

HIGH SEASON PER WK
£415.00–£760.00

Loudview Barn, Preston

contact Mr & Mrs Oliver & Ness Starkey, Loudview Barn, Rams Clough Farm, Thornley, Preston PR3 2TN **t** (01995) 61476 **e** loudview@ic24.net

open All year
payment Cash, cheques, euros
nearest shop 4 miles
nearest pub 2 miles

Stone barn conversion in peaceful location on fellside in Forest of Bowland, enjoying exceptional views across unspoilt countryside. Accommodation in two units that can be combined. Unit 1 comprises one double, one twin and pair of bunk beds. Unit 2 comprises one double and one twin.

Unit General P Leisure

THORPE BASSETT, North Yorkshire Map ref 5D3

★★★★
SELF CATERING

Units **1**
Sleeps **4**

LOW SEASON PER WK
£313.00

HIGH SEASON PER WK
£493.00

Short breaks available Oct–Mar (3-night stay).

Wold View Cottage, Thorpe Bassett, Malton

contact Mrs Stephanie French, Wold View House, Thorpe Bassett, Malton YO17 8LU
t (01944) 758704

dalesholcot.com

open All year
payment Cash, cheques
nearest shop 1 mile
nearest pub 1 mile

Tastefully converted from owner's original farm buildings, and offering a high standard of accommodation. Underfloor heating and traditional style gas-effect wood-burning stove make the cottage warm and cosy. 1.5 acres of enclosed garden shared with owner, scenic walks, easy access to many other places of interest. Beautiful, idyllic retreat.

SAT NAV *YO17 8LU*

Unit General P S Leisure

THURSTONFIELD, Cumbria Map ref 5A2

★★★★–★★★★★
SELF CATERING

Units **6**
Sleeps **2–6**

LOW SEASON PER WK
£566.00–£650.00

HIGH SEASON PER WK
£998.00–£1,184.00

The Tranquil Otter, Thurstonfield, Carlisle

contact Nick and Tazeem Kittoe, The Tranquil Otter Ltd, The Lough, Thurstonfield CA5 6HB
t (01228) 576661 **e** info@thetranquilotter.co.uk

thetranquilotter.co.uk

open All year
payment Credit/debit cards, cash, cheques, euros
nearest shop 2 miles
nearest pub 2 miles

Well-equipped lodges with picture-book views set in private nature reserve right on the lakeshore in peaceful beauty spot. Log-burner, jacuzzi bath/sauna or hot tub. Wonderful nature (including otters). Private lakeside walks. Own rowing boat. Fly fishing. Outstanding wheelchair access with wheely boat and mobility scooter.

Unit General P S
Leisure

TIRRIL, Cumbria Map ref 5B2

★★★★-★★★★★
SELF CATERING

Units 5
Sleeps 1–9

LOW SEASON PER WK
£160.00–£550.00

HIGH SEASON PER WK
£295.00–£1,020.00

Tirril Farm Cottages, Penrith

contact David Owens, Tirril Farm Cottages, Tirril View, Penrith CA10 2JE **t** (01768) 864767
e enquiries@tirrilfarmcottages.co.uk

tirrilfarmcottages.co.uk SPECIAL OFFERS

open All year
payment Cash, cheques
nearest shop 2 miles
nearest pub less than 0.5 miles

Easily accessible, two miles from Ullswater, these tasteful barn conversions enjoy a quiet courtyard setting with outstanding views over the fells. Tirril is an attractive village with prize-winning pub/restaurant. Ideal for visiting the Lakes and Eden Valley. Short breaks welcome. Disabled-friendly cottage.

Unit General P S Leisure

TODMORDEN, West Yorkshire Map ref 4B1

★★★
SELF CATERING

Units 1
Sleeps 4

LOW SEASON PER WK
£160.00–£190.00

HIGH SEASON PER WK
£190.00–£220.00

The Cottage, Todmorden

contact Mr & Mrs Bentham, The Cottage, Causeway East Farmhouse, Lee Bottom Road, Todmorden OL14 6HH **t** (01706) 815265 **e** andrew-b_5@tiscali.co.uk

Part of a 17thC farmhouse beneath the Pennine Way. Ideal for walking and touring.

open All year
payment Cash, cheques
nearest shop 2 miles
nearest pub 0.5 miles

Unit General P Leisure

TODMORDEN, West Yorkshire Map ref 4B1

★★★★
SELF CATERING

Units 1
Sleeps 10

LOW SEASON PER WK
Min £500.00

HIGH SEASON PER WK
Max £1,200.00

Shoebroad Barn, Todmorden

contact Mrs Horsfall, Pennine House, Pennine Grove, Todmorden OL14 8AU **t** (01706) 817015 & 07966 158295 **e** thehorsfalls@beeb.net

shoebroadbarn.co.uk GUEST REVIEWS

open All year
payment Cash, cheques, euros
nearest shop 1 mile
nearest pub 1 mile

Large, well-contained barn in lovely open area with commanding views and only one mile from town centre. Secluded, yet good location for walking around Pennines. Well equipped for large family get-togethers. Home from home atmosphere with lots of space for children. Close to two good quality hilltop pubs.

ONLINE MAP

Unit General P S
Leisure

WALKERS WELCOME · CYCLISTS WELCOME

FAMILIES WELCOME

Looking for an ideal family break?

For accommodation offering additional facilities and services for a range of ages and family units, look out for the Families Welcome symbol. Owners of these properties will go out of their way to welcome families.

TODMORDEN, West Yorkshire Map ref 4B1

★★★★
SELF CATERING

Units **1**
Sleeps **4–5**

LOW SEASON PER WK
£175.00–£275.00

HIGH SEASON PER WK
£275.00–£350.00

Stannally Farm Cottage, Todmorden

contact Dineen Ann Brunt, Stannally Farm Cottage, Stannally Farm, Stoney Royd Lane OL14 8EP
t (01706) 813998 **e** bruntdennis@aol.com

Luxurious 17thC stone cottage on Calderdale Way. South-facing access, rural Pennine foothills. Convenient for town, ideal centre for walking and touring.

open All year
payment Cash, cheques, euros
nearest shop 0.5 miles
nearest pub 0.5 miles

Unit General Leisure

TORVER, Cumbria Map ref 5A3

★★★
SELF CATERING

Units **3**
Sleeps **2–5**

LOW SEASON PER WK
£240.00–£350.00

HIGH SEASON PER WK
£400.00–£575.00

Sunny Bank Mill, Coniston

contact Claire Wildsmith, Sunny Bank Mill, c/o Fayrer Garden House Hotel, Lyth Valley Road, Bowness-on-Windermere LA23 3JP **t** (015394) 47474 **e** lakescene@fayrergarden.com

sunnybankmill.com

open All year
payment Credit/debit cards, cash, cheques
nearest shop 2 miles
nearest pub 2 miles

Delightful conversion of a 300-year-old Lakeland watermill in an idyllic setting beside Torver Beck. Beautiful, tranquil location, wooded grounds, an ideal base for walking and private access to Coniston Water. Four miles from Coniston village with several shops, pubs and restaurants and, of course, the lake steamers.

Unit General Leisure

TOW LAW, Durham Map ref 5B2

★★★★
SELF CATERING

Units **1**
Sleeps **2–4**

LOW SEASON PER WK
£205.00–£385.00

HIGH SEASON PER WK
Min £385.00

Binks Cottage, Bishop Auckland

contact Mrs Amanda Simpson, Oaklea, Thornley Village, Tow Law, Bishop Auckland DL13 4PA
t (01388) 731121 **e** amanda.simpson@totalise.co.uk

binkscottage.co.uk GUEST REVIEWS · SPECIAL OFFERS

Stone cottage set on a working farm overlooking a picturesque village green. Equipped to a high standard. Central heating, towels and linen included in price.

open All year
payment Cash, cheques
nearest shop 1 mile
nearest pub 1 mile

Unit General Leisure

TOW LAW, Durham Map ref 5B2

★★★
SELF CATERING

Units **4**
Sleeps **2–13**

LOW SEASON PER WK
Min £285.00

HIGH SEASON PER WK
£350.00–£980.00

Greenwell Hill Cottages, Wolsingham

contact Mrs Karen Wilson, Greenwell Hill Cottages, Greenwell Farm, Wolsingham DL13 4PH
t (01388) 527247 **e** enquiries@greenwellhill.co.uk

greenwellfarm.co.uk

Four cottages, converted from barn stables and byre, with all modern amenities. Upstairs lounge and sitting room overlooking Wear Valley. Ideal for summer/winter breaks. Sleeps two to thirteen.

open All year
payment Credit/debit cards, cash, cheques

Unit General Leisure

Where can I get live travel information?
For the latest travel update – call the RAC on 1740 from your mobile phone.

TRAWDEN, Lancashire Map ref 4B1

★★★★
SELF CATERING

Units 1
Sleeps 5

LOW SEASON PER WK
£250.00–£300.00

HIGH SEASON PER WK
£300.00–£350.00

Far Wanless Farm Stable Cottage, Colne

contact Mrs V M or Paul Johnson, Far Wanless Farm Stable Cottage, Far Wanless Farm, Hollin Hall, Colne BB8 8QE **t** (01282) 867514

Converted from a stable and piggery on a sheep and beef farm. One double, one twin, plus z-bed. Ideal walking area close to the Brontë village of Haworth and the Yorkshire Dales.

open All year
payment Cash, cheques
nearest shop 2 miles
nearest pub 2 miles

Unit General Leisure

ULVERSTON, Cumbria Map ref 5A3

★★★★
SELF CATERING & SERVICED APARTMENTS

Units 5
Sleeps 2–17

LOW SEASON PER WK
£265.00–£990.00

HIGH SEASON PER WK
£499.00–£2,100.00

Winter weekend breaks start at £145 for 2. £840 weekend for 17. Midweek breaks from £120 for 4 nights.

Ashlack Cottages, Broughton-in-Furness, Kirkby-in-Furness

contact Amanda Keegan, Ashlack Cottages, Ashlack Hall, Grizebeck, Cumbria LA17 7XN
t (01229) 889888 & 07976 867313 **e** enquiries@ashlackcottages.co.uk

ashlackcottages.co.uk SPECIAL OFFERS

open All year
payment Credit/debit cards, cash, cheques
nearest shop 2 miles
nearest pub 0.5 miles

Five luxury holiday cottages, sleeping from 2-17, between Ulverston and Coniston, providing excellent accommodation. All the cottages are beautifully decorated, are surrounded by farmland, have wonderful views overlooking the sea, and breathtaking walks from the door.

ONLINE MAP

Unit General
Leisure

WARK, Northumberland Map ref 5B2

★★★★
SELF CATERING

Units 2
Sleeps 2–8

LOW SEASON PER WK
£212.00–£334.00

HIGH SEASON PER WK
£247.00–£494.00

Roses Bower, Hexham

contact Mr & Mrs Lewis and Susan Watson, Roses Bower Farm, Wark, Hexham NE48 3DX
t (01434) 230779 & 07710 995966 **e** info@roses-bower.co.uk

roses-bower.co.uk

A cosy cottage or a traditional farmhouse in the grounds of Roses Bower, a working sheep farm in a magnificent location on The Warksburn, within the Northumbrian National Park.

open All year
payment Cash, cheques
nearest shop 5 miles
nearest pub 5 miles

Unit General
Leisure

WARKWORTH, Northumberland Map ref 5C1

★★★★
SELF CATERING

Units 3
Sleeps 2–4

LOW SEASON PER WK
£230.00–£330.00

HIGH SEASON PER WK
£280.00–£480.00

Buston Farm Holiday Cottages, Warkworth

contact Mrs Jo Leiper, Bygate, Black Heddon, Newcastle upon Tyne NE20 0JJ **t** (01661) 881506
e stay@buston.co.uk

buston.co.uk

open All year
payment Cash, cheques
nearest shop 2 miles
nearest pub 2 miles

Situated within the unique area of the Heritage Coast, between the historical village of Warkworth and picturesque Alnmouth, Buston Farm provides the ideal base from which to discover the secrets of rural Northumberland. We offer quality cottages, all superbly equipped, with many home comforts and featuring four-poster beds. All rooms en suite.

Unit TV DVD General P Leisure

WASDALE, Cumbria Map ref 5A3

★★★★
SELF CATERING

Units 1
Sleeps 1–10

LOW SEASON PER WK
Min £350.00

HIGH SEASON PER WK
Max £550.00

WALKERS WELCOME · CYCLISTS WELCOME

Bleng Barn, Gosforth, Seascale

contact Thomas Ostle, Bleng Farms, Mill House Farm, Wellington, Seascale CA20 1BH
t 07801 862237 & 07775 512918 **e** info@blengfarms.co.uk

blengfarms.co.uk GUEST REVIEWS • SPECIAL OFFERS

This newly converted rural property on a large working farm has many traditional features and modern conveniences, providing a base for a leisurely break or a variety of activity holidays.

open All year
payment Cash, cheques, euros
nearest shop 1 mile
nearest pub 0.6 miles

Unit TV SC DVD General P S
Leisure

WATERMILLOCK-ON-ULLSWATER, Cumbria Map ref 5A3

★★★
SELF CATERING

Units 6
Sleeps 2–8

LOW SEASON PER WK
£230.00–£310.00

HIGH SEASON PER WK
£475.00–£665.00

Mellfell Cottages, Melfell House Farm, Watermillock-on-Ullswater, Penrith

contact Ben & Diane Goddard, Mellfell House Farm, Watermillock, Penrith CA11 0LS
t (017684) 86295 **e** ben@mellfell.co.uk

mellfell.co.uk

Beautiful old barns converted into holiday cottages, high above Ullswater in Lake District National Park. Log fires, gas central heating, four-poster beds, drying room. Delightful walks from door. Excellent base.

open All year
payment Cheques
nearest shop 3.5 miles
nearest pub 1.5 miles

Unit TV DVD General Leisure

WETHERBY, West Yorkshire Map ref 4B1

★★★
SELF CATERING

Units 1
Sleeps 1–2

LOW SEASON PER WK
£200.00

HIGH SEASON PER WK
£225.00

Chestnut Chase, Bramham, Wetherby

contact Chris Gibson, Chestnut Chase, 9 Prospect Bank, Wetherby LS23 6RS **t** (01937) 845781
e bob@bramham.f9.co.uk

Annexe to family home. Self-contained with fully fitted kitchen, modern bathroom. Sleeps two. Set in the heart of the historic limestone village of Bramham. Ideally situated for exploring all Yorkshire.

open All year except Christmas
payment Cash, cheques, euros
nearest shop less than 0.5 miles
nearest pub less than 0.5 miles

Unit TV DVD General P

WHINFELL, Cumbria Map ref 5B3

★★★
SELF CATERING

Units 2
Sleeps 6–9

LOW SEASON PER WK
£300.00–£450.00

HIGH SEASON PER WK
£500.00–£750.00

Topthorn Holiday Cottages, Nr Kendal

contact Mrs Diane Barnes, Topthorn Holiday Cottages, Topthorn Farm, Whinfell, Nr Kendal LA8 9EG
t (01539) 824252 **e** info.barnes@btconnect.com

topthorn.com SPECIAL OFFERS

open All year
payment Credit/debit cards, cash, cheques
nearest shop 4 miles
nearest pub 4 miles

Two new 18thC barn conversions. Outstanding views, ideal area for walking. Large garden area, patios, barbecue, wheelchair-friendly, children and pets welcome. Peaceful location yet only four miles to the market town of Kendal. Windermere and the Lakes 25 minutes away. Horse-riding centre two miles. Climbing wall, leisure centre, cinema and pubs in Kendal.

Unit General Leisure

WHITBY, North Yorkshire Map ref 5D3

★★★
SELF CATERING

Units 1
Sleeps 6

LOW SEASON PER WK
£300.00–£500.00

HIGH SEASON PER WK
£300.00–£550.00

7 Henrietta Street, Whitby

contact Mr Usher, 2 Southlands Avenue, Whitby YO21 3DY **t** (01947) 605868

The cottage is situated at the bottom of the 199 steps and sleeps six people. Most rooms have sea and harbour views. Located in the old part of the town, it is convenient for all local shops and attractions.

open All year
payment Cash, cheques

Unit General

WHITBY, North Yorkshire Map ref 5D3

★★★
SELF CATERING

Units 1
Sleeps 2

LOW SEASON PER WK
£250.00–£300.00

HIGH SEASON PER WK
£350.00–£450.00

Bolthole Cottage, Whitby

contact Kaaren Noble, Stormville, Robin Hood's Bay, Whitby YO22 4RA **t** (01947) 880063
e kaaren@noble47.freeserve.co.uk

boltholecottage.co.uk

Quiet, warm, comfortable cottage. Two minutes from harbour. Good base for walking. Bath, shower, TV, DVD and modern kitchen.

open All year
payment Cash, cheques
nearest shop less than 0.5 miles
nearest pub less than 0.5 miles

Unit General Leisure

WHITBY, North Yorkshire Map ref 5D3

★★–★★★★
SELF CATERING

Units 8
Sleeps 2–4

LOW SEASON PER WK
£145.00–£380.00

HIGH SEASON PER WK
£185.00–£510.00

Carlton House Holiday Accommodation, Whitby

contact Vicki Clayton, Carlton House Holiday Accommodation, 5 Royal Crescent West Cliff, Whitby YO21 3EJ **t** (01947) 602868 **e** info@carltonhouseapartments.co.uk

carltonhouseapartments.co.uk

The accommodation is located on West Cliff with stunning views out to sea from all the front rooms. Convenient for all amenities Whitby has to offer. Refurbished 2005.

open All year
payment Credit/debit cards, cash, cheques
nearest shop less than 0.5 miles
nearest pub less than 0.5 miles

Unit General Leisure

Looking for a wide range of facilities?

More stars means higher quality accommodation plus a greater range of facilities and services.

WHITBY, North Yorkshire Map ref 5D3

★★★
SELF CATERING

Units 1
Sleeps 1–6

LOW SEASON PER WK
£200.00–£250.00

HIGH SEASON PER WK
£250.00–£350.00

White Horse Cottage, Whitby

contact George & Steven Walker, White Horse Cottage, 5 White Horse Yard, Church Street, Whitby YO22 4BW **t** (01709) 367031

Grade II Listed building with period features situated at the rear of the White Horse and Griffin pub near market square. Gas-fired central heating.

open All year
payment Cash, cheques
nearest shop less than 0.5 miles
nearest pub less than 0.5 miles

Unit General Leisure

WHITEHAVEN, Cumbria Map ref 5A3

★★★★
SELF CATERING

Units 2
Sleeps 4–6

LOW SEASON PER WK
£265.00–£430.00

HIGH SEASON PER WK
£390.00–£530.00

Short breaks (3 nights for the price of 2) available Nov-Mar (excl Christmas and New Year).

Rosmerta & Brighida Cottages, Whitehaven

contact David & Jane Saxon, Moresby Hall, Moresby, Whitehaven CA28 6PJ **t** (01946) 696317
e info@moresbyhall.co.uk

moresbyhall.co.uk REAL-TIME BOOKING

open All year
payment Credit/debit cards, cash, cheques, euros
nearest shop 2 miles
nearest pub 0.5 miles

Cottages adjacent to Moresby Hall, a historical, Grade I Listed building (circa 1620), managed by the owners of Moresby Hall with care and attention. Superbly equipped, delightful decor, quality furnishings and deceptively spacious. Our fine reputation brings many recommendations and repeat visits from satisfied guests each year. Many extras, including a welcome grocery pack.

Unit General P Leisure

WHITEHAVEN, Cumbria Map ref 5A3

★★★★
SELF CATERING

Units 1
Sleeps 1–5

LOW SEASON PER WK
£160.00–£380.00

HIGH SEASON PER WK
£390.00–£470.00

Snowdrop Cottage, Mountain View, Whitehaven

contact Mr Mark Warbrick, Wild Acre, Summergrove, Hensingham, Whitehaven CA28 8XZ
t (01946) 814194 & 07773 052960 **e** markwarbrick@aol.com

tranquilakescottages.co.uk SPECIAL OFFERS

open All year
payment Cash, cheques
nearest shop 1 mile
nearest pub 1 mile

Snowdrop Cottage is situated high above the surrounding countryside. Panoramic views to the Western Lake District and also towards Scotland and the Isle of Man. Internally, the holiday cottage is very cosy. Exposed beams, Sky TV and DVD. The lounge is tastefully furnished and decorated to a high standard.

SAT NAV *CA28 8UN* **ONLINE MAP**

Unit General P
Leisure

Using map references

The map references refer to the colour maps at the front of this guide. The first figure is the map number, the letter and figure that follow indicate the grid reference on the map.

WIGTON, Cumbria Map ref 5A2

★★★★
SELF CATERING

Units 1
Sleeps 1–8

LOW SEASON PER WK
£258.00–£307.00

HIGH SEASON PER WK
£363.00–£452.00

Short breaks and midweek breaks.

Foxgloves, Greenrigg Farm, Wigton

contact Mr & Mrs J Kerr, Foxgloves, Greenrigg Farm, Westward, Wigton CA7 8AH
t (01697) 342676 **e** kerr_greenrigg@hotmail.com

foxglovescottagewigton.co.uk SPECIAL OFFERS

open All year
payment Cash, cheques
nearest shop 1 mile
nearest pub 1 mile

Spacious, extremely well-equipped, comfortable cottage with Aga, offering a high standard of accommodation. Superlative setting and views. Large, safe garden. Guests are welcome to explore the farm and fields where a variety of wildlife can be seen. Easy reach Lake District, Scottish Borders, Roman Wall. Children, pets very welcome.

Unit TV DVD General P S
Leisure

WINDERMERE, Cumbria Map ref 5A3

★★★★
SELF CATERING

Units 1
Sleeps 1–4

LOW SEASON PER WK
£265.00–£420.00

HIGH SEASON PER WK
£445.00–£495.00

Gavel Cottage, Windermere

Screetons, 25 Bridgegate, Howden DN14 7AA **t** (01430) 431201 **e** howden@screetons.co.uk

screetons.co.uk

Secluded period cottage situated in an elevated position close to the marina. Entrance hall, open-plan lounge (with open fire), dining area and kitchen, two bedrooms, bathroom, large garden and summerhouse.

open All year
payment Cash, cheques

Unit TV DVD General P S

WINDERMERE, Cumbria Map ref 5A3

★★★★
SELF CATERING

Units 4
Sleeps 2–6

LOW SEASON PER WK
£210.00–£450.00

HIGH SEASON PER WK
£300.00–£680.00

Heaning Barn Cottages, Heaning, Windermere, Windermere

contact Mrs Jenny Truch, Heaning Barn Cottages, Heaning, Windermere, Cumbria LA23 1JW
t (01539) 766107 **e** info@heaning.com

heaning.com GUEST REVIEWS · SPECIAL OFFERS · REAL-TIME BOOKING

Four newly refurbished cottages in converted 19thC Lakeland barn. Tranquil countryside location 1.5 miles from Windermere town. Walking/cycling from door. Central heating, new kitchens, courtyard garden, cycle store, private parking.

open All year
payment Credit/debit cards, cheques
nearest shop 1 mile
nearest pub 1 mile

Unit TV DVD General P S Leisure

WINDERMERE, Cumbria Map ref 5A3

★★★
SELF CATERING

Units 4
Sleeps 2–6

LOW SEASON PER WK
£195.00–£360.00

HIGH SEASON PER WK
£305.00–£505.00

Langdale View Apartments, Windermere

contact Julie Marsh, Langdale View Apartments, 112 Craig Walk, Windermere LA23 3AX
t (015394) 46655 **e** enquiries@langdale-view.co.uk

langdale-view.co.uk GUEST REVIEWS · SPECIAL OFFERS · REAL-TIME BOOKING

Attractive, comfortable holiday apartments with car parking. Close to village centre, lake, steamers, shops and restaurants. Fully-equipped kitchens and spacious living areas. Reduced prices for short breaks in low season.

open All year
payment Credit/debit cards, cash, cheques
nearest shop less than 0.5 miles
nearest pub less than 0.5 miles

Unit TV DVD General P S Leisure

For **key to symbols** see page 7

WINDERMERE, Cumbria Map ref 5A3

★★★★★
SELF CATERING

Units 1
Sleeps 6

LOW SEASON PER WK
£1,200.00–£1,650.00

HIGH SEASON PER WK
£1,200.00–£2,700.00

Ridding Bay Lodge, Lakeside, Newby Bridge, Ulverston

contact Ms Sheena Holden, Cumbrian Cottages, Atlantic House, Fletcher Way, Parkhouse, Carlisle CA3 0LJ **t** (01228) 599950 **e** sheena@cumbrian-cottages.co.uk

cumbrian-cottages.co.uk SPECIAL OFFERS • REAL-TIME BOOKING

open All year
payment Credit/debit cards, cash, cheques
nearest shop less than 0.5 miles
nearest pub less than 0.5 miles

Ridding Bay Lodge is a superb property of great distinction, offering a remarkable and luxurious lifestyle holiday. The lodge offers amazing uninterrupted views to Lake Windermere and the fells beyond. With private access to the lakeshore jetty, beach and tennis court. An idyllic location from which to explore all the Lake District offers.

SAT NAV *LA12 8AU* **ONLINE MAP**

Unit TV SC DVD General P S
Leisure

WINDERMERE, Cumbria Map ref 5A3

★★★
SELF CATERING

Units 3
Sleeps 1–2

LOW SEASON PER WK
£195.00–£250.00

HIGH SEASON PER WK
£280.00–£315.00

Winster House, Windermere

contact Mr Whalley, Winster House, Sunny Bank Road, Windermere LA23 2EN **t** (015394) 44723 **e** enquiries@winsterhouse.co.uk

winsterhouse.co.uk

Private parking and use of secluded garden. Five minutes' walk to shops and restaurants, ten minutes' walk to Lake Windermere. Brochure available.

open All year
payment Cash, cheques
nearest shop less than 0.5 miles
nearest pub less than 0.5 miles

Unit TV General P

WOLSINGHAM, Durham Map ref 5B2

★★★
SELF CATERING

Units 1
Sleeps 4

LOW SEASON PER WK
£155.00

HIGH SEASON PER WK
£235.00

Elvet Cottage, Wolsingham

contact Mrs Gardiner, 3 Melbourne Place, Wolsingham, Bishop Auckland DL13 3EQ **t** (01388) 527538

A cosy, two-bedroomed terraced cottage overlooking small village green in old part of Wolsingham. Excellent walking and touring centre.

open All year
payment Cash, cheques
nearest shop less than 0.5 miles
nearest pub less than 0.5 miles

Unit TV DVD General P

WOLSINGHAM, Durham Map ref 5B2

APPROVED CARAVAN HOLIDAY HOME

Units 1
Sleeps 6

LOW SEASON PER WK
£170.00–£190.00

HIGH SEASON PER WK
£170.00–£190.00

Friarside Farm Caravan, Bishop Auckland

contact Mrs Frazer, Friarside Farm Caravan, Friarside Farm, Wolsingham, Bishop Auckland DL13 3BH **t** (01388) 527724 **e** angiefrazer2002@hotmail.com

friarsidefarmcaravan.co.uk

Friarside Farm Caravan is situated in an enclosed fenced-off garden within the grounds of a working farm. Consists of one double bedroom and a single bedroom, fully equipped kitchen and lounge. Close to local attractions.

open April to October
payment Cash, cheques
nearest shop 1 mile
nearest pub 1 mile

Unit TV General P S Leisure

What shall we do today?

For ideas on places to visit, see the beginning of this regional section or go online at enjoyengland.com.

WOLSINGHAM, Durham Map ref 5B2

★★★
SELF CATERING

Units 1
Sleeps 7

LOW SEASON PER WK
£215.00–£350.00

HIGH SEASON PER WK
£350.00–£495.00

Whitfield House Cottage, Bishop Auckland

contact Mrs Margaret Shepheard, 25 Front Street, Bishop Auckland DL13 3DF **t** (01388) 527466
e enquiries@whitfieldhouse.clara.net

whitfieldhouse.clara.net

Spacious accommodation in part of an attractive Grade II* Listed Queen Anne house. Near the centre of this small town, in a designated Area of Outstanding Natural Beauty.

open All year
payment Cash, cheques, euros
nearest shop less than 0.5 miles
nearest pub less than 0.5 miles

Unit General Leisure

WOOLER, Northumberland Map ref 5B1

★★★★
SELF CATERING

Units 2
Sleeps 4–12

LOW SEASON PER WK
£450.00–£650.00

HIGH SEASON PER WK
£750.00–£1,000.00

Discounts available for early and late bookings. 20% discount on multiple bookings eg. 2 weeks or 2 cottages.

Crookhouse, Wooler

contact Mrs Lynne Holden, Crookhouse, Kirknewton, Wooler NE71 6TN **t** (01668) 216113
e stay@crookhousecottages.co.uk

crookhouse.co.uk SPECIAL OFFERS

open All year
payment Credit/debit cards, cash, cheques
nearest shop 3 miles
nearest pub 3 miles

Crookhouse is a small, traditional Northumbrian steading providing superior accommodation in a secluded, tranquil location with outstanding views of the College Valley and Cheviots. Two recently renovated luxury cottages each sleeping 4-6 can easily transform into one large house to sleep 12+. Horses and dogs welcome, kennels available.

Unit General
Leisure

WOOLER, Northumberland Map ref 5B1

★★★
SELF CATERING

Units 1
Sleeps 6

LOW SEASON PER WK
£250.00–£300.00

HIGH SEASON PER WK
£400.00–£450.00

Rose Cottage, Wooler

contact Mrs Christine Andrews, 1 Littleworth Lane, Esher KT10 9PF **t** (01372) 464284
e andrews@playfactors.demon.co.uk

rosecottageselfcatering.co.uk

open April to October
payment Cash, cheques, euros
nearest shop 1 mile
nearest pub 1 mile

Old stone cottage with superb views over Glendale Valley, set amid farmland. Beautiful Northumberland beaches, castles and gardens. Edinburgh and Newcastle within easy reach, plus all the Scottish Border land. Log fires and efficient heating make it a good spring or autumn break.

SAT NAV *HE71 6SU*

Unit General Leisure

Do you have access needs?

Look for the National Accessible Scheme symbols if you have special hearing, visual or mobility needs.

WORSTON, Lancashire Map ref 4A1

★★★★
SELF CATERING

Units 2
Sleeps 1–4

LOW SEASON PER WK
£253.00–£285.00

HIGH SEASON PER WK
£342.00–£425.00

Angram Green Holiday Cottages, Clitheroe

contact Ms Christine Gorrill, Worston, Clitheroe BB7 1QB **t** (01200) 441455
e info@angramgreen.co.uk

angramgreen.co.uk

Farm-based cottages in rural Lancashire. Open beams and wood-burning stove. Stunning views across open countryside. Ideal base for walkers and cyclists. One double bedroom, one pair of child-size bunks.

open All year
payment Cash, cheques
nearest shop 2 miles
nearest pub 0.5 miles

Unit General Leisure

YORK, North Yorkshire Map ref 4C1

★★★
SELF CATERING

Units 1
Sleeps 1–5

LOW SEASON PER WK
£380.00–£480.00

HIGH SEASON PER WK
£510.00–£650.00

1 Bishops Court, York

t (01759) 307165 **e** eleanor@yorkcityholidays.co.uk

yorkcityholidays.co.uk

Bishops Court is a superb, spacious, three-bedroom house with modern furniture, all new. It is a short walk to shops and restaurants.

open All year
payment Cash, cheques
nearest shop less than 0.5 miles
nearest pub less than 0.5 miles

Unit General P

YORK, North Yorkshire Map ref 4C1

★★★★★
SELF CATERING

Units 1
Sleeps 1–6

LOW SEASON PER WK
£1,230.00

HIGH SEASON PER WK
£1,230.00

10 George Street, York

contact Mrs Heather Robinson, 3 Old Bank, Slaithwaite, Huddersfield HD7 5AR **t** (01484) 841330 & 07753 958686 **e** info@10georgestreet.co.uk

10georgestreet.co.uk REAL-TIME BOOKING

open All year
payment Credit/debit cards
nearest shop less than 0.5 miles
nearest pub less than 0.5 miles

Luxury boutique-style accommodation in a three-storey Georgian town house within the city walls, featuring highly unusual, eclectic decor. Antiques, oak panelling and floors, chandeliers and roll-top baths. Charming courtyard garden, parking for one vehicle, short breaks available, minimum two nights' stay. Top quality fittings, and goodies on arrival.

SAT NAV *YO1 9QB* **ONLINE MAP**

Unit General P

YORK, North Yorkshire Map ref 4C1

★★★★
SELF CATERING

Units 1
Sleeps 2

LOW SEASON PER WK
£325.00–£420.00

HIGH SEASON PER WK
£440.00–£550.00

24 Woodsmill Quay, York

Inyork Holidays, 11 Walmgate, York YO1 9TX **t** (01904) 632660 **e** agents@inyorkholidays.co.uk

inyorkholidays.co.uk

open All year
payment Credit/debit cards, cash, cheques

Woodsmill Quay is on the riverside and is a beautiful flat with one bedroom which overlooks the Ouse. Quietly situated, but within easy reach of the centre of York and its attractions. Private parking.

Unit TV DVD General P S

YORK, North Yorkshire Map ref 4C1

★★★
SELF CATERING

Units 1
Sleeps 1–5

LOW SEASON PER WK
£325.00–£420.00

HIGH SEASON PER WK
£440.00–£550.00

29 Richardson Street, York

Inyork Holidays, 11 Walmgate YO1 9TX **t** (01904) 632660 **e** agents@inyorkholidays.co.uk

inyorkholidays.co.uk

open All year
payment Credit/debit cards, cash, cheques

This is a very comfortable family house, a short walk from town and close to Rowntrees Park and shops. It has one double, one twin and one single room and there is also a futon if necessary. The lounge has a sofa bed, and there is a separate dining room.

Unit TV DVD General P S

YORK, North Yorkshire Map ref 4C1

★★★★★
SELF CATERING

Units 1
Sleeps 2–8

LOW SEASON PER WK
Min £295.00

Short breaks available. Discounts for smaller groups.

Abbeygate House, York

contact Mr & Mrs Halliday, 1 Grange Drive, Leeds LS18 5EQ **t** (0113) 258 9833

open All year
payment Credit/debit cards, cash, cheques
nearest shop less than 0.5 miles
nearest pub less than 0.5 miles

Superior new Georgian-style townhouse situated on prestigious Bishops Wharf riverside development overlooking medieval city walls and only a few minutes' walk along river into York. Stunning new dining-kitchen, spacious lounge with four luxurious leather sofas and south-facing balcony. New bedroom furniture. 5ft beds in two rooms. Three bathrooms, one with jacuzzi bath. Private parking.

SAT NAV *YO23 1JH*

Unit TV DVD General 6 P S Leisure

What do the star ratings mean?

Detailed information about star ratings can be found at the back of this guide.

YORK, North Yorkshire Map ref 4C1

★★★★-★★★★★
SELF CATERING

Units 5
Sleeps 1–4

LOW SEASON PER WK
£700.00–£1,400.00

HIGH SEASON PER WK
£700.00–£1,400.00

The Blue Rooms, York

contact Miss Kirsty Reid, The Blue Bicycle York Ltd, 34 Fossgate, York YO1 9TA **t** (01904) 673990
e blue-rooms@thebluebicycle.com

thebluebicycle.com

open All year
payment Credit/debit cards, cash, cheques
nearest shop less than 0.5 miles
nearest pub less than 0.5 miles

Overlooking the River Foss, The Blue Rooms occupy a secluded mews position and are equipped to the very highest standards. They offer luxury, convenience, privacy and comfort for that short romantic break or business trip. You will be welcomed on arrival with a bottle of champagne and fresh fruit basket, with our compliments.

Unit TV DVD General P S Leisure

YORK, North Yorkshire Map ref 4C1

★★★★
SELF CATERING

Units 1
Sleeps 1–4

LOW SEASON PER WK
£375.00–£475.00

HIGH SEASON PER WK
£500.00–£600.00

Crambeck Court, York

Inyork Holidays, 11 Walmgate, York YO1 9TX **t** (01904) 632660 **e** agents@inyorkholidays.co.uk

inyorkholidays.co.uk

A very attractive first-floor flat in the centre of York. En suite shower room, main bathroom, lounge with DVD, TV, CD player and video. One double, one twin. Private parking for one car.

open All year
payment Credit/debit cards, cash, cheques
nearest shop less than 0.5 miles
nearest pub less than 0.5 miles

Unit TV DVD General P

YORK, North Yorkshire Map ref 4C1

★★★
SELF CATERING

Units 1
Sleeps 2–5

LOW SEASON PER WK
£302.00–£450.00

HIGH SEASON PER WK
£402.00–£600.00

Garnet House, York

contact Mr Gordon Robinson, Garnet House, Garnet Terrace, York YO26 4XX **t** (01904) 412975 & 07973 409381 **e** herbie831@talktalk.net

Victorian three-bedroomed terrace family house, many original features, open aspects to conservation area. Twenty minutes' walk by the river into city, Free parking. Satellite TV, internet access, welcome hamper.

open All year
payment Credit/debit cards
nearest shop less than 0.5 miles
nearest pub less than 0.5 miles

Unit TV SC DVD General 1 P S
Leisure

YORK, North Yorkshire Map ref 4C1

★★–★★★
SELF CATERING

Units 6
Sleeps 2–4

LOW SEASON PER WK
£200.00–£300.00

HIGH SEASON PER WK
£250.00–£550.00

Knowle House Apartments, York

contact Greg Harrand, Knowle House Apartments, 5 Bootham Terrace, York YO30 7DH
t 0800 583 6374 **e** greg@hedleyhouse.com

hedleyhouse.com

open All year
payment Credit/debit cards, cash, cheques
nearest shop less than 0.5 miles
nearest pub less than 0.5 miles

City-centre apartments carefully maintained and recently updated next to the owners' hotel. Superbly located to explore York and the surrounding countryside. Garden jacuzzi and decked barbecue area. Off-street car parking. DVD players and DVD library. Laundry and cleaning service available. Close to bus and rail stations.

Unit General P Leisure

YORK, North Yorkshire Map ref 4C1

★★★
SELF CATERING

Units 1
Sleeps 4–10

LOW SEASON PER WK
Min £400.00

HIGH SEASON PER WK
Max £800.00

Pavilion Cottage, York

contact Mrs Heidi Whitaker, Pavilion Cottage, Shipton Road, York YO30 5RE **t** (01904) 639258 & 07974 853876 **e** pavcottage@yahoo.co.uk

pavilioncottage-holidayinyork.co.uk GUEST REVIEWS

A warm welcome awaits you. Pavilion Cottage sleeps eight to ten comfortably, has wonderful views over neighbouring cricket pitches and open countryside, yet lies close to York city centre.

open All year
payment Cash, cheques, euros
nearest shop 0.5 miles
nearest pub 0.5 miles

Unit General P
Leisure

YORK, North Yorkshire Map ref 4C1

★★★
SELF CATERING

Units 2
Sleeps 1–6

LOW SEASON PER WK
£250.00–£550.00

HIGH SEASON PER WK
£450.00–£650.00

Part-weeks available. We offer livery for up to 2 horses or ponies.

Skipwith Station Holidays, Selby

contact Mrs Lizanne Southworth, Skipwith Station, North Duffield YO8 5DE **t** (01757) 282288
e info@skipwithstation.com

skipwithstation.com REAL-TIME BOOKING

open All year
payment Cash, cheques
nearest shop 1 mile
nearest pub 1 mile

We offer elegant, stylish accommodation in two railway carriages in the grounds of the restored station. Both carriages offer contemporary and beautifully furnished interiors. Each carriage has a double bedroom, bunk room, shower room, kitchen and lounge. Views from the platform and from the lounges are across the open countryside.

ONLINE MAP

Unit General P Leisure

What if I need to cancel?

It is advisable to check the proprietor's cancellation policy in case you have to change your plans at a later date.

YORK, North Yorkshire Map ref 4C1

★★★★-★★★★★
SELF CATERING

Units **16**
Sleeps **2–7**

LOW SEASON PER WK
£225.00–£325.00

HIGH SEASON PER WK
£480.00–£790.00

York Lakeside Lodges, York

contact Mr Manasir, York Lakeside Lodges Ltd, Moor Lane, York YO24 2QU **t** (01904) 702346
e neil@yorklakesidelodges.co.uk

yorklakesidelodges.co.uk

Self-catering lodges and cottages in mature parkland around large fishing lake. Superstore across the road, coach to York centre every ten minutes.

open All year
payment Cash, cheques, euros
nearest shop less than 0.5 miles
nearest pub 0.6 miles

Unit General P Leisure

Walkers and cyclists welcome

Look out for quality-assessed accommodation displaying the Walkers Welcome and Cyclists Welcome signs.

Participants in these schemes actively encourage and support walking and cycling. In addition to special meal arrangements and helpful information, they'll provide a water supply to wash off the mud, an area for drying wet clothing and footwear, maps and books to look up cycling and walking routes and even an emergency puncture-repair kit! Bikes can also be locked up securely undercover.

The standards for these schemes have been developed in partnership with the tourist boards in Northern Ireland, Scotland and Wales, so wherever you're travelling in the UK you'll receive the same welcome.

Central England

Bedfordshire, Cambridgeshire, Derbyshire, Essex, Herefordshire, Hertfordshire, Leicestershire, Lincolnshire, Norfolk, Northamptonshire, Nottinghamshire, Rutland, Shropshire, Staffordshire, Suffolk, Warwickshire, West Midlands, Worcestershire

Clockwise: Holkham Hall, Norfolk; Royal Worcester, Worcestershire; Lincoln Cathedral, Lincolnshire

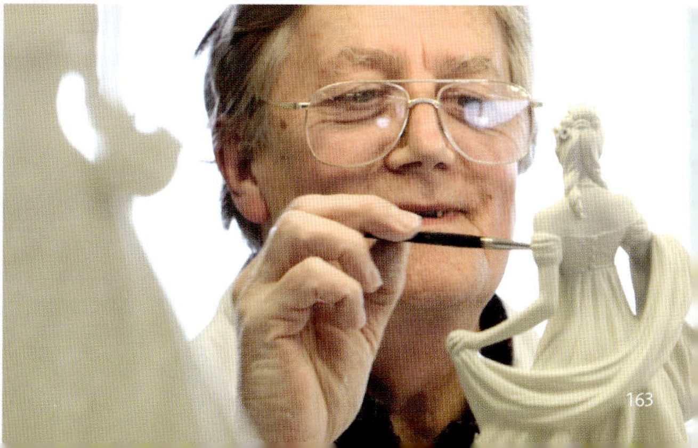

Great days out

Active pursuits, lazy days and family fun – find them all in Central England. Pull on your walking boots and challenge the Pennines, drift along the canals that criss-cross the region, follow the trail to the Major Oak in Sherwood Forest. And do come for the world-class – sometimes uniquely quirky – culture.

It's child's play

Game for anything? Then plunge in – there's such a wide choice of fun family days out. Start with a Thrill Hopper ticket giving great value access to four hair-raising theme park attractions: **Alton Towers** (try the exciting new Battle Galleons interactive water ride), **Drayton Manor Theme Park** (now with Europe's first Thomas Land for engine fiends), Tamworth **SnowDome** and **Waterworld**.

Bewilderwood, Norfolk

Next up, how about the **National Space Centre**, Leicester, where you can see if you cut it as an astronaut. Check your pulse and hit the assault course at **Conkers**, Swadlincote, in the heart of the National Forest, or tackle the zip wires and crocklebogs of **Bewilderwood**, Wroxham. Encounter lions, tigers and elephants at **Woburn Safari Park**, and get to **Dudley Zoological Gardens** for feeding time.

Good sport!

Discover natural sporting arenas to suit every pace and purpose. Walking, cycling, climbing, potholing: it's all here. Saunter along **Offa's Dyke Path**, stride part of the **Heart of England Way**, or dip into stretches of the **Pennine Way**. In the west of the region, the vistas that embrace the **Malverns** are superb. Cyclists of all ages love the flat terrain in the East of England, and you can hire bikes to explore the woodland trails at **Clumber Park**, Worksop. Mountain bikers (especially keen youngsters) can enjoy a challenge on traffic-free circular rides in **Bacton Woods**, Norfolk.

Then up the ante because action and adventure are bywords for the **Peak District and Derbyshire**. Climbers of all abilities come to grapple with limestone and gritstone crags. Potholers relish some of the most challenging caves in Britain. And if you're really more of a spectator, book your place trackside for sensational, high-octane Formula 1 racing at **Silverstone**, or have a flutter at **Newmarket**, the historical home of British horseracing.

Take the waters

Pack buckets, spades and binoculars then head for mile upon mile of sandy and shingle beaches from Essex to Lincolnshire. Hunker down in a hide along the coast at **RSPB Minsmere** to spy wading birds and waterfowl. Share the bustling delights of seaside resorts like Felixstowe, Southend-on-Sea and Great Yarmouth. For something quieter, seek out the havens of Frinton-on-Sea, Covehithe and Anderby Creek plus numerous quaint fishing villages.

Left to right: The Roaches, Staffordshire; RSPB Minsmere Nature Reserve, Suffolk

did you know... Derbyshire's Dovedale was formed from ancient coral reefs? Enjoy the ultimate ramble!

Inland, explore rivers and dykes in the **Fens**, a magical water world extending over Cambridgeshire, Lincolnshire, Norfolk and Rutland. At **Fenscape** interactive discovery centre in Spalding, learn all about the unique landscape and heritage. For lazy days with friends and family, what could be more calming than the reed-fringed waterways of the **Norfolk Broads**? When energy levels rise again, cast off for some sailing at **Rutland Water & Nature Reserve** and exhilarating watersports at **Carsington Water**.

Creative culture

With such a rich mix of history and raw natural beauty it's not surprising Central England inspires creativity. Visit the haunts of famous local lads: the **Stour Valley** of John Constable immortalised in *The Hay Wain* and **Stratford-upon-Avon** where young William Shakespeare lived – look around his birthplace then catch a performance by the **Royal Shakespeare Company**, there's nothing like Shakespeare enacted in his home town. Tour Gothic **Newstead Abbey**, full of Lord Byron's possessions and manuscripts, and gain insights into the life and music of Sir Edward Elgar at **The Elgar Birthplace Museum**, Lower Broadheath.

Today the region thrives with festivals and events ranging from classical to contemporary culture. On a musical note, Benjamin Britten's **Aldeburgh Festival** at Snape Maltings, Suffolk, is the place for classical concerts in a rural setting.

Royal Shakespeare Company, Warwickshire

The annual **DH Lawrence Festival** helps to attract thousands to the author's home town of Eastwood. Unique and quirky happenings are also to the fore, at **Whittlesea Straw Bear Festival** and **Shrewsbury's Cartoon Festival**.

Historic highlights

Linger in **Shrewsbury** to savour the historic atmosphere, or browse the streets of **Worcester** – places noted for their charming Tudor half-timbered architecture. Reach for your camera as you pass through **Much Wenlock**, one of the beautiful black and white villages of Shropshire. Castles and grand homes dot the landscape – **Warwick Castle, Hatfield House** and **Chatsworth** are favourites. For Elizabethan architecture at its most impressive, **Hardwick Hall** is hard to beat. Gothic **Lincoln Cathedral** on its lofty hill and **Lincoln Castle**, where one of only four surviving copies of Magna Carta is held, are must-visit heritage showpieces.

did you know... Lincoln Cathedral doubled as Westminster Abbey in The Da Vinci Code film?

Also step back into the area's proud industrial past, at the **Ironbridge Gorge Museums** – kids soon switch on their imaginations to design and technology at **Enginuity**. Have a chat with working craftsmen at **The Black Country Living Museum**. Trace the history of fighter planes at the **Imperial War Museum Duxford**, Europe's premier aviation museum. At the **Wedgwood Visitor Centre**, Stoke-on-Trent, you can tour the factory and throw a pot or two under the helpful eye of an expert.

Plumbread, pies and shopping

Central England serves up a mouthwatering range of distinctive foods: succulent Melton Mowbray pork pies, Red Leicester and Stilton, Lincolnshire plumbread and Bakewell pudding – often imitated, never matched. Head for Britain's food capital, pretty **Ludlow** on the Welsh borders, to discover what lures so many top chefs to the **Ludlow Marches Food and Drink Festival**. And then there's retail therapy at its most irresistible. Remember the **Bullring** in **Birmingham**? A space the size of more than 26 football pitches – all dedicated to shopping and entertainment. Soak up the colourful atmosphere of multicultural **Leicester** and try on a sari or two.

Clockwise: Imperial War Museum Duxford, Cambridgeshire; Wedgwood Visitor Centre, Staffordshire; Henry Moore Foundation, Hertfordshire

Destinations

Birmingham

A dynamic city combining a fascinating history with a world-class cultural scene. Lose yourself in shopping heaven in the stunningly remodelled Bullring, wander through the historic Jewellery Quarter then sit back and enjoy the Symphony Orchestra in the magnificent Symphony Hall. Indulge your sweet tooth at Cadbury World, or take in a major event at the NEC or NIA. You'll also find yourself at the heart of a region full of history and heritage, beautiful quaint villages and access to lush rolling countryside – Birmingham really is a gateway to the heart of England!

Cambridge

Cambridge

The name Cambridge instantly summons breathtaking images – the Backs carpeted with spring flowers, King's College Chapel, punting on the river Cam and, of course, the calm of the historic college buildings. Cambridge still has the atmosphere of a bustling market town, notwithstanding its international reputation. Explore its winding streets and splendid architecture, and choose from a range of attractions, museums, hotels, restaurants and pubs. Situated in the heart of East Anglia but less than an hour from London by high-speed rail link.

Colchester

Find internationally important treasures located in award-winning museums or visit cutting-edge contemporary galleries. It's a shopper's heaven with specialist shops and big name stores, and the range of cuisine makes Colchester a magnet for food lovers – don't miss the annual Colchester Oyster Feast.

Great Yarmouth

One of the UK's most popular seaside resorts, with an enviable mix of sandy beaches, attractions, entertainment and heritage. Beyond the seaside fun is a charming town that is steeped in history. Visit the medieval town walls, stroll the historic South Quay and discover Nelson's 'other' column. When the sun goes down colourful illuminations light up the night sky.

Hereford

In this ancient city on the banks of the River Wye, you'll find historic buildings housing modern shops and modern buildings holding historic treasures. Don't miss Hereford Cathedral with its priceless Mappa Mundi and Chained Library. Wander through the spacious High Town and the new Left Bank Village. Visit the Cider Museum to learn about Hereford's claim to be 'The Apple of England's Eye'.

Lincoln

Possessing magnificent architectural heritage, centred on its world famous Cathedral and Castle, Lincoln is a vivacious City – mixing 2,000 years of heritage with excellent shopping and lively arts and events. The Brayford Waterfront quarter is home to some of the newest places to eat and drink. Events include the famous Christmas Market and the Brayford Waterfront Festival.

Left to right: Chatsworth, Derbyshire; Alton Towers, Staffordshire

Ludlow

Ludlow

Discover the place Betjemen described as 'the loveliest town in England.' Britain's first 'slow' town is also a gastronomic capital and host to the renowned Ludlow Marches Food & Drink Festival. You'll find a host of speciality food shops, and more restaurants and inns than you can shake a cocktail stick at. To walk off lunch, stroll in the enchanting Angel Gardens, or take in a performance at the open-air theatre in the stunning medieval ruin of Ludlow Castle.

Norwich

Norwich, county town of Norfolk, is an enchanting cathedral city and a thriving modern metropolis. See some of the finest medieval architecture in Britain in the cathedral and castle, and wander an intricate network of winding streets. The city's newest centrepiece, The Forum, represents contemporary architecture at its best. You'll find excellent shopping as well as a vibrant mix of theatres, cinemas, arts festivals, exhibitions, museums, and a vast array of restaurants.

Clockwise: Brayford Waterfront, Lincoln; Colchester Castle; Birmingham

Nottingham

Nottingham is the undisputed capital of the East Midlands, boasting a sophisticated urban environment with an enviable reputation for clubs, theatres, cinemas and galleries, not to mention a deserved reputation as one of the top retail centres in the country. History is never far away, though, with reminders of Nottingham's legendary hero Robin Hood and his adversary the Sheriff of Nottingham. Explore the Castle Museum and Art Gallery, and Wollaton Hall, one of the most ornate Tudor buildings in Britain, complete with 500-acre deer park.

Peak District

The Peak District is Britain's first and most popular National Park. Roam on open moorland to the north and take in the magnificent views over the Derwent Dams. Further south, stroll alongside sparkling rivers in wildlife-rich valleys far from the hustle and bustle of town. The Peak Park Rangers lead regular guided walks – choose from long hikes to village tours. Take in the grandeur of Chatsworth House or Haddon Hall, and sample the local oatcakes with Hartington Stilton, followed by a delicious Bakewell pudding.

Stratford-upon-Avon

Unearth a magical blend of heritage and drama in and around Shakespeare's home town. Explore five houses with Shakespeare connections including Anne Hathaway's Cottage and Shakespeare's Birthplace. Visit one of England's most beautiful parish churches at Holy Trinity to see Shakespeare's grave and enjoy some of his great works performed by the world's largest classical theatre company, the RSC. Take a boat out on the River Avon, wander the boutiques, specialist stores and gift shops, and discover some of Britain's finest historic houses and gardens.

For lots more great ideas visit enjoyEngland.com/destinations

Visitor attractions

Family and Fun

Adventure Island Southend
Southend-on-Sea, Essex
(01702) 443400
adventureisland.co.uk
Great rides and attractions for all ages.

Alton Towers Theme Park
Alton, Staffordshire
0870 520 4060
altontowers.com
High-adrenalin adventure and family fun.

Banham Zoo
Banham, Norfolk
(01953) 887771
banhamzoo.co.uk
Wildlife spectacular featuring rare and endangered animals.

Bewilderwood
Wroxham, Norfolk
(01603) 783900
bewilderwood.co.uk
Treehouses, zip wires and jungle bridges.

Black Country Living Museum
Dudley, West Midlands
(0121) 557 9643
bclm.co.uk
Twenty-six acres of fascinating living history.

Cadbury World
Birmingham
0845 450 3599
cadburyworld.co.uk
Chocolate-making demonstrations and free samples.

Colchester Zoo
Stanway, Essex
(01206) 331292
colchester-zoo.com
Featuring superb cat and primate collections.

Conkers
Swadlincote, Leicestershire
(01283) 216633
visitconkers.com
Interactive adventure in the National Forest.

Coventry Transport Museum
Coventry, West Midlands
(024) 7623 4270
transport-museum.com
World-renowned exhibition of British road transport.

Drayton Manor Theme Park
Tamworth, Staffordshire
0844 472 1950
draytonmanor.co.uk
The biggest, wettest and scariest rides around.

Dudley Zoological Gardens
Dudley, West Midlands
(01384) 215313
dudleyzoo.org.uk
Lions and tigers, snakes and spiders!

Imperial War Museum Duxford
Large Visitor Attraction of the Year – Gold
near Cambridge
(01223) 835000
duxford.iwm.org.uk
The sights, sounds and power of aircraft.

Ironbridge Gorge Museums
Ironbridge, Shropshire
(01952) 884391
ironbridge.org.uk
World Heritage Site featuring ten superb museums.

National Sea Life Centre
Birmingham
(0121) 643 6777
sealifeeurope.com
Marvel at over 3,000 sea creatures.

National Space Centre
Leicester
0870 607 7223
spacecentre.co.uk
Test your abilities as an astronaut.

Nene Valley Railway
Peterborough, Cambridgeshire
(01780) 784444
nvr.org.uk
The golden age of steam comes alive.

The Poppy Line – North Norfolk Railway
Sheringham, Norfolk
(01263) 820800
nnr.co.uk
5.5 mile heritage railway through delightful countryside.

Pleasurewood Hills Leisure Park
Lowestoft, Suffolk
(01502) 586000
pleasurewoodhills.co.uk
Adrenaline-fuelled thrills and spills.

Severn Valley Railway
Bewdley, Worcestershire
(01299) 403816
svr.co.uk
Journey through 16 miles of beautiful countryside.

Twycross Zoo
Twycross, Leicestershire
(01827) 880250
twycrosszoo.com
Meet the famous gorillas, orang-utans and chimpanzees.

Warwick Castle
Warwick, Warwickshire
(01926) 406611
warwick-castle.co.uk
Enthralling medieval castle in 60-acre grounds.

Woburn Safari Park
Woburn, Bedfordshire
(01525) 290407
woburnsafari.co.uk
Wild animals just a windscreen's width away.

Heritage

Alford Manor House
Alford, Lincolnshire
(01507) 463073
alfordmanorhouse.co.uk
Britain's largest thatched manor house.

Althorp
Althorp, Northamptonshire
(01604) 770107
althorp.com
Historic Spencer family seat containing Diana exhibition.

Belton House, Park and Gardens
Belton, Lincolnshire
(01476) 566116
nationaltrust.org.uk
Fine example of Restoration country-house architecture.

Belvoir Castle
Belvoir, Leicestershire
(01476) 871002
belvoircastle.com
Fine stately home in stunning setting.

Burghley House
Stamford, Lincolnshire
(01780) 752451
burghley.co.uk
The grandest house of the Elizabethan age.

Canons Ashby House
Canons Ashby, Northamptonshire
(01327) 861900
nationaltrust.org.uk
Tranquil Elizabethan home of the Dryden family.

Chatsworth House
Bakewell, Derbyshire
(01246) 565300
chatsworth.org
One of Britain's truly great historic houses.

Doddington Hall & Gardens
Lincoln
(01522) 694308
doddingtonhall.com
Superb Elizabethan mansion set in romantic gardens.

Ely Cathedral
Ely, Cambridgeshire
(01353) 667735
cathedral.ely.anglican.org
Tour one of England's finest cathedrals.

Gainsborough Old Hall
Gainsborough, Lincolnshire
(01427) 612669
lincolnshire.gov.uk
Medieval manor house with original interiors.

Haddon Hall
Bakewell, Derbyshire
(01629) 812855
haddonhall.co.uk
Medieval and Tudor manor house with gardens.

Hardwick Hall
Chesterfield, Derbyshire
(01246) 850430
nationaltrust.org.uk
Elizabethan country house, gardens and parkland.

Hatfield House
Hatfield, Hertfordshire
(01707) 287010
hatfield-house.co.uk
Magnificent childhood home of Elizabeth I.

Hedingham Castle
Castle Hedingham, Essex
(01787) 460261
hedinghamcastle.co.uk
The finest Norman keep in England.

Hereford Cathedral
Hereford, Herefordshire
(01432) 374200
herefordcathedral.org
Magnificent cathedral housing the precious Mappa Mundi.

Holkham Hall
Wells-next-the-Sea, Norfolk
(01328) 713103
holkham.co.uk
Classic 18thC Palladian-style mansion.

Kirby Hall
Corby, Northamptonshire
(01536) 203230
Elizabethan house with superb carved decoration.

Knebworth House
Knebworth, Hertfordshire
(01438) 812661
knebworthhouse.com
Re-fashioned Tudor house in 250-acre grounds.

Lincoln Cathedral
Lincoln
(01522) 561600
lincolncathedral.com
One of Europe's finest gothic buildings.

Newstead Abbey
near Nottingham
(01623) 455900
newsteadabbey.org.uk
The ancestral home of Lord Byron.

Norwich Cathedral
Norwich, Norfolk
(01603) 218300
cathedral.org.uk
Majestic Norman cathedral with 14thC roof bosses.

Nottingham Castle
Nottingham
(0115) 915 3700
nottinghamcity.gov.uk/museums
17thC mansion on a medieval-castle site.

Rockingham Castle
Small Visitor Attraction of the Year – Silver
Rockingham, Northamptonshire
(01536) 770240
rockinghamcastle.com
Elizabethan house with splendid artworks and gardens.

Sandringham
Sandringham, Norfolk
(01553) 612908
sandringham-estate.co.uk
The country retreat of HM The Queen.

Shugborough – The Complete Working Historic Estate
Shugborough, Staffordshire
(01889) 881388
shugborough.org.uk
Fine mansion set in rare, surviving estate.

Sulgrave Manor
Sulgrave, Northamptonshire
(01295) 760205
sulgravemanor.org.uk
The home of George Washington's ancestors.

Weston Park
near Shifnal, Shropshire
(01952) 852100
weston-park.com
Charming stately home with beautiful gardens.

Woburn Abbey
Woburn, Bedfordshire
(01525) 290333
woburnabbey.co.uk
Palladian mansion set in 3,000-acre deer park.

Indoors

78 Derngate
Northampton
(01604) 603407
78derngate.org.uk
Terraced house transformed by Charles Rennie Mackintosh.

Birmingham Museum & Art Gallery
Birmingham
(0121) 303 2834
bmag.org.uk
Fine and applied arts featuring Pre-Raphaelites.

Compton Verney
Compton Verney, Warwickshire
(01926) 645500
comptonverney.org.uk
Art gallery housed in Robert Adam mansion.

The Elgar Birthplace Museum
Lower Broadheath, Worcestershire
(01905) 333224
elgarmuseum.org
Fascinating insight into the great composer's life.

Fitzwilliam Museum
Cambridge
(01223) 332900
fitzmuseum.cam.ac.uk
Internationally renowned collection of antiques and art.

Newark Castle
Newark, Nottinghamshire
(01636) 655765
newark-sherwooddc.gov.uk
Discover an exciting Civil War history.

Red House Glass Cone
Stourbridge, West Midlands
(01384) 812750
dudley.gov.uk/redhousecone
Live glassmaking, craft studios, tunnels and furnaces.

Royal Air Force Museum, Cosford
Cosford, Shropshire
(01902) 376200
rafmuseum.org
Warplanes, missiles, aero-engines and flight simulator.

Royal Shakespeare Company
Stratford-upon-Avon, Warwickshire
(01789) 403444
rsc.org.uk
Year-round performances of the great works.

Shakespeare's Birthplace
Stratford-upon-Avon, Warwickshire
(01789) 204016
shakespeare.org.uk
Acclaimed exhibition housed in Shakespeare's childhood home.

Shuttleworth Collection
Biggleswade, Bedfordshire
(01767) 627927
shuttleworth.org
Unique collection of historic aircraft.

Time and Tide – Museum of Great Yarmouth Life
Great Yarmouth, Norfolk
(01493) 743930
museums.norfolk.gov.uk
Discover a rich maritime and fishing heritage.

The Wedgwood Visitor Centre
Stoke-on-Trent, Staffordshire
(01782) 282986
thewedgwoodvisitorcentre.com
Famous pottery set in glorious Staffordshire countryside.

Outdoors

Castle Ashby Gardens
Castle Ashby, Northamptonshire
(01604) 696187
castleashby.co.uk
Capability Brown landscaped gardens and parkland.

Foxton Locks
Foxton, Leicestershire
(01908) 302500
foxtonlocks.com
Fascinating ten-lock 'staircase' climbing a 75ft hill.

Go Ape! High Wire Forest Adventure – Sherwood
Mansfield, Nottinghamshire
0845 643 9215
goape.co.uk
Rope bridges, swings and zip slides.

Peveril Castle
Castleton, Derbyshire
(01433) 620613
english-heritage.org.uk
Ruined Norman castle with impressive curtain wall.

RHS Garden Hyde Hall
Chelmsford, Essex
(01245) 400256
rhs.org.uk
28-acre hill-top garden with year-round interest.

RSPB Minsmere Nature Reserve
Saxmundham, Suffolk
(01728) 648281
rspb.org.uk
One of the RSPB's finest reserves.

Rutland Water & Nature Reserve
Oakham, Rutland
(01572) 770651
rutlandwater.org.uk
Important wildfowl sanctuary with leisure centre.

Sherwood Forest Country Park
Edwinstowe, Nottinghamshire
(01623) 823202
sherwoodforest.org.uk
Native woodland packed with adventure.

Silverstone Circuit
Silverstone, Northamptonshire
0870 4588 200
silverstone.co.uk
The home of British motor racing.

Sutton Hoo Burial Site
Woodbridge, Suffolk
(01394) 389700
nationaltrust.org.uk
Anglo-Saxon royal burial site.

The Trentham Estate
Stoke-on-Trent, Staffordshire
(01782) 646646
trentham.co.uk
One of Britain's most important historic gardens.

Welney Wetland Centre
Welney, Norfolk
(01353) 860711
wwt.org.uk
1,000-acre wetland reserve attracting wild swans.

Wrest Park
Silsoe, Bedfordshire
(01525) 860152
english-heritage.org.uk
Magnificent 18thC formal gardens with orangery.

ASSURANCE OF A GREAT DAY OUT
Attractions with this sign participate in the Visitor Attraction Quality Assurance Scheme which recognises high standards in all aspects of the visitor experience.

Events 2009

Crufts
Birmingham
the-kennel-club.org.uk
5 - 8 Mar

St George's Day Festival, Wrest Park Gardens
Silsoe
english-heritage.org.uk
Apr

Luton Carnival
Luton
luton.gov.uk
May

Southend Airshow
Southend-on-Sea
southendairshow.com
May

University of the Great Outdoors - Activity event
Ledbury
visitherefordshire.co.uk
3 - 4 May

Aldeburgh Festival of Music and the Arts
Snape
aldeburgh.co.uk
Jun

Althorp Literary Festival
Northampton
althorp.com
Jun

Stamford Shakespeare Festival
Rutland
stamfordshakespeare.co.uk
Jun - Aug

Robin Hood Festival
Nottingham
nottinghamshire.gov.uk/robinhoodfestival
Jul - Aug

Flavours of Herefordshire Food Festival
Holmer
visitherefordshire.co.uk
24 - 25 Oct

Lincoln Christmas Market
Lincoln
Dec

Regional contacts and information

For more information on accommodation, attractions, activities, events and holidays in Central England, contact one of the following regional or local tourism organisations. Their websites have a wealth of information and many produce free publications to help you get the most out of your visit.

Heart of England

Further information is available from the following organisations:

Marketing Birmingham
t (0121) 202 5115
w visitbirmingham.com

Black Country Tourism
w blackcountrytourism.co.uk

Visit Coventry & Warwickshire
t (024) 7622 7264
w visitcoventryandwarwickshire.co.uk

Visit Herefordshire
t (01432) 260621
w visitherefordshire.co.uk

Shakespeare Country
t 0870 160 7930
w shakespeare-country.co.uk

Shropshire Tourism
t (01743) 462462
w shropshiretourism.info

Destination Staffordshire
t 0870 500 4444
w enjoystaffordshire.com

Stoke-on-Trent
t (01782) 236000
w visitstoke.co.uk

Destination Worcestershire
t (01905) 728787
w visitworcestershire.org

Help before you go

To search for attractions and Tourist Information Centres on the move just text INFO to 62233, and a web link will be sent to your mobile phone.

Clockwise: Warwick Castle, Warwickshire; Rutland Water, Rutland; The Broads, Norfolk

East of England

East of England Tourism
t (01284) 727470
e info@eet.org.uk
w visiteastofengland.com

The comprehensive website is updated daily. Online brochures and information sheets can be downloaded including What's New; Major Events; Lights, Camera, Action! (film and television locations); Stars and Stripes (connections with the USA) and a range of Discovery Tours around the region.

East Midlands

The publications listed are available from the following organisations:

East Midlands Tourism
w discovereastmidlands.com
- **Discover East Midlands**

Experience Nottinghamshire
t 0844 477 5678
w visitnotts.com
- **Nottinghamshire Essential Guide, Where to Stay Guide, Stay Somewhere Different, City Breaks, Family Days Out**
- **Robin Hood Breaks**
- **Pilgrim Fathers**

Peak District and Derbyshire
t 0870 444 7275
w visitpeakdistrict.com
- **Peak District and Derbyshire Visitor Guide**
- **Peak District and Derbyshire Short Break Ideas**
- **Camping and Caravanning Guide**
- **Bess of Hardwick 400th Anniversary**

Lincolnshire
t (01522) 873800
w visitlincolnshire.com
- **Visit Lincolnshire – Destination Guide, Great days out, Gardens & Nurseries, Aviation Heritage, Good Taste**
- **Keep up with the flow**

Explore Northamptonshire
t (01604) 838800
w explorenorthamptonshire.co.uk
- **Explore Northamptonshire Visitor Guide, County Map**

Leicestershire
t 0844 888 5181
w goleicestershire.com
- **Inspiring short breaks and holidays in Leicestershire**
- **Stay, Play, Explore**
- **Great Days Out in Leicestershire**

Discover Rutland
t (01572) 653026
w discover-rutland.co.uk
- **Discover Rutland**

Tourist Information Centres

When you arrive at your destination, visit an Official Partner Tourist Information Centre for quality assured help with accommodation and information about local attractions and events, or email your request before you go. To search for attractions and Tourist Information Centres on the move just text INFO to 62233, and a web link will be sent to your mobile phone. To find a Tourist Information Centre by region visit enjoyEngland.com/find-tic.

Aldeburgh	152 High Street	(01728) 453637	atic@suffolkcoastal.gov.uk
Ashbourne	13 Market Place	(01335) 343666	ashbourneinfo@derbyshiredales.gov.uk
Ashby-de-la-Zouch	North Street	(01530) 411767	ashby.tic@nwleices.gov.uk
Bakewell	Bridge Street	(01629) 813227	bakewell@peakdistrict-npa.gov.uk
Bewdley	Load Street	(01299) 404740	bewdleytic@wyreforestdc.gov.uk
Birmingham Rotunda	150 New Street	0844 888 3883	callcentre@marketingbirmingham.com
Bishop's Stortford	The Old Monastery	(01279) 655831	tic@bishopsstortford.org
Brackley	2 Bridge Street	(01280) 700111	tic@southnorthants.gov.uk
Braintree	Market Square	(01376) 550066	tic@braintree.gov.uk
Bridgnorth	Listley Street	(01746) 763257	bridgnorth.tourism@shropshire.gov.uk
Burton upon Trent	Horninglow Street	(01283) 508111	tic@eaststaffsbc.gov.uk
Bury St Edmunds	6 Angel Hill	(01284) 764667	tic@stedsbc.gov.uk
Buxton	The Crescent	(01298) 25106	tourism@highpeak.gov.uk
Castleton	Buxton Road	(01433) 620679	castleton@peakdistrict-npa.gov.uk
Chesterfield	Rykneld Square	(01246) 345777	tourism@chesterfield.gov.uk
Church Stretton	Church Street	(01694) 723133	churchstretton.scf@shropshire.gov.uk
Colchester	Trinity Street	(01206) 282920	vic@colchester.gov.uk
Coventry Cathedral	Cathedral Ruins, 1 Hill Top	(024) 7623 4297	tic@cvone.co.uk
Coventry Ricoh	Phoenix Way	0844 873 6397	richoh@cvone.co.uk
Coventry Transport Museum	Hales Street	(024) 7622 7264	tic@cvone.co.uk
Derby	Market Place	(01332) 255802	tourism@derby.gov.uk
Felixstowe	91 Undercliff Road West	(01394) 276770	ftic@suffolkcoastal.gov.uk
Flatford	Flatford Lane	(01206) 299460	flatfordvic@babergh.gov.uk
Harwich	Iconfield Park	(01255) 506139	harwichtic@btconnect.com
Hereford	1 King Street	(01432) 268430	tic-hereford@herefordshire.gov.uk
Hunstanton	The Green	(01485) 532610	hunstanton.tic@west-norfolk.gov.uk
Ipswich	St Stephens Lane	(01473) 258070	tourist@ipswich.gov.uk
Ironbridge	Coalbrookdale	(01952) 884391	tic@ironbridge.org.uk

King's Lynn	Purfleet Quay	(01553) 763044	kings-lynn.tic@west-norfolk.gov.uk
Lavenham	Lady Street	(01787) 248207	lavenhamtic@babergh.gov.uk
Leamington Spa	The Parade	(01926) 742762	leamington@shakespeare-country.co.uk
Leek	Stockwell Street	(01538) 483741	tourism.services@staffsmoorlands.gov.uk
Leicester	7/9 Every Street	0906 294 1113**	info@goleicestershire.com
Lichfield	Castle Dyke	(01543) 412112	info@visitlichfield.com
Lincoln	9 Castle Hill	(01522) 873213	tourism@lincoln.gov.uk
Lowestoft	Royal Plain	(01502) 533600	touristinfo@waveney.gov.uk
Ludlow	Castle Street	(01584) 875053	ludlow.tourism@shropshire.gov.uk
Maldon	Coach Lane	(01621) 856503	tic@maldon.gov.uk
Malvern	21 Church Street	(01684) 892289	malvern.tic@malvernhills.gov.uk
Matlock	Crown Square	(01629) 583388	matlockinfo@derbyshiredales.gov.uk
Matlock Bath	The Pavillion	(01629) 55082	matlockbathinfo@derbyshiredales.gov.uk
Newmarket	Palace Street	(01638) 667200	tic.newmarket@forest-heath.gov.uk
Northampton	The Royal & Dernage Theatre	(01604) 838800	northampton.tic@northamptonshire enterprise.ltd.uk
Oswestry	Mile End	(01691) 662488	tic@oswestry-bc.gov.uk
Oundle	14 West Street	(01832) 274333	oundletic@east-northamptonshire.gov.uk
Peterborough	3-5 Minster Precincts	(01733) 452336	tic@peterborough.gov.uk
Ripley	Market Place	(01773) 841488	touristinformation@ambervalley.gov.uk
Ross-on-Wye	Edde Cross Street	(01989) 562768	tic-ross@herefordshire.gov.uk
Rugby	Rugby Art Gallery Museum & Library	(01788) 533217	visitor.centre@rugby.gov.uk
Saffron Walden	Market Square	(01799) 510444	tourism@uttleford.gov.uk
Shrewsbury	The Square	(01743) 281200	visitorinfo@shrewsbury.gov.uk
Sleaford	Carre Street	(01529) 414294	tic@n-kesteven.gov.uk
Solihull	Homer Road	(0121) 704 6130	artscomplex@solihull.gov.uk
Southwold	69 High Street	(01502) 724729	southwold.tic@waveney.gov.uk
Stafford	Market Street	(01785) 619619	tic@staffordbc.gov.uk
Stoke-on-Trent	Victoria Hall, Bagnall Street	(01782) 236000	stoke.tic@stoke.gov.uk
Stowmarket	The Museum of East Anglian Life	(01449) 676800	tic@midsuffolk.gov.uk
Stratford-upon-Avon	Bridgefoot	0870 160 7930	stratfordtic@shakespeare-country.co.uk
Sudbury	Market Hill	(01787) 881320	sudburytic@babergh.gov.uk
Swadlincote	West Street	(01283) 222848	Jo@sharpespotterymuseum.org.uk
Tamworth	29 Market Street	(01827) 709581	tic@tamworth.gov.uk
Warwick	Jury Street	(01926) 492212	touristinfo@warwick-uk.co.uk
Witham	61 Newland Street	(01376) 502674	ticwitham@braintree.gov.uk
Woodbridge	Station Buildings	(01394) 382240	wtic@suffolkcoastal.gov.uk
Worcester	High Street	(01905) 728787	touristinfo@cityofworcester.gov.uk

*seasonal opening

**calls to this number are charged at premium rate

enjoyEngland.com

★★★

SELF CATERING

Ratings you can trust

Wherever you see a quality rating sign, you can be sure that one of Enjoy England's professional assessors has been there before you, checking the place on your behalf – and will be there again, because every place with a national rating is assessed annually.

The star ratings reflect the quality that you're looking for when booking accommodation. All properties have to meet an extensive list of minimum requirements to take part in the scheme. From there, increased levels of quality apply. For instance, you'll find acceptable quality at one star, good to very good quality at three star and exceptional quality at five star establishments.

Quite simply, the more stars, the higher the overall level of quality you can expect to find. Establishments at higher rating levels also have to meet some additional requirements for facilities.

Minimum entry requirements include the following:

- High standards of cleanliness throughout
- Clear pricing and booking conditions
- Local information to help you make the best of your stay
- Comfortable accommodation with a range of furniture to meet your needs
- Colour television (where signal available) at no extra charge
- Kitchen equipped to meet all essential requirements.

Many self-catering establishments have a range of accommodation units in the building or on the site, and in some cases the individual units may have different star ratings. In such cases, the entry shows the range available.

where to stay in
Central England

All place names in the blue bands are shown on the maps at the front of this guide.

A complete listing of all Enjoy England assessed accommodation covered by this guide appears at the back.

Accommodation symbols

Symbols give useful information about services and facilities. On page 7 you can find a key to these symbols.

ABBERLEY, Worcestershire Map ref 4A3

★★★
SELF CATERING

Units 4
Sleeps 1–4

LOW SEASON PER WK
£175.00–£235.00

HIGH SEASON PER WK
£300.00–£400.00

Old Yates Cottages, Worcester

contact Mr & Mrs Richard & Sarah Goodman, Old Yates Cottages, Stockton Road, Abberley, Worcester WR6 6AT **t** (01299) 896500 **e** oldyates@aol.com

oldyatescottages.co.uk GUEST REVIEWS · SPECIAL OFFERS · REAL-TIME BOOKING

open All year
payment Credit/debit cards, cash, cheques
nearest shop 1 mile
nearest pub 2 miles

Cosy cottages in tranquil surroundings amidst beautiful countryside. A personal welcome awaits you. Convenient for exploring the Midlands and Welsh Borders. Contact us for colour brochure.

ONLINE MAP

Unit General
Leisure

ABBOTS BROMLEY, Staffordshire Map ref 4B3

★★★★
SELF CATERING

Units 6
Sleeps 2–10

LOW SEASON PER WK
£140.00–£365.00

HIGH SEASON PER WK
£350.00–£990.00

Blithfield Lakeside Barns, Rugeley

contact Mrs Maxine Brown, PG & MJ Brown, St Stephens Hill Farm, Steenwood Lane, Admaston, Rugeley WS15 3NQ **t** (01889) 500234 **e** maxine.brown@lineone.net

blithfieldlakesidebarns.co.uk

open All year
payment Cash, cheques, euros
nearest shop 2 miles
nearest pub 2 miles

Superb lakeside barn conversions on organic dairy farm overlooking Blithfield Reservoir, two miles from Abbots Bromley. All units have breathtaking views of the water, lakeside patios, en suite facilities and oak beams. Close to Alton Towers and Peak District. Trout and carp fishing. Walking on site, cycling and riding nearby. Excellent local pubs and restaurants.

ONLINE MAP

Unit General Leisure

ALCESTER, Warwickshire Map ref 2B1

★★★★
SELF CATERING & SERVICED APARTMENTS

Units 2
Sleeps 2–14

LOW SEASON PER WK
Min £350.00

HIGH SEASON PER WK
Max £1,680.00

Dorset House Cottage and Dorset House, Alcester

contact Mr & Mrs B Thatcher, Church Street, Alcester B49 5AJ **t** (01789) 762856
e dorsethouseaccommodation.co.uk

dorsethouseaccommodation.co.uk

open All year
payment Credit/debit cards, cash, cheques
nearest shop less than 0.5 miles
nearest pub less than 0.5 miles

Located in the centre of Alcester's historic conservation area. House and cottage are fully restored listed buildings, each well equipped and furnished with antiques. Secluded courtyard and long, walled garden lead to River Arrow and open countryside beyond. Range of shops, restaurants and other amenities within easy walking distance. Parking for four cars.

SAT NAV *B49 5AJ*

Unit General Leisure

ALDEBURGH, Suffolk Map ref 3C2

★★★★
SELF CATERING

Units 1
Sleeps 8

LOW SEASON PER WK
£450.00–£650.00

HIGH SEASON PER WK
£800.00–£1,250.00

Short breaks/long weekends available throughout the year. Discounts/last-minute deals for just couples or small groups.

3 Crespigny Road, Aldeburgh

contact Mrs J Alexander, The Old Rectory, Old Church Road, Melton, Woodbridge IP13 6DH
t (01394) 383822 **e** jenniealexander@btinternet.com

aldeburghescapes.co.uk SPECIAL OFFERS

open All year
payment Cash, cheques
nearest shop less than 0.5 miles
nearest pub less than 0.5 miles

No 3 is like the Tardis! Bungalow recently refurbished (2007) to high specification providing fantastic holiday accommodation. Sleeps eight: two king-sized doubles and two twin-bedded rooms all en suite. Modern kitchen, comfy TV lounge, large dining and sun room with sliding patio doors. Large, sunny back garden. Ample parking.

SAT NAV *IP15 5HA* **ONLINE MAP**

Unit General

ALDEBURGH, Suffolk Map ref 3C2

★★★
SELF CATERING

Units 1
Sleeps 6

LOW SEASON PER WK
£175.00–£475.00

HIGH SEASON PER WK
£475.00–£750.00

Short breaks/long weekends available throughout the year. Last-minute deals ideal for couples who want to 'get away'.

The Cottage, Crag Path, Aldeburgh

contact Mrs J Alexander, The Old Rectory, Old Church Road, Melton, Woodbridge IP13 6DH
t (01394) 383822 **e** jennialexander@btinternet.com

aldeburghescapes.co.uk SPECIAL OFFERS

open All year
payment Cash, cheques
nearest shop less than 0.5 miles
nearest pub less than 0.5 miles

Wonderful seafront cottage with amazing views of the sea. French doors opening onto Crag Path from dining room. Slees four to six. Two double bedrooms, two shower rooms (one en suite). First-floor sitting room overlooking the beach (double sofa bed). Parking outside property on Crag Path.

SAT NAV *IP15 5BS* **ONLINE MAP**

Unit General

ALDEBURGH, Suffolk Map ref 3C2

★★★★
SELF CATERING

Units 1
Sleeps 1–6

LOW SEASON PER WK
Min £350.00

HIGH SEASON PER WK
Max £750.00

Hall Cottage, Aldeburgh

contact Mrs Miriam Buchanan, Loomswood Farm, Hasketon, Woodbridge IP13 6JW **t** 07889 020654
e miriam.buchanan@gressinghamfoods.co.uk

loomscottages.co.uk

Hall Cottage, Aldeburgh is a three-bedroom semi-detached cottage recently built in period style. It offers spacious accommodation for six.

open All year
payment Cash, cheques
nearest shop 0.5 miles
nearest pub 0.5 miles

Unit General Leisure

ALDEBURGH, Suffolk Map ref 3C2

★★★★
SELF CATERING

Units 1
Sleeps 1–6

LOW SEASON PER WK
£299.00–£435.00

HIGH SEASON PER WK
£399.00–£899.00

Special offers and lower prices for less than four people.

Lower Thellusson, Aldeburgh

contact Mrs Claire Gawthrop, East Green Farm, Kelsale, Saxmundham IP17 2PH **t** (01728) 602316
e claire@eastgreen.co.uk

eastgreencottages.co.uk SPECIAL OFFERS

open All year
payment Cash, cheques
nearest shop less than 0.5 miles
nearest pub less than 0.5 miles

Situated in the heart of Aldeburgh, just 40yds from the beach, shops, restaurants and pubs. A spacious, secluded, south-facing house set in its own mature gardens with sun terrace, conservatory and ample parking. Three twin bedrooms.

Unit General Leisure

ALDEBURGH, Suffolk Map ref 3C2

★★★
SELF CATERING

Units 1
Sleeps 12–14

LOW SEASON PER WK
£1,400.00

HIGH SEASON PER WK
£2,000.00

Weekend and midweek bookings welcome.

Orlando, Aldeburgh

contact Mr Peter Hatcher, Martlesham Hall, Church Lane, Woodbridge IP12 4PQ **t** (01394) 382126
e orlando@hatcher.co.uk

hatcher.co.uk/orlando

open All year
payment Cash, cheques, euros
nearest shop less than 0.5 miles
nearest pub less than 0.5 miles

Orlando is a spacious, six-bedroom house adjacent to the beach with magnificent, panoramic views of the sea. The house is well equipped with all modern facilities. Open-plan kitchen with Aga and dining area. Two living rooms on two floors, four bathrooms. Ideal for three families. Free Wi-Fi broadband.

Unit General Leisure

Place index

If you know where you want to stay, the index by place name at the back of the guide will give you the page number listing accommodation in your chosen town, city or village. Check out the other useful indexes too.

ALDEBURGH, Suffolk Map ref 3C2

★★★★
SELF CATERING

Units 1
Sleeps 8

LOW SEASON PER WK
£350.00–£550.00

HIGH SEASON PER WK
£550.00–£1,000.00

Short breaks and long weekends available throughout the year. Discounts/last-minute deals for just couples or small groups.

Peach House, Wentworth Road, Aldeburgh

contact Mrs J Alexander, The Old Rectory, Old Church Road, Melton, Woodbridge IP13 6DH
t (01394) 383822 **e** jennialexander@btinternet.com

aldeburghescapes.co.uk SPECIAL OFFERS

open All year
payment Cash, cheques
nearest shop less than 0.5 miles
nearest pub less than 0.5 miles

Fantastic holiday accommodation. Sleeps seven. One king-sized bedroom with en suite facilities. Two double bedrooms, one of which has en suite shower, the other shares a large bathroom with the single bedroom. Large kitchen/diner and utility. Comfy TV lounge and secluded patio that gets the evening sun. Pretty private garden and kitchen. Patio for alfresco dining.

SAT NAV *IP15 5BB* **ONLINE MAP**

Unit General P

ALDEBURGH, Suffolk Map ref 3C2

★★★
SELF CATERING

Units 1
Sleeps 4

LOW SEASON PER WK
£150.00–£375.00

HIGH SEASON PER WK
£475.00–£600.00

Short breaks/long weekends available throughout the year. Last-minute deals for couples who want to 'get away'.

The Studio, King Street, Aldeburgh

contact Mrs J Alexander, The Old Rectory, Old Church Road, Woodbridge IP13 6DH
t (01394) 383822 **e** jennialexander@btinternet.com

aldeburghescapes.co.uk SPECIAL OFFERS

open All year
payment Cash, cheques
nearest shop less than 0.5 miles
nearest pub less than 0.5 miles

The Studio is light and airy, and sleeps four in a double bedroom and a twin-bedded room. There is a large bathroom which includes a separate corner shower. The smart kitchen/diner leads into a large, comfy double-bayed sitting room overlooking the high street. Entrance and studio's private garage in King Street.

SAT NAV *IP15 5AJ* **ONLINE MAP**

Unit General P

ALDEBURGH, Suffolk Map ref 3C2

★★★–★★★★
SELF CATERING

Units 12
Sleeps 2–10

LOW SEASON PER WK
Min £294.00

HIGH SEASON PER WK
Max £1,312.00

Short breaks, max 4 nights (incl Christmas and New Year, excl high season).

Thorpeness Apartments and Houses, Thorpeness

contact Mrs Lynda Griffin, Thorpeness Golf Club and Hotel, Thorpeness IP16 4NH **t** (01728) 452176
e info@thorpeness.co.uk

thorpeness.co.uk

open All year
payment Credit/debit cards, cash, cheques
nearest shop less than 0.5 miles
nearest pub less than 0.5 miles

Family apartments and houses, some with sea views. Beach, cycling and wonderful walks make up this perfect holiday. Discounted golf and tennis, excluding July and August. See website for details of individual apartments.

Unit General P Leisure

ALFORD, Lincolnshire Map ref 4D2

★★★
SELF CATERING
Units 1
Sleeps 4

LOW SEASON PER WK
£150.00–£220.00

HIGH SEASON PER WK
£280.00–£420.00

Rigsby Wold Cottage, Alford

contact Barbara Read, Rigsby House, Rigsby LN13 0AL **t** (01507) 463404
e billread2001@yahoo.com

rigsbywoldcottage.co.uk REAL-TIME BOOKING

open All year
payment Cash, cheques
nearest shop 2 miles
nearest pub 2 miles

Renovated Victorian cottage, double-glazed heated porch, kitchen/diner, lounge, cloakroom with laundry facilities. Two bedrooms, corner bath, independent shower. Wonderful countryside views, delightful birdsong, ideal for walking and cycling. Two miles to market town of Alford with its manor house and windmill. Eight miles to sandy beaches.

ONLINE MAP

Unit TV DVD General P S Leisure

ALFORD, Lincolnshire Map ref 4D2

★★★★
SELF CATERING
Units 4
Sleeps 2–6

LOW SEASON PER WK
£135.00–£245.00

HIGH SEASON PER WK
£270.00–£490.00

Woodthorpe Hall Country Cottage, Alford

contact Mrs Stubbs, Woodthorpe Hall Country Cottage, Woodthorpe, Alford LN13 0DD
t (01507) 450294 **e** enquiries@woodthorpehallleisure.co.uk

woodthorpehallleisure.co.uk

Cottages overlooking golf course. Central heating, TV and video, dishwasher, washer/dryer, fridge/freezer, microwave and telephone. Fishing, garden and aquatic centre, restaurant and bar.

open All year
payment Credit/debit cards, cash, cheques
nearest shop less than 0.5 miles
nearest pub less than 0.5 miles

Unit TV DVD General P S Leisure

ALPORT, Derbyshire Map ref 4B2

★★★★
SELF CATERING
Units 1
Sleeps 4

LOW SEASON PER WK
£450.00–£599.00

HIGH SEASON PER WK
£750.00–£899.00

Rock Cottage, Bakewell

contact Ms Janet O'Sullivan, Estate Office, Haddon Hall, Bakewell DE45 1LA **t** (01629) 810910
e janet@haddonhall.co.uk

Rock Cottage provides a very comfortable and beautifully furnished holiday home, situated on the Haddon Estate. Conveniently located for visiting Haddon Hall and Chatsworth.

open All year
payment Credit/debit cards, cash, cheques
nearest shop 1 mile
nearest pub 1 mile

Unit TV DVD General P S Leisure

ALRESFORD, Essex Map ref 3B2

★★★
SELF CATERING
Units 1
Sleeps 1–2

LOW SEASON PER WK
Min £150.00

HIGH SEASON PER WK
Min £230.00

Creek Lodge, Colchester

contact Mrs Patricia Mountney, Creek Lodge, Ford Lane, Colchester CO7 8BE **t** (01206) 825411

Tranquil riverside cottage set in extensive landscaped gardens, perfectly situated for sailing, walking and birdwatching. Only five miles from historic Colchester.

open All year
payment Cash, cheques
nearest shop 0.75 miles
nearest pub 0.75 miles

Unit TV General P

Using map references

Map references refer to the colour maps at the front of this guide.

ALSOP-EN-LE-DALE, Derbyshire Map ref 4B2

★★★★
SELF CATERING

Units 2
Sleeps 2–4

LOW SEASON PER WK
£280.00–£375.00

HIGH SEASON PER WK
£375.00–£450.00

Church Farm Cottages, Alsop en le Dale, Ashbourne

contact Mrs Christine Duffell, Church Farm, Alsop en le Dale DE6 1QP **t** (01335) 390216
e enquiries@churchfarmholidaycottages.co.uk

churchfarmholidaycottages.co.uk

Nestling at the head of one of the most beautiful, but undiscovered dales of the Peak District National Park. Our limestone barn, converted into two topsy turvy cottages, overlooks a cobbled yard, hills and copses.

open All year
payment Credit/debit cards, cash, cheques
nearest shop 7 miles
nearest pub 2 miles

Unit General P S Leisure

ALTON, Staffordshire Map ref 4B2

★★★–★★★★★
SELF CATERING

Units 10
Sleeps 2–6

LOW SEASON PER WK
£319.00–£559.00

HIGH SEASON PER WK
£379.00–£809.00

Quarry Walk Park, Alton, Stoke-on-Trent

contact Mr Ian Millican, Coppice Lane, Stoke-on-Trent ST10 1RQ **t** (01538) 723412
e quarry@quarrywalkpark.co.uk

quarrywalklodges.co.uk SPECIAL OFFERS

open All year
payment Credit/debit cards
nearest shop 1 mile
nearest pub 1 mile

For self-catering accommodation near Alton Towers and the Peak District, our lodges are set in an Area of Outstanding Natural Beauty in the Staffordshire Moorlands. Quarry Walk, with its luxurious log cabins, each with its own hot tub, is the ideal base to take a break in the countryside.

Unit General P S Leisure

ALTON, Staffordshire Map ref 4B2

★★★
SELF CATERING

Units 6
Sleeps 2–8

LOW SEASON PER WK
£250.00–£450.00

HIGH SEASON PER WK
£450.00–£600.00

The Raddle Inn, Stoke-on-Trent

contact Mr Peter Wilkinson, Quarry Bank, Hollington, Stoke-on-Trent ST10 4HQ **t** (01889) 507278
e peter@logcabin.co.uk

logcabin.co.uk

A public house/restaurant, set in the countryside, with a log cabin overlooking Croxden Abbey.

open All year
payment Credit/debit cards

Unit General P S Leisure

Don't forget www.

Web addresses throughout this guide are shown without the prefix www. Please include www. in the address line of your browser.
If a web address does not follow this style it is shown in full.

ASHBOURNE, Derbyshire Map ref 4B2

★★★★–★★★★★
SELF CATERING

Units 3
Sleeps 2–16

LOW SEASON PER WK
£373.00–£546.00

HIGH SEASON PER WK
£443.00–£1,000.00

Ancestral Barn, Ashbourne

contact Mrs Sue Fowler, Ancestral Barn, Church Farm, Stanshope, Nr Alstonefield, Ashbourne DE6 2AD **t** (01335) 310243 **e** sue@fowler89.fsnet.co.uk

dovedalecottages.co.uk

open All year
payment Cash, cheques
nearest shop 3 miles
nearest pub 1 mile

Idyllic country cottage, cosy and warm, nestling in a truly peaceful setting. Also our Ancestral Barn with luxurious canopy beds (two king-size), all en suite bathrooms, full of old-world charm, character and medieval ambience, with polished floors, rich colours and antiques. Rambles from door to Dales. Organic farm near Dovedale.

Unit TV DVD General P S Leisure

ASHBOURNE, Derbyshire Map ref 4B2

★★★★
SELF CATERING

Units 1
Sleeps 1–5

LOW SEASON PER WK
£175.00–£275.00

HIGH SEASON PER WK
£275.00–£425.00

The Nook, Kniveton, Ashbourne

contact Mrs Susan Osborn, c/o Barracca, Ivydene Close, Leicester LE9 7NR **t** (01455) 842609 **e** susan.osborn1@btinternet.com

come.to/thenook REAL-TIME BOOKING

A 250-year-old stone cottage in a conservation area, modernised but retaining a cottage charm, cosy and welcoming. Central village location near to pub serving meals. 2.5 miles from Ashbourne and Carsington Water.

open All year
payment Cash, cheques, euros
nearest shop 2 miles
nearest pub less than 0.5 miles

Unit TV SC DVD General S Leisure

ASHBOURNE, Derbyshire Map ref 4B2

★★★★
SELF CATERING

Units 2
Sleeps 2–6

LOW SEASON PER WK
£225.00–£430.00

HIGH SEASON PER WK
£430.00–£720.00

20% reduction for 2 adults booking a 3-bedroom cottage only using 1 bedroom (off-peak only).

Paddock House Farm Holiday Cottages, Alstonefield, Ashbourne

contact Mr Mark Redfern, Paddock House Farm Holiday Cottages, Alstonefield, Ashbourne DE6 2FT **t** (01335) 310282 **e** info@paddockhousefarm.co.uk

paddockhousefarm.co.uk

open All year
payment Cash, cheques
nearest shop 1.5 miles
nearest pub 1.5 miles

Luxury holiday cottages in the heart of the Peak District National Park. Cottages have either three bedrooms, two bedrooms or one bedroom. Wonderful views of the open countryside in a very peaceful location. Excellent attractions, including Alton Towers, Chatsworth and Dovedale. Pets allowed in three cottages.

Unit TV SC DVD General P S Leisure

Has every property been assessed?
All accommodation in this guide has been rated for quality, or is awaiting assessment, by a professional national tourist board assessor.

For **key to symbols** see page 7

ASHBOURNE, Derbyshire Map ref 4B2

★★★★
SELF CATERING

Units 39
Sleeps 2–8

LOW SEASON PER WK
£270.00–£550.00

HIGH SEASON PER WK
£370.00–£1,095.00

Midweek and weekend breaks available all year round (excl Christmas and New Year).

Sandybrook Country Park, Ashbourne

contact Reception, Pinelodge Holidays, Sandybrook Country Park, Buxton Road, Ashbourne DE6 2AQ **t** (01335) 300000 **e** sandybrook@pinelodgeholidays.co.uk

pinelodgeholidays.co.uk/sandybrook.ihtml GUEST REVIEWS · SPECIAL OFFERS

open All year
payment Credit/debit cards, cash, cheques
nearest shop 1 mile
nearest pub less than 0.5 miles

Set in the former grounds of Sandybrook Hall, an elegant, 19thC manor house with woodland walks and wonderful views. Luxurious, fully equipped pine lodges furnished to the highest standards. Heated indoor swimming pool with spa and sauna, indoor and outdoor play areas, restaurant and bar.

ONLINE MAP

Unit TV SC DVD General P S
Leisure

ASHBOURNE, Derbyshire Map ref 4B2

★★★★★
SELF CATERING

Units 1
Sleeps 2–4

LOW SEASON PER WK
£400.00–£450.00

HIGH SEASON PER WK
£500.00–£600.00

Thorpe Cloud View, Ashbourne

contact Mr Raymond Neilson, Thorpe Cloud View, Thorpe House, Thorpe, Ashbourne DE6 2AW
t (01335) 350215 **e** rayneilson@aol.com

a1peak.com

open All year
payment Cash, cheques
nearest shop 3 miles
nearest pub 0.5 miles

You are invited to a luxury, 18thC, detached stone barn conversion on a beautiful four-acre estate. Enjoy exclusive use of the opulent indoor swimming pool and jacuzzi. Breathtaking views of the mountains at Dovedale. Ideally located for walking, cycling, watersports, Alton Towers and many historic houses.

Unit TV DVD General P S Leisure

ASHBOURNE, Derbyshire Map ref 4B2

★★★★
SELF CATERING

Units 1
Sleeps 1–4

LOW SEASON PER WK
£200.00–£300.00

HIGH SEASON PER WK
£300.00–£400.00

Turlow Fields Farm, Hognaston, Ashbourne

contact Mandy & Adrian Hunter, Barnclose Cottage, Turlow Fields Farm, Ashbourne DE6 1PW
t (01335) 370834 **e** aahunter@uk2.net

open All year
payment Cash, cheques
nearest shop 1.5 miles
nearest pub 1 mile

Cottage on small family farm. One double bedroom, one with bunk bed (can be separated), full underfloor heating, private garden with beautiful views, private picnic areas, farm walks (with many animals to see). Carsington Water is a short, quiet walk away, and Ashbourne and Dovedale a five- to ten-minute drive.

Unit TV DVD General P S Leisure

ASHBOURNE, Derbyshire Map ref 4B2

★★★★-★★★★★
SELF CATERING

Units 4
Sleeps 2–4

LOW SEASON PER WK
£200.00–£350.00

HIGH SEASON PER WK
£275.00–£500.00

Yeldersley Hall, Ashbourne

contact Mr Andrew Bailey, Yeldersley Hall, Yeldersley, Ashbourne DE6 1LS **t** (01335) 343432

Flats in a stable block and east wing of a Georgian country house, standing in 12 acres of grounds. Ashbourne is two miles away.

open All year
payment Cash, cheques

Unit General P Leisure

ASHBY-DE-LA-ZOUCH, Leicestershire Map ref 4B3

★★★★
SELF CATERING

Units 1
Sleeps 2–5

LOW SEASON PER WK
Min £275.00

HIGH SEASON PER WK
Min £320.00

Norman's Barn, Ashby-de-la-Zouch

contact Mrs Isabel Stanley, Norman's Barn, Ingles Hill Farm, Burton Road, Ashby-de-la-Zouch LE65 2TE **t** (01530) 412224 **e** isabel_stanley@hotmail.com

normansbarn.co.uk

open All year
payment Cash, cheques
nearest shop 0.5 miles
nearest pub 0.5 miles

Luxuriously appointed barn conversion incorporating minstrels' gallery. Both double bedrooms en suite. On working farm including 130 acres of woodland walks. Easy access to M42, NEC, Calke Abbey and Castle Donington Park/Airport.

Unit General P Leisure

ASHTON, Northamptonshire Map ref 2C1

★★★★
SELF CATERING

Units 1
Sleeps 4–6

LOW SEASON PER WK
Min £350.00

Vale Farm House, Northampton

contact Mrs Zanotto, Vale Farm House, Stoke Road, Northampton NN7 2JN **t** (01604) 863697
e teresa@valefarmhouse.co.uk

valefarmhouse.co.uk

A comfortable self-catering guest annexe set in extensive farm grounds with riding stables, located in the village of Ashton between Northampton and Milton Keynes.

open All year
payment Cash, cheques, euros
nearest shop 7 miles
nearest pub 0.5 miles

Unit General 6 P Leisure

ATHERSTONE, Warwickshire Map ref 4B3

★★★★
SELF CATERING

Units 7
Sleeps 1–7

LOW SEASON PER WK
£295.00–£580.00

HIGH SEASON PER WK
£330.00–£680.00

Hipsley Farm Cottages, Atherstone

contact Mrs Ann Prosser, Hipsley Farm Cottages, Waste Farm, Hurley Common, Hurley CV9 2LR
t (01827) 872437 **e** ann@hipsley.co.uk

hipsley.co.uk

open All year
payment Credit/debit cards, cash, cheques, euros
nearest shop 1.75 miles
nearest pub 1 mile

Superb cottages carefully converted from old farm barns, each individually furnished to the highest standards. Full central heating and all linen and towels included, fully equipped laundry. Enjoy the putting green, barbecue, lovely farm walks. Within easy reach of theatres, castles, cathedrals and museums of Stratford, Warwick, Lichfield and Birmingham.

SAT NAV *CV9 2HS*

Unit General
Leisure

AYLSHAM, Norfolk Map ref 3B1

★★★★
SELF CATERING

Units 1
Sleeps 4

LOW SEASON PER WK
£325.00–£395.00

HIGH SEASON PER WK
£425.00–£575.00

Drabblegate River Cottage, Aylsham

contact Mr Peter Norton, 54 Drabblegate, Aylsham NR11 6LR **t** (01263) 732126
e bookings@norfolkrivercottage.co.uk

norfolkrivercottage.co.uk GUEST REVIEWS • SPECIAL OFFERS

Lovely beamed Norfolk cottage overlooking the River Bure. Woodburner in inglenook, double bedroom with en suite, bedroom with king-size or twin beds and nice bathroom. Spacious kitchen and separate dining room. Storage heaters.

open All year
payment Cash, cheques
nearest shop 1 mile
nearest pub 1 mile

Unit General Leisure

BACTON, Norfolk Map ref 3C1

★★★
SELF CATERING

Units 1
Sleeps 2–6

LOW SEASON PER WK
Min £238.00

HIGH SEASON PER WK
Min £550.00

Primrose Cottage, Bacton

contact Mr & Mrs Allan Epton, Coast Road, Norwich NR12 0EW **t** (01692) 650667
e holiday@cablegap.co.uk

cablegap.co.uk

open 16 February to 2 January
payment Credit/debit cards, cash, cheques
nearest shop less than 0.5 miles
nearest pub less than 0.5 miles

Newly completed two-bedroom bungalow at Cable Gap Holiday Park. Kitchen/diner/living area with sofa bed. One double and one twin room, large wetroom with walk-in shower. Fully equipped, double-glazed and centrally heated. Cable Gap is a quiet park where the owners play a major role in the day-to-day running.

Unit General

Where are the maps?

Colour maps can be found at the front of the guide. They pinpoint the location of all accommodation found in the regional sections.

BADLEY, Suffolk Map ref 3B2

★★★★
SELF CATERING

Units 1
Sleeps 7

LOW SEASON PER WK
£239.50–£399.00

HIGH SEASON PER WK
£295.00–£560.00

Singles weekend breaks to include a fantastic black tie ball or dinner disco. See website www.acrosstheroom.co.uk

The Lodge, Badley, Stowmarket

contact Ms Eleanor De Goni Parks, Doves Barn, Stowmarket Road, Badley, Stowmarket IP6 8RJ
t (01449) 722800 **e** info@acrosstheroom.co.uk

welcomecottages.co.uk

open All year
payment Cash
nearest shop 1 mile
nearest pub 1 mile

This extremely attractive detached barn conversion is stylishly furnished and offers excellent facilities. Set in the heart of the Suffolk countryside, this immaculate property provides the perfect touring base. Includes lounge, kitchen/diner, two double bedrooms. Special weekend rates available.

Unit General P Leisure

BAKEWELL, Derbyshire Map ref 4B2

★★★★
SELF CATERING

Units 1
Sleeps 1–4

LOW SEASON PER WK
£220.00–£294.00

HIGH SEASON PER WK
£422.00–£485.00

Cartwheels, Bakewell

contact Pat Heawood, 2 Leyfield Road, Dore S17 3EE **t** 07821 858640
e julianheawood@yahoo.co.uk

cottageguide.co.uk/cartwheels SPECIAL OFFERS

open All year
payment Cash, cheques, euros
nearest shop less than 0.5 miles
nearest pub less than 0.5 miles

Elegantly furnished, old stone-built cottage in heart of Derbyshire's Peak District. In beautiful Bakewell, a peaceful backwater overlooking the town, but only five minutes' walk to the centre. Two bedrooms, multi-fuel burner, big, exposed oak beam in lounge. Special parking permit provided.

Unit General Leisure

BAKEWELL, Derbyshire Map ref 4B2

★★★
SELF CATERING

Units 1
Sleeps 1–2

LOW SEASON PER WK
£180.00–£220.00

HIGH SEASON PER WK
£220.00–£300.00

The Garden Lodge, Youlgrave, Nr Bakewell

contact Mrs Irene Shimwell, The Garden Lodge, c/o Crimble House, Main Street, Youlgrave, Bakewell DE45 1UW **t** (01629) 636568 **e** irene.shimwell@hotmail.co.uk

thegardenlodgeyoulgrave.co.uk

Recently refurbished one bedroom converted architect's studio set in a private garden with views over Bradford Dale. All mod cons. A perfect base for a couple to explore the Peak District.

open All year
payment Cash, cheques
nearest shop less than 0.5 miles
nearest pub less than 0.5 miles

Unit General P

What if I need to cancel?

It's advisable to check the proprietor's cancellation policy at the time of booking in case you have to change your plans.

BAKEWELL, Derbyshire Map ref 4B2

★★★–★★★★
SELF CATERING

Units **11**
Sleeps **2–10**

LOW SEASON PER WK
£207.00–£663.00

HIGH SEASON PER WK
£393.00–£1,499.00

20% off midweek breaks outside school holidays. Last-minute special offers subject to availability. Call for details.

Haddon Grove Farm Cottages, Bakewell

contact Mr James Viner, Haddon Grove Farm Cottages, 58 Crescent Road, Sheffield S7 1HN
t 0845 634 4163 **e** haddongrovefarm@blueyonder.co.uk

haddongrovefarmcottages.co.uk GUEST REVIEWS · SPECIAL OFFERS

open All year
payment Credit/debit cards, cash, cheques
nearest shop 3 miles
nearest pub 2 miles

Newly renovated farmhouse and ten cottages with indoor heated swimming pool and games room set in three acres just outside Bakewell overlooking Lathkill Dale and beautiful countryside. Perfect setting for a perfect Peak District holiday. Ideal for groups, families, get-togethers and special occasions.

ONLINE MAP

Unit General Leisure

BAMFORD, Derbyshire Map ref 4B2

★★★★★
SELF CATERING

Units **2**
Sleeps **2–6**

LOW SEASON PER WK
£395.00–£525.00

HIGH SEASON PER WK
£730.00–£900.00

Ladybower Apartments, Hope Valley

contact Mr John Illingworth, Lady Bower Apartments, Ashopton Road, Hope Valley S33 0AZ
t (01433) 651361 **e** enquiries@ladybowerapartments.co.uk

ladybowerapartments.co.uk

open All year
payment Credit/debit cards, cash, cheques
nearest shop 0.5 miles
nearest pub 0.5 miles

Set in a glorious location, Ladybower apartments offer all the ingredients for a memorable holiday in the heart of the beautiful Peak District National Park. These stunning new apartments offer guests the luxury of material comforts on the inside and nature's wonderful landscape outside.

Unit General Leisure

BAMFORD, Derbyshire Map ref 4B2

★★★★
SELF CATERING

Units 3
Sleeps 1–4

LOW SEASON PER WK
£280.00–£350.00

HIGH SEASON PER WK
£400.00–£490.00

Shatton Hall Farm Cottages, Hope Valley

contact Mrs Angela Kellie, Shatton Hall Farm Cottages, Shatton Hall Farm, Shatton, Hope Valley S33 0BG **t** (01433) 620635 **e** ahk@peakfarmholidays.co.uk

peakfarmholidays.co.uk SPECIAL OFFERS · REAL-TIME BOOKING

open All year
payment Credit/debit cards, cash, cheques, euros
nearest shop 1.5 miles
nearest pub 1.5 miles

Comfortable barn-converted cottages, each with own garden or terrace, on this 'out of the way', beautifully situated farmstead, with good access. Waymarked woodland walks, trout lake, tennis court and gardens of interest, open National Garden Scheme. Each cottage has double and twin-bedded rooms and good-size living areas with open fires.

ONLINE MAP

Unit General P
Leisure

BARNOLDBY LE BECK, North East Lincolnshire Map ref 4D1

★★★★
SELF CATERING

Units 3
Sleeps 2–6

LOW SEASON PER WK
£175.00–£200.00

HIGH SEASON PER WK
£250.00–£320.00

Grange Farm Cottages & Riding School, Grimsby

contact Jo & Sue Jenkins, Grange Farm Cottages & Riding School, Waltham Road, Barnoldby le Beck DN37 0AR **t** (01472) 822216 **e** sueuk4000@netscape.net

grangefarmcottages.com SPECIAL OFFERS

Even non-horse riders can appreciate the tranquillity of Grange Farm Cottages. Each highly-equipped cottage has one twin and one double bedroom – a real home from home. Riding can be arranged.

open All year
payment Cash, cheques
nearest shop 2 miles
nearest pub 0.5 miles

Unit General P Leisure

BARROW UPON SOAR, Leicestershire Map ref 4C3

★★★
SELF CATERING

Units 1
Sleeps 4–6

LOW SEASON PER WK
£360.00–£390.00

HIGH SEASON PER WK
£360.00–£450.00

Kingfisher Cottage, Loughborough

contact Mr Matthews, 114 Main Street, Woodhouse Eaves, Loughborough LE12 8RZ
t (01509) 890244 **e** nikkidavid@aol.com

Semi-detached roadside cottage comprising two reception rooms, two bedrooms, two bathrooms and rear garden to canal. Quiet part of village, convenient for shops and transport. Friendly pub nearby.

open All year
payment Cash, cheques
nearest shop less than 0.5 miles
nearest pub less than 0.5 miles

Unit General 3 P
Leisure

BAWDSEY, Suffolk Map ref 3C2

★★★★★
SELF CATERING

Units 1
Sleeps 6

LOW SEASON PER WK
£484.00–£515.00

HIGH SEASON PER WK
£493.00–£917.00

Tailors House, Bawdsey, Woodbridge

contact Mr & Mrs Rawdon & Pat Saunders, Coach House, 24a The Street, Bawdsey, Nr Woodbridge IP12 3AJ **t** (01394) 411459 **e** tailors.house@tiscali.co.uk

open All year
payment Cash, cheques
nearest shop 1 mile
nearest pub 1 mile

Spacious beamed village house with inglenook fireplaces, ten minutes' walk from sea. Take foot ferry to Felixstowe or watch the sunset over the River Deben at the Ramsholt Arms. Sleeps six, lounge, dining room, kitchen, two double bedrooms en suite, one twin, bathroom, enclosed garden, pub/shop one mile. All year, holidays/short breaks.

SAT NAV *IP12 3AJ*

Unit TV SC DVD General P S
Leisure

BAYTON, Worcestershire Map ref 4A3

★★★★
SELF CATERING

Units 2
Sleeps 2–3

LOW SEASON PER WK
£180.00–£230.00

HIGH SEASON PER WK
£230.00–£280.00

WALKERS WELCOME CYCLISTS WELCOME

Church House, Kidderminster

contact Ms Maggie Gregory, Bayton, Kidderminster DY14 9LP **t** (01299) 832304
e churchhouse1@tiscali.co.uk

churchhousebayton.co.uk

Charming, period, spacious ground-floor one-bedroom accommodation. Glorious views on edge of quiet village. Ideal for walking, cycling and touring.

open All year except Christmas
payment Cash, cheques
nearest shop 1.5 miles
nearest pub 1 mile

Unit TV DVD General 4 P S Leisure

BELPER, Derbyshire Map ref 4B2

★★★
SELF CATERING

Units 1
Sleeps 1–7

LOW SEASON PER WK
Min £420.00

HIGH SEASON PER WK
Max £485.00

WALKERS WELCOME CYCLISTS WELCOME

Chevin View, Belper

contact Mrs Tracey Sowerby, Pennoch Hiron Farm, Cemetery Road, Belper DE56 1EJ
t 07773 197783 **e** traceysowerby@hotmail.com

spacelocations.co.uk GUEST REVIEWS • SPECIAL OFFERS

A luxury 200-year-old listed cottage, with a contemporary design, retaining original character features such as an open stone hearth and beamed ceilings. Situated in a quiet, central location.

open All year
payment Credit/debit cards, cash, cheques, euros
nearest shop less than 0.5 miles
nearest pub less than 0.5 miles

Unit TV SC DVD General P S Leisure

Country Code always follow the Country Code

- Be safe – plan ahead and follow any signs
- Leave gates and property as you find them
- Protect plants and animals, and take your litter home
- Keep dogs under close control
- Consider other people

BELPER, Derbyshire Map ref 4B2

★★★★
SELF CATERING

Units 1

LOW SEASON PER WK
Min £240.00

HIGH SEASON PER WK
Max £450.00

Fleet Cottage, Belper

contact Mr & Mrs Best, 66 The Fleet, Belper DE56 1NW **t** (01773) 823240 **e** janebest@inweb.co.uk

fleetcottage.fusiveweb.co.uk

open All year except Christmas
payment Credit/debit cards
nearest shop less than 0.5 miles
nearest pub less than 0.5 miles

Renovated 18thC Grade II Listed cottage, was formerly a beer house and staging inn and later a nailmaker's shop. Beamed throughout with stone-flagged floor. Lovely views and many walks from the door.

SAT NAV *DE56 1NW*

Unit General

BEWDLEY, Worcestershire Map ref 4A3

★★★★
SELF CATERING

Units 1
Sleeps 4

LOW SEASON PER WK
£300.00–£375.00

HIGH SEASON PER WK
£380.00–£475.00

Fern Cottage, Bewdley

contact Mrs Jenny Robbins, Park Lane, Bewdley DY12 2ER **t** 07899 797535
e bookings@ferncottagebewdley.co.uk

ferncottagebewdley.co.uk REAL-TIME BOOKING

A completely rebuilt cosy cottage, conveniently situated an easy walk from Bewdley's pubs, shops, restaurants, the River Severn and beautiful open countryside. Two en suite bedrooms. Private fishing by arrangement.

open All year
payment Credit/debit cards, cash, cheques, euros
nearest shop less than 0.5 miles
nearest pub less than 0.5 miles

Unit General Leisure

BEWDLEY, Worcestershire Map ref 4A3

★★★
SELF CATERING

Units 1
Sleeps 1–4

LOW SEASON PER WK
£195.00–£245.00

HIGH SEASON PER WK
£290.00–£390.00

Manor Holding, Bewdley

contact Mr & Mrs Nigel & Penny Dobson-Smyth, 32 Church Street, Hagley, Stourbridge DY9 0NA
t 07970 260010 **e** nds@landscapeconsultancy.freeserve.co.uk

Secluded 17thC farmhouse in tranquil, ancient forest (National Nature Reserve) laced with traffic-free foot, cycle and bridle paths. Enchanting, rolling countryside sprinkled with historic market towns. Near Birmingham, Ironbridge and Ludlow. GPS reference given upon booking of farmhouse.

open All year
payment Cash, cheques
nearest shop 2 miles
nearest pub 2 miles

Unit General Leisure

BEWDLEY, Worcestershire Map ref 4A3

★★★★★
SELF CATERING

Units 1
Sleeps 2

LOW SEASON PER WK
£320.00

HIGH SEASON PER WK
£420.00

The Old Barn, Bewdley

contact Mrs Jill Price, The Old Barn, Lye Head Cottage, Bewdley DY12 2UR **t** (01299) 269350
e jill_price@btinternet.com

theoldbarnbewdley.co.uk

Spacious, pretty cottage in rural location situated 0.25 miles from Wyre Forest and two miles from the Georgian riverside town of Bewdley. The cottage sleeps two. Cyclists and walkers welcome.

open All year
payment Cash, cheques
nearest shop 0.75 miles
nearest pub less than 0.5 miles

Unit General Leisure

BIGGIN-BY-HARTINGTON, Derbyshire Map ref 4B2

★★★★
SELF CATERING

Units 3
Sleeps 2

LOW SEASON PER WK
£260.00–£280.00

HIGH SEASON PER WK
£420.00–£450.00

Biggin Grange, Biggin-by-Hartington, Buxton

contact Mrs Jane Henry, Biggin by Hartington, Buxton SK17 0DJ **t** (01298) 687254
e henrys@biggingrange.co.uk

biggingrange.co.uk

open All year
payment Credit/debit cards, cash, cheques
nearest shop 2 miles
nearest pub 0.5 miles

Located in rural countryside in the grounds of the owners' 135-acre property, Biggin Grange offers complete peace and seclusion. The immaculate cottages have all been converted to a very high standard and are centrally located. All cottages have a private patio or garden with uninterrupted views of Biggin Dale.

SAT NAV *SK17 0DJ*

Unit General P S Leisure

BILLERICAY, Essex Map ref 3B3

★★★★★
SELF CATERING

Units 1
Sleeps 1–6

LOW SEASON PER WK
£500.00–£1,000.00

HIGH SEASON PER WK
£630.00–£1,100.00

5% discount for stays of 4 weeks/ 10% discount for stays of 8 weeks against 2-/ 3-bedroom options.

Pump House Apartment, Billericay

contact Mr John Bayliss, Pump House, Church Street, Billericay CM11 2TR **t** (01277) 656579
e johnwbayliss@btinternet.com

thepumphouseapartment.co.uk GUEST REVIEWS • REAL-TIME BOOKING

open All year
payment Credit/debit cards, cash, cheques, euros
nearest shop 0.75 miles
nearest pub 0.5 miles

The apartment is on two floors and luxuriously furnished, with air-conditioning. The accommodation comprises two living rooms, fully fitted kitchen/diner and the option of one, two or three bedrooms with one, two or three bath/shower rooms. Guests have use of heated outdoor pool (May to September), hot tub, gazebo and gardens. Personal supervision.

ONLINE MAP

Unit General P S
Leisure

BLAXHALL, Suffolk Map ref 3C2

★★★★
SELF CATERING

Units 1
Sleeps 1–4

LOW SEASON PER WK
£283.00

HIGH SEASON PER WK
£489.00

Primrose Cottage, Blaxhall

contact Mrs Harriet Hunter Blair, Hunter Blair Holiday Lets, Forward Green, Stowmarket IP14 5HU
t (01449) 711433 **e** enquiries@primrosecottageblaxhall.co.uk

primrosecottageblaxhall.co.uk SPECIAL OFFERS

Primrose Cottage is a charming cottage in the rural village of Blaxhall. It is furnished with lovely furniture and fittings. Private enclosed garden; a perfect holiday retreat.

open All year
payment Cash, cheques
nearest shop 2 miles
nearest pub 0.5 miles

Unit General P S Leisure

Do you have access needs?

Look for the National Accessible Scheme symbols if you have special hearing, visual or mobility needs. An index of accommodation participating in the scheme can be found at the back of this guide.

BOSTON, Lincolnshire Map ref 3A1

★★★★–★★★★★
SELF CATERING
Units 8
Sleeps 1–5
LOW SEASON PER WK
£320.00–£350.00
HIGH SEASON PER WK
£440.00–£490.00

Tastes of Lincolnshire welcome pack on weekly stays.

Elms Farm Cottages, Boston

contact Carol Emerson, Elms Farm Cottages, The Elms, Hubberts Bridge, Boston PE20 3QP
t (01205) 290840 & 07887 652021 **e** carol@elmsfarmcottages.co.uk

elmsfarmcottages.co.uk

open All year
payment Credit/debit cards, cash, cheques
nearest shop 2 miles
nearest pub less than 0.5 miles

Relax and enjoy the peaceful Lincolnshire countryside at Elms Farm Cottages with level access, woodburning stoves, en suite bedrooms and shower rooms suitable for wheelchairs. All cottages are fully equipped and furnished to a high standard. Winner of East Midlands Self Catering Holidays and Lincolnshire Tourism Accommodation of the Year 2007/8.

SAT NAV *PE20 3QP*

Unit General
Leisure

BOSTON, Lincolnshire Map ref 3A1

★★★
SELF CATERING
Units 1
Sleeps 1–4
LOW SEASON PER WK
£160.00–£250.00
HIGH SEASON PER WK
£250.00–£360.00

Somercotes, Sutterton

contact Mrs Margaret Sharp, Somercotes, Inish Fail, Orchard Close, East Hendred, Wantage OX12 8JJ **t** (01235) 833367 **e** m.l.r.sharp@btinternet.com

somercotes.biz

A comfortable bungalow with its own very large, private lawned garden and ample parking. Near to local shops and public houses. Restaurant in village.

open All year
payment Cash, cheques
nearest shop 0.5 miles
nearest pub less than 0.5 miles

Unit General

BRANCASTER, Norfolk Map ref 3B1

★★★
SELF CATERING
Units 1
Sleeps 1–6
LOW SEASON PER WK
£299.00–£545.00
HIGH SEASON PER WK
£399.00–£659.00

Cheal Cottage, Brancaster, King's Lynn

contact Mrs Janet Harrison, Field House, Little Lane, Surfleet PE11 4AZ **t** (01775) 680513

Modern, well-appointed and -equipped bungalow with three bedrooms, two bathrooms and enclosed south-facing garden and patio. Quiet location, ample parking. Beach and sailing nearby.

open All year
payment Cash, cheques
nearest shop 0.5 miles
nearest pub 0.5 miles

Unit General Leisure

BRANCASTER, Norfolk Map ref 3B1

★★★
SELF CATERING
Units 4
Sleeps 7–10
LOW SEASON PER WK
£485.00–£615.00
HIGH SEASON PER WK
£965.00–£1,250.00

Thompson Brancaster Farms, Burnham Market

contact Mrs Jane Thompson, The Hall, Brancaster, King's Lynn PE31 8AF **t** (01485) 210000
e jet@brancasterhall.co.uk

tbfholidayhomes.co.uk

Tastefully restored flint and brick farm cottages near Brancaster and Burnham Market. Fitted kitchens, linen and logs supplied. Laundry, television, patio, barbecue, tennis and stairgates.

open All year
payment Credit/debit cards, cash, cheques

Unit General
Leisure

BRANCASTER STAITHE, Norfolk Map ref 3B1

★★★–★★★★
SELF CATERING

Units 2
Sleeps 2–6

LOW SEASON PER WK
£240.00–£375.00

HIGH SEASON PER WK
£325.00–£750.00

Short breaks (weekend and midweek) available during low season or at short notice; minimum 3 nights.

Vista And Carpenters Cottages, Brancaster Staithe

contact Mrs Gloria Smith, Dale View, Main Road, Brancaster Staithe, King's Lynn, Norfolk PE31 8BY
t (01485) 210497

open All year
payment Cash, cheques
nearest shop 0.5 miles
nearest pub 0.5 miles

These lovely cottages enjoy one of the best views along the Norfolk coast (see picture). Walking down the cottage gardens you meet the saltmarsh and the Norfolk coastal path. The cottages have exposed beams and open fires as well as central heating throughout. Close to amenities. Pets welcome.

Unit General P Leisure

BRIDGNORTH, Shropshire Map ref 4A3

★★★★
SELF CATERING

Units 1
Sleeps 6

LOW SEASON PER WK
£360.00–£425.00

HIGH SEASON PER WK
£425.00–£590.00

Astbury Falls – Lodge 6, Bridgnorth

contact Mrs Jane Priest, 16 Elmhurst, Bridgnorth WV15 5DJ **t** (01746) 761622 **e** jlet05@hotmail.com

Luxury pine lodge on small select site. One double and two twin bedrooms, two bathrooms, fully equipped kitchen, comfortable open-plan living area. Decking overlooking lakes.

open All year
payment Cash, cheques
nearest shop 3 miles
nearest pub 0.5 miles

Unit General P Leisure

BRIDGNORTH, Shropshire Map ref 4A3

★★★★
SELF CATERING

Units 1
Sleeps 4

LOW SEASON PER WK
£300.00–£400.00

HIGH SEASON PER WK
£500.00–£600.00

Forge Cottage, Bridgnorth

contact Mr Dennis Price, Apley Forge, Bridgnorth WV16 4RZ **t** (01746) 762110
e apleyest@btconnect.com

apleyestate.com SPECIAL OFFERS

open All year
payment Cash, cheques, euros
nearest shop 7 miles
nearest pub 2 miles

Forge Cottage is a two-bedroom period cottage in the Severn Gorge. The property has been totally refurbished and benefits from full oil-fired central heating, ensuring a warm welcome all year round. Please go to Holiday Letting link on website for further details.

ONLINE MAP

Unit General 6 P Leisure

Check the maps for accommodation locations

Colour maps at the front pinpoint all the places where accommodation is featured within the regional sections of this guide. Pick your location and then refer to the place index at the back to find the page number.

BRIDGNORTH, Shropshire Map ref 4A3

★★★
SELF CATERING

Units 1
Sleeps 1–2

LOW SEASON PER WK
Min £140.00

HIGH SEASON PER WK
Min £180.00

The Granary, Bridgnorth

contact Mrs Sarah Allen, The Granary, The Old Vicarage, Vicarage Road, Dittons Priors, Bridgnorth WV16 6SP **t** (01746) 712272 **e** allens@oldvicditton.freeserve.co.uk

Farm granary in unspoilt South Shropshire countryside. Bridgnorth within easy reach, Ludlow 16 miles. Studio sitting room, bedroom, kitchen, bathroom. Excellent walking.

open All year
payment Cash, cheques
nearest shop 0.5 miles
nearest pub 0.5 miles

Unit General Leisure

BRIDGNORTH, Shropshire Map ref 4A3

★★★★
SELF CATERING

Units 1
Sleeps 4

LOW SEASON PER WK
£250.00–£350.00

HIGH SEASON PER WK
£350.00–£450.00

Whitford, Bridgnorth

t (01746) 764945 **e** whitford34@hotmail.com

bridgnorthholidaycottage.com

Built around 1650, this home sleeps four, is fully centrally heated and located just one street away from the centre of the lively market town of Bridgnorth.

open All year
payment Cash, cheques
nearest shop less than 0.5 miles
nearest pub less than 0.5 miles

Unit General

BRIGSLEY, North East Lincolnshire Map ref 4D1

★★★★
SELF CATERING

Units 4
Sleeps 3–4

LOW SEASON PER WK
£350.00–£400.00

HIGH SEASON PER WK
£350.00–£400.00

Prospect Farm Country Cottages, Brigsley

contact Mrs Janet Speight, Waltham Road, Brigsley DN37 0RQ **t** (01472) 826491
e prospectfarm@btconnect.com

prospectfarm.co.uk SPECIAL OFFERS

open All year
payment Credit/debit cards, cash, cheques
nearest shop 1 mile
nearest pub 1 mile

Prospect Farm is situated down a long, leafy lane which opens out onto an expanse of fields with horses grazing. A sense of peace and tranquillity surrounds the cottages. Humberside Airport 20 minutes. Ideally situated for the Lincolnshire Wolds and the seaside town of Cleethorpes.

SAT NAV *DN37 0RQ*

Unit General P Leisure

BRUISYARD, Suffolk Map ref 3C2

★★★★
SELF CATERING

Units 1
Sleeps 20

LOW SEASON PER WK
£2,500.00

HIGH SEASON PER WK
£5,500.00

Bruisyard Hall, Saxmundham

contact Mr Robert Rous, Dennington Hall Farms, Dennington IP13 8AU **t** (01728) 663205
e dennington@farmline.com

bruisyardhall.co.uk

Once a priory of the Poor Clares, this beautiful Grade II Listed house now provides all the comforts for a family holiday in secluded countryside with meadows to the front and moat and fish behind. Some en suite rooms. Ideal for weekend house parties. Also available for midweek breaks.

open All year
payment Cash, cheques

Unit General P Leisure

BURNHAM THORPE, Norfolk Map ref 3B1

★★★
SELF CATERING

Units 1
Sleeps 8–10

LOW SEASON PER WK
Min £600.00

Highfield, King's Lynn

contact Valerie Southerland, Highfield, Whitehall Farm, King's Lynn PE31 8HN **t** (01328) 738416
e barrysoutherland@aol.com

whitehallfarm-accommodation.com

A large, very spacious property, with excellent views over open countryside. Within four miles of North Norfolk coast and two miles from Burnham market.

open All year
payment Credit/debit cards, cash, cheques
nearest shop 2 miles
nearest pub 1 mile

Unit General P
Leisure

BURY ST EDMUNDS, Suffolk Map ref 3B2

★★★★-★★★★★
SELF CATERING

Units 3
Sleeps 2–6

LOW SEASON PER WK
£325.00–£434.00

HIGH SEASON PER WK
£466.00–£684.00

Culford Farm Cottages, Bury St Edmunds

contact Mr Stephen Flack, Culford Farm Cottages, Culford, Bury St Edmunds IP28 6DS
t (01284) 728334 **e** enquiries@homefarmculford.co.uk

culfordfarmcottages.co.uk GUEST REVIEWS

Unique, well-equipped farm cottages offering a pool, hot tubs (two private), and riverside walks on our peacefully located working farm with easy access to Bury St Edmunds and beyond.

open All year
payment Cash, cheques
nearest shop 2 miles
nearest pub 2 miles

Unit General P
Leisure

BURY ST EDMUNDS, Suffolk Map ref 3B2

★★★★
SELF CATERING

Units 1
Sleeps 1–2

LOW SEASON PER WK
Min £120.00

HIGH SEASON PER WK
Min £170.00

The Dower House Flat, Rattlesden, Bury St Edmunds

contact Mrs Hilary Voysey, The Dower House Flat, Clopton Green, Rattlesden, Bury St Edmunds IP30 0RN **t** (01449) 736332 **e** all@voysey.freeserve.co.uk

tiscover.co.uk

Self-contained flat in rural setting, situated between villages of Rattlesden and Woolpit. Excellent centre for touring Suffolk.

open All year except Christmas and New Year
payment Credit/debit cards
nearest shop 1.5 miles
nearest pub 1.5 miles

Unit General P

BURY ST EDMUNDS, Suffolk Map ref 3B2

★★★★
SELF CATERING

Units 1
Sleeps 1–6

LOW SEASON PER WK
£300.00

HIGH SEASON PER WK
£500.00

Short breaks available low season. 2-person discounts available.

The Old Dairy at West Lodge, Bury St Edmunds

contact Mrs Lynn Cardale, The Old Dairy at West Lodge, Bradfield St George, Bury St Edmunds IP30 0DL **t** (01284) 386327 **e** info@westlodgedairy.co.uk

westlodgedairy.co.uk

open All year
payment Cash, cheques
nearest shop 2 miles
nearest pub 1.5 miles

Sensitively restored, well equipped former dairy wing of Victorian house in parkland near historic market towns. Ground-floor double bedroom with adjacent bathroom. Upstairs double/twin and twin bedrooms, bathroom. Newly refurbished kitchen leads to enclosed courtyard. Sitting room with dining area and view of lake. Tennis court available.

SAT NAV *IP30 0DL* **ONLINE MAP**

Unit General 7 P Leisure

BUXTON, Derbyshire Map ref 4B2

★★★
SELF CATERING

Units 1
Sleeps 1–2

LOW SEASON PER WK
£290.00–£350.00

HIGH SEASON PER WK
£360.00–£450.00

Como, Buxton

contact James Freeman, 9 Lansdowne Road, Buxton SK17 6RR **t** (01298) 24275
e jim.freeman@manchester.ac.uk

luganobreaks.co.uk

Situated in a pleasant residential area close to the town centre. This delightful apartment has been furnished and equipped to a high standard, boasting very cosy accommodation. Off-road parking is available. Sorry, no pets.

open March to October
payment Cash, cheques
nearest shop 0.5 miles
nearest pub 0.5 miles

Unit General P

BUXTON, Derbyshire Map ref 4B2

★★★
SELF CATERING

Units 12
Sleeps 2–10

LOW SEASON PER WK
£270.00–£495.00

HIGH SEASON PER WK
£400.00–£735.00

Weekend and midweek breaks available all year except Christmas and New Year.

Hargate Hall, Wormhill, Buxton

contact Mr Anthony Knox, Hargate Hall, Wormhill, Buxton SK17 8TA **t** (01298) 872591
e info@hargate-hall.co.uk

hargate-hall.co.uk SPECIAL OFFERS • REAL-TIME BOOKING

open All year
payment Credit/debit cards, cash, cheques
nearest shop 3 miles
nearest pub 3 miles

A fine country house set in seven acres of parkland with twelve apartments sleeping 2-10. In total, we can sleep up to 79. Games room, open fires in most apartments, outdoor play area, barbecue area. Superb location for exploring the Peak District.

ONLINE MAP

Unit General P Leisure

BUXTON, Derbyshire Map ref 4B2

★★★
SELF CATERING

Units 1
Sleeps 4

LOW SEASON PER WK
£375.00

HIGH SEASON PER WK
£375.00

Hillside, Buxton

contact Mr David Swain, Hillside, 1 Spencer Road, Buxton SK17 9DX **t** (01298) 25451

Self-contained ground floor flat in quiet area. Seven minutes' walk to Opera House and other amenities. Equipped to highest standard. Sleeps four. Price inclusive – no meters.

open All year
payment Cash, cheques

Unit General P

BUXTON, Derbyshire Map ref 4B2

★★★★
SELF CATERING

Units **8**
Sleeps **2–5**

LOW SEASON PER WK
£340.00–£467.00

HIGH SEASON PER WK
£488.00–£651.00

Contact us for special deals on late availability. 5% discount if you arrive by public transport.

Wheeldon Trees Farm, Earl Sterndale, Buxton

contact Deborah & Martin Hofman, Earl Sterndale, Buxton SK17 0AA **t** (01298) 83219
e stay@wheeldontreesfarm.co.uk

wheeldontreesfarm.co.uk GUEST REVIEWS • SPECIAL OFFERS • REAL-TIME BOOKING

open All year
payment Credit/debit cards, cash, cheques
nearest shop 2.5 miles
nearest pub 1 mile

Relax and explore unspoilt landscapes, picturesque villages and lively market towns. 18thC dairy barn conversion, in quiet and secluded valley with fabulous views. Seven self-catering holiday cottages sleeping up to 28 (4 singles, 8 twins, 4 doubles). Newly refurbished with consideration to the environment. Communal dining and leisure facilities.

SAT NAV *SK17 0AA* **ONLINE MAP**

Unit General Leisure

CALLOW, Herefordshire Map ref 2A1

★★★★
SELF CATERING

Units **2**
Sleeps **4–6**

LOW SEASON PER WK
£190.00–£310.00

HIGH SEASON PER WK
£300.00–£430.00

The Loft and Barn at Warmhearth Cottage, Hereford

contact Louise Weir, The Loft and Barn at Warmhearth, Warmhearth, Callow, Hereford HR2 8DE
t (01432) 371517 & 07864 164938 **e** bookings@warmhearth.net

warmhearth.net SPECIAL OFFERS • REAL-TIME BOOKING

The Loft and Barn offer spacious self-catering accommodation within a converted 17thC barn. They have outstanding panoramic views of the beautiful, unspoilt Herefordshire countryside, yet are a short drive from Hereford city.

open All year
payment Cash, cheques
nearest shop 3 miles
nearest pub 3 miles

Unit General P Leisure

CAMBRIDGE, Cambridgeshire Map ref 2D1

★★★★
SELF CATERING

Units **2**
Sleeps **2–8**

LOW SEASON PER WK
£385.00–£550.00

HIGH SEASON PER WK
£490.00–£695.00

Cambridge Midsummer Apartments, Cambridge

contact Mrs Maria Fasano, Cambridge Midsummer Apartments, 4 Poynters Lodge, Chesterton Road, Cambridge CB4 1JB **t** (01223) 316074 **e** enquiry@worth-house.co.uk

cambridgemidsummerapartments.com GUEST REVIEWS • SPECIAL OFFERS

Luxurious ground-floor apartments sleeping up to four people. Fully equipped and with parking available. Ten minutes' walk to city.

open All year
payment Credit/debit cards, cash, cheques, euros
nearest shop less than 0.5 miles
nearest pub 0.5 miles

Unit General P Leisure

CASTLE ACRE, Norfolk Map ref 3B1

★★★
SELF CATERING

Units **1**
Sleeps **6**

LOW SEASON PER WK
£300.00

HIGH SEASON PER WK
£350.00

Peddars Cottage, Castle Acre

contact Mrs Angela Swindell, St Saviour's Rectory, St Saviour JE2 7NP **t** (01534) 736679
e angelaswindell@googlemail.com

castleacre.org.uk

Delightful cottage-style house in centre of village facing green. Close to castle, priory, church, river, pubs and shops.

open All year
payment Cash, cheques
nearest shop less than 0.5 miles
nearest pub less than 0.5 miles

Unit General P

CASTLE HEDINGHAM, Essex Map ref 3B2

★★★★
SELF CATERING

Units 2

LOW SEASON PER WK
Min £220.00

HIGH SEASON PER WK
Max £360.00

Rosemary Farm, Halstead

contact Mr Garry Ian Henderson, Rosemary Farm, Rosemary Lane, Halstead CO9 3AJ
t (01787) 461653

open All year
payment Cash, cheques
nearest shop 1 mile
nearest pub 1 mile

Rosemary Farm is situated in a quiet country lane within view of Hedingham Castle, former home of the De Veres, Earls of Oxford, and is a convenient base for visiting the many nearby attractions. Cottages in barn conversion offering lounge, kitchen, one and two bedrooms, shower/toilet, tiled flooring throughout, patio area, parking.

Unit General P

CASTLEMORTON, Worcestershire Map ref 2B1

★★★★
SELF CATERING

Units 1
Sleeps 1–5

LOW SEASON PER WK
£257.00–£363.00

HIGH SEASON PER WK
£457.00–£532.00

Notts Farm Cottage, Nr Malvern

contact Ms Sarah Limbrick, Druggers End, Castlemorton, Nr Malvern WR13 6JD **t** (01684) 833380
e sarah.limbrick@highcourt.demon.co.uk

malvernholidaycottage.co.uk

Charming detached barn conversion in idyllic rural setting. Two bedrooms, two bathrooms, four-poster bed, comfortable, spacious and welcoming, ideal two couples. Well behaved dogs welcome. Sorry, no smoking.

open All year
payment Cash, cheques
nearest shop 1 mile
nearest pub 1 mile

Unit General P Leisure

CASTLETON, Derbyshire Map ref 4B2

★★★★★
SELF CATERING

Units 1
Sleeps 6

LOW SEASON PER WK
£493.00–£629.00

HIGH SEASON PER WK
£697.00–£1,250.00

Mullions, Hope Valley

contact Mrs Denise Matthews, Riding House Farm, Castleton S33 8WB **t** (01433) 620257
e denise@riding-house-cottages.co.uk

riding-house-cottages.co.uk SPECIAL OFFERS

An historic and prestigious country property with fine features, log fire, magnificent views. Situated in a quiet position yet close to the village. Sleeps up to six people.

open All year
payment Cash, cheques
nearest shop less than 0.5 miles
nearest pub less than 0.5 miles

Unit General P S
Leisure

Check the maps for accommodation locations

Colour maps at the front pinpoint all the cities, towns and villages where you will find accommodation entries in the regional sections. Pick your location and then refer to the place index at the back to find the page number.

CASTLETON, Derbyshire Map ref 4B2

★★★★★
SELF CATERING

Units 2
Sleeps 2–4

LOW SEASON PER WK
£175.00–£450.00

HIGH SEASON PER WK
£450.00–£540.00

Short breaks available late Sep-Apr (excl Christmas and New Year). Last-minute short breaks may be available in high season – please phone.

Riding House Farm Cottages, Hope Valley

contact Mrs Denise Matthews, Castleton, Hope Valley S33 8WB **t** (01433) 620257
e denise@riding-house-cottages.co.uk

riding-house-cottages.co.uk

open All year
payment Cash, cheques
nearest shop 1 mile
nearest pub 1 mile

Newly converted farm cottages in the heart of the Peak District National Park. One cottage has a queen-size bed, the other has one double and one twin bedroom. Both cottages have two bathrooms and are equipped to a very high standard, with charm, character, stunning location and views.

SAT NAV *S33 8WB*

Unit TV DVD General P S Leisure

CHAPEL-EN-LE-FRITH, Derbyshire Map ref 4B2

★★★★
SELF CATERING

Units 1
Sleeps 9

LOW SEASON PER WK
£400.00–£600.00

HIGH SEASON PER WK
£800.00–£1,250.00

Saffi House, High Peak

contact Ms Carole Coe, Carole Coe Leisure, 3 Cherry Tree Court, Chapel-en-le-Frith SK23 9HF
t 0870 755 9700 **e** carole@saffihouse.co.uk

saffihouse.co.uk

Three-storey, four-bedroom property. All modern amenities, sleeps up to nine persons plus cot. Friday change-over except July and August.

open All year
payment Cash, cheques
nearest shop less than 0.5 miles
nearest pub less than 0.5 miles

Unit TV DVD General P S Leisure

CHESTERFIELD, Derbyshire Map ref 4B2

★★★★★
SELF CATERING

Units 1
Sleeps 2–4

LOW SEASON PER WK
£260.00–£390.00

HIGH SEASON PER WK
£360.00–£580.00

Special offers Nov, Dec, Jan and Feb (excl Christmas and New Year). Short breaks all year. Early booking discounts.

Pear Tree Farm Barn, Rowthorne Village, Chesterfield

contact Mel Copley, Rowthorne Village, Glapwell, Chesterfield S44 5QQ **t** (01623) 811694
e enquiries@peartreefarmbarn.co.uk

peartreefarmbarn.co.uk GUEST REVIEWS • SPECIAL OFFERS • REAL-TIME BOOKING

open All year
payment Cash, cheques
nearest shop 0.5 miles
nearest pub 0.5 miles

Luxury barn conversion in quiet conservation village. One double en suite, and one twin en suite, lounge/diner and kitchen. Full central heating and wood-burning stove. Ten minutes' walk to Hardwick Hall (National Trust). Ideally situated for visiting Peak District (Chatsworth 40 minutes). Pub and shop within walking distance.

ONLINE MAP

Unit TV DVD General P S Leisure

CHESTERFIELD, Derbyshire Map ref 4B2

★★★★
SELF CATERING

Units 1
Sleeps 1–5

LOW SEASON PER WK
£270.00–£290.00

HIGH SEASON PER WK
£300.00–£320.00

Short breaks available Oct-Mar (excl Christmas).

Ploughmans Cottage, Chesterfield

contact Mrs Margaret Fry, Ploughmans Cottage, Low Farm, Main Road, Marsh Lane S21 5RH
t (01246) 435328 **e** ploughmans.cottage@virgin.net

ploughmanscottage.com

open All year
payment Cash, cheques, euros
nearest shop 0.5 miles
nearest pub 0.5 miles

Fresh eggs from our hens, kisses from our llamas, skylarks and woodland walks. This delightful cottage is carefully and attractively maintained. It has a fenced garden with orchard, lawns, flower beds, patio and sandpit. Lovely open views and many places of interest within easy reach.

Unit TV DVD General P Leisure

CHURCH STRETTON, Shropshire Map ref 4A3

★★★★
SELF CATERING

Units 2
Sleeps 4–5

LOW SEASON PER WK
£220.00–£275.00

HIGH SEASON PER WK
£275.00–£375.00

Short breaks available from end Oct-Easter.

Lower Day Cottages, Church Stretton

contact Mr & Mrs Kirkwood, Lower Day House, Church Preen, Church Stretton SY6 7LH
t (01694) 771521 **e** bookings@lowerdayhouse.com

lowerdayhouse.com

open All year
payment Cash, cheques
nearest shop 5 miles
nearest pub 2 miles

Part of an 18thC farm courtyard, sited next to an oak-framed threshing barn. The cottages are tastefully furnished, retaining many original beams and features, with magnificent views of Wenlock Edge. Ideally suited to those seeking the real 'heart of the country'. Sorry, no smoking or pets.

ONLINE MAP

Unit TV SC DVD General P Leisure

CLEOBURY MORTIMER, Shropshire Map ref 4A3

★★★
SELF CATERING

Units 1
Sleeps 1–4

LOW SEASON PER WK
£250.00–£295.00

HIGH SEASON PER WK
£295.00–£395.00

Cherry Lodge, Cleobury Mortimer

contact Mrs Sam Adams, Cherry Cottage, Overwood, Cleobury Mortimer DY14 8LG
t (01299) 271847 **e** adamscherrycottage@yahoo.co.uk

cherry-lodge.co.uk

A beautifully appointed one-bedroom barn conversion offering high quality accommodation, situated within six acres of delightful countryside with equestrian facilities available.

open All year
payment Cash, cheques
nearest shop 3 miles
nearest pub 3 miles

Unit TV DVD General P S Leisure

Where can I get help and advice?

Tourist Information Centres offer friendly help with accommodation and holiday ideas as well as suggestions of places to visit and things to do. You'll find contact details at the beginning of each regional section.

CLEY NEXT THE SEA, Norfolk Map ref 3B1

★★★
SELF CATERING

Units 1
Sleeps 1–7

LOW SEASON PER WK
£240.00–£320.00

HIGH SEASON PER WK
£350.00–£500.00

Archway Cottage, Cley next the Sea

contact Mrs Vickey Jackson, 3a Brickendon Lane, Hertford SG13 8NU **t** (01992) 511303 & (01992) 503196

open All year
payment Cash, cheques

Pretty 18thC flint cottage, well furnished and comfortable, with four bedrooms, two bathrooms and garage. Near village centre, bird sanctuaries and the sea. Also Chantry, another similar cottage in Wells-next-the-Sea. Illustrated brochures available for both cottages.

Unit General

CLEY NEXT THE SEA, Norfolk Map ref 3B1

★★★
SELF CATERING

Units 1

LOW SEASON PER WK
£180.00–£360.00

HIGH SEASON PER WK
£360.00–£540.00

Lavender Cottage, Cley-next-the-Sea, Holt

contact Mrs M Cooke, 9 Binham Road, Warham, Well-next-the-Sea NR23 1NS **t** (01328) 710659
e lavender.cottage@hotmail.co.uk

glavenvalley.co.uk/lavendercottage/cley

A traditional flint cottage standing in the heart of Cley. It is just opposite the famous landmark Cley windmill. The cottage is a ten-minute walk to the beach.

open All year
payment Cheques
nearest shop less than 0.5 miles
nearest pub less than 0.5 miles

Unit General P

CLUN, Shropshire Map ref 4A3

★★★★
SELF CATERING

Units 2
Sleeps 2–4

LOW SEASON PER WK
£270.00–£370.00

HIGH SEASON PER WK
£390.00–£520.00

WALKERS WELCOME
CYCLISTS WELCOME

The Squire Farm, Bucknell

contact Mrs Becky Whitton, The Squire Farm, Bucknell SY7 0BW **t** (01547) 530530
e becky@squirefarm.co.uk

squirefarm.co.uk SPECIAL OFFERS

Two detached cottages on small farm in undisturbed valley. One traditionally beamed with large inglenook fireplace. Second has Japanese-style interior, with hot tub outside. Beautiful scenery and excellent walking.

open All year
payment Cash, cheques
nearest shop 3 miles
nearest pub 3 miles

Unit General P Leisure

CLUNGUNFORD, Shropshire Map ref 4A3

★★★★
SELF CATERING

Units 1
Sleeps 3

LOW SEASON PER WK
£260.00–£335.00

HIGH SEASON PER WK
£380.00–£420.00

WALKERS WELCOME
CYCLISTS WELCOME
PETS! WELCOME

Lavender Cottage, Craven Arms

contact Mrs Karin Clarke, **t** (01588) 660631 **e** kr.clarke@btinternet.com

Lavender Cottage is situated just over five miles outside Craven Arms near the lovely village of Clungunford. A cosy converted barn with one large double and one single bedroom. Full central heating and original features.

open All year
payment Cash, cheques
nearest shop 5 miles
nearest pub 2 miles

Unit General P Leisure

COMBS, Derbyshire Map ref 4B2

★★★★★
SELF CATERING

Units **1**
Sleeps **1–2**

LOW SEASON PER WK
£300.00–£330.00

HIGH SEASON PER WK
£350.00–£415.00

Pyegreave Cottage, High Peak

contact Mr & Mrs Noel & Rita Pollard, Pyegreave Cottage, High Peak SK23 9UX **t** (01298) 813444
e n.pollard@allenpollard.co.uk

holidayapartments.org

open All year
payment Credit/debit cards, cash, cheques, euros
nearest shop 3 miles
nearest pub 0.5 miles

Situated within the Peak District National Park and enjoying spectacular views, this cottage is finished and furnished to a very high standard whilst retaining original oak beams and many other interesting features. Ideal location for walking, golfing, the theatre (Buxton) or simply as an idyllic hideaway.

Unit General P S Leisure

CORPUSTY, Norfolk Map ref 3B1

★★★★★
SELF CATERING

Units **1**
Sleeps **13**

LOW SEASON PER WK
£950.00–£1,000.00

HIGH SEASON PER WK
£1,280.00–£1,700.00

Carr's Barn, Norwich

contact Mrs Marion Anthony, Pound Corner, Elms Lane, Wangford NR34 8RS **t** (01502) 578278
e info@heritagehideaways.com

carrsbarn.co.uk

open All year
payment Credit/debit cards, cash, cheques
nearest shop less than 0.5 miles
nearest pub less than 0.5 miles

A sensitively converted barn in the heart of the North Norfolk countryside between Norwich and the sea at Sheringham. Six bedrooms, four bathrooms including studio bedroom with mezzanine sleeping two-plus-two. Secluded courtyard with garden. Very near Elizabethan Blickling Hall.

Unit General P S Leisure

CRATFIELD, Suffolk Map ref 3C2

★★★★
SELF CATERING

Units **3**
Sleeps **2–10**

LOW SEASON PER WK
£250.00–£455.00

HIGH SEASON PER WK
£365.00–£595.00

Short breaks available by arrangement.

Holly Tree Farm Barns, Halesworth

contact Ms Rachel Boddy, Holly Tree Farm, Bell Green, Cratfield, Halesworth IP19 0DN
t (01986) 798062 **e** hollytreebarns@lycos.co.uk

hollytreebarns.co.uk

open All year
payment Cash, cheques
nearest shop 3 miles
nearest pub 0.5 miles

Unrivalled tranquillity in recently converted barns. Private gardens offer unbroken farmland views. Heritage Coast and unspoiled delights of Suffolk nearby. Short walk to village pub. Eleven acres of meadowland. Dogs welcome. Ample parking. Sky TV, wireless broadband. Each cottage has a sofa bed sleeping two.

Unit General P S
Leisure

For **key to symbols** see page 7

CRATFIELD, Suffolk Map ref 3C2

★★★★
SELF CATERING

Units 4
Sleeps 2–6

LOW SEASON PER WK
£200.00–£310.00

HIGH SEASON PER WK
£265.00–£550.00

Short breaks outside peak season: 3 nights for 60% of weekly price.

School Farm Cottages, Halesworth

contact Mrs Claire Sillett, School Farm, Church Road, Cratfield, Halesworth IP19 0BU
t (01986) 798844 **e** schoolfarmcotts@aol.com

schoolfarmcottages.com SPECIAL OFFERS

open All year
payment Cash, cheques
nearest shop 3 miles
nearest pub less than 0.5 miles

Welcome to our small family farm in Cratfield, a quiet north Suffolk village within easy reach of the Suffolk Heritage Coast. Relax and unwind in unspoilt Suffolk countryside; enjoy the picturesque views and walks. Facilities include pool table, football pitch, children's play area, fishing, large private garden and cycle hire.

ONLINE MAP

Unit General P Leisure

CRAVEN ARMS, Shropshire Map ref 4A3

★★★★
SELF CATERING

Units 5
Sleeps 4–12

LOW SEASON PER WK
£250.00–£600.00

HIGH SEASON PER WK
£450.00–£1,250.00

Upper Onibury Cottages, Craven Arms

contact Mrs Hickman, Upper Onibury Cottages, Upper Onibury, Craven Arms SY7 9AW
t (01584) 856206 **e** info@shropshirecottages.com

shropshirecottages.com

Charming stone barns beautifully furnished, set around central courtyard. Pretty gardens with furniture and gas barbecues. Use of heated indoor swimming pool and tennis court.

open All year
payment Cash, cheques
nearest shop 1.5 miles
nearest pub 0.5 miles

Unit General P Leisure

CRESSBROOK, Derbyshire Map ref 4B2

★★★★
SELF CATERING

Units 3
Sleeps 1–14

LOW SEASON PER WK
Min £275.00

HIGH SEASON PER WK
Max £975.00

Cressbrook Hall Self Catering Cottages, Buxton

contact Mrs Bobby Hull-Bailey, Cressbrook Hall, Cressbrook, Buxton SK17 8SY **t** (01298) 871289
e stay@cressbrookhall.co.uk

cressbrookhall.co.uk

Accommodation with a difference! Self-catering or B&B in magnificent surroundings. Special catering services and leisure facilities ensure a carefree holiday. Colour brochure.

open All year
payment Credit/debit cards, cash, cheques
nearest shop 2 miles
nearest pub 1 mile

Unit General P Leisure

CROMER, Norfolk Map ref 3C1

★–★★★
SELF CATERING

Units 5
Sleeps 2–6

LOW SEASON PER WK
£120.00–£140.00

HIGH SEASON PER WK
£280.00–£395.00

Short breaks available from Oct-Mar, 2-night stay.

Beverley House Holiday Apa, Cromer

contact Mr & Mrs Bob & Sue Collins, Beverley House Holiday Apa, 17 Alfred Road, Cromer NR27 9AN **t** (01603) 505298 & 07960 796309 **e** beverleyhouseapartments@yahoo.co.uk

broadland.com/beverleyhouse

open All year
payment Cash, cheques, euros
nearest shop less than 0.5 miles
nearest pub less than 0.5 miles

Very comfortable Victorian property, housing six well-furnished, warm and cosy self-catering apartments, some with sea view. The property retains many original period features, including marble fireplaces and high ceilings. Shops, pubs, the railway station and coaches are all within ten minutes' walk and there is on-street parking.

SAT NAV *NR27 9AN*

Unit General

CROWLAND, Lincolnshire Map ref 3A1

★★★★
SELF CATERING

Units 1
Sleeps 1–4

LOW SEASON PER WK
£290.00

HIGH SEASON PER WK
£290.00

Short breaks available from 1 night. Discounts for full-week booking. Additional discounts for bookings of 2 or more weeks.

Fen-Acre, Crowland, Peterborough

contact Mr & Mrs Michael & Julie Smith, 19 Barbers Drove, Peterborough PE6 0BE **t** (01733) 211847 **e** julie@fen-acreholidaylet.co.uk

fen-acreholidaylet.com REAL-TIME BOOKING

open All year except Christmas and New Year
payment Cash, cheques
nearest shop less than 0.5 miles
nearest pub 0.5 miles

Self-contained, gas centrally heated, modern apartment sleeps up to four persons. One double bedroom, one double sofa bed. Furnished and equipped to a high standard with all mod cons. All on one level. Parking directly outside. Ten-minute walk to shops, pubs and all village amenities.

Unit General P Leisure

DALLINGHOO, Suffolk Map ref 3C2

★★★★
SELF CATERING

Units 3
Sleeps 2–6

LOW SEASON PER WK
Min £270.00

HIGH SEASON PER WK
Max £800.00

Robins Nest, The Cottage, Carpenter's Shop, Wheelwright's, Dallinghoo

contact Mr Robert Blake, 1a Moorfield Road, Woodbridge IP12 4JN **t** (01394) 382565 & 07901 773545 **e** robert@blake4110.fsbusiness.co.uk

tiscover.co.uk

16thC cottage, converted carpenter's and wheelwright's shops – each giving privacy. Quiet rural location overlooking countryside. Each restored and converted to high standard. Ideal base for many tourist attractions. Brochures.

open All year
payment Cash, cheques
nearest shop 2 miles
nearest pub 2 miles

Unit General 5 P Leisure

Looking for a wide range of facilities?

More stars means higher quality accommodation plus a greater range of facilities and services.

DENGIE, Essex Map ref 3B3

★★★★
SELF CATERING

Units 3
Sleeps 4–6

LOW SEASON PER WK
£260.00–£285.00

HIGH SEASON PER WK
£395.00–£410.00

East Ware Farm, Tillingham, Nr Southminster

contact Mrs Lyn Ponder, Dammerwick Farm, Marsh Road, Burnham-on-Crouch CM0 8NB
t (01621) 786846 **e** lyn.ponder@btinternet.com

eastwarefarm.co.uk

Old barns converted into three fully furnished holiday cottages with en suite accommodation. Games room, courtyard, garages and shared utility room.

open All year
payment Cash, cheques
nearest shop 2 miles
nearest pub 2 miles

Unit General P S Leisure

DUDDENHOE END, Essex Map ref 2D1

★★★★
SELF CATERING

Units 1
Sleeps 2–4

LOW SEASON PER WK
£200.00–£225.00

HIGH SEASON PER WK
£250.00–£300.00

Cosh Cottage, Duddenhoe End, Saffron Walden

contact Mrs Susan Perks, The Cosh, Duddenhoe End, Saffron Walden CB11 4UX **t** (01763) 838880
e susan.perks@virgin.net

A two-bedroom cottage close to the owner's own house. Surrounded by Essex cornfields. Equipped kitchen: cooker, fridge, dishwasher, washer/dryer and microwave. Summer use of swimming pool and tennis court.

open All year
payment Cash, cheques, euros
nearest shop 6 miles
nearest pub 3 miles

Unit General P S Leisure

DUNCHURCH, Warwickshire Map ref 4C3

★★★★
SELF CATERING

Units 1
Sleeps 4

LOW SEASON PER WK
Min £450.00

HIGH SEASON PER WK
Max £650.00

Toft Manor Cottage, Rugby

contact Ms Shirley Bettinson, Toft Manor Cottage, Dunchurch, Rugby CV22 6NR **t** (01788) 810626
e shirley@toft-alpacas.co.uk

toft-alpacas.co.uk

open All year
payment Credit/debit cards, cash, cheques, euros
nearest shop 0.5 miles
nearest pub 0.5 miles

A two-double-bedroomed stable conversion set in the grounds of Toft Manor amongst a prize-winning herd of Toft alpacas. Offers outstanding views across Draycote Water, and beautiful walks amongst the alpacas.

Unit General P S Leisure

EAST RUNTON, Norfolk Map ref 3B1

★★★
SELF CATERING

Units 8
Sleeps 2–6

LOW SEASON PER WK
£220.00–£275.00

HIGH SEASON PER WK
£290.00–£550.00

Poplars Caravan And Chalet, East Runton

contact Mr & Mrs K Parfitt, Poplars Caravan & Chalet Park, East Runton NR27 9PL **t** (01263) 512892
e info@poplarscaravanandchaletpark.co.uk

tiscover.co.uk

Coastal village, brick bungalows set on edge of woodlands in peaceful spacious grounds.

open March to October
payment Cash, cheques
nearest shop 0.5 miles
nearest pub 0.5 miles

Unit General P S Leisure

What shall we do today?

For ideas on places to visit, see the beginning of this regional section or go online at enjoyengland.com.

EDWARDSTONE, Suffolk Map ref 3B2

★★★★
SELF CATERING

Units 2
Sleeps 2–6

LOW SEASON PER WK
Min £300.00

HIGH SEASON PER WK
Max £700.00

Sherbourne Farm Lodge Cottages, Sudbury

contact Mrs Anne Suckling, Sherbourne House Farm, Edwardstone, Sudbury CO10 5PD
t (01787) 210885 **e** enquiries@sherbournelodgecottages.co.uk

sherbournelodgecottages.co.uk

Located on a family farm in picturesque Suffolk, single-storey barn conversions offering quality accommodation. Kitchen/living area, wet room with bath and shower, two bedrooms (double or twin), courtyard and games barn. Disabled facilities throughout.

open All year
payment Cash, cheques
nearest shop less than 0.5 miles
nearest pub less than 0.5 miles

Unit General P Leisure

EDWARDSTONE, Suffolk Map ref 3B2

★★★
SELF CATERING

Units 2
Sleeps 1–4

LOW SEASON PER WK
£200.00–£375.00

HIGH SEASON PER WK
£250.00–£375.00

The White Horse Inn, Edwardstone

contact Mr Tom Norton, The White Horse Edwardstone LLP, The White Horse Inn, Mill Green, Edwardstone CO10 5PX **t** (01787) 211211 **e** john.norton@nortonorganic.co.uk

edwardstonewhitehorse.co.uk

The country's greenest pub, with its own wind turbine, the White Horse is on a quiet lane in Edwardstone. The cottages are located in a small field behind the pub.

open All year
payment Cash, cheques
nearest shop 2 miles

Unit General P Leisure

ELY, Cambridgeshire Map ref 3A2

★★★
SELF CATERING

Units 2
Sleeps 4–6

LOW SEASON PER WK
£380.00–£420.00

HIGH SEASON PER WK
£380.00–£420.00

7 & 9 Lisle Lane, Ely

contact Ken Davis, Forty Farmhouse, Hurdle Drove, West Row, Bury St Edmunds IP28 8RG
t (01353) 675249 & 07858 762721 **e** fortyfarmhouse@btinternet.com

Ideally placed, modern but traditional, two- and three-bedroom terrace town houses with enclosed patio garden and garage. Close to river, cathedral and market square. Private parking and walking distance to railway station.

open All year
payment Cash, cheques
nearest shop less than 0.5 miles
nearest pub less than 0.5 miles

Unit General P Leisure

ELY, Cambridgeshire Map ref 3A2

★★★
SELF CATERING

Units 1
Sleeps 5

LOW SEASON PER WK
£490.00

HIGH SEASON PER WK
£490.00–£560.00

Chiefs St Ely, Ely

contact Mrs P Coates, Cheviot House, Church End, Cambridge CB21 5PA **t** (01223) 290842
e cheviotbob@aol.com

Attractive 1930s renovated cottage-style terraced house in quiet city-centre street. Close to Cathedral and Cromwell's House. Frequent cultural events.

open All year
payment Cash, cheques, euros
nearest shop less than 0.5 miles
nearest pub less than 0.5 miles

Unit General 4 P Leisure

Do you have access needs?

Look for the National Accessible Scheme symbols if you have special hearing, visual or mobility needs.

ERPINGHAM, Norfolk Map ref 3B1

★★★
SELF CATERING

Units 4
Sleeps 2–7

LOW SEASON PER WK
£210.00–£450.00

HIGH SEASON PER WK
£380.00–£700.00

Grange Farm, Erpingham, Norwich

contact Mrs Jane Bell, Grange Farm Holidays, Scarrow Beck Farm, Erpingham, Norwich NR11 7QU
t (01263) 761241 **e** jane.bell5@btopenworld.com

grangefarmholidays.co.uk

A 17thC farmhouse and converted period farm buildings around a courtyard, all in a large garden, in the middle of an 80-acre farm beside a river. Heated indoor swimming pool. Open Christmas and New Year.

open All year
payment Cash, cheques
nearest shop 2 miles
nearest pub 0.75 miles

Unit TV General P S Leisure

EVESHAM, Worcestershire Map ref 2B1

★★★★
SELF CATERING

Units 1
Sleeps 2–6

LOW SEASON PER WK
£425.00–£495.00

HIGH SEASON PER WK
£495.00–£600.00

Thatchers End, Evesham

contact Mr & Mrs Wilson, 60 Pershore Road, Evesham WR11 2PQ **t** (01386) 446269
e trad.accom@virgin.net

http://freespace.virgin.net/trad.accom

open All year
payment Credit/debit cards, cash, cheques, euros
nearest shop less than 0.5 miles
nearest pub less than 0.5 miles

Delightful Grade II Listed thatched black and white cottage with many traditional and original period features. Spacious, tastefully furnished, all modern facilities. Large enclosed garden, patio area, garden furniture. Private and peacefully situated. Ample parking. Ideal touring base. Family-supervised. No pets. Brochures available.

Unit TV General P Leisure

EYE, Suffolk Map ref 3B2

★★★★
SELF CATERING

Units 2
Sleeps 2–6

LOW SEASON PER WK
£120.00–£230.00

HIGH SEASON PER WK
£290.00–£599.00

Log Cabin Holidays, Eye

contact Mr Peter Havers, Athelington Hall, Eye IP21 5EJ **t** (01728) 628233
e info@logcabinholidays.co.uk

logcabinholidays.co.uk SPECIAL OFFERS

open All year
payment Credit/debit cards, cash, cheques
nearest shop 1 mile
nearest pub 3 miles

Situated in an idyllic location, spacious two-bedroom lodge: one double with en suite shower and one twin with verandah and fantastic view. Breathtaking Suffolk Heritage Coast only 25 minutes away.

Unit TV General P S Leisure

It's all quality-assessed accommodation

Our commitment to quality involves wide-ranging accommodation assessment. Ratings and awards were correct at the time of going to press but may change following a new assessment. Please check at time of booking.

EYE KETTLEBY, Leicestershire Map ref 4C3

★★★★
SELF CATERING

Units 1
Sleeps 1–4

LOW SEASON PER WK
£170.00–£250.00

HIGH SEASON PER WK
£280.00–£350.00

Old Guadaloupe Cottage, Eye Kettleby, Melton Mowbray

contact Ms Sue Lomas, Old Guadaloupe, Eye Kettleby, Kirby Lane, Melton Mowbray LE14 2TS
t 07989 960588 **e** sue@suelomas.orengehome.co.uk

oldguadaloupecottage.co.uk

open All year
payment Credit/debit cards, cash, cheques
nearest shop 1 mile
nearest pub 1 mile

Cottage with hot tub. Well equipped, fitted to a high standard. Bedroom with 5ft bed. Lounge with sofa bed. Freeview TV/DVD in lounge and bedroom. Radio/CD player, hairdryer, oven/hob, fridge/freezer, washing machine, microwave. Bathroom has a large shower. On a working farm.

SAT NAV *LE14 2TS*

Unit General P Leisure

FAKENHAM, Norfolk Map ref 3B1

★★★★
SELF CATERING

Units 1
Sleeps 1–8

LOW SEASON PER WK
£340.00–£590.00

HIGH SEASON PER WK
£510.00–£890.00

Small-party reductions and short breaks available – minimum 2 nights – during non-peak times.

Pollywiggle Cottage, West Raynham, Fakenham

contact Mrs Marilyn Farnham-Smith, 79 Earlham Road, Norwich NR2 3RE **t** (01603) 471990
e marilyn@pollywigglecottage.co.uk

pollywigglecottage.co.uk GUEST REVIEWS · SPECIAL OFFERS · REAL-TIME BOOKING

open All year
payment Cash, cheques
nearest shop 4 miles
nearest pub 3 miles

Brimming with character, this pretty, well-equipped home wraps you in its cosy, comfortable interior. Nestled in secluded, rambling flower gardens, Pollywiggle lies on the fringe of a tranquil village 12 miles from the North Norfolk coast. A wealth of amenities and attractions are within an easy drive. Ramblers/cyclists are welcome.

SAT NAV *NR21 7EX* **ONLINE MAP**

Unit General P

FARNSFIELD, Nottinghamshire Map ref 4C2

★★★
SELF CATERING

Units 1
Sleeps 2

LOW SEASON PER WK
£250.00

HIGH SEASON PER WK
£250.00

The Barn, Farnsfield, Newark

contact Mrs Josephine Kitchen, Grange Cottage/The Barn, Main Street, Farnsfield NG22 8EA
t (01623) 882259 **e** jo@grange-cottage.co.uk

grange-cottage.co.uk

In two acres of gardens, The Barn has a double bedroom, bathroom, lounge/kitchen. Parking is behind electric gates. Locally are many village shops and three pubs selling food.

open All year
payment Cash, cheques, euros
nearest shop less than 0.5 miles
nearest pub less than 0.5 miles

Unit General P Leisure

Remember to check when booking

Please remember that all information in this guide has been supplied by the proprietors well in advance of publication. Since changes do sometimes occur it's a good idea to check details at the time of booking.

FINDERN, Derbyshire Map ref 4B2

★★★
SELF CATERING

Units 1
Sleeps 3–4

LOW SEASON PER WK
£250.00–£300.00

HIGH SEASON PER WK
£300.00–£400.00

Pilgrims Cottage, Findern, Derby

contact Mr & Mrs J Noon, 29 Old Hall Road, Littleover DE23 6GG **t** (01332) 769275

17thC cottage adjacent to village green, renovated to the highest standards. Comfortable lounge/dining room, well-equipped modern kitchen and shower room. Two bedrooms. Five miles from city centre.

open All year
payment Cash, cheques, euros
nearest shop less than 0.5 miles
nearest pub less than 0.5 miles

Unit General P Leisure

FOXLEY, Norfolk Map ref 3B1

★★★–★★★★
SELF CATERING

Units 9
Sleeps 3–10

LOW SEASON PER WK
£200.00–£550.00

HIGH SEASON PER WK
£350.00–£860.00

2/3-night breaks available (midweek or weekend) Oct-May, 5 nights Christmas/New Year.

Moor Farm Stable Cottages, Dereham

contact Mr Paul Davis, Moor Farm, Foxley, Dereham NR20 4QP **t** (01362) 688523
e mail@moorfarmstablecottages.co.uk

moorfarmstablecottages.co.uk

open All year
payment Cash, cheques
nearest shop 1 mile
nearest pub 0.5 miles

Located on working farm, a courtyard of two- and three-bedroomed self-catering cottages, all fully equipped and centrally heated, two specially adapted for disabled. Ideally situated for coast, Broads, Norwich, Sandringham. 365 acres of mature woodland adjoining owners' farm in which to walk. Fishing available in owners' lake close by. Pets welcome. Indoor heated swimming pool and spa.

Unit General P Leisure

FRAMLINGHAM, Suffolk Map ref 3C2

★★★★
SELF CATERING

Units 1
Sleeps 4

LOW SEASON PER WK
£199.00–£249.00

HIGH SEASON PER WK
£299.00–£349.00

10% off for 2 weeks or more. Short breaks available all year except Jun, Jul and Aug.

Courtyard Cottage, Framlingham

contact Mrs Louise Berrill, 10 Naunton Road, Woodbridge IP12 4HP **t** (01394) 388481
e info@framcottages.co.uk

framcottages.co.uk GUEST REVIEWS · SPECIAL OFFERS

open All year
payment Cash, cheques
nearest shop less than 0.5 miles
nearest pub less than 0.5 miles

Traditional Victorian cottage centrally situated in the charming market town of Framlingham. A stroll to pubs, shops, castle and mere. Close to Suffolk's Heritage Coast. Sleeps four in one double and one twin. Small secluded courtyard. Parking.

SAT NAV *IP13 9EL*

Unit General 8 P Leisure

CYCLISTS WELCOME

Fancy a cycling holiday?

For a fabulous freewheeling break, seek out accommodation participating in our Cyclists Welcome scheme. Look out for the symbol and plan your route online at nationalcyclenetwork.org.

FRETTENHAM, Norfolk Map ref 3C1

★★★
SELF CATERING

Units 2
Sleeps 1–4

LOW SEASON PER WK
£210.00–£390.00

Glebe Farm, Norwich

contact Mrs Rona Norton, Beck Farm, Off Pound Hill, Frettenham, Norwich NR12 7NF
t (01603) 897641 **e** rona.norton@btinternet.com

glebefarm-cottages.co.uk

We offer two cottages on our farm. Both are set in large gardens and offer well-equipped, comfortable, modern facilities in a picturesque rural setting with views over open countryside.

open All year
payment Cash, cheques
nearest shop 2 miles
nearest pub 1 mile

Unit General P Leisure

GAINSBOROUGH, Lincolnshire Map ref 4C2

★★★★
SELF CATERING

Units 1
Sleeps 1–6

LOW SEASON PER WK
Min £310.00

HIGH SEASON PER WK
Max £630.00

Trent House, Gainsborough

contact Mr & Mrs Knight, Riverside Approach, Gainsborough DN21 2PL **t** (01427) 612886
e knightmi79@btinternet.com

New town house, end of cul-de-sac. House and patio garden overlooking River Trent and countryside. Three bedrooms, one en suite, very well equipped. Child-friendly garden. See trenthouselets.com for details.

open All year except winter.
payment Cheques, euros
nearest shop 0.5 miles
nearest pub 0.5 miles

Unit General 1 P

GORLESTON-ON-SEA, Norfolk Map ref 3C1

★★★
SELF CATERING

Units 1
Sleeps 4

LOW SEASON PER WK
£120.00–£180.00

HIGH SEASON PER WK
£230.00–£310.00

Manor Cottage, Gorleston, Great Yarmouth

contact Mrs Margaret Ward, North Manor House, 12 Pier Plain, Gorleston, Great Yarmouth NR31 6PE **t** (01493) 669845 **e** normanward@tiscali.co.uk

wardm4.fsnet.co.uk GUEST REVIEWS

Edwardian two-bedroomed cottage attached to manor house. Quiet location between high street, beach and harbour. Parking. Near Yarmouth, Hopton, Lowestoft, Broads and nature reserves.

open All year except Christmas and New Year
payment Cash, cheques

Unit General P

GREAT CARLTON, Lincolnshire Map ref 4D2

★★★
SELF CATERING

Units 1
Sleeps 5

LOW SEASON PER WK
£160.00–£220.00

HIGH SEASON PER WK
£240.00–£320.00

Willow Farm, Louth

contact Mr James Clark, Willow Farm, Louth LN11 8JT **t** (01507) 338540

open All year
payment Cash, cheques
nearest shop 4 miles
nearest pub 2 miles

Cosy, detached bungalow in quiet, rural location. High standard of accommodation comprising one single and two twin bedrooms. Fly and coarse fishing available on site. Touring caravans welcome by arrangement. Approximately eight miles from the market town of Louth and the lovely Lincolnshire Wolds. Well situated for Cadwell Park and several golf courses.

Unit General P Leisure

What do the star ratings mean?
Detailed information about star ratings can be found at the back of this guide.

GREAT DODDINGTON, Northamptonshire Map ref 3A2

★★★★★
SELF CATERING

Units 1
Sleeps 2–4

LOW SEASON PER WK
£275.00–£590.00

HIGH SEASON PER WK
£350.00–£725.00

Short breaks available all year. Special Christmas and New Year breaks.

The Old Watermill, Great Doddington, Wellingborough

contact Anne Lowe, The Old Watermill, Hardwater Mill, Hardwater Road, Great Doddington NN29 7TD **t** (01933) 276870 **e** anne@watermillholidays.co.uk

watermillholidays.co.uk GUEST REVIEWS

open All year
payment Cash, cheques
nearest shop 1 mile
nearest pub 1 mile

A charming and historic former watermill, Grade II Listed. The well-equipped self-catering accommodation is on three floors. One four-poster double and one twin bedroom. Centrally heated. Double glazed. Plenty of old elm beams and oak floors. Pets welcome. Car park, garden, riverside walks.

SAT NAV *NN29 7TD* **ONLINE MAP**

Unit General P Leisure

GREAT DUNMOW, Essex Map ref 3B2

★★★
SELF CATERING

Units 3
Sleeps 4–6

LOW SEASON PER WK
£200.00–£350.00

HIGH SEASON PER WK
£300.00–£495.00

Short breaks available all year. Open Christmas, New Year and Easter.

The Granary, Dunmow

contact Mrs Cathy Burton, The Granary, Broxted, Dunmow CM6 2EL **t** (01371) 870821
e moorendfarm@btconnect.com

moorendfarm.com

open All year
payment Credit/debit cards, cash, cheques
nearest shop 4 miles
nearest pub 1 mile

Originally a Victorian granary, the building has now been sympathetically converted into self-contained cottages. Each cottage is extremely spacious and has a double and a twin bedroom, large bathroom, dining area and well-equipped kitchen and is supplied with everything that you may need to make your stay enjoyable.

ONLINE MAP

Unit General P Leisure

GREAT HUCKLOW, Derbyshire Map ref 4B2

★★★★
SELF CATERING

Units 1
Sleeps 2–4

LOW SEASON PER WK
£300.00–£320.00

HIGH SEASON PER WK
£320.00–£370.00

South View Cottage, Buxton

contact Mrs Maureen Waterhouse, c/o Holme Cottage, Windmill SK17 8RE **t** (01298) 871440
e mo@mmwaterhouse.demon.co.uk

cottageguide.co.uk/southviewcottage

Modernised country cottage in the hamlet of Windmill in the middle of the Peak District. Owner-maintained. Furnished and decorated to a high standard. No smoking. Lock-up garage.

open All year
payment Cash, cheques
nearest shop 2 miles
nearest pub 0.5 miles

Unit General P

WALKERS WELCOME

Do you like walking?

Walkers feel at home in accommodation participating in our Walkers Welcome scheme. Look out for the symbol. Consider walking all or part of a long-distance route – go online at nationaltrail.co.uk.

GREAT LONGSTONE, Derbyshire Map ref 4B2

★★
SELF CATERING

Units 1
Sleeps 1–2

LOW SEASON PER WK
Min £165.00

HIGH SEASON PER WK
£260.00–£280.00

Short breaks available – 3/4 nights.

Field House Cottage, Great Longstone, Nr Bakewell

contact Julia Spink, Field House, Moor Road, Great Longstone DE45 1UA **t** (01629) 640103
e juliag@lumina-solns.com

open All year except Christmas and New Year
payment Cash, cheques
nearest shop 0.5 miles
nearest pub less than 0.5 miles

Delightful open-plan, compact barn conversion in heart of Peak District. Fabulous doorstep walks/cycling on Longstone Edge, Monsal Trail etc. Visit Chatsworth, Castleton, Bakewell, Dovedale. Fully equipped kitchen, large modern shower room, spiral stairs to galleried double sleeping platform over lounge, shared garden. Pubs with food and shop within ten minutes' walk.

Unit General P Leisure

HADLEIGH, Suffolk Map ref 3B2

★★★★
SELF CATERING & SERVICED APARTMENTS

Units 1
Sleeps 6

LOW SEASON PER WK
£450.00–£550.00

HIGH SEASON PER WK
£600.00–£700.00

Lodge House, Hadleigh

contact Angela & Rod Rolfe, The Lodge, Hadleigh IP7 5AP **t** (01473) 822458
e r.rolfe@edgehall.co.uk

tiscover.co.uk

open All year
payment Cash, cheques, euros
nearest shop less than 0.5 miles
nearest pub less than 0.5 miles

Tucked away in the delightful walled garden of Edge Hall. Immaculate accommodation, perfect walks, restaurants, inns, shops, all within minutes. Provides a superb location for touring Constable Country and coast. Own patio. Ample parking. Short breaks available. Sleeps six (one twin/double on ground floor), all en suite, (one double, two singles on first floor).

SAT NAV *IP7 5AP*

Unit General P Leisure

HADLEIGH, Suffolk Map ref 3B2

★★★★
SELF CATERING

Units 3
Sleeps 1–8

LOW SEASON PER WK
£359.00–£498.00

HIGH SEASON PER WK
£629.00–£1,054.00

Short breaks available all year excl May and Oct half-terms, school summer holidays, Christmas and New Year.

Wattisham Hall Holiday Cottages, Wattisham, Ipswich

contact Jeremy and Jo Squirrell, Wattisham Hall, Wattisham, Ipswich IP7 7JX **t** (01449) 740240
e enquiries@wattishamhall.co.uk

wattishamhall.co.uk

open All year
payment Cash, cheques
nearest shop 2 miles
nearest pub 2 miles

Our charming barn conversion has beautifully furnished cottages, with exposed beams, oak floors, wood-burning stoves and plenty of character. All are well equipped with Freeview and access to Wi-Fi Internet. Enclosed patio gardens, shared games room and outdoor play area, as well as outdoor hot tub for Tithe Barn and Owls End.

Unit General P Leisure

HANLEY CASTLE, Worcestershire Map ref 2B1

★★★
SELF CATERING

Units 2
Sleeps 2–4

LOW SEASON PER WK
£175.00–£320.00

HIGH SEASON PER WK
£300.00–£460.00

3-day weekend and 4-day midweek breaks available November to March.

Whitehall Farm Holiday Cottages, Worcester

Whitehall Farm Holiday Cottages, Brotheridge Green, Worcester WR8 0BB **t** (01684) 310376
e cgpavey@aol.com

whitehalllettings.co.uk

open All year
payment Cash, cheques
nearest shop 2 miles
nearest pub 1 mile

Located in peaceful fruit-growing countryside between the Malverns and Upton upon Severn, just five minutes' drive from the Three Counties Showground, this beautifully converted 17thC barn embraces you with its old oak beams. It accommodates two (double) and four (double and twin) with facilities for walkers and cyclists.

Unit General 7 P Leisure

HARTINGTON, Derbyshire Map ref 4B2

★★★★
SELF CATERING

Units 2
Sleeps 6

LOW SEASON PER WK
£300.00–£400.00

HIGH SEASON PER WK
£400.00–£550.00

1 Staley Cottage and Victoria House, Buxton

contact Mr & Mrs Oliver, Carr Head Farm, Carr Head Lane, Penistone, Sheffield S36 7GA
t (01226) 762387

open All year
payment Cash, cheques
nearest shop 0.5 miles
nearest pub 0.5 miles

Spacious cottage with three bedrooms (two double, one twin), dining room, lounge, bathroom, shower room/wc and garden. In a pretty village near amenities, shops and restaurants. Also second property. Owner-maintained, established 23 years.

Unit General P Leisure

HARTINGTON, Derbyshire Map ref 4B2

★★★★
SELF CATERING

Units 1
Sleeps 4

LOW SEASON PER WK
£300.00–£350.00

HIGH SEASON PER WK
£375.00–£500.00

Ash Tree Cottage, Hartington, Buxton

contact Ms Clare Morson, Nettletor Farm, Mill Lane, Buxton SK17 0AN **t** (01298) 84247
e nettletorfarm@btconnect.com

Single-storey cottage, sleeps four, private parking for two cars, own contained patio and garden area, ideally located for Hartington village and the picturesque walks into the dales.

open All year
payment Cash, cheques

Unit General P Leisure

PETS! WELCOME

Where is my pet welcome?

Want to take your cherished companion with you on holiday? Proprietors participating in our Welcome Pets! scheme go out of their way to make special provision for you and your pet. Look out for the symbol.

HARTINGTON, Derbyshire Map ref 4B2

★★★★
SELF CATERING

Units 4
Sleeps 2–7

LOW SEASON PER WK
£180.00–£240.00

HIGH SEASON PER WK
£400.00–£650.00

Private farm trail weekend and short breaks available (especially Oct-Easter).

Cruck Cottage and Wolfscote Grange Cottages, Buxton

contact Mrs Jane Gibbs, Hartington, Buxton SK17 0AX **t** (01298) 84342

wolfscotegrangecottages.co.uk REAL-TIME BOOKING

open All year
payment Cash, cheques
nearest shop 2 miles
nearest pub 2 miles

The unique setting overlooking Dove Valley/Dale, with miles of rolling countryside and picture views, sells Wolfcote Cottages as the perfect place to stay. Cruck Cottage – an oak-beamed hideaway. 'No neighbours, only sheep'. Swallows Cottage – en suites, spa bathroom. Both offer comfort and character. Farm trail with freedom to roam. Central to Peak District.

SAT NAV *SK17 0AX*

Unit General P Leisure

HARTINGTON, Derbyshire Map ref 4B2

★★★
SELF CATERING

Units 1
Sleeps 2–3

LOW SEASON PER WK
£200.00–£250.00

HIGH SEASON PER WK
£270.00–£300.00

Short breaks Nov-Apr.

Stable Cottage, Nr Buxton

contact Mrs Veronica Lawrenson, Grove House, Elkstones, Buxton SK17 0LU **t** (01538) 300487
e elkstones@talk21.com

cottageguide.co.uk/peakdistrictcottage

open All year
payment Cash, cheques
nearest shop 3 miles
nearest pub 2 miles

Escape to a cosy, characterful cottage providing quality accommodation and enjoying a peaceful location within small Peak District village, set in attractive surrounding countryside with many walks in nearby Dove/Manifold valleys. Excellent base for visiting the many National Trust properties/gardens in three counties. Enclosed patio garden with sunny aspect.

Unit General P Leisure

HATHERSAGE, Derbyshire Map ref 4B2

★★★
SELF CATERING

Units 1
Sleeps 4–6

LOW SEASON PER WK
Min £250.00

HIGH SEASON PER WK
£250.00–£395.00

Pat's Cottage, Sheffield

contact Mr John Drakeford, Pat's Cottage, 110 Townhead Road, Dore, Sheffield S17 3GB
t (0114) 236 6014 & 07850 200711 **e** johnmdrakeford@hotmail.com

patscottage.co.uk

An attractive 18thC stone cottage, sympathetically refurbished, retaining original features including black beams. On the edge of the Peak District, close to Hathersage and the city of Sheffield.

open All year
payment Cash, cheques
nearest shop less than 0.5 miles
nearest pub less than 0.5 miles

Unit General P Leisure

FAMILIES WELCOME WELCOME FAMILIES

Looking for an ideal family break?

For accommodation offering additional facilities and services for a range of ages and family units, look out for the Families Welcome symbol. Owners of these properties will go out of their way to welcome families.

HATHERSAGE, Derbyshire Map ref 4B2

★★★
SELF CATERING

Units 1
Sleeps 4

LOW SEASON PER WK
£205.00–£235.00

HIGH SEASON PER WK
£275.00–£340.00

St Michael's Cottage, Hope Valley

contact Mr Hanley, Saint Michael's Environmental Education Centre, Main Road, Hathersage, Hope Valley S32 1BB **t** (01433) 650309 **e** stmichaels@nottscc.gov.uk

eess.org.uk

Cosy character cottage with one double and one twin bedroom. Dramatic scenery, walks from the door, close to all amenities.

open All year
payment Cash, cheques
nearest shop less than 0.5 miles
nearest pub less than 0.5 miles

Unit General 3 P

HAUGHLEY, Suffolk Map ref 3B2

★★★–★★★★
SELF CATERING

Units 3
Sleeps 8

LOW SEASON PER WK
£240.00–£320.00

HIGH SEASON PER WK
£300.00–£440.00

Red House Farm Cottages, Stowmarket

contact Mrs Mary Noy, Red House Farm, Haughley, Stowmarket IP14 3QP **t** (01449) 673323 **e** mary@redhousefarmhaughley.co.uk

Delightful, well-equipped cottages on small grassland farm. Ideal for exploring the many attractions in Suffolk, Norfolk and Essex.

open All year except Christmas and New Year
payment Credit/debit cards, cash, cheques
nearest shop 1 mile
nearest pub 1 mile

Unit General P S Leisure

HAYFIELD, Derbyshire Map ref 4B2

★★★★
SELF CATERING

Units 1
Sleeps 1–4

LOW SEASON PER WK
£170.00–£230.00

HIGH SEASON PER WK
£230.00–£260.00

Bowden Bridge Cottage, High Peak

contact Mrs Margrith Easter, Bowden Bridge Cottage, Hayfield, High Peak SK22 2LH **t** (01663) 743975 **e** margrith@btconnect.com

Cottage flat attached to main house, with double bedroom, lounge, kitchen, bathroom. Additional twin bedroom with washbasin available if required. Full central heating. Ideal for a Peak District walking holiday.

open All year
payment Cash, cheques
nearest shop 1 mile
nearest pub 0.5 miles

Unit General P S Leisure

HEMSBY, Norfolk Map ref 3C1

★★★
CHALET

Units 24
Sleeps 2–6

LOW SEASON PER WK
£89.00–£130.00

HIGH SEASON PER WK
£149.00–£340.00

Sunset Holiday Chalets, Hemsby and Scratby, Great Yarmouth

contact Mr Lionel Knights, 7 Green Lane, Great Yarmouth NR30 5EW **t** (01493) 720450

sunsetholidaychalets.co.uk SPECIAL OFFERS

Detached and semi-detached two-bedroom self-catering holiday chalets on holiday parks at Hemsby and Scratby, Great Yarmouth.

open 1 March to 31 October
payment Credit/debit cards, cash, cheques
nearest shop 0.5 miles

Unit General P S Leisure

Using map references

The map references refer to the colour maps at the front of this guide. The first figure is the map number, the letter and figure that follow indicate the grid reference on the map.

HEREFORD, Herefordshire Map ref 2A1

★★★★
SELF CATERING

Units 1
Sleeps 6

LOW SEASON PER WK
£400.00–£550.00

HIGH SEASON PER WK
£600.00–£850.00

Short breaks available all year. Claim a 10% discount by mentioning 'Where to Stay' or VisitBritain.

Castle Cliffe East, Hereford

contact Mr Mark Hubbard & Mr Phil Wilson, Castle Cliffe West, 14 Quay Street, Hereford HR1 2NH **t** (01432) 272096 **e** mail@castlecliffe.net

castlecliffe.net GUEST REVIEWS • SPECIAL OFFERS

open All year
payment Cash, cheques
nearest shop 0.5 miles
nearest pub 0.5 miles

Originally a medieval watergate, Castle Cliffe provides luxury accommodation which is both tranquil and convenient. Set in parkland, it has period furniture, open fires and a south-facing riverside garden. And with shops, restaurants and the cathedral within a few minutes' walk, it is the ideal place to relax and unwind.

ONLINE MAP

Unit TV SC DVD … General … P S
Leisure

HINGHAM, Norfolk Map ref 3B1

★★★★★
SELF CATERING

Units 3
Sleeps 1–12

LOW SEASON PER WK
Min £300.00

Short breaks from Fri-Mon and Mon-Fri.

White Lodge Farm Cottages, Hingham, Norwich

contact Mr & Mrs Tony Richardson, White Lodge Farm, Hardingham Road, Hingham, Norwich NR9 4LY **t** (01953) 850435 **e** vb@whitelodgefarmcottages.co.uk

whitelodgefarmcottages.co.uk GUEST REVIEWS

open All year
payment Cash, cheques
nearest shop 1 mile
nearest pub 1 mile

Self-catering accommodation seldom comes as well appointed as these three luxury cottages situated in the heart of the beautiful Norfolk countryside. The pretty village of Hingham is within walking distance.

ONLINE MAP

Unit TV DVD … General … P S
Leisure

HOLME NEXT THE SEA, Norfolk Map ref 3B1

★★★★
SELF CATERING

Units 1
Sleeps 6

LOW SEASON PER WK
£300.00–£450.00

HIGH SEASON PER WK
£475.00–£800.00

Ideal for summer and winter. Discounts for off-season short breaks, long weekends and two-person occupancy. Pets by arrangement at additional cost.

Broadwater Cottage, Holme next the Sea

contact Mrs Jayne Ransom, Vine Farm, 38 Church Street, Cambridge CB22 5DS **t** (01223) 524821 **e** vine.farm@ntlworld.com

broadwatercottage.co.uk SPECIAL OFFERS

open All year
payment Cash, cheques, euros
nearest shop 3 miles
nearest pub less than 0.5 miles

Comfortable flint, chalk and carrstone cottage in the centre of the village close to an excellent pub/restaurant with garden. The beach is a short walk across open fields with sand dunes and salt marshes beyond. Enclosed garden, conservatory, summerhouse and woodburner. One double and two twin bedrooms, shower room and bathroom. Off-road parking and garage.

SAT NAV *PE36 6LH* **ONLINE MAP**

Unit TV DVD … General … P S Leisure

HOLT, Norfolk Map ref 3B1

★★★
SELF CATERING

Units 1
Sleeps 4

LOW SEASON PER WK
£195.00–£295.00

HIGH SEASON PER WK
£340.00–£420.00

5 Carpenters Cottages, Holt

contact Mr Christopher Knights, The Hollies Farmhouse, Rushmere, Lowestoft NR33 8EP
t (01493) 842289 & (01502) 742022

Attractive 18thC flint and pantile cottage with gravelled garden area, on the edge of a pleasant market town four miles from the coast.

open April to October and Christmas
payment Cash, cheques
nearest shop less than 0.5 miles
nearest pub less than 0.5 miles

Unit General 5 P

HORNCASTLE, Lincolnshire Map ref 4D2

★★★★
SELF CATERING

Units 1
Sleeps 4

LOW SEASON PER WK
Min £400.00

HIGH SEASON PER WK
Min £475.00

Bainvalley Cottages, Horncastle

contact Wendy Harrison, Bainvalley Cottages, Manor Farm, Hemingby LN9 5QF **t** (01507) 578352
e wendy@harrison592.freeserve.co.uk

bainvalleycottages.co.uk

Built in 1910, the cottage is deceptively spacious offering a comfortable holiday home with underfloor heating and a woodburning stove. Situated within the Lincolnshire Wolds Area of Outstanding Natural Beauty. Sleeps four.

open All year
payment Cash, cheques
nearest shop 4 miles
nearest pub 0.5 miles

Unit General P S Leisure

HORNCASTLE, Lincolnshire Map ref 4D2

★★★
SELF CATERING

Units 2
Sleeps 4–6

LOW SEASON PER WK
£210.00–£258.00

HIGH SEASON PER WK
£395.00–£470.00

Special rates for booking both cottages for Christmas, New Year or any other week of the year.

Lincolnshire Wolds Cottages Ltd, Fulletby, Nr Horncastle

contact Mr John Robinson, 401 Brant Road, Waddington, Lincoln LN5 9AH **t** (01522) 876994

woldscottages.co.uk

open All year
payment Cash, cheques
nearest shop 3.5 miles
nearest pub 1.5 miles

Very pleasant converted buildings in the centre of the Lincolnshire Wolds, approximately 25 miles from the coast and Lincoln. The master bedrooms in both cottages have four-poster beds and en suites. Carpenters has its own games room. Seating is available outside with grassed areas for children to play on. An Access Statement is available on request.

Unit General P Leisure

HUNSTANTON, Norfolk Map ref 3B1

★★★★
SELF CATERING

Units 1
Sleeps 1–4

LOW SEASON PER WK
£265.00–£290.00

HIGH SEASON PER WK
£305.00–£475.00

Forget Me Not Cottage, Old Hunstanton, Hunstanton

contact Mr Gary Gibson, 11 Heron Close, Sawbridgeworth CM21 0BB **t** 07957 351250 & 07957 366745 **e** streetsaheadlettings@hotmail.com

holidayhomesnorfolk.co.uk

open All year
payment Cash, cheques
nearest shop less than 0.5 miles
nearest pub less than 0.5 miles

Beautiful two-bedroom cottage to let. Only five minutes' walk to the wide sandy beaches, and close to the extensive championship golf course behind the sand dunes. A charming property with private off-road parking at the rear for one vehicle. A small, enclosed, pretty patio garden is at the rear with patio heaters.

SAT NAV *PE36 6HX*

Unit TV SC DVD P General P Leisure

HUNSTANTON, Norfolk Map ref 3B1

★★★
SELF CATERING

Units 1
Sleeps 8

LOW SEASON PER WK
Min £415.00

HIGH SEASON PER WK
Max £950.00

Malgwyn, Old Hunstanton

contact Mrs Perdita Swift, Church Farm House, Church End, Weston Colville, Cambridge CB21 5PE **t** (01223) 290207 **e** pandp.swift@talktalk.net

cottageguide.co.uk/malgwyn

Within walking distance of a long sandy beach, two sitting rooms, kitchen, shower room, bathroom, one double, one family and one twin/ 5ft double bedroom.

open All year
payment Cash, cheques
nearest shop less than 0.5 miles
nearest pub less than 0.5 miles

Unit TV DVD General P S Leisure

ILMINGTON, Warwickshire Map ref 2B1

★★★★
SELF CATERING

Units 1
Sleeps 1–4

LOW SEASON PER WK
£220.00–£250.00

HIGH SEASON PER WK
£270.00–£300.00

Featherbed Cottage, Shipston-on-Stour

contact Mr David Price, 8 Nellands Close, Ilmington, Shipston-on-Stour CV36 4NF **t** (01608) 682215 **e** featherbedcottage@hotmail.com

Comfortable, well-equipped, two-bedroomed house in village on the edge of Cotswolds overlooking open country. Small garden. Off-season short breaks.

open All year
payment Cash, cheques
nearest shop less than 0.5 miles
nearest pub less than 0.5 miles

Unit TV General P

ILMINGTON, Warwickshire Map ref 2B1

★★★★
SELF CATERING

Units 2
Sleeps 2–4

LOW SEASON PER WK
£390.00–£420.00

HIGH SEASON PER WK
£450.00–£490.00

Special 3-night weekend and 4-night midweek break prices.

Folly Farm Self Catering, Ilmington

contact Mr Bruce McFarlane, Back Street, Ilmington, Shipston-on-Stour CV36 4LJ **t** (01608) 682425
e bruceandpam@follyfarm.co.uk

cotswold-retreats.co.uk SPECIAL OFFERS

open All year
payment Credit/debit cards, cash, cheques
nearest shop 0.5 miles
nearest pub 0.5 miles

Two luxurious, romantic self-catering studio apartments with king-sized four-poster beds and en suite bathrooms with whirlpool baths. Private entrance and secluded private garden. Five-minute walk from village pubs and shop. Wide variety of scenic walks.

SAT NAV *CV36 4LJ*

Unit General P Leisure

INGOLDSBY, Lincolnshire Map ref 3A1

★★★★
SELF CATERING

Units 1
Sleeps 1–4

LOW SEASON PER WK
£200.00–£300.00

HIGH SEASON PER WK
£300.00–£400.00

Little Scotland Farm, Ingoldsby, Grantham

contact Mrs Angela Jasinski, Little Scotland Farm, Ingoldsby, Grantham N633 4ES **t** (01476) 585494

This is the perfect base for your holiday to explore and discover Lincolnshire. Our farmhouse annexe is tastefully furnished and decorated to a very high standard. Central heating, linen included.

open All year
payment Cash, cheques
nearest shop 5 miles
nearest pub 3 miles

Unit General 10 P Leisure

IRONBRIDGE, Shropshire Map ref 4A3

★★★★
SELF CATERING

Units 2
Sleeps 4–5

LOW SEASON PER WK
£275.00–£385.00

HIGH SEASON PER WK
£440.00–£655.00

5% discount for payment in full when making your booking.

Ironbridge Holiday Cottages, Ironbridge

contact Mr Mark Shelton, 29-30 The Wharfage, Ironbridge TF8 7NH **t** 0800 633 5181 & 07977 598740 **e** info@ironbridgeholidaycottages.co.uk

ironbridgeholidaycottages.co.uk GUEST REVIEWS · SPECIAL OFFERS

open All year
payment Credit/debit cards
nearest shop less than 0.5 miles
nearest pub less than 0.5 miles

River Cottages are a pair of beautifully restored, self-catering cottages dating back to 1650, the time of the English Civil War, and are among the oldest buildings in the historic Ironbridge Gorge, right in the heart of Shropshire.

SAT NAV *TF8 7NR*

Unit General P Leisure

What if I need to cancel?

It is advisable to check the proprietor's cancellation policy in case you have to change your plans at a later date.

IRONBRIDGE, Shropshire Map ref 4A3

★★★
SELF CATERING

Units 1
Sleeps 6

LOW SEASON PER WK
£195.00–£295.00

HIGH SEASON PER WK
£350.00–£495.00

Book two consecutive weeks and receive a 10% discount off the lower-cost week.

Ironbridge Lodge, Ironbridge, Telford

contact Mrs Pamela Mundy, 16 Buildwas Road, Ironbridge, Telford TF8 7DW **t** (01952) 257242
e pam@ercallcatering.co.uk

open All year
payment Cash, cheques
nearest shop 2 miles
nearest pub less than 0.5 miles

Two-bedroom, ground-floor barn conversion with lounge, dining room and kitchen, and enclosed patio. Sleeps four plus two, and located within easy walking distance of the Iron Bridge itself and next to Dale End Park. Easy access for mobility-impaired visitors. Parking for two cars.

SAT NAV *TF8 7DW*

Unit TV DVD S General P S Leisure

KEDINGTON, Suffolk Map ref 3B2

★★★★
SELF CATERING

Units 1
Sleeps 2

LOW SEASON PER WK
£195.00–£250.00

HIGH SEASON PER WK
£250.00–£380.00

Cottage At Rowans, Kedington, Haverhill

contact Ms Cheryl Owen, Cottage At Rowans, Calford Green, Kedington, Haverhill CB9 7UN
t (01440) 702408 **e** cheryl@owen41.supanet.com

cottagesdirect.com/nfa123 REAL-TIME BOOKING

Spacious, bright, well-appointed, one-bedroom cottage with vaulted ceilings and beams. Cosy in winter. Stour Valley walks, golf and antique-hunting nearby. Garden and patio.

open All year
payment Cash, cheques, euros
nearest shop 1.5 miles
nearest pub 1 mile

Unit TV DVD General P S Leisure

KELLING, Norfolk Map ref 3B1

★★★★★
SELF CATERING

Units 1
Sleeps 8

LOW SEASON PER WK
£750.00–£1,150.00

HIGH SEASON PER WK
£1,400.00–£1,600.00

3-night midweek and weekend breaks available, out of season. Other seasonal promotions can be seen on our website.

WALKERS WELCOME · CYCLISTS WELCOME · FAMILIES WELCOME · PETS! WELCOME

Owl Place, Holt

contact Victoria Hamey, Kelling Estate Office, Kelling Hall Farms, Kelling, Holt NR25 7EW
t (01263) 712201 **e** stay@kelling-estate.co.uk

kelling-estate.co.uk SPECIAL OFFERS

open All year
payment Cash, cheques
nearest shop 2 miles
nearest pub 2 miles

Situated in an Area of Outstanding Natural Beauty. Luxury barn conversion, sleeps eight, three twin and one king with two en suite and a family bathroom. Large open plan kitchen/living room with private decked terrace. Access to indoor swimming pool, two all-weather tennis courts and children's play area.

ONLINE MAP

Unit TV SC DVD General P S
Leisure

Place index

If you know where you want to stay, the index by place name at the back of the guide will give you the page number listing accommodation in your chosen town, city or village. Check out the other useful indexes too.

KELSALE, Suffolk Map ref 3C2

★★★★
SELF CATERING

Units 4
Sleeps 4–6

LOW SEASON PER WK
£245.00–£345.00

HIGH SEASON PER WK
£345.00–£699.00

Short breaks and weekends available from £165. Tennis weekends for groups.

East Green Farm Cottages, Saxmundham

contact Claire & Robbie Gawthrop, East Green Farm Cottages, Kelsale IP17 2PH **t** (01728) 602316
e claire@eastgreen.co.uk

eastgreencottages.co.uk SPECIAL OFFERS

open All year
payment Cash, cheques
nearest shop 2 miles
nearest pub 2 miles

Between Southwold and Aldeburgh and only two miles from the beautiful Heritage Coast. The Granary, The Old Stables, The Hayloft and The Dairy are charming, spacious, fully equipped, converted barns set in the grounds of a 500-year-old farmhouse. Thirteen acres of paddocks, tennis court and outdoor swimming pool. Tennis coaching available.

Unit General
Leisure

KEMPSEY, Worcestershire Map ref 2B1

★★★★
SELF CATERING

Units 1
Sleeps 6

LOW SEASON PER WK
Min £300.00

HIGH SEASON PER WK
Max £560.00

The Barn, Beechcroft, Stonehall

contact Mrs Charlotte Underwood, The Barn, Beechcroft, Wadborough Road, Stonehall, Kempsey WR5 3QH **t** (01905) 820364 **e** info@thebarn-beechcroft.co.uk

thebarn-beechcroft.co.uk REAL-TIME BOOKING

New conversion on owner's smallholding in rural location. Original features retained, underfloor heating. Kennels and stables available. Private access, secure garden. Ideal for countryside, pubs, amenities and tourist attractions.

open All year
payment Credit/debit cards, cash, cheques
nearest shop 2.5 miles
nearest pub 0.5 miles

Unit General Leisure

KENLEY, Shropshire Map ref 4A3

★★★★
SELF CATERING

Units 2
Sleeps 2–4

LOW SEASON PER WK
£180.00–£220.00

HIGH SEASON PER WK
£280.00–£350.00

Courtyard Cottages, Shrewsbury

contact Mrs Annabel Gill, No 1 & 2 Courtyard Cottages, Lower Springs Farm, Kenley, Shrewsbury SY5 6PA **t** (01952) 510841 **e** afgill@hotmail.co.uk

stmem.com/courtyardcottages

Immaculate, recently converted cottages with exposed oak beams. Large garden and stocked trout pools in lovely, peaceful valley with panoramic views of Wenlock Edge.

open All year
payment Cash, cheques
nearest shop 3 miles
nearest pub 3 miles

Unit General Leisure

KERSEY, Suffolk Map ref 3B2

★★★★★
SELF CATERING

Units 1
Sleeps 8

LOW SEASON PER WK
£700.00–£875.00

HIGH SEASON PER WK
£1,000.00–£1,500.00

Short breaks available for 3 or 4 nights from £500.

Old Drift House, Kersey, Ipswich

contact Mrs Jill Black, 11 Poynings Close, Harpenden AL5 1JD **t** (01582) 763533 **e** ejblk@talk21.com

olddrifthouse.co.uk

open All year
payment Cash, cheques
nearest shop 2 miles
nearest pub less than 0.5 miles

15thC, Grade II Listed thatched cottage, beamed throughout, with inglenook fireplaces, bread oven and secluded garden with well – a quintessential 'chocolate-box' cottage. Set in the most picturesque village with ford and ducks by the pub. Access to Suffolk coast, Constable Country, Lavenham, Long Melford and Colchester.

Unit TV DVD General P S Leisure

KESSINGLAND, Suffolk Map ref 3C2

★★★
SELF CATERING

Units 1
Sleeps 4–5

LOW SEASON PER WK
£180.00–£190.00

HIGH SEASON PER WK
£200.00–£260.00

Kew Cottage, Lowestoft

contact Mrs Joan Gill, 46 St Georges Avenue, Northampton NN2 6JA **t** (01604) 717301
e b.s.g@btinternet.com

payment Cash, cheques, euros
nearest shop less than 0.5 miles
nearest pub less than 0.5 miles

Modernised, two-bedroomed, semi-detached cottage in the middle of village, ten minutes' walk from the sea. Large back garden with patio and seating area. Norfolk Broads three miles, Lowestoft three miles, Southwold five miles, Norwich 30 miles.

Unit TV DVD General P

KING'S LYNN, Norfolk Map ref 3B1

★★★
SELF CATERING

Units 1
Sleeps 6

LOW SEASON PER WK
Min £300.00

HIGH SEASON PER WK
£400.00–£450.00

Granary, King's Lynn

contact Mrs Ann Jones, Manor House, Churchgate Way, Terrington St Clement, King's Lynn PE34 4LZ **t** (01553) 828700 **e** rchjn957@aol.com

tiscover.co.uk

In centre of village in 15 acres. Secure walled garden with veg, fruit, barbecue. Horses and dogs welcome. Ground floor, no steps. Large shower and bath. Two beds. Sleeps six plus cot.

open All year
payment Cash, cheques
nearest shop less than 0.5 miles
nearest pub less than 0.5 miles

Unit TV General P S

Do you have access needs?

Look for the National Accessible Scheme symbols if you have special hearing, visual or mobility needs. An index of accommodation participating in the scheme can be found at the back of this guide.

KNIVETON, Derbyshire Map ref 4B2

★★★★
SELF CATERING

Units 1
Sleeps 2–4

LOW SEASON PER WK
£300.00

HIGH SEASON PER WK
£350.00

Willow Bank, Ashbourne

contact Mrs Mary Vaughan, Willow Bank, Kniveton, Ashbourne DE6 1JJ **t** (01335) 343308
e willowbank@kniveton.net

kniveton.net

Luxurious, self-contained ground-floor accommodation, one double bedroom, one twin. An acre of garden, summerhouse, stream, barbecue, lovely views. CD player, Freeview, Internet access. Pretty Peak District village, Ashbourne 15 minutes.

open All year
payment Cash, cheques
nearest shop 3 miles
nearest pub 0.5 miles

Unit General 5 P Leisure

LAMBLEY, Nottinghamshire Map ref 4C2

★★★
SELF CATERING & SERVICED APARTMENTS

Units 1
Sleeps 4

LOW SEASON PER WK
£180.00–£205.00

HIGH SEASON PER WK
£250.00–£270.00

Short and weekend breaks available. Prices on application.

Dickman's Cottage, Lambley, Nottingham

contact Mr William Marshall Smith, Springsyde, Birdcage Walk, Otley LS21 3HB **t** (01943) 462719
e marshallsmithuk@hotmail.com

dickmanscottage.co.uk

open All year
payment Cash, cheques, euros
nearest shop less than 0.5 miles
nearest pub less than 0.5 miles

Five miles north-east of Nottingham. Beamed cottage with garden. Two bedrooms – one double, one twin. TV/video, dishwasher, washer/dryer. Private parking.

Unit General P

LAVENHAM, Suffolk Map ref 3B2

★★★★
SELF CATERING

Units 6
Sleeps 2–6

LOW SEASON PER WK
£259.00–£491.00

HIGH SEASON PER WK
£422.00–£853.00

Our cosy cottages make up The Grove Farm, bookable for 2-15 guests, from 2-night short breaks upwards. Pets welcome.

Grove, Edwardstone

contact Mr Mark Scott, Priory Green, Edwardstone, Nr Lavenham, Edwardstone CO10 5PP
t (01787) 211115 **e** mark@grove-cottages.co.uk

grove-cottages.co.uk GUEST REVIEWS • SPECIAL OFFERS • REAL-TIME BOOKING

open All year
payment Credit/debit cards
nearest shop 2.8 miles
nearest pub 1 mile

Enjoy the romance of your own 300-year-old farm cottage – oak beams, open log fires, period furniture, ducks, roses and a touch of luxury. Our cottages are close to the lovely medieval Suffolk village of Lavenham – just two hours from London. Bikes free and canoes available.

ONLINE MAP

Unit General P
Leisure

Using map references

Map references refer to the colour maps at the front of this guide.

LAVENHAM, Suffolk Map ref 3B2

★★★
SELF CATERING

Units 4
Sleeps 2–6

LOW SEASON PER WK
£155.00–£325.00

HIGH SEASON PER WK
£250.00–£410.00

Maltings Farm Holiday Cottages, Bury St Edmunds

contact Mrs Rachel Bell, Maltings Farm Holiday Cottages, Bury St Edmunds IP30 0NG
t (01284) 828843 **e** tim-bell@fsbdial.co.uk

tiscover.co.uk

Situated near Lavenham in open countryside. Four charming cottages sleeping two, four and six people set around a farm courtyard.

open All year
payment Cash, cheques
nearest shop 2 miles
nearest pub 2 miles

Unit General P Leisure

LAVENHAM, Suffolk Map ref 3B2

★★★★
SELF CATERING

Units 1
Sleeps 2

LOW SEASON PER WK
£360.00

HIGH SEASON PER WK
£495.00

Weekend and midweek breaks from £271.00.

Mortimers Barn Holiday Cottage, Lavenham

contact Mrs Caroline Gove, Mortimers Barn, Nr Lavenham CO10 9ND **t** (01787) 247786
e thosegoves@aol.com

mortimersbarn.co.uk SPECIAL OFFERS • REAL-TIME BOOKING

open All year
payment Credit/debit cards, cash, cheques, euros
nearest shop 2 miles
nearest pub 1 mile

Delightful newly refurbished single-storey accommodation adjacent to owners' 15thC thatched barn, two miles from Lavenham. This is an ideal place to explore beautiful rural Suffolk, or a cosy, comfortable retreat any time of year. The decor is an eclectic mix of antiques and modern furniture. Sleeps two.

SAT NAV *CO10 9ND*

Unit General P Leisure

LAVENHAM, Suffolk Map ref 3B2

★★★
SELF CATERING

Units 1
Sleeps 2–6

LOW SEASON PER WK
Min £275.00

HIGH SEASON PER WK
Max £395.00

Old Wetherden Hall, Ipswich

contact Mrs Julie Elsden, Old Wetherden Hall, Hitcham IP7 7PZ **t** (01449) 740574
e julie.elsden@btconnect.com

oldwetherdenhall.co.uk

open All year
payment Cash, cheques
nearest shop 2 miles
nearest pub 1 mile

15thC oak-beamed house, enclosed moated site on arable farm. Beautiful, secluded setting, large garden, abundance of wildlife. Inglenook fireplace. Moat stocked with carp and other fish. Fishing available.

Unit General P Leisure

Check the maps for accommodation locations

Colour maps at the front pinpoint all the places where accommodation is featured within the regional sections of this guide. Pick your location and then refer to the place index at the back to find the page number.

For **key to symbols** see page 7

LAVENHAM, Suffolk Map ref 3B2

★★★★
SELF CATERING

Units 1
Sleeps 4

LOW SEASON PER WK
£241.00–£387.00

HIGH SEASON PER WK
£397.00–£544.00

Potash Farm Cottage, Thorpe Morieux

t (01284) 828396 & 07812 956402 **e** emmadib@aol.com

potashfarmcottage.co.uk

Comfortable cottage, idyllic country surroundings, excellent walks, abundant wildlife. One twin, one double and double sofa bed. Cosy woodburner. Enclosed private garden overlooking owner's large fenced pond. Lavenham three miles.

open All year
payment Cash, cheques, euros
nearest shop 2.5 miles
nearest pub 1.5 miles

Unit General P S
Leisure

LAVENHAM, Suffolk Map ref 3B2

★★★
SELF CATERING

Units 1
Sleeps 2

LOW SEASON PER WK
Min £294.00

HIGH SEASON PER WK
Min £336.00

Jun and Sep: 7 nights for £298. Minimum 3 nights' stay from £44 per couple, per night. 5% discount on stays of 5 nights or more.

Rector's Retreat, Ipswich

contact Mr Peter Gutteridge, The Old Convent, The Street, Ipswich IP7 7QA **t** (01449) 741557
e valandpeter@madasafish.com

tiscover.co.uk

open All year
payment Cash, cheques
nearest shop 2 miles
nearest pub 1 mile

Timber building within the curtilage of a Grade II Listed thatched cottage. Recently refurbished and renovated to provide wheelchair access. Complimentary basic provisions (milk/beverages and toiletries). The Retreat comprises a double bedroom with en suite shower, lounge/diner, kitchen, electric storage heaters. Electricity and linen included. Brochure available.

Unit General P S Leisure

LAXFIELD, Suffolk Map ref 3C2

★★★★
SELF CATERING

Units 2
Sleeps 4

LOW SEASON PER WK
£380.00–£495.00

HIGH SEASON PER WK
£550.00–£650.00

Laxfield Lodges, Laxfield, Woodbridge

contact Mrs Angie Thompson, Burnt House, Framlingham Road, Woodbridge IP13 8HE
t (01986) 798766 **e** admin@laxfieldlodges.co.uk

laxfieldlodges.co.uk GUEST REVIEWS • SPECIAL OFFERS • REAL-TIME BOOKING

Luxury self-catering holiday accommodation in authentic log cabins on our 14-acre site in the beautiful countryside of mid-Suffolk, only 25 minutes' drive from the Suffolk Heritage Coast.

open All year
payment Cash, cheques, euros
nearest shop 0.5 miles
nearest pub 0.5 miles

Unit General P S Leisure

LEAMINGTON SPA, Warwickshire Map ref 4B3

★★
SELF CATERING

Units 2
Sleeps 5

LOW SEASON PER WK
£160.00–£230.00

HIGH SEASON PER WK
£240.00–£350.00

Blackdown Farm Cottages, Leamington Spa

contact Mr & Mrs R Solt, Sandy Lane, Blackdown, Leamington Spa CV32 6QS **t** (01926) 422522
e bobby@solt.demon.co.uk

Cottages converted from farm buildings in the countryside between Leamington Spa, Kenilworth, Warwick and Coventry. Very near NAC Stoneleigh and convenient for National Exhibition Centre.

open All year
payment Cash, cheques
nearest shop 2.5 miles
nearest pub 2.5 miles

Unit General P

Has every property been assessed?

All accommodation in this guide has been rated for quality, or is awaiting assessment, by a professional national tourist board assessor.

LEAMINGTON SPA, Warwickshire Map ref 4B3

★★★★
SELF CATERING

Units 1
Sleeps 4

LOW SEASON PER WK
£275.00–£350.00

HIGH SEASON PER WK
£375.00–£450.00

Brunswick, 74a Brunswick Street, Leamington Spa

contact Ms Mary Curran, 19 Hanover Gardens, Upper Holly Walk, Leamington Spa CV32 4JW
t (01926) 420474 **e** grannycurran@aol.com

brunswickapartment.co.uk

Ground-floor two-bedroom apartment in purpose built two-apartment building, own drive and gardens. Modern, warm and fully equipped.

open All year
payment Cash, cheques
nearest shop less than 0.5 miles
nearest pub less than 0.5 miles

Unit General

LEAMINGTON SPA, Warwickshire Map ref 4B3

★★★★
SELF CATERING

Units 4
Sleeps 2–6

LOW SEASON PER WK
£240.00

HIGH SEASON PER WK
£445.00

Furzen Hill Farm, Leamington Spa

contact Mrs Christine Whitfield, Furzen Hill Farm, Coventry Road, Cubbington Heath, Leamington Spa CV32 7UJ **t** (01926) 424791 **e** christine.whitfield1@btopenworld.com

furzenhillfarmcottages.co.uk

Cottages at Cubbington, ideally situated for Warwick, Stratford-upon-Avon and NEC. Large garden. Use of hard tennis court.

open All year
payment Cash, cheques
nearest shop 1.25 miles
nearest pub 1.25 miles

Unit General Leisure

LEDBURY, Herefordshire Map ref 2B1

★★★★
SELF CATERING

Units 2
Sleeps 2

LOW SEASON PER WK
£325.00

HIGH SEASON PER WK
£325.00–£350.00

The Bee House and The Hive, Ledbury

contact Mrs Sandra Anderson, Nashend House, Bosbury, Ledbury HR8 1JU **t** (01531) 640021
e sandra@beehousecottages.co.uk

beehousecottages.co.uk

The Bee House and The Hive are two adjoining cottages located in the garden of the owner's 17thC Georgian house, outside the village of Bosbury.

open All year
payment Cash, cheques
nearest shop 2 miles
nearest pub 1 mile

Unit General

LEDBURY, Herefordshire Map ref 2B1

★★★–★★★★
SELF CATERING

Units 5
Sleeps 2–5

LOW SEASON PER WK
£200.00–£390.00

HIGH SEASON PER WK
£260.00–£499.00

3-night short breaks available all year, subject to certain booking restrictions. Please ring for details.

White House Cottages, Ledbury

contact Mrs Marianne Hills, The White House, Aylton, Ledbury HR8 2RQ **t** (01531) 670349
e bookings@whitehousecottages.co.uk

whitehousecottages.co.uk

open All year
payment Cash, cheques
nearest shop 4 miles
nearest pub 2 miles

Well-equipped, self-catering cottages situated in a small hamlet four miles west of Ledbury. Surrounded by Herefordshire's idyllic countryside, these former farm buildings have been carefully adapted to create very comfortable and individual holiday accommodation. Perfect for exploring the Wye Valley, the Malverns and surrounding area. Resident owners.

ONLINE MAP

Unit General Leisure

Where are the maps?

Colour maps can be found at the front of the guide. They pinpoint the location of all accommodation found in the regional sections.

LEDBURY, Herefordshire Map ref 2B1

★★★★★
SELF CATERING

Units 3
Sleeps 2–9

LOW SEASON PER WK
£310.00–£950.00

HIGH SEASON PER WK
£495.00–£1,700.00

Romantic breaks. 3- and 4-night breaks available.

The Woodhouse Farm Cottages, Ledbury

contact Mrs Susan Furnival, The Woodhouse, Staplow, Ledbury HR8 1NP **t** (01531) 640030
e sue@thewoodhousefarm.co.uk

thewoodhousefarm.co.uk

open All year
payment Credit/debit cards, cash, cheques
nearest shop 2 miles
nearest pub less than 0.5 miles

Tranquil retreats close to Malvern Hills. Barn Croft and The Wainhouse share 15 acres of grounds with The Woodhouse, a medieval, Grade II* Listed, semi-moated hall house. Comfortably furnished to very high standards with antiques and prints. Each cottage has a private garden. Choice of dining solutions and food hampers.

Unit General P S Leisure

LEEK, Staffordshire Map ref 4B2

★★★★
SELF CATERING

Units 1
Sleeps 4

LOW SEASON PER WK
Min £185.00

HIGH SEASON PER WK
Max £385.00

Wren Cottage, Leek

contact Mrs Elizabeth Lowe, Fairboroughs Farm, Rudyard ST13 8PR **t** (01260) 226341
e fairboroughs@talk21.com

fairboroughs.co.uk

Converted 16thC barn on working beef/sheep farm. High specification, historic features, panoramic views, fully heated. Horse-riding holidays. Convenient for Peak District, Potteries, Alton Towers. Manchester Airport 45 minutes.

open All year
payment Cash, cheques
nearest shop 3 miles
nearest pub 2 miles

Unit General P S Leisure

LINCOLN, Lincolnshire Map ref 4C2

★★★★
SELF CATERING

Units 3
Sleeps 2–4

LOW SEASON PER WK
Min £165.00

HIGH SEASON PER WK
Max £355.00

Discount for only 2 people in Corner Cottage. Short breaks sometimes available.

Old Vicarage Cottages, Nettleham

contact Mrs Susan Downs, The Old Vicarage, East Street, Lincoln LN2 2SL **t** (01522) 750819
e susan@oldvic.net

oldvic.net

open All year
payment Credit/debit cards, cash, cheques
nearest shop less than 0.5 miles
nearest pub less than 0.5 miles

Delightful old stone cottages offering spacious accommodation, equipped with everything you need including a whirlpool bath. Private gardens and off-road parking/garage. Close to the centre of this award-winning village with shops, pubs, green and picturesque beckside. Good bus service. Four miles from Lincoln – the perfect holiday location.

Unit General P S

LINCOLN, Lincolnshire Map ref 4C2

★★★
SELF CATERING

Units 3
Sleeps 1–2

LOW SEASON PER WK
Min £160.00

HIGH SEASON PER WK
Min £220.00

Saint Clements, Lincoln

contact Mrs Gill Marshall, Saint Clements Old Rectory, The Drive, Langworthgate, Lincoln LN2 4AD
t (01522) 538087 **e** info@stayatstclements.co.uk

stayatstclements.co.uk

open All year
payment Cash, cheques
nearest shop less than 0.5 miles
nearest pub less than 0.5 miles

Well-equipped, centrally heated apartments in comfortable Victorian rectory; one is twin-bedded, two are doubles. Situated down quiet drive lined with mature trees. Cathedral views, and only five minutes' walk from historic up-hill area. Plenty of car parking. A peaceful retreat in the heart of the city. Short breaks when available.

Unit General P

LINCOLN, Lincolnshire Map ref 4C2

★★★★
SELF CATERING

Units 1
Sleeps 2–4

LOW SEASON PER WK
£190.00–£275.00

HIGH SEASON PER WK
£275.00–£375.00

4 nights for the price of 3 in low season.

The Stable, Lincoln

contact Jerry & Chris Scott, Sunnyside, Lincoln Road, Lincoln LN1 2SQ **t** (01522) 730561
e jerry@lincolncottages.co.uk

lincolncottages.co.uk

open All year
payment Cash, cheques, euros
nearest shop 1.5 miles
nearest pub 1 mile

300-year-old cottage of character converted from a former stone and pantile stable. Peace and tranquillity in a conservation village, yet only six miles from the historic cathedral city of Lincoln. Tastefully furnished and decorated. Own enclosed cottage garden and views over open fields.

Unit General P S Leisure

LINCOMB, Worcestershire Map ref 4B3

★★★★
SELF CATERING

Units 1
Sleeps 1–2

LOW SEASON PER WK
£275.00–£325.00

HIGH SEASON PER WK
£375.00–£425.00

Old Tom's, Nr Stourport-on-Severn

contact Mr Andrew Symonds, Lincomb Farm, Lincomb, Stourport-on-Severn DY13 9RB
t (01299) 250241 **e** lincomb.farms@btconnect.com

experienceworcestershire.co.uk

open All year except Christmas and New Year
payment Credit/debit cards, cash, cheques
nearest shop 2 miles
nearest pub 2 miles

A new barn conversion sleeping two persons. Ground-floor property decorated and furnished to a very high standard. Solid oak floors, doors and original beams feature. Large sitting/dining area, 6ft luxury bed, 32 inch flat-panel TV with all Freeview channels and digital audio system. Woodburning stove and garage parking.

Unit General P S Leisure

LITTLE BENTLEY, Essex Map ref 3B2

★★★★
SELF CATERING

Units 1
Sleeps 4

LOW SEASON PER WK
£250.00–£350.00

HIGH SEASON PER WK
£400.00–£475.00

Short breaks available (min 3 nights). Welcome pack.

Spring Hall Cottage, Colchester

contact Mrs Tricia Maestrani, Spring Hall, Little Bentley CO7 8SR **t** (01206) 251619 & 07779 264679
e triciamaestrani@hotmail.co.uk

open All year
payment Cash, cheques, euros
nearest shop 2 miles
nearest pub 0.5 miles

Grade II Listed, 17thC thatched cottage with a wealth of character and original features including exposed beams and inglenook fireplace. Two double bedrooms, double cart lodge, 0.33-acre enclosed garden, patio area and barbecue. Ideal location for Constable Country, Manningtree, historical Harwich/Colchester and Essex coast. Excellent selection of pubs/restaurants nearby.

Unit General 5 P S Leisure

LITTLE MARCLE, Herefordshire Map ref 2B1

★★★★
SELF CATERING

Units 1
Sleeps 6

LOW SEASON PER WK
£400.00–£600.00

HIGH SEASON PER WK
£550.00–£750.00

Short breaks available.

Upper House Cottage, Little Marcle, Ledbury

contact Sarah Glanville, Upper House, Little Marcle, Ledbury HR8 2JY **t** (01531) 670125
e jimglanville@btinternet.com

holidaycottageherefordshire.com REAL-TIME BOOKING

open All year except Christmas and New Year
payment Credit/debit cards, cash, cheques
nearest shop 1.5 miles
nearest pub 1.5 miles

Fine character oak-frame cottage built in 2005, adjoining owner's home. Enjoys beautiful views, extensive wildlife and walks from the door. Fitted kitchen, three cosy bedrooms, woodburner in lounge. Many places of interest nearby – see our website for more photos/details and virtual tour. Friday changeover day.

ONLINE MAP

Unit General P S Leisure

LITTLE WALDEN, Essex Map ref 2D1

★★★
SELF CATERING

Units 4
Sleeps 3–4

LOW SEASON PER WK
£300.00

HIGH SEASON PER WK
£300.00

Orchard View Numbers 1-4, Saffron Walden

contact Mrs Maureen Chapman-Barker, Orchard View Numbers 1 - 4, Little Bowsers Farm, Bowsers Lane, Little Walden, Saffron Walden CB10 1XQ **t** (01799) 527315 **e** sales@farmerkit.co.uk

farmerkit.co.uk

1 Orchard View Cottages sleeps three. 2, 3 and 4 Orchard View Cottages each sleep four.

open All year
payment Cash, cheques
nearest shop 4 miles
nearest pub 1 mile

Unit General P Leisure

Where can I get help and advice?

Tourist Information Centres offer friendly help with accommodation and holiday ideas as well as suggestions of places to visit and things to do. You'll find contact details at the beginning of each regional section.

LITTLE WALSINGHAM, Norfolk Map ref 3B1

★★★★
SELF CATERING

Units 1
Sleeps 1–4

LOW SEASON PER WK
£280.00–£390.00

HIGH SEASON PER WK
£390.00–£490.00

The Old Coach House, Walsingham

contact Mr & Mrs Gwyn & Charlotte Pollard, c/o Baker and Mckenzie LLP, 100 New Bridge Street, London EC4V 6JA **t** (020) 7702 1814 **e** theoldcoach.house@btinternet.com

theoldcoach.house.btinternet.co.uk

Charming brick and flint coach-house conversion in the historic village of Little Walsingham, offering comfortable accommodation, with two double bedrooms, living room with woodburner and an enclosed courtyard garden.

open All year
payment Cash, cheques
nearest shop less than 0.5 miles
nearest pub less than 0.5 miles

Unit General P

LLANGARRON, Herefordshire Map ref 2A1

★★★★
SELF CATERING

Units 2
Sleeps 2–20

LOW SEASON PER WK
£200.00–£1,000.00

HIGH SEASON PER WK
£1,000.00–£3,500.00

Littlefields – Gaerfields, Ross-on-Wye

contact Mrs Jones, Littlefields - Gaerfields, Upperfields Farm, Ross-on-Wye HR9 6PQ
t (01989) 770281 **e** upperfieldsfarm1@tiscali.co.uk

upperfieldsfarm.co.uk GUEST REVIEWS • SPECIAL OFFERS

open All year
payment Cash, cheques
nearest shop 2.5 miles
nearest pub 2.5 miles

A warm welcome awaits you in Upperfields Farm in a beautifully converted barn that sleeps up to 20 with swimming pool, sauna and swim jet. Log fire, beams, stained glass, underfloor heating – everything you need for the celebration party or short-break weekend. Lovely views towards Wales and the Royal Forest of Dean.

ONLINE MAP

Unit General P S
Leisure

LONG MELFORD, Suffolk Map ref 3B2

★★★★
SELF CATERING

Units 1
Sleeps 4

LOW SEASON PER WK
Min £270.00

HIGH SEASON PER WK
Max £450.00

Short breaks available all year (subject to availability in high season).

Hope Cottage, Long Melford

contact Ms S Jamil, Hill Farm Cottage, Duffs Hill, Glemsford, Sudbury CO10 7PP **t** (01787) 282338 & 07970 808701 **e** sns.jam@tesco.net

hope-cottage-suffolk.co.uk

open All year
payment Cash, cheques, euros
nearest shop less than 0.5 miles
nearest pub less than 0.5 miles

Delightful Grade II Listed flint cottage in the heart of this historic and picturesque village. Recently renovated, retaining many traditional features. Attractively furnished to high levels of comfort. Secluded garden backing onto meadowlands. All amenities in the village are close by, including restaurants and shops.

Unit SC General P S Leisure

It's all quality-assessed accommodation

Our commitment to quality involves wide-ranging accommodation assessment. Ratings and awards were correct at the time of going to press but may change following a new assessment. Please check at time of booking.

LOUTH, Lincolnshire Map ref 4D2

★★★★–★★★★★
SELF CATERING

Units 3
Sleeps 1–24

LOW SEASON PER WK
£265.00–£655.00

HIGH SEASON PER WK
£325.00–£1,045.00

Short breaks always available. Any start day, length of stay.

Brackenborough Hall Coach House Holidays, Brackenborough, Louth

contact Mr & Mrs Paul and Flora Bennett, Brackenborough Hall, Brackenborough, Louth LN11 0NS
t (01507) 603193 & 07974 687779 **e** paulandflora@brackenboroughhall.com

brackenboroughhall.com GUEST REVIEWS • SPECIAL OFFERS

open All year
payment Credit/debit cards, cash, cheques
nearest shop 2 miles
nearest pub 2 miles

Three luxury apartments in listed 18thC coach house beside moated manor house. All original features retained. In ancient parkland on 800-acre farm. Beautiful, peaceful setting for walking, cycling, fishing, nature watching and relaxing/playing in extensive gardens. Between the Lincolnshire Wolds, coast and attractive market town of Louth. Children welcome.

SAT NAV *LN11 0NS* **ONLINE MAP**

Unit General P S
Leisure

LOUTH, Lincolnshire Map ref 4D2

★★★
SELF CATERING

Units 1
Sleeps 1–4

LOW SEASON PER WK
£200.00–£300.00

HIGH SEASON PER WK
£250.00–£350.00

Special rates for just 2 visitors. Discounted honey available.

Mill Lodge, Louth

contact Mrs P.M Cade, Benniworth House Farm, Donington on Bain, Louth LN11 9RD
t (01507) 343265

open All year
payment Cash, cheques
nearest shop 0.75 miles
nearest pub 1 mile

Ezra and Pamela Cade welcome you to a comfortable, warm, detached cottage with conservatory and garden on lovely farm/nature reserve. Fitted kitchen, open log fire. Free first snack with home-produced honey. Good footpaths join the Viking Way, open access to countryside stewardship area. Children welcome.

Unit General P S Leisure

LOUTH, Lincolnshire Map ref 4D2

★★★
SELF CATERING

Units 1
Sleeps 2–8

LOW SEASON PER WK
£349.00–£449.00

HIGH SEASON PER WK
£449.00–£689.00

Off-season short breaks available for a whistle-stop holiday.

Station Masters House, Ludborough, Grimsby

contact Graham Helm, The Old Station Yard, Station Road, Ludborough DN36 5SQ **t** (01507) 363470 & 07957 366325 **e** info@raileisure.com

raileisure.com GUEST REVIEWS • SPECIAL OFFERS • REAL-TIME BOOKING

open All year
payment Cash, cheques
nearest shop 2 miles
nearest pub 2 miles

High-quality self-catering accommodation within the Lincolnshire Wolds. Peace and tranquillity, ideal for railway, walking and cycling enthusiasts. A most unique holiday home, ideal for the larger family or family reunions, within picturesque surroundings.

ONLINE MAP

Unit General P S Leisure

LOWESTOFT, Suffolk Map ref 3C1

★
SELF CATERING

Units **1**
Sleeps **2–4**

LOW SEASON PER WK
£150.00–£200.00

HIGH SEASON PER WK
£250.00–£350.00

Marine House, Lowestoft

contact Mr & Mrs David & Teresa Conway, 416 Ashingdon Road, Rochford SS4 3EW
t (01702) 545495 & 07767 363445 **e** davidfconway@hotmail.co.uk

10marineparade.co.uk

Holiday flat overlooking the sea, close to all amenities. Lounge, bedroom, kitchen, shower, separate wc, reasonable rates, non-smoking, all-inclusive. Parking.

open All year
payment Cash, cheques, euros
nearest shop less than 0.5 miles
nearest pub less than 0.5 miles

Unit TV General 1

LOWESTOFT, Suffolk Map ref 3C1

★★★★
SELF CATERING

Units **1**
Sleeps **1–4**

LOW SEASON PER WK
Min £260.00

HIGH SEASON PER WK
Min £485.00

Pippin Cottage, Lowestoft

contact Mr Ian Crocker, Somerton House, 7 Kirkley Cliff, Lowestoft NR33 0BY **t** (01502) 565665
e pippin.somerton@btinternet.com

pippin-cottage.co.uk GUEST REVIEWS

Pippin Cottage, c1749, is set in a secluded area with private parking. Oak beams, log stove, central heating. Close to South Beach. Summer or winter, Pippin has it all.

open All year
payment Credit/debit cards, cash, cheques
nearest shop less than 0.5 miles
nearest pub less than 0.5 miles

Unit TV SC DVD Leisure

LOWESTOFT, Suffolk Map ref 3C1

★★★
SELF CATERING

Units **1**
Sleeps **5**

LOW SEASON PER WK
£250.00–£260.00

HIGH SEASON PER WK
£300.00–£370.00

Suffolk Seaside and Broadland, Lowestoft

contact Mrs Collecott, 282 Gorleston Road, Oulton, Lowestoft NR32 3AJ **t** (01502) 564396
e petecollecott@hotmail.com

Beautifully furnished, well-equipped bungalow with conservatory, garden and garage. Two bedrooms, two bathrooms, sitting room, dining room and large, fully fitted kitchen.

open All year
payment Cash, cheques
nearest shop 1 mile
nearest pub less than 0.5 miles

Unit TV General P Leisure

LUDHAM, Norfolk Map ref 3C1

★★★
SELF CATERING

Units **1**
Sleeps **4**

LOW SEASON PER WK
Min £325.00

HIGH SEASON PER WK
Max £525.00

WALKERS WELCOME CYCLISTS WELCOME

How Hill Windmill, Ludham

contact Mrs Elizabeth Ellis-Paul, The Mill House, How Hill, Ludham NR29 5PG **t** (01692) 678575

norfolkholidaywindmill.co.uk

Converted Grade II Listed grain mill built in 1824. Sleeps up to four people. Set in the peace and quiet of beautiful How Hill, the heart of the Norfolk Broads.

open All year except January and February
payment Cash, cheques
nearest shop 1.5 miles
nearest pub 1.5 miles

Unit TV DVD General 5 P Leisure

LUDLOW, Shropshire Map ref 4A3

★★★★
SELF CATERING

Units **2**
Sleeps **2–4**

LOW SEASON PER WK
£320.00–£420.00

HIGH SEASON PER WK
£320.00–£420.00

Elm Lodge Self Catering, Ludlow

contact Mrs Barbara Weaver, Fishmore, Ludlow SY8 3DP **t** (01584) 872308 **e** info@elm-lodge.org.uk

elm-lodge.org.uk

Elm Lodge/Coach House Apartments. One mile town centre. Ample on-site parking. Nine-hole golf course on site. Brochure available. Short breaks.

open All year
payment Credit/debit cards, cash, cheques

Unit TV General P Leisure

For **key to symbols** see page 7

LUDLOW, Shropshire Map ref 4A3

★★★★
SELF CATERING

Units 1
Sleeps 2–4

LOW SEASON PER WK
£335.00–£465.00

HIGH SEASON PER WK
£465.00–£535.00

Want to unwind for just a few days? 3-night weekend, 4-night midweek, or breaks tailored to your individual requirements.

Glebe Farm Cottage, Clee St Margaret

contact Mr & Mrs John & Lesley Thirlwell, Glebe Farm, Clee St Margaret SY7 9DT **t** (01584) 823349
e cottage@glebefarm.info

glebefarm.info

open All year
payment Cash, cheques
nearest shop 4.5 miles
nearest pub 5 miles

Converted detached stone granary with inglenook, exposed beams and woodburner, plus all modern comforts. In the heart of the Shropshire Hills, yet less than 20 minutes from Ludlow. Enjoy our 12 acres of flower-rich hay meadows, wildlife, stream and ponds – designated an Environmentally Sensitive Area and managed for conservation.

SAT NAV *SY7 9DT*

Unit General P Leisure

LUDLOW, Shropshire Map ref 4A3

★★★★–★★★★★
SELF CATERING

Units 3
Sleeps 4–5

LOW SEASON PER WK
£700.00–£750.00

HIGH SEASON PER WK
£1,050.00–£1,100.00

Ludlow Castle Lodgings, Ludlow

contact Helen Duce, Ludlow Castle Lodgings, Ludlow Castle, Castle Square, Ludlow SY8 1AX
t (01584) 874465 **e** hduce@ludlowcastle.com

ludlowcastle.com GUEST REVIEWS

open All year
payment Credit/debit cards, cash, cheques
nearest shop less than 0.5 miles
nearest pub less than 0.5 miles

Castle House Lodgings comprise three newly renovated apartments, full of character features and finished to the highest of standards, set within the walls of Ludlow Castle. Each apartment provides sitting room/dining room, fully equipped kitchen, two twin bedrooms and two bathrooms and a car parking space.

Unit General P Leisure

LUDLOW, Shropshire Map ref 4A3

★★★★
SELF CATERING

Units 1
Sleeps 4

LOW SEASON PER WK
£250.00–£325.00

HIGH SEASON PER WK
£350.00–£500.00

Old Harpfields Hop-Kiln, Tenbury Wells

contact Margaret & John Anderson, Old Harpfields Hop-Kiln, Old Harpfields, Burford, Tenbury Wells WR15 8HP **t** (01584) 810099 **e** john@andhow.fsnet.co.uk

harpfields-hopkiln.co.uk REAL-TIME BOOKING

Unusual, early Victorian building in unspoilt countryside south east of Ludlow. Converted and furnished to a very high standard with antiques, oak beams and logburner. Secluded courtyard and beautiful views.

open All year
payment Cash, cheques
nearest shop 2 miles
nearest pub 2 miles

Unit General P Leisure

Remember to check when booking

Please remember that all information in this guide has been supplied by the proprietors well in advance of publication. Since changes do sometimes occur it's a good idea to check details at the time of booking.

LUDLOW, Shropshire Map ref 4A3

★★★-★★★★★
SELF CATERING

Units 6
Sleeps 2–6

LOW SEASON PER WK
£210.00–£440.00

HIGH SEASON PER WK
£345.00–£500.00

Short breaks from Oct-Mar (excl holidays). 3 nights for 2, 4 nights for 3.

Sutton Court Farm Cottages, Ludlow

contact Mrs Jane Cronin, Sutton Court Farm, Little Sutton, Stanton Lacy, Ludlow SY8 2AJ
t (01584) 861305 **e** enquiries@suttoncourtfarm.co.uk

suttoncourtfarm.co.uk

open All year
payment Cash, cheques
nearest shop 6 miles
nearest pub 6 miles

Comfortable cottages set around a peaceful courtyard in the beautiful Corvedale, just five miles from historic Ludlow. World Heritage Ironbridge Gorge, Shrewsbury, Hereford and the Welsh borders all within easy reach. Short breaks available all year. Cream teas and evening meals can be ordered in advance.

SAT NAV *SY8 2AJ*

Unit General Leisure

LYDBURY NORTH, Shropshire Map ref 4A3

★★-★★★★
SELF CATERING

Units 5
Sleeps 2–8

LOW SEASON PER WK
£330.00–£550.00

HIGH SEASON PER WK
£460.00–£850.00

Walcot Hall Holiday apartments, Bishop's Castle

contact Miss Maria Higgs, Walcot Hall Holiday Apartments, Walcot Hall, Lydbury North SY7 8AZ
t (01588) 680570 **e** maria@walcotthall.com

walcothall.com

Spacious apartments with character in stately home once owned by Clive of India. Idyllic country setting with lakes, gardens and arboretum to explore. Doubles, twins and family room.

open All year
payment Cash, cheques
nearest shop 1.5 miles
nearest pub 1 mile

Unit General Leisure

MABLETHORPE, Lincolnshire Map ref 4D2

★★★
SELF CATERING

Units 1
Sleeps 1–6

LOW SEASON PER WK
Min £300.00

HIGH SEASON PER WK
Max £475.00

Dunes Cottage, Theddlethorpe St Helen

contact Sheila Morrison, Dunes cottage, Brickyard Lane, Theddlethorpe St Helen LN12 1NR
t (01507) 338342 **e** sheila.a.morrison@btopenworld.co.uk

dunesholidaycottage.co.uk

open All year
payment Cash, cheques
nearest shop 4 miles
nearest pub 2 miles

Charming 19thC cottage nestling on the edge of a National Nature Reserve. Next to the dunes with sandy beach and wonderful views from the top of the dunes to the wolds and out to sea. Offers visitors peace and tranquillity, a place to get away from the stresses and strains of modern life.

Unit General

MAER, Staffordshire Map ref 4B2

★★★★
SELF CATERING

Units 5
Sleeps 4–8

LOW SEASON PER WK
£395.00–£895.00

HIGH SEASON PER WK
£750.00–£1,150.00

Maer Estate Holiday Cottages, Newcastle-under-Lyme

Maer Estate Holiday Cottages, Newcastle-under-Lyme ST5 5EF **t** (01782) 680532
e mail@maerestateholidaycottages.co.uk

maerstateholidaycottages.co.uk

open All year
payment Credit/debit cards, cash, cheques
nearest shop 1.5 miles
nearest pub 0.5 miles

A select development of quality renovated listed cottages. Courtyard setting within the grounds of 17thC Maer Hall. Formerly the home of the Wedgwood family and in the English Heritage Register of Parks and Gardens. Seven miles from Newcastle-under-Lyme. Rural location adjoining the conservation village of Maer.

SAT NAV *ST5 5EF* **ONLINE MAP**

Unit General P Leisure

MALVERN, Worcestershire Map ref 2B1

★★★★
SELF CATERING

Units 1
Sleeps 8–10

LOW SEASON PER WK
£510.00–£525.00

HIGH SEASON PER WK
£695.00–£1,125.00

Beesoni Lodge, Malvern

contact Mrs Laura Smith, Beesoni Lodge, Beesoni Manor Farm, Hillend, Castlemorton, Malvern WR13 6BL **t** (01684) 830015 **e** beesonimanor@btconnect.com

beesonilodge.co.uk SPECIAL OFFERS

Fabulous detached barn conversion, exceptional standard, exposed beams. Sleeps eight to ten, four bedrooms (one four-poster), three bathrooms (one with spa bath). In own private grounds, stunning views of Malverns and Cotswolds.

open All year
payment Cash, cheques
nearest shop 3 miles
nearest pub 2.5 miles

Unit General P Leisure

MALVERN, Worcestershire Map ref 2B1

★★★★★
SELF CATERING

Units 2
Sleeps 4–8

LOW SEASON PER WK
£450.00–£750.00

HIGH SEASON PER WK
£650.00–£1,250.00

Netherley Hall Cottages, Malvern

contact Vivien Vos, Mathon, Malvern WR13 5LW **t** (01886) 880262
e enquiries@netherleyhallcottages.co.uk

netherleyhallcottages.co.uk

open All year
payment Cash, cheques
nearest shop 1 mile
nearest pub 2 miles

Superb, luxury self-catering cottages located on family-run farm in 700 acres of beautiful Herefordshire countryside offering marvellous woodland walks yet just 15 minutes' drive from Malvern town centre. Parkers: luxury 17thC listed four-bedroom cottage. Parker's Lodge: newly-built two-bedroom cottage. Ideal location for nature enthusiasts and birdwatchers. Broadband internet.

Unit General P Leisure

Do you like walking?

Walkers feel at home in accommodation participating in our Walkers Welcome scheme. Look out for the symbol. Consider walking all or part of a long-distance route – go online at nationaltrail.co.uk.

MALVERN, Worcestershire Map ref 2B1

★★★
SELF CATERING

Units 1
Sleeps 9

LOW SEASON PER WK
£566.00–£927.00

HIGH SEASON PER WK
£927.00–£1,279.00

Short breaks available Mar-Oct. Sat-Mon, 2 or 3-night stay.

Wayfarers Cottage, Malvern

contact Mr & Mrs John & Caroline Roslington, Wayfarers, Park Road, Malvern WR14 4BJ
t (01684) 575758 **e** info@wayfarerscottage.co.uk

wayfarerscottage.co.uk GUEST REVIEWS

open February to November and New Year
payment Cash, cheques
nearest shop 1 mile
nearest pub less than 0.5 miles

A real treat for family and friends, in attractive area rich in history and leisure activities. Spacious, extended cottage on Malvern Hills, superb views towards Wales. Parking for three cars. Library with over 1000 books. One single, two double and two twin bedrooms, bathroom, shower room, three toilets. Digital TV and computer with Wi-Fi internet. Quiet pub with good food.

SAT NAV *WR14 4BJ* **ONLINE MAP**

Unit General P S Leisure

MARKET RASEN, Lincolnshire Map ref 4D2

★★★★
SELF CATERING

Units 5
Sleeps 2–6

LOW SEASON PER WK
£190.00–£240.00

HIGH SEASON PER WK
£320.00–£439.00

Papermill Cottages, Tealby

contact Joyce Rhodes, Papermill Cottages, Vale Farm, Caistor Lane, Tealby LN8 3XN
t (01673) 838010 **e** peter.rhodes1@btinternet.com

papermillcottages.co.uk

A beautifully restored farmhouse courtyard of five cottages providing single and double self-catering accommodation to the highest standards.

open All year
payment Credit/debit cards, cash, cheques
nearest shop 0.5 miles
nearest pub 0.5 miles

Unit General P S Leisure

MATLOCK, Derbyshire Map ref 4B2

★★★★
SELF CATERING

Units 1
Sleeps 1–5

LOW SEASON PER WK
Min £220.00

HIGH SEASON PER WK
£400.00

Carpenters Cottage, Matlock

contact Bob & Iris Wilmot, c/o 8 Croft Road, Edwalton NG12 4BW **t** (0115) 923 3455 & 07967 120713 **e** bob.wilmot@merlinpoint.co.uk

carpenters-cottage.com REAL-TIME BOOKING

Fully modernised cottage within sensitively converted 18thC mill. Three bedrooms (one en suite), small, sunny garden, doorstep walks, designated private parking. Matlock is a 15-minute stroll.

open All year
payment Cash, cheques
nearest shop 0.5 miles
nearest pub 0.5 miles

Unit General P S

MATLOCK, Derbyshire Map ref 4B2

★★★-★★★★★
SELF CATERING

Units **94**
Sleeps **2–8**

LOW SEASON PER WK
£270.00–£730.00

HIGH SEASON PER WK
£470.00–£1,300.00

Midweek and weekend breaks available all year round (excl Christmas and New Year). More offers upon application.

Darwin Forest Country Park, Matlock

Darwin Forest Country Park, Darley Moor, Two Dales DE4 5LN **t** (01629) 732428
e darwin@pinelodgeholidays.co.uk

pinelodgeholidays.co.uk/darwin_forest.ihtml GUEST REVIEWS • SPECIAL OFFERS

open All year
payment Credit/debit cards, cash, cheques
nearest shop less than 0.5 miles
nearest pub less than 0.5 miles

Set in stunning woodland in the beautiful Derbyshire countryside and the Peak District. Luxurious, fully equipped pine lodges furnished to the highest standards. Indoor swimming pool, gymnasium, spa, steam room, sauna and beauty treatments, mini-golf and tennis, indoor and outdoor play areas, pub and restaurant with takeaway. Convenient shop and launderette.

ONLINE MAP

Unit General
Leisure

MATLOCK, Derbyshire Map ref 4B2

★★★
SELF CATERING

Units **1**
Sleeps **1–5**

LOW SEASON PER WK
£210.00–£270.00

HIGH SEASON PER WK
£300.00–£320.00

Eagle Cottage, Birchover, Matlock

contact Mrs Mary Prince, Eagle Cottage, c/o Haresfield House, Keeling Lane, Birchover, Matlock DE4 2BL **t** (01629) 650634 **e** maryprince@msn.com

cressbrook.co.uk/youlgve/eagle/

open All year
payment Cash, cheques
nearest shop less than 0.5 miles
nearest pub less than 0.5 miles

Quiet end-cottage in centre of small Peak District village having two pubs and a shop. Surrounded by network of public footpaths and stunning scenery in Area of Outstanding Natural Beauty. Many attractions, including stately Chatsworth House and Haddon Hall, nearby. Two rooms with double beds. Folding bed available.

SAT NAV *DE4 2BN*

Unit General P Leisure

MATLOCK, Derbyshire Map ref 4B2

★★★
SELF CATERING

Units **1**
Sleeps **1–5**

LOW SEASON PER WK
£245.00–£295.00

HIGH SEASON PER WK
£499.00–£549.00

Mansion Cottage, Crich, Matlock

contact Mrs Sally Parkin, Orchard House, Coasthill, Crich DE4 5DS **t** (01773) 857883
e info@mansioncottage.co.uk

mansioncottage.co.uk SPECIAL OFFERS • REAL-TIME BOOKING

Newly renovated, this beautiful 19thC Derbyshire stone cottage is spacious, immaculately presented and homely, retaining main original features. Totally refurbished throughout, the three bedrooms sleep four/five guests comfortably.

open All year
payment Credit/debit cards, cash, cheques
nearest shop less than 0.5 miles
nearest pub less than 0.5 miles

WALKERS WELCOME · CYCLISTS WELCOME · FAMILIES WELCOME

Unit General P Leisure

What if I need to cancel?

It's advisable to check the proprietor's cancellation policy at the time of booking in case you have to change your plans.

MATLOCK, Derbyshire Map ref 4B2

★★★★
SELF CATERING

Units 3
Sleeps 4–18

LOW SEASON PER WK
£248.00–£441.00

HIGH SEASON PER WK
£540.00–£830.00

Enjoy swimming in our heated indoor pool all year round, free to cottage guests.

Mooredge Barns, Matlock

contact Mr Barratt, Mooredge Farm, Knabb Hall Lane, Tansley, Matlock DE4 5FS **t** (01629) 583701 & 07766 074585 **e** enquiries@mooredgefarmcottages.co.uk

mooredgefarmcottages.co.uk

open All year
payment Cash, cheques
nearest shop 1 mile
nearest pub 0.5 miles

These barns are set in a very rural location down a quiet country lane, having splendid panoramic views from the grounds of the whole surrounding area with Riber Castle sitting on the horizon overlooking Matlock. Choice of cottages. Heated indoor pool.

Unit General P Leisure

MAVESYN RIDWARE, Staffordshire Map ref 4B3

★★★★★
SELF CATERING

Units 1
Sleeps 2–4

LOW SEASON PER WK
£350.00–£450.00

The Creamery at Manor Farm, Mavesyn Ridware, Nr Rugeley

contact Mrs Kate Derry, The Creamery, Mavesyn Ridware, Rugeley WS15 3QE **t** (01543) 493223 **e** katiederry@aol.com

thecreamerystaffs.com

Spacious barn conversion set within the grounds of Grade II Listed Manor Farm in the medieval hamlet of Mavesyn Ridware. Conveniently situated for easy access to Lichfield and various Midlands attractions.

open All year
payment Cash, cheques
nearest shop 1 mile
nearest pub 0.5 miles

Unit General P Leisure

MIDDLETON, Suffolk Map ref 3C2

★★★★
SELF CATERING

Units 1
Sleeps 2–4

LOW SEASON PER WK
£340.00–£390.00

HIGH SEASON PER WK
£430.00–£500.00

Short breaks available (excl Aug), min 2 nights.

The Cottage at Red Lodge Barn, Nr Saxmundham

contact Mrs Patricia Dowding, The Cottage at Red Lodge Barn, Middleton Moor, Middleton, Saxmundham IP17 3LN **t** (01728) 668100 **e** pat_roy16@hotmail.com

redlodgebarnsuffolk.co.uk

open All year
payment Cash, cheques, euros
nearest shop 1 mile
nearest pub 1 mile

Spacious, well-equipped accommodation, in an acre of grounds. Large, freshwater pond frequented by many birds. Full central heating and wood-burning stove. Many places of interest within easy reach. Five miles from Heritage Coast.

Unit General 5 P Leisure

PETS! WELCOME PETS! WELCOME

Where is my pet welcome?

Want to take your cherished companion with you on holiday? Proprietors participating in our Welcome Pets! scheme go out of their way to make special provision for you and your pet. Look out for the symbol.

MIDDLETON-BY-YOULGREAVE, Derbyshire Map ref 4B2

★★★★
SELF CATERING

Units 1
Sleeps 6

LOW SEASON PER WK
£300.00–£375.00

HIGH SEASON PER WK
£430.00–£525.00

Holly Homestead, Bakewell

contact Mr & Mrs David & Valerie Edge, Holly Homestead, c/o Ryklow, 48a Rectory Lane, Breadsall DE21 5LL **t** (01332) 830744 **e** mail@holly-homestead.co.uk

holly-homestead.co.uk SPECIAL OFFERS

open All year
payment Cash, cheques
nearest shop 1 mile
nearest pub 1 mile

Characterful, cosy Grade II Listed cottage, 250 years old, provides comfortable accommodation in beautiful and peaceful village. Two twin rooms, bathroom and one double en suite. Excellent central base for exploring, walking and cycling the Peak Park, particularly Bradford Dale, Limestone Way, High Peak Trail. Chatsworth and Haddon Hall close by. Cycle storage.

Unit General
Leisure

MILLER'S DALE, Derbyshire Map ref 4B2

★★★★
SELF CATERING

Units 1
Sleeps 9

LOW SEASON PER WK
£772.00–£847.00

HIGH SEASON PER WK
£921.00–£1,245.00

Riverside House, Miller's Dale

contact Wendy & Neil Boast, 76 Queen Elizabeth's Drive, Southgate, London N14 6RD
t (020) 8886 6324 **e** wendyboast@blueyonder.co.uk

riversidehouse-peakdistrict.co.uk GUEST REVIEWS

Spacious, detached house with lovely river views in heart of Miller's Dale. Recently modernised, well equipped, feature oak beams and exposed stone walls. Walks from door. Safe garden. Secure parking.

open All year
payment Cash, cheques
nearest shop 2 miles
nearest pub 1 mile

Unit General
Leisure

MONYASH, Derbyshire Map ref 4B2

★★★★
SELF CATERING

Units 2
Sleeps 2–5

LOW SEASON PER WK
£290.00–£320.00

HIGH SEASON PER WK
£467.00–£516.00

Sheldon Cottages, Bakewell

contact Mrs Louise Fanshawe, Sheldon Cottages, Sheldon House, Chapel Street, Bakewell DE45 1JJ
t (01629) 813067 **e** enquiries@sheldoncottages.co.uk

sheldoncottages.co.uk GUEST REVIEWS · SPECIAL OFFERS

Detached, self-catering cottage and flat in the heart of the Peak District; ideal for touring and walking. Dogs welcome in cottage by arrangement.

open All year
payment Cash, cheques
nearest shop 4 miles
nearest pub less than 0.5 miles

Unit General Leisure

MORVILLE, Shropshire Map ref 4A3

★★★★
SELF CATERING

Units 5
Sleeps 2–6

LOW SEASON PER WK
Min £200.00

HIGH SEASON PER WK
Max £600.00

Hurst Farm Cottages, Bridgnorth

contact Mr & Mrs J Brick, Hurst Farm, Morville, Bridgnorth WV16 4TF **t** (01746) 714375
e info@cottagefishingholidays.co.uk

cottagefishingholidays.co.uk

Pretty cottages overlooking lakes and open countryside. Well equipped, patios, gardens. Within east reach of Bridgnorth, Ironbridge and Much Wenlock. Coarse and fly fishing on site.

open All year
payment Cash, cheques

Unit General Leisure

MUCH WENLOCK, Shropshire Map ref 4A3

★★★★★
SELF CATERING

Units 1
Sleeps 1–6

LOW SEASON PER WK
Max £350.00

HIGH SEASON PER WK
Max £650.00

The Owl's House, Much Wenlock

contact Mrs Samantha Gray, The Owl's House, c/o Penkridge Cottage, Sheinton Road, Much Wenlock TF13 6NS **t** (01952) 728169 **e** dgray@dgray96.fsnet.co.uk

owlshouse.co.uk

open All year
payment Cash, cheques
nearest shop 2 miles
nearest pub 2 miles

Set in the heart of the Shropshire countryside, only two miles from Much Wenlock, this recently renovated and beautifully refurbished holiday cottage offers an idyllic location in which to relax and unwind. There is a herb garden and patio area, sitting amongst woodland views over the Wenlock Edge, Long Mynd and Wrekin.

Unit General 10 P S

MUCH WENLOCK, Shropshire Map ref 4A3

★★★★
SELF CATERING

Units 1
Sleeps 4

LOW SEASON PER WK
Min £295.00

HIGH SEASON PER WK
Max £495.00

Skimblescott Barn, Brockton, Much Wenlock

contact Mrs Tina Jones, Skimblescott Barn, Brockton, Skimblescott Farm, Much Wenlock TF13 6QS **t** (01746) 785664 **e** skimblescott@yahoo.co.uk

stmem.com/skimblescott-barn

Beautiful, fully equipped converted barn on working family farm. Private courtyard. Large garden with lovely views. Central for touring south Shropshire. Use of outdoor swimming pool.

open All year
payment Cash, cheques
nearest shop 4 miles
nearest pub 2 miles

Unit General P S Leisure

NARBOROUGH, Norfolk Map ref 3B1

★★★★
SELF CATERING

Units 4
Sleeps 2–6

LOW SEASON PER WK
£200.00–£405.00

HIGH SEASON PER WK
£310.00–£736.00

20% discount off all advertised prices. Phone for short-break prices.

Point House Holiday Cottages, King's Lynn

contact Ms Undine Fischer, Point House, Swaffham Road, Narborough, King's Lynn PE32 1TB **t** (01760) 338420 & 07872 064392 **e** stay@pointhousecottages.co.uk

pointhousecottages.co.uk GUEST REVIEWS · SPECIAL OFFERS · REAL-TIME BOOKING

open All year
payment Cash, cheques
nearest shop 0.5 miles
nearest pub 0.5 miles

Nestling in a peaceful and secluded woodland setting, these luxury renovated cottages offer the ideal spot to relax and unwind. Country walks in the glorious surrounding woodland start from your doorstep with an abundance of wildlife including peacocks to enjoy. Children will enjoy hours of fun in our woodland adventure activity area.

SAT NAV *PE32 1TB* **ONLINE MAP**

WALKERS WELCOME · CYCLISTS WELCOME · FAMILIES WELCOME

Unit General P S Leisure

FAMILIES WELCOME

Looking for an ideal family break?

For accommodation offering additional facilities and services for a range of ages and family units, look out for the Families Welcome symbol. Owners of these properties will go out of their way to welcome families.

NAYLAND, Suffolk Map ref 3B2

★★★★-★★★★★
SELF CATERING

Units 9
Sleeps 2–8

LOW SEASON PER WK
£260.00–£875.00

HIGH SEASON PER WK
£570.00–£1,800.00

Short breaks Oct-Easter. 3-night weekends or 4-night midweek breaks at 70% full-week rate.

Gladwins Farm, Nayland

contact Mr R Dossor, Gladwins Farm, Harpers Hill, Colchester CO6 4NU **t** (01206) 262261
e gladwinsfarm@aol.com

gladwinsfarm.co.uk SPECIAL OFFERS

open All year
payment Credit/debit cards, cash, cheques
nearest shop 0.5 miles
nearest pub less than 0.5 miles

Extensive wooded grounds in Suffolk's rolling Constable Country with marvellous views make ours a wonderful location. Charming villages and gardens to explore – not far from the sea. Heated indoor pool, sauna, hot tub, tennis, fishing, animals and playground. Pets welcome. Chelsworth and Melford cottages have private hot tubs.

ONLINE MAP

Unit General
Leisure

NEATISHEAD, Norfolk Map ref 3C1

★★★
SELF CATERING

Units 1
Sleeps 1–2

LOW SEASON PER WK
£210.00–£250.00

HIGH SEASON PER WK
£320.00–£420.00

Greengages Cottage, Neatishead, Norwich

contact Mrs Andree Davis, Threehammer Common, Neatishead, Norwich NR12 8BP
t (01692) 631176

A comfortable one-bedroom cottage in the grounds of the owner's house. A lovely, peaceful setting and conveniently located close to Horning Broad and within easy access of the North Norfolk coast.

open All year
payment Cheques, euros
nearest shop 1 mile
nearest pub 1 mile

Unit General P

NEEN SOLLARS, Shropshire Map ref 4A3

★★★★
SELF CATERING

Units 1
Sleeps 6

LOW SEASON PER WK
£230.00–£250.00

HIGH SEASON PER WK
£350.00–£420.00

Cider House, Kidderminster

contact Mrs P Kennedy, Tetstill Farm, Neen Sollars DY14 9AH **t** (01299) 270414
e email@priscillahann.co.uk

A converted farm building with 'upside down' accommodation sleeping four-six. Twin/double bed with en suite shower and double bed with bathroom next door. Own garden, 0.5 miles from Neen Sollars.

open All year
payment Cash, cheques
nearest shop 3.5 miles
nearest pub 1 mile

Unit General 5 P Leisure

NETHERSEAL, Derbyshire Map ref 4B3

★★★★
SELF CATERING

Units 2
Sleeps 2–8

LOW SEASON PER WK
£280.00–£800.00

HIGH SEASON PER WK
£320.00–£900.00

Sealbrook Farm, Swadlincote

contact Rob & Jane Kirkland, Grangewood, Swadlincote DE12 8BG **t** (01827) 373236
e info@sealbrookfarmcottages.co.uk

sealbrookfarmcottages.co.uk

Properties are in a quiet hamlet. Shops, pubs, restaurants, attractions are local, also in the heart of the National Forest. Within easy reach of motorway networks. Private off-road parking. Wi-Fi internet available.

open All year
payment Cash, cheques
nearest shop 2 miles
nearest pub 1.5 miles

Unit General P Leisure

NORFOLK BROADS

See under Aylsham, Gorleston-on-Sea, Lowestoft, Ludham, Neatishead, Oulton Broad, Stalham

NORTH SOMERCOTES, Lincolnshire Map ref 4D2

★★★★
SELF CATERING

Units 3
Sleeps 1–4

LOW SEASON PER WK
£170.00–£285.00

HIGH SEASON PER WK
£195.00–£425.00

All guests booking for a week or more will receive a complimentary £10 nursery voucher to spend as they choose.

Nursery Cottage (Meals Farm), North Somercotes, Louth

contact Mrs Linda Libell, Meals Farm, Marsh Lane, North Somercotes LN11 7NT **t** (01507) 358051 & (01507) 358256 **e** nurserycottage@hotmail.co.uk

mealsfarm.com GUEST REVIEWS

open All year
payment Cash, cheques
nearest shop 0.75 miles
nearest pub 0.75 miles

Three cottages on quiet lane leading to the sea. Lincolnshire coastal village setting with plenty to see and do nearby. Two beautiful cottages newly converted from 18thC barn, together with modern single-storey cottage also suitable for the disabled. Highest quality furnishings used throughout, luxury guaranteed. Visit our website!

SAT NAV *LN11 7NT* **ONLINE MAP**

Unit TV SC DVD General P S
Leisure

NORTON LINDSEY, Warwickshire Map ref 2B1

★★★★
SELF CATERING

Units 1
Sleeps 5

LOW SEASON PER WK
£284.00–£369.00

HIGH SEASON PER WK
£426.00–£586.00

Willow Cottage, Norton Lindsey, Warwick

contact Mrs Helen Phillips, Lower House Farm, Canada Lane, Norton Lindsey, Warwick CV35 8JH
t (01926) 842394 **e** canadalanefarm@yahoo.co.uk

willow-cottage.org.uk

open All year
payment Cash, cheques
nearest shop 2.5 miles
nearest pub 0.75 miles

Centrally heated cottage set in a quiet, rural location. Linen and heating provided. Ample parking. Lawned garden and patio.

Unit TV General P S

NOTTINGHAM, Nottinghamshire Map ref 4C2

★★★★
SELF CATERING

Units 2
Sleeps 1–4

LOW SEASON PER WK
£350.00–£400.00

HIGH SEASON PER WK
£400.00–£550.00

Short breaks available, min 3 nights.

Woodview Cottages, Owthorpe, Nottingham

contact Mrs Jane Morley, PC Morley and Son, Newfields Farm, Owthorpe NG12 3GF
t (01949) 81580 **e** enquiries@woodviewcottages.co.uk

woodviewcottages.co.uk SPECIAL OFFERS

open All year
payment Cash, cheques
nearest shop 3 miles
nearest pub 3 miles

Idyllic cottages set in picturesque gardens with woodland view surrounded by open countryside. Recently converted and tastefully furnished to complement the exposed beams/stonework. Well-equipped kitchen, comfortable living area, two bedrooms, bath/shower. Ideal touring/walking base. Located 20 minutes from Nottingham/Leicester on the edge of the Vale of Belvoir.

ONLINE MAP

Unit TV DVD General P S Leisure

OASBY, Lincolnshire Map ref 3A1

★★★★★
SELF CATERING

Units 1

LOW SEASON PER WK
£350.00–£465.00

HIGH SEASON PER WK
£525.00–£600.00

Midweek or weekend breaks available, minimum two nights.

Honeysuckle Cottage, Oasby, Grantham

contact Mrs Gill Wild, Honeysuckle Cottage, Foxdale, Mill Lane, Oasby, Grantham NG32 3NA
t (01529) 455681 & 07950 258931 **e** gillwild@foxdale-oasby.co.uk

honeysucklecottage-foxdale.co.uk

open All year
payment Cash, cheques
nearest shop 2 miles
nearest pub less than 0.5 miles

Attractive stone cottage in tranquil rural setting nestling on the edge of the quaint village of Oasby – a peaceful retreat in the Lincolnshire countryside. Two double en suite bedrooms and one twin en suite room which is disabled guest-friendly. Organic farm. Home of Oasby Horse Trials. Walks, rides. Optional stabling/grazing.

SAT NAV *NG32 3NA* **ONLINE MAP**

Unit General P Leisure

ORFORD, Suffolk Map ref 3C2

★★★★
SELF CATERING

Units 1
Sleeps 9–10

LOW SEASON PER WK
£550.00–£750.00

HIGH SEASON PER WK
£950.00–£1,255.00

Pets welcome by arrangement, £20 per pet. Large network of Suffolk Coastal Cycle Paths nearby. Access to private bird reserve by arrangement.

The Gedgrave Broom, Orford, Woodbridge

contact Mrs Ali Watson, The Groomery, Chillesford Lodge Estate, Woodbridge IP12 2AL
t (01394) 450488 **e** ab.watson@btinternet.com

tiscover.co.uk

open All year
payment Cash, cheques
nearest shop 1.5 miles
nearest pub 1.5 miles

18thC, red-brick gamekeeper's cottage with thatched roof, exposed beams and open fireplace. Very secluded edge-of-forest location with large, private, enclosed garden with barbecue and terrace. Completely tranquil, magnificent views. Includes large party/playbarn, table tennis, mini-snooker. Ideal venue for extended family groups/special celebrations, max 40 people. Suit outdoor types.

Unit
General P Leisure

OSWESTRY, Shropshire Map ref 4A3

★★★★
SELF CATERING

Units 1
Sleeps 4

LOW SEASON PER WK
Max £350.00

HIGH SEASON PER WK
Max £550.00

Free Sunday lunch for 4 at The Walls for weekly bookings.

Courtyard, Oswestry

contact Katherine Bottoms, Underhill House, Racecourse Road, Oswestry SY10 7PN
t (01691) 670066 **e** gohughes@aol.com

the-walls.co.uk

open All year
payment Credit/debit cards, cash, cheques
nearest shop 1.1 miles
nearest pub 1.1 miles

Characterful well-appointed cottage sleeping four. Both rooms double or twin and en suite. Lawn games, bikes available, large DVD/video library. Safe and peaceful but close to town. Lots of local attractions and activities, great restaurants.

ONLINE MAP

Unit General P Leisure

OSWESTRY, Shropshire Map ref 4A3

★★★★
SELF CATERING

Units 1
Sleeps 2–4

LOW SEASON PER WK
£150.00–£200.00

HIGH SEASON PER WK
£250.00–£300.00

The Stables, Morton, Oswestry

contact Mrs L M Frank, The Stables, Morton Farm, Morton, Oswestry SY10 8BE **t** (01691) 682218 **e** bookings@mortonstables.co.uk

mortonstables.co.uk

open All year
payment Cash, cheques
nearest shop 2 miles
nearest pub 1 mile

Delightful converted stable facing open countryside, across the road from our working farm. Charming bedroom with antique brass bed, French windows onto patio, and en suite shower room. Excellent fitted kitchen with washer/dryer. Comfortable sofa bed. Underfloor heating and all services included. Cosy ground-floor accommodation suitable for people with limited mobility.

Unit General P S Leisure

OULTON BROAD, Suffolk Map ref 3C1

★★★★
SELF CATERING

Units 4
Sleeps 2–18

LOW SEASON PER WK
Min £182.00

HIGH SEASON PER WK
Max £2,500.00

WALKERS WELCOME CYCLISTS WELCOME FAMILIES WELCOME PETS! WELCOME

Camps Heath Barn, Oulton, Lowestoft

contact Mr J R Overy, Camps Heath Barn, Camps Heath, Lowestoft NR32 5DW **t** (01502) 562981 & 07917 147776 **e** campsheathbarn@hotmail.co.uk

campsheathbarn.co.uk

open All year
payment Cash, cheques
nearest shop 0.5 miles
nearest pub 0.5 miles

This recently converted barn on the edge of a nature reserve provides a charming mix of traditional and modern, with spacious accommodation in the main barn and three self-contained annexes sleeping two to eighteen people. These are all furnished and equipped to please the most discerning visitor.

SAT NAV *NR32 5DW*

Unit General P S Leisure

OUNDLE, Northamptonshire Map ref 3A1

★★★–★★★★
SELF CATERING

Units 4
Sleeps 1–4

LOW SEASON PER WK
£250.00–£350.00

HIGH SEASON PER WK
£250.00–£350.00

Oundle Cottage Breaks, Oundle, Nr Peterborough

contact Mr & Mrs Simmonds, Oundle Cottage Breaks, Market Place, Oundle, Peterborough PE8 4BE **t** (01832) 275508 **e** richard@simmondsatoundle.co.uk

oundlecottagebreaks.co.uk

Self-contained units providing accommodation which forms part of the curtilage of a listed building. Non-smokers only please.

open All year except Christmas and New Year
payment Credit/debit cards, cash, cheques
nearest shop less than 0.5 miles
nearest pub less than 0.5 miles

Unit General S Leisure

PEAK DISTRICT

See under Alsop-en-le-Dale, Ashbourne, Bakewell, Bamford, Biggin-by-Hartington, Buxton, Castleton, Chapel-en-le-Frith, Cressbrook, Great Hucklow, Hartington, Hathersage, Hayfield, Middleton-by-Youlgreave, Miller's Dale, Monyash, Tideswell, Youlgreave

PELDON, Essex Map ref 3B3

★★★★
SELF CATERING

Units 1
Sleeps 4–6

LOW SEASON PER WK
£250.00–£300.00

HIGH SEASON PER WK
£350.00–£450.00

Rose Barn Cottage, Peldon, Colchester

contact Mrs Ariette Everett, Rose Barn, Mersea Road/Colchester Road, Peldon, Colchester CO5 7QJ
t (01206) 735317 **e** everettaj@aol.com

Self-catering annexe to converted barn-type property. Kitchen/dining hall, ground-floor twin bedroom and bathroom, sitting room with galleried landing to double bedroom. Set in four acres. Colchester ten minutes. Beach five minutes.

open All year except Christmas and New Year
payment Cash, cheques, euros
nearest shop 2 miles
nearest pub less than 0.5 miles

Unit General Leisure

PEMBRIDGE, Herefordshire Map ref 2A1

★★★
SELF CATERING

Units 2
Sleeps 1–4

LOW SEASON PER WK
£185.00–£280.00

HIGH SEASON PER WK
£280.00–£325.00

The Granary and The Dairy, Leominster

contact Mrs Nancy Owens, The Granary and The Dairy, The Grove, Noke Lane, Pembridge, Leominster HR6 9HP **t** (01544) 388268 **e** nancy@grovedesign.co.uk

open All year
payment Cash, cheques
nearest shop 3 miles
nearest pub 3 miles

Set in spectacular, peaceful Herefordshire countryside. Ideal for walks on Offa's Dyke, Mortimer Trail or around the farm itself. Many interesting places to visit, eg Mappa Mundi, Hereford and National Trust properties. Local horse-riding, fishing, go-karting. Warm welcome with tea tray and home bakes.

PETS! WELCOME PETS! WELCOME

Unit General Leisure

PENTNEY, Norfolk Map ref 3B1

★★★
SELF CATERING

Units 3
Sleeps 7

LOW SEASON PER WK
£250.00–£550.00

HIGH SEASON PER WK
£550.00–£750.00

Nar Valley Holiday Cottages, King's Lynn

contact Ms Rosemary de Bootman, Great Ketlam Farm, Low Road, King's Lynn PE32 1JF
t (01760) 338797 **e** info@narvalleycottagesnorfolk.co.uk

narvalleycottagesnorfolk.co.uk SPECIAL OFFERS

open All year
payment Cash, cheques
nearest shop 0.75 miles
nearest pub less than 0.5 miles

Set amidst a 230-acre farm, Nar Valley Cottages boast comfort and character in peaceful surroundings. Pentney is a picturesque village and a great base for exploring Norfolk. Enjoy country walks through woods and by the River Nar. Have a swim in the heated indoor pool, also gym and spa which is charged separately. Only 0.75 miles from A47 for good access.

ONLINE MAP

Unit General
Leisure

Using map references

The map references refer to the colour maps at the front of this guide. The first figure is the map number, the letter and figure that follow indicate the grid reference on the map.

PERSHORE, Worcestershire Map ref 2B1

★★★★
SELF CATERING

Units 1
Sleeps 2–3

LOW SEASON PER WK
£290.00–£340.00

HIGH SEASON PER WK
£400.00

Short breaks from £130. Special rates for Bank Holidays, Christmas, New Year and Cheltenham Festival.

Garth Cottage, Pershore

contact Mrs Margaret Smith, 8 Pensham Hill, Pershore WR10 3HA **t** (01386) 561213 & 07759 655717 **e** stephen.smith@homecall.co.uk

garthcottage.co.uk

open March to December
payment Cash, cheques
nearest shop 1 mile
nearest pub 0.75 miles

Delightful detached cottage in peaceful location, set in two acres of grounds in beautiful countryside, ten minutes' leisurely walk from elegant Georgian riverside town of Pershore. Use of owner's heated outdoor pool (seasonal) by arrangement. Large, airy bedroom. Double-bed settee in lounge. Oak beams and gas log-burning stove.

Unit General Leisure

PIN MILL, Suffolk Map ref 3C2

★★★
SELF CATERING

Units 1
Sleeps 4

LOW SEASON PER WK
£230.00–£360.00

HIGH SEASON PER WK
£350.00–£400.00

Alma Cottage, Ipswich

contact Mr John Pugh, Culver End, Stroud GL5 5AG **t** (01453) 872551 **e** john.pugh@talk21.com

open All year
payment Cash, cheques, euros
nearest shop 0.75 miles
nearest pub less than 0.5 miles

Located in the centre of Pin Mill, 25m from high water with uninterrupted views over the unspoilt Orwell Estuary. Pin Mill is a traditional sailing village with free public access to water. The tidal estuary and the nearby coast are ideal for families, walkers, birdwatchers and painters.

Unit General Leisure

PLUNGAR, Leicestershire Map ref 4C2

★★★
SELF CATERING

Units 1
Sleeps 2

LOW SEASON PER WK
£200.00

HIGH SEASON PER WK
£280.00

The Forge, Vale of Belvoir

contact Mrs Valerie Ridgway, The Forge, 2 Granby Lane, Plungar NG13 0JJ **t** (01949) 861355 **e** john.ridgway4@btopenworld.com

plungarforge.com

Newly converted self-contained accommodation with private patio and garden attached to a 17thC cottage. Lounge/dining room, kitchen, bedroom with double bed, and shower room with washbasin, wc and bidet.

open All year
payment Cash, cheques, euros
nearest shop 2 miles
nearest pub less than 0.5 miles

Unit General Leisure

What if I need to cancel?

It is advisable to check the proprietor's cancellation policy in case you have to change your plans at a later date.

REDE, Suffolk Map ref 3B2

★★★★
SELF CATERING & SERVICED APARTMENTS

Units **2**
Sleeps **2–6**

LOW SEASON PER WK
£225.00–£300.00

HIGH SEASON PER WK
£500.00–£650.00

Rede Hall Farm Park, Bury St Edmunds

t (01284) 850695 **e** chris@redehallfarmpark.co.uk

redehallfarmpark.co.uk

Ideal country retreat in old-fashioned farmyard. Jenny Wren has two double bedrooms and galleried twin room with its own sitting room. Nuthatch has two double en suite bedrooms and a sofa bed.

open All year
payment Cash, cheques
nearest shop 2 miles
nearest pub 2 miles

Unit General P Leisure

REEDHAM, Norfolk Map ref 3C1

★★★★
SELF CATERING

Units **3**
Sleeps **2–6**

LOW SEASON PER WK
£200.00–£400.00

HIGH SEASON PER WK
£400.00–£600.00

Riverside Properties, Reedham

contact Mrs Heather Willies, Riverside Properties, Coombe Cottage, Grayswood Road, Haslemere GU27 2BU **t** (01428) 658289 **e** rivitt@aol.com

tiscover.co.uk

One two-person and two six-person cottages in tranquil riverside location. Newly refurbished. River frontage and mooring. Swallow Cottage: one double bed. Yar Cottage and Water's Edge: two doubles, one twin.

open All year
payment Cash, cheques
nearest shop less than 0.5 miles
nearest pub less than 0.5 miles

Unit General P
Leisure

RETFORD, Nottinghamshire Map ref 4C2

★★★
SELF CATERING

Units **1**
Sleeps **1–4**

LOW SEASON PER WK
£300.00–£360.00

HIGH SEASON PER WK
£370.00–£400.00

Spruce Cottage, Ranby, Retford

t (0131) 447 6886

countrycottagesonline.net

open All year
payment Cash, cheques
nearest shop 3 miles
nearest pub 3 miles

Cottage lying in a beautiful setting surrounded by private woodland and grazing paddocks with 20 acres of private parkland for walking. One double and two single bedrooms. Warm and cosy in winter from wood-burning stove and log fire. Easy access to Sherwood Forest, Rufford Abbey and Lincoln Cathedral.

Unit General 4 P

RETFORD, Nottinghamshire Map ref 4C2

★★★
SELF CATERING

Units 1
Sleeps 4

LOW SEASON PER WK
£250.00–£300.00

HIGH SEASON PER WK
£300.00–£360.00

Westhill Cottage, Retford

t (01777) 707034 **e** holly23@tiscali.co.uk

westhillcottage.co.uk

open All year
payment Cash, cheques
nearest shop 1 mile
nearest pub 1 mile

Detached bungalow in private grounds. Fully furnished and equipped to a high standard. Two twin bedrooms with open-plan lounge/kitchen/dining room. Ideal location for historic Lincoln, Newark and Sherwood Forest. Quiet location within five minutes' walk of local shops, post office and pubs/restaurant.

Unit General P S Leisure

ROSS-ON-WYE, Herefordshire Map ref 2A1

★★★
SELF CATERING

Units 2
Sleeps 2–4

LOW SEASON PER WK
£230.00–£250.00

HIGH SEASON PER WK
£270.00–£400.00

Short breaks available Oct-Mar. 3-night stay.

The Game Larders and The Old Bakehouse, Ross-on-Wye

contact Miss Anthea McIntyre, The Game Larders and The Old Bakehouse, Wythall Estate, Bulls Hill, Ross-on-Wye HR9 5SD **t** (01989) 562688 **e** wythall@globalnet.co.uk

wythallestate.co.uk

open All year
payment Cash, cheques
nearest shop 2 miles
nearest pub 1 mile

Self-contained cottages in the wing of a 16thC manor house in a secluded setting with garden, duck pond and wooded grounds. You will enjoy peace and quiet here and see an abundance of wildlife. Well equipped and furnished in period style, the cottages are warm and comfortable.

Unit General P

RUDYARD, Staffordshire Map ref 4B2

★★★★
SELF CATERING

Units 1
Sleeps 5

LOW SEASON PER WK
£700.00–£910.00

HIGH SEASON PER WK
£700.00–£910.00

£100-£130 per night. Minimum stay 3 nights. Please phone to discuss alternative requirements.

The Bothy, Rudyard, Leek

contact Mr Andrew Mount and Miss Michelle Ash, **t** 07771 702949 & 07957 856629
e info@thebothy-rudyard.co.uk

thebothy-rudyard.co.uk

open All year
payment Cash, cheques
nearest shop 10 miles
nearest pub 3 miles

The Bothy is a secluded retreat nestling on the banks of Rudyard Lake. The perfect escape for couples and families alike. Tastefully furnished and fully equipped, no detail has been overlooked. Relax on the stunning waterfront terrace with hot tub. Complete with private pontoon and boating and fishing rights.

Unit General P S
Leisure

RUGBY, Warwickshire Map ref 4C3

★★★
SELF CATERING

Units 1
Sleeps 2–4

LOW SEASON PER WK
£250.00–£295.00

HIGH SEASON PER WK
£295.00

Lodge Farm, Long Lawford, Rugby

contact Mr & Mrs Alec & Jane Brown, Lodge Farm, Bilton Lane, Long Lawford, Rugby CV23 9DU
t (01788) 560193 **e** alec@lodgefarm.com

lodgefarm.com

Delightfully converted farm buildings in a pleasant location close to Rugby. Let nightly or weekly. Children and controlled dogs are welcome.

open All year
payment Credit/debit cards, cash, cheques, euros
nearest shop 0.5 miles
nearest pub 0.5 miles

Unit General Leisure

ST NEOTS, Cambridgeshire Map ref 2D1

★★★★★
SELF CATERING

Units 1
Sleeps 6

LOW SEASON PER WK
£480.00–£512.00

HIGH SEASON PER WK
£554.00–£796.00

Take a short break and play golf at 3 of Cambridgeshire's top golf courses at a special discounted rate.

Abbotsley Country Homes, Eynesbury Hardwicke, St Neots

contact Mr Michael Wilton-Cox, Abbotsley Country Homes, Drewels Lane, Eynesbury Hardwicke, St Neots PE19 6EF **t** (01480) 476312 **e** abbotsleyhomes@btconnect.com

abbotsleycountryhomes.co.uk REAL-TIME BOOKING

open All year
payment Cash, cheques, euros
nearest shop 3 miles
nearest pub 0.5 miles

These luxury, self-catering Norwegian log cabins overlook the stunning Cambridgeshire countryside. They are perfect for a family break, with three double bedrooms (one en suite). The lodges have classic Scandinavian styling and offer comfortable, spacious open-plan living. Adjacent to two golf courses, close to local amenities.

SAT NAV *PE19 6EF* **ONLINE MAP**

Unit General Leisure

ST OWENS CROSS, Herefordshire Map ref 2A1

★★★★★
SELF CATERING

Units 1
Sleeps 16

LOW SEASON PER WK
£1,100.00–£2,500.00

HIGH SEASON PER WK
£1,800.00–£4,000.00

Trevase Granary, Ross-on-Wye

contact Mrs Liz Pursey, Trevase Granary, Trevase Farm, St Owens Cross, Hereford HR2 8ND
t (01989) 730210 **e** stay@trevasecottages.co.uk

trevasecottages.co.uk REAL-TIME BOOKING

New, luxury barn conversion beautifully furnished and equipped. Sleeps sixteen in eight en suite bedrooms – two bedrooms for the disabled. Open plan living room for meetings. Walled garden with jacuzzi. Five-acre fishing lake.

open All year
payment Cash, cheques
nearest shop 2 miles
nearest pub 2 miles

Unit General
Leisure

SAXMUNDHAM, Suffolk Map ref 3C2

★★★★
SELF CATERING

Units 1
Sleeps 4

LOW SEASON PER WK
£290.00–£490.00

HIGH SEASON PER WK
£390.00–£490.00

Short breaks: 4 nights for the price of 3 (4 nights midweek for the price of 3 at weekends). Telephone for current offers/promotions. Wine-tastings, arts/music events locally.

Corner Cottage, Saxmundham

contact Dawn Ribnell, 35 North Road, Brentwood CM14 4UZ **t** (01277) 210551 & 07860 887653
e info@cornercottageholiday.com

cornercottageholiday.com GUEST REVIEWS · SPECIAL OFFERS

open All year
payment Cash, cheques
nearest shop less than 0.5 miles
nearest pub less than 0.5 miles

Quaint, single-storey period cottage in a quiet, friendly market town location, four miles Snape, eight miles Aldeburgh, on Suffolk Heritage Coast. Light and airy, with pleasant views from each window. Lovely feature fireplace for cosy log fires in winter. Two comfortable bedrooms. One can be arranged as either king-size double or two single beds.

SAT NAV *IP17 1BJ* **ONLINE MAP**

Unit TV DVD   General P S
Leisure

SAXMUNDHAM, Suffolk Map ref 3C2

★★★★
SELF CATERING

Units 1
Sleeps 4

LOW SEASON PER WK
£350.00–£400.00

HIGH SEASON PER WK
£450.00–£475.00

Rookery Park, Saxmundham

contact Mrs Eden McDonald, Rookery Park, Yoxford IP17 3HQ **t** (01728) 668740

tiscover.co.uk

payment Cash, cheques
nearest shop 0.5 miles
nearest pub 0.5 miles

Convenient Heritage Coast (Southwold, Dunwich, Minsmere, Snape, Aldeburgh) and rural Suffolk. Attractively furnished. Clean, spacious lounge/diner/kitchen (dishwasher, washing machine, dryer, microwave etc). One double, one twin. Large patio. Panoramic parkland views. Own grounds on 120-acre country estate. Linen, heating and lighting included. Parking. Closed 14 January to 1 March.

Unit TV DVD   General P

SHARRINGTON, Norfolk Map ref 3B1

★★★★
SELF CATERING

Units 1
Sleeps 2–4

LOW SEASON PER WK
£250.00

HIGH SEASON PER WK
£350.00–£385.00

Garden Cottage, Chequers, Sharrington

contact Mrs R M Kimmins, Chequers, Bale Road, Sharrington NR24 2PG **t** (01263) 860308
e rosemary@kimmins1.wanadoo.co.uk

tiscover.co.uk

open All year except Christmas and New Year
payment Cash, cheques
nearest shop 1 mile
nearest pub 3 miles

This high quality conversion of an 18thC building overlooks a large garden in a quiet village convenient to Holt, Blakeney, and the whole North Norfolk coast. Fitted and furnished to the highest standard. Ample parking. Private management provides a warm welcome and cares for the success of your holiday.

Unit TV   General 15 P S

For **key to symbols** see page 7

SHERINGHAM, Norfolk Map ref 3B1

★★★–★★★★★
SELF CATERING

Units 2
Sleeps 1–8

LOW SEASON PER WK
Min £169.00

HIGH SEASON PER WK
Max £899.00

Short breaks available. Reductions for Senior Citizens during winter, spring and autumn. Discounts for 2 consecutive weeks out of season.

Augusta and Bennett, Sheringham

contact Mr Trevor Claydon, Camelot House, Holt Road, Gresham NR11 8AD **t** (01263) 577560
e enquiries@sheringhamcottages.co.uk

sheringhamcottages.co.uk GUEST REVIEWS · SPECIAL OFFERS

open All year
payment Cash, cheques
nearest shop less than 0.5 miles
nearest pub less than 0.5 miles

Augusta and Bennett nestle in a peaceful conservation area between town centre and sea, only a few hundred metres from steam railway, golf course, theatre, shops, life-guarded Blue Flag beach. They offer lounge, separate dining room, kitchen, gas central heating, double-glazing. To rear are delightful gardens; patio tables, chairs, cycle storage. Off-street parking is available.

SAT NAV *NR26 8LB* **ONLINE MAP**

Unit General P Leisure

SHERWOOD FOREST

See under Retford, Southwell

SHREWSBURY, Shropshire Map ref 4A3

★★★
SELF CATERING

Units 1
Sleeps 3

LOW SEASON PER WK
£250.00–£400.00

HIGH SEASON PER WK
£300.00–£500.00

Hotspur, Shrewsbury

contact Ms Miriam Doyle, Paul Keogh Architects, Cathedral Court, New Street, Dublin 8
t 00353 1 679 1551 **e** info@pka.ie

Hotspur is a beautifully restored cottage in the centre of Shrewsbury with comfortable, well-equipped accommodation.

open All year
payment Cash, cheques
nearest shop less than 0.5 miles
nearest pub less than 0.5 miles

Unit General P Leisure

SIBSEY, Lincolnshire Map ref 3A1

★★★
SELF CATERING

Units 1
Sleeps 1–4

LOW SEASON PER WK
£200.00–£230.00

HIGH SEASON PER WK
£250.00–£280.00

Sweetbriar, Boston

contact Mrs Alison Twiddy, Sweetbriar, Main Road, Sibsey, Boston PE22 0TT **t** (01205) 750837
e twiddytowers@yahoo.co.uk

cottageguide.co.uk

One-bedroom self-catering apartment with kitchen/living room featuring one double and one sofa bed. Includes use of beautiful garden. Close to Skegness and coast, Lincoln, Lincolnshire wolds and Boston.

open All year
payment Cash, cheques
nearest shop 1 mile
nearest pub 1 mile

Unit General P Leisure

SIBTON, Suffolk Map ref 3C2

★★★★
SELF CATERING

Units 1
Sleeps 1–5

LOW SEASON PER WK
£250.00–£410.00

HIGH SEASON PER WK
£410.00–£590.00

3- and 4- night breaks available Nov-Mar (excl Christmas, New Year and Easter).

Cardinal Cottage, Sibton, Saxmundham

contact Mr & Mrs Eric Belton, Cardinal Cottage, Pouy Street, Sibton, Saxmundham IP17 2JH
t (01728) 660111 **e** jan.belton@btinternet.com

cardinalcottageholidays.co.uk GUEST REVIEWS

open All year
payment Cash, cheques
nearest shop 0.75 miles
nearest pub less than 0.5 miles

Delightfully cosy, period, timber-framed cottage with spectacular beams. Three bedrooms, sitting room, dining room, kitchen and bathroom, all fully equipped to high standard. Enclosed private garden with car park. Close Heritage Coast, Minsmere, Aldeburgh and Southwold. Ideal base for walkers and birdwatchers, or those after a quiet country retreat.

SAT NAV *IP17 2JH* **ONLINE MAP**

WELCOME FAMILIES WELCOME PETS!

Unit General P S
Leisure

SOUTH COCKERINGTON, Lincolnshire Map ref 4D2

★★★★
SELF CATERING

Units 2
Sleeps 4–5

LOW SEASON PER WK
£275.00–£325.00

HIGH SEASON PER WK
£325.00–£460.00

Grasswells Farm Holiday Cottages, Louth

contact Ms Janice Foster, Grasswells Holiday Cottages (Saddleback Leisure Ltd), Saddleback Road, Howdales, South Cockerington, Louth LN11 7DJ **t** (01507) 338508 **e** thefosters2002@talk-email.com

Single barn conversions, spacious, comfortable and well equipped. Set in three acres of grounds with private fishing lake.

open All year
payment Cash, cheques
nearest shop 3 miles
nearest pub 3 miles

Unit General P S Leisure

SOUTH COCKERINGTON, Lincolnshire Map ref 4D2

★★★
SELF CATERING

Units 3
Sleeps 2–4

LOW SEASON PER WK
£230.00–£280.00

HIGH SEASON PER WK
£290.00–£360.00

West View Cottages, Louth

contact Mr Richard Nicholson and Mrs Judith Hand, West View, South View Lane, Louth LN11 7ED
t (01507) 327209 & 07855 291185 **e** enquiries@west-view.co.uk

west-view.co.uk GUEST REVIEWS · SPECIAL OFFERS · REAL-TIME BOOKING

open All year
payment Cash, cheques
nearest shop 2 miles
nearest pub 2 miles

Beautifully converted, single-storey farm buildings tastefully decorated to a high standard. Ideally located in a quiet village with the market town of Louth four miles away. There are numerous quiet beaches along the coast (six miles). Suitable walking and cycling routes are close by. Come and relax in pleasant surroundings.

ONLINE MAP

Unit General P S Leisure

Place index

If you know where you want to stay, the index by place name at the back of the guide will give you the page number listing accommodation in your chosen town, city or village. Check out the other useful indexes too.

SOUTH MIMMS, Hertfordshire Map ref 2D1

★★–★★★
SELF CATERING

Units 3
Sleeps 2–6

LOW SEASON PER WK
£210.00–£260.00

HIGH SEASON PER WK
£240.00–£300.00

The Black Swan, Potters Bar

contact Mr Marsterson, The Black Swan, Blanche Lane, Potters Bar EN6 3PD **t** (01707) 644180
e wmarsterson@yahoo.co.uk

Cottage and self-contained flats, 16thC listed building. Rail connections at Potters Bar and London Underground at Barnet allow travel to London within 45 minutes.

open All year
payment Cash, cheques
nearest shop less than 0.5 miles
nearest pub less than 0.5 miles

Unit TV General P

SOUTHEND-ON-SEA, Essex Map ref 3B3

★★★
SELF CATERING

Units 1
Sleeps 1–5

LOW SEASON PER WK
£350.00–£450.00

HIGH SEASON PER WK
£420.00–£450.00

Everhome Apartments, Southend-on-Sea

contact Mr Malcolm Taylor, 26 Drake Road, Westcliff-on-Sea SS0 8LP **t** (01702) 434320
e malcolm-t@btconnect.com

everhome.co.uk

Lovely self-catering (two-bedroom) apartment situated in conservation area ten to fifteen minutes' walk from the sea, pier, high street, railway station (London 45 minutes), Cliffs Pavilion Theatre, restaurants and bars.

open All year
payment Credit/debit cards, cash, cheques, euros
nearest shop less than 0.5 miles
nearest pub less than 0.5 miles

Unit TV SC DVD General P

SOUTHWELL, Nottinghamshire Map ref 4C2

★★★★
SELF CATERING

Units 3
Sleeps 2–6

LOW SEASON PER WK
Min £189.00

HIGH SEASON PER WK
Max £420.00

The Hayloft, Little Tithe & Dovecote, Southwell

contact Mrs Wilson, Lodge Farm, Gorsy Lane, Morton, Fiskerton, Southwell NG25 0XH
t (01636) 830497

lodgebarns.com

open All year
payment Cash, cheques
nearest shop 1 mile
nearest pub 0.5 miles

Situated on working farm in country village of Morton, these 18thC barn conversions offer you a high standard of self-contained facilities. Twin-bedded rooms, each with shower room, fully fitted kitchen, lounge. Set in an orchard courtyard and farmland. Within walking distance of village shop, local pubs and River Trent.

Unit TV DVD General P S Leisure

SOUTHWOLD, Suffolk Map ref 3C2

★★★
SELF CATERING

Units 1
Sleeps 6

LOW SEASON PER WK
£440.00

HIGH SEASON PER WK
£695.00

11 Chester Road, Southwold

Suffolk Holidays, The Old Water Tower, The Common, Southwold IP18 6TB **t** (01502) 723571
e info@holidaysinsuffolk.co.uk

Three-bedroom house close to beach and shops. Small patio at rear. Outlook to lighthouse. Two double beds and two full-size bunk beds.

open All year
payment Cash, cheques
nearest shop less than 0.5 miles
nearest pub less than 0.5 miles

Unit TV SC DVD General P S Leisure

Looking for a wide range of facilities?
More stars means higher quality accommodation plus a greater range of facilities and services.

SOUTHWOLD, Suffolk Map ref 3C2

★★★
SELF CATERING

Units 1
Sleeps 1–6

LOW SEASON PER WK
Min £400.00

HIGH SEASON PER WK
Max £800.00

15 Stradbroke Road, Southwold

contact H A Adnams, 89 High Street, Southwold IP18 6DP **t** (01502) 723292

haadnams.com

A delightful family house, sympathetically modernised to a high standard. Situated close to the sea and within easy reach of the shops and town centre. Strictly non-smoking.

open All year
payment Credit/debit cards
nearest shop less than 0.5 miles
nearest pub less than 0.5 miles

Unit General P Leisure

SOUTHWOLD, Suffolk Map ref 3C2

★★★★
SELF CATERING

Units 1
Sleeps 6

LOW SEASON PER WK
£440.00–£645.00

HIGH SEASON PER WK
£645.00–£820.00

Off-peak short breaks available throughout the year.

Fisherman's Cottage, Southwold

contact Ms Victoria Seale, 46 Avenue Road, London N6 5DR **t** 07973 113369
e victoriaseale@btconnect.com

fishermanscottagesouthwold.co.uk

open All year
payment Cash, cheques
nearest shop less than 0.5 miles
nearest pub less than 0.5 miles

Bright, delightful terraced cottage 50yds from beach. Two receptions, one dining room (all with wood-burning stoves) leading to a small patio. Downstairs wc. Two double bedrooms (with wood-burning stoves) one with en suite shower and wc. Third bedroom with two single beds. Small bathroom, full-sized bath, separate shower, wc.

Unit General S Leisure

SOUTHWOLD, Suffolk Map ref 3C2

★★★★
SELF CATERING

Units 2
Sleeps 1–6

LOW SEASON PER WK
£190.00–£260.00

HIGH SEASON PER WK
£340.00–£470.00

Off-peak, 3- or 4-day short breaks available throughout the year (excl Bank Hols).

Poplar Hall, Southwold

contact Mrs Anna Garwood, Poplar Hall, Frostenden, Nr Southwold NR34 7JA **t** (01502) 578549

southwold.ws/poplar-hall SPECIAL OFFERS

open All year
payment Cash, cheques
nearest shop 1.5 miles
nearest pub 1.5 miles

Excellent self-catering accommodation in the grounds of 16thC thatched Poplar Hall, surrounded by quiet lanes, woods, meadows and secluded beaches. The Cottage (with double bedroom) and Lofthouse (with a double and twin) are characterful and welcoming, fully equipped and tastefully and comfortably decorated. Private gardens/patio, private parking close to units.

Unit General P S Leisure

Do you have access needs?

Look for the National Accessible Scheme symbols if you have special hearing, visual or mobility needs. An index of accommodation participating in the scheme can be found at the back of this guide.

STALHAM, Norfolk Map ref 3C1

★★★
SELF CATERING

Units 1
Sleeps 2–4

LOW SEASON PER WK
£200.00–£300.00

HIGH SEASON PER WK
£300.00–£350.00

Chapelfield Cottage Apartment, Stalham

contact Mr Gary Holmes, Chapelfield Cottage Flat, Chapel Field, Stalham NR12 9EN
t (01692) 582173 **e** chapelfield_hols@btinternet.com

chapelfieldcottage.co.uk

Holiday apartment, part of traditional pantile Norfolk cottage, ideal for couples or small family. Tranquil location close to river, only 10 minutes from Stalham. Lounge, kitchen, bathroom, bedroom.

open All year except Christmas
payment Cash, cheques
nearest shop 1 mile
nearest pub 1.2 miles

Unit General P S Leisure

STAMFORD, Lincolnshire Map ref 3A1

★★★
SELF CATERING

Units 1
Sleeps 4

LOW SEASON PER WK
£200.00–£300.00

HIGH SEASON PER WK
£300.00–£400.00

Elder Flower Cottage, Belmesthorpe, Stamford

contact Mr P & Mrs D Wilkinson, Elder Flower Cottage, Shepherds Walk, Belmesthorpe PE9 4JG
t (01780) 757188 & 07711 533204 **e** philipwdawn@btinternet.com

Spacious, detached, high-quality bungalow close to the historic town of Stamford and Rutland Water. Decorated, furnished and equipped to a high standard.

open All year
payment Cash, cheques

Unit General P Leisure

STANSTED, Essex Map ref 2D1

★★★★
SELF CATERING

Units 3
Sleeps 1–7

LOW SEASON PER WK
£360.00–£420.00

HIGH SEASON PER WK
£470.00–£560.00

The Priory, Tilty

contact Mrs Karen Thompson, Coldarbour Farm, Grange Green, Tilty CM6 2EH **t** (01371) 870547 & 07771 880077 **e** bookings@tiltypriory.co.uk

tiltypriory.co.uk

Three luxury converted self-contained listed barns in rural surroundings. Immaculately presented, stylishly equipped to the highest standards.

open All year
payment Cash, cheques
nearest shop 3 miles
nearest pub 1.5 miles

Unit General P Leisure

STANSTED MOUNTFITCHET, Essex Map ref 2D1

★★★-★★★★
SELF CATERING

Units 2
Sleeps 4–5

LOW SEASON PER WK
£200.00–£400.00

HIGH SEASON PER WK
£200.00–£400.00

Walpole Farm House, Stansted

contact Mrs Jill Walton, Walpole Farm House, Stansted CM24 8TA **t** (01279) 812265
e jill@jsawalton.demon.co.uk

walpolefarmhouse.com

An attractively converted farm building on one level with a spacious private garden, Walpole Farmhouse is conveniently located with great access to the M11 motorway and Stansted Airport.

open All year
payment Cash, cheques
nearest shop less than 0.5 miles
nearest pub less than 0.5 miles

Unit General P S

What do the star ratings mean?

For a detailed explanation of the quality and facilities represented by the stars, please refer to the information pages at the back of this guide.

STRATFORD-UPON-AVON, Warwickshire Map ref 2B1

★★★
SELF CATERING

Units **1**
Sleeps **1–2**

LOW SEASON PER WK
£260.00–£300.00

HIGH SEASON PER WK
£395.00

Flexible start days. Short breaks (3-night weekend, 4-night midweek). 10% discount for returning guests.

4 Bancroft Place, Stratford-upon-Avon

contact Mr & Mrs D Barnett, 43 Orchard Close, Stanstead Abbotts SG12 8AH **t** (01920) 871849
e carolannbarnett@yahoo.co.uk

4bancroftplace.com

open All year
payment Cash, cheques
nearest shop less than 0.5 miles
nearest pub less than 0.5 miles

Town centre, canalside, light and airy, first-floor studio apartment for two adults. Living area cleverly converts into a bedroom with fully sprung 4' 6' sofa bed. Very well equipped kitchen, shower room and hallway/dressing area. Within walking distance of everything Stratford offers. Off-road, dedicated parking for one vehicle.

Unit General P Leisure

STRATFORD-UPON-AVON, Warwickshire Map ref 2B1

★★★
SELF CATERING

Units **1**
Sleeps **1–3**

LOW SEASON PER WK
£180.00–£200.00

HIGH SEASON PER WK
£220.00–£250.00

Chestnut Cottage, Pathlow, Stratford-upon-Avon

contact Mrs Joyce Rush, Gospel Oak House, Gospel Oak Lane, Pathlow, Stratford-upon-Avon CV37 0JA **t** (01789) 292764

Set in splendid, secluded grounds by woodland, with far-reaching views. Well appointed, attractively furnished, ample parking. Two and a half miles from Stratford-upon-Avon.

open All year except Christmas and New Year
payment Cash, cheques
nearest shop 2 miles
nearest pub less than 0.5 miles

Unit General P

STRATFORD-UPON-AVON, Warwickshire Map ref 2B1

★★★★
SELF CATERING

Units **2**
Sleeps **1–6**

LOW SEASON PER WK
Max £595.00

HIGH SEASON PER WK
Max £750.00

Riverview Lodge & River Haven Lodge, Stratford-upon-Avon

t 07802 640372 **e** info@luxurylifestylelodges.co.uk

luxurylifestylelodges.co.uk

open All year
payment Cash, cheques
nearest shop less than 0.5 miles
nearest pub less than 0.5 miles

Luxury holiday retreats with decked areas overlooking the River Avon, only 0.75 miles from Stratford-upon-Avon town. A perfect base for exploring the many beautiful and historic sites of Warwickshire and the Cotswolds. Designed and decorated with style and comfort in mind.

ONLINE MAP

Unit General P Leisure

Check the maps for accommodation locations

Colour maps at the front pinpoint all the places where accommodation is featured within the regional sections of this guide. Pick your location and then refer to the place index at the back to find the page number.

SYMONDS YAT, Herefordshire Map ref 2A1

★★★
SELF CATERING

Units 9
Sleeps 2–10

LOW SEASON PER WK
£210.00–£559.00

HIGH SEASON PER WK
£294.00–£823.00

Flanesford Priory, Goodrich, Ross-on-Wye

contact Mr and Mrs Nigel & Isabel Roper, Flanesford Priory, Goodrich, Ross-on-Wye HR9 6HZ
t (01600) 890506 **e** info@flanesfordpriory.co.uk

flanesfordpriory.co.uk GUEST REVIEWS

open All year
payment Credit/debit cards, cash, cheques
nearest shop 0.5 miles
nearest pub less than 0.5 miles

Nestled between the River Wye and Goodrich Castle, this 14thC monastery contains luxury self-catering apartments complete with original ceiling beams and woodburners. Situated in the heart of the Wye Valley and beside the Forest of Dean, it is surrounded by some of the best countryside Britain has to offer.

SAT NAV *HR9 6HZ* **ONLINE MAP**

WALKERS WELCOME

Unit General P Leisure

TATTERSETT, Norfolk Map ref 3B1

★★★★
SELF CATERING

Units 5
Sleeps 4–6

LOW SEASON PER WK
£200.00–£280.00

HIGH SEASON PER WK
£400.00–£580.00

Tatt Valley Holiday Cottages, Tattersett

contact Mr Thomas Hurn, Tatt Valley Holiday Cottages, Tattersett PE31 8RT **t** (01485) 528506
e enquiries@norfolkholidayhomes.co.uk

norfolkholidayhomes.co.uk

Luxury barn conversions. High-standard accommodation with many original features. A large games barn with facilities for all ages. Situated on a working farm near to Burnham Market and the Norfolk coast.

open All year
payment Cash, cheques
nearest shop 2 miles
nearest pub 2 miles

Unit General P Leisure

TENBURY WELLS, Worcestershire Map ref 4A3

★★★★
SELF CATERING

Units 1

LOW SEASON PER WK
£500.00

HIGH SEASON PER WK
£500.00

Long Cover Cottage, Tenbury Wells

contact Mrs Eleanor Van Straaten, Holiday Cottage, Fishpool Cottage, Kyre, Tenbury Wells WR15 8RL **t** (01885) 410208 **e** ellie_vanstraaten@yahoo.co.uk

a-country-break.co.uk

open All year
payment Cash, cheques
nearest shop 3 miles
nearest pub 3 miles

A retreat from the outside world with magnificent views in all directions over the Teme and Kyre Valleys. The cottage has two double rooms and one twin. Exposed beams, oak/elm staircase, leaded light windows, Aga, woodburning stove. A network of paths and bridleways leads directly from the cottage. Badgers, woodpeckers and buzzards are regular visitors.

Unit General Leisure

Need some ideas?

Big city buzz or peaceful panoramas? Take a fresh look at England and you may be surprised at what's right on your doorstep. Explore the diversity online at enjoyengland.com

TENBURY WELLS, Worcestershire Map ref 4A3

★★★★
SELF CATERING

Units 3
Sleeps 3–8

LOW SEASON PER WK
£180.00–£379.00

HIGH SEASON PER WK
£300.00–£639.00

Rochford Park Cottages, Nr Tenbury Wells

t (01584) 781392 **e** cottages@rochfordpark.co.uk

rochfordpark.co.uk

Former farm outbuildings, now stylish, comfortable cottages suitable for couples, families, or groups of friends, situated in beautiful Teme valley. Restful places, full of character. Woodlands, lakes nearby.

open All year
payment Cash, cheques
nearest shop 3 miles
nearest pub 1.5 miles

Unit General P Leisure

THORNHAM, Norfolk Map ref 3B1

★★★
SELF CATERING

Units 1
Sleeps 5

LOW SEASON PER WK
£200.00–£280.00

HIGH SEASON PER WK
£320.00–£450.00

Malthouse Cottages, Thornham, Hunstanton

contact Mrs Leslie Rigby, Brindle Cottage, Castor PE5 7AU **t** (01733) 380399
e rigbysrushall@hotmail.co.uk

malthousecottage.co.uk

Charming, traditional Norfolk cottage with open fire in lovely coastal village with three pubs and beautiful beach. Area renowned for sailing, walking, birdwatching and golfing. Two double rooms and put-u-up. Weekend bookings available.

open All year
payment Cash, cheques
nearest shop less than 0.5 miles

Unit General Leisure

THORPENESS, Suffolk Map ref 3C2

★★★★
SELF CATERING

Units 1
Sleeps 6

LOW SEASON PER WK
£400.00–£450.00

HIGH SEASON PER WK
£740.00–£870.00

Hope Cove Cottage, Thorpeness

contact Mrs I Pearman, Hollyhock Trust, Piggotts Farm, Albury Road, Ware SG11 2HS
t (01279) 771281 **e** irene.pearman@whestates.com

tiscover.co.uk

open All year
payment Cash, cheques
nearest shop less than 0.5 miles
nearest pub less than 0.5 miles

Former stable block, now a spacious bungalow, set in a quiet village location, with large walled garden, 70yds to beach. Comfortably sleeps seven (one bunk) in three bedrooms, two bathrooms, large sitting room with cosy wood stove, TV, video, DVD. Fully fitted kitchen, dishwasher, washing machine, dryer. No pets or smoking.

Unit General P

Don't forget www.

Web addresses throughout this guide are shown without the prefix www. Please include www. in the address line of your browser. If a web address does not follow this style it is shown in full.

THORPENESS, Suffolk Map ref 3C2

★★★
SELF CATERING

Units 1
Sleeps 12

LOW SEASON PER WK
£2,040.00–£2,200.00

HIGH SEASON PER WK
£2,780.00–£3,000.00

House in the Clouds, Thorpeness

contact Mrs Le Comber, The House in the Clouds, 4 Hinde House, 14 Hinde Street, London W1U 3BG **t** (020) 7224 3615 **e** houseintheclouds@btopenworld.com

houseintheclouds.co.uk

open All year
payment Cash, cheques
nearest shop 0.5 miles
nearest pub 0.5 miles

A true family holiday in this wonderfully eccentric 'fantasy unmatched in England'. The House in the Clouds has five bedrooms, three bathrooms and unrivalled views from the 'Room at the Top'. Play billiards, snooker, table tennis, tennis and boules. Overlooking sea, golf course and Meare. Bird-watching on RSPB reserves.

Unit General P
Leisure

THURSFORD, Norfolk Map ref 3B1

★★★★
SELF CATERING

Units 1
Sleeps 5

LOW SEASON PER WK
Min £310.00

HIGH SEASON PER WK
Max £500.00

1A The Street, Fakenham

contact Ms Geraldine Rye, 1A The Street, Thursford Collection, Thursford Green, Fakenham NR21 0AS **t** (01328) 878477 **e** geraldine@thursforscollection.co.uk

thursford.com

Detached bungalow, one double bedroom with en suite bathroom and walk-in shower. One triple bedroom with separate bathroom. Sitting room, conservatory, dining room, fully equipped modern kitchen.

open All year
payment Credit/debit cards, cash, cheques
nearest shop 2 miles
nearest pub 1 mile

Unit General P

THURSFORD, Norfolk Map ref 3B1

★★★
SELF CATERING

Units 1
Sleeps 5

LOW SEASON PER WK
Max £490.00

HIGH SEASON PER WK
Max £490.00

Hayloft, Thursford

contact Mrs Ann Green, Old Coach House, Fakenham NR21 0BD **t** (01328) 878273

tiscover.co.uk

open All year
payment Cash, cheques
nearest shop 2 miles
nearest pub 1 mile

On a small, 64-acre working farm, ten miles from the unspoilt North Norfolk coast. Overlooking rolling grazing land, this unique 16thC hayloft conversion offers warmth and comfort in peaceful surroundings with owner's home across the courtyard. Birdwatching, National Trust houses, seal trips, excellent walks. Suit lovers of country life and nature.

Unit General P Leisure

Where can I get help and advice?

Tourist Information Centres offer friendly help with accommodation and holiday ideas as well as suggestions of places to visit and things to do. You'll find contact details at the beginning of each regional section.

THURSFORD, Norfolk Map ref 3B1

★★★
SELF CATERING

Units 3
Sleeps 5–6

LOW SEASON PER WK
£200.00–£250.00

HIGH SEASON PER WK
£400.00–£450.00

Station Farm Barn Holiday Cottages, Thursford

contact Mrs Sheena Walton, Norfolk Barn Holidays, Soham, Ely CB7 5BW **t** (01353) 720419
e enquiries@norfolk-barn-holidays.co.uk

norfolk-barn-holidays.co.uk

Barn conversion providing one three-bedroomed and two two-bedroomed cottages. Fully equipped for self-catering family holidays. Well situated for exploring the whole of North Norfolk.

open All year
payment Cash, cheques, euros
nearest shop 5 miles
nearest pub less than 0.5 miles

Unit General

TIDESWELL, Derbyshire Map ref 4B2

★★★
SELF CATERING

Units 1
Sleeps 4

LOW SEASON PER WK
£205.00–£215.00

HIGH SEASON PER WK
£230.00

Geil Torrs, Buxton

contact Mr Harry Buttle, Geil Torrs, Buxton Road, Buxton SK17 8QJ **t** (01298) 871302

Situated in Tideswell Dale, about 0.5 miles from the village of Tideswell, a village at the heart of the Peak District National Park.

open All year
payment Cash, cheques
nearest shop 0.5 miles
nearest pub 0.5 miles

Unit General

TIDESWELL, Derbyshire Map ref 4B2

★★★★
SELF CATERING

Units 1
Sleeps 2–4

LOW SEASON PER WK
Min £250.00

HIGH SEASON PER WK
Max £450.00

Lavender Cottage, Tideswell, Buxton

contact Ruth Wilson, 100 Graham Road, Sheffield S10 3GQ **t** (0114) 230 7857
e ruth@thewilsons100.fsnet.co.uk

lavendercottagetideswell.co.uk GUEST REVIEWS · SPECIAL OFFERS · REAL-TIME BOOKING

Recently renovated cottage with woodburning stove, flatscreen TV, walk-in power shower and bath. New soft furnishings and carpets and several pieces of antique furniture. Well equipped kitchen, dishwasher, freezer and washing machine.

open All year
payment Cash, cheques
nearest shop less than 0.5 miles
nearest pub less than 0.5 miles

Unit General

WALCOTT, Norfolk Map ref 3C1

★★★★
SELF CATERING

Units 2
Sleeps 3–6

LOW SEASON PER WK
£320.00–£440.00

HIGH SEASON PER WK
£590.00–£710.00

Tamarisk, Walcott

contact Mrs Jane Shulver, Norfolk Country Cottages, Tamarisk and Sanderling, Point House, Ridlington NR28 9TY **t** (01692) 651126 & 07879 473546 **e** pointhouse@hotmail.com

norfolkcottages.co.uk GUEST REVIEWS · SPECIAL OFFERS

Modern, semi-detached bungalow and detached house in a fine cliff-top location. Edge of village, sea in front, farmland behind. Enclosed rear gardens. Good walks. Sandy beaches.

open All year
payment Credit/debit cards, cheques
nearest shop 1 mile
nearest pub 0.75 miles

Unit General

WELLINGBOROUGH, Northamptonshire Map ref 3A2

★★★★
SELF CATERING

Units 1
Sleeps 6

LOW SEASON PER WK
Min £350.00

HIGH SEASON PER WK
Max £450.00

Short breaks available.

Friendly Lodge Cottage, Wellingborough

contact Mrs Kaye Saunders, Friendly Lodge Farm, Station Road, Raunds, Wellingborough NN9 6BT
t (01933) 461102

open All year
payment Cash, cheques
nearest shop 2 miles
nearest pub 2 miles

Modern, spacious, luxury self-catering cottage on arable farm in rolling countryside. Lounge/diner, fully equipped kitchen and utility room, three bedrooms, including ground-floor double with en suite disabled facilities. Ideally situated for many attractions and places of interest in the Heart of England.

Unit General P S Leisure

WELLS-NEXT-THE-SEA, Norfolk Map ref 3B1

★★★★
SELF CATERING

Units 1
Sleeps 6

LOW SEASON PER WK
£450.00–£535.00

HIGH SEASON PER WK
£525.00–£770.00

Bexwell, Wells-next-the-Sea

contact Mr John Stannard, Mill Lodge, Polka Road, Well-next-the-Sea NR23 1ED **t** (01328) 710752
e info@bexwellcottage.co.uk

bexwellcottage.co.uk

Charming, detached house: two en suite double bedrooms and one single; well-equipped and comfortable, spacious living accommodation and gardens. Close to town's amenities, quay and beautiful beaches. Ample parking.

open All year
payment Cash, cheques
nearest shop less than 0.5 miles
nearest pub less than 0.5 miles

Unit General P S Leisure

WELLS-NEXT-THE-SEA, Norfolk Map ref 3B1

★★★★
SELF CATERING

Units 1
Sleeps 4

HIGH SEASON PER WK
£519.00–£585.00

Gabriel Cottage, Wells-next-the-Sea

contact Dr Marie Strong, **t** (01328) 710743

tiscover.co.uk

open April to September
payment Cash, cheques

Comfortable, detached house in a quiet courtyard, 110m from main shopping street and 175m from the quayside. Two bedrooms – twin upstairs with adjacent bathroom, double downstairs with adjacent bathroom (whirlpool bath). Spacious living room. Kitchen/diner. Parking for two cars. Walled patio garden. Personally supervised.

SAT NAV *NR23 1JN*

Unit General P

It's all quality-assessed accommodation

Our commitment to quality involves wide-ranging accommodation assessment. Ratings and awards were correct at the time of going to press but may change following a new assessment. Please check at time of booking.

WELLS-NEXT-THE-SEA, Norfolk Map ref 3B1

★★★
SELF CATERING

Units 1
Sleeps 7

LOW SEASON PER WK
£390.00–£480.00

HIGH SEASON PER WK
£430.00–£530.00

Harbour Cottage, Wells-next-the-Sea

contact Mr & Mrs Simon & Trish Jackson, 233 Melton Road, Edwalton NG12 4DB **t** (0115) 923 4545
e simonnjackson@btinternet.com

harbourcottagewells.co.uk REAL-TIME BOOKING

Charming, traditional, 180-year-old three-bedroom luxury home, sensitively refurbished to a high standard. Lounge with logburner, cloakroom off, modern oak dining kitchen. Attractive south-facing patio garden. Close to all amenities. Ideal for families.

open All year
payment Cash, cheques, euros
nearest shop less than 0.5 miles
nearest pub less than 0.5 miles

Unit General Leisure

WELTON, Lincolnshire Map ref 4C2

★★★★
SELF CATERING

Units 1
Sleeps 20

LOW SEASON PER WK
£2,500.00–£3,000.00

Athina, Lincoln

contact Mrs Michelle Billington, 33 Hill Drive, Whaley Bridge, High Peak SK23 7BH
t (01663) 719661 **e** athinabookings@aol.com

athinacottage.co.uk

open All year
payment Cheques
nearest shop 0.5 miles
nearest pub 0.5 miles

Luxury, spacious ten-bedroom house in village location close to historic city of Lincoln. Heated indoor swimming pool, jacuzzi, sauna, pool and table tennis tables, board games, chess, darts, full Sky TV, DVDs, videos, books. Beautifully kept gardens with river and barbecue. Ideal for family parties and holidays.

Unit General P Leisure

WESTON RHYN, Shropshire Map ref 4A2

★★★
SELF CATERING

Units 1
Sleeps 4

LOW SEASON PER WK
£190.00–£200.00

HIGH SEASON PER WK
£200.00–£220.00

Mill Cottage, Oswestry

contact Mr & Mrs H Brannick, Mill Cottage, Mill House, The Wern, Weston Rhyn, Oswestry SY10 7ER **t** (01691) 659738

Mill Cottage is a converted 18thC barn. Set in rural surroundings with stream, very peaceful, four miles from Oswestry and the Welsh border.

open All year except Christmas and New Year
payment Cash, cheques
nearest shop 1 mile
nearest pub 0.5 miles

Unit General 4 Leisure

WHITBOURNE, Herefordshire Map ref 2B1

★★★
SELF CATERING

Units 1
Sleeps 2–11

LOW SEASON PER WK
£460.00–£530.00

HIGH SEASON PER WK
£530.00–£825.00

Crumplebury Farmhouse, Worcester

contact Ms Rachel Freeman, Longlands Farmhouse, Whitbourne, Nr Worcester WR6 5SG
t 07929 260919 **e** crumplebury@yahoo.co.uk

whitbourne-estate.co.uk/crumplebury

Personally maintained, comfortable and cosy five-bedroom farmhouse on family farm. Ideal for reunions, family gatherings, walking. Enclosed garden. Quiet. Coarse fishing available.

open All year
payment Cash, cheques
nearest shop 2 miles
nearest pub 1.5 miles

Unit General P Leisure

For **key to symbols** see page 7

WICKHAM SKEITH, Suffolk Map ref 3B2

★★★
SELF CATERING

Units 1
Sleeps 1–4

LOW SEASON PER WK
£195.00–£235.00

HIGH SEASON PER WK
£255.00–£275.00

Netus Barn, Wickham Skeith, Eye

contact Mrs Joy Homan, Street Farm, Eye IP23 8LP **t** (01449) 766275
e joygeoff@homansf.freeserve.co.uk

netusbarn.co.uk

Single-storey period barn, well-equipped kitchen-cum-living room, bathroom (shower), two twin bedrooms, disabled-friendly, parking, patio garden. Rural views. Dogs welcome.

open All year
payment Cash, cheques
nearest shop 2 miles
nearest pub 2 miles

Unit General P S Leisure

WIGSTHORPE, Northamptonshire Map ref 3A2

★★★★★
SELF CATERING

Units 3
Sleeps 2–4

LOW SEASON PER WK
£250.00–£350.00

HIGH SEASON PER WK
£350.00–£600.00

Nene Valley Cottages, Wigsthorpe

contact Heather Ball, The Cottage, Glapthorn, Northamptonshire PE8 5BQ **t** (01832) 273601 & 07962 085720 **e** stay@nenevalleycottages.co.uk

nenevalleycottages.co.uk GUEST REVIEWS

Secluded with idyllic views over the Nene Valley. Two two-bedroomed units and an interconnecting single bedroom unit equipped for the disabled. Total luxury.

open All year
payment Cash, cheques
nearest shop 4 miles
nearest pub 2 miles

Unit General P S Leisure

WITHERN, Lincolnshire Map ref 4D2

★★★
SELF CATERING

Units 6
Sleeps 2–6

LOW SEASON PER WK
£180.00–£250.00

HIGH SEASON PER WK
£250.00–£400.00

Park Farm Holidays, Withern

contact Mr & Mrs Alan & Elsie Burkitt, Park Farm Holidays, Park Farm, Withern LN13 0DF
t (01507) 450331 **e** alan@alanburkitt.wanadoo.co.uk

parkfarmholidayswithern.com

Situated just off the Wolds, seven miles from the sea. Two cottages on private road, four log cabins in woodland nearby. One mile from the village. Very peaceful. Good walking and cycling country. All are fully equipped and centrally heated. Birds and wildlife are all around.

open All year
payment Cash, cheques
nearest shop 1 mile
nearest pub 1 mile

Unit General P S Leisure

WOODBRIDGE, Suffolk Map ref 3C2

★★★
SELF CATERING

Units 1
Sleeps 4

LOW SEASON PER WK
£220.00–£250.00

HIGH SEASON PER WK
£270.00–£375.00

The Coach House, Framsden

contact Ms Nicola Deller, Hill House, Mill Hill, Framsden IP14 6HB **t** (01473) 890891
e nicoladeller@yahoo.com

open All year
payment Cash, cheques
nearest shop 3 miles
nearest pub 0.5 miles

In glorious Suffolk countryside, in front of Framsden windmill. Close to many walks/attractions and within easy reach of the coast (30 minutes) and historic market towns. Exceptionally spacious, clean, warm and well equipped. Modern kitchen with washer/dryer. Lovely views. Shared garden. Short walk to village pub. Grocery delivery by arrangement.

Unit General P S Leisure

WOODBRIDGE, Suffolk Map ref 3C2

★★★★
SELF CATERING

Units 2
Sleeps 4

LOW SEASON PER WK
Min £300.00

HIGH SEASON PER WK
Max £650.00

Old Forge and Anvil Cottage, Melton

contact Mr Robert Blake, 1a Moorfield Road, Woodbridge IP12 4JN **t** (01394) 382565 & 07901 773545 **e** robert@blake4110.fsbusiness.co.uk

tiscover.co.uk

The Old Forge, Melton is a 17thC brick and flint single-storey building sympathetically restored and converted for luxury accommodation. Anvil Cottage is a timber-framed and Essex-bordered 16thC cottage. Illustrated brochure available.

open All year
payment Cash, cheques
nearest shop less than 0.5 miles
nearest pub less than 0.5 miles

Unit General P S Leisure

WOODBRIDGE, Suffolk Map ref 3C2

★★★★-★★★★★
SELF CATERING

Units 2
Sleeps 2

LOW SEASON PER WK
Min £300.00

HIGH SEASON PER WK
Max £550.00

Quayside Holiday Cottages, Waldringfield, Woodbridge

contact Mrs Donna Morgan, Quayside, The Quay, Waldringfield, Woodbridge IP12 4QZ **t** (01473) 736724 **e** donna.morgan@quaysidecottage.com

quaysidecottage.com

open All year
payment Cheques
nearest shop 3 miles
nearest pub less than 0.5 miles

Quayside, where the River Deben literally laps outside the garden gate. Two luxury cottages to suit couples looking for something special. Waterfront views and access to fishing and secure small boat. Private car parking and bicycle store. Gentle stroll to the popular Maybush Inn. River cruises. Endless coastal walks.

Unit TV SC General P S Leisure

WOODBRIDGE, Suffolk Map ref 3C2

★★★★-★★★★★
SELF CATERING

Units 6
Sleeps 2–8

LOW SEASON PER WK
£285.00–£465.00

HIGH SEASON PER WK
£525.00–£825.00

Off-peak short breaks available (weekend – 3 nights, or midweek – 4 nights).

Windmill Lodges, Woodbridge

Windmill Lodges Ltd, Windmill Lodges Holidays, Saxtead, Woodbridge IP13 9RD **t** (01728) 685338 **e** holidays@windmilllodges.co.uk

windmilllodges.co.uk SPECIAL OFFERS · REAL-TIME BOOKING

open All year
payment Credit/debit cards, cash, cheques
nearest shop 3 miles
nearest pub 0.5 miles

Cosy log cabins nestled around our small, private fishing lake in beautiful countryside. Each lodge is extremely well equipped and features a secluded outdoor hot tub to relax in! Guests have use of our covered, heated swimming pool. Village location within walking distance of pub. Close to coast and attractions.

Unit TV General P S Leisure

Remember to check when booking

Please remember that all information in this guide has been supplied by the proprietors well in advance of publication. Since changes do sometimes occur it's a good idea to check details at the time of booking.

WOODHALL SPA, Lincolnshire Map ref 4D2

★★★★
SELF CATERING

Units 1
Sleeps 2–6

LOW SEASON PER WK
Min £240.00

HIGH SEASON PER WK
Max £330.00

Old Forge Cottage, Woodhall Spa

t (01526) 353430 **e** WoodhallBreaks@aol.com

WoodhallBreaks.com

Beautifully converted blacksmith's forge, with original beams and high ceilings. Cosy and comfortable surroundings with access to garden area. Central village location, convenient for local amenities and park.

open All year
payment Cash, cheques
nearest shop less than 0.5 miles
nearest pub less than 0.5 miles

Unit TV DVD S General P S Leisure

WOOTTON, Bedfordshire Map ref 2D1

★★★★
SELF CATERING

Units 8
Sleeps 2

LOW SEASON PER WK
Min £300.00

HIGH SEASON PER WK
Max £300.00

The Stable Yard, Wootton Green

contact Mrs Gabi Thomas, Hunters Lodge, Wootton Green MK43 9EF **t** (01234) 765351
e info@the-stableyard.co.uk

the-stableyard.co.uk SPECIAL OFFERS

open All year
payment Credit/debit cards, cash, cheques
nearest shop 2 miles
nearest pub 1 mile

We provide luxury self-catering accommodation in eight individual studio apartments suitable for business travellers, those seeking holiday accommodation or weekend breaks. Located on a working farm in the quiet village of Wootton Green. The Stable Yard offers the luxuries of a hotel with the flexibility of self-catering. Daily lets from £40.00.

SAT NAV *MK43 9EF* **ONLINE MAP**

Unit TV SC DVD General P S Leisure

WORTHAM, Suffolk Map ref 3B2

★★★★
SELF CATERING

Units 5
Sleeps 4–10

LOW SEASON PER WK
£290.00–£798.00

HIGH SEASON PER WK
£600.00–£1,743.00

Ivy House Farm, Wortham, Diss

contact Mr Paul Bradley, Ivy House Farm, Wortham, Diss IP22 1RD **t** (01379) 898395
e prjsdrad@aol.com

ivyhousefarmcottages.co.uk

open All year
payment Cash, cheques, euros
nearest shop 0.5 miles
nearest pub 2 miles

This peaceful complex, set in spacious grounds surrounded by common land in the heart of East Anglia, consists of a 17thC farmhouse and four purpose-built cottages, one of which has facilities for the disabled. Other facilities include heated indoor swimming pool and cosy barn with table-tennis, pool, piano, snooker table and library. Owners on site.

Unit TV DVD General P S
Leisure

CYCLISTS WELCOME WELCOME CYCLISTS

Fancy a cycling holiday?

For a fabulous freewheeling break, seek out accommodation participating in our Cyclists Welcome scheme. Look out for the symbol and plan your route online at nationalcyclenetwork.org.

WRENTHAM, Suffolk Map ref 3C2

★★★★
SELF CATERING

Units 1
Sleeps 1–6

LOW SEASON PER WK
Min £375.00

HIGH SEASON PER WK
Max £700.00

Discounts offered for under-occupancy. Available for long weekends – not in high season. Festively presented for Christmas and New Year lets.

Honeysuckle Cottage, Wrentham Nr Southwold, Beccles

contact Mrs Julia Price, 48 Rickmansworth Road, Watford WD18 7HT **t** (01923) 226721 & 07831 602108 **e** juliaprice@tiscali.co.uk

honeysucklecottage.net GUEST REVIEWS

open All year
payment Cash, cheques
nearest shop less than 0.5 miles
nearest pub 0.5 miles

Idyllic, spacious 16thC cottage full of charm, character and antiques – but also all the modern amenities. In the village of Wrentham, five miles from Southwold, two miles from the nearest beach. Sleeps six in three bedrooms. Children welcome. Large dining room and dining courtyard.

SAT NAV *NR34 7LR* **ONLINE MAP**

Unit TV DVD General P S Leisure

WYE VALLEY

See under Hereford, Llangarron, Ross-on-Wye, Symonds Yat

YOULGREAVE, Derbyshire Map ref 4B2

★★★
SELF CATERING

Units 1
Sleeps 2

LOW SEASON PER WK
Min £225.00

HIGH SEASON PER WK
Max £365.00

3-night breaks available Nov-Apr.

Sunnyside, Youlgreave, Bakewell

contact Ms J Steed, Falkland House, 10 New Road, Bakewell DE45 1WP **t** (01629) 636195 **e** joan.steed7@googlemail.com

open All year
payment Cash, cheques
nearest shop less than 0.5 miles
nearest pub less than 0.5 miles

Sunnyside is a homely, self-contained, very private apartment. From its patio, which is well-stocked with hanging baskets, various old farm implements and stone troughs, there are lovely views to the hills. Close to local amenities (including good pubs!), long/short walks from the door and tourist attractions (Chatsworth, Bakewell etc). Off-street parking.

Unit TV General P S

South East England

Berkshire, Buckinghamshire, East Sussex, Hampshire, Isle of Wight, Kent, Oxfordshire, Surrey, West Sussex

Clockwise: Portsmouth Historic Dockyard, Hampshire; Deal, Kent; Oxford

Great days out

The South East is your quintessential slice of England. Explore iconic chalk cliffs and 400 miles of glorious coastline, fairytale castles, colourful gardens and historic cities. Whilst singles and couples will find plenty to enjoy, this region is bursting with great family days out that the kids will treasure forever.

Enjoy the ride!

Get set, **Go Ape!** on a high-wire forest adventure course, now at Bedgebury Pinetum and Wendover Woods as well as other exciting locations across the South East. White-knuckle rides like **Thorpe Park's** Inferno and Slammer keep the thrills coming and there's always something new to try: take a dizzying spin on **Legoland Windsor's** Longboat Invader, twirl and tilt on the amazing

Paultons Park, Hampshire

Sky Swinger at **Paultons Park**, or hop aboard the spooky ghost train Horror Hotel at **Brighton Pier**. At Winchester's **Intech Science Centre and Planetarium** you can even fly through the solar system and visit a black hole. Enjoy the rides of your life!

Who killed Harold?

Explore a region that has witnessed some of the most momentous events in British history, from the Battle of Hastings in 1066 to the air raids of the Second World War. At **Battle Abbey** stand on the exact spot where tradition says King Harold fell and take the interactive audio tour of the battlefield to find out what really happened on that fateful day. Clamber aboard the world-famous HMS Victory at **Portsmouth Historic Dockyard**, then experience the challenges of the modern Navy in Action Stations.

Formidable **Dover Castle** on the Kent coast puts you right on the frontline of history: tour the **Secret Wartime Tunnels** deep beneath the gleaming White Cliffs, where the evacuation of Dunkirk was masterminded. Another of the country's dazzling landmarks, **Canterbury Cathedral**, opens the door on the infamous murder of Thomas Becket. And just for fun, why not follow in the footsteps of Morse and Lewis beneath the dreaming spires of **Oxford** to solve a fictional mystery or two?

Shore pleasures

South coast beaches keep alive all the best traditions of the seaside, with a zesty twist of watersport action. **Eastbourne**, **Bournemouth**, **Brighton** and **Margate** were popular playgrounds for the Victorians – Queen Victoria loved to escape to her Isle of Wight home, **Osborne House**. Save your small change for the slot machines on the pier where it's hot doughnuts or fish and chips all round. If you're looking for something a bit more peaceful, there are still many gems to uncover. Scamper about the sand dunes at **West Wittering**, just down the Sussex coast from **Bognor Regis**, and watch the zigzagging kitesurfers at **Pevensey Bay**. Get your own adrenalin fix at the **Calshot Activities Centre** where you can try all sorts of watersports, including sailing on the Solent.

Left to right: Hever Castle, Kent;
Royal Pavilion, Brighton, East Sussex

did you know... you're walking on 80 million years of geological history along the White Cliffs of Dover?

Castles, castles everywhere

Become king, queen, lord or lady for a day visiting the South East's magnificent castles. **Bodiam** is a picture-perfect medieval moated fortress and **Arundel** is full of priceless collections. Dreamy **Leeds** in Kent was restored by Henry VIII for his first queen, Catherine of Aragon. It might have been the ultimate romantic gesture, except that he abandoned her for his second wife, Anne Boleyn – visit Anne's beautiful childhood home, **Hever Castle**, too. **Windsor Castle** has been a royal residence for nine centuries and reflects changing royal tastes through the ages. But nothing quite prepares you for the **Royal Pavilion** at Brighton, George IV's eccentric Indian-style palace!

Follow nature's way

Kent is rightly famed as the Garden of England, so sample some real horticultural treats like **Sissinghurst Castle Garden**, lovingly created by Vita Sackville-West. Discover Kew's country garden and the Millennium Seed Bank at **Wakehurst Place**, near Haywards Heath. Follow the ancient tracks of the **South Downs Way** for an exhilarating breath of fresh air, or hop over to the **Isle of Wight** where you can cycle Round the Island in eight hours. Phew! Play hide and seek along the paths and bridleways of the **New Forest** and watch out for wild ponies as they gently graze. You'll encounter elephants and other exotic creatures at **Howletts Wild Animal Park**.

New Forest ponies

Have a Dickens of a time

Catch the buzz of a festival or event, whatever the time of year. From rock 'n' pop to hops, from rowing to sailing, from Dickens to dancing round a maypole – the rich tapestry of life. **The Brighton Festival** comes to the funky seaside town every May and is an exuberant celebration of world-class art and entertainment. If you're looking for the epitome of elegance, dress up for **Glyndebourne's** season of opera, **Royal Ascot**, **Henley Royal Regatta** or **Cowes Week** – four internationally famous spectacles.

Or join Mr Pickwick and other jolly characters in Victorian costume on the streets of Broadstairs during the **Dickens Festival**. The town was the author's favourite 'English watering place'. There's rock, pop and hip hop mixed with liberal helpings of mud at August's **Reading Festival**. And kids can always find something fantabulous to fill the school holidays at **The Roald Dahl Museum and Story Centre**, Great Missenden: from whizzpopping, hands-on science workshops to delumptious cookery classes.

Time to indulge

Had your fill of sightseeing? Then it's time to indulge! Shopaholics: head for the charming world of The Lanes, **Brighton**, to hunt out stylish gifts and antiques. Browse for hours in the country's largest second-hand bookshop, Baggins at **Rochester**. Pop into **Oxford Castle** where boutique stalls, outdoor music performances, wining and dining are set against an unusual prison backdrop. If you need to boost your energy levels, you're in just the right region, too: embark on an epicurean journey through lots of orchards, breweries and vineyards, including England's largest vineyard at **Denbies Wine Estate**. Then savour more of the genuine flavours of South East England in the oyster houses and fine restaurants.

why not... visit the world's oldest and largest occupied castle – Windsor Castle?

Clockwise: The Roald Dahl Museum and Story Centre, Buckinghamshire; Cowes, Isle of Wight; Denbies Wine Estate, Surrey

Destinations

Brighton

England's favourite seaside city, Brighton is historic, elegant and offbeat. Wander a beachfront packed with cafés and bars, then step into town for fine antiques and designer boutiques. Don't miss the Royal Pavilion, surely the most extravagant royal palace in Europe, and come in springtime for an arts festival second to none. Find the world's cuisine in over 400 restaurants, and then relax with dance, comedy or music in the thriving pub and club culture. Brighton has it all – and just 50 minutes by train from central London.

Brighton

Canterbury

Marvel with fellow 'pilgrims' from the four corners of the world as Canterbury Cathedral dominates your approach to this World Heritage Site. Let Canterbury Tales 'Medieval Misadventures' take you on a journey back to Chaucer's England. Wander traffic-free daytime streets to enjoy historic buildings and modern attractions, and then head further afield to explore the valleys, woods and coastline of this beautiful region of Kent.

Dover

Discover the rich history of Dover – 'the lock and key of England'. Tour Dover Castle and relive the epic sieges of 1216-17. Delve into the secrets contained in the Wartime Tunnels, nerve centre for the evacuation of Dunkirk. Enjoy the pier and stroll the stylish marina before heading out of town to tour the scenic beaches of White Cliffs Country.

Isle of Wight

Sixty miles of spectacular coastline, picturesque coves and safe bathing in bays of golden sand. Explore the maritime history of Cowes, the beautiful and historic town of Newport and take the family to the welcoming resorts of Shanklin and Ventnor. Follow the trail of dinosaurs, ancient tribes, Romans and monarchs.

New Forest

Roam a landscape little changed since William the Conqueror gave it his special protection over 900 years ago. Discover wild heath and dappled woodland, roaming ponies, thatched hamlets, bustling market towns, and tiny streams meandering to the sparkling expanse of the Solent. Explore great attractions too, from Buckler's Hard to the National Motor Museum Beaulieu.

Oxford

This ancient university city is both timeless and modern. Wander among its 'dreaming spires' and tranquil college quadrangles. Find national and international treasures displayed in a family of museums. Hire a punt and spend the afternoon drifting along the River Cherwell or seek out bustling shops and fashionable restaurants. Experience candlelit evensong in college chapels or Shakespeare in the park, and after dark enjoy the cosmopolitan buzz.

Left to right: Great Dixter, East Sussex; Thorpe Park, Surrey

Royal Tunbridge Wells

Portsmouth

At the heart of the city is Portsmouth Historic Dockyard where there is so much naval heritage to explore. Climb the new striking Spinnaker Tower or take a harbour tour to see naval ships. If you're after retail therapy, head for Gunwharf Quays. Portsmouth also has its own resort area, Southsea, with four miles of beach and promenade.

Royal Tunbridge Wells

Ever since the discovery of the Chalybeate Spring 400 years ago, visitors have been coming here. The health-giving waters still flow and the Pantiles, the famous colonnaded walkway, is now home to a wonderful selection of boutiques, antiques shops, bars and cafés. The village atmosphere of the old high street and Chapel Place, adds to the town's reputation as one of the most desirable destinations in the South East. Surrounded by beautiful countryside, and a wealth of castles, stately homes and gardens, there's so much to explore.

Clockwise: Portsmouth; Windsor Castle; Dover Castle

Winchester

Winchester is best known for its 11thC cathedral and the Great Hall, which for over 600 years has housed the mysterious Arthurian round table. Wander through the city's popular shopping streets, admire the architecture and enjoy quirky open air events. Home of good food, birthplace of cricket, resting place of author Jane Austen and inspiration to the many craft-makers and artists who live here, Winchester is a destination for all seasons.

Winchester Cathedral

Windsor

Explore Windsor and the Royal Borough to the west of London. Gaze at the priceless treasures in the Royal Collection at Windsor Castle, royal home and fortress for over 900 years. Henry VI founded Eton College in 1440. Lose yourself in the history of the cloisters and the chapel. Sail the rapids at Legoland's incredible Vikings' River Splash, and find peace and quiet in the rural landscape of Royal Berkshire, traversed by the timeless flow of the Thames.

For lots more great ideas visit enjoyEngland.com/destinations

Visitor attractions

Family and Fun

Blue Reef Aquarium
Hastings, East Sussex
(01424) 718776
discoverhastings.co.uk
Meet tropical sharks and giant crabs.

The Canterbury Tales
Canterbury, Kent
(01227) 479227
canterburytales.org.uk
Audiovisual recreation of life in medieval England.

Didcot Railway Centre
Didcot, Oxfordshire
(01235) 817200
didcotrailwaycentre.org.uk
Living museum of the Great Western Railway.

Dinosaur Isle
Sandown, Isle of Wight
(01983) 404344
dinosaurisle.com
Britain's first purpose-built dinosaur attraction.

Farming World
Boughton, Kent
(01227) 751144
farming-world.com
Working farm packed with family fun.

Guildford Spectrum
Guildford, Surrey
(01483) 443322
guildfordspectrum.co.uk
Olympic-sized ice rink and tenpin bowling.

Gulliver's Land
Milton Keynes, Buckinghamshire
(01925) 444888
gulliversfun.co.uk
Family magic for children aged 2-13 years.

Harbour Park
Littlehampton, West Sussex
(01903) 721200
harbourpark.com
All-weather theme park with dodgems.

The Historic Dockyard Chatham
Chatham, Kent
(01634) 823800
chdt.org.uk
Maritime heritage site with stunning architecture.

The Hop Farm Country Park
Paddock Wood, Kent
(01622) 872068
thehopfarm.co.uk
Once-working hop farm in 400 unspoilt acres.

Howletts Wild Animal Park
Canterbury, Kent
(01227) 721286
totallywild.net
Gorillas and tigers in 90-acre parkland.

Isle of Wight Zoo
Sandown, Isle of Wight
(01983) 403883
isleofwightzoo.com
Zoo specialising in big cats and primates.

LEGOLAND Windsor
Windsor, Berkshire
0870 504 0404
legoland.co.uk
More Lego bricks than you dreamed possible.

The Look Out Discovery Centre
Bracknell, Berkshire
(01344) 354400
bracknell-forest.gov.uk/lookout
Interactive science park with over 70 exhibits.

Marwell Zoological Park
Winchester, Hampshire
(01962) 777407
marwell.org.uk
Relaxing and fascinating zoological park.

Mid-Hants Railway Watercress Line
Alresford, Hampshire
(01962) 733810
watercressline.co.uk
Ten-mile steam railway through beautiful countryside.

National Motor Museum Beaulieu
Beaulieu, Hampshire
(01590) 612345
beaulieu.co.uk
Vintage cars in glorious New Forest setting.

Paultons Park
Romsey, Hampshire
(023) 8081 4442
paultonspark.co.uk
Over 50 rides for all the family.

Port Lympne Wild Animal Park, Mansion and Gardens
Lympne, Kent
(01303) 264647
totallywild.net
Rare and endangered species in 600-acre park.

Portsmouth Historic Dockyard
Portsmouth, Hampshire
(023) 9283 9766
historicdockyard.co.uk
Home to the Mary Rose and HMS Victory.

River & Rowing Museum
Henley-on-Thames, Oxfordshire
(01491) 415600
rrm.co.uk
Award-wining museum with year-round exhibitions.

The Roald Dahl Museum and Story Centre
Small Visitor Attraction of the Year - Gold
Great Missenden, Buckinghamshire
(01494) 892192
roalddahlmuseum.org
The life behind so many well-loved books.

Romney, Hythe and Dymchurch Railway
Littlestone-on-Sea, Kent
(01797) 362353
rhdr.org.uk
The world's only main line in miniature.

Thorpe Park
Chertsey, Surrey
0870 444 4466
thorpepark.com
Thrills and spills for all the family.

Weald & Downland Open Air Museum
Chichester, West Sussex
(01243) 811348
wealddown.co.uk
Rescued historic buildings in beautiful 50-acre setting.

Heritage

1066 Battle Abbey and Battlefield
Battle, East Sussex
(01424) 775705
english-heritage.org.uk
William the Conqueror's abbey commemorates the fallen.

Arundel Castle
Arundel, West Sussex
(01903) 883136
arundelcastle.org
Castle and stately home with priceless collections.

Bateman's
Burwash, East Sussex
(01435) 882302
nationaltrust.org.uk
Jacobean house, the home of Rudyard Kipling.

Blenheim Palace
Woodstock, Oxfordshire
(01993) 811091
blenheimpalace.com
Baroque palace and beautiful Capability Brown parkland.

Bodiam Castle
Bodiam, East Sussex
(01580) 830196
nationaltrust.org.uk
Magical late-medieval moated castle.

Canterbury Cathedral
Canterbury, Kent
(01227) 762862
canterbury-cathedral.org
Seat of the Archbishop of Canterbury.

Chichester Cathedral
Chichester, West Sussex
(01243) 782595
chichestercathedral.org.uk
Splendid medieval cathedral with art treasures.

Dapdune Wharf
Guildford, Surrey
(01483) 561389
nationaltrust.org.uk
Interactive exhibitions and a restored Wey barge.

Dover Castle and Secret Wartime Tunnels
Dover, Kent
(01304) 211067
english-heritage.org.uk
Historic nerve centre for Battle of Britain.

Farnham Castle
Farnham, Surrey
(01252) 721194
farnhamcastle.com
Historic home of the Bishops of Winchester.

Fishbourne Roman Palace
Chichester, West Sussex
(01243) 785859
sussexpast.co.uk/fishbourne
Remains of Roman residence with beautiful mosaics.

Goodwood House
Chichester, West Sussex
(01243) 755048
goodwood.co.uk
Stately home with superb art and furniture.

Guildford Castle
Guildford, Surrey
(01483) 444750
guildford.gov.uk
Imposing ruins and restored 12thC stone keep.

Hever Castle and Gardens
near Edenbridge, Kent
(01732) 865224
hevercastle.co.uk
Moated castle, the childhood home of Anne Boleyn.

Leeds Castle and Gardens
near Maidstone, Kent
(01622) 765400
leeds-castle.com
Medieval castle set on two islands.

Mottisfont Abbey Garden, House and Estate
Mottisfont, Hampshire
(01794) 340757
nationaltrust.org.uk
Glorious grounds of 13thC former priory.

Osborne House
East Cowes, Isle of Wight
(01983) 200022
english-heritage.org.uk
Queen Victoria's opulent seaside retreat.

Penshurst Place and Gardens
Penshurst, Kent
(01892) 870307
penshurstplace.com
Medieval manor house with Tudor gardens.

Petworth House & Park
Petworth, West Sussex
(01798) 342207
nationaltrust.org.uk
Magnificent house and internationally important art collection.

Polesden Lacey
near Dorking, Surrey
(01372) 452048
nationaltrust.org.uk
Opulent Edwardian interiors in downland setting.

Royal Pavilion
Brighton, East Sussex
(01273) 290900
royalpavilion.org.uk
King George IV's extravagant seaside palace.

Waverley Abbey
Farnham, Surrey
(01483) 252000
english-heritage.org.uk
Ruins of England's first Cistercian abbey.

Winchester Cathedral
Winchester, Hampshire
(01962) 857200
winchester-cathedral.org.uk
Magnificent medieval cathedral with soaring Gothic nave.

Windsor Castle
Windsor, Berkshire
(020) 7766 7304
royalcollection.org.uk
Official residence of HM The Queen.

Indoors

Ashford Designer Outlet
Ashford, Kent
(01233) 895900
ashforddesigneroutlet.com
One of Europe's most spectacular shopping destinations.

Bletchley Park
Bletchley, Buckinghamshire
(01908) 640404
bletchleypark.org.uk
Wartime code-breaking with the famous Enigma machines.

De La Warr Pavilion
Bexhill-on-Sea, East Sussex
(01424) 229111
dlwp.com
Superb Modernist pavilion housing theatre and gallery.

Denbies Wine Estate
Dorking, Surrey
(01306) 876616
denbiesvineyard.co.uk
Englands largest vineyard, set in 265 acres.

Dickens World
Chatham, Kent
(01634) 890421
dickensworld.co.uk
Fascinating journey through Dickens' life and times.

Gunwharf Quays
Portsmouth, Hampshire
(023) 9283 6700
gunwharf-quays.com
Innovative retail, restaurant and leisure destination.

Mercedes-Benz World
Weybridge, Surrey
0870 400 4000
mercedes-benzworld.co.uk
Thrilling driving experiences and fascinating attractions.

Pallant House Gallery
Chichester, West Sussex
(01243) 774557
pallant.org.uk
Queen Anne house holding renowned art collection.

Outdoors

Ascot Racecourse
Ascot, Berkshire
0870 727 1234
ascot.co.uk
Flat and jump racing throughout the year.

Bedgebury National Pinetum
Goudhurst, Kent
(01580) 879820
forestry.gov.uk/bedgebury
The world's finest collection of conifers.

Borde Hill Garden
Haywards Heath, West Sussex
(01444) 450326
bordehill.co.uk
Beautiful and botanically rich heritage garden.

Claremont Landscape Garden
Esher, Surrey
(01372) 467806
nationaltrust.org.uk
One of the finest English landscape gardens.

Exbury Gardens and Steam Railway
Exbury, Hampshire
(023) 8089 1203
exbury.co.uk
Vast woodland garden with circular railway.

Gardens and Grounds of Herstmonceux Castle
Herstmonceux, East Sussex
(01323) 833816
herstmonceux-castle.com
Magnificent moated castle with Elizabethan gardens.

Go Ape!
Choose from three South East locations

Bracknell, Berkshire

Leeds Castle, near Maidstone, Kent

Wendover Woods, Buckinghamshire

0845 643 9215
goape.co.uk
Rope bridges, swings and zip slides.

High Beeches Gardens
Handcross, West Sussex
(01444) 400589
highbeeches.com
Peaceful, landscaped woodland and water gardens.

Leonardslee Lakes and Gardens
Lower Beeding, West Sussex
(01403) 891212
leonardslee.com
Glorious rhododendrons and azaleas in 240-acre valley.

Loseley Park
Guildford, Surrey
(01483) 304440
loseley-park.com
Beautiful Elizabethan mansion and gardens.

Nymans Garden
Handcross, West Sussex
(01444) 405250
nationaltrust.org.uk
Romantic garden with outstanding rare tree collection.

Painshill Park
Cobham, Surrey
(01932) 868113
painshill.co.uk
Beatifully restored and renovated park with follies.

RHS Garden Wisley
Woking, Surrey
(01483) 224234
rhs.org.uk
A working encyclopedia of British gardening.

Sissinghurst Castle Garden
Sissinghurst, Kent
(01580) 710700
nationaltrust.org.uk
Celebrated gardens of enclosed compartments around mansion.

Spinnaker Tower
Portsmouth, Hampshire
(023) 9285 7520
spinnakertower.co.uk
Breathtaking views from 170m landmark.

Wakehurst Place Gardens
near Haywards Heath, West Sussex
(01444) 894066
kew.org
Kew's beautiful country garden.

ASSURANCE OF A GREAT DAY OUT
Attractions with this sign participate in the Visitor Attraction Quality Assurance Scheme which recognises high standards in all aspects of the visitor experience.

Events 2009

Sea your history
Portsmouth
seayourhistory.org.uk
Until Apr 2009

A Study in Sherlock
Portsmouth
portsmouthmuseums.co.uk
All year

New Year Steam Day
Didcot
didcotrailwaycentre.org.uk
1 Jan

Sandown Park's Golden Cup Final
Esher
sandown.co.uk
Apr

Brighton Festival
Brighton
brightonfestival.org
2 - 24 May

Derby Day at Epsom Downs Racecourse
Epsom
epsomderby.co.uk
Jun

Royal Ascot
Ascot
royalascot.co.uk
16 - 20 Jun

Henley Royal Regatta
Henley-on-Thames
hrr.co.uk
1 Jul - 5 Jul

Skandia Cowes Week
Cowes
skandiacowesweek.co.uk
1 - 8 Aug

Ringwood Carnival at Market Place and The Bickerley
Ringwood
ringwoodcarnival.org
19 Sep*

** provisional date at time of going to press*

Regional contacts and information

For more information on accommodation, attractions, activities, events and holidays in South East England, contact the regional tourism organisation below. The website has a wealth of information and you can order or download publications.

South East England

The following publications are available from Tourism South East by logging on to **visitsoutheastengland.com** or calling **(023) 8062 5400**:

Publications

- **Escape into the Countryside**
- **Distinctive Country Inns**
- **We Know Just the Place**

E-Brochures

- **Family Fun**
- **Timeless Treasures**
- **Just the Two of Us**

Clockwise: Freshwater Bay, Isle of Wight; Savill Garden, Surrey; Bewl Water, Kent; Canterbury Cathedral, Kent

Tourist Information Centres

When you arrive at your destination, visit an Official Partner Tourist Information Centre for quality assured help with accommodation and information about local attractions and events, or email your request before you go. To search for attractions and Tourist Information Centres on the move just text INFO to 62233, and a web link will be sent to your mobile phone. To find a Tourist Information Centre by region visit enjoyEngland.com/find-tic.

Bicester	Unit 86a, Bicester Village	(01869) 369055	bicester.vc@cherwell-dc.gov.uk
Brighton	Pavilion Buildings	0906 711 2255**	brighton-tourism@brighton-hove.gov.uk
Canterbury	12/13 Sun Street	(01227) 378100	canterburyinformation@canterbury.gov.uk
Chichester	29a South Street	(01243) 775888	chitic@chichester.gov.uk
Cowes	9 The Arcade	(01983) 813818	info@islandbreaks.co.uk
Dover	The Old Town Gaol	(01304) 205108	tic@doveruk.com
Hastings	Queens Square	(01424) 781111	hic@hastings.gov.uk
Newport	High Street	(01983) 813818	info@islandbreaks.co.uk
Oxford	15/16 Broad Street	(01865) 726871	tic@oxford.gov.uk
Portsmouth	Clarence Esplanade	(023) 9282 6722	vis@portsmouthcc.gov.uk
Portsmouth	The Hard	(023) 9282 6722	vis@portsmouthcc.gov.uk
Rochester	95 High Street	(01634) 843666	visitor.centre@medway.gov.uk
Royal Tunbridge Wells	The Pantiles	(01892) 515675	touristinformationcentre @tunbridgewells.gov.uk
Ryde	81-83 Union Street	(01983) 813818	info@islandbreaks.co.uk
Sandown	8 High Street	(01983) 813818	info@islandbreaks.co.uk
Shanklin	67 High Street	(01983) 813818	info@islandbreaks.co.uk
Southampton	9 Civic Centre Road	(023) 8083 3333	tourist.information@southampton.gov.uk
Winchester	High Street	(01962 840500	tourism@winchester.gov.uk
Windsor	Royal Windsor Central Station	(01753) 743900	windsor.tic@rbwm.gov.uk
Yarmouth	The Quay	(01983) 813818	info@islandbreaks.co.uk

**calls to this number are charged at premium rate

where to stay in

South East England

All place names in the blue bands are shown on the maps at the front of this guide.

A complete listing of all Enjoy England assessed accommodation covered by this guide appears at the back.

Accommodation symbols

Symbols give useful information about services and facilities. On page 7 you can find a key to these symbols.

ABINGDON, Oxfordshire Map ref 2C1

★★★★
SELF CATERING

Units 3
Sleeps 2–5

LOW SEASON PER WK
£300.00–£360.00

HIGH SEASON PER WK
£390.00–£425.00

Brook Farm Cottages, Abingdon

contact Pam Humphrey, **t** (01235) 820717 **e** info@brookfarmcottages.com

brookfarmcottages.com

Two-bedroom cottages, tastefully furnished, with own courtyard gardens. Centrally positioned for Stratford, Warwick, Windsor, London, the Cotswolds and Oxford.

open All year
payment Cash, cheques

Unit General

ALVERSTOKE, Hampshire Map ref 2C3

★★
SELF CATERING

Units 1
Sleeps 6

LOW SEASON PER WK
£360.00–£390.00

HIGH SEASON PER WK
£390.00–£450.00

28 The Avenue, Alverstoke

contact Mr Martin Lawson, 18 Upper Paddock Road, Watford WD19 4DZ **t** (01923) 244042
e martinlawson8400@aol.com

Three-bedroomed house sleeping six with pleasant garden, five minutes from Stokes Bay. Opportunities for fishing, sailing and windsurfing. Close to Portsmouth, Southampton and New Forest. On-site parking provided.

open All year
payment Cash, cheques
nearest shop less than 0.5 miles
nearest pub less than 0.5 miles

Unit General

AMBERLEY, West Sussex Map ref 2D3

★★★
SELF CATERING

Units 1
Sleeps 4

LOW SEASON PER WK
£400.00–£500.00

HIGH SEASON PER WK
£600.00

Minimum stay three nights.

Culver Cottage, Amberley, Arundel

contact Mrs Stella Kemp, Swallow Barn, The Sqaure, Amberley BN18 9SR **t** (01798) 831302 & 0033 5659 96950 **e** stellainamberley@yahoo.co.uk

visitbritain.com

open All year
payment Cash, cheques, euros
nearest shop less than 0.5 miles
nearest pub less than 0.5 miles

Culver Cottage, a charming farm cottage with pretty garden and patios, in the heart of the picturesque village of Amberley which nestles at the foot of the South Downs. There are wonderful views, thatched houses, flowering stone walls, a Norman church, Amberley Castle Hotel, pubs, restaurants and shop within walking distance.

Unit TV General S Leisure

ASHDOWN FOREST

See under Nutley

ASHFORD, Kent Map ref 3B4

★★★★★
SELF CATERING

Units 1
Sleeps 4

LOW SEASON PER WK
£350.00–£400.00

HIGH SEASON PER WK
£450.00–£600.00

Hazelhope Barn, Stalisfield, Nr Ashford

contact Mandy Southern, Hazelhope Barn, Hazelhope, Stalisfield Green, Faversham ME13 0HY **t** (01233) 713806 **e** mandy@hazelhopebarn.co.uk

hazelhopebarn.co.uk

open All year
payment Cash, cheques, euros
nearest shop 2 miles
nearest pub 0.5 miles

Excellent location. Luxury, first-floor apartment with stunning views. Built over stables in a Kent barn. Double with large, en suite shower and broadband Internet access. Large twin with adjacent bathroom. Fully fitted kitchen and separate utility room with washer/dryer. Very comfortable living/dining areas. Secure parking. Private garden with barbecue.

Unit TV SC DVD General P

BANBURY, Oxfordshire Map ref 2C1

★★★★
SELF CATERING

Units 1
Sleeps 2–4

LOW SEASON PER WK
£210.00–£360.00

HIGH SEASON PER WK
£360.00–£480.00

Mill Wheel Cottage, Banbury

contact Mrs Sheila Nichols, Mill House Farm, Banbury OX17 3QP **t** (01295) 811637

holiday-rentals.com SPECIAL OFFERS

open All year
payment Cash, cheques
nearest shop 2 miles
nearest pub 2 miles

Idyllic, private, very comfortable, well-equipped cottage on River Cherwell, converted to a high standard with original beams. Full of character, surrounded by water meadows with abundant wildlife, the ultimate in tranquillity and relaxation. Canal close by. Ideal for exploring the Cotswolds, Stratford and Oxford. Enjoy a warm welcome and personal attention.

Unit TV DVD Leisure

BATTLE, East Sussex Map ref 3B4

★★★★
SELF CATERING

Units 1
Sleeps 1–7

LOW SEASON PER WK
£250.00–£375.00

HIGH SEASON PER WK
£375.00–£495.00

Battle Field Cottage, Battle

t 07762 576495 **e** battlefieldcottage@yahoo.co.uk

battlefieldcottage.co.uk

Near Battle Abbey, East Sussex. Grade II listed beamed cottage, one double bedroom with four poster en-suite, one twin bedroom, one single, second bath/toilet. Large kitchen/diner, lounge, central heating, garden, patio, views.

open All year
payment Cash, cheques, euros
nearest shop less than 0.5 miles
nearest pub less than 0.5 miles

Unit General 4 Leisure

BATTLE, East Sussex Map ref 3B4

★★★★
SELF CATERING

Units 2
Sleeps 2–5

LOW SEASON PER WK
£250.00–£360.00

HIGH SEASON PER WK
£420.00–£470.00

Ninfield Holiday Cottages, Ninfield, Battle

contact Mr & Mrs D Godden, Moor Hall Farm, Moor Hall Drive, Ninfield, Battle TN33 9JT
t (01424) 892686 **e** jill.godden@tiscali.co.uk

ninfieldholidaycottages.co.uk SPECIAL OFFERS

Two cosy, comfortable well-equipped cottages converted from farm buildings, peacefully situated off a private drive in a picturesque location. Interesting area to explore with many varied attractions.

open All year
payment Cash, cheques
nearest shop 0.75 miles
nearest pub 0.5 miles

Unit General P Leisure

BATTLE, East Sussex Map ref 3B4

★★
SELF CATERING

Units 3
Sleeps 1–6

LOW SEASON PER WK
£220.00–£250.00

HIGH SEASON PER WK
£220.00–£250.00

Stiles Garage, Battle

t (01424) 773155 **e** stilesgarage@hotmail.com

Our holiday flats provide spacious self-contained accommodation within the heart of 1066 Country. Located in the historic town of Battle, close to town centre, attractions and mainline station.

open All year
payment Credit/debit cards, cash, cheques, euros
nearest shop less than 0.5 miles
nearest pub less than 0.5 miles

Unit General P

BIRCHINGTON, Kent Map ref 3C3

★★★★
SELF CATERING

Units 1
Sleeps 1–4

LOW SEASON PER WK
£210.00–£245.00

HIGH SEASON PER WK
£275.00–£385.00

Blue Fox Holiday, Birchington

contact Blue Fox Holidays, 6 Woodford Court, Birchington CT7 9DR **t** 07877 468851
e info@bluefoxholidays.co.uk

Comfortable and tastefully furnished, purpose-built ground-floor flat in quiet cul-de-sac with easy access to Birchington high street, local beaches and countryside.

open All year
payment Cash, cheques, euros
nearest shop less than 0.5 miles
nearest pub less than 0.5 miles

Unit General P

BIRCHINGTON, Kent Map ref 3C3

★★★★
SELF CATERING

Units 1
Sleeps 1–6

LOW SEASON PER WK
£300.00–£350.00

HIGH SEASON PER WK
£400.00–£500.00

Raleigh Cottage, Birchington

contact Mrs Jill Edwards, Raleigh Cottage, Band Box, 79 Station Road, Birchington CT7 9RE
t (01843) 841764 & (01843) 841101 **e** lou@landway99.freeserve.co.uk

birchingtonholidays.co.uk

Comfortable detached house with pleasant enclosed garden. One twin and two double bedrooms. Desirable location, two minutes to sea, shops, station. Linen provided. Off-street parking.

open All year
payment Cash, cheques
nearest shop less than 0.5 miles
nearest pub less than 0.5 miles

Unit General P Leisure

For **key to symbols** see page 7

BIRDHAM, West Sussex Map ref 2C3

★★★★★
SELF CATERING

Units 2
Sleeps 4

LOW SEASON PER WK
£400.00–£600.00

HIGH SEASON PER WK
£800.00–£850.00

Short breaks available throughout the year.

Martins Cottages, Chichester

contact Mrs Gillian Farquhar-Thomson, Martins Lane, Birdham, Chichester PO20 7AU
t (01243) 512222 **e** gillift@martinscottages.plus.com

martinscottages.co.uk SPECIAL OFFERS

open All year
payment Cash, cheques, euros
nearest shop 1 mile
nearest pub 2 miles

Two new luxury cottages situated in a three-acre meadow in the Chichester Harbour Area of Outstanding Natural Beauty. From the doorstep there are gorgeous harbour walks. Each cottage is full of sunshine and has two double bedrooms and two bathrooms. They can be linked and used as one unit.

Unit General
Leisure

BOSHAM, West Sussex Map ref 2C3

★★★★
SELF CATERING

Units 3
Sleeps 2–4

LOW SEASON PER WK
£300.00–£450.00

HIGH SEASON PER WK
£450.00–£650.00

Laneside, Chichester

contact Mr Antony Wallace, Bosham Lane, Bosham, Chichester PO18 8HL **t** (01243) 573234
e info@millstream-hotel.co.uk

millstream-hotel.co.uk

open All year
payment Credit/debit cards, cash, cheques
nearest shop 1 mile
nearest pub less than 0.5 miles

Three newly-built cottages located just 200m from the shores of Chichester Harbour. Laneside is owned and managed by the Millstream Hotel in whose AA 2 Rosette restaurant dinner can be taken. The cottages are superbly appointed and have a landscaped garden in which to relax.

Unit General Leisure

BOWLHEAD GREEN, Surrey Map ref 2C2

★★
SELF CATERING

Units 1
Sleeps 1–2

LOW SEASON PER WK
Min £125.00

HIGH SEASON PER WK
Max £145.00

Barn Flat, Godalming

contact Mrs Grace Ranson, Barn Flat, Bowlhead Green Farm, Bowlhead Green, Godalming GU8 6NW **t** (01428) 682687 **e** ranson@bowlhead.fsnet.co.uk

In a delightful hamlet, a 16thC barn conversion with exposed oak beams. Attractive, small, self-contained flat overlooking farmhouse garden. Double sofa bed, kitchenette, shower and wc. No pets.

open All year
payment Cash, cheques
nearest shop 1.25 miles
nearest pub 1.25 miles

Unit General P

Do you like walking?

Walkers feel at home in accommodation participating in our Walkers Welcome scheme. Look out for the symbol. Consider walking all or part of a long-distance route – go online at nationaltrail.co.uk.

BRADING, Isle of Wight Map ref 2C3

★★★★★
SELF CATERING

Units 1
Sleeps 8

LOW SEASON PER WK
£636.00–£895.00

HIGH SEASON PER WK
£995.00–£1,875.00

Weekend breaks (min 3 nights) price on request. Valid 3 Jan to 1 May and 25 Sept to 18 Dec, excl school holidays.

Hill Farm Barn, Brading

contact Mrs Sheila Lovegrove, Hill Farm, Carpenters Road, Brading PO36 0BB **t** (01983) 875184
e enquiries@hillfarmbrading.co.uk

hillfarmbrading.co.uk SPECIAL OFFERS • REAL-TIME BOOKING

open All year
payment Cash, cheques
nearest shop 1.25 miles
nearest pub 1.25 miles

18thC threshing barn on 1,000-acre family farm. Sleeps six in three en suite bedrooms, plus extra bedroom suitable for two children with separate bathroom. Carefully restored, retaining original features. Extensive grounds, beautiful views. Beach, sailing, pubs, restaurants one mile. St Helens, Bembridge two miles. Flexible booking. Non-smokers only.

ONLINE MAP

Unit General
Leisure

BRADING, Isle of Wight Map ref 2C3

★★★★
SELF CATERING

Units 1
Sleeps 4

LOW SEASON PER WK
£380.00–£440.00

HIGH SEASON PER WK
£512.00–£745.00

Weekends on request. Discounts for low occupancy 3 Jan to 22 May and 25 Sept to 18 Dec, excl school holidays.

Hill Farm Lodge, Brading

contact Mrs Sheila Lovegrove, Hill Farm, Carpenters Road, Brading PO36 0BB **t** (01983) 875184
e enquiries@hillfarmbrading.co.uk

hillfarmbrading.co.uk SPECIAL OFFERS • REAL-TIME BOOKING

open All year
payment Cash, cheques
nearest shop 1.25 miles
nearest pub 1.25 miles

Quality lodge on working farm, set in spectacularly southerly position, overlooking Bembridge, Brading Downs, RSPB Reserve and SSSI. Private, peaceful with plenty of garden. One mile to St Helens beach. Footpaths, sailing, fishing, golf, riding close by. Well equipped and high standard of cleanliness maintained. Sorry – no pets or smokers.

ONLINE MAP

Unit General Leisure

BRIGHSTONE, Isle of Wight Map ref 2C3

★★★–★★★★
SELF CATERING

Units 11
Sleeps 2–8

LOW SEASON PER WK
£198.00–£260.00

HIGH SEASON PER WK
£632.00–£850.00

Chilton Farm Cottages, Newport

contact Mrs Sue Fisk, Chilton Lane, Brighstone, Newport PO30 4DS **t** (01983) 740338
e info@chiltonfarm.co.uk

chiltonfarm.co.uk

Attractive stone cottages on our 800-acre dairy farm. Set in beautiful countryside close to the sea. Two tennis courts, barbecue. A warm welcome assured.

open All year
payment Credit/debit cards, cash, cheques
nearest shop 1 mile
nearest pub 1 mile

Unit General Leisure

PETS! WELCOME WELCOME PETS!

Where is my pet welcome?

Want to take your cherished companion with you on holiday? Proprietors participating in our Welcome Pets! scheme go out of their way to make special provision for you and your pet. Look out for the symbol.

For **key to symbols** see page 7

BRIGHSTONE, Isle of Wight Map ref 2C3

★★★★★
SELF CATERING

Units **2**

LOW SEASON PER WK
£350.00–£800.00

HIGH SEASON PER WK
£550.00–£1,000.00

Thorncross Farm – Rose & Pool Cottages, Brighstone

contact Mrs Russell, Thorncross Farm, Brighstone PO30 4PN **t** (01983) 740291
e info@thorncrossfarm.co.uk

thorncross-holiday-cottages.co.uk

open All year except Christmas and New Year
payment Cash, cheques
nearest shop 1 mile
nearest pub 1 mile

17thC semi-detached thatched cottages in the heart of the peaceful south west side of the island in wonderful countryside in an Area of Outstanding Natural Beauty.

SAT NAV *PO30 4PN*

Unit General P Leisure

BRIGHTON & HOVE, East Sussex Map ref 2D3

★★★★
SELF CATERING

Units **3**
Sleeps **2–4**

LOW SEASON PER WK
Max £450.00

HIGH SEASON PER WK
Max £650.00

Brighton Marina Holiday Apartments, Brighton

contact Mrs A Wills, 5 Marlborough Road, Richmond TW10 6JT **t** (020) 8940 6945
e averil.wills@london.com

brightonmarinaholidayapartments.co.uk

open All year
payment Cash, cheques, euros
nearest shop less than 0.5 miles
nearest pub less than 0.5 miles

Overlooking inner harbour with private waterside terrace or balcony. Luxury two-bedroom apartments. One twin, one double with en suite shower, bathroom, lounge/dining room, kitchen. Satellite TV, DVD, telephone, Wi-Fi broadband, private parking. Situated a mile east of Brighton, the marina boasts an extensive range of restaurants, leisure and dining facilities.

Unit General P

BROADSTAIRS, Kent Map ref 3C3

★★★–★★★★
SELF CATERING

Units **2**
Sleeps **1–6**

LOW SEASON PER WK
£250.00–£500.00

HIGH SEASON PER WK
£450.00–£650.00

Broadstairs Holiday Lets, Broadstairs

contact Linda & Harry Sear, Broadstairs Holiday Lets, Charity Farm, Eggington LU7 9PB
t (01525) 210550 **e** lindaandharrysear@yahoo.co.uk

broadstairsholidaylets.co.uk

One- and two-bedroom ground-floor apartments in conservation area of Chandos Square near seafront, Victoria Gardens, shops, restaurants. Sunny patio. Sea view from one-bedroom apartment. Short breaks out of season.

open All year
payment Cash, cheques, euros
nearest shop less than 0.5 miles
nearest pub less than 0.5 miles

Unit General

FAMILIES WELCOME

Looking for an ideal family break?

For accommodation offering additional facilities and services for a range of ages and family units, look out for the Families Welcome symbol. Owners of these properties will go out of their way to welcome families.

BROADSTAIRS, Kent Map ref 3C3

★★★★
SELF CATERING

Units 1
Sleeps 6

LOW SEASON PER WK
Min £375.00

HIGH SEASON PER WK
Max £750.00

Chandos Square, Broadstairs

contact Matthew Dove
t 07940 650023 **e** enquiries@selfcateringbroadstairs.co.uk

selfcateringbroadstairs.co.uk GUEST REVIEWS • SPECIAL OFFERS • REAL-TIME BOOKING

Comfortable, bright three-bedroom, three-bathroom apartment. Perfect position opposite wonderful sandy beach. Less that two minutes' walk to town. Very well equipped. Ideal choice for a memorable seaside holiday.

open All year
payment Cash, cheques
nearest shop less than 0.5 miles
nearest pub less than 0.5 miles

Unit General Leisure

BROADSTAIRS, Kent Map ref 3C3

★★★★
SELF CATERING

Units 1
Sleeps 2–6

LOW SEASON PER WK
£320.00–£450.00

HIGH SEASON PER WK
£520.00–£650.00

Fisherman's Cottage, Broadstairs

contact Ms Linda Spillane, 33 St James' Drive, Wandsworth, London SW17 7RN **t** (020) 8672 4150
e linda.spillane@virgin.net

fishermanscottagebroadstairs.co.uk

open All year
payment Cheques

Delightfully converted, four-storey, Grade II Listed flint cottage in Broadstairs conservation area. One minute to harbour and beach. The cottage has three bedrooms, a well-equipped kitchen and spacious living areas. The floors are linked by a wooden spiral staircase – see virtual tour on our website.

Unit General

BROOK, Isle of Wight Map ref 2C3

★★★★
SELF CATERING

Units 2
Sleeps 6

LOW SEASON PER WK
Min £260.00

HIGH SEASON PER WK
Max £955.00

Short breaks available.

Westbrook & Northbrook, Brook

contact Mrs Belinda Walters, Battersea Bridge Investments Ltd, Brook House, Brook PO30 4EJ
t (01983) 740535 & 07802 203376 **e** bookings@brookhouseiow.co.uk

brookhouseiow.co.uk

open All year
payment Cheques, euros
nearest shop 3 miles
nearest pub 0.5 miles

Two charming holiday cottages, sleeping six and four, in beautiful grounds of Brook House tucked away in the rural West Wight. Well furnished, for a comfortable and cosy holiday. A short distance from stunning National Trust beaches and downland, with some of the finest views on the Island. Within walking distance of local pub.

Unit General P
Leisure

Using map references

The map references refer to the colour maps at the front of this guide. The first figure is the map number, the letter and figure that follow indicate the grid reference on the map.

For **key to symbols** see page 7

BUCKINGHAM, Buckinghamshire Map ref 2C1

★★★★
SELF CATERING

Units **6**
Sleeps **1–9**

LOW SEASON PER WK
£225.00–£450.00

HIGH SEASON PER WK
£300.00–£575.00

Additional rooms may be added from B&B on special room-only rate.

Huntsmill Farm Holidays, Buckingham

t (01280) 704852 & 07970 871104 **e** fiona@huntsmill.com

huntsmill.com

open All year
payment Credit/debit cards, cash, cheques, euros
nearest shop 2 miles
nearest pub 2 miles

Courtyard of traditional stone, timber and slate barns, imaginatively converted from former calf sheds and pig sties, offering a high standard of accommodation. Set on a working farm in a quiet location with views of open countryside. Large gardens with easy access to footpaths. Close to Silverstone and many National Trust properties.

SAT NAV *MK18 5ND*

Unit General Leisure

BURFORD, Oxfordshire Map ref 2B1

★★★★–★★★★★
SELF CATERING

Units **2**
Sleeps **8**

LOW SEASON PER WK
£456.00–£545.00

HIGH SEASON PER WK
£756.00–£901.00

Caswell House, Brize Norton

contact Mrs Amanda Matthews, Caswell Lane, Brize Norton OX18 3NJ **t** (01993) 701064 & 07718 390867 **e** stay@caswell-house.co.uk

caswell-house.co.uk

open All year
payment Credit/debit cards, cash, cheques
nearest shop 5 miles
nearest pub 3 miles

With rural views, walled gardens, orchard, moat and extensive lawns, Caswell House provides luxurious, spacious accommodation for up to 12 guests. It has been refurbished to an excellent standard, retaining all the original rural, historic charm. An ideal relaxing retreat, with that special feeling of warmth, comfort and country-house living.

ONLINE MAP

Unit General
Leisure

BURLEY, Hampshire Map ref 2B3

★★★★
SELF CATERING

Units **1**
Sleeps **1–4**

LOW SEASON PER WK
£300.00–£450.00

HIGH SEASON PER WK
£650.00–£800.00

Barn Cottage, Burley

contact Mrs Helen Gaskell, Barn Cottage, Castle Hill Lane, Burley BH24 4HF **t** (01425) 403726 **e** gaskell425@btinternet.com

barncottageburley.co.uk SPECIAL OFFERS

Quiet, unique setting offering peace and tranquillity and yet only a mile from the village centre. Direct access into the New Forest. One double, one twin. Horses and pets welcome.

open All year
payment Credit/debit cards, cash, cheques
nearest shop 1 mile
nearest pub 1 mile

Unit General Leisure

What if I need to cancel?

It is advisable to check the proprietor's cancellation policy in case you have to change your plans at a later date.

CANTERBURY, Kent Map ref 3B3

★★★
SELF CATERING

Units 1
Sleeps 5

LOW SEASON PER WK
Min £350.00

HIGH SEASON PER WK
Max £450.00

Jubilee Lodge, Canterbury

contact Mrs S P Underwood, Dicksons Bourne, Aldington TN25 7AH **t** (01233) 720370
e juck1@aol.com

A Victorian terraced house within the city walls, with enclosed sunny garden. Only 100m walk to St Peter's Street and shops. Double, twin and single rooms. Ground-floor bathroom and bed settee.

open All year
payment Cash, cheques, euros
nearest shop less than 0.5 miles
nearest pub less than 0.5 miles

Unit General 5 Leisure

CANTERBURY, Kent Map ref 3B3

★★★
SELF CATERING

Units 5
Sleeps 2–4

LOW SEASON PER WK
£160.00–£300.00

HIGH SEASON PER WK
£300.00–£510.00

Special rates for parties requiring all the units (up to 18 people).

The Old Sawmill, Hastingleigh, Ashford

contact Mrs Caroline Gilson, The Old Sawmill, Hastingleigh, Ashford TN25 5HN **t** (01233) 750056 & 07765 963215 **e** carolinepilgrim@aol.com

hastingleighholidaylets.com

open All year
payment Credit/debit cards, cash, cheques
nearest shop 3 miles
nearest pub 0.5 miles

Five attractively converted cottages set in an Area of Outstanding Natural Beauty. Canterbury, London and France are all within easy reach. Every property is fully equipped with modern furnishings and appliances. A games room and children's play area are also on site and barbecues are available.

SAT NAV *TN25 5HN*

Unit General P Leisure

CANTERBURY, Kent Map ref 3B3

★★★★
SELF CATERING

Units 3
Sleeps 1–3

LOW SEASON PER WK
£240.00–£380.00

HIGH SEASON PER WK
£330.00–£440.00

Oriel Lodge Holiday Apartments, Canterbury

contact Mr Keith Rishworth, Oriel Lodge, 3 Queens Avenue, Canterbury CT2 8AY **t** (01227) 462845
e info@oriel-lodge.co.uk

oriel-lodge.co.uk

High-grade apartments in a peaceful Edwardian house, set in a residential area with private parking, five minutes' walk from the city centre. Weekend and short breaks all year. Broadband internet.

open All year
payment Credit/debit cards, cash, cheques
nearest shop less than 0.5 miles
nearest pub less than 0.5 miles

Unit General 6 P Leisure

Don't forget www.

Web addresses throughout this guide are shown without the prefix www. Please include www. in the address line of your browser.
If a web address does not follow this style it is shown in full.

CHICHESTER, West Sussex Map ref 2C3

★★★★★
SELF CATERING

Units 1
Sleeps 4

LOW SEASON PER WK
£350.00–£500.00

HIGH SEASON PER WK
£500.00–£700.00

Apple Barn, Runcton, Chichester

contact Mrs R Kendall, Saltham House, Saltham Lane, Runcton, Chichester PO20 1XJ
t (01243) 775997 **e** applebarn@salthamhouse.co.uk

salthamhouse.co.uk

open All year
payment Credit/debit cards, cash, cheques
nearest shop less than 0.5 miles
nearest pub 1 mile

Apple Barn is an old single-storey barn which has been converted into a luxury two-bedroom/two-bathroom holiday cottage. It is open-plan and very spacious throughout. Set in a pretty, quiet location surrounded by farmland, it is well situated for Chichester and the surrounding area.

Unit General P Leisure

CHICHESTER, West Sussex Map ref 2C3

★★★★
SELF CATERING

Units 1
Sleeps 1–6

LOW SEASON PER WK
£425.00–£595.00

HIGH SEASON PER WK
£595.00–£695.00

Short breaks available Oct-May. Reduced rates for couples Oct-May.

Cornerstones, Chichester

contact Mrs Higgins, Greenacre, Goodwood Gardens, Chichester PO20 1SP **t** (01243) 839096
e v.r.higgins@dsl.pipex.com

cornercottages.com

open All year
payment Cash, cheques
nearest shop 2 miles
nearest pub less than 0.5 miles

Sussex-style house. Two bedrooms upstairs, one downstairs. Bathroom. Separate shower room. Equipped to high standard. Double garage. Enclosed gardens. Village between Chichester and coast. Easy walks to pub/restaurant, post office/shop, church and Pagham nature reserve. Five-minute drive to Chichester. Ten minutes to Goodwood Racecourse.

Unit TV SC DVD General P

CHICHESTER, West Sussex Map ref 2C3

★★★★
SELF CATERING

Units 1
Sleeps 1–2

LOW SEASON PER WK
£235.00–£315.00

HIGH SEASON PER WK
£315.00–£350.00

Short breaks available Oct-Apr. Minimum 3 nights.

Cygnet Cottage, Chichester

contact Mrs Higgins, Greenacre, Goodwood Gardens, Chichester PO20 1SP **t** (01243) 839096
e v.r.higgins@dsl.pipex.com

cornercottages.com

open All year
payment Cash, cheques
nearest shop 2 miles
nearest pub less than 0.5 miles

Cosy one-bedroom detached cottage in village between Chichester and coast. Easy country walks to pub/restaurant, post office/shop, church and Pagham nature reserve. Fully equipped to high standard. Suntrap patio. Off-road parking. Canalside walk or five minutes' drive to historic Chichester. Ten minutes' drive to Goodwood racecourse.

Unit TV SC DVD General P S

CHICHESTER, West Sussex Map ref 2C3

★★★
SELF CATERING

Units 5
Sleeps 2–5

LOW SEASON PER WK
£273.00–£375.00

HIGH SEASON PER WK
£364.00–£599.00

Hunston Mill Cottages, Chichester

contact Mr & Mrs Ian & Lyn Potter, Hunston Mill, Selsey Road, Hunston, Chichester PO20 1AU
t (01243) 783375 **e** hunstonmillcottages@bushinternet.com

hunstonmill.co.uk

open All year
payment Cash, cheques
nearest shop 0.5 miles
nearest pub 0.5 miles

18thC windmill and adjoining buildings converted into comfortable holiday homes, set in nearly an acre of attractive gardens with barbecue. Situated in the country between the historic city of Chichester and the sea, with views over farmland, golf course and to the Downs.

Unit General Leisure

CHILHAM, Kent Map ref 3B3

★★★★
SELF CATERING

Units 2
Sleeps 2

LOW SEASON PER WK
£240.00–£290.00

HIGH SEASON PER WK
£350.00–£370.00

Short breaks available. Nov-Mar, 3-night stay.

Monckton Cottages, Canterbury

contact Mrs Helen Kirwan, Monckton Cottages, Mountain Street, Chilham, Canterbury CT4 8DG
t (01227) 730256 & 07789 431760 **e** helen@rwkirwan.plus.com

mncktoncottages.com

open All year
payment Cash, cheques, euros
nearest shop less than 0.5 miles
nearest pub less than 0.5 miles

Charming, peaceful cottages in 15thC manor set in three acres. Picturesque setting on North Downs Way overlooking Chilham Castle's parkland. Perfect for walking, exploring ancient woodland, chalk downs, Tudor village, castles. Canterbury six miles. Own large gardens, oak beams, inglenook fire/wood-burning stove. Immaculate, well equipped. Recently refitted kitchens and bathrooms.

Unit General P Leisure

CLIFTONVILLE

See under Margate

COTSWOLDS

See under Burford
See also Cotswolds in the South West England region

Country Code always follow the Country Code

- Be safe – plan ahead and follow any signs
- Leave gates and property as you find them
- Protect plants and animals, and take your litter home
- Keep dogs under close control
- Consider other people

COWES, Isle of Wight Map ref 2C3

★★★
SELF CATERING

Units 1
Sleeps 2–10

LOW SEASON PER WK
£420.00–£504.00

HIGH SEASON PER WK
£578.00–£714.00

Short breaks available on request.

The Old School House, Cowes

t 07831 514108 **e** tim@coweshouse.co.uk

coweshouse.co.uk REAL-TIME BOOKING

open All year
payment Cash, cheques
nearest shop less than 0.5 miles
nearest pub less than 0.5 miles

Unique upside-down property offering a first-floor, wooden beamed, loft-style, open-plan sitting/dining and kitchen area. One double, one twin, one bunk, two bathrooms plus two double sofa beds. Recently redecorated in a contemporary style. Conveniently located for Cowes shops, restaurants, bars and marina. Easy access to rest of island by car.

ONLINE MAP

Unit General Leisure

DYMCHURCH, Kent Map ref 3B4

★★★★★
SELF CATERING

Units 1
Sleeps 2–8

LOW SEASON PER WK
£350.00–£500.00

HIGH SEASON PER WK
£500.00–£700.00

Dymchurch House, Dymchurch

contact Mrs Uden, 53 Crescent Road, Sidcup DA15 7HW **t** (020) 8300 2100
e dymchurchhouse@btopenworld.com

open All year
payment Cash, cheques

Luxury, spacious, detached property in a prime position. Equipped to a very high standard. Ideal for superb sandy beach accessed directly via footpath. An indoor swimming pool and the famous miniature railway and village, with its children's amusement park, are all within easy walking distance. Excellent location for visiting tourist attractions.

Unit General Leisure

EPSOM, Surrey Map ref 2D2

★★★
SELF CATERING

Units 1
Sleeps 1–5

LOW SEASON PER WK
£190.00–£215.00

HIGH SEASON PER WK
£240.00–£265.00

7 Great Tattenhams, Epsom

contact Mrs Mary Willis, 7 Great Tattenhams, Epsom KT18 5RF **t** (01737) 354112

Modern, spacious, comfortably furnished first-floor flat. A good touring centre for London and the South East. Superstore nearby.

open All year
payment Cash, cheques
nearest shop less than 0.5 miles
nearest pub 0.75 miles

Unit General Leisure

EXTON, Hampshire Map ref 2C3

★★★★
SELF CATERING

Units 4
Sleeps 1–5

LOW SEASON PER WK
Max £350.00

HIGH SEASON PER WK
Max £495.00

Beacon Hill Farm Cottages, Southampton

contact Mrs Catherine Dunford, Farm Office, Beacon Hill Farm, Alton Road, Warnford, Southampton SO32 3LA **t** (01730) 829724 **e** info@beaconhillcottages.co.uk

beaconhillcottages.co.uk

Barn conversion, comprising four cottages, each with garden and barbecue. Farmland views and safe play area. Market towns, Winchester and Portsmouth easily accessible. Excellent village pub. Ideal for cyclists and walkers.

open All year
payment Cash, cheques
nearest shop 2 miles
nearest pub 2 miles

Unit General Leisure

FARINGDON, Oxfordshire Map ref 2B2

★★★★
SELF CATERING

Units 2
Sleeps 4–6

LOW SEASON PER WK
£400.00–£525.00

HIGH SEASON PER WK
£500.00–£750.00

Goodlake Barns, Faringdon

contact Mr Andrew Gantlett, Goodlake Barns, Church Farm, Church Street, Faringdon SN7 7QA
t (01367) 710112 **e** info@goodlakebarns.co.uk

goodlakebarns.co.uk

Light and spacious cottages in a picturesque village setting on an organic farm. This is a relaxing place to stay and an ideal base for exploring Oxford and the Cotswolds.

open All year
payment Credit/debit cards, cash, cheques
nearest shop 2 miles
nearest pub 2 miles

Unit TV DVD General P S Leisure

FARNHAM, Surrey Map ref 2C2

★★★★★
SELF CATERING

Units 1
Sleeps 5

LOW SEASON PER WK
£350.00–£400.00

HIGH SEASON PER WK
£450.00–£525.00

Bentley Green Farm, Bentley, Farnham

contact Mrs Glenda Powell, Bentley Green Farm, The Drift, Bentley, Farnham GU10 5JX
t (01420) 23246 **e** glenda.powell@btopenworld.com

bentleygreenfarm.co.uk

open All year
payment Cash, cheques
nearest shop 0.5 miles
nearest pub 0.5 miles

Luxury self-contained accommodation in purpose-built annexe of listed 16thC farmhouse. Set in 40 acres with outdoor swimming pool, tennis court, and fishing rights. Fully fitted and very spacious. Ideally located between Alton and Farnham with ample parking. Full details on website.

Unit TV DVD General P S
Leisure

FARNHAM, Surrey Map ref 2C2

★★★★
SELF CATERING

Units 13
Sleeps 2–6

LOW SEASON PER WK
Min £470.00

HIGH SEASON PER WK
Min £700.00

Tilford Woods, Farnham

contact Miss Victoria Heath, Tilford Woods, Tilford Road, Tilford, Farnham GU10 2DD
t (01252) 792199 **e** admin@tilfordwoods.co.uk

tilfordwoods.co.uk

Tilford Woods comprises one- to three-bedroom, fully fitted and equipped, luxury timber lodges. It is the ideal base for exploring the wonderful surrounding countryside and the many local attractions.

open All year
payment Credit/debit cards, cash, cheques
nearest shop 0.75 miles
nearest pub less than 0.5 miles

Unit TV DVD General P S
Leisure

FOLKESTONE, Kent Map ref 3B4

★★–★★★★★
SELF CATERING

Units **13**
Sleeps **2–10**

LOW SEASON PER WK
£135.00–£280.00

HIGH SEASON PER WK
£210.00–£450.00

Short breaks, Mon-Fri or Fri-Mon: low season – min £60, max £140; high season – min £125, max £255.

The Grand, Folkestone

contact Reception, The Grand, The Leas, Folkestone CT20 2XL **t** (01303) 222222
e info@grand-uk.com

grand-uk.com

open All year
payment Credit/debit cards, cash, cheques, euros
nearest shop 0.5 miles
nearest pub less than 0.5 miles

The Grand is a fine listed building situated on The Leas, the world-famous grassy cliff-top promenade running from the town centre along the southern side of the spacious and gracious west end of Folkestone. It enjoys uninterrupted views across the ever-changing seascape to France.

ONLINE MAP

Unit General P Leisure

FORDINGBRIDGE, Hampshire Map ref 2B3

★★★
SELF CATERING

Units **3**
Sleeps **2–6**

LOW SEASON PER WK
£250.00–£340.00

HIGH SEASON PER WK
£320.00–£550.00

Alderholt Mill, Fordingbridge

contact Mr & Mrs Richard & Sandra Harte, Alderholt Mill, Fordingbridge SP6 1PU **t** (01425) 653130
e alderholt-mill@zetnet.co.uk

alderholtmill.co.uk

open All year
payment Credit/debit cards, cash, cheques
nearest shop 2 miles
nearest pub 2 miles

Picturesque working water mill. The grain store has been sympathetically converted into delightful holiday apartments comprising two small ground-floor units and one large, air-conditioned first- and second-floor apartment, with a wealth of oak beams and modern-day facilities. Idyllic, rural setting. Lovely gardens, private fishing on site. Off-road parking.

Unit General 10 Leisure

FORDINGBRIDGE, Hampshire Map ref 2B3

★★★★–★★★★★
SELF CATERING

Units **8**
Sleeps **2–18**

LOW SEASON PER WK
£288.00–£1,498.00

HIGH SEASON PER WK
£298.00–£3,070.00

Burgate Manor Farm Holidays, Fordingbridge

contact Mrs Bridget Stallard, Burgate Manor Farm Holidays, Burgate Manor Farm, Burgate, Fordingbridge SP6 1LX **t** (01425) 653908 **e** info@newforestcottages.com

newforestcottages.com

New Forest/Avon Valley. Small- and medium-sized farm cottages and large, recently converted, galleried, beamed barn. Short walk pub/restaurant. Games barn. Fishing. Grazing. Beach 15 miles.

open All year
payment Cash, cheques
nearest shop 1 mile
nearest pub less than 0.5 miles

Unit General P Leisure

Place index

If you know where you want to stay, the index by place name at the back of the guide will give you the page number listing accommodation in your chosen town, city or village. Check out the other useful indexes too.

FRESHWATER, Isle of Wight Map ref 2C3

★★★
SELF CATERING

Units **29**
Sleeps **2–7**

LOW SEASON PER WK
£270.00–£430.00

HIGH SEASON PER WK
£440.00–£900.00

Fully inclusive Christmas packages available. Ferry-inclusive deals available. Subsidised child and pet rates available.

Farringford Hotel, Freshwater

contact Mr Andre Bourcier, Farringford Hotel, Bedbury Lane, Freshwater PO40 9PE
t (01983) 752500 **e** enquiries@farringford.co.uk

farringford.co.uk

open All year
payment Credit/debit cards, cash, cheques, euros
nearest shop 0.5 miles
nearest pub 0.5 miles

Once the home of Alfred Lord Tennyson, now a country-style house with self-catering units of three different styles to suit individual needs. Set within 35 acres of mature pastureland incorporating a 9-hole par 3 golf course, tennis, outdoor heated pool, bowls, Garden Restaurant and Bar.

Unit General Leisure

FUNTINGTON, West Sussex Map ref 2C3

★★★★
SELF CATERING

Units **1**
Sleeps **4**

LOW SEASON PER WK
£350.00–£400.00

HIGH SEASON PER WK
£480.00

The Courtyard, Chichester

contact Mrs Claire Hoare, Adsdean, Chichester PO18 9DN **t** (01243) 575464
e tim.hoare@farming.co.uk

adsdean.co.uk

The Courtyard is situated on a farm in a secluded courtyard, with the South Downs on the doorstep.

open All year
payment Credit/debit cards, cash, cheques
nearest shop 0.5 miles
nearest pub 0.5 miles

Unit General Leisure

GATWICK AIRPORT

See under Horsham

GLYNDE, East Sussex Map ref 2D3

★★★★
SELF CATERING

Units **9**
Sleeps **2–6**

LOW SEASON PER WK
£200.00–£480.00

HIGH SEASON PER WK
£200.00–£520.00

Caburn Cottages, Glynde

contact Mrs Rosemary Norris, Ranscombe Farm, Glynde, Nr Lewes BN8 6AA **t** (01273) 858062
e rosemary.norris@hotmail.com

caburncottages.co.uk

open All year
payment Cash, cheques, euros
nearest shop 1.5 miles
nearest pub 1.5 miles

Lovely flint and brick cottages on working farm. Very comfortable. Non-smoking. Downland walks. Close to Glyndebourne, Lewes and Brighton. Friendly welcome.

SAT NAV *BN8 6AA*

Unit General

Do you have access needs?

Look for the National Accessible Scheme symbols if you have special hearing, visual or mobility needs. An index of accommodation participating in the scheme can be found at the back of this guide.

GOSPORT, Hampshire Map ref 2C3

★★★
SELF CATERING

Units 1
Sleeps 5

LOW SEASON PER WK
Max £305.00

HIGH SEASON PER WK
Max £588.00

Eight The Mews, Gosport

contact Richard Jeal, 13 Sondes Farm, Glebe Road, Dorking RH4 3EF **t** 07771 990425
e info@eightthemews.co.uk

eightthemews.co.uk

open All year
payment Credit/debit cards, cash, cheques, euros
nearest shop 0.5 miles
nearest pub 0.5 miles

A three-bedroom self-catering town house offering accommodation for up to five people. The property is arranged over three floors, has a courtyard garden and parking for two cars. Our position in the centre of Gosport close to the ferry terminal, bus and train station makes a great spot to explore both Portsmouth and the surrounding area.

ONLINE MAP

Unit TV SC DVD General 4 P S Leisure

GOUDHURST, Kent Map ref 3B4

★★★★
SELF CATERING

Units 3
Sleeps 2–7

LOW SEASON PER WK
£285.00–£650.00

HIGH SEASON PER WK
£320.00–£795.00

Three Chimneys Farm, Cranbrook

contact Mrs Marion Fuller, Three Chimneys Farm, Bedgebury Road, Goudhurst, Cranbrook TN17 2RA **t** (01580) 212175 & 07785 734639 **e** marionfuller@threechimneysfarm.co.uk

threechimneysfarm.co.uk

open All year
payment Credit/debit cards, cash, cheques
nearest shop 2 miles
nearest pub 2 miles

Mixed farm. Spacious cottages in a beautiful location, very quiet but not isolated. Wi-Fi internet connection.

Unit TV SC DVD General P
Leisure

GUILDFORD, Surrey Map ref 2D2

★★★
SELF CATERING

Units 1
Sleeps 2–6

LOW SEASON PER WK
Min £500.00

HIGH SEASON PER WK
Min £520.00

Lavender, Guildford

contact Mr & Mrs Liew, Mandarin, Pewley Point, Guildford GU1 3SP **t** (01483) 506819 & 07906 179084 **e** shirleyliew9@hotmail.com

Well-presented, fully furnished, comfortable house, conveniently situated in town centre, close to high street shops, river, theatre, leisure facilities and railway station. Airports 40 minutes.

open All year
payment Cash, cheques

Unit TV General P

Check the maps for accommodation locations

Colour maps at the front pinpoint all the places where accommodation is featured within the regional sections of this guide. Pick your location and then refer to the place index at the back to find the page number.

GUILDFORD, Surrey Map ref 2D2

★★–★★★
SELF CATERING

Units 20
Sleeps 4–5

LOW SEASON PER WK
Min £420.00

HIGH SEASON PER WK
Max £480.00

University of Surrey, Guildford

Conference Office, University of Surrey, Guildford GU2 7XH **t** (01483) 686767
e conferences@surrey.ac.uk

surrey.ac.uk/conferences

Modern, self-contained accommodation for self-catering holidays on attractive campus. One mile from Guildford centre. Ideal base to enjoy London and South East England.

open June, July and August
payment Credit/debit cards, cash
nearest shop 0.5 miles
nearest pub 1 mile

Unit General Leisure

GUILDFORD, Surrey Map ref 2D2

★★★
SELF CATERING

Units 1
Sleeps 1–4

LOW SEASON PER WK
Min £320.00

HIGH SEASON PER WK
Max £350.00

West View, West Horsley, Guildford

contact Mrs Janet Steer, West View, Shere Road, West Horsley, Leatherhead KT24 6EW
t (01483) 284686 **e** cliveandjan@aol.com

homestead.com/2westview

open All year
payment Cash, cheques
nearest shop 0.5 miles
nearest pub 0.5 miles

Attractive, self-contained, non-smoking apartment, attached to a country house with large gardens in quiet location in Surrey Hills. Double bedroom with patio door onto private terrace. Living room with double sofa bed. Fully equipped kitchen/diner. Bathroom with shower. Close to RHS Wisley and many National Trust houses. Wi-Fi accessible.

Unit General P

HADDENHAM, Buckinghamshire Map ref 2C1

★★★★
SELF CATERING

Units 1
Sleeps 2

LOW SEASON PER WK
£400.00

HIGH SEASON PER WK
£400.00

Anvil Cottage Barn, Haddenham

contact Mrs Ann Saadi, 41 Townside, Aylesbury HP17 8AW **t** (01844) 296075
e annsaadi@hotmail.co.uk

Delightful conversion of blacksmith's forge in conservation area of picturesque Haddenham. Spacious vaulted lounge with pretty galleried sleeping area (double bed). Walking distance of shops, restaurants, pubs and station.

open All year except Christmas
payment Cash, cheques, euros
nearest shop 0.5 miles
nearest pub less than 0.5 miles

Unit General P S

For **key to symbols** see page 7

HAILSHAM, East Sussex Map ref 2D3

★★★-★★★★★
SELF CATERING

Units 5
Sleeps 4–11

LOW SEASON PER WK
Min £406.00

HIGH SEASON PER WK
Max £1,145.00

Off-peak and short breaks available (excl school holidays). Cottages £258-£710, oast house £900-£1,150.

Pekes, Chiddingly

contact Ms Eva Morris, 124 Elm Park Mansions, Park Walk, London SW10 0AR **t** (020) 7352 8088
e pekes.afa@virgin.net

pekesmanor.com

open All year
payment Cash, cheques
nearest shop 1.25 miles
nearest pub 1.25 miles

Spacious oast house, cottages and wing of Tudor manor in extensive grounds. Hard tennis court, indoor heated pool, sauna, jacuzzi, badminton. Children and pets welcome. Prices shown are for the cottages; oast house is £1,340.00-£2,000.00, excluding Christmas and New Year.

Unit General
Leisure

HAMBLE, Hampshire Map ref 2C3

★★★
SELF CATERING

Units 1

LOW SEASON PER WK
£300.00–£500.00

HIGH SEASON PER WK
£400.00–£650.00

Woodend, Bursledon

contact Mrs Woodhouse, Kew House, Kew Lane, Bursledon, Southampton SO31 8DG
t (023) 8040 2804 **e** info@woodhousecottages.co.uk

woodhousecottages.co.uk

Peaceful location, large garden with tennis court. Close to New Forest, River Hamble, Isle of Wight, Portsmouth and Southampton. Comfortable accommodation, one double, one twin. Green Tourism Silver Award for environmental awareness.

open All year
payment Cash, cheques
nearest shop 1 mile
nearest pub less than 0.5 miles

Unit General Leisure

HASTINGLEIGH, Kent Map ref 3B4

★★★★
SELF CATERING

Units 1
Sleeps 1–2

LOW SEASON PER WK
£300.00

HIGH SEASON PER WK
£300.00

Staple Farm, Hastingleigh, Ashford

contact Mr & Mrs Cliff & Betty Martindale, Staple Farm, Hastingleigh, Ashford TN25 5HF
t (01233) 750248

payment Cash, cheques
nearest shop 2.8 miles
nearest pub 1 mile

Stable conversion displaying beams and original features, yet offering all modern amenities. Situated in Area of Outstanding Natural Beauty with excellent walks from front door, including the North Downs Way. Within easy reach of Canterbury, Eurostar terminals, Channel ports of Dover and Folkestone, plus many places of historic interest.

Unit General P

HASTINGS, East Sussex Map ref 3B4

★★★
SELF CATERING

Units 1
Sleeps 6

LOW SEASON PER WK
£280.00–£380.00

HIGH SEASON PER WK
£380.00–£450.00

Short winter breaks available from £250. Discount on two-week holidays. For up-to-date information see website.

Lindsell Cottage, Hastings

contact Mr John Sydes, 27 Langham Rd, Hastings TN34 2JE **t** 07951 766 639
e jazmacuk@yahoo.co.uk

hastingsholiday.co.uk

open All year
payment Credit/debit cards, cash, cheques, euros
nearest shop less than 0.5 miles
nearest pub less than 0.5 miles

Experience the magic of the seaside in this unique fisherman's cottage. Enjoying an elevated, quiet position with inspiring views over Hastings' fishing quarter, sea, Old Town and country park. Sleeps five comfortably over four floors. Three bedrooms, first-floor wc, separate kitchen, luxury bath/shower room. Suntrap private garden. Close to all amenities.

Unit General Leisure

HENFIELD, West Sussex Map ref 2D3

★★★
SELF CATERING

Units 2
Sleeps 3–5

LOW SEASON PER WK
£300.00–£380.00

HIGH SEASON PER WK
£420.00–£460.00

Short breaks available: £200 for 2 nights, each extra night £60.

New Hall Cottage & New Hall Holiday Flat, Henfield

contact Mrs Marjorie Carreck, New Hall, New Hall Lane, Small Dole, Henfield BN5 9YJ
t (01273) 492546

newhallcottage.co.uk

open All year
payment Cash, cheques
nearest shop 0.5 miles
nearest pub 0.5 miles

Self-contained flat and 17thC cottage attached to manor house. Set in 3.5 acres of mature gardens, surrounded by farmland. Within easy reach of famous Sussex gardens – Nymans, High Beeches, Wakehurst Place, Leonardslee – and less than an hour from Wisley. Or visit Brighton, Arundel, Lewes and Chichester, South Downs and coast.

Unit General P Leisure

Where can I get help and advice?

Tourist Information Centres offer friendly help with accommodation and holiday ideas as well as suggestions of places to visit and things to do. You'll find contact details at the beginning of each regional section.

For **key to symbols** see page 7

HENLEY-ON-THAMES, Oxfordshire Map ref 2C2

★★
SELF CATERING

Units 1
Sleeps 2–6

LOW SEASON PER WK
Min £450.00

HIGH SEASON PER WK
£600.00–£700.00

First Floor Flat, Henley-on-Thames

contact Ms Caroline Bleackley, 2 River Terrace, Henley-on-Thames RG9 1BG **t** 07776 223057
e caroline.bleackley@googlemail.com

cottageguide.co.uk/carolines

Two double-bedroomed, centrally heated first-floor riverside flat in central Henley with spectacular views in a quiet Grade II Listed Regency house. Small galley kitchen, private bathroom with shower, double sofa bed and free Wi-Fi.

open All year
payment Cash, cheques

Unit General

HIGH HALDEN, Kent Map ref 3B4

★★★★
SELF CATERING

Units 2
Sleeps 2–4

LOW SEASON PER WK
£300.00–£440.00

HIGH SEASON PER WK
£450.00–£550.00

Swim for free at Tenterden Leisure Centre. Details on request.

The Granary and The Stables, High Halden, Nr Tenterden

contact Mrs Serena Maundrell, Vintage Years Company Ltd, Hales Place, High Halden, Ashford TN26 3JQ **t** (01233) 850871 & 07715 488804 **e** serena@vintage-years.co.uk

vintage-years.co.uk

open All year
payment Cash, cheques, euros
nearest shop 2 miles
nearest pub 1 mile

The Granary is beautifully converted and heavily beamed, with one double and one twin. The Stables has two en suite bedrooms on one level, one designed for wheelchair access. Both units are comfortably furnished and fully equipped. Set in ten-acre gardens, they provide tranquillity and an excellent touring base.

Unit General P Leisure

HORSHAM, West Sussex Map ref 2D2

★★★★
SELF CATERING

Units 1
Sleeps 2–4

LOW SEASON PER WK
£325.00–£400.00

HIGH SEASON PER WK
£550.00–£600.00

The Lodge, Two Mile Ash Road, Horsham

contact Mrs S Young, Ash Place Cottage, Two Mile Ash Road, Horsham RH13 0PG
t (01403) 731329 **e** richard.young6@btinternet.com

thelodgecottage.co.uk GUEST REVIEWS

open All year
payment Cash, cheques, euros
nearest shop 1 mile
nearest pub less than 0.5 miles

The Lodge is a charming self-catering holiday cottage full of character with a splash of contemporary living. Exposed oak timber a feature throughout. Set in the heart of West Sussex countryside overlooking a small lake. Close to the Downs Link, walks and cycle routes. Horsham three miles.

SAT NAV *RH13 0PG* **ONLINE MAP**

Unit General 12 P Leisure

HOVE

See under Brighton & Hove

What shall we do today?

For ideas on places to visit, see the beginning of this regional section or go online at enjoyengland.com.

HYTHE, Hampshire Map ref 2C3

★★★★
SELF CATERING

Units **1**
Sleeps **10**

LOW SEASON PER WK
£600.00–£800.00

HIGH SEASON PER WK
£1,000.00–£1,500.00

Weekend and short breaks available low season; also high season subject to availability. Reductions for 2-person occupancy.

Mullins, Hythe, New Forest

contact Ms Alison Percy, 9 Upper Mullins Lane, Hythe SO45 5AG **t** (023) 8084 5556
e alison@the-percys.co.uk

holiday-newforest.co.uk GUEST REVIEWS · SPECIAL OFFERS

open All year
payment Cash, cheques
nearest shop 0.5 miles
nearest pub 0.5 miles

Sunny house, sleeps eight to ten, private heated pool, countryside views, ample parking, four large bedrooms, three bath/shower rooms, sitting room with log fire, piano, modern and antique furniture. Nearby attractions: Beaulieu, Exbury Gardens, Lepe Beach, farmers' markets, woodland and heath walks.

Unit General P Leisure

ISLE OF WIGHT

See under Brading, Brighstone, Brook, Cowes, Freshwater, Ryde, St Helens, Seaview, Shanklin, Totland Bay, Ventnor, Whitwell, Wootton Bridge

IVINGHOE, Buckinghamshire Map ref 2D1

★★★
SELF CATERING

Units **4**
Sleeps **4–6**

LOW SEASON PER WK
£450.00–£500.00

HIGH SEASON PER WK
£500.00–£580.00

Stays of four weeks or more can attract a 10% discount on website prices.

Town Farm Holiday Cottages, Ivinghoe, Leighton Buzzard

contact Mrs Angie Leach, Town Farm Holiday Cottages, Icknield Way, Ivinghoe, Leighton Buzzard LU7 9EL **t** (01296) 668455 **e** angie@letsunlimited.com

letsunlimited.com SPECIAL OFFERS

open All year
payment Credit/debit cards, cash, cheques
nearest shop 1 mile
nearest pub 0.5 miles

We have four attractive, three-bedroom cottages with views overlooking the Chiltern Hills, which are comfortably furnished for up to six guests. The cottages are on a working farm with sheep, a pick-your-own and arable. Communal tennis court, trampoline and play area.

ONLINE MAP

Unit General P Leisure

KING'S SOMBORNE, Hampshire Map ref 2C3

★★★★
SELF CATERING

Units 4
Sleeps 1–2

LOW SEASON PER WK
Min £420.00

HIGH SEASON PER WK
Max £532.00

A discount is offered if more than 2 cottages are rented at any one booking.

Brook Farm Cottages, Stockbridge

contact Mrs Sarah de Sigley, Brook Farm House, Brook, Kings Somborne, Stockbridge SO20 6QR
t (01794) 389379

quidity.com

open All year
payment Credit/debit cards, cash, cheques, euros
nearest shop 2 miles
nearest pub 1 mile

These unique, self-contained cottages are situated in the grounds of a 16thC, Grade II Listed farmhouse. They have beamed ceilings, stone, oak and terracotta floors, and are tastefully furnished with some original works of art. The first floor has lounge, dining room and kitchen, and downstairs is a double bedroom and bathroom. One-night pricing available.

Unit TV DVD General P S Leisure

LEE-ON-THE-SOLENT, Hampshire Map ref 2C3

★★★
SELF CATERING

Units 1
Sleeps 5–6

LOW SEASON PER WK
£270.00–£350.00

HIGH SEASON PER WK
£350.00–£480.00

The Chart House, Lee-on-the-Solent

contact Mr Brook White, 6 Cambridge Road, Lee-on-the-Solent PO13 9DH **t** (023) 9255 4145
e brook.white1@btopenworld.com

lee-on-the-solentholiday.co.uk

Comfortable, detached, three-bedroomed family home, close to seafront. Enclosed patio/garden. Off-road parking. Private indoor heated pool available by arrangement.

open All year
payment Cash, cheques
nearest shop 0.5 miles
nearest pub less than 0.5 miles

Unit TV DVD General P Leisure

LEE-ON-THE-SOLENT, Hampshire Map ref 2C3

★★★
SELF CATERING

Units 1
Sleeps 1–4

LOW SEASON PER WK
£250.00–£320.00

HIGH SEASON PER WK
£350.00–£450.00

Kinderton House, Lee-on-the-Solent

contact Mrs Jean Miller, Kinderton House, 31 Marine Parade West, Lee-on-the-Solent PO13 9LW
t (023) 9255 2056

Ground-floor, seafront accommodation. Two bedrooms, kitchen, bathroom, wc, hall, good-sized lounge/diner. Fully carpeted and double-glazed. Off-road parking. Non-smokers, no pets. Wonderful views across the Solent.

open All year
payment Cash, cheques
nearest shop 0.5 miles
nearest pub 0.5 miles

Unit TV General P Leisure

LEWES, East Sussex Map ref 2D3

★★★★
SELF CATERING

Units 1
Sleeps 6

LOW SEASON PER WK
Min £500.00

HIGH SEASON PER WK
Min £575.00

The Finings, Lewes

contact Mrs Sara Gosling, The Cooperage, Castle Precincts, Lewes BN7 1YT **t** (01273) 480084
e fullofbeans@tempeh.globalnet.co.uk

Luxury self-catering, with two double/twin bedrooms, shower room, large living room with bed-settee for two. kitchen with all appliances. Central heating. Towels and linen provided. Broadband internet. No smoking.

open All year
payment Cash, cheques

Unit TV DVD General Leisure

Do you have access needs?

Look for the National Accessible Scheme symbols if you have special hearing, visual or mobility needs.

MAIDENHEAD, Berkshire Map ref 2C2

★★★★
SELF CATERING

Units 4
Sleeps 2–4

LOW SEASON PER WK
£360.00–£420.00

HIGH SEASON PER WK
£380.00–£520.00

Courtyard Cottages, Maidenhead

contact Mrs Carol Bardo, Moor Farm, Ascot Road, Holyport, Maidenhead SL6 2HY **t** (01628) 633761
e moorfm@aol.com

moorfarm.com

A 35-acre farm with easy access to London, Windsor and Ascot. Cottages converted from traditional farm buildings and furnished with antique pine. Bed and breakfast also available.

open All year
payment Cash, cheques, euros
nearest shop 0.5 miles
nearest pub less than 0.5 miles

Unit TV DVD General Leisure

MARGATE, Kent Map ref 3C3

★★★★
SELF CATERING

Units 3
Sleeps 4–6

LOW SEASON PER WK
£455.00–£595.00

HIGH SEASON PER WK
£455.00–£595.00

Midweek and nightly-stay visitors are also welcome (a nightly tariff applies). Please call for further information.

Salmestone Grange, Margate

Salmestone Grange, Nash Road, Margate CT9 4BX **t** (01843) 231161 **e** salmestonegrange@aol.com

salmestonegrange.co.uk

open All year
payment Credit/debit cards, cash, cheques
nearest shop less than 0.5 miles
nearest pub less than 0.5 miles

Unique 14thC monastic grange set in beautiful gardens. The lovingly restored apartments have many original features which capture a 'modern meets medieval' experience. Salmestone Grange is centrally located to the area's five main sandy beaches, with other tourist attractions, festivals, shopping centre and public transport also close by.

Unit TV DVD General P S Leisure

MILFORD ON SEA, Hampshire Map ref 2C3

★★★★
SELF CATERING

Units 1
Sleeps 6

LOW SEASON PER WK
£400.00–£500.00

HIGH SEASON PER WK
£500.00–£700.00

Out of season short breaks available weekends or midweek, tailored to suit your needs.

Milford Croft, Milford on Sea, Lymington

Beach Cottage, 3 Hurst Road, Milford on Sea, Lymington SO41 0PY **t** (01590) 644014
e milford.croft@yahoo.co.uk

milfordcroft.co.uk SPECIAL OFFERS • REAL-TIME BOOKING

open All year
payment Cash, cheques, euros
nearest shop 0.5 miles
nearest pub 0.5 miles

Luxurious new bungalow available all year round for up to six guests, short breaks available in low season. Located yards from beach and village centre, pubs and restaurants. Perfect for exploring New Forest. Well furnished with modern appliances, secure garden, barbecue, internet access, parking. Linen and towels provided.

SAT NAV *SO41 0PY* **ONLINE MAP**

Unit TV DVD General 7 P S Leisure

It's all quality-assessed accommodation

Our commitment to quality involves wide-ranging accommodation assessment. Ratings and awards were correct at the time of going to press but may change following a new assessment. Please check at time of booking.

MILFORD ON SEA, Hampshire Map ref 2C3

★★★
SELF CATERING

Units 1
Sleeps 5

LOW SEASON PER WK
£245.00–£320.00

HIGH SEASON PER WK
£350.00–£555.00

Windmill Cottage, Milford on Sea, Lymington

contact Mrs Perham, 14 Kivernell Road, Milford on Sea, Lymington SO41 0PQ **t** (01590) 643516

windmillcottage.info

open All year
payment Cash, cheques
nearest shop less than 0.5 miles
nearest pub less than 0.5 miles

Delightful Georgian-style house in quiet residential area close to village, sea and the New Forest. Three bedrooms – one double, one twin and one single. Recently refitted kitchen. Garage and easy parking. Five minutes' walk to village centre, good restaurants and pubs. Many places of interest nearby.

SAT NAV *SO41 0SX*

Unit General P Leisure

MOLLINGTON, Oxfordshire Map ref 2C1

★★★–★★★★★
SELF CATERING

Units 3
Sleeps 2–8

LOW SEASON PER WK
£180.00–£280.00

HIGH SEASON PER WK
£595.00–£895.00

Short breaks available on request.

The Stables, The Shippon, The Byre – Anita's Holiday Cottages, Mollington

contact Mr & Mrs Darrel & Anita Gail Jeffries, Anita's Holiday Cottages, The Yews, Church Farm, Banbury OX17 1AZ **t** (01295) 750731 **e** anitagail@btopenworld.com

cottageinthecountry.co.uk

open All year
payment Cash, cheques
nearest shop 1 mile
nearest pub less than 0.5 miles

Converted from an old cow byre, these cottages are finished to a superbly high standard. Situated in the lovely village of Mollington, within walking distance of the pub. Central to Oxford, Stratford-upon-Avon, Blenheim, Warwick and the Cotswolds. Lovely walks and cycling, even fishing close by.

Unit General P S Leisure

NEW FOREST

See under Burley, Fordingbridge, Hythe, Milford on Sea

NEWHAVEN, East Sussex Map ref 2D3

★★★
SELF CATERING

Units 3
Sleeps 2–6

LOW SEASON PER WK
£185.00–£350.00

HIGH SEASON PER WK
£310.00–£510.00

Short breaks available Oct-Mar 2 nights or more.

Barn Owls Self-Catering Apartments, Newhaven

contact Mrs Gill Canham, The Old Farmhouse, Foxhole Farm, Seaford Road BN9 0EE
t (01273) 515966 **e** gillcanham@yahoo.co.uk

barn-owls.co.uk

open All year
payment Cash, cheques
nearest shop 0.5 miles
nearest pub 1 mile

Beautiful old barn lovingly converted into three self-catering apartments each with its own individual charm, varying in size, sleeping from two to six people. Situated at the foot of the South Downs they are a wonderfully peaceful retreat. Ideal spot to discover the south coast and its surrounding countryside.

Unit General P S Leisure

NORTHIAM, East Sussex Map ref 3B4

★★★★
SELF CATERING

Units 1
Sleeps 2–5

LOW SEASON PER WK
£250.00–£325.00

HIGH SEASON PER WK
£325.00–£395.00

Hop Press Cottage, Rye

contact Ms Brenda Haines, Hop Press Cottage, Morley Farm, Beckley Road, Rye TN31 6JB
t (01797) 252011 **e** brenda@morleyfarm.co.uk

froglets.uk.com SPECIAL OFFERS • REAL-TIME BOOKING

An idyllic Grade II Listed cottage, perfect for a special break. Full gas central heating, inglenook fireplace, vaulted ceilings and pretty barbecue terrace and gardens.

open All year
payment Credit/debit cards, cash, cheques
nearest shop 1 mile
nearest pub 1 mile

Unit General P Leisure

NUTLEY, East Sussex Map ref 2D3

★★–★★★★
SELF CATERING

Units 13
Sleeps 1–5

LOW SEASON PER WK
£249.00–£595.00

HIGH SEASON PER WK
£336.00–£595.00

Whitehouse Farm Holiday Cottages, Nutley

contact Mr Keith Wilson, Whitehouse Farm Holiday Cottages, Whitehouse Farm, Uckfield TN22 3EE
t (01825) 712377 **e** keith.g.r.wilson@btinternet.com

streets-ahead.com/whitehousefarm

open All year
payment Credit/debit cards, cash, cheques
nearest shop 1.25 miles
nearest pub 1.25 miles

Former smallholding overlooking open countryside and Ashdown Forest. Shower room, kitchen/diner/lounge. Fully equipped. Wheelchair-, pet- and smoker-friendly cottages available. Spare campbeds. Ideally situated for London, castles, gardens and coast. Both Friday and Saturday turnaround.

Unit General P Leisure

OXFORD, Oxfordshire Map ref 2C1

★★★★★
SELF CATERING

Units 1
Sleeps 1–5

HIGH SEASON PER WK
£800.00–£920.00

Cherbridge Cottage, Oxford

contact Ms Laura Colman, Hill Farm, Mill Lane, Marston OX3 0QG **t** (01865) 292813 & 07976 288329 **e** laura@cherbridgecottages.co.uk

cherbridgecottages.co.uk GUEST REVIEWS

open All year
payment Credit/debit cards, cash, cheques
nearest shop 1.5 miles
nearest pub 1.5 miles

Cherbridge Cottage is part of a 1930s punting station, providing spacious holiday accommodation with en suite facilities. The secluded garden has extensive river frontage. Private punts are available, or guests are welcome to bring their own boat. Oxford city centre is easily accessible, being just two miles distant.

Unit General P
Leisure

Remember to check when booking

Please remember that all information in this guide has been supplied by the proprietors well in advance of publication. Since changes do sometimes occur it's a good idea to check details at the time of booking.

PANGBOURNE, Berkshire Map ref 2C2

★★★
SELF CATERING

Units **1**
Sleeps **5**

LOW SEASON PER WK
Min £425.00

HIGH SEASON PER WK
Max £495.00

Pay by credit card free of charge if you mention this advert. Also special monthly rates in winter.

Brambly Thatch, Nr Reading

contact Mr & Mrs Hatt, Merricroft Farming, Goring Heath, Reading RG8 7TA **t** (0118) 984 3121
e merricroft@yahoo.co.uk

open All year
payment Cash, cheques
nearest shop 2 miles
nearest pub 1 mile

Picturebook brick and flint thatched cottage on 300-acre beef and arable farm. Ideal base for visiting London, Oxford, Stonehenge and Stratford, and for sightseeing in the Thames Valley, Chilterns, Cotswolds and beyond. A warm and friendly home from home for a holiday to remember. Please telephone for quickest response.

Unit General P Leisure

PANGBOURNE, Berkshire Map ref 2C2

★★
SELF CATERING

Units **1**
Sleeps **2–3**

LOW SEASON PER WK
£185.00–£230.00

HIGH SEASON PER WK
£235.00–£250.00

Soldalen Annexe, Reading

contact Mr & Mrs John & Bente Kirk, Riverview Road, Pangbourne, Reading RG8 7AU
t (0118) 984 2924

Self-contained flat, five minutes to trains and buses for Reading, Oxford, London and village shops. Quiet location. Rural outlook.

open All year
payment Cash, cheques, euros
nearest shop 0.5 miles
nearest pub 0.5 miles

Unit General 8 P

PLAXTOL, Kent Map ref 2D2

★★★
SELF CATERING

Units **1**
Sleeps **1–6**

LOW SEASON PER WK
£250.00–£340.00

HIGH SEASON PER WK
£280.00–£430.00

Golding Hop Farm Cottage, Sevenoaks

contact Mrs Jacqueline Vincent, Golding Hop Farm, Bewley Lane, Plaxtol, Sevenoaks TN15 0PS
t (01732) 885432 **e** info@goldinghopfarm.com

goldinghopfarm.com

South-facing cottage on 12-acre cobnut farm. Quiet position but not isolated. Three bedrooms (two twin, one single), garden, all modern conveniences.

open All year
payment Cash, cheques
nearest shop 1.5 miles
nearest pub less than 0.5 miles

Unit General P Leisure

PORTSMOUTH, Hampshire Map ref 2C3

★★★★
SELF CATERING

Units **1**
Sleeps **5**

LOW SEASON PER WK
£290.00–£400.00

HIGH SEASON PER WK
£400.00–£690.00

3-day breaks considered. 2 weeks+ bookings receive a discount. Christmas tree at Christmas and Easter eggs for Easter.

Cowes View, Coastguard Cottages, Hill Head

contact Mrs Melanie Vennis, **t** (01329) 664236 **e** enquiries@cowesview.co.uk

cowesview.co.uk

open All year
payment Cash, cheques, euros
nearest shop 1.5 miles
nearest pub less than 0.5 miles

Cowes View is a delightful seaside cottage in a slightly elevated position overlooking the beach, with private access and enjoying fantastic panoramic views across the Solent to the Isle of Wight. Ideally located to visit historic Portsmouth, Southampton, New Forest and all of the heritage, countryside and culture of Hampshire.

SAT NAV *PO14 3JJ* **ONLINE MAP**

Unit General Leisure

PORTSMOUTH, Hampshire Map ref 2C3

★★★
SELF CATERING

Units 6
Sleeps 1–8

LOW SEASON PER WK
£200.00–£350.00

HIGH SEASON PER WK
£250.00–£600.00

Ocean Apartments, Southsea

contact Mrs Dawn Sait, 8-10 St Helens Parade, Southsea PO4 0RW **t** (023) 9273 4233
e ocean@portsmouth-apartments.co.uk

portsmouth-apartments.co.uk/ocean.htm

open All year
payment Credit/debit cards, cash, cheques, euros
nearest shop less than 0.5 miles
nearest pub 1 mile

Located directly on Southsea seafront with magnificent sea views. Recently refurbished. Spacious one- to four-bedroomed self-contained apartments, lift, private car parking, wireless internet. Short- and long-term bookings. More information on our website.

Unit General P Leisure

RADNAGE, Buckinghamshire Map ref 2C1

★★★
SELF CATERING

Units 1
Sleeps 2

LOW SEASON PER WK
£160.00–£175.00

HIGH SEASON PER WK
£175.00–£200.00

Golden Acres Farm, Radnage, High Wycombe

contact Mrs Julia Pitcher, Golden Acres Farm, 33 Green Lane, High Wycombe HP14 4DJ
t (01494) 483378

Self-contained, one-bedroom suite with kitchen and bathroom. Own entrance, adjacent to family farm-bungalow. Small but cosy, with lovely garden and views of open countryside. Single/twin.

open All year except Christmas
payment Cash, cheques
nearest shop 2 miles
nearest pub 0.5 miles

Unit General P

RAMSGATE, Kent Map ref 3C3

★★★★
SELF CATERING

Units 1
Sleeps 6

LOW SEASON PER WK
£350.00–£450.00

HIGH SEASON PER WK
£450.00–£650.00

Short breaks available from 2 nights upwards at discounted rates.

Harbour Cottage, Ramsgate

The Property Management Company, 8 Military Road, Ramsgate CT11 9LG **t** (01843) 596663
e enquiries@ramsgatecottage.co.uk

ramsgatecottage.co.uk SPECIAL OFFERS

open All year
payment Credit/debit cards, cash, cheques
nearest shop less than 0.5 miles
nearest pub less than 0.5 miles

Elegant, whitewashed period cottage, refurbished to the highest standards, set in Ramsgate's picturesque conservation area. Only two minutes' walk to the beach, harbour, shops and restaurants. One twin and two double bedrooms, two bathrooms, fully equipped kitchen/breakfast room, separate living and dining rooms. Two gardens and private off-street parking.

ONLINE MAP

Unit General 4 P
Leisure

ROBERTSBRIDGE, East Sussex Map ref 3B4

★★★–★★★★★
SELF CATERING

Units 4
Sleeps 2–10

LOW SEASON PER WK
£180.00–£1,000.00

HIGH SEASON PER WK
£240.00–£1,900.00

Helicopter charter (helicopter pad at property). 60ft luxury yacht charter from Eastbourne (12 guests). By arrangement.

Strawberry Hill Estate, Cripps Corner, Robertsbridge

contact Ms Margaret Parish, 1066 Leisure Breaks Ltd, The Chapel, Glengorse, Battle TN33 0TX
t (01424) 775555 **e** enquiries@1066leisure.com

1066leisure.com

open All year
payment Credit/debit cards, cash, cheques
nearest shop 1.5 miles
nearest pub 1 mile

Four properties situated on the lovely 200-acre Strawberry Hill Estate which includes a working farm, 60 acres of ancient woodland and two lakes. Farmhouse sleeps ten and cottages sleep two to three. Furnished and equipped to a high standard. Secluded rural location. Ideal base for exploring Sussex countryside and beaches.

SAT NAV *TN32 5SH*

Unit General P

ROCHESTER, Kent Map ref 3B3

★★★★
SELF CATERING

Units 6
Sleeps 5–8

LOW SEASON PER WK
£300.00–£500.00

HIGH SEASON PER WK
£550.00–£800.00

Short breaks and split weeks available.

Stable Cottages, Rochester

contact Mrs Debbie Symonds, Stable Cottages, Fenn Croft, Newland Farm Road, St Mary Hoo, Rochester ME3 8QS **t** (01634) 272439 & 07802 662702 **e** stablecottages@btinternet.com

stable-cottages.com

open All year
payment Cash, cheques
nearest shop 3 miles
nearest pub 1 mile

These luxury, oak-beamed cottages are set in 20 acres of secluded farmland close to RSPB reserve with panoramic views of the Thames. Access to motorways and ports. London/Canterbury 45 minutes. Perfect base for walking, bird-watching, sightseeing or just getting away from it all. Warm welcome. Family run. Indoor pool.

Unit General P Leisure

ROYAL TUNBRIDGE WELLS, Kent Map ref 2D2

★★★
SELF CATERING

Units 1
Sleeps 4

LOW SEASON PER WK
£260.00

HIGH SEASON PER WK
£260.00–£280.00

22 Hawkenbury Mead, Royal Tunbridge Wells

contact Mr R H Wright, Hawkenbury Farm, Hawkenbury Road, Royal Tunbridge Wells TN3 9AD
t (01892) 536977 **e** rhwright1@aol.com

A charming furnished cottage set on the outskirts of the historic spa town of Royal Tunbridge Wells.

open All year
payment Credit/debit cards, cash, cheques
nearest shop less than 0.5 miles
nearest pub less than 0.5 miles

Unit General P Leisure

WALKERS WELCOME

Do you like walking?

Walkers feel at home in accommodation participating in our Walkers Welcome scheme. Look out for the symbol. Consider walking all or part of a long-distance route – go online at nationaltrail.co.uk.

ROYAL TUNBRIDGE WELLS, Kent Map ref 2D2

★★★
SELF CATERING

Units **1**
Sleeps **8**

LOW SEASON PER WK
Min £400.00

HIGH SEASON PER WK
Max £600.00

Broad Oak House, Tunbridge Wells

contact Mrs Seymour, Broad Oak House, 9 Linden Park Road, Tunbridge Wells TN2 5QL
t (01892) 619065 **e** tina@tlctraining.co.uk

tunbridgewellsonline.com

Three-bedroom top floor flat in Victorian house. Quiet location within minutes of the Pantiles. Linen, gas and electricity included. Kitchen/living room, bathroom and three double bedrooms.

open All year
payment Cash, cheques, euros

Unit General Leisure

ROYAL TUNBRIDGE WELLS, Kent Map ref 2D2

★★★
SELF CATERING

Units **2**
Sleeps **2–4**

LOW SEASON PER WK
£270.00–£355.00

HIGH SEASON PER WK
£325.00–£385.00

Short breaks available – terms on request.

Ford Cottage, Royal Tunbridge Wells

contact Mrs Wendy Cusdin, Ford Cottage, Linden Park Road, Tunbridge Wells TN2 5QL
t (01892) 531419 **e** FordCottage@tinyworld.co.uk

fordcottage.co.uk GUEST REVIEWS

open All year
payment Credit/debit cards, cash, cheques, euros
nearest shop less than 0.5 miles
nearest pub less than 0.5 miles

Ford Cottage is a picturesque Victorian cottage three minutes' walk from the Pantiles. Self-contained studio flats with own front doors, fully fitted kitchens, en suites and showers. Off-street parking. Ideal for visiting many local gardens, castles and historic houses. Prices are for two to four people.

ONLINE MAP

Unit General Leisure

ROYAL TUNBRIDGE WELLS, Kent Map ref 2D2

★★★★
SELF CATERING

Units **6**
Sleeps **2–4**

LOW SEASON PER WK
£265.00–£300.00

HIGH SEASON PER WK
£410.00–£435.00

Itaris Properties Limited, Royal Tunbridge Wells

contact Mrs Angela May, Itaris Properties Ltd, 12 Mount Ephraim, Royal Tunbridge Wells TN4 8AS
t (01892) 511065 **e** enquiries@itaris.co.uk

itaris.co.uk

open All year
payment Cash, cheques

Royal Tunbridge Wells is surrounded by beautiful and unspoilt countryside and is the ideal location for a short break or relaxing holiday. Our self-contained and fully equipped holiday apartments are situated in the very heart of Tunbridge Wells within walking distance of its many amenities.

ONLINE MAP

Unit General

PETS! WELCOME PETS! WELCOME

Where is my pet welcome?

Want to take your cherished companion with you on holiday? Proprietors participating in our Welcome Pets! scheme go out of their way to make special provision for you and your pet. Look out for the symbol.

ROYAL TUNBRIDGE WELLS, Kent Map ref 2D2

★★★★
SELF CATERING

Units **1**

LOW SEASON PER WK
Min £270.00

HIGH SEASON PER WK
Min £420.00

Rose Cottage, Matfield, Nr. Tunbridge Wells

contact Mrs Nicky Hughes, Lodge Farm, Bramble Reed Lane, Matfield TN12 7ET **t** (01892) 722273 & 07966 524791 **e** nickyhughes7@hotmail.co.uk

lodgefarmcrosscountry.com

open All year
payment Cash, cheques
nearest shop 1 mile
nearest pub 1 mile

Tranquil and picturesque farm setting. Beautifully converted ragstone barn with private patio. Modern interior features a spiral staircase to a stunning mezzanine sleeping area. Short walk along footpath to pretty Matfield village with cricket green, pond, pubs and restaurant. Mainline train to London 3 miles.

SAT NAV *TN12 7ET*

Unit General P Leisure

RUCKINGE, Kent Map ref 3B4

★★★★
SELF CATERING

Units **1**
Sleeps **10**

LOW SEASON PER WK
Min £710.00

HIGH SEASON PER WK
Max £1,050.00

Horton Green Farmhouse, Ashford

Mulberry Cottages, Bridge Street, Wye, Ashford TN25 5ED **t** (01233) 813087
e info@mulberrycottages.com

mulberrycottages.com

Attractive, cosy, period farmhouse surrounded by fields. Refurbished to a high standard yet retaining all the charm of an historic building. Beams, inglenook fireplace, lovely gardens, large boat pond and croquet.

open All year
payment Credit/debit cards, cash, cheques, euros
nearest shop 3 miles
nearest pub 1 mile

Unit General P Leisure

RYDE, Isle of Wight Map ref 2C3

★★★★
SELF CATERING

Units **2**
Sleeps **3**

LOW SEASON PER WK
£200.00–£250.00

HIGH SEASON PER WK
£300.00–£350.00

Claverton House Self Catering, Ryde

contact Mr Metz, Claverton House Self Catering, Claverton House, 12 The Strand, Ryde PO33 1JE **t** (01983) 613015 **e** clavertonhouse@aol.com

clavertonhouse.co.uk REAL-TIME BOOKING

This beautiful holiday residence is situated in the idyllic seaside town of Ryde on the seafront. Five minutes' walk to town centre and passenger ferries, ten minutes' drive to car ferry.

open All year
payment Cash, cheques, euros
nearest shop less than 0.5 miles
nearest pub less than 0.5 miles

Unit General P

Check the maps for accommodation locations

Colour maps at the front pinpoint all the cities, towns and villages where you will find accommodation entries in the regional sections. Pick your location and then refer to the place index at the back to find the page number.

RYE, East Sussex Map ref 3B4

★★★
SELF CATERING

Units 1
Sleeps 3–4

LOW SEASON PER WK
£223.00–£302.00

HIGH SEASON PER WK
£302.00–£490.00

Chesterfield Cottage, Rye

t (01797) 222498 & 07956 280257 **e** chesterfieldcottage@virgin.net

country-holidays.co.uk GUEST REVIEWS

open All year
payment Cash, cheques
nearest shop less than 0.5 miles
nearest pub less than 0.5 miles

Charming 15thC Grade II Listed cottage by Landgate old town wall and centre of Rye. Exposed beams, open hearth, central heating, private courtyard garden. Fabulous country walks on doorstep and choice of beautiful beaches close by. Not suitable for very elderly or infirm. To locate property on website, use Property Ref 16230.

SAT NAV *TN31 7AT*

Unit General Leisure

RYE, East Sussex Map ref 3B4

★★★★
SELF CATERING

Units 2
Sleeps 2–6

LOW SEASON PER WK
£320.00–£425.00

HIGH SEASON PER WK
£425.00–£550.00

Froglets Cottage, Rye

contact Mrs Brenda Haines, Morley Farm, Beckley Road, Northiam, Rye TN31 6JB **t** (01797) 252011 **e** brenda@morleyfarm.co.uk

froglets.uk.com SPECIAL OFFERS · REAL-TIME BOOKING

A characterful Grade II Listed cottage in the heart of the conservation area and attracting many return visitors. Full gas central heating, large open log fire and personally cared for.

open All year
payment Credit/debit cards, cash, cheques

Unit General Leisure

ST HELENS, Isle of Wight Map ref 2C3

★★★★
SELF CATERING

Units 2
Sleeps 1–5

LOW SEASON PER WK
£290.00

HIGH SEASON PER WK
£640.00

The Castle, St Helens

contact Mr Jonathon Bacon, The Castle, Duver Road, St Helens PO33 1XY **t** (01983) 875993 **e** thecastle.sthelens@btinternet.com

thecastle.sthelens.btinternet.co.uk

The Castle offers two comfortable holiday lets sleeping up to five persons. Both have extensive facilities including grounds for guests' use and are within five minutes' walk of the beach.

open All year
payment Credit/debit cards, cash, cheques, euros
nearest shop less than 0.5 miles
nearest pub less than 0.5 miles

Unit General Leisure

SANDHURST, Kent Map ref 3B4

★★★★
SELF CATERING

Units 1
Sleeps 1–4

LOW SEASON PER WK
£295.00–£395.00

HIGH SEASON PER WK
£395.00–£495.00

Short breaks subject to availability.

Granary Cottage, Sandhurst, Cranbrook

contact Mary Le Pla, Court Lodge Farm, Bodiam, Robertsbridge TN32 5UJ **t** (01580) 830710 & 07733 340358 **e** office@sterlingquarterhorses.com

open All year
payment Credit/debit cards, cash, cheques, euros
nearest shop 1.2 miles
nearest pub 1.2 miles

Delightful two-bedroom single-storey cottage in idyllic farm location on a working arable and stud farm on the Kent/Sussex border. The property enjoys far-reaching views across the Rother Valley. Ideal base for walkers and families with children. Convenient for many National Trust properties and the coast.

SAT NAV *TN18 5NX*

Unit General

For **key to symbols** see page 7

SEAFORD, East Sussex Map ref 2D3

★★★★
SELF CATERING

Units 1
Sleeps 1–5

LOW SEASON PER WK
£400.00–£450.00

HIGH SEASON PER WK
£400.00–£450.00

2 Kingsway Court, Seaford

contact Mrs Pauline Gower, 6 Sunningdale Close, Southdown Road, Seaford BN25 4PF
t (01323) 895233 & 07889 310414 **e** sific@bgower.f9.co.uk

Fully equipped, spacious, semi-detached house. Gardens, balcony, parking. Five minutes from sea, open country, station and town centre. One single and two double bedrooms.

open All year except Christmas and New Year
payment Cash, cheques
nearest shop less than 0.5 miles
nearest pub less than 0.5 miles

Unit General P Leisure

SEAVIEW, Isle of Wight Map ref 2C3

★★★★
SELF CATERING

Units 1
Sleeps 2

LOW SEASON PER WK
£160.00–£220.00

HIGH SEASON PER WK
£245.00–£300.00

Studio Annexe, Seaview

contact Mr & Mrs Robin & Virginia Lobb, 38 Solent View Road, Seaview PO34 5HX
t (01983) 812180 **e** studioannexe@btinternet.com

Situated in a quiet residential area, just five minutes' walk from the beach, local shops, pubs and services.

open All year
payment Cash, cheques

Unit TV DVD General

SELSEY, West Sussex Map ref 2C3

★★★★
SELF CATERING

Units 1
Sleeps 4–8

LOW SEASON PER WK
£600.00–£850.00

HIGH SEASON PER WK
£900.00–£1,200.00

Short breaks during low season. £25 per person per night, minimum 2 nights' stay.

BeachFront House, Chichester

contact Angela Kelly, BeachFront House, 85 Bounces Road, London N9 8LD **t** 07976 957004
e angela@phoenixcommunity.co.uk

selseyretreat.co.uk SPECIAL OFFERS • REAL-TIME BOOKING

open All year
payment Credit/debit cards, cash, cheques
nearest shop 0.5 miles
nearest pub 0.5 miles

This spacious four-bedroomed house is ideal for family gatherings and special occasions. Accommodation comprising two double bedrooms and two twin bedrooms (two of the rooms are en suite). Family bathroom, study, kitchen/diner, dining room, living room, downstairs cloakroom, games room, hot tub and landscaped front and rear gardens.

SAT NAV *PO20 0UG* **ONLINE MAP**

Unit TV SC DVD General P S Leisure

SHANKLIN, Isle of Wight Map ref 2C3

★★★
SELF CATERING

Units 7
Sleeps 1–6

LOW SEASON PER WK
£220.00–£480.00

HIGH SEASON PER WK
£400.00–£810.00

WELCOME FAMILIES

Luccombe Villa, Shanklin

contact Mrs Fiona Seymour, Luccombe Villa, 9 Popham Road, Shanklin PO37 6RF **t** (01983) 862825
e info@luccombevilla.co.uk

luccombevilla.co.uk SPECIAL OFFERS

open All year
payment Cash, cheques
nearest shop less than 0.5 miles
nearest pub less than 0.5 miles

Seven self-contained holiday apartments in Shanklin Old Village. One to three bedrooms many with en suite facilities. Comfortably furnished with digital TV and DVD players. Well-equipped kitchens and separate laundry room. Plenty of parking.

SAT NAV *PO37 6RF*

Unit TV DVD General P Leisure

SHANKLIN, Isle of Wight Map ref 2C3

★★★★
SELF CATERING

Units 1
Sleeps 1–4

LOW SEASON PER WK
£200.00–£350.00

HIGH SEASON PER WK
£350.00–£550.00

Percy Cottage, Shanklin Old Village, Shanklin

contact Mr David Strugnell, Percy Cottage, Shanklin Old Village, Shanklin PO37 6NT
t (01983) 866 221 & 07752 407423 **e** dstrugnell@tiscali.co.uk

percy-cottage.co.uk

Percy Cottage is a fully equipped 18thC cottage sleeping four people and is set in the heart of Shanklin Old Village, which is close to the Chine, beach, pubs, restaurants and transport.

open All year except Christmas and New Year
payment Credit/debit cards
nearest shop less than 0.5 miles
nearest pub less than 0.5 miles

Unit General Leisure

SHELDWICH, Kent Map ref 3B3

★★★★
SELF CATERING

Units 1
Sleeps 2

LOW SEASON PER WK
£260.00–£325.00

HIGH SEASON PER WK
£350.00–£400.00

Littles Manor Farmhouse, Faversham

contact Tim Bourne, Littles Manor Farmhouse, North Street, Faversham ME13 0LP **t** (01233) 820425

open All year
payment Cash, cheques
nearest shop 2 miles
nearest pub 2 miles

Converted, fully equipped, award-winning Victorian barn in the grounds of Littles Manor Farmhouse, overlooking beautiful countryside and the sea. Easy reach of Canterbury, Calais, historic castles, golf, sea. Ideal base for walking, bird-watching and exploring the countryside. Excellent access to London and the Channel port by road and rail.

Unit General P Leisure

SOUTHAMPTON, Hampshire Map ref 2C3

★★★
SELF CATERING

Units 2
Sleeps 2

LOW SEASON PER WK
Max £168.00

HIGH SEASON PER WK
Max £205.00

Pinewood Lodge Apartments, Southampton

contact Dr Bradberry, Pinewood Lodge, Kanes Hill, Southampton SO19 6AJ **t** (023) 8040 2925
e stan.bradberry@tesco.net

self-catering-apartments-southampton.co.uk

open All year
payment Cash, cheques

Fully equipped, self-contained apartments. One double with verandah, one twin-bedded with patio. Each with separate kitchen, bathroom and lounge. Adjacent to 40 acres of heathland suitable for walking or jogging. Approximately five miles from city centre. Open throughout the year for holiday or business use. Wi-Fi access and online banking available.

SAT NAV *SO19 6AJ* **ONLINE MAP**

Unit General P

SOUTHSEA

See under Portsmouth

FAMILIES WELCOME WELCOME FAMILIES

Looking for an ideal family break?

For accommodation offering additional facilities and services for a range of ages and family units, look out for the Families Welcome symbol. Owners of these properties will go out of their way to welcome families.

STONE-IN-OXNEY, Kent Map ref 3B4

★★★★
SELF CATERING

Units 1
Sleeps 6

LOW SEASON PER WK
£295.00–£400.00

HIGH SEASON PER WK
£400.00–£700.00

Special activity weeks available. Please phone or visit website for further details.

WELCOME FAMILIES

Coldharbour Cottage, Tenterden

contact Mr Andrew Jempson, Coldharbour Cottage, Knock Hill, Stone-in-Oxney, Tenterden TN30 7JX **t** (01797) 230214 **e** stay@coldharbourcottage.co.uk

coldharbourcottage.co.uk

open All year
payment Credit/debit cards, cash, cheques
nearest shop 3 miles
nearest pub 1 mile

Old Victorian cottage recently renovated to high standard. Traditional farmhouse kitchen with Aga range cooker and baker's oven. Inglenook fireplace in dining room. Delightful Victorian parlour. Cottage situated on 62-acre farm with stunning views from garden room across valley towards the sea. Winner Tourism South East Self-Catering Holiday of The Year 2007.

Unit General P S Leisure

STORRINGTON, West Sussex Map ref 2D3

★★★–★★★★
SELF CATERING

Units 5
Sleeps 2–6

LOW SEASON PER WK
£220.00–£275.00

HIGH SEASON PER WK
£330.00–£510.00

Byre Cottages, Pulborough

contact Grahame & Gail Kittle, Byre Cottages, Sullington Manor Farm, Sullington Lane, Pulborough RH20 4AE **t** (01903) 745754 **e** kittles@waitrose.com

Cottages attractively converted from Victorian stables forming courtyard with 17thC tithe barn. Beautiful downland location on working farm. Swimming pool with springboard and slide. Tennis court. Table tennis. London 1.5 hours by train. Beaches half-hour by car.

open All year
payment Cash, cheques
nearest shop 1 mile
nearest pub 1 mile

Unit General P Leisure

SUNBURY, Surrey Map ref 2D2

★★★
SELF CATERING

Units 1
Sleeps 4

LOW SEASON PER WK
£490.00

HIGH SEASON PER WK
£560.00

85 Sundeala Close, Sunbury-on-Thames

Heathrow Apartments, 3 Barnard Close, Sunbury-on-Thames TW16 5BT **t** (01932) 786979 & 07939 543224 **e** info@heathrowapartments.biz

heathrowapartments.biz

Newly-built, comfortable, close to London Heathrow airport, Kempton Park, Hampton Court Palace, Kew Gardens, Kingston, Windsor Castle, Wimbledon, Thorpe Park, Legoland, and 30 minutes by train to central London.

open All year
payment Cash, cheques, euros
nearest shop 0.5 miles
nearest pub 0.5 miles

Unit General P S

TENTERDEN, Kent Map ref 3B4

★★★★
SELF CATERING

Units 2
Sleeps 4–5

LOW SEASON PER WK
Min £225.00

HIGH SEASON PER WK
Max £575.00

Meadow Cottage & Tamworth Cottage, Tenterden

contact Mrs Cooke, Great Prawls Farm, Stone, Tenterden TN30 7HB **t** (01797) 270539
e info@prawls.co.uk

prawls.co.uk SPECIAL OFFERS • REAL-TIME BOOKING

open All year
payment Cash, cheques
nearest shop 2 miles
nearest pub 1 mile

Lovely, detached, single-storey cottages on peaceful grass farm with views in Area of Outstanding Natural Beauty. Sandy beaches, medieval Rye and Tenterden 15 minutes. Castles, National Trust properties, bird reserves and steam trains nearby – France for a day trip! Short breaks. Brochure. See website for photos/prices/online booking form.

SAT NAV *TN30 7HB* **ONLINE MAP**

Unit General Leisure

THAME, Oxfordshire Map ref 2C1

★★★★
SELF CATERING

Units 1
Sleeps 6

LOW SEASON PER WK
£380.00–£430.00

HIGH SEASON PER WK
£480.00

The Hollies, Thame

contact Ms Julia Tanner, Little Acre, 4 High Street, Tetsworth, Thame OX9 7AT **t** (01844) 281423
e info@theholliesthame.co.uk

theholliesthame.co.uk

Beautifully appointed four-bedroomed dorma bungalow with peaceful gardens, situated in a secluded backwater near the oldest part of Thame, five minutes' walk from the centre of our historic market town.

open All year
payment Cash, cheques
nearest shop less than 0.5 miles
nearest pub less than 0.5 miles

Unit General P Leisure

TOTLAND BAY, Isle of Wight Map ref 2C3

★★★
SELF CATERING

Units 1
Sleeps 6

LOW SEASON PER WK
Min £200.00

HIGH SEASON PER WK
Max £550.00

Stonewind Farm, Totland Bay

contact Mrs Pat Hayles, Barn Cottage, Middleton, Freshwater PO40 9RW **t** (01983) 752912

Charming two-bedroom farmhouse in peaceful area with fine views. Secluded gardens with barbecue. Ten minutes' walk from villages of Totland Bay and Freshwater. The island has lots of interesting walks.

open All year
payment Cash, cheques
nearest shop 1 mile
nearest pub 1 mile

Unit General P

TUNBRIDGE WELLS

See under Royal Tunbridge Wells

VENTNOR, Isle of Wight Map ref 2C3

★★★★
SELF CATERING

Units 1
Sleeps 2–8

LOW SEASON PER WK
£500.00–£750.00

HIGH SEASON PER WK
£850.00–£1,050.00

Long weekends and short breaks (ideal for families and walkers) available off-peak.

Garden House, Ventnor

contact Mr Philip Barton, 67 Strode Road, London SW6 6BL **t** (020) 7385 7073 & 07887 848146
e philip@peoplesense.co.uk

holidaylets.net/prop_detail.asp?id=13874

open All year
payment Cash, cheques
nearest shop 0.5 miles
nearest pub 0.5 miles

Comfortable and spacious family house with pretty, secluded garden, children's playhouse, barbecue and outside eating area. Garden House provides a perfect holiday setting for families and walkers. A few minutes' walk from pretty beaches, the stunning South Wight Coastal Path, Bonchurch village and the quiet Victorian resort of Ventnor.

Unit TV DVD S General S

VENTNOR, Isle of Wight Map ref 2C3

★★★★
SELF CATERING

Units 1
Sleeps 1–4

LOW SEASON PER WK
£350.00–£400.00

HIGH SEASON PER WK
£400.00–£525.00

Ventnor Apartment, Ventnor

contact Mrs Jill Edwards, c/o Distinctive Designs, 74 High Street, Ventnor PO38 1LU
t (01983) 853555 & 07831 095407 **e** info@distinctivedesigns.co.uk

ventnorapartment.com GUEST REVIEWS

Ventnor Apartment is split-level accommodation furnished to a high standard by interior-designer owners. Centrally located in a Victorian seaside resort. Minutes from stunning coastline, Boniface Downs, beach, shops, pubs and restaurants.

open All year
payment Credit/debit cards, cash, cheques
nearest shop less than 0.5 miles
nearest pub less than 0.5 miles

Unit TV DVD General 4 P S

VENTNOR, Isle of Wight Map ref 2C3

★★★★
SELF CATERING

Units 11
Sleeps 2–6

LOW SEASON PER WK
£205.00–£255.00

HIGH SEASON PER WK
£545.00–£735.00

3-4 night short breaks available Oct-Mar. Open Christmas and New Year. Pets welcome.

Westfield Lodges & Apartments, Bonchurch

t (01983) 852268 **e** mail@westfieldlodges.co.uk

westfieldlodges.co.uk

open All year
payment Credit/debit cards, cash, cheques
nearest shop 1 mile
nearest pub 1 mile

Westfield Lodges are situated in the peaceful and historic village of Bonchurch on the south west coast of the Island. Located on a quiet, private site only five minutes from the beach.

Unit TV SC DVD General P S Leisure

Using map references

The map references refer to the colour maps at the front of this guide. The first figure is the map number, the letter and figure that follow indicate the grid reference on the map.

WHITWELL, Isle of Wight Map ref 2C3

★★★★
SELF CATERING

Units 1
Sleeps 2–6

LOW SEASON PER WK
£290.00–£400.00

HIGH SEASON PER WK
£500.00–£770.00

Maytime Cottage, Whitwell

contact Mr Jonathan McCulloch, Maytime Cottage, 5 King Edward Road, Christs Hospital, Horsham RH13 0ND **t** (01403) 211052 & 07711 807137 **e** jonty@bpmd.co.uk

maytimecottage.co.uk REAL-TIME BOOKING

open All year
payment Cash, cheques, euros
nearest shop 2 miles
nearest pub 1 mile

Spacious, well-equipped, period stone cottage in beautiful rural setting in South Wight. Large kitchen-diner, superb garden room, living room, three bedrooms, two bathrooms, enclosed rear garden and lovely views. Superb downland walks from the door. Many beaches and attractions nearby.

Unit General P Leisure

WINCHESTER, Hampshire Map ref 2C3

★★★★
SELF CATERING

Units 1
Sleeps 4

LOW SEASON PER WK
£350.00–£420.00

HIGH SEASON PER WK
£420.00–£525.00

Burwood, Winchester

contact Mrs Alice Lowery, Burwood, 128 Downs Road, South Wonston, Winchester SO21 3EH **t** (01962) 881690 **e** lowery2@btinternet.com

winchester-accommodation.com

A tastefully furnished bungalow in the village of South Wonston, north of the historic city of Winchester. Easy access to the south coast, New Forest, Oxford and London, M3, M27 and A34.

open All year
payment Cash, cheques, euros
nearest shop less than 0.5 miles
nearest pub 2 miles

Unit General 8 P S Leisure

WINCHESTER, Hampshire Map ref 2C3

★★★★
SELF CATERING

Units 1
Sleeps 3

LOW SEASON PER WK
£425.00

HIGH SEASON PER WK
£595.00

Cathedral View, Winchester

contact Mrs Sue Wustefeld, Heron Cottage, Water Lane, Bishops Sutton SO24 0AL **t** (01962) 732422 & 07708 331132 **e** help@justasksue.co.uk

cathedral-view.co.uk

In the heart of medieval Winchester, close to shops, this house provides exceptionally comfortable accommodation for two in light rooms, traditionally furnished. Roof terrace affords stunning views over cathedral. Internet access.

open All year except Christmas and New Year
payment Cash, cheques, euros
nearest shop less than 0.5 miles
nearest pub less than 0.5 miles

Unit General P S Leisure

WINCHESTER, Hampshire Map ref 2C3

★★★★
SELF CATERING

Units 1
Sleeps 1–6

LOW SEASON PER WK
Min £300.00

HIGH SEASON PER WK
Max £700.00

3-night stay: Fri-Mon. 4-night stay: Mon-Fri.

The Old Dairy, Winchester

t (01962) 868214 **e** joy_ann_waldron@hotmail.com

beechcroftfarmholiday.co.uk

open All year
payment Credit/debit cards, cash, cheques
nearest shop 1.5 miles
nearest pub 1.5 miles

Located on a working farm in a stunning setting with extensive views, this delightful former dairy offers one en suite double bedroom (5ft bed), one twin, and one room with bunk beds. Lounge/dining/kitchen and shower room. Winchester is ten minutes away. Nearby walks in Farley Mount Country Park and on the Clarendon Way.

SAT NAV *SO22 5QS* **ONLINE MAP**

Unit TV DVD S General P S

WINDSOR, Berkshire Map ref 2D2

★★★
SELF CATERING

Units 1
Sleeps 1–4

LOW SEASON PER WK
Min £495.00

HIGH SEASON PER WK
£500.00–£575.00

Flat 6 The Courtyard, Windsor

contact Mr Gavin Gordon, 5 Temple Mill Island, Marlow SL7 1SG **t** (01628) 824267
e gavingordon@totalise.co.uk

windsor-selfcatering.co.uk

open All year
payment Cash, cheques

An elegant, well-equipped, first-floor apartment (with lift) centrally situated in a quiet courtyard almost opposite Windsor Castle. One double and one twin bedroom. With direct access to Windsor High Street, the many restaurants, excellent shops, Theatre Royal and castle are only minutes away. London approximately 30 minutes. Exclusive parking.

Unit TV DVD General P

WINDSOR, Berkshire Map ref 2D2

★★★
SELF CATERING

Units 1
Sleeps 4

LOW SEASON PER WK
£450.00

HIGH SEASON PER WK
£550.00

Springfield Corner, Windsor

contact Mrs Anna Foxell, Springfield Corner, 78a Alma Road, Windsor SL4 3ET **t** (01753) 860900
e annafoxell@tiscali.co.uk

springfieldcorner.co.uk

Two-bedroom self-catering cottage. Well equipped and cosy. One double, one twin. All mod cons. Patio area, designated off-street parking. Town centre.

open All year
payment Cash, cheques, euros
nearest shop 0.5 miles
nearest pub 0.5 miles

Unit TV SC DVD General P

What if I need to cancel?

It is advisable to check the proprietor's cancellation policy in case you have to change your plans at a later date.

WOOTTON BRIDGE, Isle of Wight Map ref 2C3

★★★★
SELF CATERING

Units **11**
Sleeps **4–6**

LOW SEASON PER WK
£265.00–£630.00

HIGH SEASON PER WK
£525.00–£735.00

Creek Gardens, Ryde

contact Mrs L Samson, Creek Gardens, New Road, Wootton Bridge PO33 4JX **t** (01983) 883100
e enquiries@creekgardens.co.uk

creekgardens.co.uk

One-, two- and three-bedroom units in tranquil setting overlooking picturesque Wootton Creek on the Isle of Wight. Weekly servicing of units. Three-bedroom units include washing machine and fridge/freezer.

open All year
payment Credit/debit cards, cash, cheques
nearest shop 0.5 miles
nearest pub 0.5 miles

Unit General Leisure

London

Clockwise: Buckingham Palace; Shakespeare's Globe; Tower Bridge

Great days out

So you think you know London? Take another look because there's always another secret to discover or something new to try, as well as inspirational itineraries to follow for weekends and days out. Just remember to leave yourself with enough time for everything (a year or more should do).

Culture vulture

Does Turner turn you on? The Impressionists impress? Then London is your place. With some 70 large museums and over 30 major art galleries, it's a top culture capital. The **Museum of London** is a good start for insights into local life. Experience the Great Fire of London 1666 through the eyes of survivors – what really happened? New galleries opening 2010 include the city's 21stC story.

The National Gallery

At the **National Gallery** see famous works of art by Van Gogh, Monet and da Vinci amongst an outstanding collection of Western European paintings. Nearby, **Somerset House** is bursting with Old Master and Impressionist paintings, decorative arts and treasures from the Hermitage Museum, St Petersburg. Its Admiralty Restaurant serves delicious lunches, too. And **Tate Britain**, just along the Thames, explores over 500 years of British art.

Take a boat trip to **Greenwich** for an adventure through Britain's seafaring history at the **National Maritime Museum**. And do leave time for lesser-known gems like the **Ben Uri Gallery**, **The London Jewish Museum of Art**. Or the **Royal London Hospital Archives and Museum** telling the fascinating story of the hospital and featuring people like the unfortunate 'Elephant Man'.

Greenfingered London

Fabulous **Chelsea Flower Show** in May is a horticultural highspot of everyone's year. But at any time there are plenty of green (and every other floral colour) delights to dig into. **Kew Gardens** are the ultimate destination: over 300 acres growing more than 30,000 types of plants.

For an unusual surprise, take the train from Victoria Station to **Eltham Palace**, where 19-acre gardens combine medieval and 20thC elements. The trip to Charles Darwin's **Down House**, Orpington, also gets creative juices flowing: follow the path he paced in the beautiful gardens as he contemplated his revolutionary theories. And if you want a fragrant souvenir to take home, browse **Columbia Road Flower Market** on Sunday mornings, an absolute blaze of colour.

why not... climb the Monument (311 steps) in the City for superb views?

Left to right: South Bank; Westminster

did you know... dozens of museums and galleries are free to visit, including Tate Britain?

Ladies who lunch

London does shopping, eating and pampering so well! And, ladies, you deserve a girls' outing. Check what's chic in **Knightsbridge** and the top designer stores on the **Kings Road**. Or perfect the quirky and vintage look shopping around **Notting Hill** and **Portobello Road**. Then enjoy a leisurely lunch with **Bateaux London Restaurant Cruisers**, watching the sights drift by, or tea at **The Ritz** or **Browns**. Dinner at **The Ivy** or **Le Caprice** sounds tempting, too.

Sports galore

There's plenty of sport, too. London's great venues like **Wimbledon** – the **Lawn Tennis Museum** gives great insights into the world-famous championship. There's no need to wait for match days to enjoy a trip to **Chelsea Football Club**, the **Emirates Stadium** or **Lord's**. Behind-the-scenes tours bring to life soccer and cricket dreams. Take the kids, they love sport in the capital as well.

Luvvies London

Nearly 150 theatres raise the curtain on drama, opera, dance and more. Kick off in style with a **West End** show – ask about good deals at the tkts booth in **Leicester Square**, London's official reduced theatre ticket operation. Sip pre-performance drinks at the luvvie-friendly **French House**, **Toucan** or **Dog & Duck** pub, and digest the night's entertainment at **Joe Allen**, where you might spot a thesp or two. Next day, join a back-stage tour – the **Theatre Royal**, Drury Lane is just one venue that opens its doors. And stroll along the **South Bank**, the heart of cultural cool, to see what's on at the **Southbank Centre**. Round off with a tour of the magnificent **Shakespeare's Globe**.

Tea at Harrods

Big kids

For some family-friendly fun hop aboard the **London Eye**, rising slowly to view 55 famous landmarks across the city. Keep spirits high with a visit to the **Tower of London**, possibly the country's most haunted building – was that the scream of a ghostly nobleman being led to the executioner's block? **Hampton Court Palace** also has a host of spooks, including Henry VIII's fifth wife Catherine Howard. Who ever said history was dull?

Don't get lost in the palace's famous maze. Explore all nine decks of **HMS Belfast**, from the Captain's Bridge to the boiler and engine rooms, well below the ship's waterline. See the sick bay and operations room and imagine life on board during World War II. Who would guess you could be in a vast landscape of lagoons, lakes and ponds within 25 minutes of central London? The **London Wetland Centre** in Barnes is Europe's best urban site for watching wildlife, including hundreds of bird species. Come nose to nose with sharks and deadly stone fish at the **London Aquarium**. If you've energy to spare, let off steam in one of London's many parks. Picnic and play footie in **St James's Park** or go boating on the Serpentine in **Hyde Park**.

why not... explore Regent's Canal from Little Venice to the Docklands?

The main event

London living can be pretty high octane, no more so than for event-goers. From **Chinese New Year** Celebrations to **The Proms** to lights-on for Christmas, the calendar is packed. Gather beside the Thames for spring's **Oxford and Cambridge Boat Race**, everyone likes tradition. And a summer's evening at **Kenwood House**, Hampstead, passes perfectly at a picnic concert. Hit the streets around Ladbroke Grove for the steelbands and exuberant costumes that make **Notting Hill Carnival** swing. Admire the Golden State Coach at the **Lord Mayor's Show**, processing to the Royal Courts of Justice. And there are always those impromptu smile-breakers, like street performers around **Covent Garden**. Samuel Pepys watched a Punch and Judy show here in 1662 and open-air entertainment has flourished ever since.

Left to right: Covent Garden; Hampton Court Palace

Destinations

Covent Garden

Designer shops such as Paul Smith and Nicole Farhi, mid range shops like Karen Millen, Monsoon and Oasis and the downright quirky such as Lush, the cosmetic maker, all have a presence here. Sample the impressive array of organic cheeses at Neal's Yard or grab a table at Carluccio's Delicatessen. Settle down for some entertainment in the Piazza: music, comedy, pavement artists and jugglers. If it's culture your after, step into the magnificently refurbished Royal Opera House for a performance or a backstage tour.

Covent Garden

Greenwich

Stand with one foot in the East and one foot in the West astride the Greenwich Meridian, and set your watch by the red 'Time Ball' that drops each day at 1300hrs precisely and has done so for 170 years. There's a laid-back feel to Greenwich. Take time to browse the market stalls – crafts, antiques, records, bric-a-brac and, most famously, vintage clothing. Then pop into a riverside pub for lunch and some mellow jazz.

Kew

Stroll the finest botanic gardens in the country – 400 acres and 40,000 plant varieties. The Palm House hosts a tropical jungle of plants including bananas, pawpaws and mangoes. Marvel at the giant Amazonian water lily, aloe vera and several carnivorous plants in the Princess of Wales Conservatory where ten climatic zones are recreated. You'll find activities for children and a full calendar of special events.

Notting Hill

A colourful district filled with clubs, bars and dance venues, and now trendier than ever. Wander the celebrated Portobello Road market where over 1,500 traders compete for your custom at the Saturday antiques market. Find jewellery, silverware, paintings and more. Summertime is carnival time and the Caribbean influence has ensured the phenomenal growth of the world-famous, multi-cultural Notting Hill Carnival. Join the throng of millions – exotic costume recommended. On a quieter day, visit beautiful Holland Park, a haven of greenery with its own theatre.

Richmond

The River Thames runs through the heart of the beautiful borough of Richmond. Arrive by summer riverboat from Westminster Pier and explore the delightful village with its riverside pubs, specialist boutiques, galleries and museums. Glimpse herds of deer in the Royal parks and step into history in Henry VIII's magnificent Hampton Court Palace, the oldest Tudor palace in England. Round off your visit with a world-class rugby match at Twickenham Stadium.

Clockwise: Kenwood House; Hyde Park; Chinese New Year

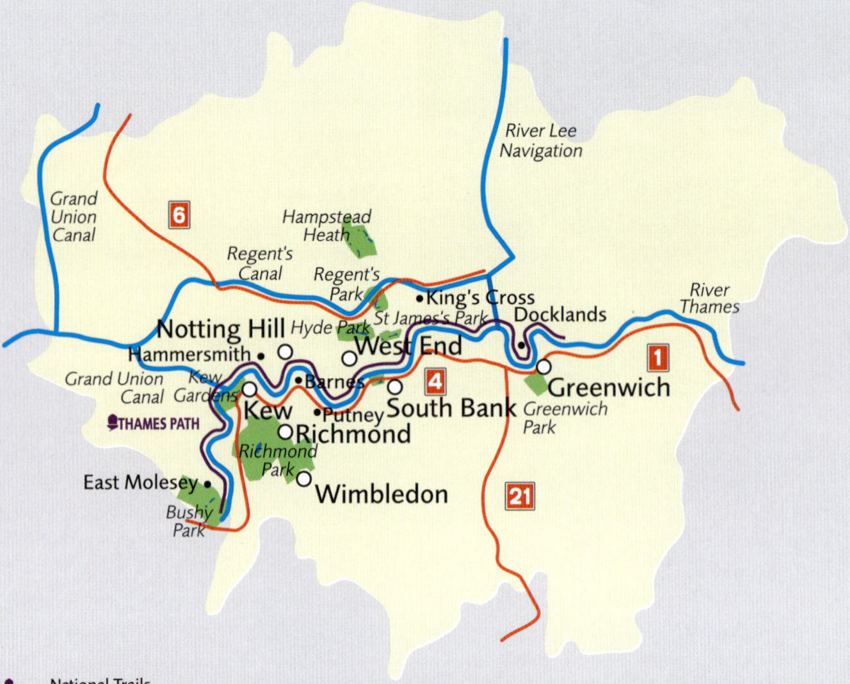

National Trails
nationaltrail.co.uk

3 Sections of the National Cycle Network
nationalcyclenetwork.org.uk

Kew Gardens

South Bank

One of London's coolest quarters, the South Bank positively teems with must-see attractions and cultural highlights. Tate Modern has gained a reputation as one of the greatest modern art galleries in the world boasting works by Moore, Picasso, Dali, Warhol and Hepworth. Take in a play at the National Theatre or Shakespeare's magnificently restored Globe, and hit the heights on British Airways London Eye, the world's highest observation wheel.

The West End

Shop in the best department stores and international designer boutiques in Oxford Street, Regent Street and Bond Street. Take lunch in a stylish eatery, and then see a major exhibition at the Royal Academy of Arts. At the heart of the West End are the landmarks of Trafalgar Square and Piccadilly Circus, and just a few minutes' stroll will take you into legendary Soho, the entertainment heart of the city, crammed with bars, pubs, clubs and restaurants.

Wimbledon

Wimbledon village is only ten miles from the centre of London but you could be in the heart of the countryside. Enjoy the open spaces of Wimbledon Common then wander along the charming high street with its unique medieval buildings, boutiques and pavement cafés. Visit the legendary All England Club where the Lawn Tennis Museum is a must-see for fans of the sport, not to mention the chance to tour the legendary Centre Court.

For lots more great ideas visit enjoyEngland.com/destinations

Clockwise: Greenwich; Notting Hill; Richmond Park

Visitor attractions

Family and Fun

Chelsea Football Club Stadium Tours
Fulham, SW6
0871 984 1955
chelseafc.com
Get behind the scenes at Stamford Bridge.

Emirates Stadium Tour and Museum
Highbury, N5
(020) 7704 4504
arsenal.com
Get to know Arsenal's stunning stadium.

HMS Belfast
Southwark, SE1
(020) 7940 6300
iwm.org.uk
A fascinating piece of British naval history.

London Aquarium
South Bank, SE1
(020) 7967 8000
londonaquarium.co.uk
Come face-to-face with two-metre long sharks.

The London Dungeon
Southwark, SE1
(020) 7403 7221
thedungeons.com
So much fun it's frightening!

London Eye
South Bank, SE1
0870 5000 600
ba-londoneye.com
The world's largest observation wheel.

London Eye River Cruise Experience
Westminster, SE1
0870 500 0600
londoneye.com
Circular cruise with fascinating live commentary.

London Wetland Centre
Barnes, SW16
(020) 8409 4400
wwt.org.uk
Europe's best urban site for watching wildlife.

Madame Tussauds and the London Planetarium
Marylebone, NW1
0870 999 0046
madame-tussauds.com/london
Meet the stars then enter the Chamber of Horrors.

National Maritime Museum
Greenwich, SE10
(020) 8858 4422
nmm.ac.uk
Over two million exhibits of seafaring history.

Royal Mews
St James Park, SW1
(020) 7766 7302
royalcollection.org.uk
One of the world's finest working stables.

Heritage

Apsley House
Piccadilly, W1
(020) 7499 5676
english-heritage.org.uk
Wellington's military memorabilia and dazzling art collection.

Buckingham Palace
SW1
(020) 7766 7300
royal.gov.uk
HM The Queen's official London residence.

Chiswick House
W4
(020) 8995 0508
english-heritage.org.uk
Glorious example of 18thC British architecture.

Eltham Palace
SE9
(020) 8294 2548
english-heritage.org.uk
Spectacular Art Deco villa and medieval hall.

Hampton Court Palace
East Molesey, KT8
0844 482 7777
hrp.org.uk
Outstanding Tudor palace with famous maze.

Kensington Palace State Apartments
W8
0844 482 7777
hrp.org.uk
Home to the Royal Ceremonial Dress Collection.

Kenwood House
Hampstead, NW3
(020) 8348 1286
english-heritage.org.uk
Beautiful 18thC villa with fine interiors.

Tower Bridge Exhibition
SE1
(020) 7403 3761
towerbridge.org.uk
Learn all about the world's most famous bridge.

Tower of London
EC3
0870 756 6060
hrp.org.uk
Crown Jewels and 900 years of history.

Indoors

Bateaux London Restaurant Cruisers
Embankment, WC2
(020) 7695 1800
bateauxlondon.com
Luxury dining and world-class live entertainment.

BBC Television Centre Tours
Shepherd's Bush, W12
0870 603 0304
bbc.co.uk/tours
Behind the scenes of world-famous television studios.

Ben Uri Art Gallery, London Jewish Museum of Art
St John's Wood, NW8
(020) 7604 3991
benuri.org.uk
Europe's only dedicated Jewish museum of art.

BFI London IMAX Cinema
Waterloo, SE1
0870 787 2525
bfi.org.uk
The ultimate big-screen experience.

British Museum
WC1
(020) 7323 8299
britishmuseum.org
One of the great museums of the world

Churchill Museum and Cabinet War Rooms
Westminster, SW1
(020) 7930 6961
iwm.org.uk
Churchill's wartime headquarters untouched since 1945.

Down House – Home of Charles Darwin
Orpington, BR6
(01689) 859119
english-heritage.org.uk
The great naturalist's home and workplace.

Hayward Gallery
South Bank, SE1
0870 380 0400
hayward.org.uk
Famous international gallery showing major exhibitions.

Imperial War Museum
Lambeth, SE1
(020) 7416 5320
iwm.org.uk
History of Britain at war since 1914.

Events 2009

New Year's Day Parade
London
londonparade.co.uk
1 Jan

Ideal Home Show
London
idealhomeshow.co.uk
20 Mar - 13 Apr

Oxford and Cambridge Boat Race
London
theboatrace.org
29 Mar

Flora London Marathon
London
london-marathon.co.uk
26 Apr

Chelsea Flower Show
London
rhs.org.uk
19 - 23 May

Wimbledon Lawn Tennis Championships
London
wimbledon.org/en_GB/index.html
Jun - Jul

The Proms
London
bbc.co.uk/proms
Jul - Sep

Notting Hill Carnival
London
rbkc.gov.uk
30 - 31 Aug

The Mayor's Thames Festival
London
thamesfestival.org
Sep

State Opening of Parliament
London
parliament.uk
Oct - Nov

Lord Mayor's Show
London
lordmayorsshow.org
Nov

Lord's Tour (MCC)
St John's Wood, NW8
(020) 7616 8595
lords.org
Guided tour of the home of cricket.

Museum of London
EC2
0870 444 3852
museumoflondon.org.uk
The world's largest urban-history museum.

National Army Museum
Chelsea, SW3
(020) 7730 0717
national-army-museum.ac.uk
The story of the British soldier.

National Portrait Gallery
WC2
(020) 7306 0055
npg.org.uk
The world's largest collection of portraits.

Natural History Museum
Kensington, SW7
(020) 7942 5000
nhm.ac.uk
World-class collections bringing the natural world to life.

Royal Air Force Museum Hendon
NW9
(020) 8205 2266
rafmuseum.org
Historic aircraft from around the world.

Royal London Hospital Archives and Museum
Whitechapel, E1
(020) 7377 7608
medicalmuseums.org
Fascinating history of Britain's largest voluntary hospital.

Royal Observatory Greenwich
SE10
(020) 8858 4422
nmm.ac.uk
Explore the history of time and astronomy.

Science Museum
Kensington, SW7
0870 870 4868
sciencemuseum.org.uk
State-of-the-art simulators, IMAX cinema and more.

Somerset House
Strand, WC2
(020) 7845 4600
somerset-house.org.uk
Arts and learning in magnificent 18thC house.

Southbank Centre
SE1
0871 663 2501
southbankcentre.co.uk
Year-round programme encompassing all the arts.

Southwark Cathedral
SE1
(020) 7367 6700
southwark.anglican.org/cathedral
London's oldest Gothic church building.

Tate Britain
Millbank, SW1
(020) 7887 8888
tate.org.uk/britain
The greatest single collection of British art.

Tate Modern
Bankside, SE1
(020) 7887 8888
tate.org.uk/modern
Britain's flagship museum of modern art.

Victoria and Albert Museum
Large Visitor Attraction of Year - Gold
Kensington, SW7
(020) 7942 2000
vam.ac.uk
World-reknowned museum, 3,000 years of art and design.

Wimbledon Lawn Tennis Museum
SW19
(020) 8946 6131
wimbledon.org/museum
Superb memorabilia and history of the game.

Outdoors

Kew Gardens (Royal Botanic Gardens)
Richmond, TW9
(020) 8332 5655
kew.org
Stunning plant collections and magnificent glasshouses.

ZSL London Zoo
Regent's Park, NW1
(020) 7722 3333
zsl.org
The hairiest and scariest animals on the planet.

ASSURANCE OF A GREAT DAY OUT
Attractions with this sign participate in the Visitor Attraction Quality Assurance Scheme which recognises high standards in all aspects of the visitor experience.

Regional contacts and information

For more information on accommodation, attractions, activities, events and holidays in London, contact Visit London. When you arrive at your destination, visit an Official Partner Tourist Information Centre for quality assured help, or email your request before you go. To search for attractions and Tourist Information Centres on the move just text INFO to 62233, and a web link will be sent to your mobile phone.

London

Go to **visitlondon.com** for all you need to know about London. Look for inspirational itineraries with great ideas for weekends and short breaks.

Or call 0870 1 LONDON (0870 1 566 366) for:

- **A London visitor information pack**
- **Visitor information on London**
  Speak to an expert for information and advice on museums, galleries, attractions, riverboat trips, sightseeing tours, theatre, shopping, eating out and much more! Or simply go to visitlondon.com.
- **Accommodation reservations**

Chelsea Flower Show

Tourist Information Centres

Britain & London Visitor Centre	1 Regent Street	0870 156636	blvcenquiries@visitlondon.com
Croydon	Katharine Street	(020) 8253 1009	tic@croydon.gov.uk
Greenwich	2 Cutty Sark Gardens	0870 608 2000	tic@greenwich.gov.uk
Lewisham	199-201 Lewisham High Street	(020) 8297 8317	tic@lewisham.gov.uk
Swanley	London Road	(01322) 614660	touristinfo@swanley.org.uk

where to stay in

London

For maps of inner and outer London, see the front of this guide.

A complete listing of all Enjoy England assessed accommodation covered by this guide appears at the back.

Accommodation symbols

Symbols give useful information about services and facilities. On page 7 you can find a key to these symbols.

INNER LONDON

LONDON E1

★★★
SELF CATERING

Units 4
Sleeps 4–6

LOW SEASON PER WK
£580.00–£775.00

HIGH SEASON PER WK
£645.00–£835.00

Discounted last-minute and long-term lets.

Hamlet UK, St Katharine Docks, Tower Hill, London

contact Ms Renata Naufal, Hamlet UK, 47 Willian Way, Letchworth SG6 2HJ **t** (01462) 678037
e hamlet_uk@globalnet.co.uk

hamletuk.com GUEST REVIEWS

open All year
payment Credit/debit cards, cash, cheques, euros
nearest shop less than 0.5 miles
nearest pub less than 0.5 miles

Friendly and personal service. Very attractive surroundings. Comfortable and clean accommodation close to public transport, supermarket, the Tower of London, Tower Bridge, the ExCeL exhibition centre and the O_2 Arena. Fully fitted kitchen, bathroom, linen and towels provided, TV, direct-dial phone, wireless broadband connection, washer/dryer, off-street parking. See guests' feedback on our website.

SAT NAV *E1W 1ND*

Unit TV ... General P S

LONDON E4

★★★
SELF CATERING

Units 2
Sleeps 4–5

LOW SEASON PER WK
£350.00–£420.00

HIGH SEASON PER WK
£350.00–£420.00

Willowside, Sewardstone

contact Mrs Roddick, Picks Farm, Sewardstone E4 7RA **t** (020) 8529 1371
e r.roddick@btconnect.com

willowsidelakes.co.uk

open All year
payment Cash, cheques
nearest shop 2.5 miles
nearest pub 1 mile

Two cottages, both one twin and one double room, kitchen, sitting room, bathroom or shower room. Sleep four and five persons. Non-smoking, all-electric, fully equipped. Large off-road car park.

WALKERS WELCOME · CYCLISTS WELCOME

Unit TV DVD ... General P S Leisure

LONDON E16

★★★★★
SELF CATERING

Units 20
Sleeps 1–6

LOW SEASON PER WK
£700.00–£1,050.00

The Grainstore, London

contact Nicky Bloom, The Grainstore, 4 Western Gateway, Royal Victoria Docks, London
t (020) 7540 9351 **e** enquiries@simplyapartments.co.uk

simplyapartments.co.uk

open All year
payment Credit/debit cards, cash, cheques
nearest shop less than 0.5 miles
nearest pub less than 0.5 miles

A selection of spacious, newly built apartments located directly in front of ExCel London. All are fully furnished and have been designed and constructed to offer a high degree of quality and specification.

Unit General

LONDON SE6

★★★–★★★★★
SELF CATERING

Units 9
Sleeps 2–10

LOW SEASON PER WK
£395.00–£800.00

HIGH SEASON PER WK
£460.00–£1,100.00

Glenthurston Self Catering Apartments, London

contact Ms Sue Halliday, 27 Canadian Avenue, London SE6 3AU **t** (020) 8690 3092
e mail@londonselfcatering.co.uk

londonselfcatering.co.uk REAL-TIME BOOKING

Two large Victorian houses converted into nine flats with use of an indoor pool and sauna. Well located for central London. Homely relaxing atmosphere. Large garden and games room. Off-street parking.

open All year
payment Credit/debit cards, cash, cheques
nearest shop less than 0.5 miles
nearest pub less than 0.5 miles

Unit General P Leisure

LONDON SE10

★★★
SELF CATERING

Units 1
Sleeps 1–7

LOW SEASON PER WK
£750.00–£1,200.00

HIGH SEASON PER WK
£850.00–£1,200.00

12 Burgos Grove, West Greenwich, London

contact Ms Dawn Harverson, 1 Egerton Drive, West Greenwich, London SE10 8JS **t** 07894 661402
e info@greenwichholidaylets.co.uk

greenwichholidaylets.co.uk GUEST REVIEWS · SPECIAL OFFERS · REAL-TIME BOOKING

open All year
payment Cash, cheques
nearest shop less than 0.5 miles
nearest pub less than 0.5 miles

Quality, serviced, family self-catering accommodation in West Greenwich, in the heart of Maritime Greenwich, World Heritage Site. 12 Burgos Grove has been decorated and furnished by artist and stylist Dawn Harverson to a high standard using The White Company linen and Designer Guild fabrics and accessories.

SAT NAV *SE10 8LL* **ONLINE MAP**

WALKERS WELCOME · CYCLISTS WELCOME · FAMILIES WELCOME · PETS! WELCOME

Unit General P
Leisure

Place index

If you know where you want to stay, the index by place name at the back of the guide will give you the page number listing accommodation in your chosen town, city or village. Check out the other useful indexes too.

LONDON SE10

★★★★
SELF CATERING

Units 1
Sleeps 1–4

LOW SEASON PER WK
£630.00–£700.00

HIGH SEASON PER WK
£630.00–£700.00

Harbour Master's House, London

contact Prof Chris French, 20 Ballast Quay, London SE10 9PD **t** (020) 8293 9597
e harbourmaster@lineone.net

http://website.lineone.net/~harbourmaster

Superb self-contained flat, part of the historic Harbour Master's House (Grade II Listed). Situated on attractive riverside enclave on the Thames in maritime Greenwich.

open All year
payment Cash, cheques
nearest shop 0.5 miles
nearest pub less than 0.5 miles

Unit TV SC DVD General P S

LONDON SW1

★★★★–★★★★★
SELF CATERING

Units 19
Sleeps 2–6

LOW SEASON PER WK
£781.00–£1,875.00

HIGH SEASON PER WK
£781.00–£1,875.00

The Apartments, London

t (020) 7589 3271 **e** sales@theapartments.co.uk

theapartments.co.uk

open All year
payment Credit/debit cards, cash, cheques
nearest shop less than 0.5 miles
nearest pub less than 0.5 miles

A selection of elegant, serviced studios and one- to two-bedroom apartments housed in prestigious Victorian buildings. Individually designed with a full range of modern amenities including broadband internet access, for the discerning, independent traveller. The apartments offer you a unique, luxurious environment combining privacy, independence and the relaxed atmosphere of home.

ONLINE MAP

Unit TV DVD General S

LONDON SW18

★★★★
SELF CATERING

Units 2
Sleeps 1–8

LOW SEASON PER WK
£570.00–£850.00

HIGH SEASON PER WK
£620.00–£890.00

Beaumont Apartments, London

contact Mr & Mrs Alan & Monica Afriat, Beaumont Apartments, 24 Combemartin Road, London SW18 5PR **t** (020) 8789 2663 **e** alan@beaumont-london-apartments.co.uk

beaumont-london-apartments.co.uk GUEST REVIEWS

Well-appointed flats in leafiest suburb within 25 minutes of West End. Close to Zone 3 Underground, Wimbledon tennis and convenient for A3, M4, M41, M25, Heathrow and Gatwick. Wi-Fi Internet.

open All year
payment Credit/debit cards, cash, cheques, euros
nearest shop less than 0.5 miles
nearest pub less than 0.5 miles

Unit TV SC DVD General P Leisure

LONDON SW20

★★★★
SELF CATERING

Units 2
Sleeps 5–6

HIGH SEASON PER WK
£682.50–£798.00

FAMILIES WELCOME

Thalia & Hebe Holiday Homes, Wimbledon, London

contact Mr & Mrs Peter & Ann Briscoe-Smith, 150 Westway, Wimbledon, London SW20 9LS
t (020) 8542 0505 **e** peter@briscoe-smith.org.uk

briscoe-smith.org.uk

Thalia and Hebe are both three-bedroomed houses in the residential suburban area of West Wimbledon. Home from home, with easy access to central London. Wi-Fi/LAN broadband.

open All year
payment Cash, cheques
nearest shop 0.5 miles
nearest pub 0.5 miles

Unit TV DVD General P S

What do the star ratings mean?

Detailed information about star ratings can be found at the back of this guide.

LONDON W1

★★–★★★
SELF CATERING

Units 10
Sleeps 2–6

LOW SEASON PER WK
£390.00–£710.00

HIGH SEASON PER WK
£400.00–£720.00

Tustin Holiday Flats, London

contact Reservation Office, 94 York Street, London W1H 1QX **t** (020) 7723 9611
e pctustinuk@btconnect.com

pctustin.com

Fully furnished, self-contained flats in central London, offering easy access to Oxford Street, places of interest and public transport.

open All year
payment Credit/debit cards, cash, cheques

Unit General

LONDON W14

★★★★
SELF CATERING

Units 1
Sleeps 2–4

LOW SEASON PER WK
£630.00

HIGH SEASON PER WK
£630.00

For bookings of more than 14 days we offer a 10% discount.

Castletown House, London

contact Mr Richard Poppleton, Castletown House, 11 Castletown Road, London W14 9HE
t (020) 7386 9423 **e** info@castletownhouse.co.uk

castletownhouse.co.uk GUEST REVIEWS · SPECIAL OFFERS · REAL-TIME BOOKING

open All year
payment Credit/debit cards, cash
nearest shop less than 0.5 miles
nearest pub less than 0.5 miles

Private apartment set in Victorian building, recently refurbished. Bedroom with balcony, lounge, kitchen, bathroom. One double bed and sofa bed in lounge. Located in West Kensington, convenient for London's main attractions. Earls Court and Olympia exhibition centres are nearby. West Kensington Underground is just a two-minute walk.

SAT NAV *W14 9HE* **ONLINE MAP**

Unit General P Leisure

OUTER LONDON

BECKENHAM

★★–★★★
SELF CATERING

Units 10
Sleeps 2–6

LOW SEASON PER WK
£250.00–£625.00

HIGH SEASON PER WK
£250.00–£625.00

Oakfield Apartments, Beckenham

t (020) 8658 4441 **e** enquiry@oakfield.co.uk

oakfield.co.uk SPECIAL OFFERS

open All year
payment Credit/debit cards, cash, cheques, euros
nearest shop less than 0.5 miles
nearest pub less than 0.5 miles

Victorian mansion with a large garden in a semi-rural setting, three minutes' walk to Eden Park rail station, 25 minutes by rail or nine miles by road to central London. Mr and Mrs Deane live on the premises and welcome children but not pets.

ONLINE MAP

Unit General P Leisure

Do you have access needs?

Look for the National Accessible Scheme symbols if you have special hearing, visual or mobility needs. An index of accommodation participating in the scheme can be found at the back of this guide.

South West England

Bristol, Cornwall, Devon, Dorset, Gloucestershire, Isles of Scilly, Somerset, Wiltshire

Clockwise: Porlock Bay, Somerset; Forest of Dean, Gloucestershire; Stonehenge, Wiltshire

Great days out

Go rock pooling in sandy coves. Indulge your love of cream teas and clotted cream fudge. Ramble along the South West Coast Path. Brave the waves surfing in Newquay. Wonder at the Cerne Abbas Giant and the stunning landscaped gardens at Stourhead. What will you do in South West England?

Refreshing rambles

The South West is truly a walker's paradise, from the gentle **Cotswold Hills** to the wilder beauty of **Exmoor** and **Dartmoor** National Parks. Spend a day or two rambling parts of the 101-mile **Cotswold Way** through quintessential English countryside and golden-stone villages. **The Two Moors Way** over Dartmoor and Exmoor takes you through moorland, wooded valleys, farmland and coastal towns. Gee up the pace pony trekking or mountain biking – the National Parks have plenty of space for both. Then feel the sea-salted breezes along the **South West Coast Path**. It stretches for 630 miles from Somerset to Dorset, opening up dramatic views of a shoreline organically sculpted by waves. Children just love stomping 185 million years of earth history underfoot along the **Jurassic Coast**, a World Heritage Site. They could even find a dinosaur print. Who's got the biggest feet?

Sea, surf and fun

How's this for the perfect antidote to hectic modern life? Genuine bucket-and-spade fun with the family, pure and simple. With more Blue Flag beaches than anywhere else in England, the region's sandy bays and sheltered coves are perfect getaways. Some stretches make thrilling waves for watersports: hit the hip centres of **Newquay**, **Bude**, **Croyde** and **Woolacombe**, great places to learn to surf or kitesurf. Try sailing and windsurfing in **Poole**. Devon's English Riviera – the bustling seaside towns of **Torquay**, **Paignton** and **Brixham** – is ideal for families and you can meet friendly coastal creatures like penguins and fur seals at **Living Coasts** in Torquay. Away from the beach quaint fishing villages, such as **Clovelly**, **Port Isaac** and **Beer**, are a picturesque maze of narrow streets and steep roads. And how's this for an unforgettable experience? Catch a play or musical at the open-air cliffside **Minack Theatre** at Porthcurno. The backdrop of sea vistas is breathtaking.

Torquay, Devon

Glorious gardens

The South West's balmy subtropical climate means exotic flora flourish, creating extraordinary gardens. Delight in the **Lost Gardens of Heligan** at Pentewan, neglected for years and now brought back to life complete with magical Jungle Garden. Take a helicopter ride to **Tresco**, one of the Scilly Isles, to browse some 20,000 luxuriant plants in the **Abbey Garden**. Explore the remarkable **Eden Project**, near St Austell, which features thousands of world plants in enormous glass biomes – and children become enthralled on the interactive trails. Then enjoy the pyrotechnic seasonal displays of trees and flowers at **Westonbirt Arboretum**,

Left to right: Eden Project, Cornwall; Salisbury Cathedral, Wiltshire

why not... cycle along Devon's 180-mile Tarka Trail, named after Henry Williamson's Tarka the Otter?

Gloucestershire; the clipped yews and cascades at **Forde Abbey and Gardens**, Dorset; and the eye-catching tableaux of lakeside temples at **Stourhead**, Wiltshire.

Yum yum!

Indulge yourself in the region's delicious specialities. Cornish pasties taste good washed down with a pint of sweet cider. Look out for Mendip Oggies, too: pasties made with pork, apple and cheese pastry. Devour mouthwatering scones straight from the oven and topped with rich clotted cream. And sample a different cheese every day: world-famous Cheddar, Double Gloucester, Somerset Brie, Dorset Blue Vinny and nettle-wrapped Cornish Yarg. Relish the best catches at **Rick Stein's Seafood Restaurant**, Padstow. Then finish your gourmet odyssey relaxing over a wine from **Three Choirs Vineyard**, Gloucestershire.

Mysterious and madcap

You're in just the right area for quirky customs and intriguing places. If you look hard enough you may spot the Witch of Wookey deep in **Wookey Hole Caves** where pagan and Christian legends intermingle. Ponder the mysteries of the ancient stone circles of **Stonehenge** and **Avebury** – just how were such enormous stones transported and arranged, and why? **Chipping Campden** in Gloucestershire is the location of the Cotswolds' unique version of the Olimpick Games: contests include shin-kicking, ouch! Meanwhile **Blackawton** in Devon hosts the annual International Worm Charming Festival. Seeing is believing!

Exmoor, Somerset

Splendid city highlights

Fill your days visiting attractions in Bristol and Bath, city neighbours yet so different. **Bristol's** maritime heritage has been channelled into the infectious vitality of the rejuvenated Harbourside of bars, eateries and sights. Clamber aboard Isambard Kingdom Brunel's **ss Great Britain**, the world's first great ocean liner. Treat the kids to an interactive science adventure at **Explore-at-Bristol** – freeze your shadow, fire a neuron, and get starry-eyed in the planetarium. Then revel in the Georgian elegance of **Bath** and tour the best-preserved Roman religious spa from the ancient world, beneath the watchful gaze of **Bath Abbey**. Dip your own toes – and more – into the natural thermal waters of the recently opened **Thermae Bath Spa**. Bliss!

why not... look for the Fossil Forest revealed at low tide near Little Bindon, Dorset?

Continue your journey with a trip to some of the West's other great cathedral cities. Stroll **Exeter's** historic Quayside; survey the medieval carvings of **Wells Cathedral's** majestic west front; wander the revitalised waterside of **Gloucester**; or take a guided tour of **Salisbury Cathedral**, its soaring spire the tallest in Britain.

More great days out

If you're looking for even more inspiration for great days out, add these to your love-to list. Have a fun time uncovering the history, sights and sounds of the railway at **Steam – Museum of the Great Western Railway** in Swindon, or take the kids on a wild animal safari at **Longleat**. Take a picnic to **Corfe Castle** whose evocative hilltop ruins recall a bold past. Or potter about on a driving tour – the scenic **Royal Forest Route** through the Forest of Dean and the **Romantic Road** via **Cheltenham** and **Cirencester** spring to mind. Floating skywards in a hot-air balloon over the countryside and llama-trekking also make memorable adventures!

Clockwise: Dartmoor, Devon; St Michael's Mount, Cornwall; ss Great Britain, Bristol

Destinations

Bath

Set in rolling countryside, less than two hours from London, this exquisite Georgian spa city was founded by the Romans and is now a World Heritage Site. Explore the compact city centre on foot and discover a series of architectural gems including the Roman baths and Pump Room, the 15thC Abbey, and stunning Royal Crescent. Follow in the footsteps of Romans and Celts and bathe in the naturally warm waters of the Thermae Bath Spa.

Bath

Bournemouth

Bournemouth is the perfect holiday and short-break destination, renowned for its seven miles of family-friendly, golden beaches, beautiful parks and gardens and cosmopolitan ambience. Enjoy the buzz of the town then head out and savour the beauty of the New Forest, the splendour of Dorset's spectacular World Heritage Jurassic Coastline, and the rolling countryside immortalised by Thomas Hardy.

Bristol

In bygone times, explorers and merchants set off on epic journeys from its harbour. Nowadays, Bristol's spirit of boldness and creativity expresses itself in art, architecture and an enviable quality of life. Take in Georgian terraces, waterfront arts centres, green spaces, great shopping and top-class restaurants. The city's heritage glitters with the work of historic figures such as Isambard Kingdom Brunel, and all set against a truly classic view – the River Avon and its dramatic gorge reaching almost into the heart of the city.

The Cotswolds

Escape to the rolling hills of the Cotswolds scattered with picturesque towns and villages built of distinctive honey-coloured limestone. Criss-cross the little bridges over the River Windrush in Bourton-on-the-Water; hunt for antiques in Stow-on-the-Wold; wander through the open-air street market of Moreton-in-Marsh and appreciate the beautifully preserved buildings in Chipping Campden and Tetbury.

Isles of Scilly

Just 20 minutes from Cornwall you'll find over 100 islands waiting to be explored– five of them inhabited: St Mary's, Tresco, St Martin's, St Agnes and Bryher. Discover fascinating prehistoric remains, rare species of birds and plant life, historic shipwrecks and some of the best beaches in Britain. Watersports, boat trips, wonderful gardens, including Tresco Abbey Gardens, keep everyone entertained.

Left to right: Corfe Castle, Dorset
Wells Cathedral, Somerset

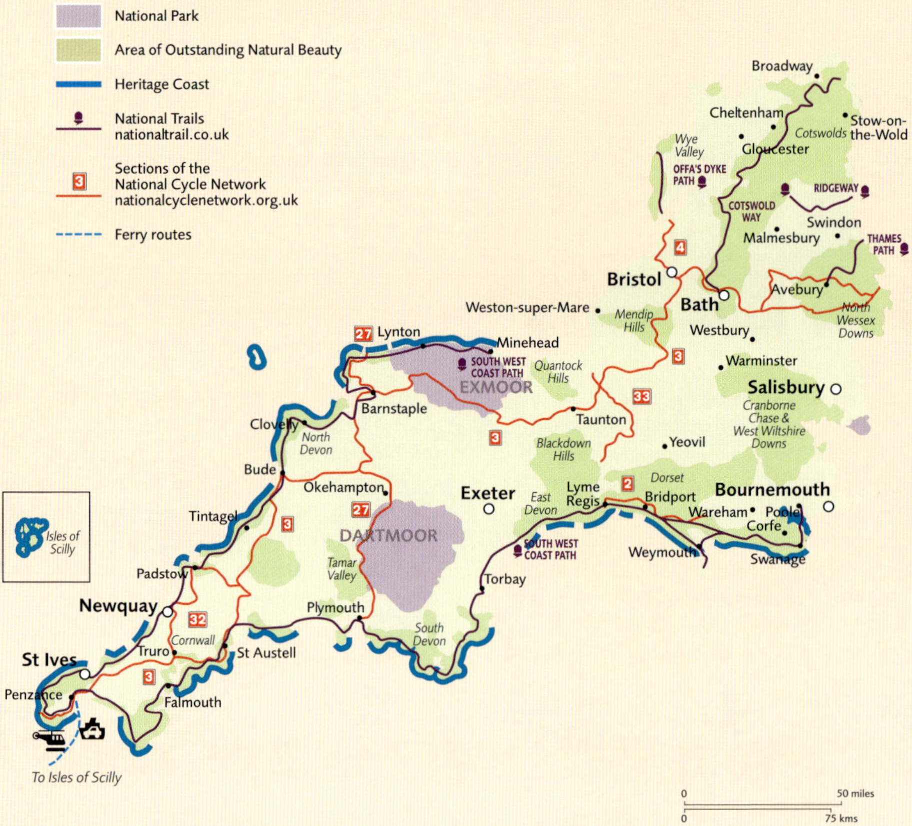

Bristol

Exeter

Devon's regional capital for culture, leisure and shopping is a vibrant city, steeped in ancient history. Don't miss the superb Decorated Gothic cathedral. Stroll along the historic Quayside, once the setting for a thriving wool trade and now a bustling riverside resort. Choose from over 700 shops, join a free Red Coat-guided city tour and dine in any one of numerous acclaimed restaurants. It's also the perfect base from which to explore the sweeping National Parks of Dartmoor and Exmoor.

Newquay

A beach paradise, stretching for seven miles, makes this one of Cornwall's premier resorts. Soaring cliffs alternate with sheltered coves, and thundering surf with secluded rock pools, smugglers' caves and soft golden sands. Whatever the weather, make a splash at Waterworld, or visit Newquay Zoo, one of the best wildlife parks in the country. Newquay offers an unforgettable holiday experience.

Clockwise: Exeter; Bournemouth; The Cotswolds

Poole

Poole is fast becoming known as the St Tropez of the south coast with its award-winning beaches, beautiful harbour, exhilarating watersports and famous pottery. Follow the Cockle Trail around the old town to discover its seafaring and trading history. Take the ferry to Brownsea Island between March and October for wonderful walks and wildlife spotting. Or relax and enjoy alfresco dining overlooking the harbour.

St Ives

What was once a small, thriving fishing village is now an internationally renowned haven for artists, attracted by the unique light. Explore the narrow streets and passageways and come upon countless galleries, studios and craft shops. Don't miss Tate St Ives and the Barbara Hepworth Museum. Enjoy the natural beauty of the harbour and explore Blue Flag beaches and coastal walks. Perfectly placed for all of West Cornwall's stunning scenery and famous attractions.

Tate, St Ives

Salisbury

Nestling in the heart of southern England, Salisbury is every bit the classic English city. The majestic cathedral boasts the tallest spire in England and rises elegantly above sweeping lawns. Wander through this medieval city and you'll find first-class visitor attractions, theatre and shopping. And, of course, no trip to Salisbury would be complete without the eight-mile pilgrimage to one of the greatest prehistoric sites in the world – Stonehenge.

For lots more great ideas visit enjoyEngland.com/destinations

Visitor attractions

Family and Fun

Babbacombe Model Village
Torquay, Devon
(01803) 315315
babbacombemodelvillage.co.uk
England in miniature in four-acre gardens.

The Big Sheep
Bideford, Devon
(01237) 472366
thebigsheep.co.uk
Family fun at the sheep races.

Blue Reef Aquarium
Newquay, Cornwall
(01637) 878134
bluereefaquarium.co.uk
Close encounters with tropical sharks and rays.

Bristol Zoo Gardens
Bristol
(0117) 974 7399
bristolzoo.org.uk
Over 400 exotic and endangered species.

Cheddar Caves & Gorge
Cheddar, Somerset
(01934) 742343
cheddarcaves.com
Britain's finest caves and deepest gorge.

Combe Martin Wildlife and Dinosaur Park
Combe Martin, Devon
(01271) 882486
dinosaur-park.com
A subtropical bird, animal and dinosaur paradise.

Dairyland Farm World
Summercourt, Cornwall
(01872) 510246
dairylandfarmworld.com
Country-life park, museum and adventure playground.

Devon's Crealy Great Adventure Park
near Exeter, Devon
(01395) 233200
crealy.co.uk
All-weather attractions and friendly animals.

Farmer Palmer's Farm Park
Poole, Dorset
(01202) 622022
farmerpalmers.co.uk
Farm activities for families with young children.

Kents Cavern Prehistoric Caves
Torquay, Devon
(01803) 215136
kents-cavern.co.uk
Britain's most important Stone Age caves.

Living Coasts
Torquay, Devon
(01803) 202470
livingcoasts.org.uk
Fascinating coastal creatures in a stunning location.

Longleat
Warminster, Wiltshire
(01985) 844400
longleat.co.uk
Lions, tigers and a stately home.

The Monkey Sanctuary Trust
Looe, Cornwall
(01503) 262532
monkeysanctuary.org
Colony of woolly monkeys.

National Marine Aquarium
Plymouth, Devon
(01752) 600301
national-aquarium.co.uk
Sharks and seahorses at Britain's biggest aquarium.

Newquay Zoo
Newquay, Cornwall
(01637) 873342
newquayzoo.org.uk
Exotic animals in subtropical lakeside gardens.

Noah's Ark Zoo Farm
Wraxall, Somerset
(01275) 852606
noahsarkzoofarm.co.uk
Hands-on animal experiences for all ages.

Paignton Zoo Environmental Park
Paignton, Devon
(01803) 697500
paigntonzoo.org.uk
Gorillas and crocodiles in 75-acre botanical gardens.

Pennywell - Devon's Farm and Wildlife Centre
Lower Dean, Devon
(01364) 642023
pennywellfarm.co.uk
The South West's biggest farm-activity park.

Woodlands Leisure Park
Blackawton, Devon
(01803) 712598
woodlandspark.com
Unique combination of indoor and outdoor attractions.

Wookey Hole Caves and Papermill
near Wells, Somerset
(01749) 672243
wookey.co.uk
Spectacular caves and working Victorian papermill.

Heritage

The Bishop's Palace & Gardens
Wells, Somerset
(01749) 678691
bishopspalacewells.co.uk
Splendid medieval palace and tranquil landscaped gardens.

Bowood House and Gardens
Chippenham, Wiltshire
(01249) 812102
bowood.org
Wonderful 18thC Robert Adam house.

Corfe Castle
Corfe Castle, Dorset
(01929) 477063
nationaltrust.org.uk
Majestic ruins of a former royal castle.

Cothay Manor & Gardens
near Wellington, Somerset
(01823) 672283
cothaymanor.co.uk
Unspoilt medieval manor and romantic gardens.

Dunster Castle
Dunster, Somerset
(01643) 821314
nationaltrust.org.uk
Romantic castle and subtropical gardens.

The Fashion Museum and Assembly Rooms
Bath, Somerset
(01225) 477789
fashionmuseum.co.uk
Fine Georgian building with world-class dress collection.

Forde Abbey and Gardens
Small Visitor Attraction of the Year – Silver
Forde Abbey, Dorset
(01460) 220231
fordeabbey.co.uk
Elegant former Cistercian monastery with gardens.

Lacock Abbey
Lacock, Wiltshire
(01249) 730459
nationaltrust.org.uk
Fine country house with medieval cloisters.

Lanhydrock
Lanhydrock, Cornwall
(01208) 265950
nationaltrust.org.uk
Re-built 17thC house with magnificent illustrated ceiling.

Lulworth Castle & Park
Wareham, Dorset
0845 450 1054
lulworth.com
Idyllic castle set in extensive park.

Montacute House
Montacute, Somerset
(01935) 823289
nationaltrust.org.uk
Renaissance manor house filled with historic treasures.

Old Wardour Castle
Tisbury, Wiltshire
(01747) 870487
english-heritage.org.uk
Unusual hexagonal ruins of a 14thC castle.

Pittville Pump Room
Cheltenham, Gloucestershire
(01242) 523852
Beautiful, imposing example of Regency architecture.

Powderham Castle
Powderham, Devon
(01626) 890243
powderham.co.uk
Restored medieval castle in beautiful deer park.

Roman Baths
Bath, Somerset
(01225) 477785
romanbaths.co.uk
Magnificent Roman temple and hot-spring baths.

St Michael's Mount
Marazion, Cornwall
(01736) 710507
stmichaelsmount.co.uk
Rocky island filled with astonishing history.

Salisbury Cathedral
Salisbury, Wiltshire
(01722) 555120
salisburycathedral.org.uk
Britain's finest 13thC gothic cathedral.

Sherborne Castle
Sherborne, Dorset
(01935) 813182
sherbornecastle.com
Tudor mansion built by Sir Walter Raleigh.

Sudeley Castle, Gardens and Exhibition
Winchcombe, Gloucestershire
(01242) 602308
sudeleycastle.co.uk
Romantic castle and restored gardens.

Tintagel Castle
Tintagel, Cornwall
(01840) 770328
english-heritage.org.uk
Evocative ruined castle on wind-swept coast.

Wells Cathedral
Wells, Somerset
(01749) 674483
wellscathedral.org.uk
Superb 12thC cathedral in Early English style.

Wilton House
Wilton, Wiltshire
(01722) 746714
wiltonhouse.com
Stunning 17thC state rooms and landscaped parkland.

Indoors

British Empire & Commonwealth Museum
Bristol
(0117) 925 4980
empiremuseum.co.uk
Explore a dramatic history and heritage.

Brunel's ss Great Britain
Bristol
(0117) 926 0680
ssgreatbritain.org
Experience life aboard Brunel's famous steam ship.

Cheltenham Art Gallery and Museum
Cheltenham, Gloucestershire
(01242) 237431
cheltenham.artgallery.museum
World-renowned Arts and Crafts Movement collection.

The China Clay Museum
Carthew, Cornwall
(01726) 850362
wheal-martyn.com
Restored clayworks in World Heritage mining landscape.

The Dinosaur Museum
Dorchester, Dorset
(01305) 269880
thedinosaurmuseum.com
Life-sized reconstructions and hands-on displays.

Dorset County Museum
Dorchester, Dorset
(01305) 262735
dorsetcountymuseum.org
The archeology and geology of Dorset.

The Dorset Teddy Bear Museum
Dorchester, Dorset
(01305) 266040
teddybearmuseum.co.uk
Featuring a family of people-sized bears.

The Edward Jenner Museum
Berkeley, Gloucestershire
(01453) 810631
jennermuseum.com
Life-story of the smallpox vaccine pioneer.

Explore-At-Bristol
Bristol
0845 345 1235
at-bristol.org.uk
An exciting hands-on science adventure.

Fleet Air Arm Museum
Yeovilton, Somerset
(01935) 840565
fleetairarm.com
See Europe's largest collection of naval aircraft.

Geevor Tin Mine
Pendeen, Cornwall
(01736) 788662
geevor.com
The largest preserved mining site in Britain.

The Museum of East Asian Art
Bath, Somerset
(01225) 464640
meaa.org.uk
Jades, bronzes and ceramics from the East.

National Maritime Museum Cornwall
Falmouth, Cornwall
(01326) 313388
nmmc.co.uk
Enthralling exhibits for landlubbers and sailors alike.

STEAM - Museum of the Great Western Railway
Swindon, Wiltshire
(01793) 466646
swindon.gov.uk/steam
Interactive story of pioneering rail company.

Tate St Ives
St Ives, Cornwall
(01736) 796226
tate.org.uk/stives
International art in striking beach-front gallery.

The Tutankhamun Exhibition
Dorchester, Dorset
(01305) 269571
tutankhamun-exhibition.co.uk
Internationally-acclaimed exhibition with perfect reconstructions.

Outdoors

Abbey House Gardens
Malmesbury, Wiltshire
(01666) 822212
abbeyhousegardens.co.uk
Wonderful displays featuring over 10,000 plants.

Eden Project
St Austell, Cornwall
(01726) 811911
edenproject.com
A global garden for the 21st century.

Hidcote Manor Garden
near Chipping Campden, Gloucestershire
(01386) 438333
nationaltrust.org.uk
Widely celebrated Arts and Crafts garden.

Land's End
Sennen, Cornwall
0871 720 0055
landsend-landmark.co.uk
Spectacular cliffs, breathtaking vistas and multi-sensory show.

The Lost Gardens of Heligan
near St Austell, Cornwall
(01726) 845100
heligan.com
Glorious 200-acre restored garden and pleasure grounds.

The Minack Theatre and Visitor Centre
Porthcurno, Cornwall
(01736) 810181
minack.com
Open-air cliff-side theatre with breathtaking views.

Painswick Rococo Garden
Painswick, Gloucestershire
(01452) 813204
rococogarden.org.uk
A flamboyant piece of English garden design.

Pecorama
Beer, Devon
(01297) 21542
peco-uk.com
Passenger-carrying miniature railway in spectacular gardens.

RHS Garden Rosemoor
Torrington, Devon
(01805) 624067
rhs.org.uk/rosemoor
Enchanting 65-acre year-round garden.

Stonehenge and Avebury World Heritage Site
near Salisbury, Wiltshire
0870 333 1181
english-heritage.org.uk
World-famous prehistoric monument.

Stourhead House and Garden
Stourton, Wiltshire
(01747) 841152
nationaltrust.org.uk
Palladian mansion with world-renowned landscape gardens.

Thermae Bath Spa
Bath, Somerset
0844 888 0848
thermaebathspa.com
Enjoy Britain's only natural thermal waters.

Trelissick Garden
near Truro, Cornwall
(01872) 862090
nationaltrust.org.uk
Tender and exotic plants in tranquil garden.

Tresco Abbey Gardens
Isles of Scilly
(01720) 424108
tresco.co.uk
Tropical garden with species from 80 countries.

Westonbirt, The National Arboretum
Westonbirt, Gloucestershire
(01666) 880220
forestry.gov.uk/westonbirt
One of the world's finest tree collections.

Wildfowl & Wetlands Trust Slimbridge
Slimbridge, Gloucestershire
(01453) 891900
wwt.org.uk
Home to an astounding array of wildlife.

Willows & Wetlands Visitor Centre
Taunton, Somerset
(01823) 490249
englishwillowbaskets.co.uk
The art of willow growing and basketmaking.

ASSURANCE OF A GREAT DAY OUT
Attractions with this sign participate in the Visitor Attraction Quality Assurance Scheme which recognises high standards in all aspects of the visitor experience.

Events 2009

Walk Scilly
Isle of Scilly
walkscilly.co.uk
Mar

Exeter Festival of South West Food & Drink
Exeter
visitsouthwest.co.uk/exeterfoodfestival
Apr

Cheese Rolling
Brockworth
cheese-rolling.co.uk
25 May

Chippenham Folk Festival
Chippenham
chippfolk.co.uk
22 - 25 May

Annual Nettle Eating Contest
Bridport
thebottleinn.co.uk
Jun

Bristol International Festival of Kites
Bristol
kite-festival.org.uk
Aug

Spirit of the Sea
Weymouth
spiritofthesea.org.uk
Aug

Falmouth Oyster Festival
Falmouth
falmouthoysterfestival.co.uk
Oct

Bath Christmas Market
Bath
bathchristmasmarket.co.uk
Nov - Dec

Tar Barrels
Ottery St Mary
otterytourism.org.uk
5 Nov

Bridgwater Guy Fawkes Carnival
Bridgwater
bridgwatercarnival.org.uk
6 Nov

Regional contacts and information

For more information on accommodation, attractions, activities, events and holidays in South West England, contact one of the following regional or local tourism organisations. Their websites have a wealth of information and many produce free publications to help you get the most out of your visit.

South West England

Visit the following websites for further information on South West England or call **01392 360050**:

- **visitsouthwest.co.uk**
- **swcp.org.uk**
- **accessiblesouthwest.co.uk**

Publications available from South West Tourism:

- **The Trencherman's Guide to Top Restaurants in South West England**
- **Adventure South West**
  Your ultimate activity and adventure guide.
- **World Heritage Map**
  Discover our World Heritage.

Clockwise: Pedn Vounder, Cornwall; Gloucester Cathedral, Gloucestershire; Lynton, Devon

Tourist Information Centres

When you arrive at your destination, visit an Official Partner Tourist Information Centre for quality assured help with accommodation and information about local attractions and events, or email your request before you go. To search for attractions and Tourist Information Centres on the move just text INFO to 62233, and a web link will be sent to your mobile phone. To find a Tourist Information Centre by region visit enjoyEngland.com/find-tic.

Avebury	Green Street	(01672) 539425	all.tic's@kennet.gov.uk
Bath	Abbey Church Yard	0906 711 2000**	tourism@bathtourism.co.uk
Bodmin	Mount Folly Square	(01208) 76616	bodmintic@visit.org.uk
Bourton-on-the-Water	Victoria Street	(01451) 820211	bourtonvic@btconnect.com
Bridport	47 South Street	(01308) 424901	bridport.tic@westdorset-dc.gov.uk
Bristol	Harbourside	0906 711 2191**	ticharbourside@destinationbristol.co.uk
Brixham	The Quay	(01803) 211 211	holiday@torbay.gov.uk
Bude	The Crescent	(01288) 354240	budetic@visitbude.info
Burnham-on-Sea	South Esplanade	(01278) 787852	burnham.tic@sedgemoor.gov.uk
Camelford*	The Clease	(01840) 212954	manager@camelfordtic.eclipse.co.uk
Cartgate	A303/A3088 Cartgate Picnic Site	(01935) 829333	cartgate.tic@southsomerset.gov.uk
Cheddar	The Gorge	(01934) 744071	cheddar.tic@sedgemoor.gov.uk
Chippenham	Market Place	(01249) 665970	tourism@chippenham.gov.uk
Chipping Campden	High Street	(01386) 841206	information@visitchippingcampden.com
Christchurch	49 High Street	(01202) 471780	enquiries@christchurchtourism.info
Cirencester	Market Place	(01285) 654180	cirencestervic@cotswold.gov.uk
Coleford	High Street	(01594) 812388	tourism@fdean.gov.uk
Corsham	31 High Street	(01249) 714660	enquiries@corshamheritage.org.uk
Devizes	Market Place	(01380) 729408	all.tic's@kennet.gov.uk
Dorchester	11 Antelope Walk	(01305) 267992	dorchester.tic@westdorset-dc.gov.uk
Falmouth	Prince of Wales Pier	(01326) 312300	info@falmouthtic.co.uk
Frome	Justice Lane	(01373) 467271	frome.tic@ukonline.co.uk
Glastonbury	9 High Street	(01458) 832954	glastonbury.tic@ukonline.co.uk
Gloucester	28 Southgate Street	(01452) 396572	tourism@gloucester.gov.uk
Looe*	Fore Street	(01503) 262072	looetic@btconnect.com
Lyme Regis	Church Street	(01297) 442138	lymeregis.tic@westdorset-dc.gov.uk
Malmesbury	Market Lane	(01666) 823748	malmesburyip@northwilts.gov.uk
Moreton-in-Marsh	High Street	(01608) 650881	moreton@cotswold.gov.uk
Padstow	North Quay	(01841) 533449	padstowtic@btconnect.com

Paignton	The Esplanade	(01803) 211 211	holiday@torbay.gov.uk
Penzance	Station Road	(01736) 362207	pztic@penwith.gov.uk
Plymouth Mayflower	3-5 The Barbican	(01752) 306330	barbicantic@plymouth.gov.uk
St Ives	The Guildhall	(01736) 796297	ivtic@penwith.gov.uk
Salisbury	Fish Row	(01722) 334956	visitorinfo@salisbury.gov.uk
Shelton Mallet	70 High Street	(01749) 345258	sheptonmallet.tic@ukonline.co.uk
Sherborne	3 Tilton Court, Digby Road	(01935) 815341	sherborne.tic@westdorset-dc.gov.uk
Somerset	Sedgemoor Services	(01934) 750833	somersetvisitorcentre@somerset.gov.uk
Stow-on-the-Wold	The Square	(01451) 831082	stowvic@cotswold.gov.uk
Street	Farm Road	(01458) 447384	street.tic@ukonline.co.uk
Stroud	George Street	(01453) 760960	tic@stroud.gov.uk
Swanage	Shore Road	(01929) 422885	mail@swanage.gov.uk
Swindon	37 Regent Street	(01793) 530328	infocentre@swindon.gov.uk
Taunton	Paul Street	(01823) 336344	tauntontic@tauntondeane.gov.uk
Tewkesbury	100 Church Street	(01684) 855043	tewkesburytic@tewkesburybc.gov.uk
Torquay	Vaughan Parade	(01803) 211 211	holiday@torbay.gov.uk
Truro	Boscawen Street	(01872) 274555	tic@truro.gov.uk
Wadebridge	Eddystone Road	0870 1223337	wadebridgetic@btconnect.com
Wareham	South Street	(01929) 552740	tic@purbeck-dc.gov.uk
Warminster	off Station Rd	(01985) 218548	visitwarminster@btconnect.com
Wells	Market Place	(01749) 672552	touristinfo@wells.gov.uk
Weston-super-Mare	Beach Lawns	(01934) 888800	westontouristinfo@n-somerset.gov.uk
Weymouth	The Esplanade	(01305) 785747	tic@weymouth.gov.uk
Winchcombe	High Street	(01242) 602925	winchcombetic@tewkesbury.gov.uk
Yeovil	Hendford	(01935) 845946/7	yeoviltic@southsomerset.gov.uk

*seasonal opening

**calls to this number are charged at premium rate

Left to right: Jurassic Coast, Dorset; Minack Theatre, Cornwall

where to stay in

South West England

All place names in the blue bands are shown on the maps at the front of this guide.

A complete listing of all Enjoy England assessed accommodation covered by this guide appears at the back.

Accommodation symbols

Symbols give useful information about services and facilities. On page 7 you can find a key to these symbols.

ADVENT, Cornwall Map ref 1B2

★★★–★★★★
SELF CATERING

Units **3**
Sleeps **2–4**

LOW SEASON PER WK
Min £170.00

HIGH SEASON PER WK
Max £480.00

Aldermoor Farm, Camelford

contact Hanne Golding, Aldermoor Farm, Advent, Camelford PL32 9QQ **t** (01840) 213366
e hanne@aldermoor.co.uk

aldermoorholidaycottages.co.uk

open All year
payment Cash, cheques
nearest shop 1.5 miles
nearest pub 1.5 miles

Wild flowers, wooded country lanes and meadows surround this secluded haven in North Cornwall. Relax and unwind in a warm and friendly atmosphere. Our cottages have all the old charms of traditionally built granite walls, log fires, four-posters and open beamed ceilings. Close to sea and majestic Bodmin Moor.

Unit General Leisure

Check the maps for accommodation locations

Colour maps at the front pinpoint all the places where accommodation is featured within the regional sections of this guide. Pick your location and then refer to the place index at the back to find the page number.

cottage heaven
Farm & Cottage
HOLIDAYS
Over 850 of the finest holiday cottages in superb coastal and rural locations throughout the West Country. View our full collection, search availability and book securely online. The perfect holiday is yours to choose!
holidaycottages.co.uk
01237 459827
devon | cornwall | somerset | dorset

Your first visit won't be your last adventure.
MARSDENS
COTTAGE HOLIDAYS
The largest selection of VisitBritain inspected holiday cottages in Devon.
Choose from over 300 cottages, sleeping up to 12, some with swimming pools.
www.marsdens.co.uk
for information and 24 hour on line booking
For a free brochure, contact holidays@marsdens.co.uk, phone 01271 813777 or write
2 The Square, Braunton, Devon EX33 2JB

ALTARNUN, Cornwall Map ref 1C2

★★★
SELF CATERING

Units 1
Sleeps 1–2

LOW SEASON PER WK
£200.00–£240.00

HIGH SEASON PER WK
£250.00–£360.00

Trenarrett Cottage, Altarnun, Launceston

contact Mrs Anne Langley, Trenarrett Cottage, Little Trenarrett, Altarnun PL15 7SY **t** (01566) 86649
e anne@trenarrett.co.uk

trenarrett.co.uk

Comfortable, well-equipped, rural cottage with one double bedroom and en suite shower. Living room with moorland view. Baby equipment, pets welcome. Secluded, quiet location, easy access all of Cornwall. Good walking.

open All year
payment Cash, cheques, euros
nearest shop 2 miles
nearest pub 1.6 miles

Unit General P S Leisure

ALTON PANCRAS, Dorset Map ref 2B3

★★★★–★★★★★
SELF CATERING

Units 4
Sleeps 4–10

LOW SEASON PER WK
£330.00–£550.00

HIGH SEASON PER WK
£500.00–£1,250.00

Bookham Court, Dorchester

contact Mr & Mrs Andrew Foot, Whiteways, Bookham, Alton Pancras, Dorchester DT2 7RP
t (01300) 345511 **e** andy.foot1@btinternet.com

bookhamcourt.co.uk GUEST REVIEWS • SPECIAL OFFERS

open All year
payment Cash, cheques
nearest shop 1 mile
nearest pub 1 mile

Luxurious and tranquil cottages with disabled access. Games room, wildlife hide, private fishing, glorious walks in Hardy Country. 20 miles from sea. Sleeps two to ten people.

Unit General P S
Leisure

ASHBURTON, Devon Map ref 1C2

Need some ideas?

Big city buzz or peaceful panoramas? Take a fresh look at England and you may be surprised at what's right on your doorstep. Explore the diversity online at enjoyengland.com

ASHBURTON, Devon Map ref 1C2

★★★
SELF CATERING

Units **14**

LOW SEASON PER WK
£155.00–£430.00

HIGH SEASON PER WK
£405.00–£665.00

See Ad on p00

Parkers Farm Cottages & Caravans, Newton Abbot

t (01364) 653008 **e** parkerscottages@btconnect.com

parkersfarm.co.uk

On friendly family-run farm. Self-catering complex with cottages and static caravans surrounded by beautiful countryside. 12 miles from the sea and close to Dartmoor National Park.

open All year
payment Credit/debit cards, cheques
nearest shop 2 miles
nearest pub 1.5 miles

Unit TV General P S Leisure

ASHBURTON, Devon Map ref 1C2

★★★★
SELF CATERING

Units **2**
Sleeps **2–4**

LOW SEASON PER WK
£230.00–£360.00

HIGH SEASON PER WK
£285.00–£430.00

Wren & Robin Cottages, Newton Abbot

contact Ms Diane Leworthy, Wren & Robin Cottages, New Cott Farm, Ashburton TQ13 7PD
t (01364) 631489 **e** newcottfarmaccom@aol.com

newcott-farm.co.uk

Enjoy Dartmoor National Park with tors, moors and tiny villages. Stress-free, plenty of fresh air. Wren/Robin Cottages are peacefully situated and beautifully furnished. Prices all-inclusive.

open All year
payment Credit/debit cards, cash, cheques
nearest shop 4 miles
nearest pub 1 mile

Unit TV DVD General 3 P S Leisure

ASHTON, Cornwall Map ref 1B3

★★★
SELF CATERING

Units **9**
Sleeps **1–4**

LOW SEASON PER WK
£120.00–£250.00

HIGH SEASON PER WK
£310.00–£490.00

3-and 4-night breaks available in off-peak periods. Call for details.

Chycarne Farm Cottages, Helston

contact Mrs Ross, Chycarne Farm Cottages, Balwest, Ashton TR13 9TE **t** (01736) 762473
e chycarnefarmcottages@hotmail.com

chycarne-farm-cottages.co.uk

payment Credit/debit cards, cash, cheques
nearest shop 1 mile
nearest pub 1 mile

Nestling in the tranquil countryside of Tregonning Hill, 17thC granite farm buildings converted into cosy self-contained cottages, set in five acres with parking. Stunning views over Mounts Bay. Located in historic World Heritage Site. Many places of interest within easy reach. Coastal and country walks. Pub/restaurant one mile. Colour brochure. Closed February, March and November.

Unit TV DVD General P Leisure

Don't forget www.

Web addresses throughout this guide are shown without the prefix www. Please include www. in the address line of your browser. If a web address does not follow this style it is shown in full.

AXMINSTER, Devon Map ref 1D2

★★★★
SELF CATERING

Units 1
Sleeps 6

LOW SEASON PER WK
£800.00

HIGH SEASON PER WK
£1,000.00–£1,200.00

Trout Lodge, Weycroft, Axminster

contact Miss Caroline Cross, 19 Hylton Road, Petersfield GU32 3JY **t** (01730) 263732
e caroline@troutlodge.co.uk

troutlodge.co.uk

open All year
payment Cash, cheques
nearest shop 1 mile
nearest pub 1 mile

In a designated Area of Outstanding Natural Beauty, this beautiful lodge is set on its own little island with 600yds of fishing on the River Axe. The accommodation comprises two twin bedrooms and one double (all en suite), an enormous living room, dining room, terrace and a well-equipped kitchen. Dogs welcome.

ONLINE MAP

Unit General P Leisure

BAMPTON, Devon Map ref 1D1

★★★
SELF CATERING

Units 1
Sleeps 4–6

LOW SEASON PER WK
£240.00–£375.00

HIGH SEASON PER WK
£375.00–£455.00

Short breaks available Oct-Mar. Min 2 nights. Prices on request. Dogs accepted by arrangement.

Wonham Barton, Bampton, Tiverton

contact Mrs Anne McLean Williams, Wonham Barton, Bampton, Tiverton EX16 9JZ
t (01398) 331312 **e** anne@wonham.wanadoo.co.uk

wonham-country-holidays.co.uk

open All year
payment Credit/debit cards, cash, cheques
nearest shop 2.5 miles
nearest pub 2.5 miles

From friendly accommodation overlooking Exe Valley, conveniently explore secretive, historic Devon, rolling moorlands and dramatic coastlines; enjoy country pursuits and leisurely cream teas. Savour 300 tranquil acres, glimpsing Exmoor red deer, soaring buzzards and traditional shepherding; share romantic scenes from TV drama and 'Landgirls', filmed here. Tell us when you're coming!

Unit General P Leisure

BARNSTAPLE, Devon Map ref 1C1

★★★
SELF CATERING

Units 8
Sleeps 2–8

LOW SEASON PER WK
£195.00–£355.00

HIGH SEASON PER WK
£460.00–£910.00

North Hill Cottages, Barnstaple

contact Mrs Carol Ann Black, North Hill, Shirwell, Barnstaple EX31 4LG **t** (01271) 850611
e info@north-hill.co.uk

north-hill.co.uk

Converted 17thC farm buildings set in eight acres of secluded gardens and meadows. Ten minutes from Barnstaple town centre.

open All year
payment Credit/debit cards
nearest shop 3 miles
nearest pub 3 miles

Unit General P
Leisure

Where can I get help and advice?

Tourist Information Centres offer friendly help with accommodation and holiday ideas as well as suggestions of places to visit and things to do. You'll find contact details at the beginning of each regional section.

BARNSTAPLE, Devon Map ref 1C1

★★★★
SELF CATERING

Units 1
Sleeps 2

HIGH SEASON PER WK
£330.00–£430.00

The Old Stables, Nr Brayford, Barnstaple

contact Mr Francis Summers, Stone Cross House, Stone Cross, Brayford, Barnstaple EX32 7PH
t (01271) 830238 **e** enquiries@the-old-stables.net

the-old-stables.net GUEST REVIEWS

Spacious and luxurious one-bedroomed cottage with private patio and garden. Situated close to Exmoor, Tarka Trail and beaches of North Devon. Off-road parking.

open April to October
payment Cash, cheques
nearest shop 3 miles
nearest pub 3 miles

Unit General P Leisure

BATH, Somerset Map ref 2B2

★★★★
SELF CATERING

Units 1
Sleeps 2

LOW SEASON PER WK
£200.00–£350.00

HIGH SEASON PER WK
£350.00–£450.00

31a Rivers Street, Bath

contact Mrs Charlotte Edge, 16 Prospect Place, Camden Road, Bath BA1 5JD **t** 07910 018751
e charls.walker@gmail.com

funlets.co.uk REAL-TIME BOOKING

open All year
payment Cash, cheques
nearest shop less than 0.5 miles
nearest pub less than 0.5 miles

A unique characterful little house in the centre of Bath, beautifully furnished with contemporary styling, 31a is perfect for the romantic couple, ardent shopper, or undaunted sightseer. Finest bed linen, fluffy towels and bathrobes complement your stay, as does a welcome pack, together with a basic larder.

SAT NAV *BA1 2QA*

Unit General Leisure

BATH, Somerset Map ref 2B2

★★★★
SELF CATERING

Units 8
Sleeps 2–6

LOW SEASON PER WK
£285.00–£645.00

HIGH SEASON PER WK
£465.00–£1,150.00

4-night midweek break (Mon-Thu) available at same price as 3-night weekend break (Fri-Sun), excl school holidays.

Church Farm Country Cottages, Bradford-on-Avon

contact Mrs Trish Bowles, Church Farm, Winsley, Bradford-on-Avon BA15 2JH **t** (01225) 722246
e stay@churchfarmcottages.com

churchfarmcottages.com GUEST REVIEWS · SPECIAL OFFERS

open All year
payment Credit/debit cards, cash, cheques, euros
nearest shop less than 0.5 miles
nearest pub less than 0.5 miles

Eight well equipped, tastefully converted single-storey cottages sleeping two, four or six. Working farm with sheep and horses. Luxurious, heated indoor swimming pool (12m x 5m), games room. Pub/shop 500m. Kennet & Avon Canal nearby for boating, cycling and walking. Regular buses. Welcome cream tea. Green Tourism Business Scheme Silver Award.

ONLINE MAP

Unit General P Leisure

It's all quality-assessed accommodation

Our commitment to quality involves wide-ranging accommodation assessment. Ratings and awards were correct at the time of going to press but may change following a new assessment. Please check at time of booking.

BATH, Somerset Map ref 2B2

★★★★–★★★★★
SELF CATERING

Units 5
Sleeps 2–4

LOW SEASON PER WK
£231.00–£366.00

HIGH SEASON PER WK
£378.00–£549.00

Fully flexible bookings and short breaks available all year round. Availability calendar and full details available on our website.

Greyfield Farm Cottages, High Littleton

contact Mrs June Merry, Greyfield Farm Cottages, Greyfield Road, High Littleton, Bristol BS39 6YQ
t (01761) 471132 **e** june@greyfieldfarm.com

greyfieldfarm.com SPECIAL OFFERS • REAL-TIME BOOKING

open All year
payment Cash, cheques, euros
nearest shop 0.5 miles
nearest pub 0.5 miles

Attractive stone cottages in peaceful, private, 3.5-acre setting overlooking the Mendips. The cottages are spacious, fully equipped, warm and very comfortable. Each enjoys its own garden/patio and adjacent safe parking. Free facilities include hot tub, sauna, fitness and barbecue centres plus video/DVD library.

ONLINE MAP

Unit General P Leisure

BEAMINSTER, Dorset Map ref 2A3

★★★
SELF CATERING

Units 3
Sleeps 4

LOW SEASON PER WK
£120.00–£210.00

HIGH SEASON PER WK
£210.00–£320.00

Greens Cross Farm, Beaminster

contact Mr & Mrs David & Lora Baker, Greens Cross Farm, Stoke Road, Beaminster DT8 3JL
t (01308) 862661 **e** greenscross@btopenworld.com

greenscrossfarm.co.uk

Well-equipped holiday units within walking distance of Beaminster in heart of Dorset and close to coast. Short winter breaks. Nearby woods and walking paths to countryside.

open All year
payment Cash, cheques
nearest shop 0.5 miles
nearest pub 0.5 miles

Unit General P Leisure

BENTHAM, Gloucestershire Map ref 2B1

★★★★★
SELF CATERING

Units 1
Sleeps 1–4

LOW SEASON PER WK
£280.00–£390.00

HIGH SEASON PER WK
£390.00–£540.00

Bridge House Cottage, Cheltenham

contact Mrs Yvonne Hodges, Church Lane, Bentham, Cheltenham GL51 4TZ **t** (01452) 862998
e yvonne@hodges0.wanadoo.co.uk

benthamcottage.co.uk

Cotswolds location. Wing of barn conversion. Heavily beamed and beautifully furnished. Own enclosed grounds including 16thC dovecote.

open All year
payment Cash, cheques
nearest shop 0.5 miles
nearest pub 0.5 miles

Unit General P Leisure

BERRYNARBOR, Devon Map ref 1C1

★★★
SELF CATERING

Units 4
Sleeps 2–7

LOW SEASON PER WK
£95.00–£301.00

HIGH SEASON PER WK
£320.00–£994.00

Smythen Farm Coastal Holiday Cottages, Ilfracombe

contact Mr & Ms Thompson & Elstone, Smythen Farm Coastal Holiday Cottages, Symthen, Sterridge Valley, Berrynarbor, Ilfracombe EX34 9TB **t** (01271) 882875
e jayne@smythenfarmholidaycottages.co.uk

smythenfarmholidaycottages.co.uk SPECIAL OFFERS

open March to January
payment Cash, cheques
nearest shop 1.5 miles
nearest pub 1.5 miles

Near golden sands with sea and coastal views. Heated, covered swimming pool in a suntrap enclosure, gardens and games room with pool table, table tennis, football machine. Tree-house on two levels. Free pony rides, ball pond and bouncy castle, 14-acre recreation field and dog walk. For colour brochure phone Jayne.

ONLINE MAP

Unit General P Leisure

BIBURY, Gloucestershire Map ref 2B1

★★★★
SELF CATERING

Units 2
Sleeps 4

LOW SEASON PER WK
£250.00–£290.00

HIGH SEASON PER WK
£310.00–£395.00

Cotteswold House Cottages, Bibury

contact Mrs Judith Underwood, Cotteswold House, Arlington, Bibury, Cirencester GL7 5ND
t (01285) 740609 **e** enquiries@cotteswoldhouse.org.uk

cotteswoldhouse.org.uk

open All year
payment Credit/debit cards, cash, cheques
nearest shop 1 mile
nearest pub 0.5 miles

Situated in this picturesque village, these delightful cottages offer tastefully furnished, spacious accommodation. Equipped to a high standard to include all the comforts of home. Heating, linen and electricity included. Private parking. No smoking/pets. An ideal centre for touring the Cotswolds and surrounding areas.

Unit General P Leisure

BIDEFORD, Devon Map ref 1C1

★★★
SELF CATERING

Units 1
Sleeps 2

LOW SEASON PER WK
£150.00–£200.00

HIGH SEASON PER WK
£200.00–£275.00

Coachmans Cottage, Monkleigh, Bideford

contact Mr & Mrs Tom & Sue Downie, Cream Tea Cottages, Staddon House, Monkleigh, Bideford EX39 5JR **t** (01805) 623670 **e** tom.downie@ukonline.co.uk

creamteacottages.co.uk GUEST REVIEWS · SPECIAL OFFERS

Charming character cottage set in traditional courtyard surroundings. Our price includes all linen, logs for the woodburner and a cream tea to help you settle in after your journey.

open All year
payment Credit/debit cards, cash, cheques
nearest shop less than 0.5 miles
nearest pub less than 0.5 miles

Unit General P Leisure

Remember to check when booking

Please remember that all information in this guide has been supplied by the proprietors well in advance of publication. Since changes do sometimes occur it's a good idea to check details at the time of booking.

BIDEFORD, Devon Map ref 1C1

★★★★
SELF CATERING

Units 3
Sleeps 4–14

LOW SEASON PER WK
£180.00–£250.00

HIGH SEASON PER WK
£250.00–£575.00

Special prices for out-of-season 3-night or weekend breaks. Please ring for details.

Cream Tea Cottages, Little Torrington, Torrington

contact Mr & Mrs Tom & Sue Downie, Staddon House, Monkleigh, Bideford EX39 5JR
t (01805) 623670 **e** tom.downie@ukonline.co.uk

creamteacottages.co.uk GUEST REVIEWS · SPECIAL OFFERS

open All year
payment Credit/debit cards, cash, cheques
nearest shop 2 miles
nearest pub 2 miles

Set in a lovely location, these cottages are converted barns dating back to the 1700s. They retain many original features but are renovated to modern standards. The properties all have french windows opening onto their own patios. There is also a play and picnic area for children.

ONLINE MAP

Unit General Leisure

BIGBURY-ON-SEA, Devon Map ref 1C3

★★★★★
SELF CATERING

Units 1
Sleeps 1–4

LOW SEASON PER WK
£451.00–£1,031.00

HIGH SEASON PER WK
£1,155.00–£1,621.00

Bargain weekend and short-stay breaks available in autumn and winter months.

Apartment 5, Burgh Island Causeway, Bigbury-on-Sea

Helpful Holidays, Mill Street, Chagford, Newton Abbot TQ13 8AW **t** (01647) 433593
e help@helpfulholidays.com

helpfulholidays.com GUEST REVIEWS · SPECIAL OFFERS · REAL-TIME BOOKING

open All year
payment Credit/debit cards, cash, cheques
nearest shop less than 0.5 miles
nearest pub less than 0.5 miles

Luxury, modern, ground-floor apartment set into cliff with panoramic southerly views from large patio. Facilities include pool, gym, sauna, cafe/bar, grassy cliff-top grounds and direct access to beautiful large sandy beach and coastal path. Popular for surfing and near golf course and village shop/post office. View www.burghislandcauseway.com

SAT NAV *TQ7 4AS* **ONLINE MAP**

Unit General
Leisure

BIGBURY-ON-SEA, Devon Map ref 1C3

★★★
SELF CATERING

Units 1
Sleeps 6

LOW SEASON PER WK
£245.00–£425.00

HIGH SEASON PER WK
£445.00–£995.00

Pictures on our website – or please phone for a brochure. Special discounts for 2 people (or 1) and out-of-season weekends.

Mount Folly Farm, Bigbury on Sea, Kingsbridge

contact Mrs Jane Tucker, Mount Folly Farm, Bigbury on Sea, Kingsbridge TQ7 4AR
t (01548) 810267 **e** chris.cathy@goosemoose.com

bigburyholidays.co.uk

open Please contact for availability
payment Cheques
nearest shop 0.5 miles
nearest pub 0.5 miles

Cliff-top position on working farm with outstanding views of Bigbury Bay. Completely self-contained, spacious wing of farmhouse. Walking distance of sandy beaches. Upstairs – two double rooms (with washbasins) and a bedroom with bunk beds. Bathroom with bath and shower. Downstairs – lounge with spectacular views and large kitchen.

SAT NAV *TQ7 4AR*

Unit General Leisure

BINEGAR, Somerset Map ref 2B2

★★★★
SELF CATERING

Units 1
Sleeps 5

LOW SEASON PER WK
£370.00–£450.00

HIGH SEASON PER WK
£495.00–£610.00

Short breaks available Oct-Mar, 2-/3-night stays.

Spindle Cottage, Binegar Green, Nr Bath

contact Mrs Angela Bunting, Spindle Cottage, Binegar Green, Binegar, Near Bath BA3 4UE
t (01749) 840497 **e** angela@spindlecottage.co.uk

spindlecottage.co.uk SPECIAL OFFERS

open All year
payment Cash, cheques
nearest shop 1 mile
nearest pub 0.5 miles

Fairy-tale 17thC cottage, high on Mendip Hills. Garden has summerhouse, gazebo, conservatory. Cottage is a place of charm and delight. Lovely sitting room with low ceiling and oak beams. Wood-burning stove. Three bedrooms: one double, one twin, one single. Wells, Glastonbury, Bath, Cheddar, Wookey Hole within easy reach.

ONLINE MAP

Unit General Leisure

BLUE ANCHOR, Somerset Map ref 1D1

★★★★
SELF CATERING

Units 3
Sleeps 2–5

LOW SEASON PER WK
£265.00–£335.00

HIGH SEASON PER WK
£335.00–£545.00

Short breaks available Nov-Mar (excl Christmas and New Year).

Huntingball Lodge, Blue Anchor

contact Mr & Mrs Brian & Kim Hall, Huntingball Lodge, Blue Anchor, Minehead TA24 6JP
t (01984) 640076

huntingball-lodge.co.uk

open All year
payment Cash, cheques
nearest shop less than 0.5 miles
nearest pub less than 0.5 miles

Elegant, quiet country house with spectacular views over the Somerset coastline and Exmoor countryside. Luxurious and spacious self-catering apartments furnished and equipped to a very high standard, each with own private patio or roof terrace. Pub/restaurant, tea rooms and convenience store within easy walking distance. Guaranteed warm welcome from the resident owners.

Unit General

BOSCASTLE, Cornwall Map ref 1B2

★★★★
SELF CATERING

Units 5
Sleeps 4–6

LOW SEASON PER WK
£195.00–£280.00

HIGH SEASON PER WK
£280.00–£630.00

Cargurra Farm, Boscastle

contact Mrs Gillian Elson, Hennett, St Juliot, Boscastle PL35 0BT **t** (01840) 261206
e gillian@cargurra.co.uk

cargurra.co.uk

open All year
payment Credit/debit cards, cash, cheques
nearest shop 2 miles
nearest pub 2 miles

Secluded farm setting within the beautiful Valency Valley where Thomas Hardy met his love. Well-appointed, traditional cottage, log fire, central heating. Spacious gardens, barbecue, games room with pool and table tennis. Wi-Fi Internet access, communal computer. Private road, ample parking. Country and coastal walks. Also, cottages converted from Victorian barn.

Unit General Leisure

BOSCASTLE, Cornwall Map ref 1B2

★★★
SELF CATERING

Units **3**
Sleeps **1–4**

LOW SEASON PER WK
£200.00–£450.00

HIGH SEASON PER WK
£300.00–£600.00

Short breaks available Oct-Mar.

Old Newham Farm, Camelford

contact Mr & Mrs Purdue, Old Newham Farm, Otterham, Camelford PL32 9SR **t** (01840) 230470
e tbg@old-newham.co.uk

old-newham.co.uk

open All year
payment Credit/debit cards, cash, cheques
nearest shop 2 miles
nearest pub 2 miles

Characterful stone cottages on peaceful 30-acre organic farm dating back to medieval times with cattle, sheep and other small animals for children. Well away from traffic down a quiet lane, the peace of the Cornish countryside only three miles from the most spectacular National Trust coastline/beaches. Internet access.

Unit General Leisure

BOURTON-ON-THE-WATER, Gloucestershire Map ref 2B1

★★★
SELF CATERING

Units **1**
Sleeps **1–6**

LOW SEASON PER WK
£460.00

HIGH SEASON PER WK
£600.00

Inglenook Cottage, Cheltenham

contact Mrs Vicki Garland, Ratcliffe House Farm, Ratcliffe House Lane, Ratcliffe Culey, Atherstone CV9 3LZ **t** (01827) 712367 & 07751 801508 **e** enquiries@ratcliffehousefarm.co.uk

holidaycottagebourton-on-the-water.co.uk

Inglenook Cottage is an old stone-built cottage, built in the Victorian era, with private courtyard garden. Centrally situated near the river. One twin, one double, bathroom and downstairs toilet/cloakroom.

open All year
payment Cash, cheques

Unit General P S Leisure

BOVEY TRACEY, Devon Map ref 1D2

★★★★
SELF CATERING

Units **1**
Sleeps **1–12**

LOW SEASON PER WK
£400.00–£700.00

HIGH SEASON PER WK
£900.00–£1,250.00

Warmhill Farm, Bovey Tracey

contact Mr W B Marnham, Warmhill Farm, Hennock, Bovey Tracey, Newton Abbot TQ13 9QH
t (01626) 833229 **e** marnham@agriplus.net

A 100-acre working farm. Superb thatched farmhouse in Dartmoor National Park. Ideal for moor and sea. Spacious and comfortable, with many old features preserved.

open All year
payment Cash, cheques
nearest shop 2 miles
nearest pub 0.5 miles

Unit General P S
Leisure

For **key to symbols** see page 7

BRADFORD-ON-AVON, Wiltshire Map ref 2B2

★★★★
SELF CATERING

Units 7
Sleeps 2–4

LOW SEASON PER WK
£220.00–£550.00

HIGH SEASON PER WK
£295.00–£845.00

Golf breaks available – Cumberwell Park Golf Club is on site. 3- and 4-night midweek and weekend breaks available.

Cumberwell Country Cottages, Bradford-on-Avon

contact Mr Alistair James, Great Cumberwell Farm, Bradford-on-Avon BA15 2PQ **t** (01225) 869230
e enquiries@cumberwellcountrycottages.com

cumberwellcountrycottages.com SPECIAL OFFERS

open All year
payment Credit/debit cards, cash, cheques
nearest shop 1 mile
nearest pub 0.5 miles

You can sample country life, town life and city life all from your stay at Cumberwell Country Cottages, situated in the peaceful Wiltshire countryside only six miles from Bath. For an idyllic country stay within reach of many attractions, Cumberwell provides the perfect location when visiting South West England.

Unit General Leisure

BRADFORD-ON-AVON, Wiltshire Map ref 2B2

★★★★★
SELF CATERING

Units 3
Sleeps 1–15

LOW SEASON PER WK
£650.00–£750.00

HIGH SEASON PER WK
£900.00–£1,300.00

Short breaks available Sep-Jun.

Fairfield Barns, Atworth

contact Mr & Mrs Taff & Gilly Thomas, Bradford Road, Atworth, Melksham SN12 8HZ
t (01225) 703585 **e** gilly@fairfieldbarns.com

fairfieldbarns.com GUEST REVIEWS · SPECIAL OFFERS

open All year
payment Credit/debit cards, cash, cheques
nearest shop less than 0.5 miles
nearest pub 0.5 miles

In a quiet village near Bath, two luxurious barn conversions with panoramic views of the Wiltshire countryside. En suite bedrooms. Also a cosy terraced cottage in the heart of the village. All superbly equipped. Use of indoor swimming pool, gym, tennis court, sauna, children's playhouse and adventure playground. Perfect for sightseeing and touring.

ONLINE MAP

Unit General
Leisure

BRATTON, Somerset Map ref 1D1

★★★★
SELF CATERING

Units 8
Sleeps 2–11

LOW SEASON PER WK
£190.00–£720.00

HIGH SEASON PER WK
£280.00–£1,295.00

Short breaks available Nov-Easter, min 3 nights.

Woodcombe Lodges, Minehead

contact Mrs Nicola Hanson, Woodcombe Lodges, Bratton Lane, Minehead TA24 8SQ
t (01643) 702789 & 07860 667325 **e** nicola@woodcombelodge.co.uk

woodcombelodge.co.uk

open All year
payment Credit/debit cards, cash, cheques
nearest shop 1 mile
nearest pub 1 mile

Timber lodges and stone cottages in a tranquil, rural setting on the edge of Exmoor National Park. Standing in a beautiful, 2.5-acre garden with wonderful views towards the wooded slopes of Exmoor. Minehead's seafront, harbour, shops etc 1.5 miles. Close to Dunster, Selworthy, Porlock and many local beauty spots.

Unit General Leisure

BRAYFORD, Devon Map ref 1C1

★★
SELF CATERING

Units 1
Sleeps 6

LOW SEASON PER WK
Min £165.00

HIGH SEASON PER WK
Max £350.00

Muxworthy Cottage, Barnstaple

contact Mrs G M Bament, Muxworthy Farm, Brayford, Barnstaple EX32 7QP **t** (01598) 710342

Secluded old-world cottage in idyllic rural location, fully equipped, with wood-burning stove. Unspoilt countryside, ideal for a peaceful holiday in the heart of Exmoor. Weekends and short breaks available.

open All year
payment Cash, cheques
nearest shop 3 miles
nearest pub 3 miles

Unit General Leisure

BRIDPORT, Dorset Map ref 2A3

★★★★
SELF CATERING

Units 10
Sleeps 2–6

LOW SEASON PER WK
£280.00–£465.00

HIGH SEASON PER WK
£480.00–£835.00

Short breaks available all year.

Rudge Farm, Bridport

contact Mr Michael Hamer, Rudge Farm, Chilcombe, Bridport DT6 4NF **t** (01308) 482630
e enquiries@rudgefarm.co.uk

rudgefarm.co.uk SPECIAL OFFERS

open All year
payment Credit/debit cards, cash, cheques
nearest shop 2 miles
nearest pub 1 mile

Rudge Farm provides a beautiful countryside location for a stress-free holiday, a short distance away from the World Heritage Coastline. The old farm buildings have been converted into comfortable and cosy cottages, ranging from one to three bedrooms. There are a number of leisure facilities on the farm, including a tennis court and games barn.

Unit General Leisure

BRIXHAM, Devon Map ref 1D2

★★★
SELF CATERING

Units 7
Sleeps 1–4

LOW SEASON PER WK
£130.00–£220.00

HIGH SEASON PER WK
£260.00–£500.00

Short breaks available Nov-Feb.

Brixham Harbourside Holiday Flats, Brixham

contact Mrs Helgard Stone, 13 Cambridge Road, Brixham TQ5 8JW **t** (01803) 851919
e david.f.stone@btinternet.com

brixham-harbourside-holiday-flats.com

open All year
payment Cash, cheques
nearest shop less than 0.5 miles
nearest pub less than 0.5 miles

Four one-bedroom, and three two-bedroom, self-contained flats. Clean, well-furnished and comfortable. Sea and harbour views of fishing boats, yachts and pleasure craft. Hot water, central heating, electricity, Freeview TV, all bed linen, towels and parking are inclusive. We do our best to make your stay a pleasant one.

Unit General Leisure

CYCLISTS WELCOME

Fancy a cycling holiday?

For a fabulous freewheeling break, seek out accommodation participating in our Cyclists Welcome scheme. Look out for the symbol and plan your route online at nationalcyclenetwork.org.

BRIXHAM, Devon **Map ref 1D2**

★★★
SELF CATERING

Units 2
Sleeps 1–4

LOW SEASON PER WK
Min £255.00

HIGH SEASON PER WK
Max £515.00

Galmpton Touring Park Cottages, Brixham

contact Mrs Pam Collins, Galmpton Touring Park Cottages, Greenway Road, Brixham TQ5 0EP
t (01803) 842066 **e** galmptontouringpark@hotmail.com

gtpcottages.co.uk

Two comfortable cottages in beautiful countryside on edge of village near Brixham. A quiet base from which to explore South Devon. Beaches and attractions nearby – lovely walks from your doorstep.

open All year
payment Credit/debit cards, cash, cheques
nearest shop 0.5 miles
nearest pub 0.5 miles

Unit General Leisure

BRIXHAM, Devon **Map ref 1D2**

★★★
SELF CATERING

Units 2
Sleeps 1–11

LOW SEASON PER WK
£190.00–£280.00

HIGH SEASON PER WK
£240.00–£490.00

Low season short breaks available.

Harbour Reach, Brixham

contact Mrs Jenny Pocock, Totley Hall Farm, Totley Hall Lane, Sheffield S17 4AA **t** (0114) 236 4761
e enquiries@harbourreachholidays.co.uk

harbourreachholidays.co.uk

open All year
payment Cash, cheques
nearest shop less than 0.5 miles
nearest pub less than 0.5 miles

The spectacular views across the harbour, Torbay and out to sea make this a perfect holiday home at any time of year. 'Harbour Reach' is excellently furnished and equipped and divided into a maisonette and flat which are let separately or jointly thereby sleeping one to 11. Phone for brochure.

Unit General

BRIXHAM, Devon **Map ref 1D2**

★★★
SELF CATERING

Units 1
Sleeps 2–6

LOW SEASON PER WK
£350.00–£450.00

HIGH SEASON PER WK
£570.00–£700.00

Overquay Cottage, Brixham

contact Mrs Moira Withey, Ranscombe House, Ranscombe Road, Brixham TQ5 9UP
t (01803) 882337 **e** info@ranscombehousehotel.co.uk

ranscombehousehotel.co.uk

open All year
payment Cash, cheques
nearest shop less than 0.5 miles
nearest pub less than 0.5 miles

Grade II Listed cottage on Brixham harbour. Sleeps six. Ground-floor: dining room, large well equipped kitchen and courtyard. First floor: sitting room with great views, double bedroom and bathroom. Second floor: two twin bedded rooms and shower room. Private off-street parking nearby. Bed linen and towels provided.

SAT NAV *TQ5 9TH* **ONLINE MAP**

Unit General Leisure

WALKERS WELCOME

Do you like walking?

Walkers feel at home in accommodation participating in our Walkers Welcome scheme. Look out for the symbol. Consider walking all or part of a long-distance route – go online at nationaltrail.co.uk.

BROADCLYST, Devon Map ref 1D2

★★★★
SELF CATERING

Units 1
Sleeps 4

LOW SEASON PER WK
£240.00–£519.00

HIGH SEASON PER WK
£609.00–£745.00

Hue's Piece, Broadclyst, Exeter

contact Mrs Anna Hamlyn, Hue's Piece, Paynes Farm, Broadclyst, Exeter EX5 3BJ **t** (01392) 466720
e annahamlyn@paynes-farm.co.uk

paynes-farm.co.uk SPECIAL OFFERS

Peaceful three-bedroomed converted barn on small friendly National Trust farm in lovely countryside yet just five miles from Exeter. Delicious farmhouse-cooked evening meals and breakfasts by arrangement.

open All year
payment Cash, cheques
nearest shop 1 mile
nearest pub 1 mile

Unit General P Leisure

BUCKLAND NEWTON, Dorset Map ref 2B3

★★★★
SELF CATERING

Units 3
Sleeps 4

LOW SEASON PER WK
£240.00–£350.00

HIGH SEASON PER WK
£375.00–£550.00

Domineys Cottages, Buckland Newton, Nr Dorchester

contact Mrs Jeanette Gueterbock, Domineys Cottages, Domineys Yard, Buckland Newton, Dorchester DT2 7BS **t** (01300) 345295 **e** cottages@domineys.com

domineys.com

open All year
payment Cash, cheques, euros
nearest shop 1 mile
nearest pub less than 0.5 miles

Delightful, Victorian, two-bedroomed cottages, comfortably furnished and equipped and maintained to highest standards. Surrounded by beautiful gardens with patios. Heated summer swimming pool. Peaceful location on village edge in heart of Hardy's Dorset. Well situated for touring Wessex, walking and country pursuits. Regret no pets. Children 5+ and babies welcome.

Unit General 5 P Leisure

BUDE, Cornwall Map ref 1C2

★★★★★
SELF CATERING

Units 1
Sleeps 4

LOW SEASON PER WK
Min £300.00

HIGH SEASON PER WK
Max £950.00

Hunters Lodge, Bude

contact Mrs Denise Congdon, Kitsham Holidays **t** (01288) 341336 **e** holidays@kitsham.co.uk

kitsham.co.uk

open All year
payment Cash, cheques
nearest shop 1.5 miles
nearest pub 1.5 miles

Delightful newly renovated barn. Slate floors, high beams, granite worktops. Plasma TV, soft lighting, patio window, own private garden, country views. Natural stone bathroom, walk-in shower. Ideal retreat for that extra special break. Near surf, sea and sands. Valley and coastal path walks. Excellent golf courses. Explore scenic Bodmin Moor or Eden Project.

Unit General P Leisure

PETS! WELCOME

Where is my pet welcome?

Want to take your cherished companion with you on holiday? Proprietors participating in our Welcome Pets! scheme go out of their way to make special provision for you and your pet. Look out for the symbol.

BUDE, Cornwall Map ref 1C2

★★★★-★★★★★
SELF CATERING

Units 5
Sleeps 2–8

LOW SEASON PER WK
£199.00–£600.00

HIGH SEASON PER WK
£500.00–£1,500.00

Ivyleaf Barton Cottages, Bude

contact Mr Robert Barrett, Ivyleaf Barton Cottages, c/o Priors Court Barn, Goose Street, Beckington BA11 6TS **t** (01288) 321237 & 07771 908108 **e** ivyleafcottages@aol.com

ivyleafbarton.co.uk

Well-equipped, cosy cottages converted from stone barns. Two sleeping two people, one sleeping four, one sleeping seven and one sleeping eight. Tennis court, adjacent golf course. Three miles to Bude. Short breaks welcome.

open All year
payment Credit/debit cards, cash, cheques, euros
nearest shop 1.5 miles
nearest pub 1.5 miles

Unit General Leisure

BUDE, Cornwall Map ref 1C2

★★★
SELF CATERING

Units 8
Sleeps 2–6

LOW SEASON PER WK
£250.00–£370.00

HIGH SEASON PER WK
£420.00–£820.00

Short breaks. Also the opportunity to book the whole manor house for special occasions or Christmas & New Year.

Langfield Manor, Bude

contact Suzanne Walker, Langfield Manor, Broadclose, Bude EX23 8DP **t** (01288) 352415
e langfieldmanor@btconnect.com

langfieldmanor.co.uk SPECIAL OFFERS

open All year
payment Credit/debit cards, cash, cheques
nearest shop 3 miles
nearest pub 3 miles

Langfield Manor is an old Edwardian house that has been converted into eight self-catering apartments, including a heated swimming pool and a full-size snooker table. It is located in a secluded corner of Bude, three minutes' walk from the shops and sandy beaches, and adjacent to Bude Golf Club.

SAT NAV *EX23 8DP*

Unit General
Leisure

BUDE, Cornwall Map ref 1C2

★★★
SELF CATERING

Units 4
Sleeps 2–4

LOW SEASON PER WK
Min £260.00

HIGH SEASON PER WK
Max £540.00

Old Lifeboat House, Bude

contact Mrs Sarah Debonnaire, Old Lifeboat House, Brendon Arms, Falcon Terrace, Bude EX23 8SD
t (01288) 354542 **e** enquiries@brendonarms.co.uk

brendonarms.co.uk

Bude's original Old Lifeboat House has been completely refurbished and now offers very comfortable self-catering accommodation to sleep two – four people. Lovely views over the canal and only a short walk to Bude's popular Summerleaze beach.

open All year
payment Credit/debit cards, cash, cheques
nearest shop less than 0.5 miles
nearest pub less than 0.5 miles

Unit General P Leisure

BUDE, Cornwall Map ref 1C2

★★★★★
SELF CATERING

Units 1
Sleeps 2

LOW SEASON PER WK
£795.00–£850.00

One4Two, Bude

contact Kathy Lawrence, One4Two, Penrhyn, Hillhead EX23 9AB **t** 07852 245967
e one4two@btconnect.com

one4two.co.uk GUEST REVIEWS • SPECIAL OFFERS

Available for short breaks of one, two or three nights only, One4Two brings romance to the West Country. One unique accommodation for one couple, together, alone. A luxury experience – anniversary, birthday – your choice!

open All year
payment Cash, cheques
nearest shop less than 0.5 miles
nearest pub less than 0.5 miles

Unit General P Leisure

BUDE, Cornwall Map ref 1C2

★★★★–★★★★★
SELF CATERING

Units 6
Sleeps 2–8

LOW SEASON PER WK
Min £240.00

HIGH SEASON PER WK
Max £1,550.00

Wooldown Farm Cottages, Marhamchurch, Bude

contact Mr & Mrs Susan Blewett, Wooldown Farm Cottages, Wooldown, Marhamchurch, Bude EX23 0HP **t** (01288) 361216 **e** holidays@wooldown.com

wooldown.com GUEST REVIEWS • SPECIAL OFFERS • REAL-TIME BOOKING

open All year
payment Cash, cheques
nearest shop less than 0.5 miles
nearest pub less than 0.5 miles

Offering a choice of delightful self-catering cottages, romantic barns for couples and larger properties perfect for families, all of which have spectacular sea views across open countryside to Widemouth Bay and Bude. We are a few minutes' walk from the village of Marhamchurch, with post office/shop and pub/restaurant.

SAT NAV *EX23 0HP* **ONLINE MAP**

Unit General P S Leisure

BURNHAM-ON-SEA, Somerset Map ref 1D1

★★★–★★★★
SELF CATERING

Units 4
Sleeps 2–9

LOW SEASON PER WK
£110.00–£175.00

HIGH SEASON PER WK
£295.00–£595.00

Special tariffs quoted for midweek and weekend breaks in low season.

Prospect Farm, Highbridge

contact Mrs Gillian Wall, Prospect Farm Holidays, Strowlands, East Brent, Highbridge TA9 4JH
t (01278) 760507

open All year
payment Cash, cheques
nearest shop less than 0.5 miles
nearest pub less than 0.5 miles

17thC, tastefully restored country cottages set amidst flower gardens and surrounded by the natural West Country beauty of the Somerset Levels, near the legendary Brent Knoll, with remains of Iron Age and Roman settlements. Two miles junction 22 M5, three miles Burnham-on-Sea. Variety of small farm animals and pets. Children welcome.

Unit General P S
Leisure

BURROWBRIDGE, Somerset Map ref 1D1

★★★
SELF CATERING

Units 1
Sleeps 2

LOW SEASON PER WK
£185.00

HIGH SEASON PER WK
£210.00

Hillview, Bridgwater

contact Mrs Rosalind Griffiths, Hillview, Stanmoor Road, Burrowbridge, Bridgwater TA7 0RX
t (01823) 698308

Compact bungalow, fully equipped and centrally heated, in its own grounds. Conservatory. Short breaks available in low season.

open All year
payment Cash, cheques
nearest shop 2 miles
nearest pub 0.75 miles

Unit General P S

FAMILIES WELCOME

Looking for an ideal family break?

For accommodation offering additional facilities and services for a range of ages and family units, look out for the Families Welcome symbol. Owners of these properties will go out of their way to welcome families.

BURTON BRADSTOCK, Dorset Map ref 2A3

★★★
SELF CATERING

Units 7
Sleeps 4–7

LOW SEASON PER WK
£220.00–£290.00

HIGH SEASON PER WK
£480.00–£610.00

Special promotion short breaks are always available in low season.

Cogden Cottages, Burton Bradstock

contact Mr Lee Connolly, Old Coastguard Holiday Park, Coast Road, Burton Bradstock, Bridport DT6 4RL **t** (01308) 897223 **e** oldcoastguard@hotmail.com

cogdencottages.co.uk

open All year
payment Credit/debit cards, cash, cheques, euros
nearest shop 0.8 miles
nearest pub 0.8 miles

Cogden Cottages provide seven two-/three-bedroom cottages remodelled from a Victorian coastguard station. Therefore, they have outstanding coastguard views of the World Heritage Jurassic coastline. Five cottages have individual decking with outdoor furniture for alfresco dining. All cottages have Freeview TV, washer/dryer, dishwasher, towels and linen provided.

Unit General Leisure

CAMELFORD, Cornwall Map ref 1B2

★★★★★
SELF CATERING

Units 3
Sleeps 2–7

LOW SEASON PER WK
£695.00–£895.00

HIGH SEASON PER WK
£895.00–£1,395.00

Couples' discount available.

Helsbury Park, Camelford

contact Mr David Wilson, The Farmhouse, Helsbury Park, Camelford PL32 9RH **t** (01840) 211726 **e** info@helsburypark.co.uk

helsburypark.co.uk GUEST REVIEWS • SPECIAL OFFERS

open All year
payment Credit/debit cards, cash, cheques
nearest shop 1 mile
nearest pub 1 mile

Award-winning, dog-friendly, luxury accommodation set in 100 acres of parkland with woods and river frontage. The cottages mix traditional character with modern comfort, including well-equipped kitchens, en suite bathrooms, log fires and four-poster beds. Situated in beautiful north Cornwall.

ONLINE MAP

Unit General
Leisure

CASTLE CARY, Somerset Map ref 2B2

★★★
SELF CATERING

Units 2
Sleeps 4

LOW SEASON PER WK
£210.00–£250.00

HIGH SEASON PER WK
£300.00–£350.00

Orchard Farm Cottages, Castle Cary

contact Mr & Mrs Dave & Helen Boyer, Orchard Farm Cottages, Cockhill, Castle Cary BA7 7NY **t** (01963) 350418 **e** boyer@orchard-farm.co.uk

orchard-farm.co.uk

open All year
payment Cash, cheques, euros
nearest shop 1.5 miles
nearest pub 1 mile

Traditional Somerset byre converted into cosy cottages providing fully equipped and comfortably furnished accommodation at a reasonable price. One cottage suitable for wheelchairs. Relax in the lawned garden or enjoy quiet country walks. Less than two miles from picturesque Castle Cary's pubs and shops. Many attractions nearby. Ideal for exploring the West Country.

ONLINE MAP

Unit General

CHAPEL AMBLE, Cornwall Map ref 1B2

★★★★
SELF CATERING

Units 2
Sleeps 2–7

LOW SEASON PER WK
Min £200.00

HIGH SEASON PER WK
Min £450.00

Homeleigh Farm Holiday Cottages, Chapel Amble, Wadebridge

contact Philip Rees, Homeleigh Farm, Chapel Amble, Wadebridge PL27 6EU **t** (01208) 812411
e homeleigh@eclipse.co.uk

eclipse.co.uk/homeleigh

Two- and three-bedroom cottages in traditional Cornish stone, on edge of village. Pub and shop 150m. Individual gardens plus six acres to play in. Pets welcome.

open All year
payment Cash, cheques
nearest shop less than 0.5 miles
nearest pub less than 0.5 miles

Unit General P
Leisure

CHARMOUTH, Dorset Map ref 1D2

★★★
SELF CATERING

Units 1
Sleeps 4

LOW SEASON PER WK
Min £250.00

HIGH SEASON PER WK
Max £650.00

10% discount for 2-week stays. Early Bird offer for bookings received before 1 Mar.

The Poplars, Charmouth

contact Mrs Jane Bremner, Wood Farm Caravan Park, Axminster Road, Bridport DT6 6BT
t (01297) 560697 **e** holiday@woodfarm.co.uk

woodfarm.co.uk

open Easter to October
payment Credit/debit cards, cash, cheques
nearest shop less than 0.5 miles
nearest pub 1 mile

With breathtaking views and superb facilities, The Poplars offers spacious, comfortable accommodation specifically designed for disabled guests. See our Heritage Coast and spectacular rural scenery.

Unit General P Leisure

CHAXHILL, Gloucestershire Map ref 2B1

★★★
SELF CATERING

Units 1
Sleeps 1–3

LOW SEASON PER WK
£175.00–£275.00

HIGH SEASON PER WK
£175.00–£490.00

Laurel Cottage, Westbury-on-Severn

contact Mr & Mrs Mark & Tasmin Terry-Lush, The Rowans, Chaxhill, Westbury-on-Severn GL14 1QP
t (01452) 760147 **e** enjoyengland@laurel-cottage.com

laurel-cottage.com

Near the Forest of Dean, Severn and Wye valleys, Laurel Cottage is attached to an 18thC farmhouse in the sleepy hamlet of Chaxhill. Modern facilities and old-world charm. Lots of activities for couples or families.

open All year
payment Credit/debit cards, cash, cheques
nearest shop less than 0.5 miles
nearest pub 1 mile

Unit General P
Leisure

CHEDDAR, Somerset Map ref 1D1

★★
SELF CATERING

Units 1
Sleeps 1–2

LOW SEASON PER WK
Min £150.00

HIGH SEASON PER WK
Min £210.00

Bradley Cross Farm, Cheddar

contact Ms Judith Credland, Bradley Cross, Cheddar BS27 3YU **t** (01934) 741771
e bradleyxfarm@btinternet.com

bradleycrossfarm.org.uk

Stone-built cottage comprising bedroom with two single beds, separate kitchen and bathroom. High on Mendip Hills, on working farm, with spectacular views. Close to West Mendip Way.

open 1 April to 1 October
payment Cash, cheques
nearest shop 1 mile
nearest pub 1 mile

Unit General P Leisure

CHEDDAR, Somerset Map ref 1D1

★★★★
SELF CATERING

Units 4
Sleeps 2–7

LOW SEASON PER WK
£240.00–£475.00

HIGH SEASON PER WK
£350.00–£750.00

Short breaks available.

Home Farm Cottages, Winscombe

contact Mr Chris Sanders, Home Farm Cottages, Barton, Winscombe BS25 1DX **t** (01934) 842078
e enquiries@homefarmcottages.com

homefarmcottages.com

open All year
payment Credit/debit cards, cash, cheques
nearest shop 2 miles
nearest pub 2 miles

Characterful, beamed, converted farm buildings, providing an ideal place to relax and an excellent base for Cheddar, Bath, Wells, Bristol and Weston-super-Mare. Many lovely walks in the area and comfortable, well-equipped cottages to return to. Set in two acres adjacent to farmhouse.

ONLINE MAP

Unit TV DVD General P S Leisure

CHEDDAR, Somerset Map ref 1D1

★★★★
SELF CATERING

Units 3
Sleeps 2

LOW SEASON PER WK
£250.00–£285.00

HIGH SEASON PER WK
£300.00–£325.00

WALKERS WELCOME CYCLISTS WELCOME

Spring Cottages, Cheddar

contact Mrs G Robinson, Spring Cottages, Spring Cottage, Venns Gate, Cheddar BS27 3LW
t (01934) 742493 **e** falcon@springcottages.co.uk

springcottages.co.uk

Charming one-bedroomed cottages in converted barn at the foot of Mendip Hills. Cheddar Gorge and caves are within walking distance. No smoking. Ample off-road parking. Dogs by arrangement.

open All year
payment Cash, cheques, euros
nearest shop 0.5 miles
nearest pub less than 0.5 miles

Unit TV General P S Leisure

CHEDDAR, Somerset Map ref 1D1

★★
SELF CATERING

Units 4
Sleeps 1–4

LOW SEASON PER WK
£160.00–£180.00

HIGH SEASON PER WK
£180.00–£200.00

Sungate Holiday Apartments, Cheddar

contact Mrs M M Fieldhouse, Pyrenmount, Parsons Way, Winscombe BS25 1BU **t** (01934) 842273 & (01934) 742264 **e** sunholapartment@btinternet.com

sungateholidayapartments.co.uk

Delightful apartments in listed Georgian house. Well furnished and equipped. Level rear entrance. In the centre of Cheddar village close to gorge and caves. Well-behaved children and pets welcome.

open All year
payment Cash, cheques, euros
nearest shop less than 0.5 miles
nearest pub less than 0.5 miles

Unit TV General P S Leisure

CHEDWORTH, Gloucestershire Map ref 2B1

★★★★
SELF CATERING

Units 1
Sleeps 2

LOW SEASON PER WK
£225.00–£275.00

HIGH SEASON PER WK
£275.00–£325.00

Short breaks available by negotiation between October and May.

The Old Post Office, Chedworth, Cheltenham

contact Mrs J Todd, The Old Village Stores, Cheap Street, Cheltenham GL54 4AA **t** (01285) 720367
e bookings@opochedworth.co.uk

opochedworth.co.uk

open All year
payment Cash, cheques
nearest shop 1 mile
nearest pub less than 0.5 miles

In Gloucestershire's Village of the Year 2007, this charming historic stone cottage offers comfort and calm. Sleeps two. Fully equipped and modernised but still retaining character features. Excellent pub and farm shop/cafe in the village. Area of Outstanding Natural Beauty, ideal for walks and touring: Cirencester, Cheltenham, Bath, Stratford, Oxford and Blenheim.

ONLINE MAP

Unit TV DVD General P Leisure

CHELTENHAM, Gloucestershire Map ref 2B1

★★★
SELF CATERING

Units 1
Sleeps 4

LOW SEASON PER WK
£240.00–£300.00

HIGH SEASON PER WK
£280.00–£350.00

Bakery Cottage, Cheltenham

contact Mrs Weller, Wortheal House, Southam Lane, Cheltenham GL52 3NY **t** (01242) 236765

Cotswold-stone cottage, gas central heating, lounge, kitchen/diner, shower and bath. Two twin bedrooms and patio.

open All year
payment Cash, cheques

Unit TV SC DVD General P

CHELTENHAM, Gloucestershire Map ref 2B1

★★★
SELF CATERING

Units 5
Sleeps 2–4

LOW SEASON PER WK
£280.00–£350.00

HIGH SEASON PER WK
£315.00–£430.00

Balcarras Farm Holiday Cottages, Cheltenham

contact Mr & Mrs David & Judith Ballinger, Balcarras Farm, London Road, Charlton Kings, Cheltenham GL52 6UT **t** (01242) 584837 **e** cottage@balcarras-farm.co.uk

balcarras-farm.co.uk

Built in 1992, around three sides of paved courtyard at rear of owners' former farmhouse, these brick-built, single-storey cottages incorporate materials from original stables and cider mill. Footpaths directly onto Cotswold Way.

open All year
payment Credit/debit cards, cash, cheques
nearest shop less than 0.5 miles
nearest pub less than 0.5 miles

Unit TV General P S Leisure

CHELTENHAM, Gloucestershire Map ref 2B1

★★★★
SELF CATERING

Units 3
Sleeps 2–6

LOW SEASON PER WK
Min £250.00

HIGH SEASON PER WK
Max £550.00

Great Coverden, Sandhurst, Nr Cheltenham

contact Mrs Deb Warren, Bengrove Farm, Base Lane, Sandhurst, Nr Cheltenham GL2 9NU
t (01452) 730231 **e** Debs@bengrovefarm.fsnet.co.uk

greatcoverden.com

Located on a farm, these converted barns with oak beams offer a high standard of spacious, well-equipped accommodation. Large gardens with fantastic views, close to many places of interest.

open All year
payment Cash, cheques, euros
nearest shop 3 miles
nearest pub 3 miles

Unit TV DVD General P S Leisure

Using map references

Map references refer to the colour maps at the front of this guide.

CHELTENHAM, Gloucestershire Map ref 2B1

★★★★
SELF CATERING

Units 3
Sleeps 8–10

LOW SEASON PER WK
£200.00–£270.00

HIGH SEASON PER WK
£300.00–£380.00

Holmer Cottages, Cheltenham

contact Mrs Jill Collins, Holmer Cottages, Haines Orchard, Woolstone, Cheltenham GL52 9RG
t (01242) 672848 **e** holmercottages@talk21.com

cottageguide.co.uk/holmercottages

Numbers 1 and 2 are charming, comfortable, rural, Edwardian cottages. Number 3 is a luxurious, independent wing of the owner's house in a peaceful hamlet.

open All year
payment Cash, cheques
nearest shop 1 mile
nearest pub 0.5 miles

Unit TV DVD General P S Leisure

CHELTENHAM, Gloucestershire Map ref 2B1

★★★
SELF CATERING

Units 1
Sleeps 1–4

LOW SEASON PER WK
£250.00–£300.00

HIGH SEASON PER WK
£300.00–£330.00

Short breaks available all year from £150.

Priory Cottage, Southam

contact Mr Ian Mant, Church Gate Southam Lane, Southam, Cheltenham GL52 3NY
t (01242) 584693 **e** iansmant@hotmail.com

countrycottagesonline.net

open All year except Christmas and New Year
payment Cash, cheques
nearest shop 1 mile
nearest pub 1 mile

Old Cotswold-stone cottage in own garden overlooking apple orchard. Cosy and warm in winter with wood-burning stove. Two bedrooms, one double, one twin; sitting room, dining room, modern fitted kitchen. Ideal base for Cheltenham, and Cotswolds Area of Outstanding Natural Beauty. Good walking country including Cotswold Way.

Unit TV DVD General 10 P S

CHIPPENHAM, Wiltshire Map ref 2B2

★★★★
SELF CATERING

Units 2
Sleeps 4–6

LOW SEASON PER WK
£225.00–£300.00

HIGH SEASON PER WK
£350.00–£450.00

Olivemead Farm Holidays, Chippenham

contact Mrs Suzanne Candy, Olivemead Farm, Olivemead Lane, Chippenham SN15 4JQ
t (01666) 510205 **e** enquiries@olivemeadfarmholidays.com

olivemeadfarmholidays.com

open All year
payment Credit/debit cards, cash, cheques
nearest shop 3 miles
nearest pub 3 miles

Imagine two delightful, comfortable, well-equipped cottages on a working farm, converted to offer the luxuries of modern living but retaining traditional features. Bed-settees available for extra guests. Perfectly positioned for days out in Wiltshire, Bath and the Cotswolds. Convenient M4. Brochure available.

Unit TV DVD General P Leisure

Using map references

The map references refer to the colour maps at the front of this guide. The first figure is the map number, the letter and figure that follow indicate the grid reference on the map.

CHIPPING CAMPDEN, Gloucestershire Map ref 2B1

★★★★
SELF CATERING

Units 1
Sleeps 1–4

LOW SEASON PER WK
£250.00–£325.00

HIGH SEASON PER WK
£350.00–£500.00

Cosy Corner, Chipping Campden

contact Mrs Pearl Brandreth, Cosy Corner, Tally Ho Cottage, Dyers Lane, Chipping Campden GL55 6EB **t** (01386) 841752 **e** pearl@mdina03.fsnet.co.uk

noelcourt.co.uk

A beautifully appointed, two-bedroom apartment (one double, one twin) situated in the centre of this historic town. Lounge with vaulted ceiling, fully equipped kitchen, bath with shower. Private parking.

open All year
payment Cash, cheques
nearest shop less than 0.5 miles

Unit TV DVD General P S Leisure

CHIPPING CAMPDEN, Gloucestershire Map ref 2B1

★★★★
SELF CATERING

Units 1
Sleeps 6

LOW SEASON PER WK
Min £550.00

HIGH SEASON PER WK
Max £920.00

Short breaks out of season/close to date – min 3 nights. Other cottages available Chipping Campden/ Broadway area – sleeping 2-6, from £290.

Orchard Cottage, Saintbury

contact Ms Sheila Rolland, Campden Cottages, Folly Cottage, Paxford, Chipping Campden GL55 6XG **t** (01386) 593315 **e** info@campdencottages.co.uk

campdencottages.co.uk

open All year
payment Credit/debit cards, cash, cheques
nearest shop 1 mile
nearest pub 1 mile

16thC Cotswold-stone cottage overlooking beautiful, peaceful countryside. Chipping Campden or Broadway three miles. Many original features including exposed beams, flagstone and wood floors, inglenook fireplace in sitting room (logs supplied), separate dining room, three bedrooms, two bathrooms. Garden, barbecue, parking. We regret no dogs. Prices excl Christmas and New Year. Wireless broadband.

ONLINE MAP

Unit TV DVD General P S Leisure

CHISELBOROUGH, Somerset Map ref 2A3

★★★★
SELF CATERING

Units 1
Sleeps 4

LOW SEASON PER WK
£275.00–£310.00

HIGH SEASON PER WK
£365.00–£490.00

Short breaks available Oct-Mar, min 2 nights. £65pn. Longer breaks negotiable.

One Fair Place, Chiselborough, Stoke-sub-Hamdon

contact Mrs Adrienne Wright, 39 The Avenue, Crowthorne RG45 6PB **t** (01344) 772461 **e** aawright@btopenworld.com

somersetcottageholidays.co.uk

open All year
payment Credit/debit cards, cash, cheques
nearest shop 1.5 miles
nearest pub less than 0.5 miles

Golden hamstone cottage in quiet, picturesque village. Wonderful walks from doorstep in lovely countryside. Many National Trust properties and well-known gardens nearby. Ideal touring area. Two bedrooms and bathroom, including shower. Freshly equipped kitchen overlooks pretty cottage garden. Very comfortable sitting room with log-burning stove. Private parking. Linen provided. Brochure.

ONLINE MAP

Unit TV SC DVD General P S

What if I need to cancel?

It is advisable to check the proprietor's cancellation policy in case you have to change your plans at a later date.

CHRISTCHURCH, Dorset Map ref 2B3

★★★
SELF CATERING

Units 4
Sleeps 2–8

LOW SEASON PER WK
£165.00–£600.00

HIGH SEASON PER WK
£220.00–£1,200.00

The Black House, Hengistbury Head, Mudeford, Bournemouth

contact Mr Andrew Brown, 51 Carbery Avenue, Bournemouth BH6 3LN **t** 07855 280191
e enquiries@theblackhouse.co.uk

theblackhouse.co.uk REAL-TIME BOOKING

open All year
payment Credit/debit cards, cash, cheques
nearest shop 0.5 miles
nearest pub 0.5 miles

Relax and enjoy The Black House holiday apartments. Beautiful location on Mudeford sandspit. One-, two- and three-bedroom apartments available all year. Right on the beach with panoramic views of harbour and sea. At the entrance to Christchurch harbour. Car-free area.

ONLINE MAP

Unit General Leisure

CHRISTCHURCH, Dorset Map ref 2B3

★★★–★★★★
SELF CATERING

Units 2
Sleeps 1–6

LOW SEASON PER WK
Min £200.00

HIGH SEASON PER WK
Min £550.00

The Coach House & The Pines, Mudeford, Christchurch

contact Miss Maggie Rose, Beehive Cottage, Swan Green, Emery Down SO43 7DT **t** 07850 668341
e info@roserentals.co.uk

roserentals.co.uk SPECIAL OFFERS

Two ideal holiday homes suitable for one- to six-person occupancy. Within walking distance of Mudeford Quay, the popular sandy Avon beach and Stampit Marsh. 'Wonderful location – we'll be back!'

open All year
payment Cash, cheques
nearest shop less than 0.5 miles
nearest pub less than 0.5 miles

Unit General P Leisure

CHRISTCHURCH, Dorset Map ref 2B3

★★★
SELF CATERING

Units 8
Sleeps 2–6

LOW SEASON PER WK
£280.00–£405.00

HIGH SEASON PER WK
£570.00–£850.00

Short breaks available Oct-mid-Mar (excl Christmas and New Year). Minimum stay 3 nights.

Riverside Park, Christchurch

contact Mrs Lisa Booth, Riverside Park, Paddlegrade Limited, 28 Willow Way, Christchurch BH23 1JJ
t (01202) 471090 **e** holidays@riversidepark.biz

riversidepark.biz SPECIAL OFFERS

open All year
payment Cash, cheques
nearest shop less than 0.5 miles
nearest pub less than 0.5 miles

Select, individual holiday houses on the River Stour, each with a balcony and patio overlooking private gardens and river. Ample car parking, riverside picnic and barbecue area. Ideally situated for riverside walks, Priory Church, quay, shops, safe sandy beaches, the New Forest, golfing and horse-riding.

ONLINE MAP

Unit General P Leisure

Place index

If you know where you want to stay, the index by place name at the back of the guide will give you the page number listing accommodation in your chosen town, city or village. Check out the other useful indexes too.

CHULMLEIGH, Devon Map ref 1C2

★★★★
SELF CATERING

Units 1
Sleeps 2

LOW SEASON PER WK
Min £238.00

HIGH SEASON PER WK
£246.00–£350.00

Deer Cott, Chulmleigh

contact Mr & Mrs George Simpson, Deer Cott, Middle Garland, Chulmleigh EX18 7DU
t (01769) 580461 **e** enquiries@deercott.co.uk

deercott.co.uk

open All year
payment Cash, cheques
nearest shop 4 miles
nearest pub 3 miles

Discover the peace and beauty of the Devonshire countryside and relax in comfortable accommodation offering every convenience for two at any time of the year. In a park-like setting of 20 acres within the Devon heartland, handy for the moors and shores. Amenities at South Molton/Barnstaple a short drive away.

Unit General P Leisure

CHURCHINFORD, Somerset Map ref 1D2

★★★★
SELF CATERING

Units 2
Sleeps 2–6

LOW SEASON PER WK
£120.00–£250.00

HIGH SEASON PER WK
£250.00–£490.00

South Cleeve Bungalows, Taunton

contact Mrs V D Manning, Churchinford, Taunton TA3 7PR **t** (01823) 601378 & 07811 362740
e enquiries@timbertopbungalows.co.uk

timbertopbungalows.co.uk

open All year
payment Cash, cheques
nearest shop 1 mile
nearest pub 1 mile

Discover all that Somerset has to offer by staying in one of our two bungalows close to the Devon border. Both are set in a rural location within easy reach of attractions and amenities. South Cleeve is equipped to a high standard with a large garden in which to view the wild birds.

Unit General P Leisure

CIRENCESTER, Gloucestershire Map ref 2B1

★★★★
SELF CATERING

Units 5
Sleeps 2–6

LOW SEASON PER WK
£170.00–£275.00

HIGH SEASON PER WK
£245.00–£540.00

Glebe Farm Holiday Lets, Cirencester

contact Mrs Polly Handover, Glebe Farm Holiday Lets, Barnsley Road, Ampney Crucis, Cirencester GL7 5DY **t** (01285) 659226 **e** enquiries@glebefarmcottages.co.uk

glebefarmcottages.co.uk

open All year
payment Cash, cheques
nearest shop 2 miles
nearest pub 1 mile

Very high standard and spacious barn conversions in the centre of the Cotswolds, two miles from Cirencester, one hour from Stratford, Bath and Oxford. Located in the grounds of the owner's house, they are beautifully furnished with antiques and pine, and retain old beams and exposed stone walls.

Unit General P Leisure

CIRENCESTER, Gloucestershire Map ref 2B1

★★★
SELF CATERING

Units 1
Sleeps 2

LOW SEASON PER WK
Min £180.00

HIGH SEASON PER WK
Max £250.00

The Tallet, Preston, Cirencester

contact Mrs Susan Spivey, The Tallet, The Old Farmhouse, Preston, Cirencester GL7 5PR
t (01285) 653405 **e** howard@spiveyfarm.co.uk

An attractive Cotswold-barn conversion on small holding, approached by outside stone steps. Beams in all rooms, which overlook farmland with a small number of livestock. Perfect for touring. Electricity included.

open May to October
payment Cash, cheques, euros
nearest shop 1.5 miles
nearest pub 3 miles

Unit General P

CLEARWELL, Gloucestershire Map ref 2A1

★★★★
SELF CATERING

Units 1
Sleeps 6

LOW SEASON PER WK
£400.00–£450.00

HIGH SEASON PER WK
£450.00–£600.00

Weekend breaks available.

Rosedean Cottage, Clearwell

contact Mrs Andrea Dombrowe, **t** (01483) 538615 **e** clearwell@gmail.com

forestofdeancottage.co.uk GUEST REVIEWS • SPECIAL OFFERS • REAL-TIME BOOKING

open All year
payment Credit/debit cards, cash, cheques, euros
nearest shop 2.5 miles
nearest pub less than 0.5 miles

Beautifully presented three-bedroom detached cottage (master en suite) situated in Wye Valley. Full range of modern appliances. Off-road parking, child-friendly enclosed garden. Lockable garage. Linen and all utilities included. Forest of Dean on doorstep. Walking, cycling, riding, canoeing, Symonds Yat, Tintern, Chepstow, Monmouth, Hay-on-Wye.

ONLINE MAP

Unit General P S Leisure

COLD ASHTON, Gloucestershire Map ref 2B2

★★★★
SELF CATERING

Units 1
Sleeps 10

LOW SEASON PER WK
£2,290.00–£3,230.00

HIGH SEASON PER WK
£3,465.00–£3,805.00

Sayres House, Nr Bath, Chippenham

contact Elaine Molyneux, Dunster Living, Halswell House, Goathurst, Somerset TA5 2DH
t 0845 208 1066 **e** info@dunsterliving.co.uk

sayreshouse.co.uk SPECIAL OFFERS • REAL-TIME BOOKING

Elegant, period Cotswold-stone house with excellent facilities and one acre of beautiful gardens with terrace and barbecue. Three double bedrooms, two triple, Aga, indoor heated swimming pool.

open All year
payment Credit/debit cards, cash, cheques
nearest shop 2 miles
nearest pub 2 miles

Unit General P S
Leisure

What do the star ratings mean?

For a detailed explanation of the quality and facilities represented by the stars, please refer to the information pages at the back of this guide.

COLYTON, Devon Map ref 1D2

★★★★★
SELF CATERING

Units 3
Sleeps 6–20

LOW SEASON PER WK
£325.00–£3,150.00

HIGH SEASON PER WK
£895.00–£5,250.00

Go to website and check online availability and last-minute deals.

Higher Wiscombe, Higher Wiscombe

contact Mr & Mrs Alistair & Lorna Handyside, Higher Wiscombe, Colyton EX24 6JF
t (01404) 871360 **e** alistair@higherwiscombe.com

higherwiscombe.com SPECIAL OFFERS

open All year
payment Credit/debit cards, cheques
nearest shop 4 miles
nearest pub 2 miles

Newly converted high-quality barn conversions with beautiful views near sea. National 'Self-Catering Holiday of the Year' plus five environmental awards. Modern luxury kitchens, crisp white linen, fluffy white towels, most bedrooms en suite. Logburners for winter evenings plus underfloor heating. All have enclosed gardens. Pool in summer.

ONLINE MAP

Unit General
Leisure

COLYTON, Devon Map ref 1D2

★★★★
SELF CATERING

Units 4
Sleeps 2–8

LOW SEASON PER WK
£155.00–£295.00

HIGH SEASON PER WK
£395.00–£725.00

Short breaks or 'Piggy Weekends'. 'Introduction to Pig-Keeping' courses. Monthly rates or longer lets Sep-Mar.

Smallicombe Farm, Colyton

contact Mrs Maggie Todd, Smallicombe Farm, Northleigh, Colyton EX24 6BU **t** (01404) 831310
e maggie_todd@yahoo.com

smallicombe.com SPECIAL OFFERS

open All year
payment Credit/debit cards, cash, cheques
nearest shop less than 0.5 miles
nearest pub 2 miles

Relax in cosy, well-equipped, award-winning converted barns enjoying idyllic rural views. Roam our ancient pastures and woodland, abounding in wildlife, with only the sights and sounds of the countryside. Close to the World Heritage Coastline. Meet our prize-winning Berkshire sows and piglets. Sample our succulent rare-breed pork.

ONLINE MAP

Unit General
Leisure

COMBE MARTIN, Devon Map ref 1C1

★★★★
SELF CATERING

Units 1
Sleeps 2–6

LOW SEASON PER WK
£250.00–£350.00

HIGH SEASON PER WK
£385.00–£550.00

Indicknowle Farm, Combe Martin, Ilfracombe

contact Mrs Susan West, Combe Martin, Long Lane, Ilfracombe EX34 0PA **t** (01271) 883980
e mark.sue@indicknowle.plus.com

indicknowlefarmholidays.co.uk

Delightfully refurbished, centrally heated cottage. Equipped to a high standard, on a small family farm producing cider, meat and honey. Peacefully situated on the edge of Exmoor National Park.

open All year
payment Cash, cheques
nearest shop 2 miles
nearest pub 3 miles

Unit General Leisure

Do you have access needs?

Look for the National Accessible Scheme symbols if you have special hearing, visual or mobility needs. An index of accommodation participating in the scheme can be found at the back of this guide.

CONSTANTINE, Cornwall Map ref 1B3

★★★★
SELF CATERING

Units 1
Sleeps 2–6

LOW SEASON PER WK
£285.00–£345.00

HIGH SEASON PER WK
£585.00–£785.00

Green Bank Cottage, Seworgan, Falmouth

contact Mrs Carole Scobie-Allin, Selective Cornish Retreats, Green Valley, Seworgan, Constantine, Falmouth. Cornwall TR11 5QN **t** (01326) 340147 & 07767 896359
e caroleselectiveretreats@yahoo.com

connexions.co.uk/schr SPECIAL OFFERS

open All year
payment Cash, cheques, euros
nearest shop 2 miles
nearest pub 4 miles

A traditional cottage in a peaceful hamlet, close to the Helford River. Well-equipped with log fire. One double, two twin bedrooms. Private use of spa, sauna and gym. Dogs welcome.

SAT NAV *TR11 5QN* **ONLINE MAP**

Unit General
Leisure

CONSTANTINE BAY, Cornwall Map ref 1B2

★★★
SELF CATERING

Units 3
Sleeps 2–4

LOW SEASON PER WK
£190.00–£220.00

HIGH SEASON PER WK
£380.00–£600.00

The Garden Cottage Holiday Flats, Padstow

contact Mrs Elizabeth Harris, Constantine Bungalow, Constantine Bay, Padstow PL28 8JQ
t (01841) 520262 **e** liz@gardencottageflats.co.uk

gardencottageflats.co.uk

Property surrounded by large garden and field, part of which is car park. Two hundred yards from beach and four miles from Padstow. Adjoins golf course and coastal path.

open March to November
payment Cash, cheques
nearest shop less than 0.5 miles
nearest pub 1 mile

Unit General Leisure

CONSTANTINE BAY, Cornwall Map ref 1B2

★★–★★★★
SELF CATERING

Units 31
Sleeps 2–6

LOW SEASON PER WK
£420.00–£1,211.00

HIGH SEASON PER WK
£840.00–£1,400.00

Trevose Golf & Country Club, Padstow

contact Mr Gammon, Trevose Golf & Country Club, Constantine Bay, Padstow PL28 8JB
t (01841) 520208 **e** info@trevose-gc.co.uk

trevose-gc.co.uk

One of England's most beautiful golf resorts situated on the north Cornish coastline with lovely views and 27 holes of superb golf (plus a short course).

open All year
payment Credit/debit cards, cash, cheques
nearest shop less than 0.5 miles
nearest pub 1.5 miles

Unit General Leisure

CORFE CASTLE, Dorset Map ref 2B3

★★★★
SELF CATERING

Units 3
Sleeps 2–10

LOW SEASON PER WK
£225.00–£400.00

HIGH SEASON PER WK
£650.00–£1,100.00

Scoles Manor, Wareham

contact Peter and Belinda Bell, Scoles Manor, Kingston, Corfe Castle, Wareham BH20 5LG
t (01929) 480312 **e** peter@scoles.co.uk

scoles.co.uk

open All year
payment Cash, cheques
nearest shop 2 miles
nearest pub 0.5 miles

Scoles Manor barns are next to historic Scoles Manor (Grade II Listed) and have been converted into beautifully appointed units. They are in a superb rural setting with 30 acres of meadows and woodlands with spectacular views over Corfe Castle and the Purbeck countryside.

ONLINE MAP

Unit General

COTSWOLDS

See under Bibury, Bourton-on-the-Water, Chedworth, Cheltenham, Chipping Campden, Cirencester, Daglingworth, Dursley, Nympsfield, Slimbridge, Stow-on-the-Wold, Upton St Leonards, Winchcombe
See also Cotswolds in the South East England region

COVERACK, Cornwall Map ref 1B3

★★★★
SELF CATERING

Units 1
Sleeps 1–2

LOW SEASON PER WK
£190.00–£300.00

HIGH SEASON PER WK
£310.00–£400.00

14 Coverack Headland, Helston

contact Mrs Anne Bradley-Smith, Dorland Cottage, The Mint, Church Lane, Bletchingley, Redhill RH1 4LP **t** (01883) 743442

coverack.org.uk

Beautiful two-person apartment. Panoramic sea views. Linen supplied. Digital flat-screen TV, VCR, DVD and tennis court. Gardens lead down to beach below.

open All year
payment Cash, cheques
nearest shop 0.5 miles
nearest pub 0.5 miles

Unit General P Leisure

CRACKINGTON HAVEN, Cornwall Map ref 1C2

★★★★
SELF CATERING

Units 5
Sleeps 2–10

LOW SEASON PER WK
£175.00–£800.00

HIGH SEASON PER WK
£250.00–£1,600.00

Higher Tresmorn, Bude

contact Ms Emma De Haan, Higher Tresmorn - BA034, Thameside, Cottage, Abingdon OX13 5DX
t (01865) 820429 **e** tresmorn@btinternet.com

highertresmorn.co.uk

This lovely medieval farmhouse and three cottages, which stand in an Area of Outstanding Natural Beauty, have delightful views over the coastline to the sea and offer an excellent standard in holiday accommodation.

open All year
payment Credit/debit cards
nearest shop 2 miles
nearest pub 2 miles

Unit General P Leisure

CRANTOCK, Cornwall Map ref 1B2

★★★
SELF CATERING

Units 1
Sleeps 4

LOW SEASON PER WK
£220.00–£395.00

HIGH SEASON PER WK
£440.00–£660.00

Churchtown Cottage, Newquay

contact Mr Millward, Churchtown Cottage, Poorhouse Lane, Crantock, Newquay TR8 5RA
t (01637) 830046 **e** info@crantockcottages.co.uk

crantockcottages.co.uk

Grade II listed cottage right in heart of village. Close to Crantock beach, shops and pubs. Two bedrooms; one with double bed, other with adult bunks. Cosy, comfortable holiday retreat.

open All year
payment Cash, cheques
nearest shop 0.75 miles
nearest pub 0.75 miles

Unit General P

CRANTOCK, Cornwall Map ref 1B2

★★★–★★★★★
SELF CATERING

Units 6
Sleeps 4–8

LOW SEASON PER WK
£189.00–£480.00

HIGH SEASON PER WK
£720.00–£2,000.00

Short breaks Nov-Mar. Christmas and New Year packages.

Crantock Holiday Cottages, Crantock

Cornwall Holiday Cottages, PO Box 24, Truro TR1 9AG **t** 0845 226 5507
e rentals@cornwall-cottages.biz

cornwall-cottages.biz GUEST REVIEWS • SPECIAL OFFERS • REAL-TIME BOOKING

open All year
payment Cash, cheques
nearest shop 1 mile
nearest pub 1 mile

Comfortable cottages, some with spectacular sea views at West Pentire; others are period properties with conservation listing located in the village; all have gardens; some have log burners; some welcome dogs; all are within easy reach of popular Crantock village and beach. Sleeping from two to eight people, all are equipped to a high standard.

ONLINE MAP

Unit General P Leisure

CROYDE, Devon Map ref 1C1

★★★
SELF CATERING

Units 2
Sleeps 2–8

LOW SEASON PER WK
£220.00–£550.00

HIGH SEASON PER WK
£365.00–£860.00

Short breaks available all year except Jul, Aug, Sep and school holidays. £50.00 off for 2 weeks or more.

Denham House & Cottages, North Buckland, Braunton

contact Mr & Mrs Bernard & Vera Sanderberg, Denham House, North Buckland, Braunton EX33 1HY
t (01271) 890297 **e** info@denhamhouse.co.uk

denhamhouse.co.uk

open All year
payment Credit/debit cards, cash, cheques
nearest shop 1 mile
nearest pub 1 mile

Barley cottage sleeps up to eight in four bedrooms and Old Granary sleeps up to four in one bedroom. Both cottages are tastefully decorated and Barley has a woodburner in the living room. The cottages are fully equipped. Facilities include parking, garden, games room and terraces. Pets welcome.

Unit General P Leisure

CULMHEAD, Somerset Map ref 1D2

★★★
SELF CATERING

Units 3
Sleeps 3–6

LOW SEASON PER WK
£200.00–£300.00

HIGH SEASON PER WK
£455.00–£695.00

Culmhead House, Culmhead, Taunton

contact Mr & Mrs Timothy & Susan Rodgers, Culmhead, Taunton TA3 7DU **t** (01823) 421073
e rodgers@culmheadhouse.com

culmheadhouse.com SPECIAL OFFERS

Beautiful Victorian manor house in ten acres of glorious parkland with wooded areas and sleepy corners. Croquet, badminton and a trampoline available or simply relax and unwind. Pets welcome by arrangement.

open All year
payment Credit/debit cards, cash, cheques, euros
nearest shop 4 miles
nearest pub 2.5 miles

Unit General P Leisure

Check the maps for accommodation locations

Colour maps at the front pinpoint all the places where accommodation is featured within the regional sections of this guide. Pick your location and then refer to the place index at the back to find the page number.

DAGLINGWORTH, Gloucestershire Map ref 2B1

★★★★
SELF CATERING

Units 1
Sleeps 2

LOW SEASON PER WK
Min £250.00

HIGH SEASON PER WK
Min £250.00

No high-season charges. Single, flat-rate tariff throughout the year.

Corner Cottage, Cirencester

contact Mrs Mary Bartlett, Brook Cottage, 23 Farm Court, Daglingworth, Cirencester GL7 7AF
t (01285) 653478

open All year
payment Cash, cheques, euros
nearest shop 2 miles
nearest pub 2 miles

Well-equipped, cosy cottage in small village. Excellent centre for exploring the Cotswolds Area of Outstanding Natural Beauty and glorious Gloucestershire. All-inclusive tariff. No hidden extras. All you need provide is food and transport. Allergy-friendly accommodation free from fur, feathers and tobacco smoke.

Unit General P

DARTMEET, Devon Map ref 1C2

★★★
SELF CATERING

Units 1
Sleeps 2–4

LOW SEASON PER WK
£240.00–£315.00

HIGH SEASON PER WK
£330.00–£465.00

Short breaks available in low season.

Coachman's Cottage, Dartmeet

contact Mrs Toni Evans, Hunter's Lodge, Dartmeet, Princetown PL20 6SG **t** (01364) 631173
e huntlodge@pobox.com

dartmeet.com

open All year
payment Credit/debit cards, cash, cheques, euros
nearest shop 4 miles
nearest pub 1 mile

Granite cottage at the meeting of the East and West Darts in the heart of Dartmoor National Park. Fully equipped kitchen/dining room. Large, comfortable lounge and spacious double/twin bedroom. Breathtaking view of the Dart Valley and surrounding tors from bedroom and patio. Immediate access to riverbank, woodland and open moorland.

SAT NAV *PL20 6SG*

Unit General P S Leisure

DARTMOOR

See under Ashburton, Bovey Tracey, Dartmeet, Moretonhampstead, Okehampton, Tavistock

DARTMOUTH, Devon Map ref 1D3

★★★
SELF CATERING

Units 4
Sleeps 2–6

LOW SEASON PER WK
£330.00–£400.00

HIGH SEASON PER WK
£420.00–£725.00

The Old Bakehouse, Dartmouth

contact Mrs Sylvia Ridalls, The Old Bakehouse, 7 Broadstone, Dartmouth TQ6 9NR
t (01803) 834585 **e** gparker@pioneerps.co.uk

oldbakehousedartmouth.co.uk

Four character cottages, with beams and old stone fireplaces. In a conservation area, two minutes from historic town centre and river. Free parking. Beach 15 minutes' drive. Dogs free. Non-smoking.

open All year
payment Credit/debit cards, cash, cheques
nearest shop less than 0.5 miles
nearest pub less than 0.5 miles

Unit General S Leisure

DAWLISH, Devon Map ref 1D2

★★★★
SELF CATERING

Units 4
Sleeps 4–6

LOW SEASON PER WK
£305.00–£349.00

HIGH SEASON PER WK
£740.00–£799.00

Short breaks early and late season. 3- or 4-night breaks at most times. Free coarse fishing Nov-Mar.

Cofton Country Cottage Holidays, Dawlish

contact Mrs Valerie Jeffery, Cofton Country Cottage Holidays, Cofton, Starcross, Exeter EX6 8RP
t (01626) 890111 **e** info@coftonholidays.co.uk

coftonholidays.co.uk SPECIAL OFFERS

open All year
payment Credit/debit cards, cash, cheques
nearest shop less than 0.5 miles
nearest pub less than 0.5 miles

On the edge of privately owned Cofton Country Holiday Park, converted 100-year-old farm buildings overlooked by ancient Cofton church. Coarse-fishing lakes. Woodland walks. Within a short drive of the Exe Estuary and Dawlish Warren. All amenities of the park available during season, including swimming pool and pub.

ONLINE MAP

Unit TV DVD General P S Leisure

DAWLISH, Devon Map ref 1D2

★★★★★
SELF CATERING

Units 1
Sleeps 4

LOW SEASON PER WK
£450.00–£550.00

HIGH SEASON PER WK
£650.00–£850.00

Great Cliff Luxury Apartment, Dawlish

contact Mr Roger Smith, 7 Lavington View, Bridgnorth WV15 6BJ **t** (01746) 769301
e rsmith@greatcliff.co.uk

greatcliff.co.uk

Great Cliff is an attractive two-bedroom luxury self-catering apartment located on the seafront in Dawlish, with spectacular views.

open All year
payment Cash, cheques
nearest shop less than 0.5 miles
nearest pub less than 0.5 miles

Unit TV DVD General P S Leisure

DAWLISH WARREN, Devon Map ref 1D2

★★★★
SELF CATERING

Units 13
Sleeps 4–6

LOW SEASON PER WK
£305.00–£349.00

HIGH SEASON PER WK
£725.00–£840.00

Short breaks early and late season. 3- or 4-night breaks at most times. Free coarse fishing Nov-Mar.

Eastdon Estate, Dawlish Warren

contact Mrs Valerie Jeffery, Cofton Country Holidays, Cofton, Starcross, Exeter EX6 8RP
t (01626) 890111 **e** info@coftonholidays.co.uk

coftonholidays.co.uk SPECIAL OFFERS

open All year
payment Credit/debit cards, cash, cheques
nearest shop 0.5 miles
nearest pub 1 mile

Luxury apartments in magnificent 18thC house and cleverly restored stable block. Also estate workers' cottage conversions at Woodside. Spectacular Exe Estuary views, surrounded by fields and 50 acres of unspoilt woodland. Quiet and restful holidays in a perfect setting. Amenities at Cofton in season.

ONLINE MAP

Unit TV DVD General P S Leisure

Where can I get help and advice?

Tourist Information Centres offer friendly help with accommodation and holiday ideas as well as suggestions of places to visit and things to do. You'll find contact details at the beginning of each regional section.

DEERHURST, Gloucestershire Map ref 2B1

★★★★
SELF CATERING

Units 2
Sleeps 2–4

LOW SEASON PER WK
Min £200.00

HIGH SEASON PER WK
Max £465.00

Short breaks available Nov-Mar (excl Christmas and New Year), min 3-night stay.

Deerhurst Cottages, Deerhurst, Tewkesbury

contact Mrs Nicole Samuel, Deerhurst Cottages, Abbots Court Farm, Deerhurst, Tewkesbury GL19 4BX **t** (01684) 275845 **e** enquiries@deerhurstcottages.co.uk

deerhurstcottages.co.uk GUEST REVIEWS

open All year
payment Credit/debit cards, cash, cheques
nearest shop 3 miles
nearest pub 1.5 miles

Deerhurst Cottages are situated on our working dairy farm, on the banks of the River Severn in the quiet village of Deerhurst. Both cottages offer comfortable, spacious and well-equipped holiday accommodation. The perfect base for exploring the Cotswolds, the Forest of Dean and the Malvern Hills.

Unit General P Leisure

DELABOLE, Cornwall Map ref 1B2

★
SELF CATERING

Units 6
Sleeps 6

LOW SEASON PER WK
£180.00–£280.00

HIGH SEASON PER WK
£320.00–£408.00

Delamere Holiday Bungalows, Delabole

contact Mrs Snowden, **t** (01895) 234144

delamerebungalows.com SPECIAL OFFERS

Traditional bungalows in lawned setting. Ideal location, panoramic country views. Sleep four – occasional five/six. Close sandy beaches. Suitable all tastes – spring/summer breaks, family holidays, exploring, surfing. No dogs.

open March to November
payment Cash, cheques
nearest shop less than 0.5 miles
nearest pub less than 0.5 miles

Unit General P S Leisure

DEVIZES, Wiltshire Map ref 2B2

★★★★
SELF CATERING

Units 1
Sleeps 6

LOW SEASON PER WK
£450.00–£525.00

HIGH SEASON PER WK
£550.00–£625.00

Fourbee, Devizes

contact Mr & Mrs Bernard & Susan Foreman, Rushley Mount, 50 High Street, Littleton Panell, Devizes SN10 4ES **t** (01380) 816919 **e** fourbeecontact@aol.com

fourbee.biz

High-quality converted self-catering accommodation in charming market town of Devizes. Ideally situated for all West Country attractions. Sleeps six en suite. Cot and highchair available. Highly recommended.

open All year
payment Cash, cheques, euros
nearest shop less than 0.5 miles
nearest pub less than 0.5 miles

Unit General P S Leisure

Country Code always follow the Country Code

- Be safe – plan ahead and follow any signs
- Leave gates and property as you find them
- Protect plants and animals, and take your litter home
- Keep dogs under close control
- Consider other people

For **key to symbols** see page 7

DEVIZES, Wiltshire Map ref 2B2

★★★★
SELF CATERING

Units 1
Sleeps 1–5

LOW SEASON PER WK
£365.00–£435.00

HIGH SEASON PER WK
£495.00–£595.00

Owls Cottage, Devizes

contact Mrs Gill Whittome, 48 White Street, Easterton, Devizes SN10 4PA **t** (01380) 818804
e gill@owls-cottage.com

owls-cottage.com

open All year
payment Credit/debit cards, cash, cheques
nearest shop 1 mile
nearest pub less than 0.5 miles

Really comfortable cottage, tastefully furnished to a high standard. Situated in private and spacious location, with outstanding downland views. Village shops and good pub within easy walking distance. Good access to White Horse/Ridgeway cycleway. Convenient Longleat, Bath, Stonehenge. Fully inclusive. A really special place to stay. Winter breaks. Brochure.

ONLINE MAP

Unit TV DVD General P S Leisure

DORCHESTER, Dorset Map ref 2B3

★★★
SELF CATERING

Units 1
Sleeps 4

HIGH SEASON PER WK
£301.00–£679.00

Wolfeton Lodge, Dorchester

contact Mrs Thimbleby, Wolfeton House, Wolfeton, Dorchester DT2 9QN **t** (01305) 263500
e kthimbleby.wolfeton@gmail.com

Idyllic lodge beside River Frome, in water meadows below historic Wolfeton House. A c1820 core with large conservatory for sitting and dining. Own garden. Sleeps four plus child.

open May to October
payment Cash, cheques
nearest shop 1 mile
nearest pub 1.5 miles

Unit TV General 8 P Leisure

DRIFFIELD, Gloucestershire Map ref 2B1

★★★★
SELF CATERING

Units 1
Sleeps 1–4

LOW SEASON PER WK
£250.00

HIGH SEASON PER WK
£350.00

The Stables, Cirencester

contact Mrs Margaret Smith, The Grange, Driffield, Cirencester GL7 5PY **t** (01285) 850641
e me_smith@btinternet.com

This spacious stable conversion is situated in a quiet, rural village, yet only five miles from Cirencester and two miles from Cotswold Water Park. Furnished to a high standard and immaculately maintained with sofa bed in lounge. Owners live opposite property. No pets.

open All year except Christmas and New Year
payment Cash, cheques
nearest shop 4 miles
nearest pub 2 miles

Unit TV DVD General P Leisure

DULVERTON, Somerset Map ref 1D1

★★★
SELF CATERING

Units 1
Sleeps 4

LOW SEASON PER WK
£236.00–£303.00

HIGH SEASON PER WK
£399.00–£504.00

Short breaks available. Fri-Mon and Mon-Fri (others by arrangement).

Paddons, Dulverton

contact Mrs Mary McMichael, Paddons, Northmoor Road, Dulverton TA22 9PW **t** (01398) 323514
e marymcmichael@waitrose.com

open All year
payment Cash, cheques, euros
nearest shop 0.5 miles
nearest pub 0.75 miles

A comfortable, newly decorated, fully equipped wing of owner's 300-year-old house comprising entrance/dining hall, sitting-room and kitchen recess, one double bedroom, one twin bedroom with river views. 0.25 miles private fishing, 12 acres private woods, pleasant garden, lovely outside sitting and barbecue areas, south facing, sun all day.

Unit TV SC DVD General P S Leisure

DURSLEY, Gloucestershire Map ref 2B2

★★★
SELF CATERING

Units 1
Sleeps 1–4

LOW SEASON PER WK
£198.00–£246.00

HIGH SEASON PER WK
£246.00–£276.00

Reduced rate out-of-season and late-availability short breaks accepted (excl Christmas and New Year).

Two Springbank, Dursley

contact Mrs Freda Jones, 32 Everlands, Cam, Dursley GL11 5NL **t** (01453) 543047
e lhandfaj32lg@surefish.co.uk

open All year
payment Cash, cheques
nearest shop 0.75 miles
nearest pub 0.75 miles

Very well-equipped and comfortable mid-terraced cottage with two bedrooms, bath and shower. Pleasant rural location near village church and open fields to rear with footpaths to nearby Cotswold Way. Within easy reach of Slimbridge WWT, Westonbirt Arboretum and Gloucestershire's many other attractions. Fully illustrated brochure available by post or email.

SAT NAV *GL11 5PD*

Unit General P Leisure

EAST LOOE, Cornwall Map ref 1C2

★★★★–★★★★★
SELF CATERING

Units 10
Sleeps 2–6

LOW SEASON PER WK
£195.00–£375.00

HIGH SEASON PER WK
£595.00–£1,500.00

Out-of-season short breaks (midweek or long weekends).

Fox Valley Cottages, Looe

contact Mr & Mrs Andy & Linda Brown, Lanlawren, Trenewan, Looe PL13 2PZ **t** (01726) 870115
e info@foxvalleycottages.co.uk

foxvalleycottages.co.uk SPECIAL OFFERS

open All year
payment Credit/debit cards, cash, cheques
nearest shop 3 miles
nearest pub 3 miles

The cottages are set in beautiful countryside – an idyllic location for your holiday in Cornwall. Indoor heated pool, spa, sauna, solarium, games room. Open fires in most of the cottages for those cosy or romantic nights in winter. Dishwashers in large cottages.

Unit General Leisure

EDMONTON, Cornwall Map ref 1B2

★★★
SELF CATERING

Units 2
Sleeps 1–4

LOW SEASON PER WK
£200.00–£350.00

HIGH SEASON PER WK
£400.00–£550.00

Quarryman's Cottages, Nr Wadebridge

contact Mr Huw Jenkins, Criafol, 17 Granville Terrace, Mountain Ash CF45 4AL **t** 07866 386611
e jenkins@choicecornishcottages.com

choicecornishcottages.com

open All year
payment Cash, cheques
nearest shop 0.5 miles
nearest pub less than 0.5 miles

These tastefully decorated cosy cottages are situated overlooking the Camel Estuary. Originally the homes of 19thC slate quarrymen, they are positioned around a stone-flagged courtyard and adjacent to a traditional Cornish inn. Twenty-minute drive from Padstow's pretty harbour and sandy beaches.

Unit General P Leisure

EXETER, Devon Map ref 1D2

★★★★
SELF CATERING

Units 7
Sleeps 6–7

LOW SEASON PER WK
£280.00–£480.00

HIGH SEASON PER WK
£400.00–£875.00

3-night stays available. Low season discounts for 1 or 2 people. Pets welcome.

Bussells Farm Cottages, Exeter

contact Andy and Lucy Hines, Bussells Farm, Huxham, Nr Stoke Canon, Exeter EX5 4EN
t (01392) 841238 **e** bussellsfarm@aol.com

bussellsfarm.co.uk SPECIAL OFFERS

open All year
payment Credit/debit cards, cash, cheques
nearest shop 1 mile
nearest pub 1 mile

Lovely barn-conversion cottages, heated outdoor swimming pool from May to September, adventure playground, well-equipped games room and excellent coarse fishing in the private lakes. We offer a wonderful base from which to explore the beautiful Exe Valley, Dartmoor, the South Devon beaches and the ancient city of Exeter.

Unit General P S
Leisure

EXETER, Devon Map ref 1D2

★★★★★
SELF CATERING

Units 1
Sleeps 4

LOW SEASON PER WK
£200.00–£380.00

HIGH SEASON PER WK
£420.00–£540.00

Coach House Farm, Exeter

contact Mr & Miss John & Polly Bale, Coach House Farm, Moor Lane, Broadclyst, Exeter EX5 3JH
t (01392) 461254 **e** selfcatering@mpprops.co.uk

open All year
payment Credit/debit cards, cash, cheques, euros
nearest shop 1 mile
nearest pub 1 mile

Surrounded by the National Trust Killerton estate, the converted stables of our Victorian coach house provide comfortable ground-floor accommodation (no steps) with private entrance and garden overlooking sheep meadows. Working arable and sheep farm. Spectacular East Devon coastline, Exmoor, Dartmoor and Exeter are easily reached. Internet access.

Unit General P

EXETER, Devon Map ref 1D2

★★★
SELF CATERING

Units 1
Sleeps 1–5

LOW SEASON PER WK
Min £260.00

HIGH SEASON PER WK
Max £525.00

Exeter Holiday Homes, Exeter

contact Mrs Gina Belcher, Exeter Holiday Homes, Southbrook Lodge, London Road, Whimple, Exeter EX5 2PQ **t** (01404) 823805 **e** gina.birchmore@btopenworld.com

exeter-holiday-homes.co.uk

Three-bedroom link house (1972): lounge, kitchen/diner, bathroom, gas central heating, paved gardens. Close to local shops, hospital and city centre. Complimentary Wi-Fi.

open All year
payment Cash, cheques
nearest shop 0.5 miles
nearest pub 0.5 miles

Unit General

It's all quality-assessed accommodation

Our commitment to quality involves wide-ranging accommodation assessment. Ratings and awards were correct at the time of going to press but may change following a new assessment. Please check at time of booking.

EXETER, Devon Map ref 1D2

★★★★ SELF CATERING

Units 1
Sleeps 6

LOW SEASON PER WK
Min £350.00

HIGH SEASON PER WK
Max £550.00

Honeysuckle End, Exeter

contact Mr & Mrs Ayre, Honeysuckle End, Ratcliffe Farm, Thorverton, Exeter EX5 5PN
t (01392) 860434 **e** ayre.ratcliffe@virgin.net

honeysuckle-end-exeter.co.uk

Thatched farmhouse, spacious and comfortable, full of original features. One mile from pretty cobbled village in Exe Valley. Central for West Country coasts and moors.

open All year
payment Cash, cheques
nearest shop 2 miles
nearest pub 1 mile

Unit General Leisure

EXFORD, Somerset Map ref 1D1

★★★ SELF CATERING

Units 1
Sleeps 6

LOW SEASON PER WK
Max £305.00

HIGH SEASON PER WK
Max £405.00

No 2 Auction Field Cottage, Exford

contact Mr & Mrs Keith & Gill Batchelor, Bulbarrow Farm, Bulbarrow, Blandford Forum DT11 0HQ
t (01258) 817801

Available all year. Short walk from village. Superb woodland and moorland walking. Very well equipped, comfortable and relaxing. An ideal base for exploring Exmoor.

open All year
payment Cash, cheques
nearest shop less than 0.5 miles
nearest pub less than 0.5 miles

Unit General P Leisure

EXFORD, Somerset Map ref 1D1

★★★ SELF CATERING

Units 1
Sleeps 4

LOW SEASON PER WK
£185.00–£280.00

HIGH SEASON PER WK
£285.00–£375.00

Holly Tree Cottage, Exford, Nr Minehead

contact Mr Chris Budd, No 1 Verandah Cottages, Newton Lane, Newton Valence, Alton GU34 3RQ
t (01420) 588577

Delightful cottage in peaceful village of Exford. Superb countryside for walking and scenic moorland views. Local inns, stores 100m.

open All year
payment Cash, cheques
nearest shop less than 0.5 miles
nearest pub less than 0.5 miles

Unit General P Leisure

EXMOOR

See under Brayford, Combe Martin, Dulverton, Exford, Luxborough, Lynton, Minehead, North Molton, Porlock, Simonsbath

FALMOUTH, Cornwall Map ref 1B3

★★★★ SELF CATERING

Units 1
Sleeps 2–4

LOW SEASON PER WK
£139.00–£255.00

HIGH SEASON PER WK
£380.00–£640.00

Country Cottage Retreats, Falmouth, Helston

contact Ralph & Ann Bailey, Country Cottage Retreats, Viscar Farm, Medlyn Moor, Helston TR13 0LF
t (01326) 340897 **e** biscarhols@amserve.net

viscarfarm-cottages.co.uk

Character cottage, recently refurnished. Stone-walled, beamed ceilings, slate floors, inglenook fireplace, brass bedsteads, furnished to high standard. Countryside location, easy reach of beaches, towns and attractions.

open All year
payment Credit/debit cards, cash, cheques
nearest shop 1.25 miles
nearest pub 1.25 miles

Unit General P Leisure

Remember to check when booking

Please remember that all information in this guide has been supplied by the proprietors well in advance of publication. Since changes do sometimes occur it's a good idea to check details at the time of booking.

FALMOUTH, Cornwall Map ref 1B3

★★★-★★★★★
SELF CATERING

Units 3
Sleeps 4–6

LOW SEASON PER WK
£500.00–£700.00

HIGH SEASON PER WK
£700.00–£950.00

Falmouth Beach Resort Apartments, Falmouth

Falmouth Beach Resort Apartments, Gyllyngvase Beach, Falmouth TR11 4NA **t** (01326) 310500
e info@falmouthbeachhotel.co.uk

bw-falmouthbeachhotel.co.uk

Self-catering units with sea views, private terraces and car parking, located adjacent to the hotel. Full use of hotel facilities, including restaurant, bar and leisure club.

open All year
payment Credit/debit cards, cash, cheques
nearest shop 0.5 miles
nearest pub 0.5 miles

Unit General P
Leisure

FALMOUTH, Cornwall Map ref 1B3

★★★
SELF CATERING

Units 6
Sleeps 2–5

LOW SEASON PER WK
£235.00–£400.00

HIGH SEASON PER WK
£425.00–£490.00

Three-day plus short breaks available out of season.

Good-Winds Holiday Apartments, Falmouth

contact Mrs Goodwin, Good-Winds Holiday Apartments, 13 Stratton Terracce, Falmouth TR11 2SY
t (01326) 313200 **e** alandnancy@goodwind64.orangehome.co.uk

open All year
payment Cash, cheques, euros
nearest shop 0.5 miles
nearest pub 0.75 miles

Modern, two-bedroom apartments with balconies having marvellous views over the harbour, River Pen and the quaint fishing village of Flushing. Under-cover parking for two cars. Walking distance to town. One double bed, two singles and extra single in three units.

Unit General P

FALMOUTH, Cornwall Map ref 1B3

★★★
SELF CATERING

Units 1
Sleeps 1–4

LOW SEASON PER WK
£140.00–£160.00

HIGH SEASON PER WK
£180.00–£340.00

Little Astra, Falmouth

contact Mrs M Welch, Wellington Terrace, Falmouth TR11 3BL **t** (01326) 319580

Ground-floor self-contained apartment with large patio and garden. Panoramic views. Close to amenities, gas, electricity and linen all included.

open All year
payment Cash, cheques
nearest shop less than 0.5 miles
nearest pub less than 0.5 miles

Unit General P

Where is my pet welcome?

Some proprietors welcome well-behaved pets. Look for the symbol in the accommodation listings.

You can also buy a copy of our popular guide – Pets Come Too! – available from good bookshops and online at visitbritaindirect.com.

FALMOUTH, Cornwall Map ref 1B3

★★★★
SELF CATERING

Units **8**
Sleeps **2–8**

LOW SEASON PER WK
£285.00–£385.00

HIGH SEASON PER WK
£760.00–£1,300.00

Short breaks available mid-September to mid-July excluding half terms and Bank Holidays. Special breaks periodically available as advertised on website.

Mylor Yacht Harbour, Falmouth

contact Miss Celeste Gagnon, Mylor Yacht Harbour, Mylor Churchtown, Penryn TR11 5UF
t (01326) 372121 **e** celeste@mylor.com

mylorharbourside.com GUEST REVIEWS · SPECIAL OFFERS

open All year
payment Credit/debit cards, cash, cheques
nearest shop 3 miles
nearest pub less than 0.5 miles

Cornwall Tourism Awards 2007 – Self Catering Establishment of the Year – Bronze Award. Award-winning harbourside cottage and apartments with unrivalled harbour facilities (restaurants, boat hire, sailing schools, marina, coast walks), private outdoor areas for each accommodation. Singles, couples, families, pets welcome. Ground-floor accessible apartment. Beautiful coastal location.

SAT NAV *TR11 5UF* **ONLINE MAP**

Unit General Leisure

FERNDOWN, Dorset Map ref 2B3

★★★★
SELF CATERING

Units **1**
Sleeps **1–8**

LOW SEASON PER WK
£415.00–£540.00

HIGH SEASON PER WK
£570.00–£1,170.00

Weekend breaks available during low seasons. Special activity weekends for golfers, etc. Fully-catered group bookings.

WALKERS WELCOME · CYCLISTS WELCOME

Birchcroft, Ferndown

contact Miss Leanne Hemingway, Dorset Cottage Holidays, 11 Tyneham Close, Sandford, Wareham BH20 7BE **t** (01929) 553443 **e** enq@dhcottages.co.uk

dhcottages.co.uk GUEST REVIEWS · SPECIAL OFFERS

open All year
payment Credit/debit cards, cash, cheques
nearest shop 0.5 miles
nearest pub 0.5 miles

A nature lover's secret hideaway, Birchcroft is surrounded by rhododendron bushes in over an acre of land. With accessible accommodation, it's large enough for two families. Terrace enjoys breathtaking local views. Deer, foxes, rabbits, and birds are often seen. Only five miles from Bournemouth beaches. Great for walkers and golfers.

SAT NAV *BH22* **ONLINE MAP**

Unit General P Leisure

FERNDOWN, Dorset Map ref 2B3

★★★
SELF CATERING

Units **1**
Sleeps **1–5**

LOW SEASON PER WK
£230.00–£305.00

HIGH SEASON PER WK
£345.00–£405.00

The Bungalow, West Moors, Ferndown

contact Mrs Annette Leach, The Bungalow, c/o 22 West Drive, Sutton SM2 7NA **t** (020) 8241 7498 & 07958 209493 **e** annette.leach@blueyonder.co.uk

geocities.com/bournemouth3/

Very attractive detached bungalow, sleeping five. Well decorated and furnished. Lies approximately five and a half miles from New Forest and seven miles from Bournemouth beach.

open May to September
payment Cash, cheques
nearest shop 1 mile
nearest pub 1 mile

Unit General P

Has every property been assessed?

All accommodation in this guide has been rated for quality, or is awaiting assessment, by a professional national tourist board assessor.

FIFEHEAD MAGDALEN, Dorset Map ref 2B3

★★
SELF CATERING

Units **4**
Sleeps **4–10**

LOW SEASON PER WK
£250.00–£500.00

HIGH SEASON PER WK
£400.00–£800.00

Middle Farm Holiday Cottages, Gillingham

contact Mrs Denise Trevor, Middle Farm, Fifehead Magdalen, Gillingham SP8 5RR **t** (01258) 820163
e trevorsmiddlefm@aol.com

middlefarmcottages-dorset.com

Recently converted, spacious character cottages, around courtyard on working family farm, bordering river and woodland. All have private parking, one bedroom on ground level and access to children's play area.

open All year
payment Cash, cheques
nearest shop 2 miles
nearest pub 3 miles

Unit TV General P S Leisure

FILLEIGH, Devon Map ref 1C1

★★
SELF CATERING

Units **1**
Sleeps **11**

LOW SEASON PER WK
£250.00–£400.00

HIGH SEASON PER WK
£500.00–£650.00

Buckingham's Leary, Barnstaple

contact Mrs Ann Bulled, Buckinghams Leary, Barnstaple EX32 0SB **t** (01598) 760204

Family-run working dairy farm. Accommodation has three bedrooms, one en suite, separate bathroom and toilet. Woodburner.

open All year
payment Cash, cheques
nearest shop 6 miles
nearest pub 2.5 miles

Unit TV DVD General S Leisure

FOREST OF DEAN

See under Clearwell, Lydney, Mitcheldean, Newland, Newnham, Yorkley

FOWEY, Cornwall Map ref 1B3

★★★★★
SELF CATERING

Units **1**
Sleeps **4**

LOW SEASON PER WK
£515.00–£751.00

HIGH SEASON PER WK
£802.00–£1,254.00

See website for prices. Weekly lettings. Saturday change-over.

Dolphins at Penlee, Fowey

contact Mr Gittus, Dolphins at Penlee, 4 Snuff Mill Walk, Bewdley DY12 2HG **t** (01299) 400447
e john.gittus@btopenworld.com

qualityholidaylets.com

open All year
payment Cash, cheques, euros
nearest shop 0.5 miles
nearest pub 0.5 miles

Exceptionally spacious first-floor apartment in a prime position. Stunning views, easy access to town, beach, cliff walks. Excellent standard of accommodation and the enviable benefit of a private parking space opposite. Readymoney Beach, which inspired Daphne Du Maurier to write Fisherman's Creek, 200yds. Pay phone provided.

Unit TV SC DVD General 5 P Leisure

FOWEY, Cornwall Map ref 1B3

★★★★
SELF CATERING

Units **1**
Sleeps **1–6**

LOW SEASON PER WK
£330.00–£350.00

HIGH SEASON PER WK
£360.00–£990.00

Duchy Cottage, Fowey

contact Mrs T J Round, 4 Diddenham Cottages, Lambwood Hill, Grazeley RG7 1JT
t (0118) 988 4256 **e** tracy@duchycottage.com

duchycottage.com SPECIAL OFFERS

A delightful Cornish cottage, well equipped for a relaxing holiday. Sleeps six, with three double bedrooms, open-plan kitchen/dining room. Just a few minutes' walk from the quay.

open All year
payment Cash, cheques
nearest shop less than 0.5 miles
nearest pub less than 0.5 miles

Unit TV SC DVD General

Where are the maps?

Colour maps can be found at the front of the guide. They pinpoint the location of all accommodation found in the regional sections.

FROME, Somerset Map ref 2B2

★★★★
SELF CATERING

Units 1
Sleeps 8

LOW SEASON PER WK
£305.00–£325.00

HIGH SEASON PER WK
£400.00–£555.00

Mill Cottage, Blatchbridge, Frome

contact Mrs Thelma Morris, Mill Cottage, Blatchbridge Mill, Frome BA11 5EJ **t** (01373) 464784

Mill Cottage is a recently-converted stable block, taking up to eight people. Situated along a private drive, overlooking open fields.

open All year
payment Cash, cheques
nearest shop 1 mile
nearest pub less than 0.5 miles

Unit General Leisure

GILLINGHAM, Dorset Map ref 2B3

★★★★
SELF CATERING

Units 1
Sleeps 2

LOW SEASON PER WK
£185.00–£195.00

HIGH SEASON PER WK
£230.00–£330.00

Woolfields Barn, Milton on Stour, Gillingham

contact Mr & Mrs Thomas, Woolfields Barn, Woolfields Farm, Milton on Stour, Gillingham SP8 5PX **t** (01747) 824729 **e** info@woolfieldsbarn.co.uk

woolfieldsbarn.co.uk

Extremely comfortable barn conversion (sleeps two), well equipped with all essentials for a peaceful and enjoyable stay in a lovely rural village. All quality linen provided. One dog welcome.

open All year except Christmas
payment Cash, cheques, euros
nearest shop 0.5 miles
nearest pub 1 mile

Unit General Leisure

GLASTONBURY, Somerset Map ref 2A2

★★★
SELF CATERING

Units 1
Sleeps 6

LOW SEASON PER WK
£180.00–£200.00

HIGH SEASON PER WK
£200.00–£450.00

Catcott Burtle Farm Cottage, Burtle, Bridgwater

contact Mrs Rosemary Tucker, Westhay Road, Burtle, Bridgwater TA7 8NE **t** (01278) 722321 **e** rosemary.tucker@virgin.net

open All year
payment Cash, cheques
nearest shop 2 miles
nearest pub less than 0.5 miles

Working farm set in small village location on Somerset Levels. The farm is between Glastonbury and Burnham-on-Sea and is ideally situated for visiting the area; sleeps six comfortably. Fishermen, birdwatchers and golfers are well catered for within the area. Within easy reach of Wells, Bath, Bristol and Taunton.

Unit General Leisure

For **key to symbols** see page 7

GLASTONBURY, Somerset Map ref 2A2

★★★
SELF CATERING

Units 8
Sleeps 2–6

LOW SEASON PER WK
£240.00–£325.00

HIGH SEASON PER WK
£475.00–£830.00

Short breaks and B&B available.

MapleLeaf Middlewick Holiday Cottages, Wick, Glastonbury

contact Ms Amanda I'Ons, Middlewick Holiday Cottages, Wick Lane, Glastonbury BA6 8JW
t (01458) 832351 **e** middlewick@btconnect.com

middlewickholidaycottages.co.uk REAL-TIME BOOKING

open All year
payment Credit/debit cards, cash, cheques
nearest shop 1.6 miles
nearest pub 2 miles

The cottages within this Grade II Listed farmstead have been restored to provide comfortable, well-equipped accommodation. Walk to Glastonbury Tor from the back door, explore the region, relax in the heated indoor swimming pool, try out the steam room or have a massage in our treatment room. Wi-Fi Internet access.

SAT NAV *BA6 8JW*

Unit General Leisure

GOONHAVERN, Cornwall Map ref 1B2

★★★
SELF CATERING

Units 5
Sleeps 5–6

LOW SEASON PER WK
£400.00–£650.00

HIGH SEASON PER WK
£650.00–£1,050.00

FAMILIES WELCOME PETS! WELCOME

Greenmeadow, Perranporth

contact Mr Ian Bodie, Green Meadow Cottages, Bridge Road, Truro TR4 9NN **t** (01872) 540483
e ianbodie@aol.com

Five cottages in a tree-lined meadow offering a quiet and relaxing environment with open beams and log fires in winter.

open All year
payment Cash, cheques, euros
nearest shop 0.5 miles
nearest pub 0.5 miles

Unit General

GORRAN HAVEN, Cornwall Map ref 1B3

★★★
SELF CATERING

Units 1
Sleeps 2–4

LOW SEASON PER WK
£200.00–£350.00

HIGH SEASON PER WK
£380.00–£540.00

Long weekends/ midweek breaks offered out of season in Nov, Feb and Mar.

Oakroyd, Gorran Haven

contact Mrs Helena Payne, Trevell, 7 Trelispen Park, St Austell PL26 6HT **t** (01726) 842546
e hrjpayne@tiscali.co.uk

open All year except Christmas and New Year
payment Cash, cheques
nearest shop less than 0.5 miles
nearest pub 0.5 miles

Comfortably furnished bungalow in quiet Cornish coastal village. Sleeps four. Ample parking. Large garden with patio. Safe, sandy beaches, harbour and shops just 150yds. South West Coast Path runs through village. Close to Heligan, Caerhays and the Eden Project. Ideal for beach holidays, walking, exploring or just pure relaxation.

Unit General Leisure

CYCLISTS WELCOME CYCLISTS WELCOME

Fancy a cycling holiday?

For a fabulous freewheeling break, seek out accommodation participating in our Cyclists Welcome scheme. Look out for the symbol and plan your route online at nationalcyclenetwork.org.

GREAT TORRINGTON, Devon Map ref 1C2

★★★★
SELF CATERING

Units 3
Sleeps 2–6

LOW SEASON PER WK
£185.00–£360.00

HIGH SEASON PER WK
£470.00–£860.00

Cloister Park Cottages, Frithelstock, Torrington

contact Mrs Melanie Goldman, Cloister Park Cottages, Cloister Park, Frithelstock, Torrington EX38 8JH **t** (01805) 622518 **e** info@cloisterpark.co.uk

cloisterpark.co.uk GUEST REVIEWS

Three cottages, all recently renovated to a high standard, set in the grounds of Cloister Park, a lovely 17thC Grade II Listed house and former vicarage surrounded by a large garden.

open All year
payment Credit/debit cards, cash, cheques
nearest shop 1.5 miles
nearest pub less than 0.5 miles

Unit General P Leisure

GREAT TORRINGTON, Devon Map ref 1C2

★★★
SELF CATERING

Units 4
Sleeps 4–6

LOW SEASON PER WK
£260.00–£310.00

HIGH SEASON PER WK
£390.00–£600.00

Stowford Lodge, Torrington

contact Mr & Mrs R Jones, Stowford Lodge, Langtree, Torrington EX38 8NU **t** (01805) 601540 **e** enq@stowfordlodge.co.uk

stowfordlodge.co.uk

Delightful stone cottages converted from Victorian farm buildings, set in six acres. Heated indoor pool. Safe and peaceful setting. Children's play area. Dogs welcome.

open All year
payment Credit/debit cards, cash, cheques
nearest shop 3 miles
nearest pub 3 miles

Unit General P Leisure

HELSTON, Cornwall Map ref 1B3

★★★
SELF CATERING

Units 2
Sleeps 1–4

LOW SEASON PER WK
£250.00–400.00

HIGH SEASON PER WK
£400.00–£490.00

Barnhaven Cottages, Polladras, Helston

contact Mrs Chris & Sue Chapman, Mary Barn, Polladras, Breage TR13 9NS **t** (01736) 763230 **e** sue@barnhaven.org

barnhaven.org

Two comfortable self-catering cottages, each sleeps four, in quiet countryside with attractive garden. Three miles south coast, seven to north, great for dog walks and beach life.

open All year
payment Cash, cheques, euros
nearest shop 1.5 miles
nearest pub 1.5 miles

Unit General P Leisure

HELSTON, Cornwall Map ref 1B3

★★★★
SELF CATERING

Units 1
Sleeps 4

LOW SEASON PER WK
£230.00–£325.00

HIGH SEASON PER WK
£400.00–£540.00

Carminowe View, Helston

contact Mr Huddleston, Carminowe View, 3 Northfield Road, Portishead BS20 8LE **t** (01275) 848899 **e** jhuddl2144@aol.com

cornwallcottage-carminoweview.co.uk

open All year
payment Cash, cheques
nearest shop 2.5 miles
nearest pub 3 miles

Overlooking Carminowe Valley and close to Loe Pool. An inverted, two-storey barn conversion with two en suite bedrooms, separate fitted kitchen and lounge and dining area. Washing/drying facilities. Central heating and wood-burning stove. Linen and towels supplied. Walled, secluded garden with seating and barbecue.

Unit General P Leisure

For **key to symbols** see page 7

HELSTON, Cornwall Map ref 1B3

★★★
SELF CATERING

Units 3
Sleeps 1–6

LOW SEASON PER WK
£150.00–£250.00

HIGH SEASON PER WK
£250.00–£450.00

Mudgeon Vean Farm Holiday Cottages, Helston

contact Mr & Mrs Trewhella, Mudgeon Vean Farm Holiday Cottages, St Martin, Helston TR12 6DB
t (01326) 231341 **e** mudgeonvean@aol.com

mudgeonvean.co.uk

open All year
payment Cash, cheques
nearest shop 1 mile
nearest pub 2 miles

Cosy cottages on small 18thC farm producing apple juice and cider, near Helford River. Equipped to high standard and personally supervised. Night storage heaters and log fires. National Trust walk to the river, outdoor play area for children, games room. Peaceful location in an Area of Outstanding Natural Beauty.

Unit General Leisure

HELSTONE, Cornwall Map ref 1B2

★★★-★★★★
SELF CATERING

Units 6
Sleeps 1–6

LOW SEASON PER WK
£250.00–£800.00

HIGH SEASON PER WK
£900.00–£1,300.00

Ideal for family reunions, group holidays etc. Catering help available. Short breaks available Oct-Mar.

Mayrose Farm, Camelford

contact Mrs Jane Maunder, Mayrose Farm, Camelford PL32 9RN **t** (01840) 213509
e info@mayrosefarmcottages.co.uk

mayrosefarmcottages.co.uk GUEST REVIEWS • SPECIAL OFFERS • REAL-TIME BOOKING

open All year
payment Credit/debit cards, cash, cheques
nearest shop 1 mile
nearest pub 2 miles

Mayrose luxury holiday cottages are set in 17 acres of fields overlooking the picturesque Allen Valley in north Cornwall. The self-catering luxury accommodation is ideal for couples and families with children and toddlers. Heated swimming pool and farm animals. Relaxed, friendly and within easy reach of sandy beaches, gardens, great houses and Bodmin Moor.

ONLINE MAP

Unit General
Leisure

HOLSWORTHY, Devon Map ref 1C2

★★★★
SELF CATERING

Units 2
Sleeps 1–4

LOW SEASON PER WK
£195.00–£295.00

HIGH SEASON PER WK
£300.00–£555.00

Dairy Cottage and Beech Barn, Thornbury, Holsworthy

contact Mrs Annie Griffiths, Bagbeare, Thornbury, Holsworthy EX22 7DF **t** (01409) 261437
e griff.bagbeare@virgin.net

selfcatering-devon.com

Dairy Cottage and Beech Barn, set in a quiet and peaceful position, furnished to a high standard, extremely well equipped, comfortable two-bedroom cottages. Vaulted ceilings, lounge/dining/kitchen area, woodburners, central heating.

open All year
payment Credit/debit cards, cheques
nearest shop 4 miles
nearest pub 4 miles

Unit General Leisure

What if I need to cancel?

It's advisable to check the proprietor's cancellation policy at the time of booking in case you have to change your plans.

HOLSWORTHY, Devon Map ref 1C2

APPROVED CARAVAN HOLIDAY HOME

Units 1
Sleeps 1–8

LOW SEASON PER WK
£150.00–£250.00

HIGH SEASON PER WK
Max £350.00

Noteworthy Caravan Holiday Home, Holsworthy

contact Mrs Julieann Snook-Bevis, Noteworthy, Bude Road, Holsworthy EX22 7JB **t** (01409) 253731 & 07811 000071 **e** enquiries@noteworthy-devon.co.uk

noteworthy-devon.co.uk

On the North Devon/Cornwall border, set in five acres of level meadow with rural views. A short drive to Bude beach.

open All year
payment Cash, cheques
nearest shop 3 miles
nearest pub 2 miles

Unit General Leisure

HONITON, Devon Map ref 1D2

★★★★★
SELF CATERING

Units 2
Sleeps 12

LOW SEASON PER WK
Min £399.00

HIGH SEASON PER WK
Max £999.00

B&B available – see website.

Bidwell Farm Cottages, Honiton

contact Mrs Patricia Wells, Bidwell Farm, Upottery, Honiton EX14 9PP **t** (01404) 861122
e pat@bidwellfarm.co.uk

bidwellfarm.co.uk GUEST REVIEWS • SPECIAL OFFERS

open All year
payment Credit/debit cards, cash, cheques, euros
nearest shop 4 miles
nearest pub 1 mile

Nestling amidst the Blackdown Hills, these cottages have been totally restored and offer superior accommodation. Stroll along sun-dappled lanes. Try local golf, horse-riding or fish our own trout pond. Sidmouth and the coast are just 30 minutes away. In winter, walk the Golden Cap and come home to a roaring log fire.

ONLINE MAP

Unit General Leisure

HONITON, Devon Map ref 1D2

★★★★
SELF CATERING

Units 2
Sleeps 2–5

LOW SEASON PER WK
£193.00–£248.00

HIGH SEASON PER WK
£468.00–£677.00

Short breaks available.

Courtmoor Farm Cottages, Upottery, Honiton

contact Mrs Rosalind Buxton, Courtmoor Farm, Upottery, Honiton EX14 9QA **t** (01404) 861565
e courtmoor.farm@btinternet.com

courtmoor.farm.btinternet.co.uk

open All year
payment Credit/debit cards, cash, cheques
nearest shop 2 miles
nearest pub 1 mile

Courtmoor Farm provides peace and tranquillity within the Blackdown Hills. Our cottages are superbly equipped providing home-from-home accommodation. We have ponies, sheep, cattle and a children's play area. There is a fitness suite and woodland nature trail for the energetic, or coarse fishing and sauna for those wanting to relax.

Unit General Leisure

WALKERS WELCOME WALKERS WELCOME

Do you like walking?

Walkers feel at home in accommodation participating in our Walkers Welcome scheme. Look out for the symbol. Consider walking all or part of a long-distance route – go online at nationaltrail.co.uk.

HUNTLEY, Gloucestershire Map ref 2B1

★★★
SELF CATERING

Units 1
Sleeps 6

LOW SEASON PER WK
£190.00–£210.00

HIGH SEASON PER WK
£220.00–£280.00

The Vineary, Gloucester

contact Mrs Ann Snow, The Vineary, Vinetree Cottage, Solomons Tump, Huntley, Gloucester GL19 3EB **t** (01452) 830006

The Vineary is a self-catering annexe to Vinetree Cottage in a quiet country lane with open views. Easy access to shop, post office and country inns.

open All year
payment Cash, cheques
nearest shop less than 0.5 miles
nearest pub less than 0.5 miles

Unit General P Leisure

ILMINSTER, Somerset Map ref 1D2

★★★
SELF CATERING

Units 1
Sleeps 1–7

LOW SEASON PER WK
£300.00–£420.00

HIGH SEASON PER WK
£500.00–£670.00

Myrtle House, Horton, Ilminster

contact Mr & Mrs Gordon & Marion Denman, 16 Challis Green, Barrington, Cambridge CB22 7RJ **t** (01223) 871294 **e** denman@myrtleonline.co.uk

myrtleonline.co.uk

Comfortable and spacious renovated farmhouse with some features dating back to 17thC. Log fire available. Adjoins fields in quiet village. Convenient for countryside and coast.

open All year
payment Credit/debit cards, cash, cheques
nearest shop less than 0.5 miles
nearest pub less than 0.5 miles

Unit General P S Leisure

ISLES OF SCILLY Map ref 1A3

★★★
SELF CATERING

Units 4
Sleeps 2–5

LOW SEASON PER WK
£200.00–£350.00

HIGH SEASON PER WK
£350.00–£725.00

Bylet Holiday Homes, St Mary's

contact Mr Williams, The Bylet, Church Road, St Mary's TR21 0NA **t** (01720) 422479 **e** thebylet@bushinternet.com

byletholidays.com SPECIAL OFFERS

A selection of properties sleeping two to five. Well furnished and equipped. Ideal 'get away from it all' short breaks out of season. Daily rates available.

open All year
payment Cash, cheques
nearest shop 0.5 miles
nearest pub 0.5 miles

Unit General S Leisure

ISLES OF SCILLY Map ref 1A3

★★★★
SELF CATERING

Units 1
Sleeps 4

LOW SEASON PER WK
£275.00–£475.00

HIGH SEASON PER WK
£525.00–£700.00

The Stable, St Martin's

contact Mrs D Williams, The Stable, Middle Town, St Martin's TR25 0QN **t** (01720) 422810 **e** fiestydee2002@yahoo.co.uk

middletownscilly.co.uk

Converted stable offering very comfortable, well-equipped and beautifully presented accommodation in quiet location. Two bedrooms (one double, one twin).

open All year
payment Cash, cheques
nearest shop 0.5 miles
nearest pub less than 0.5 miles

Unit General 10

ISLES OF SCILLY Map ref 1A3

★★★★
SELF CATERING

Units 1
Sleeps 8

LOW SEASON PER WK
£1,200.00–£1,400.00

HIGH SEASON PER WK
£1,600.00–£1,750.00

Trevean, St Mary's

contact Mrs Rosemary Sharman, Robinswood Farm, Wareham, Bere Regis BH20 7JJ **t** (01929) 471210 **e** robin@sharman0848.freeserve.co.uk

treveanislesofscilly.co.uk

Large, three-storey, granite house in town centre, two minutes to beaches. Four bedrooms (one double, three twins), 31ft lounge/diner on third floor with view over harbour.

open All year
payment Cash, cheques
nearest shop less than 0.5 miles
nearest pub less than 0.5 miles

Unit General Leisure

KILCOT, Gloucestershire Map ref 2B1

★★★★
SELF CATERING

Units 1
Sleeps 2–3

LOW SEASON PER WK
£225.00–£350.00

HIGH SEASON PER WK
£375.00–£450.00

Short breaks off-season by arrangement with owners.

Coach House, Newent

contact Mrs Jane Merritt, Coach House, Orchard House, Aston Ingham Road, Newent GL18 1NP
t (01989) 720417 **e** jane.merritt@btinternet.com

holidaycottage.uk.com

open All year
payment Cash, cheques, euros
nearest shop 1 mile
nearest pub 0.5 miles

Picturesque, quiet country cottage set in outstanding garden. Renovated autumn 2006. Accommodation comprises one twin bedroom plus large sofa bed in sitting room. Excellent base for exploring Gloucestershire, Forest of Dean, Herefordshire, Monmouthshire and Worcestershire. Small market town 1.5 miles away; good pubs close by.

Unit General P Leisure

KING'S NYMPTON, Devon Map ref 1C2

★★★★★
SELF CATERING

Units 5
Sleeps 1–5

LOW SEASON PER WK
£330.00–£500.00

HIGH SEASON PER WK
£650.00–£1,300.00

The Old Rectory, King's Nympton, Umberleigh

contact Mrs Stephanie Atkinson, King's Nympton, Umberleigh EX37 9SS **t** (01769) 580456
e info@oldrectorycottages.co.uk

theoldrectorycottages.co.uk SPECIAL OFFERS • REAL-TIME BOOKING

Five luxury self-catering cottages set in five acres of garden and parkland with an indoor heated swimming pool and children's play area.

open All year
payment Credit/debit cards, cash, cheques, euros
nearest shop 3 miles
nearest pub less than 0.5 miles

Unit General P Leisure

LACOCK, Wiltshire Map ref 2B2

★★★★
SELF CATERING

Units 2
Sleeps 2–5

LOW SEASON PER WK
£330.00–£555.00

HIGH SEASON PER WK
£330.00–£615.00

Anglers welcome at our coarse-fishing lake. Short breaks low season. Convenient for Badminton.

Cyder House and Cheese House, Lacock

contact Mr & Mrs Philip & Susan King, Cyder House and Cheese House, Wick Farm, Wick Lane, Lacock, Chippenham SN15 2LU **t** (01249) 730244 & 07813 207858
e kingsilverlands2@btinternet.com

cheeseandcyderhouses.co.uk

open All year
payment Credit/debit cards, cash, cheques
nearest shop 1.5 miles
nearest pub 1.5 miles

Tastefully converted, beamed farm building with many original features, 1.5 miles from National Trust village. Private garden with furniture and barbecue. Secluded spot with views of open countryside. Our farmhouse adjacent. Stroll to our lake. Good location for Bath (12 miles), Stonehenge, Stourhead, Longleat and Wiltshire chalk horses.

SAT NAV *SN15 2LU*

Unit General P S Leisure

Where is my pet welcome?

Want to take your cherished companion with you on holiday? Proprietors participating in our Welcome Pets! scheme go out of their way to make special provision for you and your pet. Look out for the symbol.

LANGTON MATRAVERS, Dorset Map ref 2B3

★★
SELF CATERING

Units 1
Sleeps 4–5

LOW SEASON PER WK
£245.00–£315.00

HIGH SEASON PER WK
£315.00–£385.00

Flat 5 Garfield House, Swanage

contact Miss Susan Inge, Flat A, 147 Holland Road, London W14 8AS **t** (020) 7602 4945 & 07798 500437 **e** sueinge@hotmail.com

langton-matravers.co.uk

open All year
payment Cash, cheques
nearest shop less than 0.5 miles
nearest pub less than 0.5 miles

The village of Langton Matravers is built almost entirely of the local Purbeck stone. The flat in Garfield House is spacious, traditionally furnished and homely. It has spectacular views to the Purbeck Hills and over the sea to the Isle of Wight, and is a ten-minute walk to the Jurassic Coastline.

SAT NAV *BH19 3HJ*

Unit General P S Leisure

LANGTON MATRAVERS, Dorset Map ref 2B3

★★★★
SELF CATERING

Units 1
Sleeps 1–6

LOW SEASON PER WK
£295.00–£335.00

HIGH SEASON PER WK
£590.00–£750.00

West View House, Swanage

contact Mr & Mrs Alec & Jane Brown, West View House, Bilton Lane, Long Lawford, Rugby CV23 9DU **t** (01788) 560193 **e** alec@lodgefarm.com

westviewhouse.co.uk

Carefully converted stonemason's cottage in the heart of the Jurassic Coast. Fabulous for family, walking or cycling holidays or just to escape! One double, two twins, lounge, dining, kitchen, garden, garage.

open All year
payment Credit/debit cards, cash, cheques, euros
nearest shop 1 mile
nearest pub 1 mile

Unit General P S
Leisure

LANREATH-BY-LOOE, Cornwall Map ref 1C2

★★★
SELF CATERING

Units 6
Sleeps 2–8

LOW SEASON PER WK
£170.00–£370.00

HIGH SEASON PER WK
£415.00–£650.00

Weekend and midweek short breaks available (excl Jun-Sep). Please telephone for further information.

The Old Rectory, Lanreath, Looe

contact Mrs Julie Edge, The Old Rectory, Lanreath, Looe PL13 2NU **t** (01503) 220247
e ask@oldrectory-lanreath.co.uk

oldrectory-lanreath.co.uk SPECIAL OFFERS

open All year
payment Credit/debit cards, cash, cheques
nearest shop less than 0.5 miles
nearest pub less than 0.5 miles

Georgian mansion converted into spacious, well-equipped apartments. Large, beautiful, secluded gardens with heated outdoor pool. Children's play area; table tennis. Picturesque, tranquil village with shop and pub in breathtaking countryside, minutes from pretty fishing villages and beaches. Visit stately homes and lovely gardens. Families and dogs welcome. On-site parking.

SAT NAV *PL13 2NU*

Unit General S Leisure

FAMILIES WELCOME

Looking for an ideal family break?

For accommodation offering additional facilities and services for a range of ages and family units, look out for the Families Welcome symbol. Owners of these properties will go out of their way to welcome families.

LAUNCESTON, Cornwall Map ref 1C2

★★★★
SELF CATERING

Units **8**
Sleeps **2–8**

LOW SEASON PER WK
£210.00–£385.00

HIGH SEASON PER WK
£545.00–£1,270.00

For special offers see our website.

Bamham Farm Cottages, Launceston

contact Mrs Jacki Chapman, Bamham Farm Cottages, Higher Bamham Farm, Launceston PL15 9LD
t (01566) 772141 **e** jackie@bamhamfarm.co.uk

bamhamfarm.co.uk SPECIAL OFFERS

open All year
payment Credit/debit cards, cash, cheques
nearest shop 1 mile
nearest pub 1 mile

Individually designed cottages, ideally situated in beautiful countryside one mile from Launceston, the ancient capital of Cornwall, dominated by its Norman castle. The north and south coasts are easily accessible as are both Dartmoor and Bodmin Moor. Facilities include a heated indoor swimming pool, sauna, solarium, video recorders and DVD players.

Unit General Leisure

LAUNCESTON, Cornwall Map ref 1C2

★★★★
SELF CATERING

Units **4**
Sleeps **4–6**

LOW SEASON PER WK
£150.00–£300.00

HIGH SEASON PER WK
£250.00–£600.00

Frankaborough Farm Cottages, Lifton

contact Mrs Linda Banbury, Frankaborough Farm Cottages, Lifton PL16 0JS **t** (01409) 211308
e banbury960@aol.com

devonfarmcottage.co.uk GUEST REVIEWS · SPECIAL OFFERS

Close to Devon/Cornwall border, 260-acre mixed dairy farm offering imaginative barn conversions decorated to a high standard, set in a rural location but easily accessible to the A30.

open All year
payment Cash, cheques, euros
nearest shop 4 miles
nearest pub 4 miles

Unit General
Leisure

LAUNCESTON, Cornwall Map ref 1C2

★★★–★★★★
SELF CATERING

Units **4**
Sleeps **2–4**

LOW SEASON PER WK
£140.00–£260.00

HIGH SEASON PER WK
£260.00–£480.00

Langdon Farm Holiday Cottages, Launceston

contact Mrs Fleur Rawlinson, Langdon Farm Holiday Cottages, Langdon Farm, Launceston PL15 8NW **t** (01566) 785389 **e** g.f.rawlinson@btinternet.com

langdonholidays.com SPECIAL OFFERS · REAL-TIME BOOKING

One- and two-bedroom, well-equipped cottages, four-poster beds, countryside setting, near pub, ten miles from sea. Easy drive to Eden Project. Short breaks available.

open All year
payment Credit/debit cards, cash, cheques
nearest shop 4 miles
nearest pub 1 mile

Unit General Leisure

LEE, Devon Map ref 1C1

★★★–★★★★★
SELF CATERING

Units **7**
Sleeps **2–8**

LOW SEASON PER WK
£210.00–£580.00

HIGH SEASON PER WK
£470.00–£1,030.00

Short breaks available out of school holidays. Residential craft and hobby courses second and third weeks of the month.

Lower Campscott Farm, Ilfracombe

contact Mrs Margaret Cowell, Lower Campscott Farm, Lee, Ilfracombe EX34 8LS **t** (01271) 863479
e holidays@lowercampscott.co.uk

lowercampscott.co.uk

open All year
payment Credit/debit cards, cash, cheques
nearest shop 1.5 miles
nearest pub 1.5 miles

Charming, tastefully furnished character cottages converted from our farm buildings. Everything supplied to make your stay special. Also holiday homes and lodges. Peaceful farm setting with views across the Bristol Channel. Lee and Woolacombe beaches are easily accessible.

Unit General P Leisure

LIFTON, Devon Map ref 1C2

★★★★
SELF CATERING

Units **3**
Sleeps **2–4**

LOW SEASON PER WK
£425.00–£595.00

HIGH SEASON PER WK
£695.00–£1,125.00

Short breaks available. Telephone for details.

Barbary Ball House, Lifton

contact Mr Richard Street, Barbary Ball, Lifton PL16 0AU **t** (01566) 780457
e info@devoncountrybarns.co.uk

devoncountrybarns.co.uk GUEST REVIEWS • SPECIAL OFFERS • REAL-TIME BOOKING

open All year
payment Credit/debit cards, cash, cheques
nearest shop 1.5 miles
nearest pub 0.75 miles

Exceptional barns, newly converted, set in a lush green valley. Superb views, private terraces, top-quality furnishings and equipment. Stone and slate floors, oak beams and doors, underfloor heating. Fantastic location, equidistant from the north and south coasts, twenty minutes from Dartmoor. Award-winning pubs and farm shops nearby.

SAT NAV *PL16 0AU* **ONLINE MAP**

Unit General P Leisure

LISKEARD, Cornwall Map ref 1C2

★★
SELF CATERING

Units **5**
Sleeps **2–5**

LOW SEASON PER WK
£160.00–£320.00

HIGH SEASON PER WK
£395.00–£550.00

Boturnell Barns, St Pinnock, Liskeard

contact Sue Jewell, Boturnell Barns, Boturnell Farm, St Pinnock, Liskeard PL14 4QS **t** (01579) 320880
e sue@dogs-holiday.co.uk

dogs-holiday.co.uk GUEST REVIEWS • SPECIAL OFFERS

Cosy character cottages set in 25 acres, converted from original barns with many original features – pets really welcome.

open All year
payment Credit/debit cards, cash, cheques, euros
nearest shop 3 miles
nearest pub 3 miles

Unit General P Leisure

Using map references

The map references refer to the colour maps at the front of this guide. The first figure is the map number, the letter and figure that follow indicate the grid reference on the map.

LISKEARD, Cornwall Map ref 1C2

★★★★
SELF CATERING

Units 3
Sleeps 4–6

LOW SEASON PER WK
£215.00–£255.00

HIGH SEASON PER WK
£550.00–£660.00

Hopsland Holidays, Liskeard

contact Mr & Mrs Hosken, Hopsland Holidays, Common Moor, Liskeard PL14 6EJ **t** (01579) 344480
e hopslandholidays@aol.com

hopslandholidays.co.uk

open All year
payment Cash, cheques
nearest shop 2 miles
nearest pub 2 miles

Stay in our beautiful renovated barn converted into three well-equipped cottages. Purposely converted upside down to maximize the beautiful views. 150yds from open moorland, peaceful farm setting surrounded by open fields. All cottages have oil-fired central heating, first £5 electricity, bed linen (including duvets).

ONLINE MAP

Unit General P Leisure

LONGDOWN, Devon Map ref 1D2

★★★★
SELF CATERING

Units 1
Sleeps 1–2

LOW SEASON PER WK
£225.00–£250.00

HIGH SEASON PER WK
£325.00–£385.00

Valley View, Exeter

contact Mrs Jane Steele, Valley View, Woodside, Longdown, Exeter EX6 7SR **t** (01392) 811858
e janeeileensteele@talktalk.net

Spacious self-contained annexe in lovely setting three miles outside Exeter. Large lounge-diner, fully equipped kitchen and comfortable en suite double bedroom. Good access to Dartmoor and beaches, city and university.

open All year except Christmas and New Year
payment Cash, cheques, euros
nearest shop 1.5 miles
nearest pub 1 mile

Unit General P Leisure

LOOE, Cornwall Map ref 1C2

★★★★–★★★★★
SELF CATERING

Units 8
Sleeps 2–6

LOW SEASON PER WK
£275.00–£775.00

HIGH SEASON PER WK
£855.00–£1,395.00

Special short breaks available – please call for details.

Barclay House Luxury Cottages, Looe

contact Mr Graham Brooks, Barclay House Luxury Cottages, St Martins Road, East Looe, Looe PL13 1LP **t** (01503) 262929 **e** info@barclayhouse.co.uk

barclayhouse.co.uk GUEST REVIEWS • SPECIAL OFFERS • REAL-TIME BOOKING

open All year
payment Credit/debit cards, cash, cheques
nearest shop less than 0.5 miles
nearest pub less than 0.5 miles

Luxury, award-winning holiday cottages. Breathtaking views over the Looe River valley. Heated pool nestled in a natural sun trap. Five minutes' walk to harbour, town and beach. Superb award-winning restaurant and bar/lounge on site. Gymnasium. Come stay at Barclay House, you will be glad you did!

ONLINE MAP

Unit General S
Leisure

What if I need to cancel?

It is advisable to check the proprietor's cancellation policy in case you have to change your plans at a later date.

LOOE, Cornwall Map ref 1C2

★★★★
SELF CATERING

Units 3
Sleeps 4–5

LOW SEASON PER WK
£210.00–£350.00

HIGH SEASON PER WK
£360.00–£680.00

Short breaks available Nov–Mar.

Bocaddon Holiday Cottages, Looe

contact Mrs Alison Maiklem, Bocaddon Holiday Cottages, Bocaddon Farm, Lanreath PL13 2PG
t (01503) 220192 **e** holidays@bocaddon.com

bocaddon.com

open All year
payment Credit/debit cards, cash, cheques
nearest shop 2 miles
nearest pub 2 miles

Warm, welcoming and peaceful, these tastefully converted barns on a working farm nestle deep in beautiful Cornish countryside, yet are near the famous beaches and fishing harbours of Looe, Polperro and Fowey. Walking, fishing, wonderful houses and gardens are easily available, or just relax in comfort. Very wheelchair-friendly.

Unit TV DVD General P Leisure

LOOE, Cornwall Map ref 1C2

★★★★–★★★★★
SELF CATERING

Units 5
Sleeps 2–8

LOW SEASON PER WK
£200.00–£350.00

HIGH SEASON PER WK
£350.00–£1,100.00

Short breaks from Nov–Apr (excl Christmas and New Year).

Bucklawren Farm, Looe

contact Mrs Henly, Bucklawren Farm, St Martins, Looe PL13 1NZ **t** (01503) 240738
e bucklawren@btopenworld.com

bucklawren.com

open All year
payment Credit/debit cards, cash, cheques
nearest shop 1 mile
nearest pub 3 miles

Set deep in unspoilt countryside, with a large garden and exceptional sea views, these delightful stone cottages on an award-winning farm are just one mile from the beach and three miles from the fishing port of Looe. The Granary Restaurant is on site.

Unit TV DVD General P Leisure

LOOE, Cornwall Map ref 1C2

★★★
SELF CATERING

Units 4
Sleeps 2–4

LOW SEASON PER WK
£180.00–£350.00

HIGH SEASON PER WK
£480.00–£570.00

Please contact us for out-of-season promotions.

Rivercroft Hotel & Apartments, Looe

contact Glenn, Julie and Pauline Cairns, Station Road, Looe PL13 1HL **t** (01503) 262251
e rivercroft.hotel@virgin.net

rivercrofthotel.co.uk SPECIAL OFFERS • REAL-TIME BOOKING

open All year
payment Credit/debit cards, cash, cheques
nearest shop less than 0.5 miles
nearest pub less than 0.5 miles

Combine the freedom and flexibility of self-catering with all the facilities of a hotel at the Rivercroft apartments. Stunning views, a fantastic location just minutes from the beach and picturesque harbour. The Rivercroft has been extensively refurbished and offers contemporary accommodation, stylish dining areas and a friendly atmosphere.

SAT NAV *PL13 1HL* **ONLINE MAP**

Unit TV DVD General S Leisure

LOOE, Cornwall Map ref 1C2

★★★★
SELF CATERING

Units **4**
Sleeps **2–5**

LOW SEASON PER WK
£150.00–£350.00

HIGH SEASON PER WK
£350.00–£615.00

Summercourt Coastal Cottages, Looe

contact Mr Hocking, Summercourt Coastal Cottages, Bodigga Cliff, St Martin PL13 1NZ
t (01503) 263149 **e** sccottages@freenet.co.uk

holidaycottagescornwall.tv SPECIAL OFFERS

Stone barns converted to comfortable and well-equipped cottages in a rural Area of Outstanding Natural Beauty. Close to sea and beaches.

open All year
payment Credit/debit cards, cash, cheques
nearest shop 2 miles
nearest pub 2 miles

Unit General Leisure

LOOE, Cornwall Map ref 1C2

★★★
SELF CATERING

Units **5**
Sleeps **2–5**

LOW SEASON PER WK
£173.00–£234.00

HIGH SEASON PER WK
£415.00–£722.00

Short breaks available Oct-Mar (excl Christmas and New Year), minimum 2 nights.

Talehay, Looe

contact Neil & Theresa Dennett, Talehay, Tremaine, Looe PL13 2LT **t** (01503) 220252
e infobooking@talehay.co.uk

talehay.co.uk GUEST REVIEWS · SPECIAL OFFERS

open All year
payment Credit/debit cards, cash, cheques
nearest shop 1 mile
nearest pub 1 mile

Tastefully converted and very comfortable stone holiday cottages set around 17thC non-working farmstead. Set in unspoilt, peaceful countryside with breathtaking coastal walks and beaches nearby. Close to Eden Project, Lost Gardens of Heligan and many National Trust properties. An ideal base for exploring the many varied delights of Cornwall.

ONLINE MAP

Unit General P Leisure

LOOE, Cornwall Map ref 1C2

★★★★
SELF CATERING

Units **3**
Sleeps **2–8**

LOW SEASON PER WK
Min £220.00

HIGH SEASON PER WK
Max £950.00

Woodsaws Farm, Looe

contact Mrs Ann Wills, Woodsaws Cross, Lanreath, Looe PL13 2NT **t** (01503) 220190
e ann@woodsawsfarm.co.uk

open All year
payment Credit/debit cards, cash, cheques
nearest shop 0.5 miles
nearest pub 0.5 miles

A stone-built, 19thC working mill converted into spacious and comfortable cottages, one a bungalow-style cottage in rural countryside.

Unit General P Leisure

Place index

If you know where you want to stay, the index by place name at the back of the guide will give you the page number listing accommodation in your chosen town, city or village. Check out the other useful indexes too.

LOSTWITHIEL, Cornwall Map ref 1B2

★★★–★★★★★
SELF CATERING

Units **7**
Sleeps **1–6**

LOW SEASON PER WK
£210.00–£330.00

HIGH SEASON PER WK
£330.00–£905.00

Short breaks out of season. Reduced green fees. Pets accepted in some cottages. Canoe trips available with safety boat.

Lanwithan Cottages, Lostwithiel

contact Mr V B Edward-Collins, Lanwithan Cottages, Lanwithan Road, Lostwithiel PL22 0LA
t (01208) 872444 **e** info@lanwithancottages.co.uk

lanwithancottages.co.uk

open All year
payment Cash, cheques, euros
nearest shop 0.5 miles
nearest pub 0.5 miles

Charming selection of Georgian estate cottages nestling in the Fowey Valley with two delightful waterside properties. Cottages with leaded-light windows, crackling log fires, four-poster bed and glass-topped well. Parkland, river frontage and boat. Woodland and riverside walks from your garden gate. Come and relax and soak up the Cornish atmosphere.

Unit General P
Leisure

LOSTWITHIEL, Cornwall Map ref 1B2

★★★★
SELF CATERING

Units **1**
Sleeps **1–4**

LOW SEASON PER WK
£300.00–£450.00

HIGH SEASON PER WK
£450.00–£600.00

Short weekend and midweek breaks available during spring, autumn and winter.

Trevorry, Lostwithiel

contact Ms Helen Carlisle, Trevorry Farm, Lostwithiel PL22 0JH **t** (01208) 872279
e trevorryfarm@hotmail.com

trevorry.com SPECIAL OFFERS

open All year
payment Cash, cheques
nearest shop 2 miles
nearest pub 1 mile

Trevorry Cottage, with stunning views overlooking lake and copse, offers high-quality accommodation in the heart of Cornwall. Tourist attractions close by include Eden, Heligan, Lanhydrock, Fowey, Mevagissey, Looe, Polperro and Fowey. With a wealth of glorious beaches, historic towns and fishing villages on our doorstep, Trevorry is perfect for exploring Cornwall.

SAT NAV *PL22 0JH* **ONLINE MAP**

Unit General P S Leisure

LUDGVAN, Cornwall Map ref 1A3

★★★
SELF CATERING

Units **1**
Sleeps **2–6**

LOW SEASON PER WK
Min £300.00

HIGH SEASON PER WK
Max £480.00

Nanceddan, Ludgvan, Penzance

contact Mrs Richards, Nanceddan, Ludgvan, Penzance TR20 8AN **t** (01736) 740165
e nanceddan@yahoo.co.uk

nanceddan.com GUEST REVIEWS

open Easter to October
payment Cash, cheques
nearest shop 2 miles
nearest pub 1 mile

Spacious farmhouse apartment in tranquil valley setting, midway between Penzance and St Ives. Superb views of St Michael's Mount, Mounts Bay and surrounding countryside. Nearby footpaths lead to the 14thC church. Two double rooms, one twin room. Price includes electricity, hot water, bed linen, towels (not beach), parking, wireless broadband.

ONLINE MAP

Unit General P Leisure

LUXBOROUGH, Somerset Map ref 1D1

★★★★
SELF CATERING

Units 1
Sleeps 2–10

HIGH SEASON PER WK
£210.00–£1,400.00

Pool Farm Byres, Luxborough, Watchet

contact Ms Stella Morris, Ridgeway Cottage, Southfields Road, Woldingham CR3 7BG
t (01883) 650417 & 07748 070756 **e** stella@c-prodirect.co.uk

exmoorcottage.com REAL-TIME BOOKING

open All year
payment Credit/debit cards
nearest shop 5 miles
nearest pub less than 0.5 miles

Situated in the picturesque Exmoor National Park, Pool Farm Byres is a character barn conversion with cobbled courtyard. It provides an ideal base from which to explore the delights of Exmoor. The accommodation is of a high standard, full of character and exceptionally spacious.

SAT NAV *TA23 0SJ*

Unit TV SC DVD General P S

LYDNEY, Gloucestershire Map ref 2B1

★★★
SELF CATERING

Units 5
Sleeps 4–6

LOW SEASON PER WK
£350.00–£455.00

HIGH SEASON PER WK
£700.00–£805.00

Lindors Country House, Lydney

t (01594) 530283 **e** lindors@christianguild.co.uk

christianguild.co.uk

open All year
payment Credit/debit cards, cash, cheques
nearest shop 1.5 miles
nearest pub 1 mile

Lindors Country House, five fully equipped self-catering pine lodges with magnificent views and set in nine acres of beautiful gardens. Four two-bedroom lodges (double and twin), one three-bedroom lodge (double and two twins). Free use of heated indoor swimming pool.

Unit TV DVD General P S Leisure

LYME REGIS, Dorset Map ref 1D2

★★★★★
SELF CATERING

Units 6
Sleeps 2–12

LOW SEASON PER WK
£336.00–£1,179.00

HIGH SEASON PER WK
£531.00–£2,298.00

Short breaks available Oct-May: 3 nights Fri-Mon, 4 nights Mon-Fri.

Champernhayes Cottages, Wootton Fitzpaine, Lyme Regis

contact Mr & Mrs T Dutton, Champernhayes Bookings, 22 Ringley Park Avenue, Reigate RH2 7ET
t (01297) 560853 **e** champernhayes@btinternet.com

champernhayes.com SPECIAL OFFERS

open All year
payment Credit/debit cards, cash, cheques, euros
nearest shop 2 miles
nearest pub 2 miles

Luxury accommodation set in beautiful countryside near to Jurassic Coast and beaches at Charmouth and Lyme Regis. Designated an Area of Outstanding Natural Beauty. Cottages converted from original farmhouse buildings dating back to 1482. Each cottage has its own private garden with patio and hardwood garden furniture.

SAT NAV *DT6 6DF* **ONLINE MAP**

Unit TV DVD General P S Leisure

Where can I get live travel information?
For the latest travel update – call the RAC on 1740 from your mobile phone.

For **key to symbols** see page 7

LYME REGIS, Dorset Map ref 1D2

★★★
SELF CATERING

Units 1
Sleeps 4–9

LOW SEASON PER WK
£350.00–£500.00

HIGH SEASON PER WK
£500.00–£950.00

Harbour House Flats, Lyme Regis

contact Mrs Alison Stait, Pound Cottage, Brampford Speke, Exeter EX5 5DU **t** (01392) 841507
e info@bythecobb.co.uk

bythecobb.co.uk GUEST REVIEWS · SPECIAL OFFERS

Harbour House is immediately overlooking the beach and harbour. Seafront location. Second-floor penthouse flat. Superb views over the Cobb and Lyme Bay. Three bedrooms. Large rooftop patio. Parking. Dishwasher.

open All year
payment Cheques
nearest shop less than 0.5 miles
nearest pub less than 0.5 miles

Unit General P

LYME REGIS, Dorset Map ref 1D2

★★★
SELF CATERING

Units 1
Sleeps 6–7

LOW SEASON PER WK
£250.00–£300.00

HIGH SEASON PER WK
£300.00–£500.00

Monmouth Cottage, Lyme Regis

contact Mrs W R Fisk, 28 Station Road, Crewkerne TA18 8AJ **t** (01460) 73878

A 17thC listed property in one of Lyme Regis' oldest streets. Three-storey terraced house, newly renovated inside and out. Small, sunny, walled garden up some steep steps.

open All year
payment Cash, cheques
nearest shop less than 0.5 miles
nearest pub less than 0.5 miles

Unit General

LYME REGIS, Dorset Map ref 1D2

★★★★
SELF CATERING

Units 2
Sleeps 2–4

LOW SEASON PER WK
£295.00–£420.00

HIGH SEASON PER WK
£465.00–£695.00

Short breaks available in the low season.

Sea Tree House, Lyme Regis

contact Mr David Parker, Sea Tree House, 18 Broad Street, Lyme Regis DT7 3QE **t** (01297) 442244
e seatree.house@ukonline.co.uk

lymeregis.com/seatreehouse

open All year
payment Cash, cheques
nearest shop 0.5 miles
nearest pub 0.5 miles

Romantic, elegant apartments overlooking the sea, three minutes from the beach. Spacious living room with dining area overlooking the sea. Central position giving easy access to restaurants, pubs and walks in Area of Outstanding Natural Beauty. Wi-Fi Internet. Warm, friendly welcome from owners.

Unit General P Leisure

LYME REGIS, Dorset Map ref 1D2

★★★–★★★★★
SELF CATERING

Units 3
Sleeps 6–8

LOW SEASON PER WK
£180.00–£290.00

HIGH SEASON PER WK
£295.00–£845.00

Short-break bookings a speciality and very welcome.

Westover Farm Cottages, Bridport

contact Jon Snook or Debby Snook, Westover Farm Cottages, Westover Farm, Wootton Fitzpaine, Bridport DT6 6NE **t** (01297) 560451 & (01297) 561395 **e** wfcottages@aol.com

westoverfarmcottages.co.uk SPECIAL OFFERS

open All year
payment Cash, cheques, euros
nearest shop 1.5 miles
nearest pub 1.5 miles

Lovely three-bedroomed cottages with wood-burning stoves, inglenook and open fires on edge of picturesque village. Additional three-bedroomed, stone-built cottages with adjoining games room overlooking gentle valley. Parking and large garden at all cottages. In an Area of Outstanding Natural Beauty, 1.5 miles from World Heritage Coastline.

SAT NAV *DT6 6NE*

Unit General P Leisure

LYMPSHAM, Somerset Map ref 1D1

★★
SELF CATERING

Units 4
Sleeps 2–7

LOW SEASON PER WK
£135.00–£175.00

HIGH SEASON PER WK
£255.00–£365.00

Dulhorn Farm Holiday Park, Weston-super-Mare

contact Mr & Mrs Bowden, Dulhorn Farm Holiday Park, Weston Road, Weston-super-Mare BS24 0JQ **t** (01934) 750298

On working farm. Ideal touring and fishing, country surroundings. Beaches approximately four miles. Easy access to motorway. Pets welcome. Also campsite, etc.

open Mid-February to mid-December
payment Credit/debit cards, cash, cheques
nearest shop 1.5 miles
nearest pub 1 mile

Unit General P Leisure

LYNTON, Devon Map ref 1C1

★★★
SELF CATERING

Units 3
Sleeps 2–8

LOW SEASON PER WK
£230.00–£485.00

HIGH SEASON PER WK
£520.00–£985.00

Short breaks and weekend breaks available during off-peak seasons. Special rates for advanced and late bookings.

Cloud Farm, Lynton

contact Mrs Jill Harman, Oare, Lynton EX35 6NU **t** (01598) 741234
e doonevalleyholidays@hotmail.com

doonevalleyholidays.co.uk SPECIAL OFFERS

open All year
payment Credit/debit cards, cash, cheques
nearest shop less than 0.5 miles
nearest pub 3 miles

Cloud Farm is a lovely riverside farmhouse in the heart of Exmoor's beautiful Doone Valley. The cottages, with tea room, shop, off-licence and gardens, provide an idyllic base for families and children, walkers and tourers seeking an 'away-from-it-all' break at any time of year. Riding for all ages and abilities.

ONLINE MAP

Unit General P Leisure

Do you have access needs?

Look for the National Accessible Scheme symbols if you have special hearing, visual or mobility needs. An index of accommodation participating in the scheme can be found at the back of this guide.

For **key to symbols** see page 7

LYNTON, Devon Map ref 1C1

★★★★
SELF CATERING

Units 1
Sleeps 1–2

LOW SEASON PER WK
Min £275.00

HIGH SEASON PER WK
Max £625.00

De-stressing breaks available Nov-Mar or at late availability (worth phoning!). Assistance with walking, mountain-biking, paragliding possible.

Royal Castle Lodge, Lynton

contact Mr M Wolverson, Primespot Character Cottages, c/o Stag Cottage, Holdstone Down, Combe Martin EX34 0PF **t** (01271) 882449

open All year
payment Cash, cheques, euros
nearest shop less than 0.5 miles
nearest pub less than 0.5 miles

Something special! 16thC detached, thatched cottage with rustic balcony, stable door, real fire, garden. Idyllic coastal setting in England's 'Little Switzerland'. Exmoor National Park, wooded outlook with harbour, pubs, shops within walking distance. Spectacular walks. Spotless, warm and cosy. Smoking/pets welcome downstairs. Off-season short breaks. Perfect honeymoon/anniversaries.

Unit General P Leisure

MAIDENCOMBE, Devon Map ref 1D2

★★★
SELF CATERING

Units 6
Sleeps 2–4

LOW SEASON PER WK
£230.00–£325.00

HIGH SEASON PER WK
£270.00–£570.00

Short breaks available. Low season: 20% discount for couples (except for 'Poppy' unit).

Bowden Close House, Maidencombe

contact Mrs Sarah Farquharson, Bowden Close House, Teignmouth Road, Maidencombe, Torquay TQ1 4TJ **t** (01803) 328029 **e** enquiries@bowdenclose.co.uk

bowdenclose.co.uk SPECIAL OFFERS • REAL-TIME BOOKING

open All year
payment Cash, cheques, euros
nearest shop 3 miles
nearest pub 0.5 miles

Relax in very comfortable apartments or two-storey, self-contained wings of large Victorian house overlooking Lyme Bay, four miles from Torquay. Acre of gardens with stunning views. Minutes from sheltered Maidencombe Cove and the South West Coast Path. Easy access to Dartmoor and the lovely South Devon countryside.

ONLINE MAP

Unit General Leisure

MALMESBURY, Wiltshire Map ref 2B2

★★★★
SELF CATERING

Units 1
Sleeps 5

LOW SEASON PER WK
£250.00–£450.00

HIGH SEASON PER WK
£450.00–£500.00

The Cottage, Malmesbury

contact Mrs Ross Eavis, Manor Farm, Corston, Malmesbury SN16 0HF **t** (01666) 822148
e ross@johneavis.wanadoo.co.uk

manorfarmbandb.co.uk SPECIAL OFFERS

Relax and unwind in farm surroundings. The Cottage is full of character and furnished to a very high standard. Easy access to the M4, the Cotswolds and Bath.

open All year
payment Credit/debit cards, cash, cheques
nearest shop 2 miles
nearest pub less than 0.5 miles

Unit General P

Check the maps for accommodation locations

Colour maps at the front pinpoint all the places where accommodation is featured within the regional sections of this guide. Pick your location and then refer to the place index at the back to find the page number.

MANACCAN, Cornwall Map ref 1B3

★★★–★★★★★
SELF CATERING

Units 3
Sleeps 2–17

LOW SEASON PER WK
Min £175.00

HIGH SEASON PER WK
Max £795.00

Lestowder Farm, Helston

contact Mrs Martin, Lestowder Farm, Manaccan, Helston TR12 6ES **t** (01326) 231400
e lestowderfarm@hotmail.com

lestowderfarmcottages.co.uk

Lestowder Farm cottages nestle in a very quiet, unspoilt part of Cornwall, on the south of River Helford, near coastal footpath and beach.

open All year
payment Cash, cheques, euros
nearest shop 2.5 miles
nearest pub 2.5 miles

Unit General P Leisure

MARAZION, Cornwall Map ref 1B3

★★★
SELF CATERING

Units 1
Sleeps 4

LOW SEASON PER WK
£200.00–£250.00

HIGH SEASON PER WK
£300.00–£400.00

Lowenna, Marazion

contact Mr Jelbart, Rose Hill, Marazion TR17 0HB **t** (01736) 710580

This light and spacious ground-floor apartment is set in a secluded hillside garden with spectacular views of St Michael's Mount and panoramic views of Mount's Bay.

open All year except Christmas and New Year
payment Cash, cheques, euros
nearest shop less than 0.5 miles
nearest pub less than 0.5 miles

Unit General P

MARAZION, Cornwall Map ref 1B3

★★★
SELF CATERING

Units 25
Sleeps 1–5

LOW SEASON PER WK
£170.00–£320.00

HIGH SEASON PER WK
£410.00–£850.00

£100 for 2 nights per unit in off-peak time.

Trevarthian Holiday Homes, Marazion

contact Sean Cattran, Trevarthian Holiday Homes, Trevarthian House, West End TR17 0EG
t (01736) 710100 **e** info@trevarthian.co.uk

trevarthian.co.uk SPECIAL OFFERS

open All year
payment Credit/debit cards, cash, cheques
nearest shop less than 0.5 miles
nearest pub less than 0.5 miles

High quality Victorian cottages and apartments in the prime Mount's Bay location of Marazion. Fifty yards from the beach. Superb panoramic bay views of St Michael's Mount, Mousehole, Newlyn and Penzance. A selection of the finest self-catering accommodation available. Two-minute walk to safe sandy beach, children's playground, pubs, restaurants, galleries, shops.

ONLINE MAP

Unit General P S Leisure

MARLBOROUGH, Wiltshire Map ref 2B2

★★★
SELF CATERING

Units 1
Sleeps 1–8

LOW SEASON PER WK
£300.00–£490.00

HIGH SEASON PER WK
£525.00–£650.00

Dairy Cottage, Marlborough

contact Mr & Mrs Mark and Hazel Crockford, Dairy Cottage, Browns Farm, Marlborough SN8 4ND
t (01672) 515129 & 07931 311985 **e** crockford@farming.co.uk

open All year
payment Credit/debit cards, cash, cheques
nearest shop 2 miles
nearest pub 2 miles

Dairy Cottage is situated on Browns Farm which is a working beef/arable farm set on the edge of Savernake Forest overlooking open farmland. The cottage offers peace and tranquillity for a true North Wiltshire holiday. A modern, spacious, well-equipped bungalow with open fire awaits your arrival.

Unit General P S Leisure

MAWGAN PORTH, Cornwall Map ref 1B2

★★★
SELF CATERING

Units 4
Sleeps 2–5

LOW SEASON PER WK
£200.00–£300.00

HIGH SEASON PER WK
£400.00–£600.00

Ambiance Holiday Apartments, Mawgan Porth

contact Mr Brian White, Ambiance Holiday Apartments, Trenance, Mawgan Porth TR8 4BX
t (01637) 860509 **e** brian@whiteamb.freeserve.co.uk

visitcornwall.co.uk/ambianceholidayapartments

Four self-contained apartments situated in coastal village minutes from beach, shops and coastal path. Private parking. Couples/families only.

open All year
payment Cash, cheques
nearest shop 0.5 miles
nearest pub 0.5 miles

Unit General

MAWGAN PORTH, Cornwall Map ref 1B2

APPROVED CARAVAN HOLIDAY HOME

Units 6
Sleeps 4–6

LOW SEASON PER WK
£230.00–£310.00

HIGH SEASON PER WK
£315.00–£515.00

Cosy Corner Holiday Accommodation, Newquay

contact Mr & Mrs B Lynn, Cosy Corner Holiday Accommodation, Newquay TR8 4BB
t (01637) 860611 **e** info@cosycorner.co.uk

cosycorner.co.uk SPECIAL OFFERS

open Easter to October
payment Cash, cheques
nearest shop 0.5 miles
nearest pub 0.5 miles

Situated in beautiful gardens, 200 yards from unspoilt sandy bay. Between Newquay and Padstow, an ideal location for visiting all areas of Cornwall with ease. Each caravan has a private lawn, picnic table and parking. Perfect for traditional family holidays.

Unit General P S

MAWGAN PORTH, Cornwall Map ref 1B2

★★★
SELF CATERING

Units 1
Sleeps 4

LOW SEASON PER WK
Min £140.00

HIGH SEASON PER WK
Max £305.00

Samphire, Newquay

t (01637) 860379 **e** geoffandjane@tiscali.co.uk

Comfortable, one-bedroom, ground-floor flat. Sleeps four, one twin, one double sofa bed. Fully equipped. Quiet location, large garden, parking, dogs welcome. Midway between Newquay and Padstow. Five minutes' walk to beach/coast path.

open All year
payment Cash, cheques
nearest shop 1 mile
nearest pub 1 mile

Unit General P S Leisure

MAWGAN PORTH, Cornwall Map ref 1B2

★★★★
SELF CATERING

Units 1
Sleeps 1–2

LOW SEASON PER WK
£310.00–£410.00

HIGH SEASON PER WK
£600.00–£920.00

White Lodge, Mawgan Porth, Newquay

contact Reservations, Beach Retreats, On the Beach, Watergate Bay, Newquay TR8 4AA
t (01637) 861005 & (01637) 861241 **e** kelly@beachretreats.co.uk

beachretreats.co.uk SPECIAL OFFERS · REAL-TIME BOOKING

A luxury one-bedroom, ground-floor apartment with furnished patio overlooking the beach with designated car parking. Beach 150m, shops 400m. Closed 10-29 January and 22 November-18 December.

payment Credit/debit cards, cheques, euros
nearest shop less than 0.5 miles
nearest pub less than 0.5 miles

Unit General P S Leisure

Looking for a wide range of facilities?

More stars means higher quality accommodation plus a greater range of facilities and services.

MAWNAN SMITH, Cornwall Map ref 1B3

★★★
SELF CATERING

Units 1
Sleeps 1–5

LOW SEASON PER WK
£320.00–£390.00

HIGH SEASON PER WK
£510.00–£640.00

Glen Avon, Mawnan Smith, Falmouth

contact Mr & Mrs Benney, Glen Avon, Lower Penpol, Mawnan Smith, Falmouth TR11 5LJ
t (01326) 250283 **e** annb.glen@hotmail.co.uk

cottage-cornwall.co.uk

Genuine country cottage overlooking creek on the Helford River. The perfect setting for holidays at any time of year. Within a mile of Glendurgan Garden (National Trust) and Trebah Gardens.

open All year
payment Cash, cheques
nearest shop 2 miles
nearest pub 1 mile

Unit General P Leisure

MELCOMBE BINGHAM, Dorset Map ref 2B3

★★★★
SELF CATERING

Units 1
Sleeps 1–7

LOW SEASON PER WK
£450.00–£600.00

HIGH SEASON PER WK
£675.00–£850.00

Short breaks available outside summer peak, Christmas and Easter. Min 3-night stay. Linen, towels and heating included.

Greygles, Melcombe Bingham, Dorchester

contact Mr Paul Sommerfeld, 22 Tiverton Road, London NW10 3HL **t** (020) 8969 4830
e enquiry@greygles.co.uk

greygles.co.uk

open All year
payment Cash, cheques, euros
nearest shop 0.5 miles
nearest pub 0.5 miles

Rural peace in spacious, well-equipped stone cottage with delightful views. Hardy Country, on edge of friendly village with well-known pub. Four bedrooms, one on ground floor. Log fire. Wendy house in garden. In an Area of Outstanding Natural Beauty, just off Wessex Ridgeway walkers' path. Coast, abbeys, castles, gardens, many attractions within 30 minutes' drive.

SAT NAV *DT2 7PE* **ONLINE MAP**

WALKERS WELCOME CYCLISTS WELCOME

Unit General P

MEVAGISSEY, Cornwall Map ref 1B3

★★★
SELF CATERING

Units 1
Sleeps 4

LOW SEASON PER WK
£235.00–£310.00

HIGH SEASON PER WK
£310.00–£595.00

Blue Waters, Mevagissey, St Austell

contact Mrs D Kendall, 13 Kiln Close, Mevagissey, St Austell PL26 6TP **t** (01726) 843164
e edwin.kendall@btinternet.com

Comfortable, well-equipped cottage with panoramic views of harbour and bay. Short stroll to village. Linen provided. Private parking.

open All year
payment Cash, cheques, euros
nearest shop less than 0.5 miles
nearest pub less than 0.5 miles

Unit General P S Leisure

MEVAGISSEY, Cornwall Map ref 1B3

★★★
SELF CATERING

Units 1
Sleeps 4

LOW SEASON PER WK
£200.00–£280.00

HIGH SEASON PER WK
£310.00–£410.00

Cosy Nook, Mevagissey

contact Mrs Elizabeth Rundle, Cosy Nook, Cosy Nook Annexe, Valley Road, Mevagissey PL26 6SB
t (01726) 843565

Modern two-bedroom bungalow in centre of fishing village. Accommodation includes all amenities. Linen provided. Parking for one car. Close to Heligan and Eden.

open All year
payment Cash, cheques
nearest shop less than 0.5 miles
nearest pub less than 0.5 miles

Unit General P Leisure

What shall we do today?

For ideas on places to visit, see the beginning of this regional section or go online at enjoyengland.com.

MEVAGISSEY, Cornwall Map ref 1B3

★★★★
SELF CATERING

Units 1
Sleeps 1

LOW SEASON PER WK
£375.00–£530.00

HIGH SEASON PER WK
£530.00–£680.00

Eden Cottage offers special midweek discounts and late availabilities end Sep-end Apr. Refer to website bookings.

Eden Cottage, Mevagissey, St Austell

contact Mrs Helen Whatty, Mevagissey Holiday Cottages, Mevagissey House, Vicarage Hill, Mevagissey PL26 6SZ **t** (01726) 842525 **e** hwhatty@yahoo.co.uk

edencottage.co.uk SPECIAL OFFERS · REAL-TIME BOOKING

open All year
payment Credit/debit cards, cheques
nearest shop less than 0.5 miles
nearest pub less than 0.5 miles

A charming 300-year-old, cosy but very spacious, character cottage with a modern twist in the heart of Mevagissey. Equipped with everything you will need. Ideal location for couples, families or walkers. A perfect central base, you can relax or have an energetic holiday, the choice is yours!

SAT NAV *PL26 6SS* **ONLINE MAP**

Unit General Leisure

MEVAGISSEY, Cornwall Map ref 1B3

★★★★★
SELF CATERING

Units 2
Sleeps 5

LOW SEASON PER WK
£450.00–£550.00

HIGH SEASON PER WK
£650.00–£1,099.00

Short breaks sometimes available during low season.

The Lookout and The Penthouse, Mevagissey

contact Mr Andrew Main Wilson, The Lookout and The Penthouse, The West Wing, 3 Tawsden Manor, Spout Lane, Brenchley TN2 7AS **t** (01892) 722323 & 07725 562563 **e** amw@iod.com

penthouseholidays.com GUEST REVIEWS

open All year
payment Cash, cheques, euros
nearest shop less than 0.5 miles
nearest pub less than 0.5 miles

Two magnificent luxury cliff-top apartments. Private balconies overlooking breathtaking sea and coastline panoramas. Nare Court's most spectacular and stylish properties. Spa baths, ceiling-to-floor glass windows and doors, beautifully furnished. Romantic and private, yet just five minutes' walk to restaurants and shops in picturesque Mevagissey fishing village.

Unit General 10 P Leisure

MEVAGISSEY, Cornwall Map ref 1B3

★★–★★★
SELF CATERING

Units 5
Sleeps 4–8

LOW SEASON PER WK
£200.00–£450.00

HIGH SEASON PER WK
£300.00–£700.00

Pollys Apartments, Mevagissey, St Austell

contact Mrs Diana Littlejohns, Pollys Apartments, Stanwicke, School Hill, Mevagissey PL26 6TQ **t** (01726) 843352 **e** diana@mevagisseyapartments.co.uk

mevagisseyapartments.co.uk SPECIAL OFFERS

Spacious apartments with a cottage atmosphere in Mevagissey centre, close to harbour and shops. Large, well-equipped bungalow with sheltered garden five minutes from harbour. Parking provided.

open All year
payment Cash, cheques
nearest shop less than 0.5 miles
nearest pub less than 0.5 miles

Unit General P Leisure

MILTON ABBAS, Dorset Map ref 2B3

★★★★
SELF CATERING

Units **6**
Sleeps **2–6**

LOW SEASON PER WK
£320.00–£495.00

HIGH SEASON PER WK
£415.00–£1,250.00

Luccombe Farm, Blandford Forum

contact Mr & Mrs Murray & Amanda Kayll, Luccombe Farm, Milton Abbas, Blandford Forum DT11 0BE **t** (01258) 880558 **e** mkayll@aol.com

luccombeholidays.co.uk

open All year
payment Credit/debit cards, cash, cheques
nearest shop 2 miles
nearest pub 2 miles

Comfortable converted cottages, with traditional character. Idyllic, peaceful setting in middle of proper working farm close to the historic village of Milton Abbas. Many facilities, including indoor pool.

Unit General
Leisure

MILTON ABBAS, Dorset Map ref 2B3

★★★★
SELF CATERING

Units **1**
Sleeps **2–6**

LOW SEASON PER WK
£250.00–£315.00

HIGH SEASON PER WK
£360.00–£615.00

Primrose Cottage, Blandford Forum

contact Mrs Therese Clemson, 22 Kerrfield, Winchester SO22 5EX **t** (01962) 865786
e therese.clemson@btinternet.com

miltonabbas-primrosecottage.co.uk

open All year
payment Cash, cheques

Grade II Listed, 18thC, thatched cob cottage set on the street in the unique village of Milton Abbas, created by Lord Milton. Centre of Hardy Country. Ideal for walkers and romantics.

Unit General Leisure

MINEHEAD, Somerset Map ref 1D1

★★★
SELF CATERING

Units **1**
Sleeps **5**

LOW SEASON PER WK
Min £200.00

HIGH SEASON PER WK
Min £380.00

Fishermans Cottage, Minehead

contact Mrs Martin, 57 Quay Street, Minehead TA24 5UL **t** (01643) 704263

Situated overlooking the harbour and Minehead Bay. With two bedrooms, one double, the other with double and single beds. All linen, towels and cloths provided. Electricity included.

open All year
payment Cash, cheques
nearest shop 1 mile
nearest pub less than 0.5 miles

Unit General 5 Leisure

Where can I get help and advice?

Tourist Information Centres offer friendly help with accommodation and holiday ideas as well as suggestions of places to visit and things to do. You'll find contact details at the beginning of each regional section.

MITCHELDEAN, Gloucestershire Map ref 2B1

★★★
SELF CATERING

Units 2
Sleeps 3

LOW SEASON PER WK
Min £200.00

HIGH SEASON PER WK
Max £350.00

Church Farm Holidays, Mitcheldean

contact John Verity, Church Farm, Church Lane, Abenhall, Mitcheldean GL17 0DX **t** (01594) 541211
e info@churchfarm.uk.net

churchfarm.uk.net GUEST REVIEWS • SPECIAL OFFERS • REAL-TIME BOOKING

Church Farm offers holidays for horse-riders bringing their own horses, cyclists who bring or hire cycles, walkers who wish to discover the forest using trails, and bell ringers who wish to ring at different forest towers.

open All year
payment Cash, cheques
nearest shop 1 mile
nearest pub 1 mile

Unit General Leisure

MITCHELDEAN, Gloucestershire Map ref 2B1

★★★★
SELF CATERING

Units 1
Sleeps 2

LOW SEASON PER WK
£290.00

HIGH SEASON PER WK
£325.00–£335.00

The Old Dairy, Mitcheldean

contact Lorraine Morgan, The White House, Trinity Road, Harrow Hill, Drybrook GL17 9LD
t (01594) 543737 **e** theolddairy@aic.co.uk

olddairycottage.com GUEST REVIEWS • SPECIAL OFFERS

Situated along a quiet, rural lane, The Old Dairy is a luxury cottage featuring slate floors and beamed ceilings throughout. Private patio area and parking for two vehicles.

open All year
payment Cash, cheques
nearest shop 1.5 miles
nearest pub 1.5 miles

Unit General

MODBURY, Devon Map ref 1C3

★★★★
SELF CATERING

Units 4
Sleeps 2–6

LOW SEASON PER WK
£240.00–£305.00

HIGH SEASON PER WK
£385.00–£640.00

Short breaks available 21 Sep-1 May.

Oldaport Farm Cottages, Modbury, Ivybridge

contact Miss C M Evans, Oldaport Farm Cottages, Modbury, Nr Ivybridge PL21 0TG
t (01548) 830842 **e** cathy@oldaport.com

oldaport.com GUEST REVIEWS

open All year
payment Cash, cheques
nearest shop 2.5 miles
nearest pub 2 miles

Four comfortable fully equipped cottages converted from redundant stone barns. Peaceful setting in beautiful South Hams valley on historic 70-acre working sheep farm and miniature Shetland pony stud. There is an abundance of wildlife and many fascinating walks. The South West Coast Path is nearby. Dartmoor eight miles.

SAT NAV *PL21 0TG* **ONLINE MAP**

Unit General

MONTACUTE, Somerset Map ref 2A3

★★★★
SELF CATERING

Units 1
Sleeps 4

LOW SEASON PER WK
£300.00–£340.00

HIGH SEASON PER WK
£395.00–£525.00

Far End Cottage, Montacute

contact Mrs Adrienne Wright, 39 The Avenue, Crowthorne RG45 6PB **t** (01344) 772461
e aawright@btopenworld.com

somersetcottageholidays.co.uk

Golden hamstone cottage in beautiful village. Country walks. Many NT properties and gardens nearby. Two bedrooms. Well-equipped kitchen with dishwasher. Open log fire. Lovely garden. Private parking. Linen provided. Brochure.

open All year
payment Credit/debit cards, cash, cheques
nearest shop less than 0.5 miles
nearest pub less than 0.5 miles

Unit General Leisure

MORETONHAMPSTEAD, Devon Map ref 1C2

★★★
SELF CATERING

Units 6
Sleeps 2–6

LOW SEASON PER WK
Min £165.00

HIGH SEASON PER WK
Max £535.00

Budleigh Farm, Moretonhampstead

contact Mrs Judith Harvey, Budleigh Farm, Moretonhampstead TQ13 8SB **t** (01647) 440835
e harvey@budleighfarm.co.uk

budleighfarm.co.uk

open All year
payment Credit/debit cards, cash, cheques
nearest shop 0.5 miles
nearest pub 0.5 miles

Properties created with flair from granite barns, on a farm at the end of a stunning valley – rural but not remote. Easy to find. Superb gardens, pubs of character, beaches and castles are all accessible. Superb walking country. In Dartmoor National Park.

Unit General P Leisure

MORTEHOE, Devon Map ref 1C1

★★★★★
SELF CATERING

Units 1
Sleeps 4

LOW SEASON PER WK
Min £539.00

HIGH SEASON PER WK
Max £1,074.00

Farriers End, Warcombe, Woolacombe

contact Mrs Olive Sinclair, Lee Manor Farm, Lee Manor, Lee EX34 8LR **t** (01271) 867285
e leemanor@btinternet.com

farriersend.eu

open All year
payment Cash, cheques
nearest shop 3 miles
nearest pub 2 miles

Farriers End is a truly unique property that is a magical place to relax and unwind. This stunning two-bedroom cottage is spacious with many special features and is peacefully located in an Area of Outstanding Natural Beauty on the stunning North Devon coast.

SAT NAV *EX34 7EJ*

Unit General P Leisure

MOTHECOMBE, Devon Map ref 1C3

★★★★–★★★★★
SELF CATERING

Units 7
Sleeps 5–12

LOW SEASON PER WK
£580.00–£750.00

HIGH SEASON PER WK
£1,350.00–£2,075.00

Winter breaks Nov-Mar (excl Christmas and New Year) from £150pn, minimum 3 nights. Also check our excellent weekly winter rates.

The Flete Estate Holiday Cottages, Plymouth

contact Mrs Lisa Farleigh, The Flete Estate Holiday Cottages, Haye Farm, Holbeton, Plymouth PL8 1JZ
t (01752) 830234 **e** cottages@flete.co.uk

flete.co.uk

open All year
payment Cash, cheques
nearest shop 1 mile
nearest pub 1 mile

A rural estate on the South Devon coast offering a unique selection of properties for relaxing summer holidays or refreshing midwinter breaks. Furnished to a high standard, all cottages are wonderfully secluded with gardens taking full advantage of the breathtaking scenery. A birdwatcher's paradise, guests are invited to explore the estate's woodland and estuary walks and relax on the nearby sandy beaches.

Unit General P Leisure

MULLION, Cornwall Map ref 1B3

★★★
SELF CATERING

Units 9
Sleeps 2–6

LOW SEASON PER WK
£220.00–£375.00

HIGH SEASON PER WK
£450.00–£725.00

10% discount for 2 sharing Apr-Jun (excl Easter and Spring break holiday weeks). Winter short breaks.

Trenance Farm Cottages, Helston

contact Mr & Mrs Richard, Jenny & Tamara Tyler-Street, Trenance Farm, Mullion, Helston TR12 7HB
t (01326) 240639 **e** info@trenancefarmholidays.co.uk

trenancefarmholidays.co.uk GUEST REVIEWS · SPECIAL OFFERS

open All year
payment Credit/debit cards, cash, cheques
nearest shop less than 0.5 miles
nearest pub 0.5 miles

Quality cottages, each with their own garden, converted from old farm buildings and set in 13 acres. Heated summer pool. Games rooms. Barbecues. Five minutes' walk across fields to coast and lovely walks. Swimming/surfing coves and Mullion village 0.5 miles. A peaceful location in an Area of Outstanding Natural Beauty.

Unit General Leisure

MYLOR CHURCHTOWN, Cornwall Map ref 1B3

★★★★
SELF CATERING

Units 1
Sleeps 8

LOW SEASON PER WK
£400.00–£600.00

HIGH SEASON PER WK
£700.00–£1,260.00

Penarrow Cottage, Falmouth

contact Mrs Warner, Penarrow Cottage, 54 Lemon Street, Truro TR1 2PE **t** (01872) 270199
e lemonstreetlady@aol.com

Lovely well-equipped waterside cottage in private gardens. Ample parking. Children and dogs welcome. The harbour, with restaurants, cafe/grocery, boat hire and sailing schools, is 150yds away.

open All year
payment Cheques
nearest shop less than 0.5 miles
nearest pub 3 miles

Unit General

NEW POLZEATH, Cornwall Map ref 1B2

★★★
SELF CATERING

Units 1
Sleeps 6

LOW SEASON PER WK
£350.00–£450.00

HIGH SEASON PER WK
£620.00–£750.00

Treheather, Wadebridge

contact Dr Elizabeth Mayall, Osmond House, Chestnut Crescent, Stoke Canon, Exeter EX5 4AA
t (01392) 841219

Spacious, modern bungalow. About 200yds from sandy surfing beach with rock pools. Garden, coastal walks. One double bedroom, one twin with 3ft beds, one twin with 2ft 6in beds.

open March to November
payment Cash, cheques
nearest shop 0.5 miles
nearest pub 0.5 miles

Unit General Leisure

NEWLAND, Gloucestershire Map ref 2A1

★★★
SELF CATERING

Units 1
Sleeps 2

LOW SEASON PER WK
£200.00–£245.00

HIGH SEASON PER WK
£260.00–£270.00

The Cottage, Coleford

contact Julie Pritchard, The Rookery, Newland, Coleford GL16 8NJ **t** (01594) 832986
e juliespritchard@googlemail.com

Well-equipped cosy cottage by babbling brook in beautiful village of Newland in the Forest of Dean. Private courtyard garden, barbecue, off-road parking. Sleeps two, plus one on sofa bed. Ideal location for walking. Wye Valley Walk two miles.

open All year
payment Cash, cheques
nearest shop 2.5 miles
nearest pub less than 0.5 miles

Unit General

What do the star ratings mean?

Detailed information about star ratings can be found at the back of this guide.

NEWNHAM, Gloucestershire Map ref 2B1

★★★
SELF CATERING

Units 1
Sleeps 2–6

LOW SEASON PER WK
£280.00–£400.00

HIGH SEASON PER WK
£350.00–£600.00

Short breaks welcome.

Stroods, Broadoak, Newnham

contact Miss Annabelle Gillman, Orchard Cottage, The Strood, Broadoak, Newnham GL14 1JL
t (01594) 516976 & 07710 269563 **e** annabelle@annab.entadsl.com

forestofdeancottage.com REAL-TIME BOOKING

open All year except Christmas and New Year
payment Credit/debit cards, cash, cheques, euros
nearest shop 0.5 miles
nearest pub less than 0.5 miles

Charming cottage situated close to riverside town of Newnham-on-Severn. Pleasant garden with patio area and adequate parking for three vehicles. Fitted kitchen with dishwasher and washing machine. Logburner in lounge with TV and DVD entertainment. Family bathroom and separate shower room. Conservatory and private driveway.

SAT NAV *GL14 1JL* **ONLINE MAP**

Unit General 2 P S Leisure

NEWQUAY, Cornwall Map ref 1B2

★★★★
SELF CATERING

Units 4
Sleeps 2–6

HIGH SEASON PER WK
£475.00–£995.00

Cornwall Coast Holidays, Newquay

contact Mrs Deborah Spencer-Smith, Cornwall Coast Holidays **t** (020) 8440 7518 & 07910 583050
e deborah@cornwallcoastholidays.com

cornwallcoastholidays.com

open All year
payment Cheques

Cornwall Coast Holidays offer apartments and cottages that are in the perfect location for wonderful beach holidays. The cottages are modern, and the apartments have stunning sea views. Both apartments and cottages have one en suite bathroom and are close to the town centre, golf course and other amenities.

Unit General P

NEWQUAY, Cornwall Map ref 1B2

★★★–★★★★
SELF CATERING

Units 4
Sleeps 2–8

LOW SEASON PER WK
£290.00–£520.00

HIGH SEASON PER WK
£575.00–£1,380.00

Hendra Paul Cottages, Porth, Newquay

contact Mrs Julia Schofield, Hendra Paul Cottages - BE020, Porth, Newquay TR8 4JL
t (01637) 874695 **e** info@hendrapaul.co.uk

hendrapaul.co.uk SPECIAL OFFERS

Charming cluster of four detached, beamed cottages, equipped to highest standard. Quiet countryside location, two miles Porth beach. Sleep two to eight people. Short breaks from October to May welcome.

open All year
payment Credit/debit cards, cash, cheques
nearest shop 2 miles
nearest pub 2 miles

Unit General S Leisure

It's all quality-assessed accommodation

Our commitment to quality involves wide-ranging accommodation assessment. Ratings and awards were correct at the time of going to press but may change following a new assessment. Please check at time of booking.

For **key to symbols** see page 7

NEWQUAY, Cornwall Map ref 1B2

★★★★
SELF CATERING

Units 1
Sleeps 1–5

LOW SEASON PER WK
Min £300.00

HIGH SEASON PER WK
£550.00–£700.00

Parry's Barn, Newquay

contact Mrs Sharon Rundle, Kestle Farm, Kestle Mill, Newquay TR8 4PU **t** (01637) 875798 & 07809 152582 **e** sharonrundleuk@yahoo.com

open All year
payment Cash, cheques
nearest shop 1 mile
nearest pub 0.5 miles

Beautiful converted barn, oak flooring throughout. Double bedroom with TV/DVD, twin-bedded room (extra bed, cot if required). Fully fitted kitchen with gas cooker, microwave, dishwasher and washing machine. Bathroom with shower over and wc. Lounge/diner with two large leather reclining sofas, dining table with six chairs. Fully enclosed garden, outstanding views.

Unit TV SC DVD General P S
Leisure

NEWQUAY, Cornwall Map ref 1B2

★★★★
SELF CATERING

Units 12
Sleeps 4–6

LOW SEASON PER WK
£420.00–£750.00

HIGH SEASON PER WK
£570.00–£1,200.00

Porth Veor Manor, Newquay

contact Mr Jeff Smith, Porth Way, Newquay TR7 3LW **t** (01637) 873274
e enquiries@porthveormanor.com

porthveormanor.com

Eight villas and four apartments – brand new July 2007. Two bedrooms, one with three, set in hotel grounds with full access to the restaurant, bar, pool and gardens.

open All year
payment Credit/debit cards, cash, cheques, euros
nearest shop 0.5 miles
nearest pub 0.5 miles

Unit TV SC DVD General P S Leisure

NEWQUAY, Cornwall Map ref 1B2

★★★★
SELF CATERING

Units 5
Sleeps 6

LOW SEASON PER WK
£400.00–£700.00

HIGH SEASON PER WK
£850.00–£1,530.00

Short breaks from £325.00: 4 people including fuel, linen, towels. Surfing breaks including boards, wetsuits from £175.00 per person.

Tolcarne Beach Village, Newquay

contact Mrs Veronica McCann, Narrowcliff, Newquay TR7 2QN **t** (01209) 712651 & (01637) 872489
e info@tolcarnebeach.co.uk

tolcarnebeach.co.uk GUEST REVIEWS • SPECIAL OFFERS • REAL-TIME BOOKING

open All year
payment Cash, cheques
nearest shop less than 0.5 miles
nearest pub less than 0.5 miles

Wake up, smell the fresh sea air and watch the surf roll in. Beautifully appointed luxury apartments situated right on the crescent-shaped sandy beach.

ONLINE MAP

Unit TV DVD General S Leisure

Remember to check when booking

Please remember that all information in this guide has been supplied by the proprietors well in advance of publication. Since changes do sometimes occur it's a good idea to check details at the time of booking.

NORTH MOLTON, Devon Map ref 1C1

★★–★★★
SELF CATERING

Units 3
Sleeps 2–8

LOW SEASON PER WK
Min £90.00

HIGH SEASON PER WK
Max £460.00

West Millbrook, South Molton

contact Mrs Rosemarie Courtney, West Millbrook, Twitchen, South Molton EX36 3LP
t (01598) 740382 **e** wmbselfcatering@aol.com

westmillbrook.co.uk

open All year
payment Cash, cheques
nearest shop 1.75 miles
nearest pub 1.5 miles

Farm bordering Exmoor, surrounded by pleasant gardens and beautiful, peaceful countryside. Situated a mile from North Molton village with easy access from North Devon link road. Ideal for touring Exmoor and North Devon/Somerset coast and beaches. Games room, play area. Out-of-season short breaks. Colour brochure available.

Unit General P Leisure

NYMPSFIELD, Gloucestershire Map ref 2B1

★★★
SELF CATERING

Units 1
Sleeps 1–4

LOW SEASON PER WK
Min £150.00

HIGH SEASON PER WK
Min £170.00

Crossways, Nympsfield

contact Mr & Mrs Bowen, Crossways, Tinkley Lane, Nympsfield, Stonehouse GL10 3TU
t (01453) 860309

Annexe to house, large living room, french window onto garden, fitted kitchen/diner. Twin-bedded room, bathroom. Own entrance. Fully self-contained. Private garden. Adjacent to the Cotswold Way.

open All year except Christmas and New Year
payment Cash, cheques
nearest shop 2 miles
nearest pub less than 0.5 miles

Unit General P Leisure

OKEHAMPTON, Devon Map ref 1C2

★★★★
SELF CATERING

Units 4
Sleeps 4–6

LOW SEASON PER WK
£195.00–£370.00

HIGH SEASON PER WK
£370.00–£690.00

5% discount on second (lower price) cottage if booked together. Short breaks often available (minimum 3 nights).

Beer Farm, Okehampton

contact Bob & Sue Annear, Beer Farm, Okehampton EX20 1SG **t** (01837) 840265
e info@beerfarm.co.uk

beerfarm.co.uk

open All year
payment Cash, cheques
nearest shop 1 mile
nearest pub 1.5 miles

Enjoy a peaceful holiday on our small farm situated on the northern edge of Dartmoor in mid-Devon. Comfortable and well-equipped two- and three-bedroomed cottages with DVDs and CD players. One offers accessibility for the less mobile. Games room, some covered parking. Dogs/horses by arrangement. Good walking, cycling and touring base.

Unit General P S Leisure

CYCLISTS WELCOME

Fancy a cycling holiday?

For a fabulous freewheeling break, seek out accommodation participating in our Cyclists Welcome scheme. Look out for the symbol and plan your route online at nationalcyclenetwork.org.

OKEHAMPTON, Devon Map ref 1C2

★★★★
SELF CATERING

Units 3
Sleeps 2–14

LOW SEASON PER WK
Min £225.00

HIGH SEASON PER WK
Max £1,645.00

Short breaks available out of high season.

Bowerland, Okehampton

contact Ray or Mel Quirke, East Bowerland Farm, Okehampton EX20 4LZ **t** (01837) 55979
e bowerland@devonhols.com

devonhols.com GUEST REVIEWS

open All year
payment Credit/debit cards, cash, cheques
nearest shop 1 mile

Bowerland is a traditional farmhouse with courtyard cottages on Dartmoor's doorstep. Ideally situated for a relaxing holiday in beautiful countryside but within easy reach of the many attractions of Devon and Cornwall. Good local food, superb walking, fishing, golf, cycling, tennis etc. Log fires in Old Dairy and Farmhouse.

ONLINE MAP

Unit General P
Leisure

OKEHAMPTON, Devon Map ref 1C2

★★★★
SELF CATERING

Units 1
Sleeps 2

LOW SEASON PER WK
£215.00–£443.00

HIGH SEASON PER WK
£143.00–£317.00

Heather Cottage, Okehampton

contact Yvette Martin, **t** (01837) 658820 & 07971 258040 **e** yvettemartin@btinternet.com

lastminute-cottages.co.uk/north-and-mid-devon/dem2028/ GUEST REVIEWS • SPECIAL OFFERS • REAL-TIME BOOKING

open All year
payment Credit/debit cards, cash, cheques
nearest shop less than 0.5 miles
nearest pub less than 0.5 miles

A quiet and comfortable cottage/garden flat for two featuring a locally planted verdant garden and located just five minutes' walk from Dartmoor National Park and eight to Okehampton's bustling town centre with all amenities including cinema, art gallery and Waitrose supermarket! Twin or double beds. Wireless internet connection.

SAT NAV *EX20 1EH*

Unit General P Leisure

OKEHAMPTON, Devon Map ref 1C2

★★★★
SELF CATERING

Units 4
Sleeps 4–8

LOW SEASON PER WK
£300.00–£460.00

HIGH SEASON PER WK
£360.00–£940.00

Fishing weekends based on 3 well-stocked coarse-fishing lakes.

Week Farm Country Holidays, Okehampton

contact Mrs Margaret Hockridge, Week Farm Country Holidays, Bridestowe, Okehampton EX20 4HZ
t (01837) 861221 **e** accom@weekfarmonline.com

weekfarmonline.com

open All year
payment Credit/debit cards, cash, cheques
nearest shop 1.25 miles
nearest pub 1.25 miles

Delightful barn conversions on working beef and sheep farm, furnished to high standards. Lounge, well-equipped fitted kitchens/dining areas, outdoor heated swimming pool, gardens and patio, barbecue areas. Dartmoor just a walk away. Pony-trekking, walking, cycling, fishing or just simply relaxing. Home from home. Three coarse-fishing lakes.

Unit General P
Leisure

OTTERFORD, Somerset Map ref 1D2

★★★★
SELF CATERING

Units **1**
Sleeps **1–11**

LOW SEASON PER WK
£395.00

HIGH SEASON PER WK
£750.00–£950.00

Tamarack Lodge, Chard

contact Matthew Sparks, Tamarack Lodge, Fyffett Farm, Chard TA20 3QP **t** (01823) 601270
e matthew.sparks@tamaracklodge.co.uk

tamaracklodge.co.uk GUEST REVIEWS

Luxurious log cabin-style ranch house on beautiful Blackdown Hills of Somerset. As seen on TV and in Daily Telegraph article. Suitable for disabled. Stabling available. Situated on family livestock farm. Two wildlife sites. Coast 35 minutes away.

open All year
payment Cash, cheques
nearest shop 1 mile
nearest pub 0.5 miles

Unit TV DVD General P S
Leisure

PADSTOW, Cornwall Map ref 1B2

★★★★★
SELF CATERING

Units **9**
Sleeps **2–8**

LOW SEASON PER WK
£425.00–£900.00

HIGH SEASON PER WK
£700.00–£2,300.00

Retallack Resort and Spa, Nr Padstow

contact Miranda Waldron, Retallack Resort and Spa, Winnards Perch TR9 6DE **t** (01637) 881580
e miranda@retellackresort.com

retallackresort.com GUEST REVIEWS • SPECIAL OFFERS • REAL-TIME BOOKING

open All year
payment Credit/debit cards, cash, cheques
nearest shop 1 mile
nearest pub 1 mile

A selection of two- and four-bedroom lodges, set in a luxury resort. On-site spa facilities, golf, tennis and much more for the whole family.

ONLINE MAP

Unit TV SC DVD General P S
Leisure

PADSTOW, Cornwall Map ref 1B2

★★★★
SELF CATERING

Units **2**
Sleeps **4–6**

LOW SEASON PER WK
£300.00–£325.00

HIGH SEASON PER WK
£770.00–£940.00

Sunday Cottage & School Cottage, Padstow

contact Mrs Diane Hoe, Lower Cottage, Preston on Stour, Stratford-upon-Avon CV37 8NG
t (01789) 450214 **e** mail@sundaycottage.co.uk

sundaycottage.co.uk

open All year
payment Cash, cheques
nearest shop less than 0.5 miles
nearest pub less than 0.5 miles

Beautifully restored, tastefully furnished cottages in old part of Padstow. Only three minutes' walk to the delightful harbour. Ideal location for those who appreciate comfort and quality. School Cottage has a lovely private, walled garden. Beautiful unspoilt coastline and beaches all around and many fine restaurants including four Rick Stein establishments.

Unit TV DVD General 8 P Leisure

PADSTOW, Cornwall Map ref 1B2

★★★–★★★★★
SELF CATERING

Units 4
Sleeps 1–8

LOW SEASON PER WK
£210.00–£525.00

HIGH SEASON PER WK
£540.00–£1,295.00

Special offers available upon request for low season (Nov-May) for couples and long-weekend stays.

Yellow Sands Apartments & House, Padstow

contact Mr Dakin, Yellow Sands Apartments & House, Harlyn Bay, Padstow PL28 8SE
t (01841) 520376 **e** martin@yellowsands.fsnet.co.uk

yellowsands.net SPECIAL OFFERS

open All year
payment Cash, cheques
nearest shop 1 mile
nearest pub less than 0.5 miles

Resident proprietor provides spacious, quality accommodation with stunning sea views! Just 200yds from superb sandy beach and coastal footpath in a designated Area of Outstanding Natural Beauty. Landscaped gardens. Shops and golf one mile. Historic Padstow 2.5 miles. For sightseeing daytrips, all parts of Cornwall within one hour's drive.

Unit General P S
Leisure

PADSTOW, Cornwall Map ref 1B2

★★★–★★★★★
SELF CATERING

Units 6
Sleeps 1–6

LOW SEASON PER WK
£260.00–£395.00

HIGH SEASON PER WK
£680.00–£815.00

Yellow Sands Cottages, Padstow

contact Mrs Sharon Keast, Yellow Sands Cottages, Harlyn Bay, Padstow PL28 8SE **t** (01637) 881548
e yellowsands@btinternet.com

yellowsands.co.uk

open All year
payment Cash, cheques
nearest shop 1 mile
nearest pub 0.5 miles

Cottages set in well-kept grounds, ideally situated just 250m to Harlyn's sandy shore and coastal path. Local amenities and eating houses within one mile, Padstow 2.5 miles. The cottages are fully equipped and furnished, and serviced to a high standard, providing an environment in which to sit back, relax and enjoy!

Unit General P Leisure

PAIGNTON, Devon Map ref 1D2

★★★★
SELF CATERING

Units 5
Sleeps 2–6

LOW SEASON PER WK
£185.00–£265.00

HIGH SEASON PER WK
£290.00–£625.00

Short breaks available (4 nights) except Jul & Aug. Free Wi-Fi internet access for your laptop.

All Seasons Holiday Apartments, Paignton

contact Mr Colin Livesey, 18 Garfield Road, Paignton TQ4 6AX **t** (01803) 552187
e enquiries@allseasonsholidayapartments.co.uk

allseasonsholidayapartments.co.uk SPECIAL OFFERS • REAL-TIME BOOKING

open April to October
payment Cash, cheques
nearest shop less than 0.5 miles
nearest pub less than 0.5 miles

'Ideal location, very clean, comfortable and home from home' as frequently quoted by our guests. Our high-quality apartments are all non-smoking and are situated on level ground close to the beach, shops, coach, rail and bus stations. Apartments have lounge, one or two double bedrooms, separate kitchen and full-size bathroom. Sorry no pets.

SAT NAV *TQ4 6AX* **ONLINE MAP**

Unit General P S

PAIGNTON, Devon Map ref 1D2

★★–★★★
SELF CATERING

Units 6
Sleeps 1–4

LOW SEASON PER WK
£90.00–£160.00

HIGH SEASON PER WK
£220.00–£380.00

Fairsea Holiday Flats, Paignton

contact Mr John Hallett, 12 St Andrews Road, Paignton TQ4 6HA **t** (01803) 556903
e lesleyfarrand@amserve.com

Quiet location, five minutes' walk to beaches, Quay West Water Park, harbour and town. Comfortably furnished, fully equipped, cleanliness assured.

open All year
payment Cash, cheques
nearest shop less than 0.5 miles
nearest pub less than 0.5 miles

Unit General

PAIGNTON, Devon Map ref 1D2

★★★
SELF CATERING

Units 8
Sleeps 2–8

LOW SEASON PER WK
£175.00–£420.00

HIGH SEASON PER WK
£350.00–£545.00

3-night stays available Oct-Jan (excl Christmas and New Year).

Julie Court Holiday Apartments, Paignton

Julie Court Holiday Apartments, 5 Colin Road, Paignton TQ3 2NR **t** (01803) 551012 & (01803) 551463 **e** info@juliecourt.co.uk

juliecourt.co.uk GUEST REVIEWS • SPECIAL OFFERS • REAL-TIME BOOKING

open All year
payment Credit/debit cards, cash, cheques
nearest shop less than 0.5 miles
nearest pub less than 0.5 miles

Finalist for the English Riviera Best Self-Catering Award for last two years. Regularly quoted by our guests as 'best in Paignton' and 'great for location'. Seafront position, close to all beaches, attractions, piers, cinema, coastal walks and local amenities. Quality self-catering apartments with private car park, situated on a level and quiet cul-de-sac.

SAT NAV *TQ3 2NR* **ONLINE MAP**

Unit General Leisure

PAR, Cornwall Map ref 1B3

★★★★★
SELF CATERING

Units 1
Sleeps 2–4

LOW SEASON PER WK
£399.00–£599.00

HIGH SEASON PER WK
£599.00–£899.00

Kilhallon Court Cottage

contact Anna Wright, Highland Court Lodge, Biscovey Road PL24 2HW **t** (01726) 813320
e victoria@highlandcourt.co.uk

highlandcourt.co.uk

Idyllic, luxury countryside retreat ideal for couples or family of four, plus cot. Two bedrooms, bathroom with jacuzzi spa bath/shower, open-plan kitchen, dining room, lounge. Very close to Eden Project.

open All year
payment Credit/debit cards, cash, cheques, euros
nearest shop 0.5 miles
nearest pub less than 0.5 miles

Unit General Leisure

PENZANCE, Cornwall Map ref 1A3

★★★
SELF CATERING

Units 1
Sleeps 2–4

LOW SEASON PER WK
£155.00–£225.00

HIGH SEASON PER WK
£275.00–£375.00

Crankan Flat, Penzance

contact Mr & Mrs Braybrooks, Crankan Flat, Crankan, Bone Valley TR20 8UJ **t** (01736) 351388

Peaceful three-roomed ground-floor flat in quiet gardens. Heamoor village is 0.25 miles distant, with shops, bakery, pub and post office. Excellent centre for sandy beaches, good walks and rugged coast.

open All year
payment Cash, cheques
nearest shop less than 0.5 miles
nearest pub less than 0.5 miles

Unit General Leisure

Using map references

Map references refer to the colour maps at the front of this guide.

PENZANCE, Cornwall Map ref 1A3

★★
SELF CATERING

Units 1
Sleeps 1–5

LOW SEASON PER WK
£130.00–£200.00

HIGH SEASON PER WK
£400.00–£650.00

Old Court 36, Kenegie Manor, Gulval, Penzance

contact Mrs Margaret Lewis, 6 Carter Avenue, Codsall WV8 1HQ **t** (01902) 845139
e margellen@googlemail.com

kenegie.com

Holiday house, rural setting, within beautiful grounds of country manor house. Close to St Ives. Accommodation to high standard. Sleeps five. Indoor pool, bar, sauna and tennis during season.

open All year
payment Cash, cheques
nearest shop 1 mile
nearest pub 1 mile

Unit TV DVD General Leisure

PENZANCE, Cornwall Map ref 1A3

★★★★
SELF CATERING

Units 1
Sleeps 5

LOW SEASON PER WK
£200.00–£360.00

HIGH SEASON PER WK
£360.00–£596.00

Spindrift, Penzance

contact Mrs F A Morgan, Gabbard, 16 Cuninghill Road, Inverurie AB51 3TS **t** (01467) 629597
e pjcmorgan@hotmail.com

Close to town centre and harbour, Spindrift is in a secluded location with pleasant views over Penzance harbour and Mount's Bay. All amenities are within three or four minutes' walk.

open All year
payment Cash, cheques
nearest shop 1 mile
nearest pub less than 0.5 miles

Unit TV General P Leisure

PERRANPORTH, Cornwall Map ref 1B2

★★★★
SELF CATERING

Units 1
Sleeps 1–6

LOW SEASON PER WK
£275.00–£375.00

HIGH SEASON PER WK
£430.00–£740.00

Treth Cottage, Perranporth

contact Mr & Mrs John & Jenny Cuthill, Claremont, St Georges Hill, Perranporth TR6 0JS
t (01872) 573624

Early-Victorian cottage (two double rooms, one twin) in a quiet, private location with a sheltered garden, 150m from a sandy surfing beach. Close to all amenities. Parking.

open All year
payment Cash, cheques, euros
nearest shop less than 0.5 miles
nearest pub less than 0.5 miles

Unit TV DVD General P Leisure

PLYMOUTH, Devon Map ref 1C2

★★★
SELF CATERING

Units 5
Sleeps 1–6

LOW SEASON PER WK
£250.00–£290.00

HIGH SEASON PER WK
£290.00–£350.00

One month-plus lets 15% discount.

Haddington House Apartments, Plymouth

contact Mr Fairfax Luxmoore, 42 Haddington Road, Plymouth PL2 1RR **t** (01752) 500383

abudd.co.uk

open All year
payment Credit/debit cards, cash, cheques
nearest shop less than 0.5 miles
nearest pub less than 0.5 miles

Elegant, self-contained apartments set within a large Victorian house, offering well-appointed modern facilities, tasteful decoration and furnishings. Secure parking, courtyard gardens.

SAT NAV *PL2 1RR*

Unit TV General P Leisure

PETS! WELCOME WELCOME PETS!

Where is my pet welcome?

Want to take your cherished companion with you on holiday? Proprietors participating in our Welcome Pets! scheme go out of their way to make special provision for you and your pet. Look out for the symbol.

PLYMOUTH, Devon Map ref 1C2

★★
SELF CATERING

Units 3
Sleeps 4–6

LOW SEASON PER WK
£300.00–£400.00

HIGH SEASON PER WK
£475.00–£500.00

Hoe Lodge, Plymouth

contact Mr T Miller, Hoe Apartments, Hoe Lodge, 6 Northumberland Terrace, Radford Road, Plymouth PL1 3DD **t** (01489) 557797 **e** info@hoe-apartments.co.uk

hoe-apartments.co.uk

A choice of three excellent self-catering apartments located just 200yds from Plymouth Hoe and the seafront.

open All year
payment Cash, cheques
nearest shop less than 0.5 miles
nearest pub less than 0.5 miles

Unit General Leisure

POOLE, Dorset Map ref 2B3

★★★★★
SELF CATERING

Units 10
Sleeps 2–8

LOW SEASON PER WK
£495.00–£650.00

HIGH SEASON PER WK
£690.00–£1,150.00

Special offers will appear from time to time on our website.

The Dorset Resort, Hyde, Wareham

contact Miss Jackie Langworthy, The Dorset Resort, Hyde, Wareham BH20 7NT **t** (01929) 472244 **e** resort@dorsetresort.com

dorsetresort.com

open All year
payment Credit/debit cards, cash, cheques
nearest shop 3 miles
nearest pub 3 miles

The Scandinavian-style log homes at the Dorset Resort are both beautiful and luxurious. Superbly well crafted, they are set in tranquil woodland in the heart of Dorset's stunning countryside. Each has its own sauna, log-burning stove and balcony. We are minutes from Blue Flag beaches, Jurassic Coast etc.

Unit General
Leisure

POOLE, Dorset Map ref 2B3

★★★
SELF CATERING

Units 1
Sleeps 4

LOW SEASON PER WK
£250.00–£440.00

HIGH SEASON PER WK
£440.00–£680.00

Fripps Cottage, Wimborne

contact Mrs Helen Edbrooke, Stoneleigh House, 2 Rowlands Hill, Wimborne BH21 1AN **t** (01202) 884908 **e** helen@stoneleighhouse.com

stoneleighhouse.com/frippscottage

Two-bedroom detached bungalow set in five acres in beautiful country location, close to town and coast. Large, enclosed, well-maintained garden. All mod cons, and fully equipped for a very comfortable stay.

open All year
payment Cash, cheques
nearest shop 1.5 miles
nearest pub 1 mile

Unit General Leisure

POOLE, Dorset Map ref 2B3

★★★
SELF CATERING

Units 1
Sleeps 3–5

LOW SEASON PER WK
£220.00–£350.00

HIGH SEASON PER WK
£450.00–£1,000.00

Poole Harbour Holiday Homes, Poole

contact Miss Brown, Poole Harbour Holidays, The Esplanade, Poole BH15 2BA **t** 07778 586710 & (01202) 743614 **e** stay@pooleharbourholidays.com

pooleharbourholidays.com SPECIAL OFFERS

A selection of executive accommodation around Poole Harbour, furnished to the highest standard. Double/single beds, harbour view/private courtyard, free broadband, TV/DVD/CD player, linen/towels, washing machine, microwave, parking, garden.

open All year
payment Credit/debit cards, cash, cheques, euros
nearest shop less than 0.5 miles
nearest pub less than 0.5 miles

Unit General Leisure

POOLE, Dorset Map ref 2B3

POOLE, Dorset Map ref 2B3

★★★
SELF CATERING

Units 1
Sleeps 2

LOW SEASON PER WK
Min £125.00

HIGH SEASON PER WK
Max £300.00

Sunnydale, Poole

contact Mr Ian Hull, 94 Blandford Road North, Beacon Hill, Poole BH16 6AD **t** 07880 501940
e ianhpoole@btinternet.com

Ground-floor one-bedroom flat with lounge, kitchen, bathroom, patio area. Off-road parking.

open All year
payment Cash, cheques, euros
nearest shop 0.75 miles
nearest pub 0.5 miles

Unit General Leisure

PORLOCK, Somerset Map ref 1D1

★★★
SELF CATERING

Units 1
Sleeps 2–6

LOW SEASON PER WK
£300.00–£340.00

HIGH SEASON PER WK
£360.00–£390.00

Orchard Cottage, Allerford

contact Mrs Diana Williams, Orchard Cottage, Brandish Street Farm, Brandish Street, Minehead TA24 8HR **t** (01643) 862383

open All year
payment Cash, cheques
nearest shop less than 0.5 miles
nearest pub 1 mile

Delightful, character, National Trust cottage on a traditional working farm, surrounded by beautiful scenery. Old beams, log fire, cosy, clean and comfortable. Situated near Allerford and Minehead, and central for exploring the Exmoor coast and countryside. Many attractions nearby. Village shops, pubs and restaurants five minutes' drive away. Colour brochure available.

Unit General 4 P Leisure

Check the maps for accommodation locations

Colour maps at the front pinpoint all the cities, towns and villages where you will find accommodation entries in the regional sections. Pick your location and then refer to the place index at the back to find the page number.

PORT GAVERNE, Cornwall Map ref 1B2

★★★★
SELF CATERING

Units **10**
Sleeps **2–8**

LOW SEASON PER WK
£364.00–£567.00

HIGH SEASON PER WK
£612.00–£1,254.00

3-night weekend or 4-night midweek short breaks available Jan-May, Sep-Dec.

Green Door Cottages, Port Isaac

Green Door Cottages, Port Isaac PL29 3SQ **t** (01208) 880293 **e** enquiries@greendoorcottages.co.uk

greendoorcottages.co.uk

open All year
payment Credit/debit cards, cash, cheques
nearest shop 0.5 miles
nearest pub less than 0.5 miles

A delightful collection of restored 18thC Cornish buildings built around a sunny enclosed courtyard and two lovely apartments with stunning sea views. Picturesque, tranquil cove ideal for children. Half a mile from Port Isaac, on the South West Coast Path. Polzeath beach and Camel Trail nearby. Traditional pub opposite. Dogs welcome.

ONLINE MAP

Unit General
Leisure

PORT ISAAC, Cornwall Map ref 1B2

★★★★
SELF CATERING

Units **9**
Sleeps **2–8**

LOW SEASON PER WK
£100.00–£500.00

HIGH SEASON PER WK
£540.00–£1,500.00

Trevathan Farm, Port Isaac

contact Mrs Jo Symons, Trevathan Farm, St Endellion, Port Isaac PL29 3TT **t** (01208) 880248
e symons@trevathanfarm.com

trevathanfarm.com

Beautiful cottages with countryside views, games room, fishing lake, tennis court, set on working farm. Play area and friendly animals. Beaches, golf, riding within three miles.

open All year
payment Cash, cheques
nearest shop 3 miles
nearest pub 2 miles

Unit General
Leisure

PORTHCURNO, Cornwall Map ref 1A3

★★★
SELF CATERING

Units **1**
Sleeps **1–6**

LOW SEASON PER WK
£450.00–£650.00

HIGH SEASON PER WK
£750.00–£1,100.00

Heatherlands, Porthcurno, Penzance

contact Mr Robin Newell, Holmbush, Church Road, Barcombe, Lewes BN8 5TP **t** (01273) 400153
e info@heatherlandscornwall.com

heatherlandscornwall.com

open All year
payment Cash, cheques
nearest shop 0.5 miles
nearest pub 0.5 miles

Fabulous location on South West Coast Path. Year-round appeal to families, birdwatchers, walkers. Detached granite house in Cornwall's far west, overlooking rugged coast and gorgeous, sandy Porthchapel beach. Sleeps six, full central heating, two bathrooms, three wcs, separate sitting, dining, utility rooms. Terraced grassy garden. Close to Minack Theatre.

SAT NAV *TR19 6JS*

Unit General
Leisure

Has every property been assessed?

All accommodation in this guide has been rated for quality, or is awaiting assessment, by a professional national tourist board assessor.

PORTHLEVEN, Cornwall Map ref 1B3

★★★★
SELF CATERING

Units 1
Sleeps 4

LOW SEASON PER WK
£250.00–£275.00

HIGH SEASON PER WK
£450.00–£610.00

Porthcressa, Porthleven

contact Mrs Barbara Arthur, Hillside, Fore Street, Porthleven TR13 9HJ **t** (01326) 574487
e porthcressa@orange.net

open All year except Christmas and New Year
payment Cash, cheques
nearest shop less than 0.5 miles
nearest pub less than 0.5 miles

A comfortable and beautifully maintained cottage sleeping four, a few minutes from the picturesque harbour and long stretch of beach in the fishing village of Porthleven. With its own parking and garden, it is perfectly situated for discovering the many beaches and coves around Mount's Bay and the Lizard Peninsula.

Unit TV DVD General P

PORTHTOWAN, Cornwall Map ref 1B3

★★★★★
SELF CATERING

Units 5
Sleeps 1–6

LOW SEASON PER WK
£300.00–£540.00

HIGH SEASON PER WK
£620.00–£1,490.00

Rosehill Lodges, Porthtowan

contact Mr John Barrow, Rosehill Lodges, Porthtowan TR4 8AR **t** (01209) 891920
e reception@rosehilllodges.com

rosehilllodges.com GUEST REVIEWS · SPECIAL OFFERS · REAL-TIME BOOKING

open All year
payment Credit/debit cards, cash, cheques
nearest shop 0.5 miles
nearest pub 0.5 miles

Luxurious lodges, set within a wooded valley in a Cornish seaside village just five minutes' walk to Porthtowan's Blue Flag sandy beach, pubs and restaurants. Relax and unwind with king-size beds, log burners and your own personal hot tub. Grass roofs and glass-covered decking for those stargazing nights complete the package.

ONLINE MAP

Unit TV SC DVD General P S
Leisure

PORTLAND, Dorset Map ref 2B3

★★★
SELF CATERING

Units 1
Sleeps 1–4

LOW SEASON PER WK
Min £135.00

HIGH SEASON PER WK
Max £365.00

Lilac Cottage, Portland

contact Ms Shelagh Hepple, 9 Kestrel Drive, Sandal, Wakefield WF2 6SB **t** (01924) 252522
e hepple@lilaccott171.fs.co.uk

portlandholiday.co.uk

A delightful Victorian terraced cottage with modern amenities but which retains many of its original features. Located in a highly scenic area five minutes from Church Ope Cove.

open All year
payment Cash, cheques

Unit TV General S

FAMILIES WELCOME

Looking for an ideal family break?

For accommodation offering additional facilities and services for a range of ages and family units, look out for the Families Welcome symbol. Owners of these properties will go out of their way to welcome families.

PORTLAND, Dorset Map ref 2B3

★★★★
SELF CATERING

Units 1
Sleeps 2

LOW SEASON PER WK
£175.00–£325.00

HIGH SEASON PER WK
£375.00–£450.00

Portland Hideaway, Portland

contact Mr H Marshall, 7 East Castle Avenue, Largs KA30 8JU **t** 07957 138054
e howard@bestlimited.co.uk

Romantic, spacious, peaceful, sunny studio near Portland Bill with large, private, enclosed suntrap patio garden. Secure parking. Close to shops, village pub, bistros, spectacular coastal footpaths and varied outdoor activities.

open All year
payment Cash, cheques
nearest shop less than 0.5 miles
nearest pub less than 0.5 miles

Unit General P Leisure

PORTLAND, Dorset Map ref 2B3

★★★★
SELF CATERING

Units 1
Sleeps 7

LOW SEASON PER WK
£275.00–£425.00

HIGH SEASON PER WK
£575.00–£650.00

Portland Retreat, Portland

contact Mr H Marshall, 7 East Castle Avenue, Largs KA30 8JU **t** 07957 138054
e howard@bestlimited.co.uk

Uniquely spacious, peaceful detached house near Portland Bill with conservatory and large enclosed sunny garden. Secure parking. Close to shops, village pub, sailing, diving, para sports, climbing, walks and birdwatching.

open All year
payment Cash, cheques
nearest shop less than 0.5 miles
nearest pub less than 0.5 miles

Unit General P Leisure

PORTLOE, Cornwall Map ref 1B3

★★★★
SELF CATERING

Units 1
Sleeps 1–5

LOW SEASON PER WK
£300.00–£450.00

HIGH SEASON PER WK
£450.00–£600.00

Trehaven View, Truro

contact Mr & Mrs Mlynski, Compass North, Veryan, Truro TR2 5QF **t** (01872) 501824
e julie.mlynski@virgin.net

cottageguide.co.uk/trehaven

Luxury apartment with balcony and sea views in a picturesque fishing village, Portloe, on the Roseland Peninsula.

open All year
payment Cash, cheques
nearest shop 1.5 miles
nearest pub less than 0.5 miles

Unit General P

PORTREATH, Cornwall Map ref 1B3

★★★★★
SELF CATERING

Units 3
Sleeps 1–6

LOW SEASON PER WK
£220.00–£300.00

HIGH SEASON PER WK
£300.00–£750.00

Short breaks available Oct-Mar, also discounted rates for couples, out of season.

Higher Laity Farm, Redruth

contact Mrs Lynne Drew, Higher Laity Farm, Portreath Road, Redruth TR16 4HY **t** (01209) 842317
e info@higherlaityfarm.co.uk

higherlaityfarm.co.uk SPECIAL OFFERS

open All year
payment Credit/debit cards, cash, cheques
nearest shop 1 mile
nearest pub 0.5 miles

Come and relax in our tastefully converted luxury barns. En suite bedrooms, central heating, linen provided, gas cooker, fridge/freezer, microwave, dishwasher, washer/dryer, hi-fi, video, DVD. Close to beaches and the breathtaking North Cornish coast. Ideal for walking, relaxing and exploring Cornwall. A friendly welcome is guaranteed. One cottage wheelchair accessible.

Unit General P
Leisure

Where are the maps?

Colour maps can be found at the front of the guide. They pinpoint the location of all accommodation found in the regional sections.

PORTREATH, Cornwall Map ref 1B3

★★★-★★★★★
SELF CATERING

Units 7
Sleeps 2–6

LOW SEASON PER WK
£225.00–£450.00

HIGH SEASON PER WK
£350.00–£780.00

Short breaks available from Nov to Mar.

Trengove Farm Cottages, Redruth

contact Mrs Richards, Trengove Farm, Cot Road, Illogan, Redruth TR16 4PU **t** (01209) 843008
e richards@farming.co.uk

trengovefarm.co.uk

open All year
payment Credit/debit cards, cash, cheques, euros
nearest shop 1 mile
nearest pub 1 mile

Traditional, well-equipped cottages and farmhouse on a 140-acre arable farm. Close to beautiful beaches, cliffs and countryside park, yet within easy reach of the main towns. Centrally heated, free wireless broadband available. A superb location for walking, swimming, touring or just relaxing.

SAT NAV *TR16 4PU* **ONLINE MAP**

Unit General P Leisure

PORTWRINKLE, Cornwall Map ref 1C2

★★★-★★★★★
SELF CATERING

Units 5
Sleeps 4–10

LOW SEASON PER WK
£220.00–£1,200.00

HIGH SEASON PER WK
£650.00–£2,500.00

Whitsand Bay Self Catering, Torpoint

contact J Earle, Parade House, The Parade, Liskeard PL14 6AH **t** (01579) 345688
e enwbsc@hotmail.com

whitsandbayselfcatering.co.uk

Five beautiful cottages right by the sea with unrivalled sea views and close to golf course. Indoor pool available, and one house with private pool.

open All year
payment Credit/debit cards, cash, cheques
nearest shop 0.5 miles
nearest pub 0.5 miles

Unit General P Leisure

POUGHILL, Cornwall Map ref 1C2

★★★★
SELF CATERING

Units 1
Sleeps 4

LOW SEASON PER WK
Min £300.00

HIGH SEASON PER WK
Max £750.00

Columbine Cottage, Bude

t (01942) 721003 **e** enquiries@trevalgas-columbine.co.uk

trevalgas-columbine.co.uk

Two-bedroomed self-catering contemporary cottage, part of an established holiday complex. Full bathroom and additional separate toilet. Open-plan living area with fully equipped kitchen. Wi-Fi and indoor swimming pool.

open All year
payment Cash, cheques
nearest shop 0.5 miles
nearest pub 0.5 miles

Unit General P Leisure

Where is my pet welcome?

Some proprietors welcome well-behaved pets. Look for the symbol in the accommodation listings. You can also buy a copy of our popular guide – Pets Come Too! – available from good bookshops and online at visitbritaindirect.com.

PRAA SANDS, Cornwall Map ref 1B3

★★★
SELF CATERING

Units 6
Sleeps 2–8

LOW SEASON PER WK
£295.00–£500.00

HIGH SEASON PER WK
£500.00–£1,300.00

Discounts available for smaller parties and for late availability throughout the year.

Sea Meads Holiday Homes, Penzance

contact Ms Pierpoint, Best Leisure, Old House Farm, Fulmer Road, Fulmer, Slough SL3 6HU
t (01753) 664336 **e** enquiries@bestleisure.co.uk

bestleisure.co.uk SPECIAL OFFERS • REAL-TIME BOOKING

open All year
payment Cash, cheques
nearest shop 0.5 miles
nearest pub 0.5 miles

Well-equipped detached houses, each with private garden, situated in superb subtropical position on a private estate. Spacious lounge with large patio windows. Balcony to the first floor from which to enjoy the view of the glorious mile-long Praa Sands beach, only five minutes' walk away. All houses have Wi-Fi broadband access.

SAT NAV *TR20 9TA* **ONLINE MAP**

Unit TV DVD General P S
Leisure

PUNCKNOWLE, Dorset Map ref 2A3

★★★★–★★★★★
SELF CATERING

Units 3
Sleeps 6–16

LOW SEASON PER WK
£650.00–£1,300.00

HIGH SEASON PER WK
£850.00–£3,500.00

Berwick Manor, Puncknowle Manor Farmhouse and The Carriage House, Dorchester

contact Ms Rebecca Hutchings, Puncknowle Manor Cottages, Puncknowle Manor Estate, Puncknowle, Dorchester DT2 9BX **t** (01308) 897706 **e** cottages@pknlest.com

dorset-selfcatering.co.uk

open All year
payment Cash, cheques
nearest shop 1 mile
nearest pub 0.75 miles

Located in idyllic position overlooking peaceful Bridge Valley. Just two minutes' drive from Jurassic Coast. One cottage, two large properties, adaptable for large group holidays.

Unit TV DVD General P S Leisure

RAME, Cornwall Map ref 1C3

★★★★
SELF CATERING

Units 1
Sleeps 20

LOW SEASON PER WK
£2,550.00–£4,885.00

HIGH SEASON PER WK
£4,885.00–£7,995.00

Polhawn Fort, Torpoint

contact Miss Kathryn Deakin, Polhawn Fort, Rame, Polhawn, Torpoint PL10 1LL **t** (01752) 822864

polhawnfort.com

Napoleonic fort for exclusive hire for holidays, parties and weddings – the fort has a civil wedding licence. Prices for shorter stays range from £2,595 for midweek stays to £6,795 for a summer weekend.

open All year
payment Credit/debit cards, cash, cheques
nearest shop 2 miles
nearest pub 2 miles

Unit TV DVD General P S Leisure

Using map references

The map references refer to the colour maps at the front of this guide. The first figure is the map number, the letter and figure that follow indicate the grid reference on the map.

REDRUTH, Cornwall Map ref 1B3

★★★
SELF CATERING

Units 1
Sleeps 2–6

LOW SEASON PER WK
£230.00–£300.00

HIGH SEASON PER WK
£330.00–£535.00

The Barn at Little Trefula, St Day, Redruth

contact Mr & Mrs Bill & Ann Higgins, The Barn at Little Trefula, Little Trefula Farm, Trefula, Redruth TR16 5ET **t** (01209) 820572 & 07789 044602 **e** barn@trefula.com

trefula.com SPECIAL OFFERS · REAL-TIME BOOKING

The Barn at Little Trefula, in Cornwall's historic mining country yet surrounded by fields, is a recent architect-designed conversion offering panoramic views and the perfect base for a peaceful, comfortable family holiday.

open All year
payment Credit/debit cards, cash, cheques, euros
nearest shop 0.5 miles
nearest pub less than 0.5 miles

Unit General Leisure

ROCK, Cornwall Map ref 1B2

★★★★–★★★★★
SELF CATERING

Units 7
Sleeps 2–10

LOW SEASON PER WK
£750.00–£1,000.00

HIGH SEASON PER WK
£900.00–£5,000.00

Mariners Lettings, Rock

contact Mrs Claire Stewart, Mariners Lettings Ltd, 41 Abingdon Road, London W8 6AH
t (020) 7938 2019

marinersrock.com

Luxury self-catering houses with sea views. Two minutes' walk to the beautiful Camel estuary. Fully equipped including bed linen. Dogs welcome. Open all year.

open All year
payment Credit/debit cards, cash, cheques

Unit General Leisure

RUAN HIGH LANES, Cornwall Map ref 1B3

★★★
SELF CATERING

Units 1
Sleeps 2

LOW SEASON PER WK
£200.00–£285.00

HIGH SEASON PER WK
£320.00–£420.00

The Old Loft, Ruan High Lanes

contact Mrs Delia Collins, The Old Loft, Higher Treluggan, Ruan High Lanes TR2 5LP
t (01872) 580732 **e** dee@roselandrentals.co.uk

roselandrentals.co.uk

open Easter to October, and Christmas
payment Cash, cheques
nearest shop 1.5 miles
nearest pub 1.5 miles

Cosy coach house converted to a high standard, located on the beautiful Roseland Peninsula, close to lovely beaches and picturesque coastal walks. Sleeps two, has slate patio and reserved parking space. We are close to several magnificent gardens and the Maritime Museum in Falmouth. Bed linen, towels and heating included. Children welcome by arrangement.

SAT NAV *TR2 5LP*

Unit General 1

ST AUSTELL, Cornwall Map ref 1B3

★★★–★★★★★
SELF CATERING

Units **19**
Sleeps **3–12**

LOW SEASON PER WK
£275.00–£900.00

HIGH SEASON PER WK
£650.00–£2,200.00

Short breaks Sep-May, £50 per night for 2 persons (min 3 nights).

Bosinver Farm Cottages, St Austell

contact Mrs Smith, Bosinver Farm Cottages, Trelowth, St Austell PL26 7DT **t** (01726) 72128
e reception@bosinver.co.uk

bosinver.co.uk GUEST REVIEWS • SPECIAL OFFERS • REAL-TIME BOOKING

open All year
payment Credit/debit cards, cash, cheques, euros
nearest shop 1 mile
nearest pub 1.5 miles

Best Self-Catering Establishment 2005, 2006 and 2007 – Cornwall Tourism Awards. Bosinver Farm Cottages are so nice our guests often don't want to leave. Here you can relax in real comfort, enjoy your own private garden, splash in the pool, feed the chickens, watch the wildlife, love the village feel and explore the Cornish coast and countryside.

ONLINE MAP

Unit TV DVD General P S
Leisure

ST AUSTELL, Cornwall Map ref 1B3

★★★★
SELF CATERING

Units **1**
Sleeps **2–5**

LOW SEASON PER WK
£300.00–£450.00

HIGH SEASON PER WK
£450.00–£800.00

Owls Reach, Roche, St Austell

contact Diana Pride, Owls Reach, Colbiggan Farm, Roche PL26 8LJ **t** (01208) 831597
e info@owlsreach.co.uk

owlsreach.co.uk

open All year
payment Cash, cheques, euros
nearest shop 2 miles
nearest pub 2 miles

A quiet, comfortable and elegant setting for your holiday. Detached, single-storey cottage, double glazed and centrally heated, with abundant natural light. Double/twin/single bedrooms, bathroom and shower room. Central location in peaceful countryside, adjacent to moorland – pheasants on lawn! Includes subscription to Country Club, with large indoor pool.

Unit TV DVD General P
Leisure

ST AUSTELL, Cornwall Map ref 1B3

★★★★
SELF CATERING

Units 7
Sleeps 2–6

LOW SEASON PER WK
Min £400.00

HIGH SEASON PER WK
Max £1,300.00

Short breaks available Nov-Mar inclusive. Free wireless broadband available in all the cottages.

Tregongeeves Farm Cottages, St Austell

contact Mr & Mrs John & Judith Clemo, Tregongeeves Farm Holiday Cottages, St Austell PL26 7DS
t (01726) 68202

cornwall-holidays.co.uk SPECIAL OFFERS · REAL-TIME BOOKING

open All year
payment Credit/debit cards, cash, cheques, euros
nearest shop 1 mile
nearest pub 1 mile

Tregongeeves combines quality accommodation with excellent leisure facilities. Guests enjoy exclusive, all year round use of the indoor heated swimming pool, spa bath, gym, recreation room and a professional tennis court. Being located in mid-Cornwall just off the A390 at St Austell, both coastlines are within easy reach.

ONLINE MAP

Unit General P
Leisure

ST BLAZEY, Cornwall Map ref 1B2

★★★★
SELF CATERING

Units 5
Sleeps 2

LOW SEASON PER WK
Min £250.00

HIGH SEASON PER WK
Max £450.00

Off season weekends and short breaks.

Woodmill Farm Holiday Cottages, Par

contact Mrs Michelle Hume, Woodmill Farm Holiday Cottages, Prideaux Road, St Blazey, Par PL24 2SR **t** (01726) 810171 **e** enquiries@woodmill-farm.co.uk

woodmill-farm.co.uk REAL-TIME BOOKING

open All year
payment Credit/debit cards, cash, cheques
nearest shop less than 0.5 miles
nearest pub less than 0.5 miles

A 17thC former flour mill set in seven acres on the edge of the picturesque Prideaux Wood. Eden one mile, Lost Gardens of Heligan six miles. Glorious beaches, historic ports, excellent local restaurants all within easy reach. Ideally situated to explore Cornwall. A perfect retreat at any time of year.

SAT NAV *PL24 2SR* **ONLINE MAP**

Unit General P Leisure

ST EWE, Cornwall Map ref 1B3

★★★★
SELF CATERING

Units 1
Sleeps 2–6

LOW SEASON PER WK
£350.00–£500.00

HIGH SEASON PER WK
£600.00–£850.00

Galowras Farm Cottage, St Austell

contact Dr Lisa & John Dunne, Galowras Farm Cottage, Galowras Farm, St Ewe PL26 6EW
t (01726) 842373 **e** galowras@btinternet.com

galowrasfarm.co.uk

A barn conversion providing high-quality accommodation in an idyllic situation. This is a special place in which to relax and unwind. Heligan Gardens, Eden, beaches and coastal path nearby.

open All year
payment Cash, cheques
nearest shop 2 miles
nearest pub 2 miles

Unit General P Leisure

Where can I get help and advice?

Tourist Information Centres offer friendly help with accommodation and holiday ideas as well as suggestions of places to visit and things to do. You'll find contact details at the beginning of each regional section.

ST IVES, Cornwall Map ref 1B3

★★
SELF CATERING

Units 1
Sleeps 2

LOW SEASON PER WK
£100.00–£150.00

HIGH SEASON PER WK
£185.00–£350.00

32 Porthia Road, St Ives

contact Mrs Marilyn Harry, 32 Porthia Road, St Ives TR26 2JB **t** (01736) 794986

One-bedroomed apartment for two adults. Sea views. Parking available, colour TV, twenty minutes to town on foot.

open All year except Christmas and New Year
payment Cash, cheques
nearest shop less than 0.5 miles
nearest pub less than 0.5 miles

Unit General P

ST IVES, Cornwall Map ref 1B3

★★★
SELF CATERING

Units 7
Sleeps 1–7

LOW SEASON PER WK
£190.00–£225.00

HIGH SEASON PER WK
£565.00–£745.00

Chy Mor and Premier Apartments, St Ives

contact Michael Gill, Chy Mor and Premier Apartments, Beach House, The Wharf, St Ives TR26 1LG
t (01736) 798798 **e** enquiry@stivesharbour.com

stivesharbour.com

open All year
payment Credit/debit cards, cash, cheques
nearest shop less than 0.5 miles
nearest pub less than 0.5 miles

Situated on St Ives harbour front with uninterrupted views of the harbour and bay. Visit our website.

Unit General Leisure

ST IVES, Cornwall Map ref 1B3

★★★★
SELF CATERING

Units 2
Sleeps 6

LOW SEASON PER WK
£325.00–£975.00

HIGH SEASON PER WK
£975.00–£1,350.00

Chylowen & Bluewater, St Ives

contact Miss Linda Higgins, 4 Vine Close, Bournemouth BH7 7JX **t** (01202) 258743
e lindahiggins@stivesdownalong.com

stivesdownalong.com

Our new property Bluewater is a three-bedroom fisherman's cottage with fantastic views over the harbour area of St Ives.

open All year
payment Cash, cheques

Unit General

ST IVES, Cornwall Map ref 1B3

★★★
SELF CATERING

Units 1
Sleeps 1–6

LOW SEASON PER WK
£210.00–£300.00

HIGH SEASON PER WK
£300.00–£670.00

Gran's Cottage, St Ives

contact Dorothy Edmond, Saveock Manor, Kerley, Chacewater, Truro TR4 8QR **t** (01872) 560644

Gran's Cottage, St Ives, is an all-year holiday letting cottage situated in the heart of 'Downalong' area. It is just yards from the harbour, beaches and museum. Also very close to public car parks.

open All year
payment Cash, cheques
nearest shop less than 0.5 miles
nearest pub less than 0.5 miles

Unit General

What if I need to cancel?

It's advisable to check the proprietor's cancellation policy at the time of booking in case you have to change your plans.

ST IVES, Cornwall Map ref 1B3

★★★★★
SELF CATERING

Units 1
Sleeps 1–6

LOW SEASON PER WK
Min £450.00

HIGH SEASON PER WK
Max £1,150.00

Happy Days, St Ives

contact Miss Amanda Dumbleton, **e** info@happydaysstives.co.uk

happydaysstives.co.uk GUEST REVIEWS

Happy Days is a luxury, three-bedroom, split-level penthouse apartment that sleeps up to six and overlooks the beautiful Porthminster beach in picturesque St Ives, Cornwall.

open All year
payment Cheques
nearest shop less than 0.5 miles
nearest pub less than 0.5 miles

Unit General 4 P Leisure

ST IVES, Cornwall Map ref 1B3

★★★★
SELF CATERING

Units 8
Sleeps 4–6

LOW SEASON PER WK
£295.00–£425.00

HIGH SEASON PER WK
£475.00–£765.00

Rotorua Apartments, Carbis Bay

contact Mrs Linda Roach, Rotorua Apartments, Trencrom Lane, Carbis Bay, St Ives TR26 2TD
t (01736) 795419 **e** rotorua@btconnect.com

stivesapartments.com REAL-TIME BOOKING

Holiday apartments situated in quiet, wooded lane, with heated outdoor pool and gardens. All apartments are furnished and equipped to a high standard, including dishwasher, microwave, fridge/freezer and electric cooker.

open All year
payment Credit/debit cards, cash, cheques
nearest shop 0.5 miles
nearest pub 1 mile

Unit General P Leisure

ST IVES, Cornwall Map ref 1B3

★★
SELF CATERING

Units 1
Sleeps 7–9

LOW SEASON PER WK
£360.00–£495.00

HIGH SEASON PER WK
£550.00–£758.00

The Studio, St Ives

contact Carol Holland, Little Parc Owles, Pannier Lane, Carbis Bay, St Ives TR26 2RQ
t (01736) 793015

Well-equipped five-bedroom cottage in the picturesque old fishermen's and artists' quarter of St Ives. This converted sail loft also has a spacious living room, kitchen, bath/wc and shower/wc. Non-smoking.

open All year
payment Cash, cheques
nearest shop less than 0.5 miles
nearest pub less than 0.5 miles

Unit General

ST IVES, Cornwall Map ref 1B3

★★★–★★★★★
SELF CATERING

Units 51
Sleeps 2–8

LOW SEASON PER WK
£280.00–£600.00

HIGH SEASON PER WK
£770.00–£2,280.00

Special offers available Oct-Apr. Please visit our website. Hotel from £39.95. Self-catering from £250 per week.

Tregenna Castle Self Catering, St Ives

contact Mrs Sheila Barker, Tregenna Castle Self-Catering, Treloyhan Avenue, St Ives TR26 2DE
t (01736) 795588 **e** hotel@tregenna-castle.co.uk

tregenna-castle.co.uk SPECIAL OFFERS · REAL-TIME BOOKING

open All year
payment Credit/debit cards, cash, cheques
nearest shop 0.5 miles
nearest pub less than 0.5 miles

With fantastic views over St Ives, this lovely estate is set in 72 acres of subtropical gardens with a range of traditional and modern self-catering cottages and apartments. With full use of our leisure facilities including golf, sauna, jacuzzi, squash, tennis, badminton, indoor and outdoor pools.

Unit General P
Leisure

ST IVES, Cornwall Map ref 1B3

★★★★
SELF CATERING

Units 4
Sleeps 2–6

LOW SEASON PER WK
£220.00–£370.00

HIGH SEASON PER WK
£250.00–£630.00

Trevalgan Holiday Farm, St Ives

contact Mrs Melanie Osborne, Trevalgan Holiday Farm, Trevalgan, St Ives TR26 3BJ
t (01736) 796529 **e** holidays@trevalgan.co.uk

trevalgan.co.uk

Expect excellent accommodation, breathtaking scenery and a warm welcome on this family farm close to St Ives. Cottages are toddler-friendly, decorated, furnished and equipped to a very high standard.

open All year
payment Cash, cheques
nearest shop 1.5 miles
nearest pub 1.5 miles

Unit General Leisure

ST JUST IN ROSELAND, Cornwall Map ref 1B3

★★★★
SELF CATERING

Units 3
Sleeps 1–2

LOW SEASON PER WK
£300.00–£450.00

HIGH SEASON PER WK
£450.00–£850.00

Roundhouse Barns, Nr St Mawes

contact Ms Barbara Sadler, Roundhouse Barn, St Just in Roseland, Nr St Mawes TR2 5JJ
t (01872) 580038 **e** info@roundhousebarnholidays.co.uk

roundhousebarnholidays.co.uk

open All year
payment Credit/debit cards, cash, cheques
nearest shop 4 miles
nearest pub 2 miles

Beautifully converted 17thC barn set in heart of the Roseland Peninsula. Commanding sea views from top of drive. Three very spacious one-bedroomed self-catering cottages, welcoming adults only. Complimentary Cornish cream tea on arrival. Cornish coastal path, Eden Project, St Mawes close by. Peaceful and secluded.

SAT NAV *TR2 5JJ*

WALKERS WELCOME CYCLISTS WELCOME

Unit General Leisure

ST MAWES, Cornwall Map ref 1B3

★★★
SELF CATERING

Units 1
Sleeps 1–5

LOW SEASON PER WK
£395.00–£695.00

HIGH SEASON PER WK
£395.00–£695.00

Park Cottage, St Mawes, Truro

contact Mrs Yvonne George, Lower Trestrayle, Probus, Truro TR2 4HJ **t** (01872) 530418 & 07877 867731 **e** yvonne@george031627.plus.com

acornishriver.co.uk

The cottage enjoys a superb location close to the river, shops, restaurants and village pubs in St Mawes.

open All year
payment Cash, cheques
nearest shop less than 0.5 miles
nearest pub less than 0.5 miles

Unit General

Where can I find accessible accommodation?

If you have special hearing, visual or mobility needs, there's an index of National Accessible Scheme participants featured in this guide. For more accessible accommodation buy a copy of Easy Access Britain available online at visitbritaindirect.com, and from Tourism for All on 0845 124 997 or visit tourismforall.org.uk.

For **key to symbols** see page 7

ST MERRYN, Cornwall Map ref 1B2

★★★
SELF CATERING

Units 1
Sleeps 1–6

LOW SEASON PER WK
£300.00–£500.00

HIGH SEASON PER WK
£450.00–£750.00

10% off today's rate if you book now.

138 Jasmine Way, St Merryn Holiday Village, St Merryn

contact Miss Mary-Jane Morgan, 138 Jasmine Way, Flat 2, 13 Pinfold Road, London SW16 2SL
t (020) 8355 9773 & 07768 864556 **e** haha.films@virgin.net

cornishselfcateringhols.com GUEST REVIEWS · SPECIAL OFFERS

open All year
payment Cash, cheques, euros
nearest shop 0.5 miles
nearest pub 1.5 miles

In the countryside, near local shops, bars and restaurants (including Michelin-stars). Surf the nearby beaches, play golf on championship courses, Trevose. Ten minutes to Padstow. Three bedrooms (including two doubles), fully fitted kitchen equipped with washing machine and microwave. Bath with electric shower. Parking. Front and rear garden.

ONLINE MAP

Unit General P Leisure

ST NEOT, Cornwall Map ref 1C2

★★★★
SELF CATERING

Units 3
Sleeps 2–4

LOW SEASON PER WK
£160.00–£360.00

HIGH SEASON PER WK
£320.00–£610.00

Up to 20% discount on short breaks, excl school holidays.

Badgers Holiday Cottages, St Neot, Liskeard

contact Phil & Allison Harris, Badgers Holiday Cottages, Badgers Sett, West Draynes, St Neot, Liskeard PL14 6RY **t** (01579) 320741 & 07855 807183 **e** phil.harris@btinternet.com

badgersholidaycottages.co.uk SPECIAL OFFERS

open All year
payment Cash, cheques
nearest shop 2 miles
nearest pub 2 miles

Relax in one of our three recently converted, beautiful cottages, in this tranquil and stunning area of Cornwall. All cottages have character, are comfortable, well equipped and centrally heated with own south-facing garden, set within two acres. Ideally situated for touring the South West, walking, visiting gardens and coastlines.

SAT NAV *PL14 6RY*

Unit General P Leisure

SALISBURY, Wiltshire Map ref 2B3

★★★★
SELF CATERING

Units 1
Sleeps 5

LOW SEASON PER WK
£320.00–£385.00

HIGH SEASON PER WK
£425.00–£530.00

Special rates for last minute bookings, short breaks and extended stays in off-peak periods. See website or telephone for details.

Rustic Cottage, Salisbury

contact Mrs Cheryl Beeney, 75 Church Rd, Laverstock SP1 1QS **t** (01722) 337870
e cheribeen@aol.com

rustic-cottage-salisbury.co.uk GUEST REVIEWS · SPECIAL OFFERS · REAL-TIME BOOKING

open All year
payment Credit/debit cards, cash, cheques, euros
nearest shop less than 0.5 miles
nearest pub less than 0.5 miles

Cosy, newly renovated character cottage (1810) close to historic centre of the cathedral city of Salisbury and tourist attractions of Stonehenge, the New Forest and south coast. Delightful country walks start from doorstep. Furnished and equipped throughout to high standard. Broadband connection, terraced garden, pond, large decking area with barbecue.

ONLINE MAP

Unit General 5 P Leisure

SALISBURY, Wiltshire Map ref 2B3

★★★★
SELF CATERING

Units 3
Sleeps 1–2

LOW SEASON PER WK
Max £395.00

HIGH SEASON PER WK
Max £455.00

Salisbury Apartments, Salisbury

contact Mrs Mary Webb, 50 Upper Street, West Harnham, Salisbury SP2 8LY **t** (01722) 340892 & 07759 474115 **e** enquiries@salisbury-apartments.co.uk

salisbury-apartments.co.uk GUEST REVIEWS • SPECIAL OFFERS • REAL-TIME BOOKING

Off street parking: yes. Broadband connection: yes. Welcome pack: yes. Convenient for city: yes. Best for business: yes. Lovely for leisure: yes. Salisbury Apartments say YES to all your needs.

open All year
payment Credit/debit cards, cash, cheques
nearest shop less than 0.5 miles
nearest pub less than 0.5 miles

Unit General Leisure

SALISBURY, Wiltshire Map ref 2B3

★★★★
SELF CATERING

Units 1
Sleeps 2

LOW SEASON PER WK
£275.00–£300.00

HIGH SEASON PER WK
£300.00–£375.00

Sycamore Cottage, Salisbury

contact Mr & Mrs Richard & Cilla Pickett, Melrose Cottage, Lower Road, Quidhampton, Salisbury SP2 9AS **t** (01722) 743160 **e** cilla@sycamorecottage.biz

sycamorecottage.biz

A recently converted stable offering high-quality accommodation in a lovely countryside setting. Salisbury city centre very easily accessible. Additional bedding available for children.

open All year
payment Cash, cheques
nearest shop 1 mile
nearest pub less than 0.5 miles

Unit General

SAMPFORD BRETT, Somerset Map ref 1D1

★★★
SELF CATERING

Units 2
Sleeps 4

LOW SEASON PER WK
£220.00

HIGH SEASON PER WK
£350.00–£450.00

Short breaks and weekend stays from £120 (excl Jul, Aug).

Old Rectory Coach House, Sampford Brett

contact Jan Swan, The Old Rectory, Sampford Brett, Taunton TA4 4LA **t** (01984) 633787 **e** enquiries@oldrectorycoachhouse.co.uk

oldrectorycoachhouse.co.uk SPECIAL OFFERS • REAL-TIME BOOKING

open All year
payment Cash, cheques, euros
nearest shop 1 mile
nearest pub 1 mile

Cosy and comfortable accommodation within a beautifully restored coach house. Farm View has one double bedroom and a twin room with bunks; The Elms has two double bedrooms. Ideally situated in the heart of a tranquil and pretty village, nestling between Exmoor, the Quantocks and the Somerset coast.

SAT NAV *TA4 4LA* **ONLINE MAP**

Unit General Leisure

SEATON, Devon Map ref 1D2

★★★
SELF CATERING

Units 1
Sleeps 1–4

LOW SEASON PER WK
£225.00–£325.00

HIGH SEASON PER WK
£385.00–£525.00

10% reduction for 2 persons only, throughout booking period.

West Ridge Bungalow, Seaton

contact Mrs Hildegard Fox, West Ridge Bungalow, Harepath Hill, Seaton EX12 2TA **t** (01297) 22398
e fox@foxwestridge.co.uk

cottageguide.co.uk/westridge

open March to October
payment Cash, cheques
nearest shop 0.5 miles
nearest pub 1 mile

Comfortably furnished bungalow on elevated ground in 1.5 acres of gardens. Beautiful, panoramic views of Axe Estuary and sea. Close by are Beer and Branscombe. Lyme Regis seven miles, Sidmouth ten miles. Excellent centre for touring, walking, sailing, fishing, golf. Full gas central heating, double glazing throughout.

SAT NAV *EX12 2TA*

Unit General Leisure

SEATOWN, Dorset Map ref 1D2

★★★★
SELF CATERING

Units 1
Sleeps 7

LOW SEASON PER WK
£470.00–£970.00

HIGH SEASON PER WK
£520.00–£1,150.00

3-night stays available Nov-Feb (excl Christmas and New Year).

The Guard House, Seatown, Nr Bridport

contact Mrs Charlotte Wreaves, The Guard House, Unit One, 1-11 Howie Street, London SW11 4AS
t (020) 7228 6366 **e** info@guardhouse.co.uk

guardhouse.co.uk SPECIAL OFFERS

open All year
payment Cash, cheques
nearest shop less than 0.5 miles
nearest pub less than 0.5 miles

This cosy 19thC cottage offers a high standard of accommodation with private patio gardens and log fire. Located just a stone's throw from the beach and the South West Coast Path, it offers a perfect base to explore the local area or simply to relax and enjoy the sea air.

SAT NAV *DT6 6JU* **ONLINE MAP**

PETS! WELCOME

Unit General
Leisure

SENNEN, Cornwall Map ref 1A3

★★★
SELF CATERING

Units 2
Sleeps 1–5

LOW SEASON PER WK
£200.00–£230.00

HIGH SEASON PER WK
£400.00–£440.00

3 & 4 Wesley Cottages, Nanquidno Valley, St Just, Penzance

contact Mrs J Davey, Rosteague, Raginnis Farm, Penzance TR19 6NJ **t** (01736) 731933
e wesley@raginnis.demon.co.uk

wesleyatnanquidno.co.uk

Single-storey cosy cottages with open fires. In peaceful valley with countryside/sea views. Wonderful walks/beaches. Attractions include Minack Theatre, art galleries, archaeological sites, golf, fishing, wildlife havens, theme parks and more.

open All year
payment Cash, cheques
nearest shop 2.5 miles
nearest pub 2.5 miles

Unit General Leisure

Place index

If you know where you want to stay, the index by place name at the back of the guide will give you the page number listing accommodation in your chosen town, city or village. Check out the other useful indexes too.

SENNEN COVE, Cornwall Map ref 1A3

★★★★
SELF CATERING

Units 2
Sleeps 6

LOW SEASON PER WK
£275.00–£475.00

HIGH SEASON PER WK
£475.00–£900.00

Harbour Mews, Sennen Cove, Penzance

contact Mr Jeff Hardman, Penwithern, Treen, Penzance TR19 6LQ **t** (01736) 810504
e jeff@sennencornwall.com

sennencornwall.com SPECIAL OFFERS

4 and 6 Harbour Mews, Sennen Cove. The properties are set slightly back from the Cove Road and provide everything one would expect for a stunning holiday in Sennen Cove.

open All year
payment Cash, cheques, euros
nearest shop less than 0.5 miles
nearest pub less than 0.5 miles

Unit General P Leisure

SHAFTESBURY, Dorset Map ref 2B3

★★★–★★★★★
SELF CATERING

Units 8
Sleeps 2–10

LOW SEASON PER WK
Min £190.00

HIGH SEASON PER WK
Max £687.00

Whitebridge Farm Cottages, Shaftesbury

contact Mr & Mrs Terry & Julie Neale, Whitebridge Farm, Sedgehill, Shaftesbury SP7 9JT
t (01747) 830462 **e** whitebridgefarm@btconnect.com

whitebridgeholidaycottages.co.uk

Whitebridge Farm offers eight cottages and barns converted from the original farm buildings. Ranging from one to five bedrooms, all are en suite. Fully fitted with self-catering facilities. Open all year.

open All year
payment Cash, cheques
nearest shop 3 miles
nearest pub 1 mile

Unit General Leisure

SHEPTON MONTAGUE, Somerset Map ref 2B2

★★★★
SELF CATERING

Units 1
Sleeps 1–3

LOW SEASON PER WK
£200.00–£250.00

HIGH SEASON PER WK
£300.00–£350.00

Seed House, Wincanton

contact Mrs Christina Dimond, Higher Farm, Wincanton BA9 8JJ **t** (01749) 812373
e dimond@farm24771.fsnet.co.uk

higherfarm.net

Tastefully converted from an old seed house with oak beams and stone and brick features, this cottage is situated in a delightfully rural village. One double, one single. Fully equipped.

open All year
payment Cash, cheques
nearest shop 3 miles
nearest pub less than 0.5 miles

Unit General P Leisure

SHERBORNE, Dorset Map ref 2B3

★★★
SELF CATERING

Units 1
Sleeps 4

LOW SEASON PER WK
£240.00–£300.00

HIGH SEASON PER WK
£360.00–£400.00

Blackberry Cottage, Sherborne

contact Mr John Michael Farr, 17 Marsh Lane, Yeovil BA21 3BX **t** (01935) 423148

An ideal base for discovering the delights of Dorset. This 19thC stone cottage is close to the centre of the historic town of Sherborne.

open All year
payment Cash, cheques

Unit General P

Don't forget www.

Web addresses throughout this guide are shown without the prefix www. Please include www. in the address line of your browser. If a web address does not follow this style it is shown in full.

SHERBORNE, Dorset Map ref 2B3

★★★★
SELF CATERING

Units **2**
Sleeps **1–7**

LOW SEASON PER WK
£247.00–£598.00

HIGH SEASON PER WK
£386.00–£835.00

Why not spend your next Christmas or New Year at Patson Hill? Ask about our special festive breaks!

Patson Hill Cottages, Sherborne

contact Mr & Mrs Ronald & Jill Racher, Patson Hill, Sherborne DT9 4SY **t** 0845 450 5993
e info@patsonhill.co.uk

patsonhill.co.uk SPECIAL OFFERS

open All year
payment Cash, cheques
nearest shop 2 miles
nearest pub 2 miles

Abundant views over a patchwork of fields and an idyllic location create an unequalled setting for two thoughtfully equipped holiday cottages attractively converted from a former barn on the owners' working farm. Jurassic Coast, historic houses, beautiful gardens, hill forts, safari park, interesting local shops and good walking, all accessible.

Unit General Leisure

SHERBORNE, Dorset Map ref 2B3

★★★–★★★★
SELF CATERING

Units **5**
Sleeps **2–6**

LOW SEASON PER WK
£245.00–£435.00

HIGH SEASON PER WK
£405.00–£695.00

Short breaks available – low season and late availability.

White Horse Farm, Middlemarsh, Sherborne

contact Mr & Mrs Stuart & Audrey Winterbottom, White Horse Farm, Middlemarsh, Sherborne DT9 5QN **t** (01963) 210222 **e** enquiries@whitehorsefarm.co.uk

whitehorsefarm.co.uk GUEST REVIEWS · SPECIAL OFFERS · REAL-TIME BOOKING

open Easter to October
payment Credit/debit cards, cash, cheques
nearest shop 2.5 miles
nearest pub less than 0.5 miles

Situated in rural Dorset and surrounded by miles of 'outstanding natural beauty' countryside. Four charming, featured, barn-conversion cottages and a luxurious three-bedroom farmhouse annexe within two acres of gardens and paddock with a large duck pond. Local, well-recommended inn just next door. Many places of interest nearby.

ONLINE MAP

Unit General Leisure

SIDMOUTH, Devon Map ref 1D2

★★★★
SELF CATERING

Units **1**
Sleeps **2**

LOW SEASON PER WK
£260.00–£350.00

HIGH SEASON PER WK
£385.00–£425.00

Flat 4 Western Court, Sidmouth

contact Mr G M Corr, Glendevon, Cotmaton Road, Sidmouth EX10 8QX **t** (01395) 512216
e sidmouthholidayflats@yahoo.co.uk

sidmouth-selfcatering.co.uk

A one-bedroom apartment sleeping two in the centre of Sidmouth in a quiet complex. It is close to the seafront and town centre. Modernised. Lift, garage, parking space, balcony.

open All year
payment Cash, cheques, euros
nearest shop less than 0.5 miles
nearest pub less than 0.5 miles

Unit General **P** Leisure

Do you have access needs?

Look for the National Accessible Scheme symbols if you have special hearing, visual or mobility needs. An index of accommodation participating in the scheme can be found at the back of this guide.

SIMONSBATH, Somerset Map ref 1C1

★★★★
SELF CATERING

Units 5
Sleeps 1–6

LOW SEASON PER WK
£275.00–£380.00

HIGH SEASON PER WK
£375.00–£780.00

Wintershead Farm, Simonsbath, Exmoor

contact Mrs Jane Styles, Wintershead Farm, Simonsbath, Exmoor TA24 7LF **t** (01643) 831222
e wintershead@yahoo.co.uk

wintershead.co.uk SPECIAL OFFERS

Five converted stone cottages, perfect for exploring the moor. Where a lot of the traffic has four legs, and the only street lighting is the stars above. Colour brochure.

open 14 March to 21 November
payment Cash, cheques
nearest shop 7 miles
nearest pub 3 miles

Unit General Leisure

SLIMBRIDGE, Gloucestershire Map ref 2B1

★★★★★
SELF CATERING

Units 1
Sleeps 13

LOW SEASON PER WK
£2,075.00–£2,825.00

HIGH SEASON PER WK
£3,075.00–£3,625.00

Rectory Park, Gloucester

contact Elaine Molyneux, Dunster Living, Halswell House, Goathurst TA5 2DH **t** 0845 208 1066
e info@dunsterliving.co.uk

rectorypark.co.uk SPECIAL OFFERS · REAL-TIME BOOKING

Elegant Regency rectory with excellent facilities. Six double bedrooms, one single. Extensive grounds, hot tub, croquet lawn, swings and barbecue. Home cinema, snooker table and table tennis.

open All year
payment Credit/debit cards, cash, cheques
nearest shop 3 miles
nearest pub 1 mile

Unit General P
Leisure

SNOWSHILL, Gloucestershire Map ref 2B1

★★★★★
SELF CATERING

Units 1
Sleeps 5

LOW SEASON PER WK
£285.00–£750.00

HIGH SEASON PER WK
£285.00–£750.00

Shenberrow Farm Cottage, Broadway

contact Mrs Tina Carroll, Snowshill, Broadway WR12 7JZ **t** (01386) 858359 **e** tinaacarroll@aol.com

shenberrow.co.uk

Shenberrow Farm is located in a Cotswold escarpment with stunning views. Well equipped; five boxes; dogs welcome; miles of bridleways off farm. One double, one twin.

open All year
payment Credit/debit cards, cash, cheques
nearest shop 5 miles
nearest pub 2 miles

Unit General Leisure

SOUTH PETHERTON, Somerset Map ref 1D2

★★★★
SELF CATERING

Units 1
Sleeps 4

LOW SEASON PER WK
£230.00–£280.00

HIGH SEASON PER WK
£300.00–£380.00

Tanwyn, South Petherton

contact Mr & Mrs Rodney & Ann Tanswell, St Brides Major, Bridgend CF32 0SB **t** (01656) 880524
e rodney.tanswell@btinternet.com

freewebs.com/tanwyn

Delightful semi-detached cottage in quiet picturesque village. Three bedrooms, bathroom and shower room. Well-equipped kitchen. Large garden and orchard. Good restaurant and pub nearby.

open All year except Christmas and New Year
payment Cash, cheques
nearest shop 1 mile
nearest pub less than 0.5 miles

Unit General 10 P Leisure

Check the maps for accommodation locations

Colour maps at the front pinpoint all the places where accommodation is featured within the regional sections of this guide. Pick your location and then refer to the place index at the back to find the page number.

STITHIANS, Cornwall Map ref 1B3

★★★-★★★★
SELF CATERING

Units 9
Sleeps 2–8

LOW SEASON PER WK
£175.00–£250.00

HIGH SEASON PER WK
£430.00–£750.00

Higher Trewithen Holiday Cottages, Truro

contact Mr Burgess, Higher Trewithen Holiday Cottages, Stithians, Truro TR3 7DR **t** (01209) 860863
e trewithen@talk21.com

trewithen.com

open All year
payment Cash, cheques, euros
nearest shop 2 miles
nearest pub 2 miles

Converted cottages and apartments, peacefully situated deep in the Cornish countryside. Central location within easy reach of most of Cornwall's tourist attractions. A few miles from both north and south coasts. Stithians village is five minutes by car or fifteen minutes' walk across open fields for shops and friendly pub. Dogs welcome.

Unit General P Leisure

STITHIANS, Cornwall Map ref 1B3

★★★
SELF CATERING

Units 1
Sleeps 1–4

LOW SEASON PER WK
£250.00

HIGH SEASON PER WK
£315.00

Ivory Cottage, Stithians, Truro

contact Mr & Mrs David & Daya Stafford, Carncress Farm, Carn, Stithians, Truro TR3 7AW
t (01209) 861486 **e** cottage@ivorycottage.co.uk

ivorycottage.co.uk REAL-TIME BOOKING

Pleasant cottage sleeping up to four, adjoining owner's Victorian farmhouse. Close to Truro, Falmouth, lakes and beaches. Great for walking and near to fishing and watersports centre. Pets welcome.

open All year except Christmas and New Year
payment Cash, cheques
nearest shop 1 mile
nearest pub 1 mile

Unit General P S Leisure

STOKE GABRIEL, Devon Map ref 1D2

★★★★★
SELF CATERING

Units 2
Sleeps 1–6

LOW SEASON PER WK
£395.00–£595.00

HIGH SEASON PER WK
£590.00–£995.00

Aish Cross Holiday Cottages, Totnes

contact Mrs Angela Pavey, Aish Cross House, Aish, Stoke Gabriel, Totnes TQ9 6PT
t (01803) 782022 **e** info@aishcross.co.uk

aishcross.co.uk GUEST REVIEWS · REAL-TIME BOOKING

open All year
payment Credit/debit cards, cash, cheques
nearest shop 1.5 miles
nearest pub 1.5 miles

Coach house and stable attached to lovely Regency home, offering high quality character accommodation in an Area of Outstanding Natural Beauty close to the delightful medieval market town of Totnes. The amenities of Torbay, the breathtaking South Hams coastline and the rugged Dartmoor landscape are nearby. For a virtual tour see our website.

ONLINE MAP

Unit General P S
Leisure

STOKE ST GREGORY, Somerset Map ref 1D1

★★★
SELF CATERING

Units 2
Sleeps 2–4

HIGH SEASON PER WK
£250.00–£390.00

Baileys Gallery & Baileys Barn, Taunton

contact Mr Stanley Chedzoy, Baileys Gallery, Fairholme, Stoke St Gregory, Taunton TA3 6JQ
t (01823) 490644

Converted barns. Open countryside adjacent West Sedgemoor SSSI and RSPB reserve. Spacious one and two bedroomed accommodation, comfortable lounges with woodburners and storage heaters. Well-fitted kitchens. Parking.

open April to September
payment Cash, cheques
nearest shop 1 mile
nearest pub 1 mile

Unit General P

STOKE SUB HAMDON, Somerset Map ref 1D2

★★★
SELF CATERING

Units 1
Sleeps 2

LOW SEASON PER WK
£100.00–£150.00

HIGH SEASON PER WK
£160.00–£250.00

Top o Hill, Stoke sub Hamdon

contact Mrs Mary Gane, Top o Hill, Percombe, Stoke-sub-Hamdon TA14 6RD **t** (01935) 822089

Annexe of 150-year-old house in private road, close to A303. Excellent touring base for many places of interest. Garden with garden furniture, own entrance.

open Spring to autumn
payment Cash, cheques, euros
nearest shop 1 mile
nearest pub 1 mile

Unit General P

STOW-ON-THE-WOLD, Gloucestershire Map ref 2B1

★★★★
SELF CATERING

Units 1
Sleeps 4

LOW SEASON PER WK
Min £290.00

HIGH SEASON PER WK
Min £510.00

Bottom End Cottage, Stow-on-the-Wold

contact Ms Karen Hawkes, Cottage in the Country and Cottage Holidays, Tukes Cottage, 66 West Street, Chipping Norton OX7 5ER **t** 0870 027 5930 **e** enquiries@cottageinthecountry.co.uk

cottageinthecountry.co.uk

open All year
payment Credit/debit cards, cash, cheques
nearest shop less than 0.5 miles
nearest pub less than 0.5 miles

Delightful Victorian Cotswold-stone semi-detached cottage, in a quiet street just five minutes' walk from the Market Square. Recently renovated and comfortably furnished, but retaining many original features including stripped pine doors, flagstone floors and an original range in the breakfast kitchen. Conservatory at the rear overlooks pleasant enclosed garden.

Unit General P

STOW-ON-THE-WOLD, Gloucestershire Map ref 2B1

★★★
SELF CATERING

Units 1
Sleeps 2

LOW SEASON PER WK
Min £285.00

HIGH SEASON PER WK
Max £385.00

Box Cottage, Broadwell

contact Mr Bob Johnston, Box Cottage, Poplars Barn, Evenlode, Moreton-in-Marsh GL56 0NN
t (01608) 650816 **e** enquiries@stow-cottages.co.uk

stow-cottages.co.uk

Charming well-equipped cottage in quiet village, exposed beams throughout. Good pub within a few hundred yards. Woodburning stove, logs supplied in the winter.

open All year
payment Credit/debit cards, cash, cheques
nearest shop 1.25 miles
nearest pub less than 0.5 miles

Unit General P

STOW-ON-THE-WOLD, Gloucestershire Map ref 2B1

★★★★★
SELF CATERING

Units 1
Sleeps 1–4

LOW SEASON PER WK
Min £325.00

HIGH SEASON PER WK
Min £595.00

Short breaks available (except in high season).

Broad Oak Cottages, Stow-on-the-Wold, Cheltenham

contact Mrs Wilson, Broad Oak Cottages, The Counting House, Oddington Road, Stow on the Wold, Cheltenham GL54 1AL **t** (01451) 830794 **e** mary@broadoakcottages.co.uk

broadoakcottages.co.uk

open All year
payment Cash, cheques, euros
nearest shop less than 0.5 miles
nearest pub less than 0.5 miles

May Cottage is a delightful two-bedroomed cottage all on one level and within a few minutes' walk of Stow Square. It has recently been completely renovated and extended to include a master suite with luxury bathroom, a conservatory and enlarged sitting room opening onto a patio. Parking and private garden.

SAT NAV *GL54 1AL*

Unit General P
Leisure

STOW-ON-THE-WOLD, Gloucestershire Map ref 2B1

★★★★
SELF CATERING

Units 4
Sleeps 2–4

LOW SEASON PER WK
£350.00–£650.00

HIGH SEASON PER WK
£550.00–£950.00

Cotswold Holiday Cottages, Upper Oddington, Moreton-in-Marsh

contact Wendy Hill, Cotswold Holiday Cottages, Old Mill Farm, Back Lane, Upper Oddington, Moreton-in-Marsh GL56 0XL **t** 07853 148362 **e** wendy@cotswold-holidays.com

cotswold-holidays.com

Beautifully refurbished, our cottages are equipped with all modern conveniences with interiors a blend of traditional and contemporary styling. Ideally situated for discovering the Cotswold countryside or just totally relaxing.

open All year
payment Credit/debit cards, cash, cheques
nearest shop 2 miles
nearest pub less than 0.5 miles

Unit General 8 P

STOW-ON-THE-WOLD, Gloucestershire Map ref 2B1

★★★★
SELF CATERING

Units 1
Sleeps 2–5

LOW SEASON PER WK
£295.00–£305.00

HIGH SEASON PER WK
£495.00–£505.00

Horseshoes, Stow-on-the-Wold

contact Ms Yvonne Johnston, Poplars Barn, Evenlode, Moreton-in-Marsh GL56 0NN
t (01608) 650816

stow-cottages.co.uk

Away from the hustle and bustle in a quiet lane, close to the town's many pubs and restaurants. Private parking. Ground-floor facilities, back garden with furniture. A little gem.

open All year
payment Credit/debit cards, cash, cheques
nearest shop 0.5 miles
nearest pub 0.5 miles

Unit General P

STOW-ON-THE-WOLD, Gloucestershire Map ref 2B1

★★★
SELF CATERING

Units 1
Sleeps 2–5

LOW SEASON PER WK
£285.00–£295.00

HIGH SEASON PER WK
£385.00–£460.00

Johnston Cottage & Kates, Stow-on-the-Wold

contact Mrs Yvonne Johnston, Poplars Barn, Evenlode, Moreton-in-Marsh GL56 0NN
t (01608) 650816

stow-cottages.co.uk

Charming stone terraced cottage with exposed beams and inglenook. Hanging baskets and tubs with garden furniture on terrace. Five minutes' walk from local pubs and restaurants.

open All year
payment Credit/debit cards, cash, cheques
nearest shop less than 0.5 miles
nearest pub less than 0.5 miles

Unit General P

Looking for a wide range of facilities?

More stars means higher quality accommodation plus a greater range of facilities and services.

STOW-ON-THE-WOLD, Gloucestershire Map ref 2B1

★★★
SELF CATERING

Units 1
Sleeps 4

HIGH SEASON PER WK
£240.00–£390.00

Wells Cottage, Cheltenham

contact Mr & Mrs Gwyn & Sue Williams, 24 Glebe Close, Stow-on-the-Wold, Cheltenham GL54 1DJ **t** (01451) 830045

wellscottage.co.uk

Delightful house in an Area of Outstanding Natural Beauty, close to town centre, shops and restaurants. One double, two twin bedrooms, large sitting room/diner, large kitchen, enclosed garden.

open All year
payment Cash, cheques

Unit General P Leisure

STREET, Somerset Map ref 2A2

★★★
SELF CATERING

Units 1
Sleeps 6

LOW SEASON PER WK
£290.00–£350.00

HIGH SEASON PER WK
£350.00–£500.00

Blue Lias, Street

contact Mr Mark Foot, 8 Kingston Drive, Nailsea, Bristol BS48 4RB **t** (01275) 853612
e markfoot@hotmail.com

open All year
payment Cash, cheques
nearest shop 1 mile
nearest pub 1 mile

Detached Victorian stone cottage. Fully equipped. Open fireplace, gas central heating. Town, supermarket nearby. Ideal for Glastonbury, Wells, Somerset Wetlands. Two twins, one small double with intercommunicating bunk bedroom.

Unit General P Leisure

SWANAGE, Dorset Map ref 2B3

★★★★
SELF CATERING

Units 1
Sleeps 2–10

LOW SEASON PER WK
£525.00–£900.00

HIGH SEASON PER WK
£900.00–£1,600.00

Short breaks available Oct-Apr from £395 for 3 nights.

The Quarterdeck, Swanage

contact Mr Chris Radford, The Quarterdeck **t** (020) 8144 1913 **e** enquiries@purbeckholidays.co.uk

purbeckholidays.co.uk

open All year
payment Credit/debit cards, cash, cheques
nearest shop 0.5 miles
nearest pub 0.5 miles

Spacious four-bedroom family home 400m from Swanage beach, sea views, parking. Large balcony overlooking town and bay. Refurbished in 2008 to provide modern family living. Living room, dining room, open-plan kitchen, plus games room. Five minutes' walk to beach, shops, pubs and restaurants.

SAT NAV *BH19 1PD* **ONLINE MAP**

Unit General P Leisure

Where can I get help and advice?

Tourist Information Centres offer friendly help with accommodation and holiday ideas as well as suggestions of places to visit and things to do. You'll find contact details at the beginning of each regional section.

SWANAGE, Dorset Map ref 2B3

★★★
SELF CATERING

Units 1
Sleeps 1–8

LOW SEASON PER WK
Min £300.00

HIGH SEASON PER WK
Max £700.00

Waterside, Swanage

contact Karen Dolling, 1 Abbey Mews, Isleworth TW7 5BJ **t** (020) 8560 5587 & 07985 552232
e jkdolling@hotmail.com

watersideholidaylet.co.uk

A beautifully appointed three-bedroomed ground-floor and basement flat overlooking Swange Bay, within seven metres of the shore line.

open All year
payment Cash, cheques
nearest shop less than 0.5 miles
nearest pub less than 0.5 miles

Unit General Leisure

SWIMBRIDGE, Devon Map ref 1C1

★★★★
SELF CATERING

Units 5
Sleeps 2–7

LOW SEASON PER WK
£180.00–£363.00

HIGH SEASON PER WK
£355.00–£969.00

Lower Hearson Farm, Barnstaple

contact Mr & Mrs G Pelling, Swimbridge, Barnstaple EX32 0QH **t** (01271) 830702
e info@hearsoncottagesdevon.co.uk

hearsoncottagesdevon.co.uk SPECIAL OFFERS

open All year
payment Cash, cheques
nearest shop 2 miles
nearest pub 1.5 miles

Working smallholding set in 13 acres of gardens, field and woodland. Tucked away in the heart of the North Devon countryside, perfect for a relaxing holiday. Our holiday cottages, games facilities and pool are surrounded by two acres of gardens and rolling countryside, making this a safe place for children.

Unit General Leisure

TAUNTON, Somerset Map ref 1D1

★★★
SELF CATERING

Units 1
Sleeps 5

LOW SEASON PER WK
£225.00–£345.00

HIGH SEASON PER WK
£275.00–£400.00

Short breaks available throughout the year.

Higher House, Taunton

contact Mrs Kirsten Horton, Hillcommon, Taunton TA4 1DU **t** (01823) 400570
e mail@higherhouse.co.uk

higherhouse.co.uk

open All year
payment Cash, cheques
nearest shop 1.5 miles
nearest pub less than 0.5 miles

A spacious, airy apartment on the second floor of a converted barn standing in five acres, featuring a lake, lovely gardens, as well as fields and woodland areas. Fully equipped, centrally heated and within walking distance of the pub serving tasty meals. Excellent touring base, with easy access to north and south coasts and Taunton.

Unit General Leisure

It's all quality-assessed accommodation

Our commitment to quality involves wide-ranging accommodation assessment. Ratings and awards were correct at the time of going to press but may change following a new assessment. Please check at time of booking.

TAVISTOCK, Devon Map ref 1C2

★★★
SELF CATERING

Units 1
Sleeps 2

LOW SEASON PER WK
£150.00

HIGH SEASON PER WK
£150.00

Higher Chaddlehanger Farm, Tavistock

contact Mrs Ruth Cole, The Annexe, Higher Chaddlehanger Farm, Tavistock PL19 0LG
t (01822) 810268

Holiday flatlet in farmhouse on beef and sheep farm, close to Moors. Own entrance, private garden.

open All year
payment Cash, cheques

Unit General

TAYNTON, Gloucestershire Map ref 2B1

★★★★
SELF CATERING

Units 1
Sleeps 1–2

LOW SEASON PER WK
Min £195.00

HIGH SEASON PER WK
£195.00–£300.00

Owls Barn, Gloucester

contact Mrs Barbara Goodwin, Coldcroft Farm, Glasshouse Lane, Gloucester GL19 3HJ
t (01452) 831290 **e** goodies@coldcroft.freeserve.co.uk

coldcroft.freeserve.co.uk

Owls Barn is a tastefully converted twin-bedded barn with shower, kitchen/diner and sitting room. Excellent views. Within one hour's drive of Bath, Bristol, Hereford and Worcester.

open All year
payment Cash, cheques
nearest shop less than 0.5 miles
nearest pub less than 0.5 miles

Unit General P Leisure

TEIGNGRACE, Devon Map ref 1D2

★★★
SELF CATERING

Units 2
Sleeps 4–5

LOW SEASON PER WK
£300.00–£400.00

HIGH SEASON PER WK
£400.00–£550.00

Twelve Oaks Holiday Cottages, Newton Abbot

contact Mrs Gale, Twelve Oaks Holiday Cottages, Twelve Oaks Farm, Teigngrace, Newton Abbot TQ12 6QT **t** (01626) 352769

Working 220-acre beef farm bordered by the River Teign, on the edge of the village of Teigngrace. Carefully converted cottages, each with own patio. Outdoor heated swimming pool.

open May to October
payment Credit/debit cards, cash, cheques
nearest shop 2 miles
nearest pub 1.5 miles

Unit General P Leisure

TINCLETON, Dorset Map ref 2B3

★★★★
SELF CATERING

Units 1
Sleeps 4

LOW SEASON PER WK
£350.00–£450.00

HIGH SEASON PER WK
£600.00–£950.00

Short breaks available within six weeks of arrival date. Please telephone for further information.

FAMILIES WELCOME

The Courtyard At Clyffe, Dorchester

contact Dr Ian Mew, The Courtyard At Clyffe, Brock Cottage, Clyffe House, Dorchester DT2 8QR
t 07748 417974 **e** info@tincleton.co.uk

tincleton.co.uk SPECIAL OFFERS • REAL-TIME BOOKING

open All year
payment Cash, cheques

Built in the 1840s, this cosy cottage cleverly combines period features with modern-day living, ensuring your holiday is both one of relaxation and comfort. Woodland walks are two minutes from the front door. Remarkable historic locations such at Thomas Hardy's cottage lie within a few miles of this cottage.

SAT NAV *DT2 8QR*

Unit General P S

What shall we do today?

For ideas on places to visit, see the beginning of this regional section or go online at enjoyengland.com.

TINTAGEL, Cornwall Map ref 1B2

★★★
SELF CATERING

Units 1
Sleeps 1–4

LOW SEASON PER WK
Min £110.00

HIGH SEASON PER WK
Max £410.00

Tregeath, Tintagel

contact Mrs Edwina Broad, Davina, Trevillett, Tintagel PL34 0HL **t** (01840) 770217

Old modernised detached cottage, built of stone and slate. Coal grate, six night-storage heaters, TV/DVD, payphone, microwave. One dog, no cats. Parking space. Washing machine. Separate tumble dryer.

open All year
payment Cash, cheques
nearest shop 1 mile
nearest pub 1 mile

Unit General P

TORQUAY, Devon Map ref 1D2

★★★
SELF CATERING

Units 3
Sleeps 2–6

LOW SEASON PER WK
£165.00–£320.00

HIGH SEASON PER WK
£330.00–£460.00

Short breaks available Oct-Apr, min 3 nights.

Bedford House, Torquay

contact Mrs MacDonald-Smith, Bedford House, 517 Babbacombe Road, Torquay TQ1 1HJ
t (01803) 296995 **e** bedfordhotorquay@btconnect.com

bedfordhousetorquay.co.uk

open All year
payment Credit/debit cards, cash, cheques
nearest shop less than 0.5 miles
nearest pub less than 0.5 miles

An elegant, Tudor-style house built in 1888 and set in a sunny, pleasant garden. Well situated in a conservation area, only 500m from harbour, shops and entertainment. Comfortable, self-contained and well-equipped apartments. Colour TV and microwaves. Bath or shower room. Bed linen. Guest laundry. Central heating. Private car park.

Unit General P

TORQUAY, Devon Map ref 1D2

★★★★★
SELF CATERING

Units 6
Sleeps 4–8

LOW SEASON PER WK
£900.00–£1,850.00

HIGH SEASON PER WK
£1,500.00–£2,400.00

Corbyn Lodge Apartments, Torquay

contact Reservations, c/o OJ Developments Ltd, Ilsham House, Ilsham Marine Drive, Torquay TQ1 2HT **t** (01803) 295744 **e** reservations@corbyn-lodge.co.uk

corbyn-lodge.co.uk

open All year
payment Credit/debit cards, cheques
nearest shop 0.5 miles
nearest pub less than 0.5 miles

Luxury holiday apartments in Torquay. The perfect choice for top-quality self catering accommodation in Torbay, enjoying panoramic views across the Riviera.

SAT NAV *TQ2 6QH*

Unit General P

Remember to check when booking

Please remember that all information in this guide has been supplied by the proprietors well in advance of publication. Since changes do sometimes occur it's a good idea to check details at the time of booking.

TORQUAY, Devon Map ref 1D2

★★★★★
SELF CATERING

Units 1
Sleeps 2–10

LOW SEASON PER WK
£500.00–£800.00

HIGH SEASON PER WK
£1,100.00–£1,795.00

St Christophers Holiday Home, Torquay

contact Mr David Perry, Wildewood, Meadfoot Road, Torquay TQ1 2JP **t** (01803) 297471
e enquiries@torquayholiday.com

torquayholiday.com SPECIAL OFFERS

Luxury, detached holiday home within walking distance of three beaches, town and harbour. Five bedrooms and three bathrooms. Warm and cosy in winter with central heating and woodburner. Patio and parking.

open All year
payment Cash, cheques
nearest shop less than 0.5 miles
nearest pub less than 0.5 miles

Unit General Leisure

TORQUAY, Devon Map ref 1D2

★★★
SELF CATERING

Units 19
Sleeps 1–6

LOW SEASON PER WK
£110.00–£190.00

HIGH SEASON PER WK
£390.00–£690.00

Sunningdale Apartments, Torquay

contact Mr Allan Carr, Sunningdale Apartments, 11 Babbacombe Downs Road, Torquay TQ1 3LF
t (01803) 325786 **e** allancarr@yahoo.com

sunningdaleapartments.co.uk

open All year
payment Cash, cheques, euros
nearest shop 0.5 miles
nearest pub 0.5 miles

Spacious apartments, many overlooking beach with stunning sea views. Self-contained with bathroom and shower, fitted kitchen and lounge with dining area. One or two bedrooms. Large car park, laundry room, gardens. All double glazed with central heating. Level walk to shops, restaurants, bar and theatre. Excellent touring/walking/sports centre.

Unit General Leisure

TREGREHAN MILLS, Cornwall Map ref 1B3

★★★★
SELF CATERING

Units 1
Sleeps 4

LOW SEASON PER WK
£250.00–£400.00

HIGH SEASON PER WK
£400.00–£750.00

A complimentary traditional Cornish cream tea on arrival! And free starter pack including tea, coffee, sugar, fresh bread, butter and milk.

Huel Tristram, Tregrehan Mills, St Austell

contact Mrs Sonya Rogers, Huel Tristram, Tregrehan Mills, St Austell PL25 3TQ **t** (01726) 810921
e stay@hueltristram.com

hueltristram.com SPECIAL OFFERS · REAL-TIME BOOKING

open All year
payment Cash, cheques
nearest shop 1.5 miles
nearest pub 0.5 miles

A warm welcome awaits you at Huel Tristram Cottage. Recently refurbished to a high standard but retaining much of its original charm with beamed ceilings, Rayburn stove and open fire. Just over a mile from Eden Project, ten minutes from Lost Gardens of Heligan and within easy reach of the South West Coast Path.

SAT NAV *PL25 3TQ* **ONLINE MAP**

Unit General Leisure

Do you have access needs?

Look for the National Accessible Scheme symbols if you have special hearing, visual or mobility needs.

TRURO, Cornwall Map ref 1B3

★★★-★★★★★
SELF CATERING

Units 3
Sleeps 2–6

LOW SEASON PER WK
£185.00–£310.00

HIGH SEASON PER WK
£355.00–£710.00

Clifford House, Bissoe, Truro

contact Mrs Anne Grant, Clifford House - BL027, Race Hill, Bissoe, Truro TR4 8RH **t** (01872) 863052
e enquiries@cliffordhousecottages.co.uk

cliffordhousecottages.co.uk

Very comfortable modernised cottages in countryside between Truro and Falmouth. Freeview TV, DVD player and central heating. Family-friendly and pets by arrangement. Well placed for gardens, cycling and touring.

open All year
payment Cash, cheques
nearest shop 2.5 miles
nearest pub 1 mile

Unit General P Leisure

TRURO, Cornwall Map ref 1B3

★★★★★
SELF CATERING

Units 46
Sleeps 1–7

LOW SEASON PER WK
£490.00–£870.00

HIGH SEASON PER WK
£755.00–£1,580.00

Call for short-break special offers and out-of-season discounts at Cornwall's chic country retreat.

The Valley, Carnon Downs, Truro

The Valley, Bissoe Road, Carnon Downs, Truro TR3 6LQ **t** (01872) 862194 **e** info@the-valley.co.uk

the-valley.co.uk REAL-TIME BOOKING

open All year
payment Credit/debit cards, cash, cheques, euros
nearest shop 0.5 miles
nearest pub 0.5 miles

When it's time for your next well earned break why not escape to a hidden valley and combine the service of a luxury hotel with the intimacy of your own contemporary cottage. Relax in architect-designed luxury with exclusive leisure facilities and enjoy exquisite cuisine and a superb selection of wines in the stylish Cafe Azur.

ONLINE MAP

Unit General P S
Leisure

UPTON ST LEONARDS, Gloucestershire Map ref 2B1

★★
SELF CATERING

Units 2
Sleeps 1–4

LOW SEASON PER WK
£210.00

HIGH SEASON PER WK
£300.00

Hill Farm Cottages, Gloucester

contact Mrs Margaret McLellan, Hill Farm Cottages, Hill Farm, Upton Hill, Upton St Leonards, Gloucester GL4 8DA **t** (01452) 614081

open All year
payment Cash, cheques
nearest shop less than 0.5 miles
nearest pub less than 0.5 miles

Two miles from Gloucester with panoramic views of the Cotswolds. Close to dry ski slope and golfing facilities. Ideal for walking. Country pub nearby providing food.

Unit General P Leisure

CYCLISTS WELCOME

Fancy a cycling holiday?

For a fabulous freewheeling break, seek out accommodation participating in our Cyclists Welcome scheme. Look out for the symbol and plan your route online at nationalcyclenetwork.org.

URCHFONT, Wiltshire Map ref 2B2

★★★
SELF CATERING

Units 2
Sleeps 1–4

LOW SEASON PER WK
£200.00–£250.00

HIGH SEASON PER WK
£270.00–£330.00

Breach Cottage and The Pottery, Devizes

contact Mr & Mrs Philip & Clare Milanes, Cuckoo Corner, Urchfont, Devizes SN10 4RA
t (01380) 840402 **e** info@breachhouse.co.uk

breachhouse.co.uk

Converted barns next to old farmhouse. One comprising two bedrooms and sitting room with French windows onto patio. The smaller second barn has one bedroom and own patio.

open All year except Christmas
payment Cash, cheques
nearest shop less than 0.5 miles
nearest pub less than 0.5 miles

Unit TV DVD General P

VERYAN, Cornwall Map ref 1B3

★★★★
SELF CATERING

Units 2
Sleeps 6

LOW SEASON PER WK
£275.00–£470.00

HIGH SEASON PER WK
£470.00–£790.00

Short breaks available Oct-Mar.

Trenona Farm Holidays, Veryan

contact Mrs Pamela Carbis, Trenona Farm, Ruan High Lanes, Truro TR2 5JS **t** (01872) 501339
e pam@trenonafarmholidays.co.uk

trenonafarmholidays.co.uk REAL-TIME BOOKING

open All year
payment Credit/debit cards, cash, cheques
nearest shop 1 mile
nearest pub 2 miles

The former farmhouse, and old stone workshop, have been tastefully converted to provide quality accommodation with modern furnishings and appliances for relaxing holidays on a mixed working farm on the beautiful Roseland Peninsula. Private gardens and patios. Many public gardens and attractions nearby. Children/pets welcome. Disabled access.

SAT NAV *TR2 5JS* **ONLINE MAP**

Unit TV DVD General P Leisure

WADEBRIDGE, Cornwall Map ref 1B2

★★★★
SELF CATERING

Units 4
Sleeps 2–8

LOW SEASON PER WK
£245.00–£450.00

HIGH SEASON PER WK
£450.00–£850.00

3- and 4-night breaks Oct-Apr.

WALKERS WELCOME

Tregolls Farm Cottages, Bodmin

contact Mrs Hawkey, Tregolls Farm Cottages, St Wenn, Bodmin PL30 5PG **t** (01208) 812154
e tregollsfarm@btclick.com

tregollsfarm.co.uk GUEST REVIEWS · SPECIAL OFFERS

open All year
payment Credit/debit cards, cash, cheques
nearest shop 4 miles
nearest pub 4 miles

Well-equipped holiday cottages, tastefully converted from redundant stone barns. Charming, mellow oak beams, slate window sills, fire hearths, and wonderful views of the open countryside with fields of cows and sheep grazing and a stream meandering through the valley. Pets' corner, games room, farm trail and barbecues.

ONLINE MAP

Unit TV DVD General P S Leisure

WATERGATE BAY, Cornwall Map ref 1B2

★★★★
SELF CATERING

Units 26
Sleeps 6

LOW SEASON PER WK
£360.00–£510.00

HIGH SEASON PER WK
£570.00–£1,300.00

Free-night offers selected periods for minimum 4-night stays. Great Gardens, Gourmet & Golf breaks also available.

Tregurrian Villas and Beachcombers Apartments, Watergate Bay

Beachcombers Apartments, Watergate Bay, Newquay TR8 4AB **t** (01637) 873274
e enquiries@beachcombersapartments.com

beachcombersapartments.com

open All year
payment Credit/debit cards, cash, cheques
nearest shop 2 miles
nearest pub less than 0.5 miles

Deluxe Tregurrian Villas and Beachcombers Apartments just 100/200yds from beach, four miles from Newquay. All superbly equipped one- or two-bedroom units have satellite TV. All apartments have patio or balcony, some sea view. Access to hotel amenities close by (same ownership) including bar, restaurant and pool.

Unit TV SC DVD General P S Leisure

WELLS, Somerset Map ref 2A2

★★★★
SELF CATERING

Units 1
Sleeps 1–5

LOW SEASON PER WK
£300.00–£450.00

HIGH SEASON PER WK
£475.00–£575.00

Short stays available.

Honeysuckle Cottage, Wells

contact Mrs Luana Law, Honeysuckle Cottage, Worth, Wookey, Wells BA5 1LW **t** (01749) 678971
e honeycroft2@aol.com

open All year
payment Cash, cheques
nearest shop 2 miles
nearest pub less than 0.5 miles

Barn conversion on working farm in beautiful countryside. One double en suite and one double with adjoining single bedrooms. Large bathroom upstairs, shower room downstairs. Spacious kitchen/diner/lounge leading to large patio and garden overlooking stunning Mendip Hills. All modern equipment from dishwasher to DVD.

Unit TV DVD General P S Leisure

WELLS, Somerset Map ref 2A2

★★★★
SELF CATERING

Units 1
Sleeps 1–4

LOW SEASON PER WK
£350.00–£450.00

HIGH SEASON PER WK
£450.00–£750.00

Wrinkle Mead, Wells

contact Mrs Cynthia Glass, Wrinkle Mead, Islington Farm, Wells BA5 1US **t** (01749) 673445
e islingtonfarm2004@yahoo.co.uk

islingtonfarmatwells.co.uk

open All year
payment Credit/debit cards, cash, cheques
nearest shop less than 0.5 miles
nearest pub less than 0.5 miles

Uniquely situated adjacent to The Bishop's Palace, a recent stable conversion overlooking fields and parkland, standing detached within the grounds of owner's property. Three minutes' walk to city centre. Ideal base for visiting Cheddar, Wookey Hole, Georgian Bath and National Trust properties. Excellent walking, cycling and riding on the Mendip Hills. Private parking.

Unit TV DVD General P S Leisure

WEST BAY, Dorset Map ref 2A3

★★★
SELF CATERING

Units 2
Sleeps 2–4

LOW SEASON PER WK
£220.00–£330.00

HIGH SEASON PER WK
£350.00–£420.00

Jurassic View and The Lobster Pot, Bridport

contact Mrs Frances Hunt, Spices, Stoney Lane, Curry Rivel, Langport TA10 0HY **t** (01458) 251203
e frances@holsindorset.co.uk

holsindorset.co.uk

Jurassic View, a spacious two-bedroom, south-facing apartment with balcony overlooking the sea, and the Lobster Pot, a twin-bedroom apartment overlooking the harbour. Own parking space, lift, near all amenities.

open All year
payment Cash, cheques
nearest shop less than 0.5 miles
nearest pub less than 0.5 miles

Unit TV SC General P S

WEST BAY, Dorset Map ref 2A3

★★★–★★★★★
SELF CATERING

Units 7
Sleeps 2–8

LOW SEASON PER WK
£200.00–£400.00

HIGH SEASON PER WK
£400.00–£615.00

Westpoint Apartments, Bridport

contact Mr & Mrs Slade, Westpoint Apartments, Esplanade, Bridport DT6 4HE **t** (01308) 423636
e bea@westpoint-apartments.co.uk

westpointapartments.co.uk GUEST REVIEWS · REAL-TIME BOOKING

Quality self-catering apartments on seafront overlooking sea and harbour. Fishing, 18-hole golf course, beautiful cliff walks, Thomas Hardy Country. Three- and four-day breaks available.

open All year
payment Credit/debit cards, cash, cheques
nearest shop less than 0.5 miles
nearest pub less than 0.5 miles

Unit TV DVD General 5 P S Leisure

WESTON-SUPER-MARE, Somerset Map ref 1D1

★★★★
SELF CATERING

Units 4
Sleeps 1–5

LOW SEASON PER WK
£187.00–£377.00

HIGH SEASON PER WK
£392.00–£618.00

Hope Farm Cottages, Lympsham, Nr Weston-super-Mare

contact Mrs Liz Stirk, Hope Farm Cottages, Brean Road, Lympsham, Weston-super-Mare BS24 0HA
t (01934) 750506 **e** stirkhopefarm@aol.com

hopefarmcottages.co.uk SPECIAL OFFERS

Tranquil ground-floor cottages, each with two en suites, overlooking level, landscaped courtyard. Wheelchair and other aids available. Play areas, games room, laundry. Dogs welcomed. Broadband.

open All year
payment Cash, cheques, euros
nearest shop 1 mile
nearest pub 2 miles

Unit TV DVD General P S
Leisure

WESTWARD HO!, Devon Map ref 1C1

★★★★★
SELF CATERING

Units 1
Sleeps 6

LOW SEASON PER WK
£625.00–£685.00

HIGH SEASON PER WK
£860.00–£1,395.00

3- or 4-night stays available. 25% off for couples Oct-Mar. Late booking discounts, returning customer discount.

Seascape, Nassau Court, Westward Ho!

contact Ian & Carol Gibson, 3 Wimborne Grove, Watford WD17 4JE **t** (01923) 224025
e info@devon-selfcatering-seascape.com

devon-selfcatering-seascape.com GUEST REVIEWS · SPECIAL OFFERS · REAL-TIME BOOKING

open All year
payment Cash, cheques, euros
nearest shop less than 0.5 miles
nearest pub less than 0.5 miles

Seascape is a luxurious three-bedroom apartment in Westwood Ho! Waves at high tide lap below the balcony. Sleeps six plus two plus travel cot. Beautiful views across Bideford Bay towards Lundy. Two-mile sandy beach. Rock pools. Fantastic walks in area. Golf at Royal North Devon Club included in price.

SAT NAV *EX39 1GZ* **ONLINE MAP**

Unit TV SC DVD General P S Leisure

WHIMPLE, Devon Map ref 1D2

★★★
SELF CATERING

Units 3
Sleeps 4–6

LOW SEASON PER WK
£222.00–£306.00

HIGH SEASON PER WK
£363.00–£483.00

Short breaks available throughout the year. Please ring for availability.

LSF Holiday Cottages, Exeter

contact Mrs Angela Lang, LSF Holiday Cottages, Lower Southbrook Farm, Southbrook Lane, Exeter EX5 2PG **t** (01404) 822989 **e** lowersouthbrookfarm@btinternet.com

lowersouthbrookfarm.co.uk

open All year
payment Credit/debit cards, cash, cheques
nearest shop 2 miles
nearest pub 1 mile

Clean, comfortable, well-equipped cottages in the beautiful East Devon countryside. Set in a peaceful location, yet convenient for the cathedral city of Exeter, beaches and other popular tourist attractions. Heated swimming pool and large play area for children. Fully centrally heated for early/late holidays. Brochure available.

Unit General P S Leisure

WILLERSEY, Gloucestershire Map ref 2B1

★★
SELF CATERING

Units 1
Sleeps 3

LOW SEASON PER WK
£250.00–£275.00

HIGH SEASON PER WK
£275.00–£300.00

3 Cheltenham Cottages, Broadway

contact Mrs Gillian Malin, 28 Bibsworth Avenue, Broadway WR12 7BQ **t** (01386) 853248 **e** g.malin@virgin.net

open All year
payment Cash, cheques
nearest shop less than 0.5 miles
nearest pub less than 0.5 miles

Grade II Listed Cotswold-stone cottage with countryside views. Award-winning village with excellent shops and pubs. Ideal for exploring the Cotswolds and Shakespeare Country. One double and one single. Bath and shower on ground floor. Parking off-road.

Unit General 5 Leisure

WINCHCOMBE, Gloucestershire Map ref 2B1

★★★–★★★★
SELF CATERING

Units 11
Sleeps 3–5

LOW SEASON PER WK
£270.00–£290.00

HIGH SEASON PER WK
£400.00–£620.00

Sudeley Castle Country Cottages, Cheltenham

contact Mrs Olive Byng, Castle Street, Winchcombe, Cheltenham GL54 5JA **t** (01242) 609481 **e** olive.byng@sudeley.org.uk

sudeleycastle.co.uk SPECIAL OFFERS • REAL-TIME BOOKING

open All year
payment Credit/debit cards, cash, cheques
nearest shop 0.5 miles
nearest pub 0.5 miles

Located on the Sudeley Castle estate, a small complex of 11 Cotswold stone cottages set around an open courtyard.

ONLINE MAP

Unit General P S Leisure

What do the star ratings mean?
Detailed information about star ratings can be found at the back of this guide.

WINCHCOMBE, Gloucestershire Map ref 2B1

★★★★
SELF CATERING

Units 2
Sleeps 2–4

LOW SEASON PER WK
£350.00–£450.00

HIGH SEASON PER WK
£450.00–£495.00

Traditional Accommodation, Winchcombe, Cheltenham

contact Mr & Mrs Wilson, 60 Pershore Road, Evesham WR11 2PQ **t** (01386) 446269
e trad.accom@virgin.net

http://freespace.virgin.net/trad.accom

open All year
payment Credit/debit cards, cash, cheques, euros
nearest shop 0.5 miles
nearest pub less than 0.5 miles

Courtyard setting of old traditional barns of individual style and character, finely restored to provide spacious, high-quality accommodation. Original features, quality facilities and furnishings. Gardens and patios, countryside views and private parking. Family-supervised. Ideal touring base. Regret no pets. Brochures available.

Unit General P Leisure

WINDRUSH, Gloucestershire Map ref 2B1

★★★★
SELF CATERING

Units 1
Sleeps 4

LOW SEASON PER WK
Max £395.00

HIGH SEASON PER WK
Max £495.00

Short breaks available for 3 or 4 nights. Please telephone to check availability.

Keeper's Cottage, Windrush

contact Mrs Collette Carmichael, 34 Upper High Street, Thame OX9 2DN **t** (01844) 215417 & 07730 456789 **e** enquiries@gamekeeperscottage.co.uk

gamekeeperscottage.co.uk

open All year
payment Cash, cheques
nearest shop 1 mile
nearest pub 0.5 miles

Set in peaceful rolling countryside in an Area of Outstanding Natural Beauty, Keeper's Cottage is a Grade II Listed Cotswold stone cottage dating back to the 19th century. The cottage forms part of the National Trust Sherborne Estate and enjoys stunning views across open meadow and woodland from all windows.

Unit General S Leisure

WINFORD, Somerset Map ref 2A2

★★★
SELF CATERING

Units 2
Sleeps 2–4

LOW SEASON PER WK
£190.00–£260.00

HIGH SEASON PER WK
£320.00–£450.00

Regilbury Farm, Bristol

contact Mrs Keedwell, Regilbury Farm, The Street, Regil, Winford, Bristol BS40 8BB
t (01275) 472369 **e** janekeedwell@yahoo.co.uk

regilburyfarm.co.uk

Working farm with cattle, sheep and chickens, all set in a beautiful, quiet hamlet. Wonderful rambling, lots to see. Guided walks available. Cowshed – double, Parlour – double and twin. Sorry, no pets.

open All year
payment Cash, cheques
nearest shop 2 miles
nearest pub 1 mile

Unit General P Leisure

PETS! WELCOME WELCOME PETS!

Where is my pet welcome?

Want to take your cherished companion with you on holiday? Proprietors participating in our Welcome Pets! scheme go out of their way to make special provision for you and your pet. Look out for the symbol.

For **key to symbols** see page 7

WINGFIELD, Wiltshire Map ref 2B2

★★
SELF CATERING

Units 5
Sleeps 2–4

LOW SEASON PER WK
£220.00–£290.00

HIGH SEASON PER WK
£275.00–£325.00

Short breaks available – call for prices.

Romsey Oak Cottages, Trowbridge

contact Mrs Christine Briars, Romsey Oak Cottages, Romsey Oak Farmhouse, Frome Road, Trowbridge BA14 9LS **t** (01225) 753950 **e** enquiries@romseyoakcottages.co.uk

romseyoakcottages.co.uk/intro.htm

open All year
payment Credit/debit cards, cash, cheques, euros
nearest shop 2 miles
nearest pub 1 mile

Converted farm buildings around courtyard of main house in open countryside. Bath 10 miles, Bradford-on-Avon three miles. Fully equipped kitchen, TV, heating, pay phone, laundry. Bed linen provided. Dogs accepted. Residents' garden and tennis court. Numerous good eating places and public houses nearby. Brochure available.

ONLINE MAP

Unit TV DVD General 1 P Leisure

WOOLACOMBE, Devon Map ref 1C1

★★
SELF CATERING

Units 1
Sleeps 5

LOW SEASON PER WK
£200.00–£250.00

HIGH SEASON PER WK
£300.00–£535.00

Cove Cottage Flat, Woolacombe

contact Mrs Vivien Lawrence, Sharp Rock, Mortehoe, Woolacombe EX34 7EA **t** (01271) 870403 **e** vlawrence05@aol.com

open All year
payment Cash, cheques
nearest shop 0.5 miles
nearest pub 0.5 miles

Self-contained flat with garden overlooking sandy beach. Close to South West Coast Path. Exmoor 12 miles. Ideal for children, walkers and surfers. Pets welcome. Central heating included early/late season. Parking.

Unit TV DVD General P S Leisure

YARNSCOMBE, Devon Map ref 1C1

★★★★
SELF CATERING

Units 1
Sleeps 2–4

LOW SEASON PER WK
£250.00–£350.00

HIGH SEASON PER WK
£400.00–£580.00

Swallow Barton, Yarnscombe, Barnstaple

contact Mrs Sandra Newland, Little Barton, Yarnscombe, Barnstaple EX31 3LP **t** (01769) 560583 **e** info@swallowbarton.co.uk

swallowbarton.co.uk GUEST REVIEWS · SPECIAL OFFERS · REAL-TIME BOOKING

Luxury barn conversion in a quiet, isolated, rural location conveniently situated for North Devon's beaches and tourist attractions. Two spacious bedrooms (one double, one twin). Free brochure available.

open All year
payment Cash, cheques, euros
nearest shop 5 miles
nearest pub 5 miles

Unit TV DVD General P S

FAMILIES WELCOME

Looking for an ideal family break?

For accommodation offering additional facilities and services for a range of ages and family units, look out for the Families Welcome symbol. Owners of these properties will go out of their way to welcome families.

YORKLEY, Gloucestershire Map ref 2B1

★★★
SELF CATERING

Units 1
Sleeps 6

LOW SEASON PER WK
£400.00

HIGH SEASON PER WK
£550.00–£650.00

2 Danby Cottages, Lydney

contact Gareth Lawes, c/o 23 Cotham Road South, Bristol BS6 5TZ **t** (0117) 942 2301
e glawes@tiscali.co.uk

The cottage has two double bedrooms with shared bathroom upstairs and one downstairs with a wet room. There is a large new living room with glass doors opening onto a large area of decking. The ground floor is fully accessible.

open All year except Christmas
payment Cash, cheques
nearest shop 0.5 miles
nearest pub 0.5 miles

Unit General P S Leisure

For **key to symbols** see page 7

The Channel Islands

Jersey, Guernsey, Herm, Sark and Alderney

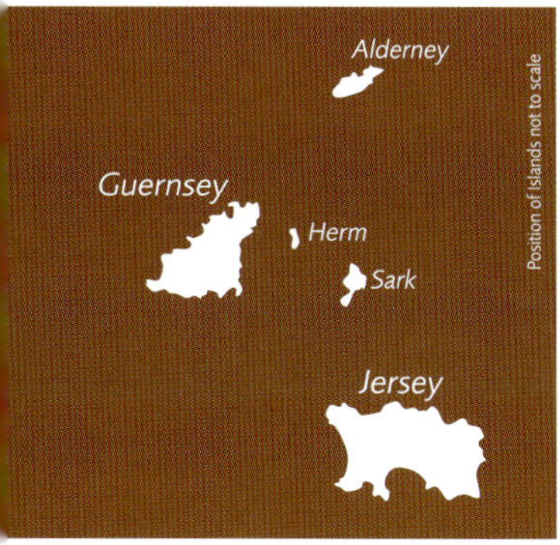

Clockwise: St Ouens Bay, Jersey; Alderney; St Peters Port, Guernsey

Great days out

The Channel Islands combine the spirit of Britain with the heart of Old Normandy in a rare fusion of English and French. Ancient customs blend with global commerce, beach and country living, the modern, the cosmopolitan and the homespun. Welcome to five distinct islands, two cultures and one memorable holiday.

Rock pools to rural treasures

Enjoy beautiful, safe sandy beaches, secret coves and rock pools, rugged harbours, stunning cliffs and fantastic flora and fauna. Inland, each island has a country character that follows the rhythm of the seasons. Sleepy lanes, private gardens, nature reserves and migrating birds are just some of the rural treasures waiting to surprise you. Take the charming Heritage Walk from **Samarès Manor** on Jersey, or spot the rare Aquatic Warbler on the wetland reserve at **La Claire Mare** on Guernsey. And with a temperate climate offering more warmth and sunshine than elsewhere in the British Isles, you'll find the islands in bloom all year round.

Bonne Nuit Bay, Jersey

Frontline history

Roll back the years to uncover Channel Island history, beginning with Neolithic Man and some of the oldest manmade structures in Europe: visit **La Hougue Bie** on Jersey, an extraordinary burial chamber and focal point for religious activity or Guernsey's Dehus Dolmen to see mysterious carvings. Twentieth-century turmoil also left its mark when the islands became bulwarks in Europe's WWII Atlantic Wall. Get a taste of daily life under occupation in the superbly preserved **Jersey War Tunnels** built by forced labour and now home to a gripping exhibition. Train your sights with the very rangefinders used by German forces in Guernsey's **Pleinmont Observation Tower**, or wander through a skilfully recreated wartime street scene at the **German Occupation Museum**.

Five lives

Each of the five islands has a distinctive personality – explore and you'll be charmed by their open welcome.

Guernsey is a heady mix of dazzling scenery and the best of contemporary living. Take inspiring walks or spend lazy days on wonderful beaches. Then explore the bustling harbour town of **St Peter Port** and let its tapestry of architectural styles tell the story of the region's changing fortunes. Here bistros, restaurants and boutiques jostle for your attention while, in the harbour, ferries are readied to take you to the sister islands. Wander through the museums at **Castle Cornet** and witness the firing of the noon day gun.

In Jersey, culture vultures will discover history at every turn, walkers will be captivated by breathtaking natural beauty and families can relax without a care on pristine beaches. In St Helier, take the Castle Ferry to the rocky islet where Sir Walter Raleigh built **Elizabeth Castle** and witness the 12-noon 'call to arms'

Left to right: Dehus Dolmen, Guernsey; Creux, Guernsey

did you know... these low-duty islands are a shopper's paradise – treat yourself!

and the firing of the castle cannon. Learn bygone skills and catch up with gossip from the time of Charles II at **Hamptonne**, a country life museum, or explore local marine ecology and learn how tides work, at the **Discovery Pier**. Jersey is also the ideal place to clear your head – come and indulge in some exhilarating outdoor sports, or simply live the life.

Herm, a tranquil island idyll that's easily reached from Guernsey by ferry, is a favourite with visitors and locals alike. No wonder: as soon as you step off the boat, the stresses of the modern world evaporate. **Alderney**, the closest island to France, feels more remote, although quickly accessible by air. Now you're in a paradise for nature lovers, where varied and rare wildlife from blonde hedgehogs to gannets share the invigorating landscapes. Refresh in the restaurants and lively pubs of the capital, **St Anne's**. Another day, step back in time in traffic-free **Sark** whose superb coastal views and picturesque rural interior can be best experienced on foot, by hired bicycle or horse and trap.

Best of two cultures

Throughout history, the islands have taken the best of Gallic and British culture: taste it now in the delicious cuisine, whether a casual snack of a fresh crab sandwich in a country pub or luxury seafood in a Michelin-starred restaurant. Norman Law, street names, surnames and local patois – a form of ancient French – give a romantic air. English conversation, the main language, extends a contemporary welcome. Stamps and currency, distinct from mainland Britain, also add to the islands' special sense of place.

Herm

Small islands, big attractions

Jersey, just 45 square miles, is packed with things to do, from shopping in the colourful town of **St Helier** to visiting the internationally famed **Durrell Wildlife Conservation Trust** to see exotic and endangered species. Delve into the island's past and rich maritime heritage at award-winning museums, unlock the secrets of **Mont Orgueil Castle**, Gorey. And plenty of attractions provide fun-filled family days out, like **Jersey Pottery** and **The Living Legend** adventure and leisure village.

Guernsey, too, embraces a wide range of must-sees, from the tiny wildlife preserve and remains of a 12th-century priory on **Lihou Island**, to museums, family activity and craft centres, quaint tearooms and top quality restaurants. Take in the extraordinary decoration of **Victor Hugo House**, where the writer of Les Misérables spent 14 years in exile, or discover the fate of ships wrecked on the infamous Hanois reefs on the rocky west coast at **Fort Grey and Shipwreck Museum**. Find out what life was like 100 years ago at the **National Trust of Guernsey Folk and Costume Museum** and thrill to the momentous events that **Castle Cornet** has witnessed.

why not... island hop to see some of the most beautiful scenery in Europe?

Walks to water-skiing

Feeling active? The islands are made for walkers! How about a slow stroll across the sands, or an energetic hike along cliff-top paths and into rocky coves. And the perfect way of taking in all the sights, sounds and smells is from the seat of a bicycle. Rent one or bring your own, enjoy a leisurely scenic ride for a few miles or gear yourself up for a more challenging route. Anglers, of course, are spoilt for choice – there's never a bad time to fish in the Channel Islands because such a wide variety of species flourish in the waters: bass to ballan wrasse, grey mullet to good old reliable garfish; something for every season.

Check the calendar for year-round high-level events like motor sports, powerboating, athletics and bowling. Watch classic cars tackle a twisting, scenic route across the island at the **Jersey Festival of Motoring** in June, then set sail for Guernsey's **Rocquaine Regatta** in August and the **Jersey Regatta** in September. Don't forget to save some energy, though – you'll need it to complete the famous Around Island Walk during Jersey's **Autumn Walking Week**. If you are looking for something a little more unusual, Guernsey hosts an **Underwater Cycling Race** in September where you can marvel at cyclists in full diving kit taking to the local outdoor bathing pools on specially modified bikes! Raise your pulse in Jersey wakeboarding, water-skiing, on banana rides, speedboat trips and ocean kayaks, or in Guernsey take an exhilarating rib ride!

Left to right: Fort Grey, Guernsey; St Brelades Bay, Jersey

Destinations

Alderney

With its rich and varied wildlife Alderney remains almost totally unaffected by the outside world, and is a paradise for nature lovers. Pull on your boots and discover over 30 miles of walks over cliffs and golden bays, across exposed commons, past Victorian fortresses and World War II batteries and alongside a scenic and challenging golf course. St Anne, the capital town, is a pretty community of colour-washed houses, cobbled streets and shops. Its magnificent church, known as 'the cathedral of the Channel Islands' is a must-see, and there are plenty of welcoming pubs and restaurants in which to relax and soak up the atmosphere.

Guernsey

Just seventy miles by fast ferry, or a short flight from mainland England, you'll find a heady mix of stunning scenery and the best of contemporary living. From its capital of St Peter Port – often regarded as the prettiest harbour in Europe – its miles of golden beaches, clear blue sea and breathtaking cliff walks to its early spring, superb seafood and fascinating history, Guernsey is the perfect mix of Continental and natural beauty.

St Peter Port, the island's capital, is a bustling harbour town in which a tapestry of architectural styles tells the story of the region's changing fortunes.

Enjoy a wide choice of dining experiences, where unsurprisingly fresh fish is in abundance. Shopping in St Peter Port is an experience not to be missed: electronic and photographic equipment, jewellery and perfume are all good, low-duty buys, and, of course, the famous Guernsey jumper. Small boutiques offer exclusive clothes, shoes and leather goods, whilst the Old Quarter is the place to find antiques. For a memorable excursion, take a trip to one of Guernsey's sister islands (Alderney, Herm or Sark) – frequent ferries run from St Peter Port harbour. And planes fly to Alderney regularly.

Herm

Disover this unspoiled paradise of sand dunes, long golden beaches, hidden bays, cliffwalks and seabreeze-combed common, just twenty minutes by boat from Guernsey. Allow yourself time to spend at least a couple of hours on Shell Beach, where clear waters lap the white sand made from millions of tiny shell fragments. It's easy to visit Herm in a day, but to really appreciate the island's charm, consider an overnight stay.

Shell Beach, Herm

Left to right: St Peter Port, Guernsey; Bluebell Valley, Guernsey; St Aubin, Jersey

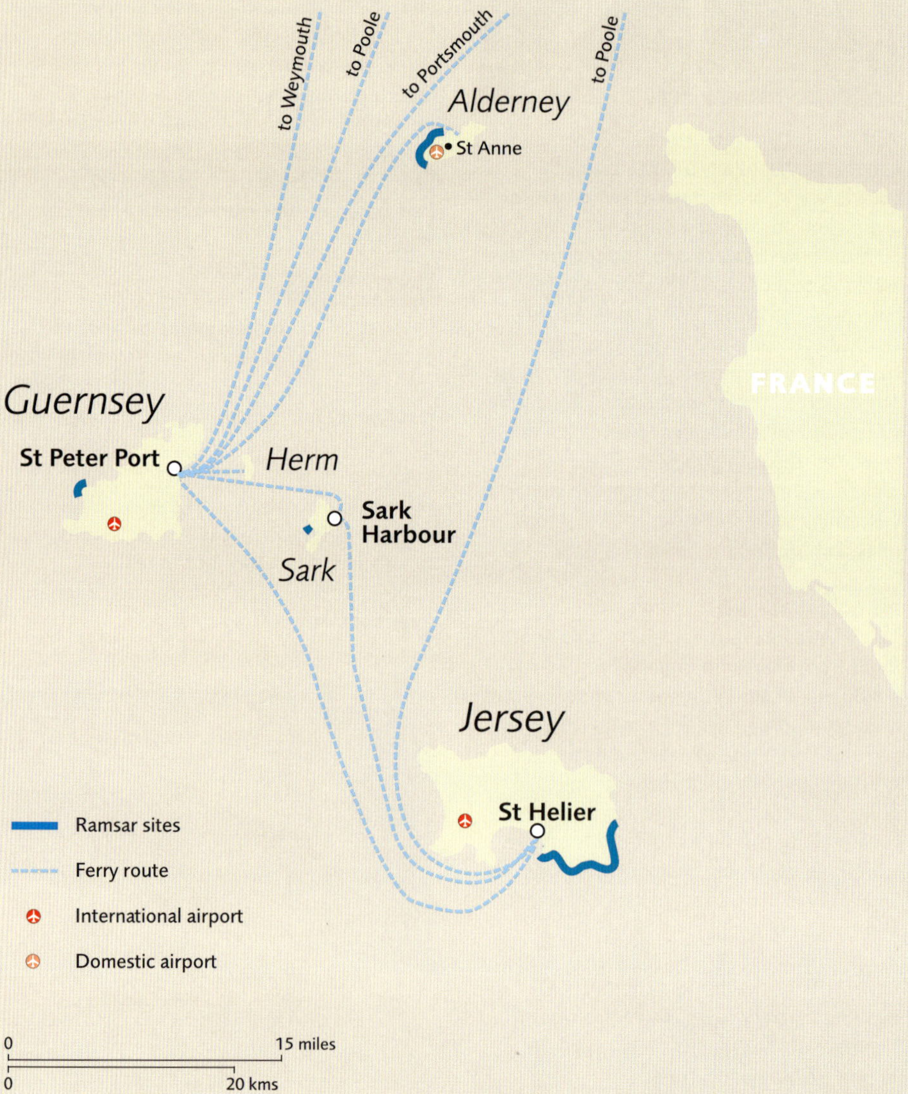

Sark

The picturesque island of Sark is the perfect escape. Traffic-free and overflowing with natural beauty, the island is easily reached by ferry from Guernsey. Take advantage of this walkers' paradise and follow one of the many coastal walks. Experience peace and tranquillity, admire wildflowers and seabirds, and feel like you have been transported to another world. If you wish to stay a little longer, there are a number of hotels and good restaurants to choose from.

Jersey

Clear water and beaches surround some 45 miles of coastline – the island's greatest natural treasure. Sweeping bays in the south give way to dramatic cliffs in the north offering spectacular scenery and stunning vistas. If food is your passion your taste buds are in for a real treat with over 170 eateries featuring Jersey's delicious local produce, top chefs and gourmet delights from around the world.

The streets of St Helier buzz with life. By day shop 'til you drop, dine al fresco whilst watching exciting street theatre or take a nautical jaunt with an appointed Blue Badge guide around the town's historic harbours. There are lots of attractions to explore, too. By night, linger in the warm evening sun in Royal Square, join theatre-goers at the Jersey Opera House or enjoy live music in one of the town's many pubs.

Hog's Back, Sark

For lots more great ideas go to visitbritain.com/destinations, visitguernsey.com and jersey.com

Clockwise: St Martin's Parish Church, Guernsey; St Lawrence, Jersey; Portelet Bay, Jersey; Rousse Tower, Guernsey

Visitor attractions

Family and Fun

aMaizin! Maze and Adventure Park
St Peter, Jersey
(01534) 482116
jerseyleisure.com
Award-winning attraction featuring maize maze, activities and entertainment.

Discovery Pier
Gorey, Jersey
(01534) 617704
eco-active.je
Interactive fun bringing Jersey's marine ecology to shore.

Guernsey Aquarium
St Peter Port, Guernsey
(01481) 723301
visitguernsey.com
Local, European and tropical marine life.

Jersey Goldsmiths and Lion Park
St Lawrence, Jersey
(01534) 482098
jerseygoldsmiths.com
Gold and gemstones set among beautiful lakes and gardens.

La Mare Wine Estate
St Mary, Jersey
(01534) 481178
lamarewineestate.com
Vineyards, winery and visitor centre with children's activities.

The Living Legend
St Peter, Jersey
(01534) 485496
jerseyslivinglegend.co.je
Adventure and leisure village packed with family fun.

Oatlands Village
St Sampson, Guernsey
(01481) 244282
Watch craftspeople at work, plus shops and café.

Samarès Manor
St Clement, Jersey
(01534) 870551
samaresmanor.com
Historic house, splendid gardens, crafts and children's activities.

Heritage

Castle Cornet
St Peter Port, Guernsey
(01481) 721657
museums.gov.gg
Ancient harbour fortress containing maritime and military museums.

Elizabeth Castle
St Helier, Jersey
(01534) 723971
jerseyheritage.com
16thC stronghold with daily call to arms.

German Occupation Museum
Forest, Guernsey
(01481) 238205
visitguernsey.com
Life during the WWII featuring authentic occupation street.

Jersey Museum and Art Gallery
St Helier, Jersey
(01534) 633300
jerseyheritage.com
Discover the history, traditions and culture of Jersey.

Jersey War Tunnels
St Lawrence, Jersey
(01534) 860808
jerseywartunnels.com
Gripping glimpse of life on Jersey under occupation.

La Hougue Bie
St Saviour, Jersey
(01534) 853823
jerseyheritage.com
One of the finest burial mounds in Europe.

La Vallette Underground Military Museum
St Peter Port, Guernsey
(01481) 722300
visitguernsey.com
Military museum housed in air-conditioned German tunnel complex.

The Little Chapel
St Andrews, Guernsey
(01481) 237200
thelittlechapel.org
Possibly the smallest chapel in the world.

Mont Orgueil Castle
Gorey, Jersey
(01534) 853292
jerseyheritage.com
Superbly preserved castle, the jewel in Jersey's crown.

Pleinmont Observation Tower
Torteval, Guernsey
(01481) 238205
visitguernsey.com
Naval observation tower used by the Germans 1942-45.

Victor Hugo House
St Peter Port, Guernsey
(01481) 721911
visitguernsey.com
Where the famous writer spent 14 years in exile.

Indoors

Fort Grey & Shipwreck Museum
Rocquaine, Guernsey
(01481) 265036
museums.gov.gg
Martello tower housing museum with many salvaged artefacts.

Guernsey Museum and Art Gallery
St Peter Port, Guernsey
(01481) 726518
museums.gov.gg
The island's natural and human history plus exhibitions.

The Guernsey Tapestry
St Peter Port, Guernsey
(01481) 727106
guernseytapestry.org.gg
Tells the 1,000-year story of Guernsey in a remarkable tapestry.

Jersey Pottery
Gorey, Jersey
(01534) 850850
jerseypottery.com
Decorate your own pottery at this famous attraction.

Maritime Museum and Occupation Tapestry
St Helier, Jersey
(01534) 811043
jerseyheritage.com
Interactive museum and famous tapestry commemorating wartime Jersey.

National Trust of Guernsey Folk and Costume Museum
Castel, Guernsey
(01481) 255384
nationaltrust-gsy.org.gg
Exhibitions and displays of old Guernsey life.

Outdoors

Durrell Wildlife
Trinity, Jersey
(01534) 860000
durrell.org
World-famous sanctuary for exotic and endangered species.

Hamptonne
St Lawrence, Jersey
(01534) 863955
jerseyheritage.com
Superbly restored farm buildings recreate rural life.

La Claire Mare
St Pierre du Bois, Guernsey
(01481) 725093
societe.org.gg
Nature reserve featuring wet grassland and reedbeds.

Le Vaux de Monel and La Varde Rock
Rocquaine, Guernsey
nationaltrust-gsy.org.gg
Naturalised garden with panoramic views over Rocquaine Bay.

Lihou Island
St Pierre du Bois, Guernsey
(01481) 266294
lihouisland.com
Unspoilt bird sanctuary reached by tidal causeway.

Events 2009

Liberation Day
Various venues, Jersey
jersey.com/liberation
9 May 2009

World Jersey Cheese Festival
Trinity, Jersey
jerseycheese.com
23 - 25 May 2009

Seafood Festival
Various venues, Guernsey
goodfoodguernsey.gg
1 - 31 Jul 2009

Out of the Blue Maritime Festival
St Helier, Jersey
jersey.com
4 - 5 Jul 2009

Battle of Flowers Carnival
St Helier, Jersey
battleofflowers.com
13 - 14 Aug 2009

Battle of Britain Week
Various venues, Guernsey
visitguernsey.com
7 - 13 Sep 2009

International Chess Festival
Vale, Guernsey
visitguernsey.com
18 - 24 Oct 2009

Guernsey Jazz Festival
St Peter Port, Guernsey
dukeofrichmond.com
30 Oct - 1 Nov 2009

La Fête dé Noué
Various venues, Jersey
jersey.com
28 Nov - 14 Dec 2009

Regional contacts and information

For more information on accommodation, attractions, activities, events and holidays in the Channel Islands, contact one of the following tourism organisations. Their websites have a wealth of information and publications to help you get the most out of your visit.

Guernsey

Guernsey Information Centre
North Esplanade, St Peter Port
Guernsey GY1 3AN
t (01481) 723552
t 0800 028 5353 (information pack request)
e enquiries@visitguernsey.com
w visitguernsey.com

Alderney

States of Alderney
PO Box 1
Alderney
GY9 3AA
t (01481) 822811

Jersey

Jersey Tourism
Liberation Place
St Helier
Jersey
JE1 1BB
t (01534) 448800
e info@jersey.com
w jersey.com

Free publications available to order from Jersey Tourism include:

- **What's on**
- **Jersey Map**
- **Walking Guide**

Clockwise: Liberation Day, Guernsey; Regatta, Guernsey; La Fête dé Noué, Jersey

Country ways

The Countryside Rights of Way Act gives people new rights to walk on areas of open countryside and registered common land.

To find out where you can go and what you can do, as well as information about taking your dog to the countryside, go online at countrysideaccess.gov.uk.

And when you're out and about...

Always follow the Country Code

- Be safe – plan ahead and follow any signs
- Leave gates and property as you find them
- Protect plants and animals, and take your litter home
- Keep dogs under close control
- Consider other people

where to stay in
The Channel Islands

For the location of the accommodation listed, refer to the maps at the front of this guide.

Accommodation symbols

Symbols give useful information about services and facilities. On page 7 you can find a key to these symbols.

GUERNSEY Map 6

★★★
SELF CATERING

Units 3
Sleeps 1–6

LOW SEASON PER WK
Min £500.00

HIGH SEASON PER WK
Max £975.00

Hotel Bon Port, St Martin

Hotel Bon Port, Moulin Huet Bay, St Martins GY4 6EW **t** (01481) 239249 **e** mail@bonport.com

bonport.com SPECIAL OFFERS

Set in the grounds of Hotel Bon Port. Two-bedroom cottages and one-bedroom apartments. Enjoy all the facilities with the independence of self-catering.

open All year
payment Credit/debit cards, cash, cheques
nearest shop 2 miles
nearest pub 1 mile

Unit General P Leisure

GUERNSEY Map 6

★★★
SELF CATERING

Units 21
Sleeps 2–5

LOW SEASON PER WK
Min £255.00

HIGH SEASON PER WK
Max £865.00

Del Mar Court, St Martin

Booking Office, Del Mar Court, Le Varclin, St Martin GY4 6AL **t** (01481) 237491
e reservations@selfcatering.co.gg

selfcatering.co.gg GUEST REVIEWS · SPECIAL OFFERS · REAL-TIME BOOKING

We are situated in a country lane above Fermain Bay yet only three minutes' drive from St Peter Port's shops and harbour. The apartments provide you will all you need for your family holiday.

open All year
payment Credit/debit cards, cash, cheques
nearest shop 1 mile
nearest pub 0.5 miles

Unit General P Leisure

Don't forget www.

Web addresses throughout this guide are shown without the prefix www. Please include www. in the address line of your browser. If a web address does not follow this style it is shown in full.

GUERNSEY Map 6

★★★-★★★★★
SELF CATERING

Units 4
Sleeps 2–4

LOW SEASON PER WK
Min £255.00

HIGH SEASON PER WK
Max £780.00

Le Douit Farm, St Martin

Del Mar Court, Le Varclin, St Martin GY4 6AL **t** (01481) 237491 **e** reservations@selfcatering.co.gg

selfcatering.co.gg GUEST REVIEWS • SPECIAL OFFERS • REAL-TIME BOOKING

open March to November
payment Credit/debit cards, cash, cheques
nearest shop 0.5 miles
nearest pub 0.5 miles

We are situated in a country lane by St Martin's Church in the ancient hamlet of La Bellieuse. You will be able to relax and unwind in these peaceful surroundings. The famous scenic cliff walks are within a one and a half mile radius giving access to over 20 miles of pedestrian paths.

SAT NAV *GY4 6RW* **ONLINE MAP**

Unit General P Leisure

JERSEY Map 6

★★★
SELF CATERING

Units 1
Sleeps 4–6

LOW SEASON PER WK
Min £495.00

HIGH SEASON PER WK
Max £990.00

The Old Forge

contact Mrs A Foley, The Old Forge, Pontorson Lane, St Clement JE2 6LG **t** (01534) 854176

oldforgejersey.co.uk

Part of a traditional Jersey granite house, the apartment consists of one double and two twin bedrooms and is suitable for between four and six people.

open All year
payment Cash, cheques
nearest shop 1 mile
nearest pub 0.5 miles

Unit General P

JERSEY Map 6

★★★★
SELF CATERING

Units 4
Sleeps 2–7

LOW SEASON PER WK
£415.00–£555.00

HIGH SEASON PER WK
£870.00–£1,550.00

La Planque Farm Country Cottages, Trinity

contact Paul Cook, La Planque Farm, La Verte Rue, Trinity JE3 5EA **t** (01534) 860773
e enquiries@laplanquefarm.com

laplanquefarm.com

Charming country cottages, three-bedroom and one-bedroom, located in idyllic and peaceful country setting. Personal, friendly hosts. See website for full details.

open All year except Christmas and New Year
payment Cash, cheques
nearest shop 1 mile
nearest pub 1 mile

Unit General P
Leisure

JERSEY Map 6

★★★-★★★★★
SELF CATERING

Units 6
Sleeps 3–8

LOW SEASON PER WK
£595.00–£1,019.00

HIGH SEASON PER WK
£860.00–£1,493.00

Samares Manor Self Catering Accommodation, St Clement

contact Sally Fleming, Samares Manor Ltd, St Clement JE3 6DJ **t** (01534) 870551
e enquiries@samaresmanor.com

samaresmanor.com

Three apartments and three cottages situated within the manor's picturesque courtyard. Registered for between three (Apt 3) and eight adults (The Forge) plus additional children. Extensive gardens accessible at all times.

open April to October
payment Credit/debit cards, cash, cheques
nearest shop 0.5 miles
nearest pub 0.5 miles

Unit General P Leisure

Self-catering agencies

This section of the guide lists agencies that have a selection of accommodation to let in various parts of the country. Some agencies specialise in a particular area or region while others have properties in all parts of England.

The agencies listed here are grouped into those which have had all properties assessed by Enjoy England and those which have had at least 50% of their properties assessed.

To obtain further information on individual properties please contact the agency or agencies direct, indicating the time of year when the accommodation is required, the number of people to be accommodated and any preferred locations.

* The agencies with an A have an advertisement in this guide.

Quality Accredited Agency Standard

As a further step towards achieving quality not only in accommodation, Enjoy England has developed a Quality Accredited Agency Standard. Agencies who are awarded the Quality Accredited Agency marque by Enjoy England are recognised as offering good customer service and peace of mind, following an assessment of their office policies, practices and procedures.

AQA®

Quality Accredited Agency

Policies, Practices & Procedures Assessed

Totally quality assessed

These agencies only promote properties that have been assessed under Enjoy England's Quality Rose assessment scheme.

AGENCIES WITH MORE THAN 100 PROPERTIES

Blakes Cottages
t 0870 078 1300
w blakes-cottages.co.uk
National agency with accommodation throughout England

Blue Chip Vacations
t (01803) 855282
e info@bluechipvacations.com
w bluechipvacations.com
Offering accommodation in Cornwall and Devon

Cornish Horizons Holiday Cottages
t (01841) 533331
e cottages@cornishhorizons.co.uk
w cornishhorizons.co.uk
Offering accommodation in North Cornwall

Country Holidays
t 0870 0781 200
w country-holidays.co.uk
National agency with accommodation throughout England

Cumbrian Cottages A
t (01228) 599960
e enquiries@cumbrian-cottages.co.uk
w cumbrian-cottages.co.uk
Offering accommodation in Cumbria – The Lake District

Dream Cottages
t (01305) 789000
e admin@dream-cottages.co.uk
w dream-cottages.co.uk
Offering accommodation in Dorset, Devon Wiltshire and Hampshire

Freedom Holiday Homes
t (01580) 720770
e mail@freedomholidayhomes.co.uk
w freedomholidayhomes.co.uk
Offering accommodation in Kent and East Sussex

Harbour Holidays, Padstow
t (01841) 533402
e contact@harbourholidays.co.uk
w harbourholidays.co.uk
Offering accommodation in Padstow, Cornwall

Lakelovers A
t (01539) 488855
e bookings@lakelovers.co.uk
w lakelovers.co.uk
Offering accommodation in Cumbria – The Lake District

Lyme Bay Holidays
t (01297) 443363
e email@lymebayholidays.co.uk
w lymebayholidays.co.uk
Offering accommodation in and around Lyme Regis, Dorset

Marsdens Cottage Holidays A
t (01271) 813777
e holidays@marsdens.co.uk
w marsdens.co.uk
Offering accommodation in North Devon

Norfolk Country Cottages
t (01603) 871872
e info@norfolkcottages.co.uk
w norfolkcottages.co.uk
Offering accommodation in Norfolk and North Suffolk

Peak Cottages
t (01142) 620777
e enquiries@peakcottages.com
w peakcottages.com
Offering accommodation in the Peak District

Suffolk Secrets
t (01502) 722717
e holidays@suffolk-secrets.co.uk
w suffolk-secrets.co.uk
Offering accommodation in Suffolk

Whitby Holiday Cottages
t (01947) 603010
e enquiries@whitbyholidaycottages.net
w whitbyholidaycottages.net
Offering accommodation in Yorkshire

AGENCIES WITH 51-100 PROPERTIES

Birds Norfolk Holiday Homes
t (01485) 534267
e shohol@birdsnorfolkholidayhomes.co.uk
w norfolkholidayhomes-birds.co.uk
Offering accommodation in Norfolk

The Coppermines & Coniston Lake Cottages
t (01539) 441765
w coppermines.co.uk
Offering accommodation in Cumbria – The Lake District

Cornish Collection
t (01503) 262736
e info@cornishcollection.co.uk
w cornishcollection.co.uk
Offering accommodation in South East Cornwall

Garden of England Cottages A
t (01892) 510117
e info@gardenofenglandcottages.co.uk
w gardenofenglandcottages.co.uk
Offering accommodation in Kent and East Sussex

Harrogate Holiday Cottages
t (01423) 523333
e bookings@harrogateholidays.co.uk
w harrogateholidays.co.uk
Offering accommodation in and around Harrogate, North Yorkshire

Holiday Homes and Cottages South West
t (01803) 299677
e holcotts@aol.com
w swcottages.co.uk
Offering accommodation in Devon and Cornwall

Home from Home Holidays
t (01983) 854340
e ventnor@crldirect.co.uk
w hfromh.co.uk
Offering accommodation on the Isle of Wight

Island Cottage Holidays
t (01929) 481555
e enq@islandcottageholidays.com
w islandcottageholidays.com
Offering accommodation on the Isle of Wight

Island Holiday Homes
t (01983) 866455
e enquiries@island-holiday-homes.net
w island-holiday-homes.net
Offering accommodation on the Isle of Wight

Island Properties
t (01720) 422082
e enquiries@scillyhols.com
w scillyhols.com
Offering accommodation on the Isle of Scilly

Lakeland Cottage Company
t (01539) 538180
e john@lakelandcottageco.com
w lakelandcottageco.com
Offering accommodation in Cumbria – The Lake District

Milkbere Cottage Holidays
t (01297) 20729
e info@milkberehols.com
w milkberehols.com
Offering accommodation on Hayling Island, Hampshire

Rock Holidays
t (01208) 863399
e info@rockholidays.co.uk
w rockholidays.co.uk
Offering accommodation in Cornwall

Roseland Holiday Cottages
t (01872) 580480
e enquiries@roselandholidaycottages.co.uk
w roselandholidaycottages.co.uk
Offering accommodation in St Mawes and Portscatho, Cornwall

AGENCIES WITH 50 PROPERTIES OR LESS

Ayia Napa Holidays
t (01736) 757237
e info@carbisbayretreats.co.uk
w carbisbayretreats.co.uk
Offering accommodation in Carbis Bay and St Ives, Cornwall

Bath Holiday Homes
t (01225) 830830
e bhh@virgin.net
w bathholidayhomes.co.uk
Offering accommodation in Bath, Somerset

Bath Holiday Rentals
t (01225) 482225
e alexa@bathholidayrentals.com
w bathholidayrentals.com
Offering accommodation in Bath

Bedwyns Holiday Accommodation
t (01723) 516700
e info@bedwyns.co.uk
w bedwyns.co.uk
Offering accommodation in and around Scarborough

Brixham Holiday Homes
t (01803) 854187
e info@brixhamholidayhomes.co.uk
w brixhamholidayhomes.com
Offering accommodation in and around Brixham

Carbis Bay Holidays
t 0800 012 2241
e enquiries@carbisbayholidays.co.uk
w carbisbayholidays.co.uk
Offering accommodation in Carbis Bay, St Ives, Cornwall

Combermere Abbey Cottages
t (01948) 662876
e cottages@combermereabbey.co.uk
w combermereabbey.co.uk
Offering accommodation in Combermere Abbey Estate, Cheshire/Shropshire border

Country Hideaways
t (01969) 663559
e info@countryhideaways.co.uk
w countryhideaways.co.uk
Offering accommodation in the Yorkshire Dales

Dorset Cottage Holidays
t (01929) 553443
e enq@dhcottages.co.uk
w dhcottages.co.uk
Offering accommodation in Dorset

Helford River Cottages [A]
t (01326) 231666
e info@helfordcottages.co.uk
w helfordcottages.co.uk
Offering accommodation in and around Helford, Cornwall

Holiday Homes Owners Services (West Wight)
t (01983) 753423
e holidayhomesiow@ic24.net
w holidayhomesiow.co.uk
Offering accommodation on the Isle of Wight

Keswick Cottages
t (01768) 778555
e info@keswickcottages.co.uk
w keswickcottages.co.uk
Offering accommodation in and around Keswick, Cumbria – The Lake District

Linstone Chine Holiday Services Ltd
t (01983) 755933
e linstone-chine@btconnect.com
w linstone-chine.com
Offering accommodation on the Isle of Wight

Millers of Hayling [A]
t (02392) 465951
e rentals@haylingproperty.co.uk
w haylingproperty.co.uk
Offering accommodation on Hayling Island, Hampshire

Miraleisure Ltd
t (01424) 730298
e infomira@waitrose.com
w miraleisure.co.uk
Offering accommodation in Bexhill-on-Sea, East Sussex

Quay Holidays [A]
t (01202) 683333
e stay@quayholidays.co.uk
w quayholidays.co.uk
Offering accommodation in South West England

Special Places in Cornwall
t (01872) 864400
e office@specialplacescornwall.co.uk
w specialplacescornwall.co.uk
Offering accommodation in Cornwall

50% quality assessed

Agencies with 50% or more of their properties officially quality assessed by VisitBritain.

Acanthus Property Letting Services
t (01502) 724033
e websales@southwold-holidays.co.uk
w southwold-holidays.co.uk
Offering accommodation in Southwold, Walberswick and Dunwich, Suffolk

Cornish Holiday Cottages
t (01326) 250339
e info@cornishholidaycottages.net
w cornishholidaycottages.net
Offering accommodation in Cornwall

Duchy Holidays Ltd
t (01872) 572971
e enquiries@duchyholidays.co.uk
w duchyholidays.co.uk
Offering accommodation in Perranporth and St Agnes, Cornwall

Northumberland Cottages
t (01665) 589434
e enquiries@northumberlandcottages.com
w northumberlandcottages.com
Offering accommodation in Northumberland

Suffolk Holidays Limited
t (01502) 723571
e sales@holidaysinsuffolk.co.uk
w holidaysinsuffolk.co.uk
Offering accommodation in Southwold, Aldeburgh and Walberswick, Suffolk

Valley Villas Ltd
t (01752) 605605
e sales@valleyvillas.com
w valleyvillas.co.uk
Offering accommodation in Cornwall

Wight Locations Ltd
t (01983) 811418
e enquiries@wightlocations.co.uk
w wightlocations.co.uk
Offering accommodation in the Isle of Wight

Yealm Holidays
t 0845 634 3490
w yealm-holidays.co.uk
Offering accommodation in South West Devon – Newton Ferrers, Noss Mayo and Yealmpton

Bank holiday dates for your diary

holiday	2009	2010
New Year's Day	1 January	1 January
Good Friday	10 April	2 April
Easter Monday	13 April	5 April
Early May Bank Holiday	4 May	3 May
Liberation Day (Channel Islands)	9 May	9 May
Spring Bank Holiday	25 May	31 May
Summer Bank Holiday	31 August	30 August
Christmas Day Holiday	25 December	27 December
Boxing Day Holiday	28 December	28 December

Enjoy England assessed accommodation

On the following pages you will find an exclusive listing of every self-catering establishment in England that has been assessed for quality by Enjoy England.

The information includes brief contact details for each place to stay, together with its star rating and classification. The listing also shows if an establishment has a National Accessible rating or participates in the Welcome schemes: Cyclists Welcome, Walkers Welcome, Welcome Pets! and Families Welcome (see the front of the guide for further information).

Accommodation is listed by region and then alphabetically by place name. Establishments may be located in, or a short distance from, the places in blue bands.

More detailed information on all the properties shown in bold can be found in the regional sections (where establishments have paid to have their details included). To find these entries please refer to the property index at the back of this guide.

The list which follows was compiled slightly later than the regional sections. For this reason you may find that, in a few instances, a star rating and quality award may differ between the two sections. This list contains the most up-to-date information and was correct at the time of going to press.

Boat accommodation

Towards the end of this section you will find details of boat accommodation quality-assessed by Enjoy England.

NORTHERN ENGLAND

ABBEYSTEAD
Lancashire

Higher Lee ★★★★
Self Catering
t (01524) 791287
w higherlee.co.uk

ACASTER MALBIS
North Yorkshire

Orchard Lodge, Acaster Malbis ★★★★ *Self Catering*
Contact: Ms Bridget Karn
t (01904) 700924 & 07766 352049
e bridget@orchardlodgeyork.co.uk
w orchardlodgeyork.co.uk

ACCRINGTON
Lancashire

Low Moorside Farm Cottage ★★★ *Self Catering*
Contact: Mr & Mrs C & E Hallworth
t (01254) 237053

Meadowtop Barn ★★★★
Self Catering
Contact: Mrs Newcombe
t (01254) 232879
e newcamuk@aol.com
w meadowtopfarm.co.uk

ACKLAM
North Yorkshire

Beck Side Cottage ★★★★
Self Catering
Contact: Margaret Phillips
t (01653) 658468

ACKLINGTON
Northumberland

Bank House Holiday Cottages, Guyzance ★★★★
Self Catering
Contact: Mr Steven Stone
t 07525 615411
e info@bankhouseholidaycottages.co.uk
w bankhouseholidaycottages.co.uk

Stable Cottage ★★★★
Self Catering
Contact: Mrs Linda Osborne
t (01670) 760320
e linda.osborne1@btopenworld.com
w wishingwellcottages.co.uk

ADLINGTON
Cheshire

Carr Cottage ★★★★
Self Catering
Contact: Mrs Isobel Worthington
t (01625) 828337
e isobel@carrhousefarm.fsnet.co.uk
w carrhousefarm.com/

AIKE
East Riding of Yorkshire

The Old Chapel ★★★
Self Catering
Sykes Cottages
t (01244) 345700
e info@sykescottages.co.uk
w sykescottages.co.uk

AINSTABLE
Cumbria

Eden Ghyll ★★★
Self Catering
Cumbrian Cottages
t (01228) 599960
e enquiries@cumbrian-cottages.co.uk
w cumbrian-cottages.co.uk

AISKEW
North Yorkshire

Courtyard Cottages, Aiskew ★★★ *Self Catering*
Contact: Mr & Mrs James & Jill Cartman
t (01677) 423689
e jill@courtyardcottages.net
w courtyardcottages.net

AISLABY
North Yorkshire

Farm Cottage ★★★
Self Catering
Whitby Holiday Cottages
t (01947) 603010
e enquiries@whitbyholidaycottages.net
w whitbyholidaycottages.net

Granary Cottage ★★★★
Self Catering
Whitby Holiday Cottages
t (01947) 603010
e enquiries@whitbyholidaycottages.net
w whitbyholidaycottages.net

Home Cottage ★★★
Self Catering
Whitby Holiday Cottages
t (01947) 603010
e enquiries@whitbyholidaycottages.net
w whitbyholidaycottages.net

Low Newbiggin House ★★★★ *Self Catering*
Contact: Miss Charlotte Etherington
t (01947) 811811
e holidays@lownewbiggin.co.uk

Pine Cottage ★★★
Self Catering
Whitby Holiday Cottages
t (01947) 603010
e enquiries@whitbyholidaycottages.net
w whitbyholidaycottages.net

Stable Cottage & Byre Cottage ★★★ *Self Catering*
Whitby Holiday Cottages
t (01947) 603010
e enquiries@whitbyholidaycottages.net
w whitbyholidaycottages.net

AKELD
Northumberland

Akeld Manor & Country Club (Aubretia Trail) ★★★★ *Self Catering*
Akeld Manor & Country Club
t (01665) 721035
e allan.group@virgin.net
w borderrose-holidays.co.uk

Akeld Manor & Country Club (Bizzie Lizzie) ★★★★
Self Catering
Akeld Manor & Country Club
t (01665) 721035
e allan.group@virgin.net
w borderrose-holidays.co.uk

Akeld Manor & Country Club (Blueberry Cottage) ★★★★ *Self Catering*
Akeld Manor & Country Club
t (01665) 721035
e allan.group@virgin.net
w borderrose-holidays.co.uk

Akeld Manor & Country Club (Catkin Cottage) ★★★★ *Self Catering*
Akeld Manor & Country Club
t (01665) 721035
e allan.group@virgin.net
w borderrose-holidays.co.uk

Akeld Manor & Country Club (The Columbine) ★★★★ *Self Catering*
Akeld Manor & Country Club
t (01665) 721035
e allan.group@virgin.net
w borderrose-holidays.co.uk

Akeld Manor & Country Club (Foxglove) ★★★★
Self Catering
Akeld Manor & Country Club
t (01665) 721035
e allan.group@virgin.net
w borderrose-holidays.co.uk

Akeld Manor & Country Club (Fresia Cottage) ★★★★ *Self Catering*
Akeld Manor & Country Club
t (01665) 721035
e allan.group@virgin.net
w borderrose-holidays.co.uk

Akeld Manor & Country Club (Holly Hocks) ★★★★
Self Catering
Akeld Manor & Country Club
t (01665) 721035
e allan.group@virgin.net
w borderrose-holidays.co.uk

Akeld Manor & Country Club (Honeysuckle Haven) ★★★★ *Self Catering*
Akeld Manor & Country Club
t (01665) 721035
e allan.group@virgin.net
w borderrose-holidays.co.uk

Akeld Manor & Country Club (Ivy Cottage) ★★★★
Self Catering
Akeld Manor & Country Club
t (01665) 721035
e allan.group@virgin.net
w borderrose-holidays.co.uk

Akeld Manor & Country Club (Lavender Cottages) ★★★★ *Self Catering*
Akeld Manor & Country Club
t (01665) 721035
e allan.group@virgin.net
w borderrose-holidays.co.uk

Akeld Manor & Country Club (Pansy Plot) ★★★★
Self Catering
Akeld Manor & Country Club
t (01665) 721035
e allan.group@virgin.net
w borderrose-holidays.co.uk

Akeld Manor & Country Club (Perry Winkle) ★★★★
Self Catering
Akeld Manor & Country Club
t (01665) 721035
e allan.group@virgin.net
w borderrose-holidays.co.uk

Akeld Manor & Country Club (Primula Patch) ★★★★
Self Catering
Akeld Manor & Country Club
t (01665) 721035
e allan.group@virgin.net
w borderrose-holidays.co.uk

Akeld Manor & Country Club (Timberwick Green) ★★★★ *Self Catering*
Akeld Manor & Country Club
t (01665) 721035
e allan.group@virgin.net
w borderrose-holidays.co.uk

ALDBROUGH
East Riding of Yorkshire

Lilac Cottage, Aldbrough ★★★★ *Self Catering*
Contact: Helen & Nick Stubbs
t (01964) 527645 & 07967 566848
e nick@seasideroad.freeserve.co.uk
w lilac-cottage.net

ALDFIELD
North Yorkshire

Mallard Cottage ★★★★
Self Catering
t (01765) 620242
w mallardgrange.co.uk

Trips Cottage ★★★
Self Catering
Contact: Valerie Leeming
t (01765) 620394
e btfarm@ppcmail.co.uk
w yorkshirebandb.co.uk

ALLENDALE
Northumberland

Allenmill Cottages ★★★★
Self Catering
Contact: Ms Emma Robson
t (01434) 683126
e info@allenmill.com
w allenmill.com

Fell View Cottage ★★★★
Self Catering
Contact: Mr & Mrs Colin & Carole Verne-Jones
t (0191) 386 9045
e colin.verne-jones@fellviewcottage.co.uk
w fellviewcottage.co.uk

Look out for establishments participating in the National Accessible Scheme

ALLENHEADS
Northumberland

Englewood ★★★
Self Catering
Sykes Cottages
t (01244) 345700
e info@sykescottages.co.uk
w sykescottages.co.uk

ALLERSTON
North Yorkshire

Dalby Station Cottage
★★★★ *Self Catering*
Contact: Vanessa Jones
t 07779 585484
e mpickard@doctors.org.uk

The Old Station ★★★★
Self Catering
Contact: Mark & Carol Benson
t (01723) 859024
e mcrbenson@aol.com
w theoldstationallerston.co.uk

Rains Farm ★★★★
Self Catering
Contact: Miss L Allanson
t (01723) 859333
e rainsholidays@btconnect.com
w rains-farm-holidays.co.uk

ALLERTHORPE
East Riding of Yorkshire

Manderlay, Allerthorpe Lakeland Park ★★★★
Self Catering
t (01759) 301444
e info@allerthorpelakelandpark.co.uk
w allerthorpelakelandpark.co.uk

ALLITHWAITE
Cumbria

Applegarth
Rating Applied For
Self Catering
Cumbrian Cottages
t (01228) 599960
e enquiries@cumbrian-cottages.co.uk
w cumbrian-cottages.co.uk

Fair View ★★★ *Self Catering*
Cumbrian Cottages
t (01228) 599960
e enquiries@cumbrian-cottages.co.uk
w cumbrian-cottages.co.uk

ALLONBY
Cumbria

Aloft Allonby ★★★
Self Catering
Cumbrian Cottages
t (01228) 599960
e enquiries@cumbrian-cottages.co.uk
w cumbrian-cottages.co.uk

Beachcomber ★★★
Self Catering
Cumbrian Cottages
t (01228) 599960
e enquiries@cumbrian-cottages.co.uk
w cumbrian-cottages.co.uk

Crookhurst Farm, Allonby
★★★★ *Self Catering*
Contact: Brenda Wilson
t (01900) 881228 & 07773 047591
e brenda@crookhurst.com
w crookhurst.com

Dickinson Place Holiday Cottages ★★★-★★★★★
Self Catering
Contact: James & Teresa Williamson
t (01900) 881440
e holidays@dickinsonplace.co.uk
w dickinsonplace.co.uk

The Old Coachmans Cottage
★★★ *Self Catering*
Cumbrian Cottages
t (01228) 599960
e enquiries@cumbrian-cottages.co.uk
w cumbrian-cottages.co.uk

Vicarage Fields Caravan Park ★★★ *Self Catering*
Contact: Mr Jeff Longton
t (01524) 850829

ALNMOUTH
Northumberland

Bilton Barns ★★★★
Self Catering
Contact: Mrs Dorothy Jackson
t (01665) 830427
e dorothy@biltonbarns.com
w biltonbarns.com

Grange Cottages – Old Watch Tower & The Coach House ★★★★ *Self Catering*
Contact: Ms Nicola Brierley
t (01665) 830783
e cottages@nccc.demon.co.uk
w northumbria-cottages.co.uk

Old Hall Cottage, High Buston Hall ★★★★★
Self Catering
Contact: Mrs Therese Atherton
t (01665) 830606
e cottage@highbuston.com
w highbuston.com

Paradise Lodge, Alnmouth
★★★★★ *Self Catering*
Contact: Ms Sandra MacDonald
Heavenly Holiday Homes
t (0191) 384 3904 & 07971 538316
e sa@heavenlyholidayhomes.co.uk
w heavenlyholidayhomes.co.uk

Platone ★★★ *Self Catering*
Contact: Mr & Mrs J & B Galbraith
t (01665) 830084
e jandbgalbraith@tiscali.co.uk
w northumberlandcottages.co.uk

Shepherds House ★★★
Self Catering
Contact: Mrs Lyn Frater
t (01665) 830361
e lynpfrater@aol.com
w cottageguide.co.uk/shepherdshouse

Sunnyside Cottage ★★★★
Self Catering
Contact: Mrs Mary Hollins
t (01665) 830330
e sunnysidecott@lineone.net
w sunnysidecott.co.uk

Wooden Farm Holiday Cottages ★★-★★★
Self Catering
Contact: Mr Gordon Farr
t (01665) 830342

ALNWICK
Northumberland

29 Bondgate Within ★★★★
Self Catering
Contact: Mr Toby Wilkie-Smith
Ridley Properties
t (0191) 230 5471
e toby@daviesbellreed.co.uk

3 Jubilee Court ★★★★
Self Catering
Contact: Mrs Jenny Robinson
t (01665) 605153
e wwr@globalnet.co.uk

7 Lower Dodds Lane ★★★
Self Catering
Contact: Mrs Helen Potts
t (01665) 711497
e hm.potts@btinternet.com

Aldyke Farm Cottages
★★★★ *Self Catering*
Contact: Mrs Laura Davison
t (01665) 510252
e laura@alndyke.co.uk
w alndyke.co.uk

Alnwick Angel ★★★
Self Catering
Contact: Mr Colin McLean
t (01665) 602315
e alnwickangel@tesco.net

Barbican View ★★★★
Self Catering
Contact: Mrs Frances Draper
t (01484) 683705
e fran.draper@virgin.net
w barbicanview.co.uk

Bog Mill Farm Holiday Cottages ★★★★-★★★★★
Self Catering
Contact: Mrs Ann Mason
t (01665) 604529
e stay@bogmill.co.uk
w bogmill.co.uk

Bolthole at Titlington Mount
★★★★ *Self Catering*
Contact: Ms Lisa Stevenson
t 07807 069576
e lisa.parisi@googlemail.com
w bolthole-in-northumberland.co.uk/

Braeside ★★★★★
Self Catering
Contact: Mrs Margaret McGregor
t (01665) 574460
e margaret@broomehillfarm.co.uk
w braesidealnwick.co.uk

Column View
Rating Applied For
Self Catering
Contact: Mrs Margaret Agan
t (01665) 602378
e philip.agan@tiscali.co.uk

Dene View Cottage and Moor Croft Cottage ★★★★
Self Catering
Contact: Mrs Margaret McGregor
t (01665) 574460
e margaret@broomehillfarm.co.uk
w broomehillfarm.co.uk

Dunelm ★★★ *Self Catering*
Contact: Mrs Val Greene
t (01529) 413148
e val.greene@btinternet.com

Farm Cottage ★★★
Self Catering
Contact: Mrs Renner
t (01665) 579266
w cottageguide.co.uk/shipleyhill

Folly Cottage ★★★
Self Catering
Contact: Mrs Joan Gilroy
t (01665) 579265

Garden Cottages ★★★★
Self Catering
Contact: Miss Andrea Tomkins
t (01665) 574129
e info@alnwickgardencottages.co.uk
w alnwickgardencottages.co.uk

Harehope Estate ★★★
Self Catering
Contact: Ms Alison Wrangham
Harehope Hall
t (01668) 217329
e aliwrangham@btconnect.com

Henhill and Birchwood Hall Cottages ★★★★
Self Catering
Northumberland Estates
Holiday Cottages
t (01668) 219941
e jane@nehc.co.uk
w alnwickcastlecottages.co.uk

Herring Sheds Cottage
★★★★★ *Self Catering*
Northumberland Estates
Holiday Cottages
t (01668) 219941
e jane@nehc.co.uk
w alnwickcastlecottages.co.uk

The Hotspur ★★★★
Self Catering
Contact: Mr & Mrs Richard & Julia Wood
t (0113) 295 9616
e stay@thehotspur.co.uk
w thehotspur.co.uk

Hufflepuff House ★★★★
Self Catering
Northumberland Cottages
t (01665) 589434
e enquiries@northumberlandcottages.com
w northumberlandcottages.co.uk

Juliet Cottage ★★★
Self Catering
Contact: Mrs Viv Butcher
t (0191) 246 1313 & 07922 082596
e viviennebutcher@yahoo.co.uk
w cottageguide.co.uk/juliet

Limpet Cottage ★★★★
Self Catering
Northumberland Estates
Holiday Cottages
t (01668) 219941
e jane@nehc.co.uk
w alnwickcastlecottages.co.uk

Loan End Cottage ★★★★
Self Catering
Contact: Ms Helen Burn
t (01665) 600914
e kmoor@doctors.org.uk
w cottageguide.co.uk/loanendcottage

Lumbylaw & Garden Cottages ★★★★
Self Catering
Contact: Mrs S Lee
t (01665) 574277
e holidays@lumbylaw.co.uk
w lumbylaw.co.uk

Moor View
Rating Applied For
Self Catering
Contact: Mrs Maureen Lorimer
t (01665) 603089
e lorimer3@tiscali.co.uk

Oakwood Apartment
★★★★ *Self Catering*
Northumbrian Cottages
t (01228) 599950
e sheena@cumbrian-cottages.co.uk
w northumbrian-cottages.info

Pugmill ★★★★ *Self Catering*
Contact: Mrs Judith Price
t (01669) 621814
e the4farm@aol.com
w pugmill.co.uk

Reiver Cottage ★★★★
Self Catering
Dales Holiday Cottages
t (01756) 790919
e info@dales-holiday-cottages.com
w dales-holiday-cottages.com

Stamford & Embleton Mill Farm Cottages ★★★★
Self Catering
Contact: Mrs Hazel Grahamslaw
t (01665) 579425
e hazelgrahamslaw@yahoo.co.uk

Village Farm
★★★-★★★★★
Self Catering
Contact: Mrs Crissy Stoker
t (01665) 575591
e crissy@villagefarmcottages.co.uk
w villagefarmcottages.co.uk

ALSTON Cumbria

Back O' The Burn ★★★★
Self Catering
Cumbrian Cottages
t (01228) 599960
e enquiries@cumbrian-cottages.co.uk
w cumbrian-cottages.co.uk

Ghyll Burn Cottage ★★★
Self Catering
t (01434) 381372

Robson's Cottage
Rating Applied For
Self Catering
Cumbrian Cottages
t (01228) 599960
e enquiries@cumbrian-cottages.co.uk
w cumbrian-cottages.co.uk

ALWINTON Northumberland

Fellside Cottage ★★★★
Self Catering
Contact: Mrs Denise Straughan
t (01670) 823042
e stay@fellsidecottcheviots.co.uk
w fellsidecottcheviots.co.uk

Stonecrop Cottage ★★★
Self Catering
Contact: Mrs Maureen Mason
t (01665) 603393
e maureenpeter10@btinternet.com
w stonecrop-alwinton.com

AMBLE Northumberland

Amble Cottages ★★★
Self Catering
Contact: Mrs Lynne Gray
t (01665) 711737
e djgray147@btinternet.com
w amblecottages.co.uk

Amblers Rest Cottage & Ground Floor Apartment
★★★ *Self Catering*
Contact: Mrs Glenys Rudd
t (01665) 714869
e amblersrest@btinternet.com
w amblersrest.co.uk

The Enchanted Cottage
★★★★ *Self Catering*
Northumbrian Cottages
t (01228) 599950
e sheena@cumbrian-cottages.co.uk
w northumbrian-cottages.info

Seashells ★★★★
Self Catering
Contact: Mr & Mrs Ian & Sue Rochester
t (01665) 713448
e ian@roch11.freeserve.co.uk
w seashellscottage.co.uk

AMBLE-BY-THE-SEA Northumberland

Coastguard Cottage ★★★★
Self Catering
Contact: Mr & Mrs N Aitchison
t (01904) 490408
e info@coastguardcottage.co.uk
w coastguardcottage.co.uk

AMBLESIDE Cumbria

1 West View ★★★★
Self Catering
Cumbrian Cottages
t (01228) 599960
e enquiries@cumbrian-cottages.co.uk
w cumbrian-cottages.co.uk

10 Badgers Rake ★★★
Self Catering
Cumbrian Cottages
t (01228) 599960
e enquiries@cumbrian-cottages.co.uk
w cumbrian-cottages.co.uk

11 Badgers Rake ★★★★
Self Catering
Cumbrian Cottages
t (01228) 599960
e enquiries@cumbrian-cottages.co.uk
w cumbrian-cottages.co.uk

11 Kings Yard ★★★
Self Catering
Hideaways
t (015394) 42435
e bookings@lakeland-hideaways.co.uk
w lakeland-hideaways.co.uk

12 Badgers Rake ★★★★
Self Catering
Cumbrian Cottages
t (01228) 599960
e enquiries@cumbrian-cottages.co.uk
w cumbrian-cottages.co.uk

20 and 21 The Falls ★★★
Self Catering
Lakelovers
t (015394) 88855
e bookings@lakelovers.co.uk
w lakelovers.co.uk

21 The Falls ★★★
Self Catering
Lakelovers
t (015394) 88855
e bookings@lakelovers.co.uk
w lakelovers.co.uk

5 Lowfield ★★★★
Self Catering
Cumbrian Cottages
t (01228) 599960
e enquiries@cumbrian-cottages.co.uk
w cumbrian-cottages.co.uk

7 Badgers Rake ★★★★
Self Catering
Cumbrian Cottages
t (01228) 599960
e enquiries@cumbrian-cottages.co.uk
w cumbrian-cottages.co.uk

9 Badgers Rake ★★★
Self Catering
Cumbrian Cottages
t (01228) 599960
e enquiries@cumbrian-cottages.co.uk
w cumbrian-cottages.co.uk

Amblers Rest ★★★★
Self Catering
Cumbrian Cottages
t (01228) 599960
e enquiries@cumbrian-cottages.co.uk
w cumbrian-cottages.co.uk

Angela's Cottage ★★★★
Self Catering
Contact: Jo Tomlinson
t (015394) 32383
e martin@waltonmount.plus.com

Appletree Cottage ★★★★
Self Catering
Cumbrian Cottages
t (01228) 599960
e enquiries@cumbrian-cottages.co.uk
w cumbrian-cottages.co.uk

Badger Cottage ★★★★
Self Catering
Cumbrian Cottages
t (01228) 599960
e enquiries@cumbrian-cottages.co.uk
w cumbrian-cottages.co.uk

Bakers Rest ★★★★
Self Catering
Lakes Cottage Holidays
t (01228) 591555
e info@lakescottageholiday.co.uk
w lakescottageholiday.co.uk

Beck and Hillside Cottages
★★★ *Self Catering*
Contact: Mrs Morris
t (0161) 790 8023
w amblesideselfcatering.co.uk

Birch Knoll ★★★★
Self Catering
Lakelovers
t (015394) 88855
e bookings@lakelovers.co.uk
w lakelovers.co.uk

Birchcroft ★★★★
Self Catering
Lakelovers
t (015394) 88855
e bookings@lakelovers.co.uk
w lakelovers.co.uk

Blelham Tarn at Neaum Crag
★★★★ *Self Catering*
Contact: Andy Witts
Pad-Lok Products Ltd
t 07740 486947
e enquiries@logcabin.bz
w logcabin.bz

Blue Hill Cottage ★★★
Self Catering
Cumbrian Cottages
t (01228) 599960
e enquiries@cumbrian-cottages.co.uk
w cumbrian-cottages.co.uk

Bluebell Cottage ★★★★
Self Catering
Lakelovers
t (015394) 88855
e bookings@lakelovers.co.uk
w lakelovers.co.uk

Bobbin Cottage ★★★
Self Catering
Lakelovers
t (015394) 88855
e bookings@lakelovers.co.uk
w lakelovers.co.uk

Bracken Howe ★★★★★
Self Catering
Cumbrian Cottages
t (01228) 599960
e enquiries@cumbrian-cottages.co.uk
w cumbrian-cottages.co.uk

Braebeck ★★★ *Self Catering*
Lakelovers
t (015394) 88855
e bookings@lakelovers.co.uk
w lakelovers.co.uk

Briar Nook ★★★★
Self Catering
Cumbrian Cottages
t (01228) 599960
e enquiries@cumbrian-cottages.co.uk
w cumbrian-cottages.co.uk

Brookfield ★★★★
Self Catering
Cumbrian Cottages
t (01228) 599960
e enquiries@cumbrian-cottages.co.uk
w cumbrian-cottages.co.uk

Buttermere ★★★
Self Catering
Lakelovers
t (015394) 88855
e bookings@lakelovers.co.uk
w lakelovers.co.uk

Buttonhole Cottage ★★★★
Self Catering
Lakelovers
t (015394) 88855
e bookings@lakelovers.co.uk
w lakelovers.co.uk

Cairn Cottage ★★★★
Self Catering
Cumbrian Cottages
t (01228) 599960
e enquiries@cumbrian-cottages.co.uk
w cumbrian-cottages.co.uk

Candleberry Cottage
★★★★ *Self Catering*
Lakelovers
t (015394) 88855
e bookings@lakelovers.co.uk
w lakelovers.co.uk

Castle Crag
Rating Applied For
Self Catering
Lakelovers
t (015394) 88855
e bookings@lakelovers.co.uk
w lakelovers.co.uk

Catsycam
Rating Applied For
Self Catering
Lakelovers
t (015394) 88855
e bookings@lakelovers.co.uk
w lakelovers.co.uk

Chanctonbury Cottage
★★★ *Self Catering*
Hideaways
t (015394) 42435
e bookings@lakeland-hideaways.co.uk
w lakeland-hideaways.co.uk

Chapel How
Rating Applied For
Self Catering
Lakelovers
t (015394) 88855
e bookings@lakelovers.co.uk
w lakelovers.co.uk

Church View ★★★★
Self Catering
Lakelovers
t (015394) 88855
e bookings@lakelovers.co.uk
w lakelovers.co.uk

Clare Cottage ★★★★
Self Catering
Cumbrian Cottages
t (01228) 599960
e enquiries@cumbrian-cottages.co.uk
w cumbrian-cottages.co.uk

Cloud Cottage ★★★★
Self Catering
Cumbrian Cottages
t (01228) 599960
e enquiries@cumbrian-cottages.co.uk
w cumbrian-cottages.co.uk

Coach House Cottage
Rating Applied For
Self Catering
Lakelovers
t (015394) 88855
e bookings@lakelovers.co.uk
w lakelovers.co.uk

Cobblestones ★★★★
Self Catering
Cumbrian Cottages
t (01228) 599960
e enquiries@cumbrian-cottages.co.uk
w cumbrian-cottages.co.uk

Cobblestones House ★★★
Self Catering
Cumbrian Cottages
t (01228) 599960
e enquiries@cumbrian-cottages.co.uk
w cumbrian-cottages.co.uk

Copper Tops ★★★★
Self Catering
Hideaways
t (015394) 42435
e bookings@lakeland-hideaways.co.uk
w lakeland-hideaways.co.uk

Cornerstones ★★★
Self Catering
Cumbrian Cottages
t (01228) 599960
e enquiries@cumbrian-cottages.co.uk
w cumbrian-cottages.co.uk

Crag View ★★★★
Self Catering
Contact: Mrs Davies
t (0151) 924 6995
e pfdavies@blueyonder.co.uk
w amblesidecottage.net

Cranford Cottage ★★★
Self Catering
Sykes Cottages
t (01244) 345700
e info@sykescottages.co.uk
w sykescottages.co.uk

Cuckoo's Nest ★★★★★
Self Catering
Lakelovers
t (015394) 88855
e bookings@lakelovers.co.uk
w lakelovers.co.uk

Derby Cottage ★★★
Self Catering
Cumbrian Cottages
t (01228) 599960
e enquiries@cumbrian-cottages.co.uk
w cumbrian-cottages.co.uk

Dower House Cottage ★★★
Self Catering
Contact: Mrs Margaret Rigg
The Dower House
t (015394) 33211

Dwarf Hall Studio ★★★
Self Catering
Cumbrian Cottages
t (01228) 599960
e enquiries@cumbrian-cottages.co.uk
w cumbrian-cottages.co.uk

Edelweiss ★★★★
Self Catering
Cumbrian Cottages
t (01228) 599960
e enquiries@cumbrian-cottages.co.uk
w cumbrian-cottages.co.uk

Eskdale ★★★★ *Self Catering*
Cumbrian Cottages
t (01228) 599960
e enquiries@cumbrian-cottages.co.uk
w cumbrian-cottages.co.uk

Fell View ★★★★
Self Catering
Cumbrian Cottages
t (01228) 599960
e enquiries@cumbrian-cottages.co.uk
w cumbrian-cottages.co.uk

Fell View
Rating Applied For
Self Catering
Lakelovers
t (015394) 88855
e bookings@lakelovers.co.uk
w lakelovers.co.uk

Fellmere ★★★★★
Self Catering
Cumbrian Cottages
t (01228) 599960
e enquiries@cumbrian-cottages.co.uk
w cumbrian-cottages.co.uk

Fellside ★★★ *Self Catering*
Lakelovers
t (015394) 88855
e bookings@lakelovers.co.uk
w lakelovers.co.uk

Gable End & Amblers Rest
★★★★ *Self Catering*
Cumbrian Cottages
t (01228) 599960
e enquiries@cumbrian-cottages.co.uk
w cumbrian-cottages.co.uk

Gale Lodge Cottage ★★★★
Self Catering
Lakelovers
t (015394) 88855
e bookings@lakelovers.co.uk
w lakelovers.co.uk

Gale Lodge Stables ★★★★
Self Catering
Lakelovers
t (015394) 88855
e bookings@lakelovers.co.uk
w lakelovers.co.uk

Galleries ★★★★
Self Catering
Cumbrian Cottages
t (01228) 599960
e enquiries@cumbrian-cottages.co.uk
w cumbrian-cottages.co.uk

The Garden Flat ★★★
Self Catering
Hideaways
t (015394) 42435
e bookings@lakeland-hideaways.co.uk
w lakedistrictholidays.net

The Gate ★★★★
Self Catering
Contact: Mike & Jan Humphreys
t (015394) 47903
e j4m7.ainke@virgin.net
w thegatetothelakes.co.uk

Ghyll Heights ★★★
Self Catering
Cumbrian Cottages
t (01228) 599960
e enquiries@cumbrian-cottages.co.uk
w cumbrian-cottages.co.uk

Ghyllside 3 ★★★
Self Catering
Cumbrian Cottages
t (01228) 599960
e enquiries@cumbrian-cottages.co.uk
w cumbrian-cottages.co.uk

Gilbertscar Foot ★★★★
Self Catering
Contact: Mr David Milne
t (015394) 32395

Le Gite ★★★ *Self Catering*
Cumbrian Cottages
t (01228) 599960
e enquiries@cumbrian-cottages.co.uk
w cumbrian-cottages.co.uk

Glenmore Cottage ★★★★
Self Catering
Cumbrian Cottages
t (01228) 599960
e enquiries@cumbrian-cottages.co.uk
w cumbrian-cottages.co.uk

Greengable ★★★★
Self Catering
Lakelovers
t (015394) 88855
e bookings@lakelovers.co.uk
w lakelovers.co.uk

Greenways ★★★
Self Catering
Lakelovers
t (015394) 88855
e bookings@lakelovers.co.uk
w lakelovers.co.uk

The Grove Cottages
★★★★-★★★★★
Self Catering
Contact: Peter Thompson
t (015394) 33074
e stay@grovecottages.com
w grovecottages.com

Halfway House ★★★★
Self Catering
Cumbrian Cottages
t (01228) 599960
e enquiries@cumbrian-cottages.co.uk
w cumbrian-cottages.co.uk

Hayrake ★★★ *Self Catering*
Cumbrian Cottages
t (01228) 599960
e enquiries@cumbrian-cottages.co.uk
w cumbrian-cottages.co.uk

Heather Cottage ★★★
Self Catering
Lakelovers
t (015394) 88855
e bookings@lakelovers.co.uk
w lakelovers.co.uk

Herald Cottage ★★★
Self Catering
Cumbrian Cottages
t (01228) 599960
e enquiries@cumbrian-cottages.co.uk
w cumbrian-cottages.co.uk

Heron Cottage
Rating Applied For
Self Catering
Lakelovers
t (015394) 88855
e bookings@lakelovers.co.uk
w lakelovers.co.uk

High View ★★★★
Self Catering
Contact: Tracy McNally
High View & Shepherds Fold
t (0161) 448 9568
e info@lakedistrictcottages.net
w lakedistrictcottages.net

High White Stones ★★★★
Self Catering
Cumbrian Cottages
t (01228) 599960
e enquiries@cumbrian-cottages.co.uk
w cumbrian-cottages.co.uk

Hillandale ★★★ *Self Catering*
Lakelovers
t (015394) 88855
e bookings@lakelovers.co.uk
w lakelovers.co.uk

Hillcrest Cottage ★★★★
Self Catering
Lakelovers
t (015394) 88855
e bookings@lakelovers.co.uk
w lakelovers.co.uk

Hole House ★★★
Self Catering
Contact: Clare Irvine
t (015394) 36106
e info@tock-how-farm.com
w tock-how-farm.com

The Hollies ★★★
Self Catering
Cumbrian Cottages
t (01228) 599960
e enquiries@cumbrian-cottages.co.uk
w cumbrian-cottages.co.uk

Hollybrook ★★★★
Self Catering
Cumbrian Cottages
t (01228) 599960
e enquiries@cumbrian-cottages.co.uk
w cumbrian-cottages.co.uk

Juniper Cottage ★★★
Self Catering
Lakelovers
t (015394) 88855
e bookings@lakelovers.co.uk
w lakelovers.co.uk

Kelsick Court ★★★
Self Catering
Cumbrian Cottages
t (01228) 599960
e enquiries@cumbrian-cottages.co.uk
w cumbrian-cottages.co.uk

Kelsick Heights ★★★★
Self Catering
Cumbrian Cottages
t (01228) 599960
e enquiries@cumbrian-cottages.co.uk
w cumbrian-cottages.co.uk

Kiln Cottage ★★★★
Self Catering
Lakelovers
t (015394) 88855
e bookings@lakelovers.co.uk
w lakelovers.co.uk

Kingfisher Cottage ★★★★
Self Catering
Lakelovers
t (015394) 88855
e bookings@lakelovers.co.uk
w lakelovers.co.uk

Kirkstone Foot Apartments
★★★★-★★★★★
Self Catering
Contact: Mrs J Tunnicliff
Kirkstone Foot Apartments Limited
t (015394) 32232
e enquiries@kirkstonefoot.co.uk
w kirkstonefoot.co.uk

The Knoll ★★★★
Self Catering
Cumbrian Cottages
t (01228) 599960
e enquiries@cumbrian-cottages.co.uk
w cumbrian-cottages.co.uk

Lakeland Cottage ★★★★
Self Catering
Lakelovers
t (015394) 88855
e bookings@lakelovers.co.uk
w lakelovers.co.uk

The Lakelands
★★★-★★★★★ *Self Catering*
Contact: Jackie Kingdom
t (015394) 33777
e lakeland@globalnet.co.uk
w the-lakelands.com

Langdale Estate Lodges
★★★★-★★★★★
Self Catering
Contact: Self Catering
The Langdale Estate
t (015394) 38012
e selfcatering@langdale.co.uk
w langdale.co.uk

Lingmell ★★★★
Self Catering
Lakelovers
t (015394) 88855
e bookings@lakelovers.co.uk
w lakelovers.co.uk

Little Robin Cottage ★★★
Self Catering
Cumbrian Cottages
t (01228) 599960
e enquiries@cumbrian-cottages.co.uk
w cumbrian-cottages.co.uk

Long Mynd ★★★
Self Catering
Cumbrian Cottages
t (01228) 599960
e enquiries@cumbrian-cottages.co.uk
w cumbrian-cottages.co.uk

Longmeadow ★★★★
Self Catering
Cumbrian Cottages
t (01228) 599960
e enquiries@cumbrian-cottages.co.uk
w cumbrian-cottages.co.uk

Loughrigg ★★★★
Self Catering
Lakelovers
t (015394) 88855
e bookings@lakelovers.co.uk
w lakelovers.co.uk

Loughrigg Brow
Rating Applied For
Self Catering
Lakelovers
t (015394) 88855
e bookings@lakelovers.co.uk
w lakelovers.co.uk

Loughrigg View ★★★★
Self Catering
Cumbrian Cottages
t (01228) 599960
e enquiries@cumbrian-cottages.co.uk
w cumbrian-cottages.co.uk

Low Fold
Rating Applied For
Self Catering
Lakelovers
t (015394) 88855
e bookings@lakelovers.co.uk
w lakelovers.co.uk

Low White Stones ★★★★
Self Catering
Cumbrian Cottages
t (01228) 599960
e enquiries@cumbrian-cottages.co.uk
w cumbrian-cottages.co.uk

Lower Wansfell ★★★
Self Catering
Lakelovers
t (015394) 88855
e bookings@lakelovers.co.uk
w lakelovers.co.uk

May Cottage
Rating Applied For
Self Catering
Lakelovers
t (015394) 88855
e bookings@lakelovers.co.uk
w lakelovers.co.uk

Mickle Moss ★★★
Self Catering
Cumbrian Cottages
t (01228) 599960
e enquiries@cumbrian-cottages.co.uk
w cumbrian-cottages.co.uk

Milestones ★★★
Self Catering
Lakelovers
t (015394) 88855
e bookings@lakelovers.co.uk
w lakelovers.co.uk

Mill Brow Farm Cottage
★★★★ *Self Catering*
Contact: Pat Long
t (015394) 33253

Nook End Annexe ★★★
Self Catering
Lakeland Cottage Comapny
t (015395) 38180
e john@lakelandcottageco.com
w lakelandcottageco.com

Nook End Farm ★★★★
Self Catering
Lakeland Cottage Comapny
t (015395) 38180
e john@lakelandcottageco.com
w lakelandcottageco.com

Nook End Garden Room
★★★ *Self Catering*
Lakeland Cottage Comapny
t (015395) 38180
e john@lakelandcottageco.com
w lakelandcottageco.com

Nook End Studio ★★★
Self Catering
Lakeland Cottage Comapny
t (015395) 38180
e john@lakelandcottageco.com
w lakelandcottageco.com

North Syke ★★★
Self Catering
Contact: Christine Fagg
North Syke Holiday Home
t 07870 576466
e chris@northsyke.co.uk
w northsyke.co.uk

Oak Cottage ★★★
Self Catering
Cumbrian Cottages
t (01228) 599960
e enquiries@cumbrian-cottages.co.uk
w cumbrian-cottages.co.uk

Oaklands ★★★ *Self Catering*
Cumbrian Cottages
t (01228) 599960
e enquiries@cumbrian-cottages.co.uk
w cumbrian-cottages.co.uk

Old Coach House ★★★
Self Catering
Cumbrian Cottages
t (01228) 599960
e enquiries@cumbrian-cottages.co.uk
w cumbrian-cottages.co.uk

Old Coachman's Cottage
★★★★ *Self Catering*
Lakelovers
t (015394) 88855
e bookings@lakelovers.co.uk
w lakelovers.co.uk

Old Oak Cottage ★★★★
Self Catering
Lakelovers
t (015394) 88855
e bookings@lakelovers.co.uk
w lakelovers.co.uk

Otters Holt Cottage ★★★★
Self Catering
Cumbrian Cottages
t (01228) 599960
e enquiries@cumbrian-cottages.co.uk
w cumbrian-cottages.co.uk

Pudding Cottage ★★★★★
Self Catering
Lakelovers
t (015394) 88855
e bookings@lakelovers.co.uk
w lakelovers.co.uk

Quaysiders Club ★★★
Serviced Apartments
t (015394) 33969
e ian@quaysiders.co.uk
w quaysiders.co.uk

Raaesbeck ★★★
Self Catering
Lakelovers
t (015394) 88855
e bookings@lakelovers.co.uk
w lakelovers.co.uk

Rattle Gill ★★★ *Self Catering*
Lakelovers
t (015394) 88855
e bookings@lakelovers.co.uk
w lakelovers.co.uk

Red Screes Cottage ★★★★
Self Catering
Lakelovers
t (015394) 88855
e bookings@lakelovers.co.uk
w lakelovers.co.uk

River Falls View ★★★★
Self Catering
Lakelovers
t (015394) 88855
e bookings@lakelovers.co.uk
w lakelovers.co.uk

Riverside Cottage 1 ★★★★
Self Catering
Lakelovers
t (015394) 88855
e bookings@lakelovers.co.uk
w lakelovers.co.uk

Riverside Cottage 3 ★★★★
Self Catering
Lakelovers
t (015394) 88855
e bookings@lakelovers.co.uk
w lakelovers.co.uk

Riverside Cottages ★★★★
Self Catering
Lakelovers
t (015394) 88855
e bookings@lakelovers.co.uk
w lakelovers.co.uk

Riverside Lodge ★★★★
Self Catering
Lakelovers
t (015394) 88855
e bookings@lakelovers.co.uk
w lakelovers.co.uk

Riverside Retreat ★★★★
Self Catering
Lakelovers
t (015394) 88855
e bookings@lakelovers.co.uk
w lakelovers.co.uk

Rock Shop Flat ★★★★
Self Catering
Contact: Louise Burhouse
Burhouse Lettings
t (01484) 485104
e flat@rock-shop.co.uk
w rock-shop.co.uk/flat

The Roost ★★★ *Self Catering*
Cumbrian Cottages
t (01228) 599960
e enquiries@cumbrian-cottages.co.uk
w cumbrian-cottages.co.uk

Roselea ★★★ *Self Catering*
Cumbrian Cottages
t (01228) 599960
e enquiries@cumbrian-cottages.co.uk
w cumbrian-cottages.co.uk

Rydal Holiday Lettings
★★★★ *Self Catering*
Contact: Amanda Rowley
t (015394) 31043
e info@steppingstonesambleside.co.uk
w steppingstonesambleside.co.uk

Rydal View Cottage
Rating Applied For
Self Catering
Cumbrian Cottages
t (01228) 599960
e enquiries@cumbrian-cottages.co.uk
w cumbrian-cottages.co.uk

Scafell ★★★★ *Self Catering*
Lakelovers
t (015394) 88855
e bookings@lakelovers.co.uk
w lakelovers.co.uk

Scandale Bridge Cottage
★★★ *Self Catering*
Lake District Inns and Cottages
t 05006 00725
e stay@lakedistrictinns.co.uk
w lakedistrictinns.co.uk

Shepherd's Fold ★★★★
Self Catering
t (0161) 448 9568

The Spinney ★★★★
Self Catering
Lakelovers
t (015394) 88855
e bookings@lakelovers.co.uk
w lakelovers.co.uk

Spring Cottage ★★★★
Self Catering
Lakelovers
t (015394) 88855
e bookings@lakelovers.co.uk
w lakelovers.co.uk

Sunset Cottage ★★★★
Self Catering
Lakelovers
t (015394) 88855
e bookings@lakelovers.co.uk
w lakelovers.co.uk

Swiss Cottage ★★★★
Self Catering
Cumbrian Cottages
t (01228) 599960
e enquiries@cumbrian-cottages.co.uk
w cumbrian-cottages.co.uk

Sycamore House ★★★
Self Catering
Cumbrian Cottages
t (01228) 599960
e enquiries@cumbrian-cottages.co.uk
w cumbrian-cottages.co.uk

Tethera ★★★ *Self Catering*
Cumbrian Cottages
t (01228) 599960
e enquiries@cumbrian-cottages.co.uk
w cumbrian-cottages.co.uk

Three Fells ★★★
Self Catering
Cumbrian Cottages
t (01228) 599960
e enquiries@cumbrian-cottages.co.uk
w cumbrian-cottages.co.uk

Top o' The Stairs ★★★
Self Catering
Cumbrian Cottages
t (01228) 599960
e enquiries@cumbrian-cottages.co.uk
w cumbrian-cottages.co.uk

Tottlebank ★★★
Self Catering
Cumbrian Cottages
t (01228) 599960
e enquiries@cumbrian-cottages.co.uk
w cumbrian-cottages.co.uk

Valentine Cottage ★★★★★
Self Catering
Lakelovers
t (015394) 88855
e bookings@lakelovers.co.uk
w lakelovers.co.uk

Violet Cottage ★★★★
Self Catering
Cumbrian Cottages
t (01228) 599960
e enquiries@cumbrian-cottages.co.uk
w cumbrian-cottages.co.uk

Walkers Cottage ★★★
Self Catering
Cumbrian Cottages
t (01228) 599960
e enquiries@cumbrian-cottages.co.uk
w cumbrian-cottages.co.uk

Wansfell ★★★★★
Self Catering
Lakeland Cottage Comapny
t (015395) 38180
e john@lakelandcottageco.com
w lakelandcottageco.com

Wansfell Heights ★★★★
Self Catering
Cumbrian Cottages
t (01228) 599960
e enquiries@cumbrian-cottages.co.uk
w cumbrian-cottages.co.uk

Wayside Cottage, Clappersgate ★★★★
Self Catering
Contact: Dennis Leech
t (024) 7667 7549 & 07712 353201
e waysidecottage@lineone.net
w waysidecottage.co.uk

Wetherlam ★★★★
Self Catering
Lakelovers
t (015394) 88855
e bookings@lakelovers.co.uk
w lakelovers.co.uk

Willow Hill ★★★★
Self Catering
Lakelovers
t (015394) 88855
e bookings@lakelovers.co.uk
w lakelovers.co.uk

Windemere ★★★
Self Catering
Hideaways
t (015394) 42435
e bookings@lakeland-hideaways.co.uk
w lakeland-hideaways.co.uk

Woodside Cottage
★★★★★ *Self Catering*
Contact: Gillian Lane
t (015394) 33215
e email@fisherbeckhotel.co.uk
w woodsidecottage-ambleside.co.uk

Woolly End ★★★★
Self Catering
Lakelovers
t (015394) 88855
e bookings@lakelovers.co.uk
w lakelovers.co.uk

AMPLEFORTH
North Yorkshire

Brackensyke Cottage
★★★★ *Self Catering*
Contact: Peter Davis
t (01904) 690465
e eazystreetpd@yahoo.co.uk
w brackensyke-ampleforth.com

The Cottage ★★★★
Self Catering
Contact: Mrs Plunkett
t (01482) 659108
e bidnbod@bidnbod.karoo.co.uk

Hillside Cottage ★★★
Self Catering
Contact: Sue Shepherd
t (01439) 788993
e sueeshepherd@btinternet.com
w cottageguide.co.uk/hillsidecottage

ANTHORN
Cumbria

Sonya's Cottage ★★★★
Self Catering
Cumbrian Cottages
t (01228) 599960
e enquiries@cumbrian-cottages.co.uk
w cumbrian-cottages.co.uk

APPERSETT
North Yorkshire

The Coach House ★★★
Self Catering
Contact: Walter Head
t (01969) 667375
e walter.head@btinternet.com

Dales Cottage ★★★
Self Catering
Contact: Deborah Allenby
t (01969) 663533
e dalescottage@yahoo.co.uk
w dales-cottage.com

APPLEBY-IN-WESTMORLAND
Cumbria

Ivy Cottage ★★★
Self Catering
t (017683) 61233

The Little House ★★★★
Self Catering
Contact: Mr & Mrs Hiscox
t (01673) 860047
e rogerhiscox@beeb.net
w thelittlehouseappleby.com

Milburn Grange Holiday Cottages, Knock ★★★
Self Catering
Contact: Russell & Debbie Clark
t (017683) 61867
e holidays@milburngrange.co.uk
w milburngrange.co.uk

The Oak Cottage ★★★
Self Catering
Cumbrian Cottages
t (01228) 599960
e enquiries@cumbrian-cottages.co.uk
w cumbrian-cottages.co.uk

The Old Smithy ★★★★
Self Catering
Contact: Kay E Smith
t (017683) 61333
e smithies.com@talk21.com

Owl Cottage ★★★
Self Catering
Dales Holiday Cottages
t (01989) 740280

The Stableblock Bungalow
Rating Applied For
Self Catering
Contact: Mrs Jo Collins
t (0151) 339 8101
e timandjo@lineone.net

Wray Cottage ★★★
Self Catering
Contact: Mrs Cowey
t (017683) 52485

APPLETHWAITE
Cumbria

Applethwaite Country House ★★★★ *Self Catering*
Contact: Tom & Gail Ryan
t (017687) 72413
e ryan@applethwaite.com
w applethwaite.com

The Manesty ★★★
Self Catering
Cumbrian Cottages
t (01228) 599960
e enquiries@cumbrian-cottages.co.uk
w cumbrian-cottages.co.uk

Merlestead ★★★★
Self Catering
Cumbrian Cottages
t (01228) 599960
e enquiries@cumbrian-cottages.co.uk
w cumbrian-cottages.co.uk

Somervell ★★★★
Self Catering
Cumbrian Cottages
t (01228) 599960
e enquiries@cumbrian-cottages.co.uk
w cumbrian-cottages.co.uk

Whiteside ★★★★
Self Catering
Lakeland Cottage Holidays
t (017687) 76065
e info@lakelandcottages.co.uk
w lakelandcottages.co.uk

APPLETON-LE-MOORS
North Yorkshire

Darley Cottage ★★★★
Self Catering
Contact: James Brooke
t (01751) 417514
e jbrooke@pottery1.fsnet.co.uk

Hamley Hagg Cottage ★★★
Self Catering
Contact: June Feaster
t (01751) 417413
e mbfiveries@appletonlemoors.fsnet.co.uk
w appletonlemoors.fsnet.co.uk

APPLETREEWICK
North Yorkshire

Fell View ★★★ *Self Catering*
Sykes Cottages
t (01244) 345700
e info@sykescottages.co.uk
w sykescottages.co.uk

ARKENGARTHDALE
North Yorkshire

Low Lock Slack Cottage
★★★ *Self Catering*
Sykes Cottages
t (01244) 345700
e info@sykescottages.co.uk
w sykescottages.co.uk

ARKHOLME
Lancashire

Lakeside Lodge 1 ★★★
Self Catering
Cumbrian Cottages
t (01228) 599960
e enquiries@cumbrian-cottages.co.uk
w cumbrian-cottages.co.uk

Lakeside Lodge 6 ★★★
Self Catering
Cumbrian Cottages
t (01228) 599960
e enquiries@cumbrian-cottages.co.uk
w cumbrian-cottages.co.uk

ARMATHWAITE
Cumbria

Castlerigg Farm Cottage
★★★ *Self Catering*
Cumbrian Cottages
t (01228) 599960
e enquiries@cumbrian-cottages.co.uk
w cumbrian-cottages.co.uk

Coombs Cottage ★★★★
Self Catering
Lakes Cottage Holidays
t (01228) 591555
e info@lakescottageholiday.co.uk
w lakescottageholiday.co.uk

Longdales Cottage ★★★
Self Catering
Cumbrian Cottages
t (01228) 599960
e enquiries@cumbrian-cottages.co.uk
w cumbrian-cottages.co.uk

ARNSIDE
Cumbria

Bay View House ★★★
Self Catering
Contact: John Jackson
t (01524) 762131

ARRATHORNE
North Yorkshire

Elmfield Cottages ★★★★
Self Catering
Contact: Mr & Mrs Lillie
t (01677) 450052
e elmfieldcottages@hotmail.com
w elmfieldcottages.co.uk

ASHTON
Cheshire

Inglenook Cottage ★★★★
Self Catering
Contact: Mrs Jenny Rowland
t (01829) 752109
e chris.n.rowland@btopenworld.com
w inglenookcottages.com

ASKHAM
Cumbria

Knipe Hall ★★★★★
Self Catering
Cumbrian Cottages
t (01228) 599960
e enquiries@cumbrian-cottages.co.uk
w cumbrian-cottages.co.uk

Park View Cottage ★★★★
Self Catering
Contact: Lyn Page
Lowther Estate Cottages
t (01931) 712577
e lyn.page@lowther.co.uk
w lowther.co.uk

Scarr View ★★★
Self Catering
Cumbrian Cottages
t (01228) 599960
e enquiries@cumbrian-cottages.co.uk
w cumbrian-cottages.co.uk

Sycamore Barn Holiday Cottage ★★★★ *Self Catering*
Contact: Ellen Pickup
t (01931) 712410
e sycamorehousebarn@btinternet.com
w sycamorehousebarn.com

ASKRIGG
North Yorkshire

Askrigg Cottages ★★★★
Self Catering
Contact: Kate Empsall
t (01969) 650565
e info@askrigg-cottages.co.uk
w askrigg-cottages.co.uk

Bear Cottage ★★★★
Self Catering
Country Hideaways
t (01969) 663559
e info@countryhideaways.co.uk
w countryhideaways.co.uk

Burn Cottage ★★★★
Self Catering
Askrigg Cottage Holidays
t (01969) 650022
e stay@askrigg.com
w askrigg.com

Cowlingholme Cottage
★★★★ *Self Catering*
Country Hideaways
t (01969) 663559
e info@countryhideaways.co.uk
w countryhideaways.co.uk

Faith Hill Cottage ★★★
Self Catering
Contact: Jennifer Kirkbride
t (01969) 650325
e allenkirkbride@hotmail.com

Lavender Cottage ★★★★
Self Catering
Contact: Sarah Deakin
t (01977) 795554
e askriggcottages@netscape.net
w askrigg.org

Lukes Barn ★★★
Self Catering
Dales Holiday Cottages
t (01756) 790919
e info@dales-holiday-cottages.com
w dales-holiday-cottages.com

Old Mill 1
Rating Applied For
Self Catering
Contact: Mrs Catherine Wernham
w askrigg-cottages.co.uk

Rook Cottage ★★★★
Self Catering
Askrigg Cottage Holidays
t (01969) 650022
e stay@askrigg.com
w askrigg.com

Rooks Cottage ★★★★
Self Catering
Askrigg Cottage Holidays
t (01969) 650022
e stay@askrigg.com
w askrigg.com

School House ★★★
Self Catering
Country Hideaways
t (01969) 663559
e info@countryhideaways.co.uk
w countryhideaways.co.uk

The Shippon ★★★★
Self Catering
Country Hideaways
t (01969) 663559
e info@countryhideaways.co.uk
w countryhideaways.co.uk

Stony Raise ★★★★
Self Catering
Yorkshire Cottages
t (01228) 406701
e enquiries@yorkshire-cottages.info
w yorkshire-cottages.info

Urlay Nook ★★★★★
Self Catering
Askrigg Cottage Holidays
t (01969) 650022
e stay@askrigg.com
w askrigg.com

ASPATRIA
Cumbria

Big White House ★★★
Self Catering
Contact: Philip Carr
Stay Lakeland
t 0845 468 0936
e info@staylakeland.co.uk
w bigwhitehouse.co.uk

Inglecroft ★★★ *Self Catering*
Cumbrian Cottages
t (01228) 599960
e enquiries@cumbrian-cottages.co.uk
w cumbrian-cottages.co.uk

Little Byre ★★★★
Self Catering
Contact: Catherine Knights
t (0191) 274 6322
e the.knights@tiscali.co.uk
w littlebyre.com

Wicket Thorn ★★★
Self Catering
Cumbrian Cottages
t (01228) 599960
e enquiries@cumbrian-cottages.co.uk
w cumbrian-cottages.co.uk

AUSTWICK
North Yorkshire

Eldroth House ★★★★
Self Catering
Holiday Cottages Yorkshire Ltd
t (01756) 700510
e brochure@holidaycotts.co.uk
w holidaycotts.co.uk

Spoutscroft Cottage
★★★★★ *Self Catering*
Contact: Christine Hartland
t (01524) 251052
e chrishartland@austwick.org
w spoutscroftcottage.co.uk

Stockdale House ★★★
Self Catering
Contact: Mrs R Hyslop
t (01729) 840234
w layhead.co.uk

BACKBARROW
Cumbria

Ben's Row Cottage ★★★
Self Catering
Cumbrian Cottages
t (01228) 599960
e enquiries@cumbrian-cottages.co.uk
w cumbrian-cottages.co.uk

High View ★★★
Self Catering
Cumbrian Cottages
t (01228) 599960
e enquiries@cumbrian-cottages.co.uk
w cumbrian-cottages.co.uk

High View Cottage
Rating Applied For
Self Catering
Cumbrian Cottages
t (01228) 599960
e enquiries@cumbrian-cottages.co.uk
w cumbrian-cottages.co.uk

Lynwood Cottage ★★★★
Self Catering
Cumbrian Cottages
t (01228) 599960
e enquiries@cumbrian-cottages.co.uk
w cumbrian-cottages.co.uk

The Old Post Office ★★★★
Self Catering
Cumbrian Cottages
t (01228) 599960
e enquiries@cumbrian-cottages.co.uk
w cumbrian-cottages.co.uk

Woodside Cottage ★★★★
Self Catering
Contact: Karen Prince
t 07758 106246
e karen@prince.ukfreedom.com
w woodside-cottage.net

BACUP
Lancashire

Oakenclough Farm ★★★
Self Catering
t (01756) 700510
e info@holidaycotts.co.uk
w oakencloughfarm.co.uk

Parrock Lumb Cottages
★★★ *Self Catering*
Contact: Mrs Moira Mitchell
t (01706) 873598
w parrocklumbcottages.co.uk

BAILEY
Cumbria

Saughs Farm Cottages
★★★-★★★★ *Self Catering*
Contact: Kevin & Jane Gray
t (01697) 748346
e kevin.graykm@btopenworld.com

BAINBRIDGE
North Yorkshire

Sykes Cottage ★★★★
Self Catering
Yorkshire Cottages
t (01228) 406701
e enquiries@yorkshire-cottages.info
w yorkshire-cottages.info

BALDERSDALE
Durham

Bluebell Barn ★★★★★
Self Catering
Contact: Mrs Moore
t (01833) 650822

Clove Lodge Cottage
★★★★ *Self Catering*
Contact: Mrs Caroline Carter
t (01833) 650030
e carolinecarter69@aol.com
w clovelodge.co.uk

Hury Lodge ★★★★
Self Catering
Contact: Mrs Alison Butler
t (01833) 650494
e info@hurylodge.co.uk
w hurylodge.co.uk

BAMBURGH
Northumberland

Adderstone Hall Country Cottages
Rating Applied For
Self Catering
Grace Darling Holidays
t (01665) 721332
e carolynalgar150@msn.com

The Blacksmiths ★★
Self Catering
Contact: Mrs Rachel Cole
t (01636) 830864
e rachelstevecole@btinternet.com

Bridge End ★★★★
Self Catering
Contact: Mr & Mrs Roger & Linda Topping
t (01670) 512115

The Bungalow ★★★★
Self Catering
Contact: Miss Eve Humphreys
t (01668) 214213
e evehumphreys@aol.com
w burtonhall.co.uk

Castle View Bungalow
★★★★ *Self Catering*
Contact: Mr & Mrs Nicol
t (01665) 720320
e ian@slatehall.freeserve.co.uk
w slatehallridingcentre.com

Coral Cottage ★★★★
Self Catering
Contact: Ms Monica Cornall
t (01665) 576890
e cornall@btinternet.com

The Cottage ★★★★
Self Catering
Contact: Mrs Turnbull
t (01668) 214494
e theturnbulls2k@btinternet.com
w holidaynorthumbria.co.uk

Dukesfield Farm Holiday Cottages
Rating Applied For
Self Catering
Grace Darling Holidays
t (01665) 721332
e carolynalgar150@msn.com

The Fairway ★★
Self Catering
Contact: Mrs Diana Middleton
t (01661) 852125
e rsmiddleton@talk21.com

Glebe House and Glebe Cottage ★★★★★
Self Catering
Contact: Mrs Maria Eliana Robinson
EMR Properties
t (01668) 214456
e stay@bamburghglebe.co.uk
w bamburghglebe.co.uk

The Granary ★★★
Self Catering
Contact: Mrs Patricia Cowen
t (01228) 560245
e cowen_home@hotmail.com
w thegranarybamburgh.co.uk

The Grove
Rating Applied For
Self Catering
Grace Darling Holidays
t (01665) 721332
e carolynalgar150@msn.com

Harelaw House ★★★★
Self Catering
Contact: Ms Zana Juppenlatz
t (01668) 215494
e zana.juppenlatz@ukonline.co.uk
w harelawhouse.ntb.org.uk

Hoppen Hall Farm Cottages
★★★★ *Self Catering*
Northumberland Estates Holiday Cottages
t (01668) 219941
e jane@nehc.co.uk
w alnwickcastlecottages.co.uk

Inglenook Cottage ★★★
Self Catering
Contact: Mrs Amanda J Moore
t (01423) 772211
e inglenookcottage@aol.com
w inglenookcottage.info

Kent Cottage and Nan Tucket ★★★★ *Self Catering*
Grace Darling Holidays
t (01665) 721332
e carolynalgar150@msn.com

Letterbox Cottage ★★★
Self Catering
Northumberland Cottages
t (01665) 589434
e enquiries@northumberlandcottages.com
w northumberlandcottages.co.uk

Millhouse Cottage ★★★★
Self Catering
Contact: Mrs Sarah Nelson
t (01665) 578361
e stay@millhouse-cottage.co.uk
w millhouse-cottage.co.uk

Outchester & Ross Farm Cottages ★★★★
Self Catering
Contact: Mrs Shirley McKie
t (01668) 213336
e enquiry@rosscottages.co.uk
w rosscottages.co.uk

Pintail
Rating Applied For
Self Catering
Contact: Mr & Mrs Graham & Jacqueline Duff
t (01669) 620661
e lynnholm@tiscali.co.uk

Point Cottages ★★★
Self Catering
Contact: Mrs Sanderson
t (0191) 266 2800
e info@bamburgh-cottages.co.uk
w bamburgh-cottages.co.uk

Seal Waters ★★★
Self Catering
Contact: Mr Peter Carr-Seaman
t (01434) 632839
e peter@carr-seaman.com
w sealwaters.com

Smugglers Court ★★★★
Self Catering
Contact: Mr Gordon Begg
t (01289) 302416
e gordonbegg@hotmail.co.uk
w budle-bay.com

Springhill Farm Holiday Accommodation, Seahouses
★★★★-★★★★★
Self Catering
Contact: Mrs Julie & Miss Sarah Gregory
t (01665) 721820
e enquiries@springhill-farm.co.uk
w springhill-farm.co.uk

Waren Lea Hall
★★★★-★★★★★
Self Catering
Contact: Carolynn Croisdale-Appleby
t (01494) 725194 & 07901 716136
e croisdaleappleby@aol.com
w selfcateringluxury.co.uk

Whinstone Cottage ★★★
Self Catering
Contact: Mrs Philippa Tait
t (0191) 285 1363

BAMPTON
Cumbria

Goosemire Cottage and Tethera ★★★★ *Self Catering*
Hideaways
t (015394) 42435
e bookings@lakeland-hideaways.co.uk
w lakedistrictholidays.net

Hollin View ★★★★
Self Catering
Contact: Caroline Entwisle
t (01253) 811867
e caroline@entwisle.co.uk
w hollinview.co.uk

Howes Beck Cottage ★★★
Self Catering
Cumbrian Cottages
t (01228) 599960
e enquiries@cumbrian-cottages.co.uk
w cumbrian-cottages.co.uk

Mews Cottage ★★★★
Self Catering
Cumbrian Cottages
t (01228) 599960
e enquiries@cumbrian-cottages.co.uk
w cumbrian-cottages.co.uk

Wheat Close ★★★★
Self Catering
Cumbrian Cottages
t (01228) 599960
e enquiries@cumbrian-cottages.co.uk
w cumbrian-cottages.co.uk

BARDEN
North Yorkshire

Hillcrest ★★★★
Self Catering
Yorkshire Cottages
t (01228) 406701
e enquiries@yorkshire-cottages.info
w yorkshire-cottages.info

BARDON MILL
Northumberland

Brownside ★★★★★
Self Catering
Contact: Mrs Ann Oliver
t (01434) 343000
e relax@brownside.co.uk

The Hott ★★★ *Self Catering*
t (01697) 741600

Keepers Cottage ★★★★★
Self Catering
Contact: Ms Jane Barnes
t (01434) 344021
e jane.barnes@bonnyrigghall.co.uk
w bonnyrigghall.co.uk

BARMBY MOOR
East Riding of Yorkshire

Northwood Coach House
★★★★ *Self Catering*
Contact: Ann Gregory
t (01759) 302305
e annjgregory@hotmail.com
w northwoodcoachhouse.co.uk

BARNARD CASTLE
Durham

5A Market Place ★★★
Self Catering
Contact: Mrs Joan Armstrong
t (01833) 690726
e joan.marketplace@gmail.com
w stay-in-teesdale.com

Boot and Shoe Cottage, Wycliffe ★★★★
Self Catering
Contact: Mrs Rachel Peat
t (01833) 627200
e info@bootandshoecottage.co.uk
w bootandshoecottage.co.uk

Cheeseborough House
★★★★ *Self Catering*
Contact: Mr & Mrs Ian & Eva Reid
t (01833) 631304
e enquiries@number34.com
w cheeseboroughs.co.uk

Dove Cottage ★★
Self Catering
Yorkshire Cottages
t (01228) 406701
e enquiries@yorkshire-cottages.info
w yorkshire-cottages.info

East Briscoe Farm Cottages
★★★★ *Self Catering*
Contact: Mr Chris Tarpey
t (01833) 650087
e one@eastbriscoe.co.uk
w eastbriscoe.co.uk

Hauxwell Grange Cottages (The Stone Byre and Curlew Cottage) ★★★★
Self Catering
Contact: Mrs Val Pearson
t (01833) 695022
e hauxwellvmp@supaworld.com
w hauxwellgrangecottages.co.uk

Riverdale Cottage ★★★★
Self Catering
Contact: Mrs Allyson Bunn
t (0191) 511 0555 & 07966 158127
e info@riverdale-cottage.co.uk
w riverdale-cottage.co.uk

Thorngate Coach House
★★★★ *Self Catering*
Contact: Mrs Clare Terry
t (01833) 637791
e info@thorngatecoachhouse.co.uk
w thorngatecoachhouse.co.uk

Wackford Squeers Cottage
★★★ *Self Catering*
Contact: Mr John Braithwaite
t (01833) 650032
e wodencraft@freenet.co.uk

Waterside (4157) ★★★★
Self Catering
Contact: Mrs Catherine Couling
t (01756) 799821
e catherine@dales-holiday-cottages.com
w dales-holiday-cottages.com

Woodland House Cottage
★★★ *Self Catering*
Contact: Mr Cliff Harding
t (01388) 710836
e cottage@woodland-house.freeserve.co.uk
w cottageguide.co.uk/woodlandhouse

BARNOLDSWICK
Lancashire

Hill Top Barn ★★★★★
Self Catering
Contact: Mrs Sharples
t (01282) 812460
e info@hilltopbarn.com
w hilltopbarn.com

BARROWFORD
Lancashire

Alondra ★★★★ *Self Catering*
t (01282) 601604

BARROWS GREEN
Cumbria

High Meadows ★★★★★
Self Catering
Cumbrian Cottages
t (01228) 599960
e enquiries@cumbrian-cottages.co.uk
w cumbrian-cottages.co.uk

BASHALL EAVES
Lancashire

Clough Bottom Farm Cottages ★★★★
Self Catering
Contact: Mrs Joanne McTiffin
t (01254) 826285
e info@cloughbottom.co.uk
w cloughbottom.co.uk

BASSENTHWAITE
Cumbria

6 Low Kiln Court ★★★
Self Catering
Cumbrian Cottages
t (01228) 599960
e enquiries@cumbrian-cottages.co.uk
w cumbrian-cottages.co.uk

Brook Cottage ★★★★
Self Catering
Cumbrian Cottages
t (01228) 599960
e enquiries@cumbrian-cottages.co.uk
w cumbrian-cottages.co.uk

Brookfield ★★★★
Self Catering
Cumbrian Cottages
t (01228) 599960
e enquiries@cumbrian-cottages.co.uk
w cumbrian-cottages.co.uk

Garries Cottage ★★★
Self Catering
Cumbrian Cottages
t (01228) 599960
e enquiries@cumbrian-cottages.co.uk
w cumbrian-cottages.co.uk

The Granary ★★★
Self Catering
Contact: Margaret Crooks
t (01697) 371524
e tmc.roadfarm@btinternet.com

Irton House Farm ★★★★
Self Catering
Contact: Mrs Almond
t (017687) 76380
e joan@irtonhousefarm.co.uk
w irtonhousefarm.com

Melbecks Holidays Homes: Skiddaw, Dodd, Dash, Randel ★★★-★★★★
Self Catering
Lakeland Cottage Holidays
t (017687) 76065
e info@lakelandcottages.co.uk
w lakelandcottages.co.uk

Mill Cottage ★★★
Self Catering
Cumbrian Cottages
t (01228) 599960
e enquiries@cumbrian-cottages.co.uk
w cumbrian-cottages.co.uk

Osprey Cottage ★★★
Self Catering
Cumbrian Cottages
t (01228) 599960
e enquiries@cumbrian-cottages.co.uk
w cumbrian-cottages.co.uk

Parkergate ★★★★
Self Catering
Contact: Ian & Jane Phillips
t (017687) 76376
e info@parkergate.co.uk
w parkergate.co.uk

Peter House Farm Cottages
★★★★ *Self Catering*
Contact: Valerie Trafford
t (017687) 76278
e info@peterhousefarm.co.uk
w peterhousefarm.co.uk

Primrose Cottage ★★★★
Self Catering
Cumbrian Cottages
t (01228) 599960
e enquiries@cumbrian-cottages.co.uk
w cumbrian-cottages.co.uk

Riggs Cottage ★★★★
Self Catering
Cumbrian Cottages
t (01228) 599960
e enquiries@cumbrian-cottages.co.uk
w cumbrian-cottages.co.uk

Robin Hood Cottage ★★★★
Self Catering
Cumbrian Cottages
t (01228) 599960
e enquiries@cumbrian-cottages.co.uk
w cumbrian-cottages.co.uk

The Ruddings ★★★
Self Catering
Cumbrian Cottages
t (01228) 599960
e enquiries@cumbrian-cottages.co.uk
w cumbrian-cottages.co.uk

South View ★★★
Self Catering
Cumbrian Cottages
t (01228) 599960
e enquiries@cumbrian-cottages.co.uk
w cumbrian-cottages.co.uk

Uldale ★★★★ *Self Catering*
Lakeland Cottage Holidays
t (017687) 76065
e info@lakelandcottages.co.uk
w lakelandcottages.co.uk

Walnut Cottage ★★★★
Self Catering
Lakeland Cottage Holidays
t (017687) 76065
e info@lakelandcottages.co.uk
w lakelandcottages.co.uk

BAYCLIFF Cumbria

Conishead House 10 ★★★★
Self Catering
Cumbrian Cottages
t (01228) 599960
e enquiries@cumbrian-cottages.co.uk
w cumbrian-cottages.co.uk

Conishead House 11 ★★★★
Self Catering
Cumbrian Cottages
t (01228) 599960
e enquiries@cumbrian-cottages.co.uk
w cumbrian-cottages.co.uk

Maskel Beach ★★
Self Catering
Cumbrian Cottages
t (01228) 599960
e enquiries@cumbrian-cottages.co.uk
w cumbrian-cottages.co.uk

BAYSDALE North Yorkshire

Baysdale Abbey ★★★★
Self Catering
Contact: Sharon Redworth
Burwarton Estates Company Limited
t (01746) 787207
e redworth@burwarton-estates.co.uk
w english-country-cottages.co.uk

BEADNELL Northumberland

17 The Haven ★★
Self Catering
Northumberland Cottages
t (01665) 589434
e enquiries@northumberlandcottages.com
w northumberlandcottages.co.uk

3 Alexandra House ★★★★
Self Catering
Contact: Mr & Mrs Steven & Ruth Lithgow
t (0191) 266 6440
e ruthlithgow@yahoo.ie
w beadnellholidays.co.uk

Alexandra Cottage ★★★★
Self Catering
Contact: Mrs Charlotte Slater
t (01661) 822337
e alexandracottage@beadnellvillage.co.uk
w beadnellvillage.co.uk/ac

Annstead Farm ★★★★
Self Catering
Contact: Mrs Susan Mellor
t (01665) 720387
e susan@annstead.co.uk
w annstead.co.uk

Beechley ★★★★
Self Catering
Contact: Mrs Deborah Baker
t (0113) 218 9176
e deb_n_ade@hotmail.com
w beadnellcottages.co.uk

Benthall Cottage
Rating Applied For
Self Catering
Contact: Ms Melanie Harrison
t 07733 230787
e melanie@seabreezecottages.co.uk
w seabreezecottages.co.uk

The Bothy, Beadnell
Rating Applied For
Self Catering
Contact: Mr & Mrs Jackie & Neil Forsyth
t (01665) 721380
e info@westfieldfarmhouse.co.uk
w thebothybeadnell.co.uk

The Bothy in the garden
★★★★ *Self Catering*
Contact: Mrs Beryl Seaward-Birchall
t (01665) 720497
e shepherds.cott@tiscali.co.uk
w shepherdscottagebeadnell.co.uk

Driftwood
Rating Applied For
Self Catering
Northumbrian Cottages
t (01228) 599950
e sheena@cumbrian-cottages.co.uk
w northumbrian-cottages.info

The Green, Beadnell ★★★★
Self Catering
Northumbrian Cottages
t (01228) 599950
e sheena@cumbrian-cottages.co.uk
w northumbrian-cottages.info

The Haven ★★★
Self Catering
Northumberland Cottages
t (01665) 589434
e enquiries@northumberlandcottages.com
w northumberlandcottages.co.uk

Low Dover Beadnell Bay
★★★★ *Self Catering*
Contact: Mrs Kath Thompson
t (01665) 720291
e enquiries@lowdover.co.uk
w lowdover.co.uk

Low Dover Beadnell Bay
Approved Caravan Holiday Home
w lowdover.co.uk

Mapleleaf Cottage ★★★
Self Catering
Contact: Mrs Susan McKenzie
t (01670) 738422 & 07950 173570
e malcolm.mckenzie@virgin.net

Mariner's Cottage ★★★★★
Self Catering
Northumberland Coastal Retreats
t (0191) 285 1272
e info@coastalretreats.co.uk
w coastalretreats.co.uk

Nook End Cottage & Driftwood Cottage
★★★★★ *Self Catering*
Northumberland Coastal Retreats
t (0191) 285 1272
e info@coastalretreats.co.uk
w coastalretreats.co.uk

Poole House ★★★★
Self Catering
Northumberland Cottages
t (01665) 589434
e enquiries@northumberlandcottages.com
w northumberlandcottages.co.uk

St Ebba's Peep ★★★★★
Self Catering
Contact: Mrs Julie Carr
t (01665) 720569
e juliecarr1@hotmail.co.uk
w beadnellhouselets.co.uk

Shore Cottage ★★★★
Self Catering
Contact: Mrs Lesley Barnett
t (01665) 833233
e d_barnettuk@yahoo.co.uk

Town Farm Cottages ★★★
Self Catering
Heritage Coast Holidays
t (01665) 604935
e info@heritagecoastholidays.co.uk
w heritagecoastholidays.co.uk

BEAL Northumberland

Bee Hill Properties
★★★★–★★★★★
Self Catering
Contact: Mr David Nesbitt
t (01289) 303425
e info@beehill.co.uk
w beehill.co.uk

BEAMISH Durham

Chapel House Studio Apartments ★★★
Self Catering
Contact: Mr John MacLennan
t (01207) 290992
e chapelhouseapartments@hotmail.co.uk
w chapelhouseapartments.co.uk

Three Arch Cottage ★★★★
Self Catering
Contact: Ms Tracey Harrison
t (0191) 370 0296
e pockerley2@btinternet.com

BEDALE North Yorkshire

High Grange Holiday Cottages ★★★★
Self Catering
Contact: Caroline Cottam
t (01677) 422740
e highgrange@yorks.net
w high-grange.co.uk

BEESTON Cheshire

The Lodge – Whitegate Farm ★★★★ *Self Catering*
Contact: Mrs Davies
t (01829) 261601
e stevedavies@euphony.net

BELFORD Northumberland

Aidan, Bede & Cuthbert
★★★★ *Self Catering*
Contact: Mr Chris Humble
Aidan, Bede & Cuthbert (Northumberland Cottages)
t (01289) 388938
e holiday@arenaproperty.com
w arenaproperty.com

Elwick Farm Cottages
★★★★ *Self Catering*
Contact: Mrs Roslyn Reay
t (01668) 213242
e w.r.reay@talk21.com
w elwickcottages.co.uk

Fenham le Moor Cottages
★★★–★★★★ *Self Catering*
Contact: Mrs Katie Burn
Fenham-le-Moor
t (01668) 213247
e enquiries@fenham-le-moor.co.uk
w fenham-le-moor.co.uk

Garden Cottage ★★★★★
Self Catering
Northumberland Coastal Retreats
t (0191) 285 1272
e info@coastalretreats.co.uk
w coastalretreats.co.uk

Gardener's Cottage ★★★★
Self Catering
Contact: Mrs Susan Comber
t (01668) 213242
e thecombers@supanet.com
w gardeners-cott.co.uk

Hollyhock House ★★★★
Self Catering
Contact: Miss Alison Turnbull
t (020) 8670 3500
e ali_turnbull@hotmail.com
w hollyhockhouse.co.uk

Kissankello Lodge ★★★★★
Self Catering
Northumberland Cottages
t (01665) 589434
e enquiries@northumberlandcottages.com
w northumberlandcottages.co.uk

The Old Mill ★★★★
Self Catering
Contact: Ms Peggy Ekeledo-Smithe info@northumberlandmill.co.uk
w northumberlandmill.co.uk

Stable Cottage ★★★★
Self Catering
t (01668) 213828

Stonefall Cottage ★★★
Self Catering
Northumberland Cottages
t (01665) 589434
e enquiries@northumberlandcottages.com
w northumberlandcottages.co.uk

Swinhoe Farm Cottages and Riding Centre ★★★
Self Catering
Contact: Mrs Valerie Nixon
t (01668) 213370
e valerie@swinhoecottages.co.uk
w swinhoecottages.co.uk

BELLERBY
North Yorkshire

Boar Cottage ★★★★
Self Catering
Contact: Bernie Gray
t (01969) 622220
e boarcott@hotmail.com
w boarcottage.co.uk

Rowan Cottage ★★★★
Self Catering
Dales Holiday Cottages
t (01756) 790919
e info@dales-holiday-cottages.com
w dales-holiday-cottages.com

Scott Cottage ★★★
Self Catering
Contact: Anne Maughan
t (01969) 622498
e scottcottage@fsmail.net
w scottcottageleyburn.co.uk

BELLINGHAM
Northumberland

Boat Farm Cottages ★★★★
Self Catering
Contact: Mrs Barbara Young
t (01434) 220989
e barbaraattheboat@hotmail.com
w boatfarm.co.uk

Buteland Bothy ★★
Self Catering
Contact: Mrs Alison Williams
t (01434) 220389
e buteland@aol.com

Conheath Cottage ★★★★
Self Catering
Contact: Mrs Zaina Riddle
t (01434) 220250
e stay@conheath.co.uk
w conheath.co.uk

Drovers Cottage ★★★★
Self Catering
Contact: Mrs Lynda Daley
t (0191) 271 6841
e lynda.daley@btinternet.co
w northumbrian-cottages.info

Riverdale Court ★★★★
Self Catering
Contact: Mr & Mrs John & Iben Cocker
t (01434) 220254
e reservations@riverdalehallhotel.co.uk
w riverdalehallhotel.co.uk

BELSAY
Northumberland

The Belsay Trust ★★★★
Self Catering
Contact: Mrs Sue Bolam
t (01661) 881206
e suebolam@belsay.com

BERRIER
Cumbria

Bells Farm ★★★
Self Catering
Cumbrian Cottages
t (01228) 599960
e enquiries@cumbrian-cottages.co.uk
w cumbrian-cottages.co.uk

The Cruck Barn ★★★
Self Catering
Cumbrian Cottages
t (01228) 599960
e enquiries@cumbrian-cottages.co.uk
w cumbrian-cottages.co.uk

Whitbarrow Holiday Village ★★★ *Self Catering*
Cumbrian Cottages
t (01228) 599960
e enquiries@cumbrian-cottages.co.uk
w cumbrian-cottages.co.uk

Whitbarrow Lodge 10 ★★★
Self Catering
Cumbrian Cottages
t (01228) 599960
e enquiries@cumbrian-cottages.co.uk
w cumbrian-cottages.co.uk

BERWICK-UPON-TWEED
Northumberland

2 The Courtyard ★★★
Self Catering
Contact: Mr & Mrs Morton
t (01289) 308737
e patmosphere@yahoo.com
w berwickselfcatering.co.uk

Ancroft Manor ★★★★
Self Catering
Northumberland Cottages
t (01665) 589434
e enquiries@northumberlandcottages.com
w northumberlandcottages.co.uk

Broadstone Cottage, Norham ★★★ *Self Catering*
Contact: Mr Edward Chantler
t (01622) 850207

Cliff Cottage ★★★★
Self Catering
Contact: Mrs Fairbairn
t (01289) 307375

Composers at Woodlands ★★★★★ *Self Catering*
Contact: Mr & Mrs Martin & Dee Colam
t (01289) 332599
e info@composers-woodlands.co.uk
w composers-woodlands.co.uk

The Cooperage ★★★★
Self Catering
Contact: Mr Chris Humble
The Cooperage (Northumberland Cottages)
t (01289) 388938
e holiday@arenaproperty.com

Ivy Cottage ★★★
Self Catering
Contact: Mr Robert Ian Heslop
t (01661) 833071
e ian@riheslop.go-plus.net

Kyloe Cabin ★★★★
Self Catering
Contact: Mr & Mrs Richard & Avril Black
t (01289) 381287
e avrilblack@aol.com
w lindisfarne.org.uk/kyloecottage/index.htm

Mill Lane Apartments ★★★★ *Self Catering*
Contact: Mr John Haswell
t (01289) 304492
e john@millane.co.uk
w millane.co.uk

Newt Cottage ★★★★
Self Catering
Contact: Mrs Karen Burn
t (01289) 388652
e kburn.huntinghall@btinternet.com
w huntinghall.co.uk

The Old Barn ★★★★
Self Catering
Contact: Mr & Mrs Richard & Susan Persse
t (01289) 306585
e r.persse-highl@amserve.com
w oldbarnhighletham.co.uk

Railway Cottage ★★★
Self Catering
Northumberland Cottages
t (01665) 589434
e enquiries@northumberlandcottages.com
w northumberlandcottages.co.uk

Smiddy Cottage ★★★★
Self Catering
Contact: Mrs June Simpson
t (01289) 386411
e june@smiddycottage.co.uk
w smiddycottage.co.uk

Snaffle Cottage
Rating Applied For
Self Catering
t (01289) 304175

Tigh Na Rudh ★★★★
Self Catering
Sykes Cottages
t (01244) 345700
e info@sykescottages.co.uk
w sykescottages.co.uk

Trevone ★★★★
Self Catering
Contact: Mr Peter Herdman
t (01289) 307524

Wellington Terrace Apartment ★★★★★
Self Catering
Contact: Mrs Aicha Fagan
t (01289) 305000
e aichafagan@hotmail.co.uk
w wellingtonterraceapartment.com

West Kyloe Cottages ★★★
Self Catering
Contact: Mrs Teresa Smalley
t (01289) 381279
e teresasmalley@westkyloe.demon.co.uk
w westkyloe.co.uk

West Longridge Cottages ★★★★–★★★★★
Self Catering
Contact: Mr Robert Whitten
t (01289) 331112
e robert@westlongridge.co.uk
w westlongridge.co.uk

West Ord Holiday Cottages ★★★–★★★★★ *Self Catering*
Contact: Mrs Carol Lang
t (01289) 386631
e stay@westord.co.uk
w westord.co.uk

Whitecroft ★★★★
Self Catering
Contact: Mrs Moira Kay
t (01289) 386066
e enquiries@whitecroftcottage.co.uk
w whitecroftcottage.co.uk

BEVERLEY
East Riding of Yorkshire

Chapel View ★★★
Self Catering
Contact: Philip Hillman
t (01482) 867465
e pcoliverhillman@hotmail.com

The Cottage ★★★★
Self Catering
Contact: Kenneth Hearne
t (01482) 868310
e knhearne@talk21.com
w akcottage.com

Foremans Cottage ★★★
Self Catering
Contact: Heather Hayward
t (01964) 550821
e heather90hayward@btinternet.com

High Farm Country Park ★★★★★ *Self Catering*
Contact: Lisa Johnson
t (01964) 543243
e info@highfarmcountrypark.co.uk
w highfarmcountrypark.co.uk

Lempicka Cottage & Apartment ★★★★
Self Catering
Contact: Linda Boyeson
Lempicka Cottage and Apartment
t (01482) 863665
e linda@lempicka.karoo.co.uk

Old Walkergate & The Cabin ★★★ *Self Catering*
Contact: Margaret Abbey
t (01482) 860005
e margaretabbey@beverleyselfcatering.co.uk
w beverleyselfcatering.co.uk

Peel Cottage ★★★
Self Catering
Contact: Mrs G Bennett
t (01482) 868506

Rudstone Walk Country Accommodation ★★–★★★★ *Self Catering*
Contact: Laura Greenwood
t (01430) 422230
e office@rudstone-walk.co.uk
w rudstone-walk.co.uk

BEWCASTLE
Cumbria

Arch View Cottages ★★★★
Self Catering
Contact: Jean James
t (01697) 748213
e jeanjames@btconnect.com
w holidaycottagescarlisle.co.uk

BEWERLEY
North Yorkshire

Briardene
Rating Applied For
Self Catering
Contact: David & Gillian Hawcroft
t (01423) 711554
e davidhawcroft@tewitfarm.co.uk
w holiday-rentals.co.uk/p84913

BILLINGTON
Lancashire

Snowdrop Cottage ★★★
Self Catering
t (01769) 580315
e jennygoldsmith@hotmail.co.uk

BINGFIELD
Northumberland

The Hytte ★★★★★
Self Catering
Contact: Mr & Mrs S R Gregory
t (01434) 672321
e sgregory001@tiscali.co.uk
w thehytte.com

BIRKENHEAD
Merseyside

Mersey View ★★★★
Serviced Apartments
Contact: Mr Nico Nicholas
t 0844 736 5899
e enquiries@merseyview.com
w merseyview.com

BIRSTWITH
North Yorkshire

3 The Square ★★★★
Self Catering
Holiday Cottages (Yorkshire) Ltd
t (01756) 700510
e brochure@holidaycotts.co.uk
w holidaycotts.co.uk

BISHOP AUCKLAND
Durham

Five Gables Cottage, Binchester ★★★★
Self Catering
Contact: Mr & Mrs Alan & Jane Barker
t (01388) 601715
e cottage@fivegables.co.uk
w fivegables.co.uk

Meadow View ref:1462
★★★ *Self Catering*
Dales Holiday Cottages
t (01756) 790919
e info@dales-holiday-cottages.com
w dales-holiday-cottages.com

BISHOP MIDDLEHAM
Durham

Bee Eater Cottage ★★★
Self Catering
Contact: Mrs Daphne Anderson
t (0191) 377 1428
e info@farnlessfarmpark.co.uk
w farnlessfarmpark.co.uk

BISHOP MONKTON
North Yorkshire

Hall Farm Cottage ★★★
Self Catering
Contact: Jennifer Barker
t (01765) 677200
e jenkenhallfarm@onetel.com
w yorkshirebandb.co.uk

The Old Telephone Exchange ★★★★★
Self Catering
Contact: Miss Vanessa Parry
t (01937) 585311
w holidayatcottages-in-yorkshire.co.uk

BISHOP THORNTON
North Yorkshire

The Courtyard at 'Dukes Place' ★★★-★★★★
Self Catering
Contact: Jaki Moorhouse
t (01765) 620229
e enquiries@dukesplace-courtyard.co.uk
w dukesplace-courtyard.co.uk

BISHOP WILTON
East Riding of Yorkshire

Grange Farm Holiday Cottages ★★★ *Self Catering*
Contact: Mr Richard & Judith Davy
t (01759) 369500
e richarddavy@supanet.com
w thegrangefarm.com

Low Callis Granary ★★★★
Self Catering
Contact: Stringer & Sons
t (01759) 368831

BISHOPDALE
North Yorkshire

Beech Cottage ★★★
Self Catering
Yorkshire Cottages
t (01228) 406701
e enquiries@yorkshire-cottages.info
w yorkshire-cottages.info

The Rookery ★★★★
Self Catering
Country Hideaways
t (01969) 663559
e info@countryhideaways.co.uk
w countryhideaways.co.uk

BISPHAM
Lancashire

Burbage Holiday Lodge ★★★★-★★★★★
Self Catering
Contact: Mr & Mrs Crewcock
t (01253) 356657
e enquires@burbageholidaylodge.co.uk
w burbageholidaygroup.co.uk

BLACKBURN
Lancashire

Serviced Apartments of Blackburn ★★★
Serviced Apartments
Contact: Mr Gordon Wright
t 07910 300 437
e servicedapartments@mac.com

BLACKO
Lancashire

Malkin Tower Farm Holiday Cottages ★★★★
Self Catering
Contact: Mrs Rachel Turner
t (01282) 699992
e info@malkintowerfarm.co.uk
w malkintowerfarm.co.uk

BLACKPOOL
Lancashire

Abingdon Holiday Apartments ★★ *Self Catering*
Contact: Mr Douglas Nelson
t (01253) 356181

The Beach House ★★★★★
Self Catering
Contact: Mrs Estelle Livesey
t (01253) 826555
e info@thebeachhouseblackpool.co.uk
w thebeachhouseblackpool.co.uk

Beachcliffe Holiday Apartments ★★★
Self Catering
Contact: Ms Maureen Checklin
t (01253) 357147
e stay@beachcliffe.com
w beachcliffe.com

The Berkeley ★★-★★★
Self Catering
Contact: Lord Lomax - Dwent
t (01253) 623218
e info@selfcatering.tv
w selfcatering.tv

Bridle Lodge Apartments
★★★ *Self Catering*
Contact: Mrs Anne Oxley
t (01253) 404117
e bridlelodge@hotmail.com
w bridlelodgeapartments.co.uk

Coast Apartments ★★★★
Self Catering
Contact: Mr & Mrs Steven & Karen Livesey
t (01253) 351377
e enquiries@coastapartments.co.uk
w coastapartments.co.uk

Crystal Lodge Apartments
★★-★★★ *Self Catering*
Contact: Mr David & Lesley Askham
t (01253) 346691
e info@crystallodge.co.uk
w crystallodge.co.uk

Empress Select Holiday Flats
★★ *Self Catering*
Contact: Mr & Mrs Woolston
t (01253) 596163
e empressselect@aol.com
w empressholidayflats.co.uk

Jade Apartments ★★★
Self Catering
Contact: Mrs Jean Long
t (01253) 341500
w jadeapartments.com

Newton Hall Apartments
Rating Applied For
Self Catering
Contact: Mrs Andrea Whittaker
t (01253) 350001
e awhittaker@partingtongroup.co.uk
w partingtons.com

Queens Mansions Holiday Apartments
★★★-★★★★★
Self Catering
Contact: Mrs Rebecca King
t (01253) 355689
w burbageholidaygroup.co.uk

San Remo Holiday Flats ★★
Self Catering
Contact: Mrs June Morgan
t (01253) 353487
e sanremoapartment@aol.com
w sanremoapartments.com

Sea Cote Holiday Flats ★★★
Self Catering
Contact: Mrs Anne Cunningham
t (01253) 354435

Stratford Holiday Apartments ★★-★★★
Self Catering
Contact: Mr Chris Taylor
t (01253) 500150
e stratford@blackpoolbreaks.com
w 500150.com

Vernon Lodge ★★★
Self Catering
Contact: Mr & Mrs Muscroft
t (01253) 403863
e andrew@vernon-hotel.co.uk
w vernon-hotel.co.uk

BLANCHLAND
Northumberland

Boltslaw Cottage ★★★★
Self Catering
Contact: Mrs Nicola Smith
t (01661) 830488
e asmith6000@aol.com
w cottageguide.co.uk/boltslaw

BLAWITH
Cumbria

Birchbank Cottage ★★★★
Self Catering
Contact: Linda Nicholson
t (01229) 885277
e birchbank@btinternet.com
w birchbank.co.uk

Blea Brows Cottage ★★★
Self Catering
The Coppermines & Coniston Lakes Cottages
t (015394) 41765
w coppermines.co.uk

BLEASDALE
Lancashire

Big Blindhurst ★★★★
Self Catering
Contact: Mrs Kelsall
t (01995) 61317
e kelsallfamily@hotmail.com
w bigblindhurstfarm.co.uk

BLENCOW
Cumbria

The Old Smithy ★★★★
Self Catering
Cumbrian Cottages
t (01228) 599960
e enquiries@cumbrian-cottages.co.uk
w cumbrian-cottages.co.uk

BOLLINGTON
Cheshire

Higher Ingersley Barn
★★★★★ *Self Catering*
Contact: Mr Peacock
t (01625) 572245
e bw.peacock@ntlworld.com
w higheringersleybarn.co.uk/

BOLSTERSTONE
South Yorkshire

Nook Farm Holiday Cottage
★★★ *Self Catering*
Contact: Jane Wainwright
t (0114) 288 3335

BOLTON ABBEY
North Yorkshire

Low Laithe Barn, Langbar
★★★★★ *Self Catering*
Contact: Susan Gray
t (01943) 609819
e info@beechhousebarns.co.uk
w beechhousebarns.co.uk

BOLTON-BY-BOWLAND
Lancashire

Corgill Farm Holiday Cottages ★★★★
Self Catering
Contact: Mr & Ms Brooks
t (01200) 47732
e info@corgillfarmholidaycottages.co.uk
w corgillfarmholidaycottages.co.uk

Fooden Farm Holiday Cottages ★★★★
Self Catering
t (01200) 447728

Springhead Farm Holiday Cottages ★★★★
Self Catering
Contact: Mrs S Lund
t (01200) 447245

BOLTON-LE-SANDS
Lancashire

Bay View ★★★ *Self Catering*
Contact: Mr John Sharples
t (01524) 822783
e acsjohn@tiscali.co.uk
w freewebs.com/bayviewlimited

De Nada ★★★★
Self Catering
Contact: Ms Allison Minto
t (01524) 824692
e allisonminto3761@hotmail.com

Waterside ★★★★
Self Catering
Contact: Mrs Hazel Wilson
t (01204) 882580
e joe@wilson882.freeserve.co.uk

BOLTONGATE
Cumbria

Bankside Cruck Barn
★★★★ *Self Catering*
Cumbrian Cottages
t (01228) 599960
e enquiries@cumbrian-cottages.co.uk
w cumbrian-cottages.co.uk

BOOTLE
Cumbria

Gardener's Cottage ★★★
Self Catering
Cumbrian Cottages
t (01228) 599960
e enquiries@cumbrian-cottages.co.uk
w cumbrian-cottages.co.uk

BOOTLE STATION
Cumbria

Station Cottage ★★★
Self Catering
Cumbrian Cottages
t (01228) 599960
e enquiries@cumbrian-cottages.co.uk
w cumbrian-cottages.co.uk

BORROWDALE
Cumbria

Barrowgate ★★ *Self Catering*
Lakeland Cottage Holidays
t (017687) 76065
e info@lakelandcottages.co.uk
w lakelandcottages.co.uk

Chapelfield ★★★★
Self Catering
Cumbrian Cottages
t (01228) 599960
e enquiries@cumbrian-cottages.co.uk
w cumbrian-cottages.co.uk

Derwent Farmhouse ★★★
Self Catering
Lakeland Cottage Holidays
t (017687) 76065
e info@lakelandcottages.co.uk
w lakelandcottages.co.uk

Hazel Bank Cottage ★★★★
Self Catering
Contact: Glen & Brenda Davies
t (017687) 77248
e enquiries@hazelbankhotel.co.uk
w hazelbankhotel.co.uk

Ivy Cottage ★★★
Self Catering
Cumbrian Cottages
t (01228) 599960
e enquiries@cumbrian-cottages.co.uk
w cumbrian-cottages.co.uk

Lodore House ★★★★★
Self Catering
Contact: Tanya Sentance
t (017687) 77285
e stay@lodorehouse.co.uk
w lodorehouse.co.uk

Maiden Moor ★★★★
Self Catering
Cumbrian Cottages
t (01228) 599960
e enquiries@cumbrian-cottages.co.uk
w cumbrian-cottages.co.uk

Rose Cottage Holiday Apartments ★★★
Self Catering
Contact: Steve Cooke
t (017687) 77678
e steve.cooke1@tiscali.co.uk
w borrowdalecottages.co.uk

BOSLEY
Cheshire

The Old Byre ★★
Self Catering
Contact: Mrs Dorothy Gilman
t (01260) 223293
e d.gilman@hotmail.co.uk
w farmstay.co.uk

Strawberry Duck Cottage
★★★ *Self Catering*
Contact: Mr B Carter
t (01260) 223591
e 2007@strawberryduckholidays.co.uk
w strawberryduckholidays.co.uk/

BOSTON SPA
West Yorkshire

Skye Cottage, Boston Spa
★★★★ *Self Catering*
Contact: Mr and Mrs David and Anne Watts
t 07941 353 202
e info@cosyhaven.co.uk
w cosyhaven.co.uk

BOTHEL
Cumbria

Limestone Lodges
★★★★-★★★★★
Self Catering
Contact: Diane Shankland
t (01697) 321674
e info@limestonelodges.co.uk
w limestonelodges.co.uk

Meadow View ★★★
Self Catering
Cumbrian Cottages
t (01228) 599960
e enquiries@cumbrian-cottages.co.uk
w cumbrian-cottages.co.uk

The Saplings Cottage ★★★
Self Catering
Lakes Cottage Holidays
t (01228) 591555
e info@lakescottageholiday.co.uk
w lakescottageholiday.co.uk

Skiddaw View Holiday Park Cottages ★★★ *Self Catering*
Contact: Mr Philip Carr
t (01697) 320919
e office@skiddawview.com
w skiddawview.co.uk/vb

BOULMER
Northumberland

Coble Cottage ★★★★
Self Catering
Contact: Mrs Lorna McQueen
t (01665) 577695
e coblecottage1@talktalk.net
w coblecottage.co.uk

North Cottage ★★★★
Self Catering
Contact: Mrs Madeleine Frater
t (01665) 577308
e frater19@hotmail.com
w northcottageboulmer.co.uk

BOUTH
Cumbria

2 Kiln Houses ★★★★
Self Catering
Lakeland Cottage Comapny
t (015395) 38180
e john@lakelandcottageco.com
w lakelandcottageco.com

Hill View ★★★★
Self Catering
Lakeland Cottage Comapny
t (015395) 38180
e john@lakelandcottageco.com
w lakelandcottageco.com

Kiln Cottage ★★★
Self Catering
Lakeland Cottage Comapny
t (015395) 38180
e john@lakelandcottageco.com
w lakelandcottageco.com

No 1 & 2 Rose Cottages
★★★★ *Self Catering*
Lakeland Cottage Comapny
t (015395) 38180
e john@lakelandcottageco.com
w lakelandcottageco.com

Yew Tree Cottage ★★★★
Self Catering
Lakeland Cottage Comapny
t (015395) 38180
e john@lakelandcottageco.com
w lakelandcottageco.com

BOWDON
Greater Manchester

The Loft ★★★★
Self Catering
t (0161) 941 7166

BOWES
Durham

Mellwaters Barn, Bowes
★★★★ *Self Catering*
Contact: Mr Andrew Tavener
t (01833) 628181
e mellwatersbarn@aol.com
w mellwatersbarn.co.uk

BOWLAND BRIDGE
Cumbria

Chase Cottage ★★★★
Self Catering
Lakelovers
t (015394) 88855
e bookings@lakelovers.co.uk
w lakelovers.co.uk

Ramblers Lodge ★★★★
Self Catering
Cumbrian Cottages
t (01228) 599960
e enquiries@cumbrian-cottages.co.uk
w cumbrian-cottages.co.uk

BOWMANSTEAD
Cumbria

Number 1 Lake View Cottages ★★★★
Self Catering
The Coppermines & Coniston Lakes Cottages
t (015394) 41765
w coppermines.co.uk

BOWNESS-ON-WINDERMERE
Cumbria

Lake View Apartment ★★★
Self Catering
Cumbrian Cottages
t (01228) 599960
e enquiries@cumbrian-cottages.co.uk
w cumbrian-cottages.co.uk

BOYNTON
East Riding of Yorkshire

No 8 Boynton ★★★★
Self Catering
Contact: Elizabeth Myhill
t (01262) 420201
e djwilson.farm@tiscali.co.uk
w no8boynton.co.uk

BRADFIELD
South Yorkshire

Cricket View, Low Bradfield
★★★ *Self Catering*
Contact: Miss Shaz Thompson
t (0114) 285 1235

BRADFIELD DALE
South Yorkshire

Thornseat Cottage ★★★
Self Catering
Peak Cottages
t (0114) 262 0777
e enquiries@peakcottages.com
w peakcottages.com

BRADSHAW
West Yorkshire

Popples Cottage ★★★★
Self Catering
Contact: Jan & Colin Huntley
t (01422) 244788
e janhuntley67@yahoo.co.uk
w popplescottage.co.uk

BRAITHWAITE
Cumbria

1 Skiddaw View ★★★
Self Catering
Cumbrian Cottages
t (01228) 599960
e enquiries@cumbrian-cottages.co.uk
w cumbrian-cottages.co.uk

Acorn Cottage ★★★
Self Catering
Cumbrian Cottages
t (01228) 599960
e enquiries@cumbrian-cottages.co.uk
w cumbrian-cottages.co.uk

Autumn Leaves ★★★★
Self Catering
Keswick Cottages
t (017687) 78555
e info@keswickcottages.co.uk
w keswickcottages.co.uk

Beech End ★★★
Self Catering
Lakeland Cottage Holidays
t (017687) 76065
e info@lakelandcottages.co.uk
w lakelandcottages.co.uk

Bridge End ★★★★
Self Catering
Contact: Denise McAdam
t (017687) 78481
e info@bridge-end-holidaycottage.co.uk
w bridge-end-holidaycottage.co.uk

Brookside Cottage ★★★★
Self Catering
Cumbrian Cottages
t (01228) 599960
e enquiries@cumbrian-cottages.co.uk
w cumbrian-cottages.co.uk

Catbells Cottage ★★★★
Self Catering
Cumbrian Cottages
t (01228) 599960
e enquiries@cumbrian-cottages.co.uk
w cumbrian-cottages.co.uk

Cosy Cottage ★★★
Self Catering
Lakeland Cottage Holidays
t (017687) 76065
e info@lakelandcottages.co.uk
w lakelandcottages.co.uk

Crown Cottage ★★★★
Self Catering
Lakeland Cottage Holidays
t (017687) 76065
e info@lakelandcottages.co.uk
w lakelandcottages.co.uk

Doves Nest ★★★
Self Catering
Cumbrian Cottages
t (01228) 599960
e enquiries@cumbrian-cottages.co.uk
w cumbrian-cottages.co.uk

Emily's Escape ★★★★
Self Catering
e dm81@blueyonder.co.uk
w dm81.pwp.blueyonder.co.uk

Highbridge Cottages
★★★★ *Self Catering*
Contact: Peter Rigg
t (017687) 80561
e riggpeter@tiscali.co.uk
w braithwaite-cottage.co.uk

Olives Cottage & Rosebank
★★★★ *Self Catering*
Keswick Cottages
t (017687) 78555
e info@keswickcottages.co.uk
w keswickcottages.co.uk

The Shieling ★★★
Self Catering
Lakeland Cottage Holidays
t (017687) 76065
e info@lakelandcottages.co.uk
w lakelandcottages.co.uk

Windrush ★★★★
Self Catering
Lakeland Cottage Holidays
t (017687) 76065
e info@lakelandcottages.co.uk
w lakelandcottages.co.uk

Wychwood ★★★
Self Catering
Lakeland Cottage Holidays
t (017687) 76065
e info@lakelandcottages.co.uk
w lakelandcottages.co.uk

BRAMPTON
Cumbria

Kingwater Coombe ★★★★
Self Catering
Cumbrian Cottages
t (01228) 599960
e enquiries@cumbrian-cottages.co.uk
w cumbrian-cottages.co.uk

Long Byres at Talkin Head
★★★ *Self Catering*
Contact: Harriet Sykes
t (01697) 73435
e stay@longbyres.co.uk
w longbyres.co.uk

South View Cottage ★★★★
Self Catering
Contact: Marie Hodgson
t (0161) 374 0110
e mariehodgson@southviewbanks.f9.co.uk

Warren Bank Cottage
★★★★★ *Self Catering*
Contact: Margie Douglas
t (01434) 607544
e margie@warrenbankcottage.com
w warrenbankcottage.com

BRANDESBURTON
East Riding of Yorkshire

Holly Cottage ★★★★
Self Catering
Yorkshire Cottages
t (01228) 406701
e enquiries@yorkshire-cottages.info
w yorkshire-cottages.info

BRANTON
Northumberland

Breamish Valley Cottages
★★★★-★★★★★
Self Catering
Contact: Mrs Michele Moralee
t (01665) 578263
e peter@breamishvalley.co.uk
w breamishvalley.co.uk

BRAWBY
North Yorkshire

The Old Cart House ★★★★
Self Catering
Contact: Anne Muir
t (01653) 668252
e theoldcarthouse@aol.com
w selfcateringcottagenorthyorks.co.uk

BRETHERDALE
Cumbria

Bretherdale Hall ★★★★
Self Catering
Cumbrian Cottages
t (01228) 599960
e enquiries@cumbrian-cottages.co.uk
w cumbrian-cottages.co.uk

BRIDEKIRK
Cumbria

Anns Hill ★★★★★
Self Catering
Contact: Vanessa Steel
t (01900) 827838
e vanessa@annshill.co.uk
w annshill.co.uk

Ellwood ★★★★★
Self Catering
Cumbrian Cottages
t (01228) 599960
e enquiries@cumbrian-cottages.co.uk
w cumbrian-cottages.co.uk

BRIDLINGTON
East Riding of Yorkshire

Acorn House ★★★
Self Catering
Contact: Mr Tony Morton
t (01262) 672451
e marieoak24@hotmail.com

Arncliffe Holiday Flats
★★-★★★ *Self Catering*
Contact: Mrs S Drew
t (01262) 677945

Ash Lee Holiday Apartments
★★-★★★ *Self Catering*
Contact: Mrs Greatorex
t (01262) 400485

Ashton Holiday Flats ★★
Self Catering
Contact: Samuel & Helen Levitt
t (01262) 675132

Bay Side Holidays ★★★★
Self Catering
Contact: Mr & Mrs Hatfield
t (01262) 609431
e bayside.bridlington@virgin.net
w baysideholidays.co.uk

Beaconsfield House ★★★
Self Catering
Contact: Mrs L Stuart
t (01262) 401482
e beaconsfield@aol.com
w beaconsfieldholidayapartments.co.uk

Bluebell Holiday Apartment
★★★ *Self Catering*
Contact: Jack Reed
t (01262) 401445

Carlton Apartments ★★★★
Self Catering
Contact: Sharon Richardson
t (01262) 672807
e info@carltonapartments.co.uk
w carltonapartments.co.uk

Contemporary Cottage Holidays ★★★★
Self Catering
Contact: Mrs Karen Lincoln-Williams
t (01262) 490667
e billlincoln@btinternet.com
w bridholidaycottages.com

East Coast Holiday Cottages
★★★ *Self Catering*
Contact: Cynthia Dean
t 0845 863 9743
e eastcoastholidaycottages@hotmail.com
w eastcoastholidaycottages.co.uk

Ellwyn Holiday Flats ★★
Self Catering
Contact: Mr & Mrs Brockbank
t (01262) 606896
e elliethodsq@supanet.com
w bridlington.net/ellwyn/business

Fairholme Holiday Flats
★-★★ *Self Catering*
Contact: Mr Geraghty
t (01262) 676269
e nicholasscott@geraghty2.fsnet.co.uk

Fir Lodge Holiday Apartments ★★★
Self Catering
Contact: Mr & Mrs Day
t (01262) 671400
e firlodgeapts@aol.com

Fountain House ★★–★★★
Self Catering
Contact: Mr Shuttleworth
t (01262) 604850
e reservations@fountainhouse.co.uk
w fountainhouseholidayflats.co.uk

The Grosvenor Holiday Flats
★★★★ *Self Catering*
Contact: Liz Otulakowski
t (01729) 830959
e anton@otulakowski.freeserve.co.uk

Hemsley Holiday Flats
★★–★★★ *Self Catering*
Contact: Mr E Halliday
Helmsley Holiday Flats
t (01262) 672603

Highcliffe Holiday Apartments
Rating Applied For
Self Catering
Contact: John Willcocks
t (01262) 674127
e info@highcliffe.net
w highcliffe.net

Imp-press Holiday Apartments ★–★★★
Self Catering
Contact: Ms A Boxer
t (01262) 608838

Marina View Holiday Apartments ★★–★★★
Self Catering
Contact: Geoff & Lynda Allanach
t (01262) 676565

Meadowfield Lodge ★★★★
Self Catering
Contact: Mr Tonks
The Marina
t (01262) 677138
e themarina8@hotmail.com
w selfcatering-bridlington.co.uk

Mount Drive Bungalow
★★★ *Self Catering*
Contact: Helen Gudgeon
23 Mount Drive
t (0113) 226 1298
e rkgudgeon@hotmail.com

North Kingsfield Holiday Cottages, Fraisthorpe
★★★★★ *Self Catering*
Contact: Peter & Helen Milner
t (01262) 673743
e helen@northkingsfield.co.uk
w northkingsfield.co.uk

Oakwell Aparthotel
★★★–★★★★ *Self Catering*
Contact: David Willaims
t (01262) 403666
e oakwellholidays@aol.com

Oakwell Holidays ★★★
Self Catering
w oakwellholidays.co.uk

Pembroke House Apartments ★★★
Self Catering
Contact: Mr Eaton
t (01262) 677376
e ampembroke@hotmail.co.uk
w pembrokehouseapartment.co.uk

The Rialto Holiday Flats
★★–★★★ *Self Catering*
Contact: Ian & Michelle Stoddard
t (01262) 677653
e mail@rialto-bridlington.co.uk
w rialto-bridlington.co.uk

Rowntree Seafront Holiday Flats ★★ *Self Catering*
Contact: Keith & Jean Barker
t (01262) 678181

Royal Court Apartments
★★★★ *Self Catering*
Contact: Jack Bath
t (01262) 604024
e royalcourtapartments@fsmail.net
w theroyalcourtapartments.co.uk

Sea View Holiday Flats ★★
Self Catering
Contact: Stanley & Margaret Benson
t (01262) 676974
e flash2@tesco.net

Winston Court Holiday Apartments ★–★★
Self Catering
Contact: Ian Read
Egsproperty
t (01262) 677819
e enquiries@winston-court.co.uk
w winston-court.co.uk

BRIGHOUSE
West Yorkshire

Modern Apartment in Brighouse ★★★
Self Catering
Contact: Kash Ijaz
t 0870 850 8514
w nomorehotels.co.uk

BRIGSTEER
Cumbria

Garden Cottage ★★★★
Self Catering
Cumbrian Cottages
t (01228) 599960
e enquiries@cumbrian-cottages.co.uk
w cumbrian-cottages.co.uk

Moss Rigg ★★★
Self Catering
Cumbrian Cottages
t (01228) 599960
e enquiries@cumbrian-cottages.co.uk
w cumbrian-cottages.co.uk

Sunnyhill ★★★★
Self Catering
Cumbrian Cottages
t (01228) 599960
e enquiries@cumbrian-cottages.co.uk
w cumbrian-cottages.co.uk

BRINSCALL
Lancashire

Moors View Cottage ★★★
Self Catering
Contact: Mrs Sheila Smith
t (01253) 853537 & 07747 808406
e fourseasonsguesthouse@talktalk.net

BROUGHTON IN FURNESS
Cumbria

Croft House ★★★★
Self Catering
Cumbrian Cottages
t (01228) 599960
e enquiries@cumbrian-cottages.co.uk
w cumbrian-cottages.co.uk

Croft House Apartment
★★★★ *Self Catering*
Cumbrian Cottages
t (01228) 599960
e enquiries@cumbrian-cottages.co.uk
w cumbrian-cottages.co.uk

Hole Beck Farm Cottages
★★★–★★★★ *Self Catering*
The Coppermines & Coniston Lakes Cottages
t (015394) 41765
w coppermines.co.uk

Long Garth Farm ★★★
Self Catering
Contact: Lynda Turner
t (01229) 716239
e enquiries@longgarthholidaycottages.co.uk
w longgarthholidaycottages.co.uk

The Old Millers Cottage
★★★★ *Self Catering*
The Coppermines & Coniston Lakes Cottages
t (015394) 41765
w coppermines.co.uk

Ring House Cottages
★★★–★★★★ *Self Catering*
Contact: Stuart & Lynda Harrison
t (01229) 716578
e info@ringhouse.co.uk
w ringhouse.co.uk

Thornthwaite Farm ★★★
Self Catering
Contact: Jean Jackson
t (01229) 716340
e info@lakedistrictcottages.co.uk
w lakedistrictcottages.co.uk

Thornthwaite Farm
Approved Caravan Holiday Home
w lakedistrictcottages.co.uk

BROUGHTON MILLS
Cumbria

Hobkin Ground Farm Cottages ★★★–★★★★
Self Catering
Contact: Janet Johnson
t (01229) 716338
e enquiries@hobkinground.co.uk
w hobkinground.co.uk

BUCKDEN
North Yorkshire

Dalegarth and The Ghyll Cottages ★★★★
Self Catering
Contact: David & Susan Lusted
t (01756) 760877
e info@dalegarth.co.uk
w dalegarth.co.uk

Rowan Cottages ★★★
Self Catering
Contact: Mr Richard Clayton
t (01274) 816966
e rick.clayton@virgin.net
w rowancottages.co.uk

BULLGILL
Cumbria

Row Moor Farm ★★★★
Self Catering
Cumbrian Cottages
t (01228) 599960
e enquiries@cumbrian-cottages.co.uk
w cumbrian-cottages.co.uk

BURLAND
Cheshire

The Stables ★★★★
Self Catering
Contact: Mrs Glenys Harris
t (01270) 524535
e info@thestables.biz

BURNESIDE
Cumbria

Mirefoot Cottages ★★★★★
Self Catering
Contact: Kate Curwen
t (01539) 720015
e kate@mirefoot.co.uk
w mirefoot.co.uk

Shepherds Nook ★★★
Self Catering
Lakeland Cottage Comapny
t (015395) 38180
e john@lakelandcottageco.com
w lakelandcottageco.com

BURNSALL
North Yorkshire

Oatcroft Farm Barn Apartment ★★★
Self Catering
Contact: Jane Stockdale
t (01756) 720268

The Sycamores ★★★★
Self Catering
Contact: Sheila Carr
DSC Holiday Lettings Ltd
t (01756) 752435
e carr@totalise.co.uk
w yorkshirenet.co.uk/stayat/mannacottage

BURNT YATES
North Yorkshire

North Gate Cottage ★★★
Self Catering
Contact: Lorraine Gilmour
Dales Holiday Cottages
t (01756) 790919
e info@dales-holiday-cottages.com
w dalesholcot.com

BURRADON
Northumberland

Keepers Cottage ★★★★
Self Catering
Contact: Mr N Forster
t (01669) 630265
e forsters.burradon@btinternet.com

Laird's Cottage ★★★★★
Self Catering
Contact: Mr David Matthews
t (0191) 251 1087
e enquiries@lairdscottage.co.uk
w lairdscottage.co.uk

BURSCOUGH
Lancashire

Moss Farm Barn ★★★★
Self Catering
Contact: Ms Rose Duncan
t (01704) 897944
w mossfarmbarn.co.uk

BURTON-IN-KENDAL
Cumbria

East Wing ★★★ *Self Catering*
Cumbrian Cottages
t (01228) 599960
e enquiries@cumbrian-cottages.co.uk
w cumbrian-cottages.co.uk

BURTON-IN-LONSDALE
North Yorkshire

Brentwood Farm Cottages
★★★★ *Self Catering*
Contact: Anita Taylor
t (01524) 262155
e info@brentwoodfarmcottages.co.uk
w brentwoodfarmcottages.co.uk

Greta Cottage ★★★★
Self Catering
Contact: Jane Burns
t (01524) 261081
e jandaburns@ktdinternet.com
w gretacottage-yorkshiredales.com

Riverside Cottage ★★★★★
Self Catering
Contact: Patricia Leverton
t (01274) 560542
e riversidecott@aol.com
w members.aol.com/riversidecott

BURY
Greater Manchester

The Old Hayloft, Holcombe
★★★ *Self Catering*
Contact: Mrs Hilditch
t (01706) 823467

Top o' th' Moor cottage
★★★★ *Self Catering*
t 07976 034196
w topofthemoorcottage.com

BURYTHORPE
North Yorkshire

The Granary ★★★★
Self Catering
Contact: Margaret Raines
t (01653) 658201
e thegranary1994@btinternet.com

Primrose Cottage and Derwent Cottage ★★★★
Self Catering
Contact: Christopher Turner
t (01653) 658336
e countryholidays@btinternet.com
w countryholidaycottages.co.uk

BUTTERMERE
Cumbria

Bridge Hotel & Self Catering Apartments ★★★★
Self Catering
Contact: John McGuire
t (017687) 70252
e enquiries@bridge-hotel.com
w bridge-hotel.com

Lanthwaite Green Farm Cottage ★★★★ *Self Catering*
Contact: John McGuire
Bridge Hotel & Self Catering Apartments
t (017687) 70252
w bridge-hotel.com

BUTTERWICK
Cumbria

Gill Barn ★★★★
Self Catering
Cumbrian Cottages
t (01228) 599960
e enquiries@cumbrian-cottages.co.uk
w cumbrian-cottages.co.uk

CALDBECK
Cumbria

The Barn, Manor Cottage
★★★★ *Self Catering*
Contact: Ann Wade
t (01697) 478214
e walterwade@tiscali.co.uk

Ellwood House ★★★
Self Catering
Cumbrian Cottages
t (01228) 599960
e enquiries@cumbrian-cottages.co.uk
w cumbrian-cottages.co.uk

Gill Beck ★★★ *Self Catering*
Cumbrian Cottages
t (01228) 599960
e enquiries@cumbrian-cottages.co.uk
w cumbrian-cottages.co.uk

Greenside Cottage ★★★
Self Catering
Cumbrian Cottages
t (01228) 599960
e enquiries@cumbrian-cottages.co.uk
w cumbrian-cottages.co.uk

High Greenrigg House Cottages ★★★★★
Self Catering
Contact: Sonia Hill
t (01697) 478430
e info@highgreenrigghouse.co.uk
w highgreenrigghouse.co.uk

Marlowe Cottage ★★★★★
Self Catering
Contact: Mrs Arkell
Marlowe Cottage Rentals
t (01697) 476417
e info@marlowecottage.co.uk
w marlowecottage.co.uk

Monkhouse Hill Cottages
★★★★-★★★★★
Self Catering
Contact: Andy & Jennifer Collard
t (01697) 476254
e cottages@monkhousehill.co.uk
w monkhousehill.co.uk

CALLALY
Northumberland

Dene Cottage ★★★★
Self Catering
Contact: Mrs Maureen Winn
t (01665) 574513

CARK IN CARTMEL
Cumbria

6 Cark House ★★★★
Self Catering
Cumbrian Cottages
t (01228) 599960
e enquiries@cumbrian-cottages.co.uk
w cumbrian-cottages.co.uk

Old Bank House
Rating Applied For
Self Catering
Contact: Mrs Maxine Bagshaw
Oxspring House Cottage
t (01226) 761186
e maxinebagshaw@madasafish.com
w old-bank-house.co.uk

CARLETON
Cumbria

Carleton Mill Cottage
★★★★ *Self Catering*
Cumbrian Cottages
t (01228) 599960
e enquiries@cumbrian-cottages.co.uk
w cumbrian-cottages.co.uk

CARLISLE
Cumbria

Bessiestown Farm Country Cottages ★★★★
Self Catering
Contact: Margaret Sisson
t (01228) 577219
e info@bessiestown.co.uk
w bessiestown.co.uk

Eden Lodge ★★★★★
Self Catering
Cumbrian Cottages
t (01228) 599960
e enquiries@cumbrian-cottages.co.uk
w cumbrian-cottages.co.uk

The Gables ★★★
Self Catering
Cumbrian Cottages
t (01228) 599960
e enquiries@cumbrian-cottages.co.uk
w cumbrian-cottages.co.uk

Meadow View, Burn Cottage & Ald Pallyards ★★★★
Self Catering
Contact: Mrs Elwen
t (01228) 577308
e info@newpallyards.freeserve.co.uk
w newpallyards.freeserve.co.uk

Old Brewery Residences
★★★ *Self Catering*
Contact: Dee Carruthers
t (01228) 597352
e deec@impacthousing.org.uk
w impacthousing.org.uk

West Cottage, Cumwhinton
★★★★ *Self Catering*
Contact: Mrs Allison Stamper
t (01228) 561600

CARLTON IN CLEVELAND
Tees Valley

Stables Cottage ★★★
Self Catering
Contact: Mr Michael Akestere michael@akester147.fsnet.co.uk

CARLTON MINIOTT
North Yorkshire

Landrace Cottage ★★★★
Self Catering
Contact: Mrs Sara Langstaff
t (01845) 525110
e sara@carthousefurniture.com
w landracecottage.co.uk

CARNFORTH
Lancashire

Deroy Cottage ★★★
Self Catering
Contact: Mr & Mrs Colin & Shirley Cross
t (01524) 733196
e colin@colincross.co.uk
w colincross.co.uk

Mansergh Farmhouse Cottages ★★★★
Self Catering
Contact: Mrs Linda Rigby
t (01524) 720129
e linda@manserghcottages.co.uk
w manserghcottages.co.uk

Old Waterslack Farm Cottages and Caravans, Silverdale ★★★ *Self Catering*
Contact: Sam Riseborough
t (01524) 720833
e bnhevey@tiscali.co.uk
w oldwaterslackfarmholidaycottages.co.uk

Pine Lake Lodges ★★★★
Self Catering
Cumbrian Cottages
t (01228) 599960
e enquiries@cumbrian-cottages.co.uk
w cumbrian-cottages.co.uk

CARPERBY
North Yorkshire

Barnbrook Ref:567 ★★★
Self Catering
Sykes Cottages
t (01244) 345700
e info@sykescottages.co.uk
w sykescottages.co.uk

Woodsomme Cottage
★★★★ *Self Catering*
Contact: Lorraine Gilmour
Dales Holiday Cottages
t (01756) 790919

CARRVILLE
Durham

62 Wantage Road ★★
Self Catering
Contact: Mr & Mrs Norman & Anne Walker
t (0191) 386 2290
e flatapar@hotmail.co.uk
w durhamflatapar.co.uk

CARTMEL
Cumbria

3 Church View ★★★★
Self Catering
Cumbrian Cottages
t (01228) 599960
e enquiries@cumbrian-cottages.co.uk
w cumbrian-cottages.co.uk

Bradlea ★★★ *Self Catering*
Cumbrian Cottages
t (01228) 599960
e enquiries@cumbrian-cottages.co.uk
w cumbrian-cottages.co.uk

Clogger Beck Cottage
★★★★ *Self Catering*
Cumbrian Cottages
t (01228) 599960
e enquiries@cumbrian-cottages.co.uk
w cumbrian-cottages.co.uk

Drakes Cottage ★★★★
Self Catering
Lakeland Cottage Comapny
t (015395) 38180
e john@lakelandcottageco.com
w lakelandcottageco.com

Ducks Haven ★★★★
Self Catering
Lakeland Cottage Comapny
t (015395) 38180
e john@lakelandcottageco.com
w lakelandcottageco.com

Grange End Cottage ★★★★
Self Catering
Contact: Simon Cleasby
Grange End Cottages
t (01524) 702955 & 07770 301709
e s.cleasby@zen.co.uk
w holidaycottagescumbria.com

The Hayloft, Nr Cartmel
★★★★ *Self Catering*
Contact: Carrie Tomlinson
t (01524) 221390
e hayloft.info@virgin.net
w hayloftcottageholidays.co.uk

Little Croft ★★★★
Self Catering
Lakeland Cottage Comapny
t (015395) 38180
e john@lakelandcottageco.com
w lakelandcottageco.com

Longlands at Cartmel
★★★-★★★★ *Self Catering*
Contact: Martin Ainscough
t (015395) 36475
e longlands@cartmel.com
w cartmel.com

Longlands Farm Cottage
★★★ *Self Catering*
Contact: Valerie Dixon
t (015395) 36406
e dixon@longlandsfarm.com
w longlandsfarmcottage.co.uk

The Old Telephone Exchange ★★★ *Self Catering*
Cumbrian Cottages
t (01228) 599960
e enquiries@cumbrian-cottages.co.uk
w cumbrian-cottages.co.uk

Wharton Barn ★★★★
Self Catering
Lakeland Cottage Comapny
t (015395) 38180
e john@lakelandcottageco.com
w lakelandcottageco.com

Wharton Cottage ★★★★
Self Catering
Cumbrian Cottages
t (01228) 599960
e enquiries@cumbrian-cottages.co.uk
w cumbrian-cottages.co.uk

Wharton House ★★★★
Self Catering
Lakeland Cottage Comapny
t (015395) 38180
e john@lakelandcottageco.com
w lakelandcottageco.com

CARTMEL FELL
Cumbria

Barrow Hollin ★★★★
Self Catering
Lakeland Cottage Comapny
t (015395) 38180
e john@lakelandcottageco.com
w lakelandcottageco.com

Danes Court Cottages
★★★★ *Self Catering*
Contact: Mr David Hoyle
t (01663) 762634
e david@disley100.freeserve.co.uk

CASTLE BOLTON
North Yorkshire

Crooked Acres ★★★★★
Self Catering
Contact: Ms Pauline Leat
t (01756) 799821
w dales-holiday-cottages.com

CASTLE CARROCK
Cumbria

Tottergill Farm
★★★★-★★★★★
Self Catering
Contact: Stephen & Joyce Wightman
t (01228) 670615
e stephen@tottergill.co.uk
w tottergill.co.uk

CASTLESIDE
Durham

Derwent Grange Cottages
★★-★★★ *Self Catering*
Contact: Mr & Mrs Elliot
Derwent Grange Farm
t (01207) 508358
e ekelliot@aol.com
w derwentgrange.co.uk

Jasmine Cottage, Castleside
★★★★ *Self Catering*
Contact: Mrs Margaret Steel
t (01207) 582703
e k.a.steel@btinternet.com
w pondfieldvillacottage.co.uk

Manor Park Cottage ★★★
Self Catering
Contact: Mr Brian Elstrop
t (01207) 501000

CATON
Lancashire

Croft (The) – Ground Floor Apartment ★★★★ *Self Catering & Serviced Apartments*
Contact: Mrs Sue Brierly-Hampton
t (01524) 770725
e suebrierly@hotmail.com

CATTERICK
North Yorkshire

The Coach House
Rating Applied For
Self Catering
Contact: Mr & Mrs C P & G Noel-Johnson
t (01748) 812110
e cllrenj@talktalk.net
w fernerycottages.co.uk

CATTON
Northumberland

Station House Flat ★★★★
Self Catering
Contact: Mr & Ms Michael & Verona Woodhouse
t (01434) 683362
e info@allendale-holidays.co.uk
w allendale-holidays.co.uk

CAWBURN
Northumberland

Rowan Cottage ★★★★
Self Catering
Contact: Mrs Margaret Swallow
t (01434) 320352
e enquiry@rowan-cottage.org.uk
w rowan-cottage.org.uk

CAWOOD
North Yorkshire

Cawood Park Holiday Cottages ★★★ *Self Catering*
Contact: Mr Andrew Pringle
t (01757) 268450
e info@cawoodpark.com
w cawoodpark.com

CAYTON
North Yorkshire

Eldin Hall – Cottage 1 ★★★
Self Catering
Bedwyn's Holiday Accommodation
t (01723) 516700
e info@bedwyns.co.uk
w bedwyns.co.uk

Eldin Hall – Cottage 2 ★★★
Self Catering
Bedwyn's Holiday Accommodation
t (01723) 516700
e info@bedwyns.co.uk
w bedwyns.co.uk

Lea Cottage ★★★
Self Catering
Bedwyn's Holiday Accommodation
t (01723) 516700
e info@bedwyns.co.uk
w bedwyns.co.uk

CHAPEL LE DALE
North Yorkshire

4 Salt Lake Cottages ★★★
Self Catering
Contact: G Lees
t (01729) 860485

Netherscar ★★ *Self Catering*
Sykes Cottages
t (01244) 345700
e info@sykescottages.co.uk
w sykescottages.co.uk

CHAPEL STILE
Cumbria

1 Lingmoor View ★★★
Self Catering
Lakes Cottage Holidays
t (01228) 591555
e info@lakescottageholiday.co.uk
w lakescottageholiday.co.uk

14 Fir Garth ★★★
Self Catering
Cumbrian Cottages
t (01228) 599960
e enquiries@cumbrian-cottages.co.uk
w cumbrian-cottages.co.uk

2 Undergarth ★★★
Self Catering
Cumbrian Cottages
t (01228) 599960
e enquiries@cumbrian-cottages.co.uk
w cumbrian-cottages.co.uk

3 Lingmoor View ★★★
Self Catering
Contact: Mr & Mrs Geoffrey & Sheila Smith
t (01756) 791779
e g.s.smith@btinternet.com

Ann's Cottage ★★★
Self Catering
Lakelovers
t (015394) 88855
e bookings@lakelovers.co.uk
w lakelovers.co.uk

Bank View ★★★
Self Catering
Lakes Cottage Holidays
t (01228) 591555
e info@lakescottageholiday.co.uk
w lakescottageholiday.co.uk

Dulcanter ★★★★
Self Catering
Cumbrian Cottages
t (01228) 599960
e enquiries@cumbrian-cottages.co.uk
w cumbrian-cottages.co.uk

Fir Garth ★★★ *Self Catering*
Cumbrian Cottages
t (01228) 599960
e enquiries@cumbrian-cottages.co.uk
w cumbrian-cottages.co.uk

Plumblands ★★★★
Self Catering
Lakes Cottage Holidays
t (01228) 591555
e info@lakescottageholiday.co.uk
w lakescottageholiday.co.uk

Thrang View ★★★★
Self Catering
Lakelovers
t (015394) 88855
e bookings@lakelovers.co.uk
w lakelovers.co.uk

Underfell ★★★★
Self Catering
Lakelovers
t (015394) 88855
e bookings@lakelovers.co.uk
w lakelovers.co.uk

CHATHILL
Northumberland

Charlton Hall Holiday Cottages ★★★★
Self Catering
Contact: Mr Robert Thorp
t (01665) 579378
e robertthorp@charltonhall.co.uk
w charltonhall.co.uk

Clover Cottage ★★★
Self Catering
Contact: Mrs Riddell
t (01665) 589263

East Cuttles & Rafters
★★★★ *Self Catering*
Grace Darling Holidays
t (01665) 721332
e carolynalgar150@msn.com

The Granary ★★★★★
Self Catering
Northumberland Coastal Retreats
t (0191) 285 1272
e info@coastalretreats.co.uk
w coastalretreats.co.uk

The Hemmel ★★★★★
Self Catering
Northumberland Coastal Retreats
t (0191) 285 1272
e info@coastalretreats.co.uk
w coastalretreats.co.uk

The Lodge and Head Gardener's House ★★★★
Self Catering
Contact: Mrs J Shirley Burnie
t (01665) 589499
e doxfordhall@aol.com
w doxfordhall.co.uk

Moo House & The Cowshed
★★★★★ *Self Catering*
Northumberland Coastal Retreats
t (0191) 285 1272
e info@coastalretreats.co.uk
w coastalretreats.co.uk

Rafters ★★★★ *Self Catering*
Grace Darling Holidays
t (01665) 721332
e carolynalgar150@msn.com

Shepherds Cottage ★★★
Self Catering
Northumberland Cottages
t (01665) 589434
e enquiries@northumberlandcottages.com
w northumberlandcottages.co.uk

CHATTON
Northumberland

Appletree Cottage ★★★★
Self Catering
Northumberland Cottages
t (01665) 589434
e enquiries@northumberlandcottages.com
w northumberlandcottages.co.uk

Chatton Park Lodge
★★★★★ *Self Catering*
Contact: Mr Paul Mattinson
t (01668) 215507
e enquiries@chattonpark.com
w chattonpark.com

Cheviot Suite ★★★★
Self Catering
Contact: Ms Tracy Fiddes
t (01289) 388830
e info@thecheviotsuite.co.uk
w thecheviotsuite.co.uk

Groom's Cottage ★★★★
Self Catering
Contact: Mrs Jane Ord
t (01668) 215247
e ord@chattonpk.fsnet.co.uk
w chattonparkfarm.co.uk

Percy Cottage ★★★
Self Catering
Contact: Mrs Helen Reed-Jones
The Property Investments
t (01668) 216556
e tonyreedjones@aol.com
w percycottage.co.uk

The Woodmill
Rating Applied For
Self Catering
Northumbrian Cottages
t (01228) 599950
e sheena@cumbrian-cottages.co.uk
w northumbrian-cottages.info

CHEADLE
Greater Manchester

AJ Estates ★★★
Self Catering
Contact: Mr David Walker
t (0161) 718 5723

CHESTER
Cheshire

Commonhall Street Apartments ★★★★
Self Catering
Contact: Ms Roslyn Bell
t (028) 3755 1974
e info@chesterholiday.com
w chesterholiday.com

Fir Tree Cottage ★★★
Self Catering
Contact: Mrs Ursula Owen
t (01244) 382681

The Garden Studio ★★★
Self Catering
Contact: Ms Carol Rannard
t (01244) 677213
e duck10@waitrose.com

Handbridge Village ★★★
Self Catering
Contact: Mrs R A Owen
t (01244) 676159

Ivy Cottage ★★ *Self Catering*
Contact: Mr Joseph Barry
t (01244) 403630
e rmd.heritage@btconnect.com
w rmd-heritage.co.uk

Kingswood Coach House
★★★ *Self Catering*
Contact: Mrs C Perry
t (01244) 851204
e caroline.m.perry@btopenworld.com

Mews Style Cottages
★★★★★ *Self Catering*
Contact: Mrs Karen Buchan
t (01745) 825880
e k.buchan@btinternet.com
w chesterholidaycottages.com

Queen's Park ★★★
Self Catering
Contact: Mrs Lilian Maddock
t (01244) 676141
e elizabethcrescent@aol.com

Spireview Apartment ★★★
Self Catering
Contact: Mr Michael Pimlott
t 07800 123964
e corkeyhomes@hotmail.com
w corkeyhomes.co.uk

Stapleford Hall Cottage
★★★ *Self Catering*
Contact: Mrs Winward
t (01829) 740202
e staplefordcottage@hotmail.com
w staplefordhallcottage.com

Wharton Lock Apartment & Balcony ★★★★ *Self Catering*
Contact: Mrs Sandra Jeffrey
Chester Canalside Holidays
t (01244) 312788
e rentals@stayinchester.com
w stayinchester.com

Wycliffe Court Apartment
★★★★ *Self Catering*
Contact: Mrs Frederika Davies
t (01244) 323204
e bookings@lavenderlodgechester.co.uk
w chester-apartment.co.uk

CHESTER-LE-STREET
Durham

Coquet Cottages
★★★★-★★★★★
Self Catering
t (0191) 388 3752
w coquetcottages.co.uk

Katie's Cottage & The Bungalow ★★★★
Self Catering
Contact: Mrs Hilary Johnson
t (0191) 410 2901
e stay@lowurpeth.co.uk
w lowurpeth.co.uk

The Old Stables ★★★★
Self Catering
Contact: Mr & Mrs Alan Cutter
t (0191) 388 7088
e staydurham@talktalk.net
w staydurham.co.uk

Plawsworth Hall Farm
★★★★ *Self Catering*
Contact: Mr Harry Johnson
t (0191) 371 0251
e plawsworth@aol.com
w plawsworth.com

CHILLINGHAM
Northumberland

Chillingham Castle
★★-★★★ *Self Catering*
Contact: Mrs Val Day
t (01668) 215359
e enquiries@chillingham-castle.com

CHIPPING
Lancashire

The Bolt Hole
Rating Applied For
Self Catering
Contact: Hazel
Cartere oceans.ah@btinternet.com
w theboltholecottage.co.uk

Fell View ★★★★
Self Catering
t (01995) 661160
e info@fellviewchipping.co.uk
w fellviewchipping.co.uk

Judd Holmes Barn ★★★★
Self Catering
Contact: Mrs Roxana Openshaw
t (01995) 61655
e info@juddholmes.co.uk
w juddholmes.co.uk

Pale Farm Cottages ★★★★
Self Catering
Contact: Mrs Lynn Ollerton
t (01772) 783082
e info@palefarmcottages.co.uk
w palefarmcottages.co.uk

Rakefoot Barn, Chaigley
★★★-★★★★ *Self Catering*
Contact: Mrs Pat Gifford
t (01995) 61332
e info@rakefootfarm.co.uk

The Waterwheel ★★★★
Self Catering
Contact: Mr Wales
t (01756) 700570
e info@holidaycotts.co.uk
w holidaycotts.co.uk

Wolfen Mill Country Retreats ★★★★-★★★★★
Self Catering
Contact: Mr Michael Lawson
t (01995) 61574
e information@wolfenmill.co.uk
w wolfenmill.co.uk

CHOP GATE
North Yorkshire

Broadfields Cottage ★★★★
Self Catering
Contact: Mrs Judith Staples
t (01642) 778384
e wkstaples@broadfields.orangehome.co.uk

Lavrock Hall Farmhouse Cottage ★★★ *Self Catering*
Contact: Jane Brack
t (01439) 798275
e info@lavrockhall.co.uk
w lavrockhall.co.uk

CHRISTON BANK
Northumberland

Rock Mill Cottage and Croft Cottage ★★★★-★★★★★
Self Catering
Contact: Mr & Mrs Jeremy & Elaine Holt
t 07714 896834
e jeremyholt@hotmail.co.uk
w rockmillholidayhomes.co.uk

CHURCHTOWN
Merseyside

Mews Cottage ★★
Self Catering
t (01704) 227222

CLAPHAM
North Yorkshire

The Old Stable ★★★★
Self Catering
Contact: Michael & Gillian Fell
t (01524) 251331
e gill@coppyhouse.co.uk
w coppyhouse.co.uk

Primrose Cottage
Rating Applied For
Self Catering
Contact: Mr Ian Beardsworthe susan.beardsworth@lineone.net

CLAPPERSGATE
Cumbria

The Clock ★★★★
Self Catering
Lakelovers
t (015394) 88855
e bookings@lakelovers.co.uk
w lakelovers.co.uk

Crag Head Cottage
★★★★★ *Self Catering*
Lakelovers
t (015394) 88855
e bookings@lakelovers.co.uk
w lakelovers.co.uk

Dove Cot ★★★★
Self Catering
Cumbrian Cottages
t (01228) 599960
e enquiries@cumbrian-cottages.co.uk
w cumbrian-cottages.co.uk

Ivy Cottage
Rating Applied For
Self Catering
Lakelovers
t (015394) 88855
e bookings@lakelovers.co.uk
w lakelovers.co.uk

The Mounting Steps ★★★★
Self Catering
Lakelovers
t (015394) 88855
e bookings@lakelovers.co.uk
w lakelovers.co.uk

The Old Dairy ★★★
Self Catering
Lakelovers
t (015394) 88855
e bookings@lakelovers.co.uk
w lakelovers.co.uk

The Pavilion ★★★★
Self Catering
Cumbrian Cottages
t (01228) 599960
e enquiries@cumbrian-cottages.co.uk
w cumbrian-cottages.co.uk

Players Hide ★★★
Self Catering
Lakelovers
t (015394) 88855
e bookings@lakelovers.co.uk
w lakelovers.co.uk

Todd Crag House ★★★★
Self Catering
Lakelovers
t (015394) 88855
e bookings@lakelovers.co.uk
w lakelovers.co.uk

CLITHEROE
Lancashire

Brownhills Cottage
★★★★★ *Self Catering*
t (01200) 420101
e info@holidaycotts.co.uk
w brownhillscottages.co.uk/

Chestnut Cottage ★★★★
Self Catering
t (01200) 440400
w holidaycotts.co.uk

Five Fells Cottage ★★★
Self Catering
Contact: Mr Roland Hailwood
t (01200) 424240
e roland.hailwood@talk21.com

Harrop Fold Cottages, Harrop Fold ★★★-★★★★
Self Catering
Contact: Mr Frank Robinson
t (01200) 447665
e robinsonharrop@aol.com
w cottagesdirect.com

Higher Gills Farm ★★★★
Self Catering
Contact: Mrs Freda Pilkington
t (01200) 445370
e pilko@highergills.co.uk
w highergills.co.uk

Hunters Rest ★★★★
Self Catering
Contact: Mrs Mary Kay
t (01254) 826304
e thekays@greengore.fsbusiness.co.uk
w huntersrestcottage.co.uk

Hydes Farm Holiday Cottages ★★★ *Self Catering*
Contact: Mrs Howard
t (01200) 446353

Saetr Cottage ★★★
Self Catering
Contact: Mrs Victoria Wood
t (01200) 447600
e victoriawood@supernet.com

Selborne Bungalow ★★★★
Self Catering
Contact: Mr Peter Hardwick
t (01200) 425157
e pbhardwick@aol.com

Weavers Cottage, West Bradford ★★★ *Self Catering*
Contact: Mr & Mrs Andrew & Susan Mackenzie
t (01200) 443122 & 07709 923715
e rafmack@hotmail.com

CLOUGHTON
North Yorkshire

Gowland Farm Holiday Cottages ★★★★
Self Catering
Contact: F J Bull
t (01723) 870924
w gowlandfarm.co.uk

Manor House ★★★
Self Catering
Contact: Mr JP Lawson
t (01723) 870455
e mrsdoreenlawson@yahoo.co.uk
w homely-holidayhomes.co.uk

'Oscar' at Station House
★★★★ *Self Catering*
Contact: Mr & Mrs Steve & Barbara Hargreaves
t (01723) 870896
e cloughtonstation@yahoo.co.uk
w cloughtonstation.co.uk

Whitby Cottages and Apartments
★★★-★★★★★
Self Catering
t (01723) 871028
w whitbycottages.com

COANWOOD
Northumberland

Mill Hill Farmhouse ★★★
Self Catering
Contact: Mrs Stephanie Wigham
t (01434) 320256
e millhill@fsmail.net
w cottageguide.co.uk/millhill

COCKERHAM
Lancashire

Near Moss Farm Holidays
★★★ *Self Catering*
t (01253) 790504
e enquiry@nearmossfarm.co.uk
w nearmossfarm.co.uk

Patty's Farm Barn ★★★★
Self Catering
Contact: Mr Christopher Parry
t (01524) 751285
e farm@pattysbarn.co.uk
w pattysfarm.co.uk

COCKERMOUTH
Cumbria

37 Kirkgate ★★★
Self Catering
Contact: Nelson & Val Chicken
39 Kirkgate
t (01900) 823236
e valandnelson@btopenworld.com
w 37kirkgate.com

Berrymeade ★★★
Self Catering
Cumbrian Cottages
t (01228) 599960
e enquiries@cumbrian-cottages.co.uk
w cumbrian-cottages.co.uk

Bridge Cottage ★★★
Self Catering
Cumbrian Cottages
t (01228) 599960
e enquiries@cumbrian-cottages.co.uk
w cumbrian-cottages.co.uk

Chestnut Cottage ★★★
Self Catering
Cumbrian Cottages
t (01228) 599960
e enquiries@cumbrian-cottages.co.uk
w cumbrian-cottages.co.uk

Church View ★★★
Self Catering
Cumbrian Cottages
t (01228) 599960
e enquiries@cumbrian-cottages.co.uk
w cumbrian-cottages.co.uk

Corner Cottage ★★★
Self Catering
Contact: Susan Hannah
W. S & S Hannah
t (01900) 822480
e suehannah@limelighting.demon.co.uk
w cottageguide.co.uk/greatbroughton

Corner House ★★★
Self Catering
Cumbrian Cottages
t (01228) 599960
e enquiries@cumbrian-cottages.co.uk
w cumbrian-cottages.co.uk

Double Dux ★★★★
Self Catering
Cumbrian Cottages
t (01228) 599960
e enquiries@cumbrian-cottages.co.uk
w cumbrian-cottages.co.uk

Fellbeck House ★★★★
Self Catering
Cumbrian Cottages
t (01228) 599960
e enquiries@cumbrian-cottages.co.uk
w cumbrian-cottages.co.uk

Garden Cottage ★★★
Self Catering
Contact: Colin Wornham
t (01900) 823531
e wornham2@aol.com
w lakesnw.co.uk/gardencottage

Ghyll Yeat ★★★★
Self Catering
Contact: Anne Haworth
t (017687) 80321
e peter_anneghyllyeat@lineone.net
w ghyllyeat.co.uk

Highside Cottage ★★★★
Self Catering
Cumbrian Cottages
t (01228) 599960
e enquiries@cumbrian-cottages.co.uk
w cumbrian-cottages.co.uk

Jenkin Cottage ★★★★
Self Catering
Contact: Margaret Teasdale
t (017687) 76387
e janet@sheepsnest.demon.co.uk
w jenkinfarm.co.uk

Low Hall Cottage ★★★★
Self Catering
Cumbrian Cottages
t (01228) 599960
e enquiries@cumbrian-cottages.co.uk
w cumbrian-cottages.co.uk

Moorside ★★★ *Self Catering*
Cumbrian Cottages
t (01228) 599960
e enquiries@cumbrian-cottages.co.uk
w cumbrian-cottages.co.uk

Packhorse Cottage ★★★★
Self Catering
Cumbrian Cottages
t (01228) 599960
e enquiries@cumbrian-cottages.co.uk
w cumbrian-cottages.co.uk

Southwaite Mill Cottages
★★★★ *Self Catering*
Contact: David & Noreen Warner
Southwaite Holidays Ltd
t (01900) 827270
e davidrwarner@hotmail.com

The Stables, Dean ★★★
Self Catering
Contact: Veronica Roper
Sunnyside
t (01254) 852027 & 07901 913812
e veronica@vroper.fsnet.co.uk
w vholidays.moonfruit.com

Stoneygate Studio ★★★★
Self Catering
Contact: Dr & Mrs Pearson
t (01900) 823595
e g.w.pearson@sky.com

Worth Cottage ★★★
Self Catering
Cumbrian Cottages
t (01228) 599960
e enquiries@cumbrian-cottages.co.uk
w cumbrian-cottages.co.uk

COCKFIELD
Durham

Daisy Cottage ★★★★
Self Catering
Contact: Mrs Jill Pegram
t (01388) 710636
e info@daisyholidaycottage.co.uk
w daisyholidaycottage.co.uk

New Cottage ★★★
Self Catering
Contact: Mrs Margaret Partridge
t (01388) 718567
e margandpatpartridge@tiscali.co.uk

Stonecroft and Swallows Nest ★★★★ *Self Catering*
Contact: Mrs Alison Tallentire
Low Lands Farm
t (01388) 718251
e info@farmholidaysuk.com
w farmholidaysuk.com

COLD KIRBY
North Yorkshire

The Cottage ★★★
Self Catering
Contact: Mrs Blythe
t (01845) 597253

COLNE
Lancashire

Heathcliff Cottage ★★★★
Self Catering
Contact: Ms Val Bennett
t (01282) 869914
e roymonk@tiscali.co.uk
w heathcliffcottage.co.uk

White Syke Farm ★★★
Self Catering
Contact: Mrs Elizabeth Haythornthwaite
t (01282) 815731

COLTHOUSE
Cumbria

The Cragg
Rating Applied For
Self Catering
Lakelovers
t (015394) 88855
e bookings@lakelovers.co.uk
w lakelovers.co.uk

Croft Head ★★★
Self Catering
Cumbrian Cottages
t (01228) 599960
e enquiries@cumbrian-cottages.co.uk
w cumbrian-cottages.co.uk

COLTON
Cumbria

Bracken Ground ★★★★
Self Catering
Cumbrian Cottages
t (01228) 599960
e enquiries@cumbrian-cottages.co.uk
w cumbrian-cottages.co.uk

Forest Field ★★★★
Self Catering
Contact: Mary Postle
t (01229) 861685
e info@forest-field.co.uk
w forest-field.co.uk

CONGLETON
Cheshire

Broomfield Barns ★★
Self Catering
Contact: Ms Anita Lockett
t (01260) 224581
w broomfieldbarns.com

The Coach House at Acorn Cottages ★★★ *Self Catering*
Contact: Mr & Mrs Mark Bullock
t (01260) 223388
e lettings@acorncottages-england.co.uk
w acorncottages-england.co.uk/

Heritage Wharf Bungalow, Scholar Green (Near Congleton) ★★★★
Self Catering
Contact: Mr Mike Dowse
t (01782) 785700
e heritage@sherbornewharf.co.uk
w heritagenarrowboats.co.uk/

CONISBROUGH
South Yorkshire

Cosy Terrace Cottage ★★
Self Catering
Contact: John Perrin
t (01709) 580612
e john@cosyterrace.co.uk
w cosyterrace.fsnet.co.uk

CONISTON
Cumbria

1 and 2 Ash Gill Cottages, Torver ★★★★ *Self Catering*
Contact: Dorothy Cowburn
Lyndene
t (01772) 612832

1 Far End Cottages ★★★
Self Catering
Contact: Jonathan Batho
Cottagescumbria.com
t (015394) 41680
e a.batho@virgin.net
w cottagescumbria.com

Bank Top ★★★★
Self Catering
The Coppermines & Coniston Lakes Cottages
t (015394) 41765
w coppermines.co.uk

Banks Ghyll Cottage ★★★★
Self Catering
The Coppermines & Coniston Lakes Cottages
t (015394) 41765
w coppermines.co.uk

Beck Yeat Cottage ★★★
Self Catering
The Coppermines & Coniston Lakes Cottages
t (015394) 41765
w coppermines.co.uk

Beech Grove ★★★★
Self Catering
t (015394) 41319

Bluebell Cottage ★★★★
Self Catering
Cumbrian Cottages
t (01228) 599960
e enquiries@cumbrian-cottages.co.uk
w cumbrian-cottages.co.uk

Bramble Cottage ★★★★
Self Catering
The Coppermines & Coniston Lakes Cottages
t (015394) 41765
w coppermines.co.uk

The Bridge Cottages ★★★★
Self Catering
The Coppermines & Coniston Lakes Cottages
t (015394) 41765
w coppermines.co.uk

Bridge End Cottage ★★★★
Self Catering
The Coppermines & Coniston Lakes Cottages
t (015394) 41765
w coppermines.co.uk

Brook Cottage ★★★
Self Catering
The Coppermines & Coniston Lakes Cottages
t (015394) 41765
w coppermines.co.uk

Brow Close Cottage ★★★
Self Catering
The Coppermines & Coniston Lakes Cottages
t (015394) 41765
w coppermines.co.uk

Campbell Apartment ★★★★ *Self Catering*
Lakeland Cottage Comapny
t (015395) 38180
e john@lakelandcottageco.com
w lakelandcottageco.com

Chapel Bank House ★★★★
Self Catering
The Coppermines & Coniston Lakes Cottages
t (015394) 41765
w coppermines.co.uk

Cherry Tree Cottage ★★★★
Self Catering
The Coppermines & Coniston Lakes Cottages
t (015394) 41765
w coppermines.co.uk

Coniston Country Cottages ★★★-★★★★★ *Self Catering*
Contact: Steve Abbott
t (015394) 41114
e enquiry@conistoncottages.co.uk
w conistoncottages.co.uk

Coniston Holidays ★★★
Self Catering
Contact: Jean Johnson
t (015394) 41319
e enquiries@conistonholidays.co.uk
w conistonholidays.co.uk

Coniston View ★★★
Self Catering
Cumbrian Cottages
t (01228) 599960
e enquiries@cumbrian-cottages.co.uk
w cumbrian-cottages.co.uk

The Coppermines Mountain Cottages ★★★-★★★★★
Self Catering
The Coppermines & Coniston Lakes Cottages
t (015394) 41765
w coppermines.co.uk

The Cottage ★★★
Self Catering
Lakeland Cottage Comapny
t (015395) 38180
e john@lakelandcottageco.com
w lakelandcottageco.com

Curdle Dub ★★ *Self Catering*
Lakelovers
t (015394) 88855
e bookings@lakelovers.co.uk
w lakelovers.co.uk

The Dairy ★★★★★
Self Catering
Lakeland Cottage Comapny
t (015395) 38180
e john@lakelandcottageco.com
w lakelandcottageco.com

Damson Cottage ★★★★
Self Catering
Cumbrian Cottages
t (01228) 599960
e enquiries@cumbrian-cottages.co.uk
w cumbrian-cottages.co.uk

Fair Snape Cottage ★★★★
Self Catering
The Coppermines & Coniston Lakes Cottages
t (015394) 41765
w coppermines.co.uk

Fernlea ★★★ *Self Catering*
Cumbrian Cottages
t (01228) 599960
e enquiries@cumbrian-cottages.co.uk
w cumbrian-cottages.co.uk

Fisherbeck Fold & Fisherbeck Nest ★★★
Self Catering
Cumbrian Cottages
t (01228) 599960
e enquiries@cumbrian-cottages.co.uk
w cumbrian-cottages.co.uk

Fisherbeck Nest ★★★
Self Catering
Cumbrian Cottages
t (01228) 599960
e enquiries@cumbrian-cottages.co.uk
w cumbrian-cottages.co.uk

Forest Cottage ★★★★
Self Catering
Lakeland Cottage Comapny
t (015395) 38180
e john@lakelandcottageco.com
w lakelandcottageco.com

Foxgloves ★★★ *Self Catering*
Lakelovers
t (015394) 88855
e bookings@lakelovers.co.uk
w lakelovers.co.uk

Gable Cottage ★★★
Self Catering
The Coppermines & Coniston Lakes Cottages
t (015394) 41765
w coppermines.co.uk

Gable End ★★★★
Self Catering
Lakeland Cottage Comapny
t (015395) 38180
e john@lakelandcottageco.com
w lakelandcottageco.com

The Gallery ★★★
Self Catering
The Coppermines & Coniston Lakes Cottages
t (015394) 41765
w coppermines.co.uk

Garden House ★★★★
Self Catering
Lakeland Cottage Comapny
t (015395) 38180
e john@lakelandcottageco.com
w lakelandcottageco.com

Gate House ★★★★
Self Catering
The Coppermines & Coniston Lakes Cottages
t (015394) 41765
w coppermines.co.uk

Grange Cottage ★★★
Self Catering
The Coppermines & Coniston Lakes Cottages
t (015394) 41765
w coppermines.co.uk

Grizedale ★★★★
Self Catering
Lakeland Cottage Comapny
t (015395) 38180
e john@lakelandcottageco.com
w lakelandcottageco.com

Hay Barn ★★★ *Self Catering*
Lakelovers
t (015394) 88855
e bookings@lakelovers.co.uk
w lakelovers.co.uk

Hay Barn Cottage & Bracken Barn Cottage ★★★
Self Catering
Lakelovers
t (015394) 88855
e bookings@lakelovers.co.uk
w lakelovers.co.uk

Hazel Cottage ★★★★
Self Catering
The Coppermines & Coniston Lakes Cottages
t (015394) 41765
w coppermines.co.uk

Heathwaite Farm Cottage
★★★ *Self Catering*
Lakeland Cottage Comapny
t (015395) 38180
e john@lakelandcottageco.com
w lakelandcottageco.com

Heathwaite Farmhouse
★★★★ *Self Catering*
Lakeland Cottage Comapny
t (015395) 38180
e john@lakelandcottageco.com
w lakelandcottageco.com

Herdwick Brow ★★★★
Self Catering
The Coppermines & Coniston Lakes Cottages
t (015394) 41765
w coppermines.co.uk

High Arnside ★★★
Self Catering
Contact: Jan Meredith
t (015394) 32261
e jmeredith@beeb.net
w higharnsidefarm.co.uk

Hollin Bank Barn ★★★
Self Catering
The Coppermines & Coniston Lakes Cottages
t (015394) 41765
w coppermines.co.uk

How Head Cottages ★★★
Self Catering
Contact: Mr & Mrs Holland
t (015394) 41594
e howhead@lineone.net
w howheadcottages.co.uk

Howhead ★★★★
Self Catering
Lakeland Cottage Comapny
t (015395) 38180
e john@lakelandcottageco.com
w lakelandcottageco.com

Kitty Crag
Rating Applied For
Self Catering
Lakelovers
t (015394) 88855
e bookings@lakelovers.co.uk
w lakelovers.co.uk

Low Howe ★★★★
Self Catering
The Coppermines & Coniston Lakes Cottages
t (015394) 41765
w coppermines.co.uk

Lower Barn ★★★
Self Catering
Lakeland Cottage Comapny
t (015395) 38180
e john@lakelandcottageco.com
w lakelandcottageco.com

Middlefield Cottage ★★★★
Self Catering
The Coppermines & Coniston Lakes Cottages
t (015394) 41765
w coppermines.co.uk

No 4 Coppermines Cottages
★★★ *Self Catering*
The Coppermines & Coniston Lakes Cottages
t (015394) 41765
w coppermines.co.uk

No1 Silverbank ★★★★★
Self Catering
Contact: Fay Gorman Hext
No 1 Silverbank
t (020) 7704 9071
e info@no1silverbank.com
w no1silverbank.com

The Old Police House
Rating Applied For
Self Catering
Lakelovers
t (015394) 88855
e bookings@lakelovers.co.uk
w lakelovers.co.uk

Old View ★★★ *Self Catering*
Cumbrian Cottages
t (01228) 599960
e enquiries@cumbrian-cottages.co.uk
w cumbrian-cottages.co.uk

One to Four Dixon Ground
★★★–★★★★ *Self Catering*
The Coppermines & Coniston Lakes Cottages
t (015394) 41765
w coppermines.co.uk

Poppy Cottage ★★★
Self Catering
The Coppermines & Coniston Lakes Cottages
t (015394) 41765
w coppermines.co.uk

Potters Wheel ★★★★
Self Catering
Cumbrian Cottages
t (01228) 599960
e enquiries@cumbrian-cottages.co.uk
w cumbrian-cottages.co.uk

Ramblers Rest ★★★★
Self Catering
Cumbrian Cottages
t (01228) 599960
e enquiries@cumbrian-cottages.co.uk
w cumbrian-cottages.co.uk

Rascal Howe Cottage ★★★
Self Catering
Cumbrian Cottages
t (01228) 599960
e enquiries@cumbrian-cottages.co.uk
w cumbrian-cottages.co.uk

Red Dell Cottage ★★★★
Self Catering
The Coppermines & Coniston Lakes Cottages
t (015394) 41765
w coppermines.co.uk

River Cottage ★★★
Self Catering
The Coppermines & Coniston Lakes Cottages
t (015394) 41765
w coppermines.co.uk

Rivington ★★★ *Self Catering*
Cumbrian Cottages
t (01228) 599960
e enquiries@cumbrian-cottages.co.uk
w cumbrian-cottages.co.uk

Rose Bank Cottage ★★★★
Self Catering
The Coppermines & Coniston Lakes Cottages
t (015394) 41765
w coppermines.co.uk

Rowan Trees ★★★★
Self Catering
The Coppermines & Coniston Lakes Cottages
t (015394) 41765
w coppermines.co.uk

Ruskin Apartment ★★★★
Self Catering
Lakeland Cottage Comapny
t (015395) 38180
e john@lakelandcottageco.com
w lakelandcottageco.com

Shelt Gill ★★★ *Self Catering*
Contact: Rosalind Dean
t 0845 009 3998
e holiday@sheltgill.co.uk
w sheltgill.co.uk

The Shieling ★★★
Self Catering
Lakelovers
t (015394) 88855
e bookings@lakelovers.co.uk
w lakelovers.co.uk

Sunbeam Cottage ★★★
Self Catering
Lakelovers
t (015394) 88855
e bookings@lakelovers.co.uk
w lakelovers.co.uk

Sunny Bank Farm ★★★★
Self Catering
Contact: Daphne Libby
t (01228) 515639
e daphne@sunnybankfarm.co.uk
w sunnybankfarm.co.uk

Sunny Brae ★★★
Self Catering
The Coppermines & Coniston Lakes Cottages
t (015394) 41765
w coppermines.co.uk

Swallow Nest 2 ★★★★
Self Catering
Cumbrian Cottages
t (01228) 599960
e enquiries@cumbrian-cottages.co.uk
w cumbrian-cottages.co.uk

Swallows Nest ★★★★
Self Catering
Cumbrian Cottages
t (01228) 599960
e enquiries@cumbrian-cottages.co.uk
w cumbrian-cottages.co.uk

Tanderra ★★★★
Self Catering
Lakeland Cottage Comapny
t (015395) 38180
e john@lakelandcottageco.com
w lakelandcottageco.com

Tent Lodge Cottage ★★★★
Self Catering
Lakeland Cottage Comapny
t (015395) 38180
e john@lakelandcottageco.com
w lakelandcottageco.com

Three Springs ★★★
Self Catering
Lakeland Cottage Comapny
t (015395) 38180
e john@lakelandcottageco.com
w lakelandcottageco.com

Thurston House & Thurston View ★★–★★★★
Self Catering
Contact: Alan Jefferson
t (01204) 419261
e alan@jefferson99.freeserve.co.uk
w thurstonhouseconiston.co.uk

Tilberthwaite Farm Cottage
★★★ *Self Catering*
Contact: Mrs D Wilkinson
t (015394) 37281
e tilberthwaite.farm@lineone.net
w tilberthwaitefarmcottage.com

Tinkler Beck Cottage
★★★★ *Self Catering*
Lakeland Cottage Comapny
t (015395) 38180
e john@lakelandcottageco.com
w lakelandcottageco.com

Tinkler Beck Farm ★★★★★
Self Catering
Lakeland Cottage Comapny
t (015395) 38180
e john@lakelandcottageco.com
w lakelandcottageco.com

Townson Ground House
★★★★ *Self Catering*
Lakeland Cottage Comapny
t (015395) 38180
e john@lakelandcottageco.com
w lakelandcottageco.com

Wetherlam ★★★
Self Catering
Lakeland Cottage Comapny
t (015395) 38180
e john@lakelandcottageco.com
w lakelandcottageco.com

Willow Tree Cottage ★★★
Self Catering
The Coppermines & Coniston Lakes Cottages
t (015394) 41765
w coppermines.co.uk

Windrush ★★★★
Self Catering
Lakeland Cottage Comapny
t (015395) 38180
e john@lakelandcottageco.com
w lakelandcottageco.com

Yewdale Cottage ★★★
Self Catering
Cumbrian Cottages
t (01228) 599960
e enquiries@cumbrian-cottages.co.uk
w cumbrian-cottages.co.uk

CORBRIDGE Northumberland

April Cottage ★★★★
Self Catering
Contact: Mrs Kate Dean
21 Woodland Close
t (01625) 861718
e peterandkatedean@btopenworld.com
w aprilcottagecorbridge.co.uk

Camellia Cottage ★★★★
Self Catering
Northumbrian Cottages
t (01228) 599950
e sheena@cumbrian-cottages.co.uk
w northumbrian-cottages.info

Garden Rooms at Dilston House ★★★★★
Self Catering
Contact: Mr Roger McKechnie
t (01434) 633653
e rogermckechnie@yahoo.co.uk
w thegardenroomsdilston.co.uk

The Hayes ★★★
Self Catering
Contact: Mrs Monica Matthews
t (01434) 632010
e camon@surfree.co.uk
w hayes-corbridge.co.uk

Hill View Cottage ★★★
Self Catering
Contact: Mrs Judith Dawson
t (0191) 416 7749
e pdm313@hotmail.co.uk
w hillview-corbridge.com

Lance-Surtees Cottage, Colwell ★★★★ *Self Catering*
Contact: Miss Dorothea Nelson
t (01884) 841320

Nosbor Cottage ★★★
Self Catering
Contact: Mrs Veronica Robson
t (01661) 871135
e nosboruk@yahoo.co.uk
w nosbor.co.uk

Oswald Cottage ★★★★
Self Catering
Contact: Mrs Hannah Harriman
t (01661) 852909
e hannahharriman@btinternet.com

Wallhouses South Farm Cottage ★★★★ *Self Catering*
Contact: Mrs Eileen Lymburn
t (01434) 672388
e loraip@aol.com

West Fell Cottage ★★★
Self Catering
Contact: Mrs Joan Smith
t (01434) 632044
e westfell@hotmail.co.uk

CORNHILL-ON-TWEED Northumberland

Melkington Lodge ★★★★★
Self Catering
Contact: Mrs Veronica Barber
t (01890) 882313
e veronicabarber@btconnect.com
w melkington.co.uk

Orchard Cottage ★★★★
Self Catering
Contact: Mrs Lucy Carroll
t (01890) 882177
e fish@till-fishing.co.uk
w till-fishing.co.uk

The Stables ★★★
Self Catering
t (01890) 882390
w thestables.cornhill.btinternet.co.uk/

Tillmouth Cottage ★★★★
Self Catering
Contact: Mrs J A Binnie
t (01289) 382482

Tithe Hill Holiday Cottages
★★★ *Self Catering*
Contact: Mrs Diana Tweedie
t (01890) 850286
e info@tithehill.co.uk
w tithehill.co.uk

West Learmouth Cottages
★★★★ *Self Catering*
Contact: Mrs Jasmin Moore
t (01665) 579425
e wwwhazelgrahamslaw@yahoo.co.uk
w westlearmouthcottages.co.uk

CORNRIGGS Durham

Cornriggs Cottages, Cowshill in Weardale
★★★★★ *Self Catering*
Contact: Mr & Mrs Harry and Janet Elliott
t (01388) 537600 & 07818 843159
e cornriggsfarm@btconnect.com
w britnett.net/lowcornriggsfarm

COTHERSTONE Durham

Brignall Mill ★★★★
Self Catering
Contact: Mr & Mrs William & Jane Weston
t (01833) 637726
e weston402@btinternet.com
w brignallmill.co.uk

Red Lion Cottage ★★★★★
Self Catering
Contact: Mr Chris Tarpey
t (01833) 650087
e one@eastbriscoe.co.uk
w redlioncottage.co.uk

Thwaite Hall ★★★
Self Catering
Contact: Mrs Audrey Wickham
t (0191) 529 3793
e keith@gate7.co.uk
w thwaitehall.com

COTTINGHAM East Riding of Yorkshire

Fairways Lodges
Rating Applied For
Self Catering
Contact: Mr David Hanson
t (01482) 846030
e david.hanson@cottinghamparks.co.uk
w cottinghamparks.co.uk

COWAN HEAD Cumbria

River View Cottage ★★★
Self Catering
Cumbrian Cottages
t (01228) 599960
e enquiries@cumbrian-cottages.co.uk
w cumbrian-cottages.co.uk

COWGILL Cumbria

Dent Station
Rating Applied For
Self Catering
Contact: Robin Hughes
t 07824 665266
w dentstation.co.uk

CRACKENTHORPE Cumbria

Meadow Ing ★★★
Self Catering
Cumbrian Cottages
t (01228) 599960
e enquiries@cumbrian-cottages.co.uk
w cumbrian-cottages.co.uk

CRAGG VALE West Yorkshire

Robin Hood Cottage ★★★
Self Catering
Contact: Elizabeth Woznicki
t 07977 459913
e liz@robinhoodcottage.co.uk
w robinhoodcottage.co.uk

CRAMLINGTON Northumberland

Burradon Farm Houses & Cottages ★★★★
Self Catering
Contact: Mrs Judith Younger
t (0191) 268 3203
e judy@burradonfarm.co.uk
w burradonfarm.co.uk

CRASTER Northumberland

Craster Pine Lodges ★★★★
Self Catering
Contact: Mr & Mrs Michael & Fyona Robson
t (01665) 576286
e pinelodges@barkpots.co.uk
w crasterpinelodges.co.uk

Craster Tower Penthouse Apartment ★★★★
Self Catering
Contact: Mrs Fiona Craster
t (01665) 576674
e stay@crastertower.co.uk
w crastertower.co.uk

Fisherman's Cottage ★★★
Self Catering
Northumberland Cottages
t (01665) 589434
e enquiries@northumberlandcottages.com
w northumberlandcottages.co.uk

Harbour Master's House
★★★★★ *Self Catering*
Northumberland Coastal Retreats
t (0191) 285 1272
e info@coastalretreats.co.uk
w coastalretreats.co.uk

Harbourside House, Craster and Low Newton ★★★★
Self Catering
Contact: Mr Geoffrey Brewis-Levie
t (01638) 604304
e brewislevie@aol.com

Hideaway Cottage ★★★★
Self Catering
Northumberland Cottages
t (01665) 589434
e enquiries@northumberlandcottages.com
w northumberlandcottages.co.uk

Rock Ville ★★★★
Self Catering
Contact: Mr & Mrs Michael & Fyona Robson
t (01665) 576286
e pinelodges@barkpots.co.uk
w rockvillecraster.co.uk

Rowan Cottage ★★★★
Self Catering
Northumberland Cottages
t (01665) 589434
e enquiries@northumberlandcottages.com
w northumberlandcottages.co.uk

Seahaven ★★★★
Self Catering
Contact: Mrs Imrie
t (01665) 602275
e seahaven-craster@hotmail.co.uk

CREWE
Cheshire

Bank Farm Cottages ★★★
Self Catering
Contact: Mrs Ann Vaughan
t (01270) 841809

CROOK
Cumbria

Brackenrigg ★★★
Self Catering
Cumbrian Cottages
t (01228) 599960
e enquiries@cumbrian-cottages.co.uk
w cumbrian-cottages.co.uk

Bronte Cottage ★★★
Self Catering
Cumbrian Cottages
t (01228) 599960
e enquiries@cumbrian-cottages.co.uk
w cumbrian-cottages.co.uk

The Hideaway ★★★
Self Catering
Lakelovers
t (015394) 88855
e bookings@lakelovers.co.uk
w lakelovers.co.uk

Lake District Disabled Holidays ★★★★
Self Catering
Contact: Stuart & Jane Higham
t (015394) 47421
w lakedistrictdisabledholidays.co.uk

The Old Coachouse
Rating Applied For
Self Catering
Lakelovers
t (015394) 88855
e bookings@lakelovers.co.uk
w lakelovers.co.uk

Outrun Nook ★★★★
Self Catering
Lakelovers
t (015394) 88855
e bookings@lakelovers.co.uk
w lakelovers.co.uk

The Sanctuary
Rating Applied For
Self Catering
Lakelovers
t (015394) 88855
e bookings@lakelovers.co.uk
w lakelovers.co.uk

Sunny Point Cottage
Rating Applied For
Self Catering
Lakelovers
t (015394) 88855
e bookings@lakelovers.co.uk
w lakelovers.co.uk

CROOKHAM
Northumberland

Askew Cottage ★★★★
Self Catering
Contact: Mrs Heather Pentland
t (01890) 820201
e hjpentland@waitrose.com

CROPTON
North Yorkshire

2 Corner Cottages ★★★
Self Catering
Contact: Mrs Jane Paterson
t (01751) 417562
e jpat.cropton@yahoo.co.uk

Beckhouse Cottages, Cropton ★★★★
Self Catering
Contact: Pam Smith
t (01751) 417235
e beckhousecottages@hotmail.com
w beckhousecottages.co.uk

High Farm Holiday Cottages ★★★★ *Self Catering*
Contact: Mrs Ruth Feaster
t (01751) 417461
e highfarmcropton@aol.com
w hhml.com/cottages/highfarmcropton.htm

Laura's Cottage
Rating Applied For
Self Catering
Contact: Ann Eddon
t (01751) 417262

CROSBY
Cumbria

The Coach House Flat ★★★★ *Self Catering*
Contact: Mr Mossom
t 07518 368441
e solwayvilla@hotmail.co.uk
w solwayvilla.com

Galloway Cottage ★★★
Self Catering
Cumbrian Cottages
t (01228) 599960
e enquiries@cumbrian-cottages.co.uk
w cumbrian-cottages.co.uk

CROSTHWAITE
Cumbria

6 Starnthwaite Ghyll ★★★★
Self Catering
Lakeland Cottage Comapny
t (015395) 38180
e john@lakelandcottageco.com
w lakelandcottageco.com

Acorn Lodge ★★★★
Self Catering
Cumbrian Cottages
t (01228) 599960
e enquiries@cumbrian-cottages.co.uk
w cumbrian-cottages.co.uk

Bega ★★★ *Self Catering*
Cumbrian Cottages
t (01228) 599960
e enquiries@cumbrian-cottages.co.uk
w cumbrian-cottages.co.uk

Bewick Lodge ★★★★
Self Catering
Cumbrian Cottages
t (01228) 599960
e enquiries@cumbrian-cottages.co.uk
w cumbrian-cottages.co.uk

Bobbin Mill Cottage ★★★★
Self Catering
Contact: Roger Green
t (015395) 68057
e rogergreen@enjoythelakes.com
w enjoythelakes.com

Corner Cottage ★★★★
Self Catering
Contact: Mary Smith
t (01744) 894196
e mary@sgcornercottage.co.uk
w sgcornercottage.co.uk

Damson Barn ★★★★
Self Catering
Cumbrian Cottages
t (01228) 599960
e enquiries@cumbrian-cottages.co.uk
w cumbrian-cottages.co.uk

Damson Fold ★★★★
Self Catering
Cumbrian Cottages
t (01228) 599960
e enquiries@cumbrian-cottages.co.uk
w cumbrian-cottages.co.uk

Ennerdale ★★★
Self Catering
Cumbrian Cottages
t (01228) 599960
e enquiries@cumbrian-cottages.co.uk
w cumbrian-cottages.co.uk

Gilpin View ★★★
Self Catering
Lakelovers
t (015394) 88855
e bookings@lakelovers.co.uk
w lakelovers.co.uk

Greenbank ★★★★
Self Catering
Contact: Jackie Gaskell
t (015395) 68598
e greenbank@nascr.net
w greenbank-cumbria.co.uk

Hill Cottage ★★★★
Self Catering
Cumbrian Cottages
t (01228) 599960
e enquiries@cumbrian-cottages.co.uk
w cumbrian-cottages.co.uk

Low Cartmell Fold ★★★
Self Catering
Cumbrian Cottages
t (01228) 599960
e enquiries@cumbrian-cottages.co.uk
w cumbrian-cottages.co.uk

Middlebank ★★★
Self Catering
Lakeland Cottage Comapny
t (015395) 38180
e john@lakelandcottageco.com
w lakelandcottageco.com

Top Bank ★★★ *Self Catering*
Lakeland Cottage Comapny
t (015395) 38180
e john@lakelandcottageco.com
w lakelandcottageco.com

Town End Cottage ★★★★
Self Catering
Contact: Brian Raine
t 07740 918380
e info@town-end-farm.co.uk
w town-end-farm.co.uk

CROSTON
Lancashire

Cockfight Barn ★★★★
Self Catering
Contact: Mr Martin Mcshane
t (01200) 420101
e info@redrosecottages.co.uk
w cockfightbarn.com

Yarrow Cottage ★★★★
Self Catering
Contact: Mrs Alison Brady
t (01772) 601190
e alison@bradyjh.fsnet.co.uk
w yarrowcottage.co.uk

CROW EDGE
South Yorkshire

Lazy Daisy's ★★★-★★★★
Self Catering
Contact: Sally Howe
t (01226) 763001
e daisyhillfarm@tiscali.co.uk
w lazydaisys.co.uk

CROWLEY
Cheshire

Fir Tree Barn Cottages ★★★★ *Self Catering*
Contact: Mr Mike Davies
t (01565) 777327
e info@firtreebarn.co.uk
w firtreebarn.co.uk

CUNSEY
Cumbria

The Barn ★★★ *Self Catering*
Lakelovers
t (015394) 88855
e bookings@lakelovers.co.uk
w lakelovers.co.uk

Deer Holm ★★★★
Self Catering
Lakeland Cottage Comapny
t (015395) 38180
e john@lakelandcottageco.com
w lakelandcottageco.com

High Cunsey ★★★★
Self Catering
Cumbrian Cottages
t (01228) 599960
e enquiries@cumbrian-cottages.co.uk
w cumbrian-cottages.co.uk

DACRE
Cumbria

Blaes Crag Cottage ★★★
Self Catering
Cumbrian Cottages
t (01228) 599960
e enquiries@cumbrian-cottages.co.uk
w cumbrian-cottages.co.uk

Dacre Cottage ★★★
Self Catering
Cumbrian Cottages
t (01228) 599960
e enquiries@cumbrian-cottages.co.uk
w cumbrian-cottages.co.uk

DACRE
North Yorkshire

Burns Farm ★★★
Self Catering
Contact: Allen & Catherine Rees
t (01423) 780217
e arees3@btinternet.com

DALSTON
Cumbria

Hall Hills ★★★★-★★★★★
Self Catering
Lakes Cottage Holidays
t (01228) 591555
e info@lakescottageholiday.co.uk
w lakescottageholiday.co.uk

DALTON
North Yorkshire

Hilltop Cottage ★★★★
Self Catering
Contact: Richard Farr
t (01833) 621234
e sue@sjfarr.freeserve.co.uk
w hilltopcottage.co.uk

Jasmine Cottage ★★★★
Self Catering
Contact: Lisa Winter
t 07904 421115
e m.winter@tesco.net

Keepers Cottage ★★★
Self Catering
Contact: Dorothy Lewis
t (01833) 621446
e dorothy.lewis@cottagesnorthyorkshire.co.uk

DALTON-ON-TEES
North Yorkshire

Pepperfield Cottage
Rating Applied For
Self Catering
Contact: Katie James
Grays Chartered Surveyors
t (01748) 829210
e katie.james@grays-cs.co.uk

DANBY
North Yorkshire

Ainthorpe Farm Cottage
★★★★ *Self Catering*
Contact: Sheila Hide
t (01287) 660358
w ainthorpefarmcottage.co.uk

Clitherbecks Farm, Danby
★★ *Self Catering*
Contact: Mrs Catherine Harland
t (01287) 660321
e nharland@clitherbecks.freeserve.co.uk
w clitherbecks.freeserve.co.uk

DARLINGTON
Tees Valley

63 Cumberland Street ★★★
Self Catering
Contact: Mrs Kathleen Reeve
t (01933) 387945
e barry.reeve1@ntlworld.com
w 63cumberlandstreet.co.uk

Pegasus Cottage ★★★
Self Catering
Contact: Mr & Mrs Stuart and Denise Chapman
t (01325) 722542
e stuart1948@msn.com
w pegasuscottage.co.uk

DEARHAM
Cumbria

Bendale Cottage ★★★★
Self Catering
Contact: Susan Harper
t (01900) 816763
e stay@bendalecottage.co.uk
w bendalecottage.co.uk

DEEPDALE
Cumbria

Willans ★★★ *Self Catering*
Contact: Kathleen Bentham
t (015396) 25285
e kathbentham@hotmail.com
w cottageguide.co.uk/willans

DELAMERE
Cheshire

Wicken Tree Farm
Rating Applied For
Self Catering
Contact: Mrs W J Appleton
t (01928) 788355
e ches@williamj99.freeserve.co.uk
w wickentreefarm.co.uk

DELPH
Greater Manchester

The Stables, Delph ★★★★
Self Catering
Contact: Mrs G Whipp
Sandbed Farm Cottage
t (01457) 871668
e gwyneth.whipp@btinternet.com
w saddleworthcottages.co.uk

DENHOLME
West Yorkshire

Blacksmiths Cottages (The Anvil) ★ *Self Catering*
Contact: Janet Nella Ackroyd
t (01274) 832850

DENSHAW
Greater Manchester

Cherry Blossom Cottage
★★★★ *Self Catering*
t (01457) 874369
w cherryclough.co.uk

Home Cottage ★★★
Self Catering
Contact: Mrs Hazel Billing
t (01457) 876527
e hazel_billi@hotmail.com

DENT
Cumbria

Buzzards Cottage ★★★★
Self Catering
Dales Holiday Cottages
t (01756) 790919
e info@dales-holiday-cottages.com
w dales-holiday-cottages.com

Clarks Cottage 4081 ★★★★
Self Catering
Dales Holiday Cottages
t (01756) 790919
e info@dales-holiday-cottages.com
w dales-holiday-cottages.com

Dragon Cottage ★★★★
Self Catering
Contact: Annette Clark
t (01785) 712386
e annetteclark43@aol.com
w dragoncottage.co.uk

Helm Byre ★★★
Self Catering
Cumbrian Cottages
t (01228) 599960
e enquiries@cumbrian-cottages.co.uk
w cumbrian-cottages.co.uk

Middleton's Cottage and Fountain Cottage, Dent
★★★ *Self Catering*
Contact: Mr & Mrs Ayers
t (01323) 870032
e candpayers@mistral.co.uk
w dentcottages.co.uk

Mire Garth ★★★
Self Catering
Contact: Jean Middleton
t (015396) 25235

Wilsey House ★★★
Self Catering
Contact: Joan Saunders
t (01487) 841556
e enquiries@wilsey.co.uk
w wilsey.co.uk

DISLEY
Cheshire

Plattwood Farm Cottage
★★★★ *Self Catering*
Contact: Mrs Emmot
t (01625) 872738
w plattwoodfarm.com

DOCKRAY
Cumbria

High Brow ★★★
Self Catering
Cumbrian Cottages
t (01228) 599960
e enquiries@cumbrian-cottages.co.uk
w cumbrian-cottages.co.uk

Lookin How ★★★★★
Self Catering
Cumbrian Cottages
t (01228) 599960
e enquiries@cumbrian-cottages.co.uk
w cumbrian-cottages.co.uk

DOLPHINHOLME
Lancashire

The Maisonette ★★★
Self Catering
Contact: Ms Donna Entwisle
t (01524) 792221

DONCASTER
South Yorkshire

Fishlake Mill
Rating Applied For
Self Catering
Contact: Graham Atha
t (01302) 841486
e info@fishlakemill.co.uk
w fishlake.co.uk

The Green Gable ★★★★
Self Catering
Contact: Trevor Smeaton
t (01302) 327782
e qjs@btconnect.com

DOVENBY
Cumbria

Sunnybrae Bungalow ★★★
Self Catering
Cumbrian Cottages
t (01228) 599960
e enquiries@cumbrian-cottages.co.uk
w cumbrian-cottages.co.uk

DOWNHAM
Lancashire

Stables Lodge Cottage ★★★
Self Catering
Contact: Mr & Mrs Loveridge
t (01200) 441242
e stableslodgecottage@yahoo.co.uk
w stableslodgecottagedownham.co.uk

DOWNHOLME
North Yorkshire

Coldstorms Farm ★★★
Self Catering
Contact: Diana Greenwood
t (01748) 822152

DOXFORD
Northumberland

Smugglers' Hide ★★★★★
Self Catering
Northumberland Coastal Retreats
t (0191) 285 1272
e info@coastalretreats.co.uk
w coastalretreats.co.uk

DRIFFIELD
East Riding of Yorkshire

Manor Farm Cottages, North Dalton ★★★ *Self Catering*
Contact: Antony & Jennie Byass
t (01377) 217324
e lanpulse@aol.com
w yorkshirewoldsholidaycottages.com

DRINGHOUSES
North Yorkshire

Mayfield ★★★★
Self Catering
Contact: Miss D Schofield
t (01904) 704571
e davidleslie@boltblue.com
w cottageholidaysonline.co.uk

DRUMBURGH
Cumbria

The Grange ★★★★
Self Catering
Contact: Sarah Hodgson
t (01228) 576551
e messrs.hodgson@tesco.net
w thegrangecottage.co.uk

DUFTON
Cumbria

Brow Farm Bed & Breakfast
★★★★ *Self Catering*
Contact: Mrs Wendy Swinbank
t (017683) 52865
e stay@browfarm.com
w browfarm.com

Holly Dene ★★★★
Self Catering
Cumbrian Cottages
t (01228) 599960
e enquiries@cumbrian-cottages.co.uk
w cumbrian-cottages.co.uk

Stag Cottage ★★★
Self Catering
Cumbrian Cottages
t (01228) 599960
e enquiries@cumbrian-cottages.co.uk
w cumbrian-cottages.co.uk

DUGGLEBY
North Yorkshire

Highbury Farm Cottage
★★★★ *Self Catering*
Contact: John & Christine Sawdon
t (01944) 738664
e john.sawdon@virgin.net
w highbury-farm-holiday-cottage.co.uk

DUNFORD BRIDGE
South Yorkshire

The Old School House ★★★
Self Catering
Contact: Mr Peter Lorimer
t (01226) 766173
e peter.heyend@virgin.net

DUNGWORTH, BRADFIELD
South Yorkshire

Rickett Field Farm ★★★★
Self Catering
Contact: Connie Shepherd
t (0114) 285 1218
w rickettfieldfarm.co.uk

DUNNINGTON
North Yorkshire

Holmfield ★★★ *Self Catering*
Contact: Mrs Ann Wilson
t (01904) 488136
e ann.wilson1@btinternet.com
w holmfieldyork.com

DUNSLEY
North Yorkshire

The Cottage
Rating Applied For
Self Catering
Whitby Holiday Cottages
t (01947) 603010
e enquiries@whitbyholidaycottages.net
w whitbyholidaycottages.net

DUNSTAN
Northumberland

Beech Cottage ★★★★
Self Catering
Contact: Mr & Mrs Mick & Karen Oxley
t (01665) 576422
e enquiries@mickoxley.com
w beech-cottage.co.uk

DURHAM

15 Mackintosh Court
★★★★ *Self Catering*
Contact: Mrs Penelope Dooley
t (01697) 342446
e mike_dooley@btconnect.com

Apt 19 Freemans Quay, Walkergate ★★★★
Self Catering
Contact: G S Hall
t (0191) 387 3001
e graham375@btinternet.com

Arbour House Bungalow and Cottage ★★★
Self Catering
Contact: Mrs Rena Hunter
t (0191) 384 2418
e enquiries@arbourhouse.co.uk
w arbourhouse.ntb.org.uk

Baxter Wood Cottages
★★★ *Self Catering*
Contact: Mr & Mrs Trevor & Tricia Jones
t (0191) 386 5820
e info@baxterwood.co.uk
w baxterwood.co.uk

Bourne Cottage
Rating Applied For
Self Catering
Contact: Mrs Judith Heron
t (0191) 372 0730
e judithheron@aol.com
w bournecottagedurham.com

City of Durham Freemans Quay Apartment ★★★★
Self Catering
Contact: Mrs Marcia Watson
t (01388) 812429 & 07779 729388
e info@cityofdurhamapartment.co.uk
w cityofdurhamapartment.co.uk

Dove Cottage ★★★★
Self Catering
t (0191) 3721 810
w durhamcottages.com

Durham City Apartment
★★★★★ *Self Catering*
Contact: Mr Ian Curry
t (0191) 371 9060
e enquiries@durhamcityapartment.co.uk
w durhamcityapartment.co.uk

Durham Oasis ★★★★★
Self Catering
Contact: Mr Ray Broadbridge
t (0191) 378 7651
e ray@nectar.uk.com
w durhamoasis.co.uk

Finney Court Apartment
★★★★ *Self Catering*
Contact: Mrs Marcia Watson
t (01388) 812429
e info@cityofdurhamapartment.co.uk
w cityofdurhamapartment.co.uk

Moonlight Apartment
★★★★★ *Self Catering*
Contact: Mr Ray Broadbridge
t (0191) 378 7651
e ray@moonlightapartment.co.uk
w moonlightapartment.co.uk

Moor End Cottage ★★★★
Self Catering
Contact: Mrs Mary Buchanan
t (0191) 384 2796
e marybnb@hotmail.com
w moorenddurham.co.uk

The Old Power House
★★★★ *Self Catering*
Contact: Mrs Anne Hall
t (0191) 387 3001
e graham375@btinternet.com
w theoldpowerhouse.co.uk

Ramside Farmhouse ★★★★
Self Catering
Contact: Ms Katherine Hunt
t (0191) 386 5282
e reservations@ramsidehallhotel.co.uk
w ramsidehallhotel.co.uk

Sands Cottages ★★★
Self Catering
Contact: Mrs Greta Hodgson
t (0191) 384 4731
e gretahodgson@btinternet.com
w sands-cottages.co.uk

Swallows' Barn ★★★★
Self Catering
Contact: Mrs Caroline Broome
t (0191) 373 7864
w holidaycott.co.uk

Sylvan House Apartment
★★★★ *Self Catering*
Contact: Mrs Marcia Watson
t (01388) 812429
e info@cityofdurhamapartment.co.uk
w cityofdurhamapartment.co.uk

Thimble Cottage ★★★
Self Catering
Contact: Mr & Mrs M Camplin
t (01302) 786524
e enquiries@oldpitcottage.co.uk

EAGLESCLIFFE
Tees Valley

Aislaby Grange Farm Cottages ★★★ *Self Catering*
Contact: Mr Andrew Hutchinson
t (01642) 782170

EAMONT BRIDGE
Cumbria

Henge Cottage ★★★
Self Catering
Cumbrian Cottages
t (01228) 599960
e enquiries@cumbrian-cottages.co.uk
w cumbrian-cottages.co.uk

EASBY
North Yorkshire

Abbey House ★★★★★
Self Catering
Contact: John Martin
t (01748) 825298
e easbycottages@hotmail.co.uk

EASINGTON
Tees Valley

Grinkle Park Farm ★★★★
Self Catering
Contact: Ms Beverley Muir
t (01287) 643087
e muir.grinkle@virgin.net

Ings Farm Cottage ★★★
Self Catering
Dales Holiday Cottages
t (01756) 790919
e info@dales-holiday-cottages.com
w dales-holiday-cottages.com

Sandstone Cottage ★★★★
Self Catering
Contact: Mrs Janet Carter
t (0113) 236 3408
e mrsjanetcarter@gmail.com

EASINGWOLD
North Yorkshire

Allerton Cottage ★★★
Self Catering
Contact: Angela Thornton
t (01347) 821912
e richdomthornton@hotmail.com

EASTFIELD
Northumberland

Seafield Lodge ★★★★
Self Catering
Contact: Mr & Mrs McCulloch
t (0113) 281 3602
e james.mcculloch@virgin.net

EBBERSTON
North Yorkshire

Cliff House, Ebberston
★★★★ *Self Catering*
Contact: Simon Morris
t (01723) 859440
e cliffhouseebberston@btinternet.com
w cliffhouse-cottageholidays.co.uk

Cow Pasture & Swallow-Tail Cottages ★★★-★★★★
Self Catering
Contact: David & Brenda Green
t (01723) 859285
e brenda@yorkshireancestors.com
w studleyhousefarm.co.uk

Nesfield Cottage ★★★★
Self Catering
Contact: Janet Wood
t (01530) 416094
e chris.wood4@virgin.net

EDDERSIDE
Cumbria

Centre Farm ★★★
Self Catering
Cumbrian Cottages
t (01228) 599960
e enquiries@cumbrian-cottages.co.uk
w cumbrian-cottages.co.uk

EDLINGHAM
Northumberland

Briar, Rose and Clematis Cottage ★★★★ *Self Catering*
Contact: Mrs Helen Wyld
t (01665) 574638
e stay@newmoorhouse.co.uk
w newmoorhouse.co.uk

The Granary Overthwarts
★★★★ *Self Catering*
Contact: Ms Alexa Reid
t (01665) 570416
e abr@rexa.co.uk

EGERTON
Cheshire

Manor Farm Holiday Cottages ★★★★
Self Catering
Contact: Mrs Jan Dilworth
t (01829) 720261
e bookings@egertonmanorfarm.co.uk
w egertonmanorfarm.co.uk

EGGLESTON
Durham

Blackthorn Cottage and Willow Cottage ★★–★★★
Self Catering
Contact: Mrs Diane Garrett
t (01708) 447260
e coldigar@talktalk.net
w teesdalecottages.co.uk

The Granary ★★★★
Self Catering
Contact: Mrs Rosemarie Gray
t (01833) 650403

Stable Court ★★★★
Self Catering
Contact: Mrs J D Broughton
t (01263) 862500

Swinkly Cottage ★★★
Self Catering
Contact: Mrs Mary Robinson
t (01388) 605620
e info@swinklycottage.co.uk
w swinklycottage.co.uk

EGREMONT
Cumbria

Howman Cottage ★★★★
Self Catering
Cumbrian Cottages
t (01228) 599960
e enquiries@cumbrian-cottages.co.uk
w cumbrian-cottages.co.uk

EGTON
North Yorkshire

Westonby Cottage ★★★
Self Catering
Contact: Joan Flintoft
t (01947) 895296

EGTON BRIDGE
North Yorkshire

Broom House Cottages, Egton Bridge ★★★–★★★★
Self Catering
Contact: David & Maria White
Broom Cottage
t (01947) 895279
e mw@broom-house.co.uk
w egton-bridge.co.uk

Key Green Farmhouse Annexe, Egton Bridge ★★★
Self Catering
Contact: Mr and Mrs Kate & Ian Johnson
t (01947) 895601
e keygreenfarmhouse@yahoo.co.uk
w keygreenfarmhouse.co.uk

ELLINGHAM
Northumberland

Coachman's Cottage
★★★★ *Self Catering*
Northumberland Cottages
t (01665) 589434
e enquiries@northumberlandcottages.com
w northumberlandcottages.co.uk

ELLONBY
Cumbria

Sycamore Cottage ★★★
Self Catering
Cumbrian Cottages
t (01228) 599960
e enquiries@cumbrian-cottages.co.uk
w cumbrian-cottages.co.uk

ELSDON
Northumberland

Dunns Farm & Bilsmoorfoot
★★★–★★★★ *Self Catering*
Contact: Mrs Mary Carruthers
t (01669) 640219
w dunnsfarm.ntb.org.uk

ELTERWATER
Cumbria

Bridge End Cottage ★★★★
Self Catering
Lakelovers
t (015394) 88855
e bookings@lakelovers.co.uk
w lakelovers.co.uk

Gunpowder Cottage ★★★★
Self Catering
Lakelovers
t (015394) 88855
e bookings@lakelovers.co.uk
w lakelovers.co.uk

Pollys Cottage
Rating Applied For
Self Catering
Lakelovers
t (015394) 88855
e bookings@lakelovers.co.uk
w lakelovers.co.uk

Wistaria Cottage ★★★
Self Catering
Contact: Mr & Mrs Beardmore
Geoff & Doreen Beardmore
t (01782) 783170
e gd.beardmore@virgin.net
w roomspr.co.uk/wistariacottagenumber3

EMBLETON
Cumbria

Derwent Lodge
Rating Applied For
Serviced Apartments
Contact: Raymond Blackburn
t (017687) 76606
e ray.dlodge@yahoo.co.uk
w thederwentlodge.com

Sunny Bank Cottage ★★★
Self Catering
Contact: Margaret Bell
t (017687) 76273

EMBLETON
Northumberland

Anvil Cottage ★★★
Self Catering
Contact: Mr George Skipper
t (01665) 576362
e skipphoto@hotmail.co.uk

Cra-na-ge ★★ *Self Catering*
Sykes Cottages
t (01244) 345700
e info@sykescottages.co.uk
w sykescottages.co.uk

Doxford Cottages ★★★★★
Self Catering
Contact: Ms Sue Pringle
t (01665) 589393
e stay@doxfordcottages.co.uk
w doxfordcottages.co.uk

Doxford Farm Cottages
★★★–★★★★ *Self Catering*
Contact: Mrs Sarah Shell
Doxford Farm
t (01665) 579348 & (01665) 579477
e doxfordfarm@hotmail.com
w doxfordfarmcottages.com

Dunstanburgh Castle Courtyard Cottages ★★
Self Catering
Contact: Mrs Tricia Bell
t (01665) 604935
w heritagecoastholidays.com

Eider ★★★★ *Self Catering*
Contact: Mrs Jan Straughan
t (01665) 830032
w cottageguide.co.uk/eidercottage/

Embleton Cottage & The Nook ★★★–★★★★
Self Catering
Contact: Mrs Ella Unwin
t (01665) 576573

Holly Cottage
Rating Applied For
Self Catering
Northumbrian Cottages
t (01228) 599950
e sheena@cumbrian-cottages.co.uk
w northumbrian-cottages.info

Mansard Cottage ★★★★
Self Catering
Contact: Mr & Mrs Nic & Pauline Grant
t (01661) 853513
e pauline.grant@btinternet.com
w mansard.cottage.btinternet.co.uk

Northumbrian Holiday Cottages ★★★ *Self Catering*
Contact: Mr & Mrs Chris Seal
t (0191) 285 6930
e seal@northumbrian-holiday-cottages.co.uk
w northumbrian-holiday-cottages.co.uk

ENDMOOR
Cumbria

Calvert Cottage ★★★★
Self Catering
Cumbrian Cottages
t (01228) 599960
e enquiries@cumbrian-cottages.co.uk
w cumbrian-cottages.co.uk

Sunrise ★★★★ *Self Catering*
Cumbrian Cottages
t (01228) 599960
e enquiries@cumbrian-cottages.co.uk
w cumbrian-cottages.co.uk

ENNERDALE
Cumbria

Routen House ★★★★
Self Catering
Contact: Mrs Joanne Green
t (01604) 626383
e joanne@routenhouse.co.uk
w routenhouse.co.uk

ESKDALE
Cumbria

Bridge End Farm Cottages
★★★★–★★★★★
Self Catering
t 0870 073 5328
w selectcottages.com

The Chalets ★★★★
Self Catering
Contact: Lisa Borrowdale & Philip Hayden
t (019467) 23128
e info@thechalets.co.uk
w thechalets.co.uk

Fisherground Farm Holidays
★★★ *Self Catering*
Contact: Ian Hall
Orchard House Holidays
t (017687) 73175
e holidays@fisherground.co.uk
w fisherground.co.uk

Old Brantrake ★★★★
Self Catering
Contact: Mr & Mrs Tyson
t (019467) 23340

Randle How ★★★★
Self Catering
Contact: Susan Wedley
t (01946) 723126
e jswedley@btinternet.com
w 3randlehowselfcatering.com

Santon House
Rating Applied For
Self Catering
Cumbrian Cottages
t (01228) 599960
e enquiries@cumbrian-cottages.co.uk
w cumbrian-cottages.co.uk

FADDILEY
Cheshire

The Roost at The Damsons
Rating Applied For
Self Catering
t 07811 511442

FADMOOR
North Yorkshire

North Farm Cottages ★★★
Self Catering
t (01751) 431934
e northfarmcottages@fsmail.net

FALSTONE
Northumberland

Station Cottage ★★★★
Self Catering
Contact: Mrs June Banks
t (01434) 240311

FAR SAWREY
Cumbria

1 & 2 Church Cottage
★★★★ *Self Catering*
Lakelovers
t (015394) 88855
e bookings@lakelovers.co.uk
w lakelovers.co.uk

Brimstock Cottage ★★★★
Self Catering
The Coppermines & Coniston Lakes Cottages
t (015394) 41765
w coppermines.co.uk

Claife Cottage ★★★
Self Catering
Contact: Mr Peter Durbin
Cumbrian Cottages
t (01228) 599960
e enquiries@cumbrian-cottages.co.uk

Drawing Room ★★★
Self Catering
The Coppermines & Coniston Lakes Cottages
t (015394) 41765
w coppermines.co.uk

Hayloft Cottage ★★★★
Self Catering
The Coppermines & Coniston Lakes Cottages
t (015394) 41765
w coppermines.co.uk

Letterbox Cottage ★★★★
Self Catering
Cumbrian Cottages
t (01228) 599960
e enquiries@cumbrian-cottages.co.uk
w cumbrian-cottages.co.uk

Sawrey Stables – Delf Suite
★★★★ *Self Catering*
Hideaways
t (015394) 42435
e bookings@lakeland-hideaways.co.uk
w lakeland-hideaways.co.uk

Sawrey Stables – The Morning Room ★★★★
Self Catering
Hideaways
t (015394) 42435
e bookings@lakeland-hideaways.co.uk
w lakeland-hideaways.co.uk

Sawrey Stables – Writing Room ★★★★ *Self Catering*
Hideaways
t (015394) 42435
e bookings@lakeland-hideaways.co.uk
w lakeland-hideaways.co.uk

Stables Cottage ★★★★
Self Catering
Lakelovers
t (015394) 88855
e bookings@lakelovers.co.uk
w lakelovers.co.uk

Tower & Knott Cottages
★★★★ *Self Catering*
The Coppermines & Coniston Lakes Cottages
t (015394) 41765
w coppermines.co.uk

FARLAM
Cumbria

Calf Close Cottage ★★★★★
Self Catering
Cumbrian Cottages
t (01228) 599960
e enquiries@cumbrian-cottages.co.uk
w cumbrian-cottages.co.uk

Tarnside Lodges
Rating Applied For
Self Catering
Contact: Anne Barnes
t (01697) 746675
e anne.barnes1@btinternet.com
w tarnsidelodges.co.uk

FARLETON
Cumbria

Knott View Barn ★★★★★
Self Catering
Contact: Mr & Mrs Ian & Anne Twiname
t (015395) 67369
e bordersales@btinternet.com

FARNDON
Cheshire

Woodpecker Cottage
★★★★ *Self Catering*
Contact: Mrs Sue Heyworth
t (01829) 270927
w woodpeckercottage.info

FELTON
Northumberland

Granary Cottage ★★★★
Self Catering
Contact: Mrs Irene Adamson
t (01665) 570205
e ireneadamson55@yahoo.co.uk
w granary-cottage.co.uk

FIELD BROUGHTON
Cumbria

Broughton Lodge Cottage
★★★★ *Self Catering*
Cumbrian Cottages
t (01228) 599960
e enquiries@cumbrian-cottages.co.uk
w cumbrian-cottages.co.uk

Broughton Lodge Farm
★★★ *Self Catering*
Cumbrian Cottages
t (01228) 599960
e enquiries@cumbrian-cottages.co.uk
w cumbrian-cottages.co.uk

Liden Lea ★★★★★
Self Catering
Lakeland Cottage Comapny
t (015395) 38180
e john@lakelandcottageco.com
w lakelandcottageco.com

FILEY
North Yorkshire

15 Mitford Place
Rating Applied For
Self Catering
Contact: Kim & James Hodgson
Hodgson's Choice
t (01904) 610351
e kim@hodgsons-choice.co.uk
w hodgsons-choice.co.uk

5 Leys Holiday Accommodation ★★★★★
Self Catering
Contact: Mrs Sonia Suggars
t 0845 094 5051
e info@5leys.co.uk
w 5leys.co.uk

84 Queen Street ★★★★
Self Catering
Contact: Deborah Whallett
t (01246) 241153
e cottageenquiries@mac.com
w filey.biz

Baxter House ★★★★
Self Catering
Contact: Mrs Anne Cooper
t (01723) 365263

The Cottages ★★★
Self Catering
Contact: Mr & Mrs David Teet
t (01723) 516620

Crescent Apartment ★★★
Self Catering
Contact: Jean & Jack Speight
t (0113) 253 8566

Crescent Apartment (No.4b)
Rating Applied For
Self Catering
Contact: Mr & Mrs C & J Thompson
t (01723) 513798

Ennerdale Holiday Flats ★★
Self Catering
Contact: Mr & Mrs C & J Thompson
Ennerdale Holiday Flats & Crescent Apart
t (01723) 513798

Fisherman Cottage ★★★
Self Catering
Contact: Mrs Annette Cavell
t (01757) 290020 & 07773 643917

Langford Villa ★★★
Self Catering
Contact: Mr & Mrs D.H Midgley
t (01723) 514813
e dhmidgley@ukonline.co.uk

Woods Holiday Flat ★★★
Self Catering
Contact: Mr & Mrs Wood
t 07913 502884
e terrywood37a@talktalk.net

FINSTHWAITE
Cumbria

Red Deer Lodge ★★★★
Self Catering
Cumbrian Cottages
t (01228) 599960
e enquiries@cumbrian-cottages.co.uk
w cumbrian-cottages.co.uk

Sheiling Barn ★★★★
Self Catering
Lakelovers
t (015394) 88855
e bookings@lakelovers.co.uk
w lakelovers.co.uk

FIRBANK
Cumbria

Goodies Farmhouse
Rating Applied For
Self Catering
Cumbrian Cottages
t (01228) 599960
e enquiries@cumbrian-cottages.co.uk
w cumbrian-cottages.co.uk

Newbarn Cottage ★★★
Self Catering
Contact: Pamela Anne Thompson
t (015396) 21278
e newfield@pentalk.org
w newbarncottage.co.uk

FITLING
East Riding of Yorkshire

Stables Cottage ★★★★
Self Catering
Contact: Patricia Cockshutt
t (01964) 527114
e stablescottage@tiscali.co.uk
w http://myweb.tiscali.co.uk/stablecottage/index.html

FLAMBOROUGH
East Riding of Yorkshire

April Cottage
Rating Applied For
Self Catering
Yorkshire Cottages
t (01228) 406701
e enquiries@yorkshire-cottages.info
w yorkshire-cottages.info

Chalk Cottage ★★★★
Self Catering
t 07766 147391
w chalkcottage.co.uk

Flamborough Rock Cottages, Flamborough
★★★ *Self Catering*
Contact: Mrs J Geraghty
t (01262) 850996
e jannicegeraghty@hotmail.com
w flamboroughrockcottages.co.uk

Hope Cottage ★★
Self Catering
Contact: Gary Asquith
t (0113) 295 7047
e louise.asquith@ntlworld.com
w holidaycottageflamborough.co.uk

FLIXTON
North Yorkshire

Castle View ★★★
Self Catering
Bedwyn's Holiday Accommodation
t (01723) 516700
e info@bedwyns.co.uk
w bedwyns.co.uk

Humble Bee Cottages
★★★★ *Self Catering*
Contact: John & Julia Warters
t (01723) 890437
e info@humblebeefarm.co.uk
w humblebeefarm.co.uk

FLOCKTON
West Yorkshire

2 The Lodge, Beaconsfield Farm, Paul Lane, Flockton Moor ★★★★★ *Self Catering*
Contact: Mr & Mrs Dale
t 07798 698 226 & (01924) 849226
e enquiries@thelodgeatflocktonmoor.co.uk
w thelodgeatflocktonmoor.co.uk

FLOOKBURGH
Cumbria

Stockdale Farm ★★★
Self Catering
Contact: Janet Fallon
South Lakes Cottages
t (01229) 889601
e enquiries@southlakes-cottages.com
w southlakes-cottages.com

FOGGATHORPE
East Riding of Yorkshire

Yellowtop Country Park
★★★★ *Self Catering*
Contact: Paula Jessop
t (01430) 860461
e paulayellowtop@aol.com
w yellowtopcountry.co.uk

FOLLIFOOT
North Yorkshire

Marlin Cottage ★★★★
Self Catering
Contact: Evelyn Clayton
t (01423) 883696
e clayton.clayton@virgin.net

Repton Green, Rudding Park
★★★★★ *Self Catering*
t (01423) 871350
e reservations@ruddingpark.com
w reptongreen.com

FORD
Northumberland

Ford Castle ★★★-★★★★
Self Catering
Contact: Mrs Karen Bartlett
t (01890) 820257
e kbartlett@northumberland.gov.uk

FORTON
Lancashire

Cleveley Mere Fishing & Lodges, Forton ★-★★★
Self Catering
Contact: Peter & Lynne Brown
Cleveley Mere Fishing Lodges
t (01524) 793644
w cleveleymere.com

Shirebank Court ★★★★
Self Catering
Contact: Mrs Hewitt
t (01524) 792179
e mail@shirebankcourt.co.uk
w shirebankcourt.co.uk

FOULRIDGE
Lancashire

Robin's Nest ★★★★
Self Catering
Contact: Mr & Mrs Phil & Jacqui Whitworth
t (01282) 415667

FOXFIELD
Cumbria

Thistle Cottage ★★★★
Self Catering
Cumbrian Cottages
t (01228) 599960
e enquiries@cumbrian-cottages.co.uk
w cumbrian-cottages.co.uk

FOXTON
Northumberland

Greybarns ★★★★
Self Catering
Northumberland Estates Holiday Cottages
t (01668) 219941
e jane@nehc.co.uk
w alnwickcastlecottages.co.uk

FROSTERLEY
Durham

Innkeepers Cottage ★★★★
Self Catering
t 07974 961620
e info@innkeeperscottage.co.uk
w innkeeperscottage.co.uk

FULFORD
North Yorkshire

Polly's Cottage ★★★★
Self Catering
Yorkshire Cottages
t (01228) 406701
e enquiries@yorkshire-cottages.info
w yorkshire-cottages.info

FYLINGDALES
North Yorkshire

Pond Farm Caravan
Approved Caravan Holiday Home
t (01947) 880441

FYLINGTHORPE
North Yorkshire

Browdale Cottage ★★★
Self Catering
Contact: Susan & Michael Earnshaw
t (01947) 880052
e thorneybrow@yorkshire.net
w thorneybrow.co.uk

Croft Farm Cottage ★★★
Self Catering
Contact: Mrs Braithwaite
t (01947) 880231
e croftfarmbb@aol.com
w robinhoodsbay.co.uk/croftfarm

GAINFORD
Durham

East Greystone Farm Cottages ★★★★-★★★★★
Self Catering
Contact: Mrs Sue Hodgson
t (01325) 730236
e sue@holidayfarmcottages.co.uk
w holidayfarmcottages.co.uk

Low Green Cottage ★★★
Self Catering
Contact: Mrs Barbara McLean
t (01833) 637594
e info@lowgreencottage.co.uk
w lowgreencottage.co.uk

River Cottage
Rating Applied For
Self Catering
Contact: Mrs Sarah Rutter
t (01325) 730059
e sarahrutter@aol.com
w rivercottagegainford.co.uk

GALGATE
Lancashire

Lakewood Cottages ★★★★
Self Catering
Contact: Mr Alec Sayer
t (01524) 751053
e alec@sayer11.freeserve.co.uk
w lakewoodcottages.co.uk

GALPHAY
North Yorkshire

West Leas Farm ★★★
Self Catering
Contact: Mrs Catherine Raw
t (01765) 658416
e raw@westleas.co.uk
w westleas.co.uk

GAMBLESBY
Cumbria

Church Court Cottages
★★★-★★★★★ *Self Catering*
Contact: Mark Cowell
t (01768) 881682
e cottages@gogamblesby.co.uk
w gogamblesby.co.uk

Cornerstones ★★★
Self Catering
Lakes Cottage Holidays
t (01228) 591555
e info@lakescottageholiday.co.uk
w lakescottageholiday.co.uk

Old Mill Barn ★★★
Self Catering
Contact: Susan Bell
t (01768) 881791
e thebellsgamblesby@btinternet.com
w oldmillbarn.co.uk

GARNETT BRIDGE
Cumbria

The Mill Cottages ★★★★
Self Catering
Cumbrian Cottages
t (01228) 599960
e enquiries@cumbrian-cottages.co.uk
w cumbrian-cottages.co.uk

Tree Tops ★★★★★
Self Catering
Cumbrian Cottages
t (01228) 599960
e enquiries@cumbrian-cottages.co.uk
w cumbrian-cottages.co.uk

GARSDALE
Cumbria

Cloughside Cottage ★★★★
Self Catering
Dales Holiday Cottages
t (01756) 790919
e info@dales-holiday-cottages.com
w dales-holiday-cottages.com

GARSTANG
Lancashire

Barnacre Cottages ★★★★★
Self Catering
Contact: Mr Terence Sharples
t (01995) 600918
e sue@barnacre-cottages.co.uk
w barnacre-cottages.co.uk

Knotts Hey Cottages, Bilsborrow ★★★
Self Catering
Contact: Mr Collinson
t (01995) 640519
e holidays@brockcottages.co.uk
w brockcottages.co.uk

GATESHEAD
Tyne and Wear

The Riding Farm ★★★★
Self Catering
Contact: Ms Louise Johnson
t (0191) 370 1868
e ridingfarm@btconnect.com
w ridingcottages.co.uk

GAYLE
North Yorkshire

Foss Cottage ★★★
Self Catering
t (01969) 667518
e brendale@watering.wanadoo.co.uk

Gayle Farmhouse ★★★
Self Catering
Dales Holiday Cottages
t (01756) 790919
e info@dales-holiday-cottages.com
w dales-holiday-cottages.com

GIGGLESWICK
North Yorkshire

2 Gildersleets ★★★★
Self Catering
Contact: Paul Griffiths
t (0161) 832 2912
e dr.paul.griffiths@hotmail.com
w 2gildersleets.co.uk

Black Horse Cottage ★★★
Self Catering
Contact: Anthony & Ann Haygarth
t (0113) 269 3960
e haygarthtony@aol.com
w black-horse-cottage.co.uk

Bookend Cottage ★★★
Self Catering
Sykes Cottages
t (01244) 345700
e info@sykescottages.co.uk
w sykescottages.co.uk

Close House Cottage Holidays ★★★ *Self Catering*
Contact: Sue Jarrom
t (01729) 822778
e chcottages@btinternet.com
w close-house.co.uk

Craven Ridge
Rating Applied For
Self Catering
t (0151) 625 3264
e bookings@holidaycottagesuk.com

Foxholes Lodge ★★★
Self Catering
Contact: Lynn Scruton
t (01729) 823505

Ivy Cottage ★★★★
Self Catering
Contact: Mr & Mrs David & Betty Hattersley
Ivy Cottage (Giggleswick) Limited
t (020) 8504 8263
e davidhattersley@aol.com

Stanton Cottage ★★★
Self Catering
Contact: Alison Boswell
t (01729) 822400
e pboswell@ukonline.co.uk

Sutcliffe Cottage Ref: 31
★★ *Self Catering*
Sykes Cottages
t (01244) 345700
e info@sykescottages.co.uk
w sykescottages.co.uk

GILCRUX
Cumbria

Ellen Hall ★★–★★★★
Self Catering
Contact: David Dunlop
t (01697) 321439
e data.dunlop@virgin.net
w cottagesmadefortwo.co.uk

GILESGATE
Durham

Fern Cottage and Rose Cottage ★★★★ *Self Catering*
t (0191) 372 1810
w durhamcottages.com

GILLAMOOR
North Yorkshire

Gales House Farm ★★★★
Self Catering
Contact: David Ward
t (01751) 431258
e cottages@gillamoor.com
w gillamoor.com

Hen House, Gillamoor
★★★★★ *Self Catering*
Contact: Maria Demkowicz
t 07786 885093
e maria@henhousecottage.co.uk
w henhousecottage.co.uk

Keepers Cottage ★★★★
Self Catering
Contact: Joan Davies
t (01751) 433129
e keri-davies@lineone.net
w yorkshireselfcatering.co.uk

GILLING EAST
North Yorkshire

Sunset Cottages ★★★★
Self Catering
Contact: Richard Kelsey
t (01347) 888654
e info@sunsetcottages.co.uk
w sunsetcottages.co.uk

GILLING WEST
North Yorkshire

Gilling Old Mill Cottages
★★★★–★★★★★
Self Catering
Contact: Hugh, Joyce and Neville Bird
Gilling Old Mill
t (01748) 822771
e admin@yorkshiredales-cottages.com
w yorkshiredales-cottages.com

Gilling Old Mill Cottages
★★★★ *Self Catering*
Contact: Mr & Mrs Bird
t (01748) 822771
e admin@yorkshiredales-cottages.com
w yorkshiredale-cottages.com

GILSLAND
Cumbria

Irthing House Cottage ★★★
Self Catering
Contact: Mr Tweddle
t (01697) 747983
e georgiashorrock@aol.com
w cottagesinnorthumberland.com

The Ostlers ★★★
Self Catering
Cumbrian Cottages
t (01228) 599960
e enquiries@cumbrian-cottages.co.uk
w cumbrian-cottages.co.uk

GILSLAND
Northumberland

Glen Garth ★★★★
Self Catering
Northumbrian Cottages
t (01228) 599950
e sheena@cumbrian-cottages.co.uk
w northumbrian-cottages.info

West Nichold Cottage
★★★★★ *Self Catering*
Contact: Mr Paul Jameson
t (01697) 747008
e stay@westnichold.co.uk
w westnichold.co.uk

GILSTEAD
West Yorkshire

Thimble, Bobbin & Shuttle
★★★ *Self Catering*
Contact: Jean Warin
t (01274) 487433
e jean.warin@nevisuk.net
w yorkshirenet.co.uk/accgde/marchcote

GISBURN
Lancashire

Coverdale Farm ★★★★
Self Catering
Contact: Mrs Mandy Pilkington
t (01200) 445265
w coverdalefarm.co.uk

Ribblesdale Park Holiday Cottages ★★★★
Self Catering
Contact: Mrs Elaine Hope
t (01200) 445227
e elaine.hope@theguyhindleygroup.com
w ribblesdalepark.com

GLAISDALE
North Yorkshire

The Studio Flat ★★★★
Self Catering
Contact: John & Mary Thompson
t (01947) 897353
e j-m.thompson.bandb@talk21.com
w postgate-farm-holidays.co.uk

Yaffles Cottage ★★★
Self Catering
Whitby Holiday Cottages
t (01947) 603010
e enquiries@whitbyholidaycottages.net
w whitbyholidaycottages.net

GLENRIDDING
Cumbria

1 Beech House Apartments
★★★★ *Self Catering*
Contact: Doreen Gash
t (0113) 250 1883
e stay@ullswaterview.co.uk
w ullswaterview.co.uk

3 High Rake ★★★
Self Catering
Cumbrian Cottages
t (01228) 599960
e enquiries@cumbrian-cottages.co.uk
w cumbrian-cottages.co.uk

Birkside Cottage ★★★
Self Catering
Cumbrian Cottages
t (01228) 599960
e enquiries@cumbrian-cottages.co.uk
w cumbrian-cottages.co.uk

Chapel Cottage ★★★★
Self Catering
Lakeland Cottage Comapny
t (015395) 38180
e john@lakelandcottageco.com
w lakelandcottageco.com

Dovedale ★★★★
Self Catering
Lakes Cottage Holidays
t (01228) 591555
e info@lakescottageholiday.co.uk
w lakescottageholiday.co.uk

Keldas View Cottage
★★★★ *Self Catering*
Contact: Ruth Teasdale
t (01768) 864204
e info@keldasviewcottage.co.uk
w keldasviewcottage.co.uk

Middle Rake ★★★
Self Catering
Cumbrian Cottages
t (01228) 599960
e enquiries@cumbrian-cottages.co.uk
w cumbrian-cottages.co.uk

Molly's Cottage ★★★★
Self Catering
Cumbrian Cottages
t (01228) 599960
e enquiries@cumbrian-cottages.co.uk
w cumbrian-cottages.co.uk

No 7 Stybarrow Terrace
★★★★ *Self Catering*
Contact: Ms Helen Beaty
t (017684) 82248
e enquiries@stybarrow.co.uk

Ullswater View Cottage
★★★ *Self Catering*
Contact: Ken Coulston
Ullswater View
t (01252) 835362
e jackcoulston@btinternet.com
w ullswaterview.com

Walkers Retreat ★★★
Self Catering
Cumbrian Cottages
t (01228) 599960
e enquiries@cumbrian-cottages.co.uk
w cumbrian-cottages.co.uk

Wallholm Cottage ★★★★
Self Catering
Cumbrian Cottages
t (01228) 599960
e enquiries@cumbrian-cottages.co.uk
w cumbrian-cottages.co.uk

Whiteside Lodge ★★★★
Self Catering
Cumbrian Cottages
t (01228) 599960
e enquiries@cumbrian-cottages.co.uk
w cumbrian-cottages.co.uk

GOATHLAND
North Yorkshire

14 Oakfield Avenue ★★★
Self Catering
Whitby Holiday Cottages
t (01947) 603010
e enquiries@whitbyholidaycottages.net
w whitbyholidaycottages.net

Eskholme Holiday Cottage
★★★★ *Self Catering*
Contact: Janet Hodgson
Eskholme
t (01924) 498154
e ffsjan@aol.com

Orchard Cottage ★★★★★
Self Catering
Dales Holiday Cottages
t (01756) 790919
e info@dales-holiday-cottages.com
w dales-holiday-cottages.com

Woodpecker Cottage
★★★★ *Self Catering*
Dales Holiday Cottages
t (01756) 790919
e info@dales-holiday-cottages.com
w dales-holiday-cottages.com

GOSFORTH
Cumbria

Potters Barn & Well Cottage
★★★★ *Self Catering*
Contact: Barbara & Dick Wright
t (01946) 725296
e dms@potters-barn.co.uk
w potters-barn.co.uk

GRANGE
Cumbria

Greystones ★★★
Self Catering
Cumbrian Cottages
t (01228) 599960
e enquiries@cumbrian-cottages.co.uk
w cumbrian-cottages.co.uk

GRANGE MOOR
West Yorkshire

The Yorkshire Barn
★★★★★ *Self Catering*
Contact: Mr Jason Noad
t (01484) 283014
e info@edenluxuryliving.co.uk

GRANGE-OVER-SANDS
Cumbria

Brook Cottage
Rating Applied For
Self Catering
Cumbrian Cottages
t (01228) 599960
e enquiries@cumbrian-cottages.co.uk
w cumbrian-cottages.co.uk

The Chalet Studio & Chalet Garden Flat ★★★
Self Catering
Contact: Margaret Wilson
t (015395) 34695
e thechalet@freeuk.com
w lakelandchalet.co.uk

Cornerways Bungalow ★★★
Self Catering
Contact: Eunice Rigg
Cornerways Bungalow & Greaves Farm
t (015395) 36329 & (015395) 36587

Devonshire House ★★★★★
Self Catering
Lakeland Cottage Comapny
t (015395) 38180
e john@lakelandcottageco.com
w lakelandcottageco.com

Dyer Dene ★★★
Self Catering
Contact: Mrs Andrews
t (01995) 602769
e dyerdene@fish.co.uk
w dyerdene.com

Hardcragg Hall
Rating Applied For
Self Catering
Cumbrian Cottages
t (01228) 599960
e enquiries@cumbrian-cottages.co.uk
w cumbrian-cottages.co.uk

Hazelwood Court ★★★★
Self Catering
Contact: Martin Stilling
t (015395) 34196
e martstilling.hazelcourt@virgin.net

Hillcrest
Rating Applied For
Self Catering
Cumbrian Cottages
t (01228) 599960
e enquiries@cumbrian-cottages.co.uk
w cumbrian-cottages.co.uk

Spring Bank Cottage ★★★★
Self Catering
Contact: Mrs Brocklebank
t (015395) 32606

Wycombe Holiday Flats
★★★ *Self Catering*
Contact: Geoff & Auriel Benson
t 0800 321 3179
e book@whf.info
w whf.info

GRANSMOOR
East Riding of Yorkshire

Fourth Farm ★★★★
Self Catering
Contact: Garry Slingsby
t (01262) 490338
e info@fourthfarm.co.uk
w fourthfarm.co.uk

Fourth Farm ★★★★
Self Catering
Contact: Mr Gary Slingsby
t (01262) 490338
e gslingsby@fwi.co.uk
w fourthfarm.co.uk

GRASMERE
Cumbria

1 Field Foot ★★★
Self Catering
Contact: Mrs J Morrison
t (01942) 236350 & (015394) 45305

14 Meadowcroft ★★★
Self Catering
Lakelovers
t (015394) 88855
e bookings@lakelovers.co.uk
w lakelovers.co.uk

2 Town Head Cottage ★★★
Self Catering
Cumbrian Cottages
t (01228) 599960
e enquiries@cumbrian-cottages.co.uk
w cumbrian-cottages.co.uk

3 Becksteps ★★★★
Self Catering
Lakelovers
t (015394) 88855
e bookings@lakelovers.co.uk
w lakelovers.co.uk

3 Dale End ★★★
Self Catering
Contact: Anne Truelove
t (015394) 35200
e paul.truelove@btinternet.com
w daleend.co.uk

3 Tarn Cottages ★★★
Self Catering
Contact: Jonathan Batho
Cottagescumbria.com
t (015394) 41680
e a.batho@virgin.net
w cottagescumbria.com

3 Town Head Cottage ★★★
Self Catering
Cumbrian Cottages
t (01228) 599960
e enquiries@cumbrian-cottages.co.uk
w cumbrian-cottages.co.uk

Acorn Cottage ★★★
Self Catering
Lakelovers
t (015394) 88855
e bookings@lakelovers.co.uk
w lakelovers.co.uk

April Cottage ★★★
Self Catering
Lakelovers
t (015394) 88855
e bookings@lakelovers.co.uk
w lakelovers.co.uk

Beck Allans Self Catering Apartments ★★★-★★★★
Self Catering
Contact: Peter & Nicola du Toit
t (015394) 35563
e mail@beckallans.com
w beckallans.com

Becksteps ★★★
Self Catering
Lakelovers
t (015394) 88855
e bookings@lakelovers.co.uk
w lakelovers.co.uk

Beechghyll ★★★★
Self Catering
Cumbrian Cottages
t (01228) 599960
e enquiries@cumbrian-cottages.co.uk
w cumbrian-cottages.co.uk

Blind Tarn ★★ *Self Catering*
Lakelovers
t (015394) 88855
e bookings@lakelovers.co.uk
w lakelovers.co.uk

Bramrigg House ★★★
Self Catering
Contact: Lana Thorne
Lake District Inns and Cottages
t 05006 00725
e stay@lakedistrictinns.co.uk
w lakedistrictinns.co.uk

Broadrayne Farm Cottages
★★★★ *Self Catering*
Contact: Mr Bev Dennison & Mrs Jo Dennison Drake
Broadrayne Farm
t (015394) 35055
e jo@grasmere-accommodation.co.uk
w grasmere-accommodation.co.uk

The Coach House ★★★★
Self Catering
Lakelovers
t (015394) 88855
e bookings@lakelovers.co.uk
w lakelovers.co.uk

The Cottage ★★★
Self Catering
Cumbrian Cottages
t (01228) 599960
e enquiries@cumbrian-cottages.co.uk
w cumbrian-cottages.co.uk

The Daffodils ★★★★
Self Catering
Lakelovers
t (015394) 88855
e bookings@lakelovers.co.uk
w lakelovers.co.uk

Dale Head Cottage ★★
Self Catering
Lakelovers
t (015394) 88855
e bookings@lakelovers.co.uk
w lakelovers.co.uk

Dove Holme ★★★
Self Catering
Lakelovers
t (015394) 88855
e bookings@lakelovers.co.uk
w lakelovers.co.uk

Easedale Studio Apartment
★★ *Self Catering*
Lakelovers
t (015394) 88855
e bookings@lakelovers.co.uk
w lakelovers.co.uk

Eller Close, Wisteria & Garden Cottage ★★★
Self Catering
Lakelovers
t (015394) 88855
e bookings@lakelovers.co.uk
w lakelovers.co.uk

Fir Tree Cottage ★★★★
Self Catering
Contact: Susan Jackson
Heart of the Lakes
t (015394) 32321

Foxtail Cot ★★★★★
Self Catering
Cumbrian Cottages
t (01228) 599960
e enquiries@cumbrian-cottages.co.uk
w cumbrian-cottages.co.uk

Ghyllburn Cottage ★★
Self Catering
Lake District Inns and Cottages
t 05006 00725
e stay@lakedistrictinns.co.uk
w lakedistrictinns.co.uk

Glen View Cottage ★★★★
Self Catering
Lakelovers
t (015394) 88855
e bookings@lakelovers.co.uk
w lakelovers.co.uk

Goody Raise ★★★
Self Catering
Lakelovers
t (015394) 88855
e bookings@lakelovers.co.uk
w lakelovers.co.uk

Grasmere Cottages ★★★★
Self Catering
Contact: Martin Wood
t (015394) 35395
e enquiries@grasmerecottage accommodation.co.uk
w grasmerecottage accommodation.co.uk

Grasmere View ★★
Self Catering
Cumbrian Cottages
t (01228) 599960
e enquiries@cumbrian-cottages.co.uk
w cumbrian-cottages.co.uk

Grey Crag Barn ★★★★★
Self Catering
Lakelovers
t (015394) 88855
e bookings@lakelovers.co.uk
w lakelovers.co.uk

Helm Crag ★★★★
Self Catering
Hideaways
t (015394) 42435
e bookings@lakeland-hideaways.co.uk
w lakedistrictholidays.net

Heron View ★★★★
Self Catering
Cumbrian Cottages
t (01228) 599960
e enquiries@cumbrian-cottages.co.uk
w cumbrian-cottages.co.uk

Hollens Farmhouse ★★★★
Self Catering
Lakes Cottage Holidays
t (01228) 591555
e info@lakescottageholiday.co.uk
w lakescottageholiday.co.uk

Holly Cottage ★★★★
Self Catering
Cumbrian Cottages
t (01228) 599960
e enquiries@cumbrian-cottages.co.uk
w cumbrian-cottages.co.uk

Kelbarrow ★★★★★
Self Catering
Lakelovers
t (015394) 88855
e bookings@lakelovers.co.uk
w lakelovers.co.uk

Lake View Holiday Apartments, Grasmere
★★★ *Self Catering*
Contact: Stephen & Michelle King
t (015394) 35384
e dms@lakeview-grasmere.com
w lakeview-grasmere.com

The Lakeside Suite
★★★★★ *Self Catering*
Cumbrian Cottages
t (01228) 599960
e enquiries@cumbrian-cottages.co.uk
w cumbrian-cottages.co.uk

Little Beeches ★★★
Self Catering
Cumbrian Cottages
t (01228) 599960
e enquiries@cumbrian-cottages.co.uk
w cumbrian-cottages.co.uk

Little Parrock ★★★★
Self Catering
Contact: Joanne Green
t (01604) 626383
e joanne@routenhouse.co.uk
w routenhouse.co.uk

Loughrigg Apartment ★★★
Self Catering
Cumbrian Cottages
t (01228) 599960
e enquiries@cumbrian-cottages.co.uk
w cumbrian-cottages.co.uk

Milly's Cottage ★★★★
Self Catering
Cumbrian Cottages
t (01228) 599960
e enquiries@cumbrian-cottages.co.uk
w cumbrian-cottages.co.uk

Nutkins Nest ★★★★★
Self Catering
Cumbrian Cottages
t (01228) 599960
e enquiries@cumbrian-cottages.co.uk
w cumbrian-cottages.co.uk

Oak Bank Apartment ★★★
Self Catering
Cumbrian Cottages
t (01228) 599960
e enquiries@cumbrian-cottages.co.uk
w cumbrian-cottages.co.uk

Old Bakers Cottage ★★★★
Self Catering
Lakes Cottage Holidays
t (01228) 591555
e info@lakescottageholiday.co.uk
w lakescottageholiday.co.uk

Old Halsteads ★★★★
Self Catering
Cumbrian Cottages
t (01228) 599960
e enquiries@cumbrian-cottages.co.uk
w cumbrian-cottages.co.uk

Poets View Cottage ★★★★
Self Catering
Cumbrian Cottages
t (01228) 599960
e enquiries@cumbrian-cottages.co.uk
w cumbrian-cottages.co.uk

Riverbank ★★★★
Self Catering
Lakelovers
t (015394) 88855
e bookings@lakelovers.co.uk
w lakelovers.co.uk

Rockwood ★★★
Self Catering
Contact: Michael Thornton
Oak Apple Barn & Rockwood
t (01344) 624896
e mikethornton@ascotgbr.freeserve.co.uk
w rockwood-lakedistrict.com

Rothay Lodge ★★★★
Self Catering
Contact: Lindsay Rogers
t (015394) 35341
e enquiries@rothay-lodge.co.uk
w rothay-lodge.co.uk

Rowan Cottage ★★★★
Self Catering
Lakes Cottage Holidays
t (01228) 591555
e info@lakescottageholiday.co.uk
w lakescottageholiday.co.uk

Swallows Cottage ★★★★
Self Catering
Lakelovers
t (015394) 88855
e bookings@lakelovers.co.uk
w lakelovers.co.uk

Tilly's Cottage ★★★★
Self Catering
Lakelovers
t (015394) 88855
e bookings@lakelovers.co.uk
w lakelovers.co.uk

Waterhey ★★★★★
Self Catering
Cumbrian Cottages
t (01228) 599960
e enquiries@cumbrian-cottages.co.uk
w cumbrian-cottages.co.uk

GRASSINGTON
North Yorkshire

6A Garrs Lane ★★★
Self Catering
Contact: Paul Borrill
t (01756) 752436 & 07709 313716
e info@grassingtonapartment.co.uk
w grassingtonapartment.co.uk

The Barn ★★★★
Self Catering
Contact: Gail Evans
t (01756) 753390
e grassington@art-by-gail.uk
w dalestay.co.uk/thebarn

Linda's Cottage ★★★
Self Catering
Yorkshire Cottages
t (01228) 406701
e enquiries@yorkshire-cottages.info
w yorkshire-cottages.info

Manna Cottage ★★★★
Self Catering
Contact: Sheila Carr
DSC Holiday Lettings Ltd
t (01756) 752435
e carr@totalise.co.uk
w yorkshirenet.co.uk/stayat/mannacottage/

Sunnyside Cottage
★★★-★★★★ *Self Catering*
Contact: Carolyn Butt
t (01756) 730391 & 07720 294391
e cosycottages@hotmail.com
w grassingtoncottages.co.uk

Theatre Cottage ★★★
Self Catering
Dales Holiday Cottages
t (01756) 790919
e info@dales-holiday-cottages.com
w dales-holiday-cottages.com

GREAT ASBY
Cumbria

Appleby View ★★★★
Self Catering
Cumbrian Cottages
t (01228) 599960
e enquiries@cumbrian-cottages.co.uk
w cumbrian-cottages.co.uk

Scalebeck Holiday Cottages, Great Asby ★★★★
Self Catering
Contact: Mr K J Budding
t (017683) 51006
e mail@scalebeckholidaycottages.com
w scalebeckholidaycottages.co.uk

GREAT AYTON
North Yorkshire

Cleve Cottage ★★★★
Self Catering
Yorkshire Cottages
t (01228) 406701
e enquiries@yorkshire-cottages.info
w yorkshire-cottages.info

The Old Stables ★★★★
Self Catering
Contact: Catherine Hawman
t (01642) 722560
e theoldstables@btopenworld.com
w cottageguide.co.uk/theoldstables

GREAT CORBY
Cumbria

Clint Head Cottage ★★★★
Self Catering
Cumbrian Cottages
t (01228) 599960
e enquiries@cumbrian-cottages.co.uk
w cumbrian-cottages.co.uk

Thackmoor House ★★★★
Self Catering
Contact: Anne McDowall
Whitehall Properties
t (01228) 514004
e anne_635@fsmail.net
w northcumbriancottages.co.uk

GREAT EDSTONE
North Yorkshire

Cowldyke Farm
★★★-★★★★ *Self Catering*
Contact: Mrs Janet Benton
t (01751) 431242
e janetbenton@btconnect.com
w cowldyke-farm.co.uk

GREAT LANGDALE
Cumbria

Crinkle Craggs ★★
Self Catering
Lakelovers
t (015394) 88855
e bookings@lakelovers.co.uk
w lakelovers.co.uk

Pye Howe ★★★ *Self Catering*
Lakelovers
t (015394) 88855
e bookings@lakelovers.co.uk
w lakelovers.co.uk

GREAT LANGTON
North Yorkshire

Stanhow Bungalow ★★★★
Self Catering
Contact: Mary Furness
t (01609) 748614
e mary.stanhow@freenet.co.uk

GREAT MUSGRAVE
Cumbria

Blandswath Cottage ★★★
Self Catering
Contact: Mrs Watson
t (017683) 41842
e watson@blandswath.freeserve.co.uk

GREAT SALKELD
Cumbria

Herbage Cottage
Rating Applied For
Self Catering
Contact: Mr & Mrs Martin & Melanie Reynolds
t (01768) 870674
e martynereynolds@yahoo.co.uk

GREAT STRICKLAND
Cumbria

The Old Cow Byre ★★★★
Self Catering
Contact: Mark Melling
t (01931) 712205
e info@taylorsfarm.co.uk
w taylorsfarm.co.uk

GREENHAUGH
Northumberland

Bought Hill Mill ★★★★
Self Catering
Contact: Mrs A Cowan
t (01434) 240373

GREENHEAD
Northumberland

Holmhead Cottage ★★★
Self Catering
Contact: Mr & Mrs Pauline & Brian Staff
t (01697) 747402
e holmhead@hadrianswall.freeserve.co.uk
w holmhead.com

GREETLAND
West Yorkshire

The Barn, Lower High Trees Farm ★★★ *Self Catering & Serviced Apartments*
Contact: Kate Griffiths
t (01422) 375205
e kate@egs.org.uk
w greetland.org.uk

GRESSINGHAM
Lancashire

Garden Cottage ★★★
Self Catering
Contact: Mrs Margaret Burrow
t (01524) 221347
e gardencottage@highsnab.freeserve.co.uk
w highsnab.freeserve.co.uk

GREWELTHORPE
North Yorkshire

Fir Tree Farm Holiday Homes, Grewelthorpe
★★★★ *Self Catering*
Contact: Eric & Jane Simpson
t (01765) 658727
e firtreefarmhouse@aol.com
w firtree-farm-holidayhomes.co.uk

GREYSTOKE
Cumbria

Blenshiel
Rating Applied For
Self Catering
Lakeland Cottage Holidays
t (017687) 76065
e info@lakelandcottages.co.uk
w lakelandcottages.co.uk

Pelican Dairy ★★★★
Self Catering
Dales Holiday Cottages
t (01756) 790919
e info@dales-holiday-cottages.com
w dales-holiday-cottages.com

Red Barn Cottages ★★★★
Self Catering
Contact: Mrs GL Jackson
t (017684) 83230
e info@redbarncottages.co.uk
w redbarncottages.co.uk

Rose Cottage ★★★★
Self Catering
Lakes Cottage Holidays
t (01228) 591555
e info@lakescottageholiday.co.uk
w lakescottageholiday.co.uk

Stable Cottage ★★★★
Self Catering
Cumbrian Cottages
t (01228) 599960
e enquiries@cumbrian-cottages.co.uk
w cumbrian-cottages.co.uk

GRINDLETON
Lancashire

Crossfold House Holiday Cottage ★★★ *Self Catering*
Contact: Mrs Sheila Hailwood
t (01200) 440178
e rodney@rhailwood.freeserve.co.uk

Foxley Bank Stables
★★★★★ *Self Catering*
Contact: Mrs Sarah Conley
t (01200) 440197
e enquiries@foxleybankstables.co.uk
w foxleybankstables.co.uk

GRINTON
North Yorkshire

Blaeberry Cottage ★★
Self Catering
Contact: Garry Hudson
t (01279) 654115
e brh@bsc.biblio.net
w blaeberry.co.uk

Feetham Holme ★★★★
Self Catering
Contact: Ian Robinson
Plantation Business Services
t (01254) 826546
e plantation@talk21.com

GRISTHORPE
North Yorkshire

Cockleshell Cottage ★★★★
Self Catering
Contact: Mrs J Bagley
t 07802 427446
e mike@msbagley.fsnet.co.uk

Dove Cottage Ref ★★★★
Self Catering
Dales Holiday Cottages
t (01756) 790919
e info@dales-holiday-cottages.com
w dales-holiday-cottages.com

Vale View ★★★ *Self Catering*
Bedwyn's Holiday Accommodation
t (01723) 516700
e info@bedwyns.co.uk
w bedwyns.co.uk

GRISTHORPE BAY
North Yorkshire

St Kitts Self Catering Holiday Flats ★★★★
Self Catering
Contact: Mr & Mrs J.R Rook
t (01430) 827661
w stkittsselfcateringholidayflats.co.uk

GRIZEBECK
Cumbria

1 Bank End ★★★
Self Catering
Cumbrian Cottages
t (01228) 599960
e enquiries@cumbrian-cottages.co.uk
w cumbrian-cottages.co.uk

GRIZEDALE
Cumbria

Dancing Beck ★★★★
Self Catering
Lakelovers
t (015394) 88855
e bookings@lakelovers.co.uk
w lakelovers.co.uk

Fairy Glen Cottage ★★★
Self Catering
Cumbrian Cottages
t (01228) 599960
e enquiries@cumbrian-cottages.co.uk
w cumbrian-cottages.co.uk

High Dale Park Barn ★★★
Self Catering
Contact: Peter Brown
t (01229) 860226
e peter@lakesweddingmusic.com
w lakesweddingmusic.com/accomm/

Windows ★★★ *Self Catering*
Lakelovers
t (015394) 88855
e bookings@lakelovers.co.uk
w lakelovers.co.uk

GROSMONT
North Yorkshire

East Farm Cottage ★★★
Self Catering
Whitby Holiday Cottages
t (01947) 603010
e enquiries@whitbyholidaycottages.net
w whitbyholidaycottages.net

Engineman's Lodge
Rating Applied For
Self Catering
Contact: Mrs Vanessa Hicking
Whitby Holiday Cottages
t (01947) 603010
e enquiries@whitbyholidaycottages.net
w whitby-cottages.co.uk

GUISBOROUGH
Tees Valley

Argument Cottage ★★★★
Self Catering
Contact: Ms Maria Wilcock
t (01287) 638716
e mariawilcock@hotmail.com
w argumentproperties.co.uk

Bousdale Old Stables
★★★★★ *Self Catering*
Contact: Miss Erica Bartram
t (01287) 633459
e erica.1@tiscali.co.uk
w bousdalefarm.co.uk

GUNNERSIDE
North Yorkshire

Dufton House ★★★
Self Catering
Contact: Annie Porter
t (01748) 886253

High Oxnop ★★★★
Self Catering
Contact: Annie Porter
t (01748) 886253

Sundale ★★ *Self Catering*
Holiday Cottages (Yorkshire) Ltd
t (01756) 700510
e brochure@holidaycotts.co.uk
w holidaycotts.co.uk

GUNNERTON
Northumberland

Southlands Farm Cottages
★★★★ *Self Catering*
Contact: Mrs Deborah McGowan
t (01434) 681464
e dee@wooshbonk.co.uk
w southlandsfarmcottages.co.uk

The Stables Cottage ★★★★
Self Catering
Contact: Mr Scott Reay
t (01434) 689942
w stablescottagelet.co.uk

HACKNESS
North Yorkshire

Granary Cottage ★★★★★
Self Catering
Contact: Julie Metcalfe
t (01723) 373461
e info@countrycottageholiday.com
w countrycottageholiday.com

Hackness Cottage ★★★
Self Catering
Contact: Mr Paul Wicks
t (01723) 871028
e spwicks@btinternet.com
w whitbycottages.com

HADSTON
Northumberland

May Lodge
Rating Applied For
Self Catering
Contact: Mrs Margaret Henderson
t (01670) 760479
e hendersonmagas@hotmail.com

HALIFAX
West Yorkshire

Cherry Tree Cottages, Barkisland ★★★★
Self Catering
Contact: Stan & Elaine Shaw
t (01422) 372662
e cherrytree@yorkshire-cottages.co.uk
w yorkshire-cottages.co.uk

The Fall ★★★ *Self Catering*
Contact: Ann Knight
t (01422) 363346

Prescott Street
Rating Applied For
Serviced Apartments
Contact: Mr Ken Forsyth
t 07789 540 577
e sales@execu-let.com
w execu-let.com

HALTON GILL
North Yorkshire

Swains Cottage (4170)
★★★ *Self Catering*
Dales Holiday Cottages
t (01756) 790919
e info@dales-holiday-cottages.com
w dales-holiday-cottages.com

HALTWHISTLE
Northumberland

Ald White Craig Farm Cottages ★-★★★
Self Catering
Contact: Mr & Mrs Newby
t (01434) 320565
e info@aldwhitecraigfarm.co.uk
w aldwhitecraigfarm.co.uk

Gibbs Hill Farm Cottages
★★★★ *Self Catering*
Contact: Mrs Valerie Gibson
t (01434) 344030
e val@gibbshillfarm.co.uk
w gibbshillfarm.co.uk

Kellah Farm Cottages
★★★-★★★★ *Self Catering*
Contact: Mrs Lesley Teasdale
t (01434) 320816
e teasdale@ukonline.co.uk
w kellah.co.uk

Milecastle Inn ★★★
Self Catering
Contact: Mr & Mrs Kevin & Clare Hind
t (01434) 321372
e clarehind@aol.com
w milecastle-inn.co.uk

Old High House Chapel
★★★ *Self Catering*
Contact: Mr Simon Williams
t (01670) 828956
e info@1750chapel.co.uk
w 1750chapel.co.uk

Whitchester Farm Cottage
★★★ *Self Catering*
Contact: Mr J M Hall
t (01434) 322855
e whitchester@ukonline.co.uk
w whitchester.co.uk

HAMBLETON
North Yorkshire

Casten Cottage ★★★
Self Catering
Sykes Cottages
t (01244) 345700
e info@sykescottages.co.uk
w sykescottages.co.uk

HAMSTERLEY
Durham

Hamsterley Cottage ★★★★
Self Catering
Contact: Mrs Margaret Christensen
t (01388) 488091
e info@dale-endhamsterleybandb.co.uk
w hamsterleycottage.co.uk

High Shipley Caravan
Approved Caravan Holiday Home
Contact: Mrs Heather Richardson
t (01388) 764620

Jasmine Cottage ★★★
Self Catering
Contact: Mrs A E Roberts
t (01388) 488630
e annee24roberts@aol.co.uk

HARBOTTLE
Northumberland

Brackenlea Cottage ★★★
Self Catering
Contact: Mr & Mrs John & Helen Dalrymple
t (01670) 519629
e info@brackenleacottage.co.uk
w brackenleacottage.co.uk

Honeysuckle Cottage ★★★
Self Catering
Contact: Mrs Jackie Bickmore
t (01669) 650348
e jackyhoney01@aol.com
w honeysuckleharbottle.ntb.org.uk

Woodhall Farm Holiday Cottage ★★★ *Self Catering*
Contact: Mrs J D Blakey
t (01669) 650245
e blakey@woodhall65.freeserve.co.uk
w woodhallcottage.co.uk

HARMBY
North Yorkshire

1,2,3 and 4 Harmby Grange Cottages ★★★★
Self Catering
Contact: Mr Jefferson
t (01969) 622559

Hillfoot House ★★
Self Catering
Contact: Mr Jones
t (01969) 623632

HARROGATE
North Yorkshire

25A West Park
Rating Applied For
Self Catering
Contact: Mr James Platt
t (01765) 635177
e james@railrover.com

Apartment 1 ★★★★
Self Catering
Contact: Mrs Hillary Mennell
t (01423) 562186
w strayside.co.uk

Ashley Cottage ★★
Self Catering
Contact: Mrs Yoko Banks
t (01423) 507474
e keith@ashleyhousehotel.com

Ashness Apartments
★★★★ *Self Catering*
Contact: Mr Spinlove & Miss H Spinlove
t (01423) 526894
e office@ashness.com
w ashness.com

Ashrigg ★★★★ *Self Catering*
Contact: Mr & Mrs Peter & Angela Holt
t (01423) 871177
e pholt@westrigg.freeserve.co.uk
w ashrigg.co.uk

The Barn@Fir Tree Farm
★★★★ *Self Catering*
Contact: Rebecca Donnelly
t (01423) 779709
e rdonnelly@ge.cokecce.com
w thebarninharrogate.co.uk

Brimham Rocks Cottages
★★★★ *Self Catering*
Contact: Chris & Deborah Gray
t (01765) 620284
e brimhamrc@yahoo.co.uk
w brimham.co.uk

Dinmore Cottages, Burnt Yates ★★★★ *Self Catering*
Contact: Denise Wales
t (01423) 770860
e aib@dinmore-cottages.freeserve.co.uk
w dinmore-cottages.co.uk

Duchy Mews ★★★★
Self Catering
Contact: Sandra Sykes
t (01423) 565109
e sandra.sykes@btopenworld.com
w duchyrentals.co.uk

The Gables
Rating Applied For
Self Catering
t (01423) 505625

Green House
Rating Applied For
Serviced Apartments
Contact: Bryan Patterson
t (01423) 524527
e stay@superiorstay.com
w superiorstay.com

Old Swan View ★★★★
Self Catering
Contact: Graham & Amanda Lloyd
Apartments of Distinction
t (01423) 538742
e info@harrogateholidayapartments.co.uk
w harrogateholidayapartments.co.uk

Regent Cottage ★★★★
Self Catering
Contact: Robert Blake
t (01394) 382565
e robert@blake4110.fsbusiness.co.uk

Rudding Estate Cottages
★★★–★★★★ *Self Catering*
Rudding Park Estate Ltd
t (01423) 844844
e info@rudding.com
w rudding.com/cottages

Rudding Gates ★★★★★
Self Catering
Contact: Jan Mackaness
Rudding Park Estate Ltd
t (01423) 844844
e info@rudding.com
w rudding.com/gates

Rudding Holiday Park ★★★
Self Catering
t (01423) 870439
e holiday-park@ruddingpark.com
w ruddingpark.com

Studley View Apartment
★★★★ *Self Catering*
Contact: Graham & Amanda Lloyd
Apartments of Distinction
t (01423) 538742
e info@harrogateholidayapartments.co.uk
w harrogateholidayapartments.co.uk

Superior Stay ★★★★★
Serviced Apartments
Contact: Sophie Hayes
t (01423) 524257
e stay@superiorstay.com
w superiorstay.com

HARTLEPOOL
Tees Valley

Mariners View
Rating Applied For
Serviced Apartments
Contact: Ms Jane Wills
t (01929) 552100
e info@stayinthenorth.co.uk
w stayinthenorth.co.uk

Waters Edge ★★★
Self Catering
Contact: Mrs Rosalie Reeder
t (01455) 284748
e rosalie.reeder@ukonline.co.uk
w cottageguide.co.uk/watersedge

HARTLEY
Cumbria

Hartley Castle Barn ★★★★
Self Catering
Contact: Sally Dixon
t (017683) 71331
e sally@hartleycastle.co.uk
w hartleycastle.co.uk

Ladthwaite Barn ★★★★
Self Catering
Contact: Anette Watt
t (017683) 71488
e anettewatt@btinternet.com
w ladthwaitebarn.co.uk

HARTSOP
Cumbria

Low Beckside ★★★
Self Catering
Contact: Shirley Thompson
Absolute Escapes Letting Ltd
t (01768) 892777
e shirley@absolute-escapes.com
w absolute-escapes.com

Willow & Grove Cottages
★★★–★★★★ *Self Catering*
Contact: Helen Griffiths
t (017684) 82647
e helen@lakes-hartsop.co.uk
w lakes-hartsop.co.uk

HARTWITH
North Yorkshire

Cow Close Barn ★★★★
Self Catering
Contact: Diana Kitzing
t (01423) 770850
e rainerkitzing@aol.com
w cowclose-barn.co.uk

HARWOOD DALE
North Yorkshire

Murk Head Holiday Cottages ★★★★
Self Catering
Contact: Mrs Joanna Gray
t (01723) 871686
e joannagray@aol.com

HAUGHTON
Cheshire

Rookery Cottage ★★★
Self Catering
Contact: Mrs G.D Burdett
t (01829) 260069
e geoff.burdett@tesco.net

HAVERIGG
Cumbria

Cockleshell Cottage ★★★
Self Catering
Cumbrian Cottages
t (01228) 599960
e enquiries@cumbrian-cottages.co.uk
w cumbrian-cottages.co.uk

Quiet Cottage ★★★
Self Catering
Contact: Mr & Mrs Haston
t (01229) 772974
e quietcottage@tiscali.co.uk

HAVERTHWAITE
Cumbria

Dairy Cottage ★★
Self Catering
Cumbrian Cottages
t (01228) 599960
e enquiries@cumbrian-cottages.co.uk
w cumbrian-cottages.co.uk

HAWES
North Yorkshire

Cherry Tree Cottage ★★★
Self Catering
Country Hideaways
t (01969) 663559
e info@countryhideaways.co.uk
w countryhideaways.co.uk

Gaudy House Farm ★★★
Self Catering
Contact: Jane Allison
t (01969) 667231
e sjane.allison@virgin.net
w gaudyhousefarm.co.uk

Jane Ann Cottage ★★
Self Catering
Contact: Mrs Irene Sunter
t (01969) 667186
e irene@overdales.co.uk
w overdales.co.uk

Pry House
Rating Applied For
Self Catering
t (01969) 667241 & 07870 415018
w pryhousefarm.co.uk

Swallowdale ★★★★
Self Catering
Contact: Lorraine Gilmour
Dales Holiday Cottages
t (01756) 790919
e info@dales-holiday-cottages.com
w dales-holiday-cottages.com

Yore View ★★★
Self Catering
Contact: Elizabeth Pedley
t (01969) 667358
e yoreviewcottage@talk21.com
w yoreview.co.uk

Yorkshire Dales Country Cottages ★★★ *Self Catering*
Contact: Brenda Stott
t (01969) 667359
e rogerstott@aol.com
w yorkshirenet.co.uk/accgde/ydcotts.htm

HAWKSHEAD
Cumbria

Barn Syke ★★★★
Self Catering
Lakelovers
t (015394) 88855
e bookings@lakelovers.co.uk
w lakelovers.co.uk

Ben Fold ★★★ *Self Catering*
Hideaways
t (015394) 42435
e bookings@lakeland-hideaways.co.uk
w lakeland-hideaways.co.uk

Birkwray Farmhouse
★★★★ *Self Catering*
Lakelovers
t (015394) 88855
e bookings@lakelovers.co.uk
w lakelovers.co.uk

The Briars ★★★★★
Self Catering
Hideaways
t (015394) 42435
e bookings@lakeland-hideaways.co.uk
w lakeland-hideaways.co.uk

Bridge View ★★★
Self Catering
Contact: Susan Dewhurst
t (015394) 36340

Broomriggs ★★★
Self Catering
Hideaways
t (015394) 42435
e bookings@lakeland-hideaways.co.uk
w lakeland-hideaways.co.uk

Columbine Cottage ★★★
Self Catering
Lakelovers
t (015394) 88855
e bookings@lakelovers.co.uk
w lakelovers.co.uk

Cowpers Barn ★★★★
Self Catering
Hideaways
t (015394) 42435
e bookings@lakeland-hideaways.co.uk
w lakeland-hideaways.co.uk

The Croft Holiday Flats, Hawkshead ★★★
Self Catering
Contact: Mrs Barr
t (015394) 36374
e enquiries@hawkshead-croft.com
w hawkshead-croft.com

Gingerbread Cottage
★★★★ *Self Catering*
Lakelovers
t (015394) 88855
e bookings@lakelovers.co.uk
w lakelovers.co.uk

High Cross ★★★★
Self Catering
Cumbrian Cottages
t (01228) 599960
e enquiries@cumbrian-cottages.co.uk
w cumbrian-cottages.co.uk

High Orchard ★★★★
Self Catering
The Coppermines & Coniston Lakes Cottages
t (015394) 41765
w coppermines.co.uk

Keen Ground Cottage ★★★
Self Catering
Lakeland Cottage Comapny
t (015395) 38180
e john@lakelandcottageco.com
w lakelandcottageco.com

Kings Yard Cottage ★★★
Self Catering
Cumbrian Cottages
t (01228) 599960
e enquiries@cumbrian-cottages.co.uk
w cumbrian-cottages.co.uk

Kingsyard ★★★ *Self Catering*
Cumbrian Cottages
t (01228) 599960
e enquiries@cumbrian-cottages.co.uk
w cumbrian-cottages.co.uk

Lantern Cottage ★★★
Self Catering
Cumbrian Cottages
t (01228) 599960
e enquiries@cumbrian-cottages.co.uk
w cumbrian-cottages.co.uk

Meadow View ★★★
Self Catering
Blakes Cottages
t 0870 336 7777
w blakes.cottages.co.uk

Oak Apple Barn ★★★★
Self Catering
Contact: Michael Thornton
Oak Apple Barn & Rockwood
t (01344) 624896
e mikethornton@ascotgbr.freeserve.co.uk
w oakapplebarn.com

Old Barn & Barn End ★★★
Self Catering
Hideaways
t (015394) 42435
e bookings@lakeland-hideaways.co.uk
w lakeland-hideaways.co.uk

The Old Loft ★★★★
Self Catering
Lakelovers
t (015394) 88855
e bookings@lakelovers.co.uk
w lakelovers.co.uk

Ramblers Roost ★★★
Self Catering
Contact: Howard King
Talcomb & Ramblers Roost
t 07973 420179
e hk.developments@virgin.net
w hkdevelopmentslakes.co.uk

Riggeswood Cottage ★★★
Self Catering
Lakelovers
t (015394) 88855
e bookings@lakelovers.co.uk
w lakelovers.co.uk

Rose Cottage
Rating Applied For
Self Catering
Lakelovers
t (015394) 88855
e bookings@lakelovers.co.uk
w lakelovers.co.uk

Rose How ★★★★
Self Catering
Hideaways
t (015394) 42435
e bookings@lakeland-hideaways.co.uk
w lakeland-hideaways.co.uk

Sergeant Man ★★★
Self Catering
Lakelovers
t (015394) 88855
e bookings@lakelovers.co.uk
w lakelovers.co.uk

Shepherds Cottage ★★★★
Self Catering
Cumbrian Cottages
t (01228) 599960
e enquiries@cumbrian-cottages.co.uk
w cumbrian-cottages.co.uk

Spinners Loft ★★★
Self Catering
Hideaways
t (015394) 42435
e bookings@lakeland-hideaways.co.uk
w lakeland-hideaways.co.uk

Swiss Cottage ★★★★
Self Catering
Hideaways
t (015394) 42435
e bookings@lakeland-hideaways.co.uk
w lakeland-hideaways.co.uk

Walker Ground Cottage
★★★★ *Self Catering*
Cumbrian Cottages
t (01228) 599960
e enquiries@cumbrian-cottages.co.uk
w cumbrian-cottages.co.uk

HAWKSHEAD HILL
Cumbria

The Old Farmhouse ★★★★
Self Catering
Lakeland Cottage Comapny
t (015395) 38180
e john@lakelandcottageco.com
w lakelandcottageco.com

Wansfell View ★★★
Self Catering
Hideaways
t (015394) 42435
e bookings@lakeland-hideaways.co.uk
w lakeland-hideaways.co.uk

HAWORTH
West Yorkshire

Bottoms Farm Cottages
★★★★ *Self Catering*
Contact: Linda Littler
t (01535) 607720
e bottomsfarm@btinternet.com

Bronte Country Cottages
★★★ *Self Catering*
Contact: Clare Pickles
t (01535) 644568
e clare@brontecountrycottages.co.uk
w brontecountrycottages.co.uk

Daisy Cottage, Haworth
★★★★ *Self Catering*
Contact: Mrs Hilary Freeman
t (01535) 644140
e hilaryanddave@yahoo.co.uk

Haworth Church Cottage
★★★ *Self Catering*
Contact: Mrs Averil Kenyon
Haworth Church Cottage Ltd
t (01535) 642264
e churchcottage@blueyonder.co.uk
w haworthchurchcottage.co.uk

Heather, Bilberry Cottage
★★★★ *Self Catering*
Contact: Janet Milner
t (01535) 644755
e janet@bronteholidays.co.uk
w bronteholidays.co.uk

Heather Cottage ★★★
Self Catering
Yorkshire Cottages
t (01228) 406701
e enquiries@yorkshire-cottages.info
w yorkshire-cottages.info

Heron Cottage, Haworth
★★★★ *Self Catering*
Contact: Janet Walker
t (01535) 648537
e jan.w@virgin.net

Hewenden Mill Cottages
★★★★–★★★★★
Self Catering
Contact: Janet Emanuel
t (01535) 274259
e info@hewendenmillcottages.co.uk
w hewendenmillcottages.co.uk

Hidden Gem ★★★
Self Catering
Contact: Christina Harte **e** info@hidden-gem.co.uk
w hidden-gem.co.uk

Loubie & Woolcombers Cottages ★★★ *Self Catering*
Contact: Barbara Clayton
t (01535) 646778
e b557clayton@btinternet.com
w haworth-cottage-rental.co.uk

Number 66 ★★★★
Self Catering
Contact: Glenda Joy
t (01535) 643008
e glendajoyuk@yahoo.co.uk
w number-66.co.uk

Penrhyn ★★★ *Self Catering*
Contact: David Smith
t (01226) 218798
e penrhynhaworth2@activemail.co.uk

September Cottage ★★★★
Self Catering
Contact: Joy Page
t (01535) 644091
e sept.cottage@btinternet.com
w robjoypagecromer.supanet.com

Weavers Cottage and Loft ★★★ *Self Catering*
Contact: Gaye Bond
Weavers Cottage & Weavers Loft
t (01535) 211184
e g.j.bond@blueyonder.co.uk
w weaverscottage-web.co.uk

HAWS BANK
Cumbria

Beckside House ★★★★
Self Catering
Contact: Martin Askew
Coniston Breaks
t (015394) 37379
e info@conistonbreaks.com
w conistonbreaks.com

Stone Leys Cottage ★★★★
Self Catering
The Coppermines & Coniston Lakes Cottages
t (015394) 41765
w coppermines.co.uk

HAWSKER
North Yorkshire

Hornblower Lodge & Holiday Cottage
Rating Applied For
Self Catering
Contact: Mr & Mrs John & Janet Evans
t (01947) 606247
e john.nunthorpe44@yahoo.com
w hornblowerlodge.co.uk

HAYDON BRIDGE
Northumberland

Braemar ★★★★
Self Catering
Contact: Mrs Cynthia Bradley
t (01434) 684622
e edenholme@btinternet.com
w edenholme.btinternet.co.uk

Langdale Cottage ★★★★
Self Catering
Contact: Mr & Mrs Richard Smith
t (01434) 688570
e langdalecottage@yahoo.co.uk

Scotch Corner ★★★★
Self Catering
Contact: Mrs Pauline Wallis
t (01434) 684061
e wallis@scotcharms.fsnet.co.uk
w scotcharms.com

HAYTON
Cumbria

The Lodge ★★★★★
Self Catering
Contact: Kath Watson
t (01228) 670215
e info@the-lodge-holiday-cottages-cumbria.co.uk
w thelodgehayton.co.uk

Plum Corner ★★★
Self Catering
Cumbrian Cottages
t (01228) 599960
e enquiries@cumbrian-cottages.co.uk
w cumbrian-cottages.co.uk

HEADS NOOK
Cumbria

Manor House Cottage ★★★★ *Self Catering*
Lakes Cottage Holidays
t (01228) 591555
e info@lakescottageholiday.co.uk
w lakescottageholiday.co.uk

HEALEY
North Yorkshire

Healey Mill Holiday Cottages ★★★★
Self Catering
Contact: Diane Fathers
t (01765) 689774
e enquiries@healeymill.co.uk
w healeymill.co.uk

Valley View ★★★
Self Catering
Yorkshire Cottages
t (01228) 406701
e enquiries@yorkshire-cottages.info
w yorkshire-cottages.info

HEALEY
Northumberland

Hilltop Barn ★★★★
Self Catering
Contact: Mrs Janet Cain
t (01434) 673647
e p.j.cain@ncl.ac.uk

HEATON
Lancashire

Whittam Barn ★★★★★
Self Catering
Contact: Mrs Susan Waldie
t (01524) 852336
e susanwaldie@aol.com
w whittambarn.co.uk

HEATON
West Yorkshire

Honeysuckle Cottage ★★★
Self Catering
Contact: Pamela Stobart
t (01274) 541181
e pameladstobart@tiscali.co.uk

HEBBURN
Tyne and Wear

26 Hazelmoor ★★★★
Self Catering
Contact: Mr Peter Goodall
t 07941 611551
e peter.goodall7@virgin.net
w stayinbritain.com/hazelmoor

HEBDEN BRIDGE
West Yorkshire

Chalet at Cairnacre ★★
Self Catering
Contact: Mrs Ruth Price
t (01422) 842861
e ruth-price@lineone.net

Croft Mill ★★★★
Self Catering
Contact: Josephine Anderson
t (01422) 846836
e andersonjosephine@btinternet.com

The Garden House ★★★
Self Catering
Contact: Mr Martin Robinson
t (01422) 842794
e manorhousestudio@talktalk.net
w manorhousestudio.co.uk

Old Town Hall Cottage ★★★★ *Self Catering*
Contact: Mrs L Finnerty
t (01422) 846559
e oldtownhallcottage@yahoo.co.uk
w cottageguide.co.uk/oldtownhallcottage

HEDDON-ON-THE-WALL
Northumberland

2 East Town House ★★★
Self Catering
Contact: Mr & Mrs Ridley and Beryl Amos
1 East Town House
t (01661) 852277

HEIGHTS
Cumbria

Berts Cottage ★★★★
Self Catering
Contact: Pauline Cleasby
t (017683) 62221
e heightsholidays@f2s.com

Meadow View ★★★★
Self Catering
t (017683) 62221

Sycamore Cottage ★★★★
Self Catering
t (017683) 51624

HELMSLEY
North Yorkshire

2 Elmslac Road ★★★
Self Catering
Contact: Mr & Mrs Richard & Dorothy Munn
t (01751) 472193

Beadlam Farm Cottage ★★★ *Self Catering*
Contact: Jenny Rooke
t (01439) 770303
e mark.rooke@farming.co.uk
w stayfarmnorth.co.uk

Bondgate Flat ★★★★
Self Catering
Contact: Margaret Kilby
t (01653) 691576
e wakilby@tiscali.co.uk

Church View ★★★★
Self Catering
Contact: Sally Ann Foster
t (01709) 852929
e sally@helmsleyhouse.co.uk
w helmsleyhouse.co.uk

The Flat, 2 Castlegate ★★★
Self Catering
Contact: Simon Laycock
Tapestry Garden
t (01904) 470028
e info@tapestrygarden.co.uk

Fleur-de-lys ★★★★
Self Catering
Contact: Mrs Pat Anderson
Mrs Anderson's Country Cottages
t (01751) 472172

Rose Beck ★★★★
Self Catering
Contact: Steph Woolhouse
t (01709) 852483
e steph.woolhouse@yahoo.co.uk
w rosebeckcottages.com

Townend Cottage ★★★★
Self Catering
Contact: Mrs Margaret Begg
Townend Farmhouse
t (01439) 770103
e margaret.begg@ukgateway.net
w visityorkshire.com

Tykes Cottage ★★★★
Self Catering
Contact: Ms Laura Barry
t (0113) 286 9735
e lpbarry@btinternet.com
w tykescottage.co.uk

Wardy's ★★★ *Self Catering*
Contact: Joanne Ward
t (01439) 770124
e jowardy@tiscali.co.uk
w jowardys.co.uk

HELPERTHORPE
North Yorkshire

The Old Dairy & The Granary ★★★★ *Self Catering*
Contact: Rozanne Startup
t (01944) 738613
e rozannestartup@aol.com
w peartreecottages.com

HELSBY
Cheshire

Courtyard Helsby ★★★★-★★★★★
Self Catering
Contact: Mr Roger Maher
t (01928) 723222
e roger.maher@thecourtyardhelsby.com
w thecourtyardhelsby.com

HELTON
Cumbria

Chapel Cottage ★★★★
Self Catering
Cumbrian Cottages
t (01228) 599960
e enquiries@cumbrian-cottages.co.uk
w cumbrian-cottages.co.uk

Talbot House & Talbot Studio ★★★-★★★★
Self Catering
Contact: Susan Calland
Lake District Cottages Helton
t (01931) 712067
e enquiries@lakedistrict-cottages.com
w lakedistrict-cottages.com

HEPPLE
Northumberland

Beech Cottage ★★★
Self Catering
Contact: Mrs Elizabeth Rogerson
t (01669) 640216
e erogerson@btinternet.com
w visitrothbury.co.uk

Cherry Tree Cottage ★★★★
Self Catering
t (01665) 574504
w visit-rothbury.co.uk

HEPTONSTALL
West Yorkshire

The Hayloft Flat ★★★
Self Catering
Contact: H M Harrison
t (01422) 843145

Loudwater Cottage ★★★
Self Catering
Contact: Shirley Taylor
t (01422) 844323 & 07799 777198

HEPWORTH
West Yorkshire

Uppergate Farm self catering ★★★★
Self Catering
Contact: Alison Booth
t (01484) 681369
e info@uppergatefarm.co.uk
w uppergatefarm.co.uk

HESKET NEWMARKET
Cumbria

Bannest Hill Cottage ★★★
Self Catering
Contact: Dr & Mrs Preston
t (017684) 84394
e stay@bannesthill.co.uk
w bannesthill.co.uk

Oak View ★★★★
Self Catering
Cumbrian Cottages
t (01228) 599960
e enquiries@cumbrian-cottages.co.uk
w cumbrian-cottages.co.uk

Ostlers Barn ★★★★★
Self Catering
Cumbrian Cottages
t (01228) 599960
e enquiries@cumbrian-cottages.co.uk
w cumbrian-cottages.co.uk

Syke House ★★★
Self Catering
Sykes Cottages
t (01244) 345700
e info@sykescottages.co.uk
w sykescottages.co.uk

HETHERSGILL
Cumbria

Newlands Farmhouse
★★★★ *Self Catering*
Cumbrian Cottages
t (01228) 599960
e enquiries@cumbrian-cottages.co.uk
w cumbrian-cottages.co.uk

HEXHAM
Northumberland

Brokenheugh Lodge & Orchard Barn ★★★★★
Self Catering
Contact: Mrs Renee Jamieson
t (01434) 684206
e stay@brokenheugh.co.uk
w brokenheugh.co.uk

Chapel House, Steel
★★★★★ *Self Catering*
Contact: Mrs Joan Liddle
t (01434) 673286
e info@chapel-house.info
w chapel-house.info

Holy Island House ★★★★★
Self Catering
Contact: Mrs Judith Youens
t (01434) 609386
e stay@holyislandhouse.co.uk
w holyislandhouse.co.uk

Kingshaw Green
Rating Applied For
Self Catering
Contact: Mr & Mrs David & Christine Thirlwell
t (01434) 606413

The Mews ★★★★
Self Catering
Contact: Mr Alan Humphreys
t (01434) 601533
e alan@kittyfriskhouse.co.uk
w northumberlandholidaylets.com

Moorgair Cottage, Slaley
★★★★ *Self Catering*
Contact: Mrs Vicki Ridley
t (01434) 673473
e g_ridley@lineone.net
w moorgair.co.uk

Old Byre ★★★★
Self Catering
Contact: Mrs Elizabeth Courage
t (01434) 673259
e info@ryehillfarm.co.uk
w ryehillfarm.co.uk

Old Church Cottages, Chollerton ★★★★
Self Catering
Contact: Mrs Marilyn Framrose
t (01434) 681930
e mframrose@chollerton-oldchurch.co.uk
w chollerton-oldchurch.co.uk

The Old Coach House Apartment ★★★★
Self Catering
Contact: Mr John Askell
t (01434) 603598
e jwcaskell@tiscali.co.uk

Rosebank Cottage ★★★
Self Catering
Contact: Mrs Francine Jukes
Appletree Cottage
t (01434) 674634
e info@rosebankcottage.co.uk
w rosebankcottage.co.uk

Sammy's Place/Broadway Apartment ★★★★
Self Catering
Contact: Mr & Mrs Ian and Susan Sibbald
9 Charlton Close
t (01434) 604143 & 07903 038623
e sammys-place@hotmail.com
w sammyshideaways.com

HIGH BENTHAM
North Yorkshire

Higher Crosdale Farmhouse
★★★★ *Self Catering*
Dales Holiday Cottages
t (01756) 790919
e info@dales-holiday-cottages.com
w dales-holiday-cottages.com

Holmes Farm Cottage
★★★★ *Self Catering*
Contact: Mrs Story
t (015242) 61198
e lucy@clucy.demon.co.uk
w holmesfarmcottage.co.uk

Lane House Farm *Approved Caravan Holiday Home*
Contact: Mrs Clapham
t (01524) 261479

HIGH CATTON
East Riding of Yorkshire

The Courtyard
★★★★-★★★★★
Self Catering
Contact: Sheila Foster
t (01759) 371374
e foster-s@sky.com
w highcattongrange.co.uk

HIGH HAWSKER
North Yorkshire

Avoncroft Cottage ★★★★
Self Catering
Contact: Mr G Calland
t (0115) 925 8412
e info@avoncroft-cottage.com
w avoncroft-cottage.com

The Old Cartshed ★★★★
Self Catering
Yorkshire Cottages
t (01228) 406701
e enquiries@yorkshire-cottages.info
w yorkshire-cottages.info

Ploughmans Cottage
★★★★ *Self Catering*
Yorkshire Cottages
t (01228) 406701
e enquiries@yorkshire-cottages.info
w yorkshire-cottages.info

Well Cottage, High Hawsker
Rating Applied For
Self Catering
Whitby Holiday Cottages
t (01947) 603010
e enquiries@whitbyholidaycottages.net
w whitbyholidaycottages.net

HIGH LORTON
Cumbria

1 & 2 Midtown Cottages
★★★★ *Self Catering*
Contact: Mr Burrell
Midtown Cottages
t (01264) 710165
e info@midtowncottages.co.uk
w midtowncottages.co.uk

Brewery House ★★★★★
Self Catering
Cumbrian Cottages
t (01228) 599960
e enquiries@cumbrian-cottages.co.uk
w cumbrian-cottages.co.uk

Dale House ★★★
Self Catering
Cumbrian Cottages
t (01228) 599960
e enquiries@cumbrian-cottages.co.uk
w cumbrian-cottages.co.uk

Grooms Cottage ★★★
Self Catering
Cumbrian Cottages
t (01228) 599960
e enquiries@cumbrian-cottages.co.uk
w cumbrian-cottages.co.uk

High Swinside Holiday Cottages ★★★ *Self Catering*
Contact: Mr Jacques Hankin
t (01900) 85206
e bookings@highswinside.demon.co.uk
w highswinside.demon.co.uk

Holemire Barn ★★★★★
Self Catering
Contact: Angela Fearfield
t (01900) 85225
e enquiries@lakelandbarn.co.uk
w lakelandbarn.co.uk

HIGH WRAY
Cumbria

Stable Cottage ★★★★
Self Catering
Contact: Sheila Briggs
t (015394) 32280
e sheila@highwrayfarm.co.uk
w highwrayfarm.co.uk

HIGHAM
Lancashire

Height Top Farm ★★★★
Self Catering
Contact: Mrs Janet Sharp
t (01282) 772009
e janet.sharp@virgin.net

HINDERWELL
North Yorkshire

Ellerby View ★★★★★
Self Catering
Contact: Shirley Donkin
t (01670) 512709
e shirley@ellerbyview.co.uk
w ellerbyview.co.uk

Hawthorne Cottage ★★★★
Self Catering
Contact: Mrs J McKitton
t (01652) 678665
e brianmckitton@btinternet.com

Meadow Lea ★★★
Self Catering
Whitby Holiday Cottages
t (01947) 603010
e enquiries@whitbyholidaycottages.net
w whitbyholidaycottages.net

HOLMBRIDGE
West Yorkshire

Heselwood Cottage ★★★
Self Catering
Contact: Mr & Mrs Chris & Jenny Brook
t (01484) 685175
e jenandchris@heselwoodcottage.co.uk
w heselwoodcottage.co.uk

Ivy Cottage ★★★
Self Catering
Contact: Ian & Joyce Bangham
t (01484) 682561
e bangham77@hotmail.com

HOLME
Cumbria

9 Holmefield ★★★
Self Catering
Contact: Jim Wilding
t (01704) 875404
w lake-district-cottage.com

HOLME
West Yorkshire

Holmfirth Cottage ★★★
Self Catering
Contact: Barry Fielder
t (01924) 275014
e thefielders@btinternet.com
w holmfirthcottage.com

HOLMFIRTH
West Yorkshire

The Barn @ Holmfirth ★★★
Self Catering
Contact: Adrian Cunliffe
t 07766 278689
e bookings@thebarnatholmfirth.co.uk
w thebarnatholmfirth.co.uk

Lane Farm Holiday Cottages ★★★★ *Self Catering*
Contact: Mrs Vivienne Howard
t (01484) 682290
e viv@lanefarmcottages.co.uk
w lanefarmcottages.co.uk

Manor Farm Cottage, Upper Denby ★★★★ *Self Catering*
Contact: Mrs C E Crossland
t (01484) 864722
e manorfarmcottage@btinternet.com
w manorfarmcottage.com

Mytholmbridge Studio Cottage ★★★★ *Self Catering*
Contact: Sue Clay
t (01484) 686642
e sue@mytholmbridge.co.uk
w mytholmbridge.co.uk

Nora Batty's Cottage ★★★
Self Catering
Contact: Neil Worthington
Nora Batty Experience
t (01274) 603750
e nw@worthingtonbrown.co.uk
w nora-batty.co.uk

Sycamore Farm Cottages ★★★-★★★★★ *Self Catering*
Contact: Frances Kaye
t (01484) 661458
e sycamorefarmcottages@hotmail.co.uk
w sycamorefamcottages.co.uk

HOLMROOK
Cumbria

Lakewood
Rating Applied For
Self Catering
Cumbrian Cottages
t (01228) 599960
e enquiries@cumbrian-cottages.co.uk
w cumbrian-cottages.co.uk

Yattus ★★★★★
Self Catering
Cumbrian Cottages
t (01228) 599960
e enquiries@cumbrian-cottages.co.uk
w cumbrian-cottages.co.uk

HOLTBY
North Yorkshire

The Apple Barn ★★★★
Self Catering
Contact: Mrs Laura Bough
t 07711 801873
e laura@thecottageholtby.co.uk
w theapplebarn.co.uk

Garden Cottage ★★★★
Self Catering
Contact: Ann Wilson
t (01904) 488089

HOLY ISLAND
Northumberland

Britannia House and The Cottage ★★★★ *Self Catering*
Contact: Mrs Katharine Tiernan
t (01665) 589322
e kmtiernan@googlemail.com
w lindisfarne-cottages.co.uk

Farne Court Cottage, Farne View Cottage ★★★
Self Catering
Contact: Mrs Batty
Waterside House
t (01387) 840122
e angelabatty@btinternet.com

Links View ★★★
Self Catering
Contact: Rachel Paine linksviewholyisland@yahoo.co.uk
w lindisfarne.org.uk/links-view

Memnon Cottage ★★★★
Self Catering
Contact: Ms Shirley Douglas
t (0161) 941 1963
e shirleyandouglas@aol.com
w memnon-cottage.co.uk

HOOLE
Cheshire

St James Apartments ★★★★ *Self Catering*
Contact: Mrs June Smith
t (01244) 315047
e reservations@babaguesthouse.co.uk
w chesterholidayrentals.co.uk

HOOLE VILLAGE
Cheshire

The Stables Holiday Cottage ★★★ *Self Catering*
Contact: Mr John Walsh
t (01244) 321767
w horsenuholidaycottage.co.uk

HORNSEA
East Riding of Yorkshire

Cherry Tree ★★★
Self Catering
Contact: Mrs Rita Leonard
t (01964) 527245 & 07720 349716
e leonardritaruth@yahoo.co.uk

Cobble Cottage ★★★
Self Catering
Contact: Nick & Jaqueline Clare
Nick & Jacqueline Clare
t (01964) 536300 & 07918 647686
e nj.clare@btinternet.com
w cobblecottage.co.uk

Two Bays ★★★ *Self Catering*
Contact: David & Patricia Fletcher
t (01422) 349844
e de.fletcher@btinternet.com

Westgate Mews ★★★
Self Catering
Contact: Catherine Walker
t (01964) 533430
e lettings@walkerhornsea.plus.com
w cottagesdirect.co.uk

HORSEHOUSE
North Yorkshire

Deer Close West
Rating Applied For
Self Catering
Country Hideaways
t (01969) 663559
e info@countryhideaways.co.uk
w countryhideaways.co.uk

HORTON IN RIBBLESDALE
North Yorkshire

Blind Beck Holiday Cottage ★★★ *Self Catering*
Contact: Heather Huddleston
t (01729) 860396
e h.huddleston@daelnet.co.uk
w blindbeck.co.uk

Poppy Cottage ★★★
Self Catering
Contact: Mrs M. Harrison
t (01729) 860311
w poppycottage.net

Selside Farm, The Byres ★★★★ *Self Catering*
Contact: Shirley Lambert
t (01729) 860367
e selsidefarm@hotmail.co.uk
w selsidefarmholidaycottage.co.uk

HORWICH
Greater Manchester

Archangelos House ★★★
Self Catering
t (01204) 692303
e enquiries@archangelos.co.uk
w archangelos.co.uk

HOVINGHAM
North Yorkshire

Home Cottage ★★★★
Self Catering
Contact: Mrs Bernadete Williams
t (01287) 630491
e r.j.williams4959@btinternet.com

HOWDEN
East Riding of Yorkshire

101 Hailgate ★★★
Self Catering
Contact: Karen Lesley Formon
t 07970 445357
e karen.formon@tiscali.co.uk

HOWGILL
Cumbria

Ash Hining Farm ★★★★
Self Catering
Cumbrian Cottages
t (01228) 599960
e enquiries@cumbrian-cottages.co.uk
w cumbrian-cottages.co.uk

Blandsgill Cottage ★★★
Self Catering
Cumbrian Cottages
t (01228) 599960
e enquiries@cumbrian-cottages.co.uk
w cumbrian-cottages.co.uk

Drawell ★★★★ *Self Catering*
Contact: Janet Postlethwaite
t (015396) 21529
e stay@drawellcottage.co.uk
w drawellcottage.co.uk

Gateside Cottage ★★★★
Self Catering
Cumbrian Cottages
t (01228) 599960
e enquiries@cumbrian-cottages.co.uk
w cumbrian-cottages.co.uk

The Whins *Approved Caravan Holiday Home*
Contact: Miss Blades
t (015396) 20581

HOYLAKE
Merseyside

AAA North Villa Apartments ★★★★ *Self Catering*
t (0151) 632 3982
w northvilla.com

HUDDERSFIELD
West Yorkshire

1535 Melting Point Cottage ★★★★★ *Self Catering*
Contact: Mrs Karen Bonnett
Melting Point Cottage
t (0118) 984 5800
e karen.bonnett@btconnect.com
w meltingpointcottage.co.uk

Castle House Farm Cottages ★★★★ *Self Catering*
Contact: Philip Coates
t (01484) 663808
e cottages@castlehousefarm.co.uk
w castlehousefarm.co.uk

Tyas Cottage ★★★★★
Self Catering
Contact: Victoria Berryman
t (01484) 841010
e vicky.berryman@gmail.com
w yorkshire-holiday.co.uk

HUGGATE
East Riding of Yorkshire

Manor House Farm ★★★
Self Catering
Contact: Barbara Macniven
t (01482) 486610
e barbara.macniven@vhey.co.uk

HUMSHAUGH
Northumberland

East Farm Cottage ★★★
Self Catering
Contact: Mrs Gwen Dodds
t (01434) 689150
e charles.dodds2@btopenworld.com

HUNMANBY
North Yorkshire

Aislaby Cottage, Hunmanby
★★★★ *Self Catering*
Contact: Suzanne Watkinson
t (0113) 250 1407
e richard.watkinson4@btinternet.com

Courtside Cottages ★★★
Self Catering
Contact: Karen Cawthorn
t (01723) 892882
e karenathunmanbyhall@fsmail.net
w courtsidecottage.co.uk

Honeysuckle Cottage ★★★
Self Catering
Dales Holiday Cottages
t (01756) 790919
e info@dales-holiday-cottages.com
w dales-holiday-cottages.com

The Old Waiting Rooms
★★★★ *Self Catering*
Contact: Karen Hubbard
t (01723) 891552
e david@dhubbard.plus.com
w oldwaitingrooms.co.uk

HUNTON
North Yorkshire

Colling Well Cottage
★★★★ *Self Catering*
Contact: Sue Tabiner
t (01677) 450742
e collingwell@hotmail.com
w collingwell.co.uk

HURST
North Yorkshire

Shiney Row Cottage ★★★
Self Catering
Dales Holiday Cottages
t (01756) 790919
e info@dales-holiday-cottages.com
w dales-holiday-cottages.com

HUTTON-LE-HOLE
North Yorkshire

The Green, Hutton-le-Hole
★★★★ *Self Catering*
t (020) 8892 9132
e info@thegreen.eu
w thegreen.eu

Halfway House Cottages
★★★★ *Self Catering*
Contact: Barbara Grabowski
t (01751) 431596
e halfwaycottages@btinternet.com
w halfwayhousecottages.co.uk

Moorland & Heather Cottages ★★★★
Self Catering
Contact: Vicki Cheney
t (01751) 417743
e moorlandcottages@btinternet.com

Primrose Hill Farmhouse
★★★ *Self Catering*
Contact: Nigel Custance
t (01751) 417752
e nigelcustance@wayah.freeserve.co.uk

HUTTON ROOF
Cumbria

Braeside Lodge ★★★
Self Catering
Lakes Cottage Holidays
t (01228) 591555
e info@lakescottageholiday.co.uk
w lakescottageholiday.co.uk

Carrock Cottages ★★★★★
Self Catering
Contact: Malcolm & Gillian Iredale
t (017684) 84111
e info@carrockcottages.co.uk
w carrockcottages.co.uk

Dukes Meadow ★★★★
Self Catering
Cumbrian Cottages
t (01228) 599960
e enquiries@cumbrian-cottages.co.uk
w cumbrian-cottages.co.uk

Dukes Meadow ★★★
Self Catering
Contact: Jane Hounsome
t (0121) 705 4381
e janeandben@hotmail.co.uk
w dukesmeadow.co.uk

Gorse Cottage ★★★
Self Catering
Cumbrian Cottages
t (01228) 599960
e enquiries@cumbrian-cottages.co.uk
w cumbrian-cottages.co.uk

HUTTON SESSAY
North Yorkshire

White Rose Holiday Cottages ★★★ *Self Catering*
Contact: Zoe Williamson
t (01845) 501180

ILDERTON
Northumberland

Coach House & Coach House Cottage ★★★
Self Catering
Contact: Mrs Margaret Sale
t (01668) 217293
e margaretsale@amserve.com

ILKLEY
West Yorkshire

Faweather Grange
★★★★-★★★★★
Self Catering
Contact: Debbie Skinn
t (01943) 878777
e skinn@attglobal.net
w faweathergrange.com

Flat 3 Carr Croft ★★★
Self Catering
Contact: Mrs C J Wiggin
t (01285) 640703
e christa-wiggin@btconnect.com

Ilkley Breaks
Rating Applied For
Self Catering
e info@ilkleybreaks.co.uk
w ilkleybreaks.co.uk

On Ilkley Moor ★★★★
Self Catering
Contact: Heather Parry
t (01943) 602383
e heather@onilkleymoor.co.uk
w onilkleymoor.co.uk

Tides Reach ★★★★
Self Catering
Yorkshire Cottages
t (01228) 406701
e enquiries@yorkshire-cottages.info
w yorkshire-cottages.info

Westwood Lodge
★★★★-★★★★★
Self Catering
Contact: Tim Edwards
t (01943) 433430
e welcome@westwoodlodge.co.uk
w westwoodlodge.co.uk

INGLEBY CROSS
North Yorkshire

The Cottage at Hill House
★★★★ *Self Catering*
Contact: Richard & Vee Kitteridge
t (01609) 882109
e kitteridge@ukgateway.net

INGLEBY GREENHOW
North Yorkshire

Ingleby Manor ★★★★
Self Catering
Contact: Christine Bianco
t (01642) 722170
e christine@inglebymanor.co.uk
w inglebymanor.co.uk

INGLETON
Durham

Mill Granary Cottages
★★★★★ *Self Catering*
Enjoy England Awards for Excellence Winner
Contact: Mr & Mrs Richard & Kate Hodgson
t (01325) 730339
e info@millgranary.co.uk
w millgranary.co.uk

INGLETON
North Yorkshire

Beech Tree Cottages
★★★★ *Self Catering*
Contact: Ms Sharon McDonald
t (01524) 241828
e beechtreecottage@aol.com
w beechtreecottages.co.uk

Doefoot ★★★★
Self Catering
Dales Holiday Cottages
t (01756) 790919
e info@dales-holiday-cottages.com
w dales-holiday-cottages.com

Holme View ★★★★
Self Catering
Contact: Lorraine Kidd
Dales Holiday Cottages
t (01756) 790919
e lundholme@btopenworld.com
w lundholmefarm.co.uk

Lundholme Farm *Approved Caravan Holiday Home*
Contact: Hilary K Lund
t (01524) 241307

The Old Laundry ★★★★
Self Catering
Contact: Ms Debby Kuhlmann
t (01524) 241843

The Tryst ★★★ *Self Catering*
Yorkshire Cottages
t (01228) 406701
e enquiries@yorkshire-cottages.info
w yorkshire-cottages.info

Warth Barn ★★★★★
Self Catering
Contact: Mrs Shula Cockett
t (01524) 241612
e thewoodman@tiscali.co.uk
w warthbarn.co.uk

INGLEWHITE
Lancashire

The Garden Cottage ★★★
Self Catering
t (01995) 640007
e info@thegarden-cottage.co.uk
w thegarden-cottage.co.uk

INGRAM
Northumberland

Cheviot Holiday Cottages
★★★★★ *Self Catering*
Contact: Mrs Trysha Stephenson
t (01665) 578236
e trysha@cheviotholidaycottages.co.uk
w cheviotholidaycottages.co.uk

INGS
Cumbria

Ings Mill Park Cottages
★★★★ *Self Catering*
Cumbrian Cottages
t (01228) 599960
e enquiries@cumbrian-cottages.co.uk
w cumbrian-cottages.co.uk

Little Ghyll Cottage ★★★★
Self Catering
Contact: Christine Ormerod
t (01539) 821274

St Annes Cottage ★★★
Self Catering
Cumbrian Cottages
t (01228) 599960
e enquiries@cumbrian-cottages.co.uk
w cumbrian-cottages.co.uk

Topiary Cottage ★★★★
Self Catering
Lakelovers
t (015394) 88855
e bookings@lakelovers.co.uk
w lakelovers.co.uk

IREBY
Cumbria

Daleside Farm ★★★★
Self Catering
t (01697) 371268

Fell Cottage ★★★★★
Self Catering
Cumbrian Cottages
t (01228) 599960
e enquiries@cumbrian-cottages.co.uk
w cumbrian-cottages.co.uk

Laundry Cottage ★★★★
Self Catering
Cumbrian Cottages
t (01228) 599960
e enquiries@cumbrian-cottages.co.uk
w cumbrian-cottages.co.uk

New Park Farm Cottages
★★★★★ *Self Catering*
t (01697) 371244
e info@newparkfarm.co.uk
w newparkfarm.co.uk

New Park Holiday Cottages
★★★★-★★★★★
Self Catering
Cumbrian Cottages
t (01228) 599960
e enquiries@cumbrian-cottages.co.uk
w cumbrian-cottages.co.uk

Old Saddler's Cottage
★★★★ *Self Catering*
Contact: Catherine Perry
t 07721 050885
e nick.perry2@btinternet.com
w oldsaddlerscottage.com

The Old Stables ★★★★
Self Catering
Cumbrian Cottages
t (01228) 599960
e enquiries@cumbrian-cottages.co.uk
w cumbrian-cottages.co.uk

Overwater Lodge ★★★★
Self Catering
Cumbrian Cottages
t (01228) 599960
e enquiries@cumbrian-cottages.co.uk
w cumbrian-cottages.co.uk

Snittlegarth 1 ★★★
Self Catering
Cumbrian Cottages
t (01228) 599960
e enquiries@cumbrian-cottages.co.uk
w cumbrian-cottages.co.uk

Snittlegarth 2 ★★★
Self Catering
Cumbrian Cottages
t (01228) 599960
e enquiries@cumbrian-cottages.co.uk
w cumbrian-cottages.co.uk

Woodlands Cottage ★★★
Self Catering
Cumbrian Cottages
t (01228) 599960
e enquiries@cumbrian-cottages.co.uk
w cumbrian-cottages.co.uk

IREBY
Lancashire

Netherbeck Farm ★★★★★
Self Catering
Yorkshire Cottages
t (01228) 406701
e enquiries@yorkshire-cottages.info
w yorkshire-cottages.info

Springfield ★★★★
Self Catering
Contact: Miss Heather Bavin
Bainbridge House
t (01524) 242501
e heather.bavin@btinternet.com
w visitnorthlancashire.co.uk

IRESHOPEBURN
Durham

Hillside Cottage ★★★
Self Catering
Contact: Mrs Sadie McMullon
t (01733) 349612
e sasmc2000@yahoo.co.uk
w hillsidecottagedurham.co.uk

IRTHINGTON
Cumbria

Farm Cottage ★★★★
Self Catering
Cumbrian Cottages
t (01228) 599960
e enquiries@cumbrian-cottages.co.uk
w cumbrian-cottages.co.uk

ISEL
Cumbria

Linskeldfield Tarn Holiday Cottages ★★★★
Self Catering
Contact: Mrs Pauline Young
t (01900) 822136
e cooleye1977@hotmail.com
w linskeldfield.co.uk

IVEGILL
Cumbria

Stable Cottage ★★★
Self Catering
Contact: Messrs Wilson
t (01697) 473327

JESMOND
Tyne and Wear

Week2Week
★★★★-★★★★★
Self Catering
Contact: Miss Kerry Wilson
t (0191) 281 3129
e tori@week2week.co.uk
w week2week.co.uk

KELD
North Yorkshire

Hillcrest Holiday Cottage
★★★ *Self Catering*
Contact: Barbara Rukin
t (01748) 886274
e babrarukin@ukonline.co.uk

Pry House Farm ★★★★
Self Catering
Askrigg Cottage Holidays
t (01969) 650022
e stay@askrigg.com
w askrigg.com

The Smithy ★★★★
Self Catering
Contact: Mrs Annette Riley
t (01969) 663716
e thesmithy@oldgoatholidays.co.uk

KENDAL
Cumbria

14 Printers Croft ★★★★
Self Catering
Cumbrian Cottages
t (01228) 599960
e enquiries@cumbrian-cottages.co.uk
w cumbrian-cottages.co.uk

3 Queens Yard ★★★★
Self Catering
Cumbrian Cottages
t (01228) 599960
e enquiries@cumbrian-cottages.co.uk
w cumbrian-cottages.co.uk

Barkinbeck Cottage ★★★
Self Catering
Contact: Mrs Ann Hamilton
t (015395) 67122
e barkinhouse@yahoo.co.uk
w barkinbeck.co.uk

Harwood Dale Cottage
★★★★ *Self Catering*
Cumbrian Cottages
t (01228) 599960
e enquiries@cumbrian-cottages.co.uk
w cumbrian-cottages.co.uk

High Swinklebank Farm
★★★ *Self Catering*
Contact: Olive Simpson
t (01539) 823682
w lakedistrictfarmhouseholidays.co.uk/highswinklebank

Moresdale Bank Cottage
★★★★ *Self Catering*
Contact: Helen Parkins
t (01539) 824227
e mclamb@ukonline.co.uk
w moresdale-bank-cottage.co.uk

Shaw End Mansion ★★★★
Self Catering
Contact: Mr & Mrs Robinson
Haveriggs Farm
t (01539) 824220
e robinson@fieldendholidays.co.uk
w fieldendholidays.co.uk

Todd Meadow ★★★
Self Catering
Cumbrian Cottages
t (01228) 599960
e enquiries@cumbrian-cottages.co.uk
w cumbrian-cottages.co.uk

The Warren Cottage ★★★★
Self Catering
Lakelovers
t (015394) 88855
e bookings@lakelovers.co.uk
w lakelovers.co.uk

Yew Tree Cottage ★★★★
Self Catering
Cumbrian Cottages
t (01228) 599960
e enquiries@cumbrian-cottages.co.uk
w cumbrian-cottages.co.uk

KENTMERE
Cumbria

Nook Cottage – Kentmere Valley ★★★ *Self Catering*
Lakeland Cottage Comapny
t (015395) 38180
e john@lakelandcottageco.com
w lakelandcottageco.com

Rawe Cottage ★★★★
Self Catering
Lakeland Cottage Comapny
t (015395) 38180
e john@lakelandcottageco.com
w lakelandcottageco.com

KESWICK
Cumbria

1 Balmoral House ★★★
Self Catering
Cumbrian Cottages
t (01228) 599960
e enquiries@cumbrian-cottages.co.uk
w cumbrian-cottages.co.uk

1 Lonsdale House ★★★★
Self Catering
Cumbrian Cottages
t (01228) 599960
e enquiries@cumbrian-cottages.co.uk
w cumbrian-cottages.co.uk

1 Windsor House ★★★★
Self Catering
Cumbrian Cottages
t (01228) 599960
e enquiries@cumbrian-cottages.co.uk
w cumbrian-cottages.co.uk

10 The Plosh ★★★★
Self Catering
Cumbrian Cottages
t (01228) 599960
e enquiries@cumbrian-cottages.co.uk
w cumbrian-cottages.co.uk

11 Burnside Park ★★★★
Self Catering
Contact: Mr Peter Durbin
Cumbrian Cottages
t (01228) 599960
e enquiries@cumbrian-cottages.co.uk

11 Howrah's Court ★★★★
Self Catering
Cumbrian Cottages
t (01228) 599960
e enquiries@cumbrian-cottages.co.uk
w cumbrian-cottages.co.uk

11 The Plosh ★★★
Self Catering
Cumbrian Cottages
t (01228) 599960
e enquiries@cumbrian-cottages.co.uk
w cumbrian-cottages.co.uk

14 Elm Court ★★★
Self Catering
Cumbrian Cottages
t (01228) 599960
e enquiries@cumbrian-cottages.co.uk
w cumbrian-cottages.co.uk

15 Elm Court ★★★★
Self Catering
Cumbrian Cottages
t (01228) 599960
e enquiries@cumbrian-cottages.co.uk
w cumbrian-cottages.co.uk

17 Greta Grove ★★★
Self Catering
Cumbrian Cottages
t (01228) 599960
e enquiries@cumbrian-cottages.co.uk
w cumbrian-cottages.co.uk

18 Elmcourt ★★★★
Self Catering
Cumbrian Cottages
t (01228) 599960
e enquiries@cumbrian-cottages.co.uk
w cumbrian-cottages.co.uk

27 Lake Road ★★★★
Self Catering
Contact: Pete & Sharon Garner
Burnside B&B
t (017687) 72639
e 27@burnside-keswick.co.uk
w 27keswickcottages.co.uk

28 Briar Rigg ★★★★
Self Catering
Contact: Emma Graham
Cumbrian Cottages
t (01228) 599960
e enquiries@cumbrian-cottages.co.uk
w cumbrian-cottages.co.uk

3 Balmoral House ★★★
Self Catering
Cumbrian Cottages
t (01228) 599960
e enquiries@cumbrian-cottages.co.uk
w cumbrian-cottages.co.uk

3 Catherine Cottages ★★★★ *Self Catering*
Cumbrian Cottages
t (01228) 599960
e enquiries@cumbrian-cottages.co.uk
w cumbrian-cottages.co.uk

3 Greta Grove ★★★★
Self Catering
Cumbrian Cottages
t (01228) 599960
e enquiries@cumbrian-cottages.co.uk
w cumbrian-cottages.co.uk

3 The Hollies ★★★★
Self Catering
Cumbrian Cottages
t (01228) 599960
e enquiries@cumbrian-cottages.co.uk
w cumbrian-cottages.co.uk

4 Lydia's Cottages ★★★
Self Catering
Contact: Jill Donington-Smith
R & J Donington-Smith
t (017687) 72919
e info@lydiascottage.co.uk
w lydiascottage.co.uk

5 Greta Side Court ★★★
Self Catering
Contact: John & Laura Atkinson
t (01204) 493138
e johnlaura3@tiscali.co.uk

5 Lonsdale House ★★★
Self Catering
Cumbrian Cottages
t (01228) 599960
e enquiries@cumbrian-cottages.co.uk
w cumbrian-cottages.co.uk

8 Greta Grove ★★★★
Self Catering
Cumbrian Cottages
t (01228) 599960
e enquiries@cumbrian-cottages.co.uk
w cumbrian-cottages.co.uk

8 Lydia's Cottages ★★★
Self Catering
Lakes Cottage Holidays
t (01228) 591555
e info@lakescottageholiday.co.uk
w lakescottageholiday.co.uk

9 Howrah's Court ★★★★
Self Catering
Cumbrian Cottages
t (01228) 599960
e enquiries@cumbrian-cottages.co.uk
w cumbrian-cottages.co.uk

Aaron Lodge ★★★★
Self Catering
Contact: Mr Robert Au
t (017687) 72541
e aurabau@hotmail.com

Abacourt & Methera Cottages ★★★★
Self Catering
Keswick Cottages
t (017687) 78555
e info@keswickcottages.co.uk
w keswickcottages.co.uk

Acorn Apartments and Acorn View ★★★★
Self Catering
t (017684) 80310
w acornselfcatering.co.uk

Acorn Lodge Cottage ★★★
Self Catering
Cumbrian Cottages
t (01228) 599960
e enquiries@cumbrian-cottages.co.uk
w cumbrian-cottages.co.uk

Alison's Cottage ★★★
Self Catering
Lakes Cottage Holidays
t (01228) 591555
e info@lakescottageholiday.co.uk
w lakescottageholiday.co.uk

Alison's View ★★★★
Self Catering
Contact: Carolyn Meachem
t (01604) 808713
e info@alisonsview.co.uk
w alisonsview.co.uk

Alvamere ★★★ *Self Catering*
Cumbrian Cottages
t (01228) 599960
e enquiries@cumbrian-cottages.co.uk
w cumbrian-cottages.co.uk

Amba ★★★ *Self Catering*
Cumbrian Cottages
t (01228) 599960
e enquiries@cumbrian-cottages.co.uk
w cumbrian-cottages.co.uk

Applecroft ★★★★
Self Catering
Cumbrian Cottages
t (01228) 599960
e enquiries@cumbrian-cottages.co.uk
w cumbrian-cottages.co.uk

Applemere ★★★★
Self Catering
Cumbrian Cottages
t (01228) 599960
e enquiries@cumbrian-cottages.co.uk
w cumbrian-cottages.co.uk

Appleside ★★★
Self Catering
Cumbrian Cottages
t (01228) 599960
e enquiries@cumbrian-cottages.co.uk
w cumbrian-cottages.co.uk

Appletree ★★★ *Self Catering*
Cumbrian Cottages
t (01228) 599960
e enquiries@cumbrian-cottages.co.uk
w cumbrian-cottages.co.uk

Ashbrooke ★★★
Self Catering
Cumbrian Cottages
t (01228) 599960
e enquiries@cumbrian-cottages.co.uk
w cumbrian-cottages.co.uk

Ashness ★★★★
Self Catering
Cumbrian Cottages
t (01228) 599960
e enquiries@cumbrian-cottages.co.uk
w cumbrian-cottages.co.uk

Ashness Apartment ★★★
Self Catering
Contact: Val Hewer
The Paddock Guest House
t (017687) 72510
e info@ashnet.net
w ashness.net

Aura ★★★★ *Self Catering*
Contact: Bill Murray
t (0161) 445 0630
e murray@swclimited.co.uk
w cottageguide.co.uk/aura

Baldisholme ★★★★
Self Catering
Cumbrian Cottages
t (01228) 599960
e enquiries@cumbrian-cottages.co.uk
w cumbrian-cottages.co.uk

Bannerdale ★★★★
Self Catering
Contact: Hazel Hutton
t (017687) 72144
e info@bannerdale.co.uk
w bannerdale.co.uk

Baxters Retreat ★★★★
Self Catering
Cumbrian Cottages
t (01228) 599960
e enquiries@cumbrian-cottages.co.uk
w cumbrian-cottages.co.uk

Bay Tree ★★★ *Self Catering*
Cumbrian Cottages
t (01228) 599960
e enquiries@cumbrian-cottages.co.uk
w cumbrian-cottages.co.uk

Beagle Cottage ★★★
Self Catering
Cumbrian Cottages
t (01228) 599960
e enquiries@cumbrian-cottages.co.uk
w cumbrian-cottages.co.uk

Beech Nut ★★★
Self Catering
Cumbrian Cottages
t (01228) 599960
e enquiries@cumbrian-cottages.co.uk
w cumbrian-cottages.co.uk

Bessy Boot ★★★★
Self Catering
Lakeland Cottage Holidays
t (017687) 76065
e info@lakelandcottages.co.uk
w lakelandcottages.co.uk

The Bield ★★★ *Self Catering*
Cumbrian Cottages
t (01228) 599960
e enquiries@cumbrian-cottages.co.uk
w cumbrian-cottages.co.uk

Birchgate Cottage ★★★★
Self Catering
Keswick Cottages
t (017687) 78555
e info@keswickcottages.co.uk
w keswickcottages.co.uk

Bleaberry ★★★ *Self Catering*
Cumbrian Cottages
t (01228) 599960
e enquiries@cumbrian-cottages.co.uk
w cumbrian-cottages.co.uk

Bleach Green Cottages No 11 ★★★ *Self Catering*
Cumbrian Cottages
t (01228) 599960
e enquiries@cumbrian-cottages.co.uk
w cumbrian-cottages.co.uk

The Blencathra ★★★
Self Catering
Cumbrian Cottages
t (01228) 599960
e enquiries@cumbrian-cottages.co.uk
w cumbrian-cottages.co.uk

Blencathra Bank ★★★
Self Catering
Cumbrian Cottages
t (01228) 599960
e enquiries@cumbrian-cottages.co.uk
w cumbrian-cottages.co.uk

Blencathra House ★★★★
Self Catering
Cumbrian Cottages
t (01228) 599960
e enquiries@cumbrian-cottages.co.uk
w cumbrian-cottages.co.uk

Bobbin Cottage ★★★★
Self Catering
Cumbrian Cottages
t (01228) 599960
e enquiries@cumbrian-cottages.co.uk
w cumbrian-cottages.co.uk

Bonshaw ★★★ *Self Catering*
Cumbrian Cottages
t (01228) 599960
e enquiries@cumbrian-cottages.co.uk
w cumbrian-cottages.co.uk

Bracken Lodge ★★★★
Self Catering
Cumbrian Cottages
t (01228) 599960
e enquiries@cumbrian-cottages.co.uk
w cumbrian-cottages.co.uk

Brackenrigg ★★★★
Self Catering
Contact: Judy & Harry Marsland
t (017687) 72258
e info@brackenrigg.com
w brackenrigg.com

Bramble Cottage ★★★★
Self Catering
Cumbrian Cottages
t (01228) 599960
e enquiries@cumbrian-cottages.co.uk
w cumbrian-cottages.co.uk

Brandelhow ★★★★
Self Catering
Cumbrian Cottages
t (01228) 599960
e enquiries@cumbrian-cottages.co.uk
w cumbrian-cottages.co.uk

Brandelhowe ★★★★
Self Catering
Cumbrian Cottages
t (01228) 599960
e enquiries@cumbrian-cottages.co.uk
w cumbrian-cottages.co.uk

Bridge Cottage ★★★
Self Catering
Cumbrian Cottages
t (01228) 599960
e enquiries@cumbrian-cottages.co.uk
w cumbrian-cottages.co.uk

Bridge Court ★★★★
Self Catering
Keswick Cottages
t (017687) 78555
e info@keswickcottages.co.uk
w keswickcottages.co.uk

Brigham Farm ★★★★
Self Catering
Contact: Mr Green
The Studio
t (017687) 79666
e selfcatering@keswickholidays.co.uk
w keswickholidays.co.uk

Brigham Row ★★★
Self Catering
Lakes Cottage Holidays
t (01228) 591555
e info@lakescottageholiday.co.uk
w lakescottageholiday.co.uk

Brow Riding ★★★
Self Catering
Cumbrian Cottages
t (01228) 599960
e enquiries@cumbrian-cottages.co.uk
w cumbrian-cottages.co.uk

Brundholme ★★★★
Self Catering
Lakes Cottage Holidays
t (01228) 591555
e info@lakescottageholiday.co.uk
w lakescottageholiday.co.uk

Brundholme Glen ★★★★
Self Catering
Cumbrian Cottages
t (01228) 599960
e enquiries@cumbrian-cottages.co.uk
w cumbrian-cottages.co.uk

Bunbury Cottage ★★★★
Self Catering
Cumbrian Cottages
t (01228) 599960
e enquiries@cumbrian-cottages.co.uk
w cumbrian-cottages.co.uk

Cairnway ★★★★
Self Catering
Cumbrian Cottages
t (01228) 599960
e enquiries@cumbrian-cottages.co.uk
w cumbrian-cottages.co.uk

Candlemas ★★★
Self Catering
Lakeland Cottage Holidays
t (017687) 76065
e info@lakelandcottages.co.uk
w lakelandcottages.co.uk

Candy Nook ★★★★
Self Catering
Keswick Cottages
t (017687) 78555
e info@keswickcottages.co.uk
w keswickcottages.co.uk

Carabara ★★★ *Self Catering*
Cumbrian Cottages
t (01228) 599960
e enquiries@cumbrian-cottages.co.uk
w cumbrian-cottages.co.uk

Carlton Cottage ★★★★
Self Catering
Cumbrian Cottages
t (01228) 599960
e enquiries@cumbrian-cottages.co.uk
w cumbrian-cottages.co.uk

Carolyn's Cottage ★★★
Self Catering
Cumbrian Cottages
t (01228) 599960
e enquiries@cumbrian-cottages.co.uk
w cumbrian-cottages.co.uk

Carthwaite ★★★★
Self Catering
Cumbrian Cottages
t (01228) 599960
e enquiries@cumbrian-cottages.co.uk
w cumbrian-cottages.co.uk

Castlerigg Manor Lodge
★★★ *Self Catering*
Cumbrian Cottages
t (01228) 599960
e enquiries@cumbrian-cottages.co.uk
w cumbrian-cottages.co.uk

Causey Pike ★★★★
Self Catering
Cumbrian Cottages
t (01228) 599960
e enquiries@cumbrian-cottages.co.uk
w cumbrian-cottages.co.uk

Causey View ★★★
Self Catering
Contact: Steve & Jo Laker
Laker District
t (017687) 74656
e lakerdistrict@ntlworld.com
w lakerdistrict.com

Central Haven ★★★★
Self Catering
Cumbrian Cottages
t (01228) 599960
e enquiries@cumbrian-cottages.co.uk
w cumbrian-cottages.co.uk

Century Cottage ★★★
Self Catering
Cumbrian Cottages
t (01228) 599960
e enquiries@cumbrian-cottages.co.uk
w cumbrian-cottages.co.uk

Chaucer Apartment ★★★★
Self Catering
Keswick Cottages
t (017687) 78555
e info@keswickcottages.co.uk
w keswickcottages.co.uk

Chaucers Nook ★★★★★
Self Catering
Cumbrian Cottages
t (01228) 599960
e enquiries@cumbrian-cottages.co.uk
w cumbrian-cottages.co.uk

Chaucers Retreat ★★★★
Self Catering
Cumbrian Cottages
t (01228) 599960
e enquiries@cumbrian-cottages.co.uk
w cumbrian-cottages.co.uk

The Coach House & Derwent Cottage Mews
★★★★★ *Self Catering*
Contact: Sue Newman
Derwent Cottage
t (017687) 74838
w derwentcottage.co.uk

Coachmans Cottage ★★★★
Self Catering
Keswick Cottages
t (017687) 78555
e info@keswickcottages.co.uk
w keswickcottages.co.uk

The Cobbles ★★★
Self Catering
Cumbrian Cottages
t (01228) 599960
e enquiries@cumbrian-cottages.co.uk
w cumbrian-cottages.co.uk

Condor ★★★★ *Self Catering*
Cumbrian Cottages
t (01228) 599960
e enquiries@cumbrian-cottages.co.uk
w cumbrian-cottages.co.uk

Conifer Cottage ★★★
Self Catering
Lakes Cottage Holidays
t (01228) 591555
e info@lakescottageholiday.co.uk
w lakescottageholiday.co.uk

Cosy Nook ★★★
Self Catering
Cumbrian Cottages
t (01228) 599960
e enquiries@cumbrian-cottages.co.uk
w cumbrian-cottages.co.uk

The Cottage ★★★
Self Catering
Contact: Mrs Margaret Beaty
t (017687) 78278

The Cottage Suite ★★★
Self Catering
Contact: Lynne Watkins
The Skiddaw Hotel
t (017687) 72071
e info@skiddawhotel.co.uk
w skiddawhotel.co.uk

Courtyard Cottages ★★★★
Self Catering
Contact: Hazel Hutton
t (017687) 72144
e info@springs-farm.co.uk
w springs-farm.co.uk

Crag View ★★★
Self Catering
Cumbrian Cottages
t (01228) 599960
e enquiries@cumbrian-cottages.co.uk
w cumbrian-cottages.co.uk

The Croft ★★★ *Self Catering*
Cumbrian Cottages
t (01228) 599960
e enquiries@cumbrian-cottages.co.uk
w cumbrian-cottages.co.uk

Croft Cottage ★★★★
Self Catering
Cumbrian Cottages
t (01228) 599960
e enquiries@cumbrian-cottages.co.uk
w cumbrian-cottages.co.uk

Croft House Holidays
★★★★ *Self Catering*
Contact: Mrs Boniface
t (017687) 73693
e holidays@crofthouselakes.co.uk
w crofthouselakes.co.uk

Croftlands Cottages, Thornthwaite ★★★★★
Self Catering
Contact: Susan McGarvie
t (017687) 78300
e info@keswickselfcateringcottage.co.uk
w keswickselfcateringcottage.co.uk

Dafffodil Bank ★★★★
Self Catering
Cumbrian Cottages
t (01228) 599960
e enquiries@cumbrian-cottages.co.uk
w cumbrian-cottages.co.uk

Dairy Lodge ★★★
Self Catering
Cumbrian Cottages
t (01228) 599960
e enquiries@cumbrian-cottages.co.uk
w cumbrian-cottages.co.uk

Darwin Cottage ★★★
Self Catering
Cumbrian Cottages
t (01228) 599960
e enquiries@cumbrian-cottages.co.uk
w cumbrian-cottages.co.uk

Denholm ★★★ *Self Catering*
Cumbrian Cottages
t (01228) 599960
e enquiries@cumbrian-cottages.co.uk
w cumbrian-cottages.co.uk

Derwent Cottage ★★★★
Self Catering
Keswick Cottages
t (017687) 78555
e info@keswickcottages.co.uk
w keswickcottages.co.uk

Derwent Cottage ★★★★
Self Catering
Contact: Susan Jackson
Heart of the Lakes
t (015394) 32321
e info@heartofthelakes.co.uk
w heartofthelakes.co.uk

Derwent House and Brandelhowe ★★★
Self Catering
Contact: Oliver & Mary Bull
Derwent House Holidays
t (01889) 505678
e thebulls@globalnet.co.uk
w dhholidays-lakes.com

Derwentwater ★★★★
Self Catering
Cumbrian Cottages
t (01228) 599960
e enquiries@cumbrian-cottages.co.uk
w cumbrian-cottages.co.uk

Dove House ★★★★
Self Catering
Contact: Peter Brackley
t 07731 398938
e dove@parkcottages.co.uk
w parkcottages.co.uk

Duck Pool ★★★
Self Catering
Lakeland Cottage Holidays
t (017687) 76065
e info@lakelandcottages.co.uk
w lakelandcottages.co.uk

Dunmallet ★★★
Self Catering
Cumbrian Cottages
t (01228) 599960
e enquiries@cumbrian-cottages.co.uk
w cumbrian-cottages.co.uk

Elm Court 11 ★★★
Self Catering
Cumbrian Cottages
t (01228) 599960
e enquiries@cumbrian-cottages.co.uk
w cumbrian-cottages.co.uk

Fell View ★★★ *Self Catering*
Cumbrian Cottages
t (01228) 599960
e enquiries@cumbrian-cottages.co.uk
w cumbrian-cottages.co.uk

Fell View Lodge ★★★
Self Catering
Cumbrian Cottages
t (01228) 599960
e enquiries@cumbrian-cottages.co.uk
w cumbrian-cottages.co.uk

The Fells ★★★★
Self Catering
Cumbrian Cottages
t (01228) 599960
e enquiries@cumbrian-cottages.co.uk
w cumbrian-cottages.co.uk

Fernbank House ★★★★★
Self Catering
Contact: Stephen Mason
Stonegarth Guest House
t (017687) 72436
e info@fernbankhouse.com
w fernbankhouse.com

Ferndale ★★ *Self Catering*
Lakeland Cottage Holidays
t (017687) 76065
e info@lakelandcottages.co.uk
w lakelandcottages.co.uk

Fieldside Lodge ★★★★
Self Catering
Cumbrian Cottages
t (01228) 599960
e enquiries@cumbrian-cottages.co.uk
w cumbrian-cottages.co.uk

The Fold ★★★ *Self Catering*
Cumbrian Cottages
t (01228) 599960
e enquiries@cumbrian-cottages.co.uk
w cumbrian-cottages.co.uk

Fornside Farm Cottages ★★★★ *Self Catering*
Contact: Robert & Pam Hall
t (017687) 79173
e cottages@fornside.co.uk
w fornside.co.uk

Fountain Cottage ★★★-★★★★★ *Self Catering*
Contact: Dr & Mrs Preston
Bannest Hill Holidays
t (017684) 84394
e stay@bannesthill.co.uk
w bannesthill.co.uk

Friars Crag ★★★
Self Catering
Cumbrian Cottages
t (01228) 599960
e enquiries@cumbrian-cottages.co.uk
w cumbrian-cottages.co.uk

Fryston Cottage ★★★★
Self Catering
Cumbrian Cottages
t (01228) 599960
e enquiries@cumbrian-cottages.co.uk
w cumbrian-cottages.co.uk

Gable Cottage ★★★
Self Catering
Cumbrian Cottages
t (01228) 599960
e enquiries@cumbrian-cottages.co.uk
w cumbrian-cottages.co.uk

Gable Cottage ★★★★
Self Catering
Contact: David & Sarah Edwards
Lake and Fell Holidays
t (01902) 846153
e enquiries@lakeandfell.co.uk
w lakeandfell.co.uk

Gabriels Cottage ★★★★
Self Catering
Cumbrian Cottages
t (01228) 599960
e enquiries@cumbrian-cottages.co.uk
w cumbrian-cottages.co.uk

Gallery Mews Cottages ★★★ *Self Catering*
Contact: Ron & Anne Monk
t (017687) 78250
e enquiries@thornthwaite.net
w thornthwaite.net

Glaramara ★★★
Self Catering
Cumbrian Cottages
t (01228) 599960
e enquiries@cumbrian-cottages.co.uk
w cumbrian-cottages.co.uk

Glen Holm
Rating Applied For
Self Catering
Cumbrian Cottages
t (01228) 599960
e enquiries@cumbrian-cottages.co.uk
w cumbrian-cottages.co.uk

Glendera ★★★ *Self Catering*
Lakeland Cottage Holidays
t (017687) 76065
e info@lakelandcottages.co.uk
w lakelandcottages.co.uk

Glenmore ★★★ *Self Catering*
Cumbrian Cottages
t (01228) 599960
e enquiries@cumbrian-cottages.co.uk
w cumbrian-cottages.co.uk

Grange Cottage Keswick ★★★★ *Self Catering*
Cumbrian Cottages
t (01228) 599960
e enquiries@cumbrian-cottages.co.uk
w cumbrian-cottages.co.uk

Green Gables ★★★★★
Self Catering
Cumbrian Cottages
t (01228) 599960
e enquiries@cumbrian-cottages.co.uk
w cumbrian-cottages.co.uk

Greenbank ★★★
Self Catering
Cumbrian Cottages
t (01228) 599960
e enquiries@cumbrian-cottages.co.uk
w cumbrian-cottages.co.uk

Greta Hall – Coach House ★★★★ *Self Catering*
Cumbrian Cottages
t (01228) 599960
e enquiries@cumbrian-cottages.co.uk
w cumbrian-cottages.co.uk

Greta Hall – Coleridge Wing ★★★★ *Self Catering*
Cumbrian Cottages
t (01228) 599960
e enquiries@cumbrian-cottages.co.uk
w cumbrian-cottages.co.uk

Greta Hall – The Old Wash House ★★★★ *Self Catering*
Cumbrian Cottages
t (01228) 599960
e enquiries@cumbrian-cottages.co.uk
w cumbrian-cottages.co.uk

Greta Side 1 ★★★
Self Catering
Cumbrian Cottages
t (01228) 599960
e enquiries@cumbrian-cottages.co.uk
w cumbrian-cottages.co.uk

Greta Side 2 ★★★
Self Catering
Cumbrian Cottages
t (01228) 599960
e enquiries@cumbrian-cottages.co.uk
w cumbrian-cottages.co.uk

Greta Side 4 ★★★
Self Catering
Cumbrian Cottages
t (01228) 599960
e enquiries@cumbrian-cottages.co.uk
w cumbrian-cottages.co.uk

Haystacks ★★★
Self Catering
Cumbrian Cottages
t (01228) 599960
e enquiries@cumbrian-cottages.co.uk
w cumbrian-cottages.co.uk

Helvellyn House Apartment ★★★ *Self Catering*
Cumbrian Cottages
t (01228) 599960
e enquiries@cumbrian-cottages.co.uk
w cumbrian-cottages.co.uk

Helvellyn Rise ★★★
Self Catering
Cumbrian Cottages
t (01228) 599960
e enquiries@cumbrian-cottages.co.uk
w cumbrian-cottages.co.uk

Herries ★★★ *Self Catering*
Lakeland Cottage Holidays
t (017687) 76065
e info@lakelandcottages.co.uk
w lakelandcottages.co.uk

High Chestnut Hill ★★★
Self Catering
Cumbrian Cottages
t (01228) 599960
e enquiries@cumbrian-cottages.co.uk
w cumbrian-cottages.co.uk

High Hill Farm Cottage
★★★★ *Self Catering*
Cumbrian Cottages
t (01228) 599960
e enquiries@cumbrian-cottages.co.uk
w cumbrian-cottages.co.uk

High Hill House ★★★★
Self Catering
Cumbrian Cottages
t (01228) 599960
e enquiries@cumbrian-cottages.co.uk
w cumbrian-cottages.co.uk

High Rigg ★★★★
Self Catering
Cumbrian Cottages
t (01228) 599960
e enquiries@cumbrian-cottages.co.uk
w cumbrian-cottages.co.uk

High Spy ★★★★
Self Catering
Contact: Alison Milner
t (01636) 831221
e milner@fearon9.fsnet.co.uk
w alisonscottages.co.uk

High Spy ★★★ *Self Catering*
Lakeland Cottage Holidays
t (017687) 76065
e info@lakelandcottages.co.uk
w lakelandcottages.co.uk

Highbank ★★★★
Self Catering
Cumbrian Cottages
t (01228) 599960
e enquiries@cumbrian-cottages.co.uk
w cumbrian-cottages.co.uk

Highcrest ★★★ *Self Catering*
Cumbrian Cottages
t (01228) 599960
e enquiries@cumbrian-cottages.co.uk
w cumbrian-cottages.co.uk

Hillside ★★★ *Self Catering*
Contact: Dr & Mrs M J & D J Wright
t (017687) 80256
e info@keswick-hillside-apts.co.uk
w keswickhillsideapartments.co.uk

Hillview ★★★★ *Self Catering*
Cumbrian Cottages
t (01228) 599960
e enquiries@cumbrian-cottages.co.uk
w cumbrian-cottages.co.uk

Holly Bank Cottage ★★★★
Self Catering
Contact: Kate Danchin
Holly Bank & Jasmine Cottages
t (01900) 822001
e enquiries@hollybankcottage.co.uk
w hollybankcottage.co.uk

Holly Cottage ★★★★
Self Catering
Contact: Richard Wilsone r.e.t. wilson@btinternet.com
w hollycottage.co.uk

Honeysuckle Cottage ★★★
Self Catering
Cumbrian Cottages
t (01228) 599960
e enquiries@cumbrian-cottages.co.uk
w cumbrian-cottages.co.uk

Horse Shoe Crag ★★★
Self Catering
Lakeland Cottage Holidays
t (017687) 76065
e info@lakelandcottages.co.uk
w lakelandcottages.co.uk

The Ivy Cottage ★★★
Self Catering
Cumbrian Cottages
t (01228) 599960
e enquiries@cumbrian-cottages.co.uk
w cumbrian-cottages.co.uk

Jane Eyres Cottage ★★★★
Self Catering
Cumbrian Cottages
t (01228) 599960
e enquiries@cumbrian-cottages.co.uk
w cumbrian-cottages.co.uk

Keswick Boat House ★★★
Self Catering
Cumbrian Cottages
t (01228) 599960
e enquiries@cumbrian-cottages.co.uk
w cumbrian-cottages.co.uk

Keswick Timeshare Limited
★★★★ *Self Catering*
Contact: Mr David Etherden
t (017687) 73591
e enquiries@keswickb.com

Keswick View ★★★
Self Catering
Contact: Andrew & Gail Newton
t 0845 680 0244
e enquiries@keswickview.co.uk
w keswickview.co.uk

Kingsfell ★★★★
Self Catering
Contact: Christine Leach
t (01462) 627291
e query@gotothelakes.co.uk
w gotothelakes.co.uk

Kingstarn ★★★★
Self Catering
Cumbrian Cottages
t (01228) 599960
e enquiries@cumbrian-cottages.co.uk
w cumbrian-cottages.co.uk

Kingstarn ★★★★ *Self Catering & Serviced Apartments*
t (01727) 853531

Kintail ★★★★★
Self Catering
Cumbrian Cottages
t (01228) 599960
e enquiries@cumbrian-cottages.co.uk
w cumbrian-cottages.co.uk

Kissing Gate ★★★
Self Catering
Cumbrian Cottages
t (01228) 599960
e enquiries@cumbrian-cottages.co.uk
w cumbrian-cottages.co.uk

Kylesku ★★★ *Self Catering*
Cumbrian Cottages
t (01228) 599960
e enquiries@cumbrian-cottages.co.uk
w cumbrian-cottages.co.uk

Lakeland View Lodge
★★★★ *Self Catering*
Contact: Les & Julie Stevens
t (017687) 72555
e lakelandview@aol.com
w lakelandview.net

Latrigg View ★★★
Self Catering
Cumbrian Cottages
t (01228) 599960
e enquiries@cumbrian-cottages.co.uk
w cumbrian-cottages.co.uk

Little Chestnut Hill ★★★
Self Catering
Lakeland Cottage Holidays
t (017687) 76065
e info@lakelandcottages.co.uk
w lakelandcottages.co.uk

Low Briery Holiday Village
★★★★ *Self Catering*
Contact: Mike Atkinson
t (017687) 72044
e lowbriery@wyrenet.co.uk
w keswick.uk.com

Loweswater ★★★
Self Catering
Cumbrian Cottages
t (01228) 599960
e enquiries@cumbrian-cottages.co.uk
w cumbrian-cottages.co.uk

Manesty View ★★★
Self Catering
Cumbrian Cottages
t (01228) 599960
e enquiries@cumbrian-cottages.co.uk
w cumbrian-cottages.co.uk

The Map House ★★★
Self Catering
Cumbrian Cottages
t (01228) 599960
e enquiries@cumbrian-cottages.co.uk
w cumbrian-cottages.co.uk

Maple Cottage ★★★★
Self Catering
Lakes Cottage Holidays
t (01228) 591555
e info@lakescottageholiday.co.uk
w lakescottageholiday.co.uk

Marley's Den ★★★★
Self Catering
Cumbrian Cottages
t (01228) 599960
e enquiries@cumbrian-cottages.co.uk
w cumbrian-cottages.co.uk

Meadow Cottage ★★★
Self Catering
Lakeland Cottage Holidays
t (017687) 76065
e info@lakelandcottages.co.uk
w lakelandcottages.co.uk

Merlebank ★★★
Self Catering
Cumbrian Cottages
t (01228) 599960
e enquiries@cumbrian-cottages.co.uk
w cumbrian-cottages.co.uk

Michaels Cottage ★★★★
Self Catering
Cumbrian Cottages
t (01228) 599960
e enquiries@cumbrian-cottages.co.uk
w cumbrian-cottages.co.uk

Mountain View ★★★
Self Catering
Cumbrian Cottages
t (01228) 599960
e enquiries@cumbrian-cottages.co.uk
w cumbrian-cottages.co.uk

Newlands View ★★★★
Self Catering
Lakeland Cottage Holidays
t (017687) 76065
e info@lakelandcottages.co.uk
w lakelandcottages.co.uk

Oaklea ★★★★ *Self Catering*
Cumbrian Cottages
t (01228) 599960
e enquiries@cumbrian-cottages.co.uk
w cumbrian-cottages.co.uk

The Old Betting Shop ★★★
Self Catering
Cumbrian Cottages
t (01228) 599960
e enquiries@cumbrian-cottages.co.uk
w cumbrian-cottages.co.uk

Olivet ★★★ *Self Catering*
Cumbrian Cottages
t (01228) 599960
e enquiries@cumbrian-cottages.co.uk
w cumbrian-cottages.co.uk

Osprey ★★★★ *Self Catering*
Keswick Cottages
t (017687) 78555
e info@keswickcottages.co.uk
w keswickcottages.co.uk

Peak View ★★★★
Self Catering
Cumbrian Cottages
t (01228) 599960
e enquiries@cumbrian-cottages.co.uk
w cumbrian-cottages.co.uk

Pine Cottage ★★★
Self Catering
Cumbrian Cottages
t (01228) 599960
e enquiries@cumbrian-cottages.co.uk
w cumbrian-cottages.co.uk

Poet's Corner ★★★★
Self Catering
Lakelovers
t (015394) 88855
e bookings@lakelovers.co.uk
w lakelovers.co.uk

Praiano ★★★★★
Self Catering
Contact: Richard Callaghan
t (01228) 562788
e callaghanrh@aol.com
w praianocottage.co.uk

Primrose Cottage ★★★★
Self Catering
Contact: Geoff & Julia Holloway
t (01473) 890035
e primrose.cott@btinternet.com
w primrose.cott.btinternet.co.uk

Ptarmigan House ★★★
Self Catering
Contact: Mrs Fursman
t (01491) 681623
e jeanfursman@hotmail.com
w ptarmiganhouse.com

Quintok ★★★★ *Self Catering*
Lakeland Cottage Holidays
t (017687) 76065
e info@lakelandcottages.co.uk
w lakelandcottages.co.uk

The Retreat ★★★
Self Catering
Cumbrian Cottages
t (01228) 599960
e enquiries@cumbrian-cottages.co.uk
w cumbrian-cottages.co.uk

Ridgemount ★★★
Self Catering
Cumbrian Cottages
t (01228) 599960
e enquiries@cumbrian-cottages.co.uk
w cumbrian-cottages.co.uk

Rivendell ★★★ *Self Catering*
Lakeland Cottage Holidays
t (017687) 76065
e info@lakelandcottages.co.uk
w lakelandcottages.co.uk

River Cottage ★★★★
Self Catering
Cumbrian Cottages
t (01228) 599960
e enquiries@cumbrian-cottages.co.uk
w cumbrian-cottages.co.uk

Rivers Edge ★★★★
Self Catering
Keswick Cottages
t (017687) 78555
e info@keswickcottages.co.uk
w keswickcottages.co.uk

Riverside Cottage ★★★★
Self Catering
Contact: Daphne Barron
t (017687) 76007
e info@riversideholidays.com
w riversideholidays.com

Robin's Nest ★★★
Self Catering
Cumbrian Cottages
t (01228) 599960
e enquiries@cumbrian-cottages.co.uk
w cumbrian-cottages.co.uk

Rose Cottage ★★★
Self Catering
Cumbrian Cottages
t (01228) 599960
e enquiries@cumbrian-cottages.co.uk
w cumbrian-cottages.co.uk

The Rowans ★★★
Self Catering
Cumbrian Cottages
t (01228) 599960
e enquiries@cumbrian-cottages.co.uk
w cumbrian-cottages.co.uk

Rowanwood ★★★
Self Catering
Contact: Mr & Mrs Davison
t (01623) 627370

Saddleback Cottage ★★★
Self Catering
Cumbrian Cottages
t (01228) 599960
e enquiries@cumbrian-cottages.co.uk
w cumbrian-cottages.co.uk

St Herbert's Cottage
★★★–★★★★★ *Self Catering*
Contact: Steve & Jo Laker
Laker District
t (017687) 74656
e lakerdistrict@ntlworld.com
w lakerdistrict.com

St Johns View ★★★
Self Catering
Cumbrian Cottages
t (01228) 599960
e enquiries@cumbrian-cottages.co.uk
w cumbrian-cottages.co.uk

San Ging ★★★★
Self Catering
Cumbrian Cottages
t (01228) 599960
e enquiries@cumbrian-cottages.co.uk
w cumbrian-cottages.co.uk

Scotts Court ★★★★
Self Catering
Contact: Mr & Mrs Peter & Pam Hodson
t (01204) 465631
e admin@6scottscourt.co.uk

Seat Howe ★★★★
Self Catering
Cumbrian Cottages
t (01228) 599960
e enquiries@cumbrian-cottages.co.uk
w cumbrian-cottages.co.uk

Serendipity ★★★
Self Catering
Cumbrian Cottages
t (01228) 599960
e enquiries@cumbrian-cottages.co.uk
w cumbrian-cottages.co.uk

Shelter Stone ★★
Self Catering
Lakeland Cottage Holidays
t (017687) 76065
e info@lakelandcottages.co.uk
w lakelandcottages.co.uk

Shepherds Corner ★★★★
Self Catering
Cumbrian Cottages
t (01228) 599960
e enquiries@cumbrian-cottages.co.uk
w cumbrian-cottages.co.uk

The Shieling ★★★★
Self Catering
Cumbrian Cottages
t (01228) 599960
e enquiries@cumbrian-cottages.co.uk
w cumbrian-cottages.co.uk

Shorley Lodge ★★★★
Self Catering
Cumbrian Cottages
t (01228) 599960
e enquiries@cumbrian-cottages.co.uk
w cumbrian-cottages.co.uk

Silene ★★★ *Self Catering*
Lakeland Cottage Holidays
t (017687) 76065
e info@lakelandcottages.co.uk
w lakelandcottages.co.uk

Skiddaw Heights ★★★★
Self Catering
Cumbrian Cottages
t (01228) 599960
e enquiries@cumbrian-cottages.co.uk
w cumbrian-cottages.co.uk

Skiddaw View ★★★★
Self Catering
Cumbrian Cottages
t (01228) 599960
e enquiries@cumbrian-cottages.co.uk
w cumbrian-cottages.co.uk

Slate Cottage ★★★★
Self Catering
Cumbrian Cottages
t (01228) 599960
e enquiries@cumbrian-cottages.co.uk
w cumbrian-cottages.co.uk

The Snug ★★★★
Self Catering
Contact: Stephen & Maria Mears
t (01325) 319142
e mariamears@hotmail.co.uk

Squirrel Cottage ★★★
Self Catering
Lakeland Cottage Holidays
t (017687) 76065
e info@lakelandcottages.co.uk
w lakelandcottages.co.uk

Stoneledges ★★★
Self Catering
Cumbrian Cottages
t (01228) 599960
e enquiries@cumbrian-cottages.co.uk
w cumbrian-cottages.co.uk

Strawberry Cottage ★★★★
Self Catering
Cumbrian Cottages
t (01228) 599960
e enquiries@cumbrian-cottages.co.uk
w cumbrian-cottages.co.uk

Sunny Cottage ★★★
Self Catering
Cumbrian Cottages
t (01228) 599960
e enquiries@cumbrian-cottages.co.uk
w cumbrian-cottages.co.uk

Sunnybank Cottage ★★★
Self Catering
Cumbrian Cottages
t (01228) 599960
e enquiries@cumbrian-cottages.co.uk
w cumbrian-cottages.co.uk

Threeways ★★★★
Self Catering
Contact: Alyson Davies
t (0116) 259 3146
e alyson@threeways-keswick.co.uk
w threeways-keswick.co.uk

The Tops ★★★★
Self Catering
Cumbrian Cottages
t (01228) 599960
e enquiries@cumbrian-cottages.co.uk
w cumbrian-cottages.co.uk

Topsey Turvey ★★★★
Self Catering
Cumbrian Cottages
t (01228) 599960
e enquiries@cumbrian-cottages.co.uk
w cumbrian-cottages.co.uk

Turners Lodge ★★★★
Self Catering
Cumbrian Cottages
t (01228) 599960
e enquiries@cumbrian-cottages.co.uk
w cumbrian-cottages.co.uk

Turners Retreat ★★★★
Self Catering
Cumbrian Cottages
t (01228) 599960
e enquiries@cumbrian-cottages.co.uk
w cumbrian-cottages.co.uk

Twentyman's Court ★★★
Self Catering
Cumbrian Cottages
t (01228) 599960
e enquiries@cumbrian-cottages.co.uk
w cumbrian-cottages.co.uk

Underne ★★★ *Self Catering*
Lakeland Cottage Holidays
t (017687) 76065
e info@lakelandcottages.co.uk
w lakelandcottages.co.uk

Underscar ★★★★★
Self Catering
Contact: Susan Jackson
Heart of the Lakes
t (015394) 32321
e info@heartofthelakes.co.uk
w heartofthelakes.co.uk

Upton Glen ★★★
Self Catering
Cumbrian Cottages
t (01228) 599960
e enquiries@cumbrian-cottages.co.uk
w cumbrian-cottages.co.uk

Vicarage Hill Apartments
★★★ *Self Catering*
Contact: Andrew & Diane Matthews
t (017687) 73324
e info@skiddawgrove.co.uk
w skiddawgrove.co.uk

Walla Crag ★★★
Self Catering
Cumbrian Cottages
t (01228) 599960
e enquiries@cumbrian-cottages.co.uk
w cumbrian-cottages.co.uk

Wendover ★★★
Self Catering
Cumbrian Cottages
t (01228) 599960
e enquiries@cumbrian-cottages.co.uk
w cumbrian-cottages.co.uk

Westies ★★★ *Self Catering*
Lakeland Cottage Holidays
t (017687) 76065
e info@lakelandcottages.co.uk
w lakelandcottages.co.uk

The White Cottage ★★★
Self Catering
Cumbrian Cottages
t (01228) 599960
e enquiries@cumbrian-cottages.co.uk
w cumbrian-cottages.co.uk

White Wicket ★★★
Self Catering
Cumbrian Cottages
t (01228) 599960
e enquiries@cumbrian-cottages.co.uk
w cumbrian-cottages.co.uk

Woodleigh ★★★★
Self Catering
Cumbrian Cottages
t (01228) 599960
e enquiries@cumbrian-cottages.co.uk
w cumbrian-cottages.co.uk

Wren Cottage ★★★★
Self Catering
Keswick Cottages
t (017687) 78555
e info@keswickcottages.co.uk
w keswickcottages.co.uk

KETTLESHULME
Greater Manchester

Townfield Farm ★★★★
Self Catering
Contact: Mrs Christine Hallam
t (01663) 733450

KETTLEWELL
North Yorkshire

Fold Farm Cottages ★★★★
Self Catering
Contact: Mrs Barbara Lambert
t (01756) 760886
e info@foldfarm.co.uk
w foldfarm.co.uk

Ghyll Cottage ★★★★
Self Catering
Contact: Richard & Anne Bush
t (01743) 351001
e ghyll_cottage_kettlewell@yahoo.co.uk
w ghyll-holiday-cottage-kettlewell.com

Heathlands ★★★
Self Catering
Dales Holiday Cottages
t (01756) 790919
e info@dales-holiday-cottages.com
w dales-holiday-cottages.com

Wayside Cottage ★★★
Self Catering
Contact: Georgina Drew
t (01296) 620017
e craig.drew@tesco.net

KIELDER
Northumberland

Kielder Lodges
★★★★–★★★★★
Self Catering
Leaplish Waterside Park
t (01434) 250294
e kielder.holidays@nwl.co.uk
w nwl.co.uk/kielder

Lightpipe Barn
Rating Applied For
Self Catering
Contact: Mr Steve Jones
t 07703 490895

KIELDER WATER
Northumberland

Calvert Trust Kielder
★★★★ *Self Catering*
t (01434) 250232
e enquiries@calvert-kielder.com
w calvert-trust.org.uk

Falstone Barns, Nr Kielder Water and Forest Park
★★★★★ *Self Catering*
Contact: Mrs Nicolette Forster
t (01434) 240251 & 07891 817185
e info@falstonebarns.com
w falstonebarns.com

KILHAM
East Riding of Yorkshire

Raven Hill Holiday Farmhouse ★★★★
Self Catering
Contact: Patricia Savile
t (01377) 267217

KILLINGTON
Cumbria

Ghyll Stile Mill Cottage
★★★ *Self Catering*
Contact: Janet & Nick Chetwood
t (015396) 21715
e janetghyll@aol.com
w ghyll-stile-mill-cottage.co.uk

Greenholme ★★★
Self Catering
Contact: Mr & Mrs Sugden
t (015396) 21153
e peter@greenholme.fsnet.co.uk
w greenholme.fsnet.co.uk

KING'S MEABURN
Cumbria

Lyvennet Cottages
★★★★–★★★★★
Self Catering
Contact: Margaret, Wendy & Janet Addison
t (01931) 714226
e wendyaddison@yahoo.com
w lyvennetcottages.co.uk

KIRBY HILL
North Yorkshire

Manor Cottage ★★★
Self Catering
Contact: Diana Whitby
t (01748) 825634
e dianawhitby@hotmail.com

KIRBY MISPERTON
North Yorkshire

2 Ducks Farm Cottages
★★★★ *Self Catering*
t (01423) 527924
w eastgatecottages.co.uk

Lendales Farm *Approved Caravan Holiday Home*
Contact: Mr Scaling
t (01653) 668220
e avvq77@dsl.pipex.com
w lendalesfarm.co.uk

KIRK MERRINGTON
Durham

Garth Cottage ★★★★
Self Catering
t (01388) 720204
w merringtongrangecottages.co.uk

Meadow Cottage ★★★★
Self Catering
Contact: Mr & Mrs John & Margaret Thompson
t (01388) 720204
e jsandm@btinternet.com
w merringtongrangecottages.co.uk

KIRKBY-IN-FURNESS
Cumbria

Sunset Cottage ★★★★
Self Catering
Contact: Janet Fallon
t (01229) 889601
e enquiries@southlakes-cottages.com
w southlakes-cottages.com

KIRKBY LONSDALE
Cumbria

Clarks Cottage ★★★★
Self Catering
Cumbrian Cottages
t (01228) 599960
e enquiries@cumbrian-cottages.co.uk
w cumbrian-cottages.co.uk

Mill House Cottages ★★★★
Self Catering
Contact: Mr R Birtwistle
t (01524) 276500
e rsvp@millhousecottages.co.uk
w millhousecottages.co.uk

The Old Stables ★★★★
Self Catering
Cumbrian Cottages
t (01228) 599960
e enquiries@cumbrian-cottages.co.uk
w cumbrian-cottages.co.uk

Rye Meadows
Rating Applied For
Self Catering
Cumbrian Cottages
t (01228) 599960
e enquiries@cumbrian-cottages.co.uk
w cumbrian-cottages.co.uk

Sellet Hall Cottages, Carnforth ★★★★
Self Catering
Contact: Mrs Hall
t (01524) 271865
e sellethall@hotmail.com
w sellethall.com

KIRKBY MALZEARD
North Yorkshire

Alma Cottage, Kirkby Malzeard ★★★★
Self Catering
Contact: Mrs Janet Barclay
t (01621) 828576
e janet@lbarclay.demon.co.uk
w almacottage.co.uk

Ashknott Cottage ★★★★
Self Catering
Contact: Sarah Manby
t (01423) 545787
e info@ashknottcottage.co.uk
w ashknottcottage.co.uk

KIRKBY STEPHEN
Cumbria

Burblet Cottage
Rating Applied For
Self Catering
Cumbrian Cottages
t (01228) 599960
e enquiries@cumbrian-cottages.co.uk
w cumbrian-cottages.co.uk

Manor Lodge ★★★★
Self Catering
Cumbrian Cottages
t (01228) 599960
e enquiries@cumbrian-cottages.co.uk
w cumbrian-cottages.co.uk

Stable Cottage ★★★★
Self Catering
Cumbrian Cottages
t (01228) 599960
e enquiries@cumbrian-cottages.co.uk
w cumbrian-cottages.co.uk

Swallow Barn (3399)
★★★★ *Self Catering*
Dales Holiday Cottages
t 0870 909 9500
e info@dales-holiday-cottages.com
w dales-holiday-cottages.com

Westmorland Cottage
Rating Applied For
Self Catering
Contact: Mr & Mrs Hiden
t 07776 276637
e hidens@supanet.com

KIRKBY THORE
Cumbria

Holme Lea ★★★
Self Catering
Contact: Alan Price
t (01603) 279713
e jprice@albatross.co.uk
w cumbriaselfcater.co.uk

KIRKBYMOORSIDE
North Yorkshire

Burton House ★★★★
Self Catering
Contact: Mrs J S Gozney
t (01777) 838246
e burtonhousekm@aol.com
w sykes2007.co.uk

Look out for establishments participating in the National Accessible Scheme

The Cornmill ★★★★
Self Catering
Contact: Chris & Karen Tinkler
t (01751) 432000
e cornmill@kirbymills.demon.co.uk
w kirbymills.demon.co.uk

Ellerslie ★★★ *Self Catering*
Contact: Elizabeth Davison
t (01751) 431112
e mail@lizdavison.com

Feversham Arms ★★★★
Self Catering
Contact: Mrs Frances Debenham
t (01751) 433206
e fevershamfarndale@hotmail.com

High Hagg Farm ★★★★
Self Catering
Contact: D.E, R.A & A Cussons
t (01751) 431428
e sylvianne@talktalkbusiness.net

Low Hagg Holidays ★★★★
Self Catering
Contact: Mr J Lee
t (01751) 430500
w longhaggfarm.com

Oak Lodge ★★★
Self Catering
Contact: Andrea Turnbull
t (01751) 431298
e turnbulls@whitehornfarm.fsnet.co.uk

Sleightholmedale Cottages
★★★★ *Self Catering*
Contact: Mrs R James
t (01751) 431942
e info@shdcottages.co.uk
w shdcottages.co.uk

Surprise View Cottage & Field Barn Cottage ★★★★
Self Catering
Contact: Mrs Ruth Wass
t (01751) 431345
e info@surpriseviewcottages.co.uk
w surpriseviewcottages.co.uk

KIRKLINTON
Cumbria

Keepers Cottage ★★★★
Self Catering
Contact: Pat Armstrong
t (01228) 791378
e info@keepers-cottage.co.uk
w keepers-cottage.co.uk

KIRKNEWTON
Northumberland

New Cottage ★★★★
Self Catering
Dales Holiday Cottages
t (01756) 790919
e info@dales-holiday-cottages.com
w dales-holiday-cottages.com

KIRKOSWALD
Cumbria

Bank House Apartment
★★★★★ *Self Catering*
Cumbrian Cottages
t (01228) 599960
e enquiries@cumbrian-cottages.co.uk
w cumbrian-cottages.co.uk

Crossfield Cottages ★★★
Self Catering
Contact: Susan Bottom
t (01768) 898711
e info@crossfieldcottages.co.uk
w crossfieldcottages.co.uk

Hazel Cottage ★★★★
Self Catering
Contact: Linda Jervis
t (01768) 897136
e hazelcottageinfo@btinternet.com
w hazelcottage.info

Howscales ★★★★
Self Catering
Contact: Liz Webster
t (01768) 898666
e liz@howscales.co.uk
w howscales.co.uk

KIRKSTALL
West Yorkshire

The Tops ★★★ *Self Catering*
Contact: Merton Miles
t (0113) 257 2197
e mertonmiles@thetops.co.uk
w thetops.co.uk

KNARESBOROUGH
North Yorkshire

Garden Apartment ★★★
Self Catering
Contact: Antje Rowinski
t (01423) 860463
e david.rowinski@ntlworld.com

The Granary ★★★★
Self Catering
Contact: Mrs Rachel Thornton
t (01423) 862325 & 07970 000068

Uncle Tom's Holiday Cabins
★★★ *Self Catering*
Contact: Pat Ridsdale
t (01423) 861397
e uncletoms@rapidial.co.uk

Watergate Lodge Holiday Apartments ★★★
Self Catering
Contact: Mr & Mrs Peter & Lesley Guest
t (01423) 864627

KNAYTON
North Yorkshire

Knayton House Cottage
★★★★★ *Self Catering*
Contact: Mr & Mrs Hopkinson
t (01845) 537822
e davidandsue@hopkinsons.freeserve.co.uk

LAITHES
Cumbria

Petterill View ★★★★
Self Catering
Cumbrian Cottages
t (01228) 599960
e enquiries@cumbrian-cottages.co.uk
w cumbrian-cottages.co.uk

LAKESIDE
Cumbria

Deer Rise ★★★★
Self Catering
Lakelovers
t (015394) 88855
e bookings@lakelovers.co.uk
w lakelovers.co.uk

Fir Tree Lodge ★★★★
Self Catering
Lakelovers
t (015394) 88855
e bookings@lakelovers.co.uk
w lakelovers.co.uk

Lakeside Lodge ★★★★
Self Catering
Lakelovers
t (015394) 88855
e bookings@lakelovers.co.uk
w lakelovers.co.uk

Landing Howe ★★★★
Self Catering
Lakelovers
t (015394) 88855
e bookings@lakelovers.co.uk
w lakelovers.co.uk

Nutwood ★★★ *Self Catering*
Lakelovers
t (015394) 88855
e bookings@lakelovers.co.uk
w lakelovers.co.uk

Woodland Vale ★★★★
Self Catering
Lakelovers
t (015394) 88855
e bookings@lakelovers.co.uk
w lakelovers.co.uk

LAMBLEY
Northumberland

Lambley Farm Cottages
★★★★ *Self Catering*
Northumbrian Cottages
t (01228) 599950
e sheena@cumbrian-cottages.co.uk
w northumbrian-cottages.info

LAMONBY
Cumbria

Half Crown Cottage ★★★★
Self Catering
Cumbrian Cottages
t (01228) 599960
e enquiries@cumbrian-cottages.co.uk
w cumbrian-cottages.co.uk

LAMPLUGH
Cumbria

2 Folly ★★★★ *Self Catering*
Contact: Alison Wilson
t (01946) 861151
e dockraynook@btinternet.com
w felldykecottageholidays.co.uk

The Spinney ★★★★★
Self Catering
Cumbrian Cottages
t (01228) 599960
e enquiries@cumbrian-cottages.co.uk
w cumbrian-cottages.co.uk

Wright Green Station House
★★★ *Self Catering*
Cumbrian Cottages
t (01228) 599960
e enquiries@cumbrian-cottages.co.uk
w cumbrian-cottages.co.uk

LANCASTER
Lancashire

Langthwaite Farm Cottages
Rating Applied For
Self Catering
Contact: Mrs Joan Deering
t (01524) 62388
w langthwaitefarmcottages.co.uk

Mulberry Cottage ★★★★
Self Catering
Contact: Ms Catherine Fatkin
t (01524) 64755
w mulberrycottages.uk.com

Parkside & Woodside
★★★★ *Self Catering*
Contact: Thomas & Jane Marshall
t (01524) 262163
e info@riversidecaravanpark.co.uk
w riversidecaravanpark.co.uk

The Stables at Glasson Dock, Conder Green ★★★
Self Catering
Contact: Mr & Mrs Quinn
t (01524) 751568
e mquinn5@conder-green.freeserve.co.uk
w condergreencottage.co.uk

LANCHESTER
Durham

Browney Cottage & Browney Close ★★★
Self Catering
Contact: Mrs Ann Darlington
t (01207) 521476
e ann@hallhillfarm.co.uk
w hallhillfarm.co.uk

Stable Cottage ★★★★
Self Catering
Dales Holiday Cottages
t (01756) 790919
e info@dales-holiday-cottages.com
w dales-holiday-cottages.com

LANEHEAD
Durham

Beckleshele ★★★★
Self Catering
Contact: Mrs Lynn Taylor
t (01388) 537683
e ltaylor_blakeleyfield@yahoo.com
w beckleshele.co.uk

LANGCLIFFE
North Yorkshire

Bear Cottage ★★★
Self Catering
Contact: Mr D Widdop
t (01729) 824363
e jayne.craig2@btopenworld.com
w bear-cottage.com

Low Fold Cottage ★★★
Self Catering
Contact: Mrs S M Nicholson
t (01491) 680154
e info@lowfoldcottage.co.uk
w lowfoldcottage.co.uk

Rose Cottage ★★★★
Self Catering
Contact: Mandy Greenwood
t (01535) 652204
e mandy_greenwood@hotmail.com
w freewebs.com/rosecottagelangcliffe

LANGDALE
Cumbria

2 & 7 Lingmoor View ★★★
Self Catering
Contact: Jonathan Batho
Cottagescumbria.com
t (015394) 41680
e a.batho@virgin.net
w cottagescumbria.com

Long House Cottages ★★★
Self Catering
Contact: Mr Grayston
t (015394) 37222
e enquiries@longhousecottages.co.uk
w longhousecottages.co.uk

Meadow Bank
★★★-★★★★ *Self Catering*
Contact: Patricia Locke
Langdale Cottages
t (0161) 928 6953
e patricia.locke@btinternet.com
w langdale-cottages.co.uk

LANGLEY
Cheshire

Pyegreave Farm Cottages
★★★ *Self Catering*
Contact: Mrs Sally Hammill
t (01260) 252325
e hammill@pyegreave.co.uk
w pyegreave.co.uk

LANGLEY-ON-TYNE
Northumberland

The Waiting Room ★★★★
Self Catering
Contact: Ms Deborah Humble
t (01434) 683030
e info@debhumble.co.uk

West Deanraw Bungalow
★★★ *Self Catering*
Contact: Mr John Drydon
t (01434) 684228
e drydon@ukonline.co.uk

LANGRIGG
Cumbria

Oaklands ★★★★★
Self Catering
Cumbrian Cottages
t (01228) 599960
e enquiries@cumbrian-cottages.co.uk
w cumbrian-cottages.co.uk

LANGTHWAITE
North Yorkshire

Arklehurst ★★★
Self Catering
Contact: Judith Dower
t (01748) 886366
e info@arkengarthdalecottage.co.uk
w arkengarthdalecottage.co.uk

LANGWATHBY
Cumbria

Byre Cottage ★★★★
Self Catering
Contact: Angela Campbell
t (017687) 73634
e angelakeswick@hotmail.co.uk
w byrecottage.co.uk

LASTINGHAM
North Yorkshire

Lastingham Holiday Cottages ★★★-★★★★
Self Catering
Contact: Andrea Cattle
t (01751) 417223
e lastinghamhols@aol.com
w members.aol.com/lastinghamhols

Old Reading Room, Lastingham ★★★★
Self Catering
t (01751) 417345
e reservations@lastinghamgrange.com
w lastinghamgrange.com

LATHOM
Lancashire

Hoscar Hall Farm ★★★★
Self Catering
t (01704) 892207
e pam@howardfamily.wanadoo.co.uk
w hoscarhallfarm.co.uk

LAVERTON
North Yorkshire

Thegns Solace ★★★
Self Catering
Yorkshire Cottages
t (01228) 406701
e enquiries@yorkshire-cottages.info
w yorkshire-cottages.info

LEALHOLM
North Yorkshire

Greenhouses Farm Cottages
★★★ *Self Catering*
Contact: Nick Eddleston
t (01947) 897486
e n_eddleston@yahoo.com
w greenhouses-farm-cottages.co.uk

Poets Cottage Holiday Flat
★★ *Self Catering*
Contact: Blanche Rees
t (01642) 532413
e reesb@btinternet.com

LEASGILL
Cumbria

Maple Cottage ★★★★ *Self Catering & Serviced Apartments*
Contact: Beverly Keatings
t (015395) 63008
e andrew.keatings@btinternet.com
w maplecottage-cumbria.co.uk

LEEDS
West Yorkshire

The Chambers ★★★★
Serviced Apartments
Contact: Karoline Newby
t (0113) 394 6379
e stay@morethanjustabed.com
w morethanjustabed.com

Harman Suites ★★★
Self Catering
Contact: Kulwinger Singh
t (0113) 295 5886 & (0113) 2622734
e info@harmansuite.co.uk
w harmansuite.co.uk

Residence 6 ★★★★★
Serviced Apartments
Bridge Street Worldwide
t (020) 7792 2222
e eileen.sexton-adams@bridgestreet.com
w bridgestreet.com

LESBURY
Northumberland

11/12 Boatmans Place
★★★★★ *Self Catering*
Contact: Mr Stephen Sharp
t (01665) 576492
w newtoncottages.co.uk

Jasmine Cottage ★★★★
Self Catering
Contact: Mr & Mrs Mike & Carol Smith
t (01665) 711360
e info@southmede.co.uk
w southmede.co.uk

Lesbury Glebe Cottage
★★★★★ *Self Catering*
Contact: Mrs D. Gillian Brunton
t (01665) 830732
e raymondbrunton@btinternet.com
w cottageguide.co.uk/lesburyglebe

LEVENS
Cumbria

The Orchard ★★★
Self Catering
Cumbrian Cottages
t (01228) 599960
e enquiries@cumbrian-cottages.co.uk
w cumbrian-cottages.co.uk

Underhill Cottage ★★★★
Self Catering
Contact: Christine Phillips
t (015395) 60298
e underhillcottage@aol.com
w southlakescottage.com

LEVISHAM
North Yorkshire

Lilac Farm ★★★-★★★★
Self Catering
Contact: Mrs Heather Eddon
t (01751) 460281
e heather@lilacfarm.f9.co.uk
w lilacfarm.f9.co.uk

LEYBURN
North Yorkshire

2 Crown Court Cottage
★★★ *Self Catering*
Contact: Roland & Diane Terry
t (01969) 624448
e dalescottages@uku.co.uk
w yorkshiredalesholidaycottages.co.uk

39 Dale Grove ★★★★
Self Catering
Contact: Susan Platts
Wensleydale Breaks
t (01274) 676886
e gplatts@ukonline.co.uk

The Bolthole ★★★★
Self Catering
Yorkshire Cottages
t (01228) 406701
e enquiries@yorkshire-cottages.info
w yorkshire-cottages.info

Bramble Lodge, Thorney Cottages ★★★ *Self Catering*
Country Hideaways
t (01969) 663559
e info@countryhideaways.co.uk
w countryhideaways.co.uk

Dales View Holiday Homes
★★★ *Self Catering*
Contact: Messrs John Chilton
t (01969) 623707 & (01969) 622808
e bookings@daleshols.co.uk
w daleshols.co.uk

Eastburn Cottage ★★★★
Self Catering
Country Hideaways
t (01969) 663559
e info@countryhideaways.co.uk
w countryhideaways.co.uk

Low Riseborough ★
Self Catering
Contact: John Rowntree
t (020) 8994 9837
e rowntreej@btinternet.com

Meadow Barn ★★★★★
Self Catering
Contact: Janice Daughters
t (01677) 450769
e admin@meadowbarn-wensleydale.co.uk
w meadowbarn-wensleydale.co.uk

Southfield Mews ★★★★
Self Catering
Yorkshire Cottages
t (01228) 406701
e enquiries@yorkshire-cottages.info
w yorkshire-cottages.info

Throstlenest Holiday Cottages ★★★ *Self Catering*
Contact: Tricia Smith
t (01969) 623694
e info@throstlenestcottages.co.uk
w throstlenestcottages.co.uk

Wensleydale House ★★★★
Self Catering
Contact: Denise Pearson
t (01969) 624229
e email@wensleydale-house.co.uk
w wensleydale-house.co.uk

LINDALE
Cumbria

Fell Cottage ★★★
Self Catering
Contact: Margaret Potts
Lindale Property
t (0161) 285 6867
e lindale.cottage@ntlworld.com
w lindale-cottage.co.uk

Inglenook Cottages & Linden Tree Cottage ★★★★
Self Catering
Hideaways
t (015394) 42435
e bookings@lakeland-hideaways.co.uk
w lakedistrictholidays.net

The Institute ★★★★
Self Catering
Lakeland Cottage Comapny
t (015395) 38180
e john@lakelandcottageco.com
w lakelandcottageco.com

Lavender Cottage ★★★★
Self Catering
Lakeland Cottage Comapny
t (015395) 38180
e john@lakelandcottageco.com
w lakelandcottageco.com

Millers Loft ★★★★
Self Catering
Lakeland Cottage Comapny
t (015395) 38180
e john@lakelandcottageco.com
w lakelandcottageco.com

LINTON
North Yorkshire

Wharfedene ★★★★
Self Catering
Contact: Elaine Liquorish
t (0115) 922 3239
e eliquorish@avernish.fsnet.co.uk

LITTLE ARROW
Cumbria

Mulberry Cottage ★★★★
Self Catering
Lakelovers
t (015394) 88855
e bookings@lakelovers.co.uk
w lakelovers.co.uk

Penny Rigg ★★★
Self Catering
The Coppermines & Coniston Lakes Cottages
t (015394) 41765
w coppermines.co.uk

LITTLE BARUGH
North Yorkshire

Ashtrees ★★★★
Self Catering
Contact: Paul Ashton
t (01653) 669596
e ashtreesinfo@btinternet.com
w ryedalecottages.co.uk

LITTLE CRAKEHALL
North Yorkshire

Watermill Cottage ★★★
Self Catering
Yorkshire Cottages
t (01228) 406701
e enquiries@yorkshire-cottages.info
w yorkshire-cottages.info

Watermill Croft ★★★★
Self Catering
Yorkshire Cottages
t (01228) 406701
e enquiries@yorkshire-cottages.info
w yorkshire-cottages.info

LITTLE LANGDALE
Cumbria

Birch House ★★★★
Self Catering
Lakelovers
t (015394) 88855
e bookings@lakelovers.co.uk
w lakelovers.co.uk

The Great Escape ★★★★
Self Catering
Lakelovers
t (015394) 88855
e bookings@lakelovers.co.uk
w lakelovers.co.uk

Hacket Forge ★★★
Self Catering
Contact: Judith Amos
t (015394) 37630
e hacketforge@btinternet.com
w amblesideonline.co.uk/display/hacket/main.html

Highfold Cottage ★★★
Self Catering
Contact: Christine Blair
t (015394) 37686
w highfoldcottage.co.uk

LITTLE OUSEBURN
North Yorkshire

Hawtree Cottage ★★★★
Self Catering & Serviced Apartments
Contact: Anne Llewellyn
t (01423) 331526
e cgllewellyn@fsmail.net

LITTLE STRICKLAND
Cumbria

Spring Bank ★★★★
Self Catering
Contact: Mrs J Ostle
t (01931) 716246
e springbank17@hotmail.com
w holidaycumbria.co.uk

LITTLE THIRKLEBY
North Yorkshire

Old Oak Cottages ★★★★
Self Catering
Contact: Amanda Tattersall
t (01845) 501258
e amanda@oldoakcottages.com
w oldoakcottages.com

LITTLEBECK
North Yorkshire

Kelp House ★★★★
Self Catering
English Country Cottages
t 0870 078 1100
w english-country-cottages.co.uk

LITTLEBOROUGH
Greater Manchester

Long Lees Farm Cottage
★★★★ *Self Catering*
t (01706) 372468
w cottageguide.co.uk/longlees/

LITTLETHORPE
North Yorkshire

Byre Cottage & Swallow Cottage ★★★★ *Self Catering*
Dales Holiday Cottages
t (01756) 790919
e info@dales-holiday-cottages.com
w dales-holiday-cottages.com

Swallow Cottage ★★★
Self Catering
Dales Holiday Cottages
t (01756) 790919
e info@dales-holiday-cottages.com
w dales-holiday-cottages.com

LITTON
North Yorkshire

Stonelands, Litton
★★★–★★★★ *Self Catering*
Contact: Brenda Cowan
Stonelands Farm Yard Cottages
t (01756) 770293
e stonelandsfarm@aol.com
w stonelandscottages.com

LIVERPOOL
Merseyside

41 Manhattan House ★★★
Serviced Apartments
Contact: Victoria Ward
t (0151) 702 9222
e info@baseproperties.com

65 – 66 The Tower Building
★★★★ *Serviced Apartments*
Contact: Victoria Ward
t (0151) 702 9222
e info@baseproperties.com

Abby Building ★★★★
Serviced Apartments
t (01606) 530246
e enquiries@servicedliverpoolapartments.co.uk
w servicedliverpoolapartments.co.uk

Albany Buildings ★★★
Self Catering
Contact: Mrs Sharon Whitehead
t (0151) 342 7711
e swhitehead@toucansurf.com

Alderley – Crosby ★★★
Self Catering
t (0151) 924 7002
e lynne_bold@hotmail.com

Blenheim Lakeside Apartments ★★★★
Self Catering
t (0151) 727 7380
e enquiries@blenheimlakesidehotel.com
w blenheimlakesidehotel.co.uk

Bridpoint Apartments
★★★★ *Serviced Apartments*
t (0151) 703 6996
w yourcitybase.co.uk

City Quay Apartments ★★★
Self Catering
t (0151) 428 5251
w cityquayapartments.co.uk

Colville Liverpool ★★★
Self Catering
t (0151) 236 6747

Dakota Buildings ★★★
Serviced Apartments
Abby Building & Dakota Buildings
t (01606) 530246
e enquiries@servicedliverpoolapartments.co.uk
w servicedliverpoolapartments.co.uk

Element 11 ★★★★
Serviced Apartments
Contact: Mr Paul Thompson
t (0151) 443 0217
e bookings@element11.co.uk
w element11.co.uk

Hudson Gardens ★★★
Serviced Apartments
Contact: Mr Keith Baldwin
t (0151) 486 3573
e keith.baldwin@hotmail.co.uk
w liverpoolcityapartments.co.uk

Imagine Apartments
Rating Applied For
Serviced Apartments
Contact: Lee James Robinson
Imagine Apartments Ltd
t 07809 557 302
e imagineapartments@talktalk.net

Imagine Apartments Ltd
★★★★ *Self Catering*
Contact: Mr Lee James Robinson
t 07809 557302
e imaginecafe@hotmail.com

International Inn Serviced Apartments ★★★
Serviced Apartments
Contact: Leah Williams
4 South Hunter Street
t (0151) 709 8135
e info@internationalinn.co.uk
w internationalinnapartments.co.uk

Karma Apartments
Rating Applied For
Serviced Apartments
Contact: Matthew Wright
Karma Apartments Ltd
t 07815 822973
e matt.wright@karmaapartments.com
w karmaapartments.com

L1 Serviced Apartments
Rating Applied For
Serviced Apartments
Contact: Kerry Bennett
St James's Place
t (0151) 224 8763
e info@l1servicedapartments.co.uk
w l1servicedapartments.co.uk

Medici Building ★★★★
Self Catering
Contact: Ms Julie Gardiner
t (01865) 321106
e greenhavenoxford@btconnect.com
w holidayhomeoxford.co.uk

Mersey Waterfront Apartments ★★★★
Self Catering
Contact: Mrs Janet Shields
t (0151) 487 7440
e merseywaterfront@aol.com
w merseywaterfrontapartments.com

Mr Alan Humphreys ★★★
Self Catering
Contact: Maria Doyle
t (0151) 428 8600
e maria@village-vets.com

Port Sunlight Village Trust, Port Sunlight ★★★★
Self Catering
Contact: Mrs Sandra Nicholls
t (0151) 644 4801
e s.nicholls@portsunlightvillage.com
w portsunlightvillage.com

Posh Pads at The Casartelli
Rating Applied For
Serviced Apartments
Contact: Mrs Gail Gillbanks
t (0151) 257 9690
e gail@thecasartelli.com
w poshpadsonline.co.uk

Premier Apartments Liverpool ★★★★
Serviced Apartments
t (0151) 227 9467
w premierapartmentsliverpool.com

The Reach ★★★
Self Catering
Contact: Mr George Hunter
t (0151) 236 0159
e hunters_cityapartments@yahoo.co.uk
w uniquecityapartments.co.uk

Trafalgar Warehouse Apartments ★★★★
Self Catering
Contact: Mr Ray Gibson
t 07715 118419
w trafalgarwarehouseapartments.co.uk

Unique City Apartments – The Reach ★★★
Serviced Apartments
Contact: Mr George Hunter
t 07884 346384
e george.hunter@littlewoods.co.uk
w uniquecityapartments.com

Waterfront Penthouse
★★★★ *Self Catering*
Contact: Mrs Muriel Simpson
t (01695) 727877 & 07860 351684
e rodmuir@btinternet.com
w stayinginliverpool.com

Waterloo Quay ★★★
Self Catering
Contact: Ms Lynne Bold
t (0151) 924 7002
e lynne_bold@hotmail.com
w alderleyselfcatering.co.uk

Westminster Chambers
★★★★ *Self Catering*
Contact: Mr Ian Kelly
t (0151) 285 9152
e ian.mandy.kelly24041968@blueyonder.co.uk

LOCKTON
North Yorkshire

Ashfield Cottages ★★★★
Self Catering
Contact: Carol Fisk
t (01751) 460218
e info@ashfieldcottages.com
w ashfieldcottages.com

The Little Barn ★★★
Self Catering
Contact: Mr James Fisk
t (01751) 460325
e judi@btinternet.com

Old Barn Cottage ★★★★
Self Catering
Contact: Lorraine Gilmour
Dales Holiday Cottages
t (01756) 790919
e info@dales-holiday-cottages.com
w dales-holiday-cottages.com

LOFTHOUSE
North Yorkshire

Edge Farm ★★★★
Self Catering
Contact: Michael O'Byrne
t (01422) 240829
e info@edgefarm.co.uk
w edgefarm.co.uk

LONG MARSTON
North Yorkshire

The Cottage ★★★
Self Catering
Contact: Mr Robert Gilmour
t (01904) 738535
e bob.gilmour@btopenworld.com
w bob.gilmour.btinternet.co.uk

LONGFRAMLINGTON
Northumberland

Dene House Farm Cottages
Rating Applied For
Self Catering
Contact: Mrs Vivien Mason
t (01665) 570665
e info@denehousefarm.com
w denehousefarm.com

Picklewood Cottage
★★★★★ *Self Catering*
Contact: Mrs Di Jevons
t (01665) 570221
e di@picklewood.info
w picklewood.info

The Red Barn ★★★★★
Self Catering
Contact: Mr & Mrs Jane & Bill Slater
t (01665) 570223
e jane@theredbarn.uk.com
w theredbarn.uk.com

LONGHORSLEY
Northumberland

Beacon Hill Farm Holidays, Longhorsley
★★★★–★★★★★
Self Catering
Contact: Mr Alun Moore
Beacon Hill Farm
t (01670) 780900 & 07802 517121
e alun@beaconhill.co.uk
w beaconhill.co.uk

Cartwheel Cottage ★★★
Self Catering
Contact: Mr & Mrs James & Sarah Chisholm
t (01665) 570661
e sarah@cartwheelcottage.com
w cartwheelcottage.com

Garrett Lee Cottage and Stable House ★★★★
Self Catering
Contact: Mrs Linda Wilson
t (01670) 788474
e info@garrettleefarm.com
w garrettleefarm.com

West Moor Farm Cottage
★★★★ *Self Catering*
Contact: Mrs Carolyn Raven
t 07816 245678
e info@westmoorfarm.co.uk
w westmoorfarm.co.uk

LONGHOUGHTON
Northumberland

Alncroft Cottage ★★★★
Self Catering
Contact: Mrs Christine Mould
t (01665) 606401
e christinemould@googlemail.com

Coast Cottage
Rating Applied For
Self Catering
Contact: Mrs Carol Slater
t (01665) 570024
e hslater4s@yahoo.co.uk

The Northumberland House
★★★★★ *Self Catering*
Contact: Mr & Mrs Michael & Jean Cockerill
t 07834 620669
e stay@thenorthumberlandhouse.co.uk
w thenorthumberlandhouse.co.uk

Rose Cottage & Croft Cottage ★★★ *Self Catering*
Contact: Mrs Margaret Forsyth
t (01665) 577227
w lowsteads.co.uk

LONGSLEDDALE
Cumbria

The Coach House ★★★
Self Catering
Contact: Jenny Farmer
t (01539) 823686
e jenyfarmer@aol.com
w capplebarrowcoachhouse.co.uk

LOTHERSDALE
North Yorkshire

Great Gib Cottage ★★★
Self Catering
Dales Holiday Cottages
t (01756) 790919
e info@dales-holiday-cottages.com
w dales-holiday-cottages.com

Street Head Farm ★★★★★
Self Catering
Contact: Julie Gooch
t (01535) 632535
e streethead@towtop.fsnet.co.uk
w towtop.co.uk

LOUGHRIGG
Cumbria

Badgers Walk ★★★
Self Catering
Lakelovers
t (015394) 88855
e bookings@lakelovers.co.uk
w lakelovers.co.uk

Crummock Water – Neaum Crag ★★★ *Self Catering*
Lakes Cottage Holidays
t (01228) 591555
e info@lakescottageholiday.co.uk
w lakescottageholiday.co.uk

The Poppies – Neaum Crag
★★★ *Self Catering*
Cumbrian Cottages
t (01228) 599960
e enquiries@cumbrian-cottages.co.uk
w cumbrian-cottages.co.uk

Ruskin Apartment ★★★
Self Catering
Cumbrian Cottages
t (01228) 599960
e enquiries@cumbrian-cottages.co.uk
w cumbrian-cottages.co.uk

LOW COTEHILL
Cumbria

Chapel House Cottage
★★★★ *Self Catering*
Cumbrian Cottages
t (01228) 599960
e enquiries@cumbrian-cottages.co.uk
w cumbrian-cottages.co.uk

Oakville Cottage ★★★★★
Self Catering
Cumbrian Cottages
t (01228) 599960
e enquiries@cumbrian-cottages.co.uk
w cumbrian-cottages.co.uk

Oakville Cottages ★★★★★
Self Catering
Cumbrian Cottages
t (01228) 599960
e enquiries@cumbrian-cottages.co.uk
w cumbrian-cottages.co.uk

LOW HAUXLEY
Northumberland

Starfish Cottage ★★★★
Self Catering
t (01282) 845284

LOW LORTON
Cumbria

Bridge End Cottage ★★★★
Self Catering
Cumbrian Cottages
t (01228) 599960
e enquiries@cumbrian-cottages.co.uk
w cumbrian-cottages.co.uk

LOW ROW
Cumbria

Cleugh Head Farm Cottage
★★★★ *Self Catering*
Cumbrian Cottages
t (01228) 599960
e enquiries@cumbrian-cottages.co.uk
w cumbrian-cottages.co.uk

LOW ROW
North Yorkshire

Birds Nest Cottage, Low Row ★★★★ *Self Catering*
Contact: Sally-Ann Wallington
t (01969) 625958
e info@yorkshiredales-cottages.net

Curlew Cottage, Low Row
★★★★ *Self Catering*
Contact: Mrs Rachel Browning
t (01634) 725273
e hillsr1@hotmail.com
w curlew-cottage.org.uk

High Smarber ★★
Self Catering
Contact: Janet Hoyle
t (01288) 406701
e rentals@swaledalecottage.com
w swaledalecottage.com

Intake Cottage ★★★
Self Catering
Contact: Dorothy Kent
t (01748) 821322
e intake@kent.go-plus.net
w intakecottageswaledale.co.uk

Sandpiper Cottage ★★★★
Self Catering
Contact: Mrs Sally-Ann Wallington
t (01969) 625958
e info@yorkshiredales-cottages.net
w yorkshiredales-cottagees.net

South View, Low Row
★★★★ *Self Catering*
Contact: John Hall
t (01748) 886545
e info@swaledaleholidays.eu
w swaledaleholidays.eu

LOW STOTT PARK
Cumbria

Fern Cottage
Rating Applied For
Self Catering
Lakelovers
t (015394) 88855
e bookings@lakelovers.co.uk
w lakelovers.co.uk

Low Mill Cottage
Rating Applied For
Self Catering
Lakelovers
t (015394) 88855
e bookings@lakelovers.co.uk
w lakelovers.co.uk

LOWESWATER
Cumbria

Crummockwater Cottages
★★★★★ *Self Catering*
Contact: Joan Warren
t (01900) 85637
e jm@crummockwatercottages.co.uk
w crummockwatercottages.co.uk

The Howe ★★★–★★★★
Self Catering
Contact: Millie Townson
t (01900) 823660
e millie@mosserhowe.freeserve.co.uk
w mosserhowe.co.uk

Low Park Cottage ★★★
Self Catering
Contact: Robert Watkins
t (01900) 85242

Loweswater Coach House
★★★★ *Self Catering*
Cumbrian Cottages
t (01228) 599960
e enquiries@cumbrian-cottages.co.uk
w cumbrian-cottages.co.uk

LOWICK
Cumbria

Bark Cottage ★★★
Self Catering
Contact: Jenny Tancock
t (01229) 885416
e barkcottage@tannerybarn.freeserve.co.uk
w tannerybarn.freeserve.co.uk

Tsukudu ★★★ *Self Catering*
Hideaways
t (015394) 42435
e bookings@lakeland-hideaways.co.uk
w lakedistrictholidays.net

LOWICK
Northumberland

Barmoor Ridge Cottage
★★★★ *Self Catering*
Contact: Mrs Patricia Adrienne Reavley
t (01289) 388226

Barmoor South Moor ★★★
Self Catering
Contact: Mrs Ann Gold
t (01289) 388205
e barryandanngold@aol.com

Cheviot Cottage ★★★
Self Catering
Contact: Ms Laura Brown
t (0191) 286 1316
e info@cheviotcottage.com
w cheviotcottage.com

The Coach House ★★★★★
Self Catering
Sykes Cottages
t (01244) 345700
e info@sykescottages.co.uk
w sykescottages.co.uk

Granary Cottage 1015
★★★★ *Self Catering*
Sykes Cottages
t (01244) 345700
e info@sykescottages.co.uk
w sykescottages.co.uk

Northcote Cottage ★★★★
Self Catering
Northumberland Cottages
t (01665) 589434
e enquiries@northumberlandcottages.com
w northumberlandcottages.co.uk

Willow Cottage ★★★★★
Self Catering
Northumberland Cottages
t (01665) 589434
e enquiries@northumberlandcottages.com
w northumberlandcottages.co.uk

LOWICK BRIDGE
Cumbria

Appletree Barn ★★★★★
Self Catering
The Coppermines & Coniston Lakes Cottages
t (015394) 41765
w coppermines.co.uk

Langholme Cottage ★★★
Self Catering
Cumbrian Cottages
t (01228) 599960
e enquiries@cumbrian-cottages.co.uk
w cumbrian-cottages.co.uk

Rose Cottage ★★★★
Self Catering
Lakeland Cottage Comapny
t (015395) 38180
e john@lakelandcottageco.com
w lakelandcottageco.com

LOWICK GREEN
Cumbria

Hidden Cottage ★★★
Self Catering
Cumbrian Cottages
t (01228) 599960
e enquiries@cumbrian-cottages.co.uk
w cumbrian-cottages.co.uk

Old Spade Forge ★★★★
Self Catering
Cumbrian Cottages
t (01228) 599960
e enquiries@cumbrian-cottages.co.uk
w cumbrian-cottages.co.uk

Thorn Cottage ★★★
Self Catering
Cumbrian Cottages
t (01228) 599960
e enquiries@cumbrian-cottages.co.uk
w cumbrian-cottages.co.uk

LOWTON
Cheshire

Orchard Cottage ★★★
Self Catering
Contact: Julia Rigby
t (01942) 671020
e johnsons.farm@tinyworld.co.uk
w johnsonsorchardcottage.co.uk

LUCKER
Northumberland

Lucker Hall Steading
★★★★–★★★★★
Self Catering
Northumberland Estates Holiday Cottages
t (01668) 219941
e jane@nehc.co.uk
w alnwickcastlecottages.co.uk

Lucker Mill ★★★★★
Self Catering
Northumberland Estates Holiday Cottages
t (01668) 219941
e jane@nehc.co.uk
w alnwickcastlecottages.co.uk

LUDDENDEN
West Yorkshire

Folly Too, Luddenden
★★★★ *Self Catering*
Contact: Mrs Gail Rowe
t (01422) 881166
e follytoo@hotmail.com
w follytoo.com

LYMM
Cheshire

Broomedge Farm Cottages
★★★★ *Self Catering*
Contact: Mrs Janet Stanhope
t (01925) 752830
e info@broomedgefarm.co.uk
w broomedgefarm.co.uk

LYTH
Cumbria

Fellside Farm, Lyth Valley
★★★ *Self Catering*
Lakelovers
t (015394) 88855
e bookings@lakelovers.co.uk
w lakelovers.co.uk

The Peat House ★★★★
Self Catering
Contact: Steven Brierley
t (015395) 68172
e enquiries@peathouse.co.uk
w peathouse.co.uk

Sarahs Cottage ★★★
Self Catering
Lakelovers
t (015394) 88855
e bookings@lakelovers.co.uk
w lakelovers.co.uk

LYTHAM ST ANNES
Lancashire

Chatsworth ★★★
Self Catering
t (01200) 442980

Christmas Cottage ★★★★
Self Catering
Contact: Mrs Elizabeth Bickerstaffe
t (01253) 713850
e enquiries@christmas-cottage-lytham.co.uk
w christmas-cottage-lytham.co.uk

The Chymes Holiday Flats
★★★ *Self Catering*
Contact: Mrs Lynn Winstanley
t (01253) 726942
e chymes@saint-annes.fsnet.co.uk

Lytham Holiday Cottage
★★★★ *Self Catering*
Contact: Mr & Mrs Llewellyn
t (01253) 739598 & 07941 866447
e cottage@llewellyns.freeserve.co.uk
w freewebs.com/lytham-holiday-cottage

Manhattan Holiday Lodge
Rating Applied For
Self Catering
t (01253) 725080

Merlewood Holiday Apartments ★★★
Self Catering
Contact: Mrs Sharon Iqbal
t (01253) 726082
w merlewoodapartments.co.uk

Stoneleigh Apartments
★★★ *Self Catering*
Contact: Ms Gillian Kilburn
t (01253) 720604
e gill@stoneleigh.net
w stoneleigh.net

York House Holiday Apartments ★★★
Self Catering
Contact: Mrs Sykes
t (01253) 721701
e info@yorkhouse.gb.com
w yorkhouse.gb.com

LYTHE
North Yorkshire

Lythe Cottage ★★★★
Self Catering
Whitby Holiday Cottages
t (01947) 603010
e enquiries@whitbyholidaycottages.net
w whitbyholidaycottages.net

Oakdene Cottage ★★★★
Self Catering
Whitby Holiday Cottages
t (01947) 603010
e enquiries@whitbyholidaycottages.net
w whitbyholidaycottages.net

MACCLESFIELD
Cheshire

Common Barn Cottages, Rainow ★★★★ *Self Catering*
Contact: Geoff & Rona Cooper
Common Barn Self-Catering Cottages
t (01625) 574878
e g_greengrass@hotmail.com
w commonbarnfarm.co.uk

Holiday Cottages North East Cheshire ★★ *Self Catering*
Contact: Mr Longden
t (01625) 875137

Lower Pethills Farm Cottage ★★★★ *Self Catering*
Contact: Mr & Mrs Greg Rowson
t (01260) 252410

Mellow Brook Cottage at Harrop Fold Farm ★★★★
Self Catering
Contact: Mrs Sue Stevenson
t (01625) 560085
e harropfold@hotmail.com
w harropfoldfarm.co.uk

Mill House Farm Cottage ★★★ *Self Catering*
Contact: Mrs Lynne Whittaker
t (01260) 226265
e lynne_whittaker@yahoo.co.uk
w geocities.com/farm_cottage

The Teachers Cottage ★★★
Self Catering
Peak Cottages
t (0114) 262 0777
e enquiries@peakcottages.com
w peakcottages.com

MALHAM
North Yorkshire

The Old School ★★★★
Self Catering
Contact: Victoria Spence
t (01729) 830445
e oldschoolmalham@btopenworld.com
w theoldschoolmalham.co.uk

MALTON
North Yorkshire

4 Wellgarth ★★ *Self Catering*
Contact: Dianne Waudby
t (01653) 697548
e diannewaudby@onetel.com

5 East Mount ★★★★
Self Catering
Contact: Mrs Susan Armitage
t (01653) 695890
w flapeastmount.co.uk

Easthorpe Lodge ★★★★
Self Catering
Contact: Mrs Rebecca A Carrie
t (01944) 710429
e info@easthorpelodge.co.uk
w easthorpelodge.co.uk

Swans Nest Cottage ★★★★
Self Catering
Contact: Yvonne Dickinson
t (01653) 694970
e swansnestcottage@hotmail.com
w cottageguide.co.uk/swansnestcottage

Walnut Garth ★★★★
Self Catering
t 07766 208348
e cas@walnutgarth.co.uk
w walnutgarth.co.uk

MANCHESTER
Greater Manchester

Atrium Apartments by Bridge Street Worldwide
★★★★ *Serviced Apartments*
Bridge Street Worldwide
t (020) 7792 2222
e eileen.sexton-adams@bridgestreet.com
w bridgestreet.com

Beetham Tower ★★★★
Serviced Apartments
Contact: Mr Justin Reyner
t (0161) 660 7701
e jreyner@citycentrechic.com

Beetham Tower ★★★★
Serviced Apartments
Staying Cool Serviced Apartments
t (0161) 832 4060
e tracey@stayingcool.com
w stayingcool.com

Blue Rainbow Apartments ★★★★-★★★★★
Serviced Apartments
t 0800 040 9730
w bluerainbowapartments.com

Castlefield – Box Works ★★★★★
Serviced Apartments
Staying Cool Serviced Apartments
t (0161) 832 4060
e tracey@stayingcool.com
w stayingcool.com

Castlefield – Burton Place ★★★★ *Serviced Apartments*
Staying Cool Serviced Apartments
t (0161) 832 4060
e tracey@stayingcool.com
w stayingcool.com

Castlefield – Moho ★★★★
Serviced Apartments
Staying Cool Serviced Apartments
t (0161) 832 4060
e tracey@stayingcool.com
w stayingcool.com

Castlefield – Timber Wharf
Rating Applied For
Serviced Apartments
Staying Cool Serviced Apartments
t (0161) 832 4060
e tracey@stayingcool.com
w stayingcool.com

Hill Quays ★★★★
Serviced Apartments
Staying Cool Serviced Apartments
t (0161) 832 4060
e tracey@stayingcool.com
w stayingcool.com

The Place Apartment Hotel, Piccadilly ★★★★
Serviced Apartments
t (0161) 778 7500
w theplacehotel.com

Premier Apartments Manchester ★★★★
Serviced Apartments
t (0161) 827 3930
w premierapartmentsmanchester.com

La Suisse Service Apartments ★★★-★★★★
Self Catering
Contact: Mr Michael Phillips
t (0161) 796 0545
e reservations@lasuisse.co.uk
w lasuisse.co.uk

MANESTY
Cumbria

The Coppice ★★
Self Catering
Lakeland Cottage Holidays
t (017687) 76065
e info@lakelandcottages.co.uk
w lakelandcottages.co.uk

Fellside Cottage ★★★
Self Catering
Contact: Peter Francis
t 07767 780850
e peter@fellsidecottage.com
w fellsidecottage.com

MARLEY HILL
Tyne and Wear

Hedley Hall Country Cottages
Rating Applied For
Self Catering
t (01207) 231835

Swallows' & 'Woodpeckers' ★★★★ *Self Catering*
Contact: Mrs Margaret Rogerson
t (01207) 232959
e maggirog@aol.com
w hedleygrange.co.uk

MARPLE
Greater Manchester

Top Lock Bungalow ★★
Self Catering
Contact: Mr & Mrs Allcard
t (0161) 427 5712

MARRICK
North Yorkshire

Curlew Cottage ★★★
Self Catering
Contact: Michael Petty
t (01740) 620723
e m.c.petty@btinternet.com
w petty.org.uk

MARSDEN
West Yorkshire

Crow Hill Cottage ★★★★★
Self Catering
Contact: Eve Wood
t (01484) 843777
e info@crowhillcottages.co.uk
w crowhillcottages.co.uk

MARSKE
North Yorkshire

Home Farm ★★★★
Self Catering
Contact: Valerie Simpson
t (01748) 824770

MARSKE-BY-THE-SEA
Tees Valley

4 Church Street ★★★
Self Catering
Contact: Mrs Barbara Mosey
t (01277) 652778
e brmosey@yahoo.co.uk

Grewgrass Lodge ★★★
Self Catering
Contact: Mrs Christine Laing
t (01642) 476255
e david.laing4@btopenworld.com
w grewgrasslodge.com

White Rose Cottage ★★★
Self Catering
Contact: Mr & Mrs Philip Phillips
t (01642) 481064
e phillipspcp@aol.com

MARTINDALE
Cumbria

Townhead Farm ★★★
Self Catering
Lakeland Cottage Comapny
t (015395) 38180
e john@lakelandcottageco.com
w lakelandcottageco.com

MARTON CUM SEWERBY
East Riding of Yorkshire

Grange Farm Cottages ★★★★ *Self Catering*
Contact: Mr & Mrs Dibb
t (01262) 671137
e richard.dibb@btclick.com
w grangefarmcottages.net

MARYPORT
Cumbria

Beach Cottage ★★★★
Self Catering
Cumbrian Cottages
t (01228) 599960
e enquiries@cumbrian-cottages.co.uk
w cumbrian-cottages.co.uk

Harbour Gates ★★★★
Self Catering
Cumbrian Cottages
t (01228) 599960
e enquiries@cumbrian-cottages.co.uk
w cumbrian-cottages.co.uk

Harbour Lights ★★★
Self Catering
Cumbrian Cottages
t (01228) 599960
e enquiries@cumbrian-cottages.co.uk
w cumbrian-cottages.co.uk

MASHAM
North Yorkshire

2A Bridge Apartments ★★★
Self Catering
Contact: James Walle jwal470@aol.com
w escapetomasham.co.uk

Barn Owl Cottage Ref:1178
★★★★ *Self Catering*
Dales Holiday Cottages
t (01756) 790919
e info@dales-holiday-cottages.com
w dales-holiday-cottages.com

The Calf Pens ★★★★
Self Catering
Contact: Mrs Keigwin
t (01765) 689499
e prue@uwclub.net

Clipstone Cottage ★★★★
Self Catering
Country Hideaways
t (01969) 663559
e info@countryhideaways.co.uk
w countryhideaways.co.uk

Craigendale Cottage ★★★★
Self Catering
Country Hideaways
t (01969) 663559
e info@countryhideaways.co.uk
w countryhideaways.co.uk

Daleside ★★★★★
Self Catering
Contact: Pam Usher
t (01765) 688277
e pamusher@btinternet.com
w self-catering-masham.co.uk

Forge Cottage ★★★★
Self Catering
Contact: Mrs Lesley Musgrave
t (01765) 689285
e forgemasham@btinternet.com
w mashamforge.co.uk

Lavender Cottage ★★★★
Self Catering
Country Hideaways
t (01969) 663559
e info@countryhideaways.co.uk
w countryhideaways.co.uk

The Mews ★★★★
Self Catering
Contact: Janet Jameson
t (01765) 689068
e jameson1@ukf.net
w themews-masham.com

The Stable Block ★★★★
Self Catering
Contact: Michelle & Columb Reid
t (01765) 688321
e mikiua@austarnet.com.au

Thorpe Cottage ★★★★
Self Catering
Contact: Ms Sarah Cussons
t (01904) 786218
e theperfectbreak@btinternet.com

Thorpe End Cottage ★★★
Self Catering
Country Hideaways
t (01969) 663559
e info@countryhideaways.co.uk
w countryhideaways.co.uk

MAULDS MEABURN
Cumbria

The Brew House
Rating Applied For
Self Catering
Contact: Ruth Tuer
t (01931) 715205
e ruth@craketreesmanor.co.uk
w craketreesmanor.co.uk

Harrys Barn ★★★★
Self Catering
Contact: Mike Eden
t (01704) 220703
e harrysbarn@hotmail.com
w harrysbarn.co.uk

MEATHOP
Cumbria

Woodlands Pine Lodges
★★★ *Self Catering*
Contact: Rosalind McTaff
t (015395) 34128
e whpl.admin@gmail.com
w whpl.co.uk

MELKINTHORPE
Cumbria

Quince Cottage ★★★★
Self Catering
Contact: Tina Ashman
t 07966 730922
e ashmantinar@aol.com

MELKRIDGE
Northumberland

Common House Farm Cottages ★★★ *Self Catering*
Contact: Mr & Mrs Richard & Louise Currie
t (01434) 321680
e stay@commonhousefarm.com
w commonhousefarm.com

Old Brewery Cottage
★★★★ *Self Catering*
Contact: Mrs Jacqueline Robson
t (01434) 320063
e jacqueline141778@aol.com
w oldbrewerycottage.com

MELLING
Lancashire

Burrow Meadows ★★★★
Self Catering
Cumbrian Cottages
t (01228) 599960
e enquiries@cumbrian-cottages.co.uk
w cumbrian-cottages.co.uk

MELMERBY
Cumbria

Alocin Cottage ★★★
Self Catering
Cumbrian Cottages
t (01228) 599960
e enquiries@cumbrian-cottages.co.uk
w cumbrian-cottages.co.uk

Fellside Cottage ★★★★
Self Catering
Cumbrian Cottages
t (01228) 599960
e enquiries@cumbrian-cottages.co.uk
w cumbrian-cottages.co.uk

MELMERBY
North Yorkshire

Mile House East ★★★★
Self Catering
Contact: Mrs Marisa McKinlay
t (01604) 770714
e info@milehouseeast.co.uk
w milehouseeast.co.uk

MELSONBY
North Yorkshire

Spencer House ★★★
Self Catering
Yorkshire Cottages
t (01228) 406701
e enquiries@yorkshire-cottages.info
w yorkshire-cottages.info

MELTHAM
West Yorkshire

Constance Cottage ★★★
Self Catering
Contact: Esposito & J B Jackman
t (01484) 851811

Millmoor Cottage ★★★★
Self Catering
Contact: Paul White
t (01484) 308995

MICKLETON
Durham

1 Syke Cottage ★★★
Self Catering
Contact: Mr John Foster
t (01833) 640132

Kirkcarrion Cottage ★★★
Self Catering
Contact: Mr John Foster
t (01833) 640132

The Old Dairy, Mickleton
★★★★ *Self Catering*
Contact: Mrs Tracey Cooke
West Pasture Farm
t (01833) 640248
e tcookes@sky.com
w teesdaleholidaycottages.co.uk

West Tofts ★★★★
Self Catering
Contact: Mrs Irene Stoddart
t (01833) 640379
e enquiries@wemmergill-farm.co.uk
w wemmergill-farm.co.uk

Whitbridge ★★★★
Self Catering
Dales Holiday Cottages
t (01756) 790919
e info@dales-holiday-cottages.com
w dales-holiday-cottages.com

MIDDLEHAM
North Yorkshire

Briar Cottage ★★★
Self Catering
Country Hideaways
t (01969) 663559
e info@countryhideaways.co.uk
w countryhideaways.co.uk

Demonicus Cottage
★★★★★ *Self Catering*
Contact: Ms Joan Macbeth
t (0191) 239 9366
e joan@middlehamcottage.com
w middlehamcottage.com

Grange Cottage ★★★★
Self Catering
Country Hideaways
t (01969) 663559
e info@countryhideaways.co.uk
w countryhideaways.co.uk

Honeykiln Cottage ★★★
Self Catering
Contact: Mrs Suter
t (0113) 269 3026
e info@honeykiln-cottage.co.uk
w honeykiln-cottage.co.uk

Jade Cottage ★★★★
Self Catering
Sykes Cottages
t (01244) 345700
e info@sykescottages.co.uk
w sykescottages.co.uk

Middle Cottage, Middleham
★★★★ *Self Catering*
Contact: Mrs Jennie Perren
t (0113) 237 1817
e jennifer.perren@btinternet.com
w yorkshire-dales-holiday-cottage.co.uk

Stonecroft ★★★★
Self Catering
Contact: Joyce Best
t (01748) 884062
e chapelfarmbb@aol.com
w middlehamcottage.co.uk

Sunnyside Cottage ★★★
Self Catering
Dales Holiday Cottages
t (01756) 790919
e info@dales-holiday-cottages.com
w dales-holiday-cottages.com

West Hill ★★★★
Self Catering
Country Hideaways
t (01969) 663559
e info@countryhideaways.co.uk
w countryhideaways.co.uk

MIDDLESBROUGH
Tees Valley

Premier Living Apartments
Rating Applied For
Self Catering
t 07896 247896

MIDDLESMOOR
North Yorkshire

Abbey Holiday Cottages
★★★★ *Self Catering*
Contact: Katrina Holmes
t (01423) 712062
e info@abbeyholidaycottages.co.uk
w abbeyholidaycottages.co.uk

MIDDLESTONE
Durham

The Chapel ★★★★
Self Catering
Contact: Mr Tony Langdale
t (01388) 810904
e tonylangdale@btconnect.com
w middlestonechapel.co.uk

MIDDLETON
North Yorkshire

Applestore Cottage
★★★★★ *Self Catering*
Contact: Noelle Thornton
t (01751) 472283
e noelle@middletonhall.org.uk

MIDDLETON-IN-TEESDALE
Durham

The Barn, Middleton-in-Teesdale ★★★★
Self Catering
Contact: Mr Alan Kitchener
t (01937) 844657
e alan.kitchener@ntlworld.com

The Barn ★★★★
Self Catering
Contact: Mrs Heather Crosby
t (01482) 869632
e judy01@judy01.karoo.co.uk

Brock Scar Cottage ★★★★
Self Catering
Contact: Mrs Winfred Gargate
t (01833) 640495
e wyngargate@btopenworld.com
w brockscar.co.uk

Bunny Cottage ★★★★
Self Catering
Contact: Mr & Mrs Karen & Anthony Slater-Davison
t (01623) 456194
e ksd1@hotmail.co.uk
w bunnycottage.co.uk

The Coach House ★★★★
Self Catering
Contact: Mrs Jenny Finn
t (01833) 640884
e info@thecoachhouse.net
w thecoachhouse.net

Country Cottage ★★★
Self Catering
Contact: Mr Burman
t (0161) 860 7123
e enquiries@robinburman.com

Dole House Apartment
★★★★ *Self Catering*
Contact: Mr Paul Callaghan
t (01833) 640950
e accommodation@middleton-in-teesdale.co.uk

Firethorn Cottage, 33 Town End ★★★ *Self Catering*
Contact: Mrs June Thompson
t (01953) 850364

Hush Cottage ★★
Self Catering
Contact: Mrs V Mulholland
t (01985) 850450
e mul.cort@btinternet.com
w cottageguide.co.uk/co-durham

Laneside, Middleton-in-Teesdale ★★★★
Self Catering
t (01833) 660207
w rabycastle.com

Meadow's Edge and Shepherd's Cottage ★★★
Self Catering
Contact: Mrs Glennis Scott
t (01833) 641334

Porter Row Cottage (4330)
★★★★ *Self Catering*
Dales Holiday Cottages
t (01756) 790919
e info@dales-holiday-cottages.com
w dales-holiday-cottages.com

Restmoor Cottage ★★★
Self Catering
Contact: Mrs Sybil Klaas
t (020) 8668 2383
e kestrel.ms@virgin.net
w klaascottages.co.uk

Snaisgill Farm Cottage ★★★
Self Catering
Contact: Mrs Susan Parmley
t (01833) 640343

Westfield Cottage ★★★★
Self Catering
Contact: Mrs Doreen Scott
t (01833) 640942

MIDDLEWICH
Cheshire

Forge Mill Farm Cottages
★★★★ *Self Catering*
Contact: Mrs Susan Moss
t (01270) 526204
e forgemill2@msn.com
w forgemillcottages.co.uk

MIDHOPESTONES
South Yorkshire

2 Old Cottages ★★★★
Self Catering
Contact: Mrs Kathleen Brookee kbrooke770@aol.com
w oldcottages.co.uk

MILBURN
Cumbria

Bramley Cottage ★★★★
Self Catering
Contact: Guy & Rose Heelis
t (017683) 61074
e guyheelis@aol.com
w uk-holiday-cottages.co.uk/bramley

Gullom Cottage ★★
Self Catering
Cumbrian Cottages
t (01228) 599960
e enquiries@cumbrian-cottages.co.uk
w cumbrian-cottages.co.uk

High Slakes ★★★★
Self Catering
t (017683) 61595
e holidays@low-howgill.co.uk
w lowhowgill.f9.co.uk

MILFIELD
Northumberland

Milfield Hill Cottage ★★★★
Self Catering
Contact: Mrs Judith Craig
t (01668) 216338
e craig@milfield1.freeserve.co.uk
w milfield-hill-cottage.co.uk

Pantile Lodge
Rating Applied For
Self Catering
Contact: Mrs Amanda Forrester
t (01668) 216535
w pantilelodge.co.uk

MILLBECK
Cumbria

2 Millbeck Cottages ★★★★
Self Catering
Cumbrian Cottages
t (01228) 599960
e enquiries@cumbrian-cottages.co.uk
w cumbrian-cottages.co.uk

3 Millbeck Cottages ★★★★
Self Catering
Contact: Richard Watson
t (01438) 869286
e r.watson@bbwlaw.biz
w flintcottagesussex.co.uk

Beck View ★★★★
Self Catering
Cumbrian Cottages
t (01228) 599960
e enquiries@cumbrian-cottages.co.uk
w cumbrian-cottages.co.uk

MILLOM
Cumbria

Combe View ★★★
Self Catering
Dales Holiday Cottages
t (01756) 790919
e info@dales-holiday-cottages.com
w dales-holiday-cottages.com

Duddon Villa ★★★★★
Self Catering
Contact: Jenny Brumby
t (01229) 775005
e paulbrumby@btinternet.com
w duddon-villa.co.uk

MILLTHROP
Cumbria

Under Rigg ★★★
Self Catering
Cumbrian Cottages
t (01228) 599960
e enquiries@cumbrian-cottages.co.uk
w cumbrian-cottages.co.uk

MINDRUM
Northumberland

Bowmont Cottage ★★
Self Catering
Contact: Mr & Mrs C Orpwood
t (01890) 850266
e s.orpwood@farmline.com
w cottageguide.co.uk/bowmonthill

MITFORD
Northumberland

The Old Blacksmiths Cottage ★★★ *Self Catering*
Contact: Mrs Pat Glass
t (01670) 512074
e blacksmith21@talktalk.net

MOORHOUSE
Cumbria

Low Moor House ★★★★
Self Catering
Cumbrian Cottages
t (01228) 599960
e enquiries@cumbrian-cottages.co.uk
w cumbrian-cottages.co.uk

MORECAMBE
Lancashire

Eden Vale Luxury Holiday Flats ★★★ *Self Catering*
Contact: Mr Jason Coombs
t 07739 008301
e jicoombs@onetel.com
w edenvalemorecambe.co.uk

Northumberland House
★★-★★★ *Self Catering*
Contact: Mr Neil Briggs
t (01524) 412039

St Ives and Rydal Mount ★★
Self Catering
Contact: Mrs Holmes
t (01524) 411858

Sandown Holiday Flats
★★★ *Self Catering*
Contact: Mr & Mrs Colin Matthews
t (01524) 410933

MORLAND
Cumbria

Hazeldene ★★★★
Self Catering
Cumbrian Cottages
t (01228) 599960
e enquiries@cumbrian-cottages.co.uk
w cumbrian-cottages.co.uk

Highgate Farm ★★★★
Self Catering
Cumbrian Cottages
t (01228) 599960
e enquiries@cumbrian-cottages.co.uk
w cumbrian-cottages.co.uk

Morland Hall ★★★★★
Self Catering
t (01931) 714715
e info@morlandhall.co.uk
w morlandhall.co.uk

MORPETH
Northumberland

Barnacre ★★★★
Self Catering
Contact: Mrs Linda Rudd
t (01670) 790116
e info@barnacre.com
w barnacre.com

The Carriage House
★★★★★ *Self Catering*
Contact: Mr Joseph Evans
t (01670) 790225
e joe@ulgham.demon.co.uk
w ulgham.demon.co.uk

Meldon Park ★★★
Self Catering
Contact: Mrs Cookson
t (01670) 772433
e mrscookson@compuserve.com
w cottageguide.co.uk/meldonpark

Micklewood Park
★★-★★★★★ *Self Catering*
Contact: Mr Mark Towers
Micklewood Park at Longhirst
t (01670) 794530
w micklewoodpark.co.uk

MOSSLEY HILL
Merseyside

17 The Firs
Rating Applied For
Serviced Apartments
Contact: Mr Stephen Shudall
t (0151) 428 1552
e steve@shudall.plus.com
w portsidecout.co.uk

Merchant Living ★★★★★
Serviced Apartments
t 0870 060 4503
e info@merchantliving.com
w merchantliving.com

MOTHERBY
Cumbria

Rowan House ★★★★
Self Catering
Cumbrian Cottages
t (01228) 599960
e enquiries@cumbrian-cottages.co.uk
w cumbrian-cottages.co.uk

Stag Cottage ★★★
Self Catering
Cumbrian Cottages
t (01228) 599960
e enquiries@cumbrian-cottages.co.uk
w cumbrian-cottages.co.uk

MUKER
North Yorkshire

Harriets and Lilac Cottage
★★★★ *Self Catering*
Contact: Mrs Margret Alderson
t (01325) 374368

Scarr House Farm ★★★★
Self Catering
Yorkshire Cottages
t (01228) 406701
e enquiries@yorkshire-cottages.info
w yorkshire-cottages.info

MUNGRISDALE
Cumbria

Near Howe Cottages
★★★ *Self Catering*
Contact: Steve & Jill Woolley
t (017687) 79678
e enquiries@nearhowe.co.uk
w nearhowe.co.uk

MURTON
Cumbria

Mini Murton Cottage ★★★
Self Catering
Cumbrian Cottages
t (01228) 599960
e enquiries@cumbrian-cottages.co.uk
w cumbrian-cottages.co.uk

MYTHOLMROYD
West Yorkshire

5 Hawksclough Farm ★★★
Self Catering
Contact: Michael Horseford
t (01422) 883257

Higher Clough Foot ★★★★
Self Catering
Contact: David Midgley
t (01422) 882577
e cloughfootbarn@tiscali.co.uk
w cloughfootbarn.co.uk

NADDLE
Cumbria

The Bungalow ★★★
Self Catering
Contact: Mrs Jane Nicholson
t (017687) 72290
e jackie@causewayfoot.co.uk

Causeway Foot *Approved Caravan Holiday Home*
Contact: Jane Nicholson
t (017687) 72290
e jackie@causewayfoot.co.uk
w causewayfoot.co.uk

NANTWICH
Cheshire

Brook Cottage ★★★★
Self Catering
Contact: Mr Robert Parton
t (01270) 522284
e robert.parton@theoutlanes.com
w theoutlanes.com

NATLAND
Cumbria

Hawes Bank ★★★★
Self Catering
Cumbrian Cottages
t (01228) 599960
e enquiries@cumbrian-cottages.co.uk
w cumbrian-cottages.co.uk

NEAR SAWREY
Cumbria

7 Broomriggs ★★★
Self Catering
Hideaways
t (015394) 42435
e bookings@lakeland-hideaways.co.uk
w lakeland-hideaways.co.uk

Broom Riggs
Rating Applied For
Self Catering
Lakelovers
t (015394) 88855
e bookings@lakelovers.co.uk
w lakelovers.co.uk

Coach House
Rating Applied For
Self Catering
Lakelovers
t (015394) 88855
e bookings@lakelovers.co.uk
w lakelovers.co.uk

Croft End Cottage ★★★★
Self Catering
Lakelovers
t (015394) 88855
e bookings@lakelovers.co.uk
w lakelovers.co.uk

Lakefield Cottage ★★★
Self Catering
Lakelovers
t (015394) 88855
e bookings@lakelovers.co.uk
w lakelovers.co.uk

Meadowcroft ★★★★
Self Catering
Lakeland Cottage Comapny
t (015395) 38180
e john@lakelandcottageco.com
w lakelandcottageco.com

Potter Cottage ★★★★★
Self Catering
Lakelovers
t (015394) 88855
e bookings@lakelovers.co.uk
w lakelovers.co.uk

Stoney Croft Cottage
Rating Applied For
Self Catering
Lakelovers
t (015394) 88855
e bookings@lakelovers.co.uk
w lakelovers.co.uk

NENTHEAD
Cumbria

Lovelady Sheilds
Rating Applied For
Self Catering
Cumbrian Cottages
t (01228) 599960
e enquiries@cumbrian-cottages.co.uk
w cumbrian-cottages.co.uk

NETHER KELLET
Lancashire

The Apartment ★★★
Self Catering
Contact: Mr Richardson
t (01524) 734969 & (01524) 736331

Ashlea Cottage ★★★★
Self Catering
Contact: Mrs Caroline Scarisbrick
t (01524) 563669
e scarisbrick825@btinternet.com

NEW HUTTON
Cumbria

Borrans Lodge *Approved Caravan Holiday Home*
Contact: Betty Pickthall
t (01539) 721753

Cragg Farm Caravan
Approved Caravan Holiday Home
Contact: Mrs Knowles
t (01539) 721760
e olive@craggfarm.com
w craggfarm.com

Hollins Farm Barn ★★★★
Self Catering
Cumbrian Cottages
t (01228) 599960
e enquiries@cumbrian-cottages.co.uk
w cumbrian-cottages.co.uk

NEWBIGGIN
North Yorkshire

School Cottage ★★★★
Self Catering
Askrigg Cottage Holidays
t (01969) 650022
e stay@askrigg.com
w askrigg.com

NEWBIGGIN-BY-THE-SEA
Northumberland

5 Sandridge ★★★
Self Catering
t (01429) 823866

Coble Cottage ★★★★
Self Catering
Contact: Ms Eva Hartley
t (01670) 817029
e stay@coblecottage.com
w coblecottage.com

Sea-ton Lodge ★★★★
Self Catering
Contact: Mrs Mary Dodds
t (01670) 816057

Tahfay House ★★★★
Self Catering
Contact: Mr Stuart Dodds
t (01670) 503597
e cozydays@tiscali.co.uk
w cozydays.co.uk

NEWBIGGIN-ON-LUNE
Cumbria

Green Bell View
★★★-★★★★ *Self Catering*
Dales Holiday Cottages
t (01756) 790919
e info@dalesholcot.com

High Lane Farm ★★★★
Self Catering
Contact: Dianne Boustead
t (015396) 23416
e dianneboustead@yahoo.co.uk

The Tower House ★★★★
Self Catering
Cumbrian Cottages
t (01228) 599960
e enquiries@cumbrian-cottages.co.uk
w cumbrian-cottages.co.uk

NEWBY
Cumbria

Mid Town Cottage and Dairy Cottage ★★★★ *Self Catering*
Contact: Alan & Margaret Wardle
Lake District Holidays
t (015395) 68074
e enquiries@lakesandvalleys.co.uk
w lakesandvalleys.co.uk

Newby Court ★★★★
Self Catering
Lakes Cottage Holidays
t (01228) 591555
e info@lakescottageholiday.co.uk
w lakescottageholiday.co.uk

NEWBY BRIDGE
Cumbria

Beech Lea ★★★★
Self Catering
Lakelovers
t (015394) 88855
e bookings@lakelovers.co.uk
w lakelovers.co.uk

Fellcroft Cottage ★★★★
Self Catering
Contact: Cath Hale
t (015395) 30316

Herdwick Retreat ★★★★
Self Catering
Lakelovers
t (015394) 88855
e bookings@lakelovers.co.uk
w lakelovers.co.uk

Old Barn Cottages
★★★★-★★★★★
Self Catering
Contact: Peter & Kathryn Harforth
t (015395) 31842
e bookings@oldbarnfarm.com
w oldbarncottages.com

Old Barn Farm
★★★★–★★★★★
Self Catering
t (015395) 31842
w oldbarnfarm.com

Woodland Cottage ★★★★
Self Catering
Contact: Mr Newton
Newby Bridge Country Caravan Park
t (015395) 31030
e info@cumbriancaravans.co.uk
w cumbriancaravans.co.uk

NEWCASTLE UPON TYNE Tyne and Wear

135 Audley Road ★★★
Self Catering
Contact: Miss Linda Wright
t (0191) 285 6374
w audleyender.fsnet.co.uk

93A Grey Street Apartments ★★★★★ *Self Catering*
Contact: Mr Michael Rea
t 07766 008498 & 07766 008498
e info@93agreystserviced apartments.co.uk
w 93agreystserviced apartments.co.uk

City Apartments Newcastle Quayside ★★★
Serviced Apartments
Contact: Ms Teresa Legg
t (0141) 419 1919
e newcastlequayside@city-apts.co.uk
w mckeverhotels.co.uk

Hanovermill
Rating Applied For
Serviced Apartments
Contact: Ms Sophie Hays
t (01423) 524527
e sophie@superiorstay.com
w superiorstay.com

Kensington House Aparthotel ★★★★
Serviced Apartments
Contact: Mrs Gillian Hall
t (0191) 281 8175
e gillian@kensingtonaparthotel.com
w kensingtonaparthotel.com

Premier Apartments Newcastle ★★★★
Serviced Apartments
Contact: Mr Matthew Whittaker
t (0191) 279 7900
e info@permierapartmentsnewcastle.com
w premierapartments newcastle.com/

Properties Unique ★★★★★
Self Catering
Contact: Mrs Vivien Lee
t (0191) 490 0789
e vivlee@propertiesunique.co.uk
w propertiesunique.com

Puffing Billy Cottage
★★★★ *Self Catering*
Northumbrian Cottages
t (01228) 599950
e sheena@cumbrian-cottages.co.uk
w northumbrian-cottages.info

River View at Three Indian Kings ★★★ *Self Catering*
Contact: Ms Deborah Prence
t (0114) 268 2200
e threeindiankings@lycos.com
w cottageguide.co.uk/threeindiankings

NEWLAND Cumbria

Heron Beck ★★★★★
Self Catering
Lakeland Cottage Comapny
t (015395) 38180
e john@lakelandcottageco.com
w lakelandcottageco.com

NEWLANDS Cumbria

Aikin ★★★ *Self Catering*
Cumbrian Cottages
t (01228) 599960
e enquiries@cumbrian-cottages.co.uk
w cumbrian-cottages.co.uk

Bawd Hall ★★★★★
Self Catering
Contact: Alison Evens
t (01900) 828189
e alison@bawdhall.co.uk
w bawdhall.co.uk

Croft Cottage ★★★★
Self Catering
Lakes Cottage Holidays
t (01228) 591555
e info@lakescottageholiday.co.uk
w lakescottageholiday.co.uk

Gill Brow Cottage ★★★
Self Catering
Contact: Anne Wilson
t (017687) 78270
e wilson_gillbrow@hotmail.com
w gillbrow-keswick.co.uk

The Oaks Apartment ★★★
Self Catering
Lakes Cottage Holidays
t (01228) 591555
e info@lakescottageholiday.co.uk
w lakescottageholiday.co.uk

NEWSHAM North Yorkshire

High Dalton Hall Cottage
★★★★ *Self Catering*
Contact: Elizabeth Jopling
t (01833) 621450
e elizabeth.jopling@btinternet.com
w cottageguide.co.uk/highdaltonhallcottage

Merok Cottage ★★★
Self Catering
Contact: Duncan Johanson
t 07790 513467
e info@acottageinyorkshire.co.uk
w acottageinyorkshire.co.uk

NEWTON-BY-THE-SEA Northumberland

3A & 3B Coastguard Cottages ★★★ *Self Catering*
Contact: Mrs Alison Cottam
t (0191) 251 2506
e coastguardcottages@hotmail.com

4 Coastguard Cottage
Rating Applied For
Self Catering
Contact: Ms Susan Jarratt
t (01242) 517772
e susanmjarratt@hotmail.com

Link House Farm Holiday Cottages, Newton-by-the-Sea ★★★★ *Self Catering*
Contact: Mrs Jayne Hellmann
t (01665) 576820
e jayne@linkhousefarm.com
w linkhousefarm.com

Newton Hall Cottages
★★★–★★★★★ *Self Catering*
Contact: Ms Claire Radford
t (01665) 576239
e cradford@apartment-luxbar.com
w newtonholidays.co.uk

Seawinds ★★★★
Self Catering
Contact: Mrs Jo Leiper
t (01661) 881506
e stay@buston.co.uk
w buston.co.uk

NEWTON-IN-BOWLAND Lancashire

Stonefold Holiday Cottage
★★★★ *Self Catering*
Contact: Ms Helen Blanc
t 07966 582834
w stonefoldholidaycottage.co.uk

NEWTON-LE-WILLOWS North Yorkshire

The Shippon ★★★★
Self Catering
Contact: Valerie Nelson
t (01677) 450227
e andrew.nelson3@virgin.net
w theshippon.co.uk

NEWTON-ON-OUSE North Yorkshire

Village Farm Cottage
★★★★ *Self Catering*
Holiday Cottages (Yorkshire) Ltd
t (01756) 700510
e brochure@holidaycotts.co.uk
w holidaycotts.co.uk

NEWTON-ON-RAWCLIFFE North Yorkshire

Keldlands Farm Cottages, Newton-on-Rawcliffe
★★★★ *Self Catering*
Contact: Jill Thomas
Holiday Homes in Yorkshire
t (01845) 597660
e info@keldlandsfarmcottages.co.uk
w keldlandsfarmcottages.co.uk

Manor Farm Cottages
★★★★ *Self Catering*
Contact: Mary Pennock
t (01284) 763568
e mpennock@ukonline.co.uk
w members.aol.com/manorfarmnewton

Sunset Cottage ★★★★
Self Catering
Contact: Pat Anderson
t (01751) 472172
e bookings@boonhill.co.uk
w boonhill.co.uk/sunset.htm

NEWTON REIGNY Cumbria

Blencathra Cottage ★★★★
Self Catering
Cumbrian Cottages
t (01228) 599960
e enquiries@cumbrian-cottages.co.uk
w cumbrian-cottages.co.uk

Gable Barn ★★★
Self Catering
Cumbrian Cottages
t (01228) 599960
e enquiries@cumbrian-cottages.co.uk
w cumbrian-cottages.co.uk

Lilac Barn ★★★★
Self Catering
Cumbrian Cottages
t (01228) 599960
e enquiries@cumbrian-cottages.co.uk
w cumbrian-cottages.co.uk

Lilac Studio ★★★★
Self Catering
Cumbrian Cottages
t (01228) 599960
e enquiries@cumbrian-cottages.co.uk
w cumbrian-cottages.co.uk

Saddleback Barn ★★★
Self Catering
Cumbrian Cottages
t (01228) 599960
e enquiries@cumbrian-cottages.co.uk
w cumbrian-cottages.co.uk

NIBTHWAITE Cumbria

Laurel House ★★★
Self Catering
Lakelovers
t (015394) 88855
e bookings@lakelovers.co.uk
w lakelovers.co.uk

Nibthwaite Grange Studio
★★★★ *Self Catering*
Lakeland Cottage Comapny
t (015395) 38180
e john@lakelandcottageco.com
w lakelandcottageco.com

The Peat House ★★★★★
Self Catering
Contact: Mr John Serginson
t (015395) 30024
e john@lakelandcottageco.com

NOMANS HEATH Cheshire

Millmoor Farm Cottages
★★★★ *Self Catering*
Contact: Mrs Sally-Ann Chesters
t (01948) 820304
e bookings@millmoorfarm.co.uk
w millmoorfarm.co.uk

NORHAM
Northumberland

Boathouse Cottage ★★★★
Self Catering
Contact: Mrs Susan Dalgety
t (01289) 382300
e susan@boathousecottage.co.uk
w boathousecottage.co.uk

Bow Well House ★★★★
Self Catering
Contact: Mr David Hogg
t (01620) 870317
e d-hogg@btconnect.com
w bordersholidays.co.uk

NORTH COWTON
North Yorkshire

Millstone ★★★ *Self Catering*
Sykes Cottages
t (01244) 345700
e info@sykescottages.co.uk
w sykescottages.co.uk

NORTH DALTON
East Riding of Yorkshire

Old Cobbler's Cottage, Driffield ★★★ *Self Catering*
Contact: Chris Wade
Waterfront Cottages
t (01377) 217662 & 07801 124264
e chris.wade@adastra-music.co.uk
w waterfrontcottages.co.uk

NORTH NEWBALD
East Riding of Yorkshire

Red House Farm ★★★★
Self Catering
Contact: Miss Nicola Willey
t (01274) 519866
e glynslinger@hotmail.co.uk
w holidaycottages-beverley.co.uk

NORTH SHIELDS
Tyne and Wear

Graham House Holiday Cottages ★★★★
Self Catering
Contact: Mr Ray Graham
t (0191) 213 6836
e ray237r@yahoo.co.uk
w tynemouthholidaycottages.co.uk

Tynemouth Luxury Holiday Apartments
Rating Applied For
Self Catering
Contact: Mr Roger John Ponton
t (0191) 296 0746
e martineau.house@ukgateway.net
w tynemouth-holiday-apartments.co.uk

NORTH SUNDERLAND
Northumberland

The Granary ★★★★
Self Catering
Northumbrian Cottages
t (01228) 599950
e sheena@cumbrian-cottages.co.uk
w northumbrian-cottages.info

The Old Granary ★★★
Self Catering
Northumberland Cottages
t (01665) 589434
e enquiries@northumberlandcottages.com
w northumberlandcottages.co.uk

Pebbles Cottage ★★★★
Self Catering
Northumberland Cottages
t (01665) 589434
e enquiries@northumberlandcottages.com
w northumberlandcottages.co.uk

The Shieling ★★★
Self Catering
Contact: Mrs Susanna Hodgson
t (01665) 721309

NORTHALLERTON
North Yorkshire

The Byre ★★★★
Self Catering
Contact: Mary Crowe
t (01609) 776072

Hill House Farm Cottages, Little Langton ★★★★
Self Catering
Contact: James Griffith
t (01609) 770643
e info@hillhousefarmcottages.com
w hillhousefarmcottages.com

NORTHWICH
Cheshire

Yew Tree Farm Apartments, Davenham ★★★-★★★★
Self Catering
t (01606) 334770 & 07794 906601
e ade@yewtreeapartments.co.uk
w yewtreeapartments.co.uk

NORTON
North Yorkshire

Anson House ★★★★
Self Catering
Contact: Susan Camacho
t (01653) 694901
e info@ansonhouseholidays.co.uk
w ansonhouseholidays.co.uk

NUN MONKTON
North Yorkshire

Lane End Barn ★★★★
Self Catering
Contact: Ms Madeline Orman
t (01423) 330217
e boo@orman25.fsnet.co.uk
w boosgotabarn.co.uk

NUNNINGTON
North Yorkshire

Muscoates Cottage ★★★★
Self Catering
t (01751) 476653

OAKENSHAW
Durham

Stockley Fell Farm Cottages ★★★★ *Self Catering*
Contact: Mr Thomas Carter
t (01388) 745938
w stockleyfellcottages.co.uk

OAKWORTH
West Yorkshire

Pine Cottage (4146) ★★★★
Self Catering
Dales Holiday Cottages
t (01756) 790919
e info@dales-holiday-cottages.com
w dales-holiday-cottages.com

OLD BYLAND
North Yorkshire

Valley View Farm Cottages ★★★★ *Self Catering*
Contact: Mrs Sally Robinson
t (01439) 798221
e sally@valleyviewfarm.com
w valleyviewfarm.com

OLD HUTTON
Cumbria

Swallow Barn ★★★
Self Catering
Cumbrian Cottages
t (01228) 599960
e enquiries@cumbrian-cottages.co.uk
w cumbrian-cottages.co.uk

OLDHAM
Greater Manchester

Clifton Cottage ★★★ *Self Catering & Serviced Apartments*
t (01457) 872098
w webstarter.easily.co.uk

ORMSKIRK
Lancashire

Tristrams Farm Holiday Cottages ★★★ *Self Catering*
Contact: Mr David Swift
t (01704) 840323

OSGODBY
North Yorkshire

Seaviews Too ★★★★
Self Catering
Contact: Mrs Rebekah Manning
t (01723) 586243 & 07972 754789
e seaviewstoo@btinternet.com
w seaviewstoo.plus.com

OSMOTHERLEY
North Yorkshire

Peelers Cottage ★★★★
Self Catering
Yorkshire Cottages
t (01228) 406701
e enquiries@yorkshire-cottages.info
w yorkshire-cottages.info

OTLEY
West Yorkshire

The Birches ★★★★
Self Catering
Contact: Liz Burrows
t 07799 142745
e lzburrows@aol.com
w chevinvista.co.uk

OTTERBURN
Northumberland

Bankfoot Cottage ★★★★
Self Catering
Contact: Mrs Kathryn Trueman
t (01670) 775410
e kstrueman@btconnect.com

Elishaw Farm Holiday Cottages ★★★★
Self Catering
Contact: Mrs Tina Brown
t (01830) 520942
e elishawfarm@btopenworld.com
w elishawfarmholidaycottages.co.uk

Woodhill Hall ★★★★★
Self Catering
Contact: Mrs Corrinne Knight
t (01830) 520657
e enquiries@woodhillhall.co.uk
w woodhillhall.co.uk

OUTGATE
Cumbria

Borwick Fold Cottages ★★★★ *Self Catering*
Contact: Mr & Mrs Johnson
t (015394) 36742
e borwickfoldcottages@tiscali.co.uk
w borwickfold.com

Claife Cottage ★★★★
Self Catering
Lakelovers
t (015394) 88855
e bookings@lakelovers.co.uk
w lakelovers.co.uk

Grizedale Cottage ★★★★
Self Catering
Lakelovers
t (015394) 88855
e bookings@lakelovers.co.uk
w lakelovers.co.uk

Honey Pot Cottage ★★★★
Self Catering
The Coppermines & Coniston Lakes Cottages
t (015394) 41765
w coppermines.co.uk

Honister Cottage ★★★★
Self Catering
Lakelovers
t (015394) 88855
e bookings@lakelovers.co.uk
w lakelovers.co.uk

Kirkstone Cottage ★★★★
Self Catering
Lakelovers
t (015394) 88855
e bookings@lakelovers.co.uk
w lakelovers.co.uk

Moss Beck ★★★★★
Self Catering
Lakeland Cottage Comapny
t (015395) 38180
e john@lakelandcottageco.com
w lakelandcottageco.com

Peacock ★★★ *Self Catering*
Cumbrian Cottages
t (01228) 599960
e enquiries@cumbrian-cottages.co.uk
w cumbrian-cottages.co.uk

Pepper Cottage ★★★
Self Catering
Lakelovers
t (015394) 88855
e bookings@lakelovers.co.uk
w lakelovers.co.uk

Rose Barn ★★★★
Self Catering
Lakelovers
t (015394) 88855
e bookings@lakelovers.co.uk
w lakelovers.co.uk

Weavers Gallery ★★★
Self Catering
Hideaways
t (015394) 42435
e bookings@lakeland-hideaways.co.uk
w lakeland-hideaways.co.uk

OUTHGILL
Cumbria

Ing Hill Barn Apartments
★★★ *Self Catering*
t (01282) 445096

The Lodge ★★★
Self Catering
Cumbrian Cottages
t (01228) 599960
e enquiries@cumbrian-cottages.co.uk
w cumbrian-cottages.co.uk

OVER KELLET
Lancashire

Lime Tree Cottage ★★
Self Catering
Contact: Mrs Greaves
t (01524) 732165

OVINGTON
Northumberland

Appletree Cottage ★★★★
Self Catering
Contact: Mrs Lesley Rowell
t (01661) 832355

Westgarth Cottage, Ovington ★★★★
Self Catering
Contact: Mrs Claire Graham
t (01661) 832202
e west.cape@btinternet.com
w west-cape-northumberland.co.uk

OXENHOPE
West Yorkshire

Hawksbridge Cottage, Oxenhope ★★★
Self Catering
Contact: Hazel Holmes
t (01535) 642203
e hazel.holmes1@virgin.net
w oxenhope-accommodation.co.uk

Honeysuckle Cottage, Oxenhope ★★★★★
Self Catering
Contact: Mrs Susan Mytum
Hardnaze Farm
t (01535) 645500
e suemytum@btinternet.com
w hardnaze.co.uk

Well Head Cottage
★★★★★ *Self Catering*
Contact: Sheena McBryde
t (01535) 647966
e sheena@brontecottages.com
w brontecottages.com

Yate Cottage, Oxenhope
★★★ *Self Catering*
Contact: Mrs Jean M M Dunn
Yate House
t (01535) 643638
e jeanandhugh@dunnyate.freeserve.co.uk
w uk-holiday-cottages.co.uk/yatecottage

PAPCASTLE
Cumbria

The Cottage ★★★★
Self Catering
Cumbrian Cottages
t (01228) 599960
e enquiries@cumbrian-cottages.co.uk
w cumbrian-cottages.co.uk

Kerria Cottage ★★★
Self Catering
Lakeland Cottage Holidays
t (017687) 76065
e info@lakelandcottages.co.uk
w lakelandcottages.co.uk

The Loft ★★★★
Self Catering
Cumbrian Cottages
t (01228) 599960
e enquiries@cumbrian-cottages.co.uk
w cumbrian-cottages.co.uk

PARK GATE
Cumbria

Line Cottage ★★★
Self Catering
The Coppermines & Coniston Lakes Cottages
t (015394) 41765
w coppermines.co.uk

PATELEY BRIDGE
North Yorkshire

Ashfield House ★★★
Self Catering
Contact: Mr Myers
t (01423) 711491
w http://freespace.virgin.net/john.myers

Helme Pasture, Old Spring Wood ★★★★ *Self Catering & Serviced Apartments*
Contact: Mrs Rosemary Helme
t (01423) 780279
e helmepasture@btinternet.com
w helmepasture.co.uk

North Oaks Farm Cottages
★★★★ *Self Catering*
Contact: Sue Loveless
t (01423) 712446
e cottages@loveless.co.uk
w northoakscottages.co.uk

Rainbows End ★★★
Self Catering
Sykes Cottages
t (01244) 345700
e info@sykescottages.co.uk
w sykescottages.co.uk

Rolling Mill Stable ★★★
Self Catering
Sykes Cottages
t (01244) 345700
e info@sykescottages.co.uk
w sykescottages.co.uk

PATRICK BROMPTON
North Yorkshire

The Parlour ★★★★
Self Catering
Contact: Mrs D Bratley
t (01677) 450229
e theparlour@butterwellfarm.com

PATTERDALE
Cumbria

Broad How ★★★★
Self Catering
Country Holidays
t 0870 192 1617
w countryholidays2007.co.uk

The Byre ★★★★
Self Catering
Contact: Chris Brown
t (017684) 82369
e brown@deepdalehall.freeserve.co.uk
w deepdalehall.co.uk

Deer How Colttages ★★★★
Self Catering
Lakeland Cottage Comapny
t (015395) 38180
e john@lakelandcottageco.com
w lakelandcottageco.com

Elm How, Cruck Barn & Eagle Cottage
★★★-★★★★ *Self Catering*
Contact: Mrs Marsden
Matson Ground Estate Co Ltd
t (015394) 45756
e info@matsonground.co.uk
w matsonground.co.uk

Hartsop Fold Holiday Lodges ★★★ *Self Catering*
Contact: Lesley Hennedy
t (015396) 22069
e bookings@hartsop-fold.co.uk
w hartsop-fold.co.uk

Stone Cottage ★★★★★
Self Catering
Enjoy England Awards for Excellence Winner
Contact: Helen Griffiths
t (01768) 482647
e helen@lakelandstonecottage.co.uk
w lakelandstonecottage.co.uk

Wordsworth Barn ★★★★★
Self Catering
Contact: Joan Martin
t (017684) 82084
e enquiries@wordsworthcottage.co.uk
w wordsworthbarn-ullswater.co.uk

PENRITH
Cumbria

Barn Croft ★★★★
Self Catering
Contact: Brenda Walton
t (017684) 86376
e brenda_walton123@btinternet.com
w barnend-cottages.co.uk

Chapel House ★★★★
Self Catering
Contact: Mr Lowis
t (01768) 898747
w glassonbycottages.co.uk

Mayburgh Lodge ★★★
Self Catering
Cumbrian Cottages
t (01228) 599960
e enquiries@cumbrian-cottages.co.uk
w cumbrian-cottages.co.uk

Monnington View ★★★
Self Catering
Lakes Cottage Holidays
t (01228) 591555
e info@lakescottageholiday.co.uk
w lakescottageholiday.co.uk

Mount Cottage ★★★★
Self Catering
Cumbrian Cottages
t (01228) 599960
e enquiries@cumbrian-cottages.co.uk
w cumbrian-cottages.co.uk

Smithy Cottage ★★★★
Self Catering
Contact: Laura Wilson
t (01768) 88241
e stay@skirwithhallcottages.co.uk
w skirwithhallcottages.co.uk

Stonefold ★★★★
Self Catering
Contact: Gill Harrington
t (01768) 866383
e gill@stonefold.co.uk
w stonefold.co.uk

Wetheral Cottages ★★★★
Self Catering
Contact: Mr J Lowrey
t (01768) 898779
e wetheralcottages@btopenworld.com
w wetheralcottages.co.uk

Wood House Lodge ★★★
Self Catering
Cumbrian Cottages
t (01228) 599960
e enquiries@cumbrian-cottages.co.uk
w cumbrian-cottages.co.uk

PENRUDDOCK
Cumbria

Beckses Cottage ★★★
Self Catering
Cumbrian Cottages
t (01228) 599960
e enquiries@cumbrian-cottages.co.uk
w cumbrian-cottages.co.uk

Green Barn ★★★
Self Catering
Cumbrian Cottages
t (01228) 599960
e enquiries@cumbrian-cottages.co.uk
w cumbrian-cottages.co.uk

Poppy, Lavender and Daisy Cottage ★★★★ *Self Catering*
Lakes Cottage Holidays
t (01228) 591555
e info@lakescottageholiday.co.uk
w lakescottageholiday.co.uk

PENTON
Cumbria

Liddel Park Country Cottages ★★★ *Self Catering*
Contact: Brian Wicklow
t (01228) 577440
e holiday@liddelpark.co.uk
w liddelpark.co.uk

PICKERING
North Yorkshire

1 Westgate ★★★★
Self Catering
Contact: Mr & Mrs S Toothill
t (01302) 770601

Beech Farm Cottages, Wrelton ★★★★-★★★★★
Self Catering
Contact: Mrs Rooney Massara
t (01751) 476612 & (01751) 476612
e massara@beechfarm.com
w beechfarm.com

Bramwood Cottages ★★★★
Self Catering
Contact: Mr John Butler
t (01751) 473446
w bramwoodguesthouse.co.uk/cottages.html

Castlegate Cottage ★★★
Self Catering
Contact: Heather Litten
Castlegate Cottages
t 07961 060273
e bookings@castlegatecottages.co.uk
w castlegatecottages.co.uk

Chappies' Cottage ★★★
Self Catering
Contact: Emma Brown
t 07979 651739
e emma@kianandemma.wanadoo.co.uk

Cinnamere Cottage
Rating Applied For
Self Catering
Contact: Steven & Caroline Herlingshaw
t (01975) 564265

Eastgate ★★★★
Self Catering
Contact: Mrs Helen Graye helen@angusgray.com

Easthill Farm House and Gardens ★★★★
Self Catering
Contact: Mrs Diane Stenton
t (01751) 474561
e info@easthill-farm-holidays.co.uk
w easthill-farm-holidays.co.uk

Eastside Cottage ★★★
Self Catering
Contact: E Evans
t (01751) 477204
e sheilaevans308@btinternet.com

High Kingthorpe Lodges ★★★★ *Self Catering*
Contact: John Tunnicliffe
t (01751) 476457
e info@kingthorpe.com
w kingthorpe.com

Hungate Cottages ★★★★
Self Catering
Contact: Mr Richard Robertson
t (01751) 476382
e holidays@hungatecottages.co.uk
w hungatecottages.co.uk

Hunny Cottage ★★★★
Self Catering
Contact: Ms Clare Chapman
t (01751) 475890
e clarechapman@kdmsolutions.co.uk

Kale Pot Cottage ★★★★
Self Catering
Contact: Diane & Mike Steele
t (01751) 476654
e mike@kalepothole.fsnet.co.uk
w northyorkmoorscottage.co.uk

Karen's Cottages ★★★
Self Catering
Contact: Karen Hill
t (01751) 473258
e hill@newmeadows.fsnet.co.uk

Keld Head Farm Cottages ★★★★ *Self Catering*
Contact: Julian & Penny Fearn
t (01751) 473974
e julian@keldheadcottages.com
w keldheadcottages.com

Kirklea Cottage ★★★★
Self Catering
Contact: Mrs Carol Hill
t (01751) 477202
e carollesleyhill@hotmail.com
w pickeringholidaycottage.co.uk

Lilac Cottage ★★★
Self Catering
Contact: Richard & Dorothy Munn
t (01751) 472193

Loand House Court ★★★★
Self Catering
Contact: Mrs Anna Wadsworth
t (01751) 472587
e loandhousecourt@tiscali.co.uk
w loandhousecourt.co.uk

Low Costa Mill Cottages ★★★★ *Self Catering*
Contact: Eileen Thomas
t (01751) 472050
e thomas@lowcostamill.freeserve.co.uk
w lowcostamill.co.uk

Lynton Cottage ★★★
Self Catering
Contact: Mrs Gough
t (01751) 473025

Mel House Cottages ★★★★
Self Catering
Contact: John and Penny Wicks
Let's Holiday, Mel House
t (01751) 475396
e holiday@letsholiday.com
w letsholiday.com

Newton Cottage ★★★
Self Catering
Contact: Tony Danks
t (01751) 477913
e mal.danks@btinternet.com

North Yorkshire Cottages ★★★★ *Self Catering*
Contact: Mrs Elaine Bedford
t (01751) 476653
e vbenq@northyorkshirecottages.co.uk
w northyorkshirecottages.co.uk/vbenq.aspx

The Old Forge Cottages ★★★ *Self Catering*
Contact: Judy French
The Old Forge
t (01751) 477399
e theoldforge1@aol.com
w forgecottages.co.uk

Pan Cottage ★★★
Self Catering
Contact: Jeff Oliver
t (01751) 473618
e pancottage@hotmail.co.uk
w pancottage.co.uk

Potter Hill ★★★
Self Catering
Contact: Michael Jones
t (020) 8853 2323
e michael@cheese-board.co.uk
w cottageguide.co.uk/potterhill

Prospect Farm Cottages ★★★ *Self Catering*
Contact: G Webster & Lynne White
t (01751) 476835
e enquiries@prospectfarmcottages.co.uk
w prospectfarmcottages.co.uk

Rawcliffe House Farm ★★★★ *Self Catering*
Contact: Duncan & Jan Allsopp
t (01751) 473292
e stay@rawcliffehousefarm.co.uk
w rawcliffehousefarm.co.uk

Sands Farm Cottages ★★★★ *Self Catering*
Contact: Mr & Mrs M & S Parkin
t (01751) 474405
e info@sandsfarmcottages.co.uk
w sandsfarmcottages.co.uk

The Sidings ★★★
Self Catering
Contact: Lloyd & Liz Varley
t (0115) 945 5543
e varleyfm@supanet.com
w pickeringcottages.co.uk

Skelton Cottage & Rowntree Cottage ★★★★ *Self Catering*
Contact: Helen Eddon
Eastgate Cottages
t (01751) 476653
e info@eastgatecottages.co.uk
w eastgatecottages.co.uk

South View Cottages ★★★-★★★★ *Self Catering*
Contact: Mr Simpson
t (01947) 604406
e info@southviewcottage.co.uk
w southviewcottages.co.uk

Stainers Farm Cottages ★★★★ *Self Catering*
Contact: Jackie Smith
t (01653) 668224
e info@stainersfarm.co.uk
w stainersfarm.co.uk

Town End Farm Cottage ★★★ *Self Catering*
Contact: Christine Fenwick
t (01751) 472713

White Lodge Cottage ★★★
Self Catering
Contact: Elizabeth Briggs
t (01751) 473897

Willows ★★★ *Self Catering*
Contact: Diana Ellis
t (01564) 779575
e diana@tanneryholidays.co.uk
w tanneryholidays.co.uk

PIERCEBRIDGE
Tees Valley

Rose Cottage ★★★★
Self Catering
Contact: Mrs Brown
t (01325) 730416
e lesliebrown.agricon@btinternet.com

PONTELAND
Northumberland

The Old Stables and The Old Tack Room ★★★
Self Catering
Contact: Miss Clare Stephenson
t (01661) 822188 & 07786 537424
e elandgreen@msn.com
w elandfarm.co.uk

POOLEY BRIDGE
Cumbria

Barton Hall Farm Holiday Cottages ★★★★
Self Catering
t (017684) 86034

Blacksmiths Cottage ★★★★
Self Catering
Cumbrian Cottages
t (01228) 599960
e enquiries@cumbrian-cottages.co.uk
w cumbrian-cottages.co.uk

Dumallard ★★★★
Self Catering
Cumbrian Cottages
t (01228) 599960
e enquiries@cumbrian-cottages.co.uk
w cumbrian-cottages.co.uk

Fell Croft ★★★ *Self Catering*
Cumbrian Cottages
t (01228) 599960
e enquiries@cumbrian-cottages.co.uk
w cumbrian-cottages.co.uk

High Winder Cottages
★★★★-★★★★★
Self Catering
Contact: Alan & Margaret Wardle
Lake District Holidays
t (015395) 68074
e enquiries@lakesandvalleys.co.uk
w lakesandvalleys.co.uk

Margaret House ★★★★
Self Catering
Cumbrian Cottages
t (01228) 599960
e enquiries@cumbrian-cottages.co.uk
w cumbrian-cottages.co.uk

Primrose Cottage ★★★★
Self Catering
Cumbrian Cottages
t (01228) 599960
e enquiries@cumbrian-cottages.co.uk
w cumbrian-cottages.co.uk

Roxby ★★★★ *Self Catering*
Cumbrian Cottages
t (01228) 599960
e enquiries@cumbrian-cottages.co.uk
w cumbrian-cottages.co.uk

The Steading, Great Strickland ★★★★
Self Catering
Contact: Mr and Mrs Yates
Yates Estates
t (0116) 237 6453
e enquiries@yatesestates.co.uk
w yatesestates.co.uk

Windy Nook ★★★★
Self Catering
Cumbrian Cottages
t (01228) 599960
e enquiries@cumbrian-cottages.co.uk
w cumbrian-cottages.co.uk

PORTINSCALE
Cumbria

1 Harney Peak ★★★★
Self Catering
Cumbrian Cottages
t (01228) 599960
e enquiries@cumbrian-cottages.co.uk
w cumbrian-cottages.co.uk

2 Harney Peak ★★★★
Self Catering
Cumbrian Cottages
t (01228) 599960
e enquiries@cumbrian-cottages.co.uk
w cumbrian-cottages.co.uk

3 Harney Peak ★★★★
Self Catering
Cumbrian Cottages
t (01228) 599960
e enquiries@cumbrian-cottages.co.uk
w cumbrian-cottages.co.uk

5 Harney Peak ★★★★
Self Catering
Cumbrian Cottages
t (01228) 599960
e enquiries@cumbrian-cottages.co.uk
w cumbrian-cottages.co.uk

6 Ladstock Hall ★★★★★
Self Catering
Cumbrian Cottages
t (01228) 599960
e enquiries@cumbrian-cottages.co.uk
w cumbrian-cottages.co.uk

Apartment 7, Harney Peak
★★★★ *Self Catering*
Contact: Kev & Jen Yates
Yates Estates
t (0116) 237 6453
e enquiries@yatesestates.co.uk
w yatesestates.co.uk

Appletree & Tawny Cottage
★★★ *Self Catering*
Keswick Cottages
t (017687) 78555
e info@keswickcottages.co.uk
w keswickcottages.co.uk

The Beeches ★★★★
Self Catering
Cumbrian Cottages
t (01228) 599960
e enquiries@cumbrian-cottages.co.uk
w cumbrian-cottages.co.uk

Borrowdale Apartment
★★★★ *Self Catering*
Keswick Cottages
t (017687) 78555
e info@keswickcottages.co.uk
w keswickcottages.co.uk

Derwentwater View ★★★★
Self Catering
Cumbrian Cottages
t (01228) 599960
e enquiries@cumbrian-cottages.co.uk
w cumbrian-cottages.co.uk

Grizedale View ★★★
Self Catering
Cumbrian Cottages
t (01228) 599960
e enquiries@cumbrian-cottages.co.uk
w cumbrian-cottages.co.uk

Jasmine Cottage ★★★
Self Catering
Cumbrian Cottages
t (01228) 599960
e enquiries@cumbrian-cottages.co.uk
w cumbrian-cottages.co.uk

Keepers Cottage ★★★★
Self Catering
Keswick Cottages
t (017687) 78555
e info@keswickcottages.co.uk
w keswickcottages.co.uk

Lingholm Gardens ★★★★
Self Catering
Keswick Cottages
t (017687) 78555
e info@keswickcottages.co.uk
w keswickcottages.co.uk

Osprey Heights ★★★★
Self Catering
Cumbrian Cottages
t (01228) 599960
e enquiries@cumbrian-cottages.co.uk
w cumbrian-cottages.co.uk

Portinscale House ★★★★
Self Catering
Lakeland Cottage Holidays
t (017687) 76065
e info@lakelandcottages.co.uk
w lakelandcottages.co.uk

Rickerby House ★★★
Self Catering
Cumbrian Cottages
t (01228) 599960
e enquiries@cumbrian-cottages.co.uk
w cumbrian-cottages.co.uk

Roseworth ★★★★
Self Catering
Cumbrian Cottages
t (01228) 599960
e enquiries@cumbrian-cottages.co.uk
w cumbrian-cottages.co.uk

Silver Hill ★★★★
Self Catering
Keswick Cottages
t (017687) 78555
e info@keswickcottages.co.uk
w keswickcottages.co.uk

Smithy Cottage ★★★
Self Catering
Cumbrian Cottages
t (01228) 599960
e enquiries@cumbrian-cottages.co.uk
w cumbrian-cottages.co.uk

Stable Cottage ★★★
Self Catering
Contact: Margaret Pope
t (017687) 75161
e pscale@btinternet.com

Swinside
Rating Applied For
Self Catering
Keswick Cottages
t (017687) 78555
e info@keswickcottages.co.uk
w keswickcottages.co.uk

Whitegates ★★★
Self Catering
Cumbrian Cottages
t (01228) 599960
e enquiries@cumbrian-cottages.co.uk
w cumbrian-cottages.co.uk

Winderwath ★★★★
Self Catering
Cumbrian Cottages
t (01228) 599960
e enquiries@cumbrian-cottages.co.uk
w cumbrian-cottages.co.uk

Woodside, Portinscale
★★★★ *Self Catering*
Contact: Mr Paul Carter
t (017687) 72702 & 07979 206925
e paulandrew40@hotmail.com
w keswickcharactercottages.co.uk

POULTON-LE-FYLDE
Lancashire

Hardhorn Breaks ★★★★
Self Catering
Contact: Mr Pawson
t (01253) 890422
e blackpoolnick@btinternet.com
w highbank-farm.com

Swans Rest Holiday Cottages ★★★★
Self Catering
Contact: Mrs Vanessa Armstrong
t (01253) 899956
w swansrest.co.uk

PRESTON
Lancashire

Bleasdale Cottages ★★★★
Self Catering
Contact: Mr Gardner
t (01995) 61343
e robert_gardner1@tiscali.co.uk
w bleasdalecottages.co.uk

PRESTON-UNDER-SCAR
North Yorkshire

Anna's Cottage at Rocky View ★★★ *Self Catering*
Country Hideaways
t (01969) 663559
e info@countryhideaways.co.uk
w countryhideaways.co.uk

Mallyan Wynd ★★★
Self Catering
Country Hideaways
t (01969) 663559
e info@countryhideaways.co.uk
w countryhideaways.co.uk

PULL WOODS
Cumbria

Pullwood Bay Estates – Blencathra ★★★★★
Self Catering
Lakelovers
t (015394) 88855
e bookings@lakelovers.co.uk
w lakelovers.co.uk

Pullwood Bay Estates – Fairfield ★★★★★
Self Catering
Lakelovers
t (015394) 88855
e bookings@lakelovers.co.uk
w lakelovers.co.uk

Pullwood Bay Estates – Great Gable ★★★★★
Self Catering
Lakelovers
t (015394) 88855
e bookings@lakelovers.co.uk
w lakelovers.co.uk

Pullwood Bay Estates – Latterbarrow ★★★★★
Self Catering
Lakelovers
t (015394) 88855
e bookings@lakelovers.co.uk
w lakelovers.co.uk

Woodside
Rating Applied For
Self Catering
Lakelovers
t (015394) 88855
e bookings@lakelovers.co.uk
w lakelovers.co.uk

QUEBEC
Durham

Hamsteels Cottages ★★★★
Self Catering
Contact: Mrs June Whitfield
t (01207) 520388
e june@hamsteelshall.co.uk
w hamsteelshall.co.uk

QUERNMORE
Lancashire

Lodge View Cottages
★★★★ *Self Catering*
Contact: Mr David Gardner
t (01524) 63109
e djkagardner@ukgateway.net
w lodgeview.co.uk

Shepherds Barn ★★★★★
Self Catering
Contact: Mr Thomas Longton
t (01524) 36867
w longtonsheepdogs.com

RAINOW
Cheshire

Coach House ★★★★★
Self Catering
Contact: Mr Ivor Williams
t (01625) 424220
e info@kerridgeendholidaycottages.co.uk
w kerridgeendholidaycottages.co.uk

RATHMELL
North Yorkshire

Gooselands Cottage ★★★★
Self Catering
Contact: Mr John Garnett
t (01729) 840291
e stay@gooselandscottages.co.uk
w gooselandscottages.co.uk

Layhead Farm Cottages
★★★★ *Self Catering*
Contact: Mrs R Hyslop
t (01729) 840234
e rosehyslop@layhead.co.uk
w layhead.co.uk

RAVENSTONEDALE
Cumbria

Oaklea Bungalow ★★★★
Self Catering
Contact: June Ellis
t (015396) 23415
e enquiries@westview-cumbria.co.uk
w westview-cumbria.co.uk

RAWMARSH
South Yorkshire

The Old Police House Annexe ★★★ *Self Catering*
Contact: Ms Lynda Baker
t (01709) 528999
e bookings@theoldpolicehouse.co.uk
w theoldpolicehouse.co.uk

REAGILL
Cumbria

Whitefold Cottage ★★★★
Self Catering
Cumbrian Cottages
t (01228) 599960
e enquiries@cumbrian-cottages.co.uk
w cumbrian-cottages.co.uk

Yew Tree Farm ★★★★★
Self Catering
Cumbrian Cottages
t (01228) 599960
e enquiries@cumbrian-cottages.co.uk
w cumbrian-cottages.co.uk

REDCAR
Tees Valley

Dovehouses ★★★
Self Catering
Contact: Mrs Carol McGovern
t (01642) 479311
e info@dovehouses.co.uk
w dovehouses.co.uk

Picknett Cottage ★★★
Self Catering
Contact: Mr Gary Hutchinson
t (01642) 291483

REDMAIN
Cumbria

Huddlestone Cottage and The Hayloft ★★★★
Self Catering
Contact: Christine Neale
t (01900) 825695
e hudcot@lakesnw.co.uk
w lakesnw.co.uk/hudcot

REDMIRE
North Yorkshire

Clematis Cottage ★★★
Self Catering
Contact: Alan Pinkney
t 07710 385103
e info@dalescottageholidays.co.uk
w dalescottageholidays.co.uk

REETH
North Yorkshire

Braeside ★★★★
Self Catering
Contact: Liz Austin
Askrigg Cottages
t (0114) 246 7599
e rentals@swaledalecottage.com
w askrigg-cottages.co.uk

Nurse Cherry Cottage
★★★★ *Self Catering*
Contact: Mr & Mrs Waller
t (01904) 798127
e info@cottagesinreeth.co.uk
w cottagesinreeth.co.uk

Swaledale Cottages ★★★★
Self Catering
Contact: Janet Hughes
t (01748) 884526
e thiernswood@talk21.com
w swaledale-cottages.co.uk

Wraycroft Holiday Cottages
★★★★ *Self Catering*
Contact: F Hodgson
t (01748) 884497
e wraycroft@rhodgson.demon.co.uk
w rhodgson.demon.co.uk

REIGHTON
North Yorkshire

Lavender Cottage ★★★★
Self Catering
Contact: Mrs Caroline Wilson
t (01262) 606665
w yorkshireheritagecoast.co.uk

St Helen's Cottage ★★★★★
Self Catering
Contact: Janice T Carter
t (01723) 882274

Sea Whispers Cottage
★★★★ *Self Catering*
Contact: David & Jean Hines
t (0115) 926 8290
e jch@spring116.fsnet.co.uk

RIBCHESTER
Lancashire

Pinfold Farm ★★★★
Self Catering
Contact: Mr Davies
t (01254) 820740
e davies-pinfold@yahoo.co.uk
w pinfoldfarm.co.uk

RICCALL
North Yorkshire

South Newlands Farm Self Catering ★★★★
Self Catering
Contact: Mrs Peggy Swann
t (01757) 248203
e southnewlandsfarm@yahoo.co.uk
w southnewlands.co.uk

RICHMOND
North Yorkshire

16 Culloden Mews ★★★
Self Catering
Contact: Robert Holmes
t (01748) 823043

Blacksmiths Cottage ★★★
Self Catering
Contact: James & Susan Melville
t (01925) 268691
e js.melville@virgin.net

The Bungalow ★★★
Self Catering
Contact: Mr & Mrs RJ & W Delf
t (01748) 823122

Coach House, Whashton
★★★★ *Self Catering*
Contact: Mrs Fairlie Turnbull
t (01748) 822276
e gandmf@tiscali.co.uk
w newskeebygrange.co.uk

Croft Cottage ★★★
Self Catering
Contact: Shirley Ann Wakeling-Stretton
t (01926) 428784 & 07939 861453
e shirlswake2@aol.com
w yorkshirecottage.org.uk

Dyson House Barn ★★★★
Self Catering
Contact: Marian Clarkson
t (01833) 627365
e dysonbarn@tinyworld.co.uk
w cottageguide.co.uk/dysonhousebarn

Fryers Cottage ★★★
Self Catering
Contact: Oliver & Valerie Blease
t (01748) 823344

High Leases Cottage ★★★★
Self Catering
Contact: Heather-Jane Hold
t (01748) 826908
e holdfamily@hotmail.com

Lions Leap ★★★★
Self Catering
Contact: Clive Haddon
t (01527) 876330
e clive_haddon@hotmail.com

Natural Retreats – Yorkshire Dales
Rating Applied For
Self Catering
Contact: Helga Pearson
t (0161) 242 2970
e helga@jmapublicrelations.com
w naturalretreats.co.uk

No. 2 South Row ★★★★
Self Catering
Askrigg Cottage Holidays
t (01969) 650022
e stay@askrigg.com
w askrigg.com

North Lodge, Stanwick St John ★★★★ *Self Catering*
Contact: Mrs Deborah Wise
t (01325) 313107
e deborah.wise@yahoo.co.uk
w yorkshiredalesholidaycottage.co.uk

Nuns Cottage ★★★
Self Catering
Contact: Mrs Judith Flint
t (01748) 822809
w nunscottage.co.uk

The Old Cello Workshop
★★★★ *Self Catering*
Contact: Marcia McLuckie
t (01748) 825525
e marcia.imij@hotmail.co.uk
w yorkshirecountryholidays.com

Tish Toms Cottage ★★★
Self Catering
Contact: Mrs Ann Hall
Tish Toms Holiday Cottages
t (01748) 822167 & (01748) 822167
e pete@catermech.co.uk
w tishtomscottages.com

RIDING MILL
Northumberland

Morningside Cottage ★★★
Self Catering
Contact: Mr Gerald & Dorothea Weldon
t (01434) 682350
e dorotheaweldon@fsmail.net
w morningside-cottage.co.uk

RILLINGTON
North Yorkshire

Thorpe Rise ★★★
Self Catering
Contact: Marilyn Legard
t (01944) 758446

RIMINGTON
Lancashire

Raikes Barn ★★★★
Self Catering
Contact: Mrs Robinson
t (01200) 445636
e elizabeth.robinson1@btinternet.com
w raikesbarn.co.uk

Tewit and Badger Cottages
★★★★ *Self Catering*
Contact: Mrs Anne Smith
t (01200) 445598
e holidays@ruralcottage.co.uk
w ruralcottage.co.uk

RIPON
North Yorkshire

Intake ★★★★ *Self Catering*
Contact: Fiona McConnell
t (01434) 632812
e kfiona@tiscali.co.uk

Pott Hall
Rating Applied For
Self Catering
Contact: Ms Helen Patchett
t (01765) 688290
e helenpatchett@breathe.com
w potthallcottages.co.uk

Waterfront House ★★★★★
Self Catering
Contact: Mrs C E Braddon
t (01423) 770704
e chris1.braddon@virgin.net
w daleshholidayripon.co.uk

ROBIN HOOD'S BAY
North Yorkshire

4 Martin's Row ★★★
Self Catering
Contact: Mrs Vanessa Hicking
Whitby Holiday Cottages
t (01947) 603010
e enquiries@whitbyholidaycottages.net
w whitby-cottages.co.uk

Coastguard Cottage ★★★★
Self Catering
Whitby Holiday Cottages
t (01947) 603010
e enquiries@whitbyholidaycottages.net
w whitbyholidaycottages.net

Farsyde Farm Cottages, Robin Hood's Bay
★★★–★★★★ *Self Catering*
Contact: Angela Green
t (01947) 880249
e farsydestud@talk21.com
w farsydefarmcottages.co.uk

Heather Croft ★★
Self Catering
Sykes Cottages
t (01244) 345700
e info@sykescottages.co.uk
w sykescottages.co.uk

Inglenook ★★★★
Self Catering
Contact: Lesley Abbott
Inglenook And Braeside Cottages
t 07939 305461
e info@inglenook-cottage.co.uk
w inglenook-cottage.co.uk

Laurel Cottage ★★★
Self Catering
Whitby Holiday Cottages
t (01947) 603010
e enquiries@whitbyholidaycottages.net
w whitbyholidaycottages.net

The White Owl Holiday Apartments ★★★
Self Catering
Contact: David & Ann Higgins
t (01947) 880879
w smoothhound.co.uk/hotels/whiteowl.html

ROCHDALE
Greater Manchester

Butterworth Hall, Milnrow
★★★★ *Self Catering*
Contact: Mrs Judith Hirst
t (01706) 882781
e judyhirst@btinternet.com
w springmill.co.uk

Pennine Cottages, Wardle
★★★ *Self Catering*
Contact: Mrs Joy Mitchell
t (01706) 379632
w hometown.aol.co.uk/penninecottage

ROGER GROUND
Cumbria

Lydia's Loft ★★★★
Self Catering
Lakelovers
t (015394) 88855
e bookings@lakelovers.co.uk
w lakelovers.co.uk

Roger Ground House
★★★★ *Self Catering*
Lakelovers
t (015394) 88855
e bookings@lakelovers.co.uk
w lakelovers.co.uk

Woodies Cottage ★★★
Self Catering
Hideaways
t (015394) 42435
e bookings@lakeland-hideaways.co.uk
w lakeland-hideaways.co.uk

ROMALDKIRK
Durham

Romaldkirk Self Catering Cottages ★★★–★★★★
Self Catering
Contact: Mrs Gwen Wall
t (01833) 650794
e richard@wall8309.freeserve.co.uk
w cottageguide.co.uk/romaldkirk

ROOKHOPE
Durham

Red Brick Barn ★★★
Self Catering
Contact: Jane Pearce
t (01388) 517844
e jane@prydale.com
w prydale.com

ROSEDALE ABBEY
North Yorkshire

Abbey House ★★★★
Self Catering
Contact: Geoff Sherwin
t (01904) 431004
e ghsherwin@aol.com
w cottageguide.co.uk/abbeyhouse

Coach House ★★★★
Self Catering
Contact: Linda Sugars
t (01751) 417283
e sevenford@aol.com
w sevenford.com

Craven Garth Holiday Cottages ★★★–★★★★
Self Catering
Contact: Ena Dent
t (01751) 417506
e ena@cravengarth.com
w cravengarth.com

The Grange Farm Cottages
★★★★ *Self Catering*
Contact: David Brown
t (01751) 417329
e dbrown329@tiscali.co.uk
w thegrangecottages.co.uk

Lily Cottage ★★★★
Self Catering
Contact: Mrs Hayley Holmes
t (01757) 210366
e info@lilycottage.eu
w lilycottage.eu

Rosedale Abbey Holiday Cottages, Rosedale Abbey
★★★★ *Self Catering*
Contact: Mrs D Collins
t (01751) 417272
e rosedalecaravanpark@moorsweb.co.uk
w rosedaleholidaycottages.co.uk

Stable Cottage ★★★
Self Catering
Contact: Chris Ewington
t (01751) 417583
e chris@medds.co.uk
w medds.co.uk

Woodlea ★★★★
Self Catering
Contact: Pauline Belt
t (01937) 831290
e p.belt@daviscoleman.com
w rosedaleholidaycottage.co.uk

ROSEDALE EAST
North Yorkshire

Hill Farm ★★★★
Self Catering
Contact: Mr & Mrs Richard & Val Cook
t (01751) 417404

ROSSENDALE
Lancashire

The Cottage, Cronkshaw Fold Farm ★★★ *Self Catering*
Contact: Ms Joy McCarthy
t (01706) 218614
e sjm@cronkshaw.co.uk
w cronkshaw.co.uk

The Old Stables, Tippett Farm ★★★★ *Self Catering*
Contact: Mrs Wendy Davison
t (01706) 224741
e wendy.davison@btopenworld.com
w tippettfarm.co.uk

ROSTHWAITE
Cumbria

Borrowdale Self Catering Holidays ★★★ *Self Catering*
Contact: Peter & Nicola Davis-Merry
t (017687) 77356
e info@kilnhow.com
w kilnhow.com

Castle Howe ★★★★
Self Catering
Lakes Cottage Holidays
t (01228) 591555
e info@lakescottageholiday.co.uk
w lakescottageholiday.co.uk

Clare's Cottage ★★
Self Catering
t (01204) 668681

High Knott ★★★
Self Catering
Cumbrian Cottages
t (01228) 599960
e enquiries@cumbrian-cottages.co.uk
w cumbrian-cottages.co.uk

Larch Cottage ★★★
Self Catering
Lakeland Cottage Holidays
t (017687) 76065
e info@lakelandcottages.co.uk
w lakelandcottages.co.uk

Lobstone ★★★ *Self Catering*
Cumbrian Cottages
t (01228) 599960
e enquiries@cumbrian-cottages.co.uk
w cumbrian-cottages.co.uk

Nokka ★★★ *Self Catering*
Cumbrian Cottages
t (01228) 599960
e enquiries@cumbrian-cottages.co.uk
w cumbrian-cottages.co.uk

Thwaite How ★★★
Self Catering
Contact: Mr & Mrs Brewerton
t (01455) 290168
e cematproperties@hotmail.com
w thwaitehow.co.uk

ROTHBURY
Northumberland

April Cottage ★★★★
Self Catering
Contact: Mr & Mrs Peter & Karina Biggers
t (01665) 603233
e hope.biggers@tiscali.co.uk
w april-cottage-rothbury.com

Bridge View House ★★★★
Self Catering
Contact: Mr Ronald Ridley
t (01670) 826807
e info@bridgeviewhouse.co.uk
w bridgeviewhouse.co.uk

Cairn Rigg ★★★★
Self Catering
Contact: Mr & Mrs Graham & Dorothy Lockwood
t (01669) 620683
e grahamlockwood@btinternet.com
w cairnrigg.co.uk

Clervaux ★★★★
Self Catering
Contact: Mrs Kathryn Reynalds
t (01669) 620784
e clervaux.rothbury@hotmail.co.uk
w clervaux.co.uk

The Cottage ★★★
Self Catering
Contact: Mrs Isabelle Anthea Wilbie-Chalk
t (01669) 620430
e enqs@wellclose.com
w wellclose.com

Deveron
Rating Applied For
Self Catering
Northumbrian Cottages
t (01228) 599950
e sheena@cumbrian-cottages.co.uk
w northumbrian-cottages.info

Ethie Lodge ★★★★
Self Catering
Contact: Mr & Mrs Graham & Dorothy Lockwood
t (01669) 620683
e grahamlockwood@btinternet.com
w cairnrigg.co.uk

Garden Cottage ★★★★
Self Catering
Contact: Mr & Mrs Roger & Dorothy Newman
t (01844) 274101
e rogerdnewman@hotmail.com

The Granary
Rating Applied For
Self Catering
t (01665) 714455
w charityhallfarm.com

Low Alwinton Cottages
★★★-★★★★ *Self Catering*
Contact: Mr & Mrs Eamon & Susan Gribben
t (0191) 420 4919
e eamongribben@blueyonder.co.uk
w lowalwinton.co.uk/

Marmic Cottage ★★★
Self Catering
Contact: Mrs Lisa Mason
t (01669) 621949

Old Stables Cottage ★★★★
Self Catering
Contact: Mrs Roz Tinlin
t (01669) 620577
e the.haven.rothbury@talk21.com
w oldstablescottage.com/

The Old Telephone Exchange ★★★★
Self Catering
Contact: Mrs Kath Scott-Foreman
t (01669) 621858
w theoldtelephoneexchange.com

The Pele Tower (wing)
★★★★★ *Self Catering*
Contact: Mr David Malia
t (01669) 620410
e davidmalia@aol.com
w thepeletower.com

Ryecroft Cottage ★★★
Self Catering
Contact: Mrs Rosalind Kerven
t (01669) 640291
e roskerven@hotmail.com

Steward Mews
Rating Applied For
Self Catering
Contact: Ms Linda Calvert
t (01669) 620315
e threebearsplay@aol.com

Tosson Tower Farm ★★★★
Self Catering
Contact: Mrs Ann Foggin
t (01669) 620228
e stay@tossontowerfarm.com
w tossontowerfarm.com

Wellstrand House ★★★
Self Catering
Contact: Mr Tim Carpenter
t (01669) 621167
e tjcarpenter@lineone.net
w northumberlandbikebreaks.co.uk/wellstrandhouse.html

Whitton Lodge ★★★★
Self Catering
Contact: Mrs Maggie Monaghan
t (01669) 620929
e maggie.monaghan@btinternet.com
w cottage-northumberland.co.uk

ROTHERHAM
South Yorkshire

Whiston Annexe ★★★
Self Catering
Contact: Rodney Marshall
t (01709) 820871
e whistonproperty@yahoo.co.uk
w whistonannex.com

RUCKCROFT
Cumbria

Ruckcroft Cottage ★★★
Self Catering
Cumbrian Cottages
t (01228) 599960
e enquiries@cumbrian-cottages.co.uk
w cumbrian-cottages.co.uk

RUFFSIDE
Durham

Winnowshill Farm Cottages
★★★ *Self Catering*
Northumbrian Cottages
t (01228) 599950
e sheena@cumbrian-cottages.co.uk
w northumbrian-cottages.info

RUSLAND
Cumbria

Stable End ★★★★
Self Catering
Lakeland Cottage Comapny
t (015395) 38180
e john@lakelandcottageco.com
w lakelandcottageco.com

Wood View & Stable End
★★★★ *Self Catering*
Lakeland Cottage Comapny
t (015395) 38180
e john@lakelandcottageco.com
w lakelandcottageco.com

RUSWARP
North Yorkshire

Croft Farm Holiday Cottages
★★★★ *Self Catering*
Contact: Ms Emma Carpenter
t (01947) 825853

Egton Cottage ★★★
Self Catering
Sykes Cottages
t (01244) 345700
e info@sykescottages.co.uk
w sykescottages.co.uk

Esk View Cottage ★★★★
Self Catering
Dales Holiday Cottages
t (01756) 790919
e info@dales-holiday-cottages.com
w dales-holiday-cottages.com

Hollybush Cottage ★★★
Self Catering
Whitby Holiday Cottages
t (01947) 603010
e enquiries@whitbyholidaycottages.net
w whitbyholidaycottages.net

Lambert Hill Cottage
★★★★ *Self Catering*
Whitby Holiday Cottages
t (01947) 603010
e enquiries@whitbyholidaycottages.net
w whitbyholidaycottages.net

SABDEN
Lancashire

Greenbank Cottages ★★★
Self Catering
Contact: Mr Gordon Greenwood
t (01254) 823064

SAIGHTON
Cheshire

The Cottage ★★★★
Self Catering
Contact: Mr P Tighe
t (01244) 332742
e trish_tighe@btinternet.com

ST BEES
Cumbria

Bootle Station House
Rating Applied For
Self Catering
Cumbrian Cottages
t (01228) 599960
e enquiries@cumbrian-cottages.co.uk
w cumbrian-cottages.co.uk

Croft Foot Cottage ★★★
Self Catering
Cumbrian Cottages
t (01228) 599960
e enquiries@cumbrian-cottages.co.uk
w cumbrian-cottages.co.uk

Springbank Farm Lodges
★★★ *Self Catering*
Contact: Carole Woodman
t (01946) 822375
e stevewoodman@talk21.com
w springbanklodges.co.uk

Tarn Flatt Cottage ★★★★
Self Catering
Contact: Janice Telfer
t (01946) 692162
e stay@tarnflattfarm.co.uk
w tarnflattfarm.co.uk

ST HELENS
Merseyside

William Court ★★★★★
Self Catering
Contact: Ms Clare Davenport
Inyork Holidays
t (01904) 632660
e agents@inyorkholidays.co.uk
w inyorkholidays.co.uk

ST JOHN'S CHAPEL
Durham

Burnbrae ★★★★
Self Catering
Contact: Mrs Ann Robson
t (01670) 518129
e annrobson@talktalk.net

ST JOHNS-IN-THE-VALE
Cumbria

Lowthwaite Cottage ★★★★
Self Catering
Cumbrian Cottages
t (01228) 599960
e enquiries@cumbrian-cottages.co.uk
w cumbrian-cottages.co.uk

The Old Hayloft ★★★
Self Catering
Contact: Mrs Sarah Chaplin-Brice
t (017687) 79242
e lbe@sjitv.freeserve.co.uk

The Studio ★★★★
Self Catering
Contact: Mr Green
t (017687) 79666
e selfcatering@keswickholidays.co.uk
w keswickholidays.co.uk

SALFORD
Greater Manchester

30 The Gallery ★★
Self Catering
t (020) 738 8993 & (020) 8675 3356
e info@kash.co.uk
w nomorehotels.co.uk

Great Northern Apartments
★★★★ *Serviced Apartments*
Contact: Mr Justin Reyner
t (0161) 660 7701
e jreyner@citycentrechic.com

The Edge ★★★★
Serviced Apartments
Staying Cool Serviced Apartments
t (0161) 832 4060
e tracey@stayingcool.com
w stayingcool.com

SALTAIRE
West Yorkshire

Glen Knoll ★★★★
Self Catering
Contact: Norman Pilsworth
t (01274) 825303
e sunderlandhpm275629@btinternet.com

Overlookers Cottage
★★★★ *Self Catering*
Contact: Anne Heald
t (01274) 774122
e saltaire_tic@yahoo.co.uk

SALTBURN-BY-THE-SEA
Tees Valley

Balmoral Apartment ★★★
Self Catering
Dales Holiday Cottages
t (01756) 790919
e info@dales-holiday-cottages.com
w dales-holiday-cottages.com

Jasmine Cottage ★★★
Self Catering
Contact: Mr Ian Savory
t (01287) 640043
e ian@savoryfamily.co.uk

Red Gables
Rating Applied For
Self Catering
Yorkshire Cottages
t (01228) 406701
e enquiries@yorkshire-cottages.info
w yorkshire-cottages.info

St Antony's ★★★
Self Catering
Contact: Ms Mary Chapman
t (01287) 622413
e mary.chapman@ntlworld.com

Tower Court ★★★★
Self Catering
Contact: Mr & Mrs Martin & Ginette Mitchell
t (01484) 530990
e mgmitchell@tower-court.co.uk
w tower-court.co.uk

Victorian Cottage ★★★
Self Catering
Contact: Mr & Mrs Stewart & Susan Morgan
t (01287) 625237
e sueandstew@saltburn-accommodation.co.uk
w saltburn-accommodation.co.uk

SALTMARSHE
East Riding of Yorkshire

Appletree Cottages ★★★★
Self Catering
Contact: Vivienne Sweeting
t (01430) 430677
e vivienne.sweeting@btinternet.com
w appletree-cottages.co.uk

SANDSEND
North Yorkshire

The Beach House Sandsend
★★★★★ *Self Catering*
Whitby Holiday Cottages
t (01947) 603010
e enquiries@whitbyholidaycottages.net
w whitbyholidaycottages.net

Eden Cottage ★★★
Self Catering
Whitby Holiday Cottages
t (01947) 603010
e enquiries@whitbyholidaycottages.net
w whitbyholidaycottages.net

The Garden Flat ★★★
Self Catering
Dales Holiday Cottages
t (01756) 790919
e info@dales-holiday-cottages.com
w dales-holiday-cottages.com

Prospect House, Flat 1 & 3
★★★★ *Self Catering*
Whitby Holiday Cottages
t (01947) 603010
e enquiries@whitbyholidaycottages.net
w whitbyholidaycottages.net

Prospect House Flat 3
★★★★ *Self Catering*
Whitby Holiday Cottages
t (01947) 603010
e enquiries@whitbyholidaycottages.net
w whitbyholidaycottages.net

Raithwaite Hall
★★★★–★★★★★
Self Catering
Contact: Amanda Pearson
t (01947) 893284
e admin@raithwaite.co.uk
w raithwaite.co.uk

Rose Cottage ★★★
Self Catering
Whitby Holiday Cottages
t (01947) 603010
e enquiries@whitbyholidaycottages.net
w whitbyholidaycottages.net

St Mary's ★★★★
Self Catering
Whitby Holiday Cottages
t (01947) 603010
e enquiries@whitbyholidaycottages.net
w whitbyholidaycottages.net

Vancouver Cottage
★★★★★ *Self Catering*
Whitby Holiday Cottages
t (01947) 603010
e enquiries@whitbyholidaycottages.net
w whitbyholidaycottages.net

SANTON BRIDGE
Cumbria

Hallflat Farm Cottages ★★★
Self Catering
Contact: Mr & Mrs I Warren
t (01946) 726233
e info@hallflatfarm.co.uk
w hallflatfarm.co.uk

Holmside Cottage ★★★
Self Catering
Cumbrian Cottages
t (01228) 599960
e enquiries@cumbrian-cottages.co.uk
w cumbrian-cottages.co.uk

SATTERTHWAITE
Cumbria

Bloomery Barn ★★★★
Self Catering
Cumbrian Cottages
t (01228) 599960
e enquiries@cumbrian-cottages.co.uk
w cumbrian-cottages.co.uk

Brackenghyll ★★★
Self Catering
Cumbrian Cottages
t (01228) 599960
e enquiries@cumbrian-cottages.co.uk
w cumbrian-cottages.co.uk

Breasty Haw ★★★★
Self Catering
Cumbrian Cottages
t (01228) 599960
e enquiries@cumbrian-cottages.co.uk
w cumbrian-cottages.co.uk

Deer Leap ★★★★
Self Catering
Cumbrian Cottages
t (01228) 599960
e enquiries@cumbrian-cottages.co.uk
w cumbrian-cottages.co.uk

Force Mill ★★★ *Self Catering*
Cumbrian Cottages
t (01228) 599960
e enquiries@cumbrian-cottages.co.uk
w cumbrian-cottages.co.uk

Force Mill Barn ★★★★
Self Catering
Lakeland Cottage Comapny
t (015395) 38180
e john@lakelandcottageco.com
w lakelandcottageco.com

Stable Cottage ★★★
Self Catering
Hideaways
t (015394) 42435
e bookings@lakeland-hideaways.co.uk
w lakeland-hideaways.co.uk

Town End Barn ★★★★
Self Catering
Cumbrian Cottages
t (01228) 599960
e enquiries@cumbrian-cottages.co.uk
w cumbrian-cottages.co.uk

Wain Garth ★★★
Self Catering
Cumbrian Cottages
t (01228) 599960
e enquiries@cumbrian-cottages.co.uk
w cumbrian-cottages.co.uk

Winnowing Barn ★★★★
Self Catering
Cumbrian Cottages
t (01228) 599960
e enquiries@cumbrian-cottages.co.uk
w cumbrian-cottages.co.uk

SAWDON
North Yorkshire

Anvil Inn ★★★★
Self Catering
t (01723) 859896

Geasea Cottage ★★★★
Self Catering
Contact: Mr & Mrs N Craig-Tyler
t (01723) 850375
w geaseacottage.co.uk

Sawdon Country Cottages
★★★★ *Self Catering*
Contact: Mrs Jennifer Worsley
t (01723) 859794
e jenny@sawdoncottages.co.uk
w sawdoncottages.co.uk

SAWLEY
North Yorkshire

Sawley Arms Cottages
★★★★ *Self Catering*
Contact: June Hawes
t (01765) 620642

SAWREY
Cumbria

Anvil Cottage ★★★
Self Catering
Cumbrian Cottages
t (01228) 599960
e enquiries@cumbrian-cottages.co.uk
w cumbrian-cottages.co.uk

Apple Tree Cottage ★★★
Self Catering
Lakelovers
t (015394) 88855
e bookings@lakelovers.co.uk
w lakelovers.co.uk

Fountain Cottage ★★★★
Self Catering
Lakelovers
t (015394) 88855
e bookings@lakelovers.co.uk
w lakelovers.co.uk

Lakefield ★★★ *Self Catering*
Lakelovers
t (015394) 88855
e bookings@lakelovers.co.uk
w lakelovers.co.uk

Meadowside ★★★★
Self Catering
Lakelovers
t (015394) 88855
e bookings@lakelovers.co.uk
w lakelovers.co.uk

Sawrey Stables ★★★★
Self Catering
Hideaways
t (015394) 42435
e bookings@lakeland-hideaways.co.uk
w lakeland-hideaways.co.uk

Sunnyside Cottage ★★★
Self Catering
Hideaways
t (015394) 42435
e bookings@lakeland-hideaways.co.uk
w lakeland-hideaways.co.uk

Town End Cottage ★★★
Self Catering
Lakelovers
t (015394) 88855
e bookings@lakelovers.co.uk
w lakelovers.co.uk

SCALBY
North Yorkshire

Away From The Madding Crowd ★★★★ *Self Catering*
Contact: Peter & Stella Ward
t (01723) 360502
e maddingcrowd@btinternet.com
w maddingcrowdcottage.com

The Croft
Rating Applied For
Self Catering
Bedwyn's Holiday Accommodation
t (01723) 516700
e info@bedwyns.co.uk
w bedwyns.co.uk

SCARBOROUGH
North Yorkshire

Abbey Holiday Flats ★★
Self Catering
Contact: C Cook
t (01262) 677819
e info@abbey-holiday-flats.co.uk
w abbey-holiday-flats.co.uk

Avenue Victoria Apartment
★★★ *Self Catering*
Bedwyn's Holiday Accommodation
t (01723) 516700
e info@bedwyns.co.uk
w bedwyns.co.uk

Avenue View Apartment
Rating Applied For
Self Catering
Bedwyn's Holiday Accommodation
t (01723) 516700
e info@bedwyns.co.uk
w bedwyns.co.uk

Avondale Holiday Flats ★★
Self Catering
Contact: Mrs Valerie Jones
t (01723) 364836

Barley Cottage ★★★
Self Catering
Bedwyn's Holiday Accommodation
t (01723) 516700
e info@bedwyns.co.uk
w bedwyns.co.uk

Bayview Holiday Flatlets
★★ *Self Catering*
Contact: Ellen Johnson
t (01723) 375139

The Beach Hut ★★★
Self Catering
Bedwyn's Holiday Accommodation
t (01723) 516700
e info@bedwyns.co.uk
w bedwyns.co.uk

Belvedere Terrace ★★★
Self Catering
Bedwyn's Holiday Accommodation
t (01723) 516700
e info@bedwyns.co.uk
w bedwyns.co.uk

Brialene Apartments
★★-★★★ *Self Catering*
Contact: Brian & Marlene Witty
t (01723) 367158
e reservations@scarborough-brialene.co.uk
w scarborough-brialene.co.uk

Brompton Holiday Flats
★★★ *Self Catering*
Contact: Kenneth Broadbent
t (01723) 364964
e info@bromptonholidayflats.co.uk
w bromptonholidayflats.co.uk

The Bungalow ★★★
Self Catering
Bedwyn's Holiday Accommodation
t (01723) 516700
e info@bedwyns.co.uk
w bedwyns.co.uk

Castle Crescent ★★★★
Self Catering
Bedwyn's Holiday Accommodation
t (01723) 516700
e info@bedwyns.co.uk
w bedwyns.co.uk

Cherry Trees Holiday Flats
★★ *Self Catering*
Contact: Una Jordan
t 07772 330437
e cherrytreesflats@hotmail.co.uk
w cherrytrees.vholiday.co.uk

Chomley Holiday Flats
Rating Applied For
Self Catering
Contact: Mr & Mrs S. Witty
t (01723) 367292
e chomleyflats@yahoo.co.uk
w iknow-yorkshire.co.uk

The Corner Pin
Rating Applied For
Self Catering
Bedwyn's Holiday Accommodation
t (01723) 516700
e info@bedwyns.co.uk
w bedwyns.co.uk

The Courtyard ★★★★
Self Catering
Bedwyn's Holiday Accommodation
t (01723) 516700
e info@bedwyns.co.uk
w bedwyns.co.uk

Cravendale Holiday Flats
★-★★★ *Self Catering*
Contact: Shirley Smith
t (01274) 871069
e shirleysflats@hotmail.com
w cravendaleflats.co.uk

Cromwell Court ★★★
Self Catering
Contact: Mrs R. Walker
t (01723) 376008
e fredjules@btinternet.com
w yorkshirecoast.co.uk/cromwell

Driftwood ★★★
Self Catering
Bedwyn's Holiday Accommodation
t (01723) 516700
e info@bedwyns.co.uk
w bedwyns.co.uk

Easby Apartment No 9
★★★★ *Self Catering*
Bedwyn's Holiday Accommodation
t (01723) 516700
e info@bedwyns.co.uk
w bedwyns.co.uk

Easby Hall Apartment 15
★★★★ *Self Catering*
Bedwyn's Holiday Accommodation
t (01723) 516700
e info@bedwyns.co.uk
w bedwyns.co.uk

East Farm Country Cottages, Scalby ★★★ *Self Catering*
Contact: Mrs J Ireland
t (01723) 353635
e joeastfarmcottages@hotmail.co.uk
w eastfarmcountrycottages.co.uk

Eldin Hall – The Gatehouse, Cayton ★★★ *Self Catering*
Bedwyn's Holiday Accommodation
t (01723) 516700
e info@bedwyns.co.uk
w bedwyns.co.uk

Elizabethan Court ★★★
Self Catering
Contact: Paula Randall
t (01423) 549436
e paularandall1@ntlworld.com

Forge Valley Cottages
★★★★ *Self Catering*
Contact: Jane Beeley
t (01723) 882284
e enquiries@forgevalleycottages.co.uk
w forgevalleycottages.co.uk

Glaisdale Holiday Flats and Cottage ★★★ *Self Catering*
Contact: Mr Michael Holliday
t (01723) 372728
e michael.holliday@tesco.net
w s-h-a.co.uk/glaisdale

Green Gables Holiday Flats
★★-★★★ *Self Catering*
Contact: Nick Jones
t (01723) 361005
e enquiries@greengablesscarborough.co.uk
w greengablesscarborough.co.uk

The Grove ★★★★
Self Catering
Bedwyn's Holiday Accommodation
t (01723) 516700
e info@bedwyns.co.uk
w bedwyns.co.uk

Harbour View Holiday Flats
★★ *Self Catering*
Contact: David Gordon Jenkinson
t (01723) 361162

The Hayloft ★★★★
Self Catering
Contact: Ingrid Flute
Ingrid Flute Holiday Accommodation
t (01723) 376777
e ingrid@ingridflute.co.uk

The Heathers ★★★
Self Catering
Bedwyn's Holiday Accommodation
t (01723) 516700
e info@bedwyns.co.uk
w bedwyns.co.uk

Lighthouse Cottage ★★
Self Catering
Bedwyn's Holiday Accommodation
t (01723) 516700
e info@bedwyns.co.uk
w bedwyns.co.uk

Lingholm Court Holiday Cottages, Lebberston
★★★★ *Self Catering*
Contact: Caroline & Stephen Woodhouse
t (01723) 586365
e info@lingholm.co.uk
w lingholm.co.uk

Little Gables ★★★
Self Catering
Bedwyn's Holiday Accommodation
t (01723) 516700
e info@bedwyns.co.uk
w bedwyns.co.uk

Lotus Mews ★★★
Self Catering
Bedwyn's Holiday Accommodation
t (01723) 516700
e info@bedwyns.co.uk
w bedwyns.co.uk

Marlborough Holiday Flats
★★-★★★ *Self Catering*
Contact: Mrs Ellard
t (01723) 373116
e julieellard@hotmail.com
w marlborough-seafront-flats.co.uk

Parade Holiday Flats
★★-★★★ *Self Catering*
Contact: Sue Sayers
t (01723) 374307
e suesayers@tesco.net

Ramsdale Lodge ★★★★
Self Catering
Contact: Mike & Louize Jones
t (01723) 503964

Red Cliff Apartment
Rating Applied For
Self Catering
Bedwyn's Holiday Accommodation
t (01723) 516700
e info@bedwyns.co.uk
w bedwyns.co.uk

Sandcastles
Rating Applied For
Self Catering
Bedwyn's Holiday Accommodation
t (01723) 516700
e info@bedwyns.co.uk
w bedwyns.co.uk

Sea Views ★★★★★
Self Catering
Contact: Mr & Mrs Hindhaugh
t (01484) 871681
e manorheath@tiscali.co.uk
w sea-views-scarborough.co.uk

Sea Vista Holiday Bungalow, Cayton Bay ★★★★
Self Catering
Contact: Mr & Mrs A Roper
t (01274) 564741
e info@sea-vista.com
w sea-vista.com

Seacliffe Holiday Flats ★★★
Self Catering
Contact: Elizabeth & David Lumley
t (01944) 728277
e dclumley@btinternet.com
w seaviewflats.co.uk

Shell Seekers Cottage
★★★★ *Self Catering*
Bedwyn's Holiday Accommodation
t (01723) 516700
e info@bedwyns.co.uk
w bedwyns.co.uk

Smugglers Rock Cottages, Ravenscar ★★★-★★★★
Self Catering
Contact: Mrs Sharon Gregson
t (01723) 870044
e info@smugglersrock.co.uk
w smugglersrock.co.uk

South Sands Apartment
★★★★ *Self Catering*
Bedwyn's Holiday Accommodation
t (01723) 516700
e info@bedwyns.co.uk
w bedwyns.co.uk

Spikers Hill Country Cottages, West Ayton ★★★
Self Catering
Contact: Janet Hutchinson
t (01723) 862537
e janet@spikershill.ndo.co.uk
w spikershill.ndo.co.uk

Starfish ★★★★ *Self Catering*
Bedwyn's Holiday Accommodation
t (01723) 516700
e info@bedwyns.co.uk
w bedwyns.co.uk

Town Farm Cottages
★★★★ *Self Catering*
Contact: Joe & Debbie Green
t (01723) 870278
e mail@greenfarming.co.uk
w greenfarming.co.uk

Two Beaches View ★★★★
Self Catering
Bedwyn's Holiday Accommodation
t (01723) 516700
e info@bedwyns.co.uk
w bedwyns.co.uk

Valley View Holiday Flats
★★ *Self Catering*
Contact: Dave & Anne Wilkinson
t (01723) 364709
e valleyview@btconnect.com
w valleyview.org.uk

Victoria's Apartment
Rating Applied For
Self Catering
Bedwyn's Holiday Accommodation
t (01723) 516700
e info@bedwyns.co.uk
w bedwyns.co.uk

White Acre ★★★★
Self Catering
Contact: J.G. Squire
JG Squire (holidays) Ltd
t (01723) 374220
e squiresc@clara.co.uk
w squiresc.clara.co.uk

Windsor Holiday Flats
★-★★★ *Self Catering*
Contact: Andrew Eadie
t 07885 638378
e andrew@windsorholidayflats.com
w windsorholidayflats.com

Wrea Head Country Cottages ★★★★
Self Catering
Contact: Richard Scales
t (01723) 375844
e info@wreahead.co.uk
w wreahead.co.uk

SCARCROFT
West Yorkshire

2 Eversley View ★★★
Self Catering
Contact: Alison Burns
t (0113) 289 3605
w eversleyview.co.uk

SCARGILL
Durham

Lodge Farm Holidays
Approved Caravan Holiday Home
Contact: Mr Gordon Thomson
t (01833) 621238
e lodgefarmhols@xemaps.com
w lodgefarmholidays.com

Thwaite Cottages ★★★★
Self Catering
Contact: Ms Julie Metcalfe
t (01723) 373461
e jmetcalfe@broadlandproperties.co.uk
w countrycottageholiday.com

SCARISBRICK
Lancashire

Shamrock Cottage ★★★★
Self Catering
Contact: Mrs Rachel Saysell
t (01704) 880513
e rachel@nwns.co.uk
w shamrock-cottage.co.uk

SCAWTON
North Yorkshire

Manor Farm Cottage ★★★
Self Catering
t (01439) 770586

SCHOLES, HOLMFIRTH
West Yorkshire

Cross Farm Barn ★★★★
Self Catering
Contact: John & Janet Armitage
t (01484) 683664
e crossfarmbarn@btconnect.com
w crossfarmbarn.co.uk

SCORTON
North Yorkshire

Lyndale ★★★ *Self Catering*
Contact: Kevin & Tracey Fogg
t (01980) 622003
e info@scortoncottage.com
w scortoncottage.com

SCOTCH CORNER
North Yorkshire

5 Cedar Grove ★★★
Self Catering
Contact: Mr & Mrs Lawson
Homely Holiday Homes
t (01723) 870455
e james@jameslawson4.wanadoo.co.uk
w homely-holidayhomes.co.uk

SCOTS GAP
Northumberland

Grangemoor Barn ★★★★
Self Catering
Contact: Mrs Jane Robson
t (01665) 589434
e enquiries@northumberlandcottages.com
w northumberlandcottages.co.uk

SEAHAM
Durham

North Pier Lodge Apartments
Rating Applied For
Self Catering
Contact: Mr Barry Giles
t (0191) 581 3512
e northpierlodge@bt.com

SEAHOUSES
Northumberland

31 Dunstan View ★★★
Self Catering
Contact: Mr & Mrs Mark & Amanda Butler
t (01665) 576586
e mrb911@hotmail.com

43 Kingsfield ★★★
Self Catering
Northumberland Cottages
t (01665) 589434
e enquiries@northumberlandcottages.com
w northumberlandcottages.co.uk

Cliff House Cottages
★★★-★★★★ *Self Catering*
t (01665) 721380
w cliffhousecottages.co.uk

Fahren House ★★★★
Self Catering
Contact: Mrs Rachel Shiel
t (01665) 721297
e rachel.dawson@virgin.net
w farne-islands.com/fahren-house/index.htm

Fishermans Mid Cottage
★★★★ *Self Catering*
Contact: Mrs Dorothy Jackson
t (01665) 830427
e dorothy@biltonbarns.com
w biltonbarns.com

Fisherman's Retreat
★★★★★ *Self Catering*
Northumberland Coastal Retreats
t (0191) 285 1272
e info@coastalretreats.co.uk
w coastalretreats.co.uk

Harbourside and Farne View
★★★★ *Self Catering*
Contact: Ms Juliet Hall
t (01661) 825819
e juliethall@harboursidecottage.co.uk
w harboursidecottage.co.uk

Harness Lodge ★★★★
Self Catering
Contact: Mr & Mrs Jackie & Neil Forsyth
t (01665) 721380
e info@westfieldfarmhouse.co.uk
w harnesslodge.co.uk

Hastings House
Rating Applied For
Self Catering
Contact: Mr & Mrs Jackie & Neil Forsyth
t (01665) 721380
e info@westfieldfarmhouse.co.uk
w hastingshouse.info

Kipper Cottage ★★★★
Self Catering
Contact: Mr & Mrs Jackie & Neil Forsyth
t (01665) 721380
e info@westfieldfarmhouse.co.uk
w kippercottage.co.uk

The Lobster Pots ★★★★
Self Catering
Contact: Mrs Julia Steel
t (0113) 239 1130
e julia@thelobsterpots.co.uk
w thelobsterpots.co.uk

Mayfield ★★★★
Self Catering
Grace Darling Holidays
t (01665) 721332
e carolynalgar150@msn.com

North East Coast Holidays
★★★ *Self Catering*
Contact: Mrs Lesley Barnett
t (01665) 833233
e d_barnettuk@yahoo.co.uk
w northeastcoastholidays.co.uk

Ocean View ★★★★
Self Catering
Northumberland Cottages
t (01665) 589434
e enquiries@northumberlandcottages.com
w northumberlandcottages.co.uk

Peregrine ★★★ *Self Catering*
Contact: Mr Chris Dempsey
t (01361) 882536 & 07711 182761
e linda@gpm-marketing.co.uk

The Plaice ★★★★★
Self Catering
Northumberland Coastal Retreats
t (0191) 285 1272
e info@coastalretreats.co.uk
w coastalretreats.co.uk

Puffin's Nest and Blue Horizon ★★★★ *Self Catering*
Grace Darling Holidays
t (01665) 721332
e carolynalgar150@msn.com

Quarry Cottage ★★★
Self Catering
Contact: Mrs Mary Alston
t (01665) 720235
e gcalston@btinernet.com

Rose Cottages ★★★★
Self Catering
Contact: Mr Michael Townsend
t (01665) 576111
e stay@dunstanburghcastlehotel.co.uk
w dunstanburghcastlehotel.co.uk

Seafarer Cottage ★★★★★
Self Catering
Northumberland Coastal Retreats
t (0191) 285 1272
e info@coastalretreats.co.uk
w coastalretreats.co.uk

Sparrowhawk ★★★★
Self Catering
Contact: Mr Chris Dempsey
t (01361) 882536
e linda@gpm-marketing.co.uk

SEAMER
North Yorkshire

Nana's Cottage ★★★
Self Catering
Yorkshire Cottages
t (01228) 406701
e enquiries@yorkshire-cottages.info
w yorkshire-cottages.info

Piglet Cottage ★★★
Self Catering
Bedwyn's Holiday Accommodation
t (01723) 516700
e info@bedwyns.co.uk
w bedwyns.co.uk

SEATHWAITE
Cumbria

2 High Moss House ★★★
Self Catering
Contact: Helen Barnard
t (0141) 423 1060
e helen@ainsdale.force9.co.uk

Hall Dunnerdale Farm Holiday Cottages ★★★
Self Catering
Contact: Ms Anne Brockbank
t (01229) 889281
e anne@hall-dunnerdale.co.uk

Rose Cottage ★★★★
Self Catering
Lakeland Cottage Comapny
t (015395) 38180
e john@lakelandcottageco.com
w lakelandcottageco.com

Tarn Foot Cottage ★★★★
Self Catering
The Coppermines & Coniston Lakes Cottages
t (015394) 41765
w coppermines.co.uk

SEATOLLER
Cumbria

The Barn ★★★★
Self Catering
Cumbrian Cottages
t (01228) 599960
e enquiries@cumbrian-cottages.co.uk
w cumbrian-cottages.co.uk

Bell Crags ★★★ *Self Catering*
Cumbrian Cottages
t (01228) 599960
e enquiries@cumbrian-cottages.co.uk
w cumbrian-cottages.co.uk

Brasscam ★★★ *Self Catering*
Cumbrian Cottages
t (01228) 599960
e enquiries@cumbrian-cottages.co.uk
w cumbrian-cottages.co.uk

Ghyllside ★★★★★
Self Catering
Cumbrian Cottages
t (01228) 599960
e enquiries@cumbrian-cottages.co.uk
w cumbrian-cottages.co.uk

Hause Gill ★★★
Self Catering
Lakeland Cottage Holidays
t (017687) 76065
e info@lakelandcottages.co.uk
w lakelandcottages.co.uk

High Stile ★★★ *Self Catering*
Lakeland Cottage Holidays
t (017687) 76065
e info@lakelandcottages.co.uk
w lakelandcottages.co.uk

Laburnum Cottage ★★★★
Self Catering
Cumbrian Cottages
t (01228) 599960
e enquiries@cumbrian-cottages.co.uk
w cumbrian-cottages.co.uk

Littlebeck ★★★ *Self Catering*
Cumbrian Cottages
t (01228) 599960
e enquiries@cumbrian-cottages.co.uk
w cumbrian-cottages.co.uk

SEATON
Durham

Slingley Cottage ★★★★
Self Catering
Contact: Mrs Anne Brough
t (0191) 526 6403
e jacksonbrough@aol.com

SEATON CAREW
Tees Valley

Ships Watch ★★★
Self Catering
Contact: Mr Glyn Sanderson
t (01429) 222660 & 07748 381943
e lynda.sanderson1@ntlworld.com

SEBERGHAM
Cumbria

Stockwell Hall Cottage
★★★★★ *Self Catering*
Cumbrian Cottages
t (01228) 599960
e enquiries@cumbrian-cottages.co.uk
w cumbrian-cottages.co.uk

SEDBERGH
Cumbria

Cobble Country Holidays
★★★-★★★★ *Self Catering*
Contact: Mrs R. Elizabeth Close
t (015396) 21000
e cobblesedbergh@yahoo.co.uk
w cobblecountry.co.uk

Dales View ★★★★
Self Catering
Cumbrian Cottages
t (01228) 599960
e enquiries@cumbrian-cottages.co.uk
w cumbrian-cottages.co.uk

Farley Croft ★★★
Self Catering
Contact: Ros Phillips
t 07949 593430
e bookings@farleycroft.com
w farleycroft.com

Fell House ★★★★
Self Catering
Contact: Stephen Wickham
t (01858) 555476
e steve@higround.co.uk
w higround.co.uk

Fells View ★★★
Self Catering
Contact: Karen Bruce-Lockhart
t 07739 639244

Helmswood Farmhouse
★★★★ *Self Catering*
Cumbrian Cottages
t (01228) 599960
e enquiries@cumbrian-cottages.co.uk
w cumbrian-cottages.co.uk

Low Foulsyke Cottage ★★★
Self Catering
Contact: Emma Middleton
t (015396) 25308
e emmalmiddleton@hotmail.com

Merlin Cottage ★★★★
Self Catering
Contact: Christine Linley
t (01539) 738677
e christine@merlincottage.com
w merlincottage.com

The Mount ★★★★
Self Catering
Contact: Suzan Sedgwick
t (015396) 20252
e sedgwick665@btinternet.com
w holidaysedbergh.co.uk

Thwaite Cottage ★★★★
Self Catering
Contact: Mrs D Parker
t (015396) 20493
e thwaitefarm@btinternet.com

Whernside View ★★★★
Self Catering
Cumbrian Cottages
t (01228) 599960
e enquiries@cumbrian-cottages.co.uk
w cumbrian-cottages.co.uk

SEDBUSK
North Yorkshire

The Coach House ★★★
Self Catering
Dales Holiday Cottages
t (01756) 790919
e info@dales-holiday-cottages.com
w dales-holiday-cottages.com

SEDGEFIELD
Durham

The Granary ★★★
Self Catering
Contact: Mr & Mrs Sam & Judith Edgoose
t (01740) 620244
e mail@toddshousefarm.co.uk
w toddshousefarm.co.uk

Sprucely Farm Cottage ★★
Self Catering
Contact: Mr Stewart Harris
t (01740) 620378
e barbara-harris@btconnect.com
w sprucelyfarmcottage.co.uk

SEDGWICK
Cumbria

Coach House ★★★★
Self Catering
Cumbrian Cottages
t (01228) 599960
e enquiries@cumbrian-cottages.co.uk
w cumbrian-cottages.co.uk

High House Barn ★★★★★
Self Catering
Cumbrian Cottages
t (01228) 599960
e enquiries@cumbrian-cottages.co.uk
w cumbrian-cottages.co.uk

Woodside ★★★★
Self Catering
Cumbrian Cottages
t (01228) 599960
e enquiries@cumbrian-cottages.co.uk
w cumbrian-cottages.co.uk

SELBY
North Yorkshire

Lund Farm Cottages ★★★★
Self Catering
Contact: Mr Chris Middleton
t (01757) 228775
e lundfarm@talktalk.net
w lundfarm.co.uk

Rusholme Cottage, Drax
★★★ *Self Catering*
Contact: Mrs Anne Roberts
t (01757) 618257
e anne@rusholmegrange.co.uk
w rusholmegrange.co.uk

SETTLE
North Yorkshire

4 St John's Row ★★★
Self Catering
Contact: Mary Sowerby
t (01943) 875552
e marysowerby@yahoo.com
w johnscottage.com

Attermire Cottage ★★★
Self Catering
Contact: Catherine Binstead
Mrs C Binstead
t (01729) 822734
e stay@attermirecottage.co.uk
w attermirecottage.co.uk

Cobweb Cottage ★★★
Self Catering
Contact: Stephen Shaw
t 07971 806627
e cobwebcottage@settle-holidays.com
w settle-holidays.com

Devonshire Flat ★★★
Self Catering
Contact: Allan Aspden
t (01729) 825781

The Folly at Settle ★★★★★
Self Catering
Contact: Pat Rand
t (01729) 822930
e m.rand@virgin.net
w follysettle.co.uk

Goldielands (4004) ★★★★
Self Catering
t (01756) 790919

Harry's Cottage ★★★
Self Catering
Contact: Wendy Porter
t (01729) 824268
e wendylou63@hotmail.com
w harryscottage.co.uk

Lock Cottage ★★★★
Self Catering
Sykes Cottages
t (01244) 345700
e info@sykescottages.co.uk
w sykescottages.co.uk

Middle Cottage ★★★
Self Catering
Contact: Mrs R Hyslop
Layhead Cottages
t (01729) 840234 & 07794 945406
e rosehyslop@layhead.co.uk
w layhead.co.uk

The Old Vicarage
Rating Applied For
Self Catering
Contact: Mr & Mrs Paul & Janice Whitehead
t (01737) 247179
e janice.whitehead@ntlworld.com

Robin Hill & Brewhouse Cottages ★★★-★★★★★
Self Catering
Contact: Mrs Jeanne Carr
t (01729) 823132
w settle-selfcatering.co.uk

SEWERBY
East Riding of Yorkshire

Bay View & Jomelage ★★★★ *Self Catering*
Contact: Tim Norman
Daisychain Holidays
t (01262) 608611
e info@daisychainholidays.co.uk
w daisychainholidays.co.uk

Field House Farm Cottages ★★★★-★★★★★
Self Catering
Contact: Mr & Mrs Foster
t (01262) 674932
e john.foster@farmline.com
w fieldhousefarmcottages.co.uk

Jessemi ★★★ *Self Catering*
Contact: Mrs Diane Pye
t (01977) 512391
e dianepye@clara.co.uk

Oakwood ★★★★
Self Catering
Contact: Josephine Hodgson
t (01977) 704942
w oakwood-sewerby.co.uk

Squirrel Lodge ★★★★
Self Catering
Contact: Anne Walker
Great Escapes Holidays LLP
t 0870 909 9500
e originalannemcg@aol.com
w dales-holiday-cottages.com

SHAP
Cumbria

The Stable, Crosby Ravensworth ★★★★
Self Catering
Contact: Mrs Christine Jackson
t (01931) 715236

SHARPERTON
Northumberland

North Sharperton Farm Cottage ★★★★ *Self Catering*
Contact: Ms Carolyn Banks
t (01669) 650321
e ormnthsharperton@bushinternet.com
w northsharperton.co.uk

SHEFFIELD
South Yorkshire

Coach House Apartment ★★★★ *Self Catering*
Peak Cottages
t (0114) 262 0777
e enquiries@peakcottages.com
w peakcottages.com

Coppice House Farm Cottage ★★★★ *Self Catering*
Contact: Pamela Revitt
t (0114) 230 1753
e info@coppicehousefarmcottage.co.uk
w coppicehousefarmcottage.co.uk

The Flat ★★★ *Self Catering*
Contact: Margaret Cox
t (0114) 221 5553

Foxholes Farm, Low Bradfield ★★-★★★
Self Catering
Contact: Rachel Hague
t (0114) 285 1383 & 07917 030602
e foxholes.farm@tiscali.co.uk
w foxholesfarm.co.uk

Moor Royd House ★★★-★★★★ *Self Catering*
Contact: Janet Hird
t (01226) 763353
e janet@moorroydhouse.freeserve.co.uk
w moorroydhouse.com

Smallshaw Farm Cottages ★★★★ *Self Catering*
Contact: James & Mary Booth
t (01226) 764271
e smallshawcottages@btinternet.com
w smallshaw.com

SHERBURN
North Yorkshire

Housemartins ★★★
Self Catering
Contact: Elissa Massie
t (01944) 710259

Westfield Granary ★★★-★★★★ *Self Catering*
Holiday Cottages (Yorkshire) Ltd
t (01756) 700510
e brochure@holidaycotts.co.uk
w holidaycotts.co.uk

SHERBURN HOUSE
Durham

The Barn ★★★★
Self Catering
Contact: Mr Peter Robson
t 07790 906965
e robsopeter@googlemail.com

SHERIFF HUTTON
North Yorkshire

The Granary ★★★★★
Self Catering
Contact: Mrs Gilly Gordon-Finlayson
t (01347) 878355
e info@cheesevatfarm.co.uk
w cheesevatfarm.co.uk

SHILBOTTLE
Northumberland

Brightfield ★★★
Self Catering
Northumberland Cottages
t (01665) 589434
e enquiries@northumberlandcottages.com
w northumberlandcottages.co.uk

SHOTLEY BRIDGE
Durham

Rivers Edge Cottage ★★★★
Self Catering
Contact: Mrs Jean Johnson
t (01207) 501194
e jean@johnson197.orangehome.co.uk

SIGGLESTHORNE
East Riding of Yorkshire

Peggy's Cottage ★★★★
Self Catering
Contact: Ms Jude Collingwood
t (01964) 535395
e p.collingwood@btinternet.com

SILLOTH
Cumbria

Glencaple ★★★★
Self Catering
Cumbrian Cottages
t (01228) 599960
e enquiries@cumbrian-cottages.co.uk
w cumbrian-cottages.co.uk

SILSDEN
West Yorkshire

Croft Cottage ★★★★
Self Catering
Contact: Philippa Cranee manorfarms@btinternet.com
w manorfarms.biz

Ford Cottage ★★★
Self Catering
Dales Holiday Cottages
t (01756) 790919
e info@dales-holiday-cottages.com
w dales-holiday-cottages.com

SILVERDALE
Lancashire

Pheasant Field ★★★
Self Catering
Sykes Cottages
t (01244) 345700
e info@sykescottages.co.uk
w sykescottages.co.uk

The Stables at Lindeth House ★★★★ *Self Catering*
Contact: Mrs Cathy Ranford
t (01524) 702121
e stables@lindethhouse.co.uk
w lindethhouse.co.uk

Swallows End ★★★
Self Catering
t (01204) 593274

Wolf House Cottages, Silverdale ★★★★-★★★★★
Self Catering
t (01524) 701573
e enquiries@wolfhousecottages.co.uk
w wolfhousecottages.co.uk

SINNINGTON
North Yorkshire

Cliff Farm Holidays
Approved Caravan Holiday Home
Contact: Mrs J Scaling
t (01751) 473792
e enquiries@clifffarmholidays.com
w clifffarmholidays.com

Corner House ★★★★
Self Catering
Contact: Norah Bessant
t (01323) 491414
e norah.bessant@btinternet.com

Sevenside Holiday Bungalow ★★★ *Self Catering*
Contact: Elizabeth Allan
t (01751) 431812
e jdallan@care4free.net
w sevensidebungalow.co.uk

SKELTON
Cumbria

Barn Owl Cottage ★★★
Self Catering
t (017684) 84538
w up-front.com

SKELTON
Tees Valley

Barn Cottage and Newbrook Cottage ★★★★ *Self Catering*
Contact: Mr Neil Goodenough
t (01287) 650288
e neilgoodenough@msn.com
w barncottage.net

SKELWITH BRIDGE
Cumbria

Colwith ★★★★ *Self Catering*
Contact: Katherine Paterson
t (01423) 501407
e colwith@tiscali.co.uk
w colwith.com

Ghyll Pool – Neaum Crag ★★★ *Self Catering*
Cumbrian Cottages
t (01228) 599960
e enquiries@cumbrian-cottages.co.uk
w cumbrian-cottages.co.uk

Hunters Moon ★★★
Self Catering
Cumbrian Cottages
t (01228) 599960
e enquiries@cumbrian-cottages.co.uk
w cumbrian-cottages.co.uk

Ivy Cottage ★★★★
Self Catering
Cumbrian Cottages
t (01228) 599960
e enquiries@cumbrian-cottages.co.uk
w cumbrian-cottages.co.uk

Mockerkin Tarn – Neaum Crag ★★★ *Self Catering*
Cumbrian Cottages
t (01228) 599960
e enquiries@cumbrian-cottages.co.uk
w cumbrian-cottages.co.uk

Ramblers Rest ★★★
Self Catering
Lakelovers
t (015394) 88855
e bookings@lakelovers.co.uk
w lakelovers.co.uk

Riversedge Cottage
Rating Applied For
Self Catering
Lakelovers
t (015394) 88855
e bookings@lakelovers.co.uk
w lakelovers.co.uk

Spindle Coppice
Rating Applied For
Self Catering
Lakelovers
t (015394) 88855
e bookings@lakelovers.co.uk
w lakelovers.co.uk

Tarn Hows ★★ *Self Catering*
Lakelovers
t (015394) 88855
e bookings@lakelovers.co.uk
w lakelovers.co.uk

Tarn Moss – Neaum Crag
★★★ *Self Catering*
Cumbrian Cottages
t (01228) 599960
e enquiries@cumbrian-cottages.co.uk
w cumbrian-cottages.co.uk

SKELWITH FOLD
Cumbria

Swallows House ★★★★★
Self Catering
Contact: Mrs Vivien Bass
Wheelwrights Holiday Cottages
t (015394) 37635
e enquiries@wheelwrights.com

SKERNE
East Riding of Yorkshire

Mulberry Cottage ★★★★
Self Catering
Contact: Gemma Dixon
t (01377) 254073
e info@mulberry-whin.com
w mulberry-whin.com

SKEUGH HEAD
North Yorkshire

Kisdon ★★★★ *Self Catering*
Yorkshire Cottages
t (01228) 406701
e enquiries@yorkshire-cottages.info
w yorkshire-cottages.info

SKIPTON
North Yorkshire

7 Elliot Street ★★★★
Self Catering
Holiday Cottages (Yorkshire) Ltd
t (01756) 700510
e brochure@holidaycotts.co.uk
w holidaycotts.co.uk

Bobbin Cottage ★★★★
Self Catering
Contact: Mrs Randell
t (01535) 632788

Causeway Cottage, Cononley ★★★★
Self Catering
Contact: Hilary Freeman
t (01535) 644140
e hilaryanddave@yahoo.co.uk

Cawder Hall Cottages
★★★-★★★★ *Self Catering*
Contact: Graham Pearson
t (01756) 791579
e info@cawderhallcottages.co.uk
w cawderhallcottages.co.uk

Craven House ★★★★
Self Catering
Contact: Mrs Joanne Rushton
t (01756) 794657
e joanne@craven-house.co.uk
w craven-house.co.uk

Fairfax Street ★★★
Self Catering
Holiday Cottages
t (01756) 700510
e info@holidaycotts.co.uk
w holidaycotts.co.uk

Ginnel Mews ★★★
Self Catering
Sykes Cottages
t (01244) 345700
e info@sykescottages.co.uk
w sykescottages.co.uk

The Lodge ★★★★
Self Catering
t (01200) 445300
w thelodgehorton.co.uk

Lower Heugh Cottage
★★★★★ *Self Catering*
Contact: T & M Nash
t (01756) 793702
w cottageguide.com

None-go-Bye Farm Cottage
★★★ *Self Catering*
Contact: Mrs M A Lawn
t (01756) 793165
e booking.nonegobye@virgin.net
w yorkshiredales.net/stayat/nonegobyefarm/index.htm

The Old Barn ★★★
Self Catering
Yorkshire Cottages
t (01228) 406701
e enquiries@yorkshire-cottages.info
w yorkshire-cottages.info

Thisledo ★★★★
Self Catering
Contact: Shelley Green
t (01756) 795024
e mail@thisledo.co.uk
w thisledo.co.uk

Whitham Cottage ★★★★
Self Catering
Yorkshire Cottages
t (01228) 406701
e enquiries@yorkshire-cottages.info
w yorkshire-cottages.info

SKIRWITH
Cumbria

Hayriggs ★★★ *Self Catering*
Cumbrian Cottages
t (01228) 599960
e enquiries@cumbrian-cottages.co.uk
w cumbrian-cottages.co.uk

SLAIDBURN
Lancashire

Burn Fell View ★★★
Self Catering
t (01200) 446654
e jeanparker@freeuk.com
w slaidburn.com/burnfellview/

Laythams Farm Cottages
★★★ *Self Catering*
Contact: Mr Ian Roger Driver
t (01200) 446454
e idriver@nildram.co.uk
w laythamsfarmcottages.co.uk

The Olde Stables ★★★★
Self Catering
Contact: Mrs Margaret Robinson
t (01200) 446240
w woodhousegatefarmcottage.co.uk

SLALEY
Northumberland

Clairmont Cottage ★★★★
Self Catering
Contact: Mr David Allsop
t (01434) 673686
e david.allsop4@which.net
w clairmontslaley.freeserve.co.uk

Combhills Farm ★★★
Self Catering
Contact: Mrs Ogle
t (01434) 673475
e margaret@ogle.entadsl.com

SLEDMERE
East Riding of Yorkshire

Life Hill Farm Cottage
★★★★ *Self Catering*
Contact: Andrew & Fay Grace
t (01377) 236224
e info@lifehillfarm.co.uk
w lifehillfarm.co.uk

SLEIGHTS
North Yorkshire

Carr View ★★★★
Self Catering
Select Holiday Homes
t (01491) 826757
e info@select-holidays-homes.co.uk
w select-holiday-homes.co.uk

Dalesview Cottage ★★★
Self Catering
Whitby Holiday Cottages
t (01947) 603010
e enquiries@whitbyholidaycottages.net
w whitbyholidaycottages.net

Groves Dyke Holiday Cottage ★★★ *Self Catering*
Contact: Niall Carson
t (01947) 810220
e relax@grovesdyke.co.uk
w grovesdyke.co.uk

The Old School House
Rating Applied For
Self Catering
Whitby Holiday Cottages
t (01947) 603010
e enquiries@whitbyholidaycottages.net
w whitbyholidaycottages.net

Rockcliffe ★★★★
Self Catering
Yorkshire Cottages
t (01228) 406701
e enquiries@yorkshire-cottages.info
w yorkshire-cottages.info

Rose Nook ★★★
Self Catering
Contact: Nicola Welford
Rose Nook Cottage
t (01947) 840726
e nicolawelford@aol.com

SLINGSBY
North Yorkshire

Cherrygarth Cottages – Hay Barn Stables ★★★★★
Self Catering
Contact: Stuart & Tracey Prest
t (01653) 628247
e s.prest@btconnect.com
w cherrygarthcottages.co.uk

Dawson Cottage ★★★
Self Catering
Contact: Julia Snowball
t (01653) 628136
e julia.snowball@amserve.com
w snowballcottage.co.uk

Home Farm Holiday Cottages ★★★★
Self Catering
Contact: Mr & Mrs Stephen Prest
t (01653) 628277
e sgprest@tiscali.co.uk
w yorkshire-holiday-cottage.co.uk

Keepers Cottage Holidays
★★★ *Self Catering*
Contact: Joanna Pavey
t (01653) 628656

SMARDALE
Cumbria

The Byre ★★★ *Self Catering*
Contact: Christina Galloway
t (017683) 71198
e leasesgall@aol.com

SNAINTON
North Yorkshire

Bramble End Cottage
★★★★ *Self Catering*
Yorkshire Cottages
t (01228) 406701
e enquiries@yorkshire-cottages.info
w yorkshire-cottages.info

Granary Cottage ★★★★
Self Catering
Contact: Mr & Mrs Jane & Kevin Wheldon
t (01723) 850402
e jane.wheldon@btinternet.com
w granary-cottage.com

Troutsdale End Cottage
★★★ *Self Catering*
Contact: Celia Tubbs
t (01723) 850620
e celiatubbs@aol.com
w troutsdale-end-cottage.co.uk

SNAPE
North Yorkshire

Jasmine Cottage ★★★
Self Catering
Contact: Colette Leyshon
t (01925) 413907
e jasminecottage@ntlworld.com

SNEATON
North Yorkshire

6 Sneaton Hall
Rating Applied For
Self Catering
Contact: Mrs Michelle Briggs
t (01274) 580225
e mbriggs@holidaybreakaway.co.uk
w holidaybreakaway.co.uk

Rose Cottage 1 ★★★
Self Catering
Whitby Holiday Cottages
t (01947) 603010
e enquiries@whitbyholidaycottages.net
w whitbyholidaycottages.net

SNEATON THORPE
North Yorkshire

Wheelhouse Cottage
★★★★ *Self Catering*
Yorkshire Cottages
t (01228) 406701
e enquiries@yorkshire-cottages.info
w yorkshire-cottages.info

SOUTH SHIELDS
Tyne and Wear

22 Hartington Terrace ★★★
Self Catering
Contact: Mrs Patricia Capps
t (01845) 578657
e mantonandpat@aol.com

Beach Haven Apartment
★★★ *Self Catering*
Contact: Mr V Cole
t (0191) 456 1802

Eccleston Road ★★★
Self Catering
Contact: Mr Tony Cole
t (0191) 456 1802

Sandhaven Beach Chalets
★★★ *Self Catering*
Contact: Mrs Christine Rowell
t (0191) 455 8319
e crowell@btconnect.com
w sandhavenchalets.co.uk

SOUTHPORT
Merseyside

4 Sandy Beach ★★★
Self Catering
Cornish Horizons Holiday Cottages
t (01841) 533331
e cottages@cornishhorizons.co.uk
w cornishhorizons.co.uk

45 Alexandra Road Holiday Flats ★ *Self Catering*
t (01704) 870137

51 Ash Street ★ *Self Catering*
Contact: Ms Pauline Meredith
t (01841) 532554
e pauline.london@btinternet.com

Barford House Apartments
★★★-★★★★ *Self Catering*
Contact: Mrs Pauline Morris
t (01704) 534454
w barfordhouse.co.uk

Beaucliffe Holiday Flats
★★★ *Self Catering*
Contact: Mrs Linda Allen
t (01704) 537207
e linda@beaucliffeholidayflats.co.uk
w beaucliffeholidayflats.co.uk

Castle Mews ★★★
Self Catering
Contact: Mr & Mrs Mike & Anne Wilsone castlemews@hotmail.co.uk
w castlemews.co.uk

Den Rae Holiday Flats ★★
Self Catering
t (01704) 530918

Holiday House
Rating Applied For
Self Catering
Contact: Mr & Mrs J. R Ramskill
t (01704) 225872
e elizabeth.mawdsley@yahooo.com

Martin Lane Farmhouse Holiday Cottages ★★★★
Self Catering
Contact: Mrs Stubbs
t (01704) 893527
e mlfhc@btinternet.com
w martinlanefarmhouse.btinternet.co.uk

Promenade Apartments
★★★★ *Self Catering*
t (01704) 541719
w promenade-apartments.co.uk

Sandcroft Holiday Flats ★
Self Catering
Contact: Mrs Edith Best
t (01704) 537497

Sandy Brook Farm ★★★
Self Catering
Contact: Mr Core
t (01704) 880337 & 07719 468712
e sandybrookfarm@lycos.co.uk
w sandybrookfarm.co.uk

SOUTHWAITE
Cumbria

Southwaite Green Farm
★★★★-★★★★★
Self Catering
Cumbrian Cottages
t (01228) 599960
e enquiries@cumbrian-cottages.co.uk
w cumbrian-cottages.co.uk

SOWERBY
North Yorkshire

Long Acre Lodge ★★★★
Self Catering
Contact: Rose Dawson
t (01845) 522360
e dawsonlongacre@aol.com
w longacrethirsk.co.uk

SOWERBY BRIDGE
West Yorkshire

Lane Ends Barn ★★★
Self Catering
Contact: Carola Ibbotson
t (01422) 833267
w laneends-selfcatering.co.uk

SPARK BRIDGE
Cumbria

Riverside Cottage ★★★
Self Catering
Cumbrian Cottages
t (01228) 599960
e enquiries@cumbrian-cottages.co.uk
w cumbrian-cottages.co.uk

Summer Hill Holidays ★★★
Self Catering
Contact: Rosemary Campbell
t (01229) 861510
e rosemary@summerhill.co.uk
w summerhill.co.uk

The Turners Cottage ★★★
Self Catering
The Coppermines & Coniston Lakes Cottages
t (015394) 41765
w coppermines.co.uk

SPARTY LEA
Northumberland

Holmcroft
Rating Applied For
Self Catering
t (01434) 683308
w allendaleselfcatering.co.uk

Isaac's Cottage ★★★
Self Catering
Contact: Mrs Heather Robson
t (01434) 685312

SPEETON
North Yorkshire

Woodbine Farm Holiday Cottages ★★★★
Self Catering
Contact: Karen Dyson
t (01723) 890783

SPITTAL
Northumberland

Beachcomber ★★★★
Self Catering
Contact: Ms P Simpson
t (01289) 306815
e priscilla.simpson@btinternet.com
w beachcomberview.co.uk

Seaview Cottage ★★★★
Self Catering
Contact: Mrs Brenda Crowcroft
t (01289) 304175
e b.crowcroft@talk21.com
w stunningseaviews.co.uk

SPROXTON
North Yorkshire

Sproxton Hall Cottages
★★★★ *Self Catering*
Contact: Mr David Bowens
t (01439) 770980
e sproxtonhallcottages@btopenworld.com

STACKHOUSE
North Yorkshire

Langcliffe Locks ★★★★
Self Catering
Contact: Colin Hibbert
t (01943) 601729
e colin.hibbert@blueyonder.co.uk
w holidaycottage.pwp.blueyonder.co.uk

STAFFIELD
Cumbria

Raven House ★★★★
Self Catering
Cumbrian Cottages
t (01228) 599960
e enquiries@cumbrian-cottages.co.uk
w cumbrian-cottages.co.uk

Staffield Hall Country Retreats ★★★★★
Self Catering
Contact: Michael & Marie Lawson
Staffield Hall
t (01995) 61574
e information@staffieldhall.co.uk
w staffieldhall.co.uk

STAINSACRE
North Yorkshire

Casa Rio ★★★ *Self Catering*
Whitby Holiday Cottages
t (01947) 603010
e enquiries@whitbyholidaycottages.net
w whitbyholidaycottages.net

Ivy Cottage ★★★
Self Catering
Contact: Mrs L Sampson
Ivy Cottage Holidays
t 07969 354475
e ivycottage@whitbyonline.co.uk
w whitbyonline.co.uk/ivy-cottage

Shalom ★★★★ *Self Catering*
Whitby Holiday Cottages
t (01947) 603010
e enquiries@whitbyholidaycottages.net
w whitbyholidaycottages.net

Sunnybrae ★★★★
Self Catering
Yorkshire Cottages
t (01228) 406701
e enquiries@yorkshire-cottages.info
w yorkshire-cottages.info

STAINTON
Cumbria

Chesnut Cottage ★★★
Self Catering
Cumbrian Cottages
t (01228) 599960
e enquiries@cumbrian-cottages.co.uk
w cumbrian-cottages.co.uk

The Cottage at Andrew House ★★★ *Self Catering*
Contact: John Brown
t (01768) 862510
e relax@andrewhousecottage.co.uk
w andrewhousecottage.co.uk

Dacre Garth ★★★★
Self Catering
Contact: Lindsay Taylor
t 0800 970 5646
e info@dacregarth.co.uk
w dacregarth.co.uk

Fairy Glenn ★★★
Self Catering
Cumbrian Cottages
t (01228) 599960
e enquiries@cumbrian-cottages.co.uk
w cumbrian-cottages.co.uk

Gibson Cottages ★★★
Self Catering
Dales Holiday Cottages
t (01756) 790919
e info@dales-holiday-cottages.com
w dales-holiday-cottages.com

Smithy Cottage ★★★★
Self Catering
Lakes Cottage Holidays
t (01228) 591555
e info@lakescottageholiday.co.uk
w lakescottageholiday.co.uk

STAINTON
Durham

Ferndale Cottage ★★★★
Self Catering
t (0191) 511 0555
w ferndalecottage.co.uk

The Old Granary ★★★★
Self Catering
t (01756) 790919
e lorraine.k@dales-holiday-cottages.com
w dales-holiday-cottages.com

STAINTONDALE
North Yorkshire

White Hall Farm Holiday Cottages ★★★ *Self Catering*
Contact: Mr & Mrs James and Celia White
t (01723) 870234
e celia@white66.fsbusiness.co.uk
w whitehallcottages.co.uk

STAIR
Cumbria

Grisdale Cottage ★★★
Self Catering
Lakeland Cottage Holidays
t (017687) 76065
e info@lakelandcottages.co.uk
w lakelandcottages.co.uk

Stair Mill ★★★ *Self Catering*
Contact: Tracey Read
t (017687) 78590
e traceyread26@btinternet.com
w stairmill.com

STAITHES
North Yorkshire

The Old Chandlers Cottage
★★★ *Self Catering*
Whitby Holiday Cottages
t (01947) 603010
e enquiries@whitbyholidaycottages.net
w whitbyholidaycottages.net

Pennysteel Cottage ★★★
Self Catering
Contact: Chris Wade
Waterfront Cottages
t (01377) 217662 & 07801 124264
e chris.wade@adastra-music.co.uk
w waterfrontcottages.co.uk

Staithes Holiday Cottages
★★★★ *Self Catering*
Contact: Maureen Selby
t (01947) 841401
e maureenselby@btinternet.com
w staithescottages.com

STAMFORD BRIDGE
East Riding of Yorkshire

The Cottage at High Catton Grange ★★★★ *Self Catering*
Contact: Sheila Foster
t (01759) 371374
e foster-s@sky.com
w highcattongrange.co.uk

STANBURY
West Yorkshire

Higher Scholes Cottage
★★★★★ *Self Catering*
Contact: Catherine O'Leary
t (01535) 646793
e info@higherscholescottage.co.uk
w higherscholescottage.co.uk

Hollies Cottage ★★★★
Self Catering
Yorkshire Cottages
t (01228) 406701
e enquiries@yorkshire-cottages.info
w yorkshire-cottages.info

Sarah's Cottage ★★★
Self Catering
Contact: Brian Fuller
t (01535) 643015
e brian.fuller2@btinternet.com
w sarahs-cottage.co.uk

STANHOPE
Durham

Eastcroft ★★★ *Self Catering*
Contact: Mrs Maureen Leach
t (01724) 868787
e dave@leach.uk.net

Lime Tree View ★★★★
Self Catering
Contact: Ms Lisa Fisher
t (024) 7651 1329
e lisa@limetreeview.co.uk
w limetreeview.co.uk

Primrose Cottage ★★
Self Catering
Contact: Mrs Vicky Reed
t (01697) 746777
e enquiries@northumbria-byways.com
w northumbria-byways.com

STANK
Cumbria

Stable Cottage & Miners Dry
★★★★ *Self Catering*
Contact: Linda Caine
t (01229) 826969
e linda@gcaine.plus.com
w southlakescottages.co.uk

STANLEY
Durham

Bushblades Farm Cottage
★★★ *Self Catering*
Contact: Mrs Pamela Gibson
t (01207) 232722

STARBOTTON
North Yorkshire

Horseshoe Cottage ★★★
Self Catering
Contact: Lynn May
t (015396) 20877
e lynnmay999@btinternet.com

Ivy Cottage ★★★★
Self Catering
Contact: Lorraine Gilmour
Dales Holiday Cottages
t (01756) 790919
e info@dales-holiday-cottages.com
w dales-holiday-cottages.com

STAVELEY
Cumbria

Avondale ★★★ *Self Catering*
Contact: Helen Hughes
t 07811 670260
e enquiries@avondale.uk.net
w avondale.uk.net

Beck View ★★★
Self Catering
Cumbrian Cottages
t (01228) 599960
e enquiries@cumbrian-cottages.co.uk
w cumbrian-cottages.co.uk

Bobbin Cottage ★★★
Self Catering
Dales Holiday Cottages
t (01756) 790919
e info@dales-holiday-cottages.com
w dales-holiday-cottages.com

Brunt Knott Farm Holiday Cottages ★★★ *Self Catering*
Contact: William & Margaret Beck
t (01539) 821030
e margaret@bruntknott.demon.co.uk
w bruntknott.demon.co.uk

The Chapel ★★★
Self Catering
Cumbrian Cottages
t (01228) 599960
e enquiries@cumbrian-cottages.co.uk
w cumbrian-cottages.co.uk

Fell Cottage ★★★★
Self Catering
Cumbrian Cottages
t (01228) 599960
e enquiries@cumbrian-cottages.co.uk
w cumbrian-cottages.co.uk

Fox Barn ★★★ *Self Catering*
Cumbrian Cottages
t (01228) 599960
e enquiries@cumbrian-cottages.co.uk
w cumbrian-cottages.co.uk

Headswood Cottage ★★★★
Self Catering
Lakelovers
t (015394) 88855
e bookings@lakelovers.co.uk
w lakelovers.co.uk

Hideaway Cottage ★★★
Self Catering
Hideaways
t (015394) 42435
e bookings@lakeland-hideaways.co.uk
w lakedistrictholidays.net

Hideaway Cottage ★★★★
Self Catering
Cumbrian Cottages
t (01228) 599960
e enquiries@cumbrian-cottages.co.uk
w cumbrian-cottages.co.uk

Meadow Cottage ★★★
Self Catering
Cumbrian Cottages
t (01228) 599960
e enquiries@cumbrian-cottages.co.uk
w cumbrian-cottages.co.uk

Reston Mill ★★★★
Self Catering
Cumbrian Cottages
t (01228) 599960
e enquiries@cumbrian-cottages.co.uk
w cumbrian-cottages.co.uk

Silver Cottage ★★★
Self Catering
Cumbrian Cottages
t (01228) 599960
e enquiries@cumbrian-cottages.co.uk
w cumbrian-cottages.co.uk

Staveley House Apartment
★★★★ *Self Catering*
Cumbrian Cottages
t (01228) 599960
e enquiries@cumbrian-cottages.co.uk
w cumbrian-cottages.co.uk

Weasel Cottage ★★★
Self Catering
Cumbrian Cottages
t (01228) 599960
e enquiries@cumbrian-cottages.co.uk
w cumbrian-cottages.co.uk

STAVELEY-IN-CARTMEL
Cumbria

April Cottage ★★★
Self Catering
Cumbrian Cottages
t (01228) 599960
e enquiries@cumbrian-cottages.co.uk
w cumbrian-cottages.co.uk

Croft Cottage ★★★
Self Catering
Lakelovers
t (015394) 88855
e bookings@lakelovers.co.uk
w lakelovers.co.uk

STILLINGTON
North Yorkshire

The Old Forge Holiday Cottage ★★★★ *Self Catering*
Contact: Annie Stirk
t (01347) 810531
e anne.stirk@btopenworld.com
w yorkholidaycottage.co.uk

STOCKSFIELD
Northumberland

The Old Bakery Cottages
★★★★ *Self Catering*
Contact: Mr & Mrs Vivien & Ron Bolton
t (01434) 633217

Old Ridley Hall ★★
Self Catering
Contact: Mrs Josephine Aldridge
t (01661) 842816
e oldridleyhall@talk21.com

STONYHURST
Lancashire

Alden Cottage ★★★★
Self Catering
t (01254) 826468
w fp.aldencottage.f9.co.uk

SUNDERLAND
Tyne and Wear

22 Topcliff ★★★
Self Catering
Contact: Mrs Bethan Farrar
t (020) 8850 4863
e cass@stayinsunderland.co.uk
w stayinsunderland.co.uk

Garden Flat ★★★
Self Catering
Contact: Mr Louis Mills
t 07973 727865
e info@sunderlandselfcatering.com
w sunderlandselfcatering.com

Hawksley House ★★★★
Serviced Apartments
t (0191) 510 9950
w hackettpropertyservicedapartments.com/index.html

Hill Head Farm ★★★★
Self Catering
Contact: Mr & Mrs William & Margaret Stewart
t (0191) 529 2076
e ask@hill-headfarm.co.uk
w hill-headfarm.co.uk

Mill View ★★★ *Self Catering*
Contact: Mrs Bethan Farrar
t (020) 8850 4863
e cass@stayinsunderland.co.uk
w stayinsunderland.co.uk

Parkside ★★★★
Self Catering
t (0191) 529 5435

Serviced Apartments at the Mowbray
Rating Applied For
Serviced Apartments
Contact: Ms Haley Sloan
t (0191) 510 9950
e haley.sloan@hackettproperty.com
w hackettproperty.com

SUTTON-ON-THE-FOREST
North Yorkshire

K M Knowlson Holiday Cottages ★★★ *Self Catering*
Contact: Heather Knowlson
t (01347) 822175
e kmkholcottyksuk@aol.com
w holidayskmkholcotts-yks.uk.com

SWARLAND
Northumberland

Four Wingates ★★★
Self Catering
Contact: Mrs M Chalk
t (01670) 788655
e northcroftmc@aol.com
w welcomenorthumberland.co.uk

Swarland Old Hall Luxury Pine Lodges ★★★★
Self Catering
Contact: Mrs Dianne Proctor
t (01670) 787642
e proctor@swarlandoldhall.fsnet.co.uk
w swarlandoldhall.co.uk

TABLEY
Cheshire

2 Waterless Brook Cottages ★★★ *Self Catering*
Contact: Mr Roger Thorp
t (01565) 734159
e rthorp@tinyworld.co.uk

TALLENTIRE
Cumbria

2 Bush Cottages ★★★★
Self Catering
Contact: Maggie Redfern
Bush Cottage
t (01946) 812091
e bushcottage@fsmail.net
w bushcottage.com

TARSET
Northumberland

Greystead Coach House ★★★★ *Self Catering*
Contact: Mrs Anne Monroe
t (01434) 240244
e wafm@greystead.fsnet.co.uk
w 2008.sytescottages.co.uk

TEBAY
Cumbria

1 Joiners Cottage ★★★
Self Catering
Cumbrian Cottages
t (01228) 599960
e enquiries@cumbrian-cottages.co.uk
w cumbrian-cottages.co.uk

Oak Tree Cottage ★★★★
Self Catering
Cumbrian Cottages
t (01228) 599960
e enquiries@cumbrian-cottages.co.uk
w cumbrian-cottages.co.uk

River View Cottage ★★★★
Self Catering
Cumbrian Cottages
t (01228) 599960
e enquiries@cumbrian-cottages.co.uk
w cumbrian-cottages.co.uk

TEMPLE SOWERBY
Cumbria

Hillview Cottage ★★★★
Self Catering
Contact: Ms Kate Blundell
t (017683) 62606
e kate@blundell73.fslife.co.uk
w hillviewcottage.com

TERRINGTON
North Yorkshire

Terrington Holiday Cottages ★★★-★★★★ *Self Catering*
Contact: Sally Goodrick
t (01653) 648370
e goodrick@terrington10.freeserve.co.uk
w terringtonholidaycottages.co.uk

THIRN
North Yorkshire

Violet Cottage ★★★★
Self Catering
Country Hideaways
t (01969) 663559
e info@countryhideaways.co.uk
w countryhideaways.co.uk

THIRSK
North Yorkshire

80 St James Green ★★★
Self Catering
Contact: Joanna Todd
t (01845) 523522

Briar Cottage & Bramble Cottage ★★★ *Self Catering*
Contact: Ms Jim Dickinson
t (01845) 597309
e jim.dickinson@btinternet.com
w rose-cottage-farm.co.uk

Fern Cottage ★★★★
Self Catering
Contact: Mrs Sal Billany
t (01845) 527056
e abillany@nildram.co.uk
w ferncottagethirsk.co.uk

The Garden Cottage, Rainton ★★★★ *Self Catering*
Contact: Mr Yates
Nursery Garden Holiday Home Park
t (01845) 577277
e nurserygardencp@talk21.com
w nurserygarden.co.uk

The Granary ★★★★
Self Catering
Contact: Mary Harrison
t (01845) 597554
e enquiries@granary-thirlby.co.uk
w granary-thirlby.co.uk

Pasture House Farm ★★★
Self Catering
Contact: Mr Arthur Bierton
t (01845) 522791

The Poplars Holiday Cottages ★★★★
Self Catering
Contact: Amanda Richards
t (01845) 522712
e amanda@thepoplarsthirsk.com
w thepoplarsthirsk.com

THORALBY
North Yorkshire

Coach House ★★★★
Self Catering
Country Hideaways
t (01969) 663559
e info@countryhideaways.co.uk
w countryhideaways.co.uk

The Garden Flat, The Old Corn Mill ★★★ *Self Catering*
Country Hideaways
t (01969) 663559
e info@countryhideaways.co.uk
w countryhideaways.co.uk

Grange Cottage ★★★
Self Catering
Country Hideaways
t (01969) 663559
e info@countryhideaways.co.uk
w countryhideaways.co.uk

May's Cottage ★★★
Self Catering
Country Hideaways
t (01969) 663559
e info@countryhideaways.co.uk
w countryhideaways.co.uk

Meadowcroft Cottage ★★★★ *Self Catering*
Contact: Chris Mason
t (01792) 280068
e mcmason@globalnet.co.uk
w meadowcroftcottage.co.uk

THORGILL
North Yorkshire

Ghyll Cottage ★★★
Self Catering
Contact: Mrs Sharon Baxter
t (01404) 815047
e maritimegs@aol.com

THORNLEY
Lancashire

Loudview Barn ★★★★
Self Catering
Contact: Mr & Mrs Oliver & Ness Starkey
t (01995) 61476
e loudview@ic24.net

Thornley Hall ★★★
Self Catering
Contact: Mrs Gill Airey
t (01995) 61243
e gillairey@hotmail.com
w thornleyhall.co.uk

THORNTHWAITE
Cumbria

3 Ladstock ★★★★
Self Catering
Cumbrian Cottages
t (01228) 599960
e enquiries@cumbrian-cottages.co.uk
w cumbrian-cottages.co.uk

5 Ladstock ★★★★
Self Catering
Cumbrian Cottages
t (01228) 599960
e enquiries@cumbrian-cottages.co.uk
w cumbrian-cottages.co.uk

7 Ladstock Hall ★★★★★
Self Catering
Cumbrian Cottages
t (01228) 599960
e enquiries@cumbrian-cottages.co.uk
w cumbrian-cottages.co.uk

Bishops View ★★★★
Self Catering
Cumbrian Cottages
t (01228) 599960
e enquiries@cumbrian-cottages.co.uk
w cumbrian-cottages.co.uk

Comb Beck ★★★-★★★★
Self Catering
Contact: Helen Davies
Comb Beck/Bleaberry Lodge
t (017687) 78097
e helen@stayinthornthwaite.co.uk
w combbeck.co.uk

The Croft at Thornwaite Hall ★★★★ *Self Catering*
Cumbrian Cottages
t (01228) 599960
e enquiries@cumbrian-cottages.co.uk
w cumbrian-cottages.co.uk

Hallgarth Barn ★★★★
Self Catering
Cumbrian Cottages
t (01228) 599960
e enquiries@cumbrian-cottages.co.uk
w cumbrian-cottages.co.uk

Harriet's Hideaway ★★★★
Self Catering
Contact: David Miller
t (0191) 488 0549
e dm81@blueyonder.co.uk
w dm81.pwp.blueyonder.co.uk

Jasmine Cottage ★★★★
Self Catering
Contact: Kate Danchin
Holly Bank & Jasmine Cottages
t (01900) 822001
e jasmine@hollybankcottage.co.uk
w hollybankcottage.co.uk

Joan's Cottage ★★★
Self Catering
Cumbrian Cottages
t (01228) 599960
e enquiries@cumbrian-cottages.co.uk
w cumbrian-cottages.co.uk

The Larches ★★★
Self Catering
Cumbrian Cottages
t (01228) 599960
e enquiries@cumbrian-cottages.co.uk
w cumbrian-cottages.co.uk

Oak Lea ★★★ *Self Catering*
Cumbrian Cottages
t (01228) 599960
e enquiries@cumbrian-cottages.co.uk
w cumbrian-cottages.co.uk

The Old School House ★★★
Self Catering
Cumbrian Cottages
t (01228) 599960
e enquiries@cumbrian-cottages.co.uk
w cumbrian-cottages.co.uk

Pen Cottage ★★★★★
Self Catering
Cumbrian Cottages
t (01228) 599960
e enquiries@cumbrian-cottages.co.uk
w cumbrian-cottages.co.uk

Seat Howe ★★★
Self Catering
Contact: Mrs Dorothy Bell
t (017687) 78371

Talcomb ★★★ *Self Catering*
Contact: Howard King
t 07973 420179
e hk.developments@virgin.net
w hkdevelopmentslakes.co.uk

Thwaite Hill Barn ★★★
Self Catering
Cumbrian Cottages
t (01228) 599960
e enquiries@cumbrian-cottages.co.uk
w cumbrian-cottages.co.uk

Thwaite Hill Cottage ★★★
Self Catering
Lakeland Cottage Holidays
t (017687) 76065
e info@lakelandcottages.co.uk
w lakelandcottages.co.uk

Vermont ★★★★
Self Catering
Cumbrian Cottages
t (01228) 599960
e enquiries@cumbrian-cottages.co.uk
w cumbrian-cottages.co.uk

Woodside Cottage ★★★★
Self Catering
Cumbrian Cottages
t (01228) 599960
e enquiries@cumbrian-cottages.co.uk
w cumbrian-cottages.co.uk

THORNTON
Lancashire

Garlands Holiday Flats ★★★
Self Catering
Contact: Mr G Powell
t (01253) 862453
e powell.geoffrey@talk21.com

Highcliffe Holiday Apartments ★★★
Self Catering
Contact: Mr Geoff Dawber
t (01253) 859017
w highcliffeapartments.co.uk

Seahawk Holiday Apartments ★★★
Self Catering
Contact: Mr & Mrs Ball
t (01253) 823957
e micar.seahawk@gmail.com
w seahawk-apartments.co.uk

THORNTON-CLEVELEYS
Lancashire

Jubilee Holiday Apartments ★★-★★★ *Self Catering*
Contact: Mrs Janet Robinson
t (01253) 856429

THORNTON DALE
North Yorkshire

Gable House ★★★★
Self Catering
Contact: Mr & Mrs Andrew & Carole Lewty
t (01924) 403716
e the.lewtys@virgin.net
w cottagegwide.co.uk/gablehouse

Hillcroft ★★★ *Self Catering*
Contact: Lily Brookfield
t (01751) 474342
w country-holidays.co.uk

The New Inn
Rating Applied For
Self Catering
Contact: Adam & Kim Shaw
t (01751) 474226
e adam.shaw2008@hotmail.co.uk
w the-new-inn.com

Station House Holiday Cottages ★★★-★★★★
Self Catering
Contact: Natalie Ellis
t (01751) 474417

THORNTON RUST
North Yorkshire

Nettle Cottage
Rating Applied For
Self Catering
Contact: Mrs Annette Riley
t (01969) 663716
e info@nettle-cottage.co.uk

The Old Goat House ★★★★
Self Catering
Contact: Annette Riley
t (01969) 663716
e info@oldgoathouse.co.uk
w oldgoathouse.co.uk

Outgang Cottage ★★★
Self Catering
Dales Holiday Cottages
t (01756) 790919
e info@dales-holiday-cottages.com
w dales-holiday-cottages.com

West Cottage ★★★
Self Catering
Country Hideaways
t (01969) 663559
e info@countryhideaways.co.uk
w countryhideaways.co.uk

THORPE BASSETT
North Yorkshire

The Old Post Office ★★★★
Self Catering
Contact: Sandra Simpson
t (01944) 758047
e ssimpsoncottages@aol.com
w ssimpsoncottages.co.uk

Wold View Cottage, Thorpe Bassett ★★★★ *Self Catering*
Contact: Mrs Stephanie French
Wold View House
t (01944) 758704
w dalesholcot.com

THRELKELD
Cumbria

Blease Barn ★★★★
Self Catering
Cumbrian Cottages
t (01228) 599960
e enquiries@cumbrian-cottages.co.uk
w cumbrian-cottages.co.uk

Blease Cottage ★★★★
Self Catering
Cumbrian Cottages
t (01228) 599960
e enquiries@cumbrian-cottages.co.uk
w cumbrian-cottages.co.uk

Blencathra ★★★
Self Catering
Lakeland Cottage Holidays
t (017687) 76065
e info@lakelandcottages.co.uk
w lakelandcottages.co.uk

Chapmere ★★★
Self Catering
Cumbrian Cottages
t (01228) 599960
e enquiries@cumbrian-cottages.co.uk
w cumbrian-cottages.co.uk

Cropple How ★★★
Self Catering
Cumbrian Cottages
t (01228) 599960
e enquiries@cumbrian-cottages.co.uk
w cumbrian-cottages.co.uk

Fell View ★★ *Self Catering*
Sykes Cottages
t (01244) 345700
e info@sykescottages.co.uk
w sykescottages.co.uk

Field Studies Council ★★★
Self Catering
Contact: Janet Elliott
t (017687) 79601
e enquiries.bl@field-studies-council.org

Heather View ★★★
Self Catering
Cumbrian Cottages
t (01228) 599960
e enquiries@cumbrian-cottages.co.uk
w cumbrian-cottages.co.uk

Kiln How Cottage ★★★★
Self Catering
Cumbrian Cottages
t (01228) 599960
e enquiries@cumbrian-cottages.co.uk
w cumbrian-cottages.co.uk

Latcrag Cottage & Caravan ★★★★ *Self Catering*
Contact: Mrs Benson
t (017687) 79256

Milerdale ★★★★
Self Catering
Cumbrian Cottages
t (01228) 599960
e enquiries@cumbrian-cottages.co.uk
w cumbrian-cottages.co.uk

The Old Manse Barn ★★★
Self Catering
Contact: Mrs L Deadman
t (017687) 79270
e jon@deadman.freeserve.co.uk
w deadman.freeserve.co.uk

The Old School House ★★★★ *Self Catering*
Contact: Lucy Swarbrick
t (0161) 928 6290
e info@cottageinthrelkeld.co.uk
w theoldschoolhousethrelkeld.co.uk

Scales View Cottages ★★★
Self Catering
Cumbrian Cottages
t (01228) 599960
e enquiries@cumbrian-cottages.co.uk
w cumbrian-cottages.co.uk

Townhead Barn ★★★
Self Catering
Lakeland Cottage Holidays
t (017687) 76065
e info@lakelandcottages.co.uk
w lakelandcottages.co.uk

Townhead Byre ★★★
Self Catering
Lakeland Cottage Holidays
t (017687) 76065
e info@lakelandcottages.co.uk
w lakelandcottages.co.uk

White Pike ★★★
Self Catering
Cumbrian Cottages
t (01228) 599960
e enquiries@cumbrian-cottages.co.uk
w cumbrian-cottages.co.uk

THRESHFIELD
North Yorkshire

No Name House ★★★
Self Catering
Contact: Mrs Marilyn Kitching
t (01756) 753049
e infononame@btinternet.com
w yorkshirenet.co.uk/stayat/nonamehouse

Wharfe Lodge ★★★
Self Catering
Contact: Mrs J Mitton
t (01494) 872572
e wharfelodge@hotmail.com
w wharfelodge.co.uk

THROPTON
Northumberland

Black Chirnells, The Cottage
★★★★ *Self Catering*
t 07747 734946
w holidaycottages northumberland.org.uk

Coach House Lynnholm
Rating Applied For
Self Catering
Contact: Mr & Mrs Graham & Jacqueline Duff
t (01669) 620661
e lynnholm@tiscali.co.uk

Mordue's Cottage & Grandma's Cottage ★★★
Self Catering
Contact: Mrs Helen Farr
t (01665) 574672
e info@lorbottle.com
w lorbottle.com

North Croft ★★★★
Self Catering
Contact: Mrs M Chalk
t (01670) 788655
e northcroftmc@aol.com

Physic Cottage ★★★★
Self Catering
Contact: Mrs Helen Duffield
t (01669) 620450
e physiccottage@aol.com
w visit-rothbury.co.uk

Westfield Cottage, Thropton
★★★★ *Self Catering*
Contact: Mr & Mrs Alastair & Catherine Hardie
t (01669) 640263
e info@westfield-cottage.co.uk
w westfield-cottage.co.uk

THURSTONFIELD
Cumbria

The Tranquil Otter, Thurstonfield
★★★★-★★★★★
Self Catering
Contact: Nick and Tazeem Kittoe
The Tranquil Otter Ltd
t (01228) 576661
e info@thetranquilotter.co.uk
w thetranquilotter.co.uk

THWAITE
North Yorkshire

Greystones ★★★★
Self Catering
Askrigg Cottage Holidays
t (01969) 650022
e stay@askrigg.com
w askrigg.com

Thwaite Farm Cottages
★★★-★★★★★ *Self Catering*
Contact: Gillian Whitehead
t (01748) 886444
e info@thwaitefarmcottages.co.uk
w thwaitefarmcottages.co.uk

Thwaitedale Cottages
★★★★ *Self Catering*
Contact: Valerie Hunter
t (01530) 272794
e info@thwaitecottages.co.uk
w thwaitecottages.co.uk

TIMBLE
North Yorkshire

The Old Dairy ★★★★
Self Catering
Contact: Alison Hartwell
Harrogate Holiday Cottages
t (01423) 523333
e bookings@harrogateholidays.co.uk
w harrogateholidays.co.uk

TIRRIL
Cumbria

Broad Ing Cottage ★★★★
Self Catering
Contact: Carol Kay
t (01423) 881886
e gjkay.tr6@ntlworld.com
w broadingcottage.co.uk

Shelterstone ★★★★
Self Catering
Cumbrian Cottages
t (01228) 599960
e enquiries@cumbrian-cottages.co.uk
w cumbrian-cottages.co.uk

Tirril Farm Cottages
★★★★-★★★★★
Self Catering
Contact: David Owens
t (01768) 864767
e enquiries@tirrilfarmcottages.co.uk
w tirrilfarmcottages.co.uk

TODMORDEN
West Yorkshire

The Cottage ★★★
Self Catering
Contact: Mr & Mrs Bentham
t (01706) 815265
e andrew-b_5@tiscali.co.uk

Lower Birks Farm ★★★★
Self Catering
Contact: Mrs Ingrid Cooper
t (01706) 814316
e ingrid@lowerbirksfarm.co.uk
w lowerbirksfarm.co.uk

Shoebroad Barn ★★★★
Self Catering
Contact: Mrs Horsfall
t (01706) 817015 & 07966 158295
e thehorsfalls@beeb.net
w shoebroadbarn.co.uk

Stannally Farm Cottage
★★★★ *Self Catering*
Contact: Dineen Ann Brunt
t (01706) 813998
e bruntdennis@aol.com

Staups Barn Holiday Cottage
★★★ *Self Catering*
Contact: Mr Crabtree
t (01706) 812730
e staups1@supanet.com

TOLLERTON
North Yorkshire

Gill Cottage ★★★★
Self Catering
Dales Holiday Cottages
t (01756) 790919
e info@dales-holiday-cottages.com
w dales-holiday-cottages.com

TORVER
Cumbria

Bankend Caravan *Approved Caravan Holiday Home*
Contact: Susan Cooper
t (015394) 41362
e sue@garth26.fsnet.co.uk
w bankendcaravan.co.uk

Braeside ★★★ *Self Catering*
Cumbrian Cottages
t (01228) 599960
e enquiries@cumbrian-cottages.co.uk
w cumbrian-cottages.co.uk

Brigg House ★★★★
Self Catering
Lakeland Cottage Comapny
t (015395) 38180
e john@lakelandcottageco.com
w lakelandcottageco.com

Daisy Cottage ★★★
Self Catering
The Coppermines & Coniston Lakes Cottages
t (015394) 41765
w coppermines.co.uk

Ellice Howe ★★★★
Self Catering
Lakelovers
t (015394) 88855
e bookings@lakelovers.co.uk
w lakelovers.co.uk

High Park Cottage ★★★★
Self Catering
The Coppermines & Coniston Lakes Cottages
t (015394) 41765
w coppermines.co.uk

Scarr Head Caravans
Approved Caravan Holiday Home
Contact: Jane Halton
t (015394) 41576
e info@scarrhead.co.uk
w scarrhead.co.uk

Scarr Head Cottage ★★★
Self Catering
Cumbrian Cottages
t (01228) 599960
e enquiries@cumbrian-cottages.co.uk
w cumbrian-cottages.co.uk

Sunny Bank Mill ★★★
Self Catering
Contact: Claire Wildsmith
t (015394) 47474
e lakescene@fayrergarden.com
w sunnybankmill.com

Torver Station Cottages
★★★ *Self Catering*
The Coppermines & Coniston Lakes Cottages
t (015394) 41765
w coppermines.co.uk

TOSSIDE
Lancashire

Crowtrees Barn ★★★★
Self Catering
Contact: Mandy Gleave
t (01729) 840278
e hol@crowtreespark.co.uk
w crowtreespark.co.uk

Primrose Cottage, Jenny Wren, Wagtail, Swallows, Lower Gill Farm ★★★★
Self Catering
t (01756) 700510
w holidaycotts.co.uk

TOTLEY RISE
South Yorkshire

Swallow Cottage ★★★★
Self Catering
Contact: Debbie Hill
t (0114) 236 7806
w peakcottages.com

TOW LAW
Durham

Binks Cottage ★★★★
Self Catering
Contact: Mrs Amanda Simpson Oaklea
t (01388) 731121
e amanda.simpson@totalise.co.uk
w binkscottage.co.uk

Greenwell Hill Cottages
★★★ *Self Catering*
Contact: Mrs Karen Wilson
t (01388) 527247
e enquiries@greenwellhill.co.uk
w greenwellfarm.co.uk

Pennine View ★★★★
Self Catering
Contact: Mrs Dawn Paterson
t (01388) 731329
e dawn@pennineview.com
w pennineview.com

TRAWDEN
Lancashire

Far Wanless Farm Stable Cottage ★★★★ *Self Catering*
Contact: Mrs V M or Paul Johnson
t (01282) 867514

TROUTBECK
Cumbria

1 and 2 Butt Hill Cottage
★★★ *Self Catering*
Lakelovers
t (015394) 88855
e bookings@lakelovers.co.uk
w lakelovers.co.uk

Applethwaite Lodge ★★★
Self Catering
Cumbrian Cottages
t (01228) 599960
e enquiries@cumbrian-cottages.co.uk
w cumbrian-cottages.co.uk

Barn Cottage ★★★
Self Catering
Lakelovers
t (015394) 88855
e bookings@lakelovers.co.uk
w lakelovers.co.uk

Blencathra Cottage
Rating Applied For
Self Catering
Contact: Sandra Woodcroft
t (017687) 79737
e lowhouse.moorend@tiscali.co.uk
w blencathracottage.co.uk

Brakenby ★★★ *Self Catering*
Cumbrian Cottages
t (01228) 599960
e enquiries@cumbrian-cottages.co.uk
w cumbrian-cottages.co.uk

Fell Cottage ★★★★
Self Catering
Lakelovers
t (015394) 88855
e bookings@lakelovers.co.uk
w lakelovers.co.uk

Gara Garth ★★★★
Self Catering
Lakelovers
t (015394) 88855
e bookings@lakelovers.co.uk
w lakelovers.co.uk

Granary Cottage ★★★
Self Catering
Cumbrian Cottages
t (01228) 599960
e enquiries@cumbrian-cottages.co.uk
w cumbrian-cottages.co.uk

Greenbank Farmhouse
★★★★★ *Self Catering*
Cumbrian Cottages
t (01228) 599960
e enquiries@cumbrian-cottages.co.uk
w cumbrian-cottages.co.uk

Limefitt Lodge ★★★
Self Catering
Cumbrian Cottages
t (01228) 599960
e enquiries@cumbrian-cottages.co.uk
w cumbrian-cottages.co.uk

Myley Ghyll ★★★★★
Self Catering
Lakelovers
t (015394) 88855
e bookings@lakelovers.co.uk
w lakelovers.co.uk

Orchard Cottage ★★★
Self Catering
Lakelovers
t (015394) 88855
e bookings@lakelovers.co.uk
w lakelovers.co.uk

Prospect Lodge ★★★
Self Catering
Cumbrian Cottages
t (01228) 599960
e enquiries@cumbrian-cottages.co.uk
w cumbrian-cottages.co.uk

Riverside
Rating Applied For
Self Catering
Lakelovers
t (015394) 88855
e bookings@lakelovers.co.uk
w lakelovers.co.uk

Riverside Farmhouse & Cottage ★★★★ *Self Catering*
Contact: Stephen Hutchinson
t 07966 486701
e riversidefarm@tiscali.co.uk
w riversidefarmholidaycottages.co.uk

Shalom ★★★ *Self Catering*
Cumbrian Cottages
t (01228) 599960
e enquiries@cumbrian-cottages.co.uk
w cumbrian-cottages.co.uk

Station House ★★★★
Self Catering
Cumbrian Cottages
t (01228) 599960
e enquiries@cumbrian-cottages.co.uk
w cumbrian-cottages.co.uk

Syke Villa ★★ *Self Catering*
Lakelovers
t (015394) 88855
e bookings@lakelovers.co.uk
w lakelovers.co.uk

Troutbeck Club Site
Approved Caravan Holiday Home
Camping & Caravanning Club
t 0845 130 7631

Troutbeck Inn Holiday Cottages ★★★★
Self Catering
Contact: Margaret Ward
t (017684) 83635
e troutbeckinn1@btconnect.com
w thetroutbeckinn.co.uk

Valley Lodge ★★★★
Self Catering
Cumbrian Cottages
t (01228) 599960
e enquiries@cumbrian-cottages.co.uk
w cumbrian-cottages.co.uk

Wee Fell Cottage ★★★★
Self Catering
Lakelovers
t (015394) 88855
e bookings@lakelovers.co.uk
w lakelovers.co.uk

Windermere Lodge
Rating Applied For
Self Catering
Contact: John Hobson
t 07976 763647
e info@windermerelodge.co.uk
w windermerelodge.co.uk

TROUTBECK BRIDGE
Cumbria

1 School Cottages ★★★
Self Catering
Cumbrian Cottages
t (01228) 599960
e enquiries@cumbrian-cottages.co.uk
w cumbrian-cottages.co.uk

3 Calgarth Cottages ★★★
Self Catering
Cumbrian Cottages
t (01228) 599960
e enquiries@cumbrian-cottages.co.uk
w cumbrian-cottages.co.uk

Barn Cottage ★★★
Self Catering
Cumbrian Cottages
t (01228) 599960
e enquiries@cumbrian-cottages.co.uk
w cumbrian-cottages.co.uk

Beckside Cottage ★★★
Self Catering
Cumbrian Cottages
t (01228) 599960
e enquiries@cumbrian-cottages.co.uk
w cumbrian-cottages.co.uk

Claife Holme ★★★★
Self Catering
Cumbrian Cottages
t (01228) 599960
e enquiries@cumbrian-cottages.co.uk
w cumbrian-cottages.co.uk

Cregary Cottage ★★★
Self Catering
Contact: Jan Kiernan
t 07834 353152
e enquiries@cregarycottage.co.uk
w cregarycottage.co.uk

Groom Cottage ★★★★
Self Catering
Cumbrian Cottages
t (01228) 599960
e enquiries@cumbrian-cottages.co.uk
w cumbrian-cottages.co.uk

Herdwick Cottage ★★★
Self Catering
Cumbrian Cottages
t (01228) 599960
e enquiries@cumbrian-cottages.co.uk
w cumbrian-cottages.co.uk

Honeymoon Lodge ★★★
Self Catering
Cumbrian Cottages
t (01228) 599960
e enquiries@cumbrian-cottages.co.uk
w cumbrian-cottages.co.uk

Howarth Cottage ★★★
Self Catering
Cumbrian Cottages
t (01228) 599960
e enquiries@cumbrian-cottages.co.uk
w cumbrian-cottages.co.uk

Lakefield ★★★ *Self Catering*
Lakelovers
t (015394) 88855
e bookings@lakelovers.co.uk
w lakelovers.co.uk

Short Nab ★★★★★
Self Catering
Cumbrian Cottages
t (01228) 599960
e enquiries@cumbrian-cottages.co.uk
w cumbrian-cottages.co.uk

Sunny Brow ★★★★
Self Catering
Lakelovers
t (015394) 88855
e bookings@lakelovers.co.uk
w lakelovers.co.uk

TUDHOE COLLIERY
Durham

Miner's Cottage ★★★
Self Catering
Contact: Mrs Jacqueline Galvin
t (01388) 721913
e lgalvin@talk21.com
w miners.cottage.btinternet.co.uk

TURTON
Greater Manchester

Clough Head Farm ★★★★
Self Catering
Contact: Mrs Ethel Houghton
t (01254) 704758
e ethelhoughton@hotmail.co.uk
w cloughheadfarm.co.uk

TWEEDMOUTH
Northumberland

Edward House ★★★★
Self Catering
Northumberland Cottages
t (01665) 589434
e enquiries@northumberlandcottages.com
w northumberlandcottages.co.uk

Marlborough Cottage
★★★★ *Self Catering*
Contact: Mr Peter Adamson
t (01289) 305293
e seaside133@onetel.com
w marlboroughcottage.info

St Andrews House ★★★
Self Catering
Contact: Mrs Katharine Tiernan
t (01665) 589322
e kmtiernan@googlemail.com
w lindisfarne-cottages.co.uk

UGTHORPE
North Yorkshire

Travellers Rest Farm Cottage
Rating Applied For
Self Catering
Yorkshire Cottages
t (01228) 406701
e enquiries@yorkshire-cottages.info
w yorkshire-cottages.info

ULDALE
Cumbria

Coach House ★★★
Self Catering
Cumbrian Cottages
t (01228) 599960
e enquiries@cumbrian-cottages.co.uk
w cumbrian-cottages.co.uk

Country Seat ★★★
Self Catering
Cumbrian Cottages
t (01228) 599960
e enquiries@cumbrian-cottages.co.uk
w cumbrian-cottages.co.uk

Knaifan Cottage ★★★
Self Catering
Cumbrian Cottages
t (01228) 599960
e enquiries@cumbrian-cottages.co.uk
w cumbrian-cottages.co.uk

The Mews ★★★★
Self Catering
Cumbrian Cottages
t (01228) 599960
e enquiries@cumbrian-cottages.co.uk
w cumbrian-cottages.co.uk

The Old School House ★★★
Self Catering
Cumbrian Cottages
t (01228) 599960
e enquiries@cumbrian-cottages.co.uk
w cumbrian-cottages.co.uk

Reservoir House ★★★
Self Catering
Cumbrian Cottages
t (01228) 599960
e enquiries@cumbrian-cottages.co.uk
w cumbrian-cottages.co.uk

ULGHAM
Northumberland

Ulgham Grange Crossing Cottage ★★★★ *Self Catering*
Contact: Mrs Gabrielle Patterson
t (01670) 790650
e gabrielle@northskeer.f9.co.uk

ULLOCK
Cumbria

Treetops Holiday Apartment ★★★★ *Self Catering*
Dales Holiday Cottages
t (01756) 790919
e info@dales-holiday-cottages.com
w dales-holiday-cottages.com

ULLSWATER
Cumbria

Land Ends Cabins ★★★
Self Catering
Contact: Mrs B Murphy
Land Ends Country Lodge
t (017684) 86438
e infolandends@btinternet.com
w landends.co.uk

Low Wood View ★★★
Self Catering
Contact: Mrs J Wear
t (017684) 82396
w ullswater-steamers.co.uk/lowwoodview

Patterdale Hall Estate, Glenridding ★★–★★★
Self Catering
Contact: Sue Kay
t (017684) 82308
e mail@patterdalehallestate.com
w patterdalehallestate.com

Townhead Cottage ★★★★
Self Catering
Lakeland Cottage Comapny
t (015395) 38180
e john@lakelandcottageco.com
w lakelandcottageco.com

ULPHA
Cumbria

Brigghouse Cottage ★★★★
Self Catering
The Coppermines & Coniston Lakes Cottages
t (015394) 41765
w coppermines.co.uk

High Kiln Bank Cottage
★★★★ *Self Catering*
Lakeland Cottage Comapny
t (015395) 38180
e john@lakelandcottageco.com
w lakelandcottageco.com

Oakbank Cottage ★★★★★
Self Catering
Cumbrian Cottages
t (01228) 599960
e enquiries@cumbrian-cottages.co.uk
w cumbrian-cottages.co.uk

Old Oak Cottage ★★★★
Self Catering
The Coppermines & Coniston Lakes Cottages
t (015394) 41765
w coppermines.co.uk

ULVERSTON
Cumbria

22 Victoria Court ★★★★
Self Catering
Contact: Katie Capstick
t (01254) 828232
e info@lake-district-holiday-home.co.uk
w lake-district-holiday-home.co.uk

Ashlack Cottages, Broughton-in-Furness
★★★★ *Self Catering & Serviced Apartments*
Contact: Amanda Keegan
t (01229) 889888 & 07976 867313
e enquiries@ashlackcottages.co.uk
w ashlackcottages.co.uk

Bark House
Rating Applied For
Self Catering
Contact: Emma Graham
Cumbrian Cottages
t (01228) 599960
e enquiries@cumbrian-cottages.co.uk
w cumbrian-cottages.co.uk

Beck Cottage ★★★
Self Catering
Hideaways
t (015394) 42435
e bookings@lakeland-hideaways.co.uk
w lakeland-hideaways.co.uk

Brookside Cottage ★★★★
Self Catering
Contact: Judith Bowers
t (0121) 459 1043
e enquiries@lakelandholidaycottage.co.uk
w lakelandholidaycottage.co.uk

Haycote Cottage ★★★★
Self Catering
Cumbrian Cottages
t (01228) 599960
e enquiries@cumbrian-cottages.co.uk
w cumbrian-cottages.co.uk

Langholme Mill Cottage
★★★ *Self Catering*
Cumbrian Cottages
t (01228) 599960
e enquiries@cumbrian-cottages.co.uk
w cumbrian-cottages.co.uk

Lile Cottage at Gleaston Water Mill ★★★★
Self Catering
Contact: Vicky Brereton
t (01229) 869244
e pigsty@watermill.co.uk
w watermill.co.uk

Marigold Barn ★★★★
Self Catering
Cumbrian Cottages
t (01228) 599960
e enquiries@cumbrian-cottages.co.uk
w cumbrian-cottages.co.uk

Orchard Cottage ★★★
Self Catering
Contact: Mr & Mrs Martin
t (01229) 463591
e brianmartin@orchardcottageulverston.co.uk
w orchardcottageulverston.co.uk

Pavilion Apartment ★★★★
Self Catering
Cumbrian Cottages
t (01228) 599960
e enquiries@cumbrian-cottages.co.uk
w cumbrian-cottages.co.uk

Phirlain Cottage ★★★
Self Catering
Cumbrian Cottages
t (01228) 599960
e enquiries@cumbrian-cottages.co.uk
w cumbrian-cottages.co.uk

Prospect Cottage ★★★
Self Catering
Cumbrian Cottages
t (01228) 599960
e enquiries@cumbrian-cottages.co.uk
w cumbrian-cottages.co.uk

Thwaite Bridge House ★★★
Self Catering
Cumbrian Cottages
t (01228) 599960
e enquiries@cumbrian-cottages.co.uk
w cumbrian-cottages.co.uk

UNDERBARROW
Cumbria

Ellerbeck ★★★★
Self Catering
Cumbrian Cottages
t (01228) 599960
e enquiries@cumbrian-cottages.co.uk
w cumbrian-cottages.co.uk

Honey Pot & Nanny Goat
★★★★★ *Self Catering*
Lakeland Cottage Comapny
t (015395) 38180
e john@lakelandcottageco.com
w lakelandcottageco.com

Nanny Goat ★★★★★
Self Catering
Lakeland Cottage Comapny
t (015395) 38180
e john@lakelandcottageco.com
w lakelandcottageco.com

Oakshead ★★★★★
Self Catering
Cumbrian Cottages
t (01228) 599960
e enquiries@cumbrian-cottages.co.uk
w cumbrian-cottages.co.uk

The Old School ★★★★
Self Catering
Cumbrian Cottages
t (01228) 599960
e enquiries@cumbrian-cottages.co.uk
w cumbrian-cottages.co.uk

UNDERSKIDDAW
Cumbria

Artists View ★★★★
Self Catering
Cumbrian Cottages
t (01228) 599960
e enquiries@cumbrian-cottages.co.uk
w cumbrian-cottages.co.uk

Brook Lodge ★★★★
Self Catering
Cumbrian Cottages
t (01228) 599960
e enquiries@cumbrian-cottages.co.uk
w cumbrian-cottages.co.uk

Derwent Lodge ★★★★
Self Catering
Cumbrian Cottages
t (01228) 599960
e enquiries@cumbrian-cottages.co.uk
w cumbrian-cottages.co.uk

Ewe Howe ★★★★
Self Catering
Cumbrian Cottages
t (01228) 599960
e enquiries@cumbrian-cottages.co.uk
w cumbrian-cottages.co.uk

Fell Foot Lodge ★★★
Self Catering
Cumbrian Cottages
t (01228) 599960
e enquiries@cumbrian-cottages.co.uk
w cumbrian-cottages.co.uk

Garth Cottage ★★★
Self Catering
Cumbrian Cottages
t (01228) 599960
e enquiries@cumbrian-cottages.co.uk
w cumbrian-cottages.co.uk

Latrigg ★★★★ *Self Catering*
Cumbrian Cottages
t (01228) 599960
e enquiries@cumbrian-cottages.co.uk
w cumbrian-cottages.co.uk

Oakfield Lodge ★★★
Self Catering
Cumbrian Cottages
t (01228) 599960
e enquiries@cumbrian-cottages.co.uk
w cumbrian-cottages.co.uk

Skiddaw Lodge ★★★★
Self Catering
Cumbrian Cottages
t (01228) 599960
e enquiries@cumbrian-cottages.co.uk
w cumbrian-cottages.co.uk

Squirrels Leap ★★★★
Self Catering
Cumbrian Cottages
t (01228) 599960
e enquiries@cumbrian-cottages.co.uk
w cumbrian-cottages.co.uk

Ullswater House ★★★★
Self Catering
Cumbrian Cottages
t (01228) 599960
e enquiries@cumbrian-cottages.co.uk
w cumbrian-cottages.co.uk

Whinny Brow ★★★
Self Catering
Cumbrian Cottages
t (01228) 599960
e enquiries@cumbrian-cottages.co.uk
w cumbrian-cottages.co.uk

WABERTHWAITE
Cumbria

Row Farm Cottage ★★★
Self Catering
Cumbrian Cottages
t (01228) 599960
e enquiries@cumbrian-cottages.co.uk
w cumbrian-cottages.co.uk

WADDINGTON
Lancashire

Hedgehog Cottage ★★★★
Self Catering
t (01200) 429557
e stephen_tasker@btinternet.com
w hedgehogcottage.co.uk

Orchard Cottages ★★★★★
Self Catering
Contact: Ms Helen Warburton
t (01200) 428501
e info@orchardcottages.co.uk
w orchardcottages.co.uk

WADSWORTH
West Yorkshire

Hebden Bridge Holiday Cottages ★★★-★★★★
Self Catering
Contact: Karen Clitheroe
t (01422) 844021
e darren.clithero@btinternet.com
w allswellfarmholidaycottages.co.uk

WAITBY
Cumbria

Waitby Longbarn ★★★★
Self Catering
Cumbrian Cottages
t (01228) 599960
e enquiries@cumbrian-cottages.co.uk
w cumbrian-cottages.co.uk

Waitby School ★★★★★
Self Catering
Cumbrian Cottages
t (01228) 599960
e enquiries@cumbrian-cottages.co.uk
w cumbrian-cottages.co.uk

WALL
Northumberland

Kiln Rigg ★★★ *Self Catering*
Contact: Mr & Mrs Ian & Lisa Burrows
t (01434) 681018
e enquires@kilnrigg.co.uk
w kilnrigg.co.uk

WALLASEY
Merseyside

Captains View ★★★★
Self Catering
t 07803 084197
w http://freespace.virgin.net/marilyn.pantoni/

Smugglers Way ★★★★
Self Catering
t (0151) 513 0709
w wirralcoastproperties.co.uk

WAREN MILL
Northumberland

2 The Maltings ★★★★
Self Catering
Contact: Mr Kiran Hingorani
t 07813 465922
e warenmill@yahoo.co.uk
w warenmill.biz

Budle Bay Penthouse ★★★★★ *Self Catering*
Northumberland Coastal Retreats
t (0191) 285 1272
e info@coastalretreats.co.uk
w coastalretreats.co.uk

Cove Cottage, Waren Mill ★★★★ *Self Catering*
Contact: Mrs Anne Lawrence
t (0191) 488 6414 & 07932 795251
e enquiries@northumberland-coast-holidays.co.uk
w northumberland-coast-holidays.co.uk

Eider Cottage ★★★★
Self Catering
Contact: Mrs Turnbull
t (01668) 214494
e theturnbulls2k@btinternet.com
w bamburghboltholes.co.uk

WARENFORD
Northumberland

1 North Farm ★★★
Self Catering
Northumberland Cottages
t (01665) 589434
e enquiries@northumberlandcottages.com
w northumberlandcottages.co.uk

Etive Cottage ★★★★
Self Catering
Contact: Mr & Mrs David & Jan Thompson
t (01668) 213233
e janet.thompson1@homecall.co.uk

WARK
Northumberland

Northumberland Cottage
Rating Applied For
Self Catering
Contact: Mr Andrew Tilley
t (01434) 230970
e andrew@atilley5.orangehome.co.uk

Rainbow Cottage ★★★
Self Catering
Contact: Mrs Susan Thorkildsen
t 07974 870622
e winston44@sky.com

Riverside Cottage ★★★
Self Catering
Contact: Mrs Stella Jackson
t (0191) 487 6531
e jackson.s9@sky.com

Roses Bower ★★★★
Self Catering
Contact: Mr & Mrs Lewis and Susan Watson
Roses Bower Farm
t (01434) 230779 & 07710 995966
e info@roses-bower.co.uk
w roses-bower.co.uk

WARKWORTH
Northumberland

Birling Vale ★★★
Self Catering
Contact: Mrs Janet Brewis
t (01665) 575222

Buston Farm Holiday Cottages ★★★★
Self Catering
Contact: Mrs Jo Leiper
t (01661) 881506
e stay@buston.co.uk
w buston.co.uk

Coquet Cottage ★★★★
Self Catering
Contact: Mrs Barbara Jean Purvis
t (01670) 786088 & 07731 883657
e fenwickpurvis@virgin.net
w northumbria-cottages.co.uk

The Loft ★★★★
Self Catering
Contact: Mrs Marie Wraith
t (01665) 711389

Magdalene House ★★★★
Self Catering
Northumberland Cottages
t (01665) 589434
e enquiries@northumberlandcottages.com
w northumberlandcottages.co.uk

Mahonia Lodge ★★★★
Self Catering
Contact: Mr Paul Smith
t (01325) 717906
e bookings@mahonialodge.co.uk
w mahonia-lodge.co.uk

Old Barns Farmhouse Holiday Cottage ★★★★
Self Catering
Contact: Mrs Jane Wilkes
t (01665) 713427
e jane.wilkes@virgin.net
w oldbarnsholidaycottage.co.uk

Rebecca House ★★★★★
Self Catering
Contact: Ms Sue Fenlon
t (01665) 830430
e suefenlon@hotmail.com
w rebeccahouse.co.uk

Riverview Cottage ★★★★★
Self Catering
Contact: Mr & Mrs Paul & Helen Skuse
t (01454) 775441
e pmskuse@hotmail.com
w riverview-warkworth.co.uk

The Shieling ★★★★
Self Catering
Contact: Mrs Carole Ann Whitefield
t (0191) 258 4347
e holidayshieling@hotmail.com
w holiday-shieling.co.uk

Southmede Cottage ★★★★
Self Catering
Contact: Mr & Mrs Mike & Carol Smith
t (01665) 711360
e info@southmede.co.uk
w southmede.co.uk

Tall Trees House ★★★★★
Self Catering
w coquetcottages.co.uk

Turnstone ★★★★
Self Catering
Contact: Mrs Sarah Morey
t (01525) 840391
e philipandsarah@hotmail.com
w turnstoneholidayhome.co.uk

Water's Edge ★★★★★
Self Catering
Contact: Mrs Mary Cooper
t (0131) 228 4309
w watersedge-warkworth.co.uk

Waterside ★★★★★
Self Catering
Contact: Mrs Julie Ringland
t (0191) 388 3752
e julieringland@btinternet.com
w coquetcottages.co.uk

Well Cottage ★★★★
Self Catering
Northumberland Cottages
t (01665) 589434
e enquiries@northumberlandcottages.com
w northumberlandcottages.co.uk

WARTON
Lancashire

Culdene, Carnforth ★★★★
Self Catering
Contact: Mrs Margaret Holmes
t (01524) 735788
e culdene@btinternet.com
w culdene.co.uk

WARWICK-ON-EDEN
Cumbria

Eva's Cottage ★★★★★
Self Catering
Cumbrian Cottages
t (01228) 599960
e enquiries@cumbrian-cottages.co.uk
w cumbrian-cottages.co.uk

Warwick Hall
★★★★-★★★★★
Self Catering
Contact: Val Marriner
t (01228) 561546
w warwickhall.org

WASDALE
Cumbria

Bleng Barn, Gosforth
★★★★ *Self Catering*
Contact: Thomas Ostle
Bleng Farms
t 07801 862237 & 07775 512918
e info@blengfarms.co.uk
w blengfarms.co.uk

WATER YEAT
Cumbria

Bee Bole House/The Farmstead/The Garden Cottage/Horseshoe Cottage
★★★★ *Self Catering*
The Coppermines & Coniston Lakes Cottages
t (015394) 41765
w coppermines.co.uk

WATERHEAD
Cumbria

Low Brow Barn ★★★★★
Self Catering
Lakelovers
t (015394) 88855
e bookings@lakelovers.co.uk
w lakelovers.co.uk

Romney Grange ★★★★
Self Catering
Lakelovers
t (015394) 88855
e bookings@lakelovers.co.uk
w lakelovers.co.uk

WATERMILLOCK-ON-ULLSWATER
Cumbria

Beauthorn Cottage ★★★
Self Catering
Hideaways
t (015394) 42435
e bookings@lakeland-hideaways.co.uk
w lakedistrictholidays.net

The Library ★★★★
Self Catering
Cumbrian Cottages
t (01228) 599960
e enquiries@cumbrian-cottages.co.uk
w cumbrian-cottages.co.uk

Loadpot ★★★★
Self Catering
Lakeland Cottage Holidays
t (017687) 76065
e info@lakelandcottages.co.uk
w lakelandcottages.co.uk

Mellfell Cottages, Mellfell House Farm, Watermillock-on-Ullswater ★★★
Self Catering
Contact: Ben & Diane Goddard
Mellfell House Farm
t (017684) 86295
e ben@mellfell.co.uk
w mellfell.co.uk

Middlegate ★★★
Self Catering
Cumbrian Cottages
t (01228) 599960
e enquiries@cumbrian-cottages.co.uk
w cumbrian-cottages.co.uk

The Old Bothy ★★★★
Self Catering
Cumbrian Cottages
t (01228) 599960
e enquiries@cumbrian-cottages.co.uk
w cumbrian-cottages.co.uk

The Quiet Site
Rating Applied For
Self Catering
e info@thequietsite.co.uk
w thequietsite.co.uk

WELBURN
North Yorkshire

Castle View ★★★
Self Catering
Contact: Michael Cockerill
t (01653) 618344

WELL
North Yorkshire

Spinners ★★★★
Self Catering
Yorkshire Cottages
t (01228) 406701
e enquiries@yorkshire-cottages.info
w yorkshire-cottages.info

WELTON
Cumbria

Green View Lodges
Rating Applied For
Self Catering
Contact: Colin Oliver
t (01697) 476230
e info@green-view-lodges.com
w green-view-lodges.com

Stay Deansgate Apartments
★★★★ *Serviced Apartments*
t (01697) 476254
w staydeansgate.co.uk

WENNINGTON
Lancashire

Easter Cottage ★★★★
Self Catering
Contact: Mrs Jenny Herd
t (01524) 221690
e info@easter-cottage.net
w easter-cottage.net

WENSLEY STATION
North Yorkshire

The Waiting Rooms ★★★★
Self Catering
Country Hideaways
t (01969) 663559
e info@countryhideaways.co.uk
w countryhideaways.co.uk

WENSLEYDALE
North Yorkshire

Clematis Cottage ★★★★
Self Catering
Contact: Mrs Anne Fawcett
Mile House Farm Country Cottages
t (01969) 667481
e milehousefarm@hotmail.com
w wensleydale.uk.com

WEST AYTON
North Yorkshire

Endeavour Loft Apartment
★★★★ *Self Catering*
Contact: Mr Paul Wicks
t (01723) 871028
e spwicks@btinternet.com
w whitbycottages.com

The Gardener's Cottage
★★★★ *Self Catering*
Yorkshire Cottages
t (01228) 406701
e enquiries@yorkshire-cottages.info
w yorkshire-cottages.info

WEST BURTON
North Yorkshire

Cherry Tree Cottage ★★★★
Self Catering
Country Hideaways
t (01969) 663559
e info@countryhideaways.co.uk
w countryhideaways.co.uk

First Floor Apartment, The Mill ★★★ *Self Catering*
Country Hideaways
t (01969) 663559
e info@countryhideaways.co.uk
w countryhideaways.co.uk

The Garden Level Apartment ★★★
Self Catering
Country Hideaways
t (01969) 663559
e info@countryhideaways.co.uk
w countryhideaways.co.uk

Grange House ★★★★
Self Catering
Contact: Zoe Mort
t (01969) 663641
e info@grangehouse.co.uk
w grangehouse.co.uk

Green Bank ★★★
Self Catering
Country Hideaways
t (01969) 663559
e info@countryhideaways.co.uk
w countryhideaways.co.uk

Green Gables Flat ★★★
Self Catering
Country Hideaways
t (01969) 663559
e info@countryhideaways.co.uk
w countryhideaways.co.uk

The Ground Floor Apartment, The Mill ★★★★
Self Catering
Country Hideaways
t (01969) 663559
e info@countryhideaways.co.uk
w countryhideaways.co.uk

Hill Top Cottage ★★★★
Self Catering
Country Hideaways
t (01969) 663559
e info@countryhideaways.co.uk
w countryhideaways.co.uk

Inglenook Cottage – Cottage in the Dales
★★★★-★★★★★
Self Catering
Contact: Diane Howarth
Cottage in the Dales
t (01256) 883633
e stay@cottageinthedales.co.uk
w cottageinthedales.co.uk

Ivy Cottage ★★★
Self Catering
Country Hideaways
t (01969) 663559
e info@countryhideaways.co.uk
w countryhideaways.co.uk

Jesmond Cottage ★★★
Self Catering
Country Hideaways
t (01969) 663559
e info@countryhideaways.co.uk
w countryhideaways.co.uk

Penny Farthings ★★★
Self Catering
Country Hideaways
t (01969) 663559
e info@countryhideaways.co.uk
w countryhideaways.co.uk

Studio Apartment, The Mill
★★★ *Self Catering*
Country Hideaways
t (01969) 663559
e info@countryhideaways.co.uk
w countryhideaways.co.uk

WEST HESLERTON
North Yorkshire

Whin Moor Cottage ★★★
Self Catering
Contact: Barbara Pease
t (01944) 738632
e juliestephenpeasewhinmoorfarm@btinternet.com
w dalesholcot.com

WEST KIRBY
Merseyside

Abbey House – Holiday/Business Apartments
★★★★ *Self Catering*
t (0151) 625 7259
w abbeyhousewestkirby.co.uk

Herons Well
Rating Applied For
Self Catering
Contact: Mrs Glynis Lavelle
t (0151) 625 1401
e glynis.lavelle@btinternet.com
w heronswell.co.uk

WEST WITTON
North Yorkshire

1 Chestnut Garth ★★★
Self Catering
Sykes Cottages
t (01244) 345700
e info@sykescottages.co.uk
w sykescottages.co.uk

Coachman's Loft ★★★★
Self Catering
Contact: Ms Carol Grieve
t (01969) 622226
w coachmansloft.co.uk

George's Cottage ★★★★
Self Catering
Contact: Ms Gill Bishop
t (01325) 243763
e agbishop46@aol.com
w yorkshiredalesholiday cottage.org.uk

Swallows Rest ★★★
Self Catering
Contact: Ingrid Arnold
t (01969) 624303
e holidaycottage2004@yahoo.com
w arnoldsholidaycottages.com

WESTWARD
Cumbria

Clea Hall ★★★★
Self Catering
Cumbrian Cottages
t (01228) 599960
e enquiries@cumbrian-cottages.co.uk
w cumbrian-cottages.co.uk

WETHERAL
Cumbria

Geltsdale ★★★★★
Self Catering
Lakes Cottage Holidays
t (01228) 591555
e info@lakescottageholiday.co.uk
w lakescottageholiday.co.uk

Hall Moor Court ★★★★
Self Catering
Lakes Cottage Holidays
t (01228) 591555
e info@lakescottageholiday.co.uk
w lakescottageholiday.co.uk

Sarah's Cottage ★★★★
Self Catering
Lakes Cottage Holidays
t (01228) 591555
e info@lakescottageholiday.co.uk
w lakescottageholiday.co.uk

WETHERBY
West Yorkshire

Chestnut Chase, Bramham
★★★ *Self Catering*
Contact: Chris Gibson
t (01937) 845781
e bob@bramham.f9.co.uk

WHALE
Cumbria

Whale Farm Cottage
★★★★★ *Self Catering*
Contact: Lyn Page
Lowther Estate Cottages
t (01931) 712577
e lyn.page@lowther.co.uk
w lowther.co.uk

WHALLEY
Lancashire

Tabgha ★★★ *Self Catering*
t (01200) 420101
e info@holidaycotts.co.uk
w holidaycotts.co.uk

WHASHTON
North Yorkshire

Mount Pleasant Farm
★★★★-★★★★★
Self Catering
Contact: Mrs Pittaway
t (01748) 822784

WHINFELL
Cumbria

Agnes Cottage ★★★★
Self Catering
Contact: Kerry Darbishire
t (01539) 824670
e stephen@stephen-darbishire.com
w agnescottage.co.uk

Pike Hill Barn ★★★★
Self Catering
Cumbrian Cottages
t (01228) 599960
e enquiries@cumbrian-cottages.co.uk
w cumbrian-cottages.co.uk

Topthorn Holiday Cottages
★★★ *Self Catering*
Contact: Mrs Diane Barnes
t (01539) 824252
e info.barnes@btconnect.com
w topthorn.com

WHITBY
North Yorkshire

1 Metropole Court ★★★★
Self Catering
Whitby Holiday Cottages
t (01947) 603010
e enquiries@whitbyholidaycottages.net
w whitbyholidaycottages.net

108 Upgang Lane ★★★
Self Catering
Whitby Holiday Cottages
t (01947) 603010
e enquiries@whitbyholidaycottages.net
w whitbyholidaycottages.net

14 Waterloo Place ★★
Self Catering
Whitby Holiday Cottages
t (01947) 603010
e enquiries@whitbyholidaycottages.net
w whitbyholidaycottages.net

15 Bagdale Court ★★★★
Self Catering
Whitby Holiday Cottages
t (01947) 603010
e enquiries@whitbyholidaycottages.net
w whitbyholidaycottages.net

16 Bagdale Court ★★★★
Self Catering
Whitby Holiday Cottages
t (01947) 603010
e enquiries@whitbyholidaycottages.net
w whitbyholidaycottages.net

2 High Stakesby Cottages
★★★★ *Self Catering*
Whitby Holiday Cottages
t (01947) 603010
e enquiries@whitbyholidaycottages.net
w whitbyholidaycottages.net

53 Cliff Street ★★★★
Self Catering
Contact: Denis & Janet Lockwood
t (01430) 810663
e denis@denislockwood.freeserve.co.uk

7 Henrietta Street ★★★
Self Catering
Contact: Mr Usher
t (01947) 605868

Abbey View ★★★★
Self Catering
Whitby Holiday Cottages
t (01947) 603010
e enquiries@whitbyholidaycottages.net
w whitbyholidaycottages.net

Abrahams Quay ★★★
Self Catering
Whitby Holiday Cottages
t (01947) 603010
e enquiries@whitbyholidaycottages.net
w whitbyholidaycottages.net

Acacia House ★★★
Self Catering
Whitby Holiday Cottages
t (01947) 603010
e enquiries@whitbyholidaycottages.net
w whitbyholidaycottages.net

Adventure Cottage
★★★★★ *Self Catering*
Contact: M Ainsworth-Hickman
t (01783) 760844
e hckmmic@aol.com

Allum Garth Cottage
★★★★ *Self Catering*
Contact: Barbara Tyerman
t (01947) 810450
e barbara@partridgenestfarm.com
w partridgenestfarm.com

Ambler Mews ★★★
Self Catering
Whitby Holiday Cottages
t (01947) 603010
e enquiries@whitbyholidaycottages.net
w whitbyholidaycottages.net

Ammonite Apartments
★★★★ *Self Catering*
Contact: Mrs Lindsey Ebbs
t (01947) 820497
e enquiries@ammonite-apartments.co.uk
w ammonite-apartments.co.uk

April Cottage ★★★
Self Catering
Whitby Holiday Cottages
t (01947) 603010
e enquiries@whitbyholidaycottages.net
w whitbyholidaycottages.net

At Long Last ★★★
Self Catering
Whitby Holiday Cottages
t (01947) 603010
e enquiries@whitbyholidaycottages.net
w whitbyholidaycottages.net

Beckside Holiday Cottage
★★★★ *Self Catering*
Contact: Kathryn Hogarth
t (01947) 897259
e jhnhogarth@aol.com

Bentley Cottages ★★★
Self Catering
Whitby Holiday Cottages
t (01947) 603010
e enquiries@whitbyholidaycottages.net
w whitbyholidaycottages.net

Berry Banks Cottage ★★★★
Self Catering
Yorkshire Cottages
t (01228) 406701
e enquiries@yorkshire-cottages.info
w yorkshire-cottages.info

Bolthole Cottage ★★★
Self Catering
Contact: Kaaren Noble
t (01947) 880063
e kaaren@noble47.freeserve.co.uk
w boltholecottage.co.uk

Borough House ★★★★
Self Catering
Contact: Julie Besford
Julie Besford (Sole Trader)
t (01430) 430963
e jdgreenhalgh@tiscali.co.uk

Bosun's Cottage ★★★
Self Catering
Contact: Susie Sykes
t (01947) 606309
e susie_sykes@btinternet.com

Bramblewick Cottage
★★★★ *Self Catering*
Yorkshire Cottages
t (01228) 406701
e enquiries@yorkshire-cottages.info
w yorkshire-cottages.info

Briarway ★★★★
Self Catering
Whitby Holiday Cottages
t (01947) 603010
e enquiries@whitbyholidaycottages.net
w whitbyholidaycottages.net

Broadings Farm Cottages
★★★★ *Self Catering*
t (01947) 601542
w broadingsfarmcottages.co.uk

The Cabin ★★ *Self Catering*
Whitby Holiday Cottages
t (01947) 603010
e enquiries@whitbyholidaycottages.net
w whitbyholidaycottages.net

Calico Cottage ★★★
Self Catering
Whitby Holiday Cottages
t (01947) 603010
e enquiries@whitbyholidaycottages.net
w whitbyholidaycottages.net

Calypso Cottage ★★
Self Catering
Whitby Holiday Cottages
t (01947) 603010
e enquiries@whitbyholidaycottages.net
w whitbyholidaycottages.net

Captain Cook's Haven
★★★-★★★★ *Self Catering*
Contact: Anne Barrowman
t (01947) 893573
w whitbyholidayhomes.co.uk

The Captains Hall ★★★
Self Catering
Whitby Holiday Cottages
t (01947) 603010
e enquiries@whitbyholidaycottages.net
w whitbyholidaycottages.net

The Captains View ★★★
Self Catering
Whitby Holiday Cottages
t (01947) 603010
e enquiries@whitbyholidaycottages.net
w whitbyholidaycottages.net

Carlton House Holiday Accommodation
★★-★★★★ *Self Catering*
Contact: Vicki Clayton
t (01947) 602868
e info@carltonhouseapartments.co.uk
w carltonhouseapartments.co.uk

Casa Romantica ★★★
Self Catering
Whitby Holiday Cottages
t (01947) 603010
e enquiries@whitbyholidaycottages.net
w whitbyholidaycottages.net

Castle View
Rating Applied For
Self Catering
Whitby Holiday Cottages
t (01947) 603010
e enquiries@whitbyholidaycottages.net
w whitbyholidaycottages.net

Church Cottage ★★★
Self Catering
Whitby Holiday Cottages
t (01947) 603010
e enquiries@whitbyholidaycottages.net
w whitbyholidaycottages.net

Clematis Cottage ★★
Self Catering
Whitby Holiday Cottages
t (01947) 603010
e enquiries@whitbyholidaycottages.net
w whitbyholidaycottages.net

Cliff House ★★ *Self Catering*
Contact: Pat Beale
Cliff House and Ryedale House
t (01947) 810534
w cliffhousewhitby.co.uk

Coble Cottage ★★★
Self Catering
Whitby Holiday Cottages
t (01947) 603010
e enquiries@whitbyholidaycottages.net
w whitbyholidaycottages.net

Cooks View ★★★★
Self Catering
Yorkshire Cottages
t (01228) 406701
e enquiries@yorkshire-cottages.info
w yorkshire-cottages.info

Cormorant View ★★★
Self Catering
Whitby Holiday Cottages
t (01947) 603010
e enquiries@whitbyholidaycottages.net
w whitbyholidaycottages.net

The Cottage ★★★
Self Catering
Whitby Holiday Cottages
t (01947) 603010
e enquiries@whitbyholidaycottages.net
w whitbyholidaycottages.net

Crows Nest Holidays ★★★
Self Catering
Contact: Mr Eric Tayler
t (01642) 492144

The Den ★★★ *Self Catering*
Whitby Holiday Cottages
t (01947) 603010
e enquiries@whitbyholidaycottages.net
w whitbyholidaycottages.net

Discovery Accommodation
★★★★ *Self Catering*
Contact: Pamela Gilmore
t (01947) 821598
w discoveryaccommodation.com

Dreaming Duck ★★★★
Self Catering
Yorkshire Cottages
t (01228) 406701
e enquiries@yorkshire-cottages.info
w yorkshire-cottages.info

East Cliff Cottages ★★★
Self Catering
Contact: Mrs C. J. Thornton
t (01274) 520392
e eastcliffcottages@btinternet.com
w eastcliffcottages.co.uk

Elizabeth House Apartments
★★★-★★★★ *Self Catering*
Contact: Mrs M. Croft
t (01947) 604168
e info@sandpiperhouse.wanadoo.co.uk
w elizabethhousewhitby.co.uk

Endeavour Cottage ★★★
Self Catering
Whitby Holiday Cottages
t (01947) 603010
e enquiries@whitbyholidaycottages.net
w whitbyholidaycottages.net

Esk Riverview ★★★★
Self Catering
Whitby Holiday Cottages
t (01947) 603010
e enquiries@whitbyholidaycottages.net
w whitbyholidaycottages.net

Esk View Cottage
Rating Applied For
Self Catering
Whitby Holiday Cottages
t (01947) 603010
e enquiries@whitbyholidaycottages.net
w whitbyholidaycottages.net

Eskcape ★★★★
Self Catering
Yorkshire Cottages
t (01228) 406701
e enquiries@yorkshire-cottages.info
w yorkshire-cottages.info

Eskside ★★★ *Self Catering*
Whitby Holiday Cottages
t (01947) 603010
e enquiries@whitbyholidaycottages.net
w whitbyholidaycottages.net

Estuary View Cottage
★★★★ *Self Catering*
Contact: Mr & Mrs Jack & Anne Cooper
t (01947) 604213
e cooperhouse14@btinternet.com
w estuaryviewcottage.co.uk

Explorers Rest ★★★★
Self Catering
Whitby Holiday Cottages
t (01947) 603010
e enquiries@whitbyholidaycottages.net
w whitbyholidaycottages.net

Fawcet House ★★★★
Self Catering
Contact: Carol Ruff
t (01947) 603760
e fawcethouse@btconnect.com
w fawcethouse.co.uk

Fayvan Holiday Apartments
★★★★ *Self Catering*
Contact: Benita & Michael Nicholson
t (01947) 604813
e fayvan.apartments@btinternet.com
w fayvan.co.uk

Fishermans Cottage ★★
Self Catering
Whitby Holiday Cottages
t (01947) 603010
e enquiries@whitbyholidaycottages.net
w whitbyholidaycottages.net

Fishermans Warehouse
★★★★ *Self Catering*
Whitby Holiday Cottages
t (01947) 603010
e enquiries@whitbyholidaycottages.net
w whitbyholidaycottages.net

Flat 1 Devonian ★★★
Self Catering
Whitby Holiday Cottages
t (01947) 603010
e enquiries@whitbyholidaycottages.net
w whitbyholidaycottages.net

Flat 2 Devonian ★★★
Self Catering
Whitby Holiday Cottages
t (01947) 603010
e enquiries@whitbyholidaycottages.net
w whitbyholidaycottages.net

Garden Court Apartment
★★★ *Self Catering*
Whitby Holiday Cottages
t (01947) 603010
e enquiries@whitbyholidaycottages.net
w whitbyholidaycottages.net

Grange Farm Holiday Cottage ★★★★ *Self Catering*
Contact: D Hooning
t (01947) 881080
e info@grangefarm.net
w grangefarm.net

Graymount House ★★★★
Self Catering
Whitby Holiday Cottages
t (01947) 603010
e enquiries@whitbyholidaycottages.net
w whitbyholidaycottages.net

Harbour Heights ★★★★
Self Catering
Yorkshire Cottages
t (01228) 406701
e enquiries@yorkshire-cottages.info
w yorkshire-cottages.info

Harbour Lights ★★★★
Self Catering
Whitby Holiday Cottages
t (01947) 603010
e enquiries@whitbyholidaycottages.net
w whitbyholidaycottages.net

Harbour View ★★★★
Self Catering
Yorkshire Cottages
t (01228) 406701
e enquiries@yorkshire-cottages.info
w yorkshire-cottages.info

Harbour View ★★★★
Self Catering
Whitby Holiday Cottages
t (01947) 603010
e enquiries@whitbyholidaycottages.net
w whitbyholidaycottages.net

Harbourside Apartments
★★★ *Self Catering*
Whitby Holiday Cottages
t (01947) 603010
e enquiries@whitbyholidaycottages.net
w whitbyholidaycottages.net

The Haven ★★★★
Self Catering
Whitby Holiday Cottages
t (01947) 603010
e enquiries@whitbyholidaycottages.net
w whitbyholidaycottages.net

Haven Cottage ★★★
Self Catering
Whitby Holiday Cottages
t (01947) 603010
e enquiries@whitbyholidaycottages.net
w whitbyholidaycottages.net

Herons Reach ★★★★
Self Catering
Whitby Holiday Cottages
t (01947) 603010
e enquiries@whitbyholidaycottages.net
w whitbyholidaycottages.net

The Hideaway ★★★
Self Catering
Whitby Holiday Cottages
t (01947) 603010
e enquiries@whitbyholidaycottages.net
w whitbyholidaycottages.net

Hideaway Cottage ★★★
Self Catering
Whitby Holiday Cottages
t (01947) 603010
e enquiries@whitbyholidaycottages.net
w whitbyholidaycottages.net

Hightrees Garden Apartment ★★★★
Self Catering
Contact: Sarah Clancy
t (01947) 601926
e seclancy@yahoo.co.uk

Huffin Cottage ★★★
Self Catering
Whitby Holiday Cottages
t (01947) 603010
e enquiries@whitbyholidaycottages.net
w whitbyholidaycottages.net

Inglenook Cottage ★★★
Self Catering
Whitby Holiday Cottages
t (01947) 603010
e enquiries@whitbyholidaycottages.net
w whitbyholidaycottages.net

Jacksons Cottage ★★★★
Self Catering
Whitby Holiday Cottages
t (01947) 603010
e enquiries@whitbyholidaycottages.net
w whitbyholidaycottages.net

Jet Apartment ★★★★
Self Catering
Whitby Holiday Cottages
t (01947) 603010
e enquiries@whitbyholidaycottages.net
w whitbyholidaycottages.net

Jet Cottage ★★★
Self Catering
Contact: Mrs Vanessa Hicking
Whitby Holiday Cottages
t (01947) 603010
e enquiries@whitby-cottages.co.uk
w whitby-cottages.co.uk

Kauri Cottage ★★★★
Self Catering
Whitby Holiday Cottages
t (01947) 603010
e enquiries@whitbyholidaycottages.net
w whitbyholidaycottages.net

Khyber Lodge ★★★
Self Catering
Contact: Mrs J Charlton
t (01947) 811531
e julie@holidayflat.co.uk

Kittiwake Cottage ★★★★
Self Catering
Whitby Holiday Cottages
t (01947) 603010
e enquiries@whitbyholidaycottages.net
w whitbyholidaycottages.net

Ladybird Cottage ★★★
Self Catering
Whitby Holiday Cottages
t (01947) 603010
e enquiries@whitbyholidaycottages.net
w whitbyholidaycottages.net

The Lair ★★★ *Self Catering*
Whitby Holiday Cottages
t (01947) 603010
e enquiries@whitbyholidaycottages.net
w whitbyholidaycottages.net

The Lamp House ★★★★
Self Catering
Whitby Holiday Cottages
t (01947) 603010
e enquiries@whitbyholidaycottages.net
w whitbyholidaycottages.net

Lantern Cottage ★★★★
Self Catering
Whitby Holiday Cottages
t (01947) 603010
e enquiries@whitbyholidaycottages.net
w whitbyholidaycottages.net

The Lobster Pot ★★★
Self Catering
Whitby Holiday Cottages
t (01947) 603010
e enquiries@whitbyholidaycottages.net
w whitbyholidaycottages.net

The Loft ★★★★
Self Catering
Whitby Holiday Cottages
t (01947) 603010
e enquiries@whitbyholidaycottages.net
w whitbyholidaycottages.net

The Lord Nelson ★★★
Self Catering
Whitby Holiday Cottages
t (01947) 603010
e enquiries@whitbyholidaycottages.net
w whitbyholidaycottages.net

Lupine Cottage ★★★
Self Catering
Whitby Holiday Cottages
t (01947) 603010
e enquiries@whitbyholidaycottages.net
w whitbyholidaycottages.net

March Court ★★★★
Self Catering
Whitby Holiday Cottages
t (01947) 603010
e enquiries@whitbyholidaycottages.net
w whitbyholidaycottages.net

Margherita Cottage ★★★★
Self Catering
Contact: Amy Wilson
t (01947) 825400
e info@margheritacottage.co.uk
w margheritacottage.co.uk

Marina Cottage ★★★
Self Catering
Whitby Holiday Cottages
t (01947) 603010
e enquiries@whitbyholidaycottages.net
w whitbyholidaycottages.net

Mariner Cottage ★★★
Self Catering
Whitby Holiday Cottages
t (01947) 603010
e enquiries@whitbyholidaycottages.net
w whitbyholidaycottages.net

Maritimus ★★★★
Self Catering
Whitby Holiday Cottages
t (01947) 603010
e enquiries@whitbyholidaycottages.net
w whitbyholidaycottages.net

Metropole Towers ★★★
Self Catering
Whitby Holiday Cottages
t (01947) 603010
e enquiries@whitbyholidaycottages.net
w whitbyholidaycottages.net

Mollymiles Cottage ★★★★
Self Catering
Whitby Holiday Cottages
t (01947) 603010
e enquiries@whitbyholidaycottages.net
w whitbyholidaycottages.net

Moor Peep ★★★★
Self Catering
Whitby Holiday Cottages
t (01947) 603010
e enquiries@whitbyholidaycottages.net
w whitbyholidaycottages.net

The Moorings ★★★★
Self Catering
Whitby Holiday Cottages
t (01947) 603010
e enquiries@whitbyholidaycottages.net
w whitbyholidaycottages.net

Mount Galleries Cottages ★★★★ *Self Catering*
Contact: Peter & Kath Weatherill
t (01947) 605508
e mountgalcot@beeb.net
w mountgalleriescottages.co.uk

Old Boatman's Shelter ★★★★ *Self Catering*
Contact: Alison Halidu
t 07876 173319
e info@oldboatmansshelter.co.uk
w oldboatmansshelter.co.uk

Old Brewery Cottage ★★★★ *Self Catering*
Whitby Holiday Cottages
t (01947) 603010
e enquiries@whitbyholidaycottages.net
w whitbyholidaycottages.net

The Old Counting House ★★★ *Self Catering*
Whitby Holiday Cottages
t (01947) 603010
e enquiries@whitbyholidaycottages.net
w whitbyholidaycottages.net

The Old Granary ★★★★
Self Catering
Contact: Mrs Jackie Richardson
t (01947) 893331

Old Lighthouse ★★★
Self Catering
Whitby Holiday Cottages
t (01947) 603010
e enquiries@whitbyholidaycottages.net
w whitbyholidaycottages.net

The Old Sweet Shop ★★★★
Self Catering
Whitby Holiday Cottages
t (01947) 603010
e enquiries@whitbyholidaycottages.net
w whitbyholidaycottages.net

Olive Tree Cottage ★★★★
Self Catering
Whitby Holiday Cottages
t (01947) 603010
e enquiries@whitbyholidaycottages.net
w whitbyholidaycottages.net

Pantiles ★★★★ *Self Catering*
Contact: Peter & Alison Lawson
t (0131) 446 0225
e pantileswhitby@blueyonder.co.uk
w pantileswhitby.pwp.blueyonder.co.uk

Park View ★★★★
Self Catering
Whitby Holiday Cottages
t (01947) 603010
e enquiries@whitbyholidaycottages.net
w whitbyholidaycottages.net

Raygill Cottage ★★★
Self Catering
Contact: John Knell
t (01423) 566280

The Red House ★★★
Self Catering
Whitby Holiday Cottages
t (01947) 603010
e enquiries@whitbyholidaycottages.net
w whitbyholidaycottages.net

Riverside ★★★★
Self Catering
Whitby Holiday Cottages
t (01947) 603010
e enquiries@whitbyholidaycottages.net
w whitbyholidaycottages.net

Riverside Retreat ★★★★
Self Catering
Whitby Holiday Cottages
t (01947) 603010
e enquiries@whitbyholidaycottages.net
w whitbyholidaycottages.net

Riverside View ★★★★
Self Catering
Whitby Holiday Cottages
t (01947) 603010
e enquiries@whitbyholidaycottages.net
w whitbyholidaycottages.net

Rockton House ★★★★
Self Catering
Whitby Holiday Cottages
t (01947) 603010
e enquiries@whitbyholidaycottages.net
w whitbyholidaycottages.net

Rusty Cottage ★★★★
Self Catering
Whitby Holiday Cottages
t (01947) 603010
e enquiries@whitbyholidaycottages.net
w whitbyholidaycottages.net

Sailing By ★★★ *Self Catering*
Whitby Holiday Cottages
t (01947) 603010
e enquiries@whitbyholidaycottages.net
w whitbyholidaycottages.net

St John's Apartment ★★★★
Self Catering
Whitby Holiday Cottages
t (01947) 603010
e enquiries@whitbyholidaycottages.net
w whitbyholidaycottages.net

St Johns World ★★★★
Self Catering
Whitby Holiday Cottages
t (01947) 603010
e enquiries@whitbyholidaycottages.net
w whitbyholidaycottages.net

Saltwick House ★★★★
Self Catering
Whitby Holiday Cottages
t (01947) 603010
e enquiries@whitbyholidaycottages.net
w whitbyholidaycottages.net

Scoresby Cottage ★★★
Self Catering
Whitby Holiday Cottages
t (01947) 603010
e enquiries@whitbyholidaycottages.net
w whitbyholidaycottages.net

Sea Views Apartment
★★★★ *Self Catering*
Whitby Holiday Cottages
t (01947) 603010
e enquiries@whitbyholidaycottages.net
w whitbyholidaycottages.net

Seagull Cottage ★★★★
Self Catering
Whitby Holiday Cottages
t (01947) 603010
e enquiries@whitbyholidaycottages.net
w whitbyholidaycottages.net

Seascape Cottage ★★★
Self Catering
Whitby Holiday Cottages
t (01947) 603010
e enquiries@whitbyholidaycottages.net
w whitbyholidaycottages.net

Seashell Cottage ★★★★
Self Catering
Contact: Mr Clive Sykes
Sykes Cottages
t (01244) 345700
e info@sykescottages.co.uk
w sykescottages.co.uk

Spiders Web ★★★
Self Catering
Whitby Holiday Cottages
t (01947) 603010
e enquiries@whitbyholidaycottages.net
w whitbyholidaycottages.net

Stable Cottage ★★★★
Self Catering
Contact: Mrs Sallie White
t (01287) 660064
e white.j@lineone.net
w stablecottage.net

Stable Cottage ★★★★
Self Catering
Contact: Martin Warner
t (01947) 602660
e info@sandfieldhousefarm.co.uk
w sandfieldhousefarm.co.uk

Starfish Accommodation
★★★★ *Self Catering*
Contact: Mrs Pam Gilmoree **e** info@discoveryaccommodation.com

Steps Cottage ★★★
Self Catering
Whitby Holiday Cottages
t (01947) 603010
e enquiries@whitbyholidaycottages.net
w whitbyholidaycottages.net

Streanaeshalch ★★★★
Self Catering
Contact: Ms Pauline Leat
Dales Holiday Cottages
t (01757) 630641
e randjbattersby@tiscali.co.uk
w holidaylettings.co.uk/rentals/whitby/51522

Suit's Us
Rating Applied For
Self Catering
Whitby Holiday Cottages
t (01947) 603010
e enquiries@whitbyholidaycottages.net
w whitbyholidaycottages.net

Swanning Off ★★★
Self Catering
Whitby Holiday Cottages
t (01947) 603010
e enquiries@whitbyholidaycottages.net
w whitbyholidaycottages.net

Swordfish Cottage ★★★★
Self Catering
Whitby Holiday Cottages
t (01947) 603010
e enquiries@whitbyholidaycottages.net
w whitbyholidaycottages.net

Thimble Cottage ★★
Self Catering
Contact: Mr & Mrs A.J. Hill
t (0114) 296 2383
e tony@tht.co.uk

Tidewatch ★★★★
Self Catering
Whitby Holiday Cottages
t (01947) 603010
e enquiries@whitbyholidaycottages.net
w whitbyholidaycottages.net

Time and Tide ★★★
Self Catering
Whitby Holiday Cottages
t (01947) 603010
e enquiries@whitbyholidaycottages.net
w whitbyholidaycottages.net

Top Floors ★★★
Self Catering
Whitby Holiday Cottages
t (01947) 603010
e enquiries@whitbyholidaycottages.net
w whitbyholidaycottages.net

The Two Belles ★★★
Self Catering
Whitby Holiday Cottages
t (01947) 603010
e enquiries@whitbyholidaycottages.net
w whitbyholidaycottages.net

Tyremans Return ★★★
Self Catering
Whitby Holiday Cottages
t (01947) 603010
e enquiries@whitbyholidaycottages.net
w whitbyholidaycottages.net

Walkers Cottage ★★★★
Self Catering
Contact: Allan & Suzanne Walker
t (01293) 885285
e a&swalker@walkerscottage.com
w walkerscottage.com

The Waterfront ★★★★
Self Catering
Whitby Holiday Cottages
t (01947) 603010
e enquiries@whitbyholidaycottages.net
w whitbyholidaycottages.net

The Watermark Apartments
★★★★ *Self Catering*
Contact: Mrs Julie Anne Purcell
t (01947) 841191
w thewatermark.net

Waters Edge ★★★★
Self Catering
Contact: Vanessa Hicking
Whitby Holiday Cootages
t (01947) 603010

Waterstead Cottage ★★★★
Self Catering
Yorkshire Cottages
t (01228) 406701
e enquiries@yorkshire-cottages.info
w yorkshire-cottages.info

Whitby Retreats – Grape Lane ★★★★ *Self Catering*
Contact: Mr & Mrs Nick & Emma Jaques
t (0113) 225 0798

White Cottages ★★★★
Self Catering
Whitby Holiday Cottages
t (01947) 603010
e enquiries@whitbyholidaycottages.net
w whitbyholidaycottages.net

White Horse Cottage ★★★
Self Catering
Contact: George & Steven Walker
t (01709) 367031

White Lodge ★★★★
Self Catering
Whitby Holiday Cottages
t (01947) 603010
e enquiries@whitbyholidaycottages.net
w whitbyholidaycottages.net

White Rose Holiday Cottages ★★★–★★★★
Self Catering
Contact: June Roberts
t (01947) 810763
e enquiries@whiterosecottages.co.uk
w whiterosecottages.co.uk

World's End Cottage ★★★
Self Catering
Contact: Ian & Teresa Cook
t 07757 162785

WHITE MOSS
Cumbria

Ladywood Lodge ★★★
Self Catering
Contact: Martin Morris
Martin Morris
t (015394) 88657
e eastbournela23@btconnect.com
w ladywood.ws

WHITEFIELD
Greater Manchester

The Standings ★★★★
Self Catering
t (0161) 796 1558

WHITEHAVEN
Cumbria

Rosmerta & Brighida Cottages ★★★★
Self Catering
Contact: David & Jane Saxon
Moresby Hall
t (01946) 696317
e info@moresbyhall.co.uk
w moresbyhall.co.uk

Snowdrop Cottage, Mountain View ★★★★
Self Catering
Contact: Mr Mark Warbrick
t (01946) 814194 & 07773 052960
e markwarbrick@aol.com
w tranquilakescottages.co.uk

Swallows Return and Owls Retreat ★★★★ *Self Catering*
Contact: James & Joyce Moore
t (01946) 64078
e mhc.moresby@virgin.net
w cottageguide.co.uk/moresby

WHITLEY BAY
Tyne and Wear

Seafront Apartments, Cullercoats ★★★–★★★★
Self Catering
Contact: Mrs Rosemary Webb
t 07977 203379
e stay@seafront.info
w seafront.info

Southcliff Apartments
★★★★ *Self Catering*
Contact: Mr Alan Heslington
t (0191) 251 3121
e southcliffapartments@theseaside.co.uk
w southcliffapartments.com

WHITTINGHAM
Northumberland

Bluebell Cottage & Granary Cottage ★★★★ *Self Catering*
Contact: Mrs Marian Charleton
t (01665) 574380
e stay@alnvalleycottages.co.uk
w alnvalleycottages.co.uk

The Lodge and the Gatehouse ★★★★
Self Catering
Contact: Mrs Jenny Sordy
t (01669) 630210
e jenny@alnhamfarm.co.uk
w alnhamfarm.co.uk

Rothlea Cottage ★★★
Self Catering
Northumberland Cottages
t (01665) 589434
e enquiries@northumberlandcottages.com
w northumberlandcottages.co.uk

WHITWELL-ON-THE-HILL
North Yorkshire

The Hay Loft ★★★
Self Catering
Contact: Anne Polley
t (01653) 618324
e anne.polley1@btopenworld.com

WHORLTON
Durham

Lavender Cottage ★★★★
Self Catering
Contact: Mr Anthony Johnson
t (01642) 483690
e enquiries@lavender-cottage.co.uk
w lavender-cottage.co.uk

WIGTON
Cumbria

Croftlands Court Self-Catering Cottages ★★★★
Self Catering
Cumbrian Cottages
t (01228) 599960
e enquiries@cumbrian-cottages.co.uk
w cumbrian-cottages.co.uk

Foxgloves, Greenrigg Farm
★★★★ *Self Catering*
Contact: Mr & Mrs J Kerr
t (01697) 342676
e kerr_greenrigg@hotmail.com
w foxglovescottagewigton.co.uk

Lane Head Apartment
★★★★ *Self Catering*
Contact: David Colborn
t (01697) 343888
e info@laneheadapartment.co.uk
w laneheadapartment.co.uk

Low Blaithwaite ★★★★
Self Catering
Cumbrian Cottages
t (01228) 599960
e enquiries@cumbrian-cottages.co.uk
w cumbrian-cottages.co.uk

Midtown House ★★★
Self Catering
Cumbrian Cottages
t (01228) 599960
e enquiries@cumbrian-cottages.co.uk
w cumbrian-cottages.co.uk

Rose Cottage ★★★
Self Catering
Cumbrian Cottages
t (01228) 599960
e enquiries@cumbrian-cottages.co.uk
w cumbrian-cottages.co.uk

South Bank ★★★★
Self Catering
Cumbrian Cottages
t (01228) 599960
e enquiries@cumbrian-cottages.co.uk
w cumbrian-cottages.co.uk

Westrigg ★★★★
Self Catering
Cumbrian Cottages
t (01228) 599960
e enquiries@cumbrian-cottages.co.uk
w cumbrian-cottages.co.uk

WILBERFOSS
East Riding of Yorkshire

Happy Days Lodges ★★★
Self Catering
Contact: Mrs Delia Kay
t 07734 972733
e info@happydayslodges.co.uk
w happydayslodges.co.uk

WILDBOARCLOUGH
Cheshire

Lower House Cottage ★★★
Self Catering
Contact: Mrs C Waller
t (01260) 227229
e sheeponthehill@aol.com

WILLASTON
Cheshire

Glenbrae ★★★★
Self Catering
t (01270) 567200

WILLINGTON
Cheshire

Delamere Cottage ★★★★
Self Catering
Contact: Mr Ernest Sidebotham
t (01829) 751628
e delamere.cottage@btinternet.com

WINCLE
Cheshire

Clough Brook Cottage
★★★★ *Self Catering*
Contact: Mr J Henshall
t (01260) 227209
e henshalls@btinternet.com
w allmeadows.co.uk/

WINDERMERE
Cumbria

1 Birchmill Cottages ★★★★
Self Catering
Lakelovers
t (015394) 88855
e bookings@lakelovers.co.uk
w lakelovers.co.uk

1 Brantfield House ★★★
Self Catering
Cumbrian Cottages
t (01228) 599960
e enquiries@cumbrian-cottages.co.uk
w cumbrian-cottages.co.uk

1 Old College Cottage
★★★★ *Self Catering*
Lakelovers
t (015394) 88855
e bookings@lakelovers.co.uk
w lakelovers.co.uk

11 Wansfell Lodge ★★★
Self Catering
Cumbrian Cottages
t (01228) 599960
e enquiries@cumbrian-cottages.co.uk
w cumbrian-cottages.co.uk

12 Meadowcroft ★★★★
Self Catering
Cumbrian Cottages
t (01228) 599960
e enquiries@cumbrian-cottages.co.uk
w cumbrian-cottages.co.uk

2 Hodge How ★★★
Self Catering
Lakeland Cottage Comapny
t (015395) 38180
e john@lakelandcottageco.com
w lakelandcottageco.com

2 Meadowcroft House
★★★★ *Self Catering*
Lakelovers
t (015394) 88855
e bookings@lakelovers.co.uk
w lakelovers.co.uk

24 Victoria Terrace ★★
Self Catering
Contact: Eileen Lishman
t (015394) 42982

27 Beechwood Close ★★★
Self Catering
Cumbrian Cottages
t (01228) 599960
e enquiries@cumbrian-cottages.co.uk
w cumbrian-cottages.co.uk

3 Woodland Grove ★★★
Self Catering
Lakelovers
t (015394) 88855
e bookings@lakelovers.co.uk
w lakelovers.co.uk

48A Quarry Rigg ★★★
Self Catering
Lakelovers
t (015394) 88855
e bookings@lakelovers.co.uk
w lakelovers.co.uk

6 Meadowcroft ★★★★
Self Catering
Cumbrian Cottages
t (01228) 599960
e enquiries@cumbrian-cottages.co.uk
w cumbrian-cottages.co.uk

Aaron's Place ★★★★
Self Catering
Cumbrian Cottages
t (01228) 599960
e enquiries@cumbrian-cottages.co.uk
w cumbrian-cottages.co.uk

The Abbey Coach House
★★★ *Self Catering*
Contact: Mrs P Bell
t (015394) 44027
e stay@abbeycoachhouse.co.uk
w abbeycoachhouse.co.uk

Abbeydale ★★★
Self Catering
Cumbrian Cottages
t (01228) 599960
e enquiries@cumbrian-cottages.co.uk
w cumbrian-cottages.co.uk

Above Cot ★★★★
Self Catering
Lakes Cottage Holidays
t (01228) 591555
e info@lakescottageholiday.co.uk
w lakescottageholiday.co.uk

Admiral's Nest ★★★
Self Catering
Cumbrian Cottages
t (01228) 599960
e enquiries@cumbrian-cottages.co.uk
w cumbrian-cottages.co.uk

Alderbeck ★★★★★
Self Catering
Lakelovers
t (015394) 88855
e bookings@lakelovers.co.uk
w lakelovers.co.uk

Alice Howe ★★★★
Self Catering
Cumbrian Cottages
t (01228) 599960
e enquiries@cumbrian-cottages.co.uk
w cumbrian-cottages.co.uk

Amberleigh House ★★★
Self Catering
Cumbrian Cottages
t (01228) 599960
e enquiries@cumbrian-cottages.co.uk
w cumbrian-cottages.co.uk

Annie's View ★★★
Self Catering
Cumbrian Cottages
t (01228) 599960
e enquiries@cumbrian-cottages.co.uk
w cumbrian-cottages.co.uk

Apple Cottage ★★★
Self Catering
Lakelovers
t (015394) 88855
e bookings@lakelovers.co.uk
w lakelovers.co.uk

April Meadow Cottage
★★★ *Self Catering*
Lakelovers
t (015394) 88855
e bookings@lakelovers.co.uk
w lakelovers.co.uk

Ash Cottage ★★★★
Self Catering
Lakelovers
t (015394) 88855
e bookings@lakelovers.co.uk
w lakelovers.co.uk

Auld Picture House ★★★★
Self Catering
Cumbrian Cottages
t (01228) 599960
e enquiries@cumbrian-cottages.co.uk
w cumbrian-cottages.co.uk

Bank Cottage ★★★★
Self Catering
Contact: Mrs Beighton
t (01474) 533028

Bannerigg ★★★★
Self Catering
Cumbrian Cottages
t (01228) 599960
e enquiries@cumbrian-cottages.co.uk
w cumbrian-cottages.co.uk

Bear's Den ★★★
Self Catering
Cumbrian Cottages
t (01228) 599960
e enquiries@cumbrian-cottages.co.uk
w cumbrian-cottages.co.uk

Beau Penny ★★★
Self Catering
Lakelovers
t (015394) 88855
e bookings@lakelovers.co.uk
w lakelovers.co.uk

Beaumont Cottages ★★★
Self Catering & Serviced Apartments
Contact: Charles Walmsley
t (015394) 45521
e beaumontcottages@aol.com
w beaumont-cottages.co.uk

Bede's Cottage ★★★★
Self Catering
Cumbrian Cottages
t (01228) 599960
e enquiries@cumbrian-cottages.co.uk
w cumbrian-cottages.co.uk

Beech Cottage ★★★
Self Catering
Cumbrian Cottages
t (01228) 599960
e enquiries@cumbrian-cottages.co.uk
w cumbrian-cottages.co.uk

Beech How Cottage ★★★
Self Catering
Lakelovers
t (015394) 88855
e bookings@lakelovers.co.uk
w lakelovers.co.uk

Beech Manor ★★★★
Self Catering
Cumbrian Cottages
t (01228) 599960
e enquiries@cumbrian-cottages.co.uk
w cumbrian-cottages.co.uk

Beechwood Apartment
★★★ *Self Catering*
Cumbrian Cottages
t (01228) 599960
e enquiries@cumbrian-cottages.co.uk
w cumbrian-cottages.co.uk

Beega Apartment ★★★
Self Catering
Cumbrian Cottages
t (01228) 599960
e enquiries@cumbrian-cottages.co.uk
w cumbrian-cottages.co.uk

The Belfrey ★★★★
Self Catering
Cumbrian Cottages
t (01228) 599960
e enquiries@cumbrian-cottages.co.uk
w cumbrian-cottages.co.uk

Belle Court ★★★★
Self Catering
Lakelovers
t (015394) 88855
e bookings@lakelovers.co.uk
w lakelovers.co.uk

Belle View – Quarry Rigg
★★★ *Self Catering*
Cumbrian Cottages
t (01228) 599960
e enquiries@cumbrian-cottages.co.uk
w cumbrian-cottages.co.uk

Biskey Howe ★★★
Self Catering
Cumbrian Cottages
t (01228) 599960
e enquiries@cumbrian-cottages.co.uk
w cumbrian-cottages.co.uk

Biskey Howe ★★★
Self Catering
Lakelovers
t (015394) 88855
e bookings@lakelovers.co.uk
w lakelovers.co.uk

Biskey Howe Cottage ★★★
Self Catering
Cumbrian Cottages
t (01228) 599960
e enquiries@cumbrian-cottages.co.uk
w cumbrian-cottages.co.uk

Black Beck Cottage
★★★★★ *Self Catering*
Cumbrian Cottages
t (01228) 599960
e enquiries@cumbrian-cottages.co.uk
w cumbrian-cottages.co.uk

Blue Ridge
Rating Applied For
Self Catering
Lakelovers
t (015394) 88855
e bookings@lakelovers.co.uk
w lakelovers.co.uk

Bluebells & Daffodils Cottage Apartment ★★★
Self Catering
Lakelovers
t (015394) 88855
e bookings@lakelovers.co.uk
w lakelovers.co.uk

Boston House ★★★★
Self Catering
Cumbrian Cottages
t (01228) 599960
e enquiries@cumbrian-cottages.co.uk
w cumbrian-cottages.co.uk

The Bothy ★★★★
Self Catering
Lakeland Cottage Comapny
t (015395) 38180
e john@lakelandcottageco.com
w lakelandcottageco.com

The Bothy ★★★
Self Catering
Cumbrian Cottages
t (01228) 599960
e enquiries@cumbrian-cottages.co.uk
w cumbrian-cottages.co.uk

Bowness Accommodation
★★★ *Self Catering*
t (015394) 88657
e eastbournela23@btconnect.com
w bowness-accommodation.co.uk

Bowness Oaks ★★★★
Self Catering
Cumbrian Cottages
t (01228) 599960
e enquiries@cumbrian-cottages.co.uk
w cumbrian-cottages.co.uk

Brackenrigg Lodge
★★★★★ *Self Catering*
Contact: Miss Lynne Bush
t (015394) 47770
e lynne@brackenriggs.co.uk

Brampton ★★★ *Self Catering*
Lakelovers
t (015394) 88855
e bookings@lakelovers.co.uk
w lakelovers.co.uk

Brantfell Cottage ★★★
Self Catering
Cumbrian Cottages
t (01228) 599960
e enquiries@cumbrian-cottages.co.uk
w cumbrian-cottages.co.uk

Brantfell Retreat ★★★
Self Catering
Cumbrian Cottages
t (01228) 599960
e enquiries@cumbrian-cottages.co.uk
w cumbrian-cottages.co.uk

Brantfield Cottage ★★★
Self Catering
Lakelovers
t (015394) 88855
e bookings@lakelovers.co.uk
w lakelovers.co.uk

Brent Cottage ★★★★
Self Catering
Lakelovers
t (015394) 88855
e bookings@lakelovers.co.uk
w lakelovers.co.uk

Briarwood ★★★
Self Catering
Cumbrian Cottages
t (01228) 599960
e enquiries@cumbrian-cottages.co.uk
w cumbrian-cottages.co.uk

Briscoe Lodge Self Catering
★★★ *Self Catering*
Contact: Janett Walker
Briscoe Lodge
t (015394) 42928
e stay@briscoelodge.co.uk
w briscoelodge.co.uk

Brook House ★★★★
Self Catering
Cumbrian Cottages
t (01228) 599960
e enquiries@cumbrian-cottages.co.uk
w cumbrian-cottages.co.uk

Brunton Lodge ★★★★
Self Catering
Lakelovers
t (015394) 88855
e bookings@lakelovers.co.uk
w lakelovers.co.uk

Bungalow One ★★★★
Self Catering
Cumbrian Cottages
t (01228) 599960
e enquiries@cumbrian-cottages.co.uk
w cumbrian-cottages.co.uk

Burnside Park ★★★★
Self Catering
Contact: Candy Philip
t 0870 046 8624
e stay@burnsidepark.co.uk
w burnsidepark.co.uk

The Burrow ★★★
Self Catering
Cumbrian Cottages
t (01228) 599960
e enquiries@cumbrian-cottages.co.uk
w cumbrian-cottages.co.uk

Burrow Cottage ★★★
Self Catering
Lakelovers
t (015394) 88855
e bookings@lakelovers.co.uk
w lakelovers.co.uk

Calgarth ★★★ *Self Catering*
Cumbrian Cottages
t (01228) 599960
e enquiries@cumbrian-cottages.co.uk
w cumbrian-cottages.co.uk

Canon's Craig ★★★★
Self Catering
Lakelovers
t (015394) 88855
e bookings@lakelovers.co.uk
w lakelovers.co.uk

Chapel House
Rating Applied For
Self Catering
Lakelovers
t (015394) 88855
e bookings@lakelovers.co.uk
w lakelovers.co.uk

Chapel House & Chapel Rest
★★★★ *Self Catering*
Lakelovers
t (015394) 88855
e bookings@lakelovers.co.uk
w lakelovers.co.uk

Cherry Tree Cottage ★★★
Self Catering
Cumbrian Cottages
t (01228) 599960
e enquiries@cumbrian-cottages.co.uk
w cumbrian-cottages.co.uk

Claife View ★★★
Self Catering
Cumbrian Cottages
t (01228) 599960
e enquiries@cumbrian-cottages.co.uk
w cumbrian-cottages.co.uk

Clara's Cottage ★★★
Self Catering
Lakelovers
t (015394) 88855
e bookings@lakelovers.co.uk
w lakelovers.co.uk

Cleabarrow Cottage ★★★★
Self Catering
Cumbrian Cottages
t (01228) 599960
e enquiries@cumbrian-cottages.co.uk
w cumbrian-cottages.co.uk

Clover Cottage ★★★
Self Catering
Lakelovers
t (015394) 88855
e bookings@lakelovers.co.uk
w lakelovers.co.uk

Cobblers Cottage ★★★★
Self Catering
Lakelovers
t (015394) 88855
e bookings@lakelovers.co.uk
w lakelovers.co.uk

Cobblestones ★★★
Self Catering
Cumbrian Cottages
t (01228) 599960
e enquiries@cumbrian-cottages.co.uk
w cumbrian-cottages.co.uk

College Gate ★★★
Self Catering
Cumbrian Cottages
t (01228) 599960
e enquiries@cumbrian-cottages.co.uk
w cumbrian-cottages.co.uk

Cooks' House ★★★★★
Self Catering
Cumbrian Cottages
t (01228) 599960
e enquiries@cumbrian-cottages.co.uk
w cumbrian-cottages.co.uk

Coppice View ★★★★
Self Catering
Lakelovers
t (015394) 88855
e bookings@lakelovers.co.uk
w lakelovers.co.uk

Corner Cottage ★★★★
Self Catering
Cumbrian Cottages
t (01228) 599960
e enquiries@cumbrian-cottages.co.uk
w cumbrian-cottages.co.uk

Cosy Nook ★★★
Self Catering
Lakelovers
t (015394) 88855
e bookings@lakelovers.co.uk
w lakelovers.co.uk

Craglands ★★★ *Self Catering*
Lakelovers
t (015394) 88855
e bookings@lakelovers.co.uk
w lakelovers.co.uk

Craigside ★★★ *Self Catering*
Lakelovers
t (015394) 88855
e bookings@lakelovers.co.uk
w lakelovers.co.uk

Crinkle Crag ★★★★
Self Catering
Cumbrian Cottages
t (01228) 599960
e enquiries@cumbrian-cottages.co.uk
w cumbrian-cottages.co.uk

Cross Cottage ★★★★
Self Catering
Cumbrian Cottages
t (01228) 599960
e enquiries@cumbrian-cottages.co.uk
w cumbrian-cottages.co.uk

Daffodils Cottage Apartment ★★★★
Self Catering
Lakelovers
t (015394) 88855
e bookings@lakelovers.co.uk
w lakelovers.co.uk

Daisy Bank Cottage ★★★
Self Catering
Cumbrian Cottages
t (01228) 599960
e enquiries@cumbrian-cottages.co.uk
w cumbrian-cottages.co.uk

December Cottage ★★★
Self Catering
Lakelovers
t (015394) 88855
e bookings@lakelovers.co.uk
w lakelovers.co.uk

Deloraine ★★★★
Self Catering
Contact: Mrs Fanstone
t (015394) 45557
e info@deloraine.demon.co.uk
w deloraine.demon.co.uk

Ecclerigg ★★★ *Self Catering*
Cumbrian Cottages
t (01228) 599960
e enquiries@cumbrian-cottages.co.uk
w cumbrian-cottages.co.uk

Elim Cottage ★★★
Self Catering
Cumbrian Cottages
t (01228) 599960
e enquiries@cumbrian-cottages.co.uk
w cumbrian-cottages.co.uk

Elterwater ★★★★
Self Catering
Cumbrian Cottages
t (01228) 599960
e enquiries@cumbrian-cottages.co.uk
w cumbrian-cottages.co.uk

Esthwaite ★★★ *Self Catering*
Cumbrian Cottages
t (01228) 599960
e enquiries@cumbrian-cottages.co.uk
w cumbrian-cottages.co.uk

Evergreen Cottage ★★★
Self Catering
Cumbrian Cottages
t (01228) 599960
e enquiries@cumbrian-cottages.co.uk
w cumbrian-cottages.co.uk

Fairfield ★★★ *Self Catering*
Cumbrian Cottages
t (01228) 599960
e enquiries@cumbrian-cottages.co.uk
w cumbrian-cottages.co.uk

Fairhaven ★★★★
Self Catering
Lakelovers
t (015394) 88855
e bookings@lakelovers.co.uk
w lakelovers.co.uk

Fellside Cottage ★★★
Self Catering
Lakelovers
t (015394) 88855
e bookings@lakelovers.co.uk
w lakelovers.co.uk

Fir Trees ★★★ *Self Catering*
Cumbrian Cottages
t (01228) 599960
e enquiries@cumbrian-cottages.co.uk
w cumbrian-cottages.co.uk

Firbank – Quarry Rigg ★★★
Self Catering
Cumbrian Cottages
t (01228) 599960
e enquiries@cumbrian-cottages.co.uk
w cumbrian-cottages.co.uk

Fireside Cottage ★★★★
Self Catering
Lakelovers
t (015394) 88855
e bookings@lakelovers.co.uk
w lakelovers.co.uk

Foxgloves ★★★ *Self Catering*
Cumbrian Cottages
t (01228) 599960
e enquiries@cumbrian-cottages.co.uk
w cumbrian-cottages.co.uk

The Galley ★★★★★
Self Catering
Lakelovers
t (015394) 88855
e bookings@lakelovers.co.uk
w lakelovers.co.uk

Gardens View ★★★
Self Catering
Lakelovers
t (015394) 88855
e bookings@lakelovers.co.uk
w lakelovers.co.uk

Garthmere ★★★★★
Self Catering
Contact: Mrs S Jackson
Heart of the Lakes
t (015394) 33110
e info@heartofthelakes.co.uk

Gavel Cottage ★★★★
Self Catering
Screetons
t (01430) 431201
e howden@screetons.co.uk
w screetons.co.uk

The Glass House ★★★★
Self Catering
Lakelovers
t (015394) 88855
e bookings@lakelovers.co.uk
w lakelovers.co.uk

Glebe Holme ★★★
Self Catering
Cumbrian Cottages
t (01228) 599960
e enquiries@cumbrian-cottages.co.uk
w cumbrian-cottages.co.uk

Gossel Ridding
Rating Applied For
Self Catering
Contact: Fay Gorman
Hexte faygorman@aol.com
w gosselridding.com

Granton Lodge ★★★★
Self Catering
Cumbrian Cottages
t (01228) 599960
e enquiries@cumbrian-cottages.co.uk
w cumbrian-cottages.co.uk

Greenrigg ★★★★
Self Catering
Cumbrian Cottages
t (01228) 599960
e enquiries@cumbrian-cottages.co.uk
w cumbrian-cottages.co.uk

Grey Cottage ★★★
Self Catering
Cumbrian Cottages
t (01228) 599960
e enquiries@cumbrian-cottages.co.uk
w cumbrian-cottages.co.uk

Greystones ★★★
Self Catering
Cumbrian Cottages
t (01228) 599960
e enquiries@cumbrian-cottages.co.uk
w cumbrian-cottages.co.uk

Havelock Cottage ★★★★
Self Catering
Cumbrian Cottages
t (01228) 599960
e enquiries@cumbrian-cottages.co.uk
w cumbrian-cottages.co.uk

Heaning Barn Cottages, Heaning, Windermere
★★★★ *Self Catering*
Contact: Mrs Jenny Truch
t (01539) 766107
e info@heaning.com
w heaning.com

Helm Farm ★★★
Self Catering
Contact: Mrs Marsden
Matson Ground Estate Co Ltd
t (015394) 45756
e info@matsonground.co.uk
w matsonground.co.uk

Hermitage Cottage ★★★
Self Catering
Lakeland Cottage Comapny
t (015395) 38180
e john@lakelandcottageco.com
w lakelandcottageco.com

Hidden Depths ★★★★★
Self Catering
Lakelovers
t (015394) 88855
e bookings@lakelovers.co.uk
w lakelovers.co.uk

Holbeck Lane Cottage
★★★★ *Self Catering*
Lakelovers
t (015394) 88855
e bookings@lakelovers.co.uk
w lakelovers.co.uk

Holburn House ★★★
Self Catering
Cumbrian Cottages
t (01228) 599960
e enquiries@cumbrian-cottages.co.uk
w cumbrian-cottages.co.uk

Holly Cottage ★★★★
Self Catering
Lakelovers
t (015394) 88855
e bookings@lakelovers.co.uk
w lakelovers.co.uk

Honeysuckle ★★★★
Self Catering
Lakeland Cottage Comapny
t (015395) 38180
e john@lakelandcottageco.com
w lakelandcottageco.com

Swallows Rest ★★★
Self Catering
Lakelovers
t (015394) 88855
e bookings@lakelovers.co.uk
w lakelovers.co.uk

Swan's Nest ★★★
Self Catering
Lakelovers
t (015394) 88855
e bookings@lakelovers.co.uk
w lakelovers.co.uk

Swirl How ★★★★
Self Catering
Lakelovers
t (015394) 88855
e bookings@lakelovers.co.uk
w lakelovers.co.uk

Swirl Howe ★★★
Self Catering
Lakelovers
t (015394) 88855
e bookings@lakelovers.co.uk
w lakelovers.co.uk

Tarn Rigg Apartment
★★★★ *Self Catering*
Cumbrian Cottages
t (01228) 599960
e enquiries@cumbrian-cottages.co.uk
w cumbrian-cottages.co.uk

The Thistles
Rating Applied For
Self Catering
Lakelovers
t (015394) 88855
e bookings@lakelovers.co.uk
w lakelovers.co.uk

Tiberthwaite ★★★★
Self Catering
Cumbrian Cottages
t (01228) 599960
e enquiries@cumbrian-cottages.co.uk
w cumbrian-cottages.co.uk

Tinkerbells ★★★★
Self Catering
Cumbrian Cottages
t (01228) 599960
e enquiries@cumbrian-cottages.co.uk
w cumbrian-cottages.co.uk

Tree Tops ★★★★
Self Catering
Lakelovers
t (015394) 88855
e bookings@lakelovers.co.uk
w lakelovers.co.uk

Treetops ★★★★
Self Catering
Contact: John Alcock
t (015394) 32819
e treetops@lakedistrictcumbria.co.uk
w lakedistrictcumbria.co.uk

Tsala ★★★★ *Self Catering*
Lakelovers
t (015394) 88855
e bookings@lakelovers.co.uk
w lakelovers.co.uk

Valentines ★★★
Self Catering
Cumbrian Cottages
t (01228) 599960
e enquiries@cumbrian-cottages.co.uk
w cumbrian-cottages.co.uk

Waterfall ★★★ *Self Catering*
Cumbrian Cottages
t (01228) 599960
e enquiries@cumbrian-cottages.co.uk
w cumbrian-cottages.co.uk

Waters Edge Villa
★★★-★★★★ *Self Catering*
Contact: Robert & Maureen Judson
t (015394) 43415
w lakewindermere.net

Wayside Cottage ★★★
Self Catering
Lakelovers
t (015394) 88855
e bookings@lakelovers.co.uk
w lakelovers.co.uk

The West Wing
Rating Applied For
Self Catering
Lakelovers
t (015394) 88855
e bookings@lakelovers.co.uk
w lakelovers.co.uk

Westwood ★★★★
Self Catering
Lakelovers
t (015394) 88855
e bookings@lakelovers.co.uk
w lakelovers.co.uk

Windermere Lodge
Rating Applied For
Self Catering
Lakelovers
t (015394) 88855
e bookings@lakelovers.co.uk
w lakelovers.co.uk

Windermere Marina Village
★★★★ *Self Catering*
Contact: Rebecca Dearden
t 0800 262902
e info@wmv.co.uk
w wmv.co.uk

Winster House ★★★
Self Catering
Contact: Mr Whalley
t (015394) 44723
e enquiries@winsterhouse.co.uk
w winsterhouse.co.uk

Woodbank
Rating Applied For
Self Catering
Lakelovers
t (015394) 88855
e bookings@lakelovers.co.uk
w lakelovers.co.uk

Woodland View ★★★
Self Catering
Cumbrian Cottages
t (01228) 599960
e enquiries@cumbrian-cottages.co.uk
w cumbrian-cottages.co.uk

Woodside Bank ★★★★
Self Catering
Lakelovers
t (015394) 88855
e bookings@lakelovers.co.uk
w lakelovers.co.uk

Woodside West ★★★★
Self Catering
Lakelovers
t (015394) 88855
e bookings@lakelovers.co.uk
w lakelovers.co.uk

Yew Tree Cottage ★★★★
Self Catering
Lakelovers
t (015394) 88855
e bookings@lakelovers.co.uk
w lakelovers.co.uk

WINSTER
Cumbria

All Seasons ★★★
Self Catering
Lakelovers
t (015394) 88855
e bookings@lakelovers.co.uk
w lakelovers.co.uk

WINSTON
Durham

Alwent Mill Cottage ★★★★
Self Catering
Contact: Mrs Libby Hampson
t (01325) 730479
e libby@alwentmill.co.uk

Strathmore Barns ★★★★
Self Catering
Contact: Mrs Marion Boyes
t (01833) 660302
e info@strathmorebarns.co.uk
w strathmorebarns.co.uk

WIRRAL
Merseyside

Mill Cottage ★★★
Self Catering
Contact: Mrs Kathleen Hogan
t (0151) 334 1193
e millnurseries@supanet.com

WITHERSLACK
Cumbria

Thornbarrow Hill Cottage
★★★ *Self Catering*
Lakeland Cottage Comapny
t (015395) 38180
e john@lakelandcottageco.com
w lakelandcottageco.com

WOLSINGHAM
Durham

Bradley Burn Holiday Cottages ★★★-★★★★
Self Catering
Contact: Mrs Judith Stephenson
t (01388) 527285
e jas@bradleyburn.co.uk
w bradleyburn.co.uk

The Convent ★★★★
Self Catering
Contact: Mr Tony Langdale
t (01388) 810904
e tonylangdale@btconnect.com

Elvet Cottage ★★★
Self Catering
Contact: Mrs Gardiner
t (01388) 527538

Friarside Farm Caravan
Approved Caravan Holiday Home
Contact: Mrs Frazer
t (01388) 527724
e angiefrazer2002@hotmail.com
w friarsidefarmcaravan.co.uk

New Hall Cottage ★★★★
Self Catering
Contact: Mrs Karen Wilson
t (01388) 527247
e enquiries@greenwellhill.co.uk
w newhall-farm.co.uk

Pasture Cottage ★★★★
Self Catering
Contact: Mrs Carolyn Ramsbotham
t (01388) 527864
e carolyn.ramsbotham@btopenworld.com
w pasturecottage.co.uk

Sandycarr Farm Cottage
★★★★ *Self Catering*
Contact: Mrs Marjorie Love
t (01388) 527249
e william@lovefarm.wanadoo.co.uk

Whitfield House Cottage
★★★ *Self Catering*
Contact: Mrs Margaret Shepheard
t (01388) 527466
e enquiries@whitfieldhouse.clara.net
w whitfieldhouse.clara.net

Willow Cottage ★★★★
Self Catering
Contact: Mr Alan Hopper
t 07977 235239
e hopperaml@aol.com
w willow-cottage-holidays.co.uk

WOMBLETON
North Yorkshire

Cruck Cottage ★★
Self Catering
Contact: Mrs Fiona Sheen
Dales Holiday Cottages
t (01756) 790919

WOODLAND
Durham

Mayland Farm Cottage
★★★ *Self Catering*
Contact: Mrs Susan Mortimer
t (01388) 718237
e john_mortimer@btinternet.com
w cottageguide.co.uk/maylandfarmcottage

WOOLER
Northumberland

Castle Hill Cottage ★★★
Self Catering
Contact: Mr James Nall-Cain
t (01582) 831083
e manussj@aol.com

Coldgate Mill ★★★★
Self Catering
Contact: Mr & Mrs Diana Stone
t (01668) 217259
e diana_coldgatemill@hotmail.com
w coldgatemill.co.uk

Criannan ★★★★
Self Catering
Contact: Mrs Sue Armstrong
t (01992) 587356
w criannan.com

Crookhouse ★★★★
Self Catering
Contact: Mrs Lynne Holden
t (01668) 216113
e stay@crookhousecottages.co.uk
w crookhouse.co.uk

Fenton Hill Farm Cottages
★★★★ *Self Catering*
Contact: Mrs Margaret Logan
t (01668) 216228
e stay@fentonhillfarm.co.uk
w fentonhillfarm.co.uk

Kimmerston Riding Centre
★★-★★★★ *Self Catering*
Contact: Mr Richard Jeffreys
t (01668) 216283
e jane@kimmerston.com
w kimmerston.com

Milfield Hill Steading
★★★★-★★★★★
Self Catering
Contact: Mrs Liz Turnbull
t (0191) 427 6203
e turnbullliz@aol.com
w english-country-cottages.co.uk

The Old Mill ★★★★
Self Catering
Contact: Mr Patrick Sheard
t (01892) 837286
e pj.sheard@virgin.net
w theoldmillwooler.co.uk

Peth Head Cottage ★★★★
Self Catering
Contact: Mr & Mrs Peter & Clare Jeffreys
t (01670) 514900
e peter@pncjeffreys.freeserve.co.uk
w pethheadcottage.co.uk

Rose Cottage ★★★
Self Catering
Contact: Mrs Christine Andrews
t (01372) 464284
e andrews@playfactors.demon.co.uk
w rosecottageselfcatering.co.uk

Swallowfields Country Cottage ★★★★ *Self Catering*
Contact: Mr Malcolm Pringle
t (01668) 283488
e stay@coldmartin.co.uk
w coldmartin.co.uk

Westnewton Estate ★★★
Self Catering
Contact: Mrs Jean Davidson
t (01668) 216077
e jd@westnewtonestate.com
w westnewtonestate.com

WORKINGTON
Cumbria

The Bird Bath ★★★
Self Catering
Cumbrian Cottages
t (01228) 599960
e enquiries@cumbrian-cottages.co.uk
w cumbrian-cottages.co.uk

WORSBROUGH
South Yorkshire

Delf Cottage ★★★★
Self Catering
Contact: Julie Elmhirst
t (01226) 282430
e julieelmhirst@hotmail.com
w delfcottage.co.uk

WORSLEY
Greater Manchester

The Cottage ★★★
Self Catering
Contact: Mr John Atherton
t (0161) 793 4157

WORSTON
Lancashire

Angram Green Holiday Cottages ★★★★
Self Catering
Contact: Ms Christine Gorrill Worston
t (01200) 441455
e info@angramgreen.co.uk
w angramgreen.co.uk

WORTLEY
South Yorkshire

Wortley Hall
Rating Applied For
Self Catering
Contact: Mr Jonathan Da Rosa
t (0114) 288 2100
e info@wortleyhall.org.uk
w wortleyhall.com

WORTON
North Yorkshire

Stoney End Cottage ★★★★
Self Catering
Contact: Mike & Pamela Hague
t (01969) 650652
e pmh@stoneyend.co.uk
w stoneyend.co.uk

WRAY
Lancashire

Wray Reading Room ★★★★
Self Catering
Contact: Mrs Janatha Anstiss
t (01772) 685735
w wrayreadingroom.com

WRELTON
North Yorkshire

Hallgarth ★★★★
Self Catering
Contact: C.A Marsh
t (01751) 476081

The Huntsman Holiday Cottages ★★★★
Self Catering
Contact: Andy & Tracy Green
t (01751) 472530
e huntsmancottages@hotmail.co.uk
w the-huntsman.net

Keld Knowle Farm *Approved Caravan Holiday Home*
t (01751) 472820

Rocklands Lodges ★★★★
Self Catering
Contact: Esmond & Jeanne Watson
t (01751) 477621
e info@rocklandslodges.co.uk
w rocklandslodges.co.uk

Vale Cottage ★★★
Self Catering
Contact: Thomas & Jean Scaling
t (01751) 473792
e jeanscaling@btinternet.com
w cottageguide.co.uk/valecottage

Wayside ★★★★
Self Catering
Contact: Mr & Mrs Kevin & Julie Honcharenko
t 07931 536209
e khoncharenko@aol.com
w wayside-cottage.org.uk

WRENBURY
Cheshire

Jasmine Cottage ★★★
Self Catering
Contact: Ms Michelle Groom
t 0845 095 6539

YANWATH
Cumbria

Amber Nook ★★★★
Self Catering
Cumbrian Cottages
t (01228) 599960
e enquiries@cumbrian-cottages.co.uk
w cumbrian-cottages.co.uk

Beech Barn ★★★
Self Catering
Cumbrian Cottages
t (01228) 599960
e enquiries@cumbrian-cottages.co.uk
w cumbrian-cottages.co.uk

Copper Beech Cottage
★★★★ *Self Catering*
Cumbrian Cottages
t (01228) 599960
e enquiries@cumbrian-cottages.co.uk
w cumbrian-cottages.co.uk

Littlewood House ★★
Self Catering
Cumbrian Cottages
t (01228) 599960
e enquiries@cumbrian-cottages.co.uk
w cumbrian-cottages.co.uk

Lyzzick Lodge ★★★★
Self Catering
Cumbrian Cottages
t (01228) 599960
e enquiries@cumbrian-cottages.co.uk
w cumbrian-cottages.co.uk

Meadow Lodge ★★★★
Self Catering
Cumbrian Cottages
t (01228) 599960
e enquiries@cumbrian-cottages.co.uk
w cumbrian-cottages.co.uk

Tillybardine Lodge ★★★
Self Catering
Cumbrian Cottages
t (01228) 599960
e enquiries@cumbrian-cottages.co.uk
w cumbrian-cottages.co.uk

YAPHAM
East Riding of Yorkshire

Wolds View Holiday Cottages ★★★★-★★★★★
Self Catering
Contact: Margaret Woodliffe
t (01759) 302172
e info@woldsview.co.uk

YARM
Tees Valley

Yarm Cottages ★★★★
Self Catering
Contact: Mrs Janice Rowley
t (01642) 787017
e info@yarmcottages.co.uk
w yarmcottages.co.uk

YARROW
Northumberland

Kielder Cottage ★★★★
Self Catering
Contact: Mrs Elaine Hunt-Vincent
t (0191) 548 7829
e ehuntvin@aol.com
w kieldercottage.co.uk

YEALAND REDMAYNE
Lancashire

Brackenthwaite Cottages
★★★-★★★★ *Self Catering*
Contact: Mrs Susan Clarke
t (015395) 63276
e info@brackenthwaite.com
w brackenthwaite.com

Greenfold Holiday Cottages
★★★★ *Self Catering*
Contact: Ms Susan Dickson
t (01524) 701508
e info@greenfoldcottages.co.uk
w greenfoldcottages.co.uk

YORK
North Yorkshire

1 Bishops Court ★★★
Self Catering
t (01759) 307165
e eleanor@yorkcityholidays.co.uk
w yorkcityholidays.co.uk

10 George Street ★★★★★
Self Catering
Contact: Mrs Heather Robinson
t (01484) 841330 & 07753 958686
e info@10georgestreet.co.uk
w 10georgestreet.co.uk

11 E Castlegate Apartments
★★★★ *Self Catering*
Contact: Mrs Maureen Hardy
t (01904) 652664

15 Stonegate Court
★★★★★ *Self Catering*
Contact: Susan Kitchener
York Luxury Holidays
t (01904) 766789
e sue@yorkluxuryholidays.co.uk
w yorkluxuryholidays.co.uk

24 Middleton House ★★★★
Self Catering
Contact: Mrs Carole Bowes
t (01845) 597334
e rce.bowes@lineone.net
w yorkcityflat.co.uk

24 Woodsmill Quay ★★★★
Self Catering
Inyork Holidays
t (01904) 632660
e agents@inyorkholidays.co.uk
w inyorkholidays.co.uk

29 Richardson Street ★★★
Self Catering
Inyork Holidays
t (01904) 632660
e agents@inyorkholidays.co.uk
w inyorkholidays.co.uk

412 Westgate Apartments
★★★★ *Self Catering*
Contact: Ms Clare Davenport
Inyork Holidays
t (01904) 632660
e agents@inyorkholidays.co.uk
w inyorkholidays.co.uk

43 Postern Close ★★★★★
Self Catering
Contact: Mrs Hilary Jones
York City Holidays
t (01904) 702043
e hilary@yorkcloisters.com
w yorkcloisters.com

44 Postern Close ★★★★
Self Catering
Contact: Christine Turner
t (01954) 201218
e c.turner@gurdon.cam.ac.uk
w yorkholidayflat.co.uk

5, 6 & 12 Monkbridge Court
★★★★ *Self Catering*
Contact: Mrs Angela Bush
5,6 & 12 Monkbridge Court
t (01759) 377579
e angelabush@monkbridge.co.uk
w monkbridge.co.uk

9 Waterfront House
★★★★★ *Self Catering*
Contact: Mr Timothy Clark
t (01945) 871336
e giles@lignacite.co.uk
w waterfrontyork.com

Abbeygate House ★★★★★
Self Catering
Contact: Mr & Mrs Halliday
t (0113) 258 9833

The Apartment In York
★★★★ *Self Catering*
Contact: Ms Rachael Hosack
t 07967 092726
e info@theapartmentinyork.co.uk
w theapartmentinyork.co.uk

Apartment No 9 ★★★★
Self Catering
Contact: Mrs Hilary Atha
Apartment No. 9
t (01904) 655571
e reservations@towerguesthouse.fsnet.co.uk
w yorkholidayhome.com

Ashling Houses ★★★★
Self Catering
Contact: Ian Addyman
t (01904) 706083
e info@yorkselfcatering.fsnet.co.uk
w yorkselfcatering.co.uk

Assam House ★★★★★
Self Catering
Contact: Ms Clare Proctor
t (01904) 700610
e info@assamhouse.co.uk
w assamhouse.co.uk

Baille Hill House ★★★★
Self Catering
Contact: Mr Chris Radford
t (01845) 597614
e enquiries@baillehillhouse.co.uk
w baillehillhouse.co.uk

Betty's York Holiday Flat
★★★ *Self Catering*
Contact: Mrs Betty Lutyens-Humfrey
t (01904) 339138
e betty@holidayflatyork.co.uk
w holidayflatyork.co.uk

Bishopgate Pavilion-Bishops Wharf ★★★★★
Self Catering
Contact: Mr John K Graham
t 07973 857187
e john@johnkgraham.com
w johnkgraham.com

The Blue Rooms
★★★★-★★★★★
Self Catering
Contact: Miss Kirsty Reid
The Blue Bicycle York Ltd
t (01904) 673990
e blue-rooms@thebluebicycle.com
w thebluebicycle.com

Bluebird
Rating Applied For
Self Catering
Contact: Laura Thompsone fabric_garment@btinternet.com

Bootham Luxury Apartment
★★★★ *Self Catering*
Contact: Mrs Dawn Eveson
t 07778 854759
e dawneveson7@aol.co.uk
w boothamluxuryapartment.co.uk

Burton Breaks ★★★
Self Catering
t (01904) 644988

Centre York Cottages ★★
Self Catering
Contact: William Richardson
t (01759) 388280
e william@centre-yorkcottages.fsnet.co.uk
w centre-yorkcottages.fsnet.co.uk

Chestnut Farm Holiday Cottages ★★★★
Self Catering
Contact: Mr Steve Smith
t (01904) 704676
e enquiries@chestnutfarmholidaypark.co.uk
w chestnutfarmholidaypark.co.uk

Classique Select Holiday Accommodation ★★★
Self Catering
Contact: Mr Rodney Inns
t (01904) 421339
w classique-york.co.uk

Cloisters Walk Holiday Accommodation ★★★
Self Catering
Contact: Mrs Vanessa Warn
Cloisters Walk
t (01904) 331479
e contact@yorkholidaylets.com
w yorkholidaylets.com

Colonia Holidays ★★★
Self Catering
Contact: Margaret Booth
t (01904) 738579

Crambeck Court ★★★★
Self Catering
Inyork Holidays
t (01904) 632660
e agents@inyorkholidays.co.uk
w inyorkholidays.co.uk

Fairfax Corner ★★★
Self Catering
Contact: Bill & Shan Rigby
t (01482) 862085
e rigby@york.netkonect.co.uk

The Garden Cottage ★★★★
Self Catering
Contact: Mrs Ann Hart
t (01904) 413353
e ann@yorkgardencottage.co.uk
w yorkgardencottage.co.uk

Garnet House ★★★
Self Catering
Contact: Mr Gordon Robinson
t (01904) 412975 & 07973 409381
e herbie831@talktalk.net

Hodgson's Choice ★★★★★
Self Catering
Contact: Mrs Kim Hodgson
t (01904) 610351
e kim@hodgsons-choice.co.uk
w hodgsons-choice.co.uk

The Juniper ★★★★★
Self Catering
Contact: Mrs Claire Waite
t 07871 728316
e claire@thejuniper.co.uk
w thejuniper.co.uk

Knowle House Apartments
★★-★★★ *Self Catering*
Contact: Greg Harrand
t 0800 583 6374
e greg@hedleyhouse.com
w hedleyhouse.com

Luxury 4 Value ★★★★
Self Catering
Contact: Mrs Colette Rogers
Luxury 4 Value – Bootham
t (01430) 861951
e coletterogers@rogersliving.com

Mayfield Cottage ★★★
Self Catering
Contact: Mrs Lorraine McDonald
t (01786) 818994
e mayfield-cottage@hotmail.co.uk
w mayfield-york.co.uk

Merchants Gate ★★★★
Self Catering
Contact: Stephen Osborne
t (01937) 574836
e oaklands.wetherby@btopenworld.com

Merricote Cottages ★★★
Self Catering
Contact: Mr Andrew Williamson
t (01904) 400256
e merricote@hotmail.com
w merricote-holiday-cottages.co.uk

Old Rectory ★★★
Self Catering
Contact: Mr & Mrs Jonathan & Adelaide Morley
t (01904) 423506
e oldrectoryyork@hotmail.co.uk
w oldrectoryyork.co.uk

The Old Stables ★★★
Self Catering
Yorkshire Cottages
t (01228) 406701
e enquiries@yorkshire-cottages.info
w yorkshire-cottages.info

Olivers of the Mount
Rating Applied For
Self Catering
Contact: Ellie Hindby-Smith
t (01904) 612119
e info@oliversofthemount.com
w oliversofthemount.com

Pavilion Cottage ★★★
Self Catering
Contact: Mrs Heidi Whitaker
t (01904) 639258 & 07974 853876
e pavcottage@yahoo.co.uk
w pavilioncottage-holidayinyork.co.uk

The Penthouse ★★★★★
Self Catering
Contact: Ms Clare Davenport
Inyork Holidays
t (01904) 632660
e agents@inyorkholidays.co.uk
w inyorkholidays.co.uk

Rowes Cottage ★★★
Self Catering
Yorkshire Cottages
t (01228) 406701
e enquiries@yorkshire-cottages.info
w yorkshire-cottages.info

St Peters Grove ★★★★
Self Catering
Contact: Ann Morrison
t (01904) 613724
e annmorrison_@hotmail.co.uk
w annapartments.com

St Peter's Quarter ★★★★★
Self Catering
Contact: Edward & Jane Wilson
t (01473) 890056
e enquiries@yorkcityhouse.com
w yorkcityhouse.com

Shambles Holiday Apartments ★★★★
Self Catering
Contact: Mrs Eileen Fletcher
t (01904) 623898
e shamblesholiday-york@tinyworld.co.uk

Skipwith Station Holidays
★★★ *Self Catering*
Contact: Mrs Lizanne Southworth
t (01757) 282288
e info@skipwithstation.com
w skipwithstation.com

Sparrow Hall Cottages ★★★
Self Catering
Contact: Nick & Pam Gaunt
t (01759) 372917
e holidays@sparrowhall.co.uk
w sparrowhall.co.uk

Swallow Hall ★★★
Self Catering
Contact: Ms Christine Scott
t (01904) 448219
e christinescutt@hotmail.co.uk
w swallowhall.co.uk

Talbot Court (Apartments 1 & 2) ★★★★★ *Self Catering*
Contact: Mrs Jane Crease
Talbot Court
t (01944) 758222
e talbotcourt@gmail.com
w talbotcourt.co.uk

Within The Walls Cottage
★★★ *Self Catering*
Contact: Mr Barry Giles
t (0115) 931 2070

York Holiday Apartments
★★★★ *Self Catering*
Contact: Mr Malcolm Bradley
t (01977) 683499
e malcolmbradley@btinternet.com
w yorkholidayapartments.co.uk

York Holiday Homes
★★★-★★★★ *Self Catering*
t (01904) 641997
w yorkholidayhomes.co.uk

York Lakeside Lodges
★★★★-★★★★★
Self Catering
Contact: Mr Manasir
York Lakeside Lodges Ltd
t (01904) 702346
e neil@yorklakesidelodges.co.uk
w yorklakesidelodges.co.uk

York Luxury Breaks ★★★★
Self Catering
Contact: Mrs Linda Waddington
t (01904) 768569

York Luxury Holidays – Stonegate Court ★★★★★
Self Catering
Contact: Mrs Susan Kitchener
York Luxury Holidays
t (01904) 766789
e sue@yorkluxuryholidays.co.uk
w yorkluxuryholidays.co.uk

York Riverside Holiday Flat
★★★★ *Self Catering*
Contact: Mr Peter & Elizabeth Jackson
t (01757) 268207 & 07885 921691
e pajack@lineone.net
w yorkriversideholidayflat.co.uk

CENTRAL ENGLAND

ABBERLEY Worcestershire

Old Yates Cottages ★★★
Self Catering
Contact: Mr & Mrs Richard & Sarah Goodman
t (01299) 896500
e oldyates@aol.com
w oldyatescottages.co.uk

ABBOTS BROMLEY Staffordshire

Blithfield Lakeside Barns
★★★★ *Self Catering*
Contact: Mrs Maxine Brown PG & MJ Brown
t (01889) 500234
e maxine.brown@lineone.net
w blithfieldlakesidebarns.co.uk

ABBOTS LENCH Worcestershire

Abbots Court Cottages
★★★★ *Self Catering & Serviced Apartments*
t (01386) 870520
w abbotscourtcottages.co.uk

ABBOTS RIPTON Cambridgeshire

Wild Goose Leys
Rating Applied For
Self Catering
Contact: Mrs Jean Burbidge
t (01487) 773349
e jean.burbidge@care4free.net
w wildgooseleys.co.uk

ABDON Shropshire

Little Cobblers Dingle ★★★
Self Catering
Contact: Mrs Josephine Brooks
t (01746) 712244
e brooks@littlecobblersdingle.co.uk
w littlecobblersdingle.co.uk

ABTHORPE Northamptonshire

Rignall Farm Barns
★★★-★★★★ *Self Catering*
Contact: Peta Jones
t (01327) 350766

ACLE Norfolk

Calm Lodge
Rating Applied For
Self Catering
Norfolk Country Cottages
t (01603) 871872
e info@norfolkcottages.co.uk
w norfolkcottages.co.uk

The Olde Chapel ★★★★
Self Catering
Norfolk Country Cottages
t (01603) 871872
e info@norfolkcottages.co.uk
w norfolkcottages.co.uk

The Retreat ★★★
Self Catering
Norfolk Country Cottages
t (01603) 871872
e info@norfolkcottages.co.uk
w norfolkcottages.co.uk

Station Cottage ★★★★
Self Catering
Contact: Mrs Deborah Mann
t (01493) 751136
w ukholidayhome.co.uk

ACTON BURNELL Shropshire

Rosehay ★★★★-★★★★★
Self Catering
Sykes Cottages
t (01244) 345700
e info@sykescottages.co.uk
w sykescottages.co.uk

ADMINGTON Warwickshire

Mole End, Admington
★★★★ *Self Catering*
Contact: Mrs Liz Hale
t (01789) 450881
e liz-hale@willowtreefarm.fslife.co.uk
w mole-end-cottage.co.uk

ALBRIGHTON Shropshire

Boningale Manor Barns
★★★★ *Self Catering*
Contact: Mrs Catherine Tummons
t (01902) 373376
e boningalemanor@aol.com
w boningalemanor.com

ALCESTER Warwickshire

The Croft Cottage ★★★★
Self Catering
Contact: Mrs Catherine Harris
t (01789) 490543
e cathy@thecroftcottage.co.uk
w thecroftcottage.co.uk

Dorset House Cottage and Dorset House ★★★★ *Self Catering & Serviced Apartments*
Contact: Mr & Mrs B Thatcher
t (01789) 762856
e book@dorsethouse.info
w cottagesdirect.com/dorsethouse

The Granary ★★★
Self Catering
Contact: Mr & Mrs Kinnersley
t (01789) 762554
e johnkinnersley@btinternet.com

Heronview ★★★★
Self Catering
Contact: Mrs Heather Bosworth
t 07875 374010
e heather@heronview.net
w heronview.net

ALCONBURY Cambridgeshire

Spring Cottages ★★★★
Self Catering
Contact: Mrs Ellicia Coulson
t (01480) 890328
e elliciaandcraig@spring-cottage.co.uk
w spring-cottage.co.uk

ALDBOROUGH Norfolk

Virginia Cottage ★★★★
Self Catering
Norfolk Country Cottages
t (01603) 871872
e info@norfolkcottages.co.uk
w norfolkcottages.co.uk

ALDEBURGH Suffolk

1 Coastguard Court ★★★
Self Catering
Suffolk Secrets
t (01502) 722717
e holidays@suffolk-secrets.co.uk
w suffolk-secrets.co.uk

17 Britten Close ★★★★
Self Catering
Contact: Miss Kim Hamblin
t 07974 074646

3 Crespigny Road ★★★★
Self Catering
Contact: Mrs J Alexander
The Old Rectory
t (01394) 383822
e jenniealexander@btinternet.com
w aldeburghescapes.co.uk

38 Lee Road ★★★★
Self Catering
Contact: Mrs Elizabeth Wagener
Cox Hill House
t (01787) 210223

Arwen Cottage ★★★★
Self Catering
Suffolk Secrets
t (01502) 722717
e holidays@suffolk-secrets.co.uk
w suffolk-secrets.co.uk

Avalon ★★★★ *Self Catering*
Suffolk Secrets
t (01502) 722717
e holidays@suffolk-secrets.co.uk
w suffolk-secrets.co.uk

Avon Cottage ★★★
Self Catering
Suffolk Secrets
t (01502) 722717
e holidays@suffolk-secrets.co.uk
w suffolk-secrets.co.uk

Beachcroft ★★★
Self Catering
Suffolk Secrets
t (01502) 722717
e holidays@suffolk-secrets.co.uk
w suffolk-secrets.co.uk

Bees Cottage ★★★
Self Catering
Suffolk Secrets
t (01502) 722717
e holidays@suffolk-secrets.co.uk
w suffolk-secrets.co.uk

Braid House ★★★
Self Catering
Contact: Miss Ying Tan
t (01728) 663432

Coastguard Court 8 ★★★
Self Catering
Contact: Mr John Mauger
t (01502) 575896
e john.mauger@blythweb.net
w blythweb.co.uk/coastguard-court

Cosy Corner ★★★
Self Catering
Contact: Ms Ann Fryer
t (01728) 453121

Cosy Nook ★★★★
Self Catering
Suffolk Secrets
t (01502) 722717
e holidays@suffolk-secrets.co.uk
w suffolk-secrets.co.uk

The Cottage, Crag Path
★★★ *Self Catering*
Contact: Mrs J Alexander
The Old Rectory
t (01394) 383822
e jennialexander@btinternet.com
w aldeburghescapes.co.uk

Dial Flat ★★ *Self Catering*
Contact: Mrs Pam Harrison
t (01728) 453212

Drift In ★★★ *Self Catering*
Suffolk Secrets
t (01502) 722717
e holidays@suffolk-secrets.co.uk
w suffolk-secrets.co.uk

Fig Tree Cottage ★★★
Self Catering
Contact: Mr Martin Jinks
Fig Tree
t (01728) 453037
w aldeburghboutiquecottages.com

The Gables ★★★★★
Self Catering
Contact: Mr Graham Thompson
t (01725) 518755
w thegablesaldeburgh.co.uk

Hall Cottage ★★★★
Self Catering
Contact: Mrs Miriam Buchanan
t 07889 020654
e miriam.buchanan@gressinghamfoods.co.uk
w loomscottages.co.uk

The Lookout ★★★★
Self Catering
Contact: Lisa Smith
New Trees
t (01728) 831488
w aldeburghlookout.co.uk

The Lookout ★★★
Self Catering
Suffolk Secrets
t (01502) 722717
e holidays@suffolk-secrets.co.uk
w suffolk-secrets.co.uk

Lower Thellusson ★★★★
Self Catering
Contact: Mrs Claire Gawthrop
East Green Farm
t (01728) 602316
e claire@eastgreen.co.uk
w eastgreencottages.co.uk

Magenta ★★★ *Self Catering*
Contact: Mr Martin Jinks
t (01728) 453037
w aldeburghboutiquecottages.com

Manor Farm Cottages
★★★★ *Self Catering*
Suffolk Secrets
t (01502) 722717
e holidays@suffolk-secrets.co.uk
w suffolk-secrets.co.uk

Mermaid Cottage ★★★★
Self Catering
Contact: Mrs Jacqueline Collier
t (01473) 735004

Moot Green House ★★★★
Self Catering
Contact: James Ellis
t (01502) 722717
e holidays@suffolk-secrets.co.uk
w suffolk-secrets.co.uk

Nightingale Cottage ★★★★
Self Catering
Suffolk Secrets
t (01502) 722717
e holidays@suffolk-secrets.co.uk
w suffolk-secrets.co.uk

Orlando ★★★ *Self Catering*
Contact: Mr Peter Hatcher
t (01394) 382126
e orlando@hatcher.co.uk
w hatcher.co.uk/orlando

Parklands ★★★★★
Self Catering
Contact: Mrs Sandra Allen
t (01728) 830139
w justsuffolk.com

Peach House, Wentworth Road ★★★★ *Self Catering*
Contact: Mrs J Alexander
The Old Rectory
t (01394) 383822
e jennialexander@btinternet.com
w aldeburghescapes.co.uk

Pembroke ★★★★
Self Catering
Contact: Mr Martin Jinks
Heron Bank
t (01728) 453037
w aldeburghboutiquecottages.com

Pilots House ★★★★
Self Catering
Suffolk Secrets
t (01502) 722717
e holidays@suffolk-secrets.co.uk
w suffolk-secrets.co.uk

The Studio, King Street
★★★ *Self Catering*
Contact: Mrs J Alexander
The Old Rectory
t (01394) 383822
e jennialexander@btinternet.com
w aldeburghescapes.co.uk

Thorpeness Apartments and Houses ★★★-★★★★
Self Catering
Contact: Mrs Lynda Griffin
t (01728) 452176
e info@thorpeness.co.uk
w thorpeness.co.uk

ALDRINGHAM Suffolk

Hillside Cottage ★★★
Self Catering
Contact: Mr Herbert Wood
t (01728) 833527
e herbert@herbertwood.wanadoo.co.uk
w fieldendbedandbreakfast.co.uk

No 3 Aldringham House
★★★★ *Self Catering*
Contact: Mr Brian Hodgkinson
t (0115) 926 7016

Yewtrees ★★★★
Self Catering
Contact: Ms Claire Webster
t (01273) 241838
w yewtreesmeadowside.com

ALFORD Lincolnshire

Rigsby Wold Cottage ★★★
Self Catering
Contact: Barbara Read
t (01507) 463404
e billread2001@yahoo.com
w rigsbywoldcottage.co.uk

Woodthorpe Hall Country Cottage ★★★★ *Self Catering*
Contact: Mrs Stubbs
t (01507) 450294
e enquiries@woodthorpehallleisure.co.uk
w woodthorpehallleisure.co.uk

ALFRETON Derbyshire

The Coach House ★★★★
Self Catering
Contact: Mr & Mrs Whitaker
t (01773) 605116
e dwhitaker@dial.pipex.com

ALKBOROUGH Lincolnshire

Corner Cottage ★★★★
Self Catering
Contact: Annette Dexter
t (01923) 330022
e annette.dexter@ntlworld.com

ALKINGTON Shropshire

Bon Accueil ★★★★★
Self Catering
t (01948) 661168
w bonaccueil.co.uk

ALL STRETTON Shropshire

The Pottery ★★★
Self Catering
t (01694) 722121
w stmem.com/the-pottery

ALLINGTON Lincolnshire

The Lodge ★★★★
Self Catering
Contact: Mrs Helen Love
t (01400) 281161
w asheslodge.co.uk

ALPORT Derbyshire

Harthill Hall
Rating Applied For
Self Catering
Contact: Ian Thompson
t (01629) 636190
e ian@harthillhall.co.uk
w harthillhall.co.uk

Peak Serenity ★★★★★
Self Catering
Contact: Mrs Christine Earl
t (01629) 650386
e maverick@sc.earl.greeserve.co.uk
w peakserenity-derbyshiredales.co.uk

Rock Cottage ★★★★
Self Catering
Contact: Ms Janet O'Sullivan
t (01629) 810910
e janet@haddonhall.co.uk

ALRESFORD Essex

Creek Lodge ★★★
Self Catering
Contact: Mrs Patricia Mountney
t (01206) 825411

ALSOP-EN-LE-DALE Derbyshire

Church Farm Cottages, Alsop en le Dale ★★★★
Self Catering
Contact: Mrs Christine Duffell
t (01335) 390216
e enquiries@churchfarmholidaycottages.co.uk
w churchfarmholidaycottages.co.uk

ALSTONEFIELD Staffordshire

Dove Cottage Fishing Lodge
★★★★★ *Self Catering*
Contact: Rupert Hignett
t (01993) 825900 & (01285) 850779
e info@dovecottages.co.uk
w dovecottages.co.uk

The Gables ★★★
Self Catering
Contact: Mr McKee
Timewell Estates Plc
t (0151) 625 3264
e timewell@rtconnect.com
w dovedale.org.uk

Gateham Grange Cottage & The Coach House
★★★-★★★★ *Self Catering*
Contact: Mrs Teresa Flower
t (01335) 310349
e gateham.grange@btinternet.com
w cressbrook.co.uk/hartingt/gateham/

The Haybarn ★★★★
Self Catering
Contact: Mrs Coralie Smith
t (01335) 310328
w cottageguide.co.uk/haybarn

Hope Farm House ★★★★★
Self Catering
Contact: Mrs R Pith-Tucker
t (01335) 310238

Rowlands Cottage ★★★★
Self Catering
Contact: Mrs Ellen Wibberley
t (01335) 310370
e rog@wibbs200.fsnet.co.uk
w cottageguide.co.uk/rowlandscottage

ALTHORNE Essex

Althorne Hall Cottages
★★★★ *Self Catering*
Contact: Mrs Mal Bass
t (01621) 740863
w althornehallcottages.co.uk

ALTON Derbyshire

Wildflower Cottages
★★★★ *Self Catering*
Contact: Mrs Susan Fewtrell
t (01246) 590052
e sue@wildflowercottages.co.uk
w wildflowercottages.co.uk

ALTON Staffordshire

The Homesteads ★★★
Self Catering
Contact: Mrs Ann Smith
t (01889) 590062

Quarry Walk Park, Alton
★★★-★★★★ *Self Catering*
Contact: Mr Ian Millican
t (01538) 723412
e quarry@quarrywalkpark.co.uk
w quarrywalklodges.co.uk

The Raddle Inn ★★★
Self Catering
Contact: Mr Peter Wilkinson
t (01889) 507278
e peter@logcabin.co.uk
w logcabin.co.uk

Rowan House ★★★★
Self Catering
Contact: Ms Emily Whitehead
t (01889) 591844
e enquiries@simplystaffordshire.co.uk
w simplystaffordshire.co.uk

ALVINGHAM Lincolnshire

The Stables Holiday Cottage
★★★★ *Self Catering*
Contact: Sheila Pinkney
t (01507) 327442
e byattsstables@btopenworld.com
w stablesholidaycottage.co.uk

AMBERGATE Derbyshire

Woodside House ★★★★
Self Catering
t (01332) 840564
e ann.wayne@derbyshire-holidays.com
w derbyshire-holidays.com/woodside

ARDLEIGH Essex

Island Lodge ★★★★
Self Catering
Contact: Mr Bill Murray
t (01206) 230943
e murrayl215@aol.com
w tiscover.co.uk

ARNOLD Nottinghamshire

The Grannary ★★★
Self Catering
Contact: Mrs Lamin
t (0115) 926 8330

ASHBOURNE Derbyshire

Ancestral Barn
★★★★-★★★★★
Self Catering
Contact: Mrs Sue Fowler
t (01335) 310243
e sue@fowler89.fsnet.co.uk
w dovedalecottages.co.uk

Ashfield and Dove Cottages
★★★ *Self Catering*
Contact: Mr Arthur Tatlow
t (01335) 324270

Borrowdale Cottage ★★★
Self Catering
Contact: Mr & Mrs Alexander
t (01763) 233216
e borrowdale.cottage@ntlworld.com
w cottageguide.co.uk/borrowdalecottage

Callow Top Cottages 1 and 2
★★★ *Self Catering*
Contact: Mrs Sue Deane
t (01335) 344020
e enquiries@callowtop.co.uk

Croft House Barn ★★★★
Self Catering
Contact: Mrs Stephanie Cadenhead
t (01538) 308125
e stephanie@crofthousebarn.co.uk
w crofthousebarn.co.uk

The Dairy
Rating Applied For
Self Catering
t (01335) 345063
e kaylivesey@yahoo.co.uk

Dove Farm ★★★★
Self Catering
Contact: Mrs Jane Stretton
t (01335) 324357
e jane@dovefarm.co.uk
w dovefarm.co.uk

Elite Holiday Cottages ★★★
Self Catering
Contact: Sue Lang
t (01335) 344065
e enquires@eliteholidaycottages.info
w eliteholidaycottages.info

Greenacres ★★★★
Self Catering
Contact: Ann Wayne
Derbyshire Holidays
t (01332) 840564
e ann.wayne@derbyshire-holidays.com
w derbyshire-holidays.com

The Grooms Quarters
★★★★★ *Self Catering*
Contact: Mr & Mrs Ray & Ann Thompson
t (01335) 324549
e ann@groomsquarters.co.uk
w groomsquarters.co.uk

Haifa ★★★★ *Self Catering*
Contact: Mr David Dudley
t (01604) 403625

Hillside Croft ★★★★★
Self Catering
Contact: Mrs Pat Walker
Offcote Grange Cottage Holidays
t (01335) 344795
e cottages@hillsidecroft.co.uk

Holme View ★★★★
Self Catering
Peak Cottages
t (0114) 262 0777
e enquiries@peakcottages.com
w peakcottages.com

The Nook, Kniveton ★★★★
Self Catering
Contact: Mrs Susan Osborn
t (01455) 842609
e susan.osborn1@btinternet.com
w come.to/thenook

The Old Laundry ★★★★★
Self Catering
Contact: Mrs Patricia Cust
t (01335) 346711
e p.cust@virgin.net
w sturston.com

Old Miller's Cottage ★★★
Self Catering
Contact: Mrs P.M. Hewitt
t (01283) 815895

The Orchards ★★★★
Self Catering
Contact: Mrs Vanessa Holland
t (01538) 308205
e rushley.farm@btinternet.com
w cottageguide.co.uk/theorchards

Paddock House Farm Holiday Cottages, Alstonefield ★★★★
Self Catering
Contact: Mr Mark Redfern
t (01335) 310282
e info@paddockhousefarm.co.uk
w paddockhousefarm.co.uk

Sandybrook Country Park
★★★★ *Self Catering*
Pinelodge Holidays
t (01335) 300000
e sandybrook@pinelodgeholidays.co.uk
w pinelodgeholidays.co.uk/sandybrook.ihtml

Slade House Farm
★★★★-★★★★★
Self Catering
Contact: Mr & Mrs Alan Philp
t (01538) 308123
e alanphilp@sladehousefarm.co.uk
w sladehousefarm.co.uk

The Tannery ★★★★
Self Catering
Peak Cottages
t (0114) 262 0777
e enquiries@peakcottages.com
w peakcottages.com

Thorpe Cloud View
★★★★★ *Self Catering*
Contact: Mr Raymond Neilson
t (01335) 350215
e rayneilson@aol.com
w a1peak.com

Turlow Fields Farm, Hognaston ★★★★
Self Catering
Contact: Mandy & Adrian Hunter
Barnclose Cottage
t (01335) 370834
e aahunter@uk2.net

Yeldersley Hall
★★★★-★★★★★
Self Catering
Contact: Mr Andrew Bailey
t (01335) 343432

ASHBY-DE-LA-ZOUCH Leicestershire

Badgers Sett ★★★
Self Catering
Contact: Mrs A E Wood
t (01670) 367723 & 07718 905251
e enquiries@badgers-sett.com
w badgers-sett.com

Norman's Barn ★★★★
Self Catering
Contact: Mrs Isabel Stanley
t (01530) 412224
e isabel_stanley@hotmail.com
w normansbarn.co.uk

Upper Rectory Farm Cottages ★★★★-★★★★★
Self Catering
Contact: Mrs Jean Corbett
t (01827) 880448
e info@upperrectoryfarmcottages.co.uk
w upperrectoryfarmcottages.co.uk

ASHDON Essex

Hill Farm Holiday Cottages
★★★ *Self Catering*
Contact: Mrs Annette Bel
t (01799) 584881
e hillfarm-holiday-cottages@hotmail.co.uk
w hillfarm-holiday-cottages.co.uk

Whitensmere Farm ★★★★
Self Catering
Contact: Mrs S Ford
t (01799) 584244
e gford@lineone.net
w holidaycottagescambridge.co.uk

ASHFORD BOWDLER Shropshire

Harvest Barn ★★★★
Self Catering
t (01584) 831707
w stmem.com/harvestbarn

ASHFORD IN THE WATER
Derbyshire

Appletree Cottage ★★★★
Self Catering
Peak Cottages
t (0114) 262 0777
e enquiries@peakcottages.com
w peakcottages.com

Ashford Farm Holiday Cottages ★★★–★★★★
Self Catering
Peak Cottages
t (0114) 262 0777
e enquiries@peakcottages.com
w peakcottages.com

Churchdale Farm ★★★★★
Self Catering
Contact: Mrs Sarah Winkworth-Smith
t (01629) 640269
e info@churchdaleholidays.co.uk
w churchdaleholidays.co.uk

Clematis Cottage ★★★
Self Catering
Contact: Bernard & Kate Armstrong
Holmedene
t (01629) 813448
e bernard.armstrong@btinternet.com

Cliff End Cottage ★★★★
Self Catering
Contact: Janet Palfreyman
t (01246) 568355
e janetpalfreyman@yahoo.co.uk

Corner Cottage ★★★★
Self Catering
Contact: Mr Tony Staley
The Barn
t (01629) 583811
e tonystaley@hotmail.com
w littlegemcottages.co.uk

End Cottage ★★★★
Self Catering
Contact: Mrs Lucy Wright
t (01629) 640136
e lucyinlongstone@hotmail.com
w endcottage.co.uk

Foxglove Cottage ★★★★
Self Catering
Peak Cottages
t (0114) 262 0777
e enquiries@peakcottages.com
w peakcottages.com

Nanny Peggy's Cottage ★★★★ *Self Catering*
Contact: Mrs Marsden
t (01629) 640576

Orchard House ★★★★
Self Catering
Contact: Mr & Mrs Marsden
t (01629) 812895
e bookings@orchardproperties.co.uk
w orchardproperties.co.uk

The Smithy ★★★★
Self Catering
Peak Cottages
t (0114) 262 0777
e enquiries@peakcottages.com
w peakcottages.com

Sunny Lea, Ashford in the Water ★★★★ *Self Catering*
Contact: Mrs D Furniss
t (01629) 815285 & 07866 329691

Thorpe Cottage ★★★
Self Catering
Peak Cottages
t (0114) 262 0777
e enquiries@peakcottages.com
w peakcottages.com

Thyme Cottage ★★★★
Self Catering
Contact: Mrs Hazel Bell
t (01246) 583564
e hazel@peak-district-holidays.co.uk
w peak-district-holidays.co.uk

Willow Cottage ★★★★
Self Catering
Contact: Mr Tony Staley
t (01629) 583811
e tonystaley@hotmail.com
w littlegemcottages.co.uk

ASHORNE
Warwickshire

The Head Gardener's Cottage ★★★★★
Self Catering
Contact: Mrs Elizabeth Struthers
t (01926) 651045
e libbystruthers@hotmail.com

ASHOVER
Derbyshire

Ashmore House Garden Apartment ★★★
Self Catering
Contact: Mr & Mrs M Thomas
t (01246) 590343
e ashmorehouse@supanet.com

Holestone Moor Barns ★★★★★ *Self Catering*
Contact: Mr & Mrs Steve & Vicki Clemerson
t (01246) 591263
e info@hmbarns.co.uk
w hmbarns.co.uk

Peasunhurst ★★★★★
Self Catering
Peak Cottages
t (0114) 262 0777
e enquiries@peakcottages.com
w peakcottages.com

Woodlands ★★★
Self Catering
Peak Cottages
t (0114) 262 0777
e enquiries@peakcottages.com
w peakcottages.com

ASHTON
Northamptonshire

Vale Farm House ★★★★
Self Catering
Contact: Mrs Zanotto
t (01604) 863697
e teresa@valefarmhouse.co.uk
w valefarmhouse.co.uk

ASTON EYRE
Shropshire

West Farm Cottage ★★★★
Self Catering
Contact: Mrs Deborah Meredith
t (01746) 714406
e deborahwestfarm@aol.com
w westfarmcottage.co.uk

ASTON-ON-CLUN
Shropshire

The Granary ★★★★
Self Catering
Contact: Mr Morgan
t (01588) 660227
e all@rowtongrange.freeserve.co.uk
w rowtongrange.co.uk

ATHERSTONE
Warwickshire

Hipsley Farm Cottages ★★★★ *Self Catering*
Contact: Mrs Ann Prosser
t (01827) 872437
e ann@hipsley.co.uk
w hipsley.co.uk

AUDLEY END
Essex

Cambridge Lodge ★★★★★
Self Catering
English Heritage
t 0870 333 1187
e holidaycottages@english-heritage.org.uk
w english-heritage.org.uk/holidaycottages

AUNBY
Lincolnshire

No 2 Clematis Cottage ★★★★–★★★★★
Self Catering
Contact: Kaye Griffin
t (01778) 590280
e info@clematiscottages.co.uk
w clematiscottages.co.uk

AVERHAM
Nottinghamshire

Flo's Cottage ★★★
Self Catering
t (01636) 672990
e floscottage@hotmail.co.uk
w grandmas-cottage.co.uk

AVON DASSETT
Warwickshire

The Limes Cottage ★★★
Self Catering
Contact: Mrs Diane Anderson-Keating
t (01295) 690245
e dianeanderson2006@yahoo.co.uk

AYLMERTON
Norfolk

Moorland Park ★★★
Self Catering
Contact: Mrs Elaine Field
t (01263) 837508
w moorlandpark.co.uk

Rodavia ★★★★ *Self Catering*
Contact: Mr & Mrs David & Rosemary Wilson
t (01263) 837338
e rodavia@hotmail.com
w villarodavia.co.uk

AYLSHAM
Norfolk

Bay Cottage ★★★★
Self Catering
Contact: Mr Stuart Clarke
t (01263) 734574
e jsclarke@colbycorner.fsnet.co.uk
w enchantingcottages.co.uk

Bure Valley Farm Stays ★★★★ *Self Catering*
Contact: Jackie Browne
t (01263) 732177
e burevalleyfarm@btconnect.com
w burevalleyfarmstay.co.uk

Drabblegate River Cottage ★★★★ *Self Catering*
Contact: Mr Peter Norton
t (01263) 732126
e bookings@norfolkrivercottage.co.uk
w norfolkrivercottage.co.uk

Old Windmill ★★★★★
Self Catering
Contact: Mr Tim Bower
t (01263) 732118
w aylshamwindmill.co.uk

AYMESTREY
Herefordshire

The Bungalow ★★★
Self Catering
Contact: Mr & Mrs T.J. Price
t (01568) 770582
e price2k@fsmail.net
w lowerlye.co.uk

BABRAHAM
Cambridgeshire

Brick Row Cottage ★★★★
Self Catering
Contact: Mr Ian Kime
t (01223) 830323
w brickrowcottage.co.uk

BACTON
Norfolk

Cobblers Cove ★★★
Self Catering
Norfolk Country Cottages
t (01603) 871872
e info@norfolkcottages.co.uk
w norfolkcottages.co.uk

Eden Cottage ★★★★
Self Catering
Norfolk Country Cottages
t (01603) 871872
e info@norfolkcottages.co.uk
w norfolkcottages.co.uk

Greenbank ★★★
Self Catering
Norfolk Country Cottages
t (01603) 871872
e info@norfolkcottages.co.uk
w norfolkcottages.co.uk

Middle Cottage ★★★
Self Catering
Norfolk Country Cottages
t (01603) 871872
e info@norfolkcottages.co.uk
w norfolkcottages.co.uk

No 2 Spindrift ★★
Self Catering
Norfolk Country Cottages
t (01603) 871872
e info@norfolkcottages.co.uk
w norfolkcottages.co.uk

Primrose Cottage ★★★
Self Catering
Contact: Mr & Mrs Allan Epton
t (01692) 650667
e holiday@cablegap.co.uk
w cablegap.co.uk

Rainbows End Park
Rating Applied For
Self Catering
Contact: Paul Whittington
t (01692) 650491
e generealmanager@rainbowsendpark.co.uk
w rainbowsendpark.co.uk

BADINGHAM Suffolk

Workhouse Cottage ★★★★
Self Catering
Contact: Mr & Mrs M Illingworth
t (01728) 688343
w workhousecottage.com

BADLEY Suffolk

Doves Barn Cottage ★★★★
Self Catering
Contact: P J Rozier
t (01449) 722606
w dovesbarncottage.co.uk

The Lodge, Badley ★★★★
Self Catering
Contact: Ms Eleanor De Goni Parks
t (01449) 722800
e info@acrosstheroom.co.uk
w welcomecottages.co.uk

BADWELL ASH Suffolk

Badwell Ash Holiday Lodges
★★★★ *Self Catering*
Contact: Jacqueline Thaokeray
t (01359) 258444
e jacquelinethackeray@btinternet.com
w badwellashlodges.co.uk

BAGNALL Staffordshire

Cordwainer Cottage ★★★
Self Catering
Contact: Mrs Muriel Buckle
t (01782) 302575
w cordwainercottage.co.uk

BAKEWELL Derbyshire

11 Catcliffe Cottage
Rating Applied For
Self Catering
Contact: Irene Thurlow
Mrs I Thurlow
t (01629) 636944
e irenethurlow@yahoo.co.uk

Anne Cottage ★★★★
Self Catering
Contact: Mr & Mrs C Kirkman
Bakewell Holidays
t (01246) 583399
e charles@bakewellholidays.com

Bakewell Holiday Cottage (Coach Cottage)
Rating Applied For
Self Catering
Contact: Mr & Mrs J Gough
Spinney Cottage
t (01628) 810112
e john@gough57.fsnet.co.uk

Barn Cottage – PK666
★★★★ *Self Catering*
Peak Cottages
t (0114) 262 0777
e enquiries@peakcottages.com
w peakcottages.com

Bay Tree Cottage ★★★★
Self Catering
Contact: Mr Philip Ryder
t 07733 308881
e baytree@smartone.co.uk
w peak-district-cottage.co.uk

Bolehill Farm Holiday Cottages ★★★-★★★★
Self Catering
Contact: Mr & Mrs Chris & Shirley Swaap
t (01629) 812359
e info8@bolehillfarm.co.uk
w bolehillfarm.co.uk

Braeside ★★★★
Self Catering
Peak Cottages
t (0114) 262 0777
e enquiries@peakcottages.com
w peakcottages.com

Brew House ★★★★
Self Catering
Contact: Mr Charles Kirkman
t (01245) 583399
e charles@bakewellholidays.com

Butts Cottage ★★★★
Self Catering
Contact: Mr & Mrs C Kirkman
Bakewell Holidays
t (01246) 583399
e charles@bakewellholidays.com

Carter's Mill Cottage
★★★★ *Self Catering*
Contact: Mr & Mrs Ian & Jane Marsden
t (01629) 812013
e marsden.millfarm@btinternet.com

Cartwheels ★★★★
Self Catering
Contact: Pat Heawood
t 07821 858640
e julianheawood@yahoo.co.uk
w cottageguide.co.uk/cartwheels

Chalice Cottage ★★★
Self Catering
Peak Cottages
t (0114) 262 0777
e enquiries@peakcottages.com
w peakcottages.com

The Chimneys ★★★★
Self Catering
Contact: Philippa Tilbrook
t (01629) 814043
e philliper@philliper.orangehome.co.uk

Clevedon ★★★ *Self Catering*
Peak Cottages
t (0114) 262 0777
e enquiries@peakcottages.com
w peakcottages.com

Dale End Farm ★★★
Self Catering
Contact: Mrs Elizabeth Hague
t (01629) 650453
e john.elizabeth.hague@talk21.com
w http://uk.geocities.com/daleendfarm@btinternet.com

Edge View ★★★★
Self Catering
Contact: Mrs Gillian Rogers
t (01629) 813336

The Garden Lodge, Youlgrave ★★★
Self Catering
Contact: Mrs Irene Shimwell
t (01629) 636568
e irene.shimwell@hotmail.co.uk
w thegardenlodgeyoulgrave.co.uk

Haddon Grove Farm Cottages ★★★-★★★★
Self Catering
Contact: Mr James Viner
t 0845 634 4163
e haddongrovefarm@blueyonder.co.uk
w haddongrovefarmcottages.co.uk

Hillside Cottage ★★★
Self Catering
Contact: Mrs Beverley Tunnicliffe
t (01629) 812752

The Manager's House
★★★★ *Self Catering*
Contact: Mr & Mrs Jonathan & Jane Snodgrass
t (01629) 650489
e enquiries@cheesefactory-cottages.co.uk
w cheesefactory-cottages.co.uk

Mill View ★★★★
Self Catering
Peak Cottages
t (0114) 262 0777
e enquiries@peakcottages.com
w peakcottages.com

Minden Cottage ★★★★
Self Catering
Peak Cottages
t (0114) 262 0777
e enquiries@peakcottages.com
w peakcottages.com

Overdale ★★★★
Self Catering
Contact: Susan & Phillip Walker
t (01623) 471369
e overdale@hotmail.co.uk
w overdale-bankside.co.uk

Peak Cottage ★★★★
Self Catering
Peak Cottages
t (0114) 262 0777
e enquiries@peakcottages.com
w peakcottages.com

Peveril Cottage ★★★★
Self Catering
Peak Cottages
t (0114) 262 0777
e enquiries@peakcottages.com
w peakcottages.com

Sherwood House Self Catering Apartments ★★★
Self Catering
t (01629) 812113

Wye Knot ★★★ *Self Catering*
Contact: Mrs Rosalyn Vahter
t (01629) 814052

Yellowcroft Dale
Rating Applied For
Self Catering
Contact: Mr Colin MacQueen
t (0114) 262 0777
e enquiries@peakcottages.com

Yuletide Cottage ★★★
Self Catering
Contact: Mrs Denise Figg
t (01629) 636234
e hillfigg@aol.com

BALDERTON Nottinghamshire

Inglenook Cottage ★★★
Self Catering
Contact: Mr Iwanciura
t (0115) 920 1973
e navana3@tiscali.co.uk

BALLIDON Derbyshire

Rachels Croft ★★★★
Self Catering
Contact: Mrs Alison Edge
t (01335) 390587
w rachelscroft.co.uk

BALSHAM Cambridgeshire

Grannies Bungalow ★★★
Self Catering
Contact: Mrs Anne Kiddy
t (01223) 893010

BAMFORD Derbyshire

Derwent View ★★★★
Self Catering
Contact: Mrs Joyce Mannion
t (01433) 651637
e jamcottage@fsmail.net
w derwentview.co.uk

Ladybower Apartments
★★★★★ *Self Catering*
Contact: Mr John Illingworth
Lady Bower Apartments
t (01433) 651361
e enquiries@ladybowerapartments.co.uk
w ladybowerapartments.co.uk

Shatton Hall Farm Cottages
★★★★ *Self Catering*
Contact: Mrs Angela Kellie
t (01433) 620635
e ahk@peakfarmholidays.co.uk
w peakfarmholidays.co.uk

Stable Cottage ★★★★★
Self Catering
Peak Cottages
t (0114) 262 0777
e enquiries@peakcottages.com
w peakcottages.com

BANHAM Norfolk

Olde Farm Cottage ★★★
Self Catering
Contact: Mrs Kathleen Girling
t (01953) 860023
w banhamandthebucks.co.uk/oldefarm

BANNINGHAM Norfolk

Bridge Bungalow ★★★★
Self Catering
Norfolk Country Cottages
t (01603) 871872
e info@norfolkcottages.co.uk
w norfolkcottages.co.uk

The Old Chapel ★★★★
Self Catering
Norfolk Country Cottages
t (01603) 871872
e info@norfolkcottages.co.uk
w norfolkcottages.co.uk

BARDWELL Suffolk

Holly House ★★★★
Self Catering
Contact: Mrs Susette Bone
t (01359) 250804
w tiscover.co.uk

BARFORD Warwickshire

The Old Barn ★★★
Self Catering
Contact: Mr Paul Hunt
t (01926) 624775
e dannihunt@btconnect.com

BARLOW Derbyshire

Mulberry Cottage ★★★★
Self Catering
Peak Cottages
t (0114) 262 0777
e enquiries@peakcottages.com
w peakcottages.com

Sycamore Cottage ★★★★
Self Catering
Contact: Mrs Liz Barrett
Sycamore Cottage (Barlow)
t (0114) 289 1071
e cottage.vacations@btopenworld.com
w cottage-vacations.co.uk

BARNEY Norfolk

The Stables ★★★
Self Catering
Contact: Mrs Christine Blackman
t (01328) 878204
e christinebblackman@googlemail.com
w tiscover.co.uk

BARNOLDBY LE BECK North East Lincolnshire

Grange Farm Cottages & Riding School ★★★★
Self Catering
Contact: Jo & Sue Jenkins
t (01472) 822216
e sueuk4000@netscape.net
w grangefarmcottages.com

BARNWELL Northamptonshire

Willow Cottage
Rating Applied For
Self Catering
Contact: Helma Grant
t (01832) 272439
e helmaveeger@aol.com

BARROW UPON SOAR Leicestershire

Kingfisher Cottage ★★★
Self Catering
Contact: Mr Matthews
t (01509) 890244
e nikkidavid@aol.com

BARTON TURF Norfolk

The Piggeries ★★★★
Self Catering
Norfolk Country Cottages
t (01603) 871872
e info@norfolkcottages.co.uk
w norfolkcottages.co.uk

BARTON-UPON-HUMBER Lincolnshire

The Cabbage Patch ★★★
Self Catering
Contact: M Martin
t 07803 504794
e monty1998@easynet.co.uk

Tilton Garth
Rating Applied For
Self Catering
Contact: Daisa Morgan
t (01652) 632313
e daisa@westfieldlakes.co.uk

BASLOW Derbyshire

Clematis Cottage ★★★★
Self Catering
Peak Cottages
t (0114) 262 0777
e enquiries@peakcottages.com
w peakcottages.com

Goose Green Cottage
★★★★ *Self Catering*
Contact: Mr & Mrs Rodgerson
t (0114) 230 8172 & 07979 004979
e i.rodgerson1@btinternet.com
w peakdistrict-nationalpark.com

Rossett Green ★★★
Self Catering
Peak Cottages
t (0114) 262 0777
e enquiries@peakcottages.com
w peakcottages.com

Stable Cottage ★★★★
Self Catering
Contact: Mrs Anne O'Connor
t (01246) 582285
e ourstablecottage@aol.com
w stablecottagebaslow.com

Tick Tock Cottage ★★★★
Self Catering
Peak Cottages
t (0114) 262 0777
e enquiries@peakcottages.com
w peakcottages.com

Toms Cottage ★★★★
Self Catering
Contact: Mr & Mrs C Kirkman
Bakewell Holidays
t (01246) 583399
e charles@bakewellholidays.com

BAWDESWELL Norfolk

Jotts Cottage ★★★★
Self Catering
Norfolk Country Cottages
t (01603) 871872
e info@norfolkcottages.co.uk
w norfolkcottages.co.uk

BAWDSEY Suffolk

Bawdsey Manor ★★★
Self Catering
Contact: Mr Niels Toettcher
t (01394) 411633
e info@bawdseymanor.co.uk

Rose Cottage
Rating Applied For
Self Catering
Suffolk Secrets
t (01502) 722717
e holidays@suffolk-secrets.co.uk
w suffolk-secrets.co.uk

Tailors House, Bawdsey
★★★★★ *Self Catering*
Contact: Mr & Mrs Rawdon & Pat Saunders
t (01394) 411459
e tailors.house@tiscali.co.uk

BAYLHAM Suffolk

Baylham House Farm Annexe ★★★ *Self Catering*
Contact: Mrs Ann Storer
t (01473) 830264
w baylham-house-farm.co.uk

BAYTON Worcestershire

Church House ★★★★
Self Catering
Contact: Ms Maggie Gregory
t (01299) 832304
e churchhouse1@tiscali.co.uk
w churchhousebayton.co.uk

BEACHAMWELL Norfolk

Rectory Holidays ★★★
Self Catering
Contact: Mrs Carole Wilson
t (01366) 328628
w beachamwellrectory.co.uk

BECCLES Suffolk

Redisham Hall ★★★★
Self Catering
t 0870 192 1617
w countryholidays2007.co.uk

BEDFORD Bedfordshire

The Dovecote ★★★★
Self Catering
Contact: Mrs Ros Northern
t (01234) 720293
e info@harroldholidays.co.uk
w harroldholidays.co.uk

BEESTON Norfolk

Holmdene Farm ★★★
Self Catering
Contact: Mrs Gaye Davidson
t (01328) 701284
w holmdenefarm.co.uk

BELPER Derbyshire

Chevin Green Farm ★★★
Self Catering
Contact: Mr Postles
t (01773) 822328
e spostles@globalnet.co.uk
w chevingreenfarm.co.uk

Chevin Side Cottage ★★★
Self Catering
Contact: Mr & Mrs Jordan
t (01773) 823144
e info@chevinhousefarmcottages.co.uk
w chevinhousefarmcottages.co.uk

Chevin View ★★★
Self Catering
Contact: Mrs Tracey Sowerby
t 07773 197783
e traceysowerby@hotmail.com
w spacelocations.co.uk

Derbyshire Holidays ★★★
Self Catering
Contact: Ann Wayne
t (01332) 840564

Fleet Cottage ★★★★
Self Catering
Contact: Mr & Mrs Best
t (01773) 823240
e janebest@inweb.co.uk
w fleetcottage.fusiveweb.co.uk

Wiggonlea Stable ★★★★
Self Catering
Contact: Mrs Spendlove
t (01773) 852344
e wiggonlea@uwclub.net
w wiggonlea.uwclub.net

BELTON Lincolnshire

Waterloo Studios ★★★
Self Catering
Contact: Rhona Repton
t (01476) 592988
e admin@stayandplaybelton.co.uk
w stayandplaybelton.co.uk

BENHALL Suffolk

1 The Beeches ★★★★
Self Catering
Suffolk Secrets
t (01502) 722717
e holidays@suffolk-secrets.co.uk
w suffolk-secrets.co.uk

BENNIWORTH Lincolnshire

Fiddledrill Barn ★★★★★
Self Catering
Contact: Sally & Ian Selby
t (01507) 313231
e infp@glebe-farm.com
w glebe-farm.com

Look out for establishments participating in the Walkers, Cyclists, Families and Welcome Pets! schemes

BERKHAMSTED
Hertfordshire

Holly Tree and Jacks Cottage ★★★ *Self Catering*
Contact: Mrs Barrington
t (01442) 843464
e rbbarrington@aol.com

Walnut Cottage ★★★★
Self Catering
Contact: Mrs Alison Knowles
t (01442) 866541
w smoothhound.co.uk/hotels/broad.html

BESTHORPE
Norfolk

The Hayloft and The Granary ★★★★ *Self Catering*
Contact: Mrs Suzanne Large
t (01953) 455589
w mayfieldbarn.co.uk

BEWDLEY
Worcestershire

The Brant ★★★★
Self Catering
Contact: Mrs Helen Robson
t (01299) 825603
e paulandhelen@hotmail.com
w thebrant.co.uk

Fern Cottage ★★★★
Self Catering
Contact: Mrs Jenny Robbins
t 07899 797535
e bookings@ferncottagebewdley.co.uk
w ferncottagebewdley.co.uk

Hobnill ★★★★ *Self Catering*
t (01299) 841238
w hobnill.co.uk

Manor Holding ★★★
Self Catering
Contact: Mr & Mrs Nigel & Penny Dobson-Smyth
t 07970 260010
e nds@landscapeconsultancy.freeserve.co.uk

The Old Barn ★★★★★
Self Catering
Contact: Mrs Jill Price
t (01299) 269350
e jill_price@btinternet.com
w theoldbarnbewdley.co.uk

Swan Cottage ★★★★
Self Catering
Contact: Mrs Mandy White
M J Services
t (01299) 401182
e mandy@swancottagebewdley.co.uk
w swancottagebewdley.co.uk

BEYTON
Suffolk

Manorflat ★★★★
Self Catering
Contact: Mr & Mrs Kay & Mark Dewsbury
t (01359) 270960

BIDFORD-ON-AVON
Warwickshire

Corner Cottage and Pathway Cottage
★★★★-★★★★★
Self Catering
Contact: Mr & Mrs Lucas
t (01789) 293932
e lucasstratford@aol.com
w lucasstratford.co.uk

Little Haven
Rating Applied For
Self Catering
Contact: Mrs Jean Cholerton
t (01789) 773653
e jcholerton@aol.com

BIGGIN-BY-HARTINGTON
Derbyshire

Biggin Grange, Biggin-by-Hartington ★★★★
Self Catering
Contact: Mrs Jane Henry
t (01298) 687254
e henrys@biggingrange.co.uk
w biggingrange.co.uk

BILLERICAY
Essex

Pump House Apartment
★★★★★ *Self Catering*
Contact: Mr John Bayliss
Pump House
t (01277) 656579
e johnwbayliss@btinternet.com
w thepumphouseapartment.co.uk

BINHAM
Norfolk

1 Abbey House ★★★★
Self Catering
Norfolk Country Cottages
t (01603) 871872
e info@norfolkcottages.co.uk
w norfolkcottages.co.uk

The Barn ★★★★
Self Catering
Norfolk Country Cottages
t (01603) 871872
e info@norfolkcottages.co.uk
w norfolkcottages.co.uk

Bettys Cottage And Bobs Cottage ★★★★-★★★★★
Self Catering
Contact: Mrs Fiona Thompson
t (01328) 830639
w tiscover.co.uk

Fairfield Cottage ★★★
Self Catering
Contact: Mrs Sheila Thornton
Apple Acre
t (01636) 830395
w tiscover.co.uk

Flat 9 Abbey House ★★★
Self Catering
Norfolk Country Cottages
t (01603) 871872
e info@norfolkcottages.co.uk
w norfolkcottages.co.uk

The Hollies ★★★★
Self Catering
Contact: Mrs Beryl Howell
t (01328) 878304

BIRCH VALE
Derbyshire

Hallishaw Cote, Birch Vale
★★★★ *Self Catering*
Contact: Mrs Jennifer Hallam
t (01663) 746155
e jenny@coldharbour.fslife.co.uk
w hallishawcote.co.uk

BIRCHER
Herefordshire

Brook House Farm Flat
★★★ *Self Catering*
Contact: Mrs Shan Smith
t (01568) 780520
e shanmsmith@aol.com

BIRCHOVER
Derbyshire

Birchover Cottages ★★★
Self Catering
Peak Cottages
t (0114) 262 0777
e enquiries@peakcottages.com
w peakcottages.com

Uppertown Byre ★★★
Self Catering
Peak Cottages
t (0114) 262 0777
e enquiries@peakcottages.com
w peakcottages.com

Uppertown Hayloft ★★★
Self Catering
Peak Cottages
t (0114) 262 0777
e enquiries@peakcottages.com
w peakcottages.com

BIRMINGHAM
West Midlands

PostBox ★★★★
Serviced Apartments
Bridge Street Worldwide
t (020) 7792 2222
e eileen.sexton-adams@bridgestreet.com
w bridgestreet.com

Premier Apartments Birmingham ★★★★
Serviced Apartments
t (0121) 666 4444
e info@premierapartmentsbirmingham.com
w premierapartmentsbirmingham.com

SACO Edgbaston ★★★★
Serviced Apartments
SACO Apartments
t (0117) 974 5936
e sarahbailey@sacaoapartments.co.uk
w sacoapartments.co.uk

SACO Livingbase ★★★★
Serviced Apartments
SACO Apartments
t (0117) 974 5936
e sarahbailey@sacaoapartments.co.uk
w sacoapartments.co.uk

Skyline ★★★★
Serviced Apartments
The Apartment Service
t (020) 8944 1444
e melanied@apartment.co.uk
w apartmentservice.com

BISHOP'S CASTLE
Shropshire

Claremont Holiday Cottages
★★★ *Self Catering*
Contact: Mrs Audrey Price
t (01588) 638170
e info@priceclaremont.co.uk
w priceclaremont.co.uk

The Firs ★★★ *Self Catering*
Sykes Cottages
t (01244) 345700
e info@sykescottages.co.uk
w sykescottages.co.uk

Mount Cottage ★★★★
Self Catering
Contact: Mrs Heather Willis
t (01588) 638288
e heather@mountcottage.co.uk
w mountcottage.co.uk

Walkmill Cottage Barn ★★★
Self Catering
t (01588) 650671
w stmem.com/walkmillcottage

BISHOPS FROME
Herefordshire

Five Bridges Cottages
★★★★ *Self Catering*
Contact: Mark & Bea Chatterton
t (01531) 640340
e fivebridgescottage@fsmail.net
w fivebridgescottage.co.uk

BISHOP'S STORTFORD
Hertfordshire

Family Stay ★★★
Self Catering
Contact: Mr & Mrs James & Louise Barrington-Brown
t (01279) 503951

Hockerill Court ★★★
Self Catering
Contact: Mr Nick Papier
t (01279) 504310
w stansted-airport-accommodation.co.uk

BISHOPSWOOD
Herefordshire

House in the Woods ★★★★
Self Catering
Contact: Paula Heath
t (01594) 860935
e hampsteaddud@btinternet.com

BLACKBROOK
Staffordshire

Nags Head Farm Cottages
★★★ *Self Catering*
Contact: Mrs A Leathem
t (01782) 680334
e nagsheadfarm@aol.com
w nagsheadfarm.co.uk

BLACKWELL
Derbyshire

Pike Barns ★★★★
Self Catering
Peak Cottages
t (0114) 262 0777
e enquiries@peakcottages.com
w peakcottages.com

BLAKENEY Norfolk

51 High Street ★★★
Self Catering
Norfolk Country Cottages
t (01603) 871872
e info@norfolkcottages.co.uk
w norfolkcottages.co.uk

Claremont House
Rating Applied For
Self Catering
Norfolk Country Cottages
t (01603) 871872
e info@norfolkcottages.co.uk
w norfolkcottages.co.uk

Currie's Cottage ★★★
Self Catering
Norfolk Country Cottages
t (01603) 871872
e info@norfolkcottages.co.uk
w norfolkcottages.co.uk

Friary ★★★ *Self Catering*
Contact: Mrs Diana Cooke
t (01603) 624827
e cookehd@paston.co.uk
w blakeney-friary.co.uk

Quayside Cottages
★★★-★★★★ *Self Catering*
Contact: Mrs Veronica Alvarez
t (01462) 768627
e veronicaalvarez@blakeneycottages.co.uk
w blakeneycottages.co.uk

Roslyn ★★★ *Self Catering*
Contact: Mrs Brenda Eke
t (01263) 860111

Seagulls ★★★★
Self Catering
Contact: Holiday Cottages
t 0870 072 3723
w english-country-cottages.co.uk

BLAXHALL Suffolk

Primrose Cottage ★★★★
Self Catering
Contact: Mrs Harriet Hunter Blair
t (01449) 711433
e enquiries@primrosecottageblaxhall.co.uk
w primrosecottageblaxhall.co.uk

Sheriff's Cottage ★★★
Self Catering
Contact: Mr & Mrs Malcolm & Viviene Browne
t (01728) 688993

BLETSOE Bedfordshire

Bourne End Farm
Rating Applied For
Self Catering
t (01234) 783184
e bourneendbandb@btconnect.com
w highfield-farm.co.uk

BLOFIELD Norfolk

The Storehouse ★★★★
Self Catering
Norfolk Country Cottages
t (01603) 871872
e info@norfolkcottages.co.uk
w norfolkcottages.co.uk

BLO'NORTON Norfolk

Fenfarm Cottage ★★★
Self Catering
Suffolk Secrets
t (01502) 722717
e holidays@suffolk-secrets.co.uk
w suffolk-secrets.co.uk

BLOXHOLM Lincolnshire

Church View Cottage
★★★★ *Self Catering*
Contact: Jane Coles
t (01526) 833055
e hospitalityjane@btinternet.com
w hospitalityjane.co.uk

The Lodge ★★ *Self Catering*
Contact: Helen Gillatt
t (01526) 860347

BLYTHBURGH Suffolk

Athel Cottage ★★★
Self Catering
Suffolk Secrets
t (01502) 722717
e holidays@suffolk-secrets.co.uk
w suffolk-secrets.co.uk

Lavender Cottage ★★★★
Self Catering
Suffolk Secrets
t (01502) 722717
e holidays@suffolk-secrets.co.uk
w suffolk-secrets.co.uk

Red Sails ★★★★★
Self Catering
Contact: Mrs Christine Baker
t (01502) 724131
w blythburgh.net/redsails/

Valleyview ★★★★
Self Catering
Suffolk Secrets
t (01502) 722717
e holidays@suffolk-secrets.co.uk
w suffolk-secrets.co.uk

BOCKLETON Worcestershire

Grafton Grove ★★★★
Self Catering
Contact: Mrs Sue Thomas
t (01568) 750602
e grafton.farm@btinternet.com
w graftonfarm.co.uk

BODENHAM Herefordshire

Bodenham Forge, Bodenham ★★★★
Self Catering
Contact: Mary & Simon Nickols
t (01568) 797144
e stay@bodenhamforge.co.uk
w bodenhamforge.co.uk

The Garden Barn ★★★
Self Catering
Contact: Julia James
t 07748 613110
e julijames1@hotmail.co.uk
w gardenbarnstudios.co.uk

BODHAM Norfolk

Hartswood Cottage ★★★★
Self Catering
Contact: Mr & Mrs Arnold
t (01582) 508281
w hartswoodcottage.mysite.orange.co.uk

BONSALL Derbyshire

Cowbell Cottage ★★★★
Self Catering
Contact: M Kehle-Cullen
t (01332) 348242
e mkehle@mac.com
w cowbellcottage.com

Hollies Cottage ★★★
Self Catering
Contact: Mrs Joy Mountney
t (01629) 823162

BOOTON Norfolk

Eliza Lodge ★★★
Self Catering
Norfolk Country Cottages
t (01603) 871872
e info@norfolkcottages.co.uk
w norfolkcottages.co.uk

BORESFORD Herefordshire

Orchard House ★★★★
Self Catering
Contact: Mrs Susan Bywater
t (01544) 260237
e enquiries@hicksfarmholidays.co.uk
w hicksfarmholidays.co.uk

BOSTON Lincolnshire

Elms Farm Cottages
★★★★-★★★★★
Self Catering
Contact: Carol Emerson
t (01205) 290840 & 07887 652021
e carol@elmsfarmcottages.co.uk
w elmsfarmcottages.co.uk

Somercotes ★★★
Self Catering
Contact: Mrs Margaret Sharp
t (01235) 833367
e m.l.r.sharp@btinternet.com
w somercotes.biz

BRACKLEY Northamptonshire

Iletts Courtyard ★★★★
Self Catering
Contact: Mrs Sally Bellingham
t (01280) 703244
e iletts@clara.co.uk
w home.clara.net/iletts

BRACON ASH Norfolk

Rectory Barn ★★★★
Self Catering
Norfolk Country Cottages
t (01603) 871872
e info@norfolkcottages.co.uk
w norfolkcottages.co.uk

BRADLEY Derbyshire

Bradley Hall
★★★★-★★★★★
Self Catering
Contact: Mrs Michele Wrigley
t (01335) 370222
e michelle@pmwproperty.com
w ashbourneselfcatering.co.uk

Briar, Bluebell & Primrose Cottages ★★★-★★★★
Self Catering
Contact: Mrs Janet Hinds
t (01335) 344504
e janethindsfarm@yahoo.co.uk
w yeldersleyoldhallfarm.co.uk

Shepherds Folly ★★★★
Self Catering
Peak Cottages
t (0114) 262 0777
e enquiries@peakcottages.com
w peakcottages.com

BRADNOP Staffordshire

Millstones ★★ *Self Catering*
Contact: Mrs Pat Edwards
t (01538) 304548
e edwards@swepme.fsnet.co.uk
w millstones.uk.com

BRADWELL Derbyshire

Smalldale ★★★★
Self Catering
Sykes Cottages
t (01244) 345700
e info@sykescottages.co.uk
w sykescottages.co.uk

BRAILSFORD Derbyshire

The Cottage at Culland Mount Farm ★★★★
Self Catering
Contact: Mrs Carolyn Phillips
t (01335) 360313
e cullandmount@tiscali.co.uk
w cullandmount.co.uk

BRAINTREE Essex

Panfield House ★★★★
Self Catering
Contact: Mrs Ursula Williamson
t (01376) 326345
w panfieldhouse.com

Red Lion Cottages 1 ★★
Self Catering
Contact: Mrs Moran McKellar Ratcliffe
t (01376) 584043

BRANCASTER Norfolk

11 Anchorage View ★★★
Self Catering
Birds Norfolk Holiday Homes
t (01485) 534267
e shohol@birdsnorfolkholidayhomes.co.uk
w norfolkholidayhomes-birds.co.uk

Look out for establishments participating in the National Accessible Scheme

Bramble ★★★★
Self Catering
Birds Norfolk Holiday Homes
t (01485) 534267
e shohol@birdsnorfolkholidayhomes.co.uk
w norfolkholidayhomes-birds.co.uk

Cheal Cottage, Brancaster ★★★ *Self Catering*
Contact: Mrs Janet Harrison
Field House
t (01775) 680513

Peddars Lodge ★★★
Self Catering
Norfolk Country Cottages
t (01603) 871872
e info@norfolkcottages.co.uk
w norfolkcottages.co.uk

Plunketts Cottage ★★★★
Self Catering
Kett Country Cottages
t (01328) 856853
e info@kettcountrycottages.co.uk
w kettcountrycottages.co.uk

Roman Way ★★★
Self Catering
Norfolk Country Cottages
t (01603) 871872
e info@norfolkcottages.co.uk
w norfolkcottages.co.uk

Russett Lodge ★★★
Self Catering
Birds Norfolk Holiday Homes
t (01485) 534267
e shohol@birdsnorfolkholidayhomes.co.uk
w norfolkholidayhomes-birds.co.uk

Sea Lodge ★★★★
Self Catering
Norfolk Country Cottages
t (01603) 871872
e info@norfolkcottages.co.uk
w norfolkcottages.co.uk

Thompson Brancaster Farms ★★★ *Self Catering*
Contact: Mrs Jane Thompson
t (01485) 210000
e jet@brancasterhall.co.uk
w tbfholidayhomes.co.uk

BRANCASTER STAITHE Norfolk

21 Dale End ★★★★
Self Catering
Contact: Mrs Debbie Clark
Stone House
t (01572) 747389
w debbieclarklettings.com

Close Cottage ★★★★
Self Catering
Norfolk Country Cottages
t (01603) 871872
e info@norfolkcottages.co.uk
w norfolkcottages.co.uk

Island Cottage ★★
Self Catering
Birds Norfolk Holiday Homes
t (01485) 534267
e shohol@birdsnorfolkholidayhomes.co.uk
w norfolkholidayhomes-birds.co.uk

Vista And Carpenters Cottages ★★★–★★★★★
Self Catering
Contact: Mrs Gloria Smith
Dale View
t (01485) 210497

Westbourne ★★★
Self Catering
Birds Norfolk Holiday Homes
t (01485) 534267
e shohol@birdsnorfolkholidayhomes.co.uk
w norfolkholidayhomes-birds.co.uk

BRANDON Suffolk

Deacons Cottage ★★
Self Catering
Contact: Mrs B D Deacon
t (01842) 828023

BRASSINGTON Derbyshire

Chapel House ★★★
Self Catering
Peak Cottages
t (0114) 262 0777
e enquiries@peakcottages.com
w peakcottages.com

The Coach House ★★★
Self Catering
Contact: Jennifer Greenleaves
t (01332) 833009
e chris@j-greenleaves.freeserve.co.uk
w holidaycottagederbyshire.com

Hillocks Barn ★★★★
Self Catering
Contact: Ms J Perkins
t 07980 868985
e info@hillocksbarn.co.uk
w hillocksbarn.co.uk

Hoe Grange Holidays ★★★★ *Self Catering*
t (01629) 540262
e info@hoegrangeholidays.co.uk
w hoegrangeholidays.co.uk

Jack's Cottage ★★★
Self Catering
Peak Cottages
t (0114) 262 0777
e enquiries@peakcottages.com
w peakcottages.com

BREDON Worcestershire

The Moretons Vacation Houses ★★★★★
Self Catering
Contact: Mrs Karen Webb
t (01684) 772294
e soutar@moretonsbredon.co.uk
w moretons-soutar.co.uk

BRIDGNORTH Shropshire

Astbury Falls – Lodge 6 ★★★★ *Self Catering*
Contact: Mrs Jane Priest
t (01746) 761622
e jlet05@hotmail.com

Bulls Head Inn ★★★
Self Catering
Contact: Mrs Norma King
t (01746) 861469
e bull_chelmarsh@btconnect.com
w bullsheadchelmarsh.co.uk

Eudon Burnell Cottages ★★★★ *Self Catering*
Contact: Mrs Margaret Crawford Clarke
t (01746) 789235
e eudon-burnell@talk21.com
w eudon.co.uk

Forge Cottage ★★★★
Self Catering
Contact: Mr Dennis Price
t (01746) 762110
e apleyest@btconnect.com
w apleyestate.com

The Granary ★★★
Self Catering
Contact: Mrs Sarah Allen
t (01746) 712272
e allens@oldvicditton.freeserve.co.uk

Jacob's Cottage ★★★★
Self Catering
Contact: Mrs Gilly Wooldridge
t (01952) 730485
e peterwulf@lineone.net
w virtual-shropshire.co.uk/jacob

Lobby Stables ★★★★ *Self Catering & Serviced Apartments*
t (01746) 789218
w shropshire-cottage.co.uk

Whitford ★★★★
Self Catering
t (01746) 764945
e whitford34@hotmail.com
w bridgnorthholidaycottage.com

BRIERLEY Herefordshire

Serafina Cottage ★★★★
Self Catering
Contact: Adam & Sarah Holt
t (01568) 620003
e aholt@lsh.co.uk

Walnut Tree Cottage ★★★★ *Self Catering*
Contact: Elaine Johnson
t (01568) 620033
e elaine@walnuttreecottage.net
w walnuttreecottage.net

BRIGSLEY North East Lincolnshire

Prospect Farm Country Cottages ★★★★
Self Catering
Contact: Mrs Janet Speight
t (01472) 826491
e prospectfarm@btconnect.com
w prospectfarm.co.uk

BRIGSTOCK Northamptonshire

The Gable End ★★★
Self Catering
Contact: Mrs Helen Clarke
t (01536) 373674
e marcus@clarke.1999.freeserve.co.uk

BRININGHAM Norfolk

Old White Horse Cottage ★★★ *Self Catering*
Kett Country Cottages
t (01328) 856853
e info@kettcountrycottages.co.uk
w kettcountrycottages.co.uk

BRISLEY Norfolk

Church Farm Cottage ★★★–★★★★ *Self Catering*
Contact: Mrs G.V Howes
t (01362) 668332
e gillhowes@yahoo.co.uk
w tiscover.co.uk

BRISTON Norfolk

Clee House ★★★★
Self Catering
Contact: Robin Burkitt
t (01263) 862133
e enquiries@glavenvalleycottages.com
w glavenvalleycottages.com

The Firs ★★★★ *Self Catering*
Contact: Mr Paul Horti
t (01277) 823204
w northnorfolkbreaks.co.uk

BROADWAY Worcestershire

Old Post Office Apartment ★★★★ *Self Catering*
t (01386) 701322

The Willows Cottages ★★★★ *Self Catering*
Contact: Mrs Deborah Williamson
t (01386) 852913
e enquiries@broadwaymanor-cottages.co.uk
w broadwaymanor-cottages.co.uk

BROBURY Herefordshire

Brobury House Cottages ★★★★ *Self Catering*
Contact: Mrs Pru Cartwright
t (01981) 500229
e enquiries@broburyhouse.co.uk
w broburyhouse.co.uk

BROCKTON Shropshire

Evergreen Cottage ★★★
Self Catering
Contact: Mr Dave Roberts
t 07808 418087
e davidroberts@fsmail.net

BROMSASH Herefordshire

Eastview ★★★★
Self Catering
Contact: Sue Powell
t (01989) 750508
e eastviewselfcatering@tiscali.co.uk
w eastviewselfcatering.co.uk

BROMYARD
Herefordshire

Boyce Holiday Cottages
★★★★ *Self Catering*
Contact: Miss Alison Richards
t (01886) 884248
e enquiries@boycecottages.co.uk
w boycecottages.co.uk

Oast House & Chaff House
★★★★ *Self Catering*
Contact: Mrs Sally Barrett
t (01885) 483262
e hodgebatch@tiscali.co.uk
w mintridge.co.uk

BROOM
Warwickshire

The Smokery House ★★★★
Self Catering
Contact: Mr Peter Cadwick
t 07710 314953
e stay@thesmokeryhouse.co.uk
w thesmokeryhouse.co.uk

BROSELEY
Shropshire

Aynsley Cottages ★★★
Self Catering
Contact: Mr & Mrs Kieth & Elsie Elcock
t (01952) 882695
e aynsleycottages@hotmail.com
w aynsleycottages.co.uk

BROSELEY WOOD
Shropshire

Rowan Tree Cottage ★★★★
Self Catering
t (01952) 881185

BRUISYARD
Suffolk

Bruisyard Hall ★★★★
Self Catering
Contact: Mr Robert Rous
t (01728) 663205
e dennington@farmline.com
w bruisyardhall.co.uk

BRUNDALL
Norfolk

Lavender Cottage ★★★★
Self Catering
Norfolk Country Cottages
t (01603) 871872
e info@norfolkcottages.co.uk
w norfolkcottages.co.uk

BRUNDISH
Suffolk

Potash Barns
Rating Applied For
Self Catering
Contact: Mr Rob Spendlove
t (01379) 384819
e enquiries@potashbarns.co.uk

BURGH
Norfolk

Corner Cottage ★★★
Self Catering
Norfolk Country Cottages
t (01603) 871872
e info@norfolkcottages.co.uk
w norfolkcottages.co.uk

BURGH-LE-MARSH
Lincolnshire

Jockhedge Cottages ★★★★
Self Catering
Contact: Karen Cumberlidge
t (01754) 810963
e karencumberlidge@hotmail.com
w jockhedge.co.uk

BURGH ON BAIN
Lincolnshire

Bainfield Lodge ★★★★
Self Catering
Contact: Marian Walker
t (01507) 313540
e dennis.walker1@btinternet.com
w bainfieldholidaylodge.co.uk

BURLEY GATE
Herefordshire

Holly Lodge ★★★
Self Catering
Contact: Nick & Trudie Meers
t (01432) 820493
e lodge@meersphoto.com
w cottageguide.co.uk/hollylodge

BURLTON
Shropshire

Oakdene Farm
Rating Applied For
Self Catering
t (01939) 270595
w oakdenefarm.co.uk

Oaks Farm ★★★★
Self Catering
Contact: Mrs Maureen Willock
t (01939) 270472

BURNHAM MARKET
Norfolk

1 Rogers Row ★★★
Self Catering
Norfolk Country Cottages
t (01603) 871872
e info@norfolkcottages.co.uk
w norfolkcottages.co.uk

2 Rogers Row ★★★
Self Catering
Norfolk Country Cottages
t (01603) 871872
e info@norfolkcottages.co.uk
w norfolkcottages.co.uk

Barley Cottage ★★★★
Self Catering
Contact: Mr & Mrs Andrew & Susan Watley
t (01277) 824854
w barleycottageburnhammarket.co.uk/

Charnwood ★★★
Self Catering
Norfolk Country Cottages
t (01603) 871872
e info@norfolkcottages.co.uk
w norfolkcottages.co.uk

The Cottage ★★★
Self Catering
Norfolk Country Cottages
t (01603) 871872
e info@norfolkcottages.co.uk
w norfolkcottages.co.uk

Croftwood ★★★★
Self Catering
Norfolk Country Cottages
t (01603) 871872
e info@norfolkcottages.co.uk
w norfolkcottages.co.uk

Easterly ★★★ *Self Catering*
Norfolk Country Cottages
t (01603) 871872
e info@norfolkcottages.co.uk
w norfolkcottages.co.uk

Fuschia Cottage ★★★
Self Catering
Norfolk Country Cottages
t (01603) 871872
e info@norfolkcottages.co.uk
w norfolkcottages.co.uk

Granary Cottage ★★★★
Self Catering
Contact: Ms Julie Levitt
t (01832) 735150
e levitt.smarter@virgin.net
w granarycottageburnhammarket.com

Maltings Cottage ★★★
Self Catering
Norfolk Country Cottages
t (01603) 871872
e info@norfolkcottages.co.uk
w norfolkcottages.co.uk

Milliners ★★★★
Self Catering
Norfolk Country Cottages
t (01603) 871872
e info@norfolkcottages.co.uk
w norfolkcottages.co.uk

Rose Cottage ★★★
Self Catering
Contact: Mrs Anne Manning
t (01328) 730775

Shielings and Ebenezer Cottage ★★★-★★★★
Self Catering
Norfolk Country Cottages
t (01603) 871872
e info@norfolkcottages.co.uk
w norfolkcottages.co.uk

Southwinds ★★★★
Self Catering
Norfolk Country Cottages
t (01603) 871872
e info@norfolkcottages.co.uk
w norfolkcottages.co.uk

Stable Cottage ★★★
Self Catering
Contact: Mrs Anne Cringle
t (01328) 738456
w cringle.org

BURNHAM THORPE
Norfolk

Cherry Tree Bungalow ★★
Self Catering
Norfolk Country Cottages
t (01603) 871872
e info@norfolkcottages.co.uk
w norfolkcottages.co.uk

Highfield ★★★ *Self Catering*
Contact: Valerie Southerland
t (01328) 738416
e barrysoutherland@aol.com
w whitehallfarm-accommodation.com

BURTON
Lincolnshire

The Conifers Guest Annexe
★★★★ *Self Catering*
Contact: Susan Gray
t (01522) 703196
e mj.grey@homecall.co.uk
w theconifers.info

BURTON OVERY
Leicestershire

Shepherds Rest Cottage
★★★★ *Self Catering*
Contact: Mrs Nicola Langton
t (0116) 259 2332
e nicola_langton@beeb.net
w shepherdsrest.org.uk

BURY ST EDMUNDS
Suffolk

15 Bridewell Lane ★★★★
Self Catering
Contact: Mr Wesley Rawdon Cushing
t (01284) 388117
w 15-bridewell-lane.co.uk

Brook Villa ★★★
Self Catering
Contact: Mr David Manning
t (01284) 764387

Court And The Granary Suites ★★★-★★★★
Self Catering
Contact: Roberta, John & Odell Truin
t (01284) 830385
w brighthousefarm.fsnet.co.uk

Culford Farm Cottages
★★★★-★★★★★
Self Catering
Contact: Mr Stephen Flack
t (01284) 728334
e enquiries@homefarmculford.co.uk
w culfordfarmcottages.co.uk

The Dower House Flat, Rattlesden ★★★★
Self Catering
Contact: Mrs Hilary Voysey
t (01449) 736332
e all@voysey.freeserve.co.uk
w tiscover.co.uk

Garden Corner ★★★★
Self Catering
Contact: Mr John Stemp
t (01284) 702848

Kitchen Flat ★★★
Self Catering
Contact: Mrs Eileen Storey
t (01284) 755744
w queequeg.demon.co.uk

The Old Dairy at West Lodge ★★★★ *Self Catering*
Contact: Mrs Lynn Cardale
t (01284) 386327
e info@westlodgedairy.co.uk
w westlodgedairy.co.uk

Oliver's Retreat ★★★
Self Catering
Contact: Mrs C Titcombe
t (01284) 766432
e christinetitcombe@bluebottle.com

Pump Lane House ★★★
Self Catering
Contact: Mrs Lucy Taylor
t (01284) 755248

BUTTERTON
Staffordshire

Megs Cottage ★★★★
Self Catering
Contact: Mrs Andrea Evans
t (01538) 304486

Swainsley Farm ★★★★★
Self Catering
Contact: Mr & Mrs Chris Snook
t (01298) 84530
e info@swainsleyfarm.co.uk
w swainsleyfarm.co.uk

BUXTON
Derbyshire

1 Rock View & The Old Stores ★★★-★★★★
Self Catering
Contact: Mrs Julie Burns
t (01298) 23374
e j.m.burns@hotmail.co.uk
w millersdaleholidaycottages.co.uk

Como ★★★ *Self Catering*
Contact: James Freeman
t (01298) 24275
e jim.freeman@manchester.ac.uk
w luganobreaks.co.uk

Corner Cottage ★★★★
Self Catering
Peak Cottages
t (0114) 262 0777
e enquiries@peakcottages.com
w peakcottages.com

Farriers ★★★★ *Self Catering*
Contact: Pam Livesley
t (0115) 922 5582
e stay@farriersbuxton.co.uk
w farriersbuxton.co.uk

Hargate Hall, Wormhill
★★★ *Self Catering*
Contact: Mr Anthony Knox
t (01298) 872591
e info@hargate-hall.co.uk
w hargate-hall.co.uk

Hillside ★★★ *Self Catering*
Contact: Mr David Swain
t (01298) 25451

Lake View ★★★
Self Catering
Contact: Mr MacQueen
Peak Cottages
t (0114) 262 0777

Market Square Apartments
★★★★ *Self Catering*
Peak Cottages
t (0114) 262 0777
e enquiries@peakcottages.com
w peakcottages.com

The Old Stables ★★★
Self Catering
t (01298) 72319
w fernfarmcottages.co.uk

The Old Stables ★★★★
Self Catering
Contact: Mr Daniel Wright
The Old Stables (Buxton)
t (01298) 25835
e suewright@surfsouth.com
w buxtonoldstables.com

Priory Lea Holiday Flats
★★-★★★ *Self Catering*
Contact: Mrs Gillian Taylor
t (01298) 23737
e priorylea@hotmail.co.uk
w cressbrook.co.uk/buxton/priorylea

Smithy's Cottage ★★★★
Self Catering
Contact: Mrs Pam Livesley
t (0115) 922 5582
e pam@smithycottage.co.uk
w smithyscottage.co.uk

Town End Apartment ★★★
Self Catering
Peak Cottages
t (0114) 262 0777
e enquiries@peakcottages.com
w peakcottages.com

Wheeldon Trees Farm, Earl Sterndale ★★★★
Self Catering
Contact: Deborah & Martin Hofman
t (01298) 83219
e stay@wheeldontreesfarm.co.uk
w wheeldontreesfarm.co.uk

BUXTON
Norfolk

The Old Stable Yard ★★★★
Self Catering
Contact: Mr B Catchpole
t (01603) 279585
w birdsplacefarm.co.uk

Snowdrops
Rating Applied For
Self Catering
Norfolk Country Cottages
t (01603) 871872
e info@norfolkcottages.co.uk
w norfolkcottages.co.uk

BYLAUGH
Norfolk

Meadowview ★★★
Self Catering
Contact: Mrs Jenny Lake
t (01362) 688584
e lakeparkfm@aol.com
w tiscover.co.uk

CAISTER-ON-SEA
Norfolk

Sand Dune Cottages ★★
Self Catering
Contact: Mr Miles Rainer
t (01493) 720352
e sand.dune.cottages@amserve.net
w eastcoastlive.co.uk

CALDECOTE
Cambridgeshire

Highfield House Annex
★★★ *Self Catering*
Contact: Mr Neville Hawkins
t (01954) 210841
w highfieldhouse.org

CALDECOTE
Northamptonshire

Home Farm
Rating Applied For
Self Catering
t (01327) 352651
e gisela@giselasbedandbreakfast.com
w giselasbedandbreakfast.com

CALDECOTT
Rutland

Wisteria Cottage & Chalet
★★★ *Self Catering*
Contact: Mrs Mel Hudson
t (01536) 771357
e enquiries@rutland-cottages.co.uk
w rutland-cottages.co.uk

CALIFORNIA
Norfolk

Cottages in Norfolk ★★★★
Self Catering
Contact: Mrs S J Sampson
t (01493) 730279
w cottages-in-norfolk.co.uk

CALLOW
Herefordshire

The Loft and Barn at Warmhearth Cottage
★★★★ *Self Catering*
Contact: Louise Weir
The Loft and Barn at Warmhearth
t (01432) 371517 & 07864 164938
e bookings@warmhearth.net
w warmhearth.net

CALVER
Derbyshire

Barn Cottage ★★★★
Self Catering
Contact: Mr Barry Finney
t (01433) 631672
e enquiries@barncottage.com
w barncottage.com

The Nurseries ★★★★
Self Catering
Contact: Dr & Mrs P Howard
t (0114) 230 8456
e dr.howard@btconnect.com
w heritageholidayhomes.com

Sunnyside ★★★
Self Catering
Peak Cottages
t (0114) 262 0777
e enquiries@peakcottages.com
w peakcottages.com

CAMBRIDGE
Cambridgeshire

18 Derby Street ★★★★
Self Catering
Contact: Mr Desmond Hirsch
t (01223) 360200
w cambridgeaccommodation.com

87 Devonshire Mews
★★★★ *Self Catering*
Contact: Mr Anton Creasy
t (01223) 709409
w cambridgeshorttermlets.co.uk

Adam and Eve Court
★★★★ *Self Catering*
Contact: Mrs Wendy Whistler
Selective Studios
t (01954) 231850
e info@selectivestudios.com
w selectivestudios.com

Alexandra Apartments
★★★★★ *Self Catering*
Contact: Mr & Mrs Nick & Julie Wright
t (01223) 500776
e info@alexandraapartments.co.uk
w alexandraapartments.co.uk

Bells Apartments ★★★
Self Catering
Contact: Mr & Mrs Diana & Tony Loizou
t (01223) 323231

Broadmeadows ★★★★
Self Catering
w accommodationcambridge.com

Cambridge Midsummer Apartments ★★★★
Self Catering
Contact: Mrs Maria Fasano
t (01223) 316074
e enquiry@worth-house.co.uk
w cambridgemidsummer apartments.com

Canonbury House & 53 Richmond Road ★★★★
Self Catering
Contact: Mr A J Kiddy
t (01799) 599272
w cambridge-vacation-homes.com

Clarence House ★★★★
Self Catering
Contact: Mr Oliver Digney
t (01223) 841294
e sdigney@clarencehouse.fsnet.co.uk
w clarencehouse.org.uk

Glebe Cottage ★★★★
Self Catering
Contact: Mrs Fiona Key
t (01954) 212895
w camcottage.co.uk

Home From Home Apartments ★★★★
Self Catering
Contact: Mrs E Fasano
t (01223) 323555
e homefromhome2@btconnect.com
w accommodationin cambridge.com

Limehouse ★★★★★
Self Catering
w accommodationcambridge.com

Nobleo
Rating Applied For
Self Catering
Contact: Mr John McPherson
t (01223) 364778
e francis_mcpherson@yahoo.co.uk

Prospero Homes
★★★★–★★★★★
Self Catering
Contact: Ms Helen Collins
t (01223) 511043 & 07771 935642
e info@prosperohomes.co.uk
w prosperohomes.co.uk

Warkworth Villa ★★★
Self Catering
Contact: Mrs Wendy Whistler
Selective Studios
t (01954) 231850
e info@selectivestudios.com
w selectivestudios.com

Your Space Apartments
★★★★ *Self Catering*
Contact: Ms Suzanne Emerson
t (01223) 315050
e bookings@yourspaceapartments.com
w yourspaceapartments.com

CANWICK
Lincolnshire

Canwick Self Catering ★★★
Self Catering
Contact: Mr Neil Murray
t (01522) 589332
e info@canwickholidayvillage.co.uk
w canwickholidayvillage.co.uk

CARDINGTON
Shropshire

Plaish Park Farm ★★★★★
Self Catering
Contact: Mrs Sara Jones
t (01694) 771262
e plaishparkfarm@hotmail.co.uk
w plaishparkfarm.co.uk

CARSINGTON
Derbyshire

Breach Farm Self Catering Cottages ★★★★
Self Catering
Contact: Mrs Michelle Wilson
t (01629) 540265
w breachfarm.co.uk

Meadow Fleck Farm
Rating Applied For
Self Catering
Contact: Mrs Josephine Haywood
t (01629) 540910
w sitchbarncottages.co.uk

Owslow Farm House ★★★
Self Catering
Contact: Mr Peter Oldfield
t (01629) 540510
e peter.oldfield@ukonline.co.uk

CASTLE ACRE
Norfolk

1 Sandles Court ★★★
Self Catering
Contact: Mrs Jane Wood
t (01760) 722455

Friars Croft ★★★
Self Catering
Contact: Mrs E McGrath
t (01362) 820408
w tiscover.co.uk

Peddars Cottage ★★★
Self Catering
Contact: Mrs Angela Swindell
t (01534) 736679
e angelaswindell@googlemail.com
w castleacre.org.uk

CASTLE HEDINGHAM
Essex

Rosemary Farm ★★★★
Self Catering
Contact: Mr Garry Ian Henderson
t (01787) 461653

CASTLEMORTON
Worcestershire

Notts Farm Cottage ★★★★
Self Catering
Contact: Ms Sarah Limbrick
t (01684) 833380
e sarah.limbrick@highcourt.demon.co.uk
w malvernholidaycottage.co.uk

CASTLETON
Derbyshire

Cliffe Cottage ★★★
Self Catering
Contact: Mr & Mrs Kenworthy
nCliffe Cottage
t (01629) 732084
e abanister@tiscali.co.uk
w cliffecottage.co.uk

Eastry Cottage ★★★★
Self Catering
Contact: Mrs Jayne Webster
t (01433) 620312
w peakdistrictnationalpark.com

Little Lilac Cottage ★★★★
Self Catering
Contact: Mrs Noorea Bassuni
t (0114) 266 1031
e booking@old-english-cottages.co.uk
w old-english-cottages.co.uk

Mullions ★★★★★
Self Catering
Contact: Mrs Denise Matthews
t (01433) 620257
e denise@riding-house-cottages.co.uk
w riding-house-cottages.co.uk

Oatcake Cottage, Castleton
★★★★ *Self Catering*
Contact: Mrs Angela Quigley
t (01433) 670014
e oatcakecottage@hotmail.com
w oatcakecottage.co.uk

Riding House Farm Cottages
★★★★★ *Self Catering*
Contact: Mrs Denise Matthews
t (01433) 620257
e denise@riding-house-cottages.co.uk
w riding-house-cottages.co.uk

Trickett Gate Barn ★★★★
Self Catering
Contact: Angela & Michael Driver
t (01433) 621590
w trickettgate.co.uk

CATFIELD
Norfolk

Church Cottage ★★★★
Self Catering
Norfolk Country Cottages
t (01603) 871872
e info@norfolkcottages.co.uk
w norfolkcottages.co.uk

CAWSTON
Norfolk

Lilac Cottage ★★★★
Self Catering
Norfolk Country Cottages
t (01603) 871872
e info@norfolkcottages.co.uk
w norfolkcottages.co.uk

Sygate Mill
Rating Applied For
Self Catering
Norfolk Country Cottages
t (01603) 871872
e info@norfolkcottages.co.uk
w norfolkcottages.co.uk

CHAPEL-EN-LE-FRITH
Derbyshire

Barn Cottage ★★★
Self Catering
Peak Cottages
t (0114) 262 0777
e enquiries@peakcottages.com
w peakcottages.com

Keepers Cottage ★★★
Self Catering
Contact: Mrs Mary Hayward
t (01298) 812845

Malcoff Farmhouse ★★★★
Self Catering
Peak Cottages
t (0114) 262 0777
e enquiries@peakcottages.com
w peakcottages.com

Rushop Hall Holiday Cottages ★★★★
Self Catering
Peak Cottages
t (0114) 262 0777
e enquiries@peakcottages.com
w peakcottages.com

Saffi House ★★★★
Self Catering
Contact: Ms Carole Coe
Carole Coe Leisure
t 0870 755 9700
e carole@saffihouse.co.uk
w saffihouse.co.uk

CHARLESWORTH
Derbyshire

Lodge Chalet ★★★★
Self Catering
Peak Cottages
t (0114) 262 0777
e enquiries@peakcottages.com
w peakcottages.com

CHEDGRAVE
Norfolk

Barn Owl Holidays ★★★
Self Catering
Contact: Mrs Rosemary Beattie
t (01508) 528786
e barnowls@bt.clara.co.uk
w barnowlholidays.co.uk

Little Willows
Rating Applied For
Self Catering
Contact: Mrs S Leigh
t (01508) 528525
e info@littlewillows.co.uk
w littlewillows.co.uk

Willow Barn ★★★★
Self Catering
Norfolk Country Cottages
t (01603) 871872
e info@norfolkcottages.co.uk
w norfolkcottages.co.uk

CHEDISTON
Suffolk

1 Town Farm Cottage
★★★★ *Self Catering*
Suffolk Secrets
t (01502) 722717
e holidays@suffolk-secrets.co.uk
w suffolk-secrets.co.uk

Mount Pleasant Farm Barn
★★★★ *Self Catering*
Contact: Ms Judith Fosset
t (01502) 578278
w heritagehideaways.co.uk

CHELMARSH
Shropshire

Dinney Farm Self Catering – Cart Cottage
★★★–★★★★★
Self Catering
t (01746) 861070

CHELMORTON
Derbyshire

Casa Dakini ★★★
Self Catering
Contact: Rebecca Menz
t (01298) 85285
e bex.menz@virgin.net
w penninebridleway accomodation.co.uk

Jollyfield Farm ★★★★
Self Catering
Peak Cottages
t (0114) 262 0777
e enquiries@peakcottages.com
w peakcottages.com

Lilac Cottage
Rating Applied For
Self Catering
Contact: Ms Goodall
t (01582) 834763
e lilaccottage@mail.com

Swallow Barn ★★★★
Self Catering
Contact: Mrs Gill Chapman
t 07891 950918
e enquiries@swallowbarn.com
w swallowbarn.com

CHELMSFORD
Essex

Bury Barn Cottage ★★★★
Self Catering
Contact: Mrs Anne Oates
t (01245) 237234
w burybarncottage.co.uk

Channel's Serviced Apartments ★★★★
Serviced Apartments
t (01245) 441547
e info@channelslodge.co.uk
w channelsserviced apartments.co.uk

CHERINGTON
Warwickshire

Steele's Cottage ★★★★
Self Catering
Contact: Mrs Carol Russell
t (01608) 686540

CHESTERFIELD
Derbyshire

20 Sanforth Street
Rating Applied For
Self Catering
Contact: Mr & Mrs Bernard & Kate Armstrong
t (01629) 813448
e bernard.armstrong@btinternet.com

Chryslinash ★★★
Self Catering
Contact: Mrs Tina Cave
t (01246) 853467
e glen.cave@sky.com

Pear Tree Cottage ★★★
Self Catering
Contact: Mrs Carol Beckett
t (01773) 872767
e carol.robbeckett@btinternet.com
w peartreecottage.co.uk

Pear Tree Farm Barn, Rowthorne Village ★★★★★
Self Catering
Contact: Mel Copley
t (01623) 811694
e enquiries@peartreefarmbarn.co.uk
w peartreefarmbarn.co.uk

Ploughmans Cottage
★★★★ *Self Catering*
Contact: Mrs Margaret Fry
t (01246) 435328
e ploughmans.cottage@virgin.net
w ploughmanscottage.com

CHINLEY
Derbyshire

Fernbank ★★★ *Self Catering*
Contact: Mrs Jean Storer
t (01298) 813458
e jeanstorer@btopenworld.com
w http://uk.geocities.com/jeanstorer@btinternet.com/

Greenacres Barn ★★★★
Self Catering
Contact: Ms Day/Mr Bennett
t (01663) 750373
e greenacresbarn@homecall.co.uk
w greenacresbarn.co.uk

Monks Meadow Cottage
★★★★ *Self Catering*
Contact: Mrs Pauline Gill
t (01663) 751267
e muriel.jackson1@btopenworld.com
w monksmeadow.co.uk

CHURCH LAWFORD
Warwickshire

The Grange ★★★
Self Catering
Contact: Mrs Lilian Reay
t (024) 7654 2133
e cwreahy@btconnect.com

CHURCH STRETTON
Shropshire

Audrey's Parkgate Cottages
★★★ *Self Catering*
Contact: Mrs Audrey Hill
t (01694) 751303
e park-gate@farmersweekly.net
w stmem.com/parkgatecottages

Botvyle Farm Holiday Cottages ★★★★
Self Catering
t (01694) 722869
w botvylefarm.co.uk

Broome Farm Cottages
★★★★★ *Self Catering*
Contact: Mrs Sarah Cavendish
t 07968 057873
e sarah@sarahcavendish.demon.co.uk
w broomefarm.co.uk

Caradoc Cottage ★★★★
Self Catering
Contact: Mrs Wendy Lewis
t (01694) 751488
e w-lewis@lineone.net
w churchstretoncottages.co.uk

Caradoc Cottages ★★★★
Self Catering
Contact: Mrs Wendy Lewis
Caradoc House
t (01694) 751488
e w-lewis@lineone.net
w churchstrettoncottages.co.uk

The Garden Flat ★★★
Self Catering
Contact: Mrs Carol Hembrow
t (01694) 723715
e cj.hembrow@ukonline.co.uk
w thegardenflatchurchstretton.co.uk

Hodghurst Cottage ★★★
Self Catering
Contact: Mrs C Forsyth
t (01694) 751403
e hodghurst@aol.com
w stmem.com/hodghurstcottage

Leasowes Cottage ★★★★
Self Catering
Contact: Mrs Margaret Harris
t (01694) 751351
e pauleasowes@btinternet.com
w stmem.com/leasowes-cottage

Lower Day Cottages ★★★★
Self Catering
Contact: Mr & Mrs Kirkwood
Lower Day House
t (01694) 771521
e bookings@lowerdayhouse.com
w lowerdayhouse.com

Middle Farm Cottages
★★★★ *Self Catering*
Contact: Mrs Anne Carter
t (01694) 751232
e anne.carter@middlefarmcottages.co.uk
w middlefarmcottages.co.uk

Ye Olde Stables ★★★★
Self Catering
Contact: Mrs Janet Tory
t (01694) 723243
e info@jinlye.co.uk
w jinlye.co.uk

The Retreat ★★★
Self Catering
Contact: Mr J Bennett
t (01694) 723370
e john@theretreatcs.co.uk
w theretreatcs.co.uk

CLACTON-ON-SEA
Essex

Pond Cottage ★★★★
Self Catering
Contact: Mrs Brenda Lord
t (01255) 820458
e brenda_lord@farming.co.uk
w earlshallfarm.info

CLAVERING
Essex

Brocking Farm Cottage
★★★★ *Self Catering*
Contact: Mr & Mrs T R & J E Gingell
t (01279) 777349
e t.gingell@btopenworld.com
w brockingfarmcottages.co.uk

CLEETHORPES
North East Lincolnshire

Beach House ★★★★
Self Catering
Contact: Ms Sarah Bottomley
t (01472) 211210
e beachhouse@cleethorpesholidays.co.uk
w cleethorpesholidays.co.uk

CLEHONGER
Herefordshire

Carramar ★★★★
Self Catering
Contact: Mr & Mrs Q Davies
t (01981) 250544
e carramar@hotmail.com

CLEOBURY MORTIMER
Shropshire

Cherry Lodge ★★★
Self Catering
Contact: Mrs Sam Adams
Cherry Cottage
t (01299) 271847
e adamscherrycottage@yahoo.co.uk
w cherry-lodge.co.uk

Cleobury Mortimer Golf Club Cottages ★★★★
Self Catering
Contact: Mrs Sara Pain
t (01299) 271112
e enquiries@cleoburygolfclub.com
w cleoburygolfclub.com

Hop Barn ★★★★
Self Catering
Contact: Mrs Birgit Jones
t (01299) 271204
e birgit.jones@onetel.net

Prescott Mill Cottage
★★★★ *Self Catering*
Contact: Mrs Wendy Etchells
t (01746) 718721
e wendy@prescott-mill-cottage.co.uk
w prescott-mill-cottage.co.uk

CLEY NEXT THE SEA
Norfolk

Archway Cottage ★★★
Self Catering
Contact: Mrs Vickey Jackson
t (01992) 511303 & (01992) 503196

Lavender Cottage, Cley-next-the-Sea ★★★
Self Catering
Contact: Mrs M Cooke
t (01328) 710659
e lavender.cottage@hotmail.co.uk
w glavenvalley.co.uk/lavendercottage/cley

Little Cottage ★★
Self Catering
Norfolk Country Cottages
t (01603) 871872
e info@norfolkcottages.co.uk
w norfolkcottages.co.uk

Mallard Cottage ★★★★
Self Catering
Contact: Miss Angela Peacock
t 07702 420735
w cleycottage.co.uk

Skylarks ★★★★
Self Catering
Contact: Mrs Nicola Arrowsmith-Brown
t (01603) 270457
e arrows270@aol.com
w cottageguide.co.uk/skylarks

Town Yard Cottage ★★★★
Self Catering
Contact: Ms C Verlander
t (01268) 730953
e carolverlander@btinternet.com
w townyardcottage.co.uk

CLIFTON UPON TEME
Worcestershire

Pitlands Farm ★★★★
Self Catering
Contact: Mrs Diane Mann
t (01886) 812220
e pitlandsfarmholidays@btopenworld.com
w pitlandsfarm.co.uk

CLIPPESBY
Norfolk

Clippesby Hall ★★★★
Self Catering
Contact: Jean, John & Sue Lindsay
t (01493) 367800
e holidays@clippesby.com
w clippesby.com

CLOPTON
Suffolk

Orchard End ★★★
Self Catering
Contact: Mr Dudley Gowland
t (01473) 737270

CLUN
Shropshire

Bramleys ★★★★
Self Catering
t (01588) 673302
w bramleysbarn.com

Dick Turpin Cottage
★★★★★ *Self Catering*
Contact: Mr Roger Wren
t (01588) 640327
e cockford.hall@virgin.net
w dickturpincottage.com

Pooh Hall Cottages
★★★★-★★★★★
Self Catering
Contact: Mrs Sue Murray
t (01588) 640075
e pooh-hall@dsl.pipex.com
w pooh-hallcottages.co.uk

The Squire Farm ★★★★
Self Catering
Contact: Mrs Becky Whitton
t (01547) 530530
e becky@squirefarm.co.uk
w squirefarm.co.uk

Tuc-Tin ★★★ *Self Catering*
Contact: Mr Charles Bremner
t 07817 370952
e info@tuc-tin.co.uk
w tuc-tin.co.uk

Wagtail Cottage ★★★★
Self Catering
Contact: Mrs Joyce Williams
t (01588) 640224
e allawala@hotmail.co.uk
w clunholidays.co.uk

Woolbury Barn ★★★★
Self Catering
Contact: Mrs Francis Morris
t (01588) 640481
w stmem.com/woolburybarn

CLUNGUNFORD
Shropshire

Lavender Cottage ★★★★
Self Catering
Contact: Mrs Karin Clarke
t (01588) 660631
e kr.clarke@btinternet.com

CLUNTON
Shropshire

Clunton Farm Granary ★★★
Self Catering
t (01588) 660120
w clunvalleyretreat.com

COALBROOKDALE
Shropshire

The Chauffeurs Flat @ No.10
★★★★ *Self Catering*
Contact: Mr Nicholas O'Shea
t (01952) 433383
e nicoshea@btinternet.com
w stmem.com/chauffeursflat

Coalbrookdale Cottages
★★★-★★★★ *Self Catering*
Contact: Mrs Mary Jones
t (01952) 433202
e mary@teakettlecottages.co.uk

Old Wynd Cottage ★★★
Self Catering
Contact: Mr & Mrs Charlie & Gail Boyce
t (01952) 432427
e info@oldwynd.co.uk
w oldwynd.co.uk

COALPORT
Shropshire

Station House Holiday Lets
★★★★ *Self Catering*
Contact: Mrs Lisa Rawlings
t (01952) 885674
e enquiries@coalportstation.com
w coalportstation.com

Thorpe House ★★★
Self Catering
t (01952) 586789
w thorpehouse.info

COCKFIELD
Suffolk

Buttons Green Farm ★★★★
Self Catering
Contact: Mr & Mrs James & Emily Ackroyd-Cooper
t (01284) 827244
w buttonsgreenfarm.com

COLBY
Norfolk

The Old Post Office ★★★★
Self Catering
Norfolk Country Cottages
t (01603) 871872
e info@norfolkcottages.co.uk
w norfolkcottages.co.uk

COLCHESTER
Essex

Acacia Cottage ★★★
Self Catering
Contact: Mrs Helen Brown
t (01206) 504048
e hc.brown@ntlworld.com
w acacia-cottages.co.uk

Castle Road Cottages
★★★★ *Self Catering*
Contact: Mrs Patsie Ford
Castle Cottages
t (01206) 262210
e patsie.ford@virgin.net
w castleroadcottages.com

The Tea House ★★★★
Self Catering
Contact: Mr & Mrs Charrington
t (01206) 330784
w layermarneytower.co.uk

COLKIRK
Norfolk

Reclaim Cottage ★★★★
Self Catering
Norfolk Country Cottages
t (01603) 871872
e info@norfolkcottages.co.uk
w norfolkcottages.co.uk

Saddlery And Hillside Cottage ★★★ *Self Catering*
Contact: Mrs Catherine Joice
t (01328) 862261
e catherine.joice@btinternet.com
w colkirkcottages.co.uk

COLLYWESTON
Northamptonshire

Slate Drift Leisure ★★★
Self Catering
Contact: Mr Roger Munro
t (01780) 444058
e rogermunro@aol.com

COLMWORTH
Bedfordshire

Colmworth Golf Course Holiday Cottages ★★★
Self Catering
Contact: Mrs Julie Vesely
t (01234) 378181
w colmworthgolfclub.co.uk

COLSTERWORTH
Lincolnshire

Farrier Cottage ★★★
Self Catering
Contact: Mrs Kathleen Clay
t (01476) 861057
e kathlen@btopenworld.com
w stablesbandb.co.uk

COLTISHALL
Norfolk

White Gable Cottage, Coltishall ★★★ *Self Catering*
Contact: Terry Holt
t (01603) 736333
w about-norfolk.com/colt/accommodation.htm

COLWALL
Herefordshire

The Threshing Barn ★★★★
Self Catering
Contact: Robin Coates
t (01684) 540284
e robin@robincoates.com
w robincoates.com

COMBS
Derbyshire

Beehive Cottage – PK682
★★★★ *Self Catering*
Peak Cottages
t (0114) 262 0777
e enquiries@peakcottages.com
w peakcottages.com

Combs Barn ★★★★
Self Catering
Peak Cottages
t (0114) 262 0777
e enquiries@peakcottages.com
w peakcottages.com

Little Oak ★★★★
Self Catering
Peak Cottages
t (0114) 262 0777
e enquiries@peakcottages.com
w peakcottages.com

Pyegreave Cottage
★★★★★ *Self Catering*
Contact: Mr & Mrs Noel & Rita Pollard
t (01298) 813444
e n.pollard@allenpollard.co.uk
w holidayapartments.org

COMBS
Suffolk

Jackbridge Cottage ★★★★
Self Catering
Contact: Ian & Teresa Pemberton
t (01449) 672177
e pembertons@jackbridgefarm.plus.com

COPDOCK
Suffolk

The Briars And Mansard Cottage ★★★★ *Self Catering*
Contact: Mrs Rosanna Steward
t (01473) 730494
w suffolkholidays.com

CORLEY
West Midlands

St Ives Lodge ★★★★
Self Catering
Contact: Mr Tim Ruffett
t (01676) 542994
e accommodation@ruffett.co.uk
w st-ives-lodge.co.uk

CORPUSTY
Norfolk

Carr's Barn ★★★★★
Self Catering
Contact: Mrs Marion Anthony
t (01502) 578278
e info@heritagehideaways.com
w carrsbarn.co.uk

CORTON
Suffolk

Barnstable Cottage
★★★★★ *Self Catering*
Contact: Mr & Mrs Laurence & Sandra Dyer
t (01502) 730716
e iggdyer@tiscali.co.uk
w tiscover.co.uk

COSTOCK
Nottinghamshire

Costock Manor Luxury Cottages ★★★★-★★★★★
Self Catering
Contact: Mr & Mrs Simblet
t (01509) 852250
e simblet@costock-manor.co.uk

COTTON
Suffolk

Coda Cottages ★★★★
Self Catering
Contact: Mrs Kate Sida-Nicholls
t (01449) 780076
w codacottages.co.uk

COVENHAM ST BARTHOLOMEW
Lincolnshire

Westfield Mews & Lodges
★★★★-★★★★★
Self Catering
Contact: Mrs J Cream
t (01507) 363217

CRANFORD
Northamptonshire

No 4 The Green
Rating Applied For
Self Catering
Contact: Mr Mark Robinson
t (01536) 330608
e sixthegreen@btinternet.com

CRANMER
Norfolk

Cranmer Country Cottages
★★★★ *Self Catering*
Contact: Mrs Lynne Johnson
t (01328) 823135
e bookings@cranmercountrycottages.co.uk
w cranmercountrycottages.co.uk

CRATFIELD
Suffolk

Holly Tree Farm Barns
★★★★ *Self Catering*
Contact: Ms Rachel Boddy
Holly Tree Farm
t (01986) 798062
e hollytreebarns@lycos.co.uk
w hollytreebarns.co.uk

Lodge Cottage ★★★★
Self Catering
Contact: Mrs Jane Brewer
t (01986) 798830
e janebrewer@ukonline.co.uk
w farmstayuk.co.uk

School Farm Cottages
★★★★ *Self Catering*
Contact: Mrs Claire Sillett
School Farm
t (01986) 798844
e schoolfarmcotts@aol.com
w schoolfarmcottages.com

CRAVEN ARMS
Shropshire

Green Farm ★★★
Self Catering
t (0151) 924 4226
w shropshirecottage4holiday.co.uk

Gwynfa, Long Meadow End
★★★ *Self Catering*
t (01588) 673375
w stmem.com/gwynfa

Highgrove Barns ★★★★
Self Catering
Contact: Mrs Christine Tromans
t (01588) 673113
e highgrovebarns@hotmail.co.uk
w highgrovebarns.co.uk

The Malt House ★★★★
Self Catering
Contact: Mrs Jean Mellings
t (01584) 873315
e jeanmellings@hotmail.com
w shropshirecottage.co.uk

Orchard Cottage ★★★★
Self Catering
Contact: Mr Peter Lewis
t (01588) 673340
e pdlewisuk@aol.com
w stmem.com/orchardcottage

Strefford Hall Self Catering – Robins & Swallows Nest
★★★★ *Self Catering*
Contact: Mrs Caroline Morgan
t (01588) 672383
w streffordhall.co.uk

Upper Onibury Cottages
★★★★ *Self Catering*
Contact: Mrs Hickman
t (01584) 856206
e info@shropshirecottages.com
w shropshirecottages.com

CRESSBROOK
Derbyshire

Cressbrook Hall Self Catering Cottages ★★★★
Self Catering
Contact: Mrs Bobby Hull-Bailey
t (01298) 871289
e stay@cressbrookhall.co.uk
w cressbrookhall.co.uk

Mill Apartment ★★★★
Self Catering
Peak Cottages
t (0114) 262 0777
e enquiries@peakcottages.com
w peakcottages.com

Monsal Dale Apartment
★★★★★ *Self Catering*
Contact: Dr & Mrs P Howard
The Nurseries
t (0114) 230 8456
e dr.howard@btconnect.com
w heritageholidayhomes.com

Owl Cottage ★★★★
Self Catering
Peak Cottages
t (0114) 262 0777
e enquiries@peakcottages.com
w peakcottages.com

CRICH
Derbyshire

1 Mansion Cottage ★★★
Self Catering
Contact: Mr Phillips
t (01773) 832485
e john.phillips@w3z.co.uk

CROMER
Norfolk

119 Kings Chalet Park ★★
Self Catering
Contact: Pamela Jonas
Country and Coast – Self Catering Holidays
t (01263) 513139

15 Clifton Park ★★★★
Self Catering
Norfolk Country Cottages
t (01603) 871872
e info@norfolkcottages.co.uk
w norfolkcottages.co.uk

1A Alexandra Court
Rating Applied For
Self Catering
Contact: Mr Matthew Harrington
t (01992) 303771
e t.harrington3@ntlworld.com

2 The Gangway ★★
Self Catering
Contact: Mrs Price
t (01992) 572672
w tiscover.co.uk

3 The Gangway ★★
Self Catering
t (01263) 512168

37 Cabbell Road
Rating Applied For
Self Catering
Norfolk Country Cottages
t (01603) 871872
e info@norfolkcottages.co.uk
w norfolkcottages.co.uk

Albion House ★★★
Self Catering
Norfolk Country Cottages
t (01603) 871872
e info@norfolkcottages.co.uk
w norfolkcottages.co.uk

Beverley House Holiday Apa
★–★★★ *Self Catering*
Contact: Mr & Mrs Bob & Sue Collins
t (01603) 505298 & 07960 796309
e beverleyhouseapartments@yahoo.co.uk
w broadland.com/beverleyhouse

Bountiful ★★★★
Self Catering
Contact: Mrs Jill Betz
t (01263) 514490
e enquiries@whisperingtrees.co.uk
w whisperingtrees.co.uk

Broadgates Cottages
★★★★ *Self Catering*
Contact: Mrs Julie Bryant
t (01263) 513290
e forestpark@netcom.co.uk
w forest-park.co.uk/cottages

Chalets 28 151 152 ★★
Self Catering
Contact: Miss Pamela Jonas
County and Coast – Self Catering Holidays
t (01263) 513139
e info@countryandcoast.co.uk
w tiscover.co.uk

Cliff Hollow ★★ *Self Catering*
Contact: Miss L Willins
t (01263) 512447
w tiscover.co.uk

Cliffside at Kings Chalet Park ★★ *Self Catering*
Contact: Mrs SA Jones
t (01692) 536281
w sloleyfarmcottages.co.uk

Coach House Cottage
★★★★ *Self Catering*
Contact: Mrs Dorothy Casburn
Grove House
t (01485) 520569
e ccasburn@britishsugar.co.uk
w tiscover.co.uk

Drift Barn Cottage ★★★
Self Catering
Contact: Mrs Daphne Payne
t (01263) 513765
w tiscover.co.uk

Flat 2 Bernard House ★★★
Self Catering
Contact: Miss Pamela Jonas
Country and Coast – Self Catering Holidays
t (01263) 513139
e info@countryandcoast.co.uk
w tiscover.co.uk

Foxglade Lodge ★★★★
Self Catering
Contact: Miss Tania Hickman
t (01263) 511028

Greenwood Holiday Cottage
★★★ *Self Catering*
Contact: Mrs Hemming
t (01263) 514139
w tiscover.co.uk

The Grove ★★★
Self Catering
Contact: Mr Paul Catton
t (01263) 512412
e thegrovecromer@btopenworld.com
w thegrovecromer.co.uk

Kings Chalet Park 123 ★★
Self Catering
Contact: Miss Pamela Jonas
Country and Coast – Self Catering Holidays
t (01263) 513139
e info@countryandcoast.co.uk
w tiscover.co.uk

Maynard House ★★★
Self Catering
Contact: Mr Adam Cade
t (01780) 720521

Old Forge ★★ *Self Catering*
Contact: Miss Pamela Jonas
Country and Coast – Self Catering Holidays
t (01263) 513139
e info@countryandcoast.co.uk
w tiscover.co.uk

Sparrow's Nest ★★★★
Self Catering
Contact: Mrs Dawn Saunt
t (01263) 838589
w sparrowsnorfolkholidaycottages.co.uk

Swallow Cottages Poppyland ★★★★
Self Catering
Contact: Mr Riches
t (01263) 577473
e poppyland@totalise.co.uk
w broadland.com/poppyland

Two The Crescent ★★★
Self Catering
Norfolk Country Cottages
t (01603) 871872
e info@norfolkcottages.co.uk
w norfolkcottages.co.uk

Westmead ★★★
Self Catering
Norfolk Country Cottages
t (01603) 871872
e info@norfolkcottages.co.uk
w norfolkcottages.co.uk

CROMFORD
Derbyshire

1 High Peak Cottages ★★★
Self Catering
Contact: Mr & Mrs David & Lorraine Wolsey
t (01629) 823402
e stay@highpeakcottage.co.uk

Willersley Barns ★★★
Self Catering
Peak Cottages
t (0114) 262 0777
e enquiries@peakcottages.com
w peakcottages.com

CROSS KEYS
Herefordshire

Dudley Cottage ★★★★
Self Catering
t (01432) 820114

CROWLAND
Lincolnshire

Fen-Acre, Crowland ★★★★
Self Catering
Contact: Mr & Mrs Michael & Julie Smith
t (01733) 211847
e julie@fen-acreholidaylet.co.uk
w fen-acreholidaylet.com

CROXTON, ST NEOTS
Cambridgeshire

Croxton Old Rectory ★★
Self Catering
Contact: Mrs Margaret Williams
t (01480) 880344

CULFORD
Suffolk

Hazelnut Cottage ★★★★
Self Catering
Contact: Mr & Mrs Roy Nieves-y-Gordo
t (01284) 728929
e nievesygordo@tiscali.co.uk

CURBAR
Derbyshire

Orchard Cottages ★★★
Self Catering
Contact: Dr Julie Morrissy
t (01433) 631885
e info@curbarcottages.com
w curbarcottages.com

CURBAR, CALVER
Derbyshire

The Old Vicarage ★★★★
Self Catering
Peak Cottages
t (0114) 262 0777
e enquiries@peakcottages.com
w peakcottages.com

CURBOROUGH
Staffordshire

The Old Haybarn Apartments ★★★★
Self Catering
Contact: Mr & Mrs Nick & Caroline Lees
t (01543) 418378
e charlie@haybarnapartments.co.uk
w haybarnapartments.co.uk

CUTTHORPE
Derbyshire

Cow Close Barn ★★★★
Self Catering
Contact: Mr & Mrs Allan & Barbara Campbell
t (01246) 272948
e cowclosebarn@hotmail.co.uk

The Saltings, Cutthorpe
★★★ *Self Catering*
Contact: Mrs Caroline Burke
t (01246) 232055
e cowclosefarm@aol.com
w cowclosefarm.com

DALLINGHOO
Suffolk

Robins Nest, The Cottage, Carpenter's Shop, Wheelwright's ★★★★
Self Catering
Contact: Mr Robert Blake
t (01394) 382565 & 07901 773545
e robert@blake4110.fsbusiness.co.uk
w tiscover.co.uk

DARLEY DALE
Derbyshire

Bumper Castle Farm ★★★★
Self Catering
Contact: Mrs Gillian Wholey
t (01629) 732534
e peakholidaycottage@hotmail.co.uk

Fircliffe Garden Cottage
★★★★ *Self Catering*
Contact: Penny Snaith
t (01629) 732910
e penny.snaith@w32.co.uk

The Tractor Shed ★★★★
Self Catering
Contact: Amy Jarvis
t (01530) 452716
e thetractorshed@ntlworld.com
w derbyshiresderbyshire.co.uk

DARLEY MOOR
Derbyshire

The Old Farmhouse ★★★
Self Catering
Contact: Shelley Littlewood
t (01629) 733838
e shelleywoodsidefarm@tiscali.co.uk

DARLINGSCOTT
Warwickshire

Sundial Wing ★★★★
Self Catering
Campden Cottages
t (01386) 593315
e info@campdencottages.co.uk
w campdencottages.co.uk

DARMSDEN
Suffolk

Burnt House Cottage ★★
Self Catering
Contact: Mr Michael Keen
t (020) 7787 6870

DARSHAM
Suffolk

Granary and The Mallards
★★★★ *Self Catering*
Contact: Mrs S Bloomfield
t (01728) 668459
e suebloomfield@btconnect.com
w holidaysatprioryfarm.co.uk

DEBACH
Suffolk

Akenfield Retreat ★★★
Self Catering
Suffolk Secrets
t (01502) 722717
e holidays@suffolk-secrets.co.uk
w suffolk-secrets.co.uk

DENGIE
Essex

East Ware Farm, Tillingham
★★★★ *Self Catering*
Contact: Mrs Lyn Ponder
t (01621) 786846
e lyn.ponder@btinternet.com
w eastwarefarm.co.uk

DENNINGTON
Suffolk

Stable Cottage ★★★
Self Catering
Contact: Mr & Mrs Derek & Jill Woodward
t (01728) 638278

DENSTON
Suffolk

Appletree Cottage ★★★
Self Catering
Suffolk Secrets
t (01502) 722717
e holidays@suffolk-secrets.co.uk
w suffolk-secrets.co.uk

DENSTONE
Staffordshire

Keepers Cottage ★★★★
Self Catering
Contact: Mr Chris Ball
t (01889) 590415
e cm_ball@yahoo.co.uk
w 4posteraccom.com

DENTON
Norfolk

Bluebell Cotage ★★★★
Self Catering
Contact: Jean Whipps
t (01986) 788360
e ca.whipps@farmline.com
w bluebellcottage.uk.com

DENVER
Norfolk

Denver Windmill ★★★
Self Catering
t (01366) 384009
e denverwm@tiscali.co.uk
w denverwindmill.co.uk

Gatehouse Cottage ★★★
Self Catering
w gatehousecottagedenver.co.uk

White House Farm
Rating Applied For
Self Catering
Birds Norfolk Holiday Homes
t (01485) 534267
e shohol@birdsnorfolkholidayhomes.co.uk
w norfolkholidayhomes-birds.co.uk

DERBY
Derbyshire

Avenue House
Rating Applied For
Self Catering
Contact: Mrs Webb
t (01332) 831387
e dwebb@gpanet.co.uk

Bank Cottage ★★★
Self Catering
Contact: Mrs Pamela Pym
t (01332) 515607

Home Farm House ★★★
Self Catering
t 0870 444 6603

The Railway Cottage ★★★
Self Catering
Contact: Ms Denise Newcomb
t (01332) 345231
e denise.newcomb@ntlworld.com

SACO Derby ★★★★
Serviced Apartments
SACO Apartments
t (0117) 974 5936
e sarahbailey@sacoapartments.co.uk
w sacoapartments.co.uk

DEREHAM
Norfolk

Maple Barns
★★★★-★★★★★
Self Catering
Contact: Mrs Hannah Jarvis
t (01362) 637260
w maple-barns.co.uk

DERSINGHAM
Norfolk

Avocet Cottage ★★★★
Self Catering
Norfolk Country Cottages
t (01603) 871872
e info@norfolkcottages.co.uk
w norfolkcottages.co.uk

Old Hall Cottage ★★★★
Self Catering
Norfolk Country Cottages
t (01603) 871872
e info@norfolkcottages.co.uk
w norfolkcottages.co.uk

Rowcroft ★★★★
Self Catering
Norfolk Country Cottages
t (01603) 871872
e info@norfolkcottages.co.uk
w norfolkcottages.co.uk

Spring Cottage ★★★
Self Catering
Birds Norfolk Holiday Homes
t (01485) 534267
e shohol@birdsnorfolkholidayhomes.co.uk
w norfolkholidayhomes-birds.co.uk

Wellswill
Rating Applied For
Self Catering
Norfolk Country Cottages
t (01603) 871872
e info@norfolkcottages.co.uk
w norfolkcottages.co.uk

DIDDLEBURY
Shropshire

Milking Barn ★★★★
Self Catering
Contact: Mr & Mrs Darren & Julie Tuskin
t (01584) 841285
e info@milkingbarn.co.uk
w milkingbarn.co.uk

DILHORNE
Staffordshire

Birchenfields Farm ★★★
Self Catering
Contact: Mr & Mrs Peter Edge
t (01538) 753972

Blakeley Barns ★★★
Self Catering
Contact: Mrs Donna Mellor
t (01782) 397800
e donna.mellor@tesco.net
w blakeleybarns.co.uk

DILLINGTON Norfolk

The Retreat ★★★★★
Self Catering
Norfolk Country Cottages
t (01603) 871872
e info@norfolkcottages.co.uk
w norfolkcottages.co.uk

DISS Norfolk

Norfolk Farm Cottages Malthouse ★★★★
Self Catering
Contact: Ms Ann Manning
Norfolk Cottages Booking Office
t (01379) 651177
e bookings@norfolkcottages.net
w norfolkcottages.net

Old Mill Farm ★★★
Self Catering
Contact: Mr & Mrs Laurence & Pauline Ward
t (01953) 681350
w oldmillfarm.co.uk

DOCKING Norfolk

2 Little Lane ★★★
Self Catering
Norfolk Country Cottages
t (01603) 871872
e info@norfolkcottages.co.uk
w norfolkcottages.co.uk

The Bungalow ★★★
Self Catering
Norfolk Country Cottages
t (01603) 871872
e info@norfolkcottages.co.uk
w norfolkcottages.co.uk

The Gallery ★★★
Self Catering
Contact: Mr Simon Barclay
Kett Country Cottages
t (01328) 856853
w kettcountrycottages.co.uk

Honeysuckle Cottage
★★★★ *Self Catering*
Contact: Miss Amanda Cox
t 07901 822621

Norfolk House and Courtyard Cottage
★★★★★ *Self Catering*
Contact: Mr & Mrs Tim & Liz Witley
t (01485) 525341
e info@escapetonorfolk.com
w escapetonorfolk.com

DODDINGTON Lincolnshire

The Stables, The Old Rectory ★★★★ *Self Catering*
Contact: Ian Macalpine-Leny
t 07810 408319
e enquiries@thestables-theoldrectory-doddington.com
w thestables-theoldrectory-doddington.com

DONINGTON Lincolnshire

The Barn ★★★ *Self Catering*
Contact: Margaret Smith
t (01775) 821242

DORSINGTON Warwickshire

Windmill Grange Cottage
★★★★ *Self Catering*
Contact: Mrs Lorna Hollis
t (01789) 720866
e lornah_windmillgrange@hotmail.com
w windmillgrange.co.uk

DOVERIDGE Derbyshire

Eaton Hall Apartments
★★★ *Self Catering*
Contact: Sue Bramley
t (01889) 565986
e doveridge-clay-sports@btinternet.com

DRAYCOTT-IN-THE-CLAY Staffordshire

Granary Court Holiday Cottages ★★★★
Self Catering
Contact: Mrs Lynne Statham
t (01283) 820917
w granarycourt.demon.co.uk

DRONFIELD Derbyshire

Hilltop Barns ★★★★
Self Catering
Peak Cottages
t (0114) 262 0777
e enquiries@peakcottages.com
w peakcottages.com

DUDDENHOE END Essex

Cosh Cottage, Duddenhoe End ★★★★ *Self Catering*
Contact: Mrs Susan Perks
t (01763) 838880
e susan.perks@virgin.net

DUFFIELD Derbyshire

Castle Orchard Cottages
★★★ *Self Catering*
Contact: Mrs Bullock
t (01332) 840516
e mail@derbyshirebreaks.com
w derbyshirebreaks.com

DUNCHURCH Warwickshire

The Cottage ★★★★
Self Catering
Contact: Mrs Paula Twigger
t (01788) 544337
e kevtwigger@aol.com
w thecottagedunchurch.co.uk

Toft Manor Cottage ★★★★
Self Catering
Contact: Ms Shirley Bettinson
t (01788) 810626
e shirley@toft-alpacas.co.uk
w toft-alpacas.co.uk

DUNMOW Essex

Bury Farm Cottages ★★★★
Self Catering
Contact: Mrs Sarah Clarke
t (01371) 872213
e sandjclarke@buryfarmcottages.co.uk
w buryfarmcottages.co.uk

DUNWICH Suffolk

Church Farm Cottage ★★★
Self Catering
Suffolk Secrets
t (01502) 722717
e holidays@suffolk-secrets.co.uk
w suffolk-secrets.co.uk

Lodge Cottage ★★★
Self Catering
Contact: Mrs Maureen Nielson
t (01728) 648388
e drbcargill@farming.co.uk
w tiscover.co.uk

Tinkers Cottage ★★★
Self Catering
Suffolk Secrets
t (01502) 722717
e holidays@suffolk-secrets.co.uk
w suffolk-secrets.co.uk

Tower Bungalow ★★★★
Self Catering
Contact: Mrs Eleanor Barnes
t (01787) 269916
e biscuitb@tiscali.co.uk
w tiscover.co.uk

EAGLE Lincolnshire

The Crossing Cottage ★★★
Self Catering
Contact: Patrick Britton
t (01673) 857290
e patrickbritton@mac.com

EARDISLAND Herefordshire

The Hopleys ★★★★
Self Catering
Contact: Mrs Elaine Lyke
t (01568) 709285
e elaine@lyke5502.freeserve.co.uk
w visitlawtonbury.co.uk

The Stables ★★★★
Self Catering
Contact: Mr & Mrs A. Priday
t (01544) 388570
e pridays@aol.com

EARL STERNDALE Derbyshire

The Cottage ★★★
Self Catering
Contact: Mr & Mrs Gary Wardle
t 07966 032079 & 07970 944795
e wag@meowd.orangehome.co.uk

EARLS COLNE Essex

Greenlands Barn ★★★★
Self Catering
Contact: Mr & Mrs Williams
t (01787) 224895
e david@greenlandsfarm.freeserve.co.uk
w greenlandsfarm.co.uk

EARLS CROOME Worcestershire

The Jockey Inn ★★★
Self Catering
t (01684) 592153
w thejockeyinn.com

EARSHAM Norfolk

Dukes Cottage ★★★
Self Catering
Norfolk Country Cottages
t (01603) 871872
e info@norfolkcottages.co.uk
w norfolkcottages.co.uk

EAST BECKHAM Norfolk

Barn House Cottage ★★★★
Self Catering
Norfolk Country Cottages
t (01603) 871872
e info@norfolkcottages.co.uk
w norfolkcottages.co.uk

EAST BERGHOLT Suffolk

Flatford Cottage ★★★
Self Catering
Contact: Mr & Mrs Paul & Debbie Goddard
t (01206) 298985
e goddard8@aol.com
w flatfordcottage.freeserves.com

EAST DEREHAM Norfolk

Clinton Cottage And Clinton House ★★★★ *Self Catering*
Contact: Mr & Mrs John & Margaret Searle
Clinton Holidays
t (01362) 692079
w norfolkcountrycottage.co.uk

EAST FIRSBY Lincolnshire

Lincolnshire Lanes Log Cabins ★★★ *Self Catering*
Contact: Robert Cox
t (01673) 878258
e info@lincolnshire-lanes.com
w lincolnshire-lanes.com

EAST HADDON Northamptonshire

East Haddon Grange Country Cottages ★★★★
Self Catering
Contact: Annie Hull
t (01604) 770368 & 07979 661122
e enquiries@easthaddongrange.co.uk
w easthaddongrange.co.uk

Mulberry Cottage ★★★★★
Self Catering
Contact: Liat Cox
t (01604) 771474
e liat3030@aol.com
w mulberrycottage.uk.com

Ryehill Cottages ★★★★
Self Catering
Contact: Margaret Widdowson
t (01604) 770990
e ryehillcottages@btinternet.co.uk
w ryehillcottages.co.uk

EAST HARLING Norfolk

Berwick Cottage ★★★★
Self Catering
Contact: Mrs Miriam Toosey
t (01787) 372343
w thelinberwicktrust.org.uk

Dove Cottage ★★★
Self Catering
Norfolk Country Cottages
t (01603) 871872
e info@norfolkcottages.co.uk
w norfolkcottages.co.uk

Tapestry Cottage ★★★
Self Catering
Contact: Mr & Mrs Terence George
t (01371) 874321
e ok_to.mark_it@virgin.net
w tapestrycottage.co.uk

EAST KIRKBY
Lincolnshire

Chesterton Cottage ★★★★
Self Catering
Contact: Mr & Mrs Raynor
t (01790) 763380

EAST RUDHAM
Norfolk

17 & 18 The Green ★★★★
Self Catering
Norfolk Country Cottages
t (01603) 871872
e info@norfolkcottages.co.uk
w norfolkcottages.co.uk

EAST RUNTON
Norfolk

Mallards Rest ★★★
Self Catering
Contact: Mrs Nicola Thompson
t (01263) 512496
w tiscover.co.uk

Poplars Caravan And Chalet ★★★ *Self Catering*
Contact: Mr & Mrs K Parfitt
t (01263) 512892
e info@poplarscaravanandchaletpark.co.uk
w tiscover.co.uk

Stable Cottage ★★★★★
Self Catering
Contact: Mr & Mrs Nick & Barbara Davies
t (01263) 515939
w incleborough-stablecottage.co.uk

Woodhill House ★★★
Self Catering
Contact: Miss Pamela Jonas
County and Coast – Self Catering Holidays
t (01263) 511028
e info@countryandcoast.co.uk
w tiscover.co.uk

EASTBRIDGE
Suffolk

Willow Farm ★★★
Self Catering
Suffolk Secrets
t (01502) 722717
e holidays@suffolk-secrets.co.uk
w suffolk-secrets.co.uk

EASTON ON THE HILL
Northamptonshire

The Old Bakery ★★★
Self Catering
Contact: Mrs Yogasundram
t (01780) 753898
e yogiandmel@theoldbakery25.freeserve.co.uk
w eastonoldbakery.co.uk

EATON
Leicestershire

Mill House Holiday Cottages ★★★★ *Self Catering*
Contact: Mrs Ursula Soar
t (01476) 870797
e belvoircottage@aol.com
w millhouseholidaycottages.co.uk

EATON-UNDER-HEYWOOD
Shropshire

Eaton Manor ★★★★
Self Catering
Contact: Mrs Nichola Madeley
t (01694) 724814
e nichola@eatonmanor.co.uk
w eatonmanor.co.uk

ECCLES-ON-SEA
Norfolk

Spencer Wall ★★★
Self Catering
Norfolk Country Cottages
t (01603) 871872
e info@norfolkcottages.co.uk
w norfolkcottages.co.uk

ECKINGTON
Worcestershire

Hillside Cottage ★★★★
Self Catering
Contact: Mrs Anne Gittins
t (01386) 750394
e anne.gittins@yahoo.co.uk
w upperclattsmore.co.uk

EDALE
Derbyshire

Ivy's Cottage ★★★★
Self Catering
Contact: Mr Khalid Qureshi
t (0161) 434 2628
e info@edalecottage.com
w edalecottage.com

Ollerbrook Cottages, Edale ★★★★–★★★★★
Self Catering
Contact: Mrs Paula Greenlees
t (01433) 670083
e ollerbrook@btinternet.com
w ollerbrook-cottages.co.uk

Taylors Croft Cottage ★★★★ *Self Catering*
Contact: Mrs Susan Favell
t (01433) 670281
e sue@skinnershall.freeserve.co.uk
w skinnershall.freeserve.co.uk

EDINGTHORPE
Norfolk

Arthur's Cottage ★★★★
Self Catering
Norfolk Country Cottages
t (01603) 871872
e info@norfolkcottages.co.uk
w norfolkcottages.co.uk

EDITH WESTON
Rutland

Corner Cottage, Edith Weston ★★★ *Self Catering*
Contact: Mrs Jo Spiegl
t (01780) 721014

Forge Cottage ★★★★
Self Catering
Contact: Ms Debbie Clark
Debbie Clark Lettings
t (01572) 747389
e debbieclark@btopenworld.com
w debbieclarklettings.com

Old School House ★★★
Self Catering
Contact: Ms Natasha Browne
e natasha@webrutland.co.uk
w webrutland.co.uk/theoldschoolhouse/

EDLASTON
Derbyshire

Church Farm Cottages ★★★
Self Catering
Contact: Mrs Lois Blake
t (01335) 348776
e adeblake@aol.com
w churchfarm-holidays.freeserve.co.uk

EDLINGTON
Lincolnshire

Edlington Hall Cottage ★★★ *Self Catering*
Contact: Louis McQuade
t (01507) 524507
e louismcquade@onetel.net
w edlingtonhallcottage.co.uk

EDWARDSTONE
Suffolk

Sherbourne Farm Lodge Cottages ★★★★
Self Catering
Contact: Mrs Anne Suckling
Sherbourne House Farm
t (01787) 210885
e enquiries@sherbournelodgecottages.co.uk
w sherbournelodgecottages.co.uk

The White Horse Inn ★★★
Self Catering
Contact: Mr Tom Norton
The White Horse Edwardstone LLP
t (01787) 211211
e john.norton@nortonorganic.co.uk
w edwardstonewhitehorse.co.uk

EDWINSTOWE
Nottinghamshire

Crow Hollow ★★★
Self Catering
t (01636) 677847
e shp18@lineone.net
w crowhollow.co.uk

EDWYN RALPH
Herefordshire

Elephant Cottage ★★★★
Self Catering
Hideaways
t (01747) 828170
e enq@hideaways.co.uk
w hideaways.co.uk

ELKINGTON
Northamptonshire

Manor Farm ★★★★
Self Catering
Contact: Mr Michael Higgott
t (01858) 575245

ELLASTONE
Staffordshire

The Byre ★★★★
Self Catering
Contact: Mrs P Longley
t (01335) 324433
e pat.longley@ulmail.net

ELLESMERE
Shropshire

The Byre, Ellesmere ★★★★
Self Catering
Contact: Mr Frank Lauriello
t (01691) 662280
e frank@myddle.net
w byre-holiday-cottage.co.uk

Teal Cottage – Shropshire Holidays ★★★★
Self Catering
t (01691) 622782
w shropshireholidays.co.uk

ELMSTEAD MARKET
Essex

Birds Farm ★★★
Self Catering
Contact: Mrs Gill Beadle
t (01206) 823838
e birdsfarm@btinternet.com
w birds-farm.co.uk

ELMSWELL
Suffolk

The Apple Store ★★★★
Self Catering
Contact: Mrs Clare Norgate
t (01359) 240333
w applestoresuffolk.co.uk

Oak Farm ★★★★★
Self Catering
Contact: Mr & Mrs Dennis & Angela Dyball
t (01359) 240263

ELSING
Norfolk

Holly Tree Cottage ★★★★
Self Catering
Norfolk Country Cottages
t (01603) 871872
e info@norfolkcottages.co.uk
w norfolkcottages.co.uk

ELTON
Derbyshire

The Stable ★★★★
Self Catering
Contact: Mrs Jean Carson
t (01629) 650359
w homesteadfarm.co.uk

Swallow Cottage ★★★★
Self Catering
Contact: Mrs Lois Clark
t (01954) 780893 & 07932 644287
e lois@swallow-cottage.co.uk
w swallow-cottage.co.uk

Two Gates Cottage & Pepperpot Cottage
Rating Applied For
Self Catering
Contact: Mr & Mrs Hirst
t (01629) 650217
e jenny.hirst@w3z.co.uk
w eltonholidays.com

ELY
Cambridgeshire

14 The Medway ★★★★
Self Catering
Contact: Mr Rowan Salger
t (01353) 658787

47a Waterside ★★★
Self Catering
Contact: Mrs Florence Nolan
t (01353) 664377

5 The Hoist ★★★★
Self Catering
Contact: Dawn Wisee dawnwise1@btconnect.com

7 & 9 Lisle Lane ★★★
Self Catering
Contact: Ken Davis
t (01353) 675249 & 07858 762721
e fortyfarmhouse@btinternet.com

Cathedral House Coach House ★★★★ *Self Catering*
Contact: Mrs Jenny Farndale
t (01353) 662124

Chiefs St Ely ★★★
Self Catering
Contact: Mrs P Coates
t (01223) 290842
e cheviotbob@aol.com

The Old Granary ★★★★★
Self Catering
Contact: Mrs Hilary Nix
t (01353) 778369
w hillhousefarm-ely.co.uk

The Pightle
Rating Applied For
Self Catering
Contact: D E Manning
t (01353) 741296

ENDON Staffordshire

Middle Cottage
Rating Applied For
Self Catering
Contact: Mike & Alison Benson
t (01782) 505089

EPPERSTONE Nottinghamshire

Eastwood Farm ★★★
Self Catering
Contact: Susan Santos
t (0115) 966 3018
e info@eastwoodfarm.co.uk
w eastwoodfarm.co.uk

EPPING Essex

Mandalay ★★★ *Self Catering*
Contact: Ms Brenda Foster
t (01992) 571828
w ukholidaycottages.biz

EPWORTH Lincolnshire

Church Lea House ★★★★
Self Catering
Contact: Katrine Barber
t (01724) 783388
e katrinebarber@btinternet.com

Newlands Holiday Cottages
★★★-★★★★ *Self Catering*
Contact: Clarissa Atkinson
t (01427) 873112
e enquiries@newlandsholidaybreaks.co.uk
w newlandsholidaybreaks.co.uk/

ERISWELL Suffolk

Church Cottage
★★★★-★★★★★
Self Catering
Contact: Ms Yolande Goode
t (01842) 890223
e estate.office@elveden.com
w elveden.com

ERPINGHAM Norfolk

The Byre
Rating Applied For
Self Catering
Norfolk Country Cottages
t (01603) 871872
e info@norfolkcottages.co.uk
w norfolkcottages.co.uk

Grange Farm, Erpingham
★★★ *Self Catering*
Contact: Mrs Jane Bell
Grange Farm Holidays
t (01263) 761241
e jane.bell5@btopenworld.com
w grangefarmholidays.co.uk

Mill House Barns ★★★
Self Catering
Norfolk Country Cottages
t (01603) 871872
e info@norfolkcottages.co.uk
w norfolkcottages.co.uk

EVESHAM Worcestershire

Thatchers End ★★★★
Self Catering
Contact: Mr & Mrs Wilson
t (01386) 446269
e trad.accom@virgin.net
w http://freespace.virgin.net/trad.accom

EWYAS HAROLD Herefordshire

Old King Street Farm
★★★★ *Self Catering*
Contact: Robert Dewar
t (01981) 240208
e info@oldkingstreetfarm.co.uk
w oldkingstreetfarm.co.uk

EXHALL Warwickshire

Glebe Farm Cottages ★★★
Self Catering
Contact: Mr Roger Albutt
t (01386) 830687
e enquiries@glebefarmcottages.net
w glebefarmcottages.net

EYAM Derbyshire

1 Lydgate Cottages ★★★★
Self Catering
Contact: Mrs Sandra Harrop
t (01925) 752118
e lydgatecottage@townfieldhouse.freeserve.co.uk

Beck Cottage ★★★★
Self Catering
Contact: Ms Becky Burton
t (0114) 250 9357
e bexburton@tiscali.co.uk
w ukpeakretreats.com

Croft View Cottage ★★★★
Self Catering
Contact: Mrs Carmichael
t (01433) 630711
e carmichaelat@hotmail.com
w croftviewcottage.co.uk

Curiosity Cottage ★★★
Self Catering
Peak Cottages
t (0114) 262 0777
e enquiries@peakcottages.com
w peakcottages.com

Dalehead Court Cottages
★★★★-★★★★★
Self Catering
Contact: Mrs Neary
t (01433) 620214
e laneside@lineone.net
w peakdistrictholidaycottages.com

Fern Cottage ★★★★
Self Catering
Contact: Mrs Jenny Vickers
t (01433) 631254
e jenny@foolowcottages.co.uk
w peak-cottages.com

Greengates ★★★★★
Self Catering
Peak Cottages
t (0114) 262 0777
e enquiries@peakcottages.com
w peakcottages.com

Lark Cottage ★★★★★
Self Catering
Contact: Mrs Hazel Bell
t (01246) 583564
e hazel@peak-district-holidays.co.uk
w peak-district-holidays.co.uk

Lea Cottage ★★★
Self Catering
Peak Cottages
t (0114) 262 0777
e enquiries@peakcottages.com
w peakcottages.com

Rose Cottage ★★
Self Catering
Peak Cottages
t (0114) 262 0777
e enquiries@peakcottages.com
w peakcottages.com

The Trap House ★★★★
Self Catering
Peak Cottages
t (0114) 262 0777
e enquiries@peakcottages.com
w peakcottages.com

EYE Suffolk

Log Cabin Holidays ★★★★
Self Catering
Contact: Mr Peter Havers
t (01728) 628233
e info@logcabinholidays.co.uk
w logcabinholidays.co.uk

Manor House Cottages
★★★-★★★★ *Self Catering*
Contact: Mrs Yvonne Mason
t (01379) 788049
e holiday@manorhousecottages.co.uk
w manorhousecottages.co.uk

EYE KETTLEBY Leicestershire

Eye Kettleby Lakes
★★★★-★★★★★
Self Catering
Contact: Ms E Lomas
t (01664) 565900
e info@eyekettlebylakes.com
w eyekettlebylakes.com

Old Guadaloupe Cottage, Eye Kettleby ★★★★
Self Catering
Contact: Ms Sue Lomas
t 07989 960588
e sue@suelomas.orengehome.co.uk
w oldguadaloupecottage.co.uk

FAIRFIELD Derbyshire

Holme Farm Bungalow
★★★★ *Self Catering*
Peak Cottages
t (0114) 262 0777
e enquiries@peakcottages.com
w peakcottages.com

FAKENHAM Norfolk

Bluebell Barn ★★★★★
Self Catering
t (01263) 862133
e enquiries@cottageconcierge.com

The Laurels ★★★
Self Catering
Norfolk Country Cottages
t (01603) 871872
e info@norfolkcottages.co.uk
w norfolkcottages.co.uk

Old Ale House Cottages
★★★ *Self Catering*
Contact: Miss Angie Hastings
t (01553) 771401
w tiscover.co.uk

The Paddocks ★★★★
Self Catering
Contact: Mr John Strahan
t (01328) 878305
e enquiries@old-brick-kilns.co.uk
w paddocks-cottages.co.uk

Pollywiggle Cottage, West Raynham ★★★★
Self Catering
Contact: Mrs Marilyn Farnham-Smith
t (01603) 471990
e marilyn@pollywigglecottage.co.uk
w pollywigglecottage.co.uk

Poppy Cottage ★★★
Self Catering
Norfolk Country Cottages
t (01603) 871872
e info@norfolkcottages.co.uk
w norfolkcottages.co.uk

Tinkerbell ★★★
Self Catering
Norfolk Country Cottages
t (01603) 871872
e info@norfolkcottages.co.uk
w norfolkcottages.co.uk

FARNSFIELD
Nottinghamshire

The Barn, Farnsfield ★★★
Self Catering
Contact: Mrs Josephine Kitchen
Grange Cottage/The Barn
t (01623) 882259
e jo@grange-cottage.co.uk
w grange-cottage.co.uk

FELBRIGG
Norfolk

Boundary Farm Cottage
★★★ *Self Catering*
Contact: Mrs Wendy Congreve
t (01406) 363618
e wcongreve@hotmail.co.uk
w tiscover.co.uk

FELIXSTOWE
Suffolk

Coach House ★★★
Self Catering
Suffolk Secrets
t (01502) 722717
e holidays@suffolk-secrets.co.uk
w suffolk-secrets.co.uk

Flat 2 ★★★ *Self Catering*
Contact: Mrs Gwen Lynch
t (01473) 328729

Honeypot Cottage ★★★
Self Catering
Contact: Mrs Theresa Adams
t (01394) 448564

Kimberley Holiday Flats ★★
Self Catering
Contact: Mrs Valerie Reed
t (01394) 672157
w tiscover.co.uk

FELMINGHAM
Norfolk

The Old Stables
Rating Applied For
Self Catering
Norfolk Country Cottages
t (01603) 871872
e info@norfolkcottages.co.uk
w norfolkcottages.co.uk

FELSTED
Essex

The Lodge
Rating Applied For
Self Catering
Contact: Mr Roger Smith
t (01371) 820271
e roger.smith21@tiscali.co.uk

FENNY BENTLEY
Derbyshire

The Priory ★★★
Self Catering
Contact: Mrs A Hughes
t (01335) 350238
e hughes.priory@virgin.net

FIELD DALLING
Norfolk

Annexe ★★★ *Self Catering*
Contact: Mrs Betty Ringer
t (01328) 830206
w tiscover.co.uk

Hard Farm Barns ★★★★
Self Catering
Contact: Mrs Angela Harcourt
t (01328) 830655
e harcog@farming.co.uk
w hardfarm.co.uk

The Little Barn ★★★★
Self Catering
Norfolk Country Cottages
t (01603) 871872
e info@norfolkcottages.co.uk
w norfolkcottages.co.uk

Lodge Cottage ★★★★
Self Catering
Norfolk Country Cottages
t (01603) 871872
e info@norfolkcottages.co.uk
w norfolkcottages.co.uk

Plough Cottage
Rating Applied For
Self Catering
Contact: Mrs Patricia Wallis
t (01328) 830017
e pmwallace1@yahoo.co.uk
w ploughhouse.co.uk

FILBY
Norfolk

1 Well Cottages ★★★
Self Catering
Norfolk Country Cottages
t (01603) 871872
e info@norfolkcottages.co.uk
w norfolkcottages.co.uk

FINCHINGFIELD
Essex

Meadow View & The Granary ★★★★ *Self Catering*
t (01371) 810315
w essexfarmholiday.co.uk

FINDERN
Derbyshire

Pilgrims Cottage, Findern
★★★ *Self Catering*
Contact: Mr & Mrs J Noon
t (01332) 769275

FINNINGHAM
Suffolk

Riverwood Cottage ★★★
Self Catering
Suffolk Secrets
t (01502) 722717
e holidays@suffolk-secrets.co.uk
w suffolk-secrets.co.uk

FISHTOFT
Lincolnshire

Earlscroft Farm ★★★★★
Self Catering
Contact: Mark Buckley
t (01205) 350426
e mark@earlscroftfarm.co.uk
w earlscroftfarm.co.uk

FLAGG
Derbyshire

Hobson Cottage ★★★★
Self Catering
Contact: P Spillane
t (01298) 85456
e liz.spillane@hotmail.co.uk
w hobsoncottage.co.uk

Taddington Barns
★★★-★★★★ *Self Catering*
Contact: Mrs Elizabeth Charboneau
t (01298) 85020 & 07974 258765
e tony@moorgrangefarm.co.uk
w moorgrangefarm.co.uk

FLASH
Staffordshire

Northfield Farm ★★★
Self Catering
Contact: Mrs Elizabeth Andrews
t (01298) 22543
e northfield@btinternet.com
w northfieldfarm.co.uk

FLECKNEY
Leicestershire

Elms Farm Holidays ★★★
Self Catering
Contact: Mrs C Greta Bentley
t (0116) 240 2238
e info@elms-farm.co.uk
w elms-farm.co.uk

FLIXTON
Suffolk

Old Rectory Cottages
★★★★ *Self Catering*
Contact: Mr Keith Parker
t (01986) 893133
e enquiries@oldrectorycottagesflixton.co.uk
w oldrectorycottagesflixton.co.uk

FOOLOW
Derbyshire

Sycamore Cottage ★★★
Self Catering
Contact: Mrs Maveen Norton
t (01433) 630186
e mnortonfoolow@aol.com
w cressbrook.co.uk/eyam

FORD
Shropshire

Church Farm Cottages ★★★
Self Catering
Contact: Mr & Mrs Alan & Margaret Bourne
t (01743) 821228
e margaret.bourne@btinternet.com
w stmem.com/churchfarmcottages

FOWNHOPE
Herefordshire

Bird's Farm Cottage ★★★
Self Catering
Contact: Mrs Margaret Edwards
t (01989) 740644
e mrsmgedwards@aol.com

FOXEARTH
Essex

Clayden's ★★★★
Self Catering
Suffolk Secrets
t (01502) 722717
e holidays@suffolk-secrets.co.uk
w suffolk-secrets.co.uk

FOXHALL
Suffolk

The Orchard, Foxhall
★★★★ *Self Catering*
Contact: Mrs Anne Pickering
t (01473) 659287
w orchardholidays.co.uk

FOXLEY
Norfolk

Moor Farm Stable Cottages
★★★-★★★★ *Self Catering*
Contact: Mr Paul Davis
t (01362) 688523
e mail@moorfarmstablecottages.co.uk
w moorfarmstablecottages.co.uk

FOXT
Staffordshire

Badger Cottage ★★★★
Self Catering
Contact: Mrs Carol Lockwood
t (01538) 266611
w rockhousefarm.org

FRAMLINGHAM
Suffolk

Ancient House ★★★★
Self Catering
Suffolk Secrets
t (01502) 722717
e holidays@suffolk-secrets.co.uk
w suffolk-secrets.co.uk

Castle House ★★★★
Self Catering
Contact: Mrs Hannah Norris
t (01728) 724403

Courtyard Cottage ★★★★
Self Catering
Contact: Mrs Louise Berrill
t (01394) 388481
e info@framcottages.co.uk
w framcottages.co.uk

Sunbeam Cottage ★★★
Self Catering
Suffolk Secrets
t (01502) 722717
e holidays@suffolk-secrets.co.uk
w suffolk-secrets.co.uk

FRESSINGFIELD
Suffolk

Hawthorn Cottage ★★★★
Self Catering
Suffolk Secrets
t (01502) 722717
e holidays@suffolk-secrets.co.uk
w suffolk-secrets.co.uk

Watsons Farm ★★★
Self Catering
Contact: Mrs Mary Hinde
t (01379) 586295
w watsonsfarm.co.uk

FRETTENHAM
Norfolk

Glebe Farm ★★★
Self Catering
Contact: Mrs Rona Norton
Beck Farm
t (01603) 897641
e rona.norton@btinternet.com
w glebefarm-cottages.co.uk

Look out for establishments participating in the National Accessible Scheme

The Old Forge ★★★★★
Self Catering
Norfolk Country Cottages
t (01603) 871872
e info@norfolkcottages.co.uk
w norfolkcottages.co.uk

FRIDAY BRIDGE
Cambridgeshire

Holly's Barn ★★★★
Self Catering
Contact: Mr & Mrs K Flint
t (01945) 860309
w woodhousefarmpark.co.uk

FRINTON-ON-SEA
Essex

Quartette ★★★ *Self Catering*
Contact: Mr Robert Bucke
Boydens
t 07010 716013
w ipsw.btinternet.co.uk/quartette.htm

FRISKNEY
Lincolnshire

Green Haven
Rating Applied For
Self Catering
t (01754) 820024
w green-havencottages.co.uk

FRISTON
Suffolk

2 Forge Cottages ★★★
Self Catering
Contact: Mrs Debbie Pickering
Knights Farm Stud
t (01621) 810833
w fristonholidaycottages.co.uk

FRITHVILLE
Lincolnshire

Carrington Court Holiday Cottages ★★★★
Self Catering
Contact: Mrs Stacey Lunn
Hawthorne House
t (01205) 750441
w carringtoncourt.co.uk

FRITTON
Norfolk

Fritton Lake Country World ★★★★ *Self Catering*
Contact: Mr Brian Humphrey
t (01493) 488208
w great-yarmouth.angle.uk.com/attractions/frittonlake.cgi

FULBOURN
Cambridgeshire

Old Chapel ★★★
Self Catering
Contact: Mrs Denise Ryder
t (01223) 881427
w stayintheoldchapel.com

FULSTOW
Lincolnshire

Enfield Farm Cottages ★★★★ *Self Catering*
Contact: Joyce Marshall
t (01507) 363268
e enquiries@enfieldfarmcottages.co.uk
w enfieldfarmcottages.co.uk

Peartree Cottage ★★★
Self Catering
Contact: Jane Thomas
t (01572) 460258
e erooke@rutland.gov.uk

Waingrove Farm Country Cottages ★★★★
Self Catering
Contact: Paul Tinker
t (01507) 363704
e ptinker.tinkernet@virgin.net
w lincolnshirecottages.com

GAINSBOROUGH
Lincolnshire

Trent House ★★★★
Self Catering
Contact: Mr & Mrs Knight
t (01427) 612886
e knightmi79@btinternet.com

GARBOLDISHAM
Norfolk

Burnside and Hawthorn Lodge ★★★★ *Self Catering*
Contact: Mrs Connie Atkins
t (01953) 688376
w alderwoodlodges.co.uk

GAYTON
Norfolk

The Annexe ★★★
Self Catering
Norfolk Country Cottages
t (01603) 871872
e info@norfolkcottages.co.uk
w norfolkcottages.co.uk

Willow Cottage ★★★★
Self Catering
Contact: Mrs S Gadsby
t (01223) 836918

GELDESTON
Norfolk

Gordan Cottage
Rating Applied For
Self Catering
Norfolk Country Cottages
t (01603) 871872
e info@norfolkcottages.co.uk
w norfolkcottages.co.uk

GIMINGHAM
Norfolk

Hollies Farm
Rating Applied For
Self Catering
Contact: Mr Neil Allsop
t (01263) 576417
e neil.allsop@btinternet.com
w holliesfarmholidaylet.co.uk

Poppy Cottage ★★★★
Self Catering
Norfolk Country Cottages
t (01603) 871872
e info@norfolkcottages.co.uk
w norfolkcottages.co.uk

GLOSSOP
Derbyshire

Rowan Tree Cottage ★★★
Self Catering
Contact: Paul & Kate Bohan
t (01457) 858786
w rowantreeglossop.co.uk

GOBOWEN
Shropshire

The Old Mill ★★–★★★
Self Catering
t (01691) 659377

GOLDICOTE
Warwickshire

Bluebell Cottage ★★★
Self Catering
Contact: Mr & Mrs Charles & Kim Wall
t (01789) 740907
e enquiries@bluebellcottagestratford.co.uk
w bluebellcottagestratford.co.uk

GORLESTON-ON-SEA
Norfolk

Manor Cottage, Gorleston ★★★ *Self Catering*
Contact: Mrs Margaret Ward
North Manor House
t (01493) 669845
e normanward@tiscali.co.uk
w wardm4.fsnet.co.uk

GOULCEBY
Lincolnshire

Bay Tree Cottage ★★★★
Self Catering
Contact: Gordon Reid
t (01507) 343230
e info@goulcebypost.co.uk
w goulcebypost.co.uk

GRANTHAM
Lincolnshire

Granary Cottage ★★★★
Self Catering
Contact: M Pepper
t (01476) 585311
e mkmaitland@hotmail.com

GREAT BARDFIELD
Essex

The Watermill Cottages ★★★★ *Self Catering*
Contact: Mr & Mrs Jonathon & Lucy Blackwell
t (01371) 811311
e blackwellsxsix@aol.com
w farmholidaysinessex.co.uk

GREAT BIRCHAM
Norfolk

Humphrey Cottage ★★★★
Self Catering
Contact: Mrs Elly Chalmers
t (01485) 578393

GREAT CARLTON
Lincolnshire

Willow Farm ★★★
Self Catering
Contact: Mr James Clark
t (01507) 338540

GREAT COMBERTON
Worcestershire

The Granary ★★★★
Self Catering
Contact: Mrs Jenny Newbury
t (01386) 710210

GREAT DODDINGTON
Northamptonshire

The Old Watermill, Great Doddington ★★★★★
Self Catering
Contact: Anne Lowe
t (01933) 276870
e anne@watermillholidays.co.uk
w watermillholidays.co.uk

GREAT DUNMOW
Essex

The Granary ★★★
Self Catering
Contact: Mrs Cathy Burton
t (01371) 870821
e moorendfarm@btconnect.com
w moorendfarm.com

GREAT EVERSDEN
Cambridgeshire

Rose Barn Cottages ★★★★
Self Catering
Contact: Mr Paul Tebbit
t (01223) 262154
w redhousefarmuk.com

GREAT HALE
Lincolnshire

The Old Stable ★★★★
Self Catering
Contact: Caroline Redmond
t (01529) 460307
e c.redmond@virgin.net
w theoldstable-greathale.co.uk

GREAT HOCKHAM
Norfolk

Old School Cottage ★★★★
Self Catering
Contact: Ms Gwen Flanders
t (01953) 498277
w 4starcottage.co.uk

GREAT HUCKLOW
Derbyshire

Burrs Cottage ★★★
Self Catering
Sykes Cottages
t (01244) 345700
e info@sykescottages.co.uk
w sykescottages.co.uk

Curlew Cottage ★★★★
Self Catering
Contact: Abigail White
t (01298) 873060
e russabi@hotmail.co.uk
w curlewcottagewindmill.co.uk

The Hayloft ★★★★
Self Catering
Contact: Mrs Margot Darley
t (01298) 871044
e margot.darley1@btinternet.com
w peakdistrictfarmhols.co.uk

South View Cottage ★★★★
Self Catering
Contact: Mrs Maureen Waterhouse
t (01298) 871440
e mo@mmwaterhouse.demon.co.uk
w cottageguide.co.uk/southviewcottage

GREAT LONGSTONE
Derbyshire

1 Harrow Cottage ★★★★
Self Catering
Peak Cottages
t (0114) 262 0777
e enquiries@peakcottages.com
w peakcottages.com

Field House Cottage, Great Longstone ★★ *Self Catering*
Contact: Julia Spink
Field House
t (01629) 640103
e juliag@lumina-solns.com

Wild Flower Cottage
★★★★ *Self Catering*
Contact: Mrs Hazel Bell
t (01246) 583564
e hazel@peak-district-holidays.co.uk
w peak-district-holidays.co.uk

GREAT MASSINGHAM
Norfolk

2 Church Cottages ★★★★
Self Catering
Norfolk Country Cottages
t (01603) 871872
e info@norfolkcottages.co.uk
w norfolkcottages.co.uk

Primrose Cottage ★★★
Self Catering
Contact: Mrs Christine Riches
t (01485) 520216
w christine-riches.com

GREAT PAXTON
Cambridgeshire

Paxton Hill House
Rating Applied For
Self Catering
Contact: Ninian Sanders
t (01480) 216237
e ninian_sanders@btinternet.com
w paxtonhillhouse.co.uk

GREAT PLUMSTEAD
Norfolk

Windfalls
Rating Applied For
Self Catering
Norfolk Country Cottages
t (01603) 871872
e info@norfolkcottages.co.uk
w norfolkcottages.co.uk

GREAT PONTON
Lincolnshire

Witham Barn ★★★★
Self Catering
Contact: Stephen. T Jackson
t (01476) 530502
e steve@jackson3985.fslife.co.uk
w withambarn.com/

GREAT SHELFORD
Cambridgeshire

Inglenook Cottage ★★★★
Self Catering
Contact: Mrs Biddy Wilkinson
t (01223) 843856
w cambridge-cottages.co.uk

GREAT SNORING
Norfolk

Church View Cottage ★★★
Self Catering
Norfolk Country Cottages
t (01603) 871872
e info@norfolkcottages.co.uk
w norfolkcottages.co.uk

Rose Cottage ★★★★
Self Catering
Contact: Mrs Gilly Paramor
t (01328) 878867
e gilly@gparamor.freeserve.co.uk
w clevencycottages.co.uk

GREAT WALSINGHAM
Norfolk

Tailors House ★★★
Self Catering
Norfolk Country Cottages
t (01603) 871872
e info@norfolkcottages.co.uk
w norfolkcottages.co.uk

GREAT YARMOUTH
Norfolk

Arrandale Apartments
★★★-★★★★ *Self Catering*
Contact: Mr Sunghuttee
t (01493) 855046
w arrandaleapartments.co.uk

The Dunes ★★★
Self Catering
Contact: Mrs Beryl Wymer
t (01493) 842584

Hadleigh Holiday Suites
★★★★ *Self Catering*
Contact: Mr Peter Meah
t (01702) 553063
e peterforhadleighsuites@talktalk.net
w hadleighholidaysuites.co.uk

Karendel Holiday Flats
★★-★★★ *Self Catering*
Contact: Mrs June Ward
t (01493) 720490

Kenwood Holiday Flats ★★
Self Catering
Contact: Mrs V Forbes
t (01493) 852740
w tiscover.co.uk

St Georges Holiday Flats ★★
Self Catering
Contact: Mr & Mrs Sungtluttee
t (01493) 842036
e st_georges_holiday_flats@msn.com

GRESHAM
Norfolk

Brencott ★★★★
Self Catering
Norfolk Country Cottages
t (01603) 871872
e info@norfolkcottages.co.uk
w norfolkcottages.co.uk

GRIMBLETHORPE
Lincolnshire

Grimblethorpe Hall Country Cottages ★★★★★
Self Catering
Contact: Mrs Annie Codling
t (01507) 313671
e enquiries@shepherdsholidaycottage.co.uk
w shepherdsholidaycottage.co.uk

GRIMSTON
Norfolk

Washpit Cottage ★★★★
Self Catering
Contact: Mrs Christine Coe
t (01485) 600334

GRINDLEFORD
Derbyshire

Rylea ★★★★ *Self Catering*
Peak Cottages
t (0114) 262 0777
e enquiries@peakcottages.com
w peakcottages.com

GRINDON
Staffordshire

Cawbrook Farm Cottage
Rating Applied For
Self Catering
Contact: Miss Nicola Distin
t (01538) 304535
e n.distin@btinternet.com

GRINSHILL
Shropshire

Amblewood Cottage
★★★★ *Self Catering*
t (01939) 220214
w stmem.com/amblewood-cottage

Barleycorn Barns ★★★★
Self Catering
Contact: Mr Neil Lewis
t (01939) 220333
e booking@barleycornbarns.co.uk
w barleycornbarns.co.uk

Chestnut Croft Cottages
★★★-★★★★ *Self Catering*
Contact: Mrs Roger & Jane Good
t (01939) 220573
e roger@goodrj.fsnet.co.uk
w chestnutcroft.co.uk

GRISTON
Norfolk

Park Farm ★★★★
Self Catering
Contact: Mrs Diane Ulrych
t (01953) 483020
e parkfarm@eidosnet.co.uk
w parkfarmbreckland.co.uk

GRUNDISBURGH
Suffolk

The Stable ★★★
Self Catering
Contact: Mrs Louisa Davies
t (01473) 738827

GUESTWICK
Norfolk

Williams Barn ★★★★
Self Catering
Contact: Ms Jayne Harrold
t (01263) 861386

GUNTHORPE
Norfolk

Chimney Cottage ★★★
Self Catering
Contact: Mr Roy Preston
t (01328) 830411
e roy@preston17.orangehome.co.uk
w tiscover.co.uk

GUNTHORPE
Nottinghamshire

Glebe Farm Cottages
★★★★ *Self Catering*
Contact: Phil Warrior
t (0115) 966 3836
e philwarrior@aol.com
w glebefarmcottages.com

HADDENHAM
Cambridgeshire

Old Porch House ★★★★
Self Catering
w oldporchhouse.co.uk

Stumps Cottage ★★★
Self Catering
Contact: Mrs JA Hill
t (01353) 740212

HADDISCOE
Norfolk

Red Mill ★★★ *Self Catering*
Contact: Mr Daniel Webster
t (01603) 472633
w listedescape.com

HADFIELD
Derbyshire

Burnswark ★★★★
Self Catering
Contact: Pat Morris
t (01457) 855667
e enquiries@burnswark.com
w burnswark.com

HADLEIGH
Suffolk

Angel Cottage ★★★★
Self Catering
Contact: Mrs Nadia Eustace
t (01473) 652356
w periodcottageholidays.co.uk

Lodge House ★★★★ *Self Catering & Serviced Apartments*
Contact: Angela & Rod Rolfe
t (01473) 822458
e r.rolfe@edgehall.co.uk
w tiscover.co.uk

Wattisham Hall Holiday Cottages, Wattisham
★★★★ *Self Catering*
Contact: Jeremy and Jo Squirrell
t (01449) 740240
e enquiries@wattishamhall.co.uk
w wattishamhall.co.uk

HAGWORTHINGHAM
Lincolnshire

Kingfisher Lodge ★★★★
Self Catering
Contact: Nick Bowser
t (01205) 870210 & 07970 128531
e office@ewbowser.com
w meridianretreats.co.uk

HALESWORTH
Suffolk

Bucks Farm Holiday Cottage
★★★★ *Self Catering*
Contact: Mrs Jo Newton
t (01986) 784216
e jo@bucksfarm.freeuk.com
w bucksfarm-holidays.co.uk

Number Sixteen ★★★★
Self Catering
Contact: Ms Fiona Coverdale
t (01763) 853325

Stable End Cottage
★★★★★ *Self Catering*
Contact: Ms Jo Jordan
t (01986) 873124
e jo@stable-end-cottage.co.uk
w stable-end-cottage.co.uk

Weavers Cottage ★★★★
Self Catering
Contact: Mrs Joyce Harper
t (01986) 872526
e paddocks@ukonline.co.uk
w halesworthcottage.co.uk

HALLINGTON
Lincolnshire

Paddy House and Blacksmith Shop ★★★★
Self Catering
Contact: Heather Canter
t (01507) 605864
e canter.hallington@virgin.net
w canter-hallington.co.uk

Look out for establishments participating in the Walkers, Cyclists, Families and Welcome Pets! schemes

HALLOW
Worcestershire

The New Cottage ★★★★
Self Catering
Contact: Mrs Doreen Jeeves
t (01905) 640953
e jeeves@thenewcottage.co.uk
w thenewcottage.co.uk

HALSTEAD
Essex

Froyz Hall Barn ★★★★
Self Catering
Contact: Mrs Judy Butler
t (01787) 476684 & 07738 147743
e judibutler@dsl.pipex.com
w froyzhall.co.uk

HALSTEAD
Leicestershire

Halstead House Farm ★★★
Self Catering
Contact: Mr John Driver
t (0116) 259 7239
e johndriver@supanet.com
w halsteadhousefarm.co.uk

HAMBLETON
Rutland

Mary's Cottage ★★★
Self Catering
Contact: Mrs Sandra Martin
t (01572) 755639

Pyghtle & Thistledown
★★★★ *Self Catering*
Contact: Mrs Cath Humphrey
t (01572) 722445
e info@rutlandwaterselfcatering.co.uk
w rutlandwaterselfcatering.co.uk

HAMPTON LOADE
Shropshire

One Lion Cottage ★★★
Self Catering
Contact: Mrs Juliet Browning
t (01746) 780404
e julietbrowning@hotmail.com

HAMPTON LUCY
Warwickshire

The Byre ★★★★
Self Catering
Contact: Mr Richard Hoare
t (01926) 624690
e richard-hoare@btconnect.com
w byre-warwick.co.uk

HANDLEY, CLAY CROSS
Derbyshire

Ridgewell Farm Holiday Cottages ★★★★
Self Catering
Contact: Mrs Ann Kerry
t (01246) 590698
e ridgewellfarm@btinternet.com

HANLEY CASTLE
Worcestershire

Rhydd Barn ★★★★
Self Catering
Contact: Miss Rosemary Boaz
t (01223) 830591
e info@rhyddbarn.co.uk
w rhyddbarn.co.uk

Whitehall Farm Holiday Cottages ★★★ *Self Catering*
t (01684) 310376
e cgpavey@aol.com
w whitehalllettings.co.uk

HANLEY SWAN
Worcestershire

Mere End Cabin ★★★★
Self Catering
Contact: Mrs Marion Bishop
t (01684) 310899
e hanleyholidays@yahoo.co.uk

HANWORTH
Norfolk

Holly Cottage
Rating Applied For
Self Catering
Norfolk Country Cottages
t (01603) 871872
e info@norfolkcottages.co.uk
w norfolkcottages.co.uk

HAPPISBURGH
Norfolk

Boundary Stables ★★★★
Self Catering
Contact: Mr Julian Burns
t (01692) 650171
e bookings@boundarystables.co.uk
w boundarystables.co.uk

Happidays
Rating Applied For
Self Catering
Norfolk Country Cottages
t (01603) 871872
e info@norfolkcottages.co.uk
w norfolkcottages.co.uk

Heather Cottage ★★★
Self Catering
Norfolk Country Cottages
t (01603) 871872
e info@norfolkcottages.co.uk
w norfolkcottages.co.uk

Lanthorn Cottage ★★★★
Self Catering
Contact: Mr Ian Brown
t (01442) 384473

Nicholson Cottage ★★★★
Self Catering
Norfolk Country Cottages
t (01603) 871872
e info@norfolkcottages.co.uk
w norfolkcottages.co.uk

The Stables ★★★★
Self Catering
Norfolk Country Cottages
t (01603) 871872
e info@norfolkcottages.co.uk
w norfolkcottages.co.uk

HARBY
Leicestershire

New Farm Holiday Cottage
★★★ *Self Catering*
Contact: Miss Ruth Stanley
t (01949) 860640

HAREWOOD END
Herefordshire

Grange Farm House
★★★★★ *Self Catering*
Gustivean Cottages
t (01579) 346473
e holidays@duchyofcornwall.gov.uk
w duchyofcornwallholidaycottages.co.uk

HARLOW
Essex

The Tythe Barn, Harlowbury Manor ★★★★ *Self Catering*
Contact: Mr & Mrs David & Marian Farningham
t (01279) 320411
w harlowbury.co.uk

HARMSTON
Lincolnshire

Keepers Cottage
Rating Applied For
Self Catering
Contact: Tony Louth
Lincoln Property Services Ltd
t (01673) 866466
e tonylouth@aol.com
w holidaysinlincoln.co.uk

HARPLEY
Norfolk

Lower Farm Self-Catering Cottages ★★★ *Self Catering*
Contact: Mrs Pippa Case
t (01485) 520541
e harpleyholidays@hotmail.co.uk
w lowerfarmholidaycottages.co.uk

HARTINGTON
Derbyshire

1 Staley Cottage and Victoria House ★★★★
Self Catering
Contact: Mr & Mrs Oliver
Carr Head Farm
t (01226) 762387

Ash Tree Cottage, Hartington ★★★★
Self Catering
Contact: Ms Clare Morson
t (01298) 84247
e nettletorfarm@btconnect.com

Beech Cottage ★★★
Self Catering
Contact: Mrs Birch
t (01298) 84532
e lesley@beechcottage99.freeserve.co.uk

Cotterill Farm Cottages
★★★★ *Self Catering*
Contact: Ms Christina Kamali
t (01298) 84447
e enquiries@cotterillfarm.co.uk
w cotterillfarm.co.uk

Cruck Cottage and Wolfscote Grange Cottages
★★★★ *Self Catering*
Contact: Mrs Jane Gibbs
t (01298) 84342
w wolfscotegrangecottages.co.uk

Dove Valley Centre ★★★★
Self Catering
Contact: Paul & Elspeth Walker
t (01298) 83282
e walker@dovevalleycentre.co.uk
w dovevalleycentre.co.uk

Grace's Cottage
Rating Applied For
Self Catering
Yorkshire Cottages
t (01228) 406701
e enquiries@yorkshire-cottages.info
w yorkshire-cottages.info

Hartington Cottages
★★★★-★★★★★
Self Catering
Contact: Mrs M Francis
t (01298) 22287
e enquiries@hartingtoncottages.co.uk
w hartingtoncottages.co.uk

Hillcrest Cottage
Rating Applied For
Self Catering
Yorkshire Cottages
t (01228) 406701
e enquiries@yorkshire-cottages.info
w yorkshire-cottages.info

Old House Farm Cottages
★★★-★★★★ *Self Catering*
Contact: Mrs Sue Flower
t (01629) 636268
e s.flower1@virgin.net

Pilsbury Barns ★★★★
Self Catering
Peak Cottages
t (0114) 262 0777
e enquiries@peakcottages.com
w peakcottages.com

Red Lion House
Rating Applied For
Self Catering
Yorkshire Cottages
t (01228) 406701
e enquiries@yorkshire-cottages.info
w yorkshire-cottages.info

Stable Cottage ★★★
Self Catering
Contact: Mrs Veronica Lawrenson
t (01538) 300487
e elkstones@talk21.com
w cottageguide.co.uk/peakdistrictcottage

HARTSHORNE
Derbyshire

Upper Hall ★★★★
Self Catering
Contact: Diane Jones
t (01332) 842750
e diane.jones@caliph.net
w derbyshire-holidays.com

HARWICH
Essex

The Coach Run ★★★★
Self Catering
Contact: Andrew Norfolk
t 07971 073938
e aanorfolk11@aol.com

HASSOP
Derbyshire

Jubilee Cottage ★★★★★
Self Catering
Contact: Mrs V Shaw
t (01629) 640631

HATHERSAGE
Derbyshire

Morley Cottage ★★★★
Self Catering
Peak Cottages
t (0114) 262 0777
e enquiries@peakcottages.com
w peakcottages.com

Morton Loft ★★★★
Self Catering
Peak Cottages
t (0114) 262 0777
e enquiries@peakcottages.com
w peakcottages.com

Pat's Cottage ★★★
Self Catering
Contact: Mr John Drakeford
t (0114) 236 6014 & 07850 200711
e johnmdrakeford@hotmail.com
w patscottage.co.uk

St Michael's Cottage ★★★
Self Catering
Contact: Mr Hanley
Saint Michael's Environmental Education Centre
t (01433) 650309
e stmichaels@nottscc.gov.uk
w eess.org.uk

HATTON
Lincolnshire

The Gables ★★★★★
Self Catering
Contact: Julia Merivale
t (01673) 858862
w thegables-hatton.co.uk

HATTON
Shropshire

The Stable ★★★★
Self Catering
Contact: Mr & Mrs Hall
t (01694) 781202
e raysarahhall@aol.com

HAUGHLEY
Suffolk

Red House Farm Cottages
★★★-★★★★★ *Self Catering*
Contact: Mrs Mary Noy
Red House Farm
t (01449) 673323
e mary@redhousefarmhaughley.co.uk

HAVERINGLAND
Norfolk

Quakerhall Barns ★★★★
Self Catering
Contact: Ms Rachel Hurlock
Barsham Barns (Norfolk) LLP
t (01328) 821744
w quakerhallbarns.co.uk

HAYFIELD
Derbyshire

Bowden Bridge Cottage
★★★★ *Self Catering*
Contact: Mrs Margrith Easter
t (01663) 743975
e margrith@btconnect.com

Cracken Cottage ★★★
Self Catering
Peak Cottages
t (0114) 262 0777
e enquiries@peakcottages.com
w peakcottages.com

Kinder Cottage ★★★
Self Catering
Peak Cottages
t (0114) 262 0777
e enquiries@peakcottages.com
w peakcottages.com

HAZELWOOD
Derbyshire

Duck Pond View ★★★★★
Self Catering
Contact: Mr & Mrs Terry & Liz Chisman
t (01773) 550686
e enquiries@duckpondview.co.uk
w duckpondview.com

HEACHAM
Norfolk

1 Canon Pot Close ★★★★
Self Catering
Contact: Mr Chris Saunders
t (01223) 832684
e mail@westcrete.co.uk

1 Sunnyside Cottages ★★★
Self Catering
Norfolk Country Cottages
t (01603) 871872
e info@norfolkcottages.co.uk
w norfolkcottages.co.uk

24 Robin Hill ★★
Self Catering
Contact: Mrs DM Gidney
t (01485) 570309
w tiscover.co.uk

3 Hall Close ★★★★
Self Catering
Contact: Mr & Mrs Walpole
t (01328) 700161
w 3hallclose.com

7 Pretoria Cottages ★★★
Self Catering
Norfolk Country Cottages
t (01603) 871872
e info@norfolkcottages.co.uk
w norfolkcottages.co.uk

Appletree Cottage ★★★★
Self Catering
Birds Norfolk Holiday Homes
t (01485) 534267
e shohol@birdsnorfolkholidayhomes.co.uk
w norfolkholidayhomes-birds.co.uk

The Beach House ★★★
Self Catering
Birds Norfolk Holiday Homes
t (01485) 534267
e shohol@birdsnorfolkholidayhomes.co.uk
w norfolkholidayhomes-birds.co.uk

Blackberry Cottage ★★★
Self Catering
Norfolk Country Cottages
t (01603) 871872
e info@norfolkcottages.co.uk
w norfolkcottages.co.uk

Carrick Cottage ★★★
Self Catering
Contact: Mrs Susan Sills
t (01485) 571369

Cedar Springs
★★★-★★★★ *Self Catering*
Contact: Mrs Antonia Howe
t (01485) 570609

Cedar Springs Chalets ★★
Self Catering
Contact: Mr & Mrs Michael & Ann Chestney
t (01328) 838341
w cottageguide.co.uk/cedarsprings

Cheney Hollow Cottages
★★★★ *Self Catering*
Contact: Ms Susan Lamb
t (01485) 572625
w cheneyhollow.co.uk

Coconut Chalet
Rating Applied For
Self Catering
Birds Norfolk Holiday Homes
t (01485) 534267
e shohol@birdsnorfolkholidayhomes.co.uk
w norfolkholidayhomes-birds.co.uk

Haydn's Retreat ★★★
Self Catering
Birds Norfolk Holiday Homes
t (01485) 534267
e shohol@birdsnorfolkholidayhomes.co.uk
w norfolkholidayhomes-birds.co.uk

Malthouse Lodge ★★★★
Self Catering
Norfolk Country Cottages
t (01603) 871872
e info@norfolkcottages.co.uk
w norfolkcottages.co.uk

Oakhill
Rating Applied For
Self Catering
Birds Norfolk Holiday Homes
t (01485) 534267
e shohol@birdsnorfolkholidayhomes.co.uk
w norfolkholidayhomes-birds.co.uk

Old Station Waiting Rooms
★★★-★★★★ *Self Catering*
Contact: Mrs Judith Clay
t (01485) 570712
w cottageguide.co.uk/waitingrooms

Painters Corner ★★★★
Self Catering
Contact: Mrs N. J. O'Callaghan
t (01485) 525381
e hideawaya1@aol.com
w heacham1.fsnet.co.uk/hideaway/accommodation_07

The Redlands ★★★★
Self Catering
Birds Norfolk Holiday Homes
t (01485) 534267
e shohol@birdsnorfolkholidayhomes.co.uk
w norfolkholidayhomes-birds.co.uk

Retreat Cottage 2 ★★★
Self Catering
Contact: Ms Clare Rooth
t (020) 7737 4515
w retreatcottage.com

Tawny Cottage ★★★★
Self Catering
t (01603) 871872

Turret House ★★★★
Self Catering
Birds Norfolk Holiday Homes
t (01485) 534267
e shohol@birdsnorfolkholidayhomes.co.uk
w norfolkholidayhomes-birds.co.uk

HEMPNALL
Norfolk

Fairstead Farmhouse
★★★★ *Self Catering*
Contact: Mrs Mary Sargent
t (01508) 530269
w morningthorpecottages.co.uk

HEMPSTEAD
Norfolk

Pine Farm Barn ★★★★
Self Catering
Norfolk Country Cottages
t (01603) 871872
e info@norfolkcottages.co.uk
w norfolkcottages.co.uk

White Horse Cottage ★★★
Self Catering
Norfolk Country Cottages
t (01603) 871872
e info@norfolkcottages.co.uk
w norfolkcottages.co.uk

HEMSBY
Norfolk

Cavalier Chalets ★★★
Chalet
Contact: Mrs B M Jermany
t (01493) 368188

Seadell Holiday Chalets
★★★ *Chalet*
t (01493) 730041
e enquiries@seadell.co.uk
w seadell.co.uk

Sunset Holiday Chalets, Hemsby and Scratby ★★★
Chalet
Contact: Mr Lionel Knights
t (01493) 720450
w sunsetholidaychalets.co.uk

Sunwright Holidays ★★
Chalet
Contact: Mrs Michelle Browne
t (01493) 304282
e sunwrightholiday@aol.com
w sunwrightholidays.com

HENLEY
Suffolk

Damerons Farm Holidays
★★★★ *Self Catering*
Contact: Mr & Mrs Wayne & Sue Leggett
t (01473) 832454
w dameronsfarmholidays.co.uk

HENLEY-IN-ARDEN
Warwickshire

Irelands Farm Cottages
★★★★ *Self Catering*
Contact: Mrs Stephanie Williams
t (01564) 792476
e stephaniewilliams1t@tiscali.co.uk
w irelandsfarmcottages.com

HEREFORD
Herefordshire

Castle Cliffe East ★★★★
Self Catering
Contact: Mr Mark Hubbard & Mr Phil Wilson
Castle Cliffe West
t (01432) 272096
e mail@castlecliffe.net
w castlecliffe.net

The Cottage ★★★★★
Self Catering
Contact: Mrs C Brooks
t (01432) 860293
e boultbeebrooks@btinternet.com

Cross In Hand Farm Cottage
★★★★ *Self Catering*
Contact: Dr J. Thornton
t (01981) 540957

Grafton Villa Farm Cottages
★★★★ *Self Catering*
Contact: Mrs Jennie Layton
t (01432) 268689
e jennielayton@ereal.net
w graftonvilla.co.uk

The Green Farm Cottage, Felton ★★★★ *Self Catering*
Contact: Shirley Simcock
t (01432) 820234
e cottage@greenfarmestate.co.uk
w greenfarmestate.co.uk

Longwood Cottage ★★★★
Self Catering
Contact: Mrs Veronica Harris
t (01989) 740248
e kenverharris@aol.com
w longwoodcottage.co.uk

Westwing ★★★★
Self Catering
Contact: Alison Warren
t (01432) 278741
e jhw.avw@tiscali.co.uk

HERTFORD
Hertfordshire

Dalmonds Barns ★★★★
Self Catering
Contact: Miss Julia Camp
t (01992) 462729
e ann.reay@virgin.net
w dalmondsbarns.com

Petasfield Cottages ★★★★
Self Catering
Contact: Miss Helen Clark
t (01992) 504201
e helen@petasfieldcottages.co.uk
w petasfieldcottages.co.uk

HESSETT
Suffolk

Heathfield, Hessett ★★★★
Self Catering
Contact: Mrs Christine Whitton Arcadia
t (01359) 271130

Wilwyn And Chapel Cottages ★★★ *Self Catering*
Contact: Mr & Mrs Chris & Nicky Glass
t (01359) 270736
w cottageguide.co.uk/hessett

HEYBRIDGE
Essex

Ivydene *Approved Caravan Holiday Home*
Contact: Mr J Wakelin
t (01954) 267190

HICKLING
Norfolk

Conifers ★★★★
Self Catering
Norfolk Country Cottages
t (01603) 871872
e info@norfolkcottages.co.uk
w norfolkcottages.co.uk

The Cottage ★★★
Self Catering
Norfolk Country Cottages
t (01603) 871872
e info@norfolkcottages.co.uk
w norfolkcottages.co.uk

Goleby's Cottage ★★★
Self Catering
Norfolk Country Cottages
t (01603) 871872
e info@norfolkcottages.co.uk
w norfolkcottages.co.uk

Kingsley Cottage ★★★★
Self Catering
Norfolk Country Cottages
t (01603) 871872
e info@norfolkcottages.co.uk
w norfolkcottages.co.uk

Neaps ★★★★ *Self Catering*
Norfolk Country Cottages
t (01603) 871872
e info@norfolkcottages.co.uk
w norfolkcottages.co.uk

Pilgrim's Chase ★★★★
Self Catering
Norfolk Country Cottages
t (01603) 871872
e info@norfolkcottages.co.uk
w norfolkcottages.co.uk

Pilgrim's Cottage ★★★
Self Catering
Norfolk Country Cottages
t (01603) 871872
e info@norfolkcottages.co.uk
w norfolkcottages.co.uk

Pilgrims Progress ★★★★
Self Catering
Norfolk Country Cottages
t (01603) 871872
e info@norfolkcottages.co.uk
w norfolkcottages.co.uk

Pilgrim's Prospect ★★★★
Self Catering
Norfolk Country Cottages
t (01603) 871872
e info@norfolkcottages.co.uk
w norfolkcottages.co.uk

Town Cottage ★★★★
Self Catering
Norfolk Country Cottages
t (01603) 871872
e info@norfolkcottages.co.uk
w norfolkcottages.co.uk

HIGH KELLING
Norfolk

Lynton Loft ★★★★
Self Catering
Norfolk Country Cottages
t (01603) 871872
e info@norfolkcottages.co.uk
w norfolkcottages.co.uk

HILL
Worcestershire

The Old Saw Barn ★★★★
Self Catering
Contact: Mrs Sarah Righton
t (01386) 860870
e oldsawbarn@righton.org.uk

HIMBLETON
Worcestershire

Phepson Farm Cottages
★★★-★★★★★
Self Catering
Contact: Mrs Patricia Havard
t (01905) 391205
e liz@phepsonfarm.co.uk
w phepsonfarm.co.uk

HINDOLVESTON
Norfolk

Pine Cottage ★★★
Self Catering
Contact: Mr Scammell
t (01707) 651734
w cheznorfolk.com

HINDRINGHAM
Norfolk

1 Field House Cottage
★★★★ *Self Catering*
Norfolk Country Cottages
t (01603) 871872
e info@norfolkcottages.co.uk
w norfolkcottages.co.uk

Juniper Cottage ★★★★★
Self Catering
Contact: Mrs Claire Waite
t 07871 728316
e claire@luxurynorfolkcottage.co.uk
w luxurynorfolkcottage.co.uk

HINGHAM
Norfolk

The Granary ★★★
Self Catering
Contact: Mrs Christine Dunnett
t (01953) 850596
w hinghamleisure.co.uk

White Lodge Farm Cottages, Hingham ★★★★★
Self Catering
Contact: Mr & Mrs Tony Richardson
White Lodge Farm
t (01953) 850435
e vb@whitelodgefarmcottages.co.uk
w whitelodgefarmcottages.co.uk

HISTON
Cambridgeshire

13 The Green ★★★★
Self Catering
Contact: Mrs Pauline Wynn
4 Eversley Close
t (01954) 250729

HITCHAM
Suffolk

Mill House Holiday Cottage
★★-★★★ *Self Catering & Serviced Apartments*
Contact: Ms Melanie Rieger
t (01449) 740315
e hitcham@aol.com
w millhouse-hitcham.co.uk

HOARWITHY
Herefordshire

The Old Mill Cottage ★★★
Self Catering
Contact: Mrs Carol Probert
t (01432) 840602
e carol.probert@virgin.net

HOCKWOLD
Norfolk

Willow Holt ★★★
Self Catering
Norfolk Country Cottages
t (01603) 871872
e info@norfolkcottages.co.uk
w norfolkcottages.co.uk

HOGNASTON
Derbyshire

Old Hall Barn ★★★
Self Catering
Peak Cottages
t (0114) 262 0777
e enquiries@peakcottages.com
w peakcottages.com

HOGSTHORPE
Lincolnshire

Helsey House Holiday Cottages ★★★★
Self Catering
Contact: Elizabeth Elvidge
t (01754) 872927
e info@helseycottages.co.uk
w helseycottages.co.uk

HOLLINGTON
Staffordshire

Old Wood Farm Barns
★★★★ *Self Catering*
Contact: Liz Bean
t (01889) 507077
e paul.bean@bt.com

HOLLINSCLOUGH
Staffordshire

Under Wilshaw Cottage
Rating Applied For
Self Catering
Contact: Bernard & Carole Selby
t (01625) 574410
e bandcselby@hotmail.com

HOLME NEXT THE SEA
Norfolk

9 Barnwell Cottages ★★★★
Self Catering
Contact: Mrs Susan Sadler
t (01485) 534991

Beach Cottage ★★★★
Self Catering
Contact: Mrs Stephanie Jones
t (01485) 525201

Broadwater Cottage ★★★★
Self Catering
Contact: Mrs Jayne Ransom
t (01223) 524821
e vine.farm@ntlworld.com
w broadwatercottage.co.uk

Brook Bungalow ★★★★
Self Catering
Contact: Mr & Mrs John & Judy Whitsed
t (01733) 380028
w brookbungalow.co.uk

Driftwood ★★★
Self Catering
Norfolk Country Cottages
t (01603) 871872
e info@norfolkcottages.co.uk
w norfolkcottages.co.uk

Rose Cottage ★★★★
Self Catering
Contact: Mrs Stephanie Hedge
t (01954) 250470
w ashtoncottages.co.uk

Sybil Cottage ★★★★
Self Catering
Birds Norfolk Holiday Homes
t (01485) 534267
e shohol@birdsnorfolkholidayhomes.co.uk
w norfolkholidayhomes-birds.co.uk

Tudor Lodge Cottage
★★★★ *Self Catering*
Birds Norfolk Holiday Homes
t (01485) 534267
e shohol@birdsnorfolkholidayhomes.co.uk
w norfolkholidayhomes-birds.co.uk

HOLT
Norfolk

5 Carpenters Cottages ★★★
Self Catering
Contact: Mr Christopher Knights
t (01493) 842289 & (01502) 742022

6 Carpenters Cottage ★★★
Self Catering
Contact: Mrs Sally Beament
t (01363) 773789

6 Letheringsett Hill ★★★★
Self Catering
Norfolk Country Cottages
t (01603) 871872
e info@norfolkcottages.co.uk
w norfolkcottages.co.uk

Albertine ★★ *Self Catering*
Contact: Helen North
t (01794) 368106

Arcadia ★★★ *Self Catering*
Contact: Mrs Elizabeth McGill
t (01932) 770207
e elizabeth@arcadia-holt.com
w tiscover.co.uk

Crowlands Cottage and 4 Carpenters Cottage ★★★
Self Catering
Contact: Mrs Julie Pell
t 07767 663938
e julie.pell@talk21.com
w tiscover.co.uk

Hill Cottage ★★★
Self Catering
Norfolk Country Cottages
t (01603) 871872
e info@norfolkcottages.co.uk
w norfolkcottages.co.uk

The Hollies ★★★
Self Catering
Contact: Miss E Allison
t (01263) 712457

Maple Cottage, Stody
★★★★ *Self Catering*
Contact: Mrs Stephanie Moore
t (01263) 861590
e mooresteph@btinternet.com

Owl Cottage ★★★★
Self Catering
Norfolk Country Cottages
t (01603) 871872
e info@norfolkcottages.co.uk
w norfolkcottages.co.uk

Rose Cottage ★★★★
Self Catering
Contact: Mrs Lisa Wickham
t (01603) 457575

Sunnyside Cottage ★★★
Self Catering
Contact: Mr Michael Drake
t (01603) 712524
e michael.drake@ukgateway.net
w tiscover.co.uk

Windy Hill ★★★
Self Catering
Norfolk Country Cottages
t (01603) 871872
e info@norfolkcottages.co.uk
w norfolkcottages.co.uk

Wood Farm Cottages
★★★-★★★★ *Self Catering*
Contact: Mrs Diana Jacob
t (01263) 587347
e info@wood-farm.com
w wood-farm.com

HOLTON
Suffolk

Swallow Barn ★★★★
Self Catering
Contact: Mrs Jackie Circus
t (01986) 874521
w valleyfarmholton.co.uk

HOLTON ST MARY
Suffolk

The Coach House ★★★★
Self Catering
Contact: Mrs A Selleck
t (01206) 298246

HOLYMOORSIDE
Derbyshire

Millclose Cottage ★★★★
Self Catering
Contact: Mr & Mrs A & S Stockton
t (01246) 567624
e allan.stockton@btinternet.com
w millclosefarm.co.uk

HONEYBOURNE
Worcestershire

Peace Haven Holiday Lets
★★★ *Self Catering*
Contact: Mrs Fiona Humphreys
t (01386) 832785
e peace.haven@btconnect.com
w peacehavenlets.com

HONING
Norfolk

Shrublands ★★★
Self Catering
Norfolk Country Cottages
t (01603) 871872
e info@norfolkcottages.co.uk
w norfolkcottages.co.uk

HOPE
Derbyshire

Chapman Farm Cottages
★★★★ *Self Catering*
Contact: Mrs Dorothy Vernon
t (01433) 620297

Farfield Farm Cottages
★★★★ *Self Catering*
Contact: Mrs Gill Elliott
t (01433) 620640
e gill.farfield@virgin.net
w farfield.gemsoft.co.uk

Hope Cottages ★★★★
Self Catering
Peak Cottages
t (0114) 262 0777
e enquiries@peakcottages.com
w peakcottages.com

Laneside Farm Holiday Cottages ★★★★
Self Catering
Contact: Mrs Dorothy Neary
t (01433) 620214
e laneside@lineone.net
w peakdistrictholidaycottages.com

Oaker Farm Cottages
★★★★ *Self Catering*
Contact: Mrs Julie Hadfield
t (01433) 621955
e julieannhadfield@hotmail.com
w oakerfarm.co.uk

HOPE-UNDER-DINMORE
Herefordshire

The Fold ★★★★
Self Catering
Contact: Zena Legge
t (01568) 611314
e info@winsleypark.co.uk
w winsleypark.co.uk

HOPE VALLEY
Derbyshire

Aston Cottages ★★★★
Self Catering
Peak Cottages
t (0114) 262 0777
e enquiries@peakcottages.com
w peakcottages.com

HOPESAY
Shropshire

Kerry Cottage ★★★
Self Catering
Contact: Mr Roger Davies
t (01588) 660487
e info@hesterworth.co.uk
w hesterworth.co.uk

HOPTON
Staffordshire

Bank Cottage
Rating Applied For
Self Catering
Contact: Mr G R Seaton
Kre-8 Ltd
t (01785) 608088
e sales@kre-8.com
w staffordshire-cottage.co.uk

HORNCASTLE
Lincolnshire

Bainvalley Cottages ★★★★
Self Catering
Contact: Wendy Harrison
t (01507) 578352
e wendy@harrison592.freeserve.co.uk
w bainvalleycottages.co.uk

Lincolnshire Wolds Cottages Ltd, Fulletby ★★★
Self Catering
Contact: Mr John Robinson
t (01522) 876994
w woldscottages.co.uk

Southolme Cottage ★★★
Self Catering
Contact: David Gresham
t (01608) 682542
e david@gartongresham.co.uk
w southolmecottage.co.uk

HORNING
Norfolk

Anchor Lodge
Rating Applied For
Self Catering
Norfolk Country Cottages
t (01603) 871872
e info@norfolkcottages.co.uk
w norfolkcottages.co.uk

Ferry Marina Ltd ★★★★
Self Catering
Contact: Mrs Sharon Reeder
t (01692) 630392
e sharon@ferry-marina.co.uk
w ferry-marina.co.uk

The Ferry Powerboat Company Limited ★★★★
Self Catering
Contact: Miss Melissa Reeder
t (01603) 782302

Heron Cottage ★★★★★
Self Catering
Contact: Mrs Gail Pitts
Premier Properties c/o
t 07788 853332
w heron-cottage.com

Heronmere ★★★★
Self Catering
Norfolk Country Cottages
t (01603) 871872
e info@norfolkcottages.co.uk
w norfolkcottages.co.uk

King Line Cottages
★★★-★★★★★ *Self Catering*
Contact: Mr Robert King
t (01692) 630297
e kingline@norfolk-broads.co.uk
w norfolk-broads.co.uk

Little River View ★★★★
Self Catering
Contact: Mrs Victoria Free
t (01245) 441981
e victoria@littleriverview.co.uk
w littleriverview.co.uk

HORRINGER
Suffolk

Garden Cottage ★★★
Self Catering
Contact: Mr Tyrone Lewis
t (01284) 735731

HORSEHAY
Shropshire

5 Pool View ★★★★
Self Catering
t (01952) 503603
w 5poolview.com

HORSEY
Norfolk

River's End ★★★
Self Catering
Norfolk Country Cottages
t (01603) 871872
e info@norfolkcottages.co.uk
w norfolkcottages.co.uk

HORSINGTON
Lincolnshire

Wayside Cottage ★★★
Self Catering
Contact: Ian Williamson
Mill Lane Holiday Cottages
t (01526) 353101
w skegness.net/woodhallspa.htm

HOVETON
Norfolk

East Wing ★★★ *Self Catering*
Norfolk Country Cottages
t (01603) 871872
e info@norfolkcottages.co.uk
w norfolkcottages.co.uk

HOWSHAM
Lincolnshire

Willow Cottages ★★★★
Self Catering
t (01652) 652549
e enquiries@willowcottages.co.uk
w willowcottages.co.uk

HULLAND WARD
Derbyshire

The Green at Hulland
★★★★ *Self Catering*
Contact: Carol A Dixon
t (01335) 372166
e carolabowler@btinternet.com
w thegreenathulland.co.uk

HUNSTANTON
Norfolk

44 Sea Lane ★★★
Self Catering
Birds Norfolk Holiday Homes
t (01485) 534267
e shohol@birdsnorfolkholidayhomes.co.uk
w norfolkholidayhomes-birds.co.uk

Albert House ★★★
Self Catering
Contact: Ms Sarah Flanagan
t (01636) 831159
e sarahflan20@aol.com
w alberthousehunstanton.co.uk

Altera ★★★★ *Self Catering*
Contact: Mrs Jean Larman
t (020) 8421 3815
w altera.mummyanddaddy.com/location.html

Ashdale House ★★★★
Self Catering
Birds Norfolk Holiday Homes
t (01485) 534267
e shohol@birdsnorfolkholidayhomes.co.uk
w norfolkholidayhomes-birds.co.uk

Beech Syde ★★★
Self Catering
Birds Norfolk Holiday Homes
t (01485) 534267
e shohol@birdsnorfolkholidayhomes.co.uk
w norfolkholidayhomes-birds.co.uk

Beeches ★★★ *Self Catering*
Contact: Mrs Julie Judd
Hunstanton Holidays
t (01485) 533981
w hunstantonholidays.co.uk

Birdwatch ★★★★
Self Catering
Birds Norfolk Holiday Homes
t (01485) 534267
e shohol@birdsnorfolkholidayhomes.co.uk
w norfolkholidayhomes-birds.co.uk

Blue Skies ★★★★
Self Catering
Contact: Ms Debbie Harrington
t (01945) 588055
e debs.harrington@btinternet.com
w hunstantonholidaycottages.co.uk

Brincliffe and Annexe
★★★★ *Self Catering*
Birds Norfolk Holiday Homes
t (01485) 534267
e shohol@birdsnorfolkholidayhomes.co.uk
w norfolkholidayhomes-birds.co.uk

Cameo Cottage ★★★
Self Catering
Birds Norfolk Holiday Homes
t (01485) 534267
e shohol@birdsnorfolkholidayhomes.co.uk
w norfolkholidayhomes-birds.co.uk

Chalet 4 ★★ *Self Catering*
Contact: Mr & Mrs Michael & Ann Chestney
t (01328) 838341

Cleeks ★★★ *Self Catering*
Birds Norfolk Holiday Homes
t (01485) 534267
e shohol@birdsnorfolkholidayhomes.co.uk
w norfolkholidayhomes-birds.co.uk

Coastguard Lookout ★★★
Self Catering
Birds Norfolk Holiday Homes
t (01485) 534267
e shohol@birdsnorfolkholidayhomes.co.uk
w norfolkholidayhomes-birds.co.uk

Dormy Cottage ★★★
Self Catering
Birds Norfolk Holiday Homes
t (01485) 534267
e shohol@birdsnorfolkholidayhomes.co.uk
w norfolkholidayhomes-birds.co.uk

Ellerslie ★★★★ *Self Catering*
Norfolk Country Cottages
t (01603) 871872
e info@norfolkcottages.co.uk
w norfolkcottages.co.uk

End Of The Road ★★★
Self Catering
Birds Norfolk Holiday Homes
t (01485) 534267
e shohol@birdsnorfolkholidayhomes.co.uk
w norfolkholidayhomes-birds.co.uk

Flat 11 ★★ *Self Catering*
Birds Norfolk Holiday Homes
t (01485) 534267
e shohol@birdsnorfolkholidayhomes.co.uk
w norfolkholidayhomes-birds.co.uk

Forget Me Not Cottage, Old Hunstanton ★★★★
Self Catering
Contact: Mr Gary Gibson
t 07957 351250 & 07957 366745
e streetsaheadlettings@hotmail.com
w holidayhomesnorfolk.co.uk

Foxgloves Cottage ★★★★
Self Catering
Contact: Terry & Lesley Heade
t (01485) 532460
e deepdenehouse@btopenworld.com
w smoothhound.co.uk/hotels/deepdene.html

Fulmars ★★★ *Self Catering*
Birds Norfolk Holiday Homes
t (01485) 534267
e shohol@birdsnorfolkholidayhomes.co.uk
w norfolkholidayhomes-birds.co.uk

The Haven ★★ *Self Catering*
Birds Norfolk Holiday Homes
t (01485) 534267
e shohol@birdsnorfolkholidayhomes.co.uk
w norfolkholidayhomes-birds.co.uk

Home Cottage ★★★
Self Catering
Birds Norfolk Holiday Homes
t (01485) 534267
e shohol@birdsnorfolkholidayhomes.co.uk
w norfolkholidayhomes-birds.co.uk

Horizons ★★★ *Self Catering*
Birds Norfolk Holiday Homes
t (01485) 534267
e shohol@birdsnorfolkholidayhomes.co.uk
w norfolkholidayhomes-birds.co.uk

Jasmine Cottage ★★★
Self Catering
Birds Norfolk Holiday Homes
t (01485) 534267
e shohol@birdsnorfolkholidayhomes.co.uk
w norfolkholidayhomes-birds.co.uk

Jordans ★★★★ *Self Catering*
Birds Norfolk Holiday Homes
t (01485) 534267
e shohol@birdsnorfolkholidayhomes.co.uk
w norfolkholidayhomes-birds.co.uk

Keepers Cottage ★★★
Self Catering
Birds Norfolk Holiday Homes
t (01485) 534267
e shohol@birdsnorfolkholidayhomes.co.uk
w norfolkholidayhomes-birds.co.uk

Kylie's Corner ★★★★
Self Catering
Birds Norfolk Holiday Homes
t (01485) 534267
e shohol@birdsnorfolkholidayhomes.co.uk
w norfolkholidayhomes-birds.co.uk

The Ladybird House ★★★★
Self Catering
Norfolk Country Cottages
t (01603) 871872
e info@norfolkcottages.co.uk
w norfolkcottages.co.uk

Lavender Cottage ★★★
Self Catering
Birds Norfolk Holiday Homes
t (01485) 534267
e shohol@birdsnorfolkholidayhomes.co.uk
w norfolkholidayhomes-birds.co.uk

Lavender Lodge ★★★★
Self Catering
Birds Norfolk Holiday Homes
t (01485) 534267
e shohol@birdsnorfolkholidayhomes.co.uk
w norfolkholidayhomes-birds.co.uk

Lighthouse Close ★★★★
Self Catering
Norfolk Country Cottages
t (01603) 871872
e info@norfolkcottages.co.uk
w norfolkcottages.co.uk

Lindoola ★★★ *Self Catering*
Birds Norfolk Holiday Homes
t (01485) 534267
e shohol@birdsnorfolkholidayhomes.co.uk
w norfolkholidayhomes-birds.co.uk

Malgwyn ★★★ *Self Catering*
Contact: Mrs Perdita Swift
t (01223) 290207
e pandp.swift@talktalk.net
w cottageguide.co.uk/malgwyn

Meadow View ★★★
Self Catering
Birds Norfolk Holiday Homes
t (01485) 534267
e shohol@birdsnorfolkholidayhomes.co.uk
w norfolkholidayhomes-birds.co.uk

Midway ★★ *Self Catering*
Birds Norfolk Holiday Homes
t (01485) 534267
e shohol@birdsnorfolkholidayhomes.co.uk
w norfolkholidayhomes-birds.co.uk

Minna Cottage ★★★
Self Catering
Contact: Mr Tony Cassie
t (01485) 532448
e tonycassie@btconnect.com
w minnacottage.com

Normanhurst ★★★
Self Catering
Birds Norfolk Holiday Homes
t (01485) 534267
e shohol@birdsnorfolkholidayhomes.co.uk
w norfolkholidayhomes-birds.co.uk

Pennot ★★★ *Self Catering*
Birds Norfolk Holiday Homes
t (01485) 534267
e shohol@birdsnorfolkholidayhomes.co.uk
w norfolkholidayhomes-birds.co.uk

Rosstyn ★★★★ *Self Catering*
Norfolk Country Cottages
t (01603) 871872
e info@norfolkcottages.co.uk
w norfolkcottages.co.uk

Roundstones ★★★
Self Catering
Birds Norfolk Holiday Homes
t (01485) 534267
e shohol@birdsnorfolkholidayhomes.co.uk
w norfolkholidayhomes-birds.co.uk

Saint Crispin ★★★
Self Catering
Contact: Mrs Lesley Poore
t (01485) 534036
e st.crispins@btinternet.com
w tiscover.co.uk

Sandbanks ★★★★
Self Catering
Birds Norfolk Holiday Homes
t (01485) 534267
e shohol@birdsnorfolkholidayhomes.co.uk
w norfolkholidayhomes-birds.co.uk

Sandpiper Cottage ★★★★
Self Catering
Birds Norfolk Holiday Homes
t (01485) 534267
e shohol@birdsnorfolkholidayhomes.co.uk
w norfolkholidayhomes-birds.co.uk

Sea Breeze ★★★
Self Catering
Birds Norfolk Holiday Homes
t (01485) 534267
e shohol@birdsnorfolkholidayhomes.co.uk
w norfolkholidayhomes-birds.co.uk

Seagull House
Rating Applied For
Self Catering
Birds Norfolk Holiday Homes
t (01485) 534267
e shohol@birdsnorfolkholidayhomes.co.uk
w norfolkholidayhomes-birds.co.uk

Serenity ★★★ *Self Catering*
Birds Norfolk Holiday Homes
t (01485) 534267
e shohol@birdsnorfolkholidayhomes.co.uk
w norfolkholidayhomes-birds.co.uk

Shorelarks ★★★★
Self Catering
Birds Norfolk Holiday Homes
t (01485) 534267
e shohol@birdsnorfolkholidayhomes.co.uk
w norfolkholidayhomes-birds.co.uk

Spindrift ★★★★
Self Catering
Birds Norfolk Holiday Homes
t (01485) 534267
e shohol@birdsnorfolkholidayhomes.co.uk
w norfolkholidayhomes-birds.co.uk

Sunny Corner ★★★
Self Catering
Birds Norfolk Holiday Homes
t (01485) 534267
e shohol@birdsnorfolkholidayhomes.co.uk
w norfolkholidayhomes-birds.co.uk

Sunset View ★★★
Self Catering
Birds Norfolk Holiday Homes
t (01485) 534267
e shohol@birdsnorfolkholidayhomes.co.uk
w norfolkholidayhomes-birds.co.uk

Surf ★★ *Self Catering*
Birds Norfolk Holiday Homes
t (01485) 534267
e shohol@birdsnorfolkholidayhomes.co.uk
w norfolkholidayhomes-birds.co.uk

Victoria House ★★★★
Self Catering
Norfolk Country Cottages
t (01603) 871872
e info@norfolkcottages.co.uk
w norfolkcottages.co.uk

Victory Cottage ★★★
Self Catering
Birds Norfolk Holiday Homes
t (01485) 534267
e shohol@birdsnorfolkholidayhomes.co.uk
w norfolkholidayhomes-birds.co.uk

Wash Sunset ★★
Self Catering
Birds Norfolk Holiday Homes
t (01485) 534267
e shohol@birdsnorfolkholidayhomes.co.uk
w norfolkholidayhomes-birds.co.uk

Westacre ★★★ *Self Catering*
Birds Norfolk Holiday Homes
t (01485) 534267
e shohol@birdsnorfolkholidayhomes.co.uk
w norfolkholidayhomes-birds.co.uk

HUNTINGFIELD
Suffolk

Corner Farm Barn ★★★★★
Self Catering
Contact: Ms Jane Morelli
t (01986) 784216
e cornerfarmholiday@btinternet.com
w cornerfarmholidays.co.uk

HUNWORTH
Norfolk

Green Farm Barn ★★★★
Self Catering
Norfolk Country Cottages
t (01603) 871872
e info@norfolkcottages.co.uk
w norfolkcottages.co.uk

Spinks Nest ★★ *Self Catering*
Contact: Mrs Angela Hampshire
t (01263) 713891
w tiscover.co.uk

HURDLOW
Derbyshire

Hurdlow Grange ★★★★
Self Catering
Peak Cottages
t (0114) 262 0777
e enquiries@peakcottages.com
w peakcottages.com

IKEN
Suffolk

Iken Barns, Bay View Barn
★★★★ *Self Catering*
Suffolk Secrets
t (01502) 722717
e holidays@suffolk-secrets.co.uk
w suffolk-secrets.co.uk

Old Stable ★★★★
Self Catering
Contact: Mrs Gunilla Hailes
t (01728) 688263

Orford Cottages ★★★★
Self Catering
Contact: Mrs Sue Cartlidge
t (01728) 687844
w orford-cottages.co.uk

ILAM
Staffordshire

Beechenhill Farm Cottages
★★★★ *Self Catering*
Contact: Mrs Sue Prince
t (01335) 310274
e beechenhill@btinternet.com
w beechenhill.co.uk

Throwley Moor Farm House & Cottages ★★★★
Self Catering
Contact: Mrs Muriel Richardson
t (01538) 308202
e throwleyhall@btinternet.com
w throwleyhallfarm.co.uk

ILMINGTON
Warwickshire

Featherbed Cottage ★★★★
Self Catering
Contact: Mr David Price
t (01608) 682215
e featherbedcottage@hotmail.com

Folly Farm Self Catering
★★★★ *Self Catering*
Contact: Mr Bruce McFarlane
t (01608) 682425
e bruceandpam@follyfarm.co.uk
w cotswold-retreats.co.uk

Woodruff Cottage ★★★★
Self Catering
Contact: Mrs Julia Gajny
t (01608) 682334
e julia@gajny.wanadoo.co.uk
w woodruffcottage.co.uk

INGHAM
Lincolnshire

3 Anyans Row ★★★
Self Catering
Contact: Mr & Mrs T Taylor
t (01427) 788023

INGHAM
Norfolk

Old Vicarage Apartment
★★★ *Self Catering*
Norfolk Country Cottages
t (01603) 871872
e info@norfolkcottages.co.uk
w norfolkcottages.co.uk

Rose Cottage ★★
Self Catering
Norfolk Country Cottages
t (01603) 871872
e info@norfolkcottages.co.uk
w norfolkcottages.co.uk

INGOLDISTHORPE
Norfolk

The Coach House ★★★★
Self Catering
Norfolk Country Cottages
t (01603) 871872
e info@norfolkcottages.co.uk
w norfolkcottages.co.uk

Foxes Croft ★★ *Self Catering*
Contact: Mrs Christine Riches
t (01485) 520216
w christine-riches.com

INGOLDMELLS
Lincolnshire

Skegness Water Leisure Park – Bungalows ★★★★
Self Catering
Contact: Ian Ellis
t (01754) 899400
e enquiries@skegnesswaterleisurepark.co.uk
w skegnesswaterleisurepark.co.uk

Summer Haven Holidays
Approved Caravan Holiday Home
Contact: Mrs Slocombe
t (01754) 873019
e info@summer-haven.co.uk
w summer-haven.co.uk

Summer Haven Holidays
★★★ *Self Catering*
Contact: Kathy Slocombe
t (01754) 873019
e info@summer-haven.co.uk
w summer-haven.co.uk

INGOLDSBY
Lincolnshire

Little Scotland Farm, Ingoldsby ★★★★
Self Catering
Contact: Mrs Angela Jasinski
t (01476) 585494

INGWORTH
Norfolk

Romarose ★★★ *Self Catering*
Norfolk Country Cottages
t (01603) 871872
e info@norfolkcottages.co.uk
w norfolkcottages.co.uk

Skipjack ★★★★
Self Catering
Norfolk Country Cottages
t (01603) 871872
e info@norfolkcottages.co.uk
w norfolkcottages.co.uk

IPSTONES
Staffordshire

Meadow Place ★★★★
Self Catering
Sykes Cottages
t (01244) 345700
e info@sykescottages.co.uk
w sykescottages.co.uk

Old Hall Farm Holiday Cottages ★★★ *Self Catering*
Contact: Mrs Ann Glover
t (01538) 266465
e info@oldhallholidaycottages.co.uk
w oldhallholidaycottages.co.uk

The Stables & The Cart Shed
★★★ *Self Catering*
Contact: Mr & Mrs Michael & Hilary Hall
t (01538) 266259
w cloughhead.co.uk

The Wolery ★★★★
Self Catering
Contact: Mr Bryan Atherton
t (01538) 266421
e bryaton@supanet.com

IRONBRIDGE
Shropshire

Benthall View ★★★
Self Catering
Contact: Mrs Beryl Eccleston
t (01952) 433408

Eley's Of Ironbridge
★★★-★★★★★ *Self Catering*
Contact: Ms Jayne Mountford
t (01952) 432030
w eleys-ironbridge.co.uk

Ironbridge Holiday Cottages
★★★★ *Self Catering*
Contact: Mr Mark Shelton
t 0800 633 5181 & 07977 598740
e info@ironbridgeholidaycottages.co.uk
w ironbridgeholidaycottages.co.uk

Ironbridge Lodge, Ironbridge ★★★
Self Catering
Contact: Mrs Pamela Mundy
t (01952) 257242
e pam@ercallcatering.co.uk

Marnwood House and School House ★★★★★
Self Catering
Contact: Miss Julie Guy
t 07831 398763
e jm@marnwood.fsnet.co.uk
w marnwoodproperty.co.uk

Paradise House Flats ★★
Self Catering
Contact: Mrs Gilbride
t (01952) 433379
e marjorie@gilbride.co.uk
w flats.gilbride.co.uk

Victoria Cottage ★★★
Self Catering
Contact: Mr Colin Thompson
t 07970 417497
e cthompson@bcs.org.uk
w ironbridgegorge.co.uk

IRSTEAD
Norfolk

Angler Cottage ★★★
Self Catering
Norfolk Country Cottages
t (01603) 871872
e info@norfolkcottages.co.uk
w norfolkcottages.co.uk

KEDINGTON
Suffolk

Cottage At Rowans ★★★★
Self Catering
Contact: Ms Cheryl Owen
t (01440) 702408
e cheryl@owen41.supanet.com
w cottagesdirect.com/nfa123

KELLING
Norfolk

Fox Hollies ★★★
Self Catering
Norfolk Country Cottages
t (01603) 871872
e info@norfolkcottages.co.uk
w norfolkcottages.co.uk

Owl Place ★★★★★
Self Catering
Contact: Victoria Hamey
t (01263) 712201
e stay@kelling-estate.co.uk
w kelling-estate.co.uk

Plough Wheel ★★★
Self Catering
Norfolk Country Cottages
t (01603) 871872
e info@norfolkcottages.co.uk
w norfolkcottages.co.uk

KELSALE
Suffolk

East Green Farm Cottages
★★★★ *Self Catering*
Contact: Claire & Robbie Gawthrop
t (01728) 602316
e claire@eastgreen.co.uk
w eastgreencottages.co.uk

KEMPSEY
Worcestershire

The Barn, Beechcroft
★★★★ *Self Catering*
Contact: Mrs Charlotte Underwood
t (01905) 820364
e info@thebarn-beechcroft.co.uk
w thebarn-beechcroft.co.uk

KENILWORTH
Warwickshire

Jackdaw Cottage & Wren's Nest ★★★★ *Self Catering*
Contact: Mrs Lynn Grierson
t (01926) 855616
e mail@kenilworthcottages.co.uk
w kenilworthcottages.co.uk

The Little Barn ★★★
Self Catering
Contact: Mrs Judith Oliver
t (01926) 850692

North Mere ★★★★
Self Catering
Contact: Mrs Tamarind Lucas
t (01926) 863134
e enquiries@northmere.co.uk
w northmere.co.uk

The Old Church House
★★★★ *Self Catering*
Contact: Mr & Mrs Tim & Maureen Bray
t (01926) 859290
e info@theoldchurchhouse.co.uk
w theoldchurchhouse.co.uk

KENLEY
Shropshire

Courtyard Cottages ★★★★
Self Catering
Contact: Mrs Annabel Gill
No 1 & 2 Courtyard Cottages
t (01952) 510841
e afgill@hotmail.co.uk
w stmem.com/courtyardcottages

KENWICK
Lincolnshire

Kenwick Lodge ★★★★
Self Catering
Contact: Kerry Bishop
t (01509) 815210
e enquiries@kenwicklodge.co.uk
w kenwicklodge.co.uk

KERSALL
Nottinghamshire

Rose and Sweet Briar Cottages ★★★ *Self Catering*
Contact: Janet Hind
t (01636) 636274
e enquiries@experiencenottinghamshire.co.uk
w roseandsweetbriar.co.uk

KERSEY
Suffolk

Old Drift House, Kersey
★★★★★ *Self Catering*
Contact: Mrs Jill Black
11 Poynings Close
t (01582) 763533
e ejblk@talk21.com
w olddrifthouse.co.uk

Wheelwrights ★★★★★
Self Catering
Contact: Mr & Mrs Peter & Doreen Gowan
t (01473) 829311
e peter@pjgowan.freeserve.co.uk
w wheelwrightscottage.co.uk

KESSINGLAND
Suffolk

11 Kessingland Cottages
★★ *Self Catering*
Contact: Mrs Carol Keane
t (01707) 330742
w tiscover.co.uk

23 Alandale Drive ★★
Self Catering
Contact: Ms Karen Foster
t (01223) 576874
e ged251@yahoo.co.uk
w tiscover.co.uk

74 The Cliff ★★ *Self Catering*
Contact: Mrs Saunders
t (01508) 538340

Clifton House ★★★★
Self Catering
Suffolk Secrets
t (01502) 722717
e holidays@suffolk-secrets.co.uk
w suffolk-secrets.co.uk

Four Winds Retreat ★★★★
Self Catering
Contact: Mr & Mrs Peter & Jane Garner
t (01502) 740044
e info@four-winds-retreat.co.uk
w four-winds-retreat.co.uk

Kew Cottage ★★★
Self Catering
Contact: Mrs Joan Gill
t (01604) 717301
e b.s.g@btinternet.com

Knights Holiday Homes
★–★★★ *Self Catering*
Contact: Mr Michael Knights
t 0800 269067
w knightsholidays.co.uk

Olympus ★★★★
Self Catering
Suffolk Secrets
t (01502) 722717
e holidays@suffolk-secrets.co.uk
w suffolk-secrets.co.uk

Spindrift ★★★ *Self Catering*
Norfolk Country Cottages
t (01603) 871872
e info@norfolkcottages.co.uk
w norfolkcottages.co.uk

KETTERING
Northamptonshire

The Villiers Suite, Cranford Hall ★★★ *Self Catering*
Contact: Mr & Mrs John Robinson
t (01536) 330248
e cranford@farmline.com
w cranfordhall.co.uk

KETTLEBURGH
Suffolk

Church Farm ★★★★
Self Catering
Contact: Mrs Anne Bater
t (01728) 723532
e jbater@suffolkonline.net
w tiscover.co.uk

KETTLESTONE
Norfolk

Caretakers Cottage ★★★★
Self Catering
Kett Country Cottages
t (01328) 856853
e info@kettcountrycottages.co.uk
w kettcountrycottages.co.uk

KETTON
Rutland

Holmes Farm ★★★
Self Catering
Contact: Mr Mary Andrew
t (01780) 720394

Randolph Cottage ★★★
Self Catering
Contact: Mrs Forster
t (01780) 720802

KILPECK
Herefordshire

The Granary ★★★★
Self Catering
Contact: Hexie & Amanda Millais
t (01981) 570209
e info@dippersmoor.com
w dippersmoor.com

Sizecroft Farm ★★★★
Self Catering
Contact: Ms V. Stockley
t (01432) 277122

KIMBOLTON
Herefordshire

Rowley Farm ★★★
Self Catering
Contact: Sue Pugh
t (01568) 611338
e lpugh@farmersweekly.net
w rowleyholidaypark.co.uk

KINETON
Warwickshire

Long Ground Barn, Kineton
★★★★★ *Self Catering*
Contact: Mrs Carolyn Gasson
t (01926) 641829
e carolyn@heartofthecountryholidays.co.uk
w heartofthecountryholidays.co.uk

Spring Hill ★★★★
Self Catering
Contact: Mr John Mayo
t (01926) 640074

KINGS CAPLE
Herefordshire

Wye Valley Cottages
★★★★ *Self Catering*
Contact: Mrs Milly Slater
t (01432) 840493
e milly@wyevalleycottages.com
w wyevalleycottages.com

KING'S CLIFFE
Northamptonshire

Maltings Cottage, King's Cliffe ★★★★ *Self Catering*
Contact: Mrs Jenny Dixon
t (01780) 470365
e kjhl_dixon@hotmail.com
w kingjohnhuntinglodge.com

KING'S LYNN
Norfolk

10 North Hirne Court ★★★
Self Catering
Contact: Miss Alison Gifford
t (01553) 763983
e alisongifford@btinternet.com

Granary ★★★ *Self Catering*
Contact: Mrs Ann Jones
t (01553) 828700
e rchjn957@aol.com
w tiscover.co.uk

Nar Valley Lodges ★★★★
Self Catering
Contact: Ms Sarah Edwards
t (01638) 721736
w narvalleylodges.co.uk

KINGTON
Herefordshire

Cider Press Cottage ★★★★
Self Catering
Contact: Mrs Lorraine Wright
t (01544) 231462

KIRK IRETON
Derbyshire

Alton Nether Farm ★★★★
Self Catering
Peak Cottages
t (0114) 262 0777
e enquiries@peakcottages.com
w peakcottages.com

Grange Cottages ★★★★
Self Catering
Contact: Mr Malcolm Race
t (01335) 370880
e cottages@w3z.co.uk
w malcolmrace.co.uk

Ivy Cottage ★★★
Self Catering
Peak Cottages
t (0114) 262 0777
e enquiries@peakcottages.com
w peakcottages.com

Millfields Farm
Rating Applied For
Self Catering
t (01335) 370222
w ashbourneselfcatering.com

KIRK LANGLEY
Derbyshire

The Cart Hovel and The Stables ★★★★ *Self Catering*
Contact: Mrs Sue Gibbs
t (01332) 824214

KIRKBY GREEN
Lincolnshire

Watermill Farm Cottages
★★★ *Self Catering*
Contact: William Stuart Ravell
t (01526) 320329
e stuart.ravell@ukonline.co.uk
w watermillfarm.net

KNIGHTCOTE
Warwickshire

Arbor Holiday & Knightcote Farm Cottages ★★★★★
Self Catering
Contact: Craig & Fiona Walker
t (01295) 770637
e fionawalker@farmcottages.com
w farmcottages.com

KNIGHTWICK
Worcestershire

Buzzard's View
Rating Applied For
Self Catering
Contact: Mr & Mrs Paul & Vicky Dodd
t (01905) 840429

KNIVETON
Derbyshire

Billy's Bothy ★★★★★
Self Catering
Contact: Mrs Pat Walker
t (01335) 344795
e enquiries@offcotegrange.com
w offcotegrange.com

Church Farm ★★★★
Self Catering
Contact: Mrs Lesley McConnachie
t (01335) 300682

Standlow Farm ★★★★
Self Catering
Contact: Mrs Michele Wrigley
Bradley Hall
t (01335) 370222
e michelle@pmwproperty.com
w ashbourneselfcatering.com

Willow Bank ★★★★
Self Catering
Contact: Mrs Mary Vaughan
t (01335) 343308
e willowbank@kniveton.net
w kniveton.net

KNOCKIN
Shropshire

The Croft ★★★★
Self Catering
t (01691) 682485
w rolly.co.uk

KNOWBURY
Shropshire

Old Vicarage Coach House
★★★ *Self Catering*
Contact: Mr Adrian Phillips
t (01584) 891749
e adriangphillips@aol.com
w knowburyoldvicarage.co.uk

LAMARSH
Essex

Hill Farm House Self Catering ★★★★
Self Catering
Contact: Mrs Brenda Greenhill
t (01787) 269905
w farmstayeastanglia.co.uk

LAMAS
Norfolk

Millers Lodge ★★★★
Self Catering
Norfolk Country Cottages
t (01603) 871872
e info@norfolkcottages.co.uk
w norfolkcottages.co.uk

LAMBLEY
Nottinghamshire

Dickman's Cottage, Lambley
★★★ *Self Catering & Serviced Apartments*
Contact: Mr William Marshall Smith
t (01943) 462719
e marshallsmithuk@hotmail.com
w dickmanscottage.co.uk

Penrhyn ★★★★
Self Catering
Contact: Jane Smith
t (0115) 931 3802
e jane_millhouse@hotmail.co.uk

LANGHAM
Norfolk

Sunnyside Cottage ★★★★
Self Catering
Contact: Mr & Mrs Trevor & Joan Shephard
t (0116) 287 2739
e info@sunnysidecottagenorfolk.co.uk
w tiscover.co.uk

LANGWORTH
Lincolnshire

The Barn ★★★ *Self Catering*
Contact: Susie Fleetwood
t (01522) 751939
e ifleet@barlings.demon.co.uk
w barlings.demon.co.uk

LAVENHAM
Suffolk

Blaize Cottages ★★★★★
Self Catering
Contact: Mr & Mrs Carol & Jim Keohane
t (01787) 247402
w blaizecottages.com

Granary Cottage ★★★★
Self Catering
Contact: Mrs Wendy Williams
t (01284) 828458

Grove ★★★★ *Self Catering*
Contact: Mr Mark Scott
t (01787) 211115
e mark@grove-cottages.co.uk
w grove-cottages.co.uk

Hour Cottage ★★★★
Self Catering
Contact: Mrs Esther Perkins
t (01277) 651843
w hourcottage.co.uk

Lavenham Cottages
★★★★★ *Self Catering*
Contact: Ms Sheila Lane
t (01284) 830771
e sheila@lavenhamcottages.co.uk
w tiscover.co.uk

Maltings Farm Holiday Cottages ★★★ *Self Catering*
Contact: Mrs Rachel Bell
t (01284) 828843
e tim-bell@fsbdial.co.uk
w tiscover.co.uk

Mortimers Barn Holiday Cottage ★★★★ *Self Catering*
Contact: Mrs Caroline Gove
t (01787) 247786
e thosegoves@aol.com
w mortimersbarn.co.uk

Old Wetherden Hall ★★★
Self Catering
Contact: Mrs Julie Elsden
t (01449) 740574
e julie.elsden@btconnect.com
w oldwetherdenhall.co.uk

Potash Farm Cottage
★★★★ *Self Catering*
t (01284) 828396 & 07812 956402
e emmadib@aol.com
w potashfarmcottage.co.uk

Rector's Retreat ★★★
Self Catering
Contact: Mr Peter Gutteridge
t (01449) 741557
e valandpeter@madasafish.com
w tiscover.co.uk

Victoria Cottage ★★★★
Self Catering
Contact: Mr Nigel & Sheila Margo
t 07931 542644
w victoriacottage-lavenham.co.uk

LAXFIELD
Suffolk

Laxfield Lodges, Laxfield
★★★★ *Self Catering*
Contact: Mrs Angie Thompson
t (01986) 798766
e admin@laxfieldlodges.co.uk
w laxfieldlodges.co.uk

The Loose Box & The Old Stables ★★★ *Self Catering*
Contact: Mr & Mrs John & Jane Reeve
t (01986) 798019
e laxfieldleisure@talk21.com
w villastables.co.uk

LAYER BRETON
Essex

Glebe Cottage
Rating Applied For
Self Catering
Contact: Jamie MacGregor
t (01206) 330522
e info@dpm2007.co.uk

LEA
Derbyshire

The Coach House ★★
Self Catering
Contact: Mr & Mrs Helme
t (01629) 534346
w coachhouselea.co.uk

LEA
Herefordshire

Moorlands ★★★
Self Catering
Contact: Mrs Jean White
t (01989) 750230
w moorlands.info

LEAMINGTON SPA
Warwickshire

8 Lansdowne Circus
★★★★★ *Self Catering*
Contact: Mrs Sheena Harris
t (01926) 773370
e bookings@lansdownecircus.co.uk
w lansdownecircus.co.uk

Barn Owl Cottage ★★★★
Self Catering
Contact: Mrs Beatrice Norman
t (01926) 614647
e bnorman@fossebarn.prestel.co.uk
w barnowlcottage.co.uk

Blackdown Farm Cottages
★★ *Self Catering*
Contact: Mr & Mrs R Solt
t (01926) 422522
e bobby@solt.demon.co.uk

Brunswick, 74a Brunswick Street ★★★★ *Self Catering*
Contact: Ms Mary Curran
t (01926) 420474
e grannycurran@aol.com
w brunswickapartment.co.uk

Furzen Hill Farm ★★★★
Self Catering
Contact: Mrs Christine Whitfield
t (01926) 424791
e christine.whitfield1@btopenworld.com
w furzenhillfarmcottages.co.uk

Wood Farm ★★★★
Self Catering
Contact: Mrs Hazel S. Hiatt
t (01926) 612270

LEATON
Shropshire

Vicarage Cottage ★★★★★
Self Catering
Contact: Mrs Joan Mansell-Jones
t (01939) 290989
e m-j@oldvicleaton.com
w oldvicleaton.com

LEDBURY
Herefordshire

The Bee House and The Hive
★★★★ *Self Catering*
Contact: Mrs Sandra Anderson
t (01531) 640021
e sandra@beehousecottages.co.uk
w beehousecottages.co.uk

Old Kennels Farm
★★★-★★★★ *Self Catering*
Contact: Mrs Jeanette Wilce
t (01531) 635024
e wilceoldkennelsfarm@btinternet.com
w oldkennelsfarm.co.uk

White House Cottages
★★★-★★★★ *Self Catering*
Contact: Mrs Marianne Hills
t (01531) 670349
e bookings@whitehousecottages.co.uk
w whitehousecottages.co.uk

The Woodhouse Farm Cottages ★★★★★
Self Catering
Contact: Mrs Susan Furnival
t (01531) 640030
e sue@thewoodhousefarm.co.uk
w thewoodhousefarm.co.uk

Woodside Lodges ★★★★
Self Catering
Contact: Ken Davies
t (01531) 670269
e info@woodsidelodges.co.uk
w woodsidelodges.co.uk

LEEK
Staffordshire

Blackshaw Grange Holiday Cottages ★★★★
Self Catering
Contact: Mrs Carolyn Williams
t (01538) 300165
e kevwilliams@btinternet.com
w btinternet.com/~blackshawgrange

Broomyshaw Country Cottages ★★-★★★
Self Catering
Contact: Graham & Joyce Saul
t (01538) 308298
e grahambroomyshaw@tiscali.co.uk
w broomyshaw.co.uk

Candy Cottage ★★★
Self Catering
Contact: Mrs Sylvia Plant
t (01538) 266243
e splantuppercadlow@hotmail.com
w cottageguide.co.uk/candycottage/

The Cottage
Rating Applied For
Self Catering
Contact: Kate Sherratt
t (01538) 385163
e reception@healthyretreat.co.uk
w healthyreatreat.co.uk

Foxtwood Cottages, Foxt
★★★★ *Self Catering*
Contact: Mr & Mrs Clive & Alison Worrall
t (01538) 266160
e info@foxtwood.co.uk
w foxtwood.co.uk

Lark's Rise ★★★
Self Catering
Contact: Mrs Laura Melland
t (01538) 304350
e newhousefarm@btinternet.com
w staffordshiremoorlandsfarmholidays.co.uk

Rosewood Cottage & Rosewood Flat ★★★
Self Catering
Contact: Mr & Mrs Edith & Alwyn Mycock
t (01538) 308213
w rosewoodcottage.co.uk

Wren Cottage ★★★★
Self Catering
Contact: Mrs Elizabeth Lowe
t (01260) 226341
e fairboroughs@talk21.com
w fairboroughs.co.uk

LEICESTER
Leicestershire

University of Leicester
Rating Applied For
Self Catering
t (0116) 271 9933
e conferences@le.ac.uk
w le.ac.uk/conference

LEINTWARDINE
Herefordshire

Dower Cottage ★★★★
Self Catering
Contact: Ms Anne & Susan Douthwaite
t (01547) 540446
e info@dower-cottage.co.uk

Oaklands Farm Cottages
★★★ *Self Catering*
Contact: Mrs Sally Ann Swift
t (01547) 540635

LEISTON
Suffolk

Studio Cottage ★★★
Self Catering
Contact: Mrs Janet Lister
t (01728) 833034

LEOMINSTER
Herefordshire

Ashton Court Farm ★★★
Self Catering
Contact: Cherry Griffiths
t (01584) 711729
e griffithsbrooches@btinternet.com

The Buzzards ★★★★
Self Catering
Contact: Ms Elaine Povey
t (01568) 708941
e holiday@thebuzzards.co.uk
w thebuzzards.co.uk

Eaton Farm Cottage ★★★
Self Catering
Contact: Mrs Audrey Pritchard
t (01568) 612095
w cottageguide.co.uk/eatonfarmcottage

LESSINGHAM
Norfolk

Grange Farm ★★★★
Self Catering
Contact: Mrs Glenda Meale
t (01359) 241143
w farmstayuk.co.uk

LEVERTON
Lincolnshire

Crewyard Cottages ★★★★
Self Catering
Contact: Colin Ash
t (01205) 871389
e gina@gina31.wanadoo.co.uk
w crewyardholidaycottages-boston.co.uk

LEYSTERS
Herefordshire

Mill House Flat ★★★
Self Catering
Contact: Mrs Elizabeth Thomas
t (01568) 750232
e thomas@woontoncourtfarm.co.uk

LICHFIELD
Staffordshire

70 Swan Mews ★★★★
Self Catering
Contact: Mrs Lucia Ratcliffe
t (01283) 791280
e stephen.ratcl@btinternet.com

Roman Way Holiday Let
★★★ *Self Catering*
Contact: Billy & Jean King
t (01543) 262759
e billyjking@aol.com

LINCOLN
Lincolnshire

5 Belle Vue Terrace ★★★
Self Catering
Contact: Christine Knight
t (01522) 520970
e john@knight9935.freeserve.co.uk

7 Neustadt Court ★★★★
Self Catering
Contact: Michele Hanby
t (01522) 539740
e m.hanby@btopenworld.com
w lincoln-accommodation.co.uk

Ashleigh ★★★ *Self Catering*
Contact: Janet Ashton
t (01903) 879763
e cwamarketing@dsl.pipex.com
w lincolnselfcatering.co.uk

Baker House
Rating Applied For
Self Catering
Contact: Tony Louth
Lincoln Property Services Ltd
t (01673) 866466
e tonylouth@aol.com
w lincolnpropertyservices.com

Bight House ★★★★
Self Catering
Contact: Mavis Sharpe
t (01522) 534477

The Cathedral View Apartment ★★★
Self Catering
Contact: Elizabeth Slingsby
t 07752 370641
e auctions@thosmawer.com
w greestoneplace.co.uk

Cliff Farm Cottage ★★★★
Self Catering
Contact: Rae Marris
t (01522) 730475
e rae.marris@farming.co.uk
w cliff-farm-cottage.co.uk

The Crown Windmill
★★★★★ *Self Catering*
Contact: Jeremy Griffin
t 07966 461887
e windymillers@btinternet.com

Danes Cottage ★★★★
Self Catering
Contact: George Gilbert
t (01522) 500359
e info@lincolncottage.co.uk
w lincolncottage.co.uk

Drury Lodge ★★★★★
Self Catering
Contact: Jon Thorne
t (01673) 866391
e jon.thorne@thorne.tv
w lincolnbreaks.com

Lincoln Town Houses
Rating Applied For
Self Catering
Contact: Alison Richards
t (01522) 530274
e lincolntownhouses@btinternet.com
w lincolntownhouses.co.uk

Martingale Cottage, Nettleham ★★★
Self Catering
Contact: P Pate
t (01522) 751795
e patsy.pate@ntlworld.com

Old Vicarage Cottages
★★★★ *Self Catering*
Contact: Mrs Susan Downs
t (01522) 750819
e susan@oldvic.net
w oldvic.net

Saint Clements ★★★
Self Catering
Contact: Mrs Gill Marshall
t (01522) 538087
e info@stayatstclements.co.uk
w stayatstclements.co.uk

The Stable ★★★★
Self Catering
t (01522) 730561
e jerry@lincolncottages.co.uk
w lincolncottages.co.uk

Willsons Cottage
Rating Applied For
Self Catering
Contact: Van Kyson
w willsonscottage.co.uk

LINCOMB
Worcestershire

Old Tom's ★★★★
Self Catering
Contact: Mr Andrew Symonds
t (01299) 250241
e lincomb.farms@btconnect.com
w experienceworcestershire.co.uk

LITCHAM
Norfolk

4 Canaan Row ★★★
Self Catering
Norfolk Country Cottages
t (01603) 871872
e info@norfolkcottages.co.uk
w norfolkcottages.co.uk

LITTLE BENTLEY
Essex

Spring Hall Cottage ★★★★
Self Catering
Contact: Mrs Tricia Maestrani
Spring Hall
t (01206) 251619 & 07779 264679
e triciamaestrani@hotmail.co.uk

LITTLE CARLTON
Lincolnshire

Garth Cottage
Rating Applied For
Self Catering
Contact: Mr & Mrs John & Margaret Nielson
t (01507) 327952
e nielsen@ycdsl.com

LITTLE DEWCHURCH
Herefordshire

The Granary ★★★★
Self Catering
Contact: Mrs Karen Tibbetts
t (01432) 840826

LITTLE FRANSHAM
Norfolk

Lyons Green and Little Flint
★★★★-★★★★★
Self Catering
Contact: Mrs Jenny Mallon
t (01362) 687649
w farmstayanglia.co.uk

LITTLE HAYFIELD
Derbyshire

Brook Cottage ★★★★
Self Catering
Contact: Mrs Diane Melland
t (01663) 746312
e brook_cottage@hotmail.com

Honeysuckle Cottage ★★★
Self Catering
Peak Cottages
t (0114) 262 0777
e enquiries@peakcottages.com
w peakcottages.com

LITTLE HENHAM
Essex

Stable Cottage ★★★
Self Catering
Contact: Mrs Kate Muskett
t (01279) 850228

LITTLE HEREFORD
Herefordshire

Cliffs Mews ★★★
Self Catering
Contact: B.R. Franklin
t (01584) 810488

LITTLE HUCKLOW
Derbyshire

Glider View Cottage ★★★★
Self Catering
Contact: Mrs Christine McMeeken
t 0870 336 8100
w english-country-cottages.co.uk

LITTLE LONGSTONE
Derbyshire

Barn End ★★★ *Self Catering*
Peak Cottages
t (0114) 262 0777
e enquiries@peakcottages.com
w peakcottages.com

Longstone Holiday Cottage
★★★-★★★★ *Self Catering*
Contact: Mrs Anne Davey
t (01629) 640542
e annie@littlelongstone.freeserve.co.uk
w longstoneholidaycottage.co.uk

Orrs Barn ★★★★
Self Catering
Peak Cottages
t (0114) 262 0777
e enquiries@peakcottages.com
w peakcottages.com

LITTLE MARCLE
Herefordshire

Upper House Cottage, Little Marcle ★★★★ *Self Catering*
Contact: Sarah Glanville
t (01531) 670125
e jimglanville@btinternet.com
w holidaycottageherefordshire.com

LITTLE SNORING
Norfolk

Jex Farm Barns ★★★★
Self Catering
Contact: Mr Stephen Harvey
t (01328) 878257 & 07979 495760
e farmerstephen@jexfarm.wanadoo.co.uk
w jexfarm.co.uk

Sunset Cottage ★★★★
Self Catering
Contact: Mr & Mrs Chris & Sue Fuller
t (01328) 878836
w tiscover.co.uk

White House Cottage And Barn ★★★ *Self Catering*
Contact: Mrs Celia Lee
t (01328) 878789
w snoringwhitehouse.co.uk/barnlodge_jn.htm

LITTLE STRETTON
Shropshire

Jessamine Cottage ★★★
Self Catering
Contact: Miss Claire Alford
t (01743) 873608
e info@strettoncottages.co.uk
w strettoncottages.co.uk

LITTLE WALDEN
Essex

Orchard View Numbers 1-4
★★★ *Self Catering*
Contact: Mrs Maureen Chapman-Barker
Orchard View Numbers 1 – 4
t (01799) 527315
e sales@farmerkit.co.uk
w farmerkit.co.uk

LITTLE WALSINGHAM
Norfolk

The Old Coach House
★★★★ *Self Catering*
Contact: Mr & Mrs Gwyn & Charlotte Pollard
c/o Baker and Mckenzie LLP
t (020) 7702 1814
e theoldcoach.house@btinternet.com
w theoldcoach.house.btinternet.co.uk

LITTLEBURY GREEN
Essex

Deer Cottage, 2 Meadow Cottages ★★★ *Self Catering*
Contact: Mrs Jane Williams
t (020) 8675 1193

LITTLEPORT
Cambridgeshire

Caves Farm Barns
★★★-★★★★ *Self Catering*
Contact: Stephen & Sue Kerridge
t (01353) 861423
w cavesfarmbarns.co.uk

LITTON
Derbyshire

Candlelight Cottage
★★★★★ *Self Catering*
Contact: Simon & Jill Wills
t (01433) 631528
e candlelightcottage@sjwills.plus.com
w candlelightcottage.co.uk

Cross View ★★★
Self Catering
Contact: Mrs Caroline Rowan-Olive
t (01727) 844169
e enquiries@cross-view.co.uk
w cross-view.co.uk

Littonfields Barn ★★★★
Self Catering
Contact: Bridget Weston
t (01298) 871738
e info@littonbarn.co.uk
w littonbarn.co.uk

LITTON MILL
Derbyshire

One Litton Mill ★★★★
Self Catering
Peak Cottages
t (0114) 262 0777
e enquiries@peakcottages.com
w peakcottages.com

Riverside Apartment
★★★★ *Self Catering*
Peak Cottages
t (0114) 262 0777
e enquiries@peakcottages.com
w peakcottages.com

Wye Apartment ★★★
Self Catering
Peak Cottages
t (0114) 262 0777
e enquiries@peakcottages.com
w peakcottages.com

LLANGARRON
Herefordshire

Little Trereece Holiday Cottages ★★★ *Self Catering*
Contact: Mark Cinderey
t (01989) 770145
e trereece@nasuwt.net
w trereececottages.co.uk

Littlefields – Gaerfields
★★★★ *Self Catering*
Contact: Mrs Jones
t (01989) 770281
e upperfieldsfarm1@tiscali.co.uk
w upperfieldsfarm.co.uk

Upper Trereece ★★★★
Self Catering
Contact: Anne Pearson
t (01604) 696889
e jgpearson@btinternet.com
w uppertrereece.co.uk

LLAWNT
Shropshire

Olde Cross Foxes ★★★★
Self Catering
Contact: Mr Trevor Upshall
t (01691) 657933
e allenbydouglas@tiscali.co.uk

LONG BUCKBY
Northamptonshire

Meadowview Cottages
★★★★ *Self Catering*
Contact: Judith Jelley
t (01327) 842205
e meadowview.cottages@farming.co.uk
w meadowviewcottages.co.uk

LONG MARSTON
Warwickshire

The Gables ★★★★
Self Catering
Contact: Mr Nigel Embery
t (024) 7669 6909

LONG MELFORD
Suffolk

4 Church Walk ★★★
Self Catering
Contact: Mr Mark Thomas
t (020) 7267 3653

Hope Cottage ★★★★
Self Catering
Contact: Ms S Jamil
Hill Farm Cottage
t (01787) 282338 & 07970 808701
e sns.jam@tesco.net
w hope-cottage-suffolk.co.uk

LONG STRATTON
Norfolk

Parsons Lodge
Rating Applied For
Self Catering
Norfolk Country Cottages
t (01603) 871872
e info@norfolkcottages.co.uk
w norfolkcottages.co.uk

LONG SUTTON
Lincolnshire

The Barn ★★★ *Self Catering*
Contact: Gary Kennedy
t (01406) 362284
e oldbakery@netbreeze.co.uk

Fen Hide
Rating Applied For
Self Catering
Contact: Ruth Ince & Sally Putterill
t (01485) 544022

LONGNOR
Staffordshire

Merril Grove Cottages
★★★★ *Self Catering*
Peak Cottages
t (0114) 262 0777
e enquiries@peakcottages.com
w peakcottages.com

Over Boothlow ★★★
Self Catering
Contact: Margaret Atkinson
t (01283) 585520
e matkinson@cbiz.freeserve.co.uk

LONGTOWN
Herefordshire

Bramley Lodge ★★★★
Self Catering
Contact: Ms Angela Lloyd
t (01981) 250250
e lloydnewbarns@tiscali.co.uk
w golden-valley.co.uk/newbarns

Court Llaca Barn
Rating Applied For
Self Catering
Contact: Mrs P M H David
t (01873) 860511
e court_llaca@btinternet.com

LOUGHBOROUGH
Leicestershire

Coach House at Quorn Lodge ★★★★ *Self Catering*
Contact: Mr Nigel Swain
t (01509) 214466
e enquiries@quorn-lodge.co.uk
w quorn-lodge.co.uk

LOUTH
Lincolnshire

All Seasons Holidays
★★★★-★★★★★
Self Catering
Contact: Adrian Budd
t (01507) 604470
e info@allseasonsuk.com
w allseasonsuk.com

Bessie's Cottage ★★★
Self Catering
Contact: Alison Boardman
t (01507) 610296
e alisonboardman2002@yahoo.co.uk
w bessiesholidaycottage.co.uk

Brackenborough Hall Coach House Holidays, Brackenborough
★★★★-★★★★★
Self Catering
Contact: Mr & Mrs Paul and Flora Bennett
t (01507) 603193 & 07974 687779
e paulandflora@brackenboroughhall.com
w brackenboroughhall.com

Canal Farm Cottages
★★★★ *Self Catering*
Contact: Mary-Anne Drinkel
t (01472) 388825
e r-ma@canalfarmcottages.co.uk
w canalfarmcottages.co.uk

The Carpenter's Lodge
★★★★ *Self Catering*
Contact: Coral Westall
t (01507) 466677
e carpenterslodge@tiscali.co.uk
w thecarpenterslodge.co.uk

Louth Holiday Home ★★★
Self Catering
Contact: Julia Mullett
t (01507) 354464
e info@louth-holidayhome.co.uk
w louth-holidayhome.co.uk

Mill Lodge ★★★
Self Catering
Contact: Mrs P.M Cade
Benniworth House Farm
t (01507) 343265

Number Nine
Rating Applied For
Self Catering
Contact: Mrs Jill Makinson-Sanders
t (01507) 600743
e numbernine@uwclub.net
w visitthewolds.uwclub.net

Railway Cottages ★★★
Self Catering
Contact: Debbie Wagstaff
t (01507) 606772
e mobile@smokebox.orangehome.co.uk
w railwaycottages.info

Station Masters House, Ludborough ★★★
Self Catering
Contact: Graham Helm
t (01507) 363470 & 07957 366325
e info@raileisure.com
w raileisure.com

Yarburgh Grove Farm ★★★
Self Catering
Contact: Alison Welsh
t (01507) 363370
e alisonjwelsh@yahoo.co.uk
w yarburghgrovefarm.co.uk

LOWER GRESHAM
Norfolk

The Cottage ★★★★
Self Catering
Contact: Mrs Karen Battrick
t (01263) 577725
e pjkbatt@tiscali.co.uk
w tiscover.co.uk

The Roost ★★★★
Self Catering
Norfolk Country Cottages
t (01603) 871872
e info@norfolkcottages.co.uk
w norfolkcottages.co.uk

LOWESTOFT
Suffolk

The Boathouse ★★★★
Self Catering
Contact: Ms Sue Roberts
t (01502) 572982
e sean@seanrobertsassociates.co.uk

Broadland Crescent ★★★★
Self Catering
Contact: Mrs Gillian Walker
t (01502) 573033
w broadlandvillage.co.uk

Glenwood ★★★★
Self Catering
Contact: Mrs Pauline Keenoy
t (01502) 585560

Lyka Sands ★★★★
Self Catering
Contact: Ms Lynne Luettschwager
t (01502) 530631
e lynne@lykas.co.uk
w tiscover.co.uk

Marine House ★ *Self Catering*
Contact: Mr & Mrs David & Teresa Conway
t (01702) 545495 & 07767 363445
e davidfconway@hotmail.co.uk
w 10marineparade.co.uk

Pippin Cottage ★★★★
Self Catering
Contact: Mr Ian Crocker
t (01502) 565665
e pippin.somerton@btinternet.com
w pippin-cottage.co.uk

Seabreeze ★★★★
Self Catering
Contact: Mrs Diane Cohen
t (01502) 582254
w tiscover.co.uk

Shaftsbury House ★★★★
Self Catering
Contact: Mrs Carol Wigg
t (01502) 568580
w tiscover.co.uk

Suffolk Seaside and Broadland ★★★
Self Catering
Contact: Mrs Collecott
t (01502) 564396
e petecollecott@hotmail.com

LUDHAM Norfolk

How Hill Windmill ★★★
Self Catering
Contact: Mrs Elizabeth Ellis-Paul
The Mill House
t (01692) 678575
w norfolkholidaywindmill.co.uk

Ludham Hall Cottage
★★★★ *Self Catering*
Contact: Mrs Alison Ritchie
t (01692) 678232
w ludhamhall.co.uk

St Benet's ★★★★
Self Catering
Norfolk Country Cottages
t (01603) 871872
e info@norfolkcottages.co.uk
w norfolkcottages.co.uk

The Tardis
Rating Applied For
Self Catering
Norfolk Country Cottages
t (01603) 871872
e info@norfolkcottages.co.uk
w norfolkcottages.co.uk

Woodbine Cottage ★★★
Self Catering
Norfolk Country Cottages
t (01603) 871872
e info@norfolkcottages.co.uk
w norfolkcottages.co.uk

LUDLOW Shropshire

Angel Barn ★★★★
Self Catering
Contact: Ms Jennifer Roberts
t (01584) 890381
e angelgardens@sy83hz.fsnet.co.uk
w stmem.com/angelbarn

Ashford Farm Cottages
★★★★ *Self Catering*
Contact: Mr & Mrs Norman & Lynda Tudge
t (01584) 831243
e cottages@ashfordfarms.co.uk
w ashfordfarms.co.uk

The Avenue Flat ★★★★
Self Catering
Contact: Mr Ron Meredith
t (01584) 831616
e ronmeredithavenue@talk21.com
w stmem.com/avenueflat

The Bakery Apartment
★★★ *Self Catering*
Contact: Ms Deborah Cook
t (01584) 872815
e pricesthebakers@btinternet.com
w pricesthebakers.co.uk

The Bindery Flat ★★★★
Self Catering
Contact: Mr Trevor Lloyd
t (01584) 876565
e info@trevorlloyd.co.uk
w trevorlloyd.co.uk/thebinderyflat

Cariad Cottage ★★★★
Self Catering
Contact: Mrs Margaret Leake
t (01584) 873418
e maragret@ludlow-cottage-lets.co.uk
w ludlow-cottage-lets.co.uk

Castle Bookshop Flat ★★★
Self Catering
t (01584) 872562
w virtualshropshire.com

Church Bank, Burrington
★★ *Self Catering*
Contact: Mrs Rosemary Laurie
t (01568) 770426
e alan@alaurie5.wanadoo.co.uk
w stmem.com/church-bank

Counties View ★★★★
Self Catering
Contact: Mrs Marguerite Maclean
t (01384) 817333
e margueritemusic@hotmail.com
w ludlowholiday.com

Criterion Cottage ★★★
Self Catering
Contact: Mrs Christine Hodgson
t (01584) 890344
w stmem.com/criterion-cottage/

Elm Lodge Self Catering
★★★★ *Self Catering*
Contact: Mrs Barbara Weaver
t (01584) 872308
e info@elm-lodge.org.uk
w elm-lodge.org.uk

Emily Place ★★★
Self Catering
Contact: Ms Melanie Chetwood
t (01298) 73807
e mail@emilyplace.co.uk
w emilyplace.co.uk

Flat 12, Castle Square ★★★
Self Catering
Contact: Mrs Marie Knowles
t (01922) 400136
e mariejknowles@btinternet.com

Flat 3 ★★★★ *Self Catering*
Contact: Mrs Wendy Petrie
t (01584) 875301
e wendypetrie@hotmail.co.uk

Garden Cottage ★★★★
Self Catering
Hideaways
t (01747) 828170
e enq@hideaways.co.uk
w hideaways.co.uk

Glebe Farm Cottage ★★★★
Self Catering
Contact: Mr & Mrs John & Lesley Thirlwell
t (01584) 823349
e cottage@glebefarm.info
w glebefarm.info

Goosefoot Barn Cottages
★★★★ *Self Catering*
Contact: Mrs Sally Loft
t (01584) 861326
e sally@goosefoot.freeserve.co.uk
w goosefootbarn.co.uk

Hazel Cottage ★★★
Self Catering
t (01584) 856342
w stmem.com/hazelcottage

Ludford View ★★★★
Self Catering
Contact: Mrs Laura Rutty
t (01584) 873249
e ludlowlet@aol.com
w ludlowlife.co.uk

Ludlow Castle Lodgings
★★★★-★★★★★
Self Catering
Contact: Helen Duce
t (01584) 874465
e hduce@ludlowcastle.com
w ludlowcastle.com

Mews Cottage ★★★
Self Catering
Contact: Mr & Mrs Lynne & Andrew Bates
t (01584) 831730
e oldchurchcottage@gmail.com
w mewscottage.com

The Mews Flat ★★★★
Self Catering
Contact: Mrs Linda Taylor
t (01584) 873609
e mrs.miggs@virgin.net
w mewsflat.co.uk

Mocktree Barns Holiday Cottages ★★★ *Self Catering*
Contact: Clive & Cynthia Prior
t (01547) 540441
e mocktreebarns@care4free.net
w mocktreeholidays.co.uk

No 1 Mortimer Court
★★★★ *Self Catering*
Contact: Mrs Carolyn Chesshire
t (01547) 540532
e bookings@ludlowholidaylets.co.uk
w ludlowholidaylets.co.uk

Old Harpfields Hop-Kiln
★★★★ *Self Catering*
Contact: Margaret & John Anderson
t (01584) 810099
e john@andhow.fsnet.co.uk
w harpfields-hopkiln.co.uk

Posthorn Cottage ★★
Self Catering
Contact: Ms Helen Davis
t (0115) 922 2383
w posthorncottage.co.uk

Ravenscourt Manor ★★★★
Self Catering
Contact: Mrs Elizabeth Purnell
t (01584) 711905
e elizabeth@ravenscourtmanor.plus.com
w smoothhound.co.uk/hotels/ravenscourt.html

Riverview Cottage ★★★★
Self Catering
t (01584) 876009
w riverview-ludlow.co.uk

Sutton Court Farm Cottages
★★★-★★★★ *Self Catering*
Contact: Mrs Jane Cronin
Sutton Court Farm
t (01584) 861305
e enquiries@suttoncourtfarm.co.uk
w suttoncourtfarm.co.uk

Toad Hall ★★★ *Self Catering*
Contact: Ms Jean Taylor
Lindidfarne
t (01584) 874161
w stayludlow.co.uk

Wandering William ★★★★
Self Catering
Contact: Mr Richard Maddicott
t (01584) 877899
e richard@maddicott.com

Whitton Farm Holiday Cottages ★★★★
Self Catering
t (01584) 890234
w whittonfarmholidaycottages.com

LUSTON Herefordshire

Meadow Lea ★★★
Self Catering
Contact: Mrs Janet Ruell
t (01568) 780262

 Look out for establishments participating in the Walkers, Cyclists, Families and Welcome Pets! schemes

LYDBURY NORTH
Shropshire

Walcot Hall Holiday apartments ★★-★★★★
Self Catering
Contact: Miss Maria Higgs
t (01588) 680570
e maria@walcotthall.com
w walcothall.com

LYNG
Norfolk

Lakeside
Rating Applied For
Self Catering
Contact: Kristina Middleton
t (01603) 879468
e kristinamiddleton@walcis.com

Stone House Farm, Lyng
★★★★ *Self Catering*
Contact: Mrs Suzan Jarvis
t (01603) 870812

LYONSHALL
Herefordshire

White Heron Properties
★★★★-★★★★★
Self Catering
Contact: Melissa Critchley
t (01544) 340383 & (01544) 340241
e info@whiteheronproperties.com
w whiteheronproperties.com

MABLETHORPE
Lincolnshire

Dunes Cottage ★★★
Self Catering
Contact: Sheila Morrison
t (01507) 338342
e sheila.a.morrison@btopenworld.co.uk
w duneshollidaycottage.co.uk

Garden Lodge ★★★
Self Catering
Contact: Barbara Lister
t (01507) 338249
e charlie.lister@btopenworld.com

Grange Cottages ★★★★
Self Catering
Contact: Ann Graves
t (01507) 450267
w grange-cottages.co.uk

MADLEY
Herefordshire

Canon Bridge House ★★★★
Self Catering
Contact: Mrs Alison Anscomb
t (01981) 251104
e timothy.anscomb4@virgin.net
w cottageguide.co.uk/canonbridge

MAER
Staffordshire

Maer Estate Holiday Cottages ★★★★
Self Catering
t (01782) 680532
e mail@maerestateholidaycottages.co.uk
w maerstateholidaycottages.co.uk

MAIDENWELL
Lincolnshire

Old School House ★★★★
Self Catering
Contact: Mary Hales
t (01507) 462350
w theoldschoolhouse.tripod.com

MALDON
Essex

Sunningdale ★★★
Self Catering
Contact: Mr & Mrs Roger & Christine Beckett
t (01621) 858235
e roger.beckett@btinternet.com
w sunningdalemaldon.co.uk

MALVERN
Worcestershire

April Cottage ★★★
Self Catering
Contact: Mrs Patricia Longmire
t (01684) 566689
e pml@peachfield.freeserve.co.uk

Beesoni Lodge ★★★★
Self Catering
Contact: Mrs Laura Smith
t (01684) 830015
e beesonimanor@btconnect.com
w beesonilodge.co.uk

Blue Cedars Annexe ★★★
Self Catering
Contact: Mrs Patricia Longmire
t (01684) 566689
e pml@peachfield.freeserve.co.uk

Clouds End ★★★
Self Catering
Contact: Ms Suzie Neill
t (01684) 578834
e suzie@cloudsend.co.uk
w cloudsend.co.uk

Como House ★★★★
Self Catering
Contact: Mr Kevin Austin
t (01684) 561486
e kevin@comohouse.co.uk
w comohouse.co.uk

The Dell House ★★★★
Self Catering
Contact: Mr Ian Burrage
t (01684) 564448
e ian@dellhouse.co.uk
w dellhouse.co.uk

Farmhouse Cottage ★★★★
Self Catering
Contact: Mrs Sue Stringer
t (01684) 566750
e cowleighpark@ukonline.co.uk
w cowleighparkfarm.co.uk

Greenbank Garden Flat
★★★ *Self Catering*
Contact: Mrs Sue Matthews
t (01684) 567328
e matthews.greenbank@virgin.net

Hidelow House Cottages
★★★★-★★★★★
Self Catering
Contact: Mrs Pauline Diplock
t (01886) 884547
e hwv@hidelow.co.uk
w hidelow.co.uk

Hillside House ★★★★
Self Catering
Contact: Ms Alison Darling
t (01684) 541736
e enquiries@hillsidehouse.uk.com
w hillsidehouse.uk.com

Holly Lodge, Earl's Croome
★★★★ *Self Catering*
Contact: Mr David Goodwin
t (01684) 592877
e sandra@hollylodge.biz
w hollylodge.biz

Marlbrook Farm ★★★
Self Catering
Contact: Mrs Liz Coles
t (01684) 310369
e liz.coles@btopenworld.com

Maynard Lodge ★★★★★
Self Catering
Contact: Mr & Mrs Michael & Elaine Roberts
t (01684) 564568
e info@maynardlodge.co.uk
w maynardlodge.co.uk

Netherley Hall Cottages
★★★★★ *Self Catering*
Contact: Vivien Vos
t (01886) 880262
e enquiries@netherleyhallcottages.co.uk
w netherleyhallcottages.co.uk

The Old Bakery ★★★
Self Catering
Contact: Mrs Judith Aldridge
t (01684) 566044
e enquiry@oldbakerymalvern.co.uk
w oldbakerymalvern.co.uk

Park View Serviced Apartment
Rating Applied For
Self Catering
t (01531) 631592
e liz@hortictraining.demon.co.uk

The Studio ★★★
Self Catering
Contact: Mrs Gwyn Sloan
t (01684) 561074
e sloaniain@hotmail.com

Wayfarers Cottage ★★★
Self Catering
Contact: Mr & Mrs John & Caroline Roslington Wayfarers
t (01684) 575758
e info@wayfarerscottage.co.uk
w wayfarerscottage.co.uk

Westhill Cottage ★★★★
Self Catering
Contact: Mrs Mary Stephens
t (01684) 566155
e mary_stephens5@hotmail.com
w westhillcottagemalvern.co.uk

Whitewells Farm Cottages
★★★★ *Self Catering*
Contact: Kate & Denis Kavanagh
t (01886) 880607
e info@whitewellsfarm.co.uk
w whitewellsfarm.co.uk

MANNINGTREE
Essex

Elmdale Garden Studio
★★★★ *Self Catering*
Contact: Lynette Edmunds
t (01206) 390046

Robins at Marsh Barn
★★★★ *Self Catering*
Contact: Mrs Margaret Lulham
t (01206) 397299
w robinsatmarshbarn.co.uk

MANSFIELD
Nottinghamshire

Blue Barn Cottage ★★★
Self Catering
Contact: June Ibbotson
t (01623) 742248
e bluebarnfarm@supanet.com

Kent Cottage & Benscott
★★★★ *Self Catering*
Grace Darling Holidays
t (01665) 721332
e carolynalgar150@msn.com

Watson Avenue ★★★★
Self Catering
Contact: Dionne Miller
t (01623) 721155
e lettings@davidblount.co.uk
w nottshouse.co.uk

MAPPLETON
Derbyshire

Hawthorn Cottage - Ashbourne ★★★★
Self Catering
Contact: Mrs J Lawrence Hawthorn Cottage
t (01925) 752220
e info@caldecotthomes.co.uk

MARDEN
Herefordshire

Litmarsh Farm ★★★★
Self Catering
Contact: Paul Trees
t (01568) 797374
e paultrees@talktalk.net

MARKET DRAYTON
Shropshire

Old Smithy Holiday Cottages ★★★★ *Self Catering & Serviced Apartments*
Contact: Mrs Carmel Simpson
t (01630) 661661
e oldsmithy@fsmail.net
w stmem.com/oldsmithyholidaycottages

MARKET HARBOROUGH
Leicestershire

Short Lodge Cottages ★★★
Self Catering
Contact: Jane Durham
t (01858) 525323

MARKET RASEN
Lincolnshire

Meadow Farm House
★★★★ *Self Catering*
Contact: Nicholas Grimshaw
t (01673) 885909
e nickgrimshaw@btconnect.com
w meadowfarmhouse.co.uk

Papermill Cottages ★★★★
Self Catering
Contact: Joyce Rhodes
t (01673) 838010
e peter.rhodes1@btinternet.com
w papermillcottages.co.uk

Pelham Arms Farm ★★★★
Self Catering
Contact: Mrs Margaret Henderson
t (01673) 828261
e pelhamarmsfarm@btinternet.com

The Stables ★★★★
Self Catering
Contact: Mr Colin Reed
t (01673) 858881
e mxrwj@ic24.net

MARSHCHAPEL
Lincolnshire

Dove Cottage ★★★★
Self Catering
Contact: June Houghton
t (01472) 388520
e june.houghton@tiscali.co.uk
w dovecottage-lincs.co.uk

MARSWORTH
Hertfordshire

Appletrees ★★★
Self Catering
t 0870 534 2342
w hoseasons.co.uk

Field House ★★★★
Self Catering
Hideaways
t (01747) 828170
e enq@hideaways.co.uk
w hideaways.co.uk

MARTIN
Lincolnshire

The Manor House Stables
★★★★ *Self Catering*
Contact: Sherry Forbes
t (01526) 378717
e sherryforbes@hotmail.com
w manorhousestables.co.uk

MATLOCK
Derbyshire

The Birds Nest & Mole End
★★★★★ *Self Catering*
Contact: Mrs Susan Shah
t (01629) 584549
e birdsnest@peakdistrictholidays.co.uk
w peakdistrictholidays.co.uk

Buttons Barn ★★★★★
Self Catering
Hideaways
t (01747) 828170
e enq@hideaways.co.uk
w hideaways.co.uk

Carpenters Cottage ★★★★
Self Catering
Contact: Bob & Iris Wilmot
t (0115) 923 3455 & 07967 120713
e bob.wilmot@merlinpoint.co.uk
w carpenters-cottage.com

Carsington Cottages Self Catering ★★★ *Self Catering*
Contact: Mr & Mrs Doug & Val Riach
t (01629) 540513
e enquiries@carsingtoncottages.co.uk
w carsingtoncottages.co.uk

Cuckoostone Cottage
Rating Applied For
Self Catering
Contact: Nancy Cobb
t (01629) 580036
e nancy.cobb@btinternet.com

Darwin Forest Country Park
★★★-★★★★ *Self Catering*
t (01629) 732428
e darwin@pinelodgeholidays.co.uk
w pinelodgeholidays.co.uk/darwin_forest.ihtml

Darwin Lake ★★★★
Self Catering
Contact: Yvonne Walker
t (01629) 735859
e enquiries@darwinlake.co.uk
w darwinlake.co.uk

Derwent House ★★★★
Self Catering
Contact: Mr Damien Fitzgerald
t (0114) 255 8646
e info@derwenthousematlock.co.uk
w derwenthousematlock.co.uk

Eagle Cottage, Birchover
★★★ *Self Catering*
Contact: Mrs Mary Prince
t (01629) 650634
e maryprince@msn.com
w cressbrook.co.uk/youlgve/eagle/

Ivy Cottage ★★★
Self Catering
Contact: Mrs Tricia Potter
t (01629) 823018
e ivy.cottage@ukgateway.net

Jewel Cottage ★★★
Self Catering
Peak Cottages
t (0114) 262 0777
e enquiries@peakcottages.com
w peakcottages.com

Lychgate Cottage ★★★★
Self Catering
Peak Cottages
t (0114) 262 0777
e enquiries@peakcottages.com
w peakcottages.com

Mansion Cottage, Crich
★★★ *Self Catering*
Contact: Mrs Sally Parkin
t (01773) 857883
e info@mansioncottage.co.uk
w mansioncottage.co.uk

Mooredge Barns ★★★★
Self Catering
Contact: Mr Barratt
t (01629) 583701 & 07766 074585
e enquiries@mooredgefarmcottages.co.uk
w mooredgefarmcottages.co.uk

Pillar Box Cottage ★★★★
Self Catering
Yorkshire Cottages
t (01228) 406701
e enquiries@yorkshire-cottages.info
w yorkshire-cottages.info

Swiss View ★★★
Self Catering
Contact: Mr William Lennox
t (01629) 582568

Thimble Cottage ★★★
Self Catering
Contact: Bernard & Kate Armstrong
Holmedene
t (01629) 813448
e bernard.armstrong@btinternet.com

MATLOCK BATH
Derbyshire

Bluebell Cottage ★★★
Self Catering
Peak Cottages
t (0114) 262 0777
e enquiries@peakcottages.com
w peakcottages.com

Derwent View ★★★
Self Catering
Contact: Mr Tim Heathcote
t (01629) 57473
e r.timheathcote@btinternet.com

Parade Apartment ★★★★
Self Catering
Peak Cottages
t (0114) 262 0777
e enquiries@peakcottages.com
w peakcottages.com

MATTERSEY
Nottinghamshire

Blaco Hill Farm Cottage
★★★★ *Self Catering*
Contact: Mrs E Lee
t (01777) 816979
e blacohillcottage@aol.com
w blacohillcottages.co.uk

MATTISHALL
Norfolk

The Old Mill ★★★
Self Catering
Norfolk Country Cottages
t (01603) 871872
e info@norfolkcottages.co.uk
w norfolkcottages.co.uk

The Swallows ★★★★
Self Catering
Norfolk Country Cottages
t (01603) 871872
e info@norfolkcottages.co.uk
w norfolkcottages.co.uk

Wayfarers Cottage ★★★★
Self Catering
Norfolk Country Cottages
t (01603) 871872
e info@norfolkcottages.co.uk
w norfolkcottages.co.uk

MAUTBY
Norfolk

Lower Wood Farm Country Cottages ★★★★-★★★★★
Self Catering
Contact: Ms Jill Nicholls
t (01493) 722523

MAVESYN RIDWARE
Staffordshire

The Creamery at Manor Farm, Mavesyn Ridware
★★★★★ *Self Catering*
Contact: Mrs Kate Derry
The Creamery
t (01543) 493223
e katiederry@aol.com
w thecreamerystaffs.com

Stable Cottage ★★★★
Self Catering
Contact: Mrs Susan Clift
t (01543) 491579
e dmsaclift@farming.co.uk
w stablecottagestaffs.co.uk

MELLIS
Suffolk

Orchard Cottage ★★★★
Self Catering
Contact: Ms Ann Young
t (01379) 788092

MELTON MOWBRAY
Leicestershire

Well Cottage and The Old Lambing Shed ★★★★
Self Catering
Contact: Mrs Anne Watchorn
t (01664) 464255
e awatchorn1314@yahoo.com

MELTON ROSS
Lincolnshire

The Old Chapel ★★★★
Self Catering
Contact: R Winning
t (01652) 680527
e rachelwinning@hotmail.com

MELVERLEY
Shropshire

River Cottage ★★★
Self Catering
Contact: Ms Joanne Trow
t (01938) 580286

MEOLE BRACE
Shropshire

Stable Cottage ★★
Self Catering
Contact: Mrs Baugh
t (01743) 236914
e sula.rayska@virgin.net
w stmem.com/stablecottage

MERTON
Norfolk

The Stables ★★★★
Self Catering
Contact: Mrs Nancy Lordon
t (01953) 880180
e nancy@lordon.co.uk
w farmholidaysnorfolk.co.uk

METHERINGHAM
Lincolnshire

Drws nesaf ★★★
Self Catering
Contact: Mr A.C. Jones
t (01526) 322558
e caradog@fish.co.uk

MICHAELCHURCH ESCLEY
Herefordshire

Holt Farm ★★★★
Self Catering
Hideaways
t (01747) 828170
e enq@hideaways.co.uk
w hideaways.co.uk

Michaelchurch House Wing
★★★ *Self Catering*
Contact: Jackie Stewart
t (01981) 510225
e jstewart@eskley.fsnet.co.uk
w golden-valley.co.uk/accdetail.asp?ent_id=75

MICKFIELD
Suffolk

Read Hall Cottage ★★★★★
Self Catering
Contact: Mr & Mrs Andrew & Andrea Stewart
t (01449) 711366
w readhall.co.uk

MIDDLETON
Derbyshire

The Barn ★★★ *Self Catering*
Contact: Mr Peter Smith
t (01629) 824519
e psmith.barn@btinternet.com
w barnaccommodation.co.uk

MIDDLETON
Suffolk

1 Stone Cottage ★★★★
Self Catering
Suffolk Secrets
t (01502) 722717
e holidays@suffolk-secrets.co.uk
w suffolk-secrets.co.uk

8 Stone Cottages ★★★
Self Catering
Suffolk Secrets
t (01502) 722717
e holidays@suffolk-secrets.co.uk
w suffolk-secrets.co.uk

The Cottage at Red Lodge Barn ★★★★ *Self Catering*
Contact: Mrs Patricia Dowding
t (01728) 668100
e pat_roy16@hotmail.com
w redlodgebarnsuffolk.co.uk

Little Glebe ★★★★
Self Catering
Suffolk Secrets
t (01502) 722717
e holidays@suffolk-secrets.co.uk
w suffolk-secrets.co.uk

Old Church Room ★★★★
Self Catering
Suffolk Secrets
t (01502) 722717
e holidays@suffolk-secrets.co.uk
w suffolk-secrets.co.uk

Rose & Stable Cottage
★★★★ *Self Catering*
Contact: Roger & Sandra Dean
t (01728) 648456
w rosefarmbarnssuffolk.co.uk

MIDDLETON-BY-YOULGREAVE
Derbyshire

Curlew Cottage ★★★★
Self Catering
Contact: Mrs Carole Brister
t (01629) 636180
w mysite.orange.co.uk/curlewatlowfield

Holly Homestead ★★★★
Self Catering
Contact: Mr & Mrs David & Valerie Edge
t (01332) 830744
e mail@holly-homestead.co.uk
w holly-homestead.co.uk

MIDDLETON SCRIVEN
Shropshire

Harry's House ★★★★
Self Catering
t (01746) 789224
w coatesfarm.co.uk

MIDDLEWOOD GREEN
Suffolk

Leys Farmhouse Annexe
★★★ *Self Catering*
Contact: Mrs Heather Trevorrow
t (01449) 711750
w leysfarmhouseannexe.co.uk

MILDENHALL
Suffolk

Coach House And Stables
★★★★ *Self Catering*
Contact: Mrs Anne Greenfield
t (01638) 711237
e orchardhouse23@aol.com
w mildenhall-bed-breakfast.co.uk

MILFORD
Derbyshire

The Garden Apartment
★★★ *Self Catering*
Contact: Ms Rosemary Timms
t (01332) 840660
e haveabreak@btinternet.com

MILLER'S DALE
Derbyshire

The Anglers Rest ★★
Self Catering
Contact: Mr Graham Yates
t (01298) 871323
e info@theanglersrest.co.uk
w theanglersrest.co.uk

Monks Retreat ★★★★
Self Catering
Contact: Mrs Pamela Wilkson
t (01298) 871306
e pamwilkson@hotmail.com
w monksdalefarm.co.uk

Riverside House ★★★★
Self Catering
Contact: Wendy & Neil Boast
t (020) 8886 6324
e wendyboast@blueyonder.co.uk
w riversidehouse-peakdistrict.co.uk

MILLTHORPE, HOLMESFIELD
Derbyshire

Millthorpe Cottage ★★★★
Self Catering
Contact: Mrs Liz Barrett
t (0114) 289 1071
e cottage.vacations@btopenworld.com
w cottage-vacations.co.uk

MILWICH
Staffordshire

Summerhill Farm Apartments ★★★★
Self Catering
Contact: Patricia Milward
t (01889) 505546
e p.milward@btinternet.com
w summerhillfarmapartments.co.uk

MINSTERLEY
Shropshire

Luckley Cottage ★★★★
Self Catering
Contact: Mrs Carolyn Sinclair
t (01743) 891469
e info@holiday-cottage-shropshire.co.uk
w holiday-cottage-shropshire.co.uk

The Old Chapel
★★★-★★★★ *Self Catering*
Contact: Mrs Jane Traies
t (01743) 891117
e jane.traies@btopenworld.com
w stmem.com/the-old-chapel

MOIRA
Leicestershire

Lakeview Lodge ★★★★
Self Catering
Contact: Mrs Carol Mallen
t (01283) 763777
e shortheathwater@aol.com
w shortheathwater.co.uk

MONTFORD BRIDGE
Shropshire

Mytton Mill House Flat
★★★ *Self Catering*
Contact: Mrs Patricia Minshall
t (01743) 850497

MONYASH
Derbyshire

The Barn ★★★★
Self Catering
Contact: Mr Tony Staley
t (01629) 583811
e tonystaley@hotmail.com
w littlegemcottages.co.uk

The Coach House ★★★★
Self Catering
Contact: Mrs Ruth Wragg
t (01629) 810434
e ruthwragg@hotmail.com
w monyash.net

Mere View ★★★★
Self Catering
Contact: Mrs Sheenagh Mudford
t (01629) 815636

Rose Cottage ★★★
Self Catering
Contact: Mrs Heather Read
t (01629) 813629

Sheldon Cottages ★★★★
Self Catering
Contact: Mrs Louise Fanshawe
t (01629) 813067
e enquiries@sheldoncottages.co.uk
w sheldoncottages.co.uk

MORNINGTHORPE
Norfolk

Friars Farm Cottage ★★★★
Self Catering
Contact: Mrs Mary Sargent
t (01508) 530269
w morningthorpecottages.co.uk

MORVILLE
Shropshire

Hurst Farm Cottages
★★★★ *Self Catering*
Contact: Mr & Mrs J Brick
t (01746) 714375
e info@cottagefishingholidays.co.uk
w cottagefishingholidays.co.uk

The Stables, 33 Morville
Rating Applied For
Self Catering
Contact: Liz Townsley
t (01746) 714040
e liz@stableaccommodation.com
w stableaccommodation.com

MUCH COWARNE
Herefordshire

Cowarne Hall Cottages
★★★★ *Self Catering*
Contact: Mr & Mrs R & M Bradbury
t (01432) 820317
e rm@cowarnehall.co.uk
w cowarnehall.co.uk

Old Bridgend Cottage
★★★★ *Self Catering*
Contact: Mrs Angela Morgan
t (020) 8942 0702
e rlmconstruction@yahoo.co.uk
w oldbridgendcottage.co.uk

MUCH MARCLE
Herefordshire

Shepherds Rest ★★★★
Self Catering
Contact: Mrs Fiona Wilcox
t (01531) 660285
e fiona@fwilcox.orangehome.co.uk
w herefordshireholidaycottage.co.uk

MUCH WENLOCK
Shropshire

3 Queen Street ★★★
Self Catering
Contact: Mrs E A Williams
t (01743) 362315 & (01743) 362315
e williams_letting@hotmail.com
w stmem.com/3queenstreet

Bramley ★★ *Self Catering*
Contact: Mrs Dee Revell
t (01952) 728153
e drevell@toucansurf.com
w stmem.com/bramley

Garden Cottage
Rating Applied For
Self Catering
t (01952) 727866
w muchwenlockcottage.co.uk

The Owl's House ★★★★★
Self Catering
Contact: Mrs Samantha Gray
t (01952) 728169
e dgray@dgray96.fsnet.co.uk
w owlshouse.co.uk

The Priory ★★★★
Self Catering
Contact: Mrs Annabel Croft
t (01952) 728280
e annabel@croftpriory.fslife.co.uk
w stmem.com/thepriory

Priory Cottage ★★★
Self Catering
Contact: Mrs Jan Cumberland
t (01952) 727386
w stmem.com/priorycottage

Skimblescott Barn, Brockton ★★★★ *Self Catering*
Contact: Mrs Tina Jones
t (01746) 785664
e skimblescott@yahoo.co.uk
w stmem.com/skimblescott-barn

Stokes Barn Cottages ★★★
Self Catering
Contact: Mrs Suzanne Hill
t (01952) 727293
e info@stokesbarn.co.uk
w stokesbarn.co.uk

MUNDESLEY
Norfolk

Anchorage ★★★
Self Catering
Norfolk Country Cottages
t (01603) 871872
e info@norfolkcottages.co.uk
w norfolkcottages.co.uk

Beach House ★★★★
Self Catering
Contact: Imogen Swallowe
t (01263) 821249
e imogenholbrook@hotmail.com
w beach-house-mundesley.co.uk

Holiday Properties Mundesley ★-★★★
Self Catering
Contact: Mr & Mrs Mark & Nadine Gray
t (01263) 720719
w holidayprops.freeuk.com

Meadow View ★★★
Self Catering
Norfolk Country Cottages
t (01603) 871872
e info@norfolkcottages.co.uk
w norfolkcottages.co.uk

Overcliff Lodge ★★★
Self Catering
Norfolk Country Cottages
t (01603) 871872
e info@norfolkcottages.co.uk
w norfolkcottages.co.uk

Wild Rose Cottage ★★★
Self Catering
Contact: Mr Graham Tuckett
t (01245) 252397
e ruffelsandtuckett@hotmail.com
w tiscover.co.uk

NANTMAWR
Shropshire

Bramble Barn ★★★★
Self Catering
t (01691) 828433
w bramblebarn.directlink.to

NARBOROUGH
Norfolk

1 Barge Cottages ★★★
Self Catering
Norfolk Country Cottages
t (01603) 871872
e info@norfolkcottages.co.uk
w norfolkcottages.co.uk

2 Barge Cottages ★★★
Self Catering
Norfolk Country Cottages
t (01603) 871872
e info@norfolkcottages.co.uk
w norfolkcottages.co.uk

The Meal House ★★★★
Self Catering
Norfolk Country Cottages
t (01603) 871872
e info@norfolkcottages.co.uk
w norfolkcottages.co.uk

Point House Holiday Cottages ★★★★
Self Catering
Contact: Ms Undine Fischer
t (01760) 338420 & 07872 064392
e stay@pointhousecottages.co.uk
w pointhousecottages.co.uk

NASSINGTON
Northamptonshire

The Lily Pad
Rating Applied For
Self Catering
Contact: Jane Thorpe-Codman
t (01780) 784394
e bookings@stamfordcottages.co.uk
w northamptonshirecottages.co.uk

NAYLAND
Suffolk

Cobblers Cottage ★★★★
Self Catering
Contact: Mr Mark Scott
t (01787) 211115
e mark@grove-cottages.co.uk
w grove-cottages.co.uk

Gladwins Farm ★★★★-★★★★★
Self Catering
Contact: Mr R Dossor
t (01206) 262261
e gladwinsfarm@aol.com
w gladwinsfarm.co.uk

NEATISHEAD
Norfolk

Beech Farm Barn ★★★★★
Self Catering
Contact: Mr Mark King
t (01692) 631258

Greengages Cottage, Neatishead ★★★
Self Catering
Contact: Mrs Andree Davis
t (01692) 631176

NEEN SOLLARS
Shropshire

Cider House ★★★★
Self Catering
Contact: Mrs P Kennedy
t (01299) 270414
e email@priscillahann.co.uk

Live & Let Live ★★★
Self Catering
Contact: Mrs Christine Ferguson
t (01299) 832391

NETHER HEYFORD
Northamptonshire

Beaver Cottage ★★★★
Self Catering
Contact: Robert Poole
t 07947 856812
e bobbobbobby@btinternet.com

NETHERSEAL
Derbyshire

Grangefields Pine Lodge ★★★★ *Self Catering*
t (01283) 761445
w grangefieldspinelodge.co.uk

Sealbrook Farm ★★★★
Self Catering
Contact: Rob & Jane Kirkland
t (01827) 373236
e info@sealbrookfarmcottages.co.uk
w sealbrookfarmcottages.co.uk

NETTLETON
Lincolnshire

Nettleton Grange ★★★
Self Catering
Contact: John Hair
t 07973 449115
e john.hair@tiscali.co.uk
w nettletongrange.co.uk

NEW MILLS
Derbyshire

Shaw Farm *Approved Caravan Holiday Home*
Contact: Mrs Nicky Burgess
t (0161) 427 1841
e nicky.burgess@talk21.com
w shawfarmhoidays.co.uk

NEWBOROUGH
Staffordshire

Poplars Farmhouse ★★★★
Self Catering
Contact: Sarah Skipper
t (01283) 575200
e sarah@skippershaulage.fsnet.co.ek

NEWHAVEN
Derbyshire

Peakfield Lodge ★★★★
Self Catering
Peak Cottages
t (0114) 262 0777
e enquiries@peakcottages.com
w peakcottages.com

NEWMARKET
Suffolk

19 Tattersalls Crescent ★★★ *Self Catering*
Contact: Ms Liz Jones
Tattersalls Crescent
t (01642) 712553
e eajones40@hotmail.com
w morleyholdings.co.uk

Belmont and Ashbourne Court ★★★ *Self Catering*
Contact: Mrs Jennie Collingridge
t (01638) 577952

NEWTON GRANGE
Derbyshire

New Hanson Bungalow ★★★★ *Self Catering*
Contact: Mrs Linda Bonsall
t (01335) 310258
e nhgfarmholiday@fsmail.net
w cressbrook.co.uk/ashborn/newhanson

NORBURY
Staffordshire

Oulton House Farm Garden Cottages ★★★★
Self Catering
Contact: Mrs Judy Palmer
t (01785) 284264
e judy@oultonhousefarm.co.uk
w oultonhousefarm.co.uk

NORMANBY-BY-SPITAL
Lincolnshire

Maggies Cottage ★★★
Self Catering
Contact: Christine Parker
t (01673) 878530
e maggiescottagelincs@yahoo.co.uk

NORTH BARSHAM
Norfolk

Barsham Barns ★★★★
Self Catering
Contact: Ms Rachel Hurlock
t (01328) 821744
e info@barshambarns.co.uk
w barshambarns.co.uk

NORTH CREAKE
Norfolk

Lavender Cottage ★★★★
Self Catering
Contact: Mr Brian Canning
t 07968 129085
e briancanning@btinternet.com
w norfolkcottagenorthcreake.co.uk

Millstone ★★★★
Self Catering
Contact: Mr & Mrs J Taylor
t (0115) 952 5441
e jeffrey.taylor5@ntlworld.com

NORTH RAUCEBY
Lincolnshire

The Bakehouse ★★★★
Self Catering
Contact: Susan Ireland
t (01529) 488396
e james.ireland@farmline.com

NORTH SOMERCOTES
Lincolnshire

Nursery Cottage (Meals Farm), North Somercotes ★★★★ *Self Catering*
Contact: Mrs Linda Libell
t (01507) 358051 & (01507) 358256
e nurserycottage@hotmail.co.uk
w mealsfarm.com

NORTH WALSHAM
Norfolk

Long Barn ★★★
Self Catering
Norfolk Country Cottages
t (01603) 871872
e info@norfolkcottages.co.uk
w norfolkcottages.co.uk

NORTH WILLINGHAM
Lincolnshire

Old Blacksmiths Cottage ★★★ *Self Catering*
Contact: Betty Burton
t (01673) 838081
e betty@oldblacksmithscottage.co.uk
w oldblacksmithscottage.co.uk

NORTH WOOTTON
Norfolk

Little Barn ★★★★
Self Catering
Contact: Mr & Mrs Cork
t (01553) 631259
w schoolfarmholidaycottage.co.uk

Winsdail ★★★★
Self Catering
Contact: Mrs Pam Goodchild
t (01485) 543639
w winsdailcottage.com

NORTHREPPS
Norfolk

Acorn Cottage ★★★★
Self Catering
Contact: Mrs Louise Strong
t (01263) 579736
e stephen.strong@virgin.net
w theholidaycottages.co.uk

Cobblestones ★★★★
Self Catering
Norfolk Country Cottages
t (01603) 871872
e info@norfolkcottages.co.uk
w norfolkcottages.co.uk

Compasses Cottage ★★★
Self Catering
Norfolk Country Cottages
t (01603) 871872
e info@norfolkcottages.co.uk
w norfolkcottages.co.uk

The Granary ★★★★★
Self Catering
Norfolk Country Cottages
t (01603) 871872
e info@norfolkcottages.co.uk
w norfolkcottages.co.uk

Manor Studio ★★★★
Self Catering
Contact: Mrs Jane Hunt
t (01263) 579126
e jane_d_hunt@yahoo.co.uk
w tiscover.co.uk

Shamrock Cottage ★★★★
Self Catering
Norfolk Country Cottages
t (01603) 871872
e info@norfolkcottages.co.uk
w norfolkcottages.co.uk

NORTON
Suffolk

Old Clavel Cottage ★★★★
Self Catering
Contact: Mrs Nancy Cockayne
t (01359) 241355
w littleclavel.co.uk

NORTON LINDSEY
Warwickshire

Willow Cottage, Norton Lindsey ★★★★ *Self Catering*
Contact: Mrs Helen Phillips
Lower House Farm
t (01926) 842394
e canadalanefarm@yahoo.co.uk
w willow-cottage.org.uk

NORWICH
Norfolk

52 Bishop Gate ★★★★
Self Catering
Norfolk Country Cottages
t (01603) 871872
e info@norfolkcottages.co.uk
w norfolkcottages.co.uk

The Hideaway ★★★★
Self Catering
Contact: Mrs Reilly
t (01603) 715052
w thehideawayinbroadland.com

Kingsley Cottage ★★★
Self Catering
Contact: Miss Valy Jules
t (01603) 628505
w selfcateringnorwich.co.uk

Mabels Cottage ★★★
Self Catering
Contact: Mrs Judy Randon
t (01508) 499279
e judy.randon@virgin.net
w mabels-cottage.co.uk

Mill House ★★★★
Self Catering
Contact: Ms Fay Godin
t (01603) 415061
w millhouse.f2s.com

Norwich Apartments ★★★★ *Self Catering*
Contact: Andrew Parker
t (01953) 601125
e info@norwichapartment.com
w norwichapartment.com

Paradise Cottage
Rating Applied For
Self Catering
Norfolk Country Cottages
t (01603) 871872
e info@norfolkcottages.co.uk
w norfolkcottages.co.uk

Poolside Lodges ★★★
Self Catering
Contact: Mrs Sally-Anne Hinkley
t (01603) 720000
e sally.hinkley@btinternet.com

Spixworth Hall Cottages ★★★★ *Self Catering*
Contact: Mrs Sheelah-Jane Cook
t (01603) 898190
w hallcottages.co.uk

NOTTINGHAM
Nottinghamshire

16 Pilcher Gate ★–★★★★
Serviced Apartments
Contact: Mr Peter Fox-Andrews
Lismar Ltd
t (0115) 986 0495
e enquiries@1hmoore.co.uk
w 16pilchergate.co.uk

---

46 Riverview ★★★
Self Catering
Contact: Margaret Hallam
t (0115) 923 3372

Premier Apartments Nottingham ★★★★
Serviced Apartments
Contact: Mr Chris Benyon
Prem Group UK Ltd
t (0151) 227 9467
e cbenyon@premgroup.com
w premierapartments nottingham.com

SACO Nottingham ★★★★
Serviced Apartments
SACO Apartments
t (0117) 974 5936
e sarahbailey@sacaoapartments.co.uk
w sacoapartments.co.uk

Woodview Cottages, Owthorpe ★★★★
Self Catering
Contact: Mrs Jane Morley
PC Morley and Son
t (01949) 81580
e enquiries@woodviewcottages.co.uk
w woodviewcottages.co.uk

NOWTON
Suffolk

Old Granary ★★★★
Self Catering
Contact: Mrs Mary Roe
t (01284) 388239

OAKAMOOR
Staffordshire

The Annexe at The Old Furnace ★★★ *Self Catering*
Contact: Mr John Higgins
t (01538) 703331
w oldfurnace.co.uk

OAKHAM
Rutland

Ashgate Annexe ★★★★
Self Catering
Contact: Mrs Isabel Lloyd Williams
t (01572) 756922
e david.lloydwilliams@homecall.co.uk

The Cat Basket ★★★★
Self Catering
Contact: Mrs Marilyn Tomalin
t (01572) 723184
e jmtomalin@onetel.com

Cromwell House ★★★
Self Catering
Contact: Peter & Linda Jonese info@cromwellhouseselfcatering.co.uk
w cromwellhouseselfcatering.co.uk

Old School Cottage, North Luffenham ★★★★
Self Catering
Contact: Mrs Handley
t (01780) 721768
e rhandley@supanet.com
w rutnet.co.uk/oldschoolcottage/

Pear Tree Cottage ★★★
Self Catering
Contact: Mrs Jane Thomas
t (01780) 460258

OASBY
Lincolnshire

Honeysuckle Cottage, Oasby ★★★★★
Self Catering
Contact: Mrs Gill Wild
t (01529) 455681 & 07950 258931
e gillwild@foxdale-oasby.co.uk
w honeysucklecottage-foxdale.co.uk

OLD BOLINGBROKE
Lincolnshire

Hope Cottages ★★★★
Self Catering
Contact: Kate Taylor
t (01673) 861412
e hopecottages@aol.com
w hopecottages.co.uk

OLD BRAMPTON
Derbyshire

Chestnut and Willow Cottages ★★★★
Self Catering
Contact: Mr & Mrs Jeffrey & Patricia Green
t (01246) 566159
e patricia_green@btconnect.com

OLD BUCKENHAM
Norfolk

Ox and Plough Cottages ★★★ *Self Catering & Serviced Apartments*
Contact: Mrs Sally Bishop
t (01953) 860004
e oxandplough.bishop@barbox.net
w oxandploughcottages.co.uk

OLD DALBY
Leicestershire

Lower Grange Farm ★★★
Self Catering
Contact: Mrs Sue Fox
t (01664) 823640

OLD HALL GREEN
Hertfordshire

High Trees Farm ★★★★
Self Catering
Contact: Mr & Mrs Andrew & Vanessa Gibson
t (01920) 438275
e stay@hightreesfarm.com
w hightreesfarm.com

OLD STRATFORD Northamptonshire

33 and 35 Brookside Close ★★★ *Self Catering*
Contact: Mrs Hepher
The Old Bakery
t (01908) 562253
e mksh@hepher.demon.co.uk

ORFORD Suffolk

47 Daphne Road ★★★
Self Catering
Suffolk Secrets
t (01502) 722717
w suffolk-secrets.co.uk

The Gedgrave Broom, Orford ★★★★ *Self Catering*
Contact: Mrs Ali Watson
t (01394) 450488
e ab.watson@btinternet.com
w tiscover.co.uk

ORWELL Cambridgeshire

Retreat ★★★★ *Self Catering*
Contact: Mrs Muriel Meikle
t (01223) 208005

OSWESTRY Shropshire

Courtyard ★★★★
Self Catering
Contact: Katherine Bottoms
t (01691) 670066
e gohughes@aol.com
w the-walls.co.uk

Cross Keys Cottage, Selattyn ★★★ *Self Catering*
Contact: Mr & Mrs Philip Rothera
t (01691) 650247
e hilda@thecrosskeys-selattyn.co.uk
w thecrosskeys-selattyn.co.uk

Hinsdale ★★ *Self Catering*
Contact: Mrs Carol Harding
t (01691) 650408
e enquiries@hinsdale.co.uk
w hinsdale.co.uk

Old Rectory Cottage ★★
Self Catering
Contact: Mrs Maggie Barnes
t (01691) 659708

The Stables, Morton ★★★★
Self Catering
Contact: Mrs L M Frank
t (01691) 682218
e bookings@mortonstables.co.uk
w mortonstables.co.uk

Tannery Cottage ★★★
Self Catering
t (01691) 654961
w http://tannery-cottage.mysite.wanadoo-members.co.uk

OULTON BROAD Suffolk

Camps Heath Barn, Oulton ★★★★ *Self Catering*
Contact: Mr J R Overy
t (01502) 562981 & 07917 147776
e campsheathbarn@hotmail.co.uk
w campsheathbarn.co.uk

Maltings Accommodation ★★★★ *Self Catering*
Contact: Mrs Caroline Coe
t (01502) 501353
e admin@ivyhousecountryhotel.co.uk
w ivyhousecountryhotel.co.uk

Sycamore Cottage ★★★★
Self Catering
Contact: Mrs Norma Barton
t (01702) 392939
e norm@davidwebb.co.uk
w normasretreat.co.uk

White House Farm ★★★
Self Catering
Contact: Mrs Sharon Hughes
t (01502) 564049
e mail@whitehousefarm.org.uk
w whitehousefarm.org.uk

OUNDLE Northamptonshire

13 Cotterstock Road ★★★
Self Catering
Contact: Mr & Mrs J S Czwortek
t (01832) 273371

The Bolt Hole ★★★★
Self Catering
Explore Accommodation
t (01832) 272298 & 07850 388109

Burnham Terrace
Rating Applied For
Self Catering
Contact: Ms Ann Fitzgerald
Global Visitor
t 0870 041 0256
e ann.fitzgerald@globalvisitor.co.uk

Orchard Cottage ★★★★
Self Catering
Contact: Ann Fitzgerald
t 0870 041 0256
e ann.fitzgerald@globalvisitor.co.uk

Oundle Cottage Breaks, Oundle ★★★-★★★★
Self Catering
Contact: Mr & Mrs Simmonds
t (01832) 275508
e richard@simmondsatoundle.co.uk
w oundlecottagebreaks.co.uk

OVER HADDON Derbyshire

Burton Manor Farm Cottages ★★★★
Self Catering
Peak Cottages
t (0114) 262 0777
e enquiries@peakcottages.com
w peakcottages.com

Dale View Cottage ★★★★
Self Catering
Peak Cottages
t (0114) 262 0777
e enquiries@peakcottages.com
w peakcottages.com

May Cottage ★★★★
Self Catering
Contact: Mrs Margaret Corbridge
t (01629) 813639

OVERSEAL Staffordshire

Bridge House
Rating Applied For
Self Catering
Contact: Mr Tom Hartley
t (01283) 763300

OVERSTRAND Norfolk

31 Harbord Road, Overstrand ★★★★
Self Catering
Contact: Mr John Langley
t (01372) 843330
w harbord.holidays.co.uk

Beaches ★★★ *Self Catering*
Contact: Miss Pamela Jonas
Country and Coast – Self Catering Holidays
t (01263) 513139

Buckthorns ★★★★
Self Catering
Contact: Mrs Mandy Reeve
t (01406) 422953
e mail@ealing74.fsnet.co.uk
w tiscover.co.uk

Green Lawn House ★★★
Self Catering
Contact: Mrs Anne Driscoll
t (01263) 576925
e info@greenlawnhouse.co.uk
w greenlawnhouse.co.uk

Poppyland Holiday Cottages ★★★★ *Self Catering*
Contact: Mrs Riches
t (01263) 577473
e poppyland@totalise.co.uk
w broadland.com/poppyland

St Paul's Lane ★★★
Self Catering
Norfolk Country Cottages
t (01603) 871872
e info@norfolkcottages.co.uk
w norfolkcottages.co.uk

OXBOROUGH Norfolk

Ferry Farm Cottage ★★★
Self Catering
Contact: Mrs Margaret Wilson
t (01366) 328287
w ferryfarm.btinternet.co.uk

OXTON Nottinghamshire

Wesley Farm Cottage ★★★★ *Self Catering*
Contact: Heather Palmer
t (0115) 965 2043
e enquiries@wesleycottage.com
w wesleycottage.com

PAKEFIELD Suffolk

Cliff Cottage ★★★
Self Catering
Contact: Mrs Thelma Bruce
t (01502) 501955
w tiscover.co.uk

PAKENHAM Suffolk

Fen House ★★★★★
Self Catering
Contact: Mrs Lynn Patterson
t (01359) 234968
w fenhouse.net

PANTON Lincolnshire

St Andrew's Church ★★★
Self Catering
Contact: Janet Haller
t (01673) 857302
e janet_haller@hotmail.com
w lincs-holiday.co.uk

PARSON DROVE Cambridgeshire

Chapel Lodge ★★★★
Self Catering
Contact: Robert & Suzanne Scrimshaw
t (01945) 700202
e robertscrimshaw@aol.com
w chapellodgeholidays.com

Warners Farm ★★★★
Self Catering
Contact: Mrs Bridget Selway
t (01945) 700077
e selwayb@aol.com
w fenhols.webeden.co.uk

PARWICH Derbyshire

Church Gates Cottage ★★★
Self Catering
Peak Cottages
t (0114) 262 0777
e enquiries@peakcottages.com
w peakcottages.com

Croft Cottage ★★★★
Self Catering
Contact: Mrs Saskia Tallis
t (01335) 390440
e enquiries@croftcottage.co.uk
w croftcottage.co.uk

Douglas's Barn ★★★★★
Self Catering
Contact: Mr & Mrs John & Marion Fuller-Sessions
t (01335) 390519
e tom@orchardfarm.demon.co.uk
w tomsbarn.co.uk

Parwich Lees Holiday Cottages ★★★ *Self Catering*
Contact: Mrs Jane Gerard-Pearse
t (01335) 390625
e ionabess@btinternet.com
w parwichlees.co.uk

Tom's Barn and Douglas's Barn ★★★★★ *Self Catering*
Contact: Marion Fuller-Sessions
t (01335) 390519
e tom@orchardfarm.demon.co.uk
w tomsbarn.co.uk

PASTON Norfolk

The Nutshell ★★★
Self Catering
Norfolk Country Cottages
t (01603) 871872
e info@norfolkcottages.co.uk
w norfolkcottages.co.uk

PEAK FOREST
Derbyshire

Bowling Green Cottage
★★★★ *Self Catering*
Peak Cottages
t (0114) 262 0777
e enquiries@peakcottages.com
w peakcottages.com

PEBWORTH
Worcestershire

Field View & Garden View
Approved Caravan Holiday Home
Contact: Marian Walters
t (01789) 720471
e chfarmdorsington@aol.com
w horseshoecottage.info

Horseshoe Cottage ★★★★
Self Catering
Contact: Marian Walters
t (01789) 720471
e chfarmdorsington@aol.com
w horseshoecottage.info

PELDON
Essex

Rose Barn Cottage, Peldon
★★★★ *Self Catering*
Contact: Mrs Ariette Everett
Rose Barn
t (01206) 735317
e everettaj@aol.com

PEMBRIDGE
Herefordshire

The Cottage at Clearbrook
★★★ *Self Catering*
Contact: Mrs Sheila Jones
t (01544) 388569
e jonescottage@aol.com

The Granary and The Dairy
★★★ *Self Catering*
Contact: Mrs Nancy Owens
t (01544) 388268
e nancy@grovedesign.co.uk

Luntley Court Farm Cottages
★★★★ *Self Catering*
Contact: Sandra Owens
t (01544) 388422
e info@luntleycourtfarm.co.uk
w luntleycourtfarm.co.uk

The Stables ★★★★
Self Catering
Contact: Mrs Jean Simmonds
t (01544) 388619
e jean@seagrasscottages.co.uk
w seagrasscottages.co.uk

Winyard Lodge ★★★★
Self Catering
Contact: Mrs Jean Gwatkin
t (01544) 388428
e ebgwatkin@aol.com

PENCOMBE
Herefordshire

Durstone Cottages ★★★
Self Catering
Contact: Ms Sarah Mulroy
t (01885) 400221
e mul@farmersweekly.net

PENKRIDGE
Staffordshire

The Coach House Cottage
★★★ *Self Catering*
Contact: Mr & Mrs Graham & A Ellis
t (01785) 712076
e gae.coachhouse@virgin.net
w coachhouse-gae.co.uk

Dalraddy Cottage ★★★★
Self Catering
Contact: Mrs Sonia Young
t 07949 721677
e sonia@dalraddycottage.co.uk
w dalraddycottage.co.uk

PENTNEY
Norfolk

Nar Valley Holiday Cottages
★★★ *Self Catering*
Contact: Ms Rosemary de Bootman
t (01760) 338797
e info@narvalleycottagesnorfolk.co.uk
w narvalleycottagesnorfolk.co.uk

Wesleyan Chapel ★★★
Self Catering
Norfolk Country Cottages
t (01603) 871872
e info@norfolkcottages.co.uk
w norfolkcottages.co.uk

PENTRICH
Derbyshire

Cherry Cottages ★★★
Self Catering
Contact: Mrs Amanda Smithe smithmandys@aol.com
w cherryholidaycottages.co.uk

PERSHORE
Worcestershire

Court Close Farm ★★★
Self Catering
Contact: Mrs Eileen Fincher
t (01386) 750297
e fincher@ukonline.co.uk

Garth Cottage ★★★★
Self Catering
Contact: Mrs Margaret Smith
t (01386) 561213 & 07759 655717
e stephen.smith@homecall.co.uk
w garthcottage.co.uk

PETTISTREE
Suffolk

Grove Stables ★★★★
Self Catering
Contact: Mrs Carol Edworthy
t (01728) 746333
w carolscottages.co.uk

PIKEHALL
Derbyshire

Roystone Grange ★★★★
Self Catering
Peak Cottages
t (0114) 262 0777
e enquiries@peakcottages.com
w peakcottages.com

Springfield Cottage ★★★★
Self Catering
Peak Cottages
t (0114) 262 0777
e enquiries@peakcottages.com
w peakcottages.com

PILLERTON HERSEY
Warwickshire

Roman Acres Cottage ★★★
Self Catering
Contact: Mrs Williams
t (01789) 740360

PILSLEY
Derbyshire

Yew Tree Cottage ★★★
Self Catering
Contact: Mrs Lisbeth Adsetts
t (01246) 853614
e eadsetts@aol.com

PIN MILL
Suffolk

Alma Cottage ★★★
Self Catering
Contact: Mr John Pugh
Culver End
t (01453) 872551
e john.pugh@talk21.com

PITCHILL
Warwickshire

New Inn Lane Holiday Cottages ★★★ *Self Catering*
Contact: Karen New
t (01386) 870073
e newinnlane@uwclub.net
w newinnlane.co.uk

PLUNGAR
Leicestershire

The Forge ★★★ *Self Catering*
Contact: Mrs Valerie Ridgway
t (01949) 861355
e john.ridgway4@btopenworld.com
w plungarforge.com

Old Wharf ★★★★★
Self Catering
Contact: Ms Elaine Pell
t (01949) 860630
e pellelaine@hotmail.com
w oldwharf.co.uk

POLSTEAD
Suffolk

Holmwood Cottage ★★★★
Self Catering
Contact: Mr Mark Scott
t (01787) 211115
e mark@grove-cottages.co.uk
w grove-cottages.co.uk

Stables ★★★ *Self Catering*
Contact: Mr Peter Crawford
t (01787) 210368

PONTRILAS
Herefordshire

Railway Cottage ★★
Self Catering
Contact: Jo Russell
t (01981) 240564
e gwrstation04@tesco.net
w golden-valley.co.uk/stationhouse

PONTSHILL
Herefordshire

Millbrook Cottages
Rating Applied For
Self Catering
Contact: Ms Karen Edwards
t (01989) 750961
e ked2064@aol.com

POTTER HEIGHAM
Norfolk

Cherry Tree Cottage ★★★★
Self Catering
Contact: Mrs C Whitehead
t (01692) 670189
e ciwhitehead@aol.com

POTTERHANWORTH
Lincolnshire

Black Horse Cottage ★★★
Self Catering
Contact: Anita Watt
t (01522) 792549
e info@blackhorsecottage.co.uk
w blackhorsecottage.co.uk

Skelghyll Cottage ★★★
Self Catering
Contact: Joan Hawes
t (01522) 790043

PRESTON ST MARY
Suffolk

Overway Cottage ★★★★
Self Catering
Contact: Miss Papillion Luck
t 07815 934182

PRESTWOOD
Staffordshire

Swallows Loft ★★★
Self Catering
Contact: Mrs Kath Robinson
t (01889) 590464
e swallowsloft@bt.connect.com
w swallows-loft.co.uk

PRINCETHORPE
Warwickshire

Stretton Lodge Barns ★★★
Self Catering
Contact: Mrs Liz Best
t (01926) 632351
e lizbest@hotmail.com

PULVERBATCH
Shropshire

Holly Grove Cottage ★★★★
Self Catering
Contact: Mrs Sue Morris
t (01743) 718300
e pulverbatch@onetel.com
w hollygrovecottage.co.uk

QUARNFORD
Derbyshire

Greens Farm ★★★
Self Catering
Contact: Mrs Sheila Kidd
t (01298) 25172
e skidd156@hotmail.com

The Studio at Adders Green
★★ *Self Catering*
Contact: Pamela Sandiford
t (01298) 237520
e pam@addersgreen.co.uk

RANWORTH
Norfolk

The Cottage ★★★
Self Catering
Norfolk Country Cottages
t (01603) 871872
e info@norfolkcottages.co.uk
w norfolkcottages.co.uk

RAUNDS
Northamptonshire

Gatehouse Annex ★★★★
Self Catering
t (01933) 626600

REDBOURN
Hertfordshire

Beeches ★★★ *Self Catering*
Contact: Mrs June Surridge
t (01582) 792638

REDE
Suffolk

Rede Hall Farm Park ★★★★
Self Catering & Serviced Apartments
t (01284) 850695
e chris@redehallfarmpark.co.uk
w redehallfarmpark.co.uk

REEDHAM
Norfolk

Norton Marsh Mill ★★★
Self Catering
Norfolk Country Cottages
t (01603) 871872
e info@norfolkcottages.co.uk
w norfolkcottages.co.uk

Riverside Properties ★★★★
Self Catering
Contact: Mrs Heather Willies
t (01428) 658289
e rivitt@aol.com
w tiscover.co.uk

REEPHAM
Norfolk

3 Church Street ★★★
Self Catering
Norfolk Country Cottages
t (01603) 871872
e info@norfolkcottages.co.uk
w norfolkcottages.co.uk

99 Tangham ★★★
Self Catering
Suffolk Secrets
t (01502) 722717
e holidays@suffolk-secrets.co.uk
w suffolk-secrets.co.uk

Bakehouse ★★★★
Self Catering
Norfolk Country Cottages
t (01603) 871872
e info@norfolkcottages.co.uk
w norfolkcottages.co.uk

Church View 3 ★★★
Self Catering
Norfolk Country Cottages
t (01603) 871872
e info@norfolkcottages.co.uk
w norfolkcottages.co.uk

RENDLESHAM
Suffolk

Bramley Cottage ★★★★
Self Catering
Contact: Mrs Priscilla Mobley
t (01394) 460716

RETFORD
Nottinghamshire

Spruce Cottage, Ranby
★★★ *Self Catering*
t (0131) 447 6886
w countrycottagesonline.net

Westhill Cottage ★★★
Self Catering
t (01777) 707034
e holly23@tiscali.co.uk
w westhillcottage.co.uk

REYDON
Suffolk

27 Nightingale Avenue
★★★ *Self Catering*
Acanthus Property Letting Services
t (01502) 724033
e websales@southwold-holidays.co.uk
w southwold-holidays.co.uk

The Ark ★★★ *Self Catering*
Suffolk Secrets
t (01502) 722717
e holidays@suffolk-secrets.co.uk
w suffolk-secrets.co.uk

Beulah ★★★★ *Self Catering*
Acanthus Property Letting Services
t (01502) 724033
e websales@southwold-holidays.co.uk
w southwold-holidays.co.uk

The Coach House ★★★
Self Catering
Contact: Mr Martyn Howard
Suffolk Secrets
t (01379) 651297
e holidays@suffolk-secrets.co.uk
w suffolk-secrets.co.uk

Field End ★★★★
Self Catering
Suffolk Secrets
t (01502) 722717
e holidays@suffolk-secrets.co.uk
w suffolk-secrets.co.uk

Goose Corner ★★★★
Self Catering
Suffolk Secrets
t (01502) 722717
e holidays@suffolk-secrets.co.uk
w suffolk-secrets.co.uk

Hilda's Cottage ★★★
Self Catering
Suffolk Holidays Ltd
t (01502) 723571
e sales@holidaysinsuffolk.co.uk
w holidaysinsuffolk.co.uk

Hurn Crag House ★★★
Self Catering
Suffolk Secrets
t (01502) 722717
e holidays@suffolk-secrets.co.uk
w suffolk-secrets.co.uk

Marigold Cottage ★★★
Self Catering
Acanthus Property Letting Services
t (01502) 724033
e websales@southwold-holidays.co.uk
w southwold-holidays.co.uk

Marram House ★★★
Self Catering
Suffolk Secrets
t (01502) 722717
e holidays@suffolk-secrets.co.uk
w suffolk-secrets.co.uk

Moorthwaite ★★★★
Self Catering
Suffolk Secrets
t (01502) 722717
e holidays@suffolk-secrets.co.uk
w suffolk-secrets.co.uk

The Old Library
Rating Applied For
Self Catering
Suffolk Secrets
t (01502) 722717
e holidays@suffolk-secrets.co.uk
w suffolk-secrets.co.uk

The Old School ★★★★
Self Catering
Suffolk Secrets
t (01502) 722717
e holidays@suffolk-secrets.co.uk
w suffolk-secrets.co.uk

Pebbles ★★★ *Self Catering*
Suffolk Secrets
t (01502) 722717
e holidays@suffolk-secrets.co.uk
w suffolk-secrets.co.uk

Scott Cottage ★★★★
Self Catering
Contact: Mrs Judith Ogden
Quorn House
w heritagehideaways.com

South View Cottage ★★★★
Self Catering
Suffolk Secrets
t (01502) 722717
e holidays@suffolk-secrets.co.uk
w suffolk-secrets.co.uk

The Spinney ★★★★
Self Catering
Suffolk Secrets
t (01502) 722717
e holidays@suffolk-secrets.co.uk
w suffolk-secrets.co.uk

Sundial ★★ *Self Catering*
Acanthus Property Letting Services
t (01502) 724033
e websales@southwold-holidays.co.uk
w southwold-holidays.co.uk

Whimbrel Cottage ★★★
Self Catering
Suffolk Secrets
t (01502) 722717
e holidays@suffolk-secrets.co.uk
w suffolk-secrets.co.uk

RICHARDS CASTLE
Shropshire

The Barn at Ryecroft
★★★★ *Self Catering*
Contact: Peter & Sue Plant
t (01584) 831224
e ryecroftbarn@hotmail.com
w ludlow.org.uk/ryecroft

Stables Flat, Richards Castle
★★★★ *Self Catering*
Contact: Mr & Mrs Sandra & David English
t (01584) 831265
e english.david@tiscali.co.uk

RIDGEWELL
Essex

The Coach House ★★★★
Self Catering
Contact: Mrs Janet Ridsdill-Smith
t 0871 479 8621
w ridgewellcoachhouse.co.uk

RINGSTEAD
Norfolk

5 Langford Cottages ★★★
Self Catering
Contact: Mr John Warham
t (01485) 512546
w thornhamcottages.co.uk

Abbotts Cottage
Rating Applied For
Self Catering
Norfolk Country Cottages
t (01603) 871872
e info@norfolkcottages.co.uk
w norfolkcottages.co.uk

April Cottage and Tamarisk
★★★★★ *Self Catering*
Contact: Mrs Laurice Jarman
t (01553) 676060
e bookings@jariard.fsnet.co.uk
w jariardltd.co.uk

RISELEY
Bedfordshire

Coldham Cottages ★★★★
Self Catering
Contact: Mrs Jean Felce
t (01234) 708489
e info@coldhamcottages.co.uk
w coldhamcottages.co.uk

ROLLESBY
Norfolk

Court House Cottage
★★★★ *Self Catering*
Contact: Julia Hawkins
t (01493) 369665
e theoldcourt@tiscali.co.uk
w courthousecottages.co.uk

Mickrandella ★★★
Self Catering
Norfolk Country Cottages
t (01603) 871872
e info@norfolkcottages.co.uk
w norfolkcottages.co.uk

ROLLESTON
Nottinghamshire

Mill Cottage ★★★
Self Catering
t (0115) 966 4015
e enquiries@rollestonmill.co.uk
w rollestonmill.co.uk

ROSS-ON-WYE
Herefordshire

Ashe Holiday Cottages
★★★-★★★★ *Self Catering*
Contact: Mrs Maria Ball
t (01989) 563336
e info@ashe-holiday-cottages.com
w ashe-holiday-cottages.com

Crispin Cottage ★★★★
Self Catering
Contact: Graham & Heather Lovett
t (01989) 567864
e heather@mlovett.orangehome.co.uk
w crispincottage.com

Farr Cottages
★★★-★★★★ *Self Catering*
Contact: Angela Farr
t (01600) 750333
e farrcottages@yahoo.com
w farrcottages.co.uk

The Game Larders and The Old Bakehouse ★★★
Self Catering
Contact: Miss Anthea McIntyre
t (01989) 562688
e wythall@globalnet.co.uk
w wythallestate.co.uk

Garden Cottage & The Granary ★★★ *Self Catering*
Contact: Carol Brewer
t (01989) 563900
e info@benhallfarm.co.uk
w benhallfarm.co.uk

India Cottage ★★★★
Self Catering
Contact: Lucy Preece
t 07775 841720
e lucy@preece.wyenet.co.uk
w wyevalleycottages.co.uk

Mainoaks Farm Cottages – Goodrich
Rating Applied For
Self Catering
Contact: Mrs P Unwin
t (01531) 650448
e mainoaks@lineone.net
w mainoaks.co.uk

Man of Ross Apartment ★★
Self Catering
Contact: David & Judy Campkin
t (0118) 957 2561
e judycampkin@yahoo.co.uk

The Olde House ★★★
Self Catering
Contact: Mrs Jane Fray
t (01989) 780383
e peter@pjfray.co.uk
w oldehouse.com

Pear Tree Cottage ★★★
Self Catering
Contact: Mrs Jenny Sanders
t (01989) 780483
e perrystonecottages@hotmail.com
w perrystonecottages.co.uk

Watchmaker's Cottage
★★★★ *Self Catering*
Contact: Mrs Jenny Clark
t (01989) 770369
e watchmakerscottage@madasafish.com

Wharton Lodge Cottages
★★★★★ *Self Catering*
Contact: Mrs Nicky Cross
t (01989) 750140
e ncross@whartonlodge.co.uk
w whartonlodge.co.uk

ROSTON
Derbyshire

Meadow Cottage – Shawley Farm ★★★★ *Self Catering*
Contact: Ms Glenys Hubbard
t (01889) 590507
e meadow_cottagederbys@hotmail.co.uk

ROUGHTON
Norfolk

The Hayloft ★★★★
Self Catering
Contact: Mr Phil Eccleston
Saffron House
t (01953) 860045
e philip.eccleston@virgin.net
w finestcottages.co.uk

Long Barn ★★★★
Self Catering
Norfolk Country Cottages
t (01603) 871872
e info@norfolkcottages.co.uk
w norfolkcottages.co.uk

Rose Cottage ★★★★
Self Catering
Norfolk Country Cottages
t (01603) 871872
e info@norfolkcottages.co.uk
w norfolkcottages.co.uk

ROWSLEY
Derbyshire

Bluebell Cottage ★★★
Self Catering
Contact: Mrs Jane Henderson
t (0114) 281 7217
e jane77@blueyonder.co.uk

The Nook ★★★ *Self Catering*
Peak Cottages
t (0114) 262 0777
e enquiries@peakcottages.com
w peakcottages.com

Swallows End ★★★
Self Catering
Peak Cottages
t (0114) 262 0777
e enquiries@peakcottages.com
w peakcottages.com

RUDYARD
Staffordshire

The Bothy, Rudyard ★★★★
Self Catering
Contact: Mr Andrew Mount and Miss Michelle Ash
t 07771 702949 & 07957 856629
e info@thebothy-rudyard.co.uk
w thebothy-rudyard.co.uk

Chacara, Rudyard ★★★★
Self Catering
Contact: Mrs Christine Gee
t (01538) 306663

RUGBY
Warwickshire

Lawford Hill Farm ★★★★
Self Catering
Contact: Mrs Susan Moses
t (01788) 542001
w lawfordhill.co.uk

Lodge Farm, Long Lawford
★★★ *Self Catering*
Contact: Mr & Mrs Alec & Jane Brown
t (01788) 560193
e alec@lodgefarm.com
w lodgefarm.com

The Saddlery ★★★★★
Self Catering
Contact: Mrs Elaine Heckford
t (01788) 890256
e office@thesaddlery.org.uk
w thesaddlery.org.uk

RUMBURGH
Suffolk

Rumburgh Farm, Swallow Lodge & Kingfisher Lodge
★★★★ *Self Catering*
Contact: Mrs Charlotte Binder
t (01986) 781351
e binder@rumburghfarm.co.uk
w rumburghfarm.co.uk

RUNCTON HOLME
Norfolk

Thorpland Manor Barns
★★★★ *Self Catering*
Contact: Mrs Mary Caley
t (01553) 810409
w thorplandmanorbarns.co.uk

RUSHBURY
Shropshire

Lilywood Cottage ★★★★
Self Catering
Contact: Mrs Ruth Lole
t (01694) 771286
e ruth.lole@talktalk.net
w stmem.com/lilywoodcottage

RUSHTON SPENCER
Staffordshire

Toft Hall ★★★★★
Self Catering
Contact: Ms Sue Norgrove-Moore
t (01260) 226609
e partyhouses@hotmail.com
w partyhouses.co.uk

RUSKINGTON
Lincolnshire

The Annexe – 4 Westcliffe Road ★★★★ *Self Catering*
Contact: Harry Pettitt
t (01526) 833857
e ipettitt@hotmail.com
w lincolnshirelet.co.uk

Orwell House Annexe ★★★
Self Catering
Contact: Elizabeth Cartwright
t (01526) 834292
e lelisian@aol.com

RYHALL
Rutland

St Johns Retreat ★★★★
Self Catering
Contact: Miss Janette McMorrow
t (01778) 590596
e enquiries@stjohnsretreat.co.uk
w stjohnsretreat.co.uk

SAFFRON WALDEN
Essex

Barn ★★★★ *Self Catering*
Contact: Mr John Goose
t (01799) 523202
w cottageguide.co.uk/the-barn

Coach House ★★★★
Self Catering
Contact: Mr John Goose
t (01799) 523202
w cottageguide.co.uk/the-coach-house

The Cottage ★★★★
Self Catering
Contact: Mr Michael Rigby
t (01799) 501373
w mcrigby.co.uk

Fisherman's Lodge ★★★★
Self Catering
Contact: Mrs Tineke Westerhuis
t (01763) 838053
w rockellsfarm.co.uk

Little Bulls Farmhouse
★★★★ *Self Catering*
Contact: Mr A Kiddy
t (01799) 599272
e ajkiddy@cambridge-vacation-homes.com
w cambridge-vacation-homes.com

ST ALBANS
Hertfordshire

17 Holmes Court ★★★★
Self Catering
w homefromholme.com

High Meadows ★★★
Self Catering
Contact: Ms Jenny Hale
t (01727) 865092
e family.hale@ntlworld.co.uk
w akomodation.co.uk

The Straw House ★★★★
Self Catering
Contact: Miss Pamela McClean
Hawk Ventures Limited
t (01727) 810673
w strawhousestalbans.co.uk

ST NEOTS
Cambridgeshire

Abbotsley Country Homes, Eynesbury Hardwicke
★★★★★ *Self Catering*
Contact: Mr Michael Wilton-Cox
t (01480) 476312
e abbotsleyhomes@btconnect.com
w abbotsleycountryhomes.co.uk

ST OSYTH
Essex

The Cartlodge at Lee Wick Farm
Rating Applied For
Self Catering
Contact: Mr Robert Clarke
t (01255) 823031
e info@leewickfarm.co.uk
w leewickfarm.co.uk

Park Hall Country Cottage
★★★★★ *Self Catering*
Contact: Trisha Ford
t (01255) 820922
e trish@parkhall.fslife.co.uk
w parkhall.info

ST OWENS CROSS
Herefordshire

Bramley Cottage ★★★★
Self Catering
Contact: Nic & Lucy Snell
t (01989) 730416
e lucy@bramleyholidaycottage.co.uk
w bramleyholidaycottage.co.uk

Trevase Granary ★★★★★
Self Catering
Contact: Mrs Liz Pursey
t (01989) 730210
e stay@trevasecottages.co.uk
w trevasecottages.co.uk

SALMONBY
Lincolnshire

Grange Farm Cottages ★★★
Self Catering
Contact: Valerie Downes
t (01507) 534101
e info@grangefarmholidaybreaks.co.uk
w grangefarmholidaybreaks.co.uk

SALTHOUSE
Norfolk

Dun Cow Public House
★★★ *Self Catering*
Contact: Mrs Kay Groom
t (01263) 740467
w theduncow-salthouse.co.uk

SALWARPE
Worcestershire

The Old Dairy ★★★★
Self Catering
Contact: Mr Mike Roberts
t (01905) 455684
e middleton-farm-fenc@talk21.com
w middletonfarm.co.uk

SANDILANDS
Lincolnshire

26 Kipling Drive ★★★
Self Catering
Contact: E Spring
t (01652) 628329
e l12spring@aol.com

SANDY
Bedfordshire

Acorn Cottage ★★★★
Self Catering
Contact: Mrs Margaret Codd
t (01767) 682332
e margaret@highfield-farm.co.uk
w highfield-farm.co.uk

SANDYHILL
Shropshire

Tall Trees
Rating Applied For
Self Catering
Contact: Mr & Mrs Roger & Rosemarie Jones
t (01743) 709503

SAXLINGHAM THORPE
Norfolk

Elmers Barn ★★★★
Self Catering
Norfolk Country Cottages
t (01603) 871872
e info@norfolkcottages.co.uk
w norfolkcottages.co.uk

Lodge Barn ★★★★
Self Catering
Norfolk Country Cottages
t (01603) 871872
e info@norfolkcottages.co.uk
w norfolkcottages.co.uk

SAXMUNDHAM
Suffolk

Albion Mill ★★★★
Self Catering
Suffolk Secrets
t (01502) 722717
e holidays@suffolk-secrets.co.uk
w suffolk-secrets.co.uk

Corner Cottage ★★★★
Self Catering
t (01277) 210551 & 07860 887653
e info@cornercottageholiday.com
w cornercottageholiday.com

Flora Cottage ★★★★
Self Catering
Suffolk Secrets
t (01502) 722717
e holidays@suffolk-secrets.co.uk
w suffolk-secrets.co.uk

Riverside Cottage ★★★
Self Catering
Suffolk Secrets
t (01502) 722717
e holidays@suffolk-secrets.co.uk
w suffolk-secrets.co.uk

Rookery Park ★★★★
Self Catering
Contact: Mrs Eden McDonald
t (01728) 668740
w tiscover.co.uk

SAXON STREET
Cambridgeshire

Syde House ★★★
Self Catering
Contact: Mrs Susan Greenwood
t (01638) 730044

SCALFORD
Leicestershire

The Bothy ★★★★
Self Catering
t (01664) 444730
e steve@robertsfarm.co.uk
w robertsfarm.co.uk

SCAMBLESBY
Lincolnshire

Brook House Barn ★★★★
Self Catering
Contact: Roger & Jucie Strawson
t (01507) 343266
e enquiry@brookhousefarm.com
w barnbreaks.co.uk

SCULTHORPE
Norfolk

1 Grove Farm Barns
★★★★★ *Self Catering*
Contact: Mrs Christine Banson
t (01328) 864427

Cottage ★★★ *Self Catering*
Contact: Mrs Margaret Chapman
t (01799) 527287
w tiscover.co.uk

Greenacre Bungalow ★★★
Self Catering
Contact: Mrs J Tuddenham
t (01328) 862858
w tiscover.co.uk

Kestrel Barn & Kingfisher Barn
Rating Applied For
Self Catering
Contact: Mr Tony Pointer
t (01328) 863965
e tony.pointer@dial.pipex.com
w piggybackbarns.com

SEA PALLING
Norfolk

The Old Cottage ★★★★
Self Catering
Norfolk Country Cottages
t (01603) 871872
e info@norfolkcottages.co.uk
w norfolkcottages.co.uk

Villa Voer ★★★ *Self Catering*
Norfolk Country Cottages
t (01603) 871872
e info@norfolkcottages.co.uk
w norfolkcottages.co.uk

SEDGEFORD
Norfolk

3 New England Cottages
★★★★ *Self Catering*
Norfolk Country Cottages
t (01603) 871872
e info@norfolkcottages.co.uk
w norfolkcottages.co.uk

Cobble Cottage ★★★★
Self Catering
Norfolk Country Cottages
t (01603) 871872
e info@norfolkcottages.co.uk
w norfolkcottages.co.uk

Highfield House ★★★★
Self Catering
Birds Norfolk Holiday Homes
t (01485) 534267
e shohol@birdsnorfolkholidayhomes.co.uk
w norfolkholidayhomes-birds.co.uk

West Lodge, Sedgeford
★★★★ *Self Catering*
Contact: Mrs Geraldine Tibbs
t (01485) 571770
w tiscover.co.uk

SELSTON
Nottinghamshire

Kinnaird ★★★★
Self Catering
Contact: Karen Barton
t (01623) 441278
e karen.barton10@btopenworld.com
w kinnaird-selston.co.uk

SEVERN STOKE
Worcestershire

Roseland Bungalow ★★★★
Self Catering
Contact: Mr & Mrs Guy & Mary Laurent
t (01905) 371463
e guy@roselandworcs.demon.co.uk
w roselandworcs.demon.co.uk

SHARDLOW
Derbyshire

The Old Workshop ★★★★
Self Catering
Contact: Mr Gary Hughes
t (01332) 792704
e theoldworkshop28@yahoo.co.uk

SHARRINGTON
Norfolk

Daubeney Cottage & The Granary ★★-★★★
Self Catering
Contact: Mrs Robin Burkitt
t (01263) 861412
e robin@daubeneyhallfarm.com
w daubeneyhallfarm.com

Gable Cottage ★★
Self Catering
Contact: Miss Mary Lakey
t (01263) 860393

Garden Cottage, Chequers
★★★★ *Self Catering*
Contact: Mrs R M Kimmins
t (01263) 860308
e rosemary@kimmins1.wanadoo.co.uk
w tiscover.co.uk

Stone Cottage ★★★
Self Catering
Norfolk Country Cottages
t (01603) 871872
e info@norfolkcottages.co.uk
w norfolkcottages.co.uk

SHEEN
Staffordshire

Bank Top Lodge ★★★★
Self Catering
Contact: Mrs Nancy Birch
t (01298) 84768

SHELDON
Derbyshire

Townend Cottage ★★★
Self Catering
Peak Cottages
t (0114) 262 0777
e enquiries@peakcottages.com
w peakcottages.com

SHELLEY
Suffolk

Ivy Tree Cottage Annexe
★★★ *Self Catering*
Contact: Mrs Hilary Lock
t (01473) 827632
w tiscover.co.uk

SHERINGHAM
Norfolk

10a Beeston Road ★★★★
Self Catering
Contact: Mr & Mrs Tricker
t (01953) 498639
e cottage.sheringham@googlemail.com

Augusta and Bennett
★★★-★★★★★ *Self Catering*
Contact: Mr Trevor Claydon
t (01263) 577560
e enquiries@sheringhamcottages.co.uk
w sheringhamcottages.co.uk

Look out for establishments participating in the National Accessible Scheme

Emmas ★★★ *Self Catering*
Norfolk Country Cottages
t (01603) 871872
e info@norfolkcottages.co.uk
w norfolkcottages.co.uk

Fishermans Cottages ★★★
Self Catering
Norfolk Country Cottages
t (01603) 871872
e info@norfolkcottages.co.uk
w norfolkcottages.co.uk

Flat 2 ★★★ *Self Catering*
Contact: Mrs Valerie Muggridge
Laburnham
t (01263) 712688

Flint Cottage ★★★
Self Catering
Contact: Mrs Christine Hyde
t (01603) 453700
e northnorfolkcottage@yahoo.co.uk
w northnorfolk-cottage.co.uk

Glendalough ★★★★
Self Catering
Contact: Mrs Janet Teather
t (01263) 825032
e janetandbrian@telinco.co.uk
w broadland.com/glendalough

Greenleas ★★★ *Self Catering*
Contact: Mr Harding
t (01263) 822054
e greenleas@talktalk.net
w greenleassheringham.com

Haven ★★★ *Self Catering*
Contact: Mrs Pam Pilkington
t (01773) 763010
e info@thehavensheringham.co.uk
w tiscover.co.uk

The Haven ★★★
Self Catering
Contact: Mrs Irene Buck
t (01263) 821281
e irene@buck1065.fsnet.co.uk
w thehavenholidayhome sheringham.com

High Lee ★★ *Self Catering*
Contact: Mrs Nelson
t (01245) 262436
w tiscover.co.uk

Ivydene ★★★ *Self Catering*
Contact: Mrs Jenny Linder
t (01263) 822990
e ivydeneholidays@tiscali.co.uk
w http://myweb.tiscali.co.uk/ivydene

Mabel Cottage ★★★
Self Catering
Norfolk Country Cottages
t (01603) 871872
e info@norfolkcottages.co.uk
w norfolkcottages.co.uk

SHERNBORNE
Norfolk

7 Mill Yard ★★★★
Self Catering
Norfolk Country Cottages
t (01603) 871872
e info@norfolkcottages.co.uk
w norfolkcottages.co.uk

The Old School Cottage
★★★★ *Self Catering*
Norfolk Country Cottages
t (01603) 871872
e info@norfolkcottages.co.uk
w norfolkcottages.co.uk

SHIFNAL
Shropshire

The Old Stable ★★★
Self Catering
Contact: Mr & Mrs R Wild
t (01952) 461136
e wildthings@raphaelsrestaurant.co.uk
w raphaelsrestaurant.co.uk

SHIMPLING
Suffolk

Maltings Farm Cottage
★★★★ *Self Catering*
Suffolk Secrets
t (01502) 722717
e holidays@suffolk-secrets.co.uk
w suffolk-secrets.co.uk

SHINGHAM
Norfolk

The Plantation ★★★★
Self Catering
t (01366) 328845
w theplantation.org

SHIPSTON-ON-STOUR
Warwickshire

Garden Cottage & Distillers Cottage ★★★ *Self Catering*
Contact: Mrs Liz Vernon Miller
t (01608) 682357
e liz@blackwellgrange.co.uk
w blackwellgrange.co.uk

Little Barn ★★★★
Self Catering
Contact: Mrs Karen Lawrence
t (01608) 684240
e johnandkaren.lawrence@ic24.net
w thelittlebarn.co.uk

SHIRLEY
Derbyshire

3 Church Cottages
Rating Applied For
Self Catering
Sykes Cottages
t (01244) 345700
e info@sykescottages.co.uk
w sykescottages.co.uk

Hall Farm Bungalow ★★★
Self Catering
Contact: Mrs Ruth Crabtree
t (01335) 360820
e sylviafoster@shirleyhallfarm.com
w shirleyhallfarm.com

SHOTLEY
Suffolk

Apartment ★★★★
Self Catering
Contact: Ms Deborah Baynes
t (01473) 788300
e deb@deborahbaynes.co.uk
w netherhall.net

Box Iron Cottage ★★★★
Self Catering
Contact: Mrs Sandra Rix
t (01277) 362912
w holidaysinsuffolk.co.uk

SHOTTERY
Warwickshire

6 Hathaway Hamlet ★★★★
Self Catering
Contact: Mr Rakesh Singh
t (01926) 810647
e rakeshmanhas@hotmail.com
w stratfordholidaylet.co.uk

Church Farm Barns
★★★★★ *Self Catering*
Contact: Mr Rakesh Singh
t (01926) 810647
e rakeshmanhas@hotmail.com
w stratfordholidaylet.co.uk

SHREWSBURY
Shropshire

12a Butcher Row ★★★★
Self Catering
Contact: Mrs Elizabeth Saxton
t 07793 604559
e butcher.row@ntlworld.com
w stmem.com/butcherrow

Barn Cottages ★★★★
Self Catering
Contact: Mr & Mrs Jon & Susan Good
t (01743) 355594
e barncottages@yahoo.co.uk
w barncottagesshrewsbury.com

Hotspur ★★★ *Self Catering*
Contact: Ms Miriam Doyle
t 00353 1 679 1551
e info@pka.ie

The Stables ★★★★
Self Catering
Contact: Ms Miriam Doylee info@pka.ie

Yews Barn ★★★★
Self Catering
Contact: Mr Glyn Passant
t (01743) 850308
e gpassant@aol.com
w yewsbarn.co.uk

SIBBERTOFT
Northamptonshire

Brook Meadow Chalets
★★★ *Self Catering*
Contact: Mary Hart
t (01858) 880886
e brookmeadow@farmline.co.uk
w brookmeadow.co.uk

SIBLE HEDINGHAM
Essex

Brickwall Farm ★★★★
Self Catering
Contact: Mrs Jean Fuller
t (01787) 460329
w brickwallfarm.co.uk

Pevors Farm Cottages
★★★★ *Self Catering*
Contact: Mrs Margaret Lewis
t (01787) 460830
w pevorsfarm.co.uk

SIBSEY
Lincolnshire

Sweetbriar ★★★
Self Catering
Contact: Mrs Alison Twiddy
t (01205) 750837
e twiddytowers@yahoo.co.uk
w cottageguide.co.uk

SIBTON
Suffolk

Bluebell, Bonny, Buttercup & Bertie ★★★★
Self Catering
Contact: Mrs Margaret Gray
t (01728) 668324
e mail@sibtonparkfarm.co.uk
w sibtonparkfarm.co.uk

Cardinal Cottage, Sibton
★★★★ *Self Catering*
Contact: Mr & Mrs Eric Belton
t (01728) 660111
e jan.belton@btinternet.com
w cardinalcottageholidays.co.uk

Mistletoe Cottage ★★★★
Self Catering
Contact: Mr & Mrs Derrick
t (01728) 668501
e owlleisure@hotmail.com

SKEGNESS
Lincolnshire

Court Royal
Rating Applied For
Self Catering
t (01754) 766408
e info@court-royal.co.uk
w court-royal.co.uk

Ingoldale Park ★★★★
Self Catering
Contact: Cathryn Whitehead
t (01754) 872335
e ingoldalepark@btopenworld.com
w ingoldmells.net

Island Holiday Apartments
★★★ *Self Catering*
Contact: Carol Haines
t (01754) 768952
e info@island-skegness.co.uk
w island-skegness.co.uk

Lyndene Holiday Apartment
★–★★★ *Self Catering*
Contact: Malcolm Bailey
t (01754) 766108
e info@lyndene-uk.com
w lyndene.co.uk

Quality Holiday Apartments
Rating Applied For
Self Catering
Contact: Judy Slater
t (01754) 763863
e info@quality-holiday-apartments.co.uk
w quality-holiday-apartments.co.uk

Spinney Lodge Holiday Flats
Rating Applied For
Self Catering
t (01754) 769789
e info@spinney-lodge.co.uk
w spinney-lodge.co.uk

Springfield Holiday Apartments ★–★★★
Self Catering
Contact: S Johnston
t (01507) 462735
e info@springfield-skegness.co.uk
w springfield-skegness.co.uk

Welcome Holiday Flats
Rating Applied For
Self Catering
Contact: Mr A P Wass
t (01754) 610704
e peterwass@onetel.com

SLOLEY
Norfolk

Piggery Cottage ★★★★
Self Catering
Contact: Mrs Ann Jones
t (01692) 536281
w sloleyfarmcottages.co.uk

SNAPE
Suffolk

Granary And The Forge ★★★★ *Self Catering*
Contact: Mrs Sally Gillett
t (01728) 688254
w croftfarmsnape.co.uk

Jubilee Cottage ★★★★
Self Catering
Suffolk Secrets
t (01502) 722717
e holidays@suffolk-secrets.co.uk
w suffolk-secrets.co.uk

Mulberry Cottage ★★★★
Self Catering
Suffolk Secrets
t (01502) 722717
e holidays@suffolk-secrets.co.uk
w suffolk-secrets.co.uk

Snape Maltings
★★★–★★★★ *Self Catering*
Contact: Miss Kate Sibthorpe
t (01728) 688303
w snapemaltings.co.uk

Squirrel Cottages
Rating Applied For
Self Catering
Contact: Caroline Beach
t (01728) 689136
e sutton144@btinternet.com
w holidaycottagessnape.co.uk

Studio Flat ★★★
Self Catering
Contact: Mrs Kathy Ball
t (01728) 688327
w churchgarage accommodation.co.uk

SNELSTON
Derbyshire

Owls Roost
Rating Applied For
Self Catering
Contact: Rachel Ward
t (01335) 324058
e ward@brookbarn.fsnet.co.uk

SNETTISHAM
Norfolk

4 The Courtyard ★★★★
Self Catering
Contact: Mrs Jennifer Overson
t (01406) 422569
w cottageguide.co.uk/4.thecourtyard

85/86 Shepherds Port
Approved Caravan Holiday Home
Contact: Ms Barbara Devonshire-Ward
Sunnyside
t (01553) 636343

Alexandra Villa ★★★★
Self Catering
Norfolk Country Cottages
t (01603) 871872
e info@norfolkcottages.co.uk
w norfolkcottages.co.uk

Bumbles ★★★ *Self Catering*
Birds Norfolk Holiday Homes
t (01485) 534267
e shohol@birdsnorfolkholidayhomes.co.uk
w norfolkholidayhomes-birds.co.uk

Carpenters Lodge ★★★
Self Catering
Contact: Mrs Marilyn Madgett
t (01485) 541580
w carpenterslodge.co.uk

Coach House Barn ★★★
Self Catering
Contact: Mrs Marion Peters-Loader
t (01485) 544902

Cobbe Court ★★★
Self Catering
Contact: Mrs Valerie Douglas
t (01485) 543986

Cursons and Fishermans Cottage ★★★★ *Self Catering*
Contact: Mrs Averil Campbell
t (01485) 541179
w campbellsofsnettisham.co.uk

Driftwood ★★★★
Self Catering
Norfolk Country Cottages
t (01603) 871872
e info@norfolkcottages.co.uk
w norfolkcottages.co.uk

Hollies Cottage and Grooms Cottage ★★★★ *Self Catering*
Contact: Mrs Elaine Aldridge
t (01485) 518760

Lavender Cottage ★★★
Self Catering
Contact: Mrs Rosa Barry
t (01485) 541280

Old Farm House Cottage
★★★★ *Self Catering*
Contact: Mrs Jacqueline Sandy
t (01485) 543106
e jacqueline.sandy@tesco.net
w tiscover.co.uk

Orangery Lodge ★★★★
Self Catering
Norfolk Country Cottages
t (01603) 871872
e info@norfolkcottages.co.uk
w norfolkcottages.co.uk

Owl Barn ★★★★
Self Catering
Birds Norfolk Holiday Homes
t (01485) 534267
e shohol@birdsnorfolkholidayhomes.co.uk
w norfolkholidayhomes-birds.co.uk

The Smithy ★★★
Self Catering
Birds Norfolk Holiday Homes
t (01485) 534267
e shohol@birdsnorfolkholidayhomes.co.uk
w norfolkholidayhomes-birds.co.uk

Southwing Snettisham House ★★★★ *Self Catering*
Norfolk Country Cottages
t (01603) 871872
e info@norfolkcottages.co.uk
w norfolkcottages.co.uk

SNITTERTON
Derbyshire

Midsummer Cottage ★★★★
Self Catering
Peak Cottages
t (0114) 262 0777
e enquiries@peakcottages.com
w peakcottages.com

Old Masson Barn ★★★★
Self Catering
Peak Cottages
t (0114) 262 0777
e enquiries@peakcottages.com
w peakcottages.com

SOHAM
Cambridgeshire

Hall Croft House ★★★
Self Catering
Contact: Ms Nadine Smith
t (01353) 722842
e nadine.smith@btconnect.com

Poppies ★★★★ *Self Catering*
Contact: Ms Roseann Allum
t (01353) 624541

SOLIHULL
West Midlands

Tudor Coppice ★★★
Serviced Apartments
Contact: Ms Dawn Barnes
t (0121) 711 7491
e dawn@solitel.co.uk
w tudorcoppice.co.uk

SOMERTON
Suffolk

Cartlodge & Granary
★★★★ *Self Catering*
Contact: Mrs Sarah Worboys
t (01284) 789241
e enquiries@francisfarmcottages.co.uk
w francisfarmcottages.co.uk

SOUTH BENFLEET
Essex

Alices Place ★★★★
Self Catering
Contact: Mr Stephen Millward
t (01268) 756283
w alices-place.co.uk

SOUTH BURLINGHAM
Norfolk

Church Farm ★★★
Self Catering
Norfolk Country Cottages
t (01603) 871872
e info@norfolkcottages.co.uk
w norfolkcottages.co.uk

SOUTH COCKERINGTON
Lincolnshire

Grasswells Farm Holiday Cottages ★★★★
Self Catering
Contact: Ms Janice Foster
Grasswells Holiday Cottages (Saddleback Leisure Ltd)
t (01507) 338508
e thefosters2002@talk-email.com

West View Cottages ★★★
Self Catering
Contact: Mr Richard Nicholson and Mrs Judith Hand
t (01507) 327209 & 07855 291185
e enquiries@west-view.co.uk
w west-view.co.uk

SOUTH MIMMS
Hertfordshire

The Black Swan ★★–★★★
Self Catering
Contact: Mr Marsterson
t (01707) 644180
e wmarsterson@yahoo.co.uk

SOUTH WALSHAM
Norfolk

Charity Barn ★★★★
Self Catering
Norfolk Country Cottages
t (01603) 871872
e info@norfolkcottages.co.uk
w norfolkcottages.co.uk

SOUTHAM
Warwickshire

The Barn ★★★★
Self Catering
t (01676) 541051
e rakeshmanhas@hotmail.com
w stratfordholidaylet.co.uk

SOUTHBURGH
Norfolk

Park Farm Barns ★★★★
Self Catering
Contact: Mrs Rosemary Bunning
t (01362) 820702
w parkfarmbarns.co.uk

SOUTHEND-ON-SEA
Essex

Everhome Apartments
★★★ *Self Catering*
Contact: Mr Malcolm Taylor
t (01702) 434320
e malcolm-t@btconnect.com
w everhome.co.uk

SOUTHMINSTER
Essex

Avonmore ★★★★
Self Catering
Contact: Mr Bull
t (01787) 280063

SOUTHWELL
Nottinghamshire

The Hayloft, Little Tithe & Dovecote ★★★★
Self Catering
Contact: Mrs Wilson
t (01636) 830497
w lodgebarns.com

Oxtonhill Cottages
Rating Applied For
Self Catering
Contact: Vivien Carter
t (0115) 965 5739
e info@oxtonhillcottages.co.uk
w oxtonhillcottages.co.uk

SOUTHWOLD
Suffolk

11 Chester Road ★★★
Self Catering
Suffolk Holidays
t (01502) 723571
e info@holidaysinsuffolk.co.uk

12b Douglas House ★★★
Self Catering
Acanthus Property Letting Services
t (01502) 724033
e websales@southwold-holidays.co.uk
w southwold-holidays.co.uk

15 Pier Avenue ★★★
Self Catering
Suffolk Secrets
t (01502) 722717
e holidays@suffolk-secrets.co.uk
w suffolk-secrets.co.uk

15 Stradbroke Road ★★★
Self Catering
89 High Street
t (01502) 723292
w haadnams.com

17 South Green ★★★
Self Catering
Suffolk Secrets
t (01502) 722717
e holidays@suffolk-secrets.co.uk
w suffolk-secrets.co.uk

20 St James Green ★★★
Self Catering
Contact: Mrs Jacquie Atkinson
t (020) 8372 1677
w visit-southwold.com/20stjamesgreen

4 Pier Court ★★ *Self Catering*
Suffolk Holidays Ltd
t (01502) 723571
e sales@holidaysinsuffolk.co.uk
w holidaysinsuffolk.co.uk

5 Blackshore Cottages
★★★★ *Self Catering*
Suffolk Secrets
t (01502) 722717
e holidays@suffolk-secrets.co.uk
w suffolk-secrets.co.uk

5 St James' Green ★★★
Self Catering
Contact: Mrs Teresa Lynch
t (020) 8422 3622
e stjamesgreen@hotmail.co.uk
w exploresouthwold.co.uk/5stjamesgreen

68 Victoria Street ★★★
Self Catering
Acanthus Property Letting Services
t (01502) 724033
e websales@southwold-holidays.co.uk
w southwold-holidays.co.uk

8 Dunwich Road ★★★★
Self Catering
Suffolk Secrets
t (01502) 722717
e holidays@suffolk-secrets.co.uk
w suffolk-secrets.co.uk

Anchor Point ★★★
Self Catering
Suffolk Secrets
t (01502) 722717
e holidays@suffolk-secrets.co.uk
w suffolk-secrets.co.uk

Blackbird Cottage ★★★
Self Catering
Suffolk Holidays Ltd
t (01502) 723571
e sales@holidaysinsuffolk.co.uk
w holidaysinsuffolk.co.uk

Blackshore Corner ★★★★
Self Catering
Suffolk Secrets
t (01502) 722717
e holidays@suffolk-secrets.co.uk
w suffolk-secrets.co.uk

Bligh Cottage ★★★
Self Catering
Suffolk Holidays Ltd
t (01502) 723571
e sales@holidaysinsuffolk.co.uk
w holidaysinsuffolk.co.uk

The Bolt Hole ★★★
Self Catering
Suffolk Secrets
t (01502) 722717
e holidays@suffolk-secrets.co.uk
w suffolk-secrets.co.uk

Castle Keep ★★★★
Self Catering
Suffolk Secrets
t (01502) 722717
e holidays@suffolk-secrets.co.uk
w suffolk-secrets.co.uk

Cautley Cottage ★★★
Self Catering
Contact: David & Caroline Goodman
t (020) 8444 7210
w southwoldcottageholidays.co.uk

Cherry Trees ★★★★
Self Catering
Suffolk Secrets
t (01502) 722717
e holidays@suffolk-secrets.co.uk
w suffolk-secrets.co.uk

Chicago Beach Villa ★★★
Self Catering
Suffolk Holidays Ltd
t (01502) 723571
e sales@holidaysinsuffolk.co.uk
w holidaysinsuffolk.co.uk

Cliff House ★★★★
Self Catering
Suffolk Secrets
t (01502) 722717
e holidays@suffolk-secrets.co.uk
w suffolk-secrets.co.uk

The Coach House and Rosemary Cottage ★★★
Self Catering
Contact: Phil & Philippa Champain
t (01502) 725414
e reydoncottages@btinternet.com
w rosemarycottage.southwold.info

Cobbler's Cottage ★★★
Self Catering
Acanthus Property Letting Services
t (01502) 724033
e websales@southwold-holidays.co.uk
w southwold-holidays.co.uk

Corner Cottage ★★★
Self Catering
HA Adnams
t (01502) 723292
w haadnamsholidaycottages.co.uk

Cottage ★★★★ *Self Catering*
Contact: Mr Trevor Thomas
t (01502) 723561

The Dolls House ★★★
Self Catering
Suffolk Secrets
t (01502) 722717
e holidays@suffolk-secrets.co.uk
w suffolk-secrets.co.uk

The Drift
Rating Applied For
Self Catering
Acanthus Property Letting Services
t (01502) 724033
e websales@southwold-holidays.co.uk
w southwold-holidays.co.uk

Eastway Cottage ★★★★
Self Catering
Acanthus Property Letting Services
t (01502) 724033
e websales@southwold-holidays.co.uk
w southwold-holidays.co.uk

Elms Mews ★★★
Self Catering
Acanthus Property Letting Services
t (01502) 724033
e websales@southwold-holidays.co.uk
w southwold-holidays.co.uk

Eversley Heights ★★★★
Self Catering
Suffolk Secrets
t (01502) 722717
e holidays@suffolk-secrets.co.uk
w suffolk-secrets.co.uk

Fairwinds ★★ *Self Catering*
HA Adnams
t (01502) 723292
w haadnamsholidaycottages.co.uk

Far Horizons ★★★★
Self Catering
Suffolk Secrets
t (01502) 722717
e holidays@suffolk-secrets.co.uk
w suffolk-secrets.co.uk

Ferry Cottage ★★★
Self Catering
Suffolk Holidays Ltd
t (01502) 723571
e sales@holidaysinsuffolk.co.uk
w holidaysinsuffolk.co.uk

Fisherman's Cottage ★★★★
Self Catering
Contact: Ms Victoria Seale
t 07973 113369
e victoriaseale@btconnect.com
w fishermanscottage southwold.co.uk

Harbour Cottage ★★★
Self Catering
Suffolk Secrets
t (01502) 722717
e holidays@suffolk-secrets.co.uk
w suffolk-secrets.co.uk

The Haven ★★★
Self Catering
Suffolk Secrets
t (01502) 722717
e holidays@suffolk-secrets.co.uk
w suffolk-secrets.co.uk

Heathside ★★★
Self Catering
Acanthus Property Letting Services
t (01502) 724033
e websales@southwold-holidays.co.uk
w southwold-holidays.co.uk

Hightide ★★★ *Self Catering*
Acanthus Property Letting Services
t (01502) 724033
e websales@southwold-holidays.co.uk
w southwold-holidays.co.uk

Holly Cottage ★★★★
Self Catering
Suffolk Secrets
t (01502) 722717
e holidays@suffolk-secrets.co.uk
w suffolk-secrets.co.uk

Hollyhocks Cottage ★★★
Self Catering
Suffolk Holidays Ltd
t (01502) 723571
e sales@holidaysinsuffolk.co.uk
w holidaysinsuffolk.co.uk

The Homestead ★★★★
Self Catering
Suffolk Secrets
t (01502) 722717
e holidays@suffolk-secrets.co.uk
w suffolk-secrets.co.uk

Horseshoe Cottage ★★★
Self Catering
Acanthus Property Letting Services
t (01502) 724033
e websales@southwold-holidays.co.uk
w southwold-holidays.co.uk

Jersey Lodge ★★★★
Self Catering
Suffolk Secrets
t (01502) 722717
e holidays@suffolk-secrets.co.uk
w suffolk-secrets.co.uk

Little Haven ★★★
Self Catering
Suffolk Holidays Ltd
t (01502) 723571
e sales@holidaysinsuffolk.co.uk
w holidaysinsuffolk.co.uk

Maisonette ★★★★
Self Catering
HA Adnams
t (01502) 723292
w haadnamsholidaycottages.co.uk

Manor Lodge ★★★★
Self Catering
Acanthus Property Letting Services
t (01502) 724033
e websales@southwold-holidays.co.uk
w southwold-holidays.co.uk

Middling ★★★★
Self Catering
Suffolk Secrets
t (01502) 722717
e holidays@suffolk-secrets.co.uk
w suffolk-secrets.co.uk

No 12 The Craighurst
★★★★ *Self Catering*
Acanthus Property Letting Services
t (01502) 724033
e websales@southwold-holidays.co.uk
w southwold-holidays.co.uk

No. 7 The Craighurst ★★★
Self Catering
Acanthus Property Letting Services
t (01502) 724033
e websales@southwold-holidays.co.uk
w southwold-holidays.co.uk

Nuage ★★★ *Self Catering*
Suffolk Holidays Ltd
t (01502) 723571
e sales@holidaysinsuffolk.co.uk
w holidaysinsuffolk.co.uk

Old Rope House ★★★★
Self Catering
Contact: Mrs Sian Mortlock
t (01502) 724769
e sian@theoldropehouse.co.uk
w theoldropehouse.co.uk

Palm House ★★★★
Self Catering
Suffolk Secrets
t (01502) 722717
e holidays@suffolk-secrets.co.uk
w suffolk-secrets.co.uk

Pebbles Cottage ★★★
Self Catering
Acanthus Property Letting Services
t (01502) 724033
e websales@southwold-holidays.co.uk
w southwold-holidays.co.uk

Pier View ★★★★
Self Catering
Suffolk Secrets
t (01502) 722717
e holidays@suffolk-secrets.co.uk
w suffolk-secrets.co.uk

Pink House ★★ *Self Catering*
Suffolk Holidays Ltd
t (01502) 723571
e sales@holidaysinsuffolk.co.uk
w holidaysinsuffolk.co.uk

Poplar Hall ★★★★
Self Catering
Contact: Mrs Anna Garwood
t (01502) 578549
w southwold.ws/poplar-hall

Poppys ★★★ *Self Catering*
Suffolk Holidays Ltd
t (01502) 723571
e sales@holidaysinsuffolk.co.uk
w holidaysinsuffolk.co.uk

Red Roofs ★★★
Self Catering
Suffolk Secrets
t (01502) 722717
e holidays@suffolk-secrets.co.uk
w suffolk-secrets.co.uk

The Reeds ★★★
Self Catering
Suffolk Secrets
t (01502) 722717
e holidays@suffolk-secrets.co.uk
w suffolk-secrets.co.uk

The Retreat ★★★
Self Catering
Acanthus Property Letting Services
t (01502) 724033
e websales@southwold-holidays.co.uk
w southwold-holidays.co.uk

Riverside ★★★ *Self Catering*
Suffolk Secrets
t (01502) 722717
e holidays@suffolk-secrets.co.uk
w suffolk-secrets.co.uk

Rutland House ★★★★★
Self Catering
Acanthus Property Letting Services
t (01502) 724033
e websales@southwold-holidays.co.uk
w southwold-holidays.co.uk

Saffron and Church Green Cottage ★★★★ *Self Catering*
t (01502) 724033

Saltings ★★★ *Self Catering*
Suffolk Secrets
t (01502) 722717
e holidays@suffolk-secrets.co.uk
w suffolk-secrets.co.uk

Seaford House ★★★
Self Catering
Suffolk Secrets
t (01502) 722717
e holidays@suffolk-secrets.co.uk
w suffolk-secrets.co.uk

Seaside House
Rating Applied For
Self Catering
Suffolk Secrets
t (01502) 722717
e holidays@suffolk-secrets.co.uk
w suffolk-secrets.co.uk

Seaward ★★★ *Self Catering*
Acanthus Property Letting Services
t (01502) 724033
e websales@southwold-holidays.co.uk
w southwold-holidays.co.uk

Shrimp Cottage ★★★
Self Catering
Suffolk Secrets
t (01502) 722717
e holidays@suffolk-secrets.co.uk
w suffolk-secrets.co.uk

Smoke House ★★
Self Catering
Suffolk Holidays Ltd
t (01502) 723571
e sales@holidaysinsuffolk.co.uk
w holidaysinsuffolk.co.uk

Solely Southwold ★★★
Self Catering
Contact: Miss Kathy Oliver
t (01502) 578383
e kathy@solely-southwold.co.uk
w solely-southwold.co.uk

Suffolk House ★★★
Self Catering
Contact: Mrs Betty Freeman
t (01502) 723742
w tiscover.co.uk

Summerly Cottage ★★★
Self Catering
Contact: David & Caroline Goodman
t (020) 8444 7210
w southwoldcottageholidays.co.uk

Tittlemouse House ★★★
Self Catering
Suffolk Secrets
t (01502) 722717
e holidays@suffolk-secrets.co.uk
w suffolk-secrets.co.uk

Trinity Cottage ★★★★
Self Catering
Acanthus Property Letting Services
t (01502) 724033
e websales@southwold-holidays.co.uk
w southwold-holidays.co.uk

Trinity Street 10 ★★★★
Self Catering
Acanthus Property Letting Services
t (01502) 724033
e websales@southwold-holidays.co.uk
w southwold-holidays.co.uk

Weathervane ★★★
Self Catering
Suffolk Secrets
t (01502) 722717
e holidays@suffolk-secrets.co.uk
w suffolk-secrets.co.uk

Weavers Cottage ★★★
Self Catering
HA Adnams
t (01502) 723292
w haadnamsholidaycottages.co.uk

The Wee House ★★★
Self Catering
Suffolk Holidays Ltd
t (01502) 723571
e sales@holidaysinsuffolk.co.uk
w holidaysinsuffolk.co.uk

Well Cottage ★★★
Self Catering
Suffolk Secrets
t (01502) 722717
e holidays@suffolk-secrets.co.uk
w suffolk-secrets.co.uk

White Cottage ★★★
Self Catering
Suffolk Secrets
t (01502) 722717
e holidays@suffolk-secrets.co.uk
w suffolk-secrets.co.uk

Whitehouse Barns ★★★★
Self Catering
Contact: Mrs Penelope Roskell-Griffiths
t (020) 8802 6258
e peneloperoskell@blueyonder.co.uk
w whitehousebarns.co.uk

SPARROWPIT
Derbyshire

Daisy Bank and Hope Cottages ★★★ *Self Catering*
Contact: Mrs Hilary Batterbee
t (01298) 813027
e mail@sparrowpit.com
w sparrowpit.com

SPILSBY
Lincolnshire

Northfields Farm Cottages
★★★ *Self Catering*
Contact: Mr W P Miller
t (01507) 588251
e chrismiller@tiscali.co.uk
w northfieldsfarmcottages.co.uk

STAINFIELD
Lincolnshire

Rural Roosts ★★★★
Self Catering
Contact: Katie Olivant
t (01526) 398492 & 07712 771102
e katie@ruralroosts.co.uk
w ruralroosts.co.uk

STAINTON BY LANGWORTH
Lincolnshire

Church Farmhouse ★★★★
Self Catering
Contact: Chris Valentine
t (01673) 862775
e churchfarmhouse2003@supanet.com
w churchfarmproperties.com

STALHAM
Norfolk

Chapelfield Cottage Apartment ★★★
Self Catering
Contact: Mr Gary Holmes
Chapelfield Cottage Flat
t (01692) 582173
e chapelfield_hols@btinternet.com
w chapelfieldcottage.co.uk

STAMFORD
Lincolnshire

Elder Flower Cottage, Belmesthorpe ★★★
Self Catering
Contact: Mr P & Mrs D Wilkinson
t (01780) 757188 & 07711 533204
e philipwdawn@btinternet.com

The Granary ★★★★
Self Catering
Contact: Mrs Katie Maitland
t (01778) 590085
e mkmaitland@hotmail.com

Nene Way Holiday Cottage, Nassington ★★★★
Self Catering
Contact: Mrs Maureen Dolby
t (01780) 783352
e dolby97@btinternet.com

Riverside View ★★★
Self Catering
Contact: Ms Tina Kirby
Universal Property
t 07752 361362
e unip@talk21.com

STANBRIDGE
Bedfordshire

Bluegate Farm Holiday Cottages ★★★★
Self Catering
Contact: Mrs Philippa Michie
t (01525) 210621
w bluegatecottages.co.uk

STANFIELD
Norfolk

Spennithorne Cottage ★★★★ *Self Catering*
Contact: Mr & Mrs Gill & Les Smith
t (01328) 700901
w spennithorne.com

STANFORD BRIDGE
Worcestershire

The Riseling ★★★★
Self Catering
t 0870 027 5930

STANHOE
Norfolk

Pilgrims ★★★ *Self Catering*
Norfolk Country Cottages
t (01603) 871872
e info@norfolkcottages.co.uk
w norfolkcottages.co.uk

Vine Cottage ★★★
Self Catering
Contact: Mrs Alyson Aronson
The Crow's Nest
t (01737) 832584
w vinecottagenorfolk.co.uk

STANSTED
Essex

The Priory ★★★★
Self Catering
Contact: Mrs Karen Thompson
t (01371) 870547 & 07771 880077
e bookings@tiltypriory.co.uk
w tiltypriory.co.uk

STANSTED MOUNTFITCHET
Essex

Walpole Farm House
★★★-★★★★ *Self Catering*
Contact: Mrs Jill Walton
t (01279) 812265
e jill@jsawalton.demon.co.uk
w walpolefarmhouse.com

STANTON
Suffolk

Cottage Farm Annexe ★★★
Self Catering
Suffolk Secrets
t (01502) 722717
e holidays@suffolk-secrets.co.uk
w suffolk-secrets.co.uk

STANTON-BY-BRIDGE
Derbyshire

Woodland Hills Court
Rating Applied For
Self Catering
Contact: David & Mary Kidd
t (01332) 863152
e info@ivy-house-farm.com
w ivy-house-farm.com

STANTON IN PEAK
Derbyshire

Rock House ★★★
Self Catering
Contact: Sandra Steverson
t (01298) 872418
e paul@rockhouse-peakdistrict.co.uk

STANTON LACY
Shropshire

Meadow Barn ★★★★★
Self Catering
Contact: Mrs Lisa Morgan
t (01584) 861249
e info@littlesuttonfarm.co.uk
w littlesuttonfarm.co.uk

STATHERN
Leicestershire

Sycamore Farm ★★★★
Self Catering
Contact: Miss Ruth Stanley
t (01949) 860640

STEWTON
Lincolnshire

Westfield Farm Cottages
★★★-★★★★ *Self Catering*
Contact: Chris Berry
t (01507) 354892
e enquiries@westfieldfarmcottages.co.uk
w westfieldfarmcottages.co.uk

STIBBARD
Norfolk

Kings Cottage Barn ★★★
Self Catering
Norfolk Country Cottages
t (01603) 871872
e info@norfolkcottages.co.uk
w norfolkcottages.co.uk

STIFFKEY
Norfolk

Bella's Cottage ★★★
Self Catering
Norfolk Country Cottages
t (01603) 871872
e info@norfolkcottages.co.uk
w norfolkcottages.co.uk

Harbour House ★★★★
Self Catering
Contact: Mr Keith Bindley
t (01603) 270637
e teresa.bindley@virgin.net
w tiscover.co.uk

Hawthorns ★★★★
Self Catering
Contact: Mrs Madeline Hickey-Smith
t (01223) 572316
e hawthorns_norfolk@hotmail.com
w hawthorns.info

Mount Tabor ★★★
Self Catering
Contact: Mrs Pat Norris
t (0161) 633 6834
e stiffkeycottage@ntlworld.com
w tiscover.co.uk

Nellie's Cottage ★★★
Self Catering
Norfolk Country Cottages
t (01603) 871872
e info@norfolkcottages.co.uk
w norfolkcottages.co.uk

Primrose Cottage ★★★
Self Catering
Contact: Mrs Pearson
t (01328) 830303
w tiscover.co.uk

Red Lion Cottages 2 ★★★
Self Catering
Contact: Ms Jane Whitaker
t (01606) 892368
e jane.pathways@virgin.net
w tiscover.co.uk

Shrimp Cottage ★★
Self Catering
Norfolk Country Cottages
t (01603) 871872
e info@norfolkcottages.co.uk
w norfolkcottages.co.uk

STILTON
Cambridgeshire

Orchard Cottage ★★★★
Self Catering
Contact: Mrs Jennifer Higgo
t (01572) 737420
w higgo.com/orchard

STIPERSTONES
Shropshire

Resting Hill ★★★
Self Catering
Contact: Mrs Marlene Rowson
t (01743) 791219
w stmem.com/restinghill

STISTED
Essex

Ballaglass ★★★★
Self Catering
Contact: Mrs Sally Dunn
t (01376) 331409

STOKE BRUERNE
Northamptonshire

3 Canalside ★★★
Self Catering
Contact: Mr Trevor Morley
t (01604) 862107
w stokebruerneboats.co.uk

STOKE-BY-NAYLAND
Suffolk

Cobbs Cottage ★★★★
Self Catering
Contact: Mr Mark Scott
t (01787) 211115
w grove-cottages.co.uk

STOKE-ON-TRENT
Staffordshire

Bank End Farm Cottage
★★★★ *Self Catering*
Contact: Mr Ken Meredith
t (01782) 502160
e pete502@btopenworld.com

Field Head Farm House Holidays ★★★★
Self Catering
Contact: Ms Janet Hudson
t (01538) 308352
e janet@field-head.co.uk
w field-head.co.uk

Lockwood Hall Farm ★★★★
Self Catering
Contact: Mrs Rebecca Sherratt
t (01538) 752270
e rebecca@lockwoodhallfarm.co.uk
w lockwoodhallfarm.co.uk

Low Roofs ★★★
Self Catering
Contact: Mrs Lesley Malkin
t (01782) 627087

Moorcourt Holiday Cottages
★★★★ *Self Catering*
Contact: Les & Vanessa Bradshawe **e** vbradshaw@moorcourtcottages.co.uk
w moorcourtcottages.co.uk

STOKE ST MILBOROUGH
Shropshire

St Milburga Chapel ★★★★
Self Catering
Contact: Mr & Mrs Claude & Wendy Bodenham
t (01584) 823626
e claude@clbodenham.com
w stmilburga-holidayhomes.com

STOURPORT-ON-SEVERN
Worcestershire

17 Lodge Cottages ★★★★
Self Catering
Contact: Mr & Mrs Stuart & Sara Peace
229 Thacker Street
e sarapeace@aapt.net.au

STOURTON
Staffordshire

The Barn ★★★ *Self Catering*
Contact: Mrs Linda Thornton
t (01384) 390520
w blackcountrystays.com

STOWMARKET
Suffolk

Barn Cottages ★★★★
Self Catering
Contact: Mrs Maria Tydeman
t (01449) 711229
w barncottages.co.uk

Kimberley Cottage ★★★
Self Catering
Contact: Mr Brian Whiting
t (01449) 677766
w kimberleyhall.biz

STRADBROKE
Suffolk

Cornhouse Cottage ★★★★
Self Catering
Contact: Mrs Charmaine Cooper
t (01379) 384256
w hepwoodcottages.co.uk

STRATFORD ST ANDREW
Suffolk

Toad Hall Flat ★★★
Self Catering
Contact: Mr Perry & Bunty Hunt
t (01728) 603463

STRATFORD ST MARY
Suffolk

Donkey Cottage ★★★
Self Catering
Suffolk Secrets
t (01502) 722717
e holidays@suffolk-secrets.co.uk
w suffolk-secrets.co.uk

STRATFORD-UPON-AVON
Warwickshire

4 Bancroft Place ★★★
Self Catering
Contact: Mr & Mrs D Barnett
t (01920) 871849
e carolannbarnett@yahoo.co.uk
w 4bancroftplace.com

4 Flower Court ★★★★
Self Catering
Contact: Mrs Rachel Liddell
No. 4 Flower Court
t (01386) 438833
e liddellrachel@aol.com
w flowercourt.co.uk

42 Shakespeare Street
★★★★ *Self Catering*
Contact: Ms Sarah Field
t (01789) 298141
e kdfield@stratfordholidaycottages.com
w stratfordholidaycottages.com

50 Ely Street
Rating Applied For
Self Catering
Hideaways
t (01747) 828170
e enq@hideaways.co.uk
w hideaways.co.uk

As You Like It
★★★-★★★★ *Self Catering*
Contact: Mr & Mrs Ian & Janet Reid
"As You Like It""
t (01789) 450266
e ian@alderminster99.freeserve.co.uk
w alderminster99.freeserve.co.uk

Chestnut Cottage, Pathlow
★★★ *Self Catering*
Contact: Mrs Joyce Rush
t (01789) 292764

The Cottage at Fosbroke House ★★★ *Self Catering*
Contact: Mrs Susan Swift
t (01789) 772327
e mark@swiftvilla.fsnet.co.uk
w smoothhound.co.uk/hotels/fosbroke.html

Crimscote Downs Farm Holiday Cottages
★★★-★★★★ *Self Catering*
Contact: Joan James
t (01789) 450275
e joan.james@tesco.net

Falcon Cottage ★★★★
Self Catering
Contact: Ms Kim Day
t (020) 8366 0237
e falconcottage@aol.com
w falcon-cottage.co.uk

Heritage Mews ★★★★★
Self Catering
Contact: Ms Val Broke-Smith
t (01564) 778649
e heritagemews@blueyonder.co.uk
w heritagemews.co.uk

No. 7 Bull Street ★★★
Self Catering
Contact: Mrs Sally-Ann Salmon
t (01675) 443613
e sallyann_salmon@yahoo.co.uk
w no7bullstreet.co.uk

Rivermeets Lodge ★★★★
Self Catering
Contact: Mr & Mrs D. Gray
t 07715 748146
e david.gray6@homecall.co.uk
w rivermeetslodge.co.uk

Riverview Lodge & River Haven Lodge ★★★★
Self Catering
t 07802 640372
e info@luxurylifestylelodges.co.uk
w luxurylifestylelodges.co.uk

Rydal Cottage ★★★★
Self Catering
Contact: Mrs Fay Frampton
t 07765 573428
e fay.fram@btopenworld.com
w stratford-selfcatering.co.uk

Stratford Cottages
★★★★ *Self Catering*
Contact: Elaine Cooke bookcottage@btinternet.com
w stratfordcottage.com

Woodcote ★★★★★ *Self Catering & Serviced Apartments*
Contact: Mr & Mrs Lucas
t (01789) 293932
e lucasstratford@aol.com
w lucasstratford.co.uk

STRENSHAM
Worcestershire

The Parlour, Home Farm, Nr Upton upon Severn ★★★★
Self Catering
Contact: Mrs Mandy Davenport
t (01684) 293685 & 07709 239652
e mdavenport@beeb.net
w parlour-cottage.co.uk

STRETTON
Rutland

Stretton Lakes ★★★★
Self Catering
Contact: Rachel Needham
t (01780) 410507
e info@strettonlakes.co.uk
w strettonlakes.co.uk

STUBWOOD
Staffordshire

Aldersbrook Cottage
★★★★ *Self Catering*
Contact: Mrs Joyce Boden
t (01889) 590253
w aldersbrookcottage.co.uk

STURTON-BY-STOW
Lincolnshire

The Apple Store ★★★★
Self Catering
Contact: Lisa Atkinson
t (01427) 787387
e info@applestorecottages.co.uk
w applestorecottages.co.uk

STUTTON
Suffolk

The Lookout ★★★★
Self Catering
Contact: John & Penny Fairrie
t (01473) 328294
w mrsjanegoodltd.co.uk

SUCKLEY
Worcestershire

Tundridge Mill ★★★★★
Self Catering
Contact: Mrs Penny Beard
t (01886) 884478
w tundridgemill.co.uk

SUTTON
Norfolk

Kingfisher Cottage & Heron Cottage ★★★★ *Self Catering*
Norfolk Country Cottages
t (01603) 871872
e info@norfolkcottages.co.uk
w norfolkcottages.co.uk

SUTTON-ON-SEA
Lincolnshire

Country Retreat Equestrian Lodges ★★★-★★★★
Self Catering
Contact: Ms Maria Spradbury
t (01507) 442631
e mariaequestrian@aol.com
w blackcatequestriancentre.co.uk

Hawthorne Farm ★★★★
Self Catering
t (01507) 472156
w turlincs.co.uk

Poplar Farm Holiday Cottages ★★★★
Self Catering
Contact: Helen Matthews
t (01507) 443112
e helen.matthews@btopenworld.com
w poplar-farm.org.uk

Sycamore Lodge Holiday Flat
Rating Applied For
Self Catering
Contact: Sheila Middleton
t (01507) 441180

SUTTON ON THE HILL
Derbyshire

The Chop House & The Hay Loft ★★★★ *Self Catering*
Contact: Keith & Joan Lennard
Windle Hill Farm Cottages
t (01283) 732377
e windlehill@btinternet.com
w windlehill.btinternet.co.uk

SWADLINCOTE
Derbyshire

Forest Lodges, Rosliston
★★★ *Self Catering*
Contact: Ms Marie Hall
t (01283) 519119
e marion@roslistonforestrycentre.co.uk
w roslistonforestrycentre.co.uk

SWAFFHAM
Norfolk

Hall Barn ★★★ *Self Catering*
Contact: Ms Brenda Wilbourn
t (01366) 328794
e brenda@hall-barn.freeserve.co.uk
w cottageguide.co.uk/hallbarn

SWANNINGTON
Norfolk

Oak Lodge & Lollipop Cottage ★★★-★★★★
Self Catering
Norfolk Country Cottages
t (01603) 871872
e info@norfolkcottages.co.uk
w norfolkcottages.co.uk

SWANTON ABBOTT
Norfolk

Lilac Barn ★★★★
Self Catering
Norfolk Country Cottages
t (01603) 871872
e info@norfolkcottages.co.uk
w norfolkcottages.co.uk

Magnolia Cottage ★★★
Self Catering
Contact: Mrs Christine Nockolds
t (01692) 538481
w tiscover.co.uk

Walnut Tree Barn ★★★★
Self Catering
Contact: Mrs Sally Page
t (01692) 538888
e sales@citibuild.co.uk
w broadland.com

SWANTON MORLEY
Norfolk

Teal Heron And Grebe Cottage, Swanton Morley
★★★ *Self Catering*
Contact: Mrs Sally Marsham
t (01362) 637300

SWAYFIELD
Lincolnshire

Greystones Lodge ★★★★
Self Catering
Contact: Claire Stanley
t (01476) 550909
e john@jstanley3.orangehome.co.uk

Woodview ★★★
Self Catering
Contact: Mrs Alison Bairsto
t (01476) 550097
e bears178@aol.com

SWINDERBY
Lincolnshire

Oaklands Retreat ★★★★
Self Catering
Contact: Michael Truelove
t (01522) 868861
e oaklandsretreat@yahoo.co.uk
w oaklandsretreat.co.uk

SWITHLAND
Leicestershire

Bybrook Lodge Self Catering Cottages ★★★★★
Self Catering
t (0116) 235 7788

SYDERSTONE
Norfolk

Croybrae ★★★★
Self Catering
Norfolk Country Cottages
t (01603) 871872
e info@norfolkcottages.co.uk
w norfolkcottages.co.uk

Harrow Barn ★★★★
Self Catering
Contact: Miss Catherine Ringer
t (01485) 578287
w norfolk-holiday-cottages.co.uk/cottage/harrowbarn.html

Swifts Cottage ★★★★
Self Catering
Contact: Mrs Mandy Gynn
t 07970 960505
w swiftscottagenorfolk.co.uk

SYMONDS YAT
Herefordshire

Flanesford Priory, Goodrich
★★★ *Self Catering*
Contact: Mr and Mrs Nigel & Isabel Roper
t (01600) 890506
e info@flanesfordpriory.co.uk
w flanesfordpriory.co.uk

Holly Tree House ★★★
Self Catering
Contact: Sue Wadley
t (01600) 772929
e sue@roscoerogersandknight.co.uk
w hollytreehouse.info

The Old Pump House ★★★
Self Catering
Contact: Mrs Sue Shergold
t (01594) 531227
e info@theoldpumphouse.co.uk
w theoldpumphouse.co.uk

Quat' Saisons ★★★
Self Catering
Contact: Howard Eason
t (01594) 543284
e info@wyevalleycottage.co.uk
w wyevalleycottage.co.uk

Wye Valley View ★★★★
Self Catering
Contact: Juliette Strefford
t (01600) 890070
e wyevalleyview@yahoo.co.uk

TADDINGTON
Derbyshire

Ash Tree Barn ★★★
Self Catering
Contact: Ms Judith Hawley
t (01298) 85453
e jah@ashtreebarn.fsnet.co.uk
w cressbrook.co.uk/tidza/ashbarn

TAMWORTH
Staffordshire

Chandlers Rest ★★★
Self Catering
Contact: Mr Malcolm Key
t 07968 550647
e malcolmk@wmtcnc.com

TANWORTH-IN-ARDEN
Warwickshire

Grange Farm Self Catering
★★★★ *Self Catering*
Contact: Miss Christine Bowen
t (01564) 742911
e enquiries@grange-farm.com
w grange-farm.com

TATTERSETT
Norfolk

The Old Dairy ★★★★
Self Catering
Norfolk Country Cottages
t (01603) 871872
e info@norfolkcottages.co.uk
w norfolkcottages.co.uk

Tatt Valley Holiday Cottages
★★★★ *Self Catering*
Contact: Mr Thomas Hurn
t (01485) 528506
e enquiries@norfolkholidayhomes.co.uk
w norfolkholidayhomes.co.uk

TATTINGSTONE
Suffolk

Cowshed ★★★★★
Self Catering
Contact: Mrs Annie Eaves
t 0870 710 8550
w suffolk-cowshed.co.uk

TEALBY
Lincolnshire

Primrose Cottage ★★★
Self Catering
Contact: Miss Diana Wood
t (01489) 559003
e diana@davenet.plus.com
w woldscottage.plus.com

TEAN
Staffordshire

Blythe Farmhouse
Rating Applied For
Self Catering
Contact: Ms Irene Bullock
t (01538) 724061
e irene@blythefarmhouse.co.uk
w blythefarmhouse.co.uk

Oakhill Holiday Homes
★★★ *Self Catering*
Contact: Mr & Mrs Philip & Hilary Williams
t (01538) 722213
e oakhillcottages@btinternet.com
w oakhillcottages.co.uk

The Old Smithy ★★★
Self Catering
Contact: Mrs Judy Dronzek
t (01889) 507249

TELFORD
Shropshire

Church Farm Self Catering
★★★ *Self Catering*
Contact: Mrs Virginia Evans
t (01952) 770381
e churchfarm49@beeb.net
w churchfarmshropshire.co.uk

Morrells Wood Farm
★★★-★★★★ *Self Catering*
Contact: Mr Derek Harper
t (01952) 510273
e derek@morrellswoodfarm.co.uk
w morrellswoodfarm.co.uk

TENBURY WELLS
Worcestershire

Long Cover Cottage ★★★★
Self Catering
Contact: Mrs Eleanor Van Straaten
Holiday Cottage
t (01885) 410208
e ellie_vanstraaten@yahoo.co.uk
w a-country-break.co.uk

Rochford Park Cottages
★★★★ *Self Catering*
t (01584) 781392
e cottages@rochfordpark.co.uk
w rochfordpark.co.uk

TERRINGTON ST CLEMENT
Norfolk

Northgate Lodge Flat ★★★
Self Catering
Contact: Mrs June Howling
t (01553) 828428

TETFORD
Lincolnshire

The Garth
★★★★-★★★★★
Self Catering
Contact: Debbie Sutcliffe
t (01507) 533697
e debbie@sutcliffell.freeserve.co.uk
w littlelondoncottages.co.uk

Grange Farm Cottages
★★★★ *Self Catering*
Contact: Sarah Stamp
t (01673) 858670
e sarahstamp@farmersweekly.net
w thegrange-lincolnshire.co.uk

TETNEY
Lincolnshire

Beech Farm Cottages
★★-★★★★ *Self Catering*
Contact: Norman Smith
t (01472) 815935
e norman@beechfarmcottages.co.uk
w beechfarmcottages.co.uk

Cedar Park ★★★★
Self Catering
Contact: Sarah Bottomley
Cedar Park Leisure Ltd.
t 07810 285111
e beachhouse@cleethorpesholidays.co.uk
w cedarparkcottages.co.uk

TEVERSAL
Nottinghamshire

Teversal Club Site *Approved*
Caravan Holiday Home
Camping & Caravanning Club
t 0845 130 7631

THAXTED
Essex

Thaxted Holiday Cottages
★★★★ *Self Catering*
Contact: Mrs Yolanda De Bono
t (01371) 830233
e enquiries@thaxtedholidaycottages.co.uk
w thaxtedholidaycottages.co.uk

THEBERTON
Suffolk

The Cottage ★★★
Self Catering
Suffolk Secrets
t (01502) 722717
e holidays@suffolk-secrets.co.uk
w suffolk-secrets.co.uk

Mizpah Cottage ★★★
Self Catering
Suffolk Secrets
t (01502) 722717
e holidays@suffolk-secrets.co.uk
w suffolk-secrets.co.uk

Pump Cottage ★★★★
Self Catering
Suffolk Secrets
t (01502) 722717
e holidays@suffolk-secrets.co.uk
w suffolk-secrets.co.uk

Teapot Hall ★★★★
Self Catering
Contact: Ms Tina Neal
t (01728) 830682
w suffolkcottagegreats.co.uk

Woodpecker Cottage ★★★
Self Catering
Suffolk Secrets
t (01502) 722717
e holidays@suffolk-secrets.co.uk
w suffolk-secrets.co.uk

THOMPSON
Norfolk

Rosemary Annexe ★★★★
Self Catering
Contact: Michael & Paula Corrie
t (01953) 488922
e rosemary.annexe@talktalk.net

THORGANBY
Lincolnshire

Little Walk Cottage
★★★-★★★★ *Self Catering*
Contact: James Milligan-Manby
t (01472) 398270
e james@thorganby.plus.com
w littlewalkcottage.co.uk

THORNAGE
Norfolk

Daisy Lodge ★★★
Self Catering
Contact: Mrs Melanie Hickling
t (01263) 761705
e primrosefarmbarns@tiscali.co.uk
w tiscover.co.uk

Well Cottage & Dairy Cottage ★★★ *Self Catering*
Norfolk Country Cottages
t (01603) 871872
e info@norfolkcottages.co.uk
w norfolkcottages.co.uk

THORNDON
Suffolk

Hestley Hall Barn ★★★★
Self Catering
Suffolk Secrets
t (01502) 722717
e holidays@suffolk-secrets.co.uk
w suffolk-secrets.co.uk

THORNHAM
Norfolk

1 West End Cottages ★★
Self Catering
Contact: Mr Hardy
t (01223) 263859

8 Malthouse Court ★★★★
Self Catering
Contact: Mr Adrian Forsell
t (01858) 565410
w forsell-property.com

Admirals Cottage ★★★★
Self Catering
Norfolk Country Cottages
t (01603) 871872
e info@norfolkcottages.co.uk
w norfolkcottages.co.uk

Brent Cottage ★★★
Self Catering
Birds Norfolk Holiday Homes
t (01485) 534267
e shohol@birdsnorfolkholidayhomes.co.uk
w norfolkholidayhomes-birds.co.uk

Captains Cottage ★★★★
Self Catering
Norfolk Country Cottages
t (01603) 871872
e info@norfolkcottages.co.uk
w norfolkcottages.co.uk

Chesnut Cottage ★★★★
Self Catering
Norfolk Country Cottages
t (01603) 871872
e info@norfolkcottages.co.uk
w norfolkcottages.co.uk

Green Side Cottage ★★★★
Self Catering
Norfolk Country Cottages
t (01603) 871872
e info@norfolkcottages.co.uk
w norfolkcottages.co.uk

Linzel Cottage ★★★★
Self Catering
Birds Norfolk Holiday Homes
t (01485) 534267
e shohol@birdsnorfolkholidayhomes.co.uk
w norfolkholidayhomes-birds.co.uk

Little Gull And Sanderling
★★★★ *Self Catering*
Contact: Mr John Warham
t (01485) 512546
e johnwarham@hotmail.com
w thornhamcottages.co.uk

Little Tern Cottage ★★★
Self Catering
Contact: Mr Misseldine
t (01353) 740297

Malthouse Cottages, Thornham ★★★
Self Catering
Contact: Mrs Leslie Rigby
Brindle Cottage
t (01733) 380399
e rigbysrushall@hotmail.co.uk
w malthousecottage.co.uk

Manor Farm Cottages
★★★★ *Self Catering*
Contact: Mrs Margaret Goddard
t (01485) 512272

The Old Garage ★★★
Self Catering
Norfolk Country Cottages
t (01603) 871872
e info@norfolkcottages.co.uk
w norfolkcottages.co.uk

Oyster Cottage
★★★-★★★★ *Self Catering*
Contact: Mrs Geraldine Tibbs
t (01485) 571770
w tiscover.co.uk

Rushmeadow Studio
★★★★ *Self Catering*
Contact: Mr Wyett
t (01485) 512372
e rushmeadow@sky.com
w rushmeadow.com

THORPE
Derbyshire

Hawthorn Studio ★★★
Self Catering
Contact: Ms Suzanne Walton
t 07740 721068
e suzanne001@btopenworld.com

The Rest ★★★★★
Self Catering
Contact: Sandy Potter
t (01773) 824060
e sandy@futurenetltd.co.uk
w derbyshirepeakcottage.co.uk

THORPE SATCHVILLE
Leicestershire

Walnut Tree Cottage
★★★★ *Self Catering*
Contact: Mrs Dee Burton
t (01664) 840638
e dee@walnut-tree-cottage.co.uk
w walnut-tree-cottage.co.uk

THORPENESS
Suffolk

2 The Dunes ★★
Self Catering
Suffolk Secrets
t (01502) 722717
e holidays@suffolk-secrets.co.uk
w suffolk-secrets.co.uk

22 North End Avenue
Rating Applied For
Self Catering
Contact: Mrs Margaret Palmer
t (01728) 454191
w cottageguide.co.uk

7, The Uplands ★★★
Self Catering
Contact: Mrs Diane Holmes
7, The Uplands
t (01728) 454648

Annie's House ★★★
Self Catering
Suffolk Secrets
t (01502) 722717
e holidays@suffolk-secrets.co.uk
w suffolk-secrets.co.uk

Beacon Hill Barn ★★★
Self Catering
Suffolk Secrets
t (01502) 722717
e holidays@suffolk-secrets.co.uk
w suffolk-secrets.co.uk

Church House ★★★
Self Catering
Suffolk Secrets
t (01502) 722717
e holidays@suffolk-secrets.co.uk
w suffolk-secrets.co.uk

Hope Cove Cottage ★★★★
Self Catering
Contact: Mrs I Pearman
Hollyhock Trust
t (01279) 771281
e irene.pearman@whestates.com
w tiscover.co.uk

Hope Cove Cottage ★★★★
Self Catering
Contact: Mrs Irene Pearman
t (01279) 771281

House in the Clouds ★★★
Self Catering
Contact: Mrs Le Comber
The House in the Clouds
t (020) 7224 3615
e houseintheclouds@btopenworld.com
w houseintheclouds.co.uk

THUNDRIDGE
Hertfordshire

Wednesday Cottage ★★★★
Self Catering
Contact: Mrs Annie Jenkins
t (01920) 465696
w wednesdaycottage.co.uk

THURLEIGH
Bedfordshire

Scald End Farm ★★
Self Catering
Contact: Mr R Towler
t (01234) 772275
e scaldendfarm@tesco.net

THURNE
Norfolk

4 Old Lion Cottages ★★★★
Self Catering
Norfolk Country Cottages
t (01603) 871872
e info@norfolkcottages.co.uk
w norfolkcottages.co.uk

THURSFORD
Norfolk

1A The Street ★★★★
Self Catering
Contact: Ms Geraldine Rye
t (01328) 878477
e geraldine@thursforscollection.co.uk
w thursford.com

Garden Barn ★★★★
Self Catering
Norfolk Country Cottages
t (01603) 871872
e info@norfolkcottages.co.uk
w norfolkcottages.co.uk

Hayloft ★★★ *Self Catering*
Contact: Mrs Ann Green
t (01328) 878273
w tiscover.co.uk

Ransome Lodge The Meadows ★★★★
Self Catering
Norfolk Country Cottages
t (01603) 871872
e info@norfolkcottages.co.uk
w norfolkcottages.co.uk

Sentinel Lodge ★★★★★
Self Catering
Norfolk Country Cottages
t (01603) 871872
e info@norfolkcottages.co.uk
w norfolkcottages.co.uk

Station Farm Barn Holiday Cottages ★★★ *Self Catering*
Contact: Mrs Sheena Walton
t (01353) 720419
e enquiries@norfolk-barn-holidays.co.uk
w norfolk-barn-holidays.co.uk

TIDESWELL
Derbyshire

Barnfield ★★★ *Self Catering*
Peak Cottages
t (0114) 262 0777
e enquiries@peakcottages.com
w peakcottages.com

Geil Torrs ★★★ *Self Catering*
Contact: Mr Harry Buttle
t (01298) 871302

Joiners Cottage ★★★
Self Catering
Peak Cottages
t (0114) 262 0777
e enquiries@peakcottages.com
w peakcottages.com

Lavender Cottage, Tideswell
★★★★ *Self Catering*
Contact: Ruth Wilson
t (0114) 230 7857
e ruth@thewilsons100.fsnet.co.uk
w lavendercottagetideswell.co.uk

Markeygate Cottages
★★★★ *Self Catering*
Contact: Mrs Melanie Greening-James
t (01298) 871260
e markeygatehouse@hotmail.com
w markeygatecottages.co.uk

Stoneycroft ★★★★
Self Catering
Sykes Cottages
t (01244) 345700
e info@sykescottages.co.uk
w sykescottages.co.uk

TINWELL
Rutland

Glebe Cottage
Rating Applied For
Self Catering
Contact: Allison Hinch
t (01780) 481228

TITLEY
Herefordshire

Newton Barn ★★★★★
Self Catering
Contact: Mr Ian Murphy
t (01749) 881611
e imurphy@allhallowsschool.co.uk
w newtonbarn.co.uk

TITTLESHALL
Norfolk

Mallards ★★★★
Self Catering
Contact: Mrs Barbara Rogers
t (01553) 617558

The Old Cartshed ★★★★
Self Catering
Contact: Mrs Margaret Daniels
t (01328) 700499

TOFTREES
Norfolk

The Dairy – Cannister Hall Barns ★★★★ *Self Catering*
Contact: Mrs Ruth Poulton
t (01480) 497422

TOLLESBURY
Essex

Fernleigh ★★★ *Self Catering*
Contact: Mrs Gillian Willson
t (01621) 868245

TOLLESHUNT KNIGHTS
Essex

Rosemary Cottage
Rating Applied For
Self Catering
Contact: Mr Adrian Tucker
t (01621) 816753

TREFONEN
Shropshire

Little Barn ★★★★
Self Catering
t (01691) 653387
w little-barn-shropshire.co.uk

TRIMINGHAM
Norfolk

Church Meadow Cottage
★★★★ *Self Catering*
Norfolk Country Cottages
t (01603) 871872
e info@norfolkcottages.co.uk
w norfolkcottages.co.uk

TRIMLEY
Suffolk

Treacle Pot Cottage ★★★
Self Catering
Contact: Mr Richard Borley
t (01394) 275367

TRIMLEY ST MARTIN
Suffolk

Oak Cottage ★★★
Self Catering
Contact: Mrs Gillian Young
t (01394) 277168
e trimleygill@btinternet.com
w tiscover.co.uk

TRUNCH
Norfolk

Robin Cottage ★★★
Self Catering
Norfolk Country Cottages
t (01603) 871872
e info@norfolkcottages.co.uk
w norfolkcottages.co.uk

TRUSTHORPE
Lincolnshire

Old Garth Holiday Cottages
★★★ *Self Catering*
Contact: Steve Lewis
t (01507) 477380
e enquiries@oldgarthcottages.co.uk
w oldgarthcottages.co.uk

TUGFORD
Shropshire

Tugford Farm Holiday Cottages & Livery
★★★-★★★★★ *Self Catering*
Contact: Mrs Bronwen Williams
t (01584) 841259
e tugfordfarm@yahoo.co.uk
w tugford.com

TUNSTALL
Suffolk

Knoll Cottage ★★★★
Self Catering
Contact: Mrs Jill Robinson
t (01728) 685084
e jill@timbertop.co.uk
w timbertop.co.uk

The Old Bakery ★★★
Self Catering
Suffolk Secrets
t (01502) 722717
e holidays@suffolk-secrets.co.uk
w suffolk-secrets.co.uk

TUNSTEAD
Norfolk

Partridge Farm Cottage
★★★★ *Self Catering*
Norfolk Country Cottages
t (01603) 871872
e info@norfolkcottages.co.uk
w norfolkcottages.co.uk

TUXFORD
Nottinghamshire

23 Ashvale Road ★★★
Self Catering
Contact: Diane Hunt
t (01777) 892776
e dianehunt08@btinternet.com

Shirehill Holiday Let ★★★
Self Catering
Contact: Elaine Benfield
t (01777) 870438
e elainebenfield@pbautoelectrics.co.uk

TWO DALES
Derbyshire

Toad Cottage ★★★★
Self Catering
Contact: Mrs Tina Boulden
t (01246) 234132
e info@toadcottage.com
w toadcottage.com

UFFORD
Suffolk

Grove Farm Cottage ★★★
Self Catering
Contact: Mrs Tricia Rolph
t (01394) 380154
w tiscover.co.uk

ULLESTHORPE
Leicestershire

Dairy Barn ★★★★
Self Catering
Contact: Mrs Donna McAllister
t (01455) 209425
e mcallisterdon5@aol.com

UPPER COLWALL
Worcestershire

Walkers End ★★★★
Self Catering
Contact: Hattie Walker
t (01684) 562597
e info@walkers-end.co.uk
w walkers-end.co.uk

UPPER HULME
Staffordshire

Hurdlow Cottage ★★★★
Self Catering
Contact: Mrs Ruth Belfield
t (01538) 300406
e robertruth@hurdlowfarm.fsnet.co.uk
w hurdlowfarm.fsnet.co.uk

Roaches Hall ★★★★
Self Catering
Contact: Ms Sue Norgrove-Moore
Party Houses Ltd
t (01260) 226609
e partyhouses@hotmail.com
w partyhouses.co.uk

Roaches Holiday Cottages
★★★ *Self Catering*
Contact: Mrs Diane & Andrew Oliver
t (01538) 300345
e diane@roachescottages.co.uk
w roachescottages.co.uk

UPPER QUINTON
Warwickshire

1 Meon View ★★★
Self Catering
Contact: Mrs Angela Rimell
t (01789) 720080
w meonview.co.uk

Gable Cottage ★★★★
Self Catering
Contact: Mr & Mrs H.D. Martine mancott@netcomuk.co.uk
w manorcottages.co.uk

UPPER SAPEY
Herefordshire

Tippins Farm ★★★★
Self Catering
w tippinsfarm.co.uk

UPPER SHERINGHAM
Norfolk

Barn Owl Cottage ★★★
Self Catering
Contact: Mr & Mrs Jim & Jackie Flynn
t (01263) 821445
e stay@visitlodgecottage.com
w visitlodgecottage.com

UPTON BISHOP
Herefordshire

Kempley Barns ★★★★★
Self Catering
Contact: Petula & Robert Skerrett
t (01989) 780772
e info@kempleybarns.co.uk
w kempleybarns.co.uk

Woodredding Farm Cottages ★★★ *Self Catering*
Contact: Brian Robbins
t (01531) 660257
e brian@woodredding.co.uk
w woodredding.co.uk

UPTON UPON SEVERN
Worcestershire

Captains Retreat ★★★★
Self Catering
Contact: Mr & Mrs Michael & Julie-Ann Cranton
White Cottage
t (01684) 592023
e michael.cranton@tesco.net

Old Market House ★★★★
Self Catering
Contact: Mr & Mrs Barry & Catherine Sparks
t (01934) 824877 & 07714 517147
e barry_sparks@hotmail.com

The Orangery at Little Boynes, Upton-upon-Severn
★★★★ *Self Catering*
Contact: Mr Chris Martin
t (01684) 594788
e info@little-boynes.co.uk
w little-boynes.co.uk

UPTON WARREN
Worcestershire

The Durrance ★★★★
Self Catering
Contact: Mrs Helen Hirons
t (01562) 777533
e helenhirons@thedurrance.co.uk
w thedurrance.co.uk

UTTOXETER
Staffordshire

Woodland Views Holiday Cottages ★★★★
Self Catering
Contact: Mrs Kate Tomlinson
t (01283) 820012
e enquiries@woodlandviews.co.uk
w woodlandviews.co.uk

WADENHOE
Northamptonshire

Woodpiece Cottage
★★★★★ *Self Catering*
Contact: Mrs K O Pollock
t (01832) 720288
e kop@khayam.org
w woodpiececottage.com

WALBERSWICK
Suffolk

6 The Terrace ★★★★
Self Catering
Contact: Ms Adelaide Boon
t (01920) 821109
w explorewalberswick.co.uk/6theterrace

Ash Cottage ★★★★
Self Catering
Suffolk Holidays Ltd
t (01502) 723571
e sales@holidaysinsuffolk.co.uk
w holidaysinsuffolk.co.uk

Drift Cottage ★★★
Self Catering
Suffolk Holidays Ltd
t (01502) 723571
e sales@holidaysinsuffolk.co.uk
w holidaysinsuffolk.co.uk

Ferry Knoll ★★★★
Self Catering
Acanthus Property Letting Services
t (01502) 724033
e websales@southwold-holidays.co.uk
w southwold-holidays.co.uk

Hollyhocks
Rating Applied For
Self Catering
Acanthus Property Letting Services
t (01502) 724033
e websales@southwold-holidays.co.uk
w southwold-holidays.co.uk

No 1 Blackshore ★★★
Self Catering
Suffolk Secrets
t (01502) 722717
e holidays@suffolk-secrets.co.uk
w suffolk-secrets.co.uk

Ryecroft ★★★★
Self Catering
Suffolk Secrets
t (01502) 722717
e holidays@suffolk-secrets.co.uk
w suffolk-secrets.co.uk

Stuckie Ben ★★★
Self Catering
Suffolk Secrets
t (01502) 722717
e holidays@suffolk-secrets.co.uk
w suffolk-secrets.co.uk

White Cottage ★★★★
Self Catering
Acanthus Property Letting Services
t (01502) 724033
e websales@southwold-holidays.co.uk
w southwold-holidays.co.uk

WALCOTT
Norfolk

Greystones ★★★
Self Catering
Norfolk Country Cottages
t (01603) 871872
e info@norfolkcottages.co.uk
w norfolkcottages.co.uk

Sanderling ★★★★
Self Catering
Norfolk Country Cottages
t (01603) 871872
e info@norfolkcottages.co.uk
w norfolkcottages.co.uk

Tamarisk ★★★★
Self Catering
Contact: Mrs Jane Shulver
Norfolk Country Cottages
t (01692) 651126 & 07879 473546
e pointhouse@hotmail.com
w norfolkcottages.co.uk

WALDRINGFIELD
Suffolk

The Cottages at Thatched Farm ★★★★ *Self Catering*
Contact: Mrs Helen Butler
t (01473) 811755
w thatchedfarm.co.uk

Low Farm Estate Services
★★★★ *Self Catering*
Contact: Miss Christine White
t (01473) 736387
w stayatlowfarm.co.uk

Windy Bank ★★
Self Catering
Contact: Mrs Rosemary Routledge
The Court
t (01275) 474472
e routledge.court@virgin.net

WALL-UNDER-HEYWOOD
Shropshire

Old Stables ★★★★
Self Catering
Contact: Mrs Helen Hartill
t (01694) 771278
e hartillhelen@aol.com

WALSINGHAM
Norfolk

1 Folgate Cottage ★★★
Self Catering
Norfolk Country Cottages
t (01603) 871872
e info@norfolkcottages.co.uk
w norfolkcottages.co.uk

16 The Hill ★★★
Self Catering
Norfolk Country Cottages
t (01603) 871872
e info@norfolkcottages.co.uk
w norfolkcottages.co.uk

End Cottage ★★★★
Self Catering
Norfolk Country Cottages
t (01603) 871872
e info@norfolkcottages.co.uk
w norfolkcottages.co.uk

Martyrs Way ★★★★
Self Catering
Norfolk Country Cottages
t (01603) 871872
e info@norfolkcottages.co.uk
w norfolkcottages.co.uk

WANGFORD
Suffolk

Corner Cottage ★★★
Self Catering
Contact: Mrs Pat Grange
t (01502) 578629
w tiscover.co.uk

Field View ★★★
Self Catering
Contact: Mrs Paula Burns
t (01788) 535505
e paulaburns@btinternet.com
w cottageguide.co.uk/fieldview

The Old Bake House ★★★★
Self Catering
Suffolk Holidays Ltd
t (01502) 723571
e sales@holidaysinsuffolk.co.uk
w holidaysinsuffolk.co.uk

Old Butchers ★★★
Self Catering
Suffolk Secrets
t (01502) 722717
e holidays@suffolk-secrets.co.uk
w suffolk-secrets.co.uk

WARDLEY
Rutland

Wardley House ★★★★
Self Catering
Contact: Mrs Ann Kanter
t (01572) 717671
e enquiries@wardleyhouse.com
w wardleyhouse.com

WARDLOW
Derbyshire

Eastview Cottage ★★★★
Self Catering
Contact: Ms LIndsey Crossley
t (0161) 449 0544
e lindseylou@btinternet.com

WARMINGTON
Northamptonshire

Papley Farm Cottages
★★★★ *Self Catering*
Contact: Joyce Lane
t (01832) 272583

WARSLOW
Staffordshire

Shay Side Barn and Cottage
★★★-★★★★ *Self Catering*
Sykes Cottages
t (01244) 345700
e info@sykescottages.co.uk
w sykescottages.co.uk

WARWICK
Warwickshire

3 Goodway Court ★★★★
Self Catering
Contact: Mr Barry Day
t 07831 550425
e info@stayinwarwick.co.uk
w stayinwarwick.co.uk

Bianca & Whitley Elm Cottages ★★★★
Self Catering
Contact: Mr Clive Bevins
t (01926) 484577
e clive.bevins@btinternet.com
w whitleyelmcottages.com

Tudor Villa ★★★★
Self Catering
Contact: Roger Mann
t (01926) 429102
e roger.mann@talktalk.net

WATERHOUSES
Staffordshire

55 Reasons
Rating Applied For
Self Catering
Peak Cottages
t (0114) 262 0777
e enquiries@peakcottages.com
w peakcottages.com

Greenside Cottages
★★★-★★★★ *Self Catering*
Sykes Cottages
t (01244) 345700
e info@sykescottages.co.uk
w sykescottages.co.uk

Hamps Hall ★★★★
Self Catering
Contact: Mrs Sue Moore
t (01260) 226609
e partyhouses@hotmail.co.uk
w hampshall.co.uk

Limestone View Cottage
Rating Applied For
Self Catering
Contact: Mrs Wendy Webster
t (01538) 308288
e wendywebster@limestoneviewfarm.freeserve.co.uk
w peakdistrictfarmhols.co.uk

WATTISFIELD
Suffolk

Jayes Holiday Cottages
★★★ *Self Catering*
Contact: Mrs Denise Williams
t (01359) 251255
w jayesholidaycottages.co.uk

WATTON
Norfolk

Fairview ★★★ *Self Catering*
Norfolk Country Cottages
t (01603) 871872
e info@norfolkcottages.co.uk
w norfolkcottages.co.uk

Stay at the Fairway ★★★★
Self Catering
Norfolk Country Cottages
t (01603) 871872
e info@norfolkcottages.co.uk
w norfolkcottages.co.uk

WAXHAM
Norfolk

Deepdale Cottages ★★★★
Self Catering
Norfolk Country Cottages
t (01603) 871872
e info@norfolkcottages.co.uk
w norfolkcottages.co.uk

WELBOURN
Lincolnshire

Hilltop Farm
Rating Applied For
Self Catering
Contact: Mr C P Overton
t (01400) 273323
e myika@biosearch.org.uk

Walker's Cottage ★★★
Self Catering
Contact: Mrs Annie Walker
t (01400) 273698
e enquiries@walkerscottage.info
w walkerscottage.info

WELFORD-ON-AVON
Warwickshire

The Granary ★★★★
Self Catering
Contact: Mr & Mrs Bruce Spink
t (01789) 750752
e bruce.spink@btopenworld.com

WELLINGBOROUGH
Northamptonshire

Friendly Lodge Cottage
★★★★ *Self Catering*
Contact: Mrs Kaye Saunders
t (01933) 461102

WELLOW
Nottinghamshire

Foliat Cottages ★★★
Self Catering
Contact: Janet Carr
t (01623) 861088
e janet.carr@farmline.com
w sherwoodforestholidaycottages.com

WELLS-NEXT-THE-SEA
Norfolk

10 Brigs Square ★★★
Self Catering
Norfolk Country Cottages
t (01603) 871872
e info@norfolkcottages.co.uk
w norfolkcottages.co.uk

14 Church Street ★★★
Self Catering
Contact: Mr Jonathon Piesse
t (01603) 744233
e randjp2004@yahoo.com
w ukcottage.com/east-of-england/14-church-street.htm

4 Monteagle House
Rating Applied For
Self Catering
Contact: Margaret Davies
t (01923) 710982
e mfdavies@hotmail.com
w wellsnorfolkaccommodation.co.uk

Annies ★★★★ *Self Catering*
Contact: Mrs Sarah Orford
t (01359) 240340
w tiscover.co.uk

Apartment 2 ★★★★
Self Catering
Birds Norfolk Holiday Homes
t (01485) 534267
e shohol@birdsnorfolkholidayhomes.co.uk
w norfolkholidayhomes-birds.co.uk

Bay Cottage ★★★
Self Catering
Norfolk Country Cottages
t (01603) 871872
e info@norfolkcottages.co.uk
w norfolkcottages.co.uk

Bexwell ★★★★ *Self Catering*
Contact: Mr John Stannard
t (01328) 710752
e info@bexwellcottage.co.uk
w bexwellcottage.co.uk

Boatyard Cottage ★★★★
Self Catering
Norfolk Country Cottages
t (01603) 871872
e info@norfolkcottages.co.uk
w norfolkcottages.co.uk

Canary Cottage ★★★
Self Catering
Contact: Ms Sally Maufe
t (01328) 710246
e branthill.farms@unicombox.co.uk
w therealaleshop.co.uk

Chantry ★★★ *Self Catering*
Contact: Mrs Vicky Jackson
t (01992) 511303
w tiscover.co.uk

Curlew Cottage ★★★★
Self Catering
Birds Norfolk Holiday Homes
t (01485) 534267
e shohol@birdsnorfolkholidayhomes.co.uk
w norfolkholidayhomes-birds.co.uk

Gabriel Cottage ★★★★
Self Catering
Contact: Dr Marie Strong
t (01328) 710743
w tiscover.co.uk

Harbour Cottage ★★★
Self Catering
Contact: Mr & Mrs Simon & Trish Jackson
t (0115) 923 4545
e simonnjackson@btinternet.com
w harbourcottagewells.co.uk

Harbour View Cottage ★★★
Self Catering
Contact: Louise Evans-Evans
t (01525) 405494
e cottageinwells@live.co.uk
w cottageinwells.tripod.com

HIdeaway House ★★★★★
Self Catering
Contact: Robin Burkitt
t (01263) 862133
e enquiries@glavenvalleycottages.com
w glavenvalleycottages.com

Honeypot Cottage ★★★
Self Catering
Contact: Mrs Joan Price
t (01328) 711982
e walker.al@talk21.com
w wells-honeypot.co.uk

Luggers Cottage ★★★★
Self Catering
Norfolk Country Cottages
t (01603) 871872
e info@norfolkcottages.co.uk
w norfolkcottages.co.uk

Monteagle 3 ★★★★
Self Catering
Norfolk Country Cottages
t (01603) 871872
e info@norfolkcottages.co.uk
w norfolkcottages.co.uk

No 5 Coastguard Cottage
★★★ *Self Catering*
Contact: Ms Sharon Asher-Smith
t (01773) 856060
e sharon.asher-smith@virgin.net
w tiscover.co.uk

Poppy Cottage ★★★
Self Catering
Contact: Mrs Christine Curtis
t (01328) 710395
w tiscover.co.uk

Quay Cottage ★★★★
Self Catering
Norfolk Country Cottages
t (01603) 871872
e info@norfolkcottages.co.uk
w norfolkcottages.co.uk

Ranters Cottage ★★★
Self Catering
Contact: Mrs Hilary Marsden St Phillips
t (01442) 872486
e ranters.cottage@tesco.net
w tiscover.co.uk

Rose Cottage ★★★
Self Catering
Contact: Mrs Madeline Rainsford
t (01328) 711463
e maddie@eastquay.co.uk
w eastquay.co.uk

Samphire Cottage ★★★★
Self Catering
Contact: Mr William Hickey
t (01223) 812743
e dbjohnson@hotmail.com
w glavenvalley.co.uk/samphirecottage/

Seashell Cottage ★★★
Self Catering
Contact: Mrs Marylou Rivett
t (01494) 681604
e marylourivett@hotmail.com
w seashellcottage.co.uk

Skylark Cottage ★★★
Self Catering
Contact: Mrs Bridget Jones
t (01507) 603852
e bridget.jones@ukgateway.net
w bridget.jones.ukgateway.net

WELTON
Lincolnshire

Athina ★★★★ *Self Catering*
Contact: Mrs Michelle Billington
t (01663) 719661
e athinabookings@aol.com
w athinacottage.co.uk

Mill Cottage ★★★★
Self Catering
Contact: Gilian Gladwin
t (01673) 860082
e gill.gladwin655@btinternet.com
w millcottageholidaylets.co.uk

WELWYN
Hertfordshire

Gamekeepers Lodge, Shire Barn ★★★★ *Self Catering*
Contact: Mrs Liz Buisman-Gaze
t (01438) 718641
w lockleyfarm.co.uk

WENHASTON
Suffolk

The Old Mill House ★★★
Self Catering
Acanthus Property Letting Services
t (01502) 724033
e websales@southwold-holidays.co.uk
w southwold-holidays.co.uk

Poplar Cottage ★★★★
Self Catering
Suffolk Secrets
t (01502) 722717
e holidays@suffolk-secrets.co.uk
w suffolk-secrets.co.uk

Rose Glen ★★★★
Self Catering
Suffolk Secrets
t (01502) 722717
e holidays@suffolk-secrets.co.uk
w suffolk-secrets.co.uk

Secret Garden ★★★
Self Catering
Suffolk Secrets
t (01502) 722717
e holidays@suffolk-secrets.co.uk
w suffolk-secrets.co.uk

WENSLEY
Derbyshire

Sid's Cottage ★★★★
Self Catering
Peak Cottages
t (0114) 262 0777
e enquiries@peakcottages.com
w peakcottages.com

Thatch Cottage ★★★★
Self Catering
Contact: Mrs Hilary Oates
t (0114) 236 5828

WEREHAM
Norfolk

Glennis's Cottage ★★★
Self Catering
Norfolk Country Cottages
t (01603) 871872
e info@norfolkcottages.co.uk
w norfolkcottages.co.uk

WESSINGTON
Derbyshire

Carr Barn Farm ★★★
Self Catering
Contact: Mandy Smithe smithmandys@aol.com
w cherryholidaycottages.co.uk

WEST BARKWITH
Lincolnshire

Glebe Farm Apartments
★★★ *Self Catering*
Contact: Stephen Campion
t (01673) 858919
e enquiries@glebeapart.co.uk
w glebeapart.co.uk

WEST BECKHAM
Norfolk

Flint Farm Cottages
★★-★★★★ *Self Catering*
Contact: Mrs Judy Wilson
t (01263) 822241
e john@mcneil-wilson.freeserve.co.uk
w tiscover.co.uk

Merry Cottage ★★★
Self Catering
Contact: Mrs Mo Teeuw
t (01406) 370012
e mo@moteeuw.co.uk
w tiscover.co.uk

WEST DEEPING
Lincolnshire

Barn Lodge
Rating Applied For
Self Catering
Contact: Mr & Mrs Michael & Sue Robinson
t (01778) 343538
e robinsonstime@aol.com

WEST FELTON
Shropshire

The Stables ★★★★
Self Catering
Contact: Mr & Mrs Edward & Kirsten Nicholas
t (01691) 610230
e edwardnicholas@freeuk.com

WEST RUDHAM
Norfolk

North Cottage ★★★
Self Catering
t 0870 070 8090
w tiscover.co.uk

WEST RUNTON
Norfolk

Roman Camp Brick Chalets
★★★ *Self Catering*
Contact: Mr John Julian
t (01263) 837256
w romancampcaravanpark.co.uk

Runton Hill Cottage ★★★★
Self Catering
Contact: Mrs Barbara Cork
t (01263) 837427
e bd.corks@btopenworld.com

St Mary's ★★★ *Self Catering*
Norfolk Country Cottages
t (01603) 871872
e info@norfolkcottages.co.uk
w norfolkcottages.co.uk

WEST WRATTING
Cambridgeshire

Bakery Cottage ★★★★
Self Catering
Contact: Mr David Denny
t (01223) 290492

WESTBURY
Shropshire

Middle Farm Barns ★★★★
Self Catering
Contact: Mrs Alison Haigh
t (01743) 884383
e alison@vennington.plus.com
w middlefarmholidays.co.uk

WESTCLIFF-ON-SEA
Essex

Thames Estuary Holiday Apartments ★★★
Self Catering
Contact: Mr Donald Watson
t (01702) 477255
w tiscover.co.uk

WESTHALL
Suffolk

Belle Grove Cottages
★★★★★ *Self Catering*
Contact: Miss Jo Jordan
t (01986) 873124

WESTHOPE
Shropshire

Westhope Country Retreats
★★★★ *Self Catering*
Contact: Mrs Marjorie Betty Manley
t (01584) 861617
e johnbett@tiscali.co.uk
w westhopecountryretreats.co.uk

WESTLETON
Suffolk

Apple Tree Cottage ★★★
Self Catering
Suffolk Secrets
t (01502) 722717
e holidays@suffolk-secrets.co.uk
w suffolk-secrets.co.uk

Briar Cottage ★★★
Self Catering
Suffolk Secrets
t (01502) 722717
e holidays@suffolk-secrets.co.uk
w suffolk-secrets.co.uk

Easter Cottage ★★★★
Self Catering
Suffolk Secrets
t (01502) 722717
e holidays@suffolk-secrets.co.uk
w suffolk-secrets.co.uk

Ebenezer House 1,3 & 5 Ebenezer Row ★★
Self Catering
Suffolk Secrets
t (01502) 722717
e holidays@suffolk-secrets.co.uk
w suffolk-secrets.co.uk

Garden House ★★★★
Self Catering
Suffolk Secrets
t (01502) 722717
e holidays@suffolk-secrets.co.uk
w suffolk-secrets.co.uk

Holly Tree Cottage ★★★★
Self Catering
Suffolk Secrets
t (01502) 722717
e holidays@suffolk-secrets.co.uk
w suffolk-secrets.co.uk

Middle Cottage ★★★★
Self Catering
Contact: Mr Richard Webster
t (01865) 558596
w suffolkcottage.net

WESTON
Shropshire

Halford Holiday Homes
★★★-★★★★★ *Self Catering*
Contact: Mr & Mrs E James
t (01588) 672382

WESTON-ON-AVON
Warwickshire

Weston Farm Cottages
★★★★-★★★★★
Self Catering
Contact: Mr & Mrs Richard Bluck
t (01789) 750688
e r.bluckwestonfarm@amserve.net
w westonfarm.co.uk

WESTON RHYN
Shropshire

Mill Cottage ★★★
Self Catering
Contact: Mr & Mrs H Brannick
t (01691) 659738

WESTON UNDERWOOD
Derbyshire

Honeysuckle Cottage
★★★★ *Self Catering*
Contact: Mrs Linda Adams
t (01335) 360352
e enquiries@parkviewfarm.co.uk
w parkviewfarm.co.uk

WETHERDEN
Suffolk

Brickwall Farm House
★★★★ *Self Catering*
Contact: Mrs Robin Bonner-Morgan
t (01359) 244118
w brickwallfarmhouse.co.uk

WETTON
Staffordshire

Old Sunday School ★★★★
Self Catering
Peak Cottages
t (0114) 262 0777
e enquiries@peakcottages.com
w peakcottages.com

WEYBOURNE
Norfolk

Appletree Cottage ★★★★
Self Catering
Norfolk Country Cottages
t (01603) 871872
e info@norfolkcottages.co.uk
w norfolkcottages.co.uk

Bolding Way Holidays
★★★★ *Self Catering*
Contact: Mr Charlie Harrison
t (01263) 588666
e holidays@boldingway.co.uk
w boldingway.co.uk

Hawthorns ★★★
Self Catering
Contact: Mrs F.P. Crane
t (01263) 821945
w hawthornslodge.co.uk

Herons Rise ★★★
Self Catering
Norfolk Country Cottages
t (01603) 871872
e info@norfolkcottages.co.uk
w norfolkcottages.co.uk

Home Farm Cottages
★★★★ *Self Catering*
Contact: Mrs Sally Middleton
t (01263) 588334
e sallymiddleton@virgin.net
w weybourne-holiday-cottage.co.uk

Lower Byre ★★★
Self Catering
Contact: Mrs Valerie James
t (01775) 760938
e valeriejames@hotmail.co.uk
w tiscover.co.uk

Poppies ★★★ *Self Catering*
Norfolk Country Cottages
t (01603) 871872
e info@norfolkcottages.co.uk
w norfolkcottages.co.uk

WHALEY BRIDGE
Derbyshire

Cote Bank Farm Cottages
★★★★ *Self Catering*
Contact: Mrs Pamela Broadhurst
t (01663) 750566
e cotebank@btinternet.com
w cotebank.co.uk

Horwich Barns ★★★★★
Self Catering
Peak Cottages
t (0114) 262 0777
e enquiries@peakcottages.com
w peakcottages.com

Nimbus House ★★★★
Self Catering
Contact: Mr & Mrs Linda Brobbin
t (01663) 734248
e lindabrobbin@hotmail.com

WHATELEY
Warwickshire

33 Rosemary Cottage ★★★
Self Catering
Contact: Mrs Violet Coles
t (01827) 280826

WHEATACRE
Norfolk

Wheatacre Hall Barns
★★★★-★★★★★
Self Catering
Contact: Mrs Joanna Burroughs
t (01502) 677208
w wheatacrehallbarns.co.uk

WHEATCROFT
Derbyshire

The Old Granary ★★★★★
Self Catering
Contact: Amanda Brown
t 05602 931292
e info@theoldgranary.net
w theoldgranary.net

WHEPSTEAD
Suffolk

Rowney Cottage ★★★
Self Catering
Contact: Mrs Kati Turner
t (01284) 735842
e nick.turner@farming.co.uk
w tiscover.co.uk

WHITBOURNE
Herefordshire

Crumplebury Farmhouse
★★★ *Self Catering*
Contact: Ms Rachel Freeman
t 07929 260919
e crumplebury@yahoo.co.uk
w whitbourne-estate.co.uk/crumplebury

Elcocks Cottage ★★★
Self Catering
Contact: Mike Hogg
t (0121) 427 1395
e mike@elcocks.net
w elcocks.net

Hareley Barn ★★★★
Self Catering
Contact: Mrs Gillian Herbert
t (01886) 884362
e holidays@hareleyfarm.fsnet.co.uk

The Olde Rectory, Whitbourne ★★★-★★★★★
Self Catering
Contact: Gilly & Cliff Poultney
t (01886) 822000
e stay@olde-rectory.co.uk
w olde-rectory.co.uk

WHITCHURCH Herefordshire

Norton Cottages ★★★★
Self Catering
Contact: Mrs Su Jackson
t (01600) 890046
e enquiries@norton-house.com
w norton-house.com

Tump Farm Holiday Cottage ★★★ *Self Catering*
Contact: Mrs Debbie Williams
t (01600) 891029
e clinwilcharmaine@hotmail.com

WHITCHURCH Shropshire

Combermere Abbey Cottages ★★★★★
Self Catering
Contact: Mrs Jean McIlroy
t (01948) 662876
e cottages@combermereabbey.co.uk
w combermereabbey.co.uk

The Park ★★★★
Self Catering
t (01948) 880669

WHITE RODING Essex

The Old Dairy ★★★★
Self Catering
Contact: Ms D Stafford
t (01279) 876056

WICKHAM MARKET Suffolk

11 Elm Road ★★★★
Self Catering
Suffolk Secrets
t (01502) 722717
e holidays@suffolk-secrets.co.uk
w suffolk-secrets.co.uk

WICKHAM SKEITH Suffolk

Netus Barn, Wickham Skeith ★★★ *Self Catering*
Contact: Mrs Joy Homan
t (01449) 766275
e joygeoff@homansf.freeserve.co.uk
w netusbarn.co.uk

WICKLEWOOD Norfolk

The Coach House ★★★★
Self Catering
Contact: Mrs Mary Gamble
t (01953) 603468
e gamble@beech.a-i-s.co.uk
w beech.a-i-s.co.uk

WIGHTON Norfolk

Nutwood Lodges ★★★★
Self Catering
Contact: Mr Jonathan Savory
t (01328) 820719
e jds@thelaurals.plus.com
w nutwoodlodges.co.uk

WIGLEY Derbyshire

Pudding Pie Barn ★★★★
Self Catering
Peak Cottages
t (0114) 262 0777
e enquiries@peakcottages.com
w peakcottages.com

WIGSTHORPE Northamptonshire

Nene Valley Cottages ★★★★ *Self Catering*
t (01832) 273601 & 07962 085720
e stay@nenevalleycottages.co.uk
w nenevalleycottages.co.uk

WILBURTON Cambridgeshire

Australia Farmhouse ★★★★ *Self Catering*
Contact: Mrs Rebecca Howard
t (01353) 740322
w sakernet.com/jameshoward

WILMCOTE Warwickshire

Pear Tree Cottage Holiday Apartments ★★★★
Self Catering
Contact: Mrs Margaret Mander
t (01789) 205889
e peartree3@hotmail.com
w peartreecot.co.uk

WINDLEY Derbyshire

The Old Cheese Factory ★★★★★ *Self Catering*
Contact: Ms Sally Wallwork
t (01773) 550947
e sawallwork@aol.com
w theoldcheesefactory.com

WING Rutland

Garden Room at Wing ★★★
Self Catering
Contact: Mr Jeffery Wilcox-Smith
t (01572) 737166
e jeffw-s@talktalk.net
w garden-room-at-wing.co.uk

WINGERWORTH Derbyshire

Spinney Top Cottage ★★★
Self Catering
Contact: Mr & Mrs Silwood & Anita Kinder
t (01246) 557979
e sil_kinder@yahoo.co.uk

WINGFIELD Suffolk

Keeleys Farm ★★★
Self Catering
Contact: Mrs Gloria Elsden
t (01379) 668409
e glori@madasafish.com
w tiscover.co.uk

WINKHILL Staffordshire

Alma Cottage ★★★★
Self Catering
Contact: Mrs Diana Cope
t (01538) 308909
e enquires@almacottage.com
w almacottage.com

WINSTER Derbyshire

Blakelow Farm Holiday Cottages ★★★★★
Self Catering
Contact: Mr Stephen Ogan
t (01629) 650814
e blakelowcottages@w3z.co.uk
w blakelowcottages.co.uk

Briar Cottage ★★★★
Self Catering
Contact: Mrs Anne Walters
t (01629) 650342
e etegfan@clara.co.uk
w cottageguide.co.uk/briarcottage

Jasmine Cottage ★★★★
Self Catering
Contact: Mrs Ann Kenworthy
t (01629) 732084
e abanister@tiscali.co.uk
w winster-cottages.co.uk

Rock Cottage ★★★★
Self Catering
Contact: Mr Christopher Higgs
t (01629) 650488
e info@peakrockcottages.co.uk
w peakrockcottages.co.uk

Ted's House ★★★★
Self Catering
Peak Cottages
t (0114) 262 0777
e enquiries@peakcottages.com
w peakcottages.com

WINTERTON-ON-SEA Norfolk

1 Prospect Place ★★★
Self Catering
Norfolk Country Cottages
t (01603) 871872
e info@norfolkcottages.co.uk
w norfolkcottages.co.uk

WIRKSWORTH Derbyshire

Hog Cottage ★★★★
Self Catering
Contact: Mrs Anna Fern
t (01625) 890001
e hogcottage@bluelagoon.co.uk
w bluelagoonproperties.co.uk

Hopton Estates ★★★★
Self Catering
Contact: Mr & Mrs Spencer & Emma Tallis
t (01629) 540458
e h.e@saqnet.co.uk

North End Cottages
Rating Applied For
Self Catering
Contact: Tamsin Ellis
t 07942 552617
e tamsin_ellis@hotmail.com
w northendcottages.co.uk

Saddler's Cottage ★★★-★★★★ *Self Catering*
Contact: Lesley Clifford
Qwirky Cottages
t (01629) 581663
w quirkycottages.co.uk

Snuffless Dip ★★★
Self Catering
Contact: Mrs Margaret Doxey
t (01629) 824466

Two China House Yard
Rating Applied For
Self Catering
Contact: Bob and Jill Rhodes
t (01629) 823623
e bandjrhodes@hotmail.com

Weathericks and Bradstone ★★★★★ *Self Catering*
Peak Cottages
t (0114) 262 0777
e enquiries@peakcottages.com
w peakcottages.com

WISBECH Cambridgeshire

Common Right Barns ★★★★ *Self Catering*
Contact: Mrs Teresa Fowler
t (01945) 410424
e teresa@commonrightbarns.co.uk
w commonrightbarns.co.uk

WISBECH ST MARY Cambridgeshire

Fenland Self Catering Holidays ★★★-★★★★★
Self Catering
Contact: Mr Michael Southern
t (01945) 410680
w fenlandselfcateringholidays.co.uk

Trafford Barns ★★★
Self Catering
Contact: Ann Desborough
t (01945) 410206
e acdesborough@aol.com
w traffordbarns.com.uk

WISSETT Suffolk

Noah's Ark ★★★★
Self Catering
Contact: Mrs Janet Craft
t (01986) 785535
e valleyfarmvineyards@tiscali.co.uk

Wissett Lodge ★★★★
Self Catering
Contact: Mrs Claire Kiddy
t (01986) 873173
e geoffrey.kiddy@farmersweekly.net
w wissettlodge.co.uk

WITHERN Lincolnshire

Park Farm Holidays ★★★
Self Catering
Contact: Mr & Mrs Alan & Elsie Burkitt
t (01507) 450331
e alan@alanburkitt.wanadoo.co.uk
w parkfarmholidayswithern.com

WITTON Norfolk

The Hideaway
Rating Applied For
Self Catering
Norfolk Country Cottages
t (01603) 871872
e info@norfolkcottages.co.uk
w norfolkcottages.co.uk

Wit's End ★★★★
Self Catering
Norfolk Country Cottages
t (01603) 871872
e info@norfolkcottages.co.uk
w norfolkcottages.co.uk

WIVETON Norfolk

Ebbtide ★ *Self Catering*
Norfolk Country Cottages
t (01603) 871872
e info@norfolkcottages.co.uk
w norfolkcottages.co.uk

Laneway Cottage ★★★
Self Catering
Contact: Mrs Catherine Joice
t (01328) 862261
e catherine.joice@btinternet.com
w colkirkcottages.co.uk

WOLFERTON Norfolk

Alice Cottage ★★★★
Self Catering
Contact: Mrs Lynn Jones
t (01485) 543611

WOOD DALLING Norfolk

St Andrews Prospect
Rating Applied For
Self Catering
Norfolk Country Cottages
t (01603) 871872
e info@norfolkcottages.co.uk
w norfolkcottages.co.uk

WOOD ENDERBY Lincolnshire

Stanhope Cottage ★★★★
Self Catering
Contact: Peter Wiggins-Davies
t (01507) 568395
e revesbyfarms@yahoo.co.uk
w revesbyestate.co.uk

WOOD NORTON Norfolk

Acorn Cottages ★★★★
Self Catering
Contact: Ms Ann Pope
t (01362) 683615
e rjpope@lineone.net
w countrysideholidays.com

Small Barn ★★★
Self Catering
Contact: Miss Jane Lister
t (01362) 684206
e hoecroft@acedial.co.uk
w hoecroft.co.uk

WOODBRIDGE Suffolk

Butley Mills ★★★★
Self Catering
Contact: Mr Glyn Evans
t (01394) 450401
w butleymills.co.uk

The Coach House ★★★
Self Catering
Contact: Ms Nicola Deller
t (01473) 890891
e nicoladeller@yahoo.com

Colston Cottages ★★★★
Self Catering
Contact: Mrs Elizabeth Bellefontaine
t (01728) 638375
w colstonhall.com

Easton Farm Park Cottages
★★★★ *Self Catering*
Contact: Miss Fiona Kerr
t (01728) 746475
w eastonfarmpark.co.uk

Old Forge and Anvil Cottage
★★★★ *Self Catering*
Contact: Mr Robert Blake
t (01394) 382565 & 07901 773545
e robert@blake4110.fsbusiness.co.uk
w tiscover.co.uk

Quayside Holiday Cottages, Waldringfield
★★★★–★★★★★
Self Catering
Contact: Mrs Donna Morgan
t (01473) 736724
e donna.morgan@quaysidecottage.com
w quaysidecottage.com

Sampsons Mill ★★★
Self Catering
Contact: Mr Gordon J. Turner
t (01728) 746791
e sampsons.mill@ntlworld.com
w tiscover.co.uk

Windmill Lodges
★★★★–★★★★★
Self Catering
Windmill Lodges Ltd
t (01728) 685338
e holidays@windmilllodges.co.uk
w windmilllodges.co.uk

WOODHALL SPA Lincolnshire

Mill Lane Holiday Cottage
★★ *Self Catering*
Contact: Ian Williamson
t (01526) 353101
w skegness.net/woodhallspa.htm

Old Forge Cottage ★★★★
Self Catering
t (01526) 353430
e WoodhallBreaks@aol.com
w WoodhallBreaks.com

WOOLHOPE Herefordshire

The Studio ★★★★
Self Catering
Contact: Martin & Beth Booth
t (01432) 860015
e mart.booth@btinternet.com

WOOLPIT Suffolk

Bothy ★★★★ *Self Catering*
Contact: Mrs Kathryn Parker
t (01359) 241143
w farmstayanglia.co.uk/grangefarm/

WOOLSCOTT Warwickshire

The Old Workshop ★★★★
Self Catering
Contact: Mrs Heather McBreen
t (01788) 522727
e heathermcbreen@yahoo.co.uk
w stayinbritain.com/theoldworkshop

WOOTTON Bedfordshire

The Stable Yard ★★★★
Self Catering
Contact: Mrs Gabi Thomas
t (01234) 765351
e info@the-stableyard.co.uk
w the-stableyard.co.uk

WORCESTER Worcestershire

The Elgar Suite ★★★★
Self Catering
Contact: Mrs Jo Rammel
t 0844 884 2624
e jo.rammell@jdr-leisure.co.uk
w jdr-leisure.co.uk

Hazeldene ★★★★
Self Catering
Contact: Mrs Vera Rogers
t (01905) 333236
e lightwood.holidays@virgin.net
w lightwoodfarm.co.uk

Maybury & Malvern View
★★★ *Self Catering*
Contact: Mrs Christine Houghton
t (01905) 333202
e r.houghton36@tiscali.co.uk
w upperlightwood.co.uk

Mill Cottage ★★★★
Self Catering
t (01905) 451554

Pool House ★★★★★
Self Catering
English Heritage
t 0870 333 1187
e holidaycottages@english-heritage.org.uk
w english-heritage.org.uk/holidaycottages

The Whitehouse ★★★★
Self Catering
Contact: Mrs Susan O'Neil
t (01886) 888743

WORKSOP Nottinghamshire

Chapel Yard Cottage ★★★
Self Catering
Contact: Mr Stephen Cotter
t (01909) 515851
e stephen.cotter@btinternet.com
w chapel-yard-cottage-whitwell.co.uk

WORMELOW Herefordshire

Old Forge Cottage ★★★
Self Catering
Contact: Mrs Shirley Wheeler
t (01981) 540625

WORMINGTON Worcestershire

Wold Cottage ★★★★
Self Catering
Contact: Mrs Maggie Campbell
t (01386) 584741
e enquiries@follycottages.co.uk
w follycottages.co.uk

WORTHAM Suffolk

Ivy House Farm, Wortham
★★★★ *Self Catering*
Contact: Mr Paul Bradley
t (01379) 898395
e prjsdrad@aol.com
w ivyhousefarmcottages.co.uk

WRANGLE Lincolnshire

Mill Farm Leisure
★★★★–★★★★★
Self Catering
Contact: Mr Gary Marston
t (01754) 820053
e gary@millfarmleisure.co.uk
w millfarmleisure.co.uk

WRENTHAM Suffolk

Honeysuckle Cottage, Wrentham Nr Southwold
★★★★ *Self Catering*
Contact: Mrs Julia Price
t (01923) 226721 & 07831 602108
e juliaprice@tiscali.co.uk
w honeysucklecottage.net

The Stables ★★★★
Self Catering
Suffolk Secrets
t (01502) 722717
e holidays@suffolk-secrets.co.uk
w suffolk-secrets.co.uk

WROOT Lincolnshire

Brook Cottage ★★★
Self Catering
Contact: M Bayes
t (01302) 772285
e bayes@brook-lodge-country-cottage.co.uk

The Granary ★★★
Self Catering
Contact: R Aconley
t (01302) 770196
e robin.aconley@tiscali.co.uk
w thegranarywroot.com

WROXHAM Norfolk

20 Trail Quay Cottages
★★★ *Self Catering*
Norfolk Country Cottages
t (01603) 871872
e info@norfolkcottages.co.uk
w norfolkcottages.co.uk

Daisy Broad Lodges and Sail Loft ★★★★ *Self Catering*
Contact: Mr Daniel Thwaites
t (01603) 782625
e daniel@barnesbrinkcraft.co.uk
w barnesbrinkcraft.co.uk

Helens ★★★ *Self Catering*
Norfolk Country Cottages
t (01603) 871872
e info@norfolkcottages.co.uk
w norfolkcottages.co.uk

Nutmeg and Plum Tree Cottages, Wroxham ★★★★
Self Catering
Contact: Mrs Jane Pond
t (01603) 782225 & 07831 258258
w eastviewfarm.co.uk

Old Farm Cottages, Tunstead ★★★★
Self Catering
Contact: Mrs Kay Paterson
t (01692) 536612
e mail@oldfarmcottages.fsnet.co.uk
w oldfarmcottages.com

WYBERTON
Lincolnshire

Westwood Lakes ★★★
Self Catering
Contact: Tracey Smith
t (01205) 355856
e enquiries@westwoodlakes.co.uk
w westwoodlakes.co.uk

WYTHALL
Worcestershire

Inkford Court Cottages
★★★-★★★★ *Self Catering*
t (01564) 822304

YARPOLE
Herefordshire

The Barn at Lower House Farm ★★★ *Self Catering*
Contact: Josie Woodfield
t (01568) 780280
e jswoodfield@tiscali.co.uk

YELDERSLEY
Derbyshire

Ladyhole House – The Coachman's Cottage
★★★★★ *Self Catering*
Contact: Mrs Rosamond Woodrow
t (01335) 342670
w ladyholehouseholidays.co.uk

YOULGREAVE
Derbyshire

April Cottage ★★★
Self Catering
Contact: Mrs L Lovell
t (01629) 636151
e l.lovell@whitepeakcottage.co.uk
w whitepeakcottage.co.uk

Bramwell Cottage
Rating Applied For
Self Catering
Contact: Ms Ali Plowright
t (01629) 636421
e ali@makingchanges.co.uk

The Cottage, Crimbles Lane, Youlgreave ★★★★
Self Catering
Contact: Carol & John Sutcliffe
t (01629) 636570
e cottage@oldschoolhall.plus.com
w thecottage-crimbleslane.co.uk

Old Stonemasons Cottage
★★★ *Self Catering*
Peak Cottages
t (0114) 262 0777
e enquiries@peakcottages.com
w peakcottages.com

Sunnyside, Youlgreave
★★★ *Self Catering*
Contact: Ms J Steed
t (01629) 636195
e joan.steed7@googlemail.com

Thyme Cottage ★★★★
Self Catering
Contact: Mrs Fiona Bradshaw
t (01543) 432739
e fiona.bradshaw@btopenworld.com

YOXFORD
Suffolk

Heather Cottage ★★★★
Self Catering
Suffolk Secrets
t (01502) 722717
e holidays@suffolk-secrets.co.uk
w suffolk-secrets.co.uk

SOUTH EAST ENGLAND

ABINGDON
Oxfordshire

Brook Farm Cottages
★★★★ *Self Catering*
Contact: Pam Humphrey
t (01235) 820717
e info@brookfarmcottages.com
w brookfarmcottages.com

Kingfisher Barn Holiday Cottages ★★★-★★★★
Self Catering
Contact: Mrs Elena Kaczmarek
t (01235) 537538
e info@kingfisherbarn.com
w kingfisherbarn.com

The Old School ★★★
Self Catering
Contact: Mrs Christine Radburn
t (01235) 531557
e gordon@theoldeschool.freeserve.co.uk

The Swallows and The Loft Apartment ★★★★★
Self Catering
Contact: Mrs Katherine Bitmead
t (01235) 831253
e theoffice@bythemeadowfarm.co.uk

The Willows ★★★★
Self Catering
Contact: Ms Beccie & Kate Bitmead
t (01235) 831253
e theoffice@bythemeadowfarm.co.uk
w bythemeadowfarm.co.uk

ADDERBURY
Oxfordshire

Hannah's Cottage at Fletcher's ★★★★
Self Catering
Contact: Mrs Charlotte Holmes
t (01295) 810308
e charlotteaholmes@hotmail.com
w holiday-rentals.com

ADGESTONE
Isle of Wight

Adgestone Club Site
Approved Caravan Holiday Home
Camping & Caravanning Club
t 0845 130 7631

ALBURY
Surrey

The Lodge at Overbrook
★★★★ *Self Catering*
t (01483) 209579

ALCISTON
East Sussex

Rose Cottage Flat ★★★
Self Catering
Freedom Holiday Homes
t (01580) 720770
e mail@freedomholidayhomes.co.uk
w freedomholidayhomes.co.uk

Southdown Barn Annexe
★★★ *Self Catering*
Freedom Holiday Homes
t (01580) 720770
e mail@freedomholidayhomes.co.uk
w freedomholidayhomes.co.uk

ALDINGTON
Kent

Peacock Studio, Aldington
★★★★ *Self Catering*
t (01233) 720452
w peacockstudio.co.uk

ALFRISTON
East Sussex

Danny Cottage ★★★★★
Self Catering
Contact: Michael & Kitty Ann
t (01323) 870406
e contact@dannycottage.co.uk
w dannycottage.co.uk

Flint Cottage ★★★★
Self Catering
Contact: Mr Richard Watson
t (01438) 359311
e r.watson@bbwlaw.biz
w flintcottagesussex.co.uk

The Pony House ★★★★
Self Catering
Contact: Mrs S Hernu
t (01323) 870303
e hernu@btinternet.com
w theponyhouse.co.uk

ALRESFORD
Hampshire

The Garden Annexe ★★★
Self Catering
Contact: Mrs Amanda Miller
t 07973 254749
e amanda@o2m.co.uk
w o2m.co.uk/millerassociates

The Gatekeeper's Lodge
★★★★ *Self Catering*
t (01962) 732829
w thegatekeeperslodge.co.uk

ALTON
Hampshire

Butts House Studio Apartment ★★★
Self Catering
t (01420) 87507
w buttshouse.com

The Coach House ★★★★
Self Catering
t (01420) 474906
w stubbsfarm.co.uk

ALVERSTOKE
Hampshire

28 The Avenue ★★
Self Catering
Contact: Mr Martin Lawson
t (01923) 244042
e martinlawson8400@aol.com

ALVERSTONE
Isle of Wight

Combe View ★★★
Self Catering
Contact: Mrs Oliver
t (01983) 403721
e gaynor@kernfarm.co.uk
w kernfarm.co.uk

AMBERLEY
West Sussex

Culver Cottage, Amberley
★★★ *Self Catering*
Contact: Mrs Stella Kemp
Swallow Barn
t (01798) 831302 & 0033 5659 96950
e stellainamberley@yahoo.co.uk
w visitbritain.com

Rosemary Cottage ★★★★
Self Catering
Contact: Mrs J Shearse sjuno@hotmail.com
w rosemarycottageholidays.co.uk

AMERSHAM
Buckinghamshire

The Barn ★★★★
Self Catering
Contact: Ms Gillian MacNeil
t 07815 045519
e gill@oldamersham.co.uk
w oldamersham.co.uk

APPLEDORE
Kent

Ashby Farms Ltd ★★-★★★
Self Catering
Contact: Mr Ashby
t (01233) 733332
w ashbyfarms.com

Cobblestone Cottage ★★★
Self Catering
Freedom Holiday Homes
t (01580) 720770
e mail@freedomholidayhomes.co.uk
w freedomholidayhomes.co.uk

Rose Cottage ★★★
Self Catering
Contact: Mrs Pauline Hunter
t (01732) 457493
e holidays@rosecottageappledore.co.uk
w rosecottageappledore.co.uk

ARUNDEL
West Sussex

Arundel Town Cottage
★★★★ *Self Catering*
Contact: Ms Sue Blaney
t 07719 817661
e arundeltowncottages@hotmail.com
w arundeltowncottages.co.uk

Castleview ★★★★
Self Catering
Contact: Ms Jeannie Gapp
t (01903) 884713
e jeanniegapp@yahoo.co.uk
w castleview-arundel.co.uk

Village Holidays ★★★★
Self Catering
Contact: Ms Carolyn Booker
t (01243) 551073
e john@villageholidays.com
w villageholidays.com

ASH
Kent

Hazelwood Lodge ★★★★
Self Catering
Garden of England Cottages
t (01892) 510117
e info@gardenofenglandcottages.co.uk
w goec.co.uk

ASHBURNHAM
East Sussex

The Stables ★★★★
Self Catering
Freedom Holiday Homes
t (01580) 720770
e mail@freedomholidayhomes.co.uk
w freedomholidayhomes.co.uk

ASHEY
Isle of Wight

Tithe Barn, Old Byre & The Cote – Little Upton Barn
★★★★★ *Self Catering*
Contact: Mrs Johnson
t (01983) 563236
e alison@littleuptonfarm.co.uk
w littleuptonfarm.co.uk

ASHFORD
Kent

Eversleigh Woodland Lodges ★★★ *Self Catering*
Contact: Mrs Chris Drury
t (01233) 733248
e enquiries@eversleighlodges.co.uk
w eversleighlodges.co.uk

Grove House Cottage
★★★★ *Self Catering*
Garden of England Cottages
t (01892) 510117
e info@gardenofenglandcottages.co.uk
w goec.co.uk

Hazelhope Barn, Stalisfield
★★★★★ *Self Catering*
Contact: Mandy Southern
t (01233) 713806
e mandy@hazelhopebarn.co.uk
w hazelhopebarn.co.uk

The Old Dairy ★★★
Self Catering
Contact: Mrs June Browning
t (01233) 750238
e browning.elmstead@talk21.com

ASHURST
Hampshire

Bramble Cottage ★★★★
Self Catering
Contact: Mrs Penny Sucharov
t (023) 8029 2266
e info@bramble-cottage.net
w bramble-cottage.net

ASTON ABBOTTS
Buckinghamshire

Orchard Cottage ★★★★
Self Catering
Contact: Ms Vera Towle
t (01296) 681714

AVINGTON
Hampshire

East Tennyson Apt – Avington Park ★★★★★
Self Catering
Hideaways
t (01747) 828170
e enq@hideaways.co.uk
w hideaways.co.uk

Park Farm Cottages
★★★★★ *Self Catering*
Contact: Mr Robert Stent
t (01962) 779955
e robert@avingtonholidays.co.uk
w avingtonholidays.co.uk

AYLESFORD
Kent

Stable Cottage At Wickham Lodge ★★★★★ *Self Catering*
Contact: Mr & Mrs Bourne
t (01622) 717267
e stablecottage73@aol.com
w wickhamlodge.co.uk

BAMPTON
Oxfordshire

Grafton Manor Wing ★★★
Self Catering
Contact: Ms Sandra Eddolls
t (01367) 810237
e sandraeddolls@btinternet.com

Haytor Cottage ★★★
Self Catering
Contact: Mrs Susan Phillips
t (01993) 850321
e smph@supanet.com

BANBURY
Oxfordshire

Little Good Lodge ★★★★
Self Catering
Contact: Ms Lynne Aries
t (01295) 750069
e bryan.aries@btopenworld.com
w littlegoodfarm.users.btopenworld.com

Mill Wheel Cottage ★★★★
Self Catering
Contact: Mrs Sheila Nichols
t (01295) 811637
w holiday-rentals.com

BARNHAM
West Sussex

Paddock Barn & West Cottage ★★★-★★★★★
Self Catering
t 0870 191 7700 & 07810 228743
w english-country-cottages.co.uk

Welldiggers ★★★★★
Self Catering
Contact: Mrs Penelope Crawford
t (01243) 555119
e welldiggers@hotmail.com
w welldiggers.co.uk

BASINGSTOKE
Hampshire

Regents Court
Rating Applied For
Serviced Apartments
Deep Blue Apartments
t 0870 770 0778
e steve@deepb.com
w deepblueapartments.com

BATTLE
East Sussex

Battle Field Cottage ★★★★
Self Catering
t 07762 576495
e battlefieldcottage@yahoo.co.uk
w battlefieldcottage.co.uk

Henley Bridge Stud ★★★
Self Catering
t (01424) 892076

Ninfield Holiday Cottages, Ninfield ★★★★ *Self Catering*
Contact: Mr & Mrs D Godden
t (01424) 892686
e jill.godden@tiscali.co.uk
w ninfieldholidaycottages.co.uk

South Lodge ★★★★★
Self Catering
English Heritage
t 0870 333 1187
e holidaycottages@english-heritage.org.uk
w english-heritage.org.uk/holidaycottages

Stiles Garage ★★
Self Catering
t (01424) 773155
e stilesgarage@hotmail.com

BEAULIEU
Hampshire

Kelmscott ★★★★
Self Catering
Contact: Mr & Mrs Steve & Tracy Cherry
t (01707) 307747
e steve@cherry.cc
w kelmscott.net

Mares Tails Cottage ★★★★
Self Catering
Contact: Mrs Barber
t (01590) 612160
e marestails1@ukonline.co.uk

Old Stables Cottage ★★★★
Self Catering
Contact: Mr & Mrs Peter & Jo Whapham
t (01590) 626707
e oldstablescott@aol.com
w oldstablescottage.co.uk

BECKLEY
East Sussex

Bixley ★★★★ *Self Catering*
Contact: Ms Philippa Bushe
t (020) 7226 9035
e tim@busheassoc.com
w bixleycottage.co.uk

Kings Bank Oast ★★★★★
Self Catering
Freedom Holiday Homes
t (01580) 720770
e mail@freedomholidayhomes.co.uk
w freedomholidayhomes.co.uk

Kingshoath Cottage ★★★★
Self Catering
Garden of England Cottages
t (01892) 510117
e info@gardenofenglandcottages.co.uk
w goec.co.uk

The Orchards ★★★
Self Catering
Freedom Holiday Homes
t (01580) 720770
e mail@freedomholidayhomes.co.uk
w freedomholidayhomes.co.uk

BEMBRIDGE
Isle of Wight

10 Sandpipers ★★★★
Self Catering
Wight Coast & Country Cottages
t (01983) 873163
e mail@wcandcc.co.uk
w wcandcc.co.uk

11 Solent Landing ★★★
Self Catering
Wight Coast & Country Cottages
t (01983) 873163
e mail@wcandcc.co.uk
w wcandcc.co.uk

2 Maritime Mews ★★★★
Self Catering
Wight Locations
t (01983) 811418
e enquiries@wightlocations.co.uk
w wightlocations.co.uk

27 Solent Landing ★★★
Self Catering
Island Holiday Homes
t (01983) 521113
e enquiries@island-holiday-homes.net
w island-holiday-homes.net

3 Harbour Strand ★★★★
Self Catering
Contact: Mrs Lisa Baskill
Home from Home Holidays
t (01983) 854340
e admin@hfromh.co.uk

4 Brooks Close ★★★
Self Catering
Island Holiday Homes
t (01983) 521113
e enquiries@island-holiday-homes.net
w island-holiday-homes.net

8 Highbury Court
Rating Applied For
Self Catering
Wight Coast & Country Cottages
t (01983) 873163
e mail@wcandcc.co.uk
w wcandcc.co.uk

Bella Vista (Wight Locations)
Rating Applied For
Self Catering
Wight Locations
t (01983) 811418
e enquiries@wightlocations.co.uk
w wightlocations.co.uk

Casa Blanca ★★★★
Self Catering
Wight Locations
t (01983) 811418
e enquiries@wightlocations.co.uk
w wightlocations.co.uk

Casa Dionisis ★★★★
Self Catering
Wight Locations
t (01983) 811418
e enquiries@wightlocations.co.uk
w wightlocations.co.uk

Castaway Cottage ★★★★
Self Catering
Contact: Mrs Christine Brooks
t (023) 9258 4616
e info@castaway-cottage.co.uk
w castaway-cottage.co.uk

Caustone
Rating Applied For
Self Catering
Wight Coast & Country Cottages
t (01983) 873163
e mail@wcandcc.co.uk
w wcandcc.co.uk

Cliff Cottage ★★★
Self Catering
Home From Home Holidays
t (01983) 854340
e ventnor@crldirect.co.uk
w hfromh.co.uk

Coastwatch Cottage ★★★
Self Catering
Wight Locations
t (01983) 811418
e enquiries@wightlocations.co.uk
w wightlocations.co.uk

Crab Cottage ★★★★
Self Catering
Wight Coast & Country Cottages
t (01983) 873163
e mail@wcandcc.co.uk
w wcandcc.co.uk

Cygnet House ★★★★
Self Catering
Wight Coast & Country Cottages
t (01983) 873163
e mail@wcandcc.co.uk
w wcandcc.co.uk

Fairhaven ★★★ *Self Catering*
Wight Coast & Country Cottages
t (01983) 873163
e mail@wcandcc.co.uk
w wcandcc.co.uk

Farm Lane Apartment
★★★★ *Self Catering*
Wight Locations
t (01983) 811418
e enquiries@wightlocations.co.uk
w wightlocations.co.uk

Flat 3 Pump Mews ★★★★
Self Catering
Contact: Mrs Janet Humphray
t (01438) 813721
e humphray@humphray.fsnet.co.uk
w mysite.orange.co.uk/pumpmews

Foreland Cottage ★★
Self Catering
Wight Coast & Country Cottages
t (01983) 873163
e mail@wcandcc.co.uk
w wcandcc.co.uk

Harbour Farm Cottages – The Water Bailiff's Cottage & The Lodge ★★★★
Self Catering
Contact: Mr & Mrs Kenneth & Deirdre Hicks
t (01983) 872610
e deirdremhicks@aol.com
w harbourfarm.co.uk

Hillway Cottage ★★★★
Self Catering
Island Cottage Holidays
t (01929) 481555
e enq@islandcottageholidays.com
w islandcottageholidays.com

Hilvana ★★ *Self Catering*
Wight Coast & Country Cottages
t (01983) 873163
e mail@wcandcc.co.uk
w wcandcc.co.uk

Holiday Home
Rating Applied For
Self Catering
Contact: Mr Jon Platt
4 / 5 Bed Detached Shanklin Home
t (01983) 873499
e jonmplatt@yahoo.co.uk

Island Cottage ★★★★★
Self Catering
Wight Coast & Country Cottages
t (01983) 873163
e mail@wcandcc.co.uk
w wcandcc.co.uk

Kingsmere ★★ *Self Catering*
Contact: Mrs Kersley
t (01983) 872778

Ledge Beach Hut ★★★
Self Catering
Wight Coast & Country Cottages
t (01983) 873163
e mail@wcandcc.co.uk
w wcandcc.co.uk

Meadow Dairy ★★★
Self Catering
Home From Home Holidays
t (01983) 854340
e ventnor@crldirect.co.uk
w hfromh.co.uk

Princessa Cottage ★★★★
Self Catering
Wight Locations
t (01983) 811418
e enquiries@wightlocations.co.uk
w wightlocations.co.uk

Seahorses ★★★
Self Catering
Wight Coast & Country Cottages
t (01983) 873163
e mail@wcandcc.co.uk
w wcandcc.co.uk

Swains Villa ★★★
Self Catering
Wight Coast & Country Cottages
t (01983) 873163
e mail@wcandcc.co.uk
w wcandcc.co.uk

Windmill Cottages ★★★★
Self Catering
Contact: Miss Lisa King
t (01983) 872875
e enquiries@windmill-inn.com
w windmillcottages.co.uk

Zanbersi
Rating Applied For
Self Catering
Wight Coast & Country Cottages
t (01983) 873163
e mail@wcandcc.co.uk
w wcandcc.co.uk

BENENDEN
Kent

Bull & Mill Cottage ★★★★
Self Catering
Freedom Holiday Homes
t (01580) 720770
e mail@freedomholidayhomes.co.uk
w freedomholidayhomes.co.uk

Forest Cottage ★★★★
Self Catering
Garden of England Cottages
t (01892) 510117
e info@gardenofenglandcottages.co.uk
w goec.co.uk

Standen Barn Cottage
★★★★ *Self Catering*
Garden of England Cottages
t (01892) 510117
e info@gardenofenglandcottages.co.uk
w goec.co.uk

BENTLEY
Hampshire

Ashfield Cottage ★★★★
Self Catering
t (01420) 22144

BEXHILL-ON-SEA
East Sussex

26 Collington Avenue
★★★★ *Self Catering*
Miraleisure Ltd
t (01424) 730298
e infomira@waitrose.com
w miraleisure.co.uk

Beachcomber Flat ★★★
Self Catering
Miraleisure Ltd
t (01424) 730298
e infomira@waitrose.com
w miraleisure.co.uk

Carlton Flat ★★ *Self Catering*
Miraleisure Ltd
t (01424) 730298
e infomira@waitrose.com
w miraleisure.co.uk

Devonshire Flat ★★★
Self Catering
Miraleisure Ltd
t (01424) 730298
e infomira@waitrose.com
w miraleisure.co.uk

Flat 1 Trent House ★★★
Self Catering
Freedom Holiday Homes
t (01580) 720770
e mail@freedomholidayhomes.co.uk
w freedomholidayhomes.co.uk

Haven Flat ★★★
Self Catering
Miraleisure Ltd
t (01424) 730298
e infomira@waitrose.com
w miraleisure.co.uk

Mulberry ★★★ *Self Catering*
Contact: Mrs Valerie Passfield
t (01424) 219204

Pavilion Flat ★★★★
Self Catering
Miraleisure Ltd
t (01424) 730298
e infomira@waitrose.com
w miraleisure.co.uk

Riviera Flat ★★★
Self Catering
Miraleisure Ltd
t (01424) 730298
e infomira@waitrose.com
w miraleisure.co.uk

Sovereign Flat ★★★
Self Catering
Miraleisure Ltd
t (01424) 730298
e infomira@waitrose.com
w miraleisure.co.uk

Sylvian ★★★ *Self Catering*
t (01424) 730302
w sylvianapartments.co.uk

Wilton Flat ★★★
Self Catering
Miraleisure Ltd
t (01424) 730298
e infomira@waitrose.com
w miraleisure.co.uk

BICESTER
Oxfordshire

Grange Farm Country Cottages ★★★★
Self Catering
Contact: Mrs Penelope Oakey
t (01869) 278778
e info@grangefarmcottages.co.uk
w grangefarmcottages.co.uk

Pimlico Farm Country Cottages ★★★★
Self Catering
Contact: Mr & Mrs John & Monica Harper
t (01869) 810306
e enquiries@pimlicofarm.co.uk

Stoke Lyne Farm Cottages, Stoke Lyne ★★★★
Self Catering
Contact: Mrs Julie Adams
t (01869) 345306
e info@stokelynefarmcottages.co.uk
w stokelynefarmcottages.co.uk

BIDDENDEN
Kent

Barclay Farmhouse Cottage ★★★★ *Self Catering*
Freedom Holiday Homes
t (01580) 720770
e mail@freedomholidayhomes.co.uk
w freedomholidayhomes.co.uk

The Bothy ★★★★
Self Catering
Freedom Holiday Homes
t (01580) 720770
e mail@freedomholidayhomes.co.uk
w freedomholidayhomes.co.uk

Gamekeeper's Lodge ★★
Self Catering
Freedom Holiday Homes
t (01580) 720770
e mail@freedomholidayhomes.co.uk
w freedomholidayhomes.co.uk

Garden Lodge ★★★★
Self Catering
Freedom Holiday Homes
t (01580) 720770
e mail@freedomholidayhomes.co.uk
w freedomholidayhomes.co.uk

Standen ★★★★
Self Catering
Freedom Holiday Homes
t (01580) 720770
e mail@freedomholidayhomes.co.uk
w freedomholidayhomes.co.uk

Willow Barn ★★★★
Self Catering
Freedom Holiday Homes
t (01580) 720770
e mail@freedomholidayhomes.co.uk
w freedomholidayhomes.co.uk

BILSINGTON
Kent

Lanary Oast ★★★★★
Self Catering
Freedom Holiday Homes
t (01580) 720770
e mail@freedomholidayhomes.co.uk
w freedomholidayhomes.co.uk

Stonecross Barn ★★★★
Self Catering
Contact: Mr & Mrs John & Jane Hickman
t (01233) 720397
w http://myweb.tiscali.co.uk/stonecrossbarn/

BINFIELD
Isle of Wight

Rijnstroom IV
Rating Applied For
Self Catering
Contact: Ms Elaine McNamara Proprietors
t 07766 501113
w welcome-cottages.com

BINFIELD HEATH
Oxfordshire

Heath View Studio ★★★★
Self Catering
Contact: Mrs Finella Woolsey
t (0118) 946 4666
e finella.woolsey@hotmail.co.uk
w woolsey.thalasoft.com

BIRCHINGTON
Kent

Blue Fox Holiday ★★★★
Self Catering
t 07877 468851
e info@bluefoxholidays.co.uk

Raleigh Cottage ★★★★
Self Catering
Contact: Mrs Jill Edwards
t (01843) 841764 & (01843) 841101
e lou@landway99.freeserve.co.uk
w birchingtonholidays.co.uk

BIRDHAM
West Sussex

Martins Cottages ★★★★★
Self Catering
Contact: Mrs Gillian Farquhar-Thomson
t (01243) 512222
e gillift@martinscottages.plus.com
w martinscottages.co.uk

BISHOPSTONE
East Sussex

Norton Farm Cottage ★★★
Self Catering
Contact: Mrs Collinson
t (01323) 897544
e norton.farm@farmline.com
w http://members.farmline.com/collinson/

BLOXHAM
Oxfordshire

Barratts Barn ★★★
Self Catering
Contact: Mr & Mrs P Cavill
t (01295) 721461
e philcav@globalnet.co.uk

BOARS HEAD
East Sussex

Foxlea ★★★★ *Self Catering*
Freedom Holiday Homes
t (01580) 720770
e mail@freedomholidayhomes.co.uk
w freedomholidayhomes.co.uk

Leggs Field Barn ★★★★
Self Catering
Garden of England Cottages
t (01892) 510117
e info@gardenofenglandcottages.co.uk
w goec.co.uk

BODLE STREET
East Sussex

Redpale Farm Cottages ★★★★-★★★★★
Self Catering
Contact: Sue Roberts
t (01323) 833613
e lettings@redpalehouse.co.uk
w redpalehouse.co.uk

BOGNOR REGIS
West Sussex

3 Coastguard Cottages
Rating Applied For
Self Catering
Contact: Carolyn Turner**e** caturner1@aol.com

7A High Trees ★★★
Self Catering
Contact: Mrs Maureen Lord
t (01248) 823891
e colin.lord@tesco.net

Aldwick Lodge ★★★★
Self Catering
Contact: Mrs Morag Bouterse
t (01243) 267445 & 07813 158445
e kees@tinyworld.co.uk
w chichesterweb.co.uk/aldwicklodge.htm

Fisherman's Cottage ★★
Self Catering
Contact: Mr & Mrs Kevin & Helen Woollan
t (01934) 750900
e waterloo.road@btinternet.com

Grange Court ★★
Self Catering
Contact: Mrs Jane Blair
t (01322) 663935

Seaview Apartment ★★
Self Catering
t (020) 8393 7636

BOLDRE
Hampshire

Orchard House The Annexe ★★★ *Self Catering*
Contact: Mrs Valerie Barnes
t (01590) 676686

Springfield Wing ★★★
Self Catering
t (01590) 672491

BONCHURCH
Isle of Wight

Hadfield Cottage ★★★★
Self Catering
Island Cottage Holidays
t (01929) 481555
e enq@islandcottageholidays.com
w islandcottageholidays.com

Uppermount ★★★★
Self Catering
Island Cottage Holidays
t (01929) 481555
e enq@islandcottageholidays.com
w islandcottageholidays.com

Wyndcliffe Holiday Apartments ★★★★
Self Catering
Contact: Mrs Rosalind Young
t (01983) 853458
e admin@wyndcliffe-holidays.com
w wyndcliffe-holidays.com

BOREHAM STREET
East Sussex

The Granary ★★★★
Self Catering
Contact: Mrs Pat Honeysett
t (01323) 833925
e thegranary@hotmail.co.uk
w granaryholiday.co.uk

BORTHWOOD
Isle of Wight

Borthwood Cottages ★★★
Self Catering
Contact: Mrs Anne Finch
t (01983) 403967
e mail@netguides.co.uk
w borthwoodcottages.co.uk

BOSHAM
West Sussex

Laneside ★★★★
Self Catering
Contact: Mr Antony Wallace
t (01243) 573234
e info@millstream-hotel.co.uk
w millstream-hotel.co.uk

The Warren ★★★
Self Catering
Contact: Mrs Gillian Odell
t (01243) 573927

BOULDNOR
Isle of Wight

Waterside ★★★★
Self Catering
Island Holiday Homes
t (01983) 521113
e enquiries@island-holiday-homes.net
w island-holiday-homes.net

BOWLHEAD GREEN
Surrey

Barn Flat ★★ *Self Catering*
Contact: Mrs Grace Ranson
t (01428) 682687
e ranson@bowlhead.fsnet.co.uk

BRADING
Isle of Wight

Charnwood Cottage ★★★★
Self Catering
Home From Home Holidays
t (01983) 854340
e ventnor@crldirect.co.uk
w hfromh.co.uk

 Look out for establishments participating in the Walkers, Cyclists, Families and Welcome Pets! schemes

Hill Farm Barn ★★★★★
Self Catering
Contact: Mrs Sheila Lovegrove
Hill Farm
t (01983) 875184
e enquiries@hillfarmbrading.co.uk
w hillfarmbrading.co.uk

Hill Farm Lodge ★★★★
Self Catering
Contact: Mrs Sheila Lovegrove
Hill Farm
t (01983) 875184
e enquiries@hillfarmbrading.co.uk
w hillfarmbrading.co.uk

BRAISHFIELD
Hampshire

Meadow Cottage & Rosie's Cottage ★★★ *Self Catering*
Contact: Mrs Wendy Graham
t (01794) 368265
e info@farleyfarmcottageholidays.com
w farleyfarmcottageholidays.com

BRAMLEY
Surrey

Converted Stable at Juniper Cottage ★★★ *Self Catering*
Contact: Mr Bob Heyes
t (01483) 893706
e convertedstable@onetel.com
w web.onetel.com/~converted_stable

Old Timbers ★★★
Self Catering
Contact: Mrs Taylor
t (01483) 893258
e jpold_timbers@hotmail.com

Orchard Paddocks ★★★★
Self Catering
t (01483) 894563
w orchardpaddocks.co.uk

BREDE
East Sussex

Eastwood Cottage ★★★★
Self Catering
Garden of England Cottages
t (01892) 510117
e info@gardenofenglandcottages.co.uk
w goec.co.uk

Goat House Cottage ★★★★
Self Catering
Garden of England Cottages
t (01892) 510117
e info@gardenofenglandcottages.co.uk
w goec.co.uk

The Hovel and The Hop House ★★★★ *Self Catering*
Garden of England Cottages
t (01892) 510117
e info@gardenofenglandcottages.co.uk
w goec.co.uk

The Old Granary ★★★★
Self Catering
Freedom Holiday Homes
t (01580) 720770
e mail@freedomholidayhomes.co.uk
w freedomholidayhomes.co.uk

BRIGHSTONE
Isle of Wight

2 The Granary ★★★★
Self Catering
Contact: Ms Teresa Herd
t 07795 078049 & 07795 078049
e brooksidecottage@ntlworld.com
w 2thegranary.co.uk

3 Sea Breeze Cottages
★★★★ *Self Catering*
Contact: Mrs Virginia Peckham
t (01983) 740993
e ginnypeckham@aol.com
w seabreeze-cottage.co.uk

Carriers Stable ★★★★
Self Catering
t (01983) 740717
w wighthols.co.uk

Casses ★★★★ *Self Catering*
Contact: Mr Nesbitt
t (01590) 679601
e jkn@casses.fsbusiness.co.uk

Chilton Farm Cottages
★★★-★★★★★ *Self Catering*
Contact: Mrs Sue Fisk
t (01983) 740338
e info@chiltonfarm.co.uk
w chiltonfarm.co.uk

Chipps Moor ★★★★
Self Catering
Island Cottage Holidays
t (01929) 481555
e enq@islandcottageholidays.com
w islandcottageholidays.com

Grange Farm Brighstone Bay
★★★ *Self Catering*
Contact: Mr & Mrs Dunjay
t (01983) 740296
e grangefarm@brighstonebay.fsnet.co.uk
w brighstonebay.fsnet.co.uk

The Mill House ★★★★★
Self Catering
Contact: Mrs Josie Gavoyannis
The Mill House (Holidays 2 Remember)
t (01825) 791055
e info@holidays2remember.co.uk
w holidays2remember.co.uk/property.php?id=1

November Cottage
★★★★★ *Self Catering*
Island Cottage Holidays
t (01929) 481555
e enq@islandcottageholidays.com
w islandcottageholidays.com

Old Rock Cottage ★★★★
Self Catering
Island Cottage Holidays
t (01929) 481555
e enq@islandcottageholidays.com
w islandcottageholidays.com

Stable Cottage ★★★★
Self Catering
Island Cottage Holidays
t (01929) 481555
e enq@islandcottageholidays.com
w islandcottageholidays.com

Thorncross Farm – Rose & Pool Cottages ★★★★★
Self Catering
Contact: Mrs Russell
t (01983) 740291
e info@thorncrossfarm.co.uk
w thorncross-holiday-cottages.co.uk

Thorncross Farm – Rose & Pool Cottages ★★★★★
Self Catering
Contact: Mrs Russell
t (01983) 740291
w thorncross-holiday-cottages.co.uk

Valentine Lodge ★★★★
Self Catering
Contact: Mrs Chris Bentley
t (01983) 740677
e chrisatblakes@btinternet.com
w valentinelodge.co.uk

BRIGHTLING
East Sussex

Great Worge Farm Barn
★★★★ *Self Catering*
Freedom Holiday Homes
t (01580) 720770
e mail@freedomholidayhomes.co.uk
w freedomholidayhomes.co.uk

BRIGHTON & HOVE
East Sussex

8 Upper Market Street ★★★
Self Catering
Contact: Mr Mark Barnes
t (020) 8979 1792

Brighton Marina Holiday Apartments ★★★★
Self Catering
Contact: Mrs A Wills
5 Marlborough Road
t (020) 8940 6945
e averil.wills@london.com
w brightonmarinaholidayapartments.co.uk

Crown Gardens ★★★★
Self Catering
Contact: Julia Harding
t 0845 094 1694
w crown-gardens.co.uk

The Edge ★★★★
Self Catering
Contact: Mr Cliff Saunderson
t (01273) 410777
e cliff64@sky.com

Flat 3 34 Brunswick Terrace
★★★★ *Self Catering*
Contact: Mr Richard Harris
Best of Brighton & Sussex Cottages Ltd
t (01273) 308779
e brightoncottages@pavilion.co.uk
w bestofbrighton.co.uk

Garden Annexe @ Florence House ★★★ *Self Catering*
Contact: Geoff Hart
t 07817 492237
e geoffhart@brightonlets.net
w brightonlets.net

Holiday Flat ★★★
Self Catering
Contact: Peter Anthony
t (01480) 495914
e peter.anthony3@ntlworld.com
w holidayflathove.co.uk

Kilcolgan Premier Bungalows, Rottingdean
★★★★★ *Self Catering*
Contact: Shaemus St George
t (020) 7250 3678
e jc.stgeorge@virgin.net
w holidaybungalowsbrighton uk.com

Palms Properties ★★★★
Self Catering
Contact: Ms Pat Lowe
t (01273) 626000
e enquiries@palmsagency.co.uk
w palmsagency.co.uk

The Patio, 3 St James's Avenue ★★★★ *Self Catering*
Contact: Mr Francis Hazel
t (01273) 676732
w brightonshortstays.co.uk

Queensbury Cottage
★★★★ *Self Catering*
Contact: Paula Hamblin
Queensbury Mews Cottage
t (01273) 270636
e info@queensburycottage.co.uk
w queensburycottage.co.uk

Spell Self Catering
★★★-★★★★ *Self Catering*
Contact: Mr Peter Ellis
t (01273) 308779 & 07707 813012
e spell.let@virgin.net
w spellselfcatering.co.uk

BROAD OAK
East Sussex

Austens Wood Annexe
★★★★ *Self Catering*
Freedom Holiday Homes
t (01580) 720770
e mail@freedomholidayhomes.co.uk
w freedomholidayhomes.co.uk

Dairy Cottage and Two Oaks
★★★-★★★★ *Self Catering*
Contact: Mr Stuart Winter
t (01892) 510117
e holidays@gardenofenglandcottages.co.uk
w gardenofenglandcottages.co.uk

Riding & Stable Cottage
★★★★ *Self Catering*
Garden of England Cottages
t (01892) 510117
e info@gardenofenglandcottages.co.uk
w goec.co.uk

Spelland Barn ★★★★★
Self Catering
Freedom Holiday Homes
t (01580) 720770
e mail@freedomholidayhomes.co.uk
w freedomholidayhomes.co.uk

BROADSTAIRS
Kent

2 Forge Cottages ★★★★
Self Catering
t (01304) 619444

Albert Cottage ★★★★
Self Catering
Freedom Holiday Homes
t (01580) 720770
e mail@freedomholidayhomes.co.uk
w freedomholidayhomes.co.uk

Beacon Light Cottage
★★★★ *Self Catering*
Contact: Patrick & Carine Vandervorst
t (03250) 423207
e beaconlight.cottage@scarlet.be
w beaconlightcottage.com

The Beeches Holiday Lets
★★★ *Self Catering*
Contact: Steven Mayhew
t (01843) 869709
e stevenmayhew@f2s.com
w thebeechesholidaylets.co.uk

Beeson Holiday House ★★★
Self Catering
Contact: Sarah Robinson
t (01635) 862918
e sarahjrobinson@yahoo.co.uk
w broadstairsholidayhome.co.uk

Bleak House Lodge ★★★★
Self Catering
Contact: Mr Connell
t (01843) 861400
e kenny.connell@btinternet.com

Broadstairs Holiday House
★★★ *Self Catering*
Contact: Lynn Bull
t (01992) 576044
e lynn.bull@tiscali.co.uk
w broadstairs-holiday-house.co.uk

Broadstairs Holiday Lets
★★★-★★★★★ *Self Catering*
Contact: Linda & Harry Sear
t (01525) 210550
e lindaandharrysear@yahoo.co.uk
w broadstairsholidaylets.co.uk

Broadstairs Holiday Lets
★★★ *Self Catering*
Contact: Linda & Harry Sear
t (01525) 210550
e lindaandharrysear@yahoo.co.uk
w broadstairsholidaylets.co.uk

Chandos Square ★★★★
Self Catering
Contact: Matthew Dove
t 07940 650023
e enquiries@selfcateringbroadstairs.co.uk
w selfcateringbroadstairs.co.uk

Chevening and Arran Bungalows ★★★★
Self Catering
Contact: Linda McDonnell
t (020) 8302 1852
e info@cheveningholiday.co.uk
w cheveningholiday.co.uk

Coachmans Flat in Reading Street ★★★ *Self Catering*
Contact: Mrs Ellen Barrett
Coachmans Flat Reading Street
t (01843) 867925
e ellen@stonar.com
w stonar.com

Fisherman's Cottage ★★★★
Self Catering
Contact: Ms Linda Spillane
t (020) 8672 4150
e linda.spillane@virgin.net
w fishermanscottage broadstairs.co.uk

The Fishermen's Cottages
★★★★ *Self Catering*
Contact: Phil & Suzanne Dennis
t (01843) 601996
e thefishermenscottages@hotmail.co.uk
w fishermenscottages.co.uk

Flat 1, 2 Prospect Place
★★★★ *Self Catering*
Freedom Holiday Homes
t (01580) 720770
e mail@freedomholidayhomes.co.uk
w freedomholidayhomes.co.uk

Flat 1 York Mansions
★★★★ *Self Catering*
Freedom Holiday Homes
t (01580) 720770
e mail@freedomholidayhomes.co.uk
w freedomholidayhomes.co.uk

Flat 3, Beach Court ★★★★
Self Catering
Freedom Holiday Homes
t (01580) 720770
e mail@freedomholidayhomes.co.uk
w freedomholidayhomes.co.uk

Inverness Flat ★★★
Self Catering
Contact: Mrs Beatrice Jones
t (01843) 867116
e rhys.maps@dsl.pipex.com

Land & Life Self Catering Apartments ★★★★
Self Catering
Contact: Mrs Simone Vince
t (01843) 867727
e info@land-and-life.de
w land-and-life.de

Lawrence Family Holidays
★★★★ *Self Catering*
Contact: Mrs J N Lawrence
t (01843) 591422
e nancy@nancylawrence.plus.com
w lawrencefamilyholidays.co.uk

Martin Holiday Homes
★★★★ *Self Catering*
Contact: Mrs Penny Martin
t (01843) 592945
e penny@martinholidays.co.uk
w martinholidays.co.uk

Martin Holiday Homes
★★★★ *Self Catering*
Contact: Mrs Penny Martin
t (01843) 592945
e penny@martinholidays.co.uk
w martinholidays.co.uk

Mertott Lodge ★★★
Self Catering
Contact: Lisa Merrill
t (01708) 859595
e broadstairsbreaks@hotmail.com
w broadstairsbreaks.co.uk

St Cuby
Rating Applied For
Self Catering
Contact: Mrs Kath Warwick
t (01304) 205653
e kathryn@kathrynbailey.wanadoo.co.uk
w stcubyholidaylet.co.uk

Sanderling Cottage ★★★★
Self Catering
Contact: Catherine Greenwood
t 07971 533220
e cath.greenwood@btinternet.com
w sanderlingcottage.co.uk

Seaview Apartment ★★★★
Self Catering
Contact: Mrs S Franks
t (01635) 873473
e mfranks@md-technology.co.uk

Stone Bay Court ★★★★
Self Catering
Contact: Gordon Crompton
t (01304) 619444
e enquiries@curlewcottages.co.uk
w beachliving.co.uk

Victoria Parade Seafront Apartment ★★★
Self Catering
Freedom Holiday Homes
t (01580) 720770
e mail@freedomholidayhomes.co.uk
w freedomholidayhomes.co.uk

BROCKENHURST
Hampshire

The Annexe ★★★★
Self Catering
t (01590) 622449
w forestlodge.info

Ashtree House ★★★★
Self Catering
Contact: Mrs Christine Hirsch
t (028) 9754 1987
e peter-hirsch@utvinternet.com
w ashtreebrockenhurst.com

Gorse Cottage ★★★★
Self Catering
Contact: Mr Julian Gilbert
t 0870 321 0020
e info@gorsecottage.co.uk
w gorsecottage.co.uk

Waterley Cottage ★★★★
Self Catering
Contact: Mrs Ann Larkin
t 0845 680 0173
e ann@brockcott.co.uk
w brockcott.co.uk

BROOK
Isle of Wight

Brook Farm Cottages ★★★
Self Catering
Contact: Mrs Fry
t (01983) 740387

The Clock House & The Clock House Cottage
★★★★ *Self Catering*
Contact: Mrs Amanda Ridler-Lee
t (01983) 741212
e clockhousebrook@btinternet.com
w clockhousebrook.co.uk

Dunsbury Farm – Cottage & Grange ★★★★ *Self Catering*
Contact: Mrs Susannah Seely
t (01983) 741325
e susannah@dunsburyfarm.co.uk
w dunsburyfarm.co.uk

Holiday Homes Owners Services: B1 ★★★★
Self Catering
Holiday Homes Owners Services (West Wight)
t (01983) 753423
e holidayhomesiow@ic24.net
w holidayhomesiow.co.uk

Holiday Homes Owners Services Ref: B4 ★★
Self Catering
Holiday Homes Owners Services (West Wight)
t (01983) 753423
e holidayhomesiow@ic24.net
w holidayhomesiow.co.uk

Sudmoor Cottage ★★★★
Self Catering
Island Cottage Holidays
t (01929) 481555
e enq@islandcottageholidays.com
w islandcottageholidays.com

Westbrook & Northbrook
★★★★ *Self Catering*
Contact: Mrs Belinda Walters
Battersea Bridge Investments Ltd
t (01983) 740535 & 07802 203376
e bookings@brookhouseiow.co.uk
w brookhouseiow.co.uk

BROOKLAND
Kent

The Granary & The Dairy
★★★★ *Self Catering*
Freedom Holiday Homes
t (01580) 720770
e mail@freedomholidayhomes.co.uk
w freedomholidayhomes.co.uk

Puddock Farm Pine Lodges
★★★★ *Self Catering*
Contact: Mrs Amanda Skinner
t (01797) 344440
e amanda_skinner@talk21.com
w puddockfarmpinelodges.co.uk

BUCKINGHAM
Buckinghamshire

Huntsmill Farm Holidays
★★★★ *Self Catering*
t (01280) 704852 & 07970 871104
e fiona@huntsmill.com
w huntsmill.com

BURFORD Oxfordshire

Candlemas ★★★★
Self Catering
t (01993) 824252
e mancott@netcomuk.co.uk
w manorcottages.co.uk

Caswell House ★★★★-★★★★★
Self Catering
Contact: Mrs Amanda Matthews
t (01993) 701064 & 07718 390867
e stay@caswell-house.co.uk
w caswell-house.co.uk

The Mill at Burford ★★★
Self Catering
t (01993) 824252
e enquiries@manorcottages.co.uk
w themillatburford.co.uk

BURGATE Hampshire

Burgate Farmhouse ★★★
Self Catering
Contact: Mrs Christine Bennett
t (01425) 655909
e admin@burgatefarm.freeserve.co.uk
w burgate.fslife.co.uk

BURLEY Hampshire

Barn Cottage ★★★★
Self Catering
Contact: Mrs Helen Gaskell
t (01425) 403726
e gaskell425@btinternet.com
w barncottageburley.co.uk

Brackenwood ★★★★
Self Catering
Contact: Mrs Ros White
t (01534) 862116
e info@forestcharm.com
w forestcharm.com

Cherry Tree Cottage ★★★
Self Catering
Contact: Mr & Mrs John & Gwen Pannell
t (01425) 402491
e che.tre-cot@virgin.net
w thecherrytreecottage.co.uk

The Dairy ★★★★
Self Catering
Contact: Mrs Carole Stewart
t (01425) 402302
e carolestewart@pobox.com
w briandix.dsl.pipex.com/great_wells/dairy.htm

Hollyhocks ★★★★★
Self Catering
Contact: Mrs Christine Outten
t (01425) 650568
e christineoutten@hotmail.co.uk

Rose Cottage ★★★
Self Catering
Contact: Mr Stephen Linney
t (01534) 857441
e splinney@rosecottage.uk.net
w rosecottage.uk.net

BURWASH COMMON East Sussex

Blackdown Cottage
Rating Applied For
Self Catering
Contact: Mr Patrick Hook
t (01435) 882943
e ph@patrickhook.com

BURWASH WEALD East Sussex

Chandlers Cottage ★★★
Self Catering
Garden of England Cottages
t (01892) 510117
e info@gardenofenglandcottages.co.uk
w goec.co.uk

CADNAM Hampshire

Kingsbridge House Retreat ★★★★ *Self Catering*
t (023) 8081 1161

CALBOURNE Isle of Wight

Holiday Homes Owners Services Ref: C1 ★★★★
Self Catering
Holiday Homes Owners Services (West Wight)
t (01983) 753423
e holidayhomesiow@ic24.net
w holidayhomesiow.co.uk

Stone Barn ★★★
Self Catering
Contact: Mrs Angela Clarke
t (01983) 531246
e ahclarke28@gmail.com

CAMBER East Sussex

Barwon Heads ★★★★
Self Catering
Contact: Mr Rick Popert
t 07764 181971
e rick.popert@byinternet.com

The Beach Retreat ★★★★
Self Catering
Contact: Ms Emma Crabtree
t (020) 7584 8996
w crabtreeandcrabtree.com/thebeach-retreat.php

Bridle Cottage & Horseshoe Cottage ★★★★ *Self Catering*
Garden of England Cottages
t (01892) 510117
e info@gardenofenglandcottages.co.uk
w goec.co.uk

Dunescape ★★★★
Self Catering
Contact: Mr Andrew J Dittone dunescape@hotmail.co.uk
w dunescape.co.uk

Laguna Beach House ★★★★ *Self Catering*
Contact: Mrs Miggie Lorraine
t (01424) 522525
e miggielorraine@hotmail.com
w camberbeachhouses.co.uk

Rye Bay Beach House ★★★★ *Self Catering*
t 07961 377365
w ryebaybeachhouse.com

'Seascape' The Beach House ★★★★ *Self Catering*
t (01797) 224754
e sea-scape@boltblue.com
w camberbeach.co.uk/seascape.html

CAMBERLEY Surrey

SACO Wentworth Place ★★★★ *Serviced Apartments*
SACO Apartments
t (0117) 974 5936
e sarahbailey@sacaoapartments.co.uk
w sacoapartments.co.uk

CANTERBURY Kent

Bell Cottage ★★★★
Self Catering
Freedom Holiday Homes
t (01580) 720770
e mail@freedomholidayhomes.co.uk
w freedomholidayhomes.co.uk

Canterbury Country Houses ★★★★★ *Self Catering*
t 07710 253690
e info@canterburyholidays.com
w canterburycountryhouses.co.uk

Jubilee Lodge ★★★
Self Catering
Contact: Mrs S P Underwood
t (01233) 720370
e juck1@aol.com

Knowlton Court Cottages ★★★-★★★★ *Self Catering*
Contact: Amy Froggatt
t (01304) 842402

The Old Sawmill, Hastingleigh ★★★
Self Catering
Contact: Mrs Caroline Gilson
t (01233) 750056 & 07765 963215
e carolinepilgrim@aol.com
w hastingleighholidaylets.com

Oriel Lodge Holiday Apartments ★★★★
Self Catering
Contact: Mr Keith Rishworth
Oriel Lodge
t (01227) 462845
e info@oriel-lodge.co.uk
w oriel-lodge.co.uk

St Mary's Cottage ★★★★
Self Catering
Contact: Mr R. Allcorn
t (01227) 450265
e r.allcorn@discovercanterbury.co.uk
w discovercanterbury.co.uk

St Michael's Place ★★★★
Self Catering
Contact: Mrs Erica Drysdale
t (020) 8398 7036
w stmichaelsplace.co.uk

The Smithy, Chilham ★★★★ *Self Catering*
t (01227) 731303
e info@smithy-cottage.com
w smithy-cottage.com

Wagoners & Shepherds Cottage
Rating Applied For
Self Catering
Contact: Ms Hazel Long
t (01227) 471513

CARISBROOKE Isle of Wight

Dairy Cottage – Luckington Farm ★★★★ *Self Catering*
Contact: Mrs Yapp
t (01983) 822951
e info@dairycottage.co.uk
w dairycottage.co.uk

Toll Cottage ★★★★
Self Catering
Contact: Mrs Siobhan Aubin
t 07967 659757
e aubinsiobhan@googlemail.com
w upthegardenpaths.com

CATHERINGTON Hampshire

Lone Barn Cottage ★★★
Self Catering
t (023) 9263 2911
w lonebarn.net

CAVERSFIELD Oxfordshire

Grooms Cottage ★★★
Self Catering
t (01869) 249307

CHALE Isle of Wight

Atherfield Green Farm Holiday Cottages ★★★★
Self Catering
Contact: Mr & Mrs Alistair Jupe
t (01983) 867613
e alistair.jupe@btinternet.com
w btinternet.com/~alistair.jupe/

The Cart House & The Milk House ★★★★ *Self Catering*
Contact: Ms Caroline Gurney-Champion
t (01983) 551368
e carthouse@gottenmanor.co.uk
w gottenmanor.co.uk

Chapel Cottage ★★★
Self Catering
Island Holiday Homes
t (01983) 521113
e enquiries@island-holiday-homes.net
w island-holiday-homes.net

Old Rectory ★★★★
Self Catering
Contact: Mrs Mary Coward
t (01983) 551393
e nigel.coward@onetel.com
w theoldrectorychale.co.uk

CHALE GREEN Isle of Wight

1 & 2 North Appleford Farm Cottages ★★★ *Self Catering*
Contact: Mr Clarke
t (01983) 721206
e admin@appleford-cottages.co.uk
w appleford-cottages.co.uk

Green Edge Holiday Cottage
★★★ *Self Catering*
Contact: Mrs Jackie Miles
t (01983) 551419
e greenedgecottage@gmail.com
w greenedgecottage.com

CHALFONT ST GILES
Buckinghamshire

Hilborough ★★★
Self Catering
t (01494) 872536

CHAPEL ROW
Berkshire

The Flat ★★★ *Self Catering*
t (0118) 971 3394

CHARLBURY
Oxfordshire

Banbury Hill Farm Cottages
★★★ *Self Catering*
Contact: Mrs Angela Widdows
t (01608) 810314
e beds@gfwiddows.f9.co.uk
w charlburyoxfordaccom.co.uk

CHART SUTTON
Kent

Brick Kiln Cottage ★★★★
Self Catering
Contact: Mrs Sue Spain
t (01622) 842490
e info@whitehousefarm-kent.co.uk
w whitehousefarm-kent.co.uk

Orchard Cottage ★★★
Self Catering
Freedom Holiday Homes
t (01580) 720770
e mail@freedomholidayhomes.co.uk
w freedomholidayhomes.co.uk

CHESSELL
Isle of Wight

Sweet Brook ★★★★
Self Catering
Island Cottage Holidays
t (01929) 481555
e enq@islandcottageholidays.com
w islandcottageholidays.com

CHICHESTER
West Sussex

12 Bishops Courtyard
★★★★ *Self Catering*
Contact: Fiona Dobbs
t 07516 762955
e fiona.dobbs@btinternet.com

Apple Barn, Runcton
★★★★★ *Self Catering*
Contact: Mrs R Kendall
Saltham House
t (01243) 775997
e applebarn@salthamhouse.co.uk
w salthamhouse.co.uk

Cornerstones ★★★★
Self Catering
Contact: Mrs Higgins
t (01243) 839096
e v.r.higgins@dsl.pipex.com
w cornercottages.com

Cygnet Cottage ★★★★
Self Catering
Contact: Mrs Higgins
t (01243) 839096
e v.r.higgins@dsl.pipex.com
w cornercottages.com

East Walls Apartment
★★★★ *Self Catering*
Contact: Mrs Pat Seager
Tanglewood
t (01243) 545168
e patriciaseager@hotmail.com
w chichesterapartment.co.uk

Honeysuckle Cottage
★★★★ *Self Catering*
Contact: Noel & Jenny Bettridge
t (01243) 779823
e noeljenny@onetel.com

Hunston Mill Cottages ★★★
Self Catering
Contact: Mr & Mrs Ian & Lyn Potter
Hunston Mill
t (01243) 783375
e hunstonmillcottages@bushinternet.com
w hunstonmill.co.uk

Lavender Cottage ★★★★
Self Catering
Contact: Ron & Pam Foden
t (01243) 771314
e rdfoden@talk21.com
w lavendercottagechichester.co.uk

New Park Studio ★★★
Self Catering
Contact: Linda Hull
t (01243) 781147
e lhull1@toucansurf.com

North Walls ★★★
Self Catering
Contact: Deborah Crampin
Oak House
t 07778 354747
e debbie@livewarehf.com
w northwalls.co.uk

Oak Apple Barn ★★★★
Self Catering
Contact: Mrs Siobain Davies
t 07763 384468
e siobain.davies@virgin.net

Quay Quarters ★★★★★
Self Catering
Contact: Mrs Lorraine Sawday
t (01243) 839900
e cottages@quayquarters.co.uk
w quayquarters.co.uk

CHIDDINGFOLD
Surrey

Prestwick Byre ★★★★
Self Catering
Contact: Mr & Mrs Paul & Valerie Mills
t (01428) 654695
e prestwick.farm@btconnect.com
w prestwickfarm.co.uk

CHIDDINGSTONE
Kent

Hay Barn & Straw Barn
★★★★ *Self Catering*
Garden of England Cottages
t (01892) 510117
e info@gardenofenglandcottages.co.uk
w goec.co.uk

CHIDHAM
West Sussex

Canute Cottages ★★★★
Self Catering
Contact: Ms Diana Beale
t (01243) 572123
e diana@canutecottages.co.uk
w canutecottages.co.uk

CHILBOLTON
Hampshire

Larch Loft ★★★★
Self Catering
Contact: Emma Way
t (01264) 860649
e stay@larchloft.co.uk
w larchloft.co.uk

CHILHAM
Kent

Monckton Cottages ★★★★
Self Catering
Contact: Mrs Helen Kirwan
t (01227) 730256 & 07789 431760
e helen@rwkirwan.plus.com
w moncktoncottages.com

CHILLERTON
Isle of Wight

Chapel Cottage ★★★
Self Catering
Island Holiday Homes
t (01983) 521113
e enquiries@island-holiday-homes.net
w island-holiday-homes.net

The Willows, ★★★
Self Catering
Contact: Mrs Muriel Burns
t (01983) 721630

CHILTON
Oxfordshire

Chilton Apartments & Cottages ★★★★
Self Catering
Contact: Mr Giles Stevens
t 0870 080 2980
e info@chiltonapartments.com
w chiltonapartments.com

CHILWORTH
Hampshire

Lavender Cottage ★★★★
Self Catering
Contact: Mrs Susan Barnes
Lavender Cottage, Chilworth
t (01788) 543932

CHIPPING NORTON
Oxfordshire

Beech House, Old Chalford
★★★★★ *Self Catering*
Contact: Mrs Dorothy Canty
t (01608) 641435
e beechhouse@chalfordpark.co.uk
w chalfordpark.co.uk

Bruern Holiday Cottages
★★★★★ *Self Catering*
Contact: Ms Frances Curtin
t (01993) 830415
e fran@bruern.co.uk
w bruern-holiday-cottages.co.uk

Dairy Cottage ★★★★
Self Catering
Contact: Mrs Janie Hextall
t (01608) 658278
e jnhh@oxhex.wanadoo.co.uk
w holiday-rental.com/dairycottage

East Churchill Holiday Cottages ★★★ *Self Catering*
Contact: Ms Miyuki Sedohara
t (01608) 641944
e miyuki@eastchurchill.com
w eastchurchill.com

Hedera Cottage ★★★★
Self Catering
Contact: Mrs Angela Richards
t (01993) 824252
e mancott@netcomuk.co.uk
w manorcottages.co.uk

CHURT
Surrey

Woodpecker Cottage
★★★★ *Self Catering*
Contact: Ms Adrienne Burgess
t 07747 145146
e adrienne@adrienneburgess.com
w martincochrane.com/woodpecker

CLAYDON
Oxfordshire

Parrots Barn ★★★★
Self Catering
Contact: Cliff & Jill Fox
t (01295) 690727
e cliff.fox@tiscali.co.uk
w parrotsbarn.co.uk

CLIFTONVILLE
Kent

Majestic Flat ★★★★
Self Catering
Contact: Yvonne Forbes
Elonville Hotel
t (01843) 298635
e yvonne.forbes@btinternet.com
w majesticholidaylettings.com

CLIMPING
West Sussex

The Dairy Cottage ★★★
Self Catering
Contact: Ms Sue Beckhurst
t (01903) 724187
e thedairy@tiscali.co.uk

COLDRED
Kent

Coldred Place ★★★★★
Self Catering
Contact: Liska Wombell
t (01304) 823533
e dwombell@hotmail.com

COLLIER STREET
Kent

Den Farm Oast Barn ★★★
Self Catering
Contact: Ms Liz Simmonds
t (01892) 730256
e liz.s@fsmail.net
w easisites.co.uk/denfarmoastbarn

COLWORTH
West Sussex

Glencroft Cottages ★★★★
Self Catering
Contact: Debbie Trust
t (01243) 532929
e glencroft.b_and_b@btinternet.com
w glencroft.biz

COMPTON
West Sussex

Yew Tree House ★★★
Self Catering
Contact: Michael & Daphne Buchanan
t (023) 9263 1248
e d.buchanan@btinternet.com

COSHAM
Hampshire

Affordable Family Holidays
Approved Caravan Holiday Home
Contact: Ms Allison Chan
t (023) 9242 2486
e awchan2002@yahoo.co.uk
w affordablefamilyholidays.co.uk

COWBEECH
East Sussex

Beechcroft, Cowbeech ★★★★★ *Self Catering*
Contact: Mr Michael Haydon
t (01435) 830237
e enquiries@beechcroft.org
w beechcroft.org

COWDEN
Kent

The Duck House ★★★★
Self Catering
t (01342) 850928
w theduckhouse.net

COWES
Isle of Wight

Belharbour ★★★★★
Self Catering
Contact: Mrs Carys Kenna
t (020) 8747 8308
e webmaster@belharbour.com
w belharbour.com

Courtmacsherry ★★★
Self Catering
Island Holiday Homes
t (01983) 521113
e enquiries@island-holiday-homes.net
w island-holiday-homes.net

Dolphin Cottage ★★★
Self Catering
Contact: Mrs Susan Brocklehurst
t (020) 8882 5606
e dolphincottage@blueyonder.co.uk
w dolphincottagecowes.co.uk

Fore & Aft Apartment ★★★★ *Self Catering*
Contact: Ms Paula Lewis
t 0870 444 8890
e holidays@redfunnel.co.uk
w redfunnel.co.uk

Gurnard Marsh ★★★★
Self Catering
Contact: Miss Michele Fisher
t 07968 437039
e mail@gurnardmarsh.co.uk
w gurnardmarsh.co.uk

Gurnard Pines ★★★★
Self Catering
Contact: Mr James Chiodini
t (01983) 292395
e info@gurnardpines.co.uk
w gurnardpines.co.uk

High Rising ★★★★★
Self Catering
Island Cottage Holidays
t (01929) 481555
e enq@islandcottageholidays.com
w islandcottageholidays.com

Little Sails ★★★
Self Catering
Contact: Mrs Sally Hedgecoe
t (01252) 722114
e sally.hedgecoe@btinternet.com
w farnham-properties.co.uk

Mariners ★★★★
Self Catering
Contact: Mrs Thomas
t (020) 8994 0856
e suziethomas47@aol.com

Medina View ★★★★
Self Catering
Contact: Mrs Jacqueline Cave
t (01983) 756300
e jacquicave@btinternet.com
w medinaviewcowes.co.uk

Medina View Cottage
Rating Applied For
Self Catering
Home From Home Holidays
t (01983) 854340
e ventnor@crldirect.co.uk
w hfromh.co.uk

Nutbourne Villa ★★★
Self Catering
Contact: Mr & Mrs Mike & Joan Vine
t (01923) 856290
e mikeandjoan.vine@btinternet.com

The Old School House ★★★
Self Catering
t 07831 514108
e tim@coweshouse.co.uk
w coweshouse.co.uk

Pebbles ★★★★ *Self Catering*
Contact: Mr Ian McLeod
t 07770 864251
e bookings@acoweshouse.co.uk
w acoweshouse.co.uk

The Pilotage ★★★★
Self Catering
Island Cottage Holidays
t (01929) 481555
e enq@islandcottageholidays.com
w islandcottageholidays.com

Point Cottages ★★★
Self Catering
Contact: Miss Louise Hall
t (01983) 280641
e louise.hall@flyingfishonline.com
w pointcottages.co.uk

Sea Axe House ★★★
Self Catering
Island Holiday Homes
t (01983) 521113
e enquiries@island-holiday-homes.net
w island-holiday-homes.net

Yachtsman's Rest ★★★
Self Catering
Contact: Mrs Janis Gorman
t (01342) 870255
e eastergorman@aol.com
w sunandsail.co.uk

CRANBROOK
Kent

1 Saltburn Cottage ★★★★
Self Catering
Freedom Holiday Homes
t (01580) 720770
e mail@freedomholidayhomes.co.uk
w freedomholidayhomes.co.uk

2 Horse Entry ★★★★
Self Catering
Freedom Holiday Homes
t (01580) 720770
e mail@freedomholidayhomes.co.uk
w freedomholidayhomes.co.uk

Bourne Farm Oast ★★★★
Self Catering
Garden of England Cottages
t (01892) 510117
e info@gardenofenglandcottages.co.uk
w goec.co.uk

Hartridge Manor Farm Byre ★★★★ *Self Catering*
Freedom Holiday Homes
t (01580) 720770
e mail@freedomholidayhomes.co.uk
w freedomholidayhomes.co.uk

Highwell Annexe ★★★★
Self Catering
Contact: Ms Linda Johnson
t (01580) 752447
e passiflora2@btinternet.com
w highwellannexe.com

The Little Barn ★★★★
Self Catering
Hideaways
t (01747) 828170
e enq@hideaways.co.uk
w hideaways.co.uk

Little Dodges ★★★★
Self Catering
Contact: Mrs Brenda Beck
Freedom Holiday Homes
t (01580) 720770
e mail@freedomholidayhomes.co.uk
w freedomholidayhomes.co.uk

Mill Cottage ★★★★
Self Catering
Garden of England Cottages
t (01892) 510117
e info@gardenofenglandcottages.co.uk
w goec.co.uk

Millhouse Granary ★★★★
Self Catering
Freedom Holiday Homes
t (01580) 720770
e mail@freedomholidayhomes.co.uk
w freedomholidayhomes.co.uk

The Old Laundry ★★★★
Self Catering
Freedom Holiday Homes
t (01580) 720770
e mail@freedomholidayhomes.co.uk
w freedomholidayhomes.co.uk

Waypost Meadow Cottage ★★★★ *Self Catering*
Freedom Holiday Homes
t (01580) 720770
e mail@freedomholidayhomes.co.uk
w freedomholidayhomes.co.uk

CROWBOROUGH
East Sussex

Cleeve Lodge ★★★★
Self Catering
Freedom Holiday Homes
t (01580) 720770
e mail@freedomholidayhomes.co.uk
w freedomholidayhomes.co.uk

The Cottage ★★★★
Self Catering
Garden of England Cottages
t (01892) 510117
e info@gardenofenglandcottages.co.uk
w goec.co.uk

Drumsell Lodge ★★★
Self Catering
Garden of England Cottages
t (01892) 510117
e info@gardenofenglandcottages.co.uk
w goec.co.uk

Hodges ★★★★★
Self Catering
Contact: Mrs Hazel Colliver
t (01892) 652386
e enquiries@hodges.uk.com
w hodges.uk.com

Keepers Lodge ★★★★
Self Catering
Garden of England Cottages
t (01892) 510117
e info@gardenofenglandcottages.co.uk
w goec.co.uk

Poundgate Park ★★★★
Self Catering
Garden of England Cottages
t (01892) 510117
e info@gardenofenglandcottages.co.uk
w goec.co.uk

The Riding ★★★★
Self Catering
Contact: Penny & Don Spearman
t (01892) 654619
e don@southerncomfort.uk.com
w southerncomfort.uk.com

Streele Farm ★★★★★
Self Catering
Contact: Mrs Jacquelyn Beesley
t (01892) 852579
e stay@compasscottages.co.uk
w compasscottages.co.uk

CROWHURST
East Sussex

Country Cottages at Park Farm, Crowhurst ★★★★
Self Catering
Contact: Mrs Joan LeMay-Edwards
t (01424) 852505
e info@parkfarmcountrycottages.co.uk
w parkfarmcountrycottages.co.uk

CRUNDALE
Kent

Farnley Little Barn ★★★★
Self Catering
Contact: Mrs Sylvia Hope
t (01227) 730510
e farnleylittlebarn@supaworld.com

Ripple Farm ★★★
Self Catering
t (01227) 730748
e ripplefarmhols@aol.com

CUDHAM
Kent

Fairmead ★★★★
Self Catering
t (01959) 532662

DALLINGTON
East Sussex

Millers Farm Cottage
★★★★ *Self Catering*
Garden of England Cottages
t (01892) 510117
e info@gardenofenglandcottages.co.uk
w goec.co.uk

DEAL
Kent

Light House Cottage
Rating Applied For
Self Catering
Freedom Holiday Homes
t (01580) 720770
e mail@freedomholidayhomes.co.uk
w freedomholidayhomes.co.uk

Pebble Cottage ★★★★
Self Catering
e enquiries@curlewcottages.co.uk

DENMEAD
Hampshire

Flint Cottage ★★★
Self Catering
t (023) 9226 6345
w http://mysite.wanadoo-members.co.uk/flintcottagehants

DODDINGTON
Kent

The Old School House
★★★★ *Self Catering*
Garden of England Cottages
t (01892) 510117
e info@gardenofenglandcottages.co.uk
w goec.co.uk

DORKING
Surrey

Bulmer Farm, Holmbury St Mary ★★★★ *Self Catering*
Contact: Mr & Mrs Graham & Sue Walker
t (01306) 731871
e enquiries@bulmerfarm.co.uk
w bulmerfarm.co.uk

Logmore Farm
Rating Applied For
Self Catering
Contact: Mr Richard Carlisle
t (01306) 885770
e rhcarlisle@gmail.com

DOVER
Kent

Meggett Farm Cottage
★★★★ *Self Catering*
Contact: Mr Simon Price
t (01303) 252764
e simon-price.dover@virgin.net
w meggettfarmcottage.co.uk

No 4 Cliffe House ★★★★
Self Catering
t (01304) 825732
e no4cliffehouse@btinternet.com
w no4cliffehouse.com

Sergeant Major's House
★★★★★ *Self Catering*
English Heritage
t 0870 333 1187
e holidaycottages@english-heritage.org.uk
w english-heritage.org.uk/holidaycottages

DUNSDEN
Oxfordshire

Ash Copse
Rating Applied For
Self Catering
Contact: Mr Hugo Ripley**e** hugo@mediaweb.co.za

DYMCHURCH
Kent

Dymchurch House ★★★★★
Self Catering
Contact: Mrs Uden
t (020) 8300 2100
e dymchurchhouse@btopenworld.com

EASEBOURNE
West Sussex

The Garden Barn ★★★★
Self Catering
Contact: Susan Clake
t (01730) 810537
e susan.clake@btinternet.com

EAST CHALLOW
Oxfordshire

Challow Hill Farm ★★★★
Self Catering
Contact: Mrs Lin Blackwell
t (01235) 765461
e info@challowhillcoachhouse.co.uk
w challowhillcoachhouse.co.uk

EAST COWES
Isle of Wight

2 Seymour Court ★★★★
Self Catering
Contact: Mr John Dean
t (01494) 677362
w cowesholidayhome.co.uk

---

28 Anchorage Way ★★★
Self Catering
Island Holiday Homes
t (01983) 521113
e enquiries@island-holiday-homes.net
w island-holiday-homes.net

No 1 Seymour Court ★★★
Self Catering
Contact: Mr & Mrs Maciw
t 07789 372371
e holiday@seymourcourt.co.uk
w seymourcourt.co.uk

Pavilion Cottage ★★★★★
Self Catering
English Heritage
t 0870 333 1187
e holidaycottages@english-heritage.org.uk
w english-heritage.org.uk/holidaycottages

EAST DEAN
East Sussex

Beachy Head Holiday Cottages ★★★★
Self Catering
Contact: Jan Smith
t (01323) 423878
e jan@beachyhead.org.uk
w beachyhead.org.uk

EAST GULDEFORD
East Sussex

The Mount ★★★★
Self Catering
Freedom Holiday Homes
t (01580) 720770
e mail@freedomholidayhomes.co.uk
w freedomholidayhomes.co.uk

EAST HAGBOURNE
Oxfordshire

The Oast House ★★★★
Self Catering
Contact: Mr Robin Harries
t (01235) 815005
w http://freespace.virgin.net/manorfarm.easthag

EAST PRESTON
West Sussex

Mariners House, East Preston ★★★★ *Self Catering*
t (01293) 871937
e derekedwards@sovereignprinters.co.uk
w marinershouse.net

EAST SUTTON
Kent

The Clockhouse
Rating Applied For
Self Catering
Contact: Brenda Beck
Freedom Holiday Homes
t (01580) 720770

EAST WITTERING
West Sussex

Fairhaven ★★★ *Self Catering*
Contact: Mr Baileys
t (01243) 672217
e anne.maddock@tiscali.co.uk
w baileys.uk.com

Southern Counties Lettings – 20 Seagate ★★★
Self Catering
Contact: Gerald Ryan
Southern Counties Lettings
t (020) 8204 1188
e info@southerncountieslettings.com
w southerncountieslettings.com

EASTBOURNE
East Sussex

Black Robin Farm ★★★★
Self Catering
Contact: Mrs Jane Higgs
t (01323) 643357
e jane_higgsbrb@yahoo.co.uk

EASTERGATE
West Sussex

Eastmere Cottage ★★
Self Catering
Contact: Mr & Mrs Jean & Bernard Lane
t (01243) 544204
e bernardlane@hotmail.com
w eastmere.com

EGERTON
Kent

Tudor Cottage ★★★★
Self Catering
Freedom Holiday Homes
t (01580) 720770
e mail@freedomholidayhomes.co.uk
w freedomholidayhomes.co.uk

ELMER
West Sussex

Pebble Cottage ★★★★
Self Catering
Contact: Mrs Sarah Picco-Barnes
Pebble Cottage, Elmer Sands
t 0870 224 5568
e sarah@pebble-cottage.co.uk
w pebble-cottage.co.uk

Sea Chalet ★★ *Self Catering*
Contact: Mrs Marilyn Appleton
Sea Chalet, Elmer Sands
t (01293) 774395
e mapleaf@talktalk.net

ELMSTED
Kent

The Dairy ★★★★
Self Catering
Freedom Holiday Homes
t (01580) 720770
e mail@freedomholidayhomes.co.uk
w freedomholidayhomes.co.uk

EMSWORTH
Hampshire

The Deckhouse ★★★★
Self Catering
Contact: Mrs Sprules
t (01883) 732144
e info@beachhutworld.com
w thedeckhouse.co.uk

Pebble Cottage ★★★★
Self Catering
Contact: Mrs Jean Buchanan
t (01243) 641452
e buchanan.j@virgin.net
w emsworthholidaycottages.co.uk

Tide Cottage ★★★
Self Catering
Contact: Mrs Candy Gourlay
t (020) 7272 8423
e candygourlay@blueyonder.co.uk
w tidecottage.co.uk

Westview Holiday Flat ★★★
Self Catering
Contact: Mrs Julia Oakley
t (01243) 373002
e joakley@onetel.com
w westviewholidayflat.co.uk

ENBORNE
Berkshire

The Cottage ★★★★
Self Catering
Contact: Sandra Edwards
t (01635) 253443

EPSOM
Surrey

7 Great Tattenhams ★★★
Self Catering
Contact: Mrs Mary Willis
t (01737) 354112

ESHER
Surrey

Lynwood Studio
Rating Applied For
Self Catering
Contact: Becky Hughes
t (020) 8339 3739
e hughesbex@sky.com

ETCHINGHAM
East Sussex

Moon Cottage, Etchingham
★★★★ *Self Catering*
Contact: Mrs Jan Harrison
t (01580) 879328
e enquiries@harrison-holidays.co.uk
w harrison-holidays.co.uk

EVERTON
Hampshire

10 Newlands Manor ★★★
Self Catering
Contact: Mrs J A Rhoden
t (01590) 642830
e newlandsmanor@tiscali.co.uk

7 Lime Grove ★★★★
Self Catering
t (01590) 642138
w oldwalls.com

Wheatley Cottage
★★★-★★★★ *Self Catering*
Contact: Mrs Jacquie Taylor
t (01590) 645217
e office@daisycottages.co.uk
w daisycottages.co.uk

EWHURST GREEN
East Sussex

Prawles Oast Barn ★★★★
Self Catering
Garden of England Cottages
t (01892) 510117
e info@gardenofenglandcottages.co.uk
w goec.co.uk

EXTON
Hampshire

Beacon Hill Farm Cottages
★★★★ *Self Catering*
Contact: Mrs Catherine Dunford
Farm Office
t (01730) 829724
e info@beaconhillcottages.co.uk
w beaconhillcottages.co.uk

FAIRLIGHT
East Sussex

Marsham Oast ★★★★★
Self Catering
Freedom Holiday Homes
t (01580) 720770
e mail@freedomholidayhomes.co.uk
w freedomholidayhomes.co.uk

FARINGDON
Oxfordshire

Goodlake Barns ★★★★
Self Catering
Contact: Mr Andrew Gantlett
t (01367) 710112
e info@goodlakebarns.co.uk
w goodlakebarns.co.uk

FARNBOROUGH
Hampshire

SACO Farnborough ★★★★
Serviced Apartments
SACO Apartments
t (0117) 974 5936
e sarahbailey@sacaoapartments.co.uk
w sacoapartments.co.uk

FARNHAM
Surrey

Bentley Green Farm, Bentley
★★★★★ *Self Catering*
Contact: Mrs Glenda Powell
t (01420) 23246
e glenda.powell@btopenworld.com
w bentleygreenfarm.co.uk

High Wray ★★★
Self Catering
Contact: Mrs Alexine G N Crawford
t (01252) 715589
e alexine@highwray73.co.uk
w highwray73.co.uk

Kilnside Farms ★★
Self Catering
Contact: Mr Bob Milton
t (01252) 710325
e bobmilton@kilnsidefarm.fsnet.co.uk

Tilford Woods ★★★★
Self Catering
Contact: Miss Victoria Heath
t (01252) 792199
e admin@tilfordwoods.co.uk
w tilfordwoods.co.uk

FAVERSHAM
Kent

The Country Retreat ★★★★
Self Catering
Contact: Mrs Maureen French
t (01795) 531257
e countryretreat1@aol.com
w syndalepark.co.uk

Monks Cottage ★★★★
Self Catering
Contact: Mr & Mrs Graham & Teresa Darby
t (01233) 740419
e info@selfcateringinkent.com
w selfcateringinkent.com

Uplees Farm ★★★★
Self Catering
Contact: Mr & Mrs Chris & Heather Flood
t (01795) 532133
e upleesfarm@businessinkent.net
w upleesfarm.co.uk

FELPHAM
West Sussex

Felpham Bungalow ★★★
Self Catering
Contact: Mrs J Yabsley
t (020) 8680 4761
e felpham.bungalow@tinyworld.co.uk

FISHBOURNE
West Sussex

The Tidings ★★★
Self Catering
Contact: Mrs Davies
t (01243) 773958

FIVE OAK GREEN
Kent

Bramley Cottage ★★★★
Self Catering
Freedom Holiday Homes
t (01580) 720770
e mail@freedomholidayhomes.co.uk
w freedomholidayhomes.co.uk

Stable Cottage ★★★★
Self Catering
Freedom Holiday Homes
t (01580) 720770
e mail@freedomholidayhomes.co.uk
w freedomholidayhomes.co.uk

FLIMWELL
Kent

Carp and Spring Lodges
Rating Applied For
Self Catering
Freedom Holiday Homes
t (01580) 720770
e mail@freedomholidayhomes.co.uk
w freedomholidayhomes.co.uk

FOLKESTONE
Kent

The Grand ★★-★★★★
Self Catering
t (01303) 222222
e info@grand-uk.com
w grand-uk.com

Merriwinds ★★★★
Self Catering
t 0870 072 6726
e ownerservices@holidaycottagesgroup.com
w varne-ridge.co.uk

FORDINGBRIDGE
Hampshire

Alderholt Mill ★★★
Self Catering
Contact: Mr & Mrs Richard & Sandra Harte
t (01425) 653130
e alderholt-mill@zetnet.co.uk
w alderholtmill.co.uk

Burgate Manor Farm Holidays ★★★-★★★★★
Self Catering
Contact: Mrs Bridget Stallard
t (01425) 653908
e info@newforestcottages.com
w newforestcottages.com

Fir Tree Farm Cottage
★★★★ *Self Catering*
Contact: Mrs Sara Proctor
t (01425) 654001
e colin.proctor@homecall.co.uk
w firtreefarmcottage.co.uk

Hucklesbrook Farm Cottages ★★★★
Self Catering
Contact: Mrs Debbie Sampson
t (01425) 653180
e jcl.sampson@btinternet.com
w newforestfarmcottages.com

Number 14 ★★ *Self Catering*
Contact: Mr Stephen Naylor
t (020) 460 8980
e ns01@gre.ac.uk
w newforesthouse.co.uk

FOXCOTTE
Hampshire

Dines Barn ★★★★★
Self Catering
Contact: Mrs Sarah Capes
t (01264) 735242
e dines@capesfarm.co.uk
w capesfarm.co.uk

FRAMFIELD
East Sussex

Great Streele Farm Cottage
★★★★ *Self Catering*
Contact: Mrs Penelope Malloy
t (01825) 890638
e mail@greatstreele.co.uk
w greatstreele.co.uk

FREELAND
Oxfordshire

Woodrush Tregarth ★★★
Self Catering
Contact: Mrs Anne Busby
t (01993) 82827
e annebusby@amserve.com

FRESHWATER
Isle of Wight

10 Dolphin Court ★★★
Self Catering
Island Holiday Homes
t (01983) 521113
e enquiries@island-holiday-homes.net
w island-holiday-homes.net

4 Afton Barns ★★★
Self Catering
Island Holiday Homes
t (01983) 521113
e enquiries@island-holiday-homes.net
w island-holiday-homes.net

4 Tennyson View
Rating Applied For
Self Catering
Island Holiday Homes
t (01983) 521113
e enquiries@island-holiday-homes.net
w island-holiday-homes.net

70 Cliff End ★★★
Self Catering
Linstone Chine Holiday Services
t (01983) 755933
e linstone-chine@btconnect.com
w linstone-chine.com

Afton Thatch & Afton Thatch Lodge
Rating Applied For
Self Catering
Contact: Mr & Mrs John & Mylene Curtis
t (020) 8995 9288
e morganhcurtis@hotmail.com
w aftonthatch.com

Applebarns Cottage, House & The Barn ★★★-★★★★
Self Catering
Contact: Mr & Mrs Poole
t (020) 8870 7632
e david_poole2000@hotmail.com
w applebarns.co.uk

Bay Close Court ★★★★
Self Catering
Contact: Ms Liz Jasper
t (01983) 721606
e info@islandviewholidays.co.uk
w islandviewholidays.co.uk

Brambles Chine 103 ★★★
Self Catering
Linstone Chine Holiday Services
t (01983) 755933
e linstone-chine@btconnect.com
w linstone-chine.com

Brambles Chine 104 ★★★
Self Catering
Linstone Chine Holiday Services
t (01983) 755933
e linstone-chine@btconnect.com
w linstone-chine.com

Brambles Chine 120 ★★★
Self Catering
Linstone Chine Holiday Services
t (01983) 755933
e linstone-chine@btconnect.com
w linstone-chine.com

Brambles Chine 128 ★★★
Self Catering & Serviced Apartments
Linstone Chine Holiday Services
t (01983) 755933
e linstone-chine@btconnect.com
w linstone-chine.com

Brambles Chine 129 ★★★
Self Catering
Linstone Chine Holiday Services
t (01983) 755933
e linstone-chine@btconnect.com
w linstone-chine.com

Brambles Chine 160 ★★★
Self Catering
Linstone Chine Holiday Services
t (01983) 755933
e linstone-chine@btconnect.com
w linstone-chine.com

Brambles Chine 166 ★★★
Self Catering
Linstone Chine Holiday Services
t (01983) 755933
e linstone-chine@btconnect.com
w linstone-chine.com

Brambles Chine 168 ★★
Self Catering
Linstone Chine Holiday Services
t (01983) 755933
e linstone-chine@btconnect.com
w linstone-chine.com

Brambles Chine 169 ★★★
Self Catering
Linstone Chine Holiday Services
t (01983) 755933
e linstone-chine@btconnect.com
w linstone-chine.com

Brambles Chine 170 ★★★
Self Catering
Linstone Chine Holiday Services
t (01983) 755933
e linstone-chine@btconnect.com
w linstone-chine.com

Brambles Chine 175 ★★★
Self Catering
Linstone Chine Holiday Services
t (01983) 755933
e linstone-chine@btconnect.com
w linstone-chine.com

Brambles Chine 176 ★
Self Catering
Linstone Chine Holiday Services
t (01983) 755933
e linstone-chine@btconnect.com
w linstone-chine.com

Brambles Chine 196 ★★★
Self Catering
Linstone Chine Holiday Services
t (01983) 755933
e linstone-chine@btconnect.com
w linstone-chine.com

Brambles Chine 222 ★★★
Self Catering
Linstone Chine Holiday Services
t (01983) 755933
e linstone-chine@btconnect.com
w linstone-chine.com

Brambles Chine 45 ★★★
Self Catering
Linstone Chine Holiday Services
t (01983) 755933
e linstone-chine@btconnect.com
w linstone-chine.com

Brambles Chine 67 ★★
Self Catering
Linstone Chine Holiday Services
t (01983) 755933
e linstone-chine@btconnect.com
w linstone-chine.com

Brambles Chine 84 ★★★
Self Catering
Linstone Chine Holiday Services
t (01983) 755933
e linstone-chine@btconnect.com
w linstone-chine.com

Brambles Chine 87 ★★
Self Catering
Linstone Chine Holiday Services
t (01983) 755933
e linstone-chine@btconnect.com
w linstone-chine.com

Brambles Chine 92 ★★
Self Catering
Linstone Chine Holiday Services
t (01983) 755933
e linstone-chine@btconnect.com
w linstone-chine.com

Brambles Chine 99 ★★★
Self Catering
Linstone Chine Holiday Services
t (01983) 755933
e linstone-chine@btconnect.com
w linstone-chine.com

Brockley Barns Cottages
★★★ *Self Catering*
Contact: Mrs Sally Munday
t (01983) 537276
e mitchellbrockley@aol.com
w brockleybarns.co.uk

Cliff End 1 ★★★
Self Catering
Linstone Chine Holiday Services
t (01983) 755933
e linstone-chine@btconnect.com
w linstone-chine.com

Cliff End 2 ★★ *Self Catering*
Linstone Chine Holiday Services
t (01983) 755933
e linstone-chine@btconnect.com
w linstone-chine.com

Cliff End 28 ★★★
Self Catering
Linstone Chine Holiday Services
t (01983) 755933
e linstone-chine@btconnect.com
w linstone-chine.com

Cliff End 36 ★★ *Self Catering*
Linstone Chine Holiday Services
t (01983) 755933
e linstone-chine@btconnect.com
w linstone-chine.com

Cliff End 71 ★★★
Self Catering
Linstone Chine Holiday Services
t (01983) 755933
e linstone-chine@btconnect.com
w linstone-chine.com

Dolphins – Bonchurch
★★★★ *Self Catering*
Island Cottage Holidays
t (01929) 481555
e enq@islandcottageholidays.com
w islandcottageholidays.com

Farringford Hotel ★★★
Self Catering
Contact: Mr Andre Bourcier
t (01983) 752500
e enquiries@farringford.co.uk
w farringford.co.uk

Freshfields (68 Cliff End)
★★★ *Self Catering*
Contact: Mr & Mrs Barry
t (01983) 529901
e jo.iow@tiscali.co.uk
w cottageguide.co.uk/freshfields

Hill View House
Rating Applied For
Self Catering
Contact: Mrs Wendy Wooff
t 07809 585654
e info@selfcateringcottage-isleofwight.co.uk
w selfcateringcottage-isleofwight.co.uk

Holiday Homes Owners Services Ref: F1 ★★★★
Self Catering
Holiday Homes Owners Services (West Wight)
t (01983) 753423
e holidayhomesiow@ic24.net
w holidayhomesiow.co.uk

Holiday Homes Owners Services Ref: F2/30 ★★
Self Catering
Holiday Homes Owners Services (West Wight)
t (01983) 753423
e holidayhomesiow@ic24.net
w holidayhomesiow.co.uk

Holiday Homes Owners Services Ref: F2/38 ★★★
Self Catering
Holiday Homes Owners Services (West Wight)
t (01983) 753423
e holidayhomesiow@ic24.net
w holidayhomesiow.co.uk

Holiday Homes Owners Services Ref: F2/48 ★★★
Self Catering
Holiday Homes Owners Services (West Wight)
t (01983) 753423
e holidayhomesiow@ic24.net
w holidayhomesiow.co.uk

Holiday Homes Owners Services Ref: F2/203 ★★★
Self Catering
Holiday Homes Owners Services (West Wight)
t (01983) 753423
e holidayhomesiow@ic24.net
w holidayhomesiow.co.uk

Holiday Homes Owners Services Ref: F5 ★★★★
Self Catering
Holiday Homes Owners Services (West Wight)
t (01983) 753423
e holidayhomesiow@ic24.net
w holidayhomesiow.co.uk

Holiday Homes Owners Services Ref: F6 ★★★★
Self Catering
Holiday Homes Owners Services (West Wight)
t (01983) 753423
e holidayhomesiow@ic24.net
w holidayhomesiow.co.uk

Holiday Homes Owners Services Ref: F10 ★★★★
Self Catering
Holiday Homes Owners Services (West Wight)
t (01983) 753423
e holidayhomesiow@ic24.net
w holidayhomesiow.co.uk

Holiday Homes Owners Services Ref: F11 ★★★★
Self Catering
Holiday Homes Owners Services (West Wight)
t (01983) 753423
e holidayhomesiow@ic24.net
w holidayhomesiow.co.uk

Holiday Homes Owners Services Ref: F12 ★★★★
Self Catering
Holiday Homes Owners Services (West Wight)
t (01983) 753423
e holidayhomesiow@ic24.net
w holidayhomesiow.co.uk

Holiday Homes Owners Services Ref: T1 ★★★★
Self Catering
Holiday Homes Owners Services (West Wight)
t (01983) 753423
e holidayhomesiow@ic24.net
w holidayhomesiow.co.uk

Holiday Homes Owners Services Ref: T2 ★★★★
Self Catering
Holiday Homes Owners Services (West Wight)
t (01983) 753423
e holidayhomesiow@ic24.net
w holidayhomesiow.co.uk

Holiday Homes Owners Services Ref: T3 ★★★★
Self Catering
Holiday Homes Owners Services (West Wight)
t (01983) 753423
e holidayhomesiow@ic24.net
w holidayhomesiow.co.uk

Holiday Homes Owners Services Ref : T4 ★★★★
Self Catering
Holiday Homes Owners Services (West Wight)
t (01983) 753423
e holidayhomesiow@ic24.net
w holidayhomesiow.co.uk

Holiday Homes Owners Services Ref: Y3 ★★★★
Self Catering
Holiday Homes Owners Services (West Wight)
t (01983) 753423
e holidayhomesiow@ic24.net
w holidayhomesiow.co.uk

Holiday Homes Owners Services Ref: Y16 ★★★★
Self Catering
Holiday Homes Owners Services (West Wight)
t (01983) 753423
e holidayhomesiow@ic24.net
w holidayhomesiow.co.uk

Holiday Homes Owners Services Ref: Y19 ★★★★
Self Catering
Holiday Homes Owners Services (West Wight)
t (01983) 753423
e holidayhomesiow@ic24.net
w holidayhomesiow.co.uk

Holiday Homes Owners Services Ref : Y22 ★★★★
Self Catering
Holiday Homes Owners Services (West Wight)
t (01983) 753423
e holidayhomesiow@ic24.net
w holidayhomesiow.co.uk

Honeysuckle Cottage Holiday Chalets ★★–★★★
Self Catering
Contact: Mrs Eve Cook
t (01983) 755131
e eve.cook@btinternet.com

Kings Lodge ★★★★★
Self Catering
Contact: Mrs Susie Sheldon
t (01983) 752347
e holidays@kingsmanorfarm.com
w kingsmanorfarm.co.uk

Little Halt Cottage ★★★★
Self Catering
Island Cottage Holidays
t (01929) 481555
e enq@islandcottageholidays.com
w islandcottageholidays.com

Mardon ★★★ *Self Catering*
Contact: Mrs Julia Sheard
t (01983) 752414

Milton Stables ★★★★
Self Catering
Home From Home Holidays
t (01983) 854340
e ventnor@crldirect.co.uk
w hfromh.co.uk

No 2 Old Coastguard Cottages ★★★ *Self Catering*
Contact: Mrs Pamela Dwyer
t (020) 8868 6568
e pamela_dwyer@btinternet.com
w oldcoastguardcottages.co.uk

Ocean View Holiday Bungalow ★★★ *Self Catering*
Linstone Chine Holiday Services
t (01983) 755933
e linstone-chine@btconnect.com
w linstone-chine.com

'Providence' 64 Brambles Chine ★★★ *Self Catering*
Linstone Chine Holiday Services
t (01983) 755933
e linstone-chine@btconnect.com
w linstone-chine.com

The Studio Apartment ★★★
Self Catering
Contact: Mr Barney Barnes
t (01983) 756661
e barney@westwightholidays.co.uk
w westwightholidays.co.uk

Sunkissed Haven ★★★
Self Catering
Contact: Mrs Elizabeth Shea
t (01780) 754112
e lizshea@hotmail.com

FRESHWATER BAY
Isle of Wight

10 Tennyson View ★★★★
Self Catering
Island Holiday Homes
t (01983) 521113
e enquiries@island-holiday-homes.net
w island-holiday-homes.net

Holiday Homes Owners Services Ref: F9 ★★★★
Self Catering
Holiday Homes Owners Services (West Wight)
t (01983) 753423
e holidayhomesiow@ic24.net
w holidayhomesiow.co.uk

FRITTENDEN
Kent

Cresslands Cottage ★★★
Self Catering
Freedom Holiday Homes
t (01580) 720770
e mail@freedomholidayhomes.co.uk
w freedomholidayhomes.co.uk

Weaversden Oast House ★★★★ *Self Catering*
Garden of England Cottages
t (01892) 510117
e info@gardenofenglandcottages.co.uk
w goec.co.uk

FROXFIELD GREEN
Hampshire

Owl Barn ★★★★
Self Catering
Contact: Mrs Valerie Hogg
t (023) 9273 0009
e valeriehogg@vhogg43.wanadoo.co.uk

FUNTINGTON
West Sussex

The Courtyard ★★★★
Self Catering
Contact: Mrs Claire Hoare
t (01243) 575464
e tim.hoare@farming.co.uk
w adsdean.co.uk

Dellfield ★★★★
Self Catering
Contact: Mr M Hall Hall
t (01243) 575244
e holidays@dellfield.com
w dellfield.com

GATCOMBE
Isle of Wight

Newbarn Country Cottages – The Parlour, The Dairy & Stable Cottages ★★★★
Self Catering
Contact: Mrs Diane Harvey
t (01983) 721202
e info@newbarncountrycottages.co.uk
w newbarncountrycottages.co.uk

GLYNDE
East Sussex

Caburn Cottages ★★★★
Self Catering
Contact: Mrs Rosemary Norris
t (01273) 858062
e rosemary.norris@hotmail.com
w caburncottages.co.uk

GODALMING
Surrey

Magpie Cottages ★★★
Self Catering
Contact: Mrs Gabrielle Mabley
t (01428) 682702
e gabrielle.mabley1@btinternet.com

GODSHILL
Hampshire

Graylands Cottage ★★★
Self Catering
Contact: Professor Tina Bruce
t (020) 8748 0611
e tinabruce@btinternet.com

Wayside ★★★★
Self Catering
Contact: Mrs Eileen Harrod
t (01425) 654892
e info@yournewforestholiday.co.uk
w yournewforestholiday.co.uk

GODSHILL
Isle of Wight

Barwick Cottages – Barwick Cottage & Lavender Cottage ★★★★ *Self Catering*
Contact: Mrs Pam Wickham
t (01983) 840787
e pam@barwickcottages.co.uk
w barwickcottages.co.uk

Bramble Cottage ★★★★
Self Catering
Island Holiday Homes
t (01983) 521113
e enquiries@island-holiday-homes.net
w island-holiday-homes.net

Coach House Studio ★★★★
Self Catering
Island Cottage Holidays
t (01929) 481555
e enq@islandcottageholidays.com
w islandcottageholidays.com

Demelza ★★★★
Self Catering
Island Cottage Holidays
t (01929) 481555
e enq@islandcottageholidays.com
w islandcottageholidays.com

Glebelands ★★★★
Self Catering
Contact: Mrs Iris Beardsall
t (01983) 840371
e enquiries@glebelands-holidays.fsnet.co.uk
w glebelands-holidays.fsnet.co.uk

Godshill Park Farm – Godshill Park Cottage, Lake View & Pheasant Cottage, Godshill ★★★★
Self Catering
Contact: Mrs Kathy Domaille
t (01983) 840781
e info@godshillparkfarm.uk.com
w godshillparkfarm.uk.com

Godshill Park House Annexe and Lodge ★★★★
Self Catering
Contact: Mrs Nora Down
t (01983) 840271
e godshillpark@yahoo.co.uk
w godshillpark.co.uk

The Hayloft ★★★★
Self Catering
Island Cottage Holidays
t (01929) 481555
e enq@islandcottageholidays.com
w islandcottageholidays.com

Lambourne View Holiday Annexe ★★★ *Self Catering*
Contact: Mrs Maureen Plumbley
t (01983) 840293

Milk Pan Farm ★★★
Self Catering
Contact: Mr Tony Morrish
t (01983) 840570
e tonymorrish@toucansurf.com
w milkpanfarm.co.uk

Milk Parlour Cottage
★★★★ *Self Catering*
Island Cottage Holidays
t (01929) 481555
e enq@islandcottageholidays.com
w islandcottageholidays.com

The Old Vicarage Apartment
★★★★ *Self Catering*
t (01983) 840270
e info@modelvillagegodshill.co.uk
w modelvillagegodshill.co.uk

Pilgrims Lodge ★★★★
Self Catering
Island Cottage Holidays
t (01929) 481555
e enq@islandcottageholidays.com
w islandcottageholidays.com

Sunnyside Cottage ★★★★
Self Catering
Contact: Mrs Sabrie Harvey
t (01983) 840283
e sunnyside@talktalk.net
w sunnyside-farm.co.uk

GODSHILL WOOD
Hampshire

The Lodge ★★★★
Self Catering
Hideaways
t (01747) 828170
e enq@hideaways.co.uk
w hideaways.co.uk

Undercastle Cottage
★★★★★ *Self Catering*
Hideaways
t (01747) 828170
e enq@hideaways.co.uk
w hideaways.co.uk

GOLDEN CROSS
East Sussex

Jasmine Windmill ★★★★
Self Catering
Freedom Holiday Homes
t (01580) 720770
e mail@freedomholidayhomes.co.uk
w freedomholidayhomes.co.uk

GORING-BY-SEA
West Sussex

37 Harwood Avenue
★★★★ *Self Catering*
t (01480) 370656
w cottageguide.co.uk

GOSPORT
Hampshire

Dolphins ★★★ *Self Catering*
Contact: Mrs Donnelly
t (023) 9258 8179

Eight The Mews ★★★
Self Catering
Contact: Richard Jeal
t 07771 990425
e info@eightthemews.co.uk
w eightthemews.co.uk

Linden House ★★★
Self Catering
Contact: Mrs F Slaven
t (01329) 848208
e harringtonsltd@aol.com
w harringtonhouses.co.uk

Number Nine ★★★
Self Catering
Contact: Mrs Claire Macaulay
t (023) 9252 8333
e enquiries@numbernine.info
w numbernine.info

Park House ★★★★
Self Catering
Contact: Mrs F Slaven
t (01329) 848208
e harringtonsltd@aol.com
w harringtonhouses.co.uk

Rivendale ★★★★★
Self Catering
t 07917 055538

GOUDHURST
Kent

3 Whitestocks Cottages
★★★★ *Self Catering*
Freedom Holiday Homes
t (01580) 720770
e mail@freedomholidayhomes.co.uk
w freedomholidayhomes.co.uk

Blackthorn Barn ★★★★
Self Catering
Freedom Holiday Homes
t (01580) 720770
e mail@freedomholidayhomes.co.uk
w freedomholidayhomes.co.uk

The Coach House ★★★★
Self Catering
Freedom Holiday Homes
t (01580) 720770
e mail@freedomholidayhomes.co.uk
w freedomholidayhomes.co.uk

Etchinghill Barn
Rating Applied For
Self Catering
Contact: Mrs Lynne Weedon
w freedomholidayhomes.co.uk

The Stables ★★★★
Self Catering
Freedom Holiday Homes
t (01580) 720770
e mail@freedomholidayhomes.co.uk
w freedomholidayhomes.co.uk

Three Chimneys Farm
★★★★ *Self Catering*
Contact: Mrs Marion Fuller
t (01580) 212175 & 07785 734639
e marionfuller@threechimneysfarm.co.uk
w threechimneysfarm.co.uk

GRAFFHAM
West Sussex

Yaffle Cottage ★★★★★
Self Catering
Contact: Mr Alex Mason
t (01798) 867553
e alex.mason@btinternet.com
w yafflecottage.com

GRAVESEND
Kent

Russell Quay ★★★★
Self Catering
Contact: T M Dickety Dickety
t (01464) 573049
e mikedickety@beeb.net
w halcyon-gifts.co.uk/holidaylet.htm

GREAT ROLLRIGHT
Oxfordshire

Butlers Hill Farm ★★★
Self Catering
Contact: Mrs L. Campbell
t (01608) 684430

GREATSTONE
Kent

Beach View ★★★
Self Catering
Garden of England Cottages
t (01892) 510117
e info@gardenofenglandcottages.co.uk
w goec.co.uk

GROOMBRIDGE
East Sussex

Primula Cottage ★★★★
Self Catering
Garden of England Cottages
t (01892) 510117
e info@gardenofenglandcottages.co.uk
w goec.co.uk

Sherlocks Cottage ★★★★
Self Catering
Freedom Holiday Homes
t (01580) 720770
e mail@freedomholidayhomes.co.uk
w freedomholidayhomes.co.uk

GUILDFORD
Surrey

Lavender ★★★ *Self Catering*
Contact: Mr & Mrs Liew Mandarin
t (01483) 506819 & 07906 179084
e shirleyliew9@hotmail.com

Rydes Hill Cottage ★★★
Self Catering
Contact: Ms Penny Wilson-Smith
t (01483) 535841
e penjws@hotmail.com
w guildfordapartment.com

Trinity Gate ★★★★
Serviced Apartments
The Apartment Service
t (020) 8944 1444
e melanied@apartment.co.uk
w apartmentservice.com

University of Surrey
★★–★★★ *Self Catering*
Conference Office
t (01483) 686767
e conferences@surrey.ac.uk
w surrey.ac.uk/conferences

West View, West Horsley
★★★ *Self Catering*
Contact: Mrs Janet Steer
t (01483) 284686
e cliveandjan@aol.com
w homestead.com/2westview

GURNARD
Isle of Wight

The Stable ★★★★
Self Catering
Contact: Mrs Clark
t (01983) 294900
e info@cowesselfcatering.co.uk
w cowesselfcatering.co.uk

HADDENHAM
Buckinghamshire

Anvil Cottage Barn ★★★★
Self Catering
Contact: Mrs Ann Saadi
t (01844) 296075
e annsaadi@hotmail.co.uk

HADLOW
Kent

4 Castle View
Rating Applied For
Self Catering
Garden of England Cottages
t (01892) 510117
e info@gardenofenglandcottages.co.uk
w goec.co.uk

HADLOW DOWN
East Sussex

The Barn Hadow Down
★★★★ *Self Catering*
Freedom Holiday Homes
t (01580) 720770
e mail@freedomholidayhomes.co.uk
w freedomholidayhomes.co.uk

HAILSHAM
East Sussex

Little Marshfoot ★★★★
Self Catering
Contact: Ms Kathryn Webster
t (01323) 844690
e kew@littlemarshfoot.biz
w littlemarshfoot.co.uk

Pekes ★★★-★★★★
Self Catering
Contact: Ms Eva Morris
t (020) 7352 8088
e pekes.afa@virgin.net
w pekesmanor.com

HALLAND
East Sussex

Little Tamberry ★★★★
Self Catering
Freedom Holiday Homes
t (01580) 720770
e mail@freedomholidayhomes.co.uk
w freedomholidayhomes.co.uk

HAMBLE
Hampshire

Woodend ★★★ *Self Catering*
Contact: Mrs Woodhouse
Kew House
t (023) 8040 2804
e info@woodhousecottages.co.uk
w woodhousecottages.co.uk

HARRIETSHAM
Kent

Tilmangate Barn ★★★★
Self Catering
Contact: Mr & Mrs Chris & Juliet Maddocks
t (01622) 843096

HASLEMERE
Surrey

The Creamery ★★★★
Self Catering
Hideaways
t (01747) 828170
e enq@hideaways.co.uk
w hideaways.co.uk

HASTINGLEIGH
Kent

Crabtree Farm ★★★★
Self Catering
Contact: Ian McLallam
t (01233) 750345
e wyncotkennels@btinternet.com
w crabtreefarm.co.uk

Staple Farm, Hastingleigh
★★★★ *Self Catering*
Contact: Mr & Mrs Cliff & Betty Martindale
t (01233) 750248

HASTINGS
East Sussex

1 Strongs Passage ★★★
Self Catering
t (01923) 226360

13 Tackle Way ★★★
Self Catering
t (01424) 437069

14 Old Humphrey Avenue
★★★ *Self Catering*
t (01296) 625780

26 Plynlimmon Road
Rating Applied For
Self Catering
Contact: Katherine McNeivee katherine.mcneive@yahoo.co.uk
w hastingsholidayhome.co.uk

Black Lantern Cottage
★★★★ *Self Catering*
Contact: Ms Vera Esdaile
t (01797) 222614
e robin.bloomfield@btinternet.com
w luxurybandbrye.co.uk

Brooklands Coach House
★★★ *Self Catering*
t (01424) 421957

Figtree House ★★★★
Self Catering
Contact: Mr & Mrs Burnham
t (01732) 453418
e rburnham@dircon.co.uk

Lindsell Cottage ★★★
Self Catering
Contact: Mr John Sydes
t 07951 766 639
e jazmacuk@yahoo.co.uk
w hastingsholiday.co.uk

Number Six ★★★
Self Catering
t (01424) 431984
w sixstanleyroad.co.uk

Rocklands Holiday Park
★★★ *Self Catering*
t (01424) 423097

St Marys Holiday Flats
★-★★ *Self Catering*
Contact: Mrs Edwards
t (01273) 556227

Spring Cottage
Rating Applied For
Self Catering
t (01580) 819542
w maximahomes.co.uk

Summer Cottage
Rating Applied For
Self Catering
t 07762 222098
e hastingsholidays@tiscali.co.uk
w http://myweb.tiscali.co.uk/hastingsholidays/index.htm

Tillys Cottage ★★★
Self Catering
Contact: Mrs Celia Conway
The Captain's Cabin
t (01494) 565493

Winchester House ★★★★
Self Catering
Freedom Holiday Homes
t (01580) 720770
e mail@freedomholidayhomes.co.uk
w freedomholidayhomes.co.uk

HAVENSTREET
Isle of Wight

The Coach House ★★★★
Self Catering
Contact: Mr Peter Dewey
t (01983) 884782
e peter.dewey@lambournes.com

HAWKHURST
Kent

Kent Bridge Croft ★★★★
Self Catering
Freedom Holiday Homes
t (01580) 720770
e mail@freedomholidayhomes.co.uk
w freedomholidayhomes.co.uk

Park Farm Chalet ★★★
Self Catering
Freedom Holiday Homes
t (01580) 720770
e mail@freedomholidayhomes.co.uk
w freedomholidayhomes.co.uk

The Stables ★★★★
Self Catering
Garden of England Cottages
t (01892) 510117
e info@gardenofenglandcottages.co.uk
w goec.co.uk

The Wrens Nest
★★★★-★★★★★
Self Catering
Contact: Mrs Lynne Rodger
t (01580) 754919

HAWKINGE
Kent

1 North Downs Cottage
★★★★-★★★★★
Self Catering
Freedom Holiday Homes
t (01580) 720770
e mail@freedomholidayhomes.co.uk
w freedomholidayhomes.co.uk

HAYLING ISLAND
Hampshire

15 Anchor Court ★★★
Self Catering
Millers of Hayling
t (023) 9246 5951
e rentals@haylingproperty.co.uk
w haylingproperty.co.uk

3 Wight View ★★★★
Self Catering
Millers of Hayling
t (023) 9246 5951
e rentals@haylingproperty.co.uk
w haylingproperty.co.uk

33 Seagrove Avenue
★★★★ *Self Catering*
Millers of Hayling
t (023) 9246 5951
e rentals@haylingproperty.co.uk
w haylingproperty.co.uk

36 Bound Lane ★★★
Self Catering
Millers of Hayling
t (023) 9246 5951
e rentals@haylingproperty.co.uk
w haylingproperty.co.uk

3A Bembridge Drive ★★★
Self Catering
Millers of Hayling
t (023) 9246 5951
e rentals@haylingproperty.co.uk
w haylingproperty.co.uk

63 North Shore Road ★★★
Self Catering
Millers of Hayling
t (023) 9246 5951
e rentals@haylingproperty.co.uk
w haylingproperty.co.uk

69 Creek Road ★★★
Self Catering
Millers of Hayling
t (023) 9246 5951
e rentals@haylingproperty.co.uk
w haylingproperty.co.uk

7 Sandybeach Estate ★★★
Self Catering
Millers of Hayling
t (023) 9246 5951
e rentals@haylingproperty.co.uk
w haylingproperty.co.uk

70 Southwold Road ★★★★
Self Catering
Millers of Hayling
t (023) 9246 5951
e rentals@haylingproperty.co.uk
w haylingproperty.co.uk

78 Sandypoint Road ★★
Self Catering
Millers of Hayling
t (023) 9246 5951
e rentals@haylingproperty.co.uk
w haylingproperty.co.uk

92 Southwood Road ★★★
Self Catering
Millers of Hayling
t (023) 9246 5951
e rentals@haylingproperty.co.uk
w haylingproperty.co.uk

92b Southwood Road ★★
Self Catering
Millers of Hayling
t (023) 9246 5951
e rentals@haylingproperty.co.uk
w haylingproperty.co.uk

HEADCORN
Kent

Wealden View Headcorn
★★★★ *Self Catering*
t (01622) 850369
w wealdenviewholidaycottage.co.uk

HEADINGTON
Oxfordshire

Mulberry Self Catering
★★★ *Self Catering*
Contact: Gordon & Nada
t (01865) 767114
e selfcatering@mulberryguesthouse.co.uk
w oxfordcity.co.uk/accom/mulberryselfcatering

HEATHFIELD
East Sussex

The Cottage ★★★★
Self Catering
Contact: Anne Reed
t (01435) 812285
e info@boringhousefarm.co.uk
w boringhousefarm.co.uk

HENFIELD
West Sussex

New Hall Cottage & New Hall Holiday Flat ★★★
Self Catering
Contact: Mrs Marjorie Carreck
New Hall
t (01273) 492546
w newhallcottage.co.uk

HENLEY-ON-THAMES
Oxfordshire

First Floor Flat ★★
Self Catering
Contact: Ms Caroline Bleackley
t 07776 223057
e caroline.bleackley@googlemail.com
w cottageguide.co.uk/carolines

Jersey Farmhouse
★★★-★★★★ *Self Catering*
Contact: Mrs Janet King
t (01491) 628486
e mjking@btinternet.com
w holiday.btinternet.co.uk

Rotherleigh House Annexe
★★★ *Self Catering*
Contact: Mrs Jane Butler
t (01491) 572776
e jvbutler57@hotmail.com
w rotherleighannexe.co.uk

The Studio ★★ *Self Catering*
Contact: Mrs Joan Kuipers
t (01491) 574760

HERNE BAY
Kent

Arlington Lodge ★★★★
Self Catering
Contact: Mr A. Webb
t (01737) 244385
e webb487@btinternet.com

Driftwood ★★★★
Self Catering
Contact: Dean Moore
t 07887 710841
e info@beaconcourt.co.uk
w beaconcourt.co.uk

Maplin Sands Holiday Apartment ★★★
Self Catering
Contact: Mrs Claire Hudson
t (01227) 360819
e claireandherbie@hotmail.co.uk
w hernebayholidayhomes.co.uk

Old Water Tower Cottage
★★★ *Self Catering*
Garden of England Cottages
t (01892) 510117
e info@gardenofenglandcottages.co.uk
w goec.co.uk

HERONS GHYLL
East Sussex

The Stables ★★★★
Self Catering
Freedom Holiday Homes
t (01580) 720770
e mail@freedomholidayhomes.co.uk
w freedomholidayhomes.co.uk

HIGH HALDEN
Kent

The Granary and The Stables, High Halden
★★★★ *Self Catering*
Contact: Mrs Serena Maundrell
Vintage Years Company Ltd
t (01233) 850871 & 07715 488804
e serena@vintage-years.co.uk
w vintage-years.co.uk

Heron and Mallard Cottages
★★★ *Self Catering*
Garden of England Cottages
t (01892) 510117
e info@gardenofenglandcottages.co.uk
w goec.co.uk

HIGH HURSTWOOD
East Sussex

Sunnymead Farm Cottages
★★★★ *Self Catering*
Contact: Joan Cooper
t (01825) 733618
e joanecuk@aol.com

HIGHMOOR
Oxfordshire

Bay Tree Cottage ★★★★
Self Catering
Contact: Ms Carolyn Wyndham
t (01491) 641229
e baytree@hotmail.com

HILDENBOROUGH
Kent

The Cottage ★★★
Self Catering
Contact: Mr Dudley Hurrell
t (01732) 832081

HOLLINGBOURNE
Kent

The Barn ★★★★-★★★★★
Self Catering
Freedom Holiday Homes
t (01580) 720770
e mail@freedomholidayhomes.co.uk
w freedomholidayhomes.co.uk

The Boat House ★★★★
Self Catering
Contact: Ms Lucy Rendle
t (01892) 615222
e enquiries@cottageonthelake.co.uk
w cottageonthelake.co.uk

Well Cottage ★★★★★
Self Catering
Contact: Mrs Angela Dixon
t (01622) 880991
e info@northdownscountrycottages.co.uk

HOLYPORT
Berkshire

Vienna ★★★ *Self Catering & Serviced Apartments*
t (01628) 411273
w jslettings.co.uk

HORAM
East Sussex

Furnace Lane Stable ★★★★
Self Catering
Garden of England Cottages
t (01892) 510117
e info@gardenofenglandcottages.co.uk
w goec.co.uk

HORDLE
Hampshire

Beech Farm House ★★★★
Self Catering
Contact: Mr Nicholas Bennett
t (01425) 620180
e enquiries@beechfarmhouse.com
w beechfarmhouse.com

HORSHAM
West Sussex

The Lodge, Two Mile Ash Road ★★★★ *Self Catering*
Contact: Mrs S Young
t (01403) 731329
e richard.young6@btinternet.com
w thelodgecottage.co.uk

Walnut Barn, Cottage and Stables ★★★★-★★★★★
Self Catering
Contact: Julian Cole
t 07730 620365
e jpcole@lineone.net
w sussexshortlets.com

HORTON HEATH
Hampshire

The Stable at Rambler Cottage ★★★★ *Self Catering*
Contact: Mrs Hilary Collins
t (023) 8060 2755
e info@stablelets.co.uk
w stablelets.co.uk

HUNTON
Kent

Woolhouse Barn ★★★★
Self Catering
Garden of England Cottages
t (01892) 510117
e info@gardenofenglandcottages.co.uk
w goec.co.uk

HURST
Hampshire

The Dairy and Parlour at Copper Beeches ★★★
Self Catering
Contact: Janet & Ian Chew
t (01730) 826662
e ianchew@torberry212.fsnet.co.uk
w copperbeeches.homecall.co.uk

Wrens Cottage ★★★★
Self Catering
Contact: Ms Rebecca Atkins
t (01730) 826842
e willowbecks@yahoo.co.uk
w wrenscottagesouthharting.co.uk

HYTHE
Hampshire

Mullins ★★★★ *Self Catering*
Contact: Ms Alison Percy
t (023) 8084 5556
e alison@the-percys.co.uk
w holiday-newforest.co.uk

Waterside Retreat ★★★★
Self Catering
Contact: Mrs Lynne Kemmish
t (023) 8081 5315
e info@watersideretreat.co.uk
w watersideretreat.co.uk

HYTHE
Kent

Hydene Cottage ★★★★
Self Catering
Freedom Holiday Homes
t (01580) 720770
e mail@freedomholidayhomes.co.uk
w freedomholidayhomes.co.uk

shortstayaway ★★★★
Self Catering
Contact: Mr & Mrs A Eatwell
t (01303) 238298
e enquiries@shortstayaway.co.uk
w shortstayaway.co.uk

Uppermill ★★★★
Self Catering
Contact: Mrs Nicola Hooshangpour
Marston Properties Ltd
t (020) 7736 7133
e nicky@marstonproperties.co.uk
w marstonproperties.co.uk

IBSLEY
Hampshire

Chocolate Box Cottage
★★★★★ *Self Catering*
Contact: Mrs F. A. Higham
t (01268) 741036 & 07768 075761
e enquiries@chocolateboxcottage.co.uk
w chocolateboxcottage.co.uk

Crofton and Fieldview
★★★★ *Self Catering*
Contact: Mrs Julie Hordle
t (01425) 471829
e crofton@tiscali.co.uk
w newforest-holidaybungalows.co.uk

ICKLESHAM
East Sussex

Garden Cottage, Stable Cottage & Broadstreet House ★★★-★★★★
Self Catering
Garden of England Cottages
t (01892) 510117
e info@gardenofenglandcottages.co.uk
w goec.co.uk

The Oast Cottage ★★★★
Self Catering
Freedom Holiday Homes
t (01580) 720770
e mail@freedomholidayhomes.co.uk
w freedomholidayhomes.co.uk

IDEN
East Sussex

Corkwood Barn ★★★
Self Catering
Freedom Holiday Homes
t (01580) 720770
e mail@freedomholidayhomes.co.uk
w freedomholidayhomes.co.uk

The Granary ★★★★
Self Catering
Freedom Holiday Homes
t (01580) 720770
e mail@freedomholidayhomes.co.uk
w freedomholidayhomes.co.uk

Riverside Cottage ★★★
Self Catering
Freedom Holiday Homes
t (01580) 720770
e mail@freedomholidayhomes.co.uk
w freedomholidayhomes.co.uk

IPING
West Sussex

The Studio ★★★
Self Catering
Contact: Miranda Granger
t (01428) 741745
e miranda@kinrose.co.uk

ITCHEN ABBAS
Hampshire

Itchen Down Farm ★★★★
Self Catering
t (01962) 779388
w itchendownfarm.co.uk

IVINGHOE
Buckinghamshire

Town Farm Holiday Cottages, Ivinghoe ★★★
Self Catering
Contact: Mrs Angie Leach
t (01296) 668455
e angie@letsunlimited.com
w letsunlimited.com

KEMSING
Kent

6 Dippers Close ★★★
Self Catering
t (01732) 761937

KENARDINGTON
Kent

Brittens Hill Cottage ★★★★
Self Catering
Contact: Pauline Sheehan
t (020) 8904 0600

KINGHAM
Oxfordshire

Cotswold Holiday Cottages Ltd ★★★★ *Self Catering*
Contact: Ms Rebecca Zamir
t (01608) 659149
e rebeccazamir@hotmail.com
w cotswold-holiday-cottages.net

KING'S SOMBORNE
Hampshire

Brook Farm Cottages
★★★★ *Self Catering*
Contact: Mrs Sarah de Sigley
t (01794) 389379
w quidity.com

By The Way Annexe ★★★
Self Catering
Contact: Dr Penny Morgan
t (01794) 388469
e bythewayannexe@yahoo.co.uk

KINGSEY
Buckinghamshire

The Stalls & Hayloft ★★★★
Self Catering
t (01844) 290808

KINGSTON
East Sussex

Nightingales ★★★★
Self Catering
Contact: Mrs Jean Hudson
t (01273) 475673
e nightingales@totalise.co.uk
w users.totalise.co.uk/~nightingales/

Roman Way ★★★★
Self Catering
Contact: Pippa & Ian Campbell
t (01273) 476583
e camp1942@aol.com

KNATTS VALLEY
Kent

Hawthorn Cottage ★★★★
Self Catering
Freedom Holiday Homes
t (01580) 720770
e mail@freedomholidayhomes.co.uk
w freedomholidayhomes.co.uk

LAGNESS
West Sussex

Lagnersh Cottage ★★★★
Self Catering
Contact: Mrs Linda Gavigan
t (01243) 268064
e gavigans@dslpipex.com
w lagnershcottage.co.uk

LAMBERHURST
Kent

Barnfield Oast Self Catering Holidays ★★★★
Self Catering
Freedom Holiday Homes
t (01580) 720770
e mail@freedomholidayhomes.co.uk
w freedomholidayhomes.co.uk

Bartley Mill Holiday Homes
★★★★ *Self Catering*
Contact: Mrs J Rogers
t (01892) 891020
e info@bartleymill.co.uk
w bartleymill.co.uk

The Hideaway
★★★-★★★★ *Self Catering*
Freedom Holiday Homes
t (01580) 720770
e mail@freedomholidayhomes.co.uk
w freedomholidayhomes.co.uk

LANGTON GREEN
Kent

Roberts House ★★★★
Self Catering
Freedom Holiday Homes
t (01580) 720770
e mail@freedomholidayhomes.co.uk
w freedomholidayhomes.co.uk

LAUGHTON
East Sussex

Laughton Granary
Rating Applied For
Self Catering
Contact: Mrs Lynne Weedon
w freedomholidayhomes.co.uk

LEAFIELD
Oxfordshire

King John's Barn ★★★★
Self Catering
Contact: Mrs Vicky Greves
t (01993) 878075
e info@kingjohnsbarn.co.uk
w kingjohnsbarn.co.uk

LEATHERHEAD
Surrey

Royal Swan ★★★★
Serviced Apartments
The Apartment Service
t (020) 8944 1444
e melanied@apartment.co.uk
w apartmentservice.com

LECKHAMPSTEAD
Buckinghamshire

The Cowshed Annexe
Rating Applied For
Self Catering
Contact: Delia Philips
t (01220) 860775
e deliaphillips@hotmail.com

LEE COMMON
Buckinghamshire

High Beeches Cottage ★★★
Self Catering
t (01494) 837246

Lower Bassibones Farm self catering ★★★★
Self Catering
Contact: Mr & Mrs hartley
t (01494) 837798
e lowerbassibones@yahoo.co.uk
w discover-real-england.com

LEE-ON-THE-SOLENT
Hampshire

The Chart House ★★★
Self Catering
Contact: Mr Brook White
t (023) 9255 4145
e brook.white1@btopenworld.com
w lee-on-the-solentholiday.co.uk

Kinderton House ★★★
Self Catering
Contact: Mrs Jean Miller
t (023) 9255 2056

LEEDS
Kent

1 & 2 Orchard View ★★★
Self Catering
Garden of England Cottages
t (01892) 510117
e info@gardenofenglandcottages.co.uk
w goec.co.uk

LENHAM
Kent

5 Lime Tree Cottages ★★★
Self Catering
Contact: Mr Peter Hasler
t (01622) 851310
e pvhasler@hotmail.com
w kentcottage.com

Apple Pye Cottage ★★★★
Self Catering
Contact: Ms Diane Leat
t (01622) 858878
e diane@bramleyknowlefarm.co.uk
w bramleyknowlefarm.co.uk

Court Lodge Cottage ★★★
Self Catering
Freedom Holiday Homes
t (01580) 720770
e mail@freedomholidayhomes.co.uk
w freedomholidayhomes.co.uk

The Olde Shoppe ★★★
Self Catering
Freedom Holiday Homes
t (01580) 720770
e mail@freedomholidayhomes.co.uk
w freedomholidayhomes.co.uk

The Pavilion ★★★★
Self Catering
Contact: Ms Alison Cannon
t (01622) 858423
e alison@bluehousefarm.co.uk
w bluehousefarm.co.uk

LEWES
East Sussex

15 Barons Walk
Rating Applied For
Self Catering
Contact: Sarah Campbell
t (01273) 479529
e campbellsarah@talktalk.net

The Finings ★★★★
Self Catering
Contact: Mrs Sara Gosling
t (01273) 480084
e fullofbeans@tempeh.globalnet.co.uk

Heath Farm, Plumpton Green ★★★★ *Self Catering*
Contact: Mrs Marilyn Hanbury
t (01273) 890712
e hanbury@heath-farm.com
w heath-farm.com

Mill Laine Barns, Offham
★★★★-★★★★★
Self Catering
Contact: Mr John Harmer
t (01273) 475473
e harmer@farming.co.uk
w milllainebarns.co.uk

Sussex Countryside Accommodation, Barcombe
★★★★ *Self Catering*
Contact: Ms Hazel Gaydon
t (01273) 400625
e bookings@crinkhouse.co.uk
w sussexcountryaccommodation.co.uk

LIMERSTONE
Isle of Wight

Monks Path ★★★★★
Self Catering
Island Cottage Holidays
t (01929) 481555
e enq@islandcottageholidays.com
w islandcottageholidays.com

LINTON
Kent

Loddington Oast ★★★★
Self Catering
Contact: Mr & Mrs Martin
t (01622) 747777
e contact@loddingtonoast.co.uk
w loddingtonoast.co.uk

LITTLEHAMPTON
West Sussex

Racing Greens Self Catering
★★★★ *Self Catering*
Contact: Mr & Mrs Alan & Eileen Thomas
t (01903) 732972
e racingreens@aol.com
w littlehampton-racing-greens.co.uk

LITTLESTONE-ON-SEA
Kent

Littlestone Court ★★★★
Self Catering
Freedom Holiday Homes
t (01580) 720770
e mail@freedomholidayhomes.co.uk
w freedomholidayhomes.co.uk

LOUDWATER
Buckinghamshire

Daisy's Cottage ★★★★
Self Catering
t (01494) 520964

LOWER BEEDING
West Sussex

Newells Farm
★★★–★★★★ *Self Catering*
Contact: Mrs Vicky Storey
t (01403) 891326
e vicky.storey@btinternet.com

LYDD ON SEA
Kent

69 Coast Drive ★★★
Self Catering
Freedom Holiday Homes
t (01580) 720770
e mail@freedomholidayhomes.co.uk
w freedomholidayhomes.co.uk

LYMINGTON
Hampshire

8 Admirals Court ★★★★
Self Catering
Contact: Mrs Mayes
t (01590) 679655
e holidays@newforestcottages.co.uk

Bourne House ★★★★
Self Catering
Contact: Mr Mare
t (01483) 772086
e jppmare@aol.com
w jppmare.ukhouse.com

Corner Cottages ★★★★
Self Catering
Contact: Mrs Ginny Neath
t (01590) 677241
e rg.neath@virgin.net
w cottagefor2.co.uk

De La Warr House ★★★★
Self Catering
Contact: Mrs Joanne Broadway
t (01590) 672785
e delawarrhouse@aol.com
w delawarrhouse.co.uk

Silk & Lace Cottages
★★★★–★★★★★
Self Catering
Contact: Mrs Anne Paterson
t 07764 607710
e anne@silkcottage.com
w silkcottage.com

South Coast Cottage ★★★
Self Catering
Contact: Ms Joanne Hill
t (01590) 679200
e joanne@jrhill.co.uk
w southcoastcottage.co.uk

Waterford Cottage ★★★★
Self Catering
Contact: Mrs Sally Sargeaunt
t (01425) 628970
w waterford-cottage.co.uk

LYNDHURST
Hampshire

95B High Street ★★★
Self Catering
Contact: Mr & Mrs John Langston
t (023) 8028 2206

Bay Tree Cottage ★★★★
Self Catering
Contact: Mrs Katrina Long
t (023) 8028 2821
e katrina.long@gmail.com
w baytreecottage.co.uk

Crowsnest Cottage ★★★★
Self Catering
t (023) 8028 3046
e booking@newforestcottage.com
w newforestcottage.com

Dairy Cottage ★★★★★
Self Catering
t (023) 8028 2629
w explorethenewforest.co.uk/dairycottage.htm

Rhubarb Cottage ★★★★
Self Catering
t (023) 8081 2753
w escapetothenewforest.co.uk

Yew Tree Cottage ★★★★
Self Catering
t (01962) 715491

Yorke Cottage ★★★★
Self Catering
Contact: Mrs H. C. Walker
t (023) 8029 2428
e helen@yorkecottage.co.uk
w yorkecottage.co.uk

MAIDENHEAD
Berkshire

11 Cadwell Drive ★★★
Self Catering
Contact: Mrs Vivien Williams
t (01628) 627370
e rvwilliams@btopenworld.com

Courtyard Cottages ★★★★
Self Catering
Contact: Mrs Carol Bardo
t (01628) 633761
e moorfm@aol.com
w moorfarm.com

Sheephouse Manor ★★★
Self Catering
Contact: Mrs Caroline Street
t (01628) 776902
e info@sheephousemanor.co.uk
w sheephousemanor.co.uk

MAIDSTONE
Kent

Heathfield House ★★★★
Self Catering
Contact: Mrs Jayne Bryant
t (01622) 765397

Old Wagon Lodge ★★★★
Self Catering
Contact: Mrs Sarah Sunnucks
t (01622) 745631
e scarytoe@kentit.net
w rankinsfarm.co.uk

The Orchard Flat, Ferlaga
★★★ *Self Catering*
Contact: Mrs Pamela Clark
t (01622) 726919
e pamclark@ferlaga.freeserve.co.uk

QL Apartments ★★★★
Self Catering
Contact: Miss Akram
t (01622) 670102
e enquiries@qlapartments.com
w qlapartments.com

Twitchers ★★★★
Self Catering
Freedom Holiday Homes
t (01580) 720770
e mail@freedomholidayhomes.co.uk
w freedomholidayhomes.co.uk

MANSTON
Kent

Annies and Well Cottage
★★★★ *Self Catering*
Contact: George Box
t (01843) 823371
e anniescottage1@aol.com
w anniescottage1.co.uk

MAPLEDURHAM
Oxfordshire

Mapledurham Holiday Cottages ★★★–★★★★
Self Catering
Contact: Mrs Lola Andrews
t (0118) 972 4292
e enquiries@mapledurham.co.uk
w mapledurham.co.uk

MARGATE
Kent

Modern House Palm Bay
★★★ *Self Catering*
Contact: Mrs Bowles
t (01732) 843396
e pat@ferryman.co.uk
w ferryman.co.uk/palmbay

Salmestone Grange ★★★★
Self Catering
t (01843) 231161
e salmestonegrange@aol.com
w salmestonegrange.co.uk

Sea View Holiday Apartments ★★★★
Self Catering
Contact: Esme Gold
t 07919 890093
e enquiries@seaviewholidayapartments.co.uk
w seaviewholidayapartments.co.uk

MEDSTEAD
Hampshire

The Barn, Medstead ★★★★
Self Catering
t (01420) 562682
w barfordfarmhouse.com

MENTMORE
Buckinghamshire

Lilly Cottage ★★★★
Self Catering
Contact: Mrs Kate Hendrickson
t (01296) 668978

MEOPHAM
Kent

Sunrise ★★★★ *Self Catering*
Contact: T M Dickety
Kites Letting Services Ltd
t (01474) 573047
e kitesletting@btconnect.com
w halcyon-gifts.co.uk/holidaylet2.htm

MERSHAM
Kent

The Barn ★★★★
Self Catering
Contact: Ms Jan Bowman
t (01233) 720345
e jan@studio2uk.com/gillfarm
w studio2uk.com/gillfarm

MERSTONE
Isle of Wight

The Barn ★★★★
Self Catering
Wight Locations
t (01983) 811418
e enquiries@wightlocations.co.uk
w wightlocations.co.uk

Chapel Cottage ★★★★
Self Catering
Contact: Mr Tony Simpson
t (01798) 872705
e jayne@chapelcottage.co.uk
w chapelcottage.co.uk

MIDHURST
West Sussex

Cowdray Park Holiday Cottages ★★★★
Self Catering
Contact: Mrs Sam Collins
t (01730) 812423
e enquiries@cowdray.co.uk
w cowdray.co.uk

MILFORD ON SEA
Hampshire

Maryland Court ★★★★
Self Catering
Contact: Mr R. J. Drake
t (01590) 643624
e robindrake@earthdesk.co.uk
w marylandcourt.co.uk

Milford Croft, Milford on Sea ★★★★ *Self Catering*
Beach Cottage
t (01590) 644014
e milford.croft@yahoo.co.uk
w milfordcroft.co.uk

Old Walls ★★★★
Self Catering
t (01590) 642138
w oldwalls.com

Windmill Cottage, Milford on Sea ★★★ *Self Catering*
Contact: Mrs Perham
t (01590) 643516
w windmillcottage.info

MINSTER-IN-THANET
Kent

Durlock Lodge
★★★–★★★★ *Self Catering*
t (01843) 821219
e david@durlocklodge.co.uk
w durlocklodge.co.uk

MINSTER LOVELL
Oxfordshire

Hill Grove Cottage ★★★★
Self Catering
Contact: Mrs Katharine Brown
t (01993) 703120
w country-accom.co.uk/hill-grove-farm/

MOLLINGTON
Oxfordshire

The Stables, The Shippon, The Byre – Anita's Holiday Cottages ★★★–★★★★
Self Catering
Contact: Mr & Mrs Darrel & Anita Gail Jeffries
Anita's Holiday Cottages
t (01295) 750731
e anitagail@btopenworld.com
w cottageinthecountry.co.uk

MONKS HORTON
Kent

Horton Cottage Annexe
★★★★ *Self Catering*
Freedom Holiday Homes
t (01580) 720770
e mail@freedomholidayhomes.co.uk
w freedomholidayhomes.co.uk

MONXTON
Hampshire

The Den at Millcroft ★★★★
Self Catering
t (01264) 710618

NEWBRIDGE
Isle of Wight

Laurel Cottage ★★★★
Self Catering
Island Cottage Holidays
t (01929) 481555
e enq@islandcottageholidays.com
w islandcottageholidays.com

NEWBURY
Berkshire

Enborne Street Farm Barn House ★★★★ *Self Catering*
t (01635) 253443

Freedom Serviced Apartments ★★★★
Serviced Apartments
Contact: Mrs N Kirby
Freedom Serviced Apartments Ltd
t (01635) 581351
e info@freedomsal.co.uk
w freedomeserviced apartments.co.uk

Newbury Apartments
★★★★★ *Self Catering*
t 07747 016478
w newburyapartments.co.uk

Peregrine Cottage ★★★★★
Self Catering
Contact: Mrs Elizabeth Knight
t (01635) 42585
e lizknight@amserve.net

NEWCHURCH
Isle of Wight

Barn Cottage ★★★
Self Catering
Contact: Mrs Corbin
t (01983) 865349
e anne.corbin@virgin.net
w wightfarmholidays.co.uk

The Brewhouse ★★★★
Self Catering
Wight Locations
t (01983) 811418
e enquiries@wightlocations.co.uk
w wightlocations.co.uk

Clematis ★★★ *Self Catering*
Contact: Mr & Mrs Alistair Jupe
t (01983) 867613
e alistair.jupe@btinternet.com
w btinternet.com/~alistair.jupe/

Knighton Gorges ★★★★
Self Catering
Island Cottage Holidays
t (01929) 481555
e enq@islandcottageholidays.com
w islandcottageholidays.com

Mersley Farm Cottages
★★★–★★★★ *Self Catering*
Contact: Mr & Mrs Colin & Jenny Boswell
t (01983) 865213
e jenny@mersleyfarm.co.uk
w mersleyfarm.co.uk

Paper Barn ★★★★
Self Catering
Island Cottage Holidays
t (01929) 481555
e enq@islandcottageholidays.com
w islandcottageholidays.com

Squire Thatchers Barn
★★★★ *Self Catering*
Island Cottage Holidays
t (01929) 481555
e enq@islandcottageholidays.com
w islandcottageholidays.com

NEWENDEN
Kent

The Bothy and The Barn
★★★★ *Self Catering*
Freedom Holiday Homes
t (01580) 720770
e mail@freedomholidayhomes.co.uk
w freedomholidayhomes.co.uk

NEWHAVEN
East Sussex

Barn Owls Self-Catering Apartments ★★★
Self Catering
Contact: Mrs Gill Canham
The Old Farmhouse
t (01273) 515966
e gillcanham@yahoo.co.uk
w barn-owls.co.uk

Kings House ★★★★
Self Catering
Garden of England Cottages
t (01892) 510117
e info@gardenofenglandcottages.co.uk
w goec.co.uk

NEWICK
East Sussex

Manor House Cottage
★★★★ *Self Catering*
Contact: Mrs Jane Roberts
t (01825) 722868
e bookings@manorhousecottage.co.uk
w manorhousecottage.co.uk

NEWPORT
Isle of Wight

2 Tennyson's View
★★★★★ *Self Catering*
Island Holiday Homes
t (01983) 521113
e enquiries@island-holiday-homes.net
w island-holiday-homes.net

Aisthorpe Farm Cottages
★★★★ *Self Catering*
Contact: Mr Paul Ancell
t (01983) 882123
e aisthorpefarm@hotmail.com
w aisthorpefarm.com

Bay Cottage (Island Holiday Homes) ★★★ *Self Catering*
Island Holiday Homes
t (01983) 521113
e enquiries@island-holiday-homes.net
w island-holiday-homes.net

The Bowling Green Apartment ★★★★★
Self Catering
English Heritage
t 0870 333 1187
e holidaycottages@english-heritage.org.uk
w english-heritage.org.uk/holidaycottages

Bramble Cottage ★★★★★
Self Catering
Island Cottage Holidays
t (01929) 481555
e enq@islandcottageholidays.com
w islandcottageholidays.com

The Cottage, Stone Farm
★★★★ *Self Catering*
Island Cottage Holidays
t (01929) 481555
e enq@islandcottageholidays.com
w islandcottageholidays.com

Dairy Cottage – Froglands Farm ★★★★ *Self Catering*
Contact: Mrs Linda Dungey
t (01983) 821027
e s.dungey@btinternet.com
w froglandsdairy.co.uk

Great East Standen Manor Cottage ★★★★ *Self Catering*
Island Cottage Holidays
t (01929) 481555
e enq@islandcottageholidays.com
w islandcottageholidays.com

Marvel Cottage ★★★★
Self Catering
Contact: Dr Steven Sweetman
t (01983) 822691
e s@mys.uk.com
w holiday-cottage-iow.co.uk

Mole Cottage 23 ★★★
Self Catering
Island Holiday Homes
t (01983) 521113
e enquiries@island-holiday-homes.net
w island-holiday-homes.net

The Old Brew House
★★★★ *Self Catering*
Island Cottage Holidays
t (01929) 481555
e enq@islandcottageholidays.com
w islandcottageholidays.com

Ye Olde Cottage ★★★★
Self Catering
Island Holiday Homes
t (01983) 521113
e enquiries@island-holiday-homes.net
w island-holiday-homes.net

Therles Cottage ★★★★
Self Catering
Island Cottage Holidays
t (01929) 481555
e enq@islandcottageholidays.com
w islandcottageholidays.com

Thornbury House ★★★
Self Catering
Island Holiday Homes
t (01983) 521113
e enquiries@island-holiday-homes.net
w island-holiday-homes.net

Tradewinds ★★★
Self Catering
Wight Locations
t (01983) 811418
e enquiries@wightlocations.co.uk
w wightlocations.co.uk

Virginia Cottage
Rating Applied For
Self Catering
Island Cottage Holidays
t (01929) 481555
e enq@islandcottageholidays.com
w islandcottageholidays.com

West Standen Farm ★★★★
Self Catering
Contact: Mr & Mrs Edwin & Sally Burt
t (01983) 522099
e weststanden@btinternet.com
w weststandenfarm.co.uk

NINFIELD
East Sussex

Little London ★★★★
Self Catering
Garden of England Cottages
t (01892) 510117
e info@gardenofenglandcottages.co.uk
w goec.co.uk

NINGWOOD
Isle of Wight

The Granary ★★★★★
Self Catering
Island Cottage Holidays
t (01929) 481555
e enq@islandcottageholidays.com
w islandcottageholidays.com

NITON
Isle of Wight

Bridge Cottage ★★★
Self Catering
Home From Home Holidays
t (01983) 854340
e ventnor@crldirect.co.uk
w hfromh.co.uk

Candleford ★★★
Self Catering
Island Holiday Homes
t (01983) 521113
e enquiries@island-holiday-homes.net
w island-holiday-homes.net

Medina ★★★ *Self Catering*
Island Holiday Homes
t (01983) 521113
e enquiries@island-holiday-homes.net
w island-holiday-homes.net

Niton Barns
Rating Applied For
Self Catering
Contact: Mr Neil Simmons
t (01983) 731506
e neil@billingsgroup.co.uk
w nitonbarns.co.uk

Pictou ★★★ *Self Catering*
Home From Home Holidays
t (01983) 854340
e ventnor@crldirect.co.uk
w hfromh.co.uk

Ramblers End ★★★★
Self Catering
Island Cottage Holidays
t (01929) 481555
e enq@islandcottageholidays.com
w islandcottageholidays.com

Scallop Shell Cottage
★★★★★ *Self Catering*
Island Cottage Holidays
t (01929) 481555
e enq@islandcottageholidays.com
w islandcottageholidays.com

Wight Heaven ★★
Self Catering
Contact: Mr John Sheppard
t (01983) 551501
e dadshep@dial.pipex.com
w wightheaven.co.uk

NOKE
Oxfordshire

Manor Barn ★★★★
Self Catering
Contact: Ms Emma Righton
t (01865) 376772
e er@oxfordshortlets.co.uk
w isisnokelets.co.uk

NORLEYWOOD
Hampshire

The Bee Garden ★★★★
Self Catering
Contact: Mr Mayes
t (01590) 679655
e holidays@newforestcottages.co.uk
w newforestcottages.co.uk/

NORTH LEIGH
Oxfordshire

Old Bakehouse ★★★★
Self Catering
Contact: Mrs Patricia Colson
t (01993) 881207
e farmerpat@btinternet.com

Wylcot Cottage ★★★★
Self Catering
Contact: Mrs Joy Crew
t (01993) 868614

NORTH NEWINGTON
Oxfordshire

Herrieff's Cottage ★★★★
Self Catering
t (01295) 738835
w herrieffscottage.co.uk

Millstream Cottages ★★★★
Self Catering
Contact: Andrew Marshall
t (01295) 730212
e lamadonett@aol.com
w themillhousebanbury.co.uk

NORTHBOURNE
Kent

New Mill ★★★★
Self Catering
Freedom Holiday Homes
t (01580) 720770
e mail@freedomholidayhomes.co.uk
w freedomholidayhomes.co.uk

NORTHIAM
East Sussex

Hop Press Cottage ★★★★
Self Catering
Contact: Ms Brenda Haines
t (01797) 252011
e brenda@morleyfarm.co.uk
w froglets.uk.com

NORTHMOOR
Oxfordshire

Rectory Farm Cottages
★★★★ *Self Catering*
Contact: Mrs Mary Anne Florey
t (01865) 300207
e pj.florey@farmline.com
w oxtowns.co.uk/rectoryfarm

NORTON
Isle of Wight

The Savoy ★★★★
Self Catering
Contact: Mr Jon Dyer
t (01983) 760355
e info@savoyholidays.co.uk
w savoyholidays.co.uk

Treetops ★★★★★
Self Catering
Island Cottage Holidays
t (01929) 481555
e enq@islandcottageholidays.com
w islandcottageholidays.com

Waters Edge ★★★★★
Self Catering
Contact: Ms Jan White
t (01983) 756401
e jan@watersedgeisleofwight.co.uk
w watersedgeisleofwight.co.uk

NUTLEY
East Sussex

The Old Cart Lodge ★★★★
Self Catering
Contact: Pauline & Peter Graves
t (01825) 712475
e grapauline@aol.com
w theoldcartlodge.co.uk

Whitehouse Farm Holiday Cottages ★★–★★★★
Self Catering
Contact: Mr Keith Wilson
t (01825) 712377
e keith.g.r.wilson@btinternet.com
w streets-ahead.com/whitehousefarm

OLD WIVES LEES
Kent

Flint Cottage ★★★★
Self Catering
Freedom Holiday Homes
t (01580) 720770
e mail@freedomholidayhomes.co.uk
w freedomholidayhomes.co.uk

OLNEY
Buckinghamshire

Hyde Farm Cottages ★★★★
Self Catering
Contact: Mrs Penny Reynolds
t (01234) 711223
e stayat.thehyde@btinternet.com

The Old Stone Barn ★★★★
Self Catering
Contact: Mr & Mrs G J Pibworth
t (01234) 711655
e info@oldstonebarn.co.uk
w oldstonebarn.co.uk

OTTERDEN
Kent

Frith Farm House ★★★★★
Self Catering
Contact: Mrs Susan Chesterfield
t (01795) 890701
e enquiries@frithfarmhouse.co.uk
w frithfarmhouse.co.uk

OWSLEBURY
Hampshire

Hensting Valley Chalet
★★★ *Self Catering*
t (01962) 777297

Lower Farm Garden Cottage
★★★★ *Self Catering*
t (01962) 777676

OXFORD
Oxfordshire

Bannisters ★★★★
Self Catering
Contact: Irene Priestly
t (01865) 251095
e bannisters@talktalk.net
w 7bannisterclose.co.uk

Cherbridge Cottage
★★★★★ *Self Catering*
Contact: Ms Laura Colman
Hill Farm
t (01865) 292813 & 07976 288329
e laura@cherbridgecottages.co.uk
w cherbridgecottages.co.uk

Green Cottage ★★★★
Self Catering
Contact: Mr & Mrs P Hankey
t (01865) 300740
e lettings@thegreen.co.uk
w oxtowns.co.uk/greencottage

The Studio ★★★★
Self Catering
t (01865) 402800

Wroxton House ★★★
Self Catering
Hideaways
t (01747) 828170
e enq@hideaways.co.uk
w hideaways.co.uk

PANGBOURNE
Berkshire

Brambly Thatch ★★★
Self Catering
Contact: Mr & Mrs Hatt
Merricroft Farming
t (0118) 984 3121
e merricroft@yahoo.co.uk

Soldalen Annexe ★★
Self Catering
Contact: Mr & Mrs John & Bente Kirk
t (0118) 984 2924

PEASE POTTAGE
West Sussex

Cottesmore Lodges ★★★★
Self Catering
Contact: Matt & Sue Rogerson
t (01293) 527759
e info@cottesmorelodges.co.uk
w cottesmorelodges.co.uk

PEASMARSH
East Sussex

Joywell Cottage ★★★★
Self Catering
Freedom Holiday Homes
t (01580) 720770
e mail@freedomholidayhomes.co.uk
w freedomholidayhomes.co.uk

PENNINGTON
Hampshire

Little Thatch ★★★★
Self Catering
Contact: Mrs Suzannah Nash
t (01582) 842831
e suzannah@littlethatchcottage.com
w littlethatchcottage.com

PETT LEVEL
East Sussex

Grace Dieu ★★★★
Self Catering
t (020) 7624 0525

PETWORTH
West Sussex

Honeysuckle Cottage
★★★★ *Self Catering*
Contact: Michelle Whitehead
t 07798 735119
e michellewhitehead@tiscali.co.uk
w honey-sucklecottage.co.uk

The Old Dairy ★★★★
Self Catering
Contact: Rosaleen Waugh
t (01798) 342900
e rosaleen@f2s.com
w theolddairy.com

PILTDOWN
East Sussex

Tom's Lodge ★★★
Self Catering
Contact: Teresa Antrobus
t (01825) 764723
e antrobus62@btinternet.com

PLAXTOL
Kent

Golding Hop Farm Cottage
★★★ *Self Catering*
Contact: Mrs Jacqueline Vincent
Golding Hop Farm
t (01732) 885432
e info@goldinghopfarm.com
w goldinghopfarm.com

PLAYDEN
East Sussex

Poppy ★★★ *Self Catering*
Freedom Holiday Homes
t (01580) 720770
e mail@freedomholidayhomes.co.uk
w freedomholidayhomes.co.uk

Saltcote Place ★★★★★
Self Catering
t (01797) 222220
w saltcote.co.uk

PORCHFIELD
Isle of Wight

Buzzard Barn ★★★★
Self Catering
Contact: K. Shynn
t (01983) 529691
e ken@buntshillbarns.co.uk
w buntshillbarns.co.uk

Heron's Ghyll ★★★★
Self Catering
Home From Home Holidays
t (01983) 854340
e ventnor@crldirect.co.uk
w hfromh.co.uk

PORTSMOUTH
Hampshire

Cowes View, Coastguard Cottages ★★★★
Self Catering
Contact: Mrs Melanie Vennis
t (01329) 664236
e enquiries@cowesview.co.uk
w cowesview.co.uk

Geminair Holiday & Business Flats ★★★ *Self Catering*
Contact: Mrs Pamela Holman
t (023) 9282 1602
e gemflat@aol.com
w gemflat.co.uk

Greenhays Business/Holiday Accommodation ★★★★
Self Catering
Contact: Mrs Christine Martin
t (023) 9273 7590
e chrismmartin@hotmail.com
w greenhays.co.uk

Helena Court Apartments
★★★ *Self Catering*
Contact: Mrs Wendy Haley
t (023) 9273 2116
e tikitouch@hotmail.com

Kenilworth Court Holiday Flats ★★★★ *Self Catering*
Contact: Mrs Teresa Sparrowhawk
t (023) 9273 4205
e kenilworthcourt@ntlworld.com
w kenilworth-court.co.uk

Lakeside Holiday & Business Apartments
Rating Applied For
Self Catering
Contact: Mrs Hamza
t 07810 436981
w lakesidesouthsea.com

Ocean Apartments ★★★
Self Catering
Contact: Mrs Dawn Sait
t (023) 9273 4233
e ocean@portsmouth-apartments.co.uk
w portsmouth-apartments.co.uk/ocean.htm

PRINCES RISBOROUGH
Buckinghamshire

Stable Cottage, Old Callow Down Farm ★★★
Self Catering
t (01844) 344416
w chilternscottage.co.uk

Windmill Farm ★★
Self Catering
t (01844) 343901

RADNAGE
Buckinghamshire

Golden Acres Farm, Radnage ★★★ *Self Catering*
Contact: Mrs Julia Pitcher
t (01494) 483378

RAMSGATE
Kent

16 Royal Road ★★★★
Self Catering
Contact: Ms D Panzetta
t 07785 733221

28 Wellington Crescent
Rating Applied For
Self Catering
Contact: Mrs Lynne Weedon
w freedomholidayhomes.co.uk

Coastguard's Cottage
★★★★ *Self Catering*
Contact: Julia Collins
t (01634) 722444
e info@coastguardscottages.co.uk
w coastguardscottages.co.uk

Hamilton House Holiday Flats ★★★ *Self Catering*
Contact: Mrs A Burridge
t (01843) 582592
e e.burridge@sky.com

Harbour Cottage ★★★★
Self Catering
The Property Management Company
t (01843) 596663
e enquiries@ramsgatecottage.co.uk
w ramsgatecottage.co.uk

Luxury Apartment ★★★★
Self Catering
Contact: Mrs J N Lawrence
Lawrence Family Holidays
t (01843) 591422
e nancy@nancylawrence.plus.com
w lawrencefamilyholidays.co.uk

Regency House ★★★★
Self Catering
Contact: Mrs Carolyn Heward
t (020) 7735 1744 & 07970 182862
e carolynheward@btinternet.com
w royalroad.co.uk

READING
Berkshire

City Gate
Rating Applied For
Serviced Apartments
Deep Blue Apartments
t 0870 770 0778
e steve@deepb.com

Kings Road
Rating Applied For
Serviced Apartments
Deep Blue Apartments
t 0870 770 0778
e steve@deepb.com
w deepblueapartments.com

McIlroy Building
Rating Applied For
Serviced Apartments
Deep Blue Apartments
t 0870 770 0778
e steve@deepb.com
w deepblueapartments.com

SACO Reading ★★★★
Serviced Apartments
SACO Apartments
t (0117) 974 5936
e sarahbailey@sacaoapartments.co.uk
w sacoapartments.co.uk

RINGWOOD
Hampshire

Karelia Holidays ★★
Self Catering
Contact: Mr Richard Gleed
t (01425) 478920
e rgleed@kareliaholidays.co.uk
w kareliaholidays.co.uk

ROBERTSBRIDGE
East Sussex

Butters Cottage ★★★★
Self Catering
Freedom Holiday Homes
t (01580) 720770
e mail@freedomholidayhomes.co.uk
w freedomholidayhomes.co.uk

The Kell ★★★★
Self Catering
Freedom Holiday Homes
t (01580) 720770
e mail@freedomholidayhomes.co.uk
w freedomholidayhomes.co.uk

Rose Cottage Studio ★★★
Self Catering
Freedom Holiday Homes
t (01580) 720770
e mail@freedomholidayhomes.co.uk
w freedomholidayhomes.co.uk

Strawberry Hill Estate
★★★-★★★★ *Self Catering*
Contact: Ms Margaret Parish
1066 Leisure Breaks Ltd
t (01424) 775555
e enquiries@1066leisure.com
w 1066leisure.com

ROCHESTER
Kent

Stable Cottages ★★★★
Self Catering
Contact: Mrs Debbie Symonds
t (01634) 272439 & 07802 662702
e stablecottages@btinternet.com
w stable-cottages.com

ROLVENDEN
Kent

The Little House Coveneys
★★★★ *Self Catering*
Contact: Mrs Jenny Field
t (01580) 241736
e field.coveneys@uwclub.net

ROOKLEY
Isle of Wight

Little Pidford Farm Cottages
★★★★ *Self Catering*
Contact: Mrs Natalie Breeze
t (01983) 721841
e pidford.farm@btinternet.com
w littlepidfordfarmcottages.co.uk

The Old Apple Store at Kennerley House & Badger's Cottage ★★★★ *Self Catering*
Contact: Mrs Carol Foote
t (01983) 842001
e carolfoote@btinternet.com
w kennerleyhouse.com

Rookley Farm Lodge
★★★★★ *Self Catering*
t (01983) 840787
w rookleyfarmlodge.co.uk

ROPLEY
Hampshire

Dairy Cottage ★★★★
Self Catering
Contact: Mr & Mrs Malcolm & Myra Neal
t (01962) 773348
e malcolm@cowgrove.co.uk

ROYAL TUNBRIDGE WELLS
Kent

1 Stable Mews ★★★
Self Catering
Freedom Holiday Homes
t (01580) 720770
e mail@freedomholidayhomes.co.uk
w freedomholidayhomes.co.uk

22 Hawkenbury Mead ★★★
Self Catering
Contact: Mr R H Wright
Hawkenbury Farm
t (01892) 536977
e rhwright1@aol.com

The Beach House ★★★
Self Catering
Contact: Ms Palmour
t (01892) 557781
e oneyeshut@onetel.com
w farmcombelane.co.uk

Broad Oak House ★★★
Self Catering
Contact: Mrs Seymour
t (01892) 619065
e tina@tlctraining.co.uk
w tunbridgewellsonline.com

Coachmans Cottage ★★★★
Self Catering
Freedom Holiday Homes
t (01580) 720770
e mail@freedomholidayhomes.co.uk
w freedomholidayhomes.co.uk

Ebenezer Cottage ★★★
Self Catering
Garden of England Cottages
t (01892) 510117
e info@gardenofenglandcottages.co.uk
w goec.co.uk

Ford Cottage ★★★
Self Catering
Contact: Mrs Wendy Cusdin
t (01892) 531419
e FordCottage@tinyworld.co.uk
w fordcottage.co.uk

Ripley Cottage ★★★★
Self Catering
Contact: Mr & Mrs Maciw
t 07789 372371
e holiday@ripleycottage.co.uk
w ripleycottage.co.uk

Royal Court & Royal Garden Apartments ★★★★
Self Catering
Contact: Mr & Mrs Graham & Kathy Blake
t (01983) 405032
e blake-rca@hotmail.com
w royalcourtgarden apartments.co.uk

St Austell ★★★ *Self Catering*
Island Holiday Homes
t (01983) 521113
e enquiries@island-holiday-homes.net
w island-holiday-homes.net

Victoria Lodge Holiday Apartments ★★★
Self Catering
Contact: Mr & Mrs Terry & Suzanne Grant
t (01983) 403209
e info@ victorialodgeapartments.co.uk
w victorialodgeapartments.co.uk

SANDWICH
Kent

Duck Cottage ★★★★
Self Catering
t (01954) 267173
e richval.lloyd@lineone.net
w duckcottage-sandwich.co.uk

Hyde-A-Way Cottage
★★★★ *Self Catering*
Contact: Mr & Mrs Ian & Gillian Hardy
t (01304) 620406
e gillhardy54@hotmail.co.uk

Primrose Cottage ★★★
Self Catering
Freedom Holiday Homes
t (01580) 720770
e mail@ freedomholidayhomes.co.uk
w freedomholidayhomes.co.uk

Thomas Paine's Cottage
★★★★ *Self Catering*
Contact: Robin Ward
t 07507 063822
e thomaspainecottage@ btopenworld.com
w thomaspaineshouse.co.uk

Updown Park Farm ★★★★
Self Catering
Contact: Mrs J R Mongomery
t (01843) 841656
e info@montgomery-cottages.co.uk
w montgomery-cottages.co.uk

Worth Village ★★★
Self Catering
Contact: Mrs Patricia Mallett
t (01304) 812276
e worthcotts@vinefarm.plus.com

SEAFORD
East Sussex

2 Kingsway Court ★★★★
Self Catering
Contact: Mrs Pauline Gower
t (01323) 895233 & 07889 310414
e sific@bgower.f9.co.uk

Dymock Farm ★★★
Self Catering
Contact: Mrs White
t (01323) 892982

SEAVIEW
Isle of Wight

2 Sandpipers ★★★★
Self Catering
Wight Locations
t (01983) 811418
e enquiries@wightlocations.co.uk
w wightlocations.co.uk

3 Pier Road
Rating Applied For
Self Catering
Wight Locations
t (01983) 811418
e enquiries@wightlocations.co.uk
w wightlocations.co.uk

33 Seaview Bay ★★★★★
Self Catering
Wight Locations
t (01983) 811418
e enquiries@wightlocations.co.uk
w wightlocations.co.uk

5 Springfield Court
★★★★★ *Self Catering*
Wight Locations
t (01983) 811418
e enquiries@wightlocations.co.uk
w wightlocations.co.uk

6 Seaview House ★★★★
Self Catering
Wight Locations
t (01983) 811418
e enquiries@wightlocations.co.uk
w wightlocations.co.uk

7 Sandpipers ★★★★
Self Catering
Wight Locations
t (01983) 811418
e enquiries@wightlocations.co.uk
w wightlocations.co.uk

The Bolthole ★★★★
Self Catering
Contact: Mrs Barbara Hughes
t (01983) 810324
e barbara_hughes@btinternet.com
w theboltholeiow.co.uk

Bonny Blink ★★★★★
Self Catering
Island Cottage Holidays
t (01929) 481555
e enq@islandcottageholidays.com
w islandcottageholidays.com

Carisbrooke ★★★★
Self Catering
Wight Locations
t (01983) 811418
e enquiries@wightlocations.co.uk
w wightlocations.co.uk

Cluniac Cottage ★★★★
Self Catering
Wight Locations
t (01983) 811418
e enquiries@wightlocations.co.uk
w wightlocations.co.uk

Clyro ★★★ *Self Catering*
Wight Locations
t (01983) 811418
e enquiries@wightlocations.co.uk
w wightlocations.co.uk

Coach House 1 ★★★★
Self Catering
Wight Locations
t (01983) 811418
e enquiries@wightlocations.co.uk
w wightlocations.co.uk

The Drey ★★★★
Self Catering
Wight Locations
t (01983) 811418
e enquiries@wightlocations.co.uk
w wightlocations.co.uk

East Gull Sands
Rating Applied For
Self Catering
Wight Locations
t (01983) 811418
e enquiries@wightlocations.co.uk
w wightlocations.co.uk

Garsdon ★★★★
Self Catering
Wight Locations
t (01983) 811418
e enquiries@wightlocations.co.uk
w wightlocations.co.uk

Hydeaway ★★★★
Self Catering
Wight Locations
t (01983) 811418
e enquiries@wightlocations.co.uk
w wightlocations.co.uk

Junipers ★★★★★
Self Catering
Wight Locations
t (01983) 811418
e enquiries@wightlocations.co.uk
w wightlocations.co.uk

Lebrel Lodge
Rating Applied For
Self Catering
Wight Locations
t (01983) 811418
e enquiries@wightlocations.co.uk
w wightlocations.co.uk

Oaks ★★★ *Self Catering*
Wight Locations
t (01983) 811418
e enquiries@wightlocations.co.uk
w wightlocations.co.uk

Old Orchard ★★★★
Self Catering
Wight Locations
t (01983) 811418
e enquiries@wightlocations.co.uk
w wightlocations.co.uk

The Old School House
Rating Applied For
Self Catering
Wight Locations
t (01983) 811418
e enquiries@wightlocations.co.uk
w wightlocations.co.uk

The Priory Coach House
★★★★★ *Self Catering*
Wight Locations
t (01983) 811418
e enquiries@wightlocations.co.uk
w wightlocations.co.uk

Studio Annexe ★★★★
Self Catering
Contact: Mr & Mrs Robin & Virginia Lobb
t (01983) 812180
e studioannexe@btinternet.com

West Ingle ★★★
Self Catering
Wight Locations
t (01983) 811418
e enquiries@wightlocations.co.uk
w wightlocations.co.uk

SEDLESCOMBE
East Sussex

Acorn Chalet ★★★★
Self Catering
Garden of England Cottages
t (01892) 510117
e info@ gardenofenglandcottages.co.uk
w goec.co.uk

The Retreat at Cherryburn
★★★★ *Self Catering*
Garden of England Cottages
t (01892) 510117
e info@ gardenofenglandcottages.co.uk
w goec.co.uk

SELSEY
West Sussex

BeachFront House ★★★★
Self Catering
Contact: Angela Kelly
t 07976 957004
e angela@phoenixcommunity.co.uk
w selseyretreat.co.uk

SEVENOAKS
Kent

Harveys ★★★ *Self Catering*
t (01732) 761862

SHALFLEET
Isle of Wight

Shalfleet Manor Farmhouse, Cottage & Barn
★★★★-★★★★★
Self Catering
Island Cottage Holidays
t (01929) 481555
e enq@islandcottageholidays.com
w islandcottageholidays.com

SHANKLIN
Isle of Wight

1 Apse Castle Cottages
★★★★ *Self Catering*
Island Cottage Holidays
t (01929) 481555
e enq@islandcottageholidays.com
w islandcottageholidays.com

12 The Priory ★★★★
Self Catering
Island Holiday Homes
t (01983) 521113
e enquiries@island-holiday-homes.net
w island-holiday-homes.net

14 The Priory
Rating Applied For
Self Catering
Island Holiday Homes
t (01983) 521113
e enquiries@island-holiday-homes.net
w island-holiday-homes.net

16 The Priory
Rating Applied For
Self Catering
Island Holiday Homes
t (01983) 521113
e enquiries@island-holiday-homes.net
w island-holiday-homes.net

2 The Stables ★★★★
Self Catering
Island Holiday Homes
t (01983) 521113
e enquiries@island-holiday-homes.net
w island-holiday-homes.net

5 The Priory ★★★
Self Catering
Island Holiday Homes
t (01983) 521113
e enquiries@island-holiday-homes.net
w island-holiday-homes.net

6 The Esplanade ★★★
Self Catering
Island Holiday Homes
t (01983) 521113
e enquiries@island-holiday-homes.net
w island-holiday-homes.net

Byre Cottage ★★★★
Self Catering
Island Cottage Holidays
t (01929) 481555
e enq@islandcottageholidays.com
w islandcottageholidays.com

Chestnut Mews Holiday Cottages ★★★★★
Self Catering
Contact: Mrs Carol Bowkis
t (01983) 861145
e chestnutmews@btinternet.com
w chestnutmews.co.uk

Dairy Cottage ★★★★
Self Catering
Contact: Mrs Justine Gertz
t (01983) 867074
e mail@isleofwightcottageholiday.com
w isleofwightcottageholiday.com

Fair Winds ★★★
Self Catering
Home From Home Holidays
t (01983) 854340
e ventnor@crldirect.co.uk
w hfromh.co.uk

Fernhurst Holiday Apartments ★★★–★★★★
Self Catering
Contact: Mrs Petcher
t (01983) 862126
e spetcher@fernhurst-apartments.co.uk
w fernhurst-apartments.co.uk

Green Gable ★★★
Self Catering
Home From Home Holidays
t (01983) 854340
e ventnor@crldirect.co.uk
w hfromh.co.uk

Groom Cottage ★★★★★
Self Catering
Island Cottage Holidays
t (01929) 481555
e enq@islandcottageholidays.com
w islandcottageholidays.com

Keats House ★★★★
Self Catering
Island Cottage Holidays
t (01929) 481555
e enq@islandcottageholidays.com
w islandcottageholidays.com

Laramie ★★★★ *Self Catering*
Contact: Mrs Sally Ranson
t (01983) 862905
e sally.ranson@tiscali.co.uk
w laramieholidayhome.co.uk

Lovecombe Cottage ★★★★
Self Catering
Island Cottage Holidays
t (01929) 481555
e enq@islandcottageholidays.com
w islandcottageholidays.com

Luccombe Villa ★★★
Self Catering
Contact: Mrs Fiona Seymour
t (01983) 862825
e info@luccombevilla.co.uk
w luccombevilla.co.uk

Lyon Court ★★★–★★★★
Self Catering
Contact: Mr & Mrs Paul & Sandra Humphreys
t (01983) 865861
e info@lyoncourtshanklin.co.uk
w lyoncourtshanklin.co.uk

Percy Cottage ★★★★
Self Catering
Contact: Mr David Strugnell
t (01983) 866 221 & 07752 407423
e dstrugnell@tiscali.co.uk
w percy-cottage.co.uk

The Priory Apartment
★★★★★ *Self Catering*
Home From Home Holidays
t (01983) 854340
e ventnor@crldirect.co.uk
w hfromh.co.uk

Rubstone Cottage ★★★★
Self Catering
Contact: Mr Haynes
t (01483) 415185
e haynesrk@talktalk.net

Summerhill Apartments
★★★★ *Self Catering*
Contact: Mrs Jean Linaker
t (01983) 862576
e jean@summerhillapts.co.uk
w summerhillapts.co.uk

Sunny Bay Apartments
★★★★ *Self Catering*
Contact: Mrs Julia Nash
t (01983) 866379
e info@sunnybayapartments.com
w sunnybayapartments.com

Upper Chine Holiday Cottages & Apartments
★★★★ *Self Catering*
Contact: Mr Danny Bowkis
t (01983) 867900
e upperchine@btconnect.com
w upperchinecottages.co.uk

YMCA Winchester House – The Lodge ★★★
Self Catering
Contact: Ms Roo Cleland
t (01489) 772215
e roo.cleland@ymca-fg.org
w ymca-fg.org/iow

SHAWFORD
Hampshire

Kingsmere Cottage ★★★★
Self Catering
Contact: Mrs Caroline Daniels
t (01962) 714876
e kingsmere@btinternet.com

SHELDWICH
Kent

Littles Manor Farmhouse
★★★★ *Self Catering*
Contact: Tim Bourne
t (01233) 820425

SHERE
Surrey

Five Pines ★★★ *Self Catering*
Contact: Ms Gill Gellatly
t (01483) 202689
e gill@lockhurst-hatch-farm.co.uk
w users.waitrose.com/~gmgellatly

SHILTON
Oxfordshire

The Chestnuts, Shilton
★★★★ *Self Catering*
Contact: Miss Christine Burton
t (01993) 844905
e chrisburtonpr@aol.com
w thechestnuts.net

SHIPBOURNE
Kent

The Old Stables ★★★★
Self Catering
t (01732) 810739
w kent-lets.co.uk

SHIPTON-UNDER-WYCHWOOD
Oxfordshire

6 Westgate ★★★★
Self Catering
Contact: Mrs Helen Harrison
t (01993) 830202

Plum Cottage ★★★★
Self Catering
Contact: Mrs Angela Richards
t (01993) 824252
e mancott@netcomuk.co.uk
w geocities.com

Turkey Cottage ★★★★
Self Catering
t 0870 027 5930
e cottage@cottageinthecountry.co.uk
w cottageinthecountry.co.uk

SHOREHAM-BY-SEA
West Sussex

140 Old Fort Road ★★★★
Self Catering
t (01273) 308779
w bestofbrighton.co.uk

SHORTGATE
East Sussex

White Lion Farm Cottages
★★★ *Self Catering*
Contact: Ms Diana Green
t (01825) 840288

SHORWELL
Isle of Wight

Brookside Cottage ★★★★
Self Catering
Contact: Ms Teresa Herd
t 07795 078049
e brooksidecottage@ntlworld.com
w brooksidecottage.info

Byre Cottage ★★★★
Self Catering
Island Holiday Homes
t (01983) 521113
e enquiries@island-holiday-homes.net
w island-holiday-homes.net

Combe Barn ★★★★★
Self Catering
Contact: Ms Jill Mears
t (01983) 741422
e claudia@combebarn.co.uk
w combebarn.co.uk

Marylands ★★★★
Self Catering
Island Cottage Holidays
t (01929) 481555
e enq@islandcottageholidays.com
w islandcottageholidays.com

Sandfoot ★★★ *Self Catering*
Island Holiday Homes
t (01983) 521113
e enquiries@island-holiday-homes.net
w island-holiday-homes.net

Stone Place Cottage ★★★
Self Catering
Home From Home Holidays
t (01983) 854340
e ventnor@crldirect.co.uk
w hfromh.co.uk

SIDLESHAM COMMON
West Sussex

Lockgate Dairy Holiday Cottages ★★★★
Self Catering
Contact: Mrs Jean Buchanan
t (01243) 641452
e holidays@lockgatedairy.co.uk
w lockgatedairy.co.uk

SISSINGHURST
Kent

Orchard Cottage ★★★★
Self Catering
Freedom Holiday Homes
t (01580) 720770
e mail@freedomholidayhomes.co.uk
w freedomholidayhomes.co.uk

SLOUGH
Berkshire

Little Acorns & Roddell Court ★★★★
Serviced Apartments
Contact: Mr Lee Owens
t (01753) 571761
e lo@capecorporation.co.uk
w heathrowapartments.co.uk

Mosaic Apartments ★★★★
Serviced Apartments
The Apartment Service
t (020) 8944 1444
e melanied@apartment.co.uk
w apartmentservice.com

SMARDEN
Kent

Braid Farm Cottages ★★★★
Self Catering
Freedom Holiday Homes
t (01580) 720770
e mail@freedomholidayhomes.co.uk
w freedomholidayhomes.co.uk

Dering Cottage ★★★★
Self Catering
Freedom Holiday Homes
t (01580) 720770
e mail@freedomholidayhomes.co.uk
w freedomholidayhomes.co.uk

SOUTHAMPTON
Hampshire

Pinewood Lodge Apartments ★★★
Self Catering
Contact: Dr Bradberry
Pinewood Lodge
t (023) 8040 2925
e stan.bradberry@tesco.net
w self-catering-apartments-southampton.co.uk

SOUTHWATER
West Sussex

Birchwood Lodge ★★★★
Self Catering
Contact: G R & J M Holding
t (01403) 731949
e nickie@holdingand.co.uk
w birchwoodlodge.co.uk

STAINES
Surrey

Thames Edge ★★★
Serviced Apartments
The Apartment Service
t (020) 8944 1444
e melanied@apartment.co.uk
w apartmentservice.com

STANDFORD
Hampshire

Standford Grange ★★★★★
Self Catering
t (01428) 751846

STAPLE
Kent

Piglet Place ★★★★
Self Catering
Contact: B. E. Barber
t (01304) 813321
e richbarber@lineone.net
w pigletplace.co.uk

STAPLECROSS
East Sussex

Mill Cottage ★★★★
Self Catering
Contact: Mrs Hend Finlay
t (01424) 427693
e millcottage06@btinternet.com
w mill-cottages.co.uk

STAPLEHURST
Kent

Basil, Thyme & Rosemary Lodges ★★★ *Self Catering*
Garden of England Cottages
t (01892) 510117
e info@gardenofenglandcottages.co.uk
w goec.co.uk

Church Cottage ★★★
Self Catering
Freedom Holiday Homes
t (01580) 720770
e mail@freedomholidayhomes.co.uk
w freedomholidayhomes.co.uk

Gardeners Cottage ★★★★
Self Catering
Freedom Holiday Homes
t (01580) 720770
e mail@freedomholidayhomes.co.uk
w freedomholidayhomes.co.uk

The Hop Barn ★★★★
Self Catering
Freedom Holiday Homes
t (01580) 720770
e mail@freedomholidayhomes.co.uk
w freedomholidayhomes.co.uk

Tudor Hurst Cottage ★★★★ *Self Catering*
Freedom Holiday Homes
t (01580) 720770
e mail@freedomholidayhomes.co.uk
w freedomholidayhomes.co.uk

STELLING MINNIS
Kent

Great Field Farm ★★★★
Self Catering
Contact: Mr Castle
t (01227) 709223
e greatfieldfarm@aol.com
w great-field-farm.co.uk

STEYNING
West Sussex

Pepperscombe Cottages ★★★★★ *Self Catering*
Contact: John & Judith Camilleri
t (01903) 813868
e john.camilleri@btconnect.com
w pepperscombecottages.com

Shepherd's Cottage ★★★
Self Catering
Contact: Steve & Cathy Davie
4 Russell's Crescent
t 05600 799385
e shepherdssteyning@btinternet.com
w shepherdssteyning.co.uk

STOCKBURY
Kent

The Old Dairy ★★★★
Self Catering
Contact: Mrs Anthony
t (01622) 884222

STOKE HAMMOND
Buckinghamshire

Pump House Barn ★★★
Self Catering
Contact: Mr & Mrs Peter & Eileen Kane & Curry
t (01525) 270858
e eileen.curry@tesco.net
w pumphousebarn.net

STONE-IN-OXNEY
Kent

Coldharbour Cottage ★★★★ *Self Catering*
Contact: Mr Andrew Jempson
t (01797) 230214
e stay@coldharbourcottage.co.uk
w coldharbourcottage.co.uk

STONEGATE
East Sussex

Bardown Farm Holiday Cottages ★★★★★
Self Catering
Contact: Mrs A Wortley
t (01580) 200452
e wortleya@aol.com
w premiercottages.co.uk/cottage.asp?id=198

Coopers Farm Cottage ★★★★★ *Self Catering*
Contact: Ms Jane Howard
t (01580) 200386
e jane@coopersfarmstonegate.co.uk

Freedom Holiday Homes ★★★ *Self Catering*
t (01580) 720770
e mail@freedomholidayhomes.co.uk
w freedomholidayhomes.co.uk

STONOR
Oxfordshire

White Pond Farm ★★★★
Self Catering
Contact: Mrs Lindy Stracey
t (01491) 638224
e info@whitepondfarm.co.uk
w whitepondfarm.co.uk

STORRINGTON
West Sussex

Byre Cottages ★★★–★★★★ *Self Catering*
Contact: Grahame & Gail Kittle
t (01903) 745754
e kittles@waitrose.com

STOWE
Buckinghamshire

The Long Barn ★★★★★
Self Catering
t (01280) 812179
w stowelongbarn.co.uk

STREAT
West Sussex

Gote Lodge ★★★★
Self Catering
Contact: Mrs Caroline Tower
t (01273) 890976
e gotestreat@btinternet.co.uk

SUNBURY
Surrey

85 Sundeala Close ★★★
Self Catering
Heathrow Apartments
t (01932) 786979 & 07939 543224
e info@heathrowapartments.biz
w heathrowapartments.biz

SWAY
Hampshire

Hackney Park ★★★
Self Catering
Contact: Mrs Helen Beale
t (01590) 682049
e hackneypark@tiscali.co.uk

Middle Cottage ★★★
Self Catering
Contact: Mrs Ann Gimeno
t (01425) 623172
e fairways@swayroad.co.uk

The Old Exchange ★★★
Self Catering
Contact: Mrs S Alborino
t (01590) 679228
e arcobaleno_1@hotmail.com
w newforestretreats.co.uk

SWERFORD
Oxfordshire

Heath Farm Holiday Cottages ★★★★–★★★★★
Self Catering
Contact: Mr & Mrs David & Nena Barbour
t (01608) 683270
e barbours@heathfarm.com
w heathfarm.com

TENTERDEN
Kent

Aylmer Cottage ★★★★
Self Catering
Freedom Holiday Homes
t (01580) 720770
e mail@freedomholidayhomes.co.uk
w freedomholidayhomes.co.uk

Malt House Barn ★★★★
Self Catering
Freedom Holiday Homes
t (01580) 720770
e mail@freedomholidayhomes.co.uk
w freedomholidayhomes.co.uk

Meadow Cottage & Tamworth Cottage ★★★★
Self Catering
Contact: Mrs Cooke
t (01797) 270539
e info@prawls.co.uk
w prawls.co.uk

THAME
Oxfordshire

The Hollies ★★★★
Self Catering
Contact: Ms Julia Tanner
t (01844) 281423
e info@theholliesthame.co.uk
w theholliesthame.co.uk

Honeysuckle Cottage ★★★
Self Catering
t (01844) 208697

Meadowbrook Farm Holiday Cottages ★★★★
Self Catering
Contact: Mrs Diana Wynn
t (01844) 212116
e rdwynn@ukonline.co.uk
w meadowbrookfarm.co.uk

THURNHAM Kent

Cobham Manor Farmhouse
Rating Applied For
Self Catering
Contact: Mrs Lynne Weedon
w freedomholidayhomes.co.uk

TICEHURST East Sussex

Chequers Cottage ★★★
Self Catering
Freedom Holiday Homes
t (01580) 720770
e mail@freedomholidayhomes.co.uk
w freedomholidayhomes.co.uk

TIPTOE Hampshire

Brockhills Farm ★★★★
Self Catering
Contact: Mr David Turner
t 07769 502214
w brockhillsfarm.co.uk/

TONBRIDGE Kent

10 The Lyons ★★★★
Self Catering
Garden of England Cottages
t (01892) 510117
e info@gardenofenglandcottages.co.uk
w goec.co.uk

88 Avebury Avenue (Castle View) ★★★★ *Self Catering*
Freedom Holiday Homes
t (01580) 720770
e mail@freedomholidayhomes.co.uk
w freedomholidayhomes.co.uk

Goldhill Mill Cottages
★★★★★ *Self Catering*
t (01732) 851626
w goldhillmillcottages.com

Grapevine Lodge ★★★
Self Catering
Garden of England Cottages
t (01892) 510117
e info@gardenofenglandcottages.co.uk
w goec.co.uk

The Little Dairy ★★★
Self Catering
Garden of England Cottages
t (01892) 510117
e info@gardenofenglandcottages.co.uk
w goec.co.uk

Postern Park Stable ★★★★
Self Catering
Garden of England Cottages
t (01892) 510117
e info@gardenofenglandcottages.co.uk
w goec.co.uk

The Roundel ★★★
Self Catering
Freedom Holiday Homes
t (01580) 720770
e mail@freedomholidayhomes.co.uk
w freedomholidayhomes.co.uk

Waters Edge ★★★★
Self Catering
Garden of England Cottages
t (01892) 510117
e info@gardenofenglandcottages.co.uk
w goec.co.uk

TOTLAND BAY Isle of Wight

33 Hurst Point View ★★★
Self Catering
Island Holiday Homes
t (01983) 521113
e enquiries@island-holiday-homes.net
w island-holiday-homes.net

Alum Bay House – Keats Wing ★★★★ *Self Catering*
Island Cottage Holidays
t (01929) 481555
e enq@islandcottageholidays.com
w islandcottageholidays.com

Craiglea Holiday Cottage
★★★★ *Self Catering*
Contact: Mr Lawrence Brown
t (01865) 875890
e enquiries@iowcottage.co.uk
w iowcottage.co.uk

Holiday Homes Owners Services Ref: T6 ★★★★
Self Catering
Holiday Homes Owners Services (West Wight)
t (01983) 753423
e holidayhomesiow@ic24.net
w holidayhomesiow.co.uk

Island View Bungalows
★★★★ *Self Catering*
Contact: Ms Liz Jasper
t (01983) 721606
e info@islandviewholidays.co.uk
w islandviewholidays.co.uk

Priestley ★★★★
Self Catering
Island Cottage Holidays
t (01929) 481555
e enq@islandcottageholidays.com
w islandcottageholidays.com

Seawinds ★★ *Self Catering*
Contact: Mrs Jacquie Simmonds
t (01983) 752772
e enquiries@buttercuphouse.co.uk

Stonewind Farm ★★★
Self Catering
Contact: Mrs Pat Hayles
t (01983) 752912

Totland Bay Apartment
★★★★ *Self Catering*
Contact: Mr & Mrs R & S Knights
t (01273) 584601
e sj.knights@virgin.net
w totlandbayapartment.co.uk

TOYS HILL Kent

Tan House Barn
Rating Applied For
Self Catering
Contact: Mrs Glynis E Cook
t (01732) 750129
e glynis.cook@hotmail.co.uk

TUDELEY Kent

Latters Farm Barn ★★★★
Self Catering
Garden of England Cottages
t (01892) 510117
e info@gardenofenglandcottages.co.uk
w goec.co.uk

Latters Oast ★★★★
Self Catering
Garden of England Cottages
t (01892) 510117
e info@gardenofenglandcottages.co.uk
w goec.co.uk

TURVILLE Oxfordshire

Old Rose Cottage ★★★★
Self Catering
t 07793 097520
w chilterncountrycottages.com

TWYFORD Hampshire

Embessy Cottage ★★★★
Self Catering
Contact: Mrs Caroline Rees
t (01962) 712921
e cjrees@onetel.com
w holiday-rentals.co.uk

UDIMORE East Sussex

Finlay Cottage ★★★
Self Catering
Garden of England Cottages
t (01892) 510117
e info@gardenofenglandcottages.co.uk
w goec.co.uk

UNDERRIVER Kent

Hopefield Cottage ★★★★
Self Catering
Contact: Ms Carol Lawrence
t (01732) 833181
e carol@hopefieldcottage.co.uk
w hopefieldcottage.co.uk

UPCHURCH Kent

The Old Stable ★★★
Self Catering
Garden of England Cottages
t (01892) 510117
e info@gardenofenglandcottages.co.uk
w goec.co.uk

VENTNOR Isle of Wight

1 Cleeve Court ★★★
Self Catering
Island Holiday Homes
t (01983) 521113
e enquiries@island-holiday-homes.net
w island-holiday-homes.net

1 Pier View ★★★
Self Catering
Island Holiday Homes
t (01983) 521113
e enquiries@island-holiday-homes.net
w island-holiday-homes.net

13 Westfield Bungalow
Rating Applied For
Self Catering
Island Holiday Homes
t (01983) 521113
e enquiries@island-holiday-homes.net
w island-holiday-homes.net

2 Cleeve Court ★★★
Self Catering
Island Holiday Homes
t (01983) 521113
e enquiries@island-holiday-homes.net
w island-holiday-homes.net

3 Riviera ★★★★
Self Catering
Contact: Mrs Carole Holway
t (01892) 521986
e carole@ancerspa.co.uk
w beachhomeventnor.com

64 South Street ★★★
Self Catering
Island Holiday Homes
t (01983) 521113
e enquiries@island-holiday-homes.net
w island-holiday-homes.net

Baltija ★★★ *Self Catering*
Island Holiday Homes
t (01983) 521113
e enquiries@island-holiday-homes.net
w island-holiday-homes.net

Bank End Farm – Beachcombers, Lobster Pot, Fisherman's Cottage, The Swallows & Swifts ★★★★
Self Catering
Contact: Mrs Clare Watson
t (01983) 852649
e enquiries@bankendfarm.co.uk
w bankendfarm.co.uk

Barn End (Home From Home Holidays) ★★★★
Self Catering
Home From Home Holidays
t (01983) 854340
e ventnor@crldirect.co.uk
w hfromh.co.uk

Bermuda House ★★★★
Self Catering
Contact: Mr John Allen
t (020) 7385 1394
e enquiries@ventnorselfcatering.co.uk
w ventnorselfcatering.co.uk

Blue Downs View ★★★
Self Catering
Home From Home Holidays
t (01983) 854340
e ventnor@crldirect.co.uk
w hfromh.co.uk

Bonchurch Cottage ★★★★
Self Catering
Contact: Mr Michael Edwards
t 0845 230 6780
e info@distinctivedesigns.co.uk
w bonchurchcottage.com

Breakers Sound
Rating Applied For
Self Catering
Island Holiday Homes
t (01983) 521113
e enquiries@island-holiday-homes.net
w island-holiday-homes.net

The Brewhouse ★★★
Self Catering
Island Holiday Homes
t (01983) 521113
e enquiries@island-holiday-homes.net
w island-holiday-homes.net

Castle Cottage ★★★★
Self Catering
Island Cottage Holidays
t (01929) 481555
e enq@islandcottageholidays.com
w islandcottageholidays.com

Church Place ★★★★
Self Catering
Home From Home Holidays
t (01983) 854340
e ventnor@crldirect.co.uk
w hfromh.co.uk

Clarence House Holiday Apartments ★★★★
Self Catering
Contact: Mr Will Glover
t (01983) 852875
e clarencehouseh@aol.com
w iowholidayapartments.co.uk

Cliff Cottage ★★★★
Self Catering
Island Cottage Holidays
t (01929) 481555
e enq@islandcottageholidays.com
w islandcottageholidays.com

Cliff Cottage ★★★
Self Catering
Home From Home Holidays
t (01983) 854340
e ventnor@crldirect.co.uk
w hfromh.co.uk

The Clock House ★★★★
Self Catering
Island Cottage Holidays
t (01929) 481555
e enq@islandcottageholidays.com
w islandcottageholidays.com

Coastguards
Rating Applied For
Self Catering
Island Holiday Homes
t (01983) 521113
e enquiries@island-holiday-homes.net
w island-holiday-homes.net

Cornerstone Garden Apartment – West Apartment ★★★★
Self Catering
Contact: Mrs Sophie Harris
t (01983) 853421
e info@ventnorapartments.co.uk
w ventnorapartments.co.uk

Cove Cottage ★★★
Self Catering
Home From Home Holidays
t (01983) 854340
e ventnor@crldirect.co.uk
w hfromh.co.uk

Crow's Nest ★★
Self Catering
Home From Home Holidays
t (01983) 854340
e ventnor@crldirect.co.uk
w hfromh.co.uk

Dolphins House ★★★★
Self Catering
Island Holiday Homes
t (01983) 521113
e enquiries@island-holiday-homes.net
w island-holiday-homes.net

Dudley House ★★★★
Self Catering
Home From Home Holidays
t (01983) 854340
e ventnor@crldirect.co.uk
w hfromh.co.uk

East Wing, Dean Farm ★★★★ *Self Catering*
Contact: Mrs Nicola Attrill
t (01983) 731475
e nicola@deanfarmholidays.wanadoo.co.uk
w deanfarm.co.uk

Eden Cottage ★★★
Self Catering
Home From Home Holidays
t (01983) 854340
e ventnor@crldirect.co.uk
w hfromh.co.uk

Fernleigh House ★★★★★
Self Catering
Home From Home Holidays
t (01983) 854340
e ventnor@crldirect.co.uk
w hfromh.co.uk

Fernwood Cottage ★★★★
Self Catering
Home From Home Holidays
t (01983) 854340
e ventnor@crldirect.co.uk
w hfromh.co.uk

Flat 1 Esplanade House ★★★ *Self Catering*
Island Holiday Homes
t (01983) 521113
e enquiries@island-holiday-homes.net
w island-holiday-homes.net

The Furlongs ★★★
Self Catering
Home From Home Holidays
t (01983) 854340
e ventnor@crldirect.co.uk
w hfromh.co.uk

Garden House ★★★★
Self Catering
Contact: Mr Philip Barton
67 Strode Road
t (020) 7385 7073 & 07887 848146
e philip@peoplesense.co.uk
w holidaylets.net/prop_detail.asp?id=13874

Garfield Holiday Flats ★★★
Self Catering
Contact: Mrs Stead
t (01983) 854084

Glenlyn ★★★ *Self Catering*
Contact: Mr Stritton
t (01983) 852244
e eversleyhotel@yahoo.co.uk
w eversleyhotel.com

Heathland Cottage ★★★★
Self Catering
Home From Home Holidays
t (01983) 854340
e ventnor@crldirect.co.uk
w hfromh.co.uk

Isle of Wight Luxury Apartments ★★★★★
Self Catering
Contact: Mrs Jo Acheson
t (01983) 721519
e jo@isleofwightluxuryapartments.co.uk
w isleofwightluxuryapartments.co.uk

Ivy Cottage ★★★★
Self Catering
Contact: Mr & Mrs Peter & Madeline Newton
t (01983) 853378
e peter.newton@talktalk.net
w thenewtons.info

Ivy Cottage ★★★
Self Catering
Home From Home Holidays
t (01983) 854340
e ventnor@crldirect.co.uk
w hfromh.co.uk

Jules Cottage ★★★★
Self Catering
Home From Home Holidays
t (01983) 854340
e ventnor@crldirect.co.uk
w hfromh.co.uk

Langonnet, Seaview ★★★★
Self Catering
Island Cottage Holidays
t (01929) 481555
e enq@islandcottageholidays.com
w islandcottageholidays.com

Little Thatch ★★★★
Self Catering
Home From Home Holidays
t (01983) 854340
e ventnor@crldirect.co.uk
w hfromh.co.uk

Lonicera ★★★★
Self Catering
Home From Home Holidays
t (01983) 854340
e ventnor@crldirect.co.uk
w hfromh.co.uk

Magnum Hall ★★★★
Self Catering
Home From Home Holidays
t (01983) 854340
e ventnor@crldirect.co.uk
w hfromh.co.uk

Maple Cottage ★★★★
Self Catering
Contact: Mrs Sarah Merry
t 07970 073339
e s.merry2@ntlworld.com
w ventnorholidaycottage.co.uk

Marina Apartments ★★★★
Self Catering
Contact: Mr & Mrs Peter & Helen Redding
t (01983) 852802
e information@marinaapartments.co.uk
w marinaapartments.co.uk

Marula ★★★ *Self Catering*
Home From Home Holidays
t (01983) 854340
e ventnor@crldirect.co.uk
w hfromh.co.uk

Millers Rock ★★★★
Self Catering
Contact: Mrs Jayne Simpson
t (01798) 872705
e jayne@millersrock.co.uk
w millersrock.co.uk

Oceanwave ★★★
Self Catering
Contact: Mrs Jean Ellis
t (01763) 246678
e fredrick.ellis@ntlworld.com
w cottageguide.co.uk/oceanwave

The Old Cottage ★★★★★
Self Catering
Island Cottage Holidays
t (01929) 481555
e enq@islandcottageholidays.com
w islandcottageholidays.com

Orchard Cottage ★★★
Self Catering
Home From Home Holidays
t (01983) 854340
e ventnor@crldirect.co.uk
w hfromh.co.uk

The Palms ★★★★
Self Catering
Home From Home Holidays
t (01983) 854340
e ventnor@crldirect.co.uk
w hfromh.co.uk

Park Lodge ★★★★
Self Catering
Island Cottage Holidays
t (01929) 481555
e enq@islandcottageholidays.com
w islandcottageholidays.com

Petit Tor ★★★★
Self Catering
Home From Home Holidays
t (01983) 854340
e ventnor@crldirect.co.uk
w hfromh.co.uk

Richmond Apartments – Sea Breeze & Sea View ★★★★
Self Catering
Home From Home Holidays
t (01983) 854340
e ventnor@crldirect.co.uk
w hfromh.co.uk

Richmond Arms and Apartments ★★★★
Self Catering
t (01983) 855674

Royal Marine House ★★★★
Self Catering
Contact: Mr Wetherill
t (01962) 878722
e aventa-architects@btconnect.com
w royalmarinehouse.co.uk

St Boniface View ★★★★
Self Catering
Contact: Mr Ian Surry
t (020) 8882 2004
e book@ventnorcottages.com
w ventnorcottages.com

St Catherines View ★★★
Self Catering
Home From Home Holidays
t (01983) 854340
e ventnor@crldirect.co.uk
w hfromh.co.uk

Sea View Holiday Bungalow
★★★ *Self Catering*
Contact: Mrs Anne Rutherford
t (020) 8676 8671
e annierutherford@btopenworld.com
w cottageguide.co.uk/iowseaview

Seaview ★★★ *Self Catering*
Contact: Mr Peter Smithers
t (01953) 602477
e janet@4sol.co.uk
w isleofwightholidays.com

Seaview Cottage ★★★
Self Catering
Home From Home Holidays
t (01983) 854340
e ventnor@crldirect.co.uk
w hfromh.co.uk

Stoneplace Cottage ★★★
Self Catering
Home From Home Holidays
t (01983) 854340
e ventnor@crldirect.co.uk
w hfromh.co.uk

Trelawney ★★★
Self Catering
Home From Home Holidays
t (01983) 854340
e ventnor@crldirect.co.uk
w hfromh.co.uk

Ventnor Apartment ★★★★
Self Catering
Contact: Mrs Jill Edwards
t (01983) 853555 & 07831 095407
e info@distinctivedesigns.co.uk
w ventnorapartment.com

Ventnor Holiday Villas ★★★
Chalet
Contact: Mr Stephen King
t (01983) 852973
e sales@ventnorholidayvillas.co.uk
w ventnorholidayvillas.co.uk

Ventnor Holiday Villas ★★★
Self Catering
Contact: Mr Stephen King
t (01983) 852973
e sales@ventnorholidayvillas.co.uk
w ventnorholidayvillas.co.uk

Verbena Cottage ★★★
Self Catering
Home From Home Holidays
t (01983) 854340
e ventnor@crldirect.co.uk
w hfromh.co.uk

Veryan ★★★★ *Self Catering*
Home From Home Holidays
t (01983) 854340
e ventnor@crldirect.co.uk
w hfromh.co.uk

Weir Cottage ★★★★★
Self Catering
Home From Home Holidays
t (01983) 854340
e ventnor@crldirect.co.uk
w hfromh.co.uk

Westfield Lodges & Apartments ★★★★
Self Catering
t (01983) 852268
e mail@westfieldlodges.co.uk
w westfieldlodges.co.uk

Westgate Cottage ★★★
Self Catering
Island Holiday Homes
t (01983) 521113
e enquiries@island-holiday-homes.net
w island-holiday-homes.net

Woodcliffe Holiday Apartments ★★★
Self Catering
Contact: Mr Bryce Wilson
t (01983) 852397
e bryce.wilson@virgin.net
w woodcliffe.net

VINES CROSS
East Sussex

Cannon Barn ★★★★
Self Catering
Contact: Anne Reed
t (01435) 812285
e info@boringhousefarm.co.uk
w boringhousefarm.co.uk

Dairy Shorthorn & Friesian Cottages ★★★★
Self Catering
Freedom Holiday Homes
t (01580) 720770
e mail@freedomholidayhomes.co.uk
w freedomholidayhomes.co.uk

WADHURST
East Sussex

Dewhurst Cottage ★★★★
Self Catering
Freedom Holiday Homes
t (01580) 720770
e mail@freedomholidayhomes.co.uk
w freedomholidayhomes.co.uk

WALMER
Kent

Cottage In Deal ★★
Self Catering
Contact: Mr Alan Haye alan.hay@t-online.de

Fisherman's Cottage ★★
Self Catering
Contact: Catherine Tsoukkas
t (020) 8874 2170
e tsoukkast@aol.com

The Garden Cottage
★★★★★ *Self Catering*
English Heritage
t 0870 333 1187
e holidaycottages@english-heritage.org.uk
w english-heritage.org.uk/holidaycottages

The Greenhouse ★★★★
Self Catering
English Heritage
t 0870 333 1187
e holidaycottages@english-heritage.org.uk
w english-heritage.org.uk/holidaycottages

The Gulls Holiday Apartment ★★★★
Self Catering
Contact: Sandra & Ken Upton
The Gardeners Rest
t (01304) 371449
e ken@holidaysdeal.co.uk
w holidaysdeal.co.uk

Shipwrech Cottage ★★★
Self Catering
Contact: Mrs Janice Twaits
t (020) 8524 3320

WALTHAM
Kent

Springfield Cottage and Springfield Barn ★★★
Self Catering
Garden of England Cottages
t (01892) 510117
e info@gardenofenglandcottages.co.uk
w goec.co.uk

WALTON-ON-THAMES
Surrey

Guest Wing ★★★★
Self Catering
Contact: Mr Richard Dominy
t (01932) 241223

WARBLETON
East Sussex

Well Cottage ★★★★
Self Catering
Garden of England Cottages
t (01892) 510117
e info@gardenofenglandcottages.co.uk
w goec.co.uk

WAREHORNE
Kent

Tuckers Farm ★★★★
Self Catering
Freedom Holiday Homes
t (01580) 720770 & 07796 878733
e mail@freedomholidayhomes.co.uk
w freedomholidayhomes.co.uk

WARSASH
Hampshire

Foredeck Holiday Cottage
★★★★ *Self Catering*
Contact: Mr Peter Wilson
t (01489) 581208
e pete@s-wilson.fsnet.co.uk
w foredeck-holiday-cottage.co.uk

WARTLING
East Sussex

The Coach House ★★★★
Self Catering
Contact: Helen Enock
t (01323) 832131
e helen.enock@btinternet.com
w thecoachhousewartling.com

WELLOW
Isle of Wight

Jubilee Villa ★★★★
Self Catering
t (01983) 760327
w coastandcountry.eu

Mattingley Farm – Blakes Barn & Dairy Cottages
★★★★ *Self Catering*
Contact: Mr & Mrs Nelson
t (01983) 760503
e heather@mattingleyfarm.co.uk
w mattingleyfarm.co.uk

Warren Holidays – Brook Cottage & Mrs Tiggywinkle Cottage ★★★★ *Self Catering*
Contact: Mrs Anne Longford
t (01983) 883364
e anne.longford@btinternet.com
w warrenholidays.com

WEST ASHLING
West Sussex

Hills Cottage ★★★★
Self Catering
Contact: Virginia & Alan Jack
t (01243) 574382
e hills.cottage@btinternet.com
w hillscottage.com

WEST MARDEN
West Sussex

Barley Cottage
★★★★–★★★★★
Self Catering
Contact: Mrs Carole Edney
t (023) 9263 1761
e carole.edney@btinternet.com
w barleycottage.co.uk

The Old Stables ★★★★★
Self Catering
Contact: Mrs Carole Edney
t (023) 9263 1761
e carole.edney@btinternet.com
w theoldstables.net

WEST PECKHAM
Kent

Beech Farmhouse ★★★★
Self Catering
Contact: Mr & Mrs Wooldridge
t (01622) 812360

WESTBOURNE
West Sussex

2 Longcopse Cottages
★★★★ *Self Catering*
Contact: Mrs Di Ashe
t (01243) 379296
e di@longcopsecottage.co.uk
w longcopsecottage.co.uk

WESTBROOK
Kent

The Cottage ★★★
Self Catering
Contact: Mr Smith
t (01843) 834545
w cornerwyse-cottage.co.uk

WESTCOTT
Surrey

Deerhurst Cottage ★★★★
Self Catering
Contact: Mrs Lindy Reif
t (01306) 888070
e lindyjo@hotmail.co.uk
w deerhurst-cottage.co.uk

The Garden Flat ★★★★
Self Catering
Contact: Mrs Louise Scillitoe-Brown
t (01306) 883838
e gardenflat@chartfield.biz
w chartfield.biz

WESTERHAM
Kent

The Barn at Bombers
★★★★★ *Self Catering*
Contact: Mr & Mrs Roy & Brigitte Callow
t (01959) 573471
e roy@bombers-farm.co.uk
w bombers-farm.co.uk

WESTFIELD
East Sussex

Byre ★★★★ *Self Catering*
Contact: Mr Paul Masters
t (01424) 882371
e byre@pattletons.co.uk
w pattletons.co.uk

WEYBRIDGE
Surrey

Cleve Place ★★★★
Serviced Apartments
The Apartment Service
t (020) 8944 1444
e melanied@apartment.co.uk
w apartmentservice.com

Nurses Cottages ★★★★
Self Catering
Contact: Mrs Terrie Fisher
t (01932) 228720
e info@the-fisher.freeserve.co.uk
w nursescottages.co.uk

WHITSTABLE
Kent

3 Harbour Mews ★★★★
Self Catering
Contact: Mrs Lynn Buckle
t (01227) 792781
e lynn.buckle@tiscali.co.uk
w 3harbourmews.co.uk

Acorns ★★★★ *Self Catering*
Contact: Ms Elaine Kirkaldie
t (01227) 275077
e info@acornswillowwood.co.uk
w acornswillowwood.co.uk

Beach View ★★★
Self Catering
Contact: Mrs Deborah Mylcrist
t (01227) 277883
e deborah@mylcrist.co.uk
w mylcrist.googlepaces.com

Coastguard's Cottage
★★★★ *Self Catering*
t (01304) 619444
e enquiries@curlewcottages.co.uk
w curlewcottages.co.uk

Flat 31 Grand Pavilion
★★★★ *Self Catering*
Contact: Mr Robert Gough
t (01227) 779066
e bobgough57@aol.com
w stayinwhitstable.co.uk

No 4 Knots Yard ★★★★
Self Catering
Freedom Holiday Homes
t (01580) 720770
e mail@freedomholidayhomes.co.uk
w freedomholidayhomes.co.uk

Pebble Cottage & Fishermans Loft ★★★★
Self Catering
Contact: Mrs Pamela Burke
Pebble Cottage & The Loft
t 0845 370 9009
e info@pebblecottage.co.uk
w pebblecottage.co.uk

Sea Street Cottage
Rating Applied For
Self Catering
Freedom Holiday Homes
t (01580) 720770
e mail@freedomholidayhomes.co.uk
w freedomholidayhomes.co.uk

Surfers Cove ★★★
Self Catering
Contact: Mrs Mylcrist
Sufers Cove
t (01227) 272261
e deborah@mylcrist.co.uk
w mylcrist.googlepages.com/home

Trappers End ★★★
Self Catering
Contact: Mrs J Reed
t (020) 8942 0342
e janette.reed@blueyonder.co.uk

Whitepost ★★★★★
Self Catering
t (01227) 272741
e 4seasons123@supanet.com
w 4whitepost.co.uk

WHITWELL
Isle of Wight

Ash Farm ★★★★
Self Catering
Island Holiday Homes
t (01983) 521113
e enquiries@island-holiday-homes.net
w island-holiday-homes.net

The Barn ★★★ *Self Catering*
Home From Home Holidays
t (01983) 854340
e ventnor@crldirect.co.uk
w hfromh.co.uk

Brook Lodge ★★★★
Self Catering
Island Cottage Holidays
t (01929) 481555
e enq@islandcottageholidays.com
w islandcottageholidays.com

Downcourt Manor Farm Cottage ★★★★ *Self Catering*
Contact: Mr Andrew Aylwin
t (01983) 730329
e a.j.aylwin@btinternet.com
w downcourtmanorfarm.co.uk

Fossil Cottage ★★★★
Self Catering
Island Cottage Holidays
t (01929) 481555
e enq@islandcottageholidays.com
w islandcottageholidays.com

Hedgerow Cottage ★★★★
Self Catering
Island Cottage Holidays
t (01929) 481555
e enq@islandcottageholidays.com
w islandcottageholidays.com

Hillrise ★★★ *Self Catering*
Island Holiday Homes
t (01983) 521113
e enquiries@island-holiday-homes.net
w island-holiday-homes.net

Kitty's Loft ★★★★
Self Catering
Contact: Miss Barbara Williams
t (01983) 551705
e barbara.williams@kittysloft.co.uk
w kittysloft.co.uk

Maytime Cottage ★★★★
Self Catering
Contact: Mr Jonathan McCulloch
t (01403) 211052 & 07711 807137
e jonty@bpmd.co.uk
w maytimecottage.co.uk

Old Chapel House
Rating Applied For
Self Catering
Island Cottage Holidays
t (01929) 481555
e enq@islandcottageholidays.com
w islandcottageholidays.com

The Old Dairy – Lower Dolcoppice Farm ★★★
Self Catering
Contact: Mrs Esther Denham
t (01983) 551445
e dolcoppice@wightfarmholidays.co.uk
w wightfarmholidays.co.uk

Pyrmont Cottage ★★★
Self Catering
Contact: Mrs Dawn Dall
Pyrmont Cottage (Island Holiday Homes)
t (01983) 521113
e enquiries@island-holiday-homes.net
w island-holiday-homes.net

Stockbridge Monor East Wing ★★★★ *Self Catering*
Island Cottage Holidays
t (01929) 481555
e enq@islandcottageholidays.com
w islandcottageholidays.com

Whitwell Station ★★★
Self Catering
Contact: Mrs Julia Carter
t (01983) 730667
e enqs@whitwellstation.co.uk
w whitwellstation.co.uk

Willow Bank ★★★
Self Catering
Contact: Mrs Eldridge
t (01258) 473327
e geoff-eldridge@onetel.com

Wren Cottage ★★★★
Self Catering
Island Holiday Homes
t (01983) 521113
e enquiries@island-holiday-homes.net
w island-holiday-homes.net

WICKHAM
Hampshire

Meonwood Annexe ★★★
Self Catering
Contact: Mrs Susan Wells
t (01329) 834130
e sjwells@meonwood.co.uk

WILMINGTON
East Sussex

Wishing Well Cottage
★★★★ *Self Catering*
Contact: Barry Taylor
t (01323) 487967
e cottage@crosswayshotel.co.uk
w crosswayshotel.co.uk

WINCHELSEA BEACH
East Sussex

Tamarix ★★★ *Self Catering*
t (01892) 528538

WINCHESTER
Hampshire

1 Abbotts Court Mews
★★★★ *Self Catering*
Contact: Mr Richard Wetherill
t (01962) 878722
e aventaarchitects@btconnect.com
w abbottscourtmews.co.uk

87 Christchurch Road
★★★★ *Self Catering*
Contact: Mrs Elisabeth Peacocke
t (01962) 854902
e liz@peacocke.wanadoo.co.uk
w cottageguide.co.uk

The Annexe: Carole Wilkins
★★★ *Self Catering*
Contact: Ms Carole Wilkins
t (01962) 883341
e acannexe@hotmail.co.uk

Burwood ★★★★
Self Catering
Contact: Mrs Alice Lowery
t (01962) 881690
e lowery2@btinternet.com
w winchester-accommodation.com

Cathedral View ★★★★
Self Catering
Contact: Mrs Sue Wustefeld
t (01962) 732422 & 07708 331132
e help@justasksue.co.uk
w cathedral-view.co.uk

City Centre Cottages: No. 32
★★★★ *Self Catering*
Contact: Mr Andrew Lattimore
t (01962) 820330
e andrew.lattimore@number32.co.uk
w number32.co.uk/landingviavisitwinchester.aspx

City Centre Cottages: Wool Cottage ★★★★ *Self Catering*
Contact: Ms Desiree Ratcliffe
t (01962) 820330
e desiree.ratcliffe@wool-cottage.co.uk
w wool-cottage.co.uk

Mallard Cottage ★★★★
Self Catering
Contact: Mrs Tricia Simpkin
t (01962) 853002
e bookings@mallardcottage.co.uk
w mallardcottage.co.uk

Mews House ★★★★
Self Catering
t (01438) 715497
w geocities.com

No. 37 ★★★★★
Self Catering
t (01962) 820330

No.38 ★★★★★ *Self Catering*
t (01962) 820330

The Old Dairy ★★★★
Self Catering
t (01962) 868214
e joy_ann_waldron@hotmail.com
w beechcroftfarmholiday.co.uk

South Winchester Lodges ★★★★★ *Self Catering*
Contact: Ms Lesley Ross
t (01962) 820490
e info@golfholidaywinchester.com
w southwinchesterlodges.co.uk

WINDSOR
Berkshire

Flat 6 The Courtyard ★★★
Self Catering
Contact: Mr Gavin Gordon
t (01628) 824267
e gavingordon@totalise.co.uk
w windsor-selfcatering.co.uk

9 The Courtyard ★★★
Self Catering
Contact: Mrs JH Hitchcock
t (01753) 545005
e enquiries@staywindsor.co.uk
w staywindsor.co.uk

Castle Mews Apartment ★★★★ *Self Catering*
Contact: Mr Duncan Gordon
t 07939 513384
e bookings@royalwindsorlets.com

Dorney Self-Catering Apartments ★★ *Self Catering*
Contact: Miss Sarah Everitt
t (01753) 827037
e sarah@troppo.uk.com
w troppo.uk.com

Knights Place
Rating Applied For
Serviced Apartments
Deep Blue Apartments
t 0870 770 0778
e steve@deepb.com
w deepblueapartments.com

Manor View Apartment ★★★ *Self Catering*
Contact: Mrs Clare Smith
t (01344) 485658
e manorview@care4free.net
w manorview.care4free.net

Springfield Corner ★★★
Self Catering
Contact: Mrs Anna Foxell
t (01753) 860900
e annafoxell@tiscali.co.uk
w springfieldcorner.co.uk

WINGHAM
Kent

Cornerways ★★★★
Self Catering
Contact: Ms Maureen Jones
t 07956 807689
e maureen.a.jones@ntlworld.com
w cornerwayscottage.com

WISBOROUGH GREEN
West Sussex

Milestone Cottage ★★★
Self Catering
Contact: Roger & Heather Richards
t (01403) 700130
e rvrichards@milestonecottage.freeserve.co.uk

WITNEY
Oxfordshire

Grove Farm Cotswold Cottages ★★★★
Self Catering
Contact: Mr & Mrs J R Bowtell
t (01993) 843755
e jrbowtell@aol.com
w grovefarmcotswoldcottages.co.uk

Little Barn ★★★★
Self Catering
Contact: Mrs Sissel Harrison
t (01993) 706632
e booking@stablebarn.co.uk
w stablebarn.co.uk

Sighs Cottage ★★★
Self Catering
Contact: Mr Peter Crowther
t (01993) 709596
e pjccrowth@hotmail.com

Swallows Nest ★★★★
Self Catering
Contact: Mrs Jan Strainge
t (01993) 704919
e jan@strainge.fsnet.co.uk

WITTERSHAM
Kent

Pospect Cottage ★★★★
Self Catering
Garden of England Cottages
t (01892) 510117
e info@gardenofenglandcottages.co.uk
w goec.co.uk

Stocks Farm Oast ★★★★
Self Catering
Contact: Mrs Kate Gale
t (01797) 270895
e galekate@yahoo.co.uk

The White Cottage ★★★★
Self Catering
Freedom Holiday Homes
t (01580) 720770
e mail@freedomholidayhomes.co.uk
w freedomholidayhomes.co.uk

WOKINGHAM
Berkshire

Lily Court
Rating Applied For
Serviced Apartments
Deep Blue Apartments
t 0870 770 0778
e steve@deepb.com
w deepblueapartments.com

WOODCHURCH
Kent

Acorn and Squirrel Cottages ★★★★ *Self Catering*
Freedom Holiday Homes
t (01580) 720770
e mail@freedomholidayhomes.co.uk
w freedomholidayhomes.co.uk

The Stable ★★★★
Self Catering
Contact: Mrs Carol Vant
t (01233) 860388
e carol.vant@thestablecottage.co.uk
w thestablecottage.co.uk

WOODGREEN
Hampshire

Sunset Place ★★★★
Self Catering
Contact: Mrs Lupita Cadman
t (01725) 512009
e lupita_cadman@yahoo.co.uk
w cottage-crest.co.uk

WOODNESBOROUGH
Kent

Sonnet Cottage ★★
Self Catering
Freedom Holiday Homes
t (01580) 720770
e mail@freedomholidayhomes.co.uk
w freedomholidayhomes.co.uk

WOODSTOCK
Oxfordshire

Little Peacock House ★★★★ *Self Catering*
Contact: Mr & Mrs Oliver
t (01993) 811430
e clive@blenheimgate.co.uk

WOOTTON BRIDGE
Isle of Wight

Bodwen Corner
Rating Applied For
Self Catering
Island Holiday Homes
t (01983) 521113
e enquiries@island-holiday-homes.net
w island-holiday-homes.net

Creek Gardens ★★★★
Self Catering
Contact: Mrs L Samson
t (01983) 883100
e enquiries@creekgardens.co.uk
w creekgardens.co.uk

The Fens ★★★ *Self Catering*
Island Holiday Homes
t (01983) 521113
e enquiries@island-holiday-homes.net
w island-holiday-homes.net

Grange Farm Cottages ★★★-★★★★ *Self Catering*
Contact: Mrs Rosemarie Horne
t (01983) 882147
e info@grange-farm-holidays.co.uk
w grange-farm-holidays.co.uk

Heron View ★★★★
Self Catering
Home From Home Holidays
t (01983) 854340
e ventnor@crldirect.co.uk
w hfromh.co.uk

Lushington Villa
Rating Applied For
Self Catering
Contact: Mrs Wanda Sartini
t (01983) 882367

Totland
Rating Applied For
Self Catering
Island Holiday Homes
t (01983) 521113
e enquiries@island-holiday-homes.net
w island-holiday-homes.net

Wootton Keepers Cottage ★★★ *Self Catering*
Island Cottage Holidays
t (01929) 481555
e enq@islandcottageholidays.com
w islandcottageholidays.com

WORTHING
West Sussex

11 Reigate Road ★★★
Self Catering
Promenade Holiday Homes
t (01903) 877047
e anne@promenade-holidays.fsbusiness.co.uk
w promenadeholidayhomes.co.uk

2 Knightsbridge House ★★★ *Self Catering*
Contact: Ms Greta Paull
t (020) 8530 2336

4 Wordsworth Road ★★★★
Self Catering
Promenade Holiday Homes
t (01903) 877047
e anne@promenade-holidays.fsbusiness.co.uk
w promenadeholidayhomes.co.uk

6 Heene Terrace ★★★
Self Catering
Promenade Holiday Homes
t (01903) 877047
e anne@promenade-holidays.fsbusiness.co.uk
w promenadeholidayhomes.co.uk

Aldine House ★★★
Self Catering
t (01903) 266980
w aldine.org.uk

Beccles Court ★★
Self Catering
t (01903) 238582

Exmoor House ★
Self Catering
Contact: Mr & Mrs A R Harrison
t (01903) 208856
w exmoorhouse.co.uk

Flat 1A Heene Court Mansions ★★★ *Self Catering*
Promenade Holiday Homes
t (01903) 877047
e anne@promenade-holidays.fsbusiness.co.uk
w promenadeholidayhomes.co.uk

Holiday Bungalow West Worthing ★★★ *Self Catering*
Contact: Mr Haynese graham.haynes@tele2.ch

Navarino Flat ★★★
Self Catering
Contact: Mrs C Hanton
t (01903) 205984
e c.hanton@cwctv.net

Rustington Bungalow ★★★
Self Catering
Promenade Holiday Homes
t (01903) 877047
e anne@promenade-holidays.fsbusiness.co.uk
w promenadeholidayhomes.co.uk

WRAYSBURY
Berkshire

Splash Windmill, Windmill House and Orange Cottage ★★★-★★★★ *Self Catering*
Contact: Mrs Sylvia Neal
The Oast Barn
t (01784) 481598
e bandb@oastbarn.com
w oastbarn.com

WROXALL
Isle of Wight

The Annexe, Clevelands Country House ★★★★
Self Catering
Contact: Mrs Anna Wooldridge
t (01983) 855449
e info@isleofwightwalks.co.uk
w isleofwightwalks.co.uk

Appuldurcombe Holiday Cottages ★★★-★★★★
Self Catering
Contact: Mrs Jane Owen
t (01983) 840188
e jane@appuldurcombe.co.uk
w appuldurcombe.co.uk

Dairy Barn & Rew Farmhouse ★★★★★
Self Catering
Contact: Mrs Sally Richards - EN
t (01983) 855163
e sheepwashcottage@btinternet.com
w wightfarmholidays.co.uk

Little Span Farm ★★★
Self Catering
Contact: Mrs Felicity Corry
t 0800 298 5819
e info@spanfarm.co.uk
w spanfarm.co.uk

Malmesbury Cottage ★★★★ *Self Catering*
Contact: Mr Tony Simpson
t (01798) 872705
e jayne@chapelcottage.co.uk
w malmesburycottage.co.uk

Manor Bottom ★★★★
Self Catering
Contact: Ms Dorothy Boswell
t (020) 7686 2696
e dorothy.boswell@virgin.net
w manorbottom.co.uk

Sundown ★★★ *Self Catering*
Home From Home Holidays
t (01983) 854340
e ventnor@crldirect.co.uk
w hfromh.co.uk

YALDING
Kent

Bridge Cottage ★★★★
Self Catering
Garden of England Cottages
t (01892) 510117
e info@gardenofenglandcottages.co.uk
w goec.co.uk

YARMOUTH
Isle of Wight

Alma Cottage ★★★
Self Catering
Island Holiday Homes
t (01983) 521113
e enquiries@island-holiday-homes.net
w island-holiday-homes.net

The Boat House Holiday Apartments ★★★
Self Catering
Contact: Mr John Brady
t (01983) 754718

Holiday Homes Owners Services Ref: Y5 ★★★★
Self Catering
Holiday Homes Owners Services (West Wight)
t (01983) 753423
e holidayhomesiow@ic24.net
w holidayhomesiow.co.uk

Holiday Homes Owners Services Ref: Y18 ★★★★
Self Catering
Holiday Homes Owners Services (West Wight)
t (01983) 753423
e holidayhomesiow@ic24.net
w holidayhomesiow.co.uk

Holiday Homes Owners Services Ref: Y9 ★★★★
Self Catering
Holiday Homes Owners Services (West Wight)
t (01983) 753423
e holidayhomesiow@ic24.net
w holidayhomesiow.co.uk

Little Stables at Chessell, Chessell ★★★★
Self Catering
Contact: Mr & Mrs Aiden & Louise Collins
t (01983) 531248
e aiden.collins@pottery-cafe.com
w chessellpotterybarns.co.uk

River Cottage ★★★★
Self Catering
Contact: Mr Nigel Howell
t (01983) 760553
e nigel@isle-wight.co.uk
w isle-wight.co.uk

LONDON

INNER LONDON

E1

Hamlet UK, St Katharine Docks, Tower Hill ★★★
Self Catering
Contact: Ms Renata Naufal
t (01462) 678037
e hamlet_uk@globalnet.co.uk
w hamletuk.com

E4

Willowside ★★★
Self Catering
Contact: Mrs Roddick
t (020) 8529 1371
e r.roddick@btconnect.com
w willowsidelakes.co.uk

E14

Bridge House-London Docklands ★★★★★
Self Catering
Contact: Mr John Graham
t 07973 857187
e john@johnkgraham.com
w johnkgraham.com

Canary Central ★★★★
Serviced Apartments
Go Native
t (020) 7313 6147
e richard.whittaker@gonative.co.uk
w gonative.co.uk

Canary Central by Bridge Street Worldwide ★★★★
Serviced Apartments
Bridge Street Worldwide
t (020) 7792 2222
e eileen.sexton-adams@bridgestreet.com
w bridgestreet.com

Canary South ★★★★
Serviced Apartments
Contact: Mr Peter Morgan
Clarendon Serviced Apartments
t (01784) 489217
e peterm@clarendonuk.com
w clarendonuk.com

Circus Apartments by Bridge Street Worldwide ★★★★ *Serviced Apartments*
Bridge Street Worldwide
t (020) 7792 2222
e eileen.sexton-adams@bridgestreet.com
w bridgestreet.com

Corona Apartments by Bridge Street Worldwide ★★★★ *Serviced Apartments*
Bridge Street Worldwide
t (020) 7792 2222
e eileen.sexton-adams@bridgestreet.com
w bridgestreet.com

Discovery Dock ★★★★
Serviced Apartments
The Apartment Service
t (020) 8944 1444
e melanied@apartment.co.uk
w apartmentservice.com

Fraser Place Canary Wharf ★★★★-★★★★★
Serviced Apartments
Frasers Hospitality
t (020) 7341 5595
e valerie.dhieux@frasershospitality.com
w frasershospitality.com

Ionian Apartment ★★★★
Self Catering
Contact: Ms Christine James
t (01902) 843545
e enquiries@vacationsinlondon.co.uk
w vacationsinlondon.co.uk

Ontario Tower ★★★★
Serviced Apartments
Go Native
t (020) 7313 6147
e richard.whittaker@gonative.co.uk
w gonative.co.uk

River Thames Apartment ★★★★ *Self Catering*
t (020) 8530 2336
w riverthamesapartment.co.uk

Riverside ★★★★
Self Catering
Contact: Ms Christine James
t (01902) 843545
e christine@capstansq.fsnet.co.uk
w vacationsinlondon.com

Zenith House by Bridge Street Worldwide ★★★★
Serviced Apartments
Bridge Street Worldwide
t (020) 7792 2222
e eileen.sexton-adams@bridgestreet.com
w bridgestreet.com

E16

The Grainstore ★★★★★
Self Catering
Contact: Nicky Bloom
t (020) 7540 9351
e enquiries@simplyapartments.co.uk
w simplyapartments.co.uk

EC1

Carthusian House ★★★★
Serviced Apartments
City Apartments Ltd
t (020) 7726 2626
e dsmith@cityaparts.com
w cityaparts.com

Dickinson Court ★★★★
Serviced Apartments
The Apartment Service
t (020) 8944 1444
e melanied@apartment.co.uk
w apartmentservice.com

Hills Chambers ★★★
Serviced Apartments
City Apartments Ltd
t (020) 7726 2626
e dsmith@cityaparts.com
w cityaparts.com

Horseshoe Court ★★★★
Serviced Apartments
The Apartment Service
t (020) 8944 1444
e melanied@apartment.co.uk
w apartmentservice.com

London House
★★★-★★★★
Serviced Apartments
City Apartments Ltd
t (020) 7726 2626
e dsmith@cityaparts.com
w cityaparts.com

Market View by Bridge Street Worldwide ★★★★
Serviced Apartments
Bridge Street Worldwide
t (020) 7792 2222
e eileen.sexton-adams@bridgestreet.com
w bridgestreet.com

Newbury House ★★★★
Serviced Apartments
City Apartments Ltd
t (020) 7726 2626
e dsmith@cityaparts.com
w cityaparts.com

Saffron Heights and St John Street ★★★
Serviced Apartments
Go Native
t (020) 7313 6147
e richard.whittaker@gonative.co.uk
w gonative.co.uk

St Paul's ★★★★
Serviced Apartments
Go Native
t (020) 7313 6147
e richard.whittaker@gonative.co.uk
w gonative.co.uk

EC3

Creechurch Lane by Bridge Street Worldwide ★★★
Serviced Apartments
Bridge Street Worldwide
t (020) 7792 2222
e eileen.sexton-adams@bridgestreet.com
w bridgestreet.com

East House ★★★
Serviced Apartments
City Apartments Ltd
t (020) 7726 2626
e dsmith@cityaparts.com
w cityaparts.com

Pepys Street by Bridge Street Worldwide ★★★
Serviced Apartments
Bridge Street Worldwide
t (020) 7792 2222
e eileen.sexton-adams@bridgestreet.com
w bridgestreet.com

Tower Hill ★★★★
Serviced Apartments
Go Native
t (020) 7313 6147
e richard.whittaker@gonative.co.uk
w gonative.co.uk

EC4

Evangelist House
Rating Applied For
Serviced Apartments
Deep Blue Apartments
t 0870 770 0778
e steve@deepb.com
w deepblueapartments.com

Fleet Street
Rating Applied For
Serviced Apartments
Deep Blue Apartments
t 0870 770 0778
e steve@deepb.com
w deepblueapartments.com

Globe View ★★★
Serviced Apartments
City Apartments Ltd
t (020) 7726 2626
e dsmith@cityaparts.com
w cityaparts.com

Kings Wardrobe by Bridge Street Worldwide ★★★★
Serviced Apartments
Bridge Street Worldwide
t (020) 7792 2222
e eileen.sexton-adams@bridgestreet.com
w bridgestreet.com

Pleydell House ★★★
Serviced Apartments
City Apartments Ltd
t (020) 7726 2626
e dsmith@cityaparts.com
w cityaparts.com

Printers Inn by Bridge Street Worldwide ★★★
Serviced Apartments
Bridge Street Worldwide
t (020) 7792 2222
e eileen.sexton-adams@bridgestreet.com
w bridgestreet.com

Watling Street ★★★
Serviced Apartments
The Apartment Service
t (020) 8944 1444
e melanied@apartment.co.uk
w apartmentservice.com

N7

Carena Holiday Apartments
★★★ *Self Catering*
Contact: Mr M Chouthi
t (020) 7607 7453
e deo.chouthi@btopenworld.com

N21

The Old Bakery ★★★★
Self Catering
Contact: Ms Nina Anstee
t (020) 8882 6255
e oldbakerylondon@tiscali.co.uk
w oldbakerylondon.co.uk

SE1

Empire Square East ★★★★
Serviced Apartments
The Apartment Service
t (020) 8944 1444
e melanied@apartment.co.uk
w apartmentservice.com

Empire Square West ★★★★
Serviced Apartments
The Apartment Service
t (020) 8944 1444
e melanied@apartment.co.uk
w apartmentservice.com

Flat One London – Tower Bridge ★★★★★
Self Catering
Contact: Mr Nico Bardon
t (020) 7403 7112
e nicobardon@aol.com
w flatone.co.uk

SE3

Sunfields ★★★ *Self Catering*
Contact: Mrs Jacqui Poole
t (020) 8858 1420
e jacqui.poole@nhs.net

SE6

Glenthurston Self Catering Apartments ★★★-★★★★
Self Catering
Contact: Ms Sue Halliday
t (020) 8690 3092
e mail@londonselfcatering.co.uk
w londonselfcatering.co.uk

SE10

12 Burgos Grove, West Greenwich ★★★
Self Catering
Contact: Ms Dawn Harverson
t 07894 661402
e info@greenwichholidaylets.co.uk
w greenwichholidaylets.co.uk

Harbour Master's House
★★★★ *Self Catering*
Contact: Prof Chris French
t (020) 8293 9597
e harbourmaster@lineone.net
w http://website.lineone.net/~harbourmaster

SE23

Dovetail House ★★★★
Self Catering
Contact: Ms Ruth Jenkins
t (020) 8291 0924
e dovetailhouse@aol.com
w dovetailhouse.com

SW1

The Apartments
★★★★-★★★★★
Self Catering
t (020) 7589 3271
e sales@theapartments.co.uk
w theapartments.co.uk

Club Suites
★★★★-★★★★★ *Self Catering & Serviced Apartments*
t (020) 7730 9131
w sloaneclub.co.uk

Phoenix House ★★★★★
Serviced Apartments
Gloucester Park Apartments
t (020) 737 3144
e reservations@chevalgroup.com
w chevalgroup.com

Piccadilly Circus ★★★
Serviced Apartments
Go Native
t (020) 7313 6147
e richard.whittaker@gonative.co.uk
w gonative.co.uk

SW3

The Apartments ★★★★
Self Catering
t (020) 7589 3271
w theapartments.co.uk

Beaufort House ★★★★★
Serviced Apartments
t (020) 7758 42600
e info@beaufortapartments.co.uk
w beaufortapartments.co.uk

SW7

Fraser Place Queens Gate
★★★ *Serviced Apartments*
Frasers Hospitality
t (020) 7341 5595
e valerie.dhieux@frasershospitality.com
w frasershospitality.com

Fraser Suites Kensington
★★★★★
Serviced Apartments
Frasers Hospitality
t (020) 7341 5595
e valerie.dhieux@frasershospitality.com
w frasershospitality.com

Gloucester Park Apartments
★★★★★
Serviced Apartments
t (020) 737 3144
e reservations@chevalgroup.com
w chevalgroup.com

Hyde Park Gate ★★★★★
Serviced Apartments
Gloucester Park Apartments
t (020) 737 3144
e reservations@chevalgroup.com
w chevalgroup.com

SW10

Fraser Place Chelsea ★★★★
Serviced Apartments
Frasers Hospitality
t (020) 7341 5595
e valerie.dhieux@frasershospitality.com
w frasershospitality.com

SW18

Beaumont Apartments
★★★★ *Self Catering*
Contact: Mr & Mrs Alan & Monica Afriat
t (020) 8789 2663
e alan@beaumont-london-apartments.co.uk
w beaumont-london-apartments.co.uk

SW19

The Courtyard ★★★★
Serviced Apartments
The Apartment Service
t (020) 8944 1444
e melanied@apartment.co.uk
w apartmentservice.com

SW20

Thalia & Hebe Holiday Homes, Wimbledon ★★★★
Self Catering
Contact: Mr & Mrs Peter & Ann Briscoe-Smith
t (020) 8542 0505
e peter@briscoe-smith.org.uk
w briscoe-smith.org.uk

W1

Cleary House ★★★★
Serviced Apartments
City Apartments Ltd
t (020) 7726 2626
e dsmith@cityaparts.com
w cityaparts.com

Durweston House
Rating Applied For
Serviced Apartments
Deep Blue Apartments
t 0870 770 0778
e steve@deepb.com
w deepblueapartments.com

Tustin Holiday Flats
★★-★★★ *Self Catering*
Contact: Reservation Office
t (020) 7723 9611
e pctustinuk@btconnect.com
w pctustin.com

W2

Spring Street
Rating Applied For
Serviced Apartments
Deep Blue Apartments
t 0870 770 0778
e steve@deepb.com
w deepblueapartments.com

W5

Clarendon House Apartments ★★★★
Self Catering
Contact: Mrs Anne Pedley
t (020) 8567 0314
e clarendon48house@tiscali.co.uk
w clarendonhouseapartments.co.uk

W8

51 Kensington Court
★★★★ *Serviced Apartments*
t (020) 7937 2030
e bookings@kensingtoncourt.co.uk
w kensingtoncourt.co.uk

Fraser Residence Prince of Wales Terrace ★★★★★
Serviced Apartments
Frasers Hospitality
t (020) 7341 5595
e valerie.dhieux@frasershospitality.com
w frasershospitality.com

W14

Castletown House ★★★★
Self Catering
Contact: Mr Richard Poppleton
t (020) 7386 9423
e info@castletownhouse.co.uk
w castletownhouse.co.uk

WC1

Brownlow Mews ★★★
Serviced Apartments
Go Native
t (020) 7313 6147
e richard.whittaker@gonative.co.uk
w gonative.co.uk

OUTER LONDON

BECKENHAM

Oakfield Apartments
★★-★★★ *Self Catering*
t (020) 8658 4441
e enquiry@oakfield.co.uk
w oakfield.co.uk

CROYDON

Credible Apartments
★★★★ *Serviced Apartments*
Contact: Larissa Jennings
Credible Apartments Ltd
t (020) 8662 2900
e enquiries@credibleapartments.co.uk
w credibleapartments.co.uk

HAMPTON COURT

Moores Place ★★★
Self Catering
Contact: Mr Mark Barnes
t (020) 8979 1792

HAMPTON WICK

Marina Place ★★★★
Serviced Apartments
The Apartment Service
t (020) 8944 1444
e melanied@apartment.co.uk
w apartmentservice.com

HOUNSLOW

London Cottage ★★★★
Self Catering
Contact: Mr Sreemal Perera
t (020) 8570 1103
e sreemalperera@aol.com
w srlettings.com

PINNER

Moss Cottage ★★★★
Self Catering
Contact: Mrs Barbara Le Quesne
t (020) 8868 5507
e bemail2@aol.com
w moss-lane-cottages.com

RICHMOND

Carna Court
Rating Applied For
Serviced Apartments
Deep Blue Apartments
t 0870 770 0778
e steve@deepb.com
w deepblueapartments.com

Clarendon House & Gardens
★★★★ *Serviced Apartments*
Contact: Mr Peter Morgan
Clarendon Serviced Apartments
t (01784) 489217
e peterm@clarendonuk.com
w clarendonuk.com

Friston House ★★★
Self Catering
Contact: Mr Arthur Shipp
t (020) 8948 6620
e shipplets@ukgateway.net
w shipplets.com

Tersha Street
Rating Applied For
Serviced Apartments
Deep Blue Apartments
t 0870 770 0778
e steve@deepb.com
w deepblueapartments.com

SOUTH WEST ENGLAND

ABBOTSBURY Dorset

The Cottage ★★★
Self Catering
Contact: Mrs Val Dredge
t (01305) 871462
e val@thecottage-abbotsbury.co.uk
w thecottage-abbotsbury.co.uk

Elworth Farmhouse Cottages ★★★★-★★★★★
Self Catering
Contact: Mrs Christine Wade
t (01305) 871693
e elworthfarmhouse@aol.com
w elworth-farmhouse.co.uk

Gorwell Farm Cottages
★★★★ *Self Catering*
Contact: Mrs Mary Pengelly
t (01305) 871401
e mary@gorwellfarm.co.uk
w gorwellfarm.co.uk

The Old Coastguards Cottages ★★★★
Self Catering
Contact: Mr & Mrs John & Cheryl Varley
t (01305) 871335
e enquiries@oldcoastguards.com
w oldcoastguards.com

ABBOTSHAM Devon

Bowood Farm Cottages
★★★★ *Self Catering*
Toad Hall Cottages
t (01548) 853089
e thc@toadhallcottages.com
w toadhallcottages.co.uk

ADVENT Cornwall

Aldermoor Farm
★★★-★★★★ *Self Catering*
Contact: Hanne Golding
t (01840) 213366
e hanne@aldermoor.co.uk
w aldermoorholidaycottages.co.uk

Steppes Farm Holiday Cottages ★★★★
Self Catering
Contact: Mrs K J Briggs
t (01840) 212214
e enquiries@steppesfarmholidaycottages.co.uk

Widewalls Barn ★★★★
Self Catering
Contact: Mrs Pauline Metters
t (01840) 211284
e widewalls@idnet.freemail.co.uk
w widewalls.co.uk

ALBASTON Cornwall

Todsworthy Farm Holidays
★★★★ *Self Catering*
Contact: Mr Pellow
t (01822) 834744
w todsworthyfarmholidays.co.uk

ALDERTON Gloucestershire

Rectory Farm Cottages
★★★★ *Self Catering*
Contact: Mr & Mrs Peter & Margaret Burton
t (01242) 620455
e peterannabel@hotmail.com
w rectoryfarmcottages.co.uk

ALHAMPTON Somerset

The Woodshed ★★★★
Self Catering
t (01749) 860386
w alhamptoncottages.co.uk

ALLERFORD Somerset

Lynch Country House ★★★
Self Catering
Contact: Mr & Mrs Daniels
t (01643) 862800
e admin@lynchcountryhouse.co.uk
w lynchcountryhouse.co.uk

The Pack Horse
★★★-★★★★ *Self Catering*
Contact: Mr & Mrs Linda & Brian Garner
t (01643) 862475
e holidays@thepackhorse.net
w thepackhorse.net

ALTARNUN Cornwall

Trenarrett Cottage, Altarnun
★★★ *Self Catering*
Contact: Mrs Anne Langley
t (01566) 86649
e anne@trenarrett.co.uk
w trenarrett.co.uk

ALTON PANCRAS Dorset

Bookham Court
★★★★-★★★★★
Self Catering
Contact: Mr & Mrs Andrew Foot
t (01300) 345511
e andy.foot1@btinternet.com
w bookhamcourt.co.uk

Look out for establishments participating in the National Accessible Scheme

AMBERLEY
Gloucestershire

The Squirrels ★★★
Self Catering
Contact: Mrs Valerie Bowen
t (01453) 836940
e valerie.bowen@btinternet.com

AMESBURY
Wiltshire

The Stables ★★★
Self Catering
Contact: Mrs Anna Thatcher
t (01980) 670557
e anna.thatcher@tiscali.co.uk
w cottageguide.co.uk/thestables-netheravon

AMPNEY CRUCIS
Gloucestershire

Plum Tree Cottage ★★★★
Self Catering
Contact: Mrs Janet Williams
t (01793) 752540
e janet.p.williams@btinternet.com
w plumtreecottage-cotswolds.co.uk

APPERLEY
Gloucestershire

The Coal House Riverside Apartment ★★★★
Self Catering
Contact: Mrs Kay MacDonald
t (01452) 780211
e enquiries@theriversideapartment.co.uk
w theriversideapartment.co.uk

APPLEDORE
Devon

18 Nassau, Westward Ho!
★★★★★ *Self Catering*
Blue Chip Vacations
t (01803) 855282
e info@bluechipvacations.com
w bluechipvacations.com

Corner Cottage ★★★
Self Catering
Marsdens Cottage Holidays
t (01271) 813777
e holidays@marsdens.co.uk
w marsdens.co.uk

Crab Apple Cottage ★★★
Self Catering
Marsdens Cottage Holidays
t (01271) 813777
e holidays@marsdens.co.uk
w marsdens.co.uk

Fishermans Cottage ★★★
Self Catering
Marsdens Cottage Holidays
t (01271) 813777
e holidays@marsdens.co.uk
w marsdens.co.uk

Rivers View ★★★★
Self Catering
Marsdens Cottage Holidays
t (01271) 813777
e holidays@marsdens.co.uk
w marsdens.co.uk

Shore Leave ★★★★
Self Catering
Farm & Cottage Holidays
t (01237) 459827
e enquiries@farmcott.co.uk
w holidaycottages.co.uk

South Corner Cottage
★★★★★ *Self Catering*
Farm & Cottage Holidays
t (01237) 459827
e enquiries@farmcott.co.uk
w holidaycottages.co.uk

The Waterfront ★★★★
Self Catering
Farm & Cottage Holidays
t (01237) 459827
e enquiries@farmcott.co.uk
w holidaycottages.co.uk

Waters Edge
Rating Applied For
Self Catering
Contact: Mrs JAnet Cornwell
t (01271) 813777
e karen@marsdens.eclipse.co.uk

ASHBURTON
Devon

Parkers Farm Cottages & Caravans ★★★ *Self Catering*
t (01364) 653008
e parkerscottages@btconnect.com
w parkersfarm.co.uk

Wren & Robin Cottages
★★★★ *Self Catering*
Contact: Mrs Margaret Phipps
t (01364) 631421
e newcottfarmaccom@aol.com
w newcott-farm.co.uk

ASHFORD
Devon

Ashford Holt Cottage ★★
Self Catering
Toad Hall Cottages
t (01548) 853089
e thc@toadhallcottages.com
w toadhallcottages.co.uk

Helliers Farm ★★★★
Self Catering
Contact: Mrs Lancaster
t (01548) 550689
w helliersfarm.co.uk

Incledon Barn ★★★
Self Catering
Marsdens Cottage Holidays
t (01271) 813777
e holidays@marsdens.co.uk
w marsdens.co.uk

Strand House ★★★★
Self Catering
Marsdens Cottage Holidays
t (01271) 813777
e holidays@marsdens.co.uk
w marsdens.co.uk

ASHPRINGTON
Devon

Hill Quay ★★★★
Self Catering
Toad Hall Cottages
t (01548) 853089
e thc@toadhallcottages.com
w toadhallcottages.co.uk

ASHREIGNEY
Devon

Northcott Barton Farm Holiday Cottage ★★★★
Self Catering
Contact: Mrs Gay
t (01769) 520259
e sandra@northcottbarton.co.uk
w northcottbarton.co.uk

ASHTON
Cornwall

Chycarne Farm Cottages
★★★ *Self Catering*
Contact: Mrs Ross
t (01736) 762473
e chycarnefarmcottages@hotmail.com
w chycarne-farm-cottages.co.uk

ASHTON KEYNES
Wiltshire

Derry Barn ★★★★
Self Catering
Contact: Mrs June Bull
t (01285) 861264
e derrybarn@live.co.uk
w derrybarn.co.uk

ASHWATER
Devon

Blagdon Farm Country Holidays ★★★★-★★★★★
Self Catering
Contact: Mr & Mrs Clark
t (01409) 211509
e info@blagdon-farm.co.uk
w blagdon-farm.co.uk

Braddon Cottages and Forest ★★★-★★★★
Self Catering
Farm & Cottage Holidays
t (01237) 459827
e enquiries@farmcott.co.uk
w holidaycottages.co.uk

ASKERSWELL
Dorset

Court Farm Cottages
★★★★ *Self Catering*
Contact: Mrs Rebecca Bryan
t (01308) 485668
e courtfarmcottages@eclipse.co.uk
w eclipse.co.uk/courtfarmcottages/webpg2

West Hembury Farm
★★★★ *Self Catering*
Contact: Mrs MacEwan
t (01308) 485289
e hunt@westhembury.com
w westhembury.com

Wheatsheaf Cottage ★★★
Self Catering
Dream Cottages
t (01305) 789000
e admin@dream-cottages.co.uk
w dream-cottages.co.uk

ATHELHAMPTON
Dorset

River Cottage ★★★★
Self Catering
Contact: Miss Tracy Winder
t (01305) 848363
e enquiry@athelhampton.co.uk
w athelhampton.co.uk

AWLISCOMBE
Devon

Breezes ★★★ *Self Catering*
Milkbere Cottage Holidays
t (01297) 20729
e info@milkberehols.com
w milkberehols.com

Godford Farm ★★★★
Self Catering
Contact: Mrs Sally Lawrence
t (01404) 42825
e lawrencesally@hotmail.com
w devon-farm-holidays.co.uk

Ivedon Farm ★★★★
Self Catering
Contact: Mrs Nichola Pring
t (01404) 43088
e nicholapring1@onetel.com
w ivedonfarm.com

AWRE
Gloucestershire

The Priory Cottages ★★★★
Self Catering
Hideaways
t (01747) 828170
e enq@hideaways.co.uk
w hideaways.co.uk

AXBRIDGE
Somerset

Waterfront Farm Cottage
★★★★ *Self Catering*
Contact: Mrs Marina Parrett
t (01934) 733202
e badgworthfarm@aol.com
w waterfrontfarm.co.uk

AXMINSTER
Devon

Beavor Grange Farm ★★★
Self Catering
Milkbere Cottage Holidays
t (01297) 20729
e info@milkberehols.com
w milkberehols.com

Cider Room Cottage ★★★★
Self Catering
Contact: Mrs Pat Steele
t (01404) 881558
e ciderroomcottage@rscontracting.co.uk

The Coach House ★★★
Self Catering
Lyme Bay Holidays
t (01297) 443363
e email@lymebayholidays.co.uk
w lymebayholidays.co.uk

Furzeleigh House Country Cottages and Gardens
★★★★ *Self Catering*
Contact: Mrs Elizabeth Kenyon
t (01297) 34448
e e.kenyon@tesco.net
w devoncottages-furzeleigh.co.uk

The Orangery ★★★★
Self Catering
Lyme Bay Holidays
t (01297) 443363
e email@lymebayholidays.co.uk
w lymebayholidays.co.uk

The Peach House ★★★★
Self Catering
Lyme Bay Holidays
t (01297) 443363
e email@lymebayholidays.co.uk
w lymebayholidays.co.uk

Primrose Cottage ★★★★
Self Catering
Milkbere Cottage Holidays
t (01297) 20729
e info@milkberehols.com
w milkberehols.com

Trout Lodge, Weycroft
★★★★ *Self Catering*
Contact: Miss Caroline Cross
19 Hylton Road
t (01730) 263732
e caroline@troutlodge.co.uk
w troutlodge.co.uk

AYLESBEARE
Devon

Alpine Park Cottages
★★★-★★★★ *Self Catering*
Contact: Mr & Mrs Sally & Curtis Mynard
t (01395) 233619
e enquiries@alpineparkcottages.co.uk
w alpineparkcottages.co.uk

AYR
Cornwall

Rosebank ★★★ *Self Catering*
Contact: Mrs Kay Davidson
t (01736) 797152
e info@rosebankholidayflats.co.uk
w rosebankholidayflats.co.uk

BABBACOMBE
Devon

Sunnybank ★★★
Self Catering
Holiday Homes and Cottages South West
t (01803) 299677
e holcotts@aol.com
w swcottages.co.uk

Willow Cottage ★★★
Self Catering
Holiday Homes and Cottages South West
t (01803) 299677
e holcotts@aol.com
w swcottages.co.uk

BAMPTON
Devon

Manor Mill House ★★★★
Self Catering
Contact: Mrs Diane Holland
t (01398) 332318
e ejjholland@tiscali.co.uk

Westbrook House ★★★
Self Catering
Contact: Mrs Patricia Currie
t (01398) 331418
e info@westbrookhouse.co.uk
w westbrookhouse.co.uk

Wonham Barton, Bampton
★★★ *Self Catering*
Contact: Mrs Anne McLean Williams
t (01398) 331312
e anne@wonham.wanadoo.co.uk
w wonham-country-holidays.co.uk

BARBROOK
Devon

New Mill Farm ★★★★
Self Catering
Contact: Mr Jim Bingham
t (01598) 753341
e info@outovercott.co.uk
w outovercott.co.uk

The Old Mill House ★★★★
Self Catering
t (01598) 763514

Woodside ★★★
Self Catering
Contact: Mrs Sally Gunn
t (01598) 753298
e woodside@salian.fsnet.co.uk

BARNSTAPLE
Devon

Coombe Cottage, Goodleigh
★★★★ *Self Catering*
Contact: Mr & Mrs Karen & John Talbot
t (0118) 976 0449
e karen@coombecottage.co.uk

Corffe Holiday Cottages
★★★★ *Self Catering*
Contact: Mr Christopher Wheeler-Grix
t (01271) 342588
e corffe@tiscali.co.uk

Country Ways
★★★-★★★★ *Self Catering*
Contact: Mrs Kate Price
t (01769) 560503
e kate@country-ways.net
w country-ways.net

Hartpiece Farm ★★★★
Self Catering
Contact: Ms Heather Lindsey c/o JFA Ltd
t (01628) 637111
e heather@jfaexport.co.uk
w hartpiece.co.uk

North Hill Cottages ★★★
Self Catering
Contact: Mrs Carol Ann Black
t (01271) 850611
e info@north-hill.co.uk
w north-hill.co.uk

The Old Stables, Nr Brayford ★★★★
Self Catering
Contact: Mr Francis Summers
t (01271) 830238
e enquiries@the-old-stables.net
w the-old-stables.net

Willesleigh Farm ★★★★
Self Catering
Contact: Mr & Mrs Charles & Anne Esmond-Cole
t (01271) 343763

BATCOMBE
Somerset

The Acorns ★★★
Self Catering
Contact: Mrs Anne Loxton
t (01749) 830328

The Coach House ★★★★
Self Catering
Contact: Mr & Mrs Michael & Anne Page
t (01749) 850372
e info@boordsfarm.co.uk
w boordsfarm.co.uk

BATH
Somerset

17 Upper Hedgemead Road
★★★★ *Self Catering*
Bath Holiday Homes
t (01225) 830830
e bhh@virgin.net
w bathholidayhomes.co.uk

1st Floor 14 Portland Place
★★★ *Self Catering*
Bath Holiday Homes
t (01225) 830830
e bhh@virgin.net
w bathholidayhomes.co.uk

27 Park Street ★★★★
Self Catering
Bath Holiday Rentals
t (01225) 482225
e alexa@bathholidayrentals.com
w bathholidayrentals.com

31a Rivers Street ★★★★
Self Catering
Contact: Mrs Charlotte Edge
t 07910 018751
e charls.walker@gmail.com
w funlets.co.uk

4 Albion Terrace ★★★★
Self Catering
Contact: Mrs Stella West-Harling
t 07830 342420
w bathselfcatering.net

Abbey Heights ★★★★
Self Catering
Contact: Mrs Sue Wright
t (01225) 428558
e stay@threeabbeygreen.com
w abbeyheights.com

The Admirals House ★★★★
Self Catering
Bath Holiday Homes
t (01225) 830830
e bhh@virgin.net
w bathholidayhomes.co.uk

BHR/Alfred Street ★★★★
Self Catering
Bath Holiday Rentals
t (01225) 482225
e alexa@bathholidayrentals.com
w bathholidayrentals.com

Barton Buildings ★★★★
Self Catering
Bath Holiday Rentals
t (01225) 482225
e alexa@bathholidayrentals.com
w bathholidayrentals.com

Bath Spa Apartments Beau Street ★★★ *Self Catering*
Contact: Mr O Flaherty
t (01225) 310005
e info@bathspaapartments.co.uk
w bath-selfcatering.com

Bath View Apartment
★★★★ *Self Catering*
Contact: Ms Jette Baker
t (01225) 421683
e info@bathviewapartment.co.uk
w bathviewapartment.co.uk

The Beeches Farmhouse – Pig Wig Cottages ★★★★
Self Catering
t (01225) 865170
w beeches-farmhouse.co.uk

BHH/2502 Blakes on the Circus ★★★★ *Self Catering*
Bath Holiday Rentals
t (01225) 482225
e alexa@bathholidayrentals.com
w bathholidayrentals.com

Calverley Wing ★★★
Self Catering
Contact: Mrs Jenny John
t (01225) 833387
e tandjjohn@aol.com
w calverleywing.co.uk

BHR/Camden Crescent
★★★★ *Self Catering*
Bath Holiday Rentals
t (01225) 482225
e alexa@bathholidayrentals.com
w bathholidayrentals.com

BHR/Catharine Place
★★★★ *Self Catering*
Bath Holiday Rentals
t (01225) 482225
e alexa@bathholidayrentals.com
w bathholidayrentals.com

BHR/Catharine Place Garden ★★★★ *Self Catering*
Bath Holiday Rentals
t (01225) 482225
e alexa@bathholidayrentals.com
w bathholidayrentals.com

Cavendish Place ★★★★
Self Catering
Bath Holiday Rentals
t (01225) 482225
e alexa@bathholidayrentals.com
w bathholidayrentals.com

Church Farm Country Cottages ★★★★
Self Catering
Contact: Mrs Trish Bowles
Church Farm
t (01225) 722246
e stay@churchfarmcottages.com
w churchfarmcottages.com

Circus View ★★★★
Self Catering
Contact: Mrs Deborah Challinor
t (020) 7835 1962
e deborah@circusview.co.uk
w circusview.co.uk

BHH/2503 City Centre Mews ★★★ *Self Catering*
Bath Holiday Homes
t (01225) 830830
e bhh@virgin.net
w bathholidayhomes.co.uk

BHH/1658 City Centre, Top Floor Flat ★★★ *Self Catering*
Bath Holiday Homes
t (01225) 830830
e bhh@virgin.net
w bathholidayhomes.co.uk

BHH/2606 City Centre Town House ★★★★
Self Catering
Bath Holiday Homes
t (01225) 830830
e bhh@virgin.net
w bathholidayhomes.co.uk

Coach House ★★★★
Self Catering
Contact: Mrs Marilyn Quiggin
t (01225) 311341
e mq@bathselfcatering.fsnet.co.uk
w bathselfcatering.fsnet.co.uk

Elwin House
Rating Applied For
Self Catering
Contact: Joelle & Kim Davenport
t (020) 7289 9446
e eyho@dial.pipex.com

Flat 2 ★★ *Self Catering*
Contact: Miss Sophie Rosser-Rees
t (01225) 723545
e srosserrees@hotmail.com

Forum Square ★★★★
Self Catering
Contact: Mr & Mrs Paul & Susan Swainbank
t 07764 143946
e sue.forum@btinternet.com
w bathholidayhome.com

Fountain House ★★★
Self Catering
Contact: Ms Kim Lake
t 07973 722374
e kim@kimlake.plus.com
w bathcentral.co.uk

The Garden Apartment
★★★★ *Self Catering*
Bath Holiday Rentals
t (01225) 482225
e alexa@bathholidayrentals.com
w bathholidayrentals.com

BHH/1877 Georgian Cottage in Bath
Rating Applied For
Self Catering
Bath Holiday Homes
t (01225) 830830
e bhh@virgin.net
w bathholidayhomes.co.uk

BHH/2082 Georgian Flat, City Centre ★★★
Self Catering
Bath Holiday Homes
t (01225) 830830
e bhh@virgin.net
w bathholidayhomes.co.uk

BHH/2292 Georgian flat, Gt. Pulteney Street ★★★★
Self Catering
Bath Holiday Homes
t (01225) 830830
e bhh@virgin.net
w bathholidayhomes.co.uk

BHH/945 Georgian Flat, Park Street ★★★
Self Catering
Bath Holiday Homes
t (01225) 830830
e bhh@virgin.net
w bathholidayhomes.co.uk

BHR/Gloucester Street
★★★★ *Self Catering*
Bath Holiday Rentals
t (01225) 482225
e alexa@bathholidayrentals.com
w bathholidayrentals.com

Grand View ★★★★★
Self Catering
t (01225) 464238
w laurastownhouseapartments.co.uk

Greyfield Farm Cottages
★★★★–★★★★★
Self Catering
Contact: Mrs June Merry
t (01761) 471132
e june@greyfieldfarm.com
w greyfieldfarm.com

Ground Floor Apartment, Portland Place ★★★★
Self Catering
Contact: Mrs Lou Bonham
t (01548) 511471
e bonhams@btinternet.com
w bathapartment.co.uk

Harington's Apartment
★★★★ *Self Catering*
t (01225) 461728
w haringtonshotel.co.uk

Henrietta Gardens ★★★★
Self Catering
Hideaways
t (01747) 828170
e enq@hideaways.co.uk
w hideaways.co.uk

BHR/Henrietta Villas
★★★★ *Self Catering*
Bath Holiday Rentals
t (01225) 482225
e alexa@bathholidayrentals.com
w bathholidayrentals.com

BHR/Lakeside Apartment Mews ★★★★ *Self Catering*
Bath Holiday Rentals
t (01225) 482225
e alexa@bathholidayrentals.com
w bathholidayrentals.com

BHH/1869 Maisonette, the Circus ★★★★ *Self Catering*
Bath Holiday Homes
t (01225) 830830
e bhh@virgin.net
w bathholidayhomes.co.uk

Margaret's Building Apartment ★★★★
Self Catering
Hideaways
t (01747) 828170
e enq@hideaways.co.uk
w hideaways.co.uk

Marlborough Buildings
Rating Applied For
Self Catering
Bath Holiday Rentals
t (01225) 482225
e alexa@bathholidayrentals.com
w bathholidayrentals.com

Marlborough Heights
★★★★ *Self Catering*
Bath Holiday Rentals
t (01225) 482225
e alexa@bathholidayrentals.com
w bathholidayrentals.com

Marlborough House ★★★★
Self Catering
Bath Holiday Rentals
t (01225) 482225
e alexa@bathholidayrentals.com
w bathholidayrentals.com

BHH/1981 Modern Bungalow, Lansdown Slopes
★★★ *Self Catering*
Bath Holiday Homes
t (01225) 830830
e bhh@virgin.net
w bathholidayhomes.co.uk

BHH/944 Modern Flat, Parkside Setting ★★★
Self Catering
Bath Holiday Homes
t (01225) 830830
e bhh@virgin.net
w bathholidayhomes.co.uk

Nailey Cottages ★★★★
Self Catering
Contact: Mrs Brett Gardner
t (01225) 852989
e cottages@naileyfarm.co.uk
w naileyfarm.co.uk

BHH/2396 New Georgian flat ★★★ *Self Catering*
Bath Holiday Homes
t (01225) 830830
e bhh@virgin.net
w bathholidayhomes.co.uk

Parkside Apartment ★★★★
Self Catering
Contact: Mrs Mary Cooper
t (01225) 421097
e mjc@parksideapartment.co.uk
w parksideapartment.co.uk

Providence Cottage ★★★★
Self Catering
Bath Holiday Rentals
t (01225) 482225
e alexa@bathholidayrentals.com
w bathholidayrentals.com

Queens Parade ★★★★
Self Catering
Bath Holiday Rentals
t (01225) 482225
e alexa@bathholidayrentals.com
w bathholidayrentals.com

Riverside Apartment ★★★
Self Catering
Contact: Mr Graham Wilson
t (01225) 337968
e rabath@btinternet.com
w rabath.co.uk

Royal Crescent LGF ★★★★
Self Catering
Bath Holiday Rentals
t (01225) 482225
e alexa@bathholidayrentals.com
w bathholidayrentals.com

Russel Street Apartment
★★★★ *Self Catering*
Contact: Mrs Clare Margaret Travers
t (01225) 312011
e traversa@aol.com
w bathbreaks.co.uk

SACO Bath ★★★★
Serviced Apartments
SACO Apartments
t (0117) 974 5936
e sarahbailey@sacaoapartments.co.uk
w sacoapartments.co.uk

Second Floor Flat ★★★★
Self Catering
Contact: Mrs Lindsay Bishop
t (01276) 29033
e lindsay.bishop@btopenworld.com
w bath-flat.co.uk

Sheylors Farm ★★★★★
Self Catering
t (01225) 743922
w thestablescottage.co.uk

Spring Farm Holiday Cottages ★★★–★★★★
Self Catering
Contact: Mrs Sue Brown
t (01761) 435524
e suebrown@springfarmcottages.co.uk
w springfarmcottages.co.uk

Sydney Mews ★★★★
Self Catering
Bath Holiday Rentals
t (01225) 482225
e alexa@bathholidayrentals.com
w bathholidayrentals.com

Time-2-Relax-Holidays
★★★★★ *Self Catering*
Contact: Ms Sue Thornton
t (01305) 837474
e sue@eastwoodquay.freeserve.co.uk
w timetorelax.co.uk

Upper Maisonette 38 Bathwick Street ★★★
Self Catering
Contact: Mr Nicholas De Villiers Kuun
t (01225) 319972

Woods Way ★★★★
Self Catering
Bath Holiday Rentals
t (01225) 482225
e alexa@bathholidayrentals.com
w bathholidayrentals.com

BATHEALTON
Somerset

Woodlands Farm ★★★★
Self Catering
Contact: Mrs Joan Greenway
t (01984) 623271
w woodlandsfarm-holidays.co.uk

BATHEASTON
Somerset

Avondale Riverside, Batheaston ★★★★★
Self Catering
Contact: Mr & Mrs Pecchia
t (01225) 852226 & 07929 842504
e sheilapex@questmusic.co.uk
w riversapart.co.uk

The Malthouse ★★★★
Self Catering
Contact: Mr David Burke
t 07803 513084
w dpburke.co.uk/themalthouse.html

BATHFORD
Somerset

Avon Cottage Studio ★★★
Self Catering
Contact: Mr Henrik Bebber
t (01225) 858490
e info@avoncottagestudio.co.uk
w avoncottagestudio.co.uk

BATHWICK
Somerset

9 St Johns Road ★★★★
Self Catering
Contact: Mrs Sue Moss
t (01245) 223016
e sue.moss2@btopenworld.com
w bathvisit.co.uk

BHH/1452 Mews House
★★★★ *Self Catering*
Bath Holiday Homes
t (01225) 830830
e bhh@virgin.net
w bathholidayhomes.co.uk

BEAMINSTER
Dorset

The Cottage ★★★
Self Catering
Contact: Ms Trish Mitchell
t (01308) 863054
e trish@northbuckham.fsnet.co.uk
w northbuckhamfarm.co.uk

Greens Cross Farm ★★★
Self Catering
Contact: Mr & Mrs David & Lora Baker
t (01308) 862661
e greenscross@btopenworld.com
w greenscrossfarm.co.uk

Lewesdon Farm Holidays
★★★★ *Self Catering*
Contact: Mr & Mrs Micheal & Linda Smith
t (01308) 868270
e lewesdonfarmholiday@tinyonline.co.uk
w lewesdonfarmholidays.co.uk

Orchard End, Hooke ★★★★
Self Catering
Contact: Mrs Pauline Wallbridge
t (01308) 862619
e enquiries@watermeadowhouse.co.uk
w watermeadowhouse.co.uk

The Sawmill ★★★★
Self Catering
Lyme Bay Holidays
t (01297) 443363
e email@lymebayholidays.co.uk
w lymebayholidays.co.uk

Stable Cottage ★★★★
Self Catering
Contact: Mrs Diana Clarke
t (01308) 862305
e meerhay@aol.com
w meerhay.co.uk

BEER
Devon

Carpenters Cottage ★★★
Self Catering
Milkbere Cottage Holidays
t (01297) 20729
e info@milkberehols.com
w milkberehols.com

Chaffcombe Lodge ★★★★
Self Catering
t (01395) 519866
w holidaysdevon.com

Church View ★★★
Self Catering
Milkbere Cottage Holidays
t (01297) 20729
e info@milkberehols.com
w milkberehols.com

Hooknell House ★★★★
Self Catering
Milkbere Cottage Holidays
t (01297) 20729
e info@milkberehols.com
w milkberehols.com

BEESANDS
Devon

Kimberley Cottage ★★★
Self Catering
Toad Hall Cottages
t (01548) 853089
e thc@toadhallcottages.com
w toadhallcottages.co.uk

BEESON
Devon

Beeson Farm Holiday Cottages ★★★★
Self Catering
Contact: Mr & Mrs Robin & Veronica Cross
t (01548) 581270
e info@beesonhols.co.uk
w beesonhols.co.uk

BENTHAM
Gloucestershire

Bridge House Cottage
★★★★★ *Self Catering*
Contact: Mrs Yvonne Hodges
t (01452) 862998
e yvonne@hodges0.wanadoo.co.uk
w benthamcottage.co.uk

BERRY HEAD
Devon

Berry Head Cottage ★★★★
Self Catering
Brixham Holiday Homes Ltd
t (01803) 854187
e info@brixhamholidayhomes.co.uk
w brixhamholidayhomes.co.uk

BERRYNARBOR
Devon

Adventure Cottage
Rating Applied For
Self Catering
Marsdens Cottage Holidays
t (01271) 813777
e holidays@marsdens.co.uk
w marsdens.co.uk

Buzzards Roost ★★★★
Self Catering
Marsdens Cottage Holidays
t (01271) 813777
e holidays@marsdens.co.uk
w marsdens.co.uk

Cairn Cottage ★★★★
Self Catering
Marsdens Cottage Holidays
t (01271) 813777
e holidays@marsdens.co.uk
w marsdens.co.uk

Deers Leap ★★★★
Self Catering
Marsdens Cottage Holidays
t (01271) 813777
e holidays@marsdens.co.uk
w marsdens.co.uk

Derrivale ★★★★
Self Catering
Marsdens Cottage Holidays
t (01271) 813777
e holidays@marsdens.co.uk
w marsdens.co.uk

Lee Copse ★★★
Self Catering
Marsdens Cottage Holidays
t (01271) 813777
e holidays@marsdens.co.uk
w marsdens.co.uk

Smythen Farm Coastal Holiday Cottages ★★★
Self Catering
Contact: Mr & Ms Thompson & Elstone
t (01271) 882875
e jayne@smythenfarmholidaycottages.co.uk
w smythenfarmholidaycottages.co.uk

BERWICK ST JAMES
Wiltshire

Rose Cottage ★★★
Self Catering
Contact: Mr & Mrs J Read
t (01722) 328934

BERWICK ST JOHN
Wiltshire

Bramble Cottage Annexe
★★★ *Self Catering*
Hideaways
t (01747) 828170
e enq@hideaways.co.uk
w hideaways.co.uk

Easton Farm Cottages
★★★★ *Self Catering*
Hideaways
t (01747) 828170
e enq@hideaways.co.uk
w hideaways.co.uk

BETTISCOMBE
Dorset

Conway Cottage ★★★
Self Catering
Contact: Mrs Margaret Smith
t (01308) 868313
e henry.smith3@virgin.net
w conway-cottage.co.uk

BIBURY
Gloucestershire

5 Jubilee Court ★★★
Self Catering
Contact: Mrs Helen Holroyd
t (01285) 711433
e reservations@biburyholidayflat.com
w biburyholidayflat.com

Bibury Holiday Cottages
★★★★ *Self Catering*
Contact: Mr & Mrs R Hedgeland
t (01285) 740314
e info@biburyholidaycottages.com
w biburyholidaycottages.com

Cotteswold House Cottages
★★★★ *Self Catering*
Contact: Mrs Judith Underwood
Cotteswold House
t (01285) 740609
e enquiries@cotteswoldhouse.org.uk
w cotteswoldhouse.org.uk

BIDDESTONE
Wiltshire

Barn End ★★★★
Self Catering
Contact: Mrs Jenny Davis
t (01249) 712104
e jennyandbob@biddestone.com
w bathselfcatering.com/barnend/listing.html

BIDEFORD
Devon

2 Longbridge Warf ★★★★
Self Catering
Contact: Mr & Mrs John & Ann Whitten
t (01409) 281859
e joanol@btinternet.com

Coachmans Cottage, Monkleigh ★★★
Self Catering
Contact: Mr & Mrs Tom & Sue Downie
Cream Tea Cottages
t (01805) 623670
e tom.downie@ukonline.co.uk
w creamteacottages.co.uk

Cream Tea Cottages, Little Torrington ★★★★
Self Catering
Contact: Mr & Mrs Tom & Sue Downie
Staddon House
t (01805) 623670
e tom.downie@ukonline.co.uk
w creamteacottages.co.uk

Georges Cottage
Rating Applied For
Self Catering
Marsdens Cottage Holidays
t (01271) 813777
e holidays@marsdens.co.uk
w marsdens.co.uk

Little Melville Holiday Cottage ★★★★ *Self Catering*
Contact: Mr Bernard Moore
t (01237) 471140
e litmelcot@yahoo.com
w littlemelville.co.uk

Peppercombe Holt ★★★★
Self Catering
Marsdens Cottage Holidays
t (01271) 813777
e holidays@marsdens.co.uk
w marsdens.co.uk

Pillhead Cottage ★★★★
Self Catering
Toad Hall Cottages
t (01548) 853089
e thc@toadhallcottages.com
w toadhallcottages.co.uk

Pillhead Farm ★★★★
Self Catering
Contact: Mr Richard Hill
t (01237) 479337
e hill@pillheadfarm.fsnet.co.uk

Salterns Lodge ★★★★★
Self Catering
Marsdens Cottage Holidays
t (01271) 813777
e holidays@marsdens.co.uk
w marsdens.co.uk

West Hele ★★★★
Self Catering
Contact: Mrs Lorna Hicks
t (01237) 451044
e lorna.hicks@virgin.net
w westhele.co.uk

West Webbery Cottage
★★★ *Self Catering*
Contact: Mr & Mrs Jonathan & Siana Yewdall
t (01237) 429294
e jonnie@yewdall.force9.co.uk
w westwebbery.co.uk

BIGBURY-ON-SEA
Devon

1 Sharpland Crest ★★★
Self Catering
Contact: Mrs Amanda Hough
t (01392) 438234
e amandahough@talk21.com

3 Sandbanks ★★★★★
Self Catering
Blue Chip Vacations
t (01803) 855282
e info@bluechipvacations.com
w bluechipvacations.com

Apartment 5, Burgh Island Causeway ★★★★★
Self Catering
Helpful Holidays
t (01647) 433593
e help@helpfulholidays.com
w helpfulholidays.com

Mount Folly Farm, Bigbury on Sea ★★★ *Self Catering*
Contact: Mrs Jane Tucker
t (01548) 810267
e chris.cathy@goosemoose.com
w bigburyholidays.co.uk

Seascape ★★★★
Self Catering
Blue Chip Vacations
t (01803) 855282
e info@bluechipvacations.com
w bluechipvacations.com

BINEGAR
Somerset

The Beanacre Barn ★★★★
Self Catering
Contact: Ms Susan M Griffin
t (01749) 841628
e enquiries@beanacrebarn.co.uk
w beanacrebarn.co.uk

Spindle Cottage, Binegar Green ★★★★ *Self Catering*
Contact: Mrs Angela Bunting
t (01749) 840497
e angela@spindlecottage.co.uk
w spindlecottage.co.uk

BISHOP SUTTON
Somerset

The Trebartha Apartment
★★★★ *Self Catering*
Contact: Mrs Sally Catchpole
t (01275) 333845
e sally@thetrebartha.co.uk
w thetrebartha.co.uk

BISHOP'S CAUNDLE
Dorset

The Tallett ★★★
Self Catering
Dream Cottages
t (01305) 789000
e admin@dream-cottages.co.uk
w dream-cottages.co.uk

BISHOP'S TAWTON
Devon

Four Rose Cottage ★★★★
Self Catering
Marsdens Cottage Holidays
t (01271) 813777
e holidays@marsdens.co.uk
w marsdens.co.uk

BISHOPSTEIGNTON
Devon

Hillcrest Cottage Bishopsteignton ★★★★
Self Catering
Blue Chip Vacations
t (01803) 855282
e info@bluechipvacations.com
w bluechipvacations.com

BISLEY
Gloucestershire

Coopers Cottage ★★★
Self Catering
Contact: Mr & Mrs Michael & Liz Flint
t (01452) 770289
e flint.bisley@btinternet.com

BLACK TORRINGTON
Devon

Old Post Office ★★★
Self Catering
Toad Hall Cottages
t (01548) 853089
e thc@toadhallcottages.com
w toadhallcottages.co.uk

BLACKAWTON
Devon

Lower Collaton Farm
★★★★ *Self Catering*
Contact: Mr & Mrs James & Rosie Mussen
t (01803) 712260
e mussen@lower-collaton-farm.co.uk
w lower-collaton-farm.co.uk

Middle Way Farm ★★★
Self Catering
w middle-wadstay-farm.com

Sheplegh Court, No 11
★★★ *Self Catering*
Contact: Mrs Lisa Crowther
t (01234) 219299
e lisa@sanddunesandsaltyair.co.uk
w sanddunesandsaltyair.co.uk

BLACKFORD
Somerset

Giffords Barn ★★★★★
Self Catering
Contact: Mr Peter Jefferies
t (01963) 440390
e jefferies100@tiscali.co.uk
w premiercottages.co.uk

BLAISDON
Gloucestershire

St Michaels
Rating Applied For
Self Catering
Contact: Nicky Charlesworth
St. Michaels
t (01452) 830278
e nickcharlesworth@waitrose.com

BLANDFORD FORUM
Dorset

Houghton Lodge ★★★★★
Self Catering
Contact: Mrs Clarice Fiander-Norman
t (01258) 882170
e enquiries@houghtonlodge.com
w houghtonlodge.com

BLISLAND
Cornwall

Bridge Pool Cottage ★★★★
Self Catering
Contact: Mr & Mrs Sobey
t (01579) 343382
e tandksobey@hotmail.co.uk

Moss Cottage Barn ★★★★
Self Catering
Contact: Mr Collins
t (01208) 850766
e stevecollins@smcsales.com

Torr House Cottages
★★★★ *Self Catering*
Contact: Mr & Mrs Wilson
t (01208) 851601
e contact@torrhousecottages.co.uk
w torrhousecottages.co.uk

BLOCKLEY
Gloucestershire

Arreton Cottage ★★★★
Self Catering
Contact: Mrs Gloria Baylis
t (01386) 701077
e bandb@arreton.demon.co.uk
w arreton.demon.co.uk

Briar Cottage ★★★★
Self Catering
Campden Cottages
t (01386) 593315
e info@campdencottages.co.uk
w campdencottages.co.uk

Oak House ★★★★★
Self Catering
t (01386) 593603
e michael@bigcottage.com
w bigcottage.com

Rosemary Cottage ★★★★
Self Catering
Campden Cottages
t (01386) 593315
e info@campdencottages.co.uk
w campdencottages.co.uk

Skylark Cottage ★★★★
Self Catering
Contact: Mrs Ruth Lucas
t (01451) 832575
e lucas@okwa.demon.co.uk
w skylarkcottage.co.uk

BLUE ANCHOR
Somerset

Huntingball Lodge ★★★★
Self Catering
Contact: Mr & Mrs Brian & Kim Hall
t (01984) 640076
w huntingball-lodge.co.uk

Primrose Hill Holidays, Blue Anchor ★★★★ *Self Catering*
Contact: Mrs Jo Halliday
t (01643) 821200
e info@primrosehillholidays.co.uk
w primrosehillholidays.co.uk

BODMIN
Cornwall

Blossom Cottage ★★★★
Self Catering
Contact: Mrs Chapman**e** enquiry@blossomcottage.co.uk
w blossomcottage.co.uk

Fox Park Farm Cottages
Rating Applied For
Self Catering
Contact: Mr Stephen Slater
t (01208) 831044
e info@foxparkfarm.co.uk
w foxparkfarm.co.uk

Glynn Barton Cottages
★★★★ *Self Catering*
Contact: Ms Orr
t (01208) 821375

Great Brightor Farm ★★★★
Self Catering
Contact: Mr & Mrs Frank & Kay Chapman
t (01208) 850464

The Honeypot ★★★★
Self Catering
Contact: Kim Roscoe
t (01208) 77553
e kim@thehoneypot-bodmin.co.uk
w thehoneypot-bodmin.co.uk

Lanjew Park ★★★★
Self Catering
Contact: Mrs Elaine Biddick
t (01726) 890214
e biddick@lanjew.co.uk
w lanjewholidays.co.uk

Rhind Street Barns ★★★★
Self Catering
Contact: Pat Spear
t (01208) 269029
e pat@rhindstreetbarns.co.uk
w rhindstreetbarns.co.uk

BODREAN
Cornwall

Apple Orchard Bungalow
★★★★ *Self Catering*
Farm & Cottage Holidays
t (01237) 459827
e enquiries@farmcott.co.uk
w holidaycottages.co.uk

BOKIDDICK
Cornwall

Bokiddick Farm Cottages
★★★★★ *Self Catering*
Contact: Mr & Mrs Trevor & Gill Hugo
t (01208) 831481
e gillhugo@bokiddickfarm.co.uk
w bokiddickfarm.co.uk

BOLINGEY
Cornwall

Middlemarch ★★★
Self Catering
Duchy Holidays
t (01872) 572971
e enquiries@duchyholidays.co.uk
w duchyholidays.co.uk

BOSCASTLE
Cornwall

Anneth Lowen ★★★★
Self Catering
Contact: Mrs Kay Dougan
Kernow Holidays
t (01483) 765446
e info@annethlowen.co.uk

The Boat House ★★★★
Self Catering
Contact: Sue Venning
t (01840) 250113
e suevenning@hotmail.co.uk
w cornwall-online.co.uk

Boscastle Holidays
★★★-★★★★ *Self Catering*
Contact: Mrs Congdon
t (01840) 250233
e info@boscastleholidays.co.uk
w boscastleholidays.co.uk

Cardew Farmhouse ★★★★
Self Catering
Contact: Mrs Liz Brewer
t (01804) 250854
e cardew@lineone.net
w cardewfarmhouse.co.uk

Cargurra Farm ★★★★
Self Catering
Contact: Mrs Gillian Elson
t (01840) 261206
e gillian@cargurra.co.uk
w cargurra.co.uk

Courtyard Farm Cottages
★★★★ *Self Catering*
Contact: Mr & Mrs Compton
t (01840) 261256
e courtyard.farm@virgin.net
w courtyardfarmcottages.com

The Garden Place, Boscastle
★★★★ *Self Catering*
Contact: Mrs C Knox
t (01840) 250817
e celia.knox@btinternet.com

Home Farm Cottage ★★★★
Self Catering
Contact: Mrs Jackie Haddy
t (01840) 250195
e homefarm.boscastle@tiscali.co.uk
w homefarm-boscastle.co.uk

Jarvies
Rating Applied For
Self Catering
Powells Cottage Holidays
t (01834) 812791
e info@powells.co.uk
w powells.co.uk

Jordan Vale ★★★-★★★★
Self Catering
Contact: Mrs Scott
t (01840) 250463
e sues-cott@lineone.net
w jordanvale.net

Lewarne ★★★ *Self Catering*
Contact: Mr Ian Purvis
t (01676) 534648

Lundy View ★★★
Self Catering
Contact: Mrs Sue Venning
t (01840) 250113
e lundynewboscastle@fsmail.net

No 4 Pennally Cottage ★★
Self Catering
Contact: Mrs Janet Welch
t (01322) 522240

Old Newham Farm ★★★
Self Catering
Contact: Mr & Mrs Purdue
t (01840) 230470
e tbg@old-newham.co.uk
w old-newham.co.uk

The Olde Carpenters Cottage ★★★★★
Self Catering
Contact: Mrs Jackie Haddy
t (01840) 250195
e homefarm.boscastle@tiscali.co.uk
w homefarm-boscastle.co.uk

Paradise Farm Cottage
★★★ *Self Catering*
Contact: Mrs Hancock
t (01840) 250528

Penrose ★★★ *Self Catering*
Contact: Mrs Cowling
t (01840) 230135
e rosemarie@cowling135.freeserve.co.uk

Seagull Barn ★★★
Self Catering
Cornish Seaview Cottages
t (01428) 723819
e enquiries@cornishseaviewcottages.co.uk
w cornishseaviewcottages.co.uk

Tregatherall Farm Cottages
★★★★ *Self Catering*
Contact: Mrs Seldon
t (01840) 250277
e ness7tregatherall@yahoo.co.uk
w tregatherallfarm.co.uk

Trewannett Bungalow ★★★
Self Catering
Contact: Mr & Mrs Sleep
t (01840) 250295

Venn Down Farmhouse Apartments ★★★★
Self Catering
Contact: Mrs Diane Bentall
t (01840) 250599
e venndownfarmhouse@uk2.net
w venndownfarmhouse.co.uk

Westerings ★★★
Self Catering
Contact: Mrs Shirley Wakelin
t (01840) 250314
e shirley@westeringsholidays.co.uk
w westeringsholidays.co.uk

BOURNEMOUTH
Dorset

Southmoor ★★★★
Self Catering
Contact: Mr Martyn Clatworthy
t (01202) 298775

BOURTON-ON-THE-WATER
Gloucestershire

Acorn Cottage ★★★★
Self Catering
Contact: Mrs Ann Oakes
t (01386) 870727
e ann@oakescottages.co.uk
w oakescottages.co.uk

Annes Cottage ★★★★
Self Catering
Contact: Mrs Ann Oakes
t (01386) 870727
e ann@oakescottages.co.uk
w oakescottages.co.uk

The Coach House of the Dower House ★★
Self Catering
Contact: Mrs Philomena Adams
t (01451) 820629

Farncombe Cottage ★★★★
Self Catering
Contact: Mrs Julia Wright
t (01451) 820120
e julia@farncombecotswolds.com
w farncombecotswolds.com

Greenleighs
Rating Applied For
Self Catering
Contact: Mr & Mrs S Robb
t (01451) 810291
e robbmob@btinternet.com
w cotswoldholidaylets.com

Inglenook Cottage ★★★
Self Catering
Contact: Mrs Vicki Garland
Ratcliffe House Farm
t (01827) 712367 & 07751 801508
e enquiries@ratcliffehousefarm.co.uk
w holidaycottagebourton-on-the-water.co.uk

Magnolia Cottage Apartment ★★★★
Self Catering
Contact: Mr & Mrs Janice & Michael Cotterill
t (01451) 821841
e cotterillmj@hotmail.com
w cottageguide.co.uk/magnolia

Southlands Cottage ★★★
Self Catering
Contact: Mr & Mrs David & Christine Hutchman
t (01451) 821987
e christine.hutchman@btopenworld.com
w southlands-bb.co.uk

Tagmoor Hollow Apartment
★★★★ *Self Catering*
Contact: Mrs Grace Bennett
t (01451) 821307

Well Cottage ★★★★
Self Catering
Contact: Mr & Mrs Bette Roberts
t (01451) 824059

Windrush Apartments ★★★
Self Catering
Contact: Mr & Mrs Arthur & Gill Perry
t 07710 404942
e arthurandgill@aol.com
w windrushapartments.co.uk

Wrights Cottage ★★★★
Self Catering
Contact: Mrs Gloria Marsh
t (01451) 820568
e gloria.marsh@ntlworld.com

BOVEY TRACEY
Devon

Pottery Leat Cottage
★★★★★ *Self Catering*
Contact: Mr Smith
t (01326) 555555
e enquiries@classic.co.uk
w classic.co.uk

Tracey Cottage ★★★★
Self Catering
Holiday Homes and Cottages South West
t (01803) 299677
e holcotts@aol.com
w swcottages.co.uk

Warmhill Farm ★★★★
Self Catering
Contact: Mr W B Marnham
t (01626) 833229
e marnham@agriplus.net

BOX
Wiltshire

The Haybarn Alcombe Manor ★★★★ *Self Catering*
Contact: Dr Caroline Morley
t (01225) 742291

BRADFORD LEIGH
Wiltshire

Merkins Farm Cottages
★★★★ *Self Catering*
Contact: Mrs Hayley Painter
t (01225) 865249
w merkinsfarmcottages.co.uk

BRADFORD-ON-AVON
Wiltshire

Bridge Cottage ★★★★
Self Catering
t (01225) 866129
w bridgecottage.org

Cumberwell Country Cottages ★★★★
Self Catering
Contact: Mr Alistair James
t (01225) 869230
e enquiries@cumberwellcountrycottages.com
w cumberwellcountrycottages.com

Fairfield Barns ★★★★★
Self Catering
Contact: Mr & Mrs Taff & Gilly Thomas
t (01225) 703585
e gilly@fairfieldbarns.com
w fairfieldbarns.com

Kemble Cottage ★★★★
Self Catering
t (01225) 309399
e info@kemble-cottage.co.uk
w kemble-cottage.co.uk

Lock View Cottage ★★★★
Self Catering
t (01225) 865607
w lockviewcottage.co.uk

BRADIFORD
Devon

Carpenters Cottage ★★★★
Self Catering
Marsdens Cottage Holidays
t (01271) 813777
e holidays@marsdens.co.uk
w marsdens.co.uk

Shippen Cottage ★★★★
Self Catering
Marsdens Cottage Holidays
t (01271) 813777
e holidays@marsdens.co.uk
w marsdens.co.uk

BRADNINCH
Devon

Highdown Organic Farm
★★★★ *Self Catering*
Contact: Mrs Vallis
t (01392) 881028
e svallis@highdownfarm.co.uk
w highdownfarm.co.uk

BRADWORTHY
Devon

Calf Barn ★★★★
Self Catering
t (01409) 241597

BRANKSOME PARK
Dorset

Grovefield Manor ★★★
Self Catering
w grovefieldmanor.co.uk

BRANSCOMBE
Devon

The Haven ★★★★
Self Catering
Milkbere Cottage Holidays
t (01297) 20729
e info@milkberehols.com
w milkberehols.com

The Nook ★★★★
Self Catering
Milkbere Cottage Holidays
t (01297) 20729
e info@milkberehols.com
w milkberehols.com

Terry Holt ★★★★
Self Catering
Milkbere Cottage Holidays
t (01297) 20729
e info@milkberehols.com
w milkberehols.com

BRATTON
Somerset

Woodcombe Lodges ★★★★
Self Catering
Contact: Mrs Nicola Hanson
t (01643) 702789 &
07860 667325
e nicola@woodcombelodge.co.uk
w woodcombelodge.co.uk

BRATTON FLEMING
Devon

Capelands Farm ★★★
Self Catering
Toad Hall Cottages
t (01548) 853089
e thc@toadhallcottages.com
w toadhallcottages.co.uk

BRAUNTON
Devon

1 Millhouse Cottage ★★★
Self Catering
Marsdens Cottage Holidays
t (01271) 813777
e holidays@marsdens.co.uk
w marsdens.co.uk

2 Millhouse Cottage ★★★
Self Catering
Marsdens Cottage Holidays
t (01271) 813777
e holidays@marsdens.co.uk
w marsdens.co.uk

Bay Tree ★★★★
Self Catering
Marsdens Cottage Holidays
t (01271) 813777
e holidays@marsdens.co.uk
w marsdens.co.uk

Beach Walk ★★★
Self Catering
Marsdens Cottage Holidays
t (01271) 813777
e holidays@marsdens.co.uk
w marsdens.co.uk

Bowden House ★★★★
Self Catering
Marsdens Cottage Holidays
t (01271) 813777
e holidays@marsdens.co.uk
w marsdens.co.uk

Britton Lodge ★★★
Self Catering
Marsdens Cottage Holidays
t (01271) 813777
e holidays@marsdens.co.uk
w marsdens.co.uk

Broadgate Byre ★★★★
Self Catering
Marsdens Cottage Holidays
t (01271) 813777
e holidays@marsdens.co.uk
w marsdens.co.uk

Buckland Manor Cottage
★★★ *Self Catering*
Marsdens Cottage Holidays
t (01271) 813777
e holidays@marsdens.co.uk
w marsdens.co.uk

Buckland Mews ★★★
Self Catering
Marsdens Cottage Holidays
t (01271) 813777
e holidays@marsdens.co.uk
w marsdens.co.uk

Florin Cottage ★★★★
Self Catering
Marsdens Cottage Holidays
t (01271) 813777
e holidays@marsdens.co.uk
w marsdens.co.uk

Garden Flat ★★★
Self Catering
Marsdens Cottage Holidays
t (01271) 813777
e holidays@marsdens.co.uk
w marsdens.co.uk

Goadgates ★★★
Self Catering
Marsdens Cottage Holidays
t (01271) 813777
e holidays@marsdens.co.uk
w marsdens.co.uk

Gull Rock ★★ *Self Catering*
t (01271) 813777
e holidays@marsdens.co.uk
w marsdens.co.uk

Hope Cottage ★★★★★
Self Catering
Marsdens Cottage Holidays
t (01271) 813777
e holidays@marsdens.co.uk
w marsdens.co.uk

Incledon Farmhouse ★★★
Self Catering
Marsdens Cottage Holidays
t (01271) 813777
e holidays@marsdens.co.uk
w marsdens.co.uk

Leacroft ★★★ *Self Catering*
Marsdens Cottage Holidays
t (01271) 813777
e holidays@marsdens.co.uk
w marsdens.co.uk

Little Comfort Farm ★★★
Self Catering
Contact: Mrs Jackie Milsom
t (01271) 812414
e enquiries@littlecomfortfarm.co.uk
w littlecomfortfarm.co.uk

Living Waters
Rating Applied For
Self Catering
Contact: Mrs Janet Cornwell
t (01271) 813777
e karen@marsdens.eclipse.co.uk

Mercaston Cottage ★★★
Self Catering
Marsdens Cottage Holidays
t (01271) 813777
e holidays@marsdens.co.uk
w marsdens.co.uk

Moor Lane Cottage ★★★★
Self Catering
Marsdens Cottage Holidays
t (01271) 813777
e holidays@marsdens.co.uk
w marsdens.co.uk

Rockham ★★★★★
Self Catering
Marsdens Cottage Holidays
t (01271) 813777
e holidays@marsdens.co.uk
w marsdens.co.uk

St Brannocks Hill ★★★
Self Catering
Marsdens Cottage Holidays
t (01271) 813777
e holidays@marsdens.co.uk
w marsdens.co.uk

Saunton Beach Villas ★★
Self Catering
Contact: Mrs Clare Oliver
t (01271) 892002

Sunnyside Cottage ★★★★
Self Catering
Marsdens Cottage Holidays
t (01271) 813777
e holidays@marsdens.co.uk
w marsdens.co.uk

Valentines Cottage ★★★★
Self Catering
Marsdens Cottage Holidays
t (01271) 813777
e holidays@marsdens.co.uk
w marsdens.co.uk

Well Cottage ★★★★
Self Catering
Marsdens Cottage Holidays
t (01271) 813777
e holidays@marsdens.co.uk
w marsdens.co.uk

Willowfield Lake Cottages
★★★★ *Self Catering*
Contact: Ms Helen Larcombe
t (01271) 814346
e info@willowfieldlakecottages.co.uk
w willowfieldlake.com

Windspray ★★★
Self Catering
Marsdens Cottage Holidays
t (01271) 813777
e holidays@marsdens.co.uk
w marsdens.co.uk

BRAYFORD
Devon

Muxworthy Cottage ★★
Self Catering
Contact: Mrs G M Bament
Muxworthy Farm
t (01598) 710342

BREAGE
Cornwall

Hillsdale Holiday Cottages
★★★ *Self Catering*
Contact: Mr & Mrs Adam Fornear
t (01736) 763466
e hillsdale@btinternet.com
w hillsdalecottages.co.uk

Little Tolmennor Barn
★★★★ *Self Catering*
Contact: Mrs Jayne Lake
t (01736) 763250
e info@littletolmennorbarn.co.uk
w littletolmennorbarn.co.uk

BREAM
Gloucestershire

Sequoia Lodge ★★★★
Self Catering
Contact: Debbie Wilkie
t (01594) 564789
e debbie@sequoialodge.co.uk
w sequoialodge.co.uk

BREAN
Somerset

42 Hill View ★★ *Self Catering*
Contact: Miss Barbara Cromey
t (0117) 977 0015
w hillview-brean.co.uk/

Gadara Bungalow ★★★
Self Catering
Contact: Mr Trevor Hicks
t (01278) 751263
e trevor@diamondfarm42.freeserve.co.uk
w diamondfarm.co.uk

BREMHILL
Wiltshire

Little Barn & Lavender Cottages ★★★★
Self Catering
Contact: Mrs Yvonne Buckley
t (01249) 811837
e yandpcottages@hotmail.co.uk
w yandpcottages.co.uk

BRENT KNOLL
Somerset

West Croft Farm Dairy Cottage ★★ *Self Catering*
Contact: Mrs Janet Harris
t (01278) 760259
e erica@westcroftcider.com

BRENTOR
Devon

The Smithy ★★★
Self Catering
Holiday Homes and Cottages South West
t (01803) 299677
e holcotts@aol.com
w swcottages.co.uk

BRIDGWATER
Somerset

Ash-Wembdon Farm Cottages ★★★★
Self Catering
Contact: Mr Clarence Rowe
t (01278) 453097
e c.a.rowe@btinternet.com
w ukcottageholiday.com

Nelson Cottage ★★★★
Self Catering
Contact: Mr & Mrs Robbins
t (01278) 453492
e robbinsm@bridgwater.ac.uk

BRIDPORT
Dorset

17 Bramble Drive ★★★
Self Catering
Contact: Mrs C Fielder
t (01344) 303370

34 Bedford Terrace ★★★★
Self Catering
Lyme Bay Holidays
t (01297) 443363
e email@lymebayholidays.co.uk
w lymebayholidays.co.uk

4 Bedford Place ★★★
Self Catering
Contact: Mr Jonathan Bourbon
t (01308) 424160

4 Brydian Mews ★★★★
Self Catering
Contact: Stephen & Virginia Rutherford
t (01872) 870446
e sandvrutherford@hotmail.co.uk

Aviary Cottage ★★★
Self Catering
Dream Cottages
t (01305) 789000
e admin@dream-cottages.co.uk
w dream-cottages.co.uk

Captains House ★★★★
Self Catering
Dream Cottages
t (01305) 789000
e admin@dream-cottages.co.uk
w dream-cottages.co.uk

Chideock Cottage ★★★
Self Catering
t (01604) 457612

Church Cottage ★★★
Self Catering
Lyme Bay Holidays
t (01297) 443363
e email@lymebayholidays.co.uk
w lymebayholidays.co.uk

Clear View ★★★
Self Catering
Dream Cottages
t (01305) 789000
e admin@dream-cottages.co.uk
w dream-cottages.co.uk

Coneygar Bungalow ★★★
Self Catering
Contact: Mrs Janet Grimwood
t (01308) 485314

Fern Down Farm
★★★-★★★★ *Self Catering*
Contact: Mr David Solly
t (01300) 320810
e pdnsolly@hotmail.com

Ganders Cottage ★★★
Self Catering
Contact: Mrs Pauline Bale
t (01308) 424321
e bale@highwayfarm.co.uk
w highwayfarm.co.uk

Hayday ★★★★ *Self Catering*
Contact: Mrs Day
t (01308) 424438
w haydaycottage.co.uk

Lancombes House
★★★-★★★★ *Self Catering*
Contact: Mr Adrian Semmence
t (01308) 485375
e info@lancombes-house.co.uk
w lancombes-house.co.uk

Quayside Apartment
★★★★ *Self Catering*
Dream Cottages
t (01305) 789000
e admin@dream-cottages.co.uk
w dream-cottages.co.uk

Rudge Farm ★★★★
Self Catering
Contact: Mr Michael Hamer
t (01308) 482630
e enquiries@rudgefarm.co.uk
w rudgefarm.co.uk

Strongate Cottage ★★★
Self Catering
Contact: Mrs Sandra Huxter
t (01308) 488295
e sandra@thecharnleys.co.uk

Sunset ★★★ *Self Catering*
Contact: Mr Dan Walker
t (01308) 423363
e cdan@walker42.freeserve.co.uk

BRIMPSFIELD
Gloucestershire

Brimpsfield Farmhouse
★★★ *Self Catering*
Contact: Mrs Valerie Partridge
t (01452) 863568

BRISTOL
City of Bristol

The Coach House ★★★★
Self Catering
t (01275) 464635
w coachhousebackwell.co.uk

Premier Apartments Bristol
★★★-★★★★
Serviced Apartments
t (0117) 954 4800
w premierapartmentsbristol.com

Redland Flat ★★★
Self Catering
t (020) 8450 6761

SACO House – Victoria Street ★★★
Serviced Apartments
SACO Apartment
t (0117) 974 5936
e sarahbailey@sacaoapartments.co.uk
w sacoapartments.co.uk

SACO West India House
★★★★ *Serviced Apartments*
SACO Apartments
t (0117) 974 5936
e sarahbailey@sacaoapartments.co.uk
w sacoapartments.co.uk

St Matthews House ★★★
Self Catering
t (01454) 227321

BRIXHAM
Devon

1 Dolphin Court, Brixham
★★★★ *Self Catering*
Blue Chip Vacations
t (01803) 855282
e info@bluechipvacations.com
w bluechipvacations.com

1 Fishermans Loft, Brixham
★★★ *Self Catering*
Blue Chip Vacations
t (01803) 855282
e info@bluechipvacations.com
w bluechipvacations.com

1 Hosgood Steps ★★★★
Self Catering
Blue Chip Vacations
t (01803) 855282
e info@bluechipvacations.com
w bluechipvacations.com

10 Pochin House ★★★★
Self Catering
Blue Chip Vacations
t (01803) 855282
e info@bluechipvacations.com
w bluechipvacations.com

15 Moorings Reach
★★★★★ *Self Catering*
Blue Chip Vacations
t (01803) 855282
e info@bluechipvacations.com
w bluechipvacations.com

18 Moorings Reach
★★★★★ *Self Catering*
Blue Chip Vacations
t (01803) 855282
e info@bluechipvacations.com
w bluechipvacations.com

2 Dolphin Court ★★★★
Self Catering
Blue Chip Vacations
t (01803) 855282
e info@bluechipvacations.com
w bluechipvacations.com

2 Fishermans Loft ★★★
Self Catering
Blue Chip Vacations
t (01803) 855282
e info@bluechipvacations.com
w bluechipvacations.com

20 Moorings Reach ★★★★
Self Catering
Blue Chip Vacations
t (01803) 855282
e info@bluechipvacations.com
w bluechipvacations.com

28 Moorings Reach
★★★★★ *Self Catering*
Blue Chip Vacations
t (01803) 855282
e info@bluechipvacations.com
w bluechipvacations.com

3 Linden Court ★★★
Self Catering
Blue Chip Vacations
t (01803) 855282
e info@bluechipvacations.com
w bluechipvacations.com

3 Moorings Reach ★★★★★
Self Catering
Blue Chip Vacations
t (01803) 855282
e info@bluechipvacations.com
w bluechipvacations.com

31 Higher Street ★★★★
Self Catering
Blue Chip Vacations
t (01803) 855282
e info@bluechipvacations.com
w bluechipvacations.com

32 Moorings Reach
★★★★★ *Self Catering*
Blue Chip Vacations
t (01803) 855282
e info@bluechipvacations.com
w bluechipvacations.com

33 Southview ★★★★
Self Catering
Blue Chip Vacations
t (01803) 855282
e info@bluechipvacations.com
w bluechipvacations.com

4 Wall Park Road ★★★★
Self Catering
Blue Chip Vacations
t (01803) 855282
e info@bluechipvacations.com
w bluechipvacations.com

42 Moorings Reach
★★★★★ *Self Catering*
Blue Chip Vacations
t (01803) 855282
e info@bluechipvacations.com
w bluechipvacations.com

44 Moorings Reach
★★★★★ *Self Catering*
Blue Chip Vacations
t (01803) 855282
e info@bluechipvacations.com
w bluechipvacations.com

5 Harbour View Close ★★★
Self Catering
Blue Chip Vacations
t (01803) 855282
e info@bluechipvacations.com
w bluechipvacations.com

50 Moorings Reach
★★★★★ *Self Catering*
Blue Chip Vacations
t (01803) 855282
e info@bluechipvacations.com
w bluechipvacations.com

54 Moorings Reach
★★★★★ *Self Catering*
Blue Chip Vacations
t (01803) 855282
e info@bluechipvacations.com
w bluechipvacations.com

55 Moorings Reach ★★★★
Self Catering
Blue Chip Vacations
t (01803) 855282
e info@bluechipvacations.com
w bluechipvacations.com

56 Moorings Reach
★★★★★ *Self Catering*
Blue Chip Vacations
t (01803) 855282
e info@bluechipvacations.com
w bluechipvacations.com

57 Moorings Reach ★★★★
Self Catering
Blue Chip Vacations
t (01803) 855282
e info@bluechipvacations.com
w bluechipvacations.com

60 Moorings Reach
★★★★★ *Self Catering*
Blue Chip Vacations
t (01803) 855282
e info@bluechipvacations.com
w bluechipvacations.com

62 Moorings Reach
★★★★★ *Self Catering*
Blue Chip Vacations
t (01803) 855282
e info@bluechipvacations.com
w bluechipvacations.com

64 Moorings Reach
★★★★★ *Self Catering*
Blue Chip Vacations
t (01803) 855282
e info@bluechipvacations.com
w bluechipvacations.com

7 Marina Court ★★★
Self Catering
Blue Chip Vacations
t (01803) 855282
e info@bluechipvacations.com
w bluechipvacations.com

9 Dolphin Court ★★★★
Self Catering
Blue Chip Vacations
t (01803) 855282
e info@bluechipvacations.com
w bluechipvacations.com

9 Ranscombe Road ★★★★
Self Catering
Blue Chip Vacations
t (01803) 855282
e info@bluechipvacations.com
w bluechipvacations.com

Admirals Rest ★★★★
Self Catering
Holiday Homes and Cottages South West
t (01803) 299677
e holcotts@aol.com
w swcottages.co.uk

Anchorage ★★★
Self Catering
Brixham Holiday Homes Ltd
t (01803) 854187
e info@brixhamholidayhomes.co.uk
w brixhamholidayhomes.co.uk

Badgers Run ★★★★
Self Catering
Blue Chip Vacations
t (01803) 855282
e info@bluechipvacations.com
w bluechipvacations.com

Beech House ★★★★
Self Catering
Holiday Homes and Cottages South West
t (01803) 299677
e holcotts@aol.com
w swcottages.co.uk

Berry Head ★★★
Self Catering
Holiday Homes and Cottages South West
t (01803) 299677
e holcotts@aol.com
w swcottages.co.uk

Blue Chip Vacations – Moorings Reach ★★★★★
Self Catering
Blue Chip Vacations
t (01803) 855282
e info@bluechipvacations.com
w bluechipvacations.com

Blue Sails, Brixham ★★★★
Self Catering
Blue Chip Vacations
t (01803) 855282
e info@bluechipvacations.com
w bluechipvacations.com

The Bluenose ★★★
Self Catering
Brixham Holiday Homes Ltd
t (01803) 854187
e info@brixhamholidayhomes.co.uk
w brixhamholidayhomes.co.uk

Brandywine House ★★★★
Self Catering
Blue Chip Vacations
t (01803) 855282
e info@bluechipvacations.com
w bluechipvacations.com

Brixham Harbourside Holiday Flats ★★★
Self Catering
Contact: Mrs Helgard Stone
t (01803) 851919
e david.f.stone@btinternet.com
w brixham-harbourside-holiday-flats.com

Captain's Quarters and Gulls' Nest ★★★★★
Self Catering
Contact: Mrs Maggie Sycamore
t (01803) 855282
e info@bluechipvacations.com
w bluechipvacations.com

Castaway Cottage ★★★
Self Catering
Brixham Holiday Homes Ltd
t (01803) 854187
e info@brixhamholidayhomes.co.uk
w brixhamholidayhomes.co.uk

Celeste Cottage ★★★
Self Catering
Brixham Holiday Homes Ltd
t (01803) 854187
e info@brixhamholidayhomes.co.uk
w brixhamholidayhomes.co.uk

Charlotte Cottage ★★★★
Self Catering
Blue Chip Vacations
t (01803) 855282
e info@bluechipvacations.com
w bluechipvacations.com

Chiseldon Farm Annexe
★★★★ *Self Catering*
Brixham Holiday Homes Ltd
t (01803) 854187
e info@brixhamholidayhomes.co.uk
w brixhamholidayhomes.co.uk

Christley
Rating Applied For
Self Catering
Holiday Homes and Cottages South West
t (01803) 299677
e holcotts@aol.com
w swcottages.co.uk

Cliff Cottage ★★★
Self Catering
Brixham Holiday Homes Ltd
t (01803) 854187
e info@brixhamholidayhomes.co.uk
w brixhamholidayhomes.co.uk

Coastguard Cottage ★★★★
Self Catering
Brixham Holiday Homes Ltd
t (01803) 854187
e info@brixhamholidayhomes.co.uk
w brixhamholidayhomes.co.uk

Compass Cottage ★★★
Self Catering
Brixham Holiday Homes Ltd
t (01803) 854187
e info@brixhamholidayhomes.co.uk
w brixhamholidayhomes.co.uk

Cotehayes, Torquay ★★★★
Self Catering
Blue Chip Vacations
t (01803) 855282
e info@bluechipvacations.com
w bluechipvacations.com

The Crab Pot ★★★
Self Catering
Blue Chip Vacations
t (01803) 855282
e info@bluechipvacations.com
w bluechipvacations.com

Creels, Brixham ★★★★
Self Catering
Blue Chip Vacations
t (01803) 855282
e info@bluechipvacations.com
w bluechipvacations.com

Devon Court Holiday Flats
★★ *Self Catering*
Contact: Mr Robin Hooker
t (01803) 853748
e robinhooker@devoncoast.com
w devoncourt.info

Farthing Cottage ★★★
Self Catering
Brixham Holiday Homes Ltd
t (01803) 854187
e info@brixhamholidayhomes.co.uk
w brixhamholidayhomes.co.uk

Fernleigh ★★★★
Self Catering
Blue Chip Vacations
t (01803) 855282
e info@bluechipvacations.com
w bluechipvacations.com

Ferrymans Ensign Cottage
★★★ *Self Catering*
Blue Chip Vacations
t (01803) 855282
e info@bluechipvacations.com
w bluechipvacations.com

Fisherman's Cottage ★★★
Self Catering
Blue Chip Vacations
t (01803) 855282
e info@bluechipvacations.com
w bluechipvacations.com

Fortune Cottage ★★★★
Self Catering
Brixham Holiday Homes Ltd
t (01803) 854187
e info@brixhamholidayhomes.co.uk
w brixhamholidayhomes.co.uk

Galmpton Touring Park Cottages ★★★ *Self Catering*
Contact: Mrs Pam Collins
t (01803) 842066
e galmptontouringpark@hotmail.com
w gtpcottages.co.uk

Halcyon ★★★ *Self Catering*
Blue Chip Vacations
t (01803) 855282
e info@bluechipvacations.com
w bluechipvacations.com

Harbour House ★★★
Self Catering
t (01963) 440390

Harbour Reach ★★★
Self Catering
Contact: Mrs Jenny Pocock
t (0114) 236 4761
e enquiries@harbourreachholidays.co.uk
w harbourreachholidays.co.uk

Harbour View ★★★
Self Catering
Brixham Holiday Homes Ltd
t (01803) 854187
e info@brixhamholidayhomes.co.uk
w brixhamholidayhomes.co.uk

Harbour View – South West Cottages ★★★★
Self Catering
Holiday Homes and Cottages South West
t (01803) 299677
e holcotts@aol.com
w swcottages.co.uk

Heath Court ★★★
Self Catering
Brixham Holiday Homes Ltd
t (01803) 854187
e info@brixhamholidayhomes.co.uk
w brixhamholidayhomes.co.uk

High Hopes ★★★★
Self Catering
Brixham Holiday Homes Ltd
t (01803) 854187
e info@brixhamholidayhomes.co.uk
w brixhamholidayhomes.co.uk

High Life ★★★ *Self Catering*
Brixham Holiday Homes Ltd
t (01803) 854187
e info@brixhamholidayhomes.co.uk
w brixhamholidayhomes.co.uk

Hylands ★★★ *Self Catering*
Brixham Holiday Homes Ltd
t (01803) 854187
e info@brixhamholidayhomes.co.uk
w brixhamholidayhomes.co.uk

Jasmine Cottage ★★
Self Catering
Blue Chip Vacations
t (01803) 855282
e info@bluechipvacations.com
w bluechipvacations.com

Jasmine Cottage ★★★★
Self Catering
Brixham Holiday Homes Ltd
t (01803) 854187
e info@brixhamholidayhomes.co.uk
w brixhamholidayhomes.co.uk

Jericho Cottage, Brixham ★★★★ *Self Catering*
Blue Chip Vacations
t (01803) 855282
e info@bluechipvacations.com
w bluechipvacations.com

Keel House ★★ *Self Catering*
Brixham Holiday Homes Ltd
t (01803) 854187
e info@brixhamholidayhomes.co.uk
w brixhamholidayhomes.co.uk

Kynance ★★★★
Self Catering
Blue Chip Vacations
t (01803) 855282
e info@bluechipvacations.com
w bluechipvacations.com

Lantau, Brixham ★★★★★
Self Catering
Blue Chip Vacations
t (01803) 855282
e info@bluechipvacations.com
w bluechipvacations.com

Lantern Cottage ★★★
Self Catering
Brixham Holiday Homes Ltd
t (01803) 854187
e info@brixhamholidayhomes.co.uk
w brixhamholidayhomes.co.uk

Lighthouse View ★★★
Self Catering
Brixham Holiday Homes Ltd
t (01803) 854187
e info@brixhamholidayhomes.co.uk
w brixhamholidayhomes.co.uk

Linden Court ★★★★
Self Catering
Blue Chip Vacations
t (01803) 855282
e info@bluechipvacations.com
w bluechipvacations.com

Lobster Pot Cottage ★★
Self Catering
Brixham Holiday Homes Ltd
t (01803) 854187
e info@brixhamholidayhomes.co.uk
w brixhamholidayhomes.co.uk

Lorna ★★★ *Self Catering*
Brixham Holiday Homes Ltd
t (01803) 854187
e info@brixhamholidayhomes.co.uk
w brixhamholidayhomes.co.uk

Marina Watch ★★★★
Self Catering
Holiday Homes and Cottages South West
t (01803) 299677
e holcotts@aol.com
w swcottages.co.uk

The Mizzen ★★★
Self Catering
Brixham Holiday Homes Ltd
t (01803) 854187
e info@brixhamholidayhomes.co.uk
w brixhamholidayhomes.co.uk

Monkbarns Annexe ★★★
Self Catering
Brixham Holiday Homes Ltd
t (01803) 854187
e info@brixhamholidayhomes.co.uk
w brixhamholidayhomes.co.uk

Moonlit Waters ★★★
Self Catering
Brixham Holiday Homes Ltd
t (01803) 854187
e info@brixhamholidayhomes.co.uk
w brixhamholidayhomes.co.uk

Mooring Reach Townhouse 16 ★★★★★ *Self Catering*
Blue Chip Vacations
t (01803) 855282
e info@bluechipvacations.com
w bluechipvacations.com

Mooring Reach TownHouse 41 ★★★★★ *Self Catering*
Blue Chip Vacations
t (01803) 855282
e info@bluechipvacations.com
w bluechipvacations.com

Newlands ★★★★
Self Catering
Brixham Holiday Homes Ltd
t (01803) 854187
e info@brixhamholidayhomes.co.uk
w brixhamholidayhomes.co.uk

North Winds ★★★★
Self Catering
Brixham Holiday Homes Ltd
t (01803) 854187
e info@brixhamholidayhomes.co.uk
w brixhamholidayhomes.co.uk

The Old Boat House ★★★★
Self Catering
Blue Chip Vacations
t (01803) 855282
e info@bluechipvacations.com
w bluechipvacations.com

Overquay Cottage ★★★
Self Catering
Contact: Mrs Moira Withey
t (01803) 882337
e info@ranscombehousehotel.co.uk
w ranscombehousehotel.co.uk

Oyster Catcher ★★★
Self Catering
Blue Chip Vacations
t (01803) 855282
e info@bluechipvacations.com
w bluechipvacations.com

Palm Cottage ★★★★
Self Catering
Blue Chip Vacations
t (01803) 855282
e info@bluechipvacations.com
w bluechipvacations.com

Pilgrim's Cottage ★★★★
Self Catering
Brixham Holiday Homes Ltd
t (01803) 854187
e info@brixhamholidayhomes.co.uk
w brixhamholidayhomes.co.uk

Pilot's Perch ★★★★
Self Catering
Blue Chip Vacations
t (01803) 855282
e info@bluechipvacations.com
w bluechipvacations.com

Pilots Rest, Brixham ★★★★★ *Self Catering*
Blue Chip Vacations
t (01803) 855282
e info@bluechipvacations.com
w bluechipvacations.com

Sea View Cottage
Rating Applied For
Self Catering
Holiday Homes and Cottages South West
t (01803) 299677
e holcotts@aol.com
w swcottages.co.uk

Sea View Terrace ★★★
Self Catering
Brixham Holiday Homes Ltd
t (01803) 854187
e info@brixhamholidayhomes.co.uk
w brixhamholidayhomes.co.uk

Seacat Cottage ★★★★
Self Catering
Holiday Homes and Cottages South West
t (01803) 299677
e holcotts@aol.com
w swcottages.co.uk

Seascape ★★★★
Self Catering
Blue Chip Vacations
t (01803) 855282
e info@bluechipvacations.com
w bluechipvacations.com

Seaway ★★★★ *Self Catering*
Blue Chip Vacations
t (01803) 855282
e info@bluechipvacations.com
w bluechipvacations.com

Serendipity ★★★
Self Catering
Holiday Homes and Cottages South West
t (01803) 299677
e holcotts@aol.com
w swcottages.co.uk

Skerrie Cottage ★★★
Self Catering
Brixham Holiday Homes Ltd
t (01803) 854187
e info@brixhamholidayhomes.co.uk
w brixhamholidayhomes.co.uk

Spyglass ★★★ *Self Catering*
Brixham Holiday Homes Ltd
t (01803) 854187
e info@brixhamholidayhomes.co.uk
w brixhamholidayhomes.co.uk

Station Hill
Rating Applied For
Self Catering
Holiday Homes and Cottages South West
t (01803) 299677
e holcotts@aol.com
w swcottages.co.uk

Sunset Cottage ★★★
Self Catering
Brixham Holiday Homes Ltd
t (01803) 854187
e info@brixhamholidayhomes.co.uk
w brixhamholidayhomes.co.uk

Top Gallant ★★★★
Self Catering
Brixham Holiday Homes Ltd
t (01803) 854187
e info@brixhamholidayhomes.co.uk
w brixhamholidayhomes.co.uk

Torbay Holiday Chalets ★★
Self Catering
Contact: Mr & Mrs Martyn & Jane Swift
t (01803) 853313

Torbay House ★★★
Self Catering
Brixham Holiday Homes Ltd
t (01803) 854187
e info@brixhamholidayhomes.co.uk
w brixhamholidayhomes.co.uk

Torfrey Cottage ★★★
Self Catering
Brixham Holiday Homes Ltd
t (01803) 854187
e info@brixhamholidayhomes.co.uk
w brixhamholidayhomes.co.uk

Trade Winds ★★★
Self Catering
Brixham Holiday Homes Ltd
t (01803) 854187
e info@brixhamholidayhomes.co.uk
w brixhamholidayhomes.co.uk

Tranquillity ★★★
Self Catering
Brixham Holiday Homes Ltd
t (01803) 854187
e info@brixhamholidayhomes.co.uk
w brixhamholidayhomes.co.uk

We Want A Holiday
Approved Caravan Holiday Home
Contact: Ms Karyn Easton
t (01803) 853465
e karyn@paranormality.com
w wewantaholiday.co.uk

White Cottage ★★★★★
Self Catering
Brixham Holiday Homes Ltd
t (01803) 854187
e info@brixhamholidayhomes.co.uk
w brixhamholidayhomes.co.uk

White Sails ★★★
Self Catering
Brixham Holiday Homes Ltd
t (01803) 854187
e info@brixhamholidayhomes.co.uk
w brixhamholidayhomes.co.uk

BROAD CAMPDEN
Gloucestershire

Green Cottage ★★★★
Self Catering
Campden Cottages
t (01386) 593315
e info@campdencottages.co.uk
w campdencottages.co.uk

Lion Cottage ★★★
Self Catering
Contact: Mrs Barbara Rawcliffe
t (01386) 840077

BROADCLYST
Devon

Hue's Piece, Broadclyst
★★★★ *Self Catering*
Contact: Mrs Anna Hamlyn
t (01392) 466720
e annahamlyn@paynes-farm.co.uk
w paynes-farm.co.uk

BROADHEMBURY
Devon

Hembury Court ★★★★★
Self Catering
Contact: Mr & Mrs Robert & Amanda Persey
t (01404) 841444
e persey@upcottfarm.fsnet.co.uk
w hembury-court-barns.co.uk

BROADMAYNE
Dorset

Fryermayne Tallet ★★★★
Self Catering
Contact: Mrs Ruth Goldsack
t (01305) 852414
e rugold@lineone.net

Holcombe Valley Cottages
★★★ *Self Catering*
Contact: Mr & Mrs Peter & Jane Davies
t (01305) 852817
e holvalcots@aol.com
w holcombe-cottages.co.uk

BROADOAK
Dorset

Grazeland Cottage ★★★★
Self Catering
Dream Cottages
t (01305) 789000
e admin@dream-cottages.co.uk
w dream-cottages.co.uk

Stoke Mill Farm ★★★
Self Catering
Contact: Mrs Anthea Bay
t (01308) 868036
w stokemillholidays.co.uk

BROADWELL
Gloucestershire

April Cottage ★★★★
Self Catering
t (01629) 814440

BROADWINDSOR
Dorset

Broadmead House ★★★★
Self Catering
Contact: Mr David Guilor
t (01308) 459851
e broadmeadhouse.enquiries@virgin.net
w broadmeadhouse.co.uk

BROADWOOD KELLY
Devon

Colehouse Farm ★★★★★
Self Catering
Contact: Mrs Louise Jackson
t (01837) 83230
e info@colehousefarm-devon.co.uk
w colehousefarm-devon.co.uk

BROMHAM
Wiltshire

Park Farm Cottages ★★★
Self Catering
Contact: Mrs Valerie Bourne
t (01380) 850966
e valandtom2003@aol.com
w park-farm-cottages.co.uk

Wayside Lodges, Chittoe
★★★ *Self Catering*
Contact: Mr Jonathan Seed
t (01380) 850695 & 07770 774463
e mail@jandlseed.co.uk
w waysideofwiltshire.co.uk

BROMPTON REGIS
Somerset

The Studio by the Lake
★★★ *Self Catering*
Contact: Mrs Barbra Buckley
t (01398) 371112
e buckley@hillfarmhouse.freeserve.co.uk
w thestudiobythelake.co.uk

Weatherham Farm Cottages
★★★★ *Self Catering*
Contact: Mrs Anne Caldwell
t (01398) 371303
e enquiries@weatherhamfarm.co.uk
w weatherhamfarm.co.uk

BROMSBERROW HEATH
Gloucestershire

Honeysuckle Cottage
★★★★ *Self Catering*
Contact: Mrs Wendy Hooper
t (01531) 650360
e ws.hooper@btopenworld.com
w honeysuckle-cottage-rent.co.uk

BROUGHTON GIFFORD
Wiltshire

Church Farm Holiday Cottages ★★★★
Self Catering
Contact: Mrs Sharon Hooper
t (01225) 783413

BRUTON
Somerset

Redlynch Farmhouse
★★★★ *Self Catering*
Contact: Mrs A Froud
t (01749) 812795
e angelafroud@hotmail.com

BRYHER
Isles of Scilly

Atlanta Holiday Accommodation ★★★
Self Catering
Contact: Mrs Gillian Langdon
t (01720) 422823

Glenhope & Atlanta
★★★–★★★★ *Self Catering*
Contact: Mrs Amy Langdon
t (01720) 423136
e langdon.glenhope@virgin.net

Hebe, Fernside & Shippen Cottage
Rating Applied For
Self Catering
Contact: Mrs Kristine Taylor
t (01720) 422862
w bryher-ios.co.uk/vf

Hillside Farm ★★★★
Self Catering
Contact: Mrs Ruth Jenkins
t (01720) 423156
e ruthbryher@aol.com
w bryher-ios.co.uk/hf

South Hill ★★★ *Self Catering*
Contact: Mrs Bennett
t (01720) 422411
e marianbennett@excite.co.uk

The White House ★★★
Self Catering
Contact: Mr Bushell
t (01720) 422010

BUCKFASTLEIGH
Devon

Well Barn
Rating Applied For
Self Catering
Contact: Ms Bella Rogers
t (01803) 762409
w wellbarn.com

BUCKLAND BREWER
Devon

Adipit ★★★★ *Self Catering*
Powells Cottage Holidays
t (01834) 812791
e info@powells.co.uk
w powells.co.uk

BUCKLAND FILLEIGH
Devon

Modbury Cottage ★★★★
Self Catering
Marsdens Cottage Holidays
t (01271) 813777
e holidays@marsdens.co.uk
w marsdens.co.uk

BUCKLAND IN THE MOOR
Devon

Pine Lodge ★★★
Self Catering
Holiday Homes and Cottages South West
t (01803) 299677
e holcotts@aol.com
w swcottages.co.uk

BUCKLAND NEWTON
Dorset

Church Farm Stables
★★★★ *Self Catering*
Contact: Mr & Mrs Neville Archer
t (01300) 345315
e enquiries@staydorset.co.uk
w staydorset.co.uk

Domineys Cottages, Buckland Newton ★★★★
Self Catering
Contact: Mrs Jeanette Gueterbock
t (01300) 345295
e cottages@domineys.com
w domineys.com

BUDE
Cornwall

4 Brightlands Apartments
★★★ *Self Catering*
Contact: Mrs Gill Tawse
t (01428) 682565
e gilliantawse@btinternet.com
w brightlandsbude.co.uk

5 & 11 Brightlands ★★★
Self Catering
Contact: Mrs Lynn Western
t (020) 8319 3508
e brightlands511@btinternet.com
w brightlands511.co.uk

Atlantic View Bungalows
★★★ *Self Catering*
Contact: Mr & Mrs Chris & Brenda Raven
t (01288) 361716
e enquiries@atlanticview.co.uk
w atlanticview.co.uk

Bithecutt Cottage ★★★★
Self Catering
Contact: Ms Christine Jurkiewicz
t (01288) 352199
e chrisjurk@aol.com

Bramble Cottage ★★★★
Self Catering
Contact: Ms Jane Campbell
t (023) 8084 4425
e jane.campbell@talk21.com
w bramblecottage.net

Broomhill Manor Country Estate ★★★★–★★★★★
Self Catering
Contact: Mr Alan Biggs
t (01288) 352940
e admin@broomhillmanor.co.uk
w broomhillmanor.co.uk

Captains Cottage ★★★★
Self Catering
Contact: Sarah Debonaire
t (01288) 354542
e enquiries@brendonarms.co.uk
w brendonarms.co.uk

Cherril ★★★ *Self Catering*
Holiday Homes and Cottages South West
t (01803) 299677
e holcotts@aol.com
w swcottages.co.uk

Forda Lodges & Cottages
★★★★-★★★★★
Self Catering
Contact: Mr & Mrs Jim & Gillian Chibbett
t (01288) 321413
e info@forda.co.uk
w forda.co.uk

Glebe House Cottages Limited ★★★★ *Self Catering*
Contact: Mr & Mrs James Varley
t (01288) 381272
e etc@glebehousecottages.co.uk
w glebehousecottages.co.uk

Harbour Loft ★★★
Self Catering
Contact: Maggie & Terry Martin
t (01288) 352082
e terence.r.martin@googlemail.com
w harbourloft.co.uk

Hunters Lodge ★★★★★
Self Catering
Contact: Mrs Denise Congdon
Kitsham Holidays
t (01288) 341336
e holidays@kitsham.co.uk
w kitsham.co.uk

Ivyleaf Barton Cottages
★★★★-★★★★★
Self Catering
Contact: Mr Robert Barrett
t (01288) 321237 & 07771 908108
e ivyleafcottages@aol.com
w ivyleafbarton.co.uk

Ivyleaf Combe ★★★★
Self Catering
Contact: Mr & Mrs Tony & Kathy Cheeseman
t (01288) 321323
e tony@ivyleafcombe.com
w ivyleafcombe.com

Kennacott Court
★★★★-★★★★★
Self Catering
Contact: Mr & Mrs Myers
t (01288) 362000
w kennacottcourt.co.uk

Langfield Manor ★★★
Self Catering
Contact: Suzanne Walker
t (01288) 352415
e langfieldmanor@btconnect.com
w langfieldmanor.co.uk

Little Orchard ★★★
Self Catering
Contact: Mrs Patricia Gosney
t (01288) 355617
e den_oldorchard@lineone.net

Lower Northcott ★★★★
Self Catering
Contact: Mr & Mrs C Trewin
t (01288) 361494
e mary@courtfarm-holidays.co.uk
w courtfarm-holidays.co.uk

Mornish Apartments
★★★★ *Self Catering*
Contact: Mr & Mrs John & Julia Hilder
t (01288) 352972
e mornishholidays@btconnect.com
w mornishapartments.co.uk

Neet Cottage ★★★ *Self Catering & Serviced Apartments*
Contact: Mr & Mrs Ian & Carolyn Harrison
t (01288) 361877
e widemouthfarm@tiscali.co.uk
w widemouth-farm.co.uk

Old Lifeboat House ★★★
Self Catering
Contact: Mrs Sarah Debonnaire
t (01288) 354542
e enquiries@brendonarms.co.uk
w brendonarms.co.uk

One4Two ★★★★★
Self Catering
Contact: Kathy Lawrence
t 07852 245967
e one4two@btconnect.com
w one4two.co.uk

Penhalt Farm ★★★
Self Catering
Contact: Mr & Mrs Marks
t (01288) 361210
e denandjennie@penhaltfarm.fsnet.co.uk
w penhaltfarm.co.uk

Penrhyn ★★★ *Self Catering*
Contact: Mr Brett
t (01288) 355039

Quinceborough Farm
★★★★ *Self Catering*
Farm & Cottage Holidays
t (01237) 459827
e enquiries@farmcott.co.uk
w holidaycottages.co.uk

St Annes Bungalow ★★★
Self Catering
Contact: Mrs Gwendoline Britten
t (024) 7669 2410

Stable Cottages ★★★
Self Catering
Contact: Ms Gregory
t (01288) 354237

West Woolley Barns ★★★★
Self Catering
Contact: Mr David Tidman
t (01288) 331202
e info@westwoolleyfarm.co.uk
w westwoolleyfarm.co.uk

Wild Pigeon Holidays ★★★
Self Catering
Contact: Mrs Anne Longley
t (01288) 353839

Woodlands Farm Holidays
★★★★-★★★★★
Self Catering
Contact: Ms Sandra Webb
t (01288) 331689
e woodlandsholiday@aol.com
w woodlandsfarmholidays.co.uk

Wooldown Farm Cottages, Marhamchurch
★★★★-★★★★★
Self Catering
Contact: Mr & Mrs Susan Blewett
t (01288) 361216
e holidays@wooldown.com
w wooldown.com

BUDLEIGH SALTERTON
Devon

Christophers ★★★★★
Self Catering
Contact: Mr & Mrs James Crill
t (01395) 567135
e info@thethatchedcottagecompany.co.uk
w thethatchedcottagecompany.co.uk

Pebble Cottage ★★★★★
Self Catering
Contact: Mrs S Walker
t (01395) 567676
e info@thethatchedcottagecompany.co.uk
w thethatchedcottagecompany.co.uk

Sunnymead ★★★★
Self Catering
Sweetcombe Cottage Holidays
t (01395) 512130
e enquiries@sweetcombe-ch.co.uk
w sweetcombe-ch.co.uk

BUDOCK WATER
Cornwall

Overdene ★★★ *Self Catering*
Cornish Holiday Cottages
t (01326) 250339
e emily@cornishholidaycottages.net
w cornishholidaycottages.net

Penmorvah Cottages
★★★★ *Self Catering*
Contact: Mr & Mrs Risely
t (01326) 250277
e reception@penmorvah.co.uk
w penmorvah.co.uk

BUGLE
Cornwall

Higher Menadew Farm Cottages ★★★★-★★★★★
Self Catering
Contact: Mr & Mrs Higman
t (01726) 850310
e mail@stayingincornwall.com
w stayingincornwall.com

BURCOMBE
Wiltshire

The Old Vicarage ★★★★
Self Catering
t (01722) 743154

BURCOTT
Somerset

Burcott Inn ★★★
Self Catering
t (01749) 673874
w burcottinn.co.uk

BURLAWN
Cornwall

Pengelly Farm Caravan
Approved Caravan Holiday Home
Contact: Mrs Estelle Hodge
t (01208) 814217
e hodgepete@hotmail.com
w pengellyfarm.co.uk

Wren Cottage ★★
Self Catering
Harbour Holidays
t (01841) 533402
e contact@harbourholidays.co.uk
w harbourholidays.co.uk

BURNHAM-ON-SEA
Somerset

14 Cheddar Close *Approved Caravan Holiday Home*
Contact: Mr Gary Ballinger
t (01453) 763566

Hurn Farm ★★★
Self Catering
Contact: Mrs Holdom
t (01278) 751418
e hurnfarm@hurnfarmcottages.co.uk

Kingsway ★★★ *Self Catering*
Contact: Mr Simon Morris
t (01237) 479146
e simon@holidaycottages.co.uk

Little Walton ★★★★
Self Catering
Contact: Mrs Patricia Harris
t (01278) 780034
e waltonhousebnb@aol.com
w waltonhousebnb.co.uk

Prospect Farm
★★★-★★★★ *Self Catering*
Contact: Mrs Gillian Wall
Prospect Farm Holidays
t (01278) 760507

Stoddens Farm Holiday Cottages
Rating Applied For
Self Catering
Contact: Mrs Anna Penfold
t (01278) 786564
e stoddens-cottage@btconnect.com

BURROWBRIDGE
Somerset

Hillview ★★★ *Self Catering*
Contact: Mrs Rosalind Griffiths
t (01823) 698308

BURTON
Dorset

Brook End ★★★★
Self Catering
Contact: Mr Martin Bateman
t (01202) 252572
e lynne.bateman@hotmail.co.uk
w hornbeams.net

BURTON BRADSTOCK
Dorset

Apple Tree Cottage ★★★
Self Catering
Dream Cottages
t (01305) 789000
e admin@dream-cottages.co.uk
w dream-cottages.co.uk

Berwick House ★★★★
Self Catering
Dream Cottages
t (01305) 789000
e admin@dream-cottages.co.uk
w dream-cottages.co.uk

Chesil Beach Lodge ★★★
Self Catering
Contact: Mrs Loveridge
t (01308) 897428
e enquiries@chesilbeachlodge.co.uk
w chesilbeachlodge.co.uk

Cliff Farm ★★★ *Self Catering*
Dream Cottages
t (01305) 789000
e admin@dream-cottages.co.uk
w dream-cottages.co.uk

Cogden Cottages ★★★
Self Catering
Contact: Mr Lee Connolly
t (01308) 897223
e oldcoastguard@hotmail.com
w cogdencottages.co.uk

The Doves ★★★
Self Catering
Dream Cottages
t (01305) 789000
e admin@dream-cottages.co.uk
w dream-cottages.co.uk

Fig Tree Cottage ★★★
Self Catering
Dream Cottages
t (01305) 789000
e admin@dream-cottages.co.uk
w dream-cottages.co.uk

Hillview Bungalow ★★★
Self Catering
Dream Cottages
t (01305) 789000
e admin@dream-cottages.co.uk
w dream-cottages.co.uk

Jasmine Cottage ★★★
Self Catering
Dream Cottages
t (01305) 789000
e admin@dream-cottages.co.uk
w dream-cottages.co.uk

Lilac Cottage ★★★★
Self Catering
Dream Cottages
t (01305) 789000
e admin@dream-cottages.co.uk
w dream-cottages.co.uk

Little Berwick ★★★
Self Catering
Dream Cottages
t (01305) 789000
e admin@dream-cottages.co.uk
w dream-cottages.co.uk

Manor Lodge ★★★★★
Self Catering
Lyme Bay Holidays
t (01297) 443363
e email@lymebayholidays.co.uk
w lymebayholidays.co.uk

Poppa's Cottage ★★
Self Catering
Dream Cottages
t (01305) 789000
e admin@dream-cottages.co.uk
w dream-cottages.co.uk

Quay Town House ★★★★★
Self Catering
Dream Cottages
t (01305) 789000
e admin@dream-cottages.co.uk
w dream-cottages.co.uk

Rolling Hills ★★★
Self Catering
Dream Cottages
t (01305) 789000
e admin@dream-cottages.co.uk
w dream-cottages.co.uk

BUSH
Cornwall

Willow Valley Holiday park ★★★ *Self Catering*
t (01288) 353104

BUTCOMBE
Somerset

Butcombe Farm ★★★
Self Catering
t (01761) 462380
w butcombe-farm.demon.co.uk

BUTLEIGH WOOTTON
Somerset

Little Broadway ★★
Self Catering
Contact: Mrs Mary Butt
t (01458) 442824

CALLINGTON
Cornwall

8 Manor Combe ★★★
Self Catering
Blue Chip Vacations
t (01803) 855282
e info@bluechipvacations.com
w bluechipvacations.com

Berrio Mill Farm Holiday Cottages ★★★★
Self Catering
Contact: Ivan & Carolyn Callanan
t (01579) 363252
e enquiries@berriomill.co.uk
w berriomill.co.uk

Cadson Manor Farm ★★★★
Self Catering
Contact: Mrs Brenda Crago
t (01579) 383969
e brenda.crago@btclick.com
w cadsonmanor.co.uk

Valley Lodge
Rating Applied For
Self Catering
Holiday Homes and Cottages South West
t (01803) 299677
e holcotts@aol.com
w swcottages.co.uk

CAMBORNE
Cornwall

Dromona ★★★ *Self Catering*
Contact: Mr & Mrs Brian & Elizabeth Jackson
t (01209) 713644
e elizabeth@dromona.fsnet.co.uk

Mill Cottage ★★★★
Self Catering
t (01209) 832276
e drymmill@btinternet.com
w drymmill.com

CAMELFORD
Cornwall

2 Chapel Court ★★★
Self Catering
Cornish Horizons Holiday Cottages
t (01841) 533331
e cottages@cornishhorizons.co.uk
w cornishhorizons.co.uk

Culloden Farmhouse ★★★★ *Self Catering*
Contact: Mr & Mrs Balaam
t (01840) 211128
e debbie_balaam@msn.com
w cullodenfarmhouse.co.uk

Helsbury Park ★★★★★
Self Catering
Contact: Mr David Wilson
t (01840) 211726
e info@helsburypark.co.uk
w helsburypark.co.uk

Juliots Well Cottages ★★★★ *Self Catering*
Contact: Mr & Mrs Boundy
t (01840) 213302
e juliotswell@holidaysincornwall.net
w holidaysincornwall.net

Swallows Cottage ★★★★
Self Catering
Contact: Mr & Mrs Elsey
t (01840) 212212
e info@swallows-cottage-boscastle.co.uk
w swallows-cottage-boscastle.co.uk

CANNARDS GRAVE
Somerset

Enniskerry ★★★★
Self Catering
Contact: Mrs Gillian Love
t (01344) 623079
e gandt@thelovescottage.co.uk
w thelovescottage.co.uk

CANNINGTON
Somerset

The Courtyard ★★★★–★★★★★
Self Catering
Contact: Mrs Dyer
t (01278) 653442
e dyerfarm@aol.com
w dyerfarm.co.uk

CANNOP
Gloucestershire

Woodside Cottage ★★★
Self Catering
Contact: Helen R Evans
Evans Holiday Cottages
t (01594) 861119
e helen@peakedrockscottage.fsnet.co.uk
w evansholidays.co.uk

CANONSTOWN
Cornwall

Eider House ★★★★
Self Catering
Cornish Gems
t 0844 800 2813
w cornishgems.com/holiday-cottages/the_eider_house.html

CARBIS BAY
Cornwall

10 Carrack Gladden ★★★
Self Catering
Ayia Napa Holidays
t (01736) 757237
e info@carbisbayretreats.co.uk
w carbisbayretreats.co.uk

12 Carrack Gladden ★★★
Self Catering
Ayia Napa Holidays
t (01736) 757237
e info@carbisbayretreats.co.uk
w carbisbayretreats.co.uk

15 Carrack Gladden ★★★★
Self Catering
Ayia Napa Holidays
t (01736) 757237
e info@carbisbayretreats.co.uk
w carbisbayretreats.co.uk

16 tryhornek ★★★★
Self Catering
Ayia Napa Holidays
t (01736) 757237
e info@carbisbayretreats.co.uk
w carbisbayretreats.co.uk

2 Atlantic Watch ★★★★
Self Catering
Ayia Napa Holidays
t (01736) 757237
e info@carbisbayretreats.co.uk
w carbisbayretreats.co.uk

20 Gwel Marten ★★★★
Self Catering
t (01736) 794686

205 Carbis Beach Apartments ★★★★
Self Catering
Ayia Napa Holidays
t (01736) 757237
e info@carbisbayretreats.co.uk
w carbisbayretreats.co.uk

206 Carbis Beach Apartments ★★★★
Self Catering
Ayia Napa Holidays
t (01736) 757237
e info@carbisbayretreats.co.uk
w carbisbayretreats.co.uk

3 Carrack Gladden ★★★
Self Catering
Ayia Napa Holidays
t (01736) 757237
e info@carbisbayretreats.co.uk
w carbisbayretreats.co.uk

3 Spinnakers ★★★★★
Self Catering
Ayia Napa Holidays
t (01736) 757237
e info@carbisbayretreats.co.uk
w carbisbayretreats.co.uk

38 Compass Point ★★★★
Self Catering
Ayia Napa Holidays
t (01736) 757237
e info@carbisbayretreats.co.uk
w carbisbayretreats.co.uk

4 Carrack Gladden ★★★★
Self Catering
Ayia Napa Holidays
t (01736) 757237
e info@carbisbayretreats.co.uk
w carbisbayretreats.co.uk

4 Riviera Apartments
★★★★ *Self Catering*
Ayia Napa Holidays
t (01736) 757237
e info@carbisbayretreats.co.uk
w carbisbayretreats.co.uk

5 Carrack Gladden ★★★
Self Catering
Ayia Napa Holidays
t (01736) 757237
e info@carbisbayretreats.co.uk
w carbisbayretreats.co.uk

7 Carrack Gladden ★★★
Self Catering
Ayia Napa Holidays
t (01736) 757237
e info@carbisbayretreats.co.uk
w carbisbayretreats.co.uk

7 Riviera Apartment ★★★
Self Catering
Ayia Napa Holidays
t (01736) 757237
e info@carbisbayretreats.co.uk
w carbisbayretreats.co.uk

8 Riviera Apartments
★★★★ *Self Catering*
Ayia Napa Holidays
t (01736) 757237
e info@carbisbayretreats.co.uk
w carbisbayretreats.co.uk

Aquamarine ★★★★★ *Self Catering & Serviced Apartments*
Carbis Bay Holidays
t 0800 012 2241
e enquiries@carbisbayholidays.co.uk
w carbisbayholidays.co.uk

Azure ★★★★★ *Self Catering*
Carbis Bay Holidays
t 0800 012 2241
e enquiries@carbisbayholidays.co.uk
w carbisbayholidays.co.uk

Bay View ★★★★★
Self Catering
Carbis Bay Holidays
t 0800 012 2241
e enquiries@carbisbayholidays.co.uk
w carbisbayholidays.co.uk

Beach Retreat ★★★★★
Self Catering
Carbis Bay Holidays
t 0800 012 2241
e enquiries@carbisbayholidays.co.uk
w carbisbayholidays.co.uk

Brambles Apartment ★★★
Self Catering
Contact: Mrs Suzanne Wild
t (01736) 793667
e brambles05@tiscali.co.uk

Cardinal Point ★★★★★
Self Catering
Carbis Bay Holidays
t 0800 012 2241
e enquiries@carbisbayholidays.co.uk
w carbisbayholidays.co.uk

Castaways ★★★★★
Self Catering
Carbis Bay Holidays
t 0800 012 2241
e enquiries@carbisbayholidays.co.uk
w carbisbayholidays.co.uk

Celeste ★★★★★
Self Catering
Carbis Bay Holidays
t 0800 012 2241
e enquiries@carbisbayholidays.co.uk
w carbisbayholidays.co.uk

Chapel View ★★★★★
Self Catering
Ayia Napa Holidays
t (01736) 757237
e info@carbisbayretreats.co.uk
w carbisbayretreats.co.uk

Dolphin Watch ★★★★ *Self Catering & Serviced Apartments*
Carbis Bay Holidays
t 0800 012 2241
e enquiries@carbisbayholidays.co.uk
w carbisbayholidays.co.uk

Fernhill Lodge ★★★★★
Self Catering
Carbis Bay Holidays
t 0800 012 2241
e enquiries@carbisbayholidays.co.uk
w carbisbayholidays.co.uk

Gennaker ★★★★★
Self Catering
Carbis Bay Holidays
t 0800 012 2241
e enquiries@carbisbayholidays.co.uk
w carbisbayholidays.co.uk

Genoa ★★★★★
Self Catering
Carbis Bay Holidays
t 0800 012 2241
e enquiries@carbisbayholidays.co.uk
w carbisbayholidays.co.uk

Godrevy View ★★★★
Self Catering
Carbis Bay Holidays
t 0800 012 2241
e enquiries@carbisbayholidays.co.uk
w carbisbayholidays.co.uk

Ivory ★★★★★ *Self Catering*
Carbis Bay Holidays
t 0800 012 2241
e enquiries@carbisbayholidays.co.uk
w carbisbayholidays.co.uk

James ★★★★ *Self Catering*
Contact: Mr & Mrs Jamie & Felicity Robertson
t (01736) 794718
e info@jamiesstives.co.uk
w jamiesstives.co.uk

Lodge 1A Carrack Gladden
★★★ *Self Catering*
Ayia Napa Holidays
t (01736) 757237
e info@carbisbayretreats.co.uk
w carbisbayretreats.co.uk

Lodge 1B Carrack Gladden
★★★ *Self Catering*
Ayia Napa Holidays
t (01736) 757237
e info@carbisbayretreats.co.uk
w carbisbayretreats.co.uk

Longships ★★★★
Self Catering
Carbis Bay Holidays
t 0800 012 2241
e enquiries@carbisbayholidays.co.uk
w carbisbayholidays.co.uk

The Lookout ★★★★★
Self Catering
Golds Coastal Holidays
t (01543) 274424
e enquiries@golds-hire.co.uk
w golds-hire.co.uk

Moonstone ★★★★★
Self Catering
Carbis Bay Holidays
t 0800 012 2241
e enquiries@carbisbayholidays.co.uk
w carbisbayholidays.co.uk

Morvah ★★★★★
Self Catering
Carbis Bay Holidays
t 0800 012 2241
e enquiries@carbisbayholidays.co.uk
w carbisbayholidays.co.uk

The Penthouse ★★★★
Self Catering
Carbis Bay Holidays
t 0800 012 2241
e enquiries@carbisbayholidays.co.uk
w carbisbayholidays.co.uk

Portside ★★★★★
Self Catering
Carbis Bay Holidays
t 0800 012 2241
e enquiries@carbisbayholidays.co.uk
w carbisbayholidays.co.uk

Sandpiper ★★★★★
Self Catering
Carbis Bay Holidays
t 0800 012 2241
e enquiries@carbisbayholidays.co.uk
w carbisbayholidays.co.uk

Sapphire ★★★★★
Self Catering
Carbis Bay Holidays
t 0800 012 2241
e enquiries@carbisbayholidays.co.uk
w carbisbayholidays.co.uk

Sea Breeze ★★★★
Self Catering
Carbis Bay Holidays
t 0800 012 2241
e enquiries@carbisbayholidays.co.uk
w carbisbayholidays.co.uk

Silver Sands ★★★★★
Self Catering
Carbis Bay Holidays
t 0800 012 2241
e enquiries@carbisbayholidays.co.uk
w carbisbayholidays.co.uk

Slipstream ★★★★★
Self Catering
Carbis Bay Holidays
t 0800 012 2241
e enquiries@carbisbayholidays.co.uk
w carbisbayholidays.co.uk

Sowena ★★★★★
Self Catering
Carbis Bay Holidays
t 0800 012 2241
e enquiries@carbisbayholidays.co.uk
w carbisbayholidays.co.uk

Starboard ★★★★★
Self Catering
Carbis Bay Holidays
t 0800 012 2241
e enquiries@carbisbayholidays.co.uk
w carbisbayholidays.co.uk

Turquarze ★★★★★
Self Catering
Carbis Bay Holidays
t 0800 012 2241
e enquiries@carbisbayholidays.co.uk
w carbisbayholidays.co.uk

Viridian ★★★★★
Self Catering
Carbis Bay Holidays
t 0800 012 2241
e enquiries@carbisbayholidays.co.uk
w carbisbayholidays.co.uk

Waves ★★★★ *Self Catering*
Carbis Bay Holidays
t 0800 012 2241
e enquiries@carbisbayholidays.co.uk
w carbisbayholidays.co.uk

White Horses
Rating Applied For
Self Catering
Carbis Bay Holidays
t 0800 012 2241
e enquiries@carbisbayholidays.co.uk
w carbisbayholidays.co.uk

White Sails ★★★★★
Self Catering
Carbis Bay Holidays
t 0800 012 2241
e enquiries@carbisbayholidays.co.uk
w carbisbayholidays.co.uk

White Water
Rating Applied For
Self Catering
Carbis Bay Holidays
t 0800 012 2241
e enquiries@carbisbayholidays.co.uk
w carbisbayholidays.co.uk

CARDINHAM
Cornwall

Welltown ★★★★
Self Catering
Contact: Mr & Mrs David & Angela Willams
t (01208) 821653
e daveange@waitrose.com
w bodminmoor.co.uk/welltown

CARLYON BAY
Cornwall

The Pavillion ★★★★★
Self Catering
Contact: Mr Jeff Taylor
t (01726) 815496
e holidays@thepavillioncarlyonbay.co.uk
w thepavillioncarlyonbay.co.uk

CARNHELL GREEN
Cornwall

Poachers Leat ★★★
Self Catering
Valley Villas Ltd
t (01752) 605605
e sales@valleyvillas.com
w valleyvillas.co.uk

CARNMENELLIS
Cornwall

The Old Vicarage ★★★
Self Catering
t (01209) 860570

CARNON DOWNS
Cornwall

Higher Tresithick Barn
★★★★ *Self Catering*
t (01872) 864400
e office@specialplacescornwall.co.uk
w specialplacescornwall.co.uk

CASTLE CARY
Somerset

The Ancient Barn and The Old Stables ★★★★
Self Catering
Contact: Ms Anthea Peppin
t (01963) 351288
e bookings@medievalbarn.co.uk
w medievalbarn.co.uk

Clanville Manor Tallet and Lone Oak Cottage ★★★★
Self Catering
Contact: Mrs Snook
t (01963) 350124
e info@clanvillemanor.co.uk
w clanvillemanor.co.uk

Orchard Farm Cottages
★★★ *Self Catering*
Contact: Mr & Mrs Dave & Helen Boyer
t (01963) 350418
e boyer@orchard-farm.co.uk
w orchard-farm.co.uk

CERNE ABBAS
Dorset

Old Gaol Cottage ★★★★★
Self Catering
Contact: Mrs Nicky Willis
t (01308) 863868
e nickywillis@tesco.net
w dorsetcottage.org

Wancombe Cottage ★★★★
Self Catering
Contact: Mr & Mrs Tom & Karen Handley
t (01300) 341158
e info@wancombe.co.uk
w wancombe.co.uk

CHACEWATER
Cornwall

Kilhellan ★★★ *Self Catering*
Contact: Mrs Moon
t (01872) 560328
e info@kilhellan.co.uk
w kilhellan.freeserve.co.uk

Morwenna Lodge ★★★
Self Catering
Holiday Homes and Cottages South West
t (01803) 299677
e holcotts@aol.com
w swcottages.co.uk

Unity Cottage at Valley View Barn, Creegbrawse ★★★★
Self Catering
Contact: Miss Gail Cooper
t (01209) 820136
e enquires@valleyviewbarn.co.uk
w valleyviewbarn.co.uk

CHALLACOMBE
Devon

Shoulsbarrow Farm ★★★★
Self Catering
Farm & Cottage Holidays
t (01237) 459827
e enquiries@farmcott.co.uk
w holidaycottages.co.uk

South Barton Cottage
★★★★ *Self Catering*
Farm & Cottage Holidays
t (01237) 459827
e enquiries@farmcott.co.uk
w holidaycottages.co.uk

Swincombe Mill ★★★★★
Self Catering
Contact: Mr & Mrs Mark & Lindsey Roberts
t (01598) 763514
e woolhanger@aol.com
w woolhanger.co.uk

Whitefield Barton ★★★
Self Catering
Contact: Mrs Rosemarie Kingdon
t (01598) 763271
e whitefieldbartonfarm@tiscali.co.uk
w exmoor-holidays.co.uk

CHAPEL
Cornwall

No. 1 Gustivean Cottages
★★★★★ *Self Catering*
Gustivean Cottages
t (01579) 346473
e holidays@duchyofcornwall.gov.uk
w duchyofcornwallholidaycottages.co.uk

No. 2 Gustivean Cottages
★★★★★ *Self Catering*
Gustivean Cottages
t (01579) 346473
e holidays@duchyofcornwall.gov.uk
w duchyofcornwallholidaycottages.co.uk

CHAPEL AMBLE
Cornwall

Ambledown Cottage
★★★★★ *Self Catering*
t 0870 585 1155

Homeleigh Farm Holiday Cottages, Chapel Amble
★★★★ *Self Catering*
Contact: Philip Rees
t (01208) 812411
e homeleigh@eclipse.co.uk
w eclipse.co.uk/homeleigh

The Olde House,Chapel Amble ★★★-★★★★
Self Catering
Contact: Mr A Hawkey
t (01208) 813219
e info@theoldehouse.co.uk
w theoldehouse.co.uk

Rooke Country Cottages Chapel Amble ★★★★★
Self Catering
Contact: Mrs Gill Reskelly
t (01208) 880368
e info@rookecottages.com
w rookecottages.com

CHARDSTOCK
Devon

Canterbury Cottage ★★★★
Self Catering
Contact: Ms Kate Looker
t (01395) 567676

Little Tythcote ★★★
Self Catering
Milkbere Cottage Holidays
t (01297) 20729
e info@milkberehols.com
w milkberehols.com

Tytherleigh Primrose ★★★
Self Catering
Milkbere Cottage Holidays
t (01297) 20729
e info@milkberehols.com
w milkberehols.com

CHARLTON
Wiltshire

Old Park Farm Holiday Cottages ★★★★
Self Catering
Contact: Mrs Ruth Baker
t (01666) 577274
e baker_richard@lineone.net
w theoldparkfarm.co.uk

CHARMOUTH
Dorset

11 Barney's Close ★★★★
Self Catering
Lyme Bay Holidays
t (01297) 443363
e email@lymebayholidays.co.uk
w lymebayholidays.co.uk

11 Queens Walk ★★★★
Self Catering
Lyme Bay Holidays
t (01297) 443363
e email@lymebayholidays.co.uk
w lymebayholidays.co.uk

3 Firlands ★★★ *Self Catering*
Lyme Bay Holidays
t (01297) 443363
e email@lymebayholidays.co.uk
w lymebayholidays.co.uk

3 Riverside Cottage ★★★★
Self Catering
Lyme Bay Holidays
t (01297) 443363
e email@lymebayholidays.co.uk
w lymebayholidays.co.uk

4 Mill View ★★★
Self Catering
Lyme Bay Holidays
t (01297) 443363
e email@lymebayholidays.co.uk
w lymebayholidays.co.uk

41 Fernhill ★★★
Self Catering
Lyme Bay Holidays
t (01297) 443363
e email@lymebayholidays.co.uk
w lymebayholidays.co.uk

5 Barneys Close ★★★★
Self Catering
Lyme Bay Holidays
t (01297) 443363
e email@lymebayholidays.co.uk
w lymebayholidays.co.uk

50 Fernhill Heights ★★★★
Self Catering
Lyme Bay Holidays
t (01297) 443363
e email@lymebayholidays.co.uk
w lymebayholidays.co.uk

7 Double Common ★★★
Self Catering
Lyme Bay Holidays
t (01297) 443363
e email@lymebayholidays.co.uk
w lymebayholidays.co.uk

9 Double Common ★★★★
Self Catering
Lyme Bay Holidays
t (01297) 443363
e email@lymebayholidays.co.uk
w lymebayholidays.co.uk

The Barn – W4368 ★★★★
Self Catering
Lyme Bay Holidays
t (01297) 443363
e email@lymebayholidays.co.uk
w lymebayholidays.co.uk

Beachcomber ★★★★
Self Catering
Dream Cottages
t (01305) 789000
e admin@dream-cottages.co.uk
w dream-cottages.co.uk

Befferlands Farm ★★★★★
Self Catering
Lyme Bay Holidays
t (01297) 443363
e email@lymebayholidays.co.uk
w lymebayholidays.co.uk

Bridge House ★★★
Self Catering
Lyme Bay Holidays
t (01297) 443363
e email@lymebayholidays.co.uk
w lymebayholidays.co.uk

Charleston Holiday Cottages
★★★ *Self Catering*
t (01297) 560053

Coach House ★★★
Self Catering
Lyme Bay Holidays
t (01297) 443363
e email@lymebayholidays.co.uk
w lymebayholidays.co.uk

Dolphin House ★★★★
Self Catering
Lyme Bay Holidays
t (01297) 443363
e email@lymebayholidays.co.uk
w lymebayholidays.co.uk

Double Common ★★★★
Self Catering
Lyme Bay Holidays
t (01297) 443363
e email@lymebayholidays.co.uk
w lymebayholidays.co.uk

Fernhill Heights ★★★
Self Catering
Lyme Bay Holidays
t (01297) 443363
e email@lymebayholidays.co.uk
w lymebayholidays.co.uk

Fernhill Heights ★★★
Self Catering
Lyme Bay Holidays
t (01297) 443363
e email@lymebayholidays.co.uk
w lymebayholidays.co.uk

Flinstones ★★★★
Self Catering
Lyme Bay Holidays
t (01297) 443363
e email@lymebayholidays.co.uk
w lymebayholidays.co.uk

Fountain's Mead ★★★★
Self Catering
Lyme Bay Holidays
t (01297) 443363
e email@lymebayholidays.co.uk
w lymebayholidays.co.uk

Greenhayes ★★★
Self Catering
Lyme Bay Holidays
t (01297) 443363
e email@lymebayholidays.co.uk
w lymebayholidays.co.uk

Jasmine Cottage ★★★
Self Catering
Lyme Bay Holidays
t (01297) 443363
e email@lymebayholidays.co.uk
w lymebayholidays.co.uk

Lias Lea ★★★ *Self Catering*
Lyme Bay Holidays
t (01297) 443363
e email@lymebayholidays.co.uk
w lymebayholidays.co.uk

Little Catherston Farm ★★★
Self Catering
Contact: Mrs R J White
t (01297) 560550
e joyce.white1@btopenworld.com
w catherstonfarm-bungalows.co.uk

Little Haven ★★★★
Self Catering
Lyme Bay Holidays
t (01297) 443363
e email@lymebayholidays.co.uk
w lymebayholidays.co.uk

The Lodge ★★★★
Self Catering
Lyme Bay Holidays
t (01297) 443363
e email@lymebayholidays.co.uk
w lymebayholidays.co.uk

Nutwood ★★★★
Self Catering
Lyme Bay Holidays
t (01297) 443363
e email@lymebayholidays.co.uk
w lymebayholidays.co.uk

Penderel ★★★★
Self Catering
Lyme Bay Holidays
t (01297) 443363
e email@lymebayholidays.co.uk
w lymebayholidays.co.uk

The Poplars ★★★
Self Catering
Contact: Mrs Jane Bremner
t (01297) 560697
e holiday@woodfarm.co.uk
w woodfarm.co.uk

Portland House ★★★
Self Catering
Lyme Bay Holidays
t (01297) 443363
e email@lymebayholidays.co.uk
w lymebayholidays.co.uk

The Pottery Flat ★★★
Self Catering
Lyme Bay Holidays
t (01297) 443363
e email@lymebayholidays.co.uk
w lymebayholidays.co.uk

Riverway ★★★ *Self Catering*
Lyme Bay Holidays
t (01297) 443363
e email@lymebayholidays.co.uk
w lymebayholidays.co.uk

Shoe & Stocking ★★★
Self Catering
Lyme Bay Holidays
t (01297) 443363
e email@lymebayholidays.co.uk
w lymebayholidays.co.uk

Smiths Farm Cottages ★★★
Self Catering
Contact: Mrs Mandy Harvey
t (01297) 560167
e smithscottages@btinternet.com
w http://uk.geocities.com/smithsfarmcottages

Stonehayes Garden Flat
Rating Applied For
Self Catering
t (01297) 561462

Swiss Cottage ★★★★
Self Catering
Lyme Bay Holidays
t (01297) 443363
e email@lymebayholidays.co.uk
w lymebayholidays.co.uk

Tillicum ★★★ *Self Catering*
Lyme Bay Holidays
t (01297) 443363
e email@lymebayholidays.co.uk
w lymebayholidays.co.uk

Vine Cottage ★★★★
Self Catering
Lyme Bay Holidays
t (01297) 443363
e email@lymebayholidays.co.uk
w lymebayholidays.co.uk

Wistaria Cottage ★★★
Self Catering
Lyme Bay Holidays
t (01297) 443363
e email@lymebayholidays.co.uk
w lymebayholidays.co.uk

CHAXHILL
Gloucestershire

Laurel Cottage ★★★
Self Catering
Contact: Mr & Mrs Mark & Tasmin Terry-Lush
t (01452) 760147
e enjoyengland@laurel-cottage.com
w laurel-cottage.com

CHEDDAR
Somerset

Bradley Cross Farm ★★
Self Catering
Contact: Ms Judith Credland
t (01934) 741771
e bradleyxfarm@btinternet.com
w bradleycrossfarm.org.uk

Home Farm Cottages
★★★★ *Self Catering*
Contact: Mr Chris Sanders
t (01934) 842078
e enquiries@homefarmcottages.com
w homefarmcottages.com

Hope Cottage
Rating Applied For
Self Catering
Contact: Mr David Holmese book@cheddarcottages.co.uk
w cheddarcottages.co.uk

Orchard Court & Bungalow
★★★★ *Self Catering*
Contact: Mrs Carol Roberts
t (01934) 742116

Somerleaze Lodge, Wookey
★★★★ *Self Catering*
Contact: Marlene & Victoria Carse Jones
t (01749) 673859
w cottagesdirect.com

Spring Cottages ★★★★
Self Catering
Contact: Mrs G Robinson
t (01934) 742493
e falcon@springcottages.co.uk
w springcottages.co.uk

Sungate Holiday Apartments ★★ *Self Catering*
Contact: Mrs M M Fieldhouse
Pyrenmount
t (01934) 842273 & (01934) 742264
e sunholapartment@btinternet.com
w sungateholidayapartments.co.uk

Uplands Cottages
Rating Applied For
Self Catering
Contact: Mrs Webb
t (01934) 842257
w uplandscottages.co.uk

CHEDWORTH
Gloucestershire

The Old Post Office, Chedworth ★★★★
Self Catering
Contact: Mrs J Todd
The Old Village Stores
t (01285) 720367
e bookings@opochedworth.co.uk
w opochedworth.co.uk

CHEDZOY
Somerset

Bramley Lodge ★★★★★
Self Catering
Contact: Mrs Judith Denning
t (01278) 423201
e temple_farm@hotmail.com
w bramleylodge.co.uk

CHELTENHAM
Gloucestershire

April Cottage ★★★★★
Self Catering
Contact: Mrs Christine Gannon
t (01242) 252128
e chris.gannon@talktalk.net
w aprilcottagecheltenham.co.uk

Look out for establishments participating in the National Accessible Scheme

Bakery Cottage ★★★
Self Catering
Contact: Mrs Weller
t (01242) 236765

Balcarras Farm Holiday Cottages ★★★ *Self Catering*
Contact: Mr & Mrs David & Judith Ballinger
Balcarras Farm
t (01242) 584837
e cottage@balcarras-farm.co.uk
w balcarras-farm.co.uk

Butlers Studios ★★★
Self Catering
Contact: Mr Guy Hunter
t (01242) 570771
e info@butlers-hotel.co.uk
w butlers-hotel.co.uk

Cheltenham Apartments ★★★★-★★★★★
Self Catering
Contact: Mrs Sophie Thompson
t (01242) 227579
e cheltapartments@aol.com
w cheltenhamapartments.co.uk

Coxhorne Farm Holiday Cottage ★★★ *Self Catering*
Contact: Mr & Mrs Close
t (01242) 236599

The Furrow ★★★★
Self Catering
Contact: Mrs Valerie Hughes
t (01451) 850733
e hughes@thefurrow.freeserve.co.uk
w cotswoldholiday.co.uk

The Garden Flat ★★★★
Self Catering
Contact: Mrs Dorcas Jones
t (01242) 584337
e info@garden-flat.co.uk
w garden-flat.co.uk/

Great Coverden, Sandhurst ★★★★ *Self Catering*
Contact: Mrs Deb Warren
Bengrove Farm
t (01452) 730231
e Debs@bengrovefarm.fsnet.co.uk
w greatcoverden.com

Holmer Cottages ★★★★
Self Catering
Contact: Mrs Jill Collins
t (01242) 672848
e holmercottages@talk21.com
w cottageguide.co.uk/holmercottages

Imperial Gate Luxury Penthouse
Rating Applied For
Self Catering
t (01531) 631592

Mayville House ★★
Self Catering
Contact: Mrs Rani Boyal
t (01242) 587345
e rani_kaur_boyal@hotmail.com
w cheltenhamapartments.org.uk

The Old Dairy ★★★★
Self Catering
Contact: Mr & Mrs Rickie & Jennie Gauld
t (01242) 676003
e rickieg@btinternet.com
w cotswoldcottages.btinternet.co.uk

Priory Cottage ★★★
Self Catering
Contact: Mr Ian Mant
t (01242) 584693
e iansmant@hotmail.com
w countrycottagesonline.net

Top Flat ★★★ *Self Catering*
Contact: Mr & Mrs Morris
t (01454) 227322
e cotswold.cottage@btopenworld.com
w cotswoldcottage.net/

The Vergus ★★★
Self Catering
Contact: Mrs Rita Preen
t (01242) 680511
e ritapreen@yahoo.co.uk
w vergus.co.uk

Vine Court ★★★★
Self Catering
Contact: Mrs Linda Hennessy
t (01242) 222403
e lindyhennessy@hotmail.com

Willoughby House Apartments ★★★-★★★★★
Self Catering
Contact: Mr & Mrs F P Eckermann
t (01242) 522798
e bookings@willoughbyhouse.com
w willoughbyhouse.com

CHERITON BISHOP
Devon

The Garden House ★★★★★
Self Catering
Contact: Mr Peter Benjamin
t (01647) 24848
e peter@medlandmanor.com

CHEW MAGNA
Somerset

Woodbarn Farm Cottages ★★★-★★★★ *Self Catering*
Contact: Mrs Judi Hasell
t (01275) 332599
e woodbarnfarm@hotmail.com
w smoothhound.co.uk/hotels/woodbarn.html

CHICKERELL
Dorset

Honey Church Cottage ★★★ *Self Catering*
Dream Cottages
t (01305) 789000
e admin@dream-cottages.co.uk
w dream-cottages.co.uk

Tidmoor Cottages ★★★★
Self Catering
Contact: Ms Townsend
t (01305) 787867
e sarah@tidmoorstables.co.uk
w tidmoorstables.co.uk

CHIDEOCK
Dorset

Ash Cottage ★★★
Self Catering
Contact: Mrs Isabel Morgan
t (0117) 962 9126
e isabel@isabelmorgan.co.uk
w dorsetcottage.net

Brook Cottage ★★★★
Self Catering
Lyme Bay Holidays
t (01297) 443363
e email@lymebayholidays.co.uk
w lymebayholidays.co.uk

Cedar Cottage ★★★
Self Catering
Contact: Mr David Roberts
t (0117) 370 6580
e info@cedarcottage.biz
w cedarcottage.biz

Chideock Cottage ★★★★
Self Catering
Contact: Mrs Pauline Bale
t (01308) 424321
e bale@highwayfarm.co.uk
w chideockcottage.co.uk

Frying Pan ★★★★
Self Catering
Dream Cottages
t (01305) 789000
e admin@dream-cottages.co.uk
w dream-cottages.co.uk

Greystones Cottage ★★★★
Self Catering
Lyme Bay Holidays
t (01297) 443363
e email@lymebayholidays.co.uk
w lymebayholidays.co.uk

CHILCOMBE
Dorset

Cherry Tree Cottage ★★★
Self Catering
Dream Cottages
t (01305) 789000
e admin@dream-cottages.co.uk
w dream-cottages.co.uk

CHILLINGTON
Devon

Chillihols ★★★★
Self Catering
Contact: Mrs Chris Fox
t (01548) 580010
e chris.fox4@btinternet.com
w chillihols.com

CHILTON TRINITY
Somerset

Chilton Farm ★★★★
Self Catering
w farmcott.co.uk

Lower Lakes ★★★★
Self Catering
Contact: Mr Stuart Key
t (01278) 453357
w lowerlakesholidays.co.uk

CHIPPENHAM
Wiltshire

London Road Guest Accommodation ★★★★
Self Catering
Contact: Mrs Jean Collom
t (01249) 656828
e mikecollom60@gmail.com
w chippenhambedand breakfast.co.uk

Nut Tree Cottage ★★★
Self Catering
Contact: Mrs Margaret Payne
t (01249) 782354

Olivemead Farm Holidays ★★★★ *Self Catering*
Contact: Mrs Suzanne Candy
Olivemead Farm
t (01666) 510205
e enquiries@olivemeadfarmholidays.com
w olivemeadfarmholidays.com

CHIPPING CAMPDEN
Gloucestershire

Bank Cottage ★★★★
Self Catering
Contact: Mr Robert Hutsby
t (01789) 841525
e robert.hutsby@btinternet.com
w chipping-campden-holiday-cottages.co.uk

Box Tree Cottage ★★★
Self Catering
Contact: Mr Robert Hutsby
t (01789) 841525
e robert.hutsby@btinternet.com
w chipping-campden-holiday-cottages.co.uk

Chapter Cottage ★★★★
Self Catering
Contact: Mrs Jan Revers
t (01386) 841450
w perpetuare.com

Cosy Corner ★★★★
Self Catering
Contact: Mrs Pearl Brandreth
t (01386) 841752
e pearl@mdina03.fsnet.co.uk
w noelcourt.co.uk

Cotswold Charm ★★★★
Self Catering
Contact: Mr & Miss Michael & Margaret Haines
t (01386) 840164
e info@cotswoldcharm.co.uk
w cotswoldcharm.co.uk

Cotswold Cottages ★★★★
Self Catering
Contact: Mrs Jane Whitehouse
t (01386) 840835
e jane_whitehouse@hotmail.com
w cotswoldcottages.uk.com

Cow Fair ★★★★
Self Catering
Contact: Mrs Whitehouse
t (01386) 840835
e jane_whitehouse@hotmail.com
w cotswoldcottages.uk.com

Croftsbrook ★★★
Self Catering
Contact: Mr David Birch
t (01386) 840682
e david@crofsbrook.co.uk
w croftsbrook.co.uk

Dragon House ★★★★
Self Catering
Campden Cottages
t (01386) 593315
e info@campdencottages.co.uk
w campdencottages.co.uk

Grafton Mews ★★★★
Self Catering
Campden Cottages
t (01386) 593315
e info@campdencottages.co.uk
w campdencottages.co.uk

Honeysuckle Cottage
★★★★ *Self Catering*
Contact: Mrs Kate Daly
t (0121) 426 6310 & 07905 497211
e stjohn.daly@blueyonder.co.uk
w thecountrycottage.co.uk

Ingleside Cottage ★★★★
Self Catering
Campden Cottages
t (01386) 593315
e info@campdencottages.co.uk
w campdencottages.co.uk

Little Thatch ★★★★
Self Catering
Contact: Mrs Dorothy Gadsby
t (01386) 840234
e info@littlethatchcampden.co.uk
w littlethatchcampden.co.uk

Orchard Cottage ★★★★
Self Catering
Campden Cottages
t (01386) 593315
e info@campdencottages.co.uk
w campdencottages.co.uk

Rosary Cottage ★★★★
Self Catering
Campden Cottages
t (01386) 593315
e info@campdencottages.co.uk
w campdencottages.co.uk

Sansons Cottage ★★★★
Self Catering
Campden Cottages
t (01386) 593315
e info@campdencottages.co.uk
w campdencottages.co.uk

Spring Cottage ★★★★
Self Catering
Campden Cottages
t (01386) 593315
e info@campdencottages.co.uk
w campdencottages.co.uk

Walkers Retreat ★★★
Self Catering
Contact: Mrs Whitehouse
t (01386) 840835
e jane_whitehouse@hotmail.com
w cotswoldcottages.uk.com

Whistlers Cottage ★★★★
Self Catering
Contact: Mr Robert Hutsby
t (01789) 841525
e robert.hutsby@btinternet.com
w chipping-campden-holiday-cottages.co.uk

CHISELBOROUGH
Somerset

One Fair Place, Chiselborough ★★★★
Self Catering
Contact: Mrs Adrienne Wright
t (01344) 772461
e aawright@btopenworld.com
w somersetcottageholidays.co.uk

CHITTLEHAMPTON
Devon

Thatch Cottage ★★★★
Self Catering
Contact: Miss L J Power Owner
t (01564) 776972

CHRISTCHURCH
Dorset

The Annexe ★★★
Self Catering
Contact: Mrs Marylyn Etheridge
t (01202) 484475

The Black House, Hengistbury Head, Mudeford ★★★ *Self Catering*
Contact: Mr Andrew Brown
t 07855 280191
e enquiries@theblackhouse.co.uk
w theblackhouse.co.uk

The Causeway ★–★★
Self Catering
Contact: Mrs Liz Knight
t (01202) 470149
e tmscauseway@tiscali.co.uk
w knightscauseway.co.uk

The Coach House, Mudeford
★★★★ *Self Catering*
Contact: Miss Maggie Rose
t 07850 668341
e info@roserentals.co.uk
w roserentals.co.uk

Cumberland Lodge
★★–★★★ *Self Catering*
Contact: Mr Paul Williamson
t (01425) 280275
e mail07@cumberland-lodge.co.uk
w cumberland-lodge.co.uk/info

The Holiday Cottage ★★★
Self Catering
Contact: Mr & Mrs John Brewer
t (01202) 420673

Mallard Cottage ★★★
Self Catering
Contact: Mrs Pam Pearce
t (01202) 475967
e mallardcottage@live.co.uk

Pedralves ★★★ *Self Catering*
Contact: Mrs Kenney
t (01425) 273858

The Quarterdeck ★★★★
Self Catering
Contact: Mrs Julie Harman
t 07779 593205
e julieharman@btinternet.com

Renee's ★★★ *Self Catering*
Contact: Mrs G Curling
t (01425) 280875
w highcliffe-mudeford.com

Riverbank Holidays ★★★
Self Catering
Contact: Mr & Mrs Gibson
t (01202) 477813

Riverside Park ★★★
Self Catering
Contact: Mrs Lisa Booth
t (01202) 471090
e holidays@riversidepark.biz
w riversidepark.biz

Saffron ★★★ *Self Catering*
Contact: Mrs Rosemary Broadey
t (01425) 277507
e rosemary@broadey.net
w saffronholiday.co.uk

Suhaili ★★★★ *Self Catering*
Contact: Ms Sally Derham-Wilkes
t (01425) 279102
e info@suhaili.biz
w suhaili.biz

Sundrone ★★★ *Self Catering*
t (01425) 272461

Two Rivers Reach ★★★
Self Catering
Contact: Ms Sandra Hayward
t 07789 908173
e sandshayward@yahoo.co.uk
w tworiversreach.com

CHRISTCHURCH
Gloucestershire

Glenwood ★★★
Self Catering
Contact: Mrs Harvey
t (01594) 833128
e joanlouiseharvey@hotmail.co.uk

CHUDLEIGH
Devon

Ashmead ★★★★★
Self Catering
Blue Chip Vacations
t (01803) 855282
e info@bluechipvacations.com
w bluechipvacations.com

CHULMLEIGH
Devon

Bealy Court Holiday Cottages ★★★★–★★★★★
Self Catering
Contact: Ms I Henderson
t (01769) 580312
e bealycourt@mac.com
w bealycourt.co.uk

Deer Cott ★★★★
Self Catering
Contact: Mr & Mrs George Simpson
t (01769) 580461
e enquiries@deercott.co.uk
w deercott.co.uk

CHURCHILL
Somerset

Bartholomew's Beautiful Barns ★★★–★★★★
Self Catering
Contact: Mrs Maxine Bartholomew
t (01934) 852043
e bbb.beechbarn@btinternet.com
w bartholomews-beautiful-barns.co.uk

CHURCHINFORD
Somerset

South Cleeve Bungalows
★★★★ *Self Catering*
Contact: Mrs V D Manning
t (01823) 601378 & 07811 362740
e enquiries@timbertopbungalows.co.uk
w timbertopbungalows.co.uk

CHURCHSTANTON
Somerset

Craigend Cottage ★★★★
Self Catering
Contact: Ms Julie Nagle
t (01823) 601441
e julieannenagle@aol.com
w craigendcottagesomerset.co.uk

CIRENCESTER
Gloucestershire

Flowers Barn ★★★★
Self Catering
Contact: Mrs Tina Barton
t (01285) 658145
e enquiries@duntisbourne.com
w duntisbourne.com

Glebe Farm Holiday Lets
★★★★ *Self Catering*
Contact: Mrs Polly Handover
t (01285) 659226
e enquiries@glebefarmcottages.co.uk
w glebefarmcottages.co.uk

Jago's Cottage
Rating Applied For
Self Catering
Contact: Liz Richens
t (01285) 651349
e info@cirencesterselfcatering.co.uk
w cirencesterselfcatering.co.uk

The Tallet, Preston ★★★
Self Catering
Contact: Mrs Susan Spivey
t (01285) 653405
e howard@spiveyfarm.co.uk

Warrens Gorse Cottages
★★★ *Self Catering*
Contact: Mrs Nanette Randall
t (01285) 831261

CLEARWELL
Gloucestershire

Rosedean Cottage ★★★★
Self Catering
Contact: Mrs Andrea Dombrowe
t (01483) 538615
e clearwell@gmail.com
w forestofdeancottage.co.uk

Stank Farm ★★★
Self Catering
Contact: Louise Salter
t (01594) 832203
e louise@stankfarmholidays.co.uk
w stankfarmholidays.co.uk

Wainlete ★★★★
Self Catering
Contact: Ms Jayne Rogerse j.r.environmental@hotmail.co.uk
w royalforestofdeancottage.co.uk

CLIFTON City of Bristol

Bristol Serviced Apartments ★★★★★ *Self Catering*
Contact: Mrs Kim White
t (0117) 974 1414
e bsapartments@aol.com
w bristolservicedapartments.co.uk

CLOVELLY Devon

Buttery Barn ★★★★
Self Catering
Marsdens Cottage Holidays
t (01271) 813777
e holidays@marsdens.co.uk
w marsdens.co.uk

Carriage House ★★★★
Self Catering
Marsdens Cottage Holidays
t (01271) 813777
e holidays@marsdens.co.uk
w marsdens.co.uk

The Long Barn ★★★★
Self Catering
Contact: Mrs Jones
t (01327) 831129
e caroline@jones-pattishall.freeserve.co.uk
w enjoyourhomes.com

COBERLEY Gloucestershire

Seven Springs Cottages ★★★ *Self Catering*
Contact: Miss Marcie Stokes
t (01242) 870385
e mail@sevenspringscottages.com
w sevenspringscottages.com

COCKLAKE Somerset

Ashton Cottages ★★★★
Self Catering
Contact: Mrs Ashley Ribi
t (01934) 712157
e info@ashtoncottages.net
w ashtoncottages.net

COFFINSWELL Devon

Willa Cottage ★★★★
Self Catering
Contact: Mr Tim Whitehouse
t (01803) 875078
e tim@willacottage.com
w willacottage.com

COLD ASHTON Gloucestershire

Sayres House, Nr Bath ★★★★ *Self Catering*
Contact: Elaine Molyneux
Dunster Living
t 0845 208 1066
e info@dunsterliving.co.uk
w sayreshouse.co.uk

COLDRIDGE Devon

The Linhay at Lower Chilverton ★★★★
Self Catering
Contact: Ms Wendy Harmsorth
t (01363) 83318
e wendyharmsworth@aol.com
w lowerchilverton.co.uk

COLEFORD Gloucestershire

Little Millend ★★★
Self Catering
Hideaways
t (01747) 828170
e enq@hideaways.co.uk
w hideaways.co.uk

COLEHILL Dorset

Brightside Cottage ★★★
Self Catering
Contact: Mrs Claire Nash
t (01202) 849044
e brightside49@btinternet.com
w brightsidecottage.co.uk

COLYFORD Devon

Apple Garth ★★★★★
Self Catering
Milkbere Cottage Holidays
t (01297) 20729
e info@milkberehols.com
w milkberehols.com

Bryher ★★★★ *Self Catering*
Contact: Mrs Stephanie Sawer
t (01297) 551093
e info@devoncottage-bryher.co.uk
w devoncottage-bryher.co.uk

The Manor House ★★★★★
Self Catering
Contact: Mr Matthew Waters
t 07943 260129
e stay@oldmanorcottages.co.uk
w oldmanorcottages.co.uk

Whitwell Farm Cottages ★★★★ *Self Catering*
Contact: Mr Mike Williams
t 0800 092 0419
e 100755.66@compuserve.com
w a5star.co.uk

COLYTON Devon

Barritshayes Farm Cottages ★★★★ *Self Catering*
Contact: Mr & Mrs Gordon & Liz Lindsay
t (01297) 552485
e info@barritshayes.co.uk
w barritshayes.co.uk

Bonehayne Farm Cottage ★★★ *Self Catering*
Contact: Mrs Gould
t (01404) 871416 & (01404) 871416
e gould@bonehayne.co.uk
w bonehayne.co.uk

Higher Wiscombe ★★★★★
Self Catering
Contact: Mr & Mrs Alistair & Lorna Handyside
t (01404) 871360
e alistair@higherwiscombe.com
w higherwiscombe.com

Little Haven ★★★★
Self Catering
Contact: Mrs Elizabeth Mills
t (01297) 553811
e liz.mills@btopenworld.com

Lovehayne Farm Cottages ★★★★ *Self Catering*
Contact: Mrs Philippa Bignell
t (01404) 871216
e stay@lovehayne.co.uk
w lovehayne.co.uk

Malt House ★★★
Self Catering
Milkbere Cottage Holidays
t (01297) 20729
e info@milkberehols.com
w milkberehols.com

Smallicombe Farm ★★★★
Self Catering
Contact: Mrs Maggie Todd
t (01404) 831310
e maggie_todd@yahoo.com
w smallicombe.com

COMBE MARTIN Devon

1 Stattens Cottages ★★★
Self Catering
Contact: Mrs Peggy Crees
t (01483) 488790
e info@cottagesindevon.com
w cottagesindevon.com

Beech & Ash Cottages ★★★★ *Self Catering*
Marsdens Cottage Holidays
t (01271) 813777
e holidays@marsdens.co.uk
w marsdens.co.uk

Bosun's Cottage, Combe Martin Harbour ★★★
Self Catering
Contact: Mr & Mrs Martin & Margaret Wolverson
Primespot Character Cottages
t (01271) 882449

Coulscott House, Combe Martin ★★★★ *Self Catering*
Contact: Mrs Susan Jay
t (01271) 883339
e stay@coulscott.co.uk
w coulscott.co.uk

The Elms ★★★ *Self Catering*
Marsdens Cottage Holidays
t (01271) 813777
e holidays@marsdens.co.uk
w marsdens.co.uk

Hangman Path ★★★★
Self Catering
Contact: Mr Simon Chappell
t (01625) 523673
e landlord@combe-martin.net
w combe-martin.net

Hillside ★★★★ *Self Catering*
Marsdens Cottage Holidays
t (01271) 813777
e holidays@marsdens.co.uk
w marsdens.co.uk

Holdstone ★★★
Self Catering
Marsdens Cottage Holidays
t (01271) 813777
e holidays@marsdens.co.uk
w marsdens.co.uk

Indicknowle Farm, Combe Martin ★★★★ *Self Catering*
Contact: Mrs Susan West
t (01271) 883980
e mark.sue@indicknowle.plus.com
w indicknowlefarmholidays.co.uk

Lynton Cottage ★★★★
Self Catering
Marsdens Cottage Holidays
t (01271) 813777
e holidays@marsdens.co.uk
w marsdens.co.uk

Newberry View ★★★★
Self Catering
Marsdens Cottage Holidays
t (01271) 813777
e holidays@marsdens.co.uk
w marsdens.co.uk

Prospect Cottage ★★★
Self Catering
Marsdens Cottage Holidays
t (01271) 813777
e holidays@marsdens.co.uk
w marsdens.co.uk

Riverside ★★★★
Self Catering
Marsdens Cottage Holidays
t (01271) 813777
e holidays@marsdens.co.uk
w marsdens.co.uk

Sea Breeze ★★★★★
Self Catering
Marsdens Cottage Holidays
t (01271) 813777
e holidays@marsdens.co.uk
w marsdens.co.uk

Yetland Farm Cottages ★★★★ *Self Catering*
Contact: Mr & Mrs Alan & Alison Balcombe
t (01271) 883655
e enquiries@yetlandfarmcottages.co.uk
w yetlandfarmcottages.co.uk

COMBEINTEIGNHEAD Devon

The Old Bakery ★★★
Self Catering
Holiday Homes and Cottages South West
t (01803) 299677
e holcotts@aol.com
w swcottages.co.uk

COMPTON ABDALE Gloucestershire

Southwold Barn ★★★★★
Self Catering
Contact: Mrs Emma Doyle
t (01242) 890147
e emma@southwoldfarm.co.uk
w southwoldbarn.co.uk

COMPTON DUNDON Somerset

Chapel Barn ★★★★
Self Catering
Contact: Mrs Diana Napper
t (01458) 442962
e diana@chapel-barn.co.uk
w chapel-barn.co.uk

Wisteria Cottage ★★★★
Self Catering
Contact: Mrs Georgina Baston
t (01458) 442848
e david.bastone@tbg.me.uk
w thewisteriacottage.co.uk

CONNOR DOWNS
Cornwall

Gwithian Holidays ★★★
Self Catering
Contact: Mr Trevor & Tyson Greenaway
t (01736) 755493
e gonesurfin74@hotmail.com
w gwithianholidays.com

Trevaskis Dairy ★★★★
Self Catering
Contact: Ms Strachey
t (01209) 613750
e julie@trevaskis-dairy.co.uk
w trevaskis-dairy.co.uk

CONSTANTINE
Cornwall

Bosryn
Rating Applied For
Self Catering
Cornish Holiday Cottages
t (01326) 250339
e emily@cornishholidaycottages.net
w cornishholidaycottages.net

Calmanasc (Sail Loft)
★★★★ *Self Catering*
Cornish Holiday Cottages
t (01326) 250339
e emily@cornishholidaycottages.net
w cornishholidaycottages.net

Chynoweth ★★★★
Self Catering
Contact: Mrs Eileen Combellack
t (01326) 340196

The Fuchsia's ★★★
Self Catering
Contact: Mr Hooton
t (01322) 339115

Green Bank Cottage, Seworgan ★★★★
Self Catering
Contact: Mrs Carole Scobie-Allin
Selective Cornish Retreats
t (01326) 340147 & 07767 896359
e caroleselectiveretreats@yahoo.com
w connexions.co.uk/schr

Owl Cottage ★★★★
Self Catering
t (01326) 340493
e sara@owlcottageholidays.co.uk
w owlcottageholidays.co.uk

Trevean
Rating Applied For
Self Catering
Cornish Holiday Cottages
t (01326) 250339
e emily@cornishholidaycottages.net
w cornishholidaycottages.net

Willow Barn ★★★★
Self Catering
t (01326) 340883
w cornishcottageholidays.co.uk

CONSTANTINE BAY
Cornwall

2 Harvest Moon Apartments
★★★★ *Self Catering*
Cornish Horizons Holiday Cottages
t (01841) 533331
e cottages@cornishhorizons.co.uk
w cornishhorizons.co.uk

7 Sandhills ★★ *Self Catering*
Contact: Linda Harker
t (01962) 890701

Boskenna Apartment ★★★
Self Catering
Cornish Horizons Holiday Cottages
t (01841) 533331
e cottages@cornishhorizons.co.uk
w cornishhorizons.co.uk

Bumblers, Constantine Bay
★★★ *Self Catering*
Contact: Mrs Penny Gibson
t (01732) 863121
e partridgefarm@talk21.com

Costilloes ★★★ *Self Catering*
Cornish Horizons Holiday Cottages
t (01841) 533331
e cottages@cornishhorizons.co.uk
w cornishhorizons.co.uk

Cowries and The Lodge
★★★ *Self Catering*
Cornish Horizons Holiday Cottages
t (01841) 533331
e cottages@cornishhorizons.co.uk
w cornishhorizons.co.uk

The Dunes ★★★
Self Catering
Cornish Horizons Holiday Cottages
t (01841) 533331
e cottages@cornishhorizons.co.uk
w cornishhorizons.co.uk

Flat 12 Sandhills, Constantine Bay ★★★
Self Catering
Contact: Mrs M Hull
t (01752) 772519
e mariehull1@btinternet.com

Flat 9, Sandhills ★★
Self Catering
Contact: Mandy France
t (01276) 677600
e mandy.france@ntlworld.com

The Garden Cottage Holiday Flats ★★★ *Self Catering*
Contact: Mrs Elizabeth Harris
t (01841) 520262
e liz@gardencottageflats.co.uk
w gardencottageflats.co.uk

The Greens ★★★
Self Catering
Cornish Horizons Holiday Cottages
t (01841) 533331
e cottages@cornishhorizons.co.uk
w cornishhorizons.co.uk

Hilda's ★★★★ *Self Catering*
Cornish Horizons Holiday Cottages
t (01841) 533331
e cottages@cornishhorizons.co.uk
w cornishhorizons.co.uk

Kalundu ★★★★
Self Catering
Cornish Horizons Holiday Cottages
t (01841) 533331
e cottages@cornishhorizons.co.uk
w cornishhorizons.co.uk

Kernyk ★★★ *Self Catering*
Cornish Horizons Holiday Cottages
t (01841) 533331
e cottages@cornishhorizons.co.uk
w cornishhorizons.co.uk

Kittiwake ★★★★
Self Catering
Cornish Horizons Holiday Cottages
t (01841) 533331
e cottages@cornishhorizons.co.uk
w cornishhorizons.co.uk

Lower Trevelyan ★★★
Self Catering
Cornish Horizons Holiday Cottages
t (01841) 533331
e cottages@cornishhorizons.co.uk
w cornishhorizons.co.uk

Newlands ★★★★
Self Catering
Harbour Holidays
t (01841) 533402
e contact@harbourholidays.co.uk
w harbourholidays.co.uk

Pippins & Dinas View ★★★
Self Catering
Cornish Horizons Holiday Cottages
t (01841) 533331
e cottages@cornishhorizons.co.uk
w cornishhorizons.co.uk

Porth Clyne ★★★
Self Catering
Cornish Horizons Holiday Cottages
t (01841) 533331
e cottages@cornishhorizons.co.uk
w cornishhorizons.co.uk

Quilletts ★★★★
Self Catering
Cornish Horizons Holiday Cottages
t (01841) 533331
e cottages@cornishhorizons.co.uk
w cornishhorizons.co.uk

Treberta ★★★★
Self Catering
Harbour Holidays
t (01841) 533402
e contact@harbourholidays.co.uk
w harbourholidays.co.uk

Trefebus ★★★★
Self Catering
Cornish Horizons Holiday Cottages
t (01841) 533331
e cottages@cornishhorizons.co.uk
w cornishhorizons.co.uk

Trefoil ★★★ *Self Catering*
Cornish Horizons Holiday Cottages
t (01841) 533331
e cottages@cornishhorizons.co.uk
w cornishhorizons.co.uk

Treglos Bungalow & Apartments ★★★–★★★★
Self Catering
Contact: Mr Barlow
t (01841) 520727
e stay@tregloshotel.com
w tregloshotel.com

Treglyn ★★ *Self Catering*
Cornish Horizons Holiday Cottages
t (01841) 533331
e cottages@cornishhorizons.co.uk
w cornishhorizons.co.uk

Treless ★★★★ *Self Catering*
Cornish Horizons Holiday Cottages
t (01841) 533331
e cottages@cornishhorizons.co.uk
w cornishhorizons.co.uk

Trevose Golf & Country Club ★★–★★★★
Self Catering
Contact: Mr Gammon
t (01841) 520208
e info@trevose-gc.co.uk
w trevose-gc.co.uk

Turnstones ★★ *Self Catering*
Cornish Horizons Holiday Cottages
t (01841) 533331
e cottages@cornishhorizons.co.uk
w cornishhorizons.co.uk

COOPERS HILL
Gloucestershire

Hay Barn Cottage ★★★★
Self Catering
Contact: Mr & Mrs Millington
t (01452) 862237
e johnjomillington@hotmail.com

CORFE CASTLE
Dorset

7 West Street ★★★
Self Catering
Contact: Mrs Fiona Wake-Walker
t (01929) 480048
e 2wwfeet@tiscali.co.uk
w cottagepurbeck.co.uk

Farriers Lodge ★★★★
Self Catering
Contact: Mrs Eileen van Lelyveld
t (01929) 480386
w farrierslodge.corfe-castle.co.uk

Look out for establishments participating in the National Accessible Scheme

Knaveswell Farm Cottage
★★★ *Self Catering*
Contact: Mrs Jo Dyer
t (01929) 422918
e joanna.dyer5@btinternet.com
w knaveswellfarmcottage.co.uk

Oddity Cottage ★★★
Self Catering
Dorset Cottage Holidays
t (01929) 553443
e enq@dhcottages.co.uk
w dhcottages.co.uk

St George's Cottage ★★★
Self Catering
Dorset Cottage Holidays
t (01929) 553443
e enq@dhcottages.co.uk
w dhcottages.co.uk

Scoles Manor ★★★★
Self Catering
Contact: Peter and Belinda Bell
t (01929) 480312
e peter@scoles.co.uk
w scoles.co.uk

CORSCOMBE
Dorset

Underhill Farm Holidays Meadow Rise ★★★★
Self Catering
Contact: Mrs Joanna Vassie
t (01935) 891245
e vassie@underhillfarm.co.uk
w underhillfarm.co.uk

CORSHAM
Wiltshire

Barnacle Goose ★★★★
Self Catering
t (01225) 869438
e stephanie@barnaclegoose.co.uk
w barnaclegoose.co.uk

Linleys Farm Cottages
★★★★ *Self Catering*
t (01249) 715578

The Ostlers House ★★★★★
Self Catering
Contact: Mr & Mrs Andy & Stella Collett
t (01225) 812700
e reservations@theostlershouse.co.uk
w theostlershouse.co.uk

Wadswick Barns ★★★★
Self Catering
Contact: Mr & Mrs Tim & Carolyn Barton
t (01225) 810733
e barns@wadswick.co.uk
w wadswick.co.uk

CORSLEY
Wiltshire

Lavender Lodge ★★★★
Self Catering
Contact: Mrs Debbie Rickhuss
t (01373) 832829
e rickhuss@tiscali.co.uk
w lavenderlodgecorsley.co.uk

COSSINGTON
Somerset

Cossington Park, Cossington
★★★★ *Self Catering*
Contact: Ms Lesley Pinnell
t (01278) 429852 & 07977 040579
e info@cossingtonpark.com
w cossingtonpark.com

COTLEIGH
Devon

Authers Cottage ★★★★
Self Catering
Milkbere Cottage Holidays
t (01297) 20729
e info@milkberehols.com
w milkberehols.com

COVE
Devon

Springdale ★★★★
Self Catering
Contact: Mrs J Hudson
t (01398) 332089
e jane.hudson@ludomino.co.uk
w home.btconnect.com/ludomino-ltd

COVERACK
Cornwall

14 Coverack Headland
★★★★ *Self Catering*
Contact: Mrs Anne Bradley-Smith
Dorland Cottage, The Mint
t (01883) 743442
w coverack.org.uk

CRACKINGTON HAVEN
Cornwall

9 Lundy Drive ★★★★
Self Catering
Contact: Mrs Anderson
t (01840) 230504
e paul@panderson60.freeserve.co.uk

Bremor Holiday Bungalows and Cottages ★★★
Self Catering
Contact: Mrs Rogers
t (01840) 230340
e cornishbreaks@bremorholidays.wanadoo.co.uk
w bremorholidays.co.uk

Higher Tresmorn ★★★★
Self Catering
Contact: Ms Emma De Haan
Higher Tresmorn – BA034
t (01865) 820429
e tresmorn@btinternet.com
w highertresmorn.co.uk

Longstones ★★★★
Self Catering
Farm & Cottage Holidays
t (01237) 459827
e enquiries@farmcott.co.uk
w holidaycottages.co.uk

St John's View ★★★★★
Self Catering
Contact: Mr Steven Barker
St Johns View
t (01905) 641290
e book@stjohnsview.co.uk
w stjohnsview.co.uk

Trelay Farm Cottages
Rating Applied For
Self Catering
Contact: Mr Ben Oubridge
t (01840) 230901
e ben@climatefriendly.co.uk
w climatefriendly.co.uk/holidays

Trenannick Cottages
★★★-★★★★ *Self Catering*
Contact: Ms Harrison
t (01566) 781443
e lorraine.trenannick@i12.com
w trenannickcottages.co.uk

Trevigue Cottages ★★★★
Self Catering
Contact: Ms Gayle Crocker
t (01840) 230418
e trevigue@talk21.com

Treworgie Barton
★★★★-★★★★★
Self Catering
Contact: Nigel & Norma Warner
t (01840) 230233
e info@treworgie.co.uk
w treworgie.co.uk

CRANTOCK
Cornwall

Basil Cottage ★★★★
Self Catering
t (01637) 831127
w surfs-view.co.uk

Churchtown Cottage ★★★
Self Catering
Contact: Mr Millward
t (01637) 830046
e info@crantockcottages.co.uk
w crantockcottages.co.uk

Crantock Holiday Cottages
★★★-★★★★ *Self Catering*
t 0845 226 5507
e rentals@cornwall-cottages.biz
w cornwall-cottages.biz

Great Weston Farmhouse
★★★ *Self Catering*
Contact: Ms Delia Mills
t 0845 226 5507
e rentals@milco.biz
w crantock-cottages.biz

Pentire Green ★★★
Self Catering
Powells Cottage Holidays
t (01834) 812791
e info@powells.co.uk
w powells.co.uk

CRAPSTONE
Devon

Midway ★★★★ *Self Catering*
Contact: Mrs Susan Eggins
t (01752) 733221
e sueandmikeeggins@hotmail.co.uk
w midwayhouse.co.uk

CREDITON
Devon

Creedy Manor ★★★★
Self Catering
Contact: Mrs Sandra Turner
t (01363) 772684
e sandra@creedymanor.com
w creedymanor.com

Rudge Rew Cottage ★★★★
Self Catering
Contact: Mrs Christine Bailey
t (01363) 877309
e rudgerewfarm@btinternet.com
w rudgerew.co.uk

White Witches and Stable Lodge ★★★★ *Self Catering*
Contact: Mrs Gillian Gillbard
t (01884) 860278
e gillbard@eclipse.co.uk
w eclipse.co.uk/helebarton

CROSCOMBE
Somerset

Millview
Rating Applied For
Self Catering
Contact: Mr & Mrs P Riley
t (01628) 481239
e kirbyjeanne@hotmail.com

CROWLAS
Cornwall

Millers Loft ★★★
Self Catering
Farm & Cottage Holidays
t (01237) 459827
e enquiries@farmcott.co.uk
w holidaycottages.co.uk

Rosehendra ★★★★
Self Catering
Contact: Mrs Paula Tennant
t (020) 8399 0518
e tennantdesign@blueyonder.co.uk
w rosehendra.com

CROYDE
Devon

Ashdene ★★★★★
Self Catering
Marsdens Cottage Holidays
t (01271) 813777
e holidays@marsdens.co.uk
w marsdens.co.uk

Bon Accord ★★★★★
Self Catering
Marsdens Cottage Holidays
t (01271) 813777
e holidays@marsdens.co.uk
w marsdens.co.uk

Bramleys ★★★ *Self Catering*
Marsdens Cottage Holidays
t (01271) 813777
e holidays@marsdens.co.uk
w marsdens.co.uk

Broad-De ★★★★
Self Catering
Marsdens Cottage Holidays
t (01271) 813777
e holidays@marsdens.co.uk
w marsdens.co.uk

Bryher Lee ★★★★
Self Catering
Marsdens Cottage Holidays
t (01271) 813777
e holidays@marsdens.co.uk
w marsdens.co.uk

Caen House ★★★★★
Self Catering
Marsdens Cottage Holidays
t (01271) 813777
e holidays@marsdens.co.uk
w marsdens.co.uk

Cock Rock Cottage ★★★★
Self Catering
Marsdens Cottage Holidays
t (01271) 813777
e holidays@marsdens.co.uk
w marsdens.co.uk

Davids Cottage ★★★★
Self Catering
Marsdens Cottage Holidays
t (01271) 813777
e holidays@marsdens.co.uk
w marsdens.co.uk

Denham House & Cottages, North Buckland ★★★
Self Catering
Contact: Mr & Mrs Bernard & Vera Sanderberg
Denham House
t (01271) 890297
e info@denhamhouse.co.uk
w denhamhouse.co.uk

Distant Point ★★★★
Self Catering
Marsdens Cottage Holidays
t (01271) 813777
e holidays@marsdens.co.uk
w marsdens.co.uk

The Dunes ★★★★
Self Catering
Marsdens Cottage Holidays
t (01271) 813777
e holidays@marsdens.co.uk
w marsdens.co.uk

Duneside ★★★★
Self Catering
Marsdens Cottage Holidays
t (01271) 813777
e holidays@marsdens.co.uk
w marsdens.co.uk

Embleton ★★★★
Self Catering
Marsdens Cottage Holidays
t (01271) 813777
e holidays@marsdens.co.uk
w marsdens.co.uk

Great Close ★★★★
Self Catering
Marsdens Cottage Holidays
t (01271) 813777
e holidays@marsdens.co.uk
w marsdens.co.uk

Hillview ★★★★ *Self Catering*
Marsdens Cottage Holidays
t (01271) 813777
e holidays@marsdens.co.uk
w marsdens.co.uk

Honeycott ★★★
Self Catering
Marsdens Cottage Holidays
t (01271) 813777
e holidays@marsdens.co.uk
w marsdens.co.uk

The Lodge ★★★★
Self Catering
Marsdens Cottage Holidays
t (01271) 813777
e holidays@marsdens.co.uk
w marsdens.co.uk

Lundy Lodge ★★★★
Self Catering
Marsdens Cottage Holidays
t (01271) 813777
e holidays@marsdens.co.uk
w marsdens.co.uk

The Mallows ★★★
Self Catering
Marsdens Cottage Holidays
t (01271) 813777
e holidays@marsdens.co.uk
w marsdens.co.uk

Marigold Cottage ★★★★
Self Catering
Marsdens Cottage Holidays
t (01271) 813777
e holidays@marsdens.co.uk
w marsdens.co.uk

Oceanside ★★★
Self Catering
Marsdens Cottage Holidays
t (01271) 813777
e holidays@marsdens.co.uk
w marsdens.co.uk

The Reeds ★★★★★
Self Catering
Marsdens Cottage Holidays
t (01271) 813777
e holidays@marsdens.co.uk
w marsdens.co.uk

Rowan Cottage ★★★★
Self Catering
Marsdens Cottage Holidays
t (01271) 813777
e holidays@marsdens.co.uk
w marsdens.co.uk

Sands End ★★★★
Self Catering
Marsdens Cottage Holidays
t (01271) 813777
e holidays@marsdens.co.uk
w marsdens.co.uk

Seahaven ★★★★
Self Catering
Marsdens Cottage Holidays
t (01271) 813777
e holidays@marsdens.co.uk
w marsdens.co.uk

Summer Breeze ★★★★
Self Catering
Marsdens
t (01271) 813777
e enquiries@marsdens.co.uk
w marsdens.co.uk

Sunnyside ★★★★
Self Catering
Marsdens Cottage Holidays
t (01271) 813777
e holidays@marsdens.co.uk
w marsdens.co.uk

Suntana ★★★ *Self Catering*
Marsdens Cottage Holidays
t (01271) 813777
e holidays@marsdens.co.uk
w marsdens.co.uk

Surfers Retreat ★★★★
Self Catering
Marsdens Cottage Holidays
t (01271) 813777
e holidays@marsdens.co.uk
w marsdens.co.uk

Sweets Cottage ★★★★
Self Catering
Marsdens Cottage Holidays
t (01271) 813777
e holidays@marsdens.co.uk
w marsdens.co.uk

Swell ★★★★ *Self Catering*
Marsdens Cottage Holidays
t (01271) 813777
e holidays@marsdens.co.uk
w marsdens.co.uk

Westside ★★★★
Self Catering
Marsdens Cottage Holidays
t (01271) 813777
e holidays@marsdens.co.uk
w marsdens.co.uk

Withyside ★★★★
Self Catering
Marsdens Cottage Holidays
t (01271) 813777
e holidays@marsdens.co.uk
w marsdens.co.uk

CRUGMEER
Cornwall

Old Lifeboat Station ★★★
Self Catering
Harbour Holidays
t (01841) 533402
e contact@harbourholidays.co.uk
w harbourholidays.co.uk

Webbers
Rating Applied For
Self Catering
Contact: Nicky Stanley
Harbour Holidays
t (01841) 532402
e contact@harbourholidays.co.uk
w harbourholidays.co.uk

CUBERT
Cornwall

Cromwell House ★★★
Self Catering
Contact: Mrs Sue Mills
t (024) 7646 3840
e enquiries@cromwellhouse.co.uk
w cromwellhouse.co.uk

Elfadore ★★★ *Self Catering*
Contact: Mrs Clegg
t (01637) 830640

CUCKLINGTON
Somerset

Hale Farm ★★★
Self Catering
Contact: Mrs David
t (01963) 33342

CULMHEAD
Somerset

Culmhead House, Culmhead ★★★ *Self Catering*
Contact: Mr & Mrs Timothy & Susan Rodgers
t (01823) 421073
e rodgers@culmheadhouse.com
w culmheadhouse.com

CURRY MALLET
Somerset

Buzzards View ★★★★
Self Catering
Contact: Major Ian Hill
t (01823) 480436
e majianhil@lineone.net
w crimsonhillfarm.co.uk

CURY
Cornwall

Treloskan Farm ★★★
Self Catering
t (01326) 240493

DAGLINGWORTH
Gloucestershire

Corner Cottage ★★★★
Self Catering
Contact: Mrs Mary Bartlett
t (01285) 653478

DALWOOD
Devon

Millwater Cottage ★★★
Self Catering
Dream Cottages
t (01305) 789000
e admin@dream-cottages.co.uk
w dream-cottages.co.uk

Riverbank Cottage ★★★
Self Catering
Dream Cottages
t (01305) 789000
e admin@dream-cottages.co.uk
w dream-cottages.co.uk

DARTINGTON
Devon

Billany ★★★ *Self Catering*
t (01237) 479146
e enquiries@farmcott.co.uk
w holidaycottages.co.uk

DARTMEET
Devon

Coachman's Cottage ★★★
Self Catering
Contact: Mrs Toni Evans
t (01364) 631173
e huntlodge@pobox.com
w dartmeet.com

DARTMOUTH
Devon

1 The Pottery ★★★★★
Self Catering
Blue Chip Vacations
t (01803) 855282
e info@bluechipvacations.com
w bluechipvacations.com

---

21 Dart Marina ★★★★★
Self Catering
Blue Chip Vacations
t (01803) 855282
e info@bluechipvacations.com
w bluechipvacations.com

---

25 Dart Marina
Rating Applied For
Self Catering
Blue Chip Vacations
t (01803) 855282
e info@bluechipvacations.com
w bluechipvacations.com

---

9 Dart Marina ★★★★★
Self Catering
Blue Chip Vacations
t (01803) 855282
e info@bluechipvacations.com
w bluechipvacations.com

Dartwood, Dartmouth ★★★★★ *Self Catering*
Blue Chip Vacations
t (01803) 855282
e info@bluechipvacations.com
w bluechipvacations.com

Ferry View ★★★★
Self Catering
Contact: Mrs Sarah Hammett
t (01392) 461268
e jarvishayes@btopenworld.com
w ferryviewdartmouth.co.uk

Harbour Heights ★★★★
Self Catering
Contact: Mrs Buckingham
t 07815 824821
w dartmouthholiday.co.uk

Higher Bowden Holiday Cottages ★★★★
Self Catering
Contact: Mrs Linda Horne
t (01803) 770745
e lin@higherbowden.com
w higherbowden.com

The Old Bakehouse ★★★
Self Catering
Contact: Mrs Sylvia Ridalls
t (01803) 834585
e gparker@pioneerps.co.uk
w oldbakehousedartmouth.co.uk

Wychwood, Dartmouth
★★★★★ *Self Catering*
Blue Chip Vacations
t (01803) 855282
e info@bluechipvacations.com
w bluechipvacations.com

DAVIDSTOW
Cornwall

4 Inny Vale ★★★
Self Catering
Contact: Mr & Mrs Adams
w valevacations.co.uk

Emily's Cottage ★★★★
Self Catering
Contact: Clare Kavanagh
t 07979 772520
e emilyscottage@hotmail.co.uk
w holidaylets.net/properties/25544

Treworra Barton Cottages
★★★★ *Self Catering*
Contact: Mr Andy Ryan
t (01840) 261798
e andy@treworra.co.uk
w treworra.co.uk

DAWLISH
Devon

1 Great Cliff, Dawlish
★★★★★ *Self Catering*
Blue Chip Vacations
t (01803) 855282
e info@bluechipvacations.com
w bluechipvacations.com

13 Great Cliff ★★★★★
Self Catering
Blue Chip Vacations
t (01803) 855282
e info@bluechipvacations.com
w bluechipvacations.com

2 Great Cliff ★★★★
Self Catering
Blue Chip Vacations
t (01803) 855282
e info@bluechipvacations.com
w bluechipvacations.com

6 Henty Close ★★★★
Self Catering
Blue Chip Vacations
t (01803) 855282
e info@bluechipvacations.com
w bluechipvacations.com

Blenheim
Rating Applied For
Self Catering
Contact: Mrs Ann Ferris
t (01626) 862372
e theblenheim@btinternet.com
w theblenheim.uk.net

Brookdale ★★★★
Self Catering
Holiday Homes and Cottages South West
t (01803) 299677
e holcotts@aol.com
w swcottages.co.uk

Cofton Country Cottage Holidays ★★★★
Self Catering
Contact: Mrs Valerie Jeffery
t (01626) 890111
e info@coftonholidays.co.uk
w coftonholidays.co.uk

Duckaller Farm *Approved Caravan Holiday Home*
Contact: Mrs Roz Partridge
t (01626) 863132
e holidays@duckallerfarm.co.uk
w duckallerfarm.co.uk

Erminhurst ★★★
Self Catering
Holiday Homes and Cottages South West
t (01803) 299677
e holcotts@aol.com
w swcottages.co.uk

Great Cliff Luxury Apartment ★★★★★
Self Catering
Contact: Mr Roger Smith
t (01746) 769301
e rsmith@greatcliff.co.uk
w greatcliff.co.uk

Rockstone ★★★★
Self Catering
Holiday Homes and Cottages South West
t (01803) 299677
e holcotts@aol.com
w swcottages.co.uk

Twin Cottage ★★★
Self Catering
Holiday Homes and Cottages South West
t (01803) 299677
e holcotts@aol.com
w swcottages.co.uk

DAWLISH WARREN
Devon

32 Devondale ★★★
Self Catering
Contact: Mr Martin Wheeler
t 0800 075 5651
e holiday@dawlish-warren.com
w dawlish-warren.com

Baichal on Welcome Family Holiday Park ★★
Self Catering
Contact: Mr Robert Bailey
t (01626) 773737
e baichalinfo@btconnect.com
w baichal.com

Cosy Lets ★★★ *Self Catering*
Contact: Mr Chris Mallee
t (0121) 354 1886
e chris.mallee@btinternet.com
w dawlishwarrenholidayhome.co.uk/

Devondale Court No. 24
★★★ *Self Catering*
Contact: Mrs Teresa Code
t (01392) 881545
e tesscode@hotmail.com
w dawlishwarren.org.uk

Eastdon Estate ★★★★
Self Catering
Contact: Mrs Valerie Jeffery
Cofton Country Holidays
t (01626) 890111
e info@coftonholidays.co.uk
w coftonholidays.co.uk

Red Rock Holidays
Rating Applied For
Self Catering
Contact: Mr Barry Cunliffe
t (01628) 862269
e redrock@hotmail.co.uk

DEERHURST
Gloucestershire

Deerhurst Cottages, Deerhurst ★★★★
Self Catering
Contact: Mrs Nicole Samuel
t (01684) 275845
e enquiries@deerhurstcottages.co.uk
w deerhurstcottages.co.uk

DELABOLE
Cornwall

Badeca Cottage ★★★
Self Catering
Contact: Angela Bakewell
t (01288) 354537
e info@badecasprings.com
w badecasprings.com

Delamere Holiday Bungalows ★ *Self Catering*
Contact: Mrs Snowden
t (01895) 234144
w delamerebungalows.com

Ruby Cottage ★★★
Self Catering
Contact: Ms Sabina Dziurman
t 07725 567666
e enquiries@rubycottage.net
w rubycottage.net

DEVIOCK
Cornwall

4 Celtic Shores ★★★★★
Self Catering
Cornish Collection Ltd
t (01503) 262736
e enquiries@cornishcollections.co.uk
w cornishcollection.co.uk

9 Celtic Shores ★★★★
Self Catering
Cornish Collection Ltd
t (01503) 262736
e enquiries@cornishcollections.co.uk
w cornishcollection.co.uk

DEVIZES
Wiltshire

Abbotts Ball Farm Cottage
★★★ *Self Catering*
Contact: Mrs V Hazel Hobbs
t (01380) 721661
e hobbs@abbottsballfarm.com
w abbottsballfarm.com

Caen View ★★★★
Self Catering
Contact: Mrs Linda Austin
t (01380) 859343

The Derby ★★★
Self Catering
Contact: Mrs Janet Tyler
t (01380) 850523
e kingsplayfarming@btinternet.com

Fourbee ★★★★
Self Catering
Contact: Mr & Mrs Bernard & Susan Foreman
t (01380) 816919
e fourbeecontact@aol.com
w fourbee.biz

The Gatehouse ★★★★
Self Catering
Contact: Mrs Laura Stratton
t (01380) 725283
e info@visitdevizes.co.uk

Owls Cottage ★★★★
Self Catering
Contact: Mrs Gill Whittome
t (01380) 818804
e gill@owls-cottage.com
w owls-cottage.com

Tichborne's Farm Cottages
★★★★ *Self Catering*
Contact: Mr & Mrs Jon & Judy Nash
t (01380) 862971
e info@tichbornes.co.uk
w tichbornes.co.uk

DEVORAN
Cornwall

Anne's Cottage ★★★
Self Catering
Special Places in Cornwall
t (01872) 864400
e office@specialplacescornwall.co.uk
w specialplacescornwall.co.uk

Charlton, Mrs E, Devoran
★★ *Self Catering*
Contact: Mrs Elizabeth Charlton
t (01872) 864188

Tinners ★★★ *Self Catering*
Special Places in Cornwall
t (01872) 864400
e office@specialplacescornwall.co.uk
w specialplacescornwall.co.uk

DILTON MARSH
Wiltshire

Cottage Next Door ★★★★
Self Catering
Contact: Mrs P Traves
t (01373) 825480
e pattraves@btinternet.com
w cottage-next-door.co.uk

DINTON
Wiltshire

The Cottage, Marshwood Farm ★★★★ *Self Catering*
Contact: Mrs Fiona Lockyer
t (01722) 716334
e marshwood1@btconnect.com
w marshwoodfarm.co.uk

Fitz Farm Cottage ★★★
Self Catering
Hideaways
t (01747) 828170
e enq@hideaways.co.uk
w hideaways.co.uk

The Flat, Honeysuckle Homestead ★★ *Self Catering*
Contact: Mr David Kirby
t (01722) 717887
e honeysuckle@dinton21.freeserve.co.uk
w honeysucklehomestead.co.uk

DIPTFORD
Devon

Fletcher's Combe Barn
★★★★ *Self Catering*
Contact: Mr Simon Harrington
t (01548) 821152
e enq@fletcherscombe.co.uk

Higher Beneknowle
★★★★★ *Self Catering*
Toad Hall Cottages
t (01548) 853089
e thc@toadhallcottages.com
w toadhallcottages.co.uk

Ley Farm ★★★ *Self Catering*
Contact: Mrs Sophia Hendy
t (01548) 821200

DITTISHAM Devon

Cobwebs ★★★★
Self Catering
Dart Valley Cottages
t (01803) 771127
e enquiries@dartvalleycottages.co.uk
w dartvalleycottages.co.uk

Sarah Elliots ★★★★
Self Catering
Dart Valley Cottages
t (01803) 771127
e enquiries@dartvalleycottages.co.uk
w dartvalleycottages.co.uk

Smugglers Cottage ★★★
Self Catering
Toad Hall Cottages
t (01548) 853089
e thc@toadhallcottages.com
w toadhallcottages.co.uk

Wild Oat House ★★★★
Self Catering
Dart Valley Cottages
t (01803) 771127
e enquiries@dartvalleycottages.co.uk
w dartvalleycottages.co.uk

DOBWALLS Cornwall

An Penty ★★★★
Self Catering
Farm & Cottage Holidays
t (01237) 459827
e enquiries@farmcott.co.uk
w holidaycottages.co.uk

West Tremabe Holiday Cottages ★★★ *Self Catering*
Contact: Mr & Mrs Kirk
t (01579) 321863
e christine.j.foster@btopenworld.com
w west-tremabe-cottages.co.uk

DOLTON Devon

Ham Farm
★★★★-★★★★★
Self Catering
Contact: Mr & Mrs Cobbledick
t (01805) 624000
e info@hamfarm.co.uk
w hamfarm.co.uk

Vine Cottage ★★★★
Self Catering
Contact: Mrs Susan Marshall
t (01252) 524156
e samandjcm@aol.com
w vinecottagedevon.co.uk

DORCHESTER Dorset

Beaufort Cottages ★★★
Self Catering
Dream Cottages
t (01305) 789000
e admin@dream-cottages.co.uk
w dream-cottages.co.uk

Damers Cottage
★★★-★★★★★ *Self Catering*
Contact: Mrs Rosemary Hodder
t (01305) 852205
e info@cottage-holidays-dorset.co.uk
w cottage-holidays-dorset.co.uk

Hardy Country Cottages
★★★★ *Self Catering*
t (01305) 889222
w hardycountrycottages.co.uk

Hastings Farm Cottages
★★★★ *Self Catering*
Contact: Mr David Hills
t (01305) 848627
e enq@dorsetfarmcottages.co.uk
w dorsetfarmcottages.co.uk

Molly's Cottage ★★★
Self Catering
Contact: Mr & Mrs Tim & Sue Stiles
t (01300) 341514
e info@mollys-cottage.co.uk
w mollys-cottage.co.uk

Swallows ★★★★★
Self Catering
Contact: Mrs Pippa James
t (01305) 889338
e hugojames@ukonline.co.uk
w dovehousedorset.co.uk

Wolfeton Lodge ★★★
Self Catering
Contact: Mrs Thimbleby
Wolfeton House
t (01305) 263500
e kthimbleby.wolfeton@gmail.com

Woodlands Cottage ★★★
Self Catering
Dream Cottages
t (01305) 789000
e admin@dream-cottages.co.uk
w dream-cottages.co.uk

DOUBLEBOIS Cornwall

The Old Farmhouse ★★★
Self Catering
Contact: Jason Wood
t 07931 377608
e jason_nicholas_wood@hotmail.com

DOWLISH FORD Somerset

3 New Buildings ★★★
Self Catering
Contact: Mrs Hillary Mead
t (01460) 61996

DOWNDERRY Cornwall

The Chalet ★★ *Self Catering*
Contact: Mr Nicholas Burns
t (01752) 302895

Derry View ★★★
Self Catering
Cornish Collection Ltd
t (01503) 262736
e enquiries@cornishcollections.co.uk
w cornishcollection.co.uk

Looe Island View
Rating Applied For
Self Catering
Valley Villas Ltd
t (01752) 605605
e sales@valleyvillas.com
w valleyvillas.co.uk

Seagulls ★★★ *Self Catering*
Valley Villas Ltd
t (01752) 605605
e sales@valleyvillas.com
w valleyvillas.co.uk

Treguna Cottage ★★★
Self Catering
Valley Villas Ltd
t (01752) 605605
e sales@valleyvillas.com
w valleyvillas.co.uk

DOWNINGTON Gloucestershire

The Gallery ★★★★
Self Catering
Contact: Mr Martin Forbes
t (01367) 253393
e mas.forbes@btopenworld.com
w thegallerybridgehouse.co.uk

DRAYCOTT Gloucestershire

Wellacres House ★★★★★
Self Catering
t (01386) 593603
e michael@bigcottage.com
w bigcottage.com

DRAYCOTT Somerset

Martindale ★★★
Self Catering
Contact: Mr & Mrs Dance
t (01934) 742811
e helen@martindale-cottage.co.uk
w martindale-cottage.co.uk

Rowan Cottage ★★★
Self Catering
t (01708) 470897
w cheddarcottages.com

DREWSTEIGNTON Devon

East Underdown ★★★★★
Self Catering
Contact: Mr Tim Clarke
t (01647) 231339
e eastunderdown@googlemail.com
w eastunderdown.co.uk/

DRIFFIELD Gloucestershire

The Stables ★★★★
Self Catering
Contact: Mrs Margaret Smith
t (01285) 850641
e me_smith@btinternet.com

DRYBROOK Gloucestershire

Coach House ★★★
Self Catering
Contact: Gill Marfell
t (01594) 542278
e gill@marfell.net
w marfell.net

DULOE Cornwall

Penquite Country Cottages
★★★ *Self Catering*
Contact: Mr & Mrs M Welch
t (01503) 220260
e stay@penquitecountrycottages.co.uk
w penquitecountrycottages.co.uk

DULVERTON Somerset

Anstey Mills Cottages
★★★★ *Self Catering*
Contact: Mrs Doris Braukmann-Pugsley
t (01398) 341329
e ansteymills@yahoo.com
w ansteymillscottagedevon.co.uk

Hayloft Cottage ★★★
Self Catering
Marsdens Cottage Holidays
t (01271) 813777
e holidays@marsdens.co.uk
w marsdens.co.uk

Melton House ★★★
Self Catering
Marsdens Cottage Holidays
t (01271) 813777
e holidays@marsdens.co.uk
w marsdens.co.uk

Paddons ★★★ *Self Catering*
Contact: Mrs Mary McMichael
t (01398) 323514
e marymcmichael@waitrose.com

Venford Cottage ★★★★
Self Catering
Contact: Mr Harley Stratton
t (01398) 341308
e harleyhstratton@aol.com
w venfordcottage.co.uk

Whitehall House ★★★★
Self Catering
Contact: Mr Kevin Reeves
t (01329) 665792
e kevin.reeves4@ntlworld.com
w whitehallhouse.f9.co.uk

Woolcotts Cross Cottage
★★★★ *Self Catering*
Contact: Mr Iain Joyce
t (01398) 371456
e iainjoyce@freeola.com
w woolcotts.com

DUNSTER Somerset

The Courtyard Flats ★★★
Self Catering
Contact: Mrs G Harwood
t (01643) 821485
e harwoods.dunster@ntlworld.com

Duddings Country Cottages
★★★★ *Self Catering*
Contact: Mr Richard Tilke
t (01643) 841123
e richard@duddings.co.uk
w duddings.co.uk

Grooms Cottage ★★★★
Self Catering
Contact: Mrs Disney
t (01643) 821497

DUNTISBOURNE ROUSE
Gloucestershire

Swallow Barns ★★★★★
Self Catering
Contact: Mr & Mrs Anthony & Jean Merrett
t (01285) 651031
e anthony.merrett@homecall.co.uk
w cottageinthecountry.co.uk

DURSLEY
Gloucestershire

The Stable ★★★★
Self Catering
Contact: Mr David Randall
t (01453) 860728
e thegranary@fsmail.net

Two Springbank ★★★
Self Catering
Contact: Mrs Freda Jones
32 Everlands
t (01453) 543047
e lhandfaj32lg@surefish.co.uk

EAST ALLINGTON
Devon

Flear Farm Cottages
★★★★-★★★★★
Self Catering
Contact: Mr Steven Dix
t (01548) 521227
e flearfarm@btinternet.com
w flearfarm.co.uk

Higher Coombe Farm Cottages ★★★★
Self Catering
Toad Hall Cottages
t (01548) 853089
e thc@toadhallcottages.com
w toadhallcottages.co.uk

Pitt Farm ★★★★
Self Catering
Contact: Mr & Mrs Christopher & Denise Bates
t (01548) 521234
e info@pitt-farm.co.uk
w pitt-farm.co.uk

Winnowers ★★★★
Self Catering
Toad Hall Cottages
t (01548) 853089
e thc@toadhallcottages.com
w toadhallcottages.co.uk

EAST BUDLEIGH
Devon

10 Brookside ★★★★
Self Catering
Sweetcombe Cottage Holidays
t (01395) 512130
e enquiries@sweetcombe-ch.co.uk
w sweetcombe-ch.co.uk

Brook Cottage ★★★★
Self Catering
Contact: Mrs Jo Simons
t (01242) 574031
e josimons@tesco.net
w brookcottagebudleigh.co.uk

Stable Cottage ★★★★
Self Catering
Sweetcombe Cottage Holidays
t (01395) 512130
e enquiries@sweetcombe-ch.co.uk
w sweetcombe-ch.co.uk

Yew Tree Cottage ★★★
Self Catering
Sweetcombe Cottage Holidays
t (01395) 512130
e enquiries@sweetcombe-ch.co.uk
w sweetcombe-ch.co.uk

EAST CHILLA
Devon

Orchard Keeper's Cottage
★★★★★ *Self Catering*
Contact: Linda Davis
t (01409) 221991
e info@west-lake.co.uk
w west-lake.co.uk

EAST CHINNOCK
Somerset

Weston House ★★★★
Self Catering
Contact: Mrs Susan Gliddon
t (01935) 863712
e sue@westonhouse.net
w westonhouse.net

EAST HILL
Devon

The Hay House ★★★★
Self Catering
Contact: Mrs Catherine Oates
t (01404) 812122
e catherine@blacklakefarm.com
w blacklakefarm.com

Mazzard Farm
Rating Applied For
Self Catering
t (01404) 815492
e info@mazzardfarm.com
w mazzardfarm.com

Mazzard Farm
Rating Applied For
Self Catering
Contact: Ruud Jansen Venneboer
t (01404) 815492
e info@mazzardfarm.com
w mazzardfarm.com

EAST KNIGHTON
Dorset

Dairy House Cottage ★★★
Self Catering
Dream Cottages
t (01305) 789000
e admin@dream-cottages.co.uk
w dream-cottages.co.uk

Lovers Knot ★★★
Self Catering
Dream Cottages
t (01305) 789000
e admin@dream-cottages.co.uk
w dream-cottages.co.uk

Oaktree Cottage ★★★
Self Catering
Dream Cottages
t (01305) 789000
e admin@dream-cottages.co.uk
w dream-cottages.co.uk

EAST KNOYLE
Wiltshire

The Old Piggery
Rating Applied For
Self Catering
Hideaways
t (01747) 828170
e enq@hideaways.co.uk
w hideaways.co.uk

Spring Cottage ★★★
Self Catering
Hideaways
t (01747) 828170
e enq@hideaways.co.uk
w hideaways.co.uk

EAST LOOE
Cornwall

7 Harbourside Apartments
★★★★ *Self Catering*
Cornish Collection Ltd
t (01503) 262736
e enquiries@cornishcollections.co.uk
w cornishcollection.co.uk

Admiralty Court Apartments
★★★★ *Self Catering*
Contact: Mrs Sheila Summers
t (01503) 264617
e admiraltycourt@hotmail.co.uk

Fox Valley Cottages
★★★★-★★★★★
Self Catering
Contact: Mr & Mrs Andy & Linda Brown
Lanlawren
t (01726) 870115
e info@foxvalleycottages.co.uk
w foxvalleycottages.co.uk

Quay View ★★★★
Self Catering
Contact: Miss Tonia Lewis
t (01503) 265377 & (01503) 265377
e quayview@looebakery.co.uk
w quayview.cornwall.uk.net

Quayside ★★★ *Self Catering*
Contact: Mrs Butters
t (01503) 262533

Seagull ★★★ *Self Catering*
Cornish Collection Ltd
t (01503) 262736
e enquiries@cornishcollections.co.uk
w cornishcollection.co.uk

EAST PORTHOLLAND
Cornwall

The Boat House ★★★★★
Self Catering
Niche Retreats
t (01209) 861745
e jackie@nicheretreats.co.uk
w nicheretreats.co.uk

EAST PORTLEMOUTH
Devon

Meadow Barn Cottage ★★★
Self Catering
Toad Hall Cottages
t (01548) 853089
e thc@toadhallcottages.com
w toadhallcottages.co.uk

EAST PRAWLE
Devon

Station Officers House
★★★★★ *Self Catering*
Contact: Mr Daniel Dovar
t (020) 7421 5567
e daniel@sohouse.co.uk
w stationofficershouse.co.uk

EAST STOUR
Dorset

The Crown Inn Apartments
★★★ *Self Catering*
Contact: Mr Samuel Holmes
t (01747) 838866
e crown.inn@tiscali.co.uk
w go.to/thecrowninn

EASTERTON
Wiltshire

Stable End ★★★
Self Catering
Contact: Mrs Anne Blagbrough
t (01380) 812426
e anne@ablagbrough.fsnet.co.uk

EBRINGTON
Gloucestershire

Pump Cottage ★★★
Self Catering
Contact: Mr Robert Hutsby
t (01789) 841525
e robert.hutsby@btinternet.com
w chipping-campden-holiday-cottages.co.uk

Tythe Barn Cottage ★★★★
Self Catering
Contact: Mrs Michelle Sharp
t (01386) 854824
e info@tythebarn.co.uk
w tythebarn.co.uk

EDINGTON
Wiltshire

Greengrove Cottage ★★★★
Self Catering
t 0870 534 2342
e mail@hoseasons.co.uk
w hoseasons.co.uk

EDMONTON
Cornwall

5 & 8 Quarryman's Cottages
★★★ *Self Catering*
Contact: Mr R Hoole
t (01709) 370034
e bobhoole@blueyonder.co.uk

Quarryman's Cottages ★★★
Self Catering
Contact: Mr Huw Jenkins
t 07866 386611
e jenkins@choicecornishcottages.com
w choicecornishcottages.com

Squirrel Cottage ★★★
Self Catering
Contact: Jon and Gail
t 07968 033927
w sunshinecottages.com

Willow Cottage ★★★★
Self Catering
Contact: Mr David Oram
t (01709) 530128
e droram@btopenworld.com

EGGESFORD
Devon

Trenchard Farm Granary Cottage
Rating Applied For
Self Catering
Contact: Jackie Skinner
t (01363) 83746
e jackieskinner22@gmail.com

ELKSTONE
Gloucestershire

The Dolls House ★★★
Self Catering
Contact: Mrs Marion Cooch
t (01242) 870244
e marioncooch@hotmail.co.uk

ELTON
Gloucestershire

Red Barn Holiday Cottages
★★★ *Self Catering*
Contact: Paul Williams
t (01594) 762030
e supreme@gotadsl.co.uk
w redbarn-holidays.co.uk

ENGLISH BICKNOR
Gloucestershire

Upper Tump Farm ★★★
Self Catering
Contact: Marion Merrett
t (01594) 860072

ERMINGTON
Devon

Lakeside Cottage ★★★★★
Self Catering
Contact: Mr & Mrs R P & P J M Longman
t (01548) 830168

ETLOE
Gloucestershire

Oatfield Country Cottages
★★★★-★★★★★
Self Catering
Contact: Alison Gray
t (01594) 510372
w oatfieldfarm.co.uk

EVENLODE
Gloucestershire

2 Rose Terrace ★★★★
Self Catering
Contact: Ms Richards
t (01993) 824252
e mancott@netcomuk.co.uk
w manorcottages.co.uk

EWEN
Gloucestershire

The Annexe ★★★★
Self Catering
Contact: Mrs Nora Beale
t (01285) 770325
e nbeale5537@aol.co.uk
w shootershillcottage.co.uk

EXBOURNE
Devon

Lower Cadham Farm
★★★★★ *Self Catering*
Contact: Mrs Jan Jopling
t (01837) 851288
e sales@trotterscottage.co.uk
w trotterscottage.co.uk

Woodhall Holiday Barns
★★★★ *Self Catering*
Contact: Mr Kevin Brown-Martin
t (01837) 810771
e kb-m@fsmail.net

EXETER
Devon

Augusta Court ★★★★★
Self Catering
Contact: Ms Juliet Ware
t (01392) 477727
e enquiries@wareedwards.co.uk
w wareedwards.com

Bussells Farm Cottages
★★★★ *Self Catering*
Contact: Andy and Lucy Hines
Bussells Farm
t (01392) 841238
e bussellsfarm@aol.com
w bussellsfarm.co.uk

Coach House Farm
★★★★★ *Self Catering*
Contact: Mr & Miss John & Polly Bale
t (01392) 461254
e selfcatering@mpprops.co.uk

Exeter Holiday Homes ★★★
Self Catering
Contact: Mrs Gina Belcher
t (01404) 823805
e gina.birchmore@btopenworld.com
w exeter-holiday-homes.co.uk

The Garden House ★★★★
Self Catering
Contact: Mr & Mrs Hugh & Anna Evans
t (01392) 211286
e enquiries@realcakes.co.uk
w exeterholidaycottage.co.uk

Honeysuckle End ★★★★
Self Catering
Contact: Mr & Mrs Ayre
t (01392) 860434
e ayre.ratcliffe@virgin.net
w honeysuckle-end-exeter.co.uk

Mr Sage, Exeter Holiday Homes ★★★ *Self Catering*
Contact: Mr William Sage
Exeter Holiday Homes
t (01392) 271668
e gina.birchmore@btopenworld.com
w exeter-holiday-homes.co.uk

Woodham ★★★★
Self Catering
Contact: Mrs Gibb
t (01392) 273451
e carysgibb@yahoo.co.uk

EXFORD
Somerset

No 2 Auction Field Cottage
★★★ *Self Catering*
Contact: Mr & Mrs Keith & Gill Batchelor
t (01258) 817801

Court Farm ★★★-★★★★
Self Catering
Contact: Mrs Beth Horstmann
t (01643) 831207
e beth@courtfarm.co.uk
w courtfarm.co.uk

Holly Tree Cottage, Exford
★★★ *Self Catering*
Contact: Mr Chris Budd
t (01420) 588577

Riscombe Farm Holiday Cottages and Stabling, Exford ★★★★ *Self Catering*
Contact: Mr & Mrs Brian & Leone Martin
t (01643) 831480
e info@riscombe.co.uk
w riscombe.co.uk

Rocks Bungalow ★★★★
Self Catering
Contact: Mrs Kathryn Tucker
t (01643) 831213
e enquiries@stetfold.wanadoo.co.uk
w rocksbungalow.co.uk

Stilemoor Bungalow ★★★★
Self Catering
Contact: Mrs Joan Atkins
t (01643) 831564
e info@stilemoorexmoor.co.uk
w stilemoorexmoor.co.uk

Westermill Farm ★★★
Self Catering
Contact: Mr Oliver Edwards
t (01643) 831238
e swt@westermill.com
w westermill.com

EXMOUTH
Devon

1 Windjammer Court
★★★★★ *Self Catering*
Blue Chip Vacations
t (01803) 855282
e info@bluechipvacations.com
w bluechipvacations.com

2 & 4 Channel View ★★★★
Self Catering
Contact: Mr & Mrs Cliff & Sandra Lenn
t (01395) 222555
e holiday@channelview.eu
w channelview.eu

Little Magnolia ★★★
Self Catering
Sweetcombe Cottage Holidays
t (01395) 512130
e enquiries@sweetcombe-ch.co.uk
w sweetcombe-ch.co.uk

Pilot Cottage ★★★★
Self Catering
Contact: Mr & Mrs Woods
t (01395) 222882
e seahorse@exmouth.net
w exmouth.net

Saxonbury Annexe ★★★★
Self Catering
Contact: Dr & Mrs John & Josephine Elliott
t (01395) 264323
e elliottjojohn@aol.com
w saxonburyselfcatering.co.uk

EYPE
Dorset

The Cabin ★★★★
Self Catering
Lyme Bay Holidays
t (01297) 443363
e email@lymebayholidays.co.uk
w lymebayholidays.co.uk

Railway Cottage ★★★
Self Catering
Dream Cottages
t (01305) 789000
e admin@dream-cottages.co.uk
w dream-cottages.co.uk

Sealark ★★★ *Self Catering*
Contact: Mrs Jill Sharp
t (01308) 425902
e jill@eypehouse.co.uk
w eypechaletpark.co.uk

FAIRFORD
Gloucestershire

Wishbone Cottage ★★★★
Self Catering
Contact: Mr & Mrs Simon & Karen Priestman
t (01285) 713133
e karen@wishbonecottage.co.uk
w wishbonecottage.co.uk

FALMOUTH
Cornwall

28 Kimberley Park Road
★★★★ *Self Catering*
Cornish Holiday Cottages
t (01326) 250339
e emily@cornishholidaycottages.net
w cornishholidaycottages.net

47 Upper Stables
Rating Applied For
Self Catering
Holiday Cornwall
t (01326) 250278
e enquiries@holidaycornwall.co.uk
w holidaycornwall.co.uk

65 Lower Maen Cottage
★★★★ *Self Catering*
Holiday Cornwall
t (01326) 250278
e enquiries@holidaycornwall.co.uk
w holidaycornwall.co.uk

69 Maen Barn
Rating Applied For
Self Catering
Holiday Cornwall
t (01326) 250278
e enquiries@holidaycornwall.co.uk
w holidaycornwall.co.uk

73 Upper Barn
Rating Applied For
Self Catering
Holiday Cornwall
t (01326) 250278
e enquiries@holidaycornwall.co.uk
w holidaycornwall.co.uk

8 Marine Crescent ★★
Self Catering
Contact: Mrs Spong
t (01702) 712596 & 07989 653639
e rcspong@hotmail.com

Anchorage Apartments
★★★ *Self Catering*
Contact: Mr & Mrs Cain
t (01326) 312164
e anchorapts@aol.com
w anchorageapartments.co.uk

Bay View Self Catering – BK094 ★★★ *Self Catering*
Contact: Mrs Walker
t (01326) 312429
e bay.viewfalmouth@btinternet.com
w bayviewselfcatering.co.uk

Blue Harbour ★★★
Self Catering
Cornish Holiday Cottages
t (01326) 250339
e emily@cornishholidaycottages.net
w cornishholidaycottages.net

Boslowen ★★★★
Self Catering
Special Places in Cornwall
t (01872) 864400
e office@specialplacescornwall.co.uk
w specialplacescornwall.co.uk

Captain's Corner ★★★★
Self Catering
Special Places in Cornwall
t (01872) 864400
e office@specialplacescornwall.co.uk
w specialplacescornwall.co.uk

Captain's Lookout ★★★
Self Catering
Contact: Mr Fishwick
t (01326) 312651
e mfishwick@aol.com

Clipper Cottage ★★★★
Self Catering
Cornish Holiday Cottages
t (01326) 250339
e emily@cornishholidaycottages.net
w cornishholidaycottages.net

Country Cottage Retreats, Falmouth ★★★★
Self Catering
Contact: Ralph & Ann Bailey
t (01326) 340897
e biscarhols@amserve.net
w viscarfarm-cottages.co.uk

The Custodian's House
★★★★★ *Self Catering*
English Heritage
t 0870 333 1187
e holidaycottages@english-heritage.org.uk
w english-heritage.org.uk/holidaycottages

Falmouth Beach Resort Apartments ★★★-★★★★
Self Catering
t (01326) 310500
e info@falmouthbeachhotel.co.uk
w bw-falmouthbeachhotel.co.uk

The Foredeck ★★★★★
Self Catering
Contact: Mr Myles Yallop
t (01934) 844131
e myles.yallop@btinternet.com
w theforedeck.com

Good-Winds Holiday Apartments ★★★
Self Catering
Contact: Mrs Goodwin
t (01326) 313200
e alandnancy@goodwind64.orangehome.co.uk

Harbour View
Rating Applied For
Self Catering
Cornish Holiday Cottages
t (01326) 250339
e emily@cornishholidaycottages.net
w cornishholidaycottages.net

Harbour View ★★★★★
Self Catering
Contact: Ross Barnese info@cornwallpremierlets.co.uk
w cornwallpremierlets.co.uk

Harbour's Reach, Falmouth
★★★★ *Self Catering*
Contact: Mr Tim Pearce
t 07710 252583
e info@falmouth-waterfront-holidays.co.uk
w falmouth-waterfront-holidays.co.uk

Kinbrae Holiday Apartments
★★★ *Self Catering*
Contact: Mr & Mrs Primrose
t (01326) 315529
e kinbrae.apartments@btinternet.com

Little Astra ★★★
Self Catering
Contact: Mrs M Welch
t (01326) 319580

Little Garden Cottage
Rating Applied For
Self Catering
Contact: Mr S Barrett
t (01326) 218444
e sacbar2004@yahoo.com

Mistral, Falmouth ★★★★
Self Catering
Contact: Julie Drage
Mistral
t (01326) 372248
e mistral.port@virgin.net
w cornwall-online.co.uk

Mylor Yacht Harbour
★★★★ *Self Catering*
Contact: Miss Celeste Gagnon
t (01326) 372121
e celeste@mylor.com
w mylorharbourside.com

Parklands ★★★ *Self Catering*
Contact: Mrs Jenny Simmons
t (01277) 654425
e parklands@sky.com
w parklandsbungalow.co.uk

Pendra Loweth Holiday Cottages ★★★ *Self Catering*
t (01326) 312190
w pendra.co.uk

Penmere ★★★ *Self Catering*
Contact: Paul & Karen Ravenhill
t (01865) 513572
e ravenhill@clara.co.uk

The Pink House ★★★★
Self Catering
Special Places in Cornwall
t (01872) 864400
e office@specialplacescornwall.co.uk
w specialplacescornwall.co.uk

Southcroft ★★★
Self Catering
Contact: Mrs Janet Stuthridge
t (01326) 314361
e anthonystuthridge@yahoo.co.uk

Spinnakers
Rating Applied For
Self Catering
Cornish Holiday Cottages
t (01326) 250339
e emily@cornishholidaycottages.net
w cornishholidaycottages.net

Tall Ships
Rating Applied For
Self Catering
Contact: Ms Kim McLellan
Cornish Holiday Cottages
t (01326) 250339
e kim@cornishholidaycottages.net
w cornishholidaycottages.net/get_property.php?p=94

Tredova, Falmouth ★★★
Self Catering
Contact: Mrs V J Challands
t (01509) 554641
e the_challands@ntlworld.com

Water's Edge ★★★★★
Self Catering
Contact: Tracey Rist
t (0116) 259 0164
e tracy@cornwallapartmentholidays.co.uk
w cornwallapartmentholidays.co.uk

White Sails ★★★
Self Catering
Cornish Holiday Cottages
t (01326) 250339
e emily@cornishholidaycottages.net
w cornishholidaycottages.net

Wodehouse Place ★★★
Self Catering
Contact: Ms Shelagh Spear
t (01326) 314311

FARWAY Devon

Church Approach Cottages
★★★ *Self Catering*
Contact: Mrs Sheila Lee
t (01404) 871383
e lizlee@eclipse.co.uk
w churchapproach.co.uk

Idehill Cottages
Rating Applied For
Self Catering
Toad Hall Cottages
t (01548) 853089
e thc@toadhallcottages.com
w toadhallcottages.co.uk

FAULKLAND Somerset

The Green Farm ★★★★★
Self Catering
Contact: Mrs Anne Gatley
t (01373) 834331
e anne@gatleyemail.co.uk
w bathholidaycottage.co.uk

Lime Kiln Farm ★★★★★
Self Catering
Contact: Mrs Merinda Kendall
t (01373) 834305
e lime_kiln@hotmail.com
w limekilnfarm.co.uk

FEOCK Cornwall

Carrick Treath
Rating Applied For
Self Catering
Cornish Holiday Cottages
t (01326) 250339
e emily@cornishholidaycottages.net
w cornishholidaycottages.net

Lilypond Cottage ★★★
Self Catering
Special Places in Cornwall
t (01872) 864400
e office@specialplacescornwall.co.uk
w specialplacescornwall.co.uk

Seaview Farm Cottage ★★★
Self Catering
Special Places in Cornwall
t (01872) 864400
e office@specialplacescornwall.co.uk
w specialplacescornwall.co.uk

Trelissick East ★★★★★
Self Catering
Special Places in Cornwall
t (01872) 864400
e office@specialplacescornwall.co.uk
w specialplacescornwall.co.uk

Trolver Farm ★★★★
Self Catering
Cornish Holiday Cottages
t (01326) 250339
e emily@cornishholidaycottages.net
w cornishholidaycottages.net

FERNDOWN Dorset

Birchcroft ★★★★
Self Catering
Contact: Miss Leanne Hemingway
Dorset Cottage Holidays
t (01929) 553443
e enq@dhcottages.co.uk
w dhcottages.co.uk

The Bungalow, West Moors
★★★ *Self Catering*
Contact: Mrs Annette Leach
t (020) 8241 7498 & 07958 209493
e annette.leach@blueyonder.co.uk
w geocities.com/bournemouth3/

Church Farm ★★★
Self Catering
Contact: Mr Andrew Ross
t (01202) 579515
w churchfarmcottages.co.uk

FIFEHEAD MAGDALEN Dorset

Middle Farm Holiday Cottages ★★ *Self Catering*
Contact: Mrs Denise Trevor
t (01258) 820163
e trevorsmiddlefm@aol.com
w middlefarmcottages-dorset.com

FILLEIGH Devon

Buckingham's Leary ★★
Self Catering
Contact: Mrs Ann Bulled
t (01598) 760204

FISHPOND Dorset

Coombe Ridge ★★★★
Self Catering
Lyme Bay Holidays
t (01297) 443363
e email@lymebayholidays.co.uk
w lymebayholidays.co.uk

FLUSHING
Cornwall

Clottage ★★★★
Self Catering
Special Places in Cornwall
t (01872) 864400
e office@specialplacescornwall.co.uk
w specialplacescornwall.co.uk

Packet Cottage ★★★★
Self Catering
Special Places in Cornwall
t (01872) 864400
e office@specialplacescornwall.co.uk
w specialplacescornwall.co.uk

Quay Cottage ★★★
Self Catering
Special Places in Cornwall
t (01872) 864400
e office@specialplacescornwall.co.uk
w specialplacescornwall.co.uk

Sea Pie Cottage ★★★★
Self Catering
Special Places in Cornwall
t (01872) 864400
e office@specialplacescornwall.co.uk
w specialplacescornwall.co.uk

Trevissome House Marine
★★ *Self Catering*
Contact: Mr John Kulpa
t (01326) 374605
e info@trevissomehouse.com
w trevissomehouse.com

Waterside House ★★★★
Self Catering
Special Places in Cornwall
t (01872) 864400
e office@specialplacescornwall.co.uk
w specialplacescornwall.co.uk

FOLKE
Dorset

Folke Manor Farm Cottages, Folke ★★★★ *Self Catering*
Contact: Mr & Mrs John & Carol Perrett
t (01963) 210731 & 07929 139472
e folkemanorfarm@aol.com

Little Glebe ★★★★
Self Catering
Contact: Mr S Friar
t (01963) 210337
e glebe.house@hotmail.com
w glebehouse-dorset.co.uk

FONTMELL MAGNA
Dorset

Brooklands Barn ★★★★
Self Catering
Contact: Mr & Mrs McNulty
t (01747) 812544
e info@brooklandsbarncottage.co.uk
w traditionaldorsetcottages.co.uk/brooklandsbarn.htm

FORRABURY
Cornwall

Sunnybank ★★★
Self Catering
Contact: Helen Young
t (020) 8894 6722
e helen.young@tufts.edu
w boscastlecottage.com

FORTUNESWELL
Dorset

Cama Cottage ★★★
Self Catering
Dream Cottages
t (01305) 789000
e admin@dream-cottages.co.uk
w dream-cottages.co.uk

Ocean Views ★★★
Self Catering
Contact: Mr Charles Gollop
t (020) 8408 9800
e charles@oceanviews.uk.com
w oceanviews.uk.com

Parkers Cottage ★★★
Self Catering
Dream Cottages
t (01305) 789000
e admin@dream-cottages.co.uk
w dream-cottages.co.uk

FOWEY
Cornwall

17a St Fimbarrus Road
★★★ *Self Catering*
t (01726) 832211
e hillandson@talk21.com
w foweyharbourcottages.co.uk

Carnethic House ★★★★★
Self Catering
Contact: Mrs M B Allison
t (01726) 833687
e carenethichouse@hotmail.co.uk
w carnethicapartments.co.uk

Chy Vounder and Rose Villa
★★ *Self Catering*
Contact: Mr David Hill
Fowey Harbour Cottages (W Hill & Son)
t (01726) 832211
e hillandson@talk21.com
w foweyharbourcottages.co.uk

Dolphins at Penlee
★★★★★ *Self Catering*
Contact: Mr Gittus
t (01299) 400447
e john.gittus@btopenworld.com
w qualityholidaylets.com

Duchy Cottage ★★★★
Self Catering
Contact: Mrs T J Round
t (0118) 988 4256
e tracy@duchycottage.com
w duchycottage.com

Lugger Cottage ★★
Self Catering
Contact: Mrs Shelagh Dolphin
St Austell Brewery Co Ltd
t (01726) 870007
e luggerinn@smallandfriendly.co.uk
w smallandfriendly.co.uk

Palm Trees ★★ *Self Catering*
t (01726) 832211
e hillandson@talk21.com
w foweyharbourcottages.co.uk

The Penthouse ★★★
Self Catering
t (01726) 832211
w foweyharbourcottages.co.uk

Polkerris ★★★ *Self Catering*
t (01726) 832211

Sideways Cottage ★★★
Self Catering
t (01726) 832211
w cottagesofcornwall.co.uk

FRADDAM
Cornwall

Deveral House ★★★
Self Catering
Contact: Mrs Ruth Trewhella
t (01736) 850730
e trewhellas@tesco.net
w deveralhouse.co.uk

FRAMPTON
Dorset

Wellbridge ★★★
Self Catering
t (01823) 491646
w wessexholidaycottages.co.uk

FRAMPTON-ON-SEVERN
Gloucestershire

Old Priest Cottage, Old Stable Cottage and The Malthouse ★★★★★
Self Catering
Contact: Mr & Mrs Mike & Caroline Williams
t (01452) 741072
e tanhouse.farm@lineone.net
w tanhouse-farm.co.uk

FRESHFORD
Somerset

The Barton Cottage ★★★
Self Catering
Contact: Mrs Foster
t (01225) 429756

Dolphin Cottage ★★★★
Self Catering
Contact: Mrs Rowena Wood
t (01225) 722100
e rowena_wood@compuserve.com
w dolphincottage.com

FRIAR WADDON
Dorset

Thelma's Cottage ★★★
Self Catering
t (01305) 816002

FRITHELSTOCK
Devon

Fuchsia Cottage ★★★
Self Catering
Contact: Mrs Ruth Blake
t (01805) 601330
e info@hollamoor.co.uk
w hollamoor.co.uk

Honeysuckle Cottage
★★★★ *Self Catering*
Farm & Cottage Holidays
t (01237) 459827
e enquiries@farmcott.co.uk
w holidaycottages.co.uk

Knaworthy ★★★★★
Self Catering
Farm & Cottage Holidays
t (01237) 459827
e enquiries@farmcott.co.uk
w holidaycottages.co.uk

FROME
Somerset

Bollow Hill Farm ★★★★
Self Catering
Contact: Mr & Mrs Mark & Emma Kaye
t (01373) 463007
e bollowhillfarm@aol.com
w farmhousecottages.co.uk

Hill View ★★ *Self Catering*
Contact: Mrs Margaret House
t (01985) 844276
e wells@packsaddle11.freeserve.co.uk

Lazy Dog Cottage ★★★★
Self Catering
Contact: Mrs Sophie Elkins
t (01373) 855275
e sophie@lazydogcottage.co.uk
w lazydogcottage.co.uk

Mill Cottage, Blatchbridge
★★★★ *Self Catering*
Contact: Mrs Thelma Morris
t (01373) 464784

St Katharine's Lodge
★★★★ *Self Catering*
Contact: Mrs Tania Maynard
t (01373) 471434
e info@stkaths.com
w stkaths.com

GALMPTON
Devon

Barnacle Cottage ★★★
Self Catering
Contact: Mrs Phyllis Norman
t (01803) 842309
e pipnorman@aol.com
w portbarnaclecottagesdevon.co.uk

Dart View ★★★ *Self Catering*
Holiday Homes and Cottages South West
t (01803) 299677
e holcotts@aol.com
w swcottages.co.uk

Georgia ★★★ *Self Catering*
Holiday Homes and Cottages South West
t (01803) 299677
e holcotts@aol.com
w swcottages.co.uk

GAUNTS COMMON
Dorset

Denbur ★★★ *Self Catering*
Contact: Mrs Susan Clarke
t (01305) 267611
e sjc@eagle-lodge.fsnet.co.uk

GEORGEHAM
Devon

Ashcroft ★★★ *Self Catering*
Marsdens Cottage Holidays
t (01271) 813777
e holidays@marsdens.co.uk
w marsdens.co.uk

Kingscote ★★★ *Self Catering*
Marsdens Cottage Holidays
t (01271) 813777
e holidays@marsdens.co.uk
w marsdens.co.uk

Pickwell Barton Cottages
★★★–★★★★ *Self Catering*
Contact: Mrs Jane Cook
t (01271) 890994
e jane@pickwellbarton.co.uk
w pickwellbarton.co.uk

Rock Cottage ★★
Self Catering
Marsdens Cottage Holidays
t (01271) 813777
e holidays@marsdens.co.uk
w marsdens.co.uk

Westcliff Cottage ★★★
Self Catering
Marsdens Cottage Holidays
t (01271) 813777
e holidays@marsdens.co.uk
w marsdens.co.uk

GILLINGHAM
Dorset

Whistley Waters ★★★
Self Catering
Contact: Mrs Cleo Campbell
t (01747) 840666
e campbell.whistley@virgin.net
w whistleywaters.co.uk

Woolfields Barn, Milton on Stour ★★★★ *Self Catering*
Contact: Mr & Mrs Thomas
t (01747) 824729
e info@woolfieldsbarn.co.uk
w woolfieldsbarn.co.uk

GLANVILLES WOOTTON
Dorset

Churchill Cottage ★★★★
Self Catering
Contact: Mrs Rachel Rich
t (01963) 210827
e family.rich@virgin.net
w churchillcottage.co.uk

The Stables ★★★★
Self Catering
t (01963) 210209
w thestablessherborne.co.uk

GLASTONBURY
Somerset

Avalon Cottage ★★★★
Self Catering
Contact: Mrs Barbara Champion
t (0121) 288 5878
e abrachampion@hotmail.com
w avaloncottageglastonbury.co.uk

Catcott Burtle Farm Cottage, Burtle ★★★ *Self Catering*
Contact: Mrs Rosemary Tucker
t (01278) 722321
e rosemary.tucker@virgin.net

Glastonbury Holiday Homes
Rating Applied For
Self Catering
Contact: Mr William Knight
t (01458) 835144
e info@glastonburyholidayhomes.com
w glastonburyholidayhomes.com

MapleLeaf Middlewick Holiday Cottages, Wick
★★★ *Self Catering*
Contact: Ms Amanda I'Ons
Middlewick Holiday Cottages
t (01458) 832351
e middlewick@btconnect.com
w middlewickholidaycottages.co.uk

St Edmunds Cottage ★★★★
Self Catering
Contact: Mrs Jeannette Heygate-Browne
t (01458) 830461
e rheygatebrowne@aol.com
w stedmundscottage.com

Whalebone Mews ★★★★
Self Catering
t (01458) 833651
w whalebonemews.co.uk

GLOUCESTER
Gloucestershire

8 Gothic Cottages ★★★★
Self Catering
t (01452) 312661
w 5stmarys.co.uk/gothic%20cottage.html

Barncastle, Pitchcombe
★★★★★ *Self Catering*
Contact: Mrs Valerie King
t (01452) 814207 & 07766 514114
e enquiries@barncastle.co.uk
w barncastle.co.uk

Middletown Farm Cottages, Upleadon ★★★★
Self Catering
Contact: Judy Elkins
t (01531) 828237
e cottages@middletownfarm.co.uk
w middletownfarm.co.uk

Sydenham House ★★★★
Self Catering
Contact: Mrs Jennifer Treasure
t (01702) 474318
e jktreasure@msn.com

GODMANSTONE
Dorset

Trinity Cottage ★★
Self Catering
Dream Cottages
t (01305) 789000
e admin@dream-cottages.co.uk
w dream-cottages.co.uk

GODNEY
Somerset

Swallow Barn ★★★★
Self Catering
Contact: Mrs Hilary Millard
t (01458) 832217
e doublegatefarm@aol.com
w doublegatefarm.com

GOLANT
Cornwall

Penquite Farm Holidays
★★★★–★★★★★
Self Catering
Contact: Mrs Ruth Varco
t (01726) 833319
e ruth@penquitefarm.co.uk
w penquitefarm.co.uk

Robins Hill ★★★★
Self Catering
Holiday Homes and Cottages South West
t (01803) 299677
e holcotts@aol.com
w swcottages.co.uk

South Torfrey Farm ★★★★
Self Catering
Contact: Mr & Mrs Andrews
t (01726) 833126
e debbie.andrews@southtorfreyfarm.com
w southtorfreyfarm.com

GOLDENBANK
Cornwall

The Strand L2A ★★★
Self Catering
Holiday Cornwall
t (01326) 250278
e enquiries@holidaycornwall.co.uk
w holidaycornwall.co.uk

GOODLEIGH
Devon

Bampfield Cottages ★★★★
Self Catering
Contact: Ms Lynda Thorne
t (01271) 346566
e enquiries@bampfieldfarm.co.uk
w bampfieldfarm.co.uk

Mistletoe Cottage ★★★
Self Catering
Contact: Mrs Linda Moore
t (01271) 321502
e www.andrew.moore777@btinternet.com

GOONHAVERN
Cornwall

Greenmeadow ★★★
Self Catering
Contact: Mr Ian Bodie
t (01872) 540483
e ianbodie@aol.com

Honeysuckle Cottage, Goonhavern ★★★★
Self Catering
Contact: Mrs Yvonne Nelson
t (01872) 540556
e yvonne158nelson@btinternet.com
w littlewatercottageholidays.co.uk

Oakridge Farm ★★★★
Self Catering
Contact: Mrs G Treleaven
t (01872) 571223
e treamble@hotmail.co.uk
w oakridgefarm.co.uk

GOONOWN
Cornwall

Goonown Barn Cottages
★★★ *Self Catering*
Contact: Mrs Butson
t (01872) 553654

Rose Cottage ★★★★
Self Catering
Contact: Helen Powell
t 07970 509825
e sales@quaintcottage.co.uk
w quaintcottage.co.uk

Shalom ★★★ *Self Catering*
Duchy Holidays
t (01872) 572971
e enquiries@duchyholidays.co.uk
w duchyholidays.co.uk

GORRAN
Cornwall

Dovecote ★★★★
Self Catering
Contact: Mrs Myra Welsh
t (01726) 842295
e treveague@btconnect.com
w treveaguefarm.co.uk

GORRAN HAVEN
Cornwall

Meadow Croft ★★★★
Self Catering
Special Places in Cornwall
t (01872) 864400
e office@specialplacescornwall.co.uk
w specialplacescornwall.co.uk

Oakroyd ★★★ *Self Catering*
Contact: Mrs Helena Payne
t (01726) 842546
e hrjpayne@tiscali.co.uk

Ryancot ★★★ *Self Catering*
Contact: Mrs Lynne Walker
t (01872) 862534
e ryancot@btinternet.com

Seamew Cottage ★★★★
Self Catering
Contact: Mr Malcolm Debbage
t (0115) 987 9184
e gorranhavencottages@hotmail.com
w gorranhavencottages.co.uk

Tregillan ★★–★★★
Self Catering
Contact: Mrs Sally Pike
t (01726) 842452
e tregillanapartment@tiscali.co.uk
w tregillanapartments.co.uk

GOVETON
Devon

Hope Cottage ★★★★
Self Catering
Toad Hall Cottages
t (01548) 853089
e thc@toadhallcottages.com
w toadhallcottages.co.uk

GRAMPOUND ROAD
Cornwall

The Garden Cottage
★★★★★ *Self Catering*
Niche Retreats
t (01209) 861745
e jackie@nicheretreats.co.uk
w nicheretreats.co.uk

GREAT ASHLEY
Wiltshire

Great Ashley Farm Cottage
★★★★ *Self Catering*
t (01225) 864563
w greatashley.co.uk

GREAT BEDWYN
Wiltshire

Little Sirron
Rating Applied For
Self Catering
t (01672) 870444

GREAT RISSINGTON
Gloucestershire

Daisy's Cottage ★★★★★
Self Catering
Contact: Ms Kate Cleverly
t (01451) 820129

GREAT TORRINGTON
Devon

Cloister Park Cottages, Frithelstock ★★★★
Self Catering
Contact: Mrs Melanie Goldman
t (01805) 622518
e info@cloisterpark.co.uk
w cloisterpark.co.uk

Stowford Lodge ★★★
Self Catering
Contact: Mr & Mrs R Jones
t (01805) 601540
e enq@stowfordlodge.co.uk
w stowfordlodge.co.uk

GUITING POWER
Gloucestershire

Little Barnfield ★★★★
Self Catering
Contact: Ms Anne Dawson
t (01451) 850664
e anne_dawson_opera@yahoo.co.uk

GULVAL
Cornwall

Barn Cottage ★★★★
Self Catering
Contact: Mr Barrie Hockley
t (01952) 415349
e barncottage@blueyonder.co.uk

Barton Woods Cottage ★★★★ *Self Catering*
t (01736) 333876
w mortimer.demon.co.uk

Mount View ★★ *Self Catering & Serviced Apartments*
t (01594) 861119

The Retreat ★★ *Self Catering & Serviced Apartments*
Contact: Mrs Evans
The Retreat – Evans Holiday Cottages
t (01594) 861119
e helen@peakedrockscottage.fsnet
w evansholidays.co.uk

Rosemorran Holiday Cottages ★★★ *Self Catering*
Contact: Mrs Shirley Leah
t (01736) 361479

GWENNAP
Cornwall

The Old Stables ★★★★★
Self Catering
Contact: Mr Mike Jeffery
t (01209) 860765
e mike@copperhouse.entadsl.com
w copperhouse.entadsl.com

GWINEAR
Cornwall

Lanyon Manor Cottages ★★★★★ *Self Catering*
Contact: Mr & Mrs Leggo
t (01736) 850795

HACCOMBE
Devon

Deer Park Barn ★★★
Self Catering
Holiday Homes and Cottages South West
t (01803) 299677
e holcotts@aol.com
w swcottages.co.uk

HALSE
Somerset

The Treehouse at West Hayes
Rating Applied For
Self Catering
Contact: Mrs Kate Rucklidge
t (01823) 431622
e kate@treehouseholidays.co.uk
w treehouseholidays.co.uk

West Hayes Barn ★★★★★
Self Catering
Contact: Mrs Kate Rucklidge
t (01823) 431622
e k.rucklidge@btinternet.com
w westhayesbarn.co.uk

HALSETOWN
Cornwall

Blackberry Cottage ★★★
Self Catering
Contact: Mrs Adams
t (0121) 354 7442
e nettieadams@blueyonder.co.uk

HARBERTON
Devon

Eastleigh Cottage ★★★★
Self Catering
Blue Chip Vacations
t (01803) 855282
e info@bluechipvacations.com
w bluechipvacations.com

HARBERTONFORD
Devon

Crowdy Mill Barn ★★★★
Self Catering
Contact: Mr Mohammed Djavanroodi
t 0870 494 6604
w countryholidays2007.co.uk

HARLYN BAY
Cornwall

The Croft ★★ *Self Catering*
Harbour Holidays
t (01841) 533402
e contact@harbourholidays.co.uk
w harbourholidays.co.uk

Flat 1 Yellow Sands ★★★
Self Catering
Harbour Holidays
t (01841) 533402
e contact@harbourholidays.co.uk
w harbourholidays.co.uk

Harlyn Farmhouse ★★★★
Self Catering
Contact: Mrs Perry
t (0117) 962 4831
e hazelperry@blueyonder.co.uk
w harlynfarmhouse.co.uk

Harlyn Inn – self catering ★★★★ *Self Catering*
Contact: Mr & Mrs Haywood
t (01841) 520207
e mail@harlyn-inn.com
w harlyn-inn.com

Polwen ★★★★ *Self Catering*
Harbour Holidays
t (01841) 533402
e contact@harbourholidays.co.uk
w harbourholidays.co.uk

Porghelly Cottage ★★★
Self Catering
Cornish Horizons Holiday Cottages
t (01841) 533331
e cottages@cornishhorizons.co.uk
w cornishhorizons.co.uk

The Red House ★★★★
Self Catering
Harbour Holidays
t (01841) 533402
e contact@harbourholidays.co.uk
w harbourholidays.co.uk

Sandpipers ★★★
Self Catering
Cornish Horizons Holiday Cottages
t (01841) 533331
e cottages@cornishhorizons.co.uk
w cornishhorizons.co.uk

Tamariska ★★★
Self Catering
Harbour Holidays
t (01841) 533402
e contact@harbourholidays.co.uk
w harbourholidays.co.uk

Trelawn
Rating Applied For
Self Catering
Cornish Horizons Holiday Cottages
t (01841) 533331
e cottages@cornishhorizons.co.uk
w cornishhorizons.co.uk

Trevoyne ★★★ *Self Catering*
Harbour Holidays
t (01841) 533402
e contact@harbourholidays.co.uk
w harbourholidays.co.uk

Trezise ★★★★ *Self Catering*
Contact: Mrs J McGrandle
t (020) 7603 3077
e jmcg@boxpress.demon.co.uk

HARTLAND
Devon

Coastguard Cottage ★★★★
Self Catering
Marsdens Cottage Holidays
t (01271) 813777
e holidays@marsdens.co.uk
w marsdens.co.uk

Longfurlong Holiday Cottages ★★★★–★★★★★
Self Catering
Contact: Mr & Mrs John & Janet Cockrill
t (01237) 441337
e longfurlong@longfurlong.eurobell.co.uk

Mettaford Farm Holiday Cottages ★★★ *Self Catering*
Contact: Mr & Mrs Stephen & Sue Hilsdon
t (01237) 441249
e mettaford@aol.com
w mettafordfarm.co.uk

The Old Dairy & Polly's Cottage ★★★–★★★★
Self Catering
Contact: Mrs Heywood
t (01237) 441268
e sue@gorvincottages.co.uk

Speke's Valley Cottages ★★★★ *Self Catering*
Contact: Mrs Sue Heywood
t (01237) 441268
e sue@spekesvalley.co.uk
w spekesvalley.co.uk

HATHERLEIGH
Devon

Lower Upcott Farm ★★★
Self Catering
Contact: Mr Ben May
t (01837) 811123
e ben@holiday-farm.co.uk
w holiday-farm.co.uk

HAWKCHURCH
Devon

Angels Farm Apartment ★★★ *Self Catering*
Contact: Mrs Anne Gibbins
t (01297) 678295
e angels.farm@virgin.net
w cottageguide.co.uk/angelsfarm

Cider Cottage 1 ★★★★
Self Catering
Lyme Bay Holidays
t (01297) 443363
e email@lymebayholidays.co.uk
w lymebayholidays.co.uk

Cider Cottage 2 ★★★★
Self Catering
Lyme Bay Holidays
t (01297) 443363
e email@lymebayholidays.co.uk
w lymebayholidays.co.uk

Orchard House Annexe ★★★★ *Self Catering*
Lyme Bay Holidays
t (01297) 443363
e email@lymebayholidays.co.uk
w lymebayholidays.co.uk

HAWKRIDGE
Somerset

West Hollowcombe Cottages ★★★★
Self Catering
Farm & Cottage Holidays
t (01237) 459827
e enquiries@farmcott.co.uk
w holidaycottages.co.uk

HAYLE
Cornwall

Brunnion Barns ★★★★
Self Catering
Hideaways
t (01747) 828170
e enq@hideaways.co.uk
w hideaways.co.uk

Chyreene Court Apartments ★★★ *Self Catering*
Contact: Miss Sarah Bailie
t (01736) 756651
e sarahbailie@hotmail.com
w chyreenecourt.co.uk

Harbourside View
Rating Applied For
Self Catering
Contact: Miss Amanda Miller
t 07967 326042
e amada@cornwallharbourviews.co.uk
w cornwallharbourviews.co.uk

Kerensa ★★★★★
Self Catering
Cornish Gems
t 0844 800 2813
w cornishgems.com/holiday-cottages/kerensa.html

Truthwall Farmhouse ★★★
Self Catering
Contact: Mrs Sheila Goldsworthy
t (01736) 850266
e truthwallfarmhouse@tiscali.co.uk
w http://myweb.tiscali.co.uk/truthwallfarmhouse

HAYTOR Devon

The Old Chapel ★★★
Self Catering
Holiday Homes and Cottages South West
t (01803) 299677
e holcotts@aol.com
w swcottages.co.uk

HEANTON Devon

Grange House ★★★★
Self Catering
Marsdens Cottage Holidays
t (01271) 813777
e holidays@marsdens.co.uk
w marsdens.co.uk

Monks Cottage ★★★
Self Catering
Marsdens Cottage Holidays
t (01271) 813777
e holidays@marsdens.co.uk
w marsdens.co.uk

HELE Devon

Hele Payne Farm Cottages
★★★★ *Self Catering*
Contact: Mrs S A Maynard
t (01392) 881530
e info@helepayne.co.uk
w helepayne.co.uk

HELFORD Cornwall

The Barns ★★★★
Self Catering
Helford River Cottages
t (01326) 231666
e info@helfordcottages.co.uk
w helfordcottages.co.uk

Bridge Cottage ★★★
Self Catering
Helford River Cottages
t (01326) 231666
e info@helfordcottages.co.uk
w helfordcottages.co.uk

The Cottage ★★★
Self Catering
Helford River Cottages
t (01326) 231666
e info@helfordcottages.co.uk
w helfordcottages.co.uk

Creek Cottage ★★★
Self Catering
Helford River Cottages
t (01326) 231666
e info@helfordcottages.co.uk
w helfordcottages.co.uk

Dowr Penty ★★★★
Self Catering
Helford River Cottages
t (01326) 231666
e info@helfordcottages.co.uk
w helfordcottages.co.uk

Laloma Cottage ★★★
Self Catering
Helford River Cottages
t (01326) 231666
e info@helfordcottages.co.uk
w helfordcottages.co.uk

Pear Tree ★★★★
Self Catering
Helford River Cottages
t (01326) 231666
e info@helfordcottages.co.uk
w helfordcottages.co.uk

Penervon House
Rating Applied For
Self Catering
Holiday Cornwall
t (01326) 250278
e enquiries@holidaycornwall.co.uk
w holidaycornwall.co.uk

Penkestle Studio ★★★
Self Catering
Helford River Cottages
t (01326) 231666
e info@helfordcottages.co.uk
w helfordcottages.co.uk

Pointside ★★★★
Self Catering
Helford River Cottages
t (01326) 231666
e info@helfordcottages.co.uk
w helfordcottages.co.uk

Popigale Cottage ★★★
Self Catering
Helford River Cottages
t (01326) 231666
e info@helfordcottages.co.uk
w helfordcottages.co.uk

Rose Cottage ★★★★
Self Catering
Helford River Cottages
t (01326) 231666
e info@helfordcottages.co.uk
w helfordcottages.co.uk

Wednesday Cottage ★★★★
Self Catering
Helford River Cottages
t (01326) 231666
e info@helfordcottages.co.uk
w helfordcottages.co.uk

Well Too ★★★★
Self Catering
Helford River Cottages
t (01326) 231666
e info@helfordcottages.co.uk
w helfordcottages.co.uk

HELFORD PASSAGE Cornwall

3c The Old Sail loft ★★★
Self Catering
Holiday Cornwall
t (01326) 250278
e enquiries@holidaycornwall.co.uk
w holidaycornwall.co.uk

5c The Courtyard ★★★
Self Catering
Holiday Cornwall
t (01326) 250278
e enquiries@holidaycornwall.co.uk
w holidaycornwall.co.uk

Flat 15D ★★★ *Self Catering*
Contact: Linda James
t (0118) 934 3310
e richardjames@tiscali.co.uk
w helfordriver.com/accommodation/15d

Lower Penavon
Rating Applied For
Self Catering
Holiday Cornwall
t (01326) 250278
e enquiries@holidaycornwall.co.uk
w holidaycornwall.co.uk

Pheasant Cottage
Rating Applied For
Self Catering
Cornish Holiday Cottages
t (01326) 250339
e emily@cornishholidaycottages.net
w cornishholidaycottages.net

Riverside
Rating Applied For
Self Catering
Holiday Cornwall
t (01326) 250278
e enquiries@holidaycornwall.co.uk
w holidaycornwall.co.uk

HELLANDBRIDGE Cornwall

Lower Helland Farm Cottages ★★★ *Self Catering*
Contact: Mrs Astrid Coad
t (01208) 72813
e cottages@lowerhellandfarm.co.uk
w lowerhellandfarm.co.uk

HELLESVEOR Cornwall

Padgy Vessa ★★★★
Self Catering
Powells Cottage Holidays
t (01834) 812791
e info@powells.co.uk
w powells.co.uk

HELSTON Cornwall

1 & 2 Hillsdale, Polladras
★★★ *Self Catering*
Contact: Mrs Chris & Sue Chapman
t (01736) 763230
e sue@barnhaven.org
w barnhaven.org

Carminowe View ★★★★
Self Catering
Contact: Mr Huddleston
t (01275) 848899
e jhuddl2144@aol.com
w cornwallcottage-carminoweview.co.uk

Mudgeon Vean Farm Holiday Cottages ★★★
Self Catering
Contact: Mr & Mrs Trewhella
t (01326) 231341
e mudgeonvean@aol.com
w mudgeonvean.co.uk

Tregathenan Country Cottages ★★★★
Self Catering
t (01326) 569840
w tregathenan.co.uk

Tregoose Farmhouse
★★★★ *Self Catering*
Contact: Mrs Hazel Bergin
t (01209) 714314
e hazel.bergin@dsl.pipex.com
w tregooselet.co.uk

HELSTONE Cornwall

Mayrose Farm
★★★-★★★★ *Self Catering*
Contact: Mrs Jane Maunder
t (01840) 213509
e info@mayrosefarmcottages.co.uk
w mayrosefarmcottages.co.uk

HEMYOCK Devon

Windover ★★★★
Self Catering
Farm & Cottage Holidays
t (01237) 459827
e enquiries@farmcott.co.uk
w holidaycottages.co.uk

HENLEY Dorset

Shepherds Cottage ★★★★
Self Catering
Dream Cottages
t (01305) 789000
e admin@dream-cottages.co.uk
w dream-cottages.co.uk

HENWOOD Cornwall

Henwood Barns ★★★
Self Catering
Contact: Miss Willisson
t (01579) 363576
e henwoodbarns@tiscali.co.uk
w henwoodbarns.co.uk

HERSHAM Cornwall

Woodhall ★★★★
Self Catering
Contact: Veronica Chouffot
t (01288) 356991
e v_chouffot@hotmail.com
w veronicachouffot.co.uk

HEYWOOD Wiltshire

Heywood Holiday Cottages
★★★★★ *Self Catering*
Contact: Mr John Boyce
t (01225) 868393
e enquiries@ashecottage-holidaylets.co.uk
w ashecottage-holidaylets.co.uk

Pine Lodge ★ *Self Catering*
Contact: Mr & Mrs Prince
t (01373) 822949
e pinelodgex@aol.com
w pinelodge.info

HIGH BICKINGTON Devon

The Corn Mill & Lee Meadow ★★★★★
Self Catering
Contact: Mrs Glenda Tucker
t (01769) 560796
w lee-barton.co.uk

Millbrook Cottages
★★★★-★★★★★
Self Catering
Contact: Miss Kate Jones
t 0800 298 2288
e kate@millbrookcottages.co.uk
w millbrookcottages.co.uk

HIGHAMPTON
Devon

The Bolt Hole ★★★★
Self Catering
Toad Hall Cottages
t (01548) 853089
e thc@toadhallcottages.com
w toadhallcottages.co.uk

Kingslake ★★★ *Self Catering*
Contact: Mrs Valerie Langdown
t (01409) 231401
e vlangdown@talk21.com
w kingslakes.co.uk

No 10 Lakeview Rise
★★★★ *Self Catering*
Contact: Mr & Mrs Peter & Margery Mathews
t (01844) 347204
e margejulepete@aol.com
w lakeviewrise.com

Orchard House & 11 Lakeside View
★★★★-★★★★★
Self Catering
Contact: Mrs Sames
t (01296) 747425
e j.l.pearce@tesco.net
w lakeviewrise.co.uk

HIGHBRIDGE
Somerset

Greenacre Place Holiday Cottage ★★★ *Self Catering*
Contact: Ms Linda White
t (01278) 785227
e info@greenacreplace.com
w greenacreplace.com

HILLERSLAND
Gloucestershire

Barn Cottage ★★★
Self Catering
Contact: Ann Dartnell
t (01594) 837115
e barnhousefd@aol.com

Mount Annexe ★★★★
Self Catering
Contact: Lucy Stevens
t (01594) 839141
e mountannexe@tiscali.co.uk

The Old Shop ★★★
Self Catering
Contact: Mrs Janice Gane
t (01594) 834474
e h.c.ganee@talk21.com

HILLFARRANCE
Somerset

The Long Barn, Hillfarrance
★★★★★ *Self Catering*
Contact: Mrs Jessica Vellacott
t (01823) 672284 & 07776 188646
e info@somersetlongbarn.co.uk
w somersetlongbarn.co.uk

HILTON
Dorset

Crown Farm ★★★
Self Catering
Contact: Mrs Pamela Crocker
t (01258) 880259

HOCKWORTHY
Devon

Quarry Hockford Barn Cottages ★★★★
Self Catering
Contact: Mr & Mrs Tod & Heather Bainbridge
t (01398) 361430
e bainbridge@quarryhockford.co.uk
w quarryhockford.co.uk

HOLBETON
Devon

Carswell Farm Cottages
★★★-★★★★★ *Self Catering*
Contact: Mrs Katherine Harding
t (01752) 830020
e enquiries@carswellcottages.com
w carswellcottages.com

HOLSWORTHY
Devon

Beech House ★★★★
Self Catering
Contact: Mrs Heard
t (01409) 253339

Dairy Cottage and Beech Barn, Thornbury ★★★★
Self Catering
Contact: Mrs Annie Griffiths
t (01409) 261437
e griff.bagbeare@virgin.net
w selfcatering-devon.com

Higher Sellick Farm Cottages ★★★★
Self Catering
Contact: Mrs Denise Grafton
t (01409) 271456
e denisegrafton@devonholidays.org
w devonholidays.org

Leworthy Cottage ★★★
Self Catering
Contact: Mrs Patricia Jennings
t (01409) 259469

Noteworthy Caravan Holiday Home *Approved Caravan Holiday Home*
Contact: Mrs Julieann Snook-Bevis
t (01409) 253731 & 07811 000071
e enquiries@noteworthy-devon.co.uk
w noteworthy-devon.co.uk

Southcombe Farm ★★★★★
Self Catering
Contact: Mrs Eileen Clark
t (01409) 253761
e relax@southcombe.net
w southcombe.net

Stanbury Wharf ★★★★
Self Catering
Contact: Scot & Sally Pawley
t (01409) 254326
e scotpawley@hotmail.co.uk
w stanburywharf-devon.com

HOLTON HEATH
Dorset

Gateway and Woodland Cottages ★★★ *Self Catering*
Contact: Mrs Liz Jones
t (01202) 631063
e facilities@holtonlee.co.uk
w holtonlee.co.uk/

HOLWORTH
Dorset

Aura Holworth ★★★
Self Catering
Dream Cottages
t (01305) 789000
e admin@dream-cottages.co.uk
w dream-cottages.co.uk

HOLYWELL
Dorset

Pippins Cottage ★★★
Self Catering
Dream Cottages
t (01305) 789000
e admin@dream-cottages.co.uk
w dream-cottages.co.uk

HOLYWELL BAY
Cornwall

Sailors Cove Bungalow
★★★ *Self Catering*
Contact: Mrs Benney
t (01637) 830031

Trevornick Cottages ★★★★
Self Catering
Contact: Mr Paul Wright
t (01637) 832906
e paul@trevornick.co.uk
w trevornickcottages.co.uk

Watership Down ★★★
Self Catering
Cornish Horizons Holiday Cottages
t (01841) 533331
e cottages@cornishhorizons.co.uk
w cornishhorizons.co.uk

HONITON
Devon

Abbots Cottage ★★★
Self Catering
Contact: Mr Douglas Acreman
t (01992) 622685
e d.acreman@tiscali.co.uk

Bidwell Farm Cottages
★★★★★ *Self Catering*
Contact: Mrs Patricia Wells
t (01404) 861122
e pat@bidwellfarm.co.uk
w bidwellfarm.co.uk

Courtmoor Farm Cottages, Upottery ★★★★
Self Catering
Contact: Mrs Rosalind Buxton
t (01404) 861565
e courtmoor.farm@btinternet.com
w courtmoor.farm.btinternet.co.uk

Odle Farm, Upottery
★★★★ *Self Catering*
Contact: Mrs Karen Marshallsay
t (01404) 861105
e info@odlefarm.co.uk
w odlefarm.co.uk

Red Doors Farm ★★★★★
Self Catering
Contact: Mr Chris Shrubb
t (01404) 890067
e info@reddoors.co.uk
w reddoors.co.uk

Sutton Barton ★★★★★
Self Catering
Contact: Mrs Teresa Cooke
t (01404) 831382
e andycooke@suttonbartonfarm.co.uk
w suttonbartonfarm.co.uk

HOPE COVE
Devon

Sanderlings, Hope Cove ★★
Self Catering
Contact: Mrs Diana Middleton
t (0118) 969 0958 & 0033 6307 25545
e diana_middleton@yahoo.com

Seascape, Hope Cove ★★★
Self Catering
Contact: Mrs Hazel Kolb
t (01285) 654781
e kolb@btinternet.com
w englishholidayhouses.co.uk

HORSINGTON
Somerset

Lois Country Cottages
★★★★ *Self Catering*
Contact: Mr & Mrs Paul & Penny Constant
t (01963) 370496
e info@loisfarm.com
w loisfarm.com

HORTON
Dorset

Old Down Cottage ★★★★
Self Catering
Contact: Mrs Pip Davidson
t (01258) 840969
e olddown@btinternet.com
w classic.co.uk

HUNTLEY
Gloucestershire

The Vineary ★★★
Self Catering
Contact: Mrs Ann Snow
t (01452) 830006

HUNTSHAW
Devon

Bowood Barn ★★★★
Self Catering
Marsdens Cottage Holidays
t (01271) 813777
e holidays@marsdens.co.uk
w marsdens.co.uk

HURN
Dorset

The Old Farmhouse ★★★
Self Catering
Contact: Mrs Jennifer Burford
t (01202) 479483

IBBERTON
Dorset

Manor House Farm Cottages
★★★★ *Self Catering*
Dream Cottages
t (01305) 789000
e admin@dream-cottages.co.uk
w dream-cottages.co.uk

ILFRACOMBE
Devon

The Admirals House ★★★★
Self Catering
Contact: Miss Marshall
t (01271) 864666
e enquiries@theadmiralshouse.co.uk
w theadmiralshouse.co.uk

Look out for establishments participating in the National Accessible Scheme

Ashmour
Rating Applied For
Self Catering
Marsdens Cottage Holidays
t (01271) 813777
e holidays@marsdens.co.uk
w marsdens.co.uk

Bath Place ★★★★
Self Catering
Marsdens Cottage Holidays
t (01271) 813777
e holidays@marsdens.co.uk
w marsdens.co.uk

Cairnside ★★★ *Self Catering*
Marsdens Cottage Holidays
t (01271) 813777
e holidays@marsdens.co.uk
w marsdens.co.uk

Capstone View ★★★★
Self Catering
Marsdens Cottage Holidays
t (01271) 813777
e holidays@marsdens.co.uk
w marsdens.co.uk

Captains House ★★★★
Self Catering
Marsdens Cottage Holidays
t (01271) 813777
e holidays@marsdens.co.uk
w marsdens.co.uk

Captains Quarters ★★★★
Self Catering
Marsdens Cottage Holidays
t (01271) 813777
e holidays@marsdens.co.uk
w marsdens.co.uk

Captains View ★★★★
Self Catering
Marsdens Cottage Holidays
t (01271) 813777
e holidays@marsdens.co.uk
w marsdens.co.uk

Clarian ★★★★ *Self Catering*
Marsdens Cottage Holidays
t (01271) 813777
e holidays@marsdens.co.uk
w marsdens.co.uk

Clover Meadows ★★★★
Self Catering
Marsdens Cottage Holidays
t (01271) 813777
e holidays@marsdens.co.uk
w marsdens.co.uk

Comyn Cottage ★★★★
Self Catering
Marsdens Cottage Holidays
t (01271) 813777
e holidays@marsdens.co.uk
w marsdens.co.uk

Comyn Lodge ★★★★
Self Catering
Marsdens Cottage Holidays
t (01271) 813777
e holidays@marsdens.co.uk
w marsdens.co.uk

Crab Cottage ★★★★
Self Catering
Contact: Mrs Janice Benny
t 0800 915 9894
e info@devonharbourcottages.co.uk
w devonharbourcottages.com

Darnley Holiday Cottages
★★★ *Self Catering*
Contact: Mrs Susan Dale
t (01271) 863955
e darnleyhotel@yahoo.co.uk
w darnleyhotel.co.uk

Ebrington Place ★★★
Self Catering
Marsdens Cottage Holidays
t (01271) 813777
e holidays@marsdens.co.uk
w marsdens.co.uk

Horizon View ★★★★
Self Catering
Marsdens Cottage Holidays
t (01271) 813777
e holidays@marsdens.co.uk
w marsdens.co.uk

The Knapps ★★★★
Self Catering
Marsdens Cottage Holidays
t (01271) 813777
e holidays@marsdens.co.uk
w marsdens.co.uk

Larkstone ★★★★
Self Catering
Marsdens Cottage Holidays
t (01271) 813777
e holidays@marsdens.co.uk
w marsdens.co.uk

The Lodge & Stables & Paddocks ★★★ *Self Catering*
Marsdens Cottage Holidays
t (01271) 813777
e holidays@marsdens.co.uk
w marsdens.co.uk

The Mill House ★★★★
Self Catering
Marsdens Cottage Holidays
t (01271) 813777
e holidays@marsdens.co.uk
w marsdens.co.uk

Norwood Holiday Flats
★★★ *Self Catering*
Contact: Mrs Betty Bulled
t (01271) 862370

Ocean View ★★★★
Self Catering
Marsdens Cottage Holidays
t (01271) 813777
e holidays@marsdens.co.uk
w marsdens.co.uk

Quay Cottage ★★★★
Self Catering
Contact: Mrs Janet Cornwell
t (01271) 813777
e karen@marsdens.eclipse.co.uk

The Round House ★★★★
Self Catering
Marsdens Cottage Holidays
t (01271) 813777
e holidays@marsdens.co.uk
w marsdens.co.uk

Sea Foam House ★★★★
Self Catering
Marsdens Cottage Holidays
t (01271) 813777
e holidays@marsdens.co.uk
w marsdens.co.uk

Sea Vista ★★★ *Self Catering*
Marsdens Cottage Holidays
t (01271) 813777
e holidays@marsdens.co.uk
w marsdens.co.uk

Somerset Villa ★★★
Self Catering
Marsdens Cottage Holidays
t (01271) 813777
e holidays@marsdens.co.uk
w marsdens.co.uk

Top Deck ★★★★
Self Catering
Marsdens Cottage Holidays
t (01271) 813777
e holidays@marsdens.co.uk
w marsdens.co.uk

Waverley ★★★★
Self Catering
Marsdens Cottage Holidays
t (01271) 813777
e holidays@marsdens.co.uk
w marsdens.co.uk

Widmouth Farm Cottages
★★★ *Self Catering*
Contact: Mrs Elizabeth Sansom
t (01271) 863743
e holidays@widmouthfarmcottages.co.uk
w widmouthfarmcottages.co.uk

Woodclose Cottage ★★★
Self Catering
Toad Hall Cottages
t (01548) 853089
e thc@toadhallcottages.com
w toadhallcottages.co.uk

ILMINSTER
Somerset

Myrtle House, Horton ★★★
Self Catering
Contact: Mr & Mrs Gordon & Marion Denman
t (01223) 871294
e denman@myrtleonline.co.uk
w myrtleonline.co.uk

INSTOW
Devon

Bath House ★★★
Self Catering
Marsdens Cottage Holidays
t (01271) 813777
e holidays@marsdens.co.uk
w marsdens.co.uk

Bosuns Haven ★★★★
Self Catering
Marsdens Cottage Holidays
t (01271) 813777
e holidays@marsdens.co.uk
w marsdens.co.uk

Chandlers Court ★★★★
Self Catering
Marsdens Cottage Holidays
t (01271) 813777
e holidays@marsdens.co.uk
w marsdens.co.uk

Driftwood ★★★
Self Catering
Marsdens Cottage Holidays
t (01271) 813777
e holidays@marsdens.co.uk
w marsdens.co.uk

Inglenook Cottage ★★★★
Self Catering
Marsdens Cottage Holidays
t (01271) 813777
e holidays@marsdens.co.uk
w marsdens.co.uk

South Corner ★★★★
Self Catering
Marsdens Cottage Holidays
t (01271) 813777
e holidays@marsdens.co.uk
w marsdens.co.uk

IPPLEPEN
Devon

Bulleigh Park Farm ★★★
Self Catering
Contact: Mrs Angela Dallyn
t (01803) 872254
e bulleigh@lineone.net
w southdevonaccommodation.co.uk

ISLE BREWERS
Somerset

Old School House ★★★★
Self Catering
Contact: Mrs Lynda Coles
t (01823) 443759
e ajcoles@supanet.com
w somerset-selfcatering.co.uk

ISLES OF SCILLY

2 Bay View Terrace ★★★
Self Catering
t (01720) 422959

3 Bay View Terrace ★★★★
Self Catering
Island Properties
t (01720) 422082
e enquiries@scillyhols.com
w scillyhols.com

7 The Strand ★★★★
Self Catering
Island Properties
t (01720) 422082
e enquiries@scillyhols.com
w scillyhols.com

An Oberva ★★ *Self Catering*
Contact: Mrs Berryman
t (01326) 574113

Bella Vista ★★★★
Self Catering
Contact: Mr & Mrs Chesterman
t (01720) 422687

Bryher ★★★★ *Self Catering*
Contact: Ms Linda Ball
t (01242) 222257
e peter.ball21@btinternet.com

Bylet Holiday Homes ★★★
Self Catering
Contact: Mr Williams
t (01720) 422479
e thebylet@bushinternet.com
w bylethholidays.com

Covean Cottage Little House
★★★ *Self Catering*
Contact: Mrs Heather Sewell
t (01720) 422620

Drinissa ★★★★ *Self Catering*
Contact: Mrs Pat Hicks
t (01720) 422028
e patriciajhicks@hotmail.co.uk

Green Pastures ★★★★
Self Catering
Contact: Mrs Tansy Tugwell
t (01342) 311354

Harbour View ★★★
Self Catering
Contact: Mr Chris Hopkins
t (01720) 422222
e chrisonscilly@aol.com
w bryher-ios.co.uk/hv

Holy Vale Holiday Houses
★★★-★★★★ *Self Catering*
Contact: Mr & Mrs John & Kay Banfield
t (01720) 422429
e johnkay@holyvale.freeserve.co.uk
w holyvale.co.uk

Leumeah House ★★
Self Catering
Island Properties
t (01720) 422082
e enquiries@scillyhols.com
w scillyhols.com

Little house ★★★★★
Self Catering
Contact: Ms Philippa Sullivan
t (01579) 346473
e holidays@duchyofcornwall.gov.uk
w duchyofcornwallholidaycottages.co.uk

Merrick ★★ *Self Catering*
Island Properties
t (01720) 422082
e enquiries@scillyhols.com
w scillyhols.com

Moonrakers Holiday Flats
★★★ *Self Catering*
Contact: Mr & Mrs R.J Gregory
t (01720) 422717
w moonrakersholidayflats.co.uk

Riviera Top Flat ★★★
Self Catering
Contact: Mrs Mary Hampton
t (0121) 378 1472

Samson ★★★ *Self Catering*
Contact: Anne Derbyshire
t (01386) 792065
e annederbyshire@hotmail.com

Samson View ★★★
Self Catering
Contact: Mrs Rebecca Douglas
t (01720) 423165
e martin.douglas3@btinternet.com

Seaways Flower Farm
★★★-★★★★ *Self Catering*
Contact: Mrs Juliet May
t (01720) 422845
e seawaysflowerfarm@btinternet.com
w seawaysfarmholidayhomes.co.uk

Serica ★★★★ *Self Catering*
Contact: Mr David Townend
t 07900 016113
e dtownend@netcomuk.co.uk
w scillyonline.co.uk/accomm/serica.html

Silverporth ★★★★
Self Catering
Island Properties
t (01720) 422082
e enquiries@scillyhols.com
w scillyhols.com

Smugglers ★★★★
Self Catering
Contact: Mrs Niki Burns
t (01720) 423677
e nikirick@yahoo.co.uk

The Stable ★★★★
Self Catering
Contact: Mrs D Williams
t (01720) 422810
e fiestydee2002@yahoo.co.uk
w middletownscilly.co.uk

Tean ★★★★ *Self Catering*
Contact: Mr & Mrs Kirby
t (01525) 210929
e susankirby1960@hotmail.co.uk

Teania ★★★★★
Self Catering
Contact: Mr & Mrs Keith & Dawn Bradford
t (01720) 423213
e dawn.davison2@btopenworld.com

Tresillian ★★★★
Self Catering
Island Properties
t (01720) 422082
e enquiries@scillyhols.com
w scillyhols.com

Trevean ★★★★ *Self Catering*
Contact: Mrs Rosemary Sharman
Robinswood Farm
t (01929) 471210
e robin@sharman0848.freeserve.co.uk
w treveanislesofscilly.co.uk

White Cottage Flat ★★
Self Catering
Island Properties
t (01720) 422082
e enquiries@scillyhols.com
w scillyhols.com

KELLOW
Cornwall

Bay Cottage ★★★
Self Catering
Cornish Collection Ltd
t (01503) 262736
e enquiries@cornishcollections.co.uk
w cornishcollection.co.uk

Boscawn ★★★★
Self Catering
Cornish Collection Ltd
t (01503) 262736
e enquiries@cornishcollections.co.uk
w cornishcollection.co.uk

Orchard Cottage ★★★★
Self Catering
Cornish Collection Ltd
t (01503) 262736
e enquiries@cornishcollections.co.uk
w cornishcollection.co.uk

Tern ★★★★ *Self Catering*
Cornish Collection Ltd
t (01503) 262736
e enquiries@cornishcollections.co.uk
w cornishcollection.co.uk

Thrift Cottage ★★★
Self Catering
Cornish Collection Ltd
t (01503) 262736
e enquiries@cornishcollections.co.uk
w cornishcollection.co.uk

KELSTON
Somerset

Coombe Barn Holidays
★★★ *Self Catering*
Contact: Mr George Cullimore
t (01225) 448757
e coombe.barn@virgin.net
w holiday-cottages-bath.co.uk

KENTISBURY
Devon

Hollacombe Farm ★★★★
Self Catering
Contact: Mrs Celia Ryall
t (01598) 763286
e martin.ryall@btinternet.com
w hollacombefarm.co.uk

Northcote Manor Farm
★★★★ *Self Catering*
Contact: Mrs Watts
t (01271) 882376
e info@northcotemanorfarm.co.uk
w northcotemanorfarm.co.uk

South Patchole Farm Cottage ★★★★ *Self Catering*
Contact: Mrs Wendy Heywood
t (01271) 883223
e wen@spcottages.fsnet.co.uk
w spcottages.fsnet.co.uk

KILCOT
Gloucestershire

Coach House ★★★★
Self Catering
Contact: Mrs Jane Merritt
t (01989) 720417
e jane.merritt@btinternet.com
w holidaycottage.uk.com

Ford Farm ★★★-★★★★
Self Catering
Contact: Martin Vick
t (01989) 720398

KILKHAMPTON
Cornwall

17 The Glade ★★
Self Catering
Contact: Ms Rebecca Webb
t (01608) 811716
e beckywebb234@btinternet.com

Bishops ★★★★ *Self Catering*
Contact: Mrs Sallie Hewitt
t (01905) 621786
e bishopsthurdon@tiscali.co.uk
w convertedchapel.co.uk

Carefree Holidays ★★★
Self Catering
Contact: Mr & Mrs Alan & Gerry Glover
t (0117) 969 3699
e gerrycarefreehols@blueyonder.co.uk
w carefree-hols.co.uk

Penhalt ★★★ *Self Catering*
Contact: Mike Babb
t (01288) 353600
e info@penhalt.co.uk
w penhalt.co.uk

Villa Nostra, Kilkhampton
★★★ *Self Catering*
Contact: Ms Lea Deely
t 07773 845663
e villanostra@btinternet.com
w villanostra.co.uk

KILLIOW
Cornwall

Nansavallan Farm House
★★★★ *Self Catering*
Special Places in Cornwall
t (01872) 864400
e office@specialplacescornwall.co.uk
w specialplacescornwall.co.uk

KILMERSDON
Somerset

The Creamery 2 & 3 ★★★★
Self Catering
Contact: Mrs Susan Knatchbull
t (01373) 812337
e richard@batchfarm.ndo.co.uk
w batchfarm.com

KILMINGTON
Devon

Little Thatch ★★★
Self Catering
Lyme Bay Holidays
t (01297) 443363
e email@lymebayholidays.co.uk
w lymebayholidays.co.uk

The Old Bakehouse
Rating Applied For
Self Catering
Lyme Bay Holidays
t (01297) 443363
e email@lymebayholidays.co.uk
w lymebayholidays.co.uk

KILMINGTON
Wiltshire

Stable Loft ★★★
Self Catering
Hideaways
t (01747) 828170
e enq@hideaways.co.uk
w hideaways.co.uk

KING'S NYMPTON
Devon

The Old Rectory, King's Nympton ★★★★★
Self Catering
Contact: Mrs Stephanie Atkinson
t (01769) 580456
e info@oldrectorycottages.co.uk
w theoldrectorycottages.co.uk

Venn Farm ★★★★
Self Catering
Contact: Mrs Pauline Cain
t (01769) 572448
e vennfarmcottages@msn.com
w vennfarm.com

KING'S STANLEY
Gloucestershire

The Barn ★★★★
Self Catering
Contact: Ms Fleur Alvares
t (01453) 824659
e thebarn@middleyard.co.uk
w middleyard.co.uk

KINGSAND
Cornwall

Alogma
Rating Applied For
Self Catering
Valley Villas Ltd
t (01752) 605605
e sales@valleyvillas.com
w valleyvillas.co.uk

The Mission Hall ★★★★
Self Catering
Valley Villas Ltd
t (01752) 605605
e sales@valleyvillas.com
w valleyvillas.co.uk

KINGSBRIDGE
Devon

2 The Moorings ★★★★★
Self Catering
Toad Hall Cottages
t (01548) 853089 &
07703 320361
e thc@toadhallcottages.com
w toadhallcottages.co.uk

6 Crabshell Quay ★★★★★
Self Catering
Blue Chip Vacations
t (01803) 855282
e info@bluechipvacations.com
w bluechipvacations.com

Malston Mill Farm Holiday Cottages ★★★★
Self Catering
Contact: Mr & Mrs Tony &
Linda Gresham
t (01548) 852518
e gresham@malstonmill.fsnet.co.uk
w malstonmill.co.uk

Seacombe ★★★
Self Catering
Toad Hall Cottages
t (01548) 853089
e thc@toadhallcottages.com
w toadhallcottages.co.uk

Sloop Cottages ★★★
Self Catering
Contact: Mr Girling
t (01548) 560810
e sloop.cottages@virgin.net
w sloopholidaycottages.co.uk

South Allington House
★★★-★★★★ *Self Catering*
Contact: Mrs Barbara Baker
t (01548) 511272
e barbara@southallingtonhouse.co.uk
w southallingtonhouse.co.uk

West Charleton Grange
★★★★★ *Self Catering*
Contact: Miss Michelle
Puncher
t (01548) 531779
e michelle@westcharletongrange.com
w westcharletongrange.com

Westcliffe ★★★★
Self Catering
Toad Hall Cottages
t (01548) 853089
e thc@toadhallcottages.com
w toadhallcottages.co.uk

KINGSDON
Somerset

The Lodge ★★★★
Self Catering
Contact: Mrs Jo Furneaux
t (01935) 841194

KINGSHEANTON
Devon

Briar Rose ★★★★
Self Catering
Marsdens Cottage Holidays
t (01271) 813777
e holidays@marsdens.co.uk
w marsdens.co.uk

The Coach House ★★★★
Self Catering
Marsdens Cottage Holidays
t (01271) 813777
e holidays@marsdens.co.uk
w marsdens.co.uk

The Welkin ★★★★
Self Catering
Marsdens Cottage Holidays
t (01271) 813777
e holidays@marsdens.co.uk
w marsdens.co.uk

KINGSTEIGNTON
Devon

Plumb Corner ★★★★
Self Catering
Holiday Homes and Cottages
South West
t (01803) 299677
e holcotts@aol.com
w swcottages.co.uk

KINGSTON
Devon

Apple Barn ★★★★
Self Catering
Toad Hall Cottages
t (01548) 853089
e thc@toadhallcottages.com
w toadhallcottages.co.uk

Thatched Cottage ★★★★
Self Catering
Toad Hall Cottages
t (01548) 853089
e thc@toadhallcottages.com
w toadhallcottages.co.uk

KINGSWEAR
Devon

1 Elm Cottage, Kingswear
★★★★ *Self Catering*
Blue Chip Vacations
t (01803) 855282
e info@bluechipvacations.com
w bluechipvacations.com

1 Inglewood Apts ★★★★
Self Catering
Blue Chip Vacations
t (01803) 855282
e info@bluechipvacations.com
w bluechipvacations.com

10 College View ★★★
Self Catering
Blue Chip Vacations
t (01803) 855282
e info@bluechipvacations.com
w bluechipvacations.com

3 The Pines, Kingswear
★★★★ *Self Catering*
Blue Chip Vacations
t (01803) 855282
e info@bluechipvacations.com
w bluechipvacations.com

Dragon's Reach ★★★★
Self Catering
Blue Chip Vacations
t (01803) 855282
e info@bluechipvacations.com
w bluechipvacations.com

The Gables, Kingswear
★★★★ *Self Catering*
Blue Chip Vacations
t (01803) 855282
e info@bluechipvacations.com
w bluechipvacations.com

Marina View, Kingswear
★★★★★ *Self Catering*
Blue Chip Vacations
t (01803) 855282
e info@bluechipvacations.com
w bluechipvacations.com

Slipway House ★★★★
Self Catering
Blue Chip Vacations
t (01803) 855282
e info@bluechipvacations.com
w bluechipvacations.com

Woodbine House, Kingswear ★★★★
Self Catering
Blue Chip Vacations
t (01803) 855282
e info@bluechipvacations.com
w bluechipvacations.com

KNOWSTONE
Devon

The Barn ★★★★
Self Catering
Contact: Mrs J.M Bray
t (01398) 341224
e west.bowden@ukf.net
w westbowden.ukf.net

LACOCK
Wiltshire

Barn Cottages ★★★★
Self Catering
Contact: Mr & Mrs Derek &
Jane Walters
t (01249) 730013
e enquiries@barncottagesatlacock.co.uk
w barncottagesatlacock.co.uk

Cyder House and Cheese House ★★★★ *Self Catering*
Contact: Mr & Mrs Philip &
Susan King
t (01249) 730244 &
07813 207858
e kingsilverlands2@btinternet.com
w cheeseandcyderhouses.co.uk

LADOCK
Cornwall

Trendeal Barn ★★★★★
Self Catering
t (01579) 346473
e holidays@duchyofcornwall.gov.uk
w duchyofcornwallholidaycottages.co.uk

LAMORNA COVE
Cornwall

Bal-Red ★★★ *Self Catering*
Contact: Miss Sarah Daniel
t (01736) 731227

LANGLEY BURRELL
Wiltshire

Cedarwood ★★★★
Self Catering
Contact: Mrs Helen Miflin
t (01249) 721500
e williammiflin@hotmail.com

LANGPORT
Somerset

Laurel Wharf ★★★★
Self Catering
Contact: Mr John Neale
t (01460) 281713
e laurelwharf@hotmail.com
w laurelwharf.co.uk

Muchelney Ham Farm, Muchelney ★★★★
Self Catering
Contact: Mr Jim Woodborne
t (01458) 250737

The Stables at Merricks Organic Farm ★★★
Self Catering
Contact: Mrs Jane Brooke
t (01458) 252901
e simon@merricksorganicfarm.co.uk
w merricksorganicfarm.co.uk

LANGRIDGE
Somerset

Langridge Studio ★★★★
Self Catering
Contact: Mr Brian Shuttleworth
t (01225) 338874
e info@langridge-studio.co.uk
w langridge-studio.co.uk

LANGTON HERRING
Dorset

Badgers Cottage ★★★
Self Catering
Dream Cottages
t (01305) 789000
e admin@dream-cottages.co.uk
w dream-cottages.co.uk

Character Farm Cottages
★★★★ *Self Catering*
Contact: Mrs Ann Mayo
t (01305) 871347
e jane@mayo.fsbusiness.co.uk
w characterfarmcottages.co.uk

Groom's Cottage ★★★★
Self Catering
Dream Cottages
t (01305) 789000
e admin@dream-cottages.co.uk
w dream-cottages.co.uk

Stepping Stones ★★★★
Self Catering
Dream Cottages
t (01305) 789000
e admin@dream-cottages.co.uk
w dream-cottages.co.uk

LANGTON MATRAVERS
Dorset

5 North Street ★★★
Self Catering
Contact: Mrs Ann Garratt
t (01959) 565145
e garratts@dsl.pipex.com
w holiday-cottage-dorset.co.uk

Bakery Cottage ★★★★
Self Catering
Dream Cottages
t (01305) 789000
e admin@dream-cottages.co.uk
w dream-cottages.co.uk

Flat 5 Garfield House ★★
Self Catering
Contact: Miss Susan Inge
Flat A
t (020) 7602 4945 & 07798 500437
e sueinge@hotmail.com
w langton-matravers.co.uk

Forge Cottage ★★★
Self Catering
Dorset Cottage Holidays
t (01929) 553443
e enq@dhcottages.co.uk
w dhcottages.co.uk

Island View ★★★
Self Catering
Dream Cottages
t (01305) 789000
e admin@dream-cottages.co.uk
w dream-cottages.co.uk

Rose Cottage ★★★
Self Catering
Contact: Mrs Helen Knight
t (01929) 425184
e info@purbeckheritage.co.uk
w purbeckheritage.co.uk

Tudor Rose ★★ *Self Catering*
Dream Cottages
t (01305) 789000
e admin@dream-cottages.co.uk
w dream-cottages.co.uk

West View House ★★★★
Self Catering
Contact: Mr & Mrs Alec & Jane Brown
t (01788) 560193
e alec@lodgefarm.com
w westviewhouse.co.uk

LANGTREE
Devon

Birchill Cottages
★★★★-★★★★★
Self Catering
Contact: Mr Simon Matthews
t (01805) 601623
e mail@birchillfarm.co.uk
w birchillfarm.co.uk

LANIVET
Cornwall

Lakeview Country Club
★★★★ *Self Catering*
Blue Chip Vacations
t (01803) 855282
e info@bluechipvacations.com
w bluechipvacations.com

LANLIVERY
Cornwall

Vitalise Churchtown
Rating Applied For
Self Catering
Contact: Tamsin Whitehead
t (01208) 872148
e fwhitehead@vitalise.org.uk
w vitalise.org.uk

LANNER
Cornwall

Hunters Lodge ★★★
Self Catering
Contact: Mr & Mrs Percy
t (01209) 218577
e anjen@anjen.co.uk
w anjen.co.uk

LANREATH-BY-LOOE
Cornwall

The Old Rectory, Lanreath
★★★ *Self Catering*
Contact: Mrs Julie Edge
t (01503) 220247
e ask@oldrectory-lanreath.co.uk
w oldrectory-lanreath.co.uk

LANSALLOS
Cornwall

Little Tregue ★★
Self Catering
Contact: Mrs Kate Kellaway
t (01503) 272758
e littletregue@hotmail.com
w littletregue.co.uk

Valleybrook Holidays
★★★-★★★★ *Self Catering*
Contact: Mr Brian Holder
t (01503) 220493
e admin@valleybrookholidays.co.uk
w valleybrookholidays.co.uk

West Kellow Farmhouse
★★★★ *Self Catering*
Contact: Mrs Evelyn Julian
t (01503) 272089
e westkellow@aol.com
w westkellow.co.uk

LAUNCESTON
Cornwall

Bamham Farm Cottages
★★★★ *Self Catering*
Contact: Mrs Jacki Chapman
t (01566) 772141
e jackie@bamhamfarm.co.uk
w bamhamfarm.co.uk

Frankaborough Farm Cottages ★★★★
Self Catering
Contact: Mrs Linda Banbury
t (01409) 211308
e banbury960@aol.com
w devonfarmcottage.co.uk

Langdon Farm Holiday Cottages ★★★-★★★★
Self Catering
Contact: Mrs Fleur Rawlinson
t (01566) 785389
e g.f.rawlinson@btinternet.com
w langdonholidays.com

Lower Dutson Farm ★★★
Self Catering
Contact: Mr & Mrs Broad
t (01566) 776456
e holidays@farm-cottage.co.uk
w farm-cottage.co.uk

Ta Mill Holidays
★★★-★★★★ *Self Catering*
Contact: Ms Helen Shopland
t (01840) 261797
e helen@tamill.co.uk
w tamill.co.uk

Trevosper Barn
★★★-★★★★ *Self Catering*
Contact: Ms Jackie Radford
t (01566) 86553
e info@trevosperholidaybarn.com
w trevosperholidaybarn.com

Wheatley Cottage and Barn
★★★★ *Self Catering*
Contact: Mrs Griffin
t (01566) 781232
e valerie@wheatleyfrm.com
w chycor.co.uk

LEE
Devon

Grange Apartment ★★★
Self Catering
Marsdens Cottage Holidays
t (01271) 813777
e holidays@marsdens.co.uk
w marsdens.co.uk

Lower Campscott Farm
★★★-★★★★★ *Self Catering*
Contact: Mrs Margaret Cowell
t (01271) 863479
e holidays@lowercampscott.co.uk
w lowercampscott.co.uk

Mill Field Cottage ★★★★
Self Catering
Marsdens Cottage Holidays
t (01271) 813777
e holidays@marsdens.co.uk
w marsdens.co.uk

Smugglers Cottage ★★★
Self Catering
Marsdens Cottage Holidays
t (01271) 813777
e holidays@marsdens.co.uk
w marsdens.co.uk

Vine Cottage ★★★★
Self Catering
Marsdens Cottage Holidays
t (01271) 813777
e holidays@marsdens.co.uk
w marsdens.co.uk

LEEDSTOWN
Cornwall

Little Pengelly Cottages
★★★-★★★★★ *Self Catering*
Contact: Miss Millichip
t (01736) 850452
e maxine@littlepengelly.co.uk
w littlepengelly.co.uk

LEIGH UPON MENDIP
Somerset

Clove Cottage ★★★★
Self Catering
Contact: Mr M Taylor
t (01373) 813426
e michelle.taylor10@btinternet.com

Fairoak Grange ★★★★
Self Catering
Contact: Mr Antony Key
t (01630) 620623
e fairoakbarns@yahoo.co.uk

LELANT
Cornwall

1 Atlantic Watch ★★★★★
Self Catering
Ayia Napa Holidays
t (01736) 757237
e info@carbisbayretreats.co.uk
w carbisbayretreats.co.uk

Badgers Den ★★★★
Self Catering
Contact: Mrs Mrs Gillian Hay
t (01209) 717980
e info@badgersden.org.uk
w badgersden.org.uk

Beersheba Brea ★★★★
Self Catering
Contact: Mrs Victoria Jelbert
t 07795 284356
e info@beersheba.co.uk
w beersheba.co.uk

Gonwin Manor Cottages
★★★★★ *Self Catering*
Contact: Mr Michael Wodskou
t (01736) 797044
e info@gonwin-manor.co.uk
w gonwin-manor.co.uk

Mount Douglas Farm Cottages ★★★★
Self Catering
Contact: Mr & Mrs Perry
t (01736) 794831
e philmd1@talktalk.net
w mountdouglascottages.co.uk

Rivavista ★★★★★
Self Catering
Cornish Gems
t 0844 800 2813
w cornishgems.com/gems-finest/riva-vista.html

Riviera 3 ★★★★
Self Catering
Ayia Napa Holidays
t (01736) 757237
e info@carbisbayretreats.co.uk
w carbisbayretreats.co.uk

Saltings View Cottage
★★★★★ *Self Catering*
Cornish Gems
t 0844 800 2813
w cornishgems.com/holiday-cottages/saltings_view.html

Trevalgan Barns ★★★★
Self Catering
Contact: Mrs Jean Osborne
t (01736) 756252
e enquiries@trevalganbarns.co.uk
w trevalganbarns.co.uk

Trevethoe Farm Cottages
★★★ *Self Catering*
Contact: Mr & Mrs Rogers
t (01736) 753279
e holidaycottages@trevethoe.co.uk
w trevethoe.co.uk

LELANT DOWNS
Cornwall

Coombe Cottage Caravan
Approved Caravan Holiday Home
Contact: Mr & Mrs Nash
t (01736) 740445

LEWDOWN
Devon

Wagon Linney & Whiterow Stables ★★★★ *Self Catering*
Farm & Cottage Holidays
t (01237) 459827
e enquiries@farmcott.co.uk
w holidaycottages.co.uk

LEZANT
Cornwall

East Penrest Barn ★★★★★
Self Catering
Contact: Mr & Mrs Jo & James Rider
t (01579) 370186
e jorider@eastpenrest.freeserve.co.uk
w cornwall-online.co.uk

LIFTON
Devon

Barbary Ball House ★★★★
Self Catering
Contact: Mr Richard Street
t (01566) 780457
e info@devoncountrybarns.co.uk
w devoncountrybarns.co.uk

LIMPLEY STOKE
Wiltshire

Iona Cottage ★★★★
Self Catering
Contact: Mr & Mrs David & Karen White
t (01225) 852360
e dc.white@ukonline.co.uk
w bath-cottages.co.uk

LISKEARD
Cornwall

48 Jade Cottage ★★★★
Self Catering
Contact: Barbara Horne
t (01788) 846241
w 48jadecottage.co.uk

Beechleigh Cottage ★★★★
Self Catering
t (01579) 342407
w tregondalefarm.co.uk

Boturnell Barns, St Pinnock
★★ *Self Catering*
Contact: Sue Jewell
t (01579) 320880
e sue@dogs-holiday.co.uk
w dogs-holiday.co.uk

Coach House Cottages
★★★★ *Self Catering*
Contact: Mr Hall
t (01579) 347755
e cottages@treworgey.co.uk
w treworgey.co.uk

Hopsland Holidays ★★★★
Self Catering
Contact: Mr & Mrs Hosken
t (01579) 344480
e hopslandholidays@aol.com
w hopslandholidays.co.uk

Lodge Barton ★★★
Self Catering
Contact: Mrs Rosanne Hodin
t (01579) 344432
e lodgebart@aol.com
w selectideas.co.uk/lodgebarton

Lower Trengale Farm
★★★★ *Self Catering*
Contact: Mr & Mrs Shears
t (01579) 321019
e enquiries@trengale.co.uk
w trengale.co.uk

Rivermead ★★★-★★★★
Self Catering
Holiday Homes and Cottages South West
t (01803) 299677
e holcotts@aol.com
w swcottages.co.uk

Trelyn Cottage ★★★
Self Catering
Contact: Ms Fisher
t (01579) 383881
e trelyn@kingfisher-training.freeserve.co.uk

LITTLE PETHERICK
Cornwall

1 Riverside
Rating Applied For
Self Catering
Cornish Horizons Holiday Cottages
t (01841) 533331
e cottages@cornishhorizons.co.uk
w cornishhorizons.co.uk

16 Rosehill Development
★★★★ *Self Catering*
Harbour Holidays
t (01841) 533402
e contact@harbourholidays.co.uk
w harbourholidays.co.uk

3 Riverside ★★★★
Self Catering
Cornish Horizons Holiday Cottages
t (01841) 533331
e cottages@cornishhorizons.co.uk
w cornishhorizons.co.uk

4 Riverside
Rating Applied For
Self Catering
Cornish Horizons Holiday Cottages
t (01841) 533331
e cottages@cornishhorizons.co.uk
w cornishhorizons.co.uk

6 Saints Way ★★★★
Self Catering
Cornish Horizons Holiday Cottages
t (01841) 533331
e cottages@cornishhorizons.co.uk
w cornishhorizons.co.uk

Creekside ★★★★
Self Catering
Cornish Horizons Holiday Cottages
t (01841) 533331
e cottages@cornishhorizons.co.uk
w cornishhorizons.co.uk

Creekside Cottage ★★★★
Self Catering
Cornish Horizons Holiday Cottages
t (01841) 533331
e cottages@cornishhorizons.co.uk
w cornishhorizons.co.uk

Driftwood ★★★★
Self Catering
Cornish Horizons Holiday Cottages
t (01841) 533331
e cottages@cornishhorizons.co.uk
w cornishhorizons.co.uk

Entwood ★★★★
Self Catering
Cornish Horizons Holiday Cottages
t (01841) 533331
e cottages@cornishhorizons.co.uk
w cornishhorizons.co.uk

Honeywood ★★★★
Self Catering
Cornish Horizons Holiday Cottages
t (01841) 533331
e cottages@cornishhorizons.co.uk
w cornishhorizons.co.uk

Pine Haven ★★★★
Self Catering
Cornish Horizons Holiday Cottages
t (01841) 533331
e cottages@cornishhorizons.co.uk
w cornishhorizons.co.uk

The Quay House ★★★
Self Catering
Contact: Mr & Mrs George & Alison Hatcher
t (01841) 540431
e quayhouse@aol.com
w quayhouse.co.uk

Swallow Court Cottage
★★★★ *Self Catering*
Contact: Mr Geoff French
t (01841) 540292
e molesworthmanor@aol.com
w molesworthmanor.co.uk

Timbers ★★★★ *Self Catering*
Cornish Horizons Holiday Cottages
t (01841) 533331
e cottages@cornishhorizons.co.uk
w cornishhorizons.co.uk

Trenant ★★★★ *Self Catering*
Cornish Horizons Holiday Cottages
t (01841) 533331
e cottages@cornishhorizons.co.uk
w cornishhorizons.co.uk

Watergate ★★★★
Self Catering
Cornish Horizons Holiday Cottages
t (01841) 533331
e cottages@cornishhorizons.co.uk
w cornishhorizons.co.uk

Waterside ★★★★
Self Catering
Cornish Horizons Holiday Cottages
t (01841) 533331
e cottages@cornishhorizons.co.uk
w cornishhorizons.co.uk

LITTLE TORRINGTON
Devon

Torridge House Cottages
★★★-★★★★ *Self Catering*
Contact: Mrs Barbara Terry
t (01805) 622542
e bookings@torridgehouse.co.uk
w torridgehouse.co.uk

LITTLEDEAN
Gloucestershire

Brambles, Littledean ★★★
Self Catering
Contact: Lynda Norman
t (01594) 827311
e lynda@searanckes.com
w forestbarnholidays.co.uk

LITTON CHENEY
Dorset

Chimney Sweep ★★★★
Self Catering
Dream Cottages
t (01305) 789000
e admin@dream-cottages.co.uk
w dream-cottages.co.uk

LIVERTON
Devon

Lookweep Farm Cottages
★★★ *Self Catering*
Contact: Mr & Mrs John & Helen Griffiths
t (01626) 833277
e holidays@lookweep.co.uk
w lookweep.co.uk

LIZARD
Cornwall

Pen Vose ★★★★
Self Catering
Toad Hall Cottages
t (01548) 853089
e thc@toadhallcottages.com
w toadhallcottages.co.uk

LOCKING
Somerset

Fermaine Garden Cottage
★★★★ *Self Catering*
Contact: Mr & Mrs David & Angela Jackson
t (01934) 820770
e david@jackson7.com
w fermainegardencottage.co.uk

LODERS
Dorset

Beachside Cottage ★★★
Self Catering
Dream Cottages
t (01305) 789000
e admin@dream-cottages.co.uk
w dream-cottages.co.uk

Farthing Cottage ★★★
Self Catering
Toad Hall Cottages
t (01548) 853089
e thc@toadhallcottages.com
w toadhallcottages.co.uk

LONDON APPRENTICE
Cornwall

Levalsa Farm ★★★-★★★★
Self Catering
Contact: Mrs Gaye Julian
t (01726) 843505
e gayejulian@hotmail.co.uk
w levalsafarm.co.uk

LONG BREDY
Dorset

Whatcombe Stables ★★★★
Self Catering
Dream Cottages
t (01305) 789000
e admin@dream-cottages.co.uk
w dream-cottages.co.uk

LONG NEWNTON
Gloucestershire

Mabels Oak Cottage ★★★
Self Catering
Contact: Mrs Ros Porter
t (01666) 504309
e cps@blackhorse.eclipse.co.uk

LONG ROCK
Cornwall

The Cottage at Heron House
★★★★ *Self Catering*
Contact: Mr James Morris-Marsham
t (01736) 711680
e susiemm@freenet.co.uk

Tregarthen Barn ★★★★★
Self Catering
t (01736) 711078
w cornishholidayspenzance.com

LONGBRIDGE DEVERILL
Wiltshire

Sturgess Farmhouse ★★★★
Self Catering
Contact: Mr Tony Ramsay
t (01985) 840329
e info@sturgessbarns.co.uk
w sturgessbarns.co.uk

LONGCOMBE
Devon

Longcombe Cottage Holidays ★★★-★★★★
Self Catering
Contact: Mrs Rita Trotman
t (01803) 863762
e enquiries@longcombe-cottages.co.uk
w longcombe-cottages.co.uk

LONGDOWN
Devon

Valley View ★★★★
Self Catering
Contact: Mrs Jane Steele
t (01392) 811858
e janeeileensteele@talktalk.net

Willhayes ★★★★
Self Catering
Contact: Mrs Joanne Summerbee
t (01392) 834943
e jo@willhayes.co.uk
w willhayes.co.uk

LOOE
Cornwall

1 Granite Henge ★★★
Self Catering
Cornish Collection Ltd
t (01503) 262736
e enquiries@cornishcollections.co.uk
w cornishcollection.co.uk

11 Granite Henge ★★★
Self Catering
Cornish Collection Ltd
t (01503) 262736
e enquiries@cornishcollections.co.uk
w cornishcollection.co.uk

11 Woburn Lodge ★★★★
Self Catering
Valley Villas Ltd
t (01752) 605605
e sales@valleyvillas.com
w valleyvillas.co.uk

11a Granite Henge ★★★
Self Catering
Cornish Collection Ltd
t (01503) 262736
e enquiries@cornishcollections.co.uk
w cornishcollection.co.uk

16 Woburn Lodge ★★★★
Self Catering
Valley Villas Ltd
t (01752) 605605
e sales@valleyvillas.com
w valleyvillas.co.uk

2 Admiralty Court ★★
Self Catering
t (01503) 269086
w cornishmanagementservices.co.uk

3 Granite Henge ★★★
Self Catering
Cornish Collection Ltd
t (01503) 262736
e enquiries@cornishcollections.co.uk
w cornishcollection.co.uk

4 Granite Henge ★★★
Self Catering
Cornish Collection Ltd
t (01503) 262736
e enquiries@cornishcollections.co.uk
w cornishcollection.co.uk

4 Harbourside ★★★
Self Catering
Cornish Collection Ltd
t (01503) 262736
e enquiries@cornishcollections.co.uk
w cornishcollection.co.uk

6 Harbourside ★★★
Self Catering
Cornish Collection Ltd
t (01503) 262736
e enquiries@cornishcollections.co.uk
w cornishcollection.co.uk

7 Granite Henge ★★★
Self Catering
Cornish Collection Ltd
t (01503) 262736
e enquiries@cornishcollections.co.uk
w cornishcollection.co.uk

8 Harbourside Apartment
Rating Applied For
Self Catering
Cornish Collection Ltd
t (01503) 262736
e enquiries@cornishcollections.co.uk
w cornishcollection.co.uk

A Wee House
Rating Applied For
Self Catering
Contact: Molly Gorman
t (01503) 269207
e mollyandminnie@hotmail.co.uk
w weehouse-looe.co.uk

Avalon ★★★★ *Self Catering*
Cornish Collection Ltd
t (01503) 262736
e enquiries@cornishcollections.co.uk
w cornishcollection.co.uk

Barclay House Luxury Cottages ★★★★-★★★★★
Self Catering
Contact: Mr Graham Brooks
t (01503) 262929
e info@barclayhouse.co.uk
w barclayhouse.co.uk

Bellevue ★★★ *Self Catering*
Cornish Collection Ltd
t (01503) 262736
e enquiries@cornishcollections.co.uk
w cornishcollection.co.uk

Bocaddon Holiday Cottages
★★★★ *Self Catering*
Contact: Mrs Alison Maiklem
t (01503) 220192
e holidays@bocaddon.com
w bocaddon.com

The Brentons ★★★
Self Catering
Contact: Mrs Hocking
t (01503) 262469
e deshocking@hotmail.com

Bucklawren Farm
★★★★-★★★★★
Self Catering
Contact: Mrs Henly
t (01503) 240738
e bucklawren@btopenworld.com
w bucklawren.com

Captain's Retreat ★★★
Self Catering
Cornish Collection Ltd
t (01503) 262736
e enquiries@cornishcollections.co.uk
w cornishcollection.co.uk

Carpenter's Cottage ★★
Self Catering
Cornish Collection Ltd
t (01503) 262736
e enquiries@cornishcollections.co.uk
w cornishcollection.co.uk

Clipper House, Main Sail, Crows Nest ★★★-★★★★
Self Catering
Contact: Mrs French
t (01503) 262754
e rfrenchclipper@aol.com
w clipperhouse.co.uk

Coldrinnick Cottages
★★★-★★★★ *Self Catering*
Contact: Mrs Chapman
t (01503) 220251
e coldrinnick@safe2say.com
w cornishcottage.net

Crylla Valley Cottages
★★★★ *Self Catering*
Contact: Mr Matt Walsh
t (01752) 851133 & (01752) 851666
e sales@cryllacottages.co.uk
w cryllacottages.co.uk

Drifters ★★★★ *Self Catering*
Cornish Collection Ltd
t (01503) 262736
e enquiries@cornishcollections.co.uk
w cornishcollection.co.uk

Ebbtide ★★★★ *Self Catering*
Cornish Collection Ltd
t (01503) 262736
e enquiries@cornishcollections.co.uk
w cornishcollection.co.uk

Enfield Cottages ★★★
Self Catering
Contact: Mrs T Hopkinson
t (01909) 540225
e enquiries@enfieldcottages.com
w enfieldcottages.com

Harbourside Holiday Flats
★★★ *Self Catering*
Contact: Mr & Mrs Pope
t (01503) 262926

Hendra Farm Cottages
★★★★ *Self Catering*
Contact: Mrs Senara Higgs
t (01503) 220701
e info@hendrafarmcottages.co.uk
w hendrafarmcottages.co.uk

Highwood ★★★★
Self Catering
Contact: Mrs Beatrix Windle
t (01483) 277894
e beatrix@talk21.com
w cornwall-online.co.uk

Inverlooe 2a ★★★★
Self Catering
Cornish Collection Ltd
t (01503) 262736
e enquiries@cornishcollections.co.uk
w cornishcollection.co.uk

Journey's End ★★★★
Self Catering
Cornish Collection Ltd
t (01503) 262736
e enquiries@cornishcollections.co.uk
w cornishcollection.co.uk

Lantau Cottage ★★★★
Self Catering
Valley Villas Ltd
t (01752) 605605
e sales@valleyvillas.com
w valleyvillas.co.uk

Lemain Garden Apartments
★★★-★★★★ *Self Catering*
Contact: Mr & Mrs Alan Palin
t (01579) 321103
e sales@lemain.com
w lemain.com

Little Cottage ★★★
Self Catering
Contact: Mrs Tolputt
t (01503) 220315
w lesquite-polperro.fsnet.co.uk

Mariner's Rest ★★★
Self Catering
Cornish Collection Ltd
t (01503) 262736
e enquiries@cornishcollections.co.uk
w cornishcollection.co.uk

Osborne House ★★★★
Self Catering
Valley Villas Ltd
t (01752) 605605
e sales@valleyvillas.com
w valleyvillas.co.uk

Penhallow ★★★★
Self Catering
Cornish Collection Ltd
t (01503) 262736
e enquiries@cornishcollections.co.uk
w cornishcollection.co.uk

Petroc ★★★ *Self Catering*
Cornish Collection Ltd
t (01503) 262736
e enquiries@cornishcollections.co.uk
w cornishcollection.co.uk

The Quarry ★★★
Self Catering
Cornish Collection Ltd
t (01503) 262736
e enquiries@cornishcollections.co.uk
w cornishcollection.co.uk

Rivercroft Hotel & Apartments ★★★
Self Catering
Contact: Glenn, Julie and Pauline Cairns
t (01503) 262251
e rivercroft.hotel@virgin.net
w rivercrofthotel.co.uk

Riverside ★★★ *Self Catering*
Cornish Collection Ltd
t (01503) 262736
e enquiries@cornishcollections.co.uk
w cornishcollection.co.uk

Rock Tower Apartment 10
★★★ *Self Catering*
Cornish Collection Ltd
t (01503) 262736
e enquiries@cornishcollections.co.uk
w cornishcollection.co.uk

Rock Tower Apartment 11
★★★ *Self Catering*
Cornish Collection Ltd
t (01503) 262736
e enquiries@cornishcollections.co.uk
w cornishcollection.co.uk

Rock Tower Apartment 12
★★★★ *Self Catering*
Cornish Collection Ltd
t (01503) 262736
e enquiries@cornishcollections.co.uk
w cornishcollection.co.uk

Rock Tower Apartment 4
★★★ *Self Catering*
Cornish Collection Ltd
t (01503) 262736
e enquiries@cornishcollections.co.uk
w cornishcollection.co.uk

Rock Tower Apartment 6
★★★ *Self Catering*
Cornish Collection Ltd
t (01503) 262736
e enquiries@cornishcollections.co.uk
w cornishcollection.co.uk

Rock Tower Apartment 7
★★★ *Self Catering*
Cornish Collection Ltd
t (01503) 262736
e enquiries@cornishcollections.co.uk
w cornishcollection.co.uk

Rockabye Cottage ★★
Self Catering
Contact: Mr & Mrs Birch
t (0118) 971 3378
w rockabyecottage.co.uk

Rosemary ★★★ *Self Catering*
Cornish Collection Ltd
t (01503) 262736
e enquiries@cornishcollections.co.uk
w cornishcollection.co.uk

The Sail-Loft ★★★
Self Catering
Contact: Mrs Melissa Hocking
t (01503) 262182
e deshocking@hotmail.com
w sail-loft.com

St Martins Apartment
★★★★ *Self Catering*
Cornish Collection Ltd
t (01503) 262736
e enquiries@cornishcollections.co.uk
w cornishcollection.co.uk

Siang Talay ★★★★
Self Catering
Cornish Collection Ltd
t (01503) 262736
e enquiries@cornishcollections.co.uk
w cornishcollection.co.uk

Spinnaker ★★★
Self Catering
Contact: Mrs Vaughan
t (0121) 241 7652 & 07981 629464
e bagginziz@tiscali.co.uk
w spinnaker-looe.co.uk

Stonemasons ★★
Self Catering
Cornish Collection Ltd
t (01503) 262736
e enquiries@cornishcollections.co.uk
w cornishcollection.co.uk

Summercourt Coastal Cottages ★★★★
Self Catering
Contact: Mr Hocking
t (01503) 263149
e sccottages@freenet.co.uk
w holidaycottagescornwall.tv

Sundew ★★★★ *Self Catering*
Cornish Collection Ltd
t (01503) 262736
e enquiries@cornishcollections.co.uk
w cornishcollection.co.uk

Talehay ★★★ *Self Catering*
Contact: Neil & Theresa Dennett
t (01503) 220252
e infobooking@talehay.co.uk
w talehay.co.uk

Trecan Farm Cottages
★★★-★★★★ *Self Catering*
Contact: Mrs Pugh
t (01503) 220768
e richardpugh@trecan.fsnet.co.uk
w trecanfarmcottages.co.uk

Trentwith ★★★ *Self Catering*
Cornish Collection Ltd
t (01503) 262736
e enquiries@cornishcollections.co.uk
w cornishcollection.co.uk

Trewith Holiday Cottages
★-★★★★ *Self Catering*
Contact: Mr & Mrs Higgins
t (01503) 262184
e holiday-cottages@trewith.freeserve.co.uk
w trewith.freeserve.co.uk

Treworgey Cottages
★★★★ *Self Catering*
Contact: Mr & Mrs Wright
t (01503) 262730
e treworgey@enterprise.net
w cornishdreamcottages.co.uk

Tudor Lodges ★★★★
Self Catering
Contact: Mrs Tudor
t (01579) 320344
e mollytudor@aol.com
w tudorlodges.co.uk

Vine Cottage ★★★
Self Catering
Cornish Collection Ltd
t (01503) 262736
e enquiries@cornishcollections.co.uk
w cornishcollection.co.uk

Woodsaws Farm ★★★★
Self Catering
Contact: Mrs Ann Wills
t (01503) 220190
e ann@woodsawsfarm.co.uk

Wringworthy Cottages
★★★★ *Self Catering*
Contact: Mr & Mrs Michael & Kim Spencer
t (01503) 240685
e holidays@wringworthy.co.uk
w wringworthy.co.uk

LOSTWITHIEL
Cornwall

Brean Park ★★★★★
Self Catering
Contact: Mrs Janet Hoskin
t (01208) 872184
e breanpark@btconnect.com
w breanpark.co.uk

Chark Country Holidays
★★★★ *Self Catering*
Contact: Mrs Jenny Littleton
t (01208) 871118
e charkholidays@tiscali.co.uk
w charkcountryholidays.co.uk

Hartswheal Barn
★★★-★★★★ *Self Catering*
t (01208) 873419
w connexions.co.uk/hartswheal/index.htm

Lanwithan Cottages
★★★-★★★★ *Self Catering*
Contact: Mr V B Edward-Collins
t (01208) 872444
e info@lanwithancottages.co.uk
w lanwithancottages.co.uk

Restormel Cottage
★★★★★ *Self Catering*
Contact: Mr Scott
t (01579) 343149
e holidays@duchyofcornwall.gov.uk
w duchyofcornwallholidaycottages.co.uk

Tredethick Farm Cottages
★★★★ *Self Catering*
Contact: Mr & Mrs Reed
t (01208) 873618
e holidays@tredethick.co.uk
w tredethick.co.uk

Trevorry ★★★★
Self Catering
Contact: Ms Helen Carlisle
t (01208) 872279
e trevorryfarm@hotmail.com
w trevorry.com

LOWER APPERLEY
Gloucestershire

Rofield Barn ★★★★★
Self Catering
Contact: Mrs Hazel Lewis
t (01452) 780323
e jeremy@tewkbury.freeserve.co.uk
w rofieldbarn.com

LOWER BAGBER
Dorset

Kite Cottage ★★★
Self Catering
Contact: Mr & Mrs Ian & Kate Osman
t (01963) 371710
e enquiries@alovelyplacetostay.co.uk
w alovelyplacetostay.co.uk

LOWER METHERELL
Cornwall

Linden Lea ★★★★
Self Catering
Holiday Homes and Cottages South West
t (01803) 299677
e holcotts@aol.com
w swcottages.co.uk

LOWER SOUDLEY
Gloucestershire

Beechwood Bungalow
Rating Applied For
Self Catering
Contact: Mrs J E Anderton
t (01594) 825864
e raanderton@ntlworld.com

LOWTON
Somerset

Bee's Cottage ★★★★
Self Catering
Farm & Cottage Holidays
t (01237) 459827
e enquiries@farmcott.co.uk
w holidaycottages.co.uk

LUDGVAN
Cornwall

Mount View Cottage ★★★
Self Catering
Contact: Mrs Wallis
t (01736) 711425
w eglos.co.uk

Nanceddan, Ludgvan ★★★
Self Catering
Contact: Mrs Richards
t (01736) 740165
e nanceddan@yahoo.co.uk
w nanceddan.com

LUXBOROUGH
Somerset

Lower Coombe Royal
★★★★★ *Self Catering*
Contact: Mrs Susi Titchener
t (01548) 852880
e retreats@lowercoomberoyal.co.uk
w lowercoomberoyal.co.uk

The Old Granary ★★★★
Self Catering
Contact: Mr & Mrs Ivan & Anne Simpson
t (01984) 640909
e theoldgranaryexmoor@yahoo.co.uk
w granarycottage.co.uk

Pool Farm Byres, Luxborough ★★★★
Self Catering
Contact: Ms Stella Morris
t (01883) 650417 & 07748 070756
e stella@c-prodirect.co.uk
w exmoorcottage.com

Westcott Lodge and Mill Cottage ★★★★ *Self Catering*
Contact: Mr Derek Gregory
t (01984) 641285
e westcottlodge@freeuk.com
w westcottlodge.co.uk/

LYDBROOK
Gloucestershire

Greenway Cottage ★★★
Self Catering
Contact: Mr Paul Hayes
t (01594) 860075
w gardencafe.co.uk

Royal Spring Cottage ★★★
Self Catering
Contact: Peter Crawley
t (01594) 860492
e royalspringinn@aol.com

LYDEARD ST LAWRENCE
Somerset

The Cottage ★★★
Self Catering
Toad Hall Cottages
t (01548) 853089
e thc@toadhallcottages.com
w toadhallcottages.co.uk

Oaklea House ★★★★
Self Catering
Contact: Mrs Peta-Elaine Barker
t (01984) 667373
e barker@oakleahouse.fsnet.co.uk
w oakleaholidays.co.uk

LYDNEY
Gloucestershire

Bream Cross Farm ★★★
Self Catering
Contact: Mr Reeks
t (01594) 562208

The Coach House, Deanfield
★★★★ *Self Catering*
Contact: Chris Preest
t (01594) 562256
e deanfieldbb@aol.com
w deanfield.org.uk

Highbury Coach House
★★★ *Self Catering*
Contact: Anthony Midgley
t (01594) 842339
e info@highburycoachhouse.co.uk
w highburycoachhouse.co.uk

Lindors Country House
★★★ *Self Catering*
t (01594) 530283
e lindors@christianguild.co.uk
w christianguild.co.uk

The Old Pumphouse ★★★★
Self Catering
Hideaways
t (01747) 828170
e enq@hideaways.co.uk
w hideaways.co.uk

LYME REGIS
Dorset

1 Coppers Knapp ★★★★
Self Catering
Lyme Bay Holidays
t (01297) 443363
e email@lymebayholidays.co.uk
w lymebayholidays.co.uk

1 Studley Gardens ★★★★
Self Catering
Lyme Bay Holidays
t (01297) 443363
e email@lymebayholidays.co.uk
w lymebayholidays.co.uk

1 Wellhayes ★★★
Self Catering
Lyme Bay Holidays
t (01297) 443363
e email@lymebayholidays.co.uk
w lymebayholidays.co.uk

10 Coombe Street ★★★
Self Catering
Lyme Bay Holidays
t (01297) 443363
e email@lymebayholidays.co.uk
w lymebayholidays.co.uk

12 Mill Green ★★★★
Self Catering
Lyme Bay Holidays
t (01297) 443363
e email@lymebayholidays.co.uk
w lymebayholidays.co.uk

14 Mill Green ★★★
Self Catering
Lyme Bay Holidays
t (01297) 443363
e email@lymebayholidays.co.uk
w lymebayholidays.co.uk

15 Broad Street ★★★★
Self Catering
Lyme Bay Holidays
t (01297) 443363
e email@lymebayholidays.co.uk
w lymebayholidays.co.uk

16 Sherborne Lane ★★★
Self Catering
Lyme Bay Holidays
t (01297) 443363
e email@lymebayholidays.co.uk
w lymebayholidays.co.uk

19 Church Street ★★★★
Self Catering
Contact: Mrs Tracey Barclay
Askew House
t (01297) 560617
e info@lymeregiscottages.co.uk
w lymeregiscottages.co.uk

2 Clappentail ★★★★
Self Catering
Lyme Bay Holidays
t (01297) 443363
e email@lymebayholidays.co.uk
w lymebayholidays.co.uk

2 Coombe Street ★★★
Self Catering
Lyme Bay Holidays
t (01297) 443363
e email@lymebayholidays.co.uk
w lymebayholidays.co.uk

2 Kersbrook Gardens
★★★★ *Self Catering*
Lyme Bay Holidays
t (01297) 443363
e email@lymebayholidays.co.uk
w lymebayholidays.co.uk

2 Portland Lodge
Rating Applied For
Self Catering
Lyme Bay Holidays
t (01297) 443363
e email@lymebayholidays.co.uk
w lymebayholidays.co.uk

2 Riverside Cottages
★★★★ *Self Catering*
Lyme Bay Holidays
t (01297) 443363
e email@lymebayholidays.co.uk
w lymebayholidays.co.uk

22a Sherborne Lane ★★★★
Self Catering
Lyme Bay Holidays
t (01297) 443363
e email@lymebayholidays.co.uk
w lymebayholidays.co.uk

23 Lym Close ★★★
Self Catering
Lyme Bay Holidays
t (01297) 443363
e email@lymebayholidays.co.uk
w lymebayholidays.co.uk

26 Coombe Street ★★★
Self Catering
Lyme Bay Holidays
t (01297) 443363
e email@lymebayholidays.co.uk
w lymebayholidays.co.uk

3 Buckfields ★★★★
Self Catering
Lyme Bay Holidays
t (01297) 443363
e email@lymebayholidays.co.uk
w lymebayholidays.co.uk

3 Chard House ★★★
Self Catering
Lyme Bay Holidays
t (01297) 443363
e email@lymebayholidays.co.uk
w lymebayholidays.co.uk

3 Dolphin Cottages ★★★
Self Catering
Lyme Bay Holidays
t (01297) 443363
e email@lymebayholidays.co.uk
w lymebayholidays.co.uk

3 Portland Lodge ★★★★
Self Catering
Lyme Bay Holidays
t (01297) 443363
e email@lymebayholidays.co.uk
w lymebayholidays.co.uk

30 Coombe Street ★★★★
Self Catering
Lyme Bay Holidays
t (01297) 443363
e email@lymebayholidays.co.uk
w lymebayholidays.co.uk

31 Sherborne Lane ★★★
Self Catering
Lyme Bay Holidays
t (01297) 443363
e email@lymebayholidays.co.uk
w lymebayholidays.co.uk

34a Coombe Street ★★★
Self Catering
Lyme Bay Holidays
t (01297) 443363
e email@lymebayholidays.co.uk
w lymebayholidays.co.uk

39 Fernhill ★★★★
Self Catering
Lyme Bay Holidays
t (01297) 443363
e email@lymebayholidays.co.uk
w lymebayholidays.co.uk

4 Buckfields ★★★★
Self Catering
Lyme Bay Holidays
t (01297) 443363
e email@lymebayholidays.co.uk
w lymebayholidays.co.uk

4 Coram Court ★★★★★
Self Catering
Lyme Bay Holidays
t (01297) 443363
e email@lymebayholidays.co.uk
w lymebayholidays.co.uk

4 East Cliff ★★★
Self Catering
Lyme Bay Holidays
t (01297) 443363
e email@lymebayholidays.co.uk
w lymebayholidays.co.uk

4 Lymbrook Cottages ★★★
Self Catering
Contact: Mrs Karen Start
t (01799) 522096

44 Henrys Way ★★★★
Self Catering
Lyme Bay Holidays
t (01297) 443363
e email@lymebayholidays.co.uk
w lymebayholidays.co.uk

44/45 Coombe Street
★★★★ *Self Catering*
Lyme Bay Holidays
t (01297) 443363
e email@lymebayholidays.co.uk
w lymebayholidays.co.uk

47 Fernhill ★★★★
Self Catering
Lyme Bay Holidays
t (01297) 443363
e email@lymebayholidays.co.uk
w lymebayholidays.co.uk

48 Fernhill ★★★★
Self Catering
Lyme Bay Holidays
t (01297) 443363
e email@lymebayholidays.co.uk
w lymebayholidays.co.uk

49 Fernhill Heights ★★★
Self Catering
Lyme Bay Holidays
t (01297) 443363
e email@lymebayholidays.co.uk
w lymebayholidays.co.uk

49a Broad Street ★★★
Self Catering
Lyme Bay Holidays
t (01297) 443363
e email@lymebayholidays.co.uk
w lymebayholidays.co.uk

5 Buckfields ★★★★
Self Catering
Lyme Bay Holidays
t (01297) 443363
e email@lymebayholidays.co.uk
w lymebayholidays.co.uk

54 Henrys Way ★★★★
Self Catering
Lyme Bay Holidays
t (01297) 443363
e email@lymebayholidays.co.uk
w lymebayholidays.co.uk

55 Church Street ★★★★
Self Catering
Lyme Bay Holidays
t (01297) 443363
e email@lymebayholidays.co.uk
w lymebayholidays.co.uk

6 Bay View Court ★★★
Self Catering
Lyme Bay Holidays
t (01297) 443363
e email@lymebayholidays.co.uk
w lymebayholidays.co.uk

6 Coppers Knapp ★★★★
Self Catering
Lyme Bay Holidays
t (01297) 443363
e email@lymebayholidays.co.uk
w lymebayholidays.co.uk

6 Silver Street ★★★★
Self Catering
Lyme Bay Holidays
t (01297) 443363
e email@lymebayholidays.co.uk
w lymebayholidays.co.uk

7 Clappentail Park ★★★★
Self Catering
Lyme Bay Holidays
t (01297) 443363
e email@lymebayholidays.co.uk
w lymebayholidays.co.uk

7 Coram Mews ★★★★★
Self Catering
Lyme Bay Holidays
t (01297) 443363
e email@lymebayholidays.co.uk
w lymebayholidays.co.uk

7 Portland Lodge ★★★★
Self Catering
Lyme Bay Holidays
t (01297) 443363
e email@lymebayholidays.co.uk
w lymebayholidays.co.uk

7 Silver Street ★★★★
Self Catering
Lyme Bay Holidays
t (01297) 443363
e email@lymebayholidays.co.uk
w lymebayholidays.co.uk

7 Windsor Terrace ★★★★
Self Catering
Lyme Bay Holidays
t (01297) 443363
e email@lymebayholidays.co.uk
w lymebayholidays.co.uk

8 Buckfields ★★★★
Self Catering
Lyme Bay Holidays
t (01297) 443363
e email@lymebayholidays.co.uk
w lymebayholidays.co.uk

Alwyns ★★★ *Self Catering*
Lyme Bay Holidays
t (01297) 443363
e email@lymebayholidays.co.uk
w lymebayholidays.co.uk

Apartment 1 & 2 Malvern House ★★★★ *Self Catering*
Lyme Bay Holidays
t (01297) 443363
e email@lymebayholidays.co.uk
w lymebayholidays.co.uk

Apartment 2 Malvern House
★★★★ *Self Catering*
Lyme Bay Holidays
t (01297) 443363
e email@lymebayholidays.co.uk
w lymebayholidays.co.uk

Apartment 3 ★★★★
Self Catering
Lyme Bay Holidays
t (01297) 443363
e email@lymebayholidays.co.uk
w lymebayholidays.co.uk

Appletree Cottage ★★★
Self Catering
Lyme Bay Holidays
t (01297) 443363
e email@lymebayholidays.co.uk
w lymebayholidays.co.uk

Appletrees ★★★★
Self Catering
Contact: Mr Charles Teall
t (01608) 641304
e teall@salfordmill.com
w salfordmill.com

Apt 2, Argyle House ★★★★
Self Catering
Lyme Bay Holidays
t (01297) 443363
e email@lymebayholidays.co.uk
w lymebayholidays.co.uk

Apt 3 Coram Tower ★★★★
Self Catering
Lyme Bay Holidays
t (01297) 443363
e email@lymebayholidays.co.uk
w lymebayholidays.co.uk

Argyle House ★★★
Self Catering
Lyme Bay Holidays
t (01297) 443363
e email@lymebayholidays.co.uk
w lymebayholidays.co.uk

Armada Guest House ★★★
Self Catering
t (01297) 445785

Bay View Court – B4357
★★★★ *Self Catering*
Lyme Bay Holidays
t (01297) 443363
e email@lymebayholidays.co.uk
w lymebayholidays.co.uk

Benwick – B4232 ★★★★
Self Catering
Lyme Bay Holidays
t (01297) 443363
e email@lymebayholidays.co.uk
w lymebayholidays.co.uk

Blacksmiths Cottage ★★★★
Self Catering
Lyme Bay Holidays
t (01297) 443363
e email@lymebayholidays.co.uk
w lymebayholidays.co.uk

Blue Horizons ★★★
Self Catering
Lyme Bay Holidays
t (01297) 443363
e email@lymebayholidays.co.uk
w lymebayholidays.co.uk

The Boat House ★★★
Self Catering
Lyme Bay Holidays
t (01297) 443363
e email@lymebayholidays.co.uk
w lymebayholidays.co.uk

The Bookie ★★★
Self Catering
Lyme Bay Holidays
t (01297) 443363
e email@lymebayholidays.co.uk
w lymebayholidays.co.uk

Bowercroft ★★★★
Self Catering
Contact: Mr V M Simpson
t (01483) 283234
e psvms@tiscali.co.uk

Bramcote Garden Apartment ★★★★
Self Catering
Contact: Mrs Rosalind Price
t (01297) 442924
e fnr.price@virgin.net
w bramcotelymeregis.com

Brewers Cottage ★★★★
Self Catering
Lyme Bay Holidays
t (01297) 443363
e email@lymebayholidays.co.uk
w lymebayholidays.co.uk

The Bungalow ★★★
Self Catering
Lyme Bay Holidays
t (01297) 443363
e email@lymebayholidays.co.uk
w lymebayholidays.co.uk

La Casa ★★★ *Self Catering*
Contact: Mr Royston Davies
t (01297) 445362
e holiday-agency@lymeregis.com
w lymeregis.com/tlha

Champernhayes Cottages, Wootton Fitzpaine
★★★★★ *Self Catering*
Contact: Mr & Mrs T Dutton
Champernhayes Bookings
t (01297) 560853
e champernhayes@btinternet.com
w champernhayes.com

Church Cliff ★★★★
Self Catering
Lyme Bay Holidays
t (01297) 443363
e email@lymebayholidays.co.uk
w lymebayholidays.co.uk

Cleve House ★★★
Self Catering
Lyme Bay Holidays
t (01297) 443363
e email@lymebayholidays.co.uk
w lymebayholidays.co.uk

Cliff Cottage ★★★
Self Catering
Contact: Mrs sue Rose
t (01420) 472512 & 07816 872101
w lymeregistourism.co.uk

Coach House ★★★★
Self Catering
Lyme Bay Holidays
t (01297) 443363
e email@lymebayholidays.co.uk
w lymebayholidays.co.uk

Cockwell Cross Cottage
★★★★ *Self Catering*
Lyme Bay Holidays
t (01297) 443363
e email@lymebayholidays.co.uk
w lymebayholidays.co.uk

Coombe House Flat ★★★★
Self Catering
Contact: Mrs Dympna Duncan
t (01297) 443849
e dymps@coombe-house.co.uk
w coombe-house.co.uk

The Cormorants ★★★★
Self Catering
Lyme Bay Holidays
t (01297) 443363
e email@lymebayholidays.co.uk
w lymebayholidays.co.uk

The Cottagee ★★★★
Self Catering
Lyme Bay Holidays
t (01297) 443363
e email@lymebayholidays.co.uk
w lymebayholidays.co.uk

The Cottage ★★★
Self Catering
Lyme Bay Holidays
t (01297) 443363
e email@lymebayholidays.co.uk
w lymebayholidays.co.uk

Dolphin Cottage ★★★
Self Catering
Lyme Bay Holidays
t (01297) 443363
e email@lymebayholidays.co.uk
w lymebayholidays.co.uk

Driftwood ★★★
Self Catering
Lyme Bay Holidays
t (01297) 443363
e email@lymebayholidays.co.uk
w lymebayholidays.co.uk

Faraway ★★★★
Self Catering
Lyme Bay Holidays
t (01297) 443363
e email@lymebayholidays.co.uk
w lymebayholidays.co.uk

Flat 1 Pyne House ★★★
Self Catering
Lyme Bay Holidays
t (01297) 443363
e email@lymebayholidays.co.uk
w lymebayholidays.co.uk

The Gables Holiday Apartments ★★★
Self Catering
Contact: Mr & Mrs Alan & Christine Simpson
t (01297) 442536
e simpson100@tiscali.co.uk
w thegableslymeregis.co.uk

Gallery Cottage ★★★
Self Catering
Lyme Bay Holidays
t (01297) 443363
e email@lymebayholidays.co.uk
w lymebayholidays.co.uk

Garden Studio ★★★★
Self Catering
Lyme Bay Holidays
t (01297) 443363
e email@lymebayholidays.co.uk
w lymebayholidays.co.uk

Garston ★★★ *Self Catering*
Contact: Ms Liz Wood
t (020) 8340 8795
e lizfromlyme@yahoo.co.uk

Greystones Flat ★★★★
Self Catering
Contact: Mrs Joan Gollop
t (01297) 443678
e greystones.flat@btopenworld.com
w lymebreak.co.uk

Gulls Nest ★★★
Self Catering
Lyme Bay Holidays
t (01297) 443363
e email@lymebayholidays.co.uk
w lymebayholidays.co.uk

Harbour House Flats ★★★
Self Catering
Contact: Mrs Alison Stait
t (01392) 841507
e info@bythecobb.co.uk
w bythecobb.co.uk

The Haven ★★★
Self Catering
Lyme Bay Holidays
t (01297) 443363
e email@lymebayholidays.co.uk
w lymebayholidays.co.uk

Haye Farm Bungalow, Stables, Hayloft & Dairy
★★★–★★★★ *Self Catering*
Contact: Mr & Mrs Richard & Michelle Trim
t (01297) 442400
e richard@rtrim.wanadoo.co.uk
w hayefarmholidays.com

Hesselhaye ★★★
Self Catering
Lyme Bay Holidays
t (01297) 443363
e email@lymebayholidays.co.uk
w lymebayholidays.co.uk

Highbanks ★★★★
Self Catering
Lyme Bay Holidays
t (01297) 443363
e email@lymebayholidays.co.uk
w lymebayholidays.co.uk

Honeymoon Cottage
★★★★ *Self Catering*
Lyme Bay Holidays
t (01297) 443363
e email@lymebayholidays.co.uk
w lymebayholidays.co.uk

Horn Tavern ★★★★
Self Catering
Lyme Bay Holidays
t (01297) 443363
e email@lymebayholidays.co.uk
w lymebayholidays.co.uk

Hove To ★★★ *Self Catering*
Lyme Bay Holidays
t (01297) 443363
e email@lymebayholidays.co.uk
w lymebayholidays.co.uk

Hoymer Villas, Apartment 2
★★★ *Self Catering*
Lyme Bay Holidays
t (01297) 443363
e email@lymebayholidays.co.uk
w lymebayholidays.co.uk

Ilex Cottage ★★★
Self Catering
Contact: Mr Royston Davies
t (01297) 445362
e holiday-agency@lymeregis.com
w lymeregis.com/tlha

Ingot Cottage ★★★★
Self Catering
Lyme Bay Holidays
t (01297) 443363
e email@lymebayholidays.co.uk
w lymebayholidays.co.uk

Ivy Cottage ★★★
Self Catering
Lyme Bay Holidays
t (01297) 443363
e email@lymebayholidays.co.uk
w lymebayholidays.co.uk

Kamloops and Nanaimo Apartments ★★★
Self Catering
Contact: Mr Sweet
t (0117) 968 1866
e sw55t@msn.com
w lymeregis.com/kamloops

Kelly Bray ★★★
Self Catering
Lyme Bay Holidays
t (01297) 443363
e email@lymebayholidays.co.uk
w lymebayholidays.co.uk

Langmoor House ★★★★
Self Catering
Lyme Bay Holidays
t (01297) 443363
e email@lymebayholidays.co.uk
w lymebayholidays.co.uk

Little Cleve ★★★★
Self Catering
Contact: Mr Alister Mackenzie
t (01761) 221554

Little Croft ★★★
Self Catering
Lyme Bay Holidays
t (01297) 443363
e email@lymebayholidays.co.uk
w lymebayholidays.co.uk

Little Jordan ★★★★
Self Catering
Lyme Bay Holidays
t (01297) 443363
e email@lymebayholidays.co.uk
w lymebayholidays.co.uk

Little Thatch ★★★
Self Catering
Lyme Bay Holidays
t (01297) 443363
e email@lymebayholidays.co.uk
w lymebayholidays.co.uk

Lucerne Apartment ★★★★
Self Catering
Contact: Mr O Lovell
t (01297) 443752

Madeira Cottage ★★★
Self Catering
Contact: Mr Andrew Marriner
t 07976 439069
e andrew.marriner@btopenworld.com
w madeiracottage.co.uk

Mermaid Cottage ★★★
Self Catering
Lyme Bay Holidays
t (01297) 443363
e email@lymebayholidays.co.uk
w lymebayholidays.co.uk

Mermaid House ★★★★
Self Catering
Lyme Bay Holidays
t (01297) 443363
e email@lymebayholidays.co.uk
w lymebayholidays.co.uk

Monmouth Cottage ★★★
Self Catering
Contact: Mrs W R Fisk
t (01460) 73878

Old Symes Cottages ★★★★
Self Catering
Contact: Mr & Mrs John & Kathleen Brennan
t (01297) 35982
e brennans@oldsymes.fsnet.co.uk
w oldsymescottages.co.uk

The Old Watch House
★★★★ *Self Catering*
Contact: Mrs Sarah Wilkinson
t (01305) 262505
e old-watch-house@lymeregis.com
w lymeregis.com/old-watch-house

One Coram Tower ★★★★
Self Catering
Contact: Ms Antoinette Delaney-Ellwood
t (01297) 442559
e reservations@onecoramtower.co.uk
w onecoramtower.co.uk

Panorama ★★★ *Self Catering*
Lyme Bay Holidays
t (01297) 443363
e email@lymebayholidays.co.uk
w lymebayholidays.co.uk

Pippin ★★★★ *Self Catering*
Lyme Bay Holidays
t (01297) 443363
e email@lymebayholidays.co.uk
w lymebayholidays.co.uk

Pooles Court House ★★★
Self Catering
Lyme Bay Holidays
t (01297) 443363
e email@lymebayholidays.co.uk
w lymebayholidays.co.uk

Radium ★★★★ *Self Catering*
Lyme Bay Holidays
t (01297) 443363
e email@lymebayholidays.co.uk
w lymebayholidays.co.uk

River Cottage ★★★★
Self Catering
Lyme Bay Holidays
t (01297) 443363
e email@lymebayholidays.co.uk
w lymebayholidays.co.uk

Riverview ★★★ *Self Catering*
Lyme Bay Holidays
t (01297) 443363
e email@lymebayholidays.co.uk
w lymebayholidays.co.uk

Rose Cottage ★★★★
Self Catering
Lyme Bay Holidays
t (01297) 443363
e email@lymebayholidays.co.uk
w lymebayholidays.co.uk

Roselands ★★★★
Self Catering
Lyme Bay Holidays
t (01297) 443363
e email@lymebayholidays.co.uk
w lymebayholidays.co.uk

Ross House ★★★
Self Catering
Lyme Bay Holidays
t (01297) 443363
e email@lymebayholidays.co.uk
w lymebayholidays.co.uk

The Rowan ★★★★
Self Catering
Lyme Bay Holidays
t (01297) 443363
e email@lymebayholidays.co.uk
w lymebayholidays.co.uk

Sandstones ★★★★
Self Catering
Lyme Bay Holidays
t (01297) 443363
e email@lymebayholidays.co.uk
w lymebayholidays.co.uk

Sea Tree House ★★★★
Self Catering
Contact: Mr David Parker
t (01297) 442244
e seatree.house@ukonline.co.uk
w lymeregis.com/seatreehouse

Seaview ★★★ *Self Catering*
Lyme Bay Holidays
t (01297) 443363
e email@lymebayholidays.co.uk
w lymebayholidays.co.uk

Seaward ★★★★
Self Catering
Lyme Bay Holidays
t (01297) 443363
e email@lymebayholidays.co.uk
w lymebayholidays.co.uk

Seven Steps ★★★★
Self Catering
Lyme Bay Holidays
t (01297) 443363
e email@lymebayholidays.co.uk
w lymebayholidays.co.uk

Sheepwash Green, Fishpond Bottom ★★★★ *Self Catering*
t (01297) 678598
w sheepwashgreen.co.uk

Sheerings ★★★ *Self Catering*
Lyme Bay Holidays
t (01297) 443363
e email@lymebayholidays.co.uk
w lymebayholidays.co.uk

Sherwood House ★★★
Self Catering
Lyme Bay Holidays
t (01297) 443363
e email@lymebayholidays.co.uk
w lymebayholidays.co.uk

Silver Cottage ★★★
Self Catering
Lyme Bay Holidays
t (01297) 443363
e email@lymebayholidays.co.uk
w lymebayholidays.co.uk

Skerries ★★★ *Self Catering*
Lyme Bay Holidays
t (01297) 443363
e email@lymebayholidays.co.uk
w lymebayholidays.co.uk

Snail House ★★★★
Self Catering
Lyme Bay Holidays
t (01297) 443363
e email@lymebayholidays.co.uk
w lymebayholidays.co.uk

Stable Cottage ★★★★
Self Catering
Lyme Bay Holidays
t (01297) 443363
e email@lymebayholidays.co.uk
w lymebayholidays.co.uk

Sundail House ★★★★
Self Catering
Lyme Bay Holidays
t (01297) 443363
e email@lymebayholidays.co.uk
w lymebayholidays.co.uk

Valentine Cottage ★★★
Self Catering
Lyme Bay Holidays
t (01297) 443363
e email@lymebayholidays.co.uk
w lymebayholidays.co.uk

Victoria House ★★★
Self Catering
Lyme Bay Holidays
t (01297) 443363
e email@lymebayholidays.co.uk
w lymebayholidays.co.uk

The Walk ★★★ *Self Catering*
Lyme Bay Holidays
t (01297) 443363
e email@lymebayholidays.co.uk
w lymebayholidays.co.uk

Watersmeet ★★★★
Self Catering
Lyme Bay Holidays
t (01297) 443363
e email@lymebayholidays.co.uk
w lymebayholidays.co.uk

Weighbridge Cottage ★★★
Self Catering
Lyme Bay Holidays
t (01297) 443363
e email@lymebayholidays.co.uk
w lymebayholidays.co.uk

Weirside ★★★ *Self Catering*
Lyme Bay Holidays
t (01297) 443363
e email@lymebayholidays.co.uk
w lymebayholidays.co.uk

Westover Farm Cottages
★★★-★★★★ *Self Catering*
Contact: Jon Snook or Debby Snook
t (01297) 560451 & (01297) 561395
e wfcottages@aol.com
w westoverfarmcottages.co.uk

Whitewaves ★★★
Self Catering
Lyme Bay Holidays
t (01297) 443363
e email@lymebayholidays.co.uk
w lymebayholidays.co.uk

Woodville Apartment ★★★
Self Catering
Lyme Bay Holidays
t (01297) 443363
e email@lymebayholidays.co.uk
w lymebayholidays.co.uk

LYMPSHAM
Somerset

Dulhorn Farm Holiday Park
★★ *Self Catering*
Contact: Mr & Mrs Bowden
t (01934) 750298

Lower Farm House ★★★★
Self Catering
Contact: Mr & Mrs Roy & Christine Ball
t (01934) 750206
e holidays@lowerfarmcottages.co.uk
w lowerfarmcottages.co.uk

LYNMOUTH
Devon

Clooneavin Holidays ★★★
Self Catering
Contact: Mrs Gill Davidson Richmond
t (01598) 753334
e relax@clooneavinholidays.co.uk
w clooneavinholidays.co.uk

Gable Cottage ★★★★
Self Catering
Marsdens Cottage Holidays
t (01271) 813777
e holidays@marsdens.co.uk
w marsdens.co.uk

Harbour Roost ★★★★
Self Catering
Marsdens Cottage Holidays
t (01271) 813777
e holidays@marsdens.co.uk
w marsdens.co.uk

The Hideaway ★★★★
Self Catering
Marsdens Cottage Holidays
t (01271) 813777
e holidays@marsdens.co.uk
w marsdens.co.uk

The Lodge at Myrtleberry
★★★ *Self Catering*
Marsdens Cottage Holidays
t (01271) 813777
e holidays@marsdens.co.uk
w marsdens.co.uk

Myrtle Cottage ★★★
Self Catering
Marsdens Cottage Holidays
t (01271) 813777
e holidays@marsdens.co.uk
w marsdens.co.uk

Ottery Cottage ★★★★
Self Catering
Marsdens Cottage Holidays
t (01271) 813777
e holidays@marsdens.co.uk
w marsdens.co.uk

Wilrose ★★★ *Self Catering*
Marsdens Cottage Holidays
t (01271) 813777
e holidays@marsdens.co.uk
w marsdens.co.uk

Woodside ★★★★
Self Catering
Marsdens Cottage Holidays
t (01271) 813777
e holidays@marsdens.co.uk
w marsdens.co.uk

LYNTON
Devon

28 Castle Heights ★★★★★
Self Catering
Select Holiday Homes
t (01491) 826757
e info@select-holidays-homes.co.uk
w select-holiday-homes.co.uk

Bakers Court ★★★
Self Catering
Marsdens Cottage Holidays
t (01271) 813777
e holidays@marsdens.co.uk
w marsdens.co.uk

Buttershaw Cottage ★★★★
Self Catering
Marsdens Cottage Holidays
t (01271) 813777
e holidays@marsdens.co.uk
w marsdens.co.uk

Byways ★★★★ *Self Catering*
Marsdens Cottage Holidays
t (01271) 813777
e holidays@marsdens.co.uk
w marsdens.co.uk

Castle Heights ★★★★
Self Catering
Marsdens Cottage Holidays
t (01271) 813777
e holidays@marsdens.co.uk
w marsdens.co.uk

Cloud Farm ★★★
Self Catering
Contact: Mrs Jill Harman
Oare
t (01598) 741234
e doonevalleyholidays@hotmail.com
w doonevalleyholidays.co.uk

Hewitts Bay View ★★★★
Self Catering
Marsdens Cottage Holidays
t (01271) 813777
e holidays@marsdens.co.uk
w marsdens.co.uk

Hewitts Retreat ★★★
Self Catering
Marsdens Cottage Holidays
t (01271) 813777
e holidays@marsdens.co.uk
w marsdens.co.uk

Keepers Cottage ★★★★★
Self Catering
Marsdens Cottage Holidays
t (01271) 813777
e holidays@marsdens.co.uk
w marsdens.co.uk

Lyn Cottage ★★★
Self Catering
Marsdens Cottage Holidays
t (01271) 813777
e holidays@marsdens.co.uk
w marsdens.co.uk

Lyn House ★★★
Self Catering
Contact: Mr & Mrs Gardiner
t (01598) 752229
e lynhouse@btinternet.com
w lynhouse.co.uk

Royal Castle Lodge ★★★★
Self Catering
Contact: Mr M Wolverson
Primespot Character Cottages
t (01271) 882449

The Smithy ★★★★
Self Catering
Select Holiday Homes
t (01491) 826757
e info@select-holidays-homes.co.uk
w select-holiday-homes.co.uk

West Lyn Farmhouse
★★★★ *Self Catering*
Contact: Mr Paul Spratley
t (01598) 753618
e info@westlynfarm.co.uk
w westlynfarm.co.uk

LYPIATT
Gloucestershire

Well Close Cottage ★★★★
Self Catering
Contact: Ms Jayne Davie
t (01285) 760225
e jayne.davie@btinternet.com
w wellclosecottage.co.uk

LYTCHETT MATRAVERS
Dorset

Purbeck View Cottage
★★★★ *Self Catering*
Dorset Cottage Holidays
t (01929) 553443
e enq@dhcottages.co.uk
w dhcottages.co.uk

MAENPORTH
Cornwall

31 Lower Stables ★★★★
Self Catering
Holiday Cornwall
t (01326) 250278
e enquiries@holidaycornwall.co.uk
w holidaycornwall.co.uk

41 Lower Stables Cottage
Rating Applied For
Self Catering
Holiday Cornwall
t (01326) 250278
e enquiries@holidaycornwall.co.uk
w holidaycornwall.co.uk

44 Upper Stables
Rating Applied For
Self Catering
Holiday Cornwall
t (01326) 250278
e enquiries@holidaycornwall.co.uk
w holidaycornwall.co.uk

52 Upper Stables ★★★★
Self Catering
Holiday Cornwall
t (01326) 250278
e enquiries@holidaycornwall.co.uk
w holidaycornwall.co.uk

59 Monterey Cottage
★★★★ *Self Catering*
Holiday Cornwall
t (01326) 250278
e enquiries@holidaycornwall.co.uk
w holidaycornwall.co.uk

63 Lower Maen Cottage
★★★★ *Self Catering*
Holiday Cornwall
t (01326) 250278
e enquiries@holidaycornwall.co.uk
w holidaycornwall.co.uk

88 Keepers Barn
Rating Applied For
Self Catering
Holiday Cornwall
t (01326) 250278
e enquiries@holidaycornwall.co.uk
w holidaycornwall.co.uk

Arvor
Rating Applied For
Self Catering
Holiday Cornwall
t (01326) 250278
e enquiries@holidaycornwall.co.uk
w holidaycornwall.co.uk

Cove 1 ★★★★ *Self Catering*
Holiday Cornwall
t (01326) 250278
e enquiries@holidaycornwall.co.uk
w holidaycornwall.co.uk

Cove 2 ★★★★ *Self Catering*
Holiday Cornwall
t (01326) 250278
e enquiries@holidaycornwall.co.uk
w holidaycornwall.co.uk

Crags 15
Rating Applied For
Self Catering
Holiday Cornwall
t (01326) 250278
e enquiries@holidaycornwall.co.uk
w holidaycornwall.co.uk

The Penthouse ★★★★
Self Catering
Holiday Cornwall
t (01326) 250278
e enquiries@holidaycornwall.co.uk
w holidaycornwall.co.uk

Ridges 10 ★★★★
Self Catering
Holiday Cornwall
t (01326) 250278
e enquiries@holidaycornwall.co.uk
w holidaycornwall.co.uk

Ridges 11 ★★★★
Self Catering
Holiday Cornwall
t (01326) 250278
e enquiries@holidaycornwall.co.uk
w holidaycornwall.co.uk

Ridges 2 ★★★★
Self Catering
Holiday Cornwall
t (01326) 250278
e enquiries@holidaycornwall.co.uk
w holidaycornwall.co.uk

Sea Breeze ★★★
Self Catering
Cornish Holiday Cottages
t (01326) 250339
e emily@cornishholidaycottages.net
w cornishholidaycottages.net

Tregullow ★★★★
Self Catering
Cornish Holiday Cottages
t (01326) 250339
e emily@cornishholidaycottages.net
w cornishholidaycottages.net

MAIDEN NEWTON
Dorset

Lancombe Country Cottages
★★★★ *Self Catering*
Contact: Mr Myles Provis
t (01300) 320562
e info@lancombe.co.uk
w lancombe.co.uk

The Retreat ★★★
Self Catering
Contact: Mr & Mrs S & Jane Bevis
t (01300) 320090
e jane.bevis@virgin.com

MAIDENCOMBE
Devon

Bowden Close House ★★★
Self Catering
Contact: Mrs Sarah Farquharson
t (01803) 328029
e enquiries@bowdenclose.co.uk
w bowdenclose.co.uk

Langley Coach House
★★★★ *Self Catering*
Holiday Homes and Cottages South West
t (01803) 299677
e holcotts@aol.com
w swcottages.co.uk

Mouse Cottage ★★★
Self Catering
Contact: Mrs Christine Davies
t (01803) 316655
e mousecottage@hotmail.com
w mousecottage.co.uk

MALBOROUGH
Devon

Church Gate Cottage
★★★★ *Self Catering*
Toad Hall Cottages
t (01548) 853089
e thc@toadhallcottages.com
w toadhallcottages.co.uk

MALMESBURY
Wiltshire

The Cottage ★★★★
Self Catering
Contact: Mrs Ross Eavis
t (01666) 822148
e ross@johneavis.wanadoo.co.uk
w manorfarmbandb.co.uk

Foundry Flat ★★★
Self Catering
Contact: Mr & Mrs Ratcliffe
t (01666) 824093
e foundryflat@fsmail.net
w ratcliffeandson.co.uk

MANACCAN
Cornwall

Flushing Cove Cottage
★★★★ *Self Catering*
Contact: Mrs Ablewhite
t (01243) 535266
e michael.ablewhite@btopenworld.com
w flushingcove-gillan.net

Gillan Cove House ★★★★
Self Catering
Contact: Mr & Mrs Ingram
t (01491) 612434
e ingram@greenfieldfarm.fsnet.co.uk
w gillancovehouse.co.uk

Lestowder Farm
★★★-★★★★ *Self Catering*
Contact: Mrs Martin
t (01326) 231400
e lestowderfarm@hotmail.com
w lestowderfarmcottages.co.uk

West Minster Cottage
★★★★ *Self Catering*
t (01326) 231666
w helfordcottages.co.uk

MANATON
Devon

Beckaford Cottage ★★★★
Self Catering
Toad Hall Cottages
t (01548) 853089
e thc@toadhallcottages.com
w toadhallcottages.co.uk

MANSTON
Dorset

Northwood Cottages
★★★★ *Self Catering*
Contact: Mr & Mrs Jonathan & Poppy Sewell
t (01258) 472666
e info@northwoodcottages.co.uk
w northwoodcottages.co.uk

MARAZION
Cornwall

Arizona & Tuscany ★★★
Self Catering
Contact: Mrs Dawn Senior
t (01736) 710222

Lowenna ★★★ *Self Catering*
Contact: Mr Jelbart
t (01736) 710580

Ocean Studios ★★★★
Self Catering
Contact: Mrs Heather Wenn
t (01736) 711040
e enquiries@mountsbayhouse.co.uk
w mountsbayhouse.co.uk

Rosevidney Manor Cottages
★★★★ *Self Catering*
Contact: Mrs Vanessa Withers
t (01736) 740811
e gary@rosevidneymanor.co.uk
w rosevidneymanor.co.uk

St Aubyn Estates
★★★★-★★★★★
Self Catering
Contact: Mrs Clare Sandry
t (01736) 710507
e godolphin@manor-office.co.uk
w staubynestates.co.uk

Sea Retreat Holiday Cottages ★★★★
Self Catering
Contact: Mrs Sally Laird
t (0118) 984 5500
e sallylaird@talk21.com
w sea-retreat.com

Tregew Holiday Bungalows
★★★ *Self Catering*
Contact: Mr Rodney Pool
t (01736) 710247

Trevarthian Holiday Homes
★★★ *Self Catering*
Contact: Sean Cattran
t (01736) 710100
e info@trevarthian.co.uk
w trevarthian.co.uk

Wheal Rodney Self-Catering Bungalows ★★ *Self Catering*
Contact: Miss Samatha Kitchen
t (01736) 710605
e reception@whealrodney.co.uk
w whealrodney.co.uk

MARHAMCHURCH
Cornwall

Budds Barns at Titson
★★★★ *Self Catering*
Contact: Mr & Mrs David & Carol Richardson
t (01288) 361339
e relax@buddsbarns.co.uk
w buddsbarns.co.uk

Court Farm Holidays
★★★★ *Self Catering*
Contact: Mr Trewin
t (01288) 361494
e info@courtfarm-holidays.co.uk
w courtfarm-holidays.co.uk

Endsleigh Cottage ★★★★
Self Catering
Contact: Simon & Denise Sheldon
t (01452) 617966
e info@endsleighcottage.com
w endsleighcottage.com

The Old Stable
★★★-★★★★ *Self Catering*
Contact: Mr & Mrs Laurence & Sylvia Henry
t (01288) 361727
e lozandsyl@henryex23.freeserve.co.uk
w crackinggoodspot.co.uk

Trelay Farmhouse ★★★★
Self Catering
Contact: Lucy Ellison
Farm & Cottage Holidays
t (01237) 479146
e enquiries@farmcott.co.uk
w farmcott.co.uk

MARK
Somerset

Pear Tree Cottage ★★★
Self Catering
Contact: Mrs Susan Slocombe
t (01278) 641228
e sslocombe1@dclonline.net

MARKET LAVINGTON
Wiltshire

The Barn
Rating Applied For
Self Catering
Contact: S B Sidebottom
t (01380) 813639
e spc.stewart@btinternet.com

MARLBOROUGH
Wiltshire

Dairy Cottage ★★★
Self Catering
Contact: Mr & Mrs Mark and Hazel Crockford
t (01672) 515129 & 07931 311985
e crockford@farming.co.uk

MARLDON
Devon

Compton Pool Farm (Farmhouse) ★★★★★
Self Catering
Contact: Mr & Mrs John & Ann Stocks
t (01803) 872241
e info@comptonpool.co.uk
w comptonpool.co.uk

Lower Tor Cottage ★★★★
Self Catering
Holiday Homes and Cottages South West
t (01803) 299677
e holcotts@aol.com
w swcottages.co.uk

Millmans Cottages
★★★-★★★★ *Self Catering*
Contact: Mrs Tina Girard
t (01803) 558213
e tina@millmans-farm.co.uk
w millmanscottages.co.uk

The Retreat ★★★★★
Self Catering
Holiday Homes and Cottages South West
t (01803) 299677
e holcotts@aol.com
w swcottages.co.uk

Wildwoods ★★★
Self Catering
Holiday Homes and Cottages South West
t (01803) 299677
e holcotts@aol.com
w swcottages.co.uk

MARSHFIELD
Gloucestershire

Kissing Gate Cottage
★★★★ *Self Catering*
t (01225) 891732
w kissinggatecottage.co.uk

MARTINHOE
Devon

Ivy Cottage ★★★★
Self Catering
Marsdens Cottage Holidays
t (01271) 813777
e holidays@marsdens.co.uk
w marsdens.co.uk

MARTINSTOWN
Dorset

Hope Cottage ★★★
Self Catering
Dream Cottages
t (01305) 789000
e admin@dream-cottages.co.uk
w dream-cottages.co.uk

MARTOCK
Somerset

Anne's Place ★★★
Self Catering
Country Holidays
t 0845 604 3900
w country-holidays.co.uk

MAWGAN
Cornwall

Le An Marghas ★★★
Self Catering
Helford River Cottages
t (01326) 231666
e info@helfordcottages.co.uk
w helfordcottages.co.uk

Trelowarren Estate Ltd
★★★★★ *Self Catering*
Contact: Mrs Angie Coombes
t (01326) 222105
e sales@trelowarren.com
w trelowarren.com

MAWGAN PORTH
Cornwall

1, 2 and 3 Merlin Apartments ★★★★
Self Catering
Cornish Horizons Holiday Cottages
t (01841) 533331
e cottages@cornishhorizons.co.uk
w cornishhorizons.co.uk

3 Sandy Beach ★★★
Self Catering
Cornish Horizons Holiday Cottages
t (01841) 533331
e cottages@cornishhorizons.co.uk
w cornishhorizons.co.uk

5 Sandy Beach ★★★
Self Catering
Cornish Horizons Holiday Cottages
t (01841) 533331
e cottages@cornishhorizons.co.uk
w cornishhorizons.co.uk

6 White Lodge ★★★★
Self Catering
t (01208) 895216

8 Europa Court ★★
Self Catering
Contact: Mr Alan Malin
t (01788) 811179
e alan@abcdholidays.com
w abcdholidays.com

Alderly Edge ★★★★
Self Catering
Cornish Horizons Holiday Cottages
t (01841) 533331
e cottages@cornishhorizons.co.uk
w cornishhorizons.co.uk

Ambiance Holiday Apartments ★★★
Self Catering
Contact: Mr Brian White
t (01637) 860509
e brian@whiteamb.freeserve.co.uk
w visitcornwall.co.uk/ambianceholidayapartments

Apartment 2 Whitelodge
★★★★ *Self Catering*
Harbour Holidays
t (01841) 533402
e contact@harbourholidays.co.uk
w harbourholidays.co.uk

Cosy Corner Holiday Accommodation *Approved Caravan Holiday Home*
Contact: Mr & Mrs B Lynn
t (01637) 860611
e info@cosycorner.co.uk
w cosycorner.co.uk

Merlin Farm Holiday Cottages ★★★ *Self Catering*
Contact: Mr Darrel Wheeler
t (01637) 860236
e info@merlinfarm.co.uk
w merlinfarm.co.uk

Samphire ★★★ *Self Catering*
t (01637) 860379
e geoffandjane@tiscali.co.uk

White Lodge, Mawgan Porth
★★★★ *Self Catering*
Beach Retreats
t (01637) 861005 & (01637) 861241
e kelly@beachretreats.co.uk
w beachretreats.co.uk

MAWNAN SMITH
Cornwall

2 Shute Hill ★★★
Self Catering
Cornish Holiday Cottages
t (01326) 250339
e emily@cornishholidaycottages.net
w cornishholidaycottages.net

Bosilliac Holiday Cottage
Rating Applied For
Self Catering
Contact: Mrs Lorna Crewes
t (01326) 250307
e lorna@rosemerrynfarm.co.uk
w rosemerrynfarm.co.uk

Brynn Cottage
Rating Applied For
Self Catering
Cornish Holiday Cottages
t (01326) 250339
e emily@cornishholidaycottages.net
w cornishholidaycottages.net

Gardeners Cottage
Rating Applied For
Self Catering
Holiday Cornwall
t (01326) 250278
e enquiries@holidaycornwall.co.uk
w holidaycornwall.co.uk

Glen Avon, Mawnan Smith
★★★ *Self Catering*
Contact: Mr & Mrs Benney
t (01326) 250283
e annb.glen@hotmail.co.uk
w cottage-cornwall.co.uk

Helford Point ★★★★
Self Catering
Cornish Holiday Cottages
t (01326) 250339
e emily@cornishholidaycottages.net
w cornishholidaycottages.net

Pedn Billy
Rating Applied For
Self Catering
Holiday Cornwall
t (01326) 250278
e enquiries@holidaycornwall.co.uk
w holidaycornwall.co.uk

Roebuck Vilas 3
Rating Applied For
Self Catering
Cornish Holiday Cottages
t (01326) 250339
e emily@cornishholidaycottages.net
w cornishholidaycottages.net

Rose Cottage 1
Rating Applied For
Self Catering
Cornish Holiday Cottages
t (01326) 250339
e emily@cornishholidaycottages.net
w cornishholidaycottages.net

Rose Cottage 3
Rating Applied For
Self Catering
Cornish Holiday Cottages
t (01326) 250339
e emily@cornishholidaycottages.net
w cornishholidaycottages.net

Selangor ★★★★
Self Catering
Cornish Holiday Cottages
t (01326) 250339
e emily@cornishholidaycottages.net
w cornishholidaycottages.net

Shepherds Close ★★★★
Self Catering
t (01237) 479146
e info@holidaycottages.co.uk
w holidaycottages.co.uk

Tranquebar ★★★★
Self Catering
Cornish Holiday Cottages
t (01326) 250339
e emily@cornishholidaycottages.net
w cornishholidaycottages.net

Trembath ★★★★
Self Catering
Cornish Holiday Cottages
t (01326) 250339
e emily@cornishholidaycottages.net
w cornishholidaycottages.net

MEETH
Devon

The Shuteslades ★★★★
Self Catering
t (01805) 804783
w shuteslade.co.uk

MELBURY ABBAS
Dorset

Melbury Vale Cottages
★★★ *Self Catering*
t 07730 955593
e enquiries@melburyvaleco.co.uk
w melburyvaleco.co.uk

MELCOMBE BINGHAM
Dorset

Greygles, Melcombe Bingham ★★★★
Self Catering
Contact: Mr Paul Sommerfeld
t (020) 8969 4830
e enquiry@greygles.co.uk
w greygles.co.uk

MELKSHAM
Wiltshire

Moorlands ★★★★
Self Catering
t (01225) 702155
w moorlandsuk.co.uk

MEMBURY
Devon

Chesnut Cottage ★★★★
Self Catering
Lyme Bay Holidays
t (01297) 443363
e email@lymebayholidays.co.uk
w lymebayholidays.co.uk

Hazel Cottage ★★★★
Self Catering
Lyme Bay Holidays
t (01297) 443363
e email@lymebayholidays.co.uk
w lymebayholidays.co.uk

Holly Cottage ★★★★
Self Catering
Lyme Bay Holidays
t (01297) 443363
e email@lymebayholidays.co.uk
w lymebayholidays.co.uk

Lea Hill ★★★★ *Self Catering*
Contact: Mrs Susan Avis
t (01404) 881881
e reception@leahill.co.uk
w leahill.co.uk

Old Orchard Cottage
★★★★ *Self Catering*
Lyme Bay Holidays
t (01297) 443363
e email@lymebayholidays.co.uk
w lymebayholidays.co.uk

MENHENIOT
Cornwall

Hayloft Courtyard Cottages
★★★★ *Self Catering*
Contact: Miss Michelle Eastwood
t (01503) 240879
e courtyardcottage@btconnect.com
w hayloftcourtyardcottages.com

Trewint Farm ★★★★
Self Catering
Contact: Mrs Rowe
t (01579) 347155
e holidays@trewintfarm.co.uk
w trewintfarm.co.uk

MERE
Wiltshire

The Coach House ★★★
Self Catering
Hideaways
t (01747) 828170
e enq@hideaways.co.uk
w hideaways.co.uk

MESHAW
Devon

Meadowside Barn ★★★★★
Self Catering
Marsdens Cottage Holidays
t (01271) 813777
e holidays@marsdens.co.uk
w marsdens.co.uk

Orchard Cottage ★★★★
Self Catering
Marsdens Cottage Holidays
t (01271) 813777
e holidays@marsdens.co.uk
w marsdens.co.uk

MEVAGISSEY
Cornwall

Blue Waters, Mevagissey
★★★ *Self Catering*
Contact: Mrs D Kendall
t (01726) 843164
e edwin.kendall@btinternet.com

Cosy Nook ★★★
Self Catering
Contact: Mrs Elizabeth Rundle
t (01726) 843565

Eden Cottage, Mevagissey
★★★★ *Self Catering*
Contact: Mrs Helen Whatty
Mevagissey Holiday Cottages
t (01726) 842525
e hwhatty@yahoo.co.uk
w edencottage.co.uk

Look Out ★★★ *Self Catering*
t (01726) 843641

The Lookout and The Penthouse ★★★★★
Self Catering
Contact: Mr Andrew Main Wilson
t (01892) 722323 & 07725 562563
e amw@iod.com
w penthouseholidays.com

Ocean's Edge ★★★★★
Self Catering
Contact: Mrs Tracey Rist
t (0116) 259 0164
e tracy@cornwallapartmentholidays.co.uk
w cornwallapartmentholidays.co.uk

Pollys Apartments, Mevagissey ★★-★★★
Self Catering
Contact: Mrs Diana Littlejohns
t (01726) 843352
e diana@mevagisseyapartments.co.uk
w mevagisseyapartments.co.uk

Treleaven Farm Cottages
★★★★ *Self Catering*
Contact: Mrs Linda Hennah
t (01726) 843558
e linda.hennah@btinternet.com
w treleavenfarm.co.uk

MIDDLE MARWOOD
Devon

Greenhill
Rating Applied For
Self Catering
Contact: Mrs Janet Cornwell
t (01271) 813777
e karen@marsdens.eclipse.co.uk

MILLBROOK
Cornwall

Stone Farm ★★★-★★★★
Self Catering
Contact: Mrs Blake
t (01752) 822267
w farmcott.co.uk

MILLENDREATH
Cornwall

79 Hillside Villa ★★★
Self Catering
Contact: Miss Anne Brennan
t (01749) 678000
e annebrennan@uwclub.net
w villainlooe.velnet.co.uk

May Lane House ★★★★
Self Catering
Cornish Collection Ltd
t (01503) 262736
e enquiries@cornishcollections.co.uk
w cornishcollection.co.uk

MILTON ABBAS
Dorset

Luccombe Farm ★★★★
Self Catering
Contact: Mr & Mrs Murray & Amanda Kayll
t (01258) 880558
e mkayll@aol.com
w luccombeholidays.co.uk

Primrose Cottage ★★★★
Self Catering
Contact: Mrs Therese Clemson
t (01962) 865786
e therese.clemson@btinternet.com
w miltonabbas-primrosecottage.co.uk

MINCHINHAMPTON
Gloucestershire

Vine House Flat ★★★
Self Catering
Contact: Mrs Veronica Finn
t (01453) 884437
e finnatminch@aol.com

MINEHEAD
Somerset

Anchor Cottage ★★★★
Self Catering
Contact: Dr John Malin
t (01643) 707529
e jmalin@btinternet.com
w anchorcottageminehead.co.uk

Chapel Cottage ★★★★
Self Catering
Contact: Ms Carolynn Thompson
t (01788) 810275
e stay@chapelcottage-exmoor.co.uk
w chapelcottage-exmoor.co.uk

Dome Flat ★★★★
Self Catering
Contact: Mr Lowin
t (01895) 236972

Dove Cottage ★★★
Self Catering
Contact: Mr Waterman
t (020) 8882 4920

Fishermans Cottage ★★★
Self Catering
Contact: Mrs Martin
t (01643) 704263

The Freight Shed ★★★
Self Catering
Contact: Mr & Mrs Alison & Duncan Waller
t (01643) 851386
e info@exmoorwildlifesafaris.co.uk
w exmoorwildlifesafaris.co.uk

Harbour View ★★★
Self Catering
Marsdens Cottage Holidays
t (01271) 813777
e holidays@marsdens.co.uk
w marsdens.co.uk

Holmbush ★★ *Self Catering*
Toad Hall Cottages
t (01548) 853089
e thc@toadhallcottages.com
w toadhallcottages.co.uk

Marshfield Flat ★★★★
Self Catering
Contact: Mr Clive Lister
t (020) 8786 8406
e c.lister7@ntl.world.com
w marshfield-apartment.co.uk

La Mer ★★★★ *Self Catering*
Contact: Mrs Audrey Bowden
t (01643) 704405
w whatsonexmoor.co.uk/la-mer/

Merlin House Holiday Apartments, Blue Anchor
★★★ *Self Catering*
Contact: Mrs Penny Marshall-Rush
t (01643) 822014
e merlinhouseholiday apartments@fsmail.net
w merlinhouseholiday apartments.co.uk

Minehead Thatched Cottages ★★★★
Self Catering
Contact: Mrs Brenda Parks
t (01643) 704939
e ted.parks@virgin.net
w mineheadthatchedcottages.co.uk

Old Black Boy Cottage ★★★
Self Catering
Contact: Mr & Mrs Harvey
t (01643) 705016

Quay Cottage ★★★★
Self Catering
Contact: Ms Cate Teideman
t (01844) 354082
e quaycottage@gmail.com
w quaycottage.googlepages.com/

Seagate Cottage ★★★★
Self Catering
Contact: Mr Roger Ball
t (01935) 881436
e roger.ball@ukonline.co.uk

MISERDEN
Gloucestershire

Sudgrove Cottages
★★★-★★★★ *Self Catering*
Contact: Mr & Mrs Martin & Carol Ractliffe
t (01285) 821322
e enquiries@sudgrovecottages.co.uk
w sudgrovecottages.co.uk

MITCHELDEAN
Gloucestershire

Church Farm Holidays ★★★
Self Catering
Contact: John Verity
t (01594) 541211
e info@churchfarm.uk.net
w churchfarm.uk.net

The Old Dairy ★★★★
Self Catering
Contact: Lorraine Morgan
t (01594) 543737
e theolddairy@aic.co.uk
w olddairycottage.com

Sunnyside ★★★★
Self Catering
Contact: Lindsey Webster
t 07980 311708
e websterlindsey@googlemail.com
w sunnyside-cottage.com

MODBURY
Devon

Old Traine Barn and Old Traine Cottage
★★★★-★★★★★
Self Catering
Toad Hall Cottages
t (01548) 853089
e thc@toadhallcottages.com
w toadhallcottages.co.uk

Oldaport Farm Cottages, Modbury ★★★★
Self Catering
Contact: Miss C M Evans
t (01548) 830842
e cathy@oldaport.com
w oldaport.com

MONKTON WYLD
Dorset

Little Goyle ★★★★
Self Catering
Lyme Bay Holidays
t (01297) 443363
e email@lymebayholidays.co.uk
w lymebayholidays.co.uk

The Thatch ★★★★
Self Catering
Lyme Bay Holidays
t (01297) 443363
e email@lymebayholidays.co.uk
w lymebayholidays.co.uk

MONTACUTE
Somerset

Far End Cottage ★★★★
Self Catering
Contact: Mrs Adrienne Wright
t (01344) 772461
e aawright@btopenworld.com
w somersetcottageholidays.co.uk

MORCOMBELAKE
Dorset

Rookery Cottage ★★★
Self Catering
Lyme Bay Holidays
t (01297) 443363
e email@lymebayholidays.co.uk
w lymebayholidays.co.uk

Upalong Studio ★★★
Self Catering
Lyme Bay Holidays
t (01297) 443363
e email@lymebayholidays.co.uk
w lymebayholidays.co.uk

MORETON
Dorset

Brickyard Cottage ★★★
Self Catering
Dream Cottages
t (01305) 789000
e admin@dream-cottages.co.uk
w dream-cottages.co.uk

The Courtyard ★★★
Self Catering
Contact: Mrs Jane Lofts
t (01305) 853499
e famlofts@aol.com
w heartofdorset.co.uk

Glebe Cottage ★★
Self Catering
Contact: Mrs Carol Gibbens
t (01929) 462468
e glebeho@btinternet.com
w heartofdorset.co.uk

Moreton Club Site ★★
Self Catering
Camping & Caravanning Club
t 0845 130 7631

MORETON-IN-MARSH
Gloucestershire

Brookside ★★★
Self Catering
Contact: Mrs Ward
t (01509) 646135
e rosemaryanne.ward@virgin.net

The Flat ★★★★ *Self Catering*
Campden Cottages
t (01386) 593315
e info@campdencottages.co.uk
w campdencottages.co.uk

Horseshoe Cottage ★★★★
Self Catering
Contact: Mr & Mrs McHale
t (01451) 831556
w horseshoecottagelower oddington.co.uk

The Knoll ★★★ *Self Catering*
Contact: Ms Josie Gavoyannis
t (01825) 791055
e info@holidays2remember.co.uk
w holidays2remember.co.uk

The Laurels ★★★
Self Catering
Contact: Mrs Sandra Billinger
t (01608) 650299
e gandsib@dialstart.net

Little Milton ★★★★
Self Catering
Contact: Mrs Heather Bates
t (01386) 701163
e info@miltonview.co.uk
w miltonview.co.uk

Michaelmas Daisy Cottage
★★★ *Self Catering*
Contact: Mrs Alexander
t (01993) 830484
e rosemaryalex@onetel.com
w rosemaryscottages.co.uk

Sarum ★★★★ *Self Catering*
Contact: Mrs Jo Brooks
t (01608) 650821
e jobrooks41@btinternet.com
w sarumbungalow.co.uk

Twinkle Toes Cottage
★★★★ *Self Catering*
Contact: Mrs Christine Gowing
t (01608) 658579
e kcgowing@talk21.com
w cottagejustfortwo.co.uk

MORETONHAMPSTEAD
Devon

Budleigh Farm ★★★
Self Catering
Contact: Mrs Judith Harvey
t (01647) 440835
e harvey@budleighfarm.co.uk
w budleighfarm.co.uk

Yarningale ★★★
Self Catering
Contact: Mrs Sarah Radcliffe
t (01647) 440560
e sally.radcliffe@virgin.net

MORTEHOE
Devon

8 Devon Beach Court
★★★★ *Self Catering*
Marsdens Cottage Holidays
t (01271) 813777
e holidays@marsdens.co.uk
w marsdens.co.uk

Beach Break ★★★★★
Self Catering
Marsdens Cottage Holidays
t (01271) 813777
e holidays@marsdens.co.uk
w marsdens.co.uk

Cobblestone Cottage
★★★★ *Self Catering*
Marsdens Cottage Holidays
t (01271) 813777
e holidays@marsdens.co.uk
w marsdens.co.uk

Combesgate and Barricane
★★★ *Self Catering*
Marsdens Cottage Holidays
t (01271) 813777
e holidays@marsdens.co.uk
w marsdens.co.uk

Combesgate House ★★★
Self Catering
Contact: Mr & Mrs Keith & Virginia Sprason
t (01562) 883038
e combesgate.house@virgin.net
w combesgate.fsnet.co.uk

Farriers End, Warcombe
★★★★★ *Self Catering*
Contact: Mrs Olive Sinclair
t (01271) 867285
e leemanor@btinternet.com
w farriersend.eu

The Grange ★★★★
Self Catering
Contact: Mr & Mrs Peter & Jill Lawley
t (01271) 870580
e the-grange-mortehoe@supanet.com
w thegrangemortehoe.co.uk

Homestead Cottage ★★★
Self Catering
Marsdens Cottage Holidays
t (01271) 813777
e holidays@marsdens.co.uk
w marsdens.co.uk

Lower Deck ★★★★
Self Catering
Marsdens Cottage Holidays
t (01271) 813777
e holidays@marsdens.co.uk
w marsdens.co.uk

Mailscot & Wykeham ★★
Self Catering
Marsdens Cottage Holidays
t (01271) 813777
e holidays@marsdens.co.uk
w marsdens.co.uk

Rosemary Cottage ★★★
Self Catering
Marsdens Cottage Holidays
t (01271) 813777
e holidays@marsdens.co.uk
w marsdens.co.uk

Schooners ★★★★★
Self Catering
Marsdens Cottage Holidays
t (01271) 813777
e holidays@marsdens.co.uk
w marsdens.co.uk

Seaview Cottage ★★★
Self Catering
Marsdens Cottage Holidays
t (01271) 813777
e holidays@marsdens.co.uk
w marsdens.co.uk

Yarde ★★★★ *Self Catering*
Marsdens Cottage Holidays
t (01271) 813777
e holidays@marsdens.co.uk
w marsdens.co.uk

MORWENSTOW Cornwall

Cordena ★★★ *Self Catering*
Contact: Mr & Mrs Peter & Rosie Willoughby
t (01732) 833196
e peter.willoughby@btopenworld.com

Cory Farm Cottages ★★★★
Self Catering
Contact: Mrs Tape
t (01288) 331735
e info@coryfarmcottages.co.uk
w coryfarmcottages.co.uk

Jacques Cottages ★★★
Self Catering
Contact: Diane Costall
t (01273) 400742
e dianecostall@onetel.net

MOTHECOMBE Devon

The Flete Estate Holiday Cottages ★★★★-★★★★★
Self Catering
Contact: Mrs Lisa Farleigh
t (01752) 830234
e cottages@flete.co.uk
w flete.co.uk

MOUNT HAWKE Cornwall

Ropers Walk Barns ★★★★
Self Catering
Contact: Mrs Elizabeth Pollard
t (01209) 891632
e peterandliz@roperswalkbarns.co.uk
w roperswalkbarns.co.uk

MOUSEHOLE Cornwall

4 & 6 The Wharf & 11 Keigwin Place ★★
Self Catering
Contact: Mrs Dawn Davey
t (01736) 731264

Fern Cottage ★★★
Self Catering
Contact: Mrs Stephens
t (01736) 731363
e stephens@churleys.freeserve.co.uk

Kernyk Cottage ★★★
Self Catering
Contact: Mrs Gay Kendall
t (01736) 732532
e mrs_g_kendall@hotmail.com

The Little Net Loft ★★★ *Self Catering & Serviced Apartments*
Contact: Mr Martin King
t (020) 8220 4538
e martin.king90@ntlworld.com
w thelittlenetloft.co.uk

Mole Cottage ★★★★
Self Catering
Contact: Mrs Jacqui Benson
t (01527) 832186
e enquiries@mousehole.org.uk
w mousehole.org.uk

The Old Standard
★★★-★★★★★ *Self Catering*
t (01264) 850234
w oldstandard.co.uk

Penzer Cottage ★★★
Self Catering
Contact: Mrs Regina MacDonald
t (01753) 854395 & 07769 741018
e info@penzercottage.co.uk
w penzercottage.co.uk

Poldark Cottage ★★★
Self Catering
Contact: Ms Christine Brown-Miller
t (01736) 330609
e brownmiller@btinternet.com

Trevean Cottage ★★★
Self Catering
Contact: Mr David Coleman
t (01736) 731699
e jex5@hotmail.com

Wootton Gray ★★★★
Self Catering
Contact: Mrs Jenifer Bower
1 Low Lee Road
t (01491) 575297

MUDDIFORD Devon

Ashtree Cottage ★★★★
Self Catering
Marsdens Cottage Holidays
t (01271) 813777
e holidays@marsdens.co.uk
w marsdens.co.uk

Home Park Cottage
★★★★★ *Self Catering*
Marsdens Cottage Holidays
t (01271) 813777
e holidays@marsdens.co.uk
w marsdens.co.uk

Rose Cottage ★★★★
Self Catering
Marsdens Cottage Holidays
t (01271) 813777
e holidays@marsdens.co.uk
w marsdens.co.uk

Walnut Tree Cottage
★★★★ *Self Catering*
Marsdens Cottage Holidays
t (01271) 813777
e holidays@marsdens.co.uk
w marsdens.co.uk

MUDEFORD Dorset

Crouch Cottage ★★★★
Self Catering
Contact: Mrs Julia Crouch
t (01202) 530540
w crouchcottage.co.uk

Victoria Cottage ★★★★
Self Catering
Dream Cottages
t (01305) 789000
e admin@dream-cottages.co.uk
w dream-cottages.co.uk

MULLION Cornwall

2 Coastguard Cottage ★★★
Self Catering
Toad Hall Cottages
t (01548) 853089
e thc@toadhallcottages.com
w toadhallcottages.co.uk

Carleon ★★★ *Self Catering*
t (01326) 240333
w mullioncottages.com

Lampra Mill ★★★★
Self Catering
Contact: Mr Michael Carter
t (01326) 240512
e michael@lampramill.co.uk
w lampramill.co.uk

Poltesco ★★★ *Self Catering*
t (01326) 240333
w mullioncottages.com

Porthpradnack ★★★★
Self Catering
t (01326) 240333

Puffin ★★★ *Self Catering*
t (020) 8270 9756

Trenance Farm Cottages
★★★ *Self Catering*
Contact: Mr & Mrs Richard, Jenny & Tamara Tyler-Street
t (01326) 240639
e info@trenancefarmholidays.co.uk
w trenancefarmholidays.co.uk

Trewenna & Scrumpy Cottage ★★★★ *Self Catering*
Farm & Cottage Holidays
t (01237) 459827
e enquiries@farmcott.co.uk
w holidaycottages.co.uk

MYLOR Cornwall

Acorn Cottage
Rating Applied For
Self Catering
Cornish Holiday Cottages
t (01326) 250339
e emily@cornishholidaycottages.net
w cornishholidaycottages.net

Carsawsan Cottage ★★★★
Self Catering
Contact: Mrs Victoria Whitworth
t (01872) 552042
e vic.whit@btinternet.com
w homesandcottages.co.uk/property/carsawsancottage

Little Albion Cottage
★★★★ *Self Catering*
Contact: Mr Patrick Polglase
t (01326) 373607
e patrickpolglase@aol.com
w cottageholidayscornwall.co.uk

Tulip Tree Cottage ★★★★
Self Catering
Special Places in Cornwall
t (01872) 864400
e office@specialplacescornwall.co.uk
w specialplacescornwall.co.uk

MYLOR BRIDGE Cornwall

Tilly's Cottage ★★★★
Self Catering
Contact: Mrs Jo Spencer
t (01872) 864400
e office@specialplacescornwall.co.uk
w specialplacescornwall.co.uk

MYLOR CHURCHTOWN Cornwall

Mimosa Cottage ★★★★
Self Catering
Special Places in Cornwall
t (01872) 864400
e office@specialplacescornwall.co.uk
w specialplacescornwall.co.uk

Penarrow Cottage ★★★★
Self Catering
Contact: Mrs Warner
t (01872) 270199
e lemonstreetlady@aol.com

NANCLEDRA Cornwall

Chypons Farm ★★★★
Self Catering
Contact: Mrs Jennifer Sharp
t (01736) 740303
e b.sharp13@virgin.net
w chyponsfarm.co.uk

Look out for establishments participating in the National Accessible Scheme

Higher Chellew Cottages
★★★ *Self Catering*
Contact: Mrs Glynis Maidment
t (01736) 364532
e higherchellew@btinternet.com
w higherchellew.co.uk

NANSTALLON Cornwall

The Gate House ★★★★
Self Catering
Contact: Mike Hamley
t (01208) 74291
e mikekathhamley@clara.co.uk
w trailcottage.co.uk

Stables Cottage ★★★★
Self Catering
Contact: Mr Allan Knowles
t (01208) 831636
e lower.mulberry@btinternet.com
w http://uk.geocities.com/lower.mulberry@btinternet.com

NAUNTON Gloucestershire

Aylworth Manor ★★★★
Self Catering
Contact: Dr & Mrs John & Joanna Ireland
t (01451) 850850
e jeaireland@aol.com
w aylworthmanor.co.uk

NETHERBURY Dorset

Little Thatch ★★★★
Self Catering
Dream Cottages
t (01305) 789000
e admin@dream-cottages.co.uk
w dream-cottages.co.uk

NETTLECOMBE Dorset

Wren Cottage ★★★★
Self Catering
Lyme Bay Holidays
t (01297) 443363
e email@lymebayholidays.co.uk
w lymebayholidays.co.uk

NETTLETON Wiltshire

Fosse Farmhouse Cottages
★★★★ *Self Catering*
t (01249) 782286
e caroncooper@compuserve.com
w fossefarmhouse.com

NEW POLZEATH Cornwall

4 PenireRocks ★★★★
Self Catering
Rock Holidays
t (01208) 863399
e info@rockholidays.co.uk
w rockholidays.co.uk

5 Pentire Rocks ★★★★
Self Catering
Rock Holidays
t (01208) 863399
e info@rockholidays.co.uk
w rockholidays.co.uk

6 Pentire Rocks ★★★★
Self Catering
Rock Holidays
t (01208) 863399
e info@rockholidays.co.uk
w rockholidays.co.uk

Atlantic View Holidays
★★★-★★★★★
Self Catering
Contact: Dr Garthwaitee enquiries@atlanticview.net
w atlanticview.net

Polzeath Court
Rating Applied For
Self Catering
Contact: Mary Knowles
t (01283) 702217
e mandmknowles@hotmail.com

Touchstone ★★★
Self Catering
Rock Holidays
t (01208) 863399
e info@rockholidays.co.uk
w rockholidays.co.uk

Treheather ★★★
Self Catering
Contact: Dr Elizabeth Mayall
t (01392) 841219

NEWENT Gloucestershire

The George Hotel ★★★
Self Catering
Contact: Mr Rhodri Yeandle
t (01531) 820203
e enquiries@georgehotel.uk.com
w georgehotel.uk.com

NEWLAND Gloucestershire

Birchamp Coach House
★★★★ *Self Catering*
Contact: Karen Davies
t (01594) 833143
e karen@birchamphouse.co.uk
w birchamphouse.co.uk

The Coach House ★★★★★
Self Catering
Contact: Alison Bassett
t (01594) 832808
e ali.bassett@craigdam.net
w craigdam.net

The Cottage ★★★
Self Catering
Contact: Julie Pritchard
t (01594) 832986
e juliespritchard@googlemail.com

NEWLYN Cornwall

Christmas Cottage ★★★★
Self Catering
Contact: Mr & Mrs R Date
t (0117) 962 0399
e enquiries@christmascottagenewlyn.com
w christmascottagenewlyn.com

Harbour View ★★★
Self Catering
Contact: Mr Nick Boden
t 07780 778074
e harbourviewcornwall@gmail.com
w web.mac.com/harbourviewcornwall

Palm Cottage ★★★★
Self Catering
t (015395) 30629
w palmcottagecornwall.co.uk

Silver Seas ★★★
Self Catering
Contact: Mrs Toms
t (01736) 368007

NEWMILL Cornwall

Little Bosulval ★★★★
Self Catering
Contact: Mr Paul Hanson
t (01736) 366024
e littlebosuval@btinternet.com
w littlebosulval.co.uk

NEWNHAM Gloucestershire

Stroods, Broadoak ★★★
Self Catering
Contact: Miss Annabelle Gillman
t (01594) 516976 & 07710 269563
e annabelle@annab.entadsl.com
w forestofdeancottage.com

NEWQUAY Cornwall

1 Spinnakers ★★★★
Self Catering
Pentire Properties
t (01302) 350000
e info@staynewquay.com
w staynewquay.com

10 Horizons, Newquay
★★★★ *Self Catering*
Blue Chip Vacations
t (01803) 855282
e info@bluechipvacations.com
w bluechipvacations.com

12 Harvest Moon Apartments ★★★★
Self Catering
Cornish Horizons Holiday Cottages
t (01841) 533331
e cottages@cornishhorizons.co.uk
w cornishhorizons.co.uk

12 Horizons, Newquay
★★★★ *Self Catering*
Blue Chip Vacations
t (01803) 855282
e info@bluechipvacations.com
w bluechipvacations.com

12 The Vista, Newquay
★★★ *Self Catering*
Blue Chip Vacations
t (01803) 855282
e info@bluechipvacations.com
w bluechipvacations.com

12A Pentire Heights ★★★★
Self Catering
Pentire Properties
t (01302) 350000
e info@staynewquay.com
w staynewquay.com

14 The Vista ★★★★
Self Catering
Blue Chip Vacations
t (01803) 855282
e info@bluechipvacations.com
w bluechipvacations.com

15 The Vista, Newquay
★★★★★ *Self Catering*
Blue Chip Vacations
t (01803) 855282
e info@bluechipvacations.com
w bluechipvacations.com

16 Horizons ★★★★
Self Catering
Blue Chip Vacations
t (01803) 855282
e info@bluechipvacations.com
w bluechipvacations.com

16 Spinnakers ★★★★
Self Catering
Pentire Properties
t (01302) 350000
e info@staynewquay.com
w staynewquay.com

18 Spinnakers ★★★★
Self Catering
Pentire Properties
t (01302) 350000
e info@staynewquay.com
w staynewquay.com

24 Horizons ★★★★
Self Catering
Blue Chip Vacations
t (01803) 855282
e info@bluechipvacations.com
w bluechipvacations.com

24 The Spinnakers ★★★★★
Self Catering
Blue Chip Vacations
t (01803) 855282
e info@bluechipvacations.com
w bluechipvacations.com

25 Waves Apartment
★★★★ *Self Catering*
Blue Chip Vacations
t (01803) 855282
e info@bluechipvacations.com
w bluechipvacations.com

27 Horizons ★★★★
Self Catering
Blue Chip Vacations
t (01803) 855282
e info@bluechipvacations.com
w bluechipvacations.com

270 North Apartment 4
Rating Applied For
Self Catering
Contact: Mr & Mrs Higgins
t (01752) 564404
e chrisatbeacon@btinternet.com
w fistralbeachapartment.co.uk

3 Harbour View
Rating Applied For
Self Catering
Blue Chip Vacations
t (01803) 855282
e info@bluechipvacations.com
w bluechipvacations.com

3 The Vista, Newquay
★★★★★ *Self Catering*
Blue Chip Vacations
t (01803) 855282
e info@bluechipvacations.com
w bluechipvacations.com

30 Surfview ★★★★
Self Catering
Pentire Properties
t (01302) 350000
e info@staynewquay.com
w staynewquay.com

4 Barrowfield View ★★★★
Self Catering
Contact: Mr Paul McAdam
t (0161) 486 9259
e paulmcadam@lineone.net
w newquaybeachretreat.co.uk

4 The Vista ★★★★★
Self Catering
Contact: Mrs Maggie Sycamore
t (01803) 855282
e sylvia@bluechipvacations.com
w bluechipvacations.com

42 Surfview ★★★
Self Catering
Pentire Properties
t (01302) 350000
e info@staynewquay.com
w staynewquay.com

46 Surfview ★★★
Self Catering
Pentire Properties
t (01302) 350000
e info@staynewquay.com
w staynewquay.com

5 Far Horizons ★★★★
Self Catering
Pentire Properties
t (01302) 350000
e info@staynewquay.com
w staynewquay.com

5 Harbour View
Rating Applied For
Self Catering
Blue Chip Vacations
t (01803) 855282
e info@bluechipvacations.com
w bluechipvacations.com

5 Pentire Heights ★★★★
Self Catering
Pentire Properties
t (01302) 350000
e info@staynewquay.com
w staynewquay.com

59 Tretherras Road
Approved Caravan Holiday Home
t (01637) 873891
w newquaycaravans.co.uk

6 Spinnakers ★★★★
Self Catering
Pentire Properties
t (01302) 350000
e info@staynewquay.com
w staynewquay.com

7 Trehellan Heights ★★★★
Self Catering
Blue Chip Vacations
t (01803) 855282
e info@bluechipvacations.com
w bluechipvacations.com

8 Harbour View
Rating Applied For
Self Catering
Blue Chip Vacations
t (01803) 855282
e info@bluechipvacations.com
w bluechipvacations.com

8 Pentire Heights ★★★★
Self Catering
Pentire Properties
t (01302) 350000
e info@staynewquay.com
w staynewquay.com

9 Trehellan Heights ★★★★
Self Catering
Blue Chip Vacations
t (01803) 855282
e info@bluechipvacations.com
w bluechipvacations.com

Apartment 2 – The Vista
★★★★★ *Self Catering*
t (01270) 883445
w pentireholidays.co.uk

Atlantic Reach ★★★
Self Catering
Blue Chip Vacations
t (01803) 855282
e info@bluechipvacations.com
w bluechipvacations.com

The Batch & Baywatch ★★★
Self Catering
t (01935) 83553
w http://mysite.wanadoo-members.co.uk/newquaybatch

The Beach House ★★★★
Self Catering
t (0117) 330 6956
w thebeachhousenewquay.co.uk

Beach House, Porth View & Surf Side ★★★★
Self Catering
Cornish Seaview Cottages
t (01428) 723819
e enquiries@cornishseaviewcottages.co.uk
w cornishseaviewcottages.co.uk

Beachbreak
Rating Applied For
Self Catering
Pentire Properties
t (01302) 350000
e info@staynewquay.com
w staynewquay.com

Boatman's Loft ★★★
Self Catering
Cornish Horizons Holiday Cottages
t (01841) 533331
e cottages@cornishhorizons.co.uk
w cornishhorizons.co.uk

C2 Bay Apartments
Rating Applied For
Self Catering
Pentire Properties
t (01302) 350000
e info@staynewquay.com
w staynewquay.com

Carols Cornwall Holidays
Approved Caravan Holiday Home
t (01726) 890291
w carolscornwallholidays.co.uk

Chatsworth Apartments
★★★★ *Self Catering*
Contact: Mrs Maureen Cornwall
t (01637) 876001
e bookings@chatsworthapartments.co.uk
w chatsworthapartments.co.uk

Cheviot Holiday Apartments
★★★★ *Self Catering*
Contact: Mr Brian Biscard
t (01637) 872712
e info@cheviotnewquay.co.uk
w cheviotnewquay.co.uk

Cornwall Coast Holidays
★★★★ *Self Catering*
Contact: Mrs Deborah Spencer-Smith
t (020) 8440 7518 & 07910 583050
e deborah@cornwallcoastholidays.com
w cornwallcoastholidays.com

Cornwall Coast Holidays
★★★★ *Self Catering*
Contact: Mrs Deborah Spencer-Smith
t (020) 8440 7518
e enquiries@cornwallcoastholidays.com
w cornwallcoastholidays.com

Degembris Cottage ★★★★
Self Catering
Contact: Mrs Kathy Woodley
t (01872) 510555
e kathy@degembris.co.uk
w degembris.co.uk

Fiddlers Green
Rating Applied For
Self Catering
Pentire Properties
t (01302) 350000
e info@staynewquay.com
w staynewquay.com

Fishermans View
Rating Applied For
Self Catering
Contact: Ms Nicola Emanuel
t (01637) 831127
e nicolaemanuel@aol.com
w surfs-view.co.uk

Fistral Cottage ★★★★
Self Catering
Contact: Mrs Sophie Banks
t (0121) 373 1388
e fistral-cottage@blueyonder.co.uk
w fistral-cottage.co.uk

Fistral House ★★★★
Self Catering
Pentire Properties
t (01302) 350000
e info@staynewquay.com
w staynewquay.com

Fistral, Watergate and Town Apartments ★★★★
Self Catering
t (01452) 312661
w 5stmarys.co.uk

Flip Flops
Rating Applied For
Self Catering
Cornish Horizons Holiday Cottages
t (01841) 533331
e cottages@cornishhorizons.co.uk
w cornishhorizons.co.uk

Green Waters ★★★★
Self Catering
Contact: Mrs Ruth Pullen
t (01637) 873551
e bernardruth.pullen@homecall.co.uk

Harris Caravans *Approved Caravan Holiday Home*
Contact: Mrs Maggi Faulkner
t (01803) 868336
e holidays@2seashore.co.uk
w 2seashore.co.uk

Harris Cottage ★★★★★
Self Catering
Gustivean Cottages
t (01579) 346473
e holidays@duchyofcornwall.gov.uk
w duchyofcornwallholidaycottages.co.uk

Hendra Paul Cottages, Porth
★★★–★★★★ *Self Catering*
Contact: Mrs Julia Schofield
Hendra Paul Cottages – BE020
t (01637) 874695
e info@hendrapaul.co.uk
w hendrapaul.co.uk

Kingswood ★★★
Self Catering
Contact: Mr Steven Wibberley
t (024) 7632 8886

Manuels Farm
★★★–★★★★ *Self Catering*
Contact: Mr James Wilson
t (01637) 878300
e james@manuelsfarm.co.uk
w manuelsfarm.co.uk

No. 3 Atlantic Reach ★★★
Self Catering
t (01637) 870578
w atlantic-reach-newquay-no3.co.uk

On The Rocks ★★
Self Catering
t (01872) 575228
w attheseaside.freeuk.com

Parry's Barn ★★★★
Self Catering
Contact: Mrs Sharon Rundle
t (01637) 875798 & 07809 152582
e sharonrundleuk@yahoo.com

Pebbles Beach House
Rating Applied For
Self Catering
Pentire Properties
t (01302) 350000
e info@staynewquay.com
w staynewquay.com

Pentire Heights ★★★
Self Catering
Cornish Horizons Holiday Cottages
t (01841) 533331
e cottages@cornishhorizons.co.uk
w cornishhorizons.co.uk

Porth Veor Manor ★★★★
Self Catering
Contact: Mr Jeff Smith
t (01637) 873274
e enquiries@porthveormanor.com
w porthveormanor.com

Sandy Beach Apartments, 2, 3, 4, 5 ★★★ *Self Catering*
Cornish Horizons Holiday Cottages
t (01841) 533331
e cottages@cornishhorizons.co.uk
w cornishhorizons.co.uk

Seascape ★★★ *Self Catering*
Contact: Mr & Mrs Selleck
t (01752) 862372
e surfamber@tiscali.co.uk

Seascape ★★★★
Self Catering
Special Places in Cornwall
t (01872) 864400
e office@specialplacescornwall.co.uk
w specialplacescornwall.co.uk

Spindrift Apartment ★★★
Self Catering
Contact: Mr Taylor
t (01293) 882557
e info@spindriftapts.co.uk
w spindriftapts.co.uk

Spindrift Holiday Flat ★★★
Self Catering
t (0116) 288 4703

The Spinnakers ★★★★
Self Catering
Cornish Horizons Holiday Cottages
t (01841) 533331
e cottages@cornishhorizons.co.uk
w cornishhorizons.co.uk

Tolcarne Beach Village
★★★★ *Self Catering*
Contact: Mrs Veronica McCann
t (01209) 712651 & (01637) 872489
e info@tolcarnebeach.co.uk
w tolcarnebeach.co.uk

Towan Place ★★★★★
Self Catering
Blue Chip Vacations
t (01803) 855282
e info@bluechipvacations.com
w bluechipvacations.com

Towan Vean ★★★
Self Catering
Cornish Horizons Holiday Cottages
t (01841) 533331
e cottages@cornishhorizons.co.uk
w cornishhorizons.co.uk

Trenance Hol Park Caravan 224 *Approved Caravan Holiday Home*
t (01637) 830134

Trenance Holiday Park
Approved Caravan Holiday Home
Contact: Mr R Dickerson
t (01637) 875311

Trenance Holiday Park (Anderson) *Approved Caravan Holiday Home*
t (01637) 876124

Trendrean Farm Barns
★★★★ *Self Catering*
Contact: Mr Ivor Marshall
t (01208) 813228
e ivor.gill@btopenworld.com
w trendreanfarmbarns.co.uk

Trewollack House ★★★★★
Self Catering
Gustivean Cottages
t (01579) 346473
e holidays@duchyofcornwall.gov.uk
w duchyofcornwallholidaycottages.co.uk

Woodpecker Cottage ★★
Self Catering
Contact: Mr & Mrs Rumsey
t (01637) 852073

NEWTON ABBOT
Devon

Copper Beech Cottage
Rating Applied For
Self Catering
Holiday Homes and Cottages South West
t (01803) 299677
e holcotts@aol.com
w swcottages.co.uk

Dawlish Villas
Rating Applied For
Self Catering
Contact: Sharon & Steve Bray
t (01626) 334783
e info@dawlishwarrenvillas.co.uk
w dawlishwarrenvillas.co.uk

Pound Cottage 2
Rating Applied For
Self Catering
Holiday Homes and Cottages South West
t (01803) 299677
e holcotts@aol.com
w swcottages.co.uk

The Pound House
Rating Applied For
Self Catering
Holiday Homes and Cottages South West
t (01803) 299677
e holcotts@aol.com
w swcottages.co.uk

NEWTON FERRERS
Devon

Myrtle ★★★ *Self Catering*
Contact: Mrs Vivienne Summers
t 0845 634 3490
w yealm-holidays.co.uk

NEWTON POPPLEFORD
Devon

The Lodge ★★★★
Self Catering
Sweetcombe Cottage Holidays
t (01395) 512130
e enquiries@sweetcombe-ch.co.uk
w sweetcombe-ch.co.uk

Umbrella Cottage ★★★
Self Catering
Contact: Mrs Margaret Woodley
t (01395) 568687

NEWTON ST LOE
Somerset

Pennsylvania Farm ★★★★
Self Catering
Contact: Mr & Mrs Ian & Pat Foster
t (01223) 12451
e enquiries@pennsylvaniafarm.co.uk
w pennsylvaniafarm.co.uk

NEWTON TRACEY
Devon

Litchardon Rose ★★★
Self Catering
Marsdens Cottage Holidays
t (01271) 813777
e holidays@marsdens.co.uk
w marsdens.co.uk

NOMANSLAND
Devon

Middlewick Barton ★★★★
Self Catering
Contact: Miss Penny Lockwood
t (01884) 861693
e middlewick.barton@tiscali.co.uk
w middlewick-barton-devon.co.uk

NORTH CHERITON
Somerset

Fives Court Cottage ★★★★
Self Catering
Contact: Mr Edward & Heather Martin
t (01963) 32777
w fivescourtcottage.co.uk

NORTH CHIDEOCK
Dorset

Hell Barn Cottages ★★★
Self Catering
Contact: Mr & Mrs Shigeaki & Diana Takezoe
t (01297) 489589
e diana@hellbarn.co.uk
w hellbarn.co.uk

NORTH HILL
Cornwall

The Granary at Eastgate Barn ★★★★ *Self Catering*
Contact: Ms Goodman
t (01566) 782573
e jill@eastgatebarn.co.uk

NORTH MOLTON
Devon

Court Farm Cottages
Rating Applied For
Self Catering
Marsdens Cottage Holidays
t (01271) 813777
e holidays@marsdens.co.uk
w marsdens.co.uk

The Hayloft ★★★★
Self Catering
Marsdens Cottage Holidays
t (01271) 813777
e holidays@marsdens.co.uk
w marsdens.co.uk

Jasmine Cottage ★★★★
Self Catering
Marsdens Cottage Holidays
t (01271) 813777
e holidays@marsdens.co.uk
w marsdens.co.uk

West Millbrook ★★–★★★
Self Catering
Contact: Mrs Rosemarie Courtney
t (01598) 740382
e wmbselfcatering@aol.com
w westmillbrook.co.uk

NORTH NEWTON
Somerset

Dragonfly Barn ★★★★
Self Catering
t (01278) 661513
w dragonflybarn.com

Swallow Barn and Heron Barn ★★★ *Self Catering*
Contact: Mrs Paula Mitchell
t (01278) 661518
e paula@greathousebarns.com
w holidaysinsomerset.co.uk

NORTH TAMERTON
Cornwall

Hill Cottage ★★★★
Self Catering
Contact: Mr & Mrs Green
t (01409) 253093
e enquiries@selfcateringcottagesdevon.co.uk
w selfcateringcottagesdevon.co.uk

Tamar Valley Cottages
★★★★ *Self Catering*
Contact: Mr & Mrs Rhodes
t (01409) 271284
e smrhodes@btinternet.com
w tamarvalleycottages.co.uk

NORTH TAWTON
Devon

Cider Cottage ★★★★
Self Catering
Contact: Mrs Susan Bartlett
t (01837) 89002
e sue@yeo-farm.com
w yeo-farm.com

NORTH WHILBOROUGH
Devon

Long Barn Luxury Holiday Cottages ★★★★★
Self Catering
Contact: Mr Peter Tidman
t (01803) 875044
e ros@longbarncottages.co.uk
w longbarncottages.co.uk

NORTHAM
Devon

Atlantis ★★★★ *Self Catering*
Marsdens Cottage Holidays
t (01271) 813777
e holidays@marsdens.co.uk
w marsdens.co.uk

Nautilus 16 ★★★★★
Self Catering
Select Holiday Homes
t (01491) 826757
e info@select-holidays-homes.co.uk
w select-holiday-homes.co.uk

Nautilus 6 ★★★★★
Self Catering
Select Holiday Homes
t (01491) 826757
e info@select-holidays-homes.co.uk
w select-holiday-homes.co.uk

Nemo ★★★★ *Self Catering*
Marsdens Cottage Holidays
t (01271) 813777
e holidays@marsdens.co.uk
w marsdens.co.uk

Northam Cottage ★★★★
Self Catering
Marsdens Cottage Holidays
t (01271) 813777
e holidays@marsdens.co.uk
w marsdens.co.uk

Point Break ★★★★
Self Catering
Marsdens Cottage Holidays
t (01271) 813777
e holidays@marsdens.co.uk
w marsdens.co.uk

Seafield ★★★★ *Self Catering*
Farm & Cottage Holidays
t (01237) 459827
e enquiries@farmcott.co.uk
w holidaycottages.co.uk

NORTHLEACH
Gloucestershire

Cotteswold Cottage, Northleach ★★★
Self Catering
Contact: Mr David Atkinson
t (01451) 860493
e cotteswoldhouse@aol.com
w cotteswoldhouse.com

The Guggle
★★★-★★★★★
Self Catering
Contact: Mrs Emma Doyle
t (01242) 890394
e emma@paddockbarn.co.uk
w theguggle.co.uk

NORTHLEIGH
Devon

Chilcombe ★★★
Self Catering
Milkbere Cottage Holidays
t (01297) 20729
e info@milkberehols.com
w milkberehols.com

Northleigh Farm ★★★★
Self Catering
Contact: Mr & Mrs Simon & Sue Potter
t (01404) 871217
e simon-potter@msn.com
w northleighfarm.co.uk

NORTHLEW
Devon

Glen Cottage ★★★★
Self Catering
Holiday Homes and Cottages South West
t (01803) 299677
e holcotts@aol.com
w swcottages.co.uk

NORTON BAVANT
Wiltshire

The Bolthole ★★★
Self Catering
Contact: Mrs Lynne Ersser
t (01985) 840271
e mikeersser@freeuk.com

NORTON SUB HAMDON
Somerset

Little Norton Mill ★★★★
Self Catering
Contact: Mrs Julie Allard
t (01935) 881337
e p.allard190@btinternet.com
w littlenortonmill.co.uk

NOSS MAYO
Devon

9 The Malt House ★★★
Self Catering
Contact: Mrs Vivienne Summers
t 0845 634 3490
w yealm-holidays.co.uk

NOTTINGTON
Dorset

April's Cottage ★★★
Self Catering
Dream Cottages
t (01305) 789000
e admin@dream-cottages.co.uk
w dream-cottages.co.uk

NOTTON
Dorset

Notton Hill Barn Holiday Cottages ★★★★
Self Catering
Contact: Mr & Mrs D Smith
t (01300) 321299
e stay@nottonhillbarncottages.co.uk
w nottonhillbarncottages.co.uk

NUNNEY
Somerset

Riverside Cottage ★★★★
Self Catering
Contact: Mrs Clare Hulley
t (01373) 836480
w nunney.net

NYMPSFIELD
Gloucestershire

Crossways ★★★
Self Catering
Contact: Mr & Mrs Bowen
t (01453) 860309

OAKRIDGE
Gloucestershire

Watercombe House
★★★★★ *Self Catering*
Contact: Mrs Julia Murray
t (01453) 840278
e watercombehouse@btconnect.com
w watercombehouse.com

OGWELL
Devon

Rydon Ball ★★★★
Self Catering
Holiday Homes and Cottages South West
t (01803) 299677
e holcotts@aol.com
w swcottages.co.uk

OKEFORD FITZPAINE
Dorset

The Garden House
Rating Applied For
Self Catering
Hideaways
t (01747) 828170
e enq@hideaways.co.uk
w hideaways.co.uk

Nutmeg Cottage ★★★
Self Catering
Contact: Mrs Eve Wood
t (01258) 860146
e enquiries@nutmegcottage.net
w nutmegcottage.net

OKEHAMPTON
Devon

Beer Farm ★★★★
Self Catering
Contact: Bob & Sue Annear
t (01837) 840265
e info@beerfarm.co.uk
w beerfarm.co.uk

Bowerland ★★★★
Self Catering
Contact: Ray or Mel Quirke
t (01837) 55979
e bowerland@devonhols.com
w devonhols.com

East Hook Holiday Cottages
★★-★★★★★ *Self Catering*
t (01837) 52305
w easthook-holiday-cottages.co.uk

Fourwinds Self-Catering Properties ★★★
Self Catering
t (01837) 55785
w 4windsholidays.co.uk

Heather Cottage ★★★★
Self Catering
Contact: Yvette Martin
t (01837) 658820 & 07971 258040
e yvettemartin@btinternet.com
w lastminute-cottages.co.uk/north-and-mid-devon/dem2028/

The Linney ★★★★
Self Catering
Milkbere Cottage Holidays
t (01297) 20729
e info@milkberehols.com
w milkberehols.com

Little Bidlake Barns ★★★★
Self Catering
Contact: Mrs Joanna Down
t (01837) 861233
e bidlakefrm@aol.com
w dartmoor-holiday-cottages.co.uk

Week Farm Country Holidays ★★★★
Self Catering
Contact: Mrs Margaret Hockridge
t (01837) 861221
e accom@weekfarmonline.com
w weekfarmonline.com

ORCHARDLEIGH
Somerset

Orchardleigh Estate
★★-★★★★ *Self Catering*
Contact: Mr Charlie Beardall
t (01373) 472550
e info@orchardleighcottages.net
w orchardleighholidays.net

OSMINGTON
Dorset

Emmies Cottage ★★★★
Self Catering
Dream Cottages
t (01305) 789000
e admin@dream-cottages.co.uk
w dream-cottages.co.uk

Honeybun ★★★★
Self Catering
Dream Cottages
t (01305) 789000
e admin@dream-cottages.co.uk
w dream-cottages.co.uk

L'Atelier ★★★★
Self Catering
Dream Cottages
t (01305) 789000
e admin@dream-cottages.co.uk
w dream-cottages.co.uk

Lavender Cottage ★★★★
Self Catering
Dorset Cottage Holidays
t (01929) 553443
e enq@dhcottages.co.uk
w dhcottages.co.uk

Overlond ★★★ *Self Catering*
Dream Cottages
t (01305) 789000
e admin@dream-cottages.co.uk
w dream-cottages.co.uk

OSMINGTON MILLS
Dorset

Smugglers Cottage ★★★
Self Catering
Dream Cottages
t (01305) 789000
e admin@dream-cottages.co.uk
w dream-cottages.co.uk

Vine Cottage ★★★
Self Catering
Dream Cottages
t (01305) 789000
e admin@dream-cottages.co.uk
w dream-cottages.co.uk

OTHERY
Somerset

Willows Cottage and Levels Cottage ★★★★ *Self Catering*
Contact: Mrs Christine Ellis
t (01823) 698166
e ellis@bagenham.freeserve.co.uk
w bagenhamfarm.co.uk

OTTERFORD
Somerset

Tamarack Lodge ★★★★
Self Catering
Contact: Matthew Sparks
t (01823) 601270
e matthew.sparks@tamaracklodge.co.uk
w tamaracklodge.co.uk

OTTERHAM
Cornwall

Saint Tinney Farm Holidays
★★★★ *Self Catering*
t (01840) 261274

OTTERTON
Devon

The Old Barn ★★★★
Self Catering
Sweetcombe Cottage Holidays
t (01395) 512130
e enquiries@sweetcombe-ch.co.uk
w sweetcombe-ch.co.uk

Otter Barn ★★★★
Self Catering
Sweetcombe Cottage Holidays
t (01395) 512130
e enquiries@sweetcombe-ch.co.uk
w sweetcombe-ch.co.uk

Rosemead ★★★★
Self Catering
Sweetcombe Cottage Holidays
t (01395) 512130
e enquiries@sweetcombe-ch.co.uk
w sweetcombe-ch.co.uk

OTTERY ST MARY
Devon

Waxway Farm ★★★★
Self Catering
Contact: Mr Patrick Roberts
t (01404) 813688
e cottages@waxwayfarm.co.uk
w waxwayfarm.co.uk

OVER COMPTON
Dorset

Meadow View Barn
Rating Applied For
Self Catering
Contact: Mr Anthony Kinch
t (01993) 843315
e info@meadowviewbarn.co.uk
w meadowviewbarn.co.uk

Uplands ★★★ *Self Catering*
Contact: Mr & Mrs Brake
t (01935) 477043
e info@uplandsholidayhome.co.uk
w uplandsholidayhome.co.uk

OWLPEN
Gloucestershire

Owlpen Manor
★★★-★★★★ *Self Catering*
Contact: Mrs Jayne Simmons
t (01453) 860261
e sales@owlpen.com
w owlpen.com

OXENTON
Gloucestershire

Crane Hill ★★★ *Self Catering*
Contact: Mrs Helen Beardsell
t (01242) 673631

OZLEWORTH
Gloucestershire

Hill Mill Cottage ★★★★
Self Catering
Contact: Mrs Nash
t (01453) 842401
e pnash@hillmillcottage.co.uk
w hillmillcottage.co.uk

PADSTOW
Cornwall

1 Meadow Court ★★★★
Self Catering
Contact: Ms Nicky Stanley
w harbourholidays.co.uk

1 Meadow Way ★★★★
Self Catering
Harbour Holidays
t (01841) 533402
e contact@harbourholidays.co.uk
w harbourholidays.co.uk

1 Oak Terrace ★★★★
Self Catering
Harbour Holidays
t (01841) 533402
e contact@harbourholidays.co.uk
w harbourholidays.co.uk

10 Church Lane ★★★
Self Catering
Harbour Holidays
t (01841) 533402
e contact@harbourholidays.co.uk
w harbourholidays.co.uk

10 Meadow Court ★★★★
Self Catering
Contact: Miss Nicola Stanley
t (01841) 533402
e contact@harbourholidays.co.uk

10 Porthilly View ★★★
Self Catering
Harbour Holidays
t (01841) 533402
e contact@harbourholidays.co.uk
w harbourholidays.co.uk

10/12 Broad Street, 2/5 Mill Road ★★★ *Self Catering*
Contact: Mrs Susan Farr
t (01454) 614861

12 Glynn Road ★★★★
Self Catering
Harbour Holidays
t (01841) 533402
e contact@harbourholidays.co.uk
w harbourholidays.co.uk

12 Netherton Road ★★★
Self Catering
Cornish Horizons Holiday Cottages
t (01841) 533331
e cottages@cornishhorizons.co.uk
w cornishhorizons.co.uk

14 Cross Street ★★★
Self Catering
Cornish Horizons Holiday Cottages
t (01841) 533331
e cottages@cornishhorizons.co.uk
w cornishhorizons.co.uk

15 Netherton Road ★★★
Self Catering
Cornish Horizons Holiday Cottages
t (01841) 533331
e cottages@cornishhorizons.co.uk
w cornishhorizons.co.uk

17 Netherton Road ★★★★
Self Catering
Harbour Holidays
t (01841) 533402
e contact@harbourholidays.co.uk
w harbourholidays.co.uk

18 Glynn Road ★★★★
Self Catering
Harbour Holidays
t (01841) 533402
e contact@harbourholidays.co.uk
w harbourholidays.co.uk

19 High Street ★★★★★
Self Catering
Contact: Nicky Stanley
t (01841) 532555
e sales@jackie-stanley.co.uk

2 Rose Terrace ★★★★
Self Catering
Harbour Holidays
t (01841) 533402
e contact@harbourholidays.co.uk
w harbourholidays.co.uk

2 The Strand ★★★
Self Catering
Contact: Nicky Stanley
t (01841) 532402
e contact@harbourholidays.co.uk
w harbourholidays.co.uk

21 New Street ★★★★★
Self Catering
Harbour Holidays
t (01841) 533402
e contact@harbourholidays.co.uk
w harbourholidays.co.uk

22 Church Street ★★★
Self Catering
Harbour Holidays
t (01841) 533402
e contact@harbourholidays.co.uk
w harbourholidays.co.uk

22 Egerton Road ★★★
Self Catering
Harbour Holidays
t (01841) 533402
e contact@harbourholidays.co.uk
w harbourholidays.co.uk

23 Treverbyn Road ★★★
Self Catering
Harbour Holidays
t (01841) 533402
e contact@harbourholidays.co.uk
w harbourholidays.co.uk

25 Old School Court ★★★★
Self Catering
Harbour Holidays
t (01841) 533402
e contact@harbourholidays.co.uk
w harbourholidays.co.uk

25 Sarahs View ★★★
Self Catering
Harbour Holidays
t (01841) 533402
e contact@harbourholidays.co.uk
w harbourholidays.co.uk

26 Church Lane ★★★
Self Catering
Cornish Horizons Holiday Cottages
t (01841) 533331
e cottages@cornishhorizons.co.uk
w cornishhorizons.co.uk

3 Red Brick Building ★★★
Self Catering
Harbour Holidays
t (01841) 533402
e contact@harbourholidays.co.uk
w harbourholidays.co.uk

34 Sarah's View ★★★
Self Catering
Contact: Mrs Thomas
t (01841) 532243

35 Duke Street ★★★★
Self Catering
Harbour Holidays
t (01841) 533402
e contact@harbourholidays.co.uk
w harbourholidays.co.uk

4 Broad Street ★★★
Self Catering
Harbour Holidays
t (01841) 533402
e contact@harbourholidays.co.uk
w harbourholidays.co.uk

4 Towans ★★★★
Self Catering
Harbour Holidays
t (01841) 533402
e contact@harbourholidays.co.uk
w harbourholidays.co.uk

5 Little Dinas ★★★★
Self Catering
Harbour Holidays
t (01841) 533402
e contact@harbourholidays.co.uk
w harbourholidays.co.uk

54 Raleigh Close ★★★
Self Catering
Harbour Holidays
t (01841) 533402
e contact@harbourholidays.co.uk
w harbourholidays.co.uk

6 Meadow Court ★★★★
Self Catering
Cornish Horizons Holiday Cottages
t (01841) 533331
e cottages@cornishhorizons.co.uk
w cornishhorizons.co.uk

6 Waterside ★★★
Self Catering
t (01841) 532555
e contact@harbourholidays.co.uk
w harbourholidays.co.uk

62 Sarahs View ★★★
Self Catering
Contact: Mrs Amey
t (01202) 258769
e kathry.amey1@ntlworld.com

68 Church Street ★★★★★
Self Catering
Harbour Holidays
t (01841) 533402
e contact@harbourholidays.co.uk
w harbourholidays.co.uk

7/9 Grove Place ★★★
Self Catering
Harbour Holidays
t (01841) 533402
e contact@harbourholidays.co.uk
w harbourholidays.co.uk

9 New Street ★★★★★
Self Catering
Harbour Holidays
t (01841) 533402
e contact@harbourholidays.co.uk
w harbourholidays.co.uk

Armsyde ★★★ *Self Catering*
Cornish Horizons Holiday Cottages
t (01841) 533331
e cottages@cornishhorizons.co.uk
w cornishhorizons.co.uk

The Backs ★★★★
Self Catering
Harbour Holidays
t (01841) 533402
e contact@harbourholidays.co.uk
w harbourholidays.co.uk

Barn Cottage ★★★
Self Catering
Harbour Holidays
t (01841) 533402
e contact@harbourholidays.co.uk
w harbourholidays.co.uk

Baxters Cottage ★★★★
Self Catering
Cornish Horizons Holiday Cottages
t (01841) 533331
e cottages@cornishhorizons.co.uk
w cornishhorizons.co.uk

Bay Tree Cottage ★★★★
Self Catering
Cornish Horizons Holiday Cottages
t (01841) 533331
e cottages@cornishhorizons.co.uk
w cornishhorizons.co.uk

Beau Vista ★★★★
Self Catering
Cornish Seaview Cottages
t (01428) 723819
e enquiries@cornishseaviewcottages.co.uk
w cornishseaviewcottages.co.uk

Bellagio – Padstow ★★★★
Self Catering
Contact: Nigel & Jane Sellar
t (01902) 840094
e janesellar@tiscali.co.uk
w padstowlets.com

Blair House ★★★★
Self Catering
Harbour Holidays
t (01841) 533402
e contact@harbourholidays.co.uk
w harbourholidays.co.uk

Bobbins ★★★★
Self Catering
Harbour Holidays
t (01841) 533402
e contact@harbourholidays.co.uk
w harbourholidays.co.uk

Bos Keun Lowen ★★★★
Self Catering
Cornish Horizons Holiday Cottages
t (01841) 533331
e cottages@cornishhorizons.co.uk
w cornishhorizons.co.uk

Broomleaf Cottage ★★★
Self Catering
Cornish Horizons Holiday Cottages
t (01841) 533331
e cottages@cornishhorizons.co.uk
w cornishhorizons.co.uk

Byre Cottage ★★★★
Self Catering
Contact: Nancy Banbury
t (01841) 532287

Camellia Cottage ★★★
Self Catering
Cornish Horizons Holiday Cottages
t (01841) 533331
e cottages@cornishhorizons.co.uk
w cornishhorizons.co.uk

Catherine's
Rating Applied For
Self Catering
Cornish Horizons Holiday Cottages
t (01841) 533331
e cottages@cornishhorizons.co.uk
w cornishhorizons.co.uk

Coachyard Mews & Thyme Cottage ★★–★★★
Self Catering
Contact: Mr Andrews
t (01841) 521198
e raideanltd@aol.com
w holidayinpadstow.co.uk

Cormorant ★★★
Self Catering
Harbour Holidays
t (01841) 533402
e contact@harbourholidays.co.uk
w harbourholidays.co.uk

Coxwain Cottage ★★★★
Self Catering
Harbour Holidays
t (01841) 533402
e contact@harbourholidays.co.uk
w harbourholidays.co.uk

Crenella Barn ★★★
Self Catering
Harbour Holidays
t (01841) 533402
e contact@harbourholidays.co.uk
w harbourholidays.co.uk

Dennis Farm Apartment ★★★ *Self Catering*
Harbour Holidays
t (01841) 533402
e contact@harbourholidays.co.uk
w harbourholidays.co.uk

Dingly Dell ★★ *Self Catering*
Harbour Holidays
t (01841) 533402
e contact@harbourholidays.co.uk
w harbourholidays.co.uk

Dodo's Cottage ★★★★
Self Catering
Harbour Holidays
t (01841) 533402
e contact@harbourholidays.co.uk
w harbourholidays.co.uk

Dove Cottage ★★
Self Catering
Harbour Holidays
t (01841) 533402
e contact@harbourholidays.co.uk
w harbourholidays.co.uk

The Drang House ★★★
Self Catering
Harbour Holidays
t (01841) 533402
e contact@harbourholidays.co.uk
w harbourholidays.co.uk

Driftwood Cottage ★★★★
Self Catering
Contact: Mrs Sarah Moore
t (01332) 695222
e sarakmoore@hotmail.com
w padstowcottagecompany.co.uk

The Dukes ★★★
Self Catering
Cornish Horizons Holiday Cottages
t (01841) 533331
e cottages@cornishhorizons.co.uk
w cornishhorizons.co.uk

Dursley Cottage ★★★★
Self Catering
Contact: Little Gem lettings
t (01841) 540447
e enquiries@littlegemlettings.co.uk
w littlegemlettings.co.uk

Ellies Den ★★★ *Self Catering*
Harbour Holidays
t (01841) 533402
e contact@harbourholidays.co.uk
w harbourholidays.co.uk

Estuary View ★★★
Self Catering
Harbour Holidays
t (01841) 533402
e contact@harbourholidays.co.uk
w harbourholidays.co.uk

Estuary View 26 ★★★★★
Self Catering
Harbour Holidays
t (01841) 533402
e contact@harbourholidays.co.uk
w harbourholidays.co.uk

Exbury House ★★★
Self Catering
Harbour Holidays
t (01841) 533402
e contact@harbourholidays.co.uk
w harbourholidays.co.uk

Felwyn ★★★ *Self Catering*
Cornish Horizons Holiday Cottages
t (01841) 533331
e cottages@cornishhorizons.co.uk
w cornishhorizons.co.uk

Fieldview
Rating Applied For
Self Catering
Contact: Mrs Susie Cocker
t (01494) 433872
e susiecocker@aol.com
w padstowcottagecompany.co.uk

Fishermans Cottage ★★★★
Self Catering
Harbour Holidays
t (01841) 533402
e contact@harbourholidays.co.uk
w harbourholidays.co.uk

Flat 3 The Old Bakehouse ★★★★ *Self Catering*
Harbour Holidays
t (01841) 533402
e contact@harbourholidays.co.uk
w harbourholidays.co.uk

Fuchsia Cottage ★★★
Self Catering
Contact: Mrs Gill Burgess
Fuchsia Cottage – Padstow
t (01841) 532633
e info@padstowcottagecompany.co.uk
w padstowcottagecompany.co.uk

Grove Cottage ★★★
Self Catering
Contact: Mr Ian Cathcart
t (01432) 275084
e ian@cathcarti.freeserve.co.uk
w padstowcottages.info

Harbour Cottage ★★★★
Self Catering
Cornish Horizons Holiday Cottages
t (01841) 533331
e cottages@cornishhorizons.co.uk
w cornishhorizons.co.uk

Harbour Holidays ★★★
Self Catering
Contact: Miss Nicky Stanley
t (01841) 533402
e contact@harbourholidays.co.uk
w harbourholidays.co.uk

Harlyn Place ★★★★
Self Catering
Contact: Nicky Stanley
Harbour Holidays
t (01841) 533402
e admin@harbourholidays.co.uk
w harbourholidays.co.uk

Hensby ★★★ *Self Catering*
Harbour Holidays
t (01841) 533402
e contact@harbourholidays.co.uk
w harbourholidays.co.uk

Hidden Cottage ★★★★★
Self Catering
Harbour Holidays
t (01841) 533402
e contact@harbourholidays.co.uk
w harbourholidays.co.uk

Hideaway Cottage ★★★★
Self Catering
Contact: Mr Nick Sutton
t (01234) 353499
e dnl.holidays@ntlworld.com
w dnlholidays.co.uk

Honey Cottage ★★★
Self Catering
Harbour Holidays
t (01841) 533402 & 07932 604943
e contact@harbourholidays.co.uk
w harbourholidays.co.uk

Honeysuckle Cottage ★★★
Self Catering
Contact: Colin & Debbie Clarkee cchaulage@lineone.net
w honeysucklecottage padstow.co.uk

Honeysuckle Cottage
★★★★ *Self Catering*
Harbour Holidays
t (01841) 533402
e contact@harbourholidays.co.uk
w harbourholidays.co.uk

House Martins ★★★
Self Catering
Cornish Horizons Holiday Cottages
t (01841) 533331
e cottages@cornishhorizons.co.uk
w cornishhorizons.co.uk

Jasmine Cottage ★★★★
Self Catering
Harbour Holidays
t (01841) 533402
e contact@harbourholidays.co.uk
w harbourholidays.co.uk

Joan's Cottage ★★–★★★★
Self Catering
Contact: Mr & Mrs Evans
t (01841) 532814
e info@symply-padstow.co.uk
w symplypadstow.co.uk

Kernyck Cottage ★★★★
Self Catering
Contact: Robert & Sue Norfolk
t (01841) 532902
e susan@padstowecho.wanadoo.co.uk

Kittiwake Cottage ★★★
Self Catering
Harbour Holidays
t (01841) 533402
e contact@harbourholidays.co.uk
w harbourholidays.co.uk

Lalapanzi ★★★★★
Self Catering
Harbour Holidays
t (01841) 533402
e contact@harbourholidays.co.uk
w harbourholidays.co.uk

Lantern House ★★★
Self Catering
Contact: Mr Wright
t (01841) 532566
e alkwright@wright3840.fslife.co.uk
w padstowlive.com

Lawn Cottage ★★★★
Self Catering
Contact: Mrs Heather Buckingham
t (01675) 464936
e heather@bprops.co.uk
w buckinghamproperties.co.uk

Lazy Days ★★★ *Self Catering*
Harbour Holidays
t (01841) 533402
e contact@harbourholidays.co.uk
w harbourholidays.co.uk

Lelissick ★★★ *Self Catering*
Harbour Holidays
t (01841) 533402
e contact@harbourholidays.co.uk
w harbourholidays.co.uk

Little Dolphins ★★★
Self Catering
Cornish Horizons Holiday Cottages
t (01841) 533331
e cottages@cornishhorizons.co.uk
w cornishhorizons.co.uk

Little Dukes ★★ *Self Catering*
Cornish Horizons Holiday Cottages
t (01841) 533331
e cottages@cornishhorizons.co.uk
w cornishhorizons.co.uk

Little Haven ★★★
Self Catering
Contact: Mr Andrew Cousins
t (0118) 932 8116
e andycousins@hotmail.com
w stay-in-padstow.co.uk

Little Penty ★★★
Self Catering
Cornish Horizons Holiday Cottages
t (01841) 533331
e cottages@cornishhorizons.co.uk
w cornishhorizons.co.uk

Lobster House ★★★
Self Catering
Harbour Holidays
t (01841) 533402
e contact@harbourholidays.co.uk
w harbourholidays.co.uk

The Lobster Pot ★★★
Self Catering
Contact: Kay Wood
t (01841) 540226
e kaywood@onetel.net.uk

Lobsterpots ★★★–★★★★
Self Catering
Cornish Horizons Holiday Cottages
t (01841) 533331
e cottages@cornishhorizons.co.uk
w cornishhorizons.co.uk

Lodderick
Rating Applied For
Self Catering
Contact: Ms Nicky Stanley
Harbour Holidays
t (01841) 533402
e admin@harbourholidays.co.uk
w harbourholidays.co.uk

The Lodge ★★★★
Self Catering
Harbour Holidays
t (01841) 533402
e contact@harbourholidays.co.uk
w harbourholidays.co.uk

Market Square Holiday Apartments ★★★–★★★★
Self Catering
Contact: Mrs Higgins
t (01208) 813379
e msh@padstow.com
w padstow.com

Maypole Cottages
★★★–★★★★ *Self Catering*
Harbour Holidays
t (01841) 533402
e contact@harbourholidays.co.uk
w harbourholidays.co.uk

Mena-Gwins ★★★★
Self Catering
Cornish Horizons Holiday Cottages
t (01841) 533331
e cottages@cornishhorizons.co.uk
w cornishhorizons.co.uk

Merrymeet ★★★★
Self Catering
Contact: Ms Nicky Stanley
Harbour Holidays
t (01841) 533402
e admin@harbourholidays.co.uk
w harbourholidays.co.uk

Mevagh ★★★★ *Self Catering*
Harbour Holidays
t (01841) 533402
e contact@harbourholidays.co.uk
w harbourholidays.co.uk

Middle Street Apartments
★★★ *Self Catering*
Contact: Mrs Joan Hull
t (01841) 533545
e jim@jwhull.fsnet.co.uk

Miss Mopsy's ★★★★★
Self Catering
Harbour Holidays
t (01841) 533402
e contact@harbourholidays.co.uk
w harbourholidays.co.uk

The Old Bakery ★★★★
Self Catering
Contact: Mr Tippett
t (01841) 532885
e tonytwprops@aol.com
w twproperties.co.uk

The Old Coach House ★★★
Self Catering
Harbour Holidays
t (01841) 533402
e contact@harbourholidays.co.uk
w harbourholidays.co.uk

Ossmill Cottage ★★★
Self Catering
Cornish Horizons Holiday Cottages
t (01841) 533331
e cottages@cornishhorizons.co.uk
w cornishhorizons.co.uk

Overcliff ★★★ *Self Catering*
Contact: Mr Hammond
t (01858) 545386

Pebble Cottage ★★★★
Self Catering
Harbour Holidays
t (01841) 533402
e contact@harbourholidays.co.uk
w harbourholidays.co.uk

Pebbles Cottage ★★★
Self Catering
Contact: Mrs Gill Burgess
t (01841) 532633
e info@padstowcottagecompany.co.uk
w padstowcottagecompany.co.uk

Penlyn ★★★★ *Self Catering*
Harbour Holidays
t (01841) 533402
e contact@harbourholidays.co.uk
w harbourholidays.co.uk

Pensers ★★★★ *Self Catering*
Harbour Holidays
t (01841) 533402
e contact@harbourholidays.co.uk
w harbourholidays.co.uk

Pentyre House, 1, 2, 4 & 5
★★★★ *Self Catering*
Cornish Horizons Holiday Cottages
t (01841) 533331
e cottages@cornishhorizons.co.uk
w cornishhorizons.co.uk

Periwinkle Cottage ★★★
Self Catering
Contact: Mrs Debbie Barnes
t (01841) 533838
e mail@padstowholidaycottage.co.uk
w padstowholidaycottage.co.uk

Perriwinkle ★★★
Self Catering
Cornish Horizons Holiday Cottages
t (01841) 533331
e cottages@cornishhorizons.co.uk
w cornishhorizons.co.uk

Pinmill Cottage ★★★
Self Catering
Harbour Holidays
t (01841) 533402
e contact@harbourholidays.co.uk
w harbourholidays.co.uk

Pippits ★★★ *Self Catering*
Harbour Holidays
t (01841) 533402
e contact@harbourholidays.co.uk
w harbourholidays.co.uk

Polbrea ★★★★ *Self Catering*
Harbour Holidays
t (01841) 533402
e contact@harbourholidays.co.uk
w harbourholidays.co.uk

Portloe ★★ *Self Catering*
Harbour Holidays
t (01841) 533402
e contact@harbourholidays.co.uk
w harbourholidays.co.uk

Primrose House ★★★★
Self Catering
Cornish Horizons Holiday Cottages
t (01841) 533331
e cottages@cornishhorizons.co.uk
w cornishhorizons.co.uk

Puffin Cottage ★★★
Self Catering
Harbour Holidays
t (01841) 533402
e contact@harbourholidays.co.uk
w harbourholidays.co.uk

Puffins ★★★★ *Self Catering*
Cornish Horizons Holiday Cottages
t (01841) 533331
e cottages@cornishhorizons.co.uk
w cornishhorizons.co.uk

Quayside Cottage ★★★
Self Catering
Contact: Mrs Andrea Richards
t (01841) 532429
e andrearichards@btinternet.com
w stayinpadstow.co.uk

Raleigh Cottage ★★★★
Self Catering
Contact: Mrs Gill Burgess
t (01841) 532633
e info@padstowcottagecompany.co.uk
w padstowcottagecompany.co.uk

Retallack Resort and Spa
★★★★★ *Self Catering*
Contact: Miranda Waldron
t (01637) 881580
e miranda@retellackresort.com
w retallackresort.com

Rhetts ★★★ *Self Catering*
Harbour Holidays
t (01841) 533402
e contact@harbourholidays.co.uk
w harbourholidays.co.uk

Rockview ★★★★
Self Catering
Harbour Holidays
t (01841) 533402
e contact@harbourholidays.co.uk
w harbourholidays.co.uk

Rose Cottage ★★★
Self Catering
Harbour Holidays
t (01841) 533402
e contact@harbourholidays.co.uk
w harbourholidays.co.uk

Rosehill Cottage ★★★
Self Catering
Harbour Holidays
t (01841) 533402
e contact@harbourholidays.co.uk
w harbourholidays.co.uk

Sable Cottage & Chiff Chaff
★★★ *Self Catering*
Contact: Mrs Daw
t (0117) 907 9348
e denisedaw@blueyonder.co.uk
w sablecottage.co.uk

Sail Loft ★★ *Self Catering*
Harbour Holidays
t (01841) 533402
e contact@harbourholidays.co.uk
w harbourholidays.co.uk

St Edmund's Cottage
★★★★ *Self Catering*
Contact: Ms Pauline Meredith
t (01841) 532554
e pauline.london@btinternet.com

Sandbanks ★★★★
Self Catering
Contact: Alyson & Gary Heath
t (024) 7667 2504
e gheath@hiaint.com
w crw.co.uk/holidays

Sarahs Lane 8 ★★★★
Self Catering
Cornish Horizons Holiday Cottages
t (01841) 533331
e cottages@cornishhorizons.co.uk
w cornishhorizons.co.uk

The School House ★★★★
Self Catering
Contact: Mr & Mrs Wilson
The School House Padstow
t (01208) 812640
e holidayat.theschoolhouse@virgin.net

Seagulls Cottage ★★★
Self Catering
Contact: Mr David Whitehead
t (01480) 213961
e evie.thomas@hotmail.co.uk
w padstowcottagecompany.co.uk

Seal Cottage ★★★
Self Catering
Harbour Holidays
t (01841) 533402
e contact@harbourholidays.co.uk
w harbourholidays.co.uk

Serendipity ★★★
Self Catering
Harbour Holidays
t (01841) 533402
e contact@harbourholidays.co.uk
w harbourholidays.co.uk

Shore Lodge ★★★
Self Catering
Harbour Holidays
t (01841) 533402
e contact@harbourholidays.co.uk
w harbourholidays.co.uk

The Slate House ★★★
Self Catering
Harbour Holidays
t (01841) 533402
e contact@harbourholidays.co.uk
w harbourholidays.co.uk

Squirrels ★★★ *Self Catering*
Cornish Horizons Holiday Cottages
t (01841) 533331
e cottages@cornishhorizons.co.uk
w cornishhorizons.co.uk

Stable Cottage ★★★★
Self Catering
Contact: Mrs Hagley
t (01841) 532874
e info@padstowcottages.co.uk
w padstowcottages.co.uk

Stella Maris ★★★
Self Catering
Contact: Mrs Linda Green
t (01841) 533592
e lesnlinda@hotmail.co.uk
w padstowholidayhouse.com

Stone Cottage ★★
Self Catering
Contact: Mr Richardson
Stone Cottage – Padstow
t (01923) 226218
e james.richardson@u-psud.fr

The Strand ★★★
Self Catering
Contact: Mrs Brown
t (01208) 821611
e info@strandpadstow.co.uk
w strandpadstow.co.uk

Summer Court ★★★★
Self Catering
Contact: Mr Whitehead
t (0113) 286 0036
e john@summercourt.info
w summercourt.info

Sunbeam Cottage Self Catering ★★★★
Self Catering
Contact: Miss Wendy Gidlow
t (01841) 533447
e wendy@wgidlow.fsnet.co.uk
w sunbeam-cottage.co.uk

Sundance ★★★ *Self Catering*
Harbour Holidays
t (01841) 533402
e contact@harbourholidays.co.uk
w harbourholidays.co.uk

Sunday Cottage & School Cottage **★★★★ *Self Catering***
Contact: Mrs Diane Hoe
Lower Cottage
t (01789) 450214
e mail@sundaycottage.co.uk
w sundaycottage.co.uk

Sunnyhill Cottage ★★★★
Self Catering
Harbour Holidays
t (01841) 533402
e contact@harbourholidays.co.uk
w harbourholidays.co.uk

Sunrise Cottage
Rating Applied For
Self Catering
Contact: Mrs Ann Walker
t (01384) 221295

T Sandt ★★★ *Self Catering*
Cornish Horizons Holiday Cottages
t (01841) 533331
e cottages@cornishhorizons.co.uk
w cornishhorizons.co.uk

Teal ★★ *Self Catering*
Harbour Holidays
t (01841) 533402
e contact@harbourholidays.co.uk
w harbourholidays.co.uk

Teazers ★★★ *Self Catering*
Harbour Holidays
t (01841) 533402
e contact@harbourholidays.co.uk
w harbourholidays.co.uk

Tides ★★★★ *Self Catering*
Cornish Horizons Holiday Cottages
t (01841) 533331
e cottages@cornishhorizons.co.uk
w cornishhorizons.co.uk

Tregenza ★★★ *Self Catering*
Harbour Holidays
t (01841) 533402
e contact@harbourholidays.co.uk
w harbourholidays.co.uk

Tregirls ★★★–★★★★
Self Catering
Contact: Mrs Watson Smyth
t (01841) 532648
e watson.smyth@farmline.com
w padstowfarmfoods.biz

Trelawney ★★★
Self Catering
Contact: Mrs Gill Burgess
t (01841) 532633
e info@padstowcottagecompany.co.uk
w padstowcottagecompany.co.uk

Trevorrick Farm Cottages
★★★★ *Self Catering*
Contact: Mrs Benwell
t (01841) 540574
e info@trevorrick.co.uk
w trevorrick.co.uk

White Horses ★★★★
Self Catering
Harbour Holidays
t (01841) 533402
e contact@harbourholidays.co.uk
w harbourholidays.co.uk

Yellow Sands Apartments & House ★★★–★★★★
Self Catering
Contact: Mr Dakin
t (01841) 520376
e martin@yellowsands.fsnet.co.uk
w yellowsands.net

Yellow Sands Cottages
★★★–★★★★ *Self Catering*
Contact: Mrs Sharon Keast
t (01637) 881548
e yellowsands@btinternet.com
w yellowsands.co.uk

PAIGNTON
Devon

1 Belvedere ★★★★
Self Catering
Blue Chip Vacations
t (01803) 855282
e info@bluechipvacations.com
w bluechipvacations.com

1 Marine Court ★★★★
Self Catering
Blue Chip Vacations
t (01803) 855282
e info@bluechipvacations.com
w bluechipvacations.com

1 Roundham Heights
★★★★ *Self Catering*
Blue Chip Vacations
t (01803) 855282
e info@bluechipvacations.com
w bluechipvacations.com

1 Vista Apartments ★★★★
Self Catering
Blue Chip Vacations
t (01803) 855282
e info@bluechipvacations.com
w bluechipvacations.com

Look out for establishments participating in the National Accessible Scheme

10 Sunhill Apts ★★★★
Self Catering
Blue Chip Vacations
t (01803) 855282
e info@bluechipvacations.com
w bluechipvacations.com

10 Vista Apartments ★★★★
Self Catering
Blue Chip Vacations
t (01803) 855282
e info@bluechipvacations.com
w bluechipvacations.com

11 Sunhill Apts ★★★★
Self Catering
Blue Chip Vacations
t (01803) 855282
e info@bluechipvacations.com
w bluechipvacations.com

14 Vista Apartments ★★★★
Self Catering
Blue Chip Vacations
t (01803) 855282
e info@bluechipvacations.com
w bluechipvacations.com

15 Belvedere Court ★★★★
Self Catering
Blue Chip Vacations
t (01803) 855282
e info@bluechipvacations.com
w bluechipvacations.com

16 Belvedere Court ★★★★
Self Catering
Blue Chip Vacations
t (01803) 855282
e info@bluechipvacations.com
w bluechipvacations.com

17 Belvedere Court ★★★★
Self Catering
Blue Chip Vacations
t (01803) 855282
e info@bluechipvacations.com
w bluechipvacations.com

18 Belvedere Court ★★★★
Self Catering
Blue Chip Vacations
t (01803) 855282
e info@bluechipvacations.com
w bluechipvacations.com

19 Esplanade Court ★★★
Self Catering
Blue Chip Vacations
t (01803) 855282
e info@bluechipvacations.com
w bluechipvacations.com

19 Tor Sands ★★★★
Self Catering
Blue Chip Vacations
t (01803) 855282
e info@bluechipvacations.com
w bluechipvacations.com

2 Carlton Manor ★★★★
Self Catering
Blue Chip Vacations
t (01803) 855282
e info@bluechipvacations.com
w bluechipvacations.com

20 Belvedere Apartment
★★★★ *Self Catering*
Blue Chip Vacations
t (01803) 855282
e info@bluechipvacations.com
w bluechipvacations.com

20 Tor Sands, Paignton
★★★★ *Self Catering*
Blue Chip Vacations
t (01803) 855282
e info@bluechipvacations.com
w bluechipvacations.com

24 Esplanade Court ★★★
Self Catering
Blue Chip Vacations
t (01803) 855282
e info@bluechipvacations.com
w bluechipvacations.com

26 New Esplanade Court
★★★ *Self Catering*
Contact: Mr Baron Elliott
t (01803) 528078
e bazzy_elliott@hotmail.com

3 Roundham Heights
★★★★ *Self Catering*
Blue Chip Vacations
t (01803) 855282
e info@bluechipvacations.com
w bluechipvacations.com

3 Vista Apartments ★★★★
Self Catering
Blue Chip Vacations
t (01803) 855282
e info@bluechipvacations.com
w bluechipvacations.com

31 Esplanade Court ★★★★
Self Catering
Blue Chip Vacations
t (01803) 855282
e info@bluechipvacations.com
w bluechipvacations.com

38 Esplanade Court ★★★
Self Catering
Blue Chip Vacations
t (01803) 855282
e info@bluechipvacations.com
w bluechipvacations.com

4 Belvedere Court ★★★★★
Self Catering
Blue Chip Vacations
t (01803) 855282
e info@bluechipvacations.com
w bluechipvacations.com

5 Carlton Manor ★★★★
Self Catering
Blue Chip Vacations
t (01803) 855282
e info@bluechipvacations.com
w bluechipvacations.com

50 Esplanade Court ★★★
Self Catering
Blue Chip Vacations
t (01803) 855282
e info@bluechipvacations.com
w bluechipvacations.com

6 Carlton Manor ★★
Self Catering
Blue Chip Vacations
t (01803) 855282
e info@bluechipvacations.com
w bluechipvacations.com

6 Vista Apartments ★★★★
Self Catering
Blue Chip Vacations
t (01803) 855282
e info@bluechipvacations.com
w bluechipvacations.com

7 Roundham Heights
★★★★★ *Self Catering*
Blue Chip Vacations
t (01803) 855282
e info@bluechipvacations.com
w bluechipvacations.com

8 Belvedere Court ★★★★
Self Catering
Blue Chip Vacations
t (01803) 855282
e info@bluechipvacations.com
w bluechipvacations.com

8 Vista Apartments ★★★★
Self Catering
Blue Chip Vacations
t (01803) 855282
e info@bluechipvacations.com
w bluechipvacations.com

Above Deck ★★★★
Self Catering
Holiday Homes and Cottages South West
t (01803) 299677
e holcotts@aol.com
w swcottages.co.uk

Acacia Holiday Apartments
★★★ *Self Catering*
Contact: Mrs Bertha Bright
t (01803) 554022
w acaciaholidayapartments.co.uk

All Seasons Holiday Apartments ★★★★
Self Catering
Contact: Mr Colin Livesey
t (01803) 552187
e enquiries@allseasonsholidayapartments.co.uk
w allseasonsholidayapartments.co.uk

Alpenrose Holiday Apartments ★★★
Self Catering
Contact: Mrs Margaret Taylor
t (01803) 558430
e alpenrose@blueyonder.co.uk
w alpenrose.myby.co.uk

Anglesea House ★★★
Self Catering
Contact: Mr & Miss Tapley
t (01803) 555006
e chubblywood@tiscali.co.uk

Beachside ★★★
Self Catering
Holiday Homes and Cottages South West
t (01803) 299677
e holcotts@aol.com
w swcottages.co.uk

Beachway Holiday Flats ★★
Self Catering
Contact: Mr Edwin Toms
t (01803) 555717

Bedford Holiday Flats ★★★
Self Catering
Contact: Mr & Mrs S Dunster
t (01803) 557737
e info@bedfordholidayflats.co.uk
w bedfordholidayflats.co.uk

Big Tree Holiday Flats ★★★
Self Catering
Contact: Mrs Pam Siddall
t (01803) 559559
e bigtree@talktalkbusiness.net
w bigtreeholidayflats.co.uk

Bosuns Cottage ★★★★
Self Catering
Holiday Homes and Cottages South West
t (01803) 299677
e holcotts@aol.com
w swcottages.co.uk

Broadsands
Rating Applied For
Self Catering
Holiday Homes and Cottages South West
t (01803) 299677
e holcotts@aol.com
w swcottages.co.uk

Broadshade Holiday Flats
★★–★★★ *Self Catering*
Contact: Mr & Mrs John & Dot Barber
t (01803) 559647
w broadshade.com

Camelot
Rating Applied For
Self Catering
Holiday Homes and Cottages South West
t (01803) 299677
e holcotts@aol.com
w swcottages.co.uk

Compton Pool Farm
★★★★★ *Self Catering*
Enjoy England Awards for Excellence Winner
Contact: Mr & Mrs John & Ann Stocks
t (01803) 872241
e enquiries@comptonpool.co.uk
w comptonpool.co.uk

Cove Cottage ★★★
Self Catering
Contact: Mr & Mrs Graham & Lynn Humphries
t (01886) 880217
e covecottagepaignton@talktalk.net
w covecottagepaignton.co.uk

Cranmore Lodge ★★★
Self Catering
Contact: Mr & Mrs David & Lynda McDermott
t (01803) 556278
e cranlodge@btopenworld.com
w cranmorelodge.co.uk

The Daisies ★★★
Self Catering
Holiday Homes and Cottages South West
t (01803) 299677
e holcotts@aol.com
w swcottages.co.uk

Denby House Holiday Apartments ★★★
Self Catering
Contact: Mr & Mrs Brian & Lina Ford
t (01803) 559121
e lina@denbyhouse.co.uk
w denbyhouse.co.uk

Fairsea Holiday Flats
★★–★★★ *Self Catering*
Contact: Mr John Hallett
t (01803) 556903
e lesleyfarrand@amserve.com

Fortescue ★★★ *Self Catering*
Holiday Homes and Cottages South West
t (01803) 299677
e holcotts@aol.com
w swcottages.co.uk

Glencoe Holiday Flats ★★★
Self Catering
Contact: Mrs Patricia Jill Ayles
t (01803) 557727
e info@glencoeapartments.com
w glencoeapartments.com

Grange View One ★★★★
Self Catering
Holiday Homes and Cottages South West
t (01803) 299677
e holcotts@aol.com
w swcottages.co.uk

Grange View Two ★★★★
Self Catering
Holiday Homes and Cottages South West
t (01803) 299677
e holcotts@aol.com
w swcottages.co.uk

H & H Caravans *Approved Caravan Holiday Home*
Contact: Mr Mel Higgs
t (01803) 605320
e hhcaravans@tiscali.co.uk
w handhcaravanstorbay.co.uk

Harbourside Holiday Apartments ★★★
Self Catering
Contact: Mrs Kathleen Quaid
t (01803) 550181
e harbour.side@tiscali.co.uk

Harwin Apartments
★★★-★★★★ *Self Catering*
Contact: Mr & Mrs S Gorman
t (01803) 558771
e harwin@blueyonder.co.uk
w harwinapartments.co.uk

Harwood Lodge ★★★★
Self Catering
Contact: Mr & Mrs Holgate
t (01803) 391538
e denise@harwoodlodge.co.uk
w harwoodlodge.co.uk

Hillside ★★★★ *Self Catering*
Blue Chip Vacations
t (01803) 855282
e info@bluechipvacations.com
w bluechipvacations.com

Hudson's Bay ★★★
Self Catering
Contact: Mr & Mrs Roy Kinder
t (01803) 664455
e enquiries@hudsonsbayholidayapartments.co.uk
w hudsonsbayholidayapartments.co.uk

Julie Court Holiday Apartments ★★★
Self Catering
t (01803) 551012 & (01803) 551463
e info@juliecourt.co.uk
w juliecourt.co.uk

Kimberley Holiday Flats
★★-★★★ *Self Catering*
Contact: Mr Nigel Boon
t (01803) 551576
e nigelboon@sky.com
w kimberleyholidayflats.co.uk

Lott's View ★★★★
Self Catering
Blue Chip Vacations
t (01803) 855282
e info@bluechipvacations.com
w bluechipvacations.com

Monkey Puzzle Lodge ★★★
Self Catering
Holiday Homes and Cottages South West
t (01803) 299677
e holcotts@aol.com
w swcottages.co.uk

Newbarn Farm Cottages
★★★★ *Self Catering*
Contact: Mr & Ms Soley
t (01803) 553602
e info@newbarnfarm.com
w newbarnfarm.com

One Braeside Mews, Paignton ★★★★★
Self Catering
Blue Chip Vacations
t (01803) 855282
e info@bluechipvacations.com
w bluechipvacations.com

Orchard View ★★★★
Self Catering
Blue Chip Vacations
t (01803) 855282
e info@bluechipvacations.com
w bluechipvacations.com

Pier View
Rating Applied For
Self Catering
Holiday Homes and Cottages South West
t (01803) 299677
e holcotts@aol.com
w swcottages.co.uk

Preston Down ★★★
Self Catering
Holiday Homes and Cottages South West
t (01803) 299677
e holcotts@aol.com
w swcottages.co.uk

Primley ★★★ *Self Catering*
Holiday Homes and Cottages South West
t (01803) 299677
e holcotts@aol.com
w swcottages.co.uk

Priory Cottages ★★★★
Self Catering
Blue Chip Vacations
t (01803) 855282
e info@bluechipvacations.com
w bluechipvacations.com

Riviera Caravans *Approved Caravan Holiday Home*
Contact: Mr & Mrs Hogger
t (01756) 601762

St Mary Mead ★★★★
Self Catering
Holiday Homes and Cottages South West
t (01803) 299677
e holcotts@aol.com
w swcottages.co.uk

San Remo Holiday Apartments ★★★
Self Catering
Contact: Mr & Mrs Christopher & Elizabeth Hannant
t (01803) 550293
e sanremo@f2s.com
w sanremopaignton.co.uk

Sandmoor Holiday Apartments ★★★
Self Catering
Contact: Mr & Mrs Rita & Brian Ellis
t (01803) 525909
e sandmoors@yahoo.co.uk
w sandmoorholidayapartments.co.uk

Sandpiper – South West Cottages ★★★★
Self Catering
Holiday Homes and Cottages South West
t (01803) 299677
e holcotts@aol.com
w swcottages.co.uk

Sea View ★★★ *Self Catering*
Holiday Homes and Cottages South West
t (01803) 299677
e holcotts@aol.com
w swcottages.co.uk

Singers Bay View ★★★
Self Catering
Holiday Homes and Cottages South West
t (01803) 299677
e holcotts@aol.com
w swcottages.co.uk

Sowenna ★★★ *Self Catering*
Holiday Homes and Cottages South West
t (01803) 299677
e holcotts@aol.com
w swcottages.co.uk

Stanley House ★★★
Self Catering
Contact: Mr & Mrs C & D Baldry
t (01803) 557173
e stanley.baldry@tiscali.co.uk
w stanleyhouseholidayapartments.co.uk

Suncrest ★★★ *Self Catering*
Contact: Mr Neil Carr
t (01803) 665571
e neilcarr@fsmail.net

Sunnybeach Holiday Flats
★★-★★★ *Self Catering*
Contact: Mr & Mrs David & Jane Schaedll
t (01803) 558729
e j.shadell@btconnect.com
w sunny-beach.co.uk

Torbay Berkeley Hotel ★★
Self Catering
Contact: Mr Booth
t (01803) 558226
e enquries@thm.co.uk
w torbayberkeleyhotel.co.uk

Torbay Caravans *Approved Caravan Holiday Home*
Contact: Mr & Mrs Colin & Mair Thomas
t (01685) 849193
e mycol_@hotmail.com
w torbaycaravans.co.uk

Tregarth Holiday Flats ★★
Self Catering
Contact: Mr Barry Haskins
t (01803) 558458
e tregarthpaignton@aol.com
w tregarthpaignton.co.uk

Woodland Park ★★★★
Self Catering
Holiday Homes and Cottages South West
t (01803) 299677
e holcotts@aol.com
w swcottages.co.uk

PANCRASWEEK
Devon

Woodland View ★★★★
Self Catering
Contact: Mrs Alison Parmley
t (01288) 381423
e alison@elmparkfarm.co.uk
w elmparkfarm.co.uk

PAR
Cornwall

Hidden Valley Gardens
★★★★ *Self Catering*
t (01208) 873225
w hiddenvalleygardens.co.uk

Kilhallon Court Cottage
★★★★★ *Self Catering*
Contact: Anna Wright
t (01726) 813320
e victoria@highlandcourt.co.uk
w highlandcourt.co.uk

Oceanblue Holidays
Rating Applied For
Self Catering
Contact: Mrs Suzanne Skerry
t (01872) 572602

PARKEND
Gloucestershire

The Barracks ★★★
Self Catering
Contact: Rachel Capon
t 07824 555805
e rachel_capon2@hotmail.com

PARRACOMBE
Devon

Dunbar Cottage ★★★
Self Catering
Marsdens Cottage Holidays
t (01271) 813777
e holidays@marsdens.co.uk
w marsdens.co.uk

Little Barn ★★★★
Self Catering
Marsdens Cottage Holidays
t (01271) 813777
e holidays@marsdens.co.uk
w marsdens.co.uk

The Swallows ★★★★★
Self Catering
Marsdens Cottage Holidays
t (01271) 813777
e holidays@marsdens.co.uk
w marsdens.co.uk

Woodcote ★★★★
Self Catering
Marsdens Cottage Holidays
t (01271) 813777
e holidays@marsdens.co.uk
w marsdens.co.uk

PAULTON
Somerset

2 Newtown Chapel ★★★★
Self Catering
t (01761) 417986

PAXFORD
Gloucestershire

Fox Cottage ★★★★
Self Catering
Campden Cottages
t (01386) 593315
e info@campdencottages.co.uk
w campdencottages.co.uk

PAYTON
Somerset

Little Owl Barn ★★★★
Self Catering
Contact: Mr & Mrs A Brodie
t (01823) 660602
e holidays@paytonfarm.com
w paytonfarm.com

PEASEDOWN ST JOHN
Somerset

The Orangery ★★★★
Self Catering
Hideaways
t (01747) 828170
e enq@hideaways.co.uk
w hideaways.co.uk

PELYNT
Cornwall

Cartole Cottages
★★★-★★★★ *Self Catering*
Contact: Mr & Mrs Taylor
t (01503) 220956
e info@cartole.co.uk
w cartole.co.uk

Tower Lodge ★★★
Self Catering
Cornish Collection Ltd
t (01503) 262736
e enquiries@cornishcollections.co.uk
w cornishcollection.co.uk

Tremaine Green Country Cottages ★★★ *Self Catering*
Contact: Mr Spreckley
t (01503) 220333
e stay@tremaine-green.co.uk
w tremainegreen.co.uk

PENDEEN
Cornwall

Merthyr Farm Cottages
★★★ *Self Catering*
Contact: Mrs Susan Wilson
t (01769) 573335
e merthyrfarmcottages@hotmail.com
w merthyrfarmcottages.co.uk

Trewellard Manor Farm Cottages ★★★★
Self Catering
Contact: Mrs Marion Bailey
t (01736) 788526
e marionbbailey@hotmail.com
w trewellardmanor.co.uk

PENDOGGETT
Cornwall

Mays Cottage ★★★★★
Self Catering
Contact: Mrs Julia Payne
t (01823) 432615
e enquiries@scarletgreen.com

PENHALLOW
Cornwall

2 White House ★★★
Self Catering
Around Kernow Holidays
t (01872) 571575
e info@ak-hols.co.uk
w ak-hols.co.uk

Crowji Sorn ★★★
Self Catering
Around Kernow Holidays
t (01872) 571575
e info@ak-hols.co.uk
w ak-hols.co.uk

PENRYN
Cornwall

1 Tresooth Court ★★★★
Self Catering
Cornish Holiday Cottages
t (01326) 250339
e emily@cornishholidaycottages.net
w cornishholidaycottages.net

Anchor Loft ★★★★★
Self Catering
Cornish Holiday Cottages
t (01326) 250339
e emily@cornishholidaycottages.net
w cornishholidaycottages.net

Bell Cottage ★★★
Self Catering
Contact: Mrs Penny Snow
t (01326) 376466
e alpensnow@clara.co.uk

Pampaluna ★★ *Self Catering*
Contact: Mr & Mrs Lawrence
t (01326) 373203
e pat-bern@tinyworld.co.uk

PENSFORD
Somerset

Leigh Farm ★ *Self Catering*
Contact: Mrs Smart
t (01761) 490281

Park Farm Country Cottages
★★★★ *Self Catering*
Contact: Mr & Mrs Gary & Fiona Sweet
t (01275) 833350

PENTEWAN
Cornwall

The Old Inn ★★★
Self Catering
t (01937) 580217
w inncornwall.com

Seabarn ★★★★
Self Catering
Blue Chip Vacations
t (01803) 855282
e info@bluechipvacations.com
w bluechipvacations.com

PENZANCE
Cornwall

57 Daniel Place ★★
Self Catering
Contact: Mrs Michell
t (01720) 422409
e lensylv@care-4free.net

Boscrowan Farm ★★★★★
Self Catering
Contact: Mrs Elizabeth Harris
t (01736) 332396
e elizabeth@boscrowan.co.uk
w boscrowan.co.uk

Boskennal Farm ★★★★
Self Catering
Contact: Mrs Beryl Richards
t (01736) 740293
e alan@boskennal.fsnet.co.uk
w boskennalbarns.com

Chy Nessa ★★★
Self Catering
Contact: Mrs Shirley Keene
t (01736) 366697
e chynessa@netscape.net
w chynessa.co.uk

Chyandaunce and Chyancrowse (Gulval Cottages) ★★★ *Self Catering*
Contact: Mrs Joan Sampson
t (01242) 232769
e tjwsampson@aol.com
w gulvalcottages.co.uk

Country View ★★★
Self Catering
Contact: Mr & Mrs Tony Wright
t (01354) 638282
e tony@wright113.freeserve.co.uk
w wright113.freeserve.co.uk

Crankan Flat ★★★
Self Catering
Contact: Mr & Mrs Braybrooks
t (01736) 351388

Cresta House ★★★★
Self Catering
Contact: Mrs Samantha Wardman
t (01736) 333144
e info@crestahouse-cornwall.co.uk
w crestahouse-cornwall.co.uk

Ivy Cottage ★★★
Self Catering
Contact: Mr Barry Chadwick
t (01736) 332540
e pirate15@totalise.co.uk
w ivycottage.174.com

Kymaurah Cottages ★★★★
Self Catering
Contact: Mr & Mrs Philip & Zoe Manley
t (01736) 732266
e zoeanphil@aol.com
w 2lamorna.co.uk

Old Court 36, Kenegie Manor, Gulval ★★
Self Catering
Contact: Mrs Margaret Lewis
t (01902) 845139
e margellen@googlemail.com
w kenegie.com

The Old Farmhouse & The Granary ★★★★★
Self Catering
Contact: Mrs Vivienne Hall
t (01736) 810516
e halls@chegwiddenfarm.com
w chegwiddenfarm.com

Penzance Seafront Cottage
★★★ *Self Catering*
Contact: Mrs Blewett
t (01736) 361741

Rospannel Farm ★★★
Self Catering
Contact: Mrs Rosemary Hocking
t (01736) 810262
e gbernard@v21.me.uk
w rospannel.com

Saddle Cottage ★★★★
Self Catering
Contact: Mr Philip Ward
t (01736) 763815
e phil@forward.supanet.com

St Anthonys Cottage ★★★
Self Catering
Contact: Mrs Christine Feiler
t (01736) 359000
e christine.feiler@virgin.net

Spindrift ★★★★
Self Catering
Contact: Mrs F A Morgan
t (01467) 629597
e pjcmorgan@hotmail.com

Wharf Apartments ★★★★
Self Catering
Contact: Mrs Penny O'Neill
t (01736) 366888 & (01736) 332315
e info@wharfapartments.com
w wharfapartments.com

PERRANARWORTHAL
Cornwall

Devichoys Farmhouse
★★★★★ *Self Catering*
Cornish Holiday Cottages
t (01326) 250339
e emily@cornishholidaycottages.net
w cornishholidaycottages.net

Granny's Farmhouse
★★★★★ *Self Catering*
Contact: Mrs Rhiannon Fraser
t (01872) 863724
e grannysfarmhouse@cosawes.com
w grannysfarmhouse.co.uk

PERRANCOOMBE
Cornwall

Grey Roofs ★★★
Self Catering
Duchy Holidays
t (01872) 572971
e enquiries@duchyholidays.co.uk
w duchyholidays.co.uk

PERRANPORTH
Cornwall

12 Penvenen ★★★
Self Catering
Duchy Holidays
t (01872) 572971
e enquiries@duchyholidays.co.uk
w duchyholidays.co.uk

14 Wheal Ramoth ★★★
Self Catering
Duchy Holidays
t (01872) 572971
e enquiries@duchyholidays.co.uk
w duchyholidays.co.uk

15 Wheal Ramoth ★★★
Self Catering
Duchy Holidays
t (01872) 572971
e enquiries@duchyholidays.co.uk
w duchyholidays.co.uk

2 Lower Hill Crest ★★★★★
Self Catering
Contact: Mr & Mrs Williams
t (01872) 862573
e fiveatuplands@aol.co.uk

2 Wheal Ramoth ★★★
Self Catering
Duchy Holidays
t (01872) 572971
e enquiries@duchyholidays.co.uk
w duchyholidays.co.uk

45 St Pirans Apartment ★★
Self Catering
Duchy Holidays
t (01872) 572971
e enquiries@duchyholidays.co.uk
w duchyholidays.co.uk

6 St Pirans Apartment ★★
Self Catering
Duchy Holidays
t (01872) 572971
e enquiries@duchyholidays.co.uk
w duchyholidays.co.uk

7 Penhale
Rating Applied For
Self Catering
Around Kernow Holidays
t (01872) 571575
e info@ak-hols.co.uk
w ak-hols.co.uk

73 Perran Sands ★★★
Self Catering
Around Kernow Holidays
t (01872) 571575
e info@ak-hols.co.uk
w ak-hols.co.uk

74 Perran Sands ★★★
Self Catering
Around Kernow Holidays
t (01872) 571575
e info@ak-hols.co.uk
w ak-hols.co.uk

Amberley ★★★ *Self Catering*
Duchy Holidays
t (01872) 572971
e enquiries@duchyholidays.co.uk
w duchyholidays.co.uk

Beach View ★★★
Self Catering
Duchy Holidays
t (01872) 572971
e enquiries@duchyholidays.co.uk
w duchyholidays.co.uk

Chy Kerensa ★★
Self Catering
Duchy Holidays
t (01872) 572971
e enquiries@duchyholidays.co.uk
w duchyholidays.co.uk

Collyn ★★ *Self Catering*
Around Kernow Holidays
t (01872) 571575
e info@ak-hols.co.uk
w ak-hols.co.uk

Conifers ★★★★
Self Catering
Duchy Holidays
t (01872) 572971
e enquiries@duchyholidays.co.uk
w duchyholidays.co.uk

Cregaminnis ★★★
Self Catering
Duchy Holidays
t (01872) 572971
e enquiries@duchyholidays.co.uk
w duchyholidays.co.uk

Droskyn Castle 12 ★★★
Self Catering
Duchy Holidays
t (01872) 572971
e enquiries@duchyholidays.co.uk
w duchyholidays.co.uk

Fishermans Cottage ★★★
Self Catering
Duchy Holidays
t (01872) 572971
e enquiries@duchyholidays.co.uk
w duchyholidays.co.uk

Milly May
Rating Applied For
Self Catering
Around Kernow Holidays
t (01872) 571575
e info@ak-hols.co.uk
w ak-hols.co.uk

Pemberley ★★★
Self Catering
Duchy Holidays
t (01872) 572971
e enquiries@duchyholidays.co.uk
w duchyholidays.co.uk

Penhale 1 ★★★ *Self Catering*
Duchy Holidays
t (01872) 572971
e enquiries@duchyholidays.co.uk
w duchyholidays.co.uk

Penhale 3 ★★★ *Self Catering*
Duchy Holidays
t (01872) 572971
e enquiries@duchyholidays.co.uk
w duchyholidays.co.uk

Penhale Villa ★★★★
Self Catering
Contact: Mrs Lauretta Wrighte lauretta@btconnect.com
w cornwall-breaks.co.uk

Rock View ★★★
Self Catering
Duchy Holidays
t (01872) 572971
e enquiries@duchyholidays.co.uk
w duchyholidays.co.uk

The Rosery ★★★
Self Catering
Duchy Holidays
t (01872) 572971
e enquiries@duchyholidays.co.uk
w duchyholidays.co.uk

Seabreaze ★★★
Self Catering
Duchy Holidays
t (01872) 572971
e enquiries@duchyholidays.co.uk
w duchyholidays.co.uk

Seathrift ★★★ *Self Catering*
Duchy Holidays
t (01872) 572971
e enquiries@duchyholidays.co.uk
w duchyholidays.co.uk

Seaview (Liskey Hill) ★★★
Self Catering
Duchy Holidays
t (01872) 572971
e enquiries@duchyholidays.co.uk
w duchyholidays.co.uk

Smugglers ★★ *Self Catering*
Duchy Holidays
t (01872) 572971
e enquiries@duchyholidays.co.uk
w duchyholidays.co.uk

Strand House Apartment
★★★ *Self Catering*
Around Kernow Holidays
t (01872) 571575
e info@ak-hols.co.uk
w ak-hols.co.uk

Trenwith ★★★★
Self Catering
Around Kernow Holidays
t (01872) 571575
e info@ak-hols.co.uk
w ak-hols.co.uk

Trerice Holiday Barn No 1
★★★★ *Self Catering*
Duchy Holidays
t (01872) 572971
e enquiries@duchyholidays.co.uk
w duchyholidays.co.uk

Trerice Holiday Barn No 2
★★★★ *Self Catering*
Duchy Holidays
t (01872) 572971
e enquiries@duchyholidays.co.uk
w duchyholidays.co.uk

Trerice Holiday Barn No 3
★★★★ *Self Catering*
Duchy Holidays
t (01872) 572971
e enquiries@duchyholidays.co.uk
w duchyholidays.co.uk

Treth Cottage ★★★★
Self Catering
Contact: Mr & Mrs John & Jenny Cuthill
Claremont
t (01872) 573624

Ventonvaise 3 ★★★
Self Catering
Duchy Holidays
t (01872) 572971
e enquiries@duchyholidays.co.uk
w duchyholidays.co.uk

Wheal Ramoth 12 ★★★
Self Catering
Duchy Holidays
t (01872) 572971
e enquiries@duchyholidays.co.uk
w duchyholidays.co.uk

PERRANWELL STATION
Cornwall

Lymington Snug ★★★★
Self Catering
Special Places in Cornwall
t (01872) 864400
e office@specialplacescornwall.co.uk
w specialplacescornwall.co.uk

Postbox Cottage ★★★★
Self Catering
Special Places in Cornwall
t (01872) 864400
e office@specialplacescornwall.co.uk
w specialplacescornwall.co.uk

Woodpeckers ★★★
Self Catering
Special Places in Cornwall
t (01872) 864400
e office@specialplacescornwall.co.uk
w specialplacescornwall.co.uk

PERRANZABULOE
Cornwall

9 White House Court
★★★★ *Self Catering*
Duchy Holidays
t (01872) 572971
e enquiries@duchyholidays.co.uk
w duchyholidays.co.uk

PETROCKSTOW
Devon

Off The Beaten Track
★★★★ *Self Catering*
Contact: Mrs Ruth Kelsey
t (01837) 811762
e kelsey.kelsey@btconnect.com
w off-the-beaten-track.co.uk

PHILLACK
Cornwall

Beach View House ★★★★
Self Catering
Golds Coastal Holidays
t (01543) 274424
e enquiries@golds-hire.co.uk
w golds-hire.co.uk

Chymoresk ★★★★★
Self Catering
Golds Coastal Holidays
t (01543) 274424
e enquiries@golds-hire.co.uk
w golds-hire.co.uk

Elova ★★★ *Self Catering & Serviced Apartments*
Contact: Mrs Terrill
Elova F71
t (01209) 612214

Greenduke & Saltair ★★★
Self Catering
t (01209) 716535

Morryp ★★★★ *Self Catering*
Contact: Mr David Jolly
t (01209) 719770
e enquiries@rivieresunsetholidays.com
w rivieresunsetholidays.com

Toms Holidays
Rating Applied For
Chalet
Contact: Mr & Mrs Downton
t (01736) 753010
e sales@tomsholidays.co.uk

PHILLEIGH
Cornwall

Bos Eglos ★★★★
Self Catering
Portscatho Holidays
t (01326) 270900
e info@portscathoholidays.co.uk
w portscathoholidays.co.uk

Lemon Chapel Cottage
★★★ *Self Catering*
Portscatho Holidays
t (01326) 270900
e info@portscathoholidays.co.uk
w portscathoholidays.co.uk

PILLATON Cornwall

Kernock Cottages ★★★★
Self Catering
Contact: Mr Hugh Bailey
t (01579) 350435
e hughbeth@kernockcottages.com

Upalong & Downalong
★★★★ *Self Catering*
Contact: Mr & Mrs Barnicoat
t (01579) 350141
e trefenten@beeb.net
w trefenten.co.uk

PILTON Somerset

Shire Cottage & Cider Barn
★★★★ *Self Catering*
Contact: Mrs Holly Corfield
t (01749) 890107
e info@bournefarmcottages.co.uk
w bournefarmcottages.co.uk

PLYMOUTH Devon

28 Century Quay
Rating Applied For
Self Catering
Blue Chip Vacations
t (01803) 855282
e info@bluechipvacations.com
w bluechipvacations.com

Barbican Base ★★★★
Self Catering
Contact: Mr Matthew Treglown
t 07825 277811
e mtreglown@hotmail.com
w plymouthholidays.co.uk

Haddington House Apartments ★★★
Self Catering
Contact: Mr Fairfax Luxmoore
t (01752) 500383
w abudd.co.uk

Hoe Lodge ★★ *Self Catering*
Contact: Mr T Miller
Hoe Apartments
t (01489) 557797
e info@hoe-apartments.co.uk
w hoe-apartments.co.uk

Traine Farm Cottages
★★★★ *Self Catering*
Contact: Mrs Sheila Rowland
t (01752) 862264
e traine.cottages@btopenworld.com
w traine-holiday-cottages.co.uk

POLBATHIC Cornwall

Higher Tredis Farm ★★
Self Catering
Contact: Mrs Cindy Rice
t (01503) 230184
e cindyrice@btopenworld.com
w cornishfarmholidays.com

POLPERRO Cornwall

Classy Cottages ★★★★★
Self Catering
Contact: Mr & Mrs Nicolle
t 07000 423000 & 07000 423000
e nicole@classycottages.co.uk
w classycottages.co.uk

Crumplehorn Cottages
★★★–★★★★ *Self Catering*
Contact: Mr & Mrs Collings
t (01503) 262523
e enquiries@crumplehorncottages.co.uk
w crumplehorncottages.co.uk

East Cliff Cottage ★★★
Self Catering
Contact: Mrs Ruth Puckey
t (01503) 272324

Landaviddy Manor
★★★–★★★★ *Self Catering*
Contact: Mr & Mrs Derx
t (01752) 812812
e annyaderx@hotmail.com
w legendholidays.co.uk

Lucys ★★★★ *Self Catering*
Contact: Mrs Leftly
t (01503) 272271
e info@leftly.com
w polperrocottages.com

Polhaven ★★★★
Self Catering
Contact: Mr Warner
t (01453) 832491
e polhaven@btinternet.com

POLRUAN Cornwall

Tommys ★★★ *Self Catering*
Contact: Mrs Sheila Mary Walter
t (01305) 871246
e enquiries@tommys-polruan.co.uk
w tommys-polruan.co.uk

POLZEATH Cornwall

14 Westward Flats ★★★
Self Catering
Rock Holidays
t (01208) 863399
e info@rockholidays.co.uk
w rockholidays.co.uk

Chough – 5 Polzeath Gardens ★★★★
Self Catering
Rock Holidays
t (01208) 863399
e info@rockholidays.co.uk
w rockholidays.co.uk

Garden Flat ★★ *Self Catering*
Rock Holidays
t (01208) 863399
e info@rockholidays.co.uk
w rockholidays.co.uk

Godolphin House ★★★★
Self Catering
Rock Holidays
t (01208) 863399
e info@rockholidays.co.uk
w rockholidays.co.uk

Honeysuckle Hill ★★★★★
Self Catering
Contact: Mrs Carolyn Crutcher
t (01306) 631568
e carrie@crutchersfarm.freeserve.co.uk
w honeysucklehill.co.uk

Jalouise ★★★★ *Self Catering*
Rock Holidays
t (01208) 863399
e info@rockholidays.co.uk
w rockholidays.co.uk

Jay – 2 Garden Bungalows
★★★ *Self Catering*
Rock Holidays
t (01208) 863399
e info@rockholidays.co.uk
w rockholidays.co.uk

Manna Place ★★★★
Self Catering
Contact: Mrs Ann Jones
t (01208) 863258
e anniepolzeath@hotmail.com
w mannaplace.co.uk

Marford Flat ★★★★
Self Catering
Rock Holidays
t (01208) 863399
e info@rockholidays.co.uk
w rockholidays.co.uk

Marmarra ★★★ *Self Catering*
Rock Holidays
t (01208) 863399
e info@rockholidays.co.uk
w rockholidays.co.uk

Palm Trees ★★★★
Self Catering
Rock Holidays
t (01208) 863399
e info@rockholidays.co.uk
w rockholidays.co.uk

Pentire Flat ★★ *Self Catering*
Rock Holidays
t (01208) 863399
e info@rockholidays.co.uk
w rockholidays.co.uk

The Point ★★★★★
Self Catering
Rock Holidays
t (01208) 863399
e info@rockholidays.co.uk
w rockholidays.co.uk

Polbilly ★★★★★
Self Catering
Contact: Mr Richard Jones
t (01208) 863397
e swseeds@tiscali.co.uk
w cornwall-online.co.uk

Polmeor & Trehenlie ★★★
Self Catering
Contact: Mrs Angwin
t (01208) 726847 & (01208) 75243
e sangwin@tiscali.co.uk

Robin – 1 Garden Bungalows ★★★
Self Catering
Rock Holidays
t (01208) 863399
e info@rockholidays.co.uk
w rockholidays.co.uk

Stonechat & Pendragon
★★★ *Self Catering*
Contact: Mrs Smith
t (01208) 863172
e info@polzeathcottages.com
w polzeathcottages.com

Tides Reach & Waves End
★★★★ *Self Catering*
Contact: Zoe Leese
t 07717 222574
e zoom@leese.org
w polzeathholidaycottages.co.uk

Trehanoo House & Bungalow Annexe, Polzeath
★★★ *Self Catering*
Contact: Ms Kate Buckingham
t (01672) 541120
e katebuckingham@waitrose.com

Trehenlie, Polzeath ★★★
Self Catering
Contact: Mrs June Angwin
t (01208) 75243
e steve@angwin.fsnet.co.uk

Trelevan ★★ *Self Catering*
Rock Holidays
t (01208) 863399
e info@rockholidays.co.uk
w rockholidays.co.uk

Tywardale Cottage Polzeath
★★★ *Self Catering*
Contact: Mr & Mrs Swann
t (01208) 862721
e sheilaandgeoff@sky.com

White Rose ★★★
Self Catering
Contact: Mrs Corinne Lee
t (01208) 862070

PONSANOOTH Cornwall

Gadles Farm Cottages
★★★★ *Self Catering*
Contact: Mr Trevor Howe
t (01872) 863214
e info@gadlesfarmholidays.co.uk
w gadlesfarmholidays.co.uk

Whispers Holiday Apartment ★★★
Self Catering
Contact: Ms Linda Croxford-Turner
t (01872) 863904
e linda@whispersofcornwall.co.uk
w whispersofcornwall.co.uk

POOLE Dorset

1 Dolphin Quays ★★★★★
Self Catering
Quay Holidays
t (01202) 683333
e stay@quayholidays.co.uk
w quayholidays.co.uk

16 Lander Close ★★★★
Self Catering
Quay Holidays
t (01202) 683333
e stay@quayholidays.co.uk
w quayholidays.co.uk

1 Murre House
Rating Applied For
Self Catering
Quay Holidays
t (01202) 683333
e stay@quayholidays.co.uk
w quayholidays.co.uk

14 Lander Close
Rating Applied For
Self Catering
Quay Holidays
t (01202) 683333
e stay@quayholidays.co.uk
w quayholidays.co.uk

17 Broomhill Way
Rating Applied For
Self Catering
Quay Holidays
t (01202) 683333
e stay@quayholidays.co.uk
w quayholidays.co.uk

21 Stone Close
Rating Applied For
Self Catering
Quay Holidays
t (01202) 683333
e stay@quayholidays.co.uk
w quayholidays.co.uk

30 Harbour Reach ★★★★★
Self Catering
Quay Holidays
t (01202) 683333
e stay@quayholidays.co.uk
w quayholidays.co.uk

32 Dolphin Quays ★★★★★
Self Catering
Quay Holidays
t (01202) 683333
e stay@quayholidays.co.uk
w quayholidays.co.uk

35 Harbour Reach ★★★★★
Self Catering
Quay Holidays
t (01202) 683333
e stay@quayholidays.co.uk
w quayholidays.co.uk

36 Catalina Drive ★★★
Self Catering
Quay Holidays
t (01202) 683333
e stay@quayholidays.co.uk
w quayholidays.co.uk

36 Harbour Reach ★★★★★
Self Catering
Quay Holidays
t (01202) 683333
e stay@quayholidays.co.uk
w quayholidays.co.uk

38 Dolphin Quays ★★★★
Self Catering
Quay Holidays
t (01202) 683333
e stay@quayholidays.co.uk
w quayholidays.co.uk

4 Gosling Close ★★★★
Self Catering
Lyme Bay Holidays
t (01297) 443363
e email@lymebayholidays.co.uk
w lymebayholidays.co.uk

42 Dolphin Quays ★★★★
Self Catering
Quay Holidays
t (01202) 683333
e stay@quayholidays.co.uk
w quayholidays.co.uk

43 Vallis Close ★★★
Self Catering
Contact: Miss Cheryl Pilley
t (01784) 452563
w pooleholidays.com

45 Dolphin Quays
Rating Applied For
Self Catering
Quay Holidays
t (01202) 683333
e stay@quayholidays.co.uk
w quayholidays.co.uk

48 Cataline Drive ★★★
Self Catering
Quay Holidays
t (01202) 683333
e stay@quayholidays.co.uk
w quayholidays.co.uk

5 Dolphin Quays ★★★★★
Self Catering
Quay Holidays
t (01202) 683333
e stay@quayholidays.co.uk
w quayholidays.co.uk

5 Rowes Warehouse ★★★★
Self Catering
Quay Holidays
t (01202) 683333
e stay@quayholidays.co.uk
w quayholidays.co.uk

51 Salterns Point ★★★★
Self Catering
Quay Holidays
t (01202) 683333
e stay@quayholidays.co.uk
w quayholidays.co.uk

52 Dolphin Quays ★★★★★
Self Catering
Quay Holidays
t (01202) 683333
e stay@quayholidays.co.uk
w quayholidays.co.uk

53 Dolphins Quay ★★★★★
Self Catering
Quay Holidays
t (01202) 683333
e stay@quayholidays.co.uk
w quayholidays.co.uk

6 Dolphin Quays ★★★★
Self Catering
Quay Holidays
t (01202) 683333
e stay@quayholidays.co.uk
w quayholidays.co.uk

6 Mirage ★★★★★
Self Catering
Quay Holidays
t (01202) 683333
e stay@quayholidays.co.uk
w quayholidays.co.uk

60 Dolphin Quays ★★★★
Self Catering
Quay Holidays
t (01202) 683333
e stay@quayholidays.co.uk
w quayholidays.co.uk

61 Dolphin Quays ★★★★★
Self Catering
Quay Holidays
t (01202) 683333
e stay@quayholidays.co.uk
w quayholidays.co.uk

68 Dolphin Quays ★★★★★
Self Catering
Quay Holidays
t (01202) 683333
e stay@quayholidays.co.uk
w quayholidays.co.uk

73 Dolphin Quays
Rating Applied For
Self Catering
Quay Holidays
t (01202) 683333
e stay@quayholidays.co.uk
w quayholidays.co.uk

76 Aqua
Rating Applied For
Self Catering
Quay Holidays
t (01202) 683333
e stay@quayholidays.co.uk
w quayholidays.co.uk

8 Aqua ★★★★ *Self Catering*
Quay Holidays
t (01202) 683333
e stay@quayholidays.co.uk
w quayholidays.co.uk

8 Dolphin Quays ★★★★★
Self Catering
Quay Holidays
t (01202) 683333
e stay@quayholidays.co.uk
w quayholidays.co.uk

84 Dolpins Quays ★★★★★
Self Catering
Quay Holidays
t (01202) 683333
e stay@quayholidays.co.uk
w quayholidays.co.uk

89 Dolphin Quays ★★★★★
Self Catering
Quay Holidays
t (01202) 683333
e stay@quayholidays.co.uk
w quayholidays.co.uk

90 Dolphin Quays
Rating Applied For
Self Catering
Quay Holidays
t (01202) 683333
e stay@quayholidays.co.uk
w quayholidays.co.uk

Amberley ★★★ *Self Catering*
Contact: Mrs Angela Miles
t (020) 8643 5226
e amberley@lycos.co.uk
w harboursideholiday.co.uk

Baiter Park ★★★★
Self Catering
Contact: Mr David King
t (01929) 471087
e david.king@gbpltd.co.uk
w dorsetholidaylets.co.uk

Corfe View ★★★★
Self Catering
Contact: Mr Simon Gillingham
t (020) 8886 6445
e simon@corfeview.co.uk
w corfeview.co.uk

Dolphin Cottage ★★★
Self Catering
Contact: Mrs Jean Redsell
t (01322) 271848
e p.redsell@btopenworld.com

The Dorset Resort, Hyde
★★★★★ *Self Catering*
Contact: Miss Jackie Langworthy
t (01929) 472244
e resort@dorsetresort.com
w dorsetresort.com

The Egret – Harbourside Park (Baiter) ★★★
Self Catering
Contact: Mr & Mrs Cocklin
t (01202) 670046

Fisherman's View ★★★
Self Catering
Contact: Mr & Mrs John & Angela Hampton
t (01844) 344102
w poolebreaks.co.uk

Flat 6 Odyssey ★★★★★
Self Catering
Quay Holidays
t (01202) 683333
e stay@quayholidays.co.uk
w quayholidays.co.uk

Fripps Cottage ★★★
Self Catering
Contact: Mrs Helen Edbrooke
Stoneleigh House
t (01202) 884908
e helen@stoneleighhouse.com
w stoneleighhouse.com/frippscottage

Golden Sands Cottage
★★★★ *Self Catering*
Quay Holidays
t (01202) 683333
e stay@quayholidays.co.uk
w quayholidays.co.uk

Harbour Haven ★★★
Self Catering
Contact: Mr Jack Wright
t (01202) 888164
e jack.wright.1@btinternet.com
w harbourhaven.co.uk

Harbour Holidays ★★
Self Catering
Contact: Mrs Beryl Saunders
t (01202) 741637

Harbourside Retreat ★★★
Self Catering
Contact: Mrs Cheryl Pilley
t (01784) 452563
e email@pooleholidays.com
w pooleholidays.com

High Street ★★★
Self Catering
Quay Holidays
t (01202) 683333
e stay@quayholidays.co.uk
w quayholidays.co.uk

Isis House ★★★★
Self Catering
Contact: Mrs Helen Chablis
t (01202) 683333
e stay@quayholidays.co.uk
w quayholidays.co.uk

Lake View Apartments
★★★ *Self Catering*
Contact: Mr & Mrs Frederick & Angela Kingsley
t (01202) 463912
e fkings12@yahoo.co.uk

Penguin Cottage ★★★
Self Catering
Contact: Mrs Christina Harris
t (01202) 462485
e penguin.cottage@ntlworld.com

Poole Harbour Holiday Homes ★★★ *Self Catering*
Contact: Miss Brown
Poole Harbour Holidays
t 07778 586710 & (01202) 743614
e stay@pooleharbourholidays.com
w pooleharbourholidays.com

Poole Quay Holiday Flat
★★★★ *Self Catering*
Contact: Miss Manta Paterson
t 07977 457036
e holidayflat@poolequay.com
w poolequay.com/holidayflat

Quayside ★★★★
Self Catering
t (01202) 666711
w baiter.holidays.btinternet.co.uk

Quayside Close Holiday Apartments ★★★
Self Catering
Contact: Mr & Mrs David & Susan Ellison
t (01202) 764107
e quaysideclose@aol.com
w quaysidecloseapartments.co.uk

Sea Escape
Rating Applied For
Self Catering
Contact: Ms Caroline Palmer
t (01202) 622632
e cw.palmer@ntlworld.com

Sea Haven ★★★
Self Catering
Contact: Mrs Hayley Copley
t (01202) 669469
e seahaven58@aol.com
w sea-haven.co.uk

Sunnydale ★★★
Self Catering
Contact: Mr Ian Hull
t 07880 501940
e ianhpoole@btinternet.com

Tavener's Reach ★★★
Self Catering
Contact: Mrs Helen Chablis
t (01202) 683333
e stay@quayholidays.co.uk
w pooleharbourholidays.co.uk

POOLE KEYNES
Gloucestershire

Isis Cottage ★★★★
Self Catering
Contact: Mrs Vittoria Thornley
t (01285) 861303
e victoria@kemblemill.com
w kemblemill.com

Old Mill Cottages ★★★★
Self Catering
Contact: Mrs Catherine Hazell
t (01285) 821255
e catherine@oldmillcottages.fsnet.co.uk
w oldmillcottages.co.uk

The Old Stables ★★★★
Self Catering
Contact: Mr & Mrs John & Jane Hiscock
t (01285) 770271
e churchfarmholidays@hotmail.co.uk
w churchfarmholidays.co.uk

PORLOCK
Somerset

Chapel Knap Accommodation ★★★★★
Self Catering
Contact: Mrs Caroline Lister
t (01643) 862364
e chapelknap@hotmail.com
w chapelknap.co.uk

Green Chantry, Porlock
★★★★ *Self Catering*
Contact: Mrs Margaret Payton
t (01823) 698330 & 07860 135848
e maggie_payton@hotmail.com

Hartshanger Exmoor Holidays ★★★★
Self Catering
Contact: Mrs Anna Edward
t (01643) 862700
e hartshanger@lineone.net
w hartshanger.com

Orchard Cottage ★★★
Self Catering
Contact: Mrs Diana Williams
t (01643) 862383

Redway ★★★★ *Self Catering*
Marsdens Cottage Holidays
t (01271) 813777
e holidays@marsdens.co.uk
w marsdens.co.uk

Seapoint ★★★★
Self Catering
Contact: Mr Stephen Fitzgerald
t (01643) 862289
e fitzgerald@seapoint.co.uk
w seapoint.co.uk

Stag Cottage ★★★★
Self Catering
Marsdens Cottage Holidays
t (01271) 813777
e holidays@marsdens.co.uk
w marsdens.co.uk

Tanglewood ★★★★
Self Catering
Contact: Ms Glynis Heymer
t (01643) 863340
e info@tanglewoodporlock.com
w tanglewoodporlock.co.uk

The Watermill ★★★★
Self Catering
Contact: Mr & Mrs John & Diane Ames
t (01474) 879810
e john.ames1@btinternet.com
w thewatermillporlock.com

Woodside Cottage ★★
Self Catering
Contact: Mr & Mrs T Lawrence
t (01934) 732978
e woodside_cottage@hotmail.com
w woodsidecottage.biz

PORT GAVERNE
Cornwall

Carn-Awn ★★★★
Self Catering
Contact: Mrs Sandy May
t (01208) 880716
e orcades@mays364.wanadoo.co.uk
w carn-awn.co.uk

Green Door Cottages
★★★★ *Self Catering*
t (01208) 880293
e enquiries@greendoorcottages.co.uk
w greendoorcottages.co.uk

PORT ISAAC
Cornwall

Back House ★★★★
Self Catering
Harbour Holidays
t (01841) 533402
e contact@harbourholidays.co.uk
w harbourholidays.co.uk

Bay View ★★★★
Self Catering
Cornish Seaview Cottages
t (01428) 723819
e enquiries@cornishseaviewcottages.co.uk
w cornishseaviewcottages.co.uk

Driftwood ★★★★
Self Catering
Contact: Mrs Elizabeth Mewton
t (01208) 880550
e elizabeth.mewton@btinternet.com

Edwarma Cottage ★★★★
Self Catering
Rock Holidays
t (01208) 863399
e info@rockholidays.co.uk
w rockholidays.co.uk

Flat 3 The Old Bakehouse
★★★★ *Self Catering*
Contact: Nicky Stanley
t (01841) 532402
e contact@harbourholidays.co.uk
w harbourholidays.co.uk

Homer Park ★★★
Self Catering
Rock Holidays
t (01208) 863399
e info@rockholidays.co.uk
w rockholidays.co.uk

Little Sark ★★★
Self Catering
Cornish Seaview Cottages
t (01428) 723819
e enquiries@cornishseaviewcottages.co.uk
w cornishseaviewcottages.co.uk

Locarno Port Isaac
★★★-★★★★★ *Self Catering*
Contact: Mrs Daisy Hicks
t (01208) 880268
e daisyhicks@supanet.com

Oyster Bay ★★★★
Self Catering
Rock Holidays
t (01208) 863399
e info@rockholidays.co.uk
w rockholidays.co.uk

Rockpools ★★★
Self Catering
Harbour Holidays
t (01841) 533402
e contact@harbourholidays.co.uk
w harbourholidays.co.uk

Sea Holly Cottage ★★★★
Self Catering
Contact: Mrs Hayley Farrelly
t (01494) 890065
e hayley.farrelly@btconnect.com
w portisaacholidaycottage.co.uk

Spindrift ★★★ *Self Catering*
Rock Holidays
t (01208) 863399
e info@rockholidays.co.uk
w rockholidays.co.uk

Trevathan Farm ★★★★
Self Catering
Contact: Mrs Jo Symons
t (01208) 880248
e symons@trevathanfarm.com
w trevathanfarm.com

The White House ★★★
Self Catering
Contact: Dr Anthony Hambly
Bodrean Manor
t (01872) 264400
e anthonyhambly@hotmail.com

PORT PENDENNIS
Cornwall

The Anchorage ★★★★
Self Catering
Contact: Mrs Haselden
t (0151) 480 6747
e theanchorage@orange.net
w theanchorage-online.co.uk

PORTESHAM
Dorset

Sleepers ★★★ *Self Catering*
Contact: Miss Brenda Parker
t (01308) 897232
e gorselands@ukonline.co.uk
w gorselands-uk.com

PORTH
Cornwall

2 Seashore Apartment
★★★★ *Self Catering*
Blue Chip Vacations
t (01803) 855282
e info@bluechipvacations.com
w bluechipvacations.com

4 Seashore Apartment
★★★★ *Self Catering*
Blue Chip Vacations
t (01803) 855282
e info@bluechipvacations.com
w bluechipvacations.com

Quay House, Seashore
★★★★ *Self Catering*
Blue Chip Vacations
t (01803) 855282
e info@bluechipvacations.com
w bluechipvacations.com

PORTHCOTHAN
Cornwall

10 Tregella Farm ★★★★
Self Catering
Harbour Holidays
t (01841) 533402
e contact@harbourholidays.co.uk
w harbourholidays.co.uk

Gull Cottage ★★★
Self Catering
Harbour Holidays
t (01841) 533402
e contact@harbourholidays.co.uk
w harbourholidays.co.uk

Porthcothan House
★★★★★ *Self Catering*
Cornish Horizons Holiday Cottages
t (01841) 533331
e cottages@cornishhorizons.co.uk
w cornishhorizons.co.uk

PORTHCURNO
Cornwall

First and Last – Stargazey, Porthcurno ★★★★
Self Catering
Contact: Mrs Liz Trenary
t (01736) 871284
e info@firstandlastcottages.co.uk
w firstandlastcottages.co.uk

Heatherlands, Porthcurno
★★★ *Self Catering*
Contact: Mr Robin Newell
t (01273) 400153
e info@heatherlandscornwall.com
w heatherlandscornwall.com

PORTHLEVEN
Cornwall

Anchor Cottage ★★★★★
Self Catering
Niche Retreats
t (01209) 861745
e jackie@nicheretreats.co.uk
w nicheretreats.co.uk

Blue Dolphin ★★★★
Self Catering
Niche Retreats
t (01209) 861745
e jackie@nicheretreats.co.uk
w nicheretreats.co.uk

Chapel Dawns ★★★★
Self Catering
Niche Retreats
t (01209) 861745
e jackie@nicheretreats.co.uk
w nicheretreats.co.uk

Chy Kensa & Chiva-Som
★★★★ *Self Catering*
t (01326) 563198
w cornishhideaways.co.uk

Cliff House ★★★★
Self Catering
Niche Retreats
t (01209) 861745
e jackie@nicheretreats.co.uk
w nicheretreats.co.uk

Dai Mar
Rating Applied For
Self Catering
Contact: Mrs Gillian Oxford
t (020) 8445 0090
e gilloxford@yahoo.co.uk

Meadowside ★★★★
Self Catering
Contact: Mr & Mrs Orchard
t (01326) 572928

Morgolok ★★★★
Self Catering
Niche Retreats
t (01209) 861745
e jackie@nicheretreats.co.uk
w nicheretreats.co.uk

Mounts Bay ★★★★★
Self Catering
Niche Retreats
t (01209) 861745
e jackie@nicheretreats.co.uk
w nicheretreats.co.uk

Niche Retreats ★★★★
Self Catering
t (01209) 861745
e jackie@nicheretreats.co.uk
w nicheretreats.co.uk

Ocean View ★★★★
Self Catering
Niche Retreats
t (01209) 861745
e jackie@nicheretreats.co.uk
w nicheretreats.co.uk

Porthcressa ★★★★
Self Catering
Contact: Mrs Barbara Arthur
t (01326) 574487
e porthcressa@orange.net

Porthleven Harbour & Dock Company ★★★–★★★★
Self Catering
Contact: Mrs Tisdale
t (01326) 574270
e kathy-phd@btconnect.com
w porthlevenholidaycottages.co.uk

St Elvans ★★★★
Self Catering
Niche Retreats
t (01209) 861745
e jackie@nicheretreats.co.uk
w nicheretreats.co.uk

Sea Breezes House
★★★★–★★★★★
Self Catering
t (01326) 563198
w abovebeachcottages.co.uk

Sea Cottage ★★★★
Self Catering
Contact: Mrs Janice Benney
t (01326) 563198
e seacottage@sandpebbles.com
w cornishhideaways.co.uk

W Oliver Allen & Sons
★★–★★★ *Self Catering*
Contact: Mr Paul Allen
t (01326) 562222
e paul@porth-leven.com
w porth-leven.com

PORTHPEAN
Cornwall

Treburthick House ★★★
Self Catering
Contact: Mrs Sarah Lawson
t (020) 7402 3296
e sarahlawson@iol.ie
w cornwallseaside.co.uk

PORTHTOWAN
Cornwall

Atlantic View Apartment, Porthtowan ★★★
Self Catering
Contact: Mr & Mrs Angove
t 07745 177654
e robertangove@btconnect.com
w cornwallapartment.co.uk

Ocean Breeze ★★
Self Catering
Duchy Holidays
t (01872) 572971
e enquiries@duchyholidays.co.uk
w duchyholidays.co.uk

Old Basset Cottage ★★★★
Self Catering
Contact: Mr Garrick Furr
t (01209) 890334
e kfurr@whealbasset.fsnet.co.uk
w geocities.com

Polvenna ★★★ *Self Catering*
Contact: Mrs Claire Smethurst
t (0117) 974 4882
e clairesandmichaels@hotmail.com

Rosehill Lodges ★★★★★
Self Catering
Contact: Mr John Barrow
t (01209) 891920
e reception@rosehilllodges.com
w rosehilllodges.com

Sea Echoes ★★★
Self Catering
Around Kernow Holidays
t (01872) 571575
e info@ak-hols.co.uk
w ak-hols.co.uk

Stones Throw ★★
Self Catering
Duchy Holidays
t (01872) 572971
e enquiries@duchyholidays.co.uk
w duchyholidays.co.uk

Whispering Waves 18 ★★★
Self Catering
Duchy Holidays
t (01872) 572971
e enquiries@duchyholidays.co.uk
w duchyholidays.co.uk

Whispering Waves 20 ★★★
Self Catering
Duchy Holidays
t (01872) 572971
e enquiries@duchyholidays.co.uk
w duchyholidays.co.uk

PORTLAND
Dorset

Alpen Rose ★★★★
Self Catering
Dream Cottages
t (01305) 789000
e admin@dream-cottages.co.uk
w dream-cottages.co.uk

The Belenes ★★★★
Self Catering
Dream Cottages
t (01305) 789000
e admin@dream-cottages.co.uk
w dream-cottages.co.uk

Breeze Cottage ★★★★
Self Catering
Dream Cottages
t (01305) 789000
e admin@dream-cottages.co.uk
w dream-cottages.co.uk

Cove Cottage ★★★★
Self Catering
Contact: Mrs Helen Wilson
t (01305) 824161
e helenportland@hotmail.com
w portlandholiday.co.uk

Cozi Cottage ★★★
Self Catering
Dream Cottages
t (01305) 789000
e admin@dream-cottages.co.uk
w dream-cottages.co.uk

Inglenook Cottage ★★★
Self Catering
Dream Cottages
t (01305) 789000
e admin@dream-cottages.co.uk
w dream-cottages.co.uk

Lilac Cottage ★★★
Self Catering
Contact: Ms Shelagh Hepple
t (01924) 252522
e hepple@lilaccott171.fs.co.uk
w portlandholiday.co.uk

Little Owl Cottage ★★★
Self Catering
Dream Cottages
t (01305) 789000
e admin@dream-cottages.co.uk
w dream-cottages.co.uk

Old Coastguard Cottage
★★★ *Self Catering*
Contact: Mr John Bunday
t (023) 8086 6421

The Old Higher Lighthouse
★★★★ *Self Catering*
Contact: Mrs Fran Lockyer
t (01305) 822300
e franlockyer@clara.co.uk
w oldhigherlighthouse.com

Polly's Cottage ★★★
Self Catering
Contact: Mr & Mrs Thompson
t (0117) 968 2167
e sarah.mail@blueyonder.co.uk
w portlandholiday.co.uk

Portland Hideaway ★★★★
Self Catering
Contact: Mr H Marshall
t 07957 138054
e howard@bestlimited.co.uk

Portland Holiday Home
★★★ *Self Catering*
Contact: Mrs Amanda Jones
t (01305) 861044
e mandy1311.jones@virgin.net

Portland Retreat ★★★★
Self Catering
Contact: Mr H Marshall
t 07957 138054
e howard@bestlimited.co.uk

Primrose Cottage ★★
Self Catering
Contact: Mrs Elaine Taylor
t (01305) 780640
e ejtaylor2@tiscali.co.uk
w primrosecottageportland.co.uk

Quarries Reach ★★★★
Self Catering
Dream Cottages
t (01305) 789000
e admin@dream-cottages.co.uk
w dream-cottages.co.uk

Sunset Cottage ★★★★
Self Catering
Dream Cottages
t (01305) 789000
e admin@dream-cottages.co.uk
w dream-cottages.co.uk

Westcliff ★★★★
Self Catering
Dream Cottages
t (01305) 789000
e admin@dream-cottages.co.uk
w dream-cottages.co.uk

PORTLOE Cornwall

8 Coast ★★ *Self Catering*
Contact: Mrs Mary Twiss
t (01404) 812858

Beach Hill Cottage
★★-★★★ *Self Catering*
Roseland Holiday Cottages
t (01872) 580480
e enquiries@roselandholidaycottages.co.uk
w roselandholidaycottages.co.uk

Chapel House
Rating Applied For
Self Catering
Portscatho Holidays
t (01326) 270900
e info@portscathoholidays.co.uk
w portscathoholidays.co.uk

Cove Cottage ★★★
Self Catering
Roseland Holiday Cottages
t (01872) 580480
e enquiries@roselandholidaycottages.co.uk
w roselandholidaycottages.co.uk

Dolphin Cottage ★★★
Self Catering
Roseland Holiday Cottages
t (01872) 580480
e enquiries@roselandholidaycottages.co.uk
w roselandholidaycottages.co.uk

Farm Cottage ★★★
Self Catering
Roseland Holiday Cottages
t (01872) 580480
e enquiries@roselandholidaycottages.co.uk
w roselandholidaycottages.co.uk

Gull Rock Cottage ★★★★
Self Catering
Roseland Holiday Cottages
t (01872) 580480
e enquiries@roselandholidaycottages.co.uk
w roselandholidaycottages.co.uk

Heartsease ★★★★
Self Catering
Roseland Holiday Cottages
t (01872) 580480
e enquiries@roselandholidaycottages.co.uk
w roselandholidaycottages.co.uk

Mara ★★★★ *Self Catering*
Roseland Holiday Cottages
t (01872) 580480
e enquiries@roselandholidaycottages.co.uk
w roselandholidaycottages.co.uk

Ocean View ★★★
Self Catering
Roseland Holiday Cottages
t (01872) 580480
e enquiries@roselandholidaycottages.co.uk
w roselandholidaycottages.co.uk

Puckey Hill ★★★★
Self Catering
Roseland Holiday Cottages
t (01872) 580480
e enquiries@roselandholidaycottages.co.uk
w roselandholidaycottages.co.uk

Trehaven View ★★★★
Self Catering
Contact: Mr & Mrs Mlynski
t (01872) 501824
e julie.mlynski@virgin.net
w cottageguide.co.uk/trehaven

PORTREATH Cornwall

Ayshe ★★★ *Self Catering*
Holiday Homes and Cottages South West
t (01803) 299677
e holcotts@aol.com
w swcottages.co.uk

Bassets Acre ★★★
Self Catering
Contact: Mr & Mrs Christ
t (01209) 842367
e bassetsacre@freenet.co.uk
w bassetsacre.co.uk

Cornish Harbourside Holidays ★★★-★★★★
Self Catering
t (01209) 820089
w cornish-harbourside-holidays.co.uk/ctb.asp

Cornwall Holiday Homes
★★★ *Self Catering*
Contact: Mrs Cousins
t (01209) 715358
e cwllholidayhomes@talk21.com
w cornwall-holidayhomes.co.uk

The Gatehouse ★★★
Self Catering
Contact: Mr & Mrs Hamer
t (01209) 843218
e rhhjb@aol.com

Gulls Roost ★★★★★
Self Catering
Golds Coastal Holidays
t (01543) 274424
e enquiries@golds-hire.co.uk
w golds-hire.co.uk

Harbour Retreat ★★★
Self Catering
Around Kernow Holidays
t (01872) 571575
e info@ak-hols.co.uk
w ak-hols.co.uk

Higher Laity Farm ★★★★★
Self Catering
Contact: Mrs Lynne Drew
t (01209) 842317
e info@higherlaityfarm.co.uk
w higherlaityfarm.co.uk

The Moorings ★★★
Self Catering
Powells Cottage Holidays
t (01834) 812791
e info@powells.co.uk
w powells.co.uk

The Moorings ★★★
Self Catering
Contact: Mr Michael Coles
t (01208) 880224
e mikesgscoles@aol.com
w gaverneholidays.co.uk

Sea Spray ★★★★
Self Catering
Golds Coastal Holidays
t (01543) 274424
e enquiries@golds-hire.co.uk
w golds-hire.co.uk

Trengove Farm Cottages
★★★-★★★★★
Self Catering
Contact: Mrs Richards
t (01209) 843008
e richards@farming.co.uk
w trengovefarm.co.uk

PORTSCATHO Cornwall

10 Wellington Terrace ★★★
Self Catering
Roseland Holiday Cottages
t (01872) 580480
e enquiries@roselandholidaycottages.co.uk
w roselandholidaycottages.co.uk

14 The Square ★★★
Self Catering
Portscatho Holidays
t (01326) 270900
e info@portscathoholidays.co.uk
w portscathoholidays.co.uk

2 Old School Cottages
★★★★ *Self Catering*
Roseland Holiday Cottages
t (01872) 580480
e enquiries@roselandholidaycottages.co.uk
w roselandholidaycottages.co.uk

3 Jubliee Place ★★★
Self Catering
Portscatho Holidays
t (01326) 270900
e info@portscathoholidays.co.uk
w portscathoholidays.co.uk

3 Shute Meadow ★★★★
Self Catering
Roseland Holiday Cottages
t (01872) 580480
e enquiries@roselandholidaycottages.co.uk
w roselandholidaycottages.co.uk

4 Jubilee Place ★★★★
Self Catering
Contact: Mrs Pat Willins
t (01562) 822161
e derek@willins.fsbusiness.co.uk
w roselandcottage.co.uk

5 Harbour Court ★★★
Self Catering
Portscatho Holidays
t (01326) 270900
e info@portscathoholidays.co.uk
w portscathoholidays.co.uk

9 Wellington Terrace ★★★
Self Catering
Roseland Holiday Cottages
t (01872) 580480
e enquiries@roselandholidaycottages.co.uk
w roselandholidaycottages.co.uk

Alicias Barn ★★★★
Self Catering
Roseland Holiday Cottages
t (01872) 580480
e enquiries@roselandholidaycottages.co.uk
w roselandholidaycottages.co.uk

Antigua ★★★ *Self Catering*
Roseland Holiday Cottages
t (01872) 580480
e enquiries@roselandholidaycottages.co.uk
w roselandholidaycottages.co.uk

Apsley's Cottage ★★★
Self Catering
Portscatho Holidays
t (01326) 270900
e info@portscathoholidays.co.uk
w portscathoholidays.co.uk

Bermuda Cottage ★★★
Self Catering
Portscatho Holidays
t (01326) 270900
e info@portscathoholidays.co.uk
w portscathoholidays.co.uk

The Boathouse ★★★
Self Catering
Portscatho Holidays
t (01326) 270900
e info@portscathoholidays.co.uk
w portscathoholidays.co.uk

Carrick Lodge ★★★
Self Catering
Portscatho Holidays
t (01326) 270900
e info@portscathoholidays.co.uk
w portscathoholidays.co.uk

Chick Cottage & The Beach House ★★★★ *Self Catering*
Roseland Holiday Cottages
t (01872) 580480
e enquiries@roselandholidaycottages.co.uk
w roselandholidaycottages.co.uk

Chywartha ★★★
Self Catering
Roseland Holiday Cottages
t (01872) 580480
e enquiries@roselandholidaycottages.co.uk
w roselandholidaycottages.co.uk

Coast Cottage ★★★★
Self Catering
Roseland Holiday Cottages
t (01872) 580480
e enquiries@roselandholidaycottages.co.uk
w roselandholidaycottages.co.uk

C-Side ★★★★ *Self Catering*
Roseland Holiday Cottages
t (01872) 580480
e enquiries@roselandholidaycottages.co.uk
w roselandholidaycottages.co.uk

Cuilan ★★★★ *Self Catering*
Roseland Holiday Cottages
t (01872) 580480
e enquiries@roselandholidaycottages.co.uk
w roselandholidaycottages.co.uk

Dormer Cottage & Byways ★★★ *Self Catering*
Roseland Holiday Cottages
t (01872) 580480
e enquiries@roselandholidaycottages.co.uk
w roselandholidaycottages.co.uk

Garden Cottage & Gull Loft ★★★★ *Self Catering*
Roseland Holiday Cottages
t (01872) 580480
e enquiries@roselandholidaycottages.co.uk
w roselandholidaycottages.co.uk

Haloyon ★★★★
Self Catering
Roseland Holiday Cottages
t (01872) 580480
e enquiries@roselandholidaycottages.co.uk
w roselandholidaycottages.co.uk

Hera ★★★★ *Self Catering*
Roseland Holiday Cottages
t (01872) 580480
e enquiries@roselandholidaycottages.co.uk
w roselandholidaycottages.co.uk

High Curgurrell ★★★★
Self Catering
Roseland Holiday Cottages
t (01872) 580480
e enquiries@roselandholidaycottages.co.uk
w roselandholidaycottages.co.uk

Hillside Cottage ★★★
Self Catering
Roseland Holiday Cottages
t (01872) 580480
e enquiries@roselandholidaycottages.co.uk
w roselandholidaycottages.co.uk

Jacaranda Apartment & Bungalow ★★★ *Self Catering*
Roseland Holiday Cottages
t (01872) 580480
e enquiries@roselandholidaycottages.co.uk
w roselandholidaycottages.co.uk

Lan Y Mor ★★★
Self Catering
Portscatho Holidays
t (01326) 270900
e info@portscathoholidays.co.uk
w portscathoholidays.co.uk

Lapwing ★★★ *Self Catering*
Portscatho Holidays
t (01326) 270900
e info@portscathoholidays.co.uk
w portscathoholidays.co.uk

Linhay Cottage ★★★★
Self Catering
Roseland Holiday Cottages
t (01872) 580480
e enquiries@roselandholidaycottages.co.uk
w roselandholidaycottages.co.uk

Lugger End ★★★
Self Catering
Roseland Holiday Cottages
t (01872) 580480
e enquiries@roselandholidaycottages.co.uk
w roselandholidaycottages.co.uk

Maralane ★★★ *Self Catering*
Roseland Holiday Cottages
t (01872) 580480
e enquiries@roselandholidaycottages.co.uk
w roselandholidaycottages.co.uk

Morgwyn ★★★ *Self Catering*
Roseland Holiday Cottages
t (01872) 580480
e enquiries@roselandholidaycottages.co.uk
w roselandholidaycottages.co.uk

Morvast ★★★ *Self Catering*
Special Places in Cornwall
t (01872) 864400
e office@specialplacescornwall.co.uk
w specialplacescornwall.co.uk

Nampara ★★★★
Self Catering
Roseland Holiday Cottages
t (01872) 580480
e enquiries@roselandholidaycottages.co.uk
w roselandholidaycottages.co.uk

Nangwedhen ★★★
Self Catering
Roseland Holiday Cottages
t (01872) 580480
e enquiries@roselandholidaycottages.co.uk
w roselandholidaycottages.co.uk

The Old School House ★★★
Self Catering
Roseland Holiday Cottages
t (01872) 580480
e enquiries@roselandholidaycottages.co.uk
w roselandholidaycottages.co.uk

Opal Cottage ★★★
Self Catering
Roseland Holiday Cottages
t (01872) 580480
e enquiries@roselandholidaycottages.co.uk
w roselandholidaycottages.co.uk

Pengerein ★★★ *Self Catering*
Portscatho Holidays
t (01326) 270900
e info@portscathoholidays.co.uk
w portscathoholidays.co.uk

Pengerrans ★★★★
Self Catering
Roseland Holiday Cottages
t (01872) 580480
e enquiries@roselandholidaycottages.co.uk
w roselandholidaycottages.co.uk

Pollaughan Farm ★★★★-★★★★★
Self Catering
Contact: Mrs Valerie Penny
t (01872) 580150
e pollaughan@yahoo.co.uk
w pollaughan.co.uk

Porthcurnick Lodge ★★★
Self Catering
Roseland Holiday Cottages
t (01872) 580480
e enquiries@roselandholidaycottages.co.uk
w roselandholidaycottages.co.uk

Porthgate
Rating Applied For
Self Catering
Portscatho Holidays
t (01326) 270900
e info@portscathoholidays.co.uk
w portscathoholidays.co.uk

Roseland Lodge ★★★
Self Catering
Roseland Holiday Cottages
t (01872) 580480
e enquiries@roselandholidaycottages.co.uk
w roselandholidaycottages.co.uk

Roses Cottage
Rating Applied For
Self Catering
Portscatho Holidays
t (01326) 270900
e info@portscathoholidays.co.uk
w portscathoholidays.co.uk

Rosteague Farm Cottage ★★★ *Self Catering*
Portscatho Holidays
t (01326) 270900
e info@portscathoholidays.co.uk
w portscathoholidays.co.uk

Rosteague Lodge ★★★
Self Catering
Portscatho Holidays
t (01326) 270900
e info@portscathoholidays.co.uk
w portscathoholidays.co.uk

Scath
Rating Applied For
Self Catering
Portscatho Holidays
t (01326) 270900
e info@portscathoholidays.co.uk
w portscathoholidays.co.uk

Seabreeze ★★★
Self Catering
Roseland Holiday Cottages
t (01872) 580480
e enquiries@roselandholidaycottages.co.uk
w roselandholidaycottages.co.uk

Seacroft ★★★ *Self Catering*
Roseland Holiday Cottages
t (01872) 580480
e enquiries@roselandholidaycottages.co.uk
w roselandholidaycottages.co.uk

Shambles ★★★ *Self Catering*
Roseland Holiday Cottages
t (01872) 580480
e enquiries@roselandholidaycottages.co.uk
w roselandholidaycottages.co.uk

Spindrift ★★★★
Self Catering
Roseland Holiday Cottages
t (01872) 580480
e enquiries@roselandholidaycottages.co.uk
w roselandholidaycottages.co.uk

Sunday House West ★★★★
Self Catering
Roseland Holiday Cottages
t (01872) 580480
e enquiries@roselandholidaycottages.co.uk
w roselandholidaycottages.co.uk

Trevellas
Rating Applied For
Self Catering
Portscatho Holidays
t (01326) 270900
e info@portscathoholidays.co.uk
w portscathoholidays.co.uk

Waterside House ★★★★
Self Catering
Roseland Holiday Cottages
t (01872) 580480
e enquiries@roselandholidaycottages.co.uk
w roselandholidaycottages.co.uk

Wilbury Cottage ★★★
Self Catering
Roseland Holiday Cottages
t (01872) 580480
e enquiries@roselandholidaycottages.co.uk
w roselandholidaycottages.co.uk

PORTWRINKLE Cornwall

Westway ★★★ *Self Catering*
Contact: Mrs Susan Irving
t (020) 8769 7988
e susanirving@btinternet.com
w westwaycottage.co.uk

Whitsand Bay Self Catering
★★★-★★★★ *Self Catering*
Contact: J Earle
Parade House
t (01579) 345688
e enwbsc@hotmail.com
w whitsandbayselfcatering.co.uk

POTTERNE Wiltshire

Stroud Hill Farm Holidays
★★★ *Self Catering*
Contact: Mrs Helen Straker
t (01380) 720371
e helenstraker@aol.com

POUGHILL Cornwall

1 Brightlands Apartments
★★★★ *Self Catering*
Contact: Mrs Justine Sames
t (01296) 747425
e j.l.pearce@tesco.net
w lakeviewrise.co.uk

Columbine Cottage ★★★★
Self Catering
t (01942) 721003
e enquiries@trevalgas-columbine.co.uk
w trevalgas-columbine.co.uk

Trevalgas Farm Cottages
★★★-★★★★ *Self Catering*
Contact: Sally Eccles
t 07976 440659
e stable@trevalgascottages.co.uk
w trevalgascottages.co.uk

POULSHOT Wiltshire

Higher Green Farm Cottages
★★★★ *Self Catering*
Contact: Mrs Eve Curnow
t (01380) 828239
e info@highergreenfarmcottages.com
w highergreenfarmcottages.com

POUNDSGATE Devon

Bramblemoor Cottage
★★★★ *Self Catering*
Contact: Mrs Helen Hull
t (01364) 631410
e helen.hull@eclipse.co.uk
w bramblemoor.fsworld.co.uk

POUNDSTOCK Cornwall

Herds Cottage ★★★
Self Catering
Contact: Ms Doris Toon
t (01288) 361448
e herdscottage@tiscali.co.uk

Penfound Lodge Farm Holiday Cottage ★★★
Self Catering
Contact: Ms Julie Hodgson
t (01288) 355040
e admin@myholidaycottagecornwall.co.uk
w myholidaycottagecornwall.co.uk

PRAA SANDS Cornwall

Clipper Cove ★★★★★
Self Catering
Valley Villas Ltd
t (01752) 605605
e sales@valleyvillas.com
w valleyvillas.co.uk

The Penthouse,Clipper Cove (Praa Sands) ★★★★★
Self Catering
Contact: Mrs Jenny Cruse
The Penthouse, Clipper Cove (Praa Sands)
t (01736) 761838
e cornwall@adventure-sports.co.uk
w adventure-sports.co.uk/cornwall

Sea Meads Holiday Homes
★★★ *Self Catering*
Contact: Ms Pierpoint
Best Leisure
t (01753) 664336
e enquiries@bestleisure.co.uk
w bestleisure.co.uk

PRAZE-AN-BEEBLE Cornwall

Hayloft (At Drym Farm)
★★★★★ *Self Catering*
Contact: Ms Jan Bright
t (01209) 831039
e drymfarm@hotmail.co.uk
w drymfarm.co.uk

PRESTBURY Gloucestershire

Church Court Cottages
★★★★-★★★★★
Self Catering
Contact: Ms Maureen Fardon
t (01242) 573277
e maureen.fardon@tenvig.com
w churchcourtcottages.co.uk

Home Farm Cottages
★★★★ *Self Catering*
Contact: Mr Charles Banwell
t (01242) 583161

PRESTON Dorset

Bella Rosa ★★★
Self Catering
Dream Cottages
t (01305) 789000
e admin@dream-cottages.co.uk
w dream-cottages.co.uk

Fisherbridge Cottage
★★★★ *Self Catering*
Dream Cottages
t (01305) 789000
e admin@dream-cottages.co.uk
w dream-cottages.co.uk

Riverside House ★★★★
Self Catering
Dream Cottages
t (01305) 789000
e admin@dream-cottages.co.uk
w dream-cottages.co.uk

Shingle Cottage ★★★
Self Catering
Dream Cottages
t (01305) 789000
e admin@dream-cottages.co.uk
w dream-cottages.co.uk

PROBUS Cornwall

Coal Harbour Cottage ★★★
Self Catering
Contact: Mrs Lucas
t (01726) 843918
e jill@mpfarm.aquiss.com
w probuscottage.vispa.com

PUDDINGTON Devon

Rose Cottage ★★★
Self Catering
Hideaways
t (01747) 828170
e enq@hideaways.co.uk
w hideaways.co.uk

PUDDLETOWN Dorset

5 The Stables ★★★★
Self Catering
Lyme Bay Holidays
t (01297) 443363
e email@lymebayholidays.co.uk
w lymebayholidays.co.uk

Weatherbury Cottages
★★★★ *Self Catering*
Contact: Mr & Mrs Clive Howes
t (01305) 848358
e enquiries@weatherburycottages.co.uk
w weatherburycottages.co.uk

PUNCKNOWLE Dorset

Berwick Manor, Puncknowle Manor Farmhouse and The Carriage House
★★★★-★★★★★
Self Catering
Contact: Ms Rebecca Hutchings
Puncknowle Manor Cottages
t (01308) 897706
e cottages@pknlest.com
w dorset-selfcatering.co.uk

Prosperous Cottage ★★
Self Catering
Dream Cottages
t (01305) 789000
e admin@dream-cottages.co.uk
w dream-cottages.co.uk

PURSE CAUNDLE Dorset

Orchard Cottage ★★★★
Self Catering
Contact: Mr Charles Perry
t (01295) 811540
e charles@astroh.co.uk
w ruraldorset.co.uk

PUTFORD Devon

Old Teddy House ★★★★
Self Catering
Farm & Cottage Holidays
t (01237) 459827
e enquiries@farmcott.co.uk
w holidaycottages.co.uk

PUTSBOROUGH Devon

Flat 1 Clifton Court ★★★★
Self Catering
Marsdens Cottage Holidays
t (01271) 813777
e holidays@marsdens.co.uk
w marsdens.co.uk

Flat 11 Clifton Court ★★★★
Self Catering
Marsdens Cottage Holidays
t (01271) 813777
e holidays@marsdens.co.uk
w marsdens.co.uk

Flat 18 Clifton Court ★★★★
Self Catering
Marsdens Cottage Holidays
t (01271) 813777
e holidays@marsdens.co.uk
w marsdens.co.uk

Flat 19 Clifton Court ★★★★
Self Catering
Marsdens Cottage Holidays
t (01271) 813777
e holidays@marsdens.co.uk
w marsdens.co.uk

Flat 22 Clifton Court ★★★
Self Catering
Marsdens Cottage Holidays
t (01271) 813777
e holidays@marsdens.co.uk
w marsdens.co.uk

Flat 24 Clifton Court ★★★★
Self Catering
Marsdens Cottage Holidays
t (01271) 813777
e holidays@marsdens.co.uk
w marsdens.co.uk

Flat 27 Clifton Court ★★★★
Self Catering
Marsdens Cottage Holidays
t (01271) 813777
e holidays@marsdens.co.uk
w marsdens.co.uk

Flat 30 Clifton Court ★★★★
Self Catering
Marsdens Cottage Holidays
t (01271) 813777
e holidays@marsdens.co.uk
w marsdens.co.uk

Flat 31 Clifton Court ★★★
Self Catering
Marsdens Cottage Holidays
t (01271) 813777
e holidays@marsdens.co.uk
w marsdens.co.uk

Flat 32 Clifton Court ★★★★
Self Catering
Marsdens Cottage Holidays
t (01271) 813777
e holidays@marsdens.co.uk
w marsdens.co.uk

Flat 7 Clifton court ★★★★
Self Catering
Marsdens Cottage Holidays
t (01271) 813777
e holidays@marsdens.co.uk
w marsdens.co.uk

Flat 8, Clifton Court ★★★★
Self Catering
Marsdens Cottage Holidays
t (01271) 813777
e holidays@marsdens.co.uk
w marsdens.co.uk

Flats 28 and 30 Clifton Court ★★★ *Self Catering*
Marsdens Cottage Holidays
t (01271) 813777
e holidays@marsdens.co.uk
w marsdens.co.uk

PYMORE
Dorset

Rowan Tree ★★★★
Self Catering
Lyme Bay Holidays
t (01297) 443363
e email@lymebayholidays.co.uk
w lymebayholidays.co.uk

QUINTRELL DOWNS
Cornwall

Old Chapel ★★★
Self Catering
Contact: Mrs Selina Kilker
t (01637) 875654
e info@theoldchapelnewquay.co.uk
w theoldchapelnewquay.co.uk

QUOIT
Cornwall

Walhalla ★★★ *Self Catering*
Harbour Holidays
t (01841) 533402
e contact@harbourholidays.co.uk
w harbourholidays.co.uk

RADSTOCK
Somerset

Charlton Farm Cottage ★★★★ *Self Catering*
Contact: Mr & Mrs Anthony & Vanessa Dutton
t (01761) 437761
e anthony@charltonfarm.com
w charltonfarm.com

RAME
Cornwall

Polhawn Fort ★★★★
Self Catering
Contact: Miss Kathryn Deakin
t (01752) 822864
w polhawnfort.com

RAMPISHAM
Dorset

Stable Cottage ★★★★
Self Catering
Contact: Mr & Mrs James & Diane Read
t (01935) 83555
e usatschoolhouse@aol.com

READY TOKEN
Gloucestershire

Hartwell Farm Cottages ★★★★ *Self Catering*
Contact: Mrs Caroline Mann
t (01285) 740210
e ec.mann@btinternet.com
w selfcateringcotswolds.com

REDBROOK
Gloucestershire

The Old Bakery, Redbrook ★★★★ *Self Catering*
Contact: Sylvia Adcock
t (01600) 713675
e bookings@the-old-bakery.com
w the-old-bakery.com

REDLYNCH
Wiltshire

New Forest Edge Holiday Cottages ★★★★
Self Catering
Contact: Mrs Candy Newman
t (01725) 511516
e forestedge@hotmail.co.uk
w newforestedge.co.uk

REDRUTH
Cornwall

The Barn at Little Trefula, St Day ★★★ *Self Catering*
Contact: Mr & Mrs Bill & Ann Higgins
t (01209) 820572 & 07789 044602
e barn@trefula.com
w trefula.com

Bettyscot ★★★ *Self Catering*
t (01209) 315319

The Gables Cottage ★★★★
Self Catering
Contact: Mrs Shiona King
t (01209) 822294
e enquiries@higher-trevethan.co.uk
w higher-trevethan.co.uk

RESTRONGUET
Cornwall

Regatta Cottage ★★★★
Self Catering
Special Places in Cornwall
t (01872) 864400
e office@specialplacescornwall.co.uk
w specialplacescornwall.co.uk

RIDDLECOMBE
Devon

Manor Farm ★★★★
Self Catering
Contact: Mrs Eveline Gay
t (01769) 520335
e eve@cottwoodvalley.fsnet.co.uk
w riddlecombe-manor.co.uk

RINGSTEAD
Dorset

The Creek ★★★
Self Catering
Contact: Mrs Fisher
t (01305) 852251
e michaelandfreda@btinternet.com

Pitt Cottage ★★★
Self Catering
Dream Cottages
t (01305) 789000
e admin@dream-cottages.co.uk
w dream-cottages.co.uk

Upton Farm ★★★★★
Self Catering
Contact: Mr & Mrs Davis
t (01305) 853970
e alan@uptonfarm.co.uk
w uptonfarm.co.uk

ROBOROUGH
Devon

Whitsleigh Barn ★★★★
Self Catering
Contact: Mrs Elizabeth Basey-Fisher
t (01805) 603286
e ebf@whitsleighdevon.co.uk
w whitsleighdevon.co.uk

ROCK
Cornwall

Little Thrift ★★★★
Self Catering
Contact: Mr Richard Jones
t (01208) 863397
e swseeds@tiscali.co.uk
w cornwall-online.co.uk

Mariners Lettings ★★★★–★★★★★
Self Catering
Contact: Mrs Claire Stewart
Mariners Lettings Ltd
t (020) 7938 2019
w marinersrock.com

Seamist ★★★★ *Self Catering*
Contact: Diana Bullivant
t (01208) 831336
e diana@dbullivant.fsnet.co.uk

The Studio ★★★
Self Catering
Contact: Mrs Ann Gregan
t (01208) 862410
e ann.nca@internet-today.co.uk

Trevethan ★★★★
Self Catering
Rock Holidays
t (01208) 863399
e info@rockholidays.co.uk
w rockholidays.co.uk

Tristan House ★★★
Self Catering
Roserrow Lettings
t (01208) 863000
e mail@roserrow.co.uk
w roserrow.co.uk

Tzitzikama Lodge Self Catering ★★★★
Self Catering
Contact: Mr & Mrs Cox
t (01208) 862839
e tzitzikama.lodge@btinternet.com
w cornwall-online.co.uk

ROCOMBE
Devon

Sunshine Cottage ★★★
Self Catering
Lyme Bay Holidays
t (01297) 443363
e email@lymebayholidays.co.uk
w lymebayholidays.co.uk

RODNEY STOKE
Somerset

Cider Barrel Cottage ★★★★
Self Catering
Contact: Mrs Kathy Longhurst
t (01749) 870322
e don@longhurst16.freeserve.co.uk

ROSUDGEON
Cornwall

Broom Farm Cottage ★★★
Self Catering
Contact: Mr & Mrs Ray Markham
t (01736) 763738
e broomfarmcottage@tiscali.co.uk

Cuddan Rose ★★★
Self Catering
Contact: Mrs Foy
t (01736) 763856
e marianfoy@prussia-cove-holiday.com
w prussia-cove-holiday.com

Rosudgeon Farm ★★★★
Self Catering
t (01702) 475075
w rosudgeonfarm.com

ROUSDON
Devon

12 The Gardens ★★★★
Self Catering
Lyme Bay Holidays
t (01297) 443363
e email@lymebayholidays.co.uk
w lymebayholidays.co.uk

2 Old Home Farm ★★★
Self Catering
Lyme Bay Holidays
t (01297) 443363
e email@lymebayholidays.co.uk
w lymebayholidays.co.uk

3 The Bothy ★★★
Self Catering
Lyme Bay Holidays
t (01297) 443363
e email@lymebayholidays.co.uk
w lymebayholidays.co.uk

3 The Gardens ★★★★
Self Catering
Lyme Bay Holidays
t (01297) 443363
e email@lymebayholidays.co.uk
w lymebayholidays.co.uk

3 Home Farm South ★★★★
Self Catering
Lyme Bay Holidays
t (01297) 443363
e email@lymebayholidays.co.uk
w lymebayholidays.co.uk

The Forge ★★★★
Self Catering
Lyme Bay Holidays
t (01297) 443363
e email@lymebayholidays.co.uk
w lymebayholidays.co.uk

Peek House ★★★★★
Self Catering
Contact: Mrs Judith Ellard
t (01297) 444734
e judith@peakhouse.co.uk
w peekhouse.co.uk

ROWDE
Wiltshire

The Canal Barn ★★★★
Self Catering
Contact: Mr & Mrs Patrick & Louise Dawe-Lane
t (01380) 728883
e mail@canalbarn.co.uk
w canalbarn.co.uk

Foxhangers Canalside Holidays *Approved Caravan Holiday Home*
t (01380) 828254
w foxhangers.com

RUAN HIGH LANES
Cornwall

Carne Cottage ★★★★★
Self Catering
Portscatho Holidays
t (01326) 270900
e info@portscathoholidays.co.uk
w portscathoholidays.co.uk

Folly's ★★★★ *Self Catering*
Roseland Holiday Cottages
t (01872) 580480
e enquiries@roselandholidaycottages.co.uk
w roselandholidaycottages.co.uk

Lambourne Vineyard Cottage ★★★★ *Self Catering*
Contact: Mr & Mrs Graham & Ann Sherat
t (01872) 501212
e graham@lambournevineyard.co.uk
w lambournevineyard.co.uk

The Little Barn ★★★★
Self Catering
Roseland Holiday Cottages
t (01872) 580480
e enquiries@roselandholidaycottages.co.uk
w roselandholidaycottages.co.uk

The Old Loft ★★★
Self Catering
Contact: Mrs Delia Collins
t (01872) 580732
e dee@roselandrentals.co.uk
w roselandrentals.co.uk

Ruan Mill
Rating Applied For
Self Catering
Portscatho Holidays
t (01326) 270900
e info@portscathoholidays.co.uk
w portscathoholidays.co.uk

Trelagossick Farm ★★★
Self Catering
Contact: Mrs Carbis
t (01872) 501338
e enquiries@trelagossickfarm.co.uk
w trelagossickfarm.co.uk

Trelagossick Farm – Barnowl Cottage ★★★★ *Self Catering*
Contact: Mrs Rachel Carbis
t (01872) 501338
e enquiries@trelagossickfarm.co.uk
w trelagossickfarm.co.uk

RUAN MINOR
Cornwall

Seascape, Cadgwith ★★★★
Self Catering
Contact: Mr & Mrs George
t (01326) 341195
e jgfamily@btinternet.com
w seascapecornwall.co.uk

Treal Farm Holidays ★★★★
Self Catering
t (01326) 290668
w trealfarm.co.uk

RUARDEAN
Gloucestershire

Anne's Cottage ★★★★
Self Catering
Contact: Anne Seager
t (01594) 543217
e anneseager@aol.com
w annescottage.ik.com

Deansbrook ★★★★
Self Catering
Contact: Annette Daly
t (01384) 873527
e ald1207@aol.com

RUMFORD
Cornwall

Corner Cottage ★★
Self Catering
Harbour Holidays
t (01841) 533402
e contact@harbourholidays.co.uk
w harbourholidays.co.uk

ST AGNES
Cornwall

Badgers Rest ★★★
Self Catering
Duchy Holidays
t (01872) 572971
e enquiries@duchyholidays.co.uk
w duchyholidays.co.uk

Bolster Farm Cottage ★★★★ *Self Catering*
Contact: Mrs Niki Lillie
t (01872) 552187
e niki@bolsterfarm.co.uk
w bolsterfarm.co.uk

Croft Cottage ★★★★
Self Catering
Contact: Mrs Sawle
t (01872) 553381
e beaconcottagefarm@lineone.net
w beaconcottagefarmholidays.co.uk

Old School House 7 ★★★
Self Catering
Duchy Holidays
t (01872) 572971
e enquiries@duchyholidays.co.uk
w duchyholidays.co.uk

The Owl House ★★★★
Self Catering
Contact: Ms Hicks
t (01872) 553644
e enquiries@the-owl-house.co.uk
w the-owl-house.co.uk

Palmvale Holidays ★★★★★
Self Catering
Contact: Mr Williams
t (01872) 552234
e duchy.holidays@virgin.net
w palmvaleholidays.co.uk

Pen Mor Cottage ★★★
Self Catering
Duchy Holidays
t (01872) 572971
e enquiries@duchyholidays.co.uk
w duchyholidays.co.uk

Rose Cottage 2 ★★★
Self Catering
Duchy Holidays
t (01872) 572971
e enquiries@duchyholidays.co.uk
w duchyholidays.co.uk

Tregease ★★★ *Self Catering & Serviced Apartments*
Contact: Mr Simmons
t 07890 3332 1601

ST AGNES
Isles of Scilly

Periglis Cottage ★★★
Self Catering
Contact: Mr Jimmy Paget-Brown
t (01720) 422366
e pagetbro@aol.com

ST AUSTELL
Cornwall

Bayview House, St. Austell ★★★★ *Self Catering*
Blue Chip Vacations
t (01803) 855282
e info@bluechipvacations.com
w bluechipvacations.com

Bosinver Farm Cottages ★★★–★★★★ *Self Catering*
Contact: Mrs Smith
t (01726) 72128
e reception@bosinver.co.uk
w bosinver.co.uk

Circle of Friends ★★
Self Catering
Contact: Mr & Mrs Taylor
t (01726) 70786
e gayleforce2006@hotmail.com
w gayleforce2006evelynn.spaces.com

The Engine House ★★★★★
Self Catering
Niche Retreats
t (01209) 861745
e jackie@nicheretreats.co.uk
w nicheretreats.co.uk

Holly Bank, London Apprentice ★★★
Self Catering
Contact: Mr & Mrs McGuffie
t (01726) 69316
e mcguffspindrift@hotmail.com
w spindrift-guesthouse.co.uk

Lanjeth Farm Holiday Cottages ★★★★
Self Catering
Contact: Ms Anita Webber
t (01726) 68438
e anita@cornwall-holidays.uk.com
w cornwall-holidays.uk.com

Nanjeath Farm ★★★★
Self Catering
Contact: Mr & Mrs Sandercock
t (01726) 70666
e jill@nanjeath.co.uk
w nanjeath.co.uk

Owls Reach, Roche ★★★★
Self Catering
Contact: Diana Pride
t (01208) 831597
e info@owlsreach.co.uk
w owlsreach.co.uk

Poltarrow Farm Cottages ★★★★–★★★★★
Self Catering
t (01726) 67111
w poltarrow.co.uk

Southfield ★★★★
Self Catering
Contact: Mrs Treleaven
t (01726) 75819
e bookings@southfieldselfcatering.co.uk

Tor View Accommodation ★★★★ *Self Catering*
Contact: Mrs Hugo
t (01726) 850340
e torview@btopenworld.co.uk
w torviewcentre.co.uk

Tregongeeves Farm Cottages ★★★★
Self Catering
Contact: Mr & Mrs John & Judith Clemo
Tregongeeves Farm Holiday Cottages
t (01726) 68202
w cornwall-holidays.co.uk

ST BLAZEY
Cornwall

Cornhill Farm Cottages ★★★★ *Self Catering*
Contact: Mrs Kay Carne
t (01726) 815700
e enquiries@cornhillfarmcottages.co.uk
w cornhillfarmcottages.co.uk

Prideaux Farm Cottages ★★★–★★★★ *Self Catering*
Contact: Mrs Watson
t (01726) 817304
e kathywatson@prideauxhouse.com

Woodmill Farm Holiday Cottages ★★★★
Self Catering
Contact: Mrs Michelle Hume
t (01726) 810171
e enquiries@woodmill-farm.co.uk
w woodmill-farm.co.uk

ST BLAZEY GATE
Cornwall

Windsworth Holiday Bungalows ★★★
Self Catering
Contact: Mrs Pat Wheeler
t (01726) 815352
e info@windsworth.co.uk
w windsworth.co.uk

ST BREOCK
Cornwall

Pawton Mill Farmhouse ★★★★★ *Self Catering*
Contact: Mrs Philippa Sullivan
t (01579) 346473
e holidays@duchyofcornwall.gov.uk
w duchyofcornwallholidaycottages.co.uk

ST BREWARD
Cornwall

Darrynane Cottages ★★★
Self Catering
Contact: Mrs Angela Clark
t (01208) 850885
e enquiries@darrynane.co.uk
w darrynane.com

Mellon Farm (formerly Meadowside) ★★★★
Self Catering
Contact: Mr & Mrs Feasey
t (01208) 851497
e feasymellon@aol.com
w mellonfarm.co.uk

ST BRIAVELS
Gloucestershire

Rodmore Lodge ★★★★
Self Catering
Contact: David James
t (01594) 529778
e info@rodmore-lodge.co.uk
w rodmore-lodge.co.uk

Rookery Barn ★★★★
Self Catering
Contact: Mrs Heather James
Rookery Barn – Hoseasons
t (01594) 837992
w rookerybarn.net

ST BURYAN
Cornwall

3 The Green ★★★
Self Catering
Contact: Ms Sally Follett
t (01736) 364892

Boskenna Home Farm ★★★★★ *Self Catering*
Contact: Ms Julia Hosking
t (01736) 810705
e julia@boskenna.co.uk
w boskenna.co.uk

Tredinney Farm, Self Catering ★★★ *Self Catering*
Contact: Mrs Rosemary Warren
t (01736) 810352
e rosemary.warren@btopenworld.com
w tredinneyfarm.co.uk

Tregurnow Holiday Cottages ★★★★★ *Self Catering*
t (01736) 810255
w lamorna.biz

ST CLETHER
Cornwall

Forget-me-not Farm Holidays ★★★★
Self Catering
Contact: Mrs Sheila Kempthorne
t (01566) 86284
e holidays@trefranck.co.uk
w forget-me-not-farm-holidays.co.uk

ST COLUMB
Cornwall

The Chalet Dennis Farm, Nr Tregonetha ★★★
Self Catering
Contact: Mr David Chambers
t (01637) 881200
e davidandgay.chambers@dennisfarm.co.uk
w dennisfarm.co.uk

Tregatillian Cottages ★★★
Self Catering
Cornish Horizons Holiday Cottages
t (01841) 533331
e cottages@cornishhorizons.co.uk
w cornishhorizons.co.uk

ST DAY
Cornwall

Manor Farmhouse ★★★★
Self Catering
Contact: Mr Murray Nelson
t (01209) 822066
e muzoe@homecall.co.uk

ST ENDELLION
Cornwall

Tolraggott Farm Cottages ★★★★ *Self Catering*
Contact: Mrs Harris
t (01208) 880927

Trentinney Farm Holiday Cottages ★★★–★★★★★
Self Catering
Contact: Mr Richard Mably
t (01208) 880564
e stay@trentinney.co.uk
w trentinney.co.uk

ST ERTH
Cornwall

The Brambles ★★★
Self Catering
Contact: Mrs Alma Barnett
t (01736) 753331
e david.alma1@virgin.net

Chy-an-Heyl ★★★
Self Catering
Contact: Mr & Mrs Derek Ripper
t (0117) 073 8733
e info@firstcottage.com
w firstcottage.com

Trewinnard Manor, St Erth ★★★★ *Self Catering*
Contact: Mrs Farnaby
t (020) 7730 2351
e treninnardmandy@yahoo.co.uk

Wisteria and Trehaven ★★★ *Self Catering*
Contact: Mrs Cynthia Lawson-Smith
t (01736) 740977
e cynthia@lawsonsmith.freeserve.co.uk

ST ERTH PRAZE
Cornwall

Trescowe Cottages ★★★
Self Catering
Contact: Mrs Veronica Froggett
t (01736) 753823
e crofterscottage@hotmail.com

ST ERVAN
Cornwall

The Nooke ★★★★★
Self Catering
Contact: Mrs Reskelly
t (01841) 540559

Treleigh Manor Farm ★★★
Self Catering
Contact: Mrs M Old
t (01841) 540075

Trenouth Cottage ★★★★
Self Catering
Harbour Holidays
t (01841) 533402
e contact@harbourholidays.co.uk
w harbourholidays.co.uk

ST EVAL
Cornwall

6 Lerwick Road ★★★★
Self Catering
Harbour Holidays
t (01841) 533402
e contact@harbourholidays.co.uk
w harbourholidays.co.uk

The Malt House ★★★★★
Self Catering
Harbour Holidays
t (01841) 533402
e contact@harbourholidays.co.uk
w harbourholidays.co.uk

Skiber An Hyli
Rating Applied For
Self Catering
Contact: Lee Payne
t (01564) 774929
e paynelee56@aol.com

Springfield ★★★
Self Catering
Harbour Holidays
t (01841) 533402
e contact@harbourholidays.co.uk
w harbourholidays.co.uk

Trelorna ★★★ *Self Catering*
t (01841) 540992
e lornacknott@yahoo.co.uk

ST EWE
Cornwall

Galowras Farm Cottage ★★★★ *Self Catering*
Contact: Dr Lisa & John Dunne
t (01726) 842373
e galowras@btinternet.com
w galowrasfarm.co.uk

ST GILES ON THE HEATH
Devon

Cross Green Cottages ★★★★ *Self Catering*
Contact: Mrs Ginette Nobbs
t (01566) 784216
e crossgreen@btconnect.com
w crossgreen-cottages.co.uk

ST GLUVIAS
Cornwall

Glengarth ★★★ *Self Catering*
Contact: Mrs Newing
t (01872) 863209

ST HILARY
Cornwall

Ennys ★★★★ *Self Catering*
t (01736) 740262

ST ISSEY
Cornwall

Bertie's Barn ★★★★
Self Catering
Cornish Horizons Holiday Cottages
t (01841) 533331
e cottages@cornishhorizons.co.uk
w cornishhorizons.co.uk

Blable Farm Barns ★★★★★
Self Catering
Contact: Mrs Roberts
t (01208) 815813
e blablefarm@btclick.com
w blablefarmbarns.co.uk

Cannalidgey Villa Farm Cottages ★★★ *Self Catering*
Contact: Mrs Old
t (01208) 812276
e cannalidgey@btinternet.com

Hawksland Mill ★★★★
Self Catering
Contact: Mr & Mrs Jenkins
t (01208) 815404
e hjc@hawkslandmill.co.uk
w 4starcottages.co.uk

Lotties Cottage ★★★★
Self Catering
Cornish Horizons Holiday Cottages
t (01841) 533331
e cottages@cornishhorizons.co.uk
w cornishhorizons.co.uk

Marshall Barn ★★★★
Self Catering
Harbour Holidays
t (01841) 533402
e contact@harbourholidays.co.uk
w harbourholidays.co.uk

Rose End Cottage ★★★
Self Catering
Harbour Holidays
t (01841) 533402
e contact@harbourholidays.co.uk
w harbourholidays.co.uk

The Roundhouse ★★★★★
Self Catering
Cornish Horizons Holiday Cottages
t (01841) 533331
e cottages@cornishhorizons.co.uk
w cornishhorizons.co.uk

The Snug ★★★★
Self Catering
Harbour Holidays
t (01841) 533402
e contact@harbourholidays.co.uk
w harbourholidays.co.uk

Sunflower Cottage ★★★★
Self Catering
Contact: Mrs Simpkin
t 07879 611647
w cornwall-online.co.uk

Trelow Barton/Trelow Farmhouse ★★★★–★★★★★
Self Catering
Farm & Cottage Holidays
t (01237) 459827
e enquiries@farmcott.co.uk
w holidaycottages.co.uk

Valencia Cottage ★★★
Self Catering
Cornish Horizons Holiday Cottages
t (01841) 533331
e cottages@cornishhorizons.co.uk
w cornishhorizons.co.uk

ST IVES
Cornwall

32 Porthia Road ★★
Self Catering
Contact: Mrs Marilyn Harry
t (01736) 794986

9 Ayr Lane ★★★
Self Catering
Contact: Ms Sue Kibby
t (020) 8870 3228
e sue.kibby@btinternet.com
w btinternet.com/~stives.cottage

Ashtrees ★★★ *Self Catering*
Contact: Mrs Paula Oates
t (01736) 793078
e paula_o@hotmail.co.uk

Ayr Holiday Homes ★★★
Self Catering
Contact: Mr Baragwanath
t (01736) 795855
e recept@ayrholidaypark.co.uk
w ayrholidaypark.co.uk

Big Picture Holidays ★★★
Self Catering
Contact: Mrs Sarah Parker
t (01237) 422637
e sarah@bigpictureholidays.co.uk
w bigpictureholidays.co.uk

Blue View Apartment ★★★
Self Catering
Contact: Mrs Ylenia Haase
t 07967 101339
e stay@seahorseflat.com
w theblueview.co.uk

By The Beach ★★★
Self Catering
Contact: Mrs Sarah Bulmer
t (01564) 794483
e sarah.bulmer@hotmail.com
w bythebeachstives.com

Casa Bella ★★★★
Self Catering
Contact: Mrs C Perry
t (01736) 793370

Cheriton Self Catering ★★★–★★★★★ *Self Catering*
Contact: Mr Alec Luke
t (01736) 795083

Chy An Eglos Apartments ★★★ *Self Catering*
Contact: Mr David Eddy
t (01736) 795542
e david.eddy@chy-an-eglos.co.uk
w chy-an-eglos.co.uk

Chy Menydh / Chy Mor
Rating Applied For
Self Catering
Contact: Ms Helen Partridge
t (01803) 866307
e helen@hpartridge5.orangehome.co.uk
w chymenydh.co.uk

Chy Mor and Premier Apartments ★★★
Self Catering
Contact: Michael Gill
t (01736) 798798
e enquiry@stivesharbour.com
w stivesharbour.com

Chylowen & Bluewater ★★★★ *Self Catering*
Contact: Miss Linda Higgins
t (01202) 258743
e lindahiggins@stivesdownalong.com
w stivesdownalong.com

Cornish Cottage ★★★
Self Catering
Contact: Mrs Ylenia Haase
t 07967 101339
e stay@seahorseflat.com
w stivesselfcatering.com

Fishermans Cottage ★★★
Self Catering
Contact: Mr & Mrs D Langridge
t (01858) 535534
e davidlangridge1940@btinternet.com
w langridge-cottages.freeservers.com

Flat 4, Barnoon Terrace ★★
Self Catering
Contact: Mrs Bruce
t (01803) 862164
e haroldlechat@hotmail.com
w vivs-flat.co.uk

Grannys ★★ *Self Catering*
Contact: Mrs Ann Renowden
t (01736) 796360

Gran's Cottage ★★★
Self Catering
Contact: Dorothy Edmond
t (01872) 560644

Gulls Nest
Rating Applied For
Self Catering
Contact: Mrs Kay Livesey
t (01335) 345063
e kaylivesey@yahoo.co.uk

Gulls Nest ★★★
Self Catering
Contact: Mrs Diana Watts
t (01736) 797969
e djgullsnest@aol.com

Happy Days ★★★★★
Self Catering
Contact: Miss Amanda Dumbletone info@happydaysstives.co.uk
w happydaysstives.co.uk

Higher Trowan ★★★★
Self Catering
Ayia Napa Holidays
t (01736) 757237
e info@carbisbayretreats.co.uk
w carbisbayretreats.co.uk

Holiday Home ★★
Self Catering
t (01736) 786006

Joshua's Cottage ★★★★
Self Catering
t (01453) 832318

Langridge Holiday Cottages ★★★ *Self Catering*
t (01858) 535534

Lifeboat Inn Flat ★★★
Self Catering
Contact: Miss Kellie McKeown
t (01736) 794123
e lifeboatinn@staustellbrewery.co.uk
w smallandfriendly.co.uk

The Look Out ★★★★
Self Catering
t (0121) 552 0011
w thelookoutstives.co.uk

Lowenna ★★★ *Self Catering*
Contact: Mrs Jemima Mitchell
t (01558) 685815
e mynydddu@aol.com

Lower Carnstabba Farm House (Toad Hall) ★★★
Self Catering
Contact: Mr Dixon
t 084536 5139
e enquiries@cornishcollections.co.uk
w cornishcollection.co.uk

Lower Trowan ★★★★
Self Catering
Ayia Napa Holidays
t (01736) 757237
e info@carbisbayretreats.co.uk
w carbisbayretreats.co.uk

Ocean Loft ★★★★
Self Catering
Contact: Mrs Emma Haase
t (01736) 795207
e stay@oceanloft.co.uk
w oceanloft.co.uk

Orla-Mo ★★★★
Self Catering
Contact: Mrs Anne Broome
t 0845 644 2833
e info@surfives.co.uk
w surfives.co.uk

Pier House ★★★★★
Self Catering
Cornish Gems
t 0844 800 2813
w cornishgems.com/gems-finest/pier_house.html

Rotorua Apartments ★★★★
Self Catering
Contact: Mrs Linda Roach
t (01736) 795419
e rotorua@btconnect.com
w stivesapartments.com

Sailfish Cottage ★★★★★
Self Catering
t (01736) 793830
w sailfishcottage.co.uk

St Nicholas Cottage ★★★★
Self Catering
t (01736) 797090
w stnicholascottage.co.uk

St Nicholas Court ★★★–★★★★★ *Self Catering*
Contact: Mr Williams
t (023) 8026 7939
e stnicholascourt@ntworld.com
w stnicholascourt.com

Samphire House ★★★★
Self Catering
Powells Cottage Holidays
t (01834) 812791
e info@powells.co.uk
w powells.co.uk

Sea Horse Flat ★★★
Self Catering
Contact: Mrs Ylenia Haase
t 07967 101339
e stay@seahorseflat.com
w seahorseflat.com

Sea Shells ★★★★★
Self Catering
Ayia Napa Holidays
t (01736) 757237
e info@carbisbayretreats.co.uk
w carbisbayretreats.co.uk

Seawater ★★★★★
Self Catering
Contact: Mr Alan Spencer
t (01736) 791857
e alan@seawater.org.uk
w seawater.org.uk

Serenity ★★★★★
Self Catering
Carbis Bay Holidays
t 0800 012 2241
e enquiries@carbisbayholidays.co.uk
w carbisbayholidays.co.uk

Star Gazy ★★★★
Self Catering
Contact: Mrs Sandra Fenn
t (01424) 882607
e sandra@northlands.co.uk
w star-gazy.co.uk

The Studio ★★ *Self Catering*
Contact: Carol Holland
Little Parc Owles
t (01736) 793015

Surf Break ★★★
Self Catering
Contact: Mrs Pat Butler
t (01736) 793114
e iankangaroo@hotmail.com

Trecillian Barn Self Catering Holidays ★★★ *Self Catering*
Contact: Mrs Jeanette Harling
t (01736) 795132
e jmharling@jmharing.f9.co.uk
w stives-accommodation.co.uk

Tregenna Castle Self Catering ★★★–★★★★★
Self Catering
Contact: Mrs Sheila Barker
Tregenna Castle Self-Catering
t (01736) 795588
e hotel@tregenna-castle.co.uk
w tregenna-castle.co.uk

Trevalgan Holiday Farm ★★★★ *Self Catering*
Contact: Mrs Melanie Osborne
t (01736) 796529
e holidays@trevalgan.co.uk
w trevalgan.co.uk

Well Cottage ★★★
Self Catering
Contact: Mrs Rosalind Bibbey
t (01736) 799209
e ros_bibbey@hotmail.com

Wigeon Watch ★★★★★
Self Catering
Cornish Gems
t 0844 800 2813
w cornishgems.com/holiday-cottages/wigeon-watch.html

ST JULIOT
Cornwall

The Hayloft ★★★★★
Self Catering
Contact: Mrs Nicola Collings
t (01840) 250218
e hayloftbarn@hotmail.com
w hayloftbarn.co.uk

ST JUST
Cornwall

Meadow Cottage ★★★★
Self Catering
Contact: Miss Michelle Woolcock
t (01736) 788455
e enquiries@commerical-hotel.co.uk
w selfcateringcottagecornwall.co.uk

Willoughby ★★★★
Self Catering
Contact: Mr & Mrs Hickman
t (01709) 328236
w willoughbycornwall.co.uk

ST JUST-IN-PENWITH
Cornwall

Swallow's End ★★★★
Self Catering
Contact: Mr David Beer
t (01736) 787011
e enquiries@westcornwalllets.co.uk
w westcornwalllets.co.uk

ST JUST IN ROSELAND
Cornwall

April Cottage
Rating Applied For
Self Catering
Portscatho Holidays
t (01326) 270900
e info@portscathoholidays.co.uk
w portscathoholidays.co.uk

Bar Point ★★★ *Self Catering*
Portscatho Holidays
t (01326) 270900
e info@portscathoholidays.co.uk
w portscathoholidays.co.uk

Bentley's Cottage
Rating Applied For
Self Catering
Portscatho Holidays
t (01326) 270900
e info@portscathoholidays.co.uk
w portscathoholidays.co.uk

Ros Creek Cottage ★★★★
Self Catering
Special Places in Cornwall
t (01872) 864400
e office@specialplacescornwall.co.uk
w specialplacescornwall.co.uk

Rose Haven Cottages ★★★★ *Self Catering*
Contact: Mr & Mrs Eccles
t (01326) 270795
e eccles@rosehavencottages.co.uk
w rosehavencottages.co.uk

Roundhouse Barns ★★★★
Self Catering
Contact: Ms Barbara Sadler
Roundhouse Barn
t (01872) 580038
e info@roundhousebarnholidays.co.uk
w roundhousebarnholidays.co.uk

ST KEVERNE
Cornwall

1 The Old Forge ★★★ *Self Catering & Serviced Apartments*
Contact: Mrs Elizabeth Gould
t (01865) 849000
e info@1theoldforge.co.uk
w 1theoldforge.co.uk

Ginentonic Cottage ★★★★
Self Catering
Contact: Mr & Mrs Cooper
t (01326) 280986
e info@oldtemperancehouse.co.uk
w oldtemperancehouse.co.uk

Trewillis Farm ★★★★
Self Catering
Farm & Cottage Holidays
t (01237) 459827
e enquiries@farmcott.co.uk
w holidaycottages.co.uk

ST KEW
Cornwall

Keats Cottage ★★
Self Catering
Contact: Mrs Susan Coster
t (01208) 880332

Lane End Farm ★★★
Self Catering
Contact: Mrs Linda Monk
t (01208) 880013
e nabmonk@tiscali.co.uk

Skisdon ★★★★ *Self Catering*
Contact: Mr Tim Honeywill
t (01208) 841372
e tim580208@aol.com
w skisdon.com

Treharrock Farm Cottages Pendoggett ★★★★
Self Catering
Contact: Mrs Emerald Quinn
t (01208) 880517
e treharrockfarmcottages@btinternet.com
w treharrockfarmcottages.com

ST KEW HIGHWAY
Cornwall

Bull's Court
Rating Applied For
Self Catering
Contact: Mrs Mary Hibbett
t (01208) 841114
e mary.hibbert@homecall.co.uk

November Cottage ★★★★
Self Catering
Cornish Horizons Holiday Cottages
t (01841) 533331
e cottages@cornishhorizons.co.uk
w cornishhorizons.co.uk

ST KEYNE
Cornwall

Summertime ★★★★
Self Catering
Cornish Collection Ltd
t (01503) 262736
e enquiries@cornishcollections.co.uk
w cornishcollection.co.uk

ST LEONARDS
Dorset

Ivy Holiday Home *Approved Caravan Holiday Home*
Contact: Mrs Pengelly
t (023) 8044 0007

ST LEVAN
Cornwall

Fern Cottage, Treen ★★★★
Self Catering
Contact: Mr Ian Norbury
t (01923) 223013
e ian.norbury@ukgateway.net
w homepage.ntlworld.com/ian.norbury/

Lands End Vineries ★★
Self Catering
t (01736) 871437

Lan-Pedn ★★★ *Self Catering*
Contact: Mr & Mrs Atter
t (01736) 810153

The Lookout ★★★
Self Catering
Contact: Mrs Barbara Ottway
t (01761) 410185
e barbara_ottway@tiscali.co.uk

Sunnymead ★★★★
Self Catering
Contact: Mr Gerard Heathcote
t (01736) 810949
e xsoft@btconnect.com
w sunnymead.biz

Trebehor Cottages ★★★★
Self Catering
Contact: Mr Richard Jeffery
t (01736) 871263
e richard@trebehorcottages.co.uk
w trebehorcottages.co.uk

Treloggan Cottage ★★★★
Self Catering
Contact: Mr & Mrs Robert & Kay George
t (01736) 810452
e robertandkay@penberth.com
w sennen-cove.com

ST MABYN
Cornwall

Polglynn Cottage, St Mabyn ★★★★★ *Self Catering*
Contact: Mr William Wareham
t (01208) 850538
e bill@polglaze.freeserve.co.uk

Rocksea Barn ★★★★
Self Catering
Contact: John Gill
t 07764 340105
e john@jgill5.wanadoo.co.uk

ST MARTIN'S
Isles of Scilly

Carron Farm ★★★
Self Catering
Contact: Mrs Julia Walder
t (01720) 422893
w carronfarm.co.uk

Churchtown Farm ★★★★
Self Catering
Contact: Mrs Julian
t (01720) 422169
e info@churchtownfarmholidays.co.uk
w churchtownfarmholidays.co.uk

Connemara Farm ★★★
Self Catering
Contact: Mr T Perkins
t (01720) 422814
e t.a.perkins@btinternet.com

Merrion's Holiday Cottage ★★★★ *Self Catering*
Contact: Mrs Valerie Thomas
t (01720) 423418
e grahamw.thomas@tiscali.co.uk

The Stables ★★★
Self Catering
Contact: Mr John Boyle
t (01326) 563811
e john@sharkbayfilms.demon.co.uk
w sharkbayfilms.com/stables.htm

ST MARYCHURCH
Devon

Sea Peep Cottage ★★★
Self Catering
Contact: Mr Nick Evans
t (01803) 292987
e enquiries@torbayaccommodation.co.uk
w torbayaccommodation.co.uk

ST MARY'S
Isles of Scilly

1 Bay View ★★★
Self Catering
Island Properties
t (01720) 422082
e enquiries@scillyhols.com
w scillyhols.com

1 Golden Bay Mansions ★★★ *Self Catering*
Island Properties
t (01720) 422082
e enquiries@scillyhols.com
w scillyhols.com

1 Pentland ★ *Self Catering*
Island Properties
t (01720) 422082
e enquiries@scillyhols.com
w scillyhols.com

1 Rosevean ★★★
Self Catering
Island Properties
t (01720) 422082
e enquiries@scillyhols.com
w scillyhols.com

1 Springfield Court ★★★
Self Catering
Island Properties
t (01720) 422082
e enquiries@scillyhols.com
w scillyhols.com

10 The Strand ★★★★
Self Catering
Island Properties
t (01720) 422082
e enquiries@scillyhols.com
w scillyhols.com

12 Silver Street and 1 Porthcressa ★★★★
Self Catering
Contact: Mrs Mills
t (01442) 262871

14 Silver Street ★★★
Self Catering
Island Properties
t (01720) 422082
e enquiries@scillyhols.com
w scillyhols.com

2 Godolphin Flats ★★★★
Self Catering
Island Properties
t (01720) 422082
e enquiries@scillyhols.com
w scillyhols.com

2 Telegraph Bungalows and Lemon Tree ★★★
Self Catering
Contact: Mrs Mumford
t (01720) 422650

22 Sally Port ★★★
Self Catering
Contact: Mr Andrew Combes
t (01823) 430057
e ajcombes@somerset.gov.uk
w scillyselfcatering.co.uk

3 Bay View ★★★
Self Catering
Island Properties
t (01720) 422082
e enquiries@scillyhols.com
w scillyhols.com

3 Spanish Ledge ★★★
Self Catering
Island Properties
t (01720) 422082
e enquiries@scillyhols.com
w scillyhols.com

4 Myrtle Cottages ★★
Self Catering
Island Properties
t (01720) 422082
e enquiries@scillyhols.com
w scillyhols.com

4 Rosevean House ★★★★
Self Catering
Contact: Mr Mark Littleford
t (01720) 423102
e booking@4roseveanhouse.co.uk
w 4roseveanhouse.co.uk

4 Silver Street ★★★
Self Catering
Contact: Mrs Julie Watt
t (01720) 423103

4 Spanish Ledge ★★
Self Catering
Island Properties
t (01720) 422082
e enquiries@scillyhols.com
w scillyhols.com

5 Myrtle Cottages ★★
Self Catering
Island Properties
t (01720) 422082
e enquiries@scillyhols.com
w scillyhols.com

5 Spanish Ledge ★★★
Self Catering
Island Properties
t (01720) 422082
e enquiries@scillyhols.com
w scillyhols.com

6 Godolphin House & 8 Buzza Street ★★★
Self Catering
Contact: Mrs Hogg
t (024) 7645 0455

6 Lower Strand ★★★★
Self Catering
Contact: Mrs Susan Richards
t (01720) 422904

7 Springfield Court ★★★
Self Catering
Island Properties
t (01720) 422082
e enquiries@scillyhols.com
w scillyhols.com

8a Buzza Street ★★★★
Self Catering
Island Properties
t (01720) 422082
e enquiries@scillyhols.com
w scillyhols.com

9 Springfield Court ★★★
Self Catering
Island Properties
t (01720) 422082
e enquiries@scillyhols.com
w scillyhols.com

The Aft Cabin ★★★
Self Catering
Contact: Mr & Mrs Terry & Elizabeth Parsons
t (01720) 422393

Ajax ★★★ *Self Catering*
Island Properties
t (01720) 422082
e enquiries@scillyhols.com
w scillyhols.com

Albany Flats & Thurleigh
★★★-★★★★ *Self Catering*
Contact: Mrs Isabel Trenear
t (01720) 422601
e itrenear@yahoo.co.uk
w scillyflats.com

Anchor Cottage ★★
Self Catering
Island Properties
t (01720) 422082
e enquiries@scillyhols.com
w scillyhols.com

Anglesea House ★★★★
Self Catering
Island Properties
t (01720) 422082
e enquiries@scillyhols.com
w scillyhols.com

Annet & Mount Flagon
★★★★ *Self Catering*
Contact: Ann Hughes
t (01425) 655729
e ann@foundryhouse.freeserve.co.uk

Ardwyn ★★★★ *Self Catering*
Contact: Mrs Gill Osborne
t (01720) 422986

Armorel Cottage ★★★★
Self Catering
Island Properties
t (01720) 422082
e enquiries@scillyhols.com
w scillyhols.com

Avoca Holiday Homes ★★★
Self Catering
Contact: Mr & Mrs Colin & Elizabeth Ridsdale
t (01720) 422656
w avocaholidayhomes.co.uk

Bar Escapade ★★
Self Catering
Island Properties
t (01720) 422082
e enquiries@scillyhols.com
w scillyhols.com

The Barn ★★★ *Self Catering*
Island Properties
t (01720) 422082
e enquiries@scillyhols.com
w scillyhols.com

Bay Tree Cottage ★★★★★
Self Catering
Island Properties
t (01720) 422082
e enquiries@scillyhols.com
w scillyhols.com

Beach House Flat
★★★-★★★★ *Self Catering*
Island Properties
t (01720) 422082
e enquiries@scillyhols.com
w scillyhols.com

Beach Mooring, Flat 1, Smugglers Ride ★★★★
Self Catering
Contact: Mrs Susan Eccles
t (01872) 580997
e norman.eccles@btopenworld.com

Beaches ★★★★★
Self Catering
Island Properties
t (01720) 422082
e enquiries@scillyhols.com
w scillyhols.com

Beggars Roost ★★
Self Catering
Contact: Mr Kenneth Peay
t (020) 8399 8364

Boswartreth ★★★
Self Catering
Island Properties
t (01720) 422082
e enquiries@scillyhols.com
w scillyhols.com

Bounty Ledge ★★★
Self Catering
Contact: Mr Raymond Jackman
t (01720) 422124

Buzza Ledge ★★★★
Self Catering
Contact: Mr Jeremy Phillips
t (01720) 422078
e jeremyphillips@rosecottagescilly.freeserve.co.uk

The Captains Cabin ★★★
Self Catering
Contact: Mrs Peggy Rowe
t (01720) 422966
e peggy@rowe55.freeserve.co.uk

Carn Thomas Cottage ★★★
Self Catering
Contact: Mrs Eileen Denton
t (01209) 860463

Carnwethers Country House
★★★★ *Self Catering*
Contact: Mrs Grace Graham
t (01720) 422415
w carnwethers.com

Christmas House ★★★
Self Catering
Contact: Mrs Jane Chiverton
t (01720) 422002
e chivy002@aol.com

Church Hall Cottage ★★★
Self Catering
Contact: Mr David Townend
t 07900 016113
e dtownend@netcomuk.co.uk

Chy Kensa ★★★★
Self Catering
Island Properties
t (01720) 422082
e enquiries@scillyhols.com
w scillyhols.com

Clemys Cottage ★★★
Self Catering
Contact: Mrs C Millard
t (01736) 363493
e cattran@btinternet.com

Cornerways ★★★★
Self Catering
Contact: Mr & Mrs Pritchard
t (01720) 422757

Dolphins ★★★ *Self Catering*
Island Properties
t (01720) 422082
e enquiries@scillyhols.com
w scillyhols.com

Dunmallard, Lower Flat
★★★ *Self Catering*
Contact: Mr & Mrs Elliot
t (01458) 272971

Ebor Cottage ★★★
Self Catering
Island Properties
t (01720) 422082
e enquiries@scillyhols.com
w scillyhols.com

Escallonia ★★★★
Self Catering
Island Properties
t (01720) 422082
e enquiries@scillyhols.com
w scillyhols.com

The Flat ★★★★ *Self Catering*
Contact: Mrs Jill May
t (01720) 422122

Flat 1 Manilla ★★★
Self Catering
Island Properties
t (01720) 422082
e enquiries@scillyhols.com
w scillyhols.com

Flat 1 Spanish Ledge ★★★
Self Catering
t (01720) 423135

Flat 2 Buccabu ★★★
Self Catering
Island Properties
t (01720) 422082
e enquiries@scillyhols.com
w scillyhols.com

Flat 2 Madura ★★★★
Self Catering
Contact: Mrs Winifred A Davis
t (01736) 757811
e fredadavis1@btinternet.com

Flat 4 Kenwyn ★★★
Self Catering
Contact: Mr & Mrs Graham & Carol Smith
t (01823) 412845

Flats 4 Pentland ★★
Self Catering
Island Properties
t (01720) 422082
e enquiries@scillyhols.com
w scillyhols.com

The Fo'c'stle ★★★
Self Catering
Contact: Mr Jeremy Dale
t (01676) 534969

Garrison Holidays
★★★-★★★★ *Self Catering*
Contact: Mr & Mrs Ted & Barbara Moulson
t (01720) 422670
e tedmoulson@aol.com
w garrisonholidays.com

Glandore Apartments
★★★★ *Self Catering*
Contact: Mr Stephen Morris
t (01720) 422535
e apartments@glandore.co.uk
w glandore.co.uk

Greystones ★★★
Self Catering
Island Properties
t (01720) 422082
e enquiries@scillyhols.com
w scillyhols.com

The Guard House ★★★★★
Self Catering
Contact: Ms Philippa Sullivan
t (01579) 346473
e holidays@duchyofcornwall.gov.uk
w duchyofcornwallholidaycottages.co.uk

Gunner Rock ★★★★
Self Catering
Contact: Mr & Mrs Heslin
t (01720) 422595

Harbour Lights 6 ★★★★
Self Catering
Contact: Mr Clifford
t (01872) 863537

Harbour Lights with Smugglers Ride
★★★-★★★★ *Self Catering*
Contact: Mr Tim Clifford Harbour Lights
t (01872) 863537
e tcclif@globalnet.co.uk
w selfcateringislesofscilly.co.uk

Harbour Walls ★★★
Self Catering
Island Properties
t (01720) 422082
e enquiries@scillyhols.com
w scillyhols.com

Haycocks ★★★ *Self Catering*
Contact: Mr Dingley
t (01720) 422082
e enquiries@islesofscillyholidays.com
w islesofscillyholidays.com

The Hideaway ★★★★
Self Catering
Contact: Mr Tim Clifford
t (01872) 863537
e tcclif@globalnet.co.uk
w selfcateringislesofscilly.co.uk

Hole in the Wall ★★
Self Catering
Island Properties
t (01720) 422082
e enquiries@scillyhols.com
w scillyhols.com

Holly Cottage ★★★★
Self Catering
Contact: Mrs Jane Chiverton
t (01720) 422002

Katrine ★★★ *Self Catering*
Island Properties
t (01720) 422082
e enquiries@scillyhols.com
w scillyhols.com

Kirklees Holiday Flat ★★★
Self Catering
Contact: Mr & Mrs Coldwell
t (01720) 422623

Kistvaen ★★★ *Self Catering*
Contact: Mrs Jane Chiverton
t (01720) 422002
e chivy002@aol.com
w kistvaen.co.uk

Lemon Tree ★★★★
Self Catering
Island Properties
t (01720) 422082
e enquiries@scillyhols.com
w scillyhols.com

The Lighthouse ★★★
Self Catering
Island Properties
t (01720) 422082
e enquiries@scillyhols.com
w scillyhols.com

Lower Anchorage ★★★★
Self Catering
Contact: Sally Thompson
t (01720) 422560

Lower Ganilly Flat ★★★
Self Catering
Island Properties
t (01720) 422082
e enquiries@scillyhols.com
w scillyhols.com

Lower Jacksons ★★★★
Self Catering
Island Properties
t (01720) 422082
e enquiries@scillyhols.com
w scillyhols.com

Lunnon Cottage, The Quillet, Medlar ★★★
Self Catering
Contact: Mrs Penny Rogers
t (01720) 422422
e jrstideford@btinternet.com

Madura 1 ★★★ *Self Catering*
Island Properties
t (01720) 422082
e enquiries@scillyhols.com
w scillyhols.com

Manilla Flats 2 ★★★
Self Catering
Contact: Mrs Frances Grottick
t (01720) 422424

Maypole Farm ★★★
Self Catering
Island Properties
t (01720) 422082
e enquiries@scillyhols.com
w scillyhols.com

Minmow Holiday Flats ★★★
Self Catering
Contact: Mr Simpson
t (01720) 422561
w scillies.freeserve.co.uk

Monaveen ★★★★
Self Catering
Contact: Mr Dingley
t (01720) 422082
w scillyhols.com

Morgelyn ★★★ *Self Catering*
Contact: Mrs Jane Lishman
t (01720) 422897
e morgelyn@sillyonline.co.uk
w morgelyn.co.uk

Morva ★★★★ *Self Catering*
Island Properties
t (01720) 422082
e enquiries@scillyhols.com
w scillyhols.com

Newfort House ★★★★
Self Catering
Island Properties
t (01720) 422082
e enquiries@scillyhols.com
w scillyhols.com

No 1 Corners ★★★★
Self Catering
Contact: Mr Ian Sibley
t (01720) 422431
e enquiries@sibleysonscilly.com
w sibleysonscilly.com/holiday

No 3 Bungalow ★★
Self Catering
Contact: Mrs Sherris
t (01720) 422496

No. 3 Godolphin House
★★★ *Self Catering*
Island Properties
t (01720) 422082
e enquiries@scillyhols.com
w scillyhols.com

The Old Cottage ★
Self Catering
Contact: Mrs Pamela Lethbridge
t (01720) 422630

Old Town Cottage ★★★★
Self Catering
Contact: Mr & Mrs Ian & Gail Sibley
t (01720) 422302
e ianandgail@oldtowncottage.wanadoo.co.uk
w sibleysonscilly.com/holiday

Peacehaven ★★★
Self Catering
Contact: Mr Bennett
t (01720) 422326

Pengarriss ★★★
Self Catering
Contact: Mrs A Walker
t (01264) 772758

Pennlyon ★★★ *Self Catering*
Contact: Mrs Marjorie Feast
t (01527) 893619

Perran ★★★★ *Self Catering*
Island Properties
t (01720) 422082
e enquiries@scillyhols.com
w scillyhols.com

Pharmacy Flat ★★★
Self Catering
Contact: Ms Helen Pearce
t (01720) 422567
e jandhpearce@tiscali.co.uk

Pilots Gig Flat ★★★★
Self Catering
Contact: Mrs Jay Holliday
t (01327) 871053

Plumb Cottage ★★★★
Self Catering
Island Properties
t (01720) 422082
e enquiries@scillyhols.com
w scillyhols.com

Porthlow Farm ★★
Self Catering
Contact: Mr Richard Woof
t (01720) 422082
e enquiries@islesofscillyholidays.com

Prospect House Flats
★★★★ *Self Catering*
Contact: Mr & Mrs Peter & Nicola Thompson
t (01720) 422948

The Retreat ★★★
Self Catering
Island Properties
t (01720) 422082
e enquiries@scillyhols.com
w scillyhols.com

Rocky Hill Chalets ★★★
Self Catering
Contact: Mrs Edwards
t (01720) 422955

Sallakee Farm ★★★
Self Catering
Contact: Mrs Mumford
t (01720) 422391

Seaview Moorings ★★★
Self Catering
Island Properties
t (01720) 422082
e enquiries@scillyhols.com
w scillyhols.com

Shamrock ★★★ *Self Catering*
Contact: Ms Tracey Guy
t (01720) 423269

Smugglers Ride 4 ★★★★
Self Catering
Contact: Mrs Clifford
t (01872) 863537

Sunny Creek ★★★
Self Catering
Island Properties
t (01720) 422082
e enquiries@scillyhols.com
w scillyhols.com

Sunnyside Holiday Flats
★★★ *Self Catering*
Contact: Mr Mike Brown
t (01720) 422903
e mike@sunnysideflats.co.uk
w sunnysideflats.co.uk

The Tardis ★★★
Self Catering
Contact: Mrs Margaret Helen Williams
t (01720) 422209

Teeki ★★★ *Self Catering*
Island Properties
t (01720) 422082
e enquiries@scillyhols.com
w scillyhols.com

Top Flat Trenoweth Farm
★★★ *Self Catering*
Contact: Mrs Christine Hosken
t (01720) 422666

Treglesyn ★★★ *Self Catering*
Contact: Dr Richard Holden
t (01943) 863260
e rick@stoneycroft27.freeserve.co.uk

Tremelethen Farm
★★★-★★★★ *Self Catering*
Contact: Mrs Sarah Hale
t (01720) 422436
e tremelethen@tiscali.co.uk

Trevessa ★★★★
Self Catering
Island Properties
t (01720) 422082
e enquiries@scillyhols.com
w scillyhols.com

Upper Flat, Dunmallard
★★★★ *Self Catering*
Contact: Mr & Mrs D J Poynter
t (0118) 940 3539

Upper Jacksons ★★★★
Self Catering
Island Properties
t (01720) 422082
e enquiries@scillyhols.com
w scillyhols.com

Verona ★★ *Self Catering*
Island Properties
t (01720) 422082
e enquiries@scillyhols.com
w scillyhols.com

Warleggan Holiday Flats
★★★ *Self Catering*
Contact: Mrs Hiron
t (01720) 422563
e enquiries@warleggan.com
w warleggan.com

The White Cottage ★★★
Self Catering
Island Properties
t (01720) 422082
e enquiries@scillyhols.com
w scillyhols.com

Wisteria & Jasmine Cottages
★★★ *Self Catering*
Contact: Claire Oyler
t (01720) 422111

ST MAWES
Cornwall

3 Tregarth Cottages
★★★★★ *Self Catering*
Portscatho Holidays
t (01326) 270900
e info@portscathoholidays.co.uk
w portscathoholidays.co.uk

4 Gibralter Terrace ★★★
Self Catering
Portscatho Holidays
t (01326) 270900
e info@portscathoholidays.co.uk
w portscathoholidays.co.uk

5 Manor Court ★★
Self Catering
Roseland Holiday Cottages
t (01872) 580480
e enquiries@roselandholidaycottages.co.uk
w roselandholidaycottages.co.uk

6 Spinnaker ★★★★
Self Catering
Portscatho Holidays
t (01326) 270900
e info@portscathoholidays.co.uk
w portscathoholidays.co.uk

The Boathouse
Rating Applied For
Self Catering
Portscatho Holidays
t (01326) 270900
e info@portscathoholidays.co.uk
w portscathoholidays.co.uk

Brackley House ★★★
Self Catering
Roseland Holiday Cottages
t (01872) 580480
e enquiries@roselandholidaycottages.co.uk
w roselandholidaycottages.co.uk

Campbell's Cottage ★★★★
Self Catering
Portscatho Holidays
t (01326) 270900
e info@portscathoholidays.co.uk
w portscathoholidays.co.uk

Chapel House East
Rating Applied For
Self Catering
Portscatho Holidays
t (01326) 270900
e info@portscathoholidays.co.uk
w portscathoholidays.co.uk

Charlies ★★★ *Self Catering*
Portscatho Holidays
t (01326) 270900
e info@portscathoholidays.co.uk
w portscathoholidays.co.uk

Chupra ★★★ *Self Catering*
Portscatho Holidays
t (01326) 270900
e info@portscathoholidays.co.uk
w portscathoholidays.co.uk

Chy Bre
Rating Applied For
Self Catering
Special Places in Cornwall
t (01872) 864400
e office@specialplacescornwall.co.uk
w specialplacescornwall.co.uk

Chy Ryn ★★★★
Self Catering
Special Places in Cornwall
t (01872) 864400
e office@specialplacescornwall.co.uk
w specialplacescornwall.co.uk

Chymor
Rating Applied For
Self Catering
Portscatho Holidays
t (01326) 270900
e info@portscathoholidays.co.uk
w portscathoholidays.co.uk

Compass ★★★★
Self Catering
Portscatho Holidays
t (01326) 270900
e info@portscathoholidays.co.uk
w portscathoholidays.co.uk

Coppers ★★★★
Self Catering
Special Places in Cornwall
t (01872) 864400
e office@specialplacescornwall.co.uk
w specialplacescornwall.co.uk

Fort House ★★★★★
Self Catering
English Heritage
t 0870 333 1187
e holidaycottages@english-heritage.org.uk
w english-heritage.org.uk/holidaycottages

The Gingerbread House
★★★★ *Self Catering*
Special Places in Cornwall
t (01872) 864400
e office@specialplacescornwall.co.uk
w specialplacescornwall.co.uk

Gulls Hill ★★★★
Self Catering
Portscatho Holidays
t (01326) 270900
e info@portscathoholidays.co.uk
w portscathoholidays.co.uk

Helm ★★★★ *Self Catering*
Portscatho Holidays
t (01326) 270900
e info@portscathoholidays.co.uk
w portscathoholidays.co.uk

High Meadows ★★★★
Self Catering
Special Places in Cornwall
t (01872) 864400
e office@specialplacescornwall.co.uk
w specialplacescornwall.co.uk

HIllside Cottage ★★★★
Self Catering
Roseland Holiday Cottages
t (01872) 580480
e enquiries@roselandholidaycottages.co.uk
w roselandholidaycottages.co.uk

Laurel Cottage/ The Studio
★★★ *Self Catering*
Roseland Holiday Cottages
t (01872) 580480
e enquiries@roselandholidaycottages.co.uk
w roselandholidaycottages.co.uk

Little Court ★★★
Self Catering
Portscatho Holidays
t (01326) 270900
e info@portscathoholidays.co.uk
w portscathoholidays.co.uk

Little Hill
Rating Applied For
Self Catering
Portscatho Holidays
t (01326) 270900
e info@portscathoholidays.co.uk
w portscathoholidays.co.uk

Little Quay ★★★★
Self Catering
Contact: Mr & Mrs Whitton
t (01326) 270769
w stmawescottage.com

Lower Fountain ★★★★
Self Catering
Special Places in Cornwall
t (01872) 864400
e office@specialplacescornwall.co.uk
w specialplacescornwall.co.uk

Manor Cottage ★★★
Self Catering
Roseland Holiday Cottages
t (01872) 580480
e enquiries@roselandholidaycottages.co.uk
w roselandholidaycottages.co.uk

Mariners ★★★★
Self Catering
Special Places in Cornwall
t (01872) 864400
e office@specialplacescornwall.co.uk
w specialplacescornwall.co.uk

The Old Bakehouse ★★★
Self Catering
Portscatho Holidays
t (01326) 270900
e info@portscathoholidays.co.uk
w portscathoholidays.co.uk

The Old Dairy ★★★
Self Catering
Portscatho Holidays
t (01326) 270900
e info@portscathoholidays.co.uk
w portscathoholidays.co.uk

The Old Dairy ★★★
Self Catering
Roseland Holiday Cottages
t (01872) 580480
e enquiries@roselandholidaycottages.co.uk
w roselandholidaycottages.co.uk

Oyster Haven ★★★★★
Self Catering
Special Places in Cornwall
t (01872) 864400
e office@specialplacescornwall.co.uk
w specialplacescornwall.co.uk

Park Cottage, St Mawes
★★★ *Self Catering*
Contact: Mrs Yvonne George
t (01872) 530418 & 07877 867731
e yvonne@george031627.plus.com
w acornishriver.co.uk

Peel Cottage ★★★★
Self Catering
Special Places in Cornwall
t (01872) 864400
e office@specialplacescornwall.co.uk
w specialplacescornwall.co.uk

Pelyn
Rating Applied For
Self Catering
Portscatho Holidays
t (01326) 270900
e info@portscathoholidays.co.uk
w portscathoholidays.co.uk

Pen An Garth ★★★★
Self Catering
Portscatho Holidays
t (01326) 270900
e info@portscathoholidays.co.uk
w portscathoholidays.co.uk

Penlee ★★★ *Self Catering*
Special Places in Cornwall
t (01872) 864400
e office@specialplacescornwall.co.uk
w specialplacescornwall.co.uk

Pier Cottage ★★★★
Self Catering
Special Places in Cornwall
t (01872) 864400
e office@specialplacescornwall.co.uk
w specialplacescornwall.co.uk

Poldhu ★★★★★
Self Catering
Portscatho Holidays
t (01326) 270900
e info@portscathoholidays.co.uk
w portscathoholidays.co.uk

Poldower ★★★ *Self Catering*
Portscatho Holidays
t (01326) 270900
e info@portscathoholidays.co.uk
w portscathoholidays.co.uk

Polmaro ★★★ *Self Catering*
Portscatho Holidays
t (01326) 270900
e info@portscathoholidays.co.uk
w portscathoholidays.co.uk

Prydes Cottage ★★★★
Self Catering
Special Places in Cornwall
t (01872) 864400
e office@specialplacescornwall.co.uk
w specialplacescornwall.co.uk

Rocklee House ★★★★
Self Catering
Special Places in Cornwall
t (01872) 864400
e office@specialplacescornwall.co.uk
w specialplacescornwall.co.uk

Roseland View
Rating Applied For
Self Catering
Portscatho Holidays
t (01326) 270900
e info@portscathoholidays.co.uk
w portscathoholidays.co.uk

Sail Cottage ★★★
Self Catering
Portscatho Holidays
t (01326) 270900
e info@portscathoholidays.co.uk
w portscathoholidays.co.uk

The Sea House ★★★
Self Catering
Portscatho Holidays
t (01326) 270900
e info@portscathoholidays.co.uk
w portscathoholidays.co.uk

Sea Star
Rating Applied For
Self Catering
Portscatho Holidays
t (01326) 270900
e info@portscathoholidays.co.uk
w portscathoholidays.co.uk

Sea View
Rating Applied For
Self Catering
Portscatho Holidays
t (01326) 270900
e info@portscathoholidays.co.uk
w portscathoholidays.co.uk

Seaspray ★★★ *Self Catering*
Roseland Holiday Cottages
t (01872) 580480
e enquiries@roselandholidaycottages.co.uk
w roselandholidaycottages.co.uk

Seaward ★★★★
Self Catering
Special Places in Cornwall
t (01872) 864400
e office@specialplacescornwall.co.uk
w specialplacescornwall.co.uk

September Cottage ★★★
Self Catering
Roseland Holiday Cottages
t (01872) 580480
e enquiries@roselandholidaycottages.co.uk
w roselandholidaycottages.co.uk

Skippers ★★★★
Self Catering
Special Places in Cornwall
t (01872) 864400
e office@specialplacescornwall.co.uk
w specialplacescornwall.co.uk

South Cottage ★★★
Self Catering
Portscatho Holidays
t (01326) 270900
e info@portscathoholidays.co.uk
w portscathoholidays.co.uk

Spinnakers ★★★
Self Catering
Portscatho Holidays
t (01326) 270900
e info@portscathoholidays.co.uk
w portscathoholidays.co.uk

Star Cottage ★★★
Self Catering
Portscatho Holidays
t (01326) 270900
e info@portscathoholidays.co.uk
w portscathoholidays.co.uk

Sunnybanks ★★★★
Self Catering
Special Places in Cornwall
t (01872) 864400
e office@specialplacescornwall.co.uk
w specialplacescornwall.co.uk

Sycamore ★★★★
Self Catering
Roseland Holiday Cottages
t (01872) 580480
e enquiries@roselandholidaycottages.co.uk
w roselandholidaycottages.co.uk

Tom Thumb Cottage ★★★
Self Catering
Roseland Holiday Cottages
t (01872) 580480
e enquiries@roselandholidaycottages.co.uk
w roselandholidaycottages.co.uk

Topdeck ★★★★
Self Catering
Special Places in Cornwall
t (01872) 864400
e office@specialplacescornwall.co.uk
w specialplacescornwall.co.uk

Tregarth Cottages ★★★★
Self Catering
Roseland Holiday Cottages
t (01872) 580480
e enquiries@roselandholidaycottages.co.uk
w roselandholidaycottages.co.uk

Trevose ★★★ *Self Catering*
Portscatho Holidays
t (01326) 270900
e info@portscathoholidays.co.uk
w portscathoholidays.co.uk

Trevu ★★★ *Self Catering*
Portscatho Holidays
t (01326) 270900
e info@portscathoholidays.co.uk
w portscathoholidays.co.uk

Uplands ★★★ *Self Catering*
Roseland Holiday Cottages
t (01872) 580480
e enquiries@roselandholidaycottages.co.uk
w roselandholidaycottages.co.uk

Upper Botreaux ★★★★
Self Catering
Portscatho Holidays
t (01326) 270900
e info@portscathoholidays.co.uk
w portscathoholidays.co.uk

Westover ★★★ *Self Catering*
Portscatho Holidays
t (01326) 270900
e info@portscathoholidays.co.uk
w portscathoholidays.co.uk

White Lodge ★★★★
Self Catering
Special Places in Cornwall
t (01872) 864400
e office@specialplacescornwall.co.uk
w specialplacescornwall.co.uk

Wiggy's ★★★ *Self Catering*
Portscatho Holidays
t (01326) 270900
e info@portscathoholidays.co.uk
w portscathoholidays.co.uk

The Workshop ★★★
Self Catering
Special Places in Cornwall
t (01872) 864400
e office@specialplacescornwall.co.uk
w specialplacescornwall.co.uk

ST MAWGAN
Cornwall

Rose Cottage ★★★★★
Self Catering
Blue Chip Vacations
t (01803) 855282
e info@bluechipvacations.com
w bluechipvacations.com

ST MELLION
Cornwall

15 Woburn Lodge ★★★★
Self Catering
Valley Villas Ltd
t (01752) 605605
e sales@valleyvillas.com
w valleyvillas.co.uk

ST MERRYN
Cornwall

121 Lily Way ★★★
Self Catering
Cornish Horizons Holiday Cottages
t (01841) 533331
e cottages@cornishhorizons.co.uk
w cornishhorizons.co.uk

138 Jasmine Way, St Merryn Holiday Village ★★★
Self Catering
Contact: Miss Mary-Jane Morgan
t (020) 8355 9773 & 07768 864556
e haha.films@virgin.net
w cornishselfcateringhols.com

5 Rose Terrace ★★★★
Self Catering
Cornish Horizons Holiday Cottages
t (01841) 533331
e cottages@cornishhorizons.co.uk
w cornishhorizons.co.uk

Angelholm ★★★
Self Catering
Cornish Horizons Holiday Cottages
t (01841) 533331
e cottages@cornishhorizons.co.uk
w cornishhorizons.co.uk

Bays Reach ★★★★
Self Catering
Cornish Horizons Holiday Cottages
t (01841) 533331
e cottages@cornishhorizons.co.uk
w cornishhorizons.co.uk

Cill Dara ★★★★
Self Catering
Harbour Holidays
t (01841) 533402
e contact@harbourholidays.co.uk
w harbourholidays.co.uk

Curlew ★★★ *Self Catering*
Cornish Horizons Holiday Cottages
t (01841) 533331
e cottages@cornishhorizons.co.uk
w cornishhorizons.co.uk

Look out for establishments participating in the National Accessible Scheme

Lanngorrow ★★★
Self Catering
Cornish Horizons Holiday Cottages
t (01841) 533331
e cottages@cornishhorizons.co.uk
w cornishhorizons.co.uk

Lantic Star ★★★
Self Catering
Cornish Horizons Holiday Cottages
t (01841) 533331
e cottages@cornishhorizons.co.uk
w cornishhorizons.co.uk

Lantic Surf ★★★
Self Catering
Cornish Horizons Holiday Cottages
t (01841) 533331
e cottages@cornishhorizons.co.uk
w cornishhorizons.co.uk

Little Gem ★★★★
Self Catering
Cornish Horizons Holiday Cottages
t (01841) 533331
e cottages@cornishhorizons.co.uk
w cornishhorizons.co.uk

Manassa ★★★ *Self Catering*
Cornish Horizons Holiday Cottages
t (01841) 533331
e cottages@cornishhorizons.co.uk
w cornishhorizons.co.uk

Meadow Lodge Annex
★★★★ *Self Catering*
Harbour Holidays
t (01841) 533402
e contact@harbourholidays.co.uk
w harbourholidays.co.uk

Point Curlew Country Holiday Estate ★★★
Self Catering
t (01305) 265487

Primrose Cottage – Treyarnon Bay ★★★★
Self Catering
Cornish Seaview Cottages
t (01428) 723819
e enquiries@cornishseaviewcottages.co.uk
w cornishseaviewcottages.co.uk

Quies ★★★ *Self Catering*
Cornish Horizons Holiday Cottages
t (01841) 533331
e cottages@cornishhorizons.co.uk
w cornishhorizons.co.uk

Rozmerrow ★★★★
Self Catering
Cornish Horizons Holiday Cottages
t (01841) 533331
e cottages@cornishhorizons.co.uk
w cornishhorizons.co.uk

St Hilary ★★★ *Self Catering*
Cornish Horizons Holiday Cottages
t (01841) 533331
e cottages@cornishhorizons.co.uk
w cornishhorizons.co.uk

Shotwood ★★★★
Self Catering
Contact: Ms Clague
t (01841) 541178

Trearth ★★★★ *Self Catering*
Cornish Horizons Holiday Cottages
t (01841) 533331
e cottages@cornishhorizons.co.uk
w cornishhorizons.co.uk

Trebiza ★★★★ *Self Catering*
Contact: Lucy Richards
t (01841) 521676
e info@seascapeholidaylets.co.uk
w seascapeholidaylets.co.uk

Tregavone Barn ★★★★
Self Catering
Farm & Cottage Holidays
t (01237) 459827
e enquiries@farmcott.co.uk
w holidaycottages.co.uk

Tregracy ★★★ *Self Catering*
Cornish Horizons Holiday Cottages
t (01841) 533331
e cottages@cornishhorizons.co.uk
w cornishhorizons.co.uk

Trevelgue ★★★ *Self Catering*
Cornish Horizons Holiday Cottages
t (01841) 533331
e cottages@cornishhorizons.co.uk
w cornishhorizons.co.uk

Twizzletwig ★★★★
Self Catering
Cornish Horizons Holiday Cottages
t (01841) 533331
e cottages@cornishhorizons.co.uk
w cornishhorizons.co.uk

Two Stiles ★★★★
Self Catering
Cornish Horizons Holiday Cottages
t (01841) 533331
e cottages@cornishhorizons.co.uk
w cornishhorizons.co.uk

Wheal Parc ★★★★
Self Catering
Cornish Horizons Holiday Cottages
t (01841) 533331
e cottages@cornishhorizons.co.uk
w cornishhorizons.co.uk

Wispa ★★★★★
Self Catering
Harbour Holidays
t (01841) 533402
e contact@harbourholidays.co.uk
w harbourholidays.co.uk

ST MINVER
Cornwall

2 Lundy House ★★★★
Self Catering
Roserrow Lettings
t (01208) 863000
e mail@roserrow.co.uk
w roserrow.co.uk

2 The Old Dairy ★★★★
Self Catering
Rock Holidays
t (01208) 863399
e info@rockholidays.co.uk
w rockholidays.co.uk

Apartment 4 ★★★★★
Self Catering
Roserrow Lettings
t (01208) 863000
e mail@roserrow.co.uk
w roserrow.co.uk

April Cottage ★★★★★
Self Catering
Rock Holidays
t (01208) 863399
e info@rockholidays.co.uk
w rockholidays.co.uk

Atlantic View ★★
Self Catering
Roserrow Lettings
t (01208) 863000
e mail@roserrow.co.uk
w roserrow.co.uk

The Bothy ★★★★
Self Catering
Roserrow Lettings
t (01208) 863000
e mail@roserrow.co.uk
w roserrow.co.uk

Breakers View ★★★★
Self Catering
Roserrow Lettings
t (01208) 863000
e mail@roserrow.co.uk
w roserrow.co.uk

Brook House ★★★★
Self Catering
Rock Holidays
t (01208) 863399
e info@rockholidays.co.uk
w rockholidays.co.uk

Bunkers Cottage ★★★★
Self Catering
Rock Holidays
t (01208) 863399
e info@rockholidays.co.uk
w rockholidays.co.uk

Caldarvan ★★★★
Self Catering
Roserrow Lettings
t (01208) 863000
e mail@roserrow.co.uk
w roserrow.co.uk

Casa Piedra Cottage ★★★★
Self Catering
Rock Holidays
t (01208) 863399
e info@rockholidays.co.uk
w rockholidays.co.uk

Cobwebs ★★★ *Self Catering*
Rock Holidays
t (01208) 863399
e info@rockholidays.co.uk
w rockholidays.co.uk

Cowrie ★★★★ *Self Catering*
Roserrow Lettings
t (01208) 863000
e mail@roserrow.co.uk
w roserrow.co.uk

The Farmhouse ★★★★
Self Catering
Rock Holidays
t (01208) 863399
e info@rockholidays.co.uk
w rockholidays.co.uk

Gearys ★★★★ *Self Catering*
Rock Holidays
t (01208) 863399
e info@rockholidays.co.uk
w rockholidays.co.uk

Glen Valley Cottage ★★★
Self Catering
Contact: Mr Richard Ellis
t (01484) 863263
e rich@glenvalleycottage.co.uk
w glenvalleycottage.co.uk

Gore's Garisson ★★★★★
Self Catering
Rock Holidays
t (01208) 863399
e info@rockholidays.co.uk
w rockholidays.co.uk

Great Bodieve Farm Barns
★★★★★ *Self Catering*
Contact: Mr & Mrs Phillips
t (01208) 814916
e enquiries@great-bodieve.co.uk
w great-bodieve.co.uk

Gwella ★★★★ *Self Catering*
Rock Holidays
t (01208) 863399
e info@rockholidays.co.uk
w rockholidays.co.uk

Hampden ★★★★★
Self Catering
Rock Holidays
t (01208) 863399
e info@rockholidays.co.uk
w rockholidays.co.uk

The Haven ★★★★★
Self Catering
Rock Holidays
t (01208) 863399
e info@rockholidays.co.uk
w rockholidays.co.uk

The Hawthorns ★★★★
Self Catering
Rock Holidays
t (01208) 863399
e info@rockholidays.co.uk
w rockholidays.co.uk

Janners Retreat ★★★
Self Catering
Roserrow Lettings
t (01208) 863000
e mail@roserrow.co.uk
w roserrow.co.uk

Keepers Cottage ★★★★
Self Catering
Rock Holidays
t (01208) 863399
e info@rockholidays.co.uk
w rockholidays.co.uk

Kensa Toll ★★★★
Self Catering
Roserrow Lettings
t (01208) 863000
e mail@roserrow.co.uk
w roserrow.co.uk

Lundy Cottage ★★★★
Self Catering
Rock Holidays
t (01208) 863399
e info@rockholidays.co.uk
w rockholidays.co.uk

Lundy House/St Agnes
★★★★ *Self Catering*
Contact: Mr & Mrs Horsfield
t (01208) 269818

Mayfield Cottage ★★★★
Self Catering
Roserrow Lettings
t (01208) 863000
e mail@roserrow.co.uk
w roserrow.co.uk

The Millhouse Barn ★★★
Self Catering
Rock Holidays
t (01208) 863399
e info@rockholidays.co.uk
w rockholidays.co.uk

Mosseyoak ★★★★
Self Catering
Rock Holidays
t (01208) 863399
e info@rockholidays.co.uk
w rockholidays.co.uk

Moyles Farm ★★★★
Self Catering
Contact: Mrs Amanda Woodward
t (01208) 862331
e mail@moylesfarm.co.uk

The Nineteenth ★★★★
Self Catering
Rock Holidays
t (01208) 863399
e info@rockholidays.co.uk
w rockholidays.co.uk

No 6 ★★★★★ *Self Catering*
Roserrow Lettings
t (01208) 863000
e mail@roserrow.co.uk
w roserrow.co.uk

Oak Tree House ★★★★
Self Catering
Rock Holidays
t (01208) 863399
e info@rockholidays.co.uk
w rockholidays.co.uk

Penhayle ★★★★
Self Catering
Rock Holidays
t (01208) 863399
e info@rockholidays.co.uk
w rockholidays.co.uk

Penkivel House ★★★★
Self Catering
Rock Holidays
t (01208) 863399
e info@rockholidays.co.uk
w rockholidays.co.uk

Penteli ★★★★ *Self Catering*
Rock Holidays
t (01208) 863399
e info@rockholidays.co.uk
w rockholidays.co.uk

Pentire ★★★★★
Self Catering
Roserrow Lettings
t (01208) 863000
e mail@roserrow.co.uk
w roserrow.co.uk

Puffin House ★★★★
Self Catering
Rock Holidays
t (01208) 863399
e info@rockholidays.co.uk
w rockholidays.co.uk

Ridgewood ★★★★
Self Catering
Rock Holidays
t (01208) 863399
e info@rockholidays.co.uk
w rockholidays.co.uk

Rose Cottage ★★★★★
Self Catering
Rock Holidays
t (01208) 863399
e info@rockholidays.co.uk
w rockholidays.co.uk

Rosewin Barn ★★★
Self Catering
Rock Holidays
t (01208) 863399
e info@rockholidays.co.uk
w rockholidays.co.uk

St Andrew's Cottage
★★★★ *Self Catering*
Rock Holidays
t (01208) 863399
e info@rockholidays.co.uk
w rockholidays.co.uk

Sandy Cottage ★★★★
Self Catering
Roserrow Lettings
t (01208) 863000
e mail@roserrow.co.uk
w roserrow.co.uk

September ★★★★
Self Catering
Rock Holidays
t (01208) 863399
e info@rockholidays.co.uk
w rockholidays.co.uk

Tamarisk ★★★★
Self Catering
Rock Holidays
t (01208) 863399
e info@rockholidays.co.uk
w rockholidays.co.uk

Thyme Cottage ★★★★
Self Catering
Roserrow Lettings
t (01208) 863000
e mail@roserrow.co.uk
w roserrow.co.uk

Tremaine ★★★★★
Self Catering
Rock Holidays
t (01208) 863399
e info@rockholidays.co.uk
w rockholidays.co.uk

Trevells ★★★ *Self Catering*
Rock Holidays
t (01208) 863399
e info@rockholidays.co.uk
w rockholidays.co.uk

Trevelver Farm Cottage
★★★ *Self Catering*
Contact: Mrs Avice Wills
t (01208) 863290

Trevose ★★★★★
Self Catering
Roserrow Lettings
t (01208) 863000
e mail@roserrow.co.uk
w roserrow.co.uk

Valerian ★★★ *Self Catering*
Roserrow Lettings
t (01208) 863000
e mail@roserrow.co.uk
w roserrow.co.uk

Webbs Retreat ★★★★
Self Catering
Rock Holidays
t (01208) 863399
e info@rockholidays.co.uk
w rockholidays.co.uk

Wedge Cottage ★★★
Self Catering
Rock Holidays
t (01208) 863399
e info@rockholidays.co.uk
w rockholidays.co.uk

Wenlock ★★★★
Self Catering
Roserrow Lettings
t (01208) 863000
e mail@roserrow.co.uk
w roserrow.co.uk

Woodbine House ★★★★★
Self Catering
Rock Holidays
t (01208) 863399
e info@rockholidays.co.uk
w rockholidays.co.uk

Woodfin ★★★ *Self Catering*
Contact: Mrs Janet Edwards
Oak & Elm Cottage
t (01483) 202478

ST NEOT
Cornwall

Badgers Holiday Cottages, St Neot ★★★★ *Self Catering*
Contact: Phil & Allison Harris
t (01579) 320741 & 07855 807183
e phil.harris@btinternet.com
w badgersholidaycottages.co.uk

ST NEWLYN EAST
Cornwall

Goonwinnow Farm Holiday Cottages ★★★★
Self Catering
Contact: Mr Andrew Murgatroyd
t (01872) 510696
e goonwinnowfarm@aol.com
w goonwinnowfarm.co.uk

Granary Cottages ★★★★
Self Catering
Contact: Mr Clark
t (01872) 510345
e trewerry.mill@talktalk.net
w trewerrymill.co.uk

ST STEPHEN
Cornwall

Court Farm Cottages
★★★★ *Self Catering*
Contact: Mr Bill Truscott
t (01726) 822727
e truscott@ctfarm.freeserve.co.uk
w courtfarmcornwall.co.uk

ST TEATH
Cornwall

26 Rosewater Park ★★★
Self Catering
Contact: Mrs Dawn Kinder
Rosewater Park
t (01633) 674388
e info@rosewaterpark.co.uk
w rosewaterpark.co.uk

Barn Farm Holidays – BC053
★★★★ *Self Catering*
Contact: Mrs Goldie
t (01208) 850912
e enquiries@barnfarmholidays.co.uk
w barnfarmholidays.co.uk

Dinnabroad Cottage ★★★★
Self Catering
Farm & Cottage Holidays
t (01237) 459827
e enquiries@farmcott.co.uk
w holidaycottages.co.uk

Higher Hendra Cottages
★★★★ *Self Catering*
Contact: Mrs Roose
t (01208) 880341
w higher-hendra.com

Mill Barn and Stable Cottage
★★★★ *Self Catering*
Contact: Mrs Julie Bailey
t (01208) 850994
e tredarrupinfo@aol.com
w tredarrup.com

ST TUDY
Cornwall

The Linhay ★★★★★
Self Catering
Contact: Mrs C.M Kingdon
t (01208) 851422
e cmkingdon@tiscali.co.uk
w stayatthelinhay.co.uk

ST VEEP
Cornwall

A Little Bit of Heaven Manelly Fleming ★★★
Self Catering
Contact: Mrs Daphne Rolling
t (01208) 872564
e daphne@alittlebitofheaven.co.uk
w alittlebitofheaven.co.uk

SALCOMBE
Devon

Coxswain's Watch ★★★★
Self Catering
Contact: Mrs Julie Powell
Robert Oulsnam & Co
t (0121) 445 3311
e barntgreen@oulsnam.net
w oulsnam.net

Dairymans Corner and Shepherds Rest ★★★
Self Catering
Contact: Mrs Anne Rossiter
t (01548) 561210
e anne@burtonfarm.co.uk
w burtonfarm.co.uk

Marine Cottage ★★★★
Self Catering
Contact: Mrs Gill Rowe
t (01242) 820213
e rowefarms@farmline.com
w salcombedevon.co.uk

SALCOMBE REGIS
Devon

Long Chimney Farm Cottages ★★★★
Self Catering
Contact: Mr & Mrs Adrian & Rowena Thomas
t (01297) 680636
e longchimney@aol.com
w longchimneyfarmcottages.co.uk

SALISBURY
Wiltshire

10 Charter Court ★★★★
Self Catering
Hideaways
t (01747) 828170
e enq@hideaways.co.uk
w hideaways.co.uk

1st Floor Apartment ★★★
Self Catering
Hideaways
t (01747) 828170
e enq@hideaways.co.uk
w hideaways.co.uk

24 Charter Court
Rating Applied For
Self Catering
Contact: Mrs Christina Walker
t (01725) 510327

Crane Street ★★★★
Self Catering
Hideaways
t (01747) 828170
e enq@hideaways.co.uk
w hideaways.co.uk

Harnham Road ★★★
Self Catering
Hideaways
t (01747) 828170
e enq@hideaways.co.uk
w hideaways.co.uk

The Hayloft, Ebblesway Courtyard ★★★★
Self Catering
Contact: Mr & Mrs Peter & Gail Smalley
t (01722) 780182
e gail@ebblesway courtyard.co.uk
w ebbleswaycourtyard.co.uk

Hen View (The Fishing Lodge) ★★★★ *Self Catering*
Contact: Mrs Victoria Dakin
t (01747) 855976
e vdakin@skymarket.org

Little Till Cottage ★★★★
Self Catering
Contact: Mr & Mrs Michael & Ninetta Hearn
t (01980) 620396
e mike@littletillcottage.com
w littletillcottage.com

Love Lane ★★★ *Self Catering*
Hideaways
t (01747) 828170
e enq@hideaways.co.uk
w hideaways.co.uk

The Old Stables ★★★★
Self Catering
Contact: Mr Giles Gould
t (01722) 349002
e mail@old-stables.co.uk
w old-stables.co.uk

Rustic Cottage ★★★★
Self Catering
Contact: Mrs Cheryl Beeney
t (01722) 337870
e cheribeen@aol.com
w rustic-cottage-salisbury.co.uk

Salisbury Apartments ★★★★ *Self Catering*
Contact: Mrs Mary Webb
t (01722) 340892 & 07759 474115
e enquiries@salisbury-apartments.co.uk
w salisbury-apartments.co.uk

Sycamore Cottage ★★★★
Self Catering
Contact: Mr & Mrs Richard & Cilla Pickett
Melrose Cottage
t (01722) 743160
e cilla@sycamorecottage.biz
w sycamorecottage.biz

Trinity Street
Rating Applied For
Self Catering
Hideaways
t (01747) 828170
e enq@hideaways.co.uk
w hideaways.co.uk

Water Lane H094 ★★★
Self Catering
Hideaways
t (01747) 828170
e enq@hideaways.co.uk
w hideaways.co.uk

Wich Hazel's Apartment, Woodfalls ★★★★
Self Catering
Contact: Mrs Ann Eveleigh
t (01725) 511599
e anneveleigh@aol.com
w wichhazel.co.uk/

Winterbourne Cottage ★★★★ *Self Catering*
Hideaways
t (01747) 828170
e enq@hideaways.co.uk
w hideaways.co.uk

SAMPFORD ARUNDEL
Somerset

Gorlegg Cottage ★★★★
Self Catering
Farm & Cottage Holidays
t (01237) 459827
e enquiries@farmcott.co.uk
w holidaycottages.co.uk

SAMPFORD BRETT
Somerset

Old Rectory Coach House ★★★ *Self Catering*
Contact: Jan Swan
t (01984) 633787
e enquiries@oldrectorycoachhouse.co.uk
w oldrectorycoachhouse.co.uk

SAMPFORD COURTENAY
Devon

Culverhayes Properties ★★★★ *Self Catering*
t (01837) 89150
w culverhayes.co.uk/

SAUL
Gloucestershire

The Old Cider House ★★★
Self Catering
Contact: Mrs Kathryn McDermott
t (01452) 741613
e mcdermott595@btinternet.com
w pridingfarm.com

SAUNTON
Devon

Knelles Retreat ★★★
Self Catering
Marsdens Cottage Holidays
t (01271) 813777
e holidays@marsdens.co.uk
w marsdens.co.uk

Little Rhu ★★★ *Self Catering*
Marsdens Cottage Holidays
t (01271) 813777
e holidays@marsdens.co.uk
w marsdens.co.uk

Rhu & Little Rhu ★★★
Self Catering
Marsdens Cottage Holidays
t (01271) 813777
e holidays@marsdens.co.uk
w marsdens.co.uk

Sandhills ★★★ *Self Catering*
Marsdens Cottage Holidays
t (01271) 813777
e holidays@marsdens.co.uk
w marsdens.co.uk

Saunton Sands Apartments ★★★-★★★★★
Self Catering
Contact: Mr David Marshall
t (01271) 322033

SEATON
Cornwall

1 Seaton Court ★★★
Self Catering
Cornish Collection Ltd
t (01503) 262736
e enquiries@cornishcollections.co.uk
w cornishcollection.co.uk

Seaton Beach House
Rating Applied For
Self Catering
Valley Villas Ltd
t (01752) 605605
e sales@valleyvillas.com
w valleyvillas.co.uk

SEATON
Devon

Birdsong ★★★ *Self Catering*
Milkbere Cottage Holidays
t (01297) 20729
e info@milkberehols.com
w milkberehols.com

Caruso ★★★ *Self Catering*
Milkbere Cottage Holidays
t (01297) 20729
e info@milkberehols.com
w milkberehols.com

Conswalk ★★★ *Self Catering*
Milkbere Cottage Holidays
t (01297) 20729
e info@milkberehols.com
w milkberehols.com

Deepdale ★★★ *Self Catering*
Milkbere Cottage Holidays
t (01297) 20729
e info@milkberehols.com
w milkberehols.com

Half Penny ★★★
Self Catering
Milkbere Cottage Holidays
t (01297) 20729
e info@milkberehols.com
w milkberehols.com

Harbour Side ★★★★
Self Catering
Contact: Mrs Hilary Bevis
t (01297) 23388

Holly Cottage
Rating Applied For
Self Catering
Milkbere Cottage Holidays
t (01297) 20729
e info@milkberehols.com
w milkberehols.com

Little Oaks ★★★★
Self Catering
Milkbere Cottage Holidays
t (01297) 20729
e info@milkberehols.com
w milkberehols.com

The Loft ★★★ *Self Catering*
Milkbere Cottage Holidays
t (01297) 20729
e info@milkberehols.com
w milkberehols.com

Manor Farm Cottages ★★★-★★★★ *Self Catering*
Contact: Mrs Parr
t (01297) 625349

Marine Place Apartments ★★★ *Self Catering*
Milkbere Cottage Holidays
t (01297) 20729
e info@milkberehols.com
w milkberehols.com

Mole Cottage ★★★★
Self Catering
Milkbere Cottage Holidays
t (01297) 20729
e info@milkberehols.com
w milkberehols.com

The Nook ★★★ *Self Catering*
Milkbere Cottage Holidays
t (01297) 20729
e info@milkberehols.com
w milkberehols.com

Pilsbury Cottage ★★★
Self Catering
Milkbere Cottage Holidays
t (01297) 20729
e info@milkberehols.com
w milkberehols.com

Pioneer ★★★ *Self Catering*
Milkbere Cottage Holidays
t (01297) 20729
e info@milkberehols.com
w milkberehols.com

Primrose ★★★ *Self Catering*
Milkbere Cottage Holidays
t (01297) 20729
e info@milkberehols.com
w milkberehols.com

Riverside ★★★★
Self Catering
Milkbere Cottage Holidays
t (01297) 20729
e info@milkberehols.com
w milkberehols.com

Sandpiper ★★★★
Self Catering
Milkbere Cottage Holidays
t (01297) 20729
e info@milkberehols.com
w milkberehols.com

Seafield ★★★★ *Self Catering*
Milkbere Cottage Holidays
t (01297) 20729
e info@milkberehols.com
w milkberehols.com

Seagulls ★★★ *Self Catering*
Milkbere Cottage Holidays
t (01297) 20729
e info@milkberehols.com
w milkberehols.com

West Acres ★★★★
Self Catering
Milkbere Cottage Holidays
t (01297) 20729
e info@milkberehols.com
w milkberehols.com

West Ridge Bungalow ★★★
Self Catering
Contact: Mrs Hildegard Fox
t (01297) 22398
e fox@foxwestridge.co.uk
w cottageguide.co.uk/westridge

Westcliff ★★★ *Self Catering*
Milkbere Cottage Holidays
t (01297) 20729
e info@milkberehols.com
w milkberehols.com

SEATOWN
Dorset

The Guard House, Seatown ★★★★ *Self Catering*
Contact: Mrs Charlotte Wreaves
t (020) 7228 6366
e info@guardhouse.co.uk
w guardhouse.co.uk

SECTOR
Devon

Brook Cottage ★★★★
Self Catering
Lyme Bay Holidays
t (01297) 443363
e email@lymebayholidays.co.uk
w lymebayholidays.co.uk

SELSLEY
Gloucestershire

Ale House Cottage ★★★
Self Catering
Contact: Ms Kate Holloway
t (01453) 872028
e holloway.kate@googlemail.com
w alehousecottage.co.uk

SEMLEY
Wiltshire

Seniors Farm Cottage ★★★★ *Self Catering*
Hideaways
t (01747) 828170
e enq@hideaways.co.uk
w hideaways.co.uk

SENNEN
Cornwall

3 & 4 Wesley Cottages, Nanquidno Valley, St Just ★★★ *Self Catering*
Contact: Mrs J Davey
t (01736) 731933
e wesley@raginnis.demon.co.uk
w wesleyatnanquidno.co.uk

Trevear Farm Cottages ★★★★ *Self Catering*
Contact: Mrs Trudi Thomas
t (01736) 731231
e thomaslamorna@googlemail.com
w trevearfarm.co.uk

SENNEN COVE
Cornwall

Dor Lewern ★★★★
Self Catering
Contact: Mr Ron Ludgate
t (020) 8452 4950
e riludgate@yahoo.com

Grassmead ★★★-★★★★
Self Catering
Contact: Mr Geoff Wood
t (0161) 308 4436
e eurofloorukltd@aol.com
w holidaylettings.co.uk/rentals/st-just/52647

Harbour Mews, Sennen Cove ★★★★ *Self Catering*
Contact: Mr Jeff Hardman
t (01736) 810504
e jeff@sennencornwall.com
w sennencornwall.com

Riviera Apartments ★★★
Self Catering
Contact: Mr & Mrs George
Riviera Apartments and Treloggan Cottage
t (01736) 810452
e robertandkay@penberth.com
w furthestwest.com

Tinker Taylor Cottage ★★★★ *Self Catering*
Contact: Mr David Paget
t (01934) 751306
e davidpagets@aol.com
w tinker-taylor.com

SHAFTESBURY
Dorset

Bowling Green Farm
Rating Applied For
Self Catering
Contact: Mr & Mrs Ian & Sue Benefer
t (01747) 811588
e bowlinggreenfarm@aol.com
w bowlinggreenfarm.co.uk

Hartgrove Farm
★★★-★★★★ *Self Catering*
Contact: Mrs Susan Smart
t (01747) 811830
e smart@hartgrovefarm.co.uk
w hartgrovefarm.co.uk

Updown Cottage ★★★★★
Self Catering
Contact: Mr & Mrs Jane & Simon Colston
t 07710 307202
e info@updowncottage.co.uk
w updowncottage.co.uk

Vale Farm Holiday Cottages ★★★-★★★★ *Self Catering*
Contact: Mr Jon Drake
t (01747) 811286
e valeholidays@tiscali.co.uk
w valeholidays.co.uk

Whitebridge Farm Cottages ★★★-★★★★ *Self Catering*
Contact: Mr & Mrs Terry & Julie Neale
Whitebridge Farm
t (01747) 830462
e whitebridgefarm@btconnect.com
w whitebridgeholidaycottages.co.uk

SHALDON
Devon

5 Shoreside ★★★★★
Self Catering
Blue Chip Vacations
t (01803) 855282
e info@bluechipvacations.com
w bluechipvacations.com

Beaulieu Apartments ★★★
Self Catering
Contact: Mr John Pile
t (01626) 872331

Centre House, Ringmore Lodge ★★★★ *Self Catering*
Contact: Mrs Chris Deacon
t (01564) 793841
e centrehouse@ringmorelodge.freeserve.co.uk
w centrehouse-ringmorelodge.co.uk

Chalet 23
Rating Applied For
Self Catering
Contact: Gaynor Diggins
t (029) 2075 3073
e chris.diggins1@virgin.net

East Cliff ★★★ *Self Catering*
Blue Chip Vacations
t (01803) 855282
e info@bluechipvacations.com
w bluechipvacations.com

Littleover ★★★★
Self Catering
Contact: Mr & Mrs Frank & Angela Hook
t (01626) 873205
e information@littleover-shaldon.co.uk
w littleover-shaldon.co.uk

Upper Deck, Shaldon ★★★
Self Catering
Blue Chip Vacations
t (01803) 855282
e info@bluechipvacations.com
w bluechipvacations.com

SHEBBEAR
Devon

Berry Barns ★★★★
Self Catering
Contact: Ms Kerry Thain
t (01409) 281859
e info@berrybarns.co.uk
w berrybarns.co.uk

SHEEPSCOMBE
Gloucestershire

Longridge Meend ★★★
Self Catering
Contact: Mr Richard Cound
t (01452) 813225
e richardcound@beeb.net

SHEEPWASH
Devon

Swardicott Farm ★★★
Self Catering
Contact: Mrs Marguerite Purser
t (01409) 231633
e m.purser@btinternet.com
w holidaycottages-devon.co.uk

SHEPTON MALLET
Somerset

Courtyard Apartment ★★★
Self Catering
Contact: Ms Ruth Pratt
t (01749) 342508
e buffiepratt@live.co.uk
w courtyardapartment.co.uk

Leigh Holt ★★★★★
Self Catering
Contact: Mrs Pamela Hoddinott
t (01749) 671271
e pam@burnthousefarmbandb.co.uk
w leighholt.co.uk

SHEPTON MONTAGUE
Somerset

Seed House ★★★★
Self Catering
Contact: Mrs Christina Dimond
t (01749) 812373
e dimond@farm24771.fsnet.co.uk
w higherfarm.net

SHERBORNE
Dorset

Blackberry Cottage ★★★
Self Catering
Contact: Mr John Michael Farr
t (01935) 423148

Millers Loft ★★★
Self Catering
Contact: Mrs Bridget Buckland
t (01963) 250380
e bandebuckland@aol.com
w millersloft.co.uk

Old Orchard Cottage
★★★★ *Self Catering*
Contact: Mrs Alexa Buckland
t (01963) 251365

Patson Hill Cottages ★★★★
Self Catering
Contact: Mr & Mrs Ronald & Jill Racher
t 0845 450 5993
e info@patsonhill.co.uk
w patsonhill.co.uk

Stable Cottage ★★★
Self Catering
t (01935) 814716

White Horse Farm, Middlemarsh ★★★-★★★★
Self Catering
Contact: Mr & Mrs Stuart & Audrey Winterbottom
t (01963) 210222
e enquiries@whitehorsefarm.co.uk
w whitehorsefarm.co.uk

SHERRINGTON
Wiltshire

Gingerbread Cottage
★★★★ *Self Catering*
Contact: Mrs Gabrielle Lewis
t (01985) 850453
e patlewis@lineone.net
w gingerbreadcottage.co.uk

SHERSTON
Wiltshire

Lantern House ★★★★★
Self Catering
Contact: Mrs Patricia Evans
t (01666) 505807
e lanternhouse@cotswolds.plus.com
w cotswolds.plus.com

SHILLINGFORD
Devon

The Fishing Lodge ★★★
Self Catering
Contact: Mrs Geraldine Newton
t (01398) 331169
e fourpondscarp@aol.com
w fourponds.com

SHIPTON MOYNE
Gloucestershire

Street Farm Cottages
★★★★ *Self Catering*
Contact: Mrs Beth Birdwood
t (01666) 880523
e beth@streetfarm.co.uk
w streetfarm.co.uk

SHIPTON OLIFFE
Gloucestershire

Paddock Barn ★★★★★
Self Catering
Contact: Mrs Doyle
t (01242) 890147
e emma@paddockbarn.co.uk
w paddockbarn.co.uk

SHREWTON
Wiltshire

Drovers' Barn ★★★
Self Catering
Hideaways
t (01747) 828170
e enq@hideaways.co.uk
w hideaways.co.uk

SHUTE
Devon

Higher Watchcombe Farmhouse and Country Cottages ★★★★
Self Catering
Contact: Mr & Mrs Paul & Jane Galloway
t (01297) 552424
e galloways@ukgateway.net
w higherwatchcombe.com

SHUTTA
Cornwall

Sunny Patch ★★★
Self Catering
Cornish Collection Ltd
t (01503) 262736
e enquiries@cornishcollections.co.uk
w cornishcollection.co.uk

SIDMOUTH
Devon

1 The Fort ★★★
Self Catering
Contact: Mr David Crooks
t (01395) 577326
e david.crooks@hlp.eclipse.co.uk

1 Hillview ★★★★
Self Catering
Sweetcombe Cottage Holidays
t (01395) 512130
e enquiries@sweetcombe-ch.co.uk
w sweetcombe-ch.co.uk

Anchor Apartment ★★★★
Self Catering
Contact: Mrs Jane Tagg
t (01392) 425858
e sidmouthanchor@yahoo.com

Anstis Court ★★★★
Self Catering
Contact: Miss Nancy Smith
t (01392) 263820
e selfcateringinsidmouth@googlemail.com
w selfcateringinsidmouth.co.uk

Bayview ★★★ *Self Catering*
Contact: Mrs Rosemary Sidwell
t (01395) 515668

Blackberry Bungalow
★★★★ *Self Catering*
Sweetcombe Cottage Holidays
t (01395) 512130
e enquiries@sweetcombe-ch.co.uk
w sweetcombe-ch.co.uk

Bohemia Villas ★★★★
Self Catering
Contact: Mrs Luisa Mellor
t (01484) 532682
e mellorfixby@yahoo.co.uk
w sidmouth-breaks.co.uk

Boswell Farm Cottages
★★★★ *Self Catering*
Contact: Mr & Mrs Brian & Linda Dillon
t (01395) 514162
e dillon@boswell-farm.co.uk
w boswell-farm.co.uk

Bulverton House – The Bakers Cottage ★★★★
Self Catering
Contact: Mr Geoffrey Roe
t (01395) 578552
e geoffroe@hotmail.com
w bulvertonhouse.co.uk

Cormorant Cottage ★★★★
Self Catering
Sweetcombe Cottage Holidays
t (01395) 512130
e enquiries@sweetcombe-ch.co.uk
w sweetcombe-ch.co.uk

Cosy Cottage ★★★
Self Catering
Contact: Mrs Pauline Flood
t (01823) 421501
e pauline.flood@btinternet.com

The Courtyard ★★★
Self Catering
Sweetcombe Cottage Holidays
t (01395) 512130
e enquiries@sweetcombe-ch.co.uk
w sweetcombe-ch.co.uk

Curlew Cottage ★★★★
Self Catering
Sweetcombe Cottage Holidays
t (01395) 512130
e enquiries@sweetcombe-ch.co.uk
w sweetcombe-ch.co.uk

Dairy Cottage ★★★
Self Catering
Sweetcombe Cottage Holidays
t (01395) 512130
e enquiries@sweetcombe-ch.co.uk
w sweetcombe-ch.co.uk

Dunscombe Manor ★★★★
Self Catering
Contact: Mrs Christina Morgan
t (01395) 513654
e info@dunscombe-manor.co
w dunscombe-manor.co.uk

Ever Rest Cottage ★★★
Self Catering
Sweetcombe Cottage Holidays
t (01395) 512130
e enquiries@sweetcombe-ch.co.uk
w sweetcombe-ch.co.uk

Flat 4 Western Court
★★★★ *Self Catering*
Contact: Mr G M Corr Glendevon
t (01395) 512216
e sidmouthholidayflats@yahoo.co.uk
w sidmouth-selfcatering.co.uk

Goldies Cottage ★★★★
Self Catering
t (01386) 833412

Littlecourt Cottages ★★★★
Self Catering
Contact: Mr Selwyn Kussman
t (01395) 515279
e admin@littlecourtcottages.com
w littlecourtcottages.com

Merrifield House (Flat 2)
★★★★ *Self Catering*
Sweetcombe Cottage Holidays
t (01395) 512130
e enquiries@sweetcombe-ch.co.uk
w sweetcombe-ch.co.uk

Poppleford ★★★
Self Catering
Sweetcombe Cottage Holidays
t (01395) 512130
e enquiries@sweetcombe-ch.co.uk
w sweetcombe-ch.co.uk

Redcliffs ★★★★
Self Catering
Sweetcombe Cottage Holidays
t (01395) 512130
e enquiries@sweetcombe-ch.co.uk
w sweetcombe-ch.co.uk

Rockcliffe ★★★★
Self Catering
Sweetcombe Cottage Holidays
t (01395) 512130
e enquiries@sweetcombe-ch.co.uk
w sweetcombe-ch.co.uk

St Davids, 1 Fortfield Terrace ★★★ *Self Catering*
Contact: Mr & Mrs George
St. Davids, 1 Fortfield Terrace
t (01395) 578173

Sidmouth Apartment
★★★★ *Self Catering*
Contact: Mr & Mrs Coates
t (01728) 842861
e kerthuapark@btinternet.co.uk
w sidmouthapartment.co.uk

Stonechat ★★★
Self Catering
Milkbere Cottage Holidays
t (01297) 20729
e info@milkberehols.com
w milkberehols.com

Tarn ★★★★ *Self Catering*
Sweetcombe Cottage Holidays
t (01395) 512130
e enquiries@sweetcombe-ch.co.uk
w sweetcombe-ch.co.uk

Treetops ★★★ *Self Catering*
Sweetcombe Cottage Holidays
t (01395) 512130
e enquiries@sweetcombe-ch.co.uk
w sweetcombe-ch.co.uk

Western Court Holiday Apartment ★★★
Self Catering
Contact: Mr & Mrs R.E. & L.V. Mitchell
t (01395) 578786
e hols@remtek46.fsnet.co.uk

Wyndham Court ★★★
Self Catering
Contact: Mr Peter Vincent
t (01395) 577973
e pvcia@aol.com
w holidaysinsidmouth.co.uk

SIMONSBATH
Somerset

Wintershead Farm, Simonsbath ★★★★
Self Catering
Contact: Mrs Jane Styles
t (01643) 831222
e wintershead@yahoo.co.uk
w wintershead.co.uk

SITHNEY
Cornwall

The Hideaway ★★★
Self Catering
Contact: Mr & Mrs Faull
t (01326) 573489
e trelissick@hotmail.com
w trelissickfarm.co.uk

SLAPTON
Devon

Beeches ★★★★
Self Catering
Toad Hall Cottages
t (01548) 853089
e thc@toadhallcottages.com
w toadhallcottages.co.uk

Blackberry Cottage ★★★★
Self Catering
Toad Hall Cottages
t (01548) 853089
e thc@toadhallcottages.com
w toadhallcottages.co.uk

Dittiscombe Holiday Cottages ★★★★
Self Catering
Contact: Mrs Ruth Saunders
t (01548) 521272
e info@dittiscombe.co.uk
w dittiscombe.co.uk

Maple Cottage ★★★
Self Catering
Toad Hall Cottages
t (01548) 853089
e thc@toadhallcottages.com
w toadhallcottages.co.uk

SLIMBRIDGE
Gloucestershire

Rectory Park ★★★★★
Self Catering
Contact: Elaine Molyneux
t 0845 208 1066
e info@dunsterliving.co.uk
w rectorypark.co.uk

SNOWSHILL
Gloucestershire

Shenberrow Farm Cottage ★★★★★ *Self Catering*
Contact: Mrs Tina Carroll
t (01386) 858359
e tinaacarroll@aol.com
w shenberrow.co.uk

SOMERFORD KEYNES
Gloucestershire

Falcon House ★★★★★
Self Catering
Contact: Ms Kareena Richards
t (020) 7720 9937
e info@falcon-house.com
w falcon-house.com

SOMERTON
Somerset

Sleepy Hollow ★★★★
Self Catering
Contact: Mrs Rhian Raine
t (01458) 850584
e paul&rhian@sleepyhollowcottages.com
w sleepyhollowcottages.com

SOUDLEY
Gloucestershire

The Cottage ★★★
Self Catering
Contact: Helen R Evans
Evans Holiday Cottages
t (01594) 861119
e helen@peakedrockscottage.fsnet.co.uk
w evansholidays.co.uk

Farriers Lodge ★★★
Self Catering
Contact: Julie Farrier
t (01452) 751044
e farrierslodge@farrier702.freeserve.co.uk
w farrierslodge.org.uk

SOUTH BOWOOD
Dorset

West Cottage ★★
Self Catering
Contact: Miss Marion Gadsby
t (01308) 488294
e marion.gadsby@btinternet.com

SOUTH BREWHAM
Somerset

Magpie Cottage ★★★★
Self Catering
Contact: Mr David Dabinett
t (01749) 850441
e david@havenfarm.co.uk
w havenfarm.co.uk

SOUTH CERNEY
Gloucestershire

Cotswold Lakeside Lodge ★★★★ *Self Catering*
t (01242) 245236
w cotswoldlakelodge.com

Cotswold Waterpark
Rating Applied For
Serviced Apartments
t (01285) 864000
w four-pillars.co.uk

Fountain View, South Cerney ★★★ *Self Catering*
Contact: Ms Jean McDonald
t 0800 043 0697
e contactus@holidaycottageisis.com
w holidaycottageisis.com

The Watermark Club ★★★-★★★★★
Self Catering
Contact: Mr Robert Cowley
t (01285) 869181
e enquiries@watermarkclub.co.uk
w watermark-holidays.com

SOUTH MILTON
Devon

Savernake ★★★
Self Catering
Contact: Miss Emily Dawson
Hall Wells Barn
e e.dawson@zoom.co.uk
w savernake-devon.com

The White Cottage ★★★★
Self Catering
Toad Hall Cottages
t (01548) 853089
e thc@toadhallcottages.com
w toadhallcottages.co.uk

SOUTH MOLTON
Devon

Bampfylde ★★★★
Self Catering
Marsdens Cottage Holidays
t (01271) 813777
e holidays@marsdens.co.uk
w marsdens.co.uk

Drewstone Farm ★★★★
Self Catering
Contact: Mrs Ruth Ley
t (01769) 572337
e ruth_ley@drewstonefarm.fsnet.co.uk
w devonself-catering.co.uk

North Lee Farm Holiday Cottages ★★★★
Self Catering
Contact: Miss Rebecca Evans
t (01598) 740248
e beck@northlee.com
w northlee.com

Stable Cottage ★★★★★
Self Catering
Contact: Mrs Victoria Huxtable
t (01598) 740130

Townhouse Barton ★★★
Self Catering
Contact: Mrs Wendy Warren
t (01769) 572467
e info@townhousebarton.co.uk
w townhousebarton.co.uk

Vicarys Mews ★★★★
Self Catering
Marsdens Cottage Holidays
t (01271) 813777
e holidays@marsdens.co.uk
w marsdens.co.uk

The Willows ★★★★
Self Catering
Marsdens Cottage Holidays
t (01271) 813777
e holidays@marsdens.co.uk
w marsdens.co.uk

SOUTH PETHERTON
Somerset

Tanwyn ★★★★ *Self Catering*
Contact: Mr & Mrs Rodney & Ann Tanswell
t (01656) 880524
e rodney.tanswell@btinternet.com
w freewebs.com/tanwyn

SOUTHLEIGH
Devon

Wiscombe Linhaye ★★★
Self Catering
Milkbere Cottage Holidays
t (01297) 20729
e info@milkberehols.com
w milkberehols.com

SPREACOMBE
Devon

Spreacombe Lodge ★★★★★ *Self Catering*
Marsdens Cottage Holidays
t (01271) 813777
e holidays@marsdens.co.uk
w marsdens.co.uk

STANTON
Gloucestershire

Charity Cottage ★★★ *Self Catering & Serviced Apartments*
Contact: Mrs Ryland
t (01386) 584339
e kennethryland@ukonline.co.uk
w myrtle-cottage.co.uk/ryland.htm

STAPLEGROVE
Somerset

The Barn ★★★★
Self Catering
Contact: Mrs Anita Harris
t (01823) 451553
e anita@higheryardefarm.co.uk
w higheryardefarm.co.uk

STAPLEY
Somerset

Willow & Bracken Lodges ★★★★★ *Self Catering*
t (01823) 672284
w sleeps12.com

STATHE
Somerset

Walkers Farm Cottages ★★★★ *Self Catering*
Contact: Mrs Dianne Tilley
t (01823) 698229
e info@walkersfarmcottages.co.uk
w walkersfarmcottages.co.uk

STAVERTON
Devon

The Kingston Estate ★★★★★ *Self Catering*
Contact: Mr Howard Turner
t (01803) 762235
e info@kingston-estate.net
w kingston-estate.net

STEEPLE ASHTON
Wiltshire

Coachmans Cottage ★★★★
Self Catering
Contact: Mrs Penny Hornsey
t (01380) 870764
e phornsey@talktalk.net
w coachmans-cottage.com

Jasmine Cottage ★★★★
Self Catering
Contact: Mr Norman Sharples
t (0121) 353 5258
e stay@jasminecottage.co.uk
w jasminecottage.co.uk

STITHIANS
Cornwall

Charis Cottage ★★★★
Self Catering
Contact: Ms Schneider
t (01209) 861003
e astondrees@hotmail.com
w chariscottage.co.uk

Higher Trewithen Holiday Cottages ★★★-★★★★
Self Catering
Contact: Mr Burgess
t (01209) 860863
e trewithen@talk21.com
w trewithen.com

Ivory Cottage, Stithians
★★★ *Self Catering*
Contact: Mr & Mrs David & Daya Stafford
t (01209) 861486
e cottage@ivorycottage.co.uk
w ivorycottage.co.uk

Kettle Cottage ★★★★
Self Catering
Contact: Mrs Barbara Simms
t (01209) 204166
e kazsimms@hotmail.co.uk

Rosies Cottage
Rating Applied For
Self Catering
Holiday Cornwall
t (01326) 250278
e enquiries@holidaycornwall.co.uk
w holidaycornwall.co.uk

STOGUMBER
Somerset

Periwinkle Cottage ★★★
Self Catering
Contact: Miss Sheila Hubbard
t (01643) 841413

STOKE FLEMING
Devon

Old Chapel
Rating Applied For
Self Catering
Blue Chip Vacations
t (01803) 855282
e info@bluechipvacations.com
w bluechipvacations.com

STOKE GABRIEL
Devon

Aish Cross Holiday Cottages
★★★★★ *Self Catering*
Contact: Mrs Angela Pavey
Aish Cross House
t (01803) 782022
e info@aishcross.co.uk
w aishcross.co.uk

Stoke House
Rating Applied For
Self Catering
Blue Chip Vacations
t (01803) 855282
e info@bluechipvacations.com
w bluechipvacations.com

STOKE ST GREGORY
Somerset

Baileys Gallery & Baileys Barn ★★★ *Self Catering*
Contact: Mr Stanley Chedzoy
Baileys Gallery
t (01823) 490644

Holly Farm Cottages ★★★★
Self Catering
Contact: Mr & Mrs Robert & Liz Hembrow
t (01823) 490828
e robhembrow@btinternet.com
w holly-farm.com

Walnut Arbour
Rating Applied For
Self Catering
t (01823) 431622

STOKE ST MARY
Somerset

Stoke Hill Studio
★★★-★★★★★ *Self Catering*
Contact: Mr Alan Coles
t (01823) 443759
e ajcoles@supanet.com
w somerset-selfcatering.co.uk

STOKE SUB HAMDON
Somerset

Blackspur Cottage ★★★★
Self Catering
Contact: Mrs Jacqueline Fisher
t (01935) 881789
e brookhouse_fishers@yahoo.co.uk

Top o Hill ★★★ *Self Catering*
Contact: Mrs Mary Gane
t (01935) 822089

West End Barn ★★★★
Self Catering
Contact: Mrs Tanya Morris
t (01935) 826540
e tanya@west-end-barn.co.uk
w west-end-barn.co.uk/

STOKEINTEIGNHEAD
Devon

Church Barn ★★★★
Self Catering
t (01626) 872433

The Granary ★★★
Self Catering
Holiday Homes and Cottages South West
t (01803) 299677
e holcotts@aol.com
w swcottages.co.uk

Mondali ★★★ *Self Catering*
Holiday Homes and Cottages South West
t (01803) 299677
e holcotts@aol.com
w swcottages.co.uk

STOKENHAM
Devon

Tilly's Tuckaway ★★★★★
Self Catering
Toad Hall Cottages
t (01548) 853089
e thc@toadhallcottages.com
w toadhallcottages.co.uk

STONEY STRATTON
Somerset

Red Tiles Barn ★★★★
Self Catering
Contact: Mr Richard Neill
t (01344) 882322
e neill.hall@care4free.net
w redtilesbarn.co.uk

Springfield Cottages ★★★★
Self Catering
Contact: Mrs Pat Allen
t (01749) 830748
e ted.allen@btinternet.com
w stayinbritain.com/springfieldcottageholidays

Stable Barn Cottage ★★★★
Self Catering
t 07749 830830

STOURPAINE
Dorset

April Cottage ★★
Self Catering
Contact: Mr John Stitt
t (01258) 458933
e stitt77@tiscali.co.uk

STOW-ON-THE-WOLD
Gloucestershire

Barn Cottage ★★★★★ *Self Catering & Serviced Apartments*
Contact: Mrs Lissa Mills
t (01451) 830947
e lissa-mills@ukonline.co.uk
w barncottagecotswolds.co.uk

Bottom End Cottage ★★★★
Self Catering
Contact: Ms Karen Hawkes
Cottage in the Country and Cottage Holidays
t 0870 027 5930
e enquiries@cottageinthecountry.co.uk
w cottageinthecountry.co.uk

Box Cottage ★★★
Self Catering
Contact: Mr Bob Johnston
t (01608) 650816
e enquiries@stow-cottages.co.uk
w stow-cottages.co.uk

Broad Oak Cottages, Stow-on-the-Wold ★★★★★
Self Catering
Contact: Mrs Wilson
t (01451) 830794
e mary@broadoakcottages.co.uk
w broadoakcottages.co.uk

The Corner Cottage
★★★-★★★★ *Self Catering*
Contact: Mr Paul Broadhead
t (01924) 255692
e info@thecornercottage.co.uk
w thecornercottage.co.uk

Cotswold Holiday Cottages, Upper Oddington ★★★★
Self Catering
Contact: Wendy Hill
t 07853 148362
e wendy@cotswold-holidays.com
w cotswold-holidays.com

Foden Lodge ★★★
Self Catering
Contact: Mr & Mrs Beryl Gypps
t (01992) 301800
e thefodenlodge@hotmail.com
w fodenlodge.co.uk

Glebe Cottage ★★★★
Self Catering
Contact: Mrs Lesley Paler
t (01483) 203375
e lesley@gbc-ca.co.uk

Horseshoes ★★★★
Self Catering
Contact: Ms Yvonne Johnston
t (01608) 650816
w stow-cottages.co.uk

Johnston Cottage & Kates
★★★ *Self Catering*
Contact: Mrs Yvonne Johnston
t (01608) 650816
w stow-cottages.co.uk

Lilac Cottage ★★★★
Self Catering
Contact: Ms Marion Anderson
t (01224) 634411
e morven@lilac-cottage.co.uk
w lilac-cottage.co.uk

Park Farm Holiday Cottages
★★★★-★★★★★
Self Catering
Contact: Mrs Tiana Ricketts
t (01451) 870568
e tiana@parkfarmholidaycottages.co.uk
w parkfarmholidaycottages.co.uk

Park House Cottage ★★★
Self Catering
Contact: Mr & Mrs George & Barbara Sutton
t (01451) 830159
e info@parkhousecottage.co.uk
w parkhousecottage.co.uk

Rose's Cottage, Broadwell
★★★★ *Self Catering*
Contact: Mr Richard Drinkwater
t (01451) 830007
e richard.drinkwater@ukonline.co.uk

Sycamore Cottage ★★★★
Self Catering
Contact: Mrs S Jones
t (01844) 208615
e suejones16@hotmail.com

Valley View ★★★★
Self Catering
Contact: Mr & Mrs Peter & Janet Craddock
t (01564) 770143
e janetcraddock25@hotmail.com
w cottageguide.co.uk/valleyview

Wells Cottage ★★★
Self Catering
Contact: Mr & Mrs Gwyn & Sue Williams
t (01451) 830045
w wellscottage.co.uk

STRATFORD SUB CASTLE
Wiltshire

Manor Cottage Holidays
★★★ *Self Catering*
Hideaways
t (01747) 828170
e enq@hideaways.co.uk
w hideaways.co.uk

Millers Barn ★★★
Self Catering
Hideaways
t (01747) 828170
e enq@hideaways.co.uk
w hideaways.co.uk

STRATTON
Cornwall

Old Sanctuary Cottages
★★★★ *Self Catering*
Contact: Mrs Berry
t (01288) 353159
e enquiries@oldsanctuarycottages.com
w oldsanctuarycottages.com

STRATTON
Dorset

Eweleaze ★★★★
Self Catering
t (01305) 263316
w wessexholidaycottages.co.uk

The Old Village Hall ★★★★
Self Catering
Contact: Miss Katherine Johnson
t (03495) 883 6849
e kayjohnson@arrakis.es
w classic.co.uk

STRATTON-ON-THE-FOSSE
Somerset

Pitcot Farm Barn Cottages ★★★★ *Self Catering*
Contact: Mrs Mary Coles
t (01761) 233108
e info@pitcotfarm.co.uk
w pitcotfarm.co.uk

STREET
Somerset

Blue Lias ★★★ *Self Catering*
Contact: Mr Mark Foot
t (01275) 853612
e markfoot@hotmail.com

Roshani ★★★★ *Self Catering*
Contact: Mrs L Turton
t (01458) 443579
e stay@avalonselfcatering.co.uk
w avalonselfcatering.co.uk

STROUD
Gloucestershire

The Coach House c/o The Old Vicarage ★★★★
Self Catering
Contact: Mrs Stella Knight
t (01453) 832265
e stella.knight@tiscali.co.uk
w cotswoldholidaycottage.co.uk

Westley Farm ★★★
Self Catering
Contact: Mr Usborne
t (01285) 760262
e cottages@westleyfarm.co.uk
w westleyfarm.co.uk

The Yew Tree ★★★
Self Catering
Contact: Mrs Elizabeth Peters
t (01453) 887980
e elizabeth.peters@tesco.net
w theyewtreestroud.co.uk

STUDLAND
Dorset

Heathland Cottage ★★★
Self Catering
Dorset Cottage Holidays
t (01929) 553443
e enq@dhcottages.co.uk
w dhcottages.co.uk

Sandyholme Garden Cottage ★★ *Self Catering*
Contact: Mrs Christine Boardman
t (01305) 265172
e j_and_c_boardman@talk21.com

STURMINSTER MARSHALL
Dorset

Parkfield Cottage ★★★
Self Catering
Contact: Mr Michael Royles
t (01258) 857804
e mikeroyles@yahoo.co.uk
w parkfieldcottage.sturminstermarshall.co.uk

SUMMERCOURT
Cornwall

13 Trehellan Heights ★★★★ *Self Catering*
Blue Chip Vacations
t (01803) 855282
e info@bluechipvacations.com
w bluechipvacations.com

SUTTON POYNTZ
Dorset

The Courthouse ★★★★
Self Catering
Dream Cottages
t (01305) 789000
e admin@dream-cottages.co.uk
w dream-cottages.co.uk

Ebenezer Cottage ★★★★
Self Catering
Contact: Mrs Cathy Varley
t 07778 524199
e info@ebenezercottage.co.uk
w ebenezercottage.co.uk

Ella Cottage ★★★★
Self Catering
Dream Cottages
t (01305) 789000
e admin@dream-cottages.co.uk
w dream-cottages.co.uk

Garland Cottage ★★★
Self Catering
Contact: Mrs Gillian Dawe
t (023) 9246 0424
e info@garlandcottage.co.uk
w garlandcottage.co.uk

Pickle Cottage ★★★
Self Catering
Dream Cottages
t (01305) 789000
e admin@dream-cottages.co.uk
w dream-cottages.co.uk

SUTTON WALDRON
Dorset

Dairy Cottage ★★★
Self Catering
Contact: Mr & Mrs S Asbury
t (01747) 811330

SWANAGE
Dorset

10 The Haven ★★★★
Self Catering
Contact: Mrs Frances Thackway
t (01929) 422715
e frances@thehavenswanage.co.uk
w virtualswanage.com/accommodation/10_the_haven/30.aspx

2 Carrants Court ★★★
Self Catering
Contact: Mrs T Leeds
t (01732) 463659
e hengistthegnome@hotmail.com

2 Chines ★★★ *Self Catering*
Contact: Mrs Caroline Grange
t (01225) 834430
e caroline@swanageholidaylet.co.uk
w swanageholidaylet.co.uk

2 Quayside Court ★★
Self Catering
Contact: Mr Michael Padfield
t (01628) 472113
e mike@thepadfields.com

2 Wilksworth Cottage ★★
Self Catering
Dream Cottages
t (01305) 789000
e admin@dream-cottages.co.uk
w dream-cottages.co.uk

2 Wordsworth Court ★★★
Self Catering
Contact: Mr Donald Pallister
t (023) 8076 9592
e pallisterdb@aol.com

27 Manwell Road ★★★
Self Catering
Contact: Mrs Jill Henstridge
t (01929) 427276
e info@swanageview.com
w swanageview.com

6 Cluny Crescent ★★★★
Self Catering
Contact: Mr David Smith
t (01929) 423333
e info@milesandson.co.uk

9 Quayside Court ★★★
Self Catering
Contact: Mr Graham Hogg
t (01454) 311178
e graham.hogg@blueyonder.co.uk
w bythequayholidays.co.uk

Acorns ★★★ *Self Catering*
Contact: Mrs Sally Lucas
t (01929) 425000
e enquiries@acornsswanage.co.uk
w acornsswanage.co.uk

Alrose Villa Holiday Apartements ★★★
Self Catering
Contact: Mr & Mrs Peter & Sally Gutteridge
t (01929) 422892
w alrosevilla.co.uk

Annexe to Stoneacre ★★★
Self Catering
Contact: Mrs Carol Brown
t (01929) 480668
e annexe_to_stoneacre@yahoo.co.uk
w annexestoneacre.co.uk

Ballard Lee ★★★
Self Catering
Contact: Mr & Mrs Ian Lever
t (01929) 551320
e ian.lever@talk21.com
w ballardholidaybungalows.co.uk

Ballard Walk ★★★
Self Catering
t (01929) 422482
w ballardwalk.co.uk

Chalkdell Cottage ★★★
Self Catering
Contact: Mr & Mrs Brian & Linda Gooding
t (01727) 831126
e chalkdell@fsmail.net

Coastguards Return ★★★★
Self Catering
Contact: Mrs Anna Morrison
t (01929) 424630
e retrieverproperties@tiscali.co.uk

Edgecroft ★★★ *Self Catering*
Dorset Cottage Holidays
t (01929) 553443
e enq@dhcottages.co.uk
w dhcottages.co.uk

Flat 13 Royal Victoria ★
Self Catering
Contact: Mr Richard Brockman
t (01962) 853088
e richard@fabrock.plus.com
w fabrock.plus.com/holidayflat

Flat 8 Sandringham Court ★★★★ *Self Catering*
Contact: Mrs Hilary Hyde
t (020) 8948 4991
e ian@mdsfg.com
w 8sandringhamcourt.co.uk

Gables Court Holiday Apartments ★★★
Self Catering
Contact: Ms Maria Thompson
t (01929) 426516
e steve.thompson@izrmail.com
w gables-apartments.co.uk

The Ketch ★★★
Self Catering
Dorset Cottage Holidays
t (01929) 553443
e enq@dhcottages.co.uk
w dhcottages.co.uk

Kings Haven Cottage ★★★
Self Catering
Dorset Cottage Holidays
t (01929) 553443
e enq@dhcottages.co.uk
w dhcottages.co.uk

Lilac Cottage ★★★
Self Catering
Contact: Mrs Jean Simmonds
t (01544) 388619
e jean@seagrasscottages.co.uk
w seagrasscottages.co.uk

Lizard's Rest ★★★★
Self Catering
Dream Cottages
t (01305) 789000
e admin@dream-cottages.co.uk
w dream-cottages.co.uk

Malverns Apartment ★★★
Self Catering
Dorset Cottage Holidays
t (01929) 553443
e enq@dhcottages.co.uk
w dhcottages.co.uk

Marston Holiday Flats ★★
Self Catering
Contact: Mrs Jackie Lane
t (01929) 422221
e marstonflats@btinternet.com
w swanageholidayflats.co.uk

Mia's Cottage ★★★★
Self Catering
Contact: Mrs Sarah Streams
t (01929) 426079
e info@swanagecottages.co.uk
w swanagecottages.co.uk

One London Row ★★★
Self Catering
Contact: Mr & Mrs Philip & Monica Sanders
t (020) 8348 9815
e info@philamonic.com
w philamonic.com

Peepsea ★★★ *Self Catering*
Dorset Cottage Holidays
t (01929) 553443
e enq@dhcottages.co.uk
w dhcottages.co.uk

The Pinnacles ★★-★★★
Self Catering
Contact: Mrs Alyson Greenfield
t (01425) 654358

Plum Tree Cottage ★★★★
Self Catering
Contact: Ms Amanda Taylor
t (020) 8355 6611
e info@purbeckholidaycottage.co.uk
w purbeckholidaycottage.co.uk

Purbeck Cliffs ★★★★
Self Catering
Contact: Mrs Sue McWilliams
t (01929) 424352
e sue@purbeckcliffs.co.uk
w purbeckcliffs.co.uk

The Quarterdeck ★★★★
Self Catering
Contact: Mr Chris Radford
t (020) 8144 1913
e enquiries@purbeckholidays.co.uk
w purbeckholidays.co.uk

St Mark's Cottage ★★★
Self Catering
t (01737) 224441

Seaside Cottage ★★★
Self Catering
Dorset Cottage Holidays
t (01929) 553443
e enq@dhcottages.co.uk
w dhcottages.co.uk

Southview Cottage ★★
Self Catering
Contact: Mr David George
t (020) 8876 1806
e davidgeorge@o2email.co.uk
w southviewcottage.co.uk

The Studio ★★★★
Self Catering
Dorset Cottage Holidays
t (01929) 553443
e enq@dhcottages.co.uk
w dhcottages.co.uk

Styre House ★★
Self Catering
Contact: Mrs Hermina Clarke
t (01929) 424209

Sunnyside ★★★
Self Catering
Contact: Mrs Elizabeth Beesley
t (01929) 422226

Sunset Penthouse Apartment ★★★★
Self Catering
Contact: Miss Kate Stracey
t (01202) 763339
e kate@quaysidedevelopments.co.uk
w swanage-apartments.co.uk

Swanage Cottage Holidays
★★★★ *Self Catering*
Contact: Mrs Janet Howells
t (01929) 421601 & 07971 552082
e bjhowells@hotmail.com
w swanagecottageholidays.co.uk

Swanwic House ★★
Self Catering
Contact: Mrs Carole Figg
t (01929) 423517

Tanglewood ★★★★
Self Catering
Dorset Cottage Holidays
t (01929) 553443
e enq@dhcottages.co.uk
w dhcottages.co.uk

Topsail House ★★★★
Self Catering
Contact: Mrs Janet Foran
t (01929) 422322
e mail@sandhaven-guest-house.co.uk
w sandhaven-guesthouse.co.uk

Waterside ★★★
Self Catering
Contact: Karen Dolling
t (020) 8560 5587 & 07985 552232
e jkdolling@hotmail.com
w watersideholidaylet.co.uk

Windjammer ★★★
Self Catering
Dorset Cottage Holidays
t (01929) 553443
e enq@dhcottages.co.uk
w dhcottages.co.uk

SWIMBRIDGE
Devon

Animal Ark Cottages
Rating Applied For
Self Catering
Contact: Mrs Lynn Marshall
t (01271) 831138
e info@animalarkcottages.co.uk
w animalarkcottages.co.uk

Heavenly House
Rating Applied For
Self Catering
Marsdens Cottage Holidays
t (01271) 813777
e holidays@marsdens.co.uk
w marsdens.co.uk

Lower Hearson Farm
★★★★ *Self Catering*
Contact: Mr & Mrs G Pelling
t (01271) 830702
e info@hearsoncottagesdevon.co.uk
w hearsoncottagesdevon.co.uk

SWINDON
Gloucestershire

Hollowmead ★★★
Self Catering
Contact: Mr Graham Moore
t 07810 626390
e grahammoore88@btinternet.com

St Magdalenes Cottage
★★★★★ *Self Catering*
Contact: Mrs Hilary Mervyn-Smith
t (01242) 511211
e hmervynsmith@hotmail.co.uk
w cottagenet.co.uk/stmagdalene.htm

SYDLING ST NICHOLAS
Dorset

Grace Cottage ★★★
Self Catering
Contact: Mrs Nicky Willis
t (01308) 863868
e nickywillis@tesco.net

SYMONDSBURY
Dorset

Chideock Cottage ★★★
Self Catering
Dream Cottages
t (01305) 789000
e admin@dream-cottages.co.uk
w dream-cottages.co.uk

Woodlanders ★★★★
Self Catering
Contact: Mrs Jackie Harris
t (01225) 335153
e jackiemharris@hotmail.co.uk
w symondsburyholiday.co.uk

TAUNTON
Somerset

The Garden Retreat ★★★★
Self Catering
Contact: Mrs Liz Thompson
t (01823) 451529
e lizthompson47@hotmail.com
w gardenretreat.co.uk

Higher House ★★★
Self Catering
Contact: Mrs Kirsten Horton
t (01823) 400570
e mail@higherhouse.co.uk
w higherhouse.co.uk

Linnets, Fitzhead ★★★★
Self Catering
Contact: Mrs Patricia Grabham
t (01823) 400658
e patricia.grabham@onetel.net
w linnetsfitzhead.co.uk

Meadowsweet Farm Cottages ★★★★
Self Catering
Contact: Miss Jacqueline McCann
t (01984) 656323
e info@meadowsweet-cottages.co.uk
w meadowsweet-cottages.co.uk

Meare Court Holiday Cottages ★★★★
Self Catering
Contact: Mrs Elizabeth Bray
t (01823) 480570
e mearecourt@farming.co.uk
w mearecourt.co.uk

The Studio ★★★★
Self Catering
Contact: Mrs Eileen Rawlings
t (01823) 331879
e ea.rawlings@virgin.net

TAVISTOCK
Devon

Dartmoor Holidays ★★★
Self Catering
Contact: Mr Christopher Boswell
t (01822) 810687
e chrisboswe@aol.com
w dartmoorholidays.co.uk

Edgemoor Cottage, Middlemoor ★★★★
Self Catering
Contact: Mrs Mary Susan Fox
t (01822) 612259
e vicky@dartmoorcottages.info
w edgemoorcottage.co.uk

Higher Chaddlehanger Farm
★★★ *Self Catering*
Contact: Mrs Ruth Cole
The Annexe
t (01822) 810268

Moorview Cottage ★★★★
Self Catering
Contact: Mrs Elaine Mackintosh
t (01822) 810271
e ejm@dartmoor-holidays.fsnet.co.uk
w dartmoor-holidays.com

Tavistock Railway Station
Rating Applied For
Self Catering
Contact: Jenny Rogers
t (01822) 610136
e jenny@tavistockrailwaystation.co.uk
w tavistockrailwaystation.co.uk

TAYNTON
Gloucestershire

Owls Barn ★★★★
Self Catering
Contact: Mrs Barbara Goodwin
t (01452) 831290
e goodies@coldcroft.freeserve.co.uk
w coldcroft.freeserve.co.uk

TEFFONT
Wiltshire

Magna Chalets ★★★
Self Catering
Contact: Mary Corrie
t (01722) 716338
e mary@corrie-deane.com
w magnachalets.co.uk

TEHIDY
Cornwall

Seven The Stables ★★★★
Self Catering
Contact: Mrs Nicola Thomas
t (01905) 621001
e nicolathomas@besidethewaves.co.uk
w besidethewaves.co.uk

TEIGNGRACE
Devon

Twelve Oaks Holiday Cottages ★★★ *Self Catering*
Contact: Mrs Gale
t (01626) 352769

TEIGNMOUTH
Devon

5 Kiniver Court ★★★★★
Self Catering
Blue Chip Vacations
t (01803) 855282
e info@bluechipvacations.com
w bluechipvacations.com

Foresters Terrace ★★★
Self Catering
Contact: Mrs Vicki Copelletti
t (01626) 879613
e vicki542@btinternet.com
w sunshine-breaks.co.uk

Gem Cottage ★★★★
Self Catering
Contact: Mrs Twigg
t (01626) 777310
e pstwigg@tiscali.co.uk
w teignmouth-holiday-cottage.co.uk

Grendons Holiday Apartments ★★★
Self Catering
Contact: Mr Charles Gray
t (01626) 773667
e grendonsholidayapt@cix.co.uk
w cottageguide.co.uk/grendons

Higher Holcombe Farm Holiday Cottages
Rating Applied For
Self Catering
Contact: Catherine Evans-Martin
t (01626) 779688
e enquiries@higherholcombefarm.co.uk
w higherholcombefarm.co.uk

Pat-A-Cake Cottage ★★★
Self Catering
Contact: Mrs Barbara Smail
t (01392) 841626
e barbarasmail@btinternet.com

Quayside Cottage ★★★
Self Catering
Holiday Homes and Cottages South West
t (01803) 299677
e holcotts@aol.com
w swcottages.co.uk

Riverside Apartment ★★★
Self Catering
Blue Chip Vacations
t (01803) 855282
e info@bluechipvacations.com
w bluechipvacations.com

The Sail Loft ★★★★
Self Catering
Contact: Mrs J R Williams
t (0117) 924 7371
e thesailloft_teignmouth@blueyonder.co.uk
w thesailloft.co.uk

Teignside Cottage ★★★★
Self Catering
Blue Chip Vacations
t (01803) 855282
e info@bluechipvacations.com
w bluechipvacations.com

TEMPLE GUITING
Gloucestershire

Springbank ★★★★★
Self Catering
Contact: Mr Kate Mather
t (01451) 850571
e springbank@landgatetg.co.uk
w landgatetg.co.uk

TETBURY
Gloucestershire

Berkeley House ★★★★★
Self Catering
Contact: Mr Nigel Stengard-Green
t (01666) 500051
e nigel@lenaproudlock.com
w lenaproudlockescapes.com

TEWKESBURY
Gloucestershire

9 Mill Bank ★★ *Self Catering*
Contact: Mr Hunt
t (01684) 276190
e billhunt@9mb.co.uk
w tewkesbury-cottage.co.uk

Courtyard Cottages ★★★★
Self Catering
Contact: Mr Herford
t (01386) 725351
e diana@uppercourt.co.uk
w uppercourt.co.uk

The Old Stable Block ★★★
Self Catering
Contact: Mr & Mrs Geoff Stringer
t (01386) 881248
e info@beckford-stores.co.uk

The Stables Rosehill Farm
★★★ *Self Catering*
Contact: Mrs Elizabeth Collinson
t (01684) 293598

THE PACKET QUAYS
Cornwall

2 Victoria Quay ★★★
Self Catering
Cornish Holiday Cottages
t (01326) 250339
e emily@cornishholidaycottages.net
w cornishholidaycottages.net

4 Jago Slip ★★★
Self Catering
Cornish Holiday Cottages
t (01326) 250339
e emily@cornishholidaycottages.net
w cornishholidaycottages.net

6 Jane's Court ★★★★
Self Catering
Cornish Holiday Cottages
t (01326) 250339
e emily@cornishholidaycottages.net
w cornishholidaycottages.net

6 Victoria Quay ★★★
Self Catering
Cornish Holiday Cottages
t (01326) 250339
e emily@cornishholidaycottages.net
w cornishholidaycottages.net

THE PLUDDS
Gloucestershire

High Beeches ★★
Self Catering
Contact: Lynda King Taylor
t (020) 7262 1531
e lktlondon@aol.com
w lyndakingtaylor.com/highbeeches/index.html

THORNCOMBE
Dorset

6 The Terrace ★★★
Self Catering
Lyme Bay Holidays
t (01297) 443363
e email@lymebayholidays.co.uk
w lymebayholidays.co.uk

Thatch Cottage ★★★★
Self Catering
Contact: Mrs Eileen Mercer
t (020) 8393 8165
e eileenjmercer@hotmail.com

THORVERTON
Devon

Fursdon House ★★★★
Self Catering
Contact: Mrs Catriona Fursdon
t (01392) 860860
e enquiries@fursdon.co.uk
w fursdon.co.uk

THREE LEGGED CROSS
Dorset

Forester's Cottage ★★★★
Self Catering
Contact: Mrs Jean Baylis
t (01202) 820203
e jeanbaylis@btinternet.com
w foresterscottages.co.uk/

The Gables ★★★
Self Catering
Contact: Mr & Mrs David Priest
t (01202) 821322
e janet@thegables3lx.com
w thegables3lx.com

Homestead Farm ★★★
Self Catering
Contact: Brigitte Pierson
t (01202) 814033
e jplgolf1@aol.com

THURLESTONE
Devon

Cob Barn ★★★★
Self Catering
Toad Hall Cottages
t (01548) 853089
e thc@toadhallcottages.com
w toadhallcottages.co.uk

Old Rectory Cottage ★★★★
Self Catering
Toad Hall Cottages
t (01548) 853089
e thc@toadhallcottages.com
w toadhallcottages.co.uk

THURLESTONE SANDS
Devon

1 Thurlestone Beach Apartment ★★★★
Self Catering
Toad Hall Cottages
t (01548) 853089
e thc@toadhallcottages.com
w toadhallcottages.co.uk

Sea Campion ★★★
Self Catering
Toad Hall Cottages
t (01548) 853089
e thc@toadhallcottages.com
w toadhallcottages.co.uk

Sea Holly ★★★★
Self Catering
Toad Hall Cottages
t (01548) 853089
e thc@toadhallcottages.com
w toadhallcottages.co.uk

Sea Lavender ★★★
Self Catering
Toad Hall Cottages
t (01548) 853089
e thc@toadhallcottages.com
w toadhallcottages.co.uk

Sea Poppy ★★★★★
Self Catering
Toad Hall Cottages
t (01548) 853089
e thc@toadhallcottages.com
w toadhallcottages.co.uk

TIMBERSCOMBE
Somerset

Avill Holidays
★★★-★★★★ *Self Catering*
t 07813 332932
w avillholidays.co.uk

TINCLETON
Dorset

The Courtyard At Clyffe
★★★★ *Self Catering*
Contact: Dr Ian Mew
t 07748 417974
e info@tincleton.co.uk
w tincleton.co.uk

The Old Dairy Cottage ★★★
Self Catering
t (01305) 848252
w the-old-barn.co.uk

Tincleton Lodge and Clyffe Dairy Cottage ★★★★★
Self Catering
Contact: Mrs Jane Coleman
t (01305) 848391
e enquiries@dorsetholidaycottages.net
w dorsetholidaycottages.net

TINTAGEL
Cornwall

Boskenna and Atlanta
★★★★ *Self Catering*
Cornish Seaview Cottages
t (01428) 723819
e enquiries@cornishseaviewcottages.co.uk
w cornishseaviewcottages.co.uk

Clifden Farm Cottages ★★★
Self Catering
Contact: Mrs Margaret Nute
t (01840) 770437
e mnute@toucansurf.com
w cornwall-online.co.uk

Halgabron Mill ★★★
Self Catering
Contact: Mr Robin Evans
t (01840) 779099
e robin@halgabronmill.co.uk
w halgabronmill.co.uk

Penpethy Holiday Cottages
★★★ *Self Catering*
Contact: Mrs Morag Steadman
t (01840) 213903

Rosemary ★★★ *Self Catering*
Contact: Mrs Mary Dyer
t (01840) 770472
e mary.dyer@virgin.net

Tregeath ★★★ *Self Catering*
Contact: Mrs Edwina Broad
t (01840) 770217

TIPTON ST JOHN
Devon

Higher Coombe Bungalow
★★★★ *Self Catering*
t (01404) 813385
e kerstinfarmer@farming.co.uk

TISBURY
Wiltshire

Mews Cottage ★★★
Self Catering
Hideaways
t (01747) 828170
e enq@hideaways.co.uk
w hideaways.co.uk

The Old Coach House ★★★
Self Catering
Hideaways
t (01747) 828170
e enq@hideaways.co.uk
w hideaways.co.uk

TIVERTON
Devon

Coombe Cottage ★★★
Self Catering
Contact: Mr & Mrs Nick & Sally Kerslake
t (01398) 351715
e sallykerslake@btinternet.com
w exmoor-holiday-cottage.co.uk

Lilac Cottage ★★★★
Self Catering
Contact: Mrs Venner
t (01884) 820226

Old Bridwell Holiday Cottages ★★★★
Self Catering
Contact: Ms Jackie Kind
t (01884) 841464
e jackie@oldbridwell.co.uk
w oldbridwell.co.uk

Tiverton Castle ★★★★
Self Catering
Contact: Mrs Alison Gordon
t (01884) 253200 & (01884) 255200
e tiverton.castle@ukf.net
w tivertoncastle.com

West Pitt Farm
★★★-★★★★ *Self Catering*
Contact: Ms Susanne Westgate
t (01884) 820296
e susannewestgate@yahoo.com
w westpittfarm.co.uk

TIVINGTON
Somerset

Tethinstone Cottage ★★★★
Self Catering
Contact: Mr Nicholas Challis
t (01643) 706757

TOLLER PORCORUM
Dorset

Froghall & Dairymaids Cottage ★★★-★★★★
Self Catering
Contact: Mrs Rosemary Gower
t (01300) 320541
e rosemarygower@hotmail.com

TOLPUDDLE
Dorset

River View Cottage ★★★★
Self Catering
Dorset Cottage Holidays
t (01929) 553443
e enq@dhcottages.co.uk
w dhcottages.co.uk

TOPSHAM
Devon

Forest End ★★★★
Self Catering
Contact: Eve Merson
t (01392) 876165
e eve@emile-et-rose.co.uk

No 22 ★★★★★ *Self Catering*
Contact: Ms Ann Maybury
t (01392) 200131
e enquiries@no22.co.uk
w no22.co.uk

Pebble Bed House
Rating Applied For
Self Catering
Contact: Ms Anna Bowen
t (01392) 875908
e anna@pebblebed.co.uk
w pebblebedhouse.co.uk

Wisteria Cottage
Rating Applied For
Self Catering
Contact: Kate Looker
t (01395) 567676
w thethatchedcottagecompany.com

TORPOINT
Cornwall

14 Celtic Shores ★★★★
Self Catering
Cornish Collection Ltd
t (01503) 262736
e enquiries@cornishcollections.co.uk
w cornishcollection.co.uk

Jackdaw Cottage ★★
Self Catering
Contact: Mrs Sartorius
t (0121) 454 0284
e aes@alucast.co.uk
w jackdawcottagecornwall.co.uk

TORQUAY
Devon

1 The Moorings ★★★
Self Catering
Blue Chip Vacations
t (01803) 855282
e info@bluechipvacations.com
w bluechipvacations.com

10 Fonthill ★★★★
Self Catering
Contact: Mrs Elizabeth Hogarth
t (0117) 956 5795
e lizhogarth@btinternet.com
w torquayholidayhomes.com

10 Manor House Apartments ★★★★★
Self Catering
Blue Chip Vacations
t (01803) 855282
e info@bluechipvacations.com
w bluechipvacations.com

11 Manor House Apts
★★★★★ *Self Catering*
Blue Chip Vacations
t (01803) 855282
e info@bluechipvacations.com
w bluechipvacations.com

12 Manor House Apts
★★★★★ *Self Catering*
Blue Chip Vacations
t (01803) 855282
e info@bluechipvacations.com
w bluechipvacations.com

15a Hesketh Crescent
★★★★★ *Self Catering*
Blue Chip Vacations
t (01803) 855282
e info@bluechipvacations.com
w bluechipvacations.com

15b Hesketh Cresent ★★★
Self Catering
Blue Chip Vacations
t (01803) 855282
e info@bluechipvacations.com
w bluechipvacations.com

21 Seaton Close
Rating Applied For
Self Catering
Blue Chip Vacations
t (01803) 855282
e info@bluechipvacations.com
w bluechipvacations.com

4 Hunters Moon ★★★★
Self Catering
Blue Chip Vacations
t (01803) 855282
e info@bluechipvacations.com
w bluechipvacations.com

5 Lisburne Place
Rating Applied For
Self Catering
Blue Chip Vacations
t (01803) 855282
e info@bluechipvacations.com
w bluechipvacations.com

5 Meadfoot Grange ★★★★
Self Catering
Contact: Mrs Maggie Sycamore
t (01803) 855282
e info@bluechipvacations.com
w bluechipvacations.com

5 The Moorings, 5 Beacon Hill ★★★ *Self Catering*
Blue Chip Vacations
t (01803) 855282
e info@bluechipvacations.com
w bluechipvacations.com

5 Rocombe Close ★★★★
Self Catering
Blue Chip Vacations
t (01803) 855282
e info@bluechipvacations.com
w bluechipvacations.com

6 Lisburne Place ★★★★★
Self Catering
Blue Chip Vacations
t (01803) 855282
e info@bluechipvacations.com
w bluechipvacations.com

6 Manor House
Rating Applied For
Self Catering
Blue Chip Vacations
t (01803) 855282
e info@bluechipvacations.com
w bluechipvacations.com

9 Hesketh Mews ★★★★★
Self Catering
Blue Chip Vacations
t (01803) 855282
e info@bluechipvacations.com
w bluechipvacations.com

Abbey Mews ★★★★
Self Catering
Holiday Homes and Cottages South West
t (01803) 299677
e holcotts@aol.com
w swcottages.co.uk

Abbey View Holiday Flats
★★★ *Self Catering*
Contact: Mr & Mrs Foss
t (01803) 293722
e abbeyflats@tiscali.co.uk
w abbeyviewholidayflats.co.uk

Acacia Apartments ★★★★
Self Catering
Blue Chip Vacations
t (01803) 855282
e info@bluechipvacations.com
w bluechipvacations.com

Appletorre House Holiday Flats ★★★ *Self Catering*
Contact: Mr & Mrs Colin & Colleen Moon
t (01803) 296430
e appletorrehols@email.com
w appletorreflats.co.uk

Atlantis Holiday Apartments
★★★-★★★★ *Self Catering*
Contact: Mrs Pauline Roberts
t (01803) 607929
e enquiry@atlantistorquay.co.uk
w atlantistorquay.co.uk

Babbacombe, Bay Fort
★★★★ *Self Catering*
Blue Chip Vacations
t (01803) 855282
e info@bluechipvacations.com
w bluechipvacations.com

Babbacombe Downs ★★★
Self Catering
Holiday Homes and Cottages South West
t (01803) 299677
e holcotts@aol.com
w swcottages.co.uk

The Balcony ★★★★★
Self Catering
Blue Chip Vacations
t (01803) 855282
e info@bluechipvacations.com
w bluechipvacations.com

Barramore Holiday Apartments
Rating Applied For
Self Catering
Contact: Mrs Ivy Scarborough
t (01803) 607105
e stay@barramore.com
w barramoreholidayapartments.co.uk

Bedford House ★★★
Self Catering
Contact: Mrs MacDonald-Smith
t (01803) 296995
e bedfordhotorquay@btconnect.com
w bedfordhousetorquay.co.uk

Belgravia Luxury Holiday Apartments ★★★★
Self Catering
Contact: Mr & Mrs Paul & Nadine Green
t (01803) 293417
e info@blha.co.uk
w blha.co.uk

Beulah Holiday Apartments
★★★ *Self Catering*
Contact: Mr & Mrs Perry
t (01803) 294410
e enquiries@thebeulah.co.uk
w thebeulah.co.uk

Boohay, Bay Fort ★★★★
Self Catering
Blue Chip Vacations
t (01803) 855282
e info@bluechipvacations.com
w bluechipvacations.com

Bosuns Cottage
Rating Applied For
Self Catering
Holiday Homes and Cottages South West
t (01803) 299677
e holcotts@aol.com
w swcottages.co.uk

Burley Court Apartments
★★★ *Self Catering*
Contact: Mr & Mrs S Palmer
t (01803) 607879
e simon@burleycourt.co.uk
w burleycourt.co.uk

Carmel, Torquay ★★★★
Self Catering
Blue Chip Vacations
t (01803) 855282
e info@bluechipvacations.com
w bluechipvacations.com

Chelston Dene Holiday Apartments ★★★
Self Catering
Contact: Mr Rod Payne
t (01803) 605180
e info@chelstondene.com
w chelstondene.com

Cliff Court Apartments
★★★★ *Self Catering*
Contact: Mrs Denise Tudor
t (01803) 294687
e info@cliffcourt.co.uk
w cliffcourt.co.uk

The Cliffs, Torquay
★★★★★ *Self Catering*
Blue Chip Vacations
t (01803) 855282
e info@bluechipvacations.com
w bluechipvacations.com

Clydesdale Apartments
★★★ *Self Catering*
Contact: Mr Terry Watson
t (01803) 292759
e info@clydesdaleapartsments.co.uk
w clydesdaleapartments.co.uk

The Coach House ★★★
Self Catering
Holiday Homes and Cottages South West
t (01803) 299677
e holcotts@aol.com
w swcottages.co.uk

Cockington, Bay Fort ★★★
Self Catering
Blue Chip Vacations
t (01803) 855282
e info@bluechipvacations.com
w bluechipvacations.com

The Corbyn ★★★★★
Self Catering
Contact: Mrs Sallie Stamp
t (01803) 215595
e reception@thecorbyn.co.uk
w thecorbyn.co.uk

Corbyn Lodge Apartments
★★★★★ *Self Catering*
Contact: Reservations c/o OJ Developments Ltd
t (01803) 295744
e reservations@corbyn-lodge.co.uk
w corbyn-lodge.co.uk

Cornerstone ★★★
Self Catering
Holiday Homes and Cottages South West
t (01803) 299677
e holcotts@aol.com
w swcottages.co.uk

Cranmere Court ★★★
Self Catering
Contact: Mrs Sally Noad
t (01803) 293173
e noad@cranmereholidayflats.co.uk
w cranmereholidayflats.co.uk

Delamere Court
★★★–★★★★ *Self Catering*
Contact: Mrs Mandy Morris
t (01803) 293428
e stay@delamerecourt.co.uk
w delamerecourt.co.uk

Fairdale ★★★★ *Self Catering*
Holiday Homes and Cottages South West
t (01803) 299677
e holcotts@aol.com
w swcottages.co.uk

Gainsborough ★★★
Self Catering
Holiday Homes and Cottages South West
t (01803) 299677
e holcotts@aol.com
w swcottages.co.uk

The Hayloft ★★★
Self Catering
Holiday Homes and Cottages South West
t (01803) 299677
e holcotts@aol.com
w swcottages.co.uk

Hesketh Mews ★★★★★
Self Catering
Holiday Homes and Cottages South West
t (01803) 299677
e holcotts@aol.com
w swcottages.co.uk

Hesketh Mews – Starboard
★★★★★ *Self Catering*
Holiday Homes and Cottages South West
t (01803) 299677
e holcotts@aol.com
w swcottages.co.uk

Ilsham ★★★ *Self Catering*
Holiday Homes and Cottages South West
t (01803) 299677
e holcotts@aol.com
w swcottages.co.uk

Kaikoura
Rating Applied For
Self Catering
Holiday Homes and Cottages South West
t (01803) 299677
e holcotts@aol.com
w swcottages.co.uk

Kingswood Holiday Flats
★★ *Self Catering*
Contact: Mr Peter Skinns
t (01803) 293164
e peter@kingswoodholidayflats.co.uk
w kingswoodholidayflats.co.uk

Little Walderlea ★★★
Self Catering
Holiday Homes and Cottages South West
t (01803) 299677
e holcotts@aol.com
w swcottages.co.uk

The Lodge
Rating Applied For
Self Catering
Holiday Homes and Cottages South West
t (01803) 299677
e holcotts@aol.com
w swcottages.co.uk

The Lookout ★★
Self Catering
Holiday Homes and Cottages South West
t (01803) 299677
e holcotts@aol.com
w swcottages.co.uk

Maidencombe, Bay Fort ★★
Self Catering
Blue Chip Vacations
t (01803) 855282
e info@bluechipvacations.com
w bluechipvacations.com

Marina View & Bay View
★★★ *Self Catering*
Holiday Homes and Cottages South West
t (01803) 299677
e holcotts@aol.com
w swcottages.co.uk

Masts B5 ★★★★
Self Catering
Blue Chip Vacations
t (01803) 855282
e info@bluechipvacations.com
w bluechipvacations.com

Masts B8 ★★★★
Self Catering
Blue Chip Vacations
t (01803) 855282
e info@bluechipvacations.com
w bluechipvacations.com

Meadcourt ★★★★
Self Catering
Holiday Homes and Cottages South West
t (01803) 299677
e holcotts@aol.com
w swcottages.co.uk

Meadfoot, Bay Fort ★★★★
Self Catering
Blue Chip Vacations
t (01803) 855282
e info@bluechipvacations.com
w bluechipvacations.com

Muntham Luxury Holiday Apartments ★★★★
Self Catering
Contact: Mr & Mrs Peter & Trudie Cross
t (01803) 292958
e muntham@btinternet.com

Palm Springs ★★★
Self Catering
Holiday Homes and Cottages South West
t (01803) 299677
e holcotts@aol.com
w swcottages.co.uk

Pentreve, Torquay ★★★★★
Self Catering
Blue Chip Vacations
t (01803) 855282
e info@bluechipvacations.com
w bluechipvacations.com

Protea, Torquay ★★★★
Self Catering
Blue Chip Vacations
t (01803) 855282
e info@bluechipvacations.com
w bluechipvacations.com

Rock House ★★★★★
Self Catering
Blue Chip Vacations
t (01803) 855282
e info@bluechipvacations.com
w bluechipvacations.com

Rooftops ★★★ *Self Catering*
Holiday Homes and Cottages South West
t (01803) 299677
e holcotts@aol.com
w swcottages.co.uk

Rose Court Holiday Apartments, Babbacombe
★★★ *Self Catering*
Contact: Mrs J Henshall
t (01803) 327203
e holidays@rosecourtorquay.co.uk
w rosecourtorquay.co.uk

Rosslyn ★★★ *Self Catering*
Contact: Mr Nick Evans
t (01803) 292987
e enquiries@torbayaccommodation.co.uk
w torbayaccommodation.co.uk

St Christophers Holiday Home ★★★★★ *Self Catering*
Contact: Mr David Perry Wildewood
t (01803) 297471
e enquiries@torquayholiday.com
w torquayholiday.com

South Sands Apartments
★★★ *Self Catering*
Contact: Mr & Mrs Paul & Deborah Moorhouse
t (01803) 293521
e info@southsands.co.uk
w southsands.co.uk

Spa Cottage ★★★
Self Catering
Holiday Homes and Cottages South West
t (01803) 299677
e holcotts@aol.com
w swcottages.co.uk

Star Delta ★★★★
Self Catering
Blue Chip Vacations
t (01803) 855282
e info@bluechipvacations.com
w bluechipvacations.com

Look out for establishments participating in the National Accessible Scheme

Suncourt ★★★ *Self Catering*
Holiday Homes and Cottages South West
t (01803) 299677
e holcotts@aol.com
w swcottages.co.uk

Sunningdale Apartments
★★★ *Self Catering*
Contact: Mr Allan Carr
t (01803) 325786
e allancarr@yahoo.com
w sunningdaleapartments.co.uk

Sunnyhill Mews ★★★★
Self Catering
Holiday Homes and Cottages South West
t (01803) 299677
e holcotts@aol.com
w swcottages.co.uk

Sunnyhill West ★★★★
Self Catering
Holiday Homes and Cottages South West
t (01803) 299677
e holcotts@aol.com
w swcottages.co.uk

Sunnyside & Silvan Lodge
★★★ *Self Catering*
t 07904 193826
e query@chilltime.biz
w chilltime.biz

Torwood Gables ★★★
Self Catering
Holiday Homes and Cottages South West
t (01803) 299677
e holcotts@aol.com
w swcottages.co.uk

Totnes Apartment ★★★★
Self Catering
Blue Chip Vacations
t (01803) 855282
e info@bluechipvacations.com
w bluechipvacations.com

Trinity ★★★★ *Self Catering*
Holiday Homes and Cottages South West
t (01803) 299677
e holcotts@aol.com
w swcottages.co.uk

Vernon Court ★★★★
Self Catering
Blue Chip Vacations
t (01803) 855282
e info@bluechipvacations.com
w bluechipvacations.com

Villa Capri ★★★
Self Catering
Contact: Mrs Jacqui Carlin-Wells
t (01803) 297959
e villcapri@btconnect.com
w villacapri.co.uk

Villa Marina ★★★★★
Self Catering
Blue Chip Vacations
t (01803) 855282
e info@bluechipvacations.com
w bluechipvacations.com

Vomero Holiday Apartments
★★★ *Self Catering*
Contact: Mr & Mrs John & Angela Bunce
t (01803) 293470
e holidays@vomero.co.uk
w vomero.co.uk

Waldon Court ★★★
Self Catering
Holiday Homes and Cottages South West
t (01803) 299677
e holcotts@aol.com
w swcottages.co.uk

Wellswood, Bay Fort
★★★★ *Self Catering*
Blue Chip Vacations
t (01803) 855282
e info@bluechipvacations.com
w bluechipvacations.com

Wellswood Park ★★★★★
Self Catering
Holiday Homes and Cottages South West
t (01803) 299677
e holcotts@aol.com
w swcottages.co.uk

Westcourt Holiday Flats
★★★ *Self Catering*
Contact: Mr John Lawton
t (01803) 311703
e westcourtholidayflats@hotmail.com
w westcourtholidayflats.co.uk

Windy Ridge ★★★
Self Catering
Blue Chip Vacations
t (01803) 855282
e info@bluechipvacations.com
w bluechipvacations.com

Wordsworth ★★★★
Self Catering
Holiday Homes and Cottages South West
t (01803) 299677
e holcotts@aol.com
w swcottages.co.uk

Wrenwood ★★★★
Self Catering
Holiday Homes and Cottages South West
t (01803) 299677
e holcotts@aol.com
w swcottages.co.uk

TORRINGTON
Devon

2 Little Silver ★★★
Self Catering
Contact: Mrs A Taylor
t (020) 8763 0796
e admin@devonshire-cottages.co.uk
w devonshire-cottages.co.uk

Hill Farm Cottages ★★★★
Self Catering
Contact: Mrs Mary Vickery
t (01805) 622432
e info@hillfarmcottages.co.uk
w hillfarmcottages.co.uk

Week Farm Flat ★★★
Self Catering
Contact: Mrs Della Bealey
t (01805) 623029
e weekfarm.flat@btinternet.com
w week-farm.co.uk

TOTNES
Devon

Barnston Caravan *Approved Caravan Holiday Home*
Contact: Ms Sarah Bulbulian
t (01548) 521274

Knowle Farm ★★★★
Self Catering
Contact: Mr & Mrs Richard & Lynn Micklewright
t (01364) 73914
e holiday@knowle-farm.co.uk
w knowle-farm.co.uk

The Little Elbow Room
★★★ *Self Catering*
Contact: Mrs Arfona Savin
t (01803) 863480
e r.savin@btinternet.com

Little Riverside ★★★
Self Catering
Contact: Mr John Hagger
t (01803) 866257
e john@littleriverside.com
w littleriverside.com

TREBETHERICK
Cornwall

Bars House ★★★
Self Catering
Contact: Dr Anthony Hambly
Bodrean Manor
t (01872) 264400
e anthonyhambly@hotmail.com

Evergreen Lodge ★★★
Self Catering
Contact: Mrs Espir
t (01483) 561951
e jo.espir@ntlworld.com
w selfcatering-evergreenlodge.com

Hillcroft Bungalow ★★★
Self Catering
Contact: Mrs Beach
t (01256) 702650
e dibeach@hotmail.com

The Millhouse ★★★★
Self Catering
Rock Holidays
t (01208) 863399
e info@rockholidays.co.uk
w rockholidays.co.uk

St Moritz Luxury Villas
★★★★ *Self Catering*
Contact: C Licsauer
t (01208) 862242
e reception@stmoritzvillas.co.uk
w stmoritzvillas.co.uk

TREDETHY
Cornwall

Brinkywell Holiday Cottages
★★★ *Self Catering*
Contact: Mr & Mrs Tocknell
Brinkywell Holidays Cottages
t (01453) 545184
e brian.tocknell@onetel.net
w brinkywell.co.uk

TREGAMERE
Cornwall

Tregamere Barton ★★★★
Self Catering
t (01637) 880222
w cornwallfarmcottages.co.uk

TREGATTA
Cornwall

Beaver Cottages ★★★
Self Catering
Contact: Mr & Mrs Luckin
t (01840) 770265
e beavercottages@virgin.net
w beavercottages.co.uk

TREGAVETHAN
Cornwall

The Mowhay at Tregavethan Manor ★★★★ *Self Catering*
Contact: Mr & Mrs Yorke
t (01872) 561735
e freddie@yorke289.fsnet.co.uk
w classic.co.uk

TREGONY
Cornwall

The Bolt Hole ★★★★
Self Catering
Contact: Miss Rebecca Nash
t (0114) 274 8821
e rebnash@yahoo.com

Garden Cottage ★★★
Self Catering
Contact: Mrs Douglass
t (01872) 530255

Lamorna Cottage ★★★★
Self Catering
Contact: Mrs Carol Salmon
t (0117) 330 6678
e carol.salmon@blueyonder.co.uk
w holidaycottage-cornwall.co.uk

Little Treworlas Farm
★★★★ *Self Catering*
Contact: Ruth Harris
t (01872) 501858
e ruth@treworlas.co.uk
w treworlas.co.uk

Tucoyse Farm Holiday Cottages ★★★ *Self Catering*
Contact: Mr & Mrs Blamey
t (01726) 843836
e penny@tucoyse.co.uk
w tucoyse.co.uk

TREGREHAN MILLS
Cornwall

Huel Tristram, Tregrehan Mills ★★★★ *Self Catering*
Contact: Mrs Sonya Rogers
t (01726) 810921
e stay@hueltristram.com
w hueltristram.com

TREKNOW
Cornwall

Parwin ★★★ *Self Catering*
Cornish Horizons Holiday Cottages
t (01841) 533331
e cottages@cornishhorizons.co.uk
w cornishhorizons.co.uk

TRELIGHTS
Cornwall

No 1 Bunts Mews ★★★★
Self Catering
Rock Holidays
t (01208) 863399
e info@rockholidays.co.uk
w rockholidays.co.uk

Resthaven-Bunts Mews
★★★★ *Self Catering*
Rock Holidays
t (01208) 863399
e info@rockholidays.co.uk
w rockholidays.co.uk

TREMAINE Cornwall

Tremaine Barn ★★★★★
Self Catering
Contact: Mr Alan Lamb
t (01566) 781636
e ctbenquiries@stay-in-cornwall.co.uk
w stay-in-cornwall.co.uk

TRENANCE Cornwall

Cuil Rathain ★★★
Self Catering
Contact: Mrs Anna Taplin
t (01841) 541046
e warmanastia@btinternet.com

Romanov ★★★★
Self Catering
Cornish Horizons Holiday Cottages
t (01841) 533331
e cottages@cornishhorizons.co.uk
w cornishhorizons.co.uk

TRENARREN Cornwall

East Wing Apartment ★★★
Self Catering
t (01726) 72954
w trevissick.co.uk

TRESCO Isles of Scilly

Boro Chalets and Cottages
★★★-★★★★ *Self Catering*
Contact: Mrs Margaret Christopher
t (01720) 422843

The Flying Boat Club
★★★★★ *Self Catering*
Contact: Mr A. Euan Rodger
t (01720) 424910
e evanrodger@tresco.co.uk
w tresco.co.uk

TRESILLIAN Cornwall

Kingfishers ★★★★
Self Catering
Special Places in Cornwall
t (01872) 864400
e office@specialplacescornwall.co.uk
w specialplacescornwall.co.uk

Penhale Cottage ★★★★★
Self Catering
Contact: Mrs Scully
t (01872) 520142
e barbara.dean@btinternet.com

TRESPARRETT Cornwall

The Cottage ★★★★
Self Catering
Contact: Mike & Sue Stickney
t (01840) 261080
e info@cottagenorthcornwall.co.uk
w cottagenorthcornwall.co.uk

TRESWITHIAN DOWNS Cornwall

Hideaway ★★★★★
Self Catering
Contact: Mr William Jenkin
t (01209) 710617
e william@jenkin9350.wanadoo.co.uk
w hideawayathighfield.co.uk

TRETHERRAS Cornwall

Trencreek Palms ★★★★
Self Catering
t (023) 9255 4738
w trencreekpalms.co.uk

TREVARRIAN Cornwall

28 Waves ★★★★
Self Catering
Blue Chip Vacations
t (01803) 855282
e info@bluechipvacations.com
w bluechipvacations.com

TREVELGUE Cornwall

2 Porth Valley Cottages
Rating Applied For
Self Catering
Cornish Horizons Holiday Cottages
t (01841) 533331
e cottages@cornishhorizons.co.uk
w cornishhorizons.co.uk

Porth Valley Cottage Holiday Bungalows 4 & 5
★★★ *Self Catering*
Contact: Miss Tracey Shirley
t (01637) 878574
e info@porthvalleycottages.co.uk
w porthvalleycottages.co.uk

TREVELLAS Cornwall

70 Perran View ★★★
Self Catering
Duchy Holidays
t (01872) 572971
e enquiries@duchyholidays.co.uk
w duchyholidays.co.uk

80 Perran View ★★★
Self Catering
Duchy Holidays
t (01872) 572971
e enquiries@duchyholidays.co.uk
w duchyholidays.co.uk

9 Perran View ★★★
Self Catering
Duchy Holidays
t (01872) 572971
e enquiries@duchyholidays.co.uk
w duchyholidays.co.uk

Perran View 12 ★★
Self Catering
Duchy Holidays
t (01872) 572971
e enquiries@duchyholidays.co.uk
w duchyholidays.co.uk

TREVONE Cornwall

1 Dobbin House ★★★★
Self Catering
Cornish Horizons Holiday Cottages
t (01841) 533331
e cottages@cornishhorizons.co.uk
w cornishhorizons.co.uk

Apartment 7 Greenwaves
★★★ *Self Catering*
Harbour Holidays
t (01841) 533402
e contact@harbourholidays.co.uk
w harbourholidays.co.uk

Avon Cottage ★★★
Self Catering
Contact: Mr Hugo Woolley
t (01841) 532426
e enquiries@woodlands-padstow.co.uk
w avoncottage.com

Bass Cottage ★★★★
Self Catering
Harbour Holidays
t (01841) 533402
e contact@harbourholidays.co.uk
w harbourholidays.co.uk

The Bothy ★★★
Self Catering
Harbour Holidays
t (01841) 533402
e contact@harbourholidays.co.uk
w harbourholidays.co.uk

The Bower ★★★
Self Catering
Harbour Holidays
t (01841) 533402
e contact@harbourholidays.co.uk
w harbourholidays.co.uk

Carrek Cottage ★★★
Self Catering
Harbour Holidays
t (01841) 533402
e contact@harbourholidays.co.uk
w harbourholidays.co.uk

Chapelfields ★★★★
Self Catering
Cornish Horizons Holiday Cottages
t (01841) 533331
e cottages@cornishhorizons.co.uk
w cornishhorizons.co.uk

Chy an Porth ★★★
Self Catering
Cornish Horizons Holiday Cottages
t (01841) 533331
e cottages@cornishhorizons.co.uk
w cornishhorizons.co.uk

Dawn ★★★ *Self Catering*
Harbour Holidays
t (01841) 533402
e contact@harbourholidays.co.uk
w harbourholidays.co.uk

Dovecote House ★★★★
Self Catering
Harbour Holidays
t (01841) 533402
e contact@harbourholidays.co.uk
w harbourholidays.co.uk

Flip Flops ★★★★
Self Catering
Harbour Holidays
t (01841) 533402
e contact@harbourholidays.co.uk
w harbourholidays.co.uk

Hill Rise ★★★ *Self Catering*
Contact: Mr Peter Alvey
t (0117) 962 5862
e hillrise1@aol.com
w cornwall-online.co.uk

Hope House ★★★★★
Self Catering
Harbour Holidays
t (01841) 533402
e contact@harbourholidays.co.uk
w harbourholidays.co.uk

Morlanar ★★★★
Self Catering
Contact: Lucy Richards
t (01841) 521676
e info@seascapeholidaylets.co.uk
w seascapeholidaylets.co.uk

Puffins Wing ★★★★
Self Catering
Cornish Horizons Holiday Cottages
t (01841) 533331
e cottages@cornishhorizons.co.uk
w cornishhorizons.co.uk

Rosben ★★★ *Self Catering*
Harbour Holidays
t (01841) 533402
e contact@harbourholidays.co.uk
w harbourholidays.co.uk

Seaboard ★★★★
Self Catering
Harbour Holidays
t (01841) 533402
e contact@harbourholidays.co.uk
w harbourholidays.co.uk

Trelyn ★★★★ *Self Catering*
Cornish Horizons Holiday Cottages
t (01841) 533331
e cottages@cornishhorizons.co.uk
w cornishhorizons.co.uk

Zanzissey ★★★★
Self Catering
Harbour Holidays
t (01841) 533402
e contact@harbourholidays.co.uk
w harbourholidays.co.uk

TREVOSE Cornwall

The Coach House ★★
Self Catering
Harbour Holidays
t (01841) 533402
e contact@harbourholidays.co.uk
w harbourholidays.co.uk

Coastguard Cottage West
★★★★ *Self Catering*
Cornish Horizons Holiday Cottages
t (01841) 533331
e cottages@cornishhorizons.co.uk
w cornishhorizons.co.uk

The Redlands ★★★★
Self Catering
Cornish Horizons Holiday Cottages
t (01841) 533331
e cottages@cornishhorizons.co.uk
w cornishhorizons.co.uk

Redlands Coachouse
★★★★ *Self Catering*
Cornish Horizons Holiday Cottages
t (01841) 533331
e cottages@cornishhorizons.co.uk
w cornishhorizons.co.uk

TREWALDER
Cornwall

Rookys Nook ★★★★
Self Catering
Contact: Mrs Liz Nathan
t (01840) 212874
e info@rookysnook.co.uk
w rookysnook.co.uk

Welch's Cottage ★★★★
Self Catering
Contact: Mrs Wendy Hester
t (01525) 405381
e w.hester@hotmail.co.uk
w welchscottage.co.uk

TREWARMETT
Cornwall

Fenta Friddle ★★★★★
Self Catering
Contact: James Scott
t (01840) 779190
e bookings@fentafriddle.com
w fentafriddle.com

TREWETHA
Cornwall

The Gwelva ★★★★
Self Catering
Rock Holidays
t (01208) 863399
e info@rockholidays.co.uk
w rockholidays.co.uk

TREWIDLAND
Cornwall

The Old Byre ★★★★
Self Catering
Contact: Mrs Patricia Francis
t (01503) 240204
e treherebarn@hotmail.co.uk

TREWOON
Cornwall

The Haven ★★★★
Self Catering
Contact: Mr Sebastian Stanley
t (01242) 584260
e sebastian.stanley@experiencecornwall.co.uk
w experiencecornwall.co.uk

TREYARNON BAY
Cornwall

Foxes ★★ *Self Catering*
Contact: Mr Peter Tapper
Foxes – Treyarnon Bay
t (01590) 674660
e peter.tapper@lafargecement.co.uk
w padstowholidayhome.co.uk

Glendurgan ★★★★
Self Catering
Harbour Holidays
t (01841) 533402
e contact@harbourholidays.co.uk
w harbourholidays.co.uk

Treyarnon Bay Farm Cottages ★★★★
Self Catering
Contact: Mr & Mrs Old
t (01841) 520653

TROON
Cornwall

Chapel Hill Farm Holidays
★★★★★ *Self Catering*
Contact: Mr Clark-Roberts
t (01208) 831706
e peterzania@btconnect.com
w chapelhillfarmholidays.co.uk

Higher Dowha Farmhouse Caravan Accommodation
Approved Caravan Holiday Home
Contact: Mrs Caroline Willoughby
t (01209) 831760
e higherdowhafarm@btinternet.com

TROWBRIDGE
Wiltshire

Hinton Lodge ★★★★
Self Catering
Contact: Mrs Gompels
t (01380) 871067
e sam@gompels.co.uk
w hintonlodge.co.uk

TRURO
Cornwall

23 Corte Mear ★★★★★
Self Catering
Blue Chip Vacations
t (01803) 855282
e info@bluechipvacations.com
w bluechipvacations.com

Ancarva Cottage ★★★
Self Catering
Special Places in Cornwall
t (01872) 864400
e office@specialplacescornwall.co.uk
w specialplacescornwall.co.uk

Chy Worval ★★★★
Self Catering
Contact: Mrs Heather Paxton
t (01872) 863950
e heather@chyworval.co.uk

Clifford House, Bissoe
★★★-★★★★ *Self Catering*
Contact: Mrs Anne Grant
Clifford House – BL027
t (01872) 863052
e enquiries@cliffordhousecottages.co.uk
w cliffordhousecottages.co.uk

The Coach House ★★★
Self Catering
Contact: Dr Hambly
t (01872) 264400
e anthonyhambly@hotmail.com
w cornishholidays.com

The Old Forge ★★★★
Self Catering
Roseland Holiday Cottages
t (01872) 580480
e enquiries@roselandholidaycottages.co.uk
w roselandholidaycottages.co.uk

Pulla Farm Holidays ★★★
Self Catering
Contact: Mrs Richards
t (01872) 863143
e enquiries@pullafarmholidays.co.uk
w pullafarmholidays.co.uk

Trelowthas, Malpas ★★★★
Self Catering
Contact: Mr Churm
w 4starcornwall.co.uk

The Valley, Carnon Downs
★★★★★ *Self Catering*
t (01872) 862194
e info@the-valley.co.uk
w the-valley.co.uk

Westward ★★★★
Self Catering
Niche Retreats
t (01209) 861745
e jackie@nicheretreats.co.uk
w nicheretreats.co.uk

TUCKENHAY
Devon

Mallard Cottage ★★★★
Self Catering
Contact: Mr R Seeley
t (01803) 732741
e ralph@pivotal.eclipse.co.uk
w mallardcottage.com

TWO WATERS FOOT
Cornwall

Bellasize Farm ★★★★
Self Catering
Valley Villas Ltd
t (01752) 605605
e sales@valleyvillas.com
w valleyvillas.co.uk

Foxglove Barn ★★★★
Self Catering
Valley Villas Ltd
t (01752) 605605
e sales@valleyvillas.com
w valleyvillas.co.uk

Gilldene Holiday Cottage
★★★★ *Self Catering*
Contact: Mr & Mrs Cliff & Sheila Walker
t (01208) 821648
e cliffnshelia@tiscali.co.uk
w gilldeneholidaycottage.com

Tregolls Farm Cottages
★★★★ *Self Catering*
Contact: Mrs Marilyn Hawkey
t (01208) 812154
e tregollsfarm@btclick.com
w tregollsfarm.co.uk

TWYNING
Gloucestershire

Hill Top ★★★★ *Self Catering*
Contact: Mr & Mrs Richardson
t (01684) 772723
e richardsonmail@easynet.co.uk
w hilltop-cottage.co.uk

TYTHERINGTON
Wiltshire

St James Court ★★★★
Self Catering
Contact: Mrs Anna Giddings
t (01985) 840568
e stjamescourt@aol.com
w wiltscottages.com

UGBOROUGH
Devon

Fowlescombe ★★★★★
Self Catering
Contact: Mr Richard Barker
t (01548) 821000
e richard@fowlescombe.com
w fowlescombe.com

Venn Farm ★★★★
Self Catering
Contact: Mrs Stephens
t (01364) 73240

ULEY
Gloucestershire

Stouts Hill Club Ltd ★★★
Self Catering
t (01453) 860134
w stoutshill.co.uk

ULLENWOOD
Gloucestershire

Ullenwood Court Cottages
★★★★ *Self Catering*
Contact: Mrs Anne Shand
t (01242) 239751

UMBERLEIGH
Devon

Little Wick ★★★★
Self Catering
Marsdens Cottage Holidays
t (01271) 813777
e holidays@marsdens.co.uk
w marsdens.co.uk

UNDERLANE
Cornwall

Wheal Sheba ★★★
Self Catering
Contact: Mrs Hilary Kneebone
t (01209) 861256

UPLODERS
Dorset

Springside & Tiddlers Cottages ★★★ *Self Catering*
Contact: Mr Alan Spargo
t (01305) 871585
e alan@aspargo.freeserve.co.uk
w springsidecottages.com

UPLOWMAN
Devon

Middle Coombe Farm ★★★
Self Catering
Contact: Mrs Angela Malyon
t (01884) 821176
e info@coombefarmwoods.co.uk
w coombefarmwoods.co.uk/

UPLYME
Devon

1 Barnes Meadow ★★★★
Self Catering
Lyme Bay Holidays
t (01297) 443363
e email@lymebayholidays.co.uk
w lymebayholidays.co.uk

3 Sherwood Apartments
★★★ *Self Catering*
Lyme Bay Holidays
t (01297) 443363
e email@lymebayholidays.co.uk
w lymebayholidays.co.uk

9 Coram Court ★★★★
Self Catering
Lyme Bay Holidays
t (01297) 443363
e email@lymebayholidays.co.uk
w lymebayholidays.co.uk

The Bower & The Bothy
★★★★ *Self Catering*
Contact: Mrs Heather Lovett
t (01297) 445185
e hal@lymeregis-accommodation.com
w lymeregis-accommodation.com

Garden Flat ★★★
Self Catering
Lyme Bay Holidays
t (01297) 443363
e email@lymebayholidays.co.uk
w lymebayholidays.co.uk

Higher Holcombe Farm Cottage ★★★★ *Self Catering*
Contact: Mrs Rosamund Duffin
t (01297) 444078
e rozduffin@hotmail.com
w higherholcombe.com

Homyer Villas ★★★★
Self Catering
Lyme Bay Holidays
t (01297) 443363
e email@lymebayholidays.co.uk
w lymebayholidays.co.uk

The Laurels ★★★★
Self Catering
Lyme Bay Holidays
t (01297) 443363
e email@lymebayholidays.co.uk
w lymebayholidays.co.uk

Lindens ★★★★ *Self Catering*
Lyme Bay Holidays
t (01297) 443363
e email@lymebayholidays.co.uk
w lymebayholidays.co.uk

Little Westhill ★★★
Self Catering
Lyme Bay Holidays
t (01297) 443363
e email@lymebayholidays.co.uk
w lymebayholidays.co.uk

Lyndale ★★★★ *Self Catering*
Contact: Miss Annie Kobus
t (01297) 443346
w lymeregis.com

Mount View ★★★
Self Catering
Lyme Bay Holidays
t (01297) 443363
e email@lymebayholidays.co.uk
w lymebayholidays.co.uk

Myrtle Cottage ★★★★
Self Catering
Contact: Mrs Gillian Leppitt
t (023) 8044 8706
e myrtle.uplyme@btinternet.com
w cottageguide.co.uk/myrtlecottage-uplyme

The Old Barn ★★★
Self Catering
Lyme Bay Holidays
t (01297) 443363
e email@lymebayholidays.co.uk
w lymebayholidays.co.uk

Old Orchard ★★★★
Self Catering
Contact: Mr George Smith
t (01297) 443172
e tvecs@aol.com

Otter View ★★★
Self Catering
Contact: Mr & Mrs Andrew & Katy Howell
t (01308) 420607
e hazelburykate@aol.com
w otterviewcottage.com

Penrith House ★★★
Self Catering
Lyme Bay Holidays
t (01297) 443363
e email@lymebayholidays.co.uk
w lymebayholidays.co.uk

Pitt White House ★★★★
Self Catering
Lyme Bay Holidays
t (01297) 443363
e email@lymebayholidays.co.uk
w lymebayholidays.co.uk

Stable Wing ★★★★
Self Catering
Lyme Bay Holidays
t (01297) 443363
e email@lymebayholidays.co.uk
w lymebayholidays.co.uk

Sunnyside Cottage ★★★★
Self Catering
Lyme Bay Holidays
t (01297) 443363
e email@lymebayholidays.co.uk
w lymebayholidays.co.uk

Yawl House & Bramleys
★★★ *Self Catering*
Lyme Bay Holidays
t (01297) 443363
e email@lymebayholidays.co.uk
w lymebayholidays.co.uk

UPOTTERY
Devon

Hoemoor Bungalow ★★★
Self Catering
Contact: Mrs Phillips
t (01823) 601265
e hoemoor@quikmail.co.uk
w hoemoorfarm.co.uk

Twistgates Farm Cottages
★★★★ *Self Catering*
Contact: Mrs Suzanne Gray
t (01404) 861173
e suzanne@twistgatesfarm.co.uk
w twistgatesfarm.co.uk

UPTON ST LEONARDS
Gloucestershire

Hill Farm Cottages ★★
Self Catering
Contact: Mrs Margaret McLellan
t (01452) 614081

UPWEY
Dorset

Chapel Cottage ★★★
Self Catering
Dream Cottages
t (01305) 789000
e admin@dream-cottages.co.uk
w dream-cottages.co.uk

Sixpenny Cottage ★★★★
Self Catering
Dream Cottages
t (01305) 789000
e admin@dream-cottages.co.uk
w dream-cottages.co.uk

Wey Valley House ★★★
Self Catering
Dream Cottages
t (01305) 789000
e admin@dream-cottages.co.uk
w dream-cottages.co.uk

URCHFONT
Wiltshire

Breach Cottage and The Pottery ★★★ *Self Catering*
Contact: Mr & Mrs Philip & Clare Milanes
t (01380) 840402
e info@breachhouse.co.uk
w breachhouse.co.uk

VERWOOD
Dorset

West Farm Lodges ★★★
Self Catering
Contact: Mr & Mrs Roger & Penny Froud
t (01202) 822263
e west.farm@virgin.net
w westfarmholidays.co.uk

VERYAN
Cornwall

1 Raglan Cottages ★★★★
Self Catering
Roseland Holiday Cottages
t (01872) 580480
e enquiries@roselandholidaycottages.co.uk
w roselandholidaycottages.co.uk

Greenbank ★★★★
Self Catering
Roseland Holiday Cottages
t (01872) 580480
e enquiries@roselandholidaycottages.co.uk
w roselandholidaycottages.co.uk

Jago Cottage ★★★★
Self Catering
Contact: Mr Treneary
t (01872) 501491
e jago@roseland.me.uk
w roseland.me.uk

Pedlars Cottage ★★★
Self Catering
Portscatho Holidays
t (01326) 270900
e info@portscathoholidays.co.uk
w portscathoholidays.co.uk

The Stables ★★★
Self Catering
Portscatho Holidays
t (01326) 270900
e info@portscathoholidays.co.uk
w portscathoholidays.co.uk

Trenona Farm Holidays
★★★★ *Self Catering*
Contact: Mrs Pamela Carbis
Trenona Farm
t (01872) 501339
e pam@trenonafarmholidays.co.uk
w trenonafarmholidays.co.uk

Veryan Club Site ★★★
Self Catering
Camping & Caravanning Club
t 0845 130 7631

VERYAN GREEN
Cornwall

Lamorran Lodge
Rating Applied For
Self Catering
Portscatho Holidays
t (01326) 270900
e info@portscathoholidays.co.uk
w portscathoholidays.co.uk

Timms Cottage ★★★
Self Catering
Contact: Mrs Kitty Eccles
t (01326) 270795
e eccles@rosehavencottages.co.uk

WADEBRIDGE
Cornwall

1 Harbour House ★★★★★
Self Catering
Contact: Rob & Gill Reskelly
t (01208) 880368
e info@harbourhouse.net
w harbourhouse.net

The Barn ★★★★
Self Catering
Cornish Horizons Holiday Cottages
t (01841) 533331
e cottages@cornishhorizons.co.uk
w cornishhorizons.co.uk

Colesent Cottages ★★★★
Self Catering
Contact: Gary & Maureen Newman
t (01208) 850112
e relax@colesent.co.uk
w colesent.co.uk

The Knap ★★★★
Self Catering
Contact: Sharon Patterson
t 07915 658556
w theknap.info

Lowenna Holiday Apartment
★★★ *Self Catering*
Contact: Mrs Katy Holmes
t (01208) 815725
e pablo.holmes@btinternet.com
w lowennahouse.co.uk

Mayfields Cottages ★★★★
Self Catering
Contact: Mrs Burgess
t (01841) 532633
w padstowcottagecompany.co.uk

Potters ★★★★ *Self Catering*
Contact: Ms Enderby
t (020) 8855 8532
e sttudycottagecornwall@yahoo.co.uk
w sttudycottagecornwall.co.uk

The Retreat ★★★-★★★★
Self Catering
Contact: Mrs Biddick
t (01726) 890214
e biddick@lanjew.co.uk

Rosehill Holiday Accommodation ★★★★
Self Catering
Cornish Horizons Holiday Cottages
t (01841) 533331
e cottages@cornishhorizons.co.uk
w cornishhorizons.co.uk

St Aldhelms Barn ★★★
Self Catering
Contact: C. Willgoss
t (01622) 813007
e m.willgo@talk21.com
w cornishbarn.com

Slate Cottage ★★★
Self Catering
Cornish Horizons Holiday Cottages
t (01841) 533331
e cottages@cornishhorizons.co.uk
w cornishhorizons.co.uk

Tern ★★★ *Self Catering*
Cornish Horizons Holiday Cottages
t (01841) 533331
e cottages@cornishhorizons.co.uk
w cornishhorizons.co.uk

Tredougann ★★★★★
Self Catering
Contact: Mr Michael Griffths
t 07918 175713
e mike@mikegriffiths.biz
w cameltrailcottage.com

Tregolls Farm Cottages
★★★★ *Self Catering*
Contact: Mrs Hawkey
t (01208) 812154
e tregollsfarm@btclick.com
w tregollsfarm.co.uk

Trewornan
Rating Applied For
Self Catering
Rock Holidays
t (01208) 863399
e info@rockholidays.co.uk
w rockholidays.co.uk

WANBOROUGH
Wiltshire

The Garden Apartment
★★★ *Self Catering*
Contact: Mrs Julie Evans
t (01793) 791395
e gardenapartment@lycos.co.uk
w swindonaccommodation.co.uk

WARBSTOW
Cornwall

Meadowview Cottage
★★★★★ *Self Catering*
Contact: Mr & Mrs Roger Bolt
t (01840) 261706
e debbie@meadowviewcottage.co.uk
w meadowviewcottage.co.uk

WAREHAM
Dorset

6 Bonnet's Lane ★★★
Self Catering
Quay Holidays
t (01202) 683333
e stay@quayholidays.co.uk
w quayholidays.co.uk

Bankgate Cottage ★★★★
Self Catering
Dorset Cottage Holidays
t (01929) 553443
e enq@dhcottages.co.uk
w dhcottages.co.uk

The Cart House ★★★★
Self Catering
Dorset Cottage Holidays
t (01929) 553443
e enq@dhcottages.co.uk
w dhcottages.co.uk

East Creech Farm House & Cottage ★★★-★★★★
Self Catering
Contact: Mrs Best
t (01929) 480519
e east.creech@virgin.net
w eastcreechfarm.co.uk

Tavern Way ★★★
Self Catering
Dream Cottages
t (01305) 789000
e admin@dream-cottages.co.uk
w dream-cottages.co.uk

Westport Cottage ★★★★
Self Catering
Dorset Cottage Holidays
t (01929) 553443
e enq@dhcottages.co.uk
w dhcottages.co.uk

WARMINSTER
Wiltshire

The Annex ★★ *Self Catering*
Contact: Mrs Sheila Allery
t (01985) 218158

Downside House ★★★★
Self Catering
Hideaways
t (01747) 828170
e enq@hideaways.co.uk
w hideaways.co.uk

Eastleigh Farm, Bishopstrow
★★★★ *Self Catering*
Contact: Mrs Roz Walker
t (01985) 212325

WARMWELL
Dorset

Beech Farm ★★★
Self Catering
Contact: Mrs Ruth Goldsack
t (01305) 852414
e rugold@lineone.net

Countryside Farm Barn
★★★ *Self Catering*
Dream Cottages
t (01305) 789000
e admin@dream-cottages.co.uk
w dream-cottages.co.uk

Misery Farm – Meadow View Barn ★★★
Self Catering
Dream Cottages
t (01305) 789000
e admin@dream-cottages.co.uk
w dream-cottages.co.uk

WASHFORD
Somerset

Monksway ★★★★★
Self Catering
Contact: Mr & Mrs Woolford
t (01491) 681229
e b.woolford@btinternet.com

WATCHET
Somerset

The Croft Holiday Cottages
★★★★-★★★★★
Self Catering
Contact: Mr & Mrs Andrew & Kirsten Musgrave
t (01984) 631121
e croftcottages@talk21.com
w cottagessomerset.com

WATERGATE BAY
Cornwall

Tregurrian Villas and Beachcombers Apartments
★★★★ *Self Catering*
Beachcombers Apartments
t (01637) 873274
e enquiries@beachcombersapartments.com
w beachcombersapartments.com

Waves ★★★★ *Self Catering*
Contact: Ms Joanne Manson
t (020) 8973 1643
e joannemanson@hotmail.co.uk

WATERMOUTH
Devon

The Nut House ★★★★
Self Catering
Marsdens Cottage Holidays
t (01271) 813777
e holidays@marsdens.co.uk
w marsdens.co.uk

WATERROW
Somerset

Exmoor Gate Lodges
★★★★ *Self Catering*
Contact: Mrs Sue Gallagher
t (01823) 672339
e bookings@oldlimekiln.freeserve.co.uk
w exmoorgatelodges.co.uk

Handley Farm ★★★★
Self Catering
Contact: Mr & Mrs George & Linda Leigh-Firbank
t (01398) 361516
e linda.handleyfarm@btinternet.com
w handleyfarm.co.uk

WEDMORE
Somerset

The Cider House
Rating Applied For
Self Catering
t (01934) 713125
w holdenhurst.co.uk/ciderhouse

The Coach House ★★★★
Self Catering
t (01934) 713125
w holdenhurst.co.uk/coachhouse

WEEK ST MARY
Cornwall

New College Barn ★★★★
Self Catering
Contact: Andrea Huxford
t (01288) 341331
e andreahuxford@hotmail.co.uk
w newcollegebarn.com

Ranelagh ★★★★
Self Catering
Contact: Mrs Dickenson
t (01288) 341134
e shdickenson@aol.com
w ranelagh.co.uk

WELCOMBE
Devon

Mead Barn Cottages, Welcombe ★★★-★★★★
Self Catering
Contact: Mr & Mrs Rob & Lisa Ireton
t (01288) 331721
e holidays@meadbarns.com
w meadbarns.com

Olde Smithy Bungalows, Welcombe ★★★
Self Catering
Contact: Mrs Sandra Millbourne
Olde Smithy Bungalows Self Catering
t (01237) 421811 & 07900 571423
e relax@oldesmithyholidays.co.uk
w oldesmithyholidays.co.uk

WELLINGTON
Somerset

Old Lime Kiln Cottages
★★★★ *Self Catering*
Contact: Mrs Sue Gallagher
t (01823) 672339
e bookings@oldlimekiln.freeserve.co.uk
w oldlimekilncottages.co.uk/

Tone Dale House ★★★★★
Self Catering
Contact: Mrs Claire Bendall
t (01823) 662673
e party@thebighouseco.com
w thebighouseco.com

WELLISFORD
Somerset

The Old Mill ★★★★★
Self Catering
Contact: Mrs Jessica Vellacott
t (01823) 672284
e info@theoldmill.me.uk
w sleeps12.com

WELLOW
Somerset

Holly Cottage & Garden Studio ★★★★ *Self Catering*
Contact: Mr Alick Bartholomew
t (01225) 840889
e enquiries@bath-holidays.co.uk
w bath-holidays.co.uk

WELLS
Somerset

Honeysuckle Cottage
★★★★ *Self Catering*
Contact: Mrs Luana Law
t (01749) 678971
e honeycroft2@aol.com

Model Farm Cottages ★★★
Self Catering
Contact: Mrs Gill Creed
t (01749) 673363
e gillcreed@aol.com
w modelfarmcottages.co.uk

The Potting Shed Holidays
★★★★ *Self Catering*
Contact: Mr John Van Bergen-Henegouwen
t (01749) 672857
e info@potingshedholidays.co.uk
w pottingshedholidays.co.uk

St Marys Lodge ★★★★
Self Catering
Contact: Mrs Jane Hughes
t (01749) 342157
e janehughes@trtopbox.net
w st-marys-lodge.co.uk

Shalom ★★★ *Self Catering*
Contact: Mrs Rees
t (01204) 418576
e rosey.rees@talk21.com
w shalomwells.co.uk

Spindlewood Lodges
★★★★ *Self Catering*
Contact: Ms Linda Norris
t (01749) 890367
e info@spindlewoodlodges.co.uk
w spindlewoodlodges.co.uk

Vicars' Close Holiday House
★★★ *Self Catering*
Contact: Mrs Debbie Jones
t (01749) 674483
e visits@wellscathedral.uk.net
w wellscathedral.org.uk

Wrinkle Mead ★★★★
Self Catering
Contact: Mrs Cynthia Glass
t (01749) 673445
e islingtonfarm2004@yahoo.co.uk
w islingtonfarmatwells.co.uk

WEMBDON
Somerset

Grange Farm Cottage
★★★★ *Self Catering*
t (01278) 452056
e grangefarm@ejeweb.com
w grangefarmcottage.co.uk

WEMBURY
Devon

Bovisand Lodge Estate – Heritage Apartments and Cottage, Bovisand ★★★★
Self Catering
t (01752) 403554
w bovisand-apartments.co.uk

WEMBWORTHY
Devon

Rose Cottage ★★★★
Self Catering
Contact: Mr William Carlyon
t (01769) 587559
e w.carlyon@btinternet.com
w devon-farm-cottage.co.uk

Taw Mill ★★★★★
Self Catering
Contact: Mr & Mrs Roger & Sheila Bowley
t (01837) 83931
e sheila@tawmill.com
w tawmill.com

WENDRON
Cornwall

Corn Loft ★★★★
Self Catering
Farm & Cottage Holidays
t (01237) 459827
e enquiries@farmcott.co.uk
w holidaycottages.co.uk

WEST ALVINGTON
Devon

Cob Cottage ★★★★
Self Catering
Toad Hall Cottages
t (01548) 853089
e thc@toadhallcottages.com
w toadhallcottages.co.uk

Easton Court ★★★★★
Self Catering
Toad Hall Cottages
t (01548) 853089
e thc@toadhallcottages.com
w toadhallcottages.co.uk

WEST ANSTEY
Devon

Dunsley Mill ★★★★
Self Catering
Contact: Mr & Mrs John & Helen Sparrow
t (01398) 341374
e helen@dunsleymill.co.uk
w dunsleymill.co.uk

WEST BAY
Dorset

11 The Boardwalk ★★★★
Self Catering
Lyme Bay Holidays
t (01297) 443363
e email@lymebayholidays.co.uk
w lymebayholidays.co.uk

13 & 18 Heron Court ★★★
Self Catering
Contact: Mrs Mary Fitzpatrick
Merlins Cottage
t (01308) 898261
e merlinscottage@aol.com
w dorset-holidays-accommodation.com

3 & 4 Chesil House ★★★★
Self Catering
Contact: Mr L Blair
t (01308) 425341
e lindseyblair@aol.com

3 The Parade ★★★
Self Catering
Contact: Mr John Daw
t (01308) 420338
e john-ann@daw6030freeserve.co.uk
w threetheparade-westbay.co.uk

8 Driftwood ★★★★
Self Catering
Lyme Bay Holidays
t (01297) 443363
e email@lymebayholidays.co.uk
w lymebayholidays.co.uk

The Boardwalk Penthouse
Rating Applied For
Self Catering
Contact: Mr & Mrs C Bourchier
t (01725) 519302
e carotalks@aol.com
w dorsetbeach.com

Flat 9 Driftwood ★★★★
Self Catering
Lyme Bay Holidays
t (01297) 443363
e email@lymebayholidays.co.uk
w lymebayholidays.co.uk

Harbour Lights ★★★
Self Catering
Dream Cottages
t (01305) 789000
e admin@dream-cottages.co.uk
w dream-cottages.co.uk

Jurassic View and The Lobster Pot ★★★
Self Catering
Contact: Mrs Frances Hunt
t (01458) 251203
e frances@holsindorset.co.uk
w holsindorset.co.uk

Sunset, 1 Riverside ★★★
Self Catering
t (01308) 458673

Thorncombe ★★★
Self Catering
Contact: Mr & Mrs Gerald & Janet Paget
t (01308) 867539
e gerry.paget@hants.gov.uk
w oas.co.uk/ukcottages/thorncombe

Westpoint Apartments
★★★–★★★★ *Self Catering*
Contact: Mr & Mrs Slade
t (01308) 423636
e bea@westpoint-apartments.co.uk
w westpointapartments.co.uk

The Yard Property ★★★
Self Catering
t (01749) 343666

WEST BEXINGTON
Dorset

Coggs Cottage ★★★★
Self Catering
Dream Cottages
t (01305) 789000
e admin@dream-cottages.co.uk
w dream-cottages.co.uk

Cranford ★★★★
Self Catering
Dream Cottages
t (01305) 789000
e admin@dream-cottages.co.uk
w dream-cottages.co.uk

Gorselands ★★★
Self Catering
Contact: Miss Brenda Parker
t (01308) 897232
w gorselands.co.uk

Tamarisk Farm Cottages
★★★–★★★★ *Self Catering*
Contact: Mrs Josephine Pearse
t (01308) 897784
e holidays@tamariskfarm.com
w tamariskfarm.com

WEST BUCKLAND
Somerset

Little Gortnell
Rating Applied For
Self Catering
Contact: Sue Attree
t (01823) 664992
e sueatt21@aol.com

WEST CHINNOCK
Somerset

Weavers Cottage ★★★★
Self Catering
Contact: Mr & Mrs Gordon & Tricia Piper
t (01935) 881370
e thepipers@btinternet.com

Yeoman Cottage ★★★
Self Catering
Contact: Mrs Marie Wheatley
t (01935) 881421
e jonwheat@aol.com
w yeomancottage.co.uk

WEST DOWN
Devon

Rock Cottage ★★★
Self Catering
Contact: Mrs Virginia Sprason
t (01562) 883038
e rock.cott@virgin.net
w devoncottage.fsnet.co.uk

WEST LOOE
Cornwall

1 New Cottage ★★★
Self Catering
Cornish Collection Ltd
t (01503) 262736
e enquiries@cornishcollections.co.uk
w cornishcollection.co.uk

1 West Quay ★★
Self Catering
Contact: Mr Gorringe
t (01202) 517329

3 West Quay House ★★★
Self Catering
Cornish Collection Ltd
t (01503) 262736
e enquiries@cornishcollections.co.uk
w cornishcollection.co.uk

4 West Quay ★★★
Self Catering
Cornish Collection Ltd
t (01503) 262736
e enquiries@cornishcollections.co.uk
w cornishcollection.co.uk

Tamarisk ★★★ *Self Catering*
Cornish Collection Ltd
t (01503) 262736
e enquiries@cornishcollections.co.uk
w cornishcollection.co.uk

WEST LULWORTH
Dorset

Advantage Point ★★★
Self Catering
Dream Cottages
t (01305) 789000
e admin@dream-cottages.co.uk
w dream-cottages.co.uk

Chestnut Court ★★★
Self Catering
Contact: Mr Zachary Stuart-Brown
t (01305) 789000
e admin@dream-cottages.co.uk
w dream-cottages.co.uk

Flat 2 Chestnut Court ★★★
Self Catering
Dream Cottages
t (01305) 789000
e admin@dream-cottages.co.uk
w dream-cottages.co.uk

Hillside House ★★★
Self Catering
Dream Cottages
t (01305) 789000
e admin@dream-cottages.co.uk
w dream-cottages.co.uk

Lulwinds ★★★★
Self Catering
Dorset Cottage Holidays
t (01929) 553443
e enq@dhcottages.co.uk
w dhcottages.co.uk

WEST MILTON
Dorset

Court House Barn
Rating Applied For
Self Catering
Contact: Anna Forrest
t (01308) 485101
e westmilton@hotmail.co.uk
w courthousefarm.com

Gore Cottage ★★★
Self Catering
Contact: Mrs E.G. Maude
t (01304) 389253
e gmaude@waitrose.com
w heartofdorset.co.uk

Pear Tree Cottage ★★★★
Self Catering
Dream Cottages
t (01305) 789000
e admin@dream-cottages.co.uk
w dream-cottages.co.uk

WEST TYTHERLEY
Dorset

Brightside Cottage Annexe
★★★ *Self Catering*
Contact: Mrs Barbara Wilks
t (01794) 341391
e barbara@hwilks.freeserve.co.uk
w brightsideholidaycottage.co.uk

WESTBURY-SUB-MENDIP
Somerset

Old Apple Loft ★★★
Self Catering
Contact: Mrs Anne Flintham
t (01749) 870557
e aflintham@toucansurf.com
w oldappleloft.co.uk

WESTHAY
Somerset

The Cider Jug ★★★
Self Catering
t (01458) 860197

The Courtyard New House Farm ★★★ *Self Catering*
Contact: Mr & Mrs Bell Bell
t (01458) 860238
e bell-bell@btconnect.com
w newhousefarmbandb.co.uk

WESTLEIGH
Devon

Langmead ★★★★
Self Catering
Marsdens Cottage Holidays
t (01271) 813777
e holidays@marsdens.co.uk
w marsdens.co.uk

WESTON
Devon

Broom Cottage ★★★★
Self Catering
Milkbere Cottage Holidays
t (01297) 20729
e info@milkberehols.com
w milkberehols.com

Cornerstone ★★★
Self Catering
Milkbere Cottage Holidays
t (01297) 20729
e info@milkberehols.com
w milkberehols.com

Garden View ★★★
Self Catering
Milkbere Cottage Holidays
t (01297) 20729
e info@milkberehols.com
w milkberehols.com

Higher Weston Farm
★★★★ *Self Catering*
Contact: Mr Euan MacFadyen
t (01395) 513741

Kirklands ★★★ *Self Catering*
Sweetcombe Cottage Holidays
t (01395) 512130
e enquiries@sweetcombe-ch.co.uk
w sweetcombe-ch.co.uk

Sandways ★★★ *Self Catering*
Milkbere Cottage Holidays
t (01297) 20729
e info@milkberehols.com
w milkberehols.com

Sea View ★★★ *Self Catering*
Milkbere Cottage Holidays
t (01297) 20729
e info@milkberehols.com
w milkberehols.com

Seagull Cottage ★★★
Self Catering
Milkbere Cottage Holidays
t (01297) 20729
e info@milkberehols.com
w milkberehols.com

Teak Cottage ★★★
Self Catering
Milkbere Cottage Holidays
t (01297) 20729
e info@milkberehols.com
w milkberehols.com

WESTON SUBEDGE
Gloucestershire

Lychgate Cottage ★★★★
Self Catering
Contact: Mr Robert Hutsby
t (01789) 841525
e robert.hutsby@btinternet.com
w chipping-campden-holiday-cottages.co.uk

WESTON-SUPER-MARE
Somerset

Beachcomber Holiday Flats
★★★★ *Self Catering*
Contact: Mrs Stephanie Rose
t (01934) 412263
e srose33@btinternet.com
w holidaysattheseaside.com

Charlton Holiday Flats ★★★
Self Catering
Contact: Mrs Deana Swords
t (01934) 751056
e enquiries@charltonholidayflats.co.uk
w charltonholidayflats.co.uk

Doubleton Farm Cottages, Hewish ★★★ *Self Catering*
Contact: Mr & Mrs John & Victoria Southwood
t (01934) 520225
e info@doubleton.com
w doubleton.com

Ellenborough Hall Holiday Flats ★★★ *Self Catering*
t (01934) 629543

Gordon Road Holiday Flats
★★ *Self Catering*
Contact: Mrs Betty Hendy
t (01278) 422465
e 424033@tiscali.co.uk

Hope Farm Cottages, Lympsham ★★★★
Self Catering
Contact: Mrs Liz Stirk
t (01934) 750506
e stirkhopefarm@aol.com
w hopefarmcottages.co.uk

Kyrenia Holiday Flats ★★★
Self Catering
Contact: Mrs Wendy Richards
t (01934) 623880

Manor House Cottages
★★★★ *Self Catering*
Contact: Mrs Hart
t (01934) 812689
e valerie@manor-house-cottages.com
w manor-house-cottages.com

Martyndale Suites ★★★
Self Catering
Contact: Ms Diane Corbett
t (01934) 631388
e diane.martyndale@btinternet.com
w martyndalesuites.com

Royal Oak Cottage ★★★
Self Catering
Contact: Mr Stephen Hotson
t (01934) 624065
e hotsonandco@btinternet.com
w royaloakcottage.com

Salisbury Court ★★★
Self Catering
Contact: Mrs Deanna Swords
t (01934) 751056
e enquiries@salisburycourt.co.uk
w salisburycourt.co.uk

Seaford Lodge Holiday Flats
★★-★★★ *Self Catering*
Contact: Miss G Wilson
t (01934) 429866
w seafordlodge.co.uk

Tidalways Holiday Flats ★★
Self Catering
Contact: Mr & Mrs Sally & Roy Thomas
t (01934) 629745
e roythomas@tidalways.fsnet.co.uk

Weston Bay Holiday Flats
★★ *Self Catering*
Contact: Mr Hui
t (01934) 628903
e westonbayhotel@btinternet.com
w westonbayhotel.co.uk

Woodview ★★★★
Self Catering
Contact: Mrs Beverly Jenkins
t (01277) 211033
e beverly.jenkins@talktalk.net
w woodview-somerset.co.uk

WESTPORT
Somerset

Wind in the Willows Cottage
★★★ *Self Catering*
Contact: Mr Baker
t (01297) 32051
e cjbaker@eggconnect.net

WESTWARD HO!
Devon

10 Nautilus Apartment
★★★★★ *Self Catering*
Select Holiday Homes
t (01491) 826757
e info@select-holidays-homes.co.uk
w select-holiday-homes.co.uk

Atlantic Spray ★★★
Self Catering
Marsdens Cottage Holidays
t (01271) 813777
e holidays@marsdens.co.uk
w marsdens.co.uk

Cloud Nine ★★★★★
Self Catering
Select Holiday Homes
t (01491) 826757
e info@select-holidays-homes.co.uk
w select-holiday-homes.co.uk

Nautilus ★★★★
Self Catering
Marsdens Cottage Holidays
t (01271) 813777
e holidays@marsdens.co.uk
w marsdens.co.uk

Pebble End ★★★★
Self Catering
Marsdens Cottage Holidays
t (01271) 813777
e holidays@marsdens.co.uk
w marsdens.co.uk

Sea Dreams ★★★★★
Self Catering
Contact: Caroline Jones
t (01327) 831129
e stephen@jones-pattishall.freeserve.co.uk
w enjoyourhomes.com

Sea Rocas ★★★★★
Self Catering
Blue Chip Vacations
t (01803) 855282
e info@bluechipvacations.com
w bluechipvacations.com

Seascape, Nassau Court
★★★★★ *Self Catering*
Contact: Ian & Carol Gibson
t (01923) 224025
e info@devon-selfcatering-seascape.com
w devon-selfcatering-seascape.com

Seaspray ★★★★
Self Catering
Contact: Tom & Sue Downie
t (01805) 623670
e tom.downie@ukonline.co.uk
w creamteacottages.co.uk

West Pusehill Farm Cottages
★★★ *Self Catering*
Contact: Mrs Rebecca Langmead
t (01237) 474622
e info@wpfcottages.co.uk
w wpfcottages.co.uk

WEYMOUTH
Dorset

15 Wedgwood Road ★★★
Self Catering
t (023) 8082 9839
w selfcateringholidays-south.co.uk

90 Old Castle Road ★★★
Self Catering
Contact: Mrs Angela Mary Blake
t (01305) 785003

Alfresco ★★★★
Self Catering
Dream Cottages
t (01305) 789000
e admin@dream-cottages.co.uk
w dream-cottages.co.uk

Apartment 1, Townbridge House ★★★★ *Self Catering*
Contact: Mr Peter Weeks
t (01249) 782713
e info@weymouthharbourholidays.co.uk
w weymouthharbourholidays.co.uk

Ashleigh Holiday Flats ★★
Self Catering
Contact: Mr Roger Littler
t (01305) 773715
e ashleighhols@btinternet.com

Ashwood ★★★★
Self Catering
Dream Cottages
t (01305) 789000
e admin@dream-cottages.co.uk
w dream-cottages.co.uk

Auberge
Rating Applied For
Self Catering
Dream Cottages
t (01305) 789000
e admin@dream-cottages.co.uk
w dream-cottages.co.uk

Azure Apartment ★★★★
Self Catering
Dream Cottages
t (01305) 789000
e admin@dream-cottages.co.uk
w dream-cottages.co.uk

Barrack Cottage ★★★★
Self Catering
Dream Cottages
t (01305) 789000
e admin@dream-cottages.co.uk
w dream-cottages.co.uk

Beach & Summer Self-Catering Accommodation
★★★★★ *Self Catering*
Contact: Mr & Mrs Graham & Barbara Dubben
t (01305) 787815
e barbara@baylodge.co.uk
w baylodge.co.uk

Beach Retreat ★★★
Self Catering
Dream Cottages
t (01305) 789000
e admin@dream-cottages.co.uk
w dream-cottages.co.uk

Bella Vista ★★★
Self Catering
Dream Cottages
t (01305) 789000
e admin@dream-cottages.co.uk
w dream-cottages.co.uk

Bittern Housea ★★★
Self Catering
Dream Cottages
t (01305) 789000
e admin@dream-cottages.co.uk
w dream-cottages.co.uk

Bowleaze New ★★★★
Self Catering
Dream Cottages
t (01305) 789000
e admin@dream-cottages.co.uk
w dream-cottages.co.uk

The Brambles ★★★
Self Catering
Dorset Cottage Holidays
t (01929) 553443
e enq@dhcottages.co.uk
w dhcottages.co.uk

Brewers Cottage ★★★★
Self Catering
Dream Cottages
t (01305) 789000
e admin@dream-cottages.co.uk
w dream-cottages.co.uk

Central Seafront Apartments ★★★
Self Catering
Contact: Mr Steve Wright
t (01305) 766744
e info@centralseafrontapartments.co.uk
w centralseafrontapartments.co.uk

Charm Properties ★★★★
Self Catering
Contact: Mrs Hannah Kearns
t (01305) 780011
e hannah@charmproperties.co.uk
w charmproperties.co.uk

Christopher Robin Holiday Flats ★★★ *Self Catering*
Contact: Mrs Davies
t (01305) 774870
e louise@christopherrobinholidayflats.co.uk
w christopherrobinholidayflats.co.uk

Churchills ★★★★
Self Catering
Dream Cottages
t (01305) 789000
e admin@dream-cottages.co.uk
w dream-cottages.co.uk

Cockleshells ★★★
Self Catering
Dream Cottages
t (01305) 789000
e admin@dream-cottages.co.uk
w dream-cottages.co.uk

Commodore's Row ★★★★
Self Catering
Dream Cottages
t (01305) 789000
e admin@dream-cottages.co.uk
w dream-cottages.co.uk

Coral Cottage ★★★★
Self Catering
Dream Cottages
t (01305) 789000
e admin@dream-cottages.co.uk
w dream-cottages.co.uk

Cove Corner ★★★★
Self Catering
Dream Cottages
t (01305) 789000
e admin@dream-cottages.co.uk
w dream-cottages.co.uk

Cove Cottage ★★★
Self Catering
Dream Cottages
t (01305) 789000
e admin@dream-cottages.co.uk
w dream-cottages.co.uk

Cove Walk Cottage ★★★★
Self Catering
Dream Cottages
t (01305) 789000
e admin@dream-cottages.co.uk
w dream-cottages.co.uk

Crescent Bay Apartments
★★★ *Self Catering*
Contact: Martin Carter
t (01305) 750123
e hi-surf@hotmail.com
w holidaysweymouth.co.uk

Crescent Cottage ★★★
Self Catering
Contact: Mrs Tracy Buckwell
t (01305) 771881
e buckwell@btinternet.com
w holidaycottagesweymouth.com

Cygnets ★★★★
Self Catering
Dream Cottages
t (01305) 789000
e admin@dream-cottages.co.uk
w dream-cottages.co.uk

Digby House ★★★
Self Catering
Dream Cottages
t (01305) 789000
e admin@dream-cottages.co.uk
w dream-cottages.co.uk

Dornare Holiday Flats ★★
Self Catering
Contact: Mrs Dorenne Fowler
t (01305) 786359
e dornare@fowler77.freeserve.co.uk

Driftwood Cottage ★★★
Self Catering
Dream Cottages
t (01305) 789000
e admin@dream-cottages.co.uk
w dream-cottages.co.uk

Fairhaven Holiday Flats & Cottage ★★ *Self Catering*
Contact: Ms Tania Hickmott
t (01305) 760100
e fairhaven@kingshotels.co.uk
w kingshotels.co.uk

The Ferryman ★★★
Self Catering
Dream Cottages
t (01305) 789000
e admin@dream-cottages.co.uk
w dream-cottages.co.uk

Fisherman's Cottage ★★★
Self Catering
Dream Cottages
t (01305) 789000
e admin@dream-cottages.co.uk
w dream-cottages.co.uk

Footprints ★★★★
Self Catering
Dream Cottages
t (01305) 789000
e admin@dream-cottages.co.uk
w dream-cottages.co.uk

Fountain Cottage ★★★★
Self Catering
Dream Cottages
t (01305) 789000
e admin@dream-cottages.co.uk
w dream-cottages.co.uk

Fuchsia's Edge ★★★
Self Catering
Dream Cottages
t (01305) 789000
e admin@dream-cottages.co.uk
w dream-cottages.co.uk

The Gables ★★★★
Self Catering
Dream Cottages
t (01305) 789000
e admin@dream-cottages.co.uk
w dream-cottages.co.uk

The Gatehouse & Malthouse
★★★★ *Self Catering*
Dream Cottages
t (01305) 789000
e admin@dream-cottages.co.uk
w dream-cottages.co.uk

George's House ★★★★
Self Catering
Dream Cottages
t (01305) 789000
e admin@dream-cottages.co.uk
w dream-cottages.co.uk

Gone Fishing ★★★★
Self Catering
Dream Cottages
t (01305) 789000
e admin@dream-cottages.co.uk
w dream-cottages.co.uk

Harbour Reach ★★★
Self Catering
Dream Cottages
t (01305) 789000
e admin@dream-cottages.co.uk
w dream-cottages.co.uk

Harbour View Bungalow
★★★★ *Self Catering*
Dream Cottages
t (01305) 789000
e admin@dream-cottages.co.uk
w dream-cottages.co.uk

Harbour Walk ★★★★
Self Catering
Dream Cottages
t (01305) 789000
e admin@dream-cottages.co.uk
w dream-cottages.co.uk

Harbour Watch
Rating Applied For
Self Catering
Dream Cottages
t (01305) 789000
e admin@dream-cottages.co.uk
w dream-cottages.co.uk

Harbourside Apartment
★★★★ *Self Catering*
Dream Cottages
t (01305) 789000
e admin@dream-cottages.co.uk
w dream-cottages.co.uk

Harbourside Cottage
★★★★ *Self Catering*
Dream Cottages
t (01305) 789000
e admin@dream-cottages.co.uk
w dream-cottages.co.uk

Harbourside Holidays
★★★-★★★★ *Self Catering*
Contact: Ms Janet Bennett
t (01305) 832134
w harboursideweymouth.co.uk

Hops House ★★★★
Self Catering
Dream Cottages
t (01305) 789000
e admin@dream-cottages.co.uk
w dream-cottages.co.uk

Horizons Views ★★★★★
Self Catering
Dream Cottages
t (01305) 789000
e admin@dream-cottages.co.uk
w dream-cottages.co.uk

Howard Cottage ★★★
Self Catering
Contact: Mrs Barbara Willy
t (01305) 871799

Iris Cottage
Rating Applied For
Self Catering
Dream Cottages
t (01305) 789000
e admin@dream-cottages.co.uk
w dream-cottages.co.uk

Island View ★★★
Self Catering
Dream Cottages
t (01305) 789000
e admin@dream-cottages.co.uk
w dream-cottages.co.uk

Jacaranda ★★★★
Self Catering
Dream Cottages
t (01305) 789000
e admin@dream-cottages.co.uk
w dream-cottages.co.uk

Kenmuire Holiday Flats
★-★★★ *Self Catering*
Contact: Mr Gary Cotterill
t (01305) 785659
w kenmuireholidayflats.co.uk

Kingsview & Alexandra House ★★-★★★
Self Catering
Contact: Ms Anne Breen
t (01305) 814741
e bookings@weymouthcottagesandflats.co.uk
w weymouthcottagesandflats.co.uk

Lavender Cottage ★★★
Self Catering
Dream Cottages
t (01305) 789000
e admin@dream-cottages.co.uk
w dream-cottages.co.uk

Lazy Days ★★★ *Self Catering*
Dream Cottages
t (01305) 789000
e admin@dream-cottages.co.uk
w dream-cottages.co.uk

Lazy Waves ★★★★
Self Catering
Contact: Mr & Mrs Dan & Julie Vockins
t (01305) 833669
e booking@monkeyholidays.co.uk
w monkeyholidays.co.uk

Lillies ★★★ *Self Catering*
Dream Cottages
t (01305) 789000
e admin@dream-cottages.co.uk
w dream-cottages.co.uk

The Little Coachouse ★★★
Self Catering
Dream Cottages
t (01305) 789000
e admin@dream-cottages.co.uk
w dream-cottages.co.uk

Little Retreat ★★★★
Self Catering
Dream Cottages
t (01305) 789000
e admin@dream-cottages.co.uk
w dream-cottages.co.uk

Little venice ★★★
Self Catering
Dream Cottages
t (01305) 789000
e admin@dream-cottages.co.uk
w dream-cottages.co.uk

Louisa Cottage ★★★★
Self Catering
Dream Cottages
t (01305) 789000
e admin@dream-cottages.co.uk
w dream-cottages.co.uk

Love Lane Cottage ★★★
Self Catering
Contact: Ms Anna Eltringham
t (020) 8656 4548
e info@holidayinweymouth.co.uk
w holidayinweymouth.co.uk

The Malthouse ★★★★
Self Catering
Dream Cottages
t (01305) 789000
e admin@dream-cottages.co.uk
w dream-cottages.co.uk

Marina View Apartment
★★★★ *Self Catering*
Dream Cottages
t (01305) 789000
e admin@dream-cottages.co.uk
w dream-cottages.co.uk

Mariner's View ★★★
Self Catering
Contact: Mrs P Brockbank
t (01454) 774645
e patriciabrockbank@yahoo.co.uk
w ferrybridgecottages.com

Mariners Way ★★★
Self Catering
Dream Cottages
t (01305) 789000
e admin@dream-cottages.co.uk
w dream-cottages.co.uk

Marlow House ★★★
Self Catering
Dream Cottages
t (01305) 789000
e admin@dream-cottages.co.uk
w dream-cottages.co.uk

Meadows Cottage ★★★★
Self Catering
Contact: Mrs Imogen Turner
t (01305) 774400
e robert@meadows24.freeserve.co.uk
w meadowscottage.com

Melcombe Apartment ★★★
Self Catering
Dorset Cottage Holidays
t (01929) 553443
e enq@dhcottages.co.uk
w dhcottages.co.uk

Mermaid House ★★★
Self Catering
Dream Cottages
t (01305) 789000
e admin@dream-cottages.co.uk
w dream-cottages.co.uk

Mistral
Rating Applied For
Self Catering
Contact: Mr M Hester
t (01305) 759109
e info@cornerstonelettings.co.uk
w weymouthholidayhomes.co.uk

Moordale Holiday Caravan
Approved Caravan Holiday Home
Contact: Mr Max Mortimer
t (01305) 786530
e mortimermax1@aol.com.

Mulberry Cottage ★★★
Self Catering
Dream Cottages
t (01305) 789000
e admin@dream-cottages.co.uk
w dream-cottages.co.uk

Nearsea ★★★★ *Self Catering*
Dream Cottages
t (01305) 789000
e admin@dream-cottages.co.uk
w dream-cottages.co.uk

Neptune House ★★★
Self Catering
Dream Cottages
t (01305) 789000
e admin@dream-cottages.co.uk
w dream-cottages.co.uk

Newberry Cottage ★★★★
Self Catering
Dream Cottages
t (01305) 789000
e admin@dream-cottages.co.uk
w dream-cottages.co.uk

The Oast House ★★★★
Self Catering
Dream Cottages
t (01305) 789000
e admin@dream-cottages.co.uk
w dream-cottages.co.uk

Ocean Reach ★★★
Self Catering
Contact: Mr Carl Labross
t (01296) 338370
e carllabross@yahoo.com

Ocean Watch ★★★★
Self Catering
Dream Cottages
t (01305) 789000
e admin@dream-cottages.co.uk
w dream-cottages.co.uk

Ocean Wave ★★★★
Self Catering
Dream Cottages
t (01305) 789000
e admin@dream-cottages.co.uk
w dream-cottages.co.uk

Oggins Edge ★★★
Self Catering
Dream Cottages
t (01305) 789000
e admin@dream-cottages.co.uk
w dream-cottages.co.uk

The Old Barley Store
★★★★ *Self Catering*
Dream Cottages
t (01305) 789000
e admin@dream-cottages.co.uk
w dream-cottages.co.uk

Old Beams ★★★★
Self Catering
Dream Cottages
t (01305) 789000
e admin@dream-cottages.co.uk
w dream-cottages.co.uk

Old Harbour Holiday Flats
★★ *Self Catering*
Contact: Mr & Mrs Anthony & Cindy Goddard
t (01305) 776674
w holidayflats.webs.com

Old Malthouse Apartments
★★★ *Self Catering*
Dream Cottages
t (01305) 789000
e admin@dream-cottages.co.uk
w dream-cottages.co.uk

Old School Cottage ★★★
Self Catering
Dream Cottages
t (01305) 789000
e admin@dream-cottages.co.uk
w dream-cottages.co.uk

One Cove Street ★★★
Self Catering
Contact: Mr Deryk Brown
t (020) 8941 6150
e derykbrown41@aol.com

Orchard Cottage ★★★
Self Catering
Contact: Miss Anne M Breen
t (01305) 814741
e bookings@weymouthcottagesandflats.co.uk
w weymouthcottagesandflats.co.uk

Paradise View ★★★
Self Catering
Dream Cottages
t (01305) 789000
e admin@dream-cottages.co.uk
w dream-cottages.co.uk

Pear Tree Cottage ★★★
Self Catering
Contact: Mr Ian Boudier
t (01305) 783188
e trelawney@freeuk.com
w trelawneyhotel.com

Pearl Cottage ★★★★
Self Catering
Dream Cottages
t (01305) 789000
e admin@dream-cottages.co.uk
w dream-cottages.co.uk

Pebble Cottage ★★★
Self Catering
Dream Cottages
t (01305) 789000
e admin@dream-cottages.co.uk
w dream-cottages.co.uk

The Pines ★★★★
Self Catering
Dream Cottages
t (01305) 789000
e admin@dream-cottages.co.uk
w dream-cottages.co.uk

Poppies Cottage ★★★★
Self Catering
Dream Cottages
t (01305) 789000
e admin@dream-cottages.co.uk
w dream-cottages.co.uk

Promenade Way ★★★
Self Catering
Dream Cottages
t (01305) 789000
e admin@dream-cottages.co.uk
w dream-cottages.co.uk

Quayside ★★★ *Self Catering*
Contact: Mr Heath
t (01753) 654676
e quayside14@aol.com
w quayside.uk.com

Queensway Apartments ★★
Self Catering
Contact: Mr Martin Kelly
t (01305) 760747
e info@queenswayapartments.co.uk
w queenswayapartments.co.uk

Redcliff View Lodge ★★★
Self Catering
Dream Cottages
t (01305) 789000
e admin@dream-cottages.co.uk
w dream-cottages.co.uk

Reefknott ★★★★
Self Catering
Contact: Mrs Susan Kay
t (0117) 932 7690
e suedental2000@yahoo.co.uk

Regency Sands ★★★★
Self Catering
Dream Cottages
t (01305) 789000
e admin@dream-cottages.co.uk
w dream-cottages.co.uk

Sailing Waters ★★★★
Self Catering
Dream Cottages
t (01305) 789000
e admin@dream-cottages.co.uk
w dream-cottages.co.uk

Salisbury Terrace ★★★
Self Catering
Contact: Mr & Mrs C M & J L Elliotte elliottbb2@btinternet.com

Sandpipers ★★★★
Self Catering
Dream Cottages
t (01305) 789000
e admin@dream-cottages.co.uk
w dream-cottages.co.uk

Savoy Holiday Flats ★★★
Self Catering
Contact: Mr Mark Taylor
t (01305) 783254
w korthals.co.uk

The Sea Nest ★★★
Self Catering
Contact: Mrs Anita Boyle
t (01305) 761380
e anita.boyle@btinternet.com

Sea Shells Holiday Flat
★★★ *Self Catering*
Contact: Mr & Mrs Duncan & Ramona Rosser
t (01305) 778540
e ramonarosser@aol.com

Sea Tower ★★★★
Self Catering
Dream Cottages
t (01305) 789000
e admin@dream-cottages.co.uk
w dream-cottages.co.uk

Sea Watch ★★★★
Self Catering
Dream Cottages
t (01305) 789000
e admin@dream-cottages.co.uk
w dream-cottages.co.uk

Seafields ★★★ *Self Catering*
Dream Cottages
t (01305) 789000
e admin@dream-cottages.co.uk
w dream-cottages.co.uk

Seafront Holiday Flats ★★
Self Catering
Contact: Mr Stephen Taylor
t (01305) 780104

Seagate ★★★★ *Self Catering*
Dream Cottages
t (01305) 789000
e admin@dream-cottages.co.uk
w dream-cottages.co.uk

Seagull Cottage ★★★
Self Catering
Dream Cottages
t (01305) 789000
e admin@dream-cottages.co.uk
w dream-cottages.co.uk

Seahorse Apartment ★★★
Self Catering
Dream Cottages
t (01305) 789000
e admin@dream-cottages.co.uk
w dream-cottages.co.uk

Seashells ★★★ *Self Catering*
Dream Cottages
t (01305) 789000
e admin@dream-cottages.co.uk
w dream-cottages.co.uk

Seastar Apartments ★★★★
Self Catering
Dream Cottages
t (01305) 789000
e admin@dream-cottages.co.uk
w dream-cottages.co.uk

Seaview Cottage & Captains Cabin ★★★ *Self Catering*
Contact: Mrs Wendy Evans
t (01305) 785037
e wenjon@onetel.com

Seaview, Seaspray, Seabreeze ★★★–★★★★
Self Catering
Dream Cottages
t (01305) 789000
e admin@dream-cottages.co.uk
w dream-cottages.co.uk

The Shanty ★★★
Self Catering
Dream Cottages
t (01305) 789000
e admin@dream-cottages.co.uk
w dream-cottages.co.uk

Shire Horse Mews ★★★
Self Catering
Dream Cottages
t (01305) 789000
e admin@dream-cottages.co.uk
w dream-cottages.co.uk

Spinnaker House ★★★
Self Catering
Dream Cottages
t (01305) 789000
e admin@dream-cottages.co.uk
w dream-cottages.co.uk

Spring Tides ★★★★
Self Catering
Dream Cottages
t (01305) 789000
e admin@dream-cottages.co.uk
w dream-cottages.co.uk

Stavordale House Holiday Apartments ★★★
Self Catering
Contact: Mr Mark Marriott
t (01305) 789004
e stavordalehouse@ukonline.co.uk
w stavordalehouse.co.uk

Stonebank Cottage ★★★★
Self Catering
Contact: Mrs Prunella Westcott
t (01305) 760120
e pushkin1932-visitswsc@yahoo.co.uk
w stonebank-chickerell.com

Summerleaze ★★
Self Catering
Contact: Mrs Julia Cole
t (01305) 777253

Sun Burst Cottage ★★★
Self Catering
Dream Cottages
t (01305) 789000
e admin@dream-cottages.co.uk
w dream-cottages.co.uk

Sunflower Cottage ★★★★
Self Catering
Dream Cottages
t (01305) 789000
e admin@dream-cottages.co.uk
w dream-cottages.co.uk

Tamarisk ★★★ *Self Catering*
Dream Cottages
t (01305) 789000
e admin@dream-cottages.co.uk
w dream-cottages.co.uk

Tamarisk Court ★★★★
Self Catering
Contact: Mrs Hilary Brain
t (01305) 786514

Tides ★★★★ *Self Catering*
Dream Cottages
t (01305) 789000
e admin@dream-cottages.co.uk
w dream-cottages.co.uk

Tintagel Court
Rating Applied For
Self Catering
Contact: Mrs Karen Albin
t (01305) 750147
e david.albin@btinternet.com

Townbridge Apartment
★★★ *Self Catering*
Dream Cottages
t (01305) 789000
e admin@dream-cottages.co.uk
w dream-cottages.co.uk

Tradewinds ★★★★
Self Catering
Dream Cottages
t (01305) 789000
e admin@dream-cottages.co.uk
w dream-cottages.co.uk

Treetops ★★★★
Self Catering
Dream Cottages
t (01305) 789000
e admin@dream-cottages.co.uk
w dream-cottages.co.uk

Upsidedown House ★★★★
Self Catering
Dream Cottages
t (01305) 789000
e admin@dream-cottages.co.uk
w dream-cottages.co.uk

Villa de la Mer ★★★
Self Catering
Dream Cottages
t (01305) 789000
e admin@dream-cottages.co.uk
w dream-cottages.co.uk

Wagonwheels ★★★
Self Catering
Dream Cottages
t (01305) 789000
e admin@dream-cottages.co.uk
w dream-cottages.co.uk

Waters Edge ★★★
Self Catering
Dream Cottages
t (01305) 789000
e admin@dream-cottages.co.uk
w dream-cottages.co.uk

Wave Crest ★★★★
Self Catering
Dream Cottages
t (01305) 789000
e admin@dream-cottages.co.uk
w dream-cottages.co.uk

Weyfarer Cottage ★★★
Self Catering
Dream Cottages
t (01305) 789000
e admin@dream-cottages.co.uk
w dream-cottages.co.uk

Weymouth Bay Holiday Apartments ★★★
Self Catering
Contact: Mrs Angela Mary Blake
t (01305) 785003

Weymouth Harbour & Beach Holidays ★★★★
Self Catering
Contact: Mr & Mrs Michael & Penny Piggin
t 07768 568057
w harbourandbeach.com

The Weymouth Seafront Holiday Flat ★★★★
Self Catering
Contact: Mr Don Whistance
t (01305) 813237
e donwhistance@rmplc.co.uk
w theflat.org.uk

Wheelwright House ★★★
Self Catering
Dream Cottages
t (01305) 789000
e admin@dream-cottages.co.uk
w dream-cottages.co.uk

White Horse House ★★★
Self Catering
Dream Cottages
t (01305) 789000
e admin@dream-cottages.co.uk
w dream-cottages.co.uk

Whitesands Seafront Apartments ★★ *Self Catering*
Contact: Mr John Watt
t (01305) 782202

Winkle Cottage ★★★
Self Catering
Dream Cottages
t (01305) 789000
e admin@dream-cottages.co.uk
w dream-cottages.co.uk

WHEAL KITTY
Cornwall

Atlantic Coast Holiday Bungalows ★★★–★★★★
Self Catering
Contact: Mr & Mrs Selby
t (01872) 552485
e atlantic.holidays@googlemail.com
w atlantic-holidays.co.uk

WHEDDON CROSS
Somerset

North Wheddon Farm
★★★★ *Self Catering*
Contact: Mr Julian Abraham
t (01225) 461634
e northwheddonfarm@aol.com
w go-exmoor.co.uk

Pembroke ★★★
Self Catering
Contact: Mrs Escott
t (01643) 841550

Triscombe Farm ★★★★
Self Catering
Contact: Mr & Mrs Ruth & Robert Brinkley
t (01643) 851227
e ruthattriscombe@aol.com
w triscombefarm.co.uk

WHIMPLE
Devon

LSF Holiday Cottages ★★★
Self Catering
Contact: Mrs Angela Lang
t (01404) 822989
e lowersouthbrookfarm@btinternet.com
w lowersouthbrookfarm.co.uk

WHITCHURCH
Devon

Challonsleigh, Whitchurch
★★★★ *Self Catering*
Contact: Mrs Vicky Fox
t (01822) 612259
e vicky@dartmoorcottage.info
w challonsleigh.co.uk

WHITCHURCH CANONICORUM
Dorset

Berehayes Farm Cottages
★★★★ *Self Catering*
Contact: Mr & Mrs Winterbourne
t (01297) 489093
e berehayes@tesco.net
w berehayes.co.uk

Bonhayes Stable ★★★
Self Catering
Lyme Bay Holidays
t (01297) 443363
e email@lymebayholidays.co.uk
w lymebayholidays.co.uk

Taphouse Farmhouse, Courthouse Farmhouse & Courthouse Dairy ★★★
Self Catering
Contact: Miss Kay Johnson
t (01297) 489375
e cardsmill@aol.com
w farmhousedorset.com

West Barn ★★★★
Self Catering
Lyme Bay Holidays
t (01297) 443363
e email@lymebayholidays.co.uk
w lymebayholidays.co.uk

WHITECROFT
Gloucestershire

Miners Cottage ★★★★
Self Catering
Contact: Karen Constantine
t (01594) 562483
e info@theminersarmswhitecroft.co.uk
w minersarmswhitecroft.co.uk

WHITFORD
Devon

Willowhayne Cottage
Rating Applied For
Self Catering
Contact: Linda Marshall
t (01297) 551077
e linmarshall@btinternet.com
w willowhayne.org.uk

WHITMINSTER
Gloucestershire

The Stable ★★★
Self Catering
Contact: Mr & Mrs A C & R M Beeby
t (01452) 740969
e thestable@jaxonsfarm.co.uk
w jaxonsfarm.co.uk

WIDCOMBE
Somerset

Highclere Holidays ★★★★
Self Catering
Contact: Mrs Elizabeth Daniel
t (01225) 465465
e liz.daniel@tiscali.co.uk
w holidayinbath.co.uk

WIDECOMBE-IN-THE-MOOR
Devon

Holwell Farm Cottages
★★★★★ *Self Catering*
Contact: Ms Philippa Hughes
t (01364) 631471
e info@holne-chase.co.uk
w holwelldartmoor.co.uk

WIDEMOUTH BAY
Cornwall

The Barns ★★★★
Self Catering
Contact: Ian & Carolyn Harrison
t (01288) 361877
e widemouthfarm@tiscali.co.uk
w widemouth-farm.co.uk

Palm Villa ★★★★
Self Catering
Farm & Cottage Holidays
t (01237) 459827
e enquiries@farmcott.co.uk
w holidaycottages.co.uk

WILLERSEY
Gloucestershire

3 Cheltenham Cottages ★★
Self Catering
Contact: Mrs Gillian Malin
28 Bibsworth Avenue
t (01386) 853248
e g.malin@virgin.net

WILLITON
Somerset

Daisy Cottage ★★★★
Self Catering
Contact: Mrs Ann Bishop
t (01984) 632657

WILLSBRIDGE
Gloucestershire

Clack Mill Farm Cottage
★★★ *Self Catering*
Contact: Ms Gaile Gay
t (0117) 932 2399
e gaile12331@aol.com
w hometown.aol.co.uk

WIMBORNE
Dorset

The Old Mill
Rating Applied For
Self Catering
Quay Holidays
t (01202) 683333
e stay@quayholidays.co.uk
w quayholidays.co.uk

WIMBORNE MINSTER
Dorset

Birdsong Cottage ★★★
Self Catering
Dorset Cottage Holidays
t (01929) 553443
e enq@dhcottages.co.uk
w dhcottages.co.uk

The Guest Suite ★★★
Self Catering
Contact: Mrs Debra Miles
t (01202) 884578
e debra.meublemarche@hotmail.com
w theguestsuite.co.uk

The Old Exchange ★★★
Self Catering
Contact: Mrs Sarah Holland
t (01258) 840809
e sarah.j.holland@talk21.com
w theoldexchange.co.uk

Suncot ★★★★ *Self Catering*
Contact: Mrs Helen Edbrooke
t (01202) 884908
e helen@stoneleighhouse.com
w stoneleighhouse.com/suncot

WINCHCOMBE
Gloucestershire

Misty View ★★★★
Self Catering
Contact: Mr Bob Turner
t (01242) 603583 & 07831 212501
e bobturner@mistyview.wanadoo.co.uk

Muir Cottage, Winchcombe
★★★★ *Self Catering*
Contact: Mr Mark Grassick
t (01242) 603124
e enquiries@thecotswoldretreat.co.uk
w thecotswoldretreat.co.uk

The Old Stables ★★★
Self Catering
Contact: Miss Jane Eayrs
t (01242) 603860

Orchard Cottage ★★★
Self Catering
Contact: Mrs S M Rolt
t (01242) 602594
e soniarolt@btinternet.com
w cottageguide.co.uk/orchard-cottage

Sudeley Castle Country Cottages ★★★-★★★★
Self Catering
Contact: Mrs Olive Byng
t (01242) 609481
e olive.byng@sudeley.org.uk
w sudeleycastle.co.uk

Traditional Accommodation, Winchcombe ★★★★
Self Catering
Contact: Mr & Mrs Wilson
t (01386) 446269
e trad.accom@virgin.net
w http://freespace.virgin.net/trad.accom

WINDMILL
Cornwall

Bryn Cottage ★★★
Self Catering
Contact: Mrs Pam Johnson
t (01442) 249998
e pammyjjohno@hotmail.co.uk

St Marina & Old Forge
★★★★-★★★★★
Self Catering
Harbour Holidays
t (01841) 533402
e contact@harbourholidays.co.uk
w harbourholidays.co.uk

WINDRUSH
Gloucestershire

Keeper's Cottage ★★★★
Self Catering
Contact: Mrs Collette Carmichael
t (01844) 215417 & 07730 456789
e enquiries@gamekeeperscottage.co.uk
w gamekeeperscottage.co.uk

WINFORD
Somerset

Regilbury Farm ★★★
Self Catering
Contact: Mrs Keedwell
t (01275) 472369
e janekeedwell@yahoo.co.uk
w regilburyfarm.co.uk

WINFRITH NEWBURGH
Dorset

Carters Barn ★★★
Self Catering
Dorset Cottage Holidays
t (01929) 553443
e enq@dhcottages.co.uk
w dhcottages.co.uk

Cherry & Willow Barn
★★★★ *Self Catering*
Dorset Cottage Holidays
t (01929) 553443
e enq@dhcottages.co.uk
w dhcottages.co.uk

Church Cottage ★★★
Self Catering
Dream Cottages
t (01305) 789000
e admin@dream-cottages.co.uk
w dream-cottages.co.uk

WINGFIELD
Wiltshire

Romsey Oak Cottages ★★
Self Catering
Contact: Mrs Christine Briars
t (01225) 753950
e enquiries@romseyoakcottages.co.uk
w romseyoakcottages.co.uk/intro.htm

WINKLEIGH
Devon

Wheatland Farm ★★★
Self Catering
Contact: Mr Ian Ripper
t (01837) 83499
e info@wheatlandfarm.co.uk
w wheatlandfarm.co.uk

WINNARDS PERCH
Cornwall

Ash Lodge ★★★★
Self Catering
Cornish Horizons Holiday Cottages
t (01841) 533331
e cottages@cornishhorizons.co.uk
w cornishhorizons.co.uk

Beech Lodge ★★★★
Self Catering
Cornish Horizons Holiday Cottages
t (01841) 533331
e cottages@cornishhorizons.co.uk
w cornishhorizons.co.uk

WINSFORD
Somerset

East Galliford ★★★
Self Catering
Contact: Mr Alexander
t (020) 8940 8078
e malcolm.alexander@interregna.com
w exmoorholidaycottages.co.uk

Karslake Cottage ★★★★
Self Catering
Marsdens Cottage Holidays
t (01271) 813777
e holidays@marsdens.co.uk
w marsdens.co.uk

Little Folly ★★★★
Self Catering
Contact: Mrs Pat Hewlett
t (01643) 851391
e adrianh@follyexmoor.co.uk
w follyexmoor.co.uk

WINSHAM
Somerset

Baytree Cottage ★★★★
Self Catering
Lyme Bay Holidays
t (01297) 443363
e email@lymebayholidays.co.uk
w lymebayholidays.co.uk

WINSON
Gloucestershire

Swan House ★★★★★
Self Catering
Contact: Mrs Patricia Langley
t (020) 995 9072
e patricia@swanhousecotswolds.co.uk
w swanhousecotswolds.co.uk

WINTERBORNE STICKLAND
Dorset

Kersin
Rating Applied For
Self Catering
Dream Cottages
t (01305) 789000
e admin@dream-cottages.co.uk
w dream-cottages.co.uk

WINTERBOURNE ABBAS
Dorset

Lavender Lodge/The Granary ★★★ *Self Catering*
Contact: Mr Graham Tobitt
t (01305) 889662
e enquiries@lgf-holidays.co.uk
w lgf-holidays.co.uk

WITCOMBE
Gloucestershire

Crickley Court Cottages
★★★★ *Self Catering*
Contact: Mr & Mrs Geoff & Lis Pilgrim-Morris
t (01452) 863634
e lispilgrimmorris@yahoo.co.uk
w crickleycourt.co.uk

WITHERIDGE
Devon

South Coombe Holiday Cottages ★★★★
Self Catering
t (01803) 814000
w westcountrycottages.co.uk

WITHINGTON
Gloucestershire

Ballingers Farmhouse Cottages ★★★★
Self Catering
Contact: Mr & Mrs Ian & Judith Pollard
t (01242) 890335
e pollardfam@compuserve.com
w ballingersfarmhouse cottages.co.uk

WITHYPOOL
Somerset

Westwater Cottage ★★★★
Self Catering
Contact: Mrs Sue Branfield
t (01643) 831360
e s.branfield@ukf.net
w westwatercottagexmoor.co.uk

WOODBURY
Devon

The Coach House ★★★★
Self Catering
Contact: Mr Paul Slade
t (01395) 233704
w tchwoodbury.co.uk

Squirrel ★★★★★
Self Catering
Contact: Mr & Mrs James Crill
t (01395) 567135
e info@thethatchedcottagecompany.co.uk
w thethatchcottagecompany.co.uk

Wodeberie Apartment, Woodbury ★★★★
Self Catering
Contact: Mrs Amanda Seale
t (01395) 239044
e info@woodmanton.co.uk
w woodmanton.co.uk

WOOKEY
Somerset

Mill Lodge ★★★★
Self Catering
Contact: Ms Lesley Burt
t (01749) 673118
e theburts@burcottmill.com
w burcottmill.com

Panniers Farm Cottage
★★★★ *Self Catering*
Contact: Mrs Gill Cumming
t (01749) 678928
e gill@panniersfarm.co.uk
w panniersfarm.co.uk

WOOLACOMBE
Devon

1 Devon Beach Court
★★★★ *Self Catering*
Marsdens Cottage Holidays
t (01271) 813777
e holidays@marsdens.co.uk
w marsdens.co.uk

1 Dolphin Court ★★★★
Self Catering
Marsdens Cottage Holidays
t (01271) 813777
e holidays@marsdens.co.uk
w marsdens.co.uk

2 Dolphin Court ★★★★
Self Catering
Marsdens Cottage Holidays
t (01271) 813777
e holidays@marsdens.co.uk
w marsdens.co.uk

5 Devon Beach ★★★★
Self Catering
Marsdens Cottage Holidays
t (01271) 813777
e holidays@marsdens.co.uk
w marsdens.co.uk

5 Little Beach ★★★★
Self Catering
Marsdens Cottage Holidays
t (01271) 813777
e holidays@marsdens.co.uk
w marsdens.co.uk

6 Little Beach ★★★★
Self Catering
Marsdens Cottage Holidays
t (01271) 813777
e holidays@marsdens.co.uk
w marsdens.co.uk

7 Little Beach ★★★
Self Catering
Marsdens Cottage Holidays
t (01271) 813777
e holidays@marsdens.co.uk
w marsdens.co.uk

The Apartment ★★★★
Self Catering
Marsdens Cottage Holidays
t (01271) 813777
e holidays@marsdens.co.uk
w marsdens.co.uk

Apartment 2 Narracott
★★★★ *Self Catering*
Marsdens Cottage Holidays
t (01271) 813777
e holidays@marsdens.co.uk
w marsdens.co.uk

Apartment 4 ★★★★
Self Catering
Marsdens Cottage Holidays
t (01271) 813777
e holidays@marsdens.co.uk
w marsdens.co.uk

Apartments 3 & 4 ★★★★
Self Catering
Marsdens Cottage Holidays
t (01271) 813777
e holidays@marsdens.co.uk
w marsdens.co.uk

Baggy Leap ★★★
Self Catering
Marsdens Cottage Holidays
t (01271) 813777
e holidays@marsdens.co.uk
w marsdens.co.uk

Barricane Sands ★★★
Self Catering
Marsdens Cottage Holidays
t (01271) 813777
e holidays@marsdens.co.uk
w marsdens.co.uk

Bay Vista ★★★★
Self Catering
Marsdens Cottage Holidays
t (01271) 813777
e holidays@marsdens.co.uk
w marsdens.co.uk

Beachcomber ★★★★
Self Catering
Marsdens Cottage Holidays
t (01271) 813777
e holidays@marsdens.co.uk
w marsdens.co.uk

Beau Rivage ★★★★
Self Catering
Marsdens Cottage Holidays
t (01271) 813777
e holidays@marsdens.co.uk
w marsdens.co.uk

Breakers ★★★★
Self Catering
Marsdens Cottage Holidays
t (01271) 813777
e holidays@marsdens.co.uk
w marsdens.co.uk

Camberley ★★★★
Self Catering
Marsdens Cottage Holidays
t (01271) 813777
e holidays@marsdens.co.uk
w marsdens.co.uk

Cove Cottage Flat ★★
Self Catering
Contact: Mrs Vivien Lawrence
t (01271) 870403
e vlawrence05@aol.com

Endsleigh ★★★★
Self Catering
Marsdens Cottage Holidays
t (01271) 813777
e holidays@marsdens.co.uk
w marsdens.co.uk

Heather Lea ★★★★
Self Catering
Marsdens Cottage Holidays
t (01271) 813777
e holidays@marsdens.co.uk
w marsdens.co.uk

Hibiscus ★★★★
Self Catering
Marsdens Cottage Holidays
t (01271) 813777
e holidays@marsdens.co.uk
w marsdens.co.uk

The Indilo ★★★★
Self Catering
Marsdens Cottage Holidays
t (01271) 813777
e holidays@marsdens.co.uk
w marsdens.co.uk

Kittiwake ★★★★
Self Catering
Marsdens Cottage Holidays
t (01271) 813777
e holidays@marsdens.co.uk
w marsdens.co.uk

Lantern House ★★★★
Self Catering
Marsdens Cottage Holidays
t (01271) 813777
e holidays@marsdens.co.uk
w marsdens.co.uk

Little Beach ★★★★
Self Catering
Marsdens Cottage Holidays
t (01271) 813777
e holidays@marsdens.co.uk
w marsdens.co.uk

Lundy Set ★★★★
Self Catering
Marsdens Cottage Holidays
t (01271) 813777
e holidays@marsdens.co.uk
w marsdens.co.uk

Marram ★★★ *Self Catering*
Marsdens Cottage Holidays
t (01271) 813777
e holidays@marsdens.co.uk
w marsdens.co.uk

Narracott Apartment 6
★★★★ *Self Catering*
Marsdens Cottage Holidays
t (01271) 813777
e holidays@marsdens.co.uk
w marsdens.co.uk

Narracott Apartment 9
★★★★★ *Self Catering*
Marsdens Cottage Holidays
t (01271) 813777
e holidays@marsdens.co.uk
w marsdens.co.uk

Oysters ★★★★ *Self Catering*
Marsdens Cottage Holidays
t (01271) 813777
e holidays@marsdens.co.uk
w marsdens.co.uk

Pebbles ★★★ *Self Catering*
Marsdens Cottage Holidays
t (01271) 813777
e holidays@marsdens.co.uk
w marsdens.co.uk

Point View ★★★★
Self Catering
Marsdens Cottage Holidays
t (01271) 813777
e holidays@marsdens.co.uk
w marsdens.co.uk

Shoreline ★★★★
Self Catering
Marsdens Cottage Holidays
t (01271) 813777
e holidays@marsdens.co.uk
w marsdens.co.uk

The Stables
Rating Applied For
Self Catering
Marsdens Cottage Holidays
t (01271) 813777
e holidays@marsdens.co.uk
w marsdens.co.uk

Swiss Cottage ★★★★
Self Catering
Marsdens Cottage Holidays
t (01271) 813777
e holidays@marsdens.co.uk
w marsdens.co.uk

Tamarin ★★★★
Self Catering
Marsdens Cottage Holidays
t (01271) 813777
e holidays@marsdens.co.uk
w marsdens.co.uk

Waves ★★★★★
Self Catering
Marsdens Cottage Holidays
t (01271) 813777
e holidays@marsdens.co.uk
w marsdens.co.uk

Waves End ★★★★
Self Catering
Marsdens Cottage Holidays
t (01271) 813777
e holidays@marsdens.co.uk
w marsdens.co.uk

WOOLFARDISWORTHY
Devon

Fairchild Cottage ★★★★★
Self Catering
Contact: Mrs Doreen Cox
t (01237) 431503
e cox5.gorrel@virgin.net

WOOLLAND
Dorset

Ellwood Cottages ★★★★
Self Catering
Contact: Mr & Mrs John & Ann Heath
t (01258) 818196
e admin@ellwoodcottages.co.uk
w ellwoodcottages.co.uk

WOOTTON BASSETT
Wiltshire

Hook Farm Cottages ★★★★
Self Catering
Contact: Mr & Mrs Richard & Jane Woolford
t (01793) 852215
e hookfarmcottages@farming.co.uk
w hookfarmcottages.co.uk

WOOTTON COURTENAY
Somerset

Exmoor View ★★★★
Self Catering
Contact: Mrs Carole Turner
t (01643) 841482
w wheddoncross.org.uk/exmoorview

Rose Cottage ★★★
Self Catering
Contact: Mr Bryan Fawcett
t (01275) 331123
e bryanfawcett@lineone.net
w exmoorose.co.uk

WOOTTON FITZPAINE
Dorset

41a Silver Street ★★★
Self Catering
Lyme Bay Holidays
t (01297) 443363
e email@lymebayholidays.co.uk
w lymebayholidays.co.uk

Cider & Barn Cottages ★★★★ *Self Catering*
Contact: Mrs Debby Snook
t (01297) 560541
e wfcottages@aol.com
w westoverfarmcottages.co.uk

East Barn ★★★★
Self Catering
Lyme Bay Holidays
t (01297) 443363
e email@lymebayholidays.co.uk
w lymebayholidays.co.uk

Hollycombe Cottage ★★★★
Self Catering
Lyme Bay Holidays
t (01297) 443363
e email@lymebayholidays.co.uk
w lymebayholidays.co.uk

Stable Cottage ★★★
Self Catering
Lyme Bay Holidays
t (01297) 443363
e email@lymebayholidays.co.uk
w lymebayholidays.co.uk

WRANTAGE
Somerset

Ludwells Barn ★★★
Self Catering
Contact: Mr Dodd
t (01823) 480316

WYCK RISSINGTON
Gloucestershire

Hope Cottage ★★★★
Self Catering
Contact: Mr & Mrs Richard & Carolyne Pye
t (01451) 822466
e hopelodgecottage@btinternet.com
w hopelodge.com

WYKE REGIS
Dorset

Church View ★★★
Self Catering
Dream Cottages
t (01305) 789000
e admin@dream-cottages.co.uk
w dream-cottages.co.uk

Still Waters ★★★
Self Catering
Dream Cottages
t (01305) 789000
e admin@dream-cottages.co.uk
w dream-cottages.co.uk

YARCOMBE
Devon

Heaven's Mouth ★★★
Self Catering
Contact: Mrs Ruth Everitt
t (01404) 861517
e ruth-everitt@supanet.com

YARLEY
Somerset

Seekings Self-Catering ★★★★ *Self Catering*
t (01749) 678402
w seekingsselfcatering.co.uk

YARNSCOMBE
Devon

Swallow Barton, Yarnscombe ★★★★
Self Catering
Contact: Mrs Sandra Newland
Little Barton
t (01769) 560583
e info@swallowbarton.co.uk
w swallowbarton.co.uk

YEO VALE
Devon

Crooked Lake Cottage ★★★
Self Catering
Toad Hall Cottages
t (01548) 853089
e thc@toadhallcottages.com
w toadhallcottages.co.uk

YORKLEY
Gloucestershire

2 Danby Cottages ★★★
Self Catering
Contact: Gareth Lawes
t (0117) 942 2301
e glawes@tiscali.co.uk

Forest of Dean Holiday Cottages ★★★ *Self Catering*
Contact: Mary Konig
t (01594) 562219
e cottages@forestofdeanholidays.co.uk
w forestofdeanholidays.co.uk

ZELAH
Cornwall

Callestock Courtyard ★★★-★★★★★
Self Catering
Contact: Mrs Down
t (01872) 540445
e liznick@littlecallestockfarm.co.uk
w callestockcoutryard.com

Little Lowarth ★★★★
Self Catering
Farm & Cottage Holidays
t (01237) 459827
e enquiries@farmcott.co.uk
w holidaycottages.co.uk

ZENNOR
Cornwall

Sener ★★ *Self Catering*
Contact: Mrs Bryan
t (0151) 648 0169

Boat accommodation

When you want to book a holiday afloat, whether for a short break or longer, you need a rating system you can trust. The Enjoy England ratings for boat accommodation are a clear guide to what to expect, in an easy-to-understand form.

Choose from nearly 1,000 quality-assessed boats in small and large fleets across England's waterways. Facilities will vary, so the following classifications will help you decide which type of boat will meet your needs:

Narrowboat

These purpose-built, traditionally decorated boats can be hired on canals and rivers, and can sleep up to 12 people. Step back in time and enjoy a very leisurely holiday cruising through the English countryside.

Cruiser

Cruisers operate mainly on the Norfolk Broads and the Thames. They range from practical, affordable craft to modern, stylish boats with accessories such as a dishwasher, DVD and flat-screen TV.

Hotel Boat

Hotel boats are generally narrowboats that are worked by a crew, so the guests can either simply relax or help if they want to. They can be booked by individuals or groups, and provide all the services of a hotel – all meals and refreshments from early morning tea to a five-course dinner in the evening. The trips are tailored to the guests and tend to be very sociable.

For more information on boating holidays visit enjoyEngland.com

Star ratings

Narrowboats and Cruisers

All narrowboats and cruisers that are awarded a star rating meet minimum standards, so you can be confident that they will adhere to statutory requirements, especially in relation to Health and Safety. All boats have a shower/bath, toilet, fridge, adequate heating and lighting, and a basic hot water supply. Bed linen will be provided.

Enjoy England professional assessors visit every year to check all the facilities and award a quality score for every aspect, including the layout and design of each boat, the quality of the galley, the sleeping cabins, bathrooms and toilet, and the cleanliness. The service offered by the boatyard staff is also assessed.

Higher star-rated boat accommodation tends to have more spacious cabins, better-presented beds, better-equipped galleys and more sophisticated toilets! The ratio of toilets to guests will improve with the higher star ratings.

Certain additional facilities and services are required at the higher star levels, some of which may be important to you:

TWO-STAR boats must provide:
- Radio/cassette player.

THREE-STAR boats must provide:
- Pump-out toilet
- Colour TV
- Central heating.

FOUR-STAR boats must provide:
- Cooker with oven, grill and four rings (two rings for four-berth boat).

FIVE-STAR boats must provide:
- Constant hot water
- Heating in bathroom
- 230V supply.

However, it is not enough to simply offer the above items to achieve the higher star ratings – the overall quality score must be achieved.

Hotel Boats

Hotel boats are assessed in the same way as hotels, with the assessor staying overnight every other year. A quality score is awarded for every aspect of the experience including the comfort of the bed, the quality of the food served on board, and, most importantly, the cleanliness. They also score the warmth of welcome and the level of care that each hotel boat offers its guests. Those that 'go the extra mile' to make every stay a special one, will be rewarded with high scores for quality.

All hotel boats have to offer the same level of facilities, except at five star, where there is a requirement for all beds to be at least 6ft in length.

Ratings made easy

★
Simple, practical, no frills

★★
Well presented and well run

★★★
Good level of quality and comfort

★★★★
Excellent standard throughout

★★★★★
Exceptional with a degree of luxury

For full details of the quality assessment schemes, go online at **enjoyengland.com/quality**

CRUISERS

Barnes Brinkcraft
★★★-★★★★★
Cruiser
Riverside Road, Norwich
NR12 8UD
t (01603) 782625
e bookings@barnesbrinkcraft.co.uk
w barnesbrinkcraft.co.uk

Caversham Boat Service
★★-★★★
Cruiser
Frys Island, Thames Side,
Reading RG1 8DG
t (0118) 957 4323

City Boats (Highcraft)
★★-★★★
Cruiser
Highcraft Marina, Griffin Lane,
Norwich NR7 0SL
t (01603) 700324
w cityboats.co.uk

Kris Cruisers
★★★★-★★★★★
Cruiser
The Waterfront, Southlea
Road, Slough SL3 9BU
t (01753) 543930

Norfolk Broads Direct-Faircraft Loynes
★★★★-★★★★★
Cruiser
The Bridge, Norwich Road,
Norwich NR12 8RX
t (01603) 782207
e info@broads.co.uk
w broads.co.uk

Norfolk Broads Direct-Herbert Woods
★-★★★★★
Cruiser
Broads Haven, Great Yarmouth
NR29 5JD
t (01692) 670711
w broads.co.uk

Sanderson Marine Craft Ltd
★★-★★★
Cruiser
Riverside, Norwich NR13 3TE
t (01493) 700242
w sandersonmarine.co.uk

Swancraft Boat Services
★★★-★★★★★
Cruiser
Benson Waterfront,
Wallingford OX10 6SL
t (01481) 836700

HOTEL BOATS

Away4awhile ★★★
Hotel Boat
3 Brindley Place, Birmingham
B1 2JB
t 0845 644 5144
e enquiries@away4awhile.com
w away4awhile.com

Duke & Duchess Cruising Co. Ltd. ★★★★
Hotel Boat
Saltisford Canal Centre,
Warwick CV34 5RJ
t 07711 836441
e info@hotelboat-holidays.co.uk
w hotelboat-holidays.co.uk

Ladyline Hotel Boats Ltd
★★★★
Hotel Boat
Stockton Road, Southam
CV47 8LD
t (01788) 553912
e ladylinehotelboats@jesney.eclipse.co.uk
w ladylinehotelboats.co.uk

My Edward Elgar
Rating applied for
Hotel Boat
Alexandra Warehouse, West
Quay, Gloucester GL1 2LG
t 0845 601 7895
e sales@englishholidaycruises.co.uk
w englishholidaycruises.co.uk

Oak & Ash Hotel Boats
★★★★
Hotel Boat
Warwick CV34 5RJ
t 07977 229103
w reedboats.co.uk

Hotel Periwinkle ★★★★
Hotel Boat
1 Isabella Street, Preston
PR3 3WL
t 07747 017263
e hotelperiwinkle@aol.com
w hotelboatperiwinkle.com

NARROWBOATS

Acton Bridge ★★★★
Narrowboat
Bartington Wharf, Northwich
CW8 4QU
t (01527) 575115
e bholidays@aol.com
w black-prince.com

Alvechurch - Alvechurch Boat Centres
★★★-★★★★★
Narrowboat
Scarfield Wharf, Scarfield Hill,
Birmingham B48 7SQ
t (0121) 445 1133
w alvechurch.com

Alvecote Marina ★★★
Narrowboat
Robeys Lane, Tamworth
B78 1AS
t (01543) 251277
w canaltime.com

Anderson Boats
★★★-★★★★
Narrowboat
Wych House Lane, Middlewich
CW10 9BQ
t (01606) 833668

Anderton - Alvechurch Boat Centres Ltd ★★★-★★★★★
Narrowboat
Anderton Marina, Uplands
Road, Northwich CW9 6AJ
t (01606) 79642
e anderton@alvechurch.com
w alvechurch.com

April Cruises ★★★★
Narrowboat
Post Lane, Stoke-on-Trent
ST9 9DT
t (01782) 878236
e p_mayer@ntlworld.com
w aprilcruises.co.uk

Aqua Narrowboat (H2O)
★★★★★
Narrowboat
6 Old Hall Drive, Derby
DE65 6DT
t (01283) 704855
e admin@aquanarrowboathire.com
w aquanarrowboathire.com

Ashby Boat Company
★★-★★★★
Narrowboat
89 Station Road, Nuneaton
CV13 6EY
t (01455) 212671
e sales@ashbyboats.co.uk
w ashbyboats.com

Autherley - Napton Narrowboats
★★★-★★★★★
Narrowboat
c/o Water Travel, Autherley
Junction, Oxley Moor Road,
Wolverhampton WV9 5HW
t (01926) 813644

Bath - Anglowelsh Boats
★★★★
Narrowboat
Sydney Wharf, Bathwick Hill,
Bath BA2 4EL
t (01225) 447276

Blackwater Meadow Marina
★★★
Narrowboat
Birch Road, Ellesmere
SY12 9DD
t (01543) 251277
w canaltime.com

Bunbury - Anglowelsh Boats
★★★-★★★★
Narrowboat
Bunbury Locks, Tarporley
CW6 9QB
t (01829) 260957

Canal Boat Escapes Applied
Narrowboat
6 Whitworth Way,
Barnoldswick BB18 6YN
t (01772) 536600

Canal Cruising Company
★★★-★★★★
Narrowboat
Crown Street, Stone ST15 8QN
t (01785) 813982
w canalcruising.co.uk

Caversham Boat Services Applied
Narrowboat
Frys Island, Thames Side,
Reading RG1 8DG
t 0870 336 8198
e blakes.boatsnw@holidaycottagesgroup.com
w cavershamboatservices.co.uk

Claymoore Navigation Ltd
★★-★★★★★
Narrowboat
The Wharf, Warrington
WA4 4BA
t (01928) 717273
w claymoore.co.uk

Copt Heath Wharf ★★★★
Narrowboat
309 Barston Lane, Solihull
B91 2SX
t (0121) 704 4464
e info@coptheathwharf.co.uk
w coptheathwharf.co.uk

Countryside Cruising Holidays Limited
★★★★
Narrowboat
c/o The Boat House,
11 Plover Close, Meir Park,
Stoke-on-Trent ST3 7FH
t (01782) 550279
e baker_arthur@hotmail.com
w countrysidecruising.co.uk

Countrywide Cruisers (Brewood) Ltd
★★★-★★★★★
Narrowboat
Wharf Lane, Stafford ST19 9BG
t (01902) 850166
w countrywide-cruisers.com

Excellence at Valley Cruises
★★★-★★★★★
Narrowboat
Springwood Haven, Mancetter
Road, Nuneaton CV10 0RZ
t (024) 7639 3333
e enquiries@valleycruises.co.uk
w valleycruises.co.uk

Eynsham (Oxford) - Anglowelsh Boats
★★★-★★★★
Narrowboat
Boat Centre, Oxford Road,
Witney OX29 4DA
t (01865) 882235

Fox Boats ★★★★★
Narrowboat
10 Marina Drive, March
PE15 0AU
t (01354) 652770
w foxboats.co.uk

Freedom Boats Ltd ★★★★
Narrowboat
Macclesfield Canal Centre,
Brook Street, Macclesfield
SK11 7AL
t (01625) 420042
w freedomboats.co.uk

Gailey - Viking Afloat
★★★★
Narrowboat
The Wharf, Watling Street,
Stafford ST19 5PR
t (01902) 790612
w viking-afloat.com

Gayton - Alvechurch Boat Centres Ltd ★★★-★★★★★
Narrowboat
Alvechurch Boats, Gayton
Marina, Blisworth Arm,
Northampton NN7 3ER
t (01604) 858685
w alvechurch.com

Great Haywood - Anglowelsh Boats
★-★★★★
Narrowboat
Mill Lane, Great Haywood, Stafford
t (01889) 881771

Heritage Narrowboats Ltd
★★★-★★★★
Narrowboat
The Marina, Kent Green, Stoke-on-Trent ST7 3JT
t (01782) 785700
w heritagenarrowboats.co.uk

Hilperton - Alvechurch Boat Centres Ltd ★★★-★★★★
Narrowboat
Hilperton Marina, Hammond Way, Trowbridge BA14 8RS
t (01225) 765243
e alvechurch@hilpertonmarina.co.uk
w alvechurch.com

Kate Boats ★★-★★★★
Narrowboat
Blue Lias Industrial Estate, Rugby Road, Southam CV47 8HN
t (01926) 492968
e molly@kateboats.co.uk
w kateboats.co.uk

Kate Boats (Warwick)
★★★-★★★★★
Narrowboat
The Boatyard, Nelson Lane, Warwick CV34 5JB
t (01926) 492968
e molly@kateboats.co.uk
w kateboats.co.uk

Lee Valley Boat Centre
★★-★★★★
Narrowboat
Old Nazeing Road, Broxbourne EN10 6LX
t (01992) 462085
e leevalleyboats@btconnect.com
w leevalleyboats.co.uk

Maestermyn Marine
★★-★★★★★
Narrowboat
Maestermyn Cruisers, Ellesmere Road, Whittington SY11 4NJ
t (01691) 662424
e enquiries@maestermyn.co.uk
w maestermyn.co.uk

Middlewich Narrowboats
★★★-★★★★
Narrowboat
Canal Terrace, Middlewich CW10 9BD
t (01606) 832460
e trish@middlewichboats.co.uk
w middlewichboats.co.uk

Mid-Wales Narrowboats
★★★-★★★★★
Narrowboat
Maestermyn Marine, Ellesmere Road, Gobowen, Whittington SY11 4NJ
t (01691) 650243
e enquiries@maestermyn.co.uk
w maestermyn.co.uk

Monkton Combe - Anglowelsh Boats
★★-★★★★
Narrowboat
Dundas Enterprises, Brassknocker Hill, Bath BA2 7JD
t (01225) 722292

Moonraker Narrowboat Company ★★★★★
Narrowboat
Watership Farm, Bath BA2 7BJ
t 07973 876891
e enquiries@moonboats.co.uk
w moonboats.co.uk

Napton - Black Prince Holidays ★★★★
Narrowboat
Wigrams Turn Marina, Shuckburgh Road, Southam CV47 8NL
t (01527) 575115
e bholidays@aol.com
w black-prince.com

Napton Narrowboats
★★★-★★★★★
Narrowboat
Napton Marina, Tomlow Road, Southam CV47 8HX
t (01926) 813644

Norbury - Anglowelsh Boats
★★★
Narrowboat
The Wharf, Norbury Junction, Norbury
t (01785) 284292

Oxfordshire Narrowboats
★★★-★★★★
Narrowboat
Heyford Wharf, Station Road, Bicester OX25 5PD
t (01869) 340348
e enquiries@oxfordshire-narrowboats.co.uk
w oxfordshire-narrowboats.co.uk

Rose Narrowboats
★★-★★★★★
Narrowboat
The Fosse Way, Stretton-under-Fosse, Rugby CV23 0PU
t (01788) 832449
w rose-narrowboats.co.uk

Rosewood Narrowboats
★★★★
Narrowboat
1 Beardwood Meadow, Blackburn BB2 7BH
t (01254) 279559
e info@rosewoodnarrowboats.co.uk
w rosewoodnarrowboats.co.uk

Rugby - Viking Afloat
★★★★
Narrowboat
Rugby Wharf, Consul Road, Rugby CV21 1PB
t (01788) 562183
e info@viking-afloat.com
w viking-afloat.com

Sally Boats Ltd
★★★-★★★★
Narrowboat
Bradford on Avon Marina, Trowbridge Road, Widbrook, Bradford-on-Avon BA15 1UD
t (01225) 864923
w sallyboats.ltd.uk

Sawley Marina ★★★★
Narrowboat
Long Eaton, Castle Donington NG10 3AE
t (0115) 973 4278
e sawleymarina@bwml.co.uk
w bwml.co.uk/index.php

Shepley Bridge Marina
★-★★★
Narrowboat
Huddersfield Road, Shepley Bridge, Mirfield WF14 9HR
t (01924) 491872
w shepleybridgemarina.com

Shire Cruisers
★★★-★★★★★
Narrowboat
The Wharf, Sowerby Bridge HX6 2AG
t (01422) 832712
e info@shirecruisers.co.uk
w shirecruisers.co.uk

Silsden Boats Holidays Ltd
★★★-★★★★
Narrowboat
Canal Wharf, Elliott Street, Keighley BD20 0DE
t (01535) 653675
w silsdenboats.com

Stoke on Trent - Black Prince Holidays ★★★★
Narrowboat
Festival Park Marina, Etruria, Stoke-on-Trent ST1 5PA
t (01527) 575115
e bholidays@aol.com
w black-prince.com

Stoke on Trent -Marine Cruises ★★★★
Narrowboat
Festival Park Marina, Etruria, Stoke-on-Trent ST1 5BS
t (01782) 201981

Stoke Prior - Black Prince Holidays ★★★★
Narrowboat
The Wharf, Hanbury Road, Bromsgrove B60 4LA
t (01527) 575115
e bholidays@aol.com
w black-prince.com

Tardebigge - Anglowelsh Boats ★★★-★★★★
Narrowboat
The Old Wharf, Bromsgrove B60 1LR
t (01527) 873898
w anglowelsh.co.uk

Union Canal Carriers (Adventure Fleet)
★★-★★★★★
Narrowboat
Braunston Pump House, Dark Lane, Daventry NN11 7HJ
t (01788) 890784

Union Wharf Marina ★★★★
Narrowboat
Leicester Road, Market Harborough LE16 7AU
t (01543) 251277
w tillermanboats.co.uk

Viking Afloat ★★★★
Narrowboat
Lowesmoor Wharf, Lowesmoor, Worcester WR1 2RS
t (01905) 610660
e info@viking-afloat.com
w viking-afloat.com

Whitchurch - Viking Afloat
★★★-★★★★
Narrowboat
Wrexham Road, Whitchurch SY13 3AA
t (01948) 662012
e viking@whitchurchmarina.com
w viking-afloat.com

Willow Wren Cruising Holidays ★★★★
Narrowboat
Rugby Wharf, Consul Road, Rugby CV21 1PB
t (01788) 562183
w willowwren.co.uk

Willow Wren Cruising Holidays (Blakes) ★★-★★★
Narrowboat
Rugby Wharf, Consul Road, Rugby CV21 1PB
t 0870 336 8198
e blakes.boatsnw@holidaycottagesgroup.com
w willowwren.co.uk

Wootton Wawen - Anglowelsh Boats
★★★-★★★★
Narrowboat
Canal Wharf, Stratford Road, Henley-in-Arden B95 6BZ
t (01564) 793427

Wrenbury - Alvechurch Boat Centres Ltd
★★★-★★★★★
Narrowboat
Wrenbury Mill, Cholmondeley Road, Nantwich CW5 8HG
t (01270) 780544
w alvechurch.com

The Wyvern Shipping Co Ltd ★★★-★★★★
Narrowboat
Rothschild Road, Leighton Buzzard LU7 2TF
t (01525) 372355
e james@canalholidays.co.uk
w canalholidays.co.uk

Further information

Clockwise: Botany Bay, Kent; Whinstone Lee Tor, Peak District, Derbyshire; Sherwood Pines Forest Park, Nottinghamshire

enjoyEngland.com
★★★
SELF CATERING

Quality assessment schemes

When you are looking for a place to stay, you need a rating system you can trust. Quality ratings are your clear guide to what to expect, in an easy-to-understand form.

National tourist board professional assessors visit all properties every year, so you can be confident that your accommodation has been thoroughly checked and rated for quality before you make a booking.

Based on the internationally recognised rating of stars, the system puts great emphasis on quality, and reflects research that shows exactly what consumers are looking for when choosing self-catering accommodation. Ratings are awarded from one to five stars – the more stars, the higher the quality and the greater the range of facilities and services provided.

Star ratings

Star ratings are the sign of quality assurance, giving you the confidence to book the accommodation that meets your expectations. All self-catering accommodation that is awarded a star rating will meet the minimum standards – so you can be confident that you will find the basic services that you would expect, such as:

- Clear information prior to booking on all aspects of the accommodation including location, facilities, prices, deposit, policies on smoking, children and cancellation etc
- No shared facilities, with the exception of a laundry room in multi-unit sites
- All appliances and furnishings will meet product safety standards for self-catering accommodation, particularly regarding fire safety
- At least one smoke alarm in the unit and a fire blanket in the kitchen
- Clear information on emergency procedures, including who to contact
- Contact details for the local doctor, dentist, chemist etc
- All statutory obligations will be met including an annual gas check and public liability insurance.

Certain additional facilities and services are required at the higher star levels, some of which may be important to you:

TWO-STAR accommodation must provide:

- Single beds which are a minimum of 3ft wide and double beds a minimum of 4ft 6in.

THREE-STAR accommodation must provide:

- Bed linen (with or without additional charge).

FOUR-STAR accommodation must provide:

- All advertised sleeping space in bedrooms (unless a studio)
- Bed linen included in the hire charge and beds are made up for arrival.

FIVE-STAR accommodation must provide:

- Full-size beds, including those for children
- At least two of the following items: tumble-dryer, telephone, Hi-Fi, video, DVD.

Some self-catering establishments offer a choice of accommodation units that may have different star ratings. In this case, the entry shows the range available.

Quality

The availability of additional facilities, such as a dishwasher or DVD, is not enough to achieve a higher star rating – the quality of the furnishings, equipment and decoration must be of a high standard. Self-catering accommodation with a lower star rating may offer some or all of the above, but to achieve the higher star ratings, the overall quality score has to be reached and exacting standards have to be met in critical areas. Consumer research has shown these critical areas to be: cleanliness, bedrooms, bathrooms, kitchens and public areas.

Advice and information

Making a booking

When enquiring about accommodation, make sure you check prices, the quality rating and other important details. You will also need to state your requirements clearly and precisely, for example:

- Arrival and departure dates, with acceptable alternatives if appropriate
- The accommodation you need
- The number of people in your party and the ages of any children
- Special requirements, such as ground-floor bathroom, garden, cot.

Booking by letter or email

Misunderstandings can easily happen over the telephone, so do request a written confirmation, together with details of any terms and conditions.

Deposits

When you book your self-catering holiday, the proprietor will normally ask you to pay a deposit immediately, and then to pay the full balance before your holiday date.

The reason for asking you to pay in advance is to safeguard the proprietor in case you decide to cancel at a late stage, or simply do not turn up. He or she may have turned down other bookings on the strength of yours, and may find it hard to re-let if you cancel.

Cancellations

Legal contract

When you accept accommodation that is offered to you, by telephone or in writing, you enter a legally binding contract with the proprietor. This means that if you cancel your booking, fail to take up the accommodation or leave early, you will probably forfeit your deposit and may expect to be charged the balance at the end of the period booked if the place cannot be re-let.

You should be advised at the time of the booking of what charges would be made in the event of cancelling the accommodation or leaving early. If this is not mentioned you should ask so that further disputes can be avoided. Where you have already paid the full amount before cancelling, the proprietor is likely to retain the money. If the accommodation is re-let, the proprietor will make a refund, normally less the amount of the deposit.

And remember, if you book by telephone and are asked for your credit card number, you should check whether the proprietor intends charging your credit card account should you later cancel your reservation. A proprietor should not be able to charge your credit card account with a cancellation unless he or she has made this clear at the time of your booking and you have agreed. However, to avoid later disputes, we suggest you check whether this is the intention.

Insurance

There are so many reasons why you might have to cancel your holiday, which is why we strongly advise people to take out a cancellation insurance policy. In fact, many self-catering agencies now insist their customers take out a policy when they book their holiday.

Arrival time

If you know you will be arriving late in the evening, it is a good idea to say so when you book. If you are delayed on your way, a telephone call to say that you will be late would be appreciated.

It is particularly important to liaise with the proprietor about key collection as he or she may not be on site.

Travelling with pets

Dogs, cats, ferrets and some other pet mammals can be brought into the UK from certain countries without having to undertake six months' quarantine on arrival provided they meet all the rules of the Pet Travel Scheme (PETS).

For full details, visit the PETS website at
w defra.gov.uk/animalh/quarantine/index.htm or contact the PETS Helpline
t +44 (0)870 241 1710
e quarantine@animalhealth.gsi.gov.uk

Ask for fact sheets which cover dogs and cats, ferrets or domestic rabbits and rodents.

There are no requirements for pets travelling directly between the UK and the Channel Islands. Pets entering Jersey or Guernsey from other countries need to be Pet Travel Scheme compliant and have a valid EU Pet Passport. For more information see jersey.com or visitguernsey.com.

What to expect

The proprietor/management is required to undertake the following:

- To maintain standards of guest care, cleanliness and service appropriate to the type of establishment;
- To describe accurately in any advertisement, brochure or other printed or electronic media, the facilities and services provided;
- To make clear to visitors exactly what is included in all prices quoted for accommodation, including taxes, and any other surcharges. Details of charges for additional services/facilities should also be made clear;
- To give a clear statement of the policy on cancellations to guests at the time of booking ie by telephone, fax, email, as well as information given in a printed format;
- To adhere to and not to exceed prices quoted at the time of booking for accommodation and other services;
- To advise visitors at the time of booking, and subsequently if any change, if the accommodation offered is in an unconnected annexe or similar and to indicate the location of such accommodation and any difference in comfort and/or amenities from accommodation in the establishment;
- To give each visitor on request details of payments due and a receipt, if required;
- To deal promptly and courteously with all enquiries, requests, bookings and correspondence from visitors;
- To ensure complaint handling procedures are in place and that complaints received are investigated promptly and courteously and that the outcome is communicated to the visitor;
- To give due consideration to the requirements of visitors with disabilities and visitors with special needs, and to make suitable provision where applicable;
- To provide public liability insurance or comparable arrangements and to comply with all applicable planning, safety and other statutory requirements;
- To allow a quality ratings assessor reasonable access to the establishment on request, to confirm the Code of Conduct is being observed.

Comments and complaints

Information

The proprietors themselves supply the descriptions of their establishments and other information for the entries (except quality ratings and awards). They have all signed a declaration that their information accurately describes their accommodation business. The publishers cannot guarantee the accuracy of information in this guide, and accept no responsibility for any error or misrepresentation.

All liability for loss, disappointment, negligence or other damage caused by reliance on the information contained in this guide, or in the event of bankruptcy or liquidation or cessation of trade of any company, individual or firm mentioned, is hereby excluded. We strongly recommend that you carefully check prices and other details when you book your accommodation.

Quality signage

All establishments displaying a quality sign have to hold current membership of a quality assessment scheme.

When an establishment is sold, the new owner has to reapply and be reassessed. In some areas the rating may be carried forward in the interim.

Problems

Of course, we hope you will not have cause for complaint, but problems do occur from time to time. If you are dissatisfied with anything, make your complaint to the management immediately. Then the management can take action at once to investigate the matter and put things right. The longer you leave a complaint, the harder it is to deal with it effectively.

In certain circumstances, the national tourist boards may look into complaints. However, they have no statutory control over establishments or their methods of operating and cannot become involved in legal or contractual matters or in seeking financial compensation.

If you do have problems that have not been resolved by the proprietor and which you would like to bring to their attention, please write to:

England – Quality in Tourism, Farncombe House, Broadway, Worcestershire WR12 7LJ

Guernsey – Quality Development Manager, Commerce and Employment Department, PO Box 459, St Martin, Guernsey GY1 6AF

Jersey – Tourism Office, Liberation Place, St Helier, Jersey JE1 1BB

About the accommodation entries

Entries

All the accommodation featured in this guide has been assessed or has applied for assessment under a quality assessment scheme.

Assessment under the EnjoyEngland Quality Rose scheme automatically entitles establishments to a listing in this guide. Start your search for a place to stay by looking in the regional sections of this guide where proprietors have paid to have their establishment featured in either a standard entry (includes description, facilities and prices) or an enhanced entry (photograph and extended details). If you can't find what you're looking for, turn to the listing section on the yellow pages for an even wider choice of accommodation.

Locations

Places to stay are generally listed under the town, city or village where they are located. If a place is in a small village, you may find it listed under a nearby town (providing it is within a seven-mile radius).

Place names are listed alphabetically within each regional section of the guide, along with the name of the ceremonial county they are in and their map reference. Complete addresses for rental properties are not given and the town(s) listed may be a distance from the actual establishment. Please check the precise location at the time of booking.

Map references

These refer to the colour location maps at the front of the guide. The first figure shown is the map number, the following letter and figure indicate the grid reference on the map. Only place names under which standard or enhanced entries (see above) feature appear on the maps. Some entries were included just before the guide went to press, so they do not appear on the maps.

Telephone numbers

Booking telephone numbers are listed below the contact address for each entry. Area codes are shown in brackets.

Prices

The prices shown are only a general guide; they were supplied to us by proprietors in summer 2008. Remember, changes may occur after the guide goes to press, so we strongly advise you to check prices when you book your accommodation.

Prices are shown in pounds sterling, including VAT where applicable, and are per unit per week.

Prices often vary through the year and may be significantly lower outside peak holiday weeks. You can get details of other bargain packages that may be available from the establishments themselves, regional tourism organisations or your local Tourist Information Centre (TIC). Your local travel agent may also have information and can help you make bookings.

Opening period

If an entry does not indicate an opening period, please check directly with the proprietor.

Symbols

The at-a-glance symbols included at the end of each entry show many of the services and facilities available at each establishment. You will find the key to these symbols on page 7.

Smoking

In the UK and the Channel Islands, it is illegal to smoke in enclosed public spaces and places of work. Smoking may be allowed in self-contained short-term rental accommodation, such as holiday cottages, flats or caravans, if the owner chooses to allow it.

If you wish to smoke, it is advisable to check whether it is allowed when you book.

Pets

Many places accept guests with dogs, but we do advise that you check this when you book, and ask if there are any extra charges or rules about exactly where your pet is allowed. The acceptance of dogs is not always extended to cats and it is strongly advised that cat owners contact the establishment well in advance. Some establishments do not accept pets at all. Pets are welcome by arrangement where you see this symbol.

The quarantine laws have changed and dogs, cats and ferrets are able to come into Britain and the Channel Islands from over 50 countries. For details of the Pet Travel Scheme (PETS) please turn to page 774.

Payment accepted

The types of payment accepted by an establishment are listed in the payment accepted section. If you plan to pay by card, check that the establishment will take your particular card before you book. Some proprietors will charge you a higher rate if you pay by credit card rather than cash or cheque. The difference is to cover the percentage paid by the proprietor to the credit card company. When you book by telephone, you may be asked for your credit card number as confirmation. But remember, the proprietor may then charge your credit card account if you cancel your booking. See under Cancellations on page 774.

Awaiting confirmation of rating

At the time of going to press some establishments featured in this guide had not yet been assessed for their rating for the year 2009 and so their new rating could not be included. Rating Applied For indicates this.

Approved Caravan Holiday Homes

Approved Caravan Holiday Homes let as individual self-catering units are included in this guide. They can be located on farms or holiday parks.

All facilities, including bathroom and toilet, are contained within the caravan and all mains services are provided. They do not have a star rating, but all caravans are assessed annually to a minimum standard.

Getting around

Travelling in London

London transport

London Underground has 12 lines, each with its own unique colour, so you can easily follow them on the Underground map. Most lines run through central London, and many serve parts of Greater London.

Buses are a quick, convenient way to travel around London, providing plenty of sightseeing opportunities on the way. There are over 6,500 buses in London operating 700 routes every day. You will need to buy a ticket before you board the bus – available from machines at the bus stop – or have a valid Oyster card (see below).

London's National Rail system stretches all over London. Many lines start at the main London railway stations (Paddington, Victoria, Waterloo, Kings Cross) with links to the tube. Trains mainly serve areas outside central London, and travel over ground.

Children usually travel free, or at reduced fare, on all public transport in London.

Oyster cards

Oyster cards can be used to pay fares on all London Underground, buses, Docklands Light Railway and trams; they are generally not valid for National Rail services in London.

Oyster cards are very easy to use – you just touch the card on sensors at stations or on buses and it always charges you the lowest fare available for your journey. You buy credit for your journey and when it runs out you simply top up with more.

Oyster is available to adults only. Children below the age of 11 can accompany adults free of charge. Children between the ages of 11 and 15 should use the standard child travel card. You can get an Oyster card at any underground station, at one of 3,000 Oyster points around London displaying the London Underground sign (usually shops), or from visitbritaindirect.com.

London congestion charge

The congestion charge is an £8 daily charge to drive in central London at certain times. Check whether the congestion charge is included in the cost of your car when you book. If your car's pick up point is in the congestion-charging zone, the company may pay the charge for the first day of your hire.

Low Emission Zone

The Low Emission Zone is an area covering most of Greater London, within which the most polluting diesel-engine vehicles are required to meet specific emissions standards. If your vehicle does not, you will need to pay a daily charge.

Vehicles affected by the Low Emission Zone are older diesel-engine lorries, buses, coaches, large vans, minibuses and other heavy vehicles such as motor caravans and motorised horse boxes. This includes vehicles registered outside of Great Britain. Cars and motorcycles are not affected by the scheme.

For more information visit tfl.gov.uk/roadusers/lez.

Rail and train travel

Britain's rail network covers all main cities and smaller regional towns. Trains on the network are operated by a few large companies running routes from London to stations all over Britain, and smaller companies running routes in regional areas. You can find up-to-the-minute information about routes, fares and train times on National Rail Enquiries (nationalrail.co.uk). For detailed information about routes and services, refer to the train operators' websites (see page 784).

Railway passes

BritRail offers a wide selection of passes and tickets giving you freedom to travel on all National Rail services. Passes can also include sleeper services, city and attraction passes and boat tours. Passes can normally be bought from travel agents outside Britain or by visiting the Britrail website (britrail.com).

Bus and coach travel

Public buses

Every city and town in Britain has a local bus service. These services are privatised and run by separate companies. The largest bus companies in Britain are First (firstgroup.com/bustravel.php), Stagecoach (stagecoachbus.com), and Arriva (arrivabus.co.uk), which run buses in most UK towns. Outside London, buses usually travel to and from the town centre or busiest part of town. Most towns have a bus station, where you'll be able to find maps and information about routes. Bus route information may also be posted at bus stops.

Tickets and fares

The cost of a bus ticket normally depends on how far you're travelling. Return fares may be available on some buses, but you usually need to buy a 'single' ticket for each individual journey.

You can buy your ticket when you board a bus, by telling the driver where you are going. One-day and weekly travel cards are available in some towns, and these can be bought from the driver or from an information centre at the bus station. Tickets are valid for each separate journey rather than for a period of time, so if you get off the bus you'll need to buy a new ticket when getting on another bus.

Domestic flights

Flying is a time-saving alternative to road or rail when it comes to travelling around Britain. Domestic flights are fast and frequent and there are 33 airports across Britain operating domestic routes. You will find airports marked on the maps at the front of this guide.

Domestic flight advice

Photo ID is required to travel on domestic flights. It is advisable to bring your passport, as not all airlines will accept other forms of photo identification.

There are very high security measures at all airports in Britain. These include restrictions on items that may be carried in hand luggage. It is important that you check with your airline prior to travel, as these restrictions may vary over time. Make sure you allow adequate time for check-in and boarding.

Cycling

Cycling is a good way to see some of Britain's best scenery and there are many networks of cycling routes. The National Cycle Network offers over 10,000 miles of walking and cycling routes connecting towns and villages, countryside and coast across the UK. For more information and routes see page 786 or visit Sustrans at sustrans.co.uk.

Think green

If you'd rather leave your car behind and travel by 'green transport' when visiting some of the attractions highlighted in this guide you'll be helping to reduce congestion and pollution as well as supporting conservation charities in their commitment to green travel.

The National Trust encourages visits made by non-car travellers. It offers admission discounts or a voucher for the tea room at a selection of its properties if you arrive on foot, cycle or public transport. (You'll need to produce a valid bus or train ticket if travelling by public transport.)

More information about The National Trust's work to encourage car-free days out can be found at nationaltrust.org.uk. Refer to the section entitled Information for Visitors.

The Channel Islands

For information about travelling to, and within, the Channel Islands go to jersey.com or visitguernsey.com.

To help you on your way you'll find a list of useful contacts at the end of this section.

England at a glance

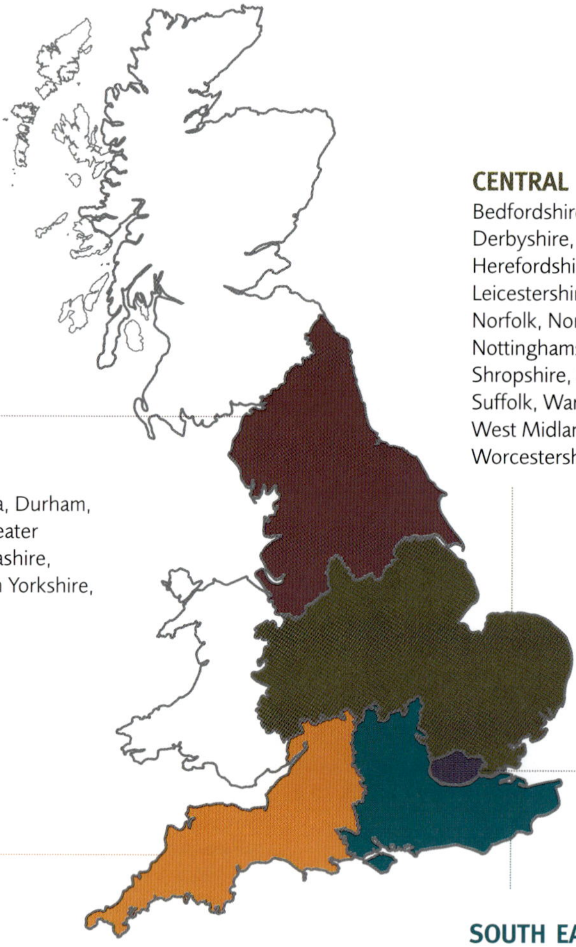

CENTRAL ENGLAND
Bedfordshire, Cambridgeshire, Derbyshire, Essex, Herefordshire, Hertfordshire, Leicestershire, Lincolnshire, Norfolk, Northamptonshire, Nottinghamshire, Rutland, Shropshire, Staffordshire, Suffolk, Warwickshire, West Midlands, Worcestershire

NORTHERN ENGLAND
Cheshire, Cumbria, Durham, East Yorkshire, Greater Manchester, Lancashire, Merseyside, North Yorkshire, Northumberland, South Yorkshire, Tees Valley, Tyne and Wear, West Yorkshire

LONDON

SOUTH WEST ENGLAND
Bristol, Cornwall, Devon, Dorset, Gloucestershire, Isles of Scilly, Somerset, Wiltshire

SOUTH EAST ENGLAND
Berkshire, Buckinghamshire, East Sussex, Hampshire, Isle of Wight, Kent, London, Oxfordshire, Surrey, West Sussex

THE CHANNEL ISLANDS
Guernsey and Jersey are not drawn to scale

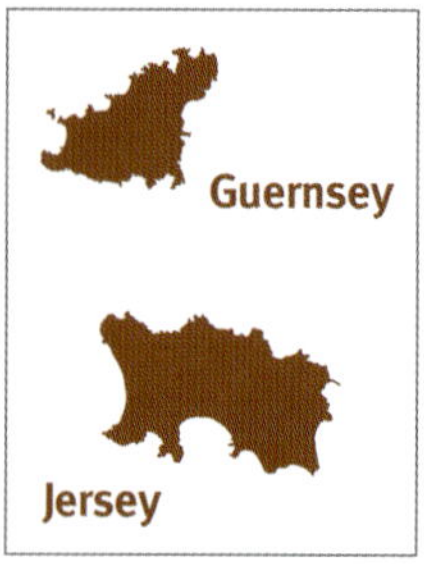

Counties and regions at a glance

If you know what county you wish to visit you'll find it in the regional section shown below.

County	Region
Bedfordshire	Central England
Berkshire	South East England
Bristol	South West England
Buckinghamshire	South East England
Cambridgeshire	Central England
Cheshire	Northern England
Cornwall	South West England
Cumbria	Northern England
Derbyshire	Central England
Devon	South West England
Dorset	South West England
Durham	Northern England
East Yorkshire	Northern England
East Sussex	South East England
Essex	Central England
Gloucestershire	South West England
Greater Manchester	Northern England
Hampshire	South East England
Herefordshire	Central England
Hertfordshire	Central England
Isle of Wight	South East England
Isles of Scilly	South West England
Kent	South East England
Lancashire	Northern England

County	Region
Leicestershire	Central England
Lincolnshire	Central England
Merseyside	Northern England
Norfolk	Central England
North Yorkshire	Northern England
Northamptonshire	Central England
Northumberland	Northern England
Nottinghamshire	Central England
Oxfordshire	South East England
Rutland	Central England
Shropshire	Central England
Somerset	South West England
South Yorkshire	Northern England
Staffordshire	Central England
Suffolk	Central England
Surrey	South East England
Tees Valley	Northern England
Tyne and Wear	Northern England
Warwickshire	Central England
West Midlands	Central England
West Sussex	South East England
West Yorkshire	Northern England
Wiltshire	South West England
Worcestershire	Central England

To help readers we do not refer to unitary authorities in this guide.

By car and by train

Distance chart

The distances between towns on the chart below are given to the nearest mile, and are measured along routes based on the quickest travelling time, making maximum use of motorways or dual-carriageway roads. The chart is based upon information supplied by the Automobile Association.

To calculate the distance in kilometres multiply the mileage by 1.6

For example: Brighton to Dover 82 miles x 1.6 =131.2 kilometres

	Aberdeen	Aberystwyth	Barnstaple	Birmingham	Brighton	Bristol	Cambridge	Cardiff	Carlisle	Carmarthen	Dorchester	Dover	Edinburgh	Exeter	Fort William	Glasgow	Gloucester	Guildford	Hereford	Holyhead	Hull	Inverness	Kendal	Leeds	Lincoln	Liverpool	Maidstone	Manchester	Middlesbrough	Newcastle	Northampton	Norwich	Nottingham	Oxford	Penzance	Perth	Peterborough	Plymouth	Portsmouth	Preston	Salisbury	Sheffield	Shrewsbury	Southampton	Stoke-on-Trent	Stranraer	Taunton	Wick	York
Aberystwyth	472
Barnstaple	608	214
Birmingham	436	124	180
Brighton	613	288	210	171
Bristol	518	130	100	90	169
Cambridge	463	215	267	97	120	170
Cardiff	537	111	128	109	202	44	203
Carlisle	236	236	371	199	376	281	256	300
Carmarthen	520	48	190	172	264	107	266	68	284
Dorchester	600	206	94	172	119	62	184	120	364	182
Dover	587	326	272	208	82	205	124	239	381	301	200
Edinburgh	126	336	471	299	476	381	333	400	100	386	463	458
Exeter	593	198	44	165	178	84	259	113	356	175	57	248	455
Fort William	156	435	570	398	576	480	456	499	199	485	562	580	137	554
Glasgow	150	332	467	295	472	377	353	396	96	382	459	477	47	451	102
Gloucester	484	113	126	56	155	36	150	63	248	125	118	192	346	110	445	343
Guildford	571	224	175	128	44	106	96	139	335	201	97	97	433	150	532	430	99
Hereford	487	79	144	59	189	54	153	59	250	85	136	225	349	129	448	346	34	133
Holyhead	464	102	339	167	345	249	259	202	228	150	331	369	326	323	425	323	215	302	156
Hull	376	227	320	139	258	230	138	250	170	311	312	262	247	304	367	266	196	239	198	218
Inverness	106	496	631	459	637	541	517	561	260	546	623	641	157	616	66	176	507	595	510	488	430
Kendal	283	189	324	153	330	234	251	254	47	240	316	354	145	309	245	143	200	288	203	181	164	307
Leeds	329	173	301	120	262	211	146	230	123	224	293	271	200	285	321	219	177	220	179	165	59	383	110
Lincoln	388	199	275	98	216	185	95	205	182	267	246	220	258	260	379	277	151	173	154	204	44	441	176	74
Liverpool	362	110	272	101	278	182	193	202	126	158	264	302	224	257	324	222	148	236	151	102	128	386	79	74	139
Maidstone	545	284	234	166	50	167	82	200	339	262	161	41	416	209	537	435	153	58	186	327	220	599	313	231	178	261
Manchester	357	134	261	89	266	171	160	190	120	184	253	290	219	245	318	216	136	224	139	125	97	380	74	44	85	34	248
Middlesbrough	276	244	357	176	318	267	197	286	95	294	349	322	146	341	283	190	232	276	235	235	89	308	84	64	122	145	280	114
Newcastle	235	275	388	207	349	298	229	317	60	325	380	353	106	372	242	153	264	307	266	266	142	267	102	95	154	176	311	145	39
Northampton	486	174	212	56	133	115	56	162	249	224	159	155	348	196	447	345	79	90	111	217	152	509	203	136	94	151	113	139	189	220
Norwich	488	278	329	160	168	233	63	266	282	328	241	172	359	313	480	378	212	160	215	321	147	542	276	174	103	240	130	185	223	254	118
Nottingham	395	162	232	51	193	142	86	161	189	223	224	210	266	216	387	285	107	151	110	178	93	449	164	77	39	112	168	71	130	161	64	119
Oxford	510	160	170	68	109	73	82	107	274	169	115	146	373	154	472	370	48	67	81	242	190	534	228	174	132	176	107	164	227	258	44	146	102
Penzance	702	308	108	274	287	193	368	222	466	284	167	357	564	109	663	562	220	259	238	434	415	726	419	403	370	367	318	356	451	482	326	433	326	265
Perth	86	388	523	351	529	433	378	453	152	438	515	503	42	507	102	64	399	486	401	379	291	114	199	245	303	278	461	275	192	150	400	404	310	426	617
Peterborough	435	204	263	86	158	173	37	193	229	255	204	162	306	248	427	325	139	115	142	225	110	489	223	121	51	159	120	132	170	201	45	78	58	86	357	351
Plymouth	633	239	62	205	218	124	299	153	397	215	98	288	495	44	594	493	151	190	169	365	346	657	350	334	301	298	249	287	382	413	257	364	257	196	78	544	288
Portsmouth	596	244	162	154	53	125	137	158	360	220	73	141	458	132	558	456	118	45	152	328	276	620	314	260	215	262	102	250	313	344	130	204	188	85	241	508	157	172
Preston	326	146	281	110	287	191	209	211	89	197	273	311	188	266	287	185	157	245	160	138	122	349	43	69	134	36	269	35	103	139	159	235	121	184	375	237	180	306	270
Salisbury	549	184	118	121	90	52	145	98	313	160	39	160	411	93	511	409	72	62	105	281	261	573	267	244	202	215	121	203	298	329	115	212	173	70	203	461	165	134	44	223
Sheffield	397	166	272	91	233	182	122	201	161	263	264	247	236	256	359	257	148	191	150	157	66	421	115	38	47	79	205	39	100	131	104	148	45	142	366	309	93	297	228	73	212
Shrewsbury	417	75	220	48	226	130	140	111	181	110	212	250	279	205	379	277	96	184	52	105	162	441	135	119	124	65	208	71	190	221	98	203	87	123	314	329	129	245	209	92	161	88
Southampton	578	225	142	135	66	106	136	140	342	201	53	152	440	111	539	437	100	49	133	309	258	601	295	241	199	243	113	232	294	325	111	204	169	67	221	489	157	152	20	252	23	209	191
Stoke-on-Trent	392	112	220	48	226	130	140	150	156	211	212	250	254	205	353	251	96	184	99	123	129	415	109	93	91	57	208	46	164	195	98	172	54	123	314	303	99	245	209	66	161	50	38	191
Stranraer	235	342	477	305	482	387	363	406	106	392	469	487	132	461	181	86	352	440	355	333	276	261	153	229	288	232	445	229	201	163	354	388	295	380	571	149	333	502	466	195	418	267	287	447	261
Taunton	560	165	50	132	160	51	226	80	323	142	45	224	422	34	521	419	77	126	96	291	272	583	277	261	228	225	185	213	309	340	183	291	184	123	144	471	215	75	114	234	70	224	172	94	172	429
Wick	207	597	732	560	738	642	618	662	361	647	724	742	258	716	166	277	608	695	610	588	531	104	408	484	543	487	700	484	409	367	609	644	550	635	826	215	589	757	721	451	673	523	542	702	516	362	684
York	323	201	314	133	275	224	154	243	116	251	306	279	193	298	314	212	189	233	192	192	38	376	91	24	79	102	237	71	51	89	146	180	87	184	408	239	125	339	269	96	254	57	146	251	120	223	265	477
LONDON	550	239	216	121	54	120	59	153	314	215	125	78	413	200	512	410	102	31	136	282	186	574	268	201	143	216	39	204	254	285	68	118	129	56	310	462	86	241	75	225	85	169	163	77	161	420	167	675	211

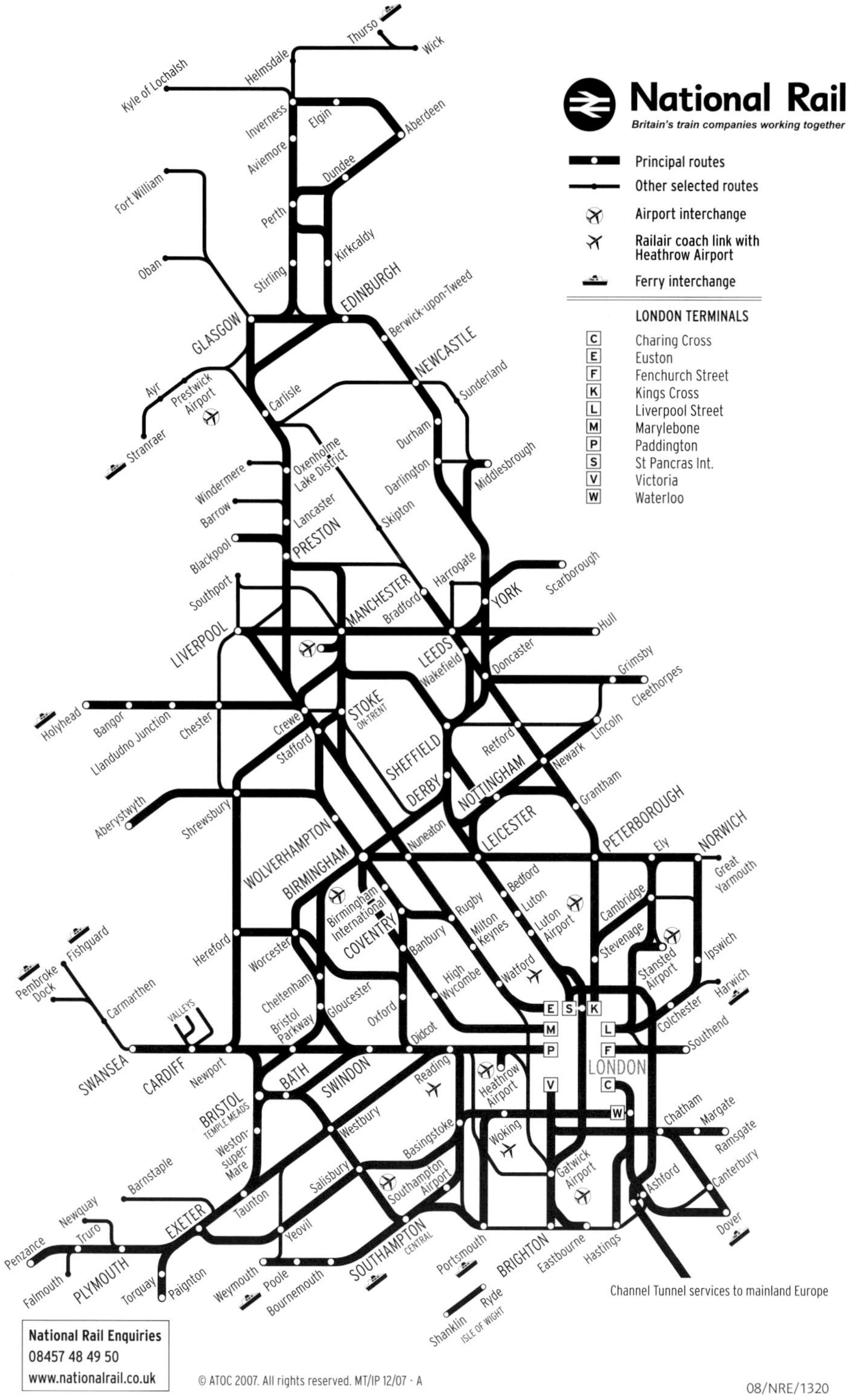
National Rail
Britain's train companies working together
Principal routes
Other selected routes
Airport interchange
Railair coach link with Heathrow Airport
Ferry interchange
LONDON TERMINALS
C Charing Cross
E Euston
F Fenchurch Street
K Kings Cross
L Liverpool Street
M Marylebone
P Paddington
S St Pancras Int.
V Victoria
W Waterloo
Thurso
Wick
Helmsdale
Kyle of Lochalsh
Inverness
Elgin
Aberdeen
Aviemore
Dundee
Fort William
Perth
Kirkcaldy
Oban
Stirling
EDINBURGH
GLASGOW
Berwick-upon-Tweed
NEWCASTLE
Ayr
Prestwick Airport
Carlisle
Sunderland
Stranraer
Durham
Oxenholme Lake District
Windermere
Darlington
Middlesbrough
Barrow
Lancaster
Skipton
Blackpool
PRESTON
Southport
Harrogate
Scarborough
YORK
MANCHESTER
Bradford
LIVERPOOL
LEEDS
Wakefield
Hull
Doncaster
Grimsby
Cleethorpes
Holyhead
Bangor
Llandudno Junction
Chester
Crewe
STOKE ON-TRENT
Stafford
SHEFFIELD
Retford
Lincoln
Newark
NOTTINGHAM
DERBY
Grantham
Aberystwyth
Shrewsbury
WOLVERHAMPTON
Nuneaton
LEICESTER
PETERBOROUGH
Ely
NORWICH
Great Yarmouth
BIRMINGHAM
Birmingham International
COVENTRY
Rugby
Bedford
Luton
Luton Airport
Cambridge
Milton Keynes
Fishguard
Pembroke Dock
Carmarthen
Hereford
Worcester
Banbury
High Wycombe
Watford
Stevenage
Stansted Airport
Ipswich
Harwich
Cheltenham
Gloucester
Oxford
Colchester
VALLEYS
Bristol Parkway
Didcot
Southend
SWANSEA
CARDIFF
Newport
BATH
SWINDON
Reading
Heathrow Airport
LONDON
BRISTOL TEMPLE MEADS
Westbury
Chatham
Margate
Ramsgate
Weston-super-Mare
Basingstoke
Woking
Canterbury
Barnstaple
Salisbury
Southampton Airport
Gatwick Airport
Ashford
Taunton
Newquay
Truro
Penzance
EXETER
Yeovil
SOUTHAMPTON CENTRAL
Dover
Falmouth
PLYMOUTH
Torquay
Paignton
Weymouth
Poole
Bournemouth
Portsmouth
BRIGHTON
Eastbourne
Hastings
Ryde
Shanklin
ISLE OF WIGHT
Channel Tunnel services to mainland Europe
National Rail Enquiries
08457 48 49 50
www.nationalrail.co.uk
© ATOC 2007. All rights reserved. MT/IP 12/07 - A
08/NRE/1320

Travel information

General travel information

Streetmap	streetmap.co.uk	
Transport Direct (a journey planner)	transportdirect.info	
Transport for London	tfl.gov.uk	(020) 7222 1234
Travel Services	departures-arrivals.com	
Traveline (public transport information)	traveline.org.uk	0870 200 2233

Bus & coach

Megabus	megabus.com	0901 331 0031
National Express	nationalexpress.com	0870 580 8080
WA Shearings	washearings.com	(01942) 823371

Car & car hire

AA	theaa.com	0870 600 0371
Green Flag	greenflag.co.uk	0845 246 1557
RAC	rac.co.uk	0870 572 2722
Alamo	alamo.co.uk	0870 400 4562*
Avis	avis.co.uk	0844 581 0147
Budget	budget.co.uk	0844 581 2231
Easycar	easycar.com	0906 333 3333
Enterprise	enterprise.com	0870 350 3000*
Hertz	hertz.co.uk	0870 844 8844*
Holiday Autos	holidayautos.co.uk	0870 400 4461
National	nationalcar.co.uk	0870 400 4581
Thrifty	thrifty.co.uk	(01494) 751500

Air

Air Southwest	airsouthwest.com	0870 043 4553
Blue Islands (Channel Islands)	blueislands.com	0845 620 2122
BMI	flybmi.com	0870 607 0555
BMI Baby	bmibaby.com	0871 224 0224
British Airways	ba.com	0844 493 0787
British International (Isles of Scilly to Penzance)	islesofscillyhelicopter.com	(01736) 363871*
Eastern Airways	easternairways.com	0870 366 9989
Easyjet	easyjet.com	0871 244 2366
Flybe	flybe.com	0871 700 2000*
Flyglobespan	flyglobespan.com	0871 271 0415*
Jet2.com	jet2.com	0871 226 1737*
Manx2	manx2.com	0871 200 0440*
Ryanair	ryanair.com	0871 246 0000
Skybus (Isles of Scilly)	islesofscilly-travel.co.uk	0845 710 5555
Thomsonfly	tomsonfly.com	0871 231 4869
VLM	flyvlm.com	0871 666 5050

Train

National Rail Enquiries	nationalrail.co.uk	0845 748 4950
Consult National Rail Enquiries for up-to-the-minute advice on journey planning, train times and service updates.		
The Trainline (online booking)	trainline.co.uk	
UK train operating companies	rail.co.uk	
Arriva Trains	arriva.co.uk	0845 748 4950
c2c	c2c-online.co.uk	0845 601 4873
Chiltern Railways	chilternrailways.co.uk	0845 600 5165
CrossCountry	crosscountrytrains.co.uk	0870 010 0084
East Midlands Trains	eastmidlandstrains.co.uk	0845 712 5678
Eurostar	eurostar.com	0870 518 6186*
First Capital Connect	firstcapitalconnect.co.uk	0845 026 4700
First Great Western	firstgreatwestern.co.uk	0845 700 0125
Gatwick Express	gatwickexpress.com	0845 850 1530
Heathrow Connect	heathrowconnect.com	0845 678 6975
Heathrow Express	heathrowexpress.com	0845 600 1515
Hull Trains	hulltrains.co.uk	0845 071 0222
Island Line	island-line.co.uk	0845 748 4950
London Midland	londonmidland.com	0844 811 0133
Merseyrail	merseyrail.org	(0151) 702 2071
National Express East Anglia	nationalexpresseastanglia.com	0845 600 7245
National Express East Coast	nationalexpresseastcoast.com	0845 722 5333
Northern Rail	northernrail.org	0845 000 0125
ScotRail	firstgroup.com/scotrail	0845 601 5929
South Eastern Trains	southeasternrailway.co.uk	0845 000 2222
South West Trains	southwesttrains.co.uk	0845 600 0650
Southern	southernrailway.com	0845 127 2920
Stansted Express	stanstedexpress.com	0845 600 7245
Translink	nirailways.co.uk	(028) 9066 6630
Transpennine Express	tpexpress.co.uk	0845 600 1671
Virgin Trains	virgintrains.co.uk	0845 722 2333*

Ferry

Ferry information	sailanddrive.com	
Condor Ferries (Channel Islands)	condorferries.co.uk	0845 609 1024*
Steam Packet Company (Isle of Man)	steam-packet.com	0871 222 1333
Isles of Scilly Travel	islesofscilly-travel.co.uk	0845 710 5555
Red Funnel (Isle of Wight)	redfunnel.co.uk	0870 444 8898
Wight Link (Isle of Wight)	wightlink.co.uk	0871 376 4342

Phone numbers listed are for general enquiries unless otherwise stated.

* Booking line only

National cycle network

Sections of the National Cycle Network are shown on the maps in this guide. The numbers on the maps will appear on the signs along your route 3 . Here are some tips about finding and using a route.

- **Research and plan your route online**
  Log on to **sustrans.org.uk** and click on 'Get cycling' to find information about routes in this guide or other routes you want to use.
- **Order a route map**
  Useful, easy-to-use maps of many of the most popular routes of the National Cycle Network are available from Sustrans, the charity behind the Network. These can be purchased online or by mail order – visit **sustransshop.co.uk** or call **0845 113 0065.**
- **Order Cycling in the UK**
  The official guide to the National Cycle Network gives details of rides all over the UK, detailing 148 routes and profiles of 43 days rides on traffic-free paths and quiet roads.

ROUTE NUMBER	ROUTE/MAP NAME	START/END OF ROUTE
South West		
3	The West Country Way	Padstow – Bristol/Bath
3 & 32	The Cornish Way	Land's End – Bude
27	The Devon Coast to Coast	Ilfracombe – Plymouth
South East		
4 & 5	Thames Valley	London – Oxford via Reading
4	Kennet & Avon	Reading – Bristol
2, 20 & 21	Downs & Weald	London – Brighton – Hastings
Central England		
5 & 54	West Midlands	Oxford – Derby via Stratford-upon-Avon
Northern England		
1	Coast & Castles South	Newcastle – Berwick-upon-Tweed – Edinburgh
7, 14 & 71	Sea to Sea (C2C)	Whitehaven/Workington – Sunderland/Newcastle upon Tyne
14	Three Rivers	Middlesbrough – Durham – South Shields
65 & Regional 52 (W2W)	Yorkshire Moors & Coast	Middlesbrough – Easingwold & Barnard Castle – Whitby
65 & 66	Yorkshire Wolds, York & Hull	Easingwold – York – Hull
68	Pennine Cycleway (South Pennines & the Dales)	Holmfirth – Appleby-in-Westmorland/Kendal
68	Pennine Cycleway North	Appleby-in-Westmorland/Penrith – Berwick-upon-Tweed
72	Hadrian's Cycleway	Ravenglass – South Shields
62 & 65	Trans Pennine Trail East	Yorkshire – North Sea
62	Trans Pennine Trail West	Irish Sea – Yorkshire
67	Trans Pennine Trail Central	Leeds – Chesterfield

National Accessible Scheme index

Establishments participating in the National Accessible Scheme are listed below – those in colour have a detailed entry in this guide. At the front of the guide you can find information about the scheme. Establishments are listed alphabetically by place name within each region.

Mobility level 1

Mobility level 1 continued

Mobility level 1 continued

Mobility level 2

Establishments in colour have a detailed entry in this guide.

Mobility level 2 continued

Mobility level 2 continued

Establishments in colour have a detailed entry in this guide.

Mobility level 3 Independent

Mobility level 3 Assisted

Mobility level 3 Assisted continued

Access Exceptional Independent

Access Exceptional Assisted

Hearing impairment level 1

Hearing impairment level 2

Visual impairment level 1

Visual impairment level 2

Establishments in colour have a detailed entry in this guide.

Walkers and cyclists welcome

Establishments participating in the Walkers Welcome and Cyclists Welcome schemes provide special facilities and actively encourage these recreations. Accommodation with a detailed entry in this guide is listed below. Place names are listed alphabetically within each region.

Walkers Welcome and Cyclists Welcome

Establishments listed here have a detailed entry in this guide.

Walkers Welcome and Cyclists Welcome continued

Walkers Welcome

Cyclists Welcome

Families and pets welcome

Establishments participating in the Families Welcome or Welcome Pets! schemes are listed below. They provide special facilities and actively encourage families or guests with pets. Establishments in bold have a detailed entry in this guide. Place names are listed alphabetically within each region.

Families and Pets Welcome

Allonby Northern England	**Crookhurst Farm ★★★★**	64
Bamburgh Northern England	**Springhill Farm Holiday Accommodation ★★★★-★★★★★**	71
Barmby Moor Northern England	**Northwood Coach House ★★★★**	72
Hutton Roof Northern England	**Carrock Cottages ★★★★★**	110
Kielder Northern England	**Kielder Lodges ★★★★-★★★★★**	113
Morpeth Northern England	**Micklewood Park ★★-★★★★**	126
Otley Northern England	**The Birches ★★★★**	129
Sandsend Northern England	**Raithwaite Hall ★★★★-★★★★★**	138
Whinfell Northern England	**Topthorn Holiday Cottages ★★★**	151
Kelling Central England	**Owl Place ★★★★★**	223
Market Rasen Central England	**Papermill Cottages ★★★★**	239
Oulton Broad Central England	**Camps Heath Barn ★★★★**	247
Sibton Central England	**Cardinal Cottage ★★★★**	255
Birdham South East England	**Martins Cottages ★★★★★**	288
London SE10	**12 Burgos Grove ★★★**	337
Crantock South West England	**Crantock Holiday Cottages ★★★-★★★★**	384
Goonhavern South West England	**Greenmeadow ★★★**	396

Families Welcome

Ambleside Northern England	**Quaysiders Club ★★★**	68
Askham Northern England	**Sycamore Barn Holiday Cottage ★★★★**	69
Cornriggs Northern England	**Cornriggs Cottages ★★★★★**	85
Grange-over-Sands Northern England	**Dyer Dene ★★★**	97
Keswick Northern England	**Croft House Holidays ★★★★**	112
Kielder Water Northern England	**Falstone Barns ★★★★★**	113
Malton Northern England	**Easthorpe Lodge ★★★★**	122
York Northern England	**Pavilion Cottage ★★★**	160
Badley Central England	**The Lodge ★★★★**	189
Bury St Edmunds Central England	**The Old Dairy at West Lodge ★★★★**	198
Louth Central England	**Brackenborough Hall Coach House Holidays ★★★★-★★★★★**	234

Families Welcome continued

Pets Welcome

Quick reference index

If you're looking for a specific facility use this index to see at-a-glance detailed accommodation entries that match your requirement. Establishments are listed alphabetically by place name within each region.

Indoor pool

Establishments listed here have a detailed entry in this guide.

Indoor pool continued

Outdoor pool

Outdoor pool continued

Tennis court(s)

Tennis court(s) continued

Index to display advertisers

Bank holiday dates for your diary

holiday	2009	2010
New Year's Day	1 January	1 January
Good Friday	10 April	2 April
Easter Monday	13 April	5 April
Early May Bank Holiday	4 May	3 May
Liberation Day (Channel Islands)	9 May	9 May
Spring Bank Holiday	25 May	31 May
Summer Bank Holiday	31 August	30 August
Christmas Day Holiday	25 December	27 December
Boxing Day Holiday	28 December	28 December

Index by property name

Accommodation with a detailed entry in this guide is listed below.

b continued

page

c

page

c continued page

d page

e page

f page

g page

h page

h continued page

i page

j page

k page

l page

m page

Establishments listed here have a detailed entry in this guide.

p continued page

q page

r page

s page

Index by place name

The following places all have detailed accommodation entries in this guide. If the place where you wish to stay is not shown, the location maps (starting on page 30) will help you to find somewhere to stay in the area.

p continued page

r page

s page

t page

u page

v page

w page

y page

Published by: Heritage House Group (Ketteringham Hall, Wymondham, Norfolk NR18 9RS; t (01603) 819420; f (01603) 814325; hhgroup.co.uk) on behalf of VisitBritain, Thames Road, Blacks Road, London W6 9EL
Publishing Manager: Tess Lugos
Production Manager: Iris Buckley
Compilation, design, copywriting, production and advertisement sales: Jackson Lowe Marketing, 3 St Andrews Place, Southover Road, Lewes, East Sussex BN7 1UP
t (01273) 487487 jacksonlowe.com
Cover design: Jamieson Eley, Nick McCann
Typesetting: Marlinzo Services, Somerset and Jackson Lowe Marketing
Accommodation maps: Based on digital map data © ESR Cartography, 2008
Touring maps: © VisitBritain 2005. National Parks, Areas of Outstanding Natural Beauty, National Trails and Heritage Coast based on information supplied by Natural England. Cycle Networks provided by Sustrans
Printing and binding: 1010 Printing International Ltd, China

Front cover: Stone Cottage, Ullswater, Cumbria
Back cover (from top)**:** The Old Drift House, Kersey, Suffolk; Quay Holidays, Poole, Dorset

Photography credits: britainonview/David Angel/ANPA/Daniel Bosworth/Martin Brent/brightononview/Alan Chandler/East Midlands Tourism/East of England Tourism/Eden Project/Rod Edwards/Damir Fabijanic/FCO/Klaus Hagmeier/Joanna Henderson/Adrian Houston/Kent Tourism Alliance/Simon Kreitem/Lee Valley Regional Park/Pawel Libera/James McCormick/McCormick-McAdam/Eric Nathan/David Noton/NWDA/Tony Pleavin/Grant Pritchard/Olivier Roques-Ro/David Sellman/Andy Sewell/Jon Spaull/Thanet District Council/Troika/Visit Chester & Cheshire/Michael Walter/Juliet White/Worcestershire County Council; Iris Buckley; cumbriaphoto.co.uk/Ben Barden/Cumbria Tourism; The Deep; Imperial War Museum North; Michael Jackson; Jersey Tourism; Allan McPhail; NTPL/Rob Judges; One NorthEast Tourism; Mark Passmore; South West News Service; Thermae Bath Spa/Matt Cardy; Visit Bristol; VisitGuernsey; visitlondonimages/britainonview

ISBN 978-0-7095-8444-5

A VisitBritain Publishing guide